ITALY

THE ROUGH GUIDE

THE ROUGH GUIDES

OTHER AVAILABLE ROUGH GUIDES

**AMSTERDAM • BARCELONA • BERLIN • BRAZIL
BRITTANY & NORMANDY • BULGARIA • CALIFORNIA & WEST COAST USA
CANADA • CRETE • CYPRUS • CZECH & SLOVAK REPUBLICS • EGYPT
EUROPE • FLORIDA • FRANCE • GERMANY • GREECE • GUATEMALA & BELIZE
HOLLAND, BELGIUM & LUXEMBOURG • HONG KONG • HUNGARY • IRELAND
ISRAEL • KENYA • MEDITERRANEAN WILDLIFE • MEXICO • MOROCCO
NEPAL • NEW YORK • NOTHING VENTURED • PARIS • PERU • POLAND
PORTUGAL • PRAGUE • PROVENCE • PYRENEES • SAN FRANCISCO
SCANDINAVIA • SICILY • SPAIN • ST PETERSBURG • THAILAND • TUNISIA
TURKEY • TUSCANY & UMBRIA • USA • VENICE • WEST AFRICA
WOMEN TRAVEL • ZIMBABWE & BOTSWANA**

FORTHCOMING

AUSTRALIA • ENGLAND & WALES • SCOTLAND

Rough Guide Credits

Series Editor: Mark Ellingham
Editorial: Martin Dunford, John Fisher, Jack Holland, Jonathan Buckley, Greg Ward, Kate Berens, Jules Brown
Production: Susanne Hillen, Gail Jammy, Andy Hilliard, Vivien Antwi
Cartography: Melissa Flack
Publicity: Richard Trillo
Finance: Celia Crowley

Many **thanks** for this edition to: Brenda Keatley, Monica Levy and Roberto Peretta, Celia Crowley, Bettie Petith, Sam Cole, Eliana Reggiori, Bruce Moffat, Stefano and all at the *Tony*, Eugenio Magnani and the Italian State Tourist Office, Emile Bruls, Marc Dubin, Les Whitehouse, Carol Lambourne, Roberto Orsi, Jonathan Degani and Maurizio, Paolo and Izaku Bortolotti, Julia Unwin, Jessica Morris, Marc Svensson, Daniel Jacobs, Flaminia Allvin, Jen Zaid, Marco and Suzy Chelo, Francesco and Daniela, Valentina, Barbara Baxter, Rupert Small, Nick and Spartaco (and Venom), Fulvia Angelino of *Enjoy Rome*. Thanks, too, to Margaret Doyle and Gareth Nash for proofreading, and to all at Rough Guides, especially everyone in the production team for their commitment and dedication... and Melissa Flack for invaluable work on the first of many Rough Guides.

Published April 1993 by Rough Guides Ltd, 1 Mercer Street, London WC2H 9QJ.
Distributed by Penguin Books, 27 Wrights Lane, London W8 5TZ.
Previous edition published by Harrap Columbus.

Typeset in Linotron Univers and Century Old Style to an original design by Andrew Oliver.
Printed in the UK by Cox & Wyman Ltd, Reading, Berks.

Illustrations in Part One and Part Three by Ed Briant; Basics illustration by Paul Leith
Contexts illustration by Tommy Yamaha

1008pp. includes index

British Library Cataloguing in Publication Data
A catalogue record for this book is available from the British Library.

ISBN 1-85828-031-1

Written and researched by

ROS BELFORD, MARTIN DUNFORD AND CELIA WOOLFREY

With additional contributions by
Robert Andrews, Jules Brown, Jonathan Buckley, Tim Jepson, Mark Ellingham, Hilary Robinson, Graziella Martina, Mark Thompson, Mike Ivy and Nicola Walker

Edited by
Martin Dunford and Jonathan Buckley

THE ROUGH GUIDES

HELP US UPDATE

We've gone to a lot of effort to ensure that this edition of *Italy: The Rough Guide* is up-to-date and accurate. However, things do change – hotels and restaurants come and go, especially in the larger cities, opening hours are notoriously fickle, and there's the ever-present danger of monuments being closed for long periods while under restoration. Any suggestions, comments or corrections toward the next edition would be much appreciated.

We'll credit all contributions, and send a copy of the next edition (or any other Rough Guide if you prefer) for the best letters. Please write to:

Martin Dunford, The Rough Guides, 1 Mercer Street, London WC2H 9QJ.

Thanks are due to all those who wrote in with comments, suggestions and criticisms of the previous edition. In no particular order, they are: Anthony Perrin, Nicola Higham and Michael Peers, Jonathan Frank, Lee Marshall, Nick Chastney, Paul Kirkwood, Rosanna M. O'Neill, Emei Loughney, Bill Thompson, Martin Easterbrook, Annabel Johnstone, Catherine Chambers and Carol Morland, Robert Stoker, Karen Jones and David Cherry, Janette Moule, Elizabeth Green, Elizabeth B. Lewis, Donna Harris, Michael J. Persellin, Elizabeth Newlands, Eduard O. Murray, Ana Sarkic, Sara Davies, Graham Anderson, Marjorie Bocking, Peter Cornish, John Humphries, A.M. Young, Mugsy May, Dominic Druce, Marion Stevens, the late Gerald Brenner, John Spial, Kenneth Bridges, S.M. Zazzi, Giacomo Bonito, David Hope, David Ronis, Phyllis Macchione, Livia Magyar, John and Kathleen Kaczmarek, K.P. Lardbon, Peter R. Hayes, Marsia Cottam, R. Healey, Amanda Wilkie, N.K. Campbell, E. Clifford, Linda Morley, Mollie Bickerstaff, Fiona Owen, Chalice Wilkerson, Nancy Altobelli, Marcella Booth, Martin Spafford, Andrew Stansfield and Elspeth French, Massimo Spiga, Jacqueline Finnegan, Nicky Moran, Mark Williams, Stephen Warburton, Alice S. Kao, Joseph Jordan, Stephen McKenna, R. Gunby, Catherine Blanchfield and Maurice Buccoliéro, Trudy and Chris Coe, Helen Jackson, David Caird, I. Scatigno, Michael Bane, P.M. Taylor, Marilyn Relf, Doreen Phillips, T.J. English, Roberta Wedge, Hamish Jack, Julie Odell, Alan Shelston, Kate Ludkin, Ruth Sullivan and Richard Hand, Agnes Hollander, R. Scott, Dee Carter, Gary Hampson, Griselda and Peter Barton, the people who live in the lower flat in London E5, A. Sword, Arun Mukherjee, Bill Rebeck, Damian Davies, Chris Tighe and Ian Wilson, Lisa Somerville, Katie Hill, Tracey Johnston, Ruth Itzhaki, Alex and Mary Carswell, Lisa Bollini, Jenny Roberts, Alison Goff, Joanna El Nemr, John C. Pinca, J.P. Dalton, Mark Lawton, J.W. Tempel, Kathrina Herren, Ellen and Alex Polsky, Lynne Cotton, Dan Estup, G. Hughes, Tracey Claxton, Julie Radcliffe, Richard Spitz, Susan Lee, Ann and Nuala O'Duffy, P.E. Field and L.F. Kelly. Apologies for anyone we may have missed... and please keep writing!

CONTENTS

INTRODUCTION

Of European countries, **Italy** is perhaps the hardest to classify. It is a modern, industrialised nation, with companies like *Fiat* and *Olivetti* market-leaders in their field. It is the harbinger of style, its designers leading the way with each season's fashions. But it is also, to an equal degree, a Mediterranean country, with all that that implies. Agricultural land covers much of the country, a lot of it, especially in the south, still owned under almost feudal conditions. In the towns and villages all over the country, life stops during the middle of the day for a siesta, and is strongly family-orientated, with an emphasis on the traditions and rituals of the Catholic church – which, notwithstanding a growing scepticism among the country's youth, still dominates people's lives here to an immediately obvious degree.

Above all Italy provokes reaction. Its people are volatile, rarely indifferent to anything, and on one and the same day you might encounter the kind of disdain dished out to tourist masses worldwide, and an hour later be treated with almost embarrassing hospitality. If there is a single national characteristic, it's to embrace life to the full: in the hundreds of local festivals taking place across the country on any given day, to celebrate a saint or the local harvest; in the importance placed on good food; in the obsession with clothes and image; and above all in the daily domestic ritual of the collective evening stroll or *passeggiata* – a sociable affair celebrated by young and old alike in every town and village across the country.

It's important to remember that Italy wasn't a unified state until 1861, and this is borne out by its regional nature. Italians often feel more loyalty to their region than the nation as a whole – something manifest in different cuisines, dialects, landscape, and often varying standards of living. There is also, of course, the country's enormous cultural legacy: Tuscany alone has more classified historical monuments than any country in the world; there are considerable remnants of the Roman empire all over the country, notably of course in Rome itself; and every region retains its own relics of an artistic tradition generally acknowledged to be the world's richest.

Yet there's no reason to be intimidated by the art and architecture. If you want to lie on a beach, there are any number of places to do it: unlike, say, Spain, development has been kept relatively under control, and many resorts are still largely the preserve of Italian tourists. Other parts of the coast, especially in the south of the country, are almost entirely undiscovered. Beaches are for the most part sandy, and doubts about the cleanliness of the water have been confined to the northern part of the Adriatic coast. Mountains, too, run the country's length – from the Alps and Dolomites in the North right along the Apennines, which form the spine of the peninsula – and are an important reference-point for most Italians: skiing and other winter sports are practised avidly, and in the five national parks, protected from the national passion for hunting, wildlife of all sorts thrives.

Italy North by South

Italy breaks down into twenty regions, which in turn divide into different provinces. Some of these regional boundaries reflect long-standing historic borders, like Tuscany, Lombardy or the Veneto; others, like Friuli-Venezia Giulia or Molise, are more recent administrative divisions, often established in recognition of quite modern distinctions. But the sharpest division is between north and south. The North is one of the most

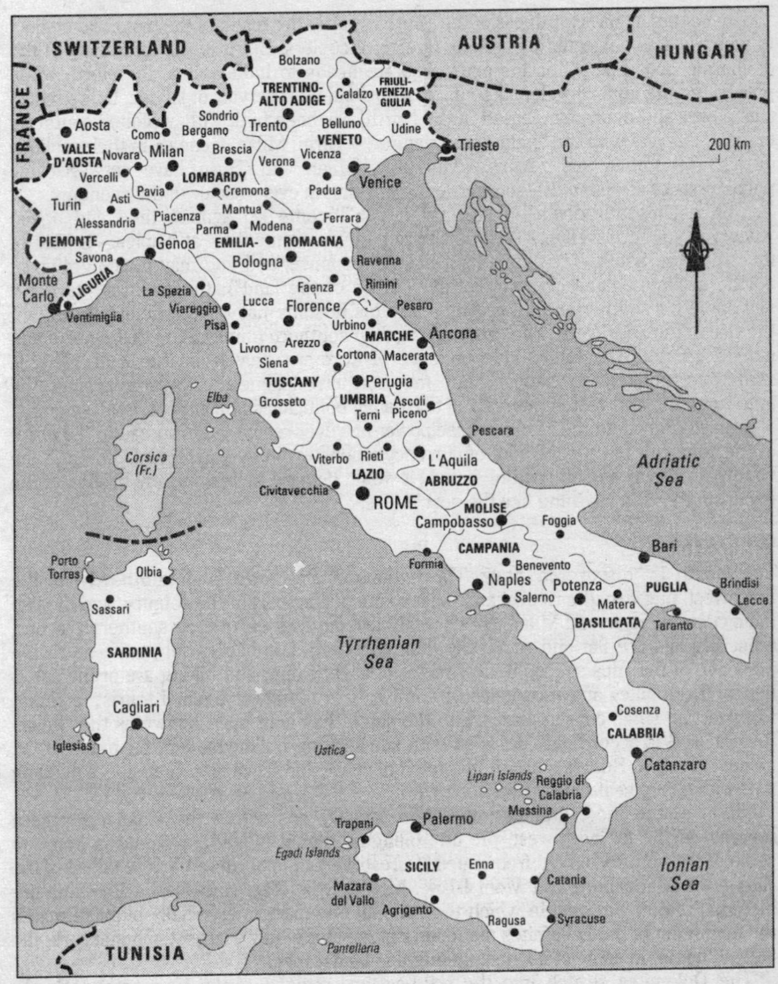

advanced industrial societies in the world, a region that despite recent hiccups is one of extraordinary economic dynamism. Its people speak Italian with the cadences of France or Germany; its "capital", Milan, is a thoroughly European city. The South, known as *il mezzogiorno*, begins somewhere between Rome and Naples, and is by contrast one of the economically most depressed areas in Europe. Its rate of unemployment (about twenty percent) is more than twice that of the North, its gross regional product about a third. And its history of absolutist regimes often seems carried over into the present by the presence of the Mafia, and the remote hand of central government in Rome. Its people are darker-skinned and speak with the cadences of the Mediterranean, the dialect sounding almost Arabic in some places; indeed its "capital" city, Naples, is often compared with Cairo.

The economic backwardness of the South is partly the result of the historical neglect to which it was subjected by various foreign occupiers. But it is also the result of the deliberate policy of politicians and corporate heads to industrialise the North while preserving the underdeveloped South as a convenient reservoir of labour. Italy's industrial power and dynamism, based in the North, has been built with exploited southerners who emigrated to the "Industrial Triangle" – Turin, Milan, Genoa – in their millions during the Fifties and Sixties. Even now, Milan and Turin have very sizeable populations of *meridionali* – southerners – working in every sector of the economy.

This north-south divide is something you'll come up against time and again, wherever you're travelling. To a northerner the mere mention of Naples – a kind of totem for the South – can provoke a hostile response; and you may notice graffiti in northern cities against *terroni* (literally "those of the land"), the offensive northern nickname for southerners. In recent years this hostility has been articulated through the rise of the *Lega Nord*, who campaign against southern immigration to the north and indeed promote the future independence of northern Italy from the south. This is somewhat unlikely to happen, but the northern league's campaign against the entrenchment and vested interests of the Italian political establishment, not to mention organised crime and the Mafia (whose power has over recent years spread to the north of the country), has gained a lot of currency among ordinary voters; and, although the country is a long way off splitting in two, it would be hard to imagine any healing of the north-south rift in anything like the near future.

Where to go

The **North** is "discovered" Italy. The regions of **Piemonte** and **Lombardy**, in the northwest, make up the richest and most cosmopolitan part of the country, and the two main centres, Turin and Milan, are its wealthiest large cities. In their southern reaches, these regions are flat and scenically dull, especially Lombardy, but in the north the presence of the Alps shapes the character of each: skiing and hiking are prime activities, and the lakes and mountains of Lombardy are long-established tourist territory. **Liguria**, the small coastal province to the south, has long been known as the "Italian Riviera" and is accordingly crowded with sun-seeking holidaymakers for much of the summer season. But it's a beautiful stretch of coast, and its capital, Genoa, is a bustling port with a long seafaring tradition.

Much of the most dramatic mountain scenery lies within the smaller northern regions. In the far northwest, the tiny bilingual region of **Valle d'Aosta** is home to some of the country's most frequented ski resorts, and is bordered by the tallest of the Alps – the Matterhorn and Mont Blanc. Moving east, **Trentino-Alto Adige**, another bilingual region, and one in which the national boundary is especially blurred, marks the beginning of the Dolomites mountain range, where Italy's largest national park, the Stelvio, lies amid some of its most memorable landscapes.

The Dolomites stretch into the northeastern regions of the **Veneto** and **Friuli-Venezia Giulia**. However here the main focus of interest is, of course, Venice: a unique city, and every bit as beautiful as its reputation would suggest – although this means you won't be alone in appreciating it. If the crowds are too much, there's also the arc of historic towns outside the city – Verona, Padua and Vicenza, all centres of interest in their own right, although rather overshadowed by their illustrious neighbour. To the south, the region of **Emilia-Romagna** has been at the heart of Italy's post-war industrial boom and has a standard of living on a par with Piemonte and Lombardy, although oddly enough it's also the traditional stronghold of the Italian Left. Its coast is popular among Italians, and Rimini is about Italy's brashest, tackiest seaside resort. You'd do better to ignore the beaches altogether and concentrate on the ancient centres of Ravenna, Ferrara and Parma and the capital, Bologna, one of Italy's liveliest, most historic but least appreciated cities.

Central Italy represents perhaps the most commonly perceived image of the country, and **Tuscany**, with its classic rolling countryside and the art-packed towns of Florence, Pisa and Siena, to name only the three best-known centres, is one of its most-visited regions. Neighbouring **Umbria** is similar in all but its relative emptiness, though it gets fuller every year, as visitors flock into towns such as Perugia, Spoleto and Assisi. Further east still, **Marche** may in time go the same way, but for the moment is comparatively untouched, its highlights being the ancient towns of Urbino and Áscoli Piceno. South of Marche, the hills begin to pucker into mountains in the twin regions of **Abruzzo** and **Molise**, Italy's first really remote area if you're travelling north to south, centring on the country's highest peak – the Gran Sasso d'Italia. Molise, particularly, is a taster of the South, as is **Lazio** to the west, in part a poor and sometimes desolate region whose often rugged landscapes contrast with the more manicured beauty of the other central regions. Lazio's real focal point, though, is **Rome**, Italy's capital and the one city in the country which owes allegiance neither to the North *or* South, its people proudly aloof from the rest of the country's squabbles. There's nowhere quite like Rome: it's a tremendous city just to *be*, and in terms of historical sights outstrips everywhere else in the country by a long way.

The **South** proper begins south of Rome, with the region of **Campania**, which is as far as many tourists get. Naples is a petulant, unforgettable city, the spiritual heart of the Italian South, and on hand nearby are some of Italy's finest ancient sites in Pompeii and Herculaneum, not to mention the country's most spectacular stretch of coast around Amalfi. **Basilicata** and **Calabria**, which make up the instep and toe of Italy's boot, are harder territory but still rewarding, the emphasis less on art, more on the landscape and quiet, unspoilt coastlines. **Puglia**, also in the "heel" of Italy, has underrated pleasures, notably the landscape of its Gargano peninsula, the souk-like quality of its capital Bari, and the Baroque glories of Lecce in the far south. As regards **Sicily**, the island is really a law unto itself, a wide mixture of attractions ranging from some of the finest preserved Hellenistic treasures in Europe, to a couple of Italy's fanciest beach resorts in Taormina and Cefalù, not to mention some gorgeous upland scenery. Come this far south and you're closer to Africa than Milan, and it shows, in the people, the architecture, and the cooking – *couscous* featuring on many menus in the west of the island. **Sardinia**, too, feels far removed from the Italian mainland, especially in its relatively undiscovered interior, although you may be content to explore its fine beaches, which are among Italy's best.

Climate: when to go

Italy's **climate** is one of the most hospitable in the world, with a general pattern of warm, dry summers and mild winters. There are, however, marked regional variations, ranging from the more temperate northern part of the country to the firmly Mediterranean south. **Summers** are hot and dry along the coastal areas, especially as you move south, cool in the major mountain areas – the Alps and Apennines. **Winters** are mild in the south of the country, Rome and below, but in the north they can be at least as cold as Britain, sometimes worse, especially across the plains of Lombardy and Emilia-Romagna, which can be very inhospitable indeed in January.

As for **when to go**, if you're planning to visit fairly touristed areas, especially beach resorts, avoid July and August, when the weather can be too hot and the crowds at their most congested; August is when the Italians go on holiday so expect the crush to be especially bad in the resorts and the scene in the major historic cities – Rome, Florence, Venice – to be slightly artificial as the only people around are fellow-tourists. The nicest time to visit, in terms of the weather and lack of crowds, is April to late June, or September and October. If you're planning to swim, however, bear in mind that only the south of the country may be warm enough outside the May–September period.

AVERAGE TEMPERATURES (°C)

	Jan	Feb	Mar	Apr	May	June	July	Aug	Sept	Oct	Nov	Dec
Ancona	5.7	5.8	9.4	13.6	17.6	22.3	24.9	24.3	21.1	16.6	12.6	7.4
Bari	8.4	8.5	10.8	13.9	17.5	21.9	24.5	24.3	21.7	18.2	14.8	10.2
Bologna	2.5	3.4	8.6	13.8	18.1	23.3	26.0	25.4	21.3	15.2	9.7	3.9
Cagliari	10.5	11.0	13.0	15.0	18.5	22.5	25.5	25.5	23.0	19.0	15.0	12.5
Florence	5.6	5.8	9.9	13.3	17.4	22.1	25.0	24.5	21.2	15.8	11.2	6.0
Genoa	8.4	8.7	11.5	14.5	17.8	21.9	24.6	25.0	21.8	18.1	13.3	9.5
Milan	1.9	3.8	8.6	13.2	17.3	22.2	24.8	23.9	20.3	13.7	8.5	3.0
Naples	8.7	8.7	11.4	14.3	18.1	22.3	24.8	24.8	22.3	18.1	14.5	10.3
Palermo	10.3	10.4	13.0	16.2	18.7	23.0	25.3	25.1	23.2	19.9	16.8	12.6
Rome	7.4	8.0	11.5	14.4	18.4	22.9	25.7	25.5	22.4	17.7	13.4	8.9
Trieste	5.3	4.8	8.6	12.9	17.1	21.2	24.0	23.8	20.8	15.6	11.0	6.3
Venice	3.8	4.1	8.2	12.6	17.1	21.2	23.6	23.3	20.4	15.1	10.5	5.0

°C = (°F - 32) multiplied by 5/9

PART ONE

THE BASICS

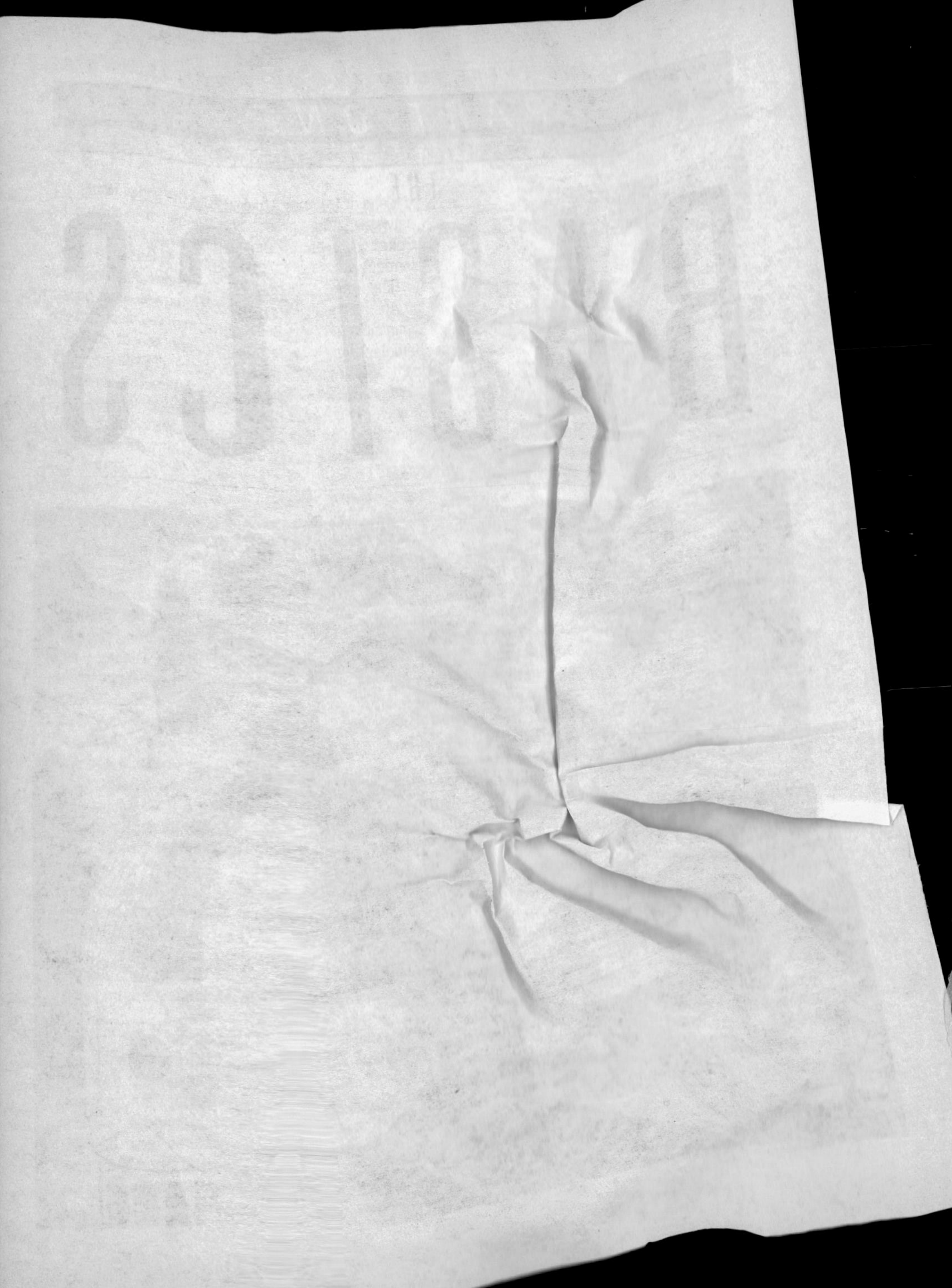

GETTING THERE FROM THE UK AND IRELAND

The easiest way to get to Italy from Britain is to fly, and prices, for charter flights at least, compare well with those for the long train journey, and even scheduled fares can prove good value. Deals change all the time, and prices depend on where you want to fly to. The majority of flights go to Milan and Rome, with usually at least one daily flight to Bologna, Pisa, Naples and Turin; onward connections are obviously possible from these gateway cities to smaller regional airports. Costs broadly reflect the distance and popularity of the place you're travelling to – flights to Milan, for instance, can be a great deal cheaper than those to Palermo.

BY PLANE

A **scheduled flight** is the most obvious, if not always the cheapest, option. The only airlines flying the Italian routes are *British Airways* and *Alitalia*, who between them fly direct from **London** Heathrow and Gatwick to Bologna (twice daily); to Milan (around 10 times daily during the week, around 8 times daily at weekends); to Naples (twice daily); to Pisa (3 times daily); to Rome (8 times daily); to Turin (around 3 times daily); and to Venice (twice daily); *British Airways* also fly from **Manchester** to Milan twice a day during the week, once daily at weekends, and to Rome once a week.

Although you can find scheduled deals for as little as £150 return in low season – broadly from the end of October through to the end of March – between April and September the cheapest **ticket** you'll get is an ordinary Apex fare, which currently goes for £250–280 to Milan, £270–300 to Rome, and £280–320 to Naples. Restrictions on Apex tickets are normally that you must book a minimum of 7 days in advance, you must stay a Saturday night abroad, and you cannot change the details of your ticket without upgrading it.

You can usually cut costs by booking through an agent, who will often be able to sell you the same scheduled seat cheaper, or do you a deal on a **direct charter** flight, although you'd be advised to make enquiries some weeks in advance during peak season. You can also approach one of the charter operators direct – see below for their details.

For discounted flights, look at the classified sections in the Sunday newspapers – the *Sunday Times* or *Observer* especially – and if you live in London, *Time Out* magazine and the *Evening Standard* newspaper. There are a number of Italian flight specialists (see below for addresses), offering a wide array of flights to a broad selection of Italian gateway cities; or you could approach a student/youth travel specialist like *Campus Travel* or *STA Travel* (again, see below for details), who offer all kinds of discounted fares. Using one of these outfits, you can reckon on paying as little as £100–120 to one of the major gateways in low season, and you should be able to find something for under £200 even during the height of summer. On a tight budget, one deal worth considering is Italy Sky-Shuttle's **"Air Coach" deals**, whereby you travel out by air and back by *Eurolines* bus from Milan or Turin after a stay of 6–12 nights. Costs can be up to 50 percent of Italy Sky-Shuttle's regular flights – basically under £100 return, even in high season.

Most agents offer **"open-jaw"** deals, whereby you can fly into one Italian city and back from another – a good idea if you want to make your way across the country, and often no more expensive than a standard charter return. Consider also a **package deal** (see below), which takes care of flights and accommodation for an all-in price. Package operators can also be a source of cheap charter flights.

AIRLINES

Alitalia, 27 Piccadilly, London W1 (☎071/602 7111).

British Airways, 75 Regent St, London W1 (☎081/897 4000).

AGENTS

CampusTravel, 52 Grosvenor Gardens, London SW1 (☎071/730 3402). Also with branches in Bristol, Cambridge, Oxford and Edinburgh.

Council Travel, 28a Poland St, London W1 (☎071/287 3377).

CTS Travel, 44 Goodge St, London W1 (☎071/637 5601).

Flight File, 49 Tottenham Court Rd, London W1 (☎071/323 1515).

Italflights, 125 High Holborn, London WC1 (☎071/405 6771).

Italia nel Mondo, 6 Palace St, London SW1 (☎071/834 7651).

Italone, 200 Tottenham Court Rd, London W1 (☎071/637 1284).

Inter-Air, Liberty House, 222 Regent St, London W1 (☎071/439 6633).

Mundus Air Travel, 5 Peter St, London W1 (☎071/437 2272).

Nouvelles Frontières, 11 Blenheim St, London W1 (☎071/629 7772).

Orion, 320 Regent St, London W1 (☎071/580 8267).

STA Travel, 86 Old Brompton Rd, London SW7; 117 Euston Rd, London NW1 (☎071/937 9921). Also with branches in Bristol, Cambridge, Oxford and Manchester.

CHARTER OPERATORS

Italy Skybus, 24 Earls Court Gardens, London SW5 (☎071/373 6055).

Italy Sky Shuttle, 227 Shepherds Bush Rd, London W6 (☎081/748 1333).

LAI, 185 Kings Cross Rd, London WC1 (☎071/837/8492).

BY TRAIN

Travelling by **train** to Italy won't save much money, certainly not if you're over 26, but it can be a more pleasurable way of getting to the country, giving the opportunity to stop off in other parts of Europe on the way. Fares vary according to the route you follow: the fastest you can reach Milan is in about 18 hours, although it can take up to 6 hours longer, while travelling all the way to Sicily can take up to 42 hours. Tickets are valid for two months, and you *can* stop off on the way, so the route you follow is obviously important. The cheapest ordinary **return fare** to Milan will cost you around £140, while to Rome you'll pay about £176 on the cheapest route; the fare is around £200 if you're going right down to Sicily.

If you're **under 26**, its possible to purchase a discounted *BIJ* ticket from London to any Italian destination, again valid for up to two months and giving as many stopovers as you like, although again this doesn't actually save very much – ten percent at most. *BIJ* tickets are available from *Eurotrain* (address above), student and youth travel agents and some high street agents. You can also arrange connecting fares at a discount from outside London, or – if you prefer – qualify for reduced price tickets if you join the train at the Channel ports. *Eurotrain* also sell *Explorer* tickets – like a rail pass, but offering a set route through Europe to Rome and Venice; prices start at £180.

All in all, if you are planning a trip through Europe, and travelling around Italy once you're there, it might be a better idea to invest in an **InterRail** pass if you're under 26. This costs £249, is valid for one month's unlimited rail travel throughout Europe, and gives discounts on cross-Channel services and some ferry routes in Europe. Once in Italy, the rail system is comprehensive and efficient, and much the best way of getting around the country. *InterRail* passes are available from British Rail stations and youth/student travel agents, and you need to have been resident in Europe for at least six months to qualify for one.

RAIL TICKET OFFICES

Eurotrain, 52 Grosvenor Gardens, London SW1 (☎071/730 8518).

International Rail Centre, Victoria Station, London SW1 (☎071/834 2345).

Italian State Railways, Marco Polo House, 3–5 Landsdowne Rd, Croydon, Surrey (☎081/686 0677).

Ultima Travel, 424 Chester Rd, Little Sutton, South Wirral, L66 3RB (☎051/339 6171).

Wasteels, 121 Wilton Rd, London SW1 (☎071/834 7066).

CROSS-CHANNEL FERRIES

Hoverspeed, Maybrook House, Queens Gardens, Dover CT17 9UQ (☎0304/240202).

P&O European Ferries, Channel House, Channel View Rd, Dover CT17 9TJ (☎0304/203388);
London (☎081/575 8555).

Sally Line, Argyle Centre, York St, Ramsgate, Kent CT11 9DS (☎0843/595522); 81 Picadilly, London W1V 9HF (☎071/858 1127).

Stena Sealink, Charter House, Park St, Ashford, Kent TN24 8EX (☎0233/647047).

Whichever method you plump for, it's well worth **reserving** a **seat**, currently about £2 for each train you travel on, and a **couchette bed** (around £10), for at least part of your journey – something you should do well in advance.

BY BUS

It's difficult to see why anyone would want to travel to Italy by **bus**. But if you do have a phobia about trains and planes, there are direct services to Turin, Milan, Bologna, Florence and Rome. The Milan service takes around 27 hours, and Rome a gruelling 36 hours. Run by *National Express Eurolines* (☎071/730 0202), coaches leave at least three times weekly during the summer: tickets to Milan cost about £117 return, to Rome £136 return, with reductions of around 10 percent for under-26s and students; children go half-price.

BY ROAD

There's no one fixed route to Italy if you're travelling under your own steam. The best cross-Channel options for most drivers and hitchers will be the standard **ferry/hovercraft** links between Dover and Calais or Boulogne (with *Hoverspeed*, *P&O* or *Stena Sealink*), Folkestone and Boulogne (*Hoverspeed*), or Ramsgate and Dunkerque (*Sally Lines*). Any travel agent can provide up-to-date schedules and make advance bookings – essential in season if you're driving. You can also contact the **ferry companies** direct – details below.

From northern France, the Alpine route, via Germany and Switzerland, is probably the shortest as the crow flies, but can be pretty arduous; most drivers hotfoot it to the south of France and then switch east into northern Italy. Certainly this is a preferable option for **hitchers**: getting rides south is notoriously difficult from the Channel ports and you're most likely to pick up a lift in the direction of Paris. From here the N7 road provides a direct – and reasonably hitchable – route south to Provence.

PACKAGE AND ORGANISED TOURS

Italy stands somewhat apart from other European package destinations: it's not especially cheap and has avoided the big hotel build-ups that have blighted parts of Spain and Greece. And it's as much a venue for specialist interest and touring holidays as sun-sand-sea packages.

That said, there's no shortage of **travel-plus-accommodation** deals on the market, and if you're keen to stay in one (or two) places, they can work out at very good value, especially if you live some way from London. Many companies offer travel at rates as competitive as you could find on your own, and any travel agent can fill you in on all the latest offers. All the usual companies – *Thomson*, etc – go to Italy, but there are a number of specialist operators too, like *Magic of Italy* or *Citalia*, with a predictably better range of holidays on offer. It's obviously cheapest to travel **out of season**, something we'd recommend anyway as the resorts and sights are much less crowded, and the weather, in the south at least, is often warm enough to swim. Prices start at around £500 per person per week for half-board in a hotel during May in Amalfi or Sorrento, though you may be able to do it a little cheaper in less popular resorts, or somewhere more downmarket like Rimini. In **high season**

SPECIALIST TOUR OPERATORS

Alternative Travel Group, 69–71 Banbury Rd, Oxford OX2 6PE (☎0865/310399). All-inclusive walking holidays in Tuscany, Umbria, and Sicily. Costly, but very well-organised.

Citalia, 50–51 Conduit St, London W1 (☎071/686 5533). Hotel and villa packages all over Italy.

Italiatours, 241 Euston Rd, London NW1 (☎071/383 3886). Package deals, city breaks, winter sun holidays and specialist Italian cuisine tours.

Italian Escapades, 227 Shepherds Bush Rd, London W6 (☎081/748 2661). A large variety of package holidays. The only specialist operator that allows you to design your own holiday from the brochure.

Italy Sky Shuttle, 227 Shepherds Bush Rd, London W6 (☎081/748 1333). Various packages, as well as good fly-drive deals.

Magic of Italy, 227 Shepherds Bush Green, London W12 (☎081/748 7575). Hotel and villa packages in Tuscany, the Amalfi coast, Sicily and Sardinia, and city breaks.

Sunvil Holidays, 7–8 Upper Square, Old Isleworth, Middx TW7 7BJ (☎081/568 4499). Hotel and villa packages, city breaks and fly-drives.

Time Off, Chester Close, Chester St, London SW1 (☎071/235 8070). Short break specialists offering holidays in Milan, Florence, Venice and Rome.

(Easter, July and August), all these prices shoot up considerably, and you can expect to pay as much as £700–1000 for a week's half-board in Amalfi, Sorrento or Taormina, although your travel agent might come up with some good, last-minute deals.

Some operators organise **specialist holidays** to Italy – walking tours, art and archaeology holidays, Italian food and wine jaunts – but they don't come cheaply: accommodation, food, local transport and the services of a guide are nearly always included, and a week's half-board holiday can cost anything from £500–700 per person. There are also many operators selling **short-break deals** to Italian cities: for these, reckon on spending from about £200 per person for three nights in Florence in a two-star hotel, upwards of £250 between March and October.

If you want to rent a car in Italy, it's well worth checking with tour operators before you leave as some **fly/drive deals** work out very cheaply. *Italian Escapades* (see above) have good prices – from about £180 a week per person in summer – but check out also *Sunvil*, *Italy Sky Shuttle* and *Italiatour*, who all offer some kind of fly-drive deal.

FROM IRELAND

No airline offers direct flights from Ireland to Italy – the cheapest way of flying from Ireland is to get to London and then catch an Italy-bound plane from there. There are numerous daily flights **from Dublin**, operated by *Ryanair*, *Aer Lingus* and *British Midland* – the cheapest are *Ryanair*, which cost from around IR£60 for a return to Luton or Stansted, though the cost of the bus and underground journeys across London may make the total cost greater than *Aer Lingus* or *British Midland* fares to Heathrow. **From Belfast**, there are *British Airways* and *British Midland* flights to Heathrow, but the cheapest service is the *Britannia Airways* run to Luton, at around £70 return. From Dublin you can slightly undercut the plane's price by getting a **Eurotrain** ticket (IR£45 return), but from Belfast you'll save nothing by taking the train and ferry. For the best youth/student deals from either city, go to *USIT* (see box below).

AIRLINES AND AGENCIES IN IRELAND

Aer Lingus, 42 Grafton St, Dublin 2 (☎01-794764); 46 Castle St, Belfast (☎0232/245 151)

British Airways, 9 Fountain Centre, College St, Belfast (☎0232/240 522).

British Midland, 54 Grafton St, Dublin 2 (☎01/798 733); Suite 2, Fountain Centre, College St, Belfast (☎0232/225 151).

Britannia Airways, no reservations office in Ireland – bookings from Luton Airport, Luton, Beds (☎0582/424 155).

Ryan Air, College Park House, 20 Nassau Street, Dublin 2 (☎01-797 444 or ☎01-770 444).

USIT, 12–21 Aston Quay, O'Connell Bridge, Dublin 2 (☎01-679 8833); Fountain Centre, College St, Belfast (☎0232/324 073).

GETTING THERE FROM AUSTRALIA & NEW ZEALAND

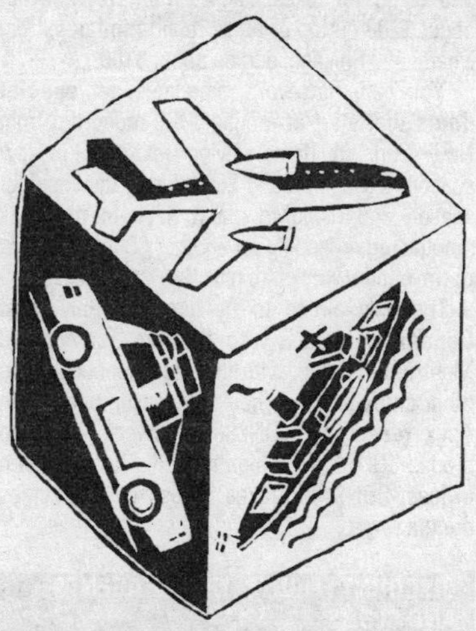

The only direct flights to Italy from Australia are to **Rome** – from Melbourne, Sydney or Auckland. Two airlines fly these routes, *Qantas* and the Indonesian carrier *Garuda*, and their fares are pretty well the same, rising from about Aus$1700 in low season to Aus$2200 in high season, although you might be able to undercut these fares slightly by shopping around, scanning the ads in the *Melbourne Age* and *Sydney Morning Herald* or approaching an agent. From New Zealand, return flights to Rome with *Garuda* or *Thai* cost from around NZ$2300 in low season to a peak of NZ$2900. One of the best agents to try is the long-established *STA*, who operate out of several branches in both Australia and New Zealand – head office addresses below. Alternatively, from either country you can always pick up whatever deal you can get to **London** and take a cheap charter to Italy from there.

STA HEAD OFFICES.

Australia: 224 Faraday St, Carlton 3053, Melbourne (☎03/347 4711).

New Zealand: 10 High St, Auckland (☎09/309 9723).

GETTING THERE FROM NORTH AMERICA

You can fly to Italy direct from a number of US and Canadian cities: the main points of entry are Rome and Milan, although there are plenty of connecting flights on to other Italian cities from those two gateways. Prices are quite competitive, making Italy a feasible entry-point for Europe as a whole. Many airlines and agents also offer "open-jaw" tickets, enabling you to fly into one Italian city and out from another.

FLIGHTS FROM USA AND CANADA

Flights to anywhere in Europe from North America are so competitive that it is hard to generalise about fares: there are so many special deals, with prices depending on the level of restrictions, which day you travel and how long you decide to go for. You can, of course, phone the airlines direct for details of ordinary **scheduled** fares. However, there are few general rules worth remembering. Firstly, it is during the low season – usually between the end of October and the end of March, excluding Christmas – that you will be able to take advantage of the most attractive offers, when airlines try and fill seats that might otherwise remain empty; fares increase somewhat in the so-called shoulder season – April and May, and September and October – while in the high season (June through to the end of August) fares will be at their highest. Throughout the year it is more expensive to fly at weekends rather than during the week. On all the airlines the cheapest fares are usually Apex or SuperApex tickets, although these often come loaded with restrictions: you must book well in advance, normally at least three weeks; there is often some kind of minimum and maximum stay, usually a minimum of a week or so, and a maximum of 30 days, you often have to spend at least one Saturday night abroad; and the tickets are often non-changeable and non-refundable once you have booked them. One thing worth knowing is that the direct scheduled fares charged by each airline don't vary as much as you might think; and you'll more often than not be basing your choice around things like flight timings, routes and gateway cities, ticket restrictions, and even the airline's reputation for comfort and service, as much as cost. It's a long flight, something like 9 hours from New York, Boston and the eastern Canadian cities, 12 hours from Chicago, and 15 hours from Los Angeles, so it's as well to be fairly comfortable and to arrive at a reasonably sociable hour.

Alitalia, the international airline of Italy, fly the widest choice of **routes between USA and Italy**. They fly direct every day from New York, Boston, Miami, Chicago and Los Angeles to Milan and Rome. As for American-based airlines, *Delta Airlines* fly daily from New York, Chicago and Los Angeles to Rome and Milan; *Trans World Airlines* fly daily from New York to Milan and Rome, and around four times a week from Los Angeles to Milan and Rome; *United Airlines* fly direct from Washington to Milan and Rome once daily.

The basic round-trip **fares**, with restrictions, do vary a little between airlines, although the only true variations start with the special offers that may be available, and even these often have a tendency to be mirrored from one carrier to another. At the time of writing, for the cheapest round-trip fare, travelling midweek in low season, you could expect to pay in the region of $650 from New York or Boston to Rome, rising to around $700 during the shoulder season, and to about $950 during the high summer months. Travelling on a weekend will normally cost you around $50 more, while you should also add on $20 or so for taxes. Flights from LA work out about $200 on top of these round-trip fares; from Miami and Chicago, add on about $100.

You can, however, sometimes get **special deals** that start at around $400 round-trip from New York to Rome, flying midweek in low season, through around $650 during the shoulder season and rising to about $750 in the peak months, again adding on another $50 if you want to travel on a weekend, plus the usual taxes.

The only airline to fly direct to Italy **from Canada** is *Alitalia* who fly from Toronto and Montréal to Rome, with the usual connections to other cities in Italy. Their low-season one-month Apex **fare** costs CDN$899 midweek, rising to around CDN$1200 in high season. Always add on at least CDN$40 in taxes. Fares from both cities are the same.

DISCOUNT FLIGHTS: TRAVEL AGENTS AND CLUBS

You can of course bypass the airlines altogether and go straight to a **travel agent**, who will at least guide you through the maze of fares even if they can't offer anything cheaper, and they will often be able to at least match any special deals the airlines are offering direct. Check the Sunday newspapers' travel sections, which are alwayss advertising discounted fares, or consult a **youth and student specialist** like *Council Travel* or *STA Travel*, who often have the best deals, and

AIRLINES

Alitalia, 666 Fifth Ave, New York, NY 10103 (☎212/582 8900 or 800/223 5730); 2055 Peel St, Montréal, PQ H3A 1V8 (☎514/842 5201); 120 Adelaide St West, Toronto, ON M5H 2E1 (☎416/363 2001).

Delta Airlines, Hartsfield Atlanta International Airport, Atlanta, GA 30320 (☎404/765 5000 or ☎800/241 4141).

Trans World Airlines, 100 South Bedford Rd, Mount Kisco, NY 10549 (☎212/290 2141 or 800/892 4141).

United Airlines, PO Box 66100, O'Hare International Airport, Chicago, IL 60666 (☎312/952 4000 or 800/538 2929).

RAIL ADDRESSES

CIE Tours International, 108 Ridgedale Ave, Morristown, NJ 07690 (☎201/292 3438 or 800/522 5258).

Italian State Railways, 666 Fifth Avenue, New York, NY 10113 (☎212/697 2100).

Rail Europe, 226–230 Westchester Ave, White Plains, NY 10604 (☎914/682 2999 or 800/438 7245); and branches in Santa Monica, San Francisco, Fort Lauderdale, Chicago, Dallas, Vancouver and Montréal.

DISCOUNT FLIGHT AGENTS, TRAVEL CLUBS, CONSOLIDATORS

Access International, 101 W 31st St, Suite 104, New York, NY 10001 (☎800/TAKE-OFF). Consolidator with good East Coast and central US deals.

Council Travel, 205 E 42nd St, New York, NY 10017 (☎212/661 1450). Head office of the nationwide US student travel organization. Branches in San Francisco, LA, Washington, New Orleans, Chicago, Seattle, Portland, Minneapolis, Boston, Atlanta and Dallas, to name only the larger ones.

Encore Short Notice, 4501 Forbes Blvd, Lanham, MD 20706 (☎301/459 8020 or 800/638 9278). East Coast travel club.

Interworld, 3400 Coral Way, Miami, FL 33145 (☎305/443 4929). Southeastern US consolidator.

Moment's Notice, 425 Madison Ave, New York, NY 10017 (☎212/486 0503). Travel club that's good for last-minute deals.

Nouvelles Frontières, 12 E 33rd St, New York, NY 10016 (☎212/779 0600); 800 bd de Maisonneuve Est, Montréal, PQ H2L 4L8 (☎514/288 9942). Main US and Canadian branches of the French discount travel outfit. Other branches in LA, San Francisco and Québec City.

STA Travel, 48 E 11th St, New York, NY 10003 (☎212/477 7166); 166 Geary St, Suite 702, San Francisco, CA 94108 (☎415/391 8407). Main US branches of the originally Australian and now worldwide specialist in independent and student travel. Other offices in LA, Boston and Honolulu.

Stand Buys, 311 W Superior St, Chicago, IL 60610 (☎800/331 0257). Good Midwestern travel club.

TFI Tours, 34 W 32nd St, New York, NY 10001 (☎212/736 1149 or 800/825 3834). The very best East Coast deals, especially worth looking into if you only want to fly one-way.

Travac, 1177 N Warson Rd, St Louis, MO 63132 (☎800/872 8800). Good central US consolidator.

Travel Avenue, 180 N Jefferson, Chicago, IL 60606 (☎312/876 1116 or 800/333 3335). Discount travel agent.

Travel Brokers, 50 Broad St, New York, NY 10004 (☎800/999 8748). New York travel club.

Travel Cuts, 187 College St, Toronto, ON M5T 1P7 (☎416/979 2406). Main office of the Canadian student travel organization. Many other offices nationwide.

Travelers Advantage, 49 Music Square, Nashville, TN 37203 (☎800/548 1116). Reliable travel club.

Unitravel, 1177 N Warson Rd, St Louis, MO 63132 (☎800/325 2027). Reliable consolidator.

Worldwide Discount Travel Club, 1674 Meridian Ave, Miami Beach, FL 33139 (☎305/534 2082).

not just for students. Another option is to contact a **discount travel club** – organizations which specialize in selling off the unsold seats of travel agents for bargain rates, often at up to half the original price, though you usually have to be a member to get the best deals. You could also try a so-called airline ticket **consolidator**, who sells the unsold seats direct from airlines, though bear in mind that discounts are usually not as high as with travel clubs and you may not get the exact flight you want.

PACKAGES AND ORGANISED TOURS

There are dozens of companies operating group travel and tours in Italy, ranging from full-blown luxury escorted tours to small groups sticking to specialized itineraries; if you're happy to stay in one (or two) places), you can also of course simply book a hotel-plus-flight deal, or, if you're keener to self-cater. rent a villa or a farmhouse for a week or two. Prices vary wildly, so check what you are getting for your money (many don't include the cost of the airfare). Reckon on paying at least $1500 for a ten-day touring vacation, up to as much as $3000 for a fourteen-day city package.

TRAVELLING VIA GREAT BRITAIN

It might be a good idea to transit **via Britain**, since there's a broad range of well-priced flights available to London from all North America, and there is a wide choice of options to Italy once there. **Flying** is the most straightforward way to get from Britain to Italy, and prices are competitive; see above for full details of flights and rail deals from Britain and Ireland. If you're interested in seeing more of Europe, the long **rail** journey may be more appealing. For students in particular there are very good deals to be had with the *InterRail* and *Eurail* passes (see above, "Getting There from the UK and Ireland", and below, "Travelling by Rail").

TRAVELLING BY RAIL

If you're interested in seeing more of Europe en route to Italy, travelling **by train** from Britain may be more appealing, though be prepared for prices comparable to air fares if you're over 26, and a shortest possible journey time of at least 18 hours from London. If you're under 26, however, a range of youth fares is available, including **BIJ youth tickets** and **Explorer** tickets (see "Getting There from Britain", above), which have to be bought in Britain, or – the most attractive option – a **Eurail Youthpass**, which gives unlimited travel in seventeen countries and costs $508 for one month or $698 for two. It must be bought before leaving home (outlets are given above), as must the other kinds of *Eurail* pass. For over-26s there's the standard **Eurail pass**, giving 15 days' first-class travel for $460, 21 days' for $598, 1 month for $728, 2 months' for $998, or 3 months' for $1260. The **Eurail Flexipass** entitles you to a number of days' first-class travel within a two-month period: 5 days for $298; 10 days for $496; 15 days for $676; the under-26s' version of this card, the **Eurail Youth Flexipass**, costs $220, $348 and $474 respectively. If you're travelling in a group, it might be worth buying the **Eurail Saverpass**, which for $390 per person gives 15 days' first-class travel for 2 or more people travelling together – or 3 or more from April to September. Finally, the **Eurail Drive Pass**, valid for any 7 days within a period of 2 months, gives you 4 days' first-class rail travel plus 3 days' car rental for $289, with options for additional days at large discounts.

Australians and Canadians can also buy *Eurail* passes, though they must again be purchased before arrival in Europe.

RED TAPE AND VISAS

British and other EC citizens can enter Italy, and stay as long as they like, simply on production of a valid passport. The temporary *British Visitor's Passport*, available over the counter at post offices, is valid for one year; full ten-year passports are available from passport offices, and you should allow around a month for delivery. Citizens of the United States, Canada, Australia and New Zealand need only a valid passport, too, but are limited to stays of three months. All other nationals should consult the relevant embassies about visa requirements.

Legally, you're required to register with the police within three days of entering Italy, though if you're staying at a hotel this will be done for you. Some policemen are more punctilious about this than ever, though others would be amazed and baffled by any attempt to register yourself down at the local police station while on holiday. If you're going to be staying for some time and working, you may as well do it; see p.44 for more details.

ITALIAN EMBASSIES AND CONSULATES

AUSTRALIA: 61–69 Macquarie St, Sydney 2000, NSW (☎02/2478 442); 509 St. Kilda Road, Melbourne (☎03/867 5744).

CANADA: 136 Beverley St, Toronto (☎416/977 1566).

IRELAND: 63–65 Northumberland Rd, Dublin (☎01/601 744); 7 Richmond Park, Belfast (☎0232/668 854).

NEW ZEALAND: 34 Grant Rd, Wellington (☎04/7473 5339).

UK: 38 Eaton Place, London SW1 (☎071/235 9371); 6 Melville Crescent, Edinburgh 3 (☎031/226 3631); 111 Picadilly, Manchester (☎061/228 7041).

USA: 690 Park Ave, New York (☎212/737 9100); 12400 Wilshire Blvd, Suite 300, Los Angeles (☎213/826 6207).

COSTS, MONEY AND BANKS

The days are long gone when Italy was a relatively cheap country to visit: the economic boom and the glut of visitors in the more touristy cities have conspired to make prices roughly on a par with the UK, and in certain cases even more expensive. Generally you'll find the poorer South much less expensive than the wealthier, more European North: as a broad guide, expect to pay most in Venice, Milan, Florence and Bologna, less in Rome, while in Naples and Sicily prices come down to fairly reasonable levels.

AVERAGE COSTS

A number of **basic things** are reasonably inexpensive: a pizza or plate of pasta with a beer (the staple cheap meal in a restaurant) will set you back £7–10 on average, though in some of the larger, more visited cities – Florence and Venice, for example – it can be difficult to find appealing venues for this; Rome and Naples, on the other hand, are no problem. Buses and trains are cheap too, the rail journey from Rome to Milan, for instance, costing just £42 for a second-class return – an eight-hour, six-hundred-kilometre trip. Drinking, by contrast, is pricey: soft drinks or coffee all cost around the same price, if not more than in Britain; a large glass of beer can cost up to £3, even more if you decide to sit down. Room rates, too, start at a bottom-line of £20 for the most basic double room in a one-star hotel, although again in Milan, Florence or Venice it's hard to find anything under £30. Overall, in central Italy, if you're watching your budget – camping, hitching a little, buying food from shops and markets – you could get by on around £20 a day; a more realistic **average daily budget** – staying in one-star hotels, taking trains and eating one cheap meal out a day – would be approaching £35, perhaps a few pounds less in the south; while to live reasonably well you probably need to spend at least £45 a day.

Bear in mind, too, that the **time of year** can make a big difference. During the height of summer, in July and August when the Italians take their holidays, hotel prices can escalate; outside the season, however, you can often negotiate much lower rates. There are few **reductions** or discounts for students or young people over 18: only a handful of museums accept ISIC cards, and buses and trains never do, although under-18s and over-65s will often be able to get to museums and archaeological sites for free.

MONEY AND BANKS

The Italian unit of **money** is the *Lira* (plural *Lire*), always abbreviated as L; for some time the rate has hovered around the L2000 to the pound sterling mark, about L1500 to the US dollar. Banknotes come in denominations of L1000, L2000, L5000, L10,000, L50,000 and L100,000, and coins as L50, L100, L200 and L500. You might also be given a telephone token or *gettone* in change, which is worth L200.

The easiest and safest way to carry your money is as **travellers' cheques**, available for a small commission (1 percent of the amount ordered) from any British high street bank and some building societies, whether or not you have an account. You'll usually – though not always – pay a small commission, too, when you **exchange money** using travellers' cheques – again around 1 percent of the amount changed, although some banks will make a standard charge per cheque regardless of its denomination – usually L5000. It's worth knowing that *Thomas Cook* offices don't charge for cashing their own cheques, and *American Express* offices don't charge for cashing anyone's cheques. Alternatively, most banks can issue current account holders with a **Eurocheque card** and chequebook, with which you can get cash from the majority of banks in Italy (including from cash-dispensing machines, which can help to avoid the queues); you'll pay a few pounds service charge but usually no commission on transactions. Major **credit and charge cards** – *Visa*, *Access*, *American Express* – are also accepted in many shops, and for cash advances in many banks. It's an idea to have at least some Italian money for when you first arrive, and you can buy *lire* in advance from British banks, though you're not supposed to exceed L400,000 in cash.

In Italy, the best place to change money or travellers' cheques is at a **bank**. There are a few banking chains that you'll find nationwide, the *Banca Nazionale del Lavoro*, *Banca d'Italia* and *Cassa di Risparmio*, as well as regional chains like the *Banca di Roma*, *Banco di Napoli* or *Banco di Sicilia*. **Banking hours** are normally Monday to Friday mornings from 8.30am until 1pm, and for an hour in the afternoon (usually 3–4pm), though there are local variations on this. Outside these times, the larger hotels will change money or travellers' cheques, although if you're staying in a reasonably large city the rate is invariably better at those times at the railway station exchange bureaux – normally open evenings and weekends. Check the city "Listings" sections for locations and specific opening hours.

If you run out of money, or there is some kind of emergency, the quickest way to get **money sent out** is to contact your bank at home and have them wire the cash to the nearest bank. You can do the same thing through *Thomas Cook* or *American Express* if there is a branch nearby. You can also have cash sent out through *Western Union* (UK ☎800/833833; North America ☎800/325 6000) to a nearby bank or post office – a process which takes 2–5 days; this is a last-ditch option, though, since commission rates are punitive.

HEALTH AND INSURANCE

EC nationals can take advantage of Italy's health services under the same terms as the residents of the country. You'll need form E111, which in theory you can get by applying on form SA30 by post, one month in advance, to any DSS office in Britain. In practice it can often be issued over the counter at a main DSS office (not an Unemployment Benefit office).

HEALTH PROBLEMS

If you need treatment, go to a **doctor** (*médico*); every town and village has one. Take your E111 with you: this should enable you to get free treatment and prescriptions for medicines at the local rate – about 10 percent of the price of the medicine. If you're looking for repeat medication, take any empty bottles or capsules with you to the doctors – the brand-names often differ.

An Italian **chemist** (*farmacia*) is well-qualified to give you advice on **minor ailments**, and to dispense prescriptions, and there's generally one open all night in the bigger towns and cities. They work on a rota system, and you should find the address of the one currently open on any *farmacia* door. There's usually a phone number you can ring for addresses – see the city "Listings" sections in the *Guide*. If you are taken **seriously ill** or involved in an **accident**, hunt out the nearest hospital and go to the *Pronto Soccorso* (casualty) section; in a real emergency phone ☎113 and ask for *ospedale* or *ambulanza*. Major railway stations and airports often have first-aid stations with qualified doctors in hand.

Try to avoid going to the **dentist** (*dentista*) while you're in Sicily. These aren't covered by the *mutua* or health service, and for the smallest problem they'll make you pay through the teeth.

INSURANCE

It might be as well to take out ordinary **travel insurance** too – certainly if you're a non-EC citizen. Before you purchase any insurance, however, check what you have already. North Americans, in particular, may find themselves covered for medical expenses and loss, and possibly loss of or damage to valuables, while abroad, as part of a family or student policy. Some credit cards, too, now offer insurance benefits if you use them to pay for your holiday tickets.

Ask about policies at any bank or travel agency. It's worth shopping around to see what's on offer since premiums vary considerably.

In Britain, as well as those policies offered by travel agents, consider using a specialist, low-priced firm like *Endsleigh* (Cranfield House, 97–107 Southampton Row, London WC1; ☎071/436 4451), who offer two weeks' basic cover in Italy for around £20. For medical treatment and drugs, keep all the bills and claim the money back later. If you have anything stolen (including money), register the loss immediately with the local police – without their report you won't be able to claim.

If transiting via Britain, **North Americans** might consider buying a policy from a British travel agent. British policies tend to be cheaper than American ones, and routinely cover thefts – which are sometimes excluded from the more health-based American policies. North Americans should in any case check carefully the insurance policies they already have before taking out a new one, since it may be that you're covered already for medical and other losses while abroad. Canadians especially are usually covered by their provincial health plans, and holders of *ISIC* cards are entitled (outside the USA) to be reimbursed for $3000-worth of accident coverage and 60 days of in-patient benefits up to $100 a day for the period the card is valid. Students may also find their health coverage extends during vacations, and many bank and charge accounts include some form of travel cover; insurance is also sometimes included if you pay for your trip with a credit card. If you do want a specific travel insurance policy, there are numerous kinds to choose from: short-term combination policies covering everything from baggage loss to broken legs are the best bet and cost around $25 for 10 days, plus $1 a day for trips of 75 days or more. One thing to bear in mind is that none of the currently available policies covers theft; they only cover loss while in the custody of an identifiable person – though even then you must make a report to the police and get their written statement. Two companies you might try are *Travel Guard*, 110 Centrepoint Drive, Steven Point, WI 54480 (☎715/345-0505 or 800/826-1300), or *Access America International*, 600 Third Ave, New York, NY 10163 (☎212/949-5960 or 800/284-8300).

INFORMATION AND MAPS

Before you leave, it's well worth dropping in at the Italian State Tourist Office (ENIT) and picking up a selection of their free maps and brochures, though don't go mad – much of what they have is available in Italy itself. Worth grabbing are any accommodation listings they may have for the area you're interested in, town plans and maps of the regions, and the useful annual *Travellers Handbook*, which, although sometimes not absolutely current, can be an indispensable reference on all aspects of the country.

TOURIST OFFICES

Most Italian towns, and main city train stations and airports, have a **tourist office** – usually either an *APT* (*Azienda Promozione Turistica*), an *EPT* (*Ente Provinciale per il Turismo*) – a provincial branch of the state organisation – an *IAT* (*Ufficio di Informazione e Accoglienza Turistica*) or an *AAST* (*Azienda Autonoma di Soggiorno e Turismo*), a smaller local outfit. All offer much the same mix of general advice and bumph, free maps and accommodation lists, though rarely do they book accommodation. Very small or out-of-the-way villages may have a tiny office known as a *Pro Loco*, which gives much the same service. Only in the larger cities and more touristed areas

ITALIAN STATE TOURIST OFFICES ABROAD

CANADA: 1 Placeville Marie, Suite 1914, Montréal, Québec H3B 3M9 (☎514/866 7667 or 866 7669)

IRELAND: 47 Merrion Square, Dublin 2 (☎01-766 397 and 766 025).

UK: 1 Princes St, London W1 (☎071/408 1254); open Monday–Friday 9am–2.30pm.

USA: 630 Fifth Ave, Suite 1565, New York, NY 10111 (☎212/245 4822/23/24); 360 Post St, Suite 801, San Francisco, CA 94108 (☎415/ 392 6206 or 392 5266).

are the staff likely to speak much English. Opening hours vary, but larger city offices are likely to be open Monday–Saturday 9am–1pm and 4–7pm, and sometimes for a short period on Sunday mornings; smaller offices may open weekdays only, while *Pro Loco* times are notoriously erratic – sometimes open for only a couple of hours a day, even in summer.

A further source of information, at any rate in larger cities, is the **Tuttocittà** booklet, given away as supplement to the main telephone directories. This carries listings and phone numbers of essential services, adverts for restaurants and shops, together with indexed maps of the appropriate city. Most bars with phones have a copy, as do hotels, or you can get a look at one in a SIP or ASST public telephone office.

MAPS

The **town plans** we've printed should be fine for most purposes, and most tourist offices give out maps of their local area for free. However, if you want an indexed town plan, *Studio FMB* cover most of the country's towns and cities, and *Falk* also do decent plans of the major cities.

For **road maps**, the *Automobile Club d'Italia* issue a reasonable free map of the country, as well as a number covering individual regions, available from the State Tourist Office (see above). The clearest and best-value large-scale commercial road map of Italy is the *Michelin* 1:1,000,000 one; *Michelin* also produce 1:400,000 maps of the north and south of Italy, and of Sicily and Sardinia that are equally good value. There are also the 1:800,000 and 1:400,000 maps produced by the *Touring Club Italiano* (*TCI*), which cover north, south and central Italy, although these are a little more expensive; *TCI* also produce excellent 1:200,000 maps of the individual regions, which are indispensable if you are confining your tour to one distinct area.

For **hiking** you'll need at least a scale 1:100,000 map, better 1:50,000 or even 1:25,000. There are a number of different series: *Studio FMB* and the *TCI* cover the major mountain areas of northern Italy to a scale of 1:50,000. If you're after something still more detailed, down to scale 1:25,000, the northwest of Italy and the Alps are covered by the *Istituto Geografico Centrale* series; central and southern Italy, including Tuscany, is covered by a series of hiking maps produced by *Multigraphic (Firenze)*, while *Tabacco* produce a good series of maps detailing the Dolomites and the northeast of the country. In Italy, the *Club Alpino Italiano* (addresses in the text – see "Milan and Rome") is a good source of hiking maps.

MAP OUTLETS IN THE UK AND NORTH AMERICA

London *Daunt Books*, 83 Marylebone High St, W1 (☎071/224 2295); *National Map Centre*, 22–24 Caxton St, SW1 (☎071/222 4945); *Stanfords*, 12–14 Long Acre, WC2 (☎071/836 1321); *The Travellers' Bookshop*, 25 Cecil Court, WC2 (☎071/836 9132).

Chicago *Rand McNally*, 444 North Michigan Ave, IL 60611 (☎312/321 1751).

New York *The Complete Traveller Bookstore*, 199 Madison Ave, NY 10016 (☎212/685 9007); *Rand McNally*, 150 East 52nd St, NY 10022 (☎212/758 7488); *Traveller's Bookstore*, 22 W 52nd St, New York, NY 10019 (☎212/664 0995).

San Francisco *The Complete Traveler Bookstore*, 3207 Filmore St, CA 92123; *Rand McNally*, 595 Market St, CA 94105 (☎415/777 3131).

Seattle *Elliot Bay Book Company*, 101 S Main St, WA 98104 (☎206/624 6600).

Toronto *Open Air Books and Maps*, 25 Toronto St, M5R 2C1 (☎416/363 0719).

Vancouver *World Wide Books and Maps*, 1247 Granville St (☎604/687 3320).

GETTING AROUND

The easiest way of travelling around Italy is by train. The Italian train system is relatively inexpensive, reasonably comprehensive, and, in the north of the country at least, fairly efficient – far preferable to the fragmented, localised and sometimes grindingly slow buses. We've detailed train, bus and ferry frequencies in the "Travel Details" section at the end of each chapter of the guide, and where it actually is a better idea to take a bus we've said as much in the text.

TRAINS

Operated by Italia State Railways, *Ferrovie dello Stato* (*FS*), there are six types of train in Italy. At the top of the range is the **ETR 450 "Pendolino"**, an exclusively first-class inter-city service on which your ticket includes seat reservation, newspapers and a meal. **Eurocity** trains connect the major Italian cities with centres such as Paris, Vienna, Hamburg and Barcelona, while **Intercity** trains link the major Italian centres; reservations are obligatory on both of these services, and a supplement in the region of 30 percent of the ordinary fare is payable. (Make sure you pay your supplement before getting on board; you'll have to cough up a far bigger surcharge to the conductor). **Espresso** trains are the common-or-garden long-distance expresses, calling only at larger stations; **Diretto** trains stop at most stations; lastly there are the **Locale** services, which stop at every place with a population higher than zero.

In addition to the routes operated by *FS*, there are a number of **privately-run lines**, using separate stations though charging similar fares. Where they're worth using, these are detailed in the text.

TIMETABLES

Obviously **timings and route information** for the *FS* network are posted up at train stations, and we give a rough idea of frequencies and journey times in the "Travel Details" sections at the end of each chapter. Otherwise the main routes (*Espresso* and upwards) are covered by *FS*'s little national pocket book, *Principali Treni*, issued twice yearly and free from most train stations; if you're travelling extensively by train, you should also pick up the free *FS* leaflets detailing individual lines (readily available from the larger stations) or invest in a copy of the twice yearly *Tutta Italia* timetable (L8000), which gives all the information you'll need; it's normally on sale at train station newspaper stands. Pay attention to the timetable notes, which may specify the dates between which some services run (*Si effetua dal . . . al . . .*), or whether a service is seasonal (*periódico*); *feriale* is the word for daily, *festivo* means a train only runs on Sundays and holidays.

FARES

Fares are very reasonable, calculated by the kilometre and thus easy to work out for each journey. The state tourist board's *Travellers Handbook* gives the prices per kilometre but as a rough guide, the single second-class one-way fare from Milan to Bari, one of the longest journeys you're ever likely to make, currently costs about L60,000. **Sleepers** are available on many long-distance services, and prices vary according to the length of journey and whether or not you're sharing. Generally, expect to pay an extra L10,000 or so for a couchette, and from about L15,000 for a place in a sleeping compartment. In summer it's often worth making a **seat reservation** on the main routes, which can get very busy; this is something you're obliged to do anyway on the faster trains.

Most stations have machines in which passengers should stamp their ticket immediately before embarking on the return leg of a journey. Look out for them at the end of the platform: if you fail to validate your ticket at a station where these machines have been fitted, you may be given a spot-fine in the region of L40,000. Bear in mind, too, that the ticket must be validated within three days of the outward journey; if you're coming back any later than that, you must buy two single tickets.

RAIL PASSES AND DISCOUNTS

The Europe-wide **InterRail** and **Eurail** passes (see "Getting There...", above,) give unlimited

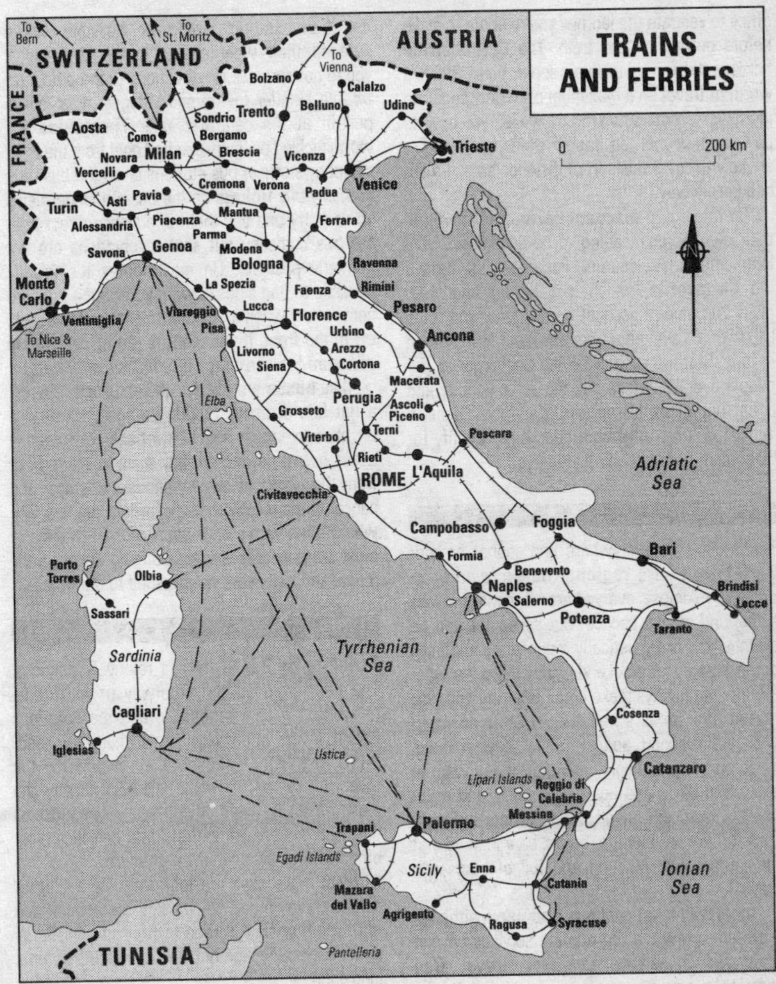

travel on the *FS* network, although you'll be liable for supplements on the faster trains.

If you're travelling exclusively in Italy by train, however, you might want to invest in one of the many rail passes available on the *FS* system. Travellers from the UK have a choice of three **Euro-Domino** passes for the Italian network, giving 3 days' unlimited rail travel for £100, 5 days' for £124, or 10 days' for £208. All these passes are available from the *International Rail Centre* or *Wasteels* (see "Getting There...", p.5, for addresses). In addition, there are three specific Italian passes, available at all the agencies listed except *Eurotrain*, and at major city train stations. The **Biglietto Turistico Libera Circolazione** is valid for unlimited travel on all *FS* trains, including *Intercity*, for 8 days its costs £88/$140, for 15 days £110/$172, for 21 days £126/$198, and for 30 days £152/$240. The **Flexi-Card** is similarly valid for all trains, and gives a certain number of days' travel within a specific period. For 4 days' travel in any 9-day period it costs £66/$105, for 8 days in 21 it costs £94/$150, and for 12 in 30 it costs £120/$190. With this card, you must get the ticket office to validate the journey you're about to make before getting on the train. The **Chilométrico** ticket, valid for up to five people, gives 3000km worth of travel on a maximum of twenty separate journeys; it costs £90/$150. However, you have to pay supplements on faster trains, and you're unlikely to cover this sort of distance on an Italian holiday anyway.

There are two **discount cards** that come into their own if you're going to be spending a very long time in the country. For under-26s there's the **Cartaverde**, which is valid for one year, gives 20 percent discount on any fare, and costs L40,000; it's available from any main train station in Italy. Stations also issue the **Cartargento**, for people over 60, which has the same validity and price, but gives 30 percent discount. Bear in mind, too, that **children** aged 4–12 qualify for 50 percent discount on all journeys.

BUSES

Trains don't go everywhere and sooner or later you'll have to use **regional buses** (*autobus* or *pullman*). Almost everywhere is connected by some kind of bus service, but schedules can be sketchy, and are drastically reduced – sometimes non-existent – at weekends, something the timetable won't always make clear. Bear in mind also that in rural areas schedules are often designed with the working and/or school day in mind, meaning a frighteningly early start if you want to catch that day's one bus out of town, and occasionally no buses at all during school holidays. Even if there are plentiful buses, bear in mind that the journey will be long and full of stops and starts.

There isn't a national **bus company**, although there are a few that do operate services beyond their own immediate area (see above). **Bus terminals** can be anywhere in larger towns, though often they're sensibly placed next door to the train station; wherever possible we've detailed their whereabouts in the text, but if you're not sure ask for directions to the *autostazione*. In smaller towns and villages, most buses pull in at the central piazza. **Timetables** are worth picking up if you can find one, from the local company's office, bus stations or on the bus. You normally buy **tickets** on the bus; on longer hauls you can try and buy them in advance direct from the bus company but seat reservations are not normally possible. On most routes it's usually possible to flag a bus down if you want a ride: the convention, when it stops, is to get on at the back, off at the front. If you want to get off, ask *posso scéndere?*; the next stop is *la próssima fermata*.

City buses are always cheap, usually costing a flat fare of about L1000; it's again normally a bit cheaper down south. Invariably you need a ticket *before* getting on; buy them in *tabacchi* or from the kiosks at bus terminals and stops, and cancel in the machine at the back of the bus. The whole thing works on a basis of trust, though in most cities checks for fare-dodging are regularly made, and hefty spot-fines issued to offenders.

MAJOR ITALIAN BUS COMPANIES

Autostradale, Piazzale Castello 1, Milan (☎02/801.161). Services around Lombardy, Liguria and the lakes.

Lazzi, Via Mercadente 2, Florence (☎055/363.041). Services around Tuscany and central Italy.

SITA, Viale del Cadorna, Florence (☎055/278.611). Services all over Italy.

CARS

Travelling **by car** in Italy is relatively painless. The roads are good, the motorway, or *autostrada*, network very comprehensive, and the notorious Italian drivers rather less erratic than their reputation suggests – though their regard for the rules of the road is sometimes lax to say the least. Basically, avoid driving in cities as much as possible; the congestion and lack of concern for other drivers can make it a nightmare.

Most motorways are toll-roads. Take a ticket as you come on and pay on exit; the amount due is flashed up on a screen in front of you. Rates aren't especially high but they can mount up on a long journey: as a general reference, you'll pay just over L15,000 driving a small car from Milan to Bologna.

As regards **documentation**, if you're bringing your own car you need a valid driving licence *plus* an Italian translation (available from the state tourist office, see "Information and Maps", p.14), and an international green card of insurance. It's compulsory to carry your car documents and passport while you're driving, and you may be required to present them if stopped by the police – not an uncommon occurrence. **Rules of the road** are straightforward: drive on the right; at junctions, where there's any ambiguity, give precedence to vehicles coming from the right; observe the speed limits – 50kph in built up areas, 110kph on country roads and on motorways during the week, 130kph on motorways at weekends); and *don't* drink and drive.

If you **break down**, dial ☎116 at the nearest phone and tell the operator where you are, the type of car and your registration number: the nearest office of the *Automobile Club d'Italia* (*ACI*), Via Marsala 8, 00185 Rome (☎06/499.8251), the Italian national motoring organisation, will be informed and they'll send someone out to fix your car – although it's not a free service, and can work out very expensive if you need a tow. For peace of mind, you might prefer to join the *ACI* outright, and so qualify for their discounted repairs scheme. Any *ACI* office in Italy can tell you where to get **spare parts** for your particular car: see the city "Listings" sections for details of local addresses.

Car rental in Italy is pricey, at a little over £200 per week for a small hatchback, with unlimited mileage. The major chains have offices in all the larger cities and at airports, train stations, etc, and addresses are detailed in the city "Listings" sections, although local firms are often more inexpensive if always not so convenient, and in any case it's normally cheapest to arrange things in advance, through agents in Britain like *Holiday Autos*, 227 Shepherds Bush Road, London W6 (☎01-748 1333), or, when you book your flight or holiday, with Italian specialists like *Italy Sky Shuttle*, 226 Shepherds Bush Road, London W6 (☎081/748 1333). Doing things this way can knock 10–20 percent off the cost per week.

Italy is also one of the most expensive countries in Europe in which to buy **petrol**, though if you take your own car you're entitled to **petrol coupons** worth 15 percent off and concessions on the motorway tolls; information from the Italian State Tourist Office. For unleaded petrol, look for the sign, "Senza Piombo" ("PB").

Never leave anything visible in the car when you're not using it, including the radio. If you're taking your own vehicle, consider installing a detachable car-radio, and always depress your aerial or else you might find it snapped off. Most cities and ports have **garages** where you can leave your car, a safe enough option. At least your car is unlikely to be stolen if it's got a right-hand drive and a foreign number-plate: they're too conspicuous to be of much use to thieves.

However you get around on the roads, bear in mind that the **traffic** can be appalling – every Italian seems to have at least two cars – and although Italians are by no means the world's worst drivers they don't win any safety prizes either. The secret really is to make it very clear what you're going to do, using your horn as much as possible, and then do it with great determination. If you're walking around, don't assume that as a pedestrian you're safe; even on crossings you can undergo some close calls. Again, the answer is to be bold, and stride straight out with great determination.

HITCHHIKING

Hitchhiking (*autostop*) is moderately possible in Italy, although less practised in the south of the country. Getting around exclusively by hitching is a chore, however, but for the odd short hop along a quiet country road, and it's more of a feasible alternative if reserved for long hauls between major cities. Remember that it's illegal to hitch on motorways – to do so would be to risk a spot-fine; stand on a slip-road or at one of the service areas. Bear in mind also that women should be *very* wary of hitching alone, particularly in the South, where male machismo predominates: pairs are best and always ask where the car is headed (*Dovè diretto?*) before you commit yourself. If you want to get out, say *Mi fa scéndere?*.

CYCLING AND MOTORBIKING

Cycling is seen as more of a sport than a way of getting around in Italy, and indeed some parts of the country aren't especially well suited to it – although in a few towns like Ferrara and Ravenna in the flat plains of Emilia it is admittedly the standard form of transport. Down south, and in the central and far northern mountains, you need a decent machine and plenty of stamina: a mountain bike would be a good bet, though you can expect to be a real curiosity in some rural places. On the islands, in major resorts and in the larger cities it's usually possible to **rent** a bike, but generally facilities for this are few and far between and you may well be better off bringing your own.

An alternative is to tour by **motorbike**, though again there are relatively few places to rent one. **Mopeds** and **scooters**, on the other hand, are relatively easy to find: everyone in Italy, from kids to grandmas, rides one of these, and, although they're not really built for any kind of long-distance travel, for shooting around towns and islands they're ideal. We've detailed outlets in the text; roughly speaking you should expect to pay up to L100,000 a day for a machine. Crash helmets are compulsory these days, though in the south at least it's a law which seems to be largely ignored.

PLANES

ATI, the domestic arm of *Alitalia*, operate **flights** all over Italy, connecting all the major cities and islands, as indeed do *Alitalia*. Really, though, it's only advisable to take a plane within Italy if you want to cover a large distance quickly: prices are quite high, pricier than even the most expensive express train, and the larger cities are all linked by fast rail night-services with sleeping cars (see p.16).

As an example of ordinary one-way fares Venice–Rome will cost you around L160,000, Milan–Naples about L200,000, although it's worth knowing that there are some tempting discounts available. Passengers under 25 qualify for a 25 percent discount on normal fares, and there are also reductions of up to 30 percent if you travel in the evening; you will get a third off the normal fare if you go on Saturday and return on Sunday, 50 percent off if you make a day return trip on a Sunday. *Alitalia* have full details.

FERRIES AND HYDROFOILS

Operated by a number of different private companies, Italy has a well-developed network of **ferries** and **hydrofoils**. Large car ferries connect the major islands of Sardinia and Sicily with the mainland ports of Genoa, Civitavecchia and Naples, while the smaller island groupings – the Tremiti islands, the Bay of Naples islands, the Pontine islands – are usually linked to a number of nearby mainland towns. There are also international links with Greece, Malta, Corsica, Spain, Tunisia, Egypt and Israel. Fares are reasonable, although on some of the more popular serices – to Sardinia, certainly – you should book well in advance in summer, especially if you're taking a vehicle across. Bear in mind also that frequencies are drastically reduced outside the summer months, and some services stop altogether. You'll find a broad guide to journey times and frequencies in the "Travel Details" section at the end of each chapter; for full up-to-date schedules, and prices, contact the local tourist office or one of the addresses below.

ITALIAN FERRY COMPANIES

Adriatica, c/o Serena Holidays, 40–42 Kenway Rd, London SW5 (☎071/373 6548/9). Ferries to Elba.

Caremar, Molo Beverello, Piazza Municipio, Naples (☎081/5551.5384). Ferries to destinations around the Bay of Naples.

Navarma, c/o Serena Holidays, 40–42 Kenway Rd, London SW5 (☎071/373 6548/9). Ferries to Elba.

Siremar, c/o Serena Holidays, 40–42 Kenway Rd, London SW5 (☎071/373 6548/9).

Snav, Via Carraciolo 13, Naples (☎081/684.288). Hydrofoils to destinations around the Bay of Naples.

SNCM, c/o Southern Ferries, 179 Piccadilly, London W1V 0BA (☎071/491 4968). Ferries from the Italian mainland to Corsica.

Tirrenia, c/o Serena Holidays, 40–42 Kenway Rd, London SW5 (☎071-373 6548/9). Ferries to Sardinia, Sicily, Corsica, Malta, Tunisia.

ACCOMMODATION

Accommodation in Italy is strictly regulated, and while never especially cheap, is at least fairly reliable: hotels are star-rated and required to post their prices clearly in each room. Most tourist offices have details of hotel rates in their town or region, and you can usually expect them to be broadly accurate. If they're not, demand to know why, and don't hesitate to report discrepancies. Whatever happens, establish the *full* price of your room *before* you accept it. In popular resorts and the major cities – Venice, Rome, Florence especially – booking ahead is often a good idea, particularly during July or August. We've given phone numbers throughout the guide for this. The phrases at the end of the book should help you get over the language barrier, but in many places you should be able to find someone who speaks at least some English.

HOTELS

Hotels in Italy come tagged with a sometimes confusing variety of names, and, although the differences have become minimal of late, you will still find the various names used for what are always basically private hotel facilities. A **locanda** is historically perhaps the most basic option, although the word is, oddly enough, sometimes appropriated these days to denote somwhere quite fancy. You will also find **pensione**, although there is nowadays very little difference between these and a regular **albergho** or **hotel**. **Prices**, as ever, vary greatly between the poor south and the wealthy north. On average, in a **one-star** hotel you can expect to pay L40–50,000 for a double without private bathroom, L50–60,000 with private facilities; and in Florence, Venice, Milan, and even Rome, it's not easy to find anything at all for much under L60,000 these days, even without private facilities. **Two-star** hotels normally cost L60,000–80,000 a double, and will usually have more (if not all) rooms with private facilities, although the rooms themselves won't always be that much better; with **three-star** places you begin to notice a difference, though in them you'll be paying a minimum of L100,000 for a double – although all rooms will have private bathrooms, and often TV and telephone as well.

In very busy places it's not unusual (as well as finding everywhere full) to have to stay for a minimum of three nights, and many proprietors will add the price of breakfast to your bill whether you want it or not; try to resist this – you can always eat more cheaply in a bar. Be warned, too, that in major resorts like Rimini you will often be forced to take half-pension in high season. You can cut costs slightly by cramming three into a double room, but on average most hotels will charge you an extra 35 percent for this. Note also that people travelling alone may often be clobbered for the price of a double room even when taking a single; check in the tourist office's listings for the officially quoted price. Again, whenever you feel you're being ripped off, don't be afraid to wave the official literature at the proprietor, or to mutter dire threats about the tourist authorities – it may have some effect.

YOUTH HOSTELS

There are around 50 official **IYHF youth hostels** in all, charging an average of L16,000 a night for a dormitory bed, and you can easily base a tour of the country around them, although for two people travelling together they don't always represent a massive saving on the cheapest double hotel room – something that's especially true once you add on the bus fare you're likely to have to fork out to reach one. If you're travelling on your own, on the other hand, hostels can work out a lot cheaper, and many have facilities – cheap restaurants, kitchens, etc – that enable you to cut costs further. In a few cases, too – notably Castroreale in Sicily, and Verona and Montagnana in the Veneto – the hostels are beautifully located and in many ways preferable to any hotel.

HOTEL PRICES

All the establishments listed in this book have been graded according to the following categories. These will often, but not always, correspond to the category laid down by the tourist authorities. Indeed they are a guide to price only, and give no indication to the facilities you might expect other than the broad outlines we give below.

Please note that the **prices** we give here are for the cheapest double room – ie without private bath – during summer.

① **Up to L20,000 per person.** Hostels, with shared facilities and dormitory accommodation. Most official IYHF youth hostels fall into this category.

② **L20–40,000 per person.** More expensive hostel accommodation, with shared facilities and dormitory beds, often in smaller, less institutional dorms, and with the option of private single and double rooms too. Religious-run institutions, welcome houses, convents, and the like, usually fall into this category.

③ **Up to L40,000.** The cheapest kind of one-star hotels; normally most rooms will have shared facilities and may be quite bleak, although rarely dangerous. You may find places in this category booked up in advance due to the fact that they're often lived in on a semi-permanent basis by students, etc.

④ **L40–60,0000** The standard one-star hotel, normally with a mixture of rooms with shared and private facilities, and in most cases comfortable enough for a shortish stay. This is probably the most commonly recommended category in this book, although in Venice, Florence and some other northern cities and resorts, you might find even one-star places at this price a little thin on the ground.

⑤ **L60–80,0000** A mixture of slightly pricier one-stars, perhaps because they have only a few rooms with shared facilities, and less expensive two-stars, which may, conversely, have a number of rooms with shared facilities. You may occasionally at this price enjoy TV and telephone too.

⑥ **L80–100,000** Two-star and three-star hotels with all the facilities you would expect at this price; generally all rooms will have private bath, and often TV and telephone too – although, again, in the larger northern cities, you may be looking at something a little more basic.

⑦ **L100–120,000** This price should get you a double room with private bath, TV and telephone pretty much everywhere in Italy, and in the south of the country and more remote places, you could be looking at something fairly swanky. We will, however, only have listed somewhere in this category if it is something reasonably special, or if there is no alternative.

⑧ **L120,000 upwards** This is a skys-the-limit price, and we have only recommended somewhere in this category if it is *really* special, if it enjoys a wonderful location, a superb site or building – perhaps an old convent or manor house – or if the service and food are just too good to miss. Bear in mind that although most places denoted by this category will cost less than L200,000, the odd unique recommendation charging an even higher price than this may have crept in for those to whom money is no object.

Virtually all of the Italian hostels are members of the official *International Youth Hostel Federation*, and strictly speaking you need to be a member of that organisation in order to use them – you can join through your home country's youth hostelling organisation (addresses below). Many hostels however allow you to join on the spot, or will simply charge you a supplement. If you choose to pay the supplement you will receive a stamp in the card they give you; once you have collected five stamps, you are deemed to have paid the membership fee.

Member or not, you will need to book ahead in the summer months, most efficiently by contacting the hostels direct at least 15 days in advance. We've listed most of the hostels in the guide, or you can get a full list from the Italian youth hostels association's travel section, *Associazione Italiana Alberghi per la Gioventù*, Via Cavour 44, 00184 Roma (☎06/487.1152).

In some cities – Rome is one – it's also possible to stay in **student accommodation** vacated by Italian students for the summer. This is usually confined to July and August, but accommodation is generally in individual rooms and can work out a lot cheaper than a straight hotel room. Again you'll need to book in advance: we've listed possible places in the text and you should contact them as far ahead as possible to be sure of a room. You will also come across accommodation operated

YOUTH HOSTEL ASSOCIATIONS

Australia *Australian Youth Hostels Association*, Level 3, 10 Mallett St, Camperdown, New South Wales 2050 (☎02/565 1699).

Canada *Canadian Hostelling Association*, 1600 James Naismith Drive, Suite 608, Gloucester, Ontario K1B 5N4 (☎613/748 5638).

England and Wales *Youth Hostel Association* (*YHA*), Trevelyan House, 8 St. Stephen's Hill, St. Alban's, Herts AL1 2DY (☎0727/55215). London shop and information office: 14 Southampton St, London WC2E 7HY (☎071/836 8542).

Ireland *An Oige*, 61 Mountjoy St, Dublin 7 (☎01/304555).

New Zealand *Youth Hostels Association of New Zealand*, PO Box 436, Christchurch 1 (☎03/799970).

Northern Ireland *Youth Hostel Association of Northern Ireland*, 56 Bradbury Place, Belfast, BT7 1RU (☎0232/324733).

Scotland *Scottish Youth Hostel Association*, 7 Glebe Crescent, Stirling, FK8 2JA (☎0786/51181).

USA *American Youth Hostels* (*AYH*), PO Box 37613, Washington, DC 200013 (☎202/783 6161).

by **religious organisations** – convents (normally for women only), welcome houses and the like, again with a mixture of dormitory and individual rooms, which can sometimes be a way of cutting costs as well as meeting like-minded people. Most operate a curfew of some sort, and you should bear in mind that they don't always work out a great deal cheaper than a bottom-line one-star hotel.

CAMPING

Camping is not as popular in Italy as it is in some European countries, but there are plenty of sites, and most of them are well-equipped. The snag is that they're expensive, and, once you've added the cost of a tent and vehicle, don't always work out a great deal cheaper than staying in a hotel or hostel. Local tourist offices have details of nearby sites, and prices range from L6000 to L9000 per person daily, plus L8000–12,000 for each caravan or tent, plus around L5000 for each vehicle. If you're camping extensively, the Tourist Club Italiano publish a comprehensive guide to campsites countrywide, *Campeggi e Villaggi Turistici*, available from bookshops before you leave or once you're there (L29,500). If you don't need something this detailed, you can obtain an abridged version, along with a location map, free of charge from *Centro Internazionale Prenotazioni, Federcampeggio*, Casella Postale 23, 50041 Calenzano, Florence (☎055/882.391). This is also the place to book places on campsites in advance.

DAY HOTELS

One peculiar Italian institution is the *albergo diurno* or **day hotel** – not as sleazy as it sounds in fact, but an establishment providing bathrooms, showers, cleaning services, hairdressers and the like for a fixed rate, usually around L7000. You'll often find them at train stations and they're usually open daily 6am–midnight. Useful for a fast clean-up if you're on the move.

VILLAS, *AGRITURISMO* AND *RIFUGI*

If you're not intending to travel around a lot it might be worth considering renting a **villa or farmhouse** for a week or two. These don't come cheap, but most are of a very high standard, and often enjoy marvellous locations. Reckon on paying around £300 a week for the average four-bedded Tuscan farmhouse, rather less in less popular regions such as Umbria or Marche. Tour operators with a selection of farmhouses and villas on their books include *CV Travel*, 43 Cadogen St, London SW3 2PR (☎071/581 0851); *Villas Italia*, Groundstar House, 390 London Rd, Crawley, W Sussex RH10 2TB (☎0293/599988)

Agriturismo is a way of doing things more cheaply, not unlike the French *gîte* system, whereby farmers let out their unused buildings to tourists through a centralised booking agency. Under this system, which is as yet fairly undiscovered, it's possible to find places for as little as L10,000 per person per night, though L20–30,000 is more usual. For a full list of properties write to *Agriturist*, Corso V. Emanuele 101, Rome (☎06/85.2342).

Finally, if you're planning on hiking and climbing, there is the ***rifugi*** network, consisting of about 500 mountain huts, owned by the *Club*

Alpino Italia, that non-members can stay in for L15–20,000 a night; there are also private *rifugi* which charge around double this. Most are fairly spartan, with bunks in unheated dorms, but their sitings can be magnificent, and usually leave you well-placed to continue your hike the next day. They are obliged to take you if you turn up on the off chance, but often it's better to book in advance, either through the local tourist office or the *Club Alpino Italia*, Via Fonseca Pimental 7, Milan (☎02/2614.1378), who can also provide a full list of huts. For more details see the note on *rifugi* at the beginning of the *Trentino-Alto Adige* chapter.

FOOD AND DRINK

Although it has long been popular primarily for its cheapness and convenience, Italian food is finally beginning to wrest some of the attention it deserves as one of the world's great cuisines. The Southern Italian diet especially, with its emphasis on fresh and plentiful fruit, vegetables and fish, is one of the healthiest in Europe, and there are few national cuisines that can boast so much variety in both ingredients and cooking methods. Wine, too, is becoming more respected, as the Italian industry's devotion to fizzy pop and characterless plonk is replaced by a new pride and a better product.

THE BASICS OF ITALIAN CUISINE

Although the twentieth century has done much to blur the **regional differences** of Italian food, they are still there – and often highly evident, the French influence strong in Piemonte, Austrian flavours in Alto Adige, and even Greek in Calabria. Also, save for the Chinese restaurants which crop up in every town, and the ubiquitous burger bars, Italy has remained largely untouched by the latter-day boom in non-indigenous eating, partly due to its lack of any substantial colonial legacy but also because of the innate chauvinism of Italian eating habits – a match for the French every time. Instead, the exotic option here is sampling cooking from other parts of the country. Milan tends to be the favourite melting-pot, with restaurants specialising in food from all regions; Rome is the only city where there's any real choice of foreign food.

Because of the feeling that every Italian cherishes at heart, that Italian food is the best in the world and that mama's is always the perfect example, many restaurants are simply an extension of the home dining table. Adventure is not common on the menu. There has been some limited experimentation with new, "trendier" ingredients like wholewheat pasta and brown rice, but the best you'd get if you asked a waiter for any such thing would be a raised eyebrow; request a wholewheat pizza and you'd certainly be laughed out of sight. Vegetarian restaurants too have been slow to catch on, the first ones appearing relatively recently, where else but in Milan. Vegetarians should know, however, that there are always plenty of non-meat choices on every menu.

Perhaps the most striking thing about eating in Italy is how deeply embedded in the culture it really is. Food is celebrated with gusto, and meals are traditional affairs of many courses that can seem to last forever, starting with an antipasto, followed by a risotto or a pasta dish, leading on to a fish or meat course, cheese, and finished with fresh fruit and coffee. Even everyday meals are a miniaturised version of the fully-blown affair. Shopping for food is a serious matter. Supermarkets have yet to make any real impact on the dominance of the traditional store in town centres, and foodstores of every description abound. Street markets, too, can be exhilarating, selling bountiful, fresh and flavoursome produce. The Italians as yet haven't adopted the heavy cropping methods which result in completely tasteless produce. Even a simple raw tomato can be a revelation.

Foods like bread and cheese are still made with an eye on quality rather than mass production; bread is still almost entirely made by small bakeries and white sliced is rare. Bread tends to get heavier, crustier and more salty the further south you go (for eating with salty hams, salami and cheeses there is "pane senza sale"). Cheese *is* often factory-produced, large firms like the Milan-based *Galbani* marketing common varieties like *Bel Paese*, *Gorgonzola* and *Taleggio*. But cheese making also remains in the hands of local farmers working to traditional recipes: local tastes are much in evidence.

BREAKFAST, SNACKS AND ICE CREAM

Most Italians start their day in a bar, their **breakfast** consisting of a coffee with hot milk, a *cappuccino* and a *cornetto* – a jam, custard or chocolate-filled croissant, which you usually help yourself to from the counter; unfilled croissants are hard to find. Breakfast in a hotel (*prima colazione*) will be a limp affair, usually worth avoiding.

At other times of the day, **sandwiches** (*panini*) can be pretty substantial, a bread stick or roll packed with any number of fillings. There are sandwich bars in larger towns and cities (*paninoteche*), and in smaller places grocer's shops (*alimentari*) will normally make you up whatever you want; you'll pay L2000–4000 each. Bars may also offer *tramezzini*, ready-made sliced white bread with mixed fillings – less appetising than the average *panino* but still tasty, and slightly cheaper at around L1500 a time. Toasted sandwiches (*toste*) are common too: in a *paninoteca* you can get whatever you want toasted; in ordinary bars it's more likely to be a variation on cheese or ham with tomato.

If you want hot takeaway food there are a number of options. It's possible to find slices of pizza (*pizza rustica* or *pizza al taglio*) pretty much everywhere, and you can get most of the things already mentioned, plus pasta, chips, even full hot meals, in a **távola calda**, a sort of stand-up snack bar that's at its best in the morning when everything is fresh. Some are self-service and have limited seating too. The bigger towns have these, and there's often one inside larger railway stations. Another alternative is a **rosticceria**. Here the speciality is spit-roast chicken but *rosticcerie* often serve fast foods such as slices of pizza, chips and hamburgers.

Other sources of quick snacks are obviously **markets**, some of which sell takeaway food from stalls, including *focacce* – oven-baked pastries topped with cheese or tomato or filled with spinach, fried offal or meat – and *arancini* or *supplì* deep-fried balls of rice with meat (*rosso*) or butter and cheese (*bianco*) filling. **Supermarkets**, also, are an obvious stop for a picnic lunch: the major department store chains, *Upim* and *Standa*, often have food halls.

Italian **ice cream** (*gelato*) is justifiably famous: a cone (*un cono*) is an indispensable accessory to the evening *passegiata*. Most bars have a fairly good selection, but for real choice go to a **gelateria**, where the range is a tribute to the Italian imagination and flair for display. You'll sometimes have to go by appearance rather than attempting to decipher their exotic names, many of which don't even mean much to Italians: often the basics – chocolate and strawberry – are best. There's no problem locating the finest *gelateria* in town – it's the one that draws the crowds, and we've noted the really special places in the text. If in doubt, go for the places that make their own ice cream, denoted by the sign, "Produzione Propria" outside.

PIZZA

Pizza is now a worldwide phenomenon, but Italy remains the best place to eat it. The creations served up here – especially in the city where pizza started, Naples – are wholly different from the soggy concoctions that have taken over the UK fast-food market. Everywhere in Italy pizza comes thin and flat, not deep-pan, and the choice of toppings is fairly limited – none of the pineapple and sweetcorn variations that have taken off in Britain and America. It's also easier, especially in the south of the country, to find pizzas cooked in the traditional way, in wood-fired ovens (*forno a legna*), rather than the squeaky-clean electric ones, so that the pizzas arrive blasted and bubbling on the surface, and with a distinctive charcoal taste.

Pizzerias range from a stand-up counter selling slices to a fully-fledged sit-down restaurant, and on the whole they don't sell much else besides pizza, soft drinks and beer. Some straight restaurants often have pizza on the menu too. A basic cheese and tomato pizza (a *margherita*) costs around L4000–6000 (sometimes less in the south, often more in the north), a fancier variety L6000–10,000, and it's quite acceptable to cut it into slices and eat it with your fingers. Check the food glossary for the different kinds of pizza.

MEALS: LUNCH AND DINNER

Full **meals** are often elaborate affairs, generally served in either a **trattoria** or a **ristorante**. Traditionally, a trattoria is a cheaper and more basic purveyor of homestyle cooking (*cucina casalinga*), while a *ristorante* is more upmarket, with aproned waiters and tablecloths, though these days the two are often interchangeable. The main differences you'll notice now are to do with opening times: often trattorias, at least in rural areas, will be open lunchtime – there won't be a menu and the waiter will simply reel off a list of what's on that day. In large towns both will be open in

REGIONAL CUISINE

Piemonte & Valle d'Aosta

Piemontese cooking gives away the region's close links with France with dishes like *fonduta* (fondue) and its preference for using butter and cream in cooking. As in most of the North, olive oil and tomatoes are relatively uncommon, although immigrants from the south to towns like Turin have brought their cooking with them. Piemonte is perhaps most famous for its truffles, the most exquisite of which come from around the town of Alba – and are ferociously expensive. Their most usual use is a few thin slices to top a dish of pasta or a risotto. Watch out too for *porcini* mushrooms, chestnuts, and, more specifically, the *bagna cauda* – a sociable local variation on the fondue in which everyone dips vegetables into a sauce of garlic, oil and anchovies. In Valle d'Aosta they prepare good rich soups like *soupe à la Valpellineuntze*, with cabbage, or *soupe à la cogneintze* – with rice.

Liguria

Liguria belongs geographically to the North, but its benign Mediterranean climate belongs further south. Its capital Genova is synonymous with pesto, the sauce made from pine nuts, basil, olive oil, pecorino and parmesan. It is usually served with linguine or trenette (long, thin pasta), but can be found with gnocchi and even in soups. Genova's links with Sardinia have also led to the adoption of pecorino in all its strengths as Liguria's favourite cheese. Seafood can be very good – Liguria is all coastline – and the region produces some fine olive oils as well as abundant quantities of chick peas. The latter are often ground to flour and made into *farinata*, a sort of cross between a pizza and an omelette. *Focaccia* – flat bread – is common too, often flavoured with olives, sage or rosemary. Pastries are excellent – Genoa is famous for its *pandolce* (sweet bread), laced with dried fruit and pine nuts.

Lombardy

The cooking of Lombardy varies even from town to town. Rice and polenta – ground maize meal, boiled and eaten hot, either on its own or as an accompaniment to a meat dish – are widely eaten, but the Alpine foothills and lakes contrast sharply with the rural plains of the Po valley and the rich urban food of Milan. *Risotto alla Milanese* is perhaps Milan's most renowned culinary export, bright yellow from saffron. *Ossobucco* (shin of veal) is another Milanese favourite, as are *biscotti* – hand-made biscuits flavoured with nuts, vanilla and lemon and sold by weight at specialist shops all over the city. *Panettone*, the soft, eggy cake with sultanas, also originated here, though now it's available all over Italy. Stuffed pastas and veal are – as in Piemonte – also popular, and again wild fungi are to be found. Some dishes, like *pizzocheri* (buckwheat noodles from the Valtellina) can be peculiarly local. Lombardy is also perhaps the largest cheese-making region in the country. As well as *Gorgonzola* and *Bel Paese* there are numerous local cheeses – the parmesan-like *Grana Padano* and the smooth rich *Mascarpone* (used in sweet dishes) are the best-known.

Trentino-Alto Adige

Trentino-Alto Adige, as its name suggests, is really two regions: Alto Adige with its unreservedly Austrian traditions, and Trentino, which mixes mountain influences with more Italian flavours from the south. Polenta is common to both, but while Italian dishes like *gnocchi* (small dumplings made from potato, flour and some-the evening, but there'll be more choice in a ristorante, which will always have a menu and sometimes a help-yourself antipasto buffet. In either, pasta dishes go for around L5000–8000, and there's never any problem just having this; the main fish or meat courses will normally be anything between L10,000 and L15,000. Bear in mind that almost everywhere you'll pay a cover charge on top of your food – the *pane e coperto* – of around L2000 a head.

Other types of eatery include places, common in tourist resorts, that bill themselves as everything – trattoria-ristorante-pizzeria – and perform no function very well, serving mediocre food that you could get much cheaper elsewhere. Look out also for spaghetterias, restaurant-bars which serve basic pasta dishes and are often the hang-out of the local youth. *Osterias* are common too, basically an old-fashioned restaurant specialising in home cooking, though be careful

times spinach and ricotta) are found in Trentino, Alto Adige turns out the decidedly Germanic *speck* (smoked pork), *knödel* (dumplings), *sauerkraut* and all manner of sweet tarts and cakes, often flavoured with apples and plums.

The Veneto/Friuli-Venezia Giulia

The Veneto vies with Lombardy for the crown of risotto making, while Venice specialises in fish and seafood, together with odd ingredients like pomegranates, pine nuts and raisins, harking back to its days as a port and merchant city. The risottos tend to be more liquid than those to the west, usually with a seafood base although peas (*bisi* in dialect) are also common, as are other seasonal vegetables – spinach, asparagus, pumpkin. The red salad leaf raddichio also has its home in the Veneto, as does the renowned Italian dessert, *tiramisu*. Polenta is eaten too, but is more common in neighbouring Friuli-Venezia-Giulia, the poorest of the northern regions, with a dialect that's almost a language of its own and culinary influences from both Austria and the former Yugoslavia. Pork in all forms features strongly, together with heavy soups of beans, rice and root vegetables. *Gnocchi* are also served in an unusual sweet-sour sauce.

Emilia-Romagna

Emilia-Romagna has a just reputation for harbouring the richest, most lavish food in Italy, its most famous specialities – parmesan cheese, egg pasta, parma ham and balsamic vinegar – quintessentially Italian in their appeal. Bologna is regarded as the gastronomic capital of Italy, and Emilia is the only true home of pasta in the North, in the form of *lasagne, tortellini* stuffed with ricotta cheese and spinach, pumpkin or pork, and other fresh pastas served with *ragù* (meat sauce), cream sauces or simply with butter and parmesan. Modena and Parma specialise in *bollito misto* – boiled meats; *alla parmigiana* usually denotes something cooked with parmesan. Romagna's cuisine is more southern in orientation. While ingredients such as butter, cheese, mushrooms, chestnuts and meat feature in Emilia, Romagna tends more to onions, garlic, olive oil and fish.

Tuscany

Tuscan cooking has been a seminal influence in Italian cuisine generally. It emphasises simplicity: meat is kept plain, often grilled, and Florentines will often profess to liking nothing better than a good *bistecca alla fiorentina* – rare grilled steak. Beans of all types are popular, white cannellini beans and chick peas most of all. They turn up in salads, with pasta (*tuoni e lampo*) or just dressed with olive oil. Chick peas can also be found in *torta di ceci*, similar to the *farinata* found in Liguria. Spinach is the essential Tuscan vegetable, often married with ricotta to make gnocchi, used as a pasta filling, and in *crespoline* (pancakes) or between two chunks of *focaccia* and eaten as a street or bar snack. *Alla fiorentina* can often mean with spinach and cheese, but don't bank on it. Soups are very popular, ranging from simple vegetable broths to thick bean *minestre*. And the region is home to Italy's most delicate olive oils. Siena is best known for its sweets – things like almond macaroons and *panforte di Siena*, a rich fruit bread.

Abruzzo/Molise

Pasta in Abruzzo often comes as the curious *maccheroni alla chitarra*, long strings cut by pressing the dough over a wired frame; typically it's eaten with a tomato and pecorino or a lamb sauce. Abruzzo food tends to be characterised by hot, strong flavours – *spaghetti aglio, olio e peperoncini* (with oil, garlic, chilli) is a favourite. Hot peppers bring their fire to all sorts of dishes. Cheeses are the ubiquitous *pecorino* and *scamorza*, a spun cheese similar to mozzarella, and often smoked.

of places that label themselves as "hosterias" – an affectation on a par with the English "Ye Olde".

Traditionally, a meal (lunch is *pranzo*, dinner is *cena*) starts with **antipasto** (literally "before the meal"), a course generally served only in *ristoranti* and consisting of various cold cuts of meat, seafood and various cold vegetable dishes. *Prosciutto* is a common antipasto dish, ham either cooked (*cotto*) or just cured and hung (*crudo*) and served alone or with mozzarella cheese. A plateful of various antipasti from a self-service buffet will set you back L8000–10,000 a head, an item chosen from the menu a few thousand less. Bear in mind that if you're moving onto pasta, let alone a main course, you may need quite an appetite to tackle this. The next course, **il primo**, consists of a soup or pasta dish, and it's fine to just eat this and nothing else. This is followed by **il secondo** – the meat or fish course, usually served alone, except for perhaps a wedge of lemon or tomato. Watch out when ordering fish, which will either be served whole or by weight: 250g is usually plenty for one person, or ask to have a look at the fish before it's cooked.

Vegetables or salads – **contorni** – are ordered and served separately, and sometimes there won't be much choice: potatoes will invariably be chips, salads either green (*verde*) or mixed (*mista*). If there's no menu, the verbal list of what's available can be bewildering; if you don't understand, just ask for what you want. Everywhere will have pasta with tomato sauce (*pomodoro*) or meat sauce (*al ragù*). Afterwards you nearly always get a choice of fresh fruit (*frutta*) and a selection of desserts (*dolci*) – sometimes just ice cream, but often more elaborate

Lazio

Lazio means only one thing – Rome, and Roman cooking, like Tuscan, is essentially simple: pasta (cut shapes like *bucatini* and *penne* are favourites), served with sauces like *all'amatriciana* (cured pork and tomato), *alla carbonara* (egg and bacon), *all'arabbiate* (hot pepper and tomato). *Fettuccine* and *gnocchi alla romana* (made with semolina and baked with tomato sauce) are also very common, not to mention all kinds of offal. *Saltimbocca*, the favourite antipasto, is veal fried with raw ham; *zampetti* are calves' trotters. Two of the most popular sauces are not used for pasta but with vegetables – *all'agro* (olive oil and lemon juice or vinegar) and *agrodolce* (sweet-sour). Pasta itself is often topped with *pecorino romano*, a hard, salty cheese with a hot, raucous flavour. Other cheeses are sheep's milk ricotta and provatura. The most common vegetables are artichokes, aubergines, courgettes and salads like *misticanza* (wild salad leaves). Rome is also one of the best places outside Naples to eat *pizza rustica*, baked on traditionally wood fires and often topped with just one embellishment – tomato, pepper, courgette, mushroom, even potato.

Umbria/Marche

Landlocked, hilly Umbria is the only area outside Piemonte where truffles are abundant, and they find their way onto eggs, pasta, fish and meat. Pork, mushrooms, game and birds are all important in Umbrian food – pork made into hams, sausage and salami, and most famously into *la porchetta*, whole suckling pig stuffed with rosemary or sage, roasted on a spit and any vegetarian's nightmare. Perugia is renowned for its pastries and chocolates. Marche is very much a rural region, its food a mixture of seafood from the long coastline and country cooking from its interior, based on locally-grown produce – tomatoes, fennel, mushrooms. Like Umbria, truffles feature, and porchetta is stuffed with garlic and fennel.

Campania

The flavour of Naples dominates the whole of Campania. Nowhere in Italy is street-food so much part of the culture. Naples is the home of the true pizza, rapidly baked in searing hot wood-fired brick ovens and running with olive oil. Pizza Neapolitana simply doesn't exist: in Naples *every* pizza is Neapolitan, and the crucial one is the *marinara*, not, as you might think, anything to do with seafood but topped with just tomato, garlic and a leaf or two of basil. Street food also comprises fried pizzas topped with a smear of tomato and a square of mozzarella; and calzone, a stuffed fried pizza with ham or cheese or vegetables. *Friggitorie* sell other fried food: heavenly *krocche* (potato croquettes), *arancini* and *fiorilli* – courgette flowers in batter. Naples is also the home of pasta and tomato sauce, made with fresh tomatoes and laced with garlic. It's a curious aspect of Neapolitan sauces that garlic, onion and parmesan are rarely combined. Aubergines and courgettes turn up endlessly in pasta sauces, as does the tomato-mozzarella pairing, the items, like, in Sicily, *cassata* – ice cream made with ricotta, *zuppa inglese* – spongecake or trifle, or fresh fruit salad (*macedonia*). The favourite way to finish an Italian meal in Britain, *zabaglione*, is sadly rarely available at any but the most upmarket places.

Italy isn't a bad country to travel in if you're a **vegetarian**. There are several pasta sauces and pizza varieties without meat, and if you eat fish and seafood you should have no problem at all. Salads, too, are fresh and good, and filling. The only real problem is one of comprehension: Italians don't *understand* someone not eating meat, and stating the obvious doesn't always get the point across. Saying you're a vegetarian (*Sono vegetariano/a*) and asking if a dish has meat in (*c'è carne dentro?*), might still turn up a poultry or *prosciutto* dish. Better is to ask what a dish is made with before you order (*com'è fatto?*), so that you can spot the non-meaty meat. Being a **vegan** you'll have a much harder time, though pizzas without cheese are a good standby, vegetable soup is usually just that and the fruit is excellent.

At the **end of the meal** ask for the bill (*il conto*). In many trattorias this doesn't amount to much more than an illegible scrap of paper, and if you want to be sure you're not being ripped off, ask to have a receipt (*ricevuta fiscale*), something all bars and restaurants are legally bound to provide anyway; indeed they – and you – can be fined if you don't take the receipt with you (the same applies to shops and bars). As well as the cover charge, service (*servizio*) will often be added, generally about 10 percent. If service isn't included you should perhaps tip about the same amount, although trattorias outside the large cities won't necessarily expect this.

latter particularly good with gnocchi (the regions to the north and of Naples are both big mozarella-producing areas). Seafood in Naples is also particularly good. Here, they love squid, octopus and mussels – clams combine with garlic and oil for *spaghetti alla vongole*, mussels are prepared as *zuppa di cozze*. Pastries are exceptionally good, too. Absolutely not to be missed is the *sfogliatella*, a flaky pastry case stuffed with ricotta and candied peel, and the Easter cake, *pastiera*, made with ricotta and wheat berries.

Calabria and Basilicata

The food of Calabria is similar to that of Campania but tends to have a rougher approach. Greek influence still pervades in the form of aubergines, swordfish and sweets incorporating figs, almonds and honey; otherwise it's the common trademarks of the South – plenty of pasta, pork and cheeses such as mozzarella, caciocavallo, mature provolone and pecorino. Basilicata is another poor region, mountainous and sparsely populated, relying on pasta, tomatoes, bread, olives and pork. A fondness for spicy food shows in the popularity of all types of peppers, and, unusually in Italy, ginger (*zenzero*), which is thrown into many dishes. Strong cheeses, like matured ricotta – to match the strength of other dishes – are favoured.

Puglia

Puglia is the land of the grape – and the wine lake. In recent years the region has exploited its hot, fertile plains to become the wealthiest part of the South and while much of its wine may be fairly basic, its olive oils are gaining much respect. Its cooking, particularly in coastal areas, has a lingering Arab-Greek feel, though bread, pasta and seafood tend to be the staples. Puglians are fond of preserved vegetables: tomatoes are sun dried and salted or boiled and bottled; mushrooms, artichokes and aubergines are submerged in oil – *sott'olio*. Hams and pork sausage feature prominently, but in the coastal areas – Bari, Taranto, Brindisi – seafood dominates, shellfish often eaten raw. Pasta in Puglia is usually *orechiette*, or "little ears".

Sicily

Sicily's food has been tinkered with by the island's endless list of invaders, from Greeks, Arabs, Normans and Spanish, even the English. Sicily is famous for its sweets, like the rich *cassata* ice cream dish, and *cannoli* – fried pastries stuffed with sweet ricotta and rolled in chocolate. Dishes like orange salads evoke North Africa; couscous is a more obvious pointer. Just as in Naples, street food is all over, things like rice balls, potato croquettes, fritters and dinky-sized pizzas made to be clutched in a hand. Rice, brought by the Arabs, is more often found here than in the rest of Italy. Naturally, fish like anchovies, sardines, tuna and swordfish are abundant, teamed often with the ever-popular pasta in dishes like *spaghetti con le sarde*. Cheeses are *pecorino*, provola, caciocavallo and, of course, the sheep's milk ricotta which goes into so many of the sweet dishes.

A LIST OF FOODS AND DISHES

Basics and snacks

Aceto	Vinegar
Aglio	Garlic
Biscotti	Biscuits
Burro	Butter
Caramelle	Sweets
Cioccolato	Chocolate
Focaccia	Oven-baked snack
Formaggio	Cheese
Frittata	Omelette
Gelato	Ice cream
Grissini	Bread sticks
Maionese	Mayonnaise
Marmellata	Jam
Olio	Oil
Olive	Olives
Pane	Bread
Pane integrale	Wholemeal bread
Panino	Bread roll/ sandwich
Patatine	Crisps
Patatine fritte	Chips
Pepe	Pepper
Pizzetta	Small cheese and tomato pizza
Riso	Rice
Sale	Salt
Uova	Eggs
Yogurt	Yoghurt
Zúcchero	Sugar
Zuppa	Soup

Pizzas

Calzone	Folded pizza, often with cheese, ham and tomato
Capricciosa	Literally "capricious"; topped with whatever they've got in the kitchen, usually including baby artichoke, ham and egg
Cardinale	Ham and olives
Funghi	Mushroom; tinned, sliced button mushrooms unless it specifies fresh mushrooms, *funghi freschi*
Frutti di mare	Seafood; usually mussels, prawns, squid and clams
Margherita	Cheese and tomato
Marinara	Tomato and garlic
Napoli/ Napoletana	Tomato, cheese, anchovy, olive oil
Quattro formaggi	"Four cheeses", usually including mozzarella, fontina, gruyère and gorgonzola
Quattro stagioni	"Four seasons"; the toppings split into four sections, usually including ham, pepper, onion, mushrooms, artichokes, olives, etc

Antipasti and starters

Antipasto misto	Starter of seafood, vegetables, and cold meats
Caponata	Mixed aubergine, olives, tomatoes
Caprese	Tomato and mozzarella cheese salad
Crespolina	Pancake, usually stuffed
Insalata di mare	Seafood salad
Insalata di riso	Rice salad
Insalata russa	Salad of diced vegetables in mayonnaise
Melanzane alla parmigiana	Aubergine with tomato and parmesan cheese
Peperonata	Green and red peppers stewed in olive oil
Pomodori ripieni	Stuffed tomatoes
Prosciutto	Ham
Salame	Salami

The first course (Il primo): soups, pasta . . .

Brodo	Clear broth
Cannelloni	Large tubes of pasta, stuffed
Farfalle	Literally bow-shaped pasta
Fettuccine	Narrow pasta ribbons
Gnocchi	Small potato and dough dumplings
Lasagne	Lasagne
Maccheroni	Tubular spaghetti
Minestrina	Any light soup
Minestrone	Thick vegetable soup
Pasta al forno	Pasta baked with minced meat, eggs, tomato and cheese
Pasta e fagioli	Pasta with beans
Pastina in brodo	Pasta pieces in clear broth
Penne	Smaller version of rigatoni
Ravioli	Ravioli
Rigatoni	Large, grooved tubular pasta
Risotto	Cooked rice dish, with sauce
Spaghetti	Spaghetti
Spaghettini	Thin spaghetti
Stracciatella	Broth with egg
Tagliatelle	Pasta ribbons, another word for fettucine
Tortellini	Small rings of pasta, stuffed with meat or cheese
Vermicelli	Thin spaghetti ("little worms")

. . . and pasta sauce (salsa)

Amatriciana	Cubed pork and tomato sauce	*Parmigiano*	Parmesan cheese
Arrabbiata	Spicy tomato sauce, with chillies	*Peperoncino*	Olive oil, garlic and fresh chillies
Bolognese	Meat sauce	*Pesto*	Sauce with ground basil, garlic and pine nuts
Burro	Butter		
Carbonara	Cream, ham and beaten egg	*Pomodoro*	Tomato sauce
Funghi	Mushroom	*Ragù*	Meat sauce
Panna	Cream	*Vóngole*	Sauce with clams

The second course (Il secondo): meat (carne) . . .

Agnello	Lamb	*Fégato*	Liver	*Pancetta*/Speck	Bacon
Bistecca	Steak	*Involtini*	Meat slices, rolled and stuffed	*Pollo*	Chicken
Carpaccio	Thin slices of raw beef			*Polpette*	Meatballs
		Lepre	Hare	*Rognoni*	Kidneys
Cervella	Brain	*Lingua*	Tongue	*Salsiccia*	Sausage
Cinghiale	Wild boar	*Maiale*	Pork	*Saltimbocca*	Veal with ham
Coniglio	Rabbit	*Manzo*	Beef	*Spezzatino*	Stew
Costolette or cotoletta	Cutlet, chop	*Mortadella*	Salami-type cured meat	*Tacchino*	Turkey
				Trippa	Tripe
Fégatini	Chicken livers	*Ossobuco*	Shin of veal	*Vitello*	Veal

. . . fish (pesce) and shellfish (crostacei)

Acciughe	Anchovies	*Gamberetti*	Shrimps	*Sampiero*	John Dory
Anguilla	Eel	*Gámberi*	Prawns	*Sarde*	Sardines
Aragosta	Lobster	*Granchio*	Crab	*Sgombro*	Mackerel
Baccalà	Dried salted cod	*Merluzzo*	Cod	*Sógliola*	Sole
Calamari	Squid	*Ostriche*	Oysters	*Tonno*	Tuna
Céfalo	Mullet	*Pesce spada*	Swordfish	*Triglie*	Red mullet
Cozze	Mussels	*Pólipo*	Octopus	*Trota*	Trout
Dentice	Sea Bream	*Rospo*	Monkfish	*Vóngole*	Clams

Vegetables (contorni), herbs (erbe aromatice) and salad (insalata)

Asparagi	Asparagus	*Cetriolo*	Cucumber	*Melanzane*	Aubergine
Basílico	Basil	*Cipolla*	Onion	*Orígano*	Oregano
Bróccoli	Broccoli	*Fagioli*	Beans	*Patate*	Potatoes
Cápperi	Capers	*Fagiolini*	Green beans	*Peperoni*	Peppers
Carciofi	Artichokes	*Finocchio*	Fennel	*Piselli*	Peas
Carciofini	Artichoke hearts	*Funghi*	Mushrooms	*Pomodori*	Tomatoes
Carotte	Carrots	*Insalata verde/ mista*	Green salad/ mixed salad	*Radicchio*	Chicory
Cavolfiori	Cauliflower			*Spinaci*	Spinach
Cávolo	Cabbage	*Lenticchie*	Lentils	*Zucchini*	Courgettes

Some terms and useful words

Affumicato	Smoked	*Al dente*	Firm, not overcooked	*Pizzaiola*	Cooked with tomato sauce
Arrosto	Roast				
Ben cotto	Well done	*Ai ferri*	Grilled without oil	*Ripieno*	Stuffed
Bollito/lesso	Boiled	*Al forno*	Baked	*Al sangue*	Rare
Alle brace	Barbecued	*Fritto*	Fried	*Allo spiedo*	On the spit
Brasato	Cooked in wine	*Grattugiato*	Grated	*Stracotto*	Braised, stewed
Cotto	Cooked (not raw)	*Alla griglia*	Grilled	*Surgelati*	Frozen
		Alla Milanese	Fried in egg and breadcrumbs	*In umido*	Stewed
Crudo	Raw				

Sweets (dolci), fruit (frutta), cheeses (formaggi) and nuts (noce)

Amaretti	Macaroons	*Gelato*	Ice cream	*Pignoli*	Pine nuts
Ananas	Pineapple	*Gorgonzola*	Soft strong blue-veined cheese	*Pistacchio*	Pistachio nut
Anguria/ Coccomero	Water melon	*Limone*	Lemon	*Provola/ Provolone*	Smooth, round mild cheese, made form buffalo or sheep's milk. Sometimes smoked.
Arance	Oranges	*Macedonia*	Fruit salad		
Banane	Bananas	*Mándorle*	Almonds		
Cacchi	Persimmons	*Mele*	Apples		
Ciliegie	Cherries	*Melone*	Melon		
Dolcelatte	Creamy blue cheese	*Mozzarella*	Soft white cheese made from buffalo's milk	*Ricotta*	Soft white sheep's cheese
Fichi	Figs			*Torta*	Cake, tart
Fichi d'India	Prickly pears	*Parmigiano*	Parmesan cheese	*Uva*	Grapes
Fontina	Northern Italian cheese, often used in cooking	*Pecorino*	Strong hard sheep's cheese	*Zabaglione*	Dessert made with eggs, sugar and marsala wine
		Pere	Pears		
Frágole	Strawberries	*Pesche*	Peaches	*Zuppa Inglese*	Trifle

Drinks

Acqua minerale	Mineral water	*Latte*	Milk	*Vino*	Wine
Aranciata	Orangeade	*Limonata*	Lemonade	*Rosso*	Red
Bicchiere	Glass	*Selz*	Soda water	*Bianco*	White
Birra	Beer	*Spremuta*	Fresh fruit juice	*Rosato*	Rosé
Bottiglia	Bottle	*Spumante*	Sparkling wine	*Secco*	Dry
Caffè	Coffee	*Succo*	Concentrated fruit juice with sugar	*Dolce*	Sweet
Cioccolata calda	Hot chocolate			*Litro*	Litre
Ghiaccio	Ice	*Tè*	Tea	*Mezzo*	Half
Granita	Iced drink, with coffee or fruit	*Tónica*	Tonic water	*Quarto*	Quarter
				Salute!	Cheers!

DRINKING

Although many Italian children are brought up on wine, there's not a great emphasis on dedicated **drinking** in Italy. You'll rarely see drunks in public, young people don't devote their nights to getting wasted, and women especially are frowned upon if they're seen to be over-indulging. Nonetheless there's a wide choice of alcoholic drinks available, often at low prices; soft drinks come in multifarious hues, thanks to the abundance of fresh fruit; and there's also mineral water and crushed-ice drinks: you'll certainly never be stuck if you want to slake your thirst.

WHERE TO DRINK

Bars are less social centres than functional places, and are all very similar to each other – brightly-lit places, with a chrome counter, a *gaggia* coffee machine and a picture of the local football team on the wall. You'll come here for **ordinary drinking**: a coffee in the morning, a quick beer, a cup of tea, but people don't generally idle away the day or evening in bars. Indeed in some more rural places it's difficult to find a bar open much after 9pm. Where it does fit into the general Meditteranean pattern is that there are no set licensing hours and children are always allowed in; there's often a telephone and you can buy snacks and ice creams as well as drinks.

Whatever you're drinking, the **procedure** is the same. It's cheapest to drink standing at the counter (there's often nowhere to sit anyway), in which case you pay first at the cash desk (*la cassa*), present your receipt (*scontrino*) to the barperson and give your order. There's always a list of prices (*listino prezzi*) behind the bar. It's customary to leave an extra L50 or L100 on the counter for the barperson, although no one will object if you don't. If there's waiter service, just sit where you like, though bear in mind that to do this will cost perhaps twice as much, especially if you sit outside (the difference is shown on the price list as *tavola*).

COFFEE, TEA, SOFT DRINKS

One of the most distinctive smells in an Italian street is that of fresh **coffee**, usually wafting out of a bar (most trattorias and pizzerias don't serve hot drinks). It's always excellent: the basic choice is either small and black (*espresso*, or just *caffé*), which costs around L1000 a cup, or white and frothy (*cappuccino*), for about L2000, but there are other varieties. If you want your *espresso* watered down ask for a *caffé lungo*; with a shot of alcohol – and you can ask for just about anything in your coffee – is *caffé corretto*; with a drop of milk is *caffé macchiato*. Although most places let you help yourself, some will lace your black coffee with sugar; if you don't want it, you can make sure by asking for *caffé senza zucchero* – though the barperson will think you're mad. Many places also now sell decaffeinated coffee (ask for *Hag*, even when it isn't); while in summer you might want to have your coffee cold (*caffé freddo*). For a real treat ask for *caffé granita* – cold coffee with crushed ice, usually topped with cream.

If you don't like coffee, there's always **tea**. In summer you can drink this cold too (*tè freddo*) – excellent for taking the heat off. Hot tea (*te caldo*) comes with lemon (*con limone*) unless you ask for milk (*con latte*). **Milk** itself is drunk hot as often as cold, or you can get it with a dash of coffee (*latte macchiato*) and sometimes as milk shakes – *frappe* or *frullati*.

Alternatively, there are various **soft drinks** (*analcoliche*) to choose from. A ***spremuta*** is a fresh fruit juice, squeezed at the bar, usually orange, lemon or grapefruit. You might need to add sugar to the lemon juice (. . . *di limone*) but the orange (. . . *d'arancia*) is invariably sweet enough on its own, especially the crimson-red variety, made from blood oranges. There's also crushed-ice ***granitas***, big in Sicily and coming in several flavours other than coffee. Otherwise there's the usual range of fizzy drinks and concentrated juices: *Coke* is as prevalent as it is everywhere; the homegrown Italian version, *Chinotto*, is less sweet – good with a slice of lemon. **Tap water** (*acqua normale*) is quite drinkable, and you won't pay for it in a bar. **Mineral water** (*acqua minerale*) is a more common choice, either still (*senza gas* or *naturale*) or sparkling (*con gas* or *frizzante*) – about L1000 a glass.

BEER AND SPIRITS

Beer (*birra*) is always a lager-type brew which usually comes in one-third or two-third litre bottles, or on draught (*alla spina*), measure for measure more expensive than the bottled variety. A small beer is a "piccola", (20cl or 25cl), a larger one (usually 40cl) a "media". The commonest and cheapest brands are the Italian *Peroni* and *Dreher*, both of which are very drinkable; if this is what you want, either state the brand name or ask for *birra nazionale* – otherwise you may be given the more expensive imported beer. You may also come across darker beers (*birra nera* or *birra rossa*), which have a sweeter, maltier taste and in appearance resemble stout or bitter.

All the usual **spirits** are on sale and known mostly by their generic names. There are also Italian brands of the main varieties: the best Italian brandies are *Stock* and *Vecchia Romagna*. A generous shot of these costs about L2000, much more for imported stuff.

The homegrown Italian firewater is **Grappa**, originally from Bassano di Grappa in the Veneto but now available just about everywhere. It's made from the leftovers from the winemaking process (skins, stalks and the like) and is something of an acquired taste; should you acquire it, it's probably the cheapest way of getting plastered.

You'll also find **fortified wines** like *Martini*, *Cinzano* and *Campari*; ask for a Campari-Soda and you'll get a ready-mixed version from a little bottle; a slice of lemon is a *spicchio di limone*, ice is *ghiaccio*. You might also try *Cynar* – believe it or not, an artichoke-based sherry often drunk as an aperitif. There's also a daunting selection of **liqueurs**. *Amaro* is a bitter after-dinner drink, *Amaretto* much sweeter with a strong taste of marzipan, *Sambuca* a sticky-sweet aniseed concoction, traditionally served with a coffee bean in it and set on fire (though only tourists are likely to experience this these days). *Strega* is another drink you'll see behind every bar – the yellow stuff in tall, elongated bottles: about as sweet as it looks but not unpleasant.

ITALIAN WINE

Just as Italy's food has suffered from stereotyped images, so too has its **wine**. *Lambrusco* has soared to second place in the best-seller list in Britain, while cheap *Soaves* and *Chianti* continue to shift units. All of which is a fair indication of the methods that until now have permeated the Italian wine industry – high yields, low prices, ship 'em out and never mind the quality.

REGIONAL WINES

The North

Piemonte rivals Tuscany as producer of Italy's finest reds. Its big names are the names of tradition – *Barolo, Barbaresco, Barbera*. These wines need ageing, and *Barolo* in particular can be very expensive. More suitable for everyday drinking are wines made from the *dolcetto* grape, notably *Dolcetto d'Alba*, drunk young and lightly chilled. Probably the most famous is the sparkling *Asti Spumante* ("Spumante" is the Italian for wines made by the champagne method) – a sweet wine, though there has been a trend in recent years to make dry spumanti. In contrast to the traditional grapes and names of Piemonte, the three northeastern regions – **Trentino-Alto Adige**, **Veneto** and **Friuli-Venezia Giulia** – have been very successful at developing wines with French and German grape varieties. Merlot, cabernet, pinot bianco, pinot grigio, müller-thurgau, riesling, chardonnay and gewürztraminer from these regions are all likely to be good, and Alto Adige in particular produces excellent fresh, aromatic whites at reasonable prices.

Names more familiar to British supermarket shelves – *Bardolino, Valpolicella* and *Soave* – are all from the Verona region and like so many Italian wines always taste better near their region of origin. **Emilia-Romagna** is synonymous with *Lambrusco*, which you could easily be forgiven for taking to be a different wine altogether from stuff you buy in Britain. Buy only DOC *Lambrusco* – it's still ridiculously cheap – and amaze yourself. **Lombardy** and **Liguria** are not well known for their wines, which is a pity, because both produce some attractive brews. Milan supermarket shelves bulge with basic wines from the *Oltrepò Pavese*, and the northern areas of Valtellina and around Brescia make good wines such as the red *Franciacorta* and the white *Cádel Bosco*, a sparkler. Liguria only really produces two wines, the crisp, dry *Cinque Terre* and the sweet *Sciacchetra* – made from partially dried grapes and prohibitively expensive.

Central Italy

Tuscany dominates central Italian winemaking, and *Chianti* can be very good, but beware of bottles that seem too cheap. It's worth genning up on vintages for reds, but most recent *Chiantis* are fairly reliable. Tuscany's two other prime reds, *Brunello di Montalcino* and *Vino Nobile di Montepulciano* can be Italy's most expensive wines – not the sort of thing you'd knock back at a trattoria. *Rosso di Montalcino* offers a more pocket-friendly option. Two common whites are *Vernaccia di San Gimignano* and the fresh *Galestro*. Tuscany is also renowned for *Vin Santo*, a sweet, strong wine into which biscuits are traditionally dipped.

Lazio, **Umbria** and **Marche** are best known for their fresh, dry whites. Umbria's *Orvieto*, once predominantly a medium sweet wine has been revived in a dry style, though the original abboccato is still available. Lazio's wine comes chiefly from the Roman hills, the best known *Est! Est! Est!* and *Frascati*, both of which can be unreliable. The best reds of these regions tend to come, like *Rosso Conero*, from Marche, though its own white, *Verdicchio dei Castelli di Jesi*, is worth a tipple.

Abruzzo produces few wines. Red wine here will almost certainly be *Montepulciano d'Abruzzo*, a strong, earthy wine; white will be *Trebbiano d'Abruzzo*. *Cerasuola* is a rosé version of Montepulciano. In **Molise** the wines are similar but the names change – *Biferno* and *Pentro*, both in white and red.

The South

Other than the odd pocket of quality, Southern wines don't enjoy a good reputation. **Puglia** perhaps sums the region up, the largest producer of wine in the country, most of which is basic stuff that goes to strengthen table wines from the North or ends up in five-litre flagons selling for a few thousand lire. There are however a number of DOC wines and one or two producers have begun to produce better wines, such as the red and rose *Castel del Monte*.

The volcanic slopes of Vesuvius in **Campania** are among the most ancient wine-producing areas in Italy, though again there's not much of note. Whites from Ischia and Capri are reliable everyday drinks, and *Lacryma Christi*, red and white, from the slopes of Vesuvius, can be reasonable. The best choices for a Campanian white are *Greco di Tufo* and *Fiano di Avellino*; for a red the only choice is *Taurasi*, a rich wine that can command high prices. The grape that produces Taurasi, *aglianico*, makes another pedigree appearance further south in **Basilicata**. *Aglianico del Vulture* is that region's only DOC, but other wines worth trying are the sweet, sparkling *Malvasia* and *Moscato*. *Cirò* is the success story of **Calabria**, an old wine which has been given some modern touches, and now shifts bottles outside its home territory. Not surprisingly, given its far-south position, Calabria also turns out sweet whites such as *Greco di Bianco*.

Sicily is of course associated mainly with the fortified *Marsala*, but the island has also made a name for itself as a producer of quality everyday wines such as *Corvo* and *Regaleali*. These names (red and white) have no classification but Corvo in particular is found all over Italy – a tribute to its quality.

The nice thing about travelling to Italy, though, is that the best wines are kept mostly for the home market. Nudged along by the DOC laws (see below), standards have been steadily increasing in recent years. Many producers have been turning their hands to making higher quality wines, and besides the finer tuning of established names such as *Barolo* and *Orvieto*, there's a good deal of experimentation going on everywhere. Southern winemakers are no longer content to see nearly all of their produce going north to beef up table-wine blends, while in Tuscany, Trentino-Alto Adige and Friuli, French grape varieties such as chardonnay, sauvignon and the pinots are joining old Italian favourites with startling success.

They don't waste drinking time in Italy with dialogue or veneration, however; neither is there much time for the snobbery associated with "serious" wine drinking in France or Britain. Light reds such as those made from the *dolcetto* grape are hauled out of the fridge in hot weather, while some full-bodied whites are drunk at near room temperature. Wine is invariably drunk with meals. It's also still very cheap, though unless your aim is to get legless as cheaply as possible, it's wise to avoid the very cheapest plonk. In restaurants you'll invariably be offered red (*rosso*) or white (*bianco*) – rarely *rose*. If you're unsure about what to order, don't be afraid to try the local stuff, sometimes served straight from the barrel, particularly down south, and often very good, and cheap at an average of around L5000 a litre. Bottled wine is pricier but still very good value; expect to pay around L10,000 a bottle in a restaurant, less than half that from a shop or supermarket. In bars you can buy a glass of wine for about L2000.

THE *DENOMINAZIONE D'ORIGINE* SYSTEM

This is the key to understanding what to look for in Italian wine, but it shouldn't be seen as any sort of guarantee. The denomination is a certification of origin, not of quality, and while it may mean a wine will be drinkable, stick to it too rigidly and you could be missing out on an awful lot.

Denomination zones are set by governmental decree. They specify where a certain named wine may be made, what grape varieties may be used, the maximum yield of grapes per hectare and how long the wine should be aged. *Vino da tavola* is simply wine that does not conform to the DOC laws, though it's not necessarily wine you'd sooner pour down the sink than drink. *Denominazione d'Origine Controllata* (DOC) guarantees the origin of the wine and that it has been made to the specification of the rules for the zone in which it's produced. *Denomin-azione d'Origine Controllata e Garantita* (DOCG) is the only designation at the moment that actually has any real meaning. Wines sold under this label not only have to conform to the ordinary DOC laws, but are also tested by government-appointed inspectors. There are only currently half a dozen or so such wines, although if the system gets up and running as is planned, there will be fifty by the year 2000.

Though it's undoubtedly true that the DOC system has helped lift standards, the laws have come under fire from both growers and critics for their rigidity, constraints and anomalies. *Chianti* for instance can be a quaffable lunchtime drink, a wine of pedigree to be treated with reverence, or – in the case of some of the 1984 harvest – it can be appalling. All have a DOC. Some claim too that the restrictions of the DOCG are losing their credibility. With big reds such as *Barolo* the ageing term can destroy all the fruitiness of the wine, while the entry of *Albana di Romagna*, a somewhat ordinary white, to DOCG status, with others to follow, has caused consternation. Increasingly, producers eager to experiment have begun to disregard the regulations and make new wines that are sometimes expensive and among Italy's best wines, though they're still offically labelled "da tavola" (the nickname "super vini da tavola" has emerged). The Sicilian *Corvo*, red and white, is perhaps the best known non-DOC label, a modern wine which goes for a little over twice the price of ordinary table plonk, and Tuscany produces some excellent table wines.

COMMUNICATIONS: POST, PHONES AND THE MEDIA

Post office opening hours are usually Monday–Saturday 8am–6.30pm; smaller towns won't have a service on a Saturday. If you want stamps, you can buy them in *tabacchi* too, as well as in some gift shops in the tourist resorts; they will often also weigh your letter. Rates to Britain are L750 for a letter, L700 for a postcard; to North America they are L1150 for a letter and L1050 for a postcard. The Italian postal system is one of the worst in Europe: if your letter is urgent consider spending the extra L3750 required to send it express. Letters can be sent poste restante to any Italian post office, by addressing them "Fermo Posta" followed by the name of the town. When picking something up take your passport, and make sure they check under middle names and initials – and every other letter when all else fails – as filing is often diabolical.

TELEPHONES

Public **telephones**, run by **SIP**, the state telephone company, come in various forms, usually with clear instructions printed on them (in English too). In the major towns, the most common type takes L100, L200 and L500 coins, as well as **telephone cards** (*carte telefoniche*), available from tabacchi and newstands for L5000 or L10,000. In larger cities you also find phones that take phonecards only, but there's always one that takes coins nearby, usually adjacent. You will also come across phones, normally in bars, that only take a *gettone* (L200), available from SIP offices, tabacchi, bars and some newstands, although these are obviously only much use for making local calls; *gettoni* are also in common use as currency. If you can't find a phone box, **bars** will often have a phone you can use (look for the red phone symbol), though these tend only to take *gettoni*.

You can make **international calls** from any booth that accepts cards, and from any other booth labelled *interurbano*; the minimum charge for an international call is L2000. The cheapest way to make international calls, however, is to get hold of a **BT Chargecard** or the card issued by **AT&T Direct Service**. Both cards are free, and they work in the same way – just ring the company's international operator (BT ☎172 0044; AT & T ☎172 1011), who will connect you free of charge and add the cost of the connected call to your domestic bill. Another alternative is to find a **SIP office** (or, less commonly, **ASST**), where you make your call from a kiosk and pay for it afterwards. Some bars have this facility too – it's called a *cabina a scatti*. Finally, you can also make metered calls from hotels, but this will cost you at least 25 percent more, unless you make the call using a BT or AT & T charge card.

INTERNATIONAL TELEPHONE CODES

For direct **international calls from Italy**, dial the country code (given below), the area code (minus its first 0), and finally the subscriber number.

UK: 0044
Australia: 0061
Ireland: 00353
New Zealand: 0064
US & Canada: 001

CODES FOR MAJOR ITALIAN CITIES

Calling Italy from abroad, dial 01039 then the area code (the major towns are listed below), then the subscriber number. If calling **long-distance within Italy**, dial 0 immediately before the area code.

Bari ☎80
Naples ☎81
Bologna ☎51
Palermo ☎91
Florence ☎55
Rome ☎6
Genoa ☎10
Turin ☎11
Milan ☎2
Venice ☎41

Phone **tariffs** are highest on weekdays between 8am and 1pm, and cheapest between 10pm and 8am all week and all day Sunday.

To make an international **reversed charge** call, ring the international operators at BT or AT & T (see above), who will connect your call free of charge, even if you don't have a charge card.

NEWSPAPERS

The **Italian press** is fairly regionally-based, but there are some newspapers that are available all over the country. The centre-left *La Repubblica* and authoritative right-slanted *Corriere della Sera* are the two most widely-read and available, published nationwide with local supplements. *L'Unità*, the party organ of the Democratic Left (formerly the Communists), has hit hard times of late, its declining appeal matched by the drop in its readership, many of whom have turned to the fresher, more radical *Il Manifesto* as an alternative. *Paese Sera*, also, is a left-wing daily read widely in the south. Of other provincial newspapers, *La Stampa* is the daily of Turin, *Il Messaggero* of Rome – both rather stuffy, establishment sheets. *Il Mattino* is the more readable organ of Naples and the Campania area, while other southern editions include the *Giornale di Sicilia* and *La Gazzetta del Sud*. Perhaps the most avidly read newspapers of all, however, are the specialist sports papers, most notably the *Corriere delle Sport* and the pink *Gazzetta dello Sport* – both essential reading if you want to get a hold on the Italian football scene.

English-language newspapers can be found for around three times their home cover price in all the larger cities and most of the more established resorts, usually a day late, though in Milan and Rome you can sometimes find the papers on the day of publication, especially those, like the *Times*, *Financial Times* and the *Guardian*, which publish a European edition. Coversely, in the remoter parts of the country it's not unusual for papers to be delayed by several days.

THE AIRWAVES: TV AND RADIO

If you get the chance, try and watch some Italian **TV**, if only to size up the pros and cons of deregulation. The three state-run channels, *RAI 1*, *2* and *3*, controlled under law by the *DC*, *PSI* and *PSD* respectively, have of late been facing a massive onslaught by independent operators, especially those owned by the Euromogul Berlusconi, whose *Canale 5* is one of the more successful of the new arrivals. Although stories of hard pornography are way overplayed, programmes with stripping housewives and the like do exist, but otherwise the output is pretty bland across the board, with the accent on ghastly quiz shows and soaps, plus a heavy smattering of American imports. The *RAI* channels, especially *RAI 3*, do however carry less advertising and at least attempt to mix the dross with above-average documentaries and news coverage.

The situation in **radio** is if anything even more anarchic, with the FM waves crowded to the extent that you continually pick up new stations whether you want to or not. This means there *are* generally some good stations if you search hard enough, but on the whole the *RAI* stations are again the more professional – though even with them daytime listening is virtually undiluted dance music.

BUSINESS HOURS, HOLIDAYS AND TOURIST SIGHTS

Most shops and businesses in Italy open from Monday to Saturday from 8 or 9am until around 1pm, and from about 4pm until 7 or 8pm, though in the north especially some offices work to a 9am–5pm day. Everything, except bars and restaurants, closes on Sunday, though you might find fish shops in some coastal towns and pasticcerias or bakers open until Sunday lunchtime.

The other factors that can disrupt your plans are **national holidays** and local **saint's days and festivals**. Local religious holidays don't generally close down shops and businesses for the whole day, but they do mean that accommodation space may be tight. The country's official national holidays, on the other hand, close everything down, except bars and restaurants. These are:

January 1

January 6 (Epiphany)

Easter Monday

April 25 (Liberation Day)

May 1 (Labour Day)

August 15 (*Ferragosto*; Assumption of the Blessed Virgin Mary)

November 1 (*Ogni Santi*; All Saints)

December 8 (Immaculate Conception of the Blessed Virgin Mary)

December 25

December 26

CHURCHES, MUSEUMS AND ARCHAEOLOGICAL SITES

The rules for visiting **churches** are much as they are all over the Mediterranean. Dress modestly, which usually means no shorts and covered shoulders for women, and try to avoid wandering around during a service. Most churches open in the early morning, around 7 or 8am for Mass, and close around noon, opening up again at 4pm and closing at 7pm or 8pm. In more obscure places, some churches will only open for early morning and evening services, while others are closed at all times except Sundays and on religious holidays.

Another problem you'll face – and this applies to the whole country – is that lots of churches, monasteries, convents and oratories are **closed for restoration** (*chiuso per restauro*). We've indicated in the text the more long-term closures, though you might be able to persuade a workman or priest/curator to show you around even if there's scaffolding everywhere.

State-run museums open daily from 9am until 2pm, Monday–Saturday, and from 9am until 1pm on Sunday; they're closed altogether on Monday. Most other museums roughly follow this pattern too, although they are more likely to open (albeit rarely) for a couple of hours in the afternoon on selected days; they are, however, also normally closed on Mondays. For smaller museums, certainly, opening hours are severely cut back during winter. The opening times of **archaeological sites** are more flexible: most sites open every day, often Sunday included, 9am until late evening – frequently specified as one hour before sunset, and thus changing according to the time of year. In winter, times are again drastically cut, if only because of the darker evenings; 4pm is a common closing time. Again they are sometimes closed on Monday. **Admission prices** for state-run museums varies between L4000 and L8000, although occasionally – the Forum in Rome, the Palazzo Ducale in Mantua, for example – the charge is as high as L10,000; under-18s and over-60s get in free on production of documentary proof – student cards are no longer accepted at most places, though it's worth a try. Some sites, churches and monasteries are nominally free to get in, though there'll be a custodian around to open things up and show you around, whom you are expected to tip – L1000 per person should do it. Otherwise expect to pay much the same as you would in a museum.

FESTIVALS AND ANNUAL EVENTS

Italy has few national festivals, but there is no shortage of celebrations, saints' days being the usual excuse for some kind of binge. All cities, small towns and villages have their local saint, who is normally paraded through the streets amid much noise and spectacle. There are no end of other occasions for a *festa* – either to commemorate a local miracle or historic event, or to show off the local products or artistic talent. Many happen at Easter, or in May, September or around Ferragosto (August 15); the local tourist office will have details and exact dates.

Recently there's also been a revival of the **carnival** (*carnevale*), the last fling before Lent, although the anarchic fun that was enjoyed in the past has generally been replaced by elegant, self-conscious affairs, with ingenious costumes and handmade masks. Venice has the most famous carnival – a well-organised event that is so popular it sometimes takes over the entire city centre – and there are other, equally large and perhaps more fun events such as at Viareggio in Tuscany and Acireale in Sicily. And smaller towns will often put on a parade. A carnival usually lasts for the five days before Ash Wednesday; because it's connected with Easter the dates can change from year to year – count on some time between the end of February and end of March.

RELIGIOUS AND TRADITIONAL FESTIVALS

Perhaps the most widespread local event in Italy is some kind of **religious procession**, some of which can be very dramatic affairs. Many – perhaps all – have strong pagan roots, marking important dates on the calendar and only relatively recently sanctified by the church. One of the best-known takes place in the small village of **Cocullo** in the Abruzzi mountains, on May 6 (Saint Dominic Abate's day), when a statue of the saint, swathed in snakes, is carried through the town – a ritual that certainly dates back to pre-Christian times. **Good Friday**, for obvious reasons, is also a popular time for processions. In many towns and villages models of Christ taken from the Cross are paraded through towns accompanied by white-robed, hooded figures singing penitential hymns. The west coast of Sicily sees many of these, as do other places across the South – **Táranto**, **Reggio**, **Bari**, **Brindisi**. On the following Saturday a procession of flagellants makes its way through **Nocera Tirinese** in Calabria. Later on in the year, big *presepi* (nativity scene) markets mark the days leading up to **Christmas** in **Naples** and **Verona** (in Naples especially *presepi* are a popular local craft), and there's a similarly large-scale *Mercato di Sant'Ambrogio* in **Milan**. At **Epiphany** (January 6) a toy and sweet fair, dedicated to the good witch *Befana*, lasts until dawn around the fountains of Piazza Navona in **Rome**. On the same day a procession of the *Rei Magi* (Three Kings) passes through **Milan**, and there are live tableaux at **Rivisondoli** in Abruzzo. There are other, less obviously purely events of celebration, marking miracles, the most famous of which is the *Festa di San Gennaro* in **Naples**, where much superstition surrounds the miraculous liquefaction of the saint's blood three times a year.

Other ritual celebrations bear less of the Church's imprint, and a Communist mayor and local bishop will jointly attend a town's saint's day celebration, where the separate motivations to make some money, have a good time and pay some spiritual dues all merge. Superstition and a desire for good luck are part of it too. In **Gubbio** there's a mad race to the Church of San Ubaldo (May 5) with the *Ceri* – three phallic wooden pillars each eight metres high. Similar obelisks are carried around in other places. On September 3 a ninety-foot tall *Macchina di Santa Rosa*, illuminated with tiny oil lamps, is paraded through **Viterbo**, and at **Nola**, near Naples, around June 22, eight *gigli* (lilies) are carried through the streets. Phallic though these may seem, the giant towers are more likely to be associated with an ancient, goddess-worshipping culture.

The number of practising Catholics in Italy is dwindling, and until recently many *feste* were dying out. But interest in many festivals has been revived over the last decade or so, especially in **pilgrimages**. These are as much social occasions as spiritual journeys, some of them more important to people than Christmas, and they still attract massive crowds. As many as a million pilgrims travel through the night, mostly on foot, to the **Shrine of the Madonna di Polsi** in the inhospitable Aspromonte mountains in Calabria. And there are other shrines and sanctuaries all over Italy, mostly in inaccessible hilltop locations, some of them visited regularly by families from the surrounding area keen for a day out, others just the subject of a once-a-year trek. **Other traditions** survive: on the **Day of the Dead** (All Saints Day) in November, children receive presents, given on behalf of dead relatives, to make them feel that the people they were close to still think of them. There are festivals which evoke local pride in tradition too, medieval contests like the *Palio* horserace in **Siena** perpetuating allegiances to certain competing clans; *Palio* races take place in a few other centres, Alba and Asti in Piemonte for example, though most have been revived more to support the tourist indiustry than anything else and can't compete with the seriousness and vigour of Siena's contest. Other towns put on crossbow and flag twirling contests, marching bands in full medieval costume accompanying the event with enthusiastic drumming.

FESTIVAL DIARY

AGRIGENTO Almond blossom festival *Feb*

ALBA *Giostra delle Centro Torri* Palio and costume parade *1st Sun in Oct*

AMALFI *Sant'Andrea*'s day *June 27*

AOSTA *Fiera di Sant'Orso* Thousand-year-old fair *End of Jan*

AREZZO *Giostra del Saracino* Jousting by knights in armour *1st Sun in Sept*

ASCOLI PICENO *Torneo della Quintana* Jousting *1st weekend in Aug*

ASSISI Holy Week celebrations *Easter*

Calendimaggio spring *festa 1st week in May*

ASTI Bareback riders from villages around take part in *Palio 3rd Sun in Sept*

BARI *Sagra di San Nicola* Pilgrims follow a boat carrying the Saint's image for a ceremony out at sea, in honour of the 47 sailors who saved his bones from raiders. *May 7–8*

BRISIGHELLA Medieval festival *End of June*

CAGLIARI *Sagra di Sant Efisio* Thousands of pilgrims accompany the Saint's statue in carts, on horseback or on foot. *May 1*

CAMOGLI *Sagra del Pesce* Procession of boats, with a fish fry-up. *2nd Sun in May*

CAMPOBASSO *Sagra dei Misteri Beginning of June*

COCULLO *Festa di San Domenico Abate* Procession through the village with a statue of the saint swathed in snakes. *May 6*

DIANO MARINA *Festival del Mare* Fireworks *Aug 15*

DOLCEACQUA *Festa di San Sebastiano* Saint's day celebrated with a tree covered with communion hosts carried through town. *Jan 20*

ENNA Celebrations for Holy Week *Easter*

FAVIGNANA (off Sicily) *La Mattanza* Ritual slaughter of tuna. *May/June*

FELTRE Medieval *Palio 1st weekend in Aug*

FLORENCE *Scoppio del Carro* Firework display in the Piazza del Duomo *Easter Sun*

Festa di San Giovanni, Fireworks and the *Gioco di Calcio Storico* – a rough-and-tumble football game played between the four quarters of the city in medieval costume. *June 24 and 28*

FOLIGNO *Torneo della Quintana* Six hundred medieval knights, in jousting contest *2nd weekend in Sept*

GENOVA *Festa di San Giovanni June 24*

GUBBIO *Festa dei Ceri May 5* Crossbow matches against San Sepolcro *Last Sun in May*

LA SPEZIA Rowing contests in *Palio del Golfo Aug*

LAVAGNA *Torta di Fieschi* Blind-Date-style festa, commemorating medieval wedding *Aug 14*

LUCCA Torchlight processions as part of *Luminaria di Santa Croce Aug 14*

LUNGRO (Calabria) Albanian celebrations *Easter*

MAROSTICA Human chess game (every even year) *2nd weekend in Sept*

MASSA MARITIMA Crossbow competition *May 24*

MILAN *Mercato di Sant'Ambrogio December*

NAPLES *Festa di San Gennaro 1st Sat of May*

Gathering in the cathedral to witness the liquefaction of the saint's blood *Sept 16, Dec 19*

NOCERA TIRINESE Flagellants' procession through the village *Easter Sat*

NORCIA (Umbria) Crossbow matches and processions *March 20–21*

NOVOLI (Lecce) Bonfires in honour of *Sant'Antonio Abate an 17*

ORVIETO *Corpus Domimi* procession *Beginning of June*

PIANA DEGLI ALBANESI Byzantine celebrations *Easter and Epiphany*

PISA *Luminaria* , Festival of Lights *June 16–17*

PISTOIA *Giostra dell Órso* Joust of the Bear *July 25*

PORTO CESAREO *Luminaria* Festival of lights *Aug 22*

ROME *Befana* Toy and sweet fair in Piazza Navona *Jan 6 (Epiphany)*

Festa de'Noantri Dancing, songs and floats in Trastevere's piazzas *July 16–24*

SAN SEPOLCRO Crossbow matches against Gubbio *2nd weekend in Sept*

SIENA *Palio* in medieval Campo *July 2, Aug 16*

TAGGIA *Festa della Maddalena* with Dance of Death in main piazza *Sun nearest to July 22*

VENICE *Carnevale* Feb/March

Il Redentore gondola procession, fireworks, to commemorate the end of a sixteenth-century plague. *3rd week in July*

Regatta 1st Sun in Sept

VENTIMIGLIA Regatta and processions *Aug 9–10*

VIAREGGIO *Carnevale Feb/March*

VITERBO Procession of the *Macchina di Santa Rosa Sept 3*

FOOD FESTIVALS

Food-inspired *feste* are more low-key affairs than the religious events, but no less enjoyable for it, usually celebrating the local speciality of the region to the accompaniment of dancing, music from a local brass band and noisy fireworks at the end of the evening. There are literally hundreds of food festivals, sometimes advertised as *sagre*, and every region has them – look in the local papers or ask at the tourist office during summer and autumn and you're bound to find something going on. Most are modest affairs, meant for the locals and little-publicised – but there are a few exceptions. In **Tivoli**, near Rome, the town's fountains run with wine on the second Sunday in October; the same happens in **Citta della Pieve** in Umbria, in April, during the *Festa dell Fontane*, and at nearby **Panicale**. Other notable events are **Orvieto**'s wine festival each June, **Bolzano**'s in the second half of March, and the truffle fair and *palio* in **Alba** on the first Sunday in October. Generally though, the smaller they are the better, giving you a chance to join in the dancing and sample the cooking.

ARTS FESTIVALS

The home-town pride that sparks off many of the food festivals also expresses itself in some of the **arts festivals** spread across Italy, particularly in the central part of the country – based in ancient amphitheatres or other ruins or marking the work of a native composer, and sometimes going on for as long as a month. Perhaps the most prestigious is the **Venice** film festival in August and September. **Spoleto**'s summer *Festival dei Due Mondi* (Festival of the Two Worlds) is also well-known, a two-month long event of classical concerts, films, ballet, street theatre and performance art, with its venue the open spaces of the ancient walled town, that is the biggest arts festival in the country nowadays. The *Sferisterio* in **Macerata** in Marche, and the Roman arena in **Verona** are two equally dramatic places to hear music in the summer months. Similarly there's the *Panatenee Pompeiane* music festival, held in the ruins of **Pompeii** during the last week of August. **Bologna**'s summer festival often tries something different, with live bands playing in its medieval palace courtyards, and screenings of soap opera or art movies in unexpected places. Other festivals remember a particular composer: Puccini's music is celebrated from the end of July to mid-August in Torre del Lago, near **Viareggio**, Rossini's in **Pésaro** from mid-August to September. And it's worth noting the dates of the Italian **opera season**, which begins in December and runs through until May or June. The principal opera houses are *la Scala*

ARTS FESTIVALS

CITTA DI CASTELLO Chamber Music Festival *Aug & Sept*

FIESOLE *Estate Fiesolana* (music, cinema, ballet, theatre) *Mid-June to Aug*

FLORENCE *Maggio Musicale Fiorentino* *May & June*

LUCCA Opera and theatre festival at Barga *Last half of July*

MESSINA International Film Festival *July*

NAPLES International Music Festival *Last half of May*

Neapolitan song contest at Piedigrotta *First half of Sept*

PERUGIA Umbria Jazz Festival *July & Aug*

RAVENNA *Basilica di San Vitale* Organ music recitals *July & Aug*

ROME Opera at Baths of Caracalla concerts at Campidoglio, in July, the Basilica of Maxentius, all summer, and the *Accademia Nazionale di Santa Cecilia* and *Accademia Filarmonica Romana* in winter *July & Aug*

SIENA *Settimane Musicale* (musical weeks) *Aug*

SORRENTO International Cinema Convention *October*

STRESA *Settimane Musicale* (Lago Maggiore) *End of Aug*

SYRACUSE Greek drama in ancient theatre *May & June*

TAORMINA International film festival concerts and plays in the Greek theatre *July & Aug*

TORINO *Settembre Musica* *Sept*

UMBÉRTIDE Rock festival *Summer*

VENICE International Film Festival *Aug & Sept*

VERONA International Film Festival *June*

VITERBO Baroque Music Festival *Mid-June to July*

in Milan, the *Teatro dell'Opera* in Rome, *La Fenice* in Venice, the *Teatro Comunale* in Florence and the *Teatro San Carlo* in Naples. But there are also other, smaller venues that have regular performances of opera throughout these months.

TROUBLE AND THE POLICE

Despite what you hear about the Mafia, most of the crime you're likely to come across in Italy is of the small-time variety, prevalent in the major cities and the south of the country, where gangs of *scippatori* or "snatchers" operate. Crowded streets or markets, and packed tourist sights, are the places to beware; *scippatori* work on foot or on scooters, disappearing before you've had time to react. As well as handbags, they whip wallets, tear off visible jewellery and, if they're really adroit, unstrap watches.

You can **minimise the risk** of this happening by being discreet: don't flash anything of value, keep a firm hand on your camera, and carry shoulderbags, as Italian women do, slung across your body. It's a good idea, too, to entrust money and credit cards to hotel managers. Never leave anything valuable in your car and try and park in car parks on well-lit, well-used streets. On the whole it's common sense to avoid badly lit areas completely at night, and deserted inner-city areas by day. Confronted with a robber, your best bet is to submit meekly: it's an excitable situation where panic can lead to violence – though very few tourists see anything of this.

THE POLICE

If it comes to the worst, you'll be forced to have some dealings with the **police**. In Italy these come in many forms, their power split ostensibly to prevent any seizure of power. You're not likely to have much contact with the **Guardia di Finanza**, responsible for investigating smuggling, tax evasion and other finance-related felonies; and the **Polizia Urbana**, or town police, are mainly concerned with directing the traffic and punishing parking offences; while the **Polizia Stradale** patrol motorways. You may, however, have dealings with the **Carabinieri**, with their military-style uniforms and white shoulder belts, who deal with general crime, public order and drug control. These are the ones Italians are most rude about, but a lot of jokes about how stupid they are stem from the usual north-south prejudice. Eighty percent of the Carabinieri are from southern Italy – joining the police is one way to climb out of the poverty trap – and they are posted away from home so as to be well out of the sphere of influence of their families (the Carabinieri is actually part of the army). The **Polizia Statale**, the other general crime-fighting branch, enjoy a fierce rivalry with the *Carabinieri*, and are the one you'll perhaps have most chance of coming into contact with, since it's to them that **thefts** should be reported. You'll find the address of the **Questura** or police station in the local telephone directory (in smaller places it may be just a local *commissariati*), and we've included details in the major city listings. The *Questura* is also where you're supposed to go to obtain a *permesso di soggiorno* **if you're staying** for any length of time, or a **visa extension** if you require one (see "Red Tape and Visas", p.11).

In any brush with the authorities, your experience will depend on the individuals you're dealing with. Apart from **topless bathing** (permitted, but don't try anything more daring) and **camping rough**, don't expect a soft touch if you're picked up for any offence, especially if it's **drugs**-related: it's not unheard-of to be stopped and searched if you're young and carry a rucksack. Drugs are generally frowned upon by everyone above a certain age, and universal hysteria about *la droga*, fuelled by the serious problem of heroin addiction all over Italy, means that any distinction between

EMERGENCIES

In an **emergency**, note the following national emergency telephone numbers.

☎112 for the police (*Carabinieri*).

☎113 for any emergency service (*Soccorso Pubblico di Emergenza*).

☎115 for the fire brigade (*Vigili del Fuoco*).

☎116 for road assistance (*Soccorso Stradale*).

the "hard" and "soft" variety has become blurred. Theoretically everything is illegal above the possession of a few grams of cannabis or marijuana "for personal use", though there's no agreed definition of what this means. In general the south of Italy is more intolerant than the north, and in any case, if found with suspicious substances you can be kept in gaol for as long as it takes for them to analyse the stuff, draw up reports and wait for the bureaucratic wheels to grind – which could be several weeks, and sometimes months. For the nearest **British consulate** see *Listings* in the Rome, Milan and Naples accounts – though bear in mind that they're unlikely to be very sympathetic, or do anything more than put you in touch with a lawyer.

SEXUAL HARASSMENT AND WOMEN IN ITALY

Customs haven't changed much over the years in many parts of Italy, even in the relatively developed North, and in the more remote parts of the country, the gap between marriage and motherhood is usually very small, about nine months, while unmarried women are carefully closeted indoors, their only escape the evening *passeggiata* – needless to say, well-chaperoned.* It's perhaps hardly surprising, then, that women tourists, radiating freedom and independence, are assumed to be easy numbers, and that Italian women have found it so hard to break the strict rules governing their conduct. The degree of freedom enjoyed by them varies from place to place: it's probably greatest in the North, where the situation is not unlike Britain or the USA, and narrowest in Calabria, Basilicata, Sardinia and Sicily, although Rome can be a nightmare, whistling and catcalling part of the capital's experience for women.

SEXUAL HARASSMENT

Italy has a reputation for **sexual harassment** against women that is well known and well founded. Generally it's worse the further south you travel, where if you're travelling on your own, or with another woman, you can expect to be tooted and hissed at in towns every time you step outside the hotel door. You're also likely to attract unwelcome attention in bars, restaurants and on the beach. This persistent pestering is not usually made with any kind of violent intent, but it's annoying and frustrating nevertheless. There are a few things you can do to ward it off, though you'll never be able to stop the car horns and hisses (the equivalent of a wolf-whistle).

Indifference is often the most effective policy, as is looking as confident as possible, a purposeful stride and directed gaze both good ways of fending off unwelcome attention. Frotteurs on buses can be a problem. To deter them, either keep your back to the wall or station yourself next to a middle-aged woman, and remonstrate noisily if someone starts rubbing up against you. Hopefully the other woman will be your ally, and

* The problem of women is closely linked to the problems of Italian men, specifically to the traditional adoration of the male-child that lingers on into adult life. After all, it is said that Jesus Christ himself was an Italian: he thought he was the son of God, lived at home till he was thirty, and thought his mother was a virgin.

give him/them a mouthful. Flashers in parks are another common occurence, and it's best to avoid hidden, leafy places. Parks are often a pick-up place, so your motives for sitting quietly in the sun may be misconstrued. This doesn't mean it's impossible to go there, just that it's more relaxing if you pick a spot where there are other people around. If all else fails, you could try hurling a few well-chosen examples of the vernacular, like *lasciátemi in pace* ("leave me alone"), *sei fesso?* ("are you stupid ?"), or *testa di cazzo* ("dickhead"). Failing that, don't hesitate to approach a policeman. Obviously, travelling with a man cuts out much of the more intense hassle, although even this won't deter the more determined onslaughts.

CONTACTS

There are women's groups all over Italy: the largest are affiliated to Italy's Democratic Left party, but campaigns against rape, for better access to abortion and towards increasing womens' skills and resources demonstrate the need for an independently active movement. There are contacts, bookshops and documentation centres in the major cities, but Italy's decentralised nature means that there are few national organisations.

Feminist papers like *Effe* and *Noi Donne* are good sources of infomation on the **women's movement**, or contact **ISIS**, Via Santa Maria dell'Anima 30, 00153 Rome, who act as a gathering group for women's organisations across the country as well as internationally. **Radio Donna** in Rome is a women's radio station (the only one in Italy), restarted after a neo-Fascist firebombing in 1979.

ARCI-Co-ordinamento Donne is the main co-ordinating body for the women's section of the *PDS* youth section, *ARCI*. They are based at Via F. Carrara 24, Rome (☎06/361.0800); other branches in the major cities are listed under *ARCI Provinciale* in the phone book. Rome, Bologna and Milan are the places with most action, although this is fairly limited: *il riflusso*, the general term to describe the fall-off in political activity since the Seventies, has affected the women's movement as it has others. The *Centro Documentazione Donne* Via Galliera 8, 40121 Bologna (☎051/233.863), the *Centro Feminista Separatista*, Via San Francesco di Sales 1a, Rome (☎06/686.4201), and the *Centro Studi Storiche sul Movimento di Liberazione delle Donne* Via Romagnosi 3, 20121 Milan (☎02/869.3911), can all put you in touch with local groups – although for a more immediate idea of what's happening, visit the women's bookshops in each of these cities (see "Listings").

Women's organisations also tend to share activities with **lesbian** groups. There's a bimonthly newsletter called *Bolletino del Connessione Lesbiche Italiane*, and a national *Lesbian Line*, based in Florence, that's open every Wednesday and Saturday 8.30–10pm (☎055/240.384), for information, advice and help.

FINDING WORK

All EC citizens are eligible to work in Italy. The two main bureaucratic requirements are a *libretto di lavoro* and *permesso di soggiorno*, respectively a work and residence permit, both available from the *Questura* (see "Trouble and the Police" p.42). For the first you must have a letter from your employers saying they are prepared to take you on, for the second (which is also necessary if you want to buy a car or have a bank acount in Italy) you'll need a passport, passport photos, and a lot of patience.

TEACHING

The obvious choice is to **teach English**, for which the demand has expanded enormously in recent years. You can do this in two ways: freelance private lessons, or through a language school. **Private lessons** generally pay best, and you can charge up to £10 an hour, though there's scope for bargaining. Advertise in bars, shop windows and local newspapers, and, most importantly, get the news around by word-of-mouth that you're looking for work, emphasising your excellent background, qualifications and experience. An advantage of private teaching is that you can start at any time of the year (summer especially is a good time for schoolchildren and students who have to retake exams in September); the main disadvantage is that it can take weeks to get off the ground, and you need enough money to support yourself until then. You'll find the best opportunities for this kind of work in the tourist resorts and the bigger towns and cities.

Teaching in schools, you start earning immediately. It usually involves more hours per week, often in the evening, at a lower rate per hour, though the amount you get depends on the school. Don't accept anything less than £5 an hour, while the bigger schools should pay much more than this. For the less reputable places, you can get away without any qualifications and a bit of bluff, but you'll need to show a *TEFL* certificate for more professional language schools. For these, it's best to apply in writing from Britain (look for the ads in the *Guardian* and *TES*, and contact the *Italian Cultural Institute* at 39 Belgrave Square, London SW1; ☎071/235 1461), preferably before the summer, though you can also find openings in September. If you're looking on the spot, sift through the yellow pages and do the rounds on foot, asking to speak to the *direttore* or his/her secretary; don't bother to try in August when everything is closed. The best teaching jobs of all are with a university as a *lettore*, a job requiring fewer hours than the language schools and generally providing a fuller pay-packet. Universities require English language teachers in most faculties and you can write to the individual faculties (addressed to *Ufficio di Personale*). Strictly speaking you could get by without any knowledge of Italian while teaching, though some definitely helps.

OTHER OPTIONS

If teaching's not up your street, there's the possibility of **courier work** in the summer, especially around the seaside resorts. These are good places for finding **bar/restaurant work** too – not the most lucrative of jobs, though you should make enough to keep you over the summer. You'll have to ask around for both types of work, and some knowledge of Italian is essential. **Au pairing** is another option: contact *Au Pairs Italy*, 46 The Rise, Sevenoaks, Kent TN13 1RJ (☎0732-461522) for more information.

DIRECTORY

ADDRESSES These are usually written as the street name followed by the number – eg Via Roma 69. *Interno* refers to the flat-number – eg interno 5 (often abbreviated as int.). Confusingly, some towns have two systems for numbering properties, one for shops and restaurants and another for business and private residences; sometimes a shop or restaurant is suffixed by the letter "r", meaning that Via Garibaldi 15r might be in an entirely different place from Via Garibaldi 15. Watch out for addresses with "s/n" rather than a street number, which refers to the fact that they have no number, or are "senza numero".

AIRPORT TAX None to pay.

BARGAINING Not really on in shops and restaurants, though you'll find you can get a "special price" for some rooms and cheap hotels if you' staying a few days, and that things like boat/bike hire and guided tours (especially out of season) are negotiable. In markets, you can if you wish haggle for everything except food.

BEACHES You'll have to pay for access to the best parts of the better beaches (referred to as lidos), plus a few thousand to hire a sun bed and shade and use the showers all day. Although technically the few metres immediately by the water cannot be sectioned off, it's debatable whether it's worth the hassle of trying to enforce your rights. During winter most beaches look like rubbish dumps, which is what they are: it's not worth anyone's while to clean them until the season starts at Easter.

BRING . . . Photographic films, which are cheaper in Britain – and wait until you get home to have them developed. An alarm clock for early morning buses is also useful, as is mosquito repellent and antiseptic cream, not to mention suntan lotion. If you're considering visiting a lot of hot, exposed archaeological sites, a water bottle is handy. And if you're camping don't forget a torch.

CAMPING GAZ Easy enough to buy for the small portable camping stoves, either from a hardware store (*ferramenta*) or camping/sports shops. You can't carry canisters on aeroplanes.

CIGARETTES The state monopoly brand – *MS* – are the most widely-smoked cigarettes, strong and aromatic, and selling for around L2600 for a packet of twenty. Younger people tend to smoke imported brands these days – all of which are slightly more expensive. You buy cigarettes from *Tabacchi*, recognisable by a sign displaying a white "T" on a black or blue background.

CONTRACEPTION Condoms (*preservativi, profilàttici*) are available over the counter from all pharmacies and some supermarkets; the Pill (*la píllola*) is available from pharmacies.

DEPARTMENT STORES There are two main nationwide chains, *Upim* and *Standa*, branches of which you'll see virtually everywhere. Neither is particularly posh, and they're good places to stock up on toiletries and other basic supplies; both stores sometimes have a food hall attached.

DISABLED TRAVELLERS Facilities aren't particul[illegible] geared towards disabled travellers, though [illegible]are helpful enough. In Britain, disabled [illegible]uld contact *Radar*, 25 Mortimer Street, [illegible]071/637 5400) to obtain a badge [illegible]park more freely. A list of tour operators who specialise in holidays for the disabled is available from the Italian State Tourist Office (see p.14 for address). There's also *Mobility International*, 228 Borough High Street, London SE11 (☎071/403 5688), which puts out a quarterly newsletter among other things that keeps up to date with developments in disabled travel; it also has a North American office and is contactable at PO Box 3551, Eugene, Oregon 97403 (☎503/343 1284).

ELECTRICITY The supply is 220V, though anything requiring 240V will work. Most plugs are two round pins: a travel plug is useful.

FOOTBALL If you are at all interested in the game, it would be a shame to leave Italy without attending a football match – it is virtually the national sport, and is followed fanatically by millions of Italians. The Italian League is split into four principal divisions, Serie A, Serie B, and Serie C1 and C2; matches are normally played on Sunday afternoons, and there is a good chance that on any weekend there will be a team from one of the above divisions playing not too far from you. Serie A is of course the most important division, comprising 18 teams; the bottom-placed 4 are relegated each season, to be replaced by the top 4 from Serie B, although there are some clubs whom it would be unimaginable to see in Serie B – teams like Juventus, Inter Milan, and the team of the moment, AC Milan, who at time of writing had not lost a game for something like 18 months. Tickets for Serie A matches are not cheap, starting at about L25,000 for "Curva" seats at each end of the ground, where the tifosi or fans go, rising to L40,000 for the "Distinti" or corner seats, up to L50–100,000 for seats in the "Tribuna", along the side of the pitch. We've given details of where to buy tickets for the major clubs, along with the basics of how to get to grounds, etc, in the city "Listings" sections. Once at the football match, get right into the atmosphere of the occasion by drinking *borghetti* – little vials of cold coffee with a drop of spirit added.

GAY LIFE Homosexuality is legal in Italy, and the age of consent is sixteen. Attitudes are most tolerant in the northern cities: Bologna is generally regarded as the gay capital, and Milan, Turin and to a lesser extent Rome all have well-developed gay nightlifes. There are a few *spiagge gay* (gay beaches) dotted along the coast, and two women-only holiday centres in Umbria. Away from the big cities, activity is more covert. You'll notice, in the south especially, that overt displays of affection between (all) men – linking arms in the *passegiata*, kissing in greeting, etc – are common. The line of what's acceptable, however, is finely drawn – in 1982 two gay men received an eight-month jail sentence for kissing in a Sicilian street. The national gay organisation, *ARCI-Gay*, Piazza di Porta Saragozza 2, PO Box 691, 40100 Bologna (☎051/436.700), affiliated to the youth section of the Communist Party, has branches in most big towns; *Babilonia* is the national gay magazine, published monthly by *Babilonia Edizioni*, PO Box 11224, 20110 Milano. For information on the situation for lesbians, see "Women in Italy", above.

KIDS Children are revered in Italy and will be made a fuss of in the street, and welcomed and catered for in bars and restaurants. Hotels normally charge around 30 percent extra to put a bed or cot in your room, although kids pay less on trains (see "Getting Around", p.16). The only hazards when travelling with kids in Italy are the summer heat and sun.

LAUNDERETTES Coin-operated launderettes, sometimes known as *tintorie*, are very rare outside large cities, and even there numbers are sparse; see the "Listings" headings of the main city sections for addresses. More common is a *lavanderia*, a service-wash laundry, but this will be expensive. Although you can usually get away with it, washing clothes in your hotel room has been known to cause problems, since in some parts of the country the plumbing can't cope with all the water. It's better to ask if there's somewhere you can wash your clothes.

PUBLIC TOILETS Almost unheard-of outside railway and bus stations, and usually the only alternative is to dive discreetly into a bar or restaurant. Carry a supply of your own paper around and don't expect anywhere to be spotless.

STUDYING IN ITALY One way of spending time in Italy is to combine a holiday with learning the language, or taking one of many summer courses on myriad aspects of Italian art and culture. There are a great many places where you can do this, usually offering language courses of varying levels of intensity for between one and three months. For a complete listing of institutions running all sorts of courses, contact the *Italian Cultural Institute*, 39 Belgrave Square, London SW1 (☎071/235 1461); 686 Park Ave, New York, NY 10021 (☎212/879-4242); 1601 Fuller St, NW Washington DC 20009 (☎202/328-5556); Suite 310, 12400 Wilshire Blvd, Los Angeles, CA 90025 (☎213/207-4737).

TAKE HOME . . . Top of the list of many Italian goodies worth taking home is a *caféteria* – the many-sided coffee-makers that cost a fortune in Britain but are actually very cheap in Italy; *Upim* and *Standa* usually have a good selection, as do markets. Obviously clothes and shoes make a tempting souvenir, too, but don't expect any bargains; in Milan, especially, prices are sky-high, though if you're in the market for designer threads, this is as cheap a place as any.

TIME Italy is always one hour ahead of Britain except for one week at the end of September when the time is the same.

VACCINATIONS None required.

WAR CEMETERIES Anzio and Cassino are just the best known of a number of fiercely contested battles on Italian soil during World War II. Information and a list of Allied cemeteries available from the *Commonwealth War Graves Commission*, 2 Marlow Road, Maidenhead, Berkshire (☎0628/34221).

WATER Safe to drink everywhere, including drinking fountains, although bottled mineral water is always more pleasant.

PART TWO

THE GUIDE

CHAPTER ONE

PIEMONTE AND VALLE D'AOSTA

Fringed by the French and Swiss Alps and grooved with mountain valleys, there are no less "Italian" regions than **Piemonte** and **Valle d'Aosta**, in the extreme northwest of the country. French was spoken in Piemonte until the end of the last century, and Valle d'Aosta remains bilingual. **Piemonte** (literally "at the foot of the mountains") is one of Italy's wealthiest regions, known for its fine wines and food and home to key Italian corporations like Fiat and Olivetti. The mighty Po River, Italy's longest, begins here, and the towns of its vast plain – which stretches right across northern Italy – are rich on both manufacturing and rice, grown on sweeping paddy fields. The region is a paradise for gastronomes and connoisseurs of vintage wines: the rolling vine-clad hills of Le Langhe and Monferrato produce classy wines like Barolo, Bardolino, Barbera and Nebbiolo, as well as the famous fizzy Asti Spumante. Martini and Cinzano are produced in and around Turin, a fusion of the region's wines with the wild herbs that grow on its mountains; and the food is Italy's richest, with much meat and game, cooked with wine or cream and butter and often enhanced with shavings of the pricey regional delicacy – white truffles.

Turin, on the main rail and road route from France to Milan, is the obvious first stop and the one place in the region that (if you're not skiing) repays a lengthy visit. It's Italy's second industrial city, but retains a splendid Baroque core and is well placed for days out. Appealing historic towns are otherwise thin on the ground. South of Turin, **Alba** and **Saluzzo** are perhaps the most enticing centres, the former a good base for visiting the wine *cantinas*, the latter convenient if you want to explore the western valleys; **Asti**, to the southeast, only really comes to life during its famous medieval Palio. For the rest, winter sports and walking are the main activities, although, except for the ascent of **Monviso** in the far west, you may find more challenges – and more spectacular views – in the adjoining region of **Valle d'Aosta**. Cut off from Switzerland and France by the highest of the Alps – **Monte Rosa**, the **Matterhorn** and **Mont Blanc** – and with a **national park** around the **Gran Paradiso** mountain, this is serious skiing and hiking country. The main town of **Aosta** itself repays a visit, and the countryside is sprinkled with **castles**.

PIEMONTE

Many of the dishes in **Piemonte**'s swankiest restaurants derive from the tables of the Piemontese aristocracy, in particular the Savoy dukes and kings who ruled the region from the eleventh century, making Turin their capital in 1574. Their presence is clearly visible today in the grandiose architecture of central Turin and in their ostentatious hunting palace at Stupenigi just outside the city.

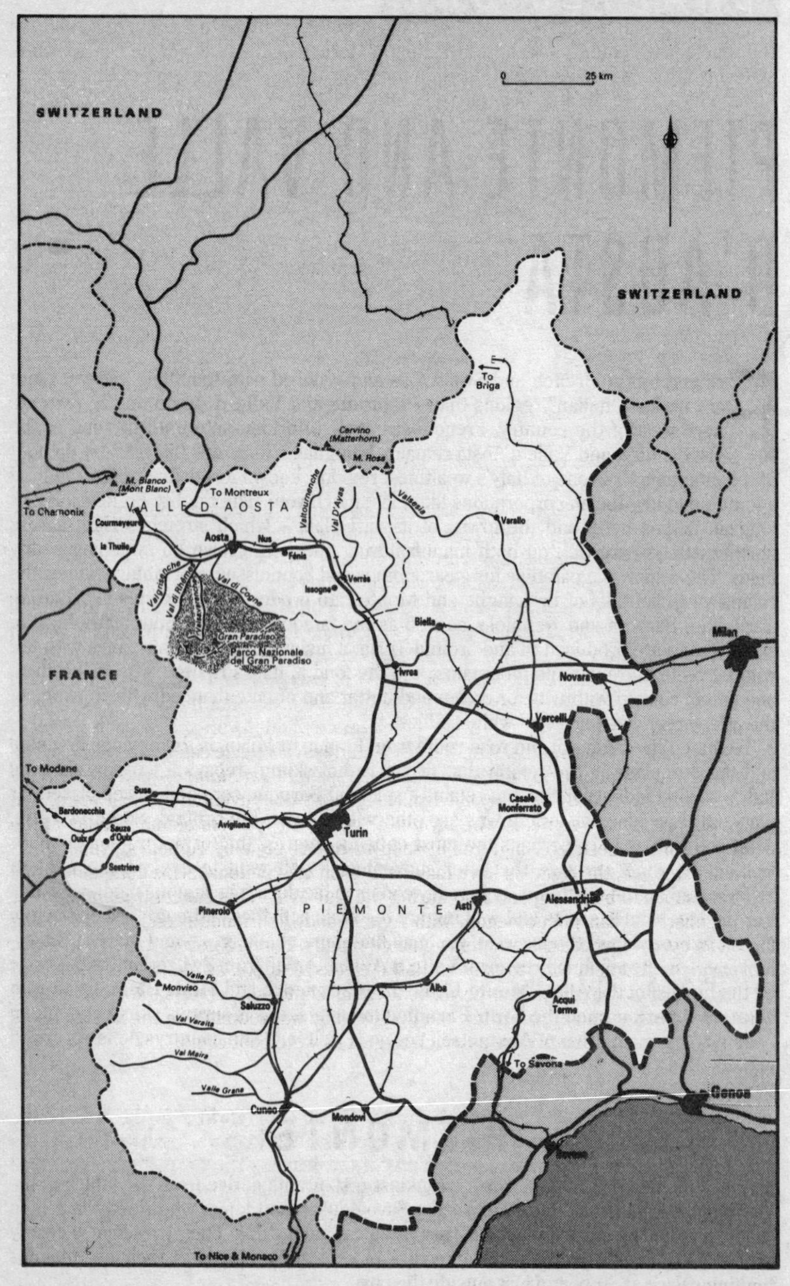
0
25 km
SWITZERLAND
SWITZERLAND
FRANCE
To Briga
Cervino (Matterhorn)
M. Rosa
M. Bianco (Mont Blanc)
To Montreux
VALLE D'AOSTA
To Chamonix
Courmayeur
la Thuile
Aosta
Nus
Fénis
Valtournenche
Val D'Ayas
Valsesia
Varallo
Verrès
Issogne
Valgrisenche
Val di Rhêmes
Val di Cogne
Gran Paradiso
Parco Nazionale del Gran Paradiso
Biella
Ivrea
Milan
Novara
Vercelli
To Modane
Susa
Bardonecchia
Casale Monferrato
Avigliana
Turin
Oulx
Sauze d'Oulx
Sestriere
Pinerolo
PIEMONTE
Asti
Alessandria
Valle Po
Monviso
Alba
Acqui Terme
Saluzzo
Val Varaita
Val Maira
To Savona
Valle Grana
Genoa
Cuneo
Mondovì
Savona
To Nice & Monaco

Piemonte – and the Savoys – were at the heart of the Italian Unification movement in the nineteenth century, which, under King Vittorio Emanuele II and the Piemontese statesman, Camillo Cavour, succeeded in dragging the various regions of Italy together under Savoy rule. Rome became the new capital, much to the disquiet of the Piemontese aristocracy and bourgeoisie, who acted quickly to save the region's not inconsiderable influence, setting up industries – Fiat and Olivetti were two – that were destined to change the face of Italian as well as Piemontese society. These days Piemonte is second only to Lombardy in national wealth and power.

Getting around Piemonte is fairly easy. The network of trains and buses is comprehensive, and your own transport is only necessary for the more out-of-the-way places. You can get to most places from Turin; Alba makes a good base for exploring Le Langhe, Saluzzo for the western valleys.

Turin (Torino)

"Do you know Turin?" said Nietzsche, "It is a city after my own heart . . . a princely residence of the seventeenth century, which has only one taste giving commands to everything, the court and its nobility. Aristocratic calm is preserved in everything: there are no nasty suburbs." Although **TURIN**'s traffic-choked streets are no longer calm, and its suburbs are as nasty as any in Italy, the city centre's gracious Baroque avenues, opulent palaces, sumptuous churches and splendid collections of Egyptian antiquities and Northern European paintings are still here – a pleasant surprise to those who might have been expecting satanic factories and little else.

Turin's suburbs were built by a new dynasty – **Fiat** (Fabbrica Italiana di Automobili Torino) – whose owner, Gianni Agnelli, is reckoned to be the most powerful man in Italy. Although the only sign of Agnelli's power appears to be the number of Fiats which cram Turin's streets (as they do those of every other Italian city), it's worth remembering that Fiat owns Lancia and Alfa Romeo too, accounting for sixty percent of the Italian car market. But there are other, more hidden, branches of the Agnelli empire. Stop for a Cinzano in one of the city's many fin de siècle cafés and you're drinking an Agnelli vermouth; buy the major local newspaper – *La Stampa* – and you're reading newsprint owned by the Agnelli family. Support the Juventus football team, and you're supporting the Agnellis who own it; or go for a *Club Med* skiing holiday at the nearby resort of Sestriere, and you'll sleep in hotels built by Agnelli's grandfather. More sinister still, the Agnellis have major stakes in international arms companies, one of which supplied both Iran and Iraq during the Gulf War. This concentration of power is a peculiarly Italian phenomenon, with Agnelli and his friends seen as a stabilising force in a country where governments change rapidly. Foreign governments often take more notice of Agnelli than they do of Italy's elected leaders: as Henry Kissinger said in 1988 – Gianni Agnelli "is the permanent establishment". Terrorists too recognised where the roots of Italian power lay: the Red Brigade was founded on the factory floors of Fiat, and Fiat executives were as much targets as were politicians.

Some history

The Torinese are accustomed to absolutism. From 1574 Turin was the seat of the Savoy Dukes, who persecuted Piemonte's Protestants and Jews, censored the press and placed education in the extreme hands of the Jesuits. The Savoys gained a royal title in 1713, and a few years later acquired Sardinia, which whetted their appetite for more territory. The second monarch, Carlo Emanuele III (who promised to "eat Italy like an artichoke"), teamed up with the liberal politician of the Risorgimento, Cavour, who used the royal family to lend credibility to the Unification movement. In 1860 Garibaldi handed over Sicily and southern Italy to Vittorio Emanuele, and though it

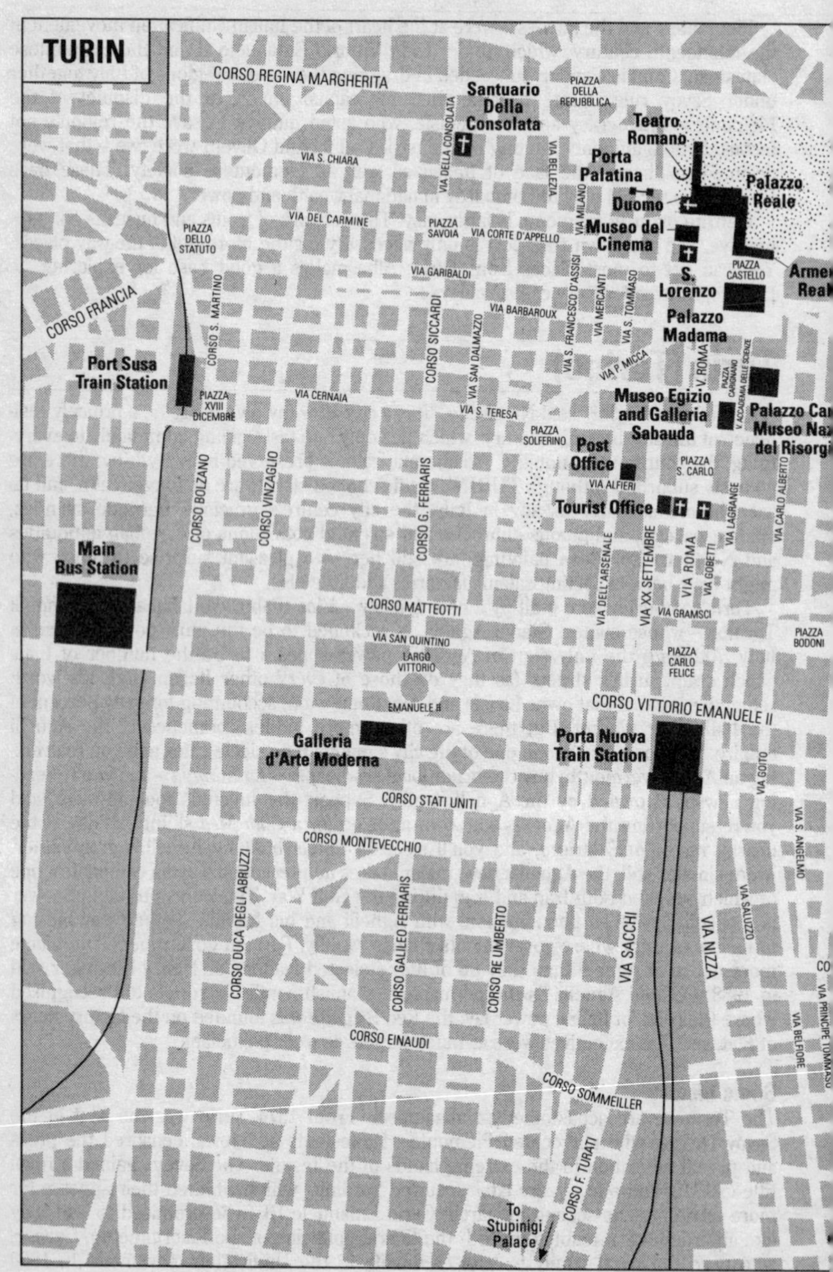
TURIN
CORSO REGINA MARGHERITA
Santuario Della Consolata
PIAZZA DELLA REPUBBLICA
Teatro Romano
Porta Palatina
Palazzo Reale
Duomo
Museo del Cinema
S. Lorenzo
PIAZZA CASTELLO
Palazzo Madama
VIA S. CHIARA
VIA DEL CARMINE
VIA DELLA CONSOLATA
VIA BELLEZIA
VIA MILANO
PIAZZA SAVOIA
VIA CORTE D'APPELLO
PIAZZA DELLO STATUTO
VIA GARIBALDI
CORSO FRANCIA
CORSO S. MARTINO
CORSO SICCARDI
VIA SAN DALMAZZO
VIA BARBAROUX
VIA S. FRANCESCO D'ASSISI
VIA MERCANTI
VIA S. TOMMASO
VIA P. MICCA
V. ROMA
Port Susa Train Station
PIAZZA XVIII DICEMBRE
VIA CERNAIA
VIA S. TERESA
Museo Egizio and Galleria Sabauda
PIAZZA CARIGNANO
V. ACCADEMIA DELLE SCIENZE
PIAZZA SOLFERINO
Post Office
PIAZZA S. CARLO
VIA ALFIERI
Tourist Office
CORSO BOLZANO
CORSO VINZAGLIO
CORSO G. FERRARIS
VIA DELL'ARSENALE
VIA XX SETTEMBRE
VIA ROMA
VIA GOBETTI
VIA LAGRANGE
VIA CARLO ALBERTO
Main Bus Station
CORSO MATTEOTTI
VIA SAN QUINTINO
VIA GRAMSCI
PIAZZA BODONI
PIAZZA CARLO FELICE
LARGO VITTORIO EMANUELE II
CORSO VITTORIO EMANUELE II
Galleria d'Arte Moderna
Porta Nuova Train Station
VIA GOITO
CORSO STATI UNITI
CORSO MONTEVECCHIO
VIA S. ANGELMO
VIA SALUZZO
CORSO DUCA DEGLI ABRUZZI
CORSO GALILEO FERRARIS
CORSO RE UMBERTO
VIA SACCHI
VIA NIZZA
VIA PRINCIPE TOMMASO
VIA BELFIORE
CORSO EINAUDI
CORSO SOMMEILLER
CORSO F. TURATI
To Stupinigi Palace

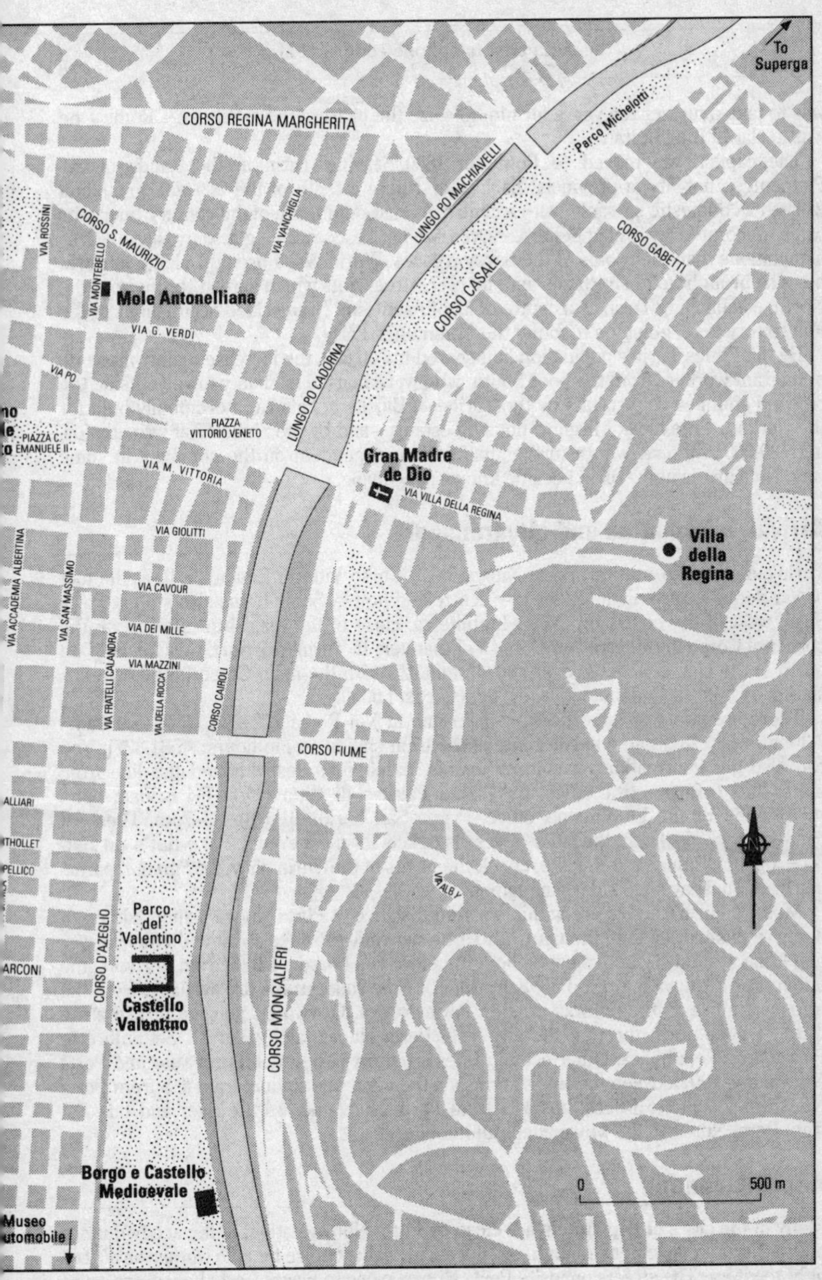
To Superga
CORSO REGINA MARGHERITA
Parco Michelotti
LUNGO PO MACHIAVELLI
CORSO S. MAURIZIO
VIA ROSSINI
VIA VANCHIGLIA
CORSO GABETTI
CORSO CASALE
VIA MONTEBELLO
Mole Antonelliana
VIA G. VERDI
VIA PO
LUNGO PO CADORNA
PIAZZA VITTORIO VENETO
PIAZZA C. EMANUELE II
Gran Madre de Dio
VIA M. VITTORIA
VIA VILLA DELLA REGINA
VIA GIOLITTI
Villa della Regina
VIA ACCADEMIA ALBERTINA
VIA SAN MASSIMO
VIA CAVOUR
VIA DEI MILLE
VIA FRATELLI CALANDRA
VIA MAZZINI
VIA DELLA ROCCA
CORSO CAIROLI
CORSO FIUME
Parco del Valentino
CORSO D'AZEGLIO
Castello Valentino
CORSO MONCALIERI
Borgo e Castello Medioevale
0
500 m
Museo
utomobile

The Turin **area telephone code** is ☎011.

was to take a further ten years for him to seize the heart of the artichoke – Rome – he was declared King of Italy.

The capital was moved to Rome in 1870, leaving Turin in the hands of the Piemontese nobility, a provincial backwater where a tenth of the 200,000 population worked as domestic servants, with a centre donned out in turn-of-the-century finery, its cafés, decorated with chandeliers, carved wood, frescoes and gilt, only slightly less ostentatious than the rooms of the Savoy palaces. World War I brought plenty of work, but also brought food shortages and, in 1917, street riots which spread throughout the North, establishing Turin as a centre of labour activism. Gramsci led occupations of the Fiat factory here, going on to found the Communist Party.

By the Fifties Turin's population had soared to 700,000, the increase mainly made up of migrant workers from the poor South, who were housed in shanty towns outside the city and shunned as peasants by the Torinese. Blocks of flats were eventually built for the workers – the bleak Mirafiori housing estates – and by the Sixties Fiat was employing 130,000 workers, with a further half million dependent on the company in some way. Not surprisingly, Turin became known as Fiatville.

Arrival, information and city transport

Turin's main **train station**, Porta Nuova, is on Corso Vittorio Emanuele II, at the foot of Via Roma – convenient for the city centre and hotels. Some trains also stop at Porta Susa, west of the centre on Corso Inghilterra, close to the main **bus station** on the corner of Corso Inghilterra and Corso V. Emanuele II. Turin's **airport**, Caselle, is 15km north of the city, connected every 30–45 minutes with the main Corso Inghilterra bus station by bus – a 45-minute journey; tickets cost L5000.

There are two **tourist offices**: a main one at Via Roma 222–226 (Mon–Sat 9am–7.30pm; ☎535.181) and a smaller one at the train station (same hours; ☎531.327). You can also get information on cultural events, exhibitions, festivals and the like from either the **Informacittà** office, on Piazza Palazzo di Città (Mon–Fri 8.30am–4pm; ☎576.5566), or the **La Vetrina** office, Piazza San Carlo 161 (Mon 3–7pm, Tues–Sat 9am–1pm; ☎5765.3740); the latter also sells tickets for most events. For **what's on listings**, opening hours and the like, check the pages of the Turin daily, *La Stampa*, particularly its Tuesday and Friday supplements.

Most of Turin's sights are within walking distance of Porta Nuova station, although if you're pushed for time the **tram and bus** network provides a fast and efficient way of getting around. Tickets must be bought before you board – L1000 from *tabacchi* (the one in Porta Nuova is open daily 8am–10pm). Free route **maps** are available from the transport office in the subway outside Porta Nuova. Of **routes** you might use a lot, tram #4 goes north through the city from Porta Nuova, along Via XX Settembre to Piazza della Repubblica. Other useful routes are tram #1 between Porta Susa and Porta Nuova, bus #60 between the two stations via the main bus station, tram #15 from Porta Nuova to Via Pietro Micca, bus #61 from Porta Nuova across the river and bus #34 from Porta Nuova to the Museo dell'Automobile.

Accommodation

Many of the city's **cheap hotels** are close by Porta Nuova station, in the seedy quarter off Via Nizza – convenient enough, but not an advisable choice for solo women as it's red light territory. The streets opposite Porta Nuova, close to Piazza Carlo Felice, are safer, although a bit more expensive, while there are also a number of fairly reasonably priced hotels in the district to the west of Piazza Castello. Wherever you decide to make for, bear in mind that demand on hotels is usually high and it's a good idea to phone in advance.

Hotels

Astoria, Via XX Settembre 4 (☎562.0653). Good-value hotel just off Piazza Carlo Felice, with very pleasant rooms, all with satellite TV, and extremely friendly management. ⑤.

Bellavista, Via Galliari 15 (☎687.989). One of the more pleasant options off Via Nizza, with decent-sized and clean rooms, though rather costly for the area. ⑤.

Bologna, Corso Vittorio Emanuele II 60 (☎562.0191). A clean two-star hotel, left of the train station, though the management isn't particularly friendly. ④.

Canelli, Via San Dalmazzo 7 (☎546.078). A neat, simple hotel, very inexpensive, close to the pedestrian area of Via Garibaldi. ③.

Europa, Piazza Castello 99 (☎544.238). Great position in an eighteenth-century palazzo. Book well in advance (around a month if possible). ⑤.

La Primula, Piazza Carignano 8 (☎535.102). Brilliantly located, with the Palazzo Carignano on the left, Teatro Carignano on the right, and good prices too. ④.

Roma & Rocca Cavour, Piazza Carlo Felice 60 (☎561.2772). Overlooking a lovely garden with a fountain, this is a three-star place with one-star prices. ④.

San Carlo, Piazza San Carlo 197 (☎553.552). A lovely position on Piazza San Carlo, and nice, very reasonably priced rooms. ④.

San Maurizio, Corso San Maurizio 31 (☎882.434). A little way east of Piazza Castello, and sometimes full during term-time, due to its proximity to the university. However, good value if you can get in. ④.

Vinzaglio, Corso Vinzaglio 12 (☎561.3793). Handily located next door to the main police station, not far from the Porta Susa train station. ④.

Hostels and campsites

Ostello Torino, Via Alby 1 (☎660.2939). Official *IYHF* hostel, with beds in clean modern dormitories for L17,000, breakfast included; dinner L12,000. Closed between Christmas and mid-February. Bus #52 from Porta Nuova.

Villa Rey, Strada Val San Martino Superiore 27 (☎819.0117). The most convenient of the city's campsites, not far from the youth hostel. Open from the end of March to the end of November. Take bus #61 from Porta Nuova, and then bus #54.

The City

The grid street-plan of Turin's Baroque centre makes it easy to find your way about. **Via Roma** is the central spine of the city, a grand affair lined with designer shops and ritzy cafés and punctuated by the city's most elegant piazzas, most notably Piazza San Carlo, close to which are some of the city's most prestigious museums. **Piazza Castello** forms a fittingly grand, if hectic, conclusion to Via Roma, with its royal palaces awash in a sea of traffic. From here you can walk in a number of directions. To the west, **Via Pietro Micca** leads to a cluster of elegant pedestrianised shopping streets, more relaxed than Via Roma and a good area to head to during the evening *passeggiata*. North lies **Piazza della Repubblica**, a vast and rather squalid square given over to a daily market. To the southeast, the shabby porticoes of **Via Po** forge down to the river, a short walk along which is the extensive **Parco del Valentino**, home to some of the city's best nightlife. Beyond lies the engaging **Museo dell'Automobile**, while the hills **across the river** are peppered with the Art Deco villas of the wealthiest Torinese. Make specific trips out here – to the **Basilica di Superga** or the **Stupinigi Palace**.

Porta Nuova and north: the Museo Egizio and Galleria Sabauda

Cars, trams and buses surge along Turin's aristocratic avenues, whipping in and out of the pompous, grimy arches. As you step out of **Porta Nuova** station, Turin's measured symmetry is immediately in evidence, although the area around is seedy, with prostitutes and street-hasslers cruising the once-elegant arcades of Via Nizza and Corso Vittorio Emanuele II. Directly opposite, embraced by curving porticoes, things pick up with the neat gardens of **Piazza Carlo Felice**, forming the gateway to **Via Roma** – still very much the stomping ground of the well heeled. Halfway down, **Piazza San Carlo** is known with some justification as the parlour of Turin, a grand and stylish open space, flanked with symmetrical porticoed buildings housing opulent cafés and decorated with buttermilk stucco reliefs and rhythmic rows of grey shutters. Holding court is an equestrian statue of the Savoy Duke, Emanuele Filiberto, raising his sword in triumph after securing Turin's independence from the French and Spanish at the battle of San Quintino in 1574, while the entrance to the square is guarded by the twin Baroque churches of **San Carlo** and **Santa Cristina**, behind which the nude statues represent Turin's two rivers – the Po and the Dora.

Around the corner from Piazza San Carlo, the **Museo Egizio**, Via Accademia delle Scienze 6 (Tues–Sun 9am–2pm; L10,000) holds a superb collection of Egyptian antiquities, gathered together in the late eighteenth century under the aegis of Carlo Emanuele III. There are gorgeously decorated mummy cases, and an intriguing assortment of everyday objects, including castanets, sandals, a linen tunic dating from 2300 BC, and even food – eggs, pomegranates and grain, recognisable despite their shrivelled, darkened state. Also interesting is the small Nubian temple dedicated by Tutmosis III to Ellesija, although the undoubted highlight is the **Tomb of Kha**, the burial chamber of a 1400 BC architect, Kha, and his wife Merit, discovered in 1906 at Deir-el-Medina, home of the architects, masons and painters of the nearby royal necropoli. The tomb contains the tools of his trade – cubits, a case for balances, pens and a writing tablet – and more ordinary daily items: a bed with a headrest, clothes, generous rations of food, even a board game to while away the posthumous hours. And to ensure that Merit continued to take care of her appearance, she was provided with a cosmetic case, wig, comb, and tweezers.

Above the museum, the **Galleria Sabauda** (Tues–Sat 9am–2pm; L6000) was built around the Savoys' private collection and is still firmly stamped with their taste – a middling miscellany of Italian paintings –work from Piemontese, Florentine, Venetian and Bolognese schools – supplemented by a fine collection of Dutch and Flemish works. Of the Italian paintings, the most interesting is the fifteenth-century *Archangel Raphael and Tobias* by Antonio and Piero Pollaiolo, an ultra-realistic work which amply demonstrates the Pollaiolo brothers' studies in anatomy. Among the first artists to do this, the brothers were once considered ahead of their time, as a look at the rarefied, almost ethereal painting of the same subject by their contemporary, Filippino Lippi, shows. The Northern European collection is more engaging. Alongside a number of French paintings, there are debauched peasant scenes by Flemish artists, notably works by Pieter Brueghel, David Teniers Jnr, and a bucolic *Amarilli and Mirtillo* by Van Dyck. Take a look too at the intriguing *Vanity of Human Life* by Jan Brueghel. On a more elevated level, Hans Memling's *Passion of Christ* tells the story of Christ's final days in a Renaissance city setting.

Piazza Castello and around

Via Roma continues north through the heart of Turin, passing some of the key monuments of the Savoys and the Italian Unification. The **Museo Nazionale del Risorgimento**, Via Accademia della Scienza 5 (Tues–Sat 9am–6.30pm, Sun 9am–12.30pm; L5000), housed in the double-fronted **Palazzo Carignano**, birthplace of

Vittorio Emanuele II, is worth a visit even if you usually give such things a miss; this was, after all, the centre of the movement and the first capital of Italy proper before it was moved to Rome. The first meetings of the Italian parliament were held in the palace's circular Chamber of the Subalpine Parliament, and the building was the power-base of leaders like Cavour, who ousted the more radical Garibaldi to an early retirement on the island of Caprera near Sardinia. It's ironic, then, that the most interesting sections of the museum are those dedicated to Garibaldi: portraits showing him as a scruffy, long-haired revolutionary, some of his clothes – an embroidered fez, a long stripey scarf and one of the famous red shirts – adopted during his exile in South America, where he trained himself by fighting in various wars of independence. These shirts became the uniform of his army of a thousand volunteers who seized southern Italy and Sicily from the Bourbons.

What Vittorio Emanuele II made of the eccentrically dressed revolutionary who secured half the kingdom for him is undocumented, but you feel sure that his residence, the **Palazzo Reale**, at the head of the sprawling, traffic-choked **Piazza Castello** (Tues–Sun 9am–2pm; guided tours only; L6000), wouldn't have impressed Garibaldi – a *nouveau riche* residence with a dull apricot facade hiding glitzy rooms gilded virtually top-to-bottom and decorated with bombastic allegorical paintings. Around the rooms you'll find comical collections of chinoiserie, with lions, cockerels and fat laughing Chinamen, a thousand-piece dinner set and a particularly tasteless vase of Meissen porcelain encrusted with golf balls and flashy birds. If this isn't enough, look in also on the seventeenth-century church of **San Lorenzo**, concealed behind the left wing of the palace. Designed by Guarini, also responsible for the Palazzo Carignano, it's scalloped with chapels, crowned by a complex dome supported on overlapping semi-circles, and lined with multicoloured marble, frescoes and stucco festoons and statuettes.

On the right-hand side of the Palazzo Reale is the **Armeria Reale** (Tues & Thurs 2.30–7.30pm, Wed, Fri, Sat & Sun 9am–2pm; L6000), a collection of armour and weapons spanning seven centuries and several continents started by King Carlo Alberto in 1837. Pride of place is given to his stuffed horse, which stands among cases of guns and swords. There's also a gallery of suits of armour and a blood-curdling collection of oriental arms, including gorgeously jewelled Turkish sheaths and intimidating Japanese masks. The same building houses the **Biblioteca Reale** (Tues, Thurs, Fri & Sat 9am–1.30pm, Mon & Wed 9am–5pm; free), which, along with countless volumes and manuscripts, has a collection of drawings by artists like Leonardo da Vinci, Bellini, Raphael, Tiepolo and Rembrandt, part of it usually on display.

Across the square from the Palazzo Reale, the **Palazzo Madama** is an altogether more appealing building, with an ornate Baroque facade by the early eighteenth-century architect, Juvarra, who also redesigned the piazza and many of the streets leading off it. Inside, the originally fifteenth-century palace incorporates parts of a thirteenth-century castle and a Roman gate, though it's currently closed for restoration and likely to remain so for some time. If it has opened by the time you read this, look in for some of the building's original furniture and frescoes, and the **Museo Civico dell'Arte Antica** – a collection that includes everything from early Christian gold jewellery and oriental ceramics to a famous *Portrait of an Unknown Man* by Antonello da Messina and an inlaid Gothic commode.

Also on the square, the otherwise dull fifteenth-century **Duomo** houses what has been called "the most remarkable forgery in history" – the **Turin Shroud**, a piece of cloth imprinted with the image of a man's body that has been claimed as the shroud in which Christ was wrapped after his crucifixion. One of the most famous medieval relics, it made world headlines in 1989 after carbon-dating tests carried out by three universities all concluded it was a fake, made between 1260 and 1390 – although no one is any the wiser about how the medieval forgers actually managed to create the image. You can't see the shroud itself, which is kept in a locked chapel built by Guarini in 1668 and topped by a fantasy spire – the church's only other remarkable feature. But a photographic reproduction, on which the face of a bearded man, crowned with thorns, is clearly visible, together with marks supposed to have been left by a double-thonged whip, spear wounds and bruises that could have been caused carrying a cross, is on show in a copy of the chapel to the left of the nave.

The only relics of Turin's days as a small Roman colony are visible from outside the duomo: the scant remains of a **theatre** and the impressive **Porta Palatina** – two sixteen-sided towers flanking an arched passageway. Beyond, the massive **Piazza della Repubblica** is another Juvarra design, though his grand plan for it is marred nowadays by seedy market buildings. The daily market here is at its best on Saturdays, when the *Balon*, or flea market, is held, home to fortune tellers (Turin is the reputed centre of Italian occult practices) and black marketeers.

Behind Piazza della Repubblica, Turin's most elaborate church, the **Santuario della Consolata**, was built to house an ancient statue of the Madonna, Maria Consolatrice, the protector of the city. Designed by Guarini, the church has an impressive decorative altar by Juvarra, and outside its pink and white Neoclassical facade there are shops crammed with votive objects, which the more devout Torinese buy to offer to the statue, housed in an ancient crypt below the church.

Down to the river: Parco del Valentino and the Museo dell'Automobile

The scruffy porticoes of Via Po lead down to the river from Via Roma, ending just before the bridge in the vast arcaded **Piazza Vittorio Veneto**. Turn off halfway down, along Via Montebello, to the **Mole Antonelliana** whose bishop's hat dome, topped by a pagoda-like spire balancing on a mini-Greek temple, is the city's most distinctive landmark. Designed as a synagogue in the nineteenth century by the eccentric architect Antonelli – who landed the town of Novara with a similar eccentricity – it's something of a white elephant today, as Turin's Jews now worship in the newer oriental-style synagogue behind Via Nizza. But it's used for occasional exhibitions, and by tourists who want a bird's-eye view of the city (Tues–Sun 9am–7pm; L3000).

Along the river from Piazza Vittorio Veneto, you're most likely to visit the riverside **Parco del Valentino** at night, as it holds some of the best of Turin's clubs. But it also makes a pleasant place to wind down after the hum of the city centre, its curving lanes, formal flower beds and fake hills covering half a million square metres – making it one of Italy's largest parks. Within the grounds are two castles, one real, the other a fake. The ornate **Castello Valentino** was another Savoy residence, mainly used for wedding feasts and other extravagant parties, and nowadays seat of the university's faculty of architecture. The **Borgo Mediovale** (daily 8am–8pm; free) – and, inside, the **Castello Mediovale** (Tues–Sat 9am–6pm, Sun 10.30am–6pm; L6000, free on Fri) – date from an industrial exhibition held in 1884, and are a synthesis of the best houses and castles of medieval Piemonte and Valle d'Aosta, built with the same materials as the originals and using the same construction techniques. You may balk at the bogusness of the thing, and it can't help but feel a little like Disneyland, but it actually conjures up a picture of life in a fifteenth-century castle far better than many of the originals, kitted out as it is with painstaking replicas of intricately carved Gothic furniture. The castle is based on those at Fénis and Verrès (see p.78 and p.79); and the frescoes are reproductions of those at Manta (see "Saluzzo" p.66).

A longish walk from here, along the river, takes you to the **Museo dell'Automobile** at Corso Unità d'Italia 40 (Tues–Sun 10am–6.30pm; L8000; bus #34 from Via Nizza) – Italy's only motor museum. Even if you know nothing about cars, this has some appeal – you'll spot models you haven't seen since your childhood and others familiar from films, as the museum traces the development from the early cars, handcrafted for a privileged minority, to the mass-produced family version. There's one of the first Fiats, a bulky 1899 model, close to a far sleeker version, built only two years later and, just three decades later, the first small Fiat family-targeted vehicle, a design which was still on the streets in the Sixties. Look also at the gleaming Isotta Franchini driven by Gloria Swanson in *Sunset Boulevard*, still with the initials of Norma Desmond, the character she played, on the side. The pride of the collection, the 1907 Itala which won the Peking-to-Paris race in the same year, is currently being prepared to try again. You can read of its adventures in Luigi Barzini's book *Peking to Paris*.

Out from the centre: the Basilica di Superga and Stupenigi Palace

South of the river, Turin fades into decrepit suburbs, beyond which lie the wooded hills that conceal the fancy villas of the city's industrialists, including that of Gianni Agnelli. For a taste of the views enjoyed by Turin's mega-rich you can take a bus (#70) up to the **Parco della Rimembranza**, with 10,000 trees planted in honour of the Torinese victims of World War I and crowned with an enormous light-flashing statue of Victory. Alternatively, head out to the grandiose Baroque **Basilica di Superga**, from which there are fine panoramas across the city to the Alps (tram #15 followed by a shuttle bus).

The basilica, yet another design from Filippo Juvarra, stands high on a hill above the rest of the city, a position that is the key to its existence. In 1706 King Vittorio Amadeo climbed the hill in order to study the positions of the French and Spanish armies who had been besieging the city for four months, and vowed that he would erect a temple to the Madonna on this site if she were to aid him in the coming battle. Turin was spared, and the king immediately set Juvarra to work, flattening the top of the hill and producing over the next 25 years the circular basilica you see today. An elegant dome, pierced by windows and supported on pairs of white columns, is flanked by delicately scalloped onion-domed towers and rises above a Greek temple entrance, though the most striking thing about the building these days is the graffiti – names dating back to the beginning of the century scratched into the interior pillars. Many Torinese come here not to pay homage to the Virgin, nor even to the splendid tombs of the Savoys, but to visit the tomb of the 1949 Torino football team, all of whom were killed when their plane crashed into the side of the hill. If you happen to go to a match between Torino and Juventus, you may well hear the sinister chant from the Juventus supporters, "Superga, Superga".

The other nearby attraction worth making a trip out of town for is the Savoys' luxurious hunting lodge, the **Palazzina Mauriziana di Caccia di Stupinigi** (Tues–Sat 9.30am–5pm, Sun 10am–1pm & 2–5pm; L6000), out to the west of the city beyond the bleak Mirafiori suburbs, purpose-built for workers at the nearby Fiat plant. This is another Juvarra creation and perhaps his finest work, a symmetrical fantasy with a generous dash of Rococo, built in the 1730s. To get here, take bus #41 from Corso Vittorio Emanuele II.

Much of the exterior of the palace is rather the worse for wear, but the interior is as luxurious as it ever was, the most extravagant room, the oval *Salone Centrale*, a dizzying triumph of optical illusion that merges fake features with real in a superb trompe l'oeil. Other rooms are decorated with hunting motifs: Diana, goddess of hunting, bathes on bedroom ceilings, hunting scenes process across walls, and even the chapel is dedicated to Saint Uberto, patron saint of the hunt. And everywhere there are opulent wall-coverings – gilded brocades, hand-painted silk, carefully inked rice paper – and delicate eighteenth-century furniture, including gilded four-posters, inlaid desks and cabinets, even a marvellous marble bath, decorated with a relief of an imperial eagle, installed by Pauline Bonaparte.

Eating, drinking and nightlife

Turin **cuisine**, influenced by the French, is guaranteed to raise cholesterol levels. Try if you can the classic winter dish, *bagna cauda* – a sauce of oil, butter, cream, garlic and anchovies into which raw and cooked vegetables are dipped. The sweets, too, are marvellous, many of them invented in the Savoy kitchens to tempt the royal palates and increase their waistlines. Sample if you dare such decadent delights as *spumone piemontese*, a mousse of marscapone cheese with rum; *panna cotta*, smooth, rich cooked cream; and light pastries like *lingue di gatto* (cat's tongues) and *baci di dama* (lady's kisses).

There are plenty of **restaurants** to try these dishes all over the city centre, as well as any number of cheaper eating places serving the kind of food you can find anywhere in the country. For food on the run, there are **snack bars** and **takeaways** on Via Nizza, some tempting **delicatessens** on Via Lagrange and a superb *rosticcerie* on Corso Vittorio Emanuele II for DIY lunches. For a drink, a snack, a pastry or in many cases an ice cream, you should also look in on one of the city's fin de siècle **cafés**, which are a Turin institution. The prices are steep, but the atmosphere normally more than compensates.

Later on in the evening, Turin's **nightlife** is more sedate than, say, that of Milan, but there is a reasonably varied mix of clubs here, and a number of decent *birrerias*, many of which have dance floors or live music.

Cafés

Baratti and Milano, Piazza Castello 29. Established in 1873 and preserving its nineteenth-century interior of mirrors, chandeliers and carved wood, in which genteel Torinese ladies sip leisurely teas. Great hot chocolate.

Al Bicerin, Piazza della Consolata 5. Good place to try a *bicerin* – a Piemontese speciality made with coffee, cream and chocolate – and lots of other things made with chocolate.

Florio, Via Po 8. Once the haunt of Cavour, this place is now visited mostly for its ice cream and real fruit sorbets.

Mulussano, Piazza San Carlo 15. A cosy café, with marble fittings and a beautiful ceiling.

Pepino, Piazza Carignano 8. Ritzy café with summer garden, famed for its ice creams. Try the violet-tasting *pinguino* or the *pezzo duro*.

Platti, Corso Vittorio Emanuele 72. Art Nouveau-furnished café that hosts art exhibitions and occasional live music.

Caffè San Carlo, Piazza San Carlo 156. Rather glitzily restored café, with gilt pilasters and an immense chandelier, that combines a restaurant and ice cream parlour.

Stratta, Piazza San Carlo 156. The oldest *confetteria* in Turin, dating back to 1836. *Marron glacé* is a speciality.

Caffè Torino, Piazza San Carlo 204. A good place for a leisurely aperitif or cocktail, of which the most popular is the *Torino*'s very own "Elvira", made with Martini, vodka and various secret ingredients.

Zucca, Via Roma 294. Pastries and *tramezzini*, plus a famous "aperitivo della casa".

Snacks, takeaways and self-service places

Frullati Varturi, Piazza Castello 15. Very central lunchtime option, with sandwiches and a wide choice of fresh local and tropical fruits, ready for the liquidiser.

Brek, Piazza Carlo Felice. Slick, high-quality self-service, with tables outside in summer.

La Ruota, Via Barbaroux 11. Good place for a quick lunch, eat in or takeaway.

Snack Bar Papillon, Via Corte d'Appello 3. Sandwiches and snacks, and full meals at around L12,000.

Rosticceria, Via Gramsci 12. Inexpensive place, very crowded at lunchtime, serving everything from *arancini* to whole roast chickens.

Restaurants

Da Amelia, Via Mercanti 6. Family-style Italian food at low prices; fixed menu for L15,000.

Biagini, Via San Tommaso 10. Restaurant specialising in Tuscan cuisine and delicious oven-baked pizzas.

Il Conte Verde, Via Bellezia 15. Serving Piemontese specialities. Try the *tartrà* – a souffle of cheese, herbs and cream.

Erewhon, Via Calandra 16. Vegetarian restaurant with good risottos, *frittate*, *farinate* and vegetables.

Le Tre Galline, Via Bellezia 37. The oldest restaurant in Turin, with a lovely old panelled interior and a fixed menu for L20,000.

La Gaia Scienza, Via Guastalla 22 (☎870.821). Formerly a *birreria*, now a pleasant restaurant with reasonably-priced food.

Peppino, Via Mercanti 9a. Good, basic food, and a fixed L15,000 menu.

Porta di Savona, Piazza Vittorio Veneto 2. Inexpensive, cheerful restaurant frequented by students.

Il Porticciolo, Via Barletta 58. Not especially central, but one of the best fish and seafood places in town – though not cheap.

Il Punto Verde, Via Belfiore 15/F. Vegetarian dishes made with organically grown vegetables at reasonable prices.

Bars and birrerias

Britannia Pub, Via C. Alberto 34 (☎543.392). A meeting-point for British expats and homesick tourists.

La Contea, Corso Quintino Sella 132 (☎812.2307). *Birreria* situated across the river that has live jazz under a trompe l'oeil fresco of a square. Food, too, served on the terrace under a pergola in summer.

Divina Commedia, Via San Donato 47 (☎488.356). Set out on three floors – Heaven, Purgatory and Hell – with music appropriate to each. Frequent gigs.

Doctor Sax, Murazzi di Lungo Po Cadorna 4 (☎878.416). African rhythms and exhibitions of contemporary art.

Clubs and discos

AEIOU, Via Spanzotti 3 (☎332.121). Off Corso Francia, this is a large, modern club in a former warehouse, with a wide selection of cocktails – and music. A good place to go if you just want to dance.

L'altra uscita, Via Avet 6 (☎471.244). Off Piazza Statuto, this is a women's café, with tea cakes and music. Open Thurs–Sun evenings only.

Hiroshima Mon Amour, Via Belfiore 24 (☎650.5287). Live music, avant-garde performances, alternative theatre and cabaret.

Portes, Via Montebello 21 (☎877.721). Club hosting Arab, African, Latin American music.

Listings

Airport information ☎577.8361.

Books If you've run out of reading matter, *Libreria Luxembourg*, Via C. Battisti 7, has an excellent range of British and American paperbacks.

Buses Most intercity and all international buses leave from the station on Corso Inghilterrra (bus #60 from Via Nizza near Porta Nuova station or from Porta Susa station). Buses to Saluzzo and Cuneo leave from the top of Corso Marconi, near the junction with Via Nizza.

Car parks The Porta Nuova car park (daily 7am–10pm; L1000 every 30min) is the most central place to leave your vehicle.

Car rental *Avis*, Corso Turati 15 (☎501.107); *Europcar*, Via Madama Cristina 72 (☎650.3603); *Hertz*, Corso Marconi 19 (☎650.4504). All these companies also have desks at Porta Nuova station and the airport.

Exchange Outside normal banking hours you can exchange money at Porta Nuova station (daily 8am–2.30pm & 3–9pm).

Football Turin's two teams, Juventus and Torino, play on Sundays at the Stadio delle Alpi, Strada Altessano 131, Continassa, Venaria Reale (☎738.0081), reachable on tram #9. You can buy tickets in advance from branches of the Banca Nazionale del Lavoro, Via XX Settembre 40.

Hospital *Ospedale Molinette*, Corso Bramante 88–90 (☎66.251); emergency medical attention (☎5747).

Laundry *Alba*, Via San Secondo 1; *Aleotti M*, Via Berthollet 18; *Peretti*, Corso Vittorio Emanuele II 73.

Markets Piazza della Repubblica is the scene of a daily fruit, veg, clothes and bric-a-brac market, and a flea market, *Balon*, takes place on Saturday mornings in the streets around; on the second Sunday of each month there's a *Gran Balon*. You can buy clothes at the market on Via Crocetta, and on Via Cassini and Via Marco Polo, Tues–Fri mornings and all day Sat.

Newspapers English-language newspapers and magazines from the newsagents in Porta Nuova station and *Libreria Internazionale de La Stampa*, Via Roma 80.

Pharmacists All-night chemists are the *Alleanza Cooperativa Torinese*, on Via Nizza (☎659.259), and *Boniscontro*, Corso Vittorio Emanuele 66 (☎538.271).

Police ☎113. Main police station at Corso Vinzaglio 10 (☎55.881).

Post office The central post office is at Via Alfieri 10 (Mon–Fri 8.30am–2.30pm, Sat 8.30am–1pm).

Shopping Via Roma for designer staples; trendier, less expensive fare in the pedestrianised streets that are bordered by Via Pietro Micca, Via Monte Pietá, Via dei Mercanti and Via San Francesco d'Assisi.

Taxis Main ranks at the stations and airport, or dial ☎5730, ☎5737, ☎5744 or ☎5748.

Telephones There's an *SIP* office on the corner of Via XX Settembre and Via Barbaroux (Mon–Sat 9am–7pm), and *ASST* offices at Via Arsenale 13bis (daily 8am–11.30pm) and at Porta Nuova (daily 8am–7.45pm).

West of Turin: the Susa and Chisone valleys

The main route to France from Turin runs through the **Susa Valley**, passing the region's main ski resorts. The one real sight, the **Sacra di San Michele**, a forbidding fortified abbey anchored atop a rocky hill, is an easy day trip from Turin. **Susa** itself, reached by a minor branch of the rail line, was once a modest Roman town and is now a modest provincial town – a pleasant stopover but with not much else to lure you.

Sacra di San Michele

Closest town to the **Sacra di San Michele** is AVIGLIANA, half an hour by train from Turin and connected with the abbey by infrequent bus. It's a grotty sort of place, though, and if you don't mind walking it's much nicer to push on to the next stop on the train route, SANT'AMBROGIO, a small village at the foot of San Michele's hill, from where it's a steep 60-90-minute hike to the abbey.

The walk is worth it, both for the views and the undeniably spooky atmosphere which surrounds the glowering abbey, reached by a long flight of stairs hewn into the rock – the *Scalone dei Morti* ("Stairs of the Dead"). Corpses used to be laid out here for local peasants to come and pay their respects – a morbid tone that's continued with the abbey buildings proper, from the Romanesque entrance arch carved with signs of the zodiac to the Gothic-Romanesque abbey church – nothing special architecturally, but a gloomy enough setting if you're in the mood for weaving Gothic horror stories.

Susa

A further 25km down the valley, **SUSA** is a possible stopover if it's late, a likeable, rather scruffy old town with a couple of very cheap **hotels**: the *Meana* (☎0122/622.280; ③), and the *Sole*, both on Piazza IV Novembre (☎0122/2474; ③).

While most of Italy was under the Romans, Susa and western Piemonte remained in the hands of the Gauls. The best known of its Gaulish leaders, Cottius, was much admired by the Romans, with whom he reached a peaceful arrangement, and there are a handful of Gaulish/Roman remains scattered around the town centre, notably in **Piazza San Giusto**, where there's a redoubtable defensive gate. The adjacent Romanesque **Cattedrale** has a fine campanile, but its most interesting features are the external frescoes – a *Crucifixion* and an *Entry into Jerusalem*. Just above the piazza, Cottius erected the **Arco di Augosto** in honour of the Roman emperor, its top decorated with a processional frieze and giving views down into a small park laid out around the remains of some **Roman Baths**. For a complete round-up of the town's ancient origins, look in on the **museum** housed in the crumbling medieval castle above the town (July & Aug Wed–Sun 9.30am–12.30pm, also 2–5pm on Thurs, Sat & Sun; Sept–June Tues–Sat 9.30am–12.30pm, also 2–5pm Thurs & Sat).

From Susa you can make an excursion to the abbey of **Novalesa**, 10km away at the foot of Rocciamelone in the Cenischia Valley, close by the French border. The church here is a relatively recent, eighteenth-century structure, but part of the cloister and walls date back to the eighth century, while the four chapels, one of which is decorated with frescoes, was built in the tenth century.

In the opposite direction, southeast, at the end of the Chisone Valley, **PINEROLO** is worth a short stop. It's a small town with a medieval centre that was for centuries the seat of the Acaia princedom, precursors of the House of Savoy. You can visit their **palace**, halfway up the hill, where you'll also find the church of **San Maurizio**, burial place of the Acaia princes, decorated with fifteenth-century frescoes. In the town centre, there's a Gothic **Duomo**, and the huge covered **Cavallerizza Caprilli** or parade ground for horses. The **Museo della Cavalleria** (Tues, Wed, Fri & Sat 9–11.15am & 3–5.15pm, Sun 9–11.15am; free), hopefully open again now after restoration, is one of only two such museums in Italy and gives a good sense of the now faded importance of the town, with displays relating to the prestigious former cavalry school of Pinerolo. There are lots of objects – uniforms, arms and spurs, trophies and documents, even a stuffed horse – pertaining to the brilliance of the horsemen and their steeds, as well as displays of bridles, horseshoes, tools and the like, and a rather sad section devoted to the tanks and jeeps that have come to replace horses in the military.

Skiing: the Piemontese resorts

Close to the French border are Piemonte's principal purpose-built ski resorts – well used by British tour operators and really far cheaper if you take a package. The snow is in any case notoriously unreliable, and resorts have been known to close down mid-season, though Sestriere has lately protected itself against the weather by installing Europe's largest artificial snow-machine.

Of the main three resorts, **BARDONECCHIA** is a weekenders' haunt, a modern resort with small chalet-style hotels. **SAUZE D'OULX**, a little way south, is known as the Benidorm of the Alps, and attracts hordes of young Brits who treat skiing as a hang-over cure. Apart from a few winding streets of old houses, it's an ugly, sprawling place, and its lift-passes are expensive, at L171,000 per week. Linked by lift to Sauze d'Oulx, **SESTRIERE** was the dream resort of Mussolini and the Fiat baron, Agnelli, though it's now very overdeveloped. Agnelli conceived of an aristocratic mountain retreat, favoured by the young and beautiful, though he was not unaware of the fast-growing tourist industry. The story goes that he insisted the height of the sinks be raised to prevent "common tourists" from pissing in them. The bland resort now dribbles over a bleak mountain, dominated by two cylindrical towers, both now owned by *Club Med*. Apart from the advantage of its snow-machine, there's little appeal to the place at all.

Saluzzo and the western valleys

A flourishing medieval town, and later the seat of one of Piemonte's few Renaissance courts, **SALUZZO**, 57km south of Turin, retains much of its period appeal. Flaking ochre-washed terraces and Renaissance houses with painted trompe l'oeil landscapes line stepped cobbled streets climbing up to a castle, now a prison. A pleasant place to stay and wander, the town has the added attraction of bus services which make it a convenient base for excursions into the Po, Varaita and Maira valleys, which cut through the foothills of the Monviso mountain towards France.

There are a few things around town worth seeing. Just below the castle, the Gothic church of **San Giovanni** has a number of thirteenth- and fourteenth-century frescoes and the tomb of the leading light of Renaissance Saluzzo, Marchese Ludovico II, anachronistically depicted like a medieval knight beneath a fancily carved canopy. Close by, the Gothic **Casa Cavassa** is a fifteenth-century palace with an arcaded courtyard that doubled as home for one of Ludovico's ministers and now houses the town's **Museo Civico** (Tues–Sun 10am–1pm & 2–6pm; L4000). Inside are period furniture and paintings, including the gorgeously gilded *Madonna della Misericordia*, with the Madonna sheltering Ludovico, his wife and the population of Saluzzo in the folds of her cloak.

That's about all there is to the town centre, but just to the south of Saluzzo, a five-minute bus ride from outside the train station, there's the **Castello di Manta** – a medieval fortress that was transformed into a refined residence by the Saluzzo marquises in the fifteenth century (Tues–Sun 10am–1pm & 2–6pm; L4000). Though from the outside it's as plain and austere as Saluzzo's castle, it's worth visiting for the late Gothic frescoes in the Baronial Hall. One of these illustrates the myth of the fountain of youth, elderly people processing towards the magical waters while others impatiently rip off their clothes to plunge in. The other, the Nine Heroes and Nine Heroines, contains idealised chivalrous courtiers and exquisite damsels, with china-pale faces and elaborate costumes, standing beneath stylised trees with coats of arms hanging from the branches.

Practicalities

Saluzzo's **tourist office** is at Via Griselda 6 (Mon–Fri 8.30am–12.30pm & 2.30–3.30pm, Sat 8.30am–noon). Of **hotels**, the *Luna* at Via Martiri della Libertá 10 (☎0175/43.707; ③) is cheap and convenient, or there's the pricier *Persico* in Vicolo Mercabilo (☎0175/42.552; ⑤), which also has a very good **restaurant**, with traditional cuisine.

Valle Po

West of Saluzzo, close to the French border, lies the source of the River Po, which flows right across industrial northern Italy, gathering the waste from its thousands of factories before finally discharging into the Adriatic. The Alpine-style resort of **CRISSOLO** lies towards the end of the valley, and you can hike (or take a minibus in summer) to the **Pian del Re**, a grassy plain around the source of the Po, walking on to the entrance of the **Pertuis de la Traversette**, a 75-metre-long tunnel (currently closed) built by Saluzzo's Marquis Ludovico, to ease the trading route into France for his mule trains. According to one theory, the pre-tunnel pass was used by Hannibal and his elephants.

Crissolo is also a good base for climbing **Monviso**, Piemonte's highest mountain, reachable by way of a long rocky scramble in about six hours from the *Quintino Sella rifugio*, two to three hours beyond the Pian del Re. Even if you don't want to scale the summit, the walk to the *rifugio* is lovely, passing a series of **mountain lakes**; or, if you prefer, it's possible to do a **circuit of the lakes**, turning off the main trail just before Lago Chiaretto, from which a path leads past Lago Superiore and back to Pian del Re. There are also **caves** near Crissolo, **Grotta del Rio Martino** above the town, with stalactites and a subterranean lake and waterfall. The quick route here takes half an hour from Crissolo but is steep; the slower, easier route takes an hour. Unless you're an experienced caver, it's advisable to go with a guide from the **tourist office** on the main square in Crissolo.

Practicalities

Crissolo's **hotels** are all on the main street. The *Albergo Serenella* at Via Provinciale 14 (☎0175/94.944; ④) is cheap and open year-round; the *Club Alpino* at Via Proviniciale 32 (☎0175/94.925; ⑤) is seasonal, as is another small hotel at Pian del Re, the *Pian del Re* (☎0175/94.967; ④). The *Quintino Sella* refuge, near the Lago Grande del Viso, is open June to September, and sometimes in winter; at all times it's advisable to phone in advance (☎0175/94.943). Most of Crissolo's **restaurants** are in the hotels, so you may find taking half-board a better deal.

Val Varaita

To the south of the Valle Po, **Val Varaita**'s only draw is the rustic-style furniture that has been produced here since the eighteenth century, when the locals decided to capitalise on the vogue among Torinese and Genovese aristocrats for building country villas in the area. The industry continues to flourish, these days patronised by wealthy Torinese weekenders, and has brought much needed prosperity to the area, though sadly its distinctly un-rustic factories and the 1980s equivalent of the country villa – fake Alpine apartment blocks – have ruined the look of the place irreparably.

Cuneo and around

There's not much to bring you to **CUNEO**, the main town of southern Piemonte and provincial capital. Its severely geometric modern centre has less appeal than its extensive bus and rail connections, and the old town – what there is left of it – is dark and gloomy. Even its one "sight", the museum (weekdays only) in the restored Gothic church of **San Francesco** behind the bus station, is only of limited interest: the collection ranges from medieval frescoes to a folk section with traditional costumes, kitchen utensils and an ancient bike.

The **tourist office** in Cuneo is at Corso Nizza 17. If you want to stay, there are a couple of reasonable **hotels**: the *Cavallo Nero* at Piazza Seminario 8 (☎62.017; ④), and the similarly priced *Ligure*, Via Savigliano 11 (☎681.942; ④).

The Valleys

What does bring people to Cuneo is the area to the south of the town, where the valleys form a popular area of sulphurous spas and summer and winter resorts. Of the main valleys, the **Valle Stura** is much visited by botanists for its many rare species of flowers; the **Valle Gesso**, whose name means gypsum or chalk, is characterised by its vast walls of limestone, unusual in Piemonte, and some of it has been set aside as the huge **Parco Naturale dell'Argentera-Valle Gesso**, in which you can stay in various refuges, take the waters at **TERME DI VALDIERI**, or visit the botanical gardens at **VALDERIA**. The **Valle del Pesio** shouldn't be missed in spring at least, when a waterfall, known for obvious reasons as the *Piss del Pesio*, is in full pelt; there's also a twelfth-century monastery, the **Certosa di Pesio**, which boasts a missionary museum. Trains to France run through the verdant **Valle Vermenagna**, part of which is given over to the **Parco Naturale di Palanfre**, visitable from **VERNANTE**. Again, the appeal is mainly botanical, with over 800 species of trees and flowers growing at some 3000m above sea level, along with lots of birds and mammals.

Val Maira, actually to the north of Cuneo but still considered one of its valleys, is a quiet and narrow valley, known as the "Emerald Valley" for its greenery; its drama is heightened if you take the bus from Cuneo, recklessly hurtling around craggy cliffs, the driver seemingly oblivious to the sheer drops below. There's not much beyond this, though the villages, with their traditional rubble and wood houses perched high above the river, are very picturesque, particularly **ELVA**, in the hills above **STROPPO** (hitch or ask in the cafés for the unofficial taxi driver). If you're walking get a **map** from Saluzzo before heading out. The best base is the small village of **PRAZZO**, where there's a hotel, the *Impero*, on Via Nazionale (☎0171/99.124; ④), which has modern, comfortable doubles and a good traditional restaurant. There are no hotels at Stroppo, just a **campsite** near the turn-off for Elva.

Mondoví: frescoes, a sanctuary and some caves

Half an hour by train from Cuneo, **MONDOVÍ** is a peculiar town. Split into two, the lower half – Breo – is sleepily suburban, while the upper half, Piazza, is an uneasy combination of crumbling medieval and exuberant Baroque. Neither are especially exciting, but the town gives access to some interesting attractions nearby – some fifteenth-century frescoes, a sanctuary and some caves.

Time in Mondoví is best spent in Piazza, built around a large square on which stand a turretted medieval palace and an exotic Baroque church, the seventeenth-century **Chiesa della Missione**, whose interior is decorated with an incredible trompe l'oeil by Andrea Pozzo, a cloudy heaven with angels seemingly suspended in mid-air. If you've time, you can laze around in the **Belvedere**, to the north of Piazza, a garden occupying the site of a thirteenth-century church destroyed except for its campanile in the last century. The campanile was used by a physicist in the eighteenth century to establish topographical measurements. Though you can't climb up, the views from the gardens stretch north to the hills of Le Langhe and south to the foothills of the Alps.

San Fiorenzo

One of the attractions of Mondoví is its vicinity to the hamlet of **BASTIA**, 10km north-east, where the church of **San Fiorenzo** – from the outside a modest rustic structure – holds some brilliantly coloured late-Gothic frescoes. Completed around 1472, and worked on by at least four artists, and they're absorbing pieces, with lively if predictable scenes from the lives of Christ and various saints, including a stunning Hell, infested with vicious monsters.

Buses run to Bastia from the train station at Mondoví but are badly timed for returning – though hitching along the main road (28bis) is fairly easy.

The Santuario di Vicoforte

A twenty-minute bus ride (from the train station) east of Mondoví, the **Santuario di Vicoforte** is another popular trip from the town, an imposing Baroque church crowned by what is claimed as the world's largest elliptical dome. It's liveliest on Sundays – like most Italian sanctuaries as much a place for a good day out as for devotions, purpose-built arcaded crescents housing restaurants, pastry, souvenir and clothes shops.

According to legend the sanctuary owes its existence to a hunter who while out in the woods discovered a pillar painted with a picture of the Madonna and Child – said, according to a second legend, to have been erected as a votive offering by a poor baker whose bread wouldn't rise. In fact, the sanctuary was begun in 1598 on the orders of King Carlo Emanuele I, and eventually finished in 1890. The frescoed pillar is nowhere to be seen, and the 36-metre dome is rather a disappointment. But the kitschy **museum** provides some compensation: a haphazard collection of ecclesiastical bric-a-brac laid out in a labyrinth of rooms around the dome and towers. The exhibits range from gaudy treasures to ceremonial costumes and photos of those cured by a visit here.

Grotta di Bossea

Twenty-four kilometres south of Vicoforte, the **Grotta di Bossea** (March–Nov 10am–noon & 2–6pm) is the third of Mondovì's surrounding attractions, a long-established underground tourist target filled with contorted stalactites and stalagmites, waterfalls and lakes and a subterranean scientific laboratory, set up to monitor the caves' population – which includes seven unique species. On display is the skeleton of the *Ursius Spelaeus*, an underground monster over three metres long and two metres high which lived here between 25,000 and 40,000 years ago. Sadly, reaching the caves without your own transport is virtually impossible, although it's often possible to hitch at weekends when the caves are busiest.

Alba and the Le Langhe hills

Northeast of Cuneo, the town of **Alba** and the surrounding Le Langhe hills mean two things to the Italians: white truffles and red wine. The region supplies some of the finest of both – the truffles are more delicate and aromatic than the black variety found further south, and the wines range from the "King of Italian reds", **Barolo**, to the light and fragrant **Nebbiolo**. There are a number of wine museums and *cantinas* in the hill-villages around Alba, best those at Barolo, Annunziata and Grinzane di Cavour – all accessible direct by bus from Alba (though to hop from one to the other you'll need to hitch).

Although these big *cantinas* all sell wine, you'll get a better deal at one of the smaller family-owned *cantinas* scattered around the region. Most of the area's very different wines all come from the same grape, Nebbiolo, and the final taste is dependent on the soil: sandy soil produces the grapes for the light red, **Nebbiolo**, calcium and mineral-rich soil those for the more robust **Barolo**.

Alba

Whether or not you want to taste wine, **ALBA** repays a visit, its central core of red-brick medieval towers, Baroque and Renaissance palaces and cobbled streets lined with gastronomic shops one of Piemonte's most alluring. And if you come in October, there's a chance to see the town's hilarious annual donkey race – a skit on nearby Asti's prestigious Palio.

Of things to see, the late-Gothic **Duomo** on the central Piazza Risorgimento has been gaudily restored and holds some fine Renaissance stalls, inlaid with cityscapes, musical instruments, and fake cupboards whose contents seem to be on the verge of falling out. But Alba is primarily a place to stroll and eat. **Via Vittorio Emanuele**, the main drag, leads up to the centre from Piazza Savona, a fine, bustling street, with the most tempting of Alba's local produce on display – wines, truffles, cheeses, weird and wonderful varieties of mushroom, and the wickedly sticky *nocciola*, a nutty, chocolatey cake. **Via Cavour** is another pleasant medieval street with plenty of wine shops, behind which the **donkey race** and displays of medieval pageantry attract the crowds during the October festival. There's also an annual **truffle festival** at the same time, when you could blow your whole budget on a knobbly truffle or a meal in one of the many swanky restaurants.

Practicalities

The **tourist office** is on Piazza Medford (Tues–Fri 9am–noon & 3.30–6.30pm, Sat 9am–noon; ☎0173/35.833) and has maps of the town and information on the surrounding area. Aside from October, when **room** rates soar, there are reasonable deals to be had at the *Leon d'Oro*, Piazza Marconi 2 (☎441.901; ④), and – cheaper still – at the *Rovej*, Via Silvio Pellico 18 (☎284.306; ③), or the *Vecchio Centro*, Via Cuneo 8 (☎441.348; ③). The best places to sample Albanese cooking are excellent *Osteria dell'Arco*, at Vicolo dell'Arco 2, off Via Vittorio Emanuele, and the *Corona Grossa* restaurant at Corso Torino 6 – though neither are cheap. If you want to save money, try the *Spaghetteria Il Girasole* on Via Maestra.

Around Alba: the Le Langhe hills

Eight kilometres south of Alba, the castle of **Grinzane di Cavour** was rented by the Cavour family in the nineteenth century and served as a weekend retreat for Camillo Cavour. Nowadays it's the seat of Piemonte's regional *enoteca*, or winery, and has a pricey restaurant specialising in local specialities. The upstairs **folk museum** (Wed–Mon 9am–noon & 2–6pm; closed Jan) holds various bits of Cavour trivia (most intimate is Camillo's wooden bedside toilet) and a surprisingly engaging display of agricultural equipment, ranging from a ferret trap and grappa distillery, to winter boots made of hay and a contraption for cleaning the cocoons of silkworms. In the afternoons there are wine-tasting sessions, and although there are inevitably some extremely expensive wines, many are affordable if you're interested in buying.

A few kilometres southwest of Grinzane, in the heart of the Le Langhe hills, **BAROLO** is the best-known name among Italian wines, its peach and ochre-washed houses set among extensive vineyards. It's a small village but is very geared up to the steady stream of wealthy gastronomes and wine connoisseurs that come here. You can visit the *Enoteca Regionale di Barolo*, housed in a flaking turreted castle on Piazza Falletti (daily except Thurs 10am–noon & 3–6.30pm; L2000, includes tasting), or indulge yourself with a night and a meal at the *Hotel Barolo* (☎0173/55.191; ⑥), whose restaurant – an imperious place with a stiff dress code – is renowned hereabouts.

Just north of Barolo, **LA MORRA** is an earthy old village, with good views over the undulating vineyards from outside the *Belvedere* restaurant and hotel on Piazza Municipio, home to the *Cantina Comunale di La Morra* (Wed–Fri 11am–noon & 2.30–5.30pm, Sat & Sun 10am–12.30pm & 2.30–6pm; free), in which you can taste and buy wine. There are also some good food shops, with a wide range of local cheeses, and if you're there on a Monday, you can pick up bargains at the market.

The *cantina* has maps of walks through the vineyards, best of which is the one to **ANNUNZIATA**, about half an hour down the hill, where there's a private wine museum, the **Museo Ratti dei Vini d'Alba** (Mon–Fri 8.30am–noon & 2.30–6pm, Sat & Sun phone in advance: ☎0173/50.185; free), housed in a Renaissance abbey next to the firm's *cantina*. Laid out in a musty cellar, this is mainly of appeal to dedicated wine buffs, although there are a number of intriguing exhibits – a massive barrel for treading grapes, a primitive wine tanker, consisting of an elongated barrel on a rickety cart, and a collection of Roman wine jugs found in the area. Best of all, there's a letter from an Arctic explorer, congratulating the Ratti on the fact that their Barolo had stood up to the rigours of travel and climate on an expedition to the North Pole.

Wine at the Ratti *cantina* is expensive, and you can only buy it in lots of six. It's far cheaper and sold in single bottles at the small family *cantina, Oberto Severino*, a kilometre or so up the road back towards La Morra. As for staying over, there are two **hotels** in La Morra – the *Italia* (☎0173/50.310; ③) on the main road, and the *Belvedere* (☎0173/50.190; ④), above the restaurant on Piazza Castello.

Asti and around

The wine connection continues in **ASTI**, 30km north of Alba and the capital of Italy's sparkling wine industry – though for most of the year Asti itself is fairly sedate, a small town, not unattractive, that only livens up in mid-September for its annual Palio. In the run-up to the event there are street banquets and a medieval market, and on the day of the race itself, the third Sunday in September, there's a thousand-strong procession of citizens dressed as their fourteenth-century ancestors, before the frenetic bare-backed horse race around the arena of the Campo del Palio – followed by the awarding of the *palio* (banner) to the winner and all night feasting and boozing. It's taken nothing like as seriously as Siena's more famous event (see *Tuscany*, Chapter Eight), and has to some extent been revived for tourists. But if you're in the area at the right time you'd be mad to miss it.

The Town

The rest of the year the Campo del Palio is a vast, bleak car park, and there's frankly not a lot to see. The arcaded **Piazza Alfieri** is official centre of the town, behind which the **Collegiata di San Secondo** (daily 7am–noon & 3.30–7pm) is dedicated to the city's patron saint, built on the site of the saint's martyrdom in the second century. Not surprisingly, there's nothing left of the second-century church but there is a fine sixth-century crypt, its columns so slender that they seem on the verge of toppling over. As for the rest of the church, it's a slick, early Gothic construction, with neat red-brick columns topped with tidily carved capitals and in the left aisle a polyptych by one of Asti's Renaissance artists, Gandolfino d'Asti. The *palio* banners are also kept here, housed in a heavily ornate Baroque chapel, along with the *Carroccio* – a sacred war chariot used in medieval times.

The main street, **Corso Alfieri**, slices through the town from the square, on the right of which the church of **San Pietro** at Corso Alfieri 2 (Tues–Sat 9am–noon & 3–6pm, Sun 10am–noon; ring for the custodian) has a circular twelfth-century **Baptistry**, now used as an exhibition space, and a **museum**, housed in what was a pilgrim's hospice, displaying an odd – and badly labelled – assortment of Roman and Egyptian artefacts. At the other end of the Corso, the **Torre Rossa** is a medieval tower with a chequered top, built on the foundations of the Roman tower in which San Secondo, a Roman soldier, was imprisoned before being killed.

Practicalities

Asti's **tourist office** is on Piazza Alfieri (Mon–Fri 9am–12.30pm & 3–6pm, Sat 9am–12.30pm; ☎50357/58.200), and has information on the Palio and maps of the town. If you're intending to go to Asti on the Palio weekend, book a **room** well in advance; at other times there should be little problem. The best of the affordable options are the conveniently sited *Cavour*, on Piazza Marconi (☎0141/50.222; ④), and the slightly cheaper *Genova*, Corso Alessandria 26 (☎593.197 or ☎54.228; ④). As somewhere renowned for its food perhaps should, Asti has a wide choice of **restaurants**, ranging from basic and cheap pizzerias like *Monna Laura*, Via Cavour 30, to places serving excellent traditional local cuisine like *Trattoria Aurora*, Viale Partigiana 58, or *Trattoria Due Lanterne*, though at either of these places you needn't spend a fortune. If you're into Asti Spumante, or want to sample the other wines of the region, there are **wine festivals** in late August and September – details from the tourist office.

Near Asti: the Abbazia di Vezzolano

Although Alba is a better base for visiting vineyards and wine museums, **COSTIGLIOLE D'ASTI**, a short bus ride south of Asti, is the centre of Asti Spumante production; it has the *Cantina dei Vini di Costigliole d'Asti*, at Via Roma 9 (open weekends only), and a predictably pricey gastronomic **restaurant** in its castle.

If you have your own transport or the patience to hitch, the **Abbazia di Vezzolano** (daily 9.30am–12.30pm & 3–6pm), in the village of **ALBUGNANO**, deep in a valley to the northwest of Asti, displays some of the area's best late-Romanesque architecture. According to legend the abbey was founded by Charlemagne, who had a religious vision on the site in the eighth century. Outside it has a fancily arcaded and sculpted facade and a secluded Romanesque cloister. Inside, there's a stone rood screen carved with expressive scenes from the life of Mary, and a row of naive, rustic-looking saints.

Alessandria, Acqui Terme and Casale Monferrato

Immediately east of Asti, the area around Alessandria is scattered with castles, though all are privately owned and only occasionally opened to the public. The one attraction of the modern, industrial provincial capital, **ALESSANDRIA**, was a museum of Borsalino hats (the kind with the dented crown, favoured by American Prohibition-era gangsters), but this has now closed, and there is no real reason to step out of the station.

ACQUI TERME, to the south, is a dreary spa town, with a steaming sulphurous spring, *La Bollente*, gurgling up in its scruffy main piazza, and a polluted river flowing through the centre. The efficacy of Acqui's spas earned the attention of Romans from Pliny to Seneca, but there's only one substantial relic from its Roman heyday – four arches of an aqueduct below the main bridge. There is also a small **museum**, with the remains of mosaics from the Roman spa, in a dilapidated castle next to the cathedral, but it's of limited interest (Tues–Sat 10am–noon & 3–6pm).

North of Asti, **CASALE MONFERRATO** has the dubious distinction of being cement capital of Italy, and it's also home to the country's most sumptuous **synagogue** – a leftover from the days when there was a sizeable Jewish population in Piemonte, most of whom had fled from Spain in the sixteenth century to escape persecution. Casale was home to nearly 200 Jewish families, who lived here in peace until Mussolini's racial laws (brought in mainly to appease Hitler) forced many to leave. The synagogue lies down an alley off Via Saloman Olmer, the first left off the main Via Roma (Sun & holidays 10am–noon & 3–5.30pm, at other times ring next door), a rich, gold-encrusted affair with a voluptuously curving pulpit and a "museum of treasures" laid out in the closed-off women's gallery.

Eastern Piemonte: Vercelli and Novara

A less typical Italian landscape than the area **east of Turin** would be difficult to imagine. The vast paddy fields here produce more rice than anywhere in Europe, on a deadly flat plain across which road and rail cut on their way to Milan. For about half the year the fields are flooded (with warm water in winter), and are at their most evocative in autumn when the weak sun filters through the mists, making the stalk-spiked waters gleam.

Whatever time of year you're here, the novelty soon wears off, and most people are only too glad to leave the area. You'd do well to follow their example, either hurrying through to Milan or Turin, or heading north, via the towns of Novara and Vercelli, to the Val Sesia – which winds up towards Monte Rosa on the Swiss border.

Vercelli

The centre of Piemonte's – indeed Europe's – rice-growing region is **VERCELLI**, usually full of businesspeople come to wheel and deal over prices in the *Borsa di Riso* or rice stock exchange. There its appeal really ends, although if you've time to spare between trains, the **Basilica of Sant'Andrea**, just across from the station, is worth a studied peek. It was built in the thirteenth century by a cardinal funded with revenues from a Cambridgeshire monastery, granted him by King Henry III as a reward for helping to establish him on the English throne. As the revenues were vast, it took only nine years to complete – an incredible feat at a time when churches frequently took over a century to build – and today it's an important church architecturally, one of the first in Italy to incorporate Gothic elements: pointed arches, slender columns shooting up to the vaults, and tall, slim conical-roofed belltowers flanking the facade.

The **Cattedrale di Sant'Eusebio**, at the end of Via Bicchieri, also deserves a visit, built on the site of a much more ancient basilica and with some fine old treasures and manuscripts in its library. Otherwise Vercelli's most atmospheric spot is **Piazza Cavour**, just off the main Corso Libertà, surrounded by pleasantly scruffy arcades and the scene of the Tuesday market. Close by, on Via Borgogna, the large **Museo Pinacoteca Borgogna** (summer Tues & Thurs 3–5.30pm; winter 2.30–5pm; all year Sat & Sun 9.30am–noon; free) holds the work of relatively unknown local artists together with the odd Brueghel and Jan Steen and some frescoes taken from local churches.

Practicalities

Vercelli's **tourist office** is at Viale Garibaldi 90 (Mon–Fri 8.30am–noon & 2.30–5.30pm, Sat 8.30am–noon). Finding a **room** in Vercelli can be a problem, with the hotels often full with rice-trade reps and the overspill from Turin's industrial fairs; it's advisable to phone in advance. The cheapest options are the *Rondinella*, Corso Gastaldi 15 (☎0161/53.835; ③), outside the bus station and a couple of minutes' walk to the right of the train station, and the *Valsesia*, at Via G. Ferraris 104 (☎0161/250.842; ④); both hotels have **restaurants** with very reasonably priced food.

Novara

NOVARA, twenty minutes further down the train line towards Milan, makes for a more elegant, unhurried stopover than Vercelli, its main street, **Corso Cavour**, neatly paved with half-moon cobbles and lined with *pasticcerias* and old-fashioned tearooms. That said, there's not much left of historic Novara: the medieval **Broletto** houses an open-air cinema in summer, and the **Duomo** is an overblown Neoclassical creation which dwarfs all around to Lilliputian proportions; inside are bits and pieces from earlier churches – a fifth-century **Baptistry** with tenth-century frescoes of the Apocalypse, and a frescoed twelfth-century chapel – both open only in the morning. A couple of blocks north, the weird three-tiered dome of the church of **San Gaudenzio** with its syringe-like spire dominates the whole town. It was built by Antonelli, a nineteenth-century architect responsible for a similar monstrosity, the *Mole* in Turin.

Novara's **tourist office** is centrally placed at at Via Dominioni 4 (Mon–Fri 8.30am–noon & 1.30–4.30pm). The cheapest **hotel** is the *Centro* (☎0321/23.232; ③), though you might prefer to splash out a bit on the much more pleasant *Parmigiano*, Via dei Cattanei 4 (☎0321/23.231; ⑤). There's a reasonable **pizzeria**, *Le Tre Lanterne*, at Via dei Tornielli 1, just off Piazza Gramsci at the end of Corso Cavour.

Northern Piemonte: Biella, Varallo and Valsesia

The main attraction of northern Piemonte is really the mountains, especially the dramatic Alpine **Valsesia**, which winds up to the foot of Monte Rosa on the Swiss border. On the way, stop off at two of the region's most visited sanctuaries, the **Santuario d'Oropa** near **Biella**, or **Sacro Monte** at **Varallo**. From here you're well poised either for Piemonte's mountains or those of Valle d'Aosta, a few kilometres west.

Biella and the Santuario d'Oropa

A short train ride northwest from Novara, the provincial capital of **BIELLA** is known for its wool industry, its periphery choked with mills and the hilltop upper town with the mansions and villas of wool barons. It's not an especially rewarding place, apart perhaps from its small medieval quarter, reachable by funicular or by strolling up its many arcaded lanes. But it does give access to the **Santuario d'Oropa**, a forty-minute bus ride northwest of Biella at the foot of Monte Mucrone. Founded in the fourth century by Saint Eusebio to house a black statue of the Madonna and Child, this is an odd sort of attraction, and can't really compete with the sanctuary at Varallo for sensation. But it's the most venerated of Piemonte's shrines, the main church an immense neo-Baroque concoction, and it's a good starting-point also for **walks** into the surrounding mountains. If you wish, you can stay at the sanctuary itself, which has around 700 rooms (phone the Biella tourist office to book – ☎015/351.128). A cable car runs regularly up Monte Mucrone as far as the (closed) *Albergo Savoia*, where a network of marked trails begins. One of the nicest and easiest is to the **Lago Mucrone**, a small mountain lake, while if you want views without too much effort you can simply walk back down to the sanctuary in about an hour. If all this seems too easy, hike up to the summit of Monte Mucrone itself – a two-hour trek.

Though you should definitely move on if you can, you may need to **stay overnight** in Biella. Be warned that the two cheap hotels are a bit seedy, best the *Monte di Varallo* at Salita Riva 2 (☎015/22.366; ④).

Varallo and Sacro Monte

Some 50km by train north of Novara, **VARALLO** marks the beginning of northern Piemonte's more picturesque reaches, a gateway to the region, surrounded by steep wooded hills and filled with Art Deco villas and Baroque palazzi. It's a pretty place in itself, very pleasant for a short visit, but most people come to see the sanctuary of **Sacro Monte**, just outside the town and connected by bus five times daily from the train station.

If you've only come for Sacro Monte you could make straight there from the station; if you want to see the town first – and it is worth a quick wander – the centre is a five-minute walk to the right along Corso Roma. On the way you pass the church of **San Gaudenzio**, spectacularly anchored to a creeper-covered cliff and surrounded by arcades. It's less impressive inside, though there's a polyptych by the sixteenth-century Varallo-born artist Gaudenzio Ferrari, responsible for much of the work at Sacro Monte. The main street, **Corso Umberto I**, lined with shuttered and balconied palaces, winds through the town from here towards the River Serio. There's more work by Gaudenzio Ferrari in the church of **Madonna delle Grazie**, where an entire wall is covered with colourful and detailed scenes from the life of Christ.

The **tourist office** is on the corner of Corso Roma and Piazza Garibaldi, at Corso Roma 41 (Tues–Fri 8.30am–noon & 2.30–6.30pm, Sat 8.30am–noon & 2.30–6pm, Sun

9am–noon). If you want to **stay over** in Varallo, the *Monte Rosa* (☎0163/51.100; ④) is a rambling, friendly and very clean hotel a brisk five-minute walk to the left of the train station.

Sacro Monte

Crowning the hill above Varallo, **Sacro Montea** is a complex of 44 chapels, each housing a 3-D tableau of painted statues against frescoed scenery representing a scene from the life of Christ. Founded in the fifteenth century by a friar anxious to popularise Catholicism in a region in which heresy was rife, Sacro Monte emphasises sensationalism and spectacle, calculated to work upon the emotions of the uneducated. The sanctuary is at its best when busy – to get a measure of its continuing popularity, you need to visit on a Sunday, when it's full of families, pensioners and nuns, all of whom picnic in the shady grounds after finishing their pilgrimage.

It's inevitably a bizarre spectacle, depicting the whole range of key biblical episodes from the Fall to Christ's birth, life and death. And the tableaux don't pull any punches: the *Massacre of the Innocents* (#11) has a floor littered with dead babies, while Herod's army prepares to spear, hack and slash more. And the chapels (#30–41) that retell the events of Christ's passion are flagrant emotional manipulation, with crazed flagellators, spitting soldiers and a series of liberally blood-splattered Christs. By the time you reach the *Road to Calvary* (#36) you almost flinch at the sight of a flaked-out Christ being viciously kicked. Dominating the central piazza of the sanctuary, the Baroque **Basilica** offers some relief, the highlight the cupola – a nice piece of optical trickery, encrusted with figures perched on bubblegum clouds.

Valsesia

From Varallo the road follows the River Sesia to the foot of multi-peaked **Monte Rosa**, whose massive bulk heads four Italian valleys and spreads north into Switzerland. **Valsesia**, the most easterly valley, is also the most dramatic – worth going for the ride even if you don't want to hike or ski.

Flanked by dark pine-wooded slopes crowned with a toothed ridge of rock, the road winds up the valley, the perspective changing at every turn. Well-touristed (mainly by Italians and Germans), traditional houses with slate roofs and wood-slatted balconies mingle with Alpine-style villas and apartments. The villages are crowded for much of the summer, and with weekend skiers in the winter. September is the quietest month, when many of the hotels close, but the weather up the mountains is unpredictable then, and hiking can be hazardous.

The Valsesia villages were founded in the thirteenth century by religious sects from the Swiss Valais, known as Walser, in search of land and the freedom to worship. There are reckoned to be around 3000 true Walsers in the valleys of Monte Rosa, and in most bars and shops you'll still hear people speaking a dialect based on ancient German. If you want to see how these isolated communities lived and worked, there's a **Walser Museum** (July & Aug only 2–6pm), a traditionally furnished seventeenth-century house in the hamlet of **PEDEMONTE**, ten minutes' walk out of Alagna.

ALAGNA, at the head of the valley, right below Monte Rosa, is the most convenient place to stay, whether you want to ski or hike. Popular and predominantly modern, it has a cluster of wood-slatted Walser houses to the south, with a tiny network of overgrown tracks winding in between them. Some houses still function as farms, with hay hanging to dry on the slats and wood stacked behind, while others are holiday homes, spilling with geraniums.

There are lots of **walks** among the foothills, all of which are well marked from Alagna. If you're interested in seeing more than mountain scenery, there's a path along 5km back down the valley to **RIVA VALDOBBIA**, whose church facade is covered with a colourful late sixteenth-century fresco of *The Last Judgement*. However, the toughest and most spectacular hikes are those on **Monte Rosa** itself. If you can afford it, it's possible to save time and energy by taking the cable car (return trip around L23,000) up to Punta Indren (3260m), from where you can walk to one of the many *rifugi*; most of these are open from June to September, but check at the tourist office in Alagna before setting out. Failing that, you could walk down into the next valley, Val Gressoney in Valle d'Aosta (see below).

All these walks involve a good deal of scree-crossing and some sobering drops, and none are to be taken lightly – you'll need a good **map** (the *FMB* map of the four Monte Rosa valleys shows all paths, *rifugi* and pistes) and you should check on the weather before setting out. There's also an ambitious long-distance circuit of Monte Rosa, starting at Alagna, taking in Val Gressoney, Val d'Ayas and Zermatt across the Swiss border: you'll need five days if you make use of ski-lifts and cable cars, and a good deal longer than that if you don't.

Skiing in the area is organised by *Monterosa Ski* who have an office in Alagna. A day pass costs L27,000, and equipment is available for hire in the village. However, the runs are narrow, and though experienced skiers can cross into Val Gressoney, it involves walking as well as off-piste skiing.

Alagna's cheapest **hotel** is the *Mirella*, in the suburb of Bonda (☎015/91.146; ④); there's also the more central but more expensive *Indren*, Via Reale Inferiore 32 (☎015/91.151; ④), and *Cristallo*, next to the **tourist office** on the appropriately named Piazza degli Alberghi (☎015/91.285).

VALLE D'AOSTA

Fringed by Europe's highest mountains, Mont Blanc, the Matterhorn and Monte Rosa, veined with valleys and studded with castles, **Valle d'Aosta** is undeniably picturesque. The central Aosta valley cuts right across the region, following the River Dora to the foot of Mont Blanc on the French border. Along the river are most of the feudal castles for which Valle d'Aosta is famed – the majority built by the Challant family who ruled the region for seven centuries. Although the castles are pretty from the outside, and easily accessible by bus or train, few are absorbing enough to warrant a special trip into the region. But as skiing and walking country, Valle d'Aosta is unsurpassed.

Valle d'Aosta is the least Italian of all the regions. Its landscape and architecture are Swiss, the official language French, and in some valleys the locals, whose ancestors emigrated from Switzerland, still speak a dialect based on German. In fact, although Italian is more widely spoken than French, bilingualism is an essential part of Valle d'Aosta's identity, which is quite distinct from other parts of the north – a distinctiveness reflected in the greater administrative and financial autonomy of the region.

Aosta, the regional capital, is the only town of any size, and though in itself unspectacular makes a good base for much of the area. As for the countryside, the main valley is for the most part rather bland, and it's in the more scenic tributary valleys that you'll want to spend most of your time. The eastern valleys are the most touristed, with ski resorts and narrow, winding roads that can get choked with holiday traffic. If you're walking, the best valleys to head for are those in the west, inside the protected zone of Italy's largest national park, the **Gran Paradiso**. The valleys here can also be busy – the mountain *rifugi* as well as the hotels get packed in summer – but development is restrained.

Getting around on public transport demands patience. Buses run from Piemonte along the main valley past most of the castles, but buses into many of the tributary valleys are rare. The road branches off at Aosta into Switzerland via the Grand-St-Bernard Pass (where you can stop to take clichéd photos of the famous dogs) and forks again some 30km further west at Pré-St-Didier: both branches run into France – the southern via the Petit-St-Bernard Pass to Chambéry, the northern to Chamonix through the Mont Blanc tunnel. Because of the border posts, the road is much used by long-distance lorries – useful for hitching, but something of an earache and eyesore. Trains are less regular and run only as far as Pré-St-Didier, but by using a combination of the two, and hitching into the less touristed tributary valleys, you can get just about everywhere.

The road to Aosta and the eastern valleys

The tributary valleys in **eastern Valle d'Aosta** have suffered most from the skiing industry, although experienced mountain hikers may be allured by the challenge of climbing Monte Rosa and the Matterhorn from **Valtournenche**. Less ambitious walkers will find most to do in the **Val Gressoney**, which still has a number of traditional villages settled by the Swiss Walsers, while in the main Aosta valley there are two of the region's more interesting castles, **Issogne** and **Fénis**.

Val Gressoney

The **Val Gressoney** is the first of the Valle d'Aosta valleys, but you could be forgiven for thinking you'd stepped into an ad-maker's Switzerland. The grass is velvety green, the River Lys crystal clear, the traditional houses wood-slatted and the modern ones gleaming Alpine chalets, while the craggy head of the valley is overlooked by one of Monte Rosa's shimmering glaciers. As you might expect from such natural advantages, the valley gets busy, especially at weekends and holidays: the walking is good, though the skiing less so, with pistes laid out on rocky slopes.

At the mouth of the valley, **PONT-ST-MARTIN** was named for the single-spanned Roman bridge that dominates the village. According to legend it was donated by the Devil in exchange for the first soul that crossed it. However, Saint Martin tricked him by sending a dog over, thus securing a bridge for the villagers and his own immortalisation in the village's name. Pont-St-Martin's usefulness as a bus and train terminus outweighs its attractiveness, and there's little reason to hang around. Buses run fairly regularly up the valley, but if there isn't one due, hitching is easy.

The valley comes into its own at **GRESSONEY-ST-JEAN** and **GRESSONEY-LA-TRINITÉ**. These are popular but attractive resorts, especially La Trinité which is close to the head of the valley. It's quieter and cheaper than St Jean, with some good, homely hotels, and makes a convenient starting-point for walks. If you want to do more than wander along the river, a track leads up to the lovely mountain lake, **Gabiet**, in two to three hours (you can go part way by ski-lift), from where you can continue over the mountain into the Valsesia, doing the descent by cable car if you're tired. Val Gressoney's Walser settlements can also be reached by footpaths from La Trinité, one of the nicest of which is **BIEL**, with some eighteenth-century houses (maps available from the tourist office). The Walsers still speak their German dialect, and French and Italian too, and the trilingual signs you'll see are not only for the benefit of tourists.

La Trinité's **tourist office** (daily 7am–7pm) is on the main piazza, across the river from the bus stop. For staying over, the *Monterosa* on Piazza Tachen (☎0125/366.120; ④), near the entrance of the village, is pleasant and cheap but closes out of season, or there's the slightly more expensive *Grizzetti* in the suburb of Edelbaden (☎0125/366.138; ④). There's a **campsite** (☎366.201) at STAFFAL, open year-round, 5km further up the valley, connected with La Trinité by shuttle bus in the skiing season – it's the starting-point for the ski-lifts across to Champoluc, in the next valley, Val d'Ayas. There are also a couple of other **campsites** just beyond Gressoney-St-Jean.

Verrès and Issogne

Buses and trains continue up the main valley to **VERRÈS**, an undistinguished village overlooked by the gloomy cube of its virtually impregnable fourteenth-century **fortress** (March 1–Nov 30 daily 9am–7pm; Oct 1–Feb 28 daily 9am–12.30pm & 2–5.30pm; closed Wed; guided tours every half-hour; L4000). This is a stark, primitive place, built by the lord of the town, Ibelto di Challant, primarily as a military stronghold. The spartan soldiers' quarters give some idea of the conditions under which they lived; the Challants' quarters are barely more comfortable, although their fortress does go down in the history books as one of the first to install a toilet. If you need a **room** in Verrès for the night, there are some very basic ones in the *Hotel Ghibli* (☎0125/929.316; ④), three minutes' walk from the train station.

Issogne

The castle at **ISSOGNE** (March 1–Nov 30 daily 9am–7pm; Oct 1–Feb 28 daily 9am–12.30pm & 2–5.30pm; closed Mon; guided tours every half-hour; L4000) is of greater interest, another residence of the Challants but a far more comfortable and civilised dwelling than its counterpart at Verrès. Few buses go there, but it's only a short walk from the bus stop outside Verrès. Set unceremoniously in the centre of Issogne village, from the outside the castle resembles a municipal building, and you'll probably wonder why you bothered to come. But the well-preserved interior is one of Valle d'Aosta's best examples of a late-Gothic ducal residence – with an arcaded courtyard, some vivid frescoes and coffered-ceilinged rooms furnished with Gothic furniture.

In the centre of the courtyard is an unusual fountain – a wrought-iron pomegranate tree with water spurting from the lower branches. The courtyard's walls are patched with painted coats of arms, and in the shelter of one of the arcades is a colourful and bustling fresco of a medieval high street. From here, guided tours take you through kitchens, a beautifully furnished dining room, a couple of chapels with ornate polyptychs, and into the Countess of Challant's bedroom, whose bedside chair conceals a commode. After seeing the castle, it's worth paying the extra to see the **exhibition of costume** – well-researched reconstructions of those worn in the courtyard frescoes.

Val d'Ayas

Branching off the main valley, and headed by the huge mass of Monte Rosa, **Val d'Ayas** is one of the region's most beautiful valleys, large, open and flanked by thickly wooded slopes. Sadly it's overwhelmed by visitors, and the tourist-geared villages are chock-full of trippers and skiers at the weekend and in season, and dead at other times of the year.

The main ski resort, **CHAMPOLUC** at the head of the valley, is connected by a series of ski-lifts to STAFFAL in the Val Gressoney. It's also the base for the tough ascent (4hr minimum; route #62) of the **Testa Grigia** (3315m) – although you can cheat on this by taking the funicular and ski-lift part of the way. From the top there's a superb view across the peaks of the Matterhorn to Mont Blanc; however, unless you can afford a guide (ask at the tourist office in Champoluc) the climb is strictly for the experienced.

BRUSSON, further down the valley, is a better base for less demanding walks. There's a trail (3hr 30min; route #6) up to seven mountain lakes, starting with a long climb through a dense wood up to a waterfall – the water drops 30m, and is most impressive in spring when the snow is melting.

Hotel *Beau Site* (☎0125/300.144; ④), on the edge of Brusson, is clean, simple and has a good restaurant. In Champoluc hotels are expensive, but the *Cre-Forné* hotel (☎0125/307.197; ③) at CREST (connected with Champoluc by funicular) is very cheap indeed. There are also **campsites** between Brusson and Champoluc.

Valtournenche and the Matterhorn (Cervino)

VALTOURNENCHE, headed by the Matterhorn, or Cervino as the Italians call it, should be one of the most spectacular of Italy's mountain valleys. Instead it's the most depressing. The international ski resort of Breuil-Cervinia is brutally ugly, and even the Matterhorn is a let-down, with tribes of skiers ensuring that its glacier is grubby for much of the year.

Breuil-Cervinia

BREUIL-CERVINIA was one of Italy's first ski resorts, built in the prewar years as part of Mussolini's drive for a healthy nation. In its day the ski-lifts, soaring to 3500m, broke all records, and its grand hotels ensured the patronage of Europe's wealthy. Today the wealthy are cossetted in modern monstrosities outside the resort, leaving the tacky streets of the purpose-built town for packaged hordes attracted by a large skiing area with lots of easy runs.

Frankly, the only reason to come here is to climb the **Matterhorn** (4476m). You'll need the *FMB* map which covers Valtournenche and the Monte Rosa valleys, and to be well equipped. There are two *rifugi* on the way, *Duca degli Abruzzi* (☎0166/949.119), open from August 1 until 30 September, two hours fifteen minutes from Breuil in ORIONDE (2800m), and the always open *Rifugio M Carrel* (no phone) – where most people stay the night – four hours beyond (3850m). From the Carrel *rifugio* it's a tough climb to the summit, even with the ropes that have been fitted along the more dangerous stretches of the route.

The less agile members of the smart set now head to **ST VINCENT**, a spa resort near the industrial town of Chatillon at the mouth of the valley. There's a famous **casino** here, but a distinct lack of Monte Carlo glitz on the streets. If you end up with time to spare between buses, the parish **church** (*Parrochiale*) is quite interesting, with the excavations of the baths of a Roman villa around the outside, some lively frescoes inside.

Nus and the Castello di Fénis

NUS, further up the main valley from Chatillon, is a small, pretty village overlooked by a ruined castle, that makes a good base for the castle of **Fénis** 2km away (March 1–Nov 30 daily 9am–7pm; Oct 1–Feb 28 daily 9am–12.30pm & 2–5.30pm; closed Tues; guided tours every half-hour; L4000). Backed by wooded hills and encircled by two rows of turreted walls, the castle is a fairy-tale cluster of towers decorated with scalloped arcades. These defences were primarily aesthetic, with the real job of protecting the valley being left to the less prettified fortresses of nearby Nus and Quart, while the Fénis branch of the Challant counts concentrated on refining their living quarters with fine Gothic frescoes.

The best of these is in the courtyard, above the elaborate twin staircase that leads to the upper storeys. A courtly Saint George rescues a damsel in distress from the clutches of a tremendous dragon, overlooked by a tribe of protective saints brandishing moral statements on curling scrolls. There are further frescoes in the Baronial Hall upstairs, which has been closed for some time. It's due to reopen this year, but the authorities are reluctant to subject the frescoes to troops of tourists.

There's a **hotel** in Fénis, *La Chatelaine* (☎0165/764.264; ④), in località Chez Sapin, open year-round. Five minutes' walk from the castle there's a **campsite**, *Les Chataigniers*, open from April to October. However, as Nus has a train station and is close to the main road for buses, you may find it more convenient to sleep there. The *Florian* (☎0165/767.968; ④), on the main street, has clean and comfortable doubles and is also open all year.

Aosta and around

AOSTA is well used to tourists. Until recently, as the capital of a duty-free region it was patronised by a steady stream of French, Swiss and Italians in search of cheap booze. Baskets of liqueurs and vermouths still line the main street, but the prices have risen and are no longer the town's main draw.

Aosta was founded by the Romans in 25 BC after they disposed of the local tribe by auctioning them off in a slave market. It was primarily a military camp, unlikely to have been particularly splendid, and in any case little survives from the era. More remains of medieval Aosta, but the town's key attraction is its position. Encircled by the **Alps**, and with access to the lovely valleys of the **Gran Paradiso National Park**, the ski resorts of **Mont Blanc**, and a sprinkling of castles in between, it's an ideal base or jumping-off point for exploring the northwest of the region, before heading on to Switzerland or France.

The Town

Centre of town is **Piazza E. Chanoux** and its smart pavement cafés, from where Via Porta Pretoriana and Via Sant'Anselmo lead east, forming the main axis of the town centre and the principal street for window-shopping and people-watching. At the far end, the **Porta Pretoria** is one of the town's most impressive sights: two parallel triple-arched gateways which formed the main entrance into the Roman town. The space in between was for soldiers to keep a check on visitors to the town, and a family of medieval nobles later made their home above it, building a tower which now houses temporary exhibitions.

North of the gate there are further relics of the Roman occupation in the **Teatro Romano** (summer daily 9am–7pm; winter daily 9.30am–noon & 2.30–4.30pm), of which an impressive section of the four-storeyed facade remains, 22m high and pierced with arched windows. Only the lower section of the auditorium or *cavea* has survived, however, and theatrical performances now take place in summer on a platform overlooking the theatre. Close by, the medieval **Torre Fromage** is now a contemporary art exhibition-space.

A short walk east of here, outside the main town walls off Via Sant'Anselmo, the church of **Sant'Orso** houses a number of tenth-century frescoes behind its dull facade, hidden up in the roof where you can examine them at close quarters from specially constructed walkways – though you'll need to find the sacristan to get up there. If you can't find him, content yourself with the fifteenth-century choir stalls, carved with a menagerie of holy men and animals, ranging from bats and monkeys to a tonsured monk. There are even better carvings on the eye-level capitals of the intimate Romanesque **cloisters** (daily except Mon 8.30am–noon & 2–5.30pm) – mostly scenes from the story of Christ, with emphasis on donkeys and sheep.

At far end of Via Sant'Anselmo, the **Arco di Augusto** was erected in 25 BC to celebrate the seizure of the territory from the local Salassi tribe and to honour Emperor Augustus, for whom the town *Augusta Praetoria* was named (Aosta is a corruption of Augusta). Though the arch loses something islanded in a sea of traffic and topped by an ugly eighteenth-century roof, it's a sturdy-looking monument, the mountains behind only adding to its measure of dignity. Beyond is a well-preserved **Roman bridge**, its single arch spanning the dried-up bed of the River Buthier.

On the other side of the centre of town, the **Foro Romano** on Piazza Giovanni XXIII is the misleading name for another Roman relic, a vaulted passage under the actual forum area, the purpose of which is unclear (summer daily 9am–7pm; winter daily 10am–noon & 2.30–4.30pm). The **Cattedrale**, next door, looks unpromising from the

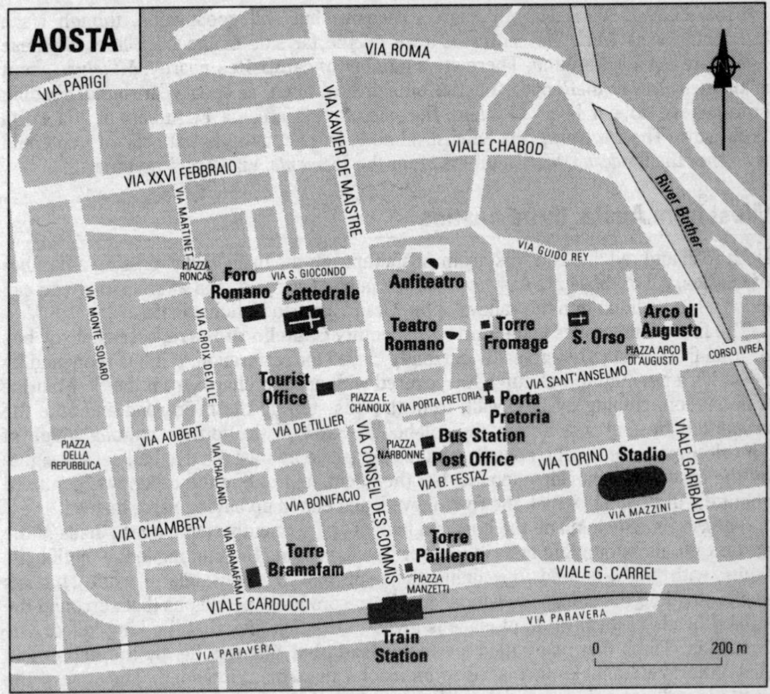

outside, but it masks a Gothic interior with even more fantastically carved choir stalls than Sant'Orso's, with a mermaid, lion and snail among the saints. Remains of a fourth-century baptistry are visible through the floor; better are the mosaics on the presbytery pavement showing the two rivers of earthly paradise and Christ, holding the sun and moon, surrounded by the symbols of the months. There are more treasures in the church's **museum** (April 1–Sept 30 Mon–Sat 10am–noon & 3–6pm, Sun 3–5.45pm) – gold-, silver- and gem-encrusted reliquaries and equally ornate chalices, crucifixes and caskets for relics.

Practicalities

Aosta's **tourist office** is at Piazza E. Chanoux 8 and has maps and other information on the town and around (June–Sept daily 9am–1pm & 3–8pm; Oct–May Mon–Sat 9am–1pm & 3–8pm, Sun 9am–1pm; ☎0165/236.627). You can get to most places within the region by bus from the **bus station** at Piazza Narbonne, but some of the more remote valleys are served by only one bus a week out of season. Trains run from the **train station** at Piazza Manzetti, south of the centre, west along the main valley only as far as Pré Saint Didier. The best bet is to arm yourself with the combined bus and train timetable from the tourist office and use both.

The first choice for a **hotel room** is *La Belle Epoque* at Via d'Avise 8, off Via Aubert (☎0165/362.276; ④), new, clean and comfortable; the *Mochetttaz*, Corso Ivrea 107 (☎0165/43.706; ④) charges around the same; while the *Pila*, Via Paravera 12b

(☎0165/43.398; ④), is slightly more expensive but still good value, though it's a ten-minute walk from the centre of town on the far side of the train line. All these hotels are open year-round. There are a number of **campsites** nearby: *Milleluci*, about a kilometre away in Roppoz, on the outskirts of town, is open year-round. Finding **somewhere to eat** is no problem; the best streets are Via E. Aubert or Via Porta Pretoriane. The *Praetoria*, Via Sant'Anselmo 9, is a family-style trattoria; or you could try either the *Moderno*, Via E. Aubert 21, or the *Piemonte*, Via Porta Praetoria 13.

West from Aosta: three castles

Both road and rail line run west from Aosta through the main valley, passing a number of **castles**. All of these are easy to reach on public transport, and after visiting you can catch a bus or hitch into the valleys of the Gran Paradiso National Park.

The first of the castles is the thirteenth-century **Castello di Sarre**, accessible by bus or train from Aosta, though sadly currently closed for restoration. If it has reopened by now, it's a ten-minute walk up a hill covered with apple orchards from the St Maurice train station; coming by bus, walk from the bus stop up the main road and take the unmarked turning just before the toll-booth. Sarre is the former hunting lodge of Vittorio Emanuele II, who actually bought the castle by mistake. He had set his sights on the castle of Aymaville opposite, but the agent sent to buy the castle was confused about the direction in which the river flowed, and ended up buying Sarre instead.

Vittorio Emanuele made the best of a bad job, permanently stamping the halls of the castle with his astounding taste in interior decor, pushing the hunting-lodge motif to its limits, with horns of wild ibex lining the main gallery, thousands of white chamois skulls studding the stuccoed festoons and horn-sprouting medallions that surround the stuffed heads of ibex. Pride of place is given to the first ibex that the king killed. The custodian claims that many died a natural death, but this was hardly the impression that Vittorio Emanuele, in his guise as macho huntsman, intended. The rest of the castle is well patronised by diehard Italian monarchists come to pay their respects to Savoy family trees, portraits and photographs and walls plastered with magazine features on the now exiled Italian royals.

Five minutes further along the rail line, the **Castello di Saint-Pierre** (mid-March–end-Sept daily 9am–7pm; L4000) perches on a rocky cliff, a crenellated and turreted castle that dates from the twelfth century but is mostly the result of a restyling in the eighteenth century. There's a small **natural history museum** inside with an array of stuffed birds, and unless this appeals you'd do well to press on.

A short walk along the main road beyond Saint-Pierre, set on a low hill above the river, and invisible from the road, **Sarriod de La Tour** (May 1–Sept 30 daily except Mon; L4000) is less a castle than a medieval tower with farm buildings built around it. It's a refreshingly rustic place, with some appealing frescoes and an archaeological museum laid out in its warren of rooms.

North from Aosta: the Col di San Bernardo

Immediately north of Aosta, the **Col di San Bernardo** (2473m) leads the way into Switzerland, named after the legendary **monastery** that provided shelter to travellers for many years and was the home of the eponymous big brown and white dogs who rescued alpine travellers in distress. The history of the mountain pass is well documented in the **museum** housed in the monastery, although you'll need your passport to visit as it's in fact situated just over the border in Switzerland. Be warned that the pass is open only during summer, although the border is open year-round by way of a tunnel.

The Gran Paradiso National Park

For some of Valle d'Aosta's most beautiful mountains and valleys you need to make for the south of the region, down to the **Parco Nazionale di Gran Paradiso** – Italy's second largest national park, spread around the valleys at the foot of 4061-metre-high Gran Paradiso mountain.

Oddly enough the park owes its foundation to King Vittorio Emanuele II, who donated his extensive hunting park to the state in 1922, ensuring that the population of ibex that he and his hunters had managed to reduce to near-extinction survived. There are now around 3500 ibex here and about 6000 chamois, living most of the year above the tree line but descending to the valleys in winter and spring. The most dramatic sightings are during the mating season in November and December, when if you're lucky you can see pairs of males fighting it out for the possession of a female. You might also see golden eagles nesting, and there are a number of rare types of alpine flower – most of which can be seen in the botanical garden in the Cogne Valley.

The park's three valleys – **Cogne**, **Valsaveranche** and **Val de Rhêmes** – are popular, but tourist development has been cautious and well organised. The hotels are good (you get far more for your money than you would in one of the nearby towns), the campsites not too vast, and there are lots of mountain *rifugi* and well-marked footpaths. Though primarily a summer resort for walkers, the cross-country skiing is also good, and every winter a 45km *Gran Paradiso Trek* is organised at Cogne (write ahead to the local tourist office for details). The starting-point for the ascent of Gran Paradiso itself is **Pont** in the Valsavarenche, while **Cogne** has a good selection of walks ranging from easy strolls to long mountain trails.

There are regular buses throughout the year from Aosta to Cogne, but Valsavarenche and Val de Rhêmes are served only by buses in summer. At other times driving or hitching into either of these valleys is easiest from the village of INTROD, about 2km from VILLENEUVE, which is on the main bus route and a walkable distance from the castles of Saint-Pierre and Sarriod de la Tour.

Val di Cogne

The **Val di Cogne** is the principal, most popular and most dramatic section of the park. Its lower reaches are narrow, the road running above the fast-flowing Grand Eyvia River overlooked by sheer wavy-ridged mountains. Further on, the valley broadens out around the main village, **COGNE**, which is surrounded by gentle green meadows and glacier-covered mountains rising beyond.

The **tourist office** here, in the centre of the village (daily 9am–12.30pm & 3–6pm, Sun 9am–12.30pm), has maps with English descriptions of walks. One of the easiest and most scenic is along the gorgeous riverside trail that winds along the valley of the Valnontey tributary, the glaciers in view for most of the way. **VALNONTEY** itself is a small village and starting-point for the walk up to the *Rifugio V. Sella* in località Lauson (open Easter–Sept; ☎0165/74.310), though this is extremely popular and you should avoid summer weekends and early August. The path passes a **botanical garden** (summer only daily 9am–noon & 2.30–6pm; L4000), with rare alpine flora, then zigzags up through a forest and down to the *rifugio*, set on a grassy mountain plain. At the small mountain Lake Lausan, half an hour's walk from the *rifugio*, you may well spot some **ibex**, especially at sunset and sunrise. Hardened hikers, who can cope with a stretch of climbing, can walk over the **Colle de Lausan** to the Val de Rhêmes.

There's a **campsite**, *Vallee de Cogne*, close to Cogne village in località Fabrique (☎0165/74.079), and two **campsites** at Valnontey – *Lo Stambecco* (☎0165/749.178) and *Gran Paradiso* (☎0165/749.204). The first is open all year, the others from June until the end of September. As for **hotels**, Cogne's cheapest hotels are the *Stambecco* (☎0165/74.068; ④), and on the main entrance road, *Du Soleil* (☎0165/74.033; ④); both are open all year round, although they can get booked up quickly in high season, and it's advisable to call ahead. **Restaurants** are pricey, but there are a couple of **takeaways** and plenty of *salumerie* which will make up sandwiches. To sit down and eat, the *Chez Moi* restaurant and pizzeria, Via Clementine 11, is OK.

Valsavarenche

Although not as spectacular as the Val di Cogne, **Valsavarenche**, the next valley west, has its own kind of beauty, attracting seasoned walkers rather than gentle amblers. The most popular route is the **ascent of Gran Paradiso**, from **PONT** at the end of the valley; though reckoned to be the easiest of the higher Alps to climb, it is nevertheless a climb rather than a hike, with no path marked beyond the *Rifugio Vittorio Emanuele* (open April 15–Sept 30; ☎0165/95.920), two and a half hours from Pont.

If you feel safer walking along footpaths, the best of the hikes are from the main village of **DEGIOZ**, otherwise known as *Valsavarenche*, up to the *Rifugio Orvielles* (2hr 30min) and then on to a series of high mountain lakes. This takes seven hours, but you can shorten it a bit by taking the path marked #3a down to Pont. Less taxing is the two-hour walk from Pont towards the glacier **Grand Etret** at the head of the valley, although the first stretch is boring.

The only **hotel** in Degioz, the *Parco Nazionale* (☎0165/95.706; ⑤), is not especially cheap, but the seasonal *Edelweiss* (☎0165/95.702; ④) in the hamlet of Bien about 25 minutes' walk away, open from June 1 until the end of September, is a little bit cheaper. Pont has the best **campsite**, *Pont Breuil* (☎0165/95.458), also open from June to September, with a fairly well stocked site shop (there's no other for miles). Best of all, in June ibex come down to graze on the grassy meadow around the tents – so have your camera at the ready in the early morning. Pont also has a bar and a hotel, the *Fior di Roccia*, open June–September (☎0165/95.478; ④). There are **places to eat** in Degioz, but at Pont you'll have to cook for yourself, or ask at one of the hotels.

Val di Rhêmes

The least touristed but most open of the valleys, **Val di Rhêmes** is also headed by glaciers. The best place to stay is **BRUIL**, a small hamlet outside Rhêmes Notre Dame at the end of the valley, from which most of the walks start. There's a fairly easy path along the river to a waterfall, the *Cascata di Goletta*, at its most spectacular after the spring snow-melt, and from here you can continue to the *Rifugio Benevolo* and the mountain lake of Goletta (open March 18–May 28 & July 1–Sept 25; ☎0165/906.143). There are only five beds, so be sure to phone before setting out. Among **hotels** in Bruil, the *Della Pineta* in the località of Artalle is open between June and September (☎0165/96.101; ④), much the same as the *Pélaud* in località Pélaud (☎0165/96.110; ④). Open for a greater part of the year is the similarly priced *Galisia* (☎0165/96.100; ④).

Arvier and Valgrisenche

Valgrisenche, a few kilometres west from Val di Rhêmes, is the wildest and least accessible of Valle d'Aosta's valleys. The only buses from Aosta into the valley are at 7am and 6pm in summer, and at 5.30am in winter, although buses and trains stop year-round at **ARVIER** at the mouth of the valley – one of the regions' most appealing villages, with a medieval core of twisting streets and stone houses alongside a gorge spanned by a Roman bridge. Arvier produces L'Enfer d'Arvier, reckoned to be the region's best wine.

Without your own transport, getting into the Valgrisenche from here is difficult: there's little traffic, especially out of season; if you have no joy hitching, try asking around in Arvier's bars. The effort, though, is worth it. A narrow valley, with rocky snow-dusted ridges rising above dark pine woods, Valgrisenche is stunning, although the upper reaches are defaced by the concrete dam of a reservoir.

In VALGRISENCHE itself, the *Frassy* hotel (☎0165/97.100; ⑤), makes a good base, although it's only open June to September. A good starting-point for **walks** is the hamlet of **BONNE** above the reservoir. These include the 4–5-hour ascent of the glaciated Testa del Rutor (3486m) via the *Rifugio Scavarda*, two hours along the path (open July 1–Sept 30). There are many other walks, but none of them is easy – you should be sure to have the *Kompass* Gran Paradiso map. The cheapest **hotel** in Bonne is the *Perret* (☎0165/97.107; ⑤), open all year and with a restaurant and bar.

The northwest: around Mont Blanc

Dominated by the year-long snowy peaks of **Mont Blanc** (Monte Bianco to the Italians), the northern reaches of Valle d'Aosta are scenically stunning but also very popular. The most sensational views are from the cable cars that glide and swoop (at times alarmingly so) across the mountain to Chamonix in France. However, the trip is expensive, even if you take a bus or hitch back to Italy through the eleven-kilometre-long Mont Blanc tunnel, and the service is often suspended because of bad weather.

La Thuile and Testa d'Arpy

If the cable car seems too pricey, you can walk up to the **Testa d'Arpy** from the sprawling resort of **LA THUILE**, on the road to the Petit-St-Bernard Pass into France, for sweeping views of the peaks and glaciers of Mont Blanc. Buses run from Pre-St-Didier at the end of the Valle d'Aosta railway line to La Thuile, from where it's just over two hours' walk by path or road to the *La Genzianella* hotel at the top of the Colle San Carlo. From here a path leads through woods to Testa d'Arpy in around ten minutes, a natural balcony with a bird's-eye view up the valley to Mont Blanc. It's well worth having a good map (*FSB* "Monte Bianco") – not so much to find your way as to identify the peaks and glaciers spread out before you.

As for La Thuile, it's an over-developed resort, and it makes sense to pass through quickly, after calling in at the **tourist office** for maps, and to sleep up the mountain at *La Genzianella* in the little hamlet of Golette (☎0165/884.137; ④), open from December 1 until April 30, and from July 1 until September 30; phone in advance to check that there's room. Of the other walks starting from the hotel the most interesting is the 45-minute hike to **Lago d'Arpy**, from where a path leads down into La Thuile.

Courmayeur and Mont Blanc

COURMAYEUR is the smartest and most popular of Valle d'Aosta's ski resorts, much used by British package operators. The skiing is good, though there's little to challenge experts, and the scenery is magnificent; but, predictably, what remains of the old village is enmeshed in a web of ersatz Alpine chalets and après-ski hang-outs.

If you want a week of skiing, you'll probably save money by taking a package anyway; if you've come to hike or take the big-dipping cable cars across to Chamonix, the most convenient place to stay is **LA PALUD**, 5km outside Courmayeur. Without your own transport, there are only three buses a day, although hitching is OK. Don't get disheartened at the number of cars of smart city skiers whizzing past you – most local people will stop.

The **cable car** (which runs June 1–Nov 1 only) starts at La Palud and travels in three stages via Punta Hellbronner and Aiguille du Midi – where there's a restaurant perched on a dizzying granite needle rock – to Chamonix. The cost from La Palud to Punta Hellbronner is L24,000 one way; you can buy a ticket at Punta Hellbronner on to Chamonix (L5000), or buy the complete La Palud–Chamonix ticket (L40,000) in advance in La Palud at the *Mont Blanc* travel agent, Piazzale Monte Bianco 3 (☎0165/841.397). There are between ten and twelve departures a day, depending on the time of year, roughly hourly starting at 8.30am – although ultimately the regularity depends on the weather. To be sure of good views, you'll need to set out early since it's usually cloudy by midday; be sure also to get there in plenty of time, especially on summer weekends, as it's much used by summer skiers. Incidentally, even if it's blazing hot in the valley, the temperature plunges to freezing-point at the top, so take some warm clothes.

There are good walks along the two valleys at the foot of the Mont Blanc glaciers, both of which have seasonal **campsites** accessible by bus from Courmayeur. Val Ferret to the west is the more interesting option – you can walk back from Frebouze over Monte de la Saxe, with some stunning views of Mont Blanc en route.

Practicalities

If you do end up having to spend a night in Courmayeur, the cheapest **hotel** is the *Agip* at Strada Regionale 76 (☎0165/842.427; ④), a motel above the *Agip* petrol station on the main road; there's also the pricier *Turistica*, off Courmayeur's main street (☎0165/846.747; ④), which also has a restaurant. The cheapest hotels in La Palud are the *Funivia* (☎0165/89.924; ④) and *La Quercia* (☎0165/89.931; ④), both open all year. Failing that, there's the extremely comfortable *Vallee Blanche* (☎0165/89.933; ⑤).

travel details

Trains

Alba to: Asti (8 daily; 1hr).

Aosta to: Pré-St-Didier (9 daily; 50min).

Asti to: Casale Monferrato (6 daily; 50min).

Cuneo to: Limone Piemonte (14 daily; 30min).

Novara to: Varallo (9 daily; 1hr 30min); Biella (10 daily; 1hr 10min).

Turin to: Vercelli (25 daily; 1hr); Novara (27 daily; 1hr 15min); Milan Centrale (19 daily; 1hr 45min); Aosta (13 daily; 1hr 45min–4hr 55min); Cuneo (9 daily; 1hr 30min); Asti (33 daily; 30min–1hr); Modane (8 daily; 1hr 25min–2hr 25min).

Verrès to: Aosta (14 daily; 30min–1hr 10min); Turin (13 daily; 1hr 10min–1hr 45min).

Buses

Alba to Barolo (6 daily; 30min); Grinzane (6 daily; hourly).

Aosta to: Cogne (5 daily; 50min); Pont Valsavarenche (3 daily; 1hr 10min); Rhêmes St Georges (3 on weekdays Sept–June; 45min; July & Aug 2 daily, going on to Rhêmes Notre Dame; 1hr); Valgrisenche (mid-June–mid-Sept 2 daily; mid-Sept–mid-June Mon, Tues & Sat only; 1hr 30min); Courmayeur (20 daily; 1hr).

Biella to: Ivrea (6 daily; 2hr 25min); Santuario di Oropa (9 daily; 40min).

Chatillon to: Breuil Cervinia (6 daily; 1hr–1hr 30min).

Cuneo to: Dronero (Val Maira) (20 daily; 35min); Valle Stura (7 daily; 1hr–1hr 20min).

Pont St Martin to: Gressoney La Trinité (7 daily; 1hr 20min).

Pré-St-Didier to: La Thuile (7 daily; 25min); Courmayeur (15 daily; 10–25min).

Saluzzo to: Cuneo (17 daily; 1hr); Val Varaita (3 daily; 1hr 15min); Crissolo (3 daily; 2hr).

Turin (Corso Marconi) to: Saluzzo (10 daily; 1hr 20min); Cuneo (8 daily; 2hr 45min).

Turin (Corso Inghilterra) to: Aosta (12 daily; 2–3hr); Ivrea (12 daily; 1hr 15min); Gressoney La Trinité (4 daily; 2hr 10min–3hr 10min); Champoluc (2 daily; 3hr 30min); Cervinia (1 daily; 2hr 15min); Courmayeur (7 daily; 3–4hr); Chamonix/Geneva (1 daily; 3hr 15min–4hr 30min); Lugano via Novara (1 daily; 3hr); Locarno (1 daily; 4hr).

Verrès to Champoluc (6 daily; 1hr 10min).

CHAPTER TWO

LIGURIA

Liguria – also known as the **Italian Riviera** – has two parts: the narrow, commercially developed strip of coast, and a mountainous hinterland of isolated villages, terraced for olives and vines. Approaching from Nice and Monaco, there's an unexpected change as you cross the border: the Italian Riviera has more variety of landscape and architecture than its French counterpart, and is generally less frenetic – though it's still extremely crowded in summer. An *autostrada* (A12) sweeps the length of the province through to Tuscany, and a main railway line follows the same route – rapid bursts of daylight between tunnels give a glimpse of the string of resorts along the coast, silver olive groves and a brilliant sea.

Chief town of the province is **Genoa**. Heavy industry and a manic traffic system make the city off-putting if you're just travelling through, but Genoa is worth spending time in for its old town, round the port. The city makes a neat division between two distinct stretches of coastline. To the west is the **Riviera del Ponente** – packed out with Italian families who book a year ahead to stay in their favourite hotel. This side of the coast has become one long ribbon of hotels, but there are places to head for: **Noli** and **Albenga** are both medieval towns; **Finale Ligure** is a pleasant resort; and **San Remo**, flanked by hillsides covered with glasshouses, is a major centre for flower growers who trade at the early morning market.

Southeast, towards Tuscany, on the **Riviera del Levante**, the coast is more rugged. Umbrella pines grow horizontally on cliff faces, and in the evening there's a glassy calm over the bays and inlets. Walks on **Monte Portofino** and in the **Cinque Terre** take you high enough through *macchia* and vineyards for views over wide gulfs. The mix of mountains and fishing villages reachable only by boat appealed to the Romantics, who "discovered" the Riviera in the eighteenth century, preparing the way for other artists and poets and the first package tourists earlier this century. Now the whole area explodes into a nightmarish ruck every July and August, with people coming to resorts like **Portofino** and **Santa Margherita Ligure** strictly for pose value.

One way to avoid this is to travel into the hinterland. Minor roads and mule tracks link villages, built spiral-fashion around hilltops, originally as protection against Saracen invasion. Further up into the mountains, the **Alta Via dei Monti Liguri** runs for 440km along the ridges, from **Ventimiglia** near the border with France, to **Ceparana**, north of La Spezia. *Club Alpino Italiano* offices in the major towns have information on refuges, and there's a guide to the trail by the *Centro Studi Unioncamere Liguri* on sale in bookshops. Base yourself at **Monesi** near Monte Saccarello, **Alberola** in the mountains near Genoa, or **Santo Stefano d'Aveto** on the border with Emilia Romagna for walking or skiing. This is one of the few areas of Liguria where hiring a car is an advantage: bus links with larger towns on the coast are good, but you need to change a few times to reach the more out-of-the-way places. You'll also be able to get to some of the mountain restaurants, which are often the best places for sampling **Ligurian cooking**. Recipes make something out of nothing – a legacy of past hardships, which have bred a reserve in the Ligurian character and given the people an undeserved reputation amongst other Italians for meanness.

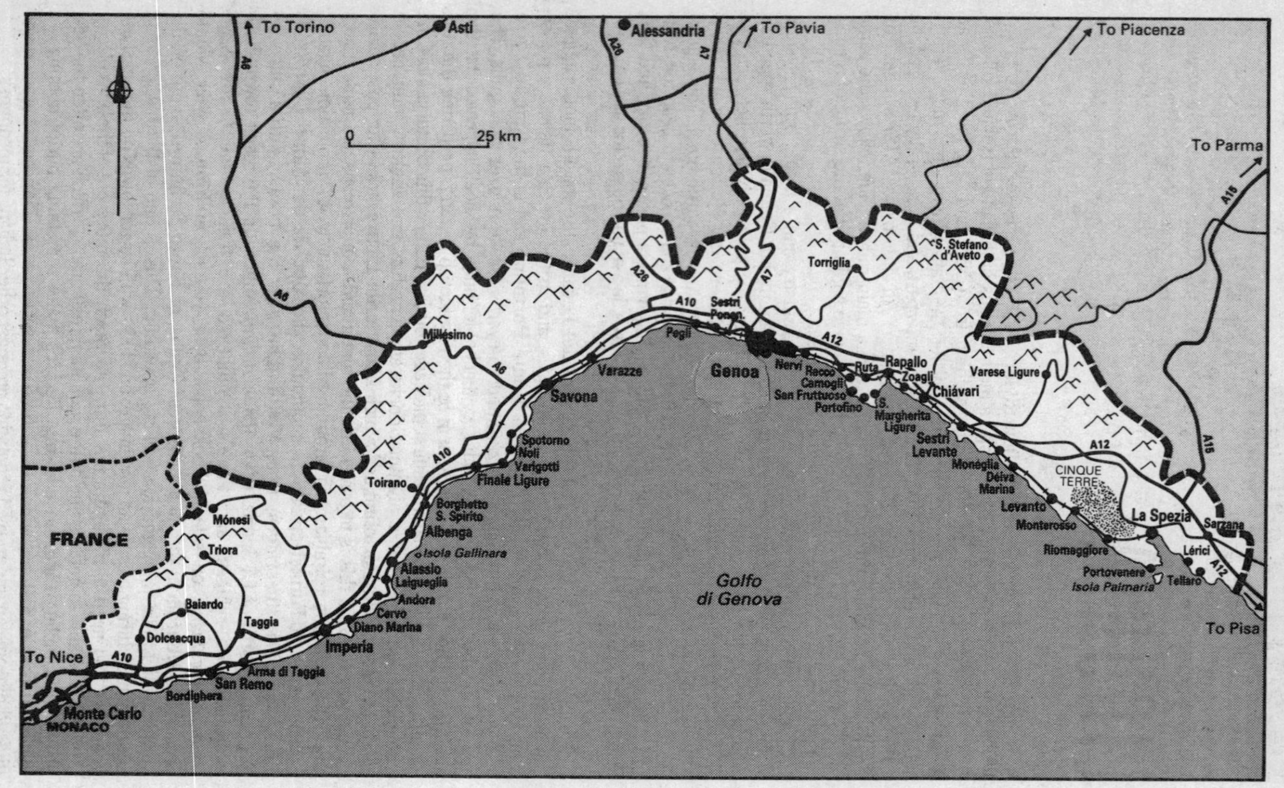
To Torino
To Piacenza
To Pavia
To Parma
Asti
Alessandria
A6
A26
A7
A10
A12
A15
25 km
FRANCE
To Nice
Monte Carlo
MONACO
Bordighera
San Remo
Arma di Taggia
Taggia
Dolceacqua
Baiardo
Triora
Mónesi
Imperia
Diano Marina
Cervo
Andora
Laigueglia
Alassio
Isola Gallinara
Albenga
Borghetto S. Spirito
Toirano
Millesimo
Finale Ligure
Varigotti
Noli
Spotorno
Savona
Varazze
Pegli
Sestri Ponen.
Genoa
Golfo di Genova
Nervi
Recco
Camogli
San Fruttuoso
Portofino
Ruta
Rapallo
Zoagli
S. Margherita Ligure
Torriglia
S. Stefano d'Aveto
Chiávari
Sestri Levante
Moneglia
Deiva Marina
Varese Ligure
Levanto
Monterosso
CINQUE TERRE
Riomaggiore
Portovenere
Isola Palmaria
La Spezia
Lérici
Tellaro
Sarzana
To Pisa

GENOA (GENOVA)

GENOA is "a place that grows upon you every day . . . it abounds in the strangest contrasts; things that are picturesque, ugly, mean, magnificent, delightful and offensive, break upon the view at every turn", wrote Dickens in 1844, and the description still fits. It's a marvellously eclectic city and it would be a big mistake to pass it by completely. At the heart of everything is the port, surrounded by a warren of alleyways which make up the medieval centre, a district which has more zest than all the coastal resorts put together.

Genoa made its money at sea, through trade, colonial exploitation and legalised piracy. By the thirteenth century it was one of the five Italian maritime republics and the implacable enemy of two of the others – Venice and Pisa. At the same time, Genoa was fighting Marseilles, the Saracens and the Sultan of Egypt as well as its own internal wars, involving the Guelphs and the Ghibellines and no fewer than four powerful families: the Doria, Fieschi, Spinola and Grimaldi. Even after the doge's election in the fourteenth century, various factions still thought power could be grabbed, and carried out several violent coups a year. Despite the shaky political climate at home, the republic forged ahead making money from its Mediterranean colonies and from merchant banking. When Columbus approached Genoa's bankers, however, no one was interested in financing his voyages – although he'd grown up in the city he had to turn to the Spanish for backing. Ironically once Columbus's explorations opened up the new Atlantic trade routes the city became something of a backwater, and "Genova La Superba" (the proud) lost much of its shine.

Later, Genoa had bigger threats from outside to worry about: France and Austria invaded in the seventeenth and eighteenth centuries, at the same time as the city lost its position as financial capital of Europe. During the Unification era, Genoa had a relatively free press and recognised at least some civil liberties. Political refugees came from more reactionary parts of Italy and the city was a base for radical thought. **Mazzini**, one of the main protagonists in Italy's unification, was born here, and in 1860 **Garibaldi**, whose family came from nearby, set sail for Sicily with his "Thousand" from the city's harbour.

Genoa is also where Italy's industrial revolution began, with steelworks and shipyards spreading where only tiny fishing villages had been before. The trade routes to the Middle East, North Africa and Spain opened Genoa up to diverse cultures, and this is still one of the more cosmopolitan cities of northern Italy. In the latter part of this century decline set in, leaving Genoa's docks empty and its steelworks without orders. All is not gloom, though, for funds which came in for the *Colombo '92 Expo* paid to renovate some of the city's late-Renaissance buildings and rejuvenate the old port area, which looks like developing into a major tourist attraction.

The repair work and tidying up hasn't sanitised the old town, though – the core of the city, between the two stations and the waterfront, is still dark and slightly threatening. Sometimes you'll see prostitutes waiting for trade down narrow alleyways, or you might accidentally surprise someone shooting up in what they thought was a safe corner. But despite the sleaze, the overriding impression is of a whole area of interest: food shops in the portals for former palaces, carpenters' workshops sandwiched between designer furniture outlets, everything surrounded by a crush of people and the inpenetrable Genoese dialect – a mixture of Neapolitan, Calabrese and Portuguese. There are enough buildings and art collections to keep you busy for several days. Worth seeking out are small medieval churches such as **San Donato** and **Santa Maria di Castello**, the **Cattedrale di San Lorenzo** with its fabulous treasury, as well as the Renaissance palaces which contain Genoa's **art collections**, with many paintings by the Flemish masters, and oriental and pre-Columbian art. But it's not all culture – other attractions include live music, theatre and cinema, and ritzy bars.

The Genoa area telephone code is ☎010.

Arrival, information and accommodation

Trains arrive from Savona at Stazione Principe, in Piazza Acquaverde, and from La Spezia and Rome at Stazione Brignole, on Piazza Verdi. Trains from Milan and Turin usually stop at both, but if you do have to travel between the two, take bus #37 or #33. At the train stations' *ATM* kiosks you can buy a 24-hour **tourist ticket** (L4000) which gives you an unlimited number of journeys on the buses and local trains; the standard one-journey bus ticket costs L1200. The **airport** is 6km away at Sestri Ponente; buses into Genoa link up with flight arrivals. Buses out to the airport leave from Piazza de Ferrari and from both train stations almost hourly.

The main **tourist office** is at Via Roma 11 (Mon–Thurs 8am–2pm & 4–6pm, Fri & Sat 8am–1pm; ☎581.407); there are also offices at Stazione Brignole (Mon–Fri 9am–noon & 3–6pm, Sat 9am–noon), Stazione Principe (same hours) and the airport (Mon–Sat 8am–noon & 2–8pm).

Accommodation

There are plenty of cheap **hotels** in the city centre, but many are grimy and depressing, and you need to look hard to find the exceptions. Good areas to try are the roads bordering the old town (Via Balbi and the roads off Via Cairoli), and Piazza Colombo and Via XX Settembre, near Stazione Brignole. The campsites within the city boundaries are ghastly – if you're camping, it's far better to stay at one of the coastal resorts and commute into Genoa.

HOTELS

Bel Soggiorno, Via XX Settembre 19 (☎581.418). The most comfortable of the budget hotels on this street. ⑤.

Bruxelles Margherita, Via XX Settembre 19/7 (☎589.191). Run-of-the-mill one-star, but tolerable for a night or two. ④.

Carletto, Via Colombo 16/4 (☎546.412). Near Stazione Brignole, with clean, plain rooms and friendly management. ⑤.

Federale, Salita San Siro 2 (☎201.729). Located off Via Cairoli, this is the cheapest place in the old town. ③.

Mediterranee, Via Cairoli 14/4 (☎206.531), Particularly good one-star, just north of the old town; bright, cheerful and run by very helpful people. ④.

Ricci, Piazza Colombo 4/8 (☎592.746). Another one-star near Stazione Brignole. ⑤.

Soana, Via XX Settembre 23 (☎562.814). Much the same as the nearby *Bruxelles Margherita*. ④.

Switzerland, Piazza Santa Brigida 16 (☎256.776). Rock-bottom prices here, off Via Balbi at the Stazione Principe end. ③.

HOSTEL

Cristoforo Colombo, Via Costanzi (☎242.2457). New *IYHF* hostel, 4km out of town – take bus #40 from Stazione Principe. Closed mid-Dec to mid-Jan. ①.

The City

Genoa's **old town** spreads outwards from the port in a confusion of tiny alleyways (*carrugi*), bordered by **Via Gramsci** along the waterfront and by **Via Balbi** and its continuations to the north. The layout of this area reflects its medieval politics. From the thirteenth to the fourteenth centuries, families marked out certain streets and

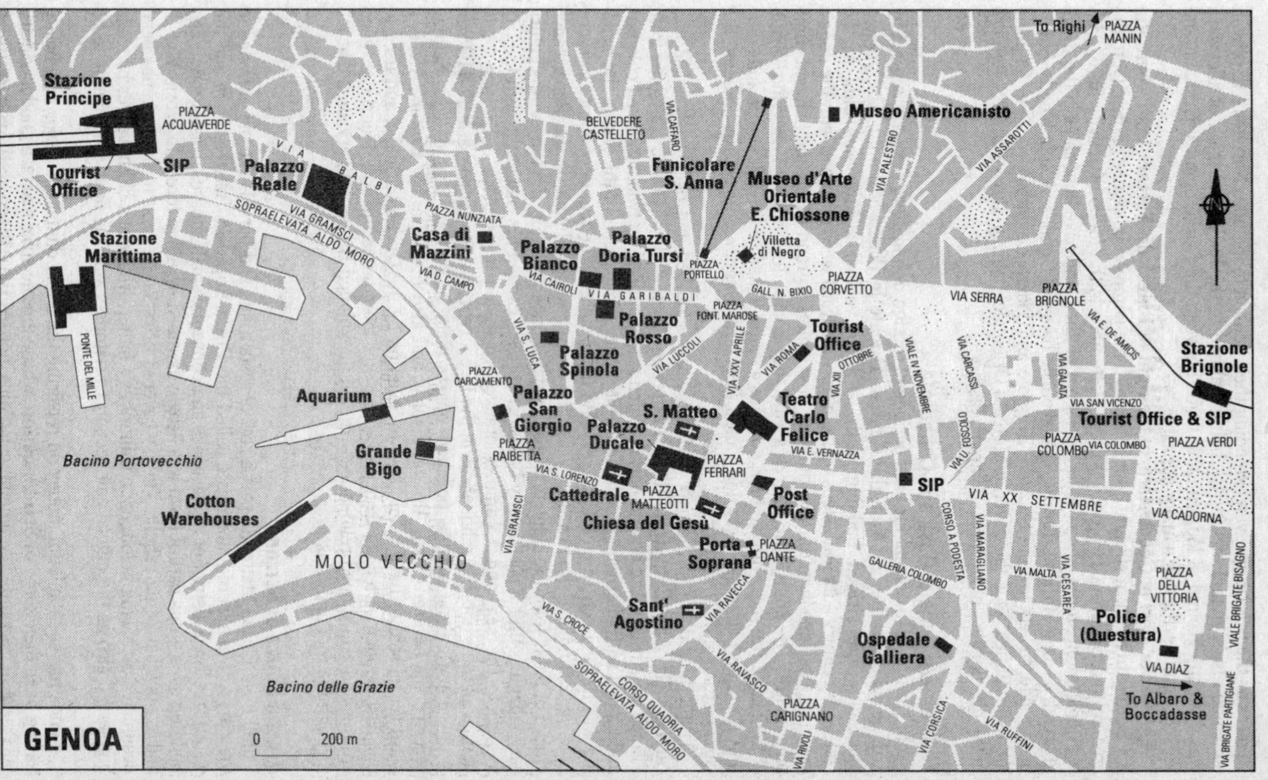
GENOA
Stazione Principe
Tourist Office
SIP
PIAZZA ACQUAVERDE
Palazzo Reale
VIA BALBI
VIA GRAMSCI
SOPRAELEVATA ALDO MORO
Stazione Marittima
PONTE DEL MILLE
Bacino Portovecchio
Cotton Warehouses
Aquarium
Grande Bigo
MOLO VECCHIO
Bacino delle Grazie
0
200 m
Casa di Mazzini
PIAZZA NUNZIATA
VIA D. CAMPO
PIAZZA CARICAMENTO
Palazzo San Giorgio
PIAZZA RAIBETTA
VIA S. LUCA
Palazzo Bianco
VIA CAIROLI
Palazzo Spinola
Palazzo Doria Tursi
VIA GARIBALDI
Palazzo Rosso
BELVEDERE CASTELLETTO
Funicolare S. Anna
VIA CAFFARO
PIAZZA PORTELLO
PIAZZA FONT. MAROSE
VIA LUCCOLI
Palazzo Ducale
S. Matteo
Cattedrale
VIA S. LORENZO
PIAZZA MATTEOTTI
Chiesa del Gesù
PIAZZA FERRARI
VIA GRAMSCI
VIA S. CROCE
Sant' Agostino
Porta Soprana
PIAZZA DANTE
VIA RAVECCA
VIA RAVASCO
CORSO QUADRIA
SOPRAELEVATA ALDO MORO
PIAZZA CARIGNANO
VIA RIVOLI
Post Office
VIA XXV APRILE
Teatro Carlo Felice
VIA E. VERNAZZA
VIA ROMA
Tourist Office
VIA XII OTTOBRE
GALL. N. BIXIO
Villetta di Negro
Museo d'Arte Orientale E. Chiossone
PIAZZA CORVETTO
Museo Americanisto
VIA PALESTRO
VIA ASSAROTTI
To Righi
PIAZZA MANIN
VIA SERRA
PIAZZA BRIGNOLE
VIA E. DE AMICIS
Stazione Brignole
Tourist Office & SIP
PIAZZA VERDI
VIA SAN VICENZO
VIA GALATA
VIA COLOMBO
PIAZZA COLOMBO
VIA CARCASSI
VIA U. FOSCOLO
VIALE IV NOVEMBRE
SIP
VIA XX SETTEMBRE
CORSO A PODESTA
GALLERIA COLOMBO
Ospedale Galliera
VIA CORSICA
VIA RUFFINI
VIA MARAGLIANO
VIA MALTA
VIA CESAREA
Police (Questura)
VIA CADORNA
PIAZZA DELLA VITTORIA
VIALE BRIGATE BISAGNO
VIA BRIGATE PARTIGIANE
VIA DIAZ
To Albaro & Boccadasse

squares as their territory, even extending their domain to include churches – to pray in someone else's chapel was to risk being stabbed in the back. The maze of alleyways was the battleground of long-running feuds between the Doria, Spinola, Grimaldi and Fieschi families, the city's major dynasties.

The **newer part** of Genoa starts to the right of **Piazza de Ferrari**, from where **Via XX Settembre** runs a straight course through the commercial centre of the city, to the area around **Stazione Brignole**. Via XX Settembre is the focus of activity here, with big department stores, shops selling designer clothes, and pavement cafés in the neon-lit arcades – one of these, *Tonitto*, is a favourite haunt of Genoese young bloods. Shops in the side streets around Stazione Brignole and Piazza Colombo are good for local food specialities, as is the covered Mercato Orientale, halfway down Via XX Settembre in the old cloisters of an Augustinian monastery.

The Palazzo Ducale, Gesù and Cattedrale

From 1384 to 1515, except for brief periods of foreign domination, Genoa was ruled by a **doge** who ran the city from the **Palazzo Ducale** in Piazza Matteotti. The present black-and-white striped building, with its huge vaulted atrium, was built in the sixteenth century – its wide steps up from the courtyard were designed with the doge's grand processions in mind. The building now makes a grand exhibition hall and shopping centre. The dour **Gesù** church across the square, designed by Pellegrino Tibaldi at the end of the sixteenth century, contains a mass of marble and gilt stucco and some fine Baroque paintings, including Guido Reni's *Assumption* and two by Rubens: the *Circumcision* and *Miracles of St Ignatius*.

Traffic files down to the port past the newly scrubbed and elaborately inlaid and carved walls of the **Cattedrale di San Lorenzo** (open all day). Gothic craftsmen from France constructed the central portal, which is surrounded by twisting, fluted columns and topped with alternating black and white stripes, but much of the rest of the building was thriftily constructed from recycled older pieces. The statue of Saint Lawrence holding a sundial is known locally as "the knife-grinder". Inside is the Renaissance chapel of Saint John the Baptist, whose remains once rested in the thirteenth-century sarcophagus. After a particularly bad storm priests carried his casket through the city to placate the sea, and a commemorative procession takes place each June 24 in honour of the saint. His reliquary is in the treasury **museum** (Tues–Sat 9.30–11.45am & 3–5.45pm) along with a polished quartz plate on which, legend says, Salome received his severed head. Also on display, and also from the first century AD, is a glass vessel said to have been given to Solomon by the Queen of Sheba, and used at the Last Supper. Artefacts from Byzantine and later times include delicate jewelled crosses and arm-shaped reliquaries – and an unexploded British artillery shell that fell through the roof in the last war.

Around Piazza di Sarzano

Uphill from Piazza Matteotti, past a row of restaurants and bars, is the old entrance to the city, a twin-towered stone gate called the **Porta Soprana**. Between here and the waterfront lies a district of monasteries and convents, small squares, wasteground and building sites – this part of town was heavily bombed by Allied forces in World War II, and is only just being rebuilt. The ivy-covered brick house next to the gate has been designated as having belonged to Columbus's father, who was a cloth weaver by trade but served also as the official gatekeeper; Christopher was the first in his family to go to sea.

Genoa has spent a lot of money on repairing the bomb damage, a major beneficiary having been the church of **Sant'Agostino**, whose mosaic spire makes a good landmark off Piazza di Sarzano. The adjoining building houses the **Museo dell'Architettura e Scultura Ligure** (Tues–Sat 9am–7pm, Sun 9am–noon; L4000, free on Sun), built

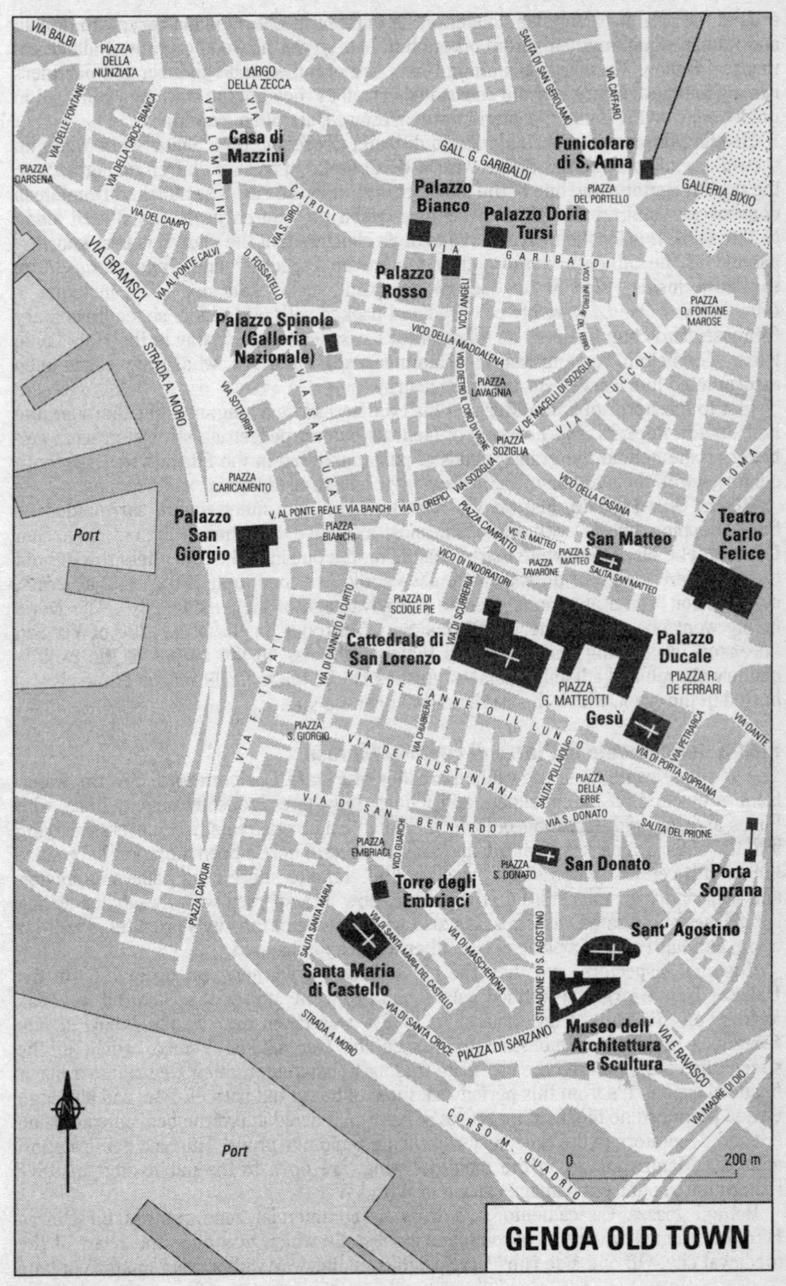
VIA BALBI
PIAZZA DELLA NUNZIATA
LARGO DELLA ZECCA
Casa di Mazzini
Funicolare di S. Anna
Palazzo Bianco
Palazzo Doria Tursi
Palazzo Rosso
Palazzo Spinola (Galleria Nazionale)
Palazzo San Giorgio
Port
Teatro Carlo Felice
San Matteo
Cattedrale di San Lorenzo
Palazzo Ducale
Gesù
San Donato
Porta Soprana
Torre degli Embriaci
Sant' Agostino
Santa Maria di Castello
Museo dell' Architettura e Scultura
0
200 m
GENOA OLD TOWN

around the original triangular cloister of the thirteenth-century monastery, with Roman and Romanesque fragments from other churches, as well as wood carvings and ancient maps of Genoa. The alleyways around here are cramped and rundown and outsiders run a gauntlet of stares and the occasional catcall as they go; the warnings you read in guidebooks on the danger to single women, though, are often overdone.

Heading down to the port, along Via di Santa Croce and then Salita Santa Maria on the right, you come across **Santa Maria di Castello**, a basilica church dating back to the twelfth century, and one of the oldest churches in the city. The attached Dominican convent was built in the fifteenth century, when the church itself was altered along Gothic lines. It is for the frescoed vaults of its cloisters that the church is best known – painted in the fifteenth century, they feature an especially fine *Annunciation*. The **museum** inside (Wed & Sat 3–5pm) has paintings by Lodovico Brea, including a *Coronation of Our Lady*, richly coloured and packed with portraits of sixteenth-century Genoese. The church served as a hostel for Crusaders on their way to the Holy Land, led by Guglielmo Testa di Maglio (Hammerhead) Embriaco, whose tower has been incorporated into a seven-storey house nearby.

Just to the north of Santa Maria is Via San Bernardo, a long, straight thoroughfare built by the Romans, and now one of Genoa's busiest pedestrian streets: grocers and bakers trade behind the grand portals of palazzi, altered in the fifteenth and sixteenth centuries with the addition of vaulted ceilings, balustraded loggias and frescoes.

Piazza San Donato, just off Via San Bernardo, is a quiet square surrounded by busy shopping streets, with one of the most attractive churches in the old town, **San Donato**. The black and white marble bands on the outside, like the others throughout the city, were a sign of prestige – families could use them only if they had a permit, awarded for "some illustrious deed to the advantage of their native city". The Doria family went one step further in **Piazza San Matteo** – on the other side of Via San Lorenzo – by carving testimonials to their worthiness on the stripes of the twelfth-century church and adjoining palaces. Andrea Doria, the most illustrious of the clan, is buried in the crypt, which the sacristan will open for you.

Piazza Caricamento to Piazza di Fontane Marose

The sea once came up to the vaulted arcades of **Piazza Caricamento**; now the waterfront is blocked off by containers and fences, but there's constant activity here, with buses arriving and departing outside the small café-restaurants and porters hurrying into the square's market from the alleyways behind. There's been a market here since the twelfth century, when small boats used to come to shore from galleys at anchor, and fruit and veg stalls still line the arcade, now interspersed with fly pitches selling sunglasses and pirated cassettes. It's also where some of the city's prostitutes wait for trade, although it's not a place where other women get hassled.

Customs inspectors, and then the city's elected governors, set up in 1260 in the **Palazzo San Giorgio**, a fortified palace built from the stones of a captured Venetian fortress on the edge of the square. In 1408 it was taken over by the *Banco di San Giorgio*, a syndicate established to finance the war against Venice, which in the sixteenth century steered the city from trading to banking, turning Genoa into a major financial capital. It's from this period that most of the grand palaces date, and although Genoa produced no outstanding artists of its own, it could afford the best portrait painters and decorators of the time, as its surviving buildings prove. The Sala dei Protettori and Sala Manica Lunga, in the medieval wing, are open to the public after massive restoration to put right damage caused in World War II.

Behind Piazza Caricamento is a thriving commercial zone centred on **Piazza Banchi**, a small square of secondhand bookstalls which was once the heart of the medieval city. Off one side runs Via Soziglia, an alleyway with a good mixture of bars and places to eat – among them *Klainguti*, an Austrian-built *salon*, selling cakes and ice cream under chandeliers. They still produce the hazelnut croissant known as a *Falstaff*, which was much esteemed by Giuseppe Verdi, who spent forty winters in Genoa – "Thanks for the Falstaff, much better than mine," he wrote to the bakers. Further along there's a shop specialising in secondhand period clothing, and a sign (*Mercato dei Pulci*) pointing to the flea market in **Piazza Lavagna**. From Piazza Soziglia it's a short stroll up to Piazza di Fontane Marose, where the city's sixteenth-century streets and palaces begin (see below).

Another exit from Piazza Banchi is the long, medieval Via San Luca. This street was in Spinola family territory, and when the last of the family died, in 1958, their palace became the **Galleria Nazionale di Palazzo Spinola** (Tues–Sat 9am–5pm, Sun & Mon 9am–1pm; L4000, free on Sun) – it's towards the far end, off Piazza Pelliceria. The Sicilian master Antonello da Messina's *Ecce Homo* might still be away for restoration, but *The Adoration of the Magi* by Joos Van Cleve, sawn into planks when stolen from the church of San Donato in the 1970s, is worth tracking down. Shops on Via San Luca sell counterfeit designer clothes and accessories; Via Luccoli, in the other direction, is the place where you'll find the real thing.

The **Museo del Risorgimento** (Tues–Sat 9am–7pm, Sun 9am–noon; L4000, free on Sun) is in this part of the old town, in the Casa Mazzini at Via Lomellini 11. **Giuseppe Mazzini** was born here in 1805, and at the age of sixteen saw political refugees begging in the streets on their way through Genoa to exile. He became the archetypal romantic hero, always dressed in black, in mourning for the failed revolution of 1821. It was his ideology which lay behind the radical revolutionary movement, and after a spell in jail he formed "Young Italy", a group dedicated to a unified country and a free sovereign state. Esoteric though his writings were, his fundamental beliefs inspired an enormous following – at one time there were 200,000 political exiles from other parts of Italy in Genoa and Turin, amongst whom Mazzinian ideals were strong. Pictures, documents and relics from Mazzini's life are on display in the museum.

Via Garibaldi and Genoa's palaces

When newly made fortunes encouraged Genoa's merchant bankers to move out of the cramped old town in the mid-sixteenth century, artisans' houses were pulled down to form the Strada Nuova, later named **Via Garibaldi**. To walk along it is to stroll through a Renaissance architect's drawing pad – sculpted facades, stucco work and medallions decorate the exterior of the three-storey palazzi, while the big courtyards are almost like private squares. Take a look, for instance, at no. 7, the sixteenth-century **Palazzo Podestà**, with its grotto and fountain. Snooty antique shops use the ground floors of some, but most of the palaces have become business and administrative offices.

Two palaces on Via Garibaldi have been turned into art galleries. **Palazzo Bianco** (Tues–Sat 9am–7pm, Sun 9am–noon; L4000, free on Sun) is the more important for its collection of paintings by Genoese artists and others who stayed here briefly, including Van Dyck and Rubens, and there's a good general collection of Flemish art too. Look for the portrait of Andrea Doria by Jan Matsys – ruler of Genoa in the early part of the sixteenth century, Doria made his reputation and fortune attacking Turkish fleets and Barbary pirate ships in the Mediterranean, and liberating the republic from the French and Spanish. Life in the streets of Genoa required as much skill and fortitude – he survived many plots on his life, several instigated by the Fieschi family.

Paintings by Titian, Caravaggio and Dürer are to be found across the road in **Palazzo Rosso** (Tues–Sat 9am–7pm, Sun 9am–noon; L4000), but it's the decor which really impresses. Looking exactly as it did on completion in 1672, the interior is bedecked with fantastic chandeliers, mirrors, an excess of gilding, and frescoed ceilings. A vast array of nativity figures is a diverting speciality. **Palazzo Doria Tursi**, a few imposing doors along, is now Genoa's town hall. Ask the custodian for a tour: the highlights are some very Genoese treasures – Paganini's favourite violin, three letters from Columbus, and the bones of one of the voyager's fingers.

The other Genoese palace worth a visit is the former residence of the Savoy kings, the **Palazzo Reale** (daily 9am–1.30pm; L4000), ten minutes' walk westward in Via Balbi. Covered galleries and arched windows which today look out over container ships once had a direct view of the sea, and the building has the feel of a summer pleasure palace – a sprung wooden floor in the ballroom, sugared-almond decor and figures floating around on Rococo ceilings. A small collection of paintings is spread through the upper storey.

The Harbour

After decades of economic decline, Genoa's **port** has been revitalised as a spin-off from the 1992 Expo, the Colombus-centred celebration of the city's heritage and potential. Cotton warehouses have been converted into exhibition spaces and a couple of stages built for waterside performances, with the "great derrick" – the **Grande Bigo** – topping the lot. A circular **elevator** (L4000) whisks visitors 200 feet up to the summit, from where you have a superb view over the city. The Grande Bigo was the brainchild of local architect Renzo Piano, best known as co-creator of the Pompidou Centre; he planned the rest of the Expo site too, linking the harbour with the rest of the old town via an underpass beneath Piazza Caricamento, thus connecting the revived port with an already thriving part of town. Shops, cafés and "Europe's Largest Aquarium" will ensure that the area has permanent appeal.

Even if you've already been up the Bigo, a **boat trip** around the harbour is fun, giving you a view of the sixteenth-century lighthouse and the Molo Vecchio, formerly the place where condemned prisoners were blessed and then hanged. You also begin to appreciate the extent of the docks: quayside and railway tracks line the basins as far west as the airport. Tours run by the *Co-operative Batterlieri* (☎265.712) leave every afternoon at about 3pm (L10,000). The **Stazione Marìttima**, a fin de siècle building from which steamers once left for New York and Buenos Aires, is now the ferry terminal for trips to Corsica, Sardinia and Sicily.

The **Ponte dei Mille** (Bridge of the Thousand), in front of the ferry terminal, was named after an episode during the Unification. It was from here that Giuseppe Garibaldi, ex-mercenary and spaghetti salesman and the ultimate guerrilla leader, persuaded his one thousand Red Shirts to set off for Sicily in two clapped-out paddle steamers, armed with just a few rifles and no ammunition. Their mission – to support a local revolution and unite the island with the mainland states – greatly annoyed some northern politicians, who didn't want anything to do with the undeveloped south. Similar attitudes are becoming increasingly prevalent in modern Italian politics.

Stazione Brignole to Sant'Anna

The small park outside the Brignole train station is fronted by **Piazza della Vittoria**, a dazzling white square built during the Fascist period, and the departure point for buses out of town. Uphill from the station, at Piazza Corvetto, buses plunge into the tunnel running underneath **Villetta di Negro**, a hill of artificial waterfalls and grottoes, topped by the **Museo d'Arte Orientale Edoardo Chiossone** (Tues–Sat 9am–5pm, Sun 9am–1.30pm; L4000, free on Sun) which holds a collection of oriental art including eighteenth-century sculpture and paintings, and samurai armour. Chiossone was a printer and engraver for the Italian mint, and on the strength of his banknote engraving skills, he was invited by the Meiji dynasty to establish the Japanese Imperial Mint. He lived in Japan from 1875 to his death in Tokyo in 1898, building up a private art collection specialising in the work of Ukoyo-e artists, the chroniclers of the Japanese stage. As well as portraits of Kabuki actors, his collection includes some fascinating pictures of the leisured classes – stylised depictions of women putting on make-up, for example, or after childbirth with kimono uncreased and not a hair out of place.

Piazza Corvetto is a major confluence of traffic and people – watch it all from the park benches, or from inside the grand **Caffè Mangini** on the corner of Via Roma, built by the Austrians in the nineteenth century. From the piazza mainly residential streets zigzag up the hills, one of which is scaled by the **funicular** which runs from Piazza del Portello, between the two road tunnels, up to the residential **Sant'Anna** district. When Genoa ran out of building space, plots for houses were hewn out of the hillside behind, like the steps of an amphitheatre, and the funicular ride shows you how it was done, as you're slowly taken past people's front windows. There's also a lift which does the same journey, leaving from Galleria Garibaldi; use ordinary bus tickets for both.

Down the hill from the funicular terminus, at Corso Solferino 39, there's an interesting collection of pre-Columbian artefacts in the **Museo Americanisto F. Lunardi** (Tues–Sat 9.30–noon & 3–5.30pm, Sun 3–5.30pm; L4000, free on Sun). Exhibits include a wonderful collection of Mayan vases from Honduras, sacrificial knives, a reconstruction of the Great Temple of the Sun of Teotihuacan, and tens of thousands of photographs. Bus #33 takes you there from Stazione Brignole.

The outskirts: Albaro, Boccadasse and the Staglieno

For a spot of relaxation, head for the suburb of **Albaro**, at the end of **Corso Italia**, a broad street which runs along the seafront beyond the *Fiera* exhibition area (bus #31 from Stazione Principe). This is the place to jog, stroll, pose, or to watch the sun set from a café table. The private **beaches** charge a small fee and provide changing areas and showers; if you don't like the look of the sea, there's an **open-air pool** at Via O. de Gaspari 39.

From Albaro, you can walk or take bus #31 or #42 to **Boccadasse**. Once an outlying fishing port, this village is now part of the city and there are boats pulled up on the pebble beach, nets hanging out to dry, stretched between windows, and some arty shops to browse around.

Much hype is expended on the view from the heights of Righi, in the hills above the city, but far more worthwhile is an outing to the **Staglieno cemetery**, across the valley from Righi. It's a veritable city of the dead, with Neoclassical porticoes and marble steps leading up to a pantheon bounded by tombs and cypress trees. One of the most sentimental monuments is the statue of Caterina Campdonico, a seller of nuts, whose life savings went to reproduce her slight, bent figure. Carved below is a poem telling how she sold her nuts in sunshine and in rain so as to gain her daily bread and propel her image into future ages. Evelyn Waugh called the Staglieno "a museum of mid-nineteenth-century bourgeois art", yet it's the melancholy atmosphere that really stays with you. It is still Genoa's major burial ground, and people come here to pay their respects to the dead and to weed the graves. To get here, take bus #34 from Piazza Annunziata, or #14 from Via XX Settembre.

Eating, drinking and nightlife

You could spend several days checking out the scores of places to **eat**, from basic trattorias to elegant nineteenth-century *caffès*. The cheapest, around the port, are often open only at lunchtime. On first impressions life after dark looks sparse – the Genoese tend to entertain at home, and if they go out, it's to somewhere like the theatre or opera. A few small **clubs and bars** have music (often live) and, during student term-time especially, small cinema clubs operate; in summer, you'd do best to head down to Albaro for the seafront cafés.

Eating

Best known of Ligurian specialities is *pesto*, made with basil, pine nuts, oil and parmesan and used as a sauce for pasta or stirred into minestrone. Others to look out for are *cima alla genovese* (stuffed veal), *burrida* (fish stew), fish *in carpione* (marinated in vinegar and herbs), and *torta pasqualina*, a spinach and cheese pie with eggs, widely served as fast food – Piazza Caricamento is especially good for **snacks**, with delicious deep-fried seafood. All over the place in the old town you'll see shops selling *farinata*, a kind of chickpea pancake. Chickpeas also feature in *zuppa di ceci*, found on practically every Genoese menu, but rarely outside Liguria.

Restaurants

Café Royal, Via di Macelli di Soziglia. Substantial informal fare, such as inexpensive steak and salad.

Caffè del Porto, Via Sottoripa 1. Down by the port, in the long portico that faces Piazza Caricamento. The anchovies with butter and the funghi and game are all good – expect to pay around L20,000.

Corona di Ferro, Vico Inferiore del Ferro 11. A must for Genoese specialities.

Florida, Via Doria. Good trattoria-pizzeria, just down the hill from Stazione Principe.

Genio, Salita San Leonardo 61. Highly regarded for Ligurian specialities – a gourmet treat of seafood, home-made pasta and pudding comes to around L40,000. Booking advisable (☎546.463). To get there, take Via Fieschi off Piazza Dante, and Salita San Leonardo is the first set of steps on the left.

Lombarda, Via San Bernardo. Serves Sardinian food and wine, at around L30,000 per person. Gets very busy.

Luciano e Mimma, Corso M. Quadrio 4. Sitting on the edge of the port, this lunchtime-only trattoria offers three courses for L14,000; in season they serve a starter which is an acquired taste – broad beans eaten with an aperitif.

Pintori, Via San Bernardo 57r. Family-run trattoria serving Sardinian specialities and vegetable dishes that are a meal in themselves: potatoes with butter and parmesan, asparagus and beans in season, and *torte di verdura*.

Puci dei Trilli, Salita Santa Maria di Castello. Reasonably priced trattoria, not far from the port.

Sâ Pesta, Via Giustiniani 16r. Well-known old-town place with excellent local dishes – get there before 7.30pm as they shut early.

Spano, Via Santa Zita 35r. Away from the old town, off Corso Buenos Aires (a continuation of Via Cadorna), this *osteria* serves *farinata* and *focaccia* as well as hearty soups, baked onions and *baccalà*.

Nightlife

The best source of information on **nightlife** is the local daily paper *Il Secolo XIX*; in summer you can supplement this with the tourist office's free guide to what's on. The student magazine *La Rosa Purpurea del Cairo* also has information on music, theatre and cinema: it's monthly and is available from some bookshops around Via Balbi in term time.

Bars and clubs

There are plenty of **bars** along the waterfront on the seamy Via Gramsci, in between the strip joints and brothels, but more relaxed places to drink can be found on the side roads off **Via XX Settembre**. If you've had enough of the local wine and are dying for a Guinness, hit the *Brittania Pub* in Vico Casana, just off Via San Lorenzo – though it's open all day, the pub is only lively at night, when it's fraternised by Genoa's foreign population as well as by Italians.

The *Centro Sociale Occupato Autogestita*, an arts centre on Via Madre di Dio, has **jazz, reggae and world music** most Fridays and Saturdays; go down the steps and alleys from Piazza di Sarzano – the centre is in an old church next to the main road. For jazz, try the *Louisiana Jazz Club* on Corso Saffi (a continuation of the waterfront Corso M. Quadrio); Genoa also has a jazz festival in July. There's live **bluegrass** on Mondays out at *The Patio*, Via Oberdan 22, Nervi (see p.100).

Open-air gigs take place in Parco Acquasola, at the Piazza Corvetto end of Viale IV Novembre; major British and American bands usually play at the *Teatro Verdi* in Sestri Ponente (see p.100).

Theatre and classical music

The brand-new *Teatro della Corte*, near Brignole station on Piazza Borgo Pila (☎570.2450), is now the main **theatre** venue in Genoa, its programmes supplemented by the *Teatro della Tosse* in Sant'Agostino and the *Teatro Politeama* at Via Martin Piaggio 4 (☎839.3589), though the latter is closed in summer.

Teatro Carlo Felice in Piazza de Ferrari (☎589.329), the replacement for a theatre that was almost entirely destroyed by bombs in 1943, is Genoa's main **opera** house; its performances are often oversubscribed, but you could be lucky. Chamber music concerts take place in some of Genoa's palaces.

Listings

Airlines *Alitalia*, Via XII Ottobre 188r (☎54.938); *British Airways*, c/o *Airsima*, Via E. Vernazza 23 (☎541.411); *TWA*, Via Cairoli 1r (☎293.858).

Airport information ☎26.901.

Banks Next to Stazione Principe in Piazza Acquaverde, along Via Balbi and at the airport.

Bicycle rental Porta delle Chiappe, Righi park – take bus #64.

Books English-language paperbacks are available from *Feltrinelli*, Via P.E. Bensa 32r and *Bozzi*, Via Cairoli 2a/r.

Bus information For city services, *ATM* (☎59.971); for provincial services *Tigullio* (☎313.851), Piazza della Vittoria.

Car rental *Hertz* (☎651.2422) and *Eurodollar* (☎651.2716), both at the airport.

Consulates *UK*, Via XII Ottobre 2 (☎564.833).

Doctor On duty Sundays and at night, (☎354.022).

Ferries *Corsica Line* and *Sardinia Ferries* are at Piazza Dante 5a (☎593.301). For crossings to Sardinia and Sicily contact *Tirrenia* at Ponte Colombo (☎258.041).

Football Genoa's premier side, the sporadically successful Sampdoria, play at the Luigi Ferraris stadium, reached by *KV* and *KM* bus from Stazione Brignole. They share the stadium with Genoa, who are expected to struggle for their place in the top league.

Hospitals Galliera, Mura delle Cappuccine 14 (☎563.2315); San Martino, Viale Benedetto XV 10 (☎35.351). For ambulance ☎595.951.

Left luggage At both train stations; L1500 for 24hr.

Pharmacists 24-hr service at *Pescetto*, Via Balbi 185r (☎262.697), near Stazione Principe, and *Ghersi*, 16–18r Corte Lambruschini (☎541.661), near Stazione Brignole.

Police Via Diaz (☎53.661).

Post office Via Boccardo 2 (Mon–Fri 8.15am–8pm, Sat 8am–1pm). Sub-post offices at both train stations, open same hours.

Taxi ☎26.96.

Telephones *SIP* at both train stations (daily 7am–10pm), and at Via XX Settembre 139 (24hr).

Train information ☎28.4081.

Travel agents *D.G. Viaggi*, Piazza San Matteo 3r, and *Guimar*, Via Balbi 192r.

Around Genoa

Genoa has spilled over the old city limits to spread around the bay, with good bus and train connections to some of its outlying parts. Popular at weekends are the parks and seaside promenade at **Nervi**, or at **Pegli** in the opposite direction, towards Savona. If you can, head **inland**, through terraced hills. They are green and lush in spring, when the blossom is out and the vines are sprouting. Several small villages make good targets, or it's possible from here to join the long-distance trail across the Ligurian mountains.

Nervi

Genoa's mainly residential suburbs extend east to **NERVI** (take a train or #15 bus from Piazza Caricamento), spread around a small harbour with one or two bars along the front. There are usually some people fishing off the rocks or paddling along in canoes, but the bulk of Nervi's visitors come for the *passeggiata*, which winds around the headland and through the gardens underneath the cliff. The **Parco Municipale**, by the main road, has an open-air cinema from June to September and a highly acclaimed ballet festival in summer. Semi-suburban though Nervi is, you still feel a long way from city life among the orange trees and the lush villa gardens.

Pegli

Out to the west of Genoa, near the airport, is the city's heavy industry, concentrated in the suburb of **Sestri Ponente**, a grim collection of blast furnaces, smelting works and housing blocks. Trains and the slow #3 buses from Stazione Principe pass through here to **PEGLI**, once a seaside town and a retreat from the city, but now engulfed by it. Although there are better places to swim further along the coast, Pegli has its own attractions, notably the **Villa Durazzo-Pallavicini**, which is set in grounds landscaped in nineteenth-century style, with fake waterfalls and pagodas. It now houses the **Museo Civico di Archeologia Ligure** (Tues–Sat 9am–5pm, Sun 9am–12.30pm; L4000), where items unearthed from cave burials in the hills along the west coast include the skeleton of a "Young Prince" with seashell crown and ceremonial dagger.

North from Genoa

Many Genoese escape the city in summer by heading for the hills inland. A narrow-gauge line runs north from Genoa's Piazza Manin to CASELLA, 12km from **Lago di Val Noci**. A small road deviates from the route to the lake and ascends the Val Brevanna to the mountainous **Parco Naturale dell'Antola**. Along the way are ancient *comunes* which the Spinola and Malaspina families, the bishops of Tortona, and the Republic of Genoa contested in medieval times. Here and there you'll see the crumbling outer walls of a castle built by one of these factions on the edge of small villages.

There are two routes over the mountains from Genoa: one to Tortona in Piemonte and the other to Piacenza in Emilia Romagna. The principal rail line follows the one to **Tortona** and Milan, tracking the *autostrada* (A7) and the SS35, passing through hillsides planted with fruit trees and vines. The long-distance **Alta Via dei Monti Liguri** dips down to the Tortona road at the Passo di Giovi, just before **BUSALLA**, a way station between Genoa and the Po Valley for hundreds of years. Should you want to explore the mountain trail, there's one **hotel** in Busalla: *Vittoria* at Via Veneto 177 (☎932.907; ④). Several trains stop there daily.

The road to **Piacenza** goes through **TORRIGLIA**, the main town of an agricultural *comune* encircled by hills; if you want to travel through the isolated land to the north, base yourself at one of its two hotels: the *Aurelio* at Piazza E. Piaggio 21 (☎944.046; ⑤), or *Della Posta*, at Via Matteotti 39 (☎944.050; ④). Further along the road lies the village of **MONTEBRUNO**, famed for its richly decorated fifteenth-century Santuario dell'Assunta (containing a Byzantine carving of the Madonna), and its mushroom-shaped chocolates called *funghetti*. Ancient copper mines, first worked in the eleventh century and revived at the beginning of this one, lie on the outskirts of **ROVEGNO** just before the border with Emilia Romagna.

THE RIVIERA DEL PONENTE

You get the most positive impression of the coast west of Genoa – the **Riviera del Ponente** – as you speed along the *autostrada*, from where the marinas and resorts are mere specks in a panorama of glittering sea and acres of glasshouses. Close up, the seaside towns from Genoa to the French border are fairly functional places, whose occasionally attractive centres are packed with hotel and apartment blocks. Yet these resorts have their good points – chiefly the sandy beaches, lower prices and lack of pretentiousness. An exceptionally mild climate means that flowering plants grow everywhere all year round, and much of the hillsides are draped with rush matting to protect the lucrative plantations of carnations and lilies.

If you can put up with the emphasis on family holidays, head for resorts such as **Finale Ligure** or **Alassio**; if not, there are the medieval ports of **Noli** and **Albenga**, and grand, crumbling **San Remo** makes a good base for travelling into the **mountain areas** behind the coast. Here, stone villages and agricultural comunes reveal the more private side of the province. Walkers can explore sections of the *Alta Via dei Monti Liguri* or loop through hill-towns like Baiardo, Apricale and Dolceacqua. And close to the French border, worth a stop before you cross, are the spectacular gardens of **La Mortola**.

Pegli to Varigotti

The resorts between Pegli and the large industrial port of Savona are inevitably affected by their proximity to two big cities. The railway, *autostrada* and trunk road all hug the coast, so ARENZANO, VARAZZE and CELLE LIGURE present an uninspiring face to the world. **SAVONA** itself is a modern city of concrete and steel architecture, and bits of the city which were bombed in the last war are now open spaces enlivened with sculpture. Via Paleocapa, an arcade of Art Nouveau buildings, leads down to the port and the alleys of the main shopping area. The **youth hostel** makes Savona a possible overnight stop: it's in an old fortress 1km from the station at Corso Giuseppe Mazzini (☎019/812.653; ①) – take bus #2.

It doesn't take much persuasion to leave the coast and head for the hills. **SASSELLO** is the most interesting of the small towns: on August 11 the streets are decorated with rose petals for the procession of the Corpus Domini, and locally produced amaretti biscuits and pecorino cheese are on sale.

Continuing west from Savona, the train emerges from the long tunnels at SPOTORNO, a soulless place with the saving grace of a long sandy beach between it and **NOLI**, 3km to the west. A tiny village now, Noli was once a maritime republic – on festivals the last flag of the Republic of Noli is flown from the **Torre Comunale**, one of its three red-brick towers. The regatta marks an important event in Noli's history, when in August 1193 the citizens bought their independence from the ruling Del Carretto family. The town retained its autonomy for over 600 years, and commemorates the deal every August with a "regatta of the districts", when consuls, warriors, pages, damsels and knights parade the streets, and crews of the long Ligurian *gozzi* boats hold a series of races.

The grid of old streets is a lively place to wander and its position – near several small beaches – makes it an appealing place to stop for a day or so. Remains of the castle and walls spread over the hill, while not far from the train station is the beautiful Romanesque church of **San Paragorio**, notable for its original crypt, fifteenth-century frescoes, a thirteenth-century bishop's throne of inlaid wood, and a twelfth-century **Volto Santo** (True Likeness) of Christ on the Cross. Some of Noli's thirteenth-century palaces have been converted into **hotels** with noisy, popular **restaurants**. *Da Ines*, Via Vignolo 1 (☎019/748.086; ⑤) is an especially convivial place to eat. For snacks, follow Via Vignolo past *Da Ines* to the first large piazza – just off here, at Via Colombo 60, is the tearoom-cum-bar *Milano*, offering over thirty different *panini*.

From Noli the Via Aurelia continues round the bay past a couple of small headlands, where the sea is inviting and the inlets accessible from the road. At nearby **VARIGOTTI** there are cheaper **places to stay** than in Noli – first choice is *Pensione Faia* at Via Orti 19 (April–Oct; ☎019/698.115; ④), though you must take full pension in July and August. Alternatively you could **camp** at *Camping Valentino* (April–Oct; ☎019/698.596), or make for the hostel at Finale Ligure, less than twenty minutes away by bus.

Finale Ligure

With nearly one hundred hotels in and around its centre, **FINALE LIGURE** is overtly committed to tourism, yet it manages to remain an attractive place. There are three parts to the town: **Finale Marina**, next to the sea, has a promenade lined with palms, and narrow shopping streets behind; **Finalpia** is the district on the Genoa side; and a couple of kilometres from the sea is the old town of **Finalborgo**, set on a slight hill. The majority of tourists in Finale Marina and Finalpia are Italian families who adhere to a formal sunbathing and mealtime schedule – only around 10pm on summer nights does the place come alive, as people pack the outdoor restaurants, seafront fairground and open-air cinema, while an extended *passeggiata* fills the promenade and the boutique-lined alley which runs the length of the old town. The bars in the vicinity of **Piazza Vittorio Emanuele II** and the adjoining **Piazza di Spagna**, the two main squares of this spread-out resort, are the points to which everyone eventually gravitates.

The bare rock faces behind the coast are particularly good for **climbing**, and are a favourite with free climbers, who gather at *Bar Gelateria Centrale* in Finalborgo's Piazza Garibaldi at weekends. (For kit and information on local routes go to *Sport Alp*, on Piazza Garibaldi.) The area's wider fame comes not from its cliffs, however, but from the **Grotte delle Arene Candide**, among Europe's most important caves for prehistoric remains. They are closed for excavation, but some finds are on display at the **Museo Archaeologico** in the cloisters of Santa Caterina in Finalborgo (Tues–Sat 10am–noon & 3–6pm, Sun 9am–noon).

Practicalities

In high season virtually all the resort's hotels insist on full pension, and not all of them are open to negotiation in quieter periods, though you should be able to find a room-only deal with a bit of effort. Outstanding among Finale Marina's central **hotels** is the friendly and lively family-run *Cirio*, Via Pertica 15, in the old part of town (☎019/692.310; ④); full pension, with bathroom, costs from L55,000 in high season – and there's also a four-berth apartment in an annexe. Slightly cheaper, but run on similar lines, is *Ferrando*, at Via Barrili 31 (☎019/692.355; ④). Two other central hotels, *Marina*, Via Barrilli 22 (☎019/692.561; ⑤) and *Giardino*, Via Pertica 49 (☎019/692.815; ⑤), are less basic, but cost around L70,000 for full pension. At the Finalpia end of town,

Albergo Italia, Via IV Novembre 8 (☎019/601.707), has its own garden, and *Ligure*, Via Veneto 30 (☎019/600.669), its own stretch of shoreline; full pension at each costs from L50,000. Rooms in **private houses** are listed by the **tourist office** on the seafront at Via San Pietro 14 (summer Mon–Sat 8am–1pm & 4–7pm, Sun 8.30am–12.30pm; winter closed Sat afternoon & all day Sun).

Cheapest options of all are the **youth hostel**, which occupies an ex-castle high above the train station in Via Generale Caviglia (mid-March to mid-Oct; ☎019/690.515; ①), or *Eurocamping Calvisio*, a well-run **campsite** at the Finalpia end (Easter–Sept; ☎019/601.240).

If you're not **eating** at the place you're staying, try *Au Quatre*, at Via Fiume 38 in Finalborgo, a relaxed trattoria with good food and music, open until midnight. In Finale Marina are *Gnabbri Trattoria*, set back next to San Giovanni Battisti just off Via Roma, one of the main alleyways running parallel with the shore. *Pizzeria Da Tonino* at 5/7 Via Bolla (between Via Pertica and the seafront) serves excellent pizzas, while dozens of open-air set-ups along the seafront sell pizzas, pasta and seafood. For more ambitious Ligurian food, jump in a taxi and head for *Osteria della Briga* in the hills above town, 5km along the road to LE MÁNIE from Finalpia. Their special dishes include *ortica* (nettle) and *tartufo nero* (black truffle) lasagne, and a choice of five or six kinds of steak; a full meal comes to around L30,000 –and you're advised to book (☎019/698.579).

Into the hills

It is worth finding transport and heading further inland. There you'll see small villages clinging to a hill, surrounded by woods; crumbling farmhouses and terraces banked up with stones growing vines. Away from the roads, you sometimes come across the occasional ox pulling a cartload of hay – the area certainly feels remote. Best of all is the food: soft cheeses preserved in oil, local wines and fruit. **Buses** inland are sporadic, but there are a few **footpaths** which take you away from the coast. One of these starts from VERZI, 5km behind Finalpia, and includes a section of the old Via Aurelia, which traverses a handful of Roman bridges along the Val Ponci. A half-day walk will bring you back down into VARIGOTTI, from where buses run half-hourly to Finale Marina. A more ambitious route, known as the **Sentieri Parlanti**, zigzags across the hills behind Noli, Finale and Borgio Verezzi – passing the *Osteria della Briga* (see above). The tourist office in Finale has information on this and other routes; proper walking maps are sold by the bookshop at Via Ghighlieri 3, between Via Pertica and Via Mazzini in Finale.

The most popular trip is to the grottoes at **TOIRANO** (daily 9am–noon & 2–5pm; L5000), set halfway up a rocky hillside just outside the village. Evidence suggests that 12,500 years ago bears and hunters penetrated this network of caves. The prehistoric human footprints in what was once mud are helpfully circled with chalk, and there's a mass of bones in the underground bear cemetery of the Grotta della Bàsura. The second set of caves, the Grotta di Santa Lucia, contains remarkable stalagmite and stalactite formations.

The daily bus service for Toirano from Finale Ligure station involves a change at BORGHETTO SAN SPIRITO, a route which takes you through **BORGIO VEREZZI**, a couple of kilometres from Finale Ligure. In the nineteenth century an artist called Brilla created an extraordinary grotto of artificial rock formations here, inside the **Santuario del Buon Consiglio**; it's open on the first Saturday of each month at 4pm, and on April 25 for the Festa della Madonna. A more conventional grotto nearby contains stalactites and stalagmites clustered around a series of beautiful underground lakes, plus remains of mammoths from half a million years ago (daily May–Sept 9am–noon & 3–6pm; Oct–April 9–11.40am & 2.30–5.35pm).

Albenga

Following the coast westwards, buses and trains take you past nurseries of artichokes and petunias, interspersed with garden gnome shops and caravan sites, before arriving at the small market town of **ALBENGA**, which sits in the middle of an exposed alluvial plain. The pebbly beach isn't worth going out of your way for, but the pleasingly business-like **old town** within the medieval walls merits a visit.

The nucleus of red-roofed buildings and thirteenth- to fourteenth-century brick **tower houses** is centred on Piazza San Michele and dominated by the **Cattedrale**. The main part of the church was built in the eleventh century and enlarged in the early fourteenth, but it has a fifth-century baptistery, constructed on the orders of Constantius III. The curator of the unengrossing **Museo Civico Ingauno** (Tues–Sun 9am–noon & 3–6pm; L2000), in the adjacent Torre Comunale, guides visitors round the baptistery, leading them across planks over the waterlogged floor. Ten-sided on the exterior yet octagonal within, the building contains fragmentary mosaics in which the Apostles are represented by twelve doves. The amphorae stacked against the walls, out of the way of the rising damp, supported the roof until the beginning of this century, and, being hollow, also augmented the acoustics.

A little way up the road from Piazza San Michele is the frescoed **Palazzo Vescovile**, which houses the cathedral treasury (Tues–Sun 9am–noon & 3–6pm). At the opposite end of the piazza is the Renaissance **Palazzo Peloso-Cepolla** (Tues–Sun 9am–noon & 3–6pm; L2000), whose tower holds items from the wreck of a Roman galley dug up from the seabed off Isola Gallinara in the 1950s. The first-century Roman port, *Album Ingaunum*, lies many layers under the present town, its centre marked by the thirteenth-century **Loggia dei Quattro Canti**, where Via delle Medgalie crosses Via Bernardo Ricci.

The bulk of the **bars and restaurants** are around Via delle Medaglie d'Oro, inland from the cathedral. For takeaway snacks, try *Puppo*, on Via Torlaro, or *Da Charlotte*, in the tiny piazza at the end of the road. There's a good *osteria* in Piazza dei Leoni, behind the baptistery, while just outside the walls, at Viale Pontelungo 26, is the popular trattoria *Lanterna Verde*. The *Pizzeria Trattoria Americana* at Via Tolaro 27 does basic trattoria food and wood-oven pizzas.

The **tourist office** (Mon–Sat 9am–noon & 3–7pm, July & Aug also Sun 9am–noon) is at Viale Martiri della Libertà 17, the road running between the bus and train stations. **Hotels** are concentrated here and by the sea: two good choices are the *Bucaniere*, right on the front (☎0182/50.220; ⑤), and *Italia*, Viale Martiri della Libertà 8–10 (☎0182/50.405; ⑤). The more attractive **campsites** lie west of Albenga: about five minutes away by the bus to Alassio is the seafront *Camping Delfino* (all year; ☎0182/51.998); five minutes further on the same bus brings you to *Camping Sant'Anna* (mid-April to mid-Oct; ☎0182/640.702), close to a pebble beach with pines and clear water.

Inland from Albenga

Several buses a day make the journey west along the terraced, semi-wooded Arroscia Valley to the ancient market town of **PIEVE DI TECO**. Formed in 1233 around a parish church, a well and a mill, it has expanded into porticoed streets of workshops and palaces and become a small industrial centre. The main reason for coming here is to make connections with **buses** further inland, but if you're here on August 15, the skittle games led by women, in commemoration of a narrow escape from a fourteenth-century Piemontese attack, are worth checking out, as is the hooded procession on the night of Good Friday.

A long bus ride further up the valley brings you to **PONTEDASSIO**, complete with a **Museo Storico degli Spaghetti**, and the village of **MENDATICA**, founded in the seventh century by refugees from the north, fleeing Lombard invasion. The latter makes a centre for trails onto Monte Saccarello, and has a couple of cheap hotels: *La Campagnola*, Via San Bernardo 28 (☎0183/38.745; ③), and *Il Torchietto*, at Piazza Roma 10 (☎0183/38.729; ③).

Alassio to Cervo

After Albenga the terrain becomes more mountainous, and the rail line and road stick close to the sea as far as **ALASSIO**, one of the more commercialised resorts along the Riviera del Ponente, with a fine four-kilometre beach. The old town centre follows the pattern of many of the other former fishing villages along the coast, with stone houses lining dark narrow alleys around the sixteenth-century Sant'Ambrogio church, with its Romanesque belltower. Alassio's sights seen, you'll probably want to head for the beach, where you can water-ski and windsurf in summer, or take a motorboat trip around the **Isola Gallinara** nature reserve, giving you a view of the cave in which Saint Martin once took refuge and of the remains of the island's Benedictine monastery.

Alassio's **tourist office** (Mon–Fri 9am–noon & 3–6.30pm, Sat 9am–noon & 3–6pm, plus Sun in summer 10am–noon) on Viale Gibb near the train station has information on the town's **hotels** – again, there are bargains to be had if you're staying for a week and want full pension, but fewer choices if you're just passing through. Out of the town's one hundred one- and two-star hotels, *Petit Chalet* at Via Adelasia 15 (☎0182/45.990), *Banksia*, Via Privata Marconi 13 (☎0182/40.504) and *Luxor*, Via P. Ferreri 59 (☎0182/42.605), are the exceptions to the full-pension rule. The alternative is to **camp**, either at *Camping Sant'Anna* (☎0182/640.702), between Alassio and Laigueglia, or the more expensive *Monti e Mare* (☎0182/643.036), 50m from the sea, off the Alassio-to-Albenga road.

You can enjoy the beach better if you move further down to **LAIGUEGLIA** (bus every 20min from Alassio), a quiet ex-fishing port with a couple of porticoed streets to wander, a large Baroque church and choice accommodation. *Hotel Mariella*, Via Dante 190 (☎0182/690.356; ⑤), combines wonderfully kitsch elegance with excellent food. Slightly higher prices are charged by the Sixties-style *Windsor Hotel*, at Via XXV Aprile 7 (☎0182/49.000; ⑤), right next to the beach. If money is in short supply, stay at *Pensione Rita*, at no. 120 on the main Via Roma (☎0182/690.400; ③). For **food**, a couple of lively places are the *Pizzeria Birreria Dante*, Via Dante 21, and *Al'Inferno*, Via Roma 45, which serves pizza and inexpensive pasta.

A walk up the steps from the junction of Via Mimosa and Via Roma takes you away from the coast through a cluster of holiday homes to the old Roman road near the top of the hill. From here, follow the *strada privata* into the woods and take the signposted path for the ruins of the **Castello di Andora** and what's rated as the best Romanesque **church** on the Riviera (45-min walk). Even if you never get to the church and castle, the walk along muletracks between olive groves and woods is one of the most appealing parts of this bit of coast, with plenty of shaded places to spend the afternoon. From the castle you can either backtrack, or walk on through the outskirts of ANDORA to its train station.

With so high a density of tourists along the coast, it's inevitable that the hillside fishing village of **CERVO**, on the other side of Capo Mele from Andora, has become primped and preened. Overlooking the houses is the rich Baroque church of **San Giovanni Battista**, dedicated to the local coral fishermen. The piazza in front of the church provides a dramatic setting for evening chamber orchestra performances in July and August, while workshops in the steep alleyways around the church sell a range of arty objects.

Imperia and around

In 1923 Mussolini joined the towns of Oneglia and Porto Maurizio to create the provincial capital of **IMPERIA**. The two halves lie on either side of the River Impero: Oneglia, to the east, is marked by large olive oil storage tanks on the harbour front, while Porto Maurizio works its way up the hillside in zigzags from the marina and beach. The main drag through town is Corso Matteotti; the **tourist office** at no. 22 (summer Mon–Sat 8am–2pm & 4–7pm; winter mornings only) has timetables for all the province's buses, many of which stop outside (tickets from the café next door). Shopping streets run parallel with Corso Matteotti, and there's a large indoor food market over the brow of the hill.

Admittedly, once you've seen this and climbed the steps round the old quarter, you've seen the sights, but Imperia is a useful place if you're looking for a **room** when everywhere else is booked up. The best area to look in is between Corso Matteotti and the sea – *Ariston*, at Via Privata Rambaldi 7 (☎0183/63.774; ④), is the most appealing of the hotels. Further down the hill, both the *Pensione Irene*, at Via Rambaldo 30 (☎0183/62.996; ④), and *Pensione Paola*, at Via Pirinoli 34 (☎0183/650.343; ④), offer full pension at very reasonable rates. *Lanterna Blù*, by the harbour at Via Scarincio 32 (☎0183/63.859), is one of the best **restaurants** in Liguria, offering innovative fish dishes and unmissable desserts at around 80,000 for a full meal.

Dolcedo

From Imperia the inland road follows an intensively cultivated valley where palm trees stand like strange oases engulfed by glasshouses, below slopes of olive trees. The bus for PRELA (every half hour) passes a couple of hilltop towns before reaching **DOLCEDO**, where a series of medieval bridges cross the River Prino, and vaulted arcades line the banks. This part of Liguria has been called "Riviera dei Fiori" – cultivated on every slope between Imperia and San Remo, and protected by glass or straw canopies, they're picked at night before being transported to San Remo flower market.

San Remo

SAN REMO's heyday as a classy resort was earlier this century, when wealthy Europeans paraded up and down the Corso Imperatrice and filled the large hotels overlooking the sea. Some of these buildings, especially near the railway station, are crumbling and grey, but others are still in pristine condition, and San Remo remains a showy town, a place with a good bit more life in it than the bland resorts up the coast.

The main road, Corso Matteotti, runs west from the central Piazza Colombo, lined with cocktail bars, gelaterias, cinemas and a selection of Paris–Milan boutiques. Neon signs down sidestreets point to private clubs and by-the-hour hotels, mixed in with a handful of expensive restaurants.

San Remo's lush gardens and parks attracted, among others, a colony of wealthy Russian exiles, who lived here at the end of the nineteenth century, ruled over by Maria Alexandrovna, consort of Tsar Alexander II. This community paid for the onion-domed **Russian Orthodox church** in Via Nuvolini (Tues, Thurs & Sat 3–6.30pm, Sun 9.30am–12.30pm & 3–6.30pm), built in the 1920s. Other relics from the same era include a ruined Art Nouveau house, complete with stained glass irises and majolica tiles, close to the junction of Via Fratelli Asquascati and Corso degli Inglese.

If you can drag yourself out of bed before 6.30am, the Via Garibaldi **flower market** is a unique experience – you'll know when you're close by the waiters running around with trays of espresso and by the plethora of woven boxes for flowers attached to the vans and Vespas outside. It's strictly for trade – lilies are bunched in fifties, for example – but no one minds bystanders as long as they don't get in the way.

An archway leads off from Piazza Colombo through to Piazza Cassini, from where you can walk up to the **old town**, called La Pigna (Fir Cone) because of the layering of the streets up the hill. **Monte Bignone**, 1300m high, towers over La Pigna and the rest of the town – a cable car from Corso Inglese, next to the market, travels up to the summit.

There isn't a lot to do in terms of galleries or museums, and even the small **beach** by the railway station is a bit mucky, but the attraction of the place is its seediness. The blue-movie cinemas, the shops selling "Souvenir of San Remo" shell lamps, the ageing cafés overlooking the marina – they all give the place some welcome sleaze after the overwhelming respectability of the rest of the coast. San Remo is also well placed for trips **inland**: the bus service is fairly good, but more options open up if you have your own wheels – bikes and Vespas are for hire at the marina and at the Piazza Colombo end of Corso Garibaldi. For advice on hiking, visit the *Club Alpino Italiano* office on Piazza Cassina (Tues & Fri 9.30–10.30pm, Wed & Sat 6–7pm).

Practicalities

The **train station** is in the western corner of town, next to the sea. An **accommodation** service operates at the *Costa Azzura* travel agency, Via Roma 19 (turn right out of the station, it's 20m after the traffic lights), where you can also exchange money. You can also get assistance across the road at the **tourist office**, Via Nuvolini 1 (Mon–Sat 8am–5pm, Sun 9am–2pm; ☎0184/571.571). The **bus station** is in front of Piazza Colombo, five minutes' walk from the train station; buy tickets from the tobacconist's opposite. Orange **trolley buses**, for transport around town and to Taggia (see overleaf), stop at the train station.

Finding a place to stay is no problem, except in August. There's a concentration of **hotels** along Corso Mombello, five minutes' walk to the right of the station – among many choices is *Mombello* at no. 49 (☎0184/501.466; ④). The two other main streets which converge at the station are Via Roma and Corso Matteotti; in Via Gioberti, between the two, you'll find the *Luce* at no. 12 (☎0184/509.096; ④), and the *Olimpia* at no. 25 (☎0184/80.093; ④). Most of the Liberty-style hotels are four- and five-star, but exceptions are *Hotel San Remo*, set back from the road at Corso Garibaldi 123 (☎0184/504.591; ⑤), and *Maristella*, Corso dell'Imperatrice 77 (☎0184/667.881; ⑤).

For **picnic** food walk along Via Palazzo, off Piazza Colombo, where four or five large shops sell spit-roasted chickens, salami, cheese and delicacies in aspic. Up in the old town, in the first street on the right as you enter from Piazza Cassini, is *Osteria della Costa*, specialising in an excellent rabbit stew – there are only a few tables, so get there around 8pm. On Via Palazzo is *Cantine San Remo*, a bar with hot food at noon and early evening. At the end of Via Palazzo and to the right you can't miss Piazza Eroi San Remesi, a car park surrounded on all sides by large pizzeria-restaurants, with so-so tourist menus – best of them is the *Pizzeria Graziella*. For **ice cream**, the pick is the *Bar-Gelateria* at Corso Garibaldi 49.

For entertainment, if you want to gross out, go to the nightly cabaret at the Liberty-style **Casinò**, or, if you're around in February, the annual "Festival of Song", which makes the Eurovision song contest look almost good. Fortunately, there's no shortage of other clubs and bars. For **live bands**, go to *Pipistrello*, a cellar bar at Piazza Borea d'Olmo 8 – to get there, turn down Via Goffredo Mameli, opposite the *Ariston* cinema on Corso Matteotti.

Inland from San Remo

Just outside San Remo are two small hilltop towns, both much visited, but rather different from each other. **BUSSANA VECCHIA** makes you want to turn round and go back home as soon as you get there. Destroyed by an earthquake in 1887, the houses are kept in an artificial state of ruin, and you can't move for rip-off galleries masquerading as artists' workshops. A far more satisfactory trip is to take the trolley bus outside San Remo station to the more sleepy **TAGGIA** (every 15min). Its long echoing alleyways are distinguished by the variety of carved slate portals with which the different families adorned their houses – some of them chipped off as fortunes dipped; the overriding sound is of cicadas in the fields around. The town's principal attraction is a collection of work by Ligurian artists in the cloister of the **San Domenico** (Mon–Sat 9.30am–noon & 3–5pm), but more thrilling is the ancient *festa* of the Magdalene, held on the Sunday closest to July 22 – it culminates in a "Dance of Death" performed by two men, traditionally from the same two families, accompanied by the local brass and woodwind band.

Baiardo and around

On the other side of Monte Bignone, past CERIANA, vines and silvery olive trees fill out a landscape which is green and lush even in the height of summer. **BAIARDO** makes the best centre if you plan to stay in this region – it's a hill-town with wide views over several valleys, reachable by bus from San Remo. No more than a few houses around a church, the village is a very relaxing place, with mule tracks and footpaths meandering through the fields and vineyards. The most central places to stay are *La Greppia* (☎0184/673.051; ⑤) and *Hotel Pineta* (☎0184/93.014; ④) – the *Pineta* also has an excellent small restaurant with dishes based on local produce such as wild boar.

Seven and a half kilometres west of Baiardo, you pass the village of APRICALE, clinging to a pinnacle of rock, with PERINALDO perched even higher in the distance. At ISOLABONA, a couple of kilometres from Apricale, you can pick up buses for Dolceacqua, Bordighera and Ventimiglia (see below).

Triora

Further into the mountains, along the heavily cultivated Argentina Valley, is the tiny village of **TRIORA**. The bus trip is worth it in itself, following the rock-strewn course of the Argentina, passing small settlements with ancient bridges, and farms linked to the main road across the valley by a rope and pulley system. Triora itself is literally the end of the road, spectacular for its setting in sight of Monte Pietradura, which stays snow-capped until April. A couple of bends below the village, a mule track leads down one mountainside and up another to **MOLINI DI TRIORA**, named after the mills which used to line the river. (You can still buy the special flat bread of the town.) In 1588, two hundred women in this isolated community were denounced as witches. Thirty were tortured, fourteen burned at the stake, and one woman committed suicide before she could be executed. The **Museo Etnografico** in Triora (June 16–Sept 15 daily 3–6pm; rest of year Sun 2.30–5.30pm) has documents from the trial and other exhibits on peasant life. Also worth seeking out is the *Baptism of Christ* by Taddeo di Bartolo, dated 1397, in the **Collegiata**'s baptistery.

Bordighera to the border

The plantation of palms surrounding the long-established resort of **BORDIGHERA** is the town's special resource – during Holy Week the Vatican uses the fronds of Bordigheran palms to the exclusion of all others. The monopoly was secured in unusual circumstances by a sea captain from the town who was visiting Rome in 1586. An obelisk which was being raised in Saint Peter's Square threatened to topple, but nobody dared disobey the pope's order for complete silence during the ceremony – nobody, that is, except the Bordigheran, whose shouted warning earned him the reward of the exclusive contract.

A cluster of medieval buildings, several alleyways of restaurants and small shops, and a Romanesque chapel make up the old town, or **Alta Bordighera** – a steep walk, or four-kilometre bus ride, away from the train station. On this steep hillside are dozens of three- and four-star grand villa hotels, beautifully kept and set in semi-tropical gardens. Katherine Mansfield rented a villa here after she had been asked to leave her hotel in San Remo, where her ill-health made the other guests nervous. Just below the nucleus of the old town there's a cool, shady park giving bird's-eye views off the headland. Below this, steps lead down to the tiny church of Sant'Ampello before descending to the water, where there are a couple of beach bars.

Dolceacqua

Buses run regularly from Bordighera and Ventimiglia to the hilltop village of **DOLCEACQUA**, visited chiefly for its excellent **Rossesse** wine, probably the best in Liguria, and olive oil. You see piles of black olives in the village at harvest, spread out on cloths on the ground before processing. The Nervia River, crossed by an elegant, single-spanned medieval bridge, runs between the two parts of town: the new part, by the main road through the valley, is called the **borgo**; the old quarter, built around the slopes of Monte Rebuffao, is the **terra**. The steep, stone alleyways of the terra are topped by a ruined castle once belonging to the Doria family, where a theatre festival is staged every July and August, as well as summer concerts. Dolceacqua is also the scene of a more ancient festival on the Sunday nearest to January 20. A laurel tree hung with coloured communion wafers like Christmas decorations is carried through the village as part of the procession of Saint Sebastian, the origins of which are rooted in ancient fertility rites. For ideas on walks in the beautiful Upper Nervia Valley ask at the **tourist office** at Via Patrioti Martiri 58 (Tues–Sat 9am–12.30pm & 4–7.30pm, Sun 9am–noon).

Ventimiglia and La Mortola

Eleven kilometres from France, **VENTIMIGLIA** is a typical border town, with a string of duty-free shops near the station, and French spoken as often as Italian. This town is the ancient city of Albintimulium, and you can still see substantial remains of its amphitheatre, which seated 5000 spectators, in Ventimiglia's northwest corner. The small **Museo Archeologico** (Tues–Sun 10am–noon & 5–7pm), close to the amphitheatre at Forte dell'Annuniziata, is also worth visiting. Modern Ventimiglia can seem on the dreary side, but livens up on Fridays when a giant **food and clothes market** takes over the town from Via della Repubblica down to the seafront. Across the river is the old quarter, where the Lombard-Romanesque **Cattedrale** and baptistery are separated from the eleventh-century church of **San Michele** by echoing alleyways and stone piazzas.

If you're stopping over, there are plenty of **hotels**: try the *Lido*, on the seafront below the old town at Via Marconi 11 (☎0184/351.473; ④), or *Villa Franca*, closer to the station at Corso Repubblica 12 (☎0184/351.871; ④).

From the junction of Via Martiri della Libertà and Via Cavour several buses a day leave for the gardens of **La Mortola** (daily summer 9am–6pm; winter 10am–4pm; L8500), set on a hillside near the frontier. Seven thousand species or more once grew in this botanical garden; now three-quarters have gone, but even on the brink of ruin it's a powerfully atmospheric place, with hidden corners and pergola-covered walks. The steeply terraced site covers 45 acres down to the sea, laid out so that vistas of grottoes and wild vegetation unfold before you. At its centre is the Islamic-style mausoleum of Sir Thomas Hanbury, the garden's creator.

A half-hour walk further up the coast road is the **frontier post** at Ponte San Luigi. A scramble down the hillside brings you to the **Balzi Rossi**, a significant prehistoric site, but visually not much more than a crevice of rock with a small museum attached (Tues–Sun summer 9am–12.30pm & 2–6.30pm; winter 9am–1pm & 2.30–6pm; L4000). Close by is the main road to France, which crosses the border at Ponte San Ludovico.

THE RIVIERA DEL LEVANTE

The stretch of coast **east from Genoa**, dubbed the **Riviera del Levante** (Riviera of the Rising Sun), is not the place to come for a relaxing beach holiday. Getting a tan in the most popular towns involves fighting for a small piece of pebble beach or concrete jetty, while the waterfront restaurants and cafés are the arenas for some highly competitive posing. Ports which once survived on the trades of navigation, fishing and coral diving have now experienced a solid thirty years of tourism; the coastline is still wild and extremely beautiful in parts, but inevitably the sense of remoteness has gone. It's pointless protesting against the stranglehold tourism has over the Riviera. Once you've accepted that wandering around ex-fishing villages with hordes of others is inevitable, you appreciate the major attractions this area still has to offer.

Away from the resorts, the cliffs and inlets are covered with pines and olive trees, best seen along the footpaths of **Monte Portofino**, on the way to **San Fruttuoso**, a short way east of Genoa. The nearby harbour towns of **Camogli** and **Santa Margherita Ligure**, painted up with trompe l'oeil balustrades and shutters, are favourite subjects for arty picture postcards, but for more nightlife you should head further along the coast to **Rapallo** and **Sestri Levante**. After Sestri, the road heads inland, bypassing the **Cinque Terre** – five fishing villages shoe-horned into inlets along the cliffs, the middle three of which are accessible only by train or boat. The main Genoa-to-La Spezia line then disappears in a series of tunnels, to emerge at the wide Golfo di Spezia. From the naval and shipbuilding port of **La Spezia** itself, there's transport to Tuscany or across the Apennines to Parma, and ferries to Bastia in Corsica.

Recco and Camogli

Allied bombing in 1944 virtually destroyed **RECCO**, and the town which has sprung up in its place is unremarkable except for the grey concrete flyover which hurdles the centre. People come here specifically to eat – some of the best **restaurants** in the province are within two or three kilometres of the town centre. If your wallet will survive an outlay of L60,000, book a table at *Manuelina*, Via Roma 300 (☎0185/720.019) – it's on the main road running north from the flyover. *Da-ö Vittorió*, at Via Roma 160 (☎0185/74.029), rivals *Manuelina* in quality and price. Eating well in Recco needn't cost a lot, however – at *La Baracchetta*, on the waterfront, superb *focaccia al formaggio* plus a carafe of house wine will set you back just L10,000.

CAMOGLI – just around the headland from Recco – was the "saltiest, roughest, most piratical little place", according to Dickens when he visited in 1884. In its day Camogli was something of a nursery for navigators and supported a fleet of 700 vessels – a force which was larger than Genoa's and once saw off Napoleon's fleet. The town's name, a contraction of *Casa Moglie* (House of Wives), comes from the days when voyages took years, and the women ran the port while the men were away. Camogli declined in the age of steam, but the crumbling arcades by the harbour and the dark flight of steps into the centre of town still have "a smell of fish, and seaweed, and old rope", although the harbour is nowadays busy with tourist ferries to San Fruttuoso, Portofino and Santa Margherita.

Punta Chiappa, across the bay, was once famous for the "ever changing colours of the sea", as guidebooks will tell you, but is now murky in places with rubbish from the yachts moored off the promontory. The flat rocks are still a popular place to bask, and plenty of people swim from here. It's also the starting-point for trails around the edge of **Monte Portofino**, and is accessible by ferry or by taking the path from San Rocco church, on the edge of Camogli. From Punta Chiappa it takes three hours to walk to San Fruttuoso and five to Portofino, along wild and beautiful clifftops.

For **places to stay**, try *La Camogliese*, Via Garibaldi 55 (☎0185/771.402; ⑥), or the slightly cheaper *Augusta*, Via P. Schiaffino 100 (☎0185/770.592; ⑤), on the edge of town as you come in by bus. The **restaurants** along the front are either expensive or bland – a better deal is *Da Fallù*, a seafood café on Salita Priaro, the flight of steps up from the harbour. The daily fruit and veg **market** takes place a few yards along the main road, in a building like a Fifties toy garage; of the food shops along the seafront, *Revello's* is the best – with queues for their *foccaccia* straight from the oven and the extravagant choux pastry *camogliese*.

On the second Sunday in May, the Camogliese celebrate the **Sagra del Pesce**, which is basically a great fry-up at the harbour. Recently it's hit problems: the authorities have said that the giant frying pan is a health hazard, and there have been allegations that frozen fish are defrosted out at sea and then passed off as fresh. On the plus side, the food is free.

Portofino and the Monte Portofino headland

PORTOFINO, at the extremity of the **Monte Portofino headland**, manages to be both attractive and off-putting at the same time. The tiny resort is a microcosm of wealthy urban life transplanted to the seaside. Once you've surveyed the expensive restaurants and lace shops by the water there's not much more to do other than watch everyone else do the same. The thing is, it is very beautiful: the slopes surrounding the bay are covered in cypress and olive trees, and a **footpath to San Fruttuoso** (about 2hr 30min) passes through vineyards and orchards, at the end of the steep flight of steps inland. Shorter walks lead to the lighthouse and the castle and church of San Giorgio, said to contain relics of the saint. Three kilometres out of the village, on the corniche road, the sparkling cove at **PARAGGI** is a good place for a swim – not exactly remote, but less formal than Portofino, with a couple of bars set back from the beach.

Staying in Portofino is expensive, even out of season – it's better to take the bus to nearby Santa Margherita Ligure or Rapallo.

Monte Portofino

At 612m, **Monte Portofino** is high enough to be interesting but not so high as to demand any hiking expertise. The trails cross slopes of wild thyme, pine and holm oak, enveloped in the constant buzz of cicadas, and loop around the headlands which fringe its base. Monte Portofino represents a goldmine for developers, but for the moment there's a ban on any building work; rumour has it that fires are started deliberately to sabotage its national park status. You can reach the coastal paths by foot from Camogli or Portofino, or take a bus to RUTA, from where you can either slog on foot to the summit, or catch another bus to PORTOFINO VETTA (see below), from where it's twenty minutes' walk to the top. On very clear days you can see as far as Corsica, or so it's said; even routinely, though, the view over successive headlands is fantastic. Not many people walk the trails, maybe because their early stages are fairly steep – but they aren't particularly strenuous, levelling off later, with plenty of places to stop.

San Fruttuoso

More rewarding than the haul to the top are the coastal paths to **SAN FRUTTUOSO** which start from Portofino Vetta (1hr 15min), Camogli (3hr) or Portofino itself (2hr 30min). What happens when you arrive depends on the time of year. If it's a summer weekend, ferries crammed with tourists will be shuttling every half-hour between the small inlet and Portofino, Santa Margherita Ligure and Rapallo in one direction, and Camogli in the other. Out of season, however, San Fruttuoso is peaceful, and an excellent place for doing nothing – wandering through the recently restored abbey, the only sounds are the waves on the beach outside. There are a couple of shack-type restaurants on the beach, and one place **to stay** – the tiny *Da Giovanni* (☎0185/770.047; ③).

The **Abbazia di San Fruttuoso di Capodimonte**, which fills the width of the bay, was originally built as a home for the relics of Saint Fructuosus, brought here after the Moorish invasion of Spain in 711. Destroyed by Saracen raids, it was rebuilt as a Benedictine abbey in 984. Among the tombs is that of one Maria Aregna, killed trying to save survivors of a warship bound for the Crimea, which had caught fire near the bay. Some of the Doria family, who gave their name to the sixteenth-century defence tower on the headland, are buried here too.

Off the headland, a bronze statue of Christ (*Cristo degli Abissi*) has been lowered eight fathoms down onto the seabed, in commemoration of divers who have lost their lives at sea. Unless you're a diver yourself you can't get down deep enough to see much of this, but there's a replica in a fish tank inside the Gothic church adjoining the abbey.

Santa Margherita Ligure

SANTA MARGHERITA LIGURE is a thoroughly attractive palm-laden small resort, which in the height of summer acts as an overspill for Portofino. In the daytime, trendy young Italians cruise the streets or whizz around the harbour on jet skis, while the rest of the family sunbathes on the minuscule pebble beach and concrete jetties, or crams the restaurants and *gelaterie*. Even if you don't have the requisite designer wardrobe, you might want to stay in Santa Margherita, as it's on the Genoa-to-La Spezia line and makes a convenient base for visiting Monte Portofino and the other coastal towns. The cheap **hotels** are friendly and pleasant. Try *Albergo Annabella* on Via Costasecca, just off Piazza Mazzini (☎0185/286.531; ④), *Albergo Fasce*, a little further up the road in Via L. Bozzo (☎0185/286.435; ④), or *La Piazzetta*, next to the seafront at Via Gramsci 1 (☎0185/286.010; ④). A refreshing exception to the expensive **restaurants** and cocktail bars is *Trattoria Baicin*, Via Algeria 5 (☎0185/286.763), with a special three-course seafood menu for L25,000.

Near the **Basilica di Santa Margherita**, which has a rich interior of gilt and Rococo paintings, you'll find the **tourist office** on Via XXV Aprile (summer daily 9am–12.30pm & 3.30–7pm; winter Mon–Sat 8–11.45am & 3.15–5.45pm); it has free footpath maps of the area. For rental of **bikes and watersports equipment**, go to *Motonoleggio*, Via Pagana 5b.

If you carry on towards Rapallo, the road cuts the corner of the first headland and drops down to a patch of beach in the bay of **SAN MICHELE DI PAGANA**. For the truly dedicated, the church here has a *Crucifixion* by Van Dyck, but the beach bars and clear water are a stronger attraction.

The Golfo di Tigullio

After the rocks and inlets which fringe Monte Portofino, the coast flattens out to form the **Golfo di Tigullio**, stretching for 28km in a wide arc. There are no quiet parts – most of the level land next to the sea has been developed, and the gulf is bracketed by the commercialised resorts of Rapallo and Sestri Levante. Chiávari and Lavagna are smaller towns, with buses into the hinterland – to the basilica at San Salvatore and, further into the mountains, to the resort of Santo Stefano d'Aveto.

Most of the train journey between Rapallo and Chiávari is through tunnels, so for an idea of what lies in between you need to take the local bus, which follows the mad coast road around several headlands. It's fairly densely built-up, although some of the villas and gardens are spectacular, surrounded by wisteria, fig trees and mini olive groves. The overriding attraction, however, is the sea, which takes on a transparent quality outside the big resorts. Brilliant turquoise coves appear and disappear in a matter of seconds as the bus takes another bend, and occasional signs point *al mare* – jump off if the fancy takes you, though you probably won't be alone when you get there.

Rapallo

RAPALLO crowds around the first bay along in the gulf, a highly developed resort with acres of glass-walled restaurants and plush hotels. Earlier this century Rapallo was a backwater, and writers in particular came for the bay's extraordinary beauty, of which you now get an inkling only early in the morning or at dusk. Caricaturist and ferocious critic of British Imperialism, Max Beerbohm lived in Rapallo for the second half of his life, and attracted a vast coterie; Ezra Pound wrote the first thirty of his *Cantos* here between 1925 and 1930. (Just to be contrary, Hemingway came to visit and said the sea was flat and boring.) The striking landmarks now are the large marina and the castle stuck out at the end of the small causeway – once a prison, now an exhibition space.

The town does have an existence separate from its tourist trade, particularly around the **old town**, a grid of cobbled streets behind the stone Saline Gate – this is the commercial centre, and venue for the Thursday **market** which overflows Piazza Cile.

The best **places to stay** in Rapallo are along the front, within sight and smell of the sea and the palm and orange trees. Recommended hotels are the *Pensione Bandoni*, Via Marsala 24 (☎0185/50.423; ④), *Vesuvio*, Via Marsala 22 (☎0185/503.48; ⑤), and the upmarket *Miro*, nearby at Lungomare V. Veneto 32 (☎0185/60.380; ⑦). *Villa Marosa* at Via Rosselli 10 (☎0185/50.668; ⑤) is another good choice, but full pension is obligatory in high season at L80,000. The *Rapallo* **campsite** is at Via S. Lazzaro 6 (June–Sept; ☎0185/262.018).

There are some fine, inexpensive trattorias in the alleys behind the mediocre seafront fish restaurants. *Da Mario*, Piazza Garibaldi 23, offers a set menu of Ligurian specialities for L35,000, with tables outside under medieval porticoes, while *U Bansin*, Via Venezia 49, has full meals around L25,000. For a costly blowout try *Zi Teresa* at Corso Italia 33 (book on ☎0185/273.418). There are some pub-type **bars** between the station and the castle, like *Taverna Paradiso* at Via Venezia 72, and *Gallo Nero* at Via Magenta 10, just up from the rotunda on the seafront.

The **tourist office** at Via Diaz 9 (daily 9.30am–12.30pm & 4–7pm) provides sketchy maps of the footpaths which head up to **MONTALLEGRO**, in the hills behind Rapallo. The less energetic could take the cable car from Via Castegneto, ten minutes' walk inland from the castle, or the bus via SAN MAURIZIO DI MONTI, where there are a couple of cheap restaurants specialising in Ligurian home cooking. The **Santuario di Montallegro**, at the top, has a superb setting, overlooking the steep, green valley, with every available space planted with terraces of olives and vegetables. It was founded in 1557 when a Byzantine icon of the Madonna appeared miraculously in the hands of one Giovanni Chichizola; a commemorative *festa* is held during the first three days of July, with the coffer of the Madonna carried through town, and a fireworks contest culminating in the mock burning of the castle.

Chiávari and around

In contrast to the rock faces and inlets which have gone before, **CHIÁVARI** faces a flat bit of coastline, featureless but for the boulder and cement breakwaters separating the marina from the sand and pebble beach. Called Clavarium (Keys) by the Romans for the access it gave them to the valleys behind the coast, Chiávari is still a good starting-point for trips into the mountains. The **bus** and **train** stations are next door to each other, just off Chiávari's main street, Corso della Libertà, which bisects a grid pattern of medieval arcades lined with food shops and macramé outlets – the craft was brought back from the East by local sailors.

Off the Corso, at Via Costaguta 2, is the **Civico Museo Archeologico** (Mon–Sat 9am–noon & 3–5.50pm, Sun 2.15–5.45pm; free) with graphics explaining such recondite matters as the intricacies of the triple flint arrowhead, backed by finds from a vast seventh- to eighth-century necropolis on the outskirts of town.

Lavagna

Occupying the other bank of the River Entella, **LAVAGNA** is a smaller, plainer version of Chiávari. Its name means "blackboard" in Italian, after the slate quarried from caves on Monte San Giacomo and used on the outside of most of Liguria's striped churches. Nothing much happens in Lavagna, with the major exception of August 14 each year, when the town hosts its own version of *Blind Date*. Hundreds of people flock to the main square to claim their piece of the giant wedding cake called the *Torta dei Fieschi*, after a thirteenth-century wedding between Opizzone Fieschi and Bianca dei Bianchi. You take a ticket, which matches up with a ticket held by someone else in the large crowd; finding your partner, according to the tourist office, "at times leads to enduring relationships".

The **Basilica di San Salvatore dei Fieschi**, a couple of kilometres north (accessible by bus from Lavagna or Chiávari), is a beautiful complex of Romanesque-Gothic buildings, adorned with pagan symbols under the eaves. Half hidden off the main road, the basilica, in its own walled square, looks down on a valley of farms and fruit trees.

Santo Stefano d'Aveto

Two routes lead inland to **SANTO STEFANO D'AVETO**: from Rapallo and from Chiávari. Both pass through isolated villages and hillsides terraced up to the snowline, with vines on the lower slopes and strange grass-hut-style canopies for covering hay. It's good countryside for hiking – especially around REZZOAGLIO and CERISOLA – and botanists will enjoy **La Riserva dell Agoraie**, a reserve of three small lakes on the northern slopes of Monte degli Abeti (1543m), with its rare plant species and 2500-year-old trees preserved in the icy water. Santo Stefano itself, the largest of the mountain resorts, is a centre for walking and skiing, with a brace of one-star **hotels** – *Genovese*, Piazza del Mercato 9 (☎0185/880.50; ④), and *San Lorenzo*, Via Marconi 26 (☎0185/880.08; ④).

Sestri Levante to the Cinque Terre

From Lavagna the road sweeps round the bay to **SESTRI LEVANTE**, one of the most commercialised resorts this side of Genoa. It consists of two bays separated by a narrow isthmus: the "Bay of Fables" (nearer the train station), said to be so named by Hans Christian Andersen, and the "Bay of Silence". Marconi conducted some of his first short-wave radio experiments at the castle between the bays in 1897, sending radio waves 19km out to warships off La Spezia. On the Bay of Fables side, the beach is wide and sandy but is packed with sunbeds and overlooked by ranks of hotels which will probably send you in the opposite direction. The Bay of Silence, on the other hand, might not exactly live up to its name in high season, but is far more pleasant, with a narrow beach and lots of fishing boats.

On the headland there are a couple of small churches, including the restored Romanesque church of San Nicolò; the adjacent park of cork oaks and other Mediterranean plants is open between May and September (closed noon–4pm). The most attractive **places to stay** are on the headland as well. *Pensione Jolanda*, Via Pozzetto 15 (☎0185/41.354; ④), has rooms with balconies; another possibility in the same range, near the Bay of Silence, is the *San Pietro*, Via Palestro 13 (☎0185/41.279). Back on the main drag, and closer to the sea, is *Locanda Trattoria L'Approdo* at Piazza Francesco Bo 17 (☎0185/42.916; ④).

Via XXV Aprile, which runs through the neck of land between the two bays and widens out onto Corso Colombo, is where you'll find the best places to **eat and drink**. *Ristorante Polpo Mario*, at no. 18, specialises in fish, and *Buon Geppin* on Corso Colombo has good fish antipasti. For **takeaway food**, from Ligurian specialities to chips and ketchup, visit the place at Via XXV Aprile 61–63, which is open restaurant hours every day. On the same road, there's a selection of wines from Liguria and the rest of Italy at *Enoteca Il Leudo* (daily until 8pm). The **nightlife** is good in Sestri, too – plenty of bars stay open until 3am, and the video bar *Ca di Ferrae*, on Via Nazionale, has **live music** on Fridays.

Inland from Sestri

Travelling inland from Sestri, buses go to **VARESE LIGURE**, a market town in the upper Val di Vara, built in a circle around a fifteenth-century castle and medieval hog-backed bridge over the River Gresino. Varese's Augustinian nuns have traditionally made an income from *scivette* – marzipan flowers. A special kind of grappa comes from here too. To see the rest of the valley you really need your own transport. If you do have a car, you can continue along 13km of switchback road to the **Passo di Cento Croci** (1053m), and loop back down to the coast, or else cross the border and make for Bedonia and Borgo Val di Taro in Emilia Romagna.

Along the coast

Once out of Sestri Levante, past the headland and the shipyards at RIVA TRIGOSO, the rail line and coastal road disappear into a set of tunnels which last almost until La Spezia. Getting around by **bus** takes time – its route loops onto the coast at the family resorts of MONÉGLIA and DÉIVA MARINA, then cuts inland, where it passes red marble quarries, olive groves and burnt-out patches of forest before coming back down to the coast at **LÉVANTO**, the last town before the Cinque Terre – an unpretentious small town with a long stretch of sand backed by beach bars. The big day here is Wednesday, when the huge general **market** draws people in from miles around.

The Cinque Terre

If you're travelling on a fast train, you'll speed through the five villages of the **Cinque Terre** without seeing much more than a few tantalising glimpses of sheer cliffs and bright turquoise water as the train dashes from one tunnel to the next. However, the stopping services on the Genoa-to-La Spezia line call at each of the five (hourly in both directions), and until the completion of the *Litoranea delle Cinque Terre*, rail is the most convenient way of getting to the villages – though there is a ferry service from La Spezia. Their comparative remoteness, and the drama of their position on tiny cliff-bound inlets, make a visit to the area a real attraction rather than just a convenient stop-over on the way to Tuscany or Rome.

Purely fishing ports originally, the Cinque Terre now also produce large quantities of wine from steeply terraced vineyards, some of which are accessible only by boat. Fishing, wine-making and olive-growing are the major occupations, though tourism is an equally visible recent addition.

RIOMAGGIORE, closest to La Spezia and one of the larger villages, is the best place to head for. Its bizarre charm lies in it being wedged impossibly into a hillside, with no two buildings on the same level. Along the cliff path which winds its way to **MANAROLA**, lemon trees flourish in every back yard, and in spring – before the sun has turned everything except the vines to dust – the cliffs are covered with wild flowers. From Manarola a less crowded and more spectacular path passes rock-cut steps leading down to the water all the way to **MONTEROSSO** (12km), largest and least attractive of the villages, and the only one with a recognisable beach. **CORNIGLIA**

and **VERNAZZA** are much the same as Riomaggiore, but on a smaller scale. A word of warning – if you follow the Italians' example and dive into the sea from the rocks, watch out for power boats whizzing past.

Reasonably priced **hotels** aren't too difficult to find – Monterosso and Riomaggiore present the best opportunities – but the only dirt-cheap accommodation is the grotty hostel run by "Mama Rosa", who pounces on backpackers at the train station. *Villa Argentina* in Riomaggiore (☎0187/920.213; ④) is the best budget hotel, but it's often full. If you ask around in the villages, you'll probably be able to find a **room** in a private house. The **restaurants** are just overdecorated ordinary trattorias with inflated cover charges to match; the only relief in Monterosso (the worst offender) is, improbably enough, a beatnik café. **Bars**, on the other hand, tend to be reasonable even in the most obvious locations.

The Golfo di Spezia

Even though La Spezia itself is a major naval and shipbuilding town, the **Golfo di Spezia** is impressive, its sweep of islands and headlands being too big for heavy industry to dominate. When everywhere else is booked up, La Spezia usually still has cheap rooms, but if you have the choice, make for the small resorts outside, linked by bus along twisting roads: Portovénere, sitting astride a spit of land on one side of the gulf, or San Terenzo, Lérici or Tellaro, lining the coast on the other.

La Spezia

Most travel guides either bypass **LA SPEZIA** or dismiss it with a few curt comments, and on the face of it it's easy to see why. It's pretty well a blank as far as art and architecture are concerned, and nobody comes here to admire the things it does have: a huge mercantile port, the largest naval base in Italy, and unsightly petrochemical and quarrying industries. Still, with its bustling market and purposeful inhabitants, La Spezia is a real town, where people do things other than cater for tourists. Although its main attraction is undoubtedly the stunning beauty of the surrounding villages – particularly the Cinque Terre to the north – its cheap hotels and restaurants make it a good base for exploration.

Sweeping around the curve of the gulf – one of Europe's best natural harbours – La Spezia is crammed between the hills and the sea. This position proved an early attraction, its strategic importance reflected in the number of Genoese castles which stud the hills. These were the town's first fortifications, yet it wasn't until Napoleon arrived that a large naval and military base developed here. The naval presence made it a prime target in World War II and the results were predictable – most of the centre had to be rebuilt after Allied bombing and is rather drab, with the exception of the modern **Cattedrale**, its boldly minimalist white tower curving against a hilly background.

In fact, the nearest La Spezia comes to anything traditional is the church of **Santa Maria**, whose facade displays attractively restrained black and white stone banding. Nestling modestly in the corner of Piazza Giulio Beverini, it was originally constructed in the 1300s and rebuilt in the seventeenth century after the city walls were expanded.

Close to the church is the town's principal raison d'être – the **Arsenale**, which was finished in 1869 and occupies a huge swathe of the southern part of town. The entrance is in Piazza Chiodo, but a visit requires a convoluted written application to the director of the complex. The **Museo Navale** (Mon–Fri 2–6pm; L2000), in the same square, contains battle relics, models and figureheads from the sixteenth century onwards. The **Museo Civico**, between the Stazione Centrale and the Arsenale at Via Curtatone 9 (Tues–Sat 8.30am–1pm & 2–6pm, Sun 9am–1pm; free) holds archaeological remains from eastern Liguria; the most striking are the simple *stele* – faces sculpted on stone slabs in the Bronze and Iron ages.

Practicalities

The **train station**, at the top end of town, is one of the main convergence points for **buses**; others are Piazza Cavour (the market place) and Piazza Chiodo. The last of these is the departure point for *ATC* buses to the Val di Magra, the Val di Vara and Tuscany. **Ferries** operate daily in summer between La Spezia and Bastia in Corsica – they're run by *Corsica Ferries*, on the Molo Italia (☎0187/21.282). Boat services to Lérici, Portovénere and its islands (Palmária and Tino), and the Cinque Terre are run by *Linea Pozzale* (☎0187/503.123) and *Linea Intur* (☎0187/30.387) both on Banchina Revel, and *Navigazione Golfo dei Poeti* on Molo Italia (☎0187/967.676).

For a list of **hotels** and a map, head for the **tourist office** at Via Mazzini 47, by the seafront. The cheaper hotels tend to be near the station – the *Parma* (☎0187/20.754; ⑤) is just to the left of the station at Via Fiume 143. The low-budget option is *Flavia*, Vicolo dello Stagno 7 (☎0187/27.465; ④).

The daily covered **market** in Piazza Cavour is a good place to buy something for a picnic; it's a huge affair on Saturday mornings. **Restaurants** cluster in the area between Via del Prione and the Arsenale, to the right as you face the sea; prices are kept low by the naval clientele, but in August the majority of them are closed for holidays. *Farinata* is available from many takeaway places, also at one or two pizzerias – try *Giulio* in Via San Agostino, just off Via del Prione. Seafood and pesto dominate trattoria menus – *Da Sandro* at Via del Prione 268 does a good line in both, while *La Posta*, Via Don Minzoni 24, is hard to beat, though the price per head can reach L50,000. There are two good places on the edge of La Spezia, on the main road to Genoa: *Antica Osteria da Caran*, Via Genoa 1, does traditional Ligurian food for around L30,000; *Al Negrao*, Via Genoa 428, serves traditional *stoccafissa* (salt cod), as well as rabbit and seafood, at the same price.

Portovénere

PORTOVÉNERE sits on the small peninsula that encloses the gulf. The bus ride from La Spezia is a frenetic affair, with some hair-raising bends, but it gives fine views of the bay and the islands of Palmária and Tino. The village is tiny, its houses perched on the cliff and along the concrete harbour, which spreads out at the end of the promontory to the medieval church of San Pietro. One of the rocky coves around its base is called "Byron's window", so called because the poet once swam across the gulf from here to visit Shelley at San Terenzo (see below).

Portovénere is firmly on the tourist trail and doesn't really cater for people travelling on a budget; the only cheapish **place to stay** is *Genio*, next to the tourist office (☎0187/900.611; ⑤). There is, though, a very good place to **eat**: *L'Antica Osteria del Carrugio* at Via Capellini 66 – it's in the shadow of the Genoese castle, built to defend the coast from the Pisans on the other side of the bay.

The most frequent island **boat trips** are to the Grotta Azzurra on Palmária and the remains of a Romanesque abbey on Tino, though it's considerably cheaper if you leave from La Spezia. Boats also run the width of the bay to Lérici.

San Terenzo and Lérici

Dockyards, foundries and bars line the coast road to the east before La Spezia gives way to some small resorts. At **SAN TERENZO** there's a good sand **beach**, but if you want to stay in high season, most of the hotels will insist on full or half-pension; about the best deal you'll get is *Leonella*, along the seafront (☎0187/970.969; ⑤). Next door but one is **Casa Magni**, where **Shelley** spent some productive months in 1822, before setting off to meet Leigh Hunt at Livorno, "full of spirits and joy", according to Mary Shelley's account; on the way back his boat, *Ariel,* went down, and Shelley drowned, aged thirty.

LÉRICI, in the next bay, is an upwardly mobile resort of seafront bars, trattorias and gift shops. The Pisans built the castle in the twelfth century, to keep out the Genoese, who were established at Portovénere on the other side of the gulf. Paths skirt the castle and cross the headland to a small cove, an alternative to the beach next to the main road on the town side. Next to the marina are stalls selling fresh coconut, a couple of bars filled with yacht crews, and some pricey restaurants. Piazza Garibaldi, behind it, acts as the **bus terminus**.

There's only one inexpensive **hotel** in Lérici – *Hotel del Golfo*, Via Gerini 37 (☎0187/967.400; ⑤) just up from the tourist office. Outdoor **pizzerias** line Lérici's harbour, an attractive setting as the sun goes down. Other places to eat are *Il Giogo*, Via O. Petriccioli 44, uphill from the seafront, which has interesting seafood and home-made desserts – make sure you arrive by 8pm as it gets packed. The elegant *La Piccola Oasi*, in the minuscule old town at Via Cavour 60, offers a simple set menu.

To Tellaro

The five-kilometre stretch of coast to Tellaro, though close to some heavily developed resorts, seems worlds apart – the water is improbably clear and the coves and inlets are irresistible places to bask. If you don't feel like walking, a bus service does the trip. Halfway along the road, huge signs direct you to a path down to a shingle and sand **beach**, surrounded by wooded slopes. Next inlet along from here is sparklingly clear FIASCHERINO, accessible along Via D.H. Lawrence (he lived here just before World War I). One of the most pleasant **campsites** on the Riviera is here – take the steps inland from the car park, turn right and *Campeggio Gianna* (Easter to late Sept; ☎0187/966.411) is in front of you, set on a terraced and shaded hillside. If it's full, try *Maralunga*, 1km out of Lérici (June–Sept; ☎0187/966.589).

Ten minutes' walk from Fiascherino is the quiet fishing village of **TELLARO**, where the road ends in a cluster of bars and a couple of **places to stay** – try *Delle Ondine* (☎0187/965.131; ⑤). The rest of the village is comparatively untouched by tourism, with stone houses packed tightly on the spur of rock over the slipway, and alleyways stalked by cats. There's no beach, but you can swim off the flat rocks at the bottom of the cliff on the other side of the slipway.

Inland to Sarzana and Luni

Immediately beyond the gulf, the hills end suddenly and give way to the flatlands of the Magra estuary (the *Bocca di Magra*), an important habitat for birds. The River Magra was once the border between Liguria and Etruria, and later between the Pisans and Genoese; thus AMÉGLIA, one of the few villages here, is well fortified and set on a hill above the plain. Nearby **SARZANA** is an unremarkable lowland town, whose medieval quarter includes a fifteenth-century citadel. Check out, too, the Romanesque church of **Sant'Andrea**, rebuilt with a Rococo interior, and the **Cattedrale di Santa Maria Assunta**, which contains a twelfth-century panel painting of the Crucifixion by Maestro Guglielmo.

Still on the plain, towards the border with Tuscany, are the remains of a Roman colony at **LUNI**, the name of which comes from a cult of the moon goddess. The shipbuilding colony, founded in 177 BC, was eventually destroyed by war and malaria; finds from villas in the Bocca di Magra are on display in the **museum** (Tues–Sun summer 9am–noon & 3–7pm; winter 9am–noon & 2–5pm; L4000). The ruined amphitheatre in the *Zona Archaeologico* (same hours as museum) is a venue for theatre and music in summer – the Sarzana-to-Carrara bus passes it.

travel details

Trains

Genoa to: Alassio (17 daily; 1hr–1hr 25min); Albenga (15 daily; 1hr 10min); Bologna (8 daily; 3hr); Bordighera (15 daily; 2hr 50min); Camogli (38 daily; 30–50min); Finale Ligure (15 daily; 1hr); Imperia (15 daily; 1hr 45min); La Spezia (hourly; 1hr 10min–2hr 10min); Milan (hourly; 2hr); Naples (9 daily; 8hr); Pisa (every 2hr; 2hr 30min); Rapallo (48 daily; 30min); Rome (every 2hr; 6hr); San Remo (17 daily; 2hr–2hr 40min); Santa Margherita (40 daily; 20min–1hr); Sestri Levante (43 daily; 40min–1hr 15min); Ventimiglia (15 daily; 2hr 55min).

Buses

Albenga to: Villanova (8 daily; 15min).

Camogli to: Ruta (hourly; 25min).

Chiavari to: Rezzoaglio (6 daily; 1hr 25min); Santo Stefano d'Aveto (6 daily; 1hr 55min).

Finale Ligure to: Borghetto Santo Spirito (every 15min; 25min); La Mánie (2 daily; 25min); Ponti Romani (2 daily; 25min).

Genoa to: Montebruno (5 daily; 1hr 35min); Rovegno (5 daily; 1hr 50min); Torriglia (hourly; 1hr 10min).

Imperia Oneglia to: Pontedassio (4 daily; 15min).

La Spezia to: Lérici (every 10min; 20min); Portovenere (every 30min; 20min).

Lérici to: Ameglia (10 daily; 35min); Sarzana (every 30min; 30min); Tellaro (every 30min; 10min).

Rapallo to: Chiávari (hourly; 30min); Montallegro (every 2hr; 40min); Portofino Vetta (4 daily; 40min); Santa Margherita (every 20min; 10min).

San Remo to: Apricale (3 daily; 40min); Baiardo (4 daily; 1hr 15min).

Santa Margherita to: Portofino (every 15min; 10min).

Savona to: Sassello (8 daily; 1hr).

Ventimiglia to: Dolceacqua (11 daily; 15min); La Mortola (9 daily; 15min); Triora (3 daily; 1hr 30min).

Ferries

Genoa to: Arbatax (2 weekly; 18hr); Cágliari (2 weekly in summer; 20hr); Olbia (3–7 weekly; 13hr); Palermo (4 weekly; 23hr); Porto Torres (daily; 12hr).

CHAPTER THREE

LOMBARDY AND THE LAKES

Lombardy, Italy's richest and most developed region, often seems to have more in common with its northern European neighbours than with the rest of Italy. Given its history, this is hardly surprising: it was ruled for almost two centuries by the French and Austrians and takes its name from the northern Lombards, who invaded the region and ousted the Romans. As a border region, accessible through numerous mountain passes, Lombardy has always been vulnerable to invasion, just as it has always profited by being a commercial crossroads. It was long viewed by northerners as the capital of Italy – emperors from Charlemagne to Napoleon came to Lombardy to be crowned king – and northern European business magnates continue to take Lombardy's capital, Milan, more seriously than Rome, the region's big businesses and banks wielding political as well as economic power across the nation.

The region's landscape has paid the price for economic success: industry chokes the peripheries of towns, sprawls across the Po plain in the south, and even spreads its polluting tentacles into the northern lakes and mountain valleys. Nonetheless Lombardy has its attractions: the upper reaches of its valleys are largely unspoilt, and there's good walking to be had in the mountains; its towns and cities all retain wanderable medieval cores; and the stunning scenery and lush vegetation of the lakes make it easy to forget that the water is polluted.

As for Lombardy's people, from the cossetted snobs of the provincial towns to Milan's workaholics, they hardly fit the popular image of Italians. In fact, they don't have much time for at least half of their compatriots: urban northerners are dismissive of the south, derisive of Rome and all too ready to exploit the so-called *terrone* (literally earth-people) – a highly insulting term for southern Italians who leave their poverty-stricken villages to find work in the north.

Milan is a natural gateway to the region, and where you may well arrive, dominating the plain that forms the southern part of Lombardy. The towns across here – **Pavia**, **Cremona**, **Mantua** – flourished during the Middle Ages and Renaissance, and retain their historical character today, albeit circled by burgeoning suburbs. To the north, Lombardy is quite different, the lakes and low mountains of the edge of the Alps sheltering fewer historic towns, though **Bergamo** and **Brescia** are notable exceptions. This has long been popular tourist territory, particularly around the lakes of **Maggiore**, **Como** and **Garda**, and is the heartland of Lombardy's monied classes; the chocolate-box image of the lake scenery is these days tarnished only slightly by encroaching industry.

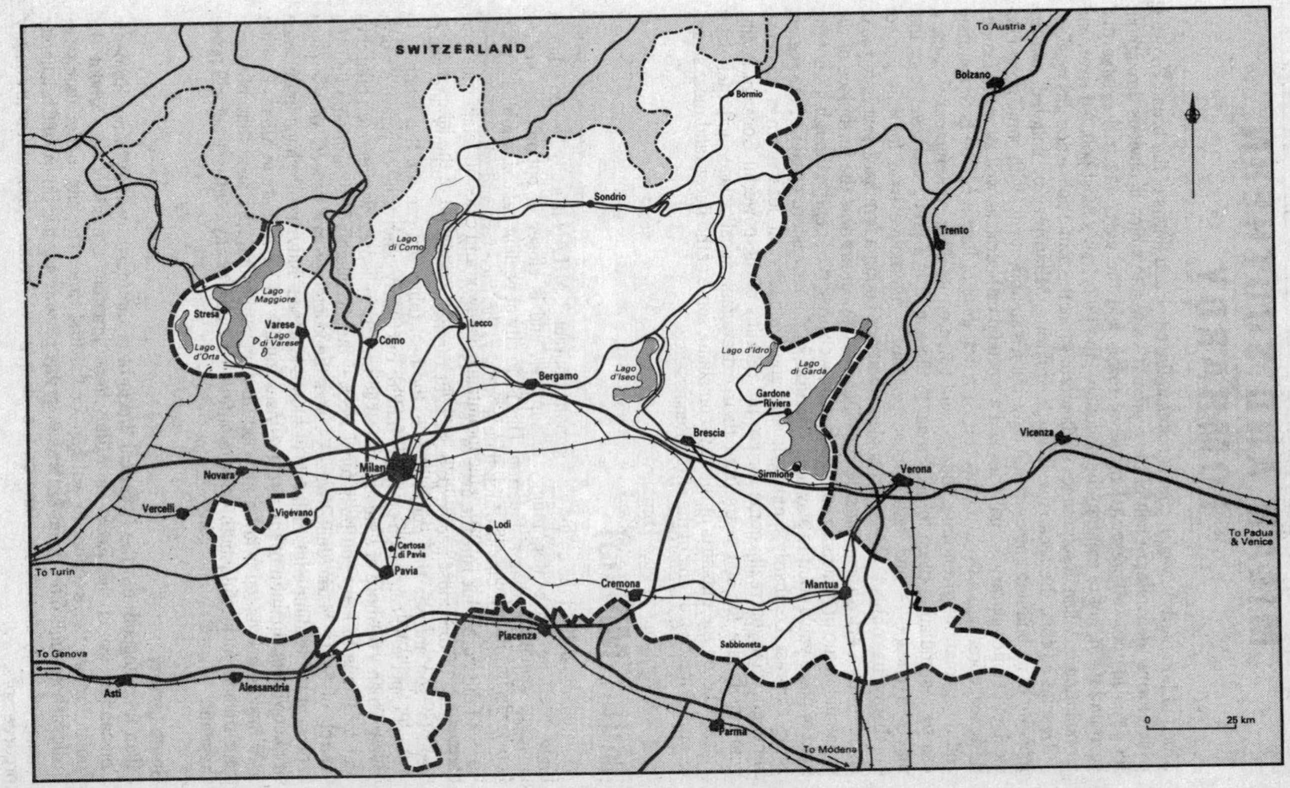
SWITZERLAND
To Austria
Bolzano
Bormio
Sondrio
Trento
Lago di Como
Lago Maggiore
Stresa
Varese
Lago di Varese
Lago d'Orta
Como
Lecco
Lago d'Idro
Lago di Garda
Bergamo
Lago d'Iseo
Gardone Riviera
Brescia
Vicenza
Milan
Novara
Vercelli
Vigevano
Sirmione
Verona
Lodi
Cartosa di Pavia
Pavia
To Turin
To Padua & Venice
Cremona
Mantua
Piacenza
Sabbioneta
To Genova
Asti
Alessandria
Parma
0
25 km
To Modena

MILAN AND SOUTHERN LOMBARDY

Much of Lombardy's wealth concentrates in the cities and towns of the broad Po plain, which forms the southern belt of the region. It's a wealth which is obvious throughout the area in the well-preserved medieval towns and the ugly industrial estates that surround them, not to mention the pollution – the Po is Italy's most polluted river, and air pollution in Milan is sometimes so dangerous that the traffic police don gas masks.

Despite all this, the area is well worth exploring. **Milan** may be polluted, and the majority of its buildings modern and ugly, but it's an upbeat city, with some great classical and contemporary art galleries and a splendid cathedral, as well as world famous designer stores and a lively nightscene. As a first taste of Italy it can be both daunting and disappointing; given time, though, and taken on its own, contemporary terms, it can be a stimulating place to be. **Pavia**, to the south, is a pretty medieval town that makes a cheaper – and rather more peaceful – alternative base for this part of Lombardy, its cobbled streets and ancient churches taking a firm back seat in terms of sights to its **Certosa**, just outside. Heading east, **Cremona** was the birthplace of the violin and home of Stradivari, and has a neat, well-preserved centre, though it's not the kind of place you'd want to stay long. **Mantua**, in the far eastern corner of the region, is by contrast Lombardy's most visually appealing city, at least from a distance, although what you really come for are the remains of the powerful Gonzaga family, who ruled here for 300 years from their extravagant ducal palace, and their later Palazzo Te, on the outskirts of the city, containing some of the finest (and most steamily erotic) fresco-painting of the entire Renaissance.

Milan (Milano)

The dynamo behind the country's "economic miracle", **MILAN** is a city like no other in Italy. It's foggy in winter, muggy in summer, and is closer in outlook, as well as distance, to London than to Palermo. This is no city of peeling palazzi, cobbled piazzas and *la dolce vita*, but one in which time is money, the pace fast, and where consumerism and the work-ethic rule the lives of its power-dressed citizens.

Because of this most people pass straight through, and if it's summer and you're keen for sun and sea this might well be the best thing you can do; the weather, in August especially, can be off-puttingly humid. But at any other time of year it's worth giving Milan a bit more of a chance. It's a historic city in its way, with enough churches and museums to keep you busy for a week – the Accademia Brera, duomo and the church of Santa Maria delle Grazie – and the contemporary aspects of the place represent the leading edge of Italy's fashion and design industry. Perhaps in defiance of the ugliness of much of the city, the visual quality of life matters in Milan. Fashion and design are taken with a passion that goes beyond the fact that they are multi-million pound industries – five minutes on a metro or city centre street will prove the point.

Some history

Milan first stepped into the historical limelight in the fourth century when Emperor Constantine issued the **Edict of Milan** here, granting Christians throughout the Roman Empire the freedom to worship for the first time. The city, under its charismatic bishop, Ambrogio (Saint Ambrose), swiftly became a major centre of Christianity – many of today's churches stand on the sites, or even retain parts, of fourth-century predecessors.

Medieval Milan rose to prominence under the ruthless regime of the Visconti dynasty, who founded what is still the city's most spectacular building, the florid late-Gothic **Duomo**, and built the first, heavily fortified nucleus of the **Castello** – which, under their successors, the Sforza, was extended to house what became one of the most luxurious courts of the Renaissance. This was a period of much building and rebuilding, notably under the last Sforza, Lodovico, who employed the architect **Bramante** to improve the city's churches and **Leonardo da Vinci** to paint *The Last Supper* and design war-machines to aid him in his struggles with foreign powers and other Italian states. Leonardo's inventions didn't prevent Milan falling to the French in 1499, marking the beginning of almost four centuries of foreign rule. Later, the Austrian Hapsburgs took control, during their time commissioning the **Teatro della Scala** and founding the **Brera** art gallery, which was filled, during Milan's short spell under Napoleon, with paintings looted from churches and private collections.

Mussolini made his mark on the city too. Arrive by train and you emerge into the massive white megalith of the central **station** built on his orders; the main tourist office is housed in one half of the pompous twin **Arengario**, from which he would address crowds gathered in Piazza Duomo. And with stark irony it was on the now major road junction of **Piazzale Loreto** that the dead dictator was strung up for display to the baying mob.

The Milan **area telephone code** is ☎02.

Arrival

Most international and domestic **trains** pull in at the main **Stazione Centrale**, north-east of the city centre on Piazza Duca d'Aosta, at the hub of the metro network on lines MM2 and MM3. Quite a few trains, especially those from stations in the Milan region – Bergamo, Pavia, Como and the other western lakes – terminate at **Garibaldi, Lambrate**, **Porta Genova** and **Nord**, all on MM2 (the metro stop for Milan Nord is "Cadorna"), although these often also stop at Centrale. International and long-distance **buses** arrive at and depart from Piazza Castello, in front of the Castello Sforzesco. Information and tickets are available from the *Autostradale* bus office on the piazza, or *Zani Viaggi* (☎867.131), on the corner of Piazza Castello and Foro Buonaparte. As for arrival **by car**, the city is encircled by a multi-laned toll road, the *Tangenzianale*, from which there are links onto the *autostradas* for Venice and Turin (A4), Genoa (A7), and the "Autostrada del Sole" (A1) for Bologna, Florence, Rome and the south.

Milan has two **airports**, both used by domestic and international traffic. The closest, **Linate**, serving mainly European flights, is just 7km from the city centre: special airport buses connect it with the air terminal on Piazza Luigi di Savoia, on the east side of Stazione Centrale, every twenty minutes between 5.40am and 7pm, and every half-hour between 7pm and 9pm; the journey takes about twenty minutes and costs L3500 one-way. Ordinary *ATM* urban transport **buses** (#73) also run every ten minutes from 5.30am until around midnight between Linate and Piazza San Babila in the city centre, and they don't take much longer; tickets cost L1100 and should be bought before you get on the bus from the airport newsagent, or, if you have change, from the ticket machine at the bus stop. The second airport, **Malpensa**, 50km away towards Lago Maggiore and serving mainly intercontinental flights, takes longer to reach: you can either take a bus direct to Stazione Centrale, an hours' journey, or catch one of the more frequent bus connections to the new air terminal at Lampugnamo station on metro line #1, a 35-minute journey – from where it's just a few stops into the centre of town. Bear in mind, too, that there's an – infrequent – connecting bus service between Linate and Malpensa.

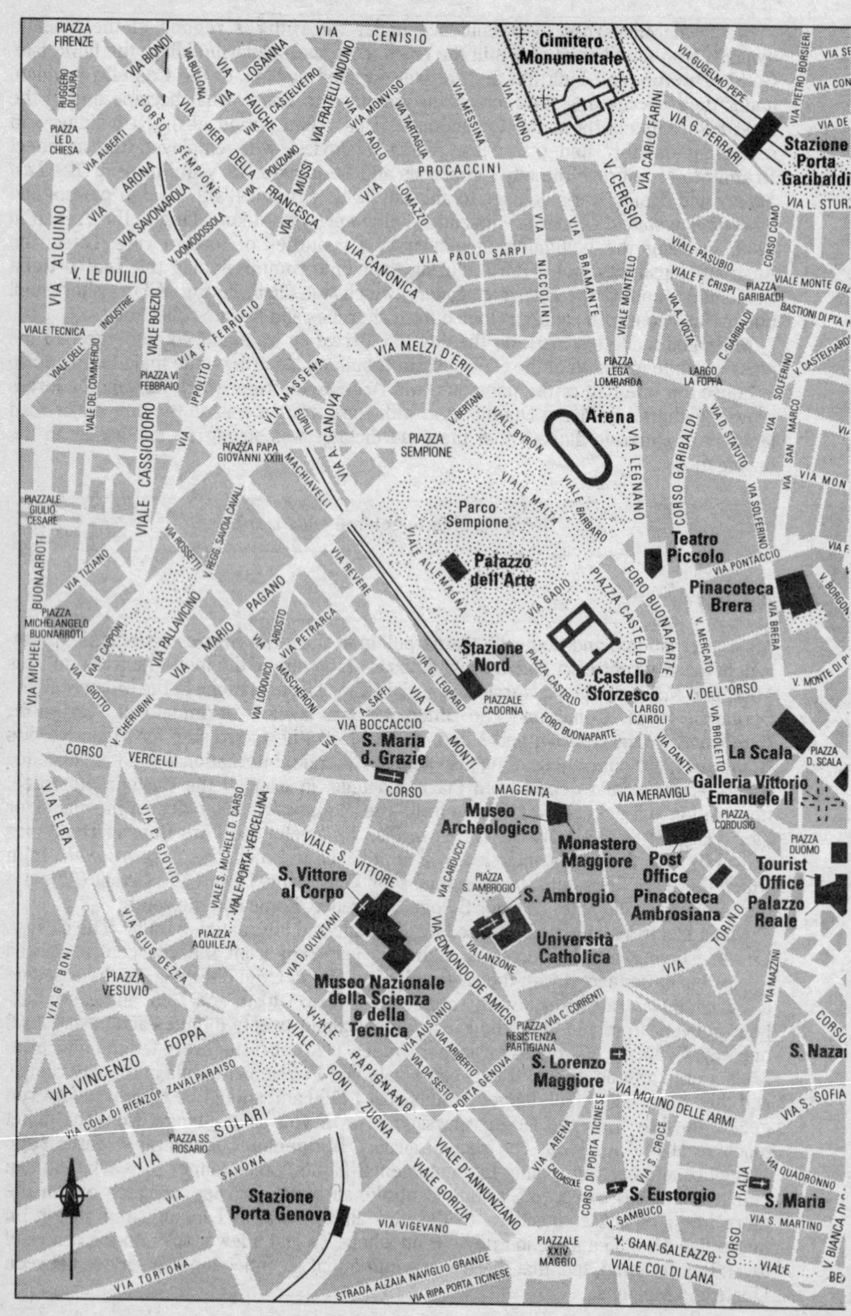
Cimitero Monumentale
Stazione Porta Garibaldi
Arena
Parco Sempione
Palazzo dell'Arte
Teatro Piccolo
Pinacoteca Brera
Stazione Nord
Castello Sforzesco
S. Maria d. Grazie
La Scala
Galleria Vittorio Emanuele II
Museo Archeologico
Monastero Maggiore
Post Office
S. Vittore al Corpo
S. Ambrogio
Pinacoteca Ambrosiana
Tourist Office
Palazzo Reale
Università Catholica
Museo Nazionale della Scienza e della Tecnica
S. Lorenzo Maggiore
S. Eustorgio
S. Maria
Stazione Porta Genova
PIAZZA FIRENZE
VIA BIONDI
VIA LOSANNA
VIA CENISIO
VIA FRATELLI INDUNO
VIA MONVISO
VIA MESSINA
VIA L. NONO
VIA CARLO FARINI
VIA G. FERRARI
VIA GUGELMO PEPE
VIA PIETRO BORSIERI
PROCACCINI
V. CERESIO
CORSO SEMPIONE
VIA ARONA
VIA SAVONAROLA
VIA ALCUINO
V. LE DUILIO
VIA PAOLO SARPI
VIA CANONICA
VIALE PASUBIO
CORSO COMO
VIALE F. CRISPI
PIAZZA GARIBALDI
VIALE MONTE GRA
VIA BRAMANTE
VIA NICCOLINI
VIALE MONTELLO
VIA MELZI D'ERIL
VIALE TECNICA
VIA BOEZIO
VIA F. FERRUCIO
PIAZZA LEGA LOMBARDA
LARGO LA FOPPA
VIA MASSENA
VIA A. CANOVA
PIAZZA SEMPIONE
VIALE BYRON
VIA LEGNANO
CORSO GARIBALDI
VIALE CASSIODORO
PIAZZA PAPA GIOVANNI XXIII
VIALE MALTA
VIALE BARBARO
VIA SOLFERINO
PIAZZALE GIULIO CESARE
VIALE ALLEMAGNA
VIA PONTACCIO
FORO BUONAPARTE
PIAZZA CASTELLO
VIA BRERA
VIA TIZIANO
VIA REVERE
VIA MARIO PAGANO
PIAZZA MICHELANGELO BUONARROTI
VIA PALLAVICINO
VIA PETRARCA
VIA G. LEOPARDI
VIA MICHEL BUONARROTI
PIAZZALE CADORNA
LARGO CAIROLI
V. DELL'ORSO
VIA BOCCACCIO
VIA DANTE
VIA BROLETTO
CORSO VERCELLI
PIAZZA D. SCALA
CORSO MAGENTA
VIA MERAVIGLI
PIAZZA CORDUSIO
VIA ELBA
VIALE S. VITTORE
PIAZZA S. AMBROGIO
PIAZZA DUOMO
VIA TORINO
PIAZZA AQUILEJA
VIA EDMONDO DE AMICIS
VIA LANZONE
VIA G. BONI
PIAZZA VESUVIO
VIA MAZZINI
PIAZZA RESISTENZA PARTIGIANA
VIA VINCENZO FOPPA
VIALE PAPIGNANO
VIA MOLINO DELLE ARMI
VIA S. SOFIA
VIA SOLARI
PIAZZA SS. ROSARIO
VIALE CONI ZUGNA
VIALE D'ANNUNZIANO
VIALE GORIZIA
CORSO DI PORTA TICINESE
VIA S. CROCE
VIA QUADRONNO
VIA SAVONA
VIA VIGEVANO
PIAZZALE XXIV MAGGIO
V. GIAN GALEAZZO
VIALE COL DI LANA
VIA S. MARTINO
VIA TORTONA
STRADA ALZAIA NAVIGLIO GRANDE
VIA RIPA PORTA TICINESE

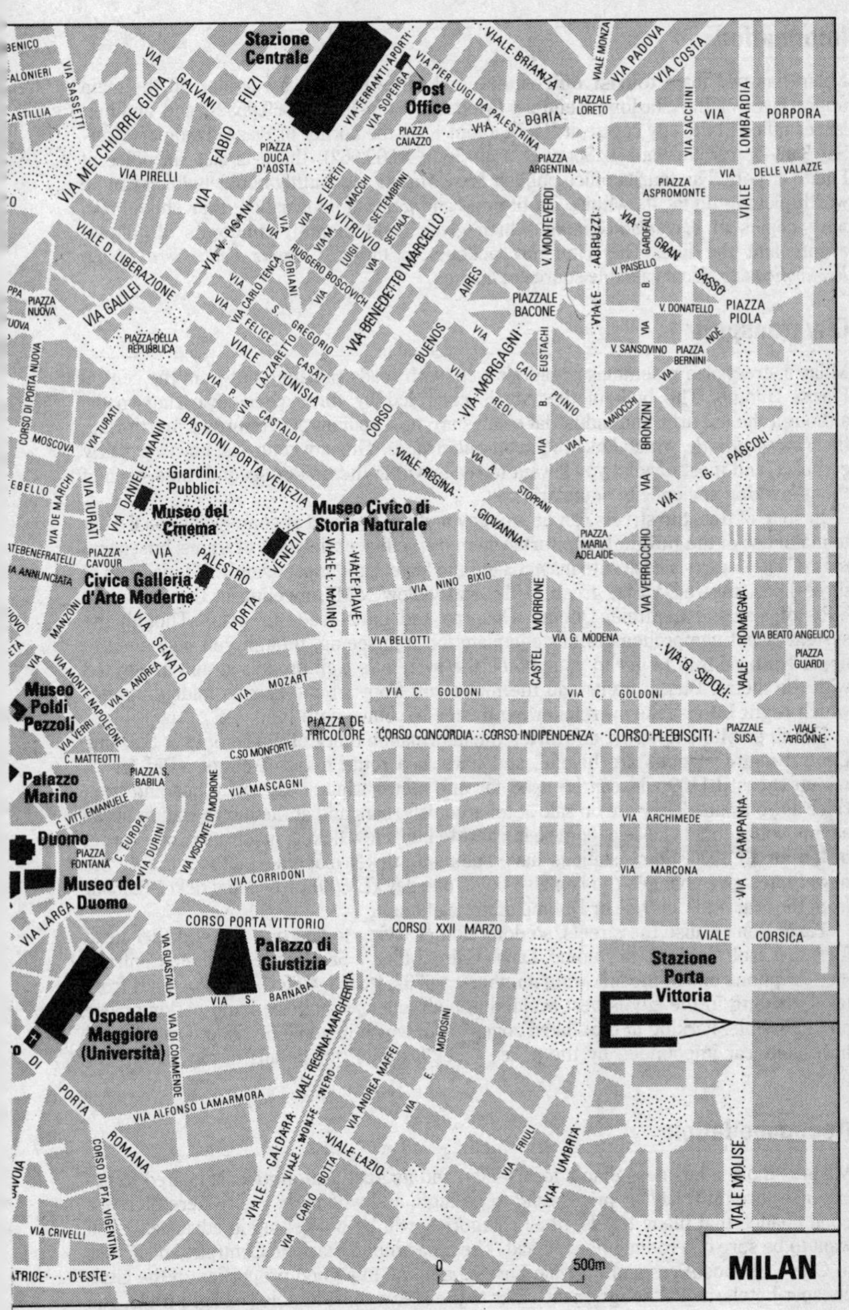
Stazione Centrale
Post Office
Museo del Cinema
Giardini Pubblici
Museo Civico di Storia Naturale
Civica Galleria d'Arte Moderne
Museo Poldi Pezzoli
Palazzo Marino
Duomo
Museo del Duomo
Palazzo di Giustizia
Ospedale Maggiore (Università)
Stazione Porta Vittoria
PIAZZA DUCA D'AOSTA
PIAZZA DELLA REPUBBLICA
PIAZZALE LORETO
PIAZZALE BACONE
PIAZZA PIOLA
PIAZZA CAVOUR
PIAZZA S. BABILA
PIAZZA FONTANA
PIAZZA DE TRICOLORE
PIAZZA MARIA ADELAIDE
PIAZZALE SUSA
VIA MELCHIORRE GIOIA
VIA PIRELLI
VIALE D. LIBERAZIONE
VIA VITRUVIO
VIA BENEDETTO MARCELLO
VIA MORGAGNI
BASTIONI PORTA VENEZIA
VIALE REGINA GIOVANNA
CORSO BUENOS AIRES
VIA PALESTRO
VIA MANZONI
VIA MONTE NAPOLEONE
VIA SENATO
CORSO PORTA VENEZIA
VIALE PIAVE
VIA NINO BIXIO
VIA C. GOLDONI
CORSO CONCORDIA
CORSO INDIPENDENZA
CORSO PLEBISCITI
C.SO MONFORTE
VIA MASCAGNI
VIA CORRIDONI
CORSO PORTA VITTORIO
CORSO XXII MARZO
VIALE CORSICA
VIA ALFONSO LAMARMORA
CORSO DI PORTA ROMANA
VIALE REGINA MARGHERITA
VIALE LAZIO
VIA UMBRIA
VIALE MOLISE
0
500m
MILAN

Information

Milan has two main **tourist offices**, one tucked away down a corridor off the main upper level of the Stazione Centrale (Mon–Sat 8am–7pm; ☎669.0532), and another, larger office in the city centre at Via Marconi 1, on the corner of Piazza Duomo (Mon–Sat 8am–8pm, Sun 9am–12.30pm & 1.30–5pm; ☎809.662); there is also an office at Linate airport. The tourist office publish *Mese Milano*, a monthly booklet which can be worth picking up for its **what's on listings** and general information; they should also have copies of *Spettacoli Milano*, which gives good monthly rundowns of cultural events and the like. The Thursday pullouts in either *Corriere della Sera* or *La Repubblica* are also a valuable source of listings.

City transport

Milan's street-plan resembles a spider's web, with roads radiating out from the central Piazza Duomo. The bulk of the city is encircled by three concentric ring roads, although the suburbs and industrial estates are now spilling out towards a fourth ring, the *Tangenzianale*, which links the main *autostradas*. The city centre is, however, fairly compact, and most of what you'll want to see is within the first or second rings, each of them marking ancient city boundaries.

In spite of this, the streets can be smoggy and packed, and at some point you'll want to make use of the **public transport** system – an efficient network of trams, buses and metro. The **metro** is easiest to master (and the fastest and most useful). It's made up of three lines, the red MM1, green MM2, and yellow MM3, meeting at the four main hubs of Stazione Centrale, Duomo, Cadorna and Lima (see our map). Though the system is not comprehensive, it's adequate for sightseeing, though you may need to use a **tram** or **bus** to get to your hotel: the system is well organised and integrated with the metro. Buses, trams and the metro run from around 6am to midnight, after which **night buses** take over, following the metro routes until 1am.

For all **public transport enquiries** the information office at the Duomo or Stazione Central metro stations are helpful, and have free route maps. **Tickets**, valid for 75 minutes, cost L1100 and can be used for one metro trip and as many bus and tram rides as you want. They are on sale at tobacconists, bars and at the metro station news-agents; most outlets close at 8pm so it's best to buy a few tickets in advance, or a carnet of ten for L11,000. Some stations have automatic ticket machines, although only the newer ones give change. You can also buy a one-day (L3800) or two-day ticket (L6600) from the Stazione Centrale or Duomo metro stations.

Taxis don't cruise the streets, so don't bother trying to flag one down. Either head for a taxi rank – on Piazza Duomo, Largo Cairoli, Piazza San Babile, Stazione Centrale, etc – or phone one of the following numbers: ☎6767, ☎5353, ☎8585, ☎8388. Apart from taxis, **driving** in the city is best avoided: the streets are congested and parking close on impossible. Parking in prohibited zones is not worth it; you'll be fined if caught and have your car impounded by the police (see "Listings" for details of city centre car parks).

Accommodation

Milan is more a business than a tourist city, and its **accommodation** is geared to the expense-account traveller: prices tend to be high, and whenever you're here there's a good chance that many hotels, of all categories, will be booked up in advance. If you want to be sure of a room, phone ahead. The area around Stazione Centrale, and across to Corso Buenos Aires and Piazzale Loreto, is home to a good proportion of the city's cheaper hotels, and although many cater to the area's considerable red light trade, you

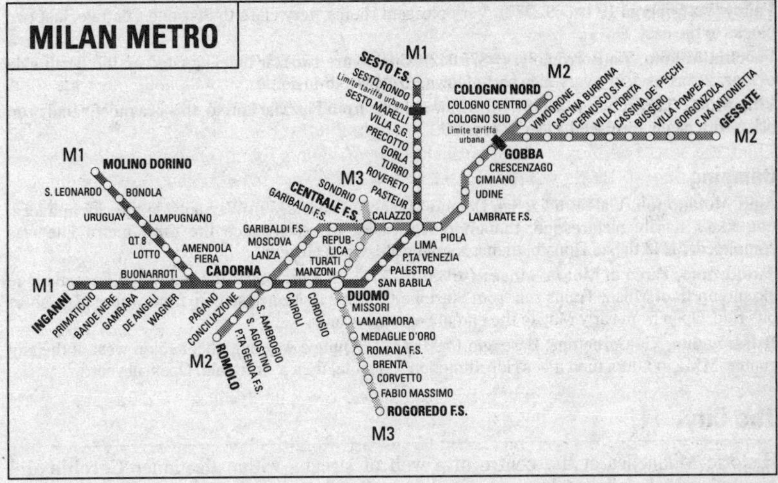

should be fine if you choose with care. We've also included a sprinkling of places in the city centre and the so-called "Città Studi" or university quarter, further east from Corso Buenos Aires.

Hostels

Ostello Piero Rotta, Via Martino Bassi 2(☎3926.7095). An official *IYHF* hostel housed in a large modern building with a garden, out in the northwest suburbs near the San Siro stadium. Open 7–9am and 5–11pm, midnight curfew. It's best to book ahead, at least in summer. MM1 to Lotto. ①.

Hotels

Antica Locanda Solferino, Via Castelfidardo 2 (☎656.905). Between the Giardini Pubblici and Parco Sempione, a fairly recently converted hotel favoured by models and lefty intellectuals. Book in advance. ⑧. MM Moscova.

Arno, Via Lazzaretto 17 (☎670.5509). Off Viale Tunisia, not far from Stazione Centrale, and packed from March to July. ⑤. Tram #4 or #11.

Arthur, Via Lazzaretto 14 (☎204.6294). Clean, spacious rooms with a touch of fading splendour. ④.

Canna, Viale Tunisia 6 (☎295.2219). Small and friendly establishment on the fifth floor of a building full of hotels. Some rooms have terraces. ④.

Città Studi, Via Saldini 24 (☎744.666). University quarter hotel that is a good deal if you get one of the rooms without bathroom. ⑦. Bus #61, #90 or #91.

Due Giardini, Via Settala 46 (☎2952.1093). Very handily placed for the station, just four blocks east down Via Scarlatti. ⑤.

London, Via Rovello 3 (☎7202.0166). Centrally placed and welcoming hotel off Via Dante, close by Castello Sforzesco, where the staff speak English. ⑥.

Rovello, Via Rovello 18a (☎8646.4654). City centre hotel, close to Castello Sforzesco, with nice rooms at two-star prices. ⑥.

San Francisco, Viale Lombardia 55 (☎236.1009). Recently renovated hotel several blocks east of Piazzale Loreto, in the student area. ⑦. Bus #56.

San Tomaso, Viale Tunisia 6 (☎2951.4747). Very popular and friendly pensione in a building full of such places. ⑤. Separate, clean bathrooms and a noticeboard crammed with testimonials from travellers.

Siena, Via P. Castaldi 17 (☎2951.4615). Stazione Centrale area hotel, with small, spotless rooms with tiled floors and shower; entrance actually on Via Lazzaretto. ⑤.

Valley, Via Soperga 19 (☎669.2777). Very pleasant rooms, very close to Stazione Centrale, just two blocks to the east. ⑤.

Vecchia Milano, Via Borromei 4 (☎875.042). City centre two-star hotel situated on the north side of Piazza Cordusio, in a very nice part of town. ⑦. MM Cordusio.

Villa Mira, Via Sacchini 19 (☎204.1618). Two blocks from Piazzale Loreto, this is a quiet, family-run place with nicely furnished, clean rooms. ④.

Camping

Agip Metanopoli, Viale Emilia, San Donato Milanese (☎537.2159). Way outside the city in a location that's hardly picturesque, though much easier to reach since the third metro line was completed. MM3 to San Donato, then a 15-min walk. Open all year.

Autodromo, Parco di Monza, Monza (☎039/387.771). In a park near the renowned Formula One circuit, north of Milan. Trains run from Stazione Centrale to Monza station, from where it's a short bus ride. Open from early May to the end of September only.

Il Bareggino, Via Corbettina, Bareggio (☎901.4417). Quite a way out, about 15km west of the city centre. MM1 to Lotto, then a bus ride, direction Magenta, then a 1km walk. Open all year.

The City

Historic Milan lies at the centre of a web of streets, within the inner **Cerchia dei Navigli**, which follows the route of the medieval city walls. **Piazza del Duomo** is perhaps the city centre's main orientation point: most of the city's major sights lie within this area, as well as the swankiest designer shops and most elegant cafés. Visits to **art galleries and museums**, the **Duomo** and other churches can be punctuated with designer window-shopping in the so-called *Quadrilatero d'Oro*, or sipping overpriced drinks among the designer-dressed clientele of the pavement cafés of the **Galleria Vittorio Emanuele** or around the **Accademia di Brera** art gallery. The second *cerchia*, the **Viali**, skirts behind the centre's two large parks – the **Parco Sempione** and **Giardini Pubblici** – to the canal sides of the **Navigli** in the south, following the tracks of defensive walls built during the Spanish occupation. Within lie the **Castello Sforzesco** and the church of **Santa Maria delle Grazie**, which has Milan's most famous painting, Leonardo's *The Last Supper*. What follows is a wedge-by-wedge account of the city: Milan is not a wanderable place, so make a judicious selection, walking a little, but where necessary hopping between places by way of the metro or other public transport.

Piazza del Duomo

The unquestioned hub of the city is **Piazza del Duomo**, a large, mostly pedestrianised square that's rarely quiet at any time of day. Harassed Milanese hurry out of the metro station deftly avoiding the pigeon-feed sellers and ice cream vendors; designer-dressed kids hang out on the steps of the cathedral; harassed tour-guides gather together their flocks; and well-preserved women stiletto-click across the square to glitzy cafés.

The **Duomo** is the world's largest Gothic cathedral, begun in 1386 under the Viscontis completed nearly five centuries later. The finishing touches to the facade were finally added in 1813, and from the outside at least it's an incredible building, notable as much for its decoration as its size and with a front that's a strange mixture of Baroque and Gothic. The marble, chosen specially by the Viscontis, comes from the quarries of Candoglia near Lago Maggiore, and continues to be used in renovation today – the fabric not surprisingly under severe attack from Milan's polluted atmosphere.

Inside the duomo, a green, almost subterranean half-light filters through the stained glass windows, lending the marble columns a bone-like hue that led the French writer Suarés to compare the interior to "the hollow of a colossal beast". By the entrance, the brass strip embedded in the pavement with the signs of the zodiac alongside is Europe's

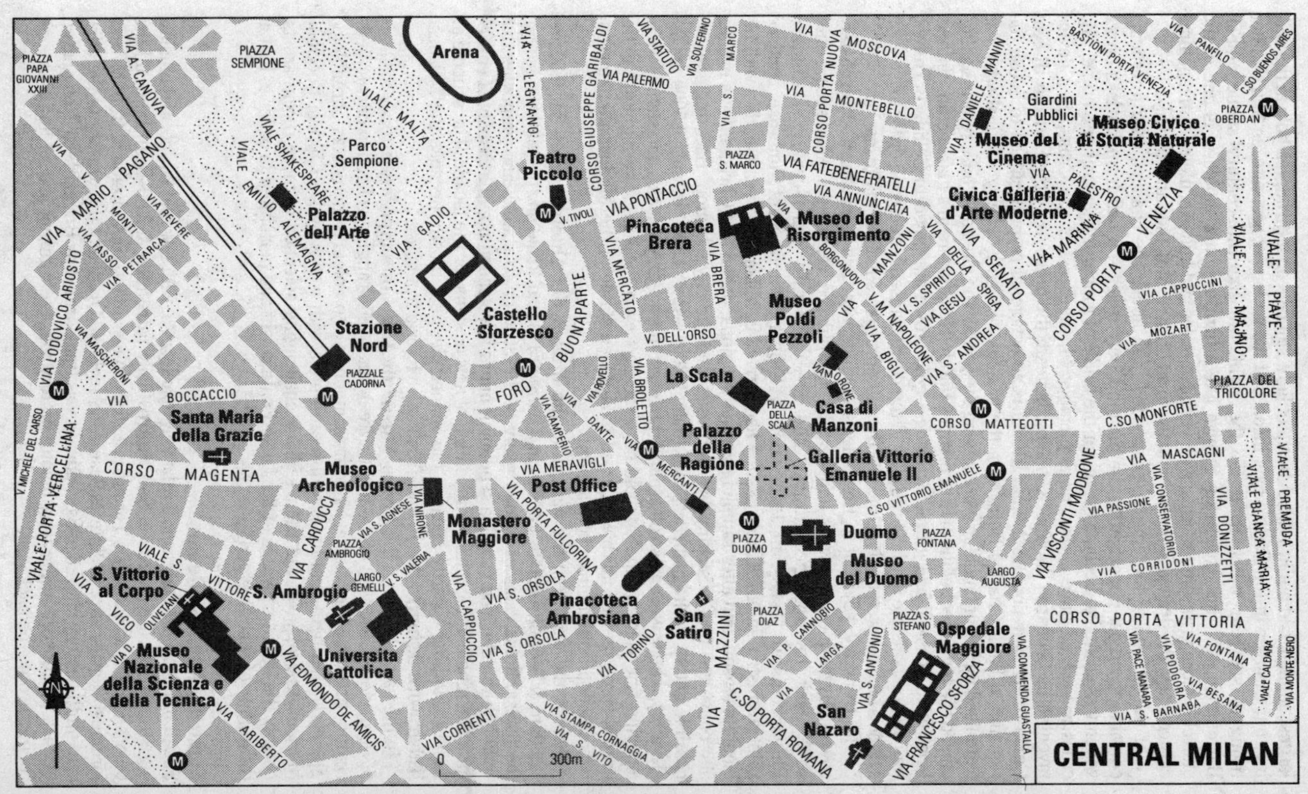
CENTRAL MILAN
Arena
Parco Sempione
Palazzo dell'Arte
Castello Sforzesco
Stazione Nord
Piazzale Cadorna
Teatro Piccolo
Pinacoteca Brera
Museo del Risorgimento
Museo Poldi Pezzoli
La Scala
Casa di Manzoni
Palazzo della Ragione
Galleria Vittorio Emanuele II
Duomo
Museo del Duomo
Piazza Duomo
Ospedale Maggiore
San Nazaro
San Satiro
Pinacoteca Ambrosiana
Post Office
Monastero Maggiore
Museo Archeologico
Universita Cattolica
S. Ambrogio
Santa Maria della Grazie
S. Vittorio al Corpo
Museo Nazionale della Scienza e della Tecnica
Giardini Pubblici
Museo del Cinema
Civica Galleria d'Arte Moderne
Museo Civico di Storia Naturale
Piazza Sempione
Piazza Papa Giovanni XXIII
Piazza S. Marco
Piazza della Scala
Piazza Fontana
Piazza Diaz
Piazza S. Stefano
Piazza Ambrogio
Piazza Oberdan
Piazza del Tricolore
Largo Augusta
Largo Gemelli
Viale Piave
Viale Majno
Viale Premuda
Viale Bianca Maria
Corso Porta Venezia
Corso Porta Vittoria
C.so Porta Romana
Corso Porta Nuova
Corso Giuseppe Garibaldi
Corso Magenta
Corso Matteotti
C.so Vittorio Emanuele
C.so Monforte
Via Manzoni
Via Brera
Via Dante
Via Torino
Via Mazzini
Via Francesco Sforza
Via Senato
Via Moscova
Via Legnano
Viale Malta
Viale Shakespeare
Viale Emilio Alemagna
Via Gadio
Foro Buonaparte
Via Carducci
Via Edmondo de Amicis
Viale Porta Vercellina
Via Lodovico Ariosto
Via A. Canova
Via Mario Pagano
Via Boccaccio
Via Meravigli
Via Porta Fulcorina
Via S. Orsola
Via Cappuccio
Via Fatebenefratelli
Via Annunciata
Via Pontaccio
Via Mercato
Via Broletto
Via Visconti Modrone
Via Donizzetti
Via Corridoni
Via Mascagni
Via Commenda Guastalla
Via Correnti
Via Stampa Cornaggia
0
300m

largest sundial, laid out in 1786. A beam of light still falls on it through a hole in the ceiling, but changes in the Earth's axis mean that it's no longer accurate, so don't bother trying to set your watch by it. To the right, the sixteenth-century statue of San Bartolomeo, with his flayed skin thrown like a toga over his shoulder, is one of the church's more gruesome statues, with veins, muscles and bones sculpted with anatomical accuracy, the draped skin retaining the form of knee, foot, toes and toenails.

At the far end of the church, suspended high above the chancel, a large crucifix contains the most important of the duomo's holy relics – a nail from Christ's cross, which was crafted to become the bit for the bridle of Emperor Constantine's horse. The cross is lowered once a year, on September 14, the Feast of the Cross, by a device invented by Leonardo da Vinci. Close by, beneath the presbytery, the **Scurolo di San Carlo** (daily 9am–noon & 2–6pm; L1000) is an octagonal crypt designed to house the remains of Saint Charles Borromeo, the zealous sixteenth-century cardinal who was canonised for his unflinching work among the poor of the city and whose reforms antagonised the higher echelons of the corrupt Church. He lies here in a glass coffin, clothed, bejewelled, masked and gloved, wearing a gold crown attributed to Cellini. Borromeo was also responsible for the large altar in the north transept, erected in order to close off a door which allowed the locals to use the cathedral as a short cut to the market.

The **treasury**, adjacent to Borromeo's resting-place, has extravagant evangelistery covers, Byzantine ivory-work and heavily embroidered vestments. After seeing this, stroll back towards the entrance and the cathedral's fourth-century **Battistero Paleocristiano** (Tues–Sun 10am–noon & 3–5pm), where Saint Ambrose baptised Saint Augustine in 387 AD. Augustine had arrived in Milan three years earlier with his illegitimate son, and after sampling various religions, pagan and Christian, was eventually converted to Christianity by Ambrose, then the city's bishop. Back outside, it's possible get up to the cathedral **roof** (daily 9.30am–4pm; L3000 to walk, L5000 for the elevator), where you can stroll around the forest of tracery, pinnacles and statues while enjoying fine views of the city and on clear days even the Alps. The highlight is the central spire, its lacy marble crowned by a gilded statue of the Madonna looking out over the bodies of the roof sunbathers.

Across the way from the cathedral, the **Museo del Duomo** (Tues–Sat 9.30am–12.30pm & 3–6pm; L5000), housed in a wing of Palazzo Reale on the southern side of the piazza, holds casts of a good many of the 3000 or so statues and gargoyles that spike the duomo. You can also see how it might have ended up, in a display of entries for a late nineteenth-century competition of new designs for the facade. The scheme all came to nothing – partly because the winner died, but mostly because the Milanese had grown attached to the duomo's distinctive hybrid frontage.

In the same building, the **Civico Museo di Arte Contemporanea** (daily 9.30am–5.30pm, closed last Mon of the month; free) has a wide-ranging collection of twentieth-century art, tastefully displayed with as much eye to colour schemes as chronology. The early twentieth century is well represented, with works by De Chirico, Boccioni, Morandi and de Pisis, but there's also a challenging selection of more recent artists, notably the bright canvases of the Lucio Fontana, slit and perforated in order to hint at the infinity of space beyond.

South of Piazza del Duomo

South of Piazza del Duomo is a relatively sparse area, with few real targets and unalluring streets. But the church of **San Satiro** (daily 9am–noon & 3.30–6pm; free), off the busy shopping street of Via Torino, is a study in ingenuity, commissioned from Milan's foremost Renaissance architect, Bramante, in 1476. Originally the oratory of the adjacent ninth-century church of San Satiro, it was transformed by Bramante to a long-naved basilica by converting the long oblong oratory into the transept and adding a trompe l'oeil apse onto the back wall.

Five minutes away, just off Via Torino at Piazza Pio 2, the **Pinacoteca Ambrosiana** – closed for restoration at time of writing but hopefully open again by now – was founded by another member of the Borromeo family, Cardinal Federico Borromeo, in the early seventeenth century. The cardinal collected ancient manuscripts, assembling one of the largest libraries in Europe, though what you come here for now is his art collection, stamped with his taste for Jan Breughel, sixteenth-century Venetians and some of the more kitschy followers of Leonardo. Among many mediocre works, there is a rare painting by Leonardo da Vinci, *Portrait of a Musician*, a cartoon by Raphael for the *School of Athens* and a Caravaggio considered to be Italy's first ever still life. The museum's quirkiest exhibit, however, is a lock of Lucrezia Borgia's hair – put for safe-keeping in a glass phial ever since Byron (having decided that her hair was the most beautiful he had ever seen) extracted one as a keepsake from the library downstairs where it used to be kept unprotected.

Cutting across Via Torino and Via Mazzini to Corso di Porta Romano, one of the city's busiest radial roads, takes you to the church of **San Nazaro** – something of a minor sight, but the severe octagonal chapel which serves as its vestibule was the family church of one of the city's better-known traitors – the condottiere Giangiacomo Trivulzio, who led the French attack on Milan to spite his rival Lodovico Sforza and was rewarded by being made the city's French governor. His tomb and those of his family are contained in niches around the walls, the inscription above Giangiacomo's reading "He who never rested now rests: silence."

Behind San Nazaro, the **Ospedale Maggiore** was once known locally as the *Ca' Granda* (Big House), an ambitious project by the Florentine architect Filarete to unite the city's numerous hospitals and charitable institutions on one site. His hopes of introducing Renaissance architecture to Milan were dampened by local architects who, as soon as Filarete returned to Florence, introduced the late-Gothic elements clearly visible on the facade. To get a clearer idea of Filarete's intentions, step inside to look at the courtyards – eight small ones formed by two crucifixes, separated by a ninth rectangular one. Today the building houses the city's university.

North of Piazza del Duomo

Almost as famous a Milanese sight as the duomo is the gaudily opulent **Galleria Vittorio Emanuele**, a cruciform glass-domed gallery designed in 1865 by Giuseppe Mengoni, who was killed when he fell from the roof a few days before the inaugural ceremony. Though the prices in its cafés are extortionate, it's worth splashing out once to indulge in some people-watching – eke your drink out for long enough and you'll see what seems like the city's whole population shove or stroll through depending on the time of day. In one of the lulls take a look at the circular mosaic of the signs of the zodiac beneath the glass cupola – it's considered good luck to stand on Taurus's testicles.

The left arm of the gallery leads towards **Piazza dei Mercanti**, the commercial centre of medieval Milan and the city's financial hub until the turn of the century, when the *Borsa* or Stock Exchange – then housed in the sixteenth-century **Palazzo dei Giureconsulti** on Via Mercanti – was moved north to Piazza degli Affari. The medieval palaces of the square were once the seats of guilds and other city organisations; now it's one of the city's more peaceful spots, dominated by the **Palazzo della Ragione** built in the early thirteenth century to celebrate Milan winning autonomy from the emperor. The upper storey was added four centuries later, by another Imperial figure, Empress Maria Theresa.

The main branch of Galleria Vittorio Emanuele leads through to Piazza della Scala and the world-famous **La Scala** opera house, designed by Piermarini and opened in 1778 with an opera by Antonio Salieri – a well-known name then, though more famous now (thanks to Peter Schaffer's play *Amadeus*) for his rivalry with Mozart than for his music. It's still to a great extent the social and cultural centre of Milan's elite, and although Sixties protests have since led to a more open official policy on the arts in Milan, remains as exclusive a venue as it ever was, with ticket prices sky-high. The small **museum** (daily 9–11.30am & 2–5.30pm, closed Sun Oct–April and when rehearsals are in progress; L5000), with its composers' death masks, plaster casts of conductors' hands, and a rugged statue of Puccini in a capacious overcoat, may be the only chance you get to see the interior.

Another big-name nineteenth-century figure lived only a block away from La Scala at Via Morone 1, just off the busy street that now bears his name. The **house of Alessandro Manzoni** (Tues–Fri 9am–noon & 2–4pm; free), who wrote *the* great Italian novel of the last century, *The Betrothed*, now contains a small museum of memorabilia, though it won't mean much if you haven't read the book.

The star attraction of this area, however, is the **Museo Poldi Pezzoli** at Via Mazoni 12 (Tues–Fri 9.30am–12.30pm & 2.30–6pm, Sat 9.30am–12.30pm & 2.30–7.30pm, Sun 9.30am–12.30pm & 2.30–6pm; L8000), comprising pieces assembled by the nineteenth-century collector, Gian Giacomo Poldi Pezzoli. Much of this is made up of rather dull rooms of clocks, watches, cutlery and jewellery, but the *Salone Dorato* upstairs contains a number of intriguing paintings, including a portrait of a portly *San Nicola da Tolentino* by Piero della Francesca, part of an altarpiece on which he worked spasmodically for fifteen years. San Nicola looks across at two works by Botticelli, one a gentle *Madonna del Libro*, among the many variations of the Madonna and Child theme which he produced at the end of the fifteenth century, the other a mesmerising *Deposition*, painted towards the end of his life in response to the monk Savonarola's crusade against his earlier, more humanistic canvases. Also in the room is one of Italy's most famous portraits, *Portrait of a Young Woman* by Pollaiuolo, whose anatomical studies are evidenced in the subtle suggestion of bone structure beneath the skin of this ideal Renaissance woman.

The Brera district and Pinacoteca di Brera

North of La Scala, **Via Brera** sets the tone for the city's arty quarter with its small galleries and art shops. There's nothing resembling an artist's garret, however: Via Brera and the streets around it are the terrain of the rich, reflected in the café prices and designer styles of those who can afford to sit outside them.

The Brera district gives its name to Milan's most prestigious art gallery, the **Pinacoteca di Brera** at Via Brera 28 (Tues–Sat 9am–5.30pm, Sun 9am–12.45pm; L8000), originally set up by Napoleon, who filled the building with works looted from the churches and aristocratic collections of French-occupied Italy, opening the museum to the public in 1809. It's a fine gallery, Milan's best by far, but it's also very large, and unless you're keen on making several exhaustive visits you need to be very selective, dipping into the collection guided by your own personal tastes.

Not surprisingly most of the museum's paintings are Italian and predate this century. The Brera does display modern work, including paintings by Modigliani, De Chirico and Carrà, but it's the Renaissance which provides the museum's core. There's a good representation of Venetian painters – works by Bonifacio and, a century later, Paolo Veronese, the latter weighing in a depiction of *Supper in the House of Simon* that got him into trouble with the Inquisition, who considered the introduction of frolicking animals and unruly kids unsuitable subject matter for a religious painting. Tintoretto's *Deposition* was more starkly in tune with requirements of the time, a scene of intense concentration and grief over Christ's body, painted in the 1560s; and Gentile Bellini's *St Mark Preaching in St Euphemia Square* introduces an exotic note, the square bustling with turbaned men, veiled women, camels and even a giraffe. There are also paintings by Gentile's follower, Carpaccio, namely *The Presentation of the Virgin* and *The Disputation of St Stephen*, while the *Pietà* by Gentile's more talented brother, Giovanni, has been deemed "one of the most moving paintings in the history of art".

Look out also for a painting by Giovanni Bellini's brother-in-law, Mantegna's *The Dead Christ*: an exercise in virtuosity really, but an ingenious one – Christ, lying on a wooden slab, viewed from the wrinkled and pierced soles of his feet upwards. Although a contemporary of Mantegna, Crivelli's work, nearby, is quite different, his paintings creating a fairyland for his pale, perfect Madonnas, hermetically sealed from the realities of time and decay.

The rooms that follow hold yet more quality work. Piero della Francesca's chill *Madonna with Angels, Saints and Federigo da Montefeltro* is the most famous painting here. But take a look too at Raphael's *Marriage of the Virgin*, whose lucid, languid Renaissance mood is in sharp contrast to the grim realism of Caravaggio's *Supper at Emmaus* – set in a dark tavern and painted a century later. Less well known but equally realistic are the paintings of Lombardy's brilliant eighteenth-century realist, Ceruti – known as *Il Pitochetto* (The Little Beggar) for his unfashionable sympathy with the poor, who stare out with reproachful dignity from his canvases. As his main champion, Roberto Longhi, said, his figures are "dangerously larger than life", not easily transformed into "gay drawing room ornaments".

Northeast from the duomo

The shopping quarter to the southeast of the Brera – the few hundred square yards bordered by Via Monte Napoleone, Via Sant'Andrea, Via Spiga and Via Borgospesso, the so-called **Quadrilatero d'Oro** – is home to the shops of all the big designer names, along with design studios and contemporary art galleries. The area is well worth a stroll, if only to observe the better-heeled Milanese searching out the perfect objet d'art for their designer pads. Indeed, to leave Milan without looking in the windows of its designer boutiques would be to miss out on a crucial aspect of the city.

Just to the north of here, the **Museo del Risorgimento** at Via Borgonuovo 23 (daily 9.30am–5.30pm, closed last Mon of the month; free) charts the course of Italian Unification through a well-presented combination of paintings, proclamations, cuttings and photographs – though as with most Italian Unification museums you need a keen knowledge of Italian (and Italian history) to appreciate it.

Along Via Fatebenefratelli from here, the heavily trafficked Piazza Cavour marks the corner of the city's oldest public park, the **Giardini Pubblici**, designed by Piermarini shortly after completing La Scala. Re-landscaped in the nineteenth century to give a more rustic look, its shady avenues and small lake are ideal for recuperating from Milan's twin doses of culture and carbon monoxide fumes. On the left side of the park, the Palazzo Dugnani houses Milan's **Museo del Cinema** in its basement (Tues–Fri 3–6pm; L4000), with an unlabelled collection of cameras, film-cutting apparatus and other equipment from the early days of cinema. The curator will do his best to persuade you to buy a catalogue, but the free leaflets are perfectly adequate, and in any case the museum isn't exactly a must. Upstairs, the **Spazio Baj** is perhaps more engaging, given over entirely to the work of the twentieth-century Milanese artist Enrico Baj, and a light-hearted change from the city's more serious museums, with primary-coloured Meccano sculptures, a series of *Personaggi* – collages using paint, glitter, card, braid and badges – aquatints for the *Hunting of the Snark* and illustrations for *Paradise Lost* – in which Adam's graffitied heart quite literally bleeds in a Picasso-meets-Disney hell inhabited by ET-like monsters. Sadly, however, it may well still be closed for restoration.

If your taste is for more conventional modern art, the **Civica Galleria d'Arte Moderne**, Via Palestro 16 (daily 9.30am–5.30pm, closed last Mon of the month; free), across the road from the park in the Villa Reale, is one of Milan's most palatable galleries, housed in Napoleon's former in-town residence, which now doubles as the civic registry office. The main building holds nineteenth-century Italian art and sculpture – striking political works by the painter Giuseppe Pellizza da Volpedo, canvases by the self-styled romantic *scapigliati* (wild-haired) movement of the late nineteenth century, impressive sculptures by Marino Marini together with a less arcane selection of paintings by Corot, Millet and various French Impressionists. Also worth a look are the works of the Futurists – Boccioni, Balla and Morandi. In the grounds, the **Padiglione d'Arte Contemporanea** (Wed–Mon 9.30am–6.30pm; free) is a venue for temporary and often prestigious exhibitions of national and international contemporary art. Overlooking the gardens, in a light airy annexe, the small **Collezione Vismara** has Picasso's *Battle of the Centaurs* – a spontaneously simple charcoal complete with finger smudges – and minor but appealing works by Matisse, Dufy and their Italian contemporaries.

On the right side of the Giardini Pubblici, the **Museo Civico di Storia Naturale**, Corso Venezia 55 (Mon–Fri 9.30am–5.30pm, Sat & Sun 9.30am–7.30pm, closed last Mon of the month; free) completes the round of museums, with a fairly predictable natural history collection. It's reckoned to be Italy's best, though really the stuffed animals and dinosaur-bits are best reserved for one of Milan's rainy afternoons.

The west: Castello Sforzesco

At the far end of Via Dante, **Castello Sforzesco** rises imperiously from the mayhem of Foro Buonaparte, a congested and distinctly un-forum-like road and bus terminus laid out by Napoleon in self-tribute. He had a vision of a grand new centre for the Italian capital, laid out along Roman lines, but he only got as far as constructing an arena, a triumphal arch and these two semicircular roads before he lost Milan to the Austrians a few years later. The arena and triumphal arch still stand behind the castle in the **Parco Sempione**, a notorious hang-out for junkies and prostitutes, while the emperor's grandiose plans for the area in front live on in name alone.

The red-brick castle, the result of numerous rebuildings, is with its crenellated towers and fortified walls one of Milan's most striking landmarks. Begun by the Viscontis, it was destroyed by mobs rebelling against their regime in 1447, and rebuilt by their successors, the Sforzas. Under Lodovico Sforza the court became one of the most powerful, luxurious and cultured of the Renaissance, renowned for its ostentatious wealth and court artists like Leonardo and Bramante. Lodovico's days of glory came to an end when Milan was invaded by the French in 1499, and from then until the end of the nineteenth century the castle was used as a barracks by successive occupying armies. A century ago it was converted into a series of museums.

The castello's buildings group around three courtyards, one of which, the Corte Ducale, formed the centre of the residential quarters which now contain the **Museo d'Arte Antica** and the **Pinacoteca del Castello** (daily 9.30am–5.30pm, closed last Mon of the month; free). The Museo d'Arte Antica holds fragments of sculpture from Milan's demolished churches and palaces, a run-of-the-mill collection saved by the inclusion of Michelangelo's *Rondanini Pietà*, which the artist worked on for the last nine years of his life. It's an unfinished but oddly powerful work, with much of the marble unpolished and a third arm (indicating a change of position for Christ's body) hanging limply from a block of stone to his right.

The first room of the **Pinacoteca**, upstairs, contains a cycle of monochrome frescoes illustrating the Griselda story from Boccaccio's *Decameron* – a catalogue of indignities inflicted by a marquis on his wife in order to test her fidelity. It was intended as a celebration of the patience and devotion of one Bianca Pellegrini, and if you decide to push on into the first room of the main picture gallery, you'll see what she looked like: Bianca was used as a model for the Madonna in a polyptych by Benedetto Bembo. In the same room are works by Bellini, Crivelli and Lippi, and one of Mantegna's last works, a dreamy evocation of the *Madonna in Glory among Angels and Saints*. There are also lots of paintings by Vincenzo Foppa, the leading artist on the Milanese scene before Leonardo da Vinci, in the next room; look out too for the polyptych by De' Tatti in which the castle makes an appearance as a fanciful setting for the crucifixion, and for Arcimboldi's bizarre *Primavera* – a portrait of a woman composed entirely of flowers, heralded as a sixteenth-century precursor of surrealism.

The castle's other museums are housed in the Sforza fortress, the **Rocchetta**, to the left of the Corte Ducale (same times). Of these, the **museum of applied arts** is of limited interest, containing wrought-iron work, ceramics, ivory and musical instruments. The small, well-displayed **Egyptian collection** in the dungeons is rather better, with impressive displays of mummies and sarcophagi, and papyrus fragments from *The Book of the Dead*. There's also a small and deftly lit **prehistoric collection**, which has as its centrepiece an assortment of finds from the Iron Age burial grounds of the Golasecca civilisation, south of Lago Maggiore.

Santa Maria delle Grazie and around

Apart from Parco Sempione, good for a wander or lakeside picnic, the area around the Castello Sforzesco has little to detain you, and there are more interesting pickings to the south, beyond the busy streets of the financial district, skirted by Corso Magenta. The **Museo Archeologico**, in the ex-Monastero Maggiore at Corso Magenta 15 (daily 9.30am–5.30pm, closed last Mon of the month; free), is well worth a visit. The displays of glass phials, kitchen utensils and jewellery from Roman Milan are compelling, and though there's a scarcity of larger objects, there is a colossal head of Jove, found near the castle, a torso of Hercules and a smattering of mosaic pavements unearthed around the city.

But what really brings visitors into this part of town is the church of **Santa Maria delle Grazie** – famous for its mural of the *Last Supper* by Leonardo da Vinci. First built as a Gothic church by the fifteenth-century architect Solari, Santa Maria delle Grazie was partially rebuilt under a dissatisfied Lodovico Sforza by the more up-to-date Bramante, who tore down Solari's chancel and replaced it with a massive dome supported by an airy Renaissance cube. Lodovico also intended to replace the nave and facade, but was unable to do so before Milan fell to the French, leaving an odd combination of styles – Solari's Gothic vaults, decorated in powdery blues, reds and ochre, illuminated by the light that floods through the windows of Bramante's dome. A side door leads into Bramante's cool and tranquil cloisters, outside of which there's a good view of the sixteen-sided drum the architect placed around his dome.

Leonardo's *Last Supper* – signposted **Cenacolo Vinciano** – covers one wall of the church's refectory (daily except Mon 9am–1.15pm; L10,000) and is one of the world's great paintings and most resonant images. Henry James likened it to an "illustrious invalid" which people visited with "leave-taking sighs and almost death-bed or tip-toe precautions"; and certainly it's hard, when you visit the painting, decayed and faded on the refectory wall and partially obscured by restorers' scaffolding, not to feel that it's the last time you'll see it. That the work survived at all is something of a miracle. Leonardo's decision to use oil paint rather than the more usual faster-drying – and longer-lasting – fresco technique led to the painting disintegrating within five years of its completion. A couple of centuries later Napoleonic troops billetted here used the wall for target practice. And in 1943 a bomb destroyed the building, amazingly leaving only the *Last Supper*'s wall standing. Well-meaning restoration over the centuries also means that little of Leonardo's original colouring has survived, but despite this the painting still retains its power. Leonardo spent two years on it, searching the streets of Milan for models. When the monks complained that the face of Judas was still unfinished, Leonardo replied that he had been searching for over a year among the city's criminals for a sufficiently evil face, and that if he didn't find one he would use the face of the prior. Whether or not Judas's face is modelled on the prior's is unrecorded, but Leonardo's Judas does seem, as Vasari wrote, "the very embodiment of treachery and inhumanity".

A couple of blocks south, the **Museo Nazionale della Scienza e della Tecnica** (daily except Mon 9.30am–4.50pm; L8000) is dedicated to Leonardo and inspired by his inventions, with reconstructions of some of his wackier contraptions, including the famous flying machine. Less compelling are the general sections of physics, astronomy, telecommunications and musical instruments, all incomprehensible to non-scientists. There are also, if you're interested in such things, collections of steam trains, aeroplanes and even an ocean liner.

The nearby church of **Sant'Ambrogio** (daily except Tues 10am–noon & 3–5pm, closed Sat afternoon; L3000) was founded in the fourth century by Milan's patron saint. Saint Ambrose, as he's known in English, is even today an important name in the city: the Milanese refer to themselves as Ambrosiani, have named a chain of banks after him, and celebrate his feast day, December 7, with the opening of the Scala season and a big street market around the church. Ambrose's remains still lie in the church's crypt, but there's nothing left of the original church in which his most famous convert, Saint Augustine, first heard him preach.

The present church, the blueprint for many of Lombardy's Romanesque basilicas, is, however, one of the city's loveliest, reached through a colonnaded quadrangle with column capitals carved with rearing horses, contorted dragons and an assortment of bizarre predators. Inside, to the left of the nave, a freestanding Byzantine pillar is topped with a "magic" bronze serpent, flicked into a loop and symbolising Aaron's rod. An ancient tradition held that on the Day of Judgment it would crawl back to the Valley of Jesophat. Look, too, at the pulpit, a superb piece of Romanesque carving decorated with reliefs of wild animals and the occasional human, most of whom are intent upon devouring one another. There are older relics further down the nave, notably the ciborium, reliefed with the figures of saints Gervasius and Protasius – martyred Roman soldiers whose clothed bodies flank that of Saint Ambrose in the crypt. A nineteenth-century autopsy revealed that they had been killed by having their throats cut. Similar investigations into Saint Ambrose's remains restored the reputation of the anonymous fifth-century artist responsible for the mosaic portrait of the saint in the Capella di San Vittorio in Ciel d'Oro (to the right of the sacristry). Until then it was assumed that Ambrose owed his skewwhiff face to a slip of the artist's hand, but the examination of his skull revealed an abnormally deep-set tooth, suggesting that his face would indeed have been slightly deformed.

Outside (entrance to the left of the choir) is Bramante's unfinished **Cortile della Canonica**. The side that Bramante did complete, a novel concoction incorporating knobbled "tree trunk" columns and a triumphal arch, was shattered by a bomb in the last war and reconstructed from the fragments. The second side was added only in 1955 and leads to a modest museum whose only memorable exhibit is Saint Ambrose's bed.

South of the centre: Navigli and Ticinese

Flanking the city's two canals, just south of the *Cerchia Viali*, the streets of the **NAVIGLI** quarter feel a long way from the city centre, their peeling houses and waterside views much sought after by the city's would-be Bohemians. A thriving inland port from the fifteenth century until the 1950s, the Naviglio Pavese – which links Milan with Pavia – and the Naviglio Grande – which runs to the west – are part of a network of rivers and canals covering the whole of Italy's northern plain, making ports or even naval bases of land-locked cities. They were also much used by travellers: the ruling families of the north used them to visit one another, Prospero and Miranda escaped along the Navigli in *The Tempest*, and they were still being used by Grand Tourists in the eighteenth century; Goethe, for example, describes the discomfort and hazards of journeying by canal. These days there's not much to do other than browsing in its artists' studios and antique shops, but it's a peaceful area, good for idle strolling, and at night its bars and clubs are among the city's best.

Back towards the centre, the **TICINESE** is another arty district, though as yet less a prey to the yuppie invasion than Navigli. On the edge of the quarter, at the bottom of Corso di Porta Ticinese, the nineteenth-century **Arco di Porta Ticinese** is an Ionic gateway on a noisy traffic island built to celebrate Napoleon's victory at Marengo – and, after his demise, dedicated to peace. Walking up the Corso, the only obvious signs of trendification are a scattering of secondhand clothes shops and the occasional club, and the musty decadence makes it one of Milan's more intriguing areas.

Ticinese also boasts two important churches. The first, **Sant'Eustorgio**, at the bottom end of the Corso, was built in the fourth century to house the bones of the Magi, said to have been brought here by Saint Ambrose. It was rebuilt in the eleventh century and virtually destroyed by Barbarossa in the twelfth century, who seized the Magi's bones and deposited them in Cologne Cathedral. Some of them were returned in 1903 and are kept in a Roman sarcophagus in the right transept. The main reason for visiting the church, however, is to see the **Portinari Chapel** commissioned from the Florentine architect Michelozzi in the 1460s by one Portinari, an agent of the Medici bank, to house the remains of Saint Peter the Martyr. Peter, one of Catholicism's less attractive saints, was banned from the Church for allegedly entertaining women in his cell, then cleared of the charge and given a job as an Inquisitor. His death was particularly nasty – he was axed in the head by a member of the sect he was persecuting – but the martyrdom led to almost immediate canonisation and the dubious honour of being deemed Patron of Inquisitors. The simple geometric design of the chapel has been credited with being Milan's first real building of the Renaissance, although it was Bramante who really developed the style. Inside, you are treated to scenes from the life of Saint Peter in frescoes by Foppa and reliefs carved on the sides of his elaborate tomb.

Further up the Corso, the fourteenth-century **Porta Ticinese** and sixteen Corinthian columns – **the Colonne di San Lorenzo**, scavenged from a Roman ruin – stand outside the church of **San Lorenzo**. It's an evocative spot – an odd contrast with the backdrop of grubby bars and rattling trams – and *the* place to hang out at night before hitting the Navigli and Ticinese clubs and bars. San Lorenzo, apparently considered by Leonardo da Vinci to be the most beautiful church in Milan, was founded in the fourth century, when it was the largest centrally planned church in the western Roman Empire. The current structure is a sixteenth-century renovation of an eleventh-century rebuilding, a shaky edifice under threat from the vibrating tramlines outside. Inside, the most interesting feature is the **Capella di San Aquilino** (usually locked, but the sacristan will open it), much of which has survived from the fourth century. There are fragments of fourth-century mosaics on the walls, including one in the left apse where the tiles have crumbled away revealing the artist's original sketches. Behind the altar steps lead down to what is left of the original foundations, a jigsaw of fragments of Roman architecture looted from an arena.

Eating

Food in workaholic Milan, at lunchtime at least, is more of a necessity than a pleasure, with the city centre dominated by *paninotece* and fast-food outlets. Don't despair, however: there are plenty of good-value – and some extremely *good* – restaurants here, and you can eat as well and as reasonably as in any other part of Italy.

Food markets and supermarkets

For real low-budget eating, there are **street markets** every day except Sunday scattered through the city, selling all the cheese, sausage and fruit you need for a picnic lunch. A complete list is given daily in the *Corriere della Sera* under the heading "Mercati". The most central **supermarkets** are *Standa* at Via Torino 37 and in Piazza Castello, and *Esselunga* at Viale Piave 38, near Porta Venezia.

Snacks, lunch, fast food

Amico, Piazza Duomo 5; Piazza San Babila; Piazza Cinque Giornate; Corso Beunos Aires at Piazza Lima. Chain of self-service restaurants that has several branches around the city centre.

Brek, Via del Duca 5; Corso Italia 3; Via Lepetit 20. Chain of good-value self-service restaurants with an excellent choice of salads and freshly cooked main courses.

Ciao, Via Dante, on the corner with Via Meravigli; Corso Europa 12; Corso Buenos Aires 7; Via Fabio Filzi 8. Citywide chain with good, reasonably priced food.

Crota Piemunteisa, Piazza Beccaria 10. Centrally placed bar and *paninoteca* with a vast array of chunky sandwiches, and wooden tables to eat and drink at.

Italy & Italy, Largo Carrobio; Corso Buenos Aires 7; Corso Venezia 7. Another chain, good for spaghetti, pizza and sparkling wine.

Latteria Unione, Via Unione 6, near the church of San Satiro on Via Torino (lunchtime only). Good for vegetarians.

Panini Giusto, Corso Garibaldi 125. Popular place on the edge of the Brera district that serves a huge selection of sandwiches. A good lunch stop between sights.

Spontini, Via Spontini 2. One kind of pizza only: tomato, cheese and anchovies on a thick, soft base served in various sized portions. Great value, and open lunchtime for lasagne as well as pizza. MM Lima or Loreto.

Restaurants

Though many restaurants in the **centre** of Milan are pricey, expense-account places, there are a few survivors from a time when the city wasn't dominated by the fashion crowd and business execs. Just outside the immediate centre, the **Ticinese** and **Navigli** areas are full of restaurants and cafés selling food; we've also included a number of options in around **Stazione Centrale and Piazzale Loreto**, since this is the part of town you're most likely to be staying in, as well as a handful of places that are simply worth going a little bit out of your way for.

CITY CENTRE

Le Briciole, Via Campieri 17. Convivial place off Piazza Castello that offers reasonable pizzas, straight meals, and a great antipasto table, not to mention a bustling atmosphere.

La Bruschetta, Piazza Beccaria 12. Two minutes from Piazza Duomo and always packed, so expect a long wait. Good location, and decent pizzas at moderate prices, and a free *bruschetta* when you eventually get a table. MM San Babila or Duomo.

Al Cantinone, Via Agnello 19. Famous old trattoria and bar, with homemade pasta, grilled meat dishes and choice wine. Not exactly leisurely dining, but good, moderately priced food – and you couldn't get more central.

Grande Italia, Via Palermo 5. Centrally placed lively restaurant serving good and well-priced pizza and *foccacce*, cooked on a wood-burning oven, as well as delicious various daily specials. Recommended.

Nabucco, Via Fiori Chiari 10. Chic little restaurant, simply furnished, whose menu encompasses a wide range of salads, imaginative fish dishes, and home-made pastries and puddings. Moderately priced.

Spaghetteria Enoteca, Via Solferino 3. Located under a clothes shop, and perhaps the cheapest place to sit down and fill up in the Brera area, with main meals for around L10,000. Closes at 7.30pm, though.

Ungherese, Largo La Foppa 5. Home-style Hungarian food in small, unpretentious surroundings, though not cheap. MM Moscova.

STAZIONE CENTRALE, PIAZZALE LORETO, AND AROUND

Abele, Via Temperenza 5. A warm, smoky atmosphere, and open until late. Risottos a speciality. Evenings only. MM Pasteur.

I Delfini, Via Lecco 7. Not worth going out of your way for, but a good choice in the Stazione Centrale area, with OK pizzas and a good antipasto bar.

Da Franco, Via Donatello 5. Tiny trattoria much frequented by students from the nearby architecture faculty. Menu always includes some fish. Last orders at 9.30pm. MM Loreto or Piola.

La Gardenia, Via P. Castaldi 4. Homely trattoria, family-run, that does good home-cooked food at low prices. Again, handy if you're staying in the station area.

La Giara, Viale Monza 10. Supremely affordable Pugliese restaurant with a very limited menu – good antipasti, grilled meats, home-made Pugliese bread and hearty wine. Eat at wooden tables and benches, which you'll have to share when things get busy.

Pasta e Fagioli, Via Venini 54. The speciality here, as the name suggests, is pasta and beans, but give their *scamorza* a go too – mozzarella grilled to a pleasant gooiness on the fire.

TICINESE/NAVIGLI AND AROUND

Artisti, Corso di Porta Ticinese 16. Near the San Lorenzo columns, a lunchtime favourite with workers and usually crowded with locals at night. Closed Sun.

Da Giulio, Corso San Gottardo 38. Lively local haunt, just off the Navigli Grande, that's both a takeaway joint and an ordinary sitdown restaurant. Has a huge array of different fish and seafood dishes, pizzas, roast chicken, polenta, etc. Good for lunch.

Mergellina, Via Molino delle Armi 48. Busy place around the corner from Porta Ticinese that serves decent pizza at low prices.

Osteria Briosca, Via Ascanio Sforza 13. Reasonably priced Ticinese restaurant with a pleasant, woody atmosphere and occasional live music.

Veneta, Corso di Porta Romana 103. Friendly place ten minutes' walk east of Corsa Porta Ticinese that specialises in Venetian food.

FURTHER AFIELD...

Rino Vecchia Napoli, Via Chevez 4. Off the beaten track, but worth the effort of getting there: Rino won the European Pizza Championship a few years ago. Good prices and a massive choice. Tram #33 or bus #56.

Rondine, Via Spartaco 2. Way out of the city centre, but with a chef from one of the most famous city restaurants. Traditional dishes, along with some more creative ones, in simple, homely surroundings. Try to get there early. Bus #84.

Stalingrado, Via Biondi 4. Long-standing politically orientated eatery that caters to a young clientele and is also open as a pub. Reasonable prices and small outside eating area for the summer. Bus #61 or #78.

Nightlife: bars, clubs, live music

Milan has perhaps Italy's best **nightlife**. This centres on two main areas: the streets around the Brerà gallery, and the canal-side Navigli and the adjacent Ticinese quarter, south of the city, where there are any number of lively bars, restaurants and night clubs, some hosting regular live bands.

The hippest time to frequent the city's **clubs** is midweek, particularly on Thursdays – at weekends out-of-towners flood in and any self-respecting Milanese trendy either stays at home or hits a bar. Many places have obscure door policies, often dependent on the whim of the bouncer; assuming you get in, you can expect to pay L15–25,000 entry, which usually includes your first drink. As for **live music**, Milan scores high on jazz, and the rock scene is relatively good by Italian standards: there are regular gigs by local bands, and the city is a stop on the circuit for big-name touring bands.

There are comprehensive **what's on listings** in the local pages of *Corriere della Sera* and *La Repubblica* on Thursdays. Look, too, in *Spettacoli Milano*, available from the tourist office, or their own *Mese Milano*.

Cafés, bars and pubs

Bar Magenta, Via Carducci 13. Twenties' decor, extremely trendy, and usually packed. Good for sandwich lunches as well as late-night drinks.

Osteria del Pallone, Via Gorizia, corner Alzaio Naviglio Grande. Old-fashioned and sometimes raucous *osteria* right on the canal.

Pois, Via Pioppette 1a. Right by the Colonne di San Lorenzo, a large trendy bar that has been around for years.

Portnoy, Via de Amicis 1. On the corner of Corso di Porta Ticinese, this is a hi-tech trendy café with regular poetry readings, art exhibitions and the like. Rather precious...

Racana Pub, Via Sannio 18. British-style pub with real ale and Guinness on draft; go there if you're feeling homesick. Out of the centre, though – bus #90 or #91.

Camparino, Piazza Duomo 21. Probably Milan's oldest bar, and the original inventor of Campari. Prices are high even by Milanese standards.

Venues and clubs

Capolinea, Via Lodovico Il Moro 119 (☎8912.2024). Founded in 1969, this place is a jazz milestone where all the best performers, Italian and foreign, have played. Named for the terminal (capolinea) of tram #19.

Club Due, Via Formentini 2 (☎873.533). Small club with a piano bar upstairs and jazz in the smoky cellar. Cocktails, champagne and wine, and pasta served until 2.30am.

City Square, Via Castelbarco 11-13 (☎5831.0682). Medium-sized venue south of the city centre, close to the Navigli canals, that hosts regular rock bands.

Hollywood, Corso Como 15 (☎659.8996). Long-established club that's popular with a trend-setting media crowd.

Leoncino, Corso Garibaldi 50 (☎802.315). Brazilian basement club with rum cocktails, milkshakes and coconut cakes.

Magia Music Meeting, Via Salutati 2 (☎481.3553). Small basement venue for new and upcoming bands.

Plastic, Viale Umbria 120 (☎743.674). Club with live and recorded music that hosts a Gothic and punky crowd.

Prego, Via Besenzanica 3 (☎4407.5653). A disco that sometimes has gigs. Each night of the week tends to host a different type of music.

Rolling Stone, Corso XXII Marzo 32 (☎733.172). Enormous hall, very loud music, sometimes used as a venue by big-name rock bands.

Scimmie, Via Ascanio Sforza 49 (☎8940.2874). Ticinese club that is one of Milan's most popular venues, with a different band every night and jazz-fusion predominating. Small, noisy and smoky. A restaurant too.

Zelig, Viale Monza 140 (☎255.1774). A slightly pretentious and overpriced venue for arty happenings, cabaret, theatre, and the like.

Opera, theatre, cinema

Many of Milan's tourists have just one reason for coming to the city – **La Scala**, Via dei Filodrammatici 2 (box office open daily 10am–1pm & 3–6pm; ☎7200.3744; fax 887.9297), one of the world's most prestigious opera houses. The opera season runs from December through to July, and there's usually also a season of classical concerts between September and November. Not surprisingly, seats for the opera sell out months in advance, though you can try and get something by writing direct to the box office, enclosing the price of a ticket in an international reply-paid coupon – this will be returned if the seats you want aren't available. There is also often a reasonable chance of picking up a seat in the gods on the day, or one of around 200 standing places; get there an hour or so before the performance starts – and good luck.

Of Milan's **theatres**, the *Teatro Piccolo* , Via Rovello 2 (☎877.663), is a classical theatre, with a traditional repertoire, and is reckoned to be one of Italy's best. *Teatro dell'Elfo*, Via Ciro Menotti 11 (☎5831.5896), reachable on bus #60, puts on more original plays. Count on paying around L30,000 for a seat at either of these places.

As for **cinema**, the *Angelicum*, Piazza Sant'Angelo 2 (☎659.2748; bus #61), shows films in the original language, usually English, often before their British release, as do the *Anteo*, Via Milazzo 9 (☎659.7732), and the *Mexico*, Via Savona 57 (☎799.913).

Listings

Airlines *Alitalia*, Via Albricci 7 (☎62.81); *Aer Lingus*, Galleria Passarella 2 (☎783.565); *American Airlines*, Piazza della Repubblica 28 (☎655.7720); *Air Canada*, Via Pisacane 44 (☎270.829); *British Airways*, Corso Italia 8 (☎809.041); *Qantas*, Piazza Velasca 4 (☎807.441).

Airport enquiries Linate ☎738.0233; Malpensa ☎749.1141.

America Express Via Brera 3 (☎85.571).

Books The *American Bookstore*, on Largo Cairoli, is probably the best source of English-language books in the city centre.

British Council Via Manzoni 38 (library open Mon 2–6pm, Tues–Thurs 10am–7.30pm, Fri 10am–6pm; ☎702.016).

Bus enquiries ☎801.161.

Car rental *Avis*, *Europcar*, *Hertz* and *Maggiore* all have desks at Stazione Centrale, and at both airports.

Car parks Central car parks include *Autosilo Diaz*, Piazza Diaz 6, just south of Piazza Duomo, *Garage Traversi*, on Via Bagutta, close to Piazza San Babila, and *Autosilo Comunale*, Via Pirelli 39, near Stazione Centrale.

Consulates *Australia*, Via Borgogna 2 (☎7601.3330); *Canada*, Via V. Pisani 19 (☎669.7451); *UK*, Via San Paolo 7 (☎723.001); *USA*, Largo Donegani 1 (☎2900.1841).

Doctors English-speaking doctors: Dr A. Ferrario, Via Tibaldi 17 (☎835.8494, 4–7pm only); Dr B. Sturlese, Via Sant'Eufemia 19 (☎805.783); Dr G. Dabbah, Via Pirandello 4 (☎469.6223).

Exchange Out of normal banking hours you can change money and travellers cheques at the Stazione Centrale office (Mon–Sat 8am–6.30pm, Sun 9am–1pm); there are also exchange facilities at both airports.

Football Milan's two teams are *Inter Milan* and *AC Milan*, who play on alternate Sundays at the San Siro stadium, Via Piccoliminni 5 (☎4870.7123), MM Lotto, then a longish walk. You can buy tickets from *Milan* games from branches of *Cariplo* banks (☎88.661), and from "Milan Point", on Largo Corsia die Servi, and for *Inter* games from branches of *Banca Popolare Milano* (☎77.001).

Gay Milan Milan is something of a focus for gays, with Italy's only gay bookshop, the *Babel Bookshop*, Via Sammartini 21. Run by a Milan-based gay publishing house, *Babilonia*, it issues a monthly magazine of the same name and makes for a good meeting-place for gay men. *Querelle*, Via de Castillia 20, is a gay bar with snacks and music; *After Dark*, Viale Certosa 134, is a disco/restaurant, with a mainly young crowd. *Nuova Idea*, Via de Castiesa 30, is the biggest gay disco in Italy; *No Ties*, Foro Buonoparte 68 (Wed–Sun 11pm–3am), is a disco-cum-restaurant whose theme is the prohibition of ties.

Hospital There is a 24-hour casualty service at the *Ospedale Maggiore Policlinico*, Via Francesco Sforza 35 (☎551.1655), a short walk from Piazza Duomo.

Laundry There's a coin-operated laundry in the Brera district, Via Anfiteatro 9. Otherwise the *tintoria* on Via Tadati, off Via Casati, which is off Corso Buenos Aires, does a full wash and dry for L11,000.

Pharmacy There is a 24-hour service in Stazione Centrale (☎669.0735), with English-speaking assistants. *Bracco*, Via Boccaccio 26 (☎469.5281), and *Duomo*, on Piazza Duomo (☎872. 2666), are sometimes open all night. Rotas are published in *Corriere del Sera*, and are usually posted on *farmacia* doors.

Police Phone ☎113. Head office at Via Fatebenefratelli 11 (☎62.261), near the Brera.

Post office Via Cordusio 4, off Piazza Cordusio – not the building marked "Poste", but around the corner (Mon–Fri 8.15am–7.40pm, Sat 8am–5.40pm, closed Sun). Telephones 7am–12.45pm.

Shopping The "Quadrilatero d'Oro" – Via Monte Napoleone and around – is the place for the big fashion designers, should you be able to afford their sky-high prices, while on the peripheries are youth-orientated shops like *Fiorucci* on Piazza San Babila; Corso Buenos Aires is home to most of the more middle-range clothes stores and chains. You can get designer cast-offs at the (early) Saturday morning market on Viale Papiniano, near the Porta Genova train station. If you're on a budget, and can't make the Papiniano market, check out the *blochisti*, or warehouses selling last season's lines at half-price; try *Gastone*, Via Vanzetti 20, *Niki*, Via Fontane 19, Zona Tribunale, or *Il Salvagente*, on Via Bronzetti.

Swimming pools *Cozzi*, Viale Tunisia 35 (☎659.9703), is perhaps the most convenient place if you're dying for a swim, close to Stazione Centrale. There's also the *Lido di Milano*, Piazzale Lotto 15 (☎36.61.00), which has both indoor and open-air pools.

Telephones International calls can be made either from the main post office (see above) or the SIP office in Galleria V. Emanuele II (daily 8am–9.30pm).

Train enquiries The Stazione Centrale office is open daily 7am–10pm (☎67.500); Stazione Nord (☎851.1608); Porta Genova (☎5810.0143); Porta Garibaldi (☎655.2708).

Travel agents *CTS*, Corso P. Ticinese 83 (☎837.2674), are the best source of train tickets, discounted flights, etc.

Women By Italian standards, Milan is not a difficult city for women. The *Libreria delle Donne* at Via Dogana 2, close to the Duomo, sells feminist literature and has information on womens' groups, events and publications. *Cicip e Ciciap*, Via Gorani 9, is a women-only café/bar/restaurant with occasional exhibitions and readings. There's also a women-only disco at *Sottomarino Giallo*, Via Donatello 2.

South of Milan: Pavia and Vigévano

Furthest west of the string of historic towns that spread across the Lombardy plain, **Pavia** and **Vigévano** are close enough to Milan to be seen on a day trip, but still retain clear identities of their own. Pavia, certainly, should not be missed if you're in Milan for any length of time, and conversely could also serve as a feasible and perhaps more palatable base for seeing the larger city. Vigévano is more of a backwater, and as such hardly a place to stay, but its central Renaissance square and ramshackle castle could make a pleasant half-day out from either Pavia or Milan.

Pavia

Medieval **PAVIA** was known as the city of a hundred towers. And although only a handful remain – one of the best collapsed last year, killing four people – the medieval aspect is still strong, with numerous Romanesque and Gothic churches tucked away in a wanderable web of narrow streets and cobbled squares. The town is not, however, stranded in the past – its ancient university continues to thrive, ensuring an animated street life and reasonably lively night scene.

Pavia reached its zenith in the Dark Ages when it was capital of the Kingdom of the Lombards. After their downfall it remained a centre of power, and the succession of emperors who ruled north Italy continued to come to the town to receive the Lombards' traditional iron crown. This all came to an end in the fourteenth century when Pavia was handed over to the Viscontis and became a satellite of Milan. The Viscontis, and later the Sforzas, did however found the university and provide the town with its prime tourist attraction – the Certosa di Pavia.

Arrival, information and accommodation

Regular trains make the half-hour journey between Pavia and Milan, but connections from Pavia to the other cities of the Lombardy plain are infrequent and slow. Once here, the centre is small and walkable and buses #3 and #6 connect the train station on the western edge of the town centre with the centre – or it's about a ten-minute walk. The **tourist office** is near the station – turn left as you leave, then right – at Via F. Filzi 2 (Mon–Sat 9.30am–12.30pm & 2.30–6pm; ☎0382/22165), and has maps of the town and other information.

Pavia's few **hotels** tend to get filled with the overspill from Milan's commercial fairs, and finding somewhere to stay can be more difficult than you might imagine, especially as there are very few cheap options. The only really reasonable alternatives are the *Splendid*, Via XX Settembre 11 (☎0382/24.703; ④), and the *Aurora*, Via Vittorio

Emanuele 25 (☎0382/23.664; ⑤). There is also a **campsite**, open from May to September, the *Ticino*, Via Mascherpa 10 (☎0382/525.362) – take bus #4 from the train station – but to be honest you'd probably be better off staying in Milan and seeing Pavia on a day trip.

The Town

It's Pavia as a whole which appeals, rather than any specific sight. Just wandering around town is the nicest way to spend time here: pick any side street and you're almost bound to stumble on something of interest – a lofty medieval tower, a pretty Romanesque or Gothic church, or just a silent, sleepy piazza. Getting lost is difficult, as long as you bear in mind that the centre is quartered by the two main streets.

One piazza that is neither sleepy nor silent is the central **Piazza della Vittoria**, a large cobbled rectangle surrounded by tatty buildings housing bars, *gelaterie* and restaurants. Steps lead down to an **underground market,** while at the square's right end the **Broletto**, medieval Pavia's town hall, abuts the rear of the rambling and unwieldy **Duomo** – an early Renaissance sprawl of protruding curves and jutting angles that was only finally completed in the 1930s. The west front of the duomo, facing **Piazza del Duomo**, is in the process of being restored following the collapse of the adjacent Torre Civica in March 1989, which killed four people.

The best of the town's churches is the Romanesque **San Michele**, a five-minute walk away on Via Cavallotti. The friezes and capitals on its broad sandstone facade are carved into a menagerie of snake-tailed fish, griffins, dragons and other beasts, some locked in a struggle with humans, representing the fight between good and evil. Look in also on the church of **San Pietro in Ciel d'Oro**, on the other side of the centre at the top of Strada Nuova, dating from 1132 and containing a superb fourteenth-century altarpiece. Nearby, the **Castello Visconteo** (daily except Mon 9am–12.15pm; L5000) was initiated by Galeazzo II Visconti in 1360, and added to by the Sforzas. The austere exterior originally housed luxurious apartments, the majority of which were in the wing of the quadrangle destroyed by the French in 1527. But the castle was used as a barracks until 1921, and although it's been restored the rooms that remain are hardly stunning. The **Museo Civico** inside includes an art gallery with a handful of Venetian paintings, an archaeology collection with Roman jewellery, pottery, and glassware, and a museum of sculpture displaying architectural fragments, mosaics and sculptures rescued from the town's demolished churches – most impressive of which are the reconstructed eleventh- and twelfth-century portals. Otherwise you'll see the castle at its best on summer evenings, when its courtyard is used for concerts, opera and dance (details from the tourist office).

The Certosa di Pavia

Ten kilometres from Pavia, the **Certosa di Pavia** (Tues–Sun 9–11.30am & 2.30–4.30/6pm; free) is one of the most extravagant monasteries in Europe, commissioned by Gian Galeazzo Visconti in 1396 as the family mausoleum. Visconti intended the church here to resemble Milan's late-Gothic cathedral. It took a century to build, and by the time it was finished tastes had changed – and the Viscontis had been replaced by the Sforzas. But the architect appointed to finish the building, Amadeo, did so in style, festooning the facade with a fantasia of inlaid marble, twisted columns and friezes that say more about the wealth of the families that financed the complex than the contemplative Carthusian order it was built for.

The Certosa is actually reachable from both Milan and Pavia, either by bus or by train. Buses are most frequent, hourly from Piazza Castello in Milan or from outside Pavia's train station, dropping you a fifteen-minute walk from the Certosa. By train, turn left out of the station and walk around the Certosa walls until you reach the entrance – also a fifteen-minute walk.

The monastery lies at the end of a tree-lined avenue, part of a former Visconti hunting range that stretched all the way from Pavia's castello. You can see the **church** unaccompanied, a Gothic building on the inside though no less splendid than the facade, its paintings, statues and vaults combining to create an almost ballroom glamour; look out for the tombs of Lodovico Il Moro and Gian Galeazzo Visconti, masterpieces of the early Renaissance. But to visit the rest of the monastery you need to join a **guided tour** (in Italian) which takes just over an hour, led by one of the monks released from the Carthusian strict vow of silence. The **small cloister** is the first stop, with fine terracotta decoration and a geometric garden around a fountain. Further on, the **great cloister** is less appealing, but offers some insight into life in the complex, surrounded on three sides by the monks' cells, each consisting of two rooms, a chapel, garden and loggia, with a bedroom above. The hatches to the side of the entrances are to enable food to be passed through without any communication. There is also a **refectory** for occasional communal eating, with a pulpit from which the Bible is read throughout the silent meal – the only diversion the frescoed ceiling. The final call is the Certosa **shop**, stocked with the famous (Chartreuse) liqueur, honey, chocolate and souvenirs. Give yourself time before leaving to sample the different varieties of liqueur at the kiosk outside the entrance – yellow is strong, green stronger.

Eating, drinking and nightlife

For a quick **lunch**, the *Bar Vittoria*, Strada Nuova 8, is a good *paninoteca*, with at least a hundred varieties of sandwich and plenty of space to sit down. For a more substantial feed in more subdued surroundings, try the *Bar del Senatore*, on Via del Senatore, off Corso Cavour. Of regular **restaurants**, the *Piedigrotta*, near the church at the far end of Via Teodolinda, does good, reasonably priced pizza and pasta, as does the *Marechiaro*, right on Piazza della Vittoria. If you're feeling flush, the *Vecchia Pavia*, by the duomo at Via Cardinale Riboldi 2, is an elegant place with adventurous local cooking – though at a price.

Vigévano

An hour by bus to the west of Pavia, **VIGÉVANO** is Lombardy at its most comfortably wealthy, a smug little town of boutiques, antique dealers and – most significantly – shoe shops. The shoe industry is Vigévano's mainstay and there are signs of the bedrock of the town's prosperity all over the centre. If you go on a Sunday, Italy's only **Shoe Museum** is open on Corso Cavour, with a collection of some of the weirdest and wackiest excesses of shoe design in the country.

As for the town itself, most of it is pretty unremarkable, and there'd be little reason to visit were it not for the **Piazza Ducale**, which is something special, surrounded on three sides by well-preserved and delicately frescoed arcades, the embodiment of Renaissance harmony. Designed by Bramante and heavily influenced by Leonardo, even the Baroque front of the duomo doesn't spoil the proportions, deftly curved to conceal the fact that the church is set at a slight angle to the square.

Otherwise the **Castello** (Tues–Sun 9.30am–12.30pm & 3–5pm) is about all Vigévano has to offer. A Visconti and later Sforza stronghold, it's been in the throes of restoration for over ten years, but its semi-dilapidated state is part of the attraction – it's largely unsupervised, especially in the mornings, which means you can go just about wherever you want, scrambling up rickety flights of steps to the upper floors, or down dank passages to the dungeons. The oldest part of the castle is the Rocca Vecchia, a fort built by the Visconti to defend the road to Milan, to which it is connected by a covered walkway. The Sforzas retained the castle's military function, but added the elegant Palazzo Ducale, still mostly unrestored, the Loggia delle Dame, an open walkway for the noblewomens' evening *passeggiata*, and the Falconiera, another open gallery used for the training of falcons but now holding the castle's most absurd sight – the tiles of a military bathroom dating from its conversion this century into a barracks. On the right of the courtyard, the stables, designed by Leonardo, offer some insight into how the Sforza troops lived and worked – cathedral-like quarters for the horses, and a loft above for soldiers and hay.

Cremona and around

A cosy provincial town situated bang in the middle of the Po plain, **CREMONA** is known for its violins. Ever since Andrea Amati established the first violin workshop here in 1566, and his son Nicola and pupils Stradivari and Guarneri continued and expanded the industry, Cremona has been a focus for the instrument, attracting both tourists and musicians worldwide. Today around a hundred violin-makers maintain the tradition started by the Amati family: there's an internationally famous school of violin-making here, and there are frequent classical concerts, as well as a string festival held every third October.

All this said, Cremona is a quiet, relatively unexciting town, and not an obvious place to spend a night, and most people treat it as a day trip from Milan or as a stopover en route to the richer pickings of Mantua or Bergamo. However, its lack of overnight visitors can be appealing in itself – certainly there are places to stay, and a small crop of pleasant restaurants – and it can be a nice idea to give yourself time to wind down here, but not long enough to get bored.

Arrival, information and accommodation

Cremona's **train station** is on Via Dante, on the northern edge of the city centre, ten minutes' walk from Piazza del Comune; bus #1 runs regularly to the centre at Piazza Cavour. Most intercity **buses** stop at the train station or at the **bus station** next door.

The **tourist office** is on the main square, opposite the duomo (Mon–Sat 9.30am–12.30pm & 3–6pm; ☎0372/21.722), and has maps, leaflets and details of classical concerts. They also have lists of violin-makers' workshops (*Botteghe Liutarie*) and will be able to tell you if the school of violin-making in Palazzo Raimondi is open for visits. They can also tell you about the **entry scheme to Cremona's main museums** – the Sala dei Violini, Museo Civico, Museo Stradivariano, Museo di Storia Naturale and Museo della Civiltà Contadina – whereby you only need buy one L5000 ticket, valid for three days, for entry to all five places.

If you want to stay over in Cremona, the cheapest **hotel** is the *Touring*, Via Palestro 3 (☎0372/36.976; ③), centrally placed close to the junction of Via Palestro and Corso Garibaldi, although this is, to be honest, slightly bleak. The *Ideale*, at Viale Trento e Trieste 2, at the junction with Corso Garibaldi (☎0372/38.668; ④), is more appealing, and has the advantage of only being a short walk from the train station. If you have a little more money, there's the *Astoria*, close to Piazza del Comune at Via Bordigallo 19, off Via Solferino (☎0372/461.616; ⑤). There's a **campsite**, the *Parco al Po*, on Via Lungo Po Europa (☎0372/27.137) – open May–September; take bus #1 (direction Viale Po) from the train station.

The City

The centre of Cremona is **Piazza del Comune**, a slightly disjointed medieval square, with a west side formed by the red-brick **Loggia dei Militia** – formerly headquarters of the town's militia – and the arched **Palazzo del Comune**, and the northeast corner-marked by the gawky Romanesque **Torazzo**, built in the mid-thirteenth century and

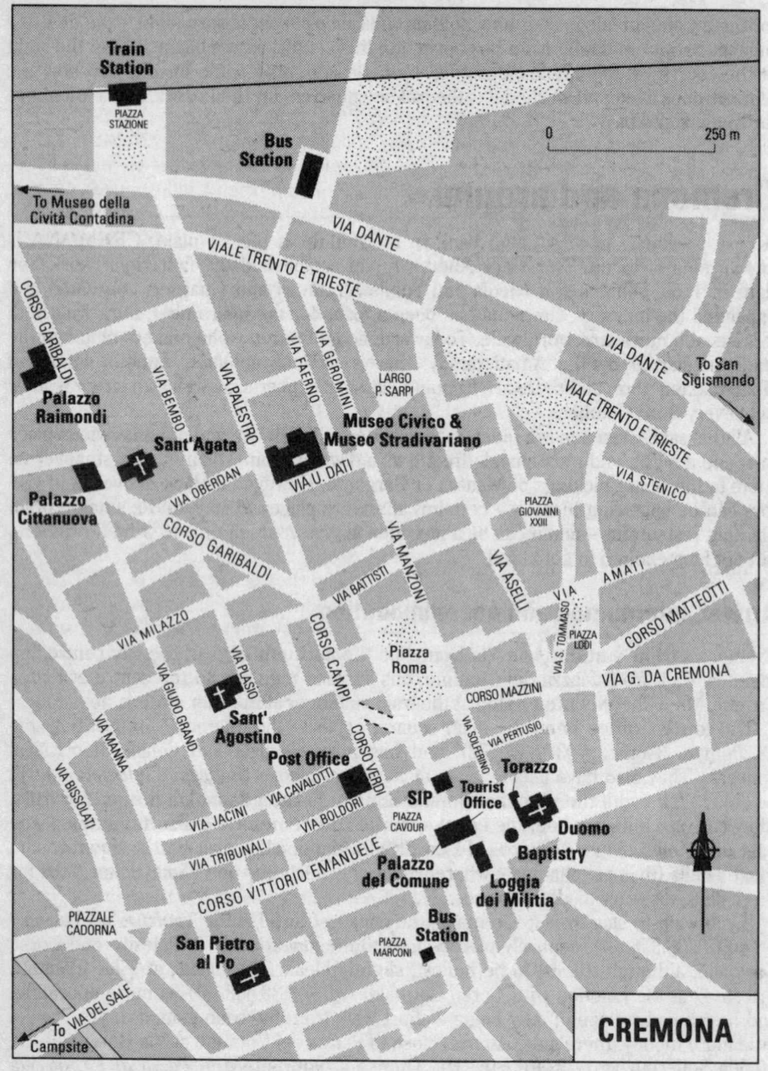

bearing a fine Renaissance clock dating from 1583. At 112m, the Torazzo claims to be Italy's highest medieval tower, and if you've the energy you can ascend for some predictably excellent views over the rest of Cremona and around (Mon–Sat 10.30am–noon & 3–6pm, Sun 10am–12.30pm; L5000). Next door, the **Duomo** is connected by way of a Renaissance loggia, a mixed-looking church, with a fine west facade made up of Classical, Romanesque and fancy Gothic features, focusing on a rose window from 1274. Originally conceived as a basilica, its transepts were added when the Gothic style became more fashionable – presumably explaining its slightly squat appearance inside. Its most significant interior features, however, are its sixteenth-century nave frescoes, including a superb trompe l'oeil by Pordenone on the west wall, showing the *Crucifixion* and *Deposition*, and the fifteenth-century pulpits, decorated with finely tortured reliefs.

Next to the duomo, the octagonal **Baptistery** dates from the late twelfth century, and is currently under restoration. Immediately opposite the duomo, the **Palazzo del Comune** has a very select exhibition of some of Cremona's most historic violins in its upstairs **Sala dei Violini** (Tues–Sat 8.30am–5pm, Sun 9am–1pm; L5000), including a very early example made by Andrea Amati in 1566 for the court of Charles IX of France, as well as later instruments by Amati's son, Guarneri, and Stradivari.

Southwest of the square, on Via Tibaldi, the church of **San Pietro al Po** has better (and more visible) frescoes; indeed its walls are coated with paintings and intricate stuccos, also dating from the sixteenth century. It's all pretty excessive, but there's sophisticated optical trickery in the trompe l'oeil work of Antonio Campi in the transept vaults. Look in also on the refectory next door for Bernadino Gatti's hearty fresco of the Feeding of the Two Thousand.

If you've come to Cremona for the violins, however, the pilastered **Palazzo Affaitati**, north of here at Via Palestro 17, is perhaps of more interest. It holds the **Museo Stradivariano** (Tues–Sat 9.30am–12.15pm & 3–5.45pm, Sun 9.30am–12.15pm; L5000), which contains models, paper patterns, tools and acoustic diagrams from Stradivari's workshop, along with more violins, violas, viols, cellos and guitars, many of which have elaborately carved scrolls, hanging impotently in glass cases. They have to be played regularly to keep them in trim, and you could try asking the custodian when the next work-out is due. In the same building (entrance around the corner in Via U. Dati), the **Museo Civico** (same hours; L5000) has yet more violins, and a bizarre collection of Garibaldi memorabilia, including a lock of his hair, shavings from his beard and a stub of his cigar; and a fragment of the Great Wall of China among the porcelain in the oriental collection. Also, among a small assortment of paintings, there's a disputed Caravaggio of an anguished Saint Francis contemplating a skull.

Eating and drinking

For **food**, *Gallery*, a self-service *tavola calda* and bar in the galleria on the southwest corner of Piazza Roma, is a decent lunch stop; *Pizzeria Stagnino*, Corso Garibaldi 85, and *Pizzeria La Pendola*, Via Voghera 5, are cheap and popular places to sit down and eat, and the city also has lots of places to try local specialities. The *Trattoria da Cerri*, Piazza Giovanni 23, off Via Aselli, and the *Ristorante Centrale*, off Via Solferino at Via Pertusio 4, are both very good, if not especially cheap. Try if you can a *bollito misto* – a mixture of boiled meats, served with Cremonese *mostarde*, consisting of fruit suspended in a sweet mustard syrup.

Around Cremona

If you liked the church of San Pietro al Po, you'll love that of **San Sigismondo** on the eastern edge of town (bus #3 from the train station, bus #2 from Piazza Cavour). Built by Francesco and Bianca Sforza in 1441 to commemorate their wedding – Cremona was Bianca's dowry – its Mannerist decor is among Italy's best, ranging from Camillo Boccaccino's soaring apse fresco to the *Pentecost* by Giulio Campi in the third bay of the nave, plagiarised from Mantegna's ceiling in the Camera degli Sposi at Mantua. Other highlights include Giulio's *Annunciation* on the entrance wall, in which Gabriel is seemingly suspended in mid-air, and the gory John the Baptist in the second left chapel, by his younger brother Antonio.

There's a rather different attraction in the opposite direction (bus #3 from the train station), the **Museo della Civiltà Contadina** (Tues–Sat 9.30am–12.15pm & 3–5.45pm Sun 9.30am–12.15pm; L5000), stuck on the edge of an industrial estate in the outskirts of town at Via Castelleone 51 and possible contender for Italy's muddiest museum. A display of agricultural history laid out in an old farm, it's a scruffy place, and sporadic labelling (in Italian only) makes working out the uses of the various pieces of agricultural apparatus virtually impossible. But the farm itself, with its row of tiny workers' cottages, the larger houses of the foreman and *padrone*, the immense stable, and the small chapel, built so that time wasn't wasted in travelling to church, is sufficient to give you a good picture of the strict hierarchy and slave-like existence that governed the lives of Italian agricultural labourers over several centuries.

Mantua and around

Aldous Huxley called it the most romantic city in the world; and with an Arabian nights skyline rising above its three encircling lakes, **MANTUA** (MANTOVA) is undeniably evocative. It was the scene of Verdi's *Rigoletto*, and its history is one of equally operatic plots, most of them perpetuated by the Gonzagas, one of Renaissance Italy's richest and most powerful families, who ruled the town for three centuries. Its centre of interlinking cobbled squares retains its medieval aspect, and there are two splendid palaces: the Palazzo Ducale, containing Mantegna's stunning fresco of the Gonzaga family and court, and Palazzo Te, whose frescoes by the flashy Mannerist Giulio Romano have entertained and outraged generations of visitors with their combination of steamy erotica and illusionistic fantasy.

But hazy sunsets reflected in tranquil lakes, and the town's melodramatic history, are only half the story. Outside the few traffic-free streets of the historic centre the roads are lined with grimy Fascist-era buildings and jammed with cars, while the outskirts have been desecrated by chemical, plastics and paper works that are reputedly responsible for lining the bed of the largest lake, Superiore, with mercury. Nevertheless, the core of the city is still appealing, especially on Thursdays when Piazza Mantegna, Piazza dell'Erbe and the streets around are filled with a large market.

The state of these same streets aroused the ire of a visiting pope in 1459, who complained that Mantua was muddy, marshy, riddled with fever and intensely hot. His host, Lodovico II Gonzaga, was spurred into action: he could do little about the heat (Mantua can still be unbearably hot and mosquito-ridden in summer) but he did give the city an elaborate facelift, ranging from paving the squares and repainting the shops, to engaging Mantegna as court artist and calling in the prestigious architectural theorist Alberti to design the monumental church of Sant'Andrea – one of the most influential buildings of the early Renaissance. Lodovico's successors continued the tradition of artistic patronage, and although most of the thousands of works of art once owned by the Gonzagas are now scattered around Europe, the town still has plenty of relics from the era.

Arrival, information and accommodation

Mantua's old centre is a ten-minute walk from the **train station** on Piazza Don E. Leoni and the **bus station**, just beyond on Piazza Mondadori, off Corso Vittorio Emanuele II. Bus #2M runs from the train station to the centre of town. The **tourist office**, in the centre of town at Piazza Mantegna 6 – the entrance is actually on Piazza dell'Erbe – (daily 9am–noon & 3–6pm; ☎0376/350.681) has maps, hotel lists and the like.

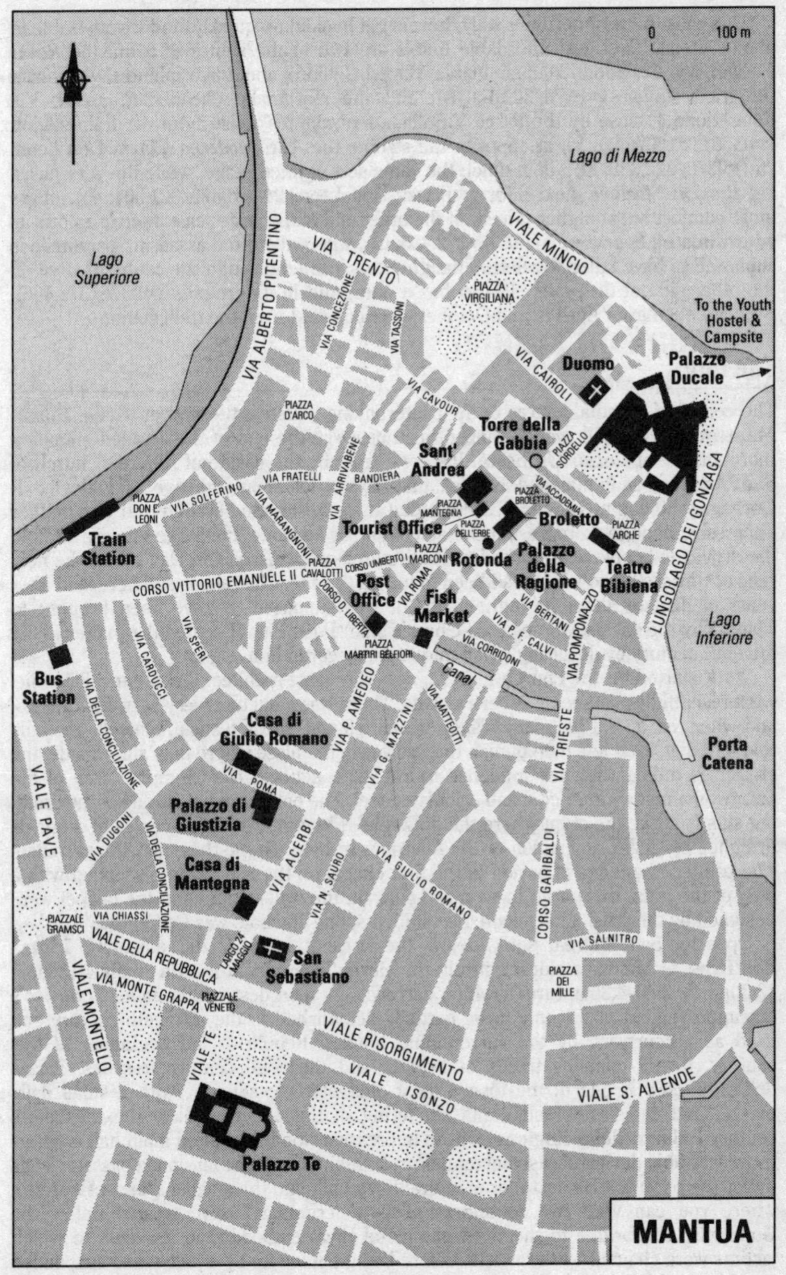
0
100 m
Lago di Mezzo
Lago Superiore
VIA ALBERTO PITENTINO
VIA TRENTO
VIALE MINCIO
PIAZZA VIRGILIANA
To the Youth Hostel & Campsite
VIA CONCEZIONE
VIA TASSONI
VIA CAIROLI
Duomo
Palazzo Ducale
VIA CAVOUR
PIAZZA D'ARCO
Torre della Gabbia
PIAZZA SORDELLO
Sant' Andrea
VIA ARRIVABENE
VIA FRATELLI BANDIERA
PIAZZA DON E. LEONI
VIA SOLFERINO
VIA MARANGNONI
PIAZZA MANTEGNA
PIAZZA BROLETTO
VIA ACCADEMIA
Broletto
Tourist Office
PIAZZA DELL'ERBE
PIAZZA ARCHE
Train Station
LUNGOLAGO DEI GONZAGA
PIAZZA CAVALOTTI
CORSO UMBERTO I
PIAZZA MARCONI
Rotonda
Palazzo della Ragione
Teatro Bibiena
CORSO VITTORIO EMANUELE II
CORSO D. LIBERTÀ
Post Office
VIA ROMA
Fish Market
VIA BERTANI
VIA POMPONAZZO
Lago Inferiore
VIA P. F. CALVI
VIA CORRIDONI
PIAZZA MARTIRI BELFIORI
Canal
VIA SPERI
VIA CARDUCCI
Bus Station
VIA DELLA CONCILIAZIONE
VIA MATTEOTTI
VIA TRIESTE
VIA P. AMEDEO
VIA G. MAZZINI
Casa di Giulio Romano
Porta Catena
VIALE PAVE
VIA POMA
Palazzo di Giustizia
VIA DUGONI
VIA DELLA CONCILIAZIONE
VIA ACERBI
VIA N. SAURO
VIA GIULIO ROMANO
Casa di Mantegna
CORSO GARIBALDI
VIA CHIASSI
PIAZZALE GRAMSCI
VIA SALNITRO
VIALE DELLA REPUBBLICA
LARGO 24 MAGGIO
San Sebastiano
PIAZZA DEI MILLE
VIALE MONTELLO
VIA MONTE GRAPPA
PIAZZALE VENETO
VIALE RISORGIMENTO
VIALE TE
VIALE ISONZO
VIALE S. ALLENDE
Palazzo Te
MANTUA

As in most parts of northern Italy, **hotels** get booked up quickly, and it's advisable to phone ahead. The most affordable hotels are two in the centre of town: the *Roma Vecchia*, Via Corridoni 20, near Piazza Martiri Belfiore, about five minutes' walk from the train station (☎0376/322.100;④), and the marginally cheaper *Rinascita*, Via Concezione 4, close by the Parco Virgiliana ten minutes' or so from the train station (☎0376/320.607; ④). Right opposite the station, the *ABC Moderno*, Piazza Don Leoni 25 (☎0376/322.329; ④), is in much the same sort of price range, while the very pleasant *Bianchi Stazione*, next door at Piazza Don Leoni 24 (☎0376/321.504; ⑥), offers more comfort but at higher prices. At the other end of the price scale, there's an official **youth hostel**, *Sparafucile* (☎0376/372.465; ①), where the hired assassin Sparafucile is supposed to have killed Rigoletto's daughter; its located through the centre of town on the other side of the water. It also has a **campsite** in its grounds (☎0376/372.465). Both are open from April to mid-October; take bus #2M from the train station.

The City

The centre of Mantua centres on four interlinking squares, the first of which, **Piazza Mantegna**, is a small, wedge-shaped open space at the end of the arcaded shopping thoroughfare of **Corso Umberto**. It's dominated by the facade of Alberti's church of **Sant'Andrea**, an unfinished basilica that says a lot about the ego of Lodovico II Gonzaga who commissioned it. He felt that the existing medieval church was neither impressive enough to represent the splendour of his state, nor large enough to hold the droves of people who flocked to Sant'Andrea every Ascension Day to see the holy relic of Christ's blood which had been found on the site. The relic is still here, and after years of dispute about its authenticity (it was supposed to have been brought to Mantua by the soldier who pierced Christ's side) Pope Pius II settled the matter in the fifteenth century by declaring it had miraculously cured him of gout.

Work started on the church in 1472, with the court architect, Luca Fancelli, somewhat resentfully overseeing Alberti's plans. There was a bitchy rivalry between the two, and when, on one of his many visits, Alberti fell and hurt a testicle, Fancelli gleefully told him that "God lets men punish themselves in the place where they sin." Inside, the church is roofed with one immense barrel vault, echoing the triumphal arch of the facade, giving it a rather cool and calculated feel. The octagonal balustrade at the crossing stands above the crypt where the holy relic is kept in two vases, copies of originals designed by Cellini and stolen by the Austrians in 1846. To see them, ask the sacristan. The painter Mantegna is buried in the first chapel on the left, his tomb topped with a bust of the artist that's said to be a self-portrait; the wall-paintings in the chapel were designed by the artist and executed by students, one of whom was Correggio.

Opposite Sant'Andrea, sunk below the present level of the adjoining **Piazza dell'Erbe**, is Mantua's oldest church, the eleventh-century **Rotonda** (daily 10.30am–12.30pm & 2.30–4.30pm; free), which narrowly escaped destruction under Lodovico's city-improvement plans, only to be partially demolished in the sixteenth century and used as a courtyard by the surrounding houses. Rebuilt at the beginning of this century, it still contains traces of twelfth- and thirteenth-century frescoes. Piazza dell'Erbe itself is one of the town's most characteristic squares, with a small daily market and cafés and restaurants sheltering in the arcades below the thirteenth-century **Palazzo della Ragione**, whose impressive wooden-waulted main hall is sometimes viewable during occasional temporary exhibitions. At the far end, a passage leads under the red-brick **Broletto**, or medieval town hall, into the smaller **Piazza Broletto**, where you can view two reminders of how "criminals" were treated under the Gonzagas. The bridge to the right has metal rings embedded in its vault, to which victims were chained by the wrists, before being hauled up by a pulley and suspended in mid-air; while on your far left – actually on the corner of Piazza Sordello – the tall medieval **Torre della Gabbia** has a cage attached in which prisoners were displayed. The Broletto itself is more generous to deserving Mantuans, and is dedicated to the city's two most famous sons: Virgil, a statue of whom overlooks the square, and Tazio Nuvolari, Italy's most celebrated racing driver, whose career is mapped in a small **museum** (Tues–Sun 9am–1pm & 3–6pm; L4000).

If you have the time, it's worth making a short diversion, off Via Broletto up Via Accademia, to the eighteenth-century **Teatro Scientifico** or **Bibiena** (Mon–Sat 9am–12.30pm & 3–5.30pm; L1000), designed by Antonio Bibiena, whose brother designed the Bayreuth Opera House. This is a much smaller theatre, at once intimate and splendid, its curving walls lined with boxes calculated to make their inhabitants more conspicuous than the performers. A thirteen-year-old Mozart gave the inaugural concert here: his impression is unrecorded, but his father was fulsome in his praise for the building, writing that he had never in his life seen anything more beautiful. Concerts are still given – details from the theatre or tourist office.

Beyond Piazza Broletto, **Piazza Sordello** is a large, sombre square, headed by the Baroque facade of the **Duomo** and flanked by grim crenellated palaces built by the Gonzagas' predecessors, the Bonalcosi. The duomo conceals a rich interior designed by Giulio Romano after the church had been gutted by fire. As for the palaces, the two on the left are now owned by the successors of Baldassare Castiglione, a relative of the Gonzagas, who made himself unpopular at the Mantuan court by setting his seminal handbook of Renaissance behaviour, *The Book of the Courtier*, in the rival court of Urbino. Opposite, the **Palazzo del Capitano** and **Magna Domus** were taken by Luigi Gonzaga when he seized Mantua from the Bonalcosi in 1328, the beginning of three hundred years of Gonzaga rule.

The Palazzo Ducale

The Palazzo del Capitano and Magna Domus form the core of the **Palazzo Ducale**, an enormous complex that was once the largest palace in Europe (Tues–Sat 9am–1pm & 2.30–5pm, Sun & Mon 9am–1pm; L10,000). At its height it covered 34,000 square metres, had a population of over a thousand, and when it was sacked by the Hapsburgs in 1630 eighty carriages were needed to carry the two thousand works of art contained in its five hundred rooms. Only a proportion of these rooms are open to visitors, and to see them you have to take a guided tour. These are fairly indiscriminate; save your energy for the rooms that deserve it.

At the time of Luigi's coup of 1328, the Gonzagas were a family of wealthy local peasants, living outside the city on vast estates with an army of retainers. On seizing power Luigi immediately nominated himself Captain of the People – an event pictured in one of the first paintings you'll see on your tour – and the role quickly became a hereditary one, eventually growing in grandeur to that of Marquis. During this time the Gonzagas did their best to make Mantua into a city which was a suitable reflection of their increasing influence, commissioning sought-after Renaissance artists like Mantegna to depict them in their finery. Lodovico II's grandson, Francesco II, further swelled the Gonzagan coffers by hiring himself out as a mercenary for various other Italian city-states – money his wife, Isabella d'Este, spent amassing a prestigious collection of paintings, sculpture and objets d'art. Under Isabella's son, Federico II, Gonzaga fortunes reached their height; his marriage to the heiress of the duchy of Monferrato procured a ducal title for the family, while he continued the policy of self-glorification by commissioning an out-of-town villa for himself and his mistress. Federico's descendants were for the most part less colourful characters, one notable exception being Vincenzo I, whose debauchery and corruption provided the inspiration for Verdi's licentious duke in *Rigoletto*. After Vincenzo's death, the now bankrupt court was forced to sell many of the family treasures to England's King Charles I (many of the works are still in the Victoria and Albert Museum) just three years before it was sacked by the Hapsburgs.

The first rooms of the palace hold the least interest. There is a thirteenth-century sculpture of a seated Virgil, a painting from 1494 by Domenico Morone showing the *Expulsion of the Bonatosi* from the square outside, and, perhaps most interestingly, the fragments of a half-finished fresco by Pisanello, discovered in 1969 behind two layers of plaster and thought to depict either an episode from an Arthurian romance or the (idealised) military exploits of the first marquis, Gianfrancesco Gonzaga. Whatever its subject, it's a powerful piece of work, charged with energy, in which faces, costumes and landscape are minutely observed.

Further on, through the *Sala dello Zodiaco*, whose late sixteenth-century ceiling is spangled with stars and constellations, is the *Salone dei Fiume* ("Room of the Rivers"), in which Baroque trompe l'oeil goes over the top to create a mock garden complete with painted creepers and two ghastly fountains surrounded by stalactites and stalagmites. The *Sala dei Specchi* ("Hall of the Mirrors") has a notice outside signed by Monteverdi, who worked as court musician to Vincenzo I and gave frequent concerts of new works – notably the world's first modern opera, *L'Orfeo*, written in 1607. Vincenzo also employed Rubens, whose *Adoration of the Magi* in the *Salone degli Arcieri*, next door, shows the Gonzaga family of 1604, including Vincenzo with his handlebar moustache. The picture was originally part of a triptych, but Napoleonic troops carried off two-thirds of it after briefly occupying the town in 1797 and chopped the remaining third into saleable chunks of portraiture. Although most have been traced, and some returned to the palazzo, there are still a few gaps. Around the room is a curious frieze of horses, glimpsed behind curtains.

The Castello di San Giorgio contains the palace's principal treasure, however: Mantegna's frescoes of the Gonzaga family – among the painter's most famous works, splendidly restored in the so-called *Camera degli Sposi* and depicting the Marquis Lodovico and his wife Barbara with their family. They're naturalistic pieces of work, giving a vivid impression of real people, of the relationships between them and of the tensions surrounding something that is happening, or about to happen. In the main one Lodovico discusses a letter with a courtier while his wife looks on; their youngest daughter leans on her mother's lap, about to bite into an apple, while an older son and daughter (possibly Barbarina) look towards the door, where an ambassador from another court is being welcomed – lending some credence to the theory that negotiations are about to take place for Barbarina's marriage. The other fresco, *The Meeting*, takes place out of doors against a landscape of weird rock formations and an imaginary city with the Gonzagan arms above the gate. Divided into three sections by fake pilasters, it shows Gonzagan retainers with dogs and a horse in attendance on Lodovico, who is welcoming his son Francesco back from Rome, where he had just become the first Gonzaga to be made a cardinal. In the background are the Holy Roman Emperor Frederick III and the King of Denmark – a selection which apparently annoyed the Duke of Milan, who was incensed that the "two most wretched men in the world" had been included while he had been omitted. Lodovico's excuse was that he would have included the Duke had he not objected so strongly to Mantegna's uncompromising portrait style. If you have time before the guide sweeps you out, have a look at the ceiling, another nice piece of trompe l'oeil, in which two women, peering down from a balustrade, have balanced a tub of plants on a pole and appear to be on the verge of letting it tumble into the room – an illusionism that was to be crucial in the development of the Gonzaga's next resident artist of any note, Giulio Romano, whose Palazzo Te – see below – should not be missed.

Finally, the private apartments of Isabella d'Este, on the ground floor, are sometimes on view. Though they once housed works by Michelangelo, Mantegna and Perugino, only the unmoveable decorations remain – inlaid cupboards and intricately carved ceilings and doors. A ruthless employer, Isabella would threaten her artists and craftsmen with the dungeon if she thought they were working too slowly, and had no compunction about bullying Mantegna on his death-bed to give her a piece of sculpture she particularly coveted. She was more deferential to Leonardo da Vinci, however, who did two drawings of her but ignored her suggestion that one be converted into a portrait of Christ. Isabella also collected dwarfs, whose job it was to cheer her up while her husband was away fighting. For centuries it was assumed that the suite of miniature rooms beyond Isabella's apartments were built for the dwarfs; in fact it's a scaled-down version of the St John Lateran basilica in Rome, built for Vincenzo.

South of the centre: to the Palazzo Te

A twenty-minute walk from the centre of Mantua, at the end of the long spine of Via Principe Amedeo and Via Acerbi, the **Palazzo Te** is the later of the city's two Gonzaga palaces, and equally compelling in its way; and you can take in a few of Mantua's more minor attractions on the way there.

The first thing to look at on the way is Giulio Romano's **Fish Market**, to the left off Piazza Martiri Belfiori, a short covered bridge over the river basically, which is still used as a market building. Following Via Principe Amedeo south, the **Casa di Giulio Romano**, off to the right at Via Poma 18, overshadowed by the monster-studded Palazzo di Giustizia, was also designed by Romano – and, like much of his Mantuan work, meant to impress the sophisticated, who would have found the licence taken with the classical rules of architecture witty and amusing. A five-minute walk away on busy Via Giovanni Acerbi, the more austere brick **Casa di Mantegna** was also designed by the artist, both as a home and private museum, and it's now used as a contemporary art-space and conference centre. If it's open, pop in and take a look at the unusual circular courtyard. Across the road, the church of **San Sebastiano** was the work of Alberti, and is famous as the first Renaissance church to be built on a central Greek cross plan. It's now a neglected, rather seedy place, however, described as "curiously pagan" by Nicholas Pevsner. Lodovico II's son was less polite: "I could not understand whether it was meant to turn out as a church, a mosque or a synagogue." If you want to look inside, the keys are available between 3pm and 5pm at Palazzo Te.

At the end of Via Giovanni Acerbi, across Viale Te, the **Palazzo Te** (Tues–Sun 10am–6pm; L10,000) was designed for playboy Federico Gonzaga and his mistress, Isabella Boschetta, by Giulio Romano; it's the artist/architect's greatest work and a renowned Renaissance pleasure dome. When the palace was built, Te – or Tejeto, as it used to be known – was an island connected to the mainland by bridge, an ideal location for an amorous retreat away from Federico's wife and the restrictions of life in the Palazzo Ducale. Built around a square courtyard originally occupied by a labyrinth, it houses modest but appealing collections of Egyptian artefacts and modern art these days, although the main reason for visiting is to see Giulio's amazing decorative scheme.

A tour of the palace is like a voyage around Giulio's imagination, a sumptuous world where very little is what it seems. In the *Camera del Sole e delle Luna*, the sun and the moon are represented by a pair of horse-drawn chariots viewed from below, giving a fine array of bottoms on the ceiling; in the *Sala dei Cavalli*, dedicated to the prime specimens from the Gonzaga stud-farm (which was also on the island), portraits of horses stand before an illusionistic background in which simulated marble, fake pilasters and mock reliefs surround views of painted landscapes through nonexistent windows. The function of the *Sala di Psiche*, further on, is undocumented, but the sultry frescoes, and the proximity to Federico's bedroom, might give a few clues, the ceiling paintings telling the story of Cupid and Psyche with some more dizzying "sotto in su" (from the bottom up) works by Giulio, among others clumsily executed by his pupils. On the walls, too, are racy pieces, covered with orgiastic wedding-feast scenes, at which drunk and languishing gods in various states of undress are attended by a menagerie of real and mythical beasts. Don't miss the severely incontinent river-god in the background, included either as a punning reference to Giulio's second name, Pippi (The Pisser), or as encouragement to Federico who according to his doctors suffered from the "obstinate retention of urine". Other scenes show Mars and Venus having a bath, Olympia about to be raped by a half-serpentine Jupiter and Pasiphae disguising herself as a cow in order to seduce a bull – all watched over by the giant Polyphemus, perched above the fireplace, clutching the pan-pipes with which he sang of his love for Galatea before murdering her lover.

Polyphemus and his fellow giants are revenged in the extraordinary *Sala dei Giganti* beyond – "the most fantastic and frightening creation of the whole Renaissance" according to the critic Frederick Hartt – showing the destruction of the giants by the gods. As if at some kind of advanced disaster movie, the destruction appears to be all around: cracking pillars, toppling brickwork, and screaming giants, mangled and crushed by great chunks of architecture, appearing to crash down into the room. Stamp your feet and you'll discover another parallel to twentieth-century cinema – the sound-effects that Giulio created by making the room into an echo chamber.

Eating, drinking and nightlife

Mantua is an easy place to **eat** well and cheaply, with plenty of reasonably priced restaurants throughout its centre, many serving Mantuan specialities like *spezzatino di Mantua* (normally donkey stew), *agnoli in brodo* (pasta stuffed with cheese and sausage in broth) or *tortelli di zucca* – pasta stuffed with pumpkin.

On a **budget**, there are a couple of decent self-service places – *Al Punto*, almost opposite the train station on Via Solferino (daily except Sun noon–2.30pm & 7.30–9.15pm), and the *Virgiliana*, Piazza Virgiliana 57, although this is only open weekday lunchtimes (noon–2pm). If all you want is a pizza, *Piedigrotto*, Corso Libertá 15, and *Bella Napoli*, Piazza Cavalotti 14, are both decent, standard pizzerias on the edge of the old town.

Among ordinary **restaurants**, with more interesting food, the *Lioncino Rosso*, just through the bridge off Piazza Broletto, is young and friendly – a good place to eat or just drink; *Da Gigi*, Via Oberdan 4, a left off Corso Umberto walking towards Piazza Mantegna, is a bright, welcoming and unpretentious eatery; *Due Cavallini*, outside the immediate centre at Via Salnitro 5, off Corso Garibaldi, is a great, affordable place to try local dishes. There's also *Trattoria del Lago*, Piazza Arche 5, which hasn't much atmosphere but is inexpensive, and it also serves traditional dishes. For just a **drink**, either before or after dinner, try *Birreria Oblo*, Via Arrivabene 50, a pubby place with a great selection of beers, almost matched by a good range of sandwiches.

Around Mantua: Sabbioneta

There's not much to see within easy reach of Mantua, and the countryside – the Mantuan plain – is for the most part flat and dull. The closest real attraction is at **GRAZIE**, a ten-minute bus ride west, where the church of **Santa Maria delle Grazie** has an interior chock-full of weird votive offerings, wax and wooden mannequins in clothes petrified with age standing in niches, surrounded by wooden hearts, breasts, hands and feet nailed up by the recipients of miracle cures. There's even a stuffed crocodile hanging from the ceiling. Alongside the church, a path leads down to the marshes, rich in rare birds and wildlife, viewable at closer quarters by booking a rowing-boat trip (☎0376/653.735 or ☎0376/311.56) the day before.

Further out, fifty minutes by bus from Mantua bus staion (4–6 daily), **SABBIONETA** is a more interesting target, an odd little place with the air of an abandoned film set, where imperious Renaissance palaces gaze blankly over deserted and dusty piazzas. The town is the result of the obsessive dream of Vespasiano Gonzaga, member of a minor branch of the Mantuan family, to create the ideal city, but it has now been abandoned by all but the oldest inhabitants, a handful of agricultural workers and the tourist board.

Sabbioneta was an anachronism even as it was being built. In the sixteenth century it was no more than an agricultural village, nominal capital of an insignificant state on the Mantuan border struggling to maintain its independence from the foreign powers who had colonised most of Lombardy. Unperturbed, its ruler, Duke Vespasiano, was keen to create an ideal state on the model of ancient Athens and Rome, and he uprooted his subjects from their farm cottages, forcing them to build and then inhabit the new city, which held a Greek and Latin Academy and a Palladian theatre as well as a couple of ducal residences. After Vespasiano's death, Sabbioneta returned to – and has remained in – its former state: a small agricultural village like hundreds of others throughout Italy.

To get inside any of the town's buildings you have to take a **guided tour**. These are arranged by the **tourist office** at Via Gonzaga 31 (daily 9.30am–noon & 2.30–5.30pm), by the main piazza and bus stop, and they start with the **Palazzo del Giardino**, Vespasiano's private residence, decorated with frescoed models of civilised behaviour, ranging from Roman emperors to the Three Graces. Next stop is the **Teatro Olimpico**, copied from Palladio's theatre of the same name in Vicenza, in which the only spectators are pallid marble gods, fake-bronze emperors and ghostly painted courtiers. The **Palazzo Ducale**, around the corner, holds painted wooden statues of four of the Gonzagas, including Vespasiano (with the ruffle and beard), sitting imperiously on horseback. What remains of the palace's decor is likewise concerned with the show of strength – frescoed elephants and friezes of eagles and lions. Close by, the **Chiesa dell'Incoronata** is remarkable mainly for its trompe l'oeil roof, which appears to be three times higher in than out – perhaps an apt comment on Vespasiano, a bronze statue of whom sits beneath, dressed as a Roman emperor and looking reluctant to leave his dream city.

NORTHERN LOMBARDY: LAKES AND MOUNTAINS

"One can't describe the beauty of the **Italian lakes**, nor would one try if one could." Henry James's, sentiment hasn't stopped generations of writers trying to describe the region in pages of purple prose. In fact, the lakes just about deserve it: their beauty *is* extravagant, and it's not surprising that the most melodramatic and romantic of Italy's opera composers – Verdi, Rossini and Bellini – rented lakeside villas to work in. British and German Romantic poets also gushed about the area, and in doing so introduced them firmly to northern European imaginations. The result: a massive influx every summer of ageing package tourists from cooler climes, come to savour the Italian dream and to take large gulps at what Keats called "the beaker of the warm south".

It would in fact be unwise to literally drink the lakes' waters. However, considerable efforts have been made in recent years to clean them up. Most *comune* have installed purification plants, and although there is still some way to go before the lakes are totally clean, swimming is safe in most areas. When it is not, the local *comune* is obliged to erect a warning notice. **Garda** is the cleanest lake, and one of the best centres in Europe for windsurfing and sailing. If water sports don't appeal, **Como** is the most scenically stunning of the lakes, the opulence of its vegetation equalled by that of villas and *palazzi*; and when such things begin to cloy, there are good hikes in its mountainous hinterland. The shores of **Maggiore** are likewise luxuriant, although many of its fin-de-siecle resorts are stodgily sedate. There are, however, some good walks, and anyone remotely interested in gardens shouldn't miss Isola Bella. Though the picture-postcard charms of Orta San Giulio, the main village on **Lago d'Orta**, ensure that it is flooded with visitors in summer, it's an appealingly restful base in spring or late autumn, and while the other minor lakes – **Lago d'Iseo** and **Lago Ledro** – are tame by comparison, you might want to stay on Iseo's islet, where there are some pleasant hikes.

The hilly terrain between the lakes is sliced up by **mountain valleys**: their lower reaches are almost inevitably choked with industry, and their rivers frequently reduced to a trickle by hydroelectric works, but the upper reaches are in parts unspoilt, with plenty of possibilities for hikes. There are also a handful of small ski resorts. There are two main cities: **Brescia**, which is really best avoided, and **Bergamo**, a much nicer place to stay, with an old walled hilltop centre that ranks as one of the loveliest in Italy. If you're lucky enough to find a room there, it's also a good base for trips to lakes Como and Iseo and the mountainous country in between.

Getting around the lakes

The three biggest lakes are all well served by ferries, which zigzag from shore to shore, docking at jetties that are usually conveniently positioned on the main lakeside piazzas or in the centre of the larger towns' promenades. The regular boats are pretty slow, and if you're in a hurry, you might want to pay extra for a hydrofoil; timings are listed in red in the timetables, which are available at all tourist offices and the ticket offices on the jetties themselves, and include a table of tariffs. Prices vary from lake to lake (Maggiore is the cheapest, with a one-stop hop costing L1300; on Garda, the most expensive lake, the same journey costs L3800) and day passes are available on all of them. However, unless you're doing two or three long journeys, they don't represent a saving.

In addition, there are fairly regular buses up and down the shores, a cheaper but far less interesting way of travelling. Timetables are often posted on bus stops, and again some of the better organised tourist offices have copies. Be warned, though, that in Garda and Maggiore, which have one shoreline in Lombardy and another in, respectively, Veneto and Piemonte, it can be impossible to get hold of timetables for the "rival" region's buses.

Lago Maggiore and Lago d'Orta

For generations of overland travellers, **LAGO MAGGIORE** has been the first taste of Italy. Road and railway from Switzerland run along its shores and, for travellers weary of the journey and the cool grandeur of the Alps, the first glimpse of Maggiore's limpid waters, gentle green hills and the hint of exotic vegetation can seem a promising taster of the country. In fact a good deal of Maggiore is dull, with the mountains set well back from its shores in its Italian stretches, and much of its southern reaches somewhat nondescript, particularly along the eastern shore.

Still, its orange blossom, vines, clear air and the verbena that flourishes on its shores continue to draw the tourists, and to stay in the most popular resorts – Pallanza, Stresa and Baveno – you'll need to book in advance in peak season. The lake has always been a favourite with the British: Queen Victoria stayed at the Villa Clara at Baveno – described by Edward Hutton in an early twentieth-century guidebook as "a replica of the Wimbledon or Putney residence of a retired tradesman" – while Robert Southey reckoned the Villa Borromeo on Isola Bella, now Maggiore's biggest tourist attraction, to be "one of the most costly efforts of bad taste in all Italy."

Predictably many of the older resorts are saturated with package tourists in season and are rather sedate places, patronised by elderly overseas visitors. Cannobio and Maccagno have perhaps more to offer – picturesque old villages in which life trundles on much as it has for centuries. In addition, both are convenient launching pads for exploring Maggiore's hilly hinterland.

The western shore

The southern reaches of the west shore of the lake are drab, but you'll have more chance of finding a room there in high season. **ARONA**, uninteresting in itself, is on the main railway line, and its cheap hotels make it a useful base for visiting the rest of the lake. The one sight here is a 100-foot-high copper statue of Saint Charles Borromeo who was born in the now ruined Castle of Arona. It's hollow, and if you don't suffer from claustrophobia you can climb up into its empty head.

If you decide to **stay** in Arona, the *Lido* campsite (☎0322/243.383) is right on the lake shore, a short walk from the train station. The cheapest hotels are the *Ponte*, Via Torini 19 (☎0322/45317; ③), and the *Antico Gallo*, Via Botelli 13 (☎0322/243137; ④).

Stresa

The Maggiore of the tourist brochures begins at **STRESA**, whose popularity as a resort began in 1906 with the construction of the Simplon Tunnel. Its elegant lakeside promenade is now trodden by elderly Brits and Germans for whose benefit the shops in its mellow old centre are stocked with banal trinkets and the cafés with overpriced drinks and snacks. At night the cobbled streets are filled with the sound of Muzak and accordion players.

The town's hotels are quite expensive, and there's not a lot to do in Stresa other than catch a boat to the Isole Borromee (something that can be just as easily done from any number of other villages), making it difficult to recommend Stresa as a base – although fans of classical might want to catch a concert or two at its prestigious **international music festival**, held annually in late August and early September. If you are here for any length of time, after strolling up and down the promenade, where the *Grand Hotel des Iles Borromees* was used as a location by Hemingway in A *Farewell to Arms*, you might want to laze around at Stresa's **Lido** (open summer only) to the north, close to the Mottarone cable car station. From here, you can also catch a cable car up **Monte Mottarone** (daily 9.20am–noon & 1.40–5.10pm; longer hours in summer; L8000 one way, L15,000 return). It's hardly the most sensational of hills, but undeserving of Ruskin's derision – he referred to it as "the stupidest of mountains" and thought the views of the Alps dull. Ruskin's mood or the weather must have been bad, for the views stretch from Monte Rosa on the Valle d'Aosta/Swiss border across to the Adamello. Its wooded western slopes are now a favourite destination for family outings, and on summer Sundays the roadside is lined with everything-but-the-kitchen-sink picnickers. There are also mountain bikes for rent (March–Oct L10,000 per hour, L25,000 per half day, L40,000 per day). Lake Orta lies on the other side of the mountain, and though it *is* possible to walk down to the lake, it's a tedious three-hour tramp.

Stresa's **tourist office**, Via Principe Tomasa 70 (Mon–Sat 8.30am–12.30pm & 3–6.15pm; Sun 9am–noon; ☎0323/30150), is a source of information on the town and around, and of programmes for the festival of classical music; tickets for this are on sale at the Cambio/excursion booking booth on the lake front, opposite the Regina Palace Hotel. Expect to pay around L25,000. If you want to **sleep** in Stresa, the cheapest option is the *Orsola*, Via Duchessa di Genova 45 (☎0323/31087; ④), three minutes' walk from the train station – turn right out of the train station; the hotel is just to the left down Via Duchessa di Genova. Otherwise *Mon Toc*, Via Duchessa di Genova 69

(☎0323/30282; ④) – turn right up Via Duchessa di Genova – is not greatly more expensive, and there are rooms above the *La Chatte* restaurant, Via Anna Maria Bolongaro 57 (☎0323/30507; ⑤). To get here, turn right out of the station and keep on straight ahead along the upper edge of the town for about ten minutes. The street is off to the left.

The best places for **full meals** are the *Papagallo*, Via Principessa Margherita 46, in which the good pizzas from a wood-fired oven compensate for the grumpy, tourist-weary waiters, and the *Ristorante Venezia*, Via Duchessa di Genova (next to the *Orsola*), which does interesting salads and risottos as well as wood-fired pizzas. For snacks and booze, the *Red Baron*, five minutes' walk along from the train station at Via Roma 63, is an amiable place run by a friendly English woman who serves up great sandwiches, hearty *bruschette* and beer on tap. Finally, don't miss the *Casa del Caffè*, Via Anna Maria Bolongaro 26, one of the town's few authentic (and cheap) bars.

The Isole Borromee

The three visitable **Isole Borromee** are all served by regular ferries, either from Piazza Marconi or Piazzale Lido, further up the lakeside promenade. Of the islands, **Isola Bella** (mid-March–late Sept daily 9am–noon & 1.30–5.30pm; Oct daily 9am–noon & 1.30–5pm: L10,000) is the best known and most gloriously excessive of all the lakes' gardens, though three centuries ago it was little more than a barren rock. In the seventeenth century Count Carlo III Borromeo decided to create an island paradise for his wife Isabella, and commissioned the architect, Angelo Crivelli, to transform it into a sumptuous Baroque oasis. Tons of soil were brought across from the mainland, a villa, fountains and statues built, white peacocks imported, and ten terraces of orange and lemon trees, camellias, magnolias, box trees, laurels and cypresses carved out. The centrepiece, however, is a four-tiered confection of shell-, mirror- and marble-encrusted grottoes, topped with a Disneyesque unicorn, mini-obelisks, stone poseurs and cute cherubs. There's more kitsch, and some ritzy rooms and furniture, in the villa – with more artificial grottoes and a collection of eighteenth-century marionettes in the cellar. Isola Bella really is worth seeing, though as Maggiore's main tourist attraction, every inch of the island *not* occupied by the palace and garden is taken up by restaurants with multilingual menus and stalls selling plastic gimcrackery.

Hemingway's favourite, **Isola dei Pescatori**, once an island of fishermen, retains a certain charm, despite the regular invasions of sightseers. Along with the obligatory trinket stands and restaurants there are a few ordinary bars and shops, and it's not a bad place to hang around for an hour or so. Ferries move on to **Isola Madre** (same hours as Isola Bella; L10,000), larger and less visited than Isola Bella, with a small, tasteful palazzo stacked with portraits of the Borromeos in a luxuriant but less contrived garden. Tiny **San Giovanni**, the fourth Borromean island, has a villa once owned by Toscanini, but is closed to the public.

Further north

If you're on a tight budget you might consider staying at **BAVENO**, up the coast from Stresa, which has ten campsites and a couple of reasonably priced hotels, and a beach backed by craggy mountains. Queen Victoria stayed at the Villa Clara (now Castello Branca) in 1879, establishing Baveno as a fashionable resort among the pre-jet set, although predictably it's now been colonised by British package operators. From here you can reach the tiny Lake Mergozzo, an arm of Maggiore, cut off from the rest of the lake by silt, or take the lovely road up to Monte Camoscio.

Again, there's not a great deal to do, though if you stay at the *Parisi* campsite (☎0323/923.156), open April–September, it's safe to swim from its narrow pebbly beach. There's a good-value **hotel** directly opposite the *imbarcadero*: the *Posta*, Piazza

Dante 16 (☎0323/924.589; ④). Alternatively there's the slightly more expensive *La Ripa*, Via Sempione 11 (☎0323/924589; ④), right on the lakeside but backed by the busy main road. Turn left out of the *imbarcadero* and follow the coast road for around five minutes. The **tourist office**, on Viale della Vittoria (Mon–Sat 9am–12.30pm & 3–6pm; Sun 9am–noon) has lists of all hotels and campsites.

Further up the lake is **PALLANZA**, which along with the industrial quarters of SUNA and INTRA makes up the town of **VERBANIA**, whose name recalls *Verbanum* – the name used by the Romans for the whole, verbena-shored lake. Verbania's winter climate is the mildest on the lake, which enabled a retired Scottish soldier, Captain Neil McEachern, to create in the Thirties the most botanically prestigious garden of all the lakes, at the **Villa Táranto** (April–Oct daily 8.30am–6.30pm; L1000). The grounds contain 20,000 species of plant, including giant Amazonian lilies, lotus blossoms, Japanese maple, and *melia azederach*, a sacred Indian tree, laid out with cool geometric accuracy around fountains and pools.

A short walk south of Villa Taranto, Pallanza's lake front is lined with manicured flower beds and dapper *gelaterias*, bars and hotels, but on the hill behind there's a more down-to-earth quarter in which the souvenir shops are almost outnumbered by *alimentari*, fruit shops and *pasticcerias*. If you want to escape the touristy lakeside bars, head up the hill to the *pasticceria Milanese*, Via Ruga 36, an unprettified wood-panelled bar with a pool table and outsize TV.

Cannobio

CANNOBIO is perhaps the most appealing place to stay on the western shore of the lake, its lakefront road of pastel-washed houses giving onto a series of stepped alleyways leading into a tightly tangled old village of stone houses. The only sight as such is the **Santuario della Pietà**, a Bramante-inspired church with a curious openwork cupola. It was built on the site of a 1522 miracle, when a picture of the *Pietà* suddenly began to bleed; shortly afterwards Cannobio remained unscathed while the plague ravished other villages nearby, and superstitious religious minds could do nothing but link the two events. Carlo Borromeo, anxious as ever to boost the morale of Catholics in the face of the snowballing power of the Protestant church, ordered a chapel to be built to house the painting. It's still there, though curiously there's no sign of blood stains.

Cannobio is well served by both ferries and buses, and you could catch one of the latter from the jetty up the Val Cannobina, a rarely visited valley punctuated by a few ancient stone-built hamlets. From FALMONTA at the end of the bus route you could walk, drive or hitch up to the winter resort of MALESCO from where you can pick up the privately run *FART* train to Locarno in Switzerland (see overleaf) .

To the far left of the lake front (as you face the village) a ramp-like street leads up to the main drag, **Via Marconi**, and at its head the SS34 coast road with the **tourist office** (Mon–Sat 9am–noon & 4.30–7pm; Sun 9am–noon) and a couple of supermarkets. Sadly, Canobbio's hotels are expensive: perhaps the best value (though not the cheapest) is the *Elvezia*, Viale Rimembranza 1 (☎0323/70142; ⑤). If it's full, try the cheaper *Giardino*, Via Veneto 24 (the SS34) (☎0323/71482; ④), or the *Canobbio* on the lake front (☎0323/71390; ⑤). As for **eating**, *Verbano*, by the lake, is one of Cannobio's more reasonable café-restaurants and as good a place as any to waste an hour or so. The *Osteria La Streccia*, also on the lake front, is worth checking out; it has a L16,000 tourist menu. Up in the village, the *Ristorante Antica Stallera*, Via P. Zacchero 7, is a pleasant and reasonably priced place for lunch or dinner, where you can eat in the garden under a vine-covered trellis. The only place to go at night is *Birreria Scurrone* on Vicolo Scurrone, reached through a tunnelling alleyway at the left end of the lake front.

Domodossola

Around 30km east of Canobbio, **DOMODOSSOLA** is a useful rail junction, although you're unlikely to do anything other than change trains there. If you're heading into Italy from Switzerland you can pick up trains to Orta there, while if you're heading north *into* Switzerland, and want an exciting train ride to Locarno, the main train station is also the terminus for private *FART* trains to Locarno. The scenery along this route is gorgeous, and, although the ride is pricier than the regular rail line, it is well worth it; *InterRail* passes are valid in any case, if you have one.

The eastern shore

In general there is little of great interest on the eastern side of Lake Maggiore, although any of the smaller centres make feasible bases for the rest of the lake, or for hiking into the hills behind. **MACCAGNO**, however, on the northeast side, is worth the trip: an ancient village stacked below a steep wooded mountain overlooked by a dour crenellated castle. Virtually untouched by tourism, it's an ideal base if you're into mountain walks or simply want to hang around keying into the everyday life of a sleepy village. One word of warning, though: many boats only call at Maccagno on request, so when you're leaving be sure to ask at the jetty to radio ahead for them to stop.

Steep narrow cobbled streets linked by flights of mossy steps squeeze between the scuffed ochre facades of houses, some still bearing frescoes of the Madonna and saints, others stencilled with ghostly signs advertising various trades. An improbably steep track leads straight out from the village into the hills, from where there are paths to the Lago Delio and Valle Veddasca. Most interestingly, you can walk to the village of CURIGLIA, beyond which, from Ponte di Piero, an acute mule track climbs to the isolated village of **MONTEVIASCO**, 500m above. There's no road to Monteviasco, and until recently the mule track was its only link with the world. Nowadays, however, there's a cable car.

Monteviasco owes its existence to a rape: it was allegedly founded by four deserters from the occupying Spanish army who abducted four girls from a neighbouring village. In fact, there are scarcely any of their descendants left in the village now – most of the covetably picturesque drystone houses have been snapped up as holiday homes.

In Maccagno the *Albergo della Torre Imperiale* on Piazza Roma (☎0332/560.142; ③), at the foot of the village near the lake, has basic doubles above a simple restaurant and bar, and there's a **campsite** on the waterfront – *Camping Lido* (☎0332/560.250).

Just to the south of Maccagno, **LUINO**, a sizeable town and tourist centre, is really only worth visiting on Wednesdays when it hosts Maggiore's biggest market. The *centro storico* (follow sign off the main road to the left of the *imbarcadero*) is no great shakes but is reasonably well stocked with food and especially wine shops. If you've spent any time in Lombardy's art galleries you may already be familiar with the work of Bernardino Luino, one of Leonardo's followers. It's assumed that he hailed from Luino, and if you like his work, you should take a look at the campanile he frescoed at the oratory of **SS Pietro e Paolo**.

Luino's **tourist office** (Mon–Sat 9am–noon & 3–7pm) is across the road from the jetty. For **food**, you could try the *pizza al trancio* outlet at Via Pellegrini 42 or the *Pizzeria Marinella*, Via Alessandro Manzoni, just of Piazza Giovanni XXIII at the top of the *centro storico*.

South of Luino, **LAVENO** (also accessible by car ferry from INTRA) specialises in bizarre attractions. At Christmas there's a floodlit underwater crypt, and, even if you're not into ceramics – its main industry – a visit to the entertainingly kitschy **museum** (daily 10am–noon & 2–6pm; L1000), 3km down the road at CERRO, is a must. The collection reaches the height of tastelessness in the gilded green aspidistra containers, a lavatory bowl decorated inside with pastoral scenes and an Art Nouveau bidet perched on a stand of leaves.

From Laveno a cable car climbs up to the **Sasso del Ferro** for great views of the Alps. On its southern slopes, but visible only from the lake, is the **Santuario di Santa Caterina del Sasso**. In the early twelfth century a wealthy moneylender, Alberto Besozzi, was sailing on the lake when his boat sank. He prayed to Saint Catherine of Alexandria and was safely washed up on shore, afterwards giving up usury and becoming a hermit in a cave on the hillside. When his prayers averted a plague the locals built a church which became popular with pilgrims, especially after a boulder fell on the roof but was miraculously wedged just above the altar instead of falling on the priest saying mass. The boulder finally crashed through in 1910, and the church remains closed for fear of further rockfalls.

Towards the foot of the lake, **ANGERA** is a sizeable village with a small, quiet beach dominated by an imposing twelfth-century castle, the **Rocca** (April 1–Oct 31 daily 8.30am–7.30pm; L8000), more appealing for the character it gives the shore than for the self-congratulatory Visconti frescoes inside – battle scenes celebrating their seizure of the Rocca from the Torriani family. Little did the Viscontis know that just over 100 years later they would lose the castle to the pious and powerful Borromeo family, who ended up owning much of the lake and producing Milan's saint, Charles Borromeo.

Lago d'Orta

The locals call **Lago d'Orta** "Cinderella", capturing perfectly the reticent beauty of this small lake with its deep blue waters and intriguing island. Unfortunately, in recent years Orta has been discovered by the package companies, so try if you can to go out of season.

Orta San Giulio and the hinterland

Occupying the tip of a peninsula on the lake's eastern shore, **ORTA SAN GIULIO** is a romantic little town where narrow cobbled streets run between pastel-washed houses and palaces with elaborate wrought-iron balconies. It is, not surprisingly, Orta's main attraction, and on summer Sundays the approach roads are jammed with traffic and the alleyways with day-trippers. Life centres on two piazzas: **Piazzetta Ernesto Ragazzoni**, where visitors congregate in three *gelaterias* (*Venus* is the best), and **Piazza Motta**, open to the lake and looking directly on to Isola San Giulio. Somewhat out of place among the pavement cafés and stalls selling gaudy plastic inflatables is the **Palazzo della Communità**, Orta's diminutive town hall, decorated with faded frescoes and supported on an arcaded loggia. From the piazza you can walk out of the village along Via Giovanotti to a lakeside promenade popular with smooching couples, or catch a boat to the island (see overleaf). Above the town is the **Sacro Monte**, 21 phoney Renaissance chapels dedicated to Saint Francis and containing some awful tableaux of painted terracotta statues acting out scenes from the saint's life against frescoed B-movie backgrounds.

Orta San Guilio's **tourist office** is at Via Olina 9-11, the narrow main street which runs through Piazzetta Ragazzoni to Piazza Motta (Tues–Sat 9am–noon & 3–5.30pm, Sun 10am–noon & 3–5pm; ☎0322/90.354). It's well organised, with bus timetables as well as information on hotels. There aren't many **hotels** in Orta San Giulio, and best choice is the creeper-draped *Antica Agnello* (☎0322/90.259; ④) just beyond Piazetta Ragazzoni. If it's full you'll pay around the same for a double in the *Conca d'Oro* on Via Fava(☎0322/90.252; ④), midway between the village and the train station. Finding reasonably priced **food** is a challenge, but the *Pizzeria Campana*, Via Giovanotti 41, isn't bad and has a neighbourly bar frequented by locals.

Isola San Giulio

Orta's highlight is the **Isola San Giulio**, a tiny island-village dominated by a severe white seminary and the tower of its twelfth-century basilica. Boats leave every fifteen minutes, and the return journey costs just L2000; the last boat back is at 7.30pm. The San Giulio of the town and island was a priest who in 390 AD decided to found a sanctuary on the island. The locals refused to row him over, as the island was supposedly seething with monsters and snakes, and Giulio is supposed to have crossed on foot using his staff as a rudder and his cloak as a sail. Once there, he banished the snakes, founded his sanctuary and earned himself a sainthood. The **Basilica** (Tues–Sun 9.30am–12.30pm & 2.30–7pm, Mon 2.30–7pm) has a redoubtable black marble pulpit, carved with venomous-looking griffins and serpents, recalling the myth. The massive vertebrae in the sacristry is said to have belonged to one of the island's dragons; scientists reckon it's a whalebone.

The Varesotto

The **Varesotto** is the least attractive but richest of the lake provinces – a major industrial region which produces everything from shoes and silk to helicopters. Its three small lakes are badly polluted, and, lying blandly on the plain, cannot compete with nearby Maggiore and Como for scenic splendour. The provincial capital, **Varese**, is worthy of a place on your itinerary only if you have to make train or bus connections, or want to visit the province's more interesting pickings at **Castiglione Olona** or **Castelseprio**.

Varese and around

VARESE is a gracious purpose-built town of gardens, marble Fifties villas and rectangular Fascist-era buildings, fringed with shoe factories. Its inhabitants are every bit as obsessed with style as the Milanese and look almost as perfect as the window-display mannequins in the designer shops that line the main street, Corso Matteotti.

The centre of town is **Piazza Monte Grappa**, not far from the city's main attraction, the formal gardens around the long, pink **Palazzo Estense**, built in the eighteenth century for the Este Dukes of Modena (daily 10am–6pm; free). Otherwise, if you're in Varese in April or October a considerable proportion of the crowds here will be Americans and Europeans come to attend the fashion shows of Milan; in fact the town's proximity to Milan means that most of its **hotels** are aimed at an expense-account clientele. However, a cheaper option is the *Stadio*, Via Bolchini 24 (☎0332/224.069; ④), which also has rooms for up to four people – and there's a reasonably priced restaurant next door. The **tourist office** at Via Carobbio 2 (Mon–Fri 9am–12.30pm & 3–7pm, Sat 9am–noon & 3–6pm) can give the full picture.

Around Varese: Castiglione Olona and Castelseprio

One of the best excursions you can make from Varese is to **CASTIGLIONE OLONA**, a Renaissance-style village just twenty minutes by bus from Varese's Piazza Kennedy (#B45), built by Cardinal Branda Castiglione in the fifteenth century and inspired by the architecture he had seen in Florence. Masolino, a pupil of Masaccio, created the limpid frescoes you can see in the hilltop **Collegiata** and its **baptistry**. And there are more frescoes in the **Casa dei Castiglioni** on the sleepy main square, including one of Vezprem, Hungary, as described to Masolino by the cardinal, who was bishop there for a while. Castiglione Olona livens up on the first Sunday in the month, when an antiques market is held.

Further along the #B45 bus route, **CASTELSEPRIO** is less attractive but worth visiting for its intriguing seventh-century church, **Santa Maria Foris Portas**, which has exotic Byzantine-style frescoes of *Christ's Infancy*, discovered during the last war by a partisan hiding in the church.

North of Varese: hiking

More attractive than the three lakes near Varese is **Lago di Ghirla**, a tarn deep in a valley, the Valganna, near the Swiss border. There's a **campsite** on the side away from the B37 road and plenty of opportunities for stiff hikes.

If you're into walking, there are a number of country and forest **treks** to the north of Varese, the most interesting of which is the haul across to MACCAGNO on Lago Maggiore. The walk starts at PORTO CERESIO at the foot of Lago Lugano near the Swiss border and takes ten days; you could, though, pick it up at any point along the route. The booklet *Via Verde Varesina*, available only in Italian from local bookstores, is useful for information on how to get to starting-points on public transport and for places to eat and stay over. The maps, however, are poor, and unless you can read its route descriptions you'll need to buy another.

Lago di Como

Of all the Italian lakes, it's the forked **Lago di Como** which comes most heavily praised. Wordsworth thought it "a treasure which the earth keeps to itself", though what he would think of the place now is anyone's guess: the lake is still surrounded by abundant vegetation but it can get very crowded and the principal towns of **Como** and **Lecco** are not these days particularly attractive destinations. At times, though, as you're zigzagging up the lake on a steamer, it can seem almost ridiculously romantic, and if you want to do more than indulge in *belle epoque* dreams, there are some great walks through the lake's mountainous hinterland – and in most places the water is clean enough for swimming. Of the lake's other towns and villages, three are outstanding: **Varenna** and **Bellagio** for unrepentant romantics and **Menaggio** if you want a pleasant, affordable base for walking, swimming or cycling.

Como town

COMO is a dispiriting town. Its position at the tip of the lake is picturesque enough, but as the nearest resort to Milan and a popular stopoff on the main road into Switzerland, it's both heavily touristed and, on the outskirts at least, fairly industrialised; and the old centre has been revamped so fussily that it has little real soul anymore. Apart from tourism, the main industry is a rarefied one – Como is the main silk-supplier for Milan's fashion designers – but it doesn't make its factories any more endearing, and you may feel inclined to bypass the place altogether for one of the lake's more attractive resorts.

Lakeside **Piazza Cavour** is a bleak space bounded by ugly metal and glass hotels and banks with a couple of pricey pavement cafés. To the left is a little lakeside park set around a curious temple, now the **Museo Alessandro Volta** (Tues–Sun 10am–noon & 3–6pm; L2000), dedicated to Como's most useful son, a pioneer in electricity who gave his name to the volt. If you're interested in such things, there are some of the instruments he used to conduct his experiments inside.

Beyond, compellingly illuminated at night, is the **Villa Olmo**, an eighteenth-century Neoclassical pile in magnificent grounds. The villa itself is a popular venue for congresses, but when the villa is delegate-free the **gardens** are open to the public (Mon–Sat 8am–6pm). Via Plinio leads up from Piazza Cavour to the **Broletto**, prettily striped in pink, white and grey, and with a fifteenth-century balcony designed for municipal orators. Next door, the splendid **Duomo** (summer daily 7.30am–noon & 3–7pm; winter daily 7am–noon & 3–7pm) was begun at the end of the fourteenth century but wasn't completed until the eighteenth, when the Baroque genius Juvarra added the cupola. The church is reckoned to be Italy's best example of Gothic-Renaissance fusion: the Gothic spirit clear in the fairy-tale pinnacles, rose windows and buffoonish gargoyles; that of the Renaissance in its portals (with rounded rather than ogival arches) and in the presence of the two pagans flanking the main west door – the Elder and Younger Plinys, both of whom were born in Como. There was nothing unusual in the sequestration of classical figures by Christians in the Renaissance, but the presence, especially of Pliny Junior, does seem somewhat inappropriate, since his only connection with Christianity was to order the assassination of two deaconesses. Inside, the Gothic aisles are hung with rich Renaissance tapestries (some woven with perspective scenes) and if you've a few spare L500 coins you could illuminate a heavy-lidded Leonardesque *Madonna* and an *Adoration of the Magi* by Luini, and a languid *Flight to Egypt* by Gaudenzio Ferrari.

The second of Como's churches, the Romanesque **Sant'Abbondio**, left along Via Regina from the main train station, struggles to hold its own in a dreary suburb. Built in the eleventh century, it was stripped of later encrustations in the nineteenth century and returned to its original simplicity. Once inside you can forget the brutal surroundings as you wander down the serene aisles to the apse with its colourful fourteenth-century frescoes, the most appealing of which depicts the Magi dreaming of Christ under striped and patterned blankets.

If you have time, head down to the lake shore to the right of Piazza Cavour, by Como Lago station, and take a **funicular** (roughly every half-hour) up to **BRUNATE**, a small hilltop resort with great views up the lake that's also a good starting-point for hikes.

Practicalities

Como has three **train stations**: Como San Giovanni, on the main line from Chiasso to Milan, and Como Borghi and Como Lago, from which trains run to Milan Nord, Saronno, Varese Nord and Novara Nord. Como Lago is, as its name suggests, on the lake shore, opposite the **ferry jetty** and across the road from the **bus station**. Como San Giovanni, ten minutes' walk from the lake and old centre, is connected with the jetty (and bus station across the road) by buses #4 and #7. Como Borghi is on the southern side of the town centre a short walk down Via Sirtori from Viale Battisti. Como's **tourist office** is situated on Piazza Cavour (Mon–Sat 9am–12.30pm & 2.30–6pm; ☎031/274.064).

The cheapest **accommodation** in Como is at the **youth hostel**, *Villa Olmo*, Via Bellinzona 2 (☎031/573800; ①). Open March–November, it serves dinner and has laundry facilities. To get there take bus #1 or #6 from Como San Giovanni or walk for twenty minutes along Via Borgo Vico (on the left as you walk down the steps from the main train station). An alternative for women is the *Ostello per la Protezione della Giovane* at Via Borgo Vico 182 (☎031/573.540; ①). Grotty as Via Borgo Vico is, it also holds some of the town's cheaper **hotels** and is conveniently close enough to Como San Giovanni. The *Dinner*, left out of San Giovanni at Via Borgo Vico 45 (☎031/570.108; ④), and the *Sole*, further along at Via Borgo Vico 91, are about as cheap as they come in Como (☎031/573.382; ④); with a little cash, you could stay more centrally at the nicely positioned *Teatro Sociale*, in a fine arcade right by the duomo at Via Maestri Comacini 8 (☎031/264.042; ④), or the two-star *Fontana*, behind Piazza Cavour at Via D. Fontana 19 (☎031/271.110; ⑤).

For **eating**, you could do worse than stay on Via Borgo Vico and join the locals in the pizzeria *Grotta Azzurra* at no. 161. The liveliest of the cheaper eateries is *La Scuderia*, Piazza Matteotti 4; the pizzas here are pretty standard, so go for something simple. Failing that, *Pizzeria Marechiaro*, Via Porta 7, close to the duomo, is a friendly enough place with reasonable pizzas and other dishes at very moderate prices. If you need something sweet, try the pastries at *Belli* on Via Vittorio Emanuele, or the ice creams at *Bolla* on Via Pietro Boldoni.

The western shore

The first port-of-call by steamer on the **western shore** of Lake Como is **CERNOBBIO** (also accessible by frequent bus from Como's Piazza Matteotti), whose main claim to fame is the nearby **Villa d'Este** hotel, a palatial sixteenth-century confection in an opulent garden which has for some time ranked among Europe's most luxurious hotels. Greta Garbo once stayed, and it still manages to fill itself with guests willing to pay L500,000 a night for the chance to wander like Garbo among the statues, fountains and grottoes of its extravagant gardens.

Although pleasant enough, Cernobbio is otherwise pretty undistinguished, though it has a good waterfront market on Wednesdays and Sundays. However, it is the starting-point for the 130-kilometre trail through the mountains on Como's west shore, known as the *Via dei Monti Lariani*. This is divided into four sections; the **tourist office**, Via Regina 33 (Mon–Sat 9.30am–12.30pm & 3–6pm; ☎031/510.198) has maps and booklets detailing the route and the various *rifugi* along the way.

Otherwise, unless you want to spend a day on the poolside at its **Lido** (summer only daily except Mon 9.30am–midnight), there's little point in dawdling. If your pockets aren't up to this, content yourself with glimpses of its gardens from the steamer. At **TORNO** on the opposite shore, where the steamer also stops, the **Villa Pliniana** was built in the sixteenth century on the site of one of Pliny the Younger's many villas. A spring behind it feeds a pool, and still gushes out at six-hour intervals as Pliny Jnr described it. Rossini composed here, and Shelley tried to rent the place, describing it as magnificent but in ruins with "ill-furnished apartments".

Further up the western shore, **ARGEGNO**'s lakeside cafés screen a hilly village of ancient houses with wooden eaves protruding over steep stepped alleyways. Served by regular ferries, it's a convenient base, as well as a peaceful place to potter around, although unfortunately its three **hotels** are not particularly cheap. The cheapest rooms are at the *Belvedere* (☎031/821116; ④); otherwise there are the pricier *Argegno*, on the lake front (☎031/821455; ⑤), or *La Griglia* (☎031/821147; ⑤).

Ferries move on from Argegno to the **Isola Comacina**, Como's only island. Anything further removed from the greenery of Maggiore's islands would be hard to imagine. Comacina, uninhabited save for a handful of artists, is a wild place where you can wander through the ruins of nine abandoned churches. One of the earliest settlements on the lake, it was conquered by the Romans, and, later, when the barbarians invaded, it became a refuge for the wealthy citizens of Como. It developed into a centre of resistance, and in the turmoil of the Middle Ages, attracted an eclectic mix of dethroned monarchs, future saints and the pirate Federico Barbarossa. Eventually it allied with Milan against Como, an unfortunate move which led to the island being sacked by Como and razed to the ground. Abandoned for centuries, it was eventually bought by a local, Auguste Caprini, who outraged Italy by selling it to the King of Belgium after World War I. Diplomatically, the King decided to return it, and the island is now administered by a joint Belgian/Italian commission, who built three houses there for artists.

Incongruously, the island has been home since 1947 to an extremely exclusive restaurant, the *Locanda dell'Isola*, whose former clients range from Arnold

Schwarzenegger and Sylvester Stallone to Ursula Andress and the Duchess of Kent. If you can't afford the L100,000 or so it will cost you to eat there, bring a picnic as the snack bar by the jetty overcharges even for simple sandwiches.

The Tremezzina

Sheltered by a headland, the shore above Isola Comacina, known as the **Tremezzina**, is where Como's climate is at its gentlest, the lake at its most tranquil and the vegetation at its most lush. Lined with cypresses and palms, it's lovely at any time, but unbeatable in spring, awash with colour and heady with the scent of flowering bushes.

LENNO, in the south of the Tremezzina, is the site of another of Pliny the Younger's villas, from which, he reported, he could fish from his bedroom window. Just inland at **MEZZEGRA** in 1944, two families of evacuees staying at the Villa Belmonte witnessed a rather different scene from their windows. A car drew up and a burly man in a black beret, nervously clutching the lapels of his coat, got out, followed by a woman and a tall pale man with a machine gun. The burly man was Mussolini, the woman his mistress, Claretta Petacci, and the tall man the partisan leader, Walter Audisio. Audisio pulled the trigger and Claretta flew at him, grasping the barrel of the gun; Audisio shot twice more, but the trigger jammed. He took his driver's machine gun and pointed it at Mussolini who said "Shoot me in the chest"; Audisio shot first at Claretta, killing her outright, and then complied with Mussolini's last request.

TREMEZZO holds some of Como's most deliciously extravagant palaces, villas and hotels, most of them painted in the good-enough-to-eat colours of Italian ice cream. It's a sedate, rather middle-aged resort, popular with Brits and Germans, and although you probably won't want to stay, it's a pleasant place to pause before or after visiting the Villa Carlotta (see below). The best place for lunch is the snappily titled *Paninoteca Birreria Bar King*, on the lakefront, which does brilliant sandwiches. If you do need to sleep here, the first choice should probably be the *Darsena* (☎0344/4042; ④) at the water's edge on the southern edge of the village.

A couple of minute's walk north along the lakeside road is the **Villa Carlotta** (April–Sept daily 9am–6pm; Oct daily 9am–11.30pm & 2–4.30pm; L6000), which has its own *imbarcadero* between Tremezzo and Cadenabbia (see below). Pink, white and Neoclassical, it was built by a Prussian princess for her daughter, Carlotta, and now houses a collection of pompous eighteenth-century statues, including Canova's meltingly romantic *Cupid & Psyche* and a frieze of Alexander entering Babylon commissioned by Napoleon – though he was exiled before he could pay for it. The bill was picked up by a count, who in return got himself included as a member of Alexander's army (he's at the end, along with the artist). The villa's greatest attraction, however, is the fourteen-acre **garden**, a beautifully ordered collection of camellias, rhododendrons and azaleas.

CADENABBIA, five minutes' walk north of the villa, has little to hold you, a rather downmarket resort that lacks Tremezza's architectural panache. Head instead to **MENAGGIO** a few kilometres further on, a bustling village and lively resort that is a good base for hiking and cycling in the mountains as well as sunbathing and swimming. The **ferry jetty** is about five minutes walk from the main square, Piazza Garibaldi, in and around which you'll find most of Menaggio's lakeside cafés and restaurants. The **tourist office** here (Mon–Sat 9am–noon & 3.30–6.30pm; ☎0344/3.2924) is unusually well organised, with practical information on the town and maps on walks in the area. Swimming in the lake is safe here, and there's a beach and vast pool at the **Lido** (late-June–mid-Sept daily 9am–7pm), as well as **water-skiing** and other waterborne activities at the *Centro Lago Service* on Via Lago Castelli (☎0344/32.003).

If you do decide to stay, Menaggio's **youth hostel**, the *Ostello La Primula* Via IV Novembre 38 (☎0344/22 017; ①), is just outside the village, overlooking the main road, and open from mid-March to mid-November. It rents out **bikes** by the day, and offers discounts at the Lido, as well as serving excellent meals for about L10,000 a head. The most convenient of the two **campsites** is the *Lido* (☎0344/31.150), open May–September. If you need a **hotel**, there are rooms above the *Vapore* restaurant (☎0344/32.229; ③) by the lake front just off Piazza Garibaldi; the restaurant also has reasonably priced meals (including a L16,000 tourist menu), or you could try the equally unpretentious *Trattoria da Gino*, Via Camozzi 16. The *gelateria* at Via Camozzi 22 makes its own ice cream, while it's worth tolerating the sour looks of the staff at the *Corona* (on the lake front near Piazza Garibaldi) for a good *frullati* or an apple pie.

There's a good selection of **hikes** to be done around Menaggio, ranging from a two-and a half hour walk to the pretty village of **CARDANO**, to the fifty-kilometre *Sentiero delle 4 Valli*, which leads through four valleys to Lake Lugano. The tourist office has descriptions of routes in English, including details of how to get to the various starting-points on public transport. You should, however, take a map as well.

The North

The next major steamer stop is **GRAVEDONA**, a not particularly pretty place, but one of the few towns on the lake as old as Como. Wordsworth set off on a moonlight hike from here, got lost, and, stuck on a rock in the middle of nowhere, was unable to sleep because he was "tormented by the stings of insects". Medieval Gravedona, along with nearby Dongo and Sorico, formed part of an independent republic, victimised in the fifteenth century by the inquisitor Peter of Verona for daring to doubt that the pope was God's earthly representative. The people got rid of Peter by hacking him to death, but the pope rewarded him for his devotion to duty by swiftly canonising him and deeming him Patron of Inquisitors. There's a prophetic twelfth-century carving in the lakeside church of **Santa Maria del Tiglio** (open July–Sept, at other times get the key from the green house on the road) – a centaur pursuing a deer, an early Christian symbol for the persecution of the Church.

If you want to stay over, the *Locanda Serenella* (☎0344/80.060; ⑤) and the *Serenella* **campsite**, beyond the church and down towards the lake, are open roughly April to September. Beyond Gravedona the lake sides flatten out and the building gets more haphazard, although as the winds are good for **sailing** and **windsurfing** there are a number of **campsites** and cheap, modern **hotels** to the north of **DOMASO** – a not unattractive small town.

The northeastern shore, Bellagio and Lecco and the central zone

The **eastern shore** of the lake, stretching from the flat marshes of the north to Como's left branch, **Lago Lecco**, overshadowed by the saw-like ridge of Monte Resegone, is often sunless and consequently less visited than the western shore. The triangle of land between the two branches – the **Central Zone** – is lusher and sunnier, busy on the coast but with plenty of quiet villages and three small lakes inland. There are fewer places to stay, however, and these are not easily accessible, except Colico, Bellano and Varenna on the main shore and Bellagio on the central triangle, which are all served by steamer and hydrofoil.

The northeastern shore

At the top end of the lake's eastern shore – opposite Gravedona – **COLICO** is the final stop for Como steamers, a small industrial centre whose only attraction is a restored eleventh-century abbey, the **Abbazia di Piona**, on the tip of the promontory just above the steamer landing. From here, steamers and hydrofoils head back down the eastern shore, stopping off at **BELLANO**, a tiny town of silk and cotton mills, near to which is a steep gorge with walkways suspended above a roaring river (Easter–Sept Thurs–Tues 9.30am–12.30pm & 1.20–5.30pm).

Further south, **VARENNA** is a relaxed, immediately likeable place, shaded by pines and planes, and with a wonderfully old-fashioned train station, whose waiting room – complete with rickety stove – looks like something out of a Thirties film set. If you're feeling energetic, you could haul up the hill to the **Castello de Vezio**, allegedly founded by the Lombard Queen Theodolinda, for some great views. If you're not, it's a short walk south along the main road to the **Villa Cipressa**, a nineteenth-century villa now occupied by a hotel. L1500 buys you access to its gardens, voluptuously terraced and swooningly scented enough to make even diehard cynics gush. After this, the gardens of the **Villa Monastero** next door (daily 10am–12.30pm & 2.30–6pm; L1500) seem tame, so it's no great hardship, if, as often happens, they are closed for conferences. Continue along the road for around a kilometre and you'll come to the miniature village of **Fiumelatte,** named after the waterfall which froths its way through its centre. If you've got the cash, it's easy to be seduced into staying at the *Villa Cipressa* (☎0341/830113; ⑦), although the rooms are more ascetic than you might imagine. Otherwise, save your money and stay at the *Sole* (☎0341/830206; ③) or the lakefront *Cavallino* (☎0341/830223; ④), whose vine-trellised terrace is the most atmospheric place to **eat**, with reasonably priced pasta and fish dishes.

Bellagio

Cradled by cypress-spiked hills on the tip of the triangle separating Como's two "legs", **BELLAGIO** has been called the most beautiful town in Italy. With a promenade planted with oleanders and limes, fin de siècle hotels painted shades of butterscotch, peach and cream, and a hilly old centre of cobbled streets and alleyways – to say nothing of its tremendous location – it's certainly a contender. Also – and this is perhaps surprising given its popularity with holiday operators – the town has not surrendered itself totally to tourism, and the everyday life of the town is very much in evidence. Bars are packed with locals, and foodstores continue to hold their own among the occasional antique, crafts or souvenir shop. If all you want to do is relax, there's really no better place.

The lake is clean enough to swim in here, which you can do from the **Lido** (May-Oct daily 8am–midnight) at the end of the promenade; you can also go water-skiing . The gardens of the **Villa Melzi** behind (daily 9am–6.30pm; L4000) are no great shakes, but it's well worth making the effort to book onto a guided tour around the gorgeous gardens of the **Villa Serbelloni**, splendidly sited on a hill above the town. Built on the site of one of Pliny the Younger's villas, it is now owned by the Rockefeller Foundation, on the hill above, and is perhaps the best place to appreciate Bellagio's genteel English air. It was once a favourite haunt of European monarchs, and it's not hard to imagine them strolling among the grottoes and statues of the extravagant garden and gushing over the views of the two branches of the lake. The sumptuously frescoed interior is closed to visitors, but there are guided tours around the **gardens** at 10.30am and 4pm (except Mon) between April 15 and October 15 (booking at the tourist office; L5000). At the foot of the hill is a classy hotel, also called *Villa Serbelloni*, whose guests numbered Churchill, recovering from the war in late 1945, and John F. Kennedy.

Bellagio's **tourist office**, on Piazza della Chiesa (Mon–Thurs 9am–noon & 2–6pm, Fri & Sat 9am–noon & 2–6.30pm), is a helpful source of information. If you're **staying**, the best-value rooms are at the *Suisse* Piazza Mazzini 8 (☎031/950335; ④), an appropriately old-style hotel on the lake front. Alternatively try the *Giardinetto*, Via Roncati 12 (☎031/950.168; ④), with a garden where you can picnic, or the *Roma*, Via Salita Grande 6 (☎031/950.424; ④), which has views of the lake.

The majority of Bellagio's **restaurants** are pricey. Try *La Grotta*, Salita Cernaia 14, clearly signposted from the lake front, which does good pizza, or splash out at *Bilacus*, on Salita Serbelloni, which is reckoned to be the town's best restaurant (be sure to avoid the very poor *Trattoria San Giacomo*). The best places for ice cream are *Il Sorbetto* at the top of Salita Serbelloni, and the *Gelateria del Borgo* at Via Garibaldi 46. If you don't want to pay over the odds for a drink at the lakeside cafés, head for the *Circolo Acli* on Via Garibaldi, where you can drink cheaply in a walled garden. Nightlife in Bellagio centres on a couple of trendy bars: *Divina Commedia* (clearly signposted off Via Garibaldi), frescoed with *putti*, poppies and dippy blond angels, where they also do good food, and *La Laterna* at Salita Serbelloni 15, an animated hang-out that serves pasta and sandwiches too.

Lecco and around

Flanked by mountains of scored granite, Como's eastern fork is austere and fjord-like, at its most atmospheric in the morning mists. The villages wedged along the shoreline are far more workaday than those of the rest of the lake, and **LECCO**, at its foot, is a drab industrial town. You certainly won't *want* to stay in Lecco, but its public transport connections are good, and there are some challenging possible hikes in the nearby mountains. Trains run to Como, Milan and Bergamo, and back up the eastern shore by way of Varenna to Sondrio, and there are buses into the mountain villages, notably **Piani Resinelli**, a good starting-point for hikes. **Buses** leave from outside the **train station**, from which it's a brisk five-minute walk from the **ferry station** (go straight down the central street, Via Cavour and across Piazza Garibaldi, to the shore and turn right). Lecco's **tourist office** is on Via N. Sauro, to the right off Piazza Garibaldi (Mon–Sat 9am–12.30pm & 2.30–6pm; ☎0341/362.360). If you need to **stay**, the *Due Torri*, Via Roma 40 (☎0341/362.425; ④), just off Piazza Garibaldi, is convenient. For **eating**, there are a number of snack bars and pizzerias around the station, though none of them are particularly special.

If you've time to kill you could pop into Lecco's **Basilica**, which boasts a set of fourteenth-century Giottesque frescoes, and the birthplace of Alessandro Manzoni, author of the great nineteenth-century novel *I Promessi Sposi* ("The Betrothed"). The **Villa Manzoni**, on Via Amendola, is open as a museum (Tues–Fri 10am–12.30pm & 2.30–5.30pm, Sat & Sun 10am–1pm).

Above Lecco at the end of the road to MALNAGA a **cable car** – and paths #1, #7 and #18 – climb up to the **Piani d'Erna**, from where trails lead further into the mountains. Alternatively, buses from outside the train station run up to **Piani Resinelli**, another starting-point for hikes. These are not Sunday afternoon strolls, and unless you are experienced, you really should get hold of a reliable walking book as well as a good map before you go. Many of the walks involve scaling a *Via Ferrata*, literally an iron road of ladders, ropes, chains, pegs and rungs fixed on to some of the steeper rock faces. Some stretches are vertical, and once you've started it's often impossible to turn back – the *Vie Ferrate* are popular and there will probably be a queue behind you. They should not be attempted solo or without proper equipment (if you don't have a harness and fall, you're unlikely to survive). Don't climb a *Via Ferrata* in a thunderstorm either; it might just become one long lightening conductor.

The Valchiavenna and Valtellina

Trains run north of Colico into the **Valchiavenna**, a flat-bottomed valley into which Lake Como extended right up until Roman times. It left behind the **Lago di Mezzola** – not worth getting off the train for, but a pleasant enough distraction before you hit the rusty corrugated iron buildings of NOVATE. Further on, you could stop at **CHIAVENNA**, at the end of the train line, to visit a *crotta*, natural cellars in the rocks (across the rail line) which have for centuries been used for maturing wine salamis, cured meats and cheeses. Most are now inns and restaurants, the most authentic of which is the *Crotto Torricelli*, where you sit at granite tables. The town otherwise is nothing special, and the old centre definitely looks best at night, but there are interesting walks up to the **Marmitte dei Giganti**, potholes formed by glaciation. The cheapest **hotel** is the *Elvezia* (☎0343/32.165; ④), but this is such a depressing place you might prefer to pay a little more and stay next door in the more civilised *Flora* (☎0343/32.254; ④). You'll see both hotels as soon as you step out of the **train station**. From Chiavenna you can catch a bus to St Moritz in Switzerland, from where the *trenino rosso* (see below) takes a scenic mountain route back across the border to Tirano.

Unless you're a keen skier, or are heading for eastern Switzerland or Trentino, there's little to draw you to the **Valtellina**, east of Lake Como, one of Italy's less appealing Alpine valleys. Cut through by road and rail, it's mined for minerals and iron ore and is prone to landslides; the last, in 1987, partially destroyed the rail line, killing several people.

The line has since been reconstructed, and runs up from Lake Como to the region's main centre, **SONDRIO**, a modern and undistinguished town, well known for its wine, which is on sale in many of the shops. The **Museo Valtellinese** (Mon–Fri 9am–noon & 2.30–5pm) is a museum of local traditions, with small art and archaeological sections. Really, you'd do better to catch a train on to **TIRANO**, a similarly bland town, but one which gives access to the private **RhB trenino rosso** through the mountains to ST MORITZ in Switzerland. *InterRail* cards are valid; otherwise the return journey costs around L40,000 (depending on the exchange rate). If you wanted, you could pick up a bus in ST MORITZ and return to Italy via Chiavenna.

Beyond Tirano, to which it's connected by bus, **BORMIO is** a snooty, unfriendly ski resort which was once an important stopover on the trade routes between Venice and Switzerland. It still retains a core of cobbled streets and frescoed palaces from the fifteenth and sixteenth centuries within a spawl of hotels for its many skiers: a very prestigious ski resort, it hosted the 1985 World Alpine Ski Championships and is now one of Europe's largest areas for summer skiing. Close by, the huge national park, the **Parco Nazionale di Stelvio**, is a good place for walks and challenging climbs as well as skiing (see Chapter Four, *Trentino-Alto Adige*). Details can be gleaned from the **tourist office** (Mon–Sat 9am–12.30pm & 2.30–6pm; Sun 9.30am–12.30pm), up the hill from the bus station just beyond the *Hotel Nazionale* – where you can also pick up maps, details of *rifugi*, and information on the town – or at the national park **visitors' centre**, Via Monte Braulio 56 (Mon–Fri 9am–12.30pm & 2–6pm; ☎0342/905.151). If you're sleeping over in Bormio, the *Villa Rina*, on the northern approach road (☎0342/901.674; ④), has reasonable doubles, but prices vary greatly with the time of year.

Bergamo

Just 50km north of Milan, yet much closer to the mountains in look and feel, **BERGAMO** is a city with a split identity, made up of two distinct parts – **Bergamo Bassa**, the lower, modern centre, and **Bergamo Alta**, clinging to the hill 1200 feet above the Lombardian plain. Bergamo Bassa is no great shakes, a mixture of faceless suburbs and pompous Neoclassical town planning; but Bergamo Alta is one of northern Italy's loveliest city centres, a favourite retreat for the work-weary Milanese, who flock here at weekends seeking solace in its fresh mountain air, wanderable streets and the lively, easy-going pace of its life.

Bergamo owes much of its magic to the Venetians, who ruled the town for over 350 years, building houses and palaces with fancy Gothic windows and adorning many a facade and open space with the Venetian lion – symbol of the republic. The most striking feature, however, is the ring of gated walls. Now worn, mellow and overgrown with creepers, these kept alien armies out until 1796, when French Revolutionary troops successfully stormed the city, throwing off centuries of Venetian rule.

Arrival and accommodation

The **train station** is right at the end of Bergamo Bassa's central avenue. To the right are the two **bus stations**: the *Stazione Autolinee*, serving all the longer distance buses, and the *SAB*, serving mostly local villages like Clusone, although there are some buses which go further afield. Bus #1 runs from the train station, and bus #3 from Viale Papa Giovanni XXIII, along the central avenue and up to Bergamo Alta. Alternatively you can get off the bus at the **funicular station** at the foot of the hill, and make the ascent by cable car for no extra charge as long as you show your bus ticket – otherwise it costs L1000.

The **tourist office** (Mon–Fri 9am–12.30pm & 2.50–6.30pm; ☎035/242.226) is a couple of minute's walk from the train station at Viale Papa Giovanni XXIII 110, and has maps and information on the town and province.

Bergamo is *not* somewhere to arrive on spec, even out of season: itinerant workers based in the new town's factories take up all the cheaper accommodation, and it's not unusual to discover that the only vacancies are in four-star hotels. There is a youth hostel, but it's currently closed; phone ☎035/342349 to see if it has re-opened; if it has, take bus #14, direction S. Colombana, and get off the stop after the modern church and the *Red Mountain* café. Bergamo's **cheaper hotels** are in Bergamo Bassa. Closest to the upper city is *Mammagrande*, Via N. Sauro 7 (☎035/218.413; ④) – bus #9a, #9b, #9c from Porta Nuova, near the Accademia Carrara. Slightly cheaper, there's the *Antica Trattoria della Brianza*, Via Broseto 61a (☎035/253.338; ③), a fifteen-minute walk to the west of the train station; take bus #11 from Porta Nuova and get off at the Esso garage. Also west of the station is the *Isabella*, Via Quarenghi 35 (☎035/237.177; ③), a friendly, family-run hotel with a pizzeria. Take Via Bonimelli from the station and walk for ten minutes. Closer to the station, though often fully booked, is the *Sant'Antonino*, Via Paleocapa 1, on the corner of Via Papa Giovanni XXIII (☎035/210.284; ④). If you have your heart set on staying in Bergamo Alta, the *Agnello d'Oro*, Via Gombito 22 (☎035/249.883; ⑤), is about the cheapest place you'll find, and has a well-regarded restaurant downstairs to boot.

The City

However you get to Bergamo, you'll arrive in **BERGAMO BASSA**, which spreads north from the railway station in an uneasy blend of Neoclassical ostentation, fascist severity and tree-lined elegance. At the heart of things, the mock-Doric temples of the **Porta Nuova** mark the entrance to **Sentierone**, a spacious piazza with gardens, surrounded by nineteenth-century arcades and frowned down upon by the **Palazzo di Giustizia**, built in the bombastic rectangular style of the Mussolini era. This is the liveliest part of the lower city, busy most of the day and especially during the evening *passeggiata*, but it has no great appeal, and you'd be wise to save your energy for **BERGAMO ALTA**, easily walkable using the **funicular** at the top end of Viale Vittorio Emanuele II, or by taking a #1 or #3 bus from the train station – both of which leave you on Piazza Mercato delle Scarpe.

Bergamo Alta

From Piazza Mercato delle Scarpe, Via Gombito leads up to **Piazza Vecchia**, enclosed by a harmonious miscellany of buildings, ranging from wrought-iron-balconied houses containing cafés and restaurants to the opulent Palladian-style civic library. Stendhal rather enthusiastically dubbed the square "the most beautiful place on earth", and certainly it's a striking open space, the most imposing building the medieval **Palazzo della Ragione**, a Venetian-Gothic style structure that stretches right across the piazza, lending a stagey feel to things, especially at night when the wrought-iron lamps are

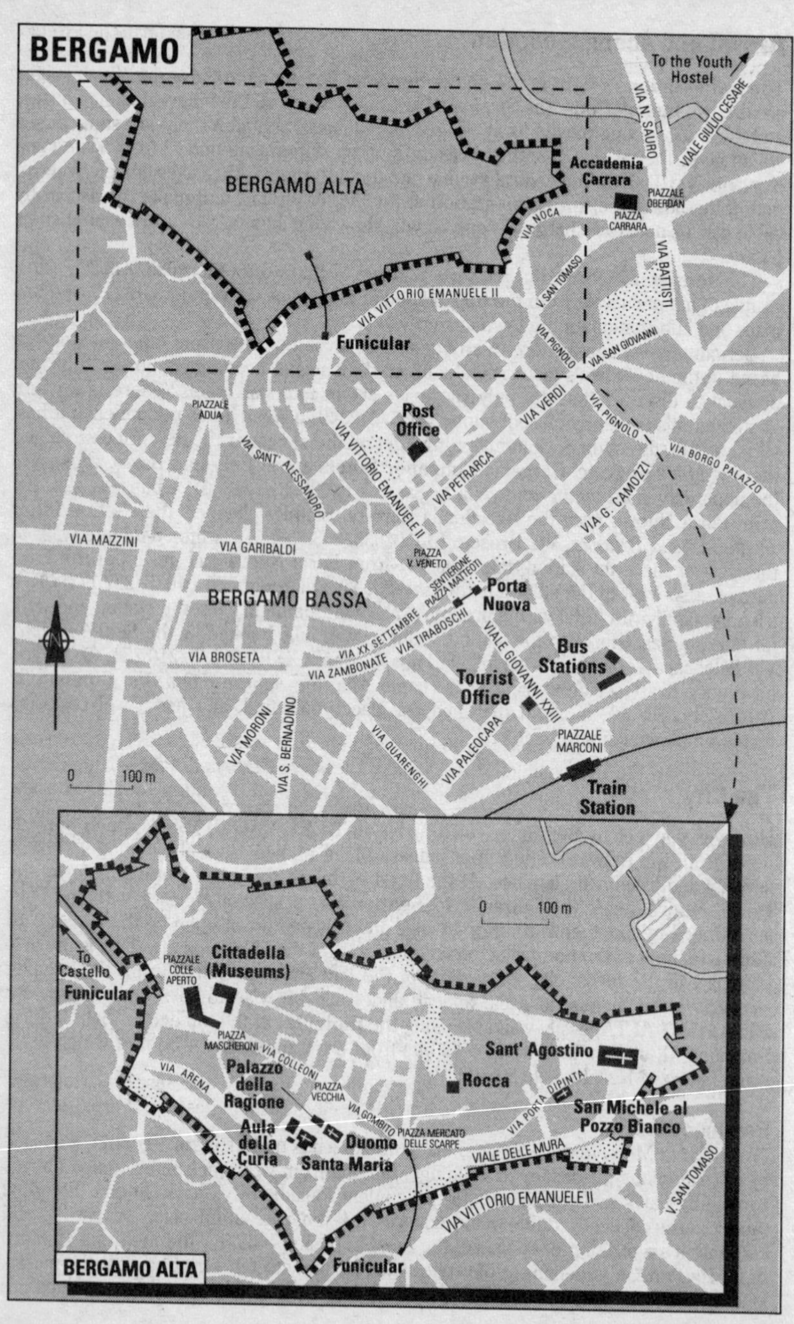
BERGAMO
To the Youth Hostel
VIA N. SAURO
VIALE GIULIO CESARE
BERGAMO ALTA
Accademia Carrara
PIAZZALE OBERDAN
PIAZZA CARRARA
VIA NOCA
V. SAN TOMASO
VIA BATTISTI
VIA VITTORIO EMANUELE II
Funicular
VIA PIGNOLO
VIA SAN GIOVANNI
PIAZZALE ADUA
Post Office
VIA VERDI
VIA PIGNOLO
VIA SANT' ALESSANDRO
VIA VITTORIO EMANUELE II
VIA PETRARCA
VIA BORGO PALAZZO
VIA G. CAMOZZI
VIA MAZZINI
VIA GARIBALDI
PIAZZA V. VENETO
SENTIERONE
PIAZZA MATTEOTTI
Porta Nuova
BERGAMO BASSA
VIA XX SETTEMBRE
VIA TIRABOSCHI
VIA BROSETA
VIA ZAMBONATE
VIALE GIOVANNI XXIII
Bus Stations
Tourist Office
VIA MORONI
VIA S. BERNADINO
VIA QUARENGHI
VIA PALEOCAPA
PIAZZALE MARCONI
Train Station
0 100 m
0 100 m
To Castello
Funicular
PIAZZALE COLLE APERTO
Cittadella (Museums)
PIAZZA MASCHERONI
VIA COLLEONI
VIA ARENA
Palazzo della Ragione
PIAZZA VECCHIA
VIA GOMBITO
PIAZZA MERCATO DELLE SCARPE
Aula della Curia
Duomo
Santa Maria
Rocca
Sant' Agostino
VIA PORTA DIPINTA
San Michele al Pozzo Bianco
VIALE DELLE MURA
VIA VITTORIO EMANUELE II
V. SAN TOMASO
Funicular
BERGAMO ALTA

switched on. Court cases used to be heard under the open arcades that form the ground floor, and, following a guilty verdict, condemned criminals were exhibited there. The piazza itself was the scene of more joyous celebrations in 1797, when the French formed the Republic of Bergamo. A "tree of liberty" was erected, and the square, carpeted with tapestries, was transformed into an open-air ballroom in which – as a symbol of the new democracy – dances were led by an aristocrat partnered by a butcher.

To the right of the Palazzo della Ragione is the entrance to the massive **Torre della Civica**, which you can ascend by lift if the repairs have been completed. Its fifteenth-century bell, which narrowly escaped being melted down by the Germans to make arms during World War II, still tolls a 180-peal curfew at 10pm every night. Afterwards, walk through the palazzo's arcades to the **Piazzetta del Duomo** and the **Duomo** on the left – though this is of less interest than the church of **Santa Maria Maggiore** in front, a rambling Romanesque church garnished with a scalloped Gothic porch crowned by two loggias sheltering statues of saints. Inside, Santa Maria is an extraordinarily elaborate church, its ceiling marzipanned with ornament in the worst tradition of Baroque excess, encrusted with gilded stucco, painted vignettes and languishing statues. There's a piece of nineteenth-century kitsch too – a monument to Donizetti, the Bergamo-based composer of highly popular romantic comedies with memorable melodies and predictable plots who died from syphilis here in 1848. As the town's most famous son, his death was much grieved, and bas-relief *putti* stamp their feet and smash their lyres in misery over the event. More subtly, the intarsia landscapes on the choir stalls – designed by Lotto, and executed by a local craftsman – are remarkable not only for their intricacy but for the incredible colour-range of the natural wood.

Even the glitziness of Santa Maria is overshadowed by the Renaissance decoration of the **Cappella Colleoni** next door (daily 9am–noon & 2–6pm). Built onto the church in the 1470s, the chapel is a gorgeously extravagant confection of pastel-coloured marble carved into an abundance of miniature arcades, balustrades and twisted columns, and capped with a mosque-like dome. Commissioned by Bartolomeo Colleoni, a Bergamo mercenary in the pay of Venice, it was designed by the Pavian sculptor Amadeo – responsible for the equally excessive Certosa di Pavia. The interior is almost as opulent, with a ceiling frescoed in the eighteenth century by Tiepolo sheltering Colleoni's sarcophagus, encrusted with reliefs and statuettes, and topped with a gleaming gilded equestrian statue. There's also the more modest tomb of his daughter, Medea, who died aged 15.

Take a look, too, at the nearby **Baptistery**, removed from the interior of Santa Maria Maggiore in the seventeenth century when christenings were transferred to the duomo. After some time in storage it was eventually reconstructed outside the **Aula della Curia** (Bishop's Court), alongside the Capella Colleoni, which contains thirteenth- and fourteenth-century frescoes of the life of Christ, including an odd scene in which Christ judges the damned, holding a dagger, Damocles-like, in his teeth. Behind, at the back of Santa Maria Maggiore, is the bulging and recently restored **Tempietto di San Croce**, dating from the tenth century.

Leading out of Piazza Vecchia, **Via Colleoni** also memorialises Bartolomeo Colleoni; it's a narrow street but one of the upper city's main pedestrian thoroughfares, lined with pastry shops selling chocolate and marzipan cakes topped with birds (*ucelli*) and leading to the brink of Bergamo Alta. At no. 9–11 is a charitable institution set up by Colleoni to provide dowries for poor women – the Venetians ruled that no woman could marry without one – that now holds a small **museum** inside, open Wednesdays from 10am until noon. At the end of Via Colleoni, Piazza Mascheroni lies at the entrance to the **Cittadella**, a military stronghold built by Barnabo Visconti that originally occupied the entire western headland. The remaining buildings now house a small theatre and two **museums**, of **archaeology** (Tues–Sun 9am–12.30pm & 2.30–6pm) and **natural history** (Tues–Sun 9am–noon & 2.30–5.30pm) – both only of interest to specialists.

There are good views from here across the **Colle Aperto** (open hill) to Bergamo Bassa, though for really outstanding views you need to walk up to the **Castello** perched on the summit of San Vigilio, which rises up from Porto San Alessandro. A funicular operates in summer but the walk is pleasant, up a steep narrow road overlooking the gardens of Bergamo's most desirable properties, and past pricey bars and restaurants. In the grounds of the castle there's a maze of underground passages to explore that used to run right down to Bergamo Alta.

Returning to the Colle Aperto, you can either walk back through the city or follow the old **walls** around its circumference – the whole circuit takes a couple of hours. The most picturesque stretch is between the Colle Aperto and Porta San Giacomo, from which a long flight of steps leads down into the lower city. Alternatively, returning through the upper city to Piazza Mercato delle Scarpe, you can climb up to the grounds of the **Rocca**, where there's a small Unification museum – worth a look before delving into the twisting streets of the **medieval quarter** below.

The Accademia Carrara

Just below the upper town, close to the city walls, the **Accademia Carrara** (Wed–Mon 9.30am–12.30pm & 2.30–5.30pm; L3000) is one of Bergamo's most important sights and among Lombardy's top quality collections of art. You can walk down here from the old city, along the steep Via Porta Dipinta and through the Porta Sant'Agostino, to see portraits by Pisanello and Botticelli, works by Giovanni Bellini and Crivelli, Carpaccio and Lotto – all carefully and imaginatively displayed with the layperson in mind. There are also paintings by the Lombard realists Foppa and Bergognone, Spanish-style portraits by Moroni, an elegant idealised *St Sebastian* by Raphael and canvases by Titian and Palma il Vecchio. Don't miss the room dedicated to works by the twentieth-century Bergamo-born sculptor Giacomo Manzù, best known for his stylised bronzes of cardinals.

Eating and drinking

Restaurant prices in Bergamo tend to be aimed at well-heeled tourists, for whom one of the town's attractions are the local bird specialities (hunting and eating the wildlife around Bergamo is a major local sport). If you're on a tight budget, the cheapest place to **eat** is the *ACLI mensa* in the *Sant'Antonino* hotel basement, and there's a self-service restaurant open lunchtimes only on Via Sant'Alessandro, a steep street packed with *birrerias* and clothes shops, climbing from the lower to the upper city. *Bar Botticelli*, in the upper town opposite the cable car station, does good-value lunches and dinners – with an *ISIC* you'll pay L12,000 for a set meal; *Vineria Cozzi*, Via Colleoni 22a, is a classy wine bar with around 300 wines and an excellent cold buffet; the *Papageno Pub*, again on Via Colleoni, does hot meals, sandwiches and salads. For cheaper and more basic sandwiches you should try *Ol Bareti* on Via Gombito, a tiny wood-panelled bar. For picnics, there is a tempting *salumeria* at Via Gombito 8, or the decadent pastries at *Dolce e Salato*, Via Gombito 4. Among ordinary restaurants you might try are *Trattoria Bernabo* on Piazza Mascheroni, outside the cittadella, which isn't too expensive, especially if you stick to pizza; *Da Franco*, also on Via Colleoni, has loads of hearty polenta dishes, and does a fixed menu for L22,000. *Da Mimmo*, on the main drag of the upper town at Via Colleoni 17, serves reasonably priced pizzas and an excellent-value tourist menu, including wine, for a little over L20,000.

Around Bergamo

Industrial development has done a pretty thorough job of ruining much of the countryside around Bergamo, particularly in the **Valle Seriana** northwest of the town, where factories and apartment blocks compete for space with forests and mountains, and rivers have been reduced to streams by hydroelectric power. Persevere, however: the upper reaches of the valley are still fairly unspoilt and easily accessible by bus from Bergamo.

Clusone

CLUSONE is the first stop worth making, a picturesque hilltop village whose **Chiesa dei Disciplini** (above the village centre, a ten-minute walk from the bus station) draws people from all over. There's little of interest inside the church, but the two fifteenth-century frescoes on its outside wall more than compensate. The upper fresco, *The Triumph of Death*, concentrates on the attitude of the wealthy towards death, with three noblemen returning from the hunt, discovering an open tomb containing the worm-infested corpses of the pope and emperor. A huge skeleton, representing Death, balances on the edge of the tomb, while other skeletons take aim at people gathered around the tomb – incorruptible figures, uninterested in the bribes being offered them. The *Dance of Death* below continues the moral tale, contrasting the corrupt upper classes with a procession of contented commoners, each dancing his way towards death quite happily, above an inscription inviting those who have genuinely served God to approach without fear and join the dance.

Clusone itself is worth a wander, especially on Mondays when the steep curving streets are taken over by a market selling local sausage and cheeses. The **tourist office** is on Piazza della Orologia, named for the fiendishly complicated sixteenth-century clock on the tower of the Palazzo Comunale. If you have the time and patience, you can work out the date, the sign of the zodiac, the duration of the night and the phase of the moon. The tourist office has information on local walks and hotels; of several one-star hotels, the cheapest is the *Gamberino* on Via Cifrondi (☎0346/21.215; ④).

Val Cavallina

From Clusone you can take a bus to Lago d'Iseo or further up the **Valle Seriana**, though this is of little interest unless you're a committed skier. Similarly the **Val Cavallina**, which has also suffered from industrial development, much of it ruined by small factories and tacky housing. The holiday area around Lago Endine isn't too bad, but you're more likely to pass through the valley only on your way up to Lago d'Iseo.

Beyond the lake, to the northwest, **Cantoniera della Presolana** is a large ski resort with some swanky hotels, dating back to the turn of the century. It has fifteeen slopes, an ice rink, ski and sled hire, and, surprisingly, a number of reasonable one-star hotels. **Val di Scalve**, beyond Presolana, is famous for the **Gorge of the Dezzo**, a narrow chasm forged by the torrents of the River Scalve, whose overhanging rocks are spectacular even if the river has been reduced to a miserable trickle by hydroelectric works.

Val Brembana

Northeast of Bergamo the **Val Brembana** follows a mountain-fringed route that was well-trodden in the Middle Ages by caravans of mules transporting minerals from the Valtellina to the cities of the plain. The road is now frequented mostly by weekend skiers heading up to FOPPOLO, and by less energetic Italians en route to **SAN**

PELLEGRINO TERME to take the waters. San Pellegrino has been Lombardy's most fashionable spa since the turn of the century, and it's from this period that its extravagant main buildings – the grand hotels and casino – date. When you tire of mock-Baroque, take the funicular up to **SAN PELLEGRINO VETTA** for fantastic views of the Alps.

Lago d'Iseo and the Val Camonica

Lago d'Iseo raises your expectations. Descending from Clusone, the road passes through steep gorges, thick forests and stark angular mountains, at the foot of which lies the lake. The fifth largest of the northern lakes, and the least known outside Italy, you'd imagine it to be more undiscovered than the others but the apartment blocks, harbourside boutiques, ice cream parlours and heavy industry of **LOVERE** put paid to any notions that Iseo might have escaped either tourist exploitation or industrialisation. This doesn't deter the Italians, who flock to Lago d'Iseo's resorts for its fish restaurants, water sports and low-key hikes, but unless any of these appeal, or you want to use it as a base for the ascent of Monte Gugliemo or for exploring the prehistoric rock carvings in the Val Camonica, there's little point in hanging around.

There is *one* retreat, the traffic-free **Monte Isola**, accessible by **ferry** (hourly) from Iseo town at the south of the lake. It's Italy's largest lake-island, over 3km long and rising to 600m. As there's a large campsite, and space in its hotels for 200 people, you're unlikely to get much solitude in high season; but out of season it's well worth a visit, either to be utterly lazy or to take a walk right around the edge of the island, for great views across the lake. There are a couple of cheap **hotels**: the *Bellavista* (☎030/988.106; ④) in the village of SIVIANO on the northwest corner of the island, and the *Sensole* (☎030/988.6203; ④) in SENSOLE. The **campsite** (☎030/988.126) is at CARZANO on the northeast tip of the island and is open year-round.

The attractions of **ISEO** town are purely practical. **Trains** from Brescia stop here, as do buses, and there's an ultra-cheap hotel above the *Il Cenacolo* bar at Via Mirolte 13 (☎030/980.136; ③), as well as a pricier but very pleasant option, the *Ambra*, Porta Gabriele Rosa 2 (☎030/980.130; ⑦). Iseo's **tourist office** at Lungolago Marroni 23 (daily 9am–12.30pm & 3–6pm; ☎030/980.209) has maps and details of walks, the most worthwhile of which is the hike from MARONE, halfway along the eastern side of the lake, up a steep and winding road to the village of ZONE. The reward is the extraordinary rock formations – soaring pinnacles formed by the erosion of the debris brought down by the glacier that gouged out the lake basin. If they look strangely familiar, it could be because Leonardo is said to have visited them, reproducing their peaks in his *Virgin of the Rocks* in the Louvre.

From Zone a track leads up to **Monte Gugliemo** (1949m), the ascent taking about three and a half hours. There's a *rifugio* near the summit: ask around in Zone before you leave to check it's open; if the warden's not there you'll be given the key.

Val Camonica: prehistoric rock carvings

Like Lago d'Iseo, the **Val Camonica** would be outstandingly beautiful were it not for the indiscriminate scattering of light industry that mars its lower reaches. Road and railway run up from the lake, following the River Oglio through the spa town of BOARIO to **CAPO DI PONTE**, whose **national park** (Tues–Sun 9am–sunset), a fifteen-minute walk from the town, contains prehistoric rock carvings spanning an incredible 8000 years – remnants from the culture of the Camuni tribe who holed up here to escape northern invaders from 5000 BC until the Romans colonised the area several thousand years later, together with the even older works that inspired the Camuni's art. There are carvings throughout the valley, but the most concentrated group is in the park, beginning with the **Great Rock** in front of the site's shop, where a set of stick-and-blob figures gives a taste of Camuni life over a 1000-year period. There are hunters, agricultural workers, a religious ceremony presided over by priests, and a Bronze Age burial in which the corpse is surrounded by his weapons and tools. To see how the civilisation developed into the Iron Age, head for Rock 35, carved with a blacksmith, and Rock 23, with a four-wheeled wagon transporting an urn. Carvings in other parts of the valley include some in the hamlet of **BEDOLINO** outside **CEMMO**, about 2km above Capo di Ponte on the other side of the Oglio, where there's a rock with a carving of a **Bronze Age map** showing huts, fields, walls, streams and canals.

Brescia and around

Famed for its arms industry and chill Fascist-era piazza, **BRESCIA** is a rather ugly industrial town, and one that is, unsurprisingly, not on most travellers' itineraries – although you may pass through on the way to Venice or up to the lakes. If you do, the architectural contrasts of its disjointed centre may provide some temporary light relief, but your overall impression will most likely be a negative one.

Arrival, information and accommodation

Brescia's main advantage is its convenience: it is on the main Milan–Verona railway line, giving you access to the cities of the Veneto, as well as those of Lombardy; local trains run up to Lecco, Lago d'Iseo, and the Camonica Valley, while the rest of the province, including the main resorts of Garda and several more distant destinations, is covered by direct buses, which leave from the two **bus terminals** outside the **train station**. This is south of the centre, a short bus ride or fifteen-minute walk from the city centre. For information, the **tourist office** is at Corso Zanardelli 34 (Mon–Thurs 8.30am–12.30pm & 3–6.30pm, Fri 8.30am–12.30pm & 3–5pm; ☎030/43.418).

If you're staying in Brescia, the best deal for **women only** is at a convent at Via Fratelli Bronzetti 17 (☎030/55.387; ①), which is very convenient and gives access to a kitchen, although it does have a 10pm curfew. Of ordinary **hotels**, *Ai Giardini*, Via Rubuffone 13, just beyond Porta Venezia (☎030/292.250; ③), is very cheap, if some way out of the centre; take bus #Q from the train station or any that runs through Porta Venezia. Other hotels include the *Calzavellia* on Via Calzavellia, off Corso Mameli (☎030/290.425; ③), and the plain but handily placed *Albergo Stazione* on Vicolo Stazione, off Viale Stazione (☎030/521.128; ④). With a little more money, you could try the *Gallo*, right on Piazza Paolo VI at Via Trieste 10 (☎030/56.252; ④), which has big airy rooms, some with balconies, or the *Nuovo Orologio*, very conveniently placed at Via Cesare Beccaria 17 (☎030/54.057; ⑤).

The City

Brescia's centre is grouped around the four piazzas beyond the main Corso Palestro. **Piazza del Mercato** is a sprawling cobbled square of more interest to the stomach than the eye – there's a weekday market, a supermarket, and small shops selling local salamis and cheeses nestling under its dark porticoes. **Piazza della Vittoria** is quite different, a disquieting reminder of the Fascist regime embodied in the clinical austerity of Piacentrini's gleaming marble rectangles. The arcades, boutiques, *gelaterie* and *pasticcerie* ensure that the square is well frequented in the *passeggiata* hour.

Alongside the post office, Via 24 Maggio leads to Brescia's pretttiest square, **Piazza della Loggia**, dating back to the fifteenth century, when the city invited Venice in to rule and protect it from Milan's power-hungry Viscontis. The Venetian influence is clearest in the fancily festooned **Loggia**, in which both Palladio and Titian had a hand, and in the **Torre dell'Orologio**, modelled on the campanile in Venice's Piazza San Marco. On the top left-hand corner is the **Porta Bruciata**, a defensive medieval tower-gate that was the scene in 1974 of a Red Brigade attack in which eight people were killed and over a hundred injured.

At the other side of Porta Bruciata, a small side street leads to **Piazza Paolo VI**, one of the few squares in Italy to have two cathedrals – though, frankly, it would have been better off without the second, a heavy Mannerist monument that took over 200 years to complete. The old twelfth-century cathedral, or **Rotonda**, is quite a different matter, a simple circular building of local stone, whose fine proportions are sadly difficult to appreciate from the outside as it is sunk below the current level of the piazza. Inside, glass set into the transept pavement reveals the remains of Roman baths (a wall and geometrical mosaics) and the apse of an eighth-century basilica which burned down in 1097. Most interesting is the fine red marble tomb of Berardo Maggi, a thirteenth-century Bishop of Brescia, opposite the entrance, decorated on one side with a full-length relief of the cleric, on the other by reliefs showing other ecclesiasts and dignitaries processing through a lively crowd of citizens to celebrate the peace Maggi had brought to the town's rival Guelph and Ghibelline factions.

Behind Piazza del Duomo, Via Mazzini leads to Via Musei, along which lie the remains of the Roman town of *Brixia*, though there's not a lot to see. There's a **theatre**, currently in the process of excavation and visible only through a wire fence. But the most substantial monument is the **Capitolino** (summer Tues–Sun 9am–noon & 2.30–5.30pm; winter 10am–12.45pm & 2–6pm; L2000), a Roman temple built in 73 AD, now reconstructed with red brick. Behind the temple are three reconstructed *celle*, probably temples to the Capitoline trinity of Jupiter, Juno and Minerva, which now house fragments of carved funerary monuments and mosaic pavements. Look also at the excellent **museum** upstairs (same hours), which has well-displayed jewellery, glassware, sculptures and bronzes, fragments of mosaic pavements and a life-sized winged Victory.

Further along Via dei Musei, the abbey of **San Salvatore** thrived from the eighth to the eighteenth century; it is currently closed for restoration, although you can still visit on guided tours (Tues–Fri 10am, 11am, 2pm and 3pm). Inside, there's a **modern art gallery** in the main building and a **museum of Christian art** in its church of **Santa Giulia**, where the prize exhibits here include a fourth-century ivory chest carved with lively biblical scenes and an eighth-century crucifix presented to the convent by Desiderius, King of the Lombards – made of wood overlaid with silver and encrusted with over 200 gems and cameos. Look also at the remains of the Byzantine **Basilica of San Salvatore**, visible through a glass screen at the back of the church.

Behind the museum, Via Piamarta climbs up the **Cydnean Hill**, the core of early Roman *Brixia*, mentioned by Catullus, though again the remains are scanty. There are a few fragments of a gate opposite the sixteenth-century church of **San Pietro in Oliveto**, so called because of the olive grove surrounding it, and the hill itself is crowned by the **Castello** – a monument to Brescia's various overlords, begun in the fifteenth century by Luchino Visconti and added to by the Venetians, French and Austrians over the years. The resultant confusion of towers, ramparts, halls and court-yards makes a good place for an atmospheric picnic, and holds Italy's largest **museum of arms** and a **model railway museum**.

More appealing perhaps is Brescia's main art gallery, the **Pinacoteca Tosio-Martinengo** – though it is sadly currently closed for restoration and its collection is mainly made up of the works of minor local artists. The works of the sixteenth-century

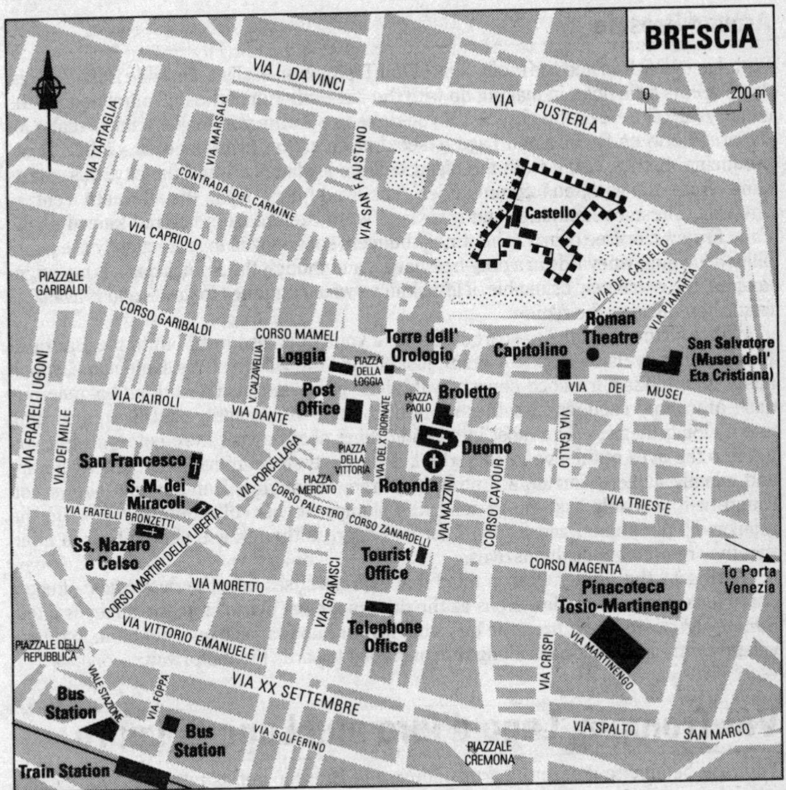

artist Romanino are worth a look, heavily influenced by Titian – as are those of the seventeenth-century realist Ceruti, who, unusually for his time, specialised in painting the poor (see "Milan", the "Accademia di Brera" p.132).

Eating, drinking and nightlife

Brescia is well endowed with **restaurants**, though none are especially cheap. If you're flat broke, *BarBar*, opposite the Rotonda, is a good place to fill up on bar snacks for free. *Bersaglieria*, at Corso Magenta 38, is the city's best pizzeria, cheap and with vegetarian pizza on a wholemeal ("integrale") base; *Ristorante Tre Merli*, Contrada del Cavaletto 8, off Corso Palestro, does a good fixed-price menu; while for a more unusual evening meal there's the natural (not vegetarian) food at *Altamira*, just off the northern end of Piazza Paolo VI on Vicolo Agostino, though this can be quite expensive. *Don Rodriguez*, Via F. Cavalotti 6, off Corso Zanardelli, is, despite the name, an ordinary Italian restaurant, with moderately priced pizza and pasta dishes. For **evenings**, there are plenty of bars and ice cream parlours around the centre, after which a good place is the *Arancia Meccanica* ("Clockwork Orange"), a student hang-out on Via Sovera at the start of Corso Mameli.

Around Brescia

With Lago di Garda and the mountains of Val Trompia so easily accessible from Brescia, there seems little point in making do with the distinctly run-of-the-mill attractions of the countryside closest to the city. But if you're keen on wine you might want to make for the area between Brescia and Lago d'Iseo, known as the **Franciacorta** – a hilly wine-producing district, rising from the bland built-up lowlands around the city, that got its name from the religious communities that lived there from the eleventh century onwards. These communities and their land were exempt from tax and known as the *Corti Franche*, or free courts. The wine-producers soon moved in, attracted by the possibility of owning vineyards in a duty-free haven, and though the Franciacorta is no longer tax-free, the extremely drinkable, if little-known wine continues to flow – and is available from shops all over the region.

With a further half-day to spare in Brescia, you could also head out to the **Badia di Rodengo** (daily 9am–noon & 3–6pm), just outside the village of the same name, which has a sumptuously frescoed church, with some gorgeous stucco-work and a generous dash of trompe l'oeil, and another room decorated with scantily clad figures surging into a cloudy heaven. The most interesting thing about a visit here is the insight you get into the lives of the five monks who live here – their primitive kitchen, tatty library and silently austere corridors. Entrance is free, although if Don Antonio shows you round he'll probably ask you to send him stamps for his collection; if you wish, the monks will put you up and feed you for no charge, although you should bear in mind that they're pretty poor themselves.

Getting to the abbey, bear in mind that express buses take the *autostrada* – keep a sharp lookout for the yellow signs as the drivers are apt not to stop; the abbey is a ten-minute signposted walk from the bus stop. If your bus is a local one, get off in Rodengo village centre and walk back along the main road towards the motorway.

Val Trompia, Lago d'Idro and Lago di Ledro

You may be able to ignore the arms industry in Brescia, but its impact is unavoidable when you pass through the **Val Trompia**, directly north of the city. The industry dates back over 400 years, started by the Venetians, keen to utilise the rich iron ore deposits of the area and to whom it became so indispensable that during the sixteenth century restrictions were actually placed on people's movements out of the region. The centre of today's (much diminished) arms industry is **GARDONE VAL TROMPIA**, where the *Beretta* company has its headquarters.

The valley beyond Gardone is crammed with industry as far as LAVONE, and hiking becomes possible only at **BOVENGNO**. From this small village paths lead up to Monte Muffetto (4hr) and, even better, to Monte Crestoso and its tiny tarns (5hr 30min), though you'll need a tent, as there are no *rifugi*. If you're without a tent, there are two *rifugi* further on – *Croce Domini* (1992m) at the head of the valley, and *Bonardi* (1743m) above the lovely Passo del Maniva. From either base you can walk down to Lago d'Idro or climb Monte Colombino, again with a couple of tarns. The map to get is the *Kompass* Carta Turistica, *Le Tre Valli Bresciane*. There are also a few cheap hotels at the ski resorts of COLLIO and SAN COLUMBANO; try the tiny *Belvedere* (☎030/927.259; ③).

From close to the *rifugio Croce Domini* a steep track climbs over into the broad Valle della Berga and up to **BAGOLINO** on the road to Lago d'Idro. Bagolino is quiet, preserving many of its medieval houses and a church, **San Rocco**, that has a startlingly realistic cycle of fifteenth-century frescoes. If you want to avoid Idro's unremarkable resorts, this is the place to stay: the *Cavallino* hotel (☎0365/99.103; ④) is quite reasonable, and buses run fairly frequently to and from the lake.

Lago d'Idro is a reasonably pretty lake, except for its marshy upper reaches where the effect is spoiled by a sand-dredger. Tourism is family-orientated, but as there's no road running along the upper reaches of the east shore, you should be able to find a quiet beach there. Although bathing in the lake is thought to induce a skin rash, few people are able to resist its cool, clear waters; there are also walks in the area if you want to do more than swim and laze around. Marked paths climb up into the hills from the east shore, and from ANFO on the west shore a track leads past the *rifugio Rosa di Baramone* to Bagolino. Again, you'll need the *Kompass* map mentioned above.

Idro's resorts are uniformly bland, but if you want to stay over, *Da Parida* (☎0365/809.026; ③) at Anfo has cheap doubles, as does the *Miralago* (☎0365/83.138) at CRONE, on the bus route, 2km from Idro town. Of the **campsites**, the most convenient are the two at Anfo and a couple at Vantone on the east shore – both on the bus route from Brescia.

Northeast from Idro, via Ponte Caffaro, you reach the point where the Austrian border ran through until 1918. From here a road leads to **Lago di Ledro** in the Val Sabbia, only 2km long and slightly less wide, and with a beauty straight out of a Swiss-kitsch postcard. Quieter than Idro, and far preferable, it has a couple of **campsites** and a **hotel**, the *Mezzolago* (☎0464/508.181; ⑤), which is open all year.

Lago di Garda

Lago di Garda is the largest and cleanest of the Italian lakes, and also the most popular. Tourism is relatively recent – beginning only this century when the road around its shores was completed – and it has little of the precious respectability that hangs over the Victorian-era resorts of Como and Maggiore. Indeed, the only celebrity English visitor to spend much time around the lake was D.H. Lawrence, whose *Twilight in Italy* details many of the lake's attractions.

For all that, Lake Garda is now firmly on the tour operators' schedules, and much of the development has been feverish; its resorts are each year invaded by a fair number of package tour Brits, as well as Germans, French and Italians attracted by some of Europe's best windsurfing and Garda's gentle climate. Winters are mild, summers tempered by breezes – the northern *sover*, which blows down the lake from midnight and through the morning, and the *ova*, blowing from the south in the afternoon and evening. Along the so-called Riviera Bresciana, on the most sheltered stretch of the western shore, are lush groves of olives, vines and citrus trees – fruits used for Garda's main products: olive oil, citrus syrups and Bardolino, Soave and Valpolicella wines. Scenically the shores of the lake are varied: the rich vegetation of its middle reaches gives way to the rugged north, where the lake narrows and is tightly enclosed by craggy mountains; the southern shores, 16km at their widest, are backed by a gentle plain.

Desenzano, Sirmione and the southern shore

Within easy striking distance of the Milan–Venice *autostrada* and railway, the **southern shore** of Lake Garda is predictably well touristed. **DESENZANO DEL GARDA**, the lake's largest town, is a major rail junction and the best starting-point for visiting Garda. Buses tend to connect with trains, and there are several ferries daily up to Riva and other resorts. Otherwise it has little to detain you. The lake front, lined with bars and restaurants, is quite attractive, though it's hard to ignore the busy main road running alongside. If you do end up with time to fill, there are spectacular views from the **castle**, and a **Roman villa** on Via Crocifisso that is definitely worth visiting, a formerly large and luxurious home that preserves some good mosaics (summer daily 9am–6.30pm; winter 9am–4pm; L4000).

A short but infrequent train ride from Desenzano, **SAN MARTINO DELLA BATTAGLIA** was the site of a famous battle, when Napoleon III and Vittorio Emanuele II defeated the Austrians in 1859. The **Torre di San Martino** (summer Wed–Mon 8am–1pm & 2–7pm; winter 9.30am–12.30pm & 1.30–4.30pm) was built in 1893 to commemorate the victory, and has paintings and sculptures of the leading figures plus a good view of the battlefield and Lake Garda from the top. Behind it is a battle museum.

Horrified by the extent of the slaughter, a Swiss man, Henry Dunant, was inspired to found the Red Cross, writing a short book, *A Memory of Solferino*, suggesting the formation of "relief societies for the purpose of having care given to the wounded in wartime, by zealous, devoted and thoroughly qualified volunteers". Dunant bankrupted himself over founding the Red Cross and was discovered in the last years of his life in a home for impoverished men. He was awarded the first ever Nobel prize, but never moved from the home. There's a monument to Dunant and the Red Cross 11km southeast of San Martino, at **SOLFERINO** – a paved path along the crest of the hill lined with tablets set into a wall, bearing the names of countries who ratified the Geneva Convention. There are also good views from the nearby fortress, and a small **museum** (same hours as Torre di San Martino, above) of battle memorabilia on the fringes of the village.

Sirmione and around

The original inhabitants of Desenzano's villa may well have come to **SIRMIONE**, spread along a narrow promontory protruding 4km into the lake, to seek cures in its sulphurous springs – it still retains the remains of a Roman spa. It is a popular spot, in a beautiful setting, though it's these days suffocated with luxury hotels, souvenir stands and lots of tourists. You're unlikely to want to stay, and in any case most of the hotels are pricey and usually full, but it's worth a brief visit to take in the town's handful of sights and laze around on the surrounding lidos.

Most people head for the **Rocca Scaligera** (summer Tues–Sun 9am–1pm & 3.30–8.30pm; winter Tues–Sun 9am–2pm; L6000), a fairy-tale castle with boxy turreted towers almost entirely surrounded by water, built by the Veronese Scaligera family in the thirteenth century when they ruled Garda. There's not much to see inside, and, although the views from its battlements are lovely, they don't really warrant the high entrance fee.

You can escape the crowds by walking out beyond the town to the peninsula's triangular and traffic-free hilly head, covered in cypresses and olive groves. The church of **San Piero** here has thirteenth-century frescoes inside, and its shady grounds make for a good picnic stop. A path leads along the edge of the peninsula, passing bubbling hot sulphur springs, to the **Lido** (May–Oct daily 8am–midnight, closed Wed in low season) where you can eat, drink, swim in the lake or sunbathe on the pontoon or nearby rocks. If you continue, you'll reach a fenced off area at the tip of the peninsula. The signs warn of landslides, but most people ignore these since the flat rocks are good for sun-soaking. Swimming or paddling is tricky, however, as underwater the rocks are slippery. There's a gate here up to the **Grotte di Catullo** (Tues–Sat 9am–6pm, Sun & Mon 9am–1pm), touted as Catullus's villa, although the white ruins are actually of a Roman spa: there's a hot sulphur spring 300m under the lake, and people still come to Sirmione to take the waters. Catullus did, however, retire to the town, coming all the way from the Black Sea by boat, hauling it overland when necessary so that he could keep it on the lake. The ruins, scattered on the hillside among ancient olive trees, are lovely, and there are superb views across the lake to the mountains. There's a small antiquarium with fragments of mosaics and frescoes, and below the site, a beach.

If you want to stay in Sirmione, booking ahead is essential in July and August. If you haven't booked, the **tourist office** by the bus station has a list of **rooms** (Mon–Fri 9am–12.30pm & 3–6.30pm), but don't count on these being free either. Of the **hotels**, the

Risorgimento, by the ferry jetty at Piazza Carducci 4–6 (☎030/916.325; ③), and *Lo Zodiaco*, Via XXV Aprile 18 (☎030/916.095; ③), a five-minute walk from the tourist office and bus station (Via XXV Aprile is the continuation of Via Marconi), are both reasonably priced and pleasant. The nearest **campsite** is the *Sirmioncino* (☎030/919.045), on the lake front, a fifteen-minute walk along Via Colombare out of town towards the mainland – though this too gets extremely crowded.

The western shore

Less built-up, and with reputedly cleaner water than the northern reaches of the lake, the lower reaches of the **western shore** are studded with campsites which make for cheap and reasonably convenient bases. If you're not heading for the campsites, only **SALÓ** is worth a stop, splendidly sited on a bay at the foot of the luxuriant Riviera Bresciana and a good place to stock up on local produce. Saló gave its name to Mussolini's short-lived last republic, instituted here after his rescue from the Abruzzi by the Nazis. Though it retains a handful of buildings from the fifteenth century – notably the duomo and town hall – when it was the Venetian Empire's main garrison town, these are unlikely to detain you for long. Better to detour 6km inland to **PUEGNAGO DEL GARDA**, where you can sample the rose wines – Grapello and Chiaretto – the **Comincioli** vineyard has been producing since the sixteenth century.

Gardone Riviera: Il Vittoriale and the village of San Michele

A few miles further up the shore **GARDONE RIVIERA** was once the most fashionable of Garda's resorts, and still retains its symbols of sophistication, though the elegant promenade, lush gardens, opulent villas and ritzy hotels now have to compete with some more recent – and less tasteful – tourist tack. It is famous for the consistency of its climate, and has Garda's most exotic botanical garden, the **Giardino Botanico Hruska** (summer only daily, 8am–7pm; L5000), laid out among artificial cliffs and streams.

Highlight of Gardone, and indeed of the whole lake, is **Il Vittoriale** (Tues–Sun 9am–12.30pm & 2–5.30pm, 6.30pm in summer; L15,000), the home of Italy's most notorious and extravagant twentieth-century writer, Gabriele D'Annunzio.

Born in 1863, D'Annunzio was no ordinary writer. He did pen some exquisite poetry and a number of novels. But he became better known as a soldier and socialite, leading his own private army and indulging in much-publicised affairs with numerous women, including the actress Eleonora Duse. When berated by his friends for treating her cruelly, he simply replied "I gave her everything, even suffering." He was a fervent supporter of Mussolini, providing the Fascist Party with their (meaningless) war-cry, *eia! eia! alalá*, though Mussolini eventually found his excessive exhibitionism an embarrassment (his boasts of eating dead babies, certainly, were bad publicity), and in 1925 presented him with this villa – ostensibly as a reward for his patriotism, in reality to shut him up.

It didn't take D'Annunzio long to transform Mussolini's Liberty-style gift into the Hollywood studio lookalike you see now. Outside, rammed into the cypress-covered hillside, is the prow of a battleship used in D'Annunzio's so-called "Fiume adventure". Fiume (now Rijeka), on the North Adriatic, had been promised to Italy before they entered World War I, but was eventually handed over to Yugoslavia instead. Incensed, D'Annunzio gathered together his army, occupied Fiume, and returned home a national hero. D'Annunzio's personality makes itself felt from the start in the two reception rooms – one a chilly and formal room for guests he didn't like, the other warm and inviting for those he did. Il Duce was apparently shown to the former, where the mirror has an inscription reputedly aimed at him – "Remember that you are made of glass and I of steel."

Nor was dining with D'Annunzio a reassuring experience: roast baby may not have featured on the menu, but in the glitzy dining room, as a warning to greedy guests, pride of place was given to a gilded and embalmed tortoise who had died of overeating. In fact D'Annunzio rarely ate with his guests, retreating instead to the *Sala di Lebbroso* where he would lie on a bier surrounded by leopard skins and contemplate death. The rest of the house is no less bizarre: the bathroom has a bathtub hemmed in by over 2000 tacky pieces of bric-a-brac; and the *Sala del Mappamondo*, as well as the huge globe for which it is named, contains an Austrian machine-gun and books including an immense version of *The Divine Comedy*. Suspended from the ceiling of the auditorium adjoining the house is the biplane which D'Annunzio used in a famous flight over Vienna in World War I.

If you want to stay over in Gardone, there are functional doubles at the *Nord*, Via Zanardelli 18 (☎0365/20.707; ④), on the main coast road by the most central bus stop. Alternatively, walk up the hill from here for a hundred metres and you'll come to the pleasantly located *Giardino*, Via Roma 31 (☎0365/21.020; ④), which, as its name suggests, has a garden. For the same price you can have a room with bath on the lakeside: head for the *Diana*, Lungolago D'Annunzio 30 (☎0365/21.815; ④), a left turn from the jetty as you step off the ferry. The pleasantest places to eat are up in the old village around Il Vittoriale: the *Bar Pizzeria Pesce* serves good, reasonably priced pizza, while, if you want to splash out, *Agli Angeli* has interesting pasta and fish courses, though you'll pay more than L50,000 for a full meal. The **tourist office** is on Via Repubblica, the cobbled street which runs down from the main road to the ferry jetty (Mon–Sat 9am–12.30pm & 3.30–6.30pm, Sun 9am–12.30pm).

San Michele

Up in the mountains behind Gardone is the little Alpine village of **SAN MICHELE**. There are six buses daily from Gardone and Saló, but as the views along the road are splendid, it's worth walking. The *Colomber Hotel* (☎0365/21.108; ④), 500m inland, is a good base if you want to do some walking to the springs and waterfalls in the surrounding hills. The owners will give suggestions for **walks**, but for more ambitious hikes, there are maps marked with footpaths available from *CAI*, Via San Carlo 17, in Saló.

Toscalano-Maderno to Limone sul Garda

A ten-minute bus ride up the coast brings you to **TOSCALANO-MADERNO**, two villages long since united by tourist sprawl. There are only two reasons for visiting. One is the regular **ferry** which plies across the lake to Garda's loveliest village, Torri del Benaco (see p.186), the other a long though narrow shingle **beach**. Beyond is **GARGNANO**, now a good place for sailing but once the headquarters of Mussolini's puppet Republic of Salò. The puppeteers were the Nazis, who placed him here largely to keep him out of harm's way. The dictator had by this time lost all credibility and he sank into depression; although he installed his mistress, Claretta Petacci, in nearby Il Vittoriale, the cold, damp rooms and heavy Nazi presence in the woods outside put paid to any passion.

Gargnano is more a working town than a resort, with a thirteenth-century church, **San Francesco**, its main sight. The columns in the cloisters are carved with citrus fruits – a reference to the fact that the Franciscans were credited with introducing the cultivation of citrus fruit to Europe.

There are citrus groves aplenty at **LIMONE SUL GARDA**, a pretty, stone-built village jammed on the slopes between the mountains and the lake. Unfortunately it's been ruined by tourism. The steep cobbled streets are lined with stalls selling souvenirs, leather jackets and sequinned T-shirts; the old stone facades are studded with plastic signs advertising restaurants and hotels; and as you elbow your way through the crowds you'll dig into more German and British than Italian ribs. Unless you're aching to eat chicken and chips, frankfurters and sauerkraut, you're better off staying away.

Riva del Garda

At the northwest tip of the lake, **RIVA DEL GARDA** is the best known of the lake's resorts. It's been a resort since the late nineteenth century and retains some stylish pastel-painted hotels, which in high season and on sunny Sundays form an elegant backdrop for a portside crammed with gaudy excursion coaches. There's an old town behind this, which is pleasant enough, but the main reason for basing yourself here is the fact that Riva boasts Garda's only youth hostel.

There's not a great deal to do or see, and the severe moated castle alongside the port was at time of writing closed for restoration (though it may have re-opened by now), but you could use Riva as a cheaper alternative to Torbole (see opposite) if your main reason for being on the lake is windsurfing.

The lake front is lined with **gelaterias and pizzerias**, and there's a good *pizza al taglio* place on Via Gazzoletti, just off the port area. For a more substantial meal try the *Vaticano*, at Via Santa Maria 8, a reasonably priced restaurant where you can eat in the garden. If you're staying at Riva you'll need a map, available from the **tourist office** in the Giardini di Porta Orientale, on the far side of the castle. There's a **youth hostel**, Piazza Cavour 10 (☎0464/554.911; ①), open from March to October, while for a **hotel** you could try the *Villa Minerva*, Viale Roma 40 (☎0464/553031; ⑤).

The eastern shore

Overlooked by the mountains of the Monte Baldo chain, the main resorts of Garda's **eastern shore** are heavily touristed. But it's worth putting up with the crowds at **Torbole** if you're a keen windsurfer, while **Malcesine** has a lovely old centre and is a good base for escapes by bike or on foot into the mountains. Further south, **Torri del Benaco** is a gorgeous old village, popular but not yet ruined by tourism, while **Garda** and **Bardolino** are bustling little resorts.

Torbole

TORBOLE, at the top of the lake, played an important role in the fifteenth-century war between the Viscontis and the Venetians, when a fleet of warships was dragged overland here and launched into the lake. Nowadays it's still the water that dominates, since Torbole is devoted almost entirely to windsurfing, its bars and fast-food joints packed with tanned young things in dazzling lycra. Windsurfing enthusiasts come here from all over Europe, and it's obvious why once you see the speed at which they skim across the water when the afternoon wind gets up. It's also a good place for beginners, and in the mornings, when the wind is gentler, the water is full of wobbling novices attempting to circle their instructors. If you want to join them, the place to go is the *Vasco Renna* (☎0464/505.993), open mid-April to mid-October, which hires out boards (L40,000 a day, L25,000 a half-day) and runs courses. A three-week beginners' course costs around L300,000.

The **tourist office** (Mon–Sat 9am–noon & 3–6pm, Sun 9am–noon) is conveniently located on the lake front between the jetty and the centre. If it's closed, there is a free phone service outside to a substantial number of the **hotels** (phone numbers are listed on a board). The *Nataly*, on Piazza Alpini (☎0464/505341; ⑤), is just off the main road on the edge of town; the *Casa Romani* (☎0464/505113; ⑤) charges about the same and is handily located just off the main road directly opposite the ferry jetty.

Malcesine

Backed by the slopes of Monte Baldo and blessed with the same windsurfer-friendly winds as Torbole, **MALCESINE**, 14km further south, nonetheless has a markedly different feel, a sedate little town popular with the over-fifties, many on UK packages. The old town is relatively appealing, although it has its inevitable share of modern hotels, bars and restaurants. Rising straight up from the water is a thirteenth-century turreted **Rocca** (summer daily 9am–1pm & 3–8pm; winter weekends only), built, like Sirmione's, by the Scaligeri family. Goethe was imprisoned here briefly in 1786, having been arrested on suspicion of being a spy – he'd been caught making sketches of the lake. The only way to get inside now is to pay L4000 to see the small natural history museum (April–Oct daily 9am–7pm; winter Sat & Sun 9am–7pm).

For more active pursuits you need to head up Monte Baldo. Although there are well-marked trails up the mountain, you can save energy by taking a **funicular** (summer daily every half-hour 8am–6.45pm; winter daily every half-hour 8am–4.45pm; L8500). If you want to mountain bike, there are wheels for hire at *G. Furioli* in Piazza Matteotti, who even transport the bikes to the top, from where you can make a panoramic descent.

The **tourist office** in Via Capitanato, running north along the lake from the port, has maps of signposted walks in the hills behind. Most **accommodation** in Malcesine gets swallowed up by package companies, however, so the choice is limited. The *Garni Catullo*, in Via Francesco e Giovanni Priori (☎045/740.0352; ④), is very reasonable, as is the *Primavera* on Via Gardesana (☎045/740 0091; ④). Many of Malcesine's restaurants are aimed at the town's German visitors, but *Mamma Ida*, Località Treera 29, has 200 varieties of pasta; the *Speck Stube*, Via Molina 1, is one of the better of the Teutonic-style eateries.

Torri del Benaco and the Punta San Vigilio

To the south of Malcesine, **TORRI DEL BENACO** is the prettiest of all the lake towns, its old centre consisting simply of one long cobbled street, Corso Dante, criss-crossed with tunnelling alleyways and lined with mellow stone *palazzi*. At one end of the street is the **castle**, illuminated at night and with a long glasshouse built along one side to protect the lemon trees inside during cold weather. Inside the castle there is a small **anthropological museum** (daily 9.30am–12.30pm; L2000). Beyond the castle, the port area is a piazza planted with limes and chestnuts, at night swinging to the strains of the live musicians at swanky pavement cafés.

There is a **Lido** in Torri (with a disco in season), but you'd probably be better off heading for the white shingle beaches at **Punta San Vigilio**, a hilly headland a short bus ride away. There's an excellent pay beach here, with sun loungers and picnic tables scattered on grassy slopes planted with pines and planes, or, if you want to save your money, you can take a footpath about 100m from the first gate to several smaller coves – one of which is unofficially nudist. There's also an extremely exclusive hotel here, which numbers Churchill and Prince Charles among its famous ex-guests. Should you happen to be on the Punta on May 25, which is the only day they're open, you could visit the immaculate formal gardens of the **Villa Guarienti**, a tidy Renaissance creation by Sanmicheli.

Torri is a fine place to stay, and there are a number of reasonable **hotels**, among them the *Belvedere* (☎045/722.5088; ⑤) and *Onda* (☎045/722.5895; ⑤), both outside the centre of the village, and the *Caminetto*, Via Gardesana (☎045/722.522; ③), on the main lake road at the south of the village, close by the **tourist office** (Mon–Sat 8.30am–1pm & 3.30–6.30pm). For **food**, *La Regata* on the lake front does hearty sandwiches, while for more refined fare you should hit *El Trincero*, Vicolo Chiesa 5, off Piazza Chiesa, a bulge in Corso Dante, whose *schiacciata* – flat bread bases topped with olive pate, or *porcini* and truffles – and sophisticated pasta dishes have a wide following. If you haven't completely baked your brain on the beach, you could speed along the path to oblivion at *Don Diego* on Via Faese, an alleyway off Corso Dante, easily recognisable by the graffitied doors, where you can drink local Bardolino wine or its notorious and moderately priced Sangria.

Garda

GARDA is a lively, flourishing resort, popular with Italians as well as foreigners, and the evening *passeggiata* along its tree-lined prom is good fun if you're into people-watching. Not long ago it was a fishing village, although now the narrow windy alleys and cottages of its old centre are studded with souvenir shops and snack bars. Even the fifteenth-century **Loggia della Losa**, originally a dock for the palace behind, is now a *gelateria*.

Like Torri, Garda is well placed for beach-bumming days on the Punta San Vigilio, but if you want to do something more energetic, there's a pleasant walk from the church of Sant Maria Maggiore up to a seventeenth-century hermitage, the **Eremo dei Camoldolesi** (Tues, Thurs, Sat 8.30am–11.30am & 2.30–4.30pm). The monks here were ousted by Napoleon in 1810, but bought the place back later in the century – though they only began to live there again in 1972. Each monk enjoys the luxury of a four-roomed house and garden.

If you want to stay, the most reasonably priced **hotels** are the *Speranza* on the central square, Piazzale Roma (☎045/725.5046; ④), and the *Vittoria* on Lungolago Regina Adelaide (☎045/725.5065; ④), near the lake just to the north of the old town (you'll see it as you drive along the main lakeside road). Otherwise, the **tourist office** on the lake front (Mon–Sat 9am–12.30pm & 3–6pm; Sun 9am–12.30pm; ☎045/725.5194) has a list of houses with **rooms to rent**. If you want to fix up somewhere like this directly, try Luigina Battistoli, Via della Libertà 11 (☎045/725.5051), Mauro Consolino, Via Monte Baldo 13 and Via Antiche Mura 4 (☎045/725.6113 and 725.5561), or Bruno Alberghini, Via Monte Baldo 71 (☎045/725.5419). There's just one **campsite**, the *Beato* on Via Monte Baldo (☎ 045/725.5273).

The best places to **eat** in Garda are outside the centre. At *Al Ponte Sel*, Via Monte Baldo 75, you can fill up on polenta, salami and cheese for less than L10,000 (including wine); *Rasole*, Via San Bernardo 95, does good, reasonably priced home-made pasta. Slightly more expensive, *La Val*, on Via Val Molini, the first left-turn along the road to Costermano, is known for its grilled trout. Garda is fairly animated at **night**: head either for the *Taverna* on the lake front just off Piazza Catullo, *Bar Taitu* on Vicolo Cieco Forni off Corso Vittorio Emanuele (the old town's main street), or to an ersatz Greek cocktail bar, perplexingly titled *Taverna Goethe*, Via delle Viole, off Via San Bernardo.

Bardolino and Lazise... and Gardaland

BARDOLINO is a spruce little resort, popular with British and German visitors, that is, as you might have guessed, the home of the light, red Bardolino wine, and the town is at its most animated between mid-September and mid-October, when the *Festa di Uva* is held. At other times of year, apart from strolling along its lush palm- and pine-planted promenade, there's not a lot to do, although the church of **San Zeno**, tucked in the corner of a dusty yard just off the main coast road, is worth a brief look. It was built in the eighth century and its Latin-cross form and high domed ceiling became a prototype for later Romanesque churches. Otherwise, concentrate on sampling Bardolino wine at the unlikely-looking *Costarica* on Via Cesare Battisti, or try the ice cream at *Cristallo* on the lake front near the ferry jetty, which sells the biggest and best ice creams on the lake, in a repertoire of flavours ranging from mascarpone to panna cotta with fresh forest fruits.

The walled village of **LAZISE**, further down the shore, was once a major Venetian port and retains a (privately owned) **castle** and, on the harbour, an arcaded medieval **customs house**. Originally used for building and repairing boats for the Venetian fleet, it was later used to house sheep whose urine was used to make nitrogen, a vital ingredient in gunpowder. Nowadays Lazise is crammed with cafés, pizzerias and *gela-*

terias and plenty of summer visitors, but it's not a bad place to escape to out of season, when it reverts to being a sleepy lakeside village. If you want to **stay**, go for the *Nereide*, on Via F. Fontana (☎045/758.0131; ④), right on the harbour. The **tourist office** (Mon–Sat 8am–2pm & 4–7pm) is also on Via F. Fontana, and has maps and leaflets about the village.

Finally, if you have kids, or just want a daft day out, you can catch a bus from any of the east shore villages to **Gardaland**, Italy's most popular theme park (March–Oct daily 9am–6pm; July & Aug noon–midnight; L20,000, children under ten L16,000; ☎045/641.0355). This is pricey, and you pay extra for some of the attractions, but its various rides and themed entertainments attract around two million visitors a year. With kids in tow, you might just want to join them.

travel details

Trains

Bergamo to: Brescia (19 daily; 1hr); Lecco (17 daily; 35min–1hr).

Brescia to: Capo di Ponte (9 daily; 2hr); Cremona (5 daily; 45min); Iseo (14 daily; 45min); Parma (6 daily; 2hr); Verona (every 30min; 50min).

Cremona to: Mantua (16 daily; 1hr).

Lecco to: Bergamo (6 daily; 40min); Sondrio (19 daily; 1hr 25min).

Milan Centrale to: Arona (10 daily; 1hr); Bergamo (5 daily; 50min); Brescia (37 daily; 1hr 10min); Certosa di Pavia (12 daily; 35min); Como (12 daily; 30min); Desenzano (16 daily; 1hr 5min–1hr 45min); Lecco (20 daily; 40min); Pavia (40 daily; 25–40min); Stresa (8 daily;1hr 20min).

Milan Lambrate to: Certosa di Pavia (7 daily; 30min); Cremona (14 daily; 1hr 30min); Pavia (8 daily; 40min).

Milan Porta Genova to: Vigévano (22 daily; 45min).

Milan Porta Garibaldi to: Bergamo (9 daily; 1hr 10min); Varese (28 daily; 11hr 10min).

Pavia to: Certosa di Pavia (18 daily; 10 min); Cremona (4 daily; 2hr 10min); Mantua (4 daily; 2hr 30min).

Sondrio to: Tirano (14 daily; 30min).

Buses

Bergamo to: Clusone (22 daily; 1[illegible]).

Brescia to: Gardone Riviera (28 daily; 1hr); Iseo (3 daily; 1hr 15min).

Como to: Argegno (16 daily; 45min); Bellagio (12 daily; 1hr 10min); Cernobbio (every 30min; 20min); Colico (6 daily; 2hr 20min); Menaggio (16 daily; 1hr 10min); Tremezzo (16 daily; 1hr); Varese (36 daily; 1hr).

Cremona to: Bergamo (4 daily; 2hr 20min); Brescia (11 daily; 1hr 25min); Iseo (2 daily; 2hr).

Gardone Riviera to: Limone (6 daily; 30min); Riva del Garda (6 daily; 50min).

Mantua to: Peschiera (9 daily; 1hr 10min); Sabbioneta (6 daily; 50min); Verona (6 daily; 1hr 20min).

Menaggio to: Lugano (10 daily; 1hr).

Milan to: Cremona (8 daily; 2hr).

Pavia to: Vigévano (11daily; 1hr).

Tirano to: Bormio (15 daily; 1hr).

Ferries

Como to: Bellagio (7 daily; 2hr); Cernobbio (24 daily; 15min); Lenno (5 daily; 1hr 40min); Varenna (5 daily; 2hr 30min).

Desenzano to: Garda (2 daily; 1hr); Gardone Riviera (up to 4 daily; 1hr 45min); Gargnano (2 daily; 2hr 30min); Malcesine (2 daily; 3hr 15min); Riva del Garda (2 daily; 4hr 10min); Saló (4 daily; 1hr 15min); Sirmione (11 daily; 20min).

Lenno to: Bellagio (5 daily; 20min); Menaggio (6 daily; 35min); Varenna (5 daily; 50min).

Stresa to: Intra (13 daily; 1hr); Isola Bella (26 daily; 5min); Isola dei Pescatori (26 daily; 10min); Isola Madre (21 daily; 20min); Pallanza (20 daily; 35min); Villa Taranto (11 daily; 45min).

Hydrofoils

Como to: Colico (10 daily; 1hr 30min). Stopping at Argegno, Tremezzo, Bellagio, Menaggio, Varenna, Gravedona.

Arona to: Locarno (2 daily; 2hr). Stopping at Stresa, Baveno, Pallanza, Intra, Luino, Cannobbio.

Pescheria to: Riva del Garda (5 daily; 2hr 15min). Stopping at Sirmione, Bardolino, Garda, Salo, Torri del Benaco, Maderno, Malcesine, Limone, Torbole.

CHAPTER FOUR

TRENTINO-ALTO ADIGE

Two quite distinct cultural entities make up the province of **Trentino-Alto Adige**. The northern half – **Alto Adige** – is Italian more in name than affiliation. It's part of the Tyrol, a mountain enclave straddling the border between Austria and Italy, and an area which sees itself as part of the German-speaking world. In **Trentino**, on the other hand, Italian is spoken everywhere, and the food and architecture belong more to Italy than to the Alps.

Austria ceded Trentino-Alto Adige to Italy at the end of World War I, a move much resented by many inhabitants of German descent, who have wanted to secede ever since. If some German speakers are unwilling to remain part of Italy, there are right-wing Italian speakers who would be equally pleased to see them go, and there's been friction between the two camps since the Sixties, when Germanic activists bombed power stations, rail lines and military installations. The government responded by occupying part of the province with troops, an economic disaster for an area dependent on tourism. Talks brought concessions and promises from central government, which satisfied some but not all, and another spate of bombings began in the Eighties, provoking a strong response from Italian right-wingers. The fascist *MSI* (*Movimento Sociale Italiano*) is nowadays the most popular party amongst Italian speakers in the province.

The region's resorts can be lethargic, but the landscape, dominated by the stark and jagged **Dolomites**, is among the most beautiful in the country. Circling the spiked towers of rock which characterise the range, a network of trails follows the ridges, varying in length from a day's walk to a two-week trek; the long-distance trails, called *Alte Vie*, can be picked up from the small resorts. The chief towns of **Trento** and **Bolzano** are the transport hubs for the region. Trento gives access to most of the western Dolomites: the **Pale di San Martino**, a cluster of enormous peaks encircling the rocky "high plain" above San Martino di Castrozza; the **Catinaccio** (or Rosengarten) range between the Val di Fassa and Bolzano; the **Gruppo di Sella**, with its *vie ferrate* (iron ladders across rock walls); and the glacier-topped **Marmolada**. Still in the western Dolomites, but with easier access from Bolzano, are the **Alpe di Siusi**, a magical plateau of grass and wetland, high above the valley. The *alpe* are enclosed by the peaks of **Sasso Lungo** (or Langkofel) and **Sciliar** (or Schlern); to the north is the quieter **Odle** (or Geisler Gruppe). Even further to the west, on the other side of Trento, are the **Dolomiti di Brenta**, a collection of wild peaks above the meadows of Valle Rendena.

The eastern Dolomites start on the opposite side of the Adige Valley, past Passo di Campolongo and Corvara, activity focusing on **Cortina d'Ampezzo**, self-styled "Queen of the Dolomite resorts" – though actually just across the regional border in the Veneto. In summer, avoid the over-populated peaks like the **Tre Cime di Lavaredo** and head for **Sorapiss** or **Monte Pelmo** to the south, or **Le Tofane** and the mountains of the **Fanes-Sennes-Braies** group to the west. In winter, Cortina comes into its own as an extremely upmarket ski resort with excellent, if expensive, facilities and a voyeuristic appeal.

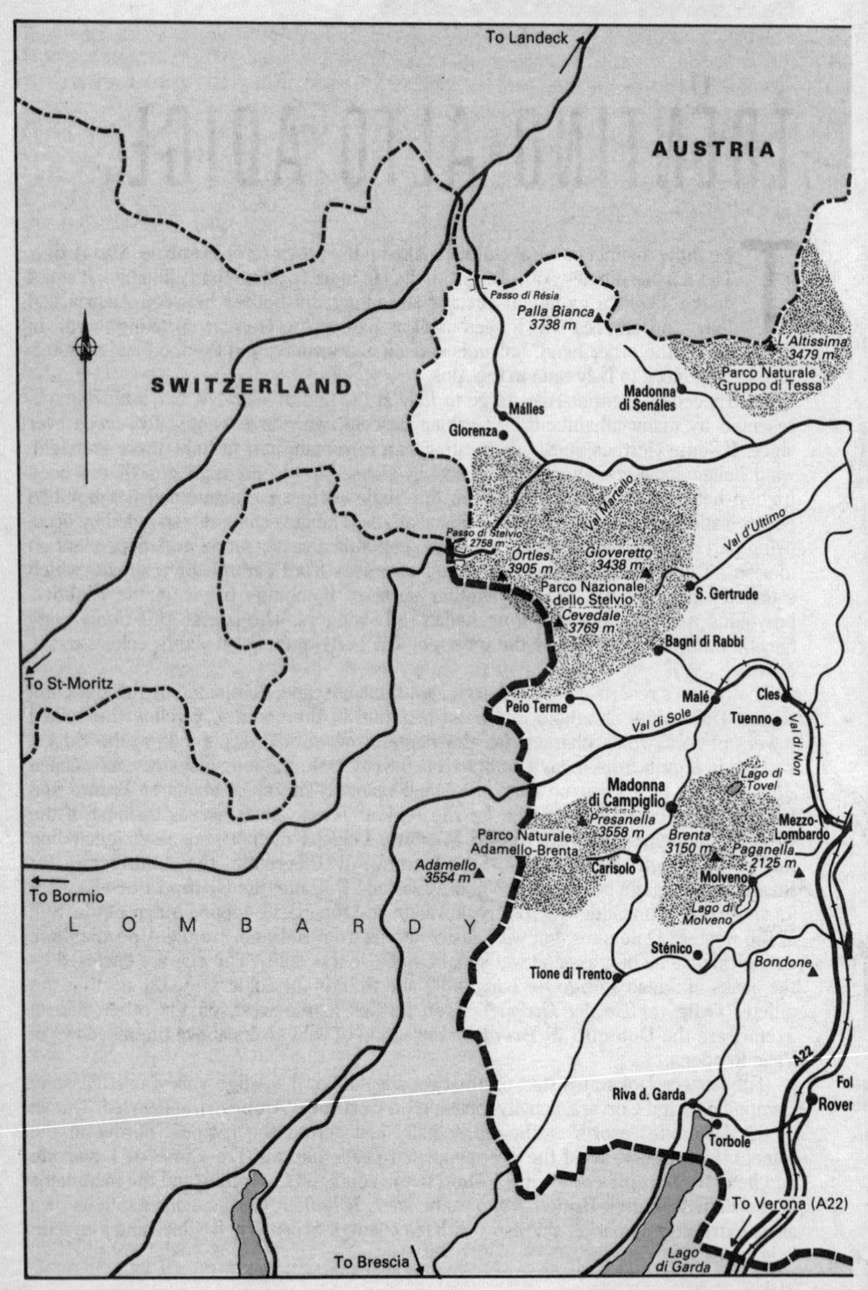

To Landeck
AUSTRIA
SWITZERLAND
Passo di Résia
Palla Bianca
3738 m
L'Altissima
3479 m
Parco Naturale
Gruppo di Tessa
Madonna
di Senáles
Málles
Glorenza
Val Martello
Val d'Ultimo
Passo di Stelvio
2758 m
Órtles
3905 m
Gioveretto
3438 m
Parco Nazionale
dello Stelvio
S. Gertrude
Cevedale
3769 m
Bagni di Rabbi
To St-Moritz
Peio Terme
Malé
Cles
Tuenno
Val di Sole
Val di Non
Madonna
di Campiglio
Lago di
Tovel
Presanella
3558 m
Parco Naturale
Adamello-Brenta
Brenta
3150 m
Paganella
2125 m
Mezzo-
Lombardo
Adamello
3554 m
Carisolo
Molveno
To Bormio
L O M B A R D Y
Lago di
Molveno
Sténico
Bondone
Tione di Trento
A22
Riva d. Garda
Rover
Torbole
To Verona (A22)
To Brescia
Lago
di Garda

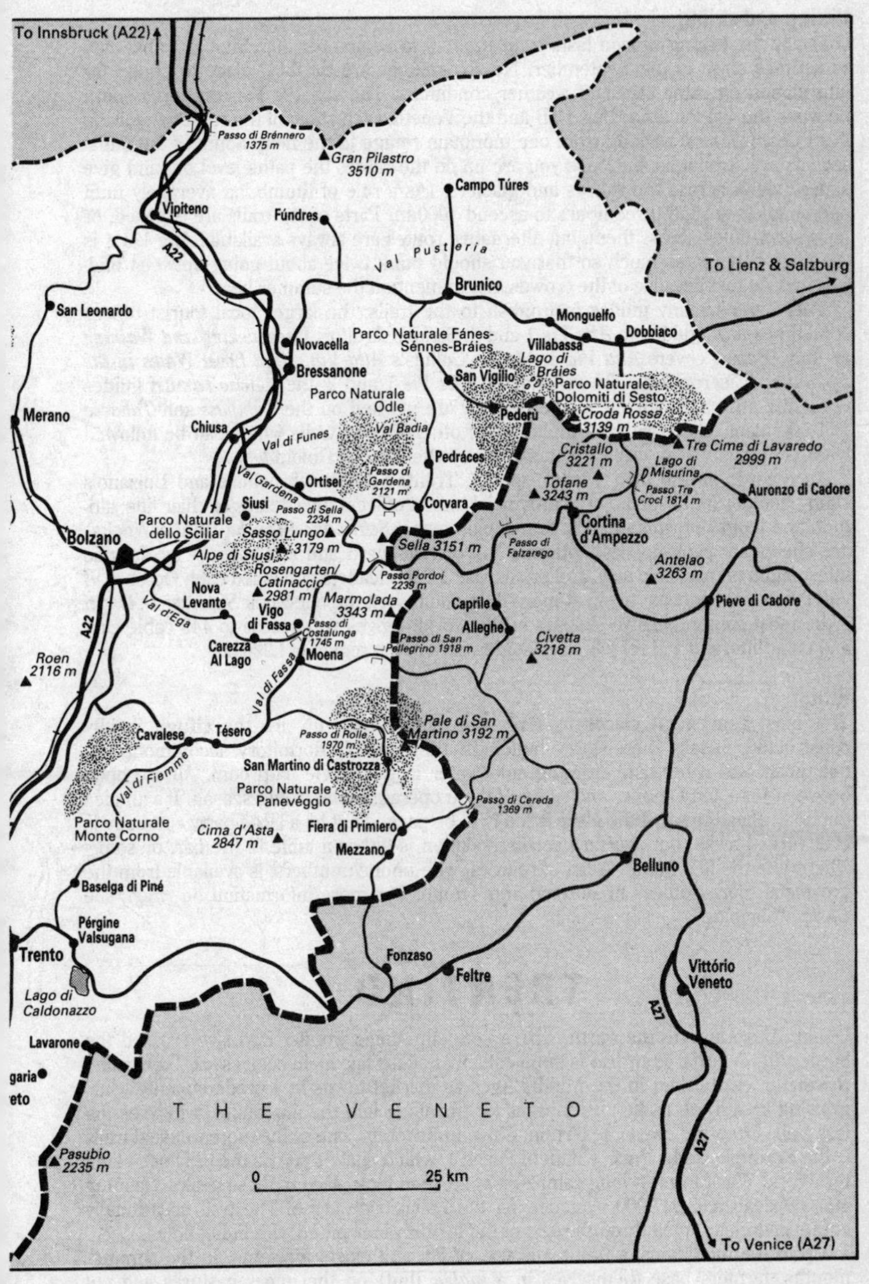
To Innsbruck (A22)
Passo di Brénnero 1375 m
Gran Pilastro 3510 m
Campo Túres
Vipiteno
Fúndres
A22
Val Pusteria
To Lienz & Salzburg
Brunico
San Leonardo
Monguelfo
Villabassa
Dobbiaco
Novacella
Parco Naturale Fánes-Sénnes-Bráies
Lago di Bráies
Bressanone
San Vigilio
Parco Naturale Dolomiti di Sesto
Parco Naturale Odle
Pederü
Croda Rossa 3139 m
Merano
Chiusa
Val di Funes
Val Badia
Tre Cime di Lavaredo 2999 m
Cristallo 3221 m
Lago di Misurina
Pedráces
Passo di Gardena 2121 m
Val Gardena
Ortisei
Tofane 3243 m
Passo Tre Croci 1814 m
Auronzo di Cadore
Siusi
Passo di Sella 2234 m
Corvara
Cortina d'Ampezzo
Parco Naturale dello Sciliar
Sasso Lungo 3179 m
Bolzano
Sella 3151 m
Passo di Falzarego
Alpe di Siusi
Antelao 3263 m
Rosengarten/ Catinaccio 2981 m
Passo Pordoi 2239 m
Nova Levante
Marmolada 3343 m
Caprile
Pieve di Cadore
Val d'Ega
Vigo di Fassa
Alleghe
Passo di Costalunga 1745 m
Passo di San Pellegrino 1918 m
Civetta 3218 m
A22
Carezza Al Lago
Moena
Roen 2116 m
Val di Fassa
Pale di San Martino 3192 m
Cavalese
Tésero
Passo di Rolle 1970 m
Val di Fiemme
San Martino di Castrozza
Parco Naturale Panevéggio
Passo di Cereda 1369 m
Parco Naturale Monte Corno
Cima d'Asta 2847 m
Fiera di Primiero
Mezzano
Belluno
Baselga di Piné
Pérgine Valsugana
Trento
Fonzaso
Feltre
Vittório Veneto
Lago di Caldonazzo
A27
Lavarone
garia
eto
THE VENETO
A27
Pasubio 2235 m
0
25 km
To Venice (A27)

Hiking and skiing

Officially the **hiking** season lasts from June 20 to September 20, although cable cars sometimes close in mid-September. Nearby refuges are the best place to phone for information on cable cars and weather conditions. The six *Alte Vie* run north–south between the Val Pusteria (Pusertal) and the Veneto, each stage of the routes requiring five to eight hours' walking from one mountain refuge to the next. Some of the initial ascents are strenuous, but once you are up on the ridges the paths level out and give superb views across the valleys and glaciers. (As a rule of thumb, an averagely unfit person takes around three hours to ascend 1000m.) Parts of the trails are exposed, or have snow fields across them, but alternative routes are always available. *Alta Via* 1 is the most popular, so much so that you should think twice about going between mid-July and August because of the crowds, not to mention the summer heat.

There aren't many guides in English to the trails: the larger local tourist offices sometimes have guides to *Alte Vie* 1 and 2; Stefano Ardito's *Backpacking and Walking in Italy* (Bradt) covers *Alta Via* 1; Martin Collins's *Alta Via: High Level Walks in the Dolomites* (Cicerone) details walks along *Alte Vie* 1 and 2; the Italian *Tamari* guides cover the others. As for maps, the *Alte Vie* are marked on the *Kompass* and *Tabacco* 1:50,000 maps, along with the multitude of other shorter trails which can be followed without guides. These maps are on sale everywhere in the Dolomites.

As regards **skiing and winter sports**, Trento's *Winters* brochure and Bolzano's skiing booklet (published by the provincial tourist offices) give details of chair lifts, altitude and length of runs in each resort, plus maps. *Settimane Bianche* (White Weeks) are cheap-rate package deals offering full or half-board and a ski-pass – for specific information on places to stay, and prices, ask for the leaflets published each October. If you take a car and want to ski at more than one resort, the one-week *Superski Dolomiti* – the most comprehensive ski-pass in the world – gives you access to 445 cable cars and chair lifts, and will set you back somewhere in the region of L220,000.

Rifugi

The most convenient places to stay once you're high up are the **rifugi**. Solidly constructed, usually three-storey buildings, they provide dormitory accommodation, hot meals and a bar, and freezing cold water in the single bathroom. All are open between June and October and some of them operate in the skiing season. It's an idea to phone ahead to see if the place is likely to be packed out by a large party – nobody is ever turned away, but overflow accommodation is either a table in the bar, or somewhere like the hen house. A list of refuges, with phone numbers, is available from the provincial tourist offices in Bolzano and Trento. For more information on *rifugi*, see *Basics*, "Sleeping".

TRENTINO

Unlike Alto Adige to the north, where you sometimes wonder if you've crossed the border into Austria, **Trentino** is unmistakably Italian. The main centres are **Trento** and **Rovereto**, established in the Middle Ages as market towns in a predominantly wine-growing area. Both make useful bases for travelling into the mountains, where countless trails cross the awesome terrain. Close to Rovereto, one of the more unusual trails is the **Sentiero della Pace** ("Path of Peace"), which snakes across the province along the World War I front. A long campaign of attrition took place in these peaks, claiming 460,000 dead and 947,000 wounded on the Italian side alone. The trail occasionally enters galleries carved through rock, or old fortifications pitted with bullet holes.

Up in the mountains, a traditional way of life still exists for some. In the summer months, farmers base themselves in a *malga* (hut) on the upper pastures and cut timber and hay, bringing their animals and wood down to the village as soon as winter starts. The first snowfall is the starting signal for Trentino's other major industry, tourism: the area is criss-crossed with ski-lifts and runs, and also offers facilities for less conventional winter sports, like ice-yachting on the lakes.

Trento

Straddling the Adige Valley, **TRENTO**, overshadowed by Monte Bondone, is a quiet provincial centre that makes one of the best bases for exploring the region, not least because of its bus services to the mountains. It's beautifully sited too, encircled by mountains and exuding a relaxed pace of life that may be a refreshing change if you've arrived from Venice, three hours away by train. It wasn't always so, however. From the tenth to the eighteenth centuries, Trento was a powerful bishopric ruled by a dynasty of princes; it was the venue of the Council of Trent in the sixteenth century, when the Catholic Church, threatened by the Reformation in northern Europe, met to plan its countermeasures – meetings which spanned a total of eighteen years. Later, throughout the nineteenth century, ownership of the city, which remained in Austrian hands, was hotly contested, and it only became properly part of Italy in 1918, after the conclusion of World War I.

Arrival, information and accommodation

Trento's main **bus** and **train stations** are almost next door to each other at Piazza Dante and Via Pozzo, and there's a second combined station, run by a private company, **Trento Malé**, ten minutes' walk away at Via Secondo da Trento 7, with trains up to Cles and the Val di Non, and buses to Madonna di Campiglio and Molveno. Tickets and information on Trento Malé connections can be had from the office at the station (☎0461/824.181).

The **tourist office** at Via Alfieri 4, across the park from the train station (Mon–Fri 8.30am–12.30pm & 3.30–6pm, Sat 9am–noon; ☎0461/980.000), has information specifically on Trento, including copies of *Viva Trento*, the monthly guide to life in the town. Another **tourist office** at Corso III Novembre 132 (Mon–Fri 8.30am–1pm & 3–6pm; ☎0461/895.111) is the main information centre for the area, with details on mountain refuges, transport, hiking and skiing possibilities, and *agriturism* in the province. Ask, too, for their free *Guida ai Trasporti nel Trentino*, which details all the bus and train schedules in the province.

For **accommodation**, try *Al Cavallino Bianco*, Via Cavour 29 (☎0461/231.342; ④), or the *Venezia*, Piazza Duomo 45 (☎0461/234.114; ⑤). Slightly cheaper, the *Port 'Aquila* at Via Cervara 66 (☎0461/982.950; ④) should have re-opened by now. There's a **youth hostel** – *Giovane Europa* – at Via Manzoni 17 (☎0461/234.567; ①), with a midnight curfew. The **campsite**, near the river at Via Lung'Adige Braille 1 (☎0461/823.562), is about twenty minutes' walk out of town; or you can take bus #2 from the station.

The Town

Trento was known as *Tridentum* to the Romans, a name celebrated by the eighteenth-century Neptune fountain in the central **Piazza Duomo**, a pleasant square ringed by arcades, shops and cafés and giving onto streets lined with frescoed palaces, many of them built in the sixteenth century when Trento was an important market town. The three most important meetings of the Council of Trent took place in the **Duomo** between 1545 and 1563. The building itself was begun in the thirteenth century, but

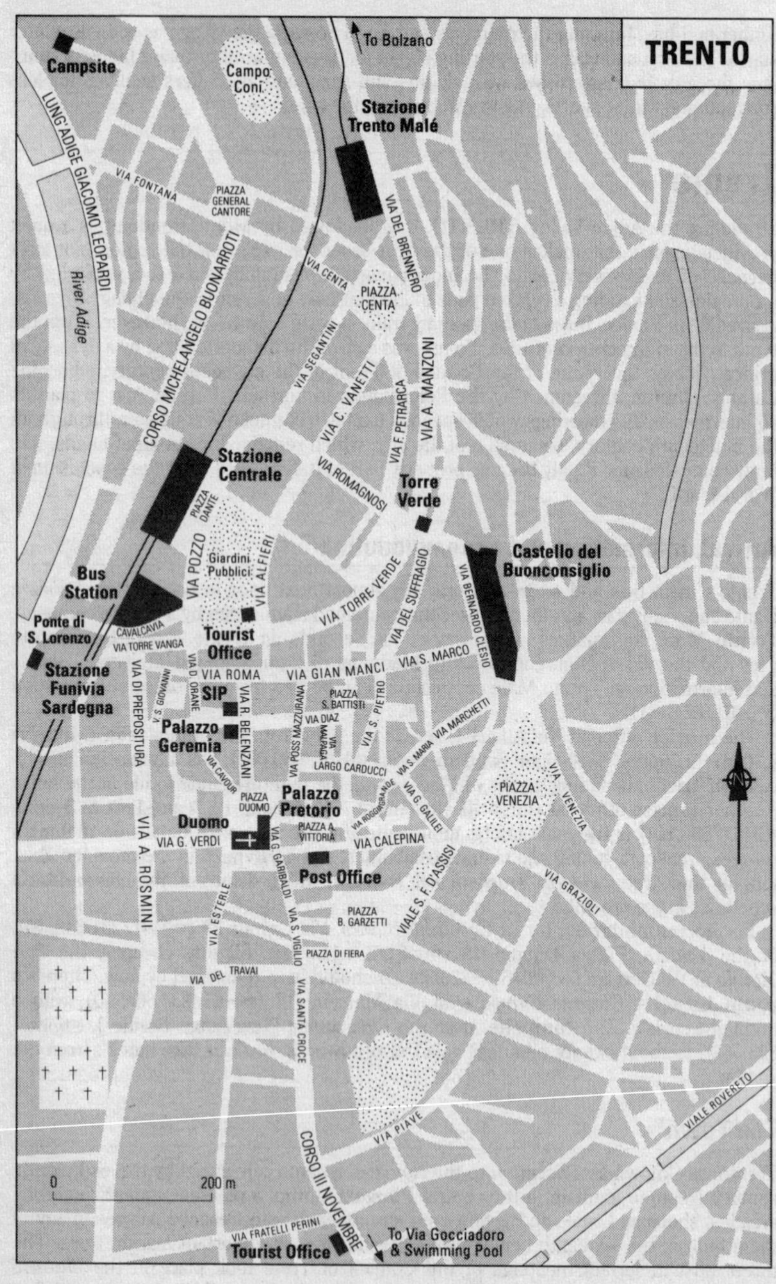
TRENTO
To Bolzano
Campsite
Campo Coni
Stazione Trento Malé
LUNG'ADIGE GIACOMO LEOPARDI
River Adige
VIA FONTANA
PIAZZA GENERAL CANTORE
VIA DEL BRENNERO
CORSO MICHELANGELO BUONARROTI
VIA CENTA
PIAZZA CENTA
VIA SEGANTINI
VIA C. VANETTI
VIA F. PETRARCA
VIA A. MANZONI
Stazione Centrale
VIA ROMAGNOSI
Torre Verde
PIAZZA DANTE
Giardini Pubblici
VIA POZZO
VIA ALFIERI
Castello del Buonconsiglio
Bus Station
VIA TORRE VERDE
VIA DEL SUFFRAGIO
VIA BERNARDO CLESIO
Ponte di S. Lorenzo
CAVALCAVIA
VIA TORRE VANGA
Tourist Office
Stazione Funivia Sardegna
VIA ROMA
VIA GIAN MANCI
VIA S. MARCO
VIA DI PREPOSITURA
V. S. GIOVANNI
VIA D. ORANE
SIP
VIA R. BELENZANI
PIAZZA S. BATTISTI
VIA DIAZ
VIA S. PIETRO
VIA MARCHETTI
Palazzo Geremia
VIA CAVOUR
VIA POSS MAZZURANA
VIA MALPAGA
LARGO CARDUCCI
VIA S. MARIA
PIAZZA VENEZIA
VIA VENEZIA
PIAZZA DUOMO
Palazzo Pretorio
VIA ROGGIA GRANDE
VIA G. GALILEI
Duomo
PIAZZA A. VITTORIA
VIA G. VERDI
VIA CALEPINA
VIA G. GARIBALDI
Post Office
VIALE S. F. D'ASSISI
VIA GRAZIOLI
VIA A. ROSMINI
VIA ESTERLE
PIAZZA B. GARZETTI
VIA S. VIGILIO
PIAZZA DI FIERA
VIA DEL TRAVAI
VIA SANTA CROCE
VIALE ROVERETO
VIA PIAVE
CORSO III NOVEMBRE
0
200 m
VIA FRATELLI PERINI
Tourist Office
To Via Gocciadoro & Swimming Pool

completed in the century of the Council. Inside, the arched, colonnaded steps flanking the nave are a dramatic touch to an otherwise plain building. There are fresco fragments in the nave and an enormous carved marble baldachino over the altar – a replica of the one in Saint Peter's – although the most interesting part lies under the church, where a medieval crypt and foundations of an early Christian basilica (built over the tomb of Saint Vigilio, the third bishop of Trento) were discovered in 1977.

The **Museo Diocesano Trentino** (Mon–Sat 9am–12.30pm & 2.30–6pm), in the neighbouring **Palazzo Pretorio** and hopefully open again now after a period of restoration, holds large annotated paintings of the sessions of the Council of Trent and some carved altarpieces from the church of San Zeno in the Val di Non. Hidden away in cell-like side rooms are some ornate reliquaries and an impressive cycle of fifteenth-century Flemish tapestries. The building is appealing in itself, too, with its fishtail battlements and heavy studded doors and a view from the upper floor of the frescoed palaces around the square.

The most powerful of the Trento princes was Bernardo Clesio, who in the late fifteenth and early sixteenth centuries built up much of the town's collection of paintings and other works of art, many of which are held in the **Castello di Buonconsiglio**, another venue of the Council of Trent, a short walk from Piazza Duomo on the eastern side of the town centre. It's two castles really: the thirteenth-century **Castelvecchio** and the extension built in 1530 called the **Magno Palazzo** (both open Tues–Sun 9am–noon & 2–5pm, summer until 5.30pm; L4000), in which several rooms frescoed with classical subjects by the Dossi brothers and Romanino lead off a quiet inner courtyard. Upstairs is the **Museo Provinciale d'Arte**, whose highlight is the *Ciclo dei Mesi* ("Cycle of the Months"), hidden at the end of a narrow passageway in the Torre d'Aquila (ask at the ticket desk to be taken there). These fifteenth-century frescoes show details from farming and courtly life; soldiers confined to barracks – the castle's role in the nineteenth century – added their own touches by scribbling on the borders and drawing in beards.

The ditch around the castle was the place of execution for two celebrated Trentese – Cesare Battisti and his comrade Fabio Filzi. Born in 1875, Battisti was a man of his times, a combination of romantic idealist and guerrilla fighter. He set up the Socialist-Irredentist newspaper *Il Popolo* as a forum for protest against Austrian rule, and used Italy's entry into World War I as an opportunity to step up his campaign to eject Austrian forces from the Tyrol. The strategem was unsuccessful: in 1916 he led an attempt to take Monte Pasubio to the south of Trento, but he was arrested by the Austrians and shot as a traitor. You can visit his and Filzi's cells in the castle, as well as a small museum to the Risorgimento and Liberation of Trentino.

Eating, drinking and nightlife

You can **eat** well in Trento and the surrounding area, feasting on unfussy local specialities like *canederli* (bread dumplings in clear broth), *torta di patate*, potato pancakes with homemade salami and cheese, and local wines like Teróldego Rotaliano, a fruity, slightly bitter red. For basic Italian cooking, *Chieste*, Via Orme 4, looks unpromising from the outside but has good pizza and pasta dishes at low prices. *Due Giganti* at Via Simonino 20 has three sections to suit all budgets, with a pizzeria, a basic restaurant and a more expensive restaurant. *Locanda Port 'Aquila*'s tiny restaurant also serves some good locally inspired food. There are two or three decent places on Via Santa Croce, while in summer you can eat outside under a pergola at *Alla Mora*, Via Roggia Grande 8, where a *piatto Trento* (consisting of a selection of local specialities) will set you back around L15,000. There's also a student *mensa* at Via Belenzani 18 – meals L7000, no ID necessary. With a great deal more money, try the pricey restaurant at the *Albergo Accademia* at Vicolo Collico 6 (☎0461/981.580), which serves marvellous local specialities. If you have transport, the *Ristorante Quattro Stagioni* in San Vito di Cognola (closed Mon) – a few kilometres above the city – is popular, with good home-made pasta.

One of the best ways to sample **local cooking** is to head for the so-called *Strada di Vino*, which tracks through vineyards parallel to the main SS12 road. At the *Trattoria Montevaccino*, up in the hills near the silver mines of Monte Calisio in the village of Montevaccino (☎0461/991.717; closed Tues & June), you can get a full meal of Trentese specialities for around L20,000. South of town, try *Marlene*, in località Margone di Ravina (☎0461/49.148; closed Thurs & June), or *Maso Comuni*, Via ai Comuni 23, Romagno, at the base of Monte Bondone (☎0461/49.135; closed Mon–Wed) – the latter a particularly friendly place with plenty of unusual local dishes.

Trento doesn't resound with **nightlife**, but there are a couple of good bars open late. *Boston Bar* at Viale San Francesco d'Assisi 8 is centre of the social whirl – American beer, loud music, and packed out all evening. *Al Picaro* on Via San Giovanni is open late and hosts live music on Friday nights.

Around Trento

Cable cars run from Ponte San Lorenzo, near Trento's bus station (every 15min; L800), to **SARDAGNA**, on the lower slopes of the towering Monte Bondone. There's some skiing in winter, and a scattering of holiday homes belonging mostly to Trentese, and commited campers might come here as an alternative to the site by the river; *Camping Mezavia* (☎0461/948.178) is two hours' trek from the top of the cable car. Also popular with people who live nearby are the resorts of **LAVARONE** and **FOLGARIA** to the south, or **PERGINE** to the west near **Lago di Caldonazzo**, where there is a free beach and lido (buses from Trento). However, if you've come from further afield, the attraction of the more distant and dramatic mountain groups may well be stronger.

Castel Beseno

The rail line south from Trento runs between the scree-covered slopes of the Adige Valley, where the only sight for miles might be a station platform in the middle of nowhere, or the blank fortifications of a castle or World War I stronghold. Hanging on an outcrop above the village of CALLIANO, 9km north of Rovereto, **Castel Beseno** is one of the few castles which have been restored and is open to the public (mid-July–mid-Sept daily 9am–noon & 2–6.30pm; rest of the year daily 9am–noon & 2–5.30pm; L2000). It's more of a fortified town than a castle in fact, spreading across the hilltop at the valley entrance and once providing a bulwark between the Venetians and the Tyrolese. A bloody but decisive battle was fought here in 1487, after which the Venetians gave up hope of seizing Trentino at all. The castle is a twenty-minute walk from the village of BESENELLO, which is connected with Trento (and Rovereto – see below) by bus. At weekends buses run all the way to the castle from Besenello's main piazza.

Rovereto and Monte Pasubio

About 45 minutes' south of Trento by bus, **ROVERETO** is the largest town in the area between Trento and Verona. The gilded lion of Saint Mark over the gateway into the old town dates from the fifteenth century, when Rovereto was an outpost of the Venetian empire, as do the extensions to the castle, now the **Museo della Guerra** (July–Sept daily 9am–7pm; rest of the year daily 9am–noon & 2–6pm; closed Dec–Feb; L3000). Along the dark stone streets of the old town on Via della Terra, the **Museo Depero** (April–Aug Tues–Sun 9am–noon & 3–6pm; rest of the year Tues–Sun 9am–noon & 2.30–5.30pm; L3000) has a collection of Futurist art ranging from Fortunato Depero's advertising designs (Campari posters among others) to semi-abstract work. Cassettes and word-pictures complement the more conventional stuff – including an evocative one of the New York subway. If you're keen to stay in Rovereto, there's a **youth hostel**, *Città di Rovereto*, at Via della Scuola 16 (☎0464/433.707; ②), 400m from the train station.

Some of the most bloody engagements of World War I took place around **Monte Pasubio**, to the southeast of Rovereto. The recently created **Sentiero della Pace** ("Path of Peace") follows the front, from the Órtles mountains east across the ranges to Marmolada, the trail littered with old bullets and barbed wire. The opposing armies dug fortresses in the rock and cut tunnels into the glaciers, but protection from enemy fire did not ensure safety – in the winter of 1916, one of the hardest in living memory, around 10,000 soldiers died in avalanches. The historian G.M. Trevelyan, commander of a British Red Cross ambulance unit in the campaign, described one fortress as "four storeys of galleries, one above the other, each grinning with cannon and machine guns. There were also medieval-looking wooden machines for pouring volleys of rock down the gullies by which the enemy might attempt to ascend . . . Our work lay, of course, at the foot of the teleferiche, or aerial railways which fed the war on those astonishing rock citadels: the sick and wounded came down the wires in cages, hundreds of feet in the air." The *Campana dei Caduti*, made out of melted-down cannon, tolls every evening in memory of the dead of both sides, from the *Colle di Miravalle* just outside Rovereto.

The Dolomiti di Brenta and the Val di Non

The sawtoothed peaks and glaciers of the **Dolomiti di Brenta**, northwest of Trento, give these ranges a rougher character than the rest of the Dolomites, yet throughout you can choose your level of walking. At around 3000m the paths are easy to follow but strenuous, while less demanding trails circle the side valleys. The range is best approached via the small resorts of **Madonna di Campiglio** or **Molveno**.

Climbers come here for the towers of Cima Tosa and Cima Brenta, the original reason for *vie delle bochette* – iron ladders knocked into the rock to give access to these ascents; their position, clinging to the rock walls, is sensational. For these *vie ferrate* you need karabiners and ropes, but no special skills are necessary for the ordinary trails, and there are enough marked footpaths for two or three days' high-altitude walking. Trento's tourist office gives a free guide to the Brenta Dolomites, in English, with details on the location of *vie delle bochette* and how long they should take.

Up the Valle Rendena

Buses from Trento to Madonna di Campiglio skirt Monte Bondone and wind their way past a series of patchy hills and villages, passing **Lago di Toblino**, just outside VEZZANO, where **Castel Toblino** – now a restaurant – sits on a spit of land jutting into the lake. The castle was the venue of a lengendary medieval love affair between one Claudia Particella and Carlo Emanuele Madruzzo, Prince-Bishop of Trento. The bishop apparently asked the pope, in vain, to allow him to leave the Church; despite this, the two lovers returned to the castle, but one night, during a trip on the lake, were drowned. Whether it was murder, accident or suicide is unknown. The story is one of those performed during Trento's summer festival of theatre in local castles.

From Lago di Toblino, the road continues west, turning into the **Valle Rendena** at **TIONE DI TRENTO**, where a more remote landscape of pasture and forest begins. This quiet valley is a good place to rest up, with a couple of small campsites reasonably close to villages; one of these is *Faè della Val Rendena* (☎0465/57.178) between Pinzolo and Sant'Antonio di Mavignola. Small churches like the lone **Sant'Antonio** just before BORZAGO are decorated with fresco cycles by Baschenis, one of the many Bergamese artists who worked in the area. At **CARISOLO**, the church of **Santo**

Stefano has frescoes of the Seven Deadly Sins on an outside wall, and others inside depicting the legend of Charlemagne's passage through the Val di Campiglio on the way to his coronation in Rome. Before Madonna, several turnings off the main road lead high up west into the Adamello range, the most beautiful being the **Val di Genova**, which begins 4.5km from Carisolo. A steep, unmetalled road takes you past several waterfalls, spectacular in spring when the snow begins to melt; the most impressive is the **Cascata di Nárdis**, where several channels spill down the granite rock walls of the mountainside. From here, it's another 13km to BÉDOLE (1614m), and a further 2–3 hours' hike from there along trail 212 to the *Rifugio Città di Trento* (☎0465/51.193) at 2480m, within reach of the Adamello glaciers.

A short way before Carisolo, at CADERZONE, there's a more restful turning off the Valle Rendena, up to Malgra Campo, from where trail 230 leads to the small lakes of **San Giuliano** and **Garzono** (two and a half hours' walk). There's a small refuge between the two – ask for keys at the bar in Caderzone.

Madonna di Campiglio

The major village in the Valle Rendena is **MADONNA DI CAMPIGLIO**, an upmarket ski resort with plenty of chair lifts and runs for all levels of skiing. **Buses** from Trento run to the main square, not far from the tourist office (Mon–Sat 9am–noon & 3–6.30pm, Sun 9am–noon; ☎0465/42.000). In summer, the climbing and walking in the Dolomiti di Brenta are superb, and you may want to stay at Madonna, if only to reach the trail heads. Luckily, out of the skiing season, Madonna tends to be deserted except for a sprinkling of walkers, and although most **hotels** expect you to want a full- or half-pension arrangement, there are often good off-season deals to be had in some of the three-star places. Madonna's best deal is *La Montanara* in the centre of the village (☎0465/41.105; ③), or there's the *Garni Bucaneve* (☎0465/41.271; ④) – follow the yellow signs for the *Rifugio Valesinalla* – and, on the same road, the more expensive *Norma Garni* (☎0465/41.110; ⑦) and *Gianna* (☎0465/41.106; ⑦).

The best way to approach the trail heads is by cable car from **Carlo Magno**, 3km north of the village centre, to GROSTÈ (mid-June–mid-Sept daily 8.30am–1pm & 2–5.30pm; L15,000 one way) – see below. Another possibility from Carlo Magno is to take *Funivia Cinque Laghi* west, to *Rifugio Pancugolo* (2064m) in the Presanella group, where the paths include a five-hour route via **Lago Ritorto** and **Lago Gelato** back down to the valley.

Near Madonna is the smaller ski resort of **PINZOLO**; ski-lift passes cover both villages, but Pinzolo has its own centre, around the church of San Vigilio, decorated with a sixteenth-century fresco of the *danse macabre*.

Trails from Grostè

Once you're at **GROSTÈ** (2437m) you can plan your own routes as long as you have a decent hiking map. The *Rifugio Graffer* at 2261m (☎0465/41.358; open Dec 1–April 30 & June 20–Sept 20), by the cable car exit, is close to the trails and has overnight accommodation. From the cable car, trail 316 sets out across boulder-strewn slopes towards refuges *Sella* and *Tuckett* (☎0465/41.226), about 5km away, where you can eat a large meal and bask on the verandah, thousands of feet above the valley.

Trail 328, which later becomes 318 (called the *Sentiero Bogani*), starts just past the refuges; there are difficult boulders to negotiate at first, but then there's an easy path which has been blasted out of the side of the rock walls. A Madonna and shrine in a small overhang commemorate the lives lost in these peaks, but by this time, about four hours from Grostè, *Rifugio Brentei* (2182m; ☎0465/41.244) is in sight, midway between Cima Brenta and Cima Tosa. There are some difficult ascents a short distance from the refuge, but it's more than likely that by this stage you won't be capable of anything other than staring across the vast ravine at the Adamello glaciers in the distance.

Next day, if you can cope with snow fields, you could either trek up to the **Bocca di Brenta** and cross over the ridge to meet trail 319 down to Molveno (3hr 30min), or simply return to Madonna via trails 318 and 316 (3hr 30min).

Molveno

The lakeside village of **MOLVENO**, surrounded by the peaks of the Brenta Alta, is a cheaper place to stay than Madonna. Although the cheapest places go quickly, particularly in high season, the **tourist office** here, at Piazza Marconi 7 (Mon–Sat 9am–12.30pm & 3–6.30pm, Sun 10am–noon; ☎0461/586.924) should be able to help you find a bed for the night for around L30,000 per person. Failing that, there's a nice **campsite**, *Campeggio Spiaggia Lago di Molveno* (☎0461/586.978), on the water's edge.

There are few **easy trails** from Molveno into the Brenta massif – paths often disappear into nothing but *vie ferrate* across the rocks; fortunately these are all marked on maps, so you just need to plan your route. If you decide to approach the Brenta group from this side, a cable car runs from the village to PRADEL (1500m), from where trails lead through the beeches and pines of the **Val delle Seghe** in the shadow of Croz dell'Altissimo (2339m). An easy circular route winds back to Molveno (2hr 30min), or technically more demanding paths take you higher up, past *Rifugio Tosa* (2439m) and *Rifugio Tommaso Pedrotti* (2491m; ☎0461/948.115).

The most prodigious of nineteenth-century climbers, Francis Fox Tuckett, opened up a difficult new route to Cima Brenta from Molveno, now known as the **Bochetta di Tuckett**. As ice axes hadn't been invented, he negotiated snow fields with a ladder and alpenstock, and carried joints of meat and bottles of wine for mountaintop breakfasts. The landscape where he "roamed amongst toppling rocks, and spires of white and brown and bronze coloured stone" is almost unchanged but for the *Bochetta*, descending from the pass down to the *Tuckett* and *Sella* refuges (see opposite). More paths skirt Cima Tosa and lead to PINZOLO via *Rifugio Dodici Apostoli* (2489m; ☎0465/51.309).

Val di Non

The steep **Val di Non**, where apple orchards cover every available terraced slope, skirts the northern edges of the Brenta group. You see the best of the valley by car, taking the turning for TUENNO off the N43 from Trento to **CLES**, at the head of the Val di Non; if you're reliant on public transport, Cles is served by buses and trains on the private Trento Malé line. Lying close to the shore of the artificial **Lago di Santa Giustina**, Cles presents a strange mixture, with a hydroelectric dam on the lake to the northeast and several (privately owned) castles around. One which merits a visit is turretted **Castel Cles**, which has good frescoes by Fogolino.

Across the lake from Cles, the **Santuario di San Romedio**, reachable by way of a 45-minute walk uphill from SANZENO (follow the signs past *Ristorante Mulino*), is a popular pilgrimage shrine, the legendary home of Romedius, a hermit who lived with his bear on the side of the cliff. The sanctuary is a complex of several churches built between the eleventh and eighteenth centuries; with its gateway and isolated position surrounded by forest, it feels like a private citadel. Votive offerings and hoards of crutches line the walls of the narrow stone stairwell up to the atmospheric highest chapel, said to be the saint's retreat. A brown bear pads rather sadly around its den on one side of the grounds.

Also from Cles, the **Parco Nazionale di Stelvio** is just an hour or so's drive via MALÉ and BAGNI DI RABBI or PEJO TERME; both are off the N42, although if you're relying on buses, access to the park is much easier from Merano (see p.209).

East of Trento

To the **east and north of Trento**, the **Val Sugana** and the **Val di Fiemme** are joined by road, making a wide loop. Halfway around, a group of stunning pinnacles and bare peaks called the **Pale di San Martino** appears: formed as a coral reef sixty million years ago, their rock is so pale it glares even at dawn. The nearest resort to the Pale is **San Martino di Castrozzo**, the terminus for buses travelling the loop in both directions.

Val Sugana

Most people take the bus along the **Val Sugana** to get to a market in one of its modern and busy towns. There's nothing to see between the towns except rows of fruit trees and vineyards, and later, as the Brenta valley closes in to become a narrow gorge, a succession of hydroelectric plants. What makes the trip interesting is the terrain to the north, in particular the **Cima d'Asta**, a mountain dotted with bright blue, icy tarns, and crossed by the *Sentiero della Pace*. You reach the westerly part of this from PANAROTTA, in the mountains above Lago di Caldonazzo, from where the trail – at this point an ancient ridgeway path and wartime patrol route – follows a course across the peaks towards Passo di Rolle (see opposite).

If you're travelling by bus from Trento to San Martino you have no choice but to travel the long way round, via FONZASO in the Veneto. By car, though, there's a short cut if you turn off at BORGO VALSUGANA, and cut through the foothills, climbing through an increasingly alpine landscape to rejoin the main road at Imer.

Imer, Mezzano, Fiero di Primiero

IMER and, a couple of kilometres north, **MEZZANO** might be archetypal tourist villages decked out with geraniums and credit card stickers. But these trappings scarcely irritate thanks to the splendour of the landscape around, the Pale di San Martino just about visible in the distance, and out to the east the peak of Sass de Mura. The valley itself is wide, with hay meadows spreading either side of the main road, and, away from the tourism, it makes a good place to rest up, with easy paths running into the foothills. One possibility is the path east from Imer along the lush Val Noana to the reservoir under the slopes of **Monte Pavione** (a 3hr 30min round trip). As far as **accommodation** goes, self-sufficiency is an advantage, as you compete with coach parties if you look for a cheap hotel. An alternative to Alpine-style hotels in the villages is *Camping Calavise*, a (well signposted) couple of kilometres off the main valley road (☎0439/67.468).

About 4km further on from Imer, **FIERO DI PRIMIERO** is a larger resort and market town. It's a major crossroads in the area, from where buses run up to the beginning of the Val Canali and to Passo Cereda (1369m). The mountains around Fiero were worked for silver from the thirteenth century, and local miners paid for the town's fifteenth-century church. Now the ranges are crossed by trails – *Alta Via* #2 dips down to the main road here, and, travelling south, regains altitude around the slopes of Monte Cimonega (2381m).

Trails to the north of Passo Cereda take you up into the **Pale di San Martino**. One path follows a long ridge of rock before passing down into **Val Canali**, described by Amelia Edwards in the nineteenth century as the most "lonely, desolate and tremendous scene . . . to be found this side of the Andes". There's now a bar and some places to camp at the head of the glen, but the valley has kept its feeling of isolation. *Rifugio Treviso* (☎0439/62.311) in Val Canali is a possible overnight stop. Another is *Cant del Gal* (☎0439/62.997; ④), which also has a good restaurant specialising in game and funghi.

A stiff ascent from *Rifugio Treviso* brings you onto the **Altopiano delle Pale** at Passo di Pradidali, where eagles can be seen circling above the barren plateau, and the silence is broken every so often by a trickle of falling stones. Once you are at this altitude, there are many possibilities for linking up with other trails across the stark upland. *Rifugio Pedrotti alla Rosetta* (2581m; ☎0439/62.567) is the nearest place with accommodation (a 2hr 30min hike north). At the refuge there's accommodation, a restaurant and bar.

San Martino and around

The road into **SAN MARTINO** twists and turns, and you feel like you're in the middle of nowhere until the resort's new hotels appear around the corner. After Cortina d'Ampezzo, San Martino is one of the smarter Dolomite resorts, but it has a more relaxed atmosphere in its cafés and a generally more unpretentious way of going about things. The **tourist office** next to the bus stop (daily 9am–12.30pm & 3–6.30pm; ☎0439/768.867) may be able to help with finding a cheapish room. Failing that, try the *Villa Marina* (☎0439/68.166; ④), or the slightly more expensive *Suisse* (☎0439/68.087; ④), whose prices include breakfast. The alternative is to pitch a tent at the village **campsite**, *Sass Maor* (☎0439/68.347).

A number of **trails** head off into the mountains; the strongest attraction is again the **Pale di San Martino**. Chair lifts and cable cars from San Martino (daily 8.30am–12.30pm & 1–4.45pm; L22,000 day return) take you up to *Rifugio Pedrotti alla Rossetta* at 2581m (☎0439/62.567), perched on the edge of the Altopiano – see above for details.

Up on the summits, either make for *Rifugio Pradidali* (2278m; ☎0439/64.180 or 64.282), a walk and descent of three hours, or climb up to **Cima della Vezzana** (3192m), the highest point in the group, with views down across the whole range – the path is difficult in places, and the round trip takes about five hours. If you prefer the relative security of a guided trek, the *Gruppo Guide Alpine*, next door to the tourist office in San Martino, runs graded excursions most days in July and August.

Parco Naturale Paneveggio

Out of San Martino, traffic files up to **Passo di Rolle**, a beautiful stretch of high moorland dotted with avalanche breaks and a few sheep. If you don't have your own transport, there are only two buses a day, but hitching is easy. At the pass, a chair lift takes you up to *Baita Segantini*, a log cabin bar from where you can see **Cimon della Pala**'s summit. It takes half an hour or so to walk back down to the pass, where there are several more bars and restaurants.

The Passo di Rolle falls within the **Parco Naturale Paneveggio**, an area of firs, rowan and larch that once provided timber for the Venetian fleet and wood for Stradivarius violins. Skirted by nature trails, it has a **visitors' centre** 7km on from the pass, outside PANEVEGGIO village, with displays on the wildlife of the area. The remoter parts of the park are where to see live specimens of the white alpine hare and the marmot – a creature resembling a large guinea pig, which stands up on its hind legs to act as sentinel for the burrow and emits a distinctive screech. After a few days trekking in the Pale, you may want to take it easy, and Paneveggio's fields are good for sunbathing and sleep. There's an unusually pleasant **campsite** next to Lago Paneveggio; the entrance is at the end of the track marked "Area della Sosta", just past the village, and the maximum stay is 24 hours.

If you're travelling by bus, there are two main choices from Paneveggio: either to finish the round trip back to Trento, or break your journey at Predazzo in the Val di Fiemme if you want to travel into the mountainous Val di Fassa.

Val di Fiemme

Once out of the confines of the park, **PREDAZZO** is the first town you come to in the **Val di Fiemme**. Hotel hoardings are ubiquitous, and even the tiniest villages hereabouts have a plan of the mountain ranges with chair lifts marked, but behind the modern Dolomites tourist industry, this is an ancient region that until the seventeenth century was virtually autonomous. A local parliament met at the *Banco de la reson*, a circle of stone benches surrounded by trees in **CAVALESE**, the next town along, and the *Magnifica Communità* of Cavalese is still relatively powerful, administering extensive communal land. Many people stop to take the cable car up to Lago Lagorai or the dozens of smaller lakes in the chain – see below for details. The **Palazzo della Communità** was the Bishop of Trento's summer palace; the building is covered in frescoes and surrounded by cobbled streets with a handful of bars and *pasticcerie*. The European witchhunt pandemic reached this valley in 1505, when eleven women were burnt at the stake in the village of DOSS DE LE STRÌE.

TESERO, halfway between the two towns, is like a smaller version of Cavalese; people drive through on their way to the mountains. Otherwise, Tesero's main attractions are a couple of *gelaterie* and the parish church, frescoed with *Cristo della Domenica* (Sabbath Christ) and symbols of everything banned on a Sunday.

South of the main road and valley, the **Catena dei Lagorai** is a group of lakes hidden in the mountains, accessible either on foot from any of the small villages along the main road or by cable car from Cavalese (daily every 15min 9am–noon & 2–5pm; L16,000). Once you're up on the ridges, either follow the paths towards Passo di Rolle, or go west. A day or two of walking west (via refuges) brings you to the Val dei Mócheni, which was colonised in medieval times by German farmers travelling south, and has kept its own language and Gothic script. The first farmers were joined later by speculators searching for the rich seams of copper and silver which lay in the mountains.

Practicalities

In the other direction, north of the valley, **Predazzo** is the turn-off for the Val di Fassa, and a good place to overnight if you're heading in this direction and want to avoid going back to Trento and retracing your steps. Of hotels, the *Cimon* (☎0462/501.691; ③) has the cheapest rooms. Failing that, try the *Laurino* (☎0462/30.151; ⑤) or *Nevada* (☎0462/41.021; ⑤) in **Cavalese**. In **Tesero**, bed and breakfast is offered by Signora Maria Canal (☎0462/84.178; ③).

The Catinaccio and Sella groups

Trails from the **Val di Fassa** take you up into ranges whose scale is unbelievable at times. These mountains make up the centre of the western Dolomites, with a number of possibilities for walking across onto the Alpe di Siusi, or towards the high Sella, Gardena and Pordoi passes. The main villages in the Val di Fassa are Moena, Vigo di Fassa and Canazei, none of which has more than a couple of thousand inhabitants, except in the winter and summer seasons, when tourists pack out the many guest houses. All three give access to the mountains and are popular with German parties, who come here for the classic Dolomite walks across the western edge of the valley, into dramatic areas such as the famous **Catinaccio** (**Rosengarten**) range. Wilderness is not the key word on the lower slopes, where the sound of overhead wires tells you another chair lift is on its way; but once you gain altitude you reach a completely different world.

Catinaccio

The long belt of sheer rock walls and towers which makes up the **Catinaccio** (Rosengarten) range gets its German name from the roses which legend says used to grow here. King Laurens, who was captured in the mountains, put a spell on the roses so that no-one would see them again by day or night, but forgot to include dawn and dusk in his curse, which is when the low sun gives the rock a roseate glow. The trails across the range are for all levels of hiking, but the going gets tough on the ridges, from where you can see as far as the Stubaier Alps, on the border with Austria. The most popular approach to **Catinaccio** is from **VIGO DI FASSA**, a bus stop on the Trento to Canazei route with a dozen or so one- and two-star hotels. Try *Cristina* (☎0462/64.109; ④), *Gambrinus* (☎0462/64.159; ④), or *Vael* (☎0462/110; ④). Alternatively, *Rifugio Roda di Vael* (☎0462/64.289) is a ninety-minute walk away from the village along trails #547 and #545.

The trek to **Torri di Váiolet** from Vigo di Fassa is the preferred route up onto the range; the cable car from the village to *Rifugio Ciampedie* (☎0462/64.432) covers most of the ascent; a well-beaten trail leads from the terminus through the woods to *Rifugio Gardeccia*. From here it's a steep walk up to a refuge under the Torri, although the severity of the ascent doesn't discourage hordes of summer Sunday walkers. A stiff zigzagging climb from here brings you to *Rifugio Re Alberto*, three hours from Ciampedie; there's also alternative accommodation nearby here at the *Rifugio Passo Santner* (☎0471/642.230) or *Rifugio Váiolet* (☎0462/63.292).

Paths lead **south** across the range and eventually down to Passo di Costalunga and the Lago di Carezza, from where you can catch a bus to Bolzano. There are more choices to the **north**, where there are a number of trails onto Monte Sciliar (Schlern), with variations in height of no more than around 500m. *Rifugio Bolzano al M. Pez* (☎0471/616.024), near the summit of Monte Sciliar, is a good two days' trek from *Rifugio Re Alberto*; you can stop overnight at *Tierser Alplhütte* (☎0471/72.952), in between the two. From Sciliar, paths descend onto the wetland plateau of the Alpi di Siusi (see below).

Canazei

CANAZEI is a relatively modern town at the head of the Val di Fassa, and it's from there that you head for the high passes – the **Gruppo di Sella** for hard trails, or the easier **Viel del Pan**, opposite Marmolada. Bus connections are virtually nonexistent, so without your own transport you have to use cable cars or hitch to get to most places. From Canazei the switchback road climbs relentlessly for 12km and is often busy with coachloads of tourists heading for the Great Dolomites Road, or cyclists making the thousand-metre ascent.

Halfway up, the cable car at PRADEL leads to **Passo di Sella** (2240m), one of the most impressive of the Dolomite passes. Paths climb from here onto the jagged peaks of the **Sasso Lungo** (Langkofel) and follow the ridges down onto the Alpi di Siusi. Even up on the summits, saxifrage grows between cracks in the rock, and the silence is broken every so often by the buzzing of a beetle. It takes two days to walk from the Sella pass, via *Rifugio Vicenza* (☎0471/77.315; open end-June–Sept 25) into the Val Gardena (Grödnertal), where there are buses to Bolzano.

Just past Pradel the road forks. The right-hand turning takes you up to **Passo Pordoi** (2242m), an astonishing vantage point between the Gruppo di Sella and Marmolada – at 3246m the highest Dolomite. The ranges and peaks in every direction are more like North America than Europe, with tough grass over the lower slopes and massive outcrops of grey rock. A small road winds downwards to Passo Folzarego, and ultimately Cortina d'Ampezzo, but Passo Pordoi itself is where many of the trails start. It's also another occasion for joining *Alta Via* #2, which dips down to the main road here. Most of the tourist buses stop at this point, so a collection of rip-off cafés and stalls have grown up around the start of the trails. The cheapest of the three **hotels** here is the *Pordoi* (☎0462/61.277; ⑤).

The Gruppo di Sella

The **Gruppo di Sella** lies to the north of Passo Pordoi, and has many fairly difficult trails. If you're a complete beginner, there's a choice of two paths: either stick to the *Alta Via* #2, which crosses from one edge of the massif to the other, or break away at Sass de Mesdi, from where a trail circles down to the Sella pass. Both routes take a couple of days, with overnight stops at *Rifugio Franco Cavazza* (Pisciaduhutte; ☎0471/836.292) or *Rifugio Boe* (Boe Hutte; ☎0471/847.303). The Sella group is an excellent place to walk, with views across the ranges down to Passo Gardena (Sellajoch, 2137m), from where Corvara and the Val Badia are within striking distance, as are the Odle (Geisler) group across the valley. Buses are few and far between up here, although you can pick up buses to Bolzano from SELVA, 11km away in the Val Gardena.

Viel del Pan

It's possible to undertake some much less ambitious walking from Passo Pordoi, starting just past the *Albergo Savoia*, again following the route of *Alta Via* #2 but in the opposite direction. A narrow path cut into the turf traverses the mountainside opposite Marmolada, where Austrian battalions hid under the glacier in 8km of gallery during World War I.

From the seventeenth century this path was on the grain-smuggling route called the **Viel del Pan** – "trail of bread" in Venetian dialect – and it remained busy enough in the nineteenth century for the Guardia di Finanza to set up armed patrols along it. The contrast between the glacier on Marmolada and the peaks of the Sella group – 360 degrees of mountain – is superb. The path descends to **Lago Fedaia**, from where there are irregular buses in summer back to Canazei. The *Rifugio Castiglioni* (☎0462/61.117) is on the edge of the reservoir. On the northern side of the ridge lies **ARABBA**, a tiny resort with small family-run hotels in the centre and in the pastures around. It's a reasonably quiet village for the moment, but there are a couple of hotels – the *Bella Vista* (☎0436/79.125; ⑤) and the *Cesamesdi* (☎0436/79.119; ⑤). The only bus service from here is the one that goes from Belluno to Corvara.

Ladini country: Corvara and the Fanes Park

This part of Italy – the meeting-point of Trentino, Alto Adige and the Veneto – is home to its own language, **Ladino**, a derivation of Latin traceable to the Roman legions who passed through on their way to subdue Celtic tribes. Ladino is unique to the Alps, and is especially prevalent in the area around the Sella group – the Val di Fassa, the Val Badia, the Val Gardena and Livinallongo. A peaceful tribe, the Ladini were constantly threatened with invasion by Germanic tribes from the north and others from the Po Valley, and their epics recount a history of battles, treachery and reversals of fortunes. Christianity later emerged as a major threat, but the Ladini absorbed and transformed the new religion, investing the new saints with the powers of more ancient female divinities. The rudimentary Castello di Thurn at San Martino di Badia, a bleak outpost of the bishop-princes of Bressanone, is testimony to the Church's attempt to keep the Val di Badia under its control. In 1452, Bishop Nicolo Cusano railed against a woman from the Val di Fassa who said she had met the goddess Diana in the woods, and there was a strong pagan undercurrent to the cult of Santa Giuliana, whose sword-wielding image is painted onto the plaster of houses in the Fassa and Badia valleys.

Relative isolation until recent years has kept the 40,000 or so Ladino-speaking people together as a culturally distinct group, even though their territory has been cut in three by the Veneto, Trentino and Alto Adige provincial boundaries. These days, however, the central town of the Ladini, **CORVARA**, is primarily a ski resort, and the most visible sign of the language is a page or two in the Ladino tongue in local newspapers. Corvara is a base for the excellent trails of the nearby Fanes park, a bus ride away, where most of the Ladini legends are based. The **tourist office** has details of **hotels** – try the *Monti Pallidi* (☎0471/836.081; ⑤) – and from outside the office a few buses leave for Brunico and Belluno. There's also a **campsite**, *Camping Colfosco* (*Colfuschg*), open all year (☎0471/836.515).

ALTO ADIGE (SÜD TIROL)

Austria officially begins at the Brenner Pass, but it can feel as though the border is some way south, around Bolzano, where the villages are Tyrolean in looks and German is spoken everywhere. **Alto Adige** (Süd Tirol) was Italy's price for cooperation with the Allies in World War I. At that time German speakers outnumbered Italian speakers by about ten to one. When the Fascists came to power, a process of Italianisation was imposed on the area: cartographers remade maps, deleting German place-names; Italian workers from other regions were encouraged to settle here; stonemasons were even brought in to chip away German inscriptions from tombstones. A great many Germans emigrated, but after World War II many still remained, and it was agreed that the region should be given some special status. A statute drawn up in 1971 deemed that two-thirds of all public jobs and houses should be reserved for German speakers (a fair reflection of the ethnic mix at the time), and that all public servants should be bilingual in German and Italian. Since then, this has been upheld, partly due to pressure from the *SVP* or the *Süd-Tiroler Volkspartein*, and funds have been channeled into the area by successive governments; unemployment is low compared with the national average, and per capita income high. However, the right-wing *MSI* (*Movimento Sociale Italiano*), who argue for repeal of the 1971 act, have gained in strength here too of late, commanding something like fifty percent of the local Italian vote in some places. The *MSI* have held rallies in Bolzano, and in 1987 managed to elect their first-ever local deputy – a lawyer who has declared Mussolini "a great man". Since then they've actively encouraged neo-Fascist sympathisers to move into the province to swell their numbers.

None of this has brought the two groups any closer together. A petty apartheid exists in the education system, for example: there are separate entrances to the German and Italian sections of the same school, and such is the division between the two communities that Italian children are sometimes actively discouraged from learning any German at all. A spate of bombings in the late Eighties increased the profile of the dispute in Italy, forcing then President Cossiga to take his holiday elsewhere, and although the terrorists were later arrested in Austria (said to be sympathetic to the secessionist cause), and the level of violence has decreased, the divisions have become deeper, with the increasingly radical *SVP* and the inflammatory *MSI* gaining in popularity broadly in line with the rise of the separatist parties in the rest of northern Italy. The only party attempting to build bridges is the recently formed *Alernative Movement*, whose German and Italian members argue against perpetuating the mutual hatreds – what they call the "lederhosen culture". With eleven percent of the vote in local elections, they have had some (limited) success.

Travelling around Alto Adige is not as eventful as it might sound from this background, and there are certainly few hints of any tension to outsiders – quite the reverse in fact, as even the big towns have a leisurely pace of life, and the high valleys are utterly peaceful. Although you can get close to some mountainous land around **Bolzano**, the provincial capital, the Dolomites region proper only begins to pay dividends once you head east, high up into the ranges between here and **Cortina d'Ampezzo**, just across the border in the Veneto. Alternatively, make for the glacial ranges to the west, in the **Ortles** group, in sight of the Swiss and Austrian Alps.

It's worth noting that provincial **bus** companies stick fairly rigidly to towns within their territory, so that some places which look like they should be easy to get to from Bolzano, say, often are not. For example, there are more frequent buses to Canazei from Trento, and this is the case for other towns in the northern part of Trentino.

Bolzano (Bozen)

Situated on the junction of the rivers Talvera (Talfer) and Isarco (Eisack) near the southern limit of the province, **BOLZANO** (BOZEN) is Alto Adige's chief town. For centuries a valley market town and way station, Bolzano's fortunes in the Middle Ages vacillated as the Counts of Tyrol and the Bishops of Trento competed for power. The town passed to the Hapsburgs in the fourteenth century, then at the turn of the nineteenth century Bavaria took control, opposed by Tyrolese patriot and military leader Andreas Hofer. His battle in 1809 to keep the Tyrol under Austrian rule was only temporarily successful, as in the same year the Austrian Emperor ceded the Tyrol to the Napoleonic kingdom of Italy. More changes followed, as Bolzano was handed back to Austria until after World War I, whereupon it passed, like the rest of the province, to Italy. Nowadays, in both winter and summer, the town is a busy tourist resort, and its pavement cafés and generally relaxed pace of life make it a good, if uneventful, place to rest up or use as a base for trips into the mountains. An unmissable pleasure is the local wine: a wine-producing area since Roman times, Bolzano is at the head of the *Strada di Vino* (*Südtiroler Weinstrasse*) which runs south to Trento, and it's especially well known for its Chardonnay.

Arrival, information and accommodation

Bolzano's **bus station**, centrally placed at Via Perathoner 4, serves most of the small villages and resorts in the province; the **train station** is a few minutes' walk south of here across Via Garibaldi. There is a **tourist office** at Piazza Walther 8 (Mon–Fri 8.30am–12.30pm & 2–6pm, Sat 9am–12.30pm; ☎0471/970.660), and another office off the square at Piazza Parrochia 11/12 (Mon–Fri 8.30am–12.30pm & 2–5.30pm; ☎0471/993.808) – their "Alpine Desk" (Mon–Fri 9am–noon & 3–5.30pm; ☎0471/993.809) has information on weather conditions and advisability of routes. The *Club Alpino Italiano* at Piazza Erbe 46 (Sun–Fri 12.30–1.30pm & 5–7pm; ☎0471/971.694) is also a good source of local hiking information.

For **places to stay**, try *Albergo Colleggio* (*Kolpinghaus*) at Via dell'Ospedale 3 (Spitalgasse; ☎0471/971.170; ⑤), a couple of minutes' walk from Piazza Walther – it's a hostel with rooms at L23,000 per person. Reasonably cheerful alternatives include the *Croce Bianco* (*Weisses Kreuz*; ☎0471/977.552; ⑤) and *Figl* (☎0471/978.412; ⑤), both on Piazza del Grano (Kornplatz). One way of escaping the summer humidity is to stay in the hills above town at Colle (Kohlern). A cable car runs there from Via Campiglio (Kamillerweg), a twenty-minute walk from the train station. The *Klaus*, Colle 14 (☎0471/971.294; ④) is one of several hotels on the same road. If you're **camping**, the *Moosbauer* site is on the main Bolzano-Merano road (☎0471/918.492).

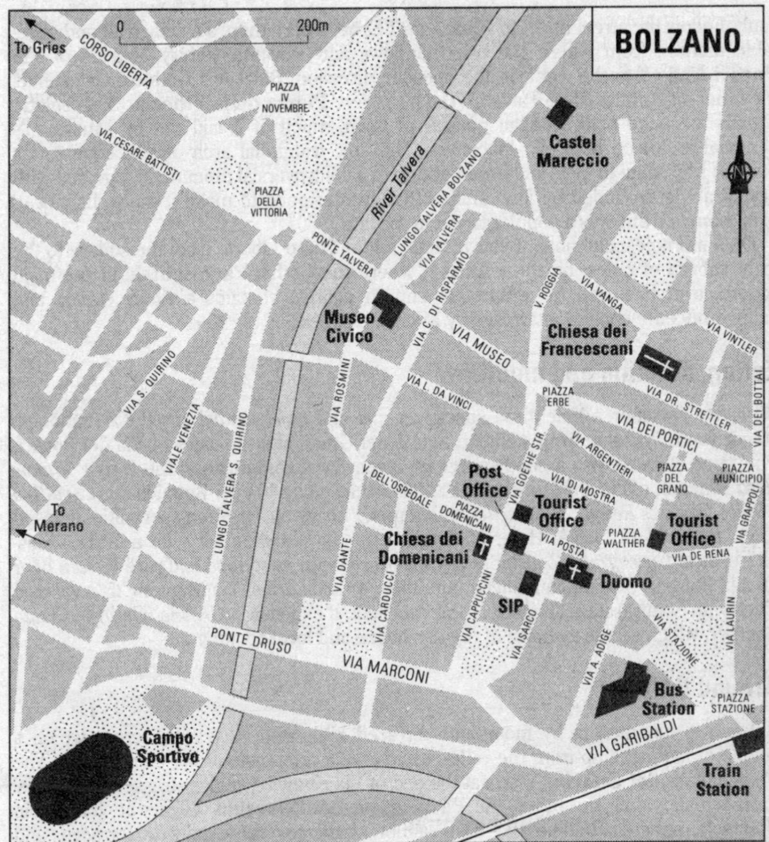

The Town

Bolzano looks part of the German-speaking world. Restaurants serve *speck*, *gulasch* and *knödel*, and bakers sell black bread and *sachertorte*. The centre of town is **Piazza Walther**, whose pavement cafés, around its statue of the *minnesinger* (troubadour) Walther von der Vogelweide, are the town's favoured meeting places. Converted into a cathedral as recently as 1964, the **Duomo** (Dom), on the edge of the square, resembles a parish church: built in the fourteenth and fifteenth centuries, and restored since bombing in World War II, it has a striking green and yellow mosaic roof and elaborately carved spire. The fourteenth-century **Franciscan church** on Via dei Francescani is also worth seeking out, embellished with a carved wooden altarpiece by Hans Klocher and with elegant, frescoed cloisters from the same period.

A couple of streets west of Piazza Walther, on Via Cappuccini, the **Chiesa dei Domenicani** (Dominican monastery) has frescoes of fifteenth-century courtly life painted on the walls of the decaying cloisters, framed by a growth of stone tracery. The Cappella di San Giovanni, built at the beginning of the fourteenth century, retains frescoes by painters of the Giotto school, including a *Triumph of Death* underneath a starry vault. Follow the street north to **Piazza dell'Erbe**, where there's a daily fruit and vegetable market, from where the oriel windows and eleventh-century arcades of **Via Portici** lead off to the right. In the opposite direction, Bolzano's Gothic quarter ends the other side of the River Talvera (Talfer), where **Piazza della Vittoria** (Siegesplatz) signals the edge of the Italian quarter of town, much of it laid out by Mussolini's personal architect, Marcello Piacentini. The epic triumphal arch on the square was built by Mussolini in 1928 and is something of a controversial monument, covered with graffiti and surrounded by low railings that are designed to make it more difficult to plant bombs – this was a popular target in the late-1980s.

On a more peaceful note, if you've time, follow Corso Libertà from the square to the leafy suburb of Gries, on the left bank, where the Gothic **Parrocchiale** in the main square, overshadowed by a Baroque church nearby, contains a richly carved and painted fifteenth-century altarpiece by Michael Pacher.

Eating, drinking and nightlife

If you're just after a lunchtime snack, *wurstel* and *apfel strudel* are the commonest **street food**, available from stalls on Piazza del Grano and the cafés of Via dei Portici. The same street is also a good source of decent local **restaurants**; the *Weisse Traube* (*Uva Bianca*), offers a set lunch for L12,000, while along Via dei Bottai is the *Cavallino Bianco* (*Weisses Rossel*), a *bierkeller* with a menu heavy on Tyrolean specialities (closed July). *Batzenhäusl*, Via A. Hofer 30, is good too, an old wine bar with a lively atmosphere, as is *Lowengrube*, Zollstanse 3 – a *bierlokal* with good food and rare *Weizen* beer on tap. For non-German-influenced fare, there's *Café Latino*, Via Marconi 25, a relaxed place with South American food, or the excellent, if expensive, *Grifone* (*Greif*) in Piazza Walther, which serves a choice of regular Italian and local cooking .

Around Bolzano

Bolzano is hemmed in by mountains terraced high with vineyards, across which a couple of footpaths up from the valley basin give a brief taste of the countryside. The **Passeggiata del Guncinà** starts at the end of Via Knoller (Knollerstrasse) near Gries' Parrocchiale, while the other, the **Passeggiata Sant'Osvaldo**, begins at Via Rencio (Rentscherstrasse), behind the train station, traverses some hillside terraces, and brings you down to the path next to the River Talvera.

Just north of the town centre, the thirteenth-century **Castello Róncolo** (Schloss Runkelstein), reachable by bus #12 from the station, is easy enough to get to, with frescoes of courtly life showing people hunting, dancing and generally having a good time, as well as a group of knights on horseback (March 1–Nov 30 Tues–Sat 10am–5pm; winter 3–6pm).

Monte Renòn (Rittner) gives a taste of the high peaks around Bolzano. A cable car ascends from Via Renòn (Rittnerstrasse) to Soprabolzano (Oberbozen), from where footpaths lead to some of the other small villages, past a forest of eroded earth pillars, half an hour's walk north of COLLALBO. If you're feeling energetic, you can attempt the summit (2260m) for a glimpse of the Dolomites to the east, or take the chair lift to **Schwarzeespitze** (2070m), a short walk from the top. A good time to come up here is in summer, around Saint Bartholomew's day (August 24), when hundreds of farmers from outlying villages congregate on Renòn for the annual horse fair. You might also visit the area north of Bolzano to **eat**; some of the farmhouses serve typical South Tyrolean dishes in their wood-panelled dining rooms. Try *Pieracher* or *Patscheiderhof* in the village of SEGNATO (SIGNAT), off the road from Bolzano to Renon, or *Noafer* in COLOGNA (GLANNING).

Merano and around

MERANO, an hour north by train from Bolzano, lies close to two great mountain ranges. The closest, the **Giogaia di Tessa** (Texelgruppe), less than 10km away, is characterised by steep traverses across pastureland, with old snow still on the slopes in summer; watercourses irrigate the south-facing slopes, planted below with vines, peach and apple trees. Further west, the **Ortles** mountains straddle the border with Valtellina – an unbelievable spread of glaciers and rocky spurs – included within the Parco Nazionale dello Stelvio, one of Italy's major national parks. Both ranges offer isolated trails, away from the tourist routes, with buses to most villages.

Merano itself sits on a bend in the River Passirio, a sedate spa town surrounded by a ring of mountains, and, incongruously, by semi-tropical plants. Mild spring and autumn weather attracted Central Europeans at the turn of the century, and a resort of fin de siècle hotels, neat gardens and promenades evolved. The town's old nucleus is **Via dei Portici**, close to the Gothic **Duomo** and fifteenth-century castle; around it are plenty of shopping streets, and the **Thermal Centre**, which still provides radioactive water cures. It's mainly a retirement resort, but you still may decide to stay in Merano for bus connections to the Parco Naturale di Tessa to the north, or the Ortles mountains in the Parco Nazionale dello Stelvio to the southwest.

Buses arrive and leave directly outside the train station. The **tourist office** at Corso Libertà 45 (Mon–Fri 8am–12.30pm & 3–6.30pm, Sat 9am–noon & 3–5pm, Sun 10am–noon; ☎0473/35.223) has details on accommodation. Two of the least expensive central hotels are the *Conca d'Oro* (☎0473/30.308; ④) and the *Santer Klause* (☎0473/34.086; ④). For **hiking**, consult the *Club Alpino Italiano* office, Corso Libertà 188, or Merano's Alpine association, the *Alpenverien Südtirol*, at Via Galilei 45, an alley off Corso Libertà. **Campers** should use *Camping Merano*, Via Piave 44 (☎0473/31.249), open late-March to early November (turn right out of the station, cross the river by way of Via Rezia and Via Piave is the third turning on the right). One of the best places to **eat** is *Weinstube Haisrainer*, Via dei Portici 102, which serves interesting Italian and Tyrolean dishes.

Parco Naturale di Tessa (Naturpark Texelgruppe)

The mountain chains around Merano belong to a separate geological period from the Dolomites, and are actually part of the Zillertaler and Ötztaler ranges of the eastern Alps. Their foothills, called the **Giogáia di Tessa** (Texelgruppe), begin immediately north of the town. Two high-level paths, the north and south sections of the **Meraner Höhenweg**, encircle this massif. The gentler **southern route** (marked as route 24 on signs) overlooks Merano, the built-up Val Venosta (Vinschgau), and the neighbouring peaks, and is crowded even out of season. The total walking time is 24 hours, and every few kilometres there's a dairy farm offering bed and breakfast, or a refuge for overnight stops. **Buses** go from Merano to the beginning of the route at Hof Unterpferl in KATHARINABERG, and to ULFAS, just west of SANKT LEONHARD, where it ends – plus several points along the way, including **Castel Tirolo**, where a cable car ascends to a couple of refuges and souvenir shops at HOCHMUTER. The castle's tenth-century frescoed chapel is worth the visit, if you can fight your way through the crowds of other tourists who pack the lanes around.

The **northern** stretch of the Meraner Höhenweg is an entirely different trail, running at a higher altitude but still below the snow line, through isolated pastures and rocky terrain. The comparative scarcity of refuges makes it necessary to plan overnight stops in advance. The first section of the trail – KATHARINABERG–MONTFERT–EISHOF – is a walk of four hours; you then pick up the path from Eishof to *Rifugio Stettiner* (3hr 30min); STETTINER to PFELDERS (3hr 30min) is the last part.

For **places to stay** in **KATHARINABERG**, try the *Katharinabergerhof* (☎0473/89.171; ④), the *Schnalsburg* (☎0473/89.145; ⑤), or the *Jaegerrast* (☎0473/89.230; ③). In **PFELDERS**, there's *Edelweiss* (☎0473/85.713; ④) and *Panorama* (☎0473/85.727; ④).

From *Rifugio Stettiner* there's another option, the **Pfelderer Höhenweg**, which runs east to the Zwickauer Shelter, crosses the path here, and traverses the pastures of Obere Schneid. There are some sheer drops down to the valley, and you need crampons above the snowline, but this is an excellent walk, with a hint of how isolated these small valleys were until recently. If you don't feel equipped for this, but want to extend the route, continue past Pfelders to ULFAS (4hr), and from there on to VIPITENO (2–3 days), where you either link up with the main Bolzano to Innsbruck railway or carry on eastwards along the **Pfunderer Höhenweg** (see p.214).

A bus travels north from Merano along the Val Passiria to **SANKT LEONHARD**, skirting the edge of the Texelgruppe, and, on the other side, Merano's ski resorts on the slopes of Punta Cervina (Hirzer Spitze). A network of paths cross the summer pastures around Sankt Leonhard: one of these leaves **SANKT MARTINO**, 4km south of Sankt Leonhard, and makes the steep ascent (2hr 30min) to **PFANDLERALM**, the home village of Andreas Hofer. Originally an innkeeper, wine merchant and cattle dealer, he fought for the Tyrol's return to Austria after it had been ceded to Bavaria in 1805. After successful uprisings against occupying Bavarian and Napoleonic troops, he became self-styled commander-in-chief of the South Tyrol, commanding strong popular support. However, larger political forces overtook him. When the Tyrol was ceded to the French by Austria's Emperor Francis I, Hofer wavered between resistance and acceptance; he was arrested in 1810 and executed under Napoleon's orders in Mantua. At Pfanderalm a memorial to him stands on the edge of the meadow.

The other road out of Sankt Leonhard follows the Val Passiria west to **MOSO** (MOOS), at the head of the Val di Plan (Pfelderer Tal). From Moso the old military road leads to **SANKT MARTIN AM SCHNEEBERG** (2hr). An eerie trail leads through a peat gulley to *Schneeberghütte* (no accommodation), surrounded by spoil heaps and ruined buildings – the remains of Europe's highest mining settlement (2355m), opened in 1660 within sight of the glaciers on Austria's Pan di Zucchero (Zuckerhütl) mountain.

Parco Nazionale dello Stelvio

The **Parco Nazionale dello Stelvio** is one of Italy's major national parks; it covers the whole **Ortles** range, and is topped by one of Europe's largest glaciers (the *Ghicciaio dei Forni*) and crossed by the Passo dello Stelvio, which misses being the highest pass in the Alps by just twelve metres. Like other places in the Alps, the park has felt the effects of tourism and is crisscrossed by ski lifts as anywhere. But it's still a remarkable place. People come here for the high trails and glacier skiing in summer, or to spot species such as the red and roe deer, elk, chamois, golden eagles and ibex. One of the best valleys for wildlife is the sheer-sided Val Zebrù, off the Valfurva, the smallest of the valleys, accessible from Bormio.

There are buses to the park's various points of access but perhaps the place to head for first is **SILANDRO** (SCHLANDERS), with its visitors' centre and information on refuges and trails.

The Valleys

Three main valley roads thread their way into the foothills of the Ortles range: Val d'Ultimo (Ultental), Val Martello (Martelltal) and Val di Solda (Suldental). A traditional place of hiding in an area renowned for mountain warfare, the isolated **Val d'Ultimo** (Ultental) was opened up this century, and buses now run from Merano to the village of SANKT GERTRUD. Around the lower slopes are startling green pastures and some ancient larches, but the main attraction of coming here lies higher up, where trails lead over rock-strewn moorland to *Rifugio Canziani* (*Höchster Hütte*; 3hr; no accommodation), dramatically surrounded by the glaciers and peaks of **Zufrittspitze**. If you're feeling less energetic, the valley is still a good place for some shorter walks, using the village as base. *Innerlahn* (☎0473/79.167; ③) is one of a handful of **hotels** in the village, while for food, you should splash out at *Genziana*, Via Fontana Bianca 116, whose French-born chef turns out amazing meals for around L50,000 a head; there are rooms available too (☎0473/79.133; ⑤).

Further west, **Val Martello** (Martelltal) is equally beautiful, its lower slopes covered with silver birches. A bus travels from Merano to Silandro, and another from Silandro into Val Martello, passing the ruins of Castel Montani and an aviary for falcons at MORTER. At the head of the valley, PARADISO DEL CEVEDALE (2088m) is one of the busiest bases for climbers and cross-country skiiers, lying close to Monte Cevedale (Zufall Spitze; 3757m) and refuges *Corsi* (*Zufall Hütte*; 2265m) and *Casati* (3266m). Other trails lead through high passes to Val d'Ultimo and Val di Solda.

One of the main roads through the park is the awe-inspiring route over the **Passo di Stelvio** (2758m) towards Bormio. A bus from Merano makes the journey to the pass (open June–Oct), passing the **Val di Solda** on the way. Base yourself at **TRAFOI**, up at 1543m, where there are a couple of good pensions: the *Sailer* (☎0473/611.710; ⑤) and the *Trafoi* (☎0473/611.728; ⑤). Alternatively, head for **SOLDA** itself, at the valley's head, where you can stay at *Pension Nives* (☎0473/75.429; ⑤). Solda is another major climbing and skiing centre, but you don't have to be experienced to attempt some of the trails. There are easy paths (2hr) up to *Rifugio Città di Milano* (*Schaubach Hütte*; 2581m; ☎0473/75.402), or more difficult trails to *Rifugio Payer* (☎0473/75.410; open July 1–Sept 30), a fantastic viewpoint and base for the ascent of **Ortles** (3905m). The Passo di Stelvio marked the frontier between Italy, Switzerland and Austria until 1918, and **Pizzo Garibaldi** (Dreisprachenspitze), a spur of rock fifteen minutes' walk from the pass, is the symbolic meeting place for the three main languages of the area. The road continues from Passo di Stelvio down through switchbacks and startling gradients to Bormio.

Alpe di Siusi (Seiser Alm)

The grasslands of the **Alpe di Siusi** (Seiser Alm), to the north of Bolzano, are Europe's largest Alpine plateau, extending over sixty square kilometres, and in an incongruous position, high above the rest of the valley under the peaks of **Sciliar** (Schlern) national park. The valley roads give you little idea of what lies above.

The bus from Bolzano goes to SIUSI, from where another service ascends to the Alpe. On the way, the road climbs through a series of loops past the Hauenstein forest, the ruins of a castle which was once the home of Osvald of Wolkenstein – the last *minnesinger* of the South Tyrol – and the onion-domed church of **San Valentino** (Saint Valentiskirchlein). Buses terminate at SALTRIA (SALTNER), at the heart of the wetlands, an area relatively untouched apart from some logging in the woods. Horses graze on the tough grass which grows up here, picking their way between the bogs and streams; small huts and clumps of pine are dotted across the plateau. Paths lead off the Alpe di Siusi to refuges in the peaks, or there are four hotels that are more or less the only buildings at Saltria: *Ritsch* is one of the simpler (☎0471/727.910; ④).

Sciliar (Schlern) and Sasso Lungo (Langkofel)

The **Parco Nazionale dello Sciliar**, which spreads over this area, is named after **Sciliar** (Schlern), a flat-topped, sheer mountain which splits into two peaks, Cima Euringer and Santner. Trails lead onto Schlern from TIRES (TIERS), FIÉ AM SCILIAR

(VÖLS AM SCHLERN) or SIUSI (SEIS), all involving long, steep climbs up to the summit (2563m). Just before the top is *Rifugio Bolzano al Monte Pez* (*Schlernhaus*; ☎0471/612.024; open June to mid-Oct), one of the original Alpine huts from the 1880s. The cable car from HOFERALP, above UMS (UMES DI FIÈ), cuts out 1000m of ascent. In summer, paths can be crowded, but the day-trippers tend to disappear back down into the valley by evening, when the teeth of **Sasso Lungo** (Langkofel) become blunted by cloud.

Trails onto Sasso Lungo spring from the path between Saltria and **Monte Pana**, above Santa Cristina in the Val Gardena (see below). Half a day's walking brings you to *Rifugio Vicenza* (*Langkofelhütte*; ☎0471/797.315; open end-June–Sept 25); from here paths lead across the mountain down to **Passo di Sella** (Sellajoch).

Val Gardena (Grödnertal)

Trails and chair lifts connect the Alpe with the **Val Gardena** (Grödnertal), a valley of squeaky-clean guest houses and a continuous stream of tourist coaches. The main village in the valley, **ORTISEI** (SAINT ULRICH), for centuries has been a big producer of hand-carved wooden toys, several families each perpetuating a particular design. Three thousand woodcarvers in the valley still make furniture and religious statues, but Ortisei, like the neighbouring villages of **SANTA CRISTINA** and **SELVA** (WOLKENSTEIN), is now mainly a ski resort, within easy reach of the **Sella Ronda**, a route of ski-runs and lifts encircling the Gruppo di Sella that make up the heart of the Dolomite skiing area. The massive circuit takes at least a day to complete. **Buses** make the journey back to Bolzano, and it's possible to hitch in the other direction towards the Passo di Sella or Passo di Gardena.

Val Isarco and Val Pusteria

The attraction of the four-hour bus trip from Bolzano to Cortina d'Ampezzo isn't so much what you see of the **Val Isarco** (Eisack) and **Val Pusteria** (Pusertal) valleys, but the access it gives to the beginning of the *Alte Vie* and quieter routes into the Val di Funes (Villnöss), the Odle group, and the isolated ridges to the north of Val Pusteria. Largely untouched by tourism, these are great places to walk. In the side valleys dippers dart in and out of the streams and the sawing of timber cuts through the air. Higher up, you're likely to see marmots, and chamoix give away their presence with a tumbling of stones.

The Val Isarco (Eisack) and around

The main village of the southern **Val Isarco** (Eisack), **CHIUSA** (KLAUSEN), is served by trains from Bolzano and Bressanone (Brixen), and buses which continue into the **Val di Funes**, a little to the north. **SANTA MADDALENA** (SANKT MAGDALENA), surrounded by tracts of pasture, lies 10km into the valley, at the base of Le Odle. This quiet village is a good place for an overnight stop: its **hotels** include the *Ranuihof* (☎0472/40.140; ④). Another bus climbs halfway up the mountain to ZANSERALM, from where it's one hour's walk to *Rifugio Genova* (☎0472/40.132; open July–Sept) at 2301m. The level paths take you above the larch forests which fill the valley, and give fantastic views of the peaks. A four-hour circular trail called the *Sentiero delle Odle* (*Adolf Munkel Weg*) traverses the grass slopes beneath the teeth of the range, from Zanseralm via SAINT ZENON to BROGLES-ALM, and back down to the valley. *Alta Via* #2 is a short walk from Saint Renon.

Bressanone (Brixen)

Alta Via #2 can also be picked up in the foothills above **BRESSANONE** (BRIXEN), whose bishops – in constant rivalry with the neighbouring Counts of Tyrol – ruled the area as an independent state for a thousand years. The complex of buildings which made up their base is still the focus of the town, on the main square of Piazza del Duomo, ten minutes' walk from the train and bus stations.

The **Duomo**, modernised in the eighteenth century, is the most imposing building in the complex – the interesting part lies to the side, in the cloisters, which were frescoed in the fourteenth century. A small room off the quadrangle contains the cathedral **treasury** (daily 10am–noon & 1–5pm), where vestments belonging to Bressanone's bishop-princes are hung. Their strong influence in the region is evident from the present given by Emperor Henry II to Bishop Albuino: a tenth-century Byzantine silk cloak, spread with the stylised eagle that was the bishop's personal emblem. The bishop's palace, next to the duomo, is now the **Museo Diocesano** (mid-March to end-Oct daily 10am–5pm; L4000), furnished in predictably grand style, with an overwhelming collection of crib scenes in the crypt.

The **tourist office** (Mon–Fri 8am–noon & 2.30–6pm, Sat 9am–noon), opposite the bus station, has information on trails around the town and further afield. **Places to stay** in the old town include *Schwarzer Adler*, Via Portici Minori 2 (Kleine Lauben; ☎0472/36.127; ④), and *Tallero*, Mercato Vecchio 35 (Altenmarktgasse; ☎0472/36.302; ④). There are two **campsites** 5km north in VARNA (VAHRN): one at Brennerstrasse 13 (☎0472/36.216), the other at Oberdorf 130 (☎0472/32.169), the latter open April–October only. Several buses travel here on weekdays, fewer at weekends. For **eating**, the narrow streets around the edge of Piazza Duomo (Dom Platz) have some old-established Tyrolean restaurants – like *Fink*, Via Portici Minori 4 – and there's a *mensa* at Via Vescovado 2. For picnic food, try the shops in the old arcades or the Monday market on Goethestrasse.

Val Pusteria (Pusertal)

The road through the **Val Pusteria** (Pusertal), a wide valley of maize fields and hay meadows, sweeps around the northern edge of the Dolomites. Most of the *Alte Vie* start from points along the main road through the valley, which is served by bus from Brunico. *Alta Via* #1 starts from Lago di Braies (Pragser Wildsee), *Alta Via* #3 from Villabassa (Niederdorf), *Alta Via* #4 from San Candido (Innichen) and *Alta Via* #5 from Sesto (Sexten). There are also lesser-known trails to the north, for example the *Alta Via di Fundres* (Pfunderer Höhenweg) – see overleaf for details.

Brunico (Bruneck)

An influx of people from the surrounding villages arrives daily in the market town of **BRUNICO** (BRUNECK), which is also the transport centre of the region, with buses along the valley and to most of the small places higher up in the hills. Brunico was home of painter and sculptor Michael Pacher: if you have some time to kill, go and look at his *Vine Madonna* in the parish church of the village of SAN LORENZO, 4km southwest of Brunico. The **tourist office**, above the **bus station** in Via Europa (Mon–Fri 8am–noon & 3–6pm, Sat 9am–noon), gives details of **places to stay**. The central *Blitzburg*, Via Europa 10 (☎0474/85.723; ④), and *Corona* (*Krone*) at Via Ragen di Sopra 8 (☎0474/85.267; ④) are reasonable options, the latter the slightly cheaper of the two. *Camping Bersaglio*, Via Dobbiaco 4 (☎0474/41.326), is open from May to September. A stopping train makes the journey along the Val Pusteria from here to the end of the line at Dobbiaco; buses from Brunico to Cortina d'Ampezzo also go through Dobbiaco.

Parco Naturale Fanes-Sennes-Braies

If you have a limited amount of time to spend in the **Parco Naturale Fanes-Sennes-Braies**, east of Brunico, you should aim for the upper slopes of **Alpe di Fanes**, where you pick up some of the best ridgeway paths. You can get here by bus from either Corvara or Brunico to LONGEGA (ZWISCHENWASSER), and then walking 4km to **SAN VIGILIO DI MAREBBE**, in a side valley, where the tourist office can advise on routes up into the mountains. A regular jeep taxi service (L7000) runs from San Vigilio to *Rifugio Fanes* (☎0474/501.097) and *Rifugio Lavarella* (☎0474/501.079), both around 2000m up on the Alpe di Fanes Piccola. Footpaths cross the grassy plateaus, past small tarns and the rocks of **Ciastel de Fanes**, home of Dolasilla, the mythical princess of the Ladini. The lakes are fed by underground streams, which you can sometimes hear, flowing deep beneath your feet.

Perhaps the best way to see the park, however, is to walk the section of *Alta Via* #1 that runs through it, a hike which takes 3–4 days, with overnight stops at refuges. The trail starts at **Lago di Braies** (Pragser Wildsee), a deep-green lake surrounded by pines, 8km off the main road through the Val Pusteria – an extraordinary place (legend says the lake is a gateway to underground caverns), although you should avoid it in July and August, when crowds descend on the trails. To get here, take a bus from Corvara to **BRUNICO** and then another bus to Dobbiaco (Toblach), asking the driver to drop you at the turnoff between MONGUELFO (WELSBERG) and VILLABASSA (NIEDERDORF), around thirty minutes later; buses also go all the way to the lake from Dobbiaco.

Also accessible from Brunico (by cable car) is the **Plan de Corones**, surrounded by jagged peaks. Here, legend has it, Dolasilla was crowned at the top of the mountain with the *raiëta* – a crystal that harnessed powerful forces.

Alta Via Val di Fundres (Pfunderer Höhenweg)

The high-level **Alta Via Val di Fundres** (Pfunderer Höhenweg) follows the ridges north of Brunico. Although it's in the lower part of the Zillertaler Alps, the path gives a feeling of the high mountains, with views across to the glaciers of Gran Pilastro (Hochfeiler) on the Austrian border. It's an exhilarating area, often with snow, ice and scorching sun in the same day. Access to the path is at Kleines Tor (2374m) on Monte Sommo (Sambock), a steep climb along path #29 from SELVA DEI MOLINI (MÜHLWALD), 24km from Brunico. The walk takes four to five days, with overnight stops in refuges or *bivacci*.

From Kleines Tor the path drops down to the Winnebach Valley, then climbs to *Fritz Walde Hütte*. A steep path crosses the Hochsagescharte Col (2650m), drops to Passenjoch (2410m) and then, after a westerly descent to *Gampes Hütte* (2223m), makes a spectacular traverse across steep pasture that eventually descends to the Eisbrugger Valley. The end of the route at VIPITENO (STERZING) is reached via BODEN and the Weitenber Valley. Early on the last day you can be descending across pasture just emerging from snow, and in the evening be eating pizza in town, listening to kids roar around on motorbikes. It's possible to do half of the walk by joining the path above FUNDRES, or the top of the Val di Valles (Valser Tal), where there's accommodation at *Brixner Hütte* (☎0472/57.131; open mid-June–mid-Sept).

Vipiteno

VIPITENO, with its geranium-filled balconies and wood-panelled old inns, is in many ways a typical Tyrolean town, although its main street, **Via Città Nuova**, lined with elegant, battlemented palazzi, erected in Renaissance times by a locally based Florentine bank, is perhaps more reminiscent of places further south. The centre of town, with its porticoed streets and **Torre di Città**, at one end of the main street, rebuilt in 1867 after fire destroyed the fifteenth-century original, make for a nice place to wander for a while, and the late-Gothic **Palazzo Comunale** on Via Città Nuova is worth a visit for its attractive galleried courtyard and a collection of fifteenth- and sixteenth-century paintings and sculptures (Mon–Sat 9am–1pm). Also worth tracking down is the **Museo Multscher**, at Piazza Città 3 (Mon–Fri 10am–noon & 3–5pm, Sat 10am–noon), near the tower, which displays the work of one Hans Multscher, a fifteenth-century sculptor and painter from Ulm. His work shows a sharp sense of realism, as exemplified in an alterpiece of 1459. You can also view his work in the parish church of **Santa Maria in Vibitin**, near the Ospedale Civile, which contains several of his carved wooden figures.

If you decide to **stay** in Vipiteno, the *Corona*, Via Città Vecchia 31 (☎0472/765.210; ⑤), offers rooms furnished in mid-nineteenth-century German style, and has an excellent, if pricey, **restaurant**.

Dobbiaco (Toblach) and around

In the eastern part of the Val Pusteria, civilisation and streams of car-borne German tourists resume at **DOBBIACO**, a stultifying resort and spa town at the junction of roads into the Val di Sesto (Sextental) and the Val di Landro (Höhlenstein Tal). The latter takes you south past Lago di Dobbiaco onto the Alemagna, the pilgrims' route from Germany to Rome. The Val di Landro bus rounds the outer peaks of the Cristallo mountain group, where the road is flanked by forest on either side, before emerging at Cortina d'Ampezzo.

Cortina d'Ampezzo

The 1956 Winter Olympics were staged at **CORTINA D'AMPEZZO** (it still has the *Pista Olimpica di Bob*), an event which began the transformation of the town from a small resort to a city in the mountains, and its main reason for existing now is the skiing season – roughly Christmas to Easter – when the population rises from 8000 to around 50,000, packing out the designer-clothes and antiques shops as well as the slopes around the city. Cortina is the Italian equivalent of Saint Moritz, attracting actors, artists, and anyone who's rich; and the place encourages a kind of Hollywood existence – taking sleighs down the mountain after a meal at *Il Meloncino*, or hiring jeeps to get to places for off-piste skiing.

The setting is stunning, surrounded by a great circle of mountains which includes Monte Pelmo and Antelao, the Gruppo delle Marmarole, and Monte Sorapiss, Cristallo and Tofane. The bad news is that staying here is prohibitively expensive, unless you manage to book a room at one of the few cheap(ish) places in town. These include *La Ginestrina*, Via Roma 55 (☎0436/860.255; ⑤), and *Albergo Cavallino*, Corso Italia 142 (☎0436/2614; ⑥), both fairly central. Women who write far enough in advance may be able to get a bed in one of the convent hostels. The names and addresses to try are: Rev. Suore Canossiane, *Casa Regina Mundi*, Località Crignes 18 (☎0436/2660); Rev. Suore Francescane, *Casa San Francesco*, Località Cianderies 7 (☎0436/2577); and Rev. Suore Missionaire dell'Eucarestia, Via XXIX Maggio 2 (☎0436/4662).

In summer, there's the option of **camping** at one of a number of sites: *Cortina* (☎0436/2483), *Dolomiti* (☎0436/2485) and *Rochetta* (☎0436/5063) are all 2km to the south, at CAMPO, while *Olympia* (☎0436/5057) is at FIAMES, 5km north. It must be said, though, that Cortina's interest lies in the people who come here to show off, and out of season the place is dead. It does have a summer hiking season of sorts, between July and September when the cable cars operate, but the ranges are less crowded from the side which lies away from the city, and are better approached from smaller resorts.

Cortina's **tourist office** is at Piazzetta San Francesco 8 (Mon–Fri 9am–noon & 3–7pm, Sat 10am–12.30pm & 3–6pm, Sun 10am–12.30pm; ☎0436/3231). Their hiking map is good, with refuge phone numbers and an indication of how long trails take to walk. Apart from the tortuous **bus** routes via Bolzano and Belluno, there are long-distance **coaches** to Cortina from Milan, Padua and Bologna; information from the **bus station** on Via Marconi, above town.

Around Cortina

Cortina is better known for trips by road and cable car than for mountain trails, with many drivers heading for the *Grande Strada delle Dolomiti* and its passes. In summer there are buses to the small lake at MISURINA and to the TRE CIME, three mountain peaks to the north of the city – both extremely busy areas in high season. The alternatives are to head south by bus towards Belluno, passing through Titian's home town of PIEVE DI CADORE, with many paintings attributed to him in the Parrocchiale. (The one most likely to be authentic is in the third chapel on the left.) Unless you hitch, it's difficult to reach the most interesting mountains in these parts. One bus route can be recommended, running from Belluno to Arabba and Corvara, via Álleghe. The lake at Álleghe was created after a huge rock avalanche in the eighteenth century – a common occurrence in the area. Álleghe gives access to the rock walls of Monte Civetta (3220m), a superb sight late in the day when the sun is low. *Rifugio Sonino*, three and a half hours' walk from Álleghe, next to the small Lago Coldai (2208m), has overnight accommodation.

travel details

Trains

Bolzano to: Bressanone (every 2hr; 40min); Chiusa (every 2hr; 30min); Merano (hourly; 40min); Vipiteno (7 daily; 1hr 10min).

Fortezza to: Brunico (9 daily; 40min); Dobbiaco (9 daily; 1hr 20min); Monguelfo (9 daily; 1hr 5min); San Candido (9 daily; 1hr 20min); Villabassa (9 daily; 1hr 10min).

Merano to: Silandro (7 daily; 40min).

Trento to: Bologna (12 daily; 3hr 10min); Bolzano (hourly; 35min); Rovereto (hourly; 15min); Venice (7 daily; 3hr 45min); Verona (hourly; 1hr 5min); Vipiteno (2 daily; 2hr).

Buses

Bolzano to: Alpe di Siusi (5 daily; 1hr 20min); Canazei (4 daily; 1hr 50min); Predazzo (7 daily; 2hr); Cortina d'Ampezzo (4 daily; 3hr 35min); Corvara (2 daily; 1hr 15min); Fiè (5 daily; 30min); Fiero di Primiero (1 daily; 3hr 45min); Lago di Carezzo (4 daily; 1hr); Merano (3 daily; 40min); Passo Costalunga (4 daily; 1hr); Saltria (5 daily; 1hr 35min); Selva (4 daily; 1hr 30min); Silandro (4 daily; 1hr); Siusi (5 daily; 45min); Vigo di Fassa (4 daily; 1hr 24min); Carezza al Lago/Passo Costalunga (2 daily; 1hr).

Bressanone to: Chiusa (3 daily; 15min); San Pietro (3 daily; 45min); Santa Maddalena (3 daily; 55min); Rifugio Zannes (3 daily; 1hr 10min).

Brunico to: Dobbiaco (7 daily; 45min); Plan de Corones cable car (9 daily; 15min); San Vigilio di Marebbe (1 daily; 55min).

Calalzo to: Belluno (12 daily; 1hr 45min); Cortina d'Ampezzo (15 daily; 1hr); Misurina (2 daily; 1hr 20min).

Chiusa to: Santa Maddalena (4 daily; 35min).

Cortina d'Ampezzo to: Belluno (5 daily; 1hr 55min); Calalzo (18 daily; 1hr); Dobbiaco (5 daily; 45min); Passo Falzarego (3 daily; 40min); Pieve di Cadore (7 daily; 50min).

Corvara to: Belluno (2 daily; 2hr 45min); Longega (8 daily; 45min).

Dobbiaco to: Villabassa/Lago Braies (4 daily; 40min).

Fiero di Primiero to: Passo di Cereda (2 daily; 25min).

Merano to: Moso (5 daily; 1hr 10min); Parcines (11 daily; 30min); Passo di Stelvio (1 daily; 3hr); Santa Caterina (3 daily; 55min); Santa Gertrude (6 daily; 1hr 25min); San Leonardo (10 daily; 50min); Silandro (hourly; 1hr 5min); Solda (2 daily; 2hr 30min).

Moso to: Plata (11 daily; 7min).

San Martino to: Passo di Rolle/Paneveggio/Predazzo (2 daily 1hr 15min).
Silandro to: Rifugio Genziana, Val Martello (2 daily; 1hr 20min).
Siusi to: Ortisei (2 daily; 45min); Saltria (6 daily; 1hr); Santa Cristina (2 daily; 1 hr 12min); Selva (2 daily; 1hr 20min); Tires (4 daily; 45min).
Trento to: Belluno (1 daily; 2hr 40min); Canazei (6 daily; 2hr 40min); Cles (Trento-Malé line; 12 daily; 1hr 15min); Madonna di Campiglio (7 daily; 2hr 10min); Molveno (Trento-Malé line; 6 daily; 2hr); Malé (Trento-Malé line; 12 daily; 1hr 35min); Rovereto (hourly; 40min); San Martino (3 daily; 3hr).

CHAPTER FIVE

VENICE AND THE VENETO

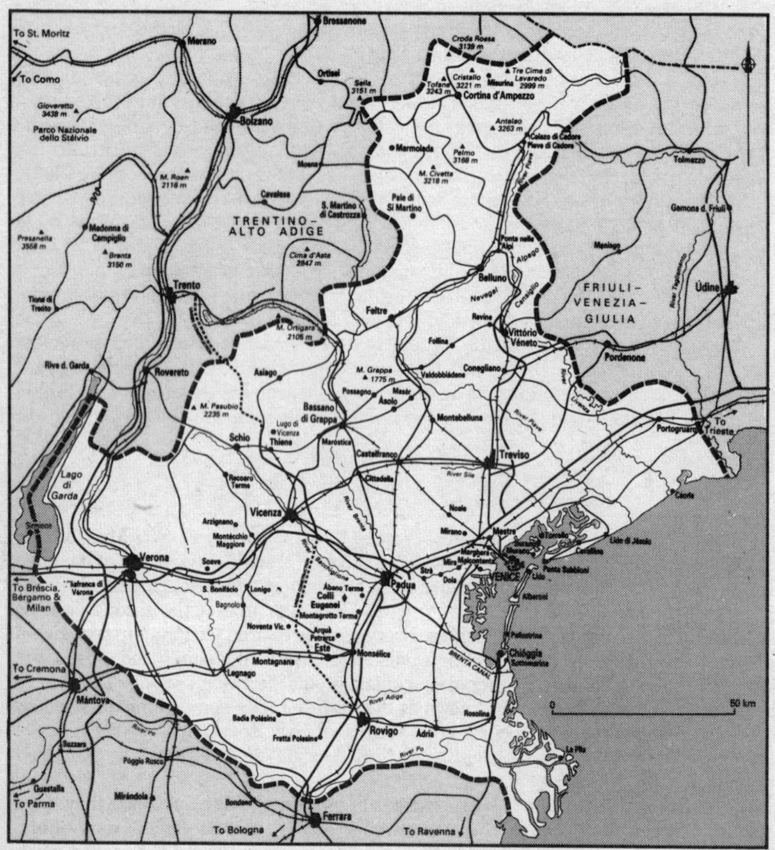

The first-time visitor to **Venice** arrives with a heavy freight of expectations, most of which turn out to be well founded. All the photographs you've seen of the Palazzo Ducale, of the Basilica di San Marco, of the palaces along the Canal Grande – they've simply been recording the extraordinary truth. All the bad things you've heard about the city turn out to be right as well. Economically and socially ossified, it is losing people by the year and plays virtually no part in the life of modern Italy. It is deluged with tourists, the annual influx exceeding Venice's population two-hundredfold – a couple of years ago things got so bad that entry into the city was barred to those who hadn't already booked a room. And it is expensive – the price of a good meal almost anywhere else in Italy will get you a lousy one in Venice, and its hoteliers make the most of a situation where demand will always far outstrip supply.

As soon as you begin to explore Venice, though, every day will bring its surprises, for this is an urban landscape so rich that you can't walk for a minute without coming across something that's worth a stop. And although it's true that Venice can be unbearably crowded, things aren't so bad beyond the magnetic field of San Marco and the kitsch-sellers of the vicinity, and in the off-season it's still possible to have parts of the centre virtually to yourself. As for keeping your costs down – Venice has plenty of markets apart from the celebrated Rialto, there are some inexpensive eating places, and you can, with planning, find a bed without spending a fortune.

Tourism is far from being the only strand to the economy of **the Veneto** – it has Italy's most productive vineyards, and at Marghera, just over the lagoon from Venice, it has the largest industrial complex in the country. But tourism is important, and the region has more tourist accommodation than any other region in Italy. After Venice, it's **Padua** and **Verona** that are the main attractions, with their masterpieces by Giotto, Donatello and Mantegna and a profusion of great buildings from Roman times to the Renaissance. None of the other towns of the Veneto can match the cultural wealth of these two former rivals to Venice, but there are nonetheless plenty of places between the plains of Polesine in the south and the mountains in the north that justify a detour – the Palladian city of **Vicenza**, for instance, or the fortified settlements of **Montagnana**, **Cittadella** and **Castelfranco**, or the idyllic upland town of **Ásolo**.

For outdoor types, much of the Veneto is dull – flatlands interrupted by gentle outcrops around Padua and Vicenza. The interesting terrain lies in its northern part, especially in the area above **Vittorio Veneto**, where the wooded slopes of the foothills – excellent for walking – soon give way to the savage precipices of the eastern Dolomites.

VENICE (VENEZIA)

The monuments which draw the largest crowds are the **Basilica di San Marco** – the mausoleum of the city's patron saint – and the **Palazzo Ducale** – the home of the doge and all the governing councils. Certainly these are the most dramatic structures in the city: the first a mosaic-clad emblem of Venice's Byzantine origins, the second perhaps the finest of all secular Gothic buildings. Every parish rewards exploration, though – a roll-call of the **churches** worth visiting would feature over fifty names, and a list of the important paintings and sculptures they contain would be twice as long. Two of the distinctively Venetian institutions known as the **Scuole** retain some of the outstanding examples of Italian Renaissance art – the **Scuola di San Rocco**, with its sequence of pictures by Tintoretto, and the **Scuola di San Giorgio degli Schiavoni**, decorated with a gorgeous sequence by Carpaccio.

Although many of the city's treasures remain in the buildings for which they were created, a sizeable number have been removed to one or other of Venice's **museums**. The one that should not be missed is the **Accademia**, an assembly of Venetian painting that consists of virtually nothing but masterpieces; other prominent collections include the museum of eighteenth-century art in the **Ca' Rezzonico**, and the **Museo Correr**, the civic museum of Venice – but again, a comprehensive list would fill a page.

The cultural heritage preserved in the museums and churches is a source of endless fascination, but you should discard your itineraries for a day and just wander – the anonymous parts of Venice reveal as much of the city's essence as the highlighted attractions. And equally indispensable for a full understanding of Venice's way of life and development are expeditions to the **northern and southern islands** of the lagoon, where the incursions of the tourist industry are on the whole less obtrusive.

A brief history

Small groups of fishermen and hunters were living on the mudbanks of the Venetian lagoon at the start of the Christian era, but it was with the barbarian invasions of the fifth century that sizeable communities began to settle on the mudbanks. The first mass migration was provoked by the arrival in the Veneto of **Attila the Hun**'s hordes in 453, and the rate of settlement accelerated a century later, when, in 568, the **Lombards** swept into northern Italy.

The loose confederation of island communes that began to develop in the sixth century owed political allegiance to Byzantium, and until the end of the seventh century its senior officials were effectively controlled by the Byzantine hierarchy of Ravenna. But with the steep increase in the population of the islands which resulted from the strengthening of the Lombard grip on the Veneto in the later seventh century, the ties with the Empire grew weaker, and in 726 the settlers chose their own leader of the provincial government – their first **doge**.

The control of Byzantium soon became no more than nominal, and the inhabitants of the lagoon signalled their independence through one great symbolic act – the theft of the body of **Saint Mark** from Alexandria in 828. Saint Mark displaced Byzantium's Saint Theodore as the city's patron, and a basilica was built alongside the doge's castle to accommodate the relics. These two buildings – the **Basilica di San Marco** and the **Palazzo Ducale** – were to remain the emblems of the Venetian state and the repository of power within the city for almost one thousand years.

Before the close of the tenth century the Venetian **trading networks** were well established through concessions granted by Byzantium in the markets of the East, and the exploitation of the waterways of northern Italy to distribute the goods from the Levant. By the early twelfth century Venetian merchants had won exemption from all tolls within the Eastern Empire and were profiting from the chaos that followed the **First Crusade**, which had been launched in 1095. Prosperity found expression in the fabric of the city: the present-day Basilica and many of its mosaics are from this period; and at the end of the century the Piazza was brought to something close to its modern shape. The **Fourth Crusade**, diverted to Constantinople by the Venetians, set the seal on their maritime empire. They brought back shiploads of treasure (including the horses of San Marco) from the **Sack of Constantinople** in 1204, but more significant was the division of the territorial spoils, which left "one quarter and half a quarter" of the Roman Empire under Venice's sway and gave the Republic a chain of ports that stretched almost without a break from the lagoon to the Black Sea.

For almost all the fourteenth century, the defeat of Genoa – Venice's main rival in the eastern markets – preoccupied Venice's rulers, who finally secured the Republic's economic and political supremacy after the defeat of the Genoese in the **War of Chioggia** (1379–80). It was during the Genoese campaigns that the **constitution** of Venice arrived at a state that was to endure until the fall of the Republic, the largest step in this evolution being the **Serrata del Maggior Consiglio** of 1297, a measure which restricted participation in the government of the city to those families already involved in it. A revolt of disgruntled aristocrats in 1310 led to the creation of the **Council of Ten** to supervise internal security – intended to be an emergency measure, it was made permanent in 1334 and became the most secretive and most feared state institution.

Venetian foreign policy was predominantly eastward-looking from the start, but a degree of intervention on the mainland was necessary to maintain its continental trade routes. By the middle of the fifteenth century, Venice was in possession of a mainland empire that was to survive virtually intact until the coming of Napoleon.

But while Venice was advancing at home, the **Ottoman Turks** were emerging as a threat to the colonial empire. Constantinople fell to the Sultan's army in 1453, and with their capture of the main fortresses of the Morea (Peloponnese) in 1499, the Turks gained control of the access to the Adriatic.

Distrust of Venice's ambitions on the mainland and fear of Turkish expansion provoked the formation of the **League of Cambrai** in 1508. Headed by Pope Julius II, Louis XII, Emperor Maximilian and the King of Spain, it pitted almost every power in Europe against the Venetians, in a pact that set out to destroy Venice's empire as a prelude to conquering the Turks. When the fighting finished in 1516, Venice's subtle diplomacy had ensured that it still possessed nearly all the land it had held a decade before, but many of the cities of the Veneto had been sacked, great swathes of the countryside ruined, and the Venetian treasury bled almost dry. Worse was to come. After Vasco da Gama's voyage to India via the Cape of Good Hope, the slow and expensive land routes across Asia to the markets of Venice could now be bypassed by the merchants of northern Europe. The economic balance of Europe now began to tilt in favour of the Portuguese, the English and the Dutch.

After the **Sack of Rome** in 1527 the whole Italian peninsula, with the sole exception of Venice, came under the domination of Emperor Charles V. Hemmed in at home, Venice saw its overseas territory further whittled away by the Turks as the century progressed: by 1529 the Ottoman Empire extended right along the southern Mediterranean to Morocco, and even the great naval success at **Lepanto** in **1571** was quickly followed by the surrender of Cyprus.

At the start of the seventeenth century a row with Rome, concerning the extent of papal jurisdiction within the Republic, culminated in 1606 with the excommunication of the entire city. After a year of arguments the **Papal Interdict** was lifted, damaging the prestige of the papacy throughout Europe. Relations with the **Hapsburgs** were no easier. The Austrian branch caused trouble by encouraging pirate raids on Venetian shipping, and in 1618 the more devious Spanish wing attempted to subvert the Venetian state by a wildly ambitious plot that has always been known as **The Spanish Conspiracy**. But the **Turks** caused the most lasting damage, taking the one remaining stronghold in the eastern Mediterranean, Crete, in 1669.

Venice in the eighteenth century became a political nonentity, reduced to pursuing a policy of unarmed neutrality. At home, the economy remained healthy, but the division between the upper stratum of the aristocracy and the ever-increasing poorer section was widening, and all attempts to dampen discontent within the city by democratising its government were stifled by the conservative elite.

Politically moribund and constitutionally ossified, Venice was renowned not as one of the great powers of Europe, but rather as its playground, a city of casinos and perpetual festivals. **Napoleon** brought the show to an end. On May 12, 1797, the Maggior Consiglio met for the last time, voting to accede to Napoleon's demand that it dismantle the machinery of government. In October, Napoleon relinquished Venice to the Austrians, but returned in 1805 to join the city to his Kingdom of Italy, and it stayed under French rule until after Waterloo. It then passed back to the Austrians again and remained a Hapsburg province until united with the Kingdom of Italy in 1866.

During the French occupation a large number of buildings were demolished to facilitate urban improvement schemes, and modernisation projects were continued under the Austrians. They created most of the *rii terrà* (infilled canals), constructed two new bridges across the Canal Grande, and built a rail link with the mainland.

Yet Venice in the nineteenth century was almost destitute. Eclipsed as an Adriatic port by Trieste (the Austrians' preference), Venice achieved large-scale expansion in the area of **tourism**, with the development of the **Lido** as Europe's most fashionable resort. It was the need for a more substantial economic base that led, in the wake of World War I, to the construction of the industrial complex on the marshland across the lagoon from Venice, at **Marghera**, a processing and refining centre to which raw materials would be brought by sea. In 1933 a road link was built to carry the workforce between Venice and the steadily expanding complex, but it was not until after World War II that Marghera's growth accelerated. The factories of Marghera are essential to the economy of the province, but they have caused terrible problems too: apart from polluting the environment of the lagoon, they have siphoned many people out of Venice and into the cheaper housing of Mestre, making Mestre-Marghera today more than three times larger than the historic centre of Venice, where the population has dropped since the last war from around 170,000 to about 80,000. No city has suffered more from the tourist industry than Venice – about 20 million people visit the city each year, and around half of those don't even stay a night – though without them Venice would barely exist at all.

The Venice area telephone code is ☎041.

Arrival, information and city transport

Flights to Venice arrive at either **Treviso** airport, 30km from Venice, or at the city's **Marco Polo** airport, on the edge of the lagoon. From the former, buses run to Treviso train station, from where there are very regular train services to Venice. Coaches (L5000) and exorbitant water taxis (L83,000) link Marco Polo to the city centre but the cheapest option by far is the *ACTV* bus #5, which runs hourly and costs just L800. There's a ticket office in the airport, but beware that they'll sell you a ticket for the coach rather than the *ACTV* bus unless you make your preference clear.

All road traffic comes into the city at **Piazzale Roma**, at the head of the Canal Grande. Two all-year *vaporetto* (water bus) services – #1 and #2 – run between the Piazzale and the San Marco area, supplemented by the #34 in summer. All three also call at Santa Lucia **train station**, the next stop along the Canal Grande. If you're coming right into Venice by **car**, you'll have to park in either the Piazzale Roma multistorey car park, or on the adjoining Tronchetto, a vast artificial island created specifically for the purpose. The queues for both can be huge – a better option in summer is to park in Mestre's municipal car park, then take a bus over the causeway.

Information

The main **tourist office** (Mon–Sat summer 8.30am–7pm; winter 8.30am–2pm; ☎522.6356) is under the Piazza's arcades, at the end farthest from the Basilica; smaller offices operate at the train station (daily 8am–8pm) and, in summer only, at Piazzale Roma. The free map distributed by the offices is fine for general orientation, but not much else. Far more useful is the English–Italian magazine *Un Ospite di Venezia*, produced weekly in summer and monthly in winter, which gives up-to-date information on exhibitions, special events and *vaporetto* timetables – it's free from the main office and from the receptions of the posher hotels.

If you're aged between fourteen and twenty-nine, the tourist offices can also issue you with a **Carta Giovani**, which entitles you to discounts at some shops and restaurants, all of which are detailed in a leaflet that comes with the card. The card is free – all you need is a passport photo.

Another card that might be worth having is the **Biglietto Cumulativo**, which for L16,000 allows you one visit to each of the following fee-charging museums: Palazzo Ducale, Museo Correr, Ca'Pésaro, Ca'Rezzonico and Museo Vetrario (Murano). It's available at each of these museums.

The transport system

Venice has two interlocking street-systems – the canals and the pavements – and contrary to what you might expect, you'll be using the latter for most of the time. Apart from services #1 and #34, which cut through the city along the Canal Grande, the water buses skirt the city centre, connecting points on the periphery and the outer islands. In most cases the speediest way of getting around is **on foot**. Distances between major sights are extremely short (you can cross the whole city in an hour), and once you've got your general bearings you'll find that navigation is not as daunting as it seems.

The water buses

A **water bus** can be the quickest way of getting between two points, though, and even in cases where it would be quicker to walk, a canal trip is sometimes the more pleasant way of covering the distance. The lack of clear numbering on many of the boats is confusing at first, but in fact the routes are pretty straightforward.

There are two basic types of boat: the **vaporetti**, which are the lumbering workhorses used on the Canal Grande stopping service and other slow routes, and the **motoscafi**, smaller vessels employed on routes where a bit of speed is needed. **Tickets** are available from most landing stages and from shops displaying the *ACTV* sign, with a flat-rate fare for any one journey on any one route. In the remoter parts of the city, though, you may not be able to find anywhere to buy a ticket, particularly after working hours; as tickets bought on board are subject to a surcharge, and there's a hefty spot-fine for not having a valid ticket, it's a good idea to keep a reserve supply. **Fares** are generally L2200 for a *vaporetto* service, L3300 for a *motoscafo*.

ACTV produce three **tourist tickets**, none of them valid on the #2 service: a **24-hour** ticket (L12,000); a **three-day** ticket (L17,000); and a **three-day "Giovani"** ticket (L13,000), available to all holders of a Carta Giovani. If you think you'll be making more than half a dozen trips, it's worth investing in a **Carta Venezia**. This costs L8000, is valid for three years and entitles you to travel for L1000/L1200 on all *ACTV* water and road buses. Take a passport photo and your passport to the *ACTV* office on Piazzale Roma (daily 6.15am–midnight), or the head office in Corte dell'Albero, near the Sant'Angelo stop on the Canal Grande (Mon–Sat 8.30am–1pm).

Timetables are posted at each stop, and details of the more important lines are included in each issue of *Un Ospite di Venezia*. The city centre services run through the night, at greatly reduced frequency after about 1am.

USEFUL WATER BUS SERVICES

#1: the so-called *accelerato*, perversely the slowest of the water buses; it starts at the Piazzale Roma, calls at all but one of the stops on the Canal Grande, works its way along the San Marco waterfront to Santa Elena, then goes over to the Lido. L2200.

#2: known as the *diretto*, the quickest way to get between San Marco and Piazzale Roma or the train station; from the station it goes to Piazzale Roma, then through the docks to the Záttere, San Marco and the Lido. L3300.

#5: known as the *circolare*, this comes in two forms. The *destra* goes from the Fondamente Nuove, through the Arsenale to San Zaccaria, zigzags between Giudecca and the Záttere, goes up to Piazzale Roma and the station, along the Canale di Cannaregio, back to the Fondamente Nuove, then over to the cemetery and Murano. The *sinistra* does the same in reverse – so if you jump on a #5, make sure you know which way round the city it's going. The *barrato* version of the #5 (shown by a 5 with a bar through it) runs from the Tronchetto to Murano only. L2200.

#12: runs to Murano, Burano and Torcello. L3300.

#34: known as the *turistico*; a limited-stop summer service from the Tronchetto car parks along the Canal Grande and across to the Lido. L2200.

#84: shuttles between the Tronchetto, Záttere, Giudecca, San Giorgio and Riva degli Schiavoni. L2200.

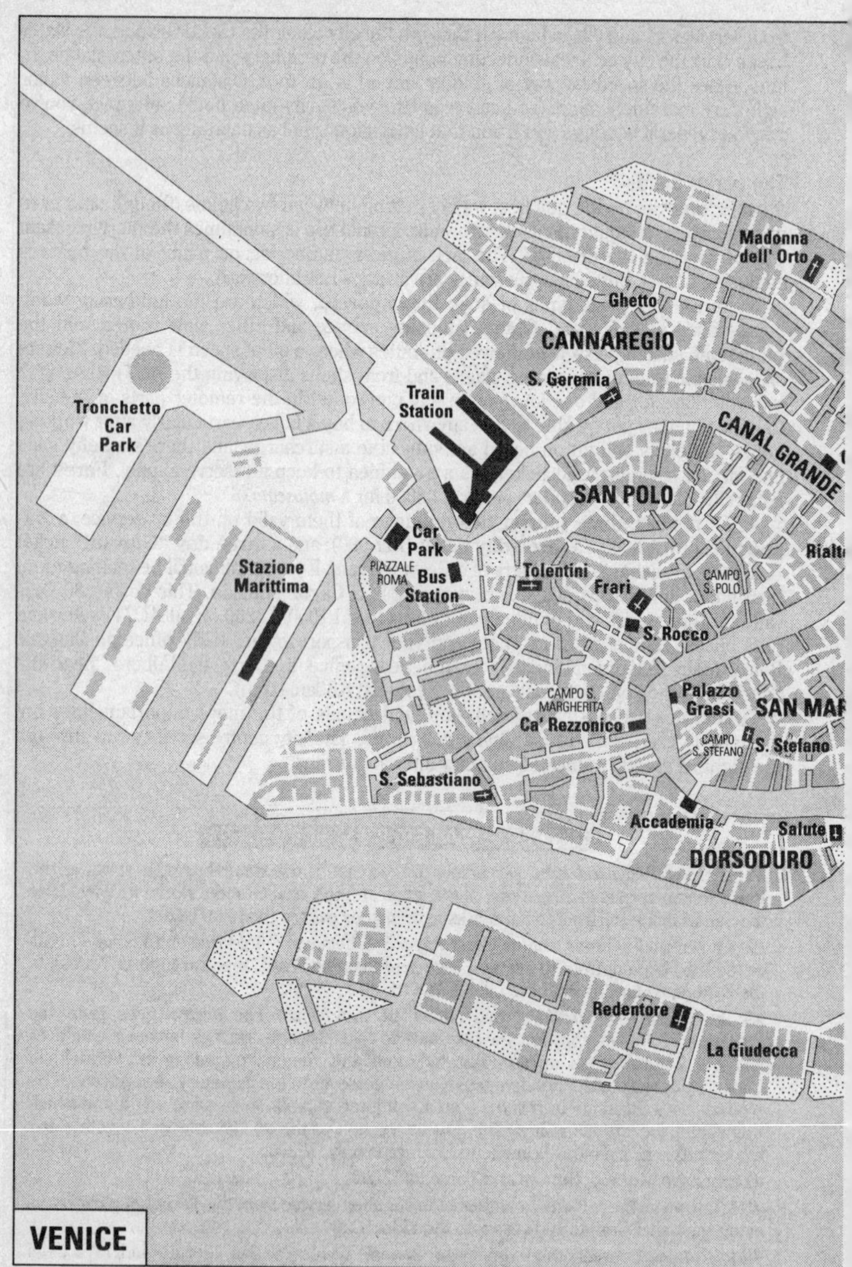
Madonna dell' Orto
Ghetto
CANNAREGIO
S. Geremia
Train Station
Tronchetto Car Park
CANAL GRANDE
SAN POLO
Car Park
PIAZZALE ROMA
Bus Station
Stazione Marittima
Tolentini
Frari
CAMPO S. POLO
S. Rocco
Palazzo Grassi
SAN MAR
CAMPO S. MARGHERITA
Ca' Rezzonico
CAMPO S. STEFANO
S. Stefano
S. Sebastiano
Accademia
Salute
DORSODURO
Redentore
La Giudecca
VENICE

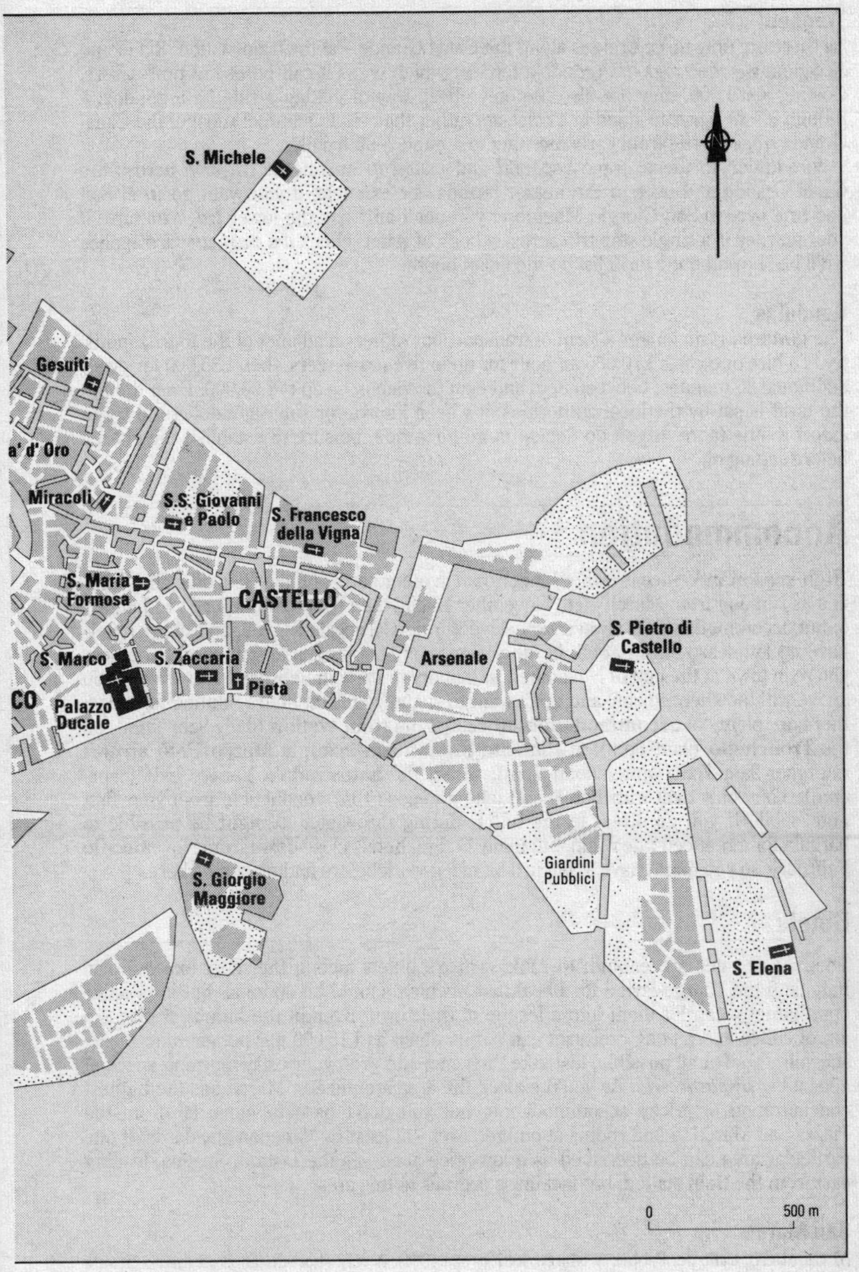
S. Michele
Gesuiti
a' d' Oro
Miracoli
S.S. Giovanni e Paolo
S. Francesco della Vigna
S. Maria Formosa
CASTELLO
S. Marco
S. Zaccaria
Pietà
CO
Palazzo Ducale
Arsenale
S. Pietro di Castello
Giardini Pubblici
S. Giorgio Maggiore
S. Elena
0
500 m

Traghetti

As there are only three bridges along the Canal Grande – at the train station, Rialto and Accademia – the *traghetti* (gondola ferries) which cross it can be useful time-savers. Costing just L500, they are also the only cheap way of getting a ride on a gondola – though it's *de rigeur* to stand in a *traghetto* rather than sit. In summer most of the Canal Grande *traghetti* run from early morning to around 7–9pm daily.

In addition to these, some *vaporetti* and *motoscafi* operate as *traghetti* across the Canal Grande and over to the nearer islands: for example, if you want go from San Zaccaria over to San Giorgio Maggiore, you need only pay the lower *traghetto* fare. If your journey is a single-stop trip across a body of water, check if a *traghetto* fare applies – it'll be shown on the tariff list on the ticket booth.

Gondolas

The **gondola** is no longer a form of transport but rather an adjunct of the tourist industry. To hire one costs L70,000 an hour for up to five passengers, then L35,000 for every additional 25 minutes; between 8pm and 8am the rate goes up to L90,000. Even though the tariff is set by the local authorities, it's been known for some gondoliers to try to extort a little more. If you do decide to go for a ride, be sure to establish the charge before setting off.

Accommodation

High season in Venice is rather longer than in other parts of Italy – it is officially classified as running from March 15 to November 15 and then from December 21 to January 6, but accommodation is always expensive during Carnevale as well, and many hotels have no low-season tariff at all. In other words, pre-booking is all but essential unless you're in town at the end of November, in January or early in February. However, if you arrive with nowhere to stay and don't want to spend your first hours hunting for a bed, there are plenty of **accommodation offices**: at the **train station** (daily 9am–9pm); on the **Tronchetto** (9am–8pm); at **Piazzale Roma** (9am–9pm); at **Marco Polo airport** (summer 9am–7pm; winter noon–7pm); and at the **autostrada's Venice exit** (8am–8pm). They only deal with hotels and take a deposit that's deductible from your first night's bill. If you go direct to the hotels during the winter it might be possible to bargain for a reduced-rate room, but many budget hotels close down from November to February, so you might have to put in a bit of leg-work before finding somewhere.

Hotels

Their basic rates are enough to rank Venice's hotels among the most expensive in Italy, and the charge levied for **breakfast** – which should be optional, but in practice often is not – can lift them into a league of their own. Even in the humblest places a jug of coffee and a puny croissant can put as much as L15,000 per person onto a one-star bill – so if at all possible, just take the room and grab your early-morning snack at a local bar or *pasticceria*. As you'd expect, the area around San Marco has the highest concentration of pricey accommodation, but you don't have to move far from the Piazza San Marco to find rooms at budget level – at least by Venetian standards. If one particular area can be described as a low-price zone, it's the Lista di Spagna, leading east from the train station, but tackiness prevails in this area.

San Marco

Al Gambero, Calle dei Fabbri, S. Marco 4687 (☎522.4384). A very short distance off the north side of the Piazza. ⑤.

Casa Petrarca, Calle delle Colonne, S. Marco 4394 (☎520.0430). The cheapest near the Piazza – but phone first, as they only have six rooms. Extremely hospitable, with English-speaking staff. ⑤.

Fiorita, Campiello Nuovo, S. Marco 3457 (☎522.8043). Just nine rooms, so again it's important to book. Welcoming management, and there's a nearby *traghetto* across the Canal Grande. ⑤.

San Samuele, Piscina S. Samuele, S. Marco 3358 (☎522.8045). Another friendly place, with rooms distinctly less shabby than some at this end of the market, if not exactly plush. ⑤.

Dorsoduro

Antico Capon, Campo S. Margherita, Dorsoduro 3004 (☎528.5292). Situated on one of the city's most atmospheric squares, in the heart of the student district. ⑤.

La Calcina, Zattere ai Gesuati, Dorsoduro 780 (☎520.6466). Unpretentious and charismatic hotel in the house where Ruskin wrote much of *The Stones of Venice*. From some of the rooms you can gaze across to Giudecca's church of the Redentore, a building that gave the old man apoplexy. ⑤.

Messner, Salute, Dorsoduro 216 (☎522.7443). Recently refurbished place close to the Salute *vaporetto* stop. ⑤.

Montin, Fondamenta di Borgo, Dorsoduro 1147 (☎522.7151). Inexpensive hotel famed for its not inexpensive restaurant. Highly recommended, but has only seven rooms. ⑤.

San Polo

Al Gallo, Calle Amao, S. Croce 197/g (☎523.6761). A few basic rooms over a pizzeria not far from the Tolentini church. ⑤.

Alex, Rio Terrà Frari, S. Polo 2606 (☎523.1341). Decorated in Sixties' style, but bearably so. Supermarket in front is useful for picnic preparations. ⑤.

Ca' Fóscari, Calle della Frescada, Dorsoduro 3888 (☎522.5817). Tucked away in a micro-alley near S. Tomà, near the university. Quiet, well decorated and relaxed. Despite its size (10 rooms), you can sometimes find a room even when all others are booked out. ⑤.

Da Bepi, Fondamenta Minotto, S. Croce 160 (☎522.6735). Run by the same family as keeps the Casa Verardo over in the Castello district, and has the same standards. ⑤.

Da Pino, Crosera S. Pantalon, Dorsoduro 3942 (☎522.3646). Very cheap hotel, in the area's main shopping street. ⑤.

Stefania, Fondamenta Tolentini, S. Croce 181 (☎520.3757). Big rooms, some with bizarre murals. ⑤.

Sturion, Calle del Sturion, S. Polo 679 (☎523.6243). Needs to be booked in advance, as it's popular with Italian families. One of the few affordable spots on the Canal Grande. ⑥.

Tivoli, Crosera S. Pantalon, Dorsoduro 3638 (☎524.2460). The biggest cheap hotel in the immediate vicinity, with 24 rooms – so often has space when the rest are full. ⑤.

Cannaregio

Adua, Lista di Spagna, Cannaregio 233/a (☎716.184). Appalling decor but humane prices. ④.

Al Gobbo, Campo S. Geremia, Cannaregio 312 (☎715.001). Rather more genteel than the nearby *Adua*, and correspondingly a touch more expensive. ⑤.

Alle Guglie, Rio Terrà S. Leonardo, Cannaregio 1523 (☎717.351). Minuscule place, with one bathroom between four rooms; the cheapest around. ④.

Bernardi Semenzato, Calle dell'Oca, Cannaregio 4366 (☎522.7257). The owners speak good English and are concerned for the welfare of impecunious young people visiting the city. Nice bars in the street and round the corner. ⑤.

Casa Carrettoni, Lista di Spagna, Cannaregio 130 (☎717.231). By a long way the most comfortable one-star in the vicinity. ⑤.

Eden, Rio Terrà della Maddalena, Cannaregio 2357 (☎720.228). In a more salubrious part of the district than the Lista di Spagna; has just eight rooms, so book ahead. One to try if you're travelling alone, as it has a few more singles than most. ⑤.

Guerrini, Lista di Spagna, Cannaregio 265 (☎715.333). About as pleasant a hotel as you can find on the Lista itself. ④.

San Geremia, Campo S. Geremia, Cannaregio 290 (☎716.245). Another good bet if you're on your own. ⑤.

Castello

Caneva, Ramo della Fava, Castello 5515 (☎522.8118). On the approach to the busy Campo S. Bartolomeo, yet very peaceful; has a private inner courtyard and overlooks the Rio della Fava. ⑤.

Casa Verardo, Ruga Giuffa, Castello 4765 (☎528.6127). Thought by many to be the best deal in the district, just a couple of minutes from San Marco. All rooms have a bath or shower. ⑤.

Rio, Campo SS. Filippo e Giacomo, Castello 4356 (☎523.4810). A couple of minutes' walk from the Piazza, so a bit of a bargain in the circumstances. ⑤.

Wildner, Riva degli Schiavoni, Castello 4161 (☎522.7463). Modest little hotel that offers some of the lowest-priced views over to San Giorgio Maggiore. ⑤.

Eastern districts

Belvedere, Via Garibaldi, Castello 1636 (☎528.5148). Far from the crowds, and usually with a room or two available, except in the height of summer. ⑤.

Sant'Anna, Corte del Bianco, Castello 269 (☎528.6466). Good for families with children, as it has rooms for three or four people and is fairly near the Giardini Pubblici. It's in a remote part of the city, beyond the far end of Via Garibaldi, but has been discovered in recent years – so book in advance. ⑤.

Toscana-Tofanelli, Via Garibaldi, Castello 1650 (☎523.5722). Spartan, but a terrific site, and with a very good trattoria. Midnight curfew. ④.

Hostels

Venice's hostels, most of which are run by religious foundations, are generally comfortable, well run and inexpensive by Venetian standards – moreover, even in the high season they might well have a place or two to spare. Each year the tourist office produces a simple typed list of all hostel accommodation in the city; if the places listed below are full up, ask for a copy of it at the San Marco branch.

Archie's House, Rio Terrà S. Leonardo, Cannaregio 1814/b (☎720.884). This cross between a hostel and a pensione has gone downhill in recent years, but is still a favourite with many budget travellers, especially US college kids. No breakfast. ①.

Domus Cavanis, Rio Terrà Foscarini, Dorsoduro 912 (☎528.7374). On the street going down the left of the Accademia. Catholic-run (ie separate male and female rooms); open June–Sept; single, double and triple rooms. ②.

Domus Civica, Calle Campazzo, S. Polo 3082 (☎721.103). A student house in winter, open to women travellers June–July & Sept–Oct. A little awkward to find: it's off Calle della Lacca, which lies to the west of San Giovanni Evangelista. Most rooms are double with running water; showers free; no breakfast; reception 7.30–11.30am; 11.30pm curfew. ②.

Foresteria Santa Fosca, Santa Maria dei Servi, Cannaregio 2372 (☎715.775). Student-run hostel in the former Servite convent, with dorm beds and double rooms. Check-in 10am–noon & 7–9pm; 11.30pm curfew. Open July & Aug. ①.

Foresteria Valdese, S. Maria Formosa, Castello 5170 (☎528.6797). Go east from the Campo Santa Maria Formosa along Calle Lunga, over the bridge forking right at the end, and it's in front of you – a real palace with flaking frescoes and a large salon. Run by Waldensians, it's principally a hostel for grown-ups, with occasional school groups. Two large dorms, and a couple of rooms for two to four people. It also has a couple of self-catering flats for three to six people, usually heavily booked. Check-in 11am–1pm and 6–8.30pm. ②.

Ostello Venezia, Fondementa delle Zitelle, Giudecca 86 (☎523.8211). Superb location looking over to San Marco. Run with a certain briskness – notices demand "perfect sobriety and cleanliness". Oct–May you can phone to book on the ansaphone 1–6pm; June–Sept personal bookings only. The waiting room opens at noon in summer and 4pm in winter for the 6pm registration. Curfew at 11pm, chucking-out time 9am. Gets so busy in July–Aug that written reservations must be made by April. If it's full, they use a local school with camp-beds as an annexe. Breakfast and sheets included in price – but remember to add the expense of the boat over to Giudecca. No kitchen, but full (and excellent) meals at L10,000. *IYHF* card necessary, but you can join on the spot for L30,000. ①.

Suore Cannosiano, Fondamenta del Ponte Piccolo, Giudecca 428 (☎522.2157). Women-only hostel near the Sant'Eufamia *vaporetto* stop. Closed 8.30am–4pm. Curfew 10.30pm. ①.

Camping

There are no inexpensive campsites in the immediate area of Venice, but perhaps the most convenient are the pair on the grim road from the airport, which at least has the benefit of frequent bus connections to Piazzale Roma: the *Marco Polo* (L20,000 per person per night) and the friendlier *Leone di San Marco* (L16,000).

The **Litorale del Cavallino**, stretching from the Punta Sabbioni to Jésolo, has sites with a total of around 60,000 places, many of them quite luxurious. The *vaporetto* #14, from the Riva degli Schiavoni to the Punta, stops close to *Marina di Venezia* (Via Montello 6; ☎966.146; April–Sept; minimum stay 3 days) and *Miramare* (Lungomare Dante Alighieri 29; ☎966.150; April–Sept). Most of the sites along the Cavallino shore are inexcusably expensive – typically L15,000 for the pitch plus L5000 per person. When you've added on the fare for the forty-minute boat trip into the city you're not left with a particularly economical proposition.

The **Lido** is a shorter ride away, but its **San Nicolò** site, at Riviera San Nicolò 65 (☎767.415), has only 150 places; an International Camping Card is necessary.

There's an all-year site back on the mainland at **Fusina** (Via Moranzani; ☎547.055), the catch here being that the direct *vaporetto* (#16) only operates in the summer; at other times you have to get the bus to the Mestre and change there. It has 1000 places.

Self-sufficient travellers used to spread their sleeping bags on the forecourt of the train station in summer, an expedient that was banned in 1987. At that point the Scuola San Caboto (Cannaregio 1104/f; ☎716.629) opened its doors to take in the displaced *saccopelisti*, as they're called. The school charges L5000 for sleeping under the stars in its garden, L8000 with your tent, L6500 with their tent, L10,000 dorm-style in the school buildings. It's open 7pm–midnight, and you have to be out by 9am. Follow the signs from the Ponte delle Guglie, on the Canale di Cannaregio.

The City

The 118 islands of central Venice are divided into six districts known as *sestieri*, and the houses within each *sestiere* are numbered in a sequence that makes sense solely to the functionaries of the post office – this explains how buildings facing each other across an alleyway can have numbers which are separated by hundreds.

The *sestiere* of **San Marco** is the zone where the majority of the essential sights are clustered, and is accordingly the most expensive and most crowded district of the city. On the east it's bordered by **Castello**, and on the north by **Cannaregio** – both of which become more residential, and poorer and quieter, the further you go from the centre. On the other side of the Canal Grande, the largest of the *sestieri* is **Dorsoduro**, stretching from the fashionable quarter at the southern tip of the canal to the docks in the west. **Santa Croce**, named after a now demolished church, roughly follows the curve of the Canal Grande from Piazzale Roma to a point just short of the Rialto, where it joins the smartest and commercially most active of the districts on this bank – **San Polo**.

To the uninitiated, the boundaries of the *sestieri* seem arbitrary, and they are of little use as a means of structuring a guide. So, although in some instances we've used *sestiere* as broad indicators of location, the boundaries of our sections have been chosen for their practicality and do not, except in the case of San Marco, exactly follow the city's official divisions.

San Marco

The section of Venice enclosed by the lower loop of the Canal Grande – a rectangle smaller than 1000 metres by 500 – is, in essence, the Venice of the travel brochures. The plush hotels are concentrated here, in the *sestiere* of **SAN MARCO**, as are the

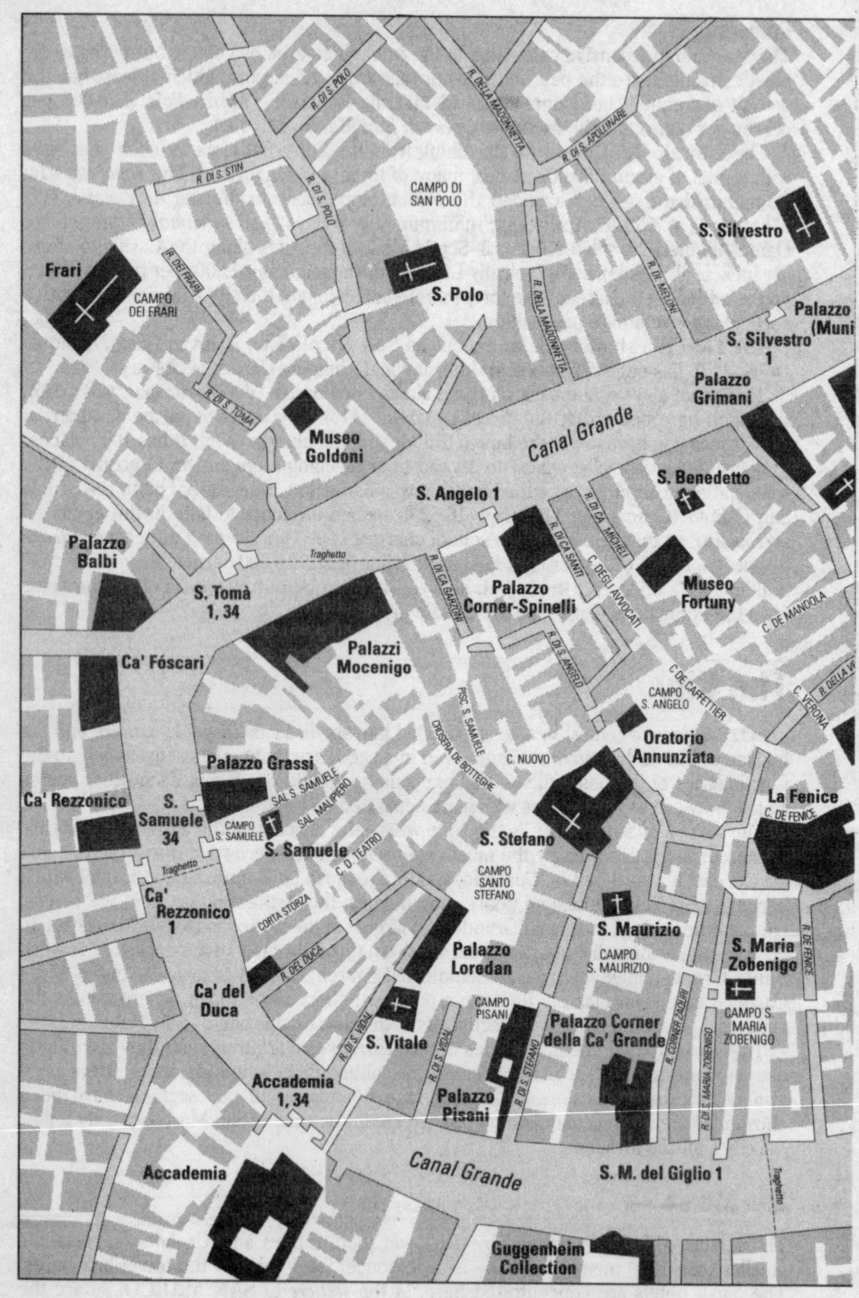
R. DI S. POLO
R. DELLA MADONNETTA
R. DI S. APOLLINARE
R. DI S. STIN
CAMPO DI SAN POLO
R. DI S. POLO
S. Silvestro
Frari
R. DEI FRARI
CAMPO DEI FRARI
S. Polo
R. DELLA MADONNETTA
R. DI MELONI
Palazzo (Muni
S. Silvestro 1
Palazzo Grimani
R. DI S. TOMÀ
Museo Goldoni
Canal Grande
S. Benedetto
S. Angelo 1
R. DI CA MICHELI
R. DI CA SANTI
Palazzo Balbi
Traghetto
C. DEGLI AVVOCATI
Museo Fortuny
R. DI CA GARZONI
Palazzo Corner-Spinelli
S. Tomà 1, 34
C. DE MANDOLA
R. DI S. ANGELO
Palazzi Mocenigo
Ca' Fóscari
C. DE CAFFETTIER
CAMPO S. ANGELO
C. VERONA
PISC. S. SAMUELE
CROSERA DE BOTTEGHE
Oratorio Annunziata
C. NUOVO
Palazzo Grassi
SAL S. SAMUELE
SAL. MALIPIERO
La Fenice
C. DE FENICE
Ca' Rezzonico
S. Samuele 34
CAMPO S. SAMUELE
S. Samuele
C. D. TEATRO
S. Stefano
Traghetto
CAMPO SANTO STEFANO
Ca' Rezzonico 1
CORTA STORZA
S. Maurizio
Palazzo Loredan
CAMPO S. MAURIZIO
S. Maria Zobenigo
R. DE FENICE
R. DEL DUCA
Ca' del Duca
CAMPO PISANI
Palazzo Corner della Ca' Grande
R. CORNER ZAGURI
CAMPO S. MARIA ZOBENIGO
R. DI S. VIDAL
S. Vitale
R. DI S. VIDAL
R. DI S. STEFANO
R. DI S. MARIA ZOBENIGO
Accademia 1, 34
Palazzo Pisani
Canal Grande
Accademia
S. M. del Giglio 1
Traghetto
Guggenheim Collection

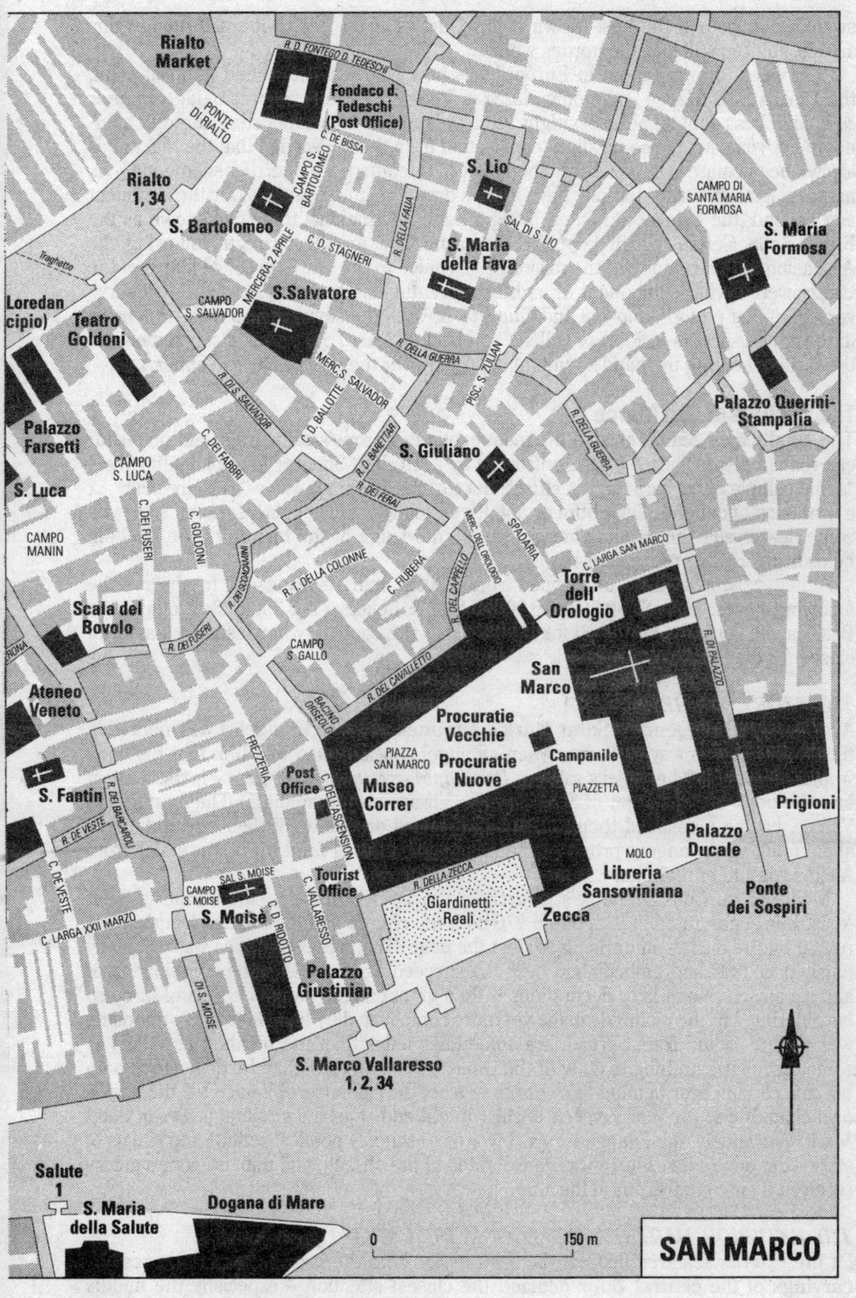
Rialto Market
R. D. FONTEGO D. TEDESCHI
Fondaco d. Tedeschi (Post Office)
PONTE DI RIALTO
C. DE BISSA
CAMPO S. BARTOLOMEO
Rialto 1, 34
S. Lio
CAMPO DI SANTA MARIA FORMOSA
S. Bartolomeo
SAL DI S. LIO
S. Maria Formosa
C. D. STAGNERI
R. DELLA FAVA
S. Maria della Fava
Traghetto
MERCERA 2 APRILE
S.Salvatore
CAMPO S. SALVADOR
Loredan
cipio)
Teatro Goldoni
R. DELLA GUERRA
PISC. S. ZULIAN
MERC. S. SALVADOR
R. DI S. SALVADOR
C. D. BALLOTTE
Palazzo Querini-Stampalia
Palazzo Farsetti
C. DEI FABBRI
R. D. BARETTAR
S. Giuliano
R. DELLA GUERRA
CAMPO S. LUCA
R. DEI FERAI
S. Luca
MERC. DELL OROLOGIO
SPADARIA
CAMPO MANIN
C. DEI FUSERI
C. GOLDONI
C. LARGA SAN MARCO
R. T. DELLA COLONNE
C. FIUBERA
R. DEL CAPPELLO
Torre dell' Orologio
Scala del Bovolo
R. DEI FUSERI
CAMPO S. GALLO
R. DI PALAZZO
San Marco
R. DEL CAVALLETTO
Ateneo Veneto
BACINO ORSEOLO
Procuratie Vecchie
PIAZZA SAN MARCO
Procuratie Nuove
Campanile
FREZZERIA
Post Office
Museo Correr
PIAZZETTA
S. Fantin
R. DEI BARCAROLI
C. DELL'ASCENSION
Prigioni
R. DE VESTE
Palazzo Ducale
MOLO
C. DE VESTE
R. DELLA ZECCA
Libreria Sansoviniana
SAL S. MOISE
Tourist Office
CAMPO S. MOISE
C. VALLARESSO
Giardinetti Reali
Ponte dei Sospiri
S. Moisè
C. D. RIDOTTO
Zecca
C. LARGA XXII MARZO
Palazzo Giustinian
DI S. MOISE
S. Marco Vallaresso 1, 2, 34
Salute 1
S. Maria della Salute
Dogana di Mare
0
150 m
SAN MARCO

swankier shops and the best-known cultural draws of the city. But small though this area is, you can still lose the hordes within it.

"The finest drawing-room in Europe" was how Napoleon described its focal point, the **Piazza San Marco** – the only *piazza* in Venice, all other squares being *campi* or *campielli*. Less genteel phrases might seem appropriate on a suffocating summer afternoon, but you can take some slight consolation from the knowledge that the Piazza has always been congested. Neither is the influx of foreigners a modern phenomenon – its parades, festivities and markets have always drawn visitors from all over the continent and beyond, the biggest attraction being a huge international trade fair known as the **Fiera della Sensa**, which kept the Piazza buzzing for the fortnight following the Ascension Day ceremony of the marriage of Venice to the sea. The coffee shops of the Piazza were a vital component of eighteenth-century high society, and the two survivors from that period – *Florian* and *Quadri* – are still the smartest and most expensive in town: an espresso in *Florian* will set you back at least L5000, plus a supplement for the thrill of hearing the band's rendition of *My Way* or the best of Lloyd-Webber.

The Basilica di San Marco

The **Basilica of San Marco** is the most exotic of Europe's cathedrals, and no visitor can remain dispassionate when confronted by it. Herbert Spencer found it loathsome – "a fine sample of barbaric architecture", but to John Ruskin it was a "treasure-heap . . . a confusion of delight". Delightful or not, it's certainly confusing, increasingly so as you come nearer and the details emerge; some knowledge of the history of the building helps bring a little order out of chaos.

Although San Marco is often open from 6.30am, tourists are asked to observe the following hours: Mon–Sat 9.30am–5.30pm, Sun & holidays 2–5.30pm. Sections of the Basilica will certainly be closed for restoration – the baptistery, for instance, has been closed for the past five years.

THE STORY OF THE BASILICA

According to the **legend of Saint Mark's annunciation**, the Evangelist was moored in the lagoon, on his way to Rome, when an angel appeared and told him that his body would rest there. (The angel's salute – *Pax tibi, Marce evangelista meus* – is the text cut into the book that the Lion of Saint Mark is always shown holding.) The founders of Venice, having persuaded themselves of the sacred ordination of their city, duly went about fulfilling the angelic prophecy, and in 828 the body of Saint Mark was stolen from Alexandria and brought here.

Modelled on Constantinople's Church of the Twelve Apostles, the shrine of Saint Mark was consecrated in 832, but in 976 both the church and the Palazzo Ducale were ruined by fire during an uprising against the doge. The present Basilica was originally finished in 1094 and embellished over the succeeding centuries. The combination of ancient structure and later decorations is, to a great extent, what makes San Marco so bewildering, but the picture is made yet more complicated by the addition of ornaments which were looted from abroad, are sometimes older than the building itself and in some cases have nothing to do with the Church. Every trophy that the doge stuck onto his church (and bear in mind this church was not the cathedral of Venice but the doge's own chapel) was proof of Venice's secular might and so of the spiritual power of Saint Mark. Conversely, the Evangelist was invoked to sanctify political actions and rituals of state – the doge's investiture was consecrated in the church, and military commanders received their commissions at the altar.

THE EXTERIOR, NARTHEX AND LOGGIA DEI CAVALLI

Of the exterior features that can be seen easily from the ground, the **Romanesque carvings** of the **central door** demand the closest attention – especially the middle arch's figures of *The Months and Seasons* and outer arch's series of *The Trades of Venice*. The carvings were begun around 1225 and finished in the early fourteenth century. Take a look also at the mosaic above the doorway on the far left – *The Arrival of the Body of St Mark* – which was made around 1260 (the only early mosaic left on the main facade) and includes the oldest known image of the Basilica.

From the Piazza you pass into the vestibule known as the **narthex**, decorated with the first of the church's **mosaics**: Old Testament scenes on the domes and arches, together with *The Madonna with Apostles and Evangelists* in the niches of the bay in front of the main door – dating from the 1060s, the oldest mosaics in San Marco.

A steep staircase goes from the church's main door up to the **Museo Marciano** and the **Loggia dei Cavalli** (L2000). Apart from giving you an all-round view which it's difficult to leave, the loggia is also the best place from which to inspect the **Gothic carvings** along the apex of the facade. The **horses** outside are replicas, the genuine articles having been removed to a room inside, allegedly to protect them from the risks of atmospheric pollution, although some cynics have insisted that the rescue mission had more to do with the marketing strategies of *Olivetti*, who sponsored the operation. Thieved from the Hippodrome of Constantinople in 1204 during the Fourth Crusade, they are probably Roman works of the second century – the only such ancient group, or *quadriga*, to have survived – and are made of a bronze which is nearly 100 percent copper.

THE INTERIOR

With its undulating floor of twelfth-century patterned marble, its plates of eastern stone on the lower walls, and its 4000 square metres of **mosaics** covering every other inch of wall and vaulting, the interior of San Marco is the most opulent of any cathedral. One visit is not enough – there's too much to take in at one go, and the shifting light reveals and hides parts of the decoration as the day progresses; try calling in for half an hour at the beginning and end of a couple of days.

The majority of the mosaics were in position by the middle of the thirteenth century; some date from the fourteenth and fifteenth centuries, and others were created in the sixteenth to replace damaged early sections. A thorough guide to them would take volumes, but an inventory of the very best might include these. On the west wall, above the door – *Christ, the Virgin and St Mark* (thirteenth century); west dome – *Pentecost* (early twelfth century); arch between west and central domes – *Crucifixion, Resurrection* (the latter a fifteenth-century copy); central dome – *Ascension*; east dome – *Religion of Christ Foretold by the Prophets*; between windows of apse – *Four Patron Saints of Venice*; north transept's dome – *Acts of St John the Evangelist*; arch to west of north transept's dome (and continued on upper part of adjacent wall) – *Life of the Virgin and Life of the Infant Christ*; wall of south aisle – *The Agony in the Garden*; west wall of south transept – *Rediscovery of the Body of St Mark*. This last scene refers to the story that Saint Mark's body was hidden during the rebuilding of the Basilica in 1063 and was not found again until 1094, when it miraculously broke through the pillar in which it had been buried.

From the south transept you can enter the **Sanctuary** (L2000), where, behind the altar, you'll find the most precious of San Marco's treasures – the **Pala d'Oro** (Golden Altar Panel). Commissioned in 976 in Constantinople, the Pala was enlarged, enriched and rearranged by Byzantine goldsmiths in 1105, then by Venetians in 1209 (to incorporate some less cumbersome loot from the Fourth Crusade) and again (finally) in 1345. The completed screen holds 83 enamel plaques, 74 enamelled roundels, 38 chiselled figures, 300 sapphires, 300 emeralds, 400 garnets, 15 rubies, 1300 pearls and a couple of hundred other stones.

In a corner of the south transept is the door of the **Treasury** (L2000), a small but dazzling line-up of chalices, reliquaries, candelabra and so on – a fair proportion of which owes its presence here to the great Constantinople robbery of 1204.

The **Baptistery** – entered from the south aisle, restorers permitting – was altered to its present form by the fourteenth-century Doge Andrea Dandolo, whose tomb (facing the door) was thought by Ruskin to have the best monumental sculpture in the city. Dandolo also ordered the creation of the **mosaics** depicting *Scenes from the Lives of Christ and John the Baptist*, works in which the hieratic formality of Byzantine art is blended with the rich detail of the Gothic.

The adjoining **Cappella Zen** was created between 1504 and 1521 by enclosing the Piazzetta entrance to the narthex, in order to house the tomb of Cardinal Giambattista Zen, whose estate was left to the city on condition that he was buried within San Marco. The late thirteenth-century **mosaics** on the vault show *Scenes from the Life of St Mark*. The chapel is sometimes known as the *Chapel of the Madonna of the Shoe*, taking its name from the *Virgin and Child* by Antonio Lombardo (1506) on the high altar.

Back in the main body of the church, there's still more to see on the lower levels of the building. Don't overlook the **rood screen**'s marble figures of *The Virgin, St Mark and the Apostles*, carved in 1394 by the dominant sculptors in Venice at that time, Jacobello and Pietro Paolo Dalle Masegne. The **pulpits** on each side of the screen were assembled in the early fourteenth century from miscellaneous panels (some from Constantinople); the new doge was presented to the people from the right-hand one. The tenth-century **Icon of the Madonna of Nicopeia** (in the chapel on east side of north transept) is the most revered religious image in Venice; it used to be one of the most revered in Constantinople. A beautiful mid-fifteenth-century mosaic cycle of *Scenes from the Life of the Virgin*, one of the earliest Renaissance works in Venice, is to be seen in the adjacent **Cappella della Madonna dei Mascoli**. And on the north side of the nave stands a marble kiosk fabricated from a variety of rare marbles to house a painting of the *Crucifix* on the altar; this arrived in Venice in 1205, and in 1290 achieved its current exalted status by spouting blood after an assault on it.

The Palazzo Ducale

The **Palazzo Ducale** (daily summer 9am–6pm; winter 9am–2pm; L8000) was far more than the residence of the doge – it was the home of all of Venice's governing councils, many of its courts, a sizeable number of its civil servants and even its prisons. The government of Venice was administered through an intricate system of elected committees and councils – a system designed to limit the power of any individual – but for the last 500 years of the Republic's existence only those families listed in the register of noble births and marriages known as the *Libro d'Oro* (Golden Book) were entitled to play a part in the system.

At the head of the network sat the **doge**, the one politician to sit on all the major councils of state and the only one elected for life; he could be immensely influential in steering policy and in making appointments, and restrictions were accordingly imposed on his actions to reduce the possibility of his abusing that influence – his letters were read by censors, for example, and he couldn't receive foreign delegations alone. The privileges of the job far outweighed the inconveniences, though, and men campaigned for years to increase their chances of election.

Like San Marco, the Palazzo Ducale has been rebuilt many times since its foundation in the first years of the ninth century. It was with the construction of a new hall for the Maggior Consiglio (Great Council) in 1340 that the Palazzo began to take on its present shape. The hall was constructed parallel to the waterfront and was inaugurated in 1419; three years later, it was decided to extend the building along the Piazzetta, copying the style of the fourteenth-century work – the slightly fatter column on the Piazzetta side, under a tondo of *Justice*, is where the two wings meet.

The principal entrance to the Palazzo – the **Porta della Carta** – is one of the most ornate Gothic works in the city. It was commissioned in 1438 by Doge Francesco Fóscari from Bartolomeo and Giovanni Bon, but the figures of Fóscari and his lion are replicas – the originals were pulverised in 1797 by the head of the stonemason's guild, as a favour to Napoleon.

The passageway into the Palazzo ends under the **Arco Fóscari**, also commissioned from the Bons by Doge Fóscari but finished a few years after his death by Antonio Rizzo and Antonio Bregno. In 1483 a fire demolished most of the wing in front of you, and led to more work for Rizzo – he designed the enormous staircase (*Scala dei Giganti*) and much of the new wing. Reconstruction continued under Pietro Lombardo, Spavento and Scarpagnino, and finally Bartolomeo Monopola, who completed the courtyard in about 1600 by extending the arcades along the other two sides.

Parts of the Palazzo Ducale can be marched through fairly briskly. Acres of canvas cover the walls, but many of the paintings are just wearisome exercises in self-aggrandisement. But other sections you will not want to rush, and, if you're there in the high season, it's a good idea to buy your ticket within half an hour of opening. A word of warning – restoration work is continually in progress in the Palazzo Ducale, and there's never any indication before you go in as to which bits are under wraps; it's a distinct possibility that some of the highlights will be hidden from view.

One of the first rooms in the palace is the **Anticollegio**, the room in which embassies had to wait before being admitted to the presence of the doge and his cabinet. As regards the quality of its paintings, this is one of the richest rooms in the Palazzo Ducale: four pictures by **Tintoretto** hang on the door walls, and facing the windows is **Veronese**'s characteristically benign *Rape of Europa*.

The cycle of paintings on the ceiling of the adjoining **Sala del Collegio** is also by Veronese, and he features strongly again in the most stupendous room in the building – the **Sala del Maggior Consiglio**. Veronese's ceiling panel of *The Apotheosis of Venice* is suspended over the dais from which the doge oversaw the sessions of the city's general assembly; the backdrop is the immense *Paradiso* painted at the end of his life by **Tintoretto**, with the aid of his son, Domenico. At the opposite end there's a curiosity: the frieze of portraits of the first 76 doges (the series continues in the *Sala dello Scrutinio* – through the door at the far end) is interrupted by a painted black veil, marking the place where **Doge Marin Falier** would have been honoured had he not conspired against the state in 1355 and been beheaded for his crime.

From here you descend quickly to the underbelly of the Venetian state, crossing the **Ponte dei Sospiri** (Bridge of Sighs) to the **prisons**. Before the construction of these cells in the early seventeenth century all prisoners were kept in the *Piombi* (the Leads), under the roof of the Palazzo Ducale, or in the *Pozzi* (the Wells) in the bottom two storeys; the new block was occupied mainly by petty criminals. If you want to see the Piombi, and the rooms in which the day-to-day administration of Venice took place, you should go on the **Itinerari Segreti del Palazzo Ducale**; a guided tour through the warren of offices and passageways that interlocks with the public rooms of the building. It's not cheap (L5000), and the guide speaks only Italian, but if you can afford it and can understand even a little of the language, it's well worth the price. Tickets can be booked by phoning ☎520.4287; posters at the entrance to the Palazzo give times.

The Campanile and Torre dell'Orologio

Most of the landscape of the Piazza dates from the great period of urban renewal which began at the end of the fifteenth century and went on for much of the following century. The one exception – excluding San Marco itself – is the **Campanile** (open daily 9.30am, closes between 3.30 and 7.30pm according to season; L3000), which began life as a lighthouse in the ninth century and was modified frequently up to the early sixteenth. The present structure is in fact a reconstruction: the original tower collapsed on July 14, 1902 – a catastrophe which injured nobody and is commemorated by faked postcard photos of the very instant of disaster. The collapse reduced to rubble the **Loggetta** at the base of the campanile, but somehow it was pieced together again;

built between 1537 and 1549 by Sansovino, it has served as a meeting-room for the nobility, a guardhouse and the place at which the state lottery was drawn. At 99 metres, the campanile is the tallest structure in the city, and from the top you can make out virtually every building, but not a single canal.

The other tower in the Piazza, the **Torre dell'Orologio**, was built between 1496 and 1506. A years'-long restoration has prevented people from taking the staircase up past the innards of the clock and onto the terrace on which the so-called *Moors* stand. Horologists would probably find the climb worthwhile, but you can watch the Moors strike the hour perfectly well from the ground.

The Procuratie and Correr museum

Away to the left of the Torre dell'Orologio stretches the **Procuratie Vecchie**; begun around 1500 by Coducci, this block housed the offices of the **Procurators of Saint Mark**, a committee of nine men whose responsibilities included the upkeep of the Basilica and other public buildings. A century or so after taking possession, the Procurators were moved to the opposite side of the Piazza, into the **Procuratie Nuove**. Napoleon converted these apartments and offices into a royal palace and then, having realised that the building lacked a ballroom, remedied the deficiency by smashing down the church of San Geminiano in order to connect the two Procuratie with a new wing for dancing.

Generally known as the **Ala Napoleonica**, this short side of the Piazza is partly occupied by the **Museo Correr** (9am–7pm; closed Tues; L5000), an immense triple-decker museum with a vast **historical collection** – coins, weapons, regalia, prints, mediocre paintings – much of which is generally heavy going unless you have an intense interest in Venetian history. The **Quadreria** on the second floor is no rival for the Accademia's collection, but does set out clearly the evolution of painting in Venice from the thirteenth century to around 1500 (though not all of its pictures are by Venetians), and it contains some gems. The *Pietà* by Cosmé Tura and the *Transfiguration* and *Dead Christ Supported by Angels* by Giovanni Bellini stand out, along with a **Carpaccio** picture usually known as *The Courtesans*, although its subjects are really a couple of late fifteenth-century bourgeois ladies dressed in a manner at which none of their contemporaries would have raised an eyebrow. There's also an appealing exhibition of the applied arts in Venice, featuring the original blocks and a print of Jacopo de'Barbari's astonishing aerial view of Venice, engraved in 1500. The final part of the Correr – the **Museo del Risorgimento** (also on the second floor) is rarely open, a fact which should grieve only worshippers of Daniele Manin, to whose rebellion against the Austrians five of the fifteen rooms are devoted.

The Piazzetta and Museo Archeologico

The **Piazzetta** – the open space between San Marco and the waterfront pavement known as the Molo – was the area where the politicians used to gather before meetings; known as the *broglio*, its wheeling and dealing probably gave rise to the English word "imbroglio". Facing the Palazzo Ducale is Sansovino's masterpiece and the most consistently admired Renaissance building in the city – the **Libreria Sansoviniana**. Work was well advanced on the building when, in December 1545, a severe frost resulted in a major collapse, a setback which landed the architect in prison for a while. Completion came in 1591, two decades after Sansovino's death.

Part of the building is given over to the **Museo Archeologico** (Tues–Sat 9am–2pm, Sun 9am–1pm; L4000), accessible through a door in the loggia. In many cities a collection of Greek and Roman sculpture as comprehensive as this one would merit a strong recommendation; in Venice you needn't feel guilty about leaving it for a rainy day. Attached to the library, with its main facade to the lagoon, Sansovino's first major building in Venice, the **Zecca** (Mint), was built between 1537 and 1545 on the site of the thirteenth-century mint. By the beginning of the fifteenth century the city's prosperity was such that the Venetian coinage was in use in every European exchange, and the doge could with some justification call Venice "the mistress of all the gold in Christendom".

The Piazzetta's two **columns** were brought here from the Levant at the end of the twelfth century, in company with a third, which fell off the barge and still lies somewhere just off the Molo. The figures perched on top are Saint Theodore, patron saint of Venice when it was dependent on Byzantium, and a Chimera, customised to look like the Lion of Saint Mark. Public executions were carried out between the columns, the techniques employed ranging from straightforward hanging to burial alive, head downwards. Superstitious Venetians avoid passing between them.

Sometimes the heads of freshly dispatched villains were mounted on the **Pietra del Bando**, the stump of porphyry at the other end of the Piazzetta, against the corner of San Marco. Its routine use, however, was as one of the two stones from which the laws of the Republic were proclaimed (the other is at the Rialto). The Pietra del Bando was brought back to Venice from Acre after the Venetian defeat of the Genoese there in 1256; the two square pillars near to it, with their fine fifth-century Syrian carving, were probably hauled away from Constantinople in 1204.

North of the Piazza

The **Mercerie**, a chain of glitzy streets that starts under the Clock Tower and finishes at the Campo San Bartolomeo, is the most direct route between the Rialto and San Marco and has therefore always been the main land thoroughfare of the city and a prime site for its shopkeepers. For those immune to the charms of window-shopping there's little reason to linger until you reach the church of **San Salvatore,** an early sixteenth-century church cleverly planned in the form of three Greek crosses placed end to end. It has a couple of Titian paintings – an altarpiece of the *Transfiguration* (1560) and an *Annunciation* (1566), whose awkwardly embarking angel is often blamed on the great man's assistants. The end of the south transept is filled by the tomb of Caterina Cornaro, who for a while was Queen of Cyprus before being manoeuvred into surrendering the island to Venice (see p.295).

The **Campo San Bartolomeo**, close to the foot of the Rialto bridge, is at its best in the evening, when it's as packed as any bar in town. For a crash-course in the Venetian character, hang around the statue of Goldoni for a while at about 7pm. If the crush gets a bit too much, you can retire to the nearby **Campo San Luca**, another after-work social centre but not as much of a pressure-cooker as San Bartolomeo.

Beyond Campo San Luca is **Campo Manin**, on the south side of which is a sign for the spiral staircase known as the **Scala del Bovolo** (*bovolo* means "snail shell" in Venetian dialect), a piece of flamboyant engineering dating from around 1500. The **Museo Fortuny** (Tues–Sun 9am–7pm; L5000) is also close at hand, similarly tucked away in a spot you'd never accidentally pass, but signposted with small eye-level posters. In addition to making his famous silk dresses, which were said to be fine enough to be threaded through a wedding ring, **Mariano Fortuny** (1871–1949) was a painter, architect, engraver, photographer, theatre designer and sculptor; the museum reflects his versatility, but you'll probably come out regretting that the museum doesn't have more of the frocks.

West of the Piazza

Although it too has its share of fashionable shops – much of the broad Calle Larga XXII Marzo, for example, is dedicated to the beautification of the well-heeled and their dwellings – the area to the **west of the Piazza** is less frenetic than the streets to the north. None of the first-division tourist sights are here, but the walk from the Piazza to the Accademia bridge, through a succession of campi each quite unlike its predecessor, isn't lacking in worthwhile diversions.

Heading west from the Piazza, you soon reach the hypnotically dreadful **San Moisè** (daily 3.30–7pm), runaway winner of any poll for the ugliest church in Venice. The facade sculpture, featuring a species of camel unknown to zoology, was created in 1668 by Heinrich Meyring; and if you think this is in dubious taste, wait till you see his altarpiece of *Mount Sinai with Moses Receiving the Tablets*.

Halfway along the Calle Larga XXII Marzo, on the right, is the Calle del Sartor da Veste, which takes you over a canal and into the Campo San Fantin, where the Renaissance church of **San Fantin** has a graceful domed apse by Sansovino. Across the campo is Venice's largest and oldest theatre, **La Fenice**, opened in December 1792. On a good day the staff will allow you a look at the auditorium, a luxuriant confection of gilt, plush and stucco, fitted out in 1836 after the place had been wrecked by fire. The opera house sets the tone of the neighbourhood, which has some of the priciest restaurants and most pretentious boutiques in town.

Back on the main road to the Accademia, another very odd church awaits – **Santa Maria Zobenigo** (or del Giglio). You can stare at this all day and still not find a single Christian image. The statues are of the five Barbaro brothers who financed the rebuilding of the church in 1678; Virtue, Honour, Fame and Wisdom hover respectfully around them; and the maps in relief depict the towns they graced in the course of their exemplary military and diplomatic careers.

The tilting campanile that soon looms into view over the vapid church of San Maurizio belongs to Santo Stefano, which stands at the end of the next campo – the **Campo Santo Stefano** (or Francesco Morosini). Large enough to hold several clusters of tourists and natives plus a kids' football match or two, the Campo Sant Stefano is always lively but never feels crowded, and has, in *Paolin*, one of the best ice cream places in Venice. To those few non-Venetians to whom his name means anything, Francesco Morosini is known as the man who lobbed a missile through the roof of the Parthenon towards the end of the seventeenth century. He lived at the Canal Grande end of the campo (no. 2802) and is buried in **Santo Stefano**, an originally thirteenth-century church, rebuilt in the fourteenth and altered again in the first half of the fifteenth; the Gothic **doorway** and the **ship's keel roof** both belong to this last phase. The best paintings are in the sacristy – *The Agony in the Garden*, *The Last Supper* and *The Washing of the Disciples' Feet*, all late works by **Tintoretto**.

Dorsoduro

Some of the finest architecture in Venice, both domestic and public, is to be found in the *sestiere* of **DORSODURO**, a situation partly attributable to the stability of its sandbanks – *Dorsoduro* means "hard back". Yet for all its attractions, not many visitors wander off the strip that runs between the main sights of the area – the Ca' Rezzonico, the Accademia and the Salute. The *sestiere* has a bafflingly complex border, so for clarity's sake we have taken the curve of the Grand Canal–Rio di Ca' Fóscari–Rio Nuovo as the boundary between Dorsoduro and the rest of central Venice.

The Galleria dell'Accademia

The **Galleria dell'Accademia** (Mon–Sat 9am–1.30pm, Sun 9am–12.30pm; L8000) is one of the finest specialist collections of European art, following the history of Venetian painting from the fourteenth to the eighteenth century. When it was established in 1807, its exhibits came largely from churches and convents that were then being suppressed; indeed, the buildings that the Accademia has occupied since then include two former religious buildings – the church of Santa Maria della Carità, rebuilt by Bartolomeo Bon in the 1440s, and the incomplete Convento dei Canonici Lateranensi, partly built by Palladio in 1561.

The Accademia is the third component – with San Marco and the Palazzo Ducale – of the triad of obligatory tourist sights in Venice, but admissions are restricted to batches of 180 people at a time. Accordingly, if you're there in high summer and don't want to wait, get over the Accademia bridge before 9am.

TO THE EARLY RENAISSANCE

The gallery is laid out in a roughly chronological succession of rooms going anticlockwise. The first room at the top of the stairs is the fifteenth-century assembly room of the Scuola, and houses works by the earliest known individual Venetian painters. **Paolo Veneziano** (from the first half of the fourteenth century) and his follower **Lorenzo Veneziano** are the most absorbing.

Room 2 moves on to works from the late fifteenth and early sixteenth centuries, with large altarpieces that are contemplative even when the scenes are far from calm. **Carpaccio**'s strange and gruesome *Crucifixion and Glorification of the Ten Thousand Martyrs of Mount Ararat* (painted around 1512) and his *Presentation of Jesus in the Temple* accompany works by **Giovanni Bellini** and **Cima da Conegliano**.

In the west room you can observe the emergence of the characteristically Venetian treatment of colour in works from the early Renaissance, but there's nothing here as exciting as the small paintings in rooms 4 and 5, a high point of the collection. Apart from an exquisite *St George* by **Mantegna**, and a series of **Giovanni Bellini** Madonnas, this section contains **Giorgione**'s enigmatic *Tempest* – nobody has ever satisfactorily explained what, if anything, is going on here, and the picture may well have been equally opaque to the person for whom it was created in 1500.

HIGH RENAISSANCE

Room 6 introduces one of the heavyweights of Venetian painting, Jacopo Robusti, called **Tintoretto**. The *Madonna dei Camerlenghi* (1566), with its sumptuously painted velvets, shows facial types still found in Venice today. Another big name represented here is **Titian** (Tiziano Vecellio), with a not particularly interesting *John the Baptist* (early 1540s). One of the most compelling paintings in the gallery is in room 7, the *Young Man in his Study* by **Lorenzo Lotto** (1528).

Room 10 is dominated by epic productions, and an entire wall is filled by **Paolo Veronese**'s *Christ in the House of Levi*. Originally called *The Last Supper*, this picture provoked a stern reaction from the Court of the Holy Office: it was too irreverent for such a holy subject, they insisted – why were there "Germans and buffoons and suchlike things in this picture? Does it appear to you fitting that at our Lord's last supper you should paint buffoons, drunkards, Germans, dwarfs, and similar indecencies?" Veronese fielded all their questions and responded simply by changing the title, which made the work acceptable. The pieces by **Tintoretto** in here include three legends of Saint Mark: *St Mark Rescues a Slave* (1548), which was the painting that made his reputation, *The Theft of the Body of St Mark* and *St Mark Saves a Saracen* (both 1560s). All of these show Tintoretto's love of energy and drama – from the physical or psychological drama of the subject matter, emphasised by the twisting poses of the people depicted, to the technical energy of his brush strokes, perception of colour and use of light. Opposite is an emotional late **Titian**, a *Pietà* (1570s) thought to be intended for his own tomb in the Frari.

THE EIGHTEENTH CENTURY

Room 11 contains a number of works by **Giambattista Tiepolo**, the most prominent painter of eighteenth-century Venice, including two shaped fragments rescued from the wreckage of the Scalzi (1743–45), and *The Translation of the Holy House of Loreto* (1743), a sketch for the same ceiling.

The following stretch of seventeenth- and eighteenth-century paintings isn't too enthralling – the highlights are portraits by **Rosalba Carriera** and interiors by **Pietro Longhi** in room 17. Carriera's work popularised the use of pastel as a medium; look for her moving *Self-Portrait in Old Age* (1740s), executed just before she went blind. Longhi is not the most brilliant of painters in the Accademia, but his illustrative work is fascinating for the insights it gives to eighteenth-century Venice. (For more, including the famous *Rhinoceros*, go to the Ca' Rezzonico; see opposite.)

THE VIVARINIS, THE BELLINIS AND CARPACCCIO

Around the corner and to the right are more works from the fifteenth and early sixteenth centuries. Pieces by the Vivarini family feature strongly; **Alvise Vivarini**'s *Santa Chiara* is outstanding. **Giovanni Bellini** is represented by four triptychs painted with workshop assistance for this church in the 1460s. The extraordinary *Blessed Lorenzo Giustinian* is by his brother, **Gentile**; one of the oldest surviving Venetian canvases, and Gentile's earliest signed work, it was possibly used as a standard in processions, which would account for its state.

The magnificent cycle of pictures painted around 1500 for the Scuola di San Giovanni Evangelista, mainly illustrating the miracles of the Relic of the Cross, is displayed in room 20, off a corridor to the left. All of the paintings are replete with fascinating local details, but particularly rich are **Carpaccio**'s *Cure of a Lunatic* and **Gentile Bellini**'s *Recovery of the Relic from the Canale di San Lorenzo* and *Procession of the Relic in the Piazza*. The next room contains a complete cycle of pictures by **Carpaccio** illustrating the *Story of Saint Ursula*, painted for the Scuola di Sant'Orsola at San Zanipolo (1490–94). Restored in the mid-1980s, the paintings form one of Italy's most unforgettable groups. The legend is that Hereus, a British prince, proposed marriage to Ursula, a Breton princess. She accepted on two conditions: that Hereus convert to Christianity, and that he should wait for three years, while she went on a pilgrimage. The pilgrimage, undertaken with a company of 11,000 virgins, ended with a massacre near Cologne by the Huns – as Ursula had been warned in a dream.

Finally, in room 24 (the former hostel of the Scuola), there's **Titian**'s *Presentation of the Virgin* (dating from 1539). It was painted for the place where it hangs, as was the triptych by **Antonio Vivarini** and **Giovanni d'Alemagna** (1446), another of the oldest Venetian canvases.

The Guggenheim and the Salute

Within five minutes' walk of the Accademia, beyond the Campo San Vio, is the unfinished Palazzo Venier dei Leoni, home of Peggy Guggenheim for thirty years until her death in 1979, now the base for the **Guggenheim Collection** (11am–6pm, plus Sat 6–9pm; closed Tues; L7000, free Sat 6–9pm). Her private collection is an eclectic, quirky choice of mainly excellent pieces from her favourite modernist movements and artists. Prime pieces include Brancusi's *Bird in Space* and *Maestra*, De Chirico's *Red Tower* and *Nostalgia of the Poet*, Max Ernst's *Robing of the Bride*, sculpture by Laurens and Lipchitz, paintings by Malevich and collages by Schwitters.

Continuing along the line of the Canal Grande, you come to Santa Maria della Salute, better known simply as the **Salute** (daily 8am–noon & 3–5pm), built to fulfil a Senate decree of October 22, 1630, that a new church would be dedicated to Mary if the city were delivered from the plague that was ravaging it – an outbreak that was to kill about a third of the population. Work began in 1631 on **Baldessare Longhena**'s design, and was completed in 1681, though the church was not consecrated until November 9, 1687, five years before Longhena's death. Thereafter, every November 21, the Signoria headed a procession from San Marco to the Salute, over a specially constructed pontoon bridge, to give thanks for the city's good health (*salute* meaning "health") – and even today the festival of the Salute is a major event on the Venetian calendar.

In 1656, a hoard of **Titian** paintings from the suppressed church of Santo Spirito were moved here and are now housed in the **sacristy** (small entrance fee). The most prominent of these is the altarpiece of *St Mark Enthroned with Saints Cosmas, Damian, Sebastian and Rocco* (the plague saints). The *Marriage at Cana*, with its dramatic lighting and perspective, is by Tintoretto (1561), featuring portraits of a number of the artist's friends.

The **Dogana di Mare** (Customs House), with its Doric facade (1676–82), occupies the spur formed by the meeting of the Canal Grande with the Giudecca canal. The gold ball, noticeable from anywhere on this busy bit of water, is a weathervane, topped by a figure representing either Justice or Fortune.

Along the Záttere to San Sebastiano

Stretching from the Punta della Dogana to the Stazione Marittima, the **Záttere** (Rafts) was originally the place where most of the bulky goods coming into Venice were unloaded – it's now a popular place to stroll on Sundays or for a picnic lunch. Its principal sight is the church of Santa Maria del Rosario, invariably known as the **Gesuati** – worth a call for its paintings by **Giambattista Tiepolo**: three ceiling frescoes of *Scenes from the Life of St Dominic* and an altarpiece of *Madonna with three Dominican Saints*.

A diversion to the right straight after the Gesuati takes you past the **squero di San Trovaso**, the busiest gondola workshop left in Venice, and on to the church of **San Trovaso**. Venetian folklore has it that this church was the only neutral ground between the rival working-class factions of the Nicolotti and the Castellani, who would celebrate intermarriages and other services here but had to use separate doors. It is a large dark church, whose paintings are properly visible only in the morning. These include **Tintoretto**'s last works, *The Adoration of the Magi* and *The Expulsion from the Temple*, flanking the high altar.

The church of **San Sebastiano**, right up by the Stazione Marittima (erratic opening hours) was built between 1505 and 1545 and was the parish church of **Paolo Veronese**, who provided most of its paintings and is buried here. He was first brought in to paint the ceiling of the sacristy with a *Coronation of the Virgin* and the *Four Evangelists*, and then the *Scenes from the Life of St Esther* on the ceiling of the church. He then painted the dome of the chancel, which is now destroyed, and with the help of his brother, Benedetto, moved on to the walls of the church and the nuns' choir. The paintings around the high altar and the organ came last, painted in the 1560s.

Ca' Rezzonico and around

From San Sebastiano it's a straightforward walk back towards the Canal Grande along Calle Avogaria and Calle Lunga San Barnaba, a route that deposits you in Campo San Barnaba, just yards from the **Ca' Rezzonico**, now the **Museo del Settecento Veneziano** – the Museum of Eighteenth-Century Venice (9am–7pm; closed Fri; L5000). Having acquired the Ca' Rezzonico in 1934, the *comune* of Venice set about furnishing and decorating it with eighteenth-century items and materials (or their closest modern equivalent), so giving the place the feel of a well-appointed house rather than of a formal museum. On the applied arts side of the collection, the plentiful and outlandish carvings by **Andrea Brustolon** are as likely to elicit revulsion as admiration. As for the paintings, the highlights are **Pietro Longhi**'s affectionate illustrations of Venice social life, and the frescoes painted towards the end of his life by **Giandomenico Tiepolo**. Although painted at a time when this type of work was going out of fashion, these frescoes of clowns and carnival scenes (created originally for his own house) are among Giandomenico's best-known images. Fans of his father's slightly more flamboyant style won't come away disappointed either.

The nearby **Campo Santa Margherita** is a wide but friendly space, with a daily **market** and a clutch of shops that contribute to the quarter's distinctive atmosphere.

The **Scuola Grande dei Carmini** (Mon–Sat 9am–noon & 3–6pm; L5000), on the west of the campo, is a showcase for Giambattista Tiepolo, whose ceiling paintings in the main upstairs hall, painted in the early 1740s, centre on a panel of *The Virgin in Glory*.

San Polo

For practical reasons, the district we have labelled **SAN POLO** covers an area over twice the size of the *sestiere* of the same name, including a huge chunk of the *sestiere* of Santa Croce and a bit of Dorsoduro and bounded by the Canal Grande and the Rio Nuovo–Rio di Ca' Fóscari. You cannot stray unwittingly over either of these canals, which is more than can be said for the boundaries of the *sestieri*.

From the Rialto to the museum of modern art

Relatively stable building land and a good defensive position drew some of the earliest lagoon settlers to the high bank (*rivo alto*) above the Canal Grande that was to develop into the **Rialto** district. While the political centre of the new city grew up around San Marco, the Rialto became the commercial zone. In the twelfth century, Europe's first state bank was opened here, and the financiers of the district were the weightiest figures on the international exchanges for the next three centuries and more. The state offices which oversaw all maritime business were here as well, and in the early sixteenth century the offices of the exchequer were installed in the new **Palazzo dei Camerlenghi**, at the foot of the Rialto bridge.

The connection between wealth and moral turpitude was exemplified by the Rialto, where the fleshpots were as busy as the cash desks. A late sixteenth-century survey showed that there were about 3000 patrician women in the city, but well over 11,000 prostitutes, the majority of them based in the banking quarter. One Rialto brothel, the *Casteletto*, was especially esteemed for the literary, musical and sexual talents of its staff, and a perennial Venetian bestseller was a catalogue giving the addresses and prices of the city's most alluring courtesans.

It was through the markets of the Rialto that Venice earned its reputation as the bazaar of Europe. Virtually anything could be bought or sold here: Italian fabrics, precious stones, silver plate and gold jewellery, spices and dyes from the Orient. Trading had been going on here for over 400 years when, in 1514, a fire destroyed everything in the area except the church. The possibility of relocating the business centre was discussed but found little favour, so reconstruction began almost straight away, the **Fabbriche Vecchie** (the arcaded buildings along the Ruga degli Orefici and around the Campo San Giacomo) being finished five years after the fire, and Sansovino's **Fabbriche Nuove** (running along the Canal Grande from Campo Cesare Battisti) following about thirty years later.

Today's Rialto market is tamer than that of Venice at its peak, but it's still one of the liveliest spots in the city, and one of the few places where it's possible to stand in a crowd and hear nothing but Italian spoken. There's a shoal of memento-sellers by the church and along the Ruga degli Orefici; the market proper lies between them and the Canal Grande – mainly fruit stalls around the **Campo San Giacomo**, vegetable stalls and butcher's shops as you go through to the **Campo Battisti**, after which you come to the fish market. (The fish market and many of the stalls close for the day at 1pm, but some stalls re-open in the late afternoon.) There are excellent cheese shops around the junction of **Ruga degli Orefici** and **Ruga Vecchia San Giovanni**; the Ruga Vecchia has a number of good *alimentari* among the kitsch-merchants.

A popular Venetian legend asserts that the city was founded on Friday, March 25, 421 AD at exactly midday; from the same legend derives the claim that the church of **San Giacomo di Rialto** (daily 10am–noon) was founded in that year, and is thus the oldest church in Venice. It might actually be the oldest; what is not disputed is that the church was rebuilt in 1071 and that parts of the present structure date from then – for instance, the interior's six columns of ancient Greek marble have eleventh-century Veneto-Byzantine capitals. As you walk away from the Rialto, following roughly the curve of the Canal Grande, you enter a district which becomes labyrinthine even by Venetian standards. A directionless stroll between the Rio delle Beccerie and the Rio di San Zan Degolà will satisfy any addict of the picturesque – you cannot walk for more than a couple of minutes without coming across a workshop crammed into a ground-floor room or a garden spilling over a canalside wall.

The church of **San Cassiano** (Mon–Sat 9.45–11.30am & 4.30–7pm) is a building you're bound to pass as you wander out of the Rialto. Don't be put off by its barn-like appearance, as it contains three paintings by **Tintoretto**: *The Resurrection*, *The Descent into Limbo* and *The Crucifixion*. The first two have been mauled by restorers, but the third is one of the greatest pictures in Venice, a startling composition dominated not by the cross but by the ladder on which the executioners stand.

Nearby, and signposted from San Cassiano, is the **Ca' Pésaro**, in which you'll find both the **Galleria d'Arte Moderna** (Tues–Sun 9am–7pm; L3000) and the **Museo Orientale** (Tues–Sat 9am–2pm, Sun 9am–1pm; L4000). Pieces bought from the Biennale make up much of the modern collection, and its backbone consists of work by a range of Italian artists, many of whom will be unfamiliar. As for the oriental galleries, the jumble of lacquer work, armour, screens, weaponry and so forth will appeal chiefly to the initiated.

Campo San Polo

The largest square in Venice after the Piazza, the **Campo San Polo** used to be the city's favourite bullfighting arena as well as the site of weekly markets and occasional fairs. Nowadays it's a combination of outdoor social centre and children's sports stadium.

The bleak interior of **San Polo** church (Mon–Sat 7.30am–noon & 4–7pm, Sun 8am–12.15pm) should be visited for a *Last Supper* by Tintoretto and Giandomenico Tiepolo's paintings of the *Stations of the Cross*, a series painted when the artist was only twenty. The sober piety of these pictures will come as a surprise if you've been to the Ca' Rezzonico, though it often seems that his interest was less in the central drama than in the society portraits which occupy the edges of the stage.

Calle Madonera, going off the campo in the direction of Rialto, is the beginning of a sequence of busy **shopping streets**, in which you'll find a couple of the best *pasticcerie* in Venice and a host of shoe and clothes shops. Salizzada San Polo and Calle dei Saoneri, on the opposite side of the campo, are effectively a continuation of these streets, which together comprise this side of the Canal Grande's answer to the Mercerie.

The Frari

The Franciscans were granted a large plot of land near San Polo in about 1250, not long after the death of Saint Francis; replacement of their first church by the present Santa Maria Gloriosa dei Frari – more generally known simply as the **Frari** (Mon–Sat 9.30am–noon & 2.30–6pm, Sun 2.30–6pm; L1000) – began in the mid-fourteenth century and took over a hundred years. This mountain of brick is not an immediately attractive building, but whatever your predilections, its collection of paintings, sculptures and monuments will get the church onto your list of Venetian highlights.

As every guide to the city points out, Venice is relatively impoverished as far as major paintings by **Titian** are concerned: apart from the Salute and the Accademia, the Frari is the only building in Venice with more than a single significant work by him. One of these – the *Assumption*, painted in 1518 – you will see almost immediately as you look towards the altar through the fifteenth-century monks' choir, a swirling, dazzling piece of compositional and colouristic bravura for which there was no precedent in Venetian art. The other Titian masterpiece here, the *Madonna di Ca' Pésaro*, is more static, but was equally innovative in its displacement of the figure of the Virgin from the centre of the picture.

Wherever you stand in the Frari, you're in front of something that deserves your attention, but three or four pieces apart from the Titians stand out from the rest. Two funerary monuments embodying the emergence in Venice of Renaissance sculptural technique flank the Titian *Assumption*: on the left the **tomb of Doge Niccolò Tron**, by Antonio Rizzo and assistants, dating from 1476; on the right, the more chaotic **tomb of Doge Francesco Fóscari**, carved shortly after Fóscari's death in 1457 by Antonio and Paolo Bregno (see p.255 for more on Fóscari). The wooden statue of *St John the Baptist*, in the chapel to the right, was commissioned from **Donatello** in 1438 by Florentine merchants in Padua; recent work has restored its luridly naturalistic appearance. On the altar of the sacristy (the site for which it was created) is a picture which alone would justify an hour in the Frari – the *Madonna and Child with SS. Nicholas of Bari, Peter, Mark and Benedict*, painted in 1488 by **Giovanni Bellini**. In the words of Henry James – "it is as solemn as it is gorgeous and as simple as it is deep."

Two massive tombs take up much of the nave. One is the bombastic **monument to Titian**, built in the mid-nineteenth century on the supposed site of his grave. He died in the 1576 plague epidemic, in around his ninetieth year, and was the only casualty of that outbreak to be given a church burial. Opposite is a tomb of similarly pompous dimensions but of redeeming peculiarity: the **Mausoleum of Canova**, erected in 1827 by pupils of the sculptor, following a design he had made for the tomb of Titian.

The Scuola di San Rocco and San Rocco church

At the rear of the Frari is a place you should on no account miss: the **Scuola Grande di San Rocco** (daily 9am–5.30pm & 3–6pm; L6000). San Rocco (Saint Roch) was attributed with the power to cure the plague and other serious illnesses, so when the saint's body was brought to Venice in 1485, this *scuola* began to profit from donations from people wishing to invoke his aid. In 1515 it commissioned this prestigious new building, and soon after its completion in 1560, work began on the decorative scheme that was to put the Scuola's rivals in the shade – a cycle of more than fifty major paintings by **Tintoretto**.

THE TINTORETTO PAINTINGS

To appreciate the evolution of Tintoretto's art you have to begin in the smaller room on the upper storey – the **Sala dell'Albergo**. In 1564 the Scuola held a competition for the contract to paint its first picture. The subject was to be *The Glorification of St Roch*, and Tintoretto won the contest by rigging up a finished painting in the very place for which the winning picture was destined – the centre of the ceiling. The protests of his rivals, who had simply submitted sketches, were to no avail. Virtually an entire wall of the Sala is occupied by the stupendous *Crucifixion*, a painting which reduced Ruskin to a state of dumbfounded wonder – his loquacious guide to the cycle concludes: "I must leave this picture to work its will on the spectator; for it is beyond all analysis, and above all praise." The pictures on the entrance wall – *Christ before Pilate, Christ Crowned with Thorns* and *The Way to Calvary* – inevitably suffer from such company, but they deserve close scrutiny, as does the easel painting of *Christ Carrying the Cross*, which is now generally thought to be an early Titian.

Tintoretto finished the Sala in 1567 and eight years later he started on the main upper hall, a project he completed in 1581. The Old Testament subjects depicted in the three large panels of the **ceiling**, with their references to the alleviation of physical suffering, are coded declarations of the Scuola's charitable activities: *Moses Striking Water from the Rock, The Miracle of the Brazen Serpent* and *The Miraculous Fall of Manna*. The paintings around the walls, all based on the New Testament, are an amazing feat of sustained inventiveness, in which every convention of perspective, lighting, colour and even anatomy is defied. A caricature of the irascible Tintoretto (with a jarful of paintbrushes) is incorporated into the trompe l'oeil carvings by the seventeenth-century sculptor **Francesco Pianta**.

The paintings on the ground floor were created between 1583 and 1587, when Tintoretto was in his late sixties. The turbulent *Annunciation* is one of the most arresting images of the event ever painted, and there are few Renaissance landscapes to match those of *The Flight into Egypt* and the small paintings of *St Mary Magdalen* and *St Mary of Egypt*.

THE CHURCH

Yet more paintings by Tintoretto adorn the neighbouring church of **San Rocco**. On the south wall of the nave you'll find *St Roch Taken to Prison*, and below it *The Pool of Bethesda* – though only the latter is definitely by Tintoretto. In the chancel are four large works, all of them difficult to see properly: the best are *St Roch Curing the Plague Victims* (lower right) and *St Roch in Prison* (lower left); the two higher pictures are *St Roch in Solitude* and *St Roch Healing the Animals*, though the second is again a doubtful attribution.

San Pantaleone

To the south of San Rocco runs the teeming Crosera San Pantalon, the atmosphere in whose shops, cafés and bars has a lot to do with the proximity of the university. Between this street and the Rio di Ca' Fóscari stands the church of **San Pantaleone**, which possesses a *Coronation of the Virgin* by Antonio Vivarini and Giovanni d'Alemagna (in the chapel to the left of the chancel) and Veronese's last painting, *San Pantaleone Healing a Boy* (second chapel on right). The church can also boast of having the most melodramatic **ceiling** in the city: *The Martyrdom and Apotheosis of San Pantaleone*. It kept **Gian Antonio Fumiani** busy from 1680 to 1704 but he never got the chance to bask in the glory of his labours – he died in a fall from the scaffolding on which he'd been working.

Cannaregio

In the northernmost section of Venice, **CANNAREGIO**, you can go from one extreme to another in a matter of minutes: it is a short distance from the bustle of the train station and the execrable Lista di Spagna to areas which, although no longer rural – *Cannaregio* comes from *canna*, meaning reed – are still among the quietest and prettiest parts of the whole city. The district also has the dubious distinction of containing the world's original ghetto.

The station area

The first building worth a look in the vicinity of the station is to the left as you come out of it – the **Scalzi** church (or Santa Maria di Nazareth). Built in the 1670s for the barefoot (*scalzi*) order of Carmelites, the interior, by Baldessare Longhena, is a joy for aficionados of the Baroque. There are frescoes by Giambattista Tiepolo in the first chapel on the left and the second on the right, but his major work in the church, the ceiling, was destroyed in 1915 by an Austrian bomb. A couple of fragments, now in the Accademia, were all that was rescued.

Foreign embassies used to be concentrated in this area, so that the Venetian authorities could keep an eye on them all together, and the **Lista di Spagna** takes its name from the Spanish embassy, which used to be at no. 168. The street is now completely given over to the tourist trade, with shops and stalls, bars, restaurants and hotels all plying for the same desperate trade. As with many major train stations, if you are hunting for trinkets, food or a bed, you'll find things cheaper elsewhere.

The church of **San Geremia** is chiefly notable for being the present home of **Saint Lucy**, martyred in Syracuse in 304, stolen from Constantinople by Venetian crusaders in 1204, and ousted from her own Palladian church in 1863 when it was demolished to build the station. Lucy tore her own eyes out after an unwanted suitor kept complimenting her on their beauty, and hence became the patron saint of eyesight: the glass case on the high altar contains her desiccated body. Architecturally, the church's main point of interest is the twelfth-century campanile, one of the oldest left in the city.

The ballroom of the **Palazzo Labia**, next door to the church, contains frescoes by Giambattista Tiepolo and his assistants (1745–50), illustrating the story of Anthony and Cleopatra. The present owners, *RAI* (the state radio service), allow the public in to see them for a couple of hours each week, but the exact times are changeable; for current hours ask at the door (or ring ☎781.111). They also record concerts here which the public can attend for free; again ask at the door or phone to reserve tickets in advance.

The **Canale di Cannaregio** was the main entrance to Venice before the road and rail bridges were built; walk along it to get to the church of **San Giobbe**. The physical afflictions with which God permitted Satan to test the faith of Job – he was smitten with "sore boils from the sole of his foot unto his crown" – made Job particularly popular with the Venetians, who suffered regularly from malaria, plague and a plethora of damp-related diseases. The church was built on the site of an oratory by the Venetian Gothic architect Antonio Gambello, later assisted by Pietro Lombardo, who introduced Tuscan Renaissance elements. Lombardo's contribution, his first work in Venice, consists of the doorway and, inside, the statues of *Saints Anthony, Bernardino and Louis* and the chancel. Its best paintings – Giovanni Bellini's *Madonna Enthroned with Saints* and Carpaccio's *Presentation in the Temple* – have been removed to the drier atmosphere of the Accademia.

The Ghetto

The Venetian **Ghetto** was in a sense the first in the world: the word comes from the Venetian dialect *getar* (to found), or *geto* (foundry), which is what this area was until 1390. It was in 1516 that all the city's Jews were ordered to move to the island of the Ghetto Nuovo, an enclave which was sealed at night by Christian curfew guards – whose wages were paid for by the Jews. Distinctive badges or caps had to be worn by all Jews, and there were various economic and social restraints on the community, although oppression was lighter in Venice than in most other parts of Europe (it was one of the few states to tolerate the Jewish religion). When Jews were expelled from Spain in 1492 and Portugal in 1497, many of them came here.

Each wave of Jewish immigrants established their own synagogues with their distinctive rites. The **Scola Levantina**, founded in 1538, and the **Scola Spagnola**, possibly founded about twenty years later, reflect the wealth of these particular groups, who were important traders within the Venetian state; the latter was redesigned around 1584 by Longhena (the profession of architect was barred to Jews), a project which influenced the alteration of the other synagogues. These two are still used today for services, and can be viewed, with the Scola Tedesca, in an informative and multilingual guided tour, organised by the **Jewish Museum** in Campo Ghetto Nuovo (10am–7pm; closed Sat; L2000). The collection is mainly of silverware and embroidery and other fabric objects.

The Ghetto looks quite different from the rest of Venice. The Jewish population rose to about 4000, and even though they were allowed to spread into the **Ghetto Vecchio** and the **Ghetto Nuovissima** there was gross overcrowding. As the Ghetto buildings were not allowed to be more than one-third higher than the surrounding houses, the result was a stack of low-ceilinged storeys – the first high-rise blocks. Napoleon removed the gates of the Ghetto in 1797 but the Austrians replaced them in 1798, and Venice's Jews didn't achieve equal rights with other Venetians until Unification with Italy in 1866.

Sant'Alvise, Madonna dell'Orto and around

The area northeast of the Ghetto is one of the most restful parts of Venice. The long *fondamente*, dotted with food shops, bars and trattorias; the red walls and green shutters of the houses; the blue and yellow hulls of the boats – together they make a scene that recalls Henry James's vision of the essence of Venice: "I simply see a narrow canal in the heart of the city – a patch of green water and a surface of pink wall."

A few minutes' north of the Ghetto stands the church of **Sant'Alvise**. Commissioned by Antonia Venier, daughter of Doge Antonio Venier, after the saint appeared to her in a vision in 1388, the church has one outstanding picture, the recently restored *The Road to Calvary* by Giambattista Tiepolo, painted in 1743. His *Crown of Thorns* and *Flagellation*, slightly earlier works, are on the right-hand wall of the nave. Under the nuns' choir, to the right as you enter the church, are eight small tempera paintings, generally known as *The Baby Carpaccios* thanks to Ruskin's speculative attribution; they do date from Carpaccio's infancy (around 1470), but they're not actually by him.

A circuitous stroll eastwards brings you to the Gothic church of **Madonna dell'Orto** (9am–noon & 3–7pm in summer; closes 5pm in winter). Dedicated to Saint Christopher in about 1350, the church was renamed after a large stone *Madonna* by Giovanni de'Santi, found discarded in a local vegetable garden (*orto*), began to work miracles; brought inside the church in 1377, the figure can still be seen (now heavily restored) in the Cappella di San Mauro. The main sculpture on the **facade** is a fifteenth-century *St Christopher* by the Florentine Nicolò di Giovanni; Bartolomeo Bon designed the portal in 1460, shortly before his death. The **interior** was messed around in the 1860s, and although some of the overpainting was removed during restoration work of the 1930s, its appearance still owes much to the nineteenth-century interference. Scraps of fresco on the arches and the painted beams give an idea of how it must have looked in the sixteenth century. This was the first church in Venice to be given a thorough restoration job after the floods of 1966; the floor was relaid, the lower walls rebuilt, chapels restored to their pre-1864 layout and all the paintings were cleaned. The *St Christopher* over the door was the first Istrian stone work to be restored in Venice.

This is Tintoretto's parish church: he is buried here, in the chapel to the right of the high altar. So too are his son and daughter, Domenico and Marietta. And there are a number of paintings by the artist here, notably the colossal *Making of the Golden Calf* and *The Last Judgment*, which flank the main altar. Others include Tintoretto's *The Presentation of the Virgin in the Temple*, at end of right aisle; *The Vision of the Cross to St Peter* and *The Beheading of St Paul*, on each side of the chancel's *Annunciation* by Palma il Giovane, and two notable works from the end of the previous century: *St John the Baptist and other Saints* by Cima da Conegliano (first altar on the right) and a *Madonna and Child* by Giovanni Bellini (first chapel on the left).

From the Ca' d'Oro to the Gesuiti

Back towards the Canal Grande, the main thoroughfare of eastern Cannaregio, the **Strada Nova**, was carved through the houses in 1871–72, and is now a bustling shopping street where you can buy anything from spaghetti to surgical trusses. Nearly halfway along is the inconspicuous *calle* named after, and leading to, the **Ca' d'Oro** – a Gothic palace, much altered by restoration, whose best feature, the facade, is in any case best seen from the water. Inside the **Galleria Giorgio Franchetti** (Mon–Sat 9am–1.30pm, Sun 9am–12.30pm; L4000) is a museum put together from the bequest of the man who owned and repaired the house at the start of this century, and from a few state collections. One of the prize exhibits is in the courtyard – Bartolomeo Bon's sculpted well-head; others include a *St Sebastian* by Mantegna and a beautifully carved *Young Couple* by Tullio Lombardo. Big names such as Tintoretto and Titian are here, but not at their best; you'll get more out of pieces from less exalted artists – for instance the views of *The Piazzetta facing San Giorgio* and *Quayside with the Salute* by Francesco Guardi.

At the eastern end of the Strada Nova you come to the Campo dei Santi Apostoli, a general meeting-point and crossroads, and the church of **Santi Apostoli**. The exterior is unexceptional, but give the interior a look for the Cappella Corner: the design of the chapel is attributed to Mauro Coducci, the altar painting of the *Communion of St Lucy* is by Giambattista Tiepolo, and the tomb of Marco Corner (father of Caterina Cornaro) is attributed to Tullio Lombardo.

Just inland from the Fondamente Nuove, the northern edge of this zone, is the **Gesuiti** church, as Santa Maria Assunta is familiarly known (daily 10am–noon & 5–7pm). The Jesuits began work on their church in 1714, and it took fifteen years to inlay the marble walls of the interior and carve its marble "curtains"; with a result that is jaw-droppingly impressive even if you hate Baroque architecture. The *Martyrdom of St Lawrence* by Titian, on the first altar on the left, is a night scene made doubly difficult to see by the lighting arrangements.

Castello

Our section of **CASTELLO** includes all the eastern section of the city, and is bounded in the northwest by the Rio dei Santi Apostoli and Rio dei Gesuiti, and in the southwest by the canal which winds from the side of the post office at the Rialto to the back of San Marco. In terms of its tourist appeal, centre stage is occupied by the huge **Santi Giovanni e Paolo**, a place saturated with the history and mythology of Venice. Within a few minutes' walk of here you will a trio of fascinating churches – **Santa Maria dei Miracoli**, **Santa Maria Formosa** and **San Zaccaria** – as well as the beguiling Carpaccio paintings in the Scuola di San Giorgio degli Schiavoni, to name just the highlights of the western part of this district.

Once the industrial hub of the city and the largest manufacturing site in Europe, the **Arsenale** area – the eastern section of the Castello *sestiere* – is now predominantly a residential quarter and has little to offer of cultural significance. It would be a mistake, however, to leave it entirely unexplored. In the summer of odd-numbered years the Biennale art show sets up shop in its custom-built pavilions here, and at other times its open spaces – the **Giardini Garibaldi, Giardini Pubblici** and **Parco della Rimembranze** – are a good antidote to the claustrophobia that overtakes most visitors to Venice at some point.

The Miracoli and around

If you head into Castello by walking north from Campo San Bartolomeo, you'll pass the cosy church of **San Giovanni Crisostomo**, built around 1500 to designs by Mauro Coducci. It has a magnificent late painting by Giovanni Bellini, *SS Jerome, Christopher and Augustine*, and a fine altarpiece by Sebastiano del Piombo – *St John Chrysostom with SS John the Baptist, Liberale, Mary Magdalen, Agnes, and Catherine*. Round the back of the church is the Corte Seconda del Milion, a tiny courtyard hemmed in by ancient buildings, one of which – nobody is sure which – was Marco Polo's family home.

Sitting on the lip of a canal just a minute to the north of Corte Seconda del Milion, the church of Santa Maria dei Miracoli – known plainly as the **Miracoli** – is one of the most attractive buildings in Europe. It was built in the 1480s to house a painting of the Madonna which was believed to have performed a number of miracles, such as reviving a man who'd spent half an hour lying at the bottom of the Giudecca canal. The church is thought to have been designed by Pietro Lombardo; certainly he and his two sons Tullio and Antonio oversaw the building and executed much of the carving. Typically for Renaissance architecture in Venice, richness of effect takes precedence over classical correctness – the Corinthian pilasters are set below the Ionic, so that the viewer can better appreciate the carving on the Corinthian.

The marble-lined interior contains some of the most intricate decorative sculpture to be seen in Venice. The half-length figures of two saints and the *Annunciation* on the balustrade of the raised galleries at the east end are attributed to Tullio Lombardo; the rest of the attributions for the carvings at this end are arguable between the two brothers and their father. Ruskin was greatly distressed by the children's heads carved to the side of the top of the altar steps – "the man who could carve a child's head so perfectly must have been wanting in all human feeling, to cut it off, and tie it by the hair to a vine leaf."

Campo Santi Giovanni e Paolo

After the Piazza, the **Campo Santi Giovanni e Paolo** – or, in its Venetian dialect form, **San Zanipolo** – is the most impressive open space in Venice. Dominated by the huge brick church from which it gets its name, it also has the most beautiful facade of any of the *scuole grandi* and one of the finest Renaissance equestrian monuments.

THE COLLEONI STATUE AND THE SCUOLA GRANDE DI SAN MARCO

The *condottiere* **Bartolomeo Colleoni** began his wayward career in Venice's army in 1429. In the succeeding years he defected to Milan, re-enlisted for Venice, fled again, and finally signed up for good in 1455 – whereupon Venice suffered an outbreak of peace which meant that in the twenty years leading up to his death in 1475 Colleoni was called upon to fight only once. When he died, Colleoni left a handsome legacy to the Republic on condition that a monument should be erected to him in the square before San Marco, an impossible proposition to Venice's rulers, with their cult of anonymity. They got around the problem with a splendid piece of disingenuousness, interpreting the will in a way that allowed them to raise the monument before the Scuola Grande di San Marco, rather than the Basilica, and still claim the money.

The commission for the monument was won by **Andrea Verrocchio** in 1481, and difficulties dogged this stage of the proceedings too. Having virtually completed the horse, Verrocchio heard that another artist was being approached to sculpt the rider, and retaliated by mutilating the work he'd done and galloping off to Florence. The matter was eventually patched up, and Verrocchio was working again on the piece when he died at the end of June 1488. **Alessandro Leopardi** was then called in to finish the work and produce the plinth for it, which he gladly did – even signing his own name on the horse's girth, and titling himself *del Cavallo*.

An unimprovable backdrop to Colleoni, the **Scuola Grande di San Marco** has provided a sumptuous facade and foyer for the Ospedale Civile since its suppression in the early nineteenth century. The facade was started by Pietro Lombardo and Giovanni Buora in 1487, and finished in 1495 by Mauro Coducci after a row between Pietro and Buoro and the Scuola. It works better in sections rather than as a unity: the perspectival panels by Tullio and Antonio Lombardo don't quite bring off the intended illusion, but only the hardhearted will not be charmed by them individually.

THE CHURCH OF SANTI GIOVANNI E PAOLO

The **church of Santi Giovanni e Paolo**, the Dominican equivalent to the Frari, was founded in 1246, rebuilt and enlarged from 1333, and finally consecrated in 1430. The sarcophagus of Doge Giacomo Tiepolo, who originally gave the site to the Dominicans, is on the left of the door outside.

The **interior** is stunning for its sheer size: 290ft long, 125ft wide at the transepts, 108ft high in the centre. It seems more spacious now than it would have up to 1682, when the wooden choir, placed similarly to that of the Frari, was demolished. The simplicity of the design, a nave with two aisles and gracefully soaring arches, is offset by the huge number of tombs and monuments around the walls. Contrary to the impression created, not all of the doges are buried here, just twenty-five of them.

The **west wall** is devoted to the Mocenigo family: above the door is the tomb of Doge Alvise Mocenigo and his wife by Pietro Lombardo (1477); to the right is the monument to Doge Giovanni Mocenigo (d.1485) by Tullio Lombardo; and on the left the superb monument to Doge Pietro Mocenigo (d.1476), by Pietro Lombardo, assisted by his sons.

In the **south aisle**, after the first altar, is the monument to the Venetian military commander Marcantonio Bragadin, to which is attached one of Venice's grisliest stories. In 1571 Bragadin was double-crossed by the Turks to whom he had been obliged to surrender Famagusta: tortured and humiliated for days by his captors, he was eventually executed by being skinned alive. Some years later the skin was brought back to Venice, and today it sits in that urn high up on the wall.

The next altar has a superb **Giovanni Bellini** polyptych, showing *St Vincent Ferrer, with SS Christopher and Sebastian*, and an *Annunciation* and *Pietà* above, still in the original frame. At the far end of this aisle, before you turn into the transept, you'll see a little shrine with the **foot of Saint Catherine of Siena**: most of her body is in Rome, her head is in her house in Siena, one foot's here, and other little relics are scattered about Italy.

The **south transept** has a painting by **Alvise Vivarini**, *Christ Carrying the Cross* (1474), and **Lorenzo Lotto**'s *Saint Antonine* (1542), painted in return for nothing more than his expenses and permission to be buried in the church. Sadly, Lotto was eventually driven from his home town by the jealousies and plots of other artists (including Titian), and died and was buried in the monastery at Loreto.

On the right of the chancel is the tomb of Doge Michele Morosini (d.1382), selected by Ruskin as "the richest monument of the Gothic period in Venice". The tomb of Doge Andrea Vendramin (d.1478), opposite, was singled out as its antithesis – only the half of the effigy's head that would be visible from below was completed by the artist, a short cut denounced by Ruskin as indicative of "an extreme of intellectual and moral degradation". Tullio Lombardo is thought to have been the culprit, with help from others – maybe his father and brother.

The **Cappella del Rosario**, at the end of the north transept, was virtually destroyed by fire in 1867; its paintings by Tintoretto, Palma il Giovane and others were lost. Of their replacements, the best are **Veronese**'s ceiling panels and *Adoration*.

Funerary sculpture is the main attraction of the **north aisle**. To the left of the sacristy door is the monument to Doge Pasquale Malipiero (d.1462) by Pietro Lombardo, one of the earliest in Renaissance style in Venice.

Santa Maria Formosa and around

South of San Zanipolo lies Campo di Santa Maria Formosa, an atmospheric square with a small but mouthwatering morning market. The church of **Santa Maria Formosa** was built by San Magno, Bishop of Oderzo in the seventh century, after a dream in which he saw a buxom (*formosa*) figure of the Madonna; the present building is another Coducci effort, dating from 1492. Palma il Vecchio's altarpiece of *St Barbara*, the church's outstanding picture, was admired by George Eliot as "an almost unique presentation of a hero-woman". Bartolomeo Vivarini's *Madonna della Misericordia*, in a side chapel, is a fine example of one of the warmest Catholic symbols – here she's shown sheltering a group of parishioners under her cloak.

The Renaissance Palazzo Querini-Stampalia, just round the corner from Santa Maria Formosa, houses the **Pinacoteca Querini-Stampalia** (Tues–Sun 10am–12.30pm; L5000). Unless you have a voracious appetite for seventeenth- and eighteenth-century Venetian painting, you'll get most pleasure from earlier pieces such as Palma il Vecchio's portraits of *Francesco Querini* and *Paola Priuli Querini* and Giovanni Bellini's *The Presentation in the Temple*. Apart from that, the main interest is in the eighteenth-century decor of the rooms.

San Zaccaria and the Riva

The Campo San Zaccaria, a few yards off the waterfront, has a more torrid past than most – the convent here was notorious for its libidinous goings-on (officials were once sent to close down the nuns' parlour, only to be met with a barrage of bricks), and in 864 Doge Pietro Tradonico was murdered here as he returned from vespers. The towering church of **San Zaccaria**, a pleasing mixture of Gothic and Renaissance, was started by Antonio Gambello and finished after his death in 1481 by Mauro Coducci, who was responsible for the facade from the first storey upwards. Inside is one of the city's most stunning altarpieces, a *Madonna and Four Saints* by Giovanni Bellini. A small fee gets you into the rebuilt remnants of the old church, the Cappella di Sant'Atanasio and Cappella di San Tarasio; here you'll find an early Tintoretto, the *Birth of John the Baptist*, and three wonderful altarpieces by Antonio Vivarini and Giovanni d'Alemagna. Floor mosaics from the ninth and twelfth centuries can be seen through panels in the present floor level, and downstairs is the spooky waterlogged ninth-century crypt.

The principal waterfront of the area, the **Riva degli Schiavoni**, stretches right back to the Molo. It's a favourite walk, particularly as the sun goes down, and many notables have lived or stayed in houses and hotels here. Petrarch and his daughter lived at no. 4145 for a while, Henry James stayed nearby at no. 4161 when he was finishing *The Portrait of a Lady*, and the *Hotel Danieli*, at the far end, has accommodated George Sand, Charles Dickens, Proust, Wagner, the ever-present Ruskin, and Tina Turner.

Halfway along the Riva stands the **Pietà** church (or Santa Maria della Visitazione), famous as the place where Vivaldi was choirmaster – he was also violin teacher to the attached orphanage. Giorgio Massari won a competition to redesign the church in 1736, and it's possible that he consulted with Vivaldi on its acoustical aspects; building didn't actually begin until 1745, and the facade was even more delayed – it was only finished in 1906. The church is still used often for concerts, and when the box office is open you can peer over the ropes at the interior, which, in its newly restored form, looks like a wedding-cake turned inside out – and it has one of Venice's most ostentatious ceiling paintings, Giambattista Tiepolo's *The Glory of Paradise*.

The Greek quarter and the Scuola di San Giorgio degli Schiavoni

Stroll north along the flank of the Pietà and you'll enter the quarter of Venice's Greek community, identifiable from a distance by the alarmingly tilted campanile of **San Giorgio dei Greci**. The Greek presence was strong in Venice from the eleventh century, and grew stronger after Constantinople's capture by the Turks in 1453; by the close of the fifteenth century they had founded their own church, college and school here. The present *scuola*, designed (like the college) by Longhena in the seventeenth century, now houses the **Museo Dipinti Sacri Bizantini** (Mon–Sat 9am–1pm & 2–5pm; L4000). Although many of the most beautiful of the exhibited works (mainly fifteenth to eighteenth century) maintain the traditions of icon painting in terms of composition and use of symbolic figures rather than attempts at realism, it's fascinating to see how some of the artists absorbed western influences. The **church** contains icons dating back to the twelfth century, and a lot of work by Michael Danaskinàs, a sixteenth-century Cretan artist.

From here it's a hundred metres or so to the **Scuola di San Giorgio degli Schiavoni**, whose ground-floor hall would get onto anyone's list of the ten most beautiful rooms in Europe (Tues–Sat 9.30am–12.30pm & 3.30–6.30pm, Sun 11am–12.30pm; L4000). Venice's resident Slavs (*Schiavoni*), most of whom were traders, set up a *scuola* to look after their interests in 1451; the present building dates from the early sixteenth century, and the whole interior looks more or less as it would have then. Entering it, you step straight from the street into the superb lower hall, the walls of which are decorated with a cycle created by Vittore Carpaccio between 1502 and 1509. Originally painted for the upstairs room, but moved here when the building was rearranged in 1551, the sequence of pictures consists chiefly of scenes from the lives of saints George, Tryphone and Jerome (the Dalmatian patron saints). Outstanding is *The Vision of St Augustine*, depicting the moment that Augustine was told in a vision of Jerome's death.

San Francesco della Vigna

Somewhat stranded on the northern edge of Castello, the church of **San Francesco della Vigna** (daily 7–11.45am & 4.45–7pm) takes its name from the vineyard that was here when the Franciscans were given the site in 1253. The present church building was begun in 1534, designed and supervised by Sansovino, but the design was modified during construction, and Palladio was later brought in to provide the facade. Although smaller than the two great mendicant churches of San Zanipolo and the Frari, it feels less welcoming – probably a simple matter of the cold colouring added to the more calculated Renaissance architecture. However, there are some fine works of art that make the trek worthwhile – but be sure to have a pocketful of coins for the (necessary) light boxes. The ones you shouldn't miss are: *SS Jerome, Bernard and Ludovic*, attributed to Antonio Vivarini (left of main door); the sculptures of *Prophets* and *Evangelists* by the Lombardo family (in the chapel left of the chancel); and the *Sacra Conversazione* by **Veronese** (fifth chapel on the north side).

The Arsenale

A corruption of the Arabic *darsin'a* (house of industry), the very name of the **Arsenale** is indicative of the strength of Venice's trading links with the eastern Mediterranean, and the workers of these dockyards and factories were the foundations upon which the city's mercantile and military supremacy rested. Construction of the Arsenale commenced in the early years of the twelfth century, and by the third decade of the fifteenth century it had become the base for some 300 shipping companies, operating around 3000 vessels in excess of 200 tons. The productivity of the Arsenale was legendary: for the visit of Henry III of France in 1574 the *Arsenalotti* built a complete ship while the state reception for the king was in progress.

Expansion of the Arsenale continued into the sixteenth century – Sanmicheli's covered dock for the state barge (the *Bucintoro*) was built in the 1540s, for example, and da Ponte's gigantic rope-factory (the *Tana*) in 1579. By then, though, the maritime strength of Venice was past its peak; militarily as well, despite the conspicuous success at Lepanto in 1571, Venice was on the wane, and the reconquest of the Morea at the end of the seventeenth century was little more than a glorious interlude in a long story of decline. When Napoleon took over the city in 1797 he burned down the wharves, sank the last *Bucintoro* and confiscated the remnant of the Venetian navy.

Under Austrian occupation the docks were reconstructed, and they stayed in continuous service until the end of 1917, when, having built a number of ships for the Italian navy in World War I, they were dismantled to prevent them being of use to the enemy. Since then it has been used by the navy for storage and repairs, but there are plans to extend the naval museum into the Arsenale buildings and to convert other parts into sports halls.

THE ARSENALE BUILDINGS AND MUSEO STORICO NAVALE

There is no public access to the Arsenale complex. You can get a look at part of it, however, from the bridge connecting the Campo Arsenale and the Fondamenta dell'Arsenale; a better view can be had by taking the *vaporetto* #5, which cuts through the oldest part of the Arsenale, taking you past Sanmichel's *Bucintoro* building, alongside which is the mouth of the *Darsena Grande*.

The main **gateway** to the Arsenale, built by Antonio Gambello in 1460, was the first structure in Venice to employ the classical vocabulary of Renaissance architecture. The four **lions** to the side of the gateway must be the most-photographed in the city: the two on the right were probably taken from Delos (at an unknown date), the left-hand one of the pair being positioned here to mark the recapture of Corfu in 1716; the larger pair were brought back from Piraeus in 1687 by Francesco Morosini after the reconquest of the Morea.

Nearby, on the other side of the Rio dell'Arsenale and facing the lagoon, is the **Museo Storico Navale** (Mon–Sat 9am–1pm; L2000). Chiefly of interest for its models of Venetian craft from the gondola to the *Bucintoro*, the museum gives a comprehensive picture of the working life of the Arsenale and the smaller boatyards of Venice; but if you want to get a taste of the city's history from a single museum visit, then you should give priority to the Correr.

San Pietro di Castello

In 1808 the greater part of the canal connecting the Bacino di San Marco to the broad inlet of the Canale di San Pietro was filled in to form what is now **Via Garibaldi**, the widest street in the city and the busiest commercial area in the eastern district. If you follow your nose along the right-hand side of the street you'll soon be crossing the Ponte di Quintavalle onto the island of **San Pietro**, once the ecclesiastical centre of Venice, nowadays a slightly down-at-heel place where the chief activity is the repairing of boats.

By 775 the settlement here had grown sufficiently to be granted the foundation of a bishopric under the authority of the Patriarch of Grado. From the beginning, the political and economic nucleus of the city was in the Rialto and San Marco areas, and the relationship between the church and the geographically remote rulers of the city was never to be close. In 1451 the first **Patriarch of Venice** was invested, but still his seat remained at Castello, and things stayed that way until 1807 (ten years after the Republic had ceased to exist), when the Patriarch was at last permitted to install himself in San Marco.

As with the Arsenale, the history of San Pietro is perhaps more interesting than what you can see. The church is basically a grandiose derivative of a plan by Palladio and has little to recommend it. The most intriguing object inside is the so-called Throne of Saint Peter (in the south aisle), a marble seat made from an Arabic funeral stone cut with texts from the Koran. The lurching campanile, rebuilt by Coducci in the 1480s, was the first tower in Venice to be clad in stone.

Sant'Elena

The island of **Sant'Elena**, the eastern limit of central Venice, was enlarged tenfold during the Austrian administration, partly to form exercise grounds for the troops. Much of the island used to be covered by the meadow of Sant'Elena, a favourite recreation area in the last century, but houses stand there now, leaving just a strip of park along the waterfront. Still, the walk out here is the nearest you'll get to country pleasures in Venice, and the **church of Sant'Elena** is worth a visit.

A church was erected here in the thirteenth century, following the acquisition of the body of Saint Helena (the mother of Constantine), and substantially rebuilt in 1435. The spartan Gothic interior has recently been restored, as have the cloister and campanile (the latter so zealously that it now looks like a power-station chimney), but the main attraction is the doorway to the church, an ensemble created in the 1470s by Antonio Rizzo. The sculptural group in the lunette – a monument to Comandante Vittore Cappello, showing him kneeling before Saint Helena – is the district's one major work of art.

The Canal Grande

The **Canal Grande** is Venice's main thoroughfare. Almost four kilometres long and between thirty and seventy metres wide (but at no point much deeper than five metres), it divides the city in half – three *sestieri* to the west and three to the east. The majority of the most important palaces in Venice stand on the Canal Grande, and the main facades of all of them are on the canalside, many properly visible only from the water. (Palaces are scattered throughout Venice, and you'll rarely come across one that wasn't built to face a canal.) The section that follows is mainly a brief guide to these palaces – the major churches and other public buildings are covered in the appropriate geographical sections.

Left Bank

The first of the major palaces to come into view is the **Palazzo Labia** (completed around 1750). The main facade of the building stretches along the Cannaregio canal, but from the Canal Grande you can see how the side wing wraps itself round the campanile of the neighbouring church – such interlocking is common in Venice, where maximum use has to be made of available space. (See p.246 for details of the interior.)

Not far beyond stands the **Palazzo Vendramin-Calergi**, built by Mauro Coducci at the start of the sixteenth century. This is the first Venetian palace constructed in accordance with the classical rules of Renaissance architecture as formulated by Alberti, and is frequently singled out as the Canal Grande's masterpiece. The round-arched windows enclosing two similar arches are identifying characteristics of Coducci's designs. Richard Wagner died here in 1883; the size of the palace can be gauged from the fact that his rented suite of fifteen rooms occupied just a part of the mezzanine level.

Just after the Rio di San Felice comes the most beguiling palace on the canal – the **Ca' d'Oro**. Incorporating fragments of a thirteenth-century palace that once stood on the site, the Ca' d'Oro was begun in the 1420s and acquired its nickname – "Golden House" – from the gilding that used to accentuate much of its carving. It now houses a large art collection, details of which are given on p.247.

Close to the far side of the Rio dei Santi Apostoli stands the **Ca' da Mosto**. The arches of the first floor and the carved panels above them are remnants of a thirteenth-century Veneto-Byzantine building, among the oldest structures to be seen on the Canal Grande. From the fifteenth to the nineteenth century this was one of Venice's most famous hotels, the *Albergo del Lion Bianco*.

As the canal turns, the **Ponte di Rialto** (Rialto Bridge) comes into view. The huge building before it, with five arches at water level, is the **Fondaco dei Tedeschi**, once the headquarters of the city's German merchants. Reconstructed in 1505 after a fire and renovated several times since (most recently to accommodate the main post office), it once had frescoes by Giorgione and Titian on its exterior walls, the remains of which are now in the Ca' d'Oro. The bridge itself was built in 1588–91, superseding a succession of wooden and sometimes unreliable structures; until 1854, when an iron bridge was built at the Accademia, this was the only point at which the Canal Grande could be crossed on foot.

Immediately before the next canal is Sansovino's first palace in Venice, the **Palazzo Dolfin-Manin**. It dates from the late 1530s, a period when other projects by him – the library, the mint and the Loggetta – were transforming the city centre. The **Palazzo Loredan** and the **Palazzo Farsetti**, standing side by side at the end of the Fondamenta del Carbon, are heavily restored thirteenth-century palaces; the former was the home of Elena Corner Piscopia, who in 1678 graduated from Padua University, so becoming the first woman to obtain a degree.

Work began on the **Palazzo Grimani** (near side of the Rio di San Luca) in 1556, to designs by Sanmicheli, but was not completed until 1575, sixteen years after his death. Ruskin, normally no fan of Renaissance architecture, made an exception for this colossal palace, calling it "simple, delicate, and sublime".

On the approach to the sharp bend in the canal (the *Volta del Canal*) there stands a line of five buildings, the first four of which belonged to the Mocenigo family. This group consists of: the **Palazzo Mocenigo-Nero**, a late sixteenth-century building; the double **Palazzo Mocenigo**, built in the eighteenth century as an extension to the Nero house, and home to Byron for a couple of years; and the **Palazzo Mocenigo Vecchio**, a Gothic palace remodelled in the seventeenth century, reputedly haunted by the ghost of the philosopher-alchemist Giordano Bruno, whose betrayal by Giovanni Mocenigo in 1592 led ultimately to his torture and execution. The fifth palace is the **Palazzo Contarini delle Figure**, named after the almost invisible figures at the water entrance.

The vast pristine building round the *Volta* is the **Palazzo Grassi**, built in 1748–72; owned by Fiat – hence the lavish renovation – it's now a conference centre and venue for Venice's glossiest exhibitions.

The Santa Maria del Giglio landing stage is virtually in the shadow of one of the Canal Grande's most imposing buildings – Sansovino's **Palazzo Corner della Ca' Grande.** The house that used to stand here was destroyed when a fire lit to dry out a stock of sugar in one of its rooms ran out of control; Sansovino's replacement was built from 1545 onwards.

Opposite the church of the Salute, squeezed into a line of fifteenth- and seventeenth-century buildings, is the narrow **Palazzo Contarini-Fasan**, a Gothic palace with unique wheel tracery on the balconies. It's popularly known as the *House of Desdemona*, for no good reason.

Right bank

The first attraction on the right bank is the **Fondaco dei Turchi**. Originally a private house, then from the 1620s until 1838 the base for Turkish traders in the city, the Fondaco was savagely restored in the last century. Whatever the shortcomings of the work, however, the building's towers and water-level arcade give a reasonably precise picture of a typical Veneto-Byzantine palace. It now houses the Museo di Storia Naturale (Natural History Museum).

A short distance beyond stands Longhena's thickly ornamented **Ca' Pésaro**, finished in 1703, long after the architect's death. Unusually, the Ca' Pésaro has a stone-clad side facade: most houses in Venice have plain brick sides, either because of the cost of stone, or to allow for a later building to be attached. It now contains the Galleria d'Arte Moderna and the Museo Orientale.

There's nothing especially engrossing now until you reach the Rialto markets, which begin with the neo-Gothic **Pescheria** (fish market), built in 1907. The older buildings which follow it, the **Fabbriche Nuove di Rialto** and (set back from the water) the **Fabbriche Vecchie di Rialto**, are by Sansovino and Scarpagnino respectively, and replaced buildings destroyed by fire in 1514. The large building at the base of the Rialto bridge is the **Palazzo dei Camerlenghi** (1525), once home to the Venetian exchequer.

The cluster of Gothic palaces at the *Volta* constitutes one of the city's architectural glories. The **Ca' Fóscari** (1435), which Ruskin thought "the noblest example in Venice" of late Gothic, was the home of Doge Francesco Fóscari, whose extraordinarily long term of office (32 years) came to an end with his forced resignation, an event partly attributable to the unrelenting feud conducted against him by the Loredan family and its allies. He died in 1457, only weeks after leaving the Palazzo Ducale. Adjoining the Ca' Fóscari are a pair of joined buildings of the same period – the **Palazzi Giustinian**. Wagner wrote the second act of *Tristan* while living here.

A little further on comes Longhena's **Ca' Rezzonico**, as gargantuan as his Ca' Pésaro but less aggressive. It was begun in 1667 as a commission from the Bon family, but their ambition exceeded their financial resources and they were obliged in 1750 to sell out to the Rezzonico, who completed the palace and even tacked a ballroom and staircase onto the back. Much of the interior of the Ca' Rezzonico is open to the public, as it houses the Museo del Settecento Veneziano. The unfinished **Palazzo dei Leoni** (soon after the Campo San Vio), would have been the largest palace on the canal, but its construction, begun in 1759, never progressed further than the first storey – probably owing to the ruinous cost. The stump of the building and the platform on which it is raised are occupied by the Guggenheim collection of modern art.

The one domestic building of note between here and the **Dogana di Mare** (Customs House) at the end of the canal is the miniature **Palazzo Dario**, two along from the Palazzo dei Leoni. Compared by Henry James to "a house of cards that hold together by a tenure it would be fatal to touch", the palace was built in the late 1480s not for a patrician family but for Giovanni Dario, a civil servant. The multicoloured marbles of the facade are characteristic of the work of the Lombardo family, and the design may actually be by the founder of the dynasty, Pietro Lombardo.

The northern islands

The islands lying to the north of Venice – **San Michele**, **Murano**, **Burano** and **Torcello** – are the places to visit when the throng of tourists in the main part of the city becomes too oppressive, and are the source of much of the glass and lace work you will have seen in many shops in Venice.

To get to them, the main *vaporetto* stop is the **Fondamente Nuove**. The *vaporetto* #5, which runs about every fifteen minutes, will take you to San Michele and Murano. For Burano and Torcello there is the *vaporetto* #12 (every 1hr–1hr 30min), which takes 45 minutes to get to Burano, from where it's a short hop to Torcello. This service can also be caught from Murano, but only from the **Faro** landing stage.

San Michele

The high brick wall around the cemetery island of **San Michele** gives way by the landing stage for the elegant white facade of **San Michele in Isola**, designed by Mauro Coducci in 1469. With this building, Coducci not only helped introduce Renaissance architecture to Venice, but also promoted the use of Istrian stone. Easy to carve yet resistant to water, it had been used as damp-proofing at ground level, but never before for a complete facade; it was to be used on the facades of most major buildings in Venice from the Renaissance onwards.

The main part of the island, through the cloisters, is the city **cemetery** (daily 8.15am–4pm), established by Napoleonic decree and nowadays maintained by the Franciscans, as is the church. The majority of Venetians lie here for just ten years or so, when their bones are dug up and removed to an ossuary and the land recycled. Only those who can afford it stay longer. The cemetery is laid out in sections – ask at the entrance for the little give-away map – the most dilapidated of which is for the Protestants (no. XV), where any admirers can find **Ezra Pound**'s grave. In section XIV are the Greek and Russian Orthodox graves, including the restrained memorial stones of **Igor and Vera Stravinsky** and the more elaborate tomb of **Serge Diaghilev** – always strewn with flowers.

Murano

Chiefly famed now as the home of Venice's **glass-blowing** industry, **Murano**'s main *fondamente* are crowded with shops selling the mostly revolting products of the furnaces. However, don't despair: Murano does have other things to offer.

The glass furnaces were moved to Murano from Venice as a safety measure in 1291, and so jealously did the Muranese guard their industrial secrets that for a long while they had the European monopoly on glass mirror-making. The glass-blowers of Murano were accorded various privileges not allowed to other artisans, such as being able to wear swords. From 1376 the offspring of a marriage between a Venetian nobleman and the daughter of a glass-worker were allowed to be entered into the Libro d'Oro, unlike the children of other cross-class matches.

Far more interesting than most of the finished products is the performance of their manufacture. There are numerous **furnaces** to visit, all free of charge on the assumption that you will then want to buy something, though you won't be pressed too hard to do so. Many of the workshops are to be found along Fondamenta dei Vereri, traditionally a glassworking centre, as the name suggests.

When the Venetian Republic fell to Napoleon in 1797, there were seventeen churches on Murano; today only two are open. The first is **San Pietro Martire**, a Dominican Gothic church begun in 1363, and largely rebuilt after a fire in 1474. Its main attraction is a large and (as ever) elegant Giovanni Bellini: the *Madonna and Child with SS Mark and Augustine, and Doge Barbarigo* (1488); a second Bellini (an *Assumption*) is at present being restored.

THE GLASS MUSEUMS

Close by, along Fondamenta Cavour, you'll find the **Museo Vetrario** in the Palazzo Giustinian (9am–7pm; closed Wed; L5000). The collection includes some Roman pieces, but the earliest surviving Murano glass dates from the fifteenth century. There are perfunctory labels in Italian only, and there is no guidebook, yet even so the exhibits often exert their own fascination – how *did* the aristocracy manage to drink in the seventeenth century? A separate room contains a fascinating exhibition on the history of Murano glass techniques, this time fully explained in English. Look out for the extraordinary *Murine in Lanna* – the technique of placing different coloured rods together to form an image in cross-section. Your entry ticket will also get you into the recently opened **Modern and Contemporary Glass Museum** on Fondamenta Manin (opposite Fondamenta Vereri; same hours as the main museum). Here they have a few pieces of functional glassware that try to look like modernist sculptures, and one or two modernist sculptures that end up looking like giant pieces of functional ware. However, there are some interesting works – like the baby by Alfredo Borbini which looks as though it's carved from lava, and the mirror with gold leaf by Piero Fornasetti.

SANTI MARIA E DONATO

Murano's main draw is the Veneto-Byzantine church of **Santi Maria e Donato**, which was founded in the seventh century and rebuilt in the twelfth (daily 8am–noon & 4–7pm). Its beautiful **mosaic floor**, dated 1141 in the nave, mingles abstract patterns with images of beasts and birds – an eagle carries off a deer; two roosters carry off a fox, slung from a pole. The church was originally dedicated to Mary, but in 1125 was re-dedicated when the relics of Saint Donato were brought here from Cephalonia. Four splendid bones from an unfortunate dragon which was slain by the holy spit of Donato are now hanging behind the altar. Above these, in the apse, is a twelfth-century **mosaic of the Madonna** and fifteenth-century frescoes of the Evangelists. A guidebook to the church is available, proceeds of which go towards restoration work.

Burano

The main route into **Burano** is a narrow street full of lace shops which soon opens out to reveal the brightly painted houses of the village itself – the colours used to be symbolic, but the meanings have got confused through time and now people paint their houses whatever colour takes their fancy.

This is still largely a fishing community, the lagoon's main yield being shellfish of various kinds, such as *vongole* (tiny clams) and small crabs. (The catch can be bought either here, on the Fondamenta Pescheria, or back in Venice, at the Rialto.) It's a solitary business; one or two people have even built themselves vulnerable-looking houses out on the slightly higher mud-flats, constructed largely from material scavenged from the lagoon tips.

As the men of Burano live mainly from the water, so the women are to a large extent dependent on **lace-making**. Making Burano-point and Venetian-point lace is extremely exacting work, both highly skilled and mind-bendingly repetitive, with an enormous toll on the eyesight. Each woman specialises in one particular stitch, and so each piece is passed from woman to woman during its construction. The skills are taught at the **Scuola dei Merletti** (Tues–Sun 9am–6pm; L5000). It's in the spacious Piazza Baldessare Galuppi and combines a lace school with a museum, and is well worth a visit before you buy anything. (Much of the work in the shops is machine produced and imported.) The school was opened in 1872 after the indigenous crafting of lace nearly died out; the museum shows work dating back to the sixteenth century, but most was produced in the past hundred years.

Torcello

Torcello has come full circle: settled as early as the fifth century, the seat of the Bishop of Altinum from 638, and the home of about 20,000 people by the fourteenth century, it was then eclipsed by Venice, and by 1600 was largely deserted. Today the total population of Torcello is about 100, and there is little visible evidence of the island's prime – two churches and a couple of buildings round a dusty square, and pottery shards half-buried in the fields.

The main reason that people come here today is to visit Venice's first cathedral, **Santa Maria Assunta** (daily 10am–12.30pm & 2–5pm; L1500). An early church on the site became a cathedral after the Bishop of Altinum arrived with other emigrants from the mainland. The present Veneto-Byzantine building is on pretty much the same plan as the seventh-century one, but it was largely rebuilt in the 860s and altered again in 1008. Inside, the waterlogged crypt is the only survival of the body of the original church; the baptistery also dates from the seventh century, but circular foundations in front of the main doors are all that remain of it.

The dominant tone of the interior is created by its watery green-grey marble columns and panelling; the mosaic floor is eleventh-century, but two wooden panels lift to reveal the original floor underneath. A stunning twelfth-century mosaic of the Madonna and Child, on a pure gold background, covers the semi-dome of the apse, resting on an eleventh-century mosaic frieze of the Apostles. In the centre of the frieze, below the window, is an image of Saint Heliodorus, the first Bishop of Altinum, whose remains were brought here by the first settlers. It's interesting to compare this image with the gold-plated face mask given to his remains in a Roman sarcophagus in front of the original seventh-century altar.

The church of **Santa Fosca** (same hours and ticket as Santa Maria) was built in the eleventh and twelfth centuries to house the body of the eponymous saint, brought to Torcello from Libya some time before 1011 and now resting under the altar. Much restored, the church retains the Greek cross form and a fine exterior apse, and inside, the elegant brick arches and cornerings leading up to its wooden dome. Despite the tourists, both these churches manage to maintain a meditative calm.

In the square outside sits the curious **chair of Attila**. Local legend has it that if you sit in it you will be wed within a year. Behind it is the **Museo dell'Estuario** (Tues–Sun 10am–12.30pm & 2–5.30pm; L3000), which includes thirteenth-century beaten gold figures, sections of mosaic heads, and jewellery. It's all nicely laid out, and worth a visit.

The southern islands

The section of the lagoon to the south of the city, enclosed by the long islands of the **Lido** and **Pellestrina**, has far fewer outcrops of solid land than the northern half: once you get past **Giudecca** and **San Giorgio Maggiore** – which are in effect detached pieces of central Venice – and clear of the smaller islands that dot the water off the middle section of the Lido, you could, on certain days, look in the direction of the mainland and think you were out in the open sea. The nearer islands are the more interesting: the farther-flung settlements of the southern lagoon have played as significant a role in the history of Venice as the better-known northern islands but nowadays they have few things going for them other than the pleasure of the trip.

San Giorgio Maggiore

The prominence of Palladio's church of **San Giorgio Maggiore** (daily 9am–noon & 2.30–5pm) almost forces you to have an opinion as to its architectural merits. Ruskin didn't much care for it: "It is impossible to conceive a design more gross, more barbarous, more childish in conception, more servile in plagiarism, more insipid in result, more contemptible under every point of rational regard." Palladio's successors were more impressed, though, and it was to prove one of the most influential Renaissance church designs.

The finely calculated proportions and Counter-Reformation austerity of the interior reminded Ruskin merely of an assembly room; in his opinion, its paintings were what justified opening the door. Two pictures by Tintoretto hang in the chancel: *The Fall of Manna* and *The Last Supper*, perhaps the most famous of all his images. They were painted as a pair in 1592–94, the last years of the artist's life; another Tintoretto of the same date – a *Deposition* – hangs in the Cappella dei Morti, approached through the door on the right of the choir.

On the left of the choir a corridor leads to the **campanile** (L2000); rebuilt in 1791 after the collapse of its predecessor, it's one of the two best vantage points in the city – the other being the campanile of San Marco.

The ex-Benedictine monastery next door to the church, now the base of the combined arts research institute, craft school and naval college known as the **Fondazione Giorgio Cini**, is one of the architectural gems of Venice. It incorporates a 128-metre-long dormitory, designed by Giovanni Buora around 1494, a double staircase and a library by Longhena, a magnificent refectory by Palladio and two adjoining cloisters, one planned by Giovanni Buora and built by his son, the other designed by Palladio. Exhibitions are regularly held at the Fondazione, and it's possible to visit the monastery at other times by ringing ☎528.9900 to make an appointment, or by persuading the custodian of your interest in Palladian architecture.

Giudecca

In the earliest records of Venice, the island of **Giudecca** was known as Spina Longa, a name clearly derived from its shape; the modern name might refer to the Jews (*Giudei*) who were based here from the late thirteenth century, or to the disruptive noble families who, from the ninth century, were shoved onto this chain of islets to keep them quiet (*giudicati* meaning "judged"). Before the banks of the Brenta became the prestigious site for one's summer abode, Giudecca was where the wealthiest aristocrats of early Renaissance Venice built their villas, and in places you can still see traces of their gardens. The present-day suburb is a strange mixture of decrepitude and vitality. The boatyards and fishing quays on the south side are interspersed with half-abandoned factories and roofless sheds, and even the side facing the city presents a remarkable economic contrast: at the western edge is the derelict neo-Gothic fortress of the

Mulino Stucky, a flour mill built in 1895, and at the other stands the *Cipriani*, the most expensive hotel in Venice.

The Franciscan church of the **Redentore** (daily 7.30am–noon & 3.30–7pm), designed by Palladio in 1577, is Giudecca's main monument. In 1575–76 Venice suffered an outbreak of bubonic plague which annihilated nearly 50,000 people – virtually a third of the city's population. The Redentore was built in thanks for Venice's deliverance, and every year until the downfall of the Republic the doge and his senators attended a mass in the church on the Feast of the Redentore to renew their declaration of gratitude. The procession walked to the church over a pontoon bridge from the Záttere, a ceremony perpetuated by the people of Venice on the third Sunday in July.

The present state of the Redentore makes an appreciation of its architectural subtleties a bit of an effort – the plaster is dowdy, statues with fairy-light haloes clutter the place and a rope prevents visitors going beyond the nave. The best paintings in the church, including a *Madonna with Child and Angels* by Alvise Vivarini, are in the sacristy, where you'll be greatly edified by a gallery of eighteenth-century wax heads of illustrious Franciscans, arranged in glass cases all round the room.

San Lazzaro degli Armeni

No foreign community has a longer pedigree in Venice than the Armenians – they were established by the end of the thirteenth century, and for around five hundred years have had a church within a few yards of the Piazza (in Calle degli Armeni). They are far less numerous now, and the most conspicuous sign of their presence is the Armenian island by the Lido, **San Lazzaro degli Armeni** (daily 3–5pm; *vaporetto* #10), identifiable from the city by the onion-shaped top of its campanile. The Roman Catholic Armenian monastery here was founded in 1717 by Manug di Pietro (known as *Mechitar* – "The Consoler"), and derived its name from the island's past function as a leper colony – Lazarus being the patron saint of lepers.

The Armenian monks have always had a reputation as scholars and linguists, and the monastery's collection of precious manuscripts and books – the former going back to the fifth century – is one of the visit's highlights, along with a Tiepolo ceiling panel and the room in which Byron stayed while lending a hand with the preparation of an Armenian–English dictionary. The tour ends in a computerised printing and typesetting hall, the nerve centre of the polyglot press which has been operating here continuously since 1789. You should leave a donation or buy something from the press – the old maps and prints of Venice are a bargain.

The Lido and the southern lagoon

For about eight centuries, the **Lido** was the focus of the annual hullaballoo of Venice's "Marriage to the Sea", when the doge went out to the Porto di Lido to drop a gold ring into the brine, and then disembarked for mass at San Nicolò al Lido. It was then an unspoilt strip of land, and remained so into the last century. Within thirty years it had become the smartest bathing resort in Italy, and although it's no longer as chic as it was when Thomas Mann set *Death in Venice* here, there's less room on its beaches now than ever before. But unless you're staying at one of the flashy hotels that stand shoulder to shoulder along the sea front, or are prepared to pay a ludicrous fee to hire one of their beach hutches for the day, you won't be allowed to get the choicest Lido sand between your toes. The ungroomed public beaches are at the northern and southern ends of the island – though why anyone should want to jeopardise his or her health in these filthy waters is a mystery.

The Film Festival occupies the Lido's Palazzo del Cinema in late August and early September, but the place has little else to recommend it – although inveterate gamblers in possession of a snappy wardrobe might want to investigate the summer Casino.

FROM THE LIDO TO CHIOGGIA

The trip across the lagoon to **Chioggia** is a more protracted business than simply taking the land bus from Piazzale Roma, but it will give you a curative dose of salt air and a good knowledge of the lagoon. From Gran Viale Santa Maria Elisabetta – the main street from the Lido landing stage to the sea front – the more or less hourly #11 bus goes down to **Alberoni**, where it drives onto a ferry for the five-minute hop to Pellestrina; the 10km to the southern tip of Pellestrina are covered by road, and then you switch from the bus to a steamer for the 25-minute crossing to Chioggia. The entire journey takes about eighty minutes and costs L4900 – but be sure to check the timetable carefully at Gran Viale Santa Maria Elisabetta – not every #11 goes all the way to Chioggia.

The fishing village of **Malamocco**, about 5km into the expedition, is the successor of the ancient settlement which in the eighth century was the capital of the lagoon confederation. In 810 the town was taken by Pepin, son of Charlemagne, and there followed one of the crucial battles in Venice's history, when Pepin's fleet, endeavouring to reach the islands that were to become Venice, became jammed in the mudbanks and was swiftly massacred. After the battle, the capital was promptly transferred to the safer islands of Rivoalto. In 1107 the old town of Malamocco was wiped out by a tidal wave. As the boat crosses from Pellestrina Cimitero to Chioggia, you get the best possible view of what could be described as the last great monument of the Republic – the **Murazzi**. This colossal wall of Istrian boulders, 4km long and 14m thick at the base, was constructed at the sides of the Porto di Chioggia to protect Venice from the battering of the sea, and did its job perfectly from the year of its completion (1782) until the flood of November 1966.

The defence of Venice is now supposedly being entrusted to the barrier that's planned to be installed below the waters of the lagoon's mouths. Nicknamed "**Moses**", the barrier is designed, like the Thames Barrier, to be raised at moments of crisis. It has consumed inordinate sums of money, is nowhere near completion (there's a fragment at Malamocco, and that's all), might well not work when it is eventually finished, and does not address the fundamental problems of the fluctuating levels of the lagoon, which are exaggerated by the shipping lanes that have been dredged across it. The press might occasionally extol the wonders of the Venice tidal barrier, but in the city itself the project arouses little except cynicism.

CHIOGGIA

In 1379 **Chioggia** was the scene of the most serious threat to Venice since Pepin's invasion, when the Genoese, after copious shedding of blood on both sides, took possession of the town. Protracted siege warfare resulted in the nearly complete destruction of medieval Chioggia before the surrender of the enemy in June 1380. From then until the arrival of Napoleon's ships nobody broke into the Venetian lagoon.

Modern Chioggia is the second largest settlement in the lagoon after Venice, and one of Italy's busiest fishing ports. It's not the most charming of places, and you can see virtually everything worth seeing in a hour's walk along the Corso del Popolo, the principal street in Chioggia's grid-iron layout. The main attractions are the **fish market** (Tues–Sat mornings) and the **Duomo**, which was Longhena's first major commission and possesses some good, if grisly, eighteenth-century paintings.

Buses run from the duomo to **Sottomarina**, Chioggia's downmarket answer to Venice's Lido. On the beaches of Sottomarina you're a fraction closer to nature than you would be on the Lido, and the resort does have one big plus – after your dip you can go back to the Corso and have a fresh seafood meal that's cheaper than any you'd find in Venice's restaurants and better than most.

The quickest way back to Venice is by bus from the duomo or Sottomarina to Piazzale Roma, but it's a dispiriting drive and only twenty minutes quicker, too.

Eating and drinking

Although there's an element of truth to Venice's reputation as a place where only the wealthy eat well, the picture is not entirely bleak for those on a tighter budget – some good-value **restaurants** do exist, it's just that they tend to be hidden away in the city's quieter places. Not surprisingly, **fish and seafood** dominate the restaurant menus. Prawns, squid and octopus are typical Venetian *antipasti*, as are Murano crabs and *sarde in saor* (marinated sardines). Dishes like eel cooked in Marsala wine, *baccalà* (salt cod) and *seppioline nere* (baby cuttlefish cooked in its own ink) are other Venetian staples, but the quintessential dish is the **risotto**, made with rice grown along the Po Valley.

Pastries and sweets are also an area of Venetian expertise. Look out for the thin oval biscuits called *baicoli*, the ring-shaped cinnamon-flavoured *bussolai* (a speciality of Burano), and *mandolato* – a cross between nougat and toffee, made with almonds. The Austrian occupation has left its mark in the form of the ubiquitous *strudel* and the cream- or jam-filled *krapfen* (doughnuts).

At the lower end of the market, the division between **bars** and restaurants is often difficult to draw – some of the places listed below under "Restaurants" are in effect grandiose bars, while some of the "Bars" have basic sit-down areas for eating. With establishments that straddle both categories, we've listed them according to which aspect of the operation draws most of the customers.

Cafés, pasticcerie and ice cream

As in every Italian city, the **cafés** are central to social life, and you'll never be more than a couple of minutes from a decent one. In addition to their marvellous local confections, many **pasticcerie** also serve coffee, but will have at most a few bar stools. Strict budgeting is further jeopardised by Venice's **gelaterie**, where ice cream comes in forms that you won't have experienced before, unless you're a seasoned traveller in Italy.

General areas in which to find good cafés and *pasticcerie* include **Campo Santa Margherita, Crosera San Pantalon**, running just south of San Rocco, and **Campiello Meloni** (between S. Polo and S. Aponal), which has a couple of excellent *pasticcerie* whose doors remain open on Sundays.

Chiusso Pierino, Salizzada dei Greci; Castello. One of a chain of "antichi pasticceri Venexiani", established in 1932 and still serving delicious cakes.

Florian, Piazza San Marco. Opened in 1720 by Florian Francesconi, and frescoed and mirrored in a passable pastiche of that period, this has long been the café to be seen in. A simple *cappuccino* will set you back around L10,000 if the band's performing, and you'll have to take out a mortgage for a cocktail.

Il Golosone, Salizzada San Lio; Castello. *Pasticceria* and bar with a glorious spread of cakes; does a delicious apple *spremute*.

Marchini, Ponte San Maurizio; San Marco. The most delicious and most expensive of Venetian *pasticcerie*, where people come on Sunday morning to buy family treats.

Nico, Záttere ai Gesuati; Dorsoduro. A high point of a wander in the area, celebrated for an artery-clogging creation called a *gianduiotto* – a paper cup with a block of praline ice cream drowned in whipped cream.

Paolin, Campo Santo Stefano; San Marco. Thought by many to be the makers of the best ice cream in Venice; certainly their pistachio is amazing, and the outside tables have one of the finest settings in the city.

Takeaways, markets and shops

The campi, parks and canalside steps make **picnicking** a pleasant alternative in Venice, and if you're venturing off to the outer islands it's often the only way of fuelling yourself. Don't try to picnic in the Piazza though – the bylaws against it are strictly enforced.

Takeaway pizza is all over the place, though most of it is pretty miserable fare. For the best and widest range of pizzas and pies go to *Cip Ciap* in Calle Mondo Nuovo, near S. Maria Formosa (Castello).

Open-air **markets** for fruit and vegetables are held in various squares every day except Sunday; check out Santa Maria Formosa, Santa Margherita, Campiello dell'Anconetta, Rio Terrà San Leonardo and the barge moored by Campo San Barnaba. The market of markets, however, is the one at the Rialto, where you can buy everything you need for an impromptu feast – it's open Monday to Saturday 8am to 1pm, with a few stalls opening again in the late afternoon.

Virtually every parish has its **alimentari** and most of them are good; one to single out is *Aliani Gastronomia* in Ruga Vecchia S. Giovanni (San Polo) – scores of cheeses, meats and salads that'll have you drooling as soon as you're through the door. Alternatively, you could get everything from one of Venice's well-hidden **supermarkets.** Most central is *Su.Ve.*, on the corner of Salizzada San Lio and Calle Mondo Nuovo (Castello); others are on Campo Santa Margherita (Dorsoduro), Rio Terrà Frari (San Polo) and Záttere Ponte Lungo (Dorsoduro).

Restaurants

Virtually every **budget restaurant** in Venice advertises a set-price *menu turistico,* which can be a cheap way of sampling Venetian specialities, but the quality and certainly the quantity won't be up to the mark of an à la carte meal. As a general rule, value for money tends to increase with the distance from San Marco; plenty of restaurants within a short radius of the Piazza offer menus that seem to be reasonable, but you'll probably find the food unappetising, the portions tiny and the service abrupt.

San Marco

Al Bacareto, Calle Crosera. Handy for the Palazzo Grassi. Best to eat standing here: excellent *risotto alla pescatore* (fisherman's risotto) and a glass of wine won't be expensive, but a sit-down meal will.

Latteria Veneziana, Calle dei Fuseri. Billed as Venice's sole vegetarian restaurant, the Latteria serves very small portions of the sort of food a carnivore rustles up when a cranky relative is due. With a full meal costing around L20,000, you could be better off with a pasta followed by a selection of vegetables at a regular restaurant.

Rosticceria San Bartolomeo, Calle della Bissa. Downstairs it's a sort of glorified snack-bar, good if you need to refuel quickly and cheaply but can't face another pizza. There's a less rudimentary restaurant upstairs, where prices are a bit higher and quality a touch better.

Self-Service Rialto, Calle del Carbon. Situated between the Rialto *vaporetto* stop and Campo San Luca, this is another option for a rapid, low-cost refill.

Vino Vino, Ponte delle Veste. This place was set up primarily as a wine bar (see overleaf), but now has a good name for quick, simple and relatively inexpensive meals.

Dorsoduro

Alle Burchielle, Fondamenta Burchielle. Simple neighbourhood trattoria, a minute's walk south of Piazzale Roma. Just ask for the day's special.

Alle Záttere, Fondamenta Záttere. Same sort of place as Da Gianni, but not quite as good. Go for the pizzas – *Primavera*, with vegetables, is recommended.

Antico Capon, Campo Santa Margherita. Wide range of pizzas including such novelties as gorgonzola and walnut.

Da Bruno, Calle Lunga San Barnaba. Cheap and homely trattoria.

Da Gianni, Fondamenta Záttere. Nicely sited restaurant-pizzeria.

Isola Misteriosa, Rio Terrà Scoazzera, just off Campo S. Margherita. This place appeals to those who wear sunglasses at midnight and never smile – it serves nice food but in small portions, and a touch overpriced. It's possible to sit and drink here when it's not full of people eating, and there's a stand-up bar.

Montin, Fondamenta di Borgo. Very highly rated, but the quality's more erratic than you'd expect for the money; you'll pay in the region of L50,000 here for what would cost L30,000 in some places. It's always been a place for the artistic set – Pound, Hemingway and Visconti, for example – and the restaurant doubles as a commercial gallery. Always book (☎522.7151).

San Trovaso, Fondamenta Priuli. A restaurant-pizzeria which serves a menu of basic Venetian dishes at prices just a little higher than rock bottom.

San Polo

Alla Madonna, Calle della Madonna. Roomy, bustling seafood restaurant. Little finesse but good value, and refreshingly varied clientele.

All'Anfora, Lista Vecchia dei Bari. An unpretentious local restaurant that's open for breakfast coffee and still going late at night, and where a woman eating alone is welcomed and not patronised. Has a pizza list, but the trattoria list is not too expensive and features dishes you might find in a Venetian home. The seafood risotto is good, as is the *spaghetti del doge*.

Alla Zucca, Ponte del Megio. Serves chiefly vegetarian dishes, and is patronised heavily by the city's students.

Alle Colonnette, Campiello del Piovan. Nudging a wall of the church of San Giacomo dell'Orio, this little trattoria is high on atmosphere, and serves good pizzas. The rest of the menu is pretty ordinary though.

Alle Oche, Calle del Tintor. Excellent pizzeria on the south side of Campo S. Giacomo dell'Orio. Has about fifty varieties to choose from, so if this doesn't do you, nothing will; on summer evenings if you're not there by 8pm you may have to queue on the pavement.

Al Sole di Napoli, Campo Santa Margherita. Cheap and very cheerful pizzeria – especially pleasant in summer, when its tables colonise the campo.

Crepizza, Calle S. Pantalon. One of the city's trendiest low-cost eateries – excellent pizzas and crêpes, buzzing atmosphere.

Da Sandro, Campiello dei Meloni. Split-site pizzeria, with rooms on both sides of the campiello and tables on the pavement. Often frenetic, though not aggressively so.

Da Silvio, Calle San Pantalon; San Polo. The best of the clutch of trattorias in this alley, with a reputation for its *tortellini*; a full meal for L30,000 is feasible.

Giardinetto, Fondamenta del Forner. Big but not impersonal trattoria-pizzeria, with wide shaded courtyard. Popular with students.

Cannaregio

Ai Promessi Sposi, Calle dell'Oca. Bar-trattoria specialising in *baccalà* and other basic traditional fish recipes.

Antica Mola, Fondamenta degli Ormesini. This family-run trattoria, near the Ghetto, is becoming trendier by the year. Good food, good value.

Bruno, Fondamenta delle Cappuccine. Very pleasant little canalside trattoria in deepest Cannaregio; tasty seafood at good prices.

Casa Mia, Calle dell'Oca, off Campo SS Apostoli. Invariably heaving with locals, who always go for the pizza list rather than the menu.

Paradiso Perduto, Fondamenta della Misericordia. Opens around noon, closes midnight or later, depending on how things are going. Fronted by a popular bar, it has a lively relaxed atmosphere, attracting students, arty types and some of the gay community.

Train Station Buffet. A good place to fill up cheaply. Open 6am–10pm daily, with self-service buffet meals 11.30am–3pm & 6.30–9.30pm, and restaurant service 11.30am–3pm.

Castello

Aciugheta, Campo Santi Filippo e Giacomo. A bar with a pizzeria-trattoria next door. The closest spot to San Marco to eat without paying through the nose.

Alla Conchiglia, Fondamenta San Lorenzo. Inexpensive trattoria-pizzeria, with tables alongside the canal.

Alla Rivetta, Ponte San Provolo, near Campo SS. Filippo e Giacomo. Excellent *sepie in nero*, best eaten *con polenta*. Getting under L30,000 might require a bit of self-restraint.

Al Mascaron, Calle Lunga Santa Maria Formosa. Arty feel and interesting bar food, but definitely two types of clientele – Italians and non-Italians – with service and prices to match. Has a good reputation among the locals though, and worth a try if you're confident with the language.

Al Milion, Corte del Milion, behind San Giovanni Crisostomo. Trattoria with bar where you can get snacks. Wide selection of Veneto wines.

Da Paolo, Campo dell'Arsenale. Tables outside in the summer, facing the Arsenale entrance. Good pizzas and *sarde in saor*; house wine not great.

Da Remigio, Salizzada dei Greci. Brilliant local trattoria, serving gorgeous homemade gnocchi. Be sure to book (☎523.0089).

Toscana, Via Garibaldi. Plain, with a tiny menu, but all dishes are good and cheap.

Bars and snacks

Stand at a Venetian **bar** any time of the day and you won't have to wait long before someone drops by for a reviving *ombra*, a tiny glass of wine customarily downed in one. Serious wine enthusiasts should sample a few *ombre* in an **enoteca**, a bar where priority is given to the range and quality of the wines (for example, *Al Volto*). Most bars also serve some kind of food, ranging from *tramezzini* to proper cooked meals.

San Marco

Al Volta, Calle Cavalli, near Campo S. Luca. An *enoteca*, or wine bar in the true sense of the word – 1300 wines from Italy and elsewhere, some cheap, many not; good snacks too.

Harry's Bar, Calle Vallaresso; San Marco. Trendiest bar in town since time immemorial; famed in equal measure for its cocktails, its sandwiches and its celebrity-league prices.

Osteria alle Botteghe, Calle delle Botteghe. Near S. Stefano. Sumptuous sandwiches, but most lunchtimes you need a shoehorn to get in the place. Closed Sun.

Vino Vino, Ponte delle Veste. Slightly posey wine bar. However, the atmosphere improves as the evening passes, and it does stock over 100 wines. Open until at least 1am; closed Tues.

Dorsoduro

Bar Novo, Calle Lunga S. Barnaba. Good spot for a lunchtime snack.

Cantina del Vino già Schiavi, Fondamenta Nani. Great wine shop and bar opposite S. Trovaso – do some sampling before you buy.

Corner Pub, Calle della Chiesa. Looks a bit like a pub, and (like *Vino Vino*) usually has a few hooray art history students from the home counties, but is authentically Venetian nonetheless. Open until 2am; closed Tues.

Da Codroma, Fondamenta Briati. The kind of place you could sit for an hour or two with a beer and a book and feel comfortable. Interesting toasted sandwiches – brie with different sauces, for example. Shows local artists, and is a venue for poetry readings and music.

Il Caffé, Campo S. Margherita. Trendy bar with so-so food.

San Polo

Antico Dolo, Ruga Vecchia S. Giovanni. A good source of wine and snacks near the Rialto.

Do Mori, Calle Do Mori, just off Ruga Vecchia S. Giovanni A narrow, standing-only bar, catering mainly for the Rialto porters and traders, and shut at lunchtime when they all nip home. Delicious snacks and terrific atmosphere. One of the best of a number of authentic bars in the market area.

Do Spade, Sottoportego delle Do Spade. Impossible to locate from a map – walk past the *Do Mori* and keep going as straight as possible. Larger than *Do Mori* (it has tables), but a very similar place.

Cannaregio

Ai Canottieri, Ponte Tre Archi. Has live music occasionally, but as usual bar prices go up to pay the band; has a restaurant section, open till midnight.

Osteria Ai Ormesini da Aldo, Fondamenta Ormesini. One of a number of bars along this canal, and an excellent place for an al fresco midday bite.

Osteria alla Ghiacciaia, Fondamenta di Cannaregio. Small local bar with an impressive kitchen. Has one main dish which changes daily. Tends to shut early.

Osteria dalla Vedova, Calle del Pistor (parallel to the Strada Nova). Run by the same family for over a century. Mouthwatering selection of *cicheti*, wide selection of wines.

Castello

Penasa, Calle delle Rasse. Possibly the best bar for a reviving measure after a tour of the Piazza – it's just a couple of minutes from the Palazzo Ducale, off the Riva degli Schiavoni.

Nightlife, shows and festivals

Except when the Carnevale is in full swing, Venice after dark is pretty moribund. That said, the city's calendar of special events is often impressive, though the bias is definitely towards high culture. To find out what's on in the way of concerts and films, check *Un Ospite di Venezia*; for news of events outside the mainstream, check the posters.

Music and theatre

Music in Venice, to all intents and purposes, means classical music – rock bands rarely come nearer than Padua. The top-bracket **music venues** are *La Fenice*, Campo S. Fantin, San Marco (☎521.0161) and the *Teatro Goldoni*, Calle Goldoni, San Marco (☎520.5422). *La Fenice* isn't as expensive as some other opera and ballet houses, but it isn't in the first division any more either. Tickets start at about L20,000, and are usually snapped up promptly. Music performances at the *Goldoni* are somewhat less frequent, but the repertoire here isn't as strait-laced, with a jazz series cropping up on the schedule every now and then.

Classical concerts are also performed at the *Palazzo Prigione Vecchie*, the *Scuola Grande di San Giovanni Evangelista* and the churches of *Santo Stefano*, *I Frari* and *La Pietà*. The state radio service records concerts at the *Palazzo Labia*, to which the public are admitted free of charge, as long as seats are reserved in advance (☎716.666).

Upbeat and downmarket from the theatre and classical concerts, some **bars** have live music: the main ones are *Paradiso Perduto* (usually jazz), *Ai Canottieri* (hot and sweaty dancing) and *Da Codroma* – addresses on the previous pages. They don't charge for entrance, but a mark-up on the drinks pays for the bands.

Exhibitions – and the Biennale

In addition to those permanent museums which hold one-off exhibitions from time to time, Venice has numerous venues for temporary shows, of which the Fiat-owned **Palazzo Grassi** maintains the highest production values. There's also the **Venice Biennale** set up in 1895 as a showpiece for international contemporary art, and held every odd-numbered year from June to September. Its permanent site in the Giardini Pubblici has pavilions for about forty countries (the largest for Italy's representatives), plus space for a thematic international exhibition. Supplementing this central part of the Biennale is the *Aperto* ("Open"), a mixed exhibition showing the work of younger, or less established artists – often more exciting than the main event. The *Aperto* takes over spaces all over the city: the salt warehouses on the Záttere, for instance, or the Corderie in the Arsenale. Over and above this, various sites throughout the city host fringe exhibitions, installations and performances, particularly in the opening weeks.

Tickets for the whole Biennale cost L10,000, but it's possible to buy tickets for individual parts of the show. Exhibits from earlier years, plus a fabulous collection of magazines and catalogues from all over the world, are kept in the **archive** in the Palazzo Corner della Regina, close to Ca' Pésaro; entrance is free.

Festivals

The Carnevale and the Film Festival might be the best publicised of the city's festivals, but the calendar is strewn with other special events, most of them with religious or commemorative origins.

CARNEVALE

The Venice **Carnevale** occupies the ten days leading up to Lent, finishing on Shrove Tuesday with a masked ball for the glitterati, and dancing in the Piazza for the plebs. Revived spontaneously in the 1970s, it is now supported by the city authorities, who now organise various pageants and performances. (Details from the San Marco tourist office.) Apart from these events, Carnevale is an endless parade. During the day people don costumes and go to the Piazza to be photographed, while business types can be seen doing their shopping in the classic white mask, black cloak and tricorne hat. In the evening some congregate in the remoter squares, while those who have spent hundreds of pounds on their costumes install themselves in the windows of *Florian*'s and pose for a while. **Masks** are on sale throughout the year in Venice, but new mask and costume shops suddenly appear during Carnevale, and Campo San Maurizio sprouts a marquee with mask-making demonstrations and a variety of designs for sale.

LA SENSA

The feast of **La Sensa** happens in May on the Sunday after Ascension Day – the latter the day on which the doge performed the wedding of Venice to the sea. The ritual has recently been revived – a distinctly feeble procession which ends with the mayor and a gang of other dignitaries getting into a present-day approximation of the *Bucintoro* (the state barge) and sailing off to the Lido. Of more interest is the **Vogalonga** (long row), held on the same day. Open to any crew in any class of rowing boat, it covers a 32-kilometre course from the Bacino di San Marco out to Burano and back; the competitors arrive at the bottom of the Canal Grande anywhere between about 11am and 3pm.

SANTA MARIA DELLA SALUTE

Named after the church of the Salute, this centuries-old feast day is a reminder of the devastating plague of 1630–31. The church was built in thanks for deliverance from the outbreak, and every November 21 since then the Venetians have processed over a pontoon bridge across the Canal Grande to give thanks for their good health, or to pray for sick friends and relatives. It offers the only chance to see the church as it was designed to be seen – with its main doors open, and with hundreds of people milling up the steps and round the building.

LA FESTA DEL REDENTORE

Another plague-related festival, this time to mark the end of the 1576 epidemic. Celebrated on the third Sunday in July, the day is centred on Palladio's church of the Redentore, which was built by way of thanksgiving for the city's escape. A bridge of boats is strung across the Giudecca canal to allow the faithful to walk over to the church, and on the Saturday night hundreds of people row out for a picnic on the water. The night ends with a grand fireworks display, after which it's traditional to make for the Lido to watch the sun rise.

THE REGATA STORICA

Held on the first Sunday in September, the **Regata Storica** is the annual trail of strength and skill for the city's gondoliers and other expert rowers. It starts with a procession of richly decorated historic craft along the Canal Grande course, their crews all decked out in period dress. Bystanders are expected to join in the support for the contestants in the main event, and may even be issued with appropriate colours.

THE FILM FESTIVAL

The **Venice Film Festival** – the world's oldest – takes place on the Lido every year in late August and early September. The tourist office will have the festival programme a few weeks in advance, as will the two cinemas where the films are shown – the main **Palazzo del Cinema** (Lungomare G. Marconi) and the **Astra** (Via Corfu). Tickets are available for the general public, but you have to go along and queue for them on the day of performance. Outside the festival season, the *Palazzo* and *Astra* are run as ordinary commercial cinemas.

Listings

Airlines *Alitalia*, Salizzada San Moisè, San Marco 1463 (☎520.0355); *British Airways*, Riva degli Schiavoni, Castello 4191 (☎528.5026); *TWA*, Salizzada San Moisè, San Marco 1475 (☎520.3219).

Airport enquiries Marco Polo airport, ☎66.1111.

Books A good general bookshop is *Goldoni*, Calle dei Fabbri, San Marco. For art books, *Fantoni Libri*, Salizzada San Luca, San Marco. For books on Venice, *Filippi Editore Venezia*, Calle della Bissa, San Marco, and Calle del Paradiso, Castello.

Bus enquiries For *ACTV* land buses ☎528.7886; for information on the city water buses ☎700.310.

Car hire The major companies have offices at Marco Polo airport and at Piazzale Roma in Venice.

Car parks Venice's car parks are at Piazzale Roma and Tronchetto, at the end of the causeway from the mainland. Additional summer facilities at Fusina, linked to Venice by a *vaporetto* service.

Consulates *UK*, Dorsoduro 1051, by the Accademia (☎522.7207). The nearest US consulate is in Milan, while travellers from Ireland, Australia, New Zealand and Canada should contact their Rome consulates.

Exchange Banks are concentrated around Campo San Bartolomeo and along Calle Larga XXII Marzo.

Hospital *Ospedale Civili Riunti di Venezia*, Campo Santi Giovanni e Paolo (☎520.5622).

Laundry *Lavaget*, Fondamenta Pescaria, off Rio Terrà San Leonardo, Cannaregio.

Left luggage Train station left-luggage desk open 24hr; L1500 per item.

Lost property If you lose something on the train or at the station call ☎716.122; on the *vaporetti* ☎780.310; in the city itself ☎520.8844.

Pharmacies A list of late-night pharmacies is printed in *Un Ospite di Venezia*, and is available by ringing ☎192.

Police Emergency ☎113; the *Questura*, for passport problems, reporting thefts and so on, is on Fondamenta San Lorenzo, Castello (☎520.0754).

Post office Central post office is in the Fondaco dei Tedeschi, by the Rialto bridge (Mon–Sat 8.15am–7pm); main branch office in Calle dell'Ascensione (Mon–Fri 8.10am–1.25pm, Sat 8.10am–noon).

Public showers *Albergo Diurnale* at the train station and in Calle dell'Ascensione (9am–7.30pm).

Telephones 24-hr booths at train station. *SIP* offices next to Rialto post office (8.15am–6.45pm) and at Piazzale Roma (8am–9.30pm).

Train enquiries ☎715.555.

THE VENETO

Virtually every acre of the Veneto bears the imprint of Venetian rule. In **Belluno**, right under the crags of the Dolomites, the style of the buildings declares the town's former allegiance. A few kilometres away, the Lion of Saint Mark looks over the central square of the hill town of **Feltre**, as it does over the market square of **Verona**, on the Veneto's western edge. On the flatlands of the Po basin (the southern border of the region) and on farming estates all over the Veneto, the elegant **villas** of the Venetian nobility are still standing.

Yet the Veneto is as diverse culturally as it is geographically. The aspects of Verona that make the city so attractive were created long before the expansion of Venice's *terra firma* empire, and in **Padua** – a university seat since the thirteenth century – the civilisation of the Renaissance displays a character quite distinct from that which evolved in Venice. Even in **Vicenza**, which reached its present form mainly during its long period of subservience, the very appearance of the streets is proof of a fundamental independence.

Nowadays this is one of Italy's wealthiest regions. Verona, Padua, Vicenza and **Treviso**, 30km north of Venice, are all major industrial and commercial centres, while intensive dairies, fruit farms and vineyards (around Conegliano, for example) have made the Veneto a leading agricultural producer too.

The Veneto's densest concentration of industry is at **Mestre** and **Marghera**, the grim conurbation through which all road and rail lines from Venice pass before spreading out over the mainland. It's less a city than an economic life-support system for Venice, and the negative impression you get on your way through is entirely justified. Some people trim their holiday expenses by staying in Mestre's cheaper hotels (Venice's tourist offices will supply addresses), but venturing further inland is a more pleasurable cost-cutting exercise.

The Brenta

The southernmost of the three main rivers that empty into the Venetian lagoon, the **Brenta** caused no end of trouble to the earliest settlers on both the mainland and the islands, with its frequent flooding and its deposits of silt. By the sixteenth century, though, the canalisation of the river had brought it under control, and it became a favoured building site for the Venetian aristocracy. Some of these Venetian villas were built as a combination of summer residence and farmhouse – many, however, were intended solely for the former function. The period from mid-June to mid-November was the season of the *villeggiatura*, when the patrician families of Venice would load their best furniture onto barges and set off for the relative coolness of the Brenta.

Around one hundred villas are left standing on the river between Padua and Venice: some are derelict, a large number are still inhabited and a handful are open to the public. Of this last category, two are outstanding – the Villa Fóscari and the Villa Pisani – both of which are easily accessible by bus from Venice: an hourly *ACTV* bus goes to the former (L1000) and the half-hourly Padua buses go past the latter (L3100). Don't be tempted by the widely advertised trip along the Brenta on board a boat named the *Burchiello*, after the vessel that used to transport the gentry to their summer abodes – it costs L98,000 and stops longer for lunch than it does at any of the villas.

The Villa Fóscari

The **Villa Fóscari** at **MALCONTENTA** (April–Oct Tues, Sat and first Sun of each month 9am–noon; L10,000) was designed in 1559 by Palladio, and is the nearest of his villas to Venice. Most of Palladio's villas fall into two broad groups: those built on cohesive farming estates, with a central low block for living quarters and wings for storage and associated uses (the Villa Barbaro at Masèr and the Villa Emo near Castelfranco); and the large, single-block villas, built for land-owners whose fields were dispersed or in some way unsuitable for the construction of a major building. The Villa Fóscari is the masterpiece of this second group, powerfully evoking the architecture of ancient Rome by its heavily rusticated exterior, its massive Ionic portico and its two-storey main hall – a space inspired by the baths of Rome.

The frescoes in the living rooms include what is said to be a portrait of a woman of the Fóscari family who was exiled here as punishment for an amorous escapade, and whose subsequent misery, according to legend, was the source of the name *Malcontenta*. The reality is more prosaic – the area was known by that name long before the Fóscari arrived, either because of some local discontent over the development of the land or because of the political *malcontenti* who used to hide out in the nearby salt marshes.

The Villa Pisani

The **Villa Pisani** (or Nazionale) at **STRA** (villa and grounds open Tues–Sun: June–Sept 9am–6pm; Oct–May 9am–1.30pm; L6000), virtually on the outskirts of Padua, looks more like a product of the *ancien régime* than a house for the Venetian gentry. Commissioned by way of celebration when Alvise Pisani was elected Doge of Venice in 1735, it was the biggest such residence to be built in Venetian territory during that century. It has appealed to megalomaniacs ever since: Napoleon bought it off the Pisani in 1807 and handed it over to Eugène Beauharnais, his stepson and Viceroy of Italy; and in 1934 it was the place chosen for the first meeting of Mussolini and Hitler.

Entry to the suite of rooms on the main floor of the villa is carefully controlled – you're shepherded round in groups of thirty – and most of what you see is unexciting. But then there's the ballroom, its ceiling covered with a fresco of *The Apotheosis of the Pisani Family*, painted by Giambattista Tiepolo at the age of 66. It's a dazzling performance, as full of blue space as it could be without falling apart; and if you're trying to puzzle out what's going on – the Pisani family, accompanied by Venice, are being courted by the Arts, Sciences and Spirits of Peace, while Fame plays a fanfare in praise of the Pisani and the Madonna looks on with appropriate pride.

Padua

Extensively reconstructed after the damage caused by bombing in the last war, and hemmed in by the sprawl which has accompanied its development as the most important economic centre of the Veneto, **PADUA** (PADOVA) is not immediately the most alluring city in northern Italy. It is, however, one of the most ancient, and plentiful evidence remains of its impressive lineage.

A Roman municipium from 45 BC, the city thrived until the barbarian onslaughts and the subsequent Lombard invasion at the start of the seventh century. Recovery was slow, but by the middle of the twelfth century, when it became a free commune, Padua was prosperous once again. The university was founded in 1221, and a decade later the city became a place of pilgrimage following the death here of Saint Anthony.

In 1337 the **Da Carrara** family established control. Under their domination, Padua's cultural eminence was secured – Giotto, Dante and Petrarch were among those attracted here – but Carraresi territorial ambitions led to conflict with Venice, and in 1405 the city's independence ended with its conquest by the neighbouring republic. Though politically nullified, Padua remained an artistic and intellectual centre: Donatello and Mantegna both worked here, and in the seventeenth century Galileo researched at the university, where the medical faculty was one of the most ambitious in Europe. With the fall of the Venetian Republic the city passed to Napoleon, who handed it over to the Austrians, after whose regime Padua was annexed to Italy 1866.

Information and accommodation

The **tourist office** is at the train station (Mon–Sat 9am–6pm, Sun 9am–noon; ☎049/875.2077). Walk straight ahead from the station for the central **post office** at Corso Garibaldi 5 (Mon–Fri 8am–8pm, Sat 8am–noon) and the 24-hour *ASST* **telephones** booths at Corso Garibaldi 7. At the main sights you can buy the Padua *biglietto unico* which costs L10,000 and allows one visit to each of the city's museums and monuments.

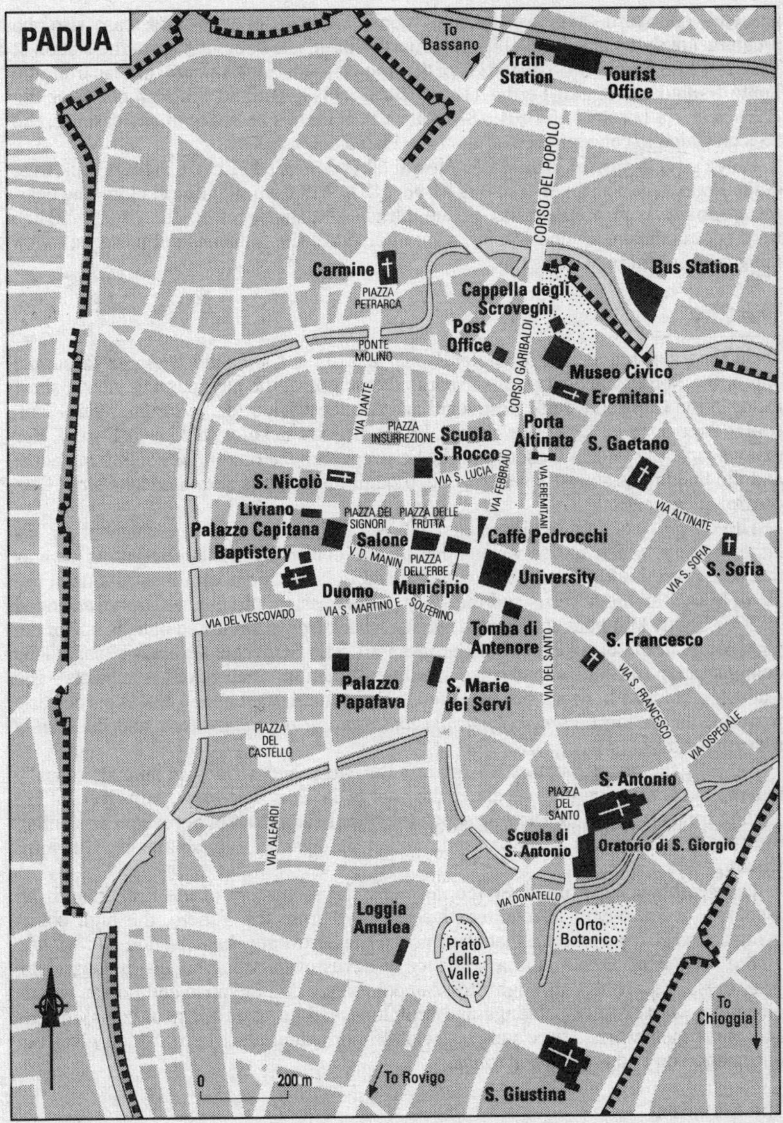

The tourist office has long lists of one-star hotels, with doubles from L38,000. A spacious, clean and friendly place is the *Albergo Pace*, near the Piazza della Frutta at Via Papafava 3 (☎049/8751566; ③); the centrally located *Verdi*, Via Dondi dell'Orologio 7 (☎049/663.450; ③) is in the same price range, as is the *Junior*, close to the station at Via L. Faggin 2 (☎049/611.756; ③). Averaging at around L20,000 more expensive is the *Bellevue*, off the Prato della Valle at Via L. Belludi 11 (☎049/875.5547; ④); it has a peaceful courtyard and well-tended rooms. A trio of two-stars can also be recommended: the large and efficiently run *Al Cason*, a few minutes from the station at Via Fra Paolo Sarpi 40 (☎049/662.636; ⑤); the pleasant *Sant'Antonio*, not far from the Ponte Molino at Via San Fermo 118 (☎049/875.1393; ④); and the *Fagiano*, near the Basilica at Via Locatelli 45 (☎049/875.3396; ⑤). If there's no space in any of these, the area on which to concentrate is around the Piazza del Santo.

Padua's *IYHF* **hostel** is at Via A. Aleardi 30 (☎049/875.2219; ①), a short walk west of the Prato della Valle – or take bus #3, #8, #12 or #18 from the train station. The nearest **campsite** is in Montegrotto Terme, Strada Romana Aponese 104 (☎049/793400; frequent trains take around 15min); a very upmarket site, it boasts not merely a swimming pool but thermal baths too.

The City

From the train station, the Corso del Popolo and Corso Garibaldi lead south through a gap in the Renaissance city walls towards the centre of the city, passing after a short distance the **Cappella degli Scrovegni** and **Museo Civico** (daily: summer 9am–7pm; winter 9am–5.30pm; L3000 for chapel; L8000 for joint ticket with Museo Civico). For many people the **Giotto frescoes** in the Scrovegni are *the* reason for coming to Padua, and the building is almost invariably full, though the crush is alleviated by a strict time control on large groups.

The chapel was commissioned in 1303 by Enrico Scrovegni in atonement for his father's usury, which was so vicious that he was denied a Christian burial. As soon as the walls were built, Giotto was commissioned to cover them with illustrations of the life of Mary, the life of Jesus and the story of the Passion; the finished cycle, arranged in three tightly knit tiers and painted against a backdrop of saturated blue, is one of the high points in the development of European art. The Scrovegni series is a marvellous demonstration of Giotto's innovative attention to the inner nature of his subjects – the exchange of looks between the two shepherds in the *Arrival of Joachim* is particularly powerful, as are the *Embrace of Joachim and Anna at the Golden Gate* and the *Visit of Mary to Elizabeth*.

Beneath the main pictures are shown the vices and virtues in human (usually female) form, while on the wall above the door is the *Last Judgement*, with rivers of fire leading from God to Hell. Directly above the door is a portrait of Scrovegni presenting the chapel; his tomb is at the far end, behind the altar with its statues by **Giovanni Pisano**.

The neighbouring **Museo Civico**, formerly the monastery of the Eremitani, is an assembly of fourteenth- to eighteenth-century art from the Veneto, the high points being a *Crucifixion* by Giotto that was once in the Scrovegni chapel, a fine *Portrait of a Young Senator* by Bellini, and a sequence of devils overcoming angels by Guariento. After these, it's a trudge through Etruscan pot-shards, dull Egyptian and Roman works, dire nineteenth-century paintings and sculpture, and an assortment of coins, medals and other metalwork. There's also a helpful information desk here, which gives out information on Padua's cultural events.

The Eremitani

The nearby church of the **Eremitani**, built at the turn of the fourteenth century, was almost completely wrecked by an Allied bombing raid in 1944 and has been fastidiously rebuilt (summer Mon–Sat 8.15am–noon & 3.30–6.30pm, Sun 9am–noon & 3.30–5.30pm; winter Mon–Sat closes 5.30pm, Sun closes 5pm). Photographs to the left of the apse show the extent of the damage, the worst aspect of which was the near-total destruction of **Mantegna**'s frescoes of the lives of Saint James and Saint Christopher – the war's severest blow to Italy's artistic heritage.

Produced between 1454 and 1457, when Mantegna was in his mid-twenties, the frescoes were unprecedented in the thoroughness with which they exploited fixed-point perspective – a concept central to Renaissance humanism, with its emphasis on the primacy of individual perception. The extent of his achievement can now be assessed only from the fuzzy photographs and the sad fragments preserved in the chapel to the right of the high altar. On the left wall is the *Martyrdom of St James*, put together from fragments found in the rubble; and on the right is the *Martyrdom of St Christopher*, which had been removed from the wall before the war.

Piazza del Santo and the Basilica

Apart from the encampment of stalls selling decorated candles and outsize souvenir rosaries, the main sight of the Piazza del Santo is Donatello's **Monument to Gattamelata** ("The Honeyed Cat"), as the *condottiere* Erasmo da Narni was known. He died in 1443 and this monument was raised ten years later, the earliest large bronze sculpture of the Renaissance. It's a direct precursor to Verrocchio's monument to Colleoni in Venice, but could hardly be more different: Gattemelata was known for his honesty and dignity, and Donatello has given us an image of comparative sensitivity and restraint, quite unlike Verrocchio's image of power through force. The modelling of the horse makes a double allusion: to the equestrian statue of Marcus Aurelius in Rome, and to the horses of San Marco.

Within eighteen months of his death, Saint Anthony had been canonised and his tomb was attracting enough pilgrims to warrant the building of the Basilica di San Antonio, or **Il Santo** (daily: summer 6.30am–7.45pm; winter 6.30am–7pm). It was not until the start of the fourteenth century that the church reached a state that enabled the saint's body to be placed in the Cappella del Santo (in the left transept). Plastered with such votive offerings as photographs of limbs healed by the saint's intervention, the shrine is irresistible to the voyeur. The chapel's more formal decoration includes a sequence of nine panels showing scenes from Saint Anthony's life; carved between 1505 and 1577, they are the most important series of relief sculpture created in sixteenth-century Italy.

Adjoining the chapel is the Cappella della Madonna Mora (named after its fourteenth-century French altar statue), which in turn lets onto the Cappella del Beato Luca, whose fourteenth-century frescoes include a lovely image of Saint James lifting a prison tower to free a prisoner. Back in the aisle, just outside the Cappella del Santo, is Padua's finest work by Pietro Lombardo, the monument to Antonio Roselli (1467). More impressive still are the high altar's bronze sculptures and reliefs by Donatello (1444–45), the works which introduced Renaissance classicism to Padua. Built onto the farthest point of the ambulatory, the Cappella del Tesoro (8am–noon & 2.30–7pm) houses the tongue and chin of Saint Anthony, kept in a head-shaped reliquary.

The south side of the Piazza

To the left as you leave the Basilica are the **Oratorio di San Giorgio** and **Scuola di Santo** (daily Feb–March & Oct–Nov 9am–12.30pm & 2.30–4.30pm; April–Sept 8.30am–12.30pm & 2.30–6.30pm; Dec–Jan 9am–12.30pm; L1000). The Oratorio was founded in 1377 as a mortuary chapel, and its frescoes by **Altichiero di Zevio** and **Jacopo Avanzi** were completed soon after. One wall is adorned by the wonderfully titled *St Lucy Remains Immoveable at an Attempt to Drag Her with the Help of Oxen to a House of Ill Repute.*

The *scuola* was founded soon after Anthony's canonisation, though this building only goes back as far as the early fifteenth century. The ground floor is still used for religious purposes, while upstairs is maintained pretty much as it would have looked in the sixteenth century, with its fine ceiling and paintings dating mainly from 1509–15. Four of the pictures are said to be by Titian.

Next door to the *scuola*, the **Museo al Santo** is used for one-off exhibitions, often drawing on the resources of the Museo Civico.

One way to relax from all this art is to stroll round the corner to the **Orto Botanico**, the oldest botanic gardens in Europe (May to mid-Sept Mon–Fri 9am–1pm & 3–6pm, Sat & Sun 9am–1pm; March, April & mid-Sept to Oct Mon–Sat 9am–1pm, Sun 9.30am–1pm; Nov–Feb Mon–Sat 9am–1pm; L3000). Planted in 1545 by the university's medical faculty as a collection of medicinal herbs, the gardens are laid out much as they were originally, and the specimens on show haven't changed too much either. Goethe came here in 1786 to see a palm tree that had been planted in 1585; the selfsame tree still stands.

The Prato della Valle and Santa Giustina

A little to the south sprawls the **Prato della Valle**, claimed to be the largest town square in Italy; it's a cheerless area, ringed by over-wide roads, and even the summer funfair does little to make it jollier.

One side is fronted by the sixteenth-century **Basilica di Santa Giustina** (Mon–Sat 7.30am–noon & 3.30–7.30pm, Sun 7am–1pm & 3.30–7.30pm). A pair of fifteenth-century griffins, one holding a knight and the other a lion, are the only notable adornments to the unclad brick facade; the freezing interior has little of interest except a huge *Martyrdom of St Justina* by Paolo Veronese (in the apse), some highly proficient carving on the choir stalls, and the sarcophagus which once contained the relics of Luke the Evangelist (apse of left transept).

More appealing are the vestiges of the church's earlier incarnations. In the right transept a stone arch opens onto the **Martyrs' Corridor**, a composite of fifth- to twelfth-century architectural fragments that leads to the **Sacellum di Santa Maria e San Prosdocimo**, burial place of Saint Prosdocimus. He was the first bishop of Padua back in the fourth century, when the church was founded, and is depicted here on a fifth-century panel. The fifteenth-century **old choir**, reached by a chain of corridors from the left-hand chapel of the right transept, has choir stalls inset with splendid marquetry panels.

To the university

Via Umberto leads towards the **university**, the main block of which is the **Palazzo del Bò** (The Ox – named after an inn that used to stand here). Established in September 1221, the University of Padua is older than any other in Italy except that of Bologna, and the coats of arms which encrust the courtyard and Great Hall attest to the social and intellectual rank of its alumni. The first permanent **anatomy theatre** was built here in 1594, a facility that doubtless greatly helped William Harvey, who went on to develop the theory of blood circulation after taking his degree here in 1602. Galileo taught physics here from 1592 to 1610, declaiming from a lectern that is still on show. And in 1678 Elena Lucrezia Corner Piscopia became the first woman to collect a university degree when she was awarded her doctorate in philosophy here – there's a statue of her in the courtyard. At the moment the Bò is undergoing a major restoration, and visits have to be arranged by phone (☎049/828.3111); controversy rages over whether the public should be allowed in *en masse* when the work is finished.

The central squares

The area north and west of the university forms the hub of the city. A little way up from the university, on the left, is the **Caffè Pedrocchi**, which used to be the city's main intellectual salon; it's no longer that, but it does have a multiplicity of functions – chic café, concert hall and conference centre.

The **Piazza delle Frutta** and **Piazza delle Erbe**, the sites of Padua's daily markets, are lined by bars, restaurants and shops. Separating them is the extraordinary **Palazzo**

della Ragione or **Salone** (Tues–Sun summer 10am–6pm; winter 10am–4pm; L4000) – at the time of its construction in the 1210s this vast hall was the largest room to have been built on top of another storey. Its decoration would once have been as astounding as its size, but the original frescoes by Giotto and his assistants were destroyed by fire in 1420, though some by Giustio de'Menabuoi have survived; most of the extant frescoes are by Nicola Miretto (1425–40). Mainly used as the city council's assembly hall, it was also a place where Padua's citizens could plead for justice – hence the appellation *della Ragione*, meaning "of reason". The gigantic wooden horse with disproportionately gigantic gonads is modelled on Donatello's *Gattamelata*, and was made for a joust in 1466.

The duomo and baptistery

Close by is Padua's **Duomo** (closed 12.30–3pm), an unlovely church whose architect cribbed his design from drawings by Michelangelo. The adjacent Romanesque **Baptistery**, though, is one of the unproclaimed delights of Padua (April–Sept Tues–Sun 9.30am–12.30pm & 2.30–6.30pm; Oct–March Tues–Sat 9.30am–12.30pm & 2.30–5.30pm, Sun 9.30am–12.30pm; L3000). Built by the Da Carraras in the thirteenth century, it's lined with fourteenth-century frescoes by Giusto de'Menabuoi, a cycle which makes a fascinating comparison with Giotto's in the Cappella degli Scrovegni. The influence of Giotto is plain, but in striving for greater realism Giusto has lost Giotto's monumentality and made some of his figures awkward and unconvincing. Yet many of the scenes are delightful, and the vibrancy of their colours, coupled with the size and relative quiet of the building, make the visit memorable.

Eating, drinking and nightlife

Catering for the midday stampede of ravenous students, Padua's bars generally produce weightier **snacks** than the routine *tremezzini* – slabs of pizza and sandwiches vast enough to satisfy a glutton are standard. A good variety of stand-up meals is offered at the *rosticceria* in Via Daniele Manin, while *La Mappa*, Via Matteotti 17, offers decent self-service fare. For a more relaxed session at only slightly greater expense, three of the best cheap **restaurants** are *Da Giovanni* at Via De Cristoforis 1, *7 Teste* at Via C. Battisti 44, and *Al Pero* on Via S. Lucia. On Piazza Cavour, *Pepen* has a wonderful range of pizzas, with seats on the square in summer. For something special, the place to go is *Vecchia Padova*, Via C. Battisti 37.

Padua's **bars** have far longer opening hours than are common in Venice – many don't close until 2am – and new places spring up as often as established ones revamp their image. Currently trendy are *Alla Ventura*, Via SS. Martino e Solferino, and *Al Coccodrillo*, Riviera S. Benedetto 154. For something a bit more hip, try the devil's grotto ambience of *Lucifer Young*, in Via Altinate. Nightlife fluctuates in synch with term time; check the posters up around the city, and particularly around the university, for details of music, theatre and such like. Of the local newspapers, the most comprehensive for **listings** is *Il Mattino*. Padua's half-dozen regular **discos** are all fairly low-octane places: liveliest are *Wag*, Via Savonarola 149, and the flashier *Extra Extra*, Via Ciamician.

South of Padua

Of the small towns to the **south of Padua** the most enticing are **Monsélice**, which has a superbly restored castle, and **Montagnana**, whose medieval town walls have survived in almost pristine form. And if you need a rest from urban pursuits, the green **Colli Euganei** (Euganean Hills) offer a pleasant excursion, while the **Po Delta**'s nature reserves and beaches are the quietest stretches of coastline in the area.

The Colli Euganei

A few kilometres to the southwest of Padua the **Colli Euganei** (Euganean Hills) rise abruptly out of the plains, their slopes patched with vineyards between the scattered villages, villas and churches. Between Padua and the hills lie the spa towns of **ÁBANO TERME** and **MONTEGROTTO TERME**, which for much of the year are crowded with people looking for cures or beauty treatment from the radioactive waters and mud baths. Largely composed of big and expensive modern hotels, these really are places to avoid unless you're hell-bent on trying to poach yourself in the hot springs.

A car is a great advantage for exploring the Colli Euganei proper, as buses are few and far between. The **villas** of the region are its major architectural attractions, but many of them remain in private hands and can only be viewed from a distance. An exception is the **Villa Barbarigo** at **VALSANZIBIO**, which is famous for its extraordinary gardens; laid out in 1699, they feature a maze and fantastical Baroque gateways (May–Sept Mon 2–6.30pm, Tues–Sat 10am–noon & 2–6.30pm, Sun 2–7.30pm; March, April & Oct daily 1.30–5.30pm; L8000).

The gem of the Colli Euganei is the medieval village of **ARQUÀ PETRARCA**, most easily reached by bus from Este or Monsélice. The poet **Francesco Petrarca** (Petrarch) spent the last summers of his life here, and this is where he died. His house still stands, and his desk and chair are still intact, as are various parts of the original fabric of the interior – though the frescoes, illustrating his works, were retouched in the seventeenth century (April–Sept Sat & Sun 9.30am–12.30pm; L5000). Petrarch's sarcophagus is in the centre of the village, with one epitaph penned by him and another by his son-in-law, who placed it here.

Monsélice

Served by nine daily trains from Padua, the attractive town of **MONSÉLICE** is far more accessible than the villages nearer to the city. In earlier times it perched on the pimple of volcanic rock round the foot of which it now winds, and you pass through the remnants of its defensive walls on your way from the train station to the central Piazza Mazzini. A little way beyond the square stands Monsélice's main sight – the **Castello di Ezzelino**, or **Ca' Marcello** (tours May 1–Nov 11 Tues, Thurs & Sat 9am, 10.30am, 3.30pm & 5pm, Sun 9am & 10.30am, plus 3.30pm & 5pm on second and third Sun of month; L5000). Dating back to the eleventh century, the house was expanded in the thirteenth century by Ezzelino da Romano, who added the square tower across the courtyard. The interior was altered by the Da Carraras in the fourteenth century, and linking the two main sections is a fifteenth-century bit added by the Marcello family. The castle's immaculate appearance is down to Count Vittorio Cini, who inherited the derelict building after it had been in the tender care of the army during World War I and sank a fortune into restoring it and furnishing each section in the appropriate style.

The **Duomo Vecchio**, higher up the hill, retains fourteenth-century fresco fragments and has a Romano-Gothic polyptych on the high altar. Just beyond it, a gateway guarded by two Venetian lions gives onto the Via Sette Chiese, a private road leading up to the **Villa Duodo** (grounds open daily March–May, Sept & Oct 8am–noon & 1.30–7pm; June–Aug 7am–12.30pm & 3.30–8pm; Nov–Feb 9am–12.30pm & 1.30–7pm). The seven churches of the road's name are a small-scale version of the seven pilgrimage churches of Rome, arranged as a line of chapels leading up to the church of **San Giorgio** at the top. Sinners could earn forgiveness by praying their way up to San Giorgio, where rows of martyred saints are arranged in wood and glass cabinets. It's not possible to go up the steps to the **Rocca** – Ezzelino's citadel – as the area is now a reserve for rare birds.

The **tourist office** is in Piazza Mazzini (daily 8.30am–12.30pm & 5–8pm). Best option for **eating** is the trattoria-pizzeria *Al Campiello*, Riviera G.B. Belzoni 2. If you want to **stay**, try the one-star *Riviera*, Riviera G.B. Belzoni 9 (☎0429/72.591; ④), or the nearby *Cadorno*, Viale Cadorno 62 (☎0429/72.002; ④).

Este

If you're dependent on public transport, about the best base from which to roam around the Colli Euganei is the ceramics-producing town of **ESTE**, on the southern edge of the range and just an eight-minute train ride from Monsélice. Sporadic buses run up into the hills from here, and there's a **tourist office** for the whole Colli Euganei in the Piazza Maggiore (Mon–Sat 9am–noon & 4–7pm).

Right out of the Piazza, you come face to face with the ruined **Castello dei Carraresi**, parts of which went to build the nearby sixteenth-century palace that now houses the **Museo Nazionale Atestino** (Tues–Sat April–Sept 9am–1pm & 3–7pm; Oct–March 9am–1pm & 3–6pm; L4000). The Veneto's outstanding collection of pre-Roman artefacts is installed on the first floor, while much of the ground floor is given over to Roman remains. The room devoted to medieval pieces includes a *Madonna and Child* by Cima that was once stolen from the church of Santa Maria della Consolazione and is now here for safekeeping.

The Baroque **Duomo**, the plan of which anticipates the Pietà in Venice, contains a huge altarpiece of *St Thecla* by G. B. Tiepolo – not one of his best, maybe because it's set in a scene of pestilence and death rather than one of his light-filled heavens.

The only one-star **hotel** in town is the *Leon d'Oro*, at Viale Fiume 20 (☎0429/2955; ⑤), but the town has a pair of two-stars charging similar rates – *Centrale*, Piazza Beatrice 16 (☎0429/3930; ⑤) and *Beatrice d'Este*, Via Rimembranze 1 (☎0429/600.533; ⑤). For **food**, try *Al Gambero*, Via d'Azeglio 6, or *Da Piero Ceschi*, Piazza Trento 16.

Montagnana

The pride of **MONTAGNANA**, fifteen minutes down the train line from Este, is its **medieval city walls**, raised by the ubiquitous Ezzelino da Romano after he had virtually flattened the town in 1242. With a circumference of nearly two kilometres and twenty-four polygonal towers spaced at regular intervals, these are among the finest medieval fortifications in the country.

Gates pierce the walls at the cardinal points of the compass, the entrances to the east and west being further reinforced by fortresses. The eastern gate (Porta Padova) is protected by the **Castello di San Zeno**, built by Ezzelino in 1242. Nearby, the **Museo Civico e Archeologico** displays objects uncovered around the town (Mon–Sat 9am–noon; L1000). On the western side, the **Rocca degli Alberi** was built by the Da Carrara clan in 1362 to keep the roads from Mantua and Verona covered.

The centre of Montagnana is the Piazza Vittorio Emanuele, dominated by the late Gothic **Duomo**; Veronese's altarpiece, a *Transfiguration*, is less engaging than the huge anonymous painting of the *Battle of Lepanto* on the left as you enter – it's said to represent accurately the ships and their positions at one point in the battle.

The **tourist office** is in the Piazza (10am–noon & 4.30–7pm, closed Tues). For **accommodation**, *Ezzelino*, Via Praterie 1 (☎0429/81.673; ④) is the best deal. The splendid **youth hostel** occupies the Rocca degli Alberi (April–mid-Oct; reception 3–11pm; ☎0429/81.076; ①); if you don't have an *IYHF* card, you can join on the spot. Many of the town's hotels have **restaurants**; for the cheapest food go to *Pizzeria al Palio*, in Piazza Trieste, but for just a little more you can eat great home-made dishes at *Da Stona*, Via Carrarese 51.

Come to Montagnana on the first Sunday in September and you'll see its **Palio** – a poor relative of the costumed horse races in Siena, but enthusiastically performed, and the day finishes with a firework display.

Rovigo and beyond

ROVIGO is the capital of the fertile and often-flooded zone between the Adige and the Po, an area known as the Polésine – "Little Mesopotamia". Trains on their way to Ferrara and Bologna from Venice call here hourly, crossing another line that runs east to west – though frankly there's little reason for coming to the town except to change trains. Should you be stuck for a couple of hours waiting for a connection, though, there are a couple of places you could visit. Maps are available from the **tourist office** at Piazza Vittorio Emanuele 3 (Tues–Sat 9.30am–12.30pm & 4–7pm).

The piazza's **Pinacoteca dei Concordi** (July & Aug Mon–Sat 10am–1pm; rest of year Mon–Fri 9.30am–noon & 3.30–7pm, Sat 9.30am–noon; free) features a few eminent artists of the Veneto – Palma il Vecchio, G. B. Piazzetta and Rosalba Carriera – in less than breathtaking form. About fifteen minutes' walk in the same direction, in Piazza San Bartolomeo, is the **Museo Civico delle Civilità in Polésine** (Mon–Sat 8.30am–12.30pm; free), the main archaeological institute for the area. This is more an assemblage of pieces unearthed by the researchers than a regular museum, and you're shown round by one of the staff, whose informed commentary makes up for the uninspiring display techniques.

Fratta Polésine

A trip to **FRATTA POLÉSINE**, 18km southwest of Rovigo, will appeal to the more ardent lovers of **Palladio**'s buildings. The **Villa Badoer** (Tues–Sun summer 9am–noon & 3–7pm; winter 10am–noon & 2–5pm; free), designed in the 1560s, is one of his most eloquent flights of architectural rhetoric, with its distinctive curving colonnades linking the porticoed house to the storage spaces at the side. None of the original furnishings is left, but restorers have uncovered the villa's sixteenth-century grotesque frescoes.

Adria and the Po Delta

Heading **eastward** from Rovigo, trains leave every couple of hours for the Po Delta and Chioggia. **ADRIA**, a sleepy town of about 20,000 inhabitants, is all that is left of the port from which the Adriatic Sea got its name. It now sits on a tributary of the Po some 25km inland, owing to heavy silting in the lagoon. The only sight is the **Museo Archeologico** in Piazzale degli Etruschi (daily April–Sept 9am–1pm & 3–7pm; Oct–March closes 6pm; L2000), which has a collection of Greek and Etruscan pieces dating from the time when Adria was a major port.

It's difficult to explore the **Po Delta** properly unless you have a car, though bikes may be hired from *Vittorio Cacciatori* at Via Bologna 1 in PORTO TOLLE – to get there you have to get a bus from LOREO, a couple of train stops after Adria. *Vittorio Cacciatori* also hires out canoes, but if you prefer a less strenuous investigation of the waterways and islets, *Marino Cacciatori*, Via Varsarvia 12, runs half-day cruises in summer for around L12,000 per person – an excellent way to observe the waterfowl and other birds of the delta's nature reserve. Resorts on the delta have done a lot to clean up their act in recent years, yet upstream the pollution of the Po continues unabated, spawning blooms of algae in the waters of the upper Adriatic.

Vicenza

Europe's largest producer of textiles and the focus of Italy's "Silicon Valley", **VICENZA** is a very sleek city, where it can seem that every second car is a BMW. Modern prosperity hasn't ruined the look of Vicenza, though. The centre of the city, still partly enclosed by medieval walls, is an amalgam of Gothic and classical buildings that today looks much as it did when the last major phase of construction came to an end at the close of the eighteenth century. This historic core is compact enough to be explored in a day, but the city and its environs really require a short stay to do them justice.

In 1404 Vicenza was absorbed by Venice, and the city's numerous Gothic palaces reflect its status as a Venetian satellite. But in the latter half of the sixteenth century the city was transformed by the work of an architect who owed nothing to Venice and whose rigorous but flexible style was to influence every succeeding generation – Andrea di Pietro della Gondola, alias **Palladio**.

Born in Padua in 1508, Palladio came to Vicenza at the age of sixteen to work as a stonecutter. At thirty he became the protegé of a local nobleman, Count Giangiorgio Trissino, who directed his architectural training, gave him his classicised name, and brought him into contact with the dominant class of Vicenza. Between 1540 and his death in 1580 Palladio created around a dozen palaces and public buildings in Vicenza – projects whose variety will surprise you if you tend to associate Palladianism with blandness. Even if you've been inclined to agree with Herbert Read's opinion that "in the back of every dying civilisation there sticks a bloody Doric column", you might well leave Vicenza converted.

The City

The main street of Vicenza, the **Corso Andrea Palladio**, cuts right through the old centre from the Piazza Castello down to the Piazza Matteotti, and is lined with palaces, all of them now occupied by shops, offices and banks. Palladio's last palace, the fragmentary **Palazzo Porto-Breganze**, stands on the far side of Piazza Castello; no. 163 on the Corso, the **Casa Cogollo**, is known as the *Casa del Palladio*, though he never lived there and few people think he designed it.

The Museo Civico and Teatro Olimpico

The Corso ends with one of the architect's most imperious buildings, the **Palazzo Chiericati** (begun in 1550), now home of the **Museo Civico** (Tues–Sat 9.30am–noon & 2.30–5pm, Sun 9.30am–noon; L3000, combined ticket for Museo Civico & Santa Corona museum L5000). The core of the picture collection is made up of Vicentine artists, none of whose work will knock you flat on your back; it's left to a few more celebrated names – Memling, Tintoretto, Veronese, Tiepolo – to make the visit memorable.

Across the Piazza Matteotti is the one building in Vicenza you shouldn't fail to go into – the **Teatro Olimpico**, the oldest indoor theatre in Europe (March 16–Oct 15 Mon–Sat 9.30am–12.20pm & 3–5.30pm, Sun 9.30am–12.20pm; Oct 16–March 15 9.30am–12.20pm & 2–4.30pm; Sun 9.30am–12.20pm; L5000). Approached in 1579 by the members of the Olympic Academy (a society dedicated to the study of the humanities) to produce a design for a permanent theatre, Palladio devised a covered amphitheatre derived from his reading of Vitruvius and his studies of Roman structures in Italy and France. He died soon after work commenced, and the scheme was then overseen by Scamozzi, who added to Palladio's design the backstage perspective of a Classical city, creating the illusion of long urban vistas by tilting the "streets" at an alarming angle. The theatre opened on March 3, 1585, with an extravagant production of *Oedipus Rex*, and is still used for plays and concerts.

The Piazza dei Signori

At the hub of the city, the **Piazza dei Signori**, stands the most awesome of Palladio's creations – the **Basilica**. Designed in the late 1540s (but not finished until the second decade of the next century), this was Palladio's first public project and secured his reputation. The monumental regularity of the Basilica disguises the fact that the Palladian building is effectively a stupendous piece of buttressing – the Doric and Ionic

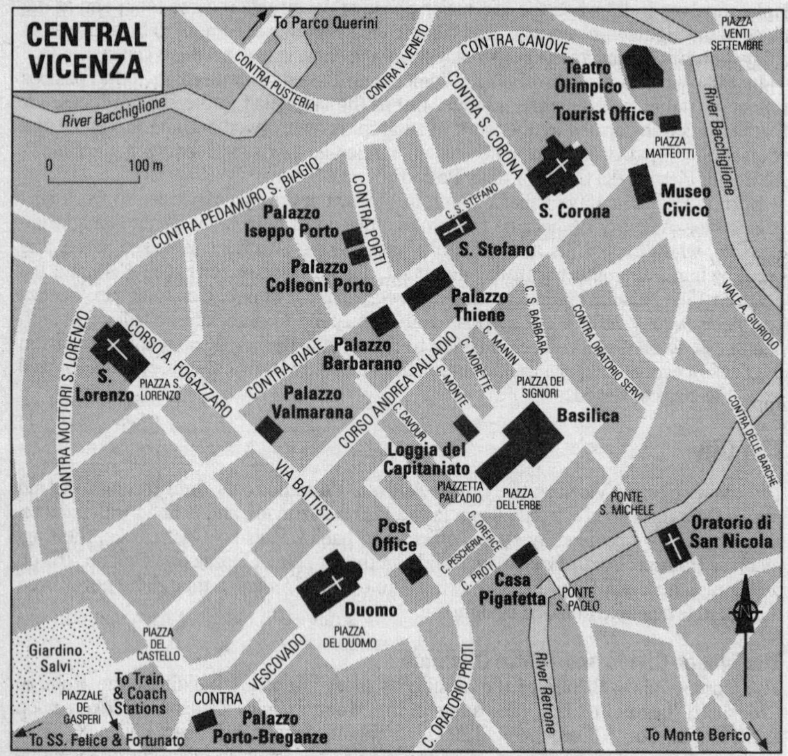

colonnades enclose the fifteenth-century hall of the city council, an unstable structure which had defied a number of attempts to prop it up before Palladio's solution was put into effect. The vast Gothic hall is often used for exhibitions (Tues–Sat 9.30am–noon & 2.30–5pm, Sun 9.30am–noon; free).

As in the sixteenth century, a daily fruit, vegetable and flower market is pitched at the back of the Basilica, in the **Piazza dell'Erbe**; if you're shopping for picnic food, you'll save money by going down the slope and over the river, where the shops are a good bit cheaper. On Tuesdays a general market spreads along the roads between the Basilica and the duomo.

A late Palladio building, the unfinished **Loggia del Capitaniato** faces the Basilica across the Piazza dei Signori. Built as accommodation for the Venetian military commander of the city, it's decorated with reliefs in celebration of the Venetian victory over the Turks at Lepanto in 1571.

The Churches

The **Duomo** was bombed flat in 1944 and carefully reconstructed after the war; it's a rather gloomy place, chiefly distinguished as one of the few Italian cathedrals to be overwhelmed by its secular surroundings. Far more interesting is **Santa Corona** (summer daily 9.30am–12.30pm & 3.30–6.30pm; winter daily 9.30am–12.30pm & 3–6pm), on the other side of the Corso Palladio (at the Piazza Matteotti end), a

Dominican church dating from the mid-thirteenth century. Here you'll find two of the three great church paintings in Vicenza – *The Baptism of Christ*, a late work by Giovanni Bellini, and *The Adoration of the Magi*, painted in 1573 by Paolo Veronese. The cloisters now house a run-of-the-mill Museo Naturalistico-Archeologico (same hours as Museo Civico; L3000, or L5000 for combined ticket).

The nearby **Santo Stefano** (daily 9–11am & 4–6.30pm) contains the third of the city's fine church paintings: Palma Vecchio's typically stolid and voluptuous *Madonna and Child with SS George and Lucy*.

Contrà Porti, Corso Fogazzaro and the parks

Santo Stefano faces a corner of the huge **Palazzo Thiene**, another of Palladio's palaces. It was planned to occupy the entire block down to Corso Palladio, but in the end work progressed no further than the addition of this wing to the existing fifteenth-century house. The facade of the old building is in Contrà Porti, a street which demonstrates the way in which the builders of Vicenza grafted new houses onto old without doing violence to the line of the street; the palaces here span two centuries, yet the overall impression is one of cohesion. Outstanding are the fourteenth-century **Palazzo Colleoni Porto** (no. 19) and Palladio's neighbouring **Palazzo Iseppo Porto**, designed a few years after the Thiene palace. The parallel Corso Fogazzaro completes the itinerary of major Palladian buildings, with the **Palazzo Valmarana** (no. 16), perhaps the most eccentric of Palladio's projects – notice the gigantic stucco figures at the sides of the facade, where you'd expect columns to be.

Contrà Porti takes you towards the Pusterla bridge and the **Parco Querini**, the biggest expanse of green in the city, enlivened by a decorative hillock populated by ducks, rabbits and peacocks. Vicenza's other refuge for the brick-wearied, the **Giardino Salvi** (at the end of the road running straight up from the train station), is a more modest and artificial affair of winding gravel paths and fountains.

The outskirts – Monte Bérico and the villas

In 1426 Vicenza was struck by bubonic plague, during the course of which outbreak the Virgin appeared twice at the summit of **Monte Bérico** – the hill on the southern edge of the city – to announce the city's deliverance. The chapel raised on the site of her appearance became a place of pilgrimage, and at the end of the seventeenth century was replaced by the present **Basilica di Monte Bérico**. Buses climb the hill from the coach station every thirty minutes or so; on foot it takes around twenty-five minutes from the centre of town.

Pilgrims regularly arrive here by the coachload, and the glossy interior of the church is immaculately maintained to receive them; a well-stocked shop in the cloister sells devotional trinkets to the faithful. The sceptical should venture into the church for Montagna's *Pietà* (in the chapel to the right of the apse) and *The Supper of St Gregory the Great* by Veronese (in the refectory). The latter, the prototype of *The Feast in the House of Levi* in Venice's Accademia, was used for bayonet practice by Austrian troops in 1848 – the small reproduction outside the refectory shows what a thorough job they did on it.

THE VILLA VALMARANA

Ten minutes' walk away from Monte Bérico is the **Villa Valmarana "ai Nani"**, an undistinguished house made extraordinary by the decorations of Giambattista and Giandomenico Tiepolo (March 15–April 30 Tues–Sat 2.30–5.30pm plus Wed, Thurs, Sat & Sun 10am–noon; May–Sept Tues–Sat 3–6pm plus same morning times; Oct–Nov 5 Tues–Sat 2–5pm plus same morning times; L5000). *Nani*, by the way, means "Dwarves", the significance of which becomes clear when you see the garden wall. To get there, go back down the hill, go along Via M. D'Azeglio for 100m, then turn right into the cobbled Via S. Bastiano, which ends at the villa.

There are two parts to the house: the Palazzina, containing six rooms frescoed with brilliant virtuosity by Giambattista (scenes based on Virgil, Tasso and Ariosto – you're handed a brief guide to the paintings at the entrance); and the Foresteria, one room of which is frescoed by Giambattista and six by Giandomenico, whose predilections are a little less heroic than his father's.

LA ROTONDA
From the Villa Valmarana the narrow Strada Valmarana descends the slope to one of Europe's most imitated buildings – Palladio's Villa Capra, known to most people as **La Rotonda** (March 15–Oct 15 Wed 10am–noon & 3–6pm; L5000, including the grounds). This is unique among Palladio's villas in that it was designed not as the main building of a farm but as a pavilion in which entertainments could be held and the landscape enjoyed. Only a tour of the lavishly decorated interior will fully reveal the subtleties of the Rotonda; the grounds (all year Tues–Sun same times; L3000) are not much more than a belt of grass round the villa, and are worth the entrance money only if you need to study the house from point-blank range.

Practicalities

The **tourist office** is alongside the entrance to the Teatro Olimpico, at Piazza Matteotti 12 (Mon–Sat 9am–12.30pm & 3–6pm, Sun 9am–12.30pm; ☎0444/320.854); when the office is shut, make use of the *Digiplan* booth next to the piazza's Bar Museo – it looks like a public toilet, but is in fact a computerised information outlet, which will print out directions, phone numbers, accommodation details and so forth, all in English.

Vicenza's one-star **hotels** are all on very noisy roads, above bars or some way out of the centre. Of the two-stars, the *Casa San Raffaele*, Viale X Giugno 10 (☎0444/323.663; ④), has the advantage of a beautiful position on the slope of Monte Bèrico. Of the two-stars close to the Piazza dei Signori, the following are worth trying – *Due Mori*, Contrà Do Rode 26 (☎0444/321.886; ⑤); *Vicenza*, Stradella dei Nodari 5 (☎0444/321.512; ④); and, friendliest of the bunch, *Palladio*, Via Oratorio dei Servi 25 (☎0444/321.072; ④). Wherever you decide to stay, ring ahead to book a room if you're going in summer or early autumn – Vicenza's popularity as a conference centre can make it tricky to find rooms, especially in September.

For a quick **snack**, the best places are *Paninoteca da Renato*, Stradella San Giacomo (between the Corso and Contrà Riale), or *La Cantinota*, Stradella del Garofalino (behind the *Corso* cinema), which offers sandwiches at lunchtimes and self-service meals in the evenings (open until 1am Mon–Fri, 2am on Sat). If you want to buy your own food, the *alimentari* of the Corso are excellent, especially *Il Ceppo* at no. 196.

First recommendation for low-cost **restaurant** eating goes to the *Antica Casa della Malvasia*, Contrà delle Morette 5, a bustling, roomy inn just off the Piazza dei Signori. The food is variable but cheap, unpretentious and genuinely regional; it has live music on Tuesdays and Thursdays; it's open till at least 1am on Fridays and Saturdays; and the bar's excellent too. Equally popular, but a shade less basic, is the *Vecchia Guardia*, at Contrà Pescheria Vecchia 11 (☎0444/321.231) – it's advisable to book at weekends. *Due Mori*, Contrà do Rode 26, and *Da Anna*, Contrà Porta Nova 41, are big and busy pizzeria-restaurants.

As for **bars** in the centre of the city, the *Firenze* on Piazzetta A. Palladio is always friendly, as is the *Malvasia* (see above), but the most popular is *Il Grottino*, under the Basilica at Piazza Erbe 2. There's a range of **cafés** and *pasticcerie* along the Corso and around the Basilica – try the excellent *Sorarù*, in the Piazzetta Andrea Palladio. Best **ice creams** in town are at *Tutto Gelato* in Contrà Frasche, between the Basilica and the duomo.

Verona

With its wealth of Roman sites and streets of pink-hued medieval buildings, the easy-going city of **VERONA** has more in the way of sights than any other place in the Veneto except Venice itself. Unlike Venice, though, it's not a city overwhelmed by the tourist industry, important though that is to the local economy. Verona is the largest city of the mainland Veneto, its economic success largely due to its position at the crossing of the major routes from Germany and Austria to central Italy and from the west to Venice and Trieste.

Verona's initial development as a **Roman** settlement was similarly due to its straddling the main east–west and north–south lines of communication. A period of decline in the wake of the disintegration of the Roman Empire was followed by revival under the Ostrogoths, who in turn were succeeded by the Franks – Charlemagne's son, Pepin, ruled his kingdom from here. By the twelfth century Verona had become a city-state, and in the following century approached the zenith of its independent existence with the rise of the **Scaligers**. Ruthless in the exercise of power, the Scaligers were at the same time energetic patrons of the arts, and many of Verona's finest buildings date from the century of their rule.

With the fall of their dynasty a time of upheaval ensued, Gian Galeazzo Visconti of Milan emerging in control of the city. Absorption into the Venetian empire came in 1405, and Venice continued to govern Verona until the arrival of Napoleon. Verona's history then shadowed that of Venice: a prolonged interlude of Austrian rule, brought to an end by the unification of Italy in 1866.

Arrival, information and accommodation

Traffic restrictions make walking the most efficient way of exploring the city, and the centre is concentrated enough to make this no great hardship. The only buses you're likely to need are the frequent #1 or #8 services (#51 or #58 in the evening) from the **train station** to the Piazza Brà, the hub of Verona; buy your ticket before you get on board, from just outside the station.

The main **tourist office** is close to the Arena at Via Leoncino 61 (summer Mon–Sat 8am–8pm, plus Sun 9am–8pm in July & Aug; winter Mon–Sat 8am–7pm; ☎045/592.828). In summer there's also an office at Piazza Erbe 42 and at the train station (same hours).

Accommodation

The most central one-star **hotels** are the *Catullo*, Via V. Catullo 1, just off Via Mazzini (☎045/800.2786; ④), and *Al Castello*, Corso Cavour 43 (☎045/800.4403; ④), but within a fairly short distance of Piazza Bra you'll find the cheaper *Armando*, Via Dietro Pallone 1 (☎045/800.026; ③), and *Volta Cittadella*, Via Volta Cittadella 8 (☎045/800.0077; ③). With many of its rooms overlooking the Piazza delle Erbe, the two-star *Hotel Aurora*, Via Pellicciai 2 (☎045/594.717; ⑤), is also recommended.

Verona's **youth hostel**, the *Ostello della Gioventù*, is at Salita Fontana del Ferro 15 (☎045/590.360; ①), a beautiful old building behind the Teatro Romano; as it's quite a walk from the centre, it's best to take bus #2 or #32 to Piazza Isolo. There's officially a 10.30pm curfew, but there's some flexibility extended to guests with concert tickets. For women, there's the option of the convent-run *Casa della Giovane*, Via Pigna 7 (☎045/596.880; ②), which has a similar curfew.

Convenient and pleasant **summer campsites** are *Campeggio Castel San Pietro*, Via Castel S. Pietro 2 (☎045/592.037; bus #3 or #15 to Via Marsala), and the small site right by the hostel.

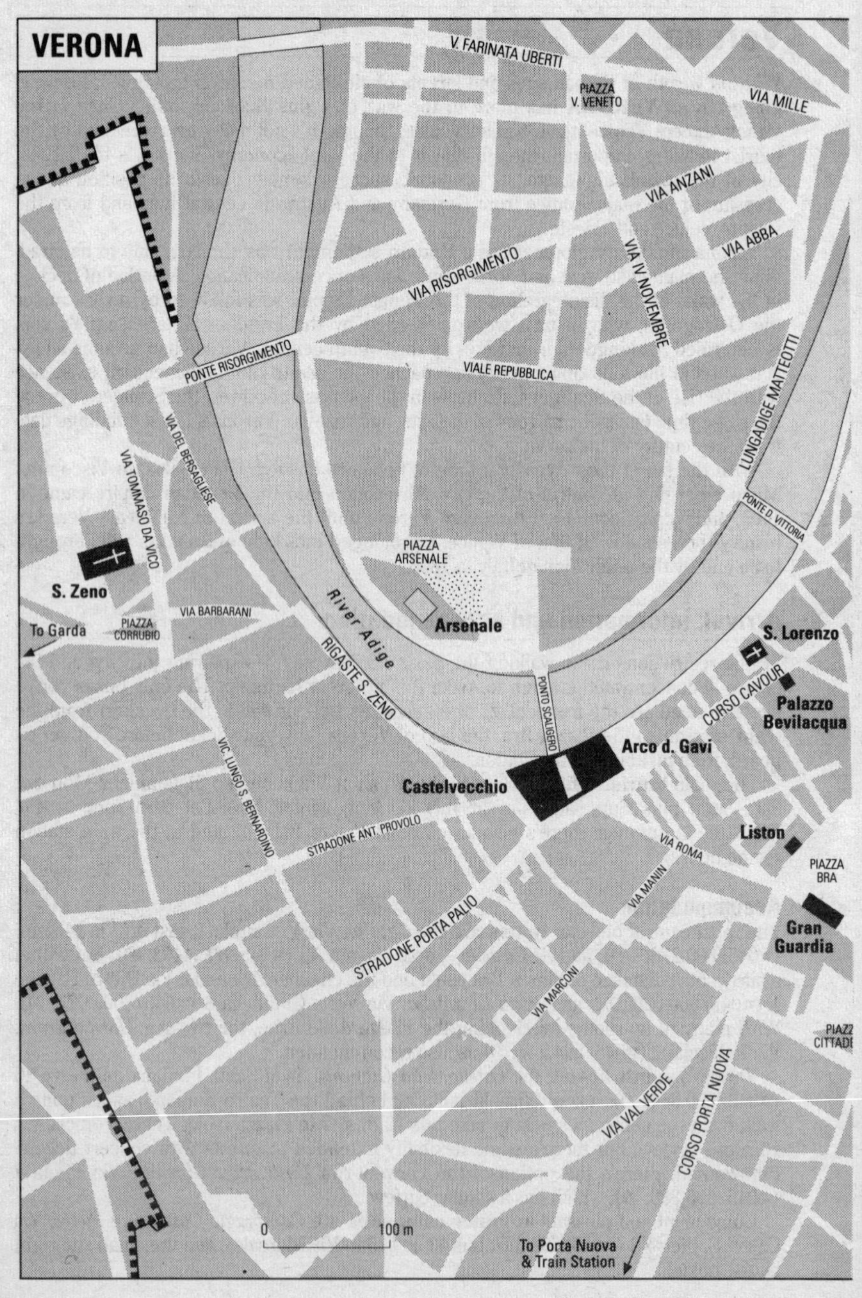
VERONA
V. FARINATA UBERTI
PIAZZA
V. VENETO
VIA MILLE
VIA ANZANI
VIA ABBA
VIA RISORGIMENTO
VIA IV NOVEMBRE
PONTE RISORGIMENTO
VIALE REPUBBLICA
LUNGADIGE MATTEOTTI
VIA DEL BERSAGLIESE
VIA TOMMASO DA VICO
PONTE D. VITTORIA
PIAZZA
ARSENALE
S. Zeno
River Adige
Arsenale
VIA BARBARANI
To Garda
PIAZZA
CORRUBIO
S. Lorenzo
RIGASTE S. ZENO
PONTO SCALIGERO
CORSO CAVOUR
Palazzo
Bevilacqua
Arco d. Gavi
Castelvecchio
VIC. LUNGO S. BERNARDINO
STRADONE ANT. PROVOLO
Liston
VIA ROMA
PIAZZA
BRA
VIA MANIN
STRADONE PORTA PALIO
Gran
Guardia
VIA MARCONI
VIA VAL VERDE
CORSO PORTA NUOVA
0
100 m
To Porta Nuova
& Train Station

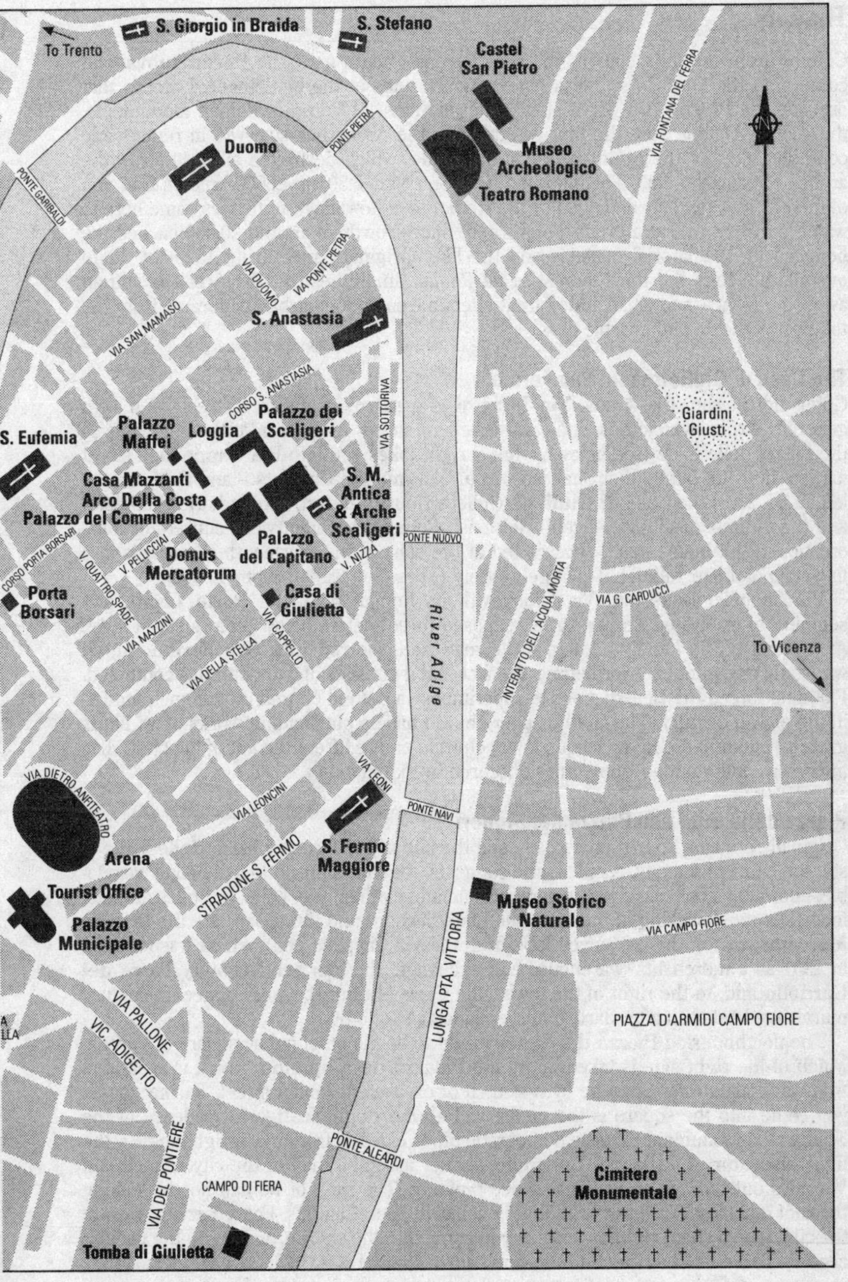
S. Giorgio in Braida
To Trento
S. Stefano
Castel San Pietro
Museo Archeologico
Teatro Romano
Duomo
PONTE PIETRA
PONTE GARIBALDI
VIA FONTANA DEL FERRA
VIA DUOMO
VIA PONTE PIETRA
VIA SAN MAMASO
S. Anastasia
CORSO S. ANASTASIA
VIA SOTTORIVA
Palazzo Maffei
Loggia
Palazzo dei Scaligeri
S. Eufemia
Giardini Giusti
Casa Mazzanti
Arco Della Costa
Palazzo del Commune
S. M. Antica & Arche Scaligeri
PONTE NUOVO
Palazzo del Capitano
Domus Mercatorum
CORSO PORTA BORSARI
V. QUATTRO SPADE
V. PELLICCIAI
V. NIZZA
Porta Borsari
Casa di Giulietta
VIA MAZZINI
VIA CAPPELLO
VIA DELLA STELLA
River Adige
INTERATTO DELL' ACQUA MORTA
VIA G. CARDUCCI
To Vicenza
VIA DIETRO ANFITEATRO
VIA LEONCINI
VIA LEONI
PONTE NAVI
Arena
S. Fermo Maggiore
STRADONE S. FERMO
Tourist Office
Palazzo Municipale
Museo Storico Naturale
VIA CAMPO FIORE
LUNGA PTA. VITTORIA
VIA PALLONE
VIC. ADIGETTO
PIAZZA D'ARMIDI CAMPO FIORE
PONTE ALEARDI
VIA DEL PONTIERE
CAMPO DI FIERA
Cimitero Monumentale
Tomba di Giulietta

The City

Coming from the train station, you pass Verona's south gate, the **Porta Nuova**, and come onto the long Corso Porta Nuova, which ends at the battlemented arches that precede the **Piazza Brà**. Here stands the mightiest of Verona's Roman monuments, the **Arena**. Dating from the first century AD, the Arena has survived in remarkable condition, despite the twelfth-century earthquake which destroyed all but four of the arches of the outer wall. The interior (Tues–Sun 8am–6.30pm; L6000, free on first Sun of month) was scarcely damaged by the tremor, and nowadays audiences come here to watch gargantuan opera productions where once crowds of around 20,000 packed the benches for gladiatorial contests and the like. Originally measuring 152m by 123m overall, and thus the third largest of all Roman amphitheatres, the Arena is still an awesome sight – and as an added treat offers a tremendous urban panorama from the topmost of the 44 pink marble tiers.

The Casa di Giulietta and San Fermo

Going north from the Arena, **Via Mazzini** is a narrow traffic-free street lined with generally expensive clothes, shoe and jewellery shops. A left turn at the end leads to the Piazza delle Erbe (see below), while a right takes you into **Via Cappello**, a street named after the family that Shakespeare turned into the Capulets – and there on the left, at no. 23, is the **Casa di Giulietta** (Juliet's House). In fact, although the "Capulets" and the "Montagues" (Montecchi) did exist, Romeo and Juliet were entirely fictional creations. The house itself, constructed at the start of the fourteenth century, is in a fine state of preservation but is largely empty (Tues–Sun 8am–6.30pm; L5000).

Via Cappello leads into Via Leoni with its Roman gate, the **Porta Leoni**, and segment of excavated Roman street, exposed three metres below today's street level. At the end of Via Leoni and across the road rises the red-brick **San Fermo** church whose inconsistent exterior betrays the fact that it consists of two churches combined. Flooding forced the Benedictines to superimpose a second church on the one founded in the eighth century. The Gothic upper church has no outstanding works of art but is graceful enough; the Romanesque lower church, entered from the left of the choir, has impressive low vaulting, sometimes obscured by exhibitions.

Piazza delle Erbe and Piazza dei Signori

Originally a major Roman crossroads and the site of the forum, **Piazza delle Erbe** is still the heart of the city. As the name suggests, the market used to sell mainly vegetables; nowadays the range has widened to include clothes, souvenirs, antiques and fast food. The most striking of the variegated buildings around the square are the **Domus Mercatorum** (on the left as you look from the Via Cappello end), which was founded in 1301 as a merchants' warehouse and exchange, the fourteenth-century **Torre del Gardello** and, to the right of the tower, the **Casa Mazzanti**, whose sixteenth-century murals are best seen after dark, under enhancing spotlights.

The neighbouring **Piazza dei Signori** used to be the chief public square of Verona. Much of the right side is taken up by the **Palazzo del Capitano**, which is separated from the Palazzo del Comune by a stretch of excavated Roman street. Facing you as you come into the square is the medieval **Palazzo degli Scaligeri**, residence of the Scaligers; a monument to more democratic times extends from it at a right angle – the fifteenth-century **Loggia del Consiglio**, former assembly hall of the city council and Verona's outstanding early Renaissance building. The rank of Roman notables along the roof includes Verona's most illustrious native poet, Catullus. For a dizzying view of the city, take a sharp right as soon as you come into the square, and go up the twelfth-century **Torre dei Lamberti** (Tues–Sun 8am–6.45pm; L4000 by lift, L3000 on foot).

The Scaliger tombs

Passing under the arch linking the Palazzo degli Scaligeri to the Palazzo del Capitano, you come to the little Romanesque church of Santa Maria Antica, in front of which are ranged the **Arche Scaligeri**, some of the most elaborate Gothic funerary monuments in Italy. Over the side entrance to the church, an equestrian statue of **Cangrande I** ("Big Dog"; d.1329) grins on the summit of his tomb's pyramidal roof; the statue is a copy, the original being displayed in the Castelvecchio (see below). The canopied tombs of the rest of the clan are enclosed within a wrought-iron palisade decorated with ladder motifs, the emblem of the Scaligers – the family name was della Scala, "scala" meaning ladder. **Mastino I** ("Mastiff"), founder of the dynasty, is buried in the simple tomb against the wall of the church; **Mastino II** is to the left of the entrance, opposite the most florid of the tombs, that of **Cansignorio** ("Top Dog"; d.1375).

Sant'Anastasia and the duomo

Going on past the Arche Scaligeri, and turning left along Via San Pietro, you come to **Sant'Anastasia**, Verona's largest church. Started in 1290 and completed in 1481, it's mainly Gothic in style, with undertones of the Romanesque. The fourteenth-century carvings of New Testament scenes around the doors are the most arresting feature of its bare exterior; the interior's highlight is Pisanello's delicately coloured fresco of *St George and the Princess* (in the sacristy), a work in which the normally martial saint appears as something of a dandy.

Verona's red-and-white-striped **Duomo** lies just round the river's bend, past the Roman **Ponte Pietra**. Consecrated in 1187, it's Romanesque in its lower parts, developing into Gothic as it goes up; the two doorways are twelfth century – look for the story of Jonah and the whale on the south porch, and the statues of Roland and Oliver, two of Charlemagne's paladins, on the west. The interior has fascinating architectural details around each chapel and on the columns – particularly fine is the Cappella Mazzanti (last on the right). In the first chapel on the left, an *Assumption* by Titian occupies an architectural frame by Sansovino, who also designed the choir.

To the Castelvecchio

After the Arena and the Teatro Romano, Verona's most impressive Roman remnant is the **Porta dei Borsari** (on the junction of Via Diaz and Corso Porta Borsari), a structure which was as great an influence on the city's Renaissance architects as the amphitheatre. Now reduced to a monumental screen straddling the road, it used to be Verona's largest Roman gate; the inscription dates it at 265, but it's almost certainly older than that.

Some way down Corso Cavour, which starts at the Porta dei Borsari, stands the **Arco dei Gavi**, a first-century Roman triumphal arch. This is your best vantage point from which to admire the **Ponte Scaligero**; built by Cangrande II between 1355 and 1375, the bridge was blown up by the Germans in 1945. The salvaged material was used for the reconstruction.

The fortress from which the bridge springs, the **Castelvecchio** (Tues–Sun 8am–6.30pm; L6000, free on first Sun of month) was commissioned by Cangrande II at around the same time, and became the stronghold for Verona's subsequent rulers. Opened as the city museum in 1925, it was damaged by bombing in World War II, but opened again after scrupulous restoration in 1964.

The Castelvecchio's collection of paintings, jewellery, weapons and other artefacts flows through a labyrinth of chambers, courtyards and passages that is fascinating to explore in itself. The equestrian figure **Cangrande I**, removed from his tomb, is strikingly displayed on an outdoor pedestal; his expression is disconcerting from close range, the simpleton's grin being difficult to reconcile with the image of the ruthless warlord. Outstanding among the paintings are two works by Jacopo Bellini, two *Madonnas* by Giovanni Bellini, another *Madonna* by Pisanello, Veronese's *Descent from the Cross*, a Tintoretto *Nativity*, a Lotto portrait and works by Giambattista and Giandomenico Tiepolo. The real joy of the museum, however, is in wandering round the medieval pieces, beautiful sculpture and frescoes by the often nameless artists of the late Middle Ages.

San Zeno Maggiore

A little over a kilometre northwest of the Castelvecchio is the **Basilica di San Zeno Maggiore**, one of the most significant Romanesque churches in northern Italy. A church was founded here, above the tomb of the city's patron saint, as early as the fifth century, but the present building and its campanile were put up in the first half of the twelfth century, with additions continuing up to the end of the fourteenth. Its large rose window, representing the Wheel of Fortune, dates from the early twelfth century, as does the magnificent portal, whose lintels bear relief sculptures representing the months – look also for Saint Zeno trampling the devil. Extraordinary bronze panels on the doors depict scenes from the Bible and the Miracles of San Zeno, their style influenced by Byzantine and Ottoman art; most of those on the left are from around 1100, most of the right-hand panels dating from a century later. Areas of the lofty and simple interior are covered with frescoes, some superimposed upon others, some defaced by ancient graffiti. Diverting though these are, the one compulsive image in the church is the high altar's luminous *Madonna and Saints* by Mantegna.

North of the Adige

On the other side of Ponte Garibaldi, and right along the embankments or through the public gardens, is **San Giorgio in Braida**, in terms of its works of art the richest of Verona's churches. A *Baptism* by Tintoretto hangs over the door, while the main altar, designed by **Sanmicheli**, incorporates a marvellous piece by **Paolo Veronese** – the *Martyrdom of St George*.

It's a short walk along the embankments, past the twelfth-century church of **Santo Stefano** and the Ponte Pietra, to the first-century BC **Teatro Romano** (Tues–Sun summer 8am–6.30pm; winter 8am–1.30pm; L5000, free on first Sun of month); much restored, the theatre is now used for concerts and plays. High above it, and reached by a rickety-looking lift, the **Museo Archeologico** (same hours & ticket) occupies the buildings of an old convent; its well-arranged collection features a number of Greek, Roman and Etruscan finds.

Eating, drinking and entertainment

Your money goes a lot further in Verona than it does in Venice: numerous **trattorias** offer full meals for under L20,000, while on almost every street corner there's a bar where a glass of house wine (red Bardolino and Valpolicella, white Soave and Custoza) costs as little as L700. **Nightlife** here is more varied too, and genuinely goes on into the night, in contrast to Venice's general late-evening shutdown.

As the Veneto produces more DOC wine than any other region in Italy, it's not surprising that Italy's main wine fair, *Vinitaly*, is held in Verona; it takes place in April, and offers infinite sampling opportunities.

Restaurants

In the centre of the city, the best value among the **restaurants** is at the *Osteria Al Duca*, Via Arche Scaligere 2b, where a genuine, no-frills meal will cost around L15,000. In the same sort of range is the restaurant at the *Al Castello* hotel (see p.283). Although it is possible to find other budget places within the historic centre, they are far more plentiful over the river on the east side of the city, in the Veronetta district. If you don't mind eating before 8pm, call in at the *Osteria ai Preti*, Via Acqua Morta 27, where the pasta and wine are cheap and musicians often drop by to play. *Pero d'Oro*, Via Ponte Pignolo 25, and *Ponte Nuovo*, Via Rocca Maggiore 8, both serve good Veronese food, as does the more expensive *Circolo Perbacco*, Via Carducci 48, which has a very attractive garden. For around L25,000 you can get a fine three-course spread at the *Dal Ropeton*, below the youth hostel at Via S. Giovanni in Valle 46.

Verona's best **pizzas** are served at *Da Salvatore*, Corso Porta Borsari 39; other central places worth trying are the *Pizzeria Corte Farina*, Corte Farina 4, and the *Pizzeria Arena*, Vicolo Tre Marchetti 1, both of which stay open until 1am. In Piazza Brà the best pizzas are those at *Pizzeria Olivo*.

Bars and gelaterie

Best of the city's **bars** is the *Osteria al Duomo*, Via Duomo 7a, a bar little changed by twentieth-century fashion and enlivened on Wednesday afternoons and Friday nights in winter by a traditional sing-along. In the same class is the nearby *Al Carro Armato*, Vicolo Gatto 2a, which has live music on Thursdays in winter. More touristy, but with a selection of wines from all over Italy, is the *Bottega dei Vini* in Vicolo Scudo di Francia, just off the north end of Via Mazzini. The central *Osteria delle Vecete*, in Via Pellicciai, also near Piazza delle Erbe, has a delicious selection of the savoury tartlets known as *bocconcini*, but unfortunately closes at 8.30pm.

The bars in the university area, around Via dell'Artigliere, attract a young crowd, while in the same district the *Campofiore* in Via Campofiore, near the university, is a favourite with Verona's **gay** population – who tend to move on to *Bar Antimo*, Via Roma 4, when the *Campofiore* is closed. Finally, for a marvellous view of Ponte Pietra and the Teatro Romano, sip a glass in the garden of the *Al Ponte* bar in Via Ponte Pietra.

For a non-alcoholic indulgence, sit outside one of the *gelaterie* in Piazza delle Erbe and give a few minutes to an incredible concoction of fruit, cream and ice cream. If you want to follow the current trend, the place to make for is *Gelateria Pampanin*, by Ponte Garibaldi.

Nightlife

Music and **theatre** are the dominant art forms in the cultural life of Verona. In July and August an opera festival takes place in the **Arena**, always featuring a no-expense-spared production of *Aida*; **big rock events** crop up on the Arena's calendar too – Bob Dylan, Sting, Tina Turner and Joe Cocker have all played it in recent years. (The booking office is in arches 8–9 of the Arena; tickets can only be reserved by post or in person.) A season of ballet and of Shakespeare and other dramatists in Italian is the principal summer fare at the **Teatro Romano**. Some of the Teatro events are free; for the rest, cheapskates who don't mind inferior acoustics can park themselves on the steps going up the hill alongside the theatre. The Teatro's box office also sells tickets for the Arena and vice versa.

Free performances by local dance and theatre groups in May can be surprisingly good, while the June **jazz festival** attracts international names, as does the **Canzone d'Autrice** festival for female singer-songwriters at the end of August.

From October to May **English-language films** are shown every Tuesday at the *Cinema Stimate* in Piazza Cittadella. The **disco** scene is much more lively than in Venice, with venues coming and going; look in the local paper, *L'Arena* (there's a copy in every bar), to find out where they are and what days they're open.

The *spettacoli* section of *L'Arena* is the best source of up-to-date information on entertainment in Verona; alternatively, call in at *Musicaviva*, Via Adigetto 6, which sells tickets for most events.

Treviso

The local tourist board are pitching it a bit high when they suggest that the waterways of **TREVISO** may remind you of Venice, but the old centre of this brisk provincial capital is certainly more alluring than you might imagine from a quick glance on your way to or from the airport. Treviso was an important town long before its assimilation by Venice in 1389, and plenty of evidence of its early stature survives in the form of Gothic churches, public buildings and, most dramatically of all, the paintings of **Tomaso da Modena** (1325–79), the major artist in north Italy in the years immediately after Giotto's death. The general townscape within Treviso's sixteenth-century walls is often appealing too – long porticoes and frescoed house facades give many of the streets an appearance quite distinct from those of other towns in the region.

The City

These features are well preserved in the main street of the centre, **Calmaggiore**, where modern commerce (epitomised by the omnipresent Benetton, a Trevisan firm) has reached the sort of compromise with the past that the Italians seem to arrange better than anyone else. Modern building techniques have played a larger part than you might think in shaping that compromise – Treviso was pounded during both world wars and on Good Friday 1944 was half destroyed in a single bombing raid.

The early thirteenth-century **Palazzo dei Trecento**, at the side of the **Piazza dei Signori**, was one casualty of 1944 – a line round the exterior shows where the restoration began. The adjoining **Palazzo del Podestà** is a nineteenth-century structure, concocted in an appropriate style.

Of more interest are the two churches at the back of the block: **San Vito** and **Santa Lucia**: the tiny, dark chapel of Santa Lucia has extensive frescoes by Tomaso da Modena and his followers; San Vito has even older paintings in the alcove through which you enter from Santa Lucia, though they're not in a good state.

The cathedral of Treviso, **San Pietro**, stands at the end of Calmaggiore (daily 7am–noon & 3–7pm). Founded in the twelfth century, San Pietro was much altered in succeeding centuries, and then rebuilt to rectify the damage of 1944. The interior is chiefly notable for the crypt – a thicket of twelfth-century columns with scraps of medieval mosaics – and the Cappella Malchiostro, with frescoes by Pordenone and an *Annunciation* by Titian.

Just over the Sile River from the railway station is the severe Dominican church of **San Nicolò**, which has frescoes dating from the thirteenth to the sixteenth century. Some of the columns are decorated with paintings by Tomaso da Modena and his school, of which the best are the *St Jerome* and *St Agnes* (by Tomaso) on the first column on your right as you enter. Equally striking, but far more graceful, is the composite *Tomb of Agostino d'Onigo* on the north wall of the chancel, created in 1500 by Antonio Rizzo (who did the sculpture) and Lorenzo Lotto (who painted the attendant pages).

The figures of Agnes and Jerome are an excellent introduction to Tomaso da Modena, but for a comprehensive demonstration of his talents you have to visit the neighbouring **Seminario**, where the chapter house is decorated with a series of forty *Portraits of Members of the Dominican Order*, executed in 1352 (Mon–Fri 9am–sunset).

The Santa Caterina district

Treviso has a second great fresco cycle by Tomaso da Modena – *The Story of the Life of Saint Ursula*, now housed in the deconsecrated church of **Santa Caterina**, on the other side of the centre from San Nicolò (Tues–Sat 9am–11.30pm & 2–4.30pm; L1000). To get into the church you have to make an appointment at the Museo Civico (call in person or ring ☎0422/51337).

The area around the church is a pleasant one, with its antiques sellers and furniture restorers, and the hubbub of the stalls around the fish market. There are a couple of other churches worth a look, too. To the north of Santa Caterina is the rebuilt thirteenth-century church of **San Francesco**, an airy building with a ship's-keel roof and patches of fresco, including a *Madonna and Saints* by Tomaso da Modena (chapel to north of chancel). To the south, at the end of Via Carlo Alberto – one of the most attractive streets in the town – stands the **Basilica di Santa Maria Maggiore**, which houses the most venerated image in Treviso, a fresco of the Madonna originally painted by Tomaso but subsequently retouched.

The Museo Civico and around

From the centre the recommended route to the **Museo Civico** on Borgo Cavour (Tues–Sat 9am–noon & 2–5pm, Sun 9am–noon; L1000) is along Via Riccati, which has a number of fine old houses. The ground floor of the museum is taken up by the archaeological collection, predominantly late Bronze Age and Roman relics; the picture collection, on the upper floor, is mediocre too, but has a few very special paintings among the dross – a *Crucifixion* by Jacopo Bassano, *Portrait of Sperone Speroni* by Titian and *Portrait of a Dominican* by Lorenzo Lotto.

Practicalities

The **tourist office** is in the Palazzo Scotti, Via Toniolo 41 (Mon–Fri 8.30am–12.30pm & 5–6pm, Sat 8.30am–noon; ☎0422/547.632); they dispense lists of the town's museums and restaurants, plus a couple of glossies on Treviso's waterways and its frescoed houses. Although Treviso itself isn't likely to tempt you to stay, you might want to use it as a base from which to strike out into the mainland, or as a fall-back if accommodation in Venice is a dead loss. There are no one-star **hotels** in the old town. Of the central two-stars, the cheapest is *Al Cuore*, Piazzale Duca d'Aosta 1 (☎0422/410.929; ④), as it's right on top of the main road and rail convergences. More comfortable is the *Beccherie*, Piazza Ancillotto 10 (☎0422/540.871; ④), a pleasant two-star right in the heart of the *centro storico*.

Treviso has a number of restaurants with very high reputations and prices to match, but there's no dearth of budget places. Good-value trattorias, in descending order of cost and quality, are: *All' Oca Bianca*, Vicolo della Torre 7; the riverside *Al Dante*, Piazza Garibaldi 6; *La Tavernetta*, a typical little trattoria at Via Manzoni 46; and the very plain *Alla Colomba*, Via Ortazzo 25.

The most popular **bars and cafés** in Treviso are those clustered underneath the Palazzo dei Trecento; two other good bars are the *Osteria dalla Elsa* on Vicolo San Gregorio, just to the south of the Piazza dei Signori, and *Scandiuzzi Secondo* on Piazza Ancillotto, which serves tasty snacks as well as cheap but fair-quality wine. For **ice cream**, drop in at the *gelateria* opposite the duomo at Piazza del Duomo 25.

Castelfranco Veneto and around

CASTELFRANCO VENETO once stood on the western edge of Treviso's territory, and battlemented brick walls that the Trevisans threw round the town in 1199 to protect it against the Paduans still encircle most of the old centre (or Castello). Of all the walled towns of the Veneto, only two – Cittadella (see overleaf) and Montagnana – bear comparison with Castelfranco, and the place would merit an expedition if it had no other attraction. But Castelfranco was also the birthplace of **Giorgione**, and possesses a painting which on its own is enough to vindicate Vasari's judgement that Giorgione's place in Venetian art is equivalent to Leonardo da Vinci's in that of Florence.

The painting in question – *The Madonna and Child with SS Francis and Liberale*, usually known simply as the *Castelfranco Madonna* – hangs in the **Duomo** (daily 9am–noon & 3–6pm), in a chapel to the right of the chancel. Giorgione is the most elusive of all the great figures of the Renaissance: including the *Castelfranco Madonna*, only six surviving paintings can indisputably be attributed to him, and so little is known about his life that legends have proliferated to fill the gaps – for instance, the story that his death in 1510, aged not more than 34, was caused by his catching the plague from a mistress. The paintings themselves have compounded the enigma, and none is more mysterious than this one, in which formal abstraction is combined with an extraordinary fidelity to physical texture, while the demeanour of the figures suggests a melancholic preoccupation. It was commissioned to commemorate Matteo Costanza, and was originally placed so that the gazes of the three figures were directed at his tombstone, which is now set into the wall to the left.

In a first-floor room of the adjacent **Casa Giorgione** there's a chiaroscuro frieze that's hopefully attributed to the artist (Tues–Sun 9am–12.30pm & 3–6pm; often closed weekday mornings in winter; free).

Practicalities

The **tourist office** is at Via Garibaldi 2 (Mon–Sat 8.30am–12.30pm & 3–7pm; Sun 8.30am–12.30pm). The cheapest **rooms** in central Castelfranco are at *Alla Speranza*, a few yards beyond the walls at Borgo Vicenza 13 (☎0423/494.480; ④); cheaper still, but about 1km outside the walls, is *All'Antica Priora*, Borgo Padova 55 (☎0423/491.764; ③). There are a few cheap trattorias in Borgo Padova, and a decent one attached to *Alla Speranza*. *Alla Torre*, a large restaurant-pizzeria at the foot of the Torrione, is as good a place as any for pizza.

Castelfranco is well connected by **rail** with all parts of the Veneto, but it's most easily approached from Treviso (25min) or Vicenza (40min) – trains run along this line on average once an hour. Connections to Venice (50min) are more sporadic – during working hours it averages out at around one every two hours. In addition there are hourly links to Padua and Trento (through Bassano), and a train to Belluno every ninety minutes.

Around Castelfranco

The major attraction within a short radius of Castelfranco is the wonderfully preserved **Cittadella**, which can be easily reached by train, as it's on the Treviso–Vicenza line. Your own transport is really needed to get to the area's other big draw, Palladio's influential villa at **Fanzolo**.

Cittadella

When Treviso turned Castelfranco into a garrison, the Paduans promptly retaliated by reinforcing the defences of **CITTADELLA**, 15km to the west, on the train line to Vicenza. The fortified walls of Cittadella were built in the first quarter of the thirteenth century, and are even more impressive than those of its neighbour. You enter the town through one of four rugged brick gateways; if you're coming from the train station it'll be the Porta Padova, the most daunting of the four, flanked by the **Torre di Malta**. The tower was built as a prison and torture chamber by the monstrous Ezzelino da Romano, known to those he terrorised in this region in the mid-thirteenth century as "The Son of Satan". His atrocities earned for himself a place in the seventh circle of Dante's *Inferno*, where he's condemned to boil eternally in a river of blood. There's not much else to Cittadella, but it's definitely worth hopping off the train for a quick circuit of the walls.

The Villa Emo at Fanzolo

Just 8km northeast of Castelfranco is **FANZOLO**, where you'll find the **Villa Emo** (Tues, Sat & Sun April–Sept 3–7pm; Oct–March 2–6pm; L6000), which Palladio designed in the 1560s for Leonardo Emo, one of the first Venetian patricians to switch his financial interests to farming. The main living rooms, as at the Villa Barbaro at Masèr, are richly frescoed, and though nobody would pretend that G. B. Zelotti's work is a match for Veronese's in the Barbaro house, few people would complain at having to stare at his creations every morning over breakfast. Two snags, though – the bus service out to the villa is woeful, and the entry charge is inexcusably high. The museum of agricultural implements installed in the old granary will set you back a further L3000, or you can pay L8000 for a combined ticket.

Bassano del Grappa and around

Situated on the Brenta River where it widens on its emergence from the hills, **BASSANO** has expanded rapidly this century, though its historic centre remains largely unspoiled by twentieth-century mistakes. It's better known for its manufactures and produce, and for the events of the two world wars (see below), than for any outstanding architecture or monuments. For centuries a major producer of ceramics and wrought iron, Bassano is also renowned for its **grappa** distilleries and delicacies such as *porcini* (dried mushrooms), white asparagus and honey.

The Town

Almost all of Bassano's sights lie between the Brenta and the train station; go much further in either direction and you'll quickly come to recently developed suburbs. Walking away from the station, you cross the orbital Viale delle Fosse to get to **Piazza Garibaldi**, one of the two main squares. Here, the cloister of the fourteenth-century church of San Francesco now houses the **Museo Civico** (Tues–Sat 10am–12.30pm & 2.30–6.30pm, Sun opens 30min later in afternoon; L2000). Downstairs the rooms are devoted to printing – for a long time one of Bassano's chief crafts – and archaeological finds. Upstairs is a collection including paintings by the da Ponte family (better known as the Bassano family), and a number of plaster works by Canova, 2000 of whose drawings are owned by the museum. There's also a room devoted to the great baritone Tito Gobbi, who was born here.

Overlooking the other side of the piazza is the **Torre Civica**, once a lookout tower for the twelfth-century inner walls, now a clock tower with spurious nineteenth-century battlements and windows. Beyond the fifteenth-century Loggia (once home of the Venetian military commander), Piazzetta Montevecchio leads to a little jumble of streets and stairways running down to the river and the **Ponte degli Alpini**. The river was first bridged at this point in the late twelfth century, and replacements or repairs have been needed at regular intervals ever since, mostly because of flooding; the present structure was designed by Palladio in 1568, and built in wood in order to make the bridge as flexible as possible. *Nardini*, a grappa distillery founded in 1779 (Tues–Sun 8am–8pm), stands at this end of the bridge; it sells the best-quality stuff and has a bar where you can sample before you select your bottle.

From here, if you follow Via Ferracina downstream for a couple of minutes you'll come to the eighteenth-century **Palazzo Sturm** (Fri 9am–noon, Sat & Sun 3–7pm; L2000), a showcase for the town's famed majolica ware.

Various streets and squares in Bassano commemorate the dead of the two world wars. The major **war memorial**, however, is out of town on **Monte Grappa**. A vast, circular, tiered edifice with a "Via Eroica" leading to a war museum, it holds 12,000

Italian and Austro-Hungarian dead; less a symbol of mourning and repentance than a declaration of future collaboration, it was built by the Fascists in 1935. Buses go up there from Bassano during the summer months.

Practicalities

The **tourist office** is opposite the train station at Largo Corona d'Italia 35 (Mon–Sat 9am–12.30pm & 3–6.45pm). For budget **accommodation**, it comes down to a choice between *Bassanello*, at Via P. Fontana 2 (☎0424/35.347; ③), or *Nuovo Mondo*, Via Vittorelli 45 (☎0424/522.010; ④), a pleasant and central two-star. As for **food**, the *Antica Osteria*, Via Matteotti 7, has good bar snacks, while *Combattini*, Via Gamba 22, is recommended for a full meal, at around L30,000. *Ottocento*, Via San Giorgio 2, is a welcoming *birreria*, though for a late-night drink the most popular spot is *Saiso*, Via Gamba 4.

Trains run from Venice to Bassano every one or two hours; the journey takes an hour. There's a useful train timetable in the centre of town on the corner of Via Guiseppi Barbieri and the piazza. **Buses** leave from Piazzale Trento, at the south end of Viale delle Fosse; the *Bar Trevizani*, on the piazzale, deals with tickets and information. Buses run to Masèr (8 daily), Maróstica (3–5 daily) and Ásolo (12–15 daily).

Maróstica

Seven kilometres to the west of Bassano (and a fifteen-minute hop on the regular bus), the walled town of **MARÓSTICA** was yet another stronghold of Ezzelino da Romano, whose fortress glowers down on the old centre from the crest of the hill of Pausolino. The Ezzelini controlled Maróstica for quite a while – Ezzelino III was preceded by Ezzelino the Stutterer and Ezzelino the Monk – but it was another despotic dynasty, the Scaligers of Verona, who constructed the **town walls** and the **Castello Inferiore** (lower castle).

Beyond the castle is Piazza Castello, the central square of the town, onto which is painted the board for the **Partita a Scacchi**, the town's principal claim to fame. The game's origin was an everyday chivalric story of rival suitors, the only unusual aspect being that the matter was decided with chess pieces rather than swords. The game was played with live pieces here in the square, and is re-enacted with great pomp on the second weekend of September of even-numbered years. Fourteenth-century costumes worn for the game are displayed in the Castello Inferiore (Sun 2–6pm; L500).

Ásolo and around

Known as "la Città dai cento orizzonti" (the city with a hundred horizons), the medieval walled town of **ÁSOLO** presides over a tightly grouped range of nearly thirty gentle peaks in the foothills of the Dolomites. In 1234 Ezzelino da Romano wrested the town from the Bishop of Treviso; on his death in 1259 the townspeople ensured that the dynasty died with him by massacring the rest of his family, who were at that time in nearby San Zenone.

The end of the fifteenth century was marked by the arrival of Caterina Cornaro (see opposite) – her celebrated court was attended by the likes of Cardinal Bembo, one of the most eminent literary figures of his day, who coined the verb *Asolare* to describe the experience of spending one's time in pleasurable aimlessness. Later writers and artists found the atmosphere equally convivial: Gabriele d'Annunzio wrote about the town, and Robert Browning's last published work – *Asolando* – was written here.

There are regular **buses** to Ásolo from Bassano; if you want to get there from Venice, it's quickest to take a train to Treviso, from where there are buses at least hourly – in addition to the direct Ásolo services, all the buses to Bassano go through Ásolo.

The Town

The bus drops you at the foot of the hill, from where a connecting minibus shuttles up into the town. Memorabilia of Ásolo's celebrated residents are gathered in the **Museo Civico** in Piazza Maggiore, which has long been in the throes of restoration but should soon be open again. Especially diverting are the portraits, photos and personal effects of **Elenora Duse**. An actress in the Sarah Bernhardt mould, Duse was almost as well known for her tempestuous love-life as for her roles in Shakespeare, Hugo and Ibsen, and she came to Ásolo to seek refuge from public gossip. Although she died in Pittsburgh while on tour in 1924, her wish was to be buried in Ásolo, and so her body was transported back here, to the church of Sant'Anna. The main interest of the art collection is provided by a pair of dubiously attributed Bellinis, a portrait of Ezzelino painted a good couple of centuries after his death and a brace of large sculptures by Canova.

The *Teatro Duse* occupies part of the **Castello**, most of which is also currently being restored. From 1489 to 1509 this was the home of **Caterina Cornaro**, one of the very few women to have played a major part in Venetian history. Born into one of Venice's most powerful families, Caterina was married to Jacques II, King of Cyprus. Within a year of the wedding Jacques was dead, and there followed nearly a decade of political pressure from Venice's rulers, who wanted to get their hands on the strategically vital island. In 1489 she was finally forced to abdicate in order to gain much-needed weapons and ships against a Turkish attack. Brought back to Venice to sign a deed "freely giving" Cyprus to the Republic, she was given the region of Ásolo as a sign of Venice's indebtedness. Eventually Ásolo too was taken away from her by the Emperor Maximilian, and she returned to seek asylum in Venice, where she died soon after, in 1510.

Practicalities

The **tourist office** is in Via Regina Cornaro, close to the Museo; they give out a map of the town which is quite handy, if not exactly a model of clarity. **Accommodation** is impossible – two luxury hotels and that's all. Ásolo does have a handful of **bars and restaurants**, though. The *Enoteca Marcello Agnoletto* is an excellent wine bar in Via Browning, while *La Papessa* in Via Pietro Bembo has a good range of pizzas plus a few other interesting dishes.

The Villa Barbaro at Masèr

Touring the villas of the Veneto, you become used to mismatches between the quality of the architecture and the quality of the decoration, but at the **Villa Barbaro** at **MASÈR** (March–Oct Tues, Sat & Sun 3–6pm; Nov–Feb Sat & Sun 2.30–5pm; L6000), a few kilometres northeast of Ásolo, you'll see the best of two of the central figures of Italian civilisation in the sixteenth century – **Palladio** and **Paolo Veronese**, whose careers crossed here and nowhere else. If you're reliant on public transport, a visit is best made by bus from Bassano via Ásolo (8 daily), or from Treviso – the services from Treviso to Ásolo (see opposite) all pass the villa.

The villa was built in the 1550s for Daniele and Marcantonio Barbaro, men whose humanist training and diverse cultural interests made the process of designing the house far more of a collaborative venture than were most of Palladio's other projects. The entire ground floor was given over to farm functions – dovecotes in the end pavilions, stables and storage space under the arcades, administrative offices on the lower floor of the central block. It's in the living quarters of the *piano nobile* that the more rarified aspect of the brothers' world is expressed, in a series of **frescoes** by Veronese that has no equal anywhere in northern Italy. The more abstruse scenes are decoded in an excellent guidebook on sale in the villa, but most of the paintings require no footnotes. The walls of the Villa Barbaro are the most resourceful display of trompe l'oeil you'll ever see – servants peer round painted doors, a dog sniffs along the base of a flat balustrade in front of a landscape of ruins, a huntsman (probably Veronese himself) steps into the house through an entrance that's a solid wall. (Inevitably it's speculated that the woman facing the hunter at the other end of the house was Veronese's mistress.)

In the grounds in front of the villa stands Palladio's **Tempietto**, the only church by him outside Venice and one of his last projects; commissioned by Marcantonio a decade after his brother's death, it was built in 1580, the year Palladio himself died.

Feltre

The historic centre of **FELTRE**, spread along a narrow ridge overlooking the modern town, owes its beguiling appearance to the calamity of 1509, when, in the course of the War of the League of Cambrai, the troops of the Imperial army decided to punish the place for its allegiance to Venice by wiping much of it from the face of the planet. The Venetians took care of the reconstruction, and within a few decades the streets looked pretty much as they do nowadays. You're not going to find architecture students on every street corner, but you'd have to travel a long way to get a better idea of how an ordinary town looked in sixteenth-century Italy.

There are no direct **trains** to Feltre from Venice, but Feltre is a stop for the twelve-daily Padua to Belluno trains, which you can intercept at Castelfranco. The journey from Padua to Feltre takes ninety minutes, and it's a further thirty to Belluno.

The Town

From the station the shortest route to the old town is to cross straight over into Viale del Piave, over Via Garibaldi (where there's a decent range of bars, restaurants and hotels) and along Via Castaldi, which brings you to the **Duomo** and **Baptistery**, at the foot of the ridge. The main objects of interest in the duomo are a sixth-century Byzantine cross and a tomb by Tullio Lombardo. At the top of the steps that go past the side of the Baptistery, on the other side of the road, is the town's south gate, under which begins a long covered flight of steps that takes you up into the heart of the old town.

You come out by the sixteenth-century Municipio, the portico of which was designed by Palladio. The keep of the medieval castello rises behind the platform of the **Piazza Maggiore.**

To the left, the main street of Feltre, **Via Mezzaterra**, slopes down to the fifteenth-century Porta Imperiale. Nearly all the houses here are sixteenth century, and several have external frescoes by the town's most important painter, Lorenzo Luzzo – better known as Il Morto da Feltre (The Dead Man), a nickname prompted by the pallor of his skin. Via L. Luzzo, the equally decorous continuation of Via Mezzaterra on the other side of the Piazza, leads to the **Museo Civico**, which contains Il Morto's *Madonna with St Vitus and St Modestus* and other pieces by him, but the building has been undergoing repairs for years, and may not yet be open. If you do manage to get in, you should also discover paintings by Cima and Gentile Bellini, and a display of Roman and Etruscan finds. Il Morto's finest work is generally held to be the fresco of the *Transfiguration* in the **Ognissanti** church; this building is very unlikely to be open in the foreseeable future, but if you want to try your luck, go out of the Porta Oria, right by the Museo, down the dip and along Borgo Ruga for a couple of hundred metres.

Feltre has another, more unusual museum – the **Museo Rizzarda** at Via del Paradiso 8, parallel to Via Mezzaterra (June–Sept Tues–Sun 10am–1pm & 4–7pm; L2000). This doubles as the town's collection of modern art and an exhibition of wrought-iron work, most of it by **Carlo Rizzarda** (1883–1931), ex-owner of the house. It might not sound appetising, but the finesse of Rizzarda's pieces is remarkable.

Practicalities

You're unlikely to need the Feltre **tourist office**, at Piazza Trento Trieste (Mon–Fri 9am–12.30pm & 3–6pm, Sat 9am–12.30pm), which is just as well, as it's one of the Veneto's less dynamic offices. Neither is it likely that you'll want a **hotel** here, but if you do, it's basically a choice between the two-star *Cavallino* at Via Garibaldi 8 (☎0439/81.547; ④), or the three-star *Nuovo Garni* at Via Fornere Pazze 5 (☎0439/2110; ⑥). For **meals**, the *Aurora*, Via Garibaldi 24, is a cheap and cheerful trattoria.

Conegliano

North of Treviso, around the amiable town of **CONEGLIANO**, the landscape ceases to be boring. The surrounding hills are patched with vineyards and the production of wine (Prosecco in particular) is central to the economy of the district. Italy's first wine-growers' college was set up in Conegliano in 1876, and today there are a couple of well-established wine routes for the tourist to explore: the *Strada dei Vini del Piave*, which runs for 68km southeast to ODERZO, and the more rewarding *Strada del Prosecco*, a 42-kilometre journey west to VALDOBBIADENE. Access to Conegliano itself is straightforward, as nearly all the regular Venice-to-Udine trains stop here.

The Town

The old centre of Conegliano, adhering to the slope of the Colle di Giano, is right in front of you as you come out of the station. The most decorative feature of Via XX Settembre – the original high street – is the unusual facade of the **Duomo**: a fourteenth-century portico, frescoed in the sixteenth century, which joins seamlessly the buildings on each side. The interior of the church has been much rebuilt, but retains fragments of fifteenth-century frescoes; the major adornment of the church, though, is the magnificent altarpiece of *The Madonna and Child with Saints and Angels*, painted in 1493 by Giambattista Cima, the most famous native of Conegliano.

Cima's birthplace, no. 24 Via G. B. Cima (at rear of duomo), has now been converted into the **Casa Museo di G. B. Cima** (Sat & Sun 4–6pm; L1000), which consists mainly of reproductions of his paintings and archaeological finds made during the restoration of the house.

The **Museo Civico** (summer Tues–Sun 9am–noon & 3.30–7pm; winter Tues–Sun 9am–noon & 2–5.30pm; L2000) is housed in the main tower of the reconstructed castello, on top of the hill. There are no masterpieces among the paintings, most of which are workshop productions, and the displays of medals, maps, war memorabilia, armour and so forth are no more fascinating than you'd expect. But two aspects of the museum lift it out of the rut: the exhibition on the upper floors devoted to *The Grape in Art*, a maniacally diligent investigation of the grape motif in every art form you could think of; and the view from the roof, after which you'll never look at a Cima painting in the same way again.

Practicalities

Conegliano's extremely helpful **tourist office** at Viale Carducci 32, in front of the station (Tues–Fri 9am–noon & 3–6pm, Sat 9am–noon; ☎0438/21.230), can give full details of the wine routes as well as the usual information. Via XX Settembre has all you'll need in the way of cafés, bars and food shops, but for one-star hotels you need to go a couple of kilometres out of town, to *Pare*, Via Vecchia Trevigiana 5 (☎0438/64.140; ④), or the nearby *Dei Mille*, Via Dei Mille 22 (☎0438/61.618; ③). The #1 bus from the train station goes by the *Pare*; both hotels have a trattoria downstairs. The *Canon d'Oro* has a fine **restaurant**, where a meal will cost around L30,000; the fish menu at *Città di Venezia*, Via XX Settembre 77, costs about L10,000 less.

Prosecco is the chief wine of the Conegliano district, and its producers compile a list of recommended outlets: two authorised bars to try in the town itself are the *Giardini* café in Piazza Duca d'Aosta and the *Al Montegan Enoteca* in Via Istria.

Vittorio Veneto

The name **VITTORIO VENETO** first appeared on the map in 1866 when, to mark the unification of Italy and honour the first king of the new country (Vittorio Emanuele II), the neighbouring towns of Cèneda and Serravalle (not previously the best of friends) were knotted together and rechristened. A new town hall was built midway along the avenue connecting the two towns, and the railway station constructed opposite, thus ensuring that the visitor steps straight from the train into a sort of no-man's-land.

Cèneda

CÈNEDA, the commercial centre of Vittorio Veneto, is primarily worth a visit for the **Museo della Battaglia**, next to the dull cathedral (May–Sept Tues–Sun 10am–noon & 4.30–6.30pm; Oct–April Tues–Sun 10am–noon & 3–5pm; L4000 includes entry to the Museo and San Lorenzo in Serravalle) – turn right out of the station and keep going until you see the sign for the centre. The museum is dedicated to the climactic Battle of Vittorio – fought in October 1918, this was the final engagement of World War I for the Italian army, which is why most towns in Italy have a Via Vittorio Veneto.

The only other building that merits a look in Cèneda is the church of **Santa Maria del Meschio**, where you'll find a splendid *Annunciation* by Andrea Previtali, a pupil of Giovanni Bellini. If you turn left off the Cèneda–Serravalle road instead of going right for the cathedral square, you'll come across it quickly.

Serravalle

SERRAVALLE, wedged in the neck of the gorge between the Col Visentin and the Cansiglio, is an entirely different proposition from its reluctant twin. Once through its southern gate you are into a town that has scarcely seen a demolition since the sixteenth century. Most of the buildings along Via Martiri della Libertà, Via Roma and Via Mazzini, and around the stage-like Piazza Marcantonio Flaminio, date from the fifteenth and sixteenth centuries – the handsomest being the shield-encrusted Loggia Serravallese. This is now the home of the **Museo del Cenedese** (May–Sept 10am–noon & 4–6.30pm; Oct–April 10am–noon & 2–5pm; closed Tues; L4000), a jumble of sculptural and archaeological bits and pieces, detached frescoes and minor paintings.

Your time is more profitably spent in **San Lorenzo dei Battuti** (May–Sept 3–4pm; Oct–April 2–3pm; closed Tues; same ticket as Museo), immediately inside the south gate, which is decorated with frescoes painted around 1450. Uncovered in 1953 and restored to rectify the damage done when Napoleon's lads used the chapel as a kitchen, this is one of the best-preserved fresco cycles in the Veneto.

Practicalities

The **tourist office**, at Piazza del Popolo 18 (Tues–Fri 9am–noon & 3–6pm, Sat 9am–noon), is best for information on the ski resorts and walking terrain around the town. There are hotels by the train station and in Cèneda, but you'll enjoy Vittorio Veneto more if you stay at the Serravalle end. Two minuscule places provide the cheapest **accommodation** here: *Al Postiglione*, Via Cavour 39 (☎0438/556.924; ③), and the extremely friendly *Vecchia Locanda*, a hundred metres up the hill at Via Tommaseo 80

(☎0438/552.121; ③). *Al Postiglione* serves some of the best **food** in town, and the *Vecchia Locanda* is good too; allow around L30,000 at the former, L25,000 at the latter. *Alla Giraffa*, Piazza Fontana 10, is a popular *gnoccoteca*, offering colossal plates of gnocchi with a variety of luscious sauces.

Belluno

The most northerly of the major towns of the Veneto, **BELLUNO** was once a strategically important ally of Venice, and today is the capital of a province which extends mainly over the eastern Dolomites. Although the urban centres to the south are not far away, Belluno's focus of attention lies clearly to the north – the network of the *Dolomiti-Bus* company radiates out from here, trains run regularly up the Piave Valley to Calalzo, and the tourist handouts are geared mostly to hikers and skiers. Just one train a day runs from Venice to Belluno directly, but it's just as quick anyway to go from Venice to Conegliano and change there; from Padua there are twelve trains daily.

Its position is Belluno's main appeal, but the old centre calls for an hour or two's exploration if you're passing through. The hub of the modern town, the spot where you'll find its most popular bars and cafés, is the wide **Piazza dei Martiri**, off the south side of which a road leads to the Piazza del Duomo, the kernel of the old town. The sixteenth-century **Duomo**, an amalgam of the Gothic and classical, and built in the pale yellow stone that is a feature of the buildings in Belluno, was designed by Tullio Lombardo; it has had to be reconstructed twice after earthquake damage, in 1873 and 1936. There are a couple of good paintings inside: one by Andrea Schiavone (first altar on right), and one by Jacopo Bassano (third altar on right). The stately **Campanile**, designed in 1743 by Filippo Juvarra, offers one of the great views of the Veneto.

Occupying one complete side of the Piazza del Duomo is the residence of the Venetian administrators of the town, the **Palazzo dei Rettori**, a frilly late fifteenth-century building dolled up with Baroque trimmings. A relic of more independent times stands on the right – the twelfth-century **Torre Civica**, all that's left of the medieval castle. Continuing round the Piazza, in Via Duomo, along the side of the town hall, you'll find the **Museo Civico** (April–Oct Tues–Sat 10am–noon & 3–6pm, Sun 10am–noon; Nov–March Tues–Fri 10am–noon & 3–6pm, Mon & Sat 10am–noon; free); the collection is strong on the work of Belluno's three best-known artists – the painters Sebastiano and Marco Ricci and the sculptor-woodcarver **Andrea Brustolon** – all of whom were born here between 1659 and 1673.

Via Duomo ends at the **Piazza del Mercato**, a tiny square hemmed in by porticoed Renaissance buildings. The principal street of the old town, **Via Mezzaterra**, goes down to the medieval **Porta Ruga** (veer left along the cobbled road about 50m from the end), from where the view up into the mountains will provide some compensation if you haven't managed to find the campanile open.

Practicalities

The **tourist office**, off Piazza dei Martiri at Via Psaro 21 (Mon–Sat 8am–1pm), is so dozy that you're better off asking for information at *ASVI Viaggi*, Piazza dei Martiri 27e (Mon–Fri 9am–12.30pm & 3–7pm, Sat 9am–12.30pm). Accommodation in Belluno is pitched at the skiing crowd, who generally aren't the type to suffer cash-flow problems. The cheapest **hotel** in town is the *Taverna*, Via Cipro 7 (☎0437/25.192; ④). For more central accommodation, there's a clutch of **hotels** on and just behind Piazza dei Martiri, of which the most reasonable is the *Centrale*, Via Loreto 2 (☎0437/943.349; ⑤). The best **restaurant** at a moderate price is *Al Sasso*, Via del Cansiglio 12; it serves local specialities at around L30,000 for a full meal. Two other genuine trattorias are close by: *Da Mara*, Piazza Mazzini 24, and *Moretto*, Via Valeriano 8 (both closed Sun).

Apart from *Dolomiti Neve* leaflets on the ski resorts of the area, *ASVI* can supply you with details of the **Alte Vie** (High Trails) of the eastern Dolomites – these are six mountain-top routes, up to nearly 200km in length, punctuated by Alpine refuges. Most popular is the *Alta Via* 1, a route right across the Dolomites from Braies to Belluno. The **Club Alpino Italiano**, at Via Ricci 1, runs several of the refuges, and is another good source of information for hikers.

If you feel like a very quick burst of Alpine exertion, it's best to head south, to the ski centre of NEVEGÀL (11km), easily reached by bus. From there you can take a chair lift up to the *Rifugio Brigata Alpina Cadore*, and then embark on the climb up the ridge to the refuge of **Col Visentin** (2hr 30min), from where you can survey the crags of the Dolomites in one direction and the waters of Venice in the other.

travel details

Trains

Conegliano to: Belluno (15 daily; 1hr–1hr 30min); Udine (30 daily; 1hr 15min); Venice (34 daily; 1hr); Vittorio Veneto (15 daily; 25min).

Padua to: Bassano (10 daily; 1hr 5min); Belluno (12 daily; 2hr); Bologna (34 daily; 1hr 25min); Feltre (12 daily; 50min); Milan (25 daily; 2hr 30min); Monsélice (9 daily; 25min); Rovigo (hourly; 40min); Venice (every 30min; 35min); Verona (25 daily; 55min); Vicenza (25 daily; 20min).

Treviso to: Castelfranco (hourly; 25min); Cittadella (hourly; 35min); Udine (hourly; 1hr 10min–1hr 30min); Venice (30 daily; 30min); Vicenza (hourly; 1hr).

Venice to: Bassano (14 daily; 1hr); Belluno (1 daily; 2hr); Bologna (19 daily; 1hr 15min–2hr); Castelfranco Veneto (every 1–2hr; 50min); Conegliano (34 daily; 1hr); Florence (4 daily; 3hr); Milan (25 daily; 2hr 50min–3hr 50min); Monsélice (6 daily; 50min); Padua (every 30min; 35min); Rovigo (19 daily; 1hr–1hr 30min); Treviso (30 daily; 30min); Trieste (14 daily; 2hr 10min); Udine (hourly; 2hr); Verona (at least 25 daily; 1hr 30min); Vicenza (25 daily; 55min); Vittorio Veneto (4 daily; 1–2hr).

Verona to: Milan (30 daily; 1hr 40min); Padua (25 daily; 50min); Venice (25 daily; 90min); Vicenza (30 daily; 30min).

Vicenza to: Castelfranco (hourly; 40min); Cittadella (hourly; 30min); Milan (30 daily; 1hr 40min); Padua (25 daily; 20min); Treviso (hourly; 1hr); Venice (25 daily; 55min); Verona (30 daily; 30min).

Buses

Bassano to: Ásolo (15 daily; 30min); Maróstica (hourly; 15min); Masèr (8 daily; 40min); Possagno (every 1–2hr; 40min).

Treviso to: Ásolo (hourly; 50min); Bassano (hourly; 1hr 20min); Padua (every 30min; 1hr 10min); Venice (every 20min; 55min).

Venice to: Malcontenta (hourly; 20min); Strà (every 30min; 45 min).

Vicenza to: Bassano (hourly; 1hr 10min); Maróstica (hourly; 40min).

CHAPTER SIX

FRIULI-VENEZIA GIULIA

The geographical complexity of **Friuli-Venezia Giulia** – over three thousand square miles of alps, limestone plateau, alluvial plain and shelving coastlands – is mirrored in its social diversity. The mountainous north is ethnically and linguistically Alpine; the old peasant culture of Friuli, though now waning, still gives a degree of coherence to the area south of the mountains; **Udine** seems Venetian, and **Grado**, slumbering in its Adriatic lagoons, Byzantine-Venetian; while **Aquileia**, a few miles north of these, is still redolent of its Roman and early Christian past. And **Trieste** itself, the regional capital, is a Hapsburg city, developed with Austrian capital to be the empire's great southern port. In spirit and appearance it is central European, more like Ljubljana in Slovenia than anywhere else in the region except **Gorizia**.

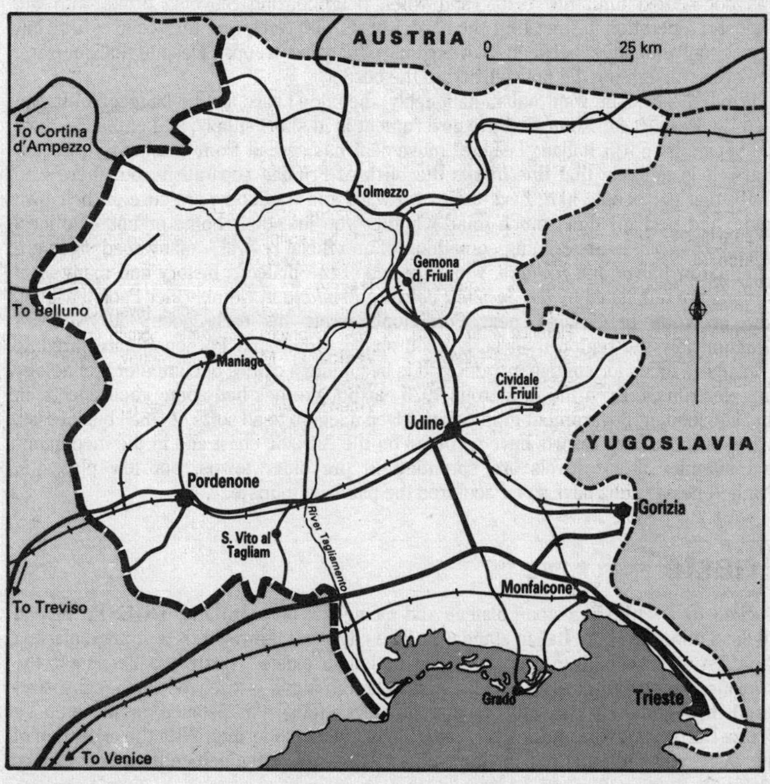

If one thing unites the different parts of the region, it's their remoteness from the conventional image of Italy, a remoteness that becomes stronger as you move east. This area has always been a bridge between the Mediterranean world and central Europe – that hazy multinational entity which begins, according to Eric Newby at least, at Monfalcone, north of Trieste. It has been invaded – sometimes enriched, often laid waste – from east and west and north, by the Romans, Huns, Goths, Lombards, Nazis and even the Cossacks. Venice in its heyday controlled the coast and plain as far as Udine; Napoleonic France succeeded the Venetian Republic, to be supplanted in turn by the Hapsburgs. Earlier this century the region saw some of the fiercest fighting of World War I on the **Carso** (the plateau behind Trieste), where artillery shells splintered the limestone into deadly shrapnel and the hills are still scarred with trenches. Vast war memorials and ossuaries punctuate the landscape: the bones of 60,000 soldiers lie at Oslavia, near Gorizia; 100,000 at Redipuglia; 25,000 in the Udine ossuary. There was less loss of life in World War II, but just as much terror. Fuelled by widespread and long-standing anti-Slavism, Italian Fascism in Trieste was especially virulent, and the city held Italy's only concentration camp. One of the strangest sideshows of the war was staged north of Udine: Cossack troops, led by White Russian officers, made an alliance with the Nazis and invaded Carnia, on the promise of a Cossack homeland among the Carnian mountains once the Reich was secure. No more invading armies have taken this road, but the last border dispute between Italy and Yugoslavia was not settled until the 1970s, and when neighbouring Slovenia broke with the Yugoslav federation in June 1991 the border posts with Italy were the scene of brief but fierce confrontations between Slovene and Yugoslav troops. Despite Italian fears, however, the fighting did not spill across the border.

While the Friulani want Italian nationality, they don't care for the baggage of Italian identity. Respect for Rome and the government is in short supply, and enthusiasm for the separatist north Italian "League" movement has spread from Lombardy in recent years. It is unlikely that this marks the birth of Friulian separatism, but there's no doubt that the people here have their own ways and traditions, are sure of their own value, and perhaps don't much mind whether you like their home or not. The local dialect, *friulano*, is undergoing something of an official revival – many road signs are bilingual in Italian and *friulano*, while studies of the dialect's history and many local variants are published by the *Società Filologica Friulana* in Udine. (Pier Paolo Pasolini, who grew up in Casarsa, near Pordenone, wrote his early poetry in *friulano*.) Economically the region is in fairly good shape: Udine and Pordenone are thriving, Trieste is a focus for container traffic and is becoming a centre of computer technology and electronics. Even the disastrous 1976 earthquake has had some good effects, in that subsequent government grants have given a leg-up to all sorts of small businesses. A few purpose-built resorts have sprouted on the Adriatic coast and in the mountains, and summer arts festivals are sprouting in the older towns, but few places in Friuli-Venezia Giulia have so far acquired the patina of tourism.

Trieste

Backed by a white limestone plateau and facing the blue Adriatic, **TRIESTE** has an idyllic setting, even by Italian standards. The city itself, however, is a strange place: a capitalist creation built to play a role that no longer exists. Trieste was *Tergeste* to the Romans, who captured it in 178 BC, but although signs of their occupancy are scattered throughout the city (the theatre off Corso Italia, for instance, or the arch by Piazza Barbacan), what strikes you straightaway is its modernity. With the exception of the castle and cathedral of San Giusto, the city's whole pre-nineteenth-century history seems dim and vague beside the massive Neoclassical architecture and confident Baroque of the **Borgo Teresiano** – the name given to the city centre, after Empress Maria Theresa (1740–80), who initiated the development.

Trieste was constructed largely with Austrian capital to serve as the Hapsburg empire's southern port, but its brief heyday drew to a close after 1918, when it finally became Italian and discovered that, for all its good intentions, Italy had no economic use for it. The city languished for sixty years, and is only now making a new role for itself. Computer-based firms are cropping up, while seaborne trade goes through the container port on the south side of Trieste, leaving the old quays as car parks.

Lying as it does on the political and ethnic fault-line between the Latin and Slavic worlds, Trieste has long been a city of political extremes. In the last century it was a hotbed of *irredentismo* – an Italian nationalist movement to "redeem" the Austrian lands of Trieste and the Trentino. After 1918 the tensions increased, leading to a strong Fascist presence in Friuli-Venezia Giulia. Yugoslavia and the Allies fought over Trieste until 1954, when the city and a connecting strip of coast were secured for Italy, though a definitive border settlement was not reached until 1975. Tito kept the Istrian peninsula, whose fearful Italian population emigrated in huge numbers – for instance, Fiume (Rijeka) lost 58,000 of its 60,000 Italians. The neo-Fascist MSI party has always done well here, and there's even a local anti-Slav party, the *Lista per Trieste*, which is sinking fast in the polls but still publicises "Slav provocation" and other supposed dangers to Italian culture. Yet nationalism provoked the development of its opposite, and there is an intense socialist tradition among Trieste's intellectuals.

Arrival, information and accommodation

Coaches from Trieste's **airport**, at Ronchi dei Legionari, terminate at the city's Piazza Libertà **bus station**, which is right by the central **train station**. The main **tourist office** is in the Castello di San Giusto (Mon–Sat 9am–1pm & 4–7pm, Sun 9am–1pm; ☎040/309.242), with an equally helpful office at the train station (same hours).

The cheapest decent **hotels** are the *Julia*, Via XXX Ottobre 5 (☎040/370.045; ④), the *Marina*, Via Galatti 14 (☎040/369.298; ④), and the *Centro*, Via Roma 13 (☎040/634.408; ④). Women and married couples can put up cheaply at the *Casa Famiglia Mater Dei*, at Strada Guardiella 8 (☎040/54.332), a convent that provides short-stay accommodation. There's also a recently restored **youth hostel**, 8km out of the city at Viale Miramare 331 (☎040/224.101; ①) – take a #6 or #36 bus from the station to Grignano. The nearest **campsite** is the *Obelisco* (☎040/211.655), 7km away in Opicina, which is on the #4 bus route and the *tranvia* (cable tramway) from Piazza Oberdan.

The City

The focal point of the city's pre-modern history, and its prime tourist site, is the hill of **San Giusto**, with its castle and cathedral. The **Castello** (daily 8am–sunset) is a fifteenth-century Venetian fortress, built near the site of the Roman forum; there's nothing much to see, but a walk round the ramparts is *de rigueur*. Its **museum** (Tues–Sun 9am–12.45pm; L3000) houses a small collection of antique weaponry. The **Cattedrale di San Giusto** (closed 3–6pm), close to the ruins of the Roman basilica, is a typically Triestine synthesis of styles. In the fourteenth century the three churches on this site were combined into one, as is obvious when you see the nave. The facade is predominantly Romanesque, but includes five Roman columns and a Gothic rose window, and the entrance pillars are fragments from a Roman tomb. Inside, between Byzantine pillars, there are fine thirteenth-century frescoes of Saint Justus, a Christian martyr killed during the persecutions of Diocletian.

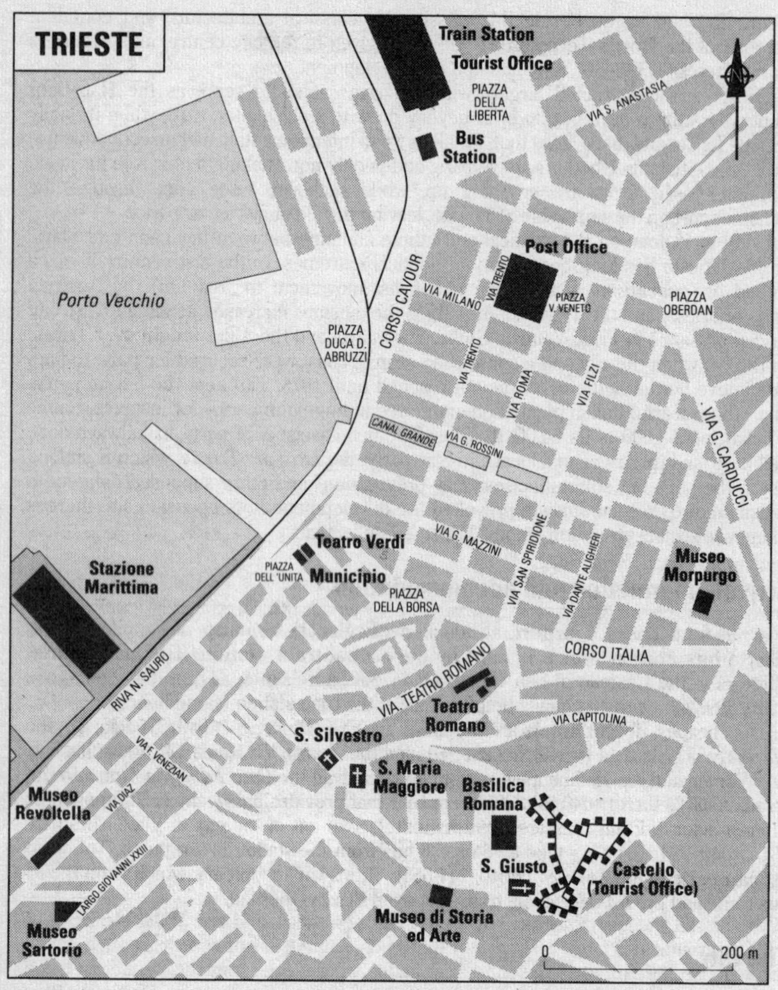

Just down the cobbled lane from the cathedral, at Via Cattedrale 15, is the **Museo di Storia ed Arte** (daily 9am–1pm; L3000), a collection of cultural plunder that embraces Himalayan sculpture, Egyptian manuscripts and Roman glass. Behind the museum, and accessible from Piazza Cattedrale, is the **Orto Lapidario**, a pleasant modernist environment in which fragments of classical statuary, pottery and inscriptions are arranged on benches and against walls, among the cow-parsley and miniature palm trees. The little Corinthian temple on the upper level contains the remains of J. J. Winckelmann (1717–68), the German archaeologist and theorist of Neoclassicism, who was murdered in Trieste by a man to whom he had shown off his collection of antique coins.

Trieste's principal museum is the **Revoltella**, Via Diaz 27, housed in a Viennese-style palazzo bequeathed to the city by the financier Baron Pasquale Revoltella in 1869. Recently re-opened after a twenty-year restoration, its combined display of stately

JOYCE IN TRIESTE

From 1905 to 1915, and again in 1919–20, **James Joyce** and his wife Nora lived in Trieste. After staying at Piazza Ponterosso 3 for a month, they moved to the third-floor flat at Via San Nicolò 30. (In 1919 the poet Umberto Saba bought a bookshop on the ground floor at the same address. The two writers seem never to have met, though they had a common friend in the novelist Italo Svevo.) There is no plaque in Via San Nicolò, but there is one on Via Bramante 4, quoting the postcard that Joyce despatched in 1915 to his brother Stanislaus, whose Irredentist sympathies had landed him in an Austrian internment camp. The postcard announced that the first chapter of James's new work, *Ulysses*, was finished.

home furnishings and Triestine paintings is well worth a look, although unfortunately access is restricted to rather sluggish guided tours – currently at 9am, 10.30am, noon, 3pm, 4.30pm and 6pm (L5000). The nearby **Museo Sartorio**, in Largo Papa Giovanni XXIII (daily 9am–1pm; L3000), has ceramics and icons downstairs and oppressive private rooms upstairs, all dark veneers, Gothic tracery and bad Venetian paintings.

A vastly more pleasant domestic interior is the **Museo Morpurgo**, north of San Giusto at Via Imbriani 5 (daily 9am–1pm; L2000). The palazzo was left to the city by the merchant and banker Mario Morpurgo di Nilma, and its apartments have not really been touched since their first decoration in the 1880s. With its sepia photographs and other memorabilia, it feels less like a museum than like a home whose owners went on holiday and never came back.

The ugliest episode of recent European history is embodied by the **Risiera di San Sabba**, on the southern flank of Trieste in Via Valmaura (daily 9am–1pm, until 7pm in May), on the #10 bus route. Once a rice-hulling plant, this was the only concentration camp in Italy. Its crematorium was installed after the German invasion of Italy in September 1943, a conversion supervised by Erwin Lambert, who had designed the death camp at Treblinka. Nobody knows exactly how many prisoners were burned at the *Risiera* before the Yugoslavs liberated the city on May 1, 1945, but a figure of 5000 is usually cited by historians. Nazism had plenty of sympathisers in this part of Italy: in 1920 Mussolini extolled the zealots of Friuli-Venezia Giulia as model Fascists, and the commander of the camp was a local man. A permanent exhibition at the *Risiera* serves as a reminder of Fascist crimes in the region.

Eating and drinking

Trieste is still the leading coffee port in the Mediterranean, and one of the pleasures of walking around the *borgo teresiano* is the unexpected scent of roasting coffee which wafts across the streets. Triestines treat coffee with great seriousness, and there's a plethora of places in which to sample the various imports. (Incidentally, if you ask for a *cappuccino* in Trieste you may well get an espresso with a dash of milk – what's known as a *macchiato* anywhere else in Italy. So ask for a *cappuccino grande* or a *caffè latte*.) As with the rest of Friuli-Venezia Giulia, the cuisine in Trieste bears central European influence – goulash, potato noodles and cheese dumplings featuring on many menus. For less formal meals, a summertime attraction are the *osmizze*, impromptu eating places offering the simplest of local produce at rock-bottom prices.

Cafés, bars and gelaterie

Trieste's favourite **café** is the *Caffè San Marco*, which has occupied its premises on Via G. Battisti for some eighty years; don't leave without at least a peek at its Art Nouveau-style interior of marble table-tops, mahogany panels, mirrors and gilt. Much of the historic style of the *Caffè Tommaseo* on Piazza Tommaseo – a rendezvous for Italian nationalists in the last century – was lost in a recent refurbishment, but it makes a pleasant if pricey refuge in the summer heat. In addition to the conventional cafés, the city centre has many *torrefazioni* – cafés which roast and sell beans, as well as grinding them; try the *Caffè Colombiana* in Via Carducci near the Via Coroneo junction, or the *Crème Caffè* in Piazza Goldoni.

Many of the city's **bars** are as glossy as the top-notch cafés. The bar in the Galleria Protti – which runs north from the Piazza Borsa, inside the *Assicurazioni Generali* building – has a Thirties' nightclub feel, while the *Caffè degli Specchi* in Piazza dell'Unita d'Italia is like the cocktail lounge of a Twenties' Cunard liner. A few bars, including the venerable *Caffè San Marco*, have occasional live music. The *Roxy Bar* and *Nutty Bar* in Via Madonnina, the *Music Club Tor Cucherna* in Via Chiauchiara, the *Tavernetta* in Via Picarda, and the *Birreria Spofford* in Via Rossetti all attract a student clientele.

For **ice cream**, the best spot is the leafy Viale XX Settembre, known as the "Aquedotto", where the citizens stroll in the evening. *Pipolo* is superb, but there are many to choose from. The Viale is sometimes less congenial at its Piazza San Giovanni end, a gathering place for young *fascisti*. The *gelateria* at Via della Madonna del Mare 8, and the *Gelateria Viti* on the Passeggio Sant'Andrea (bus #8 from the train station), are also excellent.

Snacks

For **snacks** and light meals, the most interesting places in Trieste are the *osterie*, where the landlord draws off wine by the glass from barrels stacked behind the bar. The local sparkling wine called *prosecco*, praised long ago by the Roman Empress Livia, is delicious; and *terrano*, a very sharp red wine grown only on the limestone highlands around the city, should also be tried, ideally as an accompaniment to the heavy Triestine food. The *Bar Tevere* in Via Malcanton, just behind the Piazza d'Italia, is a lively place with simple food; fried sardines or *polpette* in a bread roll, with a glass of *tocai friulano* or *malvasia*, furnish an excellent lunch. There are other *osterie* at Via delle Settefontane 13, Via Veneziana 11 and Via Carducci 34a, where there's an excellent range of bottled wines for sale too.

The *Buffet Pepi* in Via Cassa di Risparmio is a favourite student lunch-stop – offering excellent sausages and bowls of smoking sauerkraut, its cuisine emphasises Trieste's Austrian connections. Around the corner at Via San Nicolò 1b is *La Piola*, a flashier version of the same. Another student hang-out is *Notorious* in Via del Bosco – sandwiches and salads on the ground floor, and a good cheap trattoria on the first floor.

Restaurants and osmizze

For dependable Italian food, try the very popular *Trattoria dell'Antica Ghiacceretta* in Via dei Fornelli, or *Da Giovanni*, at Via S. Lazzaro 146. *Trattoria alla Palestra*, Via Madonna del Mare 18, has fine food at reasonable prices, and an English-speaking host. *L'Uva Passa*, Via F. Corridoni 2, off Piazza Garibaldi, is a bright, friendly place patronised by students. The prestige restaurant is *Antica Trattoria Suban*, at Via Comici 2; it deserves its reputation, but is pricey. Seafood can be outstanding in Trieste – it's worth making your way out to Viale Miramare for a meal at *Allo Squero*, at no. 42, or *La Marinella* at no. 323. *Branzino* and *sogliola* – sea bass and sole – are local favourites.

Decent **pizzas** can be found at *Il Barattolo* in Piazza Sant'Antonio, or at *2000* and *2001* in Via delle Settefontane. The self-service restaurant chain, *Brek*, has outlets in Via San Francesco and Via d'Alviano, and the food is good of its sort.

The thing to do in summer or early autumn is to find an **osmizza**, an informal restaurant where farmers sell their own produce, such as home-cured meats, cheese, olives, bread and wine. A frequent bonus is a stunning view over the bay of Trieste or the limestone hills behind the city. The problem with *osmizze* is that they are temporary, don't advertise, and usually lie off the beaten track – which makes them all the more worth tracking down. Your best bet is to buy a copy of the Slovene newspaper, *Primorski Dnevnik*, preferably the Sunday edition, which usually prints up-to-date lists, and if you can't make head or tail of the Slovene listings, ask someone in a tourist office or a hotel. Otherwise, just take a #44 bus from outside the station, and get off at Contovello or Prosecco, and start asking if there is an *osmizza* nearby. You'll know you are getting warm when you see arrows on clumps of leaves suspended from archways and lampposts: they point the way to the nearest *osmizza*.

Listings

Airport information ☎040/773.225 or ☎0481/77.310.

Bus information ☎040/370.160.

Car rental *Hertz*, Via Mazzini 1 (☎040/60.650).

Club Alpino Italiano Via Macchiavelli 17 (☎040/60.317).

Consulates *UK*, Vicolo delle Ville 16 (Tues & Fri 9am–12.30pm; ☎040/302.884); *USA*, Via Pellegrini 42 (Mon, Wed & Fri 10am–noon; ☎040/911.780).

Festivals and events During the summer the village of Muggia hosts an international theatre festival, and there are programmes of musical events at the castle of San Giusto. The *Verdi* opera house has a summer season. The Festa dell'Unità runs from end of July to mid-August – check the timetable in *Il Piccolo*, Trieste's daily paper, which should also have details of the festivals in the Carso villages (see below).

Hospital Ospedale Maggiore, Piazza dell'Ospedale (☎040/7761).

Laundry Via Ginnastica 36.

Police The *Questura* is on Via Teatro Romano (☎040/37.901).

Post office The main post office is in Piazza Vittorio Veneto (Mon–Sat 8am–7.30pm).

Taxis ☎040/54.533; ☎040/418.822; ☎040/772.946.

Telephones *SIP*, Viale XX Settembre 5 (daily 8am–9.30pm); *ASST*, Via Pascoli 9 (24hr).

Train information ☎040/418.207.

Travel agent *Agemar*, Piazza Duca degli Abruzzi 1a (☎040/363.737) – for ferry tickets to Grado.

Around Trieste: the Carso

The **Carso** is the Italian name for the limestone uplands which rise from the Venetian plain south of Monfalcone and eventually merge into the Istrian plateau. The border changes have put most of the Carso within Slovenia (its Slovene name is *Kras*), yet even the narrow strip inside Italy, behind Trieste, is geologically, botanically and socially distinct.

Like all limestone country, the Carso is a harsh environment, arid in summer and sometimes snowbound in winter. Its surface is studded with sink-holes, eroded by streams which sometimes reappear miles away on the coast, while in some places – near Aurisina, for instance – it is scarred with World War I trenches. The dour villages of thick-walled houses seem to hunker down against the *bora*, the northeasterly wind which blasts this area at every time of year. (When it's especially fierce, ropes are strung along the steeper streets in Trieste.)

Several bus services run up onto the Carso from Trieste – #42, #43, #44, #45 and #46. A good place to start an exploration is **BORGO GROTTA GIGANTE**, which boasts the world's largest accessible cave – 107m deep by 208m broad (guided visits April–Oct every 30min; Nov–March every hr; L8000). Whatever the temperature outside, it's a steady 11 or 12°C in the cave, so come prepared. Close to the cave is *Milic*, a pleasant trattoria, and the *Centro Sportivo Mario Ervatti* (☎040/225.047), the only bike-hire place in the area – useful should you not have a car but want to explore more of the Carso. You can make a pleasant round-trip to the Grotta Gigante by taking the old *tranvia* from Piazza Oberdan to OPICINA, and then the #45 bus, which returns via PROSECCO. The *tranvia* runs every twenty minutes between 7.30am and 8pm.

Two walks near the city can be recommended, both needing at least half a day. The **Strada Vicentina** (or *Napoleonica*) is some three kilometres long, curving along the hillside above the city, between the *Obelisco* campsite and the hamlet of BORGO NAZARIO (near Prosecco). It's a scenic but unstrenuous walk, partly shadowed by trees and partly cut through almost sheer limestone cliffs. Access couldn't be simpler: the *Obelisco* is a stop on the *tranvia*, and the Borgo Nazario end is near Via San Nazario, where the #42 and #45 buses stop on their way back to Trieste station.

The other walk, through the **Val Rosandra**, is very different. This miniature wilderness of limestone cliffs and sumac trees is the local rock-climbing headquarters. Take bus #40 to SAN DORLIGO DELLA VALLE and follow the road at the back of the square toward the hills. After half a mile or so the tarmac gives way to a path bordered on the right by Roman aqueducts. Half an hour later you see the little church of Santa Maria in Siaris, perched on a spur of rock high on the right. Beyond this is a waterfall, then the tiny hamlet of BOTTEZZA – the last habitation before the Slovene border.

From Trieste to Duino

The nearest resort to Trieste on the **Triestine Riviera** – as the twenty kilometres of coastline to Duino are optimistically known – is **BARCOLA**, connected to the city by the #6 bus service. Developed during Trieste's great days at the end of the nineteenth century, it is now really a suburb that comes to life in summer, when all Trieste seems to come here to chat, play cards, sunbathe and swim. Despite the cargo ships and tankers moored in the harbour, the water is moderately clean, and the showers are free.

Miramare

Standing at the tip of a rocky promontory 7km from Trieste, the salt-white castle of **MIRAMARE** is the area's prime tourist attraction, and a dream-castle to rank with Ludwig's in Bavaria. (Take the #36 bus from Barcola, or the train from Trieste.) The Archduke Ferdinand Maximilian, Emperor Franz Josef's younger brother, was once forced ashore here by a squall, and resolved to buy the site. He built the castle and laid out its grounds between 1856 and 1870, but never lived to see it completed – having accepted Napoleon III's offer to make him the "Emperor of Mexico", Maximilian was shot in 1867, in the line of imperial duty. His wife Charlotte went mad, and the legend was born that anyone who spends a night in Miramare will come to a bad end.

The kitsch **interior** (Mon–Fri 9am–1.30pm, Sat & Sun 9am–12.30pm, plus daily 2.30–6.30pm July–Sept; L6000) is a remarkable example of regal decadence. The "Monarchs' Salon", for instance, is embellished with portraits of the King of Norway, the Emperor of Brazil, the Czar of Russia – anyone, no matter how fraudulent or despotic, as long as he or she's a nominal monarch. This softens you up for the bedroom and its images of the most important events in the history of this area, pride of place going to the construction of the castle, of course. Other rooms are panelled and furnished like a ship's quarters, reflecting Maximilian's devotion to the Austrian navy.

Sometimes a boat runs between Trieste and Miramare – check with the tourist office. In July and August a *son et lumière* called "Maximilian of Mexico: an Emperor's Tragedy" is performed beside the sea, twice nightly on Tuesdays, Thursdays and Saturdays; the first performance on Tuesdays – at 9.30pm – is in English.

Duino and around

The village of **DUINO** (#43 bus from Trieste) is dominated by its two castles, the **Castello Vecchio** and the fifteenth-century **Castello Nuovo**, seat of the Princes of Thurn and Taxis down to the present day. It was in the latter that Rainer Maria Rilke began the great *Duino Elegies*, a work dedicated to his host, the incumbent princess. Access to the Castello Nuovo is granted only to large guided groups, but you can get into the Castello Vecchio (daily 10am–noon & 5–7pm) – now a ruined eyrie above the sea, it commands magnificent views.

The bus from Trieste goes on to **SAN GIOVANNI DEL TIMAVO**, stopping by the Gothic church of San Giovanni in Tuba, built on the site of a fifth-century basilica. A few yards away, the River Timavo surges from the limestone just below road level, the end of a subterranean course of some forty kilometres. The water is icy cold, and emerald-green fronds wave with the current in the deep pool below the spring. Despite the traffic, this is a mysterious spot. The spring is described in Virgil's *Aeneid*, and the Greek historian Strabo says there was a sacred wood here, where white horses were sacrificed to Diomedes, god-hero of the Trojan Wars.

Palmanova, Aquileia and around

Bordered by the Tagliamento in the west and the Isonzo in the east, and drained by other rivers flowing into the sandy, shallow waters at the head of the Adriatic, the triangle of flatlands **south of Udine** seems unpromising territory for a visitor – mile upon mile of maize fields, punctuated by telegraph poles, streams, level roads and newish villages. Yet the dull fields of this secretive region hide one of the most splendid surviving monuments of early Christendom, and one of Italy's most charming resorts is tucked away in the lagoons to the south. If you don't have your own transport, **buses** are the way to explore the region: buses leave Udine for Grado at least every hour, calling at Palmanova, Cervignano train station and Aquileia on the way.

Palmanova

Once ranked as the strongest fortress in all Europe, **PALMANOVA** is a massive Venetian garrison town built in 1593 in the form of a nine-pointed star, its symmetrical streets converging on a large hexagonal piazza. Guided tours are conducted through the tunnels in the fortifications, and the Museo Civico fills out the story further. Apart from this military curiosity, there is no reason to visit the town.

Aquileia

AQUILEIA was established as a Roman colony in 181 BC, its location at the eastern edge of the Venetian plain – on the bank of a navigable river a few kilometres from the sea – being ideal for defensive and trading purposes. It became the nexus for all Rome's dealings with points east and north, and by 10 BC, when the Emperor Augustus received Herod the Great here, Aquileia was the capital of the *Regio Venetia et Histria* and the fourth most important city in Italy, after Rome, Milan and Capua. In 314 the famous Patriarchate of Aquileia was founded, and under the first patriarch, Theodore, a great basilica was built. Sacked by Attila in 452 and again by the Lombards in 568, Aquileia lost the patriarchate to Grado, which was protected from invasion by its lagoons. It regained its primacy in the early eleventh century under Patriarch Poppo, who rebuilt the basilica and erected the campanile, a landmark for miles around. But regional power inevitably passed to Venice, and in 1751 Aquileia lost its patriarchate for the last time, to Udine. The sea has long since retreated, and the River Natissa is a reed-clogged stream. Aquileia is now a dusty little town of 3500 people, bisected by the main Udine-to-Grado road, but the remnants of its ancient heyday make it one of north-east Italy's most important archaeological sites.

In 1348 an earthquake destroyed much of Poppo's work on the **Basilica** (daily 8.30am–noon & 3–7pm), but the building is still superb, the Gothic elements of the reconstruction – as in the capitals and arches – harmonising perfectly with the Romanesque. The basilica's glory, though, is Theodore's mosaic pavement, which undulates the full length of the nave like a pattern of brilliant carpets. Rediscovered only this century, the mosaics are amazingly joyful and serene, combining and reconciling Christian and pagan iconography. Look for the blond angel bearing the laurel wreath and palm frond – whether it represents the Pax Romana or Christian Victory, no one can be sure. Other mosaics from Theodore's original basilica, depicting a whole bestiary, have been discovered around the base of the campanile (access from inside the basilica). The ninth-century crypt under the chancel has very beautiful soft-hued frescoes, distinctly Byzantine in form.

A couple of minutes' walk from the basilica, on the main Via Giulia Augusta, is the **Museo Archeologico** (Mon 9am–2pm, Tues–Fri 9am–6.30pm, Sat & Sun 9am–1pm & 3–6.30pm; L6000). Items relating to all aspects of Roman life are on show, from surgical needles to a reconstructed galley and statues of the gods. In all likelihood a sculpture school flourished here in the first century, which would account for the fine naturalistic busts, a collection that includes one masterpiece – an almost translucent marble head of Livia Augusta.

The **Museo Paleocristiano** (Mon–Fri 9am–2pm, Sat & Sun 9am–1pm; free), in the northern part of the town, is recommended solely for those insatiable for Roman remains. The fifteen-minute riverside walk to the museum from the basilica is pleasant though, taking you past what were once the quays of Aquileia; and from the museum you can loop back along the main road, past the forum, to the basilica and the bus stop.

The **tourist office** is in the heart of the historic quarter in Piazza Capitolo (April–Oct 9am–noon & 3.30–6pm). In the newer part of town, west of the main road, you'll find the cheapest of Aquilea's three **hotels**, the *Aquila Nera*, Piazza Garibaldi 5 (☎0431/91.045; ④). It has an excellent, inexpensive **restaurant** too. Accommodation is often available in **private houses** along Via Gemina, site of *Camping Aquileia* (May–Sept; ☎0431/91.042).

Grado

Some 11km from Aquileia, isolated among lagoons at the end of a causeway, is the ancient island-town of **GRADO**, through which Aquileia once traded with Syria, Cyprus, Arabia and Asia Minor. Highlight of the small historic centre is the sixth-century **Basilica**, notable for its Byzantine-influenced capitals and the Venetian fourteenth-century silver *pala* on the high altar. The adjacent church of Santa Maria delle Grazie is from the sixth century too.

Most of Grado, however, is a resort that extends eastwards along the sandy island. The beaches are endless, the water as warm and safe as a bath, and almost as shallow – indeed, the name of the town comes from the gentle angle of its shore. The free beaches are at the western end; if you want a locker, deckchair and shower facilities, you will have to pay a few thousand lire to one of the businesses on the Lungomare Adriatico.

Ten buses per day make the one-hour run to Udine, and there's also a half-hourly bus connection from Cervignano train station, on the Venice-to-Trieste line. The best way to visit Grado, though, is by boat from Trieste; on Tuesdays, Fridays, Saturdays and Sundays the little steamer *Dionea* calls morning and evening at the Molo Torpediniere on its way from and to the city.

Grado's **tourist office**, at Viale Dante Alighieri 68 (daily May 9.30am–4.30pm, June–Sept 8am–7pm), has details of the town's **hotels**, the majority of which are fairly expensive and often insist on your taking full pension. Two cheaper ones are the *Villa Teresa*, Via Galilei 1 (☎0431/80.467; ④), an attractively crumbling villa with a view of the lagoon, and the *Sirenetta*, Via Milano 1 (☎0431/80.404; ④), on the beachfront. Another smart one-star is the *Villa Patrizia*, in a leafy part of town at Viale Italia 19 (☎0431/80.897; ④). The best local **campsites** are at Grado Pineta, around 3km east of the town and served by regular buses – *Camping al Bosco* (☎0431/80.485), *Camping Punta Spin* (☎0431/80.732) and *Camping Europa* (☎0431/80.877). Of the many **restaurants** where you can sample Grado's fish specialities, two of the most convivial are *Al Balaor*, off Piazza XXVI Maggio at Calle Zonini 3, and *Trattoria de Toni*, in Piazza Duca d'Aosta. The pizzas are very good at the tiny *Santa Lucia*, secreted in an old-town alleyway at Calle Corbato 2. *Enoteca da Pino*, on Via Galilei, is the spot for a quick bite and a glass of wine.

Lignano

A few kilometres westwards across the lagoons lies the purpose-built resort complex of **LIGNANO**. Hemingway used to shoot duck on this sandy, pine-wooded peninsula at the mouth of the Tagliamento, but nowadays it appeals to beachniks only, and is especially popular with German tourists. Its 100,000-plus beds get booked pretty solid in summer – the **tourist office** at Via Latisana 42 will winkle out whatever hotel and campsite vacancies there are. If you do get washed up here, the wine and cakes at *Enoteca-bar Scarpa*, Vicolo Marano 9, will cheer you up. LIGNANO PINETA, 4km away, is less high-rise but equally dedicated to the beach; there's a pleasant **campsite** here, the *Pino Mare* (☎0431/428.512), a few steps from the shore on Viale Adriatico.

Gorizia

As with other towns in this region, the tranquillity of present-day **GORIZIA** (virtually midway along the Udine–Trieste rail line) belies the turbulence of its past. The castle which dominates the old centre was the power-base of the dukes of Gorizia, who ruled the area for four centuries. After their eclipse, Venice briefly ruled the town at the start of the sixteenth century, before the Hapsburgs took over. It was controlled from Vienna uninterruptedly until August 8, 1916, when the Italian army occupied it – but only until the rout at Caporetto, some 50km north. The border settlement after World War II literally split houses in Gorizia down the middle. Italy kept the town proper but lost its eastern perimeter to Yugoslavia, where the new regime resolved to build its own Gorizia: **Nova Gorica** – "New Gorizia"– is the result. The *NAŠ TITO* (OUR TITO) painted in huge letters on the hill overlooking the town also dates from the period of socialist construction, though in fact that bit of hillside is Italian territory.

The town's appearance, like that of Trieste, is distinctly central European, stamped with the authority of Empress Maria Theresa. Numerous parks and gardens – thriving in the area's mild microclimate – further enhance the fin de siècle atmosphere. Again like Trieste, it's a major shopping town for Slovenes, which explains the large number of electrical goods, clothes and food shops, and the good cafés and restaurants.

One of the finest of its Neoclassical buildings is the **Palazzo Attems** in Piazza De Amicis, which now houses the picture gallery and town archives. The building is closed "per restauro" until further notice, which is a pity, as the gallery has some nice pieces, including an altarpiece by Antonio Guardi. The **Museo di Storia e Arte** (Tues–Sun 10am–noon & 3–6pm; L4000) is in the Borgo Castello, the quarter built round the castle by the Venetians; the collection of local folkloric items and handicrafts passes a half-hour or so, but the view from the castle is more inspiring.

Probably the strangest sight in Gorizia is the crypt in the Franciscan monastery at **Castagnavizza** – Kostanjevica, rather, for the monastery lies across the border in Nova Gorica. This is the burial place of the last of the Bourbons. After Louis Philippe was ousted by the bloodless revolution of July 1830, the Bourbons were exiled from France; the family eventually arrived in Gorizia in 1836, and the Hapsburgs allowed them to stay. To judge by the impassioned entries in the visitors' book, the silence of the crypt is regularly disturbed by French royalists, whose withered bouquets line the walls. The French state must reckon that the republic is now strong enough to withstand any monarchist pressure, for it is apparently expressing interest in obtaining the return of these royal relics. The monastery was also home to Brother Stanislav Skrabec (1844–1918), an important Slovene linguist, and the library of 10,000 books includes a rare copy of the first Slovene grammar, inscribed by its author Adam Bohoric (1584). The easiest approach is to take a taxi up the hill once you're across the border; walking is the best way back. Once there, ring the bell; there's no charge, but you should offer a donation.

For information on the current status of the Palazzo Attems, ask at the **tourist office** at Galleria del Corso 100. For accommodation, there are four one-star **hotels**, the cheapest being the *Driussi*, Via Duca d'Aosta 27 (☎0481/531.693; ④).

Udine

It is fitting that the best artworks in **UDINE** are by Giambattista Tiepolo: his airy brilliance suits this town. Running beside and beneath the streets are little canals called *rogge*, diverted from the Torre and Cormor rivers, and these bright streams reflect light onto the walls and through the roadside greenery. Comfortable and bourgeois, Udine is the second city of Friuli-Venezia Giulia, and some say that although it has less than half the population of Trieste, it will gain the ascendancy sooner or later. Udine seems everything that Trieste is not – delicate, untroubled, successful. Trieste, on the other hand, has a richness of identity beside which Udine can seem as pallid as the pink-and-white facade of its famous town hall.

Along with Cividale, Tricesimo and Zuglio, Udine was one of the frontier bastions of Imperial Rome, and by the sixth century AD it was far more than a garrison colony. But it was not until the thirteenth century that it started to become a regional centre. Patriarch Bertoldo di Andechs (1218–51) can be seen as the father of Udine – he established two markets (the "old market" in Via Mercatovecchio, and the new one in Piazza Matteotti, still a marketplace), moved the patriarchate from Cividale to the castle of Udine, and set up a city council. In 1362 the dukes of Austria acquired the place by treaty, but not for long: Venice, now hungry for territory, captured Udine in 1420, after several assaults and sieges. The city was ruled by Venetian governors for almost 400 years – until 1797, when the Venetian Republic surrendered to Napoleon.

The City

Legend has it that the castle-topped hill at the heart of Udine was built by Attila's hordes, using their helmets as buckets, so that their leader could relish the spectacle of Aquileia in flames, 36km away. The place to start any exploration of Udine is at the foot of the hill, in the **Piazza Libertà**, a square whose architectural ensemble is matched by few cities in Italy. The fifteenth-century **Palazzo del Comune** is a clear homage to the Palazzo Ducale in Venice, and the clock tower facing the palazzo, built in 1527, similarly has a Venetian model – the lion on the facade and the bronze "Moors" who strike the hours on top of the tower are explicit references to the Torre dell'Orologio in Piazza San Marco. The statue at the north end of the square is a bad allegory of *Peace*, donated to the town by Emperor Franz I to commemorate the Hapsburg acquisition of Udine.

To walk up to the **Castello**, go through the **Arco Bollani**, designed by Palladio, and onward up the graceful Venetian Gothic gallery, the **Loggia del Lippomano** on the left. The sixteenth-century castello, built and decorated by local artists, houses an excellent **Museo Civico** (daily 9am–12.30pm plus Tues–Sat 3–6pm; L4000), containing works by Caravaggio, Carpaccio, Bronzino and Tiepolo.

North from the Piazza Libertà is **Via Mercatovecchio**, once the mercantile heart of the city and now the busiest shopping street. The little chapel of **Santa Maria**, incorporated into the Palazzo del Monte di Pietà in Via Mercatovecchio, is a beauty. Seen through the glass booth from the street, the interior, with its cloudy Baroque frescoes by Giulio Quaglio (1694), has a pristine, subaqueous appearance.

Due west lies the **Piazza Matteotti**, with galleries on three sides and the fine Baroque facade of San Giacomo on the fourth. The square's importance as the centre of public life in Udine is proved by the outside altar on the first-floor balcony of **San Giacomo**; mass was celebrated here on Saturdays so that selling and buying could go on uninterrupted in the market below. As well as being the town's main market, this was the setting for tournaments, plays and carnivals. The fountain in the middle of the square was designed in 1543 by Giovanni da Udine, a pupil of Raphael, who also had a hand in building the castle.

Off the south side of Piazza Libertà is the **Duomo**, a Romanesque construction that was given a Baroque refit in the eighteenth century. Altarpieces and frescoes by Giambattista Tiepolo are the main attraction – they decorate the first two chapels on the right and the chapel of the Sacrament, a little way beyond. A series of frescoes painted by Tiepolo in collaboration with his son, Giandomenico, can be seen in the tiny **Oratorio della Purità** opposite – ask the sacristan in the duomo to show you.

But Udine's outstanding works of art are the Giambattista Tiepolo frescoes in the nearby eighteenth-century **Palazzo Arcivescovile** (Mon–Fri 9am–noon; free). Painted in the late 1720s, these luminous and consummately theatrical scenes add up to a sort of Rococo epic of the Old Testament. The *Fall of the Rebel Angels* is the first work you see as you climb the staircase to the first floor; other frescoes show *Sarah and the Angel, Abraham and the Angels, Rachel, Abraham and Isaac* and the *Judgement of Solomon*.

Of the minor sights, perhaps the most enjoyable is the display of local crafts and folk art in the **Museo Friulano delle Arti e Tradizione Popolari** (Tues–Sat 9am–12.30pm & 3–6pm, Sun 9am–12.30pm; L3000), housed in the Palazzo Gorgo-Maniago in Via Viola. On the edge of the old town in Piazza Diacono, the **Galleria d'Arte Moderna** (Tues–Sat 9.30am–12.30pm & 3–6pm, Sun 9.30am–12.30pm; L3000) gives an overview of Italian art in the twentieth century, plus a glimpse of a few foreign greats.

Practicalities

Udine's **train** and **bus stations** are close together in the south of the town, on Viale Europa Unità; Via Roma leads from the train station into the centre. The **tourist office** is at Piazza I Maggio 7 (Mon–Fri 8.30am–1pm & 2.30–6pm, Sat 8.30am–1pm; ☎0432/295.972). A good, reasonable **hotel** is the *Manin*, Via Manin 5 (☎0432/501.146; ④); another in the same price range is *Al Vecchio Tram*, Piazza Garibaldi 15 (☎0432/502.516; ④). Up a notch, there's the frescoed and atmospheric *Piccolo Friuli*, Via Magrini 9 (☎0432/507.817; ⑤). Two student **hostels** in Via Zoletto (off Via Aquileia) may also be able to put you up: *Residenza Grande* (☎0432/26.058) and *Residenza Piccola* (☎0432/299.127).

Udine has scores of **restaurants**, one of the most popular being *Da Arturo*, Via Pracchiuso 75. The unpretentious *Trattoria all'Allegria*, Via Grazzano 18, does simple local dishes in the dining room beside the bar – the *gnocchi* in butter is delicious. You could also try *Ai Castagni*, Via Barigliara 271, *Al Cacciatore*, Via Cividale 638, or *Alla Ghiacciaia*, Vicolo Portello 2. The self-service *Zenit*, in Via Prefettura, may suit those in a hurry.

Students hang out in the *Manhattan* and *Arcobaleno* **bars** in Viale Palmanova, and in *St James* in Via Grazzano. The *Contarena* **disco**, in Piazza Libertà, is one of the livelier spots. Nightlife is very limited outside the university term-time, but in summer there's a busy programme of cultural events – theatre, music, dance – in and around the town.

Cividale del Friuli

Lying only 17km east of Udine and connected to it by train and bus, **CIVIDALE DEL FRIULI** is a gem of a town, much prized by the *friulani* but pretty well unknown to outsiders. It was founded in 50 BC by Julius Caesar where the Natisone Valley opens into the plain, and in the sixth century became the capital of the first Lombard duchy. In the eighth century the Patriarch of Aquileia moved here, inaugurating Cividale's most prosperous period.

The Town

The old town lies on the same side as the rail and coach stations, and the visitor need never cross the river; though a walk over the Devil's Bridge is de rigueur. Just walking around the town, within the oval ring bisected by Via Carlo Alberto and Corso Mazzini, is a pleasure; the pace of life is provincially serene, and the buildings are interesting. Cividale has been the main market town in the Natisone Valley for 200 years, and today you hear Italian, *friulano*, and Slovene dialects spoken in the street. There are some remarkable tourist sights too.

The **Tempietto Longobardo** (Mon 9am–noon, Tues–Fri 9am–noon & 3–6pm, Sat & Sun 9am–1pm), above the Natisone off Piazza San Biagio, is a uniquely fine example of Lombard art. Constructed in the eighth century, largely from older fragments, it was reduced to rubble in the terrible earthquake of 1222, so what you see now is a three-dimensional mosaic in which different styles somehow harmonise. Inside, the exquisite stucco arch around the quartet of female saints, and the luminous, smiling saints themselves, are among the most splendid surviving works of art from the eighth century; the frescoes and stalls all date from the late fourteenth century.

Two other beautiful Lombard pieces are to be found in the **Museo Cristiano**, housed in the precincts of the fifteenth-century **Duomo** (Mon–Fri 9.30am–noon & 3–6.30pm, Sat & Sun 11.30am–noon & 4.30–6.30pm). The *Altar of Ratchis* was carved for Ratchis, Duke of Cividale and King of the Lombards at Pavia, who died as a Benedictine monk at Montecassino in 759; the reliefs of *Christ in Triumph* and the *Adoration of the Magi* are delicate and haunting. The other highlight is the *Baptistery of Callisto*, named after Callisto de Treviso, the first Patriarch of Aquileia to move to Cividale. He lived here from 730 to 756 and initiated the building of the patriarchal palace, the cathedral and this octagonal baptistery, which used to stand beside the cathedral. It's constructed from older Lombard fragments, the columns and capitals dating from the fifth century.

The duomo itself houses a twelfth-century masterpiece of silversmithing: the *pala* (altarpiece) named after Pellegrino II, the Patriarch who commissioned it and donated it to the town; it depicts the Virgin seated between the archangels Michael and Gabriel, who are flanked by 25 saints and framed by saints, prophets, and the patron himself.

Also in Piazza del Duomo is the **Museo Archeologico** (Mon–Fri 9am–1.30pm, Sat & Sun 9am–12.30pm), housing a hotchpotch of local findings and treasures, including fascinating Lombard jewellery and encrusted psalters.

Just a stone's throw from the fifteenth-century Ponte del Diavolo, in Via Monastero Maggiore, is a cellar-like cavern called the *Ipogeo Celtico* (Mon 8am–1pm, Tues–Fri 8am–1pm & 3.30–5.40pm; key from the tourist office in Largo Boiani, or the *Bar al Ponte*). The hypogeum was probably used as a tomb for Celtic leaders, between the fifth and second centuries BC, but there is still some dispute whether it's artificial or was merely adapted by its users. Either way, the spectral faces carved on the walls make it a weird place.

Practicalities

The **tourist office** is on the first floor at Largo Boiani 4 (Mon–Fri 9am–1pm & 3–6pm, Sat 9am–1pm). Cividale's least expensive hotel is *Pomo d'Oro*, Piazza S. Giovanni 20 (☎0432/731.489; ④). More comfortable (and pricier), and with exceptional views, is the *Castello*, Via del Castello 20 (☎0432/733.242; ⑤) – it's a couple of kilometres north of the town, on a hill above the road to Tarcento and Faedis. The restaurant is good, and on a sunny day the terrace at the castello is the best place for a leisurely lunch, well worth the taxi trip from the town centre if you don't feel like walking.

The town's smartest **café** is the *San Marco*, opposite the tourist office in the loggia of the town hall – well placed for watching passers-by. Recommended **restaurants** are *Zorutti*, Borgo di Ponte 7, *Alla Frasca*, Via De Rubeis 10, *Al Fortino*, Via C. Alberto 46, and *Da Nardini*, Piazzetta de Portis 6.

Gemona and the Carnia

The peak district in the north of Friuli is known as the **Carnia**, a name given to it by the Celtic tribes who settled here in the fourth century BC. If you're approaching the area by road or rail from Udine, you could make a stop at **GEMONA**, a little town that was largely destroyed in the 1976 earthquake, when almost 1000 people were killed and around 15,000 houses destroyed. The historic centre, on the steep-sided hilltop, has been devotedly reconstructed, and feels disconcertingly like a film set. The cathedral, once a marvellous Romanesque-Gothic specimen, is notable for the enormous fourteenth-century statue of Saint Christopher on the facade.

Gemona is a good staging post on the way into the Carnia, with a couple of fine and inexpensive **hotels**. The better one is the *Agli Amici*, a couple of kilometres out of the centre at Via G. Odo 44 (☎0432/981.013; ④) – just take Via Piovega from the train station then follow the yellow signs; the alternative is the *Si-Si*, Via Piovega 15 (☎0432/981.158; ④). There's an excellent trattoria at the *Agli Amici*.

The Carnia proper begins north of Gemona, around the headwaters of the River Tagliamento, and comprises two distinct areas. To the west, hay meadows and orchards give way to the Alpine uplands and pastures of the **Alpi Carniche**, which share the culture of the eastern Dolomites. To the east, the high, sheer and often barren limestone peaks of the **Alpi Giulie** are divided by deep, forested valleys which radiate towards the borders with Austria in the north and Slovenia in the east. Both of these ranges are hardly known even within Italy, yet the area has a lot to offer the hiker and climber. (Linguists should get a lot out of it too, as the villagers speak strange variants of *friulano*, German and Slovene.)

If you want to plan a Carnia walking trip in advance, call in at the Udine office of the *Società Alpina Friulana*, Via Odorico da Pordenone 3 (daily 5–7.30pm plus Mon, Thurs & Fri 9–11pm; ☎0432/504.290).

Western Carnia

The lush valleys and flower-filled meadows of the **western Carnia** attract hundreds of walkers from June to September, when the numerous *refugi* are open for business. One of the best bases for the northern part of this region is the village of **ARTA TERME**, about 35km north of Gemona – there are buses direct from Udine and services from Gemona, changing at TOLMEZZO. There's cheap **accommodation** at the central

Miramonte (☎0433/920.76; ④) and *Comune Rustico* (☎0433/922.18; ④), with slightly dearer rooms at the *Gortani* (☎0433/928.754; ⑤). At PIANO D'ARTA, 1km away, you'll find another couple of one-stars – *Pensione Cozzi* (☎0433/920.39; ④) and *Edelweiss* (☎0433/920.12; ④). The **tourist office**, Via Roma 22–24 (May–Sept Mon–Sat 9am–noon & 3–6pm), has masses of information on the beautifully secluded local refuges and on the fourteen waymarked *Club Alpino* **walks** in the surrounding highlands. If these treks sound too energetic, you could always just spend L6000 on a visit to the **thermal pool** of the pagoda-style spa complex close to the tourist office.

An alternative base would be the cluster of villages that comprise **FORNI DI SOPRA**, lying about 70km northwest of Gemona at the foot of the Passo di Mauria, the mountain pass between the Carnia and the eastern Dolomites. Seven buses go there direct from Udine every day. As with Arta Terme, the **tourist office**, Via Cadore 1 (Mon–Fri 9am–12.30pm & 3–6.30pm), has lots of information on **hikes** and refuges, as well as lists of **accommodation** in town. Most of the places to stay are in VICO, a hamlet set back a little from Forni; the inexpensive choices here are the *Roma*, on Via Nazionale (☎0433/88.027; ④), and the *Centrale*, Piazza del Comune 9 (☎0433/88.062; ④). The only **campsite** hereabouts is the *Tornerai* (all year; ☎0433/88.035) 2km away in STINSANS. The Forni region is celebrated for its **food**, many of its dishes incorporating some of the wild plants found in the vicinity. The mountain refuges are excellent places to sample these local specialities. Especially good is the nearby and spectacularly sited *Varmost* (open June–Sept), on the slopes of Monte Crusicalas – it's a stiff hike up there, but there's a cable-car in operation in July and August and in the first two weeks of September. In Forni itself, the places to eat are *Pradas*, Via Nazionale 2, and the *Pizzeria Cooperativa*, close to *municipio* at Via Nazionale 36. Forni also has a branch of the *Club Alpino Italiano* at Via Roma 9 (July & Aug daily 6–7pm), which organises walks of varying degrees of difficulty.

Eastern Carnia

The place to head for in the **eastern Carnia** is **TARVISIO**, a small mountain resort 65km northeast of Gemona and just 7km from the Austrian border. Four buses a day come here from Udine, and eight trains – if you're coming by train, make sure you get out at Tarvisio Città station, perversely more central than Tarvisio Centrale.

The town receives a steady flow of Austrian visitors, who pour into town for the cheap Italian booze, the strange mix of *bierkeller* and café nightlife, and for the first-rate ski slopes. More robust types set off from here on the Carnia's one high-level **long-distance trail**: the *Traversata Carnica*, which runs all the way to Sesto, just below the border. Information on this and all other healthy Tarvisio pursuits is available from the **tourist office**, right by the bus stop on Via Roma (Mon & Sat 9am–1pm & 2.30–6.30pm, Tues–Fri 9am–12.30pm & 3–6.30pm, plus Sun in summer). The nicest play **to stay** in Tarvisio is the *Albergo Valle Verde*, just outside the village on Via Priesnig (☎0428/2342; ⑤) – it has a wonderful **restaurant** too, serving such specialities as gnocchi with smoked ricotta. The only place cheaper than this in Tarvisio itself is the *Cacciatore*, on the noisy Via Dante (☎0428/2082; ④). The nearest **campsite** is the *Dalesco* at Camporossa, 4km from Tarvisio (☎0428/2254).

For a taste of the splendours of the Alpi Giulie national park, you could hop onto one of the summer buses to the **Laghi di Fusine** – two peaceful wooded blue-green lakes within 9km of Tarvisio. The smaller of the pair, and the nearer to Tarvisio, is **Lago Inferiore**, where there's **accommodation** at the *Albergo Edelweiss* (☎0428/61.050; ④). However, the best walks are from **Lago Superiore**, a short distance up the road, from where there's a marked five-hour circular trail via the *Rifugio Zacchi* (June–Sept; ☎0428/611.95).

Udine to Pordenone

Hourly trains run west from Udine to **CODROIPO**, a peaceful little town that would have nothing to recommend it were the huge **Villa Manin** not just 3km to the south-east, where it completely dominates the little village of PASSARIANO. As the only public transport to the villa from Codroipo consists of three daily buses, the best way to get there is to walk: straight ahead from the station, and bear left in the main square – you could easily pick up a lift.

Friuli's best-known country house, the Villa Manin was built in 1738 and later enlarged for Lodovico Manin, the pitiful last doge of Venice. In 1797 Napoleon stayed here when he signed the Treaty of Campoformio, which gave Venice to Austria. The greater part of the interior, much of it coated in run-of-the-mill frescoes, is impressive solely for its size, and is used as an exhibition centre in the summer; the arena created by its great frontal galleries is used for open-air concerts. The villa contains a mediocre museum (Tues–Sun 9am–noon & 3–6pm; free) – more alluring is the ramshackle park (Thurs 2–6pm, Sat & Sun 9am–6pm), where reedy ponds, birdsong and lichen-green statues create a congenial atmosphere for an afternoon doze.

Pordenone

The westernmost of Friuli-Venezia Giulia's three large towns, **PORDENONE** is now the region's main manufacturing centre, specialising in light industries such as electronics, textiles and ceramics. The best way to see its carefully preserved historic centre is to walk along the **Corso Vittorio Emanuele** to the Gothic-Renaissance Palazzo Communale – from the train station go straight ahead along Via Mazzini, then take the second right.

Over the road from the palazzo is the **Museo Civico Ricchieri**; currently being restored, it's predominantly a second-string collection of Venetian art, but it does have a clutch of works by the finest local artist, Giovanni Antonio Sacchienze, better known simply as Il Pordenone. Many of the paintings in the museum were removed from the **Duomo** after the 1976 earthquake; the building itself, mainly a late Gothic structure, is notable only for its Romanesque campanile, and for some badly damaged frescoes by Pordenone on one of the pillars at the end of the nave. For a sense of the everyday realities of peasant life in Friuli, visit the **Museo Provinciale della Vita Contadina** (Mon–Sat 8am–2pm), a short distance along the river from the duomo in Piazza Giustiniano.

If you want to see more of Pordenone's work in his home town, search out the parish churches of Roraigrande, Torre, Villanova and Valloncello – for information about access, ask at the **tourist office**, Piazza della Motta 13. They'll also fill you in on the attractions of the surrounding area, though you really need a car to get around. The chief draw is in **SESTO AL REGHENA**, a little way south of Pordenone, where the fortified **Santa Maria in Sylvis** is one of the oldest inhabited abbeys in the world. It was founded by the Lombards in the eighth century, and has some beautiful old bas-reliefs.

travel details

Trains

Trieste to: Gorizia (13 daily; 45min); Milan (5 daily; 5hr 30min–7hr 30min); Udine (13 daily; 1hr 10min); Venice (14 daily; 2hr 10min).

Udine to: Cividale (hourly; 20min); Gemona (10 daily; 30min); Gorizia (13 daily; 30min); Palmanova (12 daily; 30min); Pordenone (hourly; 30min); Tarvisio (8 daily; 2hr); Trieste (13 daily; 1hr 10min); Venice (hourly; 2hr).

Buses

Gemona to: Tolmezzo (2 daily; 30min).

Tolmezzo to: Arta Terme (10 daily; 20min); Forni di Sopra (7 daily; 1hr 20min).

Trieste to: Duino (hourly; 30min); Gorizia (5 daily; 1hr); Udine (8 daily; 1hr).

Udine to: Aquileia (16 daily; 40min); Arta Terme (10 daily; 1hr); Cividale (20 daily; 20min); Forni di Sopra (7 daily; 2hr 10min); Gemona (9 daily; 1hr); Grado (10 daily; 1hr); Lignano (12 daily; 1hr); Palmanova (16 daily; 20min); Tarvisio (4 daily; 2hr 20min); Trieste (9 daily; 1hr).

Ferries

Trieste to: Grado (March–Sept 4 daily; 1hr 30min).

CHAPTER SEVEN

EMILIA-ROMAGNA

Set between Lombardy and Tuscany, and stretching from the Adriatic coast almost to the shores of the Mediterranean, **Emilia-Romagna** is the heartland of northern Italy. It is two provinces really: Emilia to the east and the Romagna to the west – the former Papal States, joined together after Unification. Before the papacy took charge in the area, it was a patchwork of ducal territories, ruled over by a handful of families – the Este in Ferrara and Modena, the Farnese in Piacenza and Parma, and lesser dynasties in Ravenna and Rimini – who created sparkling Renaissance courts, combining autocracy with patronage of the arts alongside a continual jockeying for power with the Church. Their castles and fortresses remain, preserved in towns with restored medieval centres which, apart from a few notable exceptions, are relatively off the tourist track, many visitors put off partly by the extreme weather (searingly hot in summer, close to freezing in winter), partly by the more immediate pleasures of Tuscany and Umbria.

The region's landscape is a varied one, ranging from the foothills of the Apennine mountains in the south to flat fields of the northern plain, the Pianura Padana, interrupted only by windbreaks of poplars, shimmering in the breeze. The area has grown wheat since Roman times, and nowadays its industry and agri-businesses are among Italy's most advanced: there are currently more pigs than people in the Po Valley, and Emilia also holds some of the most successful of the enterprises that contributed to the country's Eighties economic boom.

Carving a dead straight route through the heart of Emilia-Romagna, from Piacenza to Rimini on the coast, the **Via Emilia** is a central and obvious reference point, a Roman military road constructed in 187 BC that was part of the medieval pilgrim's route to Rome, and the way east to Ravenna and Venice. The towns that grew up along here are among Emilia's most compelling. **Bologna**, the region's capital, is one of Italy's largest cities. Despite having one of the most beautifully preserved city centres in the country, some of its finest food, and inhabitants whose openness and seemingly unflappable temperaments contrast markedly with the stressed-out Milanese, it has been relatively neglected by tourists, and most people pass straight through – definitely a mistake. Bologna also gives easy access to places like **Modena** and **Parma**, each just an hour or so away by train: wealthy provincial towns that form the smug core of Emilia and hold some of its finest and most atmospheric architecture, as well as giving access to routes south into the **Apennines**. With a car you can dip into the foothills at will from any of these points, sampling some of the cooking and visiting the local festivals; and even by bus it's possible to get a taste of the area, which at its best can be very beautiful, not at all like the functional plain to the north. If you're a keen hiker, there's the *Grand Escursione Apenninica*, a 25-day-long trek following the backbone of the range from refuge to refuge.

The north of Emilia-Romagna is less interesting than the Via Emilia stretch, the Po disgorging into the Adriatic from its bleak **delta** (which it shares with the Veneto), a desolate region of marshland and lagoons that is mainly of appeal to birdwatchers. However, **Ferrara**, just half an hour north of Bologna, is, as ex-town of the Este family, one of the most important Renaissance centres in Italy; and **Ravenna**, a short way east from here, preserves probably the finest set of Byzantine mosaics in the world in its

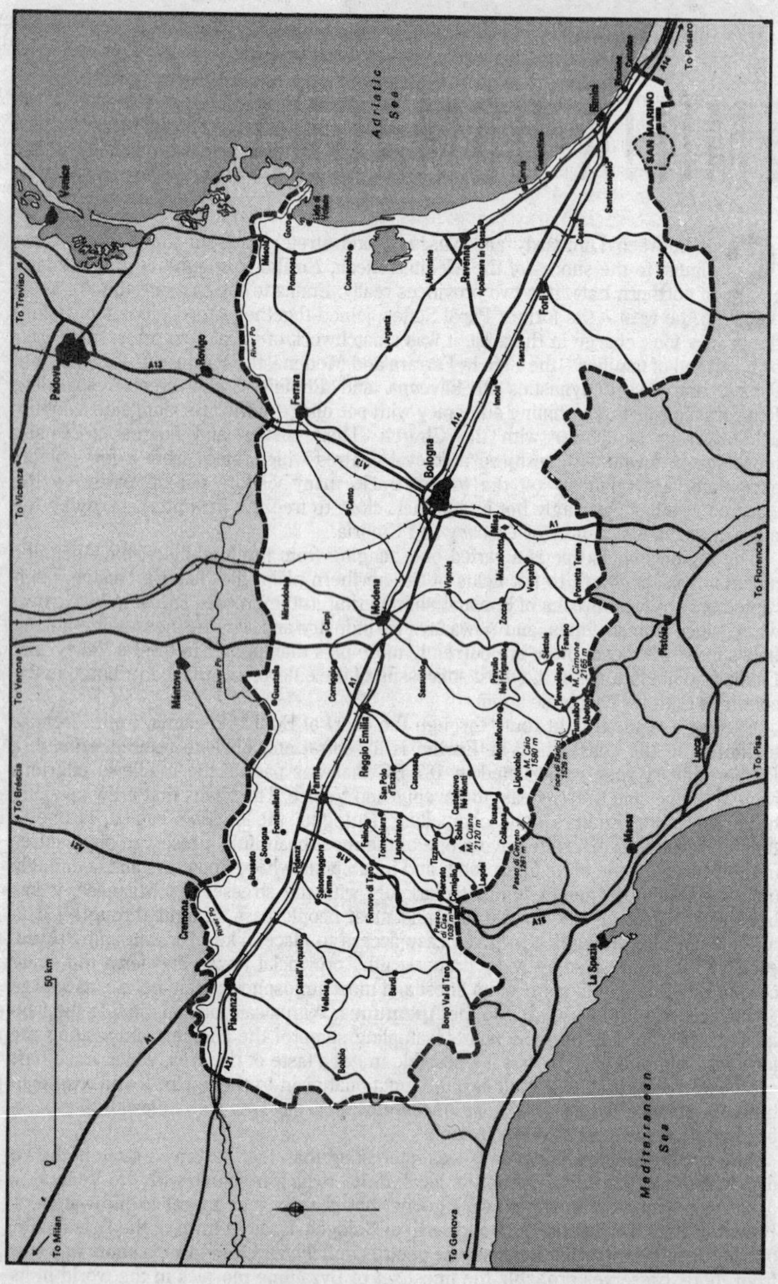

Adriatic Sea
Venice
To Treviso
Padova
Rovigo
A13
River Po
Ferrara
Mesola
Goro
Pomposa
Comacchio
Alfonsine
Argenta
Ravenna
Apollinare in Classe
Cervia
Cesenatico
Rimini
Riccione
Cattolica
To Pesaro
A14
SAN MARINO
Santarcangelo
Cesena
Sàrsina
Forlì
Faenza
Imola
Bologna
Cento
To Vicenza
To Verona
Mantova
Mirandola
Carpi
Modena
Vignola
Marzabotto
Misa
Vergato
Porretta Terme
A1
To Florence
Pistoia
Zocca
Sestola
Fanano
M. Cimone 2165 m
Pievepelago
Fiumalbo
Abetone
Pavullo Nel Frignano
Sassuolo
Correggio
Guastalla
Reggio Emilia
Montefiorino
Ligonchio
M. Cisa 1580 m
Foce di Radici 1529 m
Castelnovo Nè Monti
Canossa
San Polo d'Enza
Busana
Collagna
M. Cusna 2120 m
Schia
Tizzano
Langhirano
Torrechiara
Felino
Parma
To Brescia
A21
Busseto
Soragna
Fontanellato
Fidenza
Salsomaggiore Terme
Fornovo di Taro
Berceto
Corniglio
Lagdei
Passo di Cerreto 1261 m
Passo di Cisa 1039 m
Cremona
River Po
Piacenza
Castell'Arquato
Bardi
Borgo Val di Taro
Bobbio
50 km
To Milan
To Genova
A15
La Spezia
Massa
Lucca
To Pisa
Mediterranean Sea

churches and mausoleums. The coast south is an overdeveloped ribbon of settlement, although **Rimini**, at its southern end, provides a spark of interest, with its wild seaside strip concealing a surprisingly historic town centre.

It's worth remembering that none of this comes cheap: Emilia is a wealthy area that makes few concessions to tourists; the tone is, rather like Lombardy to the north, well mannered, well dressed and comfortable. If you need to economise, though, it would be a shame to stint when it comes to food, which is where the region excels. Emilia-Romagna is the home of quintessentially Italian food like pasta, Parma ham, salami and parmesan cheese. Lambrusco, too, hails from here, although it's a very different affair from the offerings you might be used to back home.

Bologna

Emilia's capital, **BOLOGNA**, is a boomtown of the Eighties whose computer-associated industries have brought conspicuous wealth to the old brick palaces and porticoed squares. Previously, it was best known for its food – undeniably the richest in the country – and, of course, for its politics. "Red Bologna" had been the former Italian Left's stronghold and spiritual home since the last war, and it was no chance association that it was this city's train station that was bombed by Fascist groups in 1980 in the postwar nation's worst terrorist atrocity.

After Venice, the city is among the best looking in the country. The city centre, within the circle of the central ring road, is startlingly medieval in plan, a jumble of red brick, tiled roofs and balconies radiating out from the great central square of Piazza Maggiore. There are enough monuments and curiosities for several days' leisured exploration, but Bologna is really enjoyable just for itself, its university and enlightened local government ensuring that there's always something happening – be it theatre, music, the city's strong summer festival, or just the café and bar scene, which is among northern Italy's most convivial. The only problem is expense: Bologna's latter-day affluence is reflected in a cost of living that is among Italy's highest, exceeding even Florence or Milan; nightlife, particularly, can leave your wallet steamrolled, and finding a low-priced place to stay can be very difficult.

The Bologna **area telephone code** is ☎051.

Arrival, information and city transport

Bologna's **train station** lies on the edge of the city centre at Piazza delle Medaglie d'Oro, near Porta Galleria; all long-distance buses terminate at the **bus station** (☎284.374), next door on Piazza XX Settembre. Bus #25 connects the train station and Piazza Nettuno, the city centre. The **airport** is northwest of the centre, linked to the train station by bus #91; these run approximately every twenty minutes and take around twenty minutes if the traffic is reasonably light.

For information, there are **tourist offices** at the airport (Mon–Sat 9am–1pm), at the train station (Mon–Sat 9am–12.30pm & 2.30–6pm), and a main office in the newly renovated Palazzo d'Accursio at Piazza Maggiore 6 (daily 9am–7pm; ☎239.660).

Once you're in the city centre, the best way to **get around** is to walk: the network of porticoes and small squares that make up the *centro storico* is more appealing on foot, and small enough to make buses an unnecessary expense. If you want to move quickly, or make a journey out of the centre, buses are, however, fast and frequent. Tickets cost L1200 each from *tabacchi* and are valid on as many buses as you like within one hour. Information from the booth at 1/1 Piazza Re Enzo (☎247.005 or 248.374).

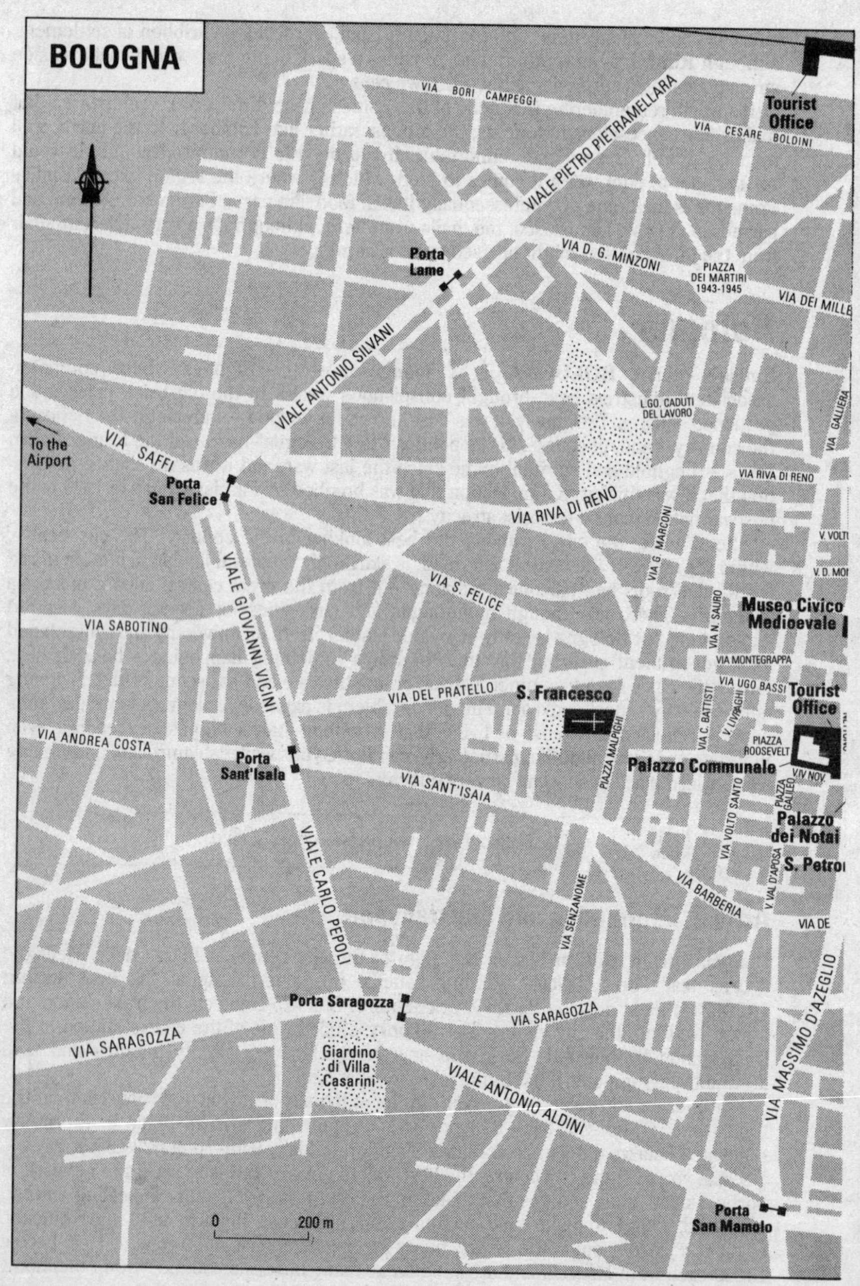
BOLOGNA
VIA BORI CAMPEGGI
VIALE PIETRO PIETRAMELLARA
Tourist Office
VIA CESARE BOLDINI
VIA D. G. MINZONI
PIAZZA DEI MARTIRI 1943-1945
VIA DEI MILLE
Porta Lame
VIALE ANTONIO SILVANI
L.GO. CADUTI DEL LAVORO
VIA GALLIERA
To the Airport
VIA SAFFI
Porta San Felice
VIA RIVA DI RENO
VIA RIVA DI RENO
VIA G. MARCONI
V. VOLTO
V. D. MO
VIA S. FELICE
VIALE GIOVANNI VICINI
VIA SABOTINO
VIA N. SAURO
Museo Civico Medioevale
VIA MONTEGRAPPA
VIA UGO BASSI
Tourist Office
VIA DEL PRATELLO
S. Francesco
VIA C. BATTISTI
V. LIVRAGHI
VIA ANDREA COSTA
PIAZZA ROOSEVELT
Porta Sant'Isaia
Palazzo Communale
PIAZZA MALPIGHI
V. IV NOV.
VIA SANT'ISAIA
PIAZZA GALILEO
VIA VOLTO SANTO
Palazzo dei Notai
VIALE CARLO PEPOLI
S. Petro
VIA SENZANOME
VIA BARBERIA
V. VAL D'APOSA
VIA DE
Porta Saragozza
VIA SARAGOZZA
VIA SARAGOZZA
VIA MASSIMO D'AZEGLIO
Giardino di Villa Casarini
VIALE ANTONIO ALDINI
0
200 m
Porta San Mamolo

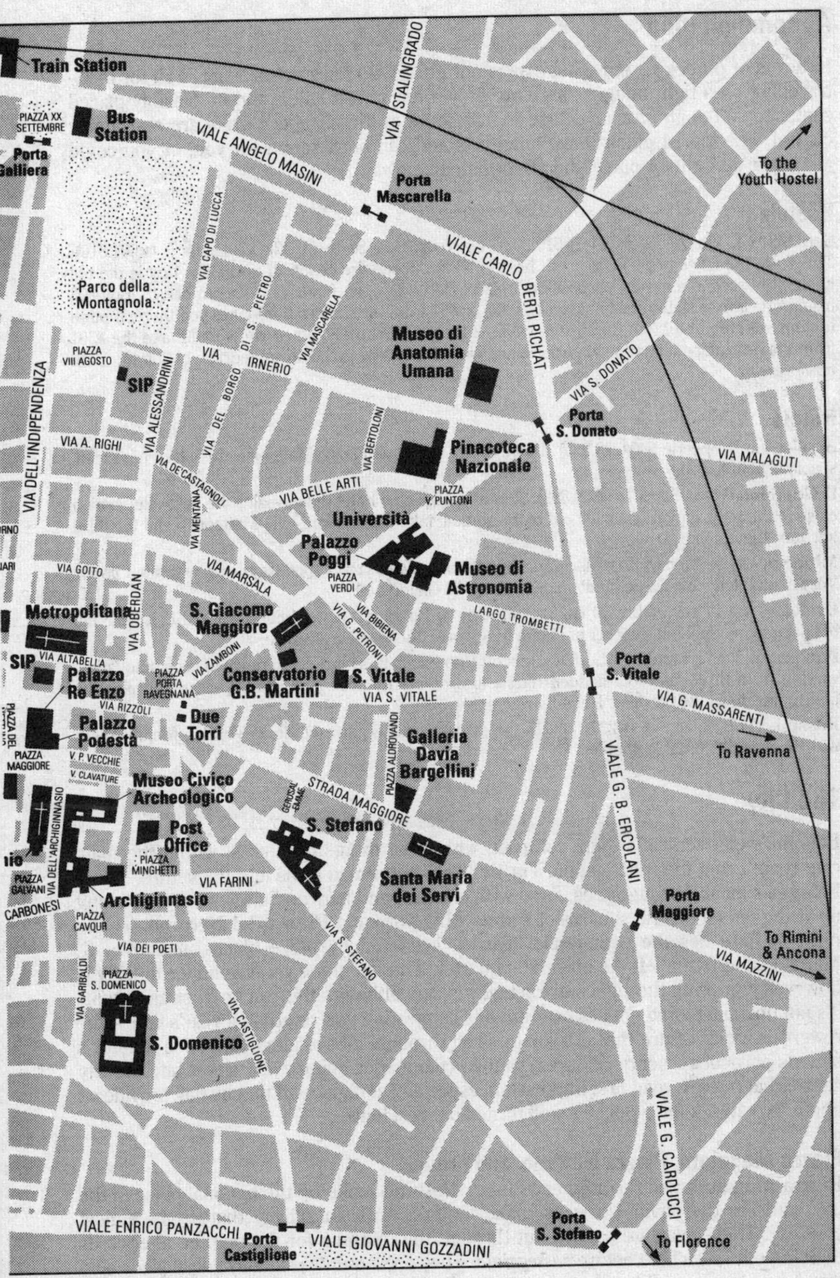
Train Station
PIAZZA XX SETTEMBRE
Bus Station
Porta Galliera
VIALE ANGELO MASINI
VIA STALINGRADO
Porta Mascarella
To the Youth Hostel
VIALE CARLO BERTI PICHAT
Parco della Montagnola
VIA CAPO DI LUCCA
VIA DEL BORGO DI S. PIETRO
VIA MASCARELLA
Museo di Anatomia Umana
PIAZZA VIII AGOSTO
VIA IRNERIO
SIP
VIA ALESSANDRINI
VIA DELL'INDIPENDENZA
VIA S. DONATO
Porta S. Donato
VIA A. RIGHI
VIA BERTOLONI
Pinacoteca Nazionale
VIA MALAGUTI
VIA DE' CASTAGNOLI
VIA MENTANA
VIA BELLE ARTI
PIAZZA V. PUNTONI
Università
Palazzo Poggi
Museo di Astronomia
VIA GOITO
VIA MARSALA
PIAZZA VERDI
VIA OBERDAN
Metropolitana
S. Giacomo Maggiore
VIA BIBIENA
VIA G. PETRONI
LARGO TROMBETTI
VIA ALTABELLA
SIP
VIA ZAMBONI
PIAZZA PORTA RAVEGNANA
Palazzo Re Enzo
Conservatorio G.B. Martini
S. Vitale
Porta S. Vitale
VIA S. VITALE
VIA G. MASSARENTI
VIA RIZZOLI
Due Torri
Palazzo Podestà
PIAZZA MAGGIORE
V. P. VECCHIE
V. CLAVATURE
VIA ALDROVANDI
Galleria Davia Bargellini
To Ravenna
VIALE G. B. ERCOLANI
Museo Civico Archeologico
STRADA MAGGIORE
VIA DELL'ARCHIGINNASIO
Post Office
S. Stefano
PIAZZA MINGHETTI
Santa Maria dei Servi
PIAZZA GALVANI
VIA FARINI
Archiginnasio
CARBONESI
PIAZZA CAVOUR
VIA S. STEFANO
Porta Maggiore
To Rimini & Ancona
VIA MAZZINI
VIA DEI POETI
PIAZZA S. DOMENICO
VIA GARIBALDI
VIA CASTIGLIONE
S. Domenico
VIALE G. CARDUCCI
VIALE ENRICO PANZACCHI
Porta Castiglione
VIALE GIOVANNI GOZZADINI
Porta S. Stefano
To Florence

Accommodation

In terms of **places to stay**, Bologna is not geared up for tourists, least of all for those travelling on a tight budget: there are only a few cheap hotels and no feasibly placed campsite, although one advantage is that some of the cheaper **hotels** are reasonably central. The tourist offices have hotel lists and can book rooms for you, or you could just make straight for one of the places listed below.

Hostels

San Sisto I, Via Viadagola 14 (☎519.202); **Le Torri-San Sisto II**, Via Viadagola 5 (☎501.810). These are the city's two official youth hostels, 6km outside the centre of town. The first is the old hostel, the second a newer, purpose-built place. Both are open January 21–December 18. Bus #93 from Porta San Donato (reachable on bus #36 or #37 from the train station) takes you there, though it stops running at 8.15pm during the week, 2.15pm on Saturday, when you should take the #301 from Via dell'Indipendenza or Via Irnerio and walk the 1500m to the hostel (curfew 11.30pm). Both places are ①.

Hotels

Apollo, Via Drapperie 5 (☎223.955). Down a tiny street off Piazza Maggiore, this place has clean, spacious doubles. ⑤.

Il Guercino, Via L. Serra 7 (☎369.893). Recently upgraded hotel that remains the best-value option close to the train station. Turn left out of the station, take the first left – Via Matteotti – and the third left after the rail line. ④.

Minerva, Via de Monari 3 (☎239.652). Friendly hotel with large, spotless rooms with tiled floors. Very central too – off Via dell'Indipendenza and Via Galleria. ⑤.

Orologio, Via IV Novembre 10 (☎231.253). One of Bologna's better hotels, housed in a beautiful old palazzo overlooking a corner of Piazza Maggiore. Book well in advance. ⑧.

Panorama, Via Livraghi 1 (☎221.802). Just off Ugo Bassi, this place has a range of accommodation, varying from three- and four-bedded rooms to ordinary doubles – all sharing clean and pleasant bathrooms down the corridor. Helpful owners. ⑤.

Rossini, Via Bibbiena 11 (☎237.716). In the student quarter, just off Piazza Verdi, a friendly place with clean and affordable doubles. ④.

The City

Bologna's city centre is quite compact, with most things of interest within the main ring road. From the train station, **Via dell'Indipendenza** leads into the centre, one of Bologna's main thoroughfares, lined with cinemas and bars and always busy, finishing up at the linked central squares of **Piazza Maggiore** and **Piazza del Nettuno.** To the right of here lies the commercial district, bordered by office blocks along Via G. Marconi, and to the left the university quarter. The one thing you will notice quickly is how well preserved the city centre actually is, and although this can be frustrating too – it's not unusual to find notices on churches suggesting you return in a year's time – the reward is a city centre that is a joy to stroll through. Above all you'll notice the city's famous porticoes – ochre-coloured, vaulted colonnades lining every street into the city centre that make a vivid first impression, especially at night, and that by day provide an unofficial catwalk for Bologna's well turned-out residents.

Piazza Maggiore, Piazza Nettuno and around

Piazza Maggiore and the adjacent **Piazza Nettuno** make up the notional pulse of the city, and are the obvious area to make for first, with an activity that seems almost constant. Their cafés are packed out through the morning for the market, afterwards thinning out just a little before *passeggiata*. They are a quintessentially social place, and they host, as you might expect, the city's principal secular and religious buildings: the church of San Petronio, Palazzo Re Enzo and Palazzo Comunale – all impressive for their bulk alone, with heavy studded holes and walls pitted with holes from the original scaffolding.

At the centre of Piazza Nettuno, the **Neptune Fountain** is a symbol of the city and target for pigeons, styled in extravagant fashion by Giambologna in 1566. Across the square, the **Palazzo Re Enzo** takes its name from its time as the prison-home of Enzo, King of Sicily, confined here by papal supporters for two decades after the Battle of Fossalta in 1249. If the building looks rather dour, it's partly thanks to controversial architect Alfonso Rubbiani, who restored (purists would say rebuilt) many of Bologna's medieval structures in the early part of this century. Next door to the Palazzo Re Enzo, **Palazzo Podestà** fills the northern side of Piazza Maggiore, built at the behest of the Bentivoglio clan, who ruled the city during the fifteenth century, before papal rule was re-established. On the piazza's western edge, the **Palazzo Comunale** gives some clue to the political shifts in power, its facade adorned by a huge statue of Pope Gregory XIII as an affirmation of papal authority. Through a small courtyard, stairs lead to the upper rooms of the palace, some of which remain in use as local government offices while others are worth visiting for their galleries of ornate furniture and paintings, which include works by Vitale da Bologna, Simone dei Crocefessi and others of the Bolognese School, as well as for the view over the square.

On the southern side of Piazza Maggiore, the church of **San Petronio** is one of the finest Gothic brick buildings in Italy, an enormous structure which was originally intended to have been larger than St Peter's in Rome, but money and land for the side aisle were diverted by the pope's man in Bologna towards a new university, and the architect Antonio di Vicenzo's plans had to be modified. You can see the beginnings of the planned side aisle on the left of the building: when they stopped work they sliced through the arch of a window and left only the bottom third of the facade decorated with the intended marble geometric patterns. There are models of what the church was supposed to look like in the museum (daily 10am–12.30pm, closed Tues & Thurs).

Notwithstanding its curtailment, San Petronio is a fine example of late fourteenth-century architecture. Above the central portal is a beautiful carving of *Madonna and Child* by visiting artist Jacopo della Quercia. Within, the side chapels contain a host of treasures, including some fifteenth-century frescoes of the *Madonna and Child* by Giovanni da Modena, and of *Heaven and Hell* by Jacopo di Paolo. The most unusual feature is the astronomical clock – a long brass meridian line set at an angle across the floor, with a hole left in the roof for the sun to shine through on the right spot.

The ornately decorated building next door to San Petronio is the Palazzo dei Notai ("Notaries") a fourteenth-century reminder that it was Bologna's legal scholars who in the Middle Ages laid the first foundations of contemporary European law. In the opposite direction, across Via dell'Archiginnasio from San Petronio, the **Palazzo dei Banchi** is more of a set-piece than a palazzo, basically a facade designed by the Renaissance architect Vignola to unify a set of medieval houses that didn't really fit with the rest of the square. Adjacent, the **Museo Civico Archeologico** (Tues–Fri 9am–2pm, Sat & Sun 9am–1pm & 3.30–7pm; L5000) is a rather stuffy museum, but has good displays of Egyptian and Roman antiquities, and an Etruscan section, drawn from finds from the Etruscan predecessor of Bologna, Felsina, that is one of the best outside Lazio. There are reliefs from tombs, vases and a bronze *situla*, richly decorated, from the fifth century BC.

Just north of the museum, **Via Clavature** – together with nearby Via Pescerie Vecchie and Via Draperie – is home to a grouping of market stalls and shops that makes for one of the city's most enticing sights and provides positive proof of Bologna's justified reputation for food. In autumn especially the market is a visual and aural feast, with fat porcini mushrooms, truffles in baskets of rice, thick rolls of mortadella, hanging pheasants, ducks and hares, and skinned frogs by the kilo. The church of **Santa Maria della Vita**, in Via Clavature, is worth a look for its outstanding *pietá* by Nicola dell'Arca – seven life-sized figures, recently moved back to this, their original site, that are among the most dramatic examples of Renaissance sculpture you'll see.

Down the street in the other direction, Bologna's university – the **Archiginnasio** – was founded at more or less the same time as Piazza Maggiore was laid out, predating the rest of Europe's universities, although it didn't get a special building until 1565, when Antonio Morandi was commissioned to construct the present building on the site until then reserved for San Petronio. Centralising the university on one site was a way of maintaining control over students at a time when the Church felt particularly threatened by the Reformation. You can wander freely into the main courtyard, covered with the coats of arms of its more famous graduates, and perhaps even attend a lecture – Umberto Eco lectures at Bologna on semiotics. It's also possible to visit the main upstairs **library**, and, most interestingly, the **Teatro Anatomico** (Mon–Fri 8.30am–1.35pm, Sat 8.30am–12.45pm) – the original medical faculty dissection theatre. Tiers of seats surround an extraordinary professor's chair, covered with a canopy supported by figures known as *gli spellati* – "the skinned ones". Not many dissections went on, due to prohibitions of the Church, but when they did (usually around carnival time), artists and the general public used to turn up as much for the social occasion as for studying the body.

Outside the old university, **Piazza Galvani** remembers the physicist Luigi Galvani with a statue. One of Bologna's more successful scientists, Galvani discovered electrical currents in animals, thereby lending his name to the English language in the word "galvanise". A few minutes south, down Via Garibaldi, is **Piazza San Domenico**, with its strange canopied tombs holding the bones of medieval law scholars. Bologna was instrumental in sorting out wrangles between the pope and the Holy Roman emperor in the tenth and eleventh centuries, earning itself the title of "La Dotta" (The Learned) and setting the basis for the university's prominent law faculties. The church of **San Domenico** was built in 1251 to house the relics of Saint Dominic, which were placed in the so-called *Arca di San Domenico*: a fifteenth-century work that was principally the creation of Nicola Pisano – though in reality many artists contributed to it. Pisano and his pupils were responsible for the reliefs illustrating the saint's life; the statues on top were the work of Pisano himself; Nicola dell'Arca was responsible for the canopy (this was the work that earned him his name); and the angel and figures of saints Proculus and Petronius were the work of a very young Michelangelo. Try also to see the **Museo di San Domenico** (daily 10am–noon & 3.30–5.30pm), whose highlight is some intricately inlaid mid-sixteenth-century choir stalls.

The university quarter

Bordered by Via Oberdan to the west and Strada Maggiore to the south, the eastern section of Bologna's *centro storico* preserves many of the older **university** departments, housed for the most part in large seventeenth- and eighteenth-century palaces. This is perhaps the most pleasant part of the city to while away the day – or night – amid a concentration of low-budget bars, restaurants and shops aimed at the student population. It is also the place to scour to find out what's on: posters plaster the walls along Via Zamboni and the lanes off it – Via delle Moline, Via Belle Arti, Via Mentana – and the bars and cafés are often promoting some happening or other.

Via Rizzoli leads into the district from Piazza Maggiore, ending up at Piazza di Porta Ravegnana, where the **Torre degli Asinelli** (daily 9am–6pm; L1000), next to the perilously leaning **Torre Garisenda**, are together known as the **Due Torri**, the remains of literally hundreds of towers that were scattered across the city during the Middle Ages. The former makes a good place from which to get an overview of the city centre and beyond, out over the red-tiled roofs across the hazy, flat plains and southern hills beyond.

Walking east from the Due Torri, Via San Stefano leads down to its medieval gateway, past a complex of four – but originally seven – churches, collectively known as **Santo Stefano**. It's an attractive complex, set in a wide piazza at the conjunction of several narrow porticoed streets. Three of the churches face on to the piazza, of which the striking polygonal church of **San Sepolcro** (closed noon–3.30pm), reached through the church of **Crocifisso**, is about the most interesting – take change for the lights. The basin in its courtyard, called "Pilate's Bowl", dates from the eighteenth century, while on the inside the bones of Saint Petronius provide a pleasingly kitsch focus, held in a tomb modelled on the church of the holy sepulchre in Jerusalem. A doorway leads from here through to **Santi Vitale e Agricola**, Bologna's oldest church, built from discarded Roman fragments in the fifth century, while the fourth church, the **Trinitá**, lies across the courtyard and is home to a small museum (daily 9am–noon & 3.30–6pm) containing a reliquary of Saint Petronius, a thirteenth-century fresco of the Massacre of the Innocents, and a handful of later paintings.

From here, follow Via Gerusalemme up to Strada Maggiore, where, a little way down on the right, the Gothic church of **Santa Maria dei Servi** dates from 1386. It's arguably Bologna's most elegant church, with a beautiful portico and fourteenth-century ceiling frescoes by Vitale da Bologna – a rare chance to see the work of the so-called "father" of Bolognese painting *in situ*. A chapel also holds a *Madonna Enthroned* by Cimabue. Across Strada Maggiore, Piazza Aldrovandi has a good daily street market, and is lined on one side by the **Museo Civico d'Arte Industriale** and **Galleria Davia Bargellini** (Tues–Sat 9am–1pm, Sun 9am–2pm; free), an eclectic mixture made up of the art collection of the Davia family and displays of textiles, glassware and furniture; the entrance is on Strada Maggiore. Further north from here, Via Petroni leads through to **Piazza Verdi**, at the heart of the university district and at lunchtimes packed with students grabbing some of the city's cheapest food. **Via Zamboni** leads off Piazza Verdi, around and along which are many of the old palaces housing various parts of the university. A large number of these buildings were decorated by members of the Bolognese academies, which were prominent in Italian art after 1600. Tibaldi, better known as an architect, turned his hand to fresco in the main building, the **Palazzo Poggi** at no. 33 (Mon–Fri 9am–12.30pm). His fresco of Ulysses here was influenced by Michelangelo's Sistine Chapel and has played a part in the well-publicised row over the latter's restoration, with art historians using Tibaldi's fresco as proof that they have got Michelangelo's colours right. On the fourth floor of the building, the **Specola** or observatory draws most people here, its small **Museo di Astronomia** (Mon–Fri 9am–5pm, Sat 9am–1pm; L5000) home to a number of eighteenth-century instruments and a frescoed map of the constellations – painted just seventy years after Galileo was imprisoned for his heretical statements about the cosmos.

A little way down Via Zamboni, in Piazza Rossini, is the church of **San Giacomo Maggiore**, a Romanesque structure begun in 1267 and enlarged over the centuries which followed. The target here is the Bentivoglio Chapel, decorated with funds provided by one Annibale Bentivoglio to celebrate the family's victory in a local feud in 1488. Lorenzo Costa painted frescoes of the *Apocalypse*, the *Triumph of Death* and a *Madonna Enthroned* as well as of the Bentivoglio family – a deceptively pious-looking lot, captured in what was a fairly innovative picture in its time for the careful characterisations of its patrons. Further frescoes by Costa, along with Francesco Francia, decorate the Oratoria di Santa Cecilia (ask the sacristan to unlock it for you); they show gory episodes from the lives of saints Cecilia and Valerian. And there's a tomb of Anton Galeazzo Bentivoglio by Quercia opposite the chapel – one of the artist's last works.

Piazza Rossini is named after the nineteenth-century composer, who studied at the **Conservatorio G. B. Martini** on the square. The library here is among the most important music libraries in Europe, with a number of original manuscripts, some of which are on display to the public along with a few paintings. Further north up Via

Zamboni, around Porta San Donato, are many of the university's largest faculties, including that of the **Museo di Anatomia Umana** at Via Irnerio 48 (Mon–Sat 9am–noon). An odd place to visit, perhaps, but it would be a shame to leave Bologna without seeing its highly idiosyncratic (and beautiful) **waxworks**. These were used until the nineteenth century for medical demonstration, and they are as startling as any art or sculpture in the city. There were two Italian schools of waxworks: the Florentine method, where they used limbs, organs and bones to make moulds to cast the wax; and the Bolognese, where everything was sculpted, even tiny veins and capillaries, which were rolled like Plasticene. The boundaries between "art" and "science" were not rigidly drawn, and in Bologna in the early eighteenth century the workshops of Anna Morandi Mazzolini and Ercole Lelli turned out figures that were much more than just clinical aids. Mazzolini, for example, created a self-portrait in the midst of a brain dissection, pulling back a scalp with wispy hairs attached; other figures, unnervingly displayed in glass cases, are modelled like classical statues, one carrying a sickle, the other a scythe.

Close by, the collection of paintings in the **Pinacoteca Nazionale** at Via Belle Arti 56 (Tues–Sat 9am–2pm, Sun 9am–10pm; L3000) may provide some light relief, concentrating mainly (though not exclusively) on the work of Bolognese artists. There are canvases by the fourteenth-century painter Vitale da Bologna, later works by Francia and Tibaldi, and paintings from the city's most productive artistic period, the early seventeenth century, when Annibale and Agostino Carracci, Guido Reni and Guercino ("The Cross-eyed") were active here.

The Metropolitana, a museum and the church of San Francesco

There's much less of interest west of Bologna's central piazzas. The city's cathedral, the **Metropolitana di San Pietro**, is on the right out of Piazza Nettuno, two blocks down Via dell'Indipendenza from Piazza Nettuno. Originally a tenth-century building, it's been rebuilt many times and is these days more enjoyable for its stately atmosphere than any particular features. The **Museo Civico Medioevale e dal Rinascimento** (Mon & Wed–Fri 9am–2pm, Sat & Sun 9am–1pm & 3.30–7pm; L5000), opposite, is of more interest, housed in the Renaissance Palazzo Fava at Via Manzoni 24 and decorated with frescoes by Carracci and members of the Bolognese School depicting the *History of Europa, Jason's Feats* and scenes from the *Aeneid*. The musuem collection itself includes bits of armour, ceramics, numerous tombs and busts of various popes and other dignitaries, and a *Madonna and Saints* by Jacopo della Quercia.

West of Piazza Nettuno, at the end of Via Ugo Bassi, the basilica of **San Francesco** (daily 6.30am–noon & 3–7pm) is a huge Gothic brick pile supported by flying buttresses that was heavily restored in the 1920s and partly rebuilt after World War II. Inside there's a beautiful and very ornate altarpiece from 1392 and a pleasant cloister.

Eating and drinking

Eating and **drinking** are the mainstays of Bolognese social life. Eating especially is important to the Bolognese: the city is known as "La Grassa" (The Fat), the result of a rich culinary tradition, and the stress laid on food here can take an extreme form. People travel a long way to eat at the top restaurants, which are said to be the best in Italy, and even the simplest restaurants and the many *osterie* often serve food of a very high standard; certainly the lack of a fancy menu or elaborate decor usually means the place is worth investigating, and you should definitely endeavour to try some local specialities while you're here – something that's perfectly feasible at moderate prices at most of the places we've listed. Handmade lasagne, tagliatelle and tortellini (small, shaped pasta with a stuffing of ham, sausage, chopped chicken, pork and veal, eggs, nutmeg and Parmesan) are excellent here and regarded with great affection by residents of Bologna, to the extent that stories have been invented to explain their origin: the first *tortellini* were made by a Bolognese innkeeper trying to re-create the beauty of Venus' navel – or so it is said.

Snacks, bars, cafés and ice cream

ACOSER, Porta Mascarella, near the Viale. Best of several student *mensas*, and open Mon–Fri 11.45am–3pm & 6.45–10pm and alternate Saturdays with *Bestial Market* (see "Clubs"). You'll need student ID for a full meal totalling around L3600. The official student bar, on the first floor of the first building on the right as you walk from Piazza Verdi along Via Zamboni, is a very friendly, noisy place to drink or have a snack. Student ID not always necessary.

Altero, Via dell'Indipendenza 33; Via Ugo Bassi 10. Part of a chain, and the best place for pizza by the slice.

Bassotto, Via Ugo Bassi 8e, with a takeaway food shop almost next door. (Mon–Fri 11.45am-2.45pm).

C'entro, Via dell'Indipendenza 45. Smart cafeteria, with tables outside in summer.

Frulé, Via Clavature. On the corner of Piazza del Francia, this is a fine place for *frullati* and ice cream.

Gianni, Via Montegrappa 11. Good place to eat ice cream, with tables outside in the summer.

Impero, Via dell'Indipendenza 39. A good place for breakfast, with excellent croissants and pastries.

Mocambo,Via d'Azeglio 1. A tiny bar where the slickest Bolognese sip their aperitifs.

Oggi Si Vola, Via Urbana 7. A macrobiotic restaurant – just the place if the "fat of Bologna" has been weighing you down.

Il Piccolo Bar-Latteria, Via Riva Reno 114, off Via Galliera. A bar with wholefood snacks.

Pino, Via Castiglione 65. The main branch of Bologna's best ice cream chain.

Bar Rosa Rose, Via Clavature 18/b. A small chic bar with meals and tables outside, popular with Bologna's new left at *aperitivo* hour.

La Torinese, Piazza Re Enzo 1. The place to go if you fancy a hot chocolate – no seats so you just stand at the counter.

Restaurants

Anna Maria, Via Belle Arti 17a. A favourite with the orchestra from the *Teatro Comunale* nearby; the *sfogline* (pasta-makers) work out front at lunchtime. Especially worth trying are the *tortellini al gorgonzola*.

Belle Arti, Via Belle Arti 14. A noisy, studenty place with friendly service and extra-large pizzas.

Boni, Via Saragozza 88. A good place to try *tortellini in brodo* (in clear broth) and other Emilian specialities, including game. The vegetable dishes and desserts are also always good.

Fantoni, Via del Pratello 11. Family-style Bolognese food on one of the oldest streets in the city.

I Gaetano, Via Bori Campeggi 7, a continuation west of Via Cesare Boldrini. Outside the town centre, this place is worth knowing about when everything else is closed. You get wonderful pizzas and big salads, as well as a good selection of fish.

Grassilli, Via del Luzzo 3. Way up in the expensive category, serving Emilian dishes that have been adapted with flair to suit modern tastes, accompanied by exceptionally good service. An experience to remember, though you'll definitely need to book ahead.

Lamma, Via dei Giudei 4. A large and popular Emilian restaurant with vaulted ceilings and an informal atmosphere.

Leon d'Oro, Via Belli Arti 17. Upscale pizzeria in the heart of the university quarter, with a wide choice of pizzas.

La Mamma, Via Zamboni 16. A long dining room with a parquet floor on the edge of the unversity quarter. A mostly youngish clientele partaking of very moderately priced pizza and pasta dishes.

Montegrappa da Nello, at the Piazza Nettuno end of Via Montegrappa. This place fills its window with examples of the season's best produce. Try the very Emilian antipasti: each *prosciutto* is described by the town it comes from. There are around half a dozen non-meat dishes on the menu too.

Nino's, Via Volturno 9 (off Via dell'Indipendenza). Pizzeria that serves a good selection of pizzas as well as home-made pasta – try the lasagne.

Rostaria Antica Brunetti, Via Caduti di Cefalonia 5. An elegant old wood-panelled restaurant on two floors, handily located close to Piazza Maggiore, that specialises in fish and seafood dishes – pizza too. Moderately priced.

Teresina, 4 Via Oberdan. A family-run restaurant serving regional dishes as well as very good southern Italian food, including fish (L40–45,000 for a full meal) with tables outside in summer.

Nightlife

Bologna has any number of chic **bars** if all you want to do is drink, most notably on and around Via Zamboni, in the student quarter. It also has a good selection of **osterie**, which have been the mainstay of Bolognese **nightlife** for several hundred years – pub-like places, open late, where you go more to drink than eat, though you can get excellent snacky (if sometimes pricey) food. The Bolognese like to go out late, around 10.30 or 11pm, and most *osterie* stay open until 2 or 3am. The city also has a good variety of **clubs**, with music to suit most tastes: the more established places are mentioned below, but check for details of what's happening, and look out for posters advertising events around the university quarter and Piazza Verdi in particular. Unlike their counterparts in other European countries, Bologna's city council encourages open-air **raves** by giving subsidies and making entrance either free or very inexpensive. They happen on weekends in summer, off Via Stalingrado in the area around the Fiera and the Parco di Nord.

As for **the arts and cultural attractions**, the city has also tried to curb the general August exodus by mounting a summer arts festival, called *Bologna Sogna* ("Bologna Dreams"), with concerts and videos at night in the courtyards of the civic buildings. *Ferragosto*, too, is a good time to be here, when everyone takes to the hills for all-night revelry in one of the parks outside town.

For **information** on all these things, get hold of the fortnightly listings magazine, *La Mongolfiera*, which has details in Italian but is easily deciphered. *Il Bo* might also be useful, a weekly with classified ads and listings, covering a wide area outside Bologna.

Osterie

Il Cantinone, Via del Pratello 56a. A lively *osteria* serving German beer in a pubby atmosphere. Food available too.

Osteria dell'Infidele, Via Gerusalemme. A tiny place which has good, inexpensive food or is fine for just drinking.

Marione, Via San Felice 137. Close to the city gate, an old, smoky and dark *osteria*, with good wine and snacks.

Da Matusel, Via Bertolini 2. Close by the university, a popular and noisy place with reasonably priced food.

Osteria del Montesino, Via del Pratello 74b. One of the best *osterie* in town, a chatty, convivial place serving a handful of snacks including substantial, Southern-inspired salads and good *crostini* (various toppings spread on fried bread). The house wine is very drinkable, though there are other, more expensive labels.

Orsa, Via Mentana 1G. Has live jazz during the winter. Try the *bruschetta*; the other dishes are fairly pricey.

Poeti, Via Poeti 1. An old palazzo which has been an *osteria* since the fifteenth century. Trades on its reputation, which means its prices are slightly inflated, although it does have occasional live music.

Senzanome, Via Senzanome 42. Off Via Saragozza, this was a favourite drinking place for cart drivers in the seventeenth century when the *osteria* was famed for its sausage – made, it is claimed, from bull's testicles. The place now serves good home-made pasta and has a wide choice of beers and wines. Arrive after 10pm if you just want to drink.

Stranamore, Via del Pratello 44a. This place can be fiercely hip at times, but sometimes an interesting experience if there's some performance art going on.

Clubs and live music venues

Bestial Market, Via dello Scale 21. A 20min walk down Via San Felice, plays a vast mix of dance, house, hardcore techno and raggamuffin. Bands play here too, from 9.30pm. Eat at the pizzeria next door for L3600 with student ID.

Café Caracol, Piazza Galileo. Centrally placed Mexican bar by the police station that's open until 2am, serves great food, and has a small dance floor. Cheap cocktails too during the club's happy hour (7.30–8.30pm).

Cassero, Porta Saragozza 2. Actually inside the city gate itself, this is a mostly male, gay club with café and bookshop open daily, bar and dancing at night, and a beautiful roof garden with some good views over the city.

Candilejas, Via Bentini 20. Most nights salsa and merengue music, other nights indie stuff. To get there take #27A bus from Piazza Nettuno to the suburb of Corticella (a 25min journey); nightbus #62 runs, on the hour, back into town.

Cantina Bentivoglio, via Mascarella 4/B. On the edge of the university quarter, and as much an *osteria* as a club. Live bands, often including jazz, play at around 9.30pm in the cellars of this sixteenth-century palazzo, where the food and wine are excellent.

La Morara, Via Giacosa 6. A slightly sleazy but fun club playing mostly indie music (starts at 10pm) with a good bar downstairs. Take #23 bus there (until midnight); to get back, the #61 night-bus stop is a ten-minute walk away.

Palazzo dei Congressi, Piazza Costituzione 5 (☎637.5165; open 3–7pm). The venue for bands commanding bigger audiences; get there on bus #23 from Piazza Maggiore. Tickets can be pricey – L40–80,000 – and can be bought from the *Minella Rock Shop*, Via Mazzini 146.

Porta di Mare, Via Sampieri. Right behind the Due Torri, with good live bands at the weekend and a Greek *taverna* downstairs.

Studios, Via Massarenti 14. Just east of the city centre (take bus #11), this is a venue for bands and dancing, as well as screenings of rarely shown US and European movies. Officially it's for *ARCI* members only, but it's unlikely you'll be turned away.

Terzo Piano, Via Giambologna 4. Occasional African and World Music nights, starting at around 10pm. Bus #14 passes the end of the road just before the *autostrada* flyover (last bus at 12.30am).

Listings

Airport enquiries ☎311.578.

American Express Piazza XX Settembre 6 (☎220.477).

Books English books from *Feltrinelli*, Via dei Guidei 6.

Bus enquiries ☎248.374.

Car rental *Avis*, Viale Tietramellara 35 (☎051/255.024); *Europcar*, Viale Masini 4 (☎051/254.126); *Hertz*, Via Amendola 17–22 (☎051/254.830). All the major companies also have desks at the airport and the train station.

Cinema *Adriano*, Via San Felice 52, shows films in their original language on Mondays; *Tiffany*, Piazza di Porta Saragozza 5, on Wednesdays.

Hospital 24hr casualty at *Ortopedico-Traumatologico Rizzoli*, Via GC Pupilli 1 (☎582.555). Bus #30.

Laundry *Lava Asciuga*, Via Irnerio 35b, is a coin-op laundry; *Lavanderia*, Via Sauro 16, off Via Ugo Bassi, will do the wash for you by the end of the day if you take it in early enough.

Markets There are a couple of great indoor food markets in the city centre: the large and lively Mercato delle Erbe, Via Ugo Bassi 2 (Mon–Sat 7.15am–1pm & 5–7pm, closed Thurs & Sat afternoon); and another on Via Clavature (same opening hours); there's also a smaller open-air market at Piazza Aldrovandi, along Strada Maggiore, closed Tuesday afternoons. Finally, there's the open-air La Montagnola market, held in Piazza VII Agosto on Fridays and Saturdays, dawn until dusk, which sells just about everything, but is especially good for new and secondhand clothes.

Pharmacy Night services rotate; look outside the *Farmacia Comunale* in Piazza Maggiore or dial ☎192.

Police In an emergency dial ☎113. Otherwise their main office is Piazza Galileo 7 (☎278.846).

Post office The city's main post office is on Piazza Minghetti (Mon–Fri 8.15am–6.30pm & Sat 8.15am–1pm).

Shops Some of Bologna's most colourful sights are inside its many food stores, particularly those between Piazza Maggiore and the Due Torri, epitomised by *Tamburini* at Via Caprarie 1, which has a sizeable array of the different ways of eating the fat of Bologna. For a supermarket, go to the *Co-op*, Via Montebello 2, behind the train station.

Swimming pool Try the one at the sports ground at Via Costa 174 (daily 9.30am–7pm).

Taxis ☎534.141 or ☎372.727.

Telephones *SIP*, Piazza VIII Agosto (24hr), or Via Fossalta 4/E (daily 8am–10pm).

Train enquiries ☎246.490.

Travel agents *CTS*, Largo Rispigli 2f (☎261.802), or *University Viaggi*, Via Zamboni 16E (☎228.584).

Women's bookshop *Librellula*, Strada Maggiore 23e.

On from Bologna: south to Tuscany

In the heat of the summer the need to get out of Bologna becomes pressing, and the hills which start almost as soon as you leave the city gates take you high enough to catch some cooling breezes. The most obvious destination for a short trip is the eighteenth-century **Santuario di Madonna di San Luca**, close on 4km outside the city but connected by way of the world's longest portico, which meanders across the hillside in a series of 666 arches – a shelter for pilgrims on the trek to the top. Bus #20 drops you at the start of the route, by Porta Saragozza southwest of the centre.

Further out, towards Tuscany, the N325 passes through **PONTECCHIO MARCONI**, where the physicist Guglielmo Marconi lived in the late nineteenth century, and from where, in 1895, he sent the first radio message ever – to his brother on the other side of the hill. Marconi lies in a specially designed mausoleum in the village, close to the remains of the boat, Elettra, from which Marconi lit up the warship Sydney while anchored in Genova in 1930. A stop here is also a convenient time to try the *crescente ripiena* (stuffed with cheese and herbs), at SASSO MARCONI, a few kilometres down the road.

The route on from here towards Pistoia is a beautiful one, taking you above the Setta Valley, past chestnut groves and small villages. It's a well-trafficked road, though, and the backroads are the greatest attraction, especially in the hills between Bologna and Modena.

MARZABOTTO, a few kilometres on from Sasso Marconi and accessible by direct bus from Bologna, is known for the massacre of 1800 people that took place here during the last war. It also sports the remains of an Etruscan town, **Misa**, just outside (daily 8am–6pm). The site marks out the residential areas, the city gates, streets and drains and fragments of foundations from temples and some tombs remain – evidence of a town of highly skilled craft workers that was much more than just a staging-post between Etruria and the Po Valley. The **museum** (daily 9am–noon & 3–6pm; L4000) contains a variety of finds, from the remains of the piped water system to household objects inscribed *mi venelus* ("I belong to Venel") or *mi Sualus* ("I belong to Sualu").

Modena and around

Though only half an hour away by train, **MODENA** has a quite distinct identity from Bologna. It proclaims itself the "spiritual capital" of Emilia, highlighting the two cities' long and sometimes intense rivalry. It's true that Modena has a number of claims to fame: its outskirts are fringed with prosperous industry – knitwear and ceramics factories make a healthy profit on the surrounding plain, and Ferrari build their prestige motor cars close by, testing the Formula 1 monsters on the racetrack at nearby

Fiorino; Pavarotti is a native of the town and gives occasional impromptu concerts in its main square; and the cathedral is considered the finest Romanesque building in the region. Of things to see, top of most people's list are the rich collections of paintings and manuscripts built up by the Este family, who decamped here from Ferrara in 1598, after it was annexed by the papal states, and ruled the town until the eighteenth century. But really the appeal of Modena is in wandering its labyrinthine old centre, finishing up the day with some good food and nightlife.

Arrival, information and accommodation

Modena's centre, marked by the main Piazza Grande, is a fifteen-minute walk from the **train station** on Piazza Dante, down the wide Corso Vittorio Emanuele II. Bus #7 connects the train station with the main street of Via Emilia. The **bus station**, for villages on the plain or in the Apennines, is on Via Fabriani, off Viale Monte Kosica, ten minutes' walk from the train station and the centre of town. The **tourist office** is just around the corner from the main square at Via Scudari 30 (Mon–Fri 9.30am–12.30pm & 3.30–6.30pm, Sat 9.30am–12.30pm; ☎059/222.482).

Modena makes a nice place to stay for a night or two, and there are a few reasonably priced **hotels** in the narrow palace-lined streets of the city centre. However, places are at a premium, especially during the summer months, and you should really book in advance whatever time of year you're here. The cheapest places in the centre of town are the rather rundown *Astoria*, Via S. Eufemia 43 (☎059/225.587; ④), and the *Bonci*, Via Ramazzini 59 (☎059/223.634; ④) – the latter the handier of the two if you're walking from the station – although the slightly pleasanter *Sole*, Via Malatesta 45 (☎059/214.245; ④), is only marginally more expensive. A step up in price, there's the *Centrale*, Via Rismondo 57 (☎059/218.808; ⑤), and, on the other side of the main spine of Via Emilia, *Hotel La Torre*, Via Cervatta 5 (☎059/222.615; ⑤). The nearest **campsite** is *International Camping Modena* (☎059/332.252) on Via Cave Ramo, Località Bruciata, halfway between Modena and Reggio Nell'Emilia; bus #19 from Viale Monte Kosica, close by the train station, takes you right there.

The Town

Modena's tight, concentric medieval centre is bisected by **Via Emilia**, which runs past the edge of **Piazza Grande**, the nominal centre of town, its stone buildings and arcades forming the focus of much of its life. Dominating the square, the twelfth-century **Duomo** is dedicated to San Geminiano, the patron saint of Modena, and is one of the finest products of the Romanesque period in Italy. Its most striking feature is the west facade, just off the piazza, whose portal is supported by two majestic lions and fringed with marvellous reliefs – the work of one Wiligelmus, who also did the larger reliefs that run along the wall. Look also at the sculpture on the south side of the church, some of which is by Wiligelmus, some – in the final arch – much later, from the fifteenth century. Inside, the duomo is a lovely Romanesque church, rising to a high choir, supported again by lions and crouched figures and friezed with polychrome reliefs depicting New Testament stories – the *Last Supper* stands out particularly. Under the choir is the plain stone coffin of San Geminiano. Have a look too at the terracotta tableaux of the *Shepherds* in the south aisle.

Close by, on Via Lanfranco, the **Museo Lapidario** (daily 9am–noon & 3–6pm) has stone bits and pieces from the duomo and around the town, while on the other side of the church, the lurching **Torre Ghirlandina** was begun at the same time as the duomo but completed 200 years later. Until recently it contained the *Seccia Rapita*, a wooden bucket stolen during a raid by the Modenese on Bologna in 1325, and often quoted to show the history of rivalry between the two towns. The Modenese, who supported Re

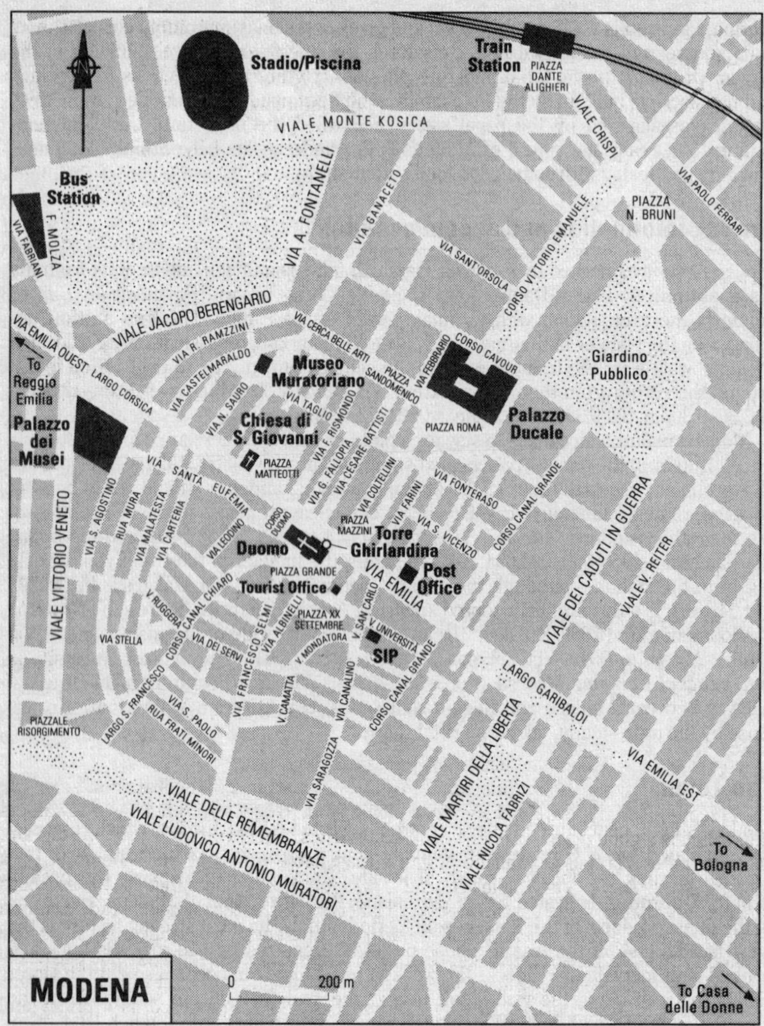

Enzo (the son of the emperor), swore enmity when the Bolognese took him prisoner after a thirteenth-century battle, liberating the bucket from Bologna until well into the next century in just one attempt to even the score. The seventeenth-century poet Tassoni wrote a mock heroic verse on the subject, which has apparently never lost its significance in people's minds, and it's still the object of occasional rag day stunts.

The other main focus for your wanderings around Modena is at the far, northwestern end of Via Emilia, a five-minute walk from Piazza Grande, where the **Palazzo dei Musei** formerly an arsenal, later a workhouse – now houses the city museums and art galleries. Through an archway lined with Roman tombstones – Piazza Matteotti was on the site of a necropolis – a staircase leads off to the right up to the **Biblioteca Estense**, on the first floor (exhibition area: daily except Sun 9am–1pm; library: Mon–Thurs 9am–7.15pm, Fri & Sat 9am–1.45pm, Sun closed). This is only partly open to non-students, but what is on display is of at least mild interest – letters between monarchs, popes and despots, with great wax seals, filed away for hundreds of years, old maps, and the prize treasure, Borso d'Este's bible, the *Bibbio Borso*, arguably the most decorated book in the world. The **Museo d'Arte Medievale e Moderne e Etnologia** (Tues–Sat 9am–1pm, Tues & Thurs also 3–6pm, Sun 10am–12.30pm & 3–6pm), on the second floor, is the newest part of the museum, with a large collection of artefacts of archaeological and artistic significance, while on the top floor, the **Galleria Estense** (Tues, Wed & Fri 9am–2pm, Thurs & Sat 9am–7.30pm, Sun 9am–1pm; L4000) is perhaps the highlight of all the collections. Made up of the picture collection of the Este family, it contains paintings of the local schools, from the early Renaissance through to the works of the Caraccis, Guercino and Guido Reni, sculptures in terracotta by Nicolo Dell'Arca, as well as portable altars, Madonnas and triptychs by lesser-known Emilian artists like Cosimo Tura, who painted the Schifanoia Palace in Ferrara. There's also a bust of Francesco d'Este by Bernini, a portrait of the same man by Velazquez, and Venetian works by Tintoretto and Veronese.

Five minutes' walk away in an undisturbed corner of town, off Via N. Sauro at Via Pomposa 1, is another museum, the **Museo Muratoriano** (daily 9am–noon). This contains possessions and works of Ludovico Antonio Muratori, the Jesuit priest, historiographer and intellectual whose ideas helped break the monopoly of the church over education in the eighteenth century.

Eating, drinking and nightlife

Like Bologna, Modena is a terrific place to **eat**, with a large array of restaurants covering the spectrum of prices. Try if you can to sample some of the local pork-based specialities, like *ciccioli* – flaky pork scratchings laid out in bars in the evening – or, in a restaurant, *zampone* (shanks of pork, boned and stuffed with minced meat) or *cotechino* – the same thing, but stuffed inside an animal bladder.

At the bottom end of the price scale, *Giusti*, Via Farini 75, a delicatessen since the seventeenth century, is a good source of picnic food; *Giusti* also run a bar, a few doors up, which is a good place for ready-made sandwiches. There is a self-service restaurant, *Il Chiostro*, at Via San Geminiano 3, and a reasonable *mensa* at Via Leodino 9. Up a notch, *Santa Lucia*, Via Taglio 61, and *Trattoria Aldini*, Via Albinelli 40, are both decent, affordable stand-bys; *Ermes*, Via Ganeceto 89, is a rough-and-ready trattoria with great food at low prices. If you want to try Modenese specialities, *Da Enzo*, Via Coltellini 17, is a nice, slightly old-fashioned place to do so – though not especially cheap; there's also *Santa Chiara*, on Via Ruggera, a swish restaurant with adventurous contemporary local cooking. Nearby *Fini*, on Largo San Francesco, is a pricey and rather upscale establishment, but the food is delectable in the extreme.

Around Modena

At first glance the countryside **around Modena** looks bland and uninviting – discount furniture and lighting stores, crumbling farmhouses the size of mansions, and factories. Further north onto the plain, wide vistas of maize fields, rows of pollarded fruit trees, vines strung up from pergolas are broken only occasionally by a line of poplar trees shimmering in the heat.

You might, however, want to venture out to visit the **Galeria Ferrari**, at Via Dino Ferrari 43 in **MARANELLO**, south of Modena (daily except Mon 9.30am–12.30pm &

3–6pm; L7000), an exhibition centre dedicated to the racing dynasty; it's reachable on bus #2 from the bus station every half an hour. On display are the cups and trophies won by the Ferrari team over the years, an assortment of Ferrari engines, along with vintage examples of the cars themselves and a reconstruction of Enzo Ferrari's study.

CARPI, the region's main centre, around 15km north, is also worth a few hours of your time. The town's central **Piazza dei Martiri** is an enormous and impressive open space, almost worth the trip alone, and the sixteenth-century **Castello del Pio**, a mass of ornamental turrets and towers, holds another interesting museum inside – the **Museo al Deportato** (Thurs, Sat & public hols only 9am–12.30pm & 3–6.30pm; free). Occupying forces in World War II held prisoners at a camp in Fossoli 6km to the north, before deporting them to Germany – the camp sheds still stand, dilapidated, in a field – and the museum has displays on the camps and the conditions for the prisoners, neatly putting them into context with information on political and racial exile. The most sobering aspect of the museum its its layout; you progress through the almost bare rooms accompanied by a long ribbon of quotes painted on the walls, taken from prisoners' letters. Some were proud to have stood by their ideals, others expressed a fear of death or surprise and frustration at dying young. Another wrote "*che la mamma nasconda il grano se non i tedeschi se lo pigliano. Addio, vostra nipote*" ("Mum should hide the grain so the Germans don't grab it. Adieu, your nephew").

The activity outside in the square provides some welcome light relief, with slick clothing stores running the length of its sixteenth-century red-brick **Portico Lungo**. At one end of the square are a couple of cafés and the bright ochre **Teatro Comunale**, at the other the Renaissance **Cattedrale** with baroque facade. *Bar Tazza d'Oro* opposite the theatre does a brisk trade (try the iced tea in summer), but for more substantial snacks head for the *Bottega della Pizza* at via Berengario 13. The rest of Carpi is unexciting so it's unlikely that you'll want to hang around town. There are trains and buses every hour to Modena, but if you do want to stay there are **rooms** to be had at *Albergo da Georgio* on Via G. Rocca (☎0531/685.365; ⑤).

About 10km northeast of Modena, and reachable by bus, **NONANTOLA** is best known for its **abbey**, founded in 752 by Anselmo – then an abbot from Lombardy, later made a saint. The abbey seems at first unprepossessing, rebuilt as it was in red-brick in the thirteenth century, but the portal more than makes up for it, flanked by stone lions and topped by carvings executed by the workshop of Wiligelmus, who worked also on Modena's and (probably) Cremona's cathedrals. The carvings tell some familiar stories, in an earthy, vernacular style, perhaps best exemplified by the figures of the asses in the nativity scene. Also featured in the series of carvings are Saint Adrian and Saint Sylvester, both of whom are buried in the monastic interior – the church is in fact dedicated to Saint Sylvester.

South of Modena

To the **south of Modena** lie the foothills of the Apennines, covered by turkey oak, hornbeam and hazel woods. Narrow roads corkscrew into the mountains, from which you can climb by foot onto the *crinale* – the backbone of the Apennine range. Trails lead along the succession of peaks above the treeline, steep slopes on either side, to some glacial lakes, although the routes are most impressive for the views they give across the breadth of Italy on either side.

For many, the main attraction of the small villages in the foothills is **food**. The tourist office can advise you on "gourmet itineraries" to find the real Modenese cuisine, but they're not really necessary: restaurant signs by the side of the road invite you in to try cuisine "*alla tua nonna*" – "like grandma used to make" – often involving mortadella, salami or *crescente* (a kind of pitta bread eaten with a mixture of dripping, garlic, rosemary and parmesan). Variations on the same theme include *gnocco fritto* – fried dough diamonds eaten with salami or ham. Higher in the mountains you can still find *ciacci* – chestnut flour pancakes, filled with ricotta and sugar – and walnuts (which should be picked on or around the night of San Giovanni, June 24) that go to make *nocino* liqueur.

Vignola, Zocca and the Riserva dei Sassi Rocca Malatina

VIGNOLA produces some of the best cherries in Italy and is an impressive sight, surrounded by acres of blossom, in April when people from all around come for the spring festival. At other times Vignola is worth a visit for its castle, the **Rocca di Vignola** (Mon–Fri 9am–noon & 3.30–7pm, Sat & Sun 10am–noon & 3.30–7pm; L3000), which is particularly well preserved, one of many castles built in the fifteenth and sixteenth centuries to defend the crossings along the River Panaro into the neighbouring state of Bologna. It is a mammoth specimen, with enormous watchtowers on each corner, and fancy brickwork — a castle style you see in other parts of Emilia.

The *Antica Osteria da Bacco*, on the main road which skirts the castle, serves classic local pasta dishes and a good *nocino* (hazlenut) liqueur. It also has an *enoteca* around the back on Via Selmi, where you can try a glass of locally produced wine, albeit in a rather serious atmosphere. If you need to **stay**, the *Eden* hotel is uninviting but the only one in town (☎059/772.847; ④).

ZOCCA, 9km away, is a quiet market town which buses from Modena, and a couple of affordable hotels, make a possible overnight stop. *Finelli*, Via Mauro Tesi 902 (☎059/987.071; ④), on the main street through town, is convenient enough; *Lenzi* Via Cavour 14 (☎059/987.039; ④), to the left off Via della Pace, is slightly more expensive, or there's a **campsite** outside town, the *Monte Questiolo*, at Via Montequestiolo 184 (☎059/987.764), open mid-June to mid-September – take Via Roma, then Via Rosola and follow the signs. One exceptionally relaxing place to stay is *Tizzano* (☎059/989.581; ④), 6km from Zocca, a former fortress farmhouse that's now an informal *osteria* with rooms. Still a working farm, it's in an unusually peaceful spot, looking across the orchards straight through to Monte Cimone, still snowcapped in spring, with only the hilltop town of MONTE CORONE between you and the mountains. The food is very good, too, and very reasonably priced. To get here, go through Monte Ombraro and take Via Lamazze out of the village; 1km further on, take the turning on the left, again signposted.

Fourteen kilometres south of Zocca, the road between CASTEL D'AINO and ABETAIA is beautiful, a lush landscape with the only sign of life an occasional farm with geese and hens scratching in a steep orchard. **MONTESE**, set back 3km from the main road, is worth a quick detour, especially around the third weekend in July, officially wild black cherry day, and from then until mid-August when there's medieval singing, dancing and classical concerts in the castle above town. The Montese **tourist office** — in reality a wooden hut in the town centre — also hires out tandems by the hour, half or full day.

The **Riserva dei Sassi Rocca Malatina** is named after the giant outcrop of rock, partly eroded into strange pinnacles and popular with climbers, located near the village of **ROCCA MALATINA** itself. If you have your own transport, take the turning off the main road for a look at **PIEVE TRÉBBIO**, an eleventh-century Romanesque church with separate polygonal baptistery and belltower, the oldest church in the Modenese Apeninnes. Much of it was reconstructed at the beginning of this century, including the facade, but plenty of intricate medieval carving remains, as well as some fine Romanesque capitals inside – though it's closed every day except Sunday.

Pievepélago and Lago Santo

A little further east, the SS12 from Modena becomes really beautiful after PAVULLO, especially in spring when the colours are startling – white blossom against bright green meadows. There is not much reason to stop until **LAMA MOCOGNO**, a little further on, where *Camping Valverde* (☎0536/44.045) is a peaceful place to camp between June and August. At **LA SANTONA**, *prodotti del sottobosco* (specialities of the woods — berries, funghi etc) are on sale in summer and autumn, when people from Bologna and the other main towns around visit, mainly to eat. **PIEVEPÉLAGO** is a modern-looking market town with a couple of inexpensive **places to stay**, of which the *Albergo Bucaneve* is the more appealing, 1km up the road from the village on Via Giardini (☎0536/71.383;⑤). Three *ATCM* buses a day make the trip here from Bologna via Vignola, six daily from Modena, and it's well worth the long journey to sample local **food**. *La Capanna Celtica*, Via Roma 24, serves an exceptional blend of Emilian and Tuscan cooking, though not especially cheaply; *Birreria-Paninoteca Il Cantuccio* is open (and lively) on Tuesdays, when practically all else is closed.

An easy path leads up to **Lago Santo**, a small lake in a large glacial basin, 150m from the bus stop, where a trail map shows you where you can walk (follow the red and white flashes painted on rocks along the way). If you want to **stay**, *Albergo-Ristorante Lago Santo* in nearby LE TAGLIOLE (☎0536/71.390; ③) is inexpensive, or there's the *Rifugio Alpino Vittoria* (open June–Sept) right next to the lake, in whose restaurant you can sample *porcini* mushrooms, game and fruits of the forest.

Séstola, Fanano and around

Buses make the trip east along the Scoltenna gorge from Pievepélago to **SÉSTOLA**, whose trattorias and hotels make it seem like a teeming metropolis compared with the tiny hamlets around. In reality, the town nucleus is quite tiny, but there are some good places to eat, including the *Ristorante Pizzeria Il Campanaccio* on Corso Libertà, which serves such mountain food as *tagliatelle ai porcini* or *porcini trifolati* and a good selection of wines at very reasonable prices. The *Sport* hotel at Via delle Ville 116 (☎0536/62.502; ⑤) is the cheapest hotel; the *Regina*, Via Cimone 23 (☎0536/62.336; ⑥), is very appealing but more expensive.

Perched at 1020m, Séstola gives good views of the countryside around; a cable car takes you even higher, so you can look back down over Séstola and its ninth-century castle (currently being restored). A 4km hike will take you up to the **Pian del Falco** (1530m), where there's accommodation at the *Baita del Sole* (☎0536/61.113; ⑤). A high path winds around the head of the Rio Vésale to **Passo del Lupo** (1550m), 4.5km later, and, soon after, the **Lago della Ninfa**, surrounded by beech and larch trees.

The wide, cultivated valley below is ideal for some easy cycling, or else climb (3hr) up to Pian Cavallaro high on Monte Cimone's slopes. A mule track south to **Madonna del Trogolino**, a seventeenth-century oratory, begins the ascent, after which you skirt Monte Carvarola and veer southwest to climb towards **Passo del Lupo** at 1550m. For a while you stay relatively level as you follow the **Cresta del Gallo** watershed, after which a westerly turning brings you into a natural rocky amphitheatre, followed by a steep ascent to **Pian Cavallaro** itself. The altitude (1827m) gives awesome views across ridge after ridge down eventually to Lombardy and the Veneto. Either retrace your steps or head down (3hr 30min) to Séstola (buses to Modena).

FANANO, just under 6km from Séstola (reachable by bus from Séstola and Modena), is a more attractive village of ancient slate-roofed houses. It's a stop on the old pilgrim's route between Modena and Pistoia, and its origins probably lie in the original Benedictine monastery founded here in 752 by Saint Anselmo. Every three years on Good Friday, a torchlight procession threads its way through the medieval streets decorated with greenery. A clutch of tiny oratories includes the **Chiesa di San Giuseppe** and **L'Oratorio del Santi Sacramento**, both with magnificent Baroque gilded wooden altars. If you decide to stay, there are half a dozen inexpensive **hotels**, including *La Pace* at Via Roma 6 (☎0536/68.865; ④) and the *Sole* at Via C. Foli 4 (☎0536/68.070; ⑤).

Montefiorino and around

A series of steep, switchback roads marks the approach to **MONTEFIORINO**, a small village often swathed in fog in spring and autumn and topped by a correspondingly grim thirteenth-century **fortress**. The seat of the partisan republic in the summer of 1944, the area was focus of some intense wartime resistance activity, its mountain farms and haylofts making ideal hide-outs. Sabotage of transport and communication links, or harbouring prisoners of war, was punishable by death, and the many people shot in reprisals are remembered in the **Museo della Repubblica** in the fortress's ground-floor rooms. For admission the best bet is to phone in advance (☎0536/965.219) or ask in one of the *comune* offices upstairs (Mon–Sat 9.30am–1pm).

From the village, you can climb by mule track (20min) to **RUBBIANO** and look at some weird stone carvings in the eleventh-century parish church of **Santa Maria** there – as all over this area, these are the work of the stonemasons of Como, renowned for their skill in the Middle Ages. Circles, spirals, wheels, all reminiscent of the sun, which can also be found in Etruscan art, symbolise light and strength and ward off darkness and evil. The highly stylised and enigmatic faces symbolically replaced the ancient custom of human sacrifices, in former times the bodies of the victims being buried in the building's foundations to appease the gods.

A side road covers the 11km from Montefiorino to **FRASSINORO**, worth the trip for a meal at *Piacentini* on the *vicolo* of the same name (☎0536/969.817; closed Thurs, booking advisable). You can eat rabbit or chicken from the garden, and home-made pasta, on a fixed-price menu in summer of around L30,000.

Reggio Emilia

Continuing north up the Via Emilia from Modena, **REGGIO EMILIA** is a quite different place from Modena, a quiet, ancient town that makes a good place to rest up for a while. It's admittedly sparse on sights, but it's a pleasant town to wander through and is a feasible jumping-off point for travelling into the Reggiano Apennines.

The Town

Reggio is built around two central squares, **Piazza Prampolini** and **Piazza San Prospero**, separated by the **Duomo**, and the **Palazzo del Municipio** with its fishtail battlements. Like other towns in the area, the centre is closed to traffic, and bicycles clatter across the cobbles from all directions. Piazza San Prospero comes alive on market days (Tues & Fri), its stalls and the shops selling a staggering array of fruit, veg, salami and cheese, including the local *parmigiano-reggiano*. Around the square, the buildings squeeze up so close to the church of **San Prospero** that they seem to have pushed it off balance and it now lurches to one side. Built in the sixteenth century, its facade is decorated with columns and statues in niches, guarded by six lions in rose-coloured Verona marble – a marked contrast to the unclad octagonal campanile next to it. Via Broletto leads through into **Piazza Prampolini**, skirting the side of the duomo, swathed in green nets and scaffolding while it's being restored. Underneath the marble tacked on in the sixteenth century, it's possible to see the church's Romanesque facade, with statues of Adam and Eve over the medieval portal, although all else that remains of the original building are the apse and enormous crypt. Inside there's a painting of the *Assumption* by Guercino and many tombs, including one for the inventor of the hourglass, Cherubino Sforzani.

At right angles to the duomo is the sugar-pink **Palazzo del Capitano del Popolo**. The tricolour was proclaimed here as the official national flag of Italy, when Napoleon's Cispadane Republic was formed in 1797. Walking north from here, the **Musei Civici** along Via Spallanzani, on the edge of Piazza della Vittoria, are made up of an eighteenth-century private collection of archaeological finds, fossils and paintings (Mon–Fri 9.30am–12.30pm). In the corner of the square, the **Galleria Parmeggiani** might also be worth a look if it hadn't been closed for the past ten years; there's nothing to suggest it will open soon, but check anyway. It's reputed to contain an important collection of Spanish, Flemish and Italian art as well as costumes and textiles. Assuming it's closed, stroll over to the church of **Madonna della Ghiara**, built in the seventeenth century and decorated with Bolognese School frescoes of scenes from the Old Testament and a *Crucifixion* scene by Guercino.

Practicalities

Reggio is on the main rail line between Bologna and Milan. The **train station** is on Piazza Marconi I, just east of the old centre; the **bus station** is on Via Raimondo Franchetti. The **tourist office** is in the main Piazza Prampolini (daily 9.30am–12.30pm & 3.30–6pm; ☎052/451.152), and there's a very helpful *Club Alpino Italia* office at Viale Mille 32 (☎052/436.685). If you're planning to stay over, be aware that **hotel** space is somewhat limited. The *Ariosto* on Via San Rocco 12 (☎052/437.320; ⑤) is a central and reasonably priced choice. There's also a **youth hostel**, 500m from the train station at Via dell'Abbadessa 8, open all year (☎052/454.795; ①). For **food**, *La Zucca*, on the southern edge of the historic centre in Piazza Fontanesi, is a good place to sample local dishes; *Condor*, at the lower end of Via Spallanzani, is a good, noisy place to eat pizza.

South of Reggio

Very much in a different vein, the foothills **south of Reggio** are cheese country: you'll see many signs along the roadside advertising the local *parmigiano-reggiano*, and the village of **CASINA**, about 20km outside Reggio on the N63 to La Spezia, holds a popular *Festa Parmigiana* in August, when the vats of cheese mixture are stirred with enormous wooden paddles. The countryside itself is a mixture of lush pastures and scraggy uplands, with some footpaths around, though there's better walking higher up in the mountains.

If you've got your own transport or are prepared to wait a long time for a lift, take the side road leading from Casina to **CANOSSA**. This was the seat of the powerful Da Canossa family, whose most famous member, the Countess Mathilda of Tuscany (*La Gran Contessa*), was a big name here in the eleventh century – unusually so in a society largely controlled by warlords and the clergy. She was known for donning armour and leading her troops into battle herself, and at the age of 43 scandalised the nobility by marrying a youth of seventeen. During the battles between Pope Gregory VII and the Holy Roman Emperor Henry IV, she supported the pope and helped draw the emperor here barefoot as a penitent to apologise to the pontiff following his excommunication. Henry was apparently left waiting outside in the snow for three days before the castle doors were opened. The remains of the **castle** (April–Sept Tues–Sun 9am–12.30pm & 3–7pm, Oct–March Tues–Sun 2.30–5pm; free) are largely thirteenth-century, but it's the location – on a rocky outcrop looking towards the mountains in one direction and over the neighbouring castle at Rossena and the towns strung out over the plain in the other – which is impressive.

People from the towns around are fond of coming out here at weekends to eat in the local restaurants, and it's a popular area for hiking or cross-country and downhill skiing. In autumn, you see people armed with plastic bags for collecting mushrooms, or filling mineral water bottles with water from the springs off the mountains. There are few specific centres to aim for, though, and you're most likely to travel along these valleys if you're driving across the Apennines to the coast. Two buses a day do the whole journey and more go part of the way – though it's not a trip to do if you're in a hurry. The road is tortuous and the viewpoint constantly changes as you switchback your way across the mountain ridges or through small villages with austere, high-walled houses backing directly onto the roadside. The best times to come are late spring and early summer – in autumn it's foggy more often than not – the fog and low cloud clearing only momentarily for a quick glimpse of chestnut grove or scree-filled riverbed hundreds of feet below.

High in the hills paths lead onto the mountain *crinale*. **CASTELNOVO NE'MONTI** in the foothills is a possible base for these. Further on, at **BUSANA**, the road forks to the left, descending through a series of hairpin bends bordered by plenty of falling rock signs, in the Secchia Valley, climbing back up the other side through CINQUECERRI to **LIGONCHIO** – another good starting-point for walks away from cable cars and ski lifts, onto nearby **Monte Cusna**. Close by here are the *Prati di Sara*, a windswept expanse of grassland with small tarns and the occasional tree. As you ascend, you have more of a view across the layers of ridges, often half-obscured in the mist. It's possible to stay overnight in some of the refuges which group along the *GEA* (*Grand Escursione Apenninica*) route, a 25-day trek which weaves its way in and out of the border between Emilia and Tuscany. If this seems too much, the *Club Alpino Italiano* office in Reggio sometimes organises weekend treks.

Parma

Generally reckoned to have the highest standard of living in Italy, **PARMA** is about as comfortable a town as you could wish for. The measured pace of its streets, the abundance of its restaurants and the general air of provincial affluence are almost cloyingly pleasant, especially if you've arrived from the South. Not surprisingly, if you're travelling on a tight budget, Parma presents a few difficulties – the cheap hotels are usually full, and, although the restaurants are excellent, food too can cost a bomb. That said, it's a friendly enough place, with plenty to see. A visit to the opera can be an experience – the audience are considered one of the toughest outside La Scala and don't pull any punches if they consider a singer to be performing badly. And the city's works of art include the legacy of two key Renaissance artists – Correggio and Parmigianino.

Arrival, information and accommodation

Parma's **train station** is fifteen minutes' walk from the central Piazza Garibaldi, or a short ride on bus #8, #9 or #12. The local **bus station** is next to the river, at the junction of Viale IV Novembre and Viale P. Toschi. The **tourist office** is on Piazza Duomo (Mon–Fri 9am–12.30pm & 3–6pm, Sat 9am–12.30pm; ☎0521/234.735). Finding a **place to stay** can be tricky, and once again you'd be well advised to book somewhere in advance. There's an official **youth hostel**, *Cittadella*, on Via Passo Buole (☎0521/581.546; ①), open April to October – take bus #9 from the station (8pm–midnight night bus #E). As for **hotels**, there are a couple of places close to Piazza Garibaldi – the *Croce di Malta*, south of the square at Borgo Palmia 8 (☎0521/235.643; ④), and the *Lazzaro*, on the other side of the square at Via XX Marzo 14 (☎0521/208.944; ④). Both have their own restaurants, of which the latter is marginally the cheaper. If you want to be near the station, the *Moderno*, Via A. Cecchi 4 (☎0521/772.647; ④), is dead opposite; the *Leon d'Oro*, Viale A. Fratti 4 (☎0521/773.182; ④), is just outside and to the left and also has its own restaurant. If all of these are full, you may have more luck on the university side of the river – take bus #3 from Piazza Garibaldi – along Via Gramsci, the main road out of town. Try the *Amorini* at Via Gramsci 37 (☎0521/983.239; ⑤), or the cheaper *Il Sole* at Via Gramsci 15 (☎0521/995.107; ④).

The Town

Parma's main street, **Via Mazzini**, and its continuation, **Strada della Repubblica**, run east from the river, past **Piazza Garibaldi** – which, together with the narrow streets and alleyways which wind to the south and west, forms the fulcrum of Parma. The mustard-coloured **Palazzo del Governatore** forms the backdrop of the square, behind which the Renaissance church of the **Madonna della Steccata** (daily 7.30am–noon & 3–6pm) was apparently built using Bramante's original plan for Saint Peter's as a model. Inside there are frescoes by a number of sixteenth-century painters, notably Parmigianino, who spent the last ten years of his life on this work, eventually being sacked for breach of contract by the disgruntled church authorities. A year later he was dead, aged 37, "an almost savage or wild man" who had become obsessed with alchemy, according to Vasari.

Five minutes' walk away – left off Strada Garibaldi – the slightly gloomy **Piazza Duomo** forms part of the old *centro episcopale*, away from the shopping streets of the commercial centre. The beautiful Lombard-Romanesque **Duomo** (daily 9am–noon & 3–7pm), dating from the eleventh century, holds earlier work by Parmigianino in its south transept, painted when the artist was a pupil of Correggio – who painted the fresco of the *Assumption* in the central cupola. Finished in 1534, this is among the most famous of Correggio's works, the Virgin Mary floating up through a sea of limbs, faces and swirling drapery that attracted some bemused comments at the time. One contemporary compared it to a "hash of frogs' legs", while Dickens, visiting much later, thought it a sight "no operative surgeon gone mad, could imagine in his wildest delirium". Correggio was paid for the painting with a sackful of small change to annoy him, since he was known to be a great miser. The story goes that he carried the sack of coins home in the heat, caught a fever and died at the age of 40. Before you leave, take a look at the relief of the *Deposition* on the west wall of the south transept, an impressive piece of work by the architect Antelami that dates from 1178. Look too at the frieze which runs the length of the nave above the arches – also by Correggio.

There's a more significant work by Benedetto Antelami outside the duomo, in the form of the octagonal **Baptistery** (daily 9am–12.30pm & 3–7pm; L3000), its pink Verona marble facing, four storeys high, encircled by a band of sculpture and topped off by some slim turrets. The three elaborately carved portals are often a meeting place in the evening. Bridging the gap between the Romanesque and Gothic styles, this is considered Antelami's finest work, built in 1196; the architect sculpted the frieze which surrounds the building, and was also responsible for the reliefs inside, including the polychrome figures above the door and a series of fourteen statues representing the months and seasons that have been painstakingly scrubbed down and restored. Take the spiral staircase to the top for a closer view of the frescoes on the rib-vaulted ceiling – by an unknown thirteenth-century artist.

There's more work by Correggio, also, in the cupola of the church of **San Giovanni Evangelista** behind the duomo (daily 6.30am–noon & 3.30–8pm) – a fresco of the *Vision of St John* at Patmos. Next door, the **Spezieria Storica di San Giovanni Evangelista**, at Borgo Pipa 1 (Tues–Sat 9am–2pm, Sun 9am–1pm; L3000), is a thirteenth-century pharmacy that preserves its medieval interior.

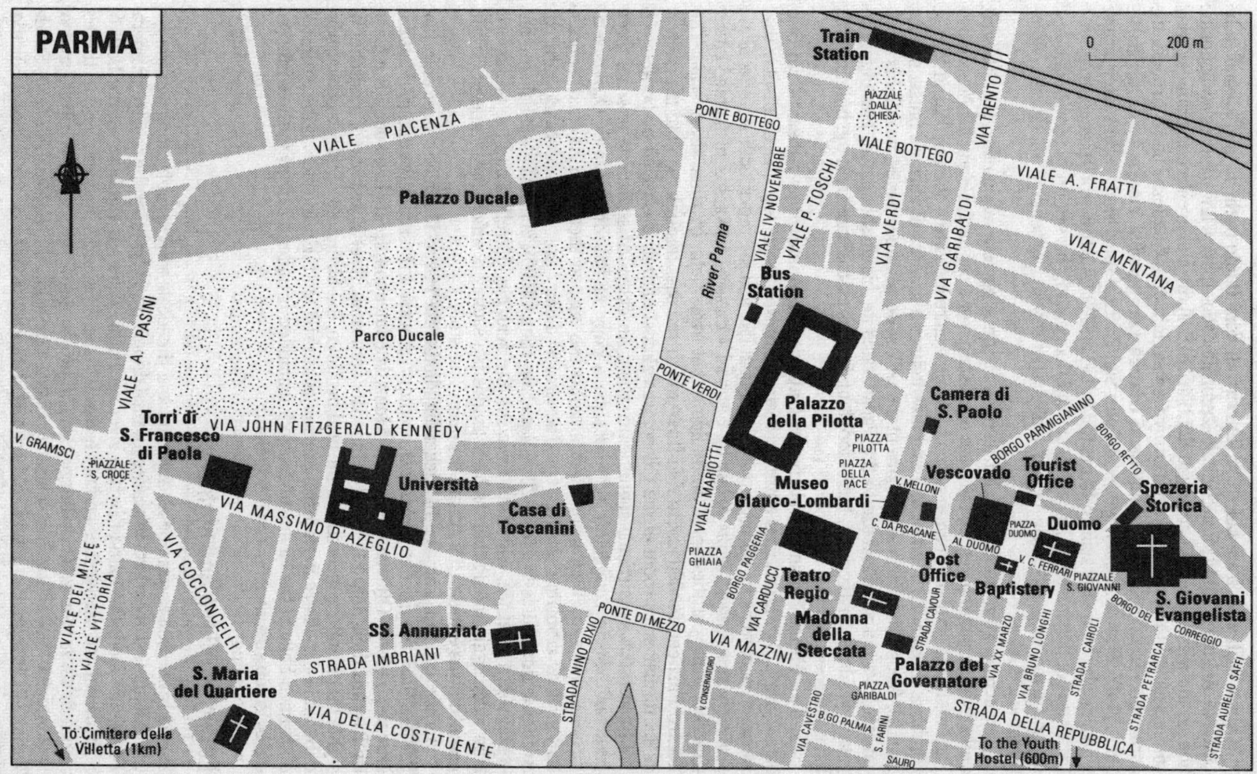
PARMA
0
200 m
Train Station
PIAZZALE DALLA CHIESA
VIA TRENTO
VIALE BOTTEGO
VIALE A. FRATTI
VIALE MENTANA
VIA GARIBALDI
VIA VERDI
VIALE P. TOSCHI
VIALE IV NOVEMBRE
PONTE BOTTEGO
River Parma
Bus Station
Palazzo della Pilotta
Camera di S. Paolo
BORGO PARMIGIANINO
BORGO RETTO
Spezeria Storica
S. Giovanni Evangelista
BORGO DEL CORREGGIO
STRADA AURELIO SAFFI
STRADA PETRARCA
PIAZZALE S. GIOVANNI
Duomo
Tourist Office
PIAZZA DUOMO
V. C. FERRARI
Vescovado
AL DUOMO
Baptistery
Post Office
V. MELLONI
C. DA PISACANE
PIAZZA PILOTTA
PIAZZA DELLA PACE
Museo Glauco-Lombardi
Teatro Regio
Madonna della Steccata
Palazzo del Governatore
STRADA CAVOUR
STRADA CAIROLI
VIA BRUNO LONGHI
VIA XX MARZO
STRADA DELLA REPUBBLICA
To the Youth Hostel (600m)
PIAZZA GARIBALDI
S. FARINI
SAURO
B.GO PALMIA
VIA CAVESTRO
VIA CARDUCCI
BORGO PAGGERIA
VIA MAZZINI
V. CONSERVATORIO
PIAZZA GHIAIA
VIALE MARIOTTI
PONTE VERDI
PONTE DI MEZZO
STRADA NINO BIXIO
Palazzo Ducale
Parco Ducale
VIALE PIACENZA
Casa di Toscanini
Università
VIA JOHN FITZGERALD KENNEDY
VIA MASSIMO D'AZEGLIO
SS. Annunziata
STRADA IMBRIANI
VIA DELLA COSTITUENTE
S. Maria del Quartiere
VIA COCCONCELLI
Torri di S. Francesco di Paola
VIALE A. PASINI
PIAZZALE S. CROCE
V. GRAMSCI
VIALE VITTORIA
VIALE DEI MILLE
To Cimitero della Villetta (1km)

A short walk west from here, the **Camera di San Paolo** in the former Benedictine Convent off Via Melloni (Mon–Sat 9am–2pm, Sun 9am–1pm), a few minutes' walk north, houses more frescoes by Correggio done in 1518; above the fireplace the abbess who commissioned the work is portrayed by Correggio as the Goddess Diana. Around the corner on Piazza della Pace, the **Museo Glauco-Lombardi** at Via Garibaldi 15 (Tues–Sat 9.30–12.30pm & 4–6pm; winter 3–5pm; Sun 9.30am–1pm; free), recalls later times, with a display of memorabilia relating to Marie-Louise of Austria, who reigned here after the defeat of her husband Napoleon at Waterloo, setting herself up here with another suitor (much to the chagrin of her exiled spouse) and expanding the Parma violet perfume industry.

Just across from here, it's hard to miss Parma's biggest monument, the **Palazzo della Pilotta**, surrounded by the wide open spaces of a car park. Begun for Alessandro Farnese in the sixteenth century, this building was reduced to a shell by World War II bombing; though it's been rebuilt and now houses a number of Parma's museums. As Paul III, Alessandro Farnese was one of the wiliest Renaissance popes, during his term annexing Parma and Piacenza to the Papal States for his dissolute son, Pierluigi. The palace was built for Pierluigi, but before long he was assassinated and the building was left unfinished.

Inside is Parma's main art gallery, the **Galleria Nazionale** (Tues–Sat 9am–2pm, Sun 9am–1pm; L10,000, includes entry to Teatro Farnese), a modern, hi-tech display that includes more work by Correggio and Parmigianino, and the remarkable *Apostles at the Sepulchre* and *Funeral of the Virgin* by Carracci – massive canvasses suspended either side of a gantry at the top of the building that overwhelm by their sheer scale. The **Teatro Farnese** (L4000 just to visit this), which you pass through to get to the gallery, in the former arms room of the palace, was almost entirely destroyed by bombing in 1944 and has been virtually rebuilt since then. An extended semicircle of seats three tiers high, made completely of wood, it's a copy of Palladio's *Teatro Olympico* at Vicenza, and as well as being (temporarily) the biggest theatre of its kind, sported Italy's first revolving stage. On the lower floor, the **Museo Nazionale di Archeologico** (Tues–Sat 9am–2pm, Sun 9am–1pm; L4000), is a less essential stop but is still worth a glance, with finds from the Etruscan city of Velleia and the prehistoric lake villages around Parma, as well as the table top on which the Emperor Trajan notched up a record of his gifts to the poor.

Across the river from the Palazzo della Pilotta, the **Parco Ducale** is a set of formal gardens laid out in the eighteenth century around the sixteenth-century **Palazzo Ducale**, built for Ottaviano Farnese (Mon–Sat 8am–noon; free). Just south, the **Casa di Toscanini** on Borgo R. Tanzi (Mon–Sat 10am–1pm; free) is just one of a number of sights that recall Parma's strong musical pedigree, the birthplace of the composer who debuted in the *Teatro Regio* here. Further south still, on the same side of the river, the embalmed body of the violinist Niccolo Paganini rests under a canopy in the **Cimitero della Villetta** (daily 8am–noon & 2–6pm).

Eating, drinking and nightlife

Parma is not well known for its nightlife, and the locals tend to prefer long sessions in the various (excellent) **restaurants**, or else dress up and head for the theatre or opera. For picnic food, the market by the river on Piazza Ghiaia is the best source both of ingredients and sandwiches and ready-made dishes at a number of *tavole calde*; there's also a small *tavola calda* at Borgo Sant'Ambrogio 2, off the Piazza Garibaldi end of Strada della Repubblica. Also close by Piazza Garibaldi, the *Enoteca Fontana*, Strada Farini 24a, is a great authentic old *enoteca*, with long wooden tables, a huge choice of different wines and a menu that includes sandwiches, steaming bowls of pasta and hot and cold daily specials – a good bet for lunch. *Trattoria Corrieri* is a popular place, tucked away off the main street at Via Conservatorio 1, and is not at all expensive; nor is *Trattoria S. Ambrogio*, Vicolo delle Piaghe 1, off Strada Farini, which has excellent fresh pasta and an all-meat menu that leans towards game. The *Croce di Malta* and *Lazzaro* hotels, both centrally placed (addresses p.341), also have decent restaurants. Up a bracket in price, opera *apassionati* eat at *Cannon d'Oro*, Via N. Sauro 3 – expensive but entertaining. For later on in the evening, *Da Quinto*, Borgo del Correggio 60, is a good *birreria* with a wide choice of beers and various hot snacks and sandwiches.

Opera is big in Parma: the *Teatro Regio*, at Via Garibaldi 16a (☎0521/795.678), is renowned for its discerning audiences. It's not unknown for supporters of one singer to gather in cliques during the opera and discuss his or her virtues with supporters of a rival. Viale Basetti, next to the river, is also the home of one of the top **theatre** companies in Europe, the *Colletivo di Parma*, who perform between October and June at the *Teatro Due*, Viale Basetti 12a (☎0521/223.024), and whose shows draw on a tradition of comedy and political theatre – Dario Fo was a founder member.

South of Parma

The countryside **around Parma** is a strange mixture: some of the major roads follow bleak gorges, skirting the edge of blank rock walls for miles; others, looking for all the world as if they lead nowhere, emerge into open meadows and orchards, rich farmland stretching far into the distance.

The famous Parma ham (*Prosciutto di Langhirano* and eaten with just butter) comes from the foothills around **LANGHIRANO**, linked by bus with Parma. The experts say the ham cures so successfully here because of the unique mixture of clear mountain air and sea breezes blowing over the Apennines from Liguria. The town itself has grown into a mass of stainless steel warehouses – there's nothing of interest unless you want to carry a haunch of meat round with you for the rest of your holiday. But the countryside around, particularly near Calestano, is beautiful.

More of a target are any of the **medieval castles** strung out across the foothills. **TORRECHIARA**, also connected with Parma by bus, has a fifteenth-century **castle** that holds a superb vantage point over the surrounding area. There are frescoes by Bembo in the *Camera d'Oro* (Tues–Sat 9am–1pm; L3000).

Apart from the rail route, the fast way over the mountains is by **autostrada**, the A15, which snakes its way in and out of a succession of tunnels, giving quick glimpses of lush, hidden valleys, vines and orchards. Women risk life and limb by climbing over the barriers to sell mushrooms on the hard shoulder: they tie plastic bags, which fill with air and act like crazy dirigible balloons, to the trees, so you can see them from a distance. Even so, lots of drivers don't and instead sail across the three lanes at the last minute, screeching to a halt to inspect the latest fruits.

The slower N62 gives access to the *crinale* of the mountains: the trails are a popular magnet for walkers these days but served a quite different purpose in the last war, when adults and children made the long journey by foot, carrying sacks of salt from the coast to trade for food. The writer Eric Newby was hidden by villagers in these mountains as an escaped prisoner of war in 1943, and his book *Love and War in the Apennines*, chronicling his experiences, best describes the beauty of the region and its stupendous views across the full width of Italy.

CORNIGLIO, reached by bus from Parma, is a centre for hiking or skiing, and there are places to stay in most villages nearby – in Bosco di Corniglio, 10km away, try the *Ghirardini* (☎0521/889.123; ④). More buses squeeze themselves round the tight bends to the small villages of MONCHIO (11km), TREFIUMI (16km) and PRATO SPILLA (23km from Corniglio), leaving you on the lower slopes of **Monte Malpasso** – glistening with small lakes and tarns.

Take a bus from Corniglio for **LAGDEI**, 14km away, from where a mule path leads up to Lago Santo – a 45-minute walk; the ski lift to the same works sporadically. There are **mountain refuges** for overnight stops at Lagdei (☎0521/889.136), and near the summit of Monte Orsaro is *Rifugio Mariotti* (☎0521/889.334). For more demanding trekking, join the *GEA* route at RIGOSO (5km from the trail), connected with Parma by three or four buses a day.

Parma to Piacenza

The Via Emilia continues west from Parma, with small towns mushrooming out from the edges of the road, but mostly it's just a ribbon of shops and roadside cafés. **FIDENZA**, the first place of any size, has a Lombard-Romanesque cathedral with a richly decorated facade worked on by followers of the Parma master, Antelami. As Fidenza was a major staging-post on the pilgrimage route to Rome, the carvings depict pilgrims and more domestic subjects: appropriately enough for such an intensive salami-producing region, strings of sausages hang over one figure; others show hunting scenes. The building itself is an important – and relatively rare – example of architecture during the Romanesque-Gothic transition period. Saint Donnino's remains (patron saint of the cathedral) lie in the crypt (daily 8am–noon & 3–7pm). If you're in the area on a Wednesday or a Saturday, don't miss the extensive market which takes over the town. **Places to eat** are good here too: *Antica Trattoria al Duomo* in Piazza Duomo serves a quality fixed-price menu for L35,000. For snacks, head for the *Birreria-Paninoteca* at the station end of Via Benedetto Bacchini.

The countryside **to the north** of here is the *bassa*, the flat, low country where Bertolucci filmed *1900*, cut by drainage ditches and open fields growing wheat and corn, sugar beet and vines. In summer it's scorching hot and almost silent, with an odd, still beauty all of its own, but generally it's seen as a place to pass through on your way to somewhere else. The small towns and villages of the region are quiet and mainly undistinguished. **SORAGNA** is a good place to be on the second Sunday in May for its grand agricultural *festa*, with local wine, cheese and salami tasting. At any time of year, the beautifully smelling *salumerie* in the main square may tempt you with an array of local produce, also available at *Birreria-Paninoteca Stella d'Oro*, on the side alley Via Mazzini. The **Rocca di Soragna** dominates this market town (April 1–Oct 21 Wed–Sun 9am–noon & 3–7pm; Nov & Mar 9am–noon & 2–5pm; closed Dec–Feb; L3000). This tenth-century palace is still owned by the local Meli Lupi family who ran the town between the fourteenth and eighteenth centuries. The dozen or so rooms are decorated with frescoes, some by Parmigianino, one of the most elegant of the early Mannerist artists – more of his work appears in Parma's churches and at the Rocca San Vitale in Fontanellato (see below). Most of the furnishings are original, from the sixteenth century.

The village of **FONTANELLATO**, a few kilometres northeast of Fidenza, was the site of the camp where Eric Newby was imprisoned, but is perhaps better known as a centre for the production of parmesan cheese. Its central square is dominated by the **Rocca San Vitale** (summer Tues–Sun 10am–12.30pm & 3–7pm; winter Tues–Sun 9.30am–12.30pm & 3–6pm; L3000), a fifteenth-century moated castle that the Sanvitale family called home until the onset of the last war. Inside there are some ancient pieces of furniture and a fresco of the legend of *Diana and Actaeon* by Parmigianino. Further north, **BUSSETO**, the home of Guiseppe Verdi, is an appealing little battlemented town that holds a few mementoes of the nineteenth-century composer in its **Museo Civico**. There's more Verdi memorabilia in the nearby village of **LE RONCOLE**, in the **house** where he was born (March–Sept Tues–Sun 9am–noon & 3–7pm; Oct & Nov Tues–Sun 9.30am–noon & 2.30–5pm; L5000), where a veritable industry has grown up around the composer's birthplace, with regular opera performances during summer. And Verdi's **villa**, a couple of kilometres outside Busseto at **SANT'AGATA DI VILLANOVA**, is open for guided tours (daily 9–11.30am & 3–4.40pm; booking on ☎0523/830.210), which include a mock-up of the Milan hotel room where he died.

South of the Via Emilia, there's the same emphasis on food and festivals in the villages as in other parts of the province: local festivals are common, cheese, bilberries, or chestnuts and mushrooms among the themes, and the whole village will turn out for a big party. With your own transport, the area is well worth dawdling through, though you can easily reach the town of **SALSOMAGGIORE TERME**, 9km from Fidenza, by train or bus. It's a major local town, popular in the region with people anxious to detoxify their systems with its springs. The domed *piscina thermale* on Via Valentini (☎0524/79.495) is a relaxed way to join in; or you can go for the full treatment either at the fabulous Art Nouveau *Terme Berzieri* (open to the general public in summer) in the town centre 100m from Piazza Libertà, or the more business-like *Terme Zoja* in Parco Mazzini, ten minutes' walk from the tourist office. Some of the grander hotels do treatments too. Out of season, the place is unsurprisingly sedate, but in summer it springs into life, mostly revolving around an almost constant *passeggiata*. There is no shortage of places to stay; the **tourist office** at Viale Romagnosi 7, off Piazza del Popolo, has a full list (Mon–Fri 8am–1pm & 3–6pm, Sat 8am–1pm & Sun 10am–12.30pm). The majority of Salsomaggiore's **hotels** open between April and November only: *Albergo Villino Cervia*, Vicolo Cervia 6, off Via Romagnosi (☎0524/572.234; ④); *Albergo Livia*, Piazzale Berzieri 6 (☎0524/573.166; ④); and *Albergo Venezia*, Vicolo Venezia 5 (☎0524/573.166; ④), are all bang in the centre of town. *Camping Arizona* (0524/66.141) between Salsomaggiore and Tabiano Bagni offers swimming pools, sports facilities and wooden bungalows as well as pitches. Café life is important in the town; there's a full complement of *gelaterie* and *pasticcerie* but not many inexpensive places (outside of the hotels) to eat. One of the few is *La Porchetta* next to the Palazzo dei Congressi, a very popular place serving massive pieces of pizza wrapped in several layers of prosciutto, or more substantial dishes including – incongruously – Tyrolean specialities.

Walks around Salsomaggiore cover some beautiful countryside: the tourist office booklet, *Carnet dell'Ospite*, details around eight routes. A 5km walk south (or a bus from Salsomaggiore to Pellegrino Parmense) takes you past the castle vineyard at **CONTIGNACO**, which sells direct to the public. On the opposite side of the road, the simple Romanesque church of **San Giovanni** contains a sixteenth-century fresco of Santa Lucia on one of its columns and other, fourteenth-century frescoes.

To the east, buses run from Salsomaggiore to the modern spa town of **TABIANO BAGNI**, from where you can get a bus or walk to **TABIANO CASTELLO**, 3km walk away, for a meal at *Locanda del Colle da Oscar* (0524/66.148), an old castle inn and staging post serving marvellous food in a warm and lively atmosphere. The castle itself is privately owned but everyone seems to ignore the keep out signs and wander into the grounds all the same.

Heading west, you can strike out on foot from Salsomaggiore across the dead flat **Parco Fluviale dell Stirone** to Castel l'Arquato, passing on the way *Azienda Agrituristica Montà dell'Orto* (0523/947.146), which offers snacks, draught wine and typical regional dishes at the weekend and on holidays. If you want to stay, there's a good place to **camp** under the trees behind the farmhouse, with cooking facilities and a shower. **CASTEL L'ARQUATO** itself lies further on, a small town with a beautiful medieval piazza, set on a hillside overlooking the Arda Valley. Among a collection of ageing buildings there is the thirteenth-century **Palazzo del Podestà**, a Romanesque basilica and the **Rocca Viscontea** from the fourteenth century, though you can only admire them from the outside. At weekends plenty of people do just that, and then repair to one of the many **restaurants and cafés** in town. *Café Trattoria Garibaldi*, just inside the old town walls, serves game and inexpensive simple dishes. The **tourist office** (daily 9.30am–12.30pm & 2.30–6pm) is on the edge of the main piazza just outside the town walls. There are a couple of very cheap **places to stay** away from the centre, notably *Locanda Le Rose* in the suburb of Case Ilariotti (0523/948.261; ③), and the *Fattoria Manaro*, a farm just before the bridge over the Arda (0523/803.738; ③), which is even cheaper, and does meals too – as well as horse-riding for L20,000 per hour.

The road continues south from here, through LUGAGNANO, following the line of the River Arda through gentle hills to **BARDI**, overshadowed by its eleventh-century **castle** on an outcrop of rock, reachable by way of one daily bus from Parma. A side turning from Lugagnano into steeper, narrower lanes takes you to **VELLEIA**, 5km west of RUSTIGAZZO (four buses a day from Piacenza), where there are the remains of a provincial Roman town, excavated in the eighteenth century (daily 9am–one hour before dusk; free). Velleia was the capital of a vast mountainous area inhabited in the first five centuries AD and named after the Ligurian tribe attracted here by the salt springs in the area. The road continues south through woods of beech to the belt of mountains – the *Apennino Piacentino* – which stretch from BOBBIO down to BORGO.

Piacenza

PIACENZA marks the end of the Via Emilia and the border with Lombardy. It's a small, unassuming city, its attractions often passed over in favour of Parma or Modena (or Cremona in Lombardy, see Chapter Three), and, despite a small industrial district across the Po, there's a definite feeling of grass growing between the tracks. Travellers are scarce enough to earn a few stares as they cross the main square, and although it's interesting enough to earn perhaps half a day of your time, you'd probably be better off staying in one of the Via Emilia's more animated centres, if not in Milan.

The Town

Piazza dei Cavalli marks the centre of town, so called because of its two famous bronze equestrian statues, one on each side of the square, often quoted as being among the finest examples of Baroque sculpture. Cast in the early part of the seventeenth century by Francesco Mochi, a pupil of Giambologna, they're impressive works certainly, convincingly poised for action. One of the riders is Alessandro Farnese, a mercenary for Philip II of Spain, the other his son Ranuccio I. Behind, the **Palazzo de Comune**, "Il Gotico", is a fine red-brick palace, built in 1280 – an elegant example of Lombard-Gothic architecture, topped by fishtail battlements.

The church of **San Francesco**, just off the square, dates from the same period and sports an imposing Gothic interior. West of here, back towards the train station, the main shopping street of **Via XX Settembre** leads down to the **Duomo**, a grand Lombard-Romanesque church that has been altered many times since it was built between 1122 and 1233. It's a lovely building inside, with a high, plain nave supported by stout columns and cupola decorated with frescoes by Guercino – though these may be more difficult to see than the fine frescoes in the transepts and apses. From the duomo, follow Via Chiapponi up to the church of **San Antonino** – known as "Il Paradiso" for the twelfth-century bas-reliefs on its portal. Beyond, a couple of minutes' walk away from here on Via San Siro, the **Galleria Ricci-Oddi** (daily except Mon 10am–noon & 3–8pm) has a collection of nineteenth-century Italian art.

The other place to visit in Piacenza is the **Museo Civico** (Tues–Sat 9am–12.30pm, Thurs also 3.30–6.30pm, Sat also 3–6pm; L4000), recently re-opened after many years under restoration. It holds displays of Romanesque and later sculpture, roomfuls of armour and weapons, lots of paintings, including a depiction of the *Madonna and Child* *with John the Baptist* by Botticelli, and, in the same room, the so-called "*fegato di Piacenza*". Very much the star exhibit of the museum, this is a bronze Etruscan representation of a sliced sheep's liver, marked with the names of Etruscan deities, that was (like real sheep livers) used to divine the future. As for the building, it's a huge affair, begun in 1558 and almost finished off by Vignola some years later for the Farnese family: one room is still decorated with heroic frescoes of Alessandro Farnese, though most were carted off to Naples by the Bourbons, where they remain.

Practicalities

The **train station** is fifteen minutes' walk west of Piazza dei Cavalli on Piazza Marconi, handily placed for two of Piacenza's cheaper **hotels**. Both of these are rather basic: the closest to the station is the *Rangoni* at Piazza Marconi 1 (☎0523/21.778; ④); the *Moderno* is five minutes' walk away – following the park on the right – at Via Tibini 31 (☎0523/29.296; ④), and has rooms for much the same price. The **tourist office** is ten minutes' walk from here, at Piazzetta dei Mercanti 10, next to Piazza dei Cavalli (daily 9am–12.30pm & 3.30–6pm, closed Thurs afternoons; ☎29.324), and has maps of the town and other information.

Piacenza is considered the gateway to Emilian cooking for people coming from Piemonte and Lombardy, but despite this **places to eat** in the centre of town are rather thin on the ground. One of the best – and most central – restaurants is *Trattoria Agnello*, right behind the Palazzo del Comune at Via Calzolai 2, an unpretentious eatery with great food and moderate prices that is justifiably very popular locally. *Ginetto*, on the other side of Piazza dei Cavalli at Piazza San Antonino 8, is more expensive, but its menu of Piacentine specialities is well worth the splurge.

The Via Emilia to Rimini

East of Bologna, the Via Emilia takes in much less of interest than it does on its way west, passing through a clutch of small towns – some of them, like Forli, industrialised and mostly postwar, others, like Faenza, with medieval piazzas surrounded by towers and embattlements. Each started life as Roman way-stations and were under the rule of the Papal States for much of their subsequent history. The lowlands to the north are farmed intensively and were the heart of the cooperative movement which spawned the now left-wing local administration. On the southern side lie hilly vineyards and pastures, and narrow gorges that lead up into the mountains and a couple of ski resorts around Monte Fumaiolo (1407m).

Ímola and Dozza

About 30km out of Bologna, **ÍMOLA** might be worth a short stop if you're heading east; it's well known as a centre for machinery and ceramic ware, and for the San Marino Grand Prix, which weaves its way through the streets of the town. It's a pleasant place, with a thirteenth-century castle and some grey-walled Renaissance palaces, but there is nothing extraordinary about it. A big new civic centre and art gallery are currently being built, until which time you can view the city's various art and historical collections in the **Palazzo dei Musei** at Via Emilia 80 – though it's only open on the first and third Sunday of each month (10am–noon; at other times phone ☎0542/34.714 for admission). If you're lucky enough to get in, the reward is an extensive display of rare plants and beetles, and a small art gallery holding work by local fifteenth- to eighteenth-century artists. If you're not, the lively *Osteria Cerchi* is a good place to **eat** unless money is no object, in which case head for the hallowed *Ristorante San*

Domenico at Via G. Sacchi 1 (☎0542/29.000), which is consistently viewed as one of the country's top restaurants. Booking is essential.

Back towards Bologna but easiest to reach by bus from Ímola, the village of **DOZZA**, set on a hill surrounded by vineyards, is a popular place for a Sunday afternoon outing, with hordes of people descending for the kitsch murals on the outside of the houses, created during the *Biennale del muro dipinto*, held every other year during the first two weeks of September (the last was in 1991). The village also has an annual *Sagra dell'Albana*, in honour of the fragrant white wine produced locally, and you can taste the local product at any time of year in an *enoteca* housed in the castle. There's a wine museum there too.

Faenza and Brisighella

East of Ímola, cypress trees and umbrella pines, gentler hills and vineyards signal the fact that you're leaving Emilia and entering the Romagna – although strictly speaking there's no clear border between the two regions. **FAENZA**, 16km from Ímola, gives its name to the faïence-ware it has been producing for the last 500 years. This style of decorated ceramic ware reached its zenith in the fifteenth and sixteenth centuries, and the town is worth a visit for the vast **Museo delle Ceramiche** alone (summer Tues–Sat 9am–7pm, Sun 9.30am–1pm; winter Tues–Sat 9am–1pm & 3–6pm, Sun 9.30am–1pm; L6000); it's at Viale Baccarini 19 – take Corso D. Baccarini from the station, and it's on the left. Its massive collection includes early work painted in the characteristic blue and ochre, and later more colourful work, often incorporating portraits and landscapes. There's a section devoted to ceramics from other parts of the world, too, including ceramic art by Picasso, Matisse and Chagall.

Faenza is still home to one of Italy's leading ceramics schools, teaching techniques of tin-glazing first introduced in the fourteenth century – the ceramics are decorated after glazing, and are given a final lead-based, lustrous wash. The town is also a major production centre, with small workshops down most of its side streets; the **tourist office** in Piazza del Popolo has details of where to buy.

The rest of Faenza is fairly ordinary, although the town's medieval centre is appealing enough. The long, crenellated, **Palazzo del Podesta** and the **Piazza del Popolo** together make up Faenza's medieval heart, linked to **Piazza Martiri di Libertà**, the main marketplace, through an archway. There's a market here on Tuesday, Thursday and Saturday mornings, when the trattorias that surround it are packed out with people. If you want to **eat**, try *Al Moro* or the *Osteria del Mercato* – both good, lively places used by the locals. The former also has accommodation. Another good time to be here is for the *Palio del Niballo* (jousting and flag twirling), which takes place on the last two Sundays in July. If you want to **stay** in Faenza, a dour but central cheap hotel is the *Torricelli*, next to the train station in Piazzale Cesare Battisti 7 (☎0546/22.287; ④).

South of Faenza, and accessible by train, the village of **BRISIGHELLA,** halfway up a hillside, is famed for its restaurants (visited by people from as far afield as Milan), and its **Via degli Asini** – a raised, covered lane once part of the town fortifications, used to protect mule trains carrying olive oil and clay for making ceramics. The medieval fortress topping the cliffs over the town was held first by the local Manfredi family, then by Cesare Borgia, the Venetians and the pope. It now houses a **Museo del Lavoro Contadino** (summer Tues–Sun 10am–noon & 3.30–7.30pm; winter Sat 2.30–4.30pm only; L2000), with objects from country life. The thirteenth-century **Torre dell'Orologio** sits on an opposite spur of rock, while below the town, down by the River Lamone, is the **Pieve del Tho** and eleventh-century church, built on top of the remains of an earlier temple to Jupiter. It's worth coming here at carnival time and in July for the *Feste Medievali* as well as the *Sagra della Polenta, del Tartufa* (truffle) *and dell'Olivo* in October, November and December respectively.

Of Brisighella's **restaurants**, *La Grotta Osteria con Uso di Cucina* (0546/81.829) serves excellent Romagnolo dishes, albeit at very high prices – although it does offer an affordable fixed-price menu; or there's the more modest *Tre Colli*, Via Gramsci 9, the other side of the level crossing below town. Brisighella's **hotels** are disappointing – all are more expensive than normal for their standard of accommodation. Stay in an *agriturismo* place instead; the **tourist office** at Via De Gasperi 6 (Mon–Fri 10am–noon & 4–6pm; ☎0546/81.166) has details of these.

Forlì

FORLÌ, administrative capital of the Romagna, is a mainly modern town with office blocks and dual carriageways around the centre, but the heart of the town is closed to traffic, and is an interesting if low-key place to visit. Benito Mussolini, who was born a few miles away at PREDAPPIO, was editor of the Forlì newspaper and spokesman of the Socialist Party's (*PSI*) radical wing before he left the town in 1912 to edit the *Avanti* paper in Milan. It's unlikely that you will want to stay in Forlì, although you might want to stop off to visit its couple of museums. For some reason the town is something of a centre for cinema history, with the **Museo Internazionale del Cinema** at Viale Libertà 37 (open by appointment Tues & Thurs 4–6pm; free; ☎0543/30.521), displaying a varied collection of film memorabilia and cinema-related exhibitions and showing special screenings. The city is also an important Romagnolo agricultural centre, its **Museo Archeologico ed Etnografico**, Corso della Repubblica 72 (Tues–Sun 9am–2pm; L3000), giving a good rundown on peasant life early this century and today.

Ferrara

Half an hour by train from Bologna, **FERRARA** was the residence of the Este dukes, an eccentric dynasty that ranked as a major political force throughout Renaissance times. The Este kept the main artists of the day (who all came to stay) in commissions, and built a town which despite a relatively small population was – and still is – one of the most elegant urban creations of the period.

When there was no heir, the Este were forced to hand over Ferrara to the papacy and leave for good. Life in Ferrara effectively collapsed. Eighteenth-century travellers found a ghost town of empty streets and canals clogged up, infested with mosquitos. Since then Ferrara has picked itself up and is now the centre of a key fruit-producing area, to which the acres of neat, pollarded trees outside town testify. It's a popular stop for tourists travelling up from Bologna to Venice, but they rarely stay, leaving the city centre enjoyably tourist-free by the evening.

Arrival, information and accommodation

Ferrara's **train station** is just west of the city walls, a fifteen-minute walk along Viale Cavour from the centre of town around the castello; buses #1, #2 and #3 run from the train station to the centre of town, of which #1 is the most direct. The **bus station** is southwest of the main square, on Corso Isonzo. The **tourist office**, right in the centre at Piazza Municipio 19 (Mon–Sat 9am–1pm & 2.30–7pm, Sun 9am–1pm; ☎0532/35.017), and has maps and bumph on the town.

Ferrara has a number of affordable **hotels**, most of them handily placed in the centre of town, although again you need to book ahead to be sure of finding a place, especially in summer. In the centre, the pleasantest place to stay is perhaps the *San Paolo*, by the river at Via Baluardi 9 (☎0532/762.040; ④); the slightly cheaper *Alfonsa*, close by the Castello at Via Padiglioni 5 (☎0532/205.726; ④), and the excellent *Casa* *degli Artisti*, in the medieval quarter at Via Vittoria 66 (☎0532/35.314; ④), are also good places to stay, while if everything else in the centre is full, the rather characterless *Nazionale*, Corso Porta Reno 32 (☎0532/35.210; ⑤), usually has rooms. If you want to be near the station, the friendly *Stazione*, in a modern block right across Piazzale Stazione and through the arch, at Piazza Castellina 1 (☎0532/56.565; ④), is perhaps the cheapest option of all, and has very nice rooms despite its unprepossessing exterior. Ferrara's **campsite**, *Estense*, is on the northeast edge of town at Via Gramicia 5; take bus #1 from the train station to Piazzale San Giovanni, from where it's a ten-minute walk.

The Town

The bulky **Castello Estense** dominates the centre of Ferrara (Tues–Sat 9am–1pm & 2–6pm, Sun 10am–6pm; L6000), built in response to a late fourteenth-century uprising and generally held at the time to be a major feat of military engineering. But behind its grim brick walls, the Este court thrived, supporting artists like Pisanello, Jacopo Bellini, Mantegna, and the poets Ariosto and Tasso. The Este dukes were a pragmatic lot, with a range of ways of raising cash, keeping tax levels just ahead of their court expenses, and boosting cashflow by selling official titles, putting up the tolls for traffic along the Po, and supplying troops for the various rulers of Naples, Milan or Florence.

The first of the **Este** to live here was Nicolò II, who commissioned the castle, though later Este were really responsible for its decoration. One of the most famous members of the family was Nicolò III d'Este, who took over in 1393. Nicolò was a well-known patron of the arts, but he was most notorious for his numerous amorous liaisons, and although the 27 children he admitted to siring seems excessive, it's likely that he was responsible for many more beyond his legitimate heir, Ercole. He was also a ruthless man, reputedly murdering his wife Parisina and son by another woman, Ugo, when he discovered that they were having an affair. Two other sons, Leonello and Borso, also became renowned characters, and together with Ercole oversaw some of Ferrara's most civilised years. Leonello was a friend of the Renaissance man, Alberti, and became a caricature of the time by consulting his horoscope before he chose what to wear in the morning. Borso loved hunting and thundered through the woods at Mesola on horseback, dressed in velvet and jewels. Ercole's children, Beatrice and Isabella, married into the Sforza and Gonzaga families, thus sealing the Este's status as one of the most glittering of Renaissance dynasties. Ercole's grandson, Alfonso I, married Lucrezia Borgia, who continued the retinue of artists and poets, patronising Titian and Ariosto – as did the last Este duke, Alfonso II, who invited Tasso and Guarini to his court.

It's hard to credit all this as you walk through the castle now, most of which is in any case used as offices nowadays and inaccessible to the public. The few rooms that you can see go some way to bringing back the days of Este magnificence, especially the *saletta* and *salone dei giochi* or games rooms, decorated by Sebastiano Filippi with vigorous scenes of wrestling, discus-throwing, ball-tossing and chariot-racing – beautifully restored and full of interest. Otherwise it's rather a cold, draughty place on the whole, perhaps at its most evocative in the dungeons, where the sound of water from the moat conjures an image of Este enemies: Ugo and Parisina were incarcerated down here before their execution, and Ferrante and Giulio Este were detained in the dungeon for most of their lives after attempting to depose Alfonso I.

Just south of here, the crenellated **Palazzo Comunale**, built in 1243 but since much altered and restored, holds statues of Nicolò III and his other son, Borso, on its facade – though they're actually twentieth-century reproductions. Walk through the arch into the pretty enclosed square of **Piazza Municipio** for a view of the rest of the building.

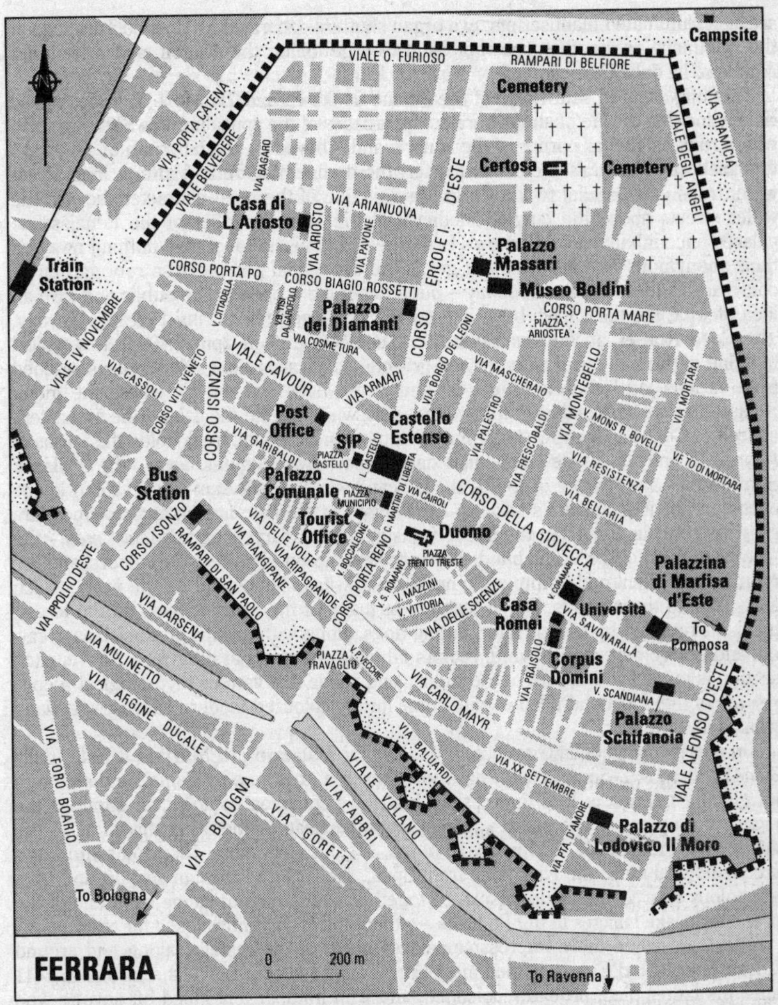

Opposite the Palazzo Comunale, the **Duomo** is a mixture of Romanesque and Gothic styles, and has an undeniably impressive facade, centring on a carved central portal that was begun in the mid-twelfth century by Wiligelmus (of Modena cathderal fame), and finished a century or so later. Much of the carving depicts the *Last Judgement*, with the damned souls grimacing on the central frieze, and Hell itself depicted on the central lunette, while below the frieze bodies climb out of their coffins. Inside, the main part of the church has the grandeur of a ballroom, with sparkling chandeliers, but is much less intriguing than the exterior carving, and it's upstairs, in the **museum** (Mon–Sat 10am–noon & 3–5pm, Sun 10am–noon; "voluntary" admission fee), that the real treasures are kept. The highlight of the collection is a set of bas-reliefs illustrating the labours of the months which formerly adorned the outside of the cathedral. There are also illuminated manuscripts, two organ shutters decorated by Cosimo Tura, one of the Annunciation, another showing Saint George killing the dragon, and a beautiful *Madonna* by della Quercia.

The long arcaded south side of the duomo flanks **Piazza Trento e Trieste**, whose rickety-looking arcade of shops heralds the arcades of the appealing **Via San Romano** which runs off the far corner of the square, and – beyond – the labyrinth of alleyways that make up Ferrara's medieval quarter; the arched **Via delle Volte**, a long street which runs east parallel to Via Carlo Mayr, is one of the most characteristic. On the wider streets above the tangled medieval district are a number of the Renaissance palaces once inhabited by Ferrara's better-heeled families. Most give nothing away by their anonymous facades – all you get is the occasional glimpse of a roof garden or courtyard inside a closing doorway – but a handful are open to the public and give an idea of what life must have been like for the privileged few during Ferrara's heyday. The **Casa Romei**, at Via Savaranola 30 (Tues–Sun 8.30am–2pm; L4000), is a typical building of the time, with frescoes and graceful courtyards alongside artefacts rescued from various local churches. Just beyond is the house, at no. 19, where the monk Savaranola was born and lived for twenty years, while behind the palace, the monastery church of **Corpus Domini** (Mon–Fri 9.30am–noon & 3–5pm; free) holds the tombs of Alfonso I and II d'Este and Lucrezia Borgia. Two minutes away, the **Palazzo Schifanoia** – the "Palace of Joy" – at Via Scandiana 23 (daily 9am–7pm; L2500) is one of the grandest of Ferrara's palaces. It belonged to the Este family, and Cosimo Tura set their court in arcadia in the frescoes inside, in the marvellous *salone dei mesi* – the "rooms of the months". The blinds here are kept closed to protect the colours, and the room seems silent and empty in comparison to what's happening on the walls, which are split into three bands. Borso features in many of the court scenes, on the lowest band, surrounded by friends and hunting dogs, along with groups of musicians, weavers and embroiderers with white rabbits nibbling the grass at their feet. Above, each section is topped with a sign of the zodiac, and above that various mythological scenes – some of them lost and filled in with some luridly coloured modern canvases showing what is missing.

On nearby Corso della Giovecca, at no. 170, the **Palazzina di Marfisa d'Este** (daily 9am–12.30pm & 2–5pm; L2000), has more frescoes, this time by Filippi, and although its gloomy interior is less impressive than the Schifanioa complex, in summer the loggia and orange grove make a retreat from the heat. In the other direction, to the south, the **Palazzo di Lodovico Il Moro**, Via XX Settembre 124, holds the city's archaeological museum, with finds from Spina, the Graeco-Etruscan seaport and trading colony near Commachio, displayed together with a dugout canoe from one of the prehistoric lake villages in the Po Delta – although it is currently closed for restoration.

There are some more impressive palaces north of the castello, along and around **Corso Ercole I d'Este** – named after Ercole I, who succeeded to the throne in 1441 after his father died, probably poisoned, and who immediately killed off anyone who was likely to be a threat. His reputation for coldness earned him the names "North Wind" and "Diamond", but he certainly got things done, consolidating his power by marrying Eleanor of Aragon, daughter of the Spanish King of Naples, and laying out the northern quarter of the city – the so-called "Herculean Addition" – on a grand scale that led to Ferrara being tagged the first modern city in Europe. He wasn't a puritanical ruler either: writers of the time describe events consisting of many hours of feasting, with sugar castles full of meat set up for the crowd to storm. The **Palazzo dei Diamanti**, a little way down the Corso on the left, named after the diamond-shaped bricks that stud its facade, was at the heart of Ercole's town-plan, and is nowadays home to the **Pinacoteca Nazionale** (Tues–Sat 9am–2pm, Sun 9am–1pm; L6000), the **Galeria Civica d'Arte Moderne** (daily 9am–7pm; L10,000), and the **Museo del Risorgimento e Della Resistenza** (Mon–Sat 9.30am–12.30pm & 3–6pm, Sun 9am–

12.30pm; L2000). You can give the latter a miss, and the rooms of the modern art gallery are often given over to temporary exhibitions. But the pinacoteca holds works from the Ferrara and Bologna schools in rooms with ornately decorated wooden ceilings, notably paintings by Dossi, Garofalo and Guercino, and a spirited St Christopher by "Il Bastianino" (Sebastian Filippo). Around the corner, at Corso Porta Mare 9, the **Palazzo Massari** (daily 9.30am–1pm & 3–6.30pm; L5000) has a small **photographic gallery** and the **Documentario della Metafisica** – a collection of transparencies of work by the *Scuola Metafisica*, the proto-surrealist group which Giorgio de'Chirico founded here in 1917. However, most of the impressive palace is given over to the **Museo Boldini**, a fairly brain-numbing collection of work by a Ferrarese nineteenth-century painter, one Giovanni Boldini.

Eating and drinking

It's relatively easy to **eat out** in Ferrara. At the bottom end of the scale, *Orsucci*, Via Garibaldi 76, and *Giuseppe*, Via Carlo Mayr 71, are takeout pizza places with a few tables if you want to sit down; *Giuseppe* is also open until 1am. *Al Postiglione*, off Corso Martiri di Libertà at Vicolo del Teatro 4, on the east side of the castello, is a *paninoteca* with any number of sandwich combinations, hot and cold, as well as home-made pasta and lots of different beers and wines – and seats (open until 9.30pm). Among regular restaurants, the *Gatto Bianco*, Via Carlo Mayr 59, and the nearby – inexplicably named – *Privacy*, Via Carlo Mayr 45, do middling pizzas and more elaborate fare at very moderate prices. *Trattoria Da Noemi*, Via Ragno 31, is an affable, family-run restaurant with a short and very simple pasta- and meat-based menu and low prices. *Trattoria-Pizzeria Piper*, Corso Porta Reno 22, a basic restaurant at the back of a bar, does excellent pasta, home-made sausage and decent local wine. *Osteria degli Angeli*, Via delle Volte 4, is a convivial *osteria*, open late, with lots of different wines and good food.

The Po Delta

"So ugly it's beautiful" is one confusing comment made about the **Po Delta**, east of Ferrara – an expanse of marshland and lagoons culminating in small fingers of land poking out into the Adriatic. Most of the traffic is just passing through, and it's not surprising that the tourist authorities have decided on some heavy promotion.

The River Po splits into several channels, reaching the sea through these wetlands. The delta has changed a great deal since Etruscan traders set up the port of Spina here in the fourth to third century BC, when the sea covered much of the land between Comacchio and Ravenna. It's now retreated by 12km, partly due to drainage schemes, and the area becomes a bit less marshy each year – something that's to the advantage of local farmers but a threat to the different varieties of sea and shore **birds** which inhabit the area. The two main lagoons – **Valli di Comacchio** and **Valle Bertuzzi** – have been designated as nature reserves to at least halt the process, and make up one of Europe's most highly regarded birdwatching areas, providing a habitat for nesting and migrating birds, including herons, egrets, curlews, avocets and terns.

Another threat to the area's wild (and human) life is **pollution**: 136,000 tonnes of nitrates, 250 tonnes of arsenic and 60 tonnes of mercury are pumped into the River Po every day; and spillages from oil refineries and nearby nuclear plants are a further cause for anxiety. Not surprisingly, the river is banned from being used for swimming, irrigation or drinking water.

Though you might not fancy it having read this, the best way to see the delta is by **boat**. There are a number of people in the surrounding area who run guided tours. Sig. Schiavi Vincensino, Via Vicolo del Farol (☎0533/99.815), or Sig. Dante Passarella, c/o

Ristorante USPA (☎0533/99.817), both in Gorino, take out boats on Sundays in summer if enough people are interested. Boats also leave from Valle Fole, south of Comacchio; ask at *Larus Viaggi* at Piazza Ugo Bassi 32 in Comacchio for details.

Comacchio

The main town of the region, **COMACCHIO** is a small fishing town intersected by a network of canals, with a famous local attraction in its triple-bridge or **Trepponti**, built in 1634, which crosses three of the canals. Comacchio is an eel-port, and you should try if you can to be here in autumn, when wriggling masses of the creatures are fished out of the canals on their way to the Sargasso Sea. There are one or two restaurants serving fixed-price menus of smoked eels (*anguille*), fish risotto, and *fritto misto*, but the best **places to eat** are out of town and inaccessible unless you've got a car.

The **beach developments** directly east of Comacchio are not particularly inviting, especially bearing in mind the proximity of the nasty waters of the Po, but it's interesting to see the cantilever nets set up either side of the channels running out to the sea. Incidentally, Comacchio's harbour is named Porto Garibaldi, after the Risorgimento hero who was left on the shore with his wife, Anita, and their companion Leggero, as the last *Garibaldini* were captured off the coast by the Austrian navy.

North of Comacchio: Pomposa Abbey and around

About twenty kilometres north of Comacchio, and connected by buses from the port and direct from Ferrara, the **Abbey of Pomposa** is about all the area has to offer in the way of orthodox sights, a lonely collection of buildings, saved from complete oblivion by the main road to Chioggia and numerous coach parties in summer. At the centre of a complex which includes a Lombard-Romanesque campanile, a chapter house and refectory is an eighth-century **Basilica** containing frescoes by Vitale di Bologna and the Bolognese school, though the abbey is better-known for one of its monks, Guido d'Arezzo, who in the early eleventh century invented the musical scale here. Only a few hundred years after Pomposa was built, it went into decline, the delta becoming marshier and malarial, and those that weren't killed off by the disease were left to scratch a living from hunting and fishing. The monks finally abandoned their abbey in the seventeenth century.

From Pomposa a minor road leads to Volano, following the **Valle Bertuzzi**, an expanse of water and small islets given over to the *Riserva Natura Pineta di Volano*. On the other side of the estuary is the **Bosco della Mesola**, an ancient wood planted by the Etruscans, now surrounded by fields of peppers and artichokes. It has been much reduced in size since it was commercially logged, but it's the only wood for miles around; deer hide out among its oak and juniper trees. It's only open at weekends (8am–dusk), and you can hire bicycles at the gate – reachable by taking a bus from Ferrara to GORO, getting off at stop no. 15 and walking the 2km back down the road to the left-hand turning.

GORO itself, the next port up the coast, is used by deep sea-drifters as well as smaller local boats, and is one of the most thriving, if bleakest, harbours along this stretch. Catches are either packed in ice and loaded directly into the container lorries, or else sold at the cooperative a few hundred yards away. In theory it's all strictly for trade but some additional private bargaining does go on at the quayside. The road from Goro inland keeps company with drainage ditches that have a water level higher than the surrounding fields. The main village here is **MÉSOLA**, where a noisy Saturday market invades the courtyard and the porticoes by the castle. From Mésola the road west follows the course of one of the Po's main channels – the *Po di Goro* – which also marks the border with the Veneto.

South of Comacchio: Alfonsine and the Museo del Senio

The countryside around the lagoons of the Valli di Comacchio is a combination of farm and marshland. Buildings are rare and the only sign of life is the odd heron or scavenging bird. **ALFONSINE**, the main centre of the area, is on the Ferrara–Ravenna rail line, although there's little to tempt you off the train. Not much of the pre-1944 town remains after a heavy World War II bombing, and only the **Museo del Senio** (daily 9am–1pm & 2–6pm, closed Sat & Sun afternoons) on Piazza della Resistenza is worth seeing. This documents the war, including the "Gothic Line" held by the Germans across the Apennines, and the role of Italian partisans in their defeat. The many objects and photographs include an esoteric collection of pictures of gates made from leftover anti-slip tank tracking (you still see lots of them around), as well as the bailey bridges used to cross the ditches and canals.

Ravenna and around

When **RAVENNA** became capital of the Western Roman Empire fifteen hundred years ago, it was more by quirk of fate than design. The Emperor Honorius, alarmed by armies invading from the north, moved his court from Milan to this obscure town on the Romagna coast around 402; it was easy to defend, surrounded by marshland, and was situated close to the port of Classis – at the time the biggest Roman naval base on the Adriatic. Honorius' anxiety proved well founded: Rome was sacked by the Goths in 410 and sunk into a decline only matched by Ravenna's ensuing prosperity, and the town became the Roman capital almost by default. Its days of glory were brief, and it too fell to the Goths in 476. However, this short period of fame had made it one of the most sought-after towns in the Mediterranean, and it wasn't long before Byzantine forces took the city from the Goths and made it into an exarchate, under the rule of Constantinople.

The Byzantine rulers were responsible for Ravenna's most glorious era, keen to outdo rival cities with magnificent palaces, churches and art, and the city became one of the most compelling cultural centres in the world. The growing importance of Venice brought some further prosperity, but the sixteenth century saw the sack of the city and its absorption into the Papal States, since when the Adriatic shoreline has receded, and an eleven-kilometre-long canal through a vast industrial complex now links Ravenna's port to the sea. But remnants of the dazzling Byzantine era are still thick on the ground aross the town, not least a set of mosaics that is generally acknowledged to be the crowning achievement of Byzantine art extant anywhere in the world.

Unlike Florence or Venice, say, tourism seems almost incidental to the life of the town, now enjoying the full advantages of jobs in chemical processing plants and oil refineries outside the old walls. Bombs levelled much of Ravenna in the last world war, but enough has survived for a couple of days' unhurried exploration. Churches and mosaics could easily monopolise your time, but foot traffic past the cafés in the main square, and noisy restaurants, make the city an appealing destination just for itself. Nightlife is sparse, but the (albeit largely family-orientated) lido towns a couple of kilometres away provide some excitement in summer.

Arrival, information and accommodation

Ravenna has a compact centre, and it's only a short, ten-minute walk from the **train station** on Piazza Farini, on the eastern edge of the centre, along Viale Farini and Via Armando Diaz to the central square, Piazza del Popolo, which with the adjoining streets makes up the old centre. The **bus station** is across the tracks behind the train station, Piazzale Aldo Moro.

There's an information office, with maps, just outside the station on the left (daily 9am–8pm), which also rents bikes, and a main **tourist office** at Via San Vitale 2 (daily 9.20am–1pm & 3–6pm; ☎0544/35.755), also with maps and assorted bumph on the town. It's worth knowing that **entry to the various churches and museums** in Ravenna is carefully controlled, and that as well as buying tickets for individual places you can also buy a single ticket that covers all the main attractions (L7000), or tickets that cover a grouping of places for L3000; it's the the latter we've given in the text. Bear in mind, too, that the opening times we have given below are summer only; expect them to be somewhat reduced between October and the beginning of April.

The district around the train station is the best place to find **somewhere to stay**. Almost opposite the station, the *Ravenna*, Via Maroncelli 12 (☎0544/212.204; ④), is very handy, as is the similarly priced *Minerva*, directly opposite at Via Maroncelli 1a (☎0544/213.711; ④). Not much further from the station, and slightly cheaper, is *Al Giaciglio*, Via Rocca Brancaleone 42 (☎0544/39.403; ④), with its own restaurant too, while in the opposite direction, behind the station, there's the pricier *Roma*, Via Candiano 26 (☎0544/420.505; ④); take a left out of the station and then left again under the foot tunnel. Not far away from here there's a **youth hostel**, the *Ostello Dante*, at Via Nicolodi 12 (☎0544/420.405; ①), though it's closed between October and March. It has some family rooms and serves evening meals. You can get there on bus #1 from outside the train station, or it's a ten-minute walk – left out of the station, left again under the tracks, follow Via Candiano and then bear right down Via T. Gulli; Via Nicolodi goes off to the right. The closest **campsite** to Ravenna is down in the nearby coastal resort of PUNTA MARINA, to which there are regular buses from the train station.

The city centre

The centre of Ravenna is without question **Piazza del Popolo**, an elegant open space, arcaded in one corner, that was laid out by the Venetians in the fifteenth century and is now filled with café tables. A few blocks south of the square, across Piazza Garibaldi on Via Alighhieri, the **Tomba di Dante** is a site of local pride, a small greyish building which was put up in the eighteenth century to enclose a previous fifteenth-century tomb. Dante had been chased out of Florence by the time he arrived in Ravenna, and he was sheltered here by the Da Polenta family – then in control of the city – while he finished his *Divine Comedy*. He died in 1381 and was laid to rest in the adjoining church of **San Francesco**, a much-restored building, elements of which date from the fourth century. File down the stairs in front of the choir for a look at the waterlogged crypt, dating from the tenth century, complete with goldfish and remnants of a mosaic floor. You might want to look in, too, on the **Museo Dantesco**, situated in San Francesco's cloister on Via Alighieri (Tues–Sat 9am–noon & 3–6pm; L3000) – though to be honest its collection of paintings, bronzes and various artefacts relating to Dante is pretty deadly unless you're absolutely fanatical about the man.

A couple of minutes' walk west of here, a grouping of buildings around **Piazza del Duomo** also has a collective interest. The **Duomo** itself, with its cylindrical – and dangerously leaning – tower, was also originally a fifth-century building, but was completely destroyed by an earthquake in 1733 and rebuilt in unexceptional style soon after. It's not particularly worth a second glance, but the **Museo Arcivescovile** (daily 9am–7pm; L3000, includes Neonian Baptistery), inside the Bishop's Palace next door, is interesting, with fragments of mosaics from around the city and the palace's sixth-century *Oratorio Sant'Andrea*, which is adorned with mosaics of birds in a meadow above a Christ dressed in the armour, cloak and gilded leather skirt of a Roman centurion. There are also fragments from the original cathedral, an ornate ivory

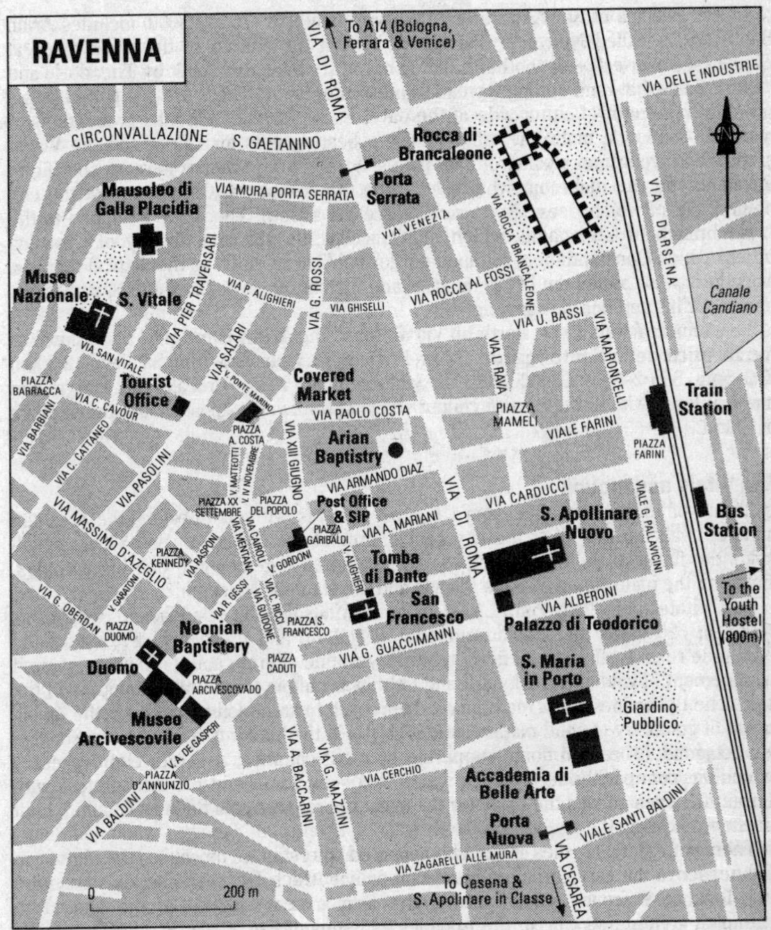

throne from Alexandria, which belonged to Bishop Maximian in the sixth century, and a circular marble calendar from the same time, used for calculating the date of Easter and related holy days according to the nineteen-year cycle of the Julian calendar.

The **Neonian Baptistery**, on the other side of the duomo (daily 9am–7pm; L3000, includes Museo Arcivescovile), is a conversion from a Roman bathhouse. The original floor level has sunk into the marshy ground, and you can still see the remains of the previous building, three metres below. The building was a logical choice: baptisms involved total immersion in those days, and the mixture of styles works well – the marble inlaid designs from the bathhouse blend in with the mosaics of prophets on the arches round the sides. Mosaics of the baptism of Christ and portraits of the twelve Apostles decorate the dome, which is made of hollow terracotta tubes.

East of here, **Via di Roma**, lined with bland, official-looking palaces, cuts right through the modern centre of Ravenna, and sees much of its traffic. Halfway up on the right, the basilica of **Sant'Apollinare Nuovo** (daily 9am–7pm; L3000, includes Arian Baptistery) – called Nuovo to distinguish it from the church of the same name at Classe (see overleaf) – is another building of the sixth century, built by Theodoric and with mosaics that rank among Ravenna's most impressive. There are just two of these, running the length of either side of the nave. Each shows ceremonial processions of martyrs – one side male, the other female – bearing gifts for Christ and the Virgin enthroned through an avenue of date palms. Some of the scenery is more specific to Ravenna: you can make out what used to be the harbour at Classe against the city behind, out of which rises Theodoric's palace. As a Goth, Theodoric belonged to the Arian branch of Christianity which didn't accept the absolute divinity of Christ, a heresy which Constantinople stamped out for political as much as theological reasons. Theodoric was painted out of the mosaics and the church re-dedicated to Saint Martin, known for his anti-heretic campaigns.

Five minutes' walk away, north up Via di Roma, the **Arian Baptistry**, also known as the **Basilica dello Santo Spirito** (Mon–Fri 9am–12.30pm & 2–7pm, Sat 9am–12.30pm & 2–5pm, Sun 2–5pm; L3000, includes Sant'Apollinare Nuovo) recalls this struggle, in name at least, with a fine mosaic ceiling showing the twelve Apostles and the baptism of Christ.

San Vitale and around

In terms of monuments, Ravenna's biggest draw is without question the area ten minutes' walk northwest of the city centre, around the basilica of San Vitale, which holds the finest of the mosaics and is now gathered together into one big complex, including the mausoleum of Galla Placida and the National Museum.

San Vitale (daily 9am–7pm; L3000, includes Mausoleo di Galla Placida), which was begun in 525 under the Roman emperor Theodoric and finished in 548 under the Byzantine ruler Justinian, is a fairly typical Byzantine church, and its Eastern-inspired arrangement of void and solid, dark and light, was unique for an Italian building of the time. The Byzantines had a mathematical approach to architecture, calling it the "application of geometry to solid matter", and it shows in the building, based on two concentric octagons, its central dome supported by eight columns, and with eight recesses extending from each side – one of which is a semicircular apse which glitters with mosaic. The design was the basis for the great church of Aghia Sofia in Istanbul, built fifteen years later.

There were definite rules about who appeared where in the mosaics – the higher up and further to the east, the more important or holy the subject. The series starts with Old Testament scenes spread across the semicircular lunettes of the choir; the triumphal arch shows Christ, the Apostles and sons of San Vitale. Further in, on the semi-dome of the apse, a beardless Christ stands between two angels, presenting a model of the church to San Vitale and Bishop Ecclesius. But what could become a rigid hierachy is enlivened by fields and rivers teeming with frogs, herons and dolphins. Of the mosaics on the side walls of the apse, the two processional panels are the best surviving portraits of the emperor Justinian and his wife Theodora – and a rich example of Byzantine mosaic technique; he's on the left, she's on the right. The small glass *tesserae* are laid in sections, alternate rows set at slightly different angles to vary reflection of light and give an impression of depth. Colour is used emblematically too, with gold backgrounds to denote either holiness or high status. As an extra sign of superiority, Justinian's foot rests on that of his general, Belisarius, who defeated the Goths holding Ravenna and reclaimed the city, while next to Theodora, on the right, is the wife of Belisarius, Antonina, and their daughter.

Theodora looks a harsh figure under her finery, and she certainly had a reputation for calculated cruelty, arranging "disappearances" of anyone who went against her.

According to the sixth-century chronicler Procopius, in his "Secret History" of the court, her rise to power was meteoric. When young she made a living as a child prostitute and circus performer with her two sisters, and later became a courtesan and an actor in bizarre sex shows. She travelled the Middle East, and when she returned brought herself to the attention of the emperor, Justinian. To the horror of the court, he rejected the well-brought up daughters of his Roman peers and lived with Theodora, giving her the rank of patrician. He was unable to marry her until his mother, the empress, was dead and the law changed; the two then embarked on a reign of staggering corruption and legalised looting.

Across the grass from the basilica is the tiny **Mausoleo di Galla Placidia** (daily 9am–7pm; L3000, includes San Vitale), named after the half-sister of Honorius, who was responsible for much of the grandeur of Ravenna's early days, though despite the name and three sarcophagi inside, it's unlikely that the building ever held her bones. Galla Placidia was taken hostage when the Goths sacked Rome, and created a scandal for the Roman world by marrying one of her kidnappers, Ataulf, going into battle with him as his army forged south. Later they reigned jointly over the Gothic kingdom; when Ataulf was assassinated the Romans took her back for a ransom of corn, after which she was obliged to marry a Roman general, Constantius. Their son formally became the Emperor Valentinian III at the age of six; as his Regent, she assumed control of the Western Empire.

Inside the building, filtered through thin alabaster windows, the light falls on mosaics which glow with a deep blue lustre, most in an earlier style than those of San Vitale, full of Roman and naturalistic motifs. Stars around a golden cross spread across the vaulted ceiling; the Gospels are four volumes on the shelves of a small cupboard, and there are symbolic representations of the Apostles – the lion of Saint Mark and the ox of Saint Luke are set in the sky at the points in which you expect to see Leo and Taurus. At each end are representations of Saint Lawrence, with the gridiron on which he was martyred, next to the Gospels, and the Good Shepherd, with one of his flock, at the entrance end.

Adjacent to San Vitale on the southern side, housed in the former cloisters of the church, the **Museo Nazionale** (Tues–Sun 8.30am–1pm; L6000) contains various items from this and later periods – fifteenth-century icons, early Byzantine glass, embroidery from Florence. Among the most eye-catching exhibits is a sixth-century statue of Hercules capturing a stag, possibly a copy of a Greek original and a very late example of classically inspired subject-matter; and the so-called "Veil of Classis", decorated with portraits of Veronese bishops of the eighth and ninth centuries.

Eating, drinking and nightlife

Central Ravenna is not exactly filled with **places to eat**, and you need to know in advance where to go to avoid lots of fruitless wandering. For lunch, the self-service *Bizantino*, just inside the covered market on Piazza A. Costa, is excellent value; the market itself is a good source of picnic supplies; *Silvano*, Via Diaz 11, just up from Piazza del Popolo, is a bar with good sandwiches; and there's a branch of the *Pizza Altero* chain at Via Camillo B. Cavour 31. In the evening, *Da Renato*, close by the cathedral square at Via R. Gessi 9, does traditional local food, specialising in funghi in autumn; nearby, towards Piazza San Francesco, *Ca' De Ven*, at Via C. Ricci 24, is a wood panelled *enoteca* with a large selection of Emilia-Romagnan wine, and some food. Behind the covered market, *La Gardela*, Via Ponte Marino 3, is a pleasant and very central eatery with a varied menu and moderate prices – ask for the daily specials; *Ristorante Scai*, Piazza Barracca 22, at the end of Via Cavour, is a roast meat and game speciality restaurant, though a moderately priced one, that serves pizzas too.

Around Ravenna: Sant'Apollinare in Classe

One stop south of Ravenna by train or bus #4, the remains of the old port of **Classe** (Mon–Fri 9am–noon) are very thin indeed – the buildings have been looted for stone and the ancient harbour has now completely disappeared under the silt of the River Uniti. One building does, however, survive – the church of **Sant'Apollinare in Classe**, which was spared because it was the burial-place of Ravenna's patron saint. It's a typical basilical church, quite large in extent, with a beautifully proportioned brick facade concealing an interior holding more fine mosaics. There's a marvellous allegorical depiction of the *Transfiguration* in the apse, with Christ represented by a large cross in a star-spangled universe, flanked by Constantine IV granting privileges to the church of Ravenna, with Sant'Apollinare pictured in prayer in a naturalistic landscape below.

It's an odd site, with an other-worldly feel quite at odds with its position close to the *autostrada*. Nearby, the **Pineta di Classe** is a long belt of umbrella pines which runs the length of the coast; the **Pineta San Vitale** runs north. This is closed to visitors during summer due to the fire risk; at other times it's a popular cycling route – though the thick belt of smog that rests over the tops of the trees destroys any bucolic appeal it might have. There's easy access to Ravenna's lido towns of **MARINA ROMEA**, **MARINA DI RAVENNA** or **PUNTA MARINA** by bus from here, resorts with some upmarket villas that make for quiet, peaceful places to stay once you have driven through Ravenna's heavy industry to get there. **PORTA CORSINI**, between Marina Romea and Marina di Ravenna, is interesting for its working port, large and modern enough to take tankers but still with old-fashioned cantilevered nets used for fishing the side channels. Just before the port, you pass the **Capanno Garibaldi**, a reconstruction of the hut in which Garibaldi hid on his epic 800-kilometre march from Rome after the fall of the short-lived Roman republic in 1849. Garibaldi's life-long partner Anita, who often fought alonside him, died on the way and he was unable to stop for long enough to bury her. After Marina Romea, take a left through the pinewoods towards the Strada Romea (SS309), where you'll find places to picnic under the umbrella pines well away from the sight of the industrial area – as well as some places for viewing the forgiving birdlife which still frequents the lagoon, which is part of the Parco Regionale Delta del Po (see above).

The coast to Rimini

From Ravenna, a slow train runs down to Rimini, past a number of resorts which blur into one after a while. It's not an enticing part of Italy, and if the sea is what you're after you may just as well push on to Rimini — compelling through its sheer excess. But if you're tempted to linger, **CERVIA** might be the place to do it, a former fishing and salt-producing village that has grown into something of a resort only in the last thirty or so years. On the first Sunday after Ascension, the town's bishop sails out into the Adriatic, accompanied by a flotilla of small boats in a ceremonial "marriage to the sea", throwing a wedding ring into the water.

Cervia's **old town** consists of a ring of porticoed houses around Piazza Garibaldi, built in the eighteenth century for the workers who worked on the salt beds a little way inland, southwest of town. At the height of production, this huge salt pan produced 500 thousand quintals (one quintal equals 100kg) of salt a year. The seventeenth-century **Torre**, just off Piazza Garibaldi, stored a mere 170 thousand quintals and is now the **Museo della Civiltà Salinara** (summer daily 8.30–11.30pm, winter Wed & Sat 4–6pm, Sun 3.30–6pm; free). Close by is Cervia's **tourist office**, in the porticoes (May–Sept daily 9am–noon & 3–6pm). For **snacks**, try the self-service *Pizzeria-Rosticceria La Terrazza* on Piazza Carlo Pisacane, which adjoins Piazza Garibaldi.

A fifteen-minute walk from Piazza Garibaldi is Cervia's main reason for a visit – acres of clean, sandy **beach**, serviced by scores of small, family-run hotels lining the grid of streets along the seafront. *Locanda Leana*, Rotonda Silvio Pellico 21 (0544/71.437; ④), is the bargain of the bunch, off Via Volturno, which runs parallel to the water, a couple of blocks back from the beach. Outside of the May–September season, the *Mussoni* hotel, above *Ristorante Al Traghetto* at Via Leoncavallo 3, by the harbour mouth (☎0544/974.136; ④), can sometimes be persuaded to open up rooms when all else is closed. Cervia's **campsites** are well-equipped places away from the town centre in PINARELLA and MILANO MARITTIMA. The closest is *Camping Adriatico* at Via Pinarella 30 (☎0544/71.537). There's a beach **tourist office** at Viale Roma 98 (mid-May–mid-Sept daily 9am–12.40pm & 3–6pm; ☎0544/974.400), and no fewer than 24 bike-hire places in all (the closest one a couple of blocks along Viale Volturno from the tourist office), not to mention any number of places with tennis, windsurfing, waterskiing and sailing facilities, on the side roads near the beach.

CESENATICO, 8km to the south, also grew up on its fishing industry, but has since developed into a large resort, with restaurants lining its central port-canal, designed by Leonardo da Vinci for Cesare Borgia in 1502. Many of the boats here are still primarily fishing vessels, but the port area is a popular place, with an attendant nightlife. There's a floating **Museo Marittima** on the canal, with a collection of old fishing and trading vessels, but otherwise nothing much to keep you if you don't go in for the grill-pan variety of sunbathing apart from a couple of good, budget **places to eat**: *La Crêpe* on Via Mazzini – two minutes walk over the canal in the Ravenna direction – offers a choice of twenty different *piadini* (the Romagnolo version of pitta bread), as well as crêpes too. A couple of doors down at no. 34, there's a good *rosticceria* serving fish kebabs, *fritto misto* and pasta dishes.

Rimini

RIMINI is one of the least pretentious towns in Italy, the archetypal seaside city, with a reputation for good if slightly sleazy fun that puts it on a par with Blackpool or Torremolinos. It's certainly brash enough to bear the comparison, and there's plenty of money in evidence; but Rimini is never tacky. Rather, it's a traditional family resort, to which some Italians return year after year, to stay in their customary *pensione* and be looked after by a hardworking *padrona di casa* as if they were her own relatives. Indeed the warmth of hoteliers in this part of Italy has undoubtedly added to the tourist industry's success.

There's also another, less savoury side to the town. Rimini is known across Italy for its fast-living and chancy nightlife, and there's a thriving hetero- and transsexual prostitution scene alongside the town's more wholesome attractions. The road between the train station and the beach can be particularly full of kerb-crawlers, and, although it's rarely dangerous, women on their own – at night at any rate – should be wary in this part of town.

Rimini was 95 percent destroyed in the last war, and the extensive beach operation you see now has been built over the last thirty years. The Adriatic slime slick hit business badly at the beginning of the 1980s, but the clean-up operation seems to have been almost completely successful. There are occasional recurrences, but nothing like the mass of gloopy algae which emptied the beaches a few years ago, and a daunting number of holidaymakers arrive once more through the city's airport. It's the beach, and the crowds and wild cruising, that you really come for – Rimini is still the country's best place to party. However, the town also has a much-ignored old centre that is worth at least a morning of your time.

Arrival, information and getting around

The **train station** is situated in the centre of Rimini, on Piazzale Cesare Battisti, ten minutes' walk from both the sea and the old centre; the town's main **bus station** is just south of here on Via Clementini. There's a **tourist office** just outside the train station (June–Sept daily 8am–8pm; Oct–May Mon–Sat 8am–2pm; ☎0541/51.480). They have a list of hotels and will help find a room, or pass you onto the *Promozione Alberghiera* – see below – except in the peak of the season (first two weeks in August), when normally you don't have a chance if you haven't booked ahead. There's another **tourist office** in the Parco dell'Indipendenza on the seafront (June–Sept daily 8am–8pm; Oct–May Mon–Sat 8am–2pm; ☎0541/51.101), which offers the same service, and a lit-up board outside showing vacancies when everything else is closed. You can also by-pass the tourist office altogether and go straight to the **Promozione Alberghiera** for somewhere to stay (Mon–Fri 9am–5pm; ☎0541/52.269; Sat & Sun ☎390.530); they have offices at the station and opposite the beach-front tourist office. The **Centro di Informazione Comunale**, in the Municipio on Piazza Cavour (Mon–Fri 8am–1pm & 2–7pm, Sat 8am–7pm; ☎0541/704.111), gives information on current cultural events, often in English.

Getting around is best done on foot, at least within the town centre. But if you need to use the buses, you're best off buying an **orange ticket**, which gives 24 hours' unlimited travel in Rimini and the surrounding area (including Santarcángelo, Riccione and Bellaria) for L3000; an eight-day ticket costs L12,000.

Accommodation

Generally speaking **accommodation** can be a problem in Rimini; prices aren't cheap, and in high season especially you often have to take full pension at hotels in Rimini, which can make it very expensive. At the beginning and end of the season (May, June, Sept), some hoteliers will negotiate a price for room only, but in the depths of low season you should bear in mind that the town is pretty much dead, and the few hotels that remain open are geared largely to people here on business. All the hotels listed here are within a five-minute walk from the beach.

One of the best of Rimini's more affordable **hotels** is the *Verudella*, Viale Tripoli 238 (☎0541/391.124; ⑤) – quite smart, with phones in rooms, and run by a friendly brother-and-sister management. Down a leafy side street between Piazzale Tripoli and Piazzale B. Croce, the *Donau*, Viale Alfieri 12 (☎0541/381.302; ⑤), does a wonderful buffet breakfast, as does the *Nancy*, Viale Leopardi 11 (☎0541/381.731; ⑤), an attractive villa in a lush garden, in a street parallel. The *Meublé Carducci*, Viale Carducci 15 (☎0541/391.780; ⑤), with doubles only, is slightly cheaper, and spotless too, down a quiet side street two blocks from Piazzale Tripoli. Cheaper still are the *Alfieri*, Viale Alfieri 10 (☎0541/381.436; ④), with more basic rooms but space to relax on the flowery deck furniture downstairs, and the *Bel Ami* at Via Metastasio 4 (☎0541/381.643; ④), in a peaceful shady side street, three blocks down from Piazzale B. Croce. You might also try booking **rooms only** in the villa with garden right on the seafront at Viale Regina Elena 20 (☎0541/391.862; ④), or at two inexpensive but basic choices – the *Capriccio Garni*, Viale Derna 22 (☎0541/390.800; ③), between Piazzale Kennedy and Piazzale Tripoli, or *Filadelfia Garni*, Viale Pola 25 (☎0541/236.79; ③), between the rail line and Piazzale Kennedy.

There's also a **youth hostel** out near the airport at MIRAMARE, at Via Flaminia 300 (☎0541/373.216), which is open May to September (bus #9 runs every 15min), although it has an 11pm curfew and you'll need to have booked. If you're camping, there are a number of **campsites** reachable by bus from Rimini station: *Camping Italia* at Via Toscanelli 112, Rivabella (☎0541/732.882), 2km along the coast, open June 1–

September 20 – take bus #2, #4 or #8 from station; *Camping Belvedere*, Via Grazia Verennin 9 at Viserbella, 5km up the coast (☎0541/720.960), open mid-June until the end of September – bus #4; and *Camping Maximum International*, Viale P. Piemonte (☎0541/372.602), next to the airport at Miramare, open May to September – bus #10 or #11. Further from the city, there are also smaller, more attractive sites, worth thinking about especially if you have your own transport – *Comunità Agro-Turistica La Ruspante* at San Ermete (☎0541/758.057), 9km from Rimini and open all year, with a swimming pool; and *Camping Green* at Via Vespucci 8, San Mauro Mare, 15km north of Rimini (☎0541/340.424), close to the beach and open mid-March to early November. The latter is also just 1km from either Gatteo a Mare or Bellária stations.

The Town

There are two parts to Rimini. The belt of land east of the rail line is taken up mostly by holiday accommodation, leading down to the main drag of souvenir shops, restaurants and video arcades, which stretches 9km north to the suburbs of Viserba and Torre Pedrera and 7km south to Miramare. Out of season, hotel windows are boarded up and neon signs wrapped in black bin liners to protect against the gales, when Rimini's activity contracts around the Parco dell'Indipendenza and the old town, inland. This is the second, often unseen part of Rimini, a ten-minute walk west from the train station – stone buildings clustered around the twin squares of Piazza Tre Martiri and Piazza Cavour, bordered by the port-canal and town ramparts.

On the southern and northern edge of the old centre respectively, the **Arco d'Augusto** and **Ponte Tiberio** sit just inside the ramparts, built at the beginning of the first century AD and BC respectively and testifying to Rimini's importance as a Roman colony. The patched-up Arco was built at the point where Via Emilia joined Via Flaminia. Rimini's other Roman remains consist of the **Anfiteatro**, of which there are sparse foundations off Via Roma, just south of the train station.

The city passed into the hands of the papacy in the eighth century and was subject to a series of disputes that left it in the hands of the Guelph family of Malatesta. Just south of the Ponte Tiberio, **Piazza Tre Martiri** and **Piazza Cavour** are the two main squares. Piazza Cavour has a statue of Pope Paul V and the Gothic **Palazzo del Podestà**; the square was rebuilt in the 1920s, and purists argue that it was ruined, although its fishtail battlements are still impressive enough. Buskers play here, and bikes and vespas converge from all directions. Opposite, beyond the sixteenth-century fountain incorporating Roman reliefs, the **Porticus Piscarias** shades bookstalls worth browsing. **Castel Sigismondo**, in the adjoining **Piazza Malatesta**, designed and built in 1446 by Sigismondo Malatesta, holds a museum of ethnography (daily 8am–1pm; L4000) – worth a look for its fine collection of Oceanic and pre-Colombian art.

The Malatesta family provide the town's best-known monument, the **Tempio Malatestiano** just east of here on Via 4 Novembre (Mon–Sat 7am–noon & 3.30–7pm, Sun 8am–1pm & 3.30pm–7pm; free), a strange-looking building, with an uncompleted facade, but generally held to be one of the masterworks of the Italian Renaissance. Transformed by Leon Battista Alberti in 1450 from a Franciscan Gothic church for Sigismondo Malatesta, a *condittiero* with an unparalled reputation for evil, it's an odd mixture of private chapel and personal monument. His long list of crimes include rape, incest, plunder and looting, not to mention the extreme oppression of his subjects. The temple kept, rather disingenuously, its dedication to Saint Francis, but this didn't fool the pope at the time, Pius II, who condemned its pagan ornaments and emphasis on Classical hedonism as "a temple of devil-worshippers".

Pius was angered enough to publicly consign Sigismondo to hell, burning an effigy of him in the streets of Rome. This had no effect on Sigismondo, who treated the church as a private memorial chapel to his great love, Isotta degli Atti. Their initials are linked in emblems all over the church, and the Malatesta armorial bearings – the elephant – appear almost as often. Trumpeting elephants, with their ears flying upwards, or elephants with their trunks entwined, decorate the screens between the side aisles and naves; chubby putti, nymphs and shepherds play, surrounded by bunches of black grapes, in a decidedly unchristian celebration of excess. There are a number of fine artworks, recently restored and very spick and span – a *Crucifix* now attributed to Giotto, friezes and reliefs by Agostino and a fresco by Piero della Francesca of Sigismondo himself. All in all it's an appropriate attraction for Rimini, its qualities of extravagance almost an emblem for a town that thrives on excess.

Eating, drinking and nightlife

As far as **eating** goes, the seafront is the best place to do it cheaply, with hundreds of pizza bars for on-your-feet refuelling. There are also some extremely ritzy places, where formal dress is obligatory, but most of the interesting restaurants are in the old town.

For **snacks**, Via Garibaldi, which leads inland from Piazza Tre Martiri, has several pizza-by-the-slice places, and a shop on Via Bonsi selling *piada* – pitta-type bread with hot fillings of mozzarella, tomato and prosciutto. The tiny *rosticceria* nearby at 117 Via S Chiara has three or four tables, usually full by 7.30pm – though it closes at 9pm; grab a variety of snacks, from well-made burgers to seafood salad, at the *Paninoteca* at Corso d'Augosto 226; there are places to sit and a good jukebox.

For **sit-down food**, *Osteria dë Börg*, at Via Forzieri 12, is definitely the place to head for first, a relaxed and moderately priced place serving Romagnolo cooking with innovations – *cappelletti* in carrot sauce, fish kebabs, meat roasted over an open fire and a dozen different vegetable dishes. *Pic-Nic*, Via Tempio Malatestiano 30, does reasonably priced pizzas, as well as pasta and crepes – and game. *L'Aquila d'Oro*, Corso Augusto 207, between Piazza Cavour and Piazza Tre Martiri, offers economical fondus and fish antipasti. *Rimini Key* has a couple of special menus for L20,000 and L27,000, as well as pizzas, and is in a prime location for watching night-time cruising along the seafront on Piazzale Croce. The *Belvedere*, on Via Molo Levante, and *Buliroun*, Piazza Kennedy 2, are both reliable places; on the other side of the Ponte Tiberio, *Il Colombo*, at Viale Tiberio 7, is a pricey fish restaurant. If you're fed up with Italian cooking, try the very affordable Chinese food at *Porta Fortuna*, Via Dante 39, between the station and the old town.

If you have transport, or are heading out to *Paradiso* (see opposite), two restaurants in the suburb of Covignano are worth a look: *Dalla Maria* at Via Grazie 81, with dependable Romagnolo cooking for L30,000, and *Grotta Rossa*, Via Grotta Rossa 13, which has much the same sort of food but at a slightly higher price. Another restaurant which merits the journey is *Bastian Contrario* (the name means "Awkward Customer"), 5km out of town at Via Marecchiese 312 in Spadarolo (bus #20), serving well-priced regional cooking. A bargain version of the same is available at *La Baracca* on the same road at no. 362.

Nightlife

Rimini's **nightlife** happens along the seafront. Above all Rimini is a place to go **clubbing**: the town has become the new Ibiza, and a favourite place for European (and Italian) ravers to head for on holiday. The evening's cruising starts at 10–11pm, along the seafront, shortly after which people then move on to the first club, either in their cool convertibles and jeeps or by a night bus called the *Blue Line*, which operates through the night and serves two routes: the first along the length of the coast, from RICCIONE to BELLARIA; the second from Rimini to Covignano for the clubs *Paradiso* and *Bandiera Gialla*. Pick up either route at Piazzale Kennedy; nightly bus passes cost L3000.

Paradiso, at Via Covignano 260 (☎0541/751.132), is perhaps the most consistently popular club, with great dance music, as well as various happenings, such as fashion shows, performances and other, often art-based events, with owner Maurizio Clemente importing DJs, designers and artists from other European countries. It's open every night in summer, and from Thursday to Sunday the rest of the year. In the same suburb, though open summer only, *Bandiera Gialla* is a weekend open-air rave – and the *Blue Line* bus takes you right there. Other places with style and good dance music are *Ethos-Mama* at Via Risorgimento 25, south of Rimini at GABICCE MARE (☎0541/961.240), and *Pascià*, Via Sardegna 30, in Riccione (☎0541/604.207). There's also *Cocoricò*, at Via Chieti 44 in Riccione, which was well known for techno until a stabbing incident temporarily closed it in 1992; it may well re-open. For up-to-date information on the club scene, check the **listings** in the fortnightly *Chiamami Città* or call in at the record store *Dischi di Importazione*, Viale Regina Elena 3, which is a good source generally on the state of play of the clubs. Incidentally, if you're pining for a pint of draught *Guinness*, the *Rose and Crown* pub, next door to *Dischi...*, will oblige.

For **quieter evenings**, *Cinema Astra*, at Via G. D'Annunzio 20, Misano Adriatico, to the south, shows alternative and re-run movies. More sedately still, there's a classical music festival throughout the summer – the *Sagra Musicale Malatestiana* – in the Tempio Malatesta. It's also worth checking to see if the independent film festivals in Bellaria (to the north) and Rimini itself are running, scheduled respectively for the third week in August and the third week in September – both appropriate events for Fellini's home town.

Listings

Airport Take bus #9B from the airport to the railway station.

Car rental *Avis*, Viale Trieste 16 (☎0541/51.256); *Europcar*, Via Giovanni XXIII 126 (☎0541/54.746); *Mondiani*, Viale Tripoli 16 (☎0541/782.646).

Doctor *Guardia Medica* on 24hr call on ☎0541/774.037. For non-emergencies, there's also a walk-in surgery at Viale Mantegazza 13 – parallel with the main road between the station and tourist office (June–Aug 9am–noon & 4–7pm; ☎0541/50.102).

Laundry *Lavanderia Italia '90*, 11e Viale Giusti, off the seafront between Piazzale Tripolo and Piazzale B Croce.

Pharmacy Via IV Novembre (daily except Thurs 8.30am–12.30pm & 4–8pm; ☎0541/24.414). When closed, it has details of all-night services posted outside.

Post office Main office on Piazza G. Cesare (Mon–Fri 8.15am–6pm, Sat 8.15am–1pm); smaller branch at Piazzale Tripoli 2 (Mon–Fri 8.10am–1.30pm, Sat 8.10–11.50am).

Taxis *Radiotaxi Cooperative* (☎0541/50.020 or ☎51.488); there's also a 24hr rank outside the station.

Telephones *SIP* at Piazza Ferrari 34 (summer daily 8am–10pm).

Travel agent *Miramare*, Via Gambalunga 28/c, does discount tickets.

Around Rimini: Santarcángelo and San Marino

The countryside around Rimini is attractive: small hilltop towns and lush gentle valleys covered with firs and chestnuts, much of which is connected to the coast by bus. **SANTARCÁNGELO**, 11km inland and easily accessible by bus or train from Rimini, is worth the short trip for its steep medieval streets and thirteenth-century **fortress** (June–Sept Tues, Thurs & Sat 10am–noon & 4–7pm). Carved into the hillside on the edge of the village are some artificial caves, a dank hide out for early Christians in the seventh century. The first two weeks of July see an **international theatre festival** here, drawing people from miles around. As an example, 1992's festival saw rituals performed by Tibetan monks, rap from Italian bands, including Bologna's *Fuckin'*

Camels 'n Effect, and an all-female *Waiting for Godot*. Get tickets from the box office in Santarcángelo's main Piazza Ganganelli (☎0541/622.224). The best bet for **accommodation** is the campsite at *La Ruspante* (see p.363), but if you need advice there's a **tourist office** at Via Montevecchi 7.

It's worth also visiting Santarcángelo for the village's restaurants, of which *Da Lazaroun* at Via del Platano 21 is recommended, as is the less refined but more affordable *Da Gigi*, Via C. Battisti 19. *Osteria della Violina*, Vicolo d'Enzi 4, occupies a seventeenth-century palazzo with internal garden, and has a cheaper section downstairs serving *piatti poveri* ("poor dishes"), which are chalked up on a board and washed down with Sangiovese wine. Booking is advisable (☎0541/620.416).

Santarcángelo is very different from the region's second tourist attraction after the beach, the **Republic of San Marino** – an unashamed tourist trap which trades on its falsely preserved autonomy. Said to have been founded around 300 AD by a monk fleeing the persecutions of Diocletian, it has its own mint, produces its own postage stamps, and has an army of around a thousand men. The ramparts and medieval-style buildings of the citadel above Borgomaggiore, also called "San Marino", restored this century, are mildly interesting; there is a crummy **waxworks museum** in Via Lapicidi Marini (April–Sept daily 8am–7pm; Oct–March daily 8.30am–12.30pm & 2–5pm; L3000), a **stamp museum** in Piazza Grande in Borgomaggiore (daily 9am–12.30pm & 2.30–6pm; L3000), and other places where you can view suits of armour, as well as tacky souvenir shops and restaurants. But really the place is a fake, and you should be prepared, too, for the opposite of the usual patience and good humour you find in other parts of the region. For the determined visitor, the walk up through town to the **rocche**, battlemented castles along the highest three ridges, is worth the effort. Below, in Borgomaggiore, is Giovanni Michelucci's "fearless and controversial" modernist church, built in the 1960s, with a roof which looks as though it pours down in waves.

travel details

Trains

Bologna to: Ancona (hourly; 1hr); Cesena (20 daily; 1hr 10min); Faenza (20 daily; 45min); Ferrara (12 daily; 30min); Fidenza (20 daily; 1hr); Florence (hourly; 1hr); Forli (20 daily; 50min); Imola (hourly; 30min); Milan (hourly; 2hr 35min); Modena (hourly; 20min); Parma (hourly; 50min); Piacenza (hourly; 1hr 20min); Reggio Emilia (hourly; 35min); Ravenna (15 daily; 1hr 25min); Rimini (hourly; 1hr 20min).

Faenza to: Brisighella (6 daily; 10min).

Fidenza to: Busseto (14 daily; 11min); Cremona (14 daily; 35min); Salsomaggiore (half-hourly; 7min).

Ferrara to: Ravenna (13 daily; 1hr 15min); Rimini (3 daily; 2hr 30min).

Modena to: Carpi (half-hourly; 12min); Mantua (8 daily; 1hr); Verona (4 daily; 1hr 30min).

Parma to: Brescia (8 daily; 1hr 45min); La Spezia (7 daily; 2hr 15min).

Piacenza to: Cremona (hourly; 30min).

Rimini to: Santarcángelo (4 daily; 8min).

Buses

Bologna to: Imola (every 15min; 1hr); Marzabotto (hourly; 15min); Porretta Terme (3 daily; 1hr 55min); Sasso Marconi (half-hourly; 45min); Vergato (hourly; 35min).

Imola to: Dozza (5 daily; 15min).

Forli to: Bertinoro (8 daily; 20min).

Modena to: Carpi (7 daily; 40min); Pievepelago (5 daily; 3hr 10min); Fanano (5 daily; 2hr); Fossoli (7 daily; 17min); Montefiorino (5 daily; 1hr 50min); Sestola (4 daily; 2hr); Vignola (5 daily; 40min).

Reggio Emilia to: Busana (4 daily; 1hr 55min); Casina (7 daily; 50min); Castelnuovo ne'Monti (13 daily; 1hr 20min); Ligonchio (2 daily; 2hr 45min).

Parma to: Bardi (5 daily; 2hr); Busseto/Le Roncole (6 daily; 1hr); Calestano (7 daily; 1hr); Corniglio (4 daily; 1hr 40min); Fontanellato (9 daily; 30min); Lagdei (1 daily; 2hr 30min); Langhirano (15 daily; 40min); Monchio (3 daily; 2hr 25min); Noceto (15 daily; 30min); Rigoso (5 daily; 2hr 20min); Roncole Verdi (8 daily; 50min);

Salsomaggiore Terme (half hourly; 1hr 5min); Soragna (8 daily; 40min); Torrechiara (15 daily; 25min).

Fidenza to: Busseto (1 daily; 2hr); Fontanellato (3 daily; 25min); Soragna (8 daily; 20min); Tabiano Castello (1 daily; 50min).

Piacenza to: Bobbio (12 daily; 1hr 15min); Castel l'Arquato (16 daily; 55min), Lugagnano (16 daily; 1hr); Rustigazzo (4 daily; 10min).

Ferrara to: Bosco della Mesola (3 daily; 1hr 20min); Comacchio (10 daily; 1hr 20min); Goro (3 daily; 1hr 30min); Pomposa Abbazia (1 daily; 2hr 45min).

Ravenna to: Classe (half-hourly; 10min); Marina Romea/Marina di Ravenna (15 daily; 20min); Mesola (2 daily; 2hr); Punta Marina (16 daily; 25min).

Rimini to: Rome (1 daily; 5hr 30min); Santarcángelo (3 daily; 25min); San Marino (12 daily; 1hr).

Salsomaggiore to: Fiorenzuola (2 daily; 45min); Tabiano Bagni (12 daily; 20min).

CHAPTER EIGHT

TUSCANY

It was in **Tuscany** that the Renaissance came to fruition, and this single fact has given the province an importance quite beyond its political significance. In the fifteenth and sixteenth centuries Tuscan artists such as Masaccio, Donatello and Michelangelo created works that have influenced painters and sculptors down to the present, and every major town in Italy reflects to some extent the ideas of Tuscan architects – Brunelleschi in particular. The country's very language bears the stamp of Tuscany, as the roots of modern Italian spring from the dialect written by Dante, Boccaccio and Petrarch, each of whom was born in the region.

For most visitors, the Tuscan **landscape**, too, is archetypally Italian. Its elements – walled towns, lines of cypress trees, rolling, vineyard-covered hills – are the classic backdrops of Renaissance art, disarmingly familiar from innumerable paintings. If the countryside of Tuscany has a fault, it's the popularity that its seductiveness has brought, and in many respects it's the lesser-known sights that prove most memorable and enjoyable: remote **monasteries** like Sant'Antimo or Monte Oliveto Maggiore, the weird **sulphur spas** of Bagno Vignoni and Saturnia, or the eerily eroded terrain of the **crete** (craters) south of Siena.

Which is not to suggest that you ignore Tuscany's established city attractions. It's true that few people react completely positively to **Florence**, which at present creates the impression that every building worth a look has been encased in scaffolding and tarpaulins. But however unappealing some of the central streets might look, there are plentiful compensations: the Uffizi gallery's masterpieces by Botticelli, Raphael, Titian, and just about every other important artist of the Renaissance; the great fresco cycles in the city churches; or the wealth of Florentine sculpture in the Bargello and Museo dell'Opera del Duomo.

Siena provokes less ambiguous reactions. Radiating from its beautiful Campo – the sloping, shell-shaped market square – this is one of the great medieval cities of Europe, almost perfectly preserved, and with superb works of art in its religious and secular buildings. The Campo is the scene, too, of Tuscany's one unmissable festival – the **Palio** – which sees bareback horse riders careering around the cobbles, amid the brightest display of pageantry this side of Rome.

The other major cities, **Pisa** and **Lucca**, provide convenient entry points to the province, either by air (Pisa's *Aeroporto Galileo Galilei* has flights from Britain) or along the Genova to Rome coastal railway. Both have medieval splendours – Pisa its Leaning Tower and cathedral ensemble, Lucca a string of Romanesque churches – though neither can quite compete with Siena's charm. The places that can are the smaller **hill towns** – the majority of them tucked away to the west or south of Siena. **San Gimignano**, the "city of the towers", is the best known, though too popular today for its own good. Better candidates for the rural Tuscan escape are the wine towns of **Montepulciano** and **Montalcino**, in each of which tourism is yet to overwhelm local character and life.

The one area where Tuscany thoroughly fails to impress is its **coastline**. On the mainland this is almost continuously developed, with overpriced and uninspired beach-

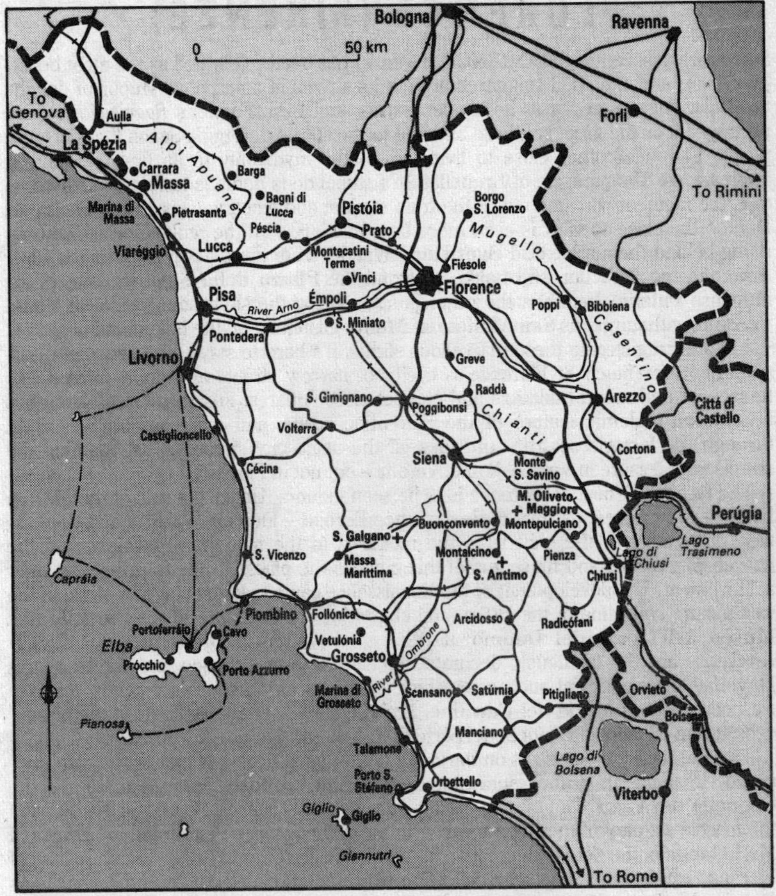

umbrella compounds filling every last scrap of sand. There is rather more going for the principal Tuscan **islands – Elba** and **Giglio** – though these also are victims of their own allure, and it's not unknown for every last campsite place to be booked through the high-season months.

The **season** is in fact a consideration in relation to everywhere remotely well known in Tuscany. Florence, especially, can be a nightmare in summer, with no clear sight-lines in the Uffizi and scrums thirty-deep round Michelangelo's *David*. Finding **accommodation** here is a major problem from April through to the end of September, and not a great deal easier elsewhere; phoning to book a room is generally essential in Tuscany, at any budget level. Beware that the province is also expensive, even by northern Italian standards, with very few hotel rooms below L50,000 a double in high season.

FLORENCE (FIRENZE)

Since early last century **FLORENCE** (Firenze) has been celebrated as the most beautiful city in Italy: Stendhal staggered around its streets in a perpetual stupor of delight; the Brownings sighed over its idyllic charms; and E.M. Forster's *Room with a View* portrayed it as the great southern antidote to the sterility of Anglo-Saxon life. For most people Florence comes close to living up to the myth only in its first, resounding impressions. The pinnacle of Brunelleschi's stupendous dome is visible over the rooftops the moment you step out of the train station, and when you reach the Piazza del Duomo the close-up view is even more breathtaking, with the multicoloured **Duomo** rising behind the marble-clad **Baptistery**. Wander from there down towards the River Arno and the attraction still holds – beyond the **Piazza della Signoria**, site of the immense **Palazzo Vecchio**, the water is spanned by the shop-laden medieval **Ponte Vecchio**, with gorgeous **San Miniato al Monte** glistening on the hill behind it.

Yet after registering these marvellous sights, it's hard to stave off a sense of disappointment, for much of Florence is a city of narrow streets and dour, fortress-like houses, of unfinished buildings and characterless squares. Restorers' scaffolding has become an endemic feature of the Florentine scene, and incessant traffic – right through the historic centre – provides all the usual city stresses. Just roaming the streets is a pleasure in Venice, Rome, Verona – but not in Florence.

The fact is, the best of Florence is to be seen indoors. Under the rule of the **Medici** family – the greatest patrons of Renaissance Europe – Florence's artists and thinkers were instigators of the shift from the medieval to the modern world-view, and the churches, galleries and museums of this city are the places to get to grips with their achievement. The development of the Renaissance can be plotted stage by stage in the vast picture collection of the **Uffizi**, and charted in the sculpture of the **Bargello**, the **Museo dell'Opera del Duomo** and the guild church of **Orsanmichele**. Equally revelatory are the fabulously decorated chapels of **Santa Croce** and **Santa Maria Novella**, forerunners of such astonishing creations as Masaccio's recently restored frescoes at **Santa Maria del Carmine**, Fra' Angelico's serene paintings in the monks' cells at **San Marco** and Andrea del Sarto's work at **Santissima Annunziata**.

The Renaissance emphasis on harmony and rational design is expressed with unrivalled eloquence in Brunelleschi's interiors of **San Lorenzo**, **Santo Spirito** and the **Cappella dei Pazzi**. The bizarre architecture of San Lorenzo's **Sagrestia Nuova** and the marble statuary of the **Accademia** – home of the *David* – display the full genius of **Michelangelo**, the dominant creative figure of sixteenth-century Italy. Every quarter of Florence can boast a church or collection worth an extended call, and the enormous **Palazzo Pitti** constitutes a museum district on its own.

A brief history

Though the Etruscan people were spread throughout Tuscany from the eighth century BC, there was no Etruscan precursor to Florence – their base in the vicinity was the hill town of Fiesole. The development of Florence itself began with the Roman colony of Florentia, established by **Julius Caesar** in 59 BC as a settlement for army veterans; the Roman grid plan is still evident in the streets between the Duomo and Piazza della Signoria. Expansion was rapid, with a steady traffic of trading vessels along the Arno providing the basis of accelerated growth in the second and third centuries AD. In 552, however, the city fell to the barbarian hordes of Totila, and less than twenty years later the Lombards stormed in, subjugating Florence to the duchy they ruled from Lucca.

By the end of the eighth century Charlemagne's Franks had taken control, with the administration being overseen by imperial margraves also based in Lucca. Over the next three hundred years Florence gained pre-eminence among the cities of Tuscany, becoming especially important as a religious centre. In 1078 Countess Mathilda of

Tuscia, one of the pope's closest allies in his struggles against the Emperor Henry IV, supervised the construction of new fortifications, and in the year of her death – 1115 – granted Florence the status of an **independent city**. The new *comune* of Florence was essentially governed by a council of one hundred men, the great majority drawn from the increasingly prosperous merchant class. In 1125 the city's dominance of the region was confirmed when it crushed its rival, Fiesole.

GUELPHS AND GHIBELLINES

Agitation from the landed nobility of the surrounding countryside was a constant fact of life in the early years of the republic, and political stability was a long time coming. The governing council was replaced in 1207 by the *Podestà*, an executive official who was traditionally a non-Florentine; around this time the first *Arti* (Guilds) were formed to promote the interests of the traders and bankers. Throughout and beyond the thirteenth century Florence was torn by conflict between the pro-imperial **Ghibelline** faction and the pro-papal **Guelphs**, a feud sparked off by a murder committed in Florence but which soon spread all over Italy. The Guelph-backed regime of the *Primo Popolo*, a government of the mercantile class, was ousted after the Florentine defeat by the Sienese army and its Ghibelline allies in 1260. By the 1280s the Guelphs were back in power through the *Secondo Popolo*, a regime run by the *Arti Maggiori* (Great Guilds). Refinement of the republican system soon followed: the exclusion of the nobility from government in 1293 was the most dramatic measure in a programme of political reforms which invested power in the *Signoria*, a council drawn from the major guilds.

Strife between the so-called "Black" and "White" factions within the Guelph camp marked the start of the fourteenth century, and worse was to come. In the 1340s the two largest banks collapsed, mainly owing to the bad debts of Edward III of England, then in 1348 the **Black Death** destroyed up to half the city's population. Thirty years later, discontent erupted among the industrial workers on whose labour the wool and cloth industries of Florence depended – the rising of the *Ciompi* (wool carders) resulted in the formation of three new guilds and direct representation for the workers. In 1382, though, an alliance of the Guelph party and the *popolo grasso* (the wealthiest merchants) took control of the city away from the guilds, a situation that lasted for four decades.

THE MEDICI

Gradually the balance shifted again, and the political rise of **Cosimo de'Medici** was to some extent due to his family's sympathies with the *popolo minuto*, the members of the lesser guilds. The Medici fortune had been made by the banking prowess of Cosimo's father, Giovanni Bicci de'Medici, and Cosimo used the power conferred by wealth to great effect, becoming the dominant figure in the city's political life, though he rarely held office himself. Through Cosimo's patronage Florence became the centre of artistic activity in Italy, an ascendancy that continued under his son, Piero il Gottoso (the Gouty), and his grandson **Lorenzo il Magnifico**. Papal resentment of Florentine independence found an echo in the jealousy of the Pazzi family, one of the city's main rivals to the Medici. However, the resulting **Pazzi conspiracy** – in which Lorenzo was wounded and his brother Giuliano murdered – only increased the esteem in which Lorenzo was held.

Before Lorenzo's death in 1492, however, the Medici bank failed, and in 1494 Lorenzo's son Piero was obliged to flee following his surrender to the invading French army of Charles VIII. For a while Florence was virtually under the control of the inspirational and ascetic monk **Girolamo Savonarola**, but he was executed as a heretic in 1498, after which the city functioned as a more democratic republic than that which the Medici had dominated. In 1512, after Florence's defeat by the Spanish, the Medici

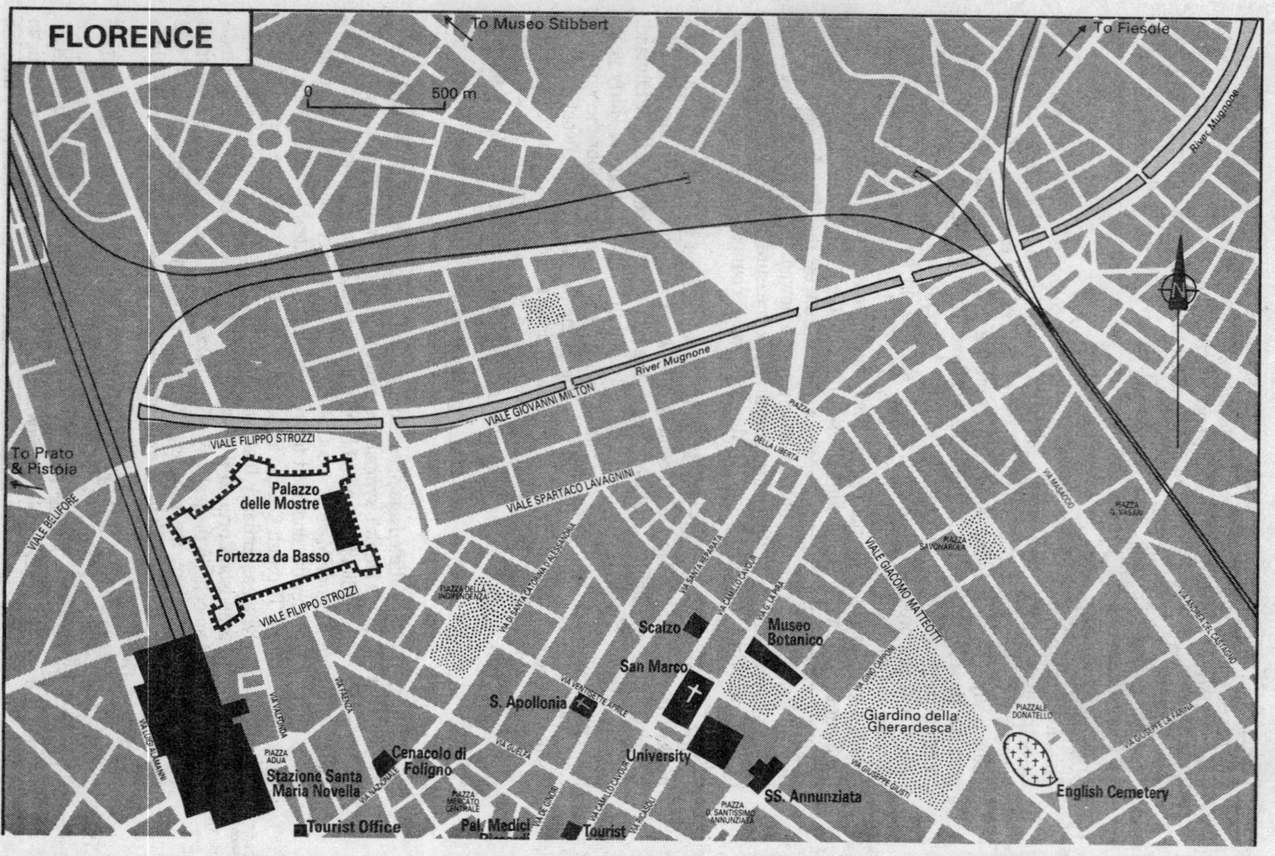
FLORENCE
To Museo Stibbert
To Fiesole
0
500 m
River Mugnone
VIALE GIOVANNI MILTON
VIALE FILIPPO STROZZI
To Prato & Pistoia
VIALE BELFIORE
Palazzo delle Mostre
Fortezza da Basso
VIALE SPARTACO LAVAGNINI
PIAZZA DELLA LIBERTÀ
VIA MASACCIO
PIAZZA G. VASARI
PIAZZA SAVONAROLA
VIALE GIACOMO MATTEOTTI
VIA ANDREA DEL CASTAGNO
PIAZZA DELLA INDIPENDENZA
VIA DI SANTA CATERINA D'ALESSANDRIA
VIA SANTA REPARATA
VIA CAMILLO CAVOUR
VIA G. LA PIRA
Scalzo
Museo Botanico
San Marco
VIA GINO CAPPONI
PIAZZALE DONATELLO
VIA GIUSEPPE LA FARINA
Giardino della Gherardesca
English Cemetery
S. Apollonia
VIA VENTISETTE APRILE
VIA VALFONDA
VIA FAENZA
VIA GUELFA
VIA LUIGI ALAMANNI
PIAZZA ADUA
Stazione Santa Maria Novella
Cenacolo di Foligno
VIA NAZIONALE
PIAZZA MERCATO CENTRALE
University
VIA GIUSEPPE GIUSTI
SS. Annunziata
PIAZZA D. SANTISSIMA ANNUNZIATA
VIA DE' GINORI
VIA RICASOLI
Tourist Office
Pal. Medici
Tourist

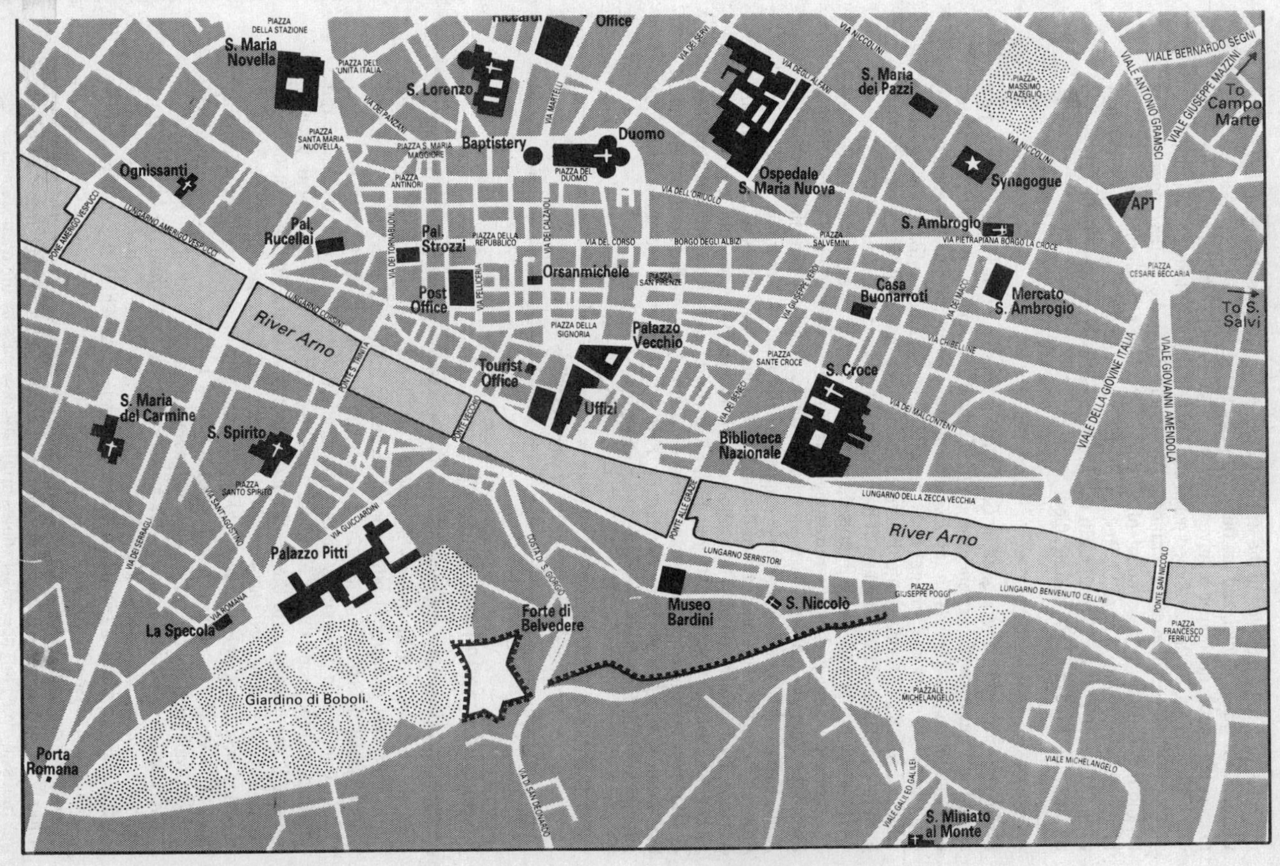
PIAZZA DELLA STAZIONE
S. Maria Novella
PIAZZA DELL'UNITA ITALIA
S. Lorenzo
Office
VIA DEI SERVI
VIA NICCOLINI
VIA DEGLI ALFANI
S. Maria dei Pazzi
PIAZZA MASSIMO D'AZEGLIO
VIALE ANTONIO GRAMSCI
VIALE GIUSEPPE MAZZINI
VIALE BERNARDO SEGNI
To Campo Marte
VIA DEI PANZANI
VIA MARTELLI
PIAZZA SANTA MARIA NOVELLA
PIAZZA S. MARIA MAGGIORE
Baptistery
Duomo
PIAZZA DEL DUOMO
Ospedale S. Maria Nuova
Synagogue
APT
Ognissanti
PIAZZA ANTINORI
VIA DELL'ORIUOLO
S. Ambrogio
VIA PIETRAPIANA BORGO LA CROCE
PONTE AMERIGO VESPUCCI
LUNGARNO AMERIGO VESPUCCI
Pal. Rucellai
Pal. Strozzi
PIAZZA DELLA REPUBBLICA
VIA DEI CALZAIOLI
VIA DEL CORSO
BORGO DEGLI ALBIZI
PIAZZA SALVEMINI
PIAZZA CESARE BECCARIA
VIA DEI TORNABUONI
Orsanmichele
PIAZZA SAN FIRENZE
VIA GIUSEPPE VERDI
Casa Buonarroti
VIA DEI MACCI
Mercato S. Ambrogio
To S. Salvi
Post Office
VIA PELLICCERIA
LUNGARNO CORSINI
River Arno
PIAZZA DELLA SIGNORIA
Palazzo Vecchio
VIA GHIBELLINE
VIALE DELLA GIOVINE ITALIA
VIALE GIOVANNI AMENDOLA
PONTE S. TRINITA
Tourist Office
PIAZZA SANTE CROCE
S. Croce
S. Maria del Carmine
PONTE VECCHIO
Uffizi
VIA DEI BENCI
VIA DEI MALCONTENTI
S. Spirito
Biblioteca Nazionale
PIAZZA SANTO SPIRITO
VIA SANT'AGOSTINO
VIA DEI SERRAGLI
VIA GUICCIARDINI
PONTE ALLE GRAZIE
LUNGARNO DELLA ZECCA VECCHIA
COSTA DI S. GIORGIO
River Arno
Palazzo Pitti
LUNGARNO SERRISTORI
PIAZZA GIUSEPPE POGGI
LUNGARNO BENVENUTO CELLINI
PONTE SAN NICCOLO
VIA ROMANA
Forte di Belvedere
Museo Bardini
S. Niccolò
PIAZZA FRANCESCO FERRUCCI
La Specola
Giardino di Boboli
PIAZZALE MICHELANGELO
Porta Romana
VIA DI SAN LEONARDO
VIALE GALILEO
VIALE MICHELANGELO
S. Miniato al Monte

returned, only to be expelled in the wake of Charles V's pillage of Rome in 1527 – Pope Clement VII was a Medici, and his humiliation by the imperial army provided the spur to eject his deeply unpopular relatives. Two years later the pendulum swung the other way – after a siege by the combined papal and imperial forces, Florence capitulated.

After the assassination of the tyrannous Alessandro de'Medici in 1537, power passed to another Cosimo, a descendant of Cosimo il Vecchio's brother. Under his rule Florence gained control of all of Tuscany; in 1570 he took the title Cosimo I, the first Grand-Duke of Tuscany. Thenceforth the Medici remained in power until 1737, when the last male Medici, Gian Gastone, died.

TO THE PRESENT

Under the terms of a treaty signed by Gian Gastone's sister, Anna Maria, Florence now passed to Francesco of Lorraine, the future Francis I of Austria. Austrian rule lasted until the coming of the French in 1799; after a fifteen-year interval of French control, the Lorraine dynasty was brought back, remaining in residence until the Risorgimento upheavals of 1859. Absorbed into the united Italian state in the following year, Florence became the capital of the Kingdom of Italy in 1861, a position it held until 1875.

The story of Florence since then is distinguished mainly by calamities. In 1944 the city was badly damaged by the retreating German army, who bombed all the bridges except the Ponte Vecchio and blew up much of the medieval city near the banks of the Arno. Even worse was the wreckage caused by the flood of November 1966, which drowned several people and caused damage to buildings and works of art which still has not been fully rectified. These monuments and paintings are the very basis of Florence's survival, a state of affairs which gives rise to considerable discontent. The development of a new industrial city (*Firenze Nuova*) between the northern suburbs and Prato – substantially underwritten by *Fiat* – is the latest and most ambitious attempt to break Florence's ever-increasing dependence on tourism.

The Florence area telephone code is ☎055.

Arrival, information and transport

A few international air services use the tiny Perètola **airport**, 5km northwest of Florence, but most of its traffic still consists of internal flights. For the foreseeable future the great majority of international incoming traffic will use **Pisa**'s Aeroporto Galileo Galilei, which is connected by a regular train service to Florence's Santa Maria Novella train station; the journey takes an hour, and tickets should be bought from the information desk inside the air terminal. If you're coming into the city by **car**, it's best to leave it some way out of the centre and take a **bus** to the station right by Santa Maria Novella – there are car parks in the centre, but these facilities are extremely busy and will cost in the region of L2000 per hour. The most central spot where you can park free of charge for an unrestricted period is Piazzale Michelangelo, thirty minutes' walk from the core of the city, high above the south bank of the River Arno.

Orientation is straightforward – it's just ten minutes' walk from the bus and train stations to Piazza del Duomo, along Via de'Panzani and Via de'Cerretani. Most of the major sights are within a few minutes of the Duomo area. Within the city, walking is generally the most efficient way of getting around, but if you want to cover a long distance in a hurry, then take one of the orange *ATAF* **buses**: tickets valid for one hour (L1000) or two hours (L1300) can be bought from *tabacchi* and from automatic machines all over Florence. Most routes originate at or pass by the train station.

The main **tourist** office, for information not just on the city but on the whole Florence province, is at **Via Cavour 1r**, a short distance north of the Duomo (Mon–Sat 8am–1.45pm; ☎276.0382). There are smaller offices, with the same unhelpful opening hours, at **Chiasso dei Baroncelli 17–19r**, just off Piazza della Signoria, and at the end of the bus ranks outside the **train station**. All these offices will give you an adequate map, leaflets on a variety of subjects, and a magazine called *Concierge Information*, which gives all the latest opening hours and entrance charges. None of these offices will book accommodation though – see below for the agencies that do.

Accommodation

Budget accommodation in Florence is a problem at most times of year – prices tend to be high and standards low, and the city's tourist invasion has scarcely any slack spots. Basically, between Easter and the start of October you're taking a risk in turning up without a pre-booked room, as it's not unknown for every one- and two-star hotel to be booked solid by the late morning.

Once you've arrived, the quickest way to get a room is to call at the train station information office to pick up a copy of the city's list of hotels (*Elenco degli Alberghi*), then get phoning from the station – the desk next to the baggage deposit sells telephone cards (*schede telefoniche*). If this sounds like too much hassle, the **Informazioni Turistiche Alberghiere**, between platforms 9 and 10 (daily 8.30am–8.15pm; ☎282.893), will make a reservation for you. In high season, though, you could spend a couple of hours queueing, and by the time you get to the front, any cheap rooms that might have been available when you arrived will probably have been taken. Their charges vary with the class of accommodation chosen, ranging from L6000 to L20,000, and you pay your first night's bill as deposit.

Should everything be booked out, the *Elenco degli Alberghi* contains addresses and phone numbers of hotels in outlying towns and indicates their accessibility by public transport. The list also details the approved **private rooms** in Florence, though these are often in dismal and distant parts of the city, and rarely undercut one-star prices.

Hotels

Even at the one-star end, prices in Florence are steep, with a high-season average in excess of L50,000, and that's without breakfast, which is virtually compulsory in summer, slapping as much as an extra L15,000 per person onto the bill. From October to April prices come down a little at some hotels, but many hotels have a single year-round tariff.

The major concentrations of one- and two-stars are within a few hundred metres of the train station, in particular along and around Via Faenza and the parallel Via Fiume, to the east of the station towards the San Lorenzo market. On the other side of the station, Via della Scala has several low-cost hotels that are often more welcoming than those to the east, and Piazza Santa Maria Novella – into which Via della Scala runs – offers a range of options, though the square is one of the city's grubbier areas at night. Generally more salubrious, if rather noisier, is Via Cavour, the main road north from the Duomo.

THE STATION AND MARKET AREAS

Anna (☎298.322); **Armonia** (☎211.146); **Azzi** (☎213.806); **Marini** (☎284.824); **Merlini** (☎212.848); and **Paola** (☎213.682), all Via Faenza 56. With most of its rooms overlooking the garden, the *Azzi* is probably the most pleasant of the six one-stars occupying the upper floors of this building. The others are all at least tolerable. All ④.

Ausonia e Rimini, Via Nazionale 24 (☎496.547). Nicely refurbished one-star halfway between the train station and the market. ④.

Concordia, Via dell'Amorino 14 (☎213.233). Extremely convenient, being located right in the heart of the market area; no private bathrooms and doesn't do breakfast. ④.

Desirée, Via Fiume 20 (☎238.2382). Overhauled to lift it into two-star status, the *Desirée* has stained-glass windows, simulated antique furniture, and a bath in every room. ⑥.

Erina, Via Fiume 17 (☎288.294). Located on the third floor of an old palazzo, with seven double rooms; open only from mid-July to mid-September. ⑤.

Tony's Inn, Via Faenza 77 (☎217.975). Run by a Canadian woman and her Italian photographer husband, so good for homesick Anglophones. ⑥.

SANTA MARIA NOVELLA AREA

Elite, Via della Scala 12 (☎215.395). Two-star run by one of the most pleasant managers in town. ⑤.

Giacobazzi, Piazza Santa Maria Novella 24 (☎294.679). Popular with Italian visitors and has only seven rooms, so usually necessary to book well in advance. ④.

Mia Casa, Piazza Santa Maria Novella 23 (☎213.061). Pleasantly ramshackle, with very helpful owners – the first choice on this square. ④.

La Romagnola and **Gigliola**, both Via della Scala 40 (☎211.597). Pick of the bunch on this street – a midnight curfew is the only drawback. With a total of 42 rooms, they often have space when the others are full. ④.

NORTH AND EAST OF THE DUOMO

Benvenuti, Via Cavour 112 (☎572.141). First-choice two-star in the university quarter. ⑥.

Brunetta, Borgo Pinti 5 (☎247.8134). Cheap and well-placed, a five-minute walk to the east of the Duomo. ④.

Donatello, Via Alfieri 9 (☎245.870). In a quiet area between Piazzale Donatello and Piazza d'Azeglio; strongly recommended – smartly renovated, airy, and run by young management. ⑤.

Genzianella, Via Cavour 112 (☎573.909). Reasonable one-star in the same building as the smarter *Benvenuti*; doesn't do breakfast. ④.

Giglio, Via Cavour 85 (☎486.621). Another serviceable two-star on this major street. ⑥.

Losanna, Via Alfieri 9 (☎245.840). Small, clean and modest one-star that shares premises with the *Donatello*. ④.

Panorama, Via Cavour 60 (☎238.2043). Pleasant one-star, but a favourite with school parties, so often fully booked. ④.

Rudy, Via San Gallo 51 (☎475.519). Somewhat quieter than the hotels on the parallel Via Cavour; 1am curfew. ④.

Savonarola, Via Matteotti 27 (☎587.824). Dependable one-star, at the limit of comfortable walking distance from the centre. ④.

Splendor, Via San Gallo 30 (☎483.427). Located in an old palazzo, this peaceful two-star is a good deal if you can get out of the exorbitant breakfast. ⑥.

Veneto, Via Santa Reparata 33 (☎294.816). Comfortable two-star, but again popular for school outings. ⑦.

THE CENTRAL AREA

Alessandra, Borgo Santi Apostoli 17 (☎283.438). Occupying a sixteenth-century palazzo and furnished in a peculiar mixture of antique and modern styles, this two-star is frequented by the fashion-show crowd, so booking is essential in September. ⑥.

Bavaria, Borgo Albizi 26 (☎234.0313). Excellent one-star installed in a sixteenth-century palazzo, with appropriate decor. ④.

Brunori, Via del Proconsolo 5 (☎289.648). Noisy and slightly run-down, but with friendly and informative owners; no single rooms. ④.

Davanzati, Via Porta Rossa 15 (☎283.414). Situated between Via Tornabuoni and Piazza della Signoria, so right in the thick of things; very good value and friendly. ④.

Zurigo, Via dell'Oriolo 17 (☎234.0644). Ordinary but clean and cheap, and just a minute or so from the Duomo. ④.

SOUTH OF THE RIVER

Bandini, Piazza Santo Spirito 9 (☎215.308). Vast rooms, gorgeous decor and great views from the top-deck loggia make this one of Florence's most attractive one-star options; no single rooms. ④.

La Scaletta, Via Guicciardini 13 (☎283.028). From the rooftop terraces you look across the Bóboli gardens in one direction and the city in the other; well worth the slightly higher outlay. ⑥.

Hostels

Florence's two official youth hostels are supplemented by a number of institutions, most of them run by religious bodies, which have sprung up in the city to provide beds for non-native students at the city's university. Out of term time – between June and October – some of these places are open to young tourists, and a couple have a few rooms to spare even during the terms. In addition to the houses listed below, there are a number of *Case dello Studente*, which are run by the university authorities and occasionally made available to visitors; for information on these, ask at the tourist office.

Istituto Gould, Via dei Serragli 49 (☎212.576). Over in Oltrarno, past Ponte alla Carrara. Reception is on the second floor, open Mon–Fri 9am–1pm & 3–7pm, all through the year. Recently renovated, the *Gould* is extremely popular, so it's wise to book in advance. ②.

Ostello Villa Camerata, Viale Righi 2 (☎610.300). A 30-min journey on the #17b bus from the train station. Tucked away in a beautiful park, the Villa Camerata is a sixteenth-century house with frescoed ceilings and a wide loggia. Doors open at 2.30pm, and if you can't be there by then, ring ahead to make sure there's a place left. If you don't have an *IYHF* card, you can buy a special guest card that's also valid in other hostels. Films in English every night; curfew at midnight. Breakfast and sheets included; optional supper at L8000; no kitchen facilities. ①.

Pio X – Artigianelli, Via dei Serragli 106 (☎225.044). Probably the cheapest option in town. Don't be put off by the huge picture of Pope Pius X at the top of the steps – the management is friendly and the atmosphere relaxed. It's open all day throughout the year, but whatever the time of year it's best to get there by 9am, as the 35 beds soon get taken. Double, triple and quadruple rooms. ①.

Santa Monaca, Via Santa Monaca 6 (☎268.338). In Oltrarno, near the *Istituto Gould*. Privately owned, so no *IYHF* card needed; open for reservations 8–9.30am and after 4pm. Kitchen facilities, free hot showers, and no maximum length of stay. Midnight curfew. Very popular. ①.

Suore Oblate dell'Assunzione, Via Borgo Pinti 15 (☎248.0582). Not far from the Duomo. Run by nuns but open to men and women, from mid-June to the end of July and throughout September (although 4–5 beds are available all year round). Midnight curfew; no breakfast. ②.

Suore Oblate dello Spirito Santo, Via Nazionale 8 (☎298.202). A few steps from the station. Run by nuns, but open to women and married couples from mid-June to October. Very clean and pleasant; beds arranged in single, double and triple rooms; midnight curfew. ②.

Campsites

Italiani e Stranieri, Viale Michelangelo 80 (☎681.1977). Open from April to October, this site is always crowded, owing to its superb hillside location. The best way to get there is by taking the #13 bus from the train station. 480 places; kitchen facilities.

Panoramico, Via Peramonda, outside Fiesole (☎599.069). Beautiful situation on a hill to the north of the city, but involves taking #7 to Fiesole and then another bus out to the site.

Villa Camerata, Viale Righi 2–4 (☎610.300). Basic site, open all year in the hostel grounds. 60 places.

FREE CAMPING

Every summer the city authorities open an *Area di Sosta*, an emergency accommodation area that usually amounts to a patch of ground sheltered by a rudimentary roof. Staying there is free, and showers are available for a small charge. At the moment the *Area di Sosta* is at the **Villa Favard**, in Via Rocca Tedalda (☎690.022), reached by the #14 or #62 bus.

The City

Greater Florence now spreads several kilometres down the Arno Valley and onto the hills north and south of the city, but the major sights are contained within an area that can be crossed on foot in little over half an hour. A short walk from the train station brings you to the **Baptistery** and **Duomo**; the area from here to **Piazza della Signoria** – site of the **Palazzo Vecchio** and the **Uffizi** – is the inner core, the area into which most of the tourists are packed. A circle drawn so that the Duomo and Uffizi stood on opposite sides of its circumference would gather in the best-preserved of Florence's medieval streets and the majority of its fashionable streets.

Immediately north of the Duomo is the **San Lorenzo** quarter, where market stalls surround one of the city's first-rank churches; within a short radius from here are the monastery of **San Marco**, with its paintings by Fra' Angelico, the **Accademia**, home of Michelangelo's *David*, and **Piazza Santissima Annunziata**, Florence's most attractive square.

The Uffizi backs onto the Arno River, over which lies the district known as **Oltrarno**, where the **Palazzo Pitti** exerts the strongest pull, followed by the churches of **Santo Spirito** and the hilltop **San Miniato al Monte**.

Close to the eastern side of Piazza del Duomo stands the **Bargello**, the main museum of sculpture; further eastwards, the area around the Franciscan church of **Santa Croce** forms a nucleus of activity. On the western side of the city, directly opposite the train station, the unmissable attraction is **Santa Maria Novella**, Florentine base of the rival Dominican order.

Piazza del Duomo

From Santa Maria Novella station, most visitors gravitate towards Piazza del Duomo, following the flow of traffic and beckoned by the pinnacle of Brunelleschi's dome, which dominates the landscape in a way unmatched by any architectural creation in any other Italian city. Yet even though the magnitude of the Duomo is apparent from a distance, the first full sight of the church and the adjacent Baptistery still comes as something of a jolt, the colours of their patterned exteriors making a startling contrast with the dun-coloured buildings around.

The Duomo (Santa Maria del Fiore)

It was some time in the seventh century when the seat of the Bishop of Florence was transferred from San Lorenzo to the ancient church which stood on the site of **Santa Maria del Fiore**, the **Duomo** of Florence. Later generations transformed that building until, in the thirteenth century, it was decided that a new cathedral was required, to reflect more accurately the wealth of the city and to put the Pisans and Sienese in their place. **Arnolfo di Cambio**, entrusted with the project in 1294, designed a massive vaulted basilica focused on a domed tribune embraced by three polygonal tribunes. Work ground to a halt immediately after his death eight years later, then was resumed under a succession of architects, each of whom roughly followed Arnolfo's plan. By 1418 the nave was finished, the tribunes were complete, and a drum was in place to bear the weight of the dome which Arnolfo had envisaged as the church's crown. The conception was magnificent: the dome was to span a distance of nearly 140 feet and rise from a base some 180 feet above the floor of the nave. It was to be the largest dome ever constructed – but nobody had yet worked out how to build the thing.

A committee of the masons' guild was set up to ponder the problem, and it was to them that **Filippo Brunelleschi** presented himself. His arrogant insistence that only he could possibly redeem the situation, and his refusal to say much more about his solution other than that he could build the dome without using scaffolding, did little to endear him to his prospective patrons. In the end, however, they relented, and Brunelleschi was given the commission on condition that he work jointly with Lorenzo Ghiberti – a partnership which did not last long, though Ghiberti's contribution to the project was probably more significant than his colleague ever admitted. On March 25, 1436 – Annunciation Day, and the Florentine New Year – the **completion of the dome** was marked by the consecration of the cathedral, a ceremony conducted by the pope. Yet the topmost piece of the dome – the lantern – was still not in place, and many were sceptical about the structure's capability to bear the weight. Other architects were consulted, but Brunelleschi again won the day; the lantern was completed in the late 1460s, when the gold ball and cross, cast by Verrocchio, was hoisted into place.

The overblown and pernickety main **facade** is a nineteenth-century imitation of a Gothic front, its marble cladding quarried from the same sources as the first builders used – white stone from Carrara, red from Maremma, green from Prato. The south side is the oldest part of the exterior, but the most attractive adornment is the *Porta della Mandorla*, on the other side. It takes its name from the oval frame (or *mandorla*) that contains the relief of *The Assumption of the Virgin*, sculpted by Nanni di Banco around 1420.

THE INTERIOR

The Duomo's interior (daily 10am–5pm) is the converse of the exterior, a vast enclosure of bare masonry. The fourth largest church in the world, it once held a congregation of 10,000 to hear Savonarola preach. The ambience is more that of a public assembly hall than of a devotional building, and it's not surprising to find that the most conspicuous pieces of painted decoration in the main body of the church are two memorials to *condottieri* on the wall of the north aisle – Uccello's **monument to Sir John Hawkwood**, painted in 1436, and Castagno's **monument to Niccolò da Tolentino**, created twenty years later. Just beyond them, Domenico do Michelino's *Dante Explaining the Divine Comedy*, painted in 1465, gives the recently completed dome a place only marginally less prominent than the mountain of Purgatory.

Judged by mere size, the major work of art in the Duomo is the fresco of *The Last Judgement* that lurks behind the restorers' planks and netting now covering the inside of the dome. A substantial number of Florentines are of the opinion that Vasari and Zuccari's effort does nothing but deface Brunelleschi's masterpiece, and want the paint stripped away. Below the fresco are seven stained-glass roundels designed by Uccello, Ghiberti, Castagno and Donatello; they are best inspected from the gallery immediately below them, which forms part of the route to the summit of the **dome** (Mon–Sat 10am–5pm; L4000). The gallery is the queasiest part of the climb, most of which winds between the brick walls of the outer and inner shells of the dome.

When you come back down to earth, be sure to take a look at the entrances to the two **sacristies**, on each side of the altar. The enamelled terracotta reliefs over the doorways are by Luca della Robbia, who also cast the doors of the north sacristy – his only works in bronze. After his brother Giuliano had been mortally stabbed on the altar steps by the Pazzi conspirators, Lorenzo de'Medici took refuge in the north sacristy, the bulk of the new doors protecting him from his would-be assassins.

In the 1960s remnants of the Duomo's predecessor, the church of **Santa Reparata**, were uncovered underneath the west end of the nave. Subsequent excavations have revealed a complicated jigsaw of Roman, palaeo-Christian and Romanesque remains, plus areas of mosaic and patches of fourteenth-century frescoes (daily 10am–5pm; L2000). The explanatory diagrams tend to intensify the confusion – to make sense of it all, refer to the detailed model standing in the further recesses of the crypt. Also discovered in the course of the dig was the **tomb of Brunelleschi**, the only Florentine ever honoured with burial inside the Duomo – his tombstone can be seen through a grille to the left of the foot of the stairs.

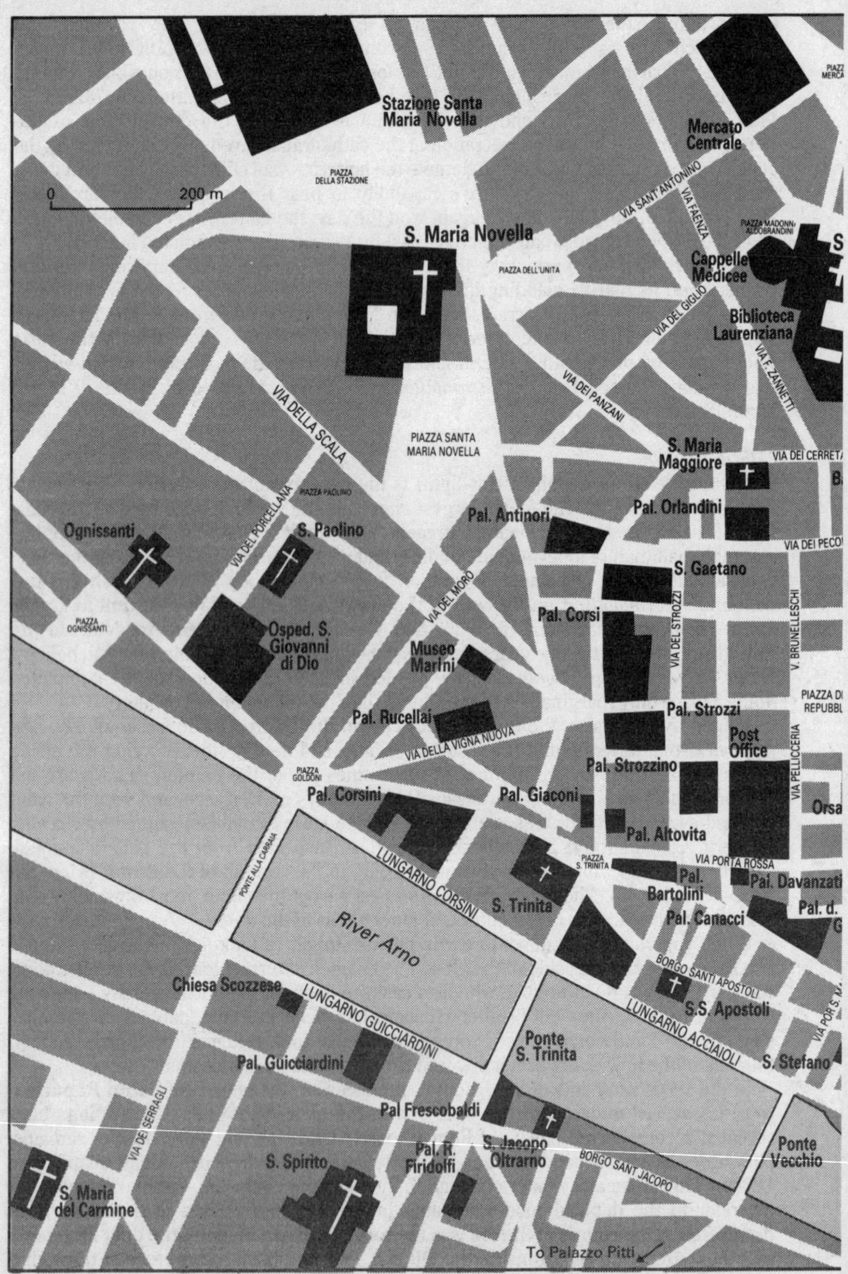
Stazione Santa Maria Novella
Mercato Centrale
PIAZZA DELLA STAZIONE
0
200 m
VIA SANT'ANTONINO
VIA FAENZA
PIAZZA MADONNA ALDOBRANDINI
S. Maria Novella
PIAZZA DELL'UNITA
Cappelle Medicee
VIA DEL GIGLIO
Biblioteca Laurenziana
VIA F. ZANNETTI
VIA DEI PANZANI
VIA DELLA SCALA
PIAZZA SANTA MARIA NOVELLA
S. Maria Maggiore
VIA DEI CERRETANI
PIAZZA PAOLINO
VIA DEL PORCELLANA
Pal. Antinori
Pal. Orlandini
Ognissanti
S. Paolino
VIA DEI PECORI
S. Gaetano
VIA DEL MORO
PIAZZA OGNISSANTI
Pal. Corsi
VIA DEL STROZZI
V. BRUNELLESCHI
Osped. S. Giovanni di Dio
Museo Marini
Pal. Strozzi
Pal. Rucellai
VIA DELLA VIGNA NUOVA
Post Office
VIA PELLICCERIA
PIAZZA GOLDONI
Pal. Strozzino
Pal. Corsini
Pal. Giaconi
Pal. Altovita
PONTE ALLA CARRAIA
LUNGARNO CORSINI
PIAZZA S. TRINITA
VIA PORTA ROSSA
Pal. Bartolini
Pal. Davanzati
S. Trinita
Pal. Canacci
River Arno
BORGO SANTI APOSTOLI
Chiesa Scozzese
LUNGARNO GUICCIARDINI
S.S. Apostoli
LUNGARNO ACCIAIOLI
Ponte S. Trinita
Pal. Guicciardini
S. Stefano
Pal Frescobaldi
VIA DEI SERRAGLI
Pal. R. Firidolfi
S. Jacopo Oltrarno
BORGO SANT JACOPO
Ponte Vecchio
S. Spirito
S. Maria del Carmine
To Palazzo Pitti

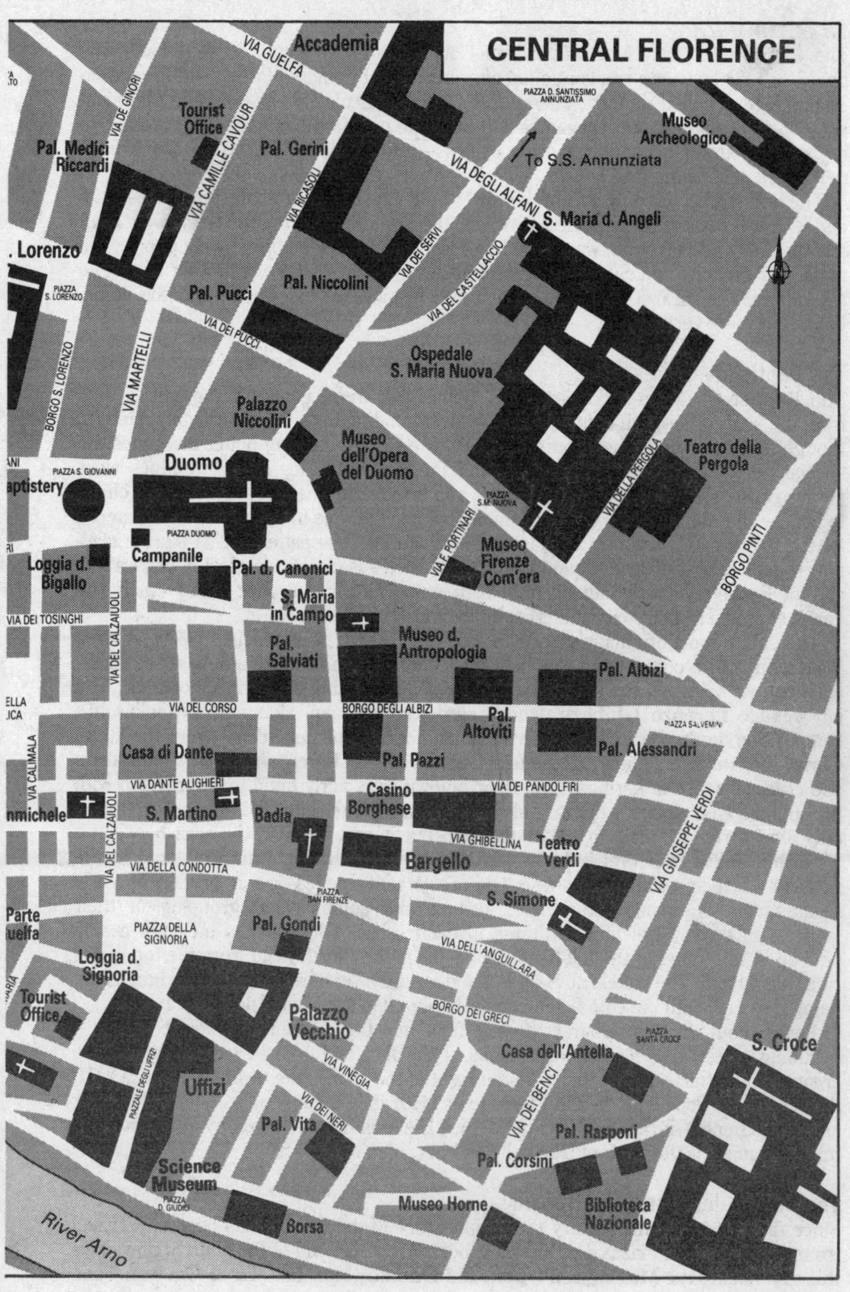
CENTRAL FLORENCE
Accademia
VIA GUELFA
PIAZZA D. SANTISSIMO ANNUNZIATA
Museo Archeologico
To S.S. Annunziata
VIA DE GINORI
Tourist Office
VIA CAMILLE CAVOUR
Pal. Gerini
Pal. Medici Riccardi
VIA RICASOLI
VIA DEGLI ALFANI
S. Maria d. Angeli
. Lorenzo
VIA DEI SERVI
VIA DEL CASTELLACCIO
PIAZZA S. LORENZO
Pal. Pucci
Pal. Niccolini
VIA DEI PUCCI
BORGO S. LORENZO
VIA MARTELLI
Ospedale S. Maria Nuova
Palazzo Niccolini
Museo dell'Opera del Duomo
Teatro della Pergola
VIA DELLA PERGOLA
Duomo
PIAZZA S. GIOVANNI
aptistery
PIAZZA S.M. NUOVA
PIAZZA DUOMO
Campanile
Loggia d. Bigallo
Pal. d. Canonici
VIA F. PORTINARI
Museo Firenze Com'era
BORGO PINTI
S. Maria in Campo
VIA DEI TOSINGHI
VIA DEL CALZAIUOLI
Museo d. Antropologia
Pal. Salviati
Pal. Albizi
VIA DEL CORSO
BORGO DEGLI ALBIZI
Pal. Altoviti
PIAZZA SALVEMINI
VIA CALIMALA
Casa di Dante
Pal. Pazzi
Pal. Alessandri
VIA DANTE ALIGHIERI
VIA DEI PANDOLFINI
Casino Borghese
nmichele
S. Martino
Badia
VIA GIUSEPPE VERDI
VIA GHIBELLINA
Teatro Verdi
Bargello
VIA DELLA CONDOTTA
PIAZZA SAN FIRENZE
S. Simone
Parte uelfa
PIAZZA DELLA SIGNORIA
Pal. Gondi
VIA DELL'ANGUILLARA
Loggia d. Signoria
Tourist Office
BORGO DEI GRECI
Palazzo Vecchio
PIAZZA SANTA CROCE
S. Croce
Casa dell'Antella
VIA VINEGIA
PIAZZALE DEGLI UFFIZI
Uffizi
VIA DEI NERI
VIA DEI BENCI
Pal. Vita
Pal. Rasponi
Pal. Corsini
Science Museum
PIAZZA D. GIUDICI
Museo Horne
Biblioteca Nazionale
Borsa
River Arno

THE CAMPANILE

The **Campanile** (daily March–Oct 9am–7.30pm; Nov–Feb 9am–5.30pm; L4000) was begun in 1334 by Giotto and continued after his death by Andrea Pisano and Francesco Talenti, who rectified the deficiencies of the artist's calculations by doubling the thickness of the walls. Erosion caused by atmospheric pollution has made it necessary to replace the tower's sculptures with copies – the originals are all in the Museo dell'Opera del Duomo (see below).

The first storey, the only part of the tower built exactly as Giotto designed it, is studded with two rows of remarkable bas-reliefs; the lower, illustrating the *Creation of Man* and the *Arts and Industries*, was carved by Pisano himself, the upper by his pupils. The figures of *Prophets* and *Sibyls* in the second-storey niches were created by Donatello and others. The parapet at the top of the tower is a less lofty viewpoint than the dome, but rather more vertiginous.

The Baptistery

The **Baptistery** (Mon–Sat 1–6pm, Sun 10am–6pm; free), generally thought to date from the sixth or seventh century, is the oldest building in the city. Strangely enough, though its origins lie in the depths of the Dark Ages, no building better illustrates the special relationship between Florence and the Roman world. The Florentines were always conscious of their Roman ancestry, and throughout the Middle Ages they chose to believe that the Baptistery was originally a Roman temple to Mars, a belief bolstered by the interior's inclusion of Roman granite columns. The pattern of its marble cladding – applied in the eleventh and twelfth centuries – is clearly classical in inspiration, and the Baptistery's most famous embellishments – its gilded bronze **doors** – mark the emergence of a self-conscious interest in the art of the ancient world.

The south door, originally placed to face the Duomo, was cast in 1336 by Andrea Pisano. In 1401 a competition was held for a commission to make a new set of doors, each entrant being set the task of creating a panel depicting the sacrifice of Isaac. The job went to **Lorenzo Ghiberti**, whose entry can be seen, alongside Brunelleschi's composition, in the Bargello. Ghiberti's north doors, depicting scenes from the life of Christ, the four Evangelists and the four Doctors of the Church, show a new naturalism and classical sense of harmony, but their innovation is fairly timid in comparison with the sublime **east doors**, which are always known as "The Gates of Paradise" – supposedly after a remark made by Michelangelo, but in fact because the area between a baptistery and a cathedral is known in Italy as the *paradiso*. Unprecedented in the subtlety of their modelling, these Old Testament scenes are a primer of early Renaissance art, using perspective, gesture and sophisticated grouping of their subjects to convey the human drama of each scene. Ghiberti has included a self-portrait in the frame of the left-hand door – his is the fourth head from the top of the right-hand band. The panels now set in the door are a set of replicas – the originals are being restored, with the completed panels displayed in the Museo dell'Opera.

Inside, both the semi-abstract mosaic floor and the magnificent mosaic ceiling – including a fearsome platoon of demons at the feet of Christ in judgement – were created in the thirteenth century. To the right of the altar is the **tomb of John XXIII**, the schismatic pope who died in Florence in 1419 while a guest of his financial adviser and close friend, Giovanni di Bicci de'Medici. His monument, draped by an illusionistic marble canopy, is the work of Donatello and his pupil Michelozzo.

The Museo dell'Opera del Duomo

Since the early fifteenth century the maintenance of the Duomo has been supervised from the building at Piazza del Duomo 9, behind the east end of the church; nowadays this also houses the **Museo dell'Opera del Duomo** (Mon–Sat March–Oct 9am–8pm;

Nov–Feb 9am–6pm; L4000), the repository of the most precious and fragile works of art from the Duomo, Baptistery and Campanile. As an overview of the sculpture of Florence it's second only to the Bargello, and is far easier to take in on a single visit.

The most arresting works in the first room are a series of sculptures by **Arnolfo di Cambio**, including a glassy-eyed *Madonna*; they were rescued from Arnolfo's unfinished facade for the Duomo, which was pulled down in the sixteenth century. Adjoining rooms are dedicated to Brunelleschi, displaying his death mask, models of the dome and a variety of tools and machines devised by the architect. At the other end of the main room, steps lead up to a display of models of suggested facades for the Duomo, and an assembly of reliquaries that can boast the jaw of Saint Jerome and the index finger of John the Baptist.

On the mezzanine level is **Michelangelo**'s anguished and angular *Pietà*, one of his last works, and intended for his own tomb – Vasari records that the face of Nicodemus is a self-portrait. Dissatisfied with the quality of the marble, Michelangelo mutilated the group by hammering off the left leg and arm of Christ; his pupil Tiberio Calcagni restored the arm, then finished off the figure of the Magdalen, turning her into a whey-faced supporting player.

Although he's represented on the lower floor as well, it's upstairs that **Donatello**, the greatest of Michelangelo's forerunners, really comes to the fore. Of the figures he carved for the Campanile, the most powerful is that of the prophet *Habbakuk*, the intensity of whose gaze prompted the sculptor to seize it and yell "Speak, speak!" Opposite poles of Donatello's temperament are represented by the haggard wooden figure of Mary Magdalen and his ornate *cantoria* (choir-loft) from the Duomo, with its playground of dancing *putti*. Opposite this is the *cantoria* created at the same time by **Luca della Robbia**, the original panels of which are displayed below the reconstructed loft; the groups of earnest young musicians embody the text from Psalm 33 inscribed on the frame: "Praise the Lord with harp. Sing unto Him with the psaltery and an instrument of ten strings."

Pisano's bas-reliefs from the Campanile are on show in one of the two adjoining rooms, while the other contains **Ghiberti**'s panels from the "Doors of Paradise" and a dazzling silver-gilt altar from the Baptistery, completed in 1480, more than a century after it was begun.

From the Duomo to the Signoria

Unless you want to construct a serpentine back-alley route, getting from Piazza del Duomo to Piazza della Signoria comes down to a choice between two streets: **Via del Proconsolo**, which leads from the eastern side of the Duomo, or **Via dei Calzaiuoli**, from the Campanile. Even the shortest stay in Florence should find time for a stroll along both, but the initial choice depends on whether it's the art you're after – in which case the former gets the nod – or the street life.

The Bargello

To get a comprehensive idea of the Renaissance achievement in Florence, two museum calls are essential: one to the Uffizi and one to the **Museo Nazionale del Bargello** (Tues–Sat 9am–2pm, Sun 9am–1pm; L6000), installed in the daunting Palazzo del Bargello, round the back of the Palazzo Vecchio on Via del Proconsolo. Nowhere else in Italy is there so full a collection of sculpture from the period, and yet the Bargello is normally uncrowded, the majority of sightseers passing it over in favour of the Accademia up the road.

The palace was built in 1255, immediately after the overthrow of the aristocratic regime, and soon became the seat of the *Podestà*, the chief magistrate. Numerous malefactors were tried, sentenced and executed here – Leonardo da Vinci stood in the street outside to make a drawing of the corpse of one of the Pazzi Conspirators, hung from the windows as an example to all traitors. The building acquired its present name in the sixteenth century, when the chief of police (the *Bargello*) was based here.

THE COLLECTION

The first part of the principal ground-floor room focuses on **Michelangelo**, within whose shadow every Florentine sculptor of the sixteenth century laboured. His first major sculpture, the lurching figure of *Bacchus*, was carved at the age of 22, seven years before his graceful *Pitti Tondo*. The bust of *Brutus* (1540), Michelangelo's sole work in the genre, is a celebration of republican virtue, made soon after the murder of the tyrannical Duke Alessandro de'Medici. Works by Michelangelo's followers and contemporaries are ranged in the immediate vicinity, most of them miniature copies of the master's creations.

The shallower and more flamboyant art of **Cellini** and **Giambologna** is exhibited in the farther section of the hall. In an arc round the preparatory model of Cellini's *Perseus* are displayed the original relief panel and four statuettes from the statue's pedestal; the huge *Bust of Cosimo I*, Cellini's first work in bronze, was a sort of technical trial for the casting of the *Perseus*. Close by Giambologna's voluptuous *Florence Defeating Pisa* – a disingenuous pretext if ever there were one – is his best-known creation, the *Mercury*, a nimble figure with no bad angles. Comic relief is provided by the reliably awful **Bandinelli**'s *Adam and Eve*, looking like a grandee and his wife taking an *au naturel* stroll through their estate.

Part two of the sculpture collection is on the other side of the Gothic courtyard, which is plastered with the coats of arms of the Podestà and contains, among many other pieces, six allegorical figures by **Ammannati** from the fountain of the Palazzo Pitti courtyard. If you're in a hurry, the motley array of fourteenth-century pieces and the adjacent collection of seals and other paraphernalia are the sections to skip.

At the top of the courtyard staircase, the first-floor loggia has been turned into an aviary for Giambologna's bronze birds, imported from the Medici villa at Castello. The nearer doorway opens into the fourteenth-century Salone del Consiglio Generale, where the presiding genius is **Donatello**. Vestiges of the Gothic manner are evident in the drapery of his marble *David* (1408), but a new emphasis on the dignity of the human spirit is embodied in the tense figure of *St George*, carved just eight years later for the tabernacle of the armourers' guild at Orsanmichele. His sexually ambiguous bronze *David*, the first freestanding nude figure since classical times, was cast in the early 1430s; the strange jubilant figure known as *Amor Atys* dates from the end of that decade.

The less complex humanism of **Luca della Robbia** is embodied in the glazed terracotta Madonnas set round the walls, while Donatello's master, **Ghiberti**, is represented by his relief of *The Sacrifice of Isaac*, his successful entry in the competition for the Baptistery doors. The treatment of the theme submitted by Brunelleschi is hung close by. Most of this floor is occupied by a collection of European and Islamic applied art, of so high a standard that it would constitute an engrossing museum in its own right; the Byzantine and medieval ivories are especially fascinating.

The sculptural display resumes upstairs with more works from the della Robbia family, in the frequently closed rooms 14 and 15. From the first of these there's access to the spectacular **armoury**; adjoining the latter is the **Sala dei Bronzetti**, Italy's best assembly of small Renaissance bronzes – with plentiful evidence of Giambologna's virtuosity at table-top scale. Lastly, room 15 is devoted mainly to Renaissance portrait busts, including **Mino da Fiesole**'s busts of Giovanni de'Medici and Piero il Gottoso (the sons of Cosimo il Vecchio), **Francesco Laurana**'s *Battista Sforza* (an interesting comparison with the della Francesca portrait in the Uffizi), and the *Woman Holding Flowers* by

Verrocchio. The centre of the room is occupied by Verrocchio's *David*, clearly influenced by Donatello's treatment of the subject, and a small bronze group of *Hercules and Antaeus* by **Antonio Pollaiuolo**, possessing a power out of all proportion to its size.

The Badìa

Across the road from the Bargello is the main entrance to the huge **Badìa Fiorentina** (daily 9am–noon & 4–6pm), which was founded late in the tenth century by Willa, widow of the Margrave of Tuscany. In the 1280s the church was overhauled, probably under the direction of Arnolfo di Cambio, architect of the Duomo and Palazzo Vecchio; later work has smothered much of the old church, but the narrow **campanile** – Romanesque at its base, Gothic higher up – has come through intact. Inside, the church itself is unremarkable save for Filippino Lippi's *Madonna and St Bernard*, immediately on the left as you enter, and the monument to Willa's son Ugo, carved in the 1470s by Mino da Fiesole, on the wall of the left transept. However, a staircase leads from the choir to the upper storey of the **Chiostro degli Aranci** (Orange Cloister – from the fruit trees that used to be grown here), brightened by a fifteenth-century fresco cycle of the life of Saint Benedict.

Along Via dei Calzaiuoli

Via dei Calzaiuoli, connecting the west edge of the Piazza della Signoria with Piazza del Duomo, is the cat-walk for the Florentine *passeggiata*. In the daytime its jewellery shops and boutiques trawl in lire by the million, while after dark it becomes a platform for palmists, tarot-readers and dreadful mime artists, who are generally overlooked by the police. The same can't be said for the mainly Senegalese street traders who used to flog their counterfeit Louis Vuitton bags and Lacoste polo shirts here. Italy has long prided itself on being a non-racist society, but the increasing numbers of impoverished Africans on Florence's streets has given this self-image its first real test. Attacks from right-wing thugs and hassle from the law has shifted the nocturnal market towards the Ponte Vecchio and the Mercato Nuovo, from where it will doubtless be displaced before too long..

Halfway down the street is the opening into **Piazza della Repubblica**, created in the last century in an attempt to give Florence the sort of grand public square that is a prerequisite for any capital city. It's an utterly characterless place, impressive solely for its size, and its four large and once-fashionable cafés – *Donnini*, *Giubbe Rosse*, *Gilli* and *Paszkowski* – similarly lack the charisma to which they aspire.

ORSANMICHELE

Several of the Bargello's exhibits were removed from Via dei Calzaiuoli's dominant building, the church of **Orsanmichele** (daily 8am–noon & 3–6.30pm), which stands foursquare as a military tower one block to the north of the Signoria. From the ninth century until the thirteenth the church of *San Michele ad hortum* stood here – hence *Orsanmichele*. Towards the end of that century a grain market was raised on the site, which was in turn replaced, after a fire in 1304, with a vast loggia that served as an oratory and a trade hall for the *Arti Maggiori*, the Great Guilds which then governed the city. In 1380 the loggia was walled in and dedicated exclusively to religious functions, while two upper storeys were added for use as emergency grain stores. Not long after, each guild was charged with decorating one of the exterior tabernacles of the building, a scheme which spanned the emergent years of the Renaissance.

At present a full restoration is in progress, so it's unlikely that all the **exterior sculpture** will be visible, but some of the major pieces – or replicas of them – should be in their rightful places. Outstanding are the following: on the east side (Via dei Calzaiuoli) – *John the Baptist* by Ghiberti, the first life-size bronze statue of the Renaissance, and *The Incredulity of St Thomas* by Verrocchio; on the north side – the *Four Crowned*

Saints by Nanni di Banco (they were four Christian sculptors executed by Diocletian for refusing to make a pagan image), and a copy of Donatello's *St George*; on the west side – *St Matthew* and *St Stephen* by Ghiberti and *St Eligius* by Nanni di Banco; on the south side – a *Madonna and Child*, probably by Giovanni Tedesco.

To get into the square nave of the church it's necessary to circumnavigate the interior's main feature, the vast **tabernacle** by **Orcagna**; carved with delicate reliefs and tiny statues, and studded with coloured marble and glass, this is the only significant sculptural work by the artist. It frames a *Madonna* painted in 1347 by **Bernardo Daddi** as a replacement for a miraculous image of the Virgin that was destroyed by the 1304 fire, and whose powers this picture is said to have inherited. The vaulted halls of the upstairs granary – one of the city's most imposing medieval interiors – are entered via a footbridge from the Palazzo dell'Arte della Lana (Wool Guild); as a rule, they are only accessible when in use as an exhibition space.

Piazza della Signoria

Even though it sets the stage for the Palazzo Vecchio and the Uffizi, Florence's main civic square – the **Piazza della Signoria** – doesn't quite live up to its role. Too many of the buildings round its edge are bland nineteenth-century efforts, now occupied by banks, and the surface of the square resembles the deck of an aircraft carrier. It looked better before the 1970s, when it was decided to restore the piazza's ancient paving stones. When the company in charge of cleaning the slabs returned the first batch, it was found that they had sandblasted chunks off them, rather than rinsing them carefully in the prescribed manner, and then some of the stones turned up in the yard of a builders' merchant and on the front drives of a few Tuscan villas. The subsequent scandal has brought corruption charges against contractors and politicians, and it's now proposed that the square be repaved with nicely weathered items, or that the new ones be hammered into a pseudo-antiquated state.

What little charm the Piazza della Signoria does possess comes from its peculiar array of statuary, a miscellany that embodies the city's political volatility. The line-up starts with Giambologna's equestrian statue of Cosimo I and continues with Ammannati's fatuous *Neptune Fountain*, and copies of Donatello's *Marzocco* (the city's heraldic lion), his *Judith and Holofernes* and Michelangelo's *David* (both originally installed here as declarations of republican solidarity). Providing a lumpen conclusion is Bandinelli's *Hercules and Cacus*, a personal emblem of Cosimo I.

The square's grace-note, the **Loggia della Signoria**, was built in the late fourteenth century as a dais for city officials during ceremonies; only in the late eighteenth century did it become a showcase for some of the city's more melodramatic sculpture. In the corner nearest the Palazzo Vecchio stands a figure that has become one of the iconic images of the Renaissance, Benvenuto Cellini's *Perseus*. The traumatic process of its casting is vividly described in Cellini's riproaring autobiography – the project seemed doomed when the molten bronze began to solidify too early, but the ever-resourceful hero saved the day by flinging all his pewter plates into the mixture. Equally attention-seeking is Giambologna's last work, *The Rape of the Sabine*, epitome of the Mannerist obsession with spiralling forms.

The Palazzo Vecchio

Florence's fortress-like town hall, the **Palazzo Vecchio** (Mon–Fri 9am–7pm, Sun 8am–1pm; L8000; last ticket 1hr before closing), was begun in the last year of the thirteenth century as the home of the *Signoria*, the highest tier of the city's republican government. Local folklore has it that the misshapen plan was not devised by the first architect (thought to be Arnolfo di Cambio), but is rather due to the fact that the Guelph government refused to encroach on land previously owned by the hated Ghibellines.

Changes in the Florentine constitution entailed alterations to the layout of the palace, the most radical overhaul coming in 1540, when Cosimo I – recently installed as Duke of Florence – moved his retinue here from the Palazzo Medici. The **Medici** were only in residence for nine years – they moved to the Palazzo Pitti, largely at the insistence of Cosimo's wife, Eleanor of Toledo – but the enlargement and refurbishment instigated by Cosimo continued throughout the period of his rule. Much of the decoration of the state rooms comprises a relentless eulogy of Cosimo and his clan, but in amongst the propaganda are some excellent works of art, including some seminal examples of Mannerism, Cosimo I's court style.

THE INTERIOR
Giorgio Vasari, court architect from 1555 until his death in 1574, was responsible for much of the sycophantic decor in the state apartments. His limited talents were given full rein in the huge **Salone dei Cinquento**, built at the end of the fifteenth century as the assembly hall for the Great Council of the penultimate republic. The production-line heroic murals, painted either by Vasari or under his direction, were executed after the failure of one of Italy's most remarkable decorative projects. Leonardo da Vinci and Michelangelo were employed to paint frescoes on opposite sides of the room; Leonardo's work was abandoned after his experimental technique went wrong, and Michelangelo's project existed only on paper when he was summoned to Rome by Pope Julius II. Michelangelo's *Victory*, facing the entrance door, was sculpted for Julius' tomb, but was donated to the Medici by the artist's nephew; Vasari installed it here to mark Cosimo's defeat of the Sienese.

A door to the right of the entrance to the hall, at the far end, opens onto the bizarre **Studiolo di Francesco I**. Created by Vasari in the 1570s and decorated by several of Florence's prominent Mannerist artists, this windowless cell was created as a retreat for the introverted son of Cosimo and Eleanor. Each of the miniature bronzes and nearly all the paintings reflect Francesco's interest in the sciences and alchemy: the entrance wall (which visitors, allowed no further than the entrance steps, can't actually see) illustrates the theme of "Earth" while the others, reading clockwise, signify "Water", "Air" and "Fire". The outstanding paintings are the two which don't fit the scheme – Bronzino's glacial portraits of the occupant's parents. (The one of Cosimo, over the door, is impossible to see.)

Bronzino's major contribution to the palace can be seen on the floor above, where Eleanor's tiny **chapel** was entirely painted by him in the 1540s. A Mannerist contemporary of Bronzino, Cecchino Salviati, produced what is widely held to be his masterpiece with the fresco cycle in the **Sala d'Udienza**, once the audience chamber of the Republic; the room also has a richly gilded ceiling by Giuliano da Maiano and assistants, and a magnificent inlaid doorway by Giuliano and his brother Benedetto, a partnership responsible for the ceiling of the adjoining **Sala dei Gigli**. Named after the lilies which adorn the room (the city's symbol), this hall was fitted out in the decade after 1475, and features frescoes by Domenico Ghirlandaio. The focus of the room now, however, is Donatello's restored *Judith and Holofernes*. Commissioned by Cosimo il Vecchio, the group originally served as a fountain in the Palazzo Medici, but was removed to the Piazza della Signoria after the expulsion of the Medici in 1494, and there displayed as a mark of vanquished tyranny.

The Uffizi

In 1560 Cosimo I asked Vasari to design a block of government offices to stand on a site then occupied by houses and a church between the Palazzo Vecchio and the river. After Vasari's death, work on the elongated U-shaped building was continued by Buontalenti, who was asked by Francesco I to glaze the upper storey so that it could house his art collection. Each of the succeeding Medici added to the family's trove of art treasures, and the accumulated collection was preserved for public inspection by the last member of the family, Anna Maria Lodovica, whose will specified that it should be left to the people of Florence and never be allowed to leave the city. Last century a large proportion of the sculpture was transferred to the Bargello, while many of the antiquities went to the Museo Archeologico, leaving the **Galleria degli Uffizi** (Tues–Sat 9am–7pm, Sun 9am–1pm; L10,000) as essentially a gallery of paintings.

In the case of the Uffizi, superlatives are simply the bare truth – this is the greatest picture gallery in Italy. So many masterpieces are collected here that it's barely possible to skate over the surface in a single visit; it makes sense to limit an initial tour to the first fifteen rooms, where the Florentine Renaissance works are concentrated, leaving the rest for another time. Only two factors impair the pleasure of the Uffizi: the lousy display of some of the paintings, and, of course, the crowds. There's little you can do about the first, but the second problem is easily overcome – be there when the doors open, or go for the last two hours.

FROM CIMABUE TO BOTTICELLI

There are scarcely any dull stretches in the Uffizi. The picture galleries are ranged on the third floor, but some remarkable exhibits are displayed on the ground floor, in rooms that once formed part of the eleventh-century church of San Pier Scheraggio: **Andrea del Castagno**'s frescoes of celebrated Florentines, for instance, and **Botticelli**'s *Sant' Agostino Altarpiece* and *Annunciation*.

Room 1, housing an assembly of antique sculptures, many of which were used as a sort of source book by Renaissance artists, is usually shut. The gestation period of the Renaissance can be studied in the following room, where three altarpieces of the *Maestà* (Madonna enthroned) by **Cimabue**, **Duccio** and **Giotto** dwarf everything around them. A high point in the comparatively conservative art of fourteenth-century Siena (**room 3**) is **Simone Martini**'s *Annunciation*, with its eloquently expansive background of plain gold. Florence's only first-rank Gothic painter, **Lorenzo Monaco**, features amid the collection of other quattrocento artists (**rooms 5 & 6**), with a majestic *Coronation of the Virgin* and an *Adoration of the Magi*; the version of the latter subject by **Gentile da Fabriano** is the epitome of International Gothic, cramming every inch of the flattened picture plane with often highly naturalistic detail.

The *Madonna with SS Francis, John the Baptist, Zenobius and Lucy* is one of only twelve known paintings by **Domenico Veneziano** (**room 7**), whose pupil **Piero della Francesca** is represented with portraits of *Federico da Montefeltro and Battista Sforza*; the portraits are backed by images of the Duke surrounded by the cardinal virtues and his wife by the theological virtues. **Paolo Uccello**'s *The Battle of San Romano* – demonstrating the artist's obsessional interest in perspectival effects – once hung in Lorenzo il Magnifico's bed chamber, in company with the depictions of the skirmish now in the Louvre and London's National Gallery. Among the plentiful works by **Filippo Lippi** in **room 8** is his *Madonna and Child with Two Angels*, one of the best-known Renaissance images of the Madonna. Close by there's a fine *Madonna* by **Botticelli**, who in the next room shares centre stage with **Antonio del Pollaiuolo**. The works upon which Botticelli's reputation rests, though, are gathered in the merged **rooms 10–14**: *Primavera*, *Birth of Venus*, *Adoration of the Magi* and *The Madonna of the Magnificat*. Even when their meaning remains opaque – and few pictures have occasioned as much scholarly argument as the *Primavera* – these paintings are irresistibly fresh in both their conception and execution, and however many reproductions you've seen of them, the experience of the actual objects always exceeds expectations. Set away from the walls is the huge *Portinari Altarpiece* by Botticelli's Flemish contemporary **Hugo van der Goes**, a work whose naturalism greatly influenced the artists of Florence.

FROM LEONARDO DA VINCI TO TITIAN

Though the Uffizi doesn't own a finished painting that's entirely by **Leonardo da Vinci**, works in **room 15** comprise a full sketch of his career. From his formative years there's the celebrated *Annunciation* (mainly by Leonardo) and the angel in profile that he painted in Verrocchio's *Baptism*, while the incomplete *Adoration of the Magi* encapsulates his later radicalism, with its vortex of figures round Mary and the infant Christ. **Room 18**, the octagonal *Tribuna*, is where the cream of the collection used to be exhibited. It now houses the most important of the **Medici sculptures**, first among which is the *Medici Venus*, a first-century BC copy of the Praxitelean *Aphrodite of Cnidos*. Also in this room are **del Sarto**'s flirtatious *Portrait of a Girl* and some chillingly precise portraits by **Bronzino** – especially compelling are *Bartolomeo Panciatichi*, *Lucrezia Panciatichi* and *Eleanor of Toledo with Giovanni de'Medici*. Vasari's portrait of Lorenzo il Magnifico and Bronzino's of Cosimo il Vecchio are deceptively immediate – each was painted long after the death of its subject.

Perugino and **Signorelli** are the principals in **room 19**, and after them comes a room largely devoted to **Cranach** and **Dürer**, including the latter's *Portrait of the Artist's Father*, his earliest authenticated painting. Highlights in the following sequence of rooms are a perplexing *Sacred Allegory* by **Giovanni Bellini**, **Holbein**'s *Portrait of Sir Richard Southwell*, and some exquisite small panels by **Memling**, and **Mantegna**. More first-rate classical pieces are clustered in the short corridor overlooking the Arno.

The main attraction in **room 25** is **Michelangelo**'s *Doni Tondo*, his only completed easel painting. Its contorted gestures and virulent colours were studied and imitated by the Mannerist painters of the sixteenth century, as can be gauged from the nearby *Moses Defending the Daughters of Jethro* by **Rosso Fiorentino**, one of the pivotal figures of the movement. Two more pieces by Rosso are on show in **room 27**, along with several works by Bronzino and the mercurial **Pontormo**, a painter whose style seems to have been in a constant state of flux. Separating the two Mannerist groups is a room containing **Andrea del Sarto**'s sultry *Madonna of the Harpies* and a number of compositions by **Raphael**, including the lovely *Madonna of the Goldfinch* and *Pope Leo X with Cardinals Giulio de'Medici and Luigi de'Rossi* – as shifty a group of ecclesiastics as ever was gathered in one frame.

Room 28 is entirely given over to another of the titanic figures of sixteenth-century art, **Titian**. His *Flora* and *A Knight of Malta* are stunning, but most eyes tend to swivel towards the celebrated *Venus of Urbino*, just about the most fleshly and provocative of all Renaissance nudes.

FROM PARMIGIANINO TO GOYA

A brief diversion through the painters of the sixteenth-century Emilian school follows, centred on **Parmigianino**, whose *Madonna of the Long Neck* is one of the definitive Mannerist creations. **Rooms 31 to 35** feature artists from Venice and the Veneto, with outstanding paintings by **Sebastiano del Piombo** (*Death of Adonis*), **GB Moroni** (*Count Pietro Secco Suardi*), **Paolo Veronese** (*Holy Family with St Barbara*) and **Tintoretto** (*Leda*).

In **room 41**, which is dominated by **Rubens** and **Van Dyck**, it's one of the less demonstrative items that makes the biggest impact – the former's *Portrait of Isabella Brandt*. Rubens' equally theatrical contemporary, **Caravaggio**, has a cluster of pieces in **room 43**, including a howling severed head of Medusa, painted onto a shield. The next room is a showcase for the portraiture of **Rembrandt** – his *Self-Portrait as an Old Man*, painted five years or so before his death, is one of his most melancholic works, its poignancy enhanced by the proximity of another self-portrait from decades earlier. Portraits also seize the attention in the following room of eighteenth-century works, especially the two of Maria Theresa painted by **Goya**. In the hall at the top of the exit stairs squats one of the city's talismans, the *Wild Boar*, a Roman copy of third-century BC Hellenistic sculpture, it was the model for the *Porcellino* fountain in the Mercato Nuovo.

THE CORRIDOIO VASARIANO

A door on the west corridor, between rooms 25 and 34, opens onto the **Corridoio Vasariano**, a passageway built by Vasari to link the Palazzo Vecchio to the Palazzo Pitti through the Uffizi. Winding its way down to the river, over the Ponte Vecchio, through the church of Santa Felicita and into the Giardino di Bóboli, it gives a fascinating series of clandestine views of the city. As if that weren't pleasure enough, the corridor is completely lined with paintings, the larger portion of which comprises a **gallery of self-portraits**. Once past the portrait of Vasari, the series proceeds chronologically, its roll-call littered with illustrious names: Andrea del Sarto, Bronzino, Bernini, Rubens, Rembrandt, Velasquez, David, Delacroix, Ingres.

Visits to the corridor have to be arranged the previous day at the gallery's offices, on the third floor near the entrance (☎218.341); tours are conducted in the morning from Tuesday to Saturday, the precise time varying with staff availability.

West of Piazza della Signoria

Despite the urban improvement schemes of the last century and the bombings of the last war, several streets in central Florence retain their medieval character, especially in the district immediately to the west of Piazza della Signoria. Forming a sort of gateway to this quarter is the **Mercato Nuovo** (summer daily 9am–7pm; winter Tues–Sat 9am–5pm), whose souvenir stalls are probably the busiest in the city; there's been a market here since the eleventh century, though the present loggia dates from the sixteenth. Usually a small group is gathered round the bronze boar known as *Il Porcellino*, trying to earn some good luck by getting a coin to fall from the animal's mouth through the grill below his head. An aimless amble through the streets beyond the thirteenth-century Palazzo di Parte Guelfa – streets such as Via delle Terme and Borgo Santi Apostoli – will give you some idea of the feel of Florence in the Middle Ages, when every important house was an urban fortress.

Palazzo Davanzati

Although it has been much restored, the fourteenth-century **Palazzo Davanzati** is the city's most authentic example of a house from that period. In the sixteenth century a loggia replaced the battlements on the roof, and the Davanzati stuck their coat of arms on the front, but otherwise the outside of the house looks much as it did when first inhabited. Nowadays the palace houses the **Museo della Casa Fiorentina Antica** (Tues–Sat 9am–2pm, Sun 9am–1pm; L4000), and virtually every room of the reconstructed interior is furnished and decorated in medieval style, using genuine artefacts assembled from a variety of sources.

Merchants' houses in the fourteenth century would typically have had elaborately **painted walls** in the main rooms, and the Palazzo Davanzati preserves some fine examples of such decor – especially in the dining room, where the imitation wall-hangings of the lower walls are patterned with a parrot motif, while the upper part depicts a row of trees. The furnishings are sparse by modern standards, but their quality rather than their quantity is the index of prosperity: the tapestries, ceramics and lacework are all beautiful examples of their craft, none more so than the Sicilian bed cover in the first-floor bedroom, woven with scenes from the story of Tristan. Perhaps the most telling sign of the wealth of the palace's first occupants, however, is the private well, from which water was drawn by a shaft connecting all five floors.

Santa Trìnita

Continuing westward past Palazzo Davanzati, Via Porta Rossa runs into Piazza Santa Trìnita, not so much a square as a widening of the city's most expensive street, Via Tornabuoni. The road crosses the Arno on the city's most stylish bridge, the **Ponte Santa Trìnita**; it was ostensibly designed by Ammannati, but the curve of its arches so closely resembles the arc of Michelangelo's Medici tombs (see p.396) that the credit probably should be his.

The antiquity of the church of **Santa Trìnita** (daily 7am–noon & 4–7pm) is evident in the Latinate pronunciation of its name – modern Italian stresses the last not the first syllable. Founded in the eleventh century, the church was rebuilt between 1250 and the end of the following century, though the inside face of the entrance wall remains from the Romanesque building. The austerity of the architecture is alleviated by a number of works of art, the best of which all date from the fifteenth century. **Lorenzo Monaco** frescoed the fourth chapel on the right and painted its *Annunciation* altarpiece, and the decoration of the Cappella Sassetti (second to the right of the altar) was undertaken by **Ghirlandaio**, who provided an altarpiece of *The Adoration of the Shepherds* and a fresco cycle depicting *Scenes from the Life of St Francis*. Set in Piazza della Signoria, the scene showing Francis receiving the rule of the order includes portraits of Lorenzo il Magnifico and Francesco Sassetti, the patron of the chapel – they are standing in the right foreground, receiving the homage of Lorenzo's sons and his protegé, the philosopher Poliziano. A powerful composition by **Luca della Robbia** – the tomb of Benozzo Federighi, Bishop of Fiesole – occupies a wall of the chapel second to the left of the altar, framed by a ceramic border of flowers and greenery.

Palazzo Strozzi and Palazzo Rucellai

The shops of Via Tornabuoni and its tributary streets are effectively out of bounds to those who don't travel first class: Versace and Armani have their outlets here, as do Ferragamo and Gucci, the best-known local firms. Conspicuous wealth is nothing new on Via Tornabuoni, for looming above everything is the vast **Palazzo Strozzi**, the last, the largest and the least subtle of Florentine Renaissance palaces. Filippo Strozzi bought and demolished a dozen town houses to make space for Giuliano da Sangallo's strong-box in stone, and the construction of it lasted from 1489 to 1536, during which time the supervision of the project passed to Cronaca.

Some of Florence's plutocrats made an impression with rather more élan. When Giovanni Rucellai – one of the richest businessmen in the city and an esteemed scholar into the bargain – decided in the 1450s to commission a new house, the architect he turned to was Leon Battista Alberti, the archetypal universal genius of the Renaissance. The **Palazzo Rucellai**, two minutes' walk from the Strozzi house in Via della Vigna Nuova, was the first palace in Florence to follow the rules of classical architecture – its tiers of pilasters, incised into smooth blocks of stone, explicitly evoke the exterior of the Colosseum. Part of the building now contains the misleadingly named **Museo della Storia della Fotografia** (10am–7.30pm; closed Wed; L5000), a selection of images from the archives of the Alinari photography company. An even more refined example of Alberti's work, the **Cappella di San Sepolcro** (open Oct–June Sat 5.30pm), is to be seen in the adjoining Cappella Rucellai; designed as the funerary monument to Giovanni Rucellai, it takes the form of a diminutive reconstruction of Jerusalem's Church of the Holy Sepulchre.

The church of San Pancrozio, of which Alberti's chapel once formed a part, has been converted into the swish **Museo Marino Marini** (June–Aug 10am–1pm & 4–7pm; Sept–May 10am–6pm; closed Tues; L4000), displaying the works left to the city in the sculptor's will a few years ago. Variations on his familiar horse-and-rider theme predominate.

Ognissanti

In medieval times a major area of cloth production – the foundation of the Florentine economy – lay in the west of the city. **Ognissanti**, the main church of this quarter, was founded in the thirteenth century by a Benedictine order whose particular monastic industry was the weaving of woollen cloth. Three hundred years later the Franciscans took it over, and the new tenure was marked by a Baroque overhaul which spared only the campanile.

The facade of the church is of historical interest as one of the earliest eruptions of the Baroque style in Florence, but the church is made appealing by earlier features – the frescoes by **Domenico Ghirlandaio** and **Sandro Botticelli**. The young face squeezed between the Madonna and the dark-cloaked man in Ghirlandaio's *Madonna della Misericordia*, over the second altar on the right, is said to be that of Amerigo Vespucci – later to set sail on voyages that would give his name to America. Just beyond this, on opposite sides of the nave, are mounted Botticelli's *St Augustine* and Ghirlandaio's more earthbound *St Jerome*, both painted in 1480. In the same year Ghirlandaio painted the bucolic *Last Supper* that covers one wall of the **refectory** (Mon, Tues & Sat 9am–noon; free), reached through the cloister.

Santa Maria Novella

Cross the road from the forecourt of the train station, and you're on the edge of a zone free from the hazards of speeding traffic and petrol fumes. On the other side of the church of Santa Maria Novella – whose back directly faces the station – lies a square with something of a lethargic backwater atmosphere, favoured as a spot for picnic lunches and after-dark loitering.

From the beguiling green and white patterns of its marble facade, you'd never guess that the church of **Santa Maria Novella** (daily 7.15–11.30am & 3.30–6pm, Sun 3.30–5pm) was the Florentine base of the Dominican order, the grim vigilantes of thirteenth-century Catholicism. A church was founded here at the end of the eleventh century, and shortly afterwards was handed over to the Dominicans, who set about altering the place to their taste. By 1360 the interior was completed, but only the lower part of the facade was finished, a state of affairs that lasted until 1456, when Giovanni Rucellai paid for Alberti to design a classicised upper storey that would blend with the older section while improving the facade's proportions.

The architects of the Gothic interior were capable of great ingenuity too – the distance between the columns diminishes with proximity to the altar, a device to make the nave seem longer from the entrance. **Masaccio**'s extraordinary fresco of *The Trinity* (1428), one of the earliest works in which perspective and classical proportion were rigorously employed, is painted onto the wall halfway down the left aisle. Nothing else in the main part of the church has quite the same impact, but the wealth of decoration at the chancel end is astounding. The **Cappella di Filippo Strozzi** (immediately to the right of the chancel) is covered by a fresco cycle commissioned by Strozzi from **Filippino Lippi** in 1486 and finished fifteen years later, after the artist's sojourn in Rome; Lippi's fantasy vision of classical ruins, in which the narrative often seems to take second place, is one of the first examples of an archaeological interest in Roman ruins. As a chronicle of fifteenth-century life in Florence, no series of frescoes is more fascinating than **Domenico Ghirlandaio**'s pictures behind the high altar; the work was commissioned by Giovanni Tornabuoni – which is why certain ladies of the Tornabuoni family are present at the birth of John the Baptist and of the Virgin.

Brunelleschi's *Crucifix*, popularly supposed to have been carved as a response to Donatello's uncouth version at Santa Croce, hangs in the Cappella Gondi, to the left of the chancel. At the end of the left transept is the raised Cappella Strozzi, whose faded frescoes by **Nardo di Cione** (1350s) include an entire wall of visual commentary on Dante's *Inferno*. The magnificent altarpiece by Nardo's brother Andrea (better known as **Orcagna**), is a piece of propaganda for the Dominicans – Christ is shown bestowing favour simultaneously on both Saint Peter and Saint Thomas Aquinas, a figure second only to Saint Dominic in the order's hierarchy.

THE CLOISTERS

Santa Maria Novella's cloisters (Mon–Thurs & Sat 9am–2pm, Sun 8am–1pm; L5000), entered to the left of the church facade, are more richly decorated than any others in Florence. **Paolo Uccello** and his workshop executed the frescoes in the Romanesque **Chiostro Verde** – look out for Uccello's windswept image of the Flood and its aftermath, on the right as you enter. The **Cappella degli Spagnuoli** (Spanish Chapel), once the chapter house, received its new name after Eleanor of Toledo reserved it for the use of her Spanish entourage; its fresco cycle by **Andrea di Firenze**, an extended depiction of the triumph of the Catholic church, was described by Ruskin as "the most noble piece of pictorial philosophy in Italy". His representation of the Duomo was purely speculative – the cycle dates from the 1360s, long before Brunelleschi even won the contract for the dome. The contemporaneous but more exposed decoration of the **Chiostrino dei Morti**, the oldest part of the complex, has not aged so robustly.

The San Lorenzo district

A couple of blocks to the east of the train station stands Florence's main food market, encircled by scores of street stalls, which spread from the vast market hall to the church of San Lorenzo – like Santa Maria Novella, a monument of major importance.

The church of San Lorenzo

Founded back in the fourth century, **San Lorenzo** (7am–noon & 3.30–6.30pm) has a good claim to be the oldest church in Florence, and for the best part of three hundred years was the city's cathedral. As this was the Medici's parish church, it inevitably benefitted from the family's patronage: in 1425 Giovanni Bicci de'Medici commissioned Brunelleschi to rebuild San Lorenzo, a move which started a long association between the family and the building. Although Michelangelo sweated to produce a scheme for San Lorenzo's facade, the bare brick of the exterior has never been clad. It's a stark, inappropriate prelude to the powerful simplicity of Brunelleschi's interior, one of the earliest Renaissance church designs.

Inside, two paintings stand out from the rest – Rosso Fiorentino's *Marriage of the Virgin* (second chapel on the right) and Filippo Lippi's *Annunciation* (in chapel on west side of the left transept). But more striking are the two **bronze pulpits** by **Donatello**. Covered in densely populated and disquieting reliefs, chiefly of scenes preceding and following the Crucifixion, these are the artist's last works, and were completed by his pupils. Close by, at the foot of the altar steps, a large disc of multicoloured marble marks the grave of Cosimo il Vecchio, the artist's main patron.

Further pieces by Donatello (who is buried in the chapel with the Lippi painting) adorn the neighbouring **Sagrestia Vecchia** (Old Sacristy). Much of the decorative work here is by Donatello – the two pairs of bronze doors, the large reliefs of *SS. Cosmas and Damian* and *SS. Lawrence and Stephen*, and the eight terracotta tondi. The table of milky marble in the centre of the room is the tomb of Cosimo il Vecchio's parents, Giovanni Bicci de'Medici and Piccarda Bueri.

THE BIBLIOTECA LAURENZIANA

At the top of the left aisle of San Lorenzo a door leads out to the cloister and the staircase going up to the **Biblioteca Laurenziana** (Mon–Sat 10am–noon; free), a crucial example of Mannerist architecture. Wishing to create a suitably grandiose home for the precious manuscripts assembled by Cosimo il Vecchio and Lorenzo il Magnifico,

Pope Clement VII (Lorenzo's nephew) asked Michelangelo to design a new Medici library in 1524.

The startling feature of the building he came up with is the **vestibule**, a room that is almost filled by a flight of steps resembling a solidified lava flow. From this deliberately eccentric space, the visitor passes into the tranquil, architecturally correct **reading room**, from where the illogically placed columns and brackets of the vestibule cannot be seen. Annual exhibitions in the connecting rooms draw on the Medici collection, which includes manuscripts as diverse as a fifth-century copy of Virgil and a treatise on architecture by Leonardo.

THE CAPPELLE MEDICEE

Michelangelo's most celebrated contribution to the San Lorenzo buildings, the **Sagrestia Nuova**, is part of the **Cappelle Medicee** (Tues–Sat 9am–2pm, Sun 9am–1pm; L8000), the entrance to which is on Piazza Madonna degli Aldobrandini. The larger of the chapels is the Cappella dei Principi (Chapel of the Princes), a marble-plated hall built as a mausoleum for Cosimo I and his ancestors. Morbid and dowdy, it was the most expensive building project ever financed by the family, and epitomises the mentality that thinks magnificence is directly proportional to expenditure.

The Sagrestia Nuova, one of the earliest Mannerist buildings, was begun in 1520 and intended as a tribute to, and subversion of, Brunelleschi's Sagrestia Vecchia. Architectural connoisseurs go into raptures over the complex cornices of the alcoves and other such sophistications, but the layperson will be drawn to the fabulous **Medici tombs**, carved by Michelangelo between 1524 and 1533. To the left is the tomb of **Lorenzo, Duke of Urbino**, the grandson of Lorenzo il Magnifico; he is depicted as a man of thought, and his sarcophagus bears figures of *Dawn* and *Dusk*, the times of day whose ambiguities appeal to the contemplative mind. Opposite is the tomb of Lorenzo il Magnifico's youngest son, **Giuliano, Duke of Nemours**; as a man of action, his character is symbolised by *Day* and *Night*. Contrary to these idealised images, Lorenzo and Giuliano were feeble individuals, and both died young and unlamented. Their effigies were intended to face the equally grand tombs of Lorenzo il Magnifico and his brother Giuliano; the only part of the project realised by Michelangelo is the serene *Madonna and Child*, the last image of the Madonna he ever sculpted.

The Markets

One of the unmissable sights of Florence is the San Lorenzo **Mercato Centrale**, built in stone, iron and glass by Giuseppe Mengoni, architect of Milan's Galleria. It opened in 1874, and a century later was given a major overhaul, reopening in 1980 with a new first floor. Butchers, *alimentari*, tripe sellers, greengrocers (on the first floor), pasta stalls, bars – they're all gathered under the one roof, all charging prices lower than you'll readily find elsewhere in the city. It's open Monday to Friday from 7am to 2pm, and on Saturdays and days immediately prior to a public holiday it opens additionally from 4 to 8pm. Get there close to the end of the working day and you'll get some good reductions. And for a taste of simple Florentine food at its best, call in at *Ottavino*, a small bar that's the established meeting-place of the market workers – it's on the Via dell'Ariento side, and is open until 1.30pm.

Each day from 8am to 7pm the streets encircling the Mercato Centrale are thronged with stalls selling bags, belts, shoes – everything, in fact, that your wardrobe might need. This is the busiest of Florence's daily **street markets**, and a half-hour's immersion in the haggling mass of customers is a pleasure for all but the irredeemably misanthropic. It's not the cheapest place in town, though – the stalls at Piazza delle Cure, just beyond Piazza della Libertà (every morning; take bus #1), and the enormous Tuesday morning market at the Cascine park, west along the Arno (bus #16), have the bargains.

The Palazzo Medici-Riccardi

On the edge of the square in front of San Lorenzo stands the **Palazzo Medici-Riccardi** (Mon, Tues & Thurs–Sat 9am–12.30pm & 3–5pm, Sun 9am–noon; free), built for Cosimo il Vecchio by Michelozzo in the 1440s. With its heavily rusticated exterior, this monolithic palace was the prototype for such houses as the Palazzo Pitti and Palazzo Strozzi, but was greatly altered in the seventeenth century by its new owners, the Riccardi family.

Of Michelozzo's original scheme, only the upstairs **chapel** remains intact, its interior covered by a colourful narrative fresco of the *Journey of the Magi*, painted around 1460 by Benozzo Gozzoli. It shows the pageant of the Compagnia dei Magi, the most patrician of the city's religious confraternities; their procession took place on Epiphany, with members of the Medici usually participating. It's known that several of the Medici household are featured in the painted procession, but putting names to these prettified faces is a problem. The man leading the cavalcade on a white horse is certainly Piero il Gottoso, sponsor of the fresco. Lorenzo il Magnifico is probably the young king in the foreground, riding the grey horse seen in full profile, while his brother, Giuliano, is probably the one preceded by the black bowman. The artist himself is in the crowd on the far left, his red beret signed with his name in gold.

A second staircase ascends from the courtyard to the **Sala di Luca Giordano**, a gilded and mirrored gallery notable for its *Madonna and Child* by Filippo Lippi, and Luca Giordano's ceiling fresco of *The Apotheosis of the Medici*, an enterprise from which one can only deduce that Giordano had no sense of shame.

The San Marco district

Much of central Florence's traffic is funnelled along **Via Cavour**, the thoroughfare connecting the Duomo area to Piazza della Libertà, a major confluence of the city's peripheral carriageways (the *viale*). Except as a place to catch buses out to Fiesole and other points north, the street has little to recommend it, but halfway along it lies **Piazza San Marco**, the core of the university district. The distinctly more youthful ambience of this area makes it a welcome refuge from the commercial hustle of inner Florence, and although one of the top tourist attractions – the Accademia – draws the coach parties out here, it has a number of sights that are often overlooked.

The Museo di San Marco

One side of the square is taken up by the Dominican convent and church of **San Marco**, recipient of Cosimo il Vecchio's most lavish patronage. In the 1430s he financed Michelozzo's enlargement of the buildings, and went on to establish a vast public library here. Abashed by the wealth he was transferring to them, the friars of San Marco suggested to Cosimo that he need not continue to support them on such a scale – to which he replied, "Never shall I be able to give God enough to set him down as my debtor." Ironically, the convent became the centre of resistance to the Medici later in the century – Girolamo Savonarola, leader of the theocratic government of Florence between the expulsion of the Medici in 1494 and his execution four years later, was prior of San Marco from 1491.

As Michelozzo was altering and expanding the convent, its walls were being decorated by one of its friars, **Fra' Angelico**, a painter in whom a medieval simplicity of mind was allied to a non-medieval sophistication of manner. Now deconsecrated, the church and convent today house the **Museo di San Marco** (Tues–Sat 9am–2pm, Sun 9am–1pm; L6000), in effect a museum dedicated to the art of Fra' Angelico.

The **Ospizio dei Pellegrini** (Pilgrims' Hospice) contains a collection of around twenty paintings by him, a large number of them brought here from other churches in

Florence. A *Deposition* and a small *Last Judgement* are outstanding – the former remarkable for its aura of tranquillity, as though the minds of its protagonists were already fixed on the Resurrection. Across the cloister, in the **Sala Capitolare**, is a powerful fresco of the *Crucifixion*, painted by Angelico and assistants in 1441. At the rear of this room, the **refectory** – with a lustrous *Last Supper* by Ghirlandaio – forms an ante-room to the **foresteria** (guest rooms), which is cluttered with architectural bits and pieces salvaged during the urban improvement schemes of the latter half of the last century.

For the drama of its setting and the lucidity of its composition, nothing matches the famous *Annunciation* at the summit of the main staircase. Right round this upper floor are ranged the 44 tiny **dormitory cells**, each frescoed either by Angelico himself or by his assistants. Most of the works in the file of cells on the left are entirely by Angelico – don't miss the *Noli me tangere* (cell 1), the *Annunciation* (cell 3), the *Transfiguration* (cell 6) and the *Coronation of the Virgin* (cell 9). In all likelihood, the marvellous *Madonna Enthroned*, on the facing wall, is by Angelico too. The incongruous monastic onlookers in several of the scenes are Saint Dominic (with the star above his head) and Saint Peter Martyr (with the split skull); the latter zealot, responsible for a massacre of Florentine heretics in the thirteenth century, is the city's home-produced Dominican saint. Michelozzo's **library**, a room that seems to exude an atmosphere of calm study, is off the corridor to the right, at the end of which is the pair of rooms used by Cosimo il Vecchio when he came here on retreat.

San Marco church, greatly altered since Michelozzo's intervention, is worth a visit for two works on the second and third altars on the right: a *Madonna and Saints*, painted in 1509 by Fra' Bartolomeo (like Fra' Angelico, a friar at the convent), and an eighth-century mosaic of *The Madonna in Prayer*, brought here from Constantinople.

The Galleria dell'Accademia

Florence's first Academy of Drawing – indeed, Europe's first – was founded in the mid-sixteenth century by Bronzino, Ammannati and Vasari. Initially based in Santissima Annunziata, this *Accademia del Disegno* moved in 1764 to Via Ricasoli 66, and soon afterwards was transformed into a general arts academy, the *Accademia di Belle Arti*. Twenty years later the Grand Duke Pietro Leopoldo founded the nearby **Galleria dell'Accademia** (Tues–Sat 9am–2pm, Sun 9am–1pm; L10,000), filling its rooms with paintings for the edification of the students. Later augmented with pieces from suppressed religious foundations and other sources, the Accademia has an impressive collection of paintings, especially of Florentine altarpieces from the fourteenth to the early sixteenth centuries. But the pictures are not what pull the crowds in numbers equalled only by the Uffizi – the attraction is the sculpture of **Michelangelo**, or rather, the **David**.

Emblem of the city's republican pride and of the illimitable ambition of the Renaissance artist, Michelangelo's *David* is nowadays also the heraldic device of touristic Florence. Yet seeing it for the first time can be something of a shock. Finished in 1504, when Michelangelo was just 29, and carved from a gigantic block of marble whose shallowness posed severe difficulties, it's an incomparable show of technical bravura. But the *David* is a piece of monumental public sculpture (it stood in the Piazza della Signoria until 1873), not a gallery exhibit: closely surveyed in the Accademia's specially built tribune, this colossal adolescent is perturbing rather than uplifting.

Michelangelo once described the process of carving as being the liberation of the form from within the stone, a notion that seems to be embodied by the remarkable unfinished **Slaves** nearby. His procedure, clearly demonstrated here, was to cut the figure as if it were a deep relief, and then to free the three-dimensional figure. Carved in the 1520s, they were intended for the tomb of Julius II; in 1564 the artist's nephew gave them to the Medici, who installed them in the grotto of the Bóboli gardens. In their midst is another unfinished work, *St Matthew*, which was started immediately after completion of the *David* as a commission from the Opera del Duomo; they actually requested a full series of Apostles, but this is the only one Michelangelo began. The *Pietà*, though labelled as a work by Michelangelo, is not thought to be by him.

Piazza Santissima Annunziata and around

Its porticoes and church make **Piazza Santissima Annunziata** the Florentines' favourite square. Until the seventeenth century the Florentine year used to begin on March 25, the Feast of the Annunciation – hence the city's predilection for paintings of the Annunciation, and the fashionableness of the Annunziata church, which is still the place for society weddings. The festival is marked by a huge fair in the square and the streets leading off it. Giambologna's final work, the **equestrian statue of Grand Duke Ferdinando I**, holds the centre of the square; it was cast by his pupil Pietro Tacca, creator of the two bizarre **fountains**, on each of which a pair of aquatic monkeys dribble water at two bewhiskered sea-slugs.

The Spedale degli Innocenti

The tone of the square is set by Brunelleschi's **Spedale degli Innocenti**, which was opened in 1445 as the first foundlings' hospital in Europe, and still incorporates an orphanage – Luca della Robbia's ceramic tondi of swaddled babies advertise the building's function. The convent, centred on two beautiful cloisters, now contains the **Museo dello Spedale degli Innocenti** (Mon, Tues & Thurs–Sat 9am–2pm, Sun 9am–1pm; L3000), a miscellany of Florentine Renaissance art including one of Luca della Robbia's most charming Madonnas and an incident-packed *Adoration of the Magi* by Ghirlandaio. No collection from this period could be anything other than interesting, but Florence has plenty of museums that you should check out before this one.

Santissima Annunziata

The church of **Santissima Annunziata** (daily 7am–12.30pm & 4–6.45pm) is the mother church of the Servite order, which was founded by seven Florentine aristocrats in 1234. Its dedication to the Virgin Annunciate took place in the fourteenth century, in recognition of its miraculous image of the Virgin: the story goes that the painting, left unfinished by the monastic artist, was completed by an angel. So many pilgrims came to adore the image that the church was rebuilt to accommodate them in the second half of the fifteenth century. The architect was Michelozzo (brother of the prior), the paymasters the Medici. In the **Chiostro dei Voti**, the atrium that Michelozzo built onto the church, are preserved some beautiful frescoes; mainly painted in the 1510s, they include a *Visitation* by Pontormo and a series by Andrea del Sarto, whose *Birth of the Virgin* achieves a perfect balance of spontaneity and geometrical order.

Much of the interior's gilt and stucco fancy dress was perpetrated in the seventeenth and eighteenth centuries, but the ornate **tabernacle** of the miraculous image, cordoned by candles and lanterns to the left of the entrance, was produced by Michelozzo. His patron, Piero di Cosimo de'Medici, made sure that nobody remained unaware of the money he sank into the shrine – an inscription in the floor reads "Costò fior. 4 mila el marmo solo" (The marble alone cost 4000 florins). The painting encased in the marble has been repainted into obscurity, and is rarely shown anyway; far more interesting are the frescoes by **Andrea del Castagno** in the first two chapels on the left – *The Vision of St Jerome* and *The Trinity*. Separated from the nave by a triumphal arch is the unusual **tribune**, begun by Michelozzo but completed to designs by Alberti; the rarely accessible chapel at the furthest point was altered by Giambologna into a monument to himself.

The adjoining **Chiostro dei Morti**, entered from the left transept, is worth visiting for Andrea del Sarto's calculatedly informal *Madonna del Sacco*, painted over the door.

The Museo Archeologico

A hundred metres from the church, on Via della Colonna, is the **Museo Archeologico** (Tues–Sat 9am–2pm, Sun 9am–1pm; L6000). This is the pre-eminent collection of its kind in north Italy, though at the moment its quality doesn't exactly shine out at you – modernisation is perpetually in progress, and they are still rectifying damage caused by the flood of 1966, so the museum generally has an *ad hoc* air about it.

The museum's special strength is its showing of **Etruscan** finds, many of them part of the Medici bequest. On the ground floor there's a varied and well-labelled display of Etruscan funerary figures and Greek statuary, but pride of place goes to the *François Vase*, an Attic krater from the sixth century BC. It's been restored twice – once after its discovery in 1845, in an Etruscan tomb at Chiusi, and again after a butter-fingered member of staff bounced it off the floor in 1900, converting it into a 638-piece jigsaw. Of comparable importance in the first-floor **Egyptian collection** is a Hittite chariot made of bone and wood and dating from the fourteenth century BC.

The rest of this floor and much of the floor above are given over to the **Etruscan, Greek and Roman collections**, arranged with variable clarity. Outstanding among the Roman pieces is the nude known as the *Idolino*, probably a copy of a fifth-century BC original. The Hellenic head of a horse, in the same room, once adorned the garden of the Palazzo Medici, where it was studied by Donatello and Verrocchio. In the long gallery stand the best of the Etruscan pieces: the *Arringatore* (Orator), the only known Etruscan large bronze from the Hellenistic period; and the *Chimera*, a triple-headed monster of the fifth century BC, much admired by Cosimo I's retinue of Mannerist artists, as well as by all subsequent connoisseurs of the bizarre. The adjoining room is a storehouse of Etruscan funerary caskets, stacked in a way that invites the visitor to pass through quickly.

The Santa Croce district

The 1966 flood permanently changed the character of the area around Santa Croce. Prior to then it had been one of the more densely populated districts of the city, packed with tenements and small workshops. Lying lower than the surrounding area, **Piazza Santa Croce** and the streets around it were devastated when the Arno burst its banks, and many of the residents moved out permanently in the following years. Leather shops and jewellers are still in evidence, but the souvenir stalls are now a more conspicuous presence.

Traditionally this has been one of the city's main arenas for festivities. The Medici used it for self-aggrandising pageants, and during the years of Savonarola's ascendancy, the square was the principal site for the ceremonial execution of heretics. It's still sometimes used as the pitch for the **Gioco di Calcio Storico**, a sort of football tournament between the city's four *quartiere*; the game is held three times in Saint John's week (last week of June), and is characterised by incomprehensible rules and a degree of violence from which the heavy sixteenth-century costumes offer inadequate protection. Tickets for the event are sold at the *Chiosco degli Sportivi* in Via de'Anselmi, off the west side of Piazza della Repubblica – by the end of May there are few left.

The church of Santa Croce

The Franciscan church of Florence, **Santa Croce** (daily 7.15am–12.30pm & 2.30–6.30pm) was begun in 1294, possibly by the architect of the Duomo, Arnolfo di Cambio. Construction was held up by a split in the Franciscan ranks and not resumed until the early fifteenth century, the period when Santa Croce acquired its status as the mausoleum of Florence's eminent citizens. Over 270 tombstones pave the floor of the church, while grander monuments commemorate the likes of Ghiberti, Michelangelo, Machiavelli, Galileo and Dante – though the last of the group is actually buried in Ravenna, where he died in exile.

A lovely relief by Antonio Rossellino surmounts one of the simpler and more eloquent tombs, attached to the first pillar on the right: it's that of **Francesco Nori**, murdered with Giuliano de'Medici by the Pazzi conspirators. Right by this is Vasari's monument to **Michelangelo**, whose body was brought back from Rome to Florence in July 1574, a return marked with a spectacular memorial service in San Lorenzo. On the opposite side of the church is the tomb of **Galileo**, built in 1737, when it was finally agreed to give the great scientist a Christian burial. Back in the right aisle, the Neoclassical cenotaph to **Dante** is immediately after the second altar, while against the third pillar there's a beautiful **pulpit** by Benedetto da Maiano, carved with scenes from the life of Saint Francis. The side door at the end of the aisle is flanked by **Donatello**'s gilded stone relief of *The Annunciation* and Bernardo Rossellino's tomb of the humanist **Leonardo Bruni**, a design which spawned innumerable imitations.

The chapels at the east end of Santa Croce are a compendium of Florentine fourteenth-century art, showing the extent of Giotto's influence and the full diversity of his followers. The **Cappella Castellani**, on the west side of the right transept, was completely frescoed in the 1480s by **Agnolo Gaddi** and his pupils, while the adjoining **Cappella Baroncelli** was decorated by Agnolo's father, **Taddeo**, a long-time assistant to Giotto himself. Taddeo's cycle features the first night scene in western painting, *The Annunciation to the Shepherds*. A doorway just inside the corridor alongside the Cappella Baroncelli opens into the **sacristy**, where the centrepiece is a *Crucifixion* by Taddeo; the tiny **Cappella Rinuccini**, separated from the sacristy by a grille, is covered with frescoes by the more solemn **Giovanni da Milano**. The corridor ends at the **Cappella Medici**, notable for its large terracotta altarpiece by Andrea della Robbia; like the corridor, the chapel was designed by Michelozzo, the Medici's favourite architect.

Both the **Cappella Peruzzi** and the **Cappella Bardi** (on the right of the chancel) are entirely covered with frescoes by **Giotto**. The former (further from the chancel), shows scenes from the lives of Saint John the Baptist and John the Evangelist; the latter, painted slightly earlier and with some assistance, features the life of Saint Francis. **Agnolo Gaddi** was responsible for all the frescoes round and above the high altar, and for the design of the stained glass in the lancet windows. The *Scenes from the Life of St Sylvester* in the **Cappella Bardi di Vernio** (the fifth after the chancel) were painted in the 1330s by **Maso di Banco**, perhaps the most inventive of Giotto's followers. At the end of the left chancel, the second **Cappella Bardi** houses a wooden *Crucifix* by **Donatello** – supposedly criticised by Brunelleschi as resembling a "peasant on the Cross".

THE CAPPELLA DEI PAZZI, CLOISTERS AND MUSEUM

If one building can be said to typify the spirit of the early Renaissance, it's Brunelleschi's **Cappella dei Pazzi**, which stands at the end of Santa Croce's first cloister (entrance to chapel, cloisters & museum: March–Sept 10am–12.30pm & 2.30–6.30pm; Oct–Feb 10am–12.30pm & 3–5pm; L3000; closed Wed). Designed in the 1430s and completed in the 1470s, several years after the architect's death, the chapel achieves an unprecedented harmony of composition and integration of decorative detail. The polychrome lining of the portico's shallow cupola is by Luca della Robbia, as is the tondo of *St Andrew* over the door; inside, Luca also produced the blue and white tondi of the *Apostles*. The vividly coloured tondi of the *Evangelists* were produced in the della Robbia workshop, possibly to designs by Donatello. The spacious **second cloister**, also by Brunelleschi, is probably the most peaceful spot in the centre of Florence.

The **Museo dell'Opera di Santa Croce**, off the first cloister, houses a miscellany of works of art, the best of which are gathered in the refectory. Cimabue's *Crucifixion* has become the emblem of the havoc caused by the 1966 flood, when eighteen feet of filthy water surged into the church, tearing the Crucifix from its mounting and stripping much of its paint away. Also in this room are Taddeo Gaddi's fresco of the *Last Supper and Crucifixion*, fragments of the Orcagna frescoes that covered Santa Croce's nave before Vasari renovated it, and Donatello's enormous gilded *St Louis of Toulouse*, made for Orsanmichele.

Casa Buonarotti

The **Casa Buonarotti** (9.30am–1.30pm; closed Tues; L5000), north of Santa Croce at Via Ghibellina 70, is enticing in name but disappointing in substance, in that it contains few items directly connected with the great man. Michelangelo did own this property, but he never lived here. He bequeathed it to his nephew, his sole descendant, whose son in turn converted part of the property into a gallery dedicated to his great-uncle. Much of the space is taken up by homages to Michelangelo, copies of works by him and portraits of him, the exciting items being confined to a few rooms on the first floor.

The two main treasures are to be found in the room to the left of the stairs: *The Madonna of the Steps* is Michelangelo's earliest known work, carved when he was no older than sixteen, and the similarly unfinished *Battle of the Centaurs* dates from immediately afterwards, when the boy was living in the Medici household. In the adjacent room you'll find the wooden model for the facade of San Lorenzo, while the room in front of the stairs houses the largest of all the sculptural models on display, the torso of a *River God* intended for the Medici chapel in San Lorenzo. To the right is a room containing a painted wooden *Crucifix* discovered in Santo Spirito in 1963; it's now generally thought to be a Michelangelo sculpture whose existence has long been known through documents, but was feared lost. In addition to these, original architectural drawings and other studies are sometimes on display, and the ground floor is often given over to specialised Michelangelo exhibitions.

Oltrarno and San Miniato

Visitors to Florence might perceive the Arno as merely a brief interruption in the urban fabric, but Florentines talk as though a ravine ran through their city. North of the river is *Arno di quà* (over here), while the other side of the river is *Arno di là* (over there) or the **Oltrarno**, a terminology which has its roots in medieval times, when a lack of bridges made the district to the south more detached than it is today. Though traditionally an artisans' quarter, the Oltrarno has always contained prosperous enclaves, and many of the ruling families chose to settle in this area. Nowadays some of the city's swankiest shops line Borgo San Jacopo, parallel to the river's southern bank, while the windows of Via Maggio are an amazing display of palatial furnishings.

FROM PONTE VECCHIO TO SANTA FELÌCITA

The direct route from the city centre to the heart of Oltrarno crosses the river on the **Ponte Vecchio**, the only bridge not mined by the retreating Nazis in 1944. Built in 1345 to replace an ancient wooden bridge, the Ponte Vecchio has always been loaded with shops propped over the water, but the monopoly of jewellers dates from 1593, when Ferdinando I ejected the butchers' stalls then in occupation. Crammed with sightseers and high-income shoppers during the day, the bridge remains busy after the shutters come down, when the street traders set out their stalls and the local lads gather round the bust of Cellini, waiting to see what the sky will let fall in the way of company.

The reason for Ferdinando's eviction notice was that the slabs of meat lay directly beneath the corridor that Vasari had constructed between the Palazzo Vecchio and Palazzo Pitti. It was to accommodate this corridor that Vasari stuck a portico onto the nearby **Santa Felìcita**, possibly the oldest church in Florence after San Lorenzo. Remodelled in the sixteenth century – when it became the Medici chapel – and in the eighteenth, the interior is worth a visit for the paintings by **Pontormo** in the Cappella Capponi (on the right, just inside the door). His *Deposition* is one of the masterworks of Florentine Mannerism, showing the lifeless body of Christ borne on a swirl of sky-blue and pink draperies.

Palazzo Pitti

Although the Medici later took possession of it, the largest palace in Florence – the **Palazzo Pitti** – still bears the name of the man for whom it was built. Luca Pitti was a prominent rival of Cosimo il Vecchio, and much of the impetus behind the building of his new house came from a desire to trump the Medici. The palace was started in around 1457, possibly using the design by Brunelleschi which the architect had intended for the Palazzo Medici but which had been rejected by Cosimo as being too grand. The central block was continually expanded up to the early seventeenth century, when it finally achieved the gargantuan bulk it has today.

All the museums in the Pitti complex are open Tues–Sat 9am–2pm & Sun 9am–1pm. The ticket for the Galleria Palatina costs L8000, as does that for the Galleria d'Arte Moderna; the ticket for the Museo degli Argenti, costing L6000, covers admission to the Galleria del Costume as well. The other collections are currently undergoing restoration. The palace garden – the Giardino di Bóboli – opens daily at 9am, closing at 6.30pm May–Sept, 5.30pm in March, April and Oct, and 4.30pm Nov – Feb, admittance L5000.

THE GALLERIA PALATINA

Many of the paintings gathered by the Medici in the seventeenth century are now arranged in the **Galleria Palatina**, a suite of 26 rooms in one first-floor wing of the palace. After the Uffizi, this is Florence's most extensive public gallery and you'll need the best part of a morning to see it properly. Stacked three deep in places, as they would have been in the days of their acquisition, the pictures conform to no ordering principle except that of making each room as varied as possible – a pleasant alternative to the didactic intent of modern museums.

The art of the sixteenth century is the Palatina's forte – in particular, the art of **Raphael** and **Titian**. There are half a dozen excellent Raphaels here, while the even larger contingent of supreme works by Titian includes a number of his most trenchant portraits – among them *Pietro Aretino*, the preening *Cardinal Ippolito de'Medici*, and the disconcerting *Portrait of an Englishman*, a picture which makes the viewer feel as closely scrutinised as was the subject. **Andrea del Sarto** is represented in strength as well, as is **Rubens**, whose *Consequences of War* packs more of a punch than most other Baroque allegories. Individual works to look out for are Fra' Bartolomeo's *Deposition*, a treatment of the same theme by Perugino, a tondo of the *Madonna and Child* by Filippo Lippi, a *Sleeping Cupid* by Caravaggio, and Cristofano Allori's *Judith and Holofernes*, incorporating portraits of the painter, his mistress and his mother.

THE PITTI'S OTHER MUSEUMS

Much of the rest of the first floor comprises the **Appartamenti Monumentali**, the Pitti's state rooms; they were completely renovated by the Dukes of Lorraine in the last century, but at the moment a restoration keeps their handiwork hidden from view.

On the floor above is the **Galleria d'Arte Moderna**, a chronological survey of primarily Tuscan art from the mid-eighteenth century to 1945. Most rewarding are the products of the *Macchiaioli*, the Italian division of the Impressionist movement; most startling, however, are the sublime specimens of sculptural kitsch, such as Antonio Ciseri's *Pregnant Nun*.

The Pitti's **Museo degli Argenti**, entered from the garden courtyard, is not – as its name implies – exclusively a museum of silverware, but a collection of luxury artefacts in general. Lorenzo il Magnifico's trove of **antique vases**, displayed in one of the four splendidly frescoed reception rooms on the ground floor, are most likely to elicit straightforward admiration. The later the date of the exhibits, though, the greater the discrepancy between the skill of the craftsman and the taste by which it was governed – by the time you reach the end of the jewellery show on the first floor, you'll have lost all capacity to be surprised or revolted.

Visitors without a specialist interest are unlikely to be riveted by the **Galleria del Costume**, housed in the Palazzina della Meridiana, the eighteenth-century southern wing of the Pitti. Here you can admire the dress that Eleanor of Toledo was buried in, but you can admire it easily enough in Bronzino's portrait of her in the Palazzo Vecchio.

THE GIARDINO DI BÓBOLI AND THE BELVEDERE

The creation of the Pitti's enormous formal garden, the **Giardino di Bóboli**, began when the Medici took possession of the Palazzo Pitti, and continued into the early seventeenth century. It is the only extensive area of greenery in the centre of the city, and thus tends to get crowded in the areas close to the gates; it gets quieter in the heart of the garden, however, as the sharp gradients of its avenues take their toll.

Of all the garden's Mannerist embellishments, the most celebrated is the **Grotta del Buontalenti**, close to the entrance to the left of the palace facade, past the turtle-back figure of Cosimo I's court dwarf (as seen on a thousand postcards). In amongst the fake stalactites are shepherds and sheep that look like calcified sponges, while embedded in the corners are replicas of Michelangelo's *Slaves*, replacing the originals that were here until 1908. In the deepest recesses of the cave, normally visible only through the railings, stands Giambologna's *Venus*, leered at by attendant imps.

The vast **amphitheatre** facing the palace courtyard was designed in the early seventeenth century as an arena for Medici festivities, the site having already been laid out by Ammannati as a garden in the shape of a Roman circus. A set piece of comparable scale is the fountain island called the **Isolotto**, which is the focal point of the far end of the gardens; it's best approached along the central cypress avenue known as the **Viottolone**, many of whose statues are Roman originals. Carry straight on from here and you'll come to the **Porta Romana** entrance, which takes its name from the fourteenth-century gate in the street outside.

It's sometimes possible to leave the gardens by the gate which leads to the precincts of the **Forte di Belvedere** (daily 9am–8pm; free), the star-shaped fortress built on the orders of Ferdinando I in 1590, ostensibly for the city's protection but really to intimidate the Grand-Duke's fellow Florentines. Art exhibitions are sometimes held in the box-like palace in the centre of the fortress, but they rarely offer any inducement to turn away from the incredible urban panorama. The road approach to the fort is from the Costa San Giorgio, which begins at the back of Santa Felicita. East from the Belvedere stretches the best-preserved stretch of Florence's fortified walls – it's followed by Via di Belvedere, an attractive if tiring route to San Miniato (see overleaf).

Santo Spirito

Some indication of the importance of the parish of Santo Spirito is given by the fact that when Florence was divided into four administrative *quartieri* in the fourteenth century, the entire area south of the Arno was given its name. The slightly seedy Piazza Santo

Spirito, with its market stalls and cafés, and the neighbouring streets, with their furniture workshops and antiques showrooms, together encapsulate the ambivalent character of Oltrarno, a character not yet compromised by the encroachments of tourism.

Don't be deterred by the vacant facade of **Santo Spirito** church: the interior, one of Brunelleschi's last projects, prompted Bernini to describe it as "the most beautiful church in the world". It's so perfectly proportioned that nothing could seem more artless, yet the plan is extremely sophisticated – a Latin cross with a continuous chain of 38 chapels round the outside and a line of 35 columns running in parallel right round the building. Unfortunately a Baroque baldachin covers the high altar, but this is the sole disruption of Brunelleschi's arrangement. The best paintings are in the transepts: in the right there's Filippino Lippi's *Nerli Altarpiece*, and in the left a *St Monica and Augustinian Nuns*, attributed to Verrocchio. Also worth a peep is the sacristy, entered through a vestibule that opens onto the left aisle; both rooms were designed at the end of the fifteenth century by Giuliano da Sangallo.

A fire in 1471 destroyed all the monastery except its refectory, now the home of the **Fondazione Salvatore Romano** (Tues–Sat 9am–2pm; Sun 8am–1pm; L3000); the collection merits a visit for its assortment of Romanesque carvings and a huge fresco of *The Crucifixion* by Orcagna and his workshop.

Santa Maria del Carmine

In 1771 fire wrecked the nearby Carmelite convent and its church of **Santa Maria del Carmine**, but somehow the flames did not damage the frescoes of the Cappella Brancacci, a cycle of paintings that makes the Carmine one of the essential sights of Florence. The decoration of the chapel was begun in 1424 by **Masolino** and **Masaccio**, the former aged 41 and the latter just 22. Within a short time the teacher was taking lessons from the supposed pupil, whose grasp of the texture of the real world, of the principles of perspective, and of the dramatic potential of the biblical texts they were illustrating, far exceeded that of his precursors. Three years later Masaccio was dead, but in the words of Vasari – "All the most celebrated sculptors and painters since Masaccio's day have become excellent and illustrious by studying their art in this chapel." Michelangelo used to come here to make drawings of Masaccio's scenes, and had his nose broken on the chapel steps by a young sculptor whom he enraged with his condescension.

The restored **Cappella Brancacci** (Mon & Wed–Sat 10am–5pm, Sun 1–5pm; L5000) is now barricaded off from the rest of the Carmine and has to be entered through the cloister; your money allows you into the chapel, in a maximum group of thirty, for an utterly inadequate fifteen minutes.

The frescoes are as startling a spectacle as the restored Sistine Chapel, the brightness and delicacy of their colours and the solidity of the figures exemplifying what Bernard Berenson singled out as the tactile quality of Florentine art. The small scene on the left of the entrance arch is the quintessence of Masaccio's art. Plenty of artists had depicted *The Expulsion of Adam and Eve* before, but none had captured the desolation of the sinners so graphically – Adam presses his hands to his face in bottomless despair, Eve raises her head and screams. Saint Peter is chief protagonist of most of the remaining scenes, two of which are especially compelling: the *Tribute Money* (on the upper left wall), a complex narrative showing Peter, under Christ's instruction, fetching money from the mouth of a fish to pay the sum demanded by the city authorities; and the scene to the left of the altar, in which the shadow of the stern saint cures the infirm as it passes over them, a miracle invested with the aura of a solemn ceremonial.

The cycle was suspended when Masaccio left for Rome, where he died, and not resumed for some sixty years, when it was completed by **Filippino Lippi**. He finished the *Raising of the Emperor's Nephew* (lower left-hand wall) and painted the lower part of the wall showing the crucifixion of the saint; his most distinctive contribution, though, is *The Release of St Peter* on the right-hand side of the entrance arch, where there's a touching intimacy in the relationship between saint and counselling angel.

San Miniato al Monte

The brilliant multicoloured facade of **San Miniato al Monte** lures troops of visitors up the hill from the south bank of the Arno, and the church more than fulfills the promise of its distant appearance. The oldest religious building in Florence after the Baptistery, San Miniato is also the finest Romanesque church in Tuscany. The church's dedicatee, Saint Minias, belonged to a Christian community which settled in Florence in the third century; according to legend, after his martyrdom his corpse was seen to carry his severed head over the river and up the hill to this spot, where a shrine was subsequently erected to him. Construction of the present building began in 1013, with the foundation of a Cluniac monastery; the gorgeous marble facade – alluding to the Baptistery in its geometrical patterning – was added towards the end of that century, though the mosaic of *Christ between the Virgin and St Minias* dates from the thirteenth.

With its choir raised on a platform above the large crypt, the interior (daily 8am–12.30pm & 2–6.15pm) is like no other in the city, and its general form has changed little since the mid-eleventh century. The main structural addition is the **Cappella del Cardinale del Portogallo**, built onto the left aisle as a memorial to Cardinal James of Lusitania, who died in Florence in 1459. His chapel is a paragon of artistic collaboration – the basic design was by Antonio Manetti (a pupil of Brunelleschi), the tomb itself was carved by Antonio Rossellino, and the terracotta decoration of the ceiling was provided by Luca della Robbia. In the lower part of the church, don't overlook the intricately patterned panels of the pavement, dating from 1207, and the tabernacle between the choir stairs, designed in 1448 by Michelozzo. The majority of the frescoes along the aisle walls were painted in the fifteenth century; the most extensive are the sacristy's *Scenes from the Life of St Benedict*, painted in the 1380s by Spinello Aretino.

Drinking, eating and entertainment

Florentines have always seemed to prefer wine to coffee, and the city can't really claim to have a café tradition like that of Rome or Paris – **bars** are both more plentiful and generally more attractive places to rest your weary limbs. In recent years Florence's gastronomic reputation has suffered under the pressure of mass tourism, and many of the locals swear there's scarcely a single genuine Tuscan **restaurant** left in the city. Certainly there's a dearth of good places to eat if you're operating on a limited budget, but a decent meal isn't hard to come by if you explore the remoter quarters. The university and the annual influx of language students and other young visitors keeps the **nightlife** lively, while **seasonal events** such as the *Maggio Musicale* maintain Florence's standing as the cultural focus of Tuscany.

Cafés, bars and pasticcerie

Pavement cafés are not really part of the Florentine scene. Smaller, less ostentatious venues are more the city's style – one-room **cafés**, **bars** and **pasticcerie**, and places that combine the functions of all three. Predictably enough, the main concentrations are to be found on the big tourist streets – Via Tornabuoni, Via de' Panzani, Via de' Cerretani, Via Por Santa Maria, Via Guicciardini and Via Calzaiuoli. To find places where prices are lower and non-Florentine faces fewer, only a little effort is needed: a short walk north from the Duomo gets you into the university area around Piazza San Marco, and it's just as easy to get over into Oltrarno, the most authentic quarter of the historic centre.

Most of the places listed in the first two sections below are at their busiest first thing in the morning, as the natives stop off on the way to work at a **café-pasticceria** for a quick coffee and a pastry such as a *budino di riso* (small rice cake) or a simple *brioche* or *cornetto* (croissant). Every other street in the centre has a café or bar of some sort; what follows is a guide to the best and the most popular.

NORTH OF THE RIVER

Caffè Strozzi, Piazza Strozzi 16r. Stylish in a posey sort of way, but the outdoor tables are good for viewing the streetlife.

Caffellatte, Via degli Alfani 39r. Housed in a former dairy shop, this is good for breakfast and brunch; features a wide range of teas.

Giacosa, Via Tornabuoni 83r. Public living room of Florence's gilded youth, this was the birthplace of the *Negroni* cocktail – equal parts Campari, sweet Martini and gin.

Gran Caffè San Marco, Piazza San Marco. Busy café-bar-*pasticceria*; a standard stopoff for the university students on their way home.

Manaresi, Via de' Lamberti 16r. In the opinion of some, the coffee roasted, milled and poured at this place, at the back of Orsanmichele, is the best in the city; serves snacks too.

Procacci, Via Tornabuoni 64r. Famous café-shop that doesn't serve coffee, just cold drinks. Its fame comes from the extraordinary truffle rolls (*tartufati*), which are delicious if not exactly filling.

Rivoire, Piazza Signoria 5r. A classy and very expensive café, with outdoor tables in summer. Specialises in chocolate and pastries: go for their *cantuccini con vin santo* – hard almond biscuits soaked in sweet white wine.

Ruggini, Via de' Neri 76r. Close to the Uffizi; smart without being intimidating.

Zatti, Borgo degli Albizi 19r. Contender for the title of best *pasticceria* in Florence.

SOUTH OF THE RIVER

Caffè, Piazza Pitti 11–12r. Right opposite the Pitti Palace, this is as elegant a café as any in the city, but you pay a fair whack for the decor – and even more for the summer outside tables.

Cennini, Borgo San Jacopo 51r. Tiny, immaculate café, with perfect coffee and pastries.

Marino, Piazza Nazario Sauro 19r. Excellent spot for a stand-up breakfast of home-made brioche and coffee.

Pasticceria Maioli, Via Guicciardini 43r. A less expensive place to stop for a home-made pastry after the rigours of the Pitti.

Late-night

Cabiria, Piazza Santo Spirito. Increasingly popular bar, with cheap beer, huge video screen, and extremely gregarious owners.

Dolce Vita, Piazza del Carmine. Trendy bar that's often a venue for small-scale art exhibitions.

Rifrullo, Via San Niccolò 55r. Calls itself a pub – indicative of its affluent young clientele – and has a garden that's open in summer. It shares the building with a small family-run *latteria* which makes ice cream on the premises.

Tiratoio, Piazza de' Nerli. Near to the *Dolce Vita*, a large easy-going place, with a couple of video jukeboxes and a wide range of food.

Video Diva, Via San Zanobi 114r. Always packed with students from the nearby university; serves good cocktails.

Snacks

Bars and cafés are far from being the only places where you can get a quick bite to eat in Florence. One of the focal points of a Florentine parish is the **vinaio**, an institution that's part wine cellar, part snack bar and part social centre, where the typical customer calls in for a quick chat, a glass of wine and a few *crostini*. Another option for a rapid filler is the **friggitoria**, a frequently nameless place serving fried food such as *polenta* (maize-cake) and croquettes. If you want something a bit less basic, there's the **rostic-**

ceria, a sort of delicatessen serving first courses and roast meat dishes; usually these are takeaway places, but there are seats at the ones we've listed. **Pizza** by the slice, a routine tourist stand-by, often amounts to just a slab of dough with a smear of tomato paste, but you can get something a touch more tasty at the addresses below. Most of the places given in this section are open from around 8am to 8pm from Monday to Saturday. Note also that *alimentari* often sell sandwiches and local delicacies, especially pastries.

All'Antico Vinaio, Via de' Neri 65r. Rough-and-ready joint, close to the Uffizi.

Alla Marchigiana, Via del Corso 60r. Good source of takeaway pizza in the centre of town.

Il Fornaio Renzo, Via Guiccardini 3. Best place for a pizza slice in the Pitti area.

Da Moreno, Via Val di Lamona. Busy *rosticceria* at the back of the *Porcellino* market.

La Mescita, Via degli Alfani 70r. Low-key student *vinaio* in the university area; serves stuffed tomatoes and a range of other vegetables in addition to the traditional *crostini*.

Friggitoria Luisa, Via Sant'Antonino 50. Sells slices of pizza as well as the traditional *friggitoria* fare.

Via de' Neri 40r. Calls itself a *friggitoria*, but in fact serves virtually nothing but pizza.

Vini e Panini i Fratelli, Via Cimatori 38r. A perfect example of the Florentine *vinaio*, just off Via Calzaiuoli.

Volta di San Pietro 5. Highly recommended *friggitoria* in a tiny alley off Borgo degli Albizi, between the Duomo and Sant'Ambrogio. Serves hamburgers, sausages and salads and you can wash your snack down with a glass of wine from *All'Antico Noè*, in front of the *friggitoria* – which also does excellent sandwiches.

Food markets and shops

An obvious and enjoyable way to cut down costs is to put together a picnic and retire to the Bóboli gardens or squares such as Piazza Santissima Annunziata, Piazza Santa Croce or Piazza Santa Maria Novella. For **provisions**, the easiest option is to call in at the **Mercato Centrale** by San Lorenzo church (Mon–Sat 7am–2pm, plus Sat 4–8pm), where everything you could possibly need can be bought under one roof – bread, ham, cheese, fruit, wine. Almost as comprehensive, and even cheaper, is the **Mercato Sant'Ambrogio** market over by Santa Croce (Mon–Fri 7am–2pm).

If you're right in the thick of the main sights with closing time approaching, **Via dei Tavolini**, off Via Calzaiuoli, is a good central street in which to assemble a picnic: *Grana Market* at 11r has a fabulous cheese selection, *Chellini* at 1r is a good *alimentari*, and *Semelino* at 18r bakes wonderful bread.

Every district has its **alimentari**, which in addition to selling the choicest Tuscan produce might also provide sandwiches. The simply named *Alimentari*, close to Santa Trìnita at Via Parione 19, prepares perhaps the most delicious sandwiches in town (eg smoked salmon and stracchino cheese), and has a few seats, so you can linger over a glass of wine. *Vera*, at the southern end of Ponte Santa Trìnita at Piazza Frescobaldi 3r, takes the prize for the ultimate Florentine deli; other excellent central *alimentari* include *Tassini* at Borgo Santi Apostoli 24r and *Alessi Paride* at Via delle Oche 27–29r.

If the stalls and the *alimentari* are shut, there's the last resort of the *Standa* **supermarkets** at Via dei Mille 140, Via Pietrapiana 42–44 and Via de' Panzi 31 (Mon 2–8pm, Tues–Sun 9am–8pm).

Restaurants

In gastronomic circles, Florentine cuisine is accorded as much reverence as Florentine art. Florentine food has always been characterised by modest raw materials and simple technique – beefsteak (*bistecca*), tripe (*trippa*) and liver (*fegato*) are typical ingredients, while grilling (*alla Fiorentina*) is a favoured method of preparation. In addition, white beans (*fagioli*) will feature on most menus, either on their own, garnished with liberal quantities of local olive oil, or as the basis of such dishes as *ribollita* soup.

Unfussy it might be, but quality cooking doesn't come cheap in Florence – most of the restaurants that meet with local approval cost L50,000-plus per person, wine included. Yet there are some decent low-budget places serving food that at least gives some idea of the region's characteristic dishes, and even the simplest trattoria should offer *bistecca alla Fiorentina*. One thing to be aware of is that many restaurants in Florence will only serve full meals – so check the menu outside if you're thinking of just popping in for a quick lunchtime plate of pasta.

As a very rough guideline, the cheapest places tend to be near the station, the best places on or near the main central streets, and the best mid-range restaurants tucked away in alleys on the north of the river or over in Oltrarno.

Station and market areas

Antichi Cancelli, Via Faenza 73r. Not a gourmet experience, but more than tolerable at the price.

Il Contadino, Via Palazzuolo 69r. Very basic meals at around L13,000; often a lot of backpackers in the queue.

Gozzi, Piazza San Lorenzo 8r. Over the road from the market, this is a fairly cheap, homely trattoria.

Mensa Universitaria, Via San Gallo 25a. Not far from the San Lorenzo market, this is the cheapest deal in town – L6500 for two-course meal plus fruit and drink. Open to all student card holders Mon–Sat noon–2.15pm and 6.45–8.45pm; closed mid-July to mid-Sept. There are smaller *mensas* at Via dei Servi 25a (same hours) and at Piazza Santissima Annunziata 2 (lunchtime only).

Da Mario, Via Rosina 2r. Popular with students and market workers, so be prepared to queue and share a table; atmosphere is friendly and the prices low.

Pepe Verde, Piazza del Mercato 17–18r. Bar/café/low-cost eatery, with mainly young clientele.

Za-za, Piazza del Mercato 26r. Has a few tables on ground level and a bigger canteen below; *fettunta con fagioli* (olive oil and white beans on bread) is something of a speciality, but it requires a strong stomach.

City centre

Antico Fattore, Via Lambertesca 1–3r. Simple Tuscan dishes dominate the menu, and the soups are particularly good; close to the Piazza della Signoria, but not as expensive as the locale might suggest. Grim service.

Aqua al Due, Via dell'Acqua 2r. Always packed, chiefly on account of its *assaggio di primi* – a succession of pasta dishes shared by everyone at the table.

Belle Donne, Via delle Belle Donne 16r. Bustling, basic trattoria with blackboard menu; especially busy at lunchtime.

Coco Lezzone, Via del Parioncino 26r. Straightforward but classy white-tiled trattoria near Santa Trìnita; go for the *porcini* (wild mushroom) pasta. A really full meal should come in at around L50,000.

I Ghibellini, Via San Pier Maggiore 8r. Inexpensive but always crowded restaurant-pizzeria, with some pleasant outside tables.

Da Gianino, Piazza dei Cimatori 4r (☎214.125). Produces wonderful home-made pastas and desserts. In summer, when tables are moved out onto the tiny square, it's essential to book.

Latini, Via Palchetti 6r. Good local fare in semi-rustic atmosphere; always busy – turn up after 8pm and you'll have to queue.

Le Mossacce, Via del Proconsolo 55r. Once the fashionable haunt of Florence's young artists, who occasionally paid for their meals with a painting or two; the bohemian element has since fled, but the food remains excellent.

Nuti, Borgo San Lorenzo 39r. Large place that claims to be the oldest trattoria in town – good pizzas, and prices are reasonable, though service can be poor.

Silvio, Via del Parione 74r. Mid-market and straightforward in its menu, this is one of the best places in town for fish.

Sostanza, Via della Porcellana 25r. Solid Tuscan fare at solid Tuscan prices – L30,000 and upwards.

Santa Croce area

Benvenuto, Via Mosca 16r, off Via de' Neri. Don't be misled by the entrance, which looks more like the doorway to a delicatessen than a trattoria; the *gnocchi* and *arista* are delicious.

Il Cibrèo, Via de' Macci 118r. Influenced by nouvelle cuisine, but not too precious; desserts are wonderful. Allow around L80,000 in the posh part of the restaurant – but round the corner in Via del Verrocchio there's the entrance to a backroom section where the menu is basically the same but the prices are far lower.

Danny Rock, Via Pandolfini 13. Looks a bit like a fast-food place with its green metal chairs but employs a French cook who creates marvellous crêpes, among other things; large suspended screens show concerts and sporting events; open until at least 1am.

La Maremmana, Via de' Macci 77r. Very good set menus from L20,000.

La Stazione di Zima, Via Ghibellina 70r. Popular vegetarian place.

Tavola Calda, Sant'Ambrogio market. A superb daytime stop for mouthwatering Tuscan dishes such as *topini di patate*, a first course of potatoes topped with a variety of sauces. A full three-course lunch costs around L20,000.

La Vie en Rose, Borgo Allegri 68r. Excellent game dishes in this cosy little restaurant, where a full meal with wine will set you back in the region of L50,000.

Oltrarno

Del Carmine, Piazza del Carmine 18r. Reasonable food, reasonable prices, charmless service.

Casalinga, Via Michelozzi 9r. About the best low-cost authentic Tuscan dishes in town; popular despite the drop-dead demeanour cultivated by the workforce.

Cinghiale Bianco, Borgo San Jacopo 43r. As the name tells you, wild boar is the pride of this mid-range restaurant.

Dante, Piazza Nazario Sauro 10r. Popular pizzeria that also serves around a dozen types of spaghetti.

Nello, Borgo Tegolaio 21r. Offers both a full and a half-portion *menu fixe* at lunchtime, an option that invariably packs the place out; in the evenings it's possible to get an excellent *à la carte* meal for under L30,000.

Oreste, Piazza Santo Spirito. A place to go to in fine weather, when it sets up its tables on the square; the *menu fixe* is usually good, as is the *salsiccia e fagioli* – sausage and beans Tuscan-style.

Dei Quattro Leoni, Via Vellutini 1r. A genuine, extremely plain trattoria with irresistible prices. As a starter try the *finocchiona*, a type of Tuscan salami.

I Raddi, Via Ardiglione 47r. One of the area's newer places, recommended for its *peposa*, veal casseroled with pepper but no salt.

Le Sorelle, Via San Niccolò 30r. Unpretentious local restaurant; specialises in salami and *penne*.

I Tarocchi, Via de' Renai 12r. Busy restaurant-pizzeria.

Alla Vecchia Bettola, Viale Lodovico Ariosto 32r. Long trestle tables give this place something of the atmosphere of a drinking den, which is what it once was; the menu is a good repertoire of Tuscan meat dishes.

Gelaterie

Devotees of Italian ice cream will find plenty of occasions to sample some wacky concoctions without straying far off the main drags – though, as with the bars and cafés, the most rewarding spots are less central.

Vivoli, Via Isola delle Stinche 7r. Operating from unprepossessing premises in a side street close to Santa Croce, this is the best ice cream maker in Florence.

Badiani, Viale dei Mille 20r. Known for its eggy *Buontalenti* ice cream, the recipe of which is known only to the proprietors; closed Tues.

Perchè No!, Via de' Tavolini 19r. Very central *gelateria*; go for the rum-laced *tiramisù* ice cream. Closed Tues.

Festival del Gelato, Via del Corso 75r. Over 100 varieties, with some very exotic combinations; good *semifreddi*. Closed Mon.

Frilli, Via San Niccolò 57. Excellent ice creams made from seasonal fruit. Closed Wed.

Nightlife and culture

After-dark Florence has a reputation for catering primarily to the middle-aged and affluent, but like every university town it has its pockets of activity, and by hanging around the San Marco area you should pick up news of any impromptu term-time events. Full details of the city's dependable venues are given below; for up-to-the-minute **information** about what's on, call in at *Box Office* at Via della Pergola 10ar, or *Contempo Records*, Via de' Neri 15r.

Florence's cultural calendar is filled out with special exhibitions and seasons of opera, theatre, ballet, and music of all varieties. You can usually find information in English about concerts and shows at the city council kiosks in Piazza Repubblica or inside the Palazzo Vecchio; otherwise, check out the tourist offices, advertising posters, and local magazines. Tickets for most events can be bought at *Box Office*.

Live music venues

Amadeus, Via Alfani 26r. Jazz and rock, plus cabaret acts on Thurs & Sun; closed Mon; membership at the door.

Chiodo fisso, Via Dante Alighieri 16r. A good spot for folk guitar music and occasionally for jazz – the wine's good as well; open every night.

Drunk Ladder, Piazza IV Novembre, Sesto Fiorentino (bus #28). Video-pub (with English beer) which hosts jazz groups from time to time; open from 8pm every night except Wed.

Genius, Via San Gallo 22r. Jazz sessions organised by the local Red Bean Jazz group, every night except Sat from 10pm; good food and drink, but the decor is off-puttingly cold.

Pegaso, Via Palazzuolo 82r. Jazz sets from 10pm to 2.30am; cheap membership.

Stonehenge, Via dell'Amorino 16r. Rock venue cum bar, operating under the slogan "Do it, then come here"; open from 10pm to 4am every night except Mon.

Clubs

Cayenna, Via Carducci 37r. Attracts a mix of student travellers and local Greens; serves beer and wine, and freshly made croissants late at night; 9pm to 1am except Tues.

Last Exit, Borgo Pinti 17r. Home of the psychedelic tendency; Tues–Sun 10pm–3am.

Liquid, Borgo Albizi 9. Vaguely underground/avant-garde, and entirely yuppie-free; the interior design is constantly changing; open from 10pm into the small hours every night.

Sfizio, Lungarno Cellini 1r. Newish place with a video jukebox inside and an open-air area close to the Arno – a drawback being the traffic between you and the river.

Discos

Flamingo, Via Pandolfi 26. The best gay disco in Florence.

Rockafè, Borgo Albizi 66r. Revamped mainstream disco; open Thurs–Sun.

Space Electronic, Via Palazzuolo 37. A favourite with young foreigners; open every night; free entry with student card.

Tenax, Via Pratese 47, Perètola. A bus-ride from the centre, this is the biggest and most popular disco, and a leading venue for bands – the cocktails are great too; open Wed– Sun.

Yab Yum, Via de' Sassetti 5r. Right in the centre, so its dance floor is heaving in summer; closed Mon.

Cinema

Florence has a large number of cinemas, but there are only a couple of places to see films undubbed: *Astro*, in Piazza San Simone (near Santa Croce), screens English-language films from Tuesday to Sunday, while *Spazio Uno*, near Santa Maria Novella at Via del Sole 10, has occasional films in English. From June to September there's a season of films on an open-air screen at the *Forte Belvedere*, above the Bóboli gardens.

Classical music

The **Maggio Musicale Fiorentino** is one of the most famous festivals of opera and classical music in Italy; confusingly, it isn't limited to May, but lasts from late April to early July. Events are staged at the *Teatro Comunale*, the *Teatro della Pergola*, the Palazzo dei Congressi, and occasionally in the Bóboli gardens. Information and tickets – usually expensive – can be obtained from the festival HQ in the *Teatro Comunale*, Corso Italia 16 (☎277.9236). The *Comunale* also has a winter concert season from November to mid-December and an opera season from then until mid-January.

Estate Fiesolana, held in Fiesole every summer, is a slightly less exclusive festival, concentrating more on chamber and symphonic music. Films and theatre groups are also featured, most events being held in the open-air *Teatro Romano*.

Listings

Airlines *Air France*, Borgo SS. Apostoli 9 (☎218.335); *Alitalia*, Lungarno Acciauoli 10–12 (☎27.888); *British Airways*, Via della Vigna Nuova 36r (☎218.655); *Lufthansa*, Via Pellicceria 6 (☎238.1450); *TWA*, Via dei Vecchietti 4 (☎284.691).

Airport enquiries *Aeroporto Galileo Galilei*, Pisa (☎050/28.088); information also from the check-in desk at Santa Maria Novella train station, platform 5 (daily 7am–8pm). Information for flights from Perètola airport: ☎373.498.

Bicycle hire *Ciao & Basta*, Costa dei Magnoli 24 (☎296.230); *Motorent*, Via Zanobi 9r(☎490.113).

Books *Feltrinelli*, Via Cavour 12r, and *Seeber*, Via Tornabuoni 68r, are the best-stocked general shops. *Paperback Exchange*, Via Fiesolana 31r, always has a good stock of English and American books; it operates an exchange scheme for second-hand books and has very friendly staff. *Il Viaggio*, Via Ghibellina 117r, specialises in travel books, guides and maps.

Bus enquiries For city services: *ATAF*, Piazza Duomo 57r (☎580.528). For state-run services all over Italy: *SITA*, Via Santa Caterina di Siena (☎214.721). For services within Tuscany and Umbria: *CLAP*, Piazza Stazione 15 (☎283.734), to Lucca and Lucca province; *CAP*, Via Nazionale 13 (☎214.637), to Prato; *CAT*, Via Fiume 2 (☎283.400), to Arezzo, Città di Castello and Sansepolcro; *COPIT*, Piazza Santa Maria Novella (☎215.451), to Pistoia, Poggio a Caiano and Vinci; *LAZZI*, Piazza Stazione 4 (☎298.840), to Empoli, Livorno, Lucca, Pisa, Pistoia, Prato and Viareggio; *RAMA* (same address and phone as *Lazzi*), to Grosseto.

Car rental *Avis*, Lungarno Torrigiani 33 (☎234.6668); *Europcar*, Borgo Ognissanti 120r (☎294.130); *Excelsior*, Via Agnelli 33 (☎293.186); *Hertz*, Via Maso Finiguerra 17r (☎298.205); *Italy by Car*, Borgo Ognissanti 134r (☎293.021); *Program*, Borgo Ognissanti 135r (☎282.916).

Consulates *Netherlands*, Via Cavour 81 (☎475.249); *UK*, Lungarno Corsini 2 (☎284.133); *US*, Lungarno Vespucci 38 (☎294.921). Travellers from Ireland, Australia, New Zealand and Canada should contact their Rome consulates.

Doctors The *Tourist Medical Service*, Via Lorenzo il Magnifico 59 (☎475.411), has English-speaking doctors on 24-hr call.

Exchange Banks are concentrated around Via Tornabuoni and Piazza della Repubblica, and some are open for a few hours on Saturday in addition to the usual hours. Otherwise try *American Express*, Via Dante Alighieri 22r (Mon–Fri 9am–6pm, Sat 9am–1pm), or the *Esercizio Promozione Turismo*, just north of Piazza Signoria at Via Condotta 42 (Mon–Sat 10am–7pm, Sun 10am–6pm).

First aid *Misericordia*, Piazza del Duomo 20 (☎212.222).

Hospital Santa Maria Nuova, Piazza Santa Maria Nuova 1 (☎27.581). If you require the services of an interpreter, the *Associazione Volontari Ospedalieri* can be called out by ringing ☎403.126; it's a volunteer organisation, and its services are free.

Laundry *Guelfa*, Via Guelfa 106n.

Left luggage Train station left-luggage desk open 24hr; L1500 per item.

Lost property Via Circondaria 19 (Mon–Wed & Fri–Sat 9am–noon; ☎367.943).

Pharmacies All-night pharmacies are as follows: *Comunale della Stazione*, at the train station; *Molteni*, Via Calzaiuoli 7r; *Taverna*, Piazza San Giovanni 20. In addition each pharmacy displays the late-night roster in its window, or you can ring ☎110 for information.

Police Emergency ☎113; urban police ☎352.141. The *Questura*, for passport problems, reporting thefts and so on, is at Via Zara 2 (☎49.771).

Post office Central post office at Via Pellicceria 8 (Mon–Fri 8.15am–7pm, Sat 8.15am–noon; telegram office open 24hr); poste restante at counters 23 & 24. Florence's main post office is at Via Pietrapiana 53–55 (same hours).

Scooter and motorbike hire *Eurodrive*, Via Alamanni 7–9 (☎298.639); *Excelsior*, Via della Scala 48ar (☎293.186); *Free Motor*, Via Santa Monica 6–8 (☎295.102); *Motorent*, Via San Zenobi 9 (☎490.113); *Program*, Borgo Ognissanti 135r (☎282.916); *Sabra*, Via Artisti 8 (☎576.256); *Vespa Rent*, Via Pisana 103r (☎715.691).

Taxis Main ranks by the train station and in Piazza della Repubblica; radio cabs ☎4798 or ☎4390.

Telephones 24-hr booths at train station, at Via Pellicceria post office, and at SIP office, Via Cavour 21r.

Train enquiries ☎278.785.

Around Florence

If you settle into Florence as a base, there's a lot to be said for a couple of days' escape to the environs. Within the area of Greater Florence, city buses run to the hill village of **Fiesole**, and to the nearest of the various **Medici villas** – originally country retreats, now all but consumed by the suburbs. Further afield, **Prato** and **Pistoia** – respectively 25 and 35 minutes distant by train or bus – each make fine day trips, with their medieval ensembles and Florentine-inspired Renaissance art. On the parallel rail lines and roads to Pisa, there are worthwhile diversions to **Vinci** – Leonardo's birthplace – and to **San Miniato**. And to the south, though requiring your own transport to explore properly, lie the hills and vineyards of **Chianti**, Italy's premier wine region and expat ghetto.

Fiesole

A long-established Florentine retreat from the summer heat and crowds, **FIESOLE** spreads over a cluster of hilltops above the Mugnone and Arno valleys, some 8km northeast of Florence. First settled in the Bronze Age, then by the Etruscans, then absorbed by the Romans, it rivalled its neighbour until the early twelfth century, when the Florentines overran the town. From that time it became a satellite of Florence, being especially favoured as a semi-rural second home for its wealthier citizens.

The #7 *ATAF* bus runs every quarter of an hour from Florence train station, through San Domenico (see overleaf) to the central square of Fiesole, Piazza Mino da Fiesole; the journey takes around twenty minutes, and costs the standard L1000. The town itself is small enough to be explored in a morning, but the country lanes of its surroundings invite a more leisurely tour, and might even tempt you to stay.

Accommodation on a tight budget is a problem, though: *Villa Sorriso*, Via Gramsci 21 (☎59.027; ⑥), is the cheapest close to the centre; about a kilometre further out, *Villa Baccano*, Via Bosconi 4 (☎59.341; ④), is a lot less expensive. Fiesole's **campsite**, *Camping Panoramico* (☎599.069), is 3km out of town in Via Peramonda; the #70 bus goes to the foot of the hill on which it's situated. The Fiesole **tourist office** (March–Oct Mon–Sat 8.30am–6.30pm; Nov–Feb closes 1.30pm) is at Piazza Mino da Fiesole 45.

The Town

Nineteenth-century restoration has ruined the exterior of the **Duomo**, on the central piazza. The interior is something like a stripped-down version of Florence's San Miniato, though there's relief from the overall austerity in the Cappella Salutati, to the right of the choir: it contains two fine pieces carved by Mino da Fiesole in the mid-fifteenth century – a panel of *The Madonna and Saints* and the tomb of Bishop Salutati.

Fiesole's other major churches, **Sant'Alessandro** and **San Francesco**, are reached by the steep Via San Francesco, which just below the churches widens into a terrace giving a remarkable panorama of Florence. Sant'Alessandro (daily 10am–noon & 3–5pm) was founded in the sixth century on the site of Etruscan and Roman temples; recent repairs have rendered the outside a whitewashed nonentity, but the beautiful *marmorino cipollino* (onion marble) columns of the basilical interior make it the most atmospheric building in Fiesole. Again, restoration has not improved the Gothic church of San Francesco (same hours), which occupies the site of the acropolis. Across one of the convent's tiny cloisters there's a chaotic museum of pieces brought back from Egypt and China by missionaries. An alternative descent back to the main square is through the public park, entered by a gate facing San Francesco's facade.

Around the back of the duomo, in Via Marini, is the entrance to the **Teatro Romano** and **Museo Archeologico** (April–Sept daily 9am–7pm; Oct–March Tues–Sun 10am–4pm; L4000). Built in the first century BC, the 3000-seater theatre was excavated towards the end of the last century and remains in good enough repair to be used for performances during the *Estate Fiesolana* festival. Most of the museum exhibits were discovered here, and encompass pieces from the Bronze Age to the Roman occupation.

San Domenico

If you've time to spare in Fiesole, wander down the narrow Via Vecchia Fiesolana, which goes by the **Villa Medici** (built for Cosimo il Vecchio by Michelozzo) on its way to the hamlet of **SAN DOMENICO**, 1500m southwest of Fiesole. Fra' Angelico was once prior of the Dominican **monastery** here, and the church retains a *Madonna and Angels* by him (first chapel on left); the chapter house also has a Fra' Angelico fresco of *The Crucifixion* (ring at no. 4 for entry).

Five minutes' walk northwest from San Domenico brings you to the **Badia Fiesolana**, Fiesole's cathedral from the ninth century to the eleventh. Cosimo il Vecchio had the church altered in the 1460s, a project which left the magnificent Romanesque facade intact while transforming the interior into a superb Renaissance building.

The Medici villas

The finest country houses of the Florentine hinterland are, predictably enough, those built for the Medici. The earliest of these grand villas were intended as fortified refuges to which the family could withdraw when the political temperature in the city became a little too hot, but by the sixteenth and seventeenth centuries, when they were established as the unchallenged rulers of the city, the villas became more ostentatious, signifying the might of the dynasty through their sheer luxuriousness. They had a financial function too: as Florence's importance as a manufacturing city began to dwindle, the Medici decided to sink some of their resources into agricultural real estate.

Villa Medicea della Petraia

The **Villa della Petraia** (bus #28 from the train station; Tues–Sun 9am–2pm; free), now hedged about by the industrial sprawl of Florence's northern edge, was adapted from a medieval castle in the 1570s and 1580s by Buontalenti, working to a commission from the future Grand-Duke Ferdinando I. The interior was altered in turn by Vittorio Emanuele II, who glassed over the interior courtyard to convert it into a ballroom; its walls are covered by a seventeenth-century fresco cycle glorifying the Medici. Giambologna's bronze statue of *Venus*, now transplanted to a small room indoors, used to adorn the marble fountain on the upper terrace of the magnificent **garden** (Tues–Sun 9am–sunset).

Villa Medicea di Castello

A little under a kilometre's walk northwest down the hill from La Petraia stands the **Villa di Castello**, which was bought in 1477 by Lorenzo and Giovanni de'Medici, second cousins of Lorenzo il Magnifico and the principal patrons of Botticelli. The fame of the villa rests on its spectacular **gardens** (Tues–Sun 9am–sunset; free), which were laid out by Tribolo for Cosimo I and completed by Buontalenti, who also redesigned the house. Delighted by its labyrinths, fountains and myriad Mannerist tricks, Montaigne judged this to be the best garden in Europe. The outstanding eccentricities are Ammannati's shivering figure of *January*, the triple-bowled fountain topped by the same artist's *Hercules and Antaeus*, and the Grotto degli Animali, an artificial cave against whose walls stands a menagerie of sculpted creatures.

Villa Medicea di Careggi

Originally a fortified farmhouse, the **Villa di Careggi** was altered by Michelozzo in the 1430s for Cosimo il Vecchio, but is particularly associated with his grandson Lorenzo il Magnifico, whose academy of Platonic scholars used to meet here. Lorenzo, his father and Cosimo all died here. The best known of all the Medici villas, it's now a nurse's home, and permission to visit the interior normally has to be obtained in advance (☎277.4329), though a request at the office inside the entrance sometimes succeeds, and the surrounding gardens and woodland can be explored freely. The #14c bus covers the 5km from the train station to the villa, or you can walk from La Petraia.

Poggio a Caiano

For the most complete image of what life was like in the Medici villas in the family's heyday, make the trip to the **Villa Medicea di Poggio a Caiano** (Tues–Sat 9am–1.30pm, Sun 9am–12.30pm; L4000), 18km northwest of Florence at the foot of Monte Albano. (Take the *COPIT* bus from Piazza Santa Maria Novella; they leave every 30min, and take around 30min.) Lorenzo il Magnifico bought a farmhouse on this site in 1480 and had it rebuilt as a classical rural palace by Giuliano da Sangallo – the only architectural project instigated by Lorenzo that has survived. Additions made by later members of the family fit well within Sangallo's design – the imposing entrance loggia, for instance, was commissioned by Lorenzo's son Giovanni, the future Pope Leo X. Inside, the focal point is the double-height *salone* which the architect made out of the original courtyard; its sixteenth-century frescoes include works by Pontormo and del Sarto. The **gardens** (Mon–Sat 9am–sunset, Sun 9am–12.30pm), modified by the Lorraine princes into an English-style landscape, contain some magnificent old trees.

Villa dell'Artimino

From Poggio e Caiano a bus runs south, past COMEANA, to the walled village of Artimino, site of the **Villa Artimino**, sometimes known as *La Ferdinanda*. Designed by Buontalenti as a hunting lodge for Ferdinando I, the villa has the appearance of a rather dandified fortress, and its most distinctive external feature has earned it the nickname "the villa of the hundred chimneys". The interior is pleasingly unpretentious but can only be visited on a pre-booked guided tour on Tuesdays (☎871.8072); in the basement there's a museum of Etruscan finds from the tombs at Comeana (Mon, Tues & Thurs–Sat 9am–12.30pm, plus Sat 3.30–6.30pm; L3000).

Pratolino

Nothing remains of Francesco I's favourite villa, the Villa Demidoff at **Pratolino**, except its expansive park, and even this is but a shadow of its earlier self (May–Sept Fri–Sun 10am–8pm; L2000). The mechanical toys, trick fountains and other practical jokes that Buontalenti installed in the grounds of Pratolino were the most ingenious ever seen, and required so much maintenance that there was a house in the grounds for the court plumbers. Only Giambologna's immense *Appennino* – a man-mountain who gushes water – survives from the original garden, but the park is still one of the pleasantest green spaces within a bus-ride of Florence. It's 12km north of the city and is served by the #25 route.

Prato

Taking its name from the meadow (*prato*) where the ancient settlement's great market used to be held, **PRATO** has long been a commercial success, and is now the third largest city in Tuscany, after Florence and Livorno. It's been Italy's chief textile city since the early Middle Ages, and even though recession has cut exports by a quarter over the last five years, it still produces three-quarters of all the woollen cloth sold from Italy. It might not feature on a list of the most attractive places in the province, but its long-time wealth has left a fair legacy of buildings and art, including Filippo Lippi's most engaging cycle of frescoes.

The *centro storico* remains enclosed within a hexagon of walls, making orientation straightforward. Buses from Florence run direct to the Piazza del Duomo. Coming from the train station you cross the Ponte della Vittoria, the bridge in front of the square, and Viale Vittorio Veneto leads you to the walls. Directly ahead, past a Henry Moore sculpture, rises the white-walled **Castello d'Imperatore** (Mon & Wed–Sat 9am–12.30pm & 3–6.30pm, Sun 9.30am–12.30pm; free), built in the thirteenth century for Emperor Frederick II. The castle is heavily restored – concerts are held in the courtyard in summer – but you can wander around the ramparts for views over the old city and the industrial suburbs. Virtually adjacent is Prato's major Renaissance monument, Giuliano Sangallo's church of **Santa Maria delle Carceri** (closed noon–4.30pm). Heavily influenced by Brunelleschi's Strozzi chapel, it makes a decorative gesture towards the Romanesque with its bands of green and white marble; the interior is lightened by an Andrea della Robbia frieze.

From here, the route to the duomo passes through the Piazza del Comune, where the **Galleria Comunale** (Mon & Wed–Sat 9.30am–12.30pm & 3–6.30pm, Sun 9.30am–12.30pm; L5000 ticket includes entry to the other two town museums) contains a ramshackle collection of Florentine art, including work by Filippo Lippi and a predella by Bernardo Daddi narrating the story of Prato's holy relic, the Girdle of the Madonna (see below). The collections fizzle out with a stream of forgettable seventeenth- and eighteenth-century pieces. A couple of blocks south of here, on Via Rinaldesca, is the **Palazzo Datini**, the fourteenth-century home of the merchant and banker Francesco di Marco Datini, whose life is superbly re-created in Iris Origo's classic study, *The Merchant of Prato*. The late Gothic building was completely frescoed inside and out; it is not open to visits, but its decoration can be glimpsed from the street.

The Piazza del Duomo, one block north of Piazza del Comune, forms an effective space for the Pisan-Romanesque facade of the **Duomo** (closed noon–4pm), distinguished by an Andrea della Robbia terracotta over the portal and, on the corner, a strange external pulpit designed by Donatello and Michelozzo, from which the Holy Girdle is displayed five times each year. The interior has three major fresco cycles. In the chapel immediately left of the entrance is **Agnolo Gaddi**'s *Legend of the Holy Girdle* (1392–95); the girdle was supposedly given by the Virgin to the ever-incredulous Thomas – who doubted the reality of her Assumption – and was brought from the Holy Land to Prato in the twelfth century. The sensuous frescoes behind the high altar were created between 1452 and 1466 by **Filippo Lippi**, and depict the martyrdoms of Saint John the Baptist and Saint Stephen. During the period of his work, Lippi – though nominally a monk – became infatuated by a young nun called Lucrezia, who later became the mother of his son, Filippino Lippi. She is said to be the model for the dancing figure of Salome, while her lover has painted himself as one of those mourning Saint Stephen – he's third from the right. The chapel to the right of the high altar has scenes from lives of the Virgin and Saint Stephen, still labelled as being by Paolo Uccello, though they don't look remotely like his work and a study of the underpainting has proved that they can't possibly be by him.

To see the heavily corroded original panels of Donatello's exterior pulpit, look in at the **Museo dell'Opera del Duomo** (Mon & Wed–Sat 9am–12.30pm & 3–6.30pm, Sun 9.30am–12.30pm), housed alongside the Duomo in the Bishop's Palace. The museum's other main treasure is Maso di Bartolomeo's tiny reliquary for the Sacred Girdle.

The third of Prato's museums, the **Museo Pittura Murale** (9am–noon; closed Tues), is a five-minute walk west of the Duomo, in the ex-monastery adjoining the mainly fourteenth-century church of San Domenico. It contains a hotch-potch of minor frescoes, culled mostly from churches in and around Prato.

Practicalities

Behind the Carceri church at Via Cairoli 48, the **tourist office** (daily 8.30am–1.30pm) provides details of the city's practicalities and many cultural events. Prato has a single one-star hotel, the *Roma*, outside the southern gate at Via Carradori 1 (☎0574/31.777; ④). If you want more comfort, try the two-star *Stella d'Italia* at Piazza Duomo 8 (☎0574/27.910; ⑤) or *Il Giglio* at Piazza San Marco 14 (☎0574/37.049; ⑤). For **food**, the *Trattoria Lapo* is a basic local place at Piazza Mercatale 140, and there are two neon-lit *birreria*-pizzeria places on the square as well.

Pistoia

The provincial capital of **PISTOIA** is one of the least visited cities in Tuscany: an unjustified ranking for this quiet, well-preserved medieval city at the base of the Apennines. Just 35 minutes by train from Florence (about the same by bus), it is an easy and enjoyable day trip – and also forms the most attractive approach to Lucca and Pisa, with both of which it has strong architectural links.

The city was known through medieval times for its feuds and was condemned by Dante, Machiavelli and Michelangelo, who referred to the Pistoese as "the enemies of heaven". An important metalworking centre, it left a legacy to the world in the pistol, originally the name of a dagger but later the label for the first local firearms. These days, Pistoia maintains its industrial tradition with a large rail plant, but is better known for the acres of garden nurseries on the slopes around. In terms of art attractions, its appeal lies in a sequence of Romanesque churches and sculpture, and, its most famous image, a superb technicolour della Robbia frieze.

The Town

Arriving by train or by bus from Florence you are just a couple of minutes' walk south of the historic centre – Viale XX Settembre points the way through the city walls. The interesting part of the city begins one block north of Piazza Treviso, at the junction with the centre's widest avenue, Corso Gramsci.

A right turn at this junction takes you to Piazza Garibaldi and the thirteenth-century church of **San Domenico**. Over the road, the **Cappella del Tau** preserves a chaos of fourteenth- and fifteenth-century frescoed scenes from the lives of Adam and Eve, Christ and various saints. A couple of doors away, in the Palazzo del Tau, there's the new **Museo Marino Marini** (Tues–Sat 9am–1pm & 3–7pm, Sun 9am–12.30pm; free), showing a selection of work by Pistoia's most famous modern son. As well as a posse of his trademark horses and riders, the museum features his forays into portraiture – subjects here include Thomas Mann, Henry Miller and Marc Chagall.

All streets north from Piazza Garibaldi link with Via Cavour, now the main street of the city's inner core but once the settlement's outer limit – as the name of the majestic **San Giovanni Fuorcivitas** ("outside the walls") proclaims. The church was founded in the eighth century, but rebuilt between the twelfth and fourteenth centuries, when it received the dazzling green and white flank that serves as its **facade**. The **interior**, though only feebly lit by the slit windows, is just as remarkable, as this is one of three Pistoia churches distinguished by pulpits showing state-of-the-art Tuscan sculpture in the thirteenth century. The **pulpit** here was carved in 1270 by a pupil of Nicola Pisano, whose son, Giovanni, executed the four figures of cardinals on the holy water stoup.

The superb medieval complex of the **Piazza del Duomo**, a short way north, gets packed to capacity just once a year, for July 25's *Giostro dell'Orso*, Pistoia's answer to the medieval shenanigans of Siena's Palio. If you have come from Pisa or Lucca, the style of the **Duomo** itself will be immediately familiar, with its tiered arcades and striped decoration of black and white marble. Set into this soberly refined front is a tunnel-vault portico of bright terracotta tiles by Andrea della Robbia, creator also of the *Madonna and Child* above the door. The interior (Mon–Sat 7am–noon & 4–7pm, Sun 7am–1pm) has an outstanding array of sculptural pieces, one of which is part of the entrance wall – a marvellous font designed by Benedetto da Maiano, showing incidents from the life of the Baptist. Off the right aisle is the Cappella di San Jacopo (L1000), endowed with one of the richest pieces of silverwork to be seen in Italy, the **Altarpiece of St James**. Weighing almost a ton and populated with 628 figures, it was begun in 1287 and completed in the fifteenth century, when Brunelleschi cast the two half-figures of prophets on the left-hand side.

Adjoining the duomo, the partly clad Palazzo dei Vescovi is now home of the small **Museo San Zeno** (tours Tues, Thurs & Fri 10am, 11.30am & 3.30pm; L2000), where the chief exhibit is Ghiberti's reliquary of Saint James. The basement has an even more modest archaeological collection, with relics from the Roman settlement. Opposite is the tall, dapper Gothic **Baptistery**, designed by Giovanni Pisano; there's nothing under the conical brick ceiling but an old font, though the vacancy is sometimes filled by commercial art shows.

On the far side of the square, the **Palazzo Comunale** contains the **Museo Civico** (Tues–Sat 9am–1pm & 3–7pm, Sun 9am–12.30pm; L4000), where the customary Tuscan welter of medieval and Renaissance pieces is counterweighted by an impressive showing of Baroque hyperactivity. To the side of the Palazzo Comunale, Ripa del Sale contains the **Museo Rospigliosi e Museo Diocesano** (Tues–Sat 10am–1pm, plus Tues, Thurs & Fri 4–7pm; L4000 or L6000 with Museo Civico), a typical small-town collection of historical and ecclesiastical oddments.

A better use of your time is to go round the back of the Palazzo Comunale, where Via Pacini is the obvious route to take to explore the northern part of the town. Across this road, on Piazza San Bartolomeo, stands **San Bartolomeo in Panatano**, residence of the earliest of Pistoia's trio of pulpits. Executed in 1250 by Guido da Como, it's a rectangular box whose principal scenes are filled with figures arrayed in level ranks like a crowd in a stadium.

The most publicised episode of the Pistoia townscape is not a church but a hospital in a square at the end of Via Pacini – the **Ospedale del Ceppo**, at the top of Via Pacini. Established in the thirteenth century, it was embellished in the fifteenth with a portico like the one Brunelleschi designed for the Innocenti in Florence. Emblazoned along its length is the feature that makes it famous – Giovanni della Robbia's startlingly colourful terracotta **frieze** of the *Theological Virtues* and the *Seven Works of Mercy*, a panoply of Renaissance types and costume.

A couple of minutes over to the west, the twelfth-century **Sant'Andrea** has a typically Pisan facade with a pair of Romanesque lions and a panel of *The Journey of the Magi* stuck onto it. The corridor-slim aisle contains the third and greatest of the pulpits, by **Giovanni Pisano**; carved in 1297, it is based on his father's design for the Pisa baptistery pulpit and only marginally less elaborate than his own slightly later work in Pisa cathedral. It shows scenes from the life of Christ and the Last Judgement, the figures carved so thickly and in such deep relief that they seem to be surging out of a limitless depth.

Practicalities

Pistoia's central **tourist office** is on Piazza del Duomo (Mon–Sat 9.30am–12.30pm & 3.30–6.30pm). The city's low tourist profile means a dearth of **accommodation** – so if you plan to stay, phone ahead. There's just one one-star hotel, the grim *Albergo Autisti*, close to Piazza Treviso at Viale Pacinotti 93 (☎0573/21.771; ④), and within the city walls there's only one two-star, the *Albergo Firenze*, a short walk west of Piazza del Duomo at Via Curtatone e Montanara 42 (☎0573/23.141; ⑤). On balance the best bets are a pair of three-stars within a minute of San Giovanni Fuorcivitas: *Leon Bianco*, Via Panciatichi 2 (☎0573/26.675; ⑤), and the *Patria*, Via Crispi 6 (☎0573/25.187; ⑤). The **restaurant** scene in Pistoia isn't a lot better: try *Le Chiavi d'Oro*, a busy and welcoming pizzeria-trattoria at Via Pacini 17–19, or the more basic *Pollo d'Oro*, Via A. Frostini 132.

Leaving Pistoia, *Lazzi* **buses** for Florence and Prato run from by the train station; *COPIT* buses for Vinci and Empoli from Piazza San Francesco. The route to Vinci goes over beautiful Monte Albano and allows a loop to Florence or Pisa if you set out early in the day.

The route to Pisa

By train, it's just an hour from Florence to Pisa – a pleasant enough journey, though with no compelling reason to stop. **Empoli** and PONTEDERA are industrial towns, the latter of no interest, the former of interest chiefly for its links north to **Vinci** and south to Siena and **San Miniato**.

Empoli

Most people limit their exploration of **EMPOLI** to a change of platforms at the train station, or a confused tour of the one-way road system. If you want to spare time for a quick look around, though, head for the central **Piazza Farinata degli Uberti**, named after the commander of the Ghibelline army of Siena which defeated the Florentine Guelphs at Montaperti in 1260. The green and white **Collegiata**, on the square, was founded as far back as the fifth century; its lower portion is the most westerly example of Florentine Romanesque architecture, the top a postwar reconstruction of a nineteenth-century imitation. The adjacent **Pinacoteca San Andrea** (Tues–Sun 9am–noon, plus Thurs–Sat 4–7pm; L3000), which has a pretty good collection of sculpture and painting, features a couple of panels by local-born Pontormo and Lorenzo di Bicci's *St Nicholas of Tolentino Saving Empoli from the Plague* – with a view of the town in the 1440s.

Vinci

Sitting on the southern slopes of Monte Albano, 11km north of Empoli, **VINCI** is inextricably associated with **Leonardo da Vinci**, who in April 1452 was born in the nearby hamlet of ARCHIANO and baptised in Vinci's church of Santa Croce. Vinci itself is a torpid place but preserves a thirteenth-century castle, in which the **Museo Leonardiano** (daily 9.30am–noon & 2.30–6pm; L5000) has been set up. It's dedicated to Leonardo the inventor and engineer, honouring him with a large and fairly imaginative display of models all reconstructed from Leonardo's notebook drawings, which are reproduced alongside the relevant contraptions. The museum doesn't do Leonardo any favours, though, in giving as much space to his half-baked jottings as to his sounder propositions – thus half a room is wasted on a mock-up of his skis for walking on water. Avoid the museum on a Sunday, when half the population of Tuscany seems to come out here. Leonardo's actual **birthplace** (Mon, Tues & Thurs–Sun 9.30am–noon & 2.30–6pm; free) is a couple of kilometres further north into the hills, a pleasant walk past fields of poppies. It's now filled with placard-size captions and a couple of reproduction drawings – otherwise there's nothing to see.

From Vinci you could make a circuit **north to Pistoia**, along a fine scenic road. Buses from Empoli pass through the village three times daily.

San Miniato

The strategic hilltop site of **SAN MINIATO**, more or less equidistant from Pisa and Florence, was given its landmark fortress by the Holy Roman Emperor Frederick II, and the imperial connection led to the nickname "San Miniato dei Tedeschi" – San Miniato of the Germans. Today San Miniato is a brusque little agricultural town, good for a couple of hours' break of journey, but unlikely to tempt anyone to give it longer.

The train station and main, predominantly modern, part of town – **San Miniato Basso** – is sited down in the valley. From here it's a steep four-kilometre climb to **San Miniato Alto**, the old quarter. If you get a **bus** from the train station, it will deposit you just below the walls in **Piazzale Dante Alighieri**, which is also the place to park. From here, once through the town gate, Via Conti rises to the **Piazza della Repubblica**, which is jazzed up by seventeenth-century *sgraffiti* on the long facade of the seminary, part of whose ground floor is a row of restored fourteenth-century shops, a rare survival. Opposite the seminary a flight of steps rises to the **Prato del Duomo**, where a tower of the imperial fortress now houses the expensive *Miravalle* hotel (☎0571/418.075; ⑥) and its more affordable restaurant.

The red brick **Duomo** itself, dedicated to Saint Genesius, the patron saint of actors, is hacked-about Romanesque, with an interior of Baroque gilding and marbling. Next door, the tiny **museum** (Sat & Sun 9am–noon & 2.30–5pm; L1000) has a *Crucifixion* by Filippo Lippi and a terracotta bust of Christ by Verrocchio. From the Prato del Duomo it's a short walk up to the tower of the **Rocca**, which was restored brick by brick after damage in the last war; the view is the main point of the climb. Dante's *Inferno* perpetuates the memory of Pier della Vigna, Frederick's treasurer, who was imprisoned and blinded here, a fate that drove him to suicide by jumping from the tower – as the inscription at its foot records.

Chianti

Ask a sample of wealthy northern Europeans to define their idea of paradise and the odds are that several will come up with something that sounds much like **Chianti**, the territory of vineyards and hill towns that stretches between Florence and Siena. Every aspect of life in Chianti is in perfect balance: the Tuscan landscape is the sort of terrain devised by painters to evoke the Golden Age; one of the most fascinating cities in the world is nearby; and, of course, the climate for most of the year is balmy, and even in the pit of winter it's rarely too grim. And on top of all this, there's the wine, the one Italian vintage everyone knows.

The British and others from similarly ill-favoured zones were long ago alerted to Chianti's charms and the rate of immigration has been so rapid since the 1960s that the region is now generally known as **"Chiantishire"**. The effects of this moneyed influx have been all too predictable – an escalation in property prices and the gentrification of some of the more picturesque villages. Yet it would be an exaggeration to say that Chianti is losing its character in the way that many of Italy's coastal towns have lost theirs – the tone of certain parts has been altered, but it's still a largely unspoilt district.

Buses from Florence and Siena connect with the more populous Chianti towns, but the only really feasible way to get to know the region is by car. Your own **transport** allows you to roam into the quieter recesses of the hills and to stop off at one of the 800-odd farms and **vineyards** to sample the local produce. If you pick up a detailed survey map of the region, you can pick out some of the innumerable miniature **lakes**, too – offering the quietest swimming you'll find anywhere in Tuscany in the summer. The best **road** to follow is the so-called *Chiantigiana* (N222), a route from Florence to Siena that passes through the most beautiful parts of Chianti.

Chianti towns

The district's heart is formed by the three small towns which constituted the fourteenth-century League of Chianti: **GAIOLE** (2hr by *SITA* bus from Florence), **RADDA IN CHIANTI** (1hr 40min) and **CASTELLINA IN CHIANTI** (1hr 35min). Castellina and Radda (Chianti's unofficial capital) are where the medieval splendour has left its clearest traces; Gaiole has become a modern market town, but its wine cooperative offers splendid tasting opportunities. Perhaps the best target for oenophiles is **GREVE** (1hr by bus from Florence), a town with a wine shop on every street and Chianti's biggest wine fair in September. If you are interested in visiting a classic Chianti *cantina*, perhaps the best to make for is the majestic **Castello di Brolio** (daily 9am–noon & 3–6pm), just outside the village of **BROLIO**, near Gaiole.

Practicalities

Hotel accommodation in Chianti is unremittingly expensive; the only low-budget options are the one-star *Girarrosto* in Radda (☎0577/738.010; ④), the one-star *Vittoria* (☎055/807.6180; ④) in TAVARNELLE VAL DI PESA, on the western edge of Chianti, the same town's youth hostel (☎055/807.7009), and the **campsites** at Castellina and the fortified town of BARBERINO VAL D'ELSA, close to Tavarnelle. Much the same goes for the area's **restaurants**. A pleasant, regular trattoria is the *Trattoria San Sano* in SAN SANO (near Gaiole), a combined restaurant, bar and general store, with tables outside – a good stop if you're driving through. *Il Molino delle Bagnaie*, a very attractive cellar in a small converted mill on the road from Gaiole to Pianella, has music most evenings – part cabaret, part Tuscan folk songs. It's middlingly expensive and, for Chianti, distinctly offbeat.

AREZZO PROVINCE

The Arno Valley upstream from Florence is a solidly industrialised district, with warehouses and manufacturing plants enclosing many of the small towns strung along the train line. The villages up on the sides of the valley often retain an appealing medieval square or a cluster of attractive buildings, but there's no very compelling stop before you reach the provincial capital of the upper Arno region, **Arezzo**, one hour's train ride from Florence. Foreign visitors come to Arezzo in their thousands for its paintings by Piero della Francesca, while Italians flock there in even greater numbers for its antiques, traded on the town's Piazza Grande in quantities scarcely matched anywhere else in the country.

In the **Casentino**, the stretch of the Arno Valley between Arezzo and the source of the river to the north, the character of the region is quite different: small hill towns such as **Poppi** and **Bibbiena** stand above a terrain of vineyards, olive groves and pastures, and business activity tends to be small-scale. For visitors on the trail of the masterpieces of Tuscan art, the essential call in the vicinity of Arezzo is **Sansepolcro**, almost on the Umbrian border to the east – the birthplace of della Francesca, it possesses two magnificent works by him. To the south of Arezzo stretches the plain of the **Valdichiana**, where picturesque if unexceptional little towns punctuate a landscape of farming estates. The ancient hill town of **Cortona** is the major attraction of this part of the province, its steep streets forming a distinctive urban landscape.

Arezzo

Occupying a site that controls the major passes of the central Apennines, **AREZZO** was one of the most important settlements of the Etruscan federation. It maintained its pre-eminence under Roman rule, and was a prosperous independent republic in the Middle Ages, until, in 1289, its Ghibelline loyalties brought about military defeat by the Guelph Florentines. This was a reversal from which it temporarily recovered, but definitive subjugation by Florence came about in 1384. In the arts, Petrarch, Pietro Aretino and Vasari, all native Aretines, brought lasting prestige to the city, yet it was an outsider who gave Arezzo its permanent Renaissance monument – Piero della Francesca, whose fresco cycle for the church of San Francesco belongs in the same category as Masaccio's frescoes in Florence and Michelangelo's in Rome.

Today Arezzo's economy rests on its innumerable jewellers and goldsmiths (the city has the world's largest gold manufacturing plant), and on its antiques industry – in the vicinity of the Piazza Grande there are showrooms filled with the sort of furniture you put in a bank vault rather than in your living room. At noon on the Saturday before the first Sunday of every month a less exclusive *Fiera Antiquaria* (Antiques Fair) pitches camp in the square, pulling in dealers from Rome and further afield. It's fun to look around, but don't expect any bargains, even among the junkier articles further out from the piazza.

The Town

There are two distinct parts to Arezzo: the **older quarter**, at the top of the hill, and the businesslike **lower town**, facing you at the exit from the train station. The bus terminal is diagonally opposite the train station. The traffic axis between the upper and lower town is Via Guido Monaco, a street which nobody walks along except to shop on it; the parallel **Corso Italia**, now pedestrianised, is the route to take up the hill and the place to hang out in the evening.

San Francesco

Off to the left of the Corso, not far from its summit, stands the building every tourist comes to Arezzo to see – the church of **San Francesco** (daily 8am–noon & 1.30–7pm). Built after 1322, the plain basilica earned its renown in the early 1450s, when the Bacci family commissioned **Piero della Francesca** to continue the decoration of the choir. The theme chosen was **The Legend of the True Cross**, a story in which the physical material of the Cross forms the link in the cycle of redemption that begins with humanity's original sin. Starting with the right wall, Piero painted the series in narrative sequence, working continuously until about 1457 – the precise chronology isn't known. However, the episodes are not arranged in narrative sequence, the artist preferring to arrange them according to the precepts of symmetry: thus the two battle scenes face each other across the chapel, rather than coming where the story dictates. As is always the case with this mystical rationalist painter, smaller-scale symmetries are present in every part of the work: the retinue of the Queen of Sheba (middle right wall) appears twice, in mirror-image arrangement, and the face of the queen is exactly the same as the face of the Empress Helena (middle left wall). This orderliness, combined with the pale light and the statuesque quality of the figures, create an atmosphere that's unique to Piero, a sense of each incident as a part of a greater plan.

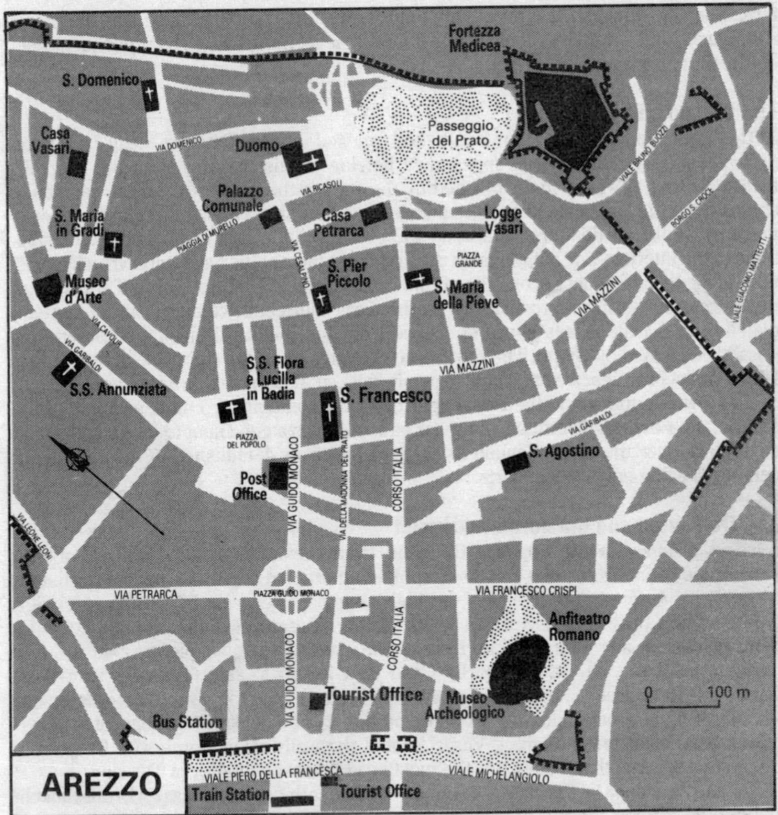

Damp has badly damaged areas of the chapel and some bits have peeled away as a result of Piero's notoriously slow working procedures. Most of the rest, however, is slowly emerging in magnificent condition from the restoration that was optimistically planned for completion in 1992, the five-hundredth anniversary of Piero's death.

Pieve di Santa Maria and the Piazza Grande

Further up the Corso stands the twelfth-century **Pieve di Santa Maria**, signposted by the fourteenth-century campanile, known locally as "the tower of the hundred holes". Its arcaded facade, elaborate yet severe, belongs to a Romanesque type associated more with Pisa and western Tuscany, and is doubly unusual in presenting its front to a narrow street rather than to the town's main square. Dating from the 1210s, the carvings of the months over the portal are a perfect Romanesque group; inside, the raised sanctuary – the oldest section of the church – supports Pietro Lorenzetti's *Madonna and Saints* polyptych, painted in 1320 and horribly restored.

The steeply sloping **Piazza Grande**, on the other side of the church, is bordered by a diverting assortment of buildings. On the west side is the apse of Santa Maria and the tiered facade of the **Palazzetto della Fraternità dei Laci**, with a Gothic ground floor and fifteenth-century upper storeys, while the northern edge is formed by **Vasari's loggia**, occupied by shops that in some instances still have their original stone counters. Socially, though, it's less than engrossing, only coming alive for the *Fiera Antiquaria*, and – more raucously – for the *Giostra del Saraceno*, a costumed joust held on the first Sunday in September.

The Duomo and around

At the highest point of the town looms the large and unfussy **Duomo** (daily 7am–noon & 3–6.30pm), its harmonious appearance belying its history. Begun in the late thirteenth century, it was virtually finished by the start of the sixteenth, but the campanile comes from the last century and the facade from this one. The stained-glass windows, made by Guillaume de Marcillat around 1520, let in so little light that his other contributions to the interior – the paintings on the first three bays of the nave – are virtually invisible. In the left aisle, just beyond the organ, is the **tomb of Bishop Guido Tarlati**, head of the *comune* during its resurgence in the early fourteenth century; the monument, plated with marble reliefs showing scenes from the militaristic bishop's career, was possibly designed by Giotto. The tiny fresco nestled against the right side of the tomb is **Piero della Francesca**'s *Magdalen*, his only work in Arezzo outside San Francesco.

The town's public park, the **Passeggio del Prato**, extends from the east end of the duomo; the **Fortezza Medicea**, at the far end, provides a good spot to take a picnic and gaze down over the town. Cosimo I's fortress here was demolished in the eighteenth century, leaving only the ramparts.

San Domenico and the northern district

A short distance in the opposite direction from the duomo is the church of **San Domenico** (daily 7am–noon & 3.30–6/7pm). Constructed mostly in the late thirteenth century, it's more striking inside – the high altar has a *Crucifix* by **Cimabue** (1260), painted when he would have been about twenty. Tatters of fifteenth- and sixteenth-century frescoes all round the church create the effect of a gigantic picture album.

Signs point the way to the nearby **Casa di Giorgio Vasari** (Tues–Sat 9am–7pm, Sun 9am–1pm; free), designed by the celebrated biographer-architect-painter for himself. Taking greater pleasure from the products of his imagination than later generations have managed to extract, Vasari coated the walls of his home with frescoes, a decorative scheme that makes this the most lurid domestic interior in Tuscany.

Down the slope, in Via San Lorentino, the fifteenth-century Palazzo Bruni-Ciocchi houses the **Museo Statale d'Arte Medioevale e Moderna** (Tues–Sat 9am–7pm, Sun 9am–1.30pm; L6000); its collection of paintings by local artists and majolica pieces dating from the thirteenth to the eighteenth centuries, generously spread over three floors of the palazzo, requires severe editorial work from the visitor.

The Museo Archeologico

All the principal sights are in the upper part, with the exception of the **Museo Archeologico** (Tues–Sat 9am–2pm, Sun 9am–1pm; L6000), which occupies part of a monastery built into the wall of the town's Roman amphitheatre, to the right of the station. The desultory remains of the amphitheatre are part of the museum, but more impressive are the marvellously coloured **coralline vases**; produced here in the first century BC, they show why the Aretines achieved their reputation as consummate craftspeople throughout the Roman world.

Practicalities

The main **tourist office** is on the edge of the train station forecourt (Mon–Fri 9am–1pm & 3.30–6.30pm, Sat 9am–1pm; ☎0575/23.952); the helpful staff speak English and have masses of information on Arezzo and its province. The EPT office for regional tourism, at Piazza Risorgimento 116 (first right off Via Guido Monaco), displays the latest information on Arezzo accommodation outside, so you can get the up-to-date essentials if you roll into town in the evening.

Because of the *Fiera*, rooms are hard to come by on the first weekend of every month, and things are bad at the end of August and beginning of September, when the *Concorso Polifonico Guido d'Arezzo* (an international choral competition) and the *Giostra del Saraceno* follow in quick succession. Best of the one-star **hotels** is the *Milano*, close to the EPT at Via Madonna del Prato 83 (☎0575/26.836; ④); if that's full, try *La Toscana*, Via M. Perennio 56 (☎0575/21.692; ④), or – definitely third choice – the *Roma*, Via V. Veneto 46 (☎0575/902.494; ④). Alternatively, there's a new **youth hostel**, the *Villa Severi*, at Via F. Redi 13 (☎0575/29.047; ①) – take bus #4.

For **restaurants**, the best deal is at the rough-and-ready *La Scaletta*, next to the main post office at Piazza del Popolo 11, which offers filling set meals at rock-bottom prices. *Da Guido*, at Via Madonna del Prato 85, is an equally basic local trattoria. An excellent place for **pizzas** is *Il Ruspante*, at Via Roma 34; it's not cheap, but the pizzas are the genuine wood-oven article. *La Buca di San Francesco*, right by San Francesco church, is your spot for high-quality Tuscan cuisine.

To Sansepolcro

Arezzo is the springboard for one of Tuscany's most rewarding art itineraries – the Piero della Francesca trail, whose other stops lie east of the city at **Monterchi** and **Sansepolcro**, the artist's birthplace. There's no train link from Arezzo, the rail approach to Sansepolcro being the private Terni–Perugia line. The *CAT* **bus** company runs seventeen services a day to Sansepolcro, all but two of which stop no nearer to Monterchi than LE VILLE, 2km to the west.

What makes **MONTERCHI** a crucial station on the della Francesca trail is his **Madonna del Parto**, the only representation in Renaissance art of the pregnant Madonna and one of the country's most revered images. For its restoration the painting was moved from its home in the cemetery chapel on the outskirts of the village to an ex-primary school in Via Reglia, when it can be viewed over the shoulders of the working technicians (Tues–Sun 9am–1pm & 2.30–7.30pm; L5000); whether it will remain here when work is completed is anyone's guess.

Sansepolcro

The *CAT* bus from Arezzo takes an hour to get to **SANSEPOLCRO**, an unassuming place which makes its way in the world as a manufacturer of lace and *Buitoni* pasta. Born here at some time in the 1410s, Piero della Francesca returned in the 1470s, having abandoned painting due to encroaching blindness, and devoted most of his time to working on his treatises *On Perspective in Painting* and *On the Five Regular Bodies*. The greatest treasure of the **Museo Civico** (daily 9.30am–1pm & 2.30–6pm; L5000) is his spectral *Resurrection* – an image which has occasioned more exotic prose than any other of his paintings. Kenneth Clark's description at least has the virtue of being provocative – "This country god, who rises in the grey light while humanity is asleep, has been worshipped ever since man first knew that the seed is not dead in the winter earth, but will force its way upwards through an iron crust." An earlier della Francesca masterpiece, the *Madonna della Misericordia*, epitomises the graceful solemnity of his work. Other pieces that attract attention are a sadistic *Martyrdom of St Quentin* by Pontormo and a painted standard by Luca Signorelli, a student of della Francesca.

Lesser art treasures are to be found in the **Duomo**, with its tenth-century carved image of the crucified Christ, and in the church of **San Lorenzo**, which has a *Deposition* by Rosso Fiorentino, painted within half a century of della Francesca's last works but seeming to belong to another world.

There is little to stay for once you have seen the *Resurrection*, so there is usually space in the town's half dozen **hotels**. Cheapest is the two-star *Orfeo*, just outside the walls at Viale Diaz 12 (☎0575/742.287; ③), but first recommendation is the three-star *Fiorentino*, Via Pacioli 60 (☎0575/740.350; ④), a comfortable and very welcoming hotel with a wonderful, no-frills **restaurant**. The last bus back to Arezzo leaves at 8pm in summer, 7.25pm in winter.

The Casentino

The **Casentino**, stretching north of Arezzo, is a lush agricultural area once it gets clear of the town's textile factories, and its high, often walled towns see few tourists. Thick woodland of oak, beech and pine covers much of the upper slopes, the remnant of the forest that used to supply the shipyards of Pisa, Livorno and Genoa, as well as the building sites of Tuscany. By **public transport**, the best target for a day trip is **Poppi**, connected to Arezzo by bus and by the private *LFI* **train** line. This line, which shares the *FS* station in Arezzo, has been undergoing repairs for the last few years, and at the time of writing trains were running only as far as SUBBIANO, from where a connecting bus continues to the rail terminus at STIA. To strike into the hills, to the monasteries of **La Verna** and **Camáldoli**, requires a car; buses do run through Bibbiena to La Verna and through Poppi to Camáldoli, but are too infrequent to make a round trip feasible.

Bibbiena and La Verna

The chief town of the Casentino, **BIBBIENA** has an attractive innermost quarter cordoned by a large tobacco factory and straggling development. The main sight is the church of **San Lorenzo**, a fifteenth-century building that contains a fair quantity of terracotta from the della Robbia workshops.

At the mountaintop site of **LA VERNA**, 23km east of Bibbiena, **Saint Francis** established a retreat in 1213 and it was here, nine years later, that he received the stigmata, a badge of sanctity bestowed on nobody before. Now a site of pilgrimage, the monastic village contains the masterpieces of **Andrea della Robbia**, in the fifteenth-century basilica and the smaller Chiesa delle Stimmate and Cappella di Santa Maria degli Angeli. The sanctuary is open to visitors daily from 6am to 8.30pm, though in midwinter the road is often impassable.

Poppi and Camáldoli

POPPI, 6km to the north of Bibbiena and plainly visible from there, is sited high above the road and train station. If you emerge at the latter, in the lower suburb of Ponte a Poppi, follow Via Dante Alighieri – a cobbled shortcut which leads to the upper town in ten minutes' walk. The old town is not much more than a couple of squares and the arcaded Via Cavour, but it is lent a monumental aspect beyond its size by the Casentino's chief landmark, the **Castello dei Conti Guidi** (Mon–Sat 9am–2pm; L3000). Built for the Guidi lords in the thirteenth century, its design is based on Florence's Palazzo Vecchio and it's likely that Arnolfo di Cambio was the architect here as well. The courtyard, with its wooden landings and beautiful staircases, is the most attractive bit of architecture in the Casentino; much of the interior is occupied by a massive library but the parts that are open to the public contain a superb array of arms and some well-preserved medieval frescoes.

At its lower end, Via Cavour climaxes at the magnificent twelfth-century **Badìa di San Fedele**; its very dark interior – locked most of the time – contains a beguiling thirteenth-century painting of the *Madonna and Child*. Opposite the *castello* is the town's one central **hotel**, the small two-star *Pension Casentino* (☎0575/529.090; ④), which also has a **restaurant**.

Just over 15km northeast of Poppi is **CAMÁLDOLI**, where, at the start of the eleventh century, Saint Romauld founded a particularly ascetic order of the Benedictines. The much rebuilt main complex is of little interest except for its sixteenth-century pharmacy, which now sells herbal products. But the countryside is beautiful – thick forests of pine and fir – and an hour's walk up the hill brings you to the original **Eremo** and its Baroque church. Only male visitors are allowed past the gate to see the twenty monastic cells at close range – women have to peer from afar.

The whole Camáldoli area is an extremely popular holiday district in summer. BADIA PRATAGLIA, 10km east of Camáldoli, is the focus of activity, with marvellous walks in all directions.

To Cortona

Travelling **south from Arezzo** you enter the **Valdichiana**, reclaimed swampland that is now prosperous cattle country, producing the much-prized Florentine *bistecca*. It's an underwhelming landscape but its flatness does at least mean that the towns on its flanks – of which **Cortona** is the most inspiring – have very long sight-lines. Unlike in the Casentino, public transport is fine. There are hourly *LFI* **buses** between Arezzo and Cortona, and stopping **trains** from Arezzo call at Camucia-Cortona station, from where a shuttle runs up to the centre of the old town. The fast Florence–Rome trains stop at TERÓNTOLA, 6km south, which is also served by a shuttle; Teróntola is the station to get off at if you are approaching from Umbria.

Looming high above the road 17km south of Arezzo are the walls and massive tower of **CASTIGLION FIORENTINO**, a fortified old town that's so far above the train station that it makes more sense to visit by bus; the half-hourly bus from Arezzo to Cortona bowls through here thirty minutes into its one-hour journey. At the navel of the *centro storico*, the elegant Piazza del Municipio, there's a modest **Pinacoteca** (Tues–Sun 10.30am–12.30pm, plus Sun 3–5pm; L3000), starring a Signorelli *Virgin with St Anne*. Opposite the palazzo is Castiglion's distinguishing feature, a **loggia** – supposedly by Vasari – which forms a picture-frame for the hills to the east.

Four kilometres south from here, the eleventh-century castle of **Montécchio Vesponi** jabs up from the horizon. Commanding a great sweep of valley, this was the base of the *condottiere* Sir John Hawkwood – he of the fresco in Florence's duomo. It is now a private residence.

Cortona

From the valley floor a five-kilometre road winds up through terraces of vines and olives to the hill town of **CORTONA**, from whose heights you can gaze over and beyond the Valdichiana, and at the sheen of Lago Trasimeno to the south. A scattering of Etruscan tombs aside, it is the medieval period that dominates the town's steep streets, the constricted ridge site having limited modern expansion to Camucia, which is where the approach road begins. Even without its art treasures, this would be a good place to rest up, with pleasant hotels, excellent restaurants, and an amazing view at night, with the villages of southern Tuscany glistening like ships' lights on a dark sea.

The bus terminus is in **Piazza Garibaldi**, from where the only level street in town, **Via Nazionale**, leads into Piazza della Repubblica, where the staircase of the squat **Palazzo del Comune** provides the grandstand for the *ragazzi* to appraise the world as it goes by. One flank of the Palazzo del Comune forms a side of **Piazza Signorelli**, named after Luca Signorelli, Cortona's most famous son – as is the peeling nineteenth-century theatre. Opposite the theatre the crude Palazzo Casali houses the **Museo dell'Accademia Etrusca** (April–Sept Tues–Sun 10am–1pm & 4–7pm; Oct–March

Tues–Sun 9am–1pm & 3–5pm; L5000), where an enormous hall contains cabinets of prized Etruscan stuff, surrounded by second-rate paintings. The major exhibit – honoured with its own bijou temple – is an Etruscan bronze lamp from the fifth century BC, its circumference decorated with alternating male and female squatting figures. Elsewhere there are ranks of Etruscan figurines, an altarpiece by Bicci di Lorenzo and masses of unlabelled domestic odds and ends. The painter Gino Severini, another native of Cortona and an acolyte of the Futurist firebrand Filippo Marinetti, gets a room to himself at the end.

Piazza Signorelli links with Piazza del Duomo, where the **Duomo** is now in such a state that it's been closed off. The couple of churches that used to face the duomo have been knocked together to house the **Museo Diocesano** (Tues–Sun April–Sept 9am–1pm & 3–6.30pm; Oct–March 9am–1pm & 3–5pm; L5000), a tiny collection of Renaissance art plus a fine Roman sarcophagus, carved with fighting centaurs. Inevitably Luca Signorelli features strongly, but more eloquent is Fra' Angelico, represented by a *Madonna, Child and Saints* and an exquisite *Annunciation*.

For the full taste of Cortona take Via Santucci from Piazza della Repubblica and clamber along Via Berrettini, past the decrepit San Francesco church. A further work by Signorelli can be found in the unassuming church of **San Nicolò**, reached by veering right across Piazza della Pescaia then going up the stepped Via San Nicolò. Ring the bell on the left-hand side wall, and the caretaker will take you to Signorelli's double-sided altarpiece – revealed by a hydraulic system that swivels the picture away from the wall.

From Piazza della Pescaia, a steep path leads to **Santa Margherita**, resting place of **Margaret of Cortona**, the town's patron saint. The daughter of a local farmer, she spent her long years of widowhood helping the poor and sick of Cortona, founding a hospital that stood close to the site of this church. Her tomb, with marble angels lifting the lid of her sarcophagus, was created in the mid-fourteenth century, and is now mounted on the wall to the left of the chancel.

The **Fortezza Medicea**, at the summit of the town, is often shut, but the area around is good ground for a picnic, looking down over ruined Etruscan and Roman walls towards Trasimeno. You could descend to Piazza Garibaldi by the stepped Via Crucis, where the Stations of the Cross are marked with booths sheltering unsubtle mosaics by Severini. A last church to check out is **San Domenico**, a minute's walk from Piazza Garibaldi, where the high altar displays a *Coronation of the Virgin* polyptych by Lorenzo di Niccolò Gerini. Below the piazza, the middle distance is occupied by the perfectly proportioned but crumbling Renaissance church of **Santa Maria del Calcinaio**. The masterpiece of Giorgio di Martini, it was begun in 1484 to enshrine a miraculous image of the Virgin that a lime burner had unearthed here.

Practicalities

The **tourist office** is at Via Nazionale 72 (Mon–Sat 8.30am–12.30pm & 3–6pm). There are half a dozen **hotels** in the town proper, only two of which could be described as budget options: the one-star *Athens*, Via S. Antonio (☎0575/603.008; ④), and the comfortable two-star *Italia*, Via Ghibellina 5 (☎0575/603.264; ⑤) – and be warned that the former is often filled by students on art and language programmes held here by the University of Athens, Georgia. However, Cortona does have an IYHF **youth hostel**, the *Ostello San Marco*, situated in the heart of the town at Via Maffei 57 (☎0575/601.392; open March 15–Sept 30; ①).

For **meals**, the liveliest and almost the cheapest place is the *Spaghetteria Fuflons*, Via Ghibellina 3. Cortona is a town where you can treat your stomach without ruining your finances, though. Best of the restaurants is probably *La Loggetta*, overlooking Piazza della Repubblica, where a memorable meal will cost around L50,000. The *Trattoria Grotta di San Francesco*, just off the piazza at Piazzetta Baldelli 3, is less self-conscious, almost as good, and far cheaper.

SIENA AND CENTRAL TUSCANY

Siena is the perfect antidote to Florence. Self-contained and still part-rural behind its medieval walls, its great attraction is its cityscape, a majestic Gothic whole that could be enjoyed without venturing into a single museum. To get anything genuine from it you'll need to stay at least one night. Too many visitors don't, romping through on a day trip that leaves no chance of easing into the life and moods of its quarters. As a provincial capital, Siena has good transport links with some of the finest sights of Tuscany. The most popular trip is to the multi-towered village of **San Gimignano**, to the northwest; it's worthwhile, though packed out in midsummer. Far fewer people take the trouble to sample the medieval and ancient Etruscan town of **Volterra**, a rewarding stop en route to Pisa.

Siena

For a hundred or so years, in the twelfth and thirteenth centuries, **SIENA** was one of the major cities of Europe. Virtually the size of Paris, it controlled most of southern Tuscany and its wool industry, dominated the trade routes between France and Rome, and maintained Italy's richest pre-Medici banks. The city also developed a highly sophisticated civic life, with its own written constitution, a quasi-democratic government, and a council responsible for as wide a range of duties as any modern city.

This era reached an apotheosis with the defeat of a much superior Florentine army at the battle of **Montaperti** in 1260. Although the result was reversed permanently nine years later, Siena embarked on an unrivalled urban development under the guidance of its mercantile governors, the **Council of Nine**. From 1287 to 1355 the city underwrote first the completion of its cathedral and then the extraordinary shell-like **Campo** – the greatest medieval square in Italy – with its exuberant **Palazzo Pubblico**.

The prosperity came to an abrupt halt with the **Black Death**, which reached Siena in May 1348. By October, when the disease exhausted its course, the population had dropped from 100,000 to 30,000. The city was never fully to recover (the population today is 60,000) and its politics, always factional, moved into a period of intrigue and chaos. The chief figures of the following century were the city's two nationally renowned saints – **Catherine** and **Bernardino** – whose mysticism exercised an enormous grip on the age, amid two further outbreaks of plague.

A period of autocratic rule under the tyrannical Pandolfo Petrucci brought a further victory over Florence, but ended with the city embroiled in ever-expanding intrigue involving the Florentines, the papacy, France, and the empire of **Charles V**. The latter proved too big a figure for the Sienese, imposing a fortress and garrison, and then, after the city had with French assistance expelled his troops, laying siege to it and the Sienese countryside. The effects of the siege (1554–55) proved more terrible even than the Black Death, with the population slumping from 40,000 to as little as 8000. Two years later, Philip II, Charles's successor, gave up Siena to **Cosimo de'Medici** in lieu of war services, and the city subsequently became part of Cosimo's Grand Duchy of Tuscany. This was the death knell. For sixty years the Sienese were forbidden even to operate banks, while control of what was now an increasingly minor provincial town reverted, under Medici patronage, to the nobles.

The lack of subsequent development, as the city slipped to little more than a market centre, explains Siena's astonishing state of preservation. Little was built and still less demolished, while allotments and vineyards occupied (as they do today) the spaces between the ancient quarters. Since the last war, however, Siena has again become prosperous, partly due to **tourism**, partly to the resurgence of the **Monte dei Paschi di Siena**. This bank, founded in Siena in 1472, is one of the major players in Italian

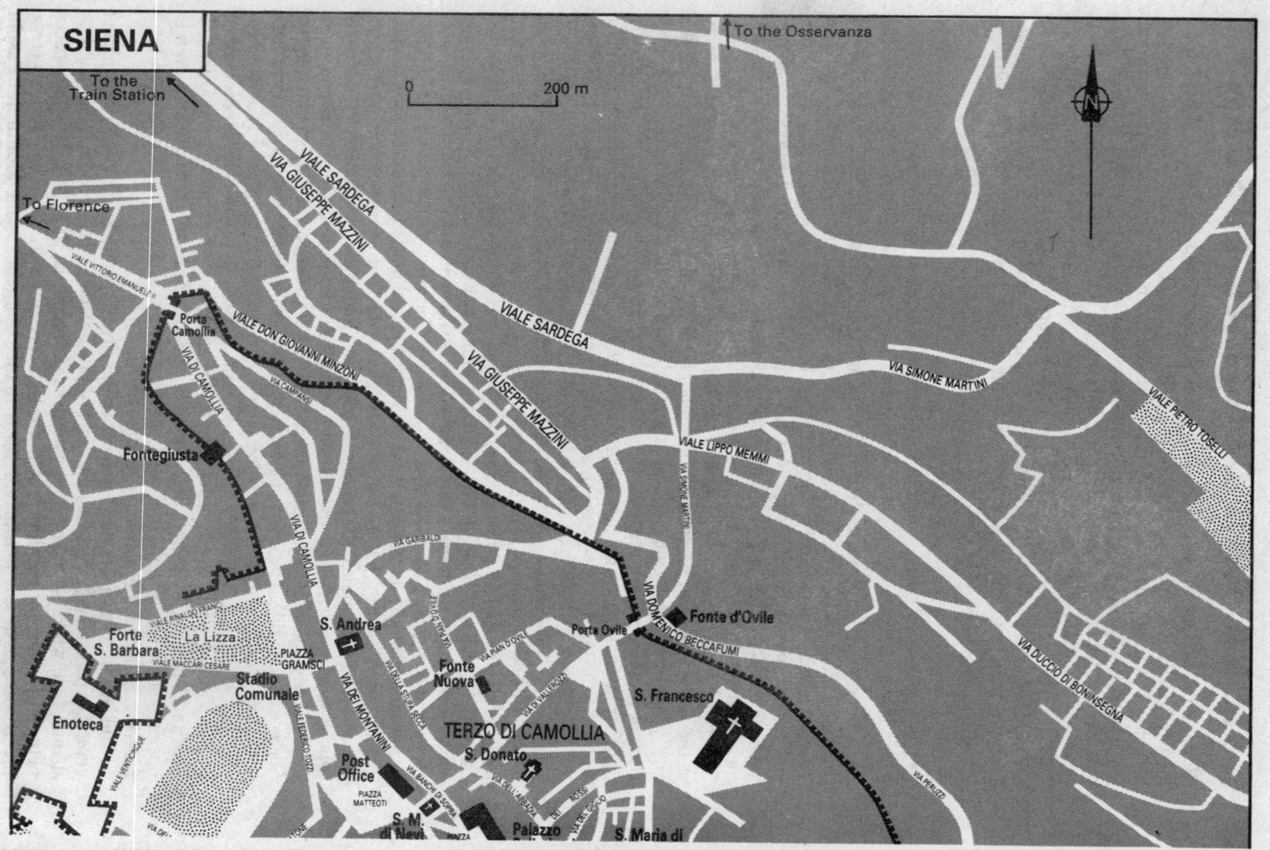
SIENA
To the Train Station
To the Osservanza
0
200 m
To Florence
VIALE SARDEGA
VIA GIUSEPPE MAZZINI
VIALE VITTORIO EMANUELE II
Porta Camollia
VIALE DON GIOVANNI MINZONI
VIA SIMONE MARTINI
VIA DI CAMOLLIA
VIA CAMPANSI
VIALE PIETRO TOSELLI
Fontegiusta
VIALE LIPPO MEMMI
VIA GARIBALDI
VIA DOMENICO BECCAFUMI
Fonte d'Ovile
Porta Ovile
S. Andrea
VIALE RINALDO FRANCI
Forte S. Barbara
La Lizza
VIALE MACCARI CESARE
PIAZZA GRAMSCI
VIA PIAN D'OVILE
VIA DELLA STUFA SECCA
Fonte Nuova
VIA DI VALLEROZZI
VIA DUCCIO DI BONINSEGNA
Stadio Comunale
S. Francesco
Enoteca
VIALE VENTICINQUE
VIALE FEDERICO TOZZI
VIA DEI MONTANINI
TERZO DI CAMOLLIA
S. Donato
Post Office
VIA BANCHI DI SOPRA
VIA DELL'ABBADIA
VIA PERUZZI
PIAZZA MATTEOTTI
S. M. di Nevi
Palazzo
S. Maria di

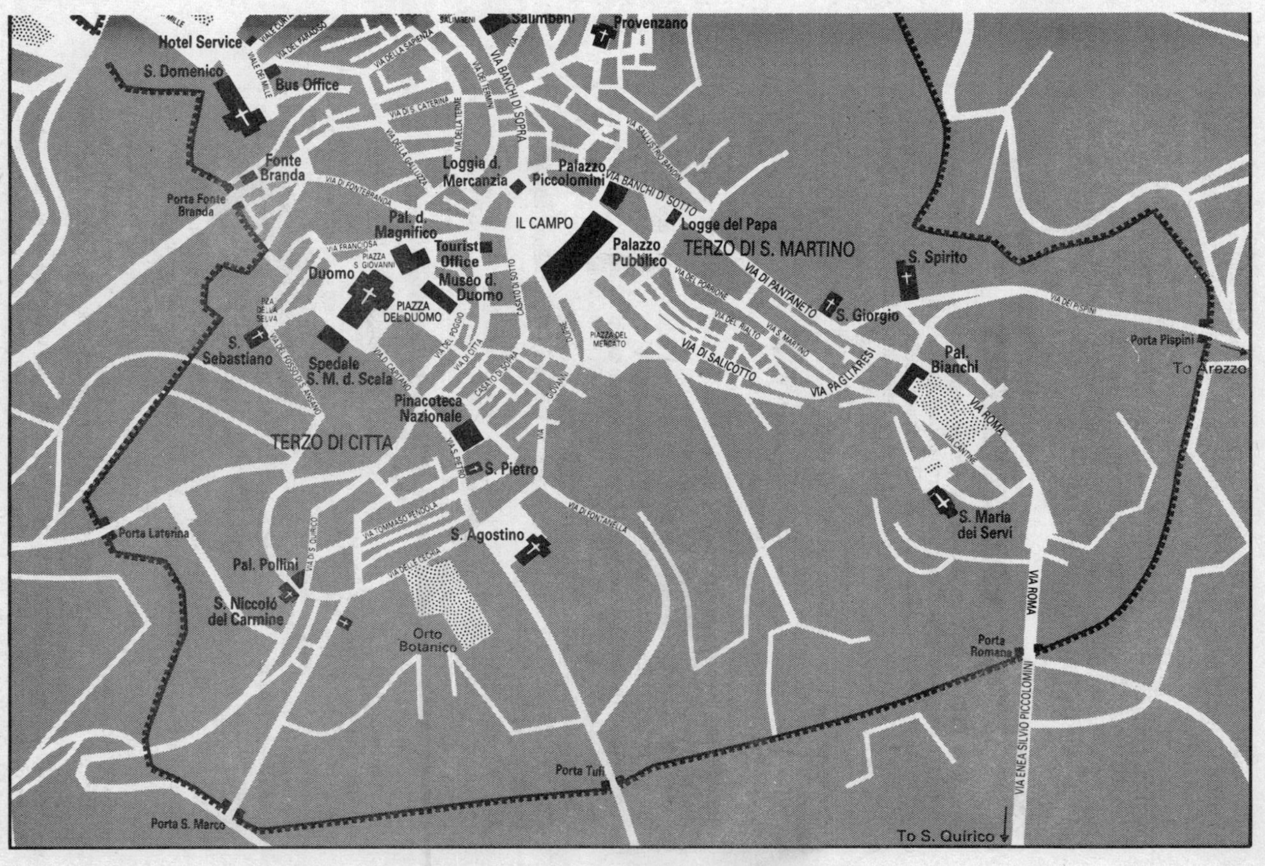
Hotel Service
S. Domenico
Bus Office
Salimbeni
Provenzano
VIA BANCHI DI SOPRA
VIA DEI TERMINI
VIA DELLA GALLUZZA
Fonte Branda
Porta Fonte Branda
VIA DI FONTEBRANDA
Loggia d. Mercanzia
Palazzo Piccolomini
VIA BANCHI DI SOTTO
VIA SALLUSTIO BANDINI
Logge del Papa
IL CAMPO
Palazzo Pubblico
TERZO DI S. MARTINO
S. Spirito
Pal. d. Magnifico
Tourist Office
Museo d. Duomo
Duomo
PIAZZA DEL DUOMO
VIA DI PANTANETO
S. Giorgio
VIA DEI PISPINI
Porta Pispini
To Arezzo
S. Sebastiano
Spedale S. M. d. Scala
PIAZZA DEL MERCATO
VIA DI SALICOTTO
VIA PAGLIARESI
Pal. Bianchi
VIA ROMA
Pinacoteca Nazionale
TERZO DI CITTA
S. Pietro
VIA DI FONTANELLA
S. Maria dei Servi
Porta Laterina
S. Agostino
Pal. Pollini
S. Niccolò del Carmine
Orto Botanico
Porta Romana
VIA ENEA SILVIO PICCOLOMINI
Porta Tufi
Porta S. Marco
To S. Quirico

finance and in its home base is by far the largest employer. It today sponsors much of the cultural life of the city, coexisting, apparently easily, with Italy's strongest **communist council**.

Tourism may have played a part in refuelling the city coffers, but it creates problems too. Siena's population is ageing, and there is little in the tourist industry to encourage the young to stay. Building on the existing strengths of the university, the council have plans for a biotechnology park and other high-tech projects – hoping to create, perhaps, a kind of Tuscan equivalent of MIT.

THE PALIO

The **Siena Palio** is the most spectacular festival event in Italy: a bareback horse race around the Campo, preceded by days of preparation, medieval pageantry and chicanery. Only ten of the *contrade* can take part in any one race; these are chosen by lot, and their horses and jockeys (who are not local) are also assigned at random. The only rule is that riders cannot interfere with each others' reins. Otherwise, anything goes: each *contrada* has a traditional rival, and ensuring that it loses is as important as winning oneself. Jockeys may be bribed to throw the race, or whip a rival or a rival's horse; *contrade* have been known to drug horses, and even to ambush a jockey on his way to the race. This is primarily a show for the Sienese: for visitors, in fact, the undercurrent of brutality, and the bragging, days-long celebration of victory, can be quite a shock.

The race has been held since at least the beginning of the fourteenth century. Originally it followed a circuit through the town, but it has been focused, since the sixteenth century, on three laps of the **Campo**, around a track covered with sand and padded with mattresses to minimise injury to horses and riders. There are two palios a year, on July 2 and August 16, with the following build-up:

June 29 and August 13: The year's horses are presented in the morning at the town hall and drawn by lot. At 7.15pm the first trial race is held in the Campo.

June 30 and August 14: Further trial races at 9am and 7.45pm.

July 1 and August 15: Two more trial races at 9am and 7.45pm, followed by a street banquet in each of the *contrade*.

July 2 and August 16: The day of the Palio opens with a final trial at 9am. In the early afternoon each *contrada* takes its horse to be blessed in its church (if the horse shits it's a good omen). At around 5pm the town hall bell begins to ring and riders and *comparse* – equerries, ensigns, pages and drummers in medieval costume – proceed to the Campo for a display of flag-twirling and other pageantry.

The race itself begins at 7.45pm in July, 7pm in August, and lasts little more than one exciting minute. There's no PA system to tell you what's going on. At the start (in the northwest corner of the Campo) all the horses except one are penned between two ropes; the free one charges the group from behind, when its rivals least expect it, and the race is on. It's a hectic and violent spectacle; a horse which throws its rider is still eligible to win. The jockeys don't stop at the finishing line, but keep going at top speed out of the Campo, pursued by a frenzied mass of supporters. The *palio* itself is a silk banner subsequently presented to the winner.

There are viciously expensive stands for dignitaries and the rich (booked months ahead), but most spectators crowd (free) into the centre of the Campo. For the best view, you need to have found a position on the inner rail by 2pm (ideally at the start and finishing line), and to keep it for the next six hours; otherwise, there's no great hurry, as you'll be able to see a certain amount from anywhere within the throng. Toilet and refreshment facilities are minimal, though very little drinking goes on in the crowd. For at least two hours you won't be able to leave the centre.

Rooms are extremely difficult to find at Palio time, and if you haven't booked, either reckon on staying up all night, or commuting in from a neighbouring town. The races are shown live on TV and repeated endlessly all evening.

The Contrade

Within the fabric of the medieval city, Siena preserves its ancient division into wards, or *contrade*. These are integral to the competition of the Palio (see box) and they also foster a unique neighbourhood identity, clearly visible as you wander around the streets. Each of the seventeen *contrade* – there were originally sixty, based on military obligations – has its own church, social centre and museum. Each, too, has an heraldic animal motif, displayed in a modern fountain-sculpture in its individual piazza. Although the social distinctions between the *contrade* today are blurred to the point of extinction, allegiance to one's *contrada* – conferred by birth – remains a strong element of civic life.

The *contrade* **museums**, with their displays of Palio trophies, are all open to visitors during the build-up to the Palio and at other times by appointment (ask the tourist office to phone). Each *contrada* also has its own annual celebration, accompanied by parades and feasts. At almost any time of year, you will see their groups of *comparse* practising flag-waving and drum-rolling in the streets.

The Siena area **phone code** is ☎0577.

Arrival, orientation and accommodation

Arriving by **bus**, you are dropped along Via Curtatone, by the church of San Domenico, from where you can see the city – dominated by the cathedral and town hall belltowers – spread out below. The **train station** is less convenient, 2km to the north-east in the valley below the city; connecting buses shuttle between here and Piazza Matteotti, at the top end of Via Curtatone. **Driving**, it's best to leave your car in the free parking area alongside the Forte di Santa Barbara, five minutes' walk from San Domenico; beyond here you have to pay for your space.

Accommodation

Finding a room is barely less of a struggle than in Florence, for although Siena gets fewer visitors it has far fewer hotels. If you haven't booked a place, make your way on arrival either to the **Cooperativa "Hotels Promotion"** booth opposite San Domenico on Via Curtatone (Mon–Sat 8.30am–7pm; ☎288.084), or to one of the **tourist offices** – the main one is at Via di Città 43 (Mon–Fri 8.30am–1pm & 3–7pm, Sat 8.30am–1pm; ☎280.551), with a branch office at no. 56 on the Campo (same hours). The booth will book you a room in any of the city's thirty regular hotels or at one of the two *residenze turistico*; the tourist offices provide lists of rooms in private houses and extremely good (and free) contour **maps** of the city and environs. Some of the **private rooms** are taken by students in term-time and others have a minimum stay of one week – but they're worth at least a try, as rates are below one-star prices.

HOTELS

Cannon d'Oro, Via Montanini 28 (☎44.321). A stylish, small, two-star hotel tucked down an alleyway east of Piazza Matteotti. ⑤.

Centrale, Via Calzoleria 24 (☎280.379). As central as the name suggests – a block north of the Campo. Large doubles, but no singles. ⑤.

Continentale, Via Banchi di Sopra 85 (☎41.451). Elegant hotel in a sixteenth-century palazzo on the main *passeggiata* route, with great marble stairways and some wonderful trompe l'oeil ceilings on the huge first-floor rooms. Highly recommended. ⑤.

Duomo, Via Stalloreggi 34 (☎289.088). Probably the best of the city's three-star hotels, located south of the duomo on the westward continuation of Via di Città. ⑦.

Garibaldi, Via Giovanni Dupre 18 (☎284.204). A good, no-nonsense *locanda*, sited above one of the city's cheapest restaurants, just south of the Campo (off to the right-hand side of the Palazzo Pubblico). Midnight curfew. Doubles only. ④.

Palazzo Ravizza, Pian dei Mantellini 34 (☎280.462). Quiet hotel in a pleasant backwater of town, near Santa Maria del Carmine. ⑤.

La Perla, Via delle Terme 25 (☎47.144). Regular *pensione*, in a very central location, two blocks north of the Campo on a street parallel to Banchi di Sopra. Curfew 1am. ④.

Piccolo Hotel Etruria,Via Donzelle 1 (☎288.088). Small, smart and central. ⑤.

Santa Caterina, Via Piccolomini 7 (☎221.105). Ten minutes' walk from the Campo, on the street that leads out of town from Porta Romana. ⑤.

La Toscana, Via Cecco Angioleri 12 (☎46.097). Atmospheric, central location on an alley behind Piazza Tolomei (on Banchi di Sopra). ⑤.

Tre Donzelle, Via Donzelle 5 (☎280.358). The *Donzelle* is right in the heart of town, just off Banchi di Sotto, north of the Campo. Good, clean rooms. 12.30am curfew. ④.

HOSTELS

Casa del Pellegrino (Santuario di Santa Caterina), Via Camporegio (☎44.177). This old pilgrim hostel behind San Domenico offers single, double and triple rooms. Curfew 11pm. ②.

Conservatori Femminili Riuniti, Via del Refugio 4 (☎280.376). Women-only hostel, off Via Roma in the Terzo di San Martino. Phone in advance to check that it's operating. ①.

Ostello della Gioventù "Guidoriccio", Via Fiorentina 89 (☎522.12). The city youth hostel is 2km northwest of the centre; take bus ##3, #10 or #15 from Piazza Matteotti or, if you're coming from Florence, ask the bus driver to let you off at "Lo Stellino" (just after the Siena city sign). IYHF card required. Curfew 11pm. ①.

CAMPING

Campeggio Siena Colleverde, Strada di Scacciapensieri 37 (☎280.044). Secure, well-maintained campsite, 2km out to the north; take bus #8 from Piazza Matteotti (last one runs at 10pm). Shop, bar and swimming pool. Open late March–late Sept.

The City

The centre of Siena is its great square, the **Campo**, built at the convergence of the city's principal roads, the **Banchi di Sopra**, **Banchi di Sotto** and **Via di Città**. Each of these roads leads out across a ridge, straddled by one of the city's three medieval *terzi*, or quarters: the **Terzo di Città** to the southwest, the **Terzo di San Martino** to the southeast, and the **Terzo di Camollia** to the north. This central core – almost entirely medieval in plan and appearance – has, since the 1960s, been effectively pedestrianised. Finding your way around is therefore simple and enjoyable; everywhere of interest is within easy walking distance.

The Campo

The Campo might seem an organic piece of city planning but in fact, when the Council of Nine began its construction in 1347, they were building on the only possible land – the old marketplace, which stood at the convergence of the city quarters but belonged to none. To build it, it was necessary to make an enormous buttress beneath the lower half of the square, where the Palazzo Pubblico, or town hall, was to be raised. The square itself was created in nine segments to commemorate the council's highly civic rule, adding to the stage-like aspect. It was, from the start, a focus of city life, the scene of executions, bullfights, communal boxing matches, and, of course, the Palio. San Bernardino preached here, too, holding before him the monogram of Christ's name – IHS – which he urged the nobles to adopt in place of their own vainglorious coats of arms. A few did so (the monogram is to be seen on various palazzi), and it was adopted by the council on the facade of the Palazzo Pubblico, alongside the city's she-wolf symbol, itself a reference to legendary foundation by the sons of Remus.

The **Palazzo Pubblico**, with its 320ft belltower, the **Torre del Mangia**, is the focus of the Campo, occupying virtually its entire south side. Its lower level of arcading is a characteristic of Sienese Gothic, as are the three-part windows, which pleased the council so much that they ordered its emulation on all other buildings on the square – and it was indeed gracefully adapted on the twelfth-century **Palazzo Sansedoni** across on the north side. The other main exterior feature of the Palazzo Pubblico is the **Cappella di Piazza**, a stone loggia set at the base of the tower, built to celebrate the end of plague in 1348.

At the highest point of the Campo the Renaissance makes a fleeting entry with the **Fonte Gaia** (Gay Fountain), designed and carved by Jacopo della Quercia in the early fifteenth century. Its panels are reproductions; the originals, badly eroded, can be seen on the rear loggia of the Palazzo Pubblico.

THE PALAZZO PUBBLICO

The Palazzo Pubblico remains in use as Siena's town hall, but its principal rooms have been converted into the **Museo Civico** (March 15–Nov 15 & Dec 27–31 Mon–Sat 9.30am–6.45pm, Sun 9.30am–12.45pm; rest of year daily 9.30am–1.30pm; L6000), entered through the courtyard to the right of the Cappella di Piazza. Off to the left of the courtyard there is separate access to the **Torre del Mangia** (daily from 10am, closing between 12.45pm and 6.15pm according to season; L4000), with its fabulous views across town and countryside. The tower takes its name from its first watchman – a glutton (*mangia*), commemorated by a statue in the courtyard.

If you have time or inclination only for one of Siena's museums, it should be the Museo Civico, a series of former public rooms, frescoed with themes integral to the secular life of the medieval city. The visit begins on the first floor, with a rather miscellaneous picture gallery and the **Sala del Risorgimento**, painted with nineteenth-century scenes of Vittorio Emanuele. The medieval interest begins as you reach the **Sala dei Priori**, frescoed by Spinello Aretino in 1407 with episodes from the life of Pope Alexander III and his conflict with Emperor Frederick Barbarossa, and, beyond it, the **Cappella del Consiglio**, frescoed by Taddeo di Bartolo a year later, and with a majestic wrought-iron screen by Jacopo della Quercia.

These are little more than a warm-up, however, to room 10, the **Sala del Mappamondo**, named after the frescoed cosmology that can just about be discerned below the fabulous **Maestà** (Virgin in Majesty) of Simone Martini. A painting of almost translucent colour, the *Maestà* was the *comune*'s first major commission for the palace and is one of Martini's earliest known works, painted at the age of thirty in 1315, though he touched up parts of the picture, following damage from damp, six years later. The richly decorative style is archetypal Sienese Gothic and its arrangement makes a fascinating comparison with the *Maestà* by Duccio, with whom Martini perhaps trained, in the cathedral museum. Martini's great innovation was the use of a canopy and a frieze of medallions which frame and organise the figures – a sense of space and hint of perspective that suggest a knowledge of Giotto's work.

The picture on the opposite wall, the *Equestrian Portrait of Guidoriccio da Fogliano*, a motif for medieval chivalric Siena, was until recently unanimously credited to Martini. Depicting the knight setting forth from his battle camp to besiege a walled hill town, it would, if it were by Simone, be accounted one of the earliest Italian portrait paintings. Art historians, however, have long puzzled over the anachronistic castles, which are much later in style than the painting's signed date of 1328. The current state of the debate is confused, with a number of historians – led by the American Gordon Moran (whom the council for a while banned from the Palazzo Pubblico) – interpreting the *Guidoriccio* as a sixteenth-century fake, and others maintaining that it is a genuine

Martini overpainted by subsequent restorers. The newly revealed fresco below the portrait, of two figures in front of a castle, is meanwhile variously attributed to Martini, Duccio and Pietro Lorenzetti.

The Palazzo Pubblico's most important frescoes are to be seen in the adjacent **Sale dei Nove**, the "Room of the Nine". These are Ambrogio Lorenzetti's *Allegories of Good and Bad Government*, commissioned in 1338 to remind the councillors of their duties. The paintings include the first-known panorama in western art, and their moral theme is expressed in a complex iconography of allegorical virtues and figures. *Good Government* is dominated by a throned figure representing the *comune*, flanked by the Virtues and with Faith, Hope and Charity buzzing about his head. To the left, Justice (with Wisdom in the air above) dispenses rewards and punishments, while below her throne Concordia advises the Republic's councillors on their duties. *Bad Government* is ruled by a horned demon, while over the city flies the figure of Fear, whose scroll reads: "Because he looks for his own good in the world, he places justice beneath tyranny. So nobody walks this road without Fear: robbery thrives inside and outside the city gates." Ironically, within a decade of the frescoes' completion, Siena was engulfed by the Black Death – in which Lorenzetti and his family were among the victims – and the city was under tyrannical government.

Some of the finest panel paintings – by Lorenzetti's contemporaries, Guido da Siena and Matteo di Giovanni – are displayed in the **Sala della Pace**, off the Sala dei Novi. Take time, too, for a visit to the rear **loggia**, where, in addition to the original panels of the Fonte Gaia, you can crane your neck to see the current (and again frescoed) council chambers. From the loggia you look down on the **Piazza del Mercato** and see how abruptly the town ends: buildings rise to the right and left for a few hundred metres along the ridges of the Terzo di San Martino and Terzo di Città, holding a rural valley in their embrace.

Terzo di San Martino

Behind the top end of the Campo, marking the start of Banchi di Sotto – the main thoroughfare through **Terzo di San Martino** – stands the **Loggia di Mercanzia**, designed as a tribune house for the merchants to do their deals. It is a fifteenth-century structure, essentially Renaissance but still reluctantly so, with its Gothic niches with saints. Following the Banchi di Sotto from here, you pass the **Palazzo Piccolomini**, a more committed Renaissance building by Bernardo Rossellino, the architect employed by the Sienese pope Pius II (Aeneas Sylvius Piccolomini) at Pienza. It now houses the **Archivio di Stato** (Mon–Fri 9am–1pm; free admission – ask at reception), which displays the painted covers of the *Tavolette di Biccherna*, the city accounts. The earlier paintings depict religious themes, but they soon move towards secular images of the city's life and events – the monks doing the audits, victories against the Florentines, the demolition of the Spanish fortress, the entry of Cosimo I.

Heading south along the parallel Via Salicotto you find yourself in the territory of the **Torre contrada**, with their museum (at no. 76) and their fountain-square a few houses beyond. This street, or Via San Martino, will bring you out towards the end of the Terzo di San Martino and to **Santa Maria dei Servi**, the Servites' massive monastic church. Inside, there are two contrasting frescoes of the *Massacre of the Innocents* – a Gothic version by Lorenzetti, in the second chapel behind the high altar, and a Renaissance treatment by Matteo di Giovani (1492) in the fifth chapel on the right. The church has fine altarpieces, too, by Lippo Memmi and Taddeo di Bartolo.

Terzo di Città

Via di Città cuts across the cathedral quarter of the city, fronted by some of Siena's finest private palazzi. The **Palazzo Chigi-Saracini** at no. 82 is a Gothic beauty, with its curved facade and back courtyard, which you're free to have a look at. The palace, closed to the public, is home to the Accademia Chigiana, which sponsors music programmes, and houses an art collection including works by Botticelli and Donatello (open Mon–Fri by appointment; ☎46.152).

Off to the left at the end of the street, Via San Pietro leads to the **Pinacoteca Nazionale** (Tues–Sat 8.30am–2pm, Sun 8.30am–1pm; L8000), housed in a fourteenth-century palace. The collection is a roll of honour of Sienese Gothic painting, though individually few of its works are up to the standards of the Martini and Lorenzetti in the Palazzo Pubblico, or the Duccio in the cathedral museum.

Keeping south from here, you pass **Sant'Agostino**, erratically open, with frescoes by Sodoma and Matteo Giovanni, and beyond it a patch of botanical garden. Looping along the **Via della Cerchia** from here makes a nice walk – and offers some good local restaurants around the church of **Santa Maria del Carmine**, a predominantly student section of the town. If you follow the Via del Fosso di San Ansano, north of the Carmine square, you find yourself on a country lane, with terraced vineyards below, before emerging at the **Selva** (rhinoceros) *contrada*'s square and church of **San Sebastiano**. Climb up the stepped Vicolo di San Girolamo and you reach the duomo.

THE DUOMO

Few buildings reveal so much of a city's history and aspirations as Siena's **Duomo**. Complete to virtually its present size around 1215, it was subjected to constant plans for expansion throughout Siena's years of medieval prosperity. An initial project, at the beginning of the fourteenth century, attempted to double its extent by building a baptistery on the slope below and using this as a foundation for a rebuilt nave, but the work ground to a halt as the walls and joints gaped under the pressure. For a while, the chapter pondered knocking down the whole building and starting from scratch to the principles of the day, but eventually they hit on a new scheme to re-orient the cathedral instead, using the existing nave as a transept and building a new nave out towards the Campo. Again cracks appeared, and then, in 1348, came the Black Death. With the population ravaged, and funds suddenly cut off, the plan was abandoned once and for all. The extension still stands at the north end of the square – a vast structure that would have created the largest church in Italy outside Rome.

The duomo as it stands, however, is a delight. Its style is an amazing conglomeration of Romanesque and Gothic, its lineaments picked out in bands of black and white marble, an idea adapted from Pisa and Lucca – though here with much more extravagant effect. The **facade** was in fact designed in 1284 by the Pisan sculptor Giovanni Pisano, who with his workshop created much of the statuary – philosophers, patriarchs, prophets, now replaced by copies. In the next century a Gothic rose window was added. The mosaics in the gables, however, had to wait until the nineteenth century, when money was found to employ Venetian artists.

The use of black and white decoration is continued in the *sgraffito* marble **pavement**, which begins outside the church and takes off into a startling sequence of 56 panels within. They were completed between 1349 and 1547, virtually every artist who worked in the city trying his hand on a design. Many are obscure to a modern audience, like Pinturicchio's *Allegory of Virtue* in the nave, a rocky island of serpents with a nude posed between a boat and the land. The finest are reckoned to be Beccafumi's *Moses Striking Water from a Rock* and *Sacrifice of Isaac*, just beyond the dome area. These are kept covered except from August 7–22.

The rest of the **interior** is equally arresting, with its line of popes' heads – the same scowling, hollow-cheeked faces cropping up repeatedly – set above the multi-striped pillars. Among the greatest individual artistic treasures are **Nicola Pisano's pulpit** – completed after his commission at Pisa and more elaborate in its high-relief details of the *Life of Jesus* and *Last Judgement* – and, in the north transept, a bronze Donatello statue of *Saint John the Baptist*. Midway along the nave, on the left, the entrance to the

Libreria Piccolomini (daily summer 9am–7pm; winter 9am–5pm; L2000) is signalled by **Pinturicchio**'s brilliantly coloured fresco of the *Coronation of Pius II*. Within the library a further ten frescoes by Pinturicchio and his pupils (who included Raphael) illustrate scenes from Pius's life – his travels to Scotland, canonisation of Saint Catherine, and officiation at the marriage of Emperor Frederick III and Eleonora of Portugal outside Siena's Porta Camollia.

THE PIAZZA AND BAPTISTERY

Opposite the cathedral is the medieval **Ospedale di Santa Maria della Scala**, still in use as a hospital, and with fifteenth-century frescoes in its Sala dei Pellegrini. The other sides of the square continue the history of Sienese power, with the **Archbishop's Palace**, the **Palazzo del Magnifico** built for Petrucci in 1508, and the **Palazzo Granducale** built later in the century for the Medici.

The **Baptistery** (Mon–Sat 9am–1pm & 3–6.30pm, Sun closes 5pm; free) is reached down a flight of steps behind the cathedral, past the opportunistic Cripta delle Statue "museum". The elaborately frescoed baptistery is fronted by an unfinished Gothic facade and houses a Renaissance **font** with panels illustrating the Baptist's life by Jacopo della Quercia (*The Angel Announcing the Baptist's Birth*), Lorenzo Ghiberti (*Baptism of Christ* and *John in Prison*) and Donatello (*Herod's Feast*).

MUSEO DELL'OPERA DEL DUOMO

After the Museo Civico, the best art in Siena is to be seen in the **Museo dell'Opera del Duomo** (daily 9am–6pm; L5000), which occupies the projected, re-oriented nave. Downstairs are Pisano's original statues from the facade. Upstairs, amid a comprehensive display of cathedral treasures, is a fine array of panels, including works by Simone Martini, Pietro Lorenzetti and Sano di Pietro, and the cathedral's original altarpiece, the stark, haunting icon known as the *Madonna dagli Occhi Grossi* (Madonna of the Big Eyes).

The painting that merits the museum admission, however, is the cathedral's second altarpiece, Duccio's *Maestà*. On its completion in 1311 this painting was taken in a ceremony that processed from Duccio's studio, then around the Campo to a special mass in the duomo; everything in the city was closed and virtually the entire population attended. This is possibly the climax of the Sienese style of painting, its iconic spirituality heightened by Duccio's attention to narrative detail in the panels of the *Life of Christ and the Virgin*, originally on the reverse but now displayed opposite.

An additional bonus to the museum is the chance to climb up onto the top of the "new nave", arguably a better vantage point than the Torre di Mangia.

San Domenico, San Francesco and the Terzo di Camollia

Monasteries were essentially rural until the beginning of the thirteenth century when the idea of an exclusively meditative retreat was displaced by the preaching orders of friars. Suddenly, in the space of a few decades, each of the orders founded monasteries on the periphery of the major Italian cities. In Siena the two greatest orders, the Dominicans and Franciscans, located themselves respectively to the west and east.

San Domenico, founded in 1125, is closely identified with Saint Catherine of Siena. On the right of the entrance is a kind of raised chapel, with a contemporary portrait of her by her friend Andrea Vanni; below are steps and a niche, where she received the stigmata. Her own chapel, on the south side of the church, has frescoes of her in ecstasy, by Sodoma, and a reliquary containing her head.

Saint Catherine's family house, where she lived as a Dominican nun, is a short distance away to the south, near the Fontebranda on Via Santa Caterina. The entrance to the **Casa Sanctuario di Santa Caterina** (daily 9am–12.30pm & 3.30–6.30pm;

L1500) is on Via Benincasa, behind. The building has been much adapted, with a Renaissance loggia and a series of oratories – one on the site of her cell – as is only fitting for Italy's patron saint and the first ever canonised woman. Her career, encompassing innumerable miracles, was pretty extraordinary in secular terms, too, reconciling Tuscan cities to each other, and persuading the pope, Gregory XI, to return to Rome from Avignon.

Catherine died in 1380, the year of the birth of Saint Bernardino, who began his preaching life at the monastic church of **San Francesco**, across the city to the east. His **Oratorio** (ring for admission), with an upper chapel frescoed by Sodoma, stands beside the main church, which, like that of the Dominicans, is vast, Gothic and austere.

Walking between these two saintly locales you'll cross the heart of business Siena. Close by Piazza Matteotti, on Banchi di Sopra, is the **Palazzo Salimbeni**, the headquarters throughout its history of the **Monte dei Paschi di Siena**. The building behind the facade is a radical 1980s design by Pierlugi Spadolini, though scarcely visible unless you can convince the doorman of an architectural interest.

North of Piazza Matteotti you enter the less monumental neighbourhood of the **Terzi di Camollia**, with a solid shopping street along **Via Montanini** and largely untouristed bars and restaurants. The church of **San Stefano** fronts one of the nicest *contrade* squares in the city, home of the Istrici or porcupine. Away to the west, the gardens of **La Lizza** lead up to the walls of the **Forte di Santa Barbara**, rebuilt on Charles V's foundations by the Medici, and housing the *Enoteca Italiana*, one of the best-stocked wine bars in the country.

Practicalities

Siena feels distinctly provincial after Florence. The main action of an evening is the **passeggiata** from Piazza Matteotti along Banchi di Sopra to the Campo – and there's not much in the way of nightlife to follow. For most visitors, though, the Campo, the city's universal gathering place, provides diversion enough, while the presence of the university ensures a bit of life in the bars, as well as a cluster of cheaper trattorie alongside the pricier tourist restaurants.

Posters for city **events** are to be seen around Piazza Matteotti or on the stepped alley leading out of Piazza del Mercato to Via di Salicotto. The local communist party organise a range of concerts (mostly rock and jazz) as part of their local *Festa dell'Unità*, and the *Monte dei Paschi* and *Accademia Chigiana* put on some impressive classical concerts throughout the year.

Picnics, snacks and ice cream

It's an easy matter to put together your own picnic, allowing a very cheap meal in the Campo or other squares – Piazza Santa Maria dei Servi is a nice spot. There is **pizza by weight** just off the Campo at *Buca di San Pietro* (see "Restaurants", overleaf) and at the bar at Via delle Terme 10, and an extravagantly stocked **deli**, the *Pizzicheria Morbidi*, at Banchi di Sotto 27. Nearby **bakeries** include the *Forno dei Galli* at Via dei Termini 45, with a fabulous selection of breads, biscuits and pastas, and the *Forno Independenza* at Piazza Independenza 27 – a block northwest of the Campo. The market building south of the Campo in Piazza del Mercato is also good for picnic provisions, while Wednesday mornings see a full-scale **market** – with food and clothing stalls – sprawling across La Lizza, below the fortress.

Among the best **bars for snacks** are *Antico Sghenghero* at Via di Città 13, which has treats like *porcini* and *tartufi* (truffle) rolls, and the main branch of *Nannini* at Banchi di Sopra 22–24, a constant call for locals with perhaps the largest range of sweet and savoury snacks.

Ice cream is bought by most Sienese at one or the other end of the *passeggiata* – either at the *Nannini Gelateria*, at the Piazza Matteotti end of Banchi di Sopra, or at *La Costearella dei Barbiri*, just off the Campo near the corner of Via di Città and Via dei Pellegrini.

Siena's famous **panforte** – a dense and delicious wedge of nuts, fruit and honey – is best bought fresh by the *etto* in any of the bakeries or the *pasticcerie* along Bianchi di Sopra; the gift-packaged slabs aren't so good.

Restaurants

Siena used to have a poor reputation for **restaurants** but over the last few years things have looked up, with a range of imaginative *osterie* opening up and a general rise in standards. For cheaper meals, you'll generally do best by walking out a little from the centre, west towards Santa Maria del Carmine, or north towards the Porta Camollia. Local **specialities** include *pici* (noodle-like pasta with toasted breadcrumbs), *salsicce secche* (dried sausages), *finocchiona* (minced pork flavoured with fennel), *capolocci* (spiced loin of pork), *pappa col pomodoro* (bread and tomato soup), *tortino di carciofi* (artichoke omelette) and *fagioli all'uccelletto* (bean and sausage stew).

Buca di San Pietro, Vicolo di San Pietro 2. On an alley behind the loggia on one of the alleys leading to the Campo, this is a very popular restaurant-pizzeria. Also takeaway pizza.

Cane e Gatto, Via Pagliaresi 6 (☎220.751). Don't be put off by the lack of any menu: this restaurant serves superb Tuscan *cucina nuova*, featuring seven sublime courses on its *menù degustazione* (L50,000). If you want to pay less, ask to take just a selection of dishes. Via Pagliaresi is southeast of the Campo, off Via di Pantaneto. Essential to book.

Mariotti da Mugolone, Via dei Pellegrini 8–12. Perfectly cooked, classic Sienese dishes, unrushed service, and a fine house wine, too. L40,000 and upwards.

Mensa Universitaria, Via Sant'Agata 1. The university canteen has full meals for around L10,000. It's a bit hidden away, on the continuation of Via G. Dupre, below the church of Sant'Agostino. Daily noon–2pm & 6.45–9pm.

La Nuova Grotta del Gallo Nero, Via del Porrione 65–67. Lively and inexpensive pizzeria and restaurant. Stays open till 1am.

Osteria Le Logge, Via del Porrione 33. Popular and very tasteful trattoria, in an old cabinet-lined *farmacia* by the Logge del Papa, east of the Campo. Excellent pasta and some unusual *secondi*. L35,000 for a full meal.

Pizzeria Carlo e Franca, Via di Pantaneto 121b. Café-like place with generous pizza and pasta at very regular prices.

Rosticceria La Mossa, Piazza Il Campo 29. An excellent value if rather basic trattoria, bang on the Campo.

La Torre, Via Salicotto 7. Friendly place off the Campo that maintains a real local trattoria feel. All types of home-made pasta, excellent grills . . . no menu, so follow the advice of the waiters. Very popular.

Transport

Leaving Siena is easiest by **bus**. From the station by San Domenico, *Lazzi* and *Tra-In* have connections throughout the province – half-hourly to Poggibonsi (for connections to San Gimignano you should buy a through ticket), and half a dozen times daily to Montalcino and Montepulciano. *Lazzi* services also run throughout the day to Florence (take a *diretto*, which arrives in 1hr), and regularly to Massa Maríttima, Volterra and Rome.

Trains are less convenient as they're slower and the station involves a connecting bus (see "Arriving"). However, Siena is linked with the Florence to Pisa line via Empoli, with Grosseto (and thence Rome) to the southwest, and there's a very pretty minor line southeast through Asciano and San Giovanni d'Asso – local stations if you fancy a hike to Monte Oliveto Maggiore (see p.449).

Listings

Banks Banks are concentrated along Banchi di Sopra: the *Banca Toscana*, at the corner of Piazza Tolomei, is worth a visit for its building alone, and there's an automatic exchange machine and computer currency display in the window of the *Monte dei Paschi* at no. 92.

Books and newspapers English-language books are to be found at the *Libreria Senese*, Via di Città 94, *Feltrinelli*, Banchi di Sopra 66, and *Bassi*, Via di Città 6–8. *Bassi* also stocks foreign newspapers and magazines.

Car and scooter hire *Autonoleggi Intercar Eurodrive*, Via San Marco 96 (☎411.48). They share office space with *Hertz*.

Phones International calls can be made from the main *SIP* office at Via dei Termini 40 (Mon–Sat 8am–8.30pm, Sun 9am–12.45pm & 3–7.45pm). Alternatively, try *Bar Centrale* (open till midnight) at Via Cecco Angiollieri 37, a block north of the Campo; you pay at the bar after making your call.

Post office The main post office is on Piazza Matteotti (Mon–Fri 8.15am–7pm, Sat 8.15am–noon).

Around Siena: approaches to San Gimignano

A possible stop if you are heading from Siena to San Gimignano – the most popular town within Siena's orbit – is the tiny fortress-village of **MONTERIGGIONI**, whose towers Dante compared to giants. The village's walls and position are its most imposing aspect: it is visible for miles, high above the autostrada. There is a good, though rather pricey restaurant, *Il Pozzo*, in the main square.

Nearby **COLLE DI VAL D'ELSA**, with its old upper town, is more interesting and has plentiful transport connections with Florence and Siena and its province. Buses stop in the main piazza of the lower town, with a couple of modest **hotels** (cheapest is the *Olimpia*; ☎0577/921.662; ④). **Colle Alta**, the upper town, is a steep climb up – and has a slightly ghost-town atmosphere with its single main street, **Via del Castello**, along a narrow ridge. It is lined with a scattering of medieval palazzi (including a tower-house, at no. 63, where the architect Arnolfo di Cambio was born) and opens out, midway along, to the Piazza del Duomo. The **Palazzo Vescovile** (ring for admission), here, has frescoes of hunting scenes by Bartolo di Fredi and a fair collection of Sienese paintings. At the far end of the street is the **Porta Nuova**, designed by the Renaissance architect Giuliano da Sangallo.

Industrial **POGGIBONSI**, by contrast, has little more than its transport links and its politics to recommend it. Conspicuously ugly alongside its Tuscan neighbours, it is reputed as the home of Italy's reddest council. Travelling by public transport in this region, you are almost bound to have a Poggibonsi halt – you'll need to change here if you're heading to San Gimignano from Siena or Florence on certain buses. The place has bars and cafés to pass the time and a cheapish hotel, but there's little else to explore.

San Gimignano

SAN GIMIGNANO – "delle Belle Torri" – is probably the best-known town in Tuscany after Florence, Pisa and Siena. Its image as a "Medieval Manhattan", with its skyline of towers, has caught the tourist imagination – helped along, no doubt, by its convenience as a day trip from Florence or Siena. The town is all that it's cracked up to be: quietly monumental, very well preserved, enticingly rural, and with a fine array of religious and secular frescoes. However, from May through to October, San Gimignano has very little life of its own, and a lot of day-trippers. If you want to get any feel for the place, beyond the level of art treasures or quaintness, you really need to come well out of season. If you can't, then aim to spend the night here – in the evenings the town takes on a very different pace and atmosphere.

Founded around the eighth century, San Gimignano was quite a force to be reckoned with by the early Middle Ages. It was controlled by two great families – the Ardinghelli and the Salvucci – and its 15,000 population (twice the present number) prospered on agricultural holdings and its position on the Lombardy to Rome pilgrim route. At its heyday, in the fourteenth century, the town's walls enclosed five monasteries, four hospitals, public baths and a brothel.

Feuds, however, had long wreaked havoc. The first Ardinghelli–Salvucci conflict erupted in 1246, and for the following century there were few years of peace. Guelph–Ghibelline loyalties provided further fuel, and whenever the town itself was united there were wars with Volterra, Poggibonsi and other nearby towns. They came to a halt only through the Black Death, which devastated the population and – as the pilgrim trade collapsed – the economy. The Ardinghelli family, despite opposition from the Salvucci, applied to Florence for the town to become a part of the city's *comune*: an appeal that was accepted by one vote – a reflection on the wariness of San Gimignano's reputation.

Subjection to Florence broke the power of the nobles and so San Gimignano was unaffected by the struggles between aristocracy and town council which racked other Tuscan towns. The towerhouses, symbolic of real control elsewhere, posed little threat – and so were not torn down; today, 15 of an original 72 survive. The town itself, further hit by plague in 1464 and 1631, passed into a rural backwater existence. At the turn of the present century, travellers spoke of it as "miserably poor", a condition that was barely romanticised by E.M. Forster, who took the town (he calls it Monteriano) as the setting for his novel *Where Angels Fear to Tread*. San Gimignano's postwar history has been one of ever-increasing affluence, through tourism and the production of an old established but recently rejuvenated white wine, **Vernaccia**.

The Town

The main entrance gate to the town, facing the bus terminal (and car park), is **Porta San Giovanni**, on the south side of town. From here **Via San Giovanni**, lined with a series of defensive palazzi, leads to the town's interlocking main squares, the Piazza della Cisterna and Piazza del Duomo. On the right of the street, about a hundred metres up, is the former church of **San Francisco** – a Romanesque building converted now, like many of the palazzi, to a *Vernaccia* cellar.

You enter the **Piazza della Cisterna** through another majestic gateway, the **Arco dei Becci**, part of the original fortifications before the town expanded in the twelfth century. The square itself is flanked by an anarchic cluster of towers and palazzi, with a thirteenth-century cistern – still functioning – in the centre. It was here, and in other streets within these inner walls, that most of the leading families had their houses. To the left of the square, beside an arch leading through to the Piazza Duomo, is one of the old Ardinghelli towers; a Salvucci rival rears up behind.

The more austere **Piazza Duomo**, off to the left, introduces further towers and civic palazzi. As you face the duomo (more properly the Collegiata, as San Gimignano no longer has a bishop), the crenellated **Palazzo del Popolo**, still the town hall, stands to your left, the older **Palazzo del Podestà** behind you. The latter's Torre della Rognosa was once set as the maximum height – 160ft – for any tower. Looking around the skyline, the rule, clearly, was not much respected.

The Collegiata

The **Collegiata**'s plain facade could hardly provide a greater contrast with the interior, one of the most comprehensively frescoed churches in Tuscany. You need a good pocketful of coins to do justice to the cycles, which fill every available space, their brilliant colours set off by Pisan-Romanesque arcades of black and white striped marble. The church is closed from 12.30 to 3pm.

The principal cycles are scenes of the Old Testament (on the left wall) and the New Testament (on the right); in the lunettes above, scenes of the Creation are paralleled by those of the Nativity. The **Old Testament** scenes, completed by Bartolo di Fredi around 1367, are full of medieval detail in the costumes, activities (*Abraham and Lot leading their flock towards Canaan*) and interiors (the bedroom of *Joseph's Dream*). The **New Testament** scenes were begun by Barna da Siena (1381) and completed by a pupil after his death – he fell from the scaffold while at work. More tightly composed than Bartolo's scenes, they impress most by the intensity of their human interraction – as with the focus of eyes in *Judas's Betrayal* and *Christ Carrying the Cross*.

An altogether different vision pervades Taddeo di Bartolo's **Last Judgement** (1393) on the inner wall of the facade and the flanking walls. This is one of the most gruesome depictions of a customarily lurid subject, with no-holds-bared delineations of the Seven Deadly Sins, including Bosch-like fantasies on lust and gluttony. Below is a comprehensively punctured *Saint Sebastian* by Benozzo Gozzoli, painted in gratitude at the end of an outbreak of plague in 1464. The chapels of the cathedral were remodelled in the mid-fifteenth century by Giuliano da Maiano, and San Gimignano made its most important Renaissance commission – a small cycle by Domenico Ghirlandaio – for the **Cappella di Santa Fina**. This is a superb work, access to which is included on a general tourist ticket (L10,000) that includes entry to the town's museums. The subject is a local saint, born in 1238, who was struck by a dreadful and incurable disease at the age of ten. She gave herself immediately to God, repented her sins (the worst seems to have been accepting an orange from a boy), and spent the five years until her death – predicted in a vision of Saint Gregory – lying on a plank on the floor.

To the left of the cathedral, an arch surmounted by a statue of San Gimignano leads into a courtyard, fronted on the near side by a loggia, with an *Annunciation* by Ghirlandaio. The rather anonymous **sacred art** and **Etruscan museums** are housed in buildings off the court, where musicians often busk in summer.

Palazzo del Popolo

A visit to the **Palazzo del Popolo** (April–Sept daily 9.30am–12.30pm & 3–6pm; Oct–March Tues–Sun 9.30am–12.30pm & 2.30–5.30pm) gives you the chance to climb the **Torre Grossa**, the highest surviving and best preserved of the towers – and the only one you can ascend. It's an impressively solid structure, with various vaults and a gallery of spectacular panoramic views .

In the same building, a number of rooms have been given over to the **Museo Civico**. The first of these, frescoed with hunting scenes, is known as the **Sala di Dante** – the poet visited as Florence's ambassador to the town in 1300, making a plea here for Guelph unity. Most of the paintings displayed are fourteenth-century works, Sienese in origin or inspiration in these years before San Gimignano passed into the Florentine Renaissance orbit. The highlight in the Sala di Dante is Lippo Memmi's *Maestà* (1317), his masterpiece, modelled on that of Simone Martini in Siena. The most fascinating and enjoyable paintings in the palazzo, however, are hidden away in a small room off the stairs. These **frescoes of wedding scenes** are unique in their subject matter, and show a tournament where the wife rides on her husband's back, followed by the lovers taking a shared bath and climbing into bed. They were completed early in the fourteenth century by the Sienese painter Memmo di Filipuccio.

The rest of the town

Heading away from the central squares and Via San Giovanni, the crowds quickly thin away. Just behind the Piazza Duomo, a signposted lane leads to the **Rocca**, the old fortress, with its one surviving tower and superb views. It was built, at local expense, by the Florentines "in order to remove every cause of evil thinking from the inhabitants" after their union with the *comune*. Later, its purpose presumably fulfilled, it was dismantled by Cosimo de' Medici. Nowadays it encloses an orchard-like public garden, with figs, olives and a well in the middle.

In the opposite direction, following the Via di Castello, east of Piazza della Cisterna, leads you past Romanesque **San Lorenzo in Ponte** (one of the few other churches kept open – with dramatic fragments of a frescoed *Last Judgement*) and the attached **Farmacia Preindustriale**. This was part of a medieval hospital and normally houses an interesting display of medicines and equipment, as well as the story of San Gimignano under plague – though at the moment the place is undergoing restoration, so many of its exhibits have been moved to Museo Civico. At the end of the street is **Via del Ponte**, almost a rural lane, which winds down between vineyards to the walls, a public well-house – the **Fonti** – and open countryside.

North from Piazza Duomo, **Via San Matteo** is one of the grandest and best preserved of the city streets, with quiet little alleyways again running down to the walls. The street ends at the **Porta San Matteo**, just inside of which an alleyway leads to the large church of **Sant'Agostino** (8am–noon & 3–5/7pm). Here the great attraction is a cycle of seventeen scenes of the *Life of Saint Augustine* by Benozzo Gozzoli (1465), behind the high altar. The reluctantly celibate saint is depicted being flogged by his teacher (Augustine recalls these punishments in his *Confessions*), studying grammar at Carthage university, and travelling to Rome to teach philosophy.

Practicalities

San Gimignano's hotels are all expensive, the cheapest being the three-star *Da Graziano* at Via San Matteo 39/a (☎0577/940.101; ⑥), but beds are not too pricey at *Locanda Il Pino* at Via San Matteo 102 (☎0577/940.415; ④). There is also a good new **youth hostel** at Via delle Fonti 1 (☎0577/941.991; reception 7.30–9.30am and 5–11.30pm; ①). Best of all, if you write or phone ahead, the **Convento di Sant'Agostino** (☎0577/940.383; ③) has a dozen or so beautiful doubles.

Full lists of rooms in **private houses** (around L50,000) are available from the **tourist office** on Piazza del Duomo (Mon–Sat 9.30am–12.30pm & 2.30–6.30pm; ☎0577/940.008). However, you might save a lot of frustration by using the *Cooperativa Turistiche* at Via S. Giovanni 125 (Mon–Sat 9.30am–12.30pm & 2.30–7.30pm, Sun closes 12.30pm; ☎0577/940.809), which arranges rooms for L3000 commission. If you want to **camp**, the nearest site is *Il Boschetto* (☎0577/940.352; reception closed 1–3pm & 8–9pm), 3km downhill at Santa Lucia. This has sporadic bus connections, a bar and shop.

There are some fairly hefty charges for sitting outside at any of the bars and **restaurants** – so take good stock of menus in advance. One of the most popular choices, a fraction cheaper than most, is *Le Vecchie Mura* at Via Piandornella 15, which offers good-value pizzas and set meals. Another reasonable option is *La Stella*, Via San Matteo 75, where the food comes fresh from the restaurant's own farm. For **snacks**, there is pizza by weight at Via San Giovanni 38, or, if you're in town on Thursday or Saturday morning, a variety of fare at the open-air **market** in Piazza del Duomo.

The townscape is entertainment enough, but from June to October San Gimignano hosts a **summer festival**, with classical concerts, theatre and films in the Rocca.

Volterra

Built on a high plateau enclosed by volcanic hills, **VOLTERRA** seems a bleak, isolated place – a surprise after the pastoralism of the region around. Etruscan Volterra (*Velathri*) was one of the earliest and most important commercial centres in Italy, flourishing through a combination of mineral resources and impregnable position, attributes which ensured its survival through the Roman and Dark Ages. Its isolation, however, was later its downfall. Under Florentine control from 1360, it proved unable to keep pace with changing and expanding patterns of trade, and the town itself began to subside, its walls and houses slipping away to the east over the *balze* (cliffs), which form a dramatic approach coming in on the Pisa road.

The town occupies less than a third of the ancient extent, essentially medieval in appearance, with cobbled and stone streets, grim palazzi and walled gateways. In summer it lives a little too exclusively on tourism, with every other shop selling alabaster ware (an Etruscan survival), but it's all atmospheric enough – and there are great views, good walks and a major Etruscan museum.

Getting to Volterra is easiest by **bus** – there are regular services from Pisa, San Gimignano, Siena and Florence. The nearest **train station** is at SALINE, 8km away (connecting bus); the rail line links to the busy coastal route between Pisa and Rome.

The Town

There is little more to Volterra than its old, walled centre, so orientation is straightforward. Buses arrive on the south side of the town at **Piazza Martiri della Libertà**, from where it's a two-minute walk to the central Piazza dei Priori.

Around Piazza dei Priori

The **Piazza dei Priori** is almost totally medieval and is flanked by the town hall, the **Palazzo dei Priori**, built in the thirteenth century and said to be the oldest such palace in Italy. It may have served as the model for Florence's Palazzo Vecchio, though the influences were reversed in later years – the facade is studded with Florentine medallions. Inside the palazzo, on the first floor, is a huge, frescoed *Annunciation* by Orcagna (Mon–Sat 9am–1pm; free).

At the back of the Palazzo dei Priori, the cathedral square seems rather down-at-heel, with the crumbling masonry of the baptistery (locked for safety) and the unfinished facade of the duomo. The **Baptistery**, built on the site of a pagan temple, makes a nod towards the Renaissance in its design, executed, like the churches of Pisa, in bands of black and white marble. The **Duomo** is a more ancient conglomerate of styles. The best of its works is a thirteenth-century sculpture of *The Deposition*, in the south transept, disarmingly repainted in its original bright colours, and a fresco of *The Magi* by Benozzo Gozzoli, forming the backdrop to a crib in the oratory off the left aisle.

Other works gathered from local churches, including one that was swallowed up by the *Balze*, are displayed in the **Museo di Arte Sacra** housed in the old bishop's palace in Via Roma and the **Pinacoteca Comunale** in Via dei Sarti, a continuation of Via Roma (daily 9.30am–1pm; L8000 with Museo Guarnacci). The former has been in restoration for some time now – if you find it open, the highlight should be Andrea della Robbia's ceramic bust of Saint Linus – a Volterran who was Saint Peter's successor as pope. The latter is a good provincial collection, worth the fee for an *Annunciation* by Signorelli and Rosso Fiorentino's agitated *Descent from the Cross*.

In the opposite direction from Piazza dei Priori, Via Porta dell'Arco runs downhill to the **Arco Etrusco**, an Etruscan gateway, third-century BC in origin, built in cyclopean blocks of stone; the three blackened and eroded lumps on its outer face are probably images of Etruscan gods. The gate was narrowly saved from German destruction in the last war, during the course of a ten-day battle between the partisans and Nazis.

The Museo Guarnacci

The Etruscan legacy is represented most importantly at the **Museo Guarnacci**, Via Don Minzoni 15 (daily April–Sept 9am–1pm & 2.30–6pm; Oct–March 10am–2pm). One of Italy's major archaeological museums, it consists entirely of local finds, including some six hundred **funerary urns**. Carved in alabaster, tufo and terracotta, they date from the fourth to first centuries BC; earlier tombs were lost as the cliffs fell to nothing. The urns follow a standard pattern: below a reclining figure of the subject, bas reliefs depict domestic events, Greek myths or simply a symbolic flower – one for a young person, two for middle-aged, three for elderly.

Unfortunately the display, grouped according to subject, is stultifyingly old-fashioned and uninstructive, and only a few pieces manage to stand out from the mass-produced ware. The best are mostly to be found on the top floor, where examples from the "golden age" of the third and second centuries BC are gathered. Among them is the much-reproduced **Gli Sposi**, a disturbing portrait scene of a supposed married couple – all piercing eyes and dreadful looks. On this floor, too, are a number of small bronze sculptures, including the extraordinary **Ombra della Sera** (Shadow of the Evening), an elongated nude which provided inspiration for the Swiss sculptor Giacometti.

The Rocca

The Medicean **Rocca** dominates the southern section of town. With its rounded bastions and central tower, it's one of the great examples of Italian military architecture – and perhaps the most overbearing Renaissance palace in the country. For the last century and a half it has been a prison for lifers and hard cases.

On the town side of the prison stretches a lush area of grass, trees and shade known as the **Parco Archeologico** (daily 8.30am–5/8pm; free). There's not much archaeology about the place – a few odd lumps of rock, said to be part of a Roman bathhouse – but it's a beautiful part of the town to lie around for a few hours, and there is a good-value café-snack bar in one corner. Rather more evidence of the past remains on the north side of town, where a **Roman theatre and bath complex** have been excavated, the latter with mosiac floors.

The Balze

To reach the Balze, follow the Via di San Lino northeast from the Piazza dei Priori. This passes the church of **San Francisco**, with fifteenth-century frescoes of the *Legend of the True Cross* by Cenni di Cenni, before leaving town through the Porta San Francisco. From here, follow Borgo Santo Stefano and its continuation, Borgo San Giusto, past the Baroque church and former abbey of **San Giusto** – its dilapidated but striking facade framed by an avenue of cypress trees.

At the **Balze** you gain a real sense of the extent of Etruscan Volterra, whose walls drop away into the chasms. Gashes in the slopes and the natural erosion of sand and clay are made more dramatic by alabaster mines, ancient and modern. Below are buried great tracts of the Etruscan and Roman city, and landslips continue – as evidenced by the locked and ruined monastery, ebbing away over the precipice.

Practicalities

The **tourist office** (daily 9am–noon) is around the corner from Piazza dei Priori at Via G. Turazza 2. **Accommodation** is poor, with just four three-star hotels and one four-star. Of the three-stars, the *Villa Nencini* (☎0588/86.386; ⑤) is the most attractive, just outside Porta San Francisco. For lesser budgets, the local *Cooperativa Nuova SCAP* fills the gap, running a **youth hostel** (☎0588/87.880; ①), a couple of hundred metres past the Etruscan museum in Via Don Minzoni, and a **campsite**, *Le Balze* (April–Sept; ☎0588/87.880), nicely positioned outside Borgo San Giusto, 1km from the city. There are also plentiful rooms at the **monastery** of San Andrea, on the northeast outskirts of the town; these are generally available if you just turn up – the views are great and charges are a modest L15,000 per person.

As a hunting centre, Volterra's gastronomic efforts are dominated by wild boar (*cinghiale*). You see stuffed heads of the unfortunate beasts throughout town, and the meat is packaged as salamis or hams, as well as roasted in the **restaurants**, alongside *lepre* (hare) and *coniglio* (rabbit). In terms of price, there's little to choose between any of the eating places, and you may as well plump for quality at the locally favoured *Ristorante Beppino*, Via delle Prigioni 15–19. Cheaper options include a lone self-service at Via Matteotti 19, *Il Pozzo degli Etruschi*, a simple trattoria at Via delle Prigioni 28–30, and a few pizzerias – there's a good one opposite the *Beppino*.

SOUTHERN TUSCANY

Southern Tuscany is the province at its best: an infinite gradation of hills, trees and cultivation that runs across the *crete* – the Sienese badlands – and through the vineyards of Montepulciano and Montalcino, before climbing into the hills around Monte Amiata. Over in the west of this region, rugged **Massa Maríttima** presides over a coastal plain that has developed since the town's inception. Inland, magnificent monastic architecture can be savoured in the tranquil settings of **San Galgano** and, a short distance east on the Montepulciano road, **Monte Oliveto Maggiore**, which boasts the additional attraction of some marvellous frescoes. Perhaps the finest of the towns of southern Tuscany is **Montepulciano**, with its independent hill-town life and a Renaissance ensemble that rivals neighbouring **Pienza**. Famous for its wine, **Montalcino** is also close to the superb abbey of **Sant'Antimo**; while further south, there are medieval centres and mountain walking at **Arcidosso** and **Abbadia San Salvatore**, the remarkable sulphur springs of **Saturnia**, and the isolated drama of **Pitigliano** and **Sovana**.

Massa Maríttima

The road south from Volterra over the mountains to **MASSA MARÍTTIMA** is little explored and scenically magnificent: classic Tuscan countryside which is given an added surreal quality by the presence of *soffioni*, hot steam geysers from which boric acid is extracted. Massa, like Volterra, has been a wealthy mining town since Roman and Etruscan times. In 1225 it saw Europe's first ever charter for the protection of miners and it still peddles a militant politics – its communist council is a major link in Italy's red belt. Maríttima (maritime) is a misnomer. It's a long time since the sea lapped the town walls, and the coast is now 19km distant across a silt-filled plain.

Crashing waves would have made the hilltop location that much more impressive. Today the road skirts a small industrial estate before the town comes into view across a whaleback of hills. Blocks of new buildings take an edge off the medieval splendours, yet tourism is now as big a part of the economy as the mines. Menus posted in English are the norm, while the estate agents push their farmhouses in fluent German. There's perhaps rather less than the hype merits, but the Piazza Garibaldi and duomo are certainly enough to warrant a visit.

Getting to Massa is no problem. There are three or four **bus** services daily from Volterra (changing at Monterotondo) plus one from Grosseto and two from Florence and Siena. The nearest **train** station is MASSA-FOLLÓNICA, 19km away on the main Pisa–Rome rail line; a bus shuttle meets the incoming trains.

The Old Town

The Old Town is divided into two. The lower, walled section, the **Città Vecchia**, is predominantly Romanesque, and has most to see. The Gothic so-called **Città Nuova**, above, is still pretty old but less a place to wander, having been built largely as a residential centre. An immensely steep but picturesque lane, Via Moncini, connects the two. For most of the Middle Ages the lower town was inhabited by a Pisan clan, the Todini, the upper by their Sienese rivals, the Pannochieschi. The Florentines collared the lot in the sixteenth century.

Most of the medieval interest centres on the **Piazza Garibaldi**, a small, eccentric and exquisite example of Tuscan town planning at the heart of the Città Vecchia. The thirteenth-century **Duomo** (8am–noon & 3–6pm) is the climax of the ensemble, set on broad steps at a dramatically oblique angle to the square, its porticoes, tiny columns and blind arcades forming a highly individual Romanesque mix with the adjoining **campanile**. The cathedral has an unusual dedication to the sixth-century Saint Cerbone; his claim to fame was to persuade a flock of geese to follow him when summoned to Rome on heresy charges.

The duomo's exterior grandeur is matched by an airy internal space, and it's worth lingering over; little else in the town compares with its simple bare stone appeal, nor its handful of artistic offerings. Check in particular the eleventh-century carvings at the rear: the grinning and cross-eyed faces have the power of primitive, almost pagan art, a dramatic contrast to the severe, polished Roman sarcophagus to the right. Take a look, too, at the *Madonna delle Grazie* at the end of the left transept, a damaged but gorgeous Sienese work attributed to Duccio or Simone Martini.

For more art you could head for the **Museo Civico** in the neighbouring Palazzo del Podestà (Tues–Sun April–Oct 10am–12.30pm & 3.30–7pm; Nov–March 9am–1pm & 3–5pm; L3000), the smaller of the two palazzi on the piazza. The fee admits you to the presence of the town's undisputed masterpiece, a *Maestà* by Ambrogio Lorenzetti, considered his finest work; Cerbone and his geese lurk in the right-hand corner.

Inevitably, given Massa's mining heritage, there is also a large – and, if you're into this sort of thing, impressive – **Miniera Museo** (tours Tues–Sun April–Sept 10am–12.30pm & 3.30–7pm; Oct–March 11am–1pm & 4–5pm), five minutes from Piazza Garibaldi on Via Corridoni. Sited appropriately enough underground, but in an old air-raid shelter rather than a mine-shaft, the museum boasts seven hundred metres of galleries, with a chronological display of the area's mining methods and equipment. You might want to couple this with a visit to the **Museo di Arte e Storia delle Miniere** (Tues–Sun 10am–12.30pm & 3.30–6pm; L2000), located on Piazza Matteotti in the Città Nuova, which houses a small collection of fossils and archive photographs of local history.

Practicalities

The **tourist office** is just off Piazza Garibaldi at Via Todini 8 (Mon–Sat 10am–12.30pm & 4–6pm). Given Massa's popularity, there are surprisingly few **places to stay**. The only central budget hotel is the one-star *Cris*, Via Roma 9–10 (☎0566/903.830; ④); the town's other two low-cost hotels, the two-star *Duca del Mare* (☎0566/902.284; ⑤) and one-star *Girifalco* (☎0566/902.177; ④) are down below on the approaches to Massa, at Via Massetana Sud 25 and Via Massetana Nord 25 respectively. The nearest **campsites** are on the coast around the modern town of FOLLONICA: *Tahiti* (May 15–Sept 30; ☎0566/60.255) at Prato Ranieri, and *Pineta del Golfo* (June–Sept; ☎0566/53.369) at Pineta di Levante.

Piazza Garibaldi has some pleasant **bars**, especially the one under the arches in the corner by Via Moncini, but its restaurants are geared straight to tourist trade. Better options include the **restaurant** at the *Hotel Cris*; the cheap and excellent-value *Vecchio Borgo*, just behind Piazza Garibaldi at Via Parenti 12; and the nearby *Roma* at Via Parenti 19, something of a tourist trap but with good food and a strange local wine from Monte Regio. For **pizza**, served at outside tables, try the *Pizzeria La Torre*, Piazza Matteotti 5; or, for a snack, the *pizza taglia* at Via Moncini 44.

San Galgano

The **Abbazzia di San Galgano**, sited midway between Massa Maríttima and Siena, is perhaps the most evocative Gothic building in all Italy – roofless, with a grass field for a nave, nebulous patches of fresco amidst the vegetation, and panoramas of the sky, clouds and hills through a rose window. If you have seen Tarkovsky's film *Nostalgia*, it will be immediately familiar from the finale.

This region south of Siena was one of the heartlands of medieval monasticism: over to the west the Benedictine order had their main house at Sant'Ántimo (see p.456), while the Vallombrosan order maintained theirs a few miles to the north at Torri. In the twelfth and thirteenth centuries, however, Cistercian San Galgano was the leading power in Tuscany. Its abbots exercised powers of arbitration in disputes between the cities, and at Siena its monks oversaw the building of the duomo and held posts as *casalinghi*, or accountants, for the *comune*. They were a mix of Italians and French – from the principal house at Cîteaux – and through them the ideas of Gothic building were imported to Italy, along with sophisticated schemes for land drainage and agriculture.

The real appeal of the abbey is its state of ruin, which is owed principally to the papacy. The Cistercians lost much of their power towards the close of the thirteenth century, during which the English *condottiere* Sir John Hawkwood took the opportunity to sack the abbey, and by 1397 the abbot was the sole occupant. During the following century it recovered its numbers for a while, until the papacy made over its income to a particularly profligate cardinal. The monks left for the last time and the building gradually decayed – the campanile collapsing dramatically during a mass attended by villagers.

On the hill above the monastery, the unusual round Romanesque church of **Monte Siepi** commemorates the spot where San Galgano – a soldier from the nearby village of Chiusdino – had a vision of Saint Michael and began his life as a hermit. The saint's sword-in-the-stone legend is depicted in one of a series of frescoes by Ambrogio Lorenzetti in the adjacent chapel.

Practicalities – and Torri

Visiting San Galgano by public **transport** involves juggling with bus times – there are two or three services daily between Massa and Siena – or hitching, which shouldn't be too difficult in summer. If you need to stay, the nearest **accommodation** to be found is at the village of PALAZZETTO, a couple of kilometres back on the road to Massa. The *Bar-Albergo Il Palazzetto* (☎0577/750.160; ④) has a good restaurant, too.

If you are driving to or from Siena, **TORRI**, 2km east of the road, is a worthwhile stop. The **Monasterio dei Santi Trinità e Mustiola** is less dramatic than San Galgano, but a fine Romanesque building nonetheless, with a triple cloister of black and white marble.

Monte Oliveto Maggiore

It takes some effort to visit the **Abbazia di Monte Oliveto Maggiore**, but the rewards are there: Tuscany's grandest monastery is sited in one of the most beautiful tracts of Sienese countryside. You approach from Buonconvento, to the west, and climb quickly into forests of pine, oak and cypress, and then into the olive groves that enclose the monastery. From the east, coming through Asciano or San Giovanni d'Asso, the road passes through a sparsely populated farming region of forever-shifting colours and cultivation – the beautiful **Crete**, "craters" or moors.

Approaching the monastery: Buonconvento

Transport to Monte Oliveto is a little difficult. The nearest village served by bus is CHIUSURE, 2km east: this has a daily departure from Siena at 2pm, returning at 7pm (Mon–Sat). It's considerably easier to get to **BUONCONVENTO**, 9km southwest, the most obvious place to stay if you are visiting the monastery and travelling on south. The town looks grittily industrial on the approach, but preserves a perfect, walled medieval village at its heart. It's an enjoyable stop, with a single **hotel-restaurant**, the *Albergo Roma* (☎0577/806.021; ⑤), inside the walls. Along the street, the Sienese Renaissance paintings in the small **Museo di Arte Sacra** (Tues–Thurs 10am–noon, Sat 10am–noon & 4–6pm, Sun 9am–1pm; L2500) include a classic Sienese altarpiece by Matteo Giovanni.

If you are driving, or leave Monte Oliveto early in the day, Montalcino or San Quírico d'Orcia (see p.455) are alternative bases for accommodation. There are regular connections to both places from Buonconvento.

The Monastery

When Pius II visited Monte Oliveto Maggiore in 1463, it was the overall scene that impressed him: the architecture, in honey-coloured Sienese brick, merging into the woods and gardens that the monks had created from the eroded chalk hills around. The monastery had been founded a century and a half earlier, in 1313, by Giovanni (later Bernardo) Tolomei, a Sienese noble. He belonged to one of the wealthiest merchant families of the region, but, in the pattern of monastic legend, was struck blind, saw visions of the Virgin, and renounced worldly life. With two companions, he came to this place – known then as the desert of Accona – and lived the life of a hermit, soon drawing a following. Within six years, the pope recognised his order – the **Olivetans**, or White Benedictines – and over the following two centuries this, their principal house, was transformed into one of the most powerful monasteries in the land. It was only in 1810, when the monastery was suppressed by Napoleon, that it fell from influence. It is today maintained by a small group of Olivetan monks, who supplement their state income with a very modern centre for the restoration of ancient books.

From the **gateway**, surmounted by a square watchtower and niches containing della Robbia terracottas, an avenue of cypresses leads to the abbey. Off to the right, at the bottom of the slope, signs direct you along a walk to the **Blessed Bernardo's grotto** – a chapel built on the site where Tolomei settled as a hermit.

The abbey itself is a huge complex, though much of it remains off limits to visitors. The entrance leads past a gift shop, selling herbal cures and liquors, to the **Chiostro Grande**, covered by the series of frescoes depicting the *Life of St Bernard*. The cycle begins on the east wall, just on the right of the door into the church. It was begun in 1497 by Signorelli, who painted nine panels (in the middle of the series) before abandoning the work for a more stimulating commission at Orvieto cathedral. His sequence starts with the scene depicting a collapsing house. The colourful if minor artist Antonio Bazzi, known as **Il Sodoma**, then took over, painting the remaining 27 scenes from 1505 to 1508. He was by all accounts a lively presence in the abbey, bringing with him part of his menagerie of pets – which included badgers, depicted at his feet in a self-portrait in the third panel. There's a sensuality in many of the secular figures: the young men especially, as befits his nickname, and the "evil women" (originally nudes, until protests from the abbot) seen tempting the monks.

The **church** was given a Baroque remodelling in the eighteenth century, and some superb stained glass in the present one. Its main treasure is the choirstalls, inlaid by Giovanni di Verona (1503) with architectural, landscape and domestic scenes (including a nod to Sodoma's pets with a cat in a window). Back in the cloister, stairs lead up to the **library**, again with carving by Giovanni; sadly, it has had to be viewed from the door since the theft of sixteen of its twenty codices in 1975.

Practicalities

The monastery is **open to visits** from 9.15am to 12.30pm and from 3.15 to 6.30pm (5.30pm in winter). At the gatehouse there is a good **café-restaurant**, and also a hostel – as is the Benedictine custom. There is, however, a minimum stay of ten days (most guests stay two to three months) and summer places are almost always taken. If you want to try your luck, phone ahead (☎0577/707.017).

Montepulciano

The highest of the Tuscan hill towns, at nearly 2000ft, **MONTEPULCIANO** is built on a narrow ridge, along which runs the **Corso**, flanked by a dark series of alleys, dropping away to the walls. Henry James, who compared it to a ship, spent most of his time here drinking: a good policy, in view of the fine local table wine and the more expensive and mature *Vino Nobile*. The town remains today one of the most enjoyable places to stay in Tuscany, set in superb walking country and maintaining a refreshingly low-key tourist profile.

Montepulciano's main **transport** links are with Chiusi. *LFI* **buses** run more or less every half-hour until 9pm to Chianciano Terme, Chiusi and Chiusi station. To the west, *TRA-IN* has seven buses daily on the circuit through Pienza, San Quírico d'Órcia, Torrenieri (change for Montalcino) and Buonconvento, with three continuing to Siena. Montepulciano's **train** station, 10km northeast, is a stop only for *locales* – better to take a train to Chiusi, then a bus from there.

The Town

Montepulciano's unusually consistent array of Renaissance palazzi and churches is a reflection of its remarkable development after 1511, when, following intermittent alliance with Siena, the town finally threw in its lot with Florence. In that year the Florentines sent **Antonio Sangallo the Elder** to rebuild the town's gates and walls, which he did so impressively that the council took him on to work on the town hall and a series of churches. The local nobles meanwhile hired him, his nephew, Antonio Sangallo the Younger, and later the Modena-born **Vignola** – a founding figure of Baroque – to work on their own palazzi. The work of this trio, totally assured in conception and execution, makes a fascinating comparison with Rossellino's work at Pienza.

The Corso: Porta al Prato to the fortress

Sangallo's first commission was Montepulciano's main gate, the **Porta al Prato**, at the north end of town. Inside the gate the **Corso** begins, the palazzi immediately making clear the town's allegiance to Florence. In the first square, beside the *Albergo Marzocco*, is a stone column bearing the heraldic lion (*marzocco*) of Florence, while across the street further lion heads decorate the **Palazzo Avignonesi** (no. 91), probably the work of Vignola. Sangallo makes a second appearance with the **Palazzo Cocconi** (no. 70), opposite the **Palazzo Bucelli** (no. 73), its base inset with Roman and Etruscan reliefs.

Just beyond this crop of palazzi is the church of **Sant'Agostino**, designed by the earlier Medici protegé, Michelozzo – who also carved the relief above the door; within are good Sienese paintings by Lorenzo di Credi and Giovanni di Paolo. Across the street a medieval **tower house**, a rare survival in Montepulciano, is surmounted by the Commedia dell'Arte figure of **Pulcinella**, who strikes out the hours on the town clock; most un-Tuscan, it is said to have been put up by an exiled bishop from Naples.

About a hundred metres further along you reach the Renaissance **Loggia di Mercato** and a fork in the roads. The Corso continues to the left past further palazzi, including Sangallo's **Palazzo Cervini**, occupied by the Banco Toscana. Beyond this, you pass the church of **Gesù**, remodelled in Baroque style by Andrea dal Pozzo, before the road turns the corner and rambles outside the town walls. Just prior to the turn – at no. 5 – is the **Casa Poliziano** (no. 5), birthplace of the Renaissance humanist and poet Angelo Ambrogini, known as Poliziano, who translated many of the Greek classics under the patronage of Lorenzo de' Medici.

Via di Poliziano loops outside the walls to the **Santa Maria dei Servi**, another Baroque job by Pozzo, before re-entering town by the old **Fortezza**, now part-occupied by houses. At the end of Via di San Donato, the last stretch back into town, you find yourself in the cathedral and town hall square, Piazza Grande.

Santa Lucia, Via del Poggio and the Museo Civico

A quicker approach to Piazza Grande would be to head right at the Loggia di Mercato. A block to the north of here, a beautiful little piazza fronts the church of **Santa Lucia**, which has a fabulous *Madonna* by Signorelli in a chapel on the right. Turning instead to the south, Via del Poggio runs down to the church of San Francesco, then the imposing Via Ricci takes over for the last stretch to the Piazza Grande; it is flanked on one side by the Renaissance **Palazzo Ricci** (housing the tourist office), on the other by the Sienese-Gothic **Palazzo Neri-Orselli**. The latter is home to the **Museo Civico** (April–Sept Tues–Sun 10.30am–12.30pm & 4–7pm; Oct–March Mon–Sat 9am–1pm; L3000), an extensive collection of small-town Gothic and Renaissance works.

The Piazza Grande

The **Piazza Grande**, the town's theatrical flourish of a main square, is built on the highest point of the ridge. Its most distinctive building is the **Palazzo Comunale**, a thirteenth-century Gothic palace to which Michelozzo added a tower and rustication in imitation of the Palazzo Vecchio in Florence. You can climb the tower for free and on those fabled clear days the view supposedly stretches to Siena, 65km northeast.

Two of the palazzi on the square were designed by Sangallo. The **Palazzo Tarugi**, by the lion and griffin fountain, is a highly innovative building, with a public loggia cut through one corner; it originally had an extension on the top floor, though this has been bricked in. More tangible pleasures await at the **Palazzo Cantucci**, one of many buildings scattered about the town that serve as *cantine* for the **wine trade**, offering *degustazione* and sale of the *Vino Nobile*.

Sangallo and his contemporaries never got around to building a facade for the **Duomo** (closed 1–3.30pm), whose plain brick pales somewhat against the neighbouring palazzi. Its interior, however, is an elegant Renaissance design, and it is scattered with superb sculptures by Michelozzo. These pieces originally comprised a tomb for a local papal secretary, the core of which remains by the door. The finest of the church's paintings, Taddeo di Bartolo's iridescent altarpiece of the *Assumption*, belongs to an earlier age when Montepulciano was within Siena's orbit.

San Biagio

Antonio da Sangallo's greatest commission came in 1518, when he was invited to design the pilgrimage church of **San Biagio** on the hillside below the town. To reach it, follow Via San Biagio out from the Porta di Grassi; it's about half an hour's walk. San Biagio was the second-largest church project of its time after Saint Peter's in Rome, and exercised Antonio until his death in 1534. The result is one of the most serene Renaissance creations in Italy, constructed from a porous travertine whose soft honey-coloured stone blends perfectly into its niche in the landscape. A deeply intellectualised building, its major architectural novelty was the use of freestanding towers (only one was completed) to flank the facade. Within, it is spoilt a little by extraneous decoration but is equally harmonious. Scarcely less perfect is the nearby **Canonica** (rectory), endowed by Sangallo with a graceful portico and double-tiered loggia.

Practicalities

Montepulciano is not a cheap place to stay. If they have space, the *Marzocco* (☎0578/757.262; ⑥) is the **hotel** to make for – an elegant nineteenth-century place with a full-size billiards table. Alternatives, at slightly lower prices, are *Albergo Duomo* just off the Piazza Grande (☎0578/757.473; ⑤), at the *Ristorante Cittino*, Vicolo della Via Nuova 2 (☎0578/757.335; ⑤), or in one of the **private houses** listed by the **tourist office** at Via Ricci 9 (Tues–Sun 10am–noon & 4–6pm; ☎0578/757.985). If you're stuck, get the bus to CHIANCIANO TERME, 8km east, a huge spa with over two hundred hotels.

The town has a good spread of **restaurants**, all of them offering local wines. Best, perhaps, is the *Trattoria Diva*, just inside the gate on Via Gracciano; it's moderately priced unless you go for a vintage *Vino Nobile* from the co-owned *enoteca* next door. Its main rival, a fraction cheaper, is *Il Cantuccio*, on an alley to the right of Via Gracciano (at no. 67). Buying your own food, there's an open-air **market**, held in the gardens outside the Porta al Prato, on Thursday mornings; this is also the site of the local **youth bar**, with table football and a jukebox through to midnight.

Chiusi

CHIUSI, 14km east of Montepulciano, is a useful transport hub, with trains and buses south to Orvieto and Rome, and north to Castiglione del Lago, Cortona and Arezzo. Though it's not really a place to make an excursion to, the Etruscan museum and cathedral are good for an hour or two if you're passing through. They stand more or less opposite each other on Via Porsenna, a short walk up from the bus stop; a tourist office is on the same street at no. 61. The train station is a further 3km east at CHIUSI SCALO, a stop on all the inter-town bus routes.

The **Museo Etrusco** (Tues–Thurs 9am–2pm, Sat & Sun 9am–1pm; L3000) ought to be good, for the region is littered with tombs. Many of the best exhibits, however, have been spirited away to Florence and Rome, and what remains is modest: numerous sarcophagi, a few terracottas with traces of ancient paint, cabinets of pots, and the odd treasure – notably the enigmatic *Gualandi Urn*. If you are interested in seeing **Etruscan tombs**, ask one of the museum guards if they'll take you to the *Tomba della Pelegrina* and *Tomba del Leone*, 3km north of the town. Other local tombs (including the more famous, frescoed *Scimmia* and *Colle*) have been locked in recent years.

At the Romanesque **Duomo** there is further evidence of Chiusi's ancient past. The building itself consists almost entirely of Etruscan and Roman blocks, while the museum (L1000) gives access to **catacombs** below – used by early Christians in the fifth century. The cathedral interior is a mass of apparent mosaic work, actually painted, in Byzantine style, in 1915.

Lago di Chiusi

Chiusi's **lake** lies 5km north of the town, reached along the road past the Etruscan tombs. It is served sporadically by bus (4 daily on weekdays) but for anyone driving, or planning to camp for a few days, it makes a fine detour, and the swimming is warm in summer. The buses run to the **restaurant-bar-campsite** *Pesce d'Oro* (☎0578/21.403), set amid trees by a small quay for rowing boats.

Practicalities

Should you want to stay, Chiusi has just one **hotel**, *La Sfinge* at Via Marconi 2 (☎0578/20.157; ④). Other cheaper hotels are clustered down at Chiusi Scalo, an unattractive suburb that makes its living from a large slaughterhouse and meat storage plant. The best budget eatery is the *Pizzeria Il Capannino*, Via Bonci 28.

Pienza, San Quírico and Bagno Vignoni

Seven daily buses ply the route between Montepulciano and Buonconvento, passing through Pienza and San Quírico d'Órcia, but a pleasant way to explore the countryside **west of Montepulciano** is to hike. Pienza is only around 11km following the old road across country through Monticchiello, while another track from Pienza winds south to the medieval baths at Bagno Vignoni. **MONTICCHIELLO** is a minor attraction in itself: a walled village, with a leaning watchtower, and a **Pieve** (key in house next door) housing fourteenth-century Sienese frescoes and a panel of the *Madonna* by Pietro Lorenzetti.

Pienza

PIENZA, as complete a Renaissance creation as any in Italy, was created as a Utopian "New Town" – and an act of considerable vanity – by **Pope Pius II**. The site was previously a small village, Cortignano, where Pius, son of an exiled Sienese family, was born. Its transformation began just a year after Pius's election, the architect being **Bernardo Rossellino**, who worked on all the major buildings under the guidance of Alberti. The cost was astronomical, but astonishingly the cathedral, papal and bishop's palaces, and the core of a town were completed in just three years.

After consecration of the cathedral in 1462, Pius issued a papal bull changing the name in his own honour and stipulating that no detail of cathedral or palaces should be changed. Pius established his papal court here, but lived just two more years, and of his successors only Pius III, his nephew, paid Pienza any regard. The city, intended to spread across the hill, never grew beyond a couple of blocks to either side of the Corso, and its population (2500 today) remained scarcely that of a village. Today it still has an air of emptiness and folly: a natural stage set, which was in fact used by Zeffirelli for his film of *Romeo and Juliet*.

There is no difficulty finding your way about. Roads, buses and cars converge on the **Piazza Dante**, just outside the main entrance gate, Porta al Murello, and from here the **Corso** leads to Rossellino's centrepiece, the **Piazza Pio II**. This is enclosed by the duomo, Palazzo Piccolomini (papal palace), Bishop's Palace, Palazzo Pubblico, and, in the corner, a fourth palace built by one of Pius's more ambitious Vatican followers – Cardinal Borgia, the future Pope Alexander VI. The square makes the usual medieval nod to Florence in its town hall, but it is otherwise entirely Renaissance in conception.

The **Duomo** (closed 1–3pm) has one of the earliest Renaissance facades in Tuscany; the interior, on Pius's orders, took inspiration from the German hall-churches he had seen on his travels, and remains essentially Gothic. The chapels house a rather indifferent series of Sienese altarpieces, commissioned by the pope and his architect from the major painters of the age – Giovanni di Paolo, Matteo di Giovanni, Vecchietta and Sano di Pietro. How long the building itself will remain standing is uncertain, as, to fit the cramped site, Rossellino had to build on sandstone that soon gives way to clay. Even before completion a crack appeared, and after an earthquake this century it has required progressively more buttressing and ties.

Pius's residence, the **Palazzo Piccolomini**, was modelled on Alberti's Palazzo Rucellai in Florence, with an imaginative addition of a triple-tiered loggia at the back. You can walk into the courtyard at any time of day. The **apartments** (Tues–Sun summer 10am–12.30pm & 4–7pm; winter 10am–12.30pm & 3–5pm; L3000) include Pius II's bedroom, library and other rooms filled with collections of weapons and medals. Further mementos of the pope – notably his embroidered cope – are to be seen, along with Sienese panels, across the piazza in the **Museo Civico** (Wed–Sun summer 10am–1pm & 4–7pm; winter 10am–1pm & 2–5pm; L3000).

From Cortignano, two earlier churches survive. **San Francesco**, adjacent to the Palazzo Piccolomini, has fourteenth-century frescoes, a cloister and panoramic snack bar above the Piccolomini gardens. Down below, ten minutes' walk to the west, is the Romanesque **Pieve** where Pius was baptised. An odd structure, with a cylindrical tower, it has a portal sculpted with knights, fish and mermaids.

Practicalities

Pienza is easiest seen as a trip out from Montepulciano, but if you want to spend the night, there are **rooms** at the *Ristorante dal Falco* (☎0578/748.551; ④) in Piazza Dante. The best **restaurants** are the *Prato*, just outside the walls on Piazza Dante, and the *Trattoria La Buca delle Fate*, Corso Il Rossellino 38. Alternatively, you can get good-value beers and *crostini* at the *Birreria Sperone Nudo* in the middle of the town, and you're spoilt for choice for picnic food as the town, centre of a region producing *pecorino* sheep's cheese, seems to have gone overboard on *alimentari* and "natural food" shops.

San Quírico d'Orcia and Bagno Vignoni

SAN QUÍRICO D'ORCIA, a rambling, part-walled village, stands at a crossroads on the Siena to Bolsena road, overlooking the Orcia and Asso valleys. It's quiet and rather decayed, with a couple of bars and an exceptionally pretty Romanesque **Collegiata**, with a delicate triptych by Sano di Pietro. The village has a small hotel, *La Patrizia* (☎0577/897.715; ⑤).

Six kilometres southeast of San Quírico, **BAGNO VIGNONI** is scarcely more than a handful of buildings around a central square. The square, however, is one of Tuscany's most memorable sights, occupied by an arcaded Renaissance **piscina**. This was built by the Medici, who, like Saint Catherine of Siena, took the sulphur cure here. The hot springs still bubble away in the bath (they formed a perfect set in Tarkovsky's film *Nostalgia*), though they are currently out of bounds for bathing.

You can, however, bathe in the sulphur springs where they emerge from the hillside below the village, or use the sulphur pool at the *Posta Marcucci* hotel (☎0577/887.112; ⑦), which allows non-residents use of the pool for L15,000 a day. The village's other hotel, *Le Terme* (☎0577/897.715; ⑤), has a marginally better restaurant.

Montalcino

MONTALCINO is another classic Tuscan hill town. Set within a full circuit of walls and watched over by a *rocca*, it looks tremendous from below; and from above the countryside around – all vineyards, orchards and olive groves – looks equally wonderful in turn. In the fifteenth century the town was for a time of great symbolic importance: the last of the Sienese *comune*, holding out against the Medici, the French and the Spanish after Siena itself had capitulated to the Florentines. This role is acknowledged at the Siena *Palio*, where the Montalcino contingent – under their medieval banner proclaiming "The Republic of Siena in Montalcino" – still take place of honour.

The town today is a quiet place, affluent in an unshowy way from its tourist trade and the production of *Brunello* wine, reckoned by many the finest in Italy. By bus, you arrive at the north end, in **Piazza Cavour**, where you can look in at the **Museo Civico** and adjacent **Museo Archeologico** (daily summer 10am–noon & 4–6pm; winter 10am–noon & 3–5pm; L3000 joint admission), both of which are rather miscellaneous collections.

From here the main street, Via Mazzini, leads to the **Piazza del Popolo**, an odd little square, set beneath the elongated tower of the town hall, based in all but its dimensions on that of Siena. An elegant double loggia, almost a reprimand in proportional architecture, occupies another side, with a wonderful and rather Germanic nineteenth-century café, the *Fiaschetteria Italiana*, opposite. There is little pressure to do anything cultural in Montalcino and the café is very much the heart of town life – the focus, inevitably, of the evening *passeggiata* along Via Mazzini.

Following Via Mazzini's continuation, Via Matteotti, or taking the steps by the foot of the town hall tower to Via Ricasoli (past Romanesque Sant'Agostino, with fourteenth-century frescoes), you emerge at the south end of town by the **Rocca** (daily 9am–1pm & 2–6pm). Impressively complete, this encloses a public park and plush **Enoteca** – a good place to sample some of the glorious *Brunello*; the *enoteca* also sells tickets giving access to the ramparts (L2000) and a glimpse at the famous banner.

To the east of the Rocca, Viale Strozzi runs just inside the walls, past plots and orchards to the distinctive Renaissance **Santuario della Madonna del Soccorso**. It's a short walk from here back down to Piazza Cavour.

Practicalities

There are just two **hotels** in Montalcino: the *Giardino*, Via Cavour 2 (☎0577/848.257; ⑤), and the shabby *Giglio*, Via Saloni 49 (☎0577/848.167; ⑥). **Private rooms** are cheaper at around L50,000: try *Idolina*, Via Mazzini 2, *Anna Affitacamere* on Via Saloni, or *Casali* on Via Spagni. In summer you might find it easier to book any type of room through the *Porposta* **accommodation bureau** at Costa del Municipio 8 (Mon–Sat 9.30am–1pm & 3.30–7pm; ☎0577/849.321) or the **tourist office** (same hours; ☎0577/848.242) opposite the Palazzo Comunale. Both charge commission. The best budget **meals** are at *Trattoria Sciame*, 9 Via Ricasoli, or the *Pizzeria-Enoteca S. Giorgio* on Via Saloni.

Buses run more or less hourly to Buonconvento and Siena, most of them via TORRENIERI, and five times daily (Mon–Sat) to Monte Amiata, passing Sant'Antimo. At Torrenieri you can also pick up one of the six daily buses to Arcidosso or the five to San Quírico and Montepulciano. For **rail connections** to Siena or Grosseto, head either to Torrenieri or to SANT'ANGELO, 9km south of Montalcino and connected by three buses daily.

Sant'Antimo

At the hamlet of CASTELNUOVE DELL'ABATE, 10km south of Montalcino, is the **Abbazia di Sant'Antimo** (daily summer 9.30am–12.30pm & 3–7pm; winter 10.30am–12.30pm & 3–6pm), a glorious, isolated Benedictine monastery which stands good comparison with San Galgano and San Salvatore. The abbey is today maintained by a small group of French Cistercians, who celebrate the Sunday mass in haunting Gregorian chant.

Little remains of the monastic buildings – a ruined refectory and chapter house are used as barns – but the **church** remains in good repair. It was built in the twelfth century, in a soft, creamy stone that reflects the season's light. Its proportions are perfect, too, the rounded apse flanked by roofed side chapels, and inside, columns running around both apse and nave. Equally delightful are the details of the **carving and frescoes**. As so often with the Romanesque, these feature animals, and have an earthy sense of humour. One of the capitals depicts Daniel in the lions' den, aloof while his fellow prisoners are crushed and eaten by romping beasts. In the sacristy, an array of primitive black-and-white frescoes include details like a rat looking up attentively at Saint Benedict, and a pair of copulating pigs. Further frescoes are to be found in some of the rooms built around the **gallery**, approached from the nave by a circular stairway.

Monte Amiata

The extinct volcano of **Monte Amiata**, at 1739m, is the highest point in southern Tuscany. Rising from the comparative desolation of the *crete*, in a succession of hills rather than a peak, it is visible for miles around. The area is basically a winter resort, with snow lingering late into the spring. Its **forests** of chestnut and fir are said, rather fancifully, to delineate the Italian flag – the white of snow, green of pine and (pushing it a bit) red of chestnuts. Around the summit there are numerous marked **hiking trails** and several *rifugi* – though they are all at least L50,000 for a double.

Abbadia San Salvatore

The centre of skiing activity is **ABBADIA SAN SALVATORE**, easiest reached by bus from Buonconvento (6 daily) or Montalcino (5 daily). The Benedictine **Abbadia**, which the village grew up around, was founded under the Lombards and rebuilt in 1036, becoming the richest in Tuscany – exceeding even Monte Oliveto Maggiore. Today only a mere fraction remains of the original establishment, and most of the surviving parts date from the Middle Ages; the highlight is a large and beautiful eighth-century crypt, its columns decorated with crude Lombard motifs.

The town around, though greatly expanded since the war, retains a Gothic and Renaissance aspect with its age-blackened buildings enclosed within castellated walls. It sees plenty of summer visitors, up here for the landscape, cool upland breezes and some good easy walking. There are quite a number of **hotels**, including half a dozen one- and two-star options. About the cheapest, and a good choice, is the small *Hotel Roma* on Via Matteotti 32 (☎0577/778.015; ④; closed Sept). For alternatives, consult the **tourist office** at Via Mentana 97.

Arcidosso and Santa Fiora

ARCIDOSSO, linked to Abbadia by six daily buses, is in a similar mould: another summer walking centre, with prosperous new development surrounding a well-preserved medieval quarter of steep narrow streets. The cheapest **place to stay** is the two-star *Hotel Giardino* at Via Risorgimento 4 (☎0564/966.406; ⑤; closed Oct–Christmas). An alternative, at similar prices, is the *Park Hotel* (☎0564/967.355), 3km out of the town at CAPERTI on the Santa Fiora road.

Good **walks around the town** could include a ramble to the nearby Romanesque **Abbadia Santa Maria ad Lamulas** and the less interesting Renaissance church of Madonna Incoronata, both passed along the way to the village of MONTELATERONE, 3km to the northwest. More demanding is the hike up **Monte Labbro** (1193m) to the south, though for drivers the summit can be reached by unmetalled road, or the ridges from the hamlet of Zancona. On the summit you can visit the ruins of a church established by Davide Lazzaretti, who claimed to be the Second Christ in the 1870s.

SANTA FIORA, also connected to Abbadia by six buses each day, is another medieval village and popular summer walking base. Its crop of buildings, flanking the hillside, is slightly more notable: the **Abbadia** and fortified **Palazzo Comunale** each have fine exteriors, and the three churches each house della Robbia terracotta work. The village has a couple of **hotels**, the best option being the *Fiora*, Via Roma 8 (☎0564/977.043; ⑤).

Saturnia, Pitigliano and Sovana

Heading **south from Arcidosso** on a winding road over the hills, you are suddenly confronted by pillars of white smoke on the hillsides. This is sulphur country, a landscape full of underground springs which are tapped at intervals to provide energy for one of Tuscany's wildest and least populated regions. The route is covered very sporadically by buses (operated by *RAMA*) but it is worth a fair amount of effort to get down to the springs at Saturnia, and, if Tuscany's surplus of tourism is beginning to wear you down, the towns beyond, on the southern borders of the province, should provide an antidote.

Terme di Saturnia

Word is spreading about the sulphurous hot springs at **SATURNIA**, as the summer crowds of battered Volkswagen campers testify. Nonetheless, they're not that easy to find. If all you want is a dip you should initially ignore the hill town and follow the road south towards Montemerano. A large **spa complex** – with fierce admission charges, a vast pool and a five-star hotel – is signposted to the left, and about 200m on (as the road takes a sharp curve) a dirt track heads off straight, unsignposted but usually signalled by a cluster of cars and vans. Two minutes' walk from here brings you to the **cascatelle**, sulphur springs which burst from the ground, forming natural rock-pool jacuzzis of warm water, in which you can lie around for hours submerged up to your neck. Entrance is unrestricted and free, but rumour has it that the water here has already been channelled through the resort's treatment centre: not a very nice thought, and perhaps enough to discourage bathing in the April to October spa season.

Practicalities

There are two daily **buses** along the road between Santa Fiore and Manciano: be sure to get out at the springs (*Le Terme*) and not at Saturnia village; hitching should be reasonably easy, as there's usually someone heading for the springs.

If you intend to **stay** near the springs, you'll need a shower to wash off the sulphur smell, which can linger for days. The nearest cheap **hotel** is the excellent two-star *Albergo-Ristorante Cascata* (☎0564/602.978; ⑤), in an isolated spot 1km down from the falls on the road to Manciano (it's signposted left on a dirt road). The nearest **campsite**, *La Ciabatta*, is four kilometres down the same road at Montemerano. In Saturnia proper – a fairly unassuming place – the better of the **hotels** is the *Villa Clodia*, tucked away in one of the village's nicer quarters at Via Italia 43 (☎0564/601.212; ⑤).

Manciano and Pitigliano

MANCIANO, an attractive market town, with a medieval quarter grouped around a Sienese fortress, is an important hub of the southern Tuscan **bus** network. *RAMA* bus services include four daily to Grosseto (via Orbetello and Albinia), three to Saturnia, one to Scansano and five to **PITIGLIANO**, which is definitely best approached along the road from Manciano. As you arrive, the town soars above you on a spectacular outcrop of tufa, its quarters linked by an awesomely imposing aqueduct. The largest settlement in this southern region of Tuscany, it was for centuries known for its flourishing Jewish community – annihilated in the last war. It has today a slightly grim grandeur, the result in part of its mighty fortress – dividing the old upper town from the more modern lower suburb – in part of the tall alleys of the old Jewish district.

Piazza Garibaldi is a good place to begin a wander around the town, flanked by the fortress and aqueduct, and with views across of houses wedged against the cliffside. The **aqueduct** and **fortress** are contemporaries, completed in the mid-sixteenth century under Sangallo the Younger, along with a complex string of fortifications; within the fortress is the Renaissance **Palazzo Orsini**.

Through the piazza you reach Via Romana and the twisting, convoluted side-alleys of the old **ghetto**. Signposts direct you to the ruins of the **synagogue** and **Jewish bakery** – behind the Baroque cathedral. Traces of **Etruscan wall** are to be seen, too, below the Porte Capisotto, on the far west end of the spur.

With its scattering of Renaissance monuments and the drama of its site, the town makes a good night's stopover. In the Piazza Petruccioli, where you'll arrive by bus or car (parking space), is the town's single **hotel**, the modern two-star *Guastini* (☎0564/616.065; ⑤), which should have space. For **meals**, try the restaurant at the *Guastini*, or the pizzeria-*birreria Chalet Il Noce* on Piazza Garibaldi, through the gateway from Piazza Petruccioli.

Sovana

SOVANA, 8km northwest of Pitigliano on a minor but highly picturesque loop road to Saturnia, was the medieval capital of this southern region. It owed part of this prosperity to the fact that the reforming Pope Gregory VII (1073–85) was born here. His family built the **Rocca**, though this apart there are few reminders of medieval splendour: malaria and susceptibility to Sienese attack brought an all too swift decline. The town today, a cluster of low buildings centred on a Romanesque church, humble Palazzo Pretorio, and small civic palaces, is tumbling down and part abandoned.

Sovana is even less visited than Pitigliano, but if you have transport it is definitely worthwhile, along with the set of **Etruscan tombs**, their facades carved from the rock, a kilometre and a half to the south. The best is the **Tomba Ildebranda**, built in the form of a temple, with a well-preserved entrance stairway.

An evocative place to stay, Sovana has two good **hotels**: the tiny *Albergo-Ristorante Etrusca* (☎0564/616.183; ⑤), opposite the Santa Maria church, and the cheaper *Hotel Scilla* (☎0564/616.531; ④), just off the piazza. Both have a **restaurant**, and there's also a pizzeria, *La Tavernetta*, midway down Via di Mezzo.

PISA, LUCCA AND THE COAST

Thanks to its Leaning Tower, **Pisa** is known in name to almost every visitor to the province, though it remains an underrated place, seen by most outsiders on a whistle-stop trip. The city bears the architectural stamp of the Middle Ages, boasting Italy's most refined medieval ensemble, the Campo dei Miracoli. Since before the time of Galileo it has had one of Italy's major universities, and its student life is a major aspect of Pisa's strong sense of identity. Furthermore, its excellent road and rail connections to Florence and to the north and south make it a good base for wider exploration.

Genteel **Lucca**, with its wonderful Romanesque churches, makes an ideal springboard to the little-explored north of Tuscany, where the majestic **Alpi Apuane** harbour the marble quarries of **Carrara**, ultimate source of many a Renaissance sculpture. Here and to the south, the **coast** is a mixed bag. Travelling down the mainland your main impression is of development and sameness: a hundred scrubby strips of hotels and campsites, their sands remorselessly staked out by beach-umbrella operators. At its best, however – out of season on the islands of **Elba** and **Giglio**, around the protected **Monti dell'Uccellina**, or the wild peninsula of **Monte Argentario** in the southern Maremma – the Tuscan shoreline is as good as any in Italy.

Pisa

Since the beginning of the age of the tourist brochure, **PISA** has been known for just one thing – the **Leaning Tower**, the favourite shorthand image for the idea of Italy. It is indeed a freakishly beautiful building, a sight whose impact no amount of prior knowledge can blunt. Yet it's just a single component of the city's amazing religious core – the **Campo dei Miracoli** – where the duomo, baptistery and Camposanto complete an unrivalled quartet of medieval masterpieces. These, and a dozen or so churches and palazzi scattered about the town, belong to Pisa's "Golden Age", from the eleventh to the thirteenth centuries, when the city, then still a port, was one of the maritime powers of the Mediterranean. The Pisan Romanesque architecture of this period, distinguished by its white and black marble facades, is complemented by some of the finest medieval sculpture in Italy, much of it from the workshops of Nicola and Giovanni Pisano.

The city's political zenith came in the second half of the eleventh century with a series of victories over the Saracens, whom the Pisans drove out from Corsica, Sardinia and the Balearic Islands. Decline set in early, however, with defeat at sea by the Genoese in 1284 followed by the silting up of the harbour. From 1406 the city was governed by Florence, whose Medici rulers re-established the University of Pisa, one of the intellectual forcing houses of the Renaissance; **Galileo**, Pisa's most famous native, was one of the teachers there. Subsequent centuries saw the city fade into provinciality, but the modern city has been revitalised by its airport and industrial suburbs and, of course, money from tourism.

The City

Coming in by **train** you arrive at the Piazza della Stazione on the south bank of the Arno; by **bus** at the nearby Piazza Vittorio Emanuele II or adjacent Piazza San Antonio. From here, the **Campo dei Miracoli** is about twenty minutes' walk, across the Ponte di Mezzo, or a five-minute bus ride (#1) from outside the train station; local bus tickets are sold at a kiosk to the left of the station as you leave. If you arrive by **car**, follow the signs to the official car park outside the Porta Nuova, just west of the Campo dei Miracoli.

The Campo dei Miracoli

Since it was first laid out, Pisa's ecclesiastical centre has been known as the **Campo dei Miracoli** (Field of Miracles), and the sight of it is as stunning today as it must have been to medieval travellers. Nowhere in Italy are the key buildings of a city arrayed with such precision, and nowhere is there so beautiful a contrast of stonework and surrounding meadow. (Admission to each of the museums on the Campo – the Museo dell'Opera, Camposanto, baptistery and Museo dell Sinopie – costs L5000, or you can buy a L12,000 general ticket for all four.)

Underneath the pavements and the turf of the Campo dei Miracoli lies a platform of saturated sandy soil, whose instability accounts for the crazy tilt of the **Leaning Tower** or Torre Pendente. Begun in 1173, the tower started to subside when it had reached just three of its eight storeys. Over the next 180 years a succession of architects continued to extend it upwards, until in 1350 Tomasso di Andrea da Pontedera completed the stack by crowning it with a bell-chamber. Galileo exploited the overhang in one of his celebrated experiments, dropping metal balls of different mass to demonstrate the constancy of gravity. Eight centuries on, the tower leans more than five metres from the upright and in 1990 was declared off-limits to visitors. The precaution may have come too late: having moved annually by about one millimetre over the last couple of decades, the tower shifted that amount in the first ten weeks of 1991 alone. In the short term, steel bands are being wrapped round the tower to prevent the base from buckling; once the bands are in place, massive weights will be hung onto the foundations to try to haul the thing back into the vertical. If it works, the tower may be open again some time in the new millennium.

The **Duomo** (daily summer 7.45am–12.45pm & 3–7pm; winter closes 5pm) was begun a century before the campanile, in 1064. With its four levels of variegated colonnades and its subtle interplay of dark grey marble and white stone, it's the archetype of the Pisan Romanesque style, a model often imitated but never surpassed. The original

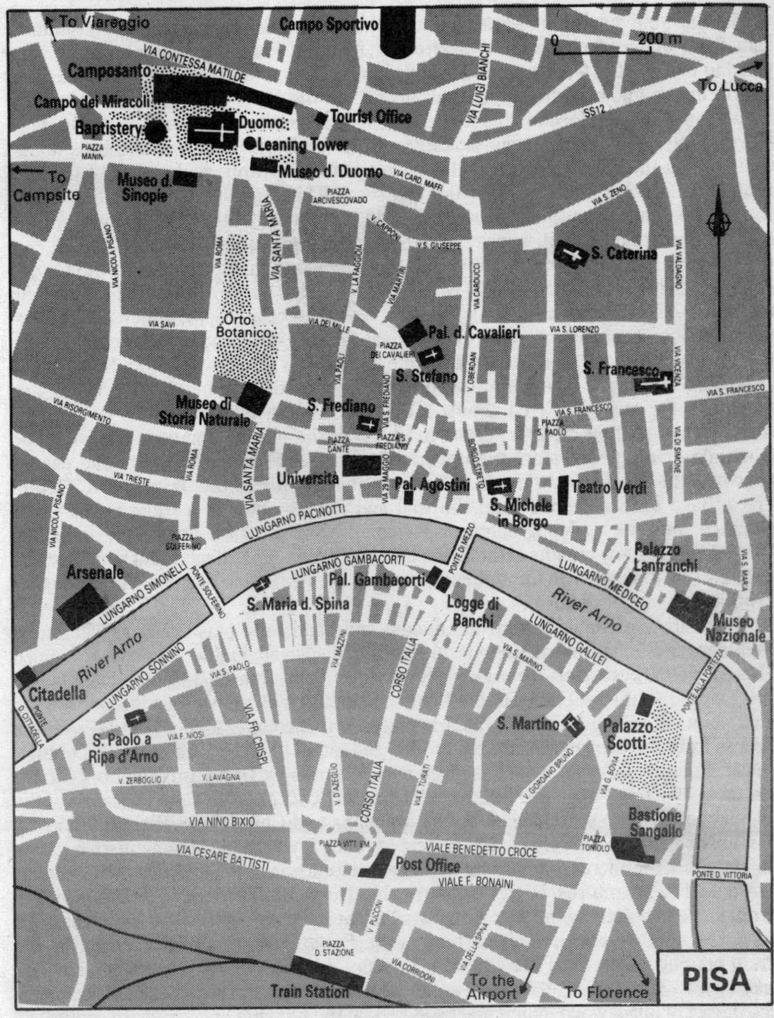

bronze doorway, the **Portale di San Ranieri**, stands opposite the Leaning Tower, and was cast around 1180 by Bonnano Pisano, first architect of the Leaning Tower. **Inside**, the impact of the crisp black and white marble of the long arcades is diminished by the redecorations carried out after a fire in 1595, but a notable survivor from the medieval building is the apse mosaic of *Christ in Majesty*, completed by Cimabue in 1302. The acknowledged highlight, however, is the **pulpit** sculpted by **Giovanni Pisano**. This was packed away after the fire, sixteenth-century Pisans evidently no longer concurring with the Latin inscription around the base, which records that Giovanni had "the art of pure sculpture . . . and would not know how to carve ugly or base things, even if he wished to". Only in 1926 was it rediscovered and put back together in the nave.

The third building of the Miracoli ensemble, the circular **Baptistery** (daily summer 8am–8pm; winter 9am–5pm), is a bizarre mix, its three storeys of Romanesque arcades peaking in a crest of Gothic pinnacles and a dome shaped like the stalk end of a lemon. Begun in the mid-twelfth century and finished in the latter half of the thirteenth by Nicola and Giovanni Pisano, this is the largest baptistery in Italy, and the plainness of the vast interior is immediately striking, with its unadorned arcades and bare dome. Overlooking the massive raised font is Nicola Pisano's **pulpit**, sculpted in 1260, half a century before his son's work in the cathedral. This was the sculptor's first major commission and manifests a classical spirit in part attributable to the influence of the court of Emperor Henry II, whose Italian power base was in Nicola's native Apulia.

The screen of sepulchral white marble running along the north edge of the Campo dei Miracoli is the perimeter wall of what has been called the most beautiful cemetery in the world – the **Camposanto** (daily Jan, Feb, Nov & Dec 9am–5pm; March & Oct 9am–6pm; April–Sept 8am–8pm). According to Pisan legend, at the end of the twelfth century the city's archbishop brought back from the Crusades a cargo of soil from Golgotha, in order that eminent Pisans might be buried in holy earth. The building enclosing this sanctified site was completed almost a century later. Incendiary bombs dropped by Allied planes on July 27, 1944, destroyed most of the cloister's famous **frescoes**: the most important survivors are the remarkable fourteenth-century cycle by the painter known as the *Maestro del Trionfo della Morte*, the **Master of the Triumph of Death**. These have been detached from the wall and put on show in a room opposite the entrance, beyond a photographic display of the Camposanto before the bombing. Painted within a few months of the Black Death of 1348 – a pestilence which hit Tuscany so badly that it was known throughout Europe as the Florentine Plague – the *Triumph* is a ruthless catalogue of horrors.

A vast array of statuary from the duomo and baptistery, plus ecclesiastical finery, paintings and other miscellaneous pieces are displayed in the recently revamped **Museo dell'Opera del Duomo** (daily summer 9am–1pm & 3–7pm; winter closes 5pm), at the southeast corner of the Campo. Sculptures by the various Pisanos are the high points of the museum, but the first pieces you encounter – Nicola and Giovanni's figures from the baptistery – are too eroded and pitted to give much of an idea of their power. Room 5, however, which is given over to works by **Giovanni Pisano**, contains the most affecting statue in Pisa, the *Madonna del Colloquio*, so called because of the intensity of the gazes exchanged by the Madonna and Child. **Nino Pisano** – no relation to Nicola and Giovanni – is the subject of room 7, where his creamy marble monuments show the increasing suavity of Pisan sculpture in the late fourteenth century. Giovanni Pisano returns in the **treasury**, his ivory *Madonna and Child* showing a remarkable ingenuity in the way it exploits the natural curve of the tusk from which it's carved. The other priceless object here is the *Pisan Cross*, which was carried by the Pisan contingent on the First Crusade. Upstairs, big and witless altarpiece paintings take up a lot of room, as do cases of ecclesiastical clothing and lavish examples of intarsia, the art of inlaid wood, much practised here in the fifteenth and sixteenth centuries.

On the south side of the Campo, the only gap in the souvenir stalls is the entrance to the **Museo delle Sinopie** (daily summer 9am–1pm & 3–7pm; winter closes 5pm). This new, well-arranged museum, created for the preliminary fresco sketches removed from the Camposanto, is not for non-specialists.

The rest of the city

Away from the Campo dei Miracoli, Pisa takes on a very different character, as few tourists penetrate far into its squares and arcaded streets, with their Romanesque churches and – especially along the Arno's banks – ranks of fine palazzi. Despite the large student population it's generally quiet, except during the summer festivals and the monthly market, when the main streets on each side of the river become one continuous bazaar.

The **Piazza dei Cavalieri** is an obvious first stop from the Campo, a large square that opens unexpectedly from the narrow backstreets. Perhaps the site of the Roman forum, it was the central civic square of medieval Pisa, before being remodelled by Vasari as the headquarters of the Knights of Saint Stephen – their palace, the curving **Palazzo dei Cavalieri**, covered in *sgraffiti* and topped with busts of the Medici, adjoins the order's church of **Santo Stefano**, designed by Vasari and housing banners captured from the Turks. On the other side of the square is the Renaissance-adapted **Palazzo dell'Orologio**, in whose tower the military leader Ugolino della Gherardesca was starved to death in 1208, with his sons and grandsons, as punishment for his alleged duplicity with the Genoese enemy – an episode described in Dante's *Inferno* and Shelley's *Tower of Famine*.

Heading from Piazza dei Cavalieri towards the Arno, Via Dini swings into the arcaded **Borgo Stretto**, Pisa's smart street, its windows glistening with desirables that seem slightly out of tune with the city's unshowy style. More typically Pisan is the **market** just off Via Dini (weekday mornings and all day Saturday), its fruit, vegetable, fish, meat and clothing stalls spilling onto the lanes around Piazza Vettovaglie.

Past the Romanesque-Gothic facade of **San Michele** – built on the site of the Roman temple to Mars – the Borgo meets the river at the traffic-knotted Piazza Garibaldi and **Ponte di Mezzo**, the city's central bridge. A left turn along Lungarno Mediceo takes you past the **Palazzo Toscanelli** (now the city archives), which was rented by Byron in 1821–22, after his expulsion from Ravenna for seditious activities. A couple of doors further along the *lungarno* is the **Museo Nazionale di San Matteo** (Tues–Sat 9am–7.30pm, Sun 9am–1.30pm; L6000), where most of the major works of art from Pisa's churches are now gathered. Fourteenth-century religious paintings make up the meat of this collection, though there's also a panel of *Saint Paul* by Masaccio, Gozzoli's strangely festive *Crucifixion* and Donatello's reliquary bust of the introspective *St Rossore*.

To the west of the Ponte di Mezzo on the more down-at-heel south side of the Arno, the rather monotonous line of palazzi is suddenly enlivened by the spry turreted oratory of **Santa Maria della Spina**. Rebuilt in 1323 by a merchant who had acquired one of the thorns (*spine*) of Christ's crown, it's the finest flourish of Pisan Gothic. Originally built closer to the river, it was moved here for fear of floods in 1871. The interior is a disappointment that visitors are usually spared by extremely erratic opening hours.

Practicalities

People tend to cover Pisa as a day trip, or stay just a night, so **accommodation** is usually not too hard to find, although many of the one-stars are used by students during term time. To pick up full hotel lists for the city and province look in at one of the **tourist offices**: to the left of the station as you leave, and in the northeast corner of the Campo dei Miracoli, close to the Leaning Tower (both Mon 3–5.30pm, Tues–Sat 9.30am–noon & 3–5.30pm, Sun 9.30am–noon; ☎050/542.344).

There are **currency exchange** bureaux at the station, the airport, and in the middle of the row of stalls at the Campo dei Miracoli. The station also has a 24-hour **telephone office** and a **left luggage office**, while the main post office is 100m away in Piazza Vittorio Emanuele.

Accommodation

The most attractive of Pisa's budget **hotels** are grouped around the Campo dei Miracoli. A definite first choice should be the elegant, old *Gronchi*, just east of the Campo in Piazza Arcivescovado (☎050/23.626; ④). Others nearby include the *Galileo*, Via Santa Maria (☎050/40.621; ④); the *Giardino*, tucked behind a self-service restaurant on Via Cammeo, by the Porta Nova (☎050/56.2101; ④); and the *Helvetia*, Via Don

G. Boschi 31 (☎050/41.232; ③). There are also a few places around Piazza Dante and Piazza dei Cavalieri in the centre of town: *Rinascente* at Via del Castelletto 28 (☎050/580.460; ④), *Serena* at Via D. Cavalca 45 (☎050/24.491; ④), and *Di Stefano*, Via S. Apollonia 35 (☎050/553.559; ④). If these are all full, you may as well reconcile yourself to the station area, where the best of the cheapies is the *Milano*, Via Mascagni 14 (☎050/23.162; ④).

The city **campsite**, *Campeggio Torre Pendente* (☎050/561.704), is 1km west of the Campo dei Miracoli at Viale delle Cascine 86 (signposted from Piazza Manin). It's a large, well maintained site, with a laundry, bar, restaurant and shop. The **youth hostel** is at Via Pietrasantina 15 (☎050/890.622; ①), a good 45 minutes' walk from the Campo – better to take the #3 bus from the station.

Restaurants

Restaurants in the environs of the Leaning Tower are not good value, but head a few blocks south, to the area **around Piazza Cavalieri and Piazza Dante**, and you find predominantly local places, many with prices reflecting student custom. One of the most popular is *Trattoria Stelio*, Piazza Dante 11, good for meals around L15,000 and impressive pizzas for a lot less. Also in this area, the modern university building on Via Martiri, off Piazza Cavalieri, houses a student **Mensa** (mid-Sept to mid-July Mon–Fri noon–2.30pm & 7–9pm; Sat & Sun noon–2.30pm). Over to the west, *Scarpellini Cassio*, Piazza Cavallotti 14, is a good *tavola calda*, while in the train station area *Il Viale*, Viale Bonaini 78, offers excellent-value seafood.

Festivals and events

The city's big traditional event is the **Gioco del Ponte**, held on June 27, when teams from the north and south banks of the city stage a series of "battles", pushing a seven-ton carriage over the Ponte di Mezzo. The event has taken place since Medici times and continues in medieval costume. Other celebrations – concerts, regattas, art events – are held around the same time, and the city has a festive feel, for most of the month, with banners, posters and pavement drawings. Most spectacular of the ancillary shows is the **Luminaria di San Raniero**, when blazing torches light up both river banks.

Among **regular events**, look out for concerts at the *Teatro Comunale Verdi*, Via Palestro, and for more off-beat and contemporary shows (even the odd rock concert) held in a former church at the end of Via San Zeno. The city also has an adventurous **arts cinema**, *Cinema Nuove*, in Piazza Stazione.

Certosa di Pisa

Of the thirty Carthusian monasteries left intact in Italy none makes a more diverting excursion than the fourteenth-century **Certosa di Pisa**, close by the village of CALCI, 12km east of Pisa. A regular *APT* bus service runs to the village from the bus station a short distance west of Piazza Vittorio Emanuele; if you're in a car, just get to the amazing Medici aqueduct – immediately visible on the eastern outskirts of the city – and follow it all the way. The guided tour of the monastery (May–Sept Tues–Sat 9am–7pm, Sun 9am–1pm; Oct–April Tues–Sat 9am–5pm, Sun 9am–1pm; L4000) gives a remarkable sense of how the building related to the lives of this order.

The size of the Certosa is startling. From the frescoed central **church** the tour passes through eleven other **chapels** in which Sunday Mass was conducted simultaneously. Looking as fresh as the day they were decorated (they have not been restored), these are strangely sybaritic interiors – all powder blue, baby pink, pale violet and pallid green. This ballroom decor contrasts with the more conventional monasticism of the **cloister** and its three-roomed cells, each of which has a self-contained garden, walled so that the monks could maintain their soul-perfecting isolation. From the cloister the tour progresses to the **refectory**, where frescoes of seminal moments in the history of the monastery are interspersed with images of the months and their associated crops – a reminder of the order's agricultural self-sufficiency.

Lucca

LUCCA is the most graceful of Tuscany's provincial capitals, set inside a ring of Renaissance walls fronted by gardens and huge bastions. The streets are dotted with palazzi and the odd tower and at intervals open onto a church square, invariably overlooked by a brilliantly decorated Romanesque facade. It's quiet without being dull, absorbs its tourists with ease, and – perhaps uniquely in Italy – has a population that chooses to ride bikes rather than cram the centre with cars.

The city lies at the heart of one of Italy's richest agricultural regions, renowned above all for the quality of its olive oil, and it has prospered since Roman times. Its heyday, however, was the eleventh to fourteenth centuries, when the silk trade brought wealth and, for a time, political power. In a brief flurry of military activity, Lucca first lost its independence to Pisa in 1314, then, under the command of a remarkable adventurer, Castruccio Castracani, itself forged an empire in the west of Tuscany. Pisa and Pistoia both fell, and, but for Castracani's untimely death in 1325, Lucca might well have taken Florence. In subsequent centuries it remained largely independent until falling into the hands of Napoleon, the Bourbons and, just prior to Italian unification, the Grand Duchy of Tuscany. Today the city is reckoned among the wealthiest in Tuscany – a prosperity based largely on high-quality olive oil and, strangely enough, lingerie.

The City

Arriving by **bus**, you'll find yourself just inside the western stretch of walls, in Piazza Verdi. The **train station** is a short way outside the walls to the south, an easy walk or short bus ride to the centre.

Confined within its walls, Lucca is a pretty easy place to get your bearings. The centre of town is ostensibly **Piazza Napoleone**, a huge expanse carved out by the Bourbons to house their administration. From here, **Via Fillungo** – the "long thread" – heads north through the heart of the medieval city to the Piazza Anfiteatro, built on the Roman arena. To the west of Via Fillungo is Lucca's social heart, **Piazza San Michele**, while to the east, fronting a rather anonymous square, is the **Duomo**. Further east still, the **Fosso** ("ditch") cuts off the quarter around **San Francesco**.

The Duomo di San Martino

It needs a double-take before you realise why the **Duomo di San Martino** (closed 3.30–6.30pm) looks odd. The city's cathedral is fronted by a severely assymetric **facade** – its right-hand arch and loggias squeezed by the belltower, which was already in place from an earlier building. Nonetheless, the building sets a tone for Lucca's Romanesque churches and little detracts from the overall grandeur, created by the repetition of tiny columns and loggias and by the stunning **atrium**, whose bas-reliefs are some of the finest sculptures in the city.

The carvings over the left-hand door – a *Deposition*, *Annunciation*, *Nativity* and *Adoration of the Magi* – are by **Nicola Pisano**, and may well be his first work after arriving in Tuscany from Apulia. Between the doors, the panels of the *Life of St Martin* (1210) are the masterpiece of the facade's architect, **Guidetto da Como**.

The **interior** is best known for the contribution of **Matteo Civitali** (1435–1501), who is represented here by a couple of fonts, the pulpits and several tombs – but his most famous work is the **Tempietto**, an unmissable gilt and marble octagon halfway down

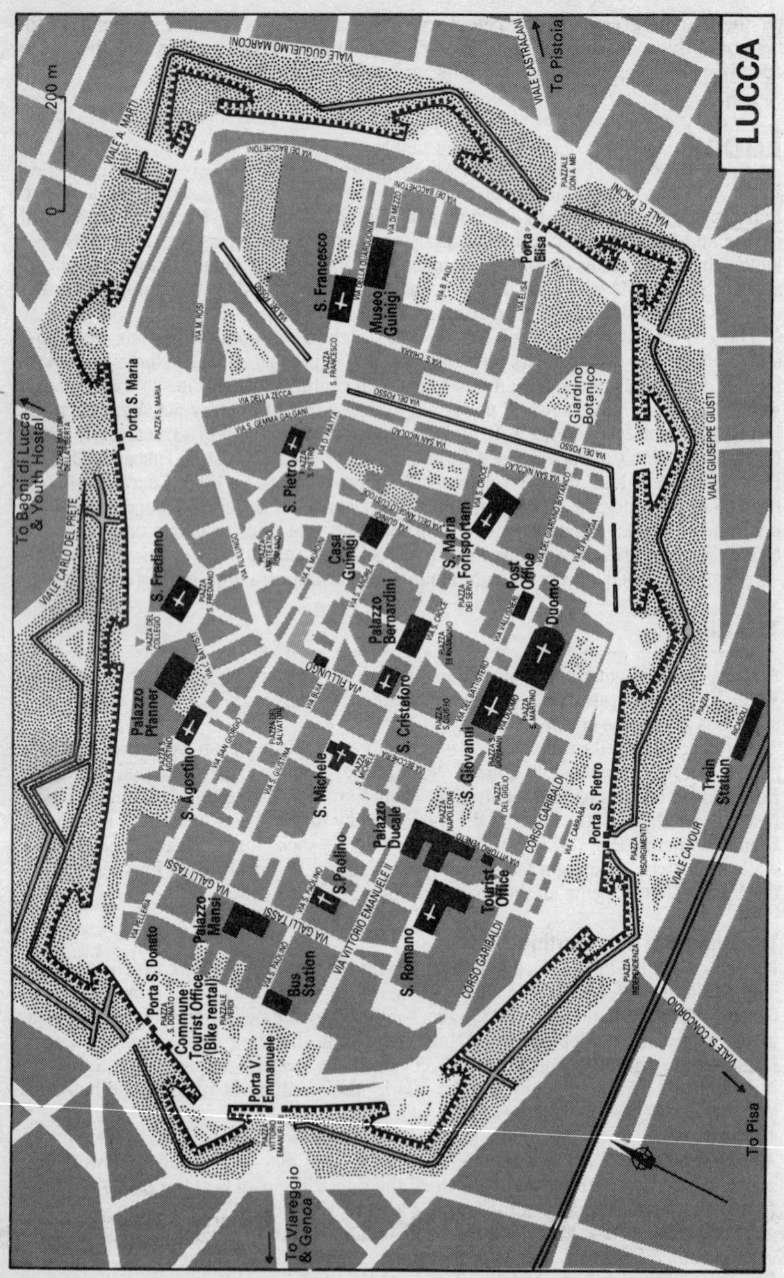
LUCCA
0
200 m
To Pistoia
To Bagni di Lucca & Youth Hostal
To Viareggio & Genoa
To Pisa
Porta S. Maria
Porta Elisa
Porta S. Pietro
Porta V. Emmanuele
Porta S. Donato
Commune Tourist Office (Bike rental)
Bus Station
Palazzo Mansi
S. Paolino
S. Romano
Tourist Office
Palazzo Ducale
S. Michele
S. Giovanni
S. Cristoforo
Palazzo Bernardini
Duomo
Post Office
S. Maria Forisportam
Casa Guinigi
S. Pietro
S. Frediano
Palazzo Pfanner
S. Agostino
S. Francesco
Museo Guinigi
Giardino Botanico
Train Station
VIALE CARLO DEL PRETE
VIALE A. MARTI
VIALE GUGLIELMO MARCONI
VIALE CASTRACANI
VIALE G. PACINI
VIALE GIUSEPPE GIUSTI
VIALE CAVOUR
VIALE S. CONCORDIO
VIA GALLI TASSI
VIA VITTORIO EMANUELE II
CORSO GARIBALDI
VIA FILLUNGO
VIA DEL FOSSO
VIA DELLA ZECCA

the church. Some fanatically intense acts of devotion are performed in front of it, directed at the **Volto Santo** (Holy Face), a cedarwood crucifix popularly said to be a true effigy of Christ carved by Nicodemus, an eyewitness to the crucifixion. Legend has it that the *Volto Santo* came to Lucca of its own volition, first journeying by boat from the Holy Land, and then brought by oxen guided by divine will – a story similar to the ecclesiastical sham of Saint James's bones at Santiago di Compostela in Spain. It may be no coincidence that it appeared during the bishopric of Anselmo di Baggio, later elevated to the papacy.

Elsewhere in the church the works of art are of less disputed origin. The finest of them is the **tomb of Ilaria del Carretto** (1410), a little beyond the Tempietto in the left transept. Considered the masterpiece of Jacopo della Quercia, it consists of a raised dais and the sculpted body of Ilaria, wife of Paolo Giunigi, one of Lucca's medieval big shots. In a touching, almost sentimental gesture, the artist has carved the family dog at her feet.

In the chapel immediately beyond the sculpture is a *Madonna and Child*, painted in 1509 by Bartolomeo della Porta, the first of several paintings – all recently restored – by surprisingly big names. The second altar on the left has a *Presentation of the Virgin* by **Bronzino** (1598), the third altar on the right has a garish *Last Supper* by **Tintoretto**, and in the sacristy off to the right, there's a superb *Madonna Enthroned with Saints* by **Domenico Ghirlandaio**.

Over Via Archivescovale from the duomo, the **Museo della Cattedrale** (Tues–Sun 10am–1pm & 2.30–5.30pm; L5000 or L7000 with San Giovanni church), is a spanking-new showcase for a generally unexceptional array of artefacts, though it does contain some unnerving Romanesque stone heads – human and equine – and some lavish metalwork, including the festive regalia for the *Volto Santo*.

San Michele – and the western quarter

Visible immediately to the west of the duomo is the church of **San Giovanni** (L3000, or L7000 with Museo della Cattedrale), where recent excavations have unearthed a tangle of architectural remains, from Roman villa mosaics to traces of a Carolingian church. Continue west from here into Piazza Napoleone, then head north, and you emerge on the site of the Roman forum, now the square surrounding **San Michele in Foro**, a church with one of Tuscany's most exquisite **facades**. The church is unfinished, as the money ran out before the body of the church could be raised to the level of the facade. The effect is wonderful, the upper loggias and the windows fronting air, supporting the figure of the archangel at their summit. Its Pisan-inspired intricacy is a triumph of poetic eccentricity, mirrored in many of Lucca's churches. Each of its myriad columns is different – some twisted, others sculpted or candy-striped. The impressive **campanile** is the city's tallest. It would be hard to follow this act and the **interior** barely tries; the best work of art is a beautifully framed painting of *SS. Jerome, Sebastian, Roch and Helena* by **Filippino Lippi**, at the end of the right-hand nave.

Giacomo Puccini was born almost opposite San Michele at Via di Poggio 30; his father and grandfather had both been organists in the church. Their home, the **Casa di Puccini** (April–Sept Tues–Sun 10am–6pm; L3000) is now a school of music and maintains a small museum containing the Steinway on which he wrote *Turandot*, some scores, photographs, even his overcoat. Students take it in turns to show visitors around and put on records of the master's compositions.

Just a couple of blocks to the west of Puccini's house, in Via Galli Tassi, the seventeenth-century Palazzo Mansi houses a **Pinacoteca Nazionale** (Tues–Sat 9am–7pm, Sun 9am–2pm; L6000). This is an indifferent collection of pictures – its only real highlight Pontormo's portrait of Alessandro de' Medici – but the palace itself is a sight: all over-the-top Rococo, which reaches its zenith in a spectacularly gilded bridal suite.

North to San Frediano

Back to the east of San Michele, **Via Fillungo** cuts through Lucca's luxury shopping district, past the **Torre delle Ore**, the city's clock tower since 1471, and the famous *Caffè di Simo*, a bar worth the price of a drink just for the turn-of-the-century ambience. Beyond, the street branches into a warren of lanes that lead to Piazza San Frediano.

San Frediano is again Pisan-Romanesque, though in place of the characteristic multiple loggias of the other great facades is a magnificent thirteenth-century mosaic of *Christ in Majesty* with the Apostles gathered below. The **interior** lives up to the facade's promise – a delicately lit, hall-like basilica, with subtly varied columns and capitals and some fine treasures. Immediately facing the door is one of the best, the **Fonta Lustrale**, a huge twelfth-century font executed by three different craftsmen. Set behind the font is an *Annunciation* by Andrea della Robbia, festooned with trailing garlands of ceramic fruit. More fine carving is displayed by the Jacopo della Quercia altarpiece and pavement tombs in the **Cappella Trenta** (fourth on the right). The best frescoes in the city, meanwhile, are to be found in the second chapel of the left aisle: **Amico Aspertini**'s sixteenth-century scenes of the *Arrival of the Volto Santo*, the *Life of St Augustine* and *The Miracle of St Frediano*. Frediano, an Irish monk, is said to have brought Christianity to Lucca in the sixth century and is depicted here saving the city from flood.

Palazzo Pfanner, Piazza del Anfiteatro and around

A short distance south of San Frediano, at Via degli Asili 33, is the **Palazzo Pfanner** (April–Sept Tues–Sun 10am–5pm; L3000), whose collection of eighteenth- and nineteenth-century costume is not of great general interest. However, its rear loggia and statued gardens are exquisite. They can be seen to equally good effect from the city walls, which also yield a good overview of another fine church, **Sant'Agostino**, currently in the throes of what looks like long-term restoration.

East of San Frediano, just off Via Fillungo, you reach the remarkable **Piazza del Anfiteatro**, aerial shots of which are featured in all Lucca's tourist literature. A ramshackle circuit of medieval buildings, as yet unprettified, it incorporates elements of the Roman amphitheatre that once stood here. The character of this quiet neighbourhood finds its best expression in the small **covered market** just north of the square in Piazza dei Carmini – distinguished by a huge brick campanile. An unappealing frontage gives way to a lovely arcaded interior of homely stalls.

A couple of blocks east is **San Pietro Somaldi**, with the usual delicate facade, this time green stone on the lower levels, topped with two tiers of Pisan marbling and small columns. The **Casa Guinigi**, south of San Pietro, is the strangest sight in Lucca's cityscape: the fifteenth-century home of Lucca's leading family, its battlemented tower is surmounted by a holm oak whose roots have grown into the room below. Much of the stolid, red-brick tower is still undergoing repairs, but from Via San Andrea you can climb up for a close look at the tree and for one of the best views over the city (April–Sept 9am–7.30pm; Oct–March 10am–4.30pm; L4500).

Continue south along Via Guinigi then left at the end of it and you come to the twelfth-century **Santa Maria Forisportam** ("outside the gate"), signalling the limit of the Roman and medieval city. Ruskin claimed that it was this church that sparked his interest in medieval architecture. The facade in fact sports just two unfinished tiers and none of its relatives' decorative columns, but it's appealing for all that, with a few carvings above the doors and the usual jutting animals high on the front.

Across the Fosso: San Francesco and the Museo Nazionale

The city's canal and parallel road, the **Via del Fosso**, mark the entry to Lucca's more lacklustre eastern margins. The most attractive part of this quarter is the **Giardino Botanico** (Tues–Sun 9am–noon & 4–7pm; L3000) at the southern end of Via del Fosso, an extensive patch of green neatly complementing the ramparts.

Otherwise, the only significant sights are in the north of this quarter, around the church of **San Francesco**, which is fronted by a relatively simple facade and adjoining a crumbling brick convent. Across the street from the back of the church is the much-restored **Villa Guinigi**, built to supplement the family's medieval town house. This is now home to the city's major museum, the **Museo Nazionale Guinigi** (Tues–Sun April–Sept 9am–7pm; Oct–March 9am–2pm; L4000), an extremely varied collection of painting, sculpture, furniture and applied arts. The lower floor is mainly sculpture and archaeological finds, with numerous Romanesque pieces and works by della Quercia and Matteo Civitali. Upstairs, the gallery moves onto paintings, with lots of big sixteenth-century canvases, and more impressive works by early Lucchese and Sienese masters, as well as fine Renaissance offerings from such as Fra' Bartolomeo.

Practicalities

Lucca is an excellent base for exploring northwest Tuscany, with Pisa, the coast and the Alpi Apuane just a short bus or train ride away. However, **accommodation** is a major problem at almost any time of year.

Information

The lone building on the north side of Piazza Verdi is the new **tourist office** (daily summer 9am–7pm, winter 9am–2pm; ☎0583/48.881), a swish affair with plenty of information. The office also hires out **bikes** (April–Sept; L10,000 per day), good for a circuit of the walls. In summer there's another small tourist office off Piazza Napoleone at Via Vittorio Emanuele 40.

Accommodation

Lucca's dozen one- and two-star **hotels** are scattered about the city, with a couple (usually the last to fill) located outside the walls. If you turn up without a booking and can't find a room, be prepared to press on to Viareggio. The cheapest hotels **within the walls** are *La Margherita*, Via San Andrea 8 (☎0583/494.146; ④), and *L'Orologio*, Via San Pierino 7 (☎0583/53.419; ④). After these, the best bet in the centre is the *Moderno*, Via Civitali 38 (☎0583/558.429; ⑤).

Two hotels that fill less quickly, two blocks east of Porta Elisa, are *Melecchi* (☎0583/950.234; ④) and *Stipino* (☎0583/495.077; ⑤), at Via Romana 37 and 109. Also **outside the walls**, 3km to the north, is the **youth hostel**, *Ostello Il Serchio* (March 1–Oct 15; ☎0583/953.686; ①): leave the city at Porta Santa Maria, go up Viale Civitali then right onto Via del Brennero – the hostel is on the left, next to a garage and opposite a heavy industrial plant. You can **camp** at the back of the hostel, should you feel so inclined.

Food and festivals

As a gastronomic centre, Lucca is packed full of delicatessens, and quality is reflected, too, in the **restaurants**. If you can afford at least L60,000, call in at the Michelin-rated *Il Buca di Sant'Antonio* at Via della Cervia 1. On a more realistic level, there's: *Trattoria da Leo*, Via Tegrimi 1, near Piazza del Salvatore; *Trattoria da Giulio*, Via del Tommaso 29, by the Palazzo Mansi; *Trattoria da Guido*, Via Battisti 28; or *Ristorante Sergio*, Via Santa Croce 44. For excellent pizza, with good beer, try *Pizzeria Queens* at Via Cenami 13, or *Pizza Italia*, just off Via Fillungo at Corte Compagni 2.

Entertainment centres on classical music and dance. During the summer there are special concerts and events as part of the *Festival di Marlia* (held at the Villa Reale, 8km towards Pistoia), and in September the focus shifts back to the city with the *Settembre Lucchese*. Both feature at least one Puccini opera, staged during the *Settembre* at the intimate **Teatro Comunale** in Piazza del Giglio. Details from the tourist office.

Viareggio to Carrara

The **Riviera della Versilia**, the coast between Viareggio and Carrara, is a more or less solid strip of resorts – none of them very attractive. It ought to be otherwise, given the 6000ft backdrop of the **Alpi Apuane**, but the beaches share the coastal plain with a railway, *autostrada* and clogged urban roads, and the water, too, is polluted. If you are passing through the region, en route to greater rewards in Liguria, **Viareggio**, the largest Tuscan resort, provides a bit of life and beach access, and Torre del Lago an opera festival. Otherwise, the only real appeal lies inland, hiking in the Alps above the marble quarrying centres of **Massa** or **Carrara**.

Viareggio and Torre del Lago

VIAREGGIO is the Biarritz of the Riviera della Versilia: a large and once elegant nineteenth-century resort, which continues to aim – with limited success – for a well-heeled clientele. It has its attractions, with a fair amount of nightlife (including big-name concerts) and some neat Art Deco buildings along the boardwalk, Passeggiata Margherita. But the beaches are privatised and charge upwards of L10,000 for admission, and in season, at least, the hotels tend to be full – and those that aren't often hold out for *pensione completa*. The one time to actively visit is during **Carnevale** (Jan 22–Feb 7), one of the liveliest in Italy. Each Sunday there's an amazing parade of floats or *carri* – colossal, lavishly designed papier-mâché models of politicians and celebrities. Outside carnival time these are displayed in the **Hangar-Carnevale** at the top end of Via Marco Polo (10.30am–noon & 4.30–7pm; free). They're very much an art form (top *carri* designers are famous), highly imaginative, and a lot of fun.

Arriving at the **train station**, 600m back from the seafront, you can pick up a map from the information office. **Buses** (*Lazzi*, *CAT* and *CLAP*) stop nearer the centre, by the Giardini d'Azeglio; turn right along the seafront, past Piazza Mazzini, and you'll find the **tourist office** at Viale Carducci 10 (daily 8.30am–noon). The biggest concentrations of budget hotels – there are over 100 one-stars – are along Via Carducci, Via Leonardo da Vinci and Via Vespucci, which run from near the train station to the seafront.

Equipped with a bike (there are several hire places in the centre), or your own transport, you could make for the public beaches, past the port area and south along the wooded road to **MARINA DI TORRE DEL LAGO**. The later stretches of sand are undeveloped, while inland, by the lake of Massaciúccoli – a protected bird reserve – is the **Villa Puccini** (half-hourly tours 10–11.30am & 3.30–5.30pm; L4000). At the town, **TORRE DEL LAGO PUCCINI**, a summer **Festival Pucciniano** presents the master's works at an open-air theatre. Torre del Lago has a huge **campsite** – to the left of the road as you arrive from Viareggio – and a single **hotel**, the *Albergo Antonio*, Via G. Puccini 260 (☎0584/341.053; ④), next to the Villa Puccini. Otherwise there's nothing but the odd restaurant and a couple of bars.

To Massa

There is little to entice a stop between Viareggio and Carrara. The coast is continuously developed, with the prettiest beaches tightly corralled by **FORTE DEI MARMI**, the Versilia's most upmarket resort.

MASSA and its port, MARINA DI MASSA, are more or less merged in a sprawl of holiday development. It is basically an Italian family resort – not very appealing, with weed-ridden beaches and shallow water a long way out to sea. The Massa **youth hostel**, however, *Ostello Apuano* (☎0585/240.288; ①), might prove useful. It is actually at Viale delle Pinete 89, Località Partaccia, most easily accessible from the Carrara-Avenza train station (take a bus from here for 3km towards Marina di Massa); there's a free beach adjacent.

Carrara

CARRARA again has its beach strip, MARINA DI CARRARA, which serves also as the port for the town's prodigious output of marble. The **marble** trade has been going here since Roman times, and sculptors from Michelangelo to Henry Moore have tramped up here in search of the perfect block. The slashes of quarries in the mountainside are clearly visible from the town, which is dominated by the trade and now finds itself at loggerheads with conservationists who want the peaks declared a national park.

The **train station** is close to the sea, with a regular bus service to the old town, where – as you'd expect – the Romanesque-Gothic **Duomo** is full of marble statuary. For the low-down on the raw material, there's a **Museo Civico di Marmo** in Via XX Settembre, 2km out of town on the road towards Marina di Carrara (May–Sept Mon–Fri 9.30am–12.30pm & 3.30–6.30pm, Sun 9.30am–12.30pm; open till 8pm in June; L2000). Run by the local Chamber of Commerce, it's an impressive display that looks at the history and production of the stone – lots of photographs, examples of different types of marble, and a room devoted to dubious examples of marble art. A bus runs there from the central Piazza Matteotti station. The most exciting display of contemporary marble, though, comes with the **Scolpire all'Aperto** (late July to early Oct), when the town invites international sculptors to create new works in the Piazza Alberica.

To get a closer view of the **quarries**, take a bus (hourly from Via Minzoni) towards **Colonnata**, just 8km from Carrara. Don't go all the way to Colonnata village, but get off at the *Visita Cave* signs by the mine, where you'll see a huge, blindingly white marble basin, its floor and sides perfectly squared by the enormous wire saws used to cut the blocks that litter the surroundings.

Marble aside, Carrara makes a pleasant stop – an integral, self-sufficient place that comes as a relief after the holiday coast. There's budget **hotel** accommodation at *Albergo da Roberto*, just north of Piazza Alberica on Via Apuana (☎0585/54.033; ④). For a more salubrious room, head for the *Michelangelo*, Corso Fratelli Rosselli 3 (☎0585/70.861; ⑥). **Restaurants** are numerous, few of them tourist-oriented. The best mid-price option is the *Roma di Prioreschi*, Piazza Cesare Battisti 1 (closed Sat). An excellent little spot for snacks is the **bar** at Via Santa Maria 12, just off Piazza Accademia.

WALKS IN THE ALPI APUANE

There are mapped-out **paths** throughout the **Alpi Apuane**, where altitudes are relatively low, conditions are generally suitable for trainers and distances short – you are never very far from a road, *rifugio* or hotel. Two **leaflets** are available from the Carrara **tourist office** at Piazza II Giugno 14. One is a disorientated "map" showing paths, refuges, roads and rivers – and nothing else; the second contains "Itineraries for Tourists", of which half a dozen at the back are for walkers.

Colonnata village marks an entrance point for walks in the Alpi Apuane, the CAI trail #38 behind the village leading to a dense web of paths around **Monte Rasore** (1422m) and **Monte Grondice** (1805m); the 1:25,000 *Multigraphic-Wanderkarte* **map** #101/102 is useful for making sense of this. As an alternative, take the SS446 north from Carrara to CAMPO CECINA (18km), where the all-year **Rifugio Carrara** (1320m; ☎0585/841.972) offers accommodation and a rather more limited and gentle selection of paths. You'll have to hitch to get there, as buses run only on Sundays.

Livorno to Piombino

If the Versilian Riviera sounds unappealing, the so-called **Etruscan Riviera**, the coast south from Livorno to Piombino, has even less going for it. The backdrop of the Alpi Apuane is replaced by the drabness of reclaimed swampland, while holiday development is, if anything, more intense. **Livorno** has some interest as a major Mediterranean port, and offers **ferry connections** to the islands of Elba and Capráia. But for itself, the mainland coast only really gets appealing way to the south, beyond **Cécina**.

Livorno

LIVORNO is, after Florence, Tuscany's largest city, and is the country's second largest port after Genoa. Heavily bombed during the last war, it is not a pretty place, but it does have the feel of a real Mediterranean port and city. This can be a welcome change from the tourist focus of so much of Tuscany, and if you are just staying a night here, en route for Elba, there are usually beds to be found.

The City

Livorno's origins go back to Roman times but the port was properly developed only under the Medici, who set out to transform it into an ideal city. Their plan is still evident in the old, central grid, enclosed by a ring of the canals (*fossi*) and guarded by a pair of fortresses.

Buses arrive at the heart of this "old town" in **Piazza Grande**; from the **train station**, 2km east, take a local bus (#1, #2 or #8) to the same square. From here it's a five-minute walk down Via Grande to the Porto Mediceo, where the ferries leave for the islands. The **Porto Mediceo** is the most picturesque area of Livorno, with fishing boats spilling back into the canals, often a liner blocking the view out to sea, and Sangallo's **Fortezza Vecchia** flanking the harbour. Further down the quay, at the centre of Piazza Micheli, is a bizarre Renaissance **statue of Ferdinando I** with four "Mori", or slaves, chained to its base. It is said to have marked the arrival of slaves to the port – which was, otherwise, one of the most liberal and cosmopolitan in the Mediterranean.

The moated, rather derelict **Fortezza Nuova** (10am–dusk; free) signals a second, lively area on the east side of the inner grid. Cross Piazza della Repubblica from here and you reach the **Mercato Americano** (Mon–Sat) in Piazza XX Settembre. The cultural endowment of stationed American troops, the stalls sell army surplus clothing, fishing and camping gear, and flick knives. For produce, the **Mercato Central** is across the canal on Via Buontalenti. The streets around Piazza XX Settembre – **Via Oberdan**, especially – are good territory for cafés, pizzerias and trattorias.

Beaches

If you just want a quick dip, **ARDENZA** – a ten-minute bus ride from Piazza della Repubblica – is the nearest beach to Livorno. It is, though, very urban and crowded, with swimming off a paved promenade, or (if you pay), a couple of concrete *bagni*. A better alternative is to head north to **TIRRÉNIA** (25min by bus), where there's a real stretch of beach, separated from the main road by pine woods, and windsurfers, and a **youth hostel**, *Ostello San Francesco* (☎050/37.442).

Practicalities

Livorno's **tourist office** is on the third floor at Piazza Cavour 6 (Mon–Fri 8.30am–12.30pm); in summer there's a small booth on the Mole Mediceo, the ferry dock. As a port, the city has a rash of cheap, basic **hotels**, some of which – around the harbour and station – are grim dives. It's best to head for the centre of the old town, especially around Corso Mazzini, where you'll find the two-star *Corsica* at no. 148 (☎0586/882.103; ⑤), and the one-star *Cremona* at no. 24 (☎0586/23.681; ③). The nearest **campsite** is *Camping Miramare* (☎0586/580.402), on the Via Aurelia past ANTIGNANO, a short distance to the south.

For **meals** the great temptation is the seafood. Among the more esteemed **trattorias** are the *Antico Moro* at Via di Franco 59, and the big, busy *La Barcarola*, Viale Carducci 63. These are relatively upmarket at around L40,000 per person, but you'll have no problem digging out a cheap neighbourhood choice such as *L'Attias* at Via Ricasoli 127 or *Trattoria Galileo* in Via delle Campare. For pizza, try *Pizzeria Umbra*, Via E. Mayer 1, or the *Rustic Inn*, Via Bosi 16.

FERRIES

Two main ferry companies operate car and passenger services to Elba (4hr), Capraia, Gorgona, Sardinia and Corsica. All the Tuscan island ferries leave from the Porto Mediceo; some Sardinia and Corsica sailings leave from the Porto Industriale (30min by bus #18). Beware that ferries are often fully booked through July and August; for the Tuscan islands, Piombino is a cheaper and more reliable point of departure.

Toremar, Via Calafati 6 (☎0586/896.372). To Elba (Portoferraio) and Capraia; once daily throughout year – twice daily on Thursdays and Saturdays in summer.

Navarma, Via Calafati 4 (☎0586/38.068). To Sardinia (Olbia); daily in season, otherwise three times a week. To Corsica (Bastia); daily from end of March to early November. Note: US citizens travelling to Corsica will need to obtain a **visa** from the French consulate at Via Montegrappa 6 (☎0586/896.368).

Cécina

Heading south from Livorno and further afield, there's little to distinguish any of the resorts, with their scrubby beaches and remorseless development. Pick of an undistinguished lot is **CÉCINA**, which marks the start of the coastal plain known as the Maremma. It has a small **museum**, in Piazza Carducci, with a few Etruscan and Roman remains, and a **tourist office** at Largo Cairoli 17, but essentially it is a place to pick up **bus** connections for Volterra, or **trains** to Saline di Volterra, from where there's a connecting bus. If these leave you stranded in town, there are cheap **rooms** at the one-star *Iolanda*, Piazza Gramsci 12 (☎0586/680.724; ④).

At **MARINA DI CÉCINA**, a quite pleasant coastal strip, there are fair sections of beach, most freely accessible save for a patch cordoned off by the local military academy. A range of **hotels** are to be found on Viale della Vittoria, among them the two-star *Miramare* (☎0586/620.295; ⑤) and *Azzurra* (☎0586/620.595; ④). To the south there's also a huge conglomeration of **campsites**.

South of Cécina, the **WWF reserve of Bolgheri** is a classic wildlife habitat, with thousands of birds spending the winter here (Oct 15–April 15 Fri & first and third Sat of the month 9am–12.30pm & 2–4.30pm).

Piombino

PIOMBINO is the nearest port to Elba, to which it has mercifully frequent ferries. The town itself is not a great place to stay – a steelworks centre, rebuilt after almost total destruction during the last war. If you come down by train, get out at CAMPIGLIA MARÍTTIMA station, from where there's a connecting train to Piombino port (don't get off at Piombino town). At the port you can pick up information and tickets; one-way fares (returns aren't sold) for Elba are L10,000 per person, and from L50,000 per car, plus five percent port tax.

The same two companies run **ferries out of Piombino** as from Livorno; both have offices by the port train station, and charge in the region of L10,000 per person:

Toremar, Calata Italia 22 (☎0586/918.080). Ferries several times daily (almost hourly in summer) to Cavo and Portoferraio (50min); less often to Rio Marina and Porto Azzurro (2hr). Also summer-only hydrofoil (*aliscafo*) to Portoferraio (25–35min).

Navarma, Viale Elba 4 (☎0565/92.133 or 918.101). Daily ferries to Portoferraio, en route to Basta (Corsica).

Elba

Mountainous **ELBA** is the third largest Italian island after Sicily and Sardinia: 29km long by 19km wide. It has exceptionally clear water, fine white sand beaches, and a lush, wooded interior, superb for walking. For decades, it had a reputation, too, as a quiet hideaway island – though it's now firmly on the package trail, with an estimated one million tourists in August. If you want to enjoy the place, or even just find a room (or campsite space), come well out of season; the climate is mild year-round and ferries run at least once daily.

Historically, Elba has been well out of the mainstream – rural, agricultural and, of course, place of exile for Napoleon, who could have seen his birthplace on Corsica from the highest point, Monte Capanne. Earlier eras saw the island exploited primarily for its iron ore – fashioned by Greeks, Carthaginians, Etruscans and Romans alike. Through later centuries control passed from Pisa to Genova and on to the Medici, Spain, Turkey and finally France: a cosmopolitan mix that has left its legacy on both architecture and cultivation.

Today, though the economy revolves almost entirely around tourism, Elba's size and topography have allowed the towns and villages to keep distinct characters. **Portoferraio** is very much the capital; **Marina di Campo**, over on the south coast, has the best beach; **Marciano** and **Poggio**, on the north, are sheltered by lush woods and give access to hikes around **Monte Capanne**. To the east, military history is evident in **Capoliveri's** hill-top position and **Porto Azzurro's** fortifications, the latter still in use to detain Elba's criminal population.

Getting round the island

Buses run to just about everywhere on the island, whether or not they're main tourist centres. The key services **from Portoferraio**, the main terminal, are to **Procchio** (21 daily), **Marina di Campo** (13 daily) and **Porto Azzurro** (12 daily); other services are more sporadic, and there are very few after 8pm. For general information on Elba bus services, contact *ATL* at Viale Elba 20, Portoferraio (☎0565/92.392). **Boats** are much used to reach out-of-the-way beaches, and are well advertised at all ports.

Bike or **moped hire** is a good way of exploring the island. Both are available from a couple of places in Portoferraio: *Rent Ghiaie*, Via Cairoli 26 (☎0565/92.666), and the more professional *Brandi Motori*, in the suburbs at Via Manganaro 11 (☎0565/92.359). Mopeds cost around L50,000 per day, bikes L25,000.

There are also several **car hire** agencies in Portoferraio: in the port area try *Maggiore*, Calata Italia (☎0565/915.368), or *Segnini*, in the same street (☎0565/916.374); in town, try *Arrighi*, Via Mercato Vecchio (☎0565/92.062). Reckon on at least L80,000 a day, and be ready for considerable summer congestion.

Portoferraio

Unless you're interested solely in beachlife, **Portoferraio** is probably the best place to stay. It is the hub of the island's roads (and transport system), has most of the life, and offers a reasonable chance of accommodation – at least outside of July and August.

Information and accommodation

The bus terminal and **tourist office** (Mon–Sat summer 8am–1pm & 3.30–7.30pm; winter 9am–1pm & 4–6pm; ☎0565/914.671) are both at Calata Italia 26, in the peeling tower block on the quay. The tourist office provides a map, bus timetable and a list of the island's hotels, apartments and campsites, and will often phone around to try and find space. So, too, will the **Associazione Albergatori** at Calata Italia 21 (summer daily 8.30am–12.30pm & 3–7pm).

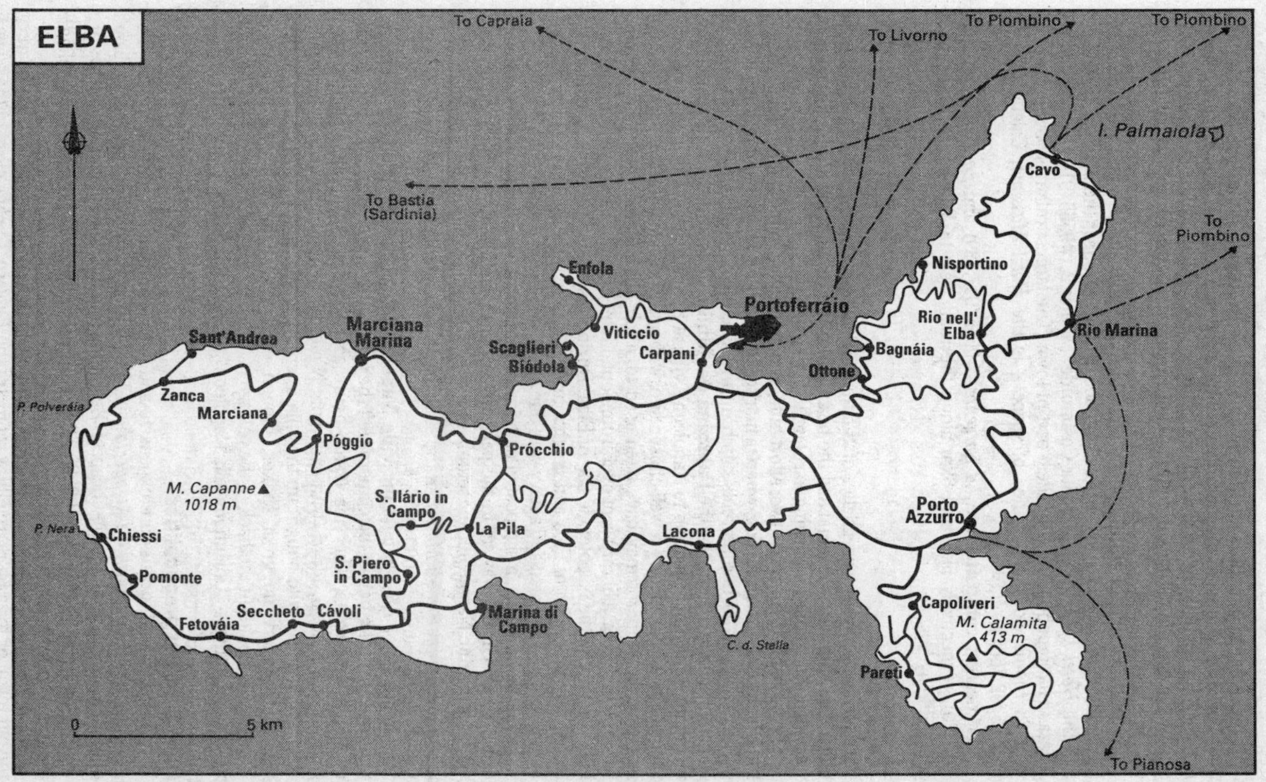
ELBA
To Capraia
To Livorno
To Piombino
To Piombino
I. Palmaiola
To Bastia (Sardinia)
Cavo
To Piombino
Enfola
Nisportino
Portoferraio
Rio nell' Elba
Rio Marina
Sant'Andrea
Marciana Marina
Scaglieri
Viticcio
Carpani
Biódola
Bagnáia
Ottone
Zanca
P. Polveráia
Marciana
Póggio
Prócchio
M. Capanne 1018 m
S. Ilário in Campo
Porto Azzurro
La Pila
Lacona
P. Nera
Chiessi
S. Piero in Campo
Pomonte
Capolíveri
Seccheto
Cávoli
M. Calamita 413 m
Marina di Campo
Fetováia
C. d. Stella
Pareti
0
5 km
To Pianosa

If these fail to turn up something – as is likely in August – tour the bars and ask about **private rooms**; in season prices are on a par with hotels. If you can get a group together, an **apartment** may work out cheaper. Bookable through the tourist office, most have two double rooms with cooking facilities, and prices from about L70,000 a day, less by the week.

Portoferraio's better **hotel** options are: *Touring*, Via Roma 13 (☎0565/915.851; ⑤); the *Villa Ombrosa*, Viale de Gasperi 3 (☎0565/92.363; ④), near the beach at Le Ghiaie; and the *Hotel L'Ape Elbana*, Salita Cosimo de' Medici 2 (☎0565/914.245; ④), just off Piazza della Repubblica in the oldest part of town. The largest relatively budget hotel – with 68 rooms, so some chance of space – is the *Hotel Massimo*, Calata Italia 23 (☎0565/92.766; ④).

The nearest **campsites** are *La Sorgente* (☎0565/917.139) and *La Enfola* (☎0565/915.390), respectively 5km and 6km along the road west to Viticcio; both are quite accessible by bus.

The Town

Portoferraio consists, essentially, of the "useful" modern part of town (with tourist office, bus stop, ferry terminal and the beach of Le Ghiaie), and the old Medicean port, with its fortifications and fishing harbour, to the east.

The walled **old town** has two, short tunnelled entrances from the quay. Just inside is the **Piazza della Repubblica**, where a market (good for beachwear and leather) is held every Friday. From here, streets climb up the side of the promontory and to one of Napoleon's exile residences, the **Palazzina dei Mulini** (Tues–Sat 9am–1.30pm; L4000, including same-day admission to Napoleon's villa at San Martino). The palace was built specifically for Napoleon – a well-chosen site, with grand views of the bay – and, though not what the emperor may have been used to, a fair old building. There's a stunning baroque bedroom, a library sent over from Fontainebleau, and various items of memorabilia – including the Napoleonic flag of Elba. During his ten-month exile, Napoleon was technically sovereign of Elba and neighbouring Pianosa. He established a small court, kept an army of 500 men and a navy with one ship, "The Inconstant".

From the Palazzina, a signposted path leads down to the small, rock-enclosed **beach** of **Le Viste**. On the way up to the palace, you pass the **Misericordia**, housing a not very worthwhile Napoleonic museum.

San Martino

Napoleon's sister Elisa bought the **Villa Napoleonica di San Martino** for a summer residence not long before the emperor left the island. It's located 6km from Portoferraio on the #1 bus route. The villa (same hours as Palazzo dei Mulini) is fronted by a Neoclassical palazzo, added (with exuberant N motifs) by Prince Demidoff, husband of Napoleon's niece, who bought up the villa to create a Napoleonic museum. Its permanent exhibits are no great shakes, though each year exhibitions are held on a Napoleonic theme. At the back of the palazzo is Napoleon's relatively modest villa, with its famous graffito – "Ubicunque felix Napoleon" (Napoleon is happy everywhere).

Food and other practicalities

Portoferraio's **restaurants** are expensive and few have food to merit the prices. The well-patronised *Pizzeria Il Castagnacciaio* in Via del Mercato Vecchio (parallel to Piazza della Repubblica) is about the cheapest. Best-known of the more upmarket choices are *La Ferrigna*, Piazza della Repubblica, and the *Trattoria La Barca* in Via Guerazzi, both at around L50,000 per head.

For **bars**, pick from any of the places around Piazza della Repubblica, the heart of the old town; or for a bit more elbow room, try the *Enoteca Torchio*, close to the square in Via dell'Amore.

The town **post office** is in Piazza Hutre, off Piazza della Repubblica; there are **public telephones** in *Bar L'Angolo*, Via Cavalieri di V. Veneto (7am–midnight). If you plan on **hiking**, the *Comunità Montana*, Viale Manzoni 4, provides a contour map of the Monte Capanne area.

Leaving Elba by ferry, it's best to book a ticket well in advance in summer – especially if you're taking a car. *Toremar* are at Calata Italia 22 (☎0565/590.018), *Navarma* just round the corner at Viale Elba 4 (☎0565/918.101). Both offices are for advance reservations; buying a ticket on the day you leave, go to the kiosks by the quay.

Eastern Elba

Eastern Elba is a distinct geographical area, basically comprising two tongues of land, each dominated by mountain ridges. Away from the main seaside centres of **Rio Marina** and **Porto Azzurro** the beaches are comparatively quiet, but much of the southern isthmus – **Monte Calamita** – was the heart of the mining industry, and is still owned by the quarrying companies. Close by, on the southern coast, **Lacona** boasts one of the island's main concentrations of **campsites**.

Portoferraio to Rio Marina

South of Portoferraio the main road divides, one spur heading west, the other east towards Porto Azzurro. West-facing **BAGNAIA**, just beyond OTTONE (off the direct road to Rio nell'Elba), is famous for its sunsets – hence the *Sunset* bar. The one **hotel** is the *Clara* (☎0565/961.077; ④). If you have the patience to drive the twisting road beyond, the twin tiny hamlets NISPORTO and NISPORTINO mark the beginning of the most unspoilt beaches and coastline on Elba's north shore. You can walk into the hills behind, or take boats out to the beaches beyond the end of the road. The only **accommodation** in the immediate vicinity is the *Camping-Villagio Sole e Mare* at Nisporto (April–Sept; ☎0565/961.059). There's a **hotel** 2km from the sea at LA GINESTRA – the three-star *La Ginestra* (☎0564/943.181; ⑤).

A narrow, scenic road climbs from Nisportino to Rio nell'Elba through La Ginestra; if you've taken the more direct route from Maggazzino you'll pass the old castle at **VOLTERRAIO**, once the strongest in Elba and now a silent and evocative ruin, with a great view over its desolate surroundings. It's a stiff climb from the road. **RIO NELL'ELBA** itself is a graceless place, though old enough in parts and almost unique in appearing to have resisted Elba's tourist boom. From its high vantage it surveys a wild countryside devastated by repeated forest fires. There's nowhere to stay, and just one place to **eat**, *Da Cipolla* in the main square (closed Tues, except in summer).

The main town on Elba's east coast is **RIO MARINA**, a ferry terminal for connections to Piombino, Portoferraio and Porto Azzurro. Tourism and a busy harbour have replaced iron ore as the sources of revenue, but this again isn't one of the better Elban towns. There's just one **hotel**, the *Rio* at Via Palestro 31 (☎0565/962.016; ④), next to the scrubby public gardens overlooking the port.

For a **beach**, head south to the hamlet of **ORTANO**, dominated by a big tourist complex, but with public sand too; there's an on-beach **campsite**, the *Canapai* (☎0564/943.271). You get to it by a turning 1500 metres back along the road to Rio nell'Elba.

Porto Azzurro to Lacona

The resort of **PORTO AZZURRO** was heavily fortified by Philip III of Spain in 1603 as protection against continual raids by the French and the Austrians. Today his fortress is the island's prison; a walk round the outer ramparts brings you to a shop selling pottery and other prison crafts. The town's small old quarter, closed to cars, centres on **Via d'Alarcon**, a bustle of bars, shops and restaurants, with traditional open-front shops and balconied houses in the cobbled area near Piazza Matteotti. The best place to swim is from the rocks east of the harbour.

Porto Azzurro's **accommodation** is limited and lacklustre: best bets are the *Belmare*, Banchina IV Novembre 21 (☎0564/95.012; ⑤), and the *Arrighi*, Via V. Veneto 18 (☎0565/95.315; ④). Otherwise enlist the help of the **information kiosk** at the junction of the Portoferraio and Rio Marino roads. The best of the **campsites** are at the small nearby resort of BARBAROSSA – the *Da Mario* and *Arrighi* sites both give straight onto the beach. For **food** there are plenty of identikit joints, the best known being the *Delfino Verde* in Lungomare Vitaliani (☎0565/95.197).

East of the road between Porto Azzuro and Capoliveri, **NAREGNO** is a small resort with a good beach, though not as good as the less accessible sand to the south at CÔTE PIANE, LISCOLINO and BUZZANCONE. None can match the village's **accommodation** possibilities, however, which include the seafront *Villa Rodriguez* (☎0565/968.423; ③), *Frank's Hotel* (☎0565/968.427; ④), and *La Voce del Mare* (☎0565/968.455; ③).

CAPOLIVERI, 3.5km south of Porto Azzurro, is the best of the towns on Elba's eastern fringe, a prosperous centre whose close-knit streets have made few concessions to tourism. Its hinterland remains undeveloped, as the mining companies have not sold their disused plots to the hoteliers – though much of the area is thus out of bounds.

Capoliveri makes an ideal base for visits to the fine **beaches** at Naregno, Morcone and Innamorata (see below). Numerous private agencies rent **apartments**, though don't expect many high-season vacancies. In town, there's just one budget **hotel**, the *Golfo Azzurro*, Via Appiani 5 (☎0565/968.167; ④). Amongst the **restaurants**, *Il Chiasso*, Via Sauro, is outstanding at around L50,000 a head. Its more reasonable rivals include *Da Beppe*, Via Roma 25, and the rustic and informal *L'Arco Vecchio*, off the main piazza.

It's better to continue to the trio of resorts at **MORCONE**, **PARETI** and **INNAMORATA**. The last is the quietest and has a fine sand and shingle beach; the other hamlets have large beaches, the one at Morcone being more regimented than its neighbour. Parking is difficult, as is **accommodation** – best head for Pareti's *Pensione Villa Miramare* (☎0565/968.673; ④).

LACONA, well round the coast to the west of Porto Azzurro, is one of the island's main camping centres, and its flat foreshore is crowded with **bars and discos** designed to cater to the beach crowd once the sun's gone down. The **campsites** to head for are *Il Lacona* (☎0565/964.161) or the nearby *Lacona Pineta* (☎0565/964.149), both set in the pine woods on the eastern arm of the Golfo di Lacona. The best-value **hotel** is the *Pensione Giardino* (☎0565/964.059; ④).

Western Elba

Western Elba's road system allows for a circular tour of the area, but many people make immediately for specific targets – usually **Marina di Campo**, with its huge beach and the island's major concentration of hotels after Portoferraio. Upmarket alternatives are offered by the north-coast resorts of **Procchio** and **Marciana Marina**, while backpackers favour the relatively uncommercialised **Énfola** area. Few visitors go inland to **Marciano**, one of Elba's nicest villages, or to the long sweep of the **western coast**, whose hamlets and beaches are amongst the island's most tranquil.

Énfola

If you want a spread of beach and a choice of **campsites** near Portoferraio, follow the scenic road below Monte Poppe to **ÉNFOLA**, where the land narrows to a 75-metre-wide isthmus with beaches on both sides. The road ends at a small car park next to the *Bar Emanuel*, where you can get down to either strip of sand. There are numerous **hotels** in the area, pick of the bunch being the three-star *Paradiso* at nearby VITICCIO (☎0565/915.385; ⑤). Énfola has a shady **campsite**, *Énfola Camping* (☎0565/915.390).

Biodola, Scaglieri and Procchio

From Viticcio a footpath runs a couple of kilometres round the coast to Scaglieri and Biodola, otherwise reached by a side road from the main highway out of Portoferraio. **BIODOLA** consists simply of a road, two big hotels and a superb **beach**; parking is difficult, so it's best to take the early morning **bus** (25min) from Portoferraio – there's a lunchtime and early evening return. Biodola's two **hotels** are very expensive, though there's a cheaper and beautifully situated *pensione* two minutes from the beach, the *Casa Rosa* (☎0565/969.931; ⑤).

SCAGLIERI is a similar sort of place but a touch livelier and more picturesque, fronted by a shop, a bar (which rents bikes and mopeds) and a **restaurant** that doubles as an evening-only pizzeria. As well as rooms at the *Albergo-Ristorante Danila* (☎0565/969.915; ④), there's a new **campsite**, the *Scaglieri* (☎0565/969.940), on the hillside.

PROCCHIO, with its buzzing bars and shops, is not a place to get away from it all, but the sea is good and the white beach excellent. However, this is a relatively expensive town, with low-cost rooms at the **hotels** *L'Edera* (☎0565/907.525; ⑤), *Monna Lisa* (☎0565/907.519; ⑤) and *Da Renzo* (☎0565/907.504; ④). Campsites don't exist.

Marciana Marina and Poggio

Further round the north coast, **MARCIANA MARINA** has the minor distinction of being the smallest *comune* in Tuscany, a status it's proud of, allowing few hotels and aiming to preserve an air of residential order away from the seafront. The traffic-filled promenade of bars, restaurants and trinket shops do nothing to lure you into staying.

Situated 5km inland from Marciana Marina, **POGGIO** is renowned for its **spring water**, the *Fonte di Napoleone*. It also has a tight medieval centre whose decorated doorways and patchwork of cheerful gardens make this an attractive place to **stay**. Best overnight option is the *Albergo-Ristorante Monte Capanne*, Via Pini 1 (☎0565/99.083; ④), in a lovely, peaceful setting. **Food** here is good and the village claims one of the island's leading restaurants, the *Publius*, Via XX Settembre 13 (☎0565/99.208) – great views, classic Tuscan cooking and steep prices.

Poggio is a good base for a **walk** to the summit of **Monte Capanne** (1018m), Elba's highest point. Before setting off, pick up the local *Comunità Montana* **map** or a less detailed equivalent on sale in Poggio and Marciana.

Marciana

The high and isolated village of **MARCIANA**, the oldest settlement on Elba, is perfectly placed between great beaches (Promonte and Sant'Andrea), mountainous interior (Monte Capanne), and a modern centre for supplies (Procchio). Its **old quarter** is a delight, too, its narrow alleys, arches, belvederes and stone stairs festooned with flowers and climbing plants. Marciana's history is encapsulated in the Roman and prehistoric remains in the small **Museo Archeologico** in Via del Pretorio (April–Sept Mon, Tues & Thurs–Sun 10am–noon & 4–7.30pm), in the **Fortezza Pisano** above the village (closed to the public), and in the palaces of the Appiani, Elba's leading fifteenth-century family, who made Marciana their home base.

The **walk** to Monte Capanne (trail #1; 3hr) passes **Santuario di San Cerbone**, on its way to the summit – the track starts from the southern tip of the village, the church appearing after an hour at the junction with trail #6. San Cerbone was buried here during a miraculous cloudburst that hid the ceremony from the Lombards who had the saint's valuable remains in their sights. If you don't want to walk up Monte Capanne, there's a popular **cable car** to the top (daily 10am–noon & 2.30–6pm; L12,000 return).

Marciana's only drawback is its shortage of **accommodation**, restricted to rented rooms and apartments available through the *Ristorante da Enzio*, Via delle Coste 12 (☎0565/901.024; ④), and the *Birreria La Porta* (☎0565/901.027; ④), in the piazza at the entrance to the village.

Sant'Andrea

The dispersed village of **SANT'ANDREA**, 6km west of Marciana, just off the coast road, is currently one of Elba's trendiest retreats, with villas and hotels creeping further into the wooded hinterland each year. It's popular with divers, drawn here by what is reputedly some of the clearest sea water around Elba. **Accommodation** is at a premium, but it's not necessarily expensive, and most is discreetly set amid almost tropical vegetation. On the beach itself there's the small *Bambu* (☎0565/908.012; ④); top hotel of the moment is *La Cernia* (☎0565/908.195; ⑥), midway between the coast and the main road.

Chiessi to Cavoli

CHIESSI and POMONTE, further round the coast road, each have a small stony beach, beautifully clear water, a rocky hinterland and little commercialism. By **FETOVAIA** you're back to beach development, but the sand is superb – and a big car park prevents some of the chaos of other Elban resorts. There's lots of apartment accommodation and several top-whack hotels. If you want somewhere central, go for *Lo Scirocco* (☎0565/987.060; ⑥); the budget choice is the *Pensione Montemerlo* (☎0565/987.061; ⑤), out of town on the hill.

Further on, **SECCHETO** is good for a swim from the rocks at the western end of town, or for tanning on the largely nudist stretch beyond. Two **hotels** have reasonable doubles: the three-star *La Stella* (☎0565/987.013; ⑤), at the end of the road to the sea, and the nearby two-star *Da Fine* (☎0565/987.017; ④). Nearby **CAVOLI** is more upmarket, though the beach is good if you don't mind the crowds. There are two similar beach-side *pensioni*, the *Lorenza* (☎0565/987.054; ⑤) and the *Conchiglia* (☎0565/987.010; ⑤).

Marina di Campo

Set in one of the island's few areas of plain, **MARINA DI CAMPO** was the first and is now the largest resort on Elba. The huge white **beach** is what makes the place popular: the water's clean, and there's space on land if you walk to the east end or out to the rockier west. There's also all the tourist frippery and **nightlife** you'd expect in any major seaside centre, with key discos and clubs changing by the month.

Pick of the numerous **hotels** are: *Pensione Elba*, Via Mascagni 43 (☎0565/97.224; ⑤); *Santa Caterina*, Viale Elba (☎0565/97.452; ⑥); and *Barracuda*, Viale Elba (☎0565/976.893; ⑥). If you arrive early in the day you might find space at one of the four **campsites**. Best deals for a **meal** are *Rosticceria Mazzarri*, at the west end of the main Via Roma, *Il Golfo* at the eastern end of the beach, *Kontiki* in the port (for fish), and *La Triglia* in Via Roma, the town's best-known restaurant.

Islands around Elba

Of the four islands around Elba, **Gorgona** and **Pianosa** house prisoners and are off limits to casual visitors; **Montecristo** is a protected nature reserve, accessible only to day-trippers from Porto Azzurro and Marina di Campo, who are confined to its beach; but **Capraia** is a rewarding place to visit, served by daily **ferry** from Livorno or Portoferraio throughout the year – twice daily on Thursdays and Saturdays in summer.

Capraia

CAPRAIA, 30km northwest of Elba, is a Mediterranean island in the old sense: unspoilt, with just a couple of hotels and one road that links the small port to the old town on the hill. Its former use as a penal colony ensured that the terrain remained largely untouched, and now – despite considerable pressure from potential hoteliers –

the local council have held back on commercial development, instead promoting the formation of a Parco Naturale to protect the island's natural heritage.

From the tiny harbour to the town of **CAPRAIA ISOLA** – the only inhabited part of the island except the port – is a gentle walk of about a kilometre; there's a bus if you're feeling lazy. The **Pro Loco**, at Via Roma 2, has a map of the island and a variety of information on wildlife, walking, accommodation and boat trips.

The main **hotel**, the four-star *Il Saracino* (☎0586/905.018; ⑦), is in the upper part of town; a far cheaper option is the small *Pensione Da Beppone* (☎0586/905.001; ④). There are, however, numerous private **rooms** and **apartments** for rent; the Pro Loco will ring around for you, or you can just wander round town and look for the signs. There's a single **campsite**, the *Le Sughere* (May 1–Sept 15; ☎0586/905.066), behind the town's small church of the Assumption. **Free camping** is feasible, but the terrain is rocky, and there's little cover or fresh water.

The best **restaurant** is *La Garitta*, up in the top of the town near the castle; run as a bar during the day, it's an informal place, dedicated to simple seafood. *Al Corsaro* is a divers' hang-out, and also opens as a pizzeria in the evenings; it closes out of season. Still in the upper town, the *Cala Rossa* is a homely trattoria.

South to Lazio: the Maremma coast

The term **Maremma** defines the entire coastal strip from Cécina as far south as Civitavecchia, well into Lazio, and extends as far east as Monte Amiata. The region was the northern heartland of the Etruscans but became depopulated in the Middle Ages as wars disrupted the drainage schemes and allowed malarial swamps to build up behind the dunes. These became almost synonymous with disease in Italy, and nineteenth-century guides devote a lot of space to advising very strongly against a visit. Today, the regional capital of **Grosseto** remains a pretty miserable city, though there are bright patches of scenery – the protected nature reserve of **Monti dell'Uccellina** – and some attractive (though upmarket) resorts around the peninsula of **Monte Argentario**. Once again, however, hotels along this strip are expensive and full in summer, so without reservations don't expect more than a camping place.

Grosseto and around

Until the mid-nineteenth century, **Grosseto** was a malaria-ridden backwater. The draining of the marshes, however, which was finally effected only under Mussolini, has transformed it into a provincial capital for the Maremma and its prosperous agricultural hinterland. The last thirty years have seen an explosion of population, and the city – heavily damaged in the war – has been virtually rebuilt.

With its characterless condominiums and commercial buildings, it is deservedly undervisited, though it is a major communications centre and you may well find yourself passing through. Most **trains** on the Genova to Rome coastal line stop here and you can change for the line to Siena or *locale* connections to Orbetello and the south, Follonica (for Massa Maríttima) and Cécina (for Saline di Volterra). Timetabling always seems to leave about an hour between trains – about all you'd want to see what remains of the old town, which you reach from the station by walking down Via Carducci, a road interrupted by an over-the-top post office and bleak piazza. The best of what survives in Grosseto is on **Piazzetta del Campanile**, where a quirky statue shows Leopoldo II protecting Mother Maremma and crushing the serpent malaria under his foot. The **Duomo** was started in 1294 but virtually nothing is left to suggest antiquity: the white and pink marble facade is a product of the nineteenth century, while the interior has suffered repeated butchery.

The best pieces from the duomo have been transferred to the **Museo Archeologico** at nearby Via Mazzini 34 (Mon & Tues–Sat 9am–1pm & 4.30–8pm; Sun 9am–12.30pm; L3000), where the second-floor **Pinacoteca** has a handful of good Sienese paintings, notably Sassetta's *Madonna of the Cherries* and a *Madonna and Child* attributed to Simone Martini. The town's only other significant work is an early *Crucifix* by Duccio in **San Francesco**, just north of the museum, also home to a few patches of fresco. From San Francesco you can walk round the **walls**, a trip of about forty minutes, and one of the more rewarding things the place has to offer.

Rusellae and Vetulonia

Etruscan enthusiasts might want to visit **Rusellae** and **Vetulonia**, two ancient sites north of Grosseto. To reach either, you really need your own transport. **RUSELLAE**, modern ROSELLE, lies 10km to the northeast, and makes a mildly diverting detour, with a forum and the odd street discernible. Twenty kilometres north of Grosseto off the Follónica road (the SS1), **VETULONIA** is a more rewarding destination. This ancient city was another member of the Etruscan federation and survived through to the Middle Ages, when it was probably destroyed during a revolt against the Pisans in the fourteenth century: blocks from its buildings are now incorporated into a village above the ruins, which stand at the road junction for BURIANO to the south.

Little of genuine Etruscan vintage remains apart from a couple of big **tombs** – the Tomba della Pietrera and the Tomba del Diavolino – though scholars claim to have unearthed an Etruscan brothel, along with lewd graffiti apparently left by the women who staffed it. Much of the area is still being excavated, and there's a small **museum** which displays the latest finds.

Perhaps the best reason for a visit to the area, though, is the fine **restaurant** in the main square of modern Vetulonia, the *Taverna Etrusca*; the regional specialities – and the views – are superb.

Marina di Grosseto and Castiglione della Pescaia

MARINA DI GROSSETO and **CASTIGLIONE DELLA PESCAIA**, Grosseto's local resorts, have the mixed blessing of broad, shelving beaches. Each is now conclusively developed, having lost its old identity as a fishing village, though they both preserve walls and towers and a bit of character. Marina is least spoilt, with a good sandy beach and pinewood hinterland, and a small tourist office at Via Piave 10, which might be able to help with rooms. Otherwise count on camping at one of the six **campsites** in the vicinity. The best are the small three-star *Rosmarina* (☎0564/36.319; open April–Sept; ⑥), on the outskirts of the town at Via delle Colonie 37, and much larger two-star *Principina* (☎0564/35.647; ⑤), 4km south at PRINCIPINA A MARE. The others are huge complexes.

Short walks along the **Pineta della Tombolo**, the pine woods between the two resorts, bring relative peace – disturbed mainly by the presence of wild boar, which you are almost certain to see. At Castiglione there are **ferries**, in season, across to the island of Giglio.

The Monti dell'Uccellina

The hills and coastline of the **MONTI DELL'UCCELLINA** are set to become a fully fledged *Parco Nazionale*, recognition for an area that is claimed to be the last virgin coastal landscape on the Italian peninsula.

The heart of the park is a hump of hills that rises suddenly from the plain, about a dozen kilometres south of Grosseto. A breathtaking piece of countryside that combines cliffs, coastal marsh, *macchia*, forest-covered hills, pristine beaches and some of the most beautiful stands of umbrella pines in the country, it is a microcosm of all that's best in the Maremma – devoid of the bars, marinas, hotels, roads and half-finished houses that have destroyed much of the Italian littoral. Kept remote for centuries by malaria and impassable swamp, it's now preserved by the determination of its owners to keep the region sacrosanct, producing an area that rewards the casual walker, bird-watcher, botanist, or anyone simply in search of unspoilt sand.

Except for the beach at MARINA DI ALBERESE, the park is open only on Wednesdays, Saturdays and Sundays from 9am to dusk, with numbers limited to 500 daily. There is no public road access – all drivers should park near the reserve headquarters in the main square at **ALBERESE** (☎0564/407.098). Without a car it is difficult to get here from Grosseto. Irregular buses run from the station every day except Sunday; otherwise it's a choice between taking a taxi from the station (L30,000) or one of the two daily **trains** to Alberese station, a four-kilometre walk from the village.

Admission to the park (L5000) secures a useless **map** and a place on an hourly **bus** which runs 10km into the hills, drops you at PRATINI (virtually just a field) and leaves you to your own devices. It's about a twenty-minute stroll from there to the beach. Really energetic types can walk all the way from Alberese; if you want to see the wildlife at dusk (the best time) you'll have to walk back anyway, as the last bus from Pratini departs at 5.30pm in summer, and even earlier at other times of the year. It'll usually take you back to Grosseto.

Orbetello and Monte Argentario

Orbetello is principally distinguished by its strange location on a narrow isthmus in the middle of the **Laguna di Orbetello**, which was formed when **Monte Argentario** became joined to the mainland by two narrow sand spits (or *tomboli*): one to the north – Tombolo di Giannella – and one to the south – Tombolo di Feniglia. Little in the place excites real attention but it has become something of a resort, thanks to its function as the gateway to the dramatic rocky outcrop of the Argentario: on summer weekends it becomes a bottleneck of cars as tourists pile in to Porto Ercole and Porto Santo Stefano, the area's chic resorts. As well as seafront attractions, the Orbetello area offers much to naturalists, its lagoon boasting a **nature reserve** renowned as the Italian bird-watchers' El Dorado.

The **train station** is 4km away at ORBETELLO SCALO, on the mainland edge of the lagoon, a prominent stop for trains on the Rome–Pisa line. There are connections for Siena (one fast service daily) and slow trains to smaller stations to the north and south. Connecting buses run from the station to the bus **terminal** just off Piazza della Repubblica; from here there are regular services to Grosseto, Porto Ercole and Porto San Stefano, as well as daily buses to Capálbio and Pitigliano.

Orbetello

ORBETELLO, like most places in this region, was once Etruscan, though its tangible history – the fortifications – is the result of a Spanish garrison in the sixteenth century. There is a provincial main drag, thronged with the usual evening *passeggiata*, and very little else. Orbetello has two one-star **hotels**: *La Perla*, Via Voluntari Sangue 10 (☎0564/863.546; ④); and the *Piccolo Parigi*, Corso d'Italia 159 (☎0564/867.233; ④), the better overall choice. The town's best budget **restaurant** is the *Pizzeria Gennaro* in Corso d'Italia. Most of the area's fourteen **campsites** are on and around the lagoon and along the main SS1 Via Aurelia: the most attractive is the all-year *Feniglia* (☎0564/831.090), the only site on the Tombolo di Feniglia.

Porto Santo Stefano and Porto Ercole

PORTO SANTO STEFANO is the more developed of the Argentario resorts, and also the more fashionable – which in Italy is a lot worse than being plain popular. Something of the charm which first brought people here, however, still shines through, despite the hotels, villas and yachts that have all but obliterated the original village. If you're on a budget, you'll probably stay only as long as it takes to get a **ferry** to the island of Giglio (see below). Information and sailing times are available from the quayside *TO.RE.MAR* office (☎0564/814.615), or the neighbouring *Maregiglio* (☎0564/812.920), or the **tourist office** at Corso Umberto 55a. **Buses** run to the port from the train station at Orbetello Scalo. Affordable **accommodation** does exist, though mainly in private rooms – for which the tourist office supplys lists.

PORTO ERCOLE is a more intimate place, with an attractive old quarter and a more genuine fishing-village atmosphere. Though founded by the Romans, its chief historical monuments are two **Spanish fortresses**, facing each other across the harbour. There's a small **tourist office** at Viale Caravaggio 67. In 1610 the street's eponym, the painter Caravaggio, keeled over with sunstroke on a beach nearby; taken to a local tavern, he soon died of a fever, and was buried in the parish church of Sant'Erasmo. Reasonably priced **hotels** in Porto Ercole are limited to the one-star *Conchiglia* in Via della Marina (☎0564/833.134; ④), and the *Albergo-Gelateria Stella Marina* in Lungomare A. Doria (☎0564/833.055; ④).

Ansedonia

Back on the mainland, **ANSEDONIA**, with another crop of Roman holiday villas and a rail station, is a last possible stop before Lazio if you're interested in Roman remains. The site of ancient **COSA** spreads over a hill just to the west of the town. Founded in 273 BC, this was one of the most important commercial centres of Roman Tuscany, and according to the historian Rutilius its population was driven out by an army of mice. The Roman walls still stand eight metres high in places, along with remains of a circuit of eighteen defensive towers, a forum, temples, and recently uncovered mosaics and wall paintings.

Giglio

The largest of the Tuscan islands after Elba, **GIGLIO** is visited by an ever-increasing number of foreign tourists and is so popular with Romans that in high season there's standing room only on the boats. Yet it's well worth making the effort to stay on this fabulous island. The rush is fairly short-lived, most visitors are day-trippers, and few of them explore the tracks across the unspoilt interior, a mix of barren rock and reforested upland. The island is rich in such **fauna** as peregrine falcons, mouflon, kestrels and buzzards, and in **wild flowers** too – this is the only place outside North Africa to shelter wild mustard.

There are eight **ferry** connections daily in summer from Porto Santo Stefano to **Giglio Porto**, four by car ferry and four by more costly hydrofoils; the rest of the year daily sailings drop to two.

Giglio Porto

Small, rock-girdled **GIGLIO PORTO** is the place you're likeliest to stay on Giglio, as it hosts eight of the island's thirteen hotels. It has no sights to be visited, but the whole scene is wonderful, the pale-coloured houses offset by a backdrop of terraced vineyards. There's a **tourist office** opposite the ferry ramp at Via Umberto I 48, which can provide details of accommodation possibilities – including a fair number of houses around the port which have **rooms to let**. The **hotels** generally offer only full board in high season, and most are open only then. A modest choice is *La Pergola*, in the port's Via Thaon de Revel (☎0564/809.051; ④).

From Giglio Porto there's a **bus** service to Giglio's two main villages, **Giglio Castello** and **Campese**.

Giglio Castello

GIGLIO CASTELLO, hidden away in the hills just under six hairpin kilometres from the port, was for a long time the island's only settlement and the sole spot safe from pirate attack. Surprisingly well preserved, its maze of arches and medieval alleyways is still surrounded by thick defensive walls. Buses from the port stop near a vine-covered patio **bar** in the large main square, also the entrance to the granite **fortress** and medieval quarter. **Accommodation** is limited to private rooms; the first bungalow up a path from the bar in the square is one possibility (☎0564/806.074). *Da Maria* in Via Casamatta is the island's best **restaurant**, though the seafood doesn't come cheap.

Giglio Campese

Sited at the western end of the island road, **GIGLIO CAMPESE** is a growing resort. It has Giglio's best **beach** – a fine stretch of sand, overlooked by a Medici tower, and curving for two kilometres from a huge phallic rock which the tourist brochures are too modest to photograph. Around the base of the tower is a modern, turreted apartment complex with a couple of restaurants, tennis courts and all manner of water-sport facilities – including diving gear for hire and lessons in how to use it.

The resort has five **hotels**, cheapest of which is *Da Giovanni*, Via di Mezzo Franco 10 (June–Sept; ☎0564/804.010; ⑤). There's also a **campsite**, the *Baia del Sole* (May–Sept; ☎0564/804.036).

travel details

Trains

Arezzo to: Assisi (2 daily; 1hr 35min); Bibbiena (hourly; 50min); Bolzano (5 daily; 7hr 30min); Camucia-Cortona (hourly; 20min); Chiusi (hourly; 1hr); Florence (hourly; 1hr); Foligno (every 2hr; 1hr 50min); Orvieto (7 daily; 1hr 20min); Perugia (every 2hr; 1hr 15min); Poppi (hourly; 57min); Rome (hourly; 1hr 40min); Terόntola (hourly; 25min); Terni (1 daily; 2hr 35min); Trento (5 daily; 7hr 30min); Udine (5 daily; 7hr); Venice (5 daily; 5hr 10min); Verona (5 daily; 7hr).

Empoli to: Florence (every 30min; 25min); Pisa (every 30min; 25min), Siena (hourly; 50min–1hr 20min).

Florence to: Ancona (hourly; 3hr 30min–6hr); Arezzo (hourly; 1hr); Assisi (11 daily; 2hr 35min); Bari (12 daily; 8hr 15min–9hr); Bologna (every 30min; 1hr–1hr 30min); Bolzano (14 daily; 4hr 10min–5hr 50min); Empoli (every 20min; 25min); Foligno (11 daily; 2hr 55min); Genoa (hourly; 3hr 10min–4hr 30min); Lecce (7 daily; 10hr 25min–12hr); Livorno (12 daily; 1hr 30min); Lucca (hourly; 1hr 5min–1hr 50min); Milan (18 daily; 2hr 50min–4hr 50min); Naples (2 daily; 4hr); Perugia (11 daily; 2hr 10min); Pisa central (every 30min; 55min); Pisa airport (hourly; 1hr); Pistoia (hourly; 30–45min); Prato (every 30min; 20min); Rimini (hourly; 2hr 30min–4hr); Rome (hourly; 2hr 15min–3hr 30min); Trieste (9 daily; 5hr–6hr 15min); Udine (10 daily; 5hr 20min–6hr); Venice-Mestre (10 daily; 2hr 45min–3hr 20min); Venice central (hourly; 3hr 25min–4hr 10min); Verona (14 daily; 2hr 40min–3hr 40min); Viareggio (hourly; 1hr 30min–2hr 25min).

Grosseto to: Cécina (10 daily; 1hr); Florence (1 daily; 2hr 20min); Livorno (15 daily; 1hr 15min); Orbetello (10 daily; 30min); Pisa (15 daily; 1hr 30min); Rome (10 daily; 1hr 30min); Siena (6 daily; 1hr 20min).

Livorno to: Florence (12 daily; 1hr 30min); La Spezia (5 daily; 1hr 20min); Pisa (every 20min; 15–30min); Rome (every 30min; 3–4hr).

Lucca to: Florence (hourly; 1hr 5min–1hr 50min); Pisa (hourly; 30min); Pistoia (hourly; 45min); Prato (hourly; 1hr); Viareggio (hourly; 30min).

Pisa to: Empoli (hourly; 35min); Florence (hourly; 1hr); Livorno (every 30min; 15min); Lucca (hourly; 30min); Viareggio (every 30min; 20min).

Pistoia to: Bologna (hourly; 1hr); Florence (hourly; 30–45min); Lucca (hourly; 45min); Viareggio (hourly; 1hr 15min).

Prato to: Bologna (10 daily; 1hr); Florence (every 30min; 20min); Lucca (hourly; 1hr); Pistoia (hourly; 15min); Viareggio (hourly; 1hr 30min).

Siena to: Asciano (12 daily; 35min); Buonconvento (6 daily; 25min); Chiusi (12 daily; 1hr 35min); Empoli (hourly; 50min–1hr 20min); Grosseto (6 daily; 1hr 20min).

Buses

Arezzo to: Cortona (hourly; 1hr); Sansepolcro (17 daily; 1hr); Città di Castello (15 daily; 1hr 30min).

Chiusi to: Montepulciano (14 daily; 45min).

Cortona to: Arezzo (hourly; 50min); Chianciano (4 daily; 1hr).

Florence to: Castellina in Chianti (1 daily; 1hr 35min); Gaiole (2 daily Mon–Fri; 2hr); Greve (around 25 daily; 1hr 5min); Poggibonsi (10 daily; 1hr 20min); Poppi (9 daily; 2hr 5min); Radda in Chianti (1 daily Mon–Sat; 1hr 40min); Siena (21 daily; 1hr–2hr 30min); Volterra (6 daily; 2hr 25min). In addition to these state-owned *SITA* services, numerous independent bus companies operate from Florence to Lucca, Pisa, Prato, Pistoia, Chianti, Arezzo, Sansepolcro, Viareggio and Grosseto.

Livorno to: Piombino (8 daily; 2hr); Pisa (every 30min; 20min).

Lucca to: Florence (30 daily; 1hr 15min); La Spezia (7 daily; 2hr 20min); Livorno (3 daily; 1hr 20min); Pisa airport (3 daily; 1hr 30min); Pisa (35 daily; 40min); Prato (9 daily; 2hr 15min); Viareggio (30 daily; 40min).

Massa Maríttima to: Piombino (2 daily; 25min); Siena (2 daily; 1hr 40min); San Galgano (2 daily; 1hr).

Montalcino to: Buonconvento (hourly; 35min); Monte Amiata (5 daily; 1hr); Siena (6 daily; 1hr).

Montepulciano to: Buonconvento (7 daily; 1hr); Chianciano (every 30min; 25min); Chiusi (every 30min; 50min); Pienza (7 daily; 20min), San Quirico (7 daily; 40min), Torrenieri (7 daily; 50min).

Pisa to: Florence (hourly; 1hr 10min); Livorno (every 30min; 20min); La Spezia (7 daily; 1hr 20min); Viareggio (hourly; 20min).

San Gimignano to: Poggibonsi (17 daily; 35min).

Siena to: Abbadia San Salvatore (3 daily; 1hr 20min); Arezzo (4 daily; 2hr); Buonconvento (10 daily; 35min); Florence (30 daily; 1hr 30min–3hr); Grosseto (4 daily; 2hr); Massa Maríttima (4 daily; 1hr 40min); Montalcino (6 daily; 1hr); Montepulciano (4 daily; 1hr 20min); San Galgano (3 daily; 40min); San Gimignano (16 daily; 1hr–1hr 30min); Volterra (6 daily; 2hr).

Viareggio to: Pisa (every 30min; 35min).

Volterra to: Florence (4 daily; 2hr); Siena (5 daily; 1hr).

Ferries

Livorno to: Capraia (1–2 daily; 3hr); Portoferraio (1–2 daily; 4hr).

Piombino to: Portoferraio (10–18 daily; 1hr).

Porto Santo Stefano to: Giglio Porto (2–8 daily; 1hr).

CHAPTER NINE

UMBRIA

Often referred to as "the green heart of Italy", **Umbria** is a beautiful region of rolling hills, woods, streams and valleys, and despite the growing number of visitors has largely retained an unspoilt air. Within its borders it also contains a dozen or so classic hill-towns, each resolutely individual and crammed with artistic and architectural treasures to rival bigger and more famous cities.

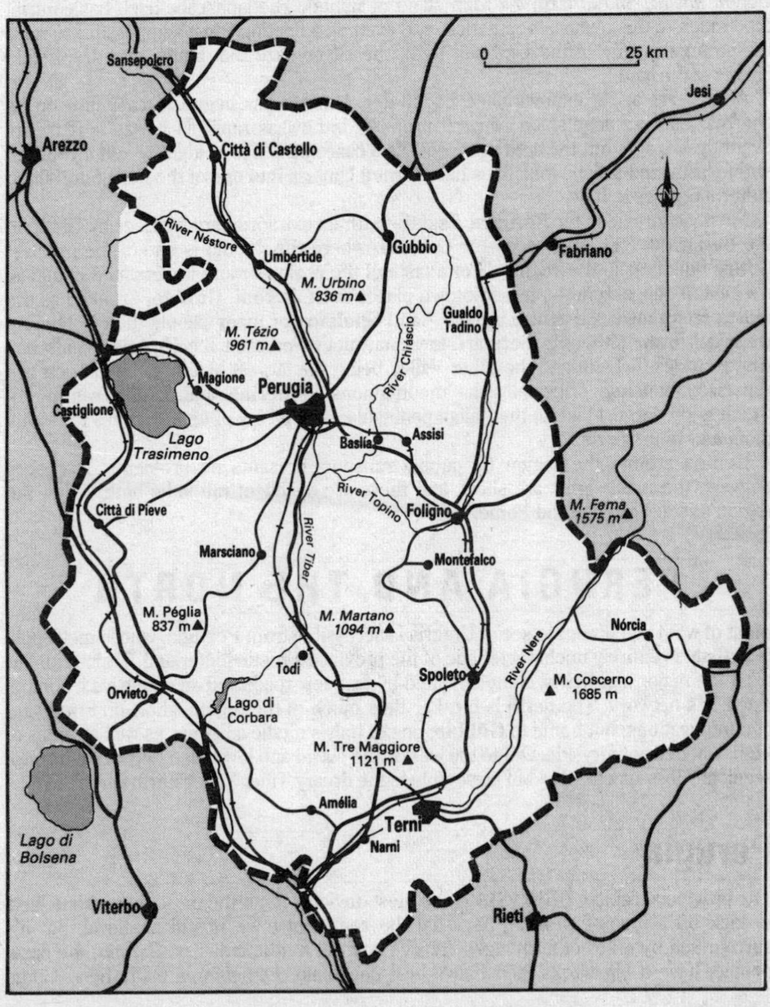

Umbria was named by the Romans after the mysterious Umbrii, a tribe cited by Pliny as the oldest in Italy, and one that controlled territory reaching into present-day Tuscany and the Marche. Their influence was mainly confined to the east of the Tiber, the darker and bleaker towns to the west – such as Perugia and Orvieto – being founded by the Etruscans, whose rise forced the Umbrii to retreat into the eastern hills. Roman domination was eventually destroyed by the barbarian invasions, in the face of which the Umbrians withdrew into fortified hill-towns, paving the way for a pattern of bloody rivalry between independent city-states that continued through the Middle Ages. Weakened by constant warfare, the towns finally fell to the papacy, entering a period of economic and cultural stagnation that has continued almost to the present day.

Historically, however, Umbria is best known as the birthplace of **Saint Francis of Assisi** and for a religious tradition that earned the region such names as *Umbra santa*, *Umbra mistica* and *la terra dei santi* (land of saints). The landscape itself has contributed much to this mystical reputation, and even on a fleeting trip it's impossible to miss the strange quality of the Umbrian light, the silver haze that hangs over the gentle curves of the land.

After years as an impoverished backwater, Umbria has begun to capitalise on its charms. Foreign acquisition of rural property is now as rapid as it was in Tuscany twenty years ago, but the area now projects a renewed sense of identity and a youthful enthusiasm, and artistic initiatives have turned Umbria into one of the most flourishing cultural centres in Italy.

Most visitors head for **Perugia**, **Assisi** – with its extraordinary frescoes by Giotto in the Basilica di San Francesco – or **Orvieto**, where the duomo is one of the greatest Gothic buildings in the country. For a taste of the region's more understated qualities, it's best to concentrate on lesser-known places such as **Todi**, **Gubbio** – ranked as the most perfect medieval centre in Italy – and **Spoleto**, for many people the outstanding Umbrian town. Although there are few unattractive parts of the Umbrian landscape (the factories of Terni and the Tiber Valley being the largest blots), some districts are especially enticing: principally the mountainous **Valnerina** and **Lago Trasimeno**, which is the largest lake in the Italian peninsula, with plenty of opportunities for swimming and watersports.

Getting around the region by public transport presents no problems. Distances between the main sights are short, and there are excellent rail links both within the region and to Florence and Rome.

PERUGIA AND THE NORTH

Most of what you'll want to see in Umbria is accessible from **Perugia**, whose metropolitan bustle is entirely uncharacteristic of the province's rustic hinterland. Trains run out to all the major highlights, complemented by fast new roads and an extensive if complicated bus network. The north is bleaker than much of the region, short on towns and communications, but home to **Gubbio**, one of Italy's medieval gems, as well as miles of high, wooded countryside. Out to the west is the placid and low-hilled **Lago Trasimeno**, scenically less spectacular, but preferable to the dreary Tiber Valley northwards.

Perugia

The provincial capital, **PERUGIA** is the most obvious, if not the most picturesque base to kick off a tour of Umbria. As usual the centre of town is still medieval, but it's surrounded by miles of fairly ugly suburbs and not a little industry. *Buitoni*, the pasta people, have a big works, and Italy's best chocolate, *Perugino*, is made here. Come summer the streets become claustrophobic and exhausting, so if your idea of Umbria is rural peace and quiet and lolling around old hill-towns – and really that's what the region is about – you probably won't want to spend a lot of time here. On the other hand there's a day's worth of good sightseeing plus some big-city attractions and the chance to catch up with other travellers.

The main draw in the summer is **Umbria Jazz**, Italy's foremost jazz event, whose line-ups may well tempt you into staying – past stars have included Miles Davis, Sting, Stan Getz, Gil Evans and Wynton Marsalis. Information and tickets are best sussed out well in advance from the tourist office (see p.493).

The presence of the **Università Italiana per Stranieri** (the Italian University for Foreigners) is another plus – set up by Mussolini to improve the image of Italy abroad, it's now run as a private concern and gives the town a welcome dash of style and an unexpectedly cosmopolitan flavour. The big state university also means there's an above-average number of films, concerts and miscellaneous cultural events, stuff you won't get elsewhere in the region.

Arrival

Arriving on the state **train** network you'll find yourself well away from the centre at **Piazza V. Veneto**: from here it's a fifteen-minute ride on bus #26, #27, #29 or #32–36 to Piazza Italia. City bus tickets (valid for 40 or 70min) are available from a small booth in the forecourt or a machine by the entrance. If you're coming on the private *FCU* lines from Todi or Terni to the south, or from Città di Castello or Sansepolcro to the north, you'll arrive at the much more central **Stazione Sant'Anna**, near the **bus terminal** at **Piazza dei Partigiani**. From this large square you can jump on one of the signed *scale mobili* (escalators) through weird subterranean streets to **Piazza Italia**.

If you're arriving by **car** be prepared for hassle: all the town's approaches are up steep hills and the signposting leaves plenty to be desired. The centre is closed to traffic at peak times, and you'll do best to leave your car at the main train station and take a bus. Alternatively you could head towards one of the big peripheral car parks – Piazza dei Partigiani, also the **bus station**, is the largest and most convenient.

The Town

Once you're safely in Piazza Italia, **orientation** is straightforward. The town hinges around a single street, the Corso Vannucci, one of the country's greatest people-watching streets, packed from dawn through to the early hours with a parade of Umbria's style-makers and style-followers. Named after the city's most celebrated artist, Pietro Vannucci, better known simply as Perugino, the Corso has the most atmospheric café in the city – the *Pasticceria Sandri* at no. 32 – and the trendiest locale – the *Café del Cambio* at no. 29.

Piazza Quattro Novembre and the Palazzo dei Priori

At the far end of the Corso Vannucci is the big and austere **Piazza Quattro Novembre** (once a Roman reservoir), backed by the plain-faced **Duomo**, now fully restored after damage caused by the 1983 earthquake. You feel maybe they shouldn't have bothered, because while the Baroque interior is big on size, it's pretty small on works of art, and comes as a disappointment after the fifteenth-century facade. As a change from pieces of the True Cross, one of the chapels contains the Virgin's "wedding ring", an unwieldy one-inch-diameter piece of agate that changes colour according to the character of the person wearing it. The Perugians keep it locked up in fifteen boxes fitted into one another like Russian dolls, each opened with a key held by a different person. It's brought out for general public edification once a year on July 30. In one of the transepts there's an urn holding the ashes of Pope Martin IV, who died in

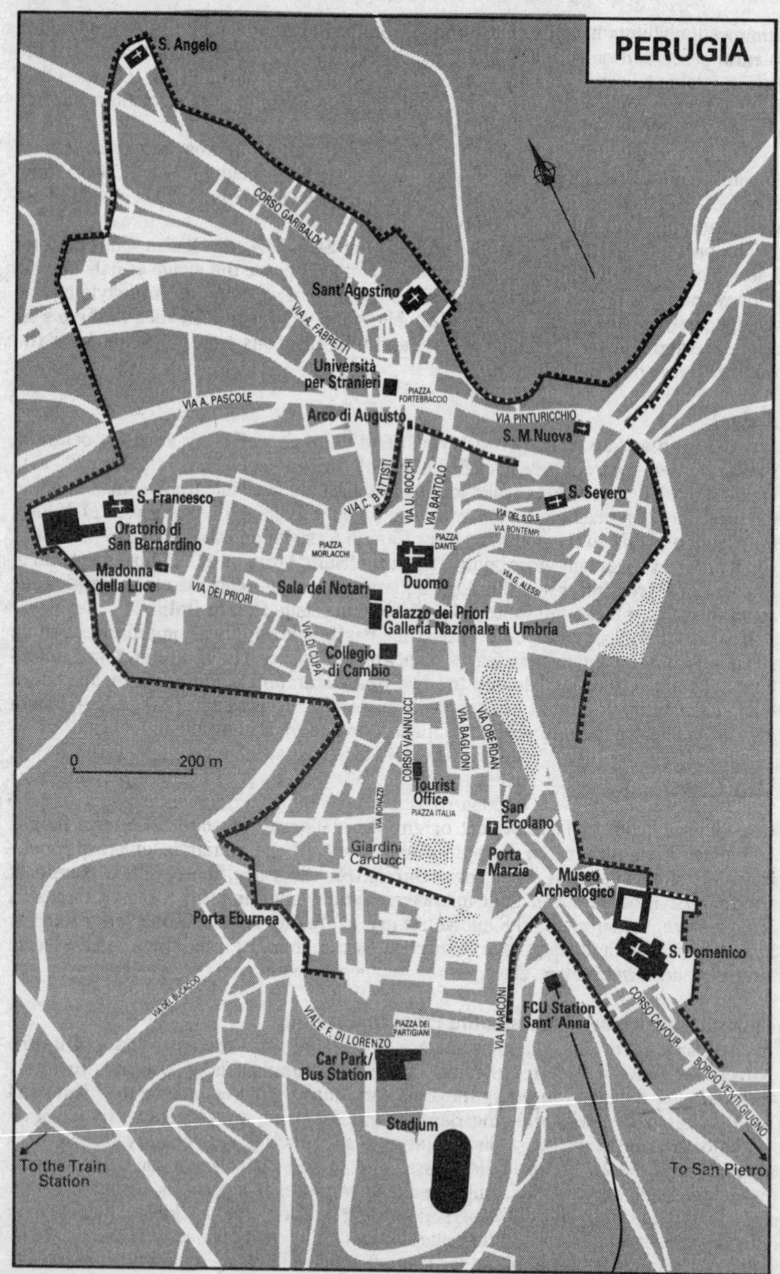
PERUGIA
S. Angelo
CORSO GARIBALDI
Sant'Agostino
VIA A. FABRETTI
Università per Stranieri
PIAZZA FORTEBRACCIO
VIA A. PASCOLE
Arco di Augusto
VIA PINTURICCHIO
S. M.Nuova
VIA C. BATTISTI
VIA U. ROCCHI
VIA BARTOLO
S. Severo
VIA DEL SOLE
VIA BONTEMPI
S. Francesco
Oratorio di San Bernardino
PIAZZA MORLACCHI
PIAZZA DANTE
Madonna della Luce
VIA DEI PRIORI
Sala dei Notari
Duomo
VIA G. ALESSI
Palazzo dei Priori
Galleria Nazionale di Umbria
VIA DI CUPA
Collegio di Cambio
CORSO VANNUCCI
VIA BAGLIONI
VIA OBERDAN
0
200 m
Tourist Office
PIAZZA ITALIA
VIA BONAZZI
San Ercolano
Giardini Carducci
Porta Marzia
Museo Archeologico
Porta Eburnea
S. Domenico
VIA DEL BULAGAIO
VIALE F. DI LORENZO
PIAZZA DEI PARTIGIANI
VIA MARCONI
FCU Station Sant' Anna
CORSO CAVOUR
BORGO VENTI GIUGNO
Car Park/ Bus Station
Stadium
To the Train Station
To San Pietro

the city after eating too many eels. Urban IV's remains are here too – he was reputedly poisoned with *aquetta*, an imaginative little brew made by rubbing white arsenic into pork fat and distilling the unpleasantness that oozes out.

Outside in the piazza (which is the town's main hang-out), the centrepiece is the **Fontana Maggiore**, designed by Fra' Bevignate, the monk who had a hand in the shaping of Orvieto's cathedral, and sculpted by the father and son team, Nicola and Giovanni Pisano. The sculptures and bas-reliefs on the two basins – now decidedly the worse for wear – describe episodes from the Old Testament, classical myth, Aesop's fables and the twelve months of the year. By some canny design work they never line up directly, encouraging you to walk round the fountain chasing a point of repose that never comes.

Just opposite rises the gaunt mass of the **Palazzo dei Priori**, hyped as one of the greatest public palaces in Italy. Sheer bulk aside, it's certainly impressive – with rows of trefoil windows (from which convicted criminals were thrown to their deaths), majestic Gothic doorway, and business-like Guelph crenellations – but the overall effect is rather grim; its real beauty derives from the overall harmony set up by the medieval buildings around it. The lawyers' meeting hall, the **Sala dei Notari** (9am–1pm & 3–6pm), at the top of the fan-shaped steps, is noted for its frescoes: lots of colour, fancy flags, swirls and no substance – but it's free to get in, so worth a quick glance.

The small **Collegio della Mercanzia** (Tues–Sat 9am–12.30pm & 2.30–5.30pm, Sun 9am–12.30pm; L2500), further down the Corso side of the palace and hidden behind an innocuous door, was the seat of the Merchants' Guild, and is covered entirely in intricate fifteenth-century panelling. The admission also gets you into the more impressive **Collegio di Cambio** a few doors down – the town's medieval money exchange – its walls superbly frescoed by Perugino at the height of his powers. They're considered the artist's masterpiece, and in true Renaissance fashion represent an attempt to fuse ancient and Christian culture. Up on the door-side wall there's a famous but unremarkable self-portrait with the artist looking like he had a bad lunch. The small chapel to the right of the Collegio is frescoed by Giannicola di Paolo (1519), the last important Umbrian painter influenced by Perugino.

The **Galleria Nazionale dell'Umbria** (Tues–Sat 9am–2pm, Sun 9am–1pm; L8000) is on the fourth floor of the palace complex, with the entrance through its opulently carved **doorway**. (You have to push past harassed-looking Perugians on their way to do battle with council bureaucracy on the other floors.) It's one of central Italy's biggest and best – a 33-room romp through the history of Umbrian painting, with one or two stunning Tuscan masterpieces (Duccio, Fra' Angelico, Piero della Francesca) thrown in for good measure. The entrance is worth every penny if you're the slightest bit interested in early and mid-Renaissance art, but be warned that a major restructuring is in progress, and the rooms devoted to Perugino and Pinturicchio – potentially the most appealing – may be closed or missing certain paintings.

North and west of Corso Vannucci

The best streets to wander around for a feel of the old city are right and left of the duomo, **Via dei Priori** being the most characteristic. In the Via della Gabbia partway down there once hung a large iron cage used to imprison thieves and sometimes even clergy. In January 1442, wrote a medieval chronicler, priest Angelo di Ferolo "was put back into the cage at midday, and it was very cold and there was much snow, and he remained there until the first day of February both night and day and that same day he was brought out dead." You can still make out long spikes on some of the lower walls, used as hooks for the heads of executed criminals. Medieval Perugia was evidently a hell of a place to be. "The most warlike of the people of Italy," wrote the historian Sismondi, "who always preferred Mars to the Muse". Male citizens played a game (and this was for pleasure) in which two teams, thickly padded in clothes stuffed with deer hair, and wearing beaked helmets, stoned each other mercilessly until the majority of the other side were dead or wounded. Children were encouraged to join in for the first two hours to promote "application and aggression".

In 1265 Perugia was also the birthplace of the **Flagellants**, who had half of Europe whipping itself into a frenzy before the movement was declared heretical. In addition to some hearty scourging they took to the streets on moonlit nights, groaning and wailing, dancing in white sheets, singing dirges and clattering human bones together, all as expiation for sin and the wrongs of the world. Then there were the infamous **Baglioni**, the medieval family who misruled the city for several generations, their spell-binding history – full of vendetta, incest, mass-slaughter – the stuff of great medieval soap opera.

Via dei Priori passes **Madonna della Luce** on the right after the medieval Torre degli Scirri, little more than a chapel dominated by an impressive altarpiece (by a follower of Perugino). It takes its name – Madonna of the Light – from the story that in 1513 a young barber swore so profusely on losing at cards that a Madonna in a wayside shrine closed her eyes in horror and kept them closed for four days. The miracle caused celebrations, processions and the building of a new church. Some way beyond is a nice patch of grass perfectly placed for relaxing with the crowd from the art school next door or for admiring Agostino di Duccio's colourful **Oratorio di San Bernardino**, whose richly embellished facade (1461) is far and away the best piece of sculpture in the city. To the right is what's left of San Francesco, once a colossal church, now ruined by centuries of earthquakes and neglect, but with a curiously jumbled and striking facade still just about standing.

From here you can wander along Via A. Pascoli, past the hideous university buildings, to the **Università Italiana per Stranieri** in Piazza Fortebraccio. The big patched-up gateway here is the **Arco di Augusto** – its lowest section one of the few remaining monuments of Etruscan Perugia. The upper remnant was added by the Romans when they captured the city in 40 BC. The university bar atmosphere is friendly and cosmopolitan – obviously a good place for contacts – but don't expect much joy out of the (surely ironically titled) Information Desk in the foyer. Posters around the place give details of concerts and English films (especially in the summer). Terms run from April to December.

About a minute's walk away on Corso Garibaldi is the sadly half-defunct **Sant'Agostino**, once Romanesque, now botched Baroque and filled with wistful signs explaining what paintings used to hang in the church before they were spirited to France by light-fingered Napoleonic troops. The missing pictures have been replaced with some horrendously inappropriate pieces of what someone somewhere obviously considers "modern art" . The church, however, is not entirely ruined: there's a beautiful choir (probably based on a drawing by Perugino) and a couple of patches of fresco on the left-hand wall, giving a tantalising idea of what the place must once have been. Next door to the left is the fifteenth-century **Oratorio di Sant'Agostino**, its ludicrously ornate ceiling looking as if it's about to erupt in an explosion of gilt, stucco and chubby plaster cherubs. Fifteen minutes' walk up the street is the fifth-century church of **Sant'Angelo**, situated in a tranquil spot and based on a circular pagan temple. The 24 columns, each made from a different stone, are from the earlier building.

Corso Cavour

The rest of Perugia's highlights are on the other side of town, grouped together on **Corso Cavour**, a busy and dustily unpleasant road in the summer, and just plain unpleasant the rest of the time. On the way over you could join the smooching couples in the small but well-kept **Giardini Carducci** (by Piazza Italia) to see why Henry James called Perugia the "little city of the infinite views". When the haze lifts – which except on crisp winter mornings isn't often – half of Umbria is laid out before you, with the mountains of Tuscany in the distance.

Below the piazza you could take a short walk past the strange octagonal church of **Sant'Ercolano** (rarely open) – built on the site where the head of Perugia's first bishop miraculously reattached itself to his body after the Goths chopped it off – and through the Porta Marzia, where a subterranean road of medieval houses (Via Baglioni Sotteranea) leads under the ruins of the Rocca Paolina (a once-enormous papal fortress destroyed by the Perugians at Unification). You come eventually to **San Domenico**.

The church, Umbria's biggest, has a desolate and unfinished air from the outside – pigeons nesting where they shouldn't, grass growing from the pinky-orange marble – but it's also pretty in a big and sad sort of way. The original Romanesque interior, however, collapsed in the sixteenth century and the Baroque replacement is vast, cold and bare, something like an EC warehouse waiting for a food-mountain. Like Sant'Agostino, however, it's full of hints as to how beautiful it must have been – nowhere more so than in the fourth chapel on the right, where a superb **carved arch** by Agostino di Duccio, spoilt only by Victorian Christmas card decorations and a doll-like Madonna. At the top of the church, to the right of the altar, is the **tomb of Benedict XI** (1324), another pope who died in Perugia, this time from eating poisoned figs. It's an elegant and well-preserved piece by one of the period's three leading sculptors: Pisano, Lorenzo Maitini or Arnolfo di Cambio, no-one knows which. There's also another good choir, and – a welcome splash of colour in the midst of all the mud-coloured paint – some impressive **stained glass** windows, the second biggest in Italy after those in Milan Cathedral.

Housed in the church's cloisters is the **Museo Archeologico Nazionale dell'Umbria** (Tues–Sat 9am–2pm, Sun 9am–1pm; L4000). Before being hammered by Augustus, Perugia was a big shot in the twelve-strong Etruscan federation of cities, which is why this museum has one of the most extensive Etruscan collections around. There's also a sizable section devoted to prehistory. If the Etruscans get you going you might try the local tombs, the **Ipogeo dei Volumni** (Tues–Sat 9am–5pm, Sun 9am–1pm; L2000), seven kilometres east of the town (bus or train to Ponte San Giovanni and then a short walk). Though the best in Umbria, they're quite small and without any of the usual racy paintings; not a patch on the graves at Tarquinia or Cerveteri (see p.634 and p.636).

Further on down the Corso Cavour, advertised by a rocket-shaped belltower, is the tenth-century basilica of **San Pietro**, the most idiosyncratic of all the town's churches. It's tangled up in a group of buildings belonging to the university's agriculture department, the none too obvious entrance being through a frescoed doorway in the far left-hand corner of the first courtyard off the road. Few churches can be so sumptuously decorated – every inch of available space being covered in gilt, paint or marble. Things appear to have been done with a sense of taste rather than to create some intimidating effect, and in the candle-lit gloom it actually feels like the sacred place it's meant to be. All the woodwork is extraordinary: **the choir** has been called the best in Italy, and there is a host of works by Perugino, Fiorenzo di Lorenzo and others.

Practicalities

The **tourist office**, in the Palazzo dei Priori at Piazza dei Priori 3 (Mon–Sat 8.30am–1.30pm & 4–7pm, Sun 9am–1pm; ☎075/23.327), is good for advice on city events and helpful in finding accommodation. There's a small summer-only office at the train station (daily 8.30am–1.30pm). At the station and in Piazza Italia you'll see some *Digiplan* machines, primed to provide tourist information on computer print-out – great in theory but almost invariably broken.

Cheap and central **accommodation** is no problem in Perugia. The **youth hostel**, two minutes from the duomo, Via Bontempi 13 (☎075/22.880; ①), is nicely situated, pleasant, and you don't need IYHF membership. It's closed from 9.30am though, and there's a midnight curfew. As for hotel rooms try *Anna*, Via dei Priori 48 (☎075/66.304; ⑤), *Piccolo*, Via Bonazzi 25 (☎075/22.987; ⑤), *Etruria*,Via della Luna 21 (☎075/237.30; ④), or *Lory*, Corso Vannucci 10 (☎075/24.266; ④). *Pensione Paola*, Via della Canapina 25 (☎075/23.816; ④), is hard to find – follow signs for the *Hotel Umbria* off the Corso and then bear left – but popular, so try to call in advance. The *Il Rocco* (☎075/798.550; open May–Sept) and *Paradise d'Été* (☎075/795.117; all year) **campsites** are 5km out of town at Colle della Trinità (#36 bus and a short uphill walk), but you're better off heading to the superior sites on Lago Trasimeno.

On the **food** front, there's a lot of *Perugino* chocolate about, plus the inevitable ice cream – try *Gelateria 2000*, Via L. Bonazzi 3 – and plenty of busy student hang-outs. Best of the budget eateries are: *La Botte*,Via Volte della Pace 31; *Tavola Calda*, Piazza Dante 16; *Pizza Medio Evo*, Via Baldo; *Trattoria Brizi*, Via Fabretti 75 – close to the Università per Stranieri; *Lo Scalino*, Via San Arcolano; *Osteria il Gufo*, Via della Viola 32; and the very large *Pizza Grimana*, Via Scortici 6 – ditto. *Café del Cambio*, Corso Vannucci 29, has good lunchtime snacks and a cheap restaurant downstairs. Best of the upmarket places is *Falchetto*, just off Piazza Dante at Via Bartolo 20.

Lago Trasimeno

The most tempting option around Perugia – whose surroundings are generally pretty bleak – is **LAGO TRASIMENO**, an ideal spot to hole up for a few days, and particularly recommended if you want to get in some swimming. It's the biggest stretch of water on the Italian peninsula, the fourth largest in Italy overall, and, though you wouldn't think so to look at it, never deeper than seven metres – hence bath-like warm water in summer. And because the tourist and fishing industries are the economic bread and butter of the surrounding towns it's also clean. Large banks of weed drift in during the summer, but the council takes care of these, dumping them with little subtlety on the shore.

A winning combination of tree-covered hills to the north, Umbria's subtle light, and miles of placid lapping water produces some magical moments, but on overcast and squally days the mood can turn melancholy. Not all the reed-lined shore is uniformly pretty either; steer clear of the northern coast recently opened up by Perugia's new motorway spur, and head for the stretches south of Magione and Castiglione if you're after relative peace and quiet. Be warned, too, that **unofficial camping** is not as easy as it looks, partly because a lot of the immediate shoreline is marshy, but mainly because many of the good spots have already been grabbed by locals.

Passingnano

PASSINGNANO, a newish town with a medieval heart, strung out along the northern shore, is the lake's most accessible point, being served by seven daily buses and by hourly trains from Perugia and Terontola. Popular with those Italians whose idea of a day out is to spend the whole day in a car, the town in summer often resembles nothing so much as a big traffic jam. In the evenings, however, when people come flooding in from the surrounding campsites, the place is jumping, with bars, discos and fish restaurants aplenty. There's a tourist office at Via Roma 38 (daily 9am–noon plus Mon–Wed & Fri–Sat 4–7pm; ☎075/827.635), and dozens of **rooms** – the best value are *Aviazione*, Via Roma 54 (☎075/827.162; ⑤), and *Beaurivage*, Via L. A. Pompili 3 (☎075/827.347; ④). The *Aviazione* also rents out bikes.

Somewhere on the coast towards Tuoro, probably at Sanguineto ("the Place of Blood") or Ossaia ("the Place of Bones") is the spot where the Romans suffered their famous clobbering at the hands of **Hannibal** in 217 BC. Hannibal was headed for Rome, having just crossed the Alps, when he was met by a Roman force under the

Consul Flaminius. Things might have gone better for Flaminius if he'd heeded the omens that piled up on the morning of battle. First he fell off his horse, next the legionary standards had to be dug out of the mud, then – and this really should have raised suspicions – the sacred chickens refused their breakfast. Poultry accompanied all Roman armies and, by some means presumably known to the legionnaire in charge of chickens, communicated the will of the gods to waiting commanders in the field. With the chickens against him Flaminius didn't stand a chance. Hannibal lured him into a masterful ambush, with the only escape a muddy retreat into the lake. Sixteen thousand Romans, including the hapless commander, were killed.

Tuoro and Castel Rigone

The shady, rambling village of **TUORO**, four kilometres west of Passingnano and a three kilometres' walk from the Trasimeno battlefield, is a quiet little place giving road access into the desolate, beautiful mountains north of the lake – the best of the scenery within easy reach of Perugia. Accommodation is tricky, though, as there's only one **hotel**, the eight-roomed *Volante*, Via 7 Martiri (☎075/826.107; ⑤). There is also a **campsite**, the *Punta Navaccia* (April–Sept; ☎075/826.357).

CASTEL RIGONE, 8km north of Tuoro, is the outstanding village in the mountains, with superb views and a small, geranium-strewn medieval centre. There are two smart, rather staid **hotels**, the better of which is the obvious *Fattoria*, Via Rigone 1 (☎075/845.322; ⑥). Each of the hotels has a cavernous **restaurant**, the only places for a bite to eat. A little outside the village is the Renaissance church **Madonna dei Miracoli**, somewhat out of place in the overall medieval context.

There's some good **walking** locally, with treks possible up Monte Castiglione on the mule track from the Passo di Gosparani (7km north of Tuoro); up Monte Acuto from GALERA or MONTEACUTO (15km northeast on the Umbértide road); or up Monte Murlo from PREGGIO, a hill-village 6km north of Castel Rigone and worth a visit in its own right. With a car, you could also cross the border into Tuscany to visit Cortona.

Castiglione del Lago

CASTIGLIONE DEL LAGO is the most appealing town on the lake and cuts a fine silhouette from other points around the shore, jutting out into the water on a fortified promontory. In the event it doesn't live up to its distant promise, but is still a friendly, unpretentious place with enough charm and action to hold anyone's interest for a couple of days – longer if all you want to do is crash out on an (albeit modest) beach. It's easy to reach by slow train either from Chiusi (heading north) or Terontola if you're coming from Arezzo or Perugia. There are also nine buses daily from Perugia.

There's a good **tourist office** in the main Piazza Mazzini (Mon 8am–1.30pm, Tues–Sat 8am–1.30pm & 3–7.30pm, Sun 9am–1pm; ☎075/952.184) whose flashiness in such a small town suggests an imminent inundation of tourists. They have a lot of reasonable but characterless **rooms** on their books, and apartments to rent on a weekly basis, usually a cheaper option if you can get a party together. Amongst the **hotels**, the top dog is the *Trasimeno*, Via Roma 174 (☎075/952.194; ⑥); more atmospheric is the two-star *Miralago*, Piazza Mazzini 6 (☎075/951.157; ⑤), with views of the lake behind. Most of the **campsites** are off the main road some way south of the town. *Lido Trasimeno* (☎075/954.120) on the shore north of the castle has good facilities (swimming, windsurfing school, sailing etc.), but it's next to a training school for police alsations. Best **eating**, outside the summer-only restaurants on the promenade, is the excellent *La Cantina*, at the lower end of Via V. Emanuele, the old town's single main street. Best **swimming** is at the public lido on the southern side of the promontory.

Eight boats daily make the trip out to the **Isola Maggiore** (L7000 return), one of the lake's three islands, a fun ride if you don't mind the crowds and some steep prices in the couple of restaurants when you get there. There's a pretty walk round the edge of the island, and you should have no problem pitching a tent when everyone else has packed up and gone home.

Panicale

The surrounding countryside is best appreciated from a reclining position on the beach. The low hills make a good scenic backdrop but they're not worth exploring, though if you have a car **PANICALE** to the south has some picture-postcard views of the lake, plus two easily missed Peruginos tucked away in the church of San Sebastiano (off Piazza Vittoria). During the town's April fiesta, thanks to some miraculous plumbing, the fountains run with wine; well worth checking out.

The Upper Tiber

Rome's great and famously polluted river, the Tiber, actually spends most of its short life in Umbria, rising in the Alpe della Luna (the mountains of the moon) above Sansepolcro. In its rather unexciting upper reaches north of Perugia – largely given over to sheep and fields of tobacco – you're faced with the familiar problem that everything you don't want to see is easily accessible and everything you do is out of reach without a car, bike or lucky hitch. The **Ferrovia Centrale Umbra** and the fast N3 to Sansepolcro are perfect for Città di Castello, the area's only town of note, after which you'll probably want to strike east on the N257 across the mountains to Urbino (70km). The best reason to follow the Tiber is to stay on the trail of **Piero della Francesca's** mysterious and unsettling masterpieces at Sansepolcro, Arezzo and Monterchi.

The region's best aspect, in fact, is not the valley but the desolate countryside on either side, regions which, like the Valnerina in the east, give the lie to the notion of Umbria as some sort of pastoral idyll. With few roads and fewer villages, but thousands of hectares of natural woodland and abandoned pasture, it teems with protected wildlife, including many rare species of birds, deer, wild boar and even wolves, now apparently pushing further up the Italian peninsula every year. **Pietralunga** and **Apecchio** to the north are the best exploring bases, with a **campsite** at Candeleto close to the former (*La Pineta*, open June to mid-Sept), but there's obviously plenty of scope for solo camping if you're geared up.

Umbertide

UMBERTIDE is largely modern and lightly industrial, having been bombed almost to oblivion in the last war, but – except in the tiny medieval centre – it doesn't come over as a place which had much going for it in the first place. It's only useful for trips into the surrounding hills, and then only if you have transport. The big castle, **Civitella Ranieri**, looms invitingly to the northeast, but it's privately owned, so don't be suckered into the steep climb for a closer look. **Mount Corona** (693m), six kilometres south, has some good views and the reasonably evocative remains of a fifteenth-century monastery. The hill-village of **MONTONE** is the one to see if you're not just passing through, thanks to a surprisingly good collection of paintings in the fifteenth-century Gothic church of San Francesco. Much further south – and with a car you could tackle this from Perugia – is the **Abbazia di Montelabate**. While the immense adjoining church of Santa Maria is second rate, the eleventh-century crypt and fourteenth-century cloisters are medieval perfection.

Città di Castello

The Church's seventh-century nickname for **CITTÀ DI CASTELLO** was "castrum felicitas" – the castle of happiness – though why, when it had been all but obliterated by Totila, is hard to fathom. Today there's nothing very cheerful about the place – unless you've drunk sufficient quantities of the local Colli Altotiberini **wines** or you happen to be in town during August for its renowned **Festival of Chamber Music**.

Once an important Roman centre – the grid-iron of streets is the only legacy – today the plain-bound site is drab and preserves only a handful of fairly mediocre medieval monuments. The town's only real merit is its ten-roomed **Pinacoteca** at Via della Cannoniera 22 (Tues–Sun 10am–noon & 4–5pm; L5000), reckoned one of the region's best after Perugia's. The collection takes in works by **Raphael, Signorelli, Ghirlandaio and Lorenzetti**, plus a wondrous *Maestà*, in Room 1, by the anonymous fourteenth-century Maestro di Città di Castello. There are also several **sculptures**, the most notable by Ghiberti, and a glittering reliquary of Florentine origin (1420).

If you stop off, then the banal reworked **Duomo** warrants a call for its museum (daily 8am–noon & 3pm–dusk; L2500), which contains the **treasure of Canoscio**, a precious hoard of sixth-century silver chalices dug up in 1932. The town's other more paltry offerings include a late Renaissance **choir**, located in San Francesco's Cappella Vitelli, and the fourteenth-century **Palazzo Comunale**, an imposing but unfinished work by Angelo da Orvieto, who was responsible for the vastly more impressive palaces in Gubbio.

Città di Castello's **tourist office** at Via Raffaele de Cesare 2b (daily 9am–1pm & 4–7pm; ☎075/855.4817) deals with the whole Upper Tiber region and so is a useful stop if you're spending any time locally. The town's top-of-the-range **hotel** is the central three-star *Tiferno*, Piazza R. Sanzio 13 (☎075/885.0331; ⑤). A cheaper option is the modern one-star *Umbria*, Via dei Galanti 4 (☎075/855.4925; ④). There's also a pleasant, rural **campsite** at LA MONTESCA, 1km west of town on the minor road to Monte San Marina – the *Montesca* (May–Sept; ☎075/855.8566).

A couple of kilometres north of Città di Castello, in the hamlet of **GARAVELLE**, is one of Umbria's best **folk museums** (daily 9.30am–noon & 3.30–6pm; free). Situated in Via Marchese Cappellett, this is basically an eighteenth-century farmhouse, preserved with all the accoutrements of daily life – pots, pans, furniture and so forth, plus a range of exhibits covering rural activities from wine-making, weaving and carpentry through to the blacksmith's forge. Totally out of context, the museum also has a **model railway collection** (Mon–Fri 3–5pm).

Gubbio

GUBBIO is the most thoroughly medieval of the Umbrian towns, an immediately likable place that's hanging onto its charm despite an ever-increasing influx of tourists. (It's being hailed – possible kiss of death – as the Umbrian Siena.) The streets are picture-book pretty, with houses of rosy-pink stone and seas of orange-tiled roofs; only the market in pricey but attractive ceramics suggests serious pandering to the town's sightseers. A broad and largely unspoilt plain stretches out in front (there's the odd quarry and cement works roundabouts, but out of sight), with the first high peaks of the Apennines rising behind, a lovely tree-covered backdrop which gives the place the feel of a mountain outpost – something it's always been in fact.

A powerful medieval commune, and always important as the gateway to Ravenna and the Adriatic (it was a key point on the Roman Via Flaminia), these days it's a town apart, not really part of Umbria, Tuscany or the Marche – the reason it's been spared the onslaught of the twentieth century and why getting here can be tricky. The best **approach** is by bus from Perugia (ten a day) or by train from Foligno to FOSSATO DI VICO, 19km away but with an hourly connecting bus service. Coming from Città di Castello or the north (Arezzo, Sansepolcro) means back-peddling to Umbertide to pick an easy hitch over the mountains. The one road, through CAMPO REGIANO, is minor but busy.

The Town

Centre-stage is the immense and austere fourteenth-century **Palazzo dei Consoli**, whose crenellated outline and 98-metre campanile command your attention for miles. Probably designed by Matteo Gattapone – also responsible for Spoleto's Ponte delle Torri – it took a couple of hundred years to build and required the levelling of vast tracts of the medieval town, mainly to accommodate the huge and windswept Piazza della Signoria. (The lesser **Palazzo Pretorio** opposite was built to the same plan.) Deliberately dominating and humbling, it was what medieval civic pride was all about, an attempt to express power and supremacy in bricks and mortar. Behind a plain square facade (there's a small hole top right where criminals were hung in a cage called *la gogna* – from *vergogna* or "shame") is a cavernous baronial hall, the Salone dell'Arengo, where council officials and leading citizens met to discuss business. The word "harangue" derives from *arengo*, so business obviously got pretty heated. It's base for the town **Museo Civico** (9am–1pm & 3–5pm; L4000), a typical miscellany, unremarkable except for the famous **Eugubine Tablets**, Umbria's most important archaeological find.

Discovered in 1444 by an illiterate shepherd, later conned into swapping priceless treasure trove for a worthless piece of land, the seven bronze tablets are more or less the only extant record of the ancient Umbrian language, a vernacular tongue without written characters. The bastardised Etruscan and Latin of their religious texts was aimed at producing a phonetic translation of the dialect using the main languages of the day. Gubbio was close to the shrine of the so-called Apennine Jove, a major pagan deity visited by pilgrims from all over Italy, so the tablets were probably the work of Roman and Etruscan priests taking advantage of the established order to impose their religious cults in a region where their languages weren't understood. Most importantly, they suggest Romans, Etruscans and Umbrians achieved some sort of coexistence, refuting a long-held belief that succeeding civilisations wiped one another out.

Restoration work permitting, admission to the museum might get you into the five-roomed **Pinacoteca** upstairs, worth a look for works by the Gubbian School – one of central Italy's earliest, and a collection of ponderous fourteenth-century furniture. Try the door at the back for views from the palace's **Loggia**. The palace also boasts 26 medieval toilets; it was the first in Italy with interior piped water.

A couple of steets above the Piazza della Signoria lurks a not very inspiring thirteenth-century **Duomo**, partly redeemed by the odd fresco, twelfth-century **stained glass**, and some arches gracefully curved to emulate the meeting of hands in prayer. There are also a pair of carved **organ lofts** that for once don't look as if they'd be more at home in a fairground. The small adjoining museum is worth five minutes, mainly for a florid Flemish cope, presented to the cathedral by Pope Marcellus II, who was born in Gubbio.

The plain-faced Gothic pile is overshadowed by the **Palazzo Ducale** opposite (Tues–Sun 9am–2pm; L3000), built over an earlier Lombard palace by the Dukes of Montefeltro as a scaled-down copy of their more famous palace in Urbino. The **courtyard** is particularly good, but most of the interior has been closed for years.

On the hillside above the town stands the **Basilica of Sant'Ubaldo**, a place Gubbians drive to for their Sunday morning walk, but pleasant enough for all that. There's a very handy bar, plenty of shady spots to crash out, and some great views (even better ones if you can be bothered to climb up to the **Rocca**). There's not much to see in the basilica itself, except the body of the town's patron saint, Saint Ubaldo, who's missing three fingers, hacked off by his manservant as a religious keepsake. You can't miss the big wooden pillars (*ceri*) featured in Gubbio's annual **Corsa dei Ceri** (May 15), little known outside Italy but second only to Siena's Palio in terms of exuberance and bizarre pageantry. The rules and rigmarole of the 900-year-old ceremony are mind-boggling, but boil down to three teams racing from Piazza della Signoria to the

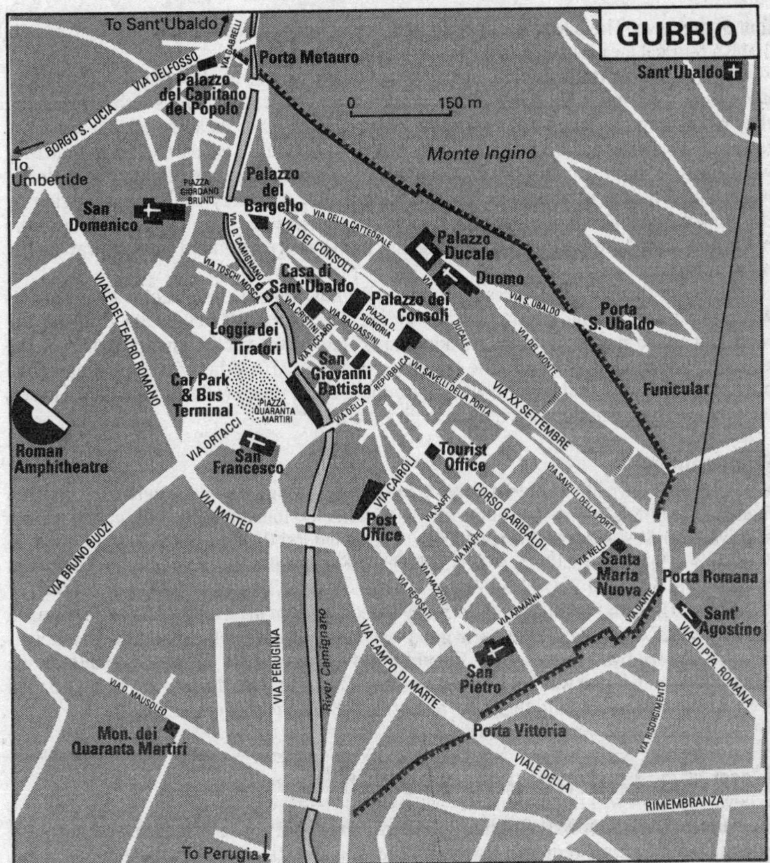

basilica, carrying the *ceri* (each representing a different saint) on wooden stretchers. The *cero* of Sant'Ubaldo always wins, the other teams having to ensure they're in the basilica before the doors are shut by the leaders. There's hours of involved ritual at either end, vast crowds and plenty of drinking. A scholarly debate rages as to whether the whole thing's intrinsically religious (commemorating the day in 1155 Ubaldo talked Barbarossa out of flattening Gubbio), or a hangover from some pagan fertility rite. Nowadays the Church not surprisingly claims it as its own, but judging by the very phallic *ceri*, and the roar that goes up when they're raised to the vertical, there's something more than religion going on.

There are several ways up to the basilica, one being via the steep track that strikes off from behind the duomo, but it's quicker and more fun to take the **funicular** from Porta Romana, over on the eastern side of town. While you're waiting you could take in more of Ottaviano Nelli's paintings, tucked away in the thirteenth-century **Sant'Agostino** and **Santa Maria Nuova** nearby. The unusually lovely *Madonna del Belvedere* (1408) in the latter is a masterpiece of the detailed and highly decorative style for which he was famous. His most majestic efforts – seventeen frescoes on the life of the Virgin – are in **San Francesco**, the big church that dominates the Piazza dei Quaranta Martiri at the foot of the town. The piazza's named in memory of forty citizens shot by the Germans in 1944, a reprisal for partisan attacks in the surrounding hills.

Gubbio's **Porte della Morte**, the "doors of death", are as controversial as the phallic *ceri*. Almost unique to the town (there are a few others in Assisi and southern France), they're narrow, bricked-up doorways wedged into the facades of its medieval townhouses (with the best examples in Via dei Consoli). The party line is that they were used to carry a coffin out of a house, and then having been tainted with death, were sealed up out of superstitious fear. Nice theory, and very Italian, but judging by the constricted stairways behind the doors, their purpose was probably defensive – the main door could be barricaded, leaving the more easily defended passageway as the only entrance.

There are dozens of picturesque odds and ends around the streets, which are as wonderfully explorable as any in the region. The **Bargello** in Via dei Consoli, the medieval police station, is worth tracking down, and gives you the chance to survey the adjacent **Fontana dei Matti** (the "fountain of the mad"), otherwise undistinguished but for the tradition that anyone walking round it three times will wind up mad. There's usually someone wondering whether to give it a go.

Practicalities

You shouldn't have any problem **staying** in Gubbio, though the place gets busy, and too many of the hotels and restaurants cater to well-heeled Italians. Check for cheap **rooms** in private houses with the **tourist office**, Piazza Odersi 6 (Mon–Sat 8.30am–1.30pm & 3–6pm, Sun 9.30am–12.30pm; ☎075/922.0693). For **hotel** accommodation, try *Locanda Galletti*, Via Piccardi 3 (☎075/927.4247; ④), *Grotta dell'Angelo*, Via Gioia 47 (☎075/927.1747; ⑤), or the popular and perfectly placed *Albergo dei Consoli* at Via dei Consoli 59 (☎075/927.3335; ⑤). There's a good selection of **eateries**, including the upper-bracket *Taverna del Lupo* at Via Repubblica 41, the touristy *Porta Tessenaca* at Via Piccardi 21, and, if you want to be outdoors, the *Trattoria San Martino* at Via dei Consoli 8. Best cheap **pizzeria** (and there are plenty) is *Il Bargello*,Via dei Consoli 37.

Gualdo Tadino and around

GUALDO TADINO, like Gubbio, is distinct from the rest of Umbria and similarly mountain-outpost in character. Sprawling over the lower slopes of the Apennines, it has a bleakly medieval centre, hedged about with light industry and unplanned housing around the station and plain below. It's easy to reach, with frequent **trains** from Foligno and Fabriano, and deserves more attention than it gets. With Umbrian and Roman origins, its single historical claim to fame was as witness to the death of Totila the Hun, who was slain by the Romans under the town walls.

The only remarkable thing about the thirteenth-century Gothic **Duomo** is that the facade has two tiers instead of Umbria's usual three; the interior, done to death in the nineteenth century, has absolutely nothing to recommend it. The **Pinacoteca**, housed in the angular San Francesco, is far more interesting, with an impressive collection for so modest a town. Much space is given to local painters such as fifteenth-century Matteo da Gualdo, but the centrepiece is a polyptych by **Nicolò Alunno**, considered unsurpassed amongst the central Italian artists before Perugino. Without the sugary quality of some Umbrian offerings – all soft-focus saints and dewy-eyed Madonnas – Alunno has a harder edge and a wider and more genuine range of emotion.

Without a lot to see or do, you'll be here for the flavour, which you could easily soak up between trains. Cheapest **rooms** if you need them are at *Centro Sociale Verde Soggiorno*, Via del Bosco 50 (☎075/916.263; ④), or at the five-roomed *Da Anna*, 5km south in BOSCHETTO (☎075/810.171; ④). The best **food** is at *Gigiotto*, Via Morone, 5.

The **tourist office** at Via Calai 39 (May–Sept Mon–Sat 9am–1pm & 3.30–7.30pm; ☎075/912.172) will fill in the gaps.

Nocera Umbra

Whether you make the fifteen-kilometre trip south to **NOCERA UMBRA** depends on whether you're sticking with Umbria, or heading to Urbino or Fabriano in the Marche. The rail links and the N3 and N76 roads are virtually the only routes east, making Gualdo an important watershed. Highly accessible, Norcera itself could just as easily be seen from Assisi, 20km away to the southwest. Hitching locally is a doddle, and there are plenty of trains. A place for a flying visit, it's yet another hill-town, middling by Umbrian standards and with a sizable new town on the valley floor to detract from its medieval charms. It's most famous for its **mineral waters**, exported worldwide, and renowned since the sixteenth century when people came from as far afield as Portugal and Turkey, lured by reputedly miraculous cures. (The biggest public **spa** is at BAGNI DI NOCERA, 4km southeast on the COLFIORITO road.)

Attractions are sparse, limited to the usual warren of streets, a nondescript fifteenth-century duomo, and an extraordinarily good **art gallery** secreted away in the church of San Francesco. Local artists predominate, as in Gualdo, and there's another big canvas attributed to Nicolò Alunno. If you've got transport, the villages and hilly countryside to the east repay aimless exploration, and there's a scenic route over to MATELICA (45km) in the Marche.

Parco Regionale del Monte Cucco

Some of Umbria's best upland scenery is to be found in the mountains east and north of Gualdo on the border with the Marche, much of it protected by the **Parco Regionale del Monte Cucco**. Where this area really scores is in its organised trails and backup for outdoor activities of every kind; if you want to don walking boots without too much fuss, this is the area to do it – and **access** is easy, with buses from Gualdo to Valsorda and from Perugia, Gualdo, Gubbio and Assisi to Costacciaro.

The southernmost base for exploration of the park is the resort of **VALSORDA** (1000m), 8km northeast of Gualdo on the southern extremity of the park. You can tackle the straightforward trek up **Serra Santa** (1421m) on a track of motorway proportions carved out by pilgrims over the years. From the summit you could drop into the spectacular **Valle del Fonno** gorge and follow it down to Gualdo. Paths follow the main ridge from Valsorda north and south, and it's feasible to walk all the way to Nocera Umbra.

Valsorda has two **hotels**: the one-star *Narciso* (☎075/913.282; ④), which also doubles as a **restaurant**, and the three-star *Stella* (☎075/913.282; ⑥). There's also a **campsite**, the one-star *Valsorda* (June–Sept; ☎075/913.261).

To get closer to the heart of the mountains you head to **COSTACCIARO**, centre for all the park's outdoor pursuits and access point for the **Grotta di Monte Cucco**, at 922 metres the fifth-deepest cave system in the world. Above, the huge, bare-sloped Monte Cucco (1566m) is the main playground for **walkers**. The best place to go if you want to get seriously wet or muddy, or just tag along with a tour party, is the **Centro Nazionale di Speleologia**, Corso Mazzini 9 (June–Sept, weekends only off-season; ☎075/917.0236), one of the country's most energetic and organised outdoor centres.

There are plenty of **accommodation** possibilities in and around Costacciaro, the best of them the *Monte Cucco da Tobia* in the Val di Ranco (☎075/917.7194; ④), a fabled mountaineers' and cavers' hang-out. Also convenient for walkers is the *Cappelloni*, Val di Ranco (May–Sept; ☎075/917.7131; ④). The park centre has **hostel** accommodation (open daily June–Sept, weekends only off-season). The nearest **campsite** is at FORNACE, 3km north of Costacciaro – *Rio Verde* (Easter–Sept; ☎075/917.0307). Freelance camping is prohibited within the *parco regionale*, but elsewhere you'll have few problems finding a discreet pitch for a tent.

ASSISI AND THE VALE OF SPOLETO

The broad southern sweep of the Vale of Spoleto constitutes Umbria's historic and spiritual heartland, boasting three or four of its most archetypal hill-towns – with **Assisi** and **Spoleto** the obvious highlights – plus great swathes of the sunny, pastoral countryside for which the region has been traditionally famous (though be prepared for the occasional blight of factories and unplanned housing). Everything is accessible from Perugia and within easy reach of the main routes, the railway to Terni and dual carriageway (N75) being particularly useful. Scenically inviting **Norcia** and the **Valnerina** are more tricky to reach, but well worth the effort – the best approach if you don't have transport is by bus from Spoleto.

Assisi

ASSISI is already too well known, thanks to **Saint Francis**, Italy's premier saint and founder of the Franciscan order – with its various splinter groups, the world's biggest. Had the man not been born here in 1182 the town wouldn't be thronged with tourists and pilgrims for ten months of the year, but then neither would it have the **Basilica of Saint Francis**, one of the greatest monuments to thirteenth- and fourteenth-century Italian art. On balance you'll probably feel it's worth putting up with the crowds and commercialism for art's sake, but you may not want to hang around once you've seen all there is to see – something which is going to take under a day. That said, Assisi quietens down in the evening, and it does retain some medieval hill-town charm. Ash

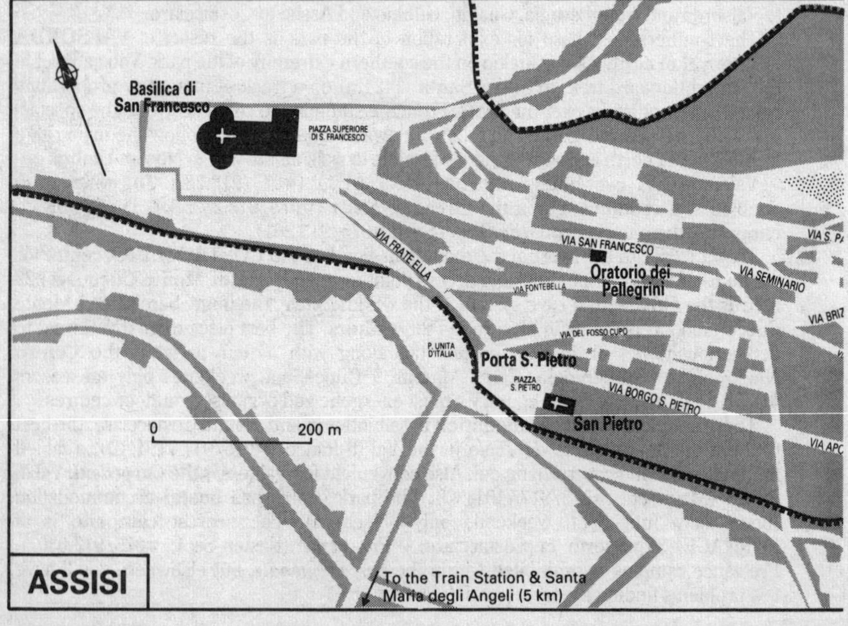

trays, key rings and other tacky paraphernalia are off-set by geranium-filled window boxes, tranquil backstreets and some lovely buildings in the muted, pinkish stone that softens all towns in this area.

Getting there is easy. **Buses** connect regularly with surrounding towns – especially Perugia – putting down and picking up in Piazza Matteotti, in the east of the town above the duomo. In addition, one bus a day leaves for Rome and two for Florence, from Piazza Unità d'Italia. There are hourly **rail** links to Foligno (via Spello) and Terontola (via Perugia), with connecting half-hourly bus services from the station to Assisi, which is 5km from its station.

The Basilica di San Francesco

Pilgrims and art lovers alike usually make straight for the **Basilica di San Francesco** (daily 6.30am–7pm), justifiably famed as Umbria's single greatest glory, and one of the most overwhelming collections of art outside a gallery anywhere in the world. Started in 1228, two years after the saint's death, and financed by donations that flooded in from all over Europe, it's not as grandiose as some religious shrines, though it still strikes you as being a long way from the embodiment of Franciscan principles. If you don't mind compromised ideals, the two churches making up the basilica – one built on top of the other – are a treat.

Most people start with Giotto in the **Upper Church**, mainly because it's the first one they come to, but the sombre **Lower Church** – down the steps to the left – comes earlier, both structurally and artistically. The complicated floor plan and claustrophobic low-lit vaults were intended to create a mood of calm and meditative introspection – an effect added to by brown-robed monks and a ban on photography, though the rules on silence are pretty much ignored by the scrums around the Cavallini frescoes. Francis

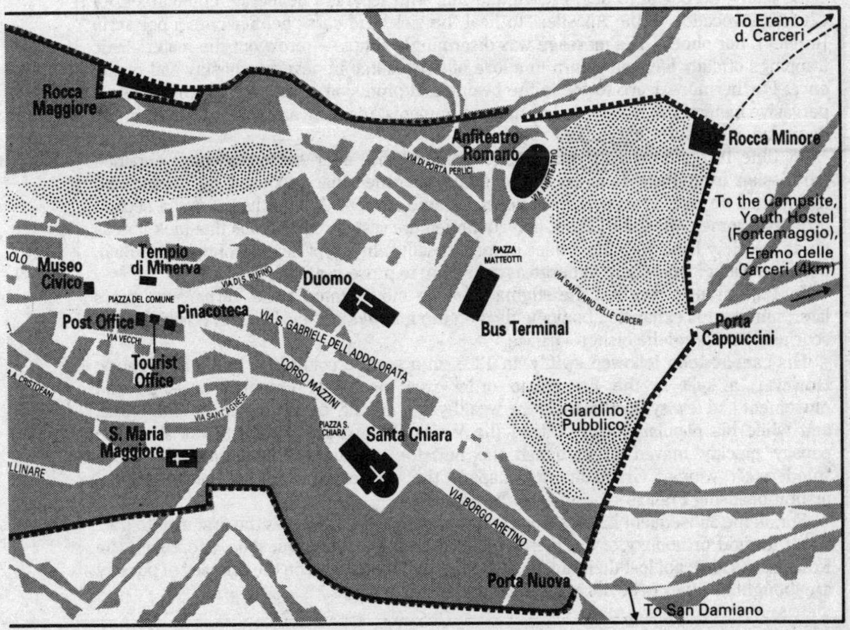

SAINT FRANCIS

Saint Francis is the most extraordinary figure that the Italian church has produced, a revolutionary spirit who took Christianity back to basics. The impact that he had upon the evolution of the Catholic Church stands without parallel, and everything he accomplished in his short life was achieved by nothing more persuasive than the power of preaching and personal example. Dante placed him alongside another Messianic figure, John the Baptist, and his appeal has remained undiminished – Mussolini, of all people, called him "il piu santo dei santi" (the most saintly of the saints).

The events of his life, though doubtless encrusted with myth, are well chronicled. He was born in Assisi in 1182, the son of a wealthy merchant and a Provençal woman – which is why he replaced his baptismal name, Giovanni, with Francesco (Little Frenchman). The Occitan literature of Provence, with its troubadour songs and courtly love poems, was later to be the making of Francis as a poet and speaker. One of the earliest writers in the vernacular, Francis laid the foundation of a great Franciscan literary tradition – his *Fioretti* and famous *Canticle to the Sun* ("brother sun . . . sister moon") stand comparison with the best of medieval verse.

In line with the standard early life of most saints, his formative years were full of drinking and womanising; he was, says one chronicler, "the first instigator of evil, and behind none in foolishness". Illness and imprisonment in a Perugian jail instilled the first seeds of contemplation. Abstinence and solitary wanderings soon followed. The call from God, the culmination of several visions, came in Assisi in 1209, when the crucifix in San Damiano bowed to him and told him to repair God's Church. Francis took the injunction literally, sold his father's stock of cloth and gave the money to Damiano's priest, who refused it.

Francis subsequently renounced his inheritance in the Piazza del Comune: before a large crowd and his outraged father, he stripped naked in a symbolic rejection of wealth and worldly shackles. Adopting the peasant's grey sackcloth (the brown Franciscan habit came later), he began to beg, preach and mix with lepers, a deliberate embodiment of Christ's invocation to the Apostles "to heal the sick, and carry neither purse, nor scrip [money], nor shoes". His message was disarmingly simple – throw out the materialistic trappings of daily life, and return to a love of God rooted in poverty, chastity and obedience. Furthermore, learn to see in the beauty and profusion of the natural world the all-pervasive hand of the Divine – a keystone of humanist thought, and a departure from the doom-laden strictures of the Dark Ages.

In time he gathered his own twelve apostles and, after some difficulty, obtained permission from Pope Innocent III to found an order that espoused no dogma and maintained no rule. Francis himself never became a priest. In 1212 he created a second order for women, the Poor Clares, and continued the vast peregrinations that took him as far as the Holy Land with the armies of the Crusades. In Egypt he confronted the Sultan, Melek el-Kamel, offering to undergo a trial by fire to prove his faith.

In 1224 Francis received the stigmata on the mountaintop at La Verna. Two years later, nursing his exhausted body, he died on the mud floor of his hovel in Assisi, having scorned the offer of the bishop's palace.

His canonisation followed swiftly, in 1228, in a service conducted by Pope Gregory. However, a split in the Franciscan order was inevitable. Francis's message and movement had few sympathisers in the wealthy and morally bankrupt papacy of the time, and while his popularity had obliged the Vatican to applaud while he was alive, the papacy quickly moved in to quash the purist elements and encourage the more "moderate" wings. Gradually it shaped the movement to its own designs, institutionalising Francis's message in the process.

For all the subsequent history, however, Francis's achievement as the first man to fracture the rigid orthodoxy of the hierarchical Church is beyond question. Moreover, the Franciscans have not lost their ideological edge, and their views on the primacy of poverty are thought by many to be out of favour with the current pope.

lies under the floor in a **crypt** only brought to light in 1818 after 52 days of digging (entrance midway down the nave). He was hidden after his funeral for safekeeping, and nowadays lies through almost continuous Masses in dozens of languages.

Frescoes cover almost every available space and span a century of continuous artistic development. Stilted early works by anonymous painters influenced by the Byzantines sit alongside Roman painters such as Cavellini, who with Cimabue pioneered the move from mosaic to naturalism and the "new" medium of fresco. They were followed by the best of the Sienese School, **Simone Martini and Pietro Lorenzetti**, whose paintings are the ones to make a real point of seeing.

Martini's frescoes are in the **Cappella di San Martino** (1322–26), the first chapel on the left as you enter the nave. He was given free rein in the chapel and every detail, right down to the floor and stained glass, follows his drawings, adding up to a unified scheme that's unique in Italy. Lorenzetti's works, dominated by a powerful *Crucifixion*, are in the transept to the left of the main altar. Vaults above the altar itself contain four magnificent frescoes, complicated but colourful allegories of the virtues on which Francis founded his order; Poverty, Chastity and Obedience. Once thought to have been the work of Giotto, they're now attributed to one of the church's army of unknown artists. Big feature in the right transept is Cimabue's over-restored *Madonna, Child and Angels with St. Francis*, a painting Ruskin described as the noblest depiction of the Virgin in Christendom. Look out for the famous portrait of Francis and for the much-reproduced fresco of Saint Clare on the wall to its left.

The more straightforward **Upper Church**, built to a light and airy Gothic plan – that was to be followed by countless Franciscan churches – is a completely different experience. It's less a church than an excuse to show off **Giotto**'s dazzling frescoes on the life of Saint Francis. *Francis Preaching to the Birds* and *Driving the Devils from Arezzo* are just two of the famous scenes reproduced worldwide on cards and posters. The cycle starts on the right-hand wall up by the main altar and continues clockwise. Giotto was still in his twenties when he accepted the commission, having been recommended for the job by Cimabue, whose own frescoes – almost ruined now by the oxidation of badly chosen pigments – fill large parts of the apse and transepts.

If time allows check out the **cloisters**, accessible from the rear right-hand side of the Lower Church, and the **Treasury** (April–Oct Tues–Sun 9.30am–noon; L2000), reached via the apse of the Lower Church. The latter, often passed by, contains a rich collection of paintings, reliquaries and general religious clutter given to the Franciscans over the centuries.

The rest of the town

Festooned with tourist trash, Via San Francesco – what else – leads back to the town centre. Halfway down on the right are the remains of the fifteenth-century **Oratorio dei Pellegrini** (daily 9am–noon & 3–8pm), the hospice for pilgrims, frescoed inside and out by local painters Mezzastris and Matteo da Gualdo – appealing but modest offerings after the basilica. The same goes for the fairly nondescript **Museo Civico** (daily 9am–1pm & 3–7pm; L2500), housed in the crypt of the now defunct church of San Nicolo. The collection includes Etruscan fragments and finds from the excavations now in progress to uncover the Roman forum, buried under the tourist-filled Piazza del Comune. The piazza is dominated by the so-called **Tempio di Minerva**, an enticing and perfectly preserved classical facade from the first century; it was the only thing Goethe was bothered about seeing when he came to Assisi – the basilica he avoided, calling it a "Babylonian pile". It's great to look at from the outside, but the interior is a seventeenth-century Baroque conversion of no interest whatsoever.

On the other side of the piazza the much-restored Palazzo Comunale contains the town's small **pinocoteca** (Tues–Sun 9am–noon & 4–7pm; L2500), whose small but worthy Renaissance collection feels like a light snack after your previous artistic gorging. Francis's birthplace is next door, marked by the dull Chiesa Nuova.

A short hike up the steep Via di San Rufino brings you to the thirteenth-century **Duomo**, with a typical and very lovely three-tiered Umbrian facade and sumptuously carved central doorway. The only point of interest in a stultifyingly boring interior is the font used to baptise Saint Francis, Saint Clare and – by an historical freak – the future Emperor Frederick II, born prematurely in a field outside the town. The cathedral makes a good point to strike off for the **Rocca Maggiore** (summer daily 9am–noon & 2–6pm; winter opening on the whim of the caretaker; L2000), one of the bigger and better-preserved in the region, with some all-embracing views after a stiff climb, though there's little reason to go inside.

Below the duomo, on the pedestrianised Piazza Santa Chiara, stands the **Basilica di Santa Chiara**, burial place of Saint Francis's devoted early companion, who at the age of seventeen founded the Order of the Poor Clares, the female wing of the Franciscans. By some peculiar and not terribly dignified quirk she's also the patron saint of television. The church was consecrated in 1265 and is a virtual facsimile of the basilica up the road, down to the simple facade and opulent rose window. Its engineering wasn't up to the same standards, however, and arches had to be added in 1351 to prevent the whole thing being undermined by crumbling foundations.

Instead of art, the scantily decorated interior has the once withered and macabrely blackened body of Chiara herself (now back from a session with a Roman saint-restorer) and a Byzantine crucifix famous for having bowed to Francis and commanded him to embark on his sacred mission to repair God's Church.

You're not long off the Francis trail in Assisi; **San Damiano** (daily 10am–6pm), a peaceful spot of genuine monastic charm, is one of its highlights. It's easily reached by taking the Borgo Aretino beyond the basilica and following signs from the Porta Nuova, a steep downhill walk of about fifteen minutes. Original home to the Poor Clares, and one of Saint Francis's favourite spots – he is thought to have written his well-known *Canticle to the Sun* here – the church, cloisters and rustic setting preserve a sense of the original Franciscan ideals of humility and simplicity often missing in the rest of the town.

From the railway station you can see the town's other major attraction, the vast and majestically uninspiring **Santa Maria degli Angeli**, built in the seventeenth century and rebuilt after an earthquake in 1832. Somewhere in its Baroque bowels are the remains of the **Porzuincola**, a tiny chapel which was effectively the first Franciscan monastery. Francis lived here after founding the Order in 1208, attracted by its then remote and wooded surroundings, and in time was joined by other monks and hermits who built a series of cells and mud huts in the vicinity. Today the church is crammed full of largely fourth-rate works of art and bears no relation to the Franciscan ideal.

After you've exhausted the myriad Francis connections, Assisi has the usual churches, Roman remains and miscellaneous odds and ends that characterise most Italian towns of similar age. If you have time you could check out the **Roman amphitheatre** near Porta Perlici (east of the duomo) or the Romanesque church of **San Pietro**, brilliantly restored for once, in Piazza San Pietro.

Practicalities

The **tourist office** is at Piazza del Comune 12 (Mon–Sat 8.30am–1pm & 3.30–6.30pm; Sun 9am–1pm; ☎075/812.450); clearly overworked, the staff do their best to help with accommodation and provide some useful maps and pamphlets. There are getting on for a hundred **hotels** in Assisi, along with a large stock of **private rooms** and **pilgrim hostels** (*Case Religiose di Ospitalità*). At most times of year this is just about adequate for the number of visitors, though advance booking is still highly advisable – it is essential if you plan to visit over Easter or during the *Festa di San Francesco* (Oct 3–4) or *Calendimaggio* (May 21–22). If booking through the tourist office, try to avoid the concentrations of rooms and hotels in Santa Maria degli Angeli or the grim village of Bastia, 4km out.

The *Italia*, Vicolo della Fortezza 2 (March–Oct; ☎075/812.625; ④), is the most central one-star hotel, in an alley off the north side of Piazza del Comune. Other good choices are: *La Rocca*, Via di P. Perlici 27 (☎075/812.284; ⑤), where half-board is obligatory; *Sole*, Corso Mazzini 35 (☎075/812.373; ⑤), a big, functional hotel one minute's walk from the Basilica di Santa Chiara, often with space when other spots are full; *Pallotta*, Via San Rufino 6 (☎075/812.307; ⑤), a seven-roomed place in a good location between the duomo and Piazza del Comune; the *Anfiteatro Romano*, Via Anfiteatro 4 (☎075/813.025; ④); and the convenient and popular *Properzio*, Via San Francesco 38 (☎075/813.188; ⑤). The IYHF **youth hostel** is in Via Valecchi (April–Oct; ☎075/813.767; ①), ten minutes' walk from Piazza San Pietro.

Multilingual tourist menus proliferate in the town's restaurants, and prices can be steep. For straight pizzas there's *Il Pozzo Romano* in Via Sant'Agnese (near Santa Chiara) and *Ristorante Pizzeria*, Via Italia 34. *Palotta*, Via San Rufino 4, is near some sticky tourist traps but reasonable and friendly – arrive early for a table. Moving upmarket, *La Fortezza*, Vicolo della Fortezza 2 (☎075/812.418), has great food but dubious decoration – it's essential to reserve in summer. *Medioevo*, Via dell'Arco dei Priori 4 (☎075/813.068), just south off the Piazza del Comune, is highly recommended for a real splurge.

Spello to Trevi

Ranged on broad terraces above the Vale of Spoleto, medieval and pink-stoned **SPELLO** is the best place for a half-hour taste of small-town Umbria if you haven't time or means to explore further, being easy to reach by road and rail (20min from Assisi or Spoleto). Emperor Augustus gave land in the adjacent valley to faithful legionaries to build themselves retirement homes, turning the town (*Hispellum*) into a sort of Roman Eastbourne in the process, an ambience it still rather retains.

The walls and three gateways are the most obvious Roman remnants. (Don't bother walking out to the paltry and overgrown remains of the old amphitheatre hidden away beyond the main road – you can see all you need to from the top of the town.) By far the most distinguished sight is **Pinturicchio's fresco cycle** in the thirteenth-century church of Santa Maria Maggiore (Piazza G. Matteotti). Number two Umbrian painter after Perugino, he left other important works in Siena (the duomo), Rome (the Sistine Chapel, Borgia apartments) and a host of churches scattered over central Italy. The frescoes themselves are fresh and glowing from recent restoration, with Pinturicchio's famous details and colouring brought out to stunning effect. Unfortunately they're behind glass, which also means you can't get a closer look at the chapel's praised but faded fifteenth-century **ceramic pavement**.

Spello makes an alternative base for Assisi, with a good range of accommodation (albeit quite pricey), fair restaurants and a small summer-only **tourist office** at Piazza Matteotti 3. *Il Cacciatore*, Via Giulia 42 (☎0742/651.141; ⑤), is an excellent-value two-star **hotel**, with fine views from some rooms; at *La Bastiglia*, Via Salnitraria 17 (☎0742/651.277; ⑥), the small but smart rooms all command a fine view. *Camping Umbria* (April to mid-Oct; ☎0742/651.772), is the nearest campsite, 2km east of town at CHIONA.

Spello's best **restaurant**, set in a vaulted medieval town house, is *La Cantina*, Via Cavour 2, a friendly local place serving plenty of regional specialities – and wonderful fresh pasta. *Il Cacciatore*, Via Giulia 42, has middling food and service, but a great terrace for summer eating.

Foligno

To move on anywhere from Spello means a trip to **FOLIGNO** and a lull in proceedings, because it's a large modern town and flat in every sense of the word. Its star turns were bombed out of existence in the war, and the place is now a mediocre provincial backwater sprawled over an unattractive plain. However, much of what's left is conveniently grouped together in the central **Piazza della Repubblica**, and as you're likely to be passing through a quick look isn't going to hurt. The town's also brimful of hotels and acts as a nodal point for trains and local village buses.

For the **tourist office** and **bus station** (Porta Romana) follow Viale Mezzetti from the train station, turn right into Piazzale Alunno and the office is in the top right-hand corner. Continue up Corso Cavour and you hit the historic centre two minutes later. The twelfth-century **Duomo** has two good Romanesque facades (there's an extra one on the side) but the interior was finished off in the eighteenth century to predictable effect. The nearby **Palazzo Trinci** is the only thing worth making a real effort to see. The Trincis were Foligno's medieval big shots, with territory and influence extending over great swathes of Umbria, and their palace is an art-filled monument to wealth and power – all frescoed stairways, carved ceilings and general opulence, most of it recently restored. Inside are a small **archaeological museum** and a **pinacoteca** with good frescoes by the fifteenth-century Gubbian painter, Ottaviano Nelli.

The only other monument which hints at Foligno's former glory is **Santa Maria Infraportas** (off Piazza San Domenico), a church of pagan origins in which Saint Peter himself is said to have conducted a Mass. Oldest bit of the current building (eighth century) is the Cappella dell'Assunta off the left nave, dominated by the town's most precious piece of art, a twelfth-century Byzantine mural.

Bevagna

BEVAGNA is quieter and less visited than Spello, but a serene backwater if ever there were one, with a windswept **central square** of absolute austere perfection. Flanked by two of Umbria's finest Romanesque churches (both untouched and creaking with age), the Piazza Silvestri dates from around the thirteenth century. The only exception is the fountain, which while blending perfectly, was installed in 1889. Look out particularly for the surreal and demented gargoyles over the doorway of the larger church, San Michele. And if it's open, check out the Palazzo Comunale, which was converted in the nineteenth century into one of Umbria's prettiest provincial theatres.

There's not a lot else to the town, other than the backwoods charm of the streets. You can take a **bus** here from Foligno (8km) or hitch easily on the road that crosses the plain. Unfortunately, though, the town has no official accommodation.

Montefalco

Short of a lucky hitch, a bus is the only way to get from Foligno to **MONTEFALCO**, a faintly forlorn medieval village, but home to a superb collection of paintings that definitely merits a morning. Its name, meaning Falcon's Mount, was glorified with the appendage "la ringhiera dell'Umbria" – the balcony of Umbria, a hyperbolic tribute to its **views**. It was also the birthplace of eight saints, good going even by Italian standards. Nowadays the town's sleepy rather than holy, with only a stupendously ugly water tower and very slight urban sprawl to take the edge off its moderate medieval appeal. The strong, blackberry-flavoured **local wine**, *Sangrantino passito*, is well worth a try; there's a good little shop in the main square for this and other liquid purchases.

The lofty location was a godsend to Spoleto's papal governors, left high, dry and terrified by the fourteenth-century defection of the popes to Avignon. They took refuge here, and their cowering presence accounts for the rich decoration of the town churches, a richness out of all proportion to the town's size. The cavernous ex-church of **San Francesco**, off the central Piazza del Comune in Via Ringhiera Umbra (Tues–

Sun 9am–noon & 3.30–6.30pm; L6000), houses the town's big feature, Benozzo Gozzoli's sumptuous **fresco cycle** on the life of Saint Francis. With Fra' Angelico, Gozzoli was one of the most prolific and influential Florentine painters to come south and show the backward Umbrians what the Renaissance was all about. Resplendent with colour and detail, the cycle copies many of the ideas and episodes from Giotto's Assisi cycle but, with 200 years of artistic know-how to draw on, is more sophisticated and more immediately appealing (if lacking Giotto's austere dignity). Amongst numerous other paintings in the church and adjoining gallery are works by most of the leading Umbrians (Perugino, Nicolò Alunno, Tiberio d'Assisi) as well as a host of more minor efforts by local fifteenth-century artists. There are more early frescoes in **Sant'Agostino** across the main piazza in Via Umberto I, where you should also look out for some revered mummified bodies – they are halfway down the nave and in a wardrobe at the top end of the left-hand nave.

The rest of the town is relatively low key and doesn't take long to see. Probably the most bizarre sight is the mummified body of Saint Clare (Santa Chiara) which languishes in the otherwise dismal church of the same name, five minutes from San Francesco in Via Verdi (this is a second Saint Clare, not to be confused with the one in Assisi). Ring a bell, and if the nuns aren't praying, they'll show you round the adjoining convent. It's a good behind-the-scenes look at monastic life, the sisters showing you the remains of the saint's heart and the scissors used to hack it out. The story goes that Christ appeared to Clare, saying the burden of carrying the Cross was becoming too heavy; Clare replied she would help by carrying it in her heart. When she was opened up, a cross-shaped piece of tissue was found on her heart. Other exhibits include three of her kidney stones, and a miraculous tree that grew from a staff planted in the garden by Christ, who appeared to her here. Apparently it's the only one of its kind growing wild in Europe; the berries are used to make rosaries and are said to have powerful medicinal qualities.

Fifty metres beyond the church, preceded by a triple-arched Renaissance porch, is the chapel of **Sant'Illuminata**, comprehensively but not terribly well frescoed by Melanzio in 1510. Keep on heading out of town, turn left at the T-junction, and fifteen minutes of tedious walking brings you to **San Fortunato**, nicely situated amongst ilix woods and noted for the frescoes by Tiberio d'Assisi (1512), in the Cappella delle Rose (left of the main courtyard). Check out the macabre bundle of blackened bones in the main church, the remains of San Fortunato himself, martyred in 390.

There's no need to spend more than a morning in Montefalco, but if you do decide to **stay**, there are two hotels in town: the tiny *Ringhiera Umbra*, Via Umberto 1 (☎0742/79.166; ④), and the nearby *Santa Chiara*, Via de Cuppis 18 (☎0742/79.114; ⑤), whose main reason for a stay is the owner's Aladdin's Cave of kitsch and memorabilia. For something grander than the *Ringhiera*'s **restaurant**, try the *Coccorone* on the corner of Largo Tempestivi and Via Fabbri (☎0742/795.35), where the chances are you'll have one of the best meals you'll ever experience in Umbria. Should you want more **information** on the town, the tourist desk inside San Francesco is more reliable than the main office in the Palazzo Comunale.

Trevi

The best way to move southwards from Foligno is by train, which skirts the plain of Spoleto and whisks past the light industrial sites that blight the whole stretch of the valley to Terni and beyond. Not many people stop before Spoleto itself, giving **TREVI** and its towering position no more than an admiring glance from the train. Its daunting inaccessibility is one of the reasons for its easy-going charm. The feeling is of a pleasant, ordinary provincial town still stuck somewhere in the Fifties, unvisited and unspoilt. Beyond it lie miles and miles of olive groves, renowned for producing central Italy's finest oil. The town's also apparently famous for its celery.

The medieval centre, looming away high on its hill, is 4km from the station, a dull and exhausting trek – take the connecting bus service instead. The **tourist office** in Via Roma off the central Piazza Mazzini (Mon–Sat 9am–1pm & 3.30–6.30pm) is invaluable for maps to the peripheral churches, which contain a sprinkling of Umbrian paintings. The most noteworthy are in **San Martino** and **Madonna delle Lacrime**, the latter containing excellent and recently restored works by Perugino and Lo Spagna. The twelfth-century **Duomo** of Sant'Emiliano at the town's highest point suffered more than usually violent nineteenth-century butchery of its innards, but is fine from the outside and conserves a series of sixteenth-century frescoes by Melanzio, a half-decent painter active in several villages locally.

The small **Museo-Pinacoteca** in Piazza Mazzini houses a predictable display of coins, ceramics and Roman trivia, and two masterpieces, a *Madonna* by Pinturicchio and a *Coronation of the Virgin* (1522) by Lo Spagna. Trevi's medieval governors commissioned the latter as a copy of a more famous work by the Florentine, Ghirlandaio, mainly because they couldn't afford the real thing. Todi's *comune* had the same economical idea and got Lo Spagna to knock them out another copy. The original is in Terni. Unfortunately you can't count on finding the museum open – hours are highly variable and often you'll have to negotiate entry in the council offices alongside.

Trevi has just one **hotel**, the *Cochetto*, Via Dogali 13 (☎0742/78.229; ⑤); downstairs is a good **restaurant**. The *Pizzeria Casavecchia*, Piazza Garibaldi 19, also has a few rooms in the same range.

FONTI DI CLITUNNO

A short hop from Trevi on the road south are the sacred **FONTI DI CLITUNNO**, an unexpected beauty spot, given the pockmarked surroundings. There's a certain amount of commercialised fuss and bother at the entrance, but the springs, streams and willow-shaded lake beyond – painted by Corot and an inspiration to poets from Virgil to Byron – are pure, languid romanticism. Faint traffic noise and the occasional mega-coach party are the only intrusions. The spa waters have attracted people since Roman times – the likes of Caligula and Claudius came here to party – but their major curative effect is allegedly the dubious one of completely removing any appetite for alcohol. Earthquakes over the years have upset many of the underground springs, so the waters aren't as plentiful as they were, but they still flow as limpid as they did in Byron's day, the "sweetest wave of the most living crystal . . . the purest god of gentle waters . . . most serene of aspect and most clear . . . a mirror and a bath for Beauty's youngest daughters." The site closes for lunch, but opens again until dusk, with a small admission charge to get in. A mini tourist office doles out background information in the summer.

A few hundred metres north is the so-called **Tempietto di Clitunno**, looking for all the world like a miniature Greek temple but actually an eighth-century Christian church, cobbled together with a mixture of idiosyncrasy, wishful thinking and old Roman columns. It's only a small, one-off novelty, but still evocative, and with the bonus inside of some faded frescoes said to be the oldest in Umbria.

Spoleto

SPOLETO is Umbria's most compelling town and many people's central-Italian favourite. Known mainly for its big **summer festival**, it's remarkable also for its thoroughgoing medievalism, an extremely pretty position, and several of Italy's most ancient Romanesque churches. Far more graceful and provincial a city than Perugia, nowadays it plays second fiddle to its long-time historical enemy, though for several centuries it was amongst the most influential of Italian towns. Two kilometres of well-preserved walls stand as testament to the one-time grandeur of its Roman colony, though its real importance dates from the sixth century when the Lombards made it the capital of one of their three Italian dukedoms. The autonomous **Duchy of Spoleto** eventually stretched to Rome, and by 890 its rulers had become powerful enough to lay claim to the Imperial throne itself, making Spoleto, for a short time at least, the capital of the entire Holy Roman Empire. Barbarossa flattened the city in a fit of pique in 1155, and in 1499 the nineteen-year-old Lucrezia Borgia was appointed governer by her father, Pope Alexander VI. After that it was one long decline until about thirty years ago, and the arrival of the festival.

The lower town

The first thing which greets you outside Spoleto's quaint Thirties-style station is a ludicrously out-of-place sculpture heralding the town's delusions of cultural grandeur – a shame, because the overall feel of the place is anything but pretentious. The lower town to which it's a gateway was badly damaged by World War II bombing, and its only real interest lies in a couple of churches, most impressively the fourth-century palaeo-Christian **San Salvatore**. If you're not into church excursions a bus runs from the station up to Piazza Libertà, the heart of the medieval town, tempting with a superb skyline of spires, tiled roofs and splashes of craggy countryside.

San Salvatore is on the outskirts of the modern suburb, half-hidden in the **town cemetery**, whose spooky glimpse of the Italian way of death provides a faintly bizarre attraction in itself. The church was built by Christian monks from the Eastern Mediterranean in the fourth century, since when it's hardly been touched. Conceived when the only models for religious buildings were Roman temples, that's pretty much what the monks came up with, the net result leaning more to primitive paganism than Christianity. The walls inside are bare, the floors covered in fallen stone, and the dusty gloom is heavy with an almost eerie antiquity. Crumbling Corinthinian columns from different ages are wedged awkwardly alongside one another, and at some point the arches in the nave were filled in to prevent total collapse. Try to visit at dusk to get the full effect.

In the vicinity is **San Ponziano**, much praised but easily ignored if it weren't for a distinctive Romanesque facade. There's also a fascinating tenth-century **crypt** if you can tempt the caretaker out of his cave-like house to show you it. The lower town's other attraction close by is the church of **San Gregorio**, started in 1069 but looking as if it was built yesterday, a result of recent cleaning and restoration. The tower and intriguing portico are made from a patchwork of fragments clearly pinched from earlier Roman remains, but it's the interior that commands most attention. Stripped back to their Romanesque state, the walls are dotted with substantial patches of fresco and interrupted by a series of unusual, rather intimidating stone confessionals. The presbytery is raised several metres above the level of the naves to allow for a masterful little **crypt**, supported by dozens of tiny pillars.

Tradition has it that somewhere under the church are the bones of ten thousand Christian martyrs killed by the Romans in the **amphitheatre** close by. There are still traces of the bloodbath visible in the military barracks up the road. No-one seems to mind if you just walk straight in; bear right from the gateway for the best remains, none of which are terribly substantial. The ever-ingenious Romans apparently constructed special gutters to drain blood from the arena into the nearby Torrente Tessino, which ran crimson as a result. Now the river's full of rubbish and a long way from being a puddle, let alone a torrent.

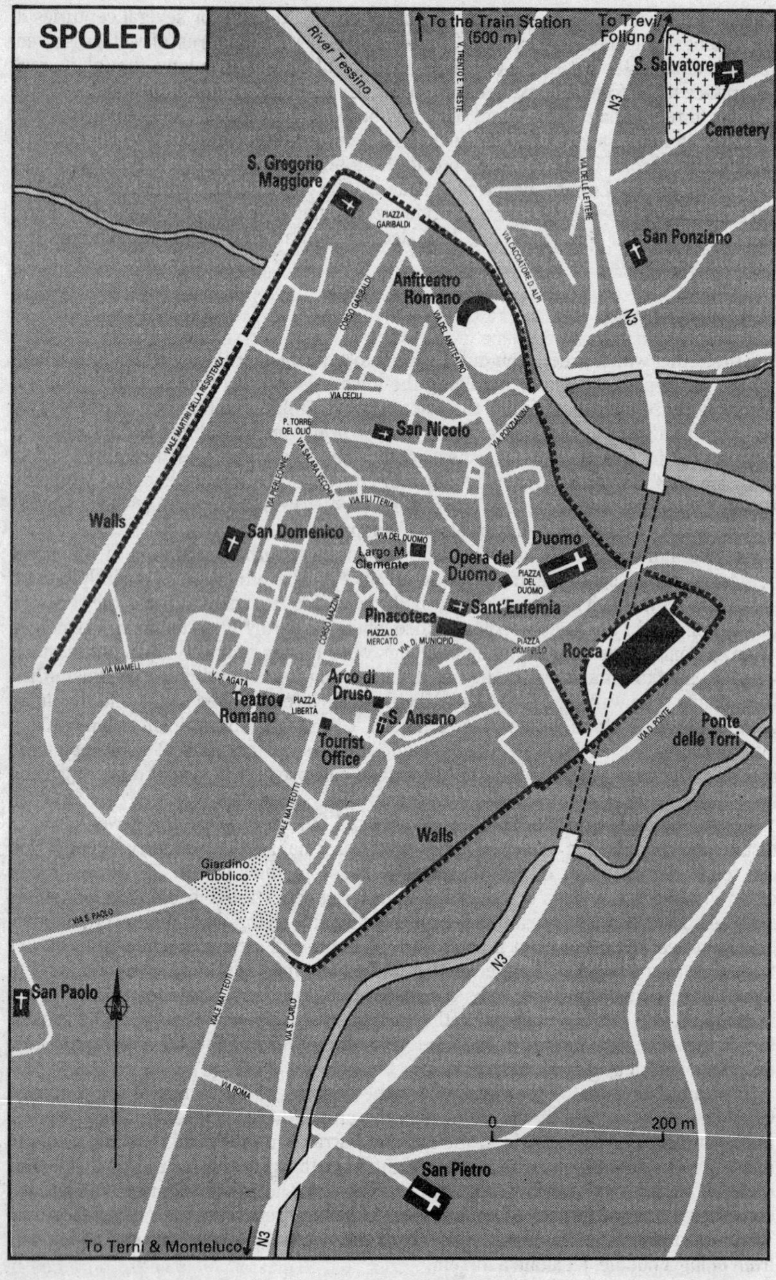
SPOLETO
To the Train Station (500 m)
To Trevi/ Foligno
River Tessino
V. TRENTO E TRIESTE
S. Salvatore
Cemetery
N3
VIA DELLE LETTERE
S. Gregorio Maggiore
PIAZZA GARIBALDI
VIA CACCIATORE D. ALPI
San Ponziano
Anfiteatro Romano
CORSO GARIBALDI
VIA DEL ANFITEATRO
VIALE MARTIRI DELLA RESISTENZA
VIA CECILI
P. TORRE DEL OLIO
San Nicolo
VIA PONZIANINA
VIA SALARA VECCHIA
VIA PERLEONE
VIA FILITTERIA
Walls
San Domenico
VIA DEL DUOMO
Largo M. Clemente
Duomo
Opera del Duomo
PIAZZA DEL DUOMO
Sant'Eufemia
Pinacoteca
PIAZZA D. MERCATO
CORSO MAZZINI
VIA D. MUNICIPIO
PIAZZA CAMPELLO
Rocca
VIA MAMELI
V. S. AGATA
Arco di Druso
Teatro Romano
PIAZZA LIBERTÀ
S. Ansano
Tourist Office
VIA D. PONTE
Ponte delle Torri
VIALE MATTEOTTI
Walls
Giardino Pubblico
VIA S. PAOLO
San Paolo
VIA S. CARLO
VIA ROMA
0
200 m
San Pietro
To Terni & Monteluco
N3

THE FESTIVAL DEI DUE MONDI

Hosting Italy's leading international arts festival, the **Festival dei Due Mondi**, has been a double-edged blessing for Spoleto – crowds and commercialism being the price it has had to pay for culture. Having already rejected thirty other Italian towns, the influential arts guru Giancarlo Menotti plumped for the town in 1958, attracted by its scenery, small venues and general good vibes. The ensuing jamboree is a great attraction if you're into music, dance or theatre, though the place forgoes a good part of its charm as a result. On top of the crowds, ticket prices for top companies and world-class performers can be off-putting, as can the jet-set, well-heeled cut of the audiences. Be warned too that while the festival's in progress you can expect packed hotels, madness in the restaurants and higher prices all round. At the same time there's an Edinburgh-type fringe and plenty of fellow travellers (plus lots of film, jazz, buskers and so on). Organisers, moreover, have recently looked to more avant-garde acts to recover the artistic edge of the festival's early days. So count on seeing some wacky shows, but be prepared for a possible fleecing in the process. Check out **tickets and information** from the **tourist office** on Piazza Libertà or the festival's own box office on Piazza del Duomo 9 (☎0743/28.120).

The upper town

There's really no single central piazza in Spoleto, but the place to head for is **Piazza Libertà**, local **bus terminal** and home to the town's tourist office. Here you are confronted by the much-restored first-century **Roman theatre** (daily 9am–1.30pm & 3–7pm; free), complete enough, if overshadowed by the gaudily painted buildings on all sides. The worst of these offenders, the church and convent of Sant'Agata, absorbed much of the stage area in the Middle Ages and houses a small **archaeological collection** of busts and stone fragments (same hours). The theatre stage, such as it is, is used for festival and other performances throughout the summer. Its past includes a grisly episode in 1319 when four hundred Guelph supporters were rounded up by the Spoletans and dumped on the stage with their throats cut; the corpses were then pushed into a pile and burnt.

Cutting into the adjoining Piazza della Fontana are more Roman remains, all far more humble than the vast wad of tourist blurb leads you to expect. Of the town's many arches from the period, the **Arco di Druso** (23 AD) straddling the entrance to the Piazza del Mercato is the only one not embedded in a wall. It was intended as a triumphal gateway to the old forum, and built to honour what must have been very minor campaign victories on the part of Drusus, son of Tiberius. The patched-up walls behind it are the city's oldest, built in the sixth century BC by the Umbrians, who otherwise are as mysterious and elusive as ever. To the right of the arch is what is described as a Roman **temple**, but unless you've a vivid imagination it's difficult to see it as anything other than a ditch. Pop into the adjacent church of **San Ansano** for a look at more of the temple, and the fresco-covered crypt, originally the home of sixth-century monks.

Nowhere do you get a better sense of Spoleto's market-town roots than in the homely **Piazza del Mercato** beyond, a fine opportunity to take in some colourful streetlife. Old women wash fruit and vegetables in a fountain, its crown embellished with a highly eccentric clock, the men drink in the bars and swap unintelligible stall-holders' gossip, and tourists make barely a dent in the proceedings. The *alimentari* on all sides are a cornucopia of goodies, with a definite bias towards truffles and sticky liqueurs (the *Amaro di Tartufo* guarantees a grim morning after).

Turning the corners of the attractive streets roundabouts, it's a short walk to the **Duomo**, whose facade of restrained elegance is one of the most memorable in the region. The careful balance of Romanesque and Renaissance elements is framed by a gently sloping piazza and lovely hanging gardens, but the broad background of sky and open countryside is what sets the seal on the whole thing. The church suffered like many in Italy from the desire of rich communities to make their wealth and power conspicuous, a desire usually realised by tearing the guts out of old churches and remodelling them in the latest style. This worked well on the thirteenth-century **facade** which has an arched portico tacked on in 1491, but less well in the interior where Pope Urban VIII's architect, Luigi Arrigucci, applied great dollops of Baroque midway through the seventeenth century. His "improvements", luckily, are eclipsed by the apse's superlative **frescoes** by the great Florentine artisit Fra' Lippo Lippi, dominated by his final masterpiece, a *Coronation of the Virgin* (1469).

He died shortly after their completion, the rumour being that he was poisoned for seducing the daughter of a local noble family, his position as a monk having had no bearing on his sexual appetite. The Spoletans, not too bothered by moral laxity, were delighted at having someone famous to put in their cathedral, being, as Vasari put it, "poorly provided with ornaments, above all with distinguished men," and so refused to send the dead artist back to Lorenzo di Medici, his Florentine patron. Interred in a **tomb** designed by his son, Filippino Lippi (now in the right transept), the corpse disappeared during restoration two centuries later, the popular theory being that it was spirited away by descendants of the compromised girl – a sort of vendetta beyond the grave.

You should also make a point of seeing the **Erioli Chapels** at the beginning of the right nave, primarily for a faded *Madonna and Child* (with Lago di Trasimeno in the background) by Pinturicchio (1497), and for the cruder frescoes in the adjoining chapel by the Sicilian artist Jacopo Santori. There's also a good **Cosmati marble floor** and the inevitable **icon**, which Barbarossa gave to the town in 1185 to try to make amends for having flattened it thirty years earlier.

The town's **museums** are minor and motley affairs, difficult to find and even harder to get into. The **Museo Civico** (10am–noon & 3–5pm, closed Tues; L2000) is at Piazza del Duomo 3, round the corner from the tiny and elegant nineteenth-century Teatro Caio Melisso. Amidst a less than absorbing collection of cannon-balls, sarcophagi, chimney breasts and other bits and pieces, only the *Lex Spoletina* merit a special mention, two Roman inscriptions which forbade the chopping down of trees in the sacred woods of **Monteluco**. The injunction must have worked because the forests, home to second-century hermits and later to Saint Francis, are still there, 8km east of the town. Take one of the hourly #9 buses from Piazza Libertà if you're not into the stiff walk, and head away from the hotel-restaurant complex and accompanying crowds into the footpaths that cross the woods. You don't have to walk far before you're alone. The views are great on a good day, and it's a welcome relief from the summer maelstrom down in Spoleto itself.

The **Pinacoteca** is stuck away in the farthest reaches of the Palazzo del Municipio, the town's council building (10am–1pm & 3–7pm; closed Tues; L3000). You're sold a ticket by a policeman from a very officious office to the right of the main entrance, and then have to wait for someone to show you around the gallery on the upper floor. The half dozen rooms are sumptuously decorated, and many of the paintings outstanding, though most are unlabelled. The best stuff is the early Umbrian work in the last of the rooms, particularly a couple of big canvases by a local follower of Perugino, **Lo Spagna**. If you're lucky enough to get an enthusiastic guide, he or she may show the remains of a Roman house nearby – admission included with the pinacoteca ticket.

The medieval town's most celebrated **church** is the twelfth-century **Sant'Eufemia**, architecturally unique in Umbria for its *matronei*, high-arched galleries above the side-naves which served the purpose of segregating women from the males in the main body of the church. It was built over the site of the eighth-century Lombard ducal palace, and appears to have been partly constructed from the remains of this and earlier Roman monuments; one or two of the completely mismatched columns are carved with distinctive Lombard motifs. The general dank solemnity of the place clearly points to an early foundation. As one of the region's Romanesque highlights it warrants a few minutes of attention – as long as you're lucky enough to find it open.

The Rocca, Ponte delle Torri and San Pietro

If you do nothing else in Spoleto you should take the short walk out to the **Ponte delle Torri**, the town's picture-postcard favourite and an astonishing piece of medieval engineering. It's best taken in as part of a circular walk around the base of the Rocca or on the longer trek out to San Pietro (see below). Within a minute of leaving shady gardens in Piazza Campello you suddenly find yourself in superb countryside, with a dramatic panorama across the Tessino gorge and south to the mountains of Castelmonte. (There's an informal little bar, on the left before the bend, to help you enjoy the views.)

The **Rocca**, everyone's idea of a cartoon castle, with towers, crenellations and sheer walls, was another in the chain of fortresses with which the tireless Cardinal Albornoz hoped to re-establish Church domination in central Italy, a primacy lost during the fourteenth-century papal exile to Avignon. It served until recently as a high-security prison – testimony to the skill of its medieval builders – and was home to, amongst others, Pope John Paul II's would-be assassin and leading members of the Red Brigade.

The **bridge** is a genuinely impressive affair, with a 240-metre span supported by ten eighty-metre arches that have been used as a launching pad by jilted lovers for six centuries. Designed by the Gubbian architect, Gattapone, who was also responsible for Gubbio's Palazzo dei Consoli, it was initially planned as an aqueduct to bring water from Monteluco, replacing an earlier Roman causeway whose design Gattopone probably borrowed and enlarged upon. In time it also became used as an escape from the Rocca when Spoleto was under siege. The remains of what used to be a covered passageway connecting the two are still visible straggling down the hillside.

It's well worth crossing the bridge and picking up the footpath that contours round into peaceful countryside within a few hundred metres, giving great views back over the gorge. Alternatively, turn right on the road and make for the church of **San Pietro**, whose facade beckons from a not-too-distant hillside. If the idea of another church doesn't appeal you can easily double back to town on the circular Via della Rocca.

Though the walk to San Pietro is a longish one (2km), it's pleasantly shady with some good glimpses of Spoleto; and far nicer, in any case, than walking through the streets in the southern part of the town. The only thing to look out for on the country road (no pavements) are crazed Italians taking the bends too fast. The church would be otherwise unremarkable were it not for the splendid **sculptures** adorning its facade. Taken with Maitini's bas-reliefs in Orvieto, they are the best Romanesque carvings in Umbria, partly Lombard in their inspiration, and drawing variously on the Gospels and medieval legend for their complicated narrative and symbolic purpose. A particularly juicy scene to look out for includes the Death of a Sinner (left series, second from the top) where the Archangel Michael abandons the sinner to a couple of demons who bind and torture him before bringing in the burning oil to finish the job. Fourth panel from the top (right series) shows a wolf disguised as a friar before a fleeing ram – a dig at dodgy monastic morals.

Practicalities

The Spoleto **tourist office** is on Piazza Libertà (daily 9am–1pm & 4–7.30pm; ☎0743/220.311). Cheap **rooms** are hard to come by when the festival's in full swing. *Pensione dell'Angelo* is central, above a busy trattoria at Via Arco del Druso 25 (☎0743/222.385; ④), but small. Otherwise try *Pensione Aurora* off Piazza Libertà, Via dell'Apollinare 4 (☎0743/220.315; ⑤), or the cheap rooms above the *Panciolle* restaurant at Via del Duomo 3–4. The lower town is very much a second choice, but there are more likely to be rooms available, and it's still handy for the medieval highlights. Addresses to try here are *Fracassa*, Via Focaroli 15 (☎0743/221.177; ③), and the noisier but recently renovated *Anfiteatro*, Via dell'Anfiteatro 14 (☎0743/49.853; ③).

Campsites are more promising. Closest is *Camping Monteluco*, (☎0743/220.358) behind San Pietro and an easy downhill walk from Piazza Libertà; open from May to September, it (officially) only has places for twenty tents. The all-year *Il Girasole* (☎0743/51.335) in the village of PETROGNANO (hourly buses from the station) is a bigger and flashier affair, with swimming pool and tennis courts (open all year).

Bargain **meals** of school-dinner quality and quantity are served up in *Ristorante Economico*, Via San Carlo 7 – between Piazza Libertà and San Pietro. There are a couple of nameless cheapies in Piazza del Mercato, at nos. 29 and 10, both catering mainly to Spoleto's workmen and market traders. The best basic trattoria is *Il Panciolle* (see above); for something more special, go to *Sabatini* at Corso Mazzini 54 or the slightly cheaper *Pentagramma*, signed off Piazza Libertà at Via T. Martini 4.

The Valnerina and Norcia

The **VALNERINA** is the most beautiful part of Umbria but is hard to get to without your own transport. Strictly translated as the "little valley of the Nera", it effectively refers to the whole eastern part of the region, a self-contained area of high mountains, poor communications, steep wooded valleys, upland villages and vast stretches of barren nothingness. Wolves still roam the summit ridges and are to be protected by a proposed (but long awaited) regional Nature Reserve. The area is a genuine "forgotten corner", deserted farms everywhere bearing witness to a century of continuous emigration.

Six **buses** daily run from Spoleto station to Norcia (1hr 15min), calling at PIEDIPATERNO (2 daily connections to MONTELEONE), BORGO CERRETO, SERRAVALLE and villages in between (timetables from the tourist office in Spoleto). Because roads are scarce, what few there are tend to be busy, so you shouldn't have too many problems **hitching**.

The beautiful and tortuous N395 road from Spoleto is virtually the only access point until you hit the "main" SS209 and the more pastoral run up the Nera Valley towards Norcia. Mountains roundabout are around 1500m high, with excellent walking, creeping up as you move eastwards to about 2500m in the **Monti Sibillini**. It's difficult to explore with any sort of plan (unless you stick to the Nera), and the best approach is follow your nose, poking into small valleys, tracing high country lanes to remote hamlets.

More deliberately, you could make for VALLO DI NERA, most archetypal of the **fortified villages** that pop up along the Lower Nera. Medieval TRIPONZO is a natural focus of communications, little more than a quaint staging post and fortified tower (and a better target than modernish CERRETO nearby). MONTELEONE is the only place of any size for miles, with a fine church, and popular with trippers.

CASCIA figures large on the map, but is disappointing in actuality, only recommendable to pilgrims in search of **Saint Rita**, whose presence – enshrined in the stupendously ugly twentieth-century **Basilica** – dominates both the new and earthquake-damaged hill-town. Rita's cult is enormous in Italy, particularly amongst women, who've virtually adopted her as their uncrowned patron saint. There's not much a woman can suffer that Rita didn't come through, which is the main reason for her "Everywoman" appeal and why she's sometimes known as the "saint of the impossible". Apparently you invoke Saint Rita when an "ordinary" miracle isn't enough. A poor child of aged parents, she endured a forced marriage, followed by eighteen years of mistreatment from an alcoholic husband, who died in a brawl weeks after repenting his evil ways. Both sons died trying to avenge their father, leaving Rita alone in the world and, as a widow, unable to become a nun. A relaxation of convent rules did eventually allow her to take holy orders, a turnaround held up as one of her "impossible" miracles.

Norcia

Small, stolid **NORCIA**, a mountain retreat if ever there were one, is the only place of any size or substance in the Valnerina. Noted on one hand as the birthplace of **Saint Benedict** – founder of western monasticism – and on the other as the producer of Italy's top **salami**, its air of shadowy desolation and low, sturdy houses (built as protection against earthquakes) are a world away from the pastoral, fairy-tale cities to the west. It's friendly and appealing, though, if you don't mind the leaden atmosphere, and if transport allows, it can be the base for some good trips into neighbouring territory, particularly the famed **Piano Grande**. A big new road over the mountains to the Marche looks set to open up the area – good news for local employment, which is scarce, but probable doom for the environment. Hang-gliders and winter sports enthusiasts are pouring in, another mixed blessing.

Taking in the town itself doesn't detain you long. Most of the action is in the central **Piazza San Benedetto**, site of the Roman forum and presided over by a statue of Benedict. The duomo you can largely forget about – its facade aside – destroyed by several earthquakes (the last big one was in 1979), and patched up to look like nothing on earth. The **Castellina** is more captivating: a papal fortress, full of gaunt medieval echoes, it's a strange bedfellow for the church of **San Benedetto**, which supposedly was built over the saint's birthplace, but more likely raised from the ruins of an earlier Roman temple. Inside there are a few paltry frescoes, nothing more. There's a tiny **tourist office** at the end of the small arched gallery to the right of the church.

Meat-eaters would be daft not to try the deservedly famous pork products. Anything that can be done to a pig, the Norcians apparently do, and supposedly better than anyone else. Even today you still see butchers in other parts of Italy called "un nurcino", after the town, a measure of its widespread notoriety. If finances stretch you could indulge in the area's prized black **truffle**. Several thousand lire will buy a light dusting over your tagliatelle. The season runs from January to April.

Cheapest **hotels** are the central nine-roomed *Da Benito*, Via Marconi 5 (☎0743/816.670; ④) and the bigger (and slightly cheaper) *Monastero S. Antonio*, Via dei Vergini 13 (☎0743/816.657; ④). The three-star *Grotta Azzurra*, Via Alfieri 12 (☎0743/816.513; ⑥), is an excellent hotel with a very good, relatively inexpensive **restaurant**, set in a medieval banqueting hall complete with suits of armour.

Around Norcia – the Piano Grande and Preci

The eerie, expansive **Piano Grande**, twenty kilometres to the east of Norcia, is definitely one of Umbria's sights, an extraordinary prairie ringed by bare, whaleback mountains and unbroken for miles and miles by tree, hedge or habitation. It's much photographed – especially in spring when it's ablaze with poppies – and was used by Zeffirelli as a setting in his Franciscan film *Brother Sun, Sister Moon*. The desperately isolated village of **CASTELLUCCIO** hangs above it at around 1400m; as the curious trickle in, it's no longer the sole reserve of shepherds, but remains an unspoilt base and the ideal starting point for any number of **mountain walks**. (Get hold of the 1:50,000 *Kompass* map no. 666 to plan routes.) Rough **camping** is no problem, and there are two one-star hotel–restaurants convenient for the plain: *La Sibilla*, in Castelluccio itself (☎0743/870.113; ④), and the newly renovated *Canapine* (☎0743/816.508) in FORCA CANAPINE, at the southern end of the Piano Grande. You might also find rooms above the *Taverna* bar, a hundred metres from the *Sibilla*. If you can't get out here, the smaller **Piano di Santa Scolastica**, due south of Norcia, will give you a watered-down idea of what you're missing.

Another worthwhile trip, if you're short of time to spend in aimless exploration, is the road north to **PRECI** and thus to VISSO in the Marche. Walled and castled Preci was known throughout Europe in the sixteenth century as a school for surgeons, their main trade being removal of kidney stones. However, they had a more notorious sideline – castrating young boys who were foolish enough to show operatic potential. A kilometre above nearby PIEDIVALLE is the beautifully sited **Abbey of San Eutizio**, one of the cradles of the Benedictine movement. Now only a twelfth-century Romanesque church stands on the site, but in its day the community of monks held sway over more than a hundred castles and local churches.

ORVIETO AND THE SOUTH

Towards its southern edge Umbria loses its pastoral mystical character and begins to feel like a flat foretaste of Rome and Lazio. **Terni**, its main focus, is a grim industrial city and little more than a watershed for regional transportation, though less than half an hour to the north are the classic hill-towns of **Orvieto** and **Todi**, too popular with tourists for their own good, perhaps, but still essential viewing. **Rail** is the key to getting about, with the single-track **FCU** branching off to Todi and thence to Perugia, complementing the **FS** line which runs down from Spoleto to connect with the Rome–Florence route at Orte. Trains from Terni via Rieti are perfect if you intend to head south into the Abruzzi. Good road links follow almost identical routes, and if you're hitching, the big junction with the AI at **Orte** – an obvious gateway in and out of the region – offers great opportunities for lifts in all directions.

Terni and around

TERNI was the unlikely birthplace of one of the world's most famous saints, **Saint Valentine**, bishop of the town until his martyrdom in 273 and now entombed in his personal basilica at San Valentino, a village two kilometres to the southwest. A less romantic city, however, would be hard to imagine. Terni's important arms and steel industries made it a natural target for Allied bombing in 1944, and eighty percent of the town was reduced to rubble, including, sadly, the best part of its Roman and medieval heritage. Rebuilding replaced what was lost with a grey grid-iron city straight out of post-war Eastern Europe; it also put the arms industry back on its feet – the gun which shot Kennedy was made here – and though the town no longer lives up to its nineteenth-century nickname of "the Manchester of Italy", high-tech weaponry and the stench of chemicals aren't the most enticing of prospects. The **tourist office** (Mon–Sat 9am–1pm & 4–7pm), should you need it, is at Viale Battisti 5 – take Viale della Stazione from the station, and Viale Battisti is 300m up, on the right.

The Marmore waterfall

The best place to make for locally is the **Cascate delle Marmore** (train or bus from Terni), created by the Romans in 271 BC when they diverted the River Velino into the Nera during drainage of marshlands to the south. The highest waterfall in Europe (at 165m), it was boosted by the damming of Lake Piediluco in 1930s to satisfy the demands of industry for cheap hydroelectric power. Pictures of the falls in full spate adorn most Umbrian tourist offices, but what they don't tell you is that the water can be turned off at the flick of a switch (in favour of electric turbines), leaving a none-too-spectacular trickle for the expectant tourist. No two sources agree on when exactly the water is likely to be switched on, but the best chances of finding it running seem to be weekend lunchtimes and evenings when there's often a *son et lumière*. From July 15 to August 11 it also does the business on weekdays, between 5 and 6.30pm. The observation platforms are below on the SS209 and above in the village of Marmore, with a steep path between the two. The green and luxuriant setting, tumbling water and the acres of gleaming polished marble add up to a spectacular show – shame about the factories round the corner, though. There's a **campsite** at Marmore, open from May to September (☎0744/67.198).

Lago di Piediluco

If you want to carry on up the Velino Valley, **Lago di Piediluco** makes an attractive target. Surrounded by steep and thickly wooded hills, it's Umbria's prettiest lake, something like a miniature version of one of the northern Alpine lakes. Very dark and deep, the water's a bit on the cold side for swimming (and in places unsafe), though it's a big sailing and canoeing centre. The **station** is at the western end, some distance from the town of **PIEDILUCO** itself (bus from Terni), but perfect if you want to put up a tent on the southern, less-visited shore, or walk the scenic minor road on this shore to Monte Caperno. There's a quay here with boats to and from Piediluco, as well as a famous four-second **echo**, constantly and enthusiastically being tested out. Piediluco is picturesque – with the lake on its doorstep it doesn't have to try too hard – but is filled by people escaping from Terni at the weekends. This said, if you're a fishing or watersports fan, or just need a quiet spot for your tent, you may want to go to ground for a couple of days. **Accommodation** can be tight: try the two-star *Lido* (☎0744/368.354; ⑤) on the lake shore at Piazza Bonanni 2, also a popular restaurant. There's a big and usually packed **campsite**, *Il Lago* (May 15–Sept 15; ☎0744/68.371). If Piediluco seems too frenetic, you could always push on to neighbouring CORNELLO or CAPOLOZZA.

To the Abbazia di San Pietro in Valle

There are further worthwhile excursions from Terni, particularly if you're making for Norcia and the Valnerina from the south rather than Spoleto. The only route is the SS209, which follows the mountainous Nera Valley almost to its head. Buses make the run up to TRIPONZO, but the valley's highlight is the Abbazia di San Pietro in Valle, 18km from Terni. You could, if tempted, stop off beforehand at ARRONE and MONTEFRANCO, the first of several spectacularly sited **fortress villages** lining the valley. The Valnerina, now desolate and sparsely populated, was once the strategic and bustling hub of communications between the Kingdom of Naples and the Dukedom of Spoleto, and later a bone of contention between the Church and Imperial armies – hence the castles.

FERENTILLO, last village before the abbey, sprawls across two barren hillsides, guarded by twin fourteenth-century towers; it merits a brief stop only if the idea of **mummies** is appealing. Grotesquely propped up in the crypt of San Stefano (signed off the main road), these bizarre figures have been preserved by dry sandy soils and dessicating exposure to wind from south-facing windows. They include two French prisoners hung during the Napoleonic wars, a hapless Chinese couple from the last century who came to Italy for their honeymoon and died of cholera instead, and a pile of cheerfully leering skulls.

Much more enjoyable is to continue five kilometres up the valley to the **Abbazia di San Pietro in Valle** (Tues–Sat 9am–12.30pm & 2–5pm; free), the real point of the exercise if you're not passing through simply for the scenery. Founded by the Lombard Duke Faroaldo II, who retired to the monastic life after being deposed by his son in 720, it was amongst the most powerful religious houses in Umbro-Romano, controlling vast tracts of land and dominating the lives of thousands of people. It's set high on the hillside near a thickly wooded cleft, the first impression being of a dull blockhouse affair, with nothing to hint at the splendour of the Lombard and Byzantine art inside. The faded **frescoes** (1190) which cover the body of the main church are the first tentative attempts to create a distinctively Italian art and move away from the stylised influence of Byzantine painting, an influence that nonetheless was to prevail until the advent of Pietro Cavallini, Cimabue and Giotto a century later. The **altar**, beautifully set off by the rose-coloured stone and rich Romanesque display all around, is a rare and important example of Lombard sculpture, carved with what look like pagan, almost Celtic figures and motifs. To each side are well-preserved Roman sarcophagi, backed by a profusion of gorgeously coloured frescoes. A doorway (not always open) to the left leads to the twelfth-century **campanile**, a Lombard import of a type common in Rome and Lazio and distinguished by fragments and reliefs salvaged from the eighth-century church. There's also a faultless double-tiered **cloister** from the twelfth century and a pricey restaurant.

By following the SS209 past the walled, medieval village of SCHEGGINO you can pick up the Spoleto road into the Valnerina, a route covered earlier on in the chapter. If you need to stay locally, Scheggino's *Albergo del Ponte*, Via del Borgo 17 (☎075/61.131; ⑤), is the best bet. Even if you're just passing through, give the excellent restaurant a try – the trout dishes are superb.

Carsulae

The building of the Via Flaminia in 220 BC between Rome and Ancona cemented Umbria's strategic importance as the crossroads of central Italy. Staging-posts and fully fledged colonies sprang up along its route, turning into modern-day Narni, Terni, Spoleto, and Spello. Some settlements, however, such as **CARSULAE**, 15km north of Terni, were subsequently abandoned in the wake of earthquakes and civil war. In its day this particular pile of stones was known as the Pompeii of central Italy, and both Tacitus and Pliny the Younger praised its beauty.

The surrounding plain, though rustic and peaceful, has little real interest, but the excavated remains are reasonably impressive. The site – the largest Roman site in Umbria – is dominated by a church, **San Damiano**, made from materials filched from the ruins (other stones and precious marbles went to build local houses), behind which runs a stretch of the original Via Flaminia, complete with grooves made by carts and chariots, part of the arched northern gate, tombs, baths, wells, an amphitheatre and all the other trappings of an ex-Roman town.

Narni and around

It's an easy half-hour hop on the train from Terni to **NARNI**, with a hilltop site jutting into the Nera Valley on a majestic spur and crowned by another of Albornoz's formidable papal fortresses. Commanding one end of a steep gorge (about ten minutes of fairly spectacular rail travel), it was once the gateway into Umbria, the last post before the Tiber Valley and the undefended road to Rome. However, while the town retains a fine medieval character, the views from its heights are marred by steel and chemical works around NARNI SCALO, the new town that's grown up in the valley below. The trick is to keep your gaze firmly fixed on the gorge side of the walls and pretend the factories don't exist.

The heart of the **old town** (bus from the station) has all the standard fittings: the medieval piazzas, the warren of streets, a modest art gallery, the usual crop of Romanesque churches, and a huge *Rocca*, currently being restored. There's a **Roman bridge** on the outskirts, the subject of considerable local hype. Goethe arrived in Narni in the middle of the night and was peeved not to have seen it; he was only missing a solitary arch in the middle of the river – just as easily viewed from the train.

In what's an appealing but relatively low-key centre, things revolve around the narrow **Piazza dei Priori**, where pride of place goes to the fourteenth-century **Palazza dei Priori**, unremarkable except for a fountain and graceful **loggia** designed by the Gubbian architect Gattapone. The gaunt and somewhat eccentric building opposite is the Palazzo del Podestà, cobbled together by amalgamating three town houses and adding some token decoration. The thirteenth-century Romanesque sculptures above the main door are worth a glance, and there's a small **Pinacoteca** on the first floor whose main feature is a superlative and much-copied canvas by Ghirlandaio. The bulk of its paintings are in the process of being moved to the gallery in the ex-church of San Domenico, just a minute away in Via Mazzini, where there are key works by Benozzo Gozzoli and Fiorenzo di Lorenzo, plus fourteenth- to sixteenth-century frescoes removed from churches in surrounding villages. The walk down to the gallery offers a chance to look at the tiny and easily overlooked church of **Santa Maria in Pensole**, unaltered since 1175 – you can still see the date above the door – and adorned across the width of its facade with a marvellous carved frieze.

The twelfth-century **Duomo** merits a brief mention, chiefly because its front steps are where the town hangs out. Inside, the Cosmati marble floor and a recently discovered ninth-century mosaic of Christ don't give much cause to linger.

There's no real reason for staying overnight in Narni, but should you want to there's a collection of cheap but uninspiring **rooms** around the station, and a **campsite** out of town at Monte del Sole (April–Oct; ☎0744/796.336). For a first-class meal, try the lovely *La Loggia* restaurant in Vicolo del Comune, just off Piazza dei Priori. The **tourist office** is at Piazza dei Priori 12 (Mon–Sat 9am–1pm & 3.30–7pm).

Amelia

AMELIA, 11km northwest of Narni and plonked on top of a sugar-loaf hilltop, is by far the most tempting local excursion if the ruins don't appeal. Though not big on monuments, it's a delightful and unvisited town, noted mainly for its extraordinary **cyclopean walls**, claimed as some of the oldest and mightiest in Italy. Supported by their own weight and comprising vast polygonal blocks up to seven metres across, they reach a height of over twenty metres in places and date back, according to early Roman historians, to the Umbrian settlement of the eleventh century BC. Most of the town's churches were ruined in the nineteenth century, and art's thin on the ground – San Giacomo's **double cloister** and a **tomb** by **Agostino di Duccio** are the only highlights – but Amelia's charm is the typically Umbrian mixture of good views, medieval streets and lovely countryside close at hand. The local speciality is a tooth-rotting combination of white figs, chocolate and crushed nuts, but for more substantial fare there are two good **restaurants**, both with **rooms** to rent – *Anita*, Via Roma 31 (☎0744/982.146; ⑤), and *Le Colonne*, Via Roma 191 (0744/983.529; ④).

If you have wheels, the run on to Orvieto along the backroads is a treat: plenty of oak forests and fine walks, and the chance to catch one of Umbria's Romanesque highlights, the twelfth-century church of **Santa Maria Assunata** at LUGNANO IN TEVERINA.

Otrícoli

OTRÍCOLI, 15km south of Narni, is almost the last town in Umbria and a reasonable miniature of all the region's hill-towns. Its medieval delights, though, are eclipsed by the remains of Roman **Otriculum**, a ramshackle collection of ruins within easy walking distance of the village. To reach them get on the main road that bypasses the village, head downhill for two hundred metres and take the signposted track that strikes off right towards the Tiber. So far no more than a trickle of tourists visits the colony – still largely unexcavated and evocatively draped in clinging undergrowth – but plans by the state to make them the centre of a big archaeological park mean they're headed for the big time.

Unusually, the settlement has no walls, mainly because it was more a pleasure garden than a defensive site, built as a sort of holiday village for Rome's hoi polloi, who travelled up from the capital by boat on the then still navigable Tiber. Turner stopped off to paint a picture (now in the Clore gallery), and in the sixteenth century Montaigne described the spot as "infinitely pleasant", though it probably won't stay that way for much longer. You can find **rooms** up in Ortrícoli at the *Pensione Umbra*, Via Roma 18 (☎0744/719.112; ④).

Todi

TODI is one of the emerging Umbrian hill-towns, at heart still a thriving and insular agricultural centre, but recently a favoured trendy retreat for Rome's arts and media types. In the way of these things the tourists can't be far behind, but neither fact should deter you from making a day trip: few places beat it for sheer location and fairy-tale medievalism. With a stunning and extremely daunting position, it makes a highly inviting prospect from below, though you'd have to have some sort of death wish to tackle the approaches on foot or on a bike. Once up, it feels as if Todi, high and isolated, cares little for the rest of the twentieth century – at least for the time being.

Getting there, and sussing out how to fit it into an itinerary, are likely to be your biggest problems. Basically you come either from Terni on the hourly *FCU* train or from Perugia, again by *FCU* or on one of the regular buses which stop below the town by the church of Santa Maria della Consolazione. Moving on, in addition to the train, there's the option of a straightforward hitch or a daily bus to Orvieto. Todi's **stations** (there are two) are both in the middle of nowhere, and buses to the centre don't always tie in with the trains. Ponte Naia, 5km distant, is marginally more convenient, but the uphill walk is a bit of a slog, so you're probably better off putting your thumb out.

The Town

The central **Piazza del Popolo** is why most people come here: just about every guidebook describes it as the most perfect medieval piazza in Italy, and it's every inch what it's claimed to be, though the cars detract and the tone's a bit more gaunt and austere than you're led to expect. The **Duomo** at the far end, atop a broad flight of steps, is the main feature – a meeting point of the last of the Romanesque and the first of the Gothic forms filtering up from France in the early fourteenth century. The square, three-tiered **facade** is inspired simplicity; just a sumptuous rose window (1520) and ornately carved doorway to embellish the pinky weathered marble – the classic example of a form found all over Umbria. Inevitably the interior is less impressive. There's some delicate nineteenth-century stained glass in the arched nave on the right, and a good altarpiece by Giannicolo di Paolo (a follower of Perugino), but an appalling sixteenth-century copy of Michelangelo's *Last Judgement* defaces the back wall, putting everything else in its dismal shadow. The strikingly carved **choir** (1530) – of incredible delicacy and precision – is the region's best, with panels at floor level near the front depicting the tools used to carve the piece.

Back in the piazza, the other key buildings are the three **public palaces**, squared off near the duomo in deliberately provocative fashion as an expression of medieval civic pride – definitely trying to put one over on the Church. The adjoining Palazzo del Capitano (1290) and adjacent Palazzo del Popolo (begun 1213) are most prominent, thanks mainly to the stone staircase which looks like it's been the scene of a thousand B-movie sword fights. Several films have actually been shot in Todi, lured by its relative proximity to Cinecittà and scenographic "authenticity". Most notable was the doomed *Cleopatra* – hence the yellowing photographs of a pouting Liz Taylor in some of the bars.

The Palazzo del Capitano houses the town's small **art gallery**, but it's been closed for "reordering" since 1977 and shows no signs of reopening. Hard to know why because it only has a couple of dozen paintings. More of a loss is the **Etrusco-Romano** museum in the same building, by all accounts a small but interesting collection, but likewise closed to the public.

The **Palazzo dei Priori** (1293–1337) is the southernmost building in the square, with all the various crenellations, battlements and mullioned windows of the other palaces, but with the difference they've just been restored. It's been the seat of all the town's various rulers and today is still the town hall; if you can look like you're on council business you should be able to peep inside. Best place to enjoy the streetlife is from the **bar** down on its right-hand side, more of a locals' local than the flashy newcomer halfway down the piazza (but which does do a good line in sandwiches).

There's not much more to Todi, but what there is is likable. Streets to the right of the duomo are quiet and dozy and worth a wander, though the single most celebrated thing in the town after the piazza is a church, **San Fortunato**. Set above some half-hearted gardens a very short stroll from the centre, it's an enormous thing given the size of the town – testimony to Todi's medieval wealth and importance. The squat, messy and clearly unfinished facade, an amalgam of Romanesque and Gothic styles, reflects the time it took to build (1292–1462) and at first glance doesn't exactly raise expectations. A florid **Gothic doorway** of arched swirls and carved craziness, however, is the first of several surprises, second of which is the enormous interior, recently highlighted by cleaning and several dazzling coats of whitewash. For once it's a light, airy and pleasing sort of size – a legacy of its Romanesque origins – rather than the aircraft-hangar dimensions that church builders seemed to indulge in for their own sake.

It marks the pinnacle of the Umbrian tradition for large vaulted churches, a style based on the smaller and basic "barn churches" common in Tuscany, which were distinguished by a single, low-pitched roof and naves and aisles of equal height. (San Domenico in Perugia is another example.) Also interesting is the increasing use of side-chapels, a habit picked up from Catalonia and southern France in the thirteenth century and made necessary by the rising demand for daily Masses as the Franciscans became a more ministering order.

There's another good **choir,** heavier and with more hints of the Baroque than the one in the duomo, as well as a few scant patches of Sienese fresco. The fresco by **Masolino di Panicale** in the sixth chapel on the right is supposed to be the best painting in the town and a good example of this rare painter's work, but these days it's in such a bad state (restoration notwithstanding) that you could easily walk past without noticing it. Some lovely **cloisters** to the rear (outside and to the right) round off a distinctive and worthwhile church.

Which is more than can be said of **Santa Maria della Consolazione**, considered the town's big draw to judge by the way it's plastered over all the tourist literature. Ninety-nine years in the making, it's a late-Renaissance effort (finished in 1607) probably built on a plan by Bramante, architect of Saint Peter's, and claimed by some to be the way he would have liked the Rome church to turn out. Victorian writers called it the best Renaissance church in Italy (pretty close to saying the best in the world). It's worth a look to judge for yourself, but certainly not a special journey.

Your time could be more enjoyably spent taking a siesta in the rambling **Giardino Pubblico**, full of shady nooks and narrow pathways, and a cut above the normal town plot. There's also a kids' playground and a very small **Rocca**, both far less noteworthy than the views, which are extensive, though usually hazy. The gardens are best tackled via the stony track to the right of San Fortunato, less of a sweat than the path which comes up from Piazza Oberdan.

Todi's tourist offerings are soon exhausted, but if you want to go the whole hog, check the so-called **niches** in Piazza del Vecchio Mercato, all that's left of the Roman colony. The town's proud of them, but they don't amount to much: four big and slightly overgrown arches of completely unknown purpose. Two minutes' walk down the lane in the lowest corner of the piazza brings you to the tiny **San Carlo** (1020), an ancient Lombard chapel well off the beaten track that's all too often locked to protect a set of frescoes by Lo Spagna. A few metres beyond the church, and next to a crumbling flower-strewn arbour, is the **Fonte Scarnabecco** (1241), an unusual arched fountain that's now all but redundant, but the town's lifeblood and social meeting place before piped water. During your wanderings look out for the **three sets of walls**, concentric rings that mark Todi's Umbrian, Roman and medieval limits. They're seen to best effect on Via Matteotti.

Practicalities

Todi is still not really geared up to deal with visitors and the **tourist office**, Piazza del Popolo 38 (daily 9am–1pm & 4–7pm; closed Sun afternoon in winter; ☎075/894.3062), seems a little surprised that anyone should want information. The office also houses **telephone** booths and bus timetables. **Rooms** are in very short supply, especially during the increasingly popular Todi Festival (first ten days of Sept). Most central and cheapest is the *Zodiaco*, Via del Crocefisso 23 (☎075/882.625; ④), one minute east of Porta Romana. Ten minutes' walk straight down the main road from Porta Romana brings you to the *Tuder*, Via Maestà dei Lombardi 13 (☎075/882.184; ⑥), an overpriced and functional place in an uninspiring spot. A short distance beyond it is the better located but rather posh *Villa Luisa*, Via A.Cortesi 147 (☎075/884.8571; ⑥).

The town's most enjoyable **restaurant** is the *Umbra*, behind the tourist office; prices are high and service can be slapdash, but the panorama from the terrace makes it all worthwhile; in season, book to be sure of an outside table (☎075/882.390). Cheaper alternatives include the excellent and unpretentious *Cavour* at Via Cavour 21 and the basic *Pizzeria-Rosticceria* off Corso Cavour in Piazza B. d'Alviano, a hundred metres from Piazza del Popolo.

Deruta and the Tiber Valley

North of Todi, the Tiber Valley broadens out into a flat plain edged with low hills and dotted with light industry. It's not somewhere you'll want to spend a lot of time, but there are one or two things worth catching if you're in no hurry to get to Perugia (though MARSCIANO, the area's main town, certainly isn't one of them).

Instead try to take in some of the hill-villages along the route – almost any you choose will boast a **Romanesque church**. Most are built over the graves of early monks and martyrs, the Tiber and Naia valleys having been amongst the earliest to be colonised by Christians fleeing Roman persecution, and thus the springboard of Umbria's powerful monastic tradition. The most rewarding churches are those you come upon by accident, in crumbling hamlets or in the midst of the ilex woods that blanket surrounding hills, but if you prefer to plan a visit the following are a cut above the rest: Viepri, Villa di San Faustino, Santa Maria in Partano, San Teranzano and the Abbazia di San Fidenzo.

If you don't get to the peripheral villages, **Madonna dei Bagni** is the one church on the main N3 bis that's definitely worth a look. Its walls are covered with hundreds of votive tiles left by pilgrims over 300 years, making a unique social document and occasionally wacky insight into the peculiarities of religious belief. Day-to-day life in the fields, the insides of houses, transport (from horse to carriage to car), clothes and so on are represented almost as cartoons, though the most entertaining tiles are those offered as thanks for "miraculous" escapes from dangerous and not so dangerous corners – a fall from a cow, a bite from a donkey, fire, flood and famine. A hundred tiles were stolen in 1980, so opening times are curtailed as a result. The best time to try is Saturday morning (when it's not unknown for coach parties to show up); otherwise ask at the tourist office in Deruta, 2km up the road.

Deruta

The town of **DERUTA** is best known for its **ceramics** and seems to be devoted to nothing else. Some of the stuff is mass-produced trash, and some pieces so big you'd need a trailer to get them home, but most is beautiful – handmade, handpainted, and by general consent, Italy's best. The Romans worked local clay, but it was the discovery of distinctive blue and yellow glazes in the fifteenth century, allied with the Moorish-influenced designs of southern Spain, that put the town on the map. Some fifty workshops traded as far afield as Britain, and pieces from the period have found their way into most of the world's major museums. Designs these days are mainly copies, with little original work, though it's still very much the place for browsing and buying if you're serious about this sort of thing. Avoid the roadside stalls and head for the workshops of the new town for best choice and prices.

The **old town** on the hill isn't particularly compelling, but there's a mildly interesting **Museo-Pinocoteca** (9am–1pm, closed Sun; L2000) alongside the tourist office in Piazza dei Consoli. Highlights of the three small rooms downstairs are paintings by Nicolò Alunno and Fiorenzo di Lorenzo, but most sections, not surprisingly, are given over to ceramics, largely unremarkable except for a **tiled floor** (1524) lifted wholesale from the town's parish church.

Torgiano

TORGIANO, 8km north, is the last worthwhile stop before Perugia. It's a fairly dull town, but home to Umbria's finest **wines**, all of them produced by Giorgio Lungarotti, one of the new breed of Italian producers. A self-made man, and now something of a national celebrity, he's put together an unexpectedly interesting **wine museum** in Via Garibaldi (daily 9am–noon & 3–7pm; L2000), a varied and comprehensive look at every aspect of viticulture and the best non-liquid reason for a visit. Wines to look out for (and they're not all cheap) include *Rubesco*, *Torre di Giano*, *Chardonnay* and *Castel Grifone*.

Orvieto

ORVIETO, out on a limb from the rest of Umbria, is perfectly placed between Rome and Florence to serve as an historical picnic for tour operators. Tourists flood into the town in their millions, drawn by the **Duomo** – one of the greatest Gothic buildings in Italy. But once its facade and Signorelli's frescoes have been admired, the town's not as exciting as guides and word of mouth make out. This is partly to do with the gloominess of the dark volcanic rock (tufa) from which it's built, and, more poetically, because it harbours something of the characteristic brooding of Etruscan towns. (It was one of the twelve-strong federation of Etruscan cities.) Two thousand years on, it's not difficult to detect a more laid-back atmosphere in the cities east of the Tiber – sunnier and easier-going chiefly because they were founded by the Umbrians, a sunnier and easier-going people. All the same Orvieto is likable, the duomo unmissable, and the rest of the town good for an enjoyable couple of hours. And there's always its renowned white **wine** if you're stuck with time on your hands.

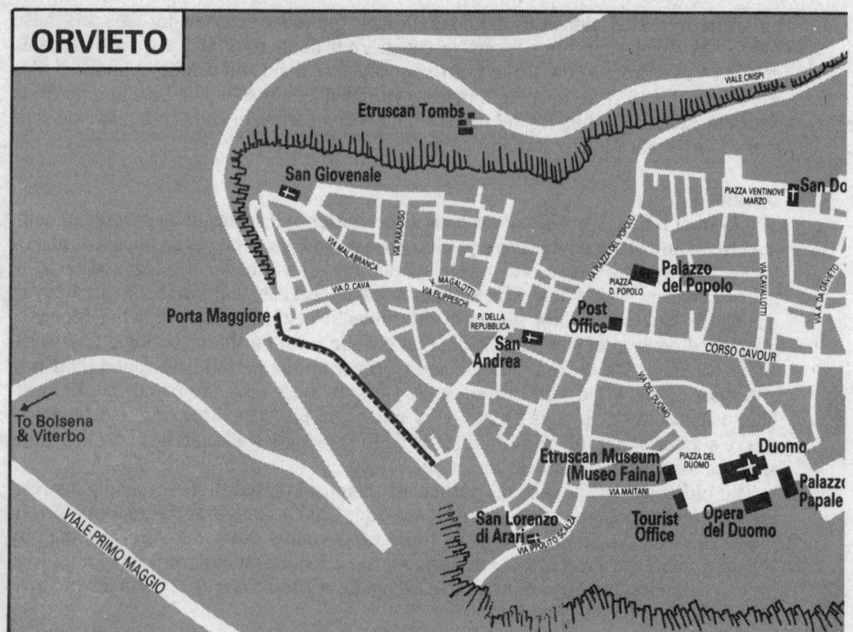

Arrival

First impressions of Orvieto from afar tend to be the ones that linger; its position is almost as remarkable and famous as its cathedral. The town, rising 300m sheer from the valley floor, sits on a tabletop plug of volcanic lava, one of four such remnants in the vicinity. It starts to look fairly average again from the dismal town around the station, but hit the twisting three-kilometre road up to the old centre and you begin to get a sense of its drama and one-off weirdness. If you arrive by train the **#1 bus** makes the regular trip from the **station** to Piazza XXIX Marzo (buy two tickets at the platform bar – one for the return leg). Local bus tickets are also valid for the old water-powered funicular from the station forecourt to Piazza Cahen. Inter-town buses take you directly to Piazza Cahen or Piazza della Repubblica, depending on the service.

The Duomo

Burckhardt described Orvieto's duomo as "the greatest and richest polychrome monument in the world", while Pope Leo XIII called it "the Golden Lily of Italian cathedrals", adding that on the Day of Judgement it would float up to heaven carried by its own beauty.

According to a tradition fostered by the Church, it was built to celebrate the so-called **Miracle of Bolsena** (1263), an event centred on a Bohemian priest travelling to Rome to shake off an heretical disbelief in transubstantiation – the idea that the body and blood of Christ are physically present in the Eucharist. While he celebrated Mass in a church near Lago di Bolsena, blood started to drip from the Host onto the *corporale*, the white linen cloth that covered the altar. The stained linen was whisked off to Pope

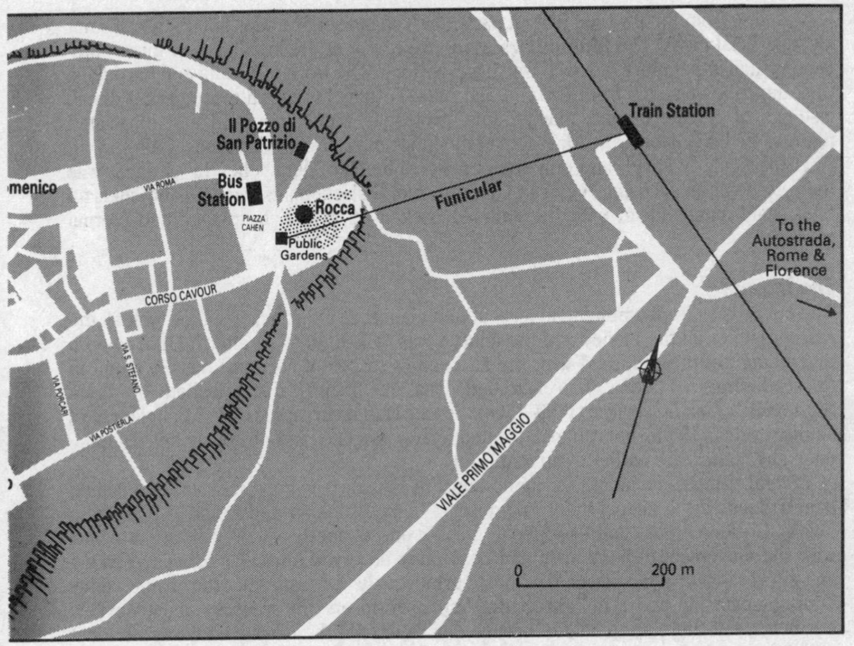

Urban IV, who like many a pope was in Orvieto to escape the heat and political hassle of Rome. He immediately proclaimed a miracle, and a year later Thomas Aquinas, no less, drew up a papal bull instigating the feast of **Corpus Domini**. The Church at the time, however, was in retreat, and the Umbrian towns were at the height of their civic expansion. It's likely that the building of an awe-inspiring cathedral in one of the region's most powerful *comunes* was less to commemorate a miracle than a shrewd piece of political opportunism designed to remind errant citizens of the papacy's power.

It was miraculous that the duomo was built at all. Medieval Orvieto was so violent that at times the population thought about giving up on it altogether. Dante wrote that its family feuds were worse than those between Verona's Montagues and Capulets – the originals for Romeo and Juliet. The building was also dogged by a committee approach to design – even the plans took thirty years to draw up. Yet though construction dragged on for three centuries and exhausted 33 architects, 152 sculptors, 68 painters, and 90 mosaicists, the final product is a surprisingly unified example of the transitional Romanesque-Gothic style. Credit for guiding the work at its most important stage goes to the Sienese architect **Lorenzo Maitini** (1330–60), with the initial plans probably drawn up by Arnolfo di Cambio, architect of the duomo and Florence's Palazzo Vecchio.

The Facade

The facade is the undoubted star-turn, owing its undeniable impact to a decorative richness just the right side of overkill. It's a riot of columns, spires, bas-reliefs, sculptures, dazzling and almost overpowering use of colour, colossally emphasised doorways and hundreds of capricious details just about held together by four enormous fluted columns.

Stunning from the dwarfed piazza, particularly at sunset or under floodlights, it's not all superficial gloss. The **four pillars** at the base, one of the highlights of fourteenth-century Italian sculpture, are well worth a close look. The work of Maitini and his pupils, they describe episodes from the Old and New Testaments in quite staggering detail: lashings of plague, famine, martyrdoms, grotesque mutilation, mad and emaciated figures, the Flagellation, the Massacre of the Innocents, strange visitations, Cain slaying Abel (particularly juicy), and only the occasional touch of light relief. In its day it was there to point an accusing finger at Orvieto's moral slackers, as the-none-too cheerful final panel makes clear, with the damned packed off to fire, brimstone and eternal misery.

The Interior

The inside is a disappointment, at least at first glance, as if the facade either took all the enthusiasm or all the money and the church was tacked on as an afterthought to prop everything else up. Adorned with the alternating stripes of coloured marble found in the cathedrals of Siena, Florence and Pisa, it's mainly distinguished by **Luca Signorelli's** *Last Judgement* (1499–1504). Some claim it surpasses even Michelangelo's similar cycle in the Sistine Chapel, painted forty years later and obviously heavily influenced by Signorelli's earlier treatment.

Several painters including Perugino and Fra' Angelico (who completed two ceiling panels) tackled the chapel before Signorelli – a free-thinking and singular artist from nearby Cortona – was commissioned to finish it off. All but the lower walls are crowded with the movement of passionate and beautifully observed muscular figures, creating an effect that's realistic and almost grotesquely fantastic at the same time. Draughtsmanship and a delight in the human form are the frescoes' most obvious attributes, but there are plenty of bizarre details to hold the narrative interest. A mass of monstrous lechery and naked writhing flesh fill the *Inferno* panel, including that of the painter's unfaithful mistress, immortalised in hell for all to see. In another an unfortunate is having his ear bitten off by a green-buttocked demon. Signorelli, suitably clad in black, has painted himself with Fra' Angelico in the lower left corner of *The Sermon of the Antichrist*, both calmly looking on as someone is garrotted at their feet.

All this overshadows the twin **Cappella del Corporale**, which contains the sacred corporale itself, locked away in a massive, jewel-encrusted casket (designed as a deliberate copy of the facade), plus some appealing frescoes by local fourteenth-century painter Ugolino di Prete, describing events connected with the Miracle of Bolsena.

The entire apse is covered in more frescoes by Ugolino, many of which were partly restored by Pinturicchio, who was eventually kicked off the job for "consuming too much gold, too much azure and too much wine". The **choir** is good, but in Umbria – which is renowned for its medieval carving – similar examples are ten a penny. Also worth a mention are an easily missed *Madonna and Child* by Gentile da Fabriano and a beautifully delicate fifteenth-century font, both near the main doors.

The rest of the town

Next to the duomo on the right as you look at it is the **Museo dell'Opera del Duomo e di Emilio Greco** (Tues–Sun summer 9am–1pm & 2–5pm; winter 9am–1pm & 2.30–4.30pm; L6000, or L10,000 with Il Pozzo), the main part of which is more charming for its atmosphere than for what it contains. There's probably no other Italian museum quite as chaotic and badly organised, though current restoration may tidy things up a bit. Imagine opening up an attic that's been sealed for centuries, and you get the idea. Amongst the meaningless stone fragments, rusty keys, moth-eaten vestments, dusty pottery and woodwormy sculptures (all unlabelled), you'll unearth one or two gems, all the better for requiring a bit of rooting around to find them. There are paintings by

Martini and Pastura (an artist from Viterbo influenced by Perugino), several important thirteenth-century sculptures by Arnolfo di Cambio and Andrea Pisano, and a lovely font filled with Escher-like carved fishes. The Emilio Greco section of the museum comprises nearly a hundred works donated to the city by the artist who created the duomo's bronze doors in the 1960s, none of them profoundly interesting.

The **Museo Etrusco** or **Museo Faina**, opposite the cathedral (Tues–Sun 9am–1pm & 3–7pm; L2000), has a predictable collection of vases and fragments excavated from local tombs. Nothing's been done to cheer up a display that would be dull at the best of times, though a bust known as the *Larth Cupures Aranthia* and a fourth-century sarcophagus are mildly interesting. The sixth-century BC **tombs** (9am–dusk; free) near Piazza Cahen are more worth tracking down – rows of massive and sombre stone graves, though with none of the grandeur or paintings of the more famous necropoli in Tarquinia and Cerveteri.

As far as the town's **churches** go, they all pale beside the duomo, though they've a lot more going for them in terms of humility. The tiny Romanesque **San Lorenzo di Arari** is the perfect antidote, built in 1291 on the site of a church destroyed by monks from nearby San Francesco because the sound of its bells got on their nerves. Four recently restored frescoes on the left of the nave describe typically traumatic scenes from the life of Saint Lawrence. There's also an Etruscan sacrificial slab which rather oddly serves as the Christian altar (*arari* meaning "altar"). From Piazzale Cacciatore there's a goodish **walk** around the city's southern walls (Via Ripa Medici) with views over to a prominent outcrop of rock in the mid-distance, part of the old volcanic crater.

Ten minutes or so brings you to **San Giovenale**, whose rustic surroundings, on the very western tip of the *rupa*, Orvieto's volcanic plateau, are a far cry from the bustle of the duomo. It's not much to look at from the outside, but the musty **medieval interior** is the best (and oldest) in the town, though virtually no-one makes the trek out to see it. The thirteenth-century Gothic transept, with its two pointed arches, rather oddly stands a metre above the rounded Romanesque nave, making for a hybrid and distinctive church, all of it exhaustively decorated with **thirteenth- and fifteenth-century frescoes**. Check out the *Tree of Life* fresco right of the main door, and the macabre *Calendar of Funeral Anniversaries* partly covered by the side entrance.

From the church back to the centre of town Via Malabranca and Via Filippeschi are the best of the **medieval streets**, all tantalising doorways and tiled roofs, but second-rate by the standards of neighbouring hill-towns. **San Andrea** is worth a mention, more for its strange twelve-sided **campanile** than the bits and pieces of the Roman and Etruscan city in the crypt. In the Piazza del Popolo, further up Corso Cavour (the town's pedestrianised main drag), there's a daily fruit and veg market plus the odd craft stall – all far more fun than the noted but forlorn ruins of the **Palazzo del Popolo**, whose long-running restoration should almost be finished.

Il Pozzo di San Patrizio (daily 8am–6pm; L5000, or L10,000 with the duomo museum) is the town's novelty act, a huge cylindrical well commissioned in 1527 by Pope Clement VII to guarantee the town's water supply during an expected siege by the Imperial army (which never came). It's a striking piece of engineering, 13m wide and 62m deep, named after its supposed similarity to the Irish cave where Saint Patrick died in 493, aged 133. Water was brought to the surface by donkeys on two broad staircases, cannily designed never to intersect. Apart from a small Etruscan tomb halfway down, however, the whole thing's simply an impressive hole in the ground.

Practicalities

The **tourist office** is at Piazza del Duomo 24 (daily 9am–1pm and 3–7pm; ☎0763/41.772), with a room-finding service and plenty of information, though they often tend to run out of the more useful stuff. Most of the town's **nightlife** and cheap **rooms** are near Piazza Cahen and down in Orvieto Scalo, the unlovely district around the station. The best low-cost central hotels are: *Duomo*, Via Maurizio 7 (☎0763/41.887; ④); the self-consciously medieval *Antico Zoppo*, Via Marabottini 2 (☎0763/40.370; ④); the very pleasant *Posta*, Via Signorelli 18 (☎0763/41.909; ④), two minutes from the duomo; and the *Italia*, Piazza del Popolo 13 (☎0763/42.065; ⑤), the biggest central place and thus likely to have space in an emergency. *Corso*, Corso Cavour 343 (☎0763/42.020; ⑤), is the best hotel near Piazza Cahen.

The nearest **campsite**, the *Orvieto*, is 10km away on Lago di Corbora (bus to Baschi/Civitella); it's a three-star job with a swimming pool, but out of the way and open only from Easter to the end of September (☎0744/950.240).

Cheap **restaurants** are grouped together at the bottom of Corso Cavour, though the best-value eating in the town is close to the duomo at the cooperatively run *CRAMST*, Via Maitini 15. Very popular with locals, it's a 450-seat canteen affair, offering a choice between restaurant and self-service pizzeria. For an appealing, friendly trattoria, try the *Grotta*, Via Signorelli 5. To sit outside, *Da Pepe*, Via Beato Angelico 4, has a nice garden and is a safe bet for a quiet unpretentious meal. Others worth a try – even though prices generally are over the odds – are *Da Anna*, Piazza Corsica 4–5, *Della Mezza Luna*, Via Ripa Serancia 3, and *Ricci*, Via Magalotti 22.

The **wine** bars around the duomo are an expensive way of sampling the well-known Orvietan white, a better wine before local producers turned to mass-production to satisfy the demands of the American market. Most bizarre place to drink or buy the stuff is in *La Bottega del Buon Vino*, halfway down the steep Via della Cave at no. 26. It's located partly in the cave from which the street gets its name and boasts an odd funnel-shaped well into the bargain; the owner offers the least enticing sales incentive in marketing history – a free postcard of the well with every purchase. The tiny adjoining restaurant is also excellent value. Finally, there's great **ice cream** at *L'Archetto*, an ivy-covered gelateria to the left of the duomo.

Around Orvieto

Moving on from Orvieto there are plenty of choices of destination. The obvious targets are Rome and Florence, both about ninety minutes away by train, but if you're in no hurry you could just as well head west into Tuscany and Lazio. There are buses from Piazza Cahen to VITERBO and BOLSENA. The road to Bolsena has some of the best **views** of Orvieto: it's where the postcard shots are taken from and was also where Turner set up his easel (the resulting picture's now in the Clore wing of the Tate Gallery).

The wooded pocket of countryside west of Orvieto around CASTEL GIORGIO is pretty enough, but probably only worth bothering with if you're in a car. Depending on the route you've taken so far you could stay in Umbria and take a slow train north through CITTÀ DELLA PIEVE or follow one of two good routes east to Todi. The first of these runs through Monte Peglia, some of the region's classic hill country.

Monte Peglia

Monte Peglia is the generic name for the triangular expanse of land that rises between the Chiani Valley in the west and the Tevere in the east. It's wild, sparse and timeless countryside, with hilltop hamlets, olives, vines, herds of white oxen and miles of deserted roads and tracks – the archetype of the pastoral lowlands you find all over the region. Although the map marks several villages, most turn out to be no more than scattered farms, many of them abandoned. The only realistic way of tackling the remoteness is by your own transport.

You'll get the best quick taste of the area on the circuitous and beautifully deserted N79 bis from Orvieto Scalo to Todi. You might be lucky and get a hitch, though most of the traffic these days takes the newer and infinitely quicker route south of Lago di Corbara. Superb initial views of Orvieto peter out as the road climbs through many a hairpin into densely wooded hill country, with occasional glimpses (haze allowing) as far as Perugia.

The best of the scenery is north of the road, where, as its name suggests, the area's woods, rivers and fields are a haven for **wildlife**. It's about the only place in Umbria you'll see otters, for example, and is well known for the variety of its birds, who owe their immunity from the Sunday morning blast-anything-that-flies fraternity to an ancient tract of land – *una bandita demeniale di caccia* – where hunting has traditionally been forbidden.

It's quicker and almost equally scenic to take the new N448 to Todi, which after meandering along the flattish southern shore of Lago di Corbara takes off into an unexpectedly dramatic **gorge** for the rest of the run onto Todi. Nobody seems willing to swim in the lake, and it's not used for any sort of watersports – and to be honest it doesn't actually look that inviting. Further on things get better, when the strange purple-red rocks of the gorge, along with sheer cliffs and forested slopes, add up to a more enticing package. The road's pretty quiet, with plenty of **camping** and picnic opportunities as the valley flattens out towards Todi.

Città della Pieve

Città della Pieve is most famous as the birthplace of Perugino (1445–1523), but it has a modicum of charm that merits a short visit in its own right. Again, you're better off in a car, for the station is a long haul from the town, and it's the sort of place that can easily be seen in an hour. From below, in the Tiber Valley, the town straggles along a distant ridge to the east, vaguely and mysteriously enticing, but once up in the streets it lacks the impact of other Umbrian towns, the chief appeal being the tiny red-bricked houses (there was no local building stone), old women knitting and a proliferation of geraniums at every window. One of the streets, Via della Baciadonna, claims to be the narrowest in Italy, the width of a "woman's kiss", the translation suggests. If you prefer your poetry liquid, the town's fountains run with wine during its April *festa*.

Otherwise its only real interest lies in the handful of **Perugino's paintings**, which lie scattered around the town's fairly dismal churches. If the small **tourist office** at Piazza Matteotti 4 is shut, there's a map of the town's few highlights outside the unremarkable duomo in Piazza Gramsci (or Piazza Plebiscito, depending on your politics).

The cathedral itself has a couple of late works which show the painter in his worst light. Perugino's reputation today, though still very high, is lower than it was in his own time, when contemporaries put him in the same bracket as Leonardo and Michelangelo. He trained with Leonardo da Vinci in Florence but largely remained faithful to the tenets of the Umbrian School – sublime misty landscapes behind ethereal religious subjects. His great facility enabled him to produce vast numbers of dewy-eyed saints and Madonnas, whose occasional absence of genuine religious sentiment horrified those who demanded sincerity above all else in devotional art. What in his youth had been profound and innovative gradually came to seem stilted and repetitive. Accused of merely replicating a successful formula, he also did nothing to discourage pupils finishing his works, adding his signature to some real shockers – especially in old age. He remains, however, one of the leading and most influential of the Renaissance painters. The painting not to miss is *The Adoration of the Magi* in **Santa Maria dei Bianchi**, considered his greatest work still resident in Italy (Napoleon removed many to the Louvre), with lesser paintings in nearby **San Antonio Abate** and **Santa Maria dei Servi**.

travel details

Trains

Assisi to: Foligno (hourly; 15min); Perugia (hourly; 25min); Spello (hourly; 10min); Terόntola (hourly; 1hr).

Città di Castello to: Perugia (hourly; 50min); Sansepolcro (hourly; 50min).

Orvieto to: Arezzo (7 daily; 1hr 20min); Chiusi (7 daily; 40min); Florence (7 daily; 1hr 30min); Rome (7 daily; 1hr 30min).

Perugia to: Assisi (hourly; 25min); Città di Castello (hourly; 50min); Deruta (hourly; 30min); Foligno (hourly; 40min); Sansepolcro (hourly; 1hr 40min); Spello (hourly; 35min); Terni (hourly; 1hr 50min); Terόntola (hourly; 40min); Todi (hourly; 50min).

Spoleto to: Foligno (15 daily; 20min); Fossato di Vico (12 daily; 1hr); Narni (10 daily; 40min); Nocera Umbra (8 daily; 40min); Perugia (1 daily; 45min); Terni (15 daily; 30min).

Buses

Assisi to: Foligno (4 daily; 50min); Gualdo Tadino (1 daily; 1hr 15min); Perugia (8 daily; 30min); Spello (4 daily; 40min).

Gubbio to: Fossato di Vico (10 daily; 30min); Perugia (10 daily; 1hr).

Norcia to: Perugia (1 daily; 1hr 30min); Spoleto (6 daily; 1hr 10min).

Orvieto to: Terni (6 daily; 1hr 40min); Todi (1 daily; 50min).

Perugia to: Assisi (12 daily; 30min); Gubbio (10 daily; 1hr); Spoleto (2 daily; 1hr 20min); Todi (5–7 daily; 1hr).

Spoleto to: Foligno (7 daily; 40min); Montefalco (4 daily; 1hr); Norcia (6 daily; 1hr 10min); Perugia (2 daily; 1hr 20min); Scheggino (5 daily; 1hr 10min); Terni (6 daily; 45min).

Todi to: Orvieto (1 daily; 50min); Perugia (5–7 daily; 1hr); Terni (8 daily; 45min).

CHAPTER TEN

MARCHE

Lying between the Apennines and the Adriatic, **Marche** is a varied region, and one you could spend weeks exploring, its mountains and valleys forming a backdrop for a series of historic towns and remote villages. Much of the region is unspoilt, particularly in the southwest between Macerata and the Sibillini Mountains, where crumbling hill-villages make atmospheric bases for hikes into the stunning **Monti Sibillini** range. Not that all of Marche is free from tourism, though; much of its coastline is studded with modern grid-plan resorts, and ranks of sun-umbrellas fill many of its beaches. The region also has a fair amount of industry, heaviest around the port of **Ancona** and along the main road and rail route into the region from Umbria.

Of Marche's larger seaside resorts, **Pésaro** is the most appealing, with a Renaissance centre maintaining its dignity behind the package-tour seafront; and to the south of Ancona is the **Cónero Riviera**, a spectacular stretch of coast, with small beaches nestling beneath the dramatic cliffs of Monte Cónero. For an upbeat resort, head south to **San Benedetto del Tronto**, with six kilometres of beach, five thousand palm trees, and numerous discos. Really, though, the most appealing – and best known – of Marche's sights are the small hilltop town of **Urbino**, with its spectacular Renaissance palace, and the fortress of **San Leo**, just across the border from San Marino. Further south, **Macerata** is a university town surrounded by lovely countryside, and, right on the regional border, **Ascoli Piceno** is a worthy stop-off on the way into Abruzzo.

Getting around on public transport is not too much of a problem, though you'll obviously save time in the remotest parts of the region with your own transport. The provincial capitals – Urbino, Pésaro, Macerata, Ancona and Áscoli Piceno – are all well served by public transport; and Ancona is also a major port for ferries to Greece – although it is not at all an attractive base in itself. In general, though, you'll get closer to the region and its people if you stay in a smaller centre. If you're hiking in the Sibillini, **Amandola** has the best bus service; if you don't mind hitching, or relying on fewer buses, **Montefortino** is a prettier base.

Urbino

During the second half of the fifteenth century, **URBINO** was one of the most prestigious courts in Europe, ruled by the remarkable Federico da Montefeltro, who employed some of the greatest artists and architects of the time to build and decorate his palace in the town. Baldassare Castiglione, whose sixteenth-century handbook of courtly behaviour, *Il Cortegiane* (The Courtier), is set in the palace, reckoned it to be the most beautiful in all Italy, and it does seem from contemporary accounts that fifteenth-century Urbino was an extraordinarily civilised place, a measured and urbane society in which life was lived without indulgence.

Nowadays Urbino is Marche's most immediately likeable town, saved from an existence as a museum-piece by its lively university. There's a refreshing, energetic feel to the place, plenty of conducive places to eat and drink, and, although its nightlife is hardly wild, there are a few music bars hosting local bands and the like.

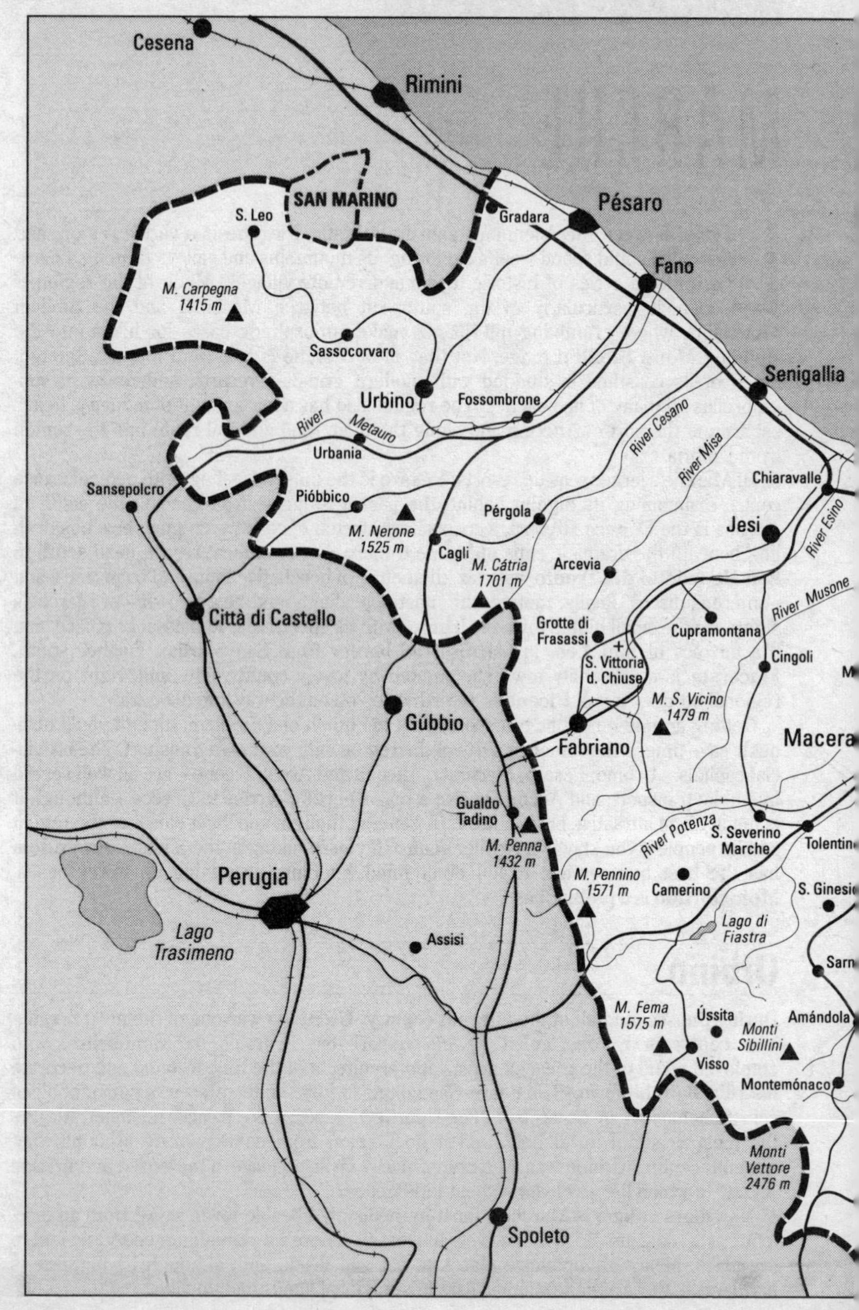
Cesena
Rimini
SAN MARINO
S. Leo
Gradara
Pésaro
Fano
M. Carpegna
1415 m
Sassocorvaro
Senigallia
Urbino
Fossombrone
River Metauro
Urbania
River Cesano
River Misa
Chiaravalle
Sansepolcro
Pióbbico
M. Nerone
1525 m
Pérgola
Jesi
River Esino
Cagli
M. Cátria
1701 m
Arcevia
River Musone
Città di Castello
Grotte di
Frasassi
Cupramontana
S. Vittoria
d. Chiuse
Cingoli
M. S. Vicino
1479 m
Gúbbio
Fabriano
Macera
Gualdo
Tadino
M. Penna
1432 m
River Potenza
S. Severino
Marche
Tolentin
Perugia
M. Pennino
1571 m
Camerino
S. Ginesi
Lago
Trasimeno
Lago di
Fiastra
Assisi
Sarn
M. Fema
1575 m
Ússita
Amándola
Monti
Sibillini
Visso
Montemónaco
Monti
Vettore
2476 m
Spoleto

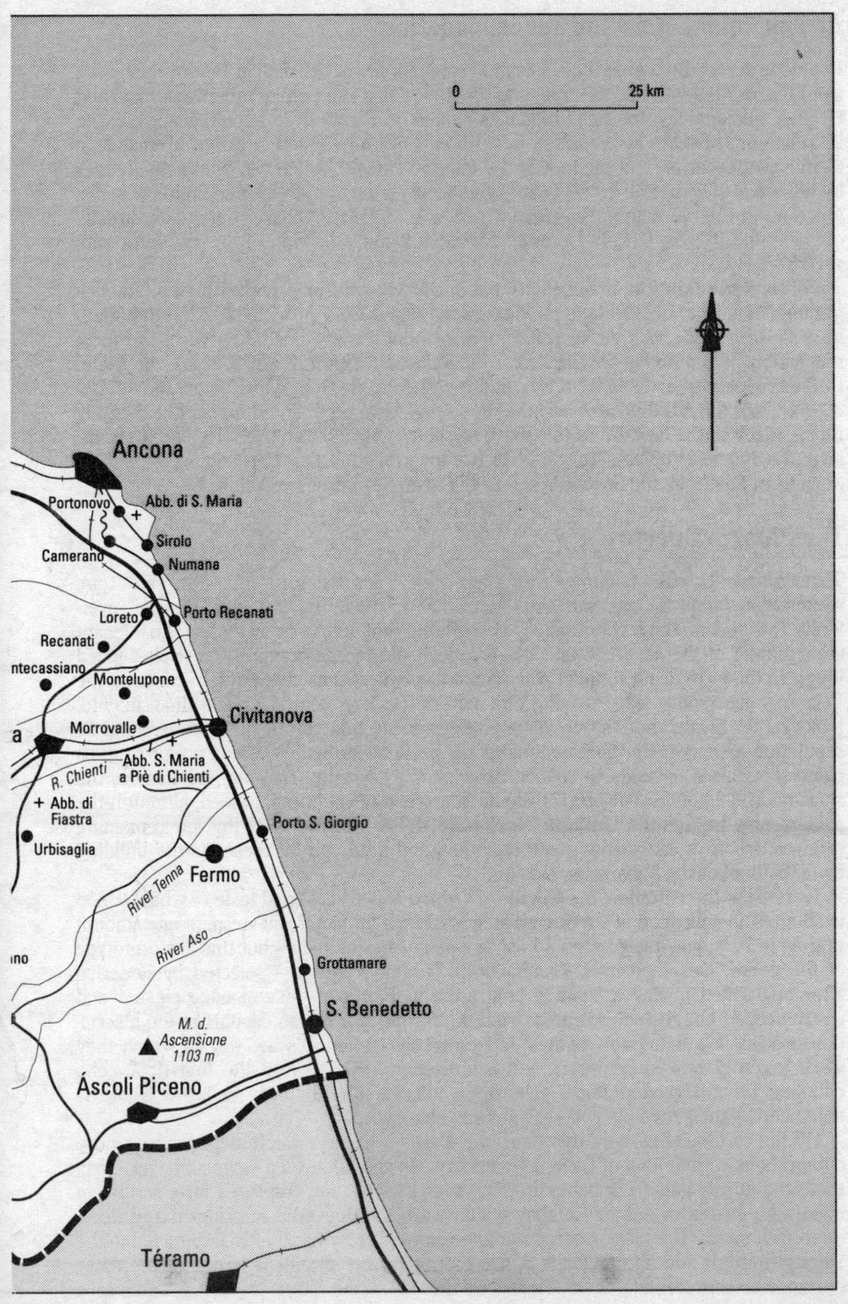
0
25 km
Ancona
Portonovo
Abb. di S. Maria
Sirolo
Camerano
Numana
Loreto
Porto Recanati
Recanati
ntecassiano
Montelupone
Civitanova
Morrovalle
a
Abb. S. Maria
a Piè di Chienti
R. Chienti
+ Abb. di
Fiastra
Porto S. Giorgio
Urbisaglia
Fermo
River Tenna
River Aso
ıno
Grottamare
S. Benedetto
M. d.
Ascensione
1103 m
Áscoli Piceno
Téramo

Arrival, information and accommodation

Urbino is served by regular buses from Pésaro, some via Urbania; in Pésaro they leave from Piazza Matteotti and the train station. Buses also run regularly between Fano and Urbino. (Incidentally, the bus timetables posted on Piazza della Repubblica are not to be relied on; best bet is to ask the bus drivers.) All buses stop in Borgo Mercatale, a terminus-cum-car park at the foot of the Palazzo Ducale, which can be reached either by lift, spiral staircase, or by way of a series of steep narrow streets and flights of steps. Once up in the old centre, the **tourist office** is at Piazza Duca Federico 35, directly opposite the Palazzo Ducale (summer Mon–Sat 9am–7pm; winter Mon–Sat 9am–2pm; ☎0722/2441).

For **accommodation**, the cheapest options are **rooms in private houses**. You can get hold of a list at the Comune on Piazza della Repubblica (☎0722/329.537), though to be sure of a place in high season you must book in advance. Otherwise, the most reasonably priced hotels are the *Fosca*, Via Rafaello 67 (☎0722/329.622; ④), the *Italia*, Corso Garibaldi 32 (☎0722/2701; ④), and the *Feltria*, Via G. de Montefeltro 18 (☎0722/328.718; ④), though the latter is some way out of town on the road to San Leo. Slightly more pricey is the *San Giovanni*, Via Barocci 13 (☎0722/2827; ⑤). There's a **campsite**, the *Pineta* (☎0722/4710), outside the town beyond San Bernadino (see p.540), open from Easter to mid-September; bus #7 (#4 on Sun) drops you close by.

The Palazzo Ducale

The **Palazzo Ducale** (summer Mon 9am–2pm, Tues–Sat 9am–7pm, Sun 9am–1pm; winter Mon–Sat 9am–2pm, Sun 9am–1pm; L8000), whose "Facciata dei Torricini" overlooks the surrounding countryside, is a fitting monument to Federico. An elegant combination of the aesthetic and the practical, the facade comprises a triple-decked loggia in the form of a triumphal arch flanked by twin defensive towers. In contrast, the Palazzo's bare south side, forming one side of the long central Piazza Rinascimento, looks rather bleak, and it's only once you get inside that you begin to understand its reputation as one of the finest buildings of the Renaissance. Whereas a tour of most palaces of this size tends to reduce the visitor to a state of crabby exhaustion, the spacious rooms of the Palazzo Ducale instil a sense of calmness. Indeed, although the palazzo now houses the **Galleria Nazionale delle Marche**, only the few remaining original Urbino works justify much attention, and until you hit these it's the building itself that makes the biggest impression.

Just inside the entrance, the **Cortile d'Onore** is your first real taste of what Urbino is about. The courtyard is not immediately striking – in fact if you've spent any amount of time in Italy, you'll have seen a host of similar ones already – but this is a prototype of the genre. Designed by Dalmatian-born Luciano Laurana – selected by Federico after he'd failed to find a suitably bold artist in Florence – it's at once elegant and restrained. Although each element, from the furling Corinthian capitals to the inscription proclaiming Federico's virtues, is exquisitely crafted, it's the way in which they work together that is Laurana's real achievement. Pilasters on the first floor echo columns on the ground floor, pale stone alternates with dark, and the whole is enhanced by the subtle interplay of light and shadow.

Off the cortile is the room that housed Federico's library, which in its day was more comprehensive than that of Oxford University. He spent fourteen years and over thirty thousand ducats gathering books from all over Europe, and employed forty scribes to make illuminated copies on kidskin, which were then covered in crimson and decorated with silver. They disappeared into the vaults of the Vatican after Urbino fell to the papacy in 1631, and all that's left of the room's former grandeur is one of the more outrageous representations of Federico's power – the Eagle of the Montefeltros

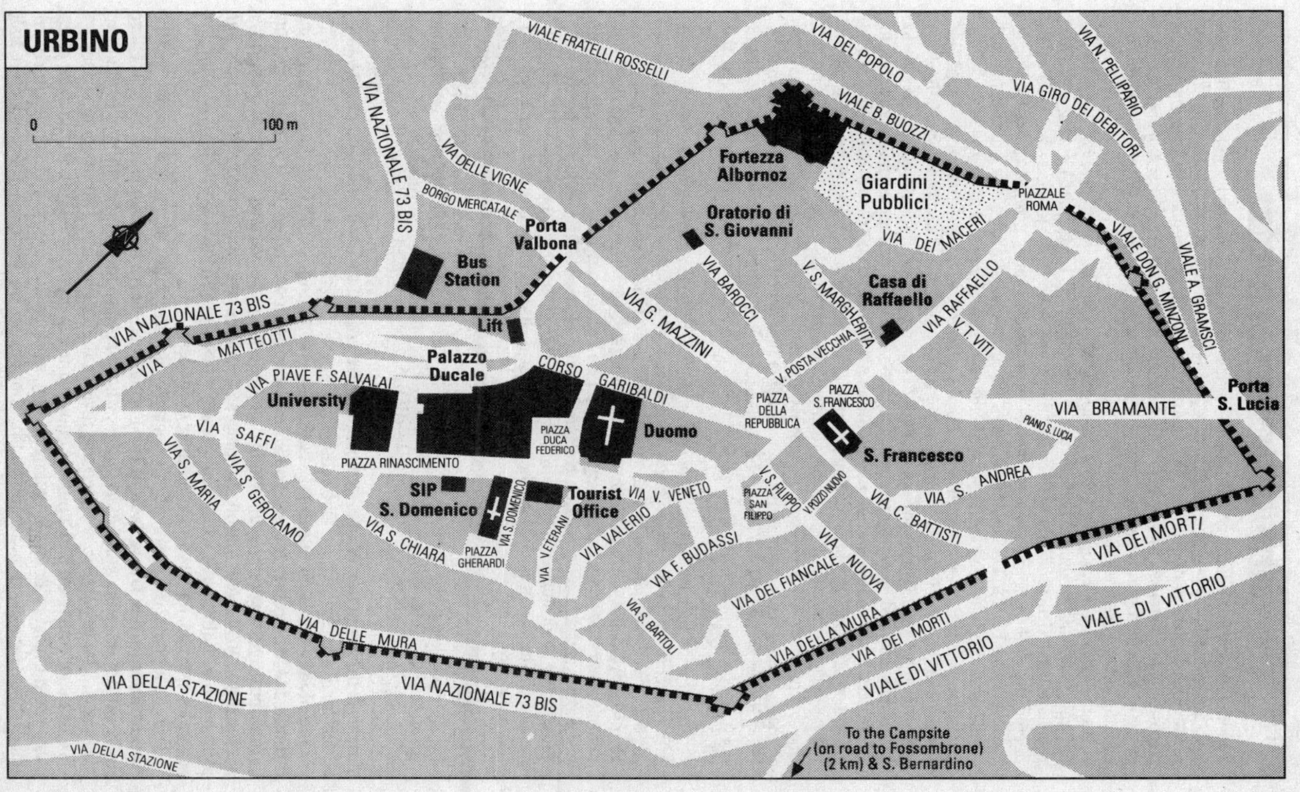

URBINO
0
100 m
VIALE FRATELLI ROSSELLI
VIA DEL POPOLO
VIA N. PELLIPARIO
VIA GIRO DEI DEBITORI
VIALE B. BUOZZI
VIA NAZIONALE 73 BIS
VIA DELLE VIGNE
BORGO MERCATALE
Porta Valbona
Fortezza Albornoz
Giardini Pubblici
PIAZZALE ROMA
Oratorio di S. Giovanni
VIA DEI MACERI
VIALE DON G. MINZONI
VIALE A. GRAMSCI
Bus Station
Casa di Raffaello
VIA BAROCCI
V. S. MARGHERITA
VIA RAFFAELLO
V. T. VITI
VIA G. MAZZINI
Lift
VIA NAZIONALE 73 BIS
MATTEOTTI
VIA
V. POSTA VECCHIA
Palazzo Ducale
CORSO GARIBALDI
VIA PIAVE F. SALVALAI
University
PIAZZA S. FRANCESCO
PIAZZA DELLA REPUBBLICA
VIA BRAMANTE
Porta S. Lucia
PIANO S. LUCIA
VIA SAFFI
PIAZZA DUCA FEDERICO
Duomo
S. Francesco
PIAZZA RINASCIMENTO
VIA S. MARIA
VIA S. GEROLAMO
SIP
S. Domenico
VIA S. DOMENICO
Tourist Office
VIA V. VENETO
V. S. FILIPPO
PIAZZA SAN FILIPPO
V. POZZO NUOVO
VIA S. ANDREA
VIA C. BATTISTI
VIA S. CHIARA
PIAZZA GHERARDI
VIA V. ETERANI
VIA VALERIO
VIA F. BUDASSI
VIA NUOVA
VIA DEL FIANCALE
VIA DEI MORTI
VIA S. BARTOLI
VIALE DI VITTORIO
VIA DELLE MURA
VIA DELLA MURA
VIA DEI MORTI
VIA DELLA STAZIONE
VIA NAZIONALE 73 BIS
VIALE DI VITTORIO
To the Campsite (on road to Fossombrone) (2 km) & S. Bernardino
VIA DELLA STAZIONE

FEDERICO DA MONTEFELTRO

Federico was a formidable soldier, a shrewd and humane ruler, and a genuine intellectual, qualities which were due in part to his education at the Mantua school of the most prestigious Renaissance teacher, Vittorino da Feltre. Poor scholars and young nobles were educated together in Vittorino's classes and were taught self-discipline and frugal living as well as the more usual Latin, maths, literature and the courtly skills of riding, dancing, and swordsmanship.

As the elder but illegitimate son of the Montefeltro family, Federico only became ruler of Urbino after his tyrannical half-brother Oddantonio was assassinated during a popular rebellion. Federico promptly arrived on the scene – fuelling rumours that he'd engineered the uprising himself – and was elected to office after promising not to punish those responsible for Oddantonio's death, to cut taxes, to provide an educational and medical service, and to allow the people some say in the election of magistrates.

Urbino was a small state with few natural resources, and a long way from any major trading routes, so selling the military services of himself and his army was Federico's only way of keeping Urbino solvent. In high demand because of his exceptional loyalty to his employers, Federico's mercenary activities yielded an annual income equivalent to £7,000,000, a substantial portion of which was used to keep taxes low, thus reducing the likelihood of social discontent during his long absences. When he was at home, he seems to have been a remarkably accessible ruler: he would leave his door open at mealtimes so that any member of his 500-strong court might speak to him between courses, and used to move around his state unarmed (unusual in a time when assassination was common), checking up on the welfare of his people. Stores of grain were brought in from Puglia, to keep prices low when the harvest failed, and "revisers" were dispatched around the villages to investigate grievances.

Between his military and political commitments, Federico found time to devote to the arts – according to his biographer, Vespasiano di Bisticci, "He delighted greatly in music . . . and maintained a fine choir with skilled musicians and many singing boys. . . . He preferred delicate to loud instruments, caring little for trombones and the like." But Federico's first love was architecture, which he considered to be the highest form of intellectual and aesthetic activity. He was a friend of the leading architectural theorist, Alberti, and according to Vespasiano his knowledge of the art was unequalled: "Though he had his architects about him, he always first realised the design and then explained the proportions and all else; indeed, to hear him discourse . . . it would seem that his chief talent lay in this art; so well he knew how to expound and carry out its principles." The Dalmation architect Luciano Laurana was scarcely known until taken up by him, and he later employed the more established Francesco di Giorgio Martini and one of the greatest of all painters and theorists of architecture, Piero della Francesca.

surrounded by tongues of fire, symbolising the artistic and spiritual gifts bestowed by Federico.

One of Italy's first monumental staircases takes you up to the first floor. Wandering through the white airy rooms, you'll see wooden doors inlaid with everything from gyroscopes and mandolins to armour, representing the various facets of Federico's personality. On carved marble fireplaces, sphinxes are juxtaposed with angels and palm trees with dolphins, while ceilings are stuccoed with such symbols of Montefeltro power as ermines, eagles and exploding grenades.

The best-preserved part of the palazzo is the suite of rooms known as the **Appartamento del Duca**, behind the Facciata dei Torricini. Displayed here is **Piero della Francesca**'s uncanny *Flagellation*, whose precise meaning continues to elude art historians. The geometric architecture divides the canvas into two unequal spaces – a slice of a cool courtyard and a perfect cube bathed in crystalline light. At the back of the cubic room Christ is almost languidly beaten, while in the foreground, in the courtyard, stand three figures, a beautiful youth, thought to be Federico's assassinated half-brother, Oddantonio, and two older men, who, if the Oddantonio identification is correct, are evil counsellors. Piero's application of mathematical principles to the representation of architecture and the human form had a profound effect on the architects of the palazzo.

No painting better embodies the notion of perfection held by Urbino's elite than *The Ideal City*, long attributed to Piero, but now thought to be by one of his followers. This famous perspective painting of a perfectly symmetrical and utterly deserted cityscape was probably intended as a design for a stage set, but sums up the desire for a civic order which mirrored that of the heavens.

Paolo Uccello's last work, the six-panelled *Profanation of the Host*, is pervaded by a fairy-tale atmosphere, possibly in reaction to the depression of getting old – shortly after completing it, he filled in his tax return with the statement "I am old, infirm and unemployed, and my wife is ill." The story is of a woman who sold a consecrated host to a Jewish merchant. She was hanged, and the merchant and his family were burned at the stake – the angels and devils are arguing over custody of the woman's soul.

In the same room is a famous portrait of Federico da Montefeltro by the Spanish artist **Pedro Berruguete**. Painted as ever in profile (having lost his right eye in battle), Federico is shown as warrior, ruler, scholar and dynast – wearing an ermine-fringed gown over his armour, he sits reading a book, with his pale and delicate son, Guidobaldo, standing at his feet. It's in the three most intimate rooms of the palazzo, however, that you get most insight into Federico's personality. A spiral staircase descends to two adjoining chapels, one dedicated to Apollo and the Muses, the other to the Christian God. This dualism typifies Renaissance neo-Platonic thought, in which mythology and Christianity were reconciled by positing a universe in which pagan deities were seen as aspects of the omnipotent Christian God.

Back on the main floor you come to the most interesting and best preserved of the palace's rooms, Federico's *Studiolo*, a triumph of illusory perspective created not with paint, but with intarsia (inlaid wood). Shelves laden with geometrical instruments appear to protrude from the walls, cupboard doors seem to swing open to reveal lines of books, a letter lies in an apparently half-open drawer. Even more remarkable are the delicately-hued landscapes of Urbino as it might appear from one of the surrounding hills, and the lifelike squirrel perching next to an equally realistic bowl of fruit. The upper half of the room is covered with 28 portraits of great men, another indication of Federico's eclecticism, as they range from Homer and Petrarch to Solomon and Saint Ambrose. (Only fourteen are originals, the rest having ended up in the Louvre.)

The rest of the town

Urbino is a lively place, and its bustling streets – a pleasant jumble of Renaissance and medieval houses – can be a welcome antidote to the rarefied atmosphere of the Palazzo Ducale. Next door to the palace, the town's **Duomo** is a pompous neoclassical replacement for Francesco di Giorgio Martini's Renaissance church, destroyed in an earthquake in 1789. The only reason for going in is to see Barocci's *Last Supper*, with Christ surrounded by the chaos of washers-up, dogs and angels. Afterwards you can wind down in one of the many bars and trattorias, or take a picnic up to the gardens within the **Fortezza Albornoz**, from where you'll get great views of the town and the countryside. Close by is the **Oratorio di San Giovanni** (daily 10am–noon & 3–5pm; L2000), behind whose unfortunate modern facade is a stunning cycle of early fifteenth-century frescoes, depicting the life of Saint John the Baptist and the Crucifixion. Vividly coloured and full of expressive detail, so different from the cool economy of later Renaissance artists, the frescoes are at their liveliest in such incidental scenes as the boozy picnic in the background of the *Baptism of the Multitude*, or the child trying to escape from its mother in the *Crucifixion*. On Via Rafaello, the **Casa di Raffaello**, the former home of Urbino's most famous son, the painter Raphael (Tues–Sat 9am–2pm, Sun 9am–1pm; L4000), is not worth the entrance fee, unless you're especially interested in fifteenth-century domestic architecture. There's just one example of Raphael's work, an early *Madonna and Child*, and apart from that the walls are covered with reproductions and minor works by his contemporaries and his father, Giovanni Santi.

There's another fine Renaissance church just outside Urbino, that of **San Bernardino**, built atop a hill 2km south of town. It's the last resting-place of the Montefeltros, whose black marble memorial stones were placed inside when it was realised that the mausoleum designed for the Palazzo Ducale was never going to get built. It was long thought to have been the work of Bramante but is now attributed to Francesco di Giorgio Martini.

Eating, drinking and nightlife

There are plenty of reasonable places to **eat** in Urbino. The cheapest deal is the university *mensa* on Piazza San Filippo, open to ISIC card-holders only. For those on a budget, there are any number of fast-food and self-service outlets; try the *Pizzeria-Bar* at Via V. Veneto 32, which does slices of pizza, sandwiches and *piadine* – a kind of unleavened bread, a bit like pitta. There are also good *crescie* (a kind of *piadina*) at the *Rosticceria Il Girarrosto* on Piazza San Francesco. The best of Urbino's sit-down pizzerias is the reasonably priced *La Rustica*, Via Nuova 3, or there's the slightly cheaper *Fosca*, Via Budassi 62. *Le Tre Piante*, Via Foro Posterula 1, just off Via Budassi, offers more interesting fare, including pasta dishes like *strozzapreti* – with sausage, cream, mushrooms and peppers – or tagliatelle with lemon and prawns; *Trattoria Leone*, on Via C. Battista (just off Piazza della Repubblica), is an authentic sidestreet place serving good home-made pasta dishes. For ice cream, go to *L'Orchidea* on Corso Garibaldi.

As for **drinking and nightlife**, the strangely named *Bosom Pub*, Via Budassi 24, has a good range of bottled beers, including Belgian classics, as well as decent sandwiches; there's also the *Oxford Pub*, Via San Domenico 1. If you're in search of live music, local bands tend to play at *Underground*, Via Barocci 16.

North of Urbino: Sassocorvaro and San Leo

The villages of northern Marche, though pleasant enough, cannot compete with the crumbling hill settlements further south, and the rarity of buses makes exploration by public transport something of an ordeal. However, two places within the region are worth the effort.

Perched above a twee artificial lake some 30km northwest of Urbino by road, **SASSOCORVARO** is dominated by one of Francesco di Giorgio Martini's most ambitious fortresses. Like San Leo (see opposite) it was built to withstand the recently invented cannon, but as the site lacked San Leo's natural advantages, Francesco was forced to find a strictly architectural solution. He did away, as far as possible, with straight walls, and built a grim and cunning fortress bulging with hourglass towers. Inside, it's something of a surprise to find an elegant Renaissance courtyard and an intimate and frescoed theatre – the fortress was built on the orders of Federico da Montefeltro for one of his *condottieri*, Ottaviano degli Ubaldini.

It's a tribute to the strength of Francesco's architecture that the fortress was selected as a safe house for some of Italy's greatest works of art during World War II, including Piero della Francesca's *Flagellation* and Giorgione's *La Tempesta*, reproductions of which are on show. There's also a **museum of folk life** (summer daily 9am–12.30pm & 3–7pm; winter Sat 2.30–6pm, Sun 9.30–12.30pm & 2.30–6pm; L3000), with displays of traditional weaving, wine-making equipment and a mock-up of an old kitchen.

San Leo

The menacing fortress of **SAN LEO** (daily 9am–noon & 2–7pm; closes at least an hour earlier in winter; L6000), clamped to the summit of a dizzy precipice in the northern tip of the Marche, has staggered generations of visitors with its intimidating beauty. Machiavelli praised it, Dante modelled the terrain of his Purgatory on it, and Pietro Bembo considered it Italy's "most beautiful implement of war". In fact it's not as impregnable as it seems, and has fallen to a succession of powers, most recently to the Fascists in World War II, who used it as an aircraft sighting post. One of the few invaders to have been repelled was Cesare Borgia, who was twice driven out of the citadel, despite having first persuaded a weak-willed retainer to give him the key.

There's been a fortress at San Leo since the Romans founded a city on the rock. Later colonisers added to it as necessary until the fifteenth century, when Federico da Montefeltro realised that it was no match for the new gunpowder-charged weapons, and set his military architect, Francesco di Giorgio Martini, the task of creating a new one. The walls were built on a slight inward slope and backed with earth, thus reducing the impact of cannonballs and providing a rampart. Three large squares were incorporated for the manoeuvring of heavy cannons, and every point was defended with firing posts. San Leo's greatest advantage, however, remained its position, which allows unwelcome visitors to be spotted from a great distance.

From the eighteenth century San Leo was used as a prison for enemies of the Vatican, of whom the most notorious was the womanising Count of Cagliostro, a self-proclaimed alchemist, miracle doctor and necromancer. At first the charismatic heretic was incarcerated in a regular prison, but on the insistence of his guards, who were terrified of his diabolic powers, he was moved to the so-called *Pozetto di Cagliostro* (Cagliostro's Well) now the fortress's most memorable sight. The only entrance was through a trap door in the ceiling, so that food could be lowered to him without the warden running the risk of engaging Cagliostro's evil eye. There was one window, triple-barred and placed so that the prisoner couldn't avoid seeing San Leo's two churches. Not that this had any effect – Cagliostro died of an apopleptic attack, unrepentant, after four years of being virtually buried alive.

As well as the fortress, there's the pleasant old village to explore. Its two churches, though they had no impact on Cagliostro, are worth a visit. The **Parrochio** was built in the ninth century, with material salvaged from a Roman temple to Jupiter by Byzantine-influenced architects from Ravenna. The capitals, dimly lit by the tiny windows, are carved with stylised foliage; also notable is the raised sanctuary, designed to impress upon the common worshippers the elevated position of their social superiors. Sunk beneath the back of the church is a sixth-century chapel founded by and later dedicated to Saint Leo, whose body lay here until 1014 when Henry II, emperor of Germany, calling in at the town on his way home from defeating the Greeks and Saracens in Rome, decided to remove it to Germany. His plans were thwarted by the horses bearing the saint's body – after a few miles they refused to go any further, so San Leo's body was left in the small village of Voghenza near Ferrara.

The heavy lid of the sarcophagus remains in the twelfth-century **Duomo**, dedicated to the saint. Like the Parrochio it's built of local sandstone and incorporates fragments from the Jupiter temple, on whose site it was raised. The best of these are the Corinthian capitals sitting on the stubby Roman columns in the raised sanctuary. Above them, vaults are supported on the heads of crouching caryatids – which are more aesthetically pleasing than structurally efficient, for the church walls and arches have been distorted by bearing the brunt of the weight. The lid of San Leo's sarcophagus is in the crypt, which is far older than the church, and was perhaps once used for pagan worship, as there are primitive pagan carvings on the wall behind the altar.

Getting to San Leo is a pain: you need to travel up the coast to Rimini (see Chapter Seven, *Emilia-Romagna*), from whose train station there are around four buses a day to the village. Once here, there's a **tourist office** at Piazza Dante 14 (Mon–Sat 8.30am–12.30pm & 3–6.30pm, Sun 9am–noon). There are only two **hotels** in San Leo, the cheaper of which is *La Rocca*, Via G. Leopardi 16 (☎0541/916.241; ④), which has a pleasant **restaurant** beneath its seven rooms.

Pésaro and around

PÉSARO is Marche's most appealing resort, a lively, even rather stylish place, which, despite its growing reputation as an international package-holiday playground, has subtly adapted its historical core to cope with the demands of being a provincial capital. Its post office is entered through the delicate portal of a Gothic church, for instance, and the bus terminus is overshadowed by an imposing fifteenth-century fort housing a prison. As well as its wanderable old centre, there is a long stretch of sandy beach, and regular connections to lesser-known towns like Gradara and Fano, making Pésaro an ideal base from which to explore the northern Marche.

The Town

The centre of town is the coolly dignified **Piazza del Popolo**, in which the rituals of the pavement café scene are played out against the cool, sharp lines of sundry Fascist-period buildings and the Renaissance restraint of the **Palazzo Ducale**. The most significant relic of Renaissance Pésaro, however, is Giovanni Bellini's magnificent *Coronation of the Virgin* polyptych, now housed in the art gallery of the **Museo Civico** (April–Sept Tues–Sat 9am–8pm, Sun 9am–1pm; Oct–March Tues–Sat 8.30am–1.30pm, Sun 9.30am–12.30pm; L5000). Painted in the 1470s for a church now known as Madonna delle Grazie (in Via San Francesco), the altarpiece situates the coronation not in some cloudy heaven, but in the countryside around Pésaro, dominated by the castle of Gradara. Fully individualised portraits of saints flank the central scene, ranging from the hesitant Saint Lawrence to the dreamy Saint Anthony. Below is a *Nativity* and scenes from the saints' lives, each set in a landscape evocative of a particular mood. Although none of the gallery's other paintings can compare with the Bellini, don't miss Marco Zoppo's *Pietà*, in which the dead Christ's muscled sensuousness prompts speculation on the artist's necrophiliac tendencies.

Renaissance Pésaro was famous for its ceramics, and the museum houses a fine collection – ranging from a Madonna and Child surrounded by pine cones, lemons and bilberries from the workshop of Andrea della Robbia, to plates decorated with an Arabian bandit and a rape scene. The most striking ceramic, however, stands above the entrance to the museum – a ferocious snake-haired Medusa by the local artist Ferruccio Mengaroni.

A block beyond the museum, the old and narrow Via Castelfidardo leads down to Pésaro's most attractive street, the porticoed Corso XI Settembre. If you want to do more than browse in its shops, take a look inside the church of **Sant'Agostino** – the choir stalls are inlaid with landscapes, Renaissance cityscapes, and, displaying a wit to rival the *studiolo* at Urbino, half-open cupboards and protruding stacks of books.

On Via Mazza, the continuation of Via Castelfidardo, is Pésaro's archaeological museum, the **Museo Oliveriano** (Mon–Sat 9.30am–12.30pm; apply at the adjacent library), with a small but unusual collection of local finds. Among the relics from the Iron Age necropolis at nearby Novilara is a child's tomb filled with miniature domestic utensils, and a tomb slab carved with pear-shaped figures rowing a square-sailed boat into battle. Even more intriguing is the collection of ex-votives – breasts, feet, heads

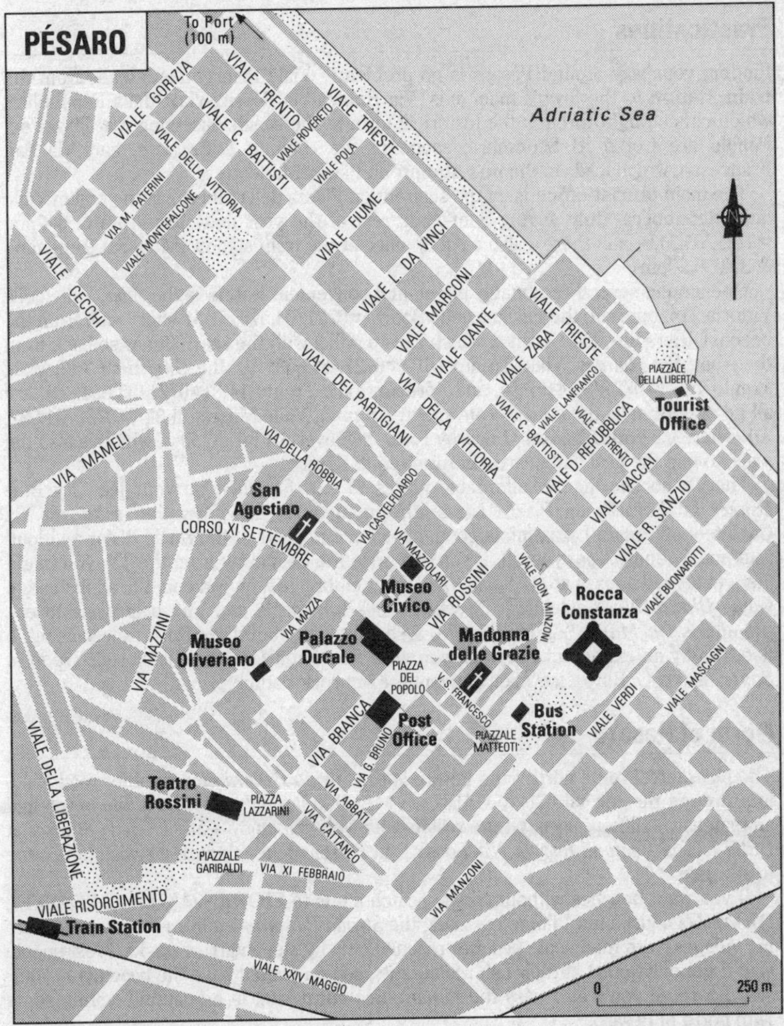

and even a dog – collected not from an early Catholic church, but from a Roman sacred grove at San Veneranda (3km from Pésaro), consecrated in the second century BC. Pride of place, however, goes to a bronze statue of a Grecian youth, exquisite even though it's a copy of a Roman copy of a fifth-century BC Greek original.

In the other direction, the tree-lined grid of gleaming stucco hotels and apartments marks Pésaro's long sandy beachfront, punctuated by a handful of Art Deco villas, including one on Piazzale Libertà whose eaves are supported by white plaster lobsters. On the way, at Via Rossini 34, the **Casa di Rossini** (opening hours erratic; L2000) houses a modest shrine of memorabilia to the composer, who was born here in 1792. The **Teatro Rossini** on Piazza Lazzarini hosts an opera festival in his honour every August.

Practicalities

Finding your way around Pésaro is no problem – Viale Risorgimento leads from the **train station** to the town's main axis, Via Branca-Via Rossini-Viale della Repubblica, which cuts straight through the historical town to the beach. Bisecting it at Piazza del Popolo are Corso XI Settembre, scene of the evening *passeggiata*, and Via San Francesco, which leads to the **bus station** on Piazza Matteotti.

The main **tourist office** is on the seafront on Piazza della Libertà, at the end of Viale della Repubblica (July & Aug 8am–8pm; rest of the year daily 9am–1pm & 3–7pm; ☎0721/69.341), and there's also a small office at the train station (Mon–Sat 9am–noon & 3.30–6.30pm).

One among several reasonably priced and convenient **hotels** is the *Alba*, Viale della Vittoria 216, opposite the Palazzo dello Sport (☎0721/64.516; ④), a short walk from the beach. Others line Viale Trento, which runs parallel with the sea 100m or so back from the front: the *Holiday*, Viale Trento 161 (☎0721/62.643; ③), the *Guglielmo Tell*, Viale Trento 195 (☎0721/32.445; ④), and *Abbazia*, Viale Trento 147 (☎0721/33.694; ④), are all good bets, as is the equally convenient *Arianna*, Viale Mascagni 84 (☎0721/31.927; ④). There's a **youth hostel** at nearby Fano (see overleaf for details), which is also the place to find the best and nearest **campsites** to Pésaro.

There's no shortage of affordable places to **eat**. For food on your feet, try *Blitz Dinner* or *Harold's* on Piazza Lazzarini; among pizzerias, *C'era una volta*, on Via Cattaneo, off Piazza Lazzarini, is good, cheap and popular, if the rustic decor and loud rock music doesn't put you off. If you can prise the chef away from the TV, you might just get served a pizza at *Da Silvo*, Via XX Settembre 161, or you could head instead to *Cigno Bianco*, Via Castelfiardo 6, which does full meals too. The best place to eat, though, is *Da Maria*, Via Mazzini 73, a chaotic, neighbourly trattoria, specialising in fish, run by an exuberant couple. If you want fish when *Da Maria* is closed, *Trattoria Sante*, on Via G. Bovio, has zilch atmosphere but rock-bottom prices.

North of Pésaro

The pleasantest route north from Pésaro is the *Strada Panoramica*, a minor road winding through the coastal hills to GABICCE MARE, a large resort with a fine beach and an expensive clifftop disco. Of the restaurants, you can enjoy a fine *brodetto di pesce* at *Dalla Ivia al Vento di Focara*, Via Fossa 1, in Fiorenzuola – though it's wise to reserve in advance.

If you want beaches without crowds, catch a bus to **FIORENZUOLA** and **CASTEL DI MEZZO**, just a few kilometres along the *Strada Panoramica* from Pésaro – tiny fishing villages, with minuscule beaches reached only by steep narrow tracks. Most people visit them only to eat at their fish restaurants, so you should have the beaches to yourself. En route you'll also pass the *Panoramica* **campsite**, in a beautiful setting some 7km north of Pésaro.

Alternatively, you can escape beaches altogether by taking a trip (organised by Pésaro's tourist office) to the sixteenth-century **Villa Imperiale** (L5000), a sumptuous mansion in extensive grounds, with rooms decorated by Bronzino and Genga. Note that the villa is normally only open to the public on one day a week, and that you have to visit by way of an organised tour.

Gradara

To the north and further inland is the castle of **GRADARA** (Mon–Sat 9am–2pm, Sun 9am–1pm; free) – not a place to go in season if you want to avoid crowds, as it's one of the main package-tour excursions. A fairy-tale confection of mellow red-brick and swallow-tail turrets, it's said to be the scene of the thirteenth-century scandal involving

Francesca da Rimini, who committed adultery with Paolo da Malatesta, her husband's brother. The lovers were killed for their transgression, and later consigned to hell by Dante – he meets their spirits in Canto V of the *Inferno*, where they are caught in a ceaseless whirlwind.

Inside the castle is a room decked out as the scene of the crime, with a sumptuously refurbished four-poster bed, fake wall hangings and an open book – Francesca tells Dante in hell that it was while reading the story of Lancelot and Guinevere that she and Paolo first succumbed to their passion. Further reminders of the story are found in two nineteenth-century paintings – one showing the lovers either dead or in a state of post-coital collapse watched by the crippled husband, the other, less ambiguous, of the naked couple. Other rooms are furnished as a torture chamber, complete with spiked iron ball, handcuffs and lances, and as the guards' room, a strange mixture of tavern and armoury. After touring the castle, it's well worth paying the extra L500 to walk round the walls for the fine views over the surrounding hills. Incidentally, Francesca's unhappy spirit is supposed to wander the castle when the moon is full.

Fano

Ten minutes away from Pésaro by half-hourly bus, **FANO** has changed since Robert Browning came here in 1848, seeking relief from the heat and crowds of Florence. Its beaches remain splendid – the sandy and sheltered Lido and the long, pebbly Sassonia – but it's become one of the Adriatic's most popular resorts. If all you want is an enjoyable beach, you might be better off heading south to the resorts of TORRETTE and MAROTTA, both easily reached by bus. If, on the other hand, you don't plan a session of uninterrupted sun-soaking and swimming, Fano is a pleasant enough place, comfortably combining its role as resort with those of small fishing port and minor historical town.

The Town

If you're coming to Fano by bus, you could ask to be dropped off at the crenellated **Porta Maggiore** and the remnants of the medieval defensive walls, on the southwestern side of the town centre. Behind them is a Roman gate, the **Arco di Augusto**, impressive despite having been truncated in the fifteenth century when Federico da Montefeltro blasted away its upper storey. You can see what it used to look like in a relief on the facade of the adjacent church of San Michele.

The Roman precursor of Fano, named *Fanum Fortunae* after its Temple of Fortune, stood at the eastern end of the *Via Flaminia*, which cut across the Apennines to Rome. The town is still built around a Roman crossroads plan: Via Arco di Augusto and Corso Matteotti follow the routes of the *cardus* and *decumanus*, and their junction is marked with a copy of a Roman milestone stating its distance from the capital (195.4 Roman miles). There are few other relics of Roman Fano, although the fifteenth-century **fountain** in the main square, along Via Mazzini, is dedicated to Fortune.

Overlooking it are the reconstructed thirteenth-century Palazzo della Ragione and the fifteenth-century **Corte Malatestiana**, dating from the time Fano was ruled by the Malatesta family. Its most notorious member was Sigismondo, whose disagreements with the pope led to the siege of Fano (when the Arco di Augusto lost its top) and his excommunication. After the death of his first wife – whom he was suspected of having poisoned – Sigismondo remarried in Fano in 1449, holding a three-day banquet in the Corte Malatestiana. Rumours about Sigismondo's sinister interest in his wives' diet revived when, seven years later, this wife also died, leaving him free to marry his long-time mistress, Isotta degli Atti. The Corte is at its best nowadays on summer evenings, when its loggias, turrets and trefoil windows provide a backdrop for concerts. Inside there's a small **museum** (July–Sept only Tues–Sun 8.30–12.30pm & 5–7pm; L3000) whose most striking exhibit is a mosaic of a winged figure riding a panther. Upstairs is the **art gallery**, worth visiting for an insight into the Victorian psyche, as it's here that you'll find Guercino's *The Guardian Angel*, a painting which entranced Browning during his stay here and inspired a poem of the same title. Expressing a wistful desire to take the place of the child depicted here learning how to pray, the gushingly sentimental poem ("And wilt thou bend me low . . . and gently tether me as thy lamb there . . .") became incredibly popular, and Italy was flooded with reproductions of the painting for holidaying Browning fans. The keenest disciples set up a club, membership of which was gained by travelling to Fano and sending the founder a postcard.

Less saccharine paintings are to be found in the Renaissance church of **Santa Maria Nuova** on Via de Pili, off the main square. The two works by Perugino, a *Madonna, Child and Saints* and an *Annunciation*, are both suffused with a calm luminosity, emanating as much from the figures as from the landscapes behind them.

A less demanding way of punctuating your sessions on the beach would be to browse through the classy shopping arcade tastefully laid out in the cloisters of the ex-convent of **San Domenico**.

Practicalities

The **train station**, where buses also stop, is ten minutes' walk from the seafront, at the end of Via Cavallotti. Fano's **tourist office**, at Via C. Battisti 10 (Mon–Fri 8am–2pm & 4–7pm, Sat 8am–1pm; ☎0721/803.354), is well organised and has good maps of the town, hotel lists and the like. There are also seasonal offices at Torrette (Via Boscamarina 10) and Marotta (Via Viale C. Colombo 30).

Hotels in Fano tend to be pricey in high season. Two of the most reasonable options are *Da Angelo*, Via G. Spontini 12, at the Lido end of town (☎0721/866.233; ④), and *Leila*, on Sassonia beach at Viale Adriatico 164 (☎0721/800.765; ③). There are plenty of **campsites** and a **youth hostel** nearby. The campsites *Norina* (☎0721/55.792) and *Marinella* (☎0721/55.795), both open from April to September, are on the coast between Pésaro and Fano, and easily reached by bus. Close by the campsites is the *Ardizio* youth hostel (☎0721/55.798), open mid-May to early September. South of Fano, there are the *Stella Maris* (☎0721/884.464) and *Torette* (☎0721/884.787) campsites, near the small resort of Torette, and many others strung along the coast in between, all easily accessible by bus from Fano.

For **eating**, apart from numerous pizzerias and snack bars, there's a cheap and earthy fish taverna, *Quinta*, in the fishing harbour at Viale – it caters mostly for fishermen and the prices reflect it. Just around the corner from the port is an even cheaper place, *Self Service del Mare* (open June–Sept), specialising in cheaper fish like sardines, anchovies and mackerel.

Senigallia

A typical family resort, with one of the Adriatic's best beaches, **SENIGALLIA** is primarily a place for beach-lazing and swimming. The town centre, though cheerful enough in season, is rather gloomy outside this period – although whenever you're around it's a conceivable base for exploring the surrounding area, and is far pleasanter than Ancona.

The town centre focuses on the rickety **Foro Annonario**, a semicircular neoclassical marketplace, behind which the imposing **Rocca Roveresca** (summer only Tues–Sat

9am–1pm & 3–7pm, Sun 9am–1pm; Aug afternoon hours 5–10pm, L4000), built for Federico da Montefeltro's son-in-law by Luciano Laurana, architect of the Palazzo Ducale in Urbino, is worth an hour of your time. Its austere exterior is embellished by white stone brackets, while inside airily elegant Renaissance halls stand above an underground warren of vaulted storage rooms and dungeons. It seems that the Rocca was rarely used as a ducal residence – the fireplaces and beautiful spiral staircase show little sign of use. The cells, though, were a different matter: converted from cannon positions when the region fell to the pope, they were designed with diminutive air-holes to inflict a slow and agonising death on their occupants. Fine views are to be had from the towers, built in the fifteenth century when the Adriatic coast was plagued by Turkish bandits.

The Rocca overlooks Senigallia's scruffy and dilapidated sixteenth-century **Palazzo Ducale**, and – more interesting – the **Palazzo Baviera**. Now the seat of the *comune*, it still contains some original furniture and wall coverings, and its ceilings – stuccoed with sixteenth-century scenes from Greek mythology, Roman history and the Old Testament – are, to say the least, sumptuous.

Practicalities

The **tourist office** (summer daily 8am–7pm; winter Mon–Fri 8am–2pm & 3.30–6.30pm; ☎071/792.2725), is behind the train station on Piazzale Morandi, a block from the beach. **Hotel** prices are on a par with the rest of Marche's resorts; bear in mind, however, that rooms are hard to come by in July and August. The cheapest hotels are to the south of the centre: among the best places to try are the *Gasthof*, Via Galilei 24 (☎071/63.375; ④), *Simona*, Via Pisa 4 (☎071/60.428; ④), *Angela*, Via Rieti 65 (☎071/63.521;④), and *Del Sole*, Lungomare Dante Alighieri 118 (☎071/62.089; ④).

With sixteen **campsites**, Senigallia is ideal if you've got a tent. Most of the hotels and all the campsites are along the coast, those to the south reached by bus #2 and those to the north by bus #1, both of which leave from the train station. If you want to be independent, there are **bikes** for hire at the Rotonda in the centre of the beach.

Senigallia's liveliest street, Corso 2 Giugno (behind the Rocca), runs down to the Foro and the grim tunnel of arcades called the Portici Ercolani, which are the best hunting grounds for cheap **snacks**. For more substantial sit-down meals, *Da Franco*, at Via Fratelli Bandiera 55, is a good deal, specialising in local dishes like *vincisgrassi*, a lasagne of ham, cream and truffles.

Ancona and around

ANCONA is a depressing place. Severely damaged by war and earthquakes, it has a few historical monuments embedded in a squalid tangle of cracked and collapsing buildings. The modern centre is a bland grid of broad avenues and palm-shaded piazzas, while the squalour of the station area, with its one-night cheap hotels, gaudy Chinese restaurants and heavy trucks travelling noisily to and from the port, will probably make you want to take the next train out. However, as the Adriatic's largest port, with regular ferries to Greece and Turkey, it's a convenient departure point, and you may just have to make the best of it.

The Town

Regular buses run along the seafront from the train station to the port, passing the pentagonal **Lazzaretto**, built within the harbour in the eighteenth century as a quarantine station for immigrants. The port itself is headed by a well-preserved Roman arch, the **Arco di Traiano**, raised in honour of Emperor Trajan, under whose rule Ancona first became a major port. Behind it is the **Arco Clementino**, a piece of architectural self-congratulation by Pope Clement XII, who made Ancona a free port in the eighteenth century and thus considered himself Trajan's equal.

On a steep hill overlooking the port rises the town's Romanesque duomo. What survives of old Ancona is spread out below it, and a wander up the hill is the pleasantest way of filling in time before your ferry leaves. At the foot of the hill is Piazza della Repubblica, from which Via della Loggia leads past the **Loggia dei Mercanti**, whose Gothic splendours are now barely discernible through layers of grime – though you can just make out the figures of medieval dignitaries and horsemen below its elaborately carved windows.

More appealing is the Romanesque church of **Santa Maria della Piazza**, its facade a fantasia of blind loggias and its portal carved with chunky figures and elegant birds. Behind the church, on Via Pizzecolli, is the town's **Pinacoteca Comunale** (Tues–Sat 10am–7pm, Sun 9am–1pm; L3000), highlight of which is Titian's *Apparition of the Virgin*, with a display charting the recently completed restoration. It's a sombre yet impassioned work, with the Virgin appearing to a rotund and fluffy-bearded bishop in a stormy sunset sky. There's also a glorious *Sacra Conversazione* by Lotto, a view of sixteenth-century Ancona by Andrea Lilli, and an exquisite yet chilling *Madonna and Child* by Carlo Crivelli, with a mean-looking Mary pinching the toe of a rather pained Christ, incongruously flanked by bunches of apples and a marrow.

Beyond the gallery is the church of **San Francesco delle Scale**, named for the steps leading up to it. Titian's *Apparition* was painted for here, but today its most remarkable work is an almost orgasmic *Assumption* by Lotto. Further up the hill, the **Museo Nazionale delle Marche** is not a bad place to spend an hour (daily 8.30am–1.30pm; L4000), its wacky moulded ceilings vaulting over a collection of finds ranging from splendid Greek red- and black-figure kraters to bright gold-leaf jewellery.

Passing the remains of the Roman amphitheatre, now capped with graffitied earthquake-shattered buildings, you climb up to the pink-and-white **Duomo** (or San Ciriaco). Though mostly built in a restrained Romanesque style, there's an outburst of Gothic exuberance in the doorway's cluster of slender columns, some plain, others twisted and carved. The simple and calm interior is built on a Greek-cross plan, enlivened by a cupola that from below resembles an elongated umbrella. The most memorable feature, however, is a screen along the edge of the raised right transept, one section of which is carved with eagles, fantastic birds and storks entwined in a tree, the other with saints.

Practicalities

Via Marconi and its continuation, Via XXIX Settembre, run straight along the coast up from the train station to the port and the centre of town. Via XXIX Settembre ends in the adjacent piazzas of Kennedy and Repubblica, from which the modern centre's three parallel avenues – Corso Stamira, Corso Garibaldi and Corso Mazzini – slice up to Piazza Cavour, while Via della Loggia runs up above the port to the alleyways of the old town. The main **bus terminus** is Piazza Cavour, connected by regular bus with the **train station** on Piazza Rossetti. The **Stazione Marittima**, where ferries dock, is connected with the train station by bus #1/4.

If you need to stay the night in Ancona (and you wouldn't want to stay any longer), there are plenty of depressing dives opposite the train station: the *Dorico* (☎071/42.761; ④), *Gino* (☎071/43.333; ⑤) and *Fiore* (☎071/43.390; ④) are all OK. There are also a couple of hotels in the modern centre: the *Centrale*, Via Marsala 10, off Corso Garibaldi (☎071/54.388; ④), and the *Astor*, on the corner of Corso Mazzini and Via Marsala (☎071/202.776; ④).

ONWARDS TO GREECE AND TURKEY

Ferries leave from the Stazione Maríttima, a couple of kilometres (bus #1/4) north of the train station, close to the centre of town. The information office here (summer daily 8am–8pm; winter daily 8am–2pm) has timetables, and each of the main ferry lines has a ticket office – a better place to buy tickets than the agencies that line the approach to the port. The main lines are *Strintzis* (☎071/286.431), who go to Corfu, Igoumenitsa and Patras, and *Minoan* (☎071/56.789), who sail to Corfu, Igoumenitsa, Patras, Piraeus, Paros, Samos, Iraklion and Kusadasi in Turkey. All **ferry** lines charge about the same; there are no discounts for holders of *InterRail* and *Eurail* passes – for these you need to go to Bríndisi. Between late-July and August you should book in advance, and you should always aim to arrive at the Stazione Maríttima a couple of hours before your ferry is due to depart. Luckily, most departures are at night, so you're unlikely to need to stay over in Ancona.

The pleasantest place to drown your sorrows in Ancona is *Sottozero* on Piazza del Plebiscito; if you're waiting for a bus on Piazza Cavour, *Caffé Cavour* is an appealing little place, doing good sandwiches and great pastries. For sit-down meals, the first choice is *La Cantineta* on Via Gramsci, just off Piazza del Plebiscito, and *Osteria del Pozzo*, on Via Bonda, also just off Piazza del Plebiscito, which does no-frills food in a no-frills environment. For more comfortable surroundings, head for *Clarice*, on an unnamed *vicolo* off Corso Garibaldi (on the right as you walk up from the sea), or the rather more expensive *Pizzeria Desidero* on Via Bernabet, just above Piazza del Plebiscito.

Inland: the Esino Valley and Fabriano

Cutting right across the Marche, the **Esino Valley** is broad and bland in the east, but narrows to a dramatic limestone gorge – the Gola di Rossa – just before the town of Fabriano and the border with Umbria. Although Fabriano and Jesi are heavily industrialised, most of the valley is given over to agriculture, and is best known for *Verdicchio*, a dry white wine produced in the hilltop villages around Jesi. What most visitors come for, however, are the vast Frassassi caves.

Jesi

Though its industrial development has led to **JESI** being known as "the little Milan of the Marche", the historic centre of the town is well preserved. Clinging to a long ridge, it's fringed by pale brown medieval walls and retains a scattering of Renaissance and Baroque palaces. One of the most majestic of these, the Palazzo Pianetti, is home of the **Pinacoteca Comunale** (Tues–Sat 9.30am–12.30pm & 4–7pm, Sun & holidays 10am–1pm; L3000). The highlight of its opulent interior is the magnificent 72-metre-long stuccoed, gilded and frescoed gallery – a rococo fantasy of shells, flowers and festoons framing cloud-backed allegorical figures. The picture collection is best known for its late works by Lotto, including the graceful *Annunciation* panels (once part of a triptych), scenes from the refreshingly assertive life of Saint Lucy, and the *Visitation*, set in a simple domestic interior. If you've time, walk to the Gothic **San Marco**, outside the town walls on Viale della Vittoria: it has some wonderful Giottoesque frescoes, including a *Crucifixion* in which every face in the crowd is individually realised and totally absorbing.

Verdicchio country

No wine is produced in Jesi itself – if you want to indulge in some wine sampling, head for the *Colonnara cantina*, at **CUPRAMONTANA**, accessible by bus from Ancona and Jesi. The *cantina* is disappointingly up-to-date, but the wines, including a champagne-like *charmant*, are generally good. The best time to visit is on the first Sunday in October, when there's a parade and dancing, and the village streets are lined with stalls of wine and food for the **grape festival**. The idea is that the harvest should begin the day after, but owing to hangovers, it's usually a couple of days before anyone feels fit enough to start work.

The Frassassi caves and San Vittore Terme

Further up the Esino Valley, just after the Gola di Rossa, a road leads up from GENGA train station to the Frassassi gorge, carved by the River Sentino, which was also responsible for creating the eighteen kilometres of caves beneath it. The largest cave of the **Grotte di Frassassi** (daily 8am–8pm; tours every 90min, every 10min on Sun, last tour 6.30pm; L10,000) was discovered only in 1971, and just over a kilometre of its caverns and tunnels are now open to the public.

As ever, the most remarkable stalactite and stalagmite formations have been named – there's a petrified Niagara Falls, a giant's head with a wonderfully Roman profile, a cave whose floor is covered with candles, complete with holders, and a set of organ pipes. (The sounds of the drips have been electronically processed and marketed as a cassette.) The vast Cave of the Great Wind, at 240m high, is one of the biggest in Europe, and large enough to contain Milan Cathedral. It's been used for a series of experiments, ranging from sensory deprivation (as a possible treatment for drug addicts) to a sociological exploration of the dynamics that developed between a group of people enclosed there for a month.

Fabriano

Famous for two things – paper-making and Gentile da Fabriano, the best of the International Gothic artists – **FABRIANO** is now heavily industrialised and a dismal town at first sight. You're most likely to pass through on your way on to Umbria and Rome, and frankly there's little reason to stop off unless it's to visit the **Museum of Paper and Watermarks** (Tues–Sat 9am–noon & 3–6pm, Sun 9am–12.30pm; L4000), housed in the ex-convent of San Domenico. The sort of place kids are dragged to on rainy days, it's owned by the biggest of Fabriano's paper mills, *Miliani*, which produces a staggering 900km of paper each day, including watermarked paper for bank notes of various currencies.

The Cónero Riviera

Just south of Ancona the white cliffs of **Monte Cónero** plunge straight into the sea, forming the northern Adriatic's most spectacular stretch of coastline. It's an easily accessible stretch, the major resorts of Portonovo, Sirolo and Numana all linked by bus from Ancona, either from the train station or Piazza Cavour. Although the beaches at Sirolo and Numana are developed, you should be able to find a quiet cove or a rocky ledge from which to swim in peace, even in high season.

Portonovo

Closest to Ancona, **PORTONOVO** nestles beneath Monte Cónero, undeveloped save for two campsites and three expensive hotels, one of which is sited in the Napoleonic fort which dominates the bay. Although its pebbly beach gets fairly busy in summer, the scenery is unbeatable, and the crowds are as nothing compared to those at Sirolo and Numana. There are also a few tiny beaches to the south, which you can reach if you're prepared to paddle and clamber. There's also a lovely Romanesque church,

Santa Maria, perched above the beach at the end of an oleander-lined path (key to the grounds from the custodian's house on the right). At present you can see it only from the outside, but this is enough – the clear light reflected from the sea bathes it in a golden glow, the shadows adding to the delicate interplay of arcades and wavily tiled roof.

Portonovo is the starting point for the **trail across Monte Cónero to Sirolo**, beginning at a stairway to the right of the *Hotel Internazionale*. Though rewarding, it's a steep and tricky hike, so don't attempt it without a map.

Portonovo is linked with Ancona by regular urban buses. If you are keen to stay, the cheapest **hotel** is the *Internazionale* (☎071/801.001; ⑥). Of the town's two **campsites**, *Camping Communale La Torre* (☎071/801.038) is slightly cheaper; if it's full, try the *Camping Club Adriatico* (☎071/801.170). Both are open June to mid-September. For food, *Da Anna*, on the beach, is a great family-run fish restaurant.

To Sirolo and Numana

The most stunning stretch of coast, a series of tiny coves at the base of Monte Cónero between Portonovo and Sirolo, is best explored by boat – they leave from both bays. You can go just for the scenery or ask to be dropped off somewhere along the way for a few hours of swimming. Particularly inviting is the small beach close to the jagged mid-sea islets of the "Due Sorelle", although you won't have it to yourself in peak season.

Sirolo and Numana are now almost as crowded in July and August as the rest of the Adriatic resorts, the main difference being that their cliff-backed beaches are more picturesque. **SIROLO** is the pleasanter of the two, with an old centre of demure, pastel-washed terraced cottages divided by neat cobbled streets. The central square, Piazza Veneto, is on the clifftop, with good views of the coast and Monte Cónero, and is home to a seasonal tourist office and a couple of bar-gelaterias. In season, buses run roughly every hour to the two beaches below, Sassi Neri and San Michele, of which San Michele, just to the north, is the better, with a section at the far end where nudism is tolerated.

NUMANA, a small port with a large pebble beach, is more developed than Sirolo, and the main reason to go is to catch a boat to the offshore islets of Due Sorelle (June–Sept roughly hourly between 9am & 3pm) for a spot of swimming and sunbathing, although there is also the added attraction of a **museum** (Tues–Sun 9am–1pm; L3000), filled mostly with relics of the Piceni tribe, who occupied the area between Senigallia and Pescara from the seventh century BC; the extent to which they were influenced by the Greeks, who set up a trading post nearby, is clearly visible in the red and black pots decorated with scenes from Greek mythology.

Happily, **hotels** are considerably cheaper in Sirolo than in Numana. The most atmospheric choice is the *Rocco*, Via Torrioni 1 (☎071/933.0558; ⑤), a short walk down the main street, Via Italia, from the piazza, a thirteenth-century inn above an upmarket restaurant where Saint Francis is alleged to have slept. Among more functional alternatives are the *Arturo*, on Via Spiaggia (☎071/933.075; ④), the *Emiliana*, Via R. Sanzio 2 (☎071/933.0932; ④), and the *Vascello*, Via Giulietti 128 (☎071/933.0533; ④). Sirolo's pleasantest campsite is the *Internazionale* (☎071/933.0884), set on tree-lined terraces on the cliffs below Piazza Veneto.

If you can afford to splurge in Sirolo, do it on a fish meal at the *Rocco*; otherwise you can **eat** more modestly at the pizzeria, *Il Grottino* on Via Ospedale, just off Via Italia, or plump for beer and sandwiches at the *Cambusa* pub on Via Galdini, a right-turn off Via Italia. For cocktails and ice creams with a sea view, there's *Il Grillo*, just below Piazza Veneto.

Loreto

One of Italy's most popular sites of pilgrimage, attracting three million visitors every year, **LORETO** owes its existence to one of the Catholic Church's more surreal legends. The story goes that in 1292, when the Muslims kicked the Crusaders out of Palestine, a band of angels flew the **house of Mary** from Nazareth to Dalmatia, and then, a few years later, whisked it across the Adriatic to Loreto. In the face of growing scepticism, the Vatican came up with the more plausible story that the Holy House was transported to Loreto on board a Crusader ship. Not surprisingly, though, this theory has not had the same hold on the Catholic imagination, and the Madonna of Loreto continues to be viewed as the patron of aviators – Lindbergh took an image of the Madonna of Loreto on his Atlantic flight in 1927, and a medallion inscribed with her image also accompanied the Apollo 9 crew. Among the Madonna of Loreto's more unlikely fans were Galileo, later denounced and imprisoned as a heretic, and Descartes, who reckoned she'd helped him refine his philosophical method. For centuries she also had military victories attributed to her – presumably she was thought to have power over projectiles – though the builders of Loreto's basilica, aware that the site was vulnerable to Turkish pirates, decided not to rely on the Madonna's defensive capabilities, and accordingly constructed a formidable fortified church here.

Loreto's treasures were indeed covetable, the most costly and idiosyncratic being a golden baby donated by Louis XIII of France, weighing exactly the same as his long-tried-for heir, the future Louis XIV. The basilica was ransacked in 1798 by Napoleonic troops, most of the plunder ending up on the shelves of the Louvre. Following Napoleon's demise, subsequent popes managed to retrieve many of the valuables, but the majority were stolen again in 1974, in what's known as the "holy theft of the century".

Numbering among its contributors such figures as Bramante, Antonio da Sangallo, Sansovino, Lotto and Luca Signorelli, the basilica is a must for anyone midly interested in the Renaissance. However, for the non-believer the atmosphere of devotional hard-sell can soon become stifling. Loreto can also be a distressing or a moving place, depending on your attitude to faith – between April and October so-called "white trains" bring the sick and terminally ill on three-day missions of hope, the main event being a mass in Piazza della Madonna, outside the basilica.

The pilgrimage site

Had it been completed according to Bramante's design, the **Piazza della Madonna** would have been an ideal Renaissance square. It still looks pretty good, although Bramante's **Palazzo Apostolico** has only two of its projected three wings, and his low facade for the basilica, designed to make its elegant dome the piazza's focal point, was never built. Instead, the dome, masked by a fluid late-Renaissance facade, is best seen from the back. Here you can see how Bacio Pontelli, who had a hand in most of the Marche's fifteenth-century military architecture, fortified the church – the loggia that runs along the sides and around the nine apses doubles as a walkway for meditating monks and a battlement, looking down over the sturdy defensive walls.

Inside the basilica

The church's **interior** (June–Sept daily 6am–8pm; Oct–May daily 6am–7pm) is the jumbled result of Bramante's, Sansovino's and Sangallo's attempts to graft Renaissance elements onto the late-Gothic structure. Clashing with the pointed arches of the nave, Loreto's raison d'être, the *Santa Casa* (Holy House), is encased in a marble cuboid designed by Bramante and encrusted with statues and reliefs. With typical Renaissance panache pagan sibyls are juxtaposed with Old Testament prophets, sharing the honour of foreseeing Mary's life, scenes from which decorate the rest of the walls. The best are by Sansovino – a *Nativity* on the south side and an *Annunciation* on the front. The sixteenth-century artists' biographer, Vasari, considered the angel in the latter "not to be made out of marble at all, but truly celestial, as though actually speaking the words *Ave Maria*."

The Holy House itself is a primitive stone building, with no foundations and only three walls – proof to believers of its authenticity (the basement and fourth wall were formed by a grotto which can still be seen in Nazareth), but evidence to sceptics of the research undertaken by its fakers. Pride of place is given to a copy of the famous *Black Madonna of Loreto* – the medieval original, once crazily attributed to Saint Luke, was destroyed in a fire in 1921. Madonna and Child are usually to be seen swathed in an ornate but ill-fitting wrap known as a dalmatic – a tradition started by Pope Pius VII in 1801 in celebration of the statue's return from the Louvre. Pope Julius II contributed the cannon shell hanging on the right wall, attributing his escape from being killed by it in the siege of Mirandola to the Madonna of Loreto's missile-deflecting powers.

One of the most recent of the church's twenty-five chapels is the **Capella Americana**, featuring a plane in recognition of the Madonna's role as patron of aviators. Of more artistic interest is the **Capella del Crocifisso** whose wooden Crucifixion is a triumph of baroque ingenuity – viewed from the left, Christ appears to be still alive; from the centre, to be drawing his last agonising breath; and from the right, to be dead. Less theatrical is the **Sagrestia di San Giovanni**, frescoed by Luca Signorelli – most striking is the *Conversion of St Paul*, with its panic-stricken courtiers. The sacristy's inlaid cupboards, featuring a jumble of trompe l'oeil bric-a-brac, are influenced by those in the *studiolo* of Urbino's palace.

Next door, in the **Capella dei Duchi di Urbino**, commissioned by the last duke, Francesco Maria II della Rovere, is an *Annunciation* Barocci, taking place before an open window through which the Palazzo Ducale can be seen. By far the most entertaining chapel, however, is the **Sagrestia di San Marco**, where vault frescoes feature Prophets who seem to be resolving the knotty problem of the sex of angels by peering up their skirts. Ezekiel looks appalled, Zacharias flushed and embarrassed, Jeremiah delighted, and David utterly overwhelmed.

To the left of the Chapel of the Crucifix, a corridor leads to the sumptuously stuccoed atrium and the **Treasury**, its vault frescoed by Pomerancio. The artist won the competition for the commission in 1604 thanks to Vatican manoeuvring, much to the chagrin of the loser, Caravaggio, who hired a cutthroat to slash Pomerancio's face. Surveying the unremarkable work Pomerancio produced, you have to suppress a feeling of regret that Caravaggio didn't select a more competent hitman.

The Museo-Pinacoteca

The items left behind in the treasury after the 1974 burglary are now kept in the **Museo-Pinacoteca** (normally Tues–Sat 9am–1pm & 3–6pm, Sun 9am–1pm) housed in the west wing of the Palazzo Apostolico, though this is unfortunately currently closed for restoration. Once it's open again, it certainly shouldn't be missed, principally for the five paintings by Lorenzo Lotto that are here, including his final work, *The Presentation in the Temple*. Plagued by neurosis and lack of money, Lotto finally joined the religious community at Loreto, and died here in 1556. Looking at *The Presentation*, with its rotund, crumbling priest and frail, almost skeletal nun, it would appear that he never found much inner peace. *Christ and the Adulteress* is an even more powerful work, with Christ surrounded by maniacally intense men and a swooning adulteress. For some light relief, take a look at the best of all the depictions of the Holy House's angel-powered flight – a fluffy-clouded fantasy by GB Tiepolo.

Practicalities

Loreto is easily accessible by **train** from Ancona; the train station is some way out of town, but connected with the centre by regular bus. The busiest periods are December 8–12 (the anniversary of the legendary flight), September 5–10, Easter, and from Christmas through to January 7; it's also pretty crowded throughout the summer, and finding accommodation can be difficult. All the cheap **hotels** are run by religious orders, the cheapest of which is that of the *Sorelle Francescane*, Via Marconi 26 (☎071/970.306; ④). If that's full, the **tourist office** at Via Solari 3 (Mon–Sat 9am–noon & 3–6pm) has a complete list. Also in Via Solari is the *Ristorante Centrale*, which does good fresh pasta.

Recanati and Porto Recanati

A few kilometres along the Macerata road from Loreto is **RECANATI**, a small town that makes a comfortable living from having been the birthplace of the opera singer Beniamino Gigli and the nineteenth-century poet Giacomo Leopardi. The visitor can wallow in Gigli memorabilia in the civic art gallery, or visit places that feature in Leopardi's poems, but if such acts of homage don't appeal, there's little point in coming to Recanati. It's attractive in a forgettable sort of way, but the precious provinciality soon becomes stultifying – Leopardi himself, though loving Recanati for its views of sea, hills and mountains, found most of its inhabitants stodgy and narrow-minded.

Recanati

On the central Piazza Leopardi, the town's **Pinacoteca Civica** (daily 9am–12.30pm & 4–6pm; free) is housed in the nineteenth-century **Palazzo Comunale**, a fussy mock-Renaissance symbol of Recanatese obtuseness – in order to build it they ripped down a fine medieval palace; all that remains of this is the vast **Torre del Borgo**, glowering down on the municipal architecture that surrounds it. Once inside the gallery you can forget all this and lose yourself in Gigli's world, evoked by costumes worn by the great tenor, presents received by him (including a walking stick from Verdi and a dagger from D'Annunzio), and, best of all, a replica of his dressing room. A crackly recording of his voice is often playing on a wind-up gramophone as accompaniment to the exhibits. The gallery itself has only two paintings worth spending time on, both by **Lotto**. There's a polyptych, complete save for its predella (which somehow ended up in the USSR), and an *Annunciation*, better known as *The Madonna of the Cat* for the cat scuttling between the Madonna and angel – thought by some critics to represent the devil.

Turning left out of the piazza, the main street leads down to the **Palazzo Leopardi** (Tues–Sun 9am–noon & 3–6pm; L2000), where the poet was born in 1798. The odd name of the square in front of it, **Piazzuola Sabato del Villagio**, comes from one of Leopardi's poems, in which he observes a typical Recanati Saturday, with "a swarm of children shouting on the piazzuola". You're almost bound to meet crowds of schoolkids here, but their elation tends to come from relief at finishing the tedious tour of Leopardi's gloomy house. The poet's lack of success with women is the best known fact about him – possibly the result of his smothering mother, who still cut up his meat for him when he was 25. Bits of poetry are affixed to a couple of houses, where women who obsessed him once lived. Leopardi sought solace for the pains of love, or rather the lack of it, in the view from the edge of town – on a good day it extends as far as the Apennines. The lower hills, which seem to roll endlessly towards the mountains, inspired his most famous poem *Colle Infinito* ("Infinite Hills"), and a plaque with a line from it has been stuck on a wall, above a heap of rocks from Naples, where he died and is buried. As the ultimate irony, the place where he came to forget his failures with women has become a lovers' lane.

Porto Recanati

If you're not familiar with either Gigli or Leopardi, you may as well head straight to **PORTO RECANATI**, the nearest resort to Loreto. With its main street, Corso Matteotti, headed by the turreted tower of a medieval castle, and an old quarter of pale stuccoed fishermans' cottages in the centre of the hotels and apartment buildings, it's one of the Adriatic's pleasanter resorts. Apart from the beach, attractions include a **sailing and windsurfing school** – details from the **tourist office** (Mon–Sat 8am–1pm & 4–8pm, Sun 10am–noon; ☎071/979.9084) on the Corso – and five discos. When you tire of the beach there's an art gallery inside the **castle**, which includes a view of Venice attributed to Turner and a portrait of a peasant at work by Millet. Even better, the castle courtyard has an arena – a wonderfully atmospheric place to see films and theatre.

There are only two cheapish **hotels**, both on Corso Matteotti – *Laura*, at no. 86 (☎071/759.1614; ⑤), and the *Cacciatore*, at no. 11 (☎071/979.9234; ④). The *Pineta* **campsite**, to the south on Viale della Repubblica, is reasonably convenient and has four-person bungalows as well. When you get **hungry** it's worth knowing that Porto Recanati is best known for its *brodetto*, a classy fish soup cooked with nine varieties of fish, spiced with saffron and served with squares of toast. If you want to splash out, the place to go is *Bianchi A. Vincenzo*, Via Garibaldi 15 on the sea front – the chef is justifiably known as the *mago del brodetto* (the "brodetto magician") and conjures up other equally delicious dishes, including delicate seafood starters and a superb fish risotto.

Macerata

A little-known provincial capital surrounded by Marche's loveliest countryside, **MACERATA** is one of the region's liveliest historical towns, thanks to its ancient university. Easy-paced and unpretentious, it's an ideal place to wind down in the evenings after exploring the province. For opera and ballet fans, its annual *Stagione Lirica*, held in Italy's best open-air venue outside Verona, is a must – in recent years it has drawn such heavyweights as Placido Domingo, Birgit Nilsson and Nureyev. And if you're the slightest bit interested in contemporary art, Macerata has a gallery that alone is reason enough for visiting the town.

The Town

Piazza della Libertà is the heart of the old town, an odd square in which the disparate buildings vie for supremacy – all of them failing. The Renaissance **Loggia dei Mercanti** was supplied by Alessandro Farnese, better known as Pope Paul III, instigator of many architectural improvements to sixteenth-century Rome; sadly he did nothing else for the square, and the loggia is elbowed out by the bland **Palazzo del Comune** and overlooked by the dull **Torre del Comune**. The dreariest feature, however, is the mournful brick facade of **San Paolo**, a deconsecrated seventeenth-century church now used as an exhibition space.

Things buzz a bit more along the main *passeggiata* route, the boutique- and bar-lined **Corso della Repubblica**, which ends at **Piazza Vittoria Veneto** and the **Pinacoteca Civica** (Mon 5–7.30pm, Tues–Sat 9am–1pm & 5–7.30pm, Sun 9am–noon; free). The collection here, ranging from the Renaissance perfectionist Crivelli to Ancona-born Futurist Cagli, isn't bad, but you might find the artworks on show in the **Palazzo Ricci**, off the square on Via Ricci, more challenging; they make up what is by any standards a good collection of Italian contemporary art (Mon–Sat 9am–1pm; free). The building and the collection are owned by a local bank. There are two thrilling sculptures by Francesco Messina – a nerve-charged nude of a dancer putting on her shoes and a leaping horse. Enrico Baj's *Military Head* depicts a general decorated with assorted fabric on a background of upholstery material, and you might see a similarly satiric intent in Manzu's bronze bas-relief of a clutch of cardinals. There's also a good cross-section of work by the Italian Futurists, followed by de Chirico's weird *Worried Muse*; de Chirico's brother, Alberto Savinio, provides the gallery's jokiest piece of social satire – a richly dressed society woman whose long neck ends in a goose's head.

Seeing the rest of Macerata's sights doesn't take long. Via Ricci leads along towards the bleak **Piazza Mazzini**, below which is the neoclassical **Sferisterio**, built in the early nineteenth century as an arena for *sphaera*, a traditional game which involved bashing a ball with an iron spiked glove. It was also used for bullfights, horse racing and mock jousts until, in 1921, the opera festival was inaugurated and the musicians took it over. It's a dismal place, not worth visiting unless to see a performance.

Up Via Ciccarelli from Piazza Mazzini, the town's **Duomo** on Piazza Strambi is no architectural triumph either – a workaday chunk of Baroque, which might have looked slightly more appetising had its facade been finished. Inside there's a statue of Macerata's patron saint, Giuliano, whose path to sainthood sounds like something out of a Sunday tabloid. He arrived home to find two people in his bed, and, thinking they were his wife and her lover, promptly killed them. Discovering he'd murdered his parents, he hacked one of his arms off in remorse – the severed limb is now kept in a church strong room, encased in a sleeve of gold and silver. The relic is displayed on request, but you need to give a day's notice.

Practicalities

Old Macerata is wrapped around a hill, surrounded by modern suburbs that are home to the train station, a ten-minute walk south at the end of Viale Don Bosco. This is connected with Piazza della Libertà by buses #2, #2a, #6 and #6c. Buses stop at the Giardini Diaz, directly below the old town on the western side, across Viale Puccinotti; some buses, however, do continue to a second, more convenient stop, from which it's a five-minute climb up stepped Piaggia delle Torre to Piazza della Libertà.

The **tourist office** is on Piazza della Libertà (Tues–Sun 9am–1pm & 4–7pm; ☎0733/45.807); and there's another, **provincial office** at Via Garibaldi 87 (same hours; ☎0733/230.449). There are very few **hotels** in Macerata, and if you're looking for somewhere fairly cheap you should normally book in advance; during the opera season (mid-July–mid-August) this is absolutely crucial. The *San Giorgio*, Via T. Lauri 6 (☎0733/232.376; ④), is the most affordable choice; otherwise there's the *Arena*, on Vicolo Sferisterio, off Piazza Mazzini (☎0733/230.931; ⑤), and the *Della Piaggia*, on Via S. Maria della Porta, off Piaggia delle Torre (☎0733/230.387; ⑤).

As for **food**, *Rusticanella Romana*, Corso della Repubblica 13, and *La Scaletta*, on the corner of Piaggia delle Torre and Via Rossi, both do decent takeaway pizza; *Narciso*, just inside the Porta Montana, is a nice place for breakfast. Further on, Macerata has an outstanding pizzeria, *Da Silvano* on Piaggia delle Torre, just off Piazza della Libertà. If you want to fill up at lunchtime, try *Trattoria Crescimbeni*, Via Crescimbeni 65, a basic, reasonably priced local place. If you've the money to indulge yourself, Macerata's most famous restaurant, *Da Secondo*, on Via Pescheria Vecchia, is worth trying; they do a superlative *vincisgrassi*, a sinfully rich lasgane, along with excellent roast lamb and pigeon. For late-night **drinking** (or indeed daytime sandwiches), there's the *Firenze* bar on Via Pescheria Vecchia, and the popular *Il Pozzo*, Via Costa 5, a student hang-out that sadly closes at around 8pm. The kitschly tropical *Maracuia*, on

Piazza V. Veneto, is a nice place to drink *al fresco* along with Macerata's young and beautiful. Seats for the **opera** are bookable at the *Biglietteria dell'Arena Sferisterio*, Piazza Mazzini 10 (☎0733/230.735 or 233.508).

East of Macerata

With its hills rising from the coast and rippling towards the Apennines, its medieval villages and scattering of Romanesque abbeys and churches, the area around Macerata is interesting to explore. You can get to most places by bus from Macerata, although if you're wanting to visit some of the more out-of-the-way hill-villages, you may find it convenient to sleep over.

The Chienti Valley

From Macerata the road and rail line run east to the coast through the **Chienti Valley**, passing through some of the region's most characteristic hill-towns and two of its finest churches. About 10km from Macerata, close to the turn-off for Morravalle, is the Romanesque church of **San Claudio al Chienti**, approached along a cypress-lined avenue. It's recently been carefully restored after years of use as a farm out-building, and appears to be none the worse for its undignified past – you'd never guess that the two cylindrical towers that flank its facade used to serve as grain silos. The upper storey, intended for church dignitaries, was entered through the elegant marble portal, while lesser mortals were directed to the tunnel-like door on the ground floor. The marble for the portal, like much of the church's fabric, was scavenged from a Roman village, Pausula, which stood on the site of the adjacent field. The interior is atmospheric enough, though there's not much to absorb you for long.

Morravalle

Above San Claudio, the hill-village of **MORRAVALLE**, skirted by a stepped street which disappears through arched gates, is worth a visit only if you have your own transport.

The main piazza, tucked away at the top, is a tightly enclosed, even claustrophobic square, which for the past six centuries has been given over to municipal business. Flanked by the eighteenth-century Palazzo del Comune and squat Palazzo del Podestà (where Italy's first pawnshop was set up by San Bernadino in 1428), is the Palazzo Lazzarini, built by those members of the Lazzarini family who survived their internecine battle for the privilege of ruling Morravalle. The palazzo, though built in the fourteenth century, incorporates an earlier Romanesque-Gothic portal, possibly taken – somewhat inappropriately, given the family history – from a local church.

Montelupone

The even more remote **MONTELUPONE** is the most memorable of the district's walled hill-villages because it appears to be on the point of collapse. The problem is subsidence, and most of its golden stone buildings are held up by medieval-looking wooden scaffolding, which makes the stepped streets and narrow alleys a pleasurable sort of obstacle course. Get there, if you can, in the early evening – the village is at its liveliest then, and looks particularly good glowing in the late sun. If it's clear, you can also catch a photographer's dream sunset from the belvedere – the view extends from Monte Cónero on the coast and across to the most beautiful of the Apennines, the Monti Sibillini.

You can get to Montelupone by (rare) bus from Macerata; if you're hitching, it's easiest from the Montelupone fork on the SS77 below Recanati. There's a reasonable **hotel**, the Moretti *Damiani*, on Via E. Fermi (☎0733/586.211; ④), which also has a restaurant.

Santa Maria a Piè di Chienti

Back in the valley, road and railway pass the ex-monastery of **Santa Maria a Piè di Chienti** just after the fork for MONTECOSARO. It was built by Cluniac monks, who came to the area in the tenth century, draining the flood-prone river into channels and creating fertile land out of what had been a fever-ridden marsh. Situated close to the coast, the monastery was vulnerable to Saracen invasions, so the monks encircled it with ditches, which could be flooded in the event of a raid. It survived until the early nineteenth century, when it was destroyed by Napoleonic troops – all that remains is the church itself. The facade was rebuilt in the eighteenth century, and the church's best external features are now its apses, decorated with fake pilasters and scalloped arcades. However, it's the interior (key from the adjacent bar) that's really special, its columns and arches bathed in the half-light that falls from the windowpanes of alabaster. After wandering around the vaulted chamber beneath the raised presbytery, and up the stairs to the galleries (narrow to ensure that they were climbed slowly, with a prayer on every step), you'll need to switch the lights on (by the right transept) to see the fifteenth-century frescoes properly. The best-preserved are in the apse, showing New Testament scenes in Renaissance settings, framed by fake mosaics and dominated by a stony-faced Christ.

Tolentino and around

Around 20km southwest of Macerata, **TOLENTINO** doesn't look much at first sight, girded as it is by ugly modern suburbs. But it improves markedly after you've crossed its turretted thirteenth-century bridge, a short way beyond which stands the **Basilica di San Nicolo**, the main reason for visiting the town. Its west front is a real feast for the eyes – a curly Baroque facade with a grinning sun instead of a rose window, and a fancily twisting Gothic portal topped by an oriental-style arch enclosing a dragon-killing saint. Inside, the most intriguing feature is the **Capellone di San Nicola**, whose Gothic frescoes create a kaleidoscope of colourful scenes of medieval life. In fact, they are episodes from the life of Christ, painted in the fourteenth century by one of Giotto's followers, known only as the *Maestro di Tolentino*. The most striking are *The Marriage at Cana*, with hefty servants carrying massive jugs of wine on their shoulders, *The Slaughter of the Innocents*, and *The Entry into Jerusalem*, in which an attempt at perspective is made by peopling the trees with miniature figures.

Just off the main piazza is the **Museo Internazionale della Cariacatura**, hopefully now reopened after restoration, which is filled with some of the world's best satirical cartoons. After this, there's not much else to detain you.

San Severino Marche

Twelve kilometres north of Tolentino lies the old, silvery-grey town of **SAN SEVERINO MARCHE**, a pretty little place whose modern centre converges on an unusual elliptical square, **Piazza del Popolo**, surrounded by porticoes. Just above the piazza on Via Salimbeni the town's art gallery, known as the **Pinacoteca Tacchi-Venturi** after a local historian (Mon–Sat 9am–1pm & 4–7pm; free) is as good a reason as any for a visit, with a quite memorable assembly of pieces. A gilded polyptych of saints by Paolo Veneziano is followed by an even more sumptuous altarpiece by Vittore Crivelli, which centres on a china-doll Madonna weighed down in heavy gold embroidery. It's the frame that really catches your eye, though – an opulent confection of scalloped arches topped with urns from which spring gesticulating ecclesiastics. Other highlights are the works by the Salimbeni brothers, who were born and worked in San Severino in the fifteenth century; they are represented by delicate and expressive frescoes detached from local churches and a wooden polyptych of *The Marriage of Saint Catherine*. In the same building is the **Museo Archaeologico**, with relics from the Roman valley town of Septempeda, whose inhabitants, driven out by barbarian invasions in the sixth century, escaped up the nearest hill to found the forerunner of San Severino.

Other works by the Salimbeni brothers adorn two of San Severino's churches. One of these, the ancient **San Lorenzo in Doliolo**, at the top of Via Salimbeni, looks slightly odd thanks to a medieval brick tower standing on top of its stone portal. The Salimbeni frescoes, illustrating the story of Saint Andrew, are on the vault of the tenth-century crypt, looking far older and more primitive than they really are because of their antique surroundings; the back part of the crypt is thought to be a pagan temple dating back to the time of the refugees from Septempeda.

The other church – actually the old cathedral – is up in **CASTELLO**, the upper part of San Severino, a long and steep walk – although there are occasional buses from the main square. A lonely, evocative place, it was here that the Romans from Septempeda came, though as Castello continued to be the hub of religious and political life until the eighteenth century, any traces of them have long been covered over. Close to its thirteenth-century walls, sheltered by a Gothic portico, is the **Fontana dei Sette Canelle**, a seven-spouted fountain where you'll occasionally see old women doing their washing. Right at the top, dwarfed by the medieval Torre del Comune, is the **Duomo Vecchio**, founded in the tenth century, but with a Romanesque-Gothic facade, simple Gothic cloisters, and a much rebuilt interior. Not surprisingly, it's lost a bit of atmosphere with all these reconstructions, but the baptistery vault still has its Salimbeni frescoes. Also worth a look are the inlaid choir stalls and tomb of the town's patron, Saint Severinus.

Ússita and hiking territory

South of San Severino, close to the border with Umbria and the Monti Sibillini, is **ÚSSITA**, a rather anonymous winter sports resort squeezed into a narrow valley at the foot of Monte Bove. Reachable by bus from Macerata, it's an accessible first base for mountain **hikes**, a 7–8km hike from the basic *Rifugio Forcella del Fargno* (open daily in Aug, Sun only June–end-Oct; ☎0733/32.071), from which there's a good choice of walks, including the ascent of the three-peaked mountain known as the **Pizzo Tre Vescovi** because it resembles three mitred bishops. The going can be tricky, as the upper peaks are covered in snow for most of the year, so you'll need a good map (*Kompass* 666 is the best), and if you can read Italian the *CAI Guida dei Monti Sibillini* is helpful, being packed with information on flora, fauna and local legends.

If you have your own transport or you don't mind road walking, you can also head up to the **Santuario di Macereto**, set on a wild high plain above Ússita. It's no rustic chapel, but a classy Bramantesque church built in the sixteenth century as a spiritual stopover for shepherds bringing their flocks up from their winter grazing grounds in the south, and is surrounded by arcaded stalls for the animals.

South of Macerata: the road to Sarnano

With the Sibillini mountains on the horizon, snow-capped for most of the year, the route south from Macerata ranks as one of the Marche's most beautiful. Ten kilometres along the road, on the edge of a dense wood, is the Romanesque-Gothic complex of a Cistercian abbey, the **Abbazia di Fiastra** (open daily in summer), adjoining which is an eighteenth-century house where Wagner once stayed. The trails through the woods are perhaps more enticing, and you should take time to see the **Museo della Civiltà Contadina** (L3500), a folk museum laid out in the abbey's low-vaulted outhouses. Among the agricultural and weaving equipment is a decorated wagon such as most farming families owned, until the middle of this century, using it as a manure cart, a wedding carriage, or whatever form of transport was needed. For some insight into the economics of marriage, take a look at the dowry lists, itemising the value of household goods. There's also a small **archaeological museum**, visitable on the same ticket, containing finds from the nearby Roman town of Urbisaglia.

A five-minute bus ride away, the site of **Urbisaglia** (or Urbs Salvia) was one of the Marche's most important Roman towns until it was sacked by Alaric in 409 AD. Its fame continued into the Middle Ages, when Dante invoked it as an example of a city fallen from glory in his *Paradiso*. So far an amphitheatre, theatre, baths and parts of the walls have been excavated, and frescoes of hunting scenes have been discovered in an underpassage.

South of Urbisaglia, the hill-town of **SAN GINESIO** is justifiably known as the balcony of the Sibillini: the panoramic view from the gardens of the Colle Ascarano, just outside the town walls, stretches from the Adriatic and Monte Cónero to the Sibillini mountains and the highest of the Apennines, the Gran Sasso in Abruzzo. There's a fair amount to see in the town itself, though as it's primarily set up as a summer health resort, you may find its hyper-cleanliness a little unreal. Its central piazza is dominated by one of the Marche's most unusual churches, the **Collegiata della Annunziata**, whose late-Gothic facade is decorated with filigree-like terracotta moulding. Rising above it are two campaniles, one capped by an onion dome, and the other by what looks like a manicured cactus. Gothic frescoes adorn some of the chapels, and the crypt has frescoes by the Salimbeni brothers – including a *Pietà* in which Mary looks completely demented and Christ is so covered with nail-holes that he appears to have chicken pox.

Sarnano

Until a few years ago, **SARNANO**, south of San Ginesio, was a poor and virtually abandoned village. Recently, however, the town has woken up to the potential of its radioactive springs, known since Roman times to have wide-ranging curative properties, and has began to develop itself into an exclusive spa resort. The medieval core, coiling in concentric circles around a gentle hill, was subtly restored, and though it's now more of a showpiece than a living village, its narrow interconnecting cobbled streets and picturesque old houses make it an ideal place for a undemanding day's wandering.

It's worth getting a map from the **tourist office** just off Piazza della Libertà in the small new town (Mon–Sat 8.30am–1.30pm & 3.30–6.30pm), before heading up through **Porta Brunforte** into old Sarnano. Just inside is the fourteenth-century church of **San Francesco**, decorated with Palestinian plates, thought to have been brought to Sarnano by souvenir-collecting Crusaders. Its convent is now the seat of the *comune*, and houses a small **Pinacoteca** (daily except Wed 3–7pm, Tues, Thurs, Sat also 9am–1pm), the major item being a *Madonna and Child* by Vittore Crivelli.

Continue climbing to the summit of the town and you hit **Piazza Alta**, once the political and religious centre. When Sarnano fell under papal rule in the sixteenth century, the limitation of local power made participation in public life lose its allure; eventually, in the last century, the underused fourteenth-century **Palazzo del Popolo** was converted into a theatre. It also proved increasingly difficult to ordain priors, as Rome refused to accept those chosen by the people, and the **Palazzo dei Priori** became the prison. These and the square's other medieval buildings are now in the process of restoration, and it's likely that the *comune* will move back here one day. At present the most interesting of the piazza's buildings is the thirteenth-century church of **Santa Maria di Piazza**, whose fifteenth-century frescoes include a figure known as the *Madonna with Angels*, for the host of celestial musicians and choristers surrounding her. The wooden statue of Christ on the altar has been saddled with one of popular tradition's looniest myths – if it's about to rain, his beard is supposed to grow. On the second Sunday in August, Santa Maria is the starting point for Sarnano's annual medieval knees-up – though apart from the costumes and processions, it has more in common with a kids' sports day, featuring a tug-of-war, pole climbing, and a race in which the competitors have to balance jugs of water on their heads.

The two most affordable **hotels** in Sarnano are the the *San Giacomo*, Via Garibaldi 88 (☎0733/657.201; ④), and *Ai Pini*, Via F. Corridoni 101 (☎0733/657.183; ④). If you want to **ski** in winter, or to spend a few summer days in the mountains, there's a small resort, SASSOTETTO, 10km away – the cheapest hotel there is *La Sibilla* (Dec–March & June–Sept; ☎0733/651.102; ④).

Southeast of Macerata: Fermo and Porto San Giorgio

Southeast of Macerata, a short distance from the coast, is the attractive old town of **FERMO**. Its web of streets is lined with medieval and Renaissance buildings, erupting out of which is a wooded peak crowned with a Romanesque-Gothic duomo. The town's most spectacular monument, however, is hidden from view – a first-century underground complex of thirty filter beds known as the **Piscina Epurtoria Romana**. Entered from Via Aceti, off the main Piazza del Popolo, it's something akin to a flooded cathedral, with its well-preserved vault and arches subtly lit, and, in the sections which remain in use, reflected in the dark, still water.

From Fermo a road descends to the resort of **PORTO SAN GIORGIO**, with a small fishing and sailing port and a long sandy beach. Its palms, pines and oleanders, and its sprinkling of Art Deco villas, make it a pleasant enough place, though the modern seafront is predictably bland. The best day to visit is on the second Sunday in July, for the *Festa del Mare*, when fish are fried in the open air in a giant frying pan – 5m across, it weighs 10,000 pounds and needs 3310 pounds of oil to fill it.

The Monti Sibillini

With a mountain lake reddened by the blood of the devil, a narrow pass known as the gorge of hell and a cave reputed to have been the lair of an enchantress, the **Monti Sibillini** are not only the most beautiful of the Apennines, but they teem with ancient legends too.

The best way of exploring the Sibillini is on foot; even if you're not a seasoned hiker there are easy but stunning trails, while for diehard backpackers there are challenging long treks, too. The most agreeable bases are the medieval hill-villages which crown the Sibillini foothills, but there are also a number of *rifugi* if you want to be closer to the starting-points for walks. Most villages are served by buses, but they're few and far between and you'll do better with your own transport.

Amándola and around

Though perhaps not the prettiest of the Sibillini hill-villages, **AMÁNDOLA** is easy to get to on public transport and makes for one of the best bases for seeing the region. Its main sight is a **Museo della Civiltà Contadina** (currently closed for restoration), housed in the ex-convent of the church of San Francesco. The collection is fascinating, ranging from wine-making and grappa-distilling apparatus to a hand-pulled ambulance and carts decorated with Fascist symbols. It's in the kitchen, though, that things really come alive – the clutter includes a jar of roasted barley (a coffee substitute), a sausage-making machine, mosquito spray, and a primitive potty and wooden baby-walker.

Otherwise, Amándola is a great place to wind down after a day's hiking. It has an excellent **youth hostel** in a newly converted eighteenth-century palazzo (☎0736/847.491) – all rooms have a bathroom, and there are plans to install individual kitchens as well – and you can spend your evenings drinking the local wine at the *osteria* below. The only other **hotel** is the *Paradiso* (☎0736/847.468; ⑥). Amándola is also a rather forward-looking place, holding an excellent week-long international **theatre festival** in the first week of September that was established a few years back by its left-leaning council. Low on pretension and high on participation, the festival overcomes language barriers with mime and movement performances and workshops – the atmosphere is irresistible, and it's well worth sticking around for the whole week.

Around Amándola

One kilometre north of Amándola is the fifteenth-century church of **Santa Maria a Piè d'Agello** – no architectural masterpiece, but a fine country church, with slots in the window sills for offerings and a few simple frescoes, though many were destroyed by the lime with which they were covered in the seventeenth century. It was thought, in plague-ridden times, that frescoes were unsanitary.

Further along the Tenna valley road you come to the abbey of **San Ruffino**, a thirteenth-century church built above catacombs. Their frescoes, dating back to the ninth and tenth centuries, indicate how long it was before Christianity was tolerated outside the main towns; in fact it wasn't until Saint Francis visited the area in the late eleventh century that Christianity took a hold and paganism finally began to decline.

Montefortino

A few kilometres south of Amándola, the hill-village of **MONTEFORTINO** is perhaps a prettier base than Amándola, touristy in season and dead quiet out – and less well served by buses. The cheapest place to stay is *Del Girone*, Via Papiri 5 (☎0736/859.219; ④). Primarily a place to wander and admire the Sibillini views, Montefortino also has a small **Pinacoteca** (Sat & Sun 10am–noon; at other times ask custodian at house no. 1, to the right of the piazza), whose chief attractions are a polyptych by Alemanno – a follower of the Crivelli who took as much delight in painting embroidery as they did – and an arresting twelfth-century portrait of a man with a pipe and candle emerging from the darkness. Appropriately, given the necromantic traditions of the area, there's also an eighteenth-century painting of *Circe* with her occult apparatus.

Montemonaco and around

A short way southeast of Montefortino, **MONTEMONACO**, a walled medieval village of cobbled streets and honey-gold houses, is close to some of the Sibillini's most legendary sights. One, the **cave of the sibyl**, whose occupant gave her name to the mountain group, is a two-hour walk west from the village, though sadly a recent rockfall blocked the entrance so there's little incentive for any but the seriously mystical to make the trip (see Chapter Thirteen, *Cumae*, for more on sibyls). The other, through the **Gola dell'Infernaccio** ("Gorge of Hell"), southwest of the village, is, however, one of the most spectacular (and easiest) walks you can do around Montemonaco; buses run by the Infernaccio fork, from where it's a three-hour walk to the gorge. Even the approach to the gorge, down a narrow valley, is evocative: silent, except for the distant roar of the River Tenna seething through the Gola. Although a straightforward walk in summer, it can be hazardous in winter, as the plaques to dead hikers on the cliffs at the entrance testify. Climbing up beyond the bridge, the path follows the river, squeezing its way under jagged overhanging rocks, accompanied by the deafening sound of raging water. After a second bridge the path forks, the lower leading to the tranquil source of the Tenna, and the upper, more interestingly, in about half an hour, to the **Hermitage of San Leonardo**, occupied by a solitary monk.

Hotels in Montemonaco are surprisingly expensive, but the *Rifugio Monte Sibilla* (open daily mid-July–mid-Sept; ☎0337/560.393; information from the *comune* at Montemonaco), close to the cave, is in any case the best base for climbing Monte Sibilla; without your own transport you'll have to walk. It lies about 6km east of the village along the path which eventually leads to the cave. As the path is only barely visible you'd be advised to take the *Kompass Monti Sibillini* map.

To do the best of the Sibillini treks, you need to travel 8km east from Montemonaco to **FOCE**, where you can stay in the *Rifugio della Montagna* (☎0736/960.327). The hike, through the **Valle del Lago di Pilato** and up to the **Lago di Pilato** and **Pizzo di Diavolo** (Devil's Peak), is fairly tough, and you'll need the *Kompass* map; and you shouldn't try the trip at all outside the high summer months, as the snows don't melt until June. If you want to extend the hike, you can camp on the shores of the lake, and the next morning climb the highest of the Sibillini peaks, **Monte Vettore**.

According to the legend of the lake, Pilate's body was dispatched from Rome on a cart pulled by two wild oxen, who climbed up into the Sibillini and ditched the corpse in the water here. In the Middle Ages it became a favourite haunt for necromancers seeking dialogues with the devil – stones inscribed with occult symbols have been found on its shores. Deciding they wanted to be rid of the magicians, the local lords one night put soldiers on guard around its shores. Nothing happened until the morning, when the soldiers discovered that the lake had turned red – assuming it was with the devil's blood, they fled. What in fact turned the water red was a mass of minuscule red *chircephalus marchesonii*, a species of fish indigenous to Asia; a shoal was left behind here millions of years ago, when the sea receded, and its descendants still thrive here.

Áscoli Piceno

ÁSCOLI PICENO owes its existence to a woodpecker that led a band of nomadic shepherds to the wedge of land between two rivers on which the city now stands. At least, that's one of the many legends to have grown up around the origins of Áscoli and the Piceni tribe for whom it is named; other versions replace the woodpecker-guide with Diomedes or the son of Saturn, and the nomadic shepherds with veterans of the Trojan War or Greek traders. Whatever the truth, the Piceni were real enough, and the relics of their civilisation suggest that they were a pretty emotional and impetuous people – writing curses on missiles before firing them, gauging the intensity of grief by measuring the volume of tears, and losing a critical battle against the Romans when they interpreted an earthquake as a sign of divine wrath, and abandoned the fight.

Today the Ascolani seem initially to be reserved, as if in obedience to the aphorisms urging moderation, hard work and reticence that are inscribed on many of their houses. However, one taste of the exuberance of the central piazza in the early evening is enough to dispel such an impression. If you come for Mardi Gras, you'll be able to participate in the Marche's most flamboyant carnival, while on the first Sunday in August there's the *Quintana*, a medieval festival which incorporates a spectacular joust.

The Town

The central **Piazza del Popolo**, the stage for the evening *passeggiata*, is the place to get the feel of Áscoli. Paved with gleaming travertine and flanked by Renaissance porticoes, it's the setting for two of the city's finest buildings, the pleasantly jumbled

Palazzo dei Capitani del Popolo and the refined Gothic San Francesco. The former was built in the thirteenth century, when the free commune of Áscoli was at its height. That anything of the building has survived is something of a miracle, for in 1535 a certain Giambattista Quieti, fearing that his rivals might seek refuge there, set fire to it. The interior was gutted but enough remained of the facade for a swift facelift to suffice. Rectangular windows were slotted into medieval arches, and a grand portal affixed, on top of which sits a statue to Pope Paul III, who reintroduced peace by replacing Quieti with a neutral outsider. Not that peace lasted long – a few years after the portal had been completed, the Ascolani, finding themselves under the rule of an overbearing papal representative, solved the problem by murdering him in the sacristy of the duomo.

When they weren't slaughtering each other, at least some of Áscoli's rulers found time to collect public money in order to finance city improvements. The sixteenth-century **loggias** that enclose the piazza are one of the results – each of a slightly different width, to correspond to the size of the contribution made by the various merchants and shopkeepers who worked there.

The church of **San Francesco**, on the other hand, was financed by the sale of a Franciscan convent outside the city, after Pope Alexander IV had given the Franciscans permission to move within its walls. Construction started in 1262 but wasn't completed until 1549, when the low cupola was added. It's a somewhat restrained church, with little to seize the attention except for the intricate west portal on Via del Trivio. Unless you need to cool and calm down after the heat and bustle of Áscoli's narrow streets, there's little point in going inside. Adjoining the south side of the church is the sixteenth-century **Loggia dei Mercanti**, sometimes attributed to Bramante. It was once the scene of commercial wheeling and dealing; there are still niches cut into the back wall in which bricks could be checked for size before being purchased. Lower-scale commerce now takes place in the cloister to the north of the church, where market stalls fill the area to which the monks would have come to meditate. The church's smaller and older cloister is far prettier and remains tranquil despite forming the garden of a Fascist-era office block.

San Vincenzo and around

Via Trivio continues up towards Piazza Ventidio Basso, the medieval commercial centre of town, now of interest for its two churches. **San Vincenzo e San Anastasio** is Áscoli's most distinctive church, with a fifteenth-century chessboard facade that was once filled out with frescoes. Beneath the mainly eleventh-century body of the building is a primitive crypt erected over a spring which was supposed to have leprosy-curing properties. Although the plunge bath is still there, the spring was diverted elsewhere in the last century.

Across the square, **San Pietro Martire** is a far less appealing building, erected by Dominican monks in the thirteenth century in order not to be outdone by their Franciscan rivals down the road. It's as austere and intimidating as Saint Peter Martyr himself, who, between founding Dominican communities like that at Áscoli, gained such a reputation as a persecutor of religious sects that he became the patron of inquisitors after his murder by a couple of so-called heretics.

The dark **Via Soderini**, leading out of the square, forms the spine of Áscoli's riverside medieval quarter. Lined with buildings out of which the occasional defensive tower sprouts, it's an evocative street, giving you a clear idea of how rigorously the town was defended. Tiny streets fan out from it, many of them spanned by covered passages which in times of siege served as escape routes and as stations from which to pour oil down onto the heads of attackers. Of the defensive tower houses, one of the best preserved is the **Palazzetto Longobardi**, a virtually windowless twelfth-century building; it's been converted into a youth hostel (see overleaf).

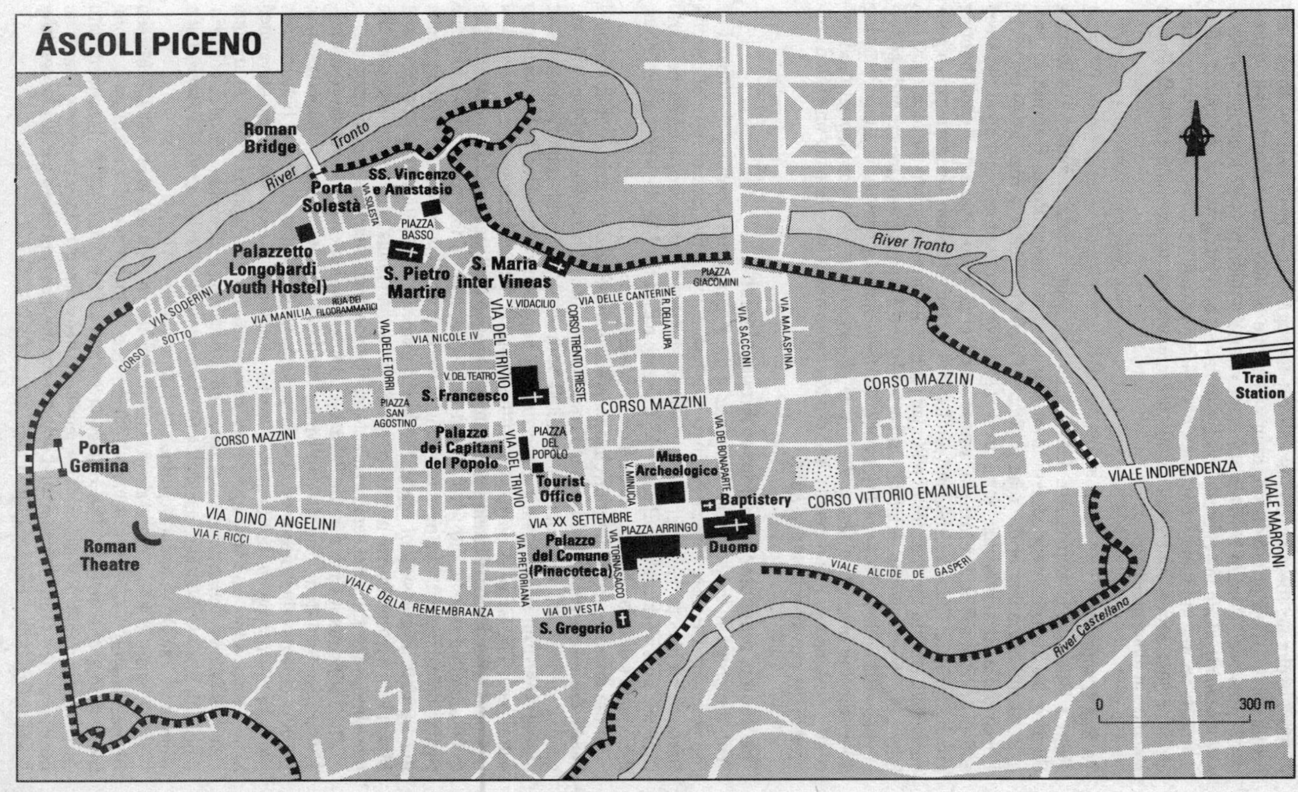
ÁSCOLI PICENO
Roman Bridge
River Tronto
Porta Solestà
VIA SOLESTA
SS. Vincenzo e Anastasio
PIAZZA BASSO
Palazzetto Longobardi (Youth Hostel)
S. Pietro Martire
S. Maria inter Vineas
River Tronto
PIAZZA GIACOMINI
VIA SODERINI
VIA MANILIA
RUA DEI FILODRAMMATICI
CORSO SOTTO
VIA DELLE TORRI
VIA NICOLE IV
V. VIDACILIO
VIA DEL TRIVIO
CORSO TRENTO TRIESTE
VIA DELLE CANTERINE
R. DELLA LUPA
VIA SACCONI
VIA MALASPINA
V. DEL TEATRO
S. Francesco
PIAZZA SAN AGOSTINO
CORSO MAZZINI
Train Station
Porta Gemina
Palazzo dei Capitani del Popolo
PIAZZA DEL POPOLO
Tourist Office
Museo Archeologico
V. MINUCIA
VIA DEI BONAPARTE
Baptistery
CORSO VITTORIO EMANUELE
VIALE INDIPENDENZA
VIALE MARCONI
VIA DINO ANGELINI
VIA F. RICCI
Roman Theatre
VIA XX SETTEMBRE
PIAZZA ARRINGO
Palazzo del Comune (Pinacoteca)
VIA PRETORIANA
VIA TORNASACCO
Duomo
VIALE ALCIDE DE GASPERI
VIALE DELLA REMEMBRANZA
VIA DI VESTA
S. Gregorio
River Castellano
0
300 m

After exploring the quarter you can cut through to the river and the thirteenth-century gate, the **Porta Solestà**, from which one of Italy's largest and most impressively preserved **Roman bridges** spans the river. An underpassage tunnels through it, and it's worth taking the effort to arrange to have it opened for you at the tourist office, as much for the uncanny experience of walking across an unseen river with traffic crossing just above your head as for the opportunity to examine colossal Roman masonry at close quarters.

To San Gregorio

There's little else of Roman Áscoli to see, except some sparse remains of a **Roman theatre**, on the southwest edge of town, close to the Roman **Porta Gemina**, or twin gate, at the beginning of the road to Rome. From the theatre a road leads up to the **Parco della Rimembranza**, for a great rooftop view of the town, and on to the steep and picturesque **Via Pretoriana**, whose small craft shops make it a good hunting ground for gifts. Close by, the fourteenth-century church of **San Gregorio** was ingeniously built around the remains of a Roman temple. Incorporated into the facade are two lofty Corinthian columns, originally imported by the Romans from Greece, and patches of *opus reticulatum* (diamond brickwork). In the adjoining convent is a tiny revolving door with the inscription *Qui si depositano gli innocenti* ("Here you deposit the innocent"), designed so that parents could remain anonymous when leaving unwanted children to the care of priests and nuns.

The duomo, pinacoteca and Museo Archaeologico

With the pregnant caryatids on the facade of the **Palazzo del Comune** overlooked by the pompous **Duomo, Piazza Arringo** is a testimony to the lack of taste of Áscoli's Baroque architects. However, as the duomo shelters what is reckoned to be Carlo Crivelli's best work, and the Palazzo del Comune one of the Marche's best art galleries, the square's daft flamboyance does have its positive side.

In the duomo's flashy interior chandeliers are suspended on strings of illuminated beads, the apse is painted with a fake Persian carpet, the pillar capitals and vault ribs are gaudily gilded, and the cupola is painted with late nineteenth-century frescoes of obscure Ascolani saints against a backdrop of impossibly blue skies and feather-mop palm trees. The **Crivelli polyptych**, in the Cappella del Sacramento, thus comes as a welcome relief. Even if Crivelli's penchant for rarefied opulence isn't to your taste, it has to be admitted that he did what he did with style, and, in this work, with admirable psychological insight. The most arresting of the ten panels is the central *Pietà*, in which the haggard expression of Mary, the bitter torment that distorts Christ's face, and Magdalene's frozen horror as she examines the wound in his hand are rendered all the more intense by the strict semicircular formation in which their heads are arranged.

The **Pinacoteca Civica** in the Palazzo Comunale (summer Mon–Fri 9am–1pm & 3–7.30pm, Sat 9am–1pm, Sun 4–8pm; winter Mon–Sat 9am–1pm, Sun 9.30am–12.30pm; L2500) contains other pieces by Crivelli, none as sophisticated or as well preserved as the duomo's polyptych, but engaging works nonetheless – one shows the sprawling baby Christ, chin in hand, apparently mesmerised by an apple. Pietro Alemanno, Crivelli's follower, contributes an *Annunciation* featuring a view of medieval Áscoli bristling with towers, and there are also a few foreign works – most notably a *Portrait of a Woman* by Van Dyck, and a *Deposition* by Rogier van der Weyden.

If you want to know more about ancient Áscoli, you should also visit the **Museo Archaeologico** (Tues–Fri 9.30am–1.30pm, Sat 3.30–5.30pm, Sun 9.30am–1.30pm; free), across the square. The collection includes Piceni projectiles inscribed with curses against their Roman enemies, jewellery, heavy bronze rings that were placed on the stomachs of dead women, and small test tube-like containers used to assess the quality of grief by measuring the volume of tears.

Practicalities

Ascoli's train station is just east of the town centre, ten minutes' walk away, left off Viale Indipendenza. The **tourist office** is on the ground floor of the Palazzo dei Capitani del Popolo on Piazza del Popolo (Mon–Fri 8.30am–1pm & 3–7pm, Sat 8.30am–12.30pm & 3–7pm, Sun 9am–1pm; ☎0736/253.045). You're likely to want to stay over, although there are few hotels and you will certainly need to book in advance. The most affordable option is a **youth hostel**, the *Ostello de' Longobardi*, open all year round and housed in a medieval tower bang in the historic centre at Via Soderini 16 (☎0736/259.007; ①). The most reasonable **hotels** are the *Piceno*, Via Minucia 10 (☎0736/252.553; ④), and the *Cantina dell'Arte*, Rua della Lupa 8 (☎0736/255.620; ④).

You can **eat** reasonably cheaply. The lively *Bella Napoli*, Via Bonaparte 18–20, off Piazza Aringo, is reckoned to be Ascoli's best pizzeria. *Al Teatro*, Via del Teatro 3, has modestly priced regular meals as well as pizzas, as does *Il Menetrello*, Via Pretoriana 32–34. For more refined fare, try the *Locanda La Monella*, Via di Vesta 28, an old inn with wooden bench tables, great wine and lots of gastronomic goodies. It's highly popular, so best to book (☎0736/255.730). For a **drink**, you could do worse than *Pub Nicolo IV*, Via Nicolo IV 13, or linger over a cocktail at the *Bistro*, Via Vidacilio 12.

The Áscoli coast

Easily accessible by bus or train from Áscoli Piceno, **SAN BENEDETTO DEL TRONTO** is the most extravagant of the Marche's resorts. Known as the "Riviera delle Palme" for the five thousand palms that shade its promenade, and with six kilometres of sandy white beach, it'll give you a hedonistic buzz if you're in the mood for beaches, discos and *passeggiata* posing; if you're not, give it a miss. There are something like a hundred **hotels**, details of which are available from the **tourist office** on Viale delle Tamerici (Mon–Sat 8am–2pm). Try *Zodiaco*, Via Tibullo 5 (☎0735/85.503; ④), 1km south of the station just off the seafront. **GROTTAMARE**, a few minutes further up the coastal rail line, is a lower-key resort on the same model, but without San Benedetto's panache. One factor that makes it worth considering, though, is the extremely cheap *Parco* hotel, at Lungomare della Repubblica 48 (☎0735/631.015; ③).

travel details

Trains

Ancona to: Loreto (13 daily; 20min).

Áscoli Piceno to: San Benedetto al Tronto (13 daily; 40min).

Macerata to: Tolentino/San Severino (13 daily; 20min/25min).

Pésaro to: Ancona (39 daily; 50min).

Buses

Amándola to: Áscoli Piceno (3 daily; 1hr 20min); Fermo (4 daily; 1hr); Montefortino (5 daily; 25min); Montemonaco (5 daily; 25min); Porto San Giorgio (4 daily; 1hr 15min).

Ancona to: Jesi (8 daily); Macerata (10 daily; 2hr); Porto Recanati (5 daily; 50min); Senigallia (23 daily; 1hr); Sirolo (20 daily; 30min).

Áscoli Piceno to: Amándola (3 daily; 1hr 20min); Montefortino (3 daily; 1hr 30min); Montemonaco (3 daily; 1hr 45min); San Benedetto al Tronto (35 daily; 50min).

Macerata to: Amándola (8 daily; 1hr 25min); Fiastra (8 daily; 15min); Loreto (8 daily; 45min); Morrovalle (5 daily; 30min); Porto Recanati (8 daily; 30min); Recanati (8 daily; 55min); Sarnano (8 daily; 1hr).

Pésaro to: Fano (every 30min; 10min); Gradara (5 daily; 15min); Marotta (7 daily; 20min); Torrette (7 daily; 15min); Urbino (11 daily; 50min).

International Ferries

Ancona to: Corfu (summer at least 1 a day; winter 2–4 weekly; 22–25hr); Igoumenitsa (summer at least 1 a day; winter 2–4 weekly; 24hr); Patras (at least 1 a day; 34hr).

CHAPTER ELEVEN

ROME AND LAZIO

Of all Italy's historic cities, it's Rome which perhaps exerts the most compelling fascination. There's arguably more to see here than in any other city in the world, with the relics of a constant two thousand-plus years of population packed into its sprawling urban area; and as a contemporary European capital, it has a feel which is quite unique. Even if you don't intend to travel any further south, it would be a great mistake to exclude it from any tour of the north of the country.

Rome is, in many ways, the ideal capital of Italy. Perfectly placed between Italy's warring north and south factions and heartily despised by both, it has long been the country's parasite, under the papacy ruling its dominions with a distant and autocratic hand, overweighted with courtiers and hangers-on, and since Unification spending money that's largely made in the prosperous North on programmes imposed on the poor and helpless South. Romans, the thinking seems to go in other Italian cities, are a lazy bunch, not to be trusted, living very nicely off the fat of the rest of the land. The Romans, for their part, are happy to agree, considering themselves a breed apart (SPQR "Sono Pordi Questi Romani") from their compatriots, with no particular allegiances, and comfortable in the belief that their city is where the things that matter happen. In fact, much of Italy's power-broking goes on elsewhere, amongst the bosses of Turin and Milan; and the politicians are often manipulated by the country's powerful industrialists. But Rome remains the proud centre of government string-pulling, the wastefulness, inefficiency and corruption of its bloated bureaucracies a national fact of life. In a city of around four million people, there are around 600,000 office workers, compared to an industrial workforce of around a sixth of that.

For the traveller, all of this is less evident than the sheer weight of history in the city, its various eras crowding in on each other to an almost overwhelming degree. Nowhere else in the world, perhaps, are you forced to take account of history in such an uncompromising way. There are, of course, the **Classical** features, most renownedly the Colosseum, the rubbly Forum and Palatine Hill; and relics from the **early Christian** period in ancient basilicas. And the fountains and churches of the **Baroque** period go a long way to determining the look of the city centre, most notably in the work of Bernini. But these are just a part of the picture, which is an almost continuous one right up to the present day, taking in **Romanesque** churches, **Renaissance** palazzi, **Rococo** fountains, right up to the ponderous buildings of **post-Unification** and the often destructive, self-publicising legacies of **Mussolini** – often all found within a few paces of each other. There are medieval churches atop early Christian basilicas above Roman palaces; houses and apartment blocks incorporate fragments of eroded Roman columns, carvings and inscriptions; roads and piazzas follow the lines of classical amphitheatres and stadia.

All of which is to say that Rome is not an easy place to absorb on one visit, and you need to approach things slowly, taking care not to try and see too much too quickly, even if you only have a few days here. Whatever you do, don't feel obliged to tramp around the ancient sites and make a dutiful visit to Saint Peter's and the Vatican. If time is short, and unless you're a real aficionado of ruins and religious art, you'll have a much better time if you stick mainly to the narrow cobbled streets and splendid piazzas

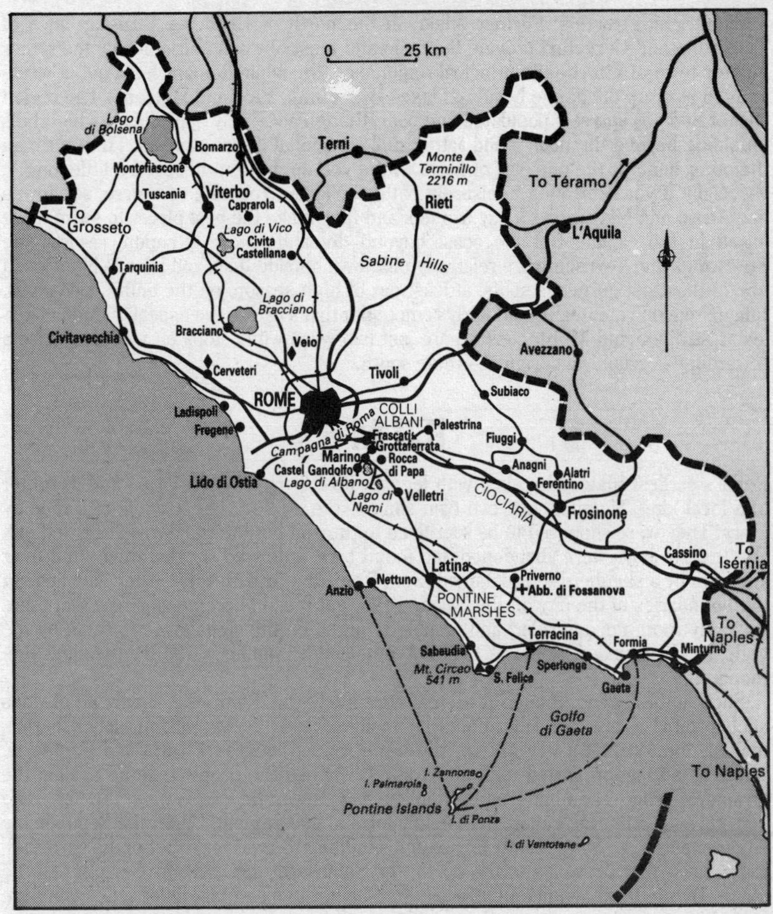

of the old centre and Trastevere. Apart from anything, it's hard to get anywhere very fast. Despite regular threats to close the city centre off to motor vehicles altogether, the congestion problem is awful and getting worse; on foot it's easy to lose a sense of direction winding about in the twisting old streets, and in any case you're so likely to see something interesting that detours and stopoffs are almost inevitable. Sturdy, comfortable shoes and loose, cool clothes – Rome can get very sticky in summer – will be your greatest assets. One further thing: don't come in August, when the city centre is half closed up and the only people in town are fellow tourists.

Beyond Rome, the region of **Lazio** inevitably pales in comparison, with relatively few centres of note and a landscape that varies from the gently undulating green hills of its northern sector to the more inhospitable mountains south and east of the capital. It's a poor region, its lack of identity the butt of a number of Italian jokes, and it's the closest you'll get to the feel of the Italian South without catching a train all the way to Naples. Much, however, is easily seen on a day trip from the capital, not least the ancient sites of **Ostia Antica** and Hadrian's villa at **Tivoli** – two of the Rome area's most important (and intriguing) sights. Further afield, in the north of Lazio the Etruscan sites of **Tarquinia** and **Cerveteri** provide the main and most obvious tourist focus, the rather gloomy town of **Viterbo** the principal regional centre; while Romans head out at weekends to soak up the gentle beauty of lakes **Bracciano**, **Vico** and **Bolsena**. The region east of Rome is sparsely populated and poor, though scenically appealing, its high hills unfolding beyond the main – and rather dull – regional centre of **Rieti**. The south, on the other hand, is the one part of Lazio where you might want to spend a little longer, especially if you're beating a leisurely path to Naples. You can, of course, see towns like **Anzio** and **Nettuno** as a day trip too, and they make the best places to swim while based in the capital. But the coast beyond demands more attention: resorts like **Sperlonga** and **Terracina** are relatively unknown outside Italy, and islands like **Ponza** one of the most gorgeous spots, at least out of high season, on the entire west coast. Inland, much is mountains and fairly remote but that's part of the appeal; the monasteries at **Subiaco** and **Montecassino** are just two worthwhile stops on what might be a rewarding – certainly an original – route south.

ROME

Rome's earliest **history** is caked with legend. Rea Silvia, a Vestal Virgin and daughter of a local king, Numitor, had two twin sons – the product, she alleged, of a rape by Mars. They were supposed to be sacrificed to the god but the ritual wasn't carried out, and the two boys were abandoned and found by a wolf, who suckled them until their adoption by a shepherd – who named them **Romulus and Remus**. Later they laid out the boundaries of the city on the Palatine Hill, but it soon became apparent that there was only room for one ruler, and, unable to agree on the signs given to them by the gods, they quarrelled, Romulus killing Remus and becoming in 753 BC the city's first monarch.

Such is the legend, though it seems more likely that Rome was simply an obvious spot to build a city: the Tiber could be easily crossed by way of the Isola Tiberina, making the location a key one on the trade routes between Etruria and Campania. Rome as a kingdom lasted until about 507 BC, when the people rose up against the tyrannical King Tarquinius and established a **Republic**, appointing the first two consuls and instituting a more democratic form of government. Under the Republic the city prospered, growing greatly in size and subduing the various tribes of the surrounding areas – the Etruscans to the north, the Sabines to the east, the Samnites to the south. By the third century BC the city had begun to extend its influence beyond the boundaries of what is now mainland Italy, pushing south into Sicily and across the ocean to Africa and Carthage, soon becoming the dominant power in the Mediterranean. Domestically, however, the history of the Republic is one of internal strife, faction fighting faction among the patrician ruling classes as everyone tried to grab a slice of the riches that were pouring into the city from its plundering expeditions abroad – and the ordinary people, or plebians, enjoying little more justice than they had under the Roman monarchs.

Following the murder of Julius Caesar, a brief period of turmoil gave way, in 27 BC, to the founding of the **Empire** under Augustus, a triumph for the new democrats over the old guard. Augustus heaved Rome into the Imperial era, determined to turn the city – as he claimed – from one of stone to one of marble, building arches, theatres and monuments of a magnificence suited to the capital of an expanding empire. The city swelled to a population of a million or more, its people housed in cramped apartment blocks or *insulae*; crime in the city was rife, and the traffic problem apparently on a par with today's, one contemporary writer complaining that the din on the streets made it impossible to get a good night's sleep. It was, however, a time of peace and prosperity, the

Roman upper classes living a life of indolent luxury, in sumptuous residences with proper plumbing and central heating, and the Empire's borders being ever more extended, reaching their maximum limits under the emperor Trajan, who died in 117 AD.

The **decline** of Rome is hard to date precisely, but it could be said to have started with the emperor Diocletian, who assumed power in 284 and divided the Empire into two parts, East and West. The first Christian emperor, Constantine, shifted the seat of power altogether in 330, and Rome's heady period as capital of the world was over, the wealthier members of the population moving east and a series of invasions by Goths in 410 AD and Vandals about forty years later only serving to quicken the city's ruin. By the sixth century the city was a devastated and infection-ridden shadow of its former self.

It was the **papacy,** under Pope Gregory I ("the Great") in 590, that rescued Rome from its demise, Gregory sending missions all over Europe to spread the word of the Church and publicise its holy relics, so drawing pilgrims – and their money – back to the city, and in time making the papacy the natural authority in Rome. The pope took the name "Pontifex Maximus" after the title of the high priest of classical times (literally "the keeper of the bridges", which were vital to the city's well-being during the Roman era). The crowning a couple of centuries later of Charlemagne as Holy Roman Emperor, with dominions spread Europe-wide but answerable to the pope, intensified the city's revival, and the pope and city became recognised as head of the Christian world.

There were times over the **next few hundred years** when the power of Rome and the papacy was weakened: Robert Guiscard, the Norman king, sacked the city in 1084; a century later, a dispute between the city and the papacy led to a series of popes relocating in Viterbo; and in 1308 the French-born Pope Clemente V transferred his court to Avignon. In the mid-fourteenth century, Cola di Rienzo seized power, setting himself up as the people's saviour from the decadent ways of the city's rulers and forming a new Roman republic. But the increasingly autocratic ways of the new ruler soon lost popularity; di Rienzo was deposed, and in 1376 Pope Gregory XI returned to Rome. As time went on, power gradually became concentrated in a handful of families, who swapped the top jobs, including the papacy itself, between them. Under the burgeoning power of the pope, the city began to take on a new aspect: churches were built, the city's pagan monuments rediscovered and preserved, and artists began to arrive in Rome to work on commissions for the latest pope, who would invariably try to outdo his predecessor's efforts with ever more glorious self-aggrandising buildings and works of art. This process reached a head during the **Renaissance** period; Bramante, Raphael and Michelangelo all worked in the city, on and off, throughout their careers. The reigns of popes Julius II and Leo X were something of a golden age, the city at the centre of Italian cultural and artistic life, and site of the creation of great works of art like the Sistine Chapel frescoes, Raphael's *Stanze* in the Vatican Palace and fine palaces like the Villa Farnesina, Palazzo Farnese and Spada, not to mention the commissioning of a new Saint Peter's as well as any number of other churches. In 1527 all was brought abruptly to an end, when the armies of the Hapsburg monarch, Charles V, swept into the city, occupying it – and wreaking havoc – for a year while Pope Clement VII cowered in the Castel Sant' Angelo.

The ensuing years were ones of yet more restoration, and perhaps because of this it's the **seventeenth century** which has left the most tangible impression on Rome today; the vigour of the counter-Reformation throwing up huge sensational monuments like the Gesù church that were designed to confound the scepticism of the new Protestant thinking. The period also saw the completion of Saint Peter's under Paul V, and the ascendancy of Gianlorenzo Bernini as the city's principal architect and sculptor under Pope Urban VIII. Many of the city's exotic fountains date from this Baroque era, as do a great many of its churches and palaces.

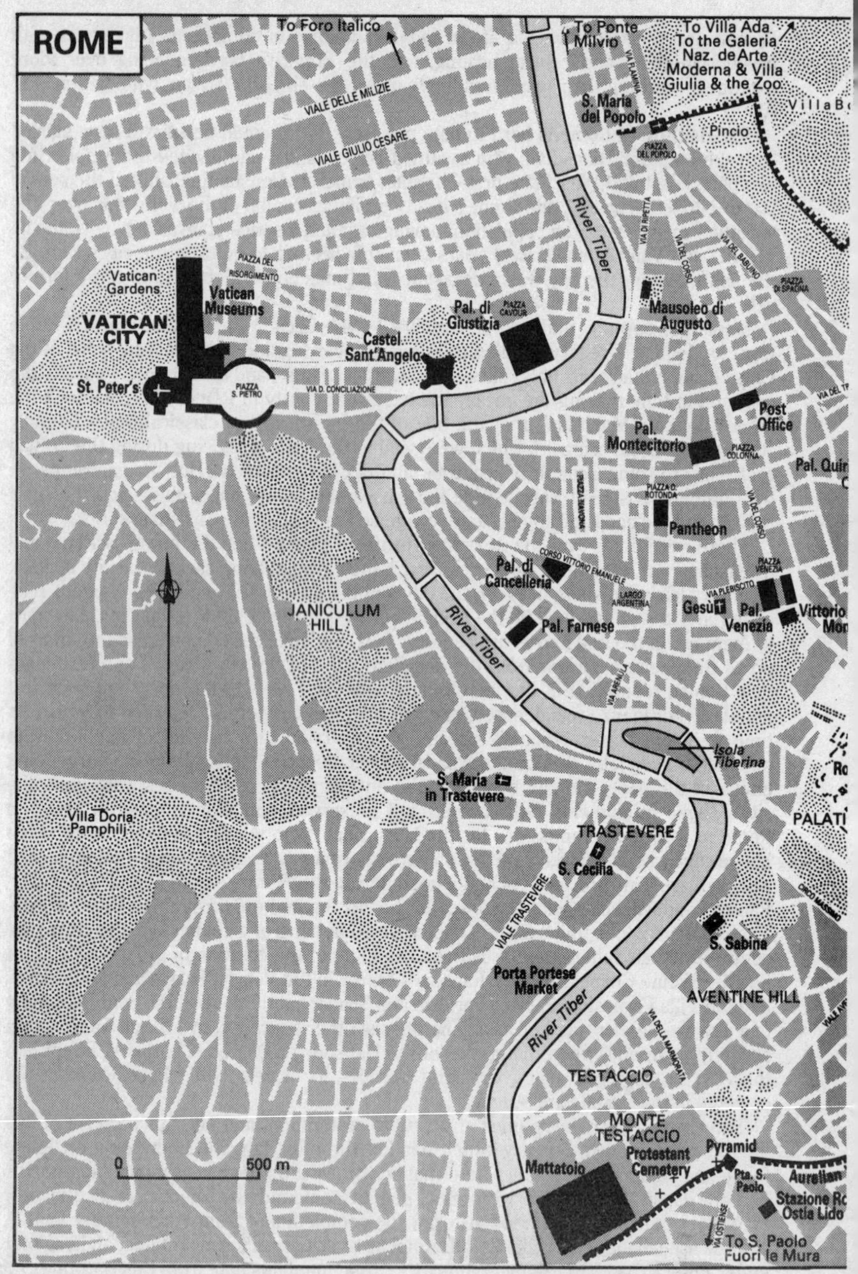

ROME
To Foro Italico
To Ponte Milvio
To Villa Ada, To the Galeria Naz. de Arte Moderna & Villa Giulia & the Zoo
VIALE DELLE MILIZIE
VIALE GIULIO CESARE
VIA FLAMINIA
S. Maria del Popolo
PIAZZA DEL POPOLO
Pincio
River Tiber
VIA DI RIPETTA
VIA DEL CORSO
VIA DEL BABUINO
PIAZZA DI SPAGNA
PIAZZA DEL RISORGIMENTO
Vatican Gardens
Vatican Museums
VATICAN CITY
Pal. di Giustizia
PIAZZA CAVOUR
Mausoleo di Augusto
Castel Sant'Angelo
St. Peter's
PIAZZA S. PIETRO
VIA D. CONCILIAZIONE
Post Office
Pal. Montecitorio
PIAZZA COLONNA
PIAZZA NAVONA
PIAZZA D. ROTONDA
Pantheon
Pal. di Cancelleria
CORSO VITTORIO EMANUELE
LARGO ARGENTINA
VIA PLEBISCITO
PIAZZA VENEZIA
Gesù
Pal. Venezia
JANICULUM HILL
Pal. Farnese
VIA ARENULA
Isola Tiberina
S. Maria in Trastevere
Villa Doria Pamphilj
TRASTEVERE
S. Cecilia
VIALE TRASTEVERE
CIRCO MASSIMO
S. Sabina
Porta Portese Market
AVENTINE HILL
VIA DELLA MARMORATA
TESTACCIO
MONTE TESTACCIO
Pyramid
Protestant Cemetery
Mattatoio
Pta. S. Paolo
VIA OSTIENSE
To S. Paolo Fuori le Mura
0
500 m

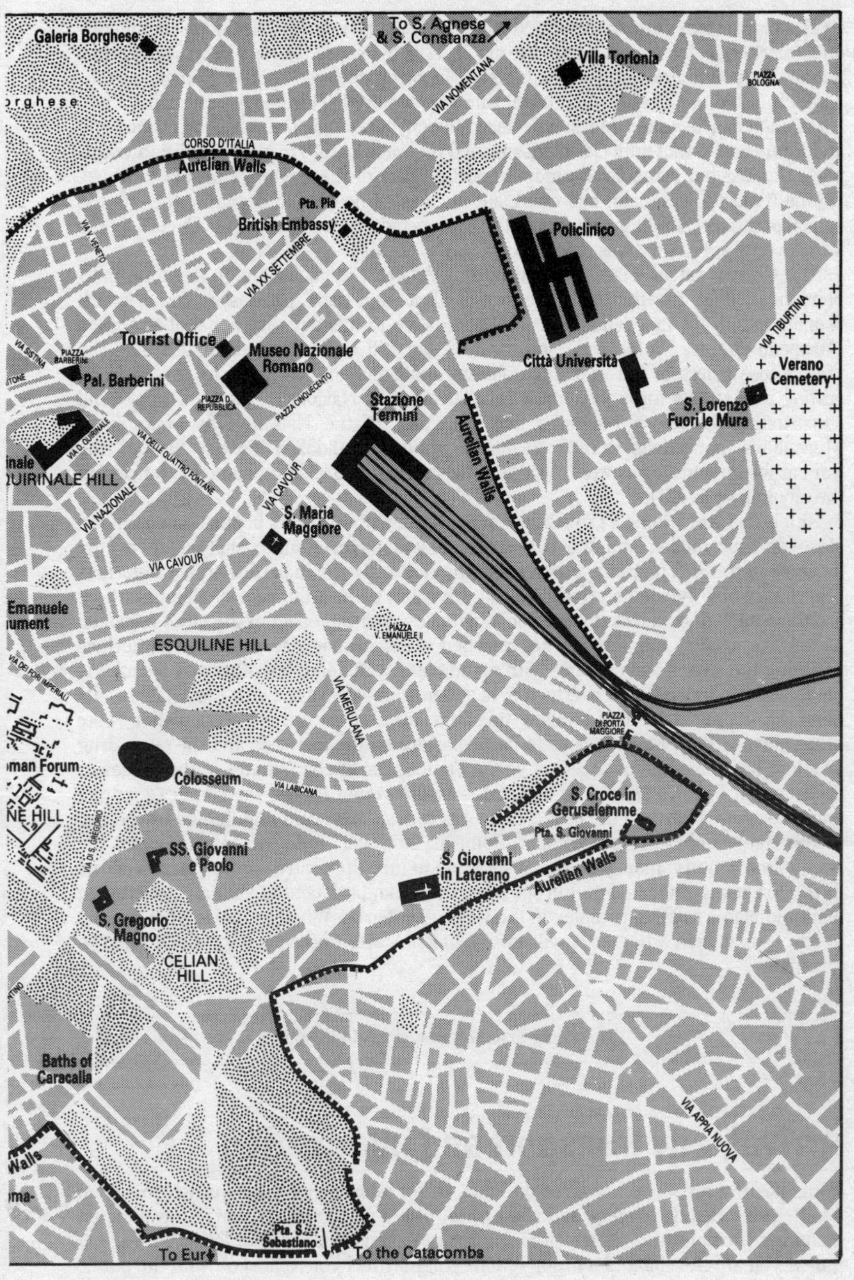

Galeria Borghese
To S. Agnese & S. Constanza
Villa Torlonia
PIAZZA BOLOGNA
VIA NOMENTANA
CORSO D'ITALIA
Aurelian Walls
Pta. Pia
British Embassy
Policlinico
VIA V. VENETO
VIA XX SETTEMBRE
VIA TIBURTINA
Tourist Office
Museo Nazionale Romano
Città Università
Verano Cemetery
PIAZZA BARBERINI
Pal. Barberini
VIA SISTINA
PIAZZA D. REPUBBLICA
PIAZZA CINQUECENTO
Stazione Termini
S. Lorenzo Fuori le Mura
VIA D. QUIRINALE
VIA DELLE QUATTRO FONTANE
Aurelian Walls
VIA CAVOUR
VIA NAZIONALE
S. Maria Maggiore
VIA CAVOUR
ESQUILINE HILL
PIAZZA V. EMANUELE II
VIA DEI FORI IMPERIALI
VIA MERULANA
PIAZZA DI PORTA MAGGIORE
Colosseum
VIA LABICANA
S. Croce in Gerusalemme
Pta. S. Giovanni
VIA DI S. GREGORIO
SS. Giovanni e Paolo
S. Giovanni in Laterano
Aurelian Walls
S. Gregorio Magno
CELIAN HILL
Baths of Caracalla
VIA APPIA NUOVA
Pta. S. Sebastiano
To Eur
To the Catacombs

The **eighteenth century** saw the decline of the papacy as a political force, a phenomenon marked by the occupation of the city in 1798 by Napoleon; Pius VI was unceremoniously sent off to France as a prisoner and Napoleon declared another Roman republic – which lasted until 1815, when papal rule was restored. Thirty-four years later a pro-Unification caucus under Mazzini declared the city a republic but was soon chased out, and Rome had to wait until Garibaldi stormed the walls in 1870 to join the **unified country** – the last but symbolically most important part of the Italian peninsula to do so. "Roma o morte", Garibaldi had cried, and he wasted no time in declaring the city the capital of the new kingdom, confining the by now quite powerless pontiff, Pius IX, in the Vatican until agreement was reached on a way to coexist.

The **Concordat of 1929** recognised the Vatican City as sovereign territory, independent of Italy, together with the key basilicas and papal palaces in Rome, which remain technically independent of the Italian state to this day. As capital of a modern European country, Rome was (some would say still is) totally unequipped, and the Piemontese rulers of the new kingdom set about building a city fit to govern from, cutting new streets through Rome's central core (Via Nazionale, Via del Tritone) and constructing grandiose buildings like the Altar of the Nation. Fifty years later, Mussolini's motivations weren't dissimilar when he bulldozed his way through the Roman forum and began work on the futuristic, self-publicising planned extension to the city known as EUR.

Since the war, Rome's growth has been steadily upwards, its population soaring to close on four million and the city centre becoming ever more snarled up by the increase in traffic. The traffic problems of the *centro storico*, in particular, are notorious – in theory only residents are allowed to drive and park in the centre, although there are thousands of counterfeit passes in existence – and the effect of the city's poisoned air on the ancient monuments has reached crisis proportions, with the authorities swathing the stones and columns with netting and scaffolding but otherwise seemingly paralysed into indecision. Poverty, too, is endemic in parts of the city, the estates on its outskirts finding it hard to swallow the huge upsurge in the city's population. Like other parts of Italy, racist attacks in particular are on the increase; and the city's drug problem has worsened over recent years. Famous for fifteen minutes in the Sixties as the home of Fellini's *Dolce Vita* and Italy's bright young things, the country's cutting edge has shifted north in the past couple of decades – a process highlighted by the rise of the right-wing Northern leagues. Rome is, however, trying to lug itself into the twenty-first century: money has been set aside to turn the centre – from Piazza Venezia to the Via Appia Antica – into Europe's largest urban park, and to shift all government institutions to a satellite complex in the western suburbs. Whether this is what the city needs – or indeed whether it will ever happen – are, however, very much open to question.

The Rome **area telephone code** is ☎06.

Arrival, city transport and information

Rome has two **airports**: Leonardo da Vinci, better known simply as **Fiumicino**, which handles all scheduled flights, and **Ciampino**, where you'll arrive if you're travelling on a charter. Taxis in from either airport are very expensive at around L75,000-plus, and unless you are travelling in a group of four you may feel you're best off with the public transport links.

From **Fiumicino** it's fairly easy: between 5.40am and midnight, trains run approximately every twenty minutes (every thirty minutes early afternoon), via Trastevere station, to Ostiense station, which is linked with the Piramide stop on metro line #B, a short ride away from Termini. Bear in mind, though, that line #B closes at 9.30pm on weekdays and 11.30pm on Saturdays and Sundays. Buses #94 and #95 from Piazzale Partigiani, directly outside the station, will take you to Piazza Venezia, or you can usually pick up at a cab on the Via Ostiense side of Piazzale Ostiense, a five-minute walk away. Alternatively, you could get off the Fiumicino train at the smaller Trastevere station, from where you can catch bus #26, #170, #718 or #719 to Largo Argentina.

From **Ciampino**, take an *ACOTRAL* bus from the terminal to the Anagnina stop of metro line #A, from where it's a twenty-minute ride to Termini. (Leaving Rome for Ciampino, be sure to take the bus marked "Aeroporto", *not* the bus for Ciampino, which only goes to Ciampino village).

Travelling by **train** from most places in Italy, you arrive at Stazione Termini, centrally placed for all parts of the city and meeting-point of the two metro lines and many city bus routes. There are other rail stations in Rome: Tiburtina is a stop for some north–south intercity trains, while selected routes around Lazio are handled by both the Laziali platform of Stazione Termini and the *ACOTRAL* station on Piazzale Flaminio – the so-called Roma-Nord line.

Arriving by **bus** could leave you in any one of a number of places around the city. The main stations include Rebibbia (Tivoli, Subiaco); Via Lepanto (Cerveteri, Civitavecchia, Bracciano area); EUR Fermi (Nettuno, Anzio, southern Lazio coast); Anagnina (Castelli Romani); Saxa Rubra (Viterbo and around). All of these stations are on a metro line, except Saxa Rubra, which is on the Roma-Nord line and connected by trains every fifteen minutes with the station at Piazzale Flaminio, on metro line #A. *Eurolines* buses from outside Italy terminate on Piazza della Repubblica.

Coming into the city **by road**, the Grande Raccordo Anulare circles the city and is connected with all of the major arteries into the city centre – the Via Cassia from the north, Via Salaria from the northeast, Via Tiburtina or Via Nomentana from the east, Via Appia Antica or Via Cristoforo Colombo from the south, and Via Aurelia from the west.

City transport

Like most Italian cities, even the larger ones, the best way to get around Rome is to **walk** – you'll see more and will better appreciate the city. The city wasn't built for motor traffic, and it shows – in the traffic jams, the pollution, and the bad tempers of its drivers. That said, its **bus service**, run by *ATAC*, is a good one – cheap, reliable and as quick as the clogged streets allow. Flat-fare **tickets**, valid for ninety minutes, cost L800 from bars with an *ATAC* sign or booths at major bus stages, and will take you as far as you want to go – cancel them in the machine by the rear doors when you get on. You can also get a one-day pass, valid on buses and the metro for L2800, or a weekly pass, also valid on both buses and metro for L10,000, both available from the booths on Piazza dei Cinquecento and Piazza del Risorgimento. It's worth knowing that there's a L50,000 spot fine for fare-dodging, and pleading a foreigner's ignorance will get you nowhere.

To sidestep the traffic, Rome also has a **metro**, though it's not as useful as you'd think, its two lines more directed at ferrying commuters out to the suburbs than transporting tourists around the city centre. Nonetheless it's much less crowded (and cooler) than the buses, and there are a few useful city centre stations: Termini is the hub of both lines, and there are stations at the Colosseum, Piazza Barberini and the Spanish Steps. Tickets cost a flat L1000. Metro maps are posted up in every station, and the *Tutto Città* has a complete list of bus and tram lines, although if you're going to use the system a lot, especially the buses, it's worth investing in the excellent detailed *ATAC* **transport map** (L6000), available from Termini newsstands and the Piazza dei Cinquecento booth.

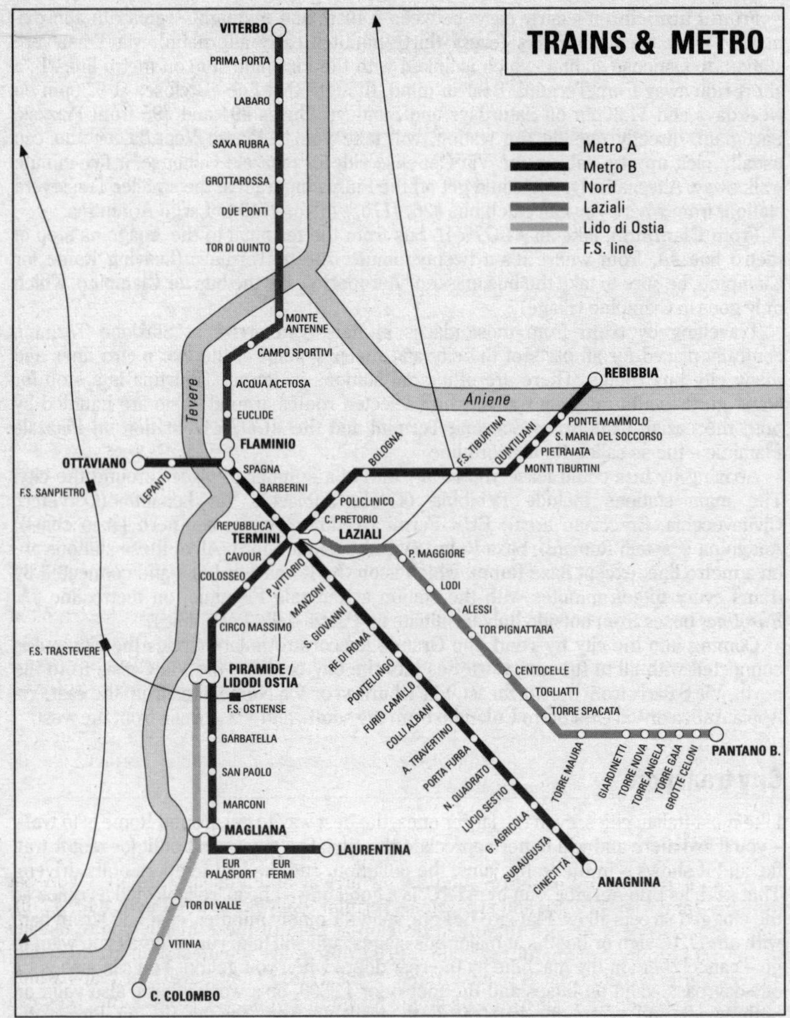

MUSEUM CARDS

It is now possible to buy **museum cards**, which are valid for selected Rome attractions, although you should study the list carefully before buying one – it is by no means comprehensive. If you decide that one would be useful, the cards are available from the Capitoline Museums, the Ara Pacis Augustae, and the Museo della Civilità Romana, among other places, and cost L13,000 for a light blue card, valid for one day, L23,000 for yellow card, valid for two consecutive days, L30,000 for an orange card, valid for four consecutive days, and L48,000 for a green card, valid for 7 consecutive days.

USEFUL BUS ROUTES

#26 Viale Trastevere–Largo Argentina–Corso del Rinascimento

#27 Stazione Trastevere–Colosseum–Termini

#44 Viale Trastevere–Largo Argentina–Piazza Venezia

#56 Via Veneto–Via del Corso–Piazza Venezia–Largo Argentina–Piazza Sonnino

#64 Termini–Piazza Venezia–Saint Peter's

#81 San Giovanni in Laterano–Colosseum–Piazza Venezia–Largo Argentina–Corso del Rinascimento

#93 Termini–Santa Maria Maggiore–Baths of Caracalla–EUR

#95 Piazza Venezia–Via del Tritone–Via Veneto–Piazzale Flaminio

#118 Colosseum–San Giovanni in Laterano–Via Appia Antica

#492 Stazione Tiburtina–Piazza Barberini–Piazza Venezia–Largo Argentina–Corso del Rinascimento–Piazza Risorgimento

The buses and the metro line #A stop around midnight, metro line #B at 9.30pm on weekdays, at 11.30pm on weekends, after which a network of **night buses** clicks into service, accessing most parts of the city through to about 5am; they normally have conductors so you can buy a ticket. During the day there are also a few **tram** routes in operation, one of which – the #30 – is a nice leisurely way to see the sights of the city centre, its route taking you on a two-hour circular meander from Piazza del Risorgimento to Piazza San Giovanni di Dio, all for L800. *ATAC* also run a city tour; see "Listings" for details.

Taxis aren't always worth taking unless you're in a group or it's late: they're often not very much quicker and they can be costly. If you want a taxi, don't try to hail one but go to a rank – central ones include Termini, Piazza Venezia, Piazza San Silvestro – or call ☎3570, ☎3875 or ☎4994. Only take a licensed yellow cab, and make sure the meter is switched on as you move off – it should start at L6400.

Finally you could also hire a **bike or scooter**. *Scoot-a-long*, Via Cavour 302 (☎678.0206), rents scooters (but not bikes); *Motonoleggio*, Via della Purificazione 66 (☎465.485), rents out scooters and bikes.

Information

There are **tourist information booths** on arrival at Fiumicino airport (Mon–Sat 8.15am–7pm; ☎6501.0255), and at Stazione Termini (daily 8.15am–7.15pm; ☎487.1270), although the heavy queues that often develop at both of these means you're usually better off heading straight for the main **tourist office,** five minutes' walk from Termini at Via Parigi 5 (Mon–Sat 8.15am–7.15pm; ☎488.3748). They have free maps which should – together with our own – be ample for finding your way around. And they can also help with accommodation needs, as well as handing out any amount of usually out-of-date bumph on Rome and around; the free booklet *Qui Roma* is quite useful and available in English, although the information is not always current. For information on Italy beyond Rome, there's also the national tourist organisation, the **ENIT**, to the right of Termini station as you come out, at Via Marghera 2 (Mon–Fri 9am–1pm; ☎497.1282).

You might be better off bypassing the official tourist offices altogether and going to **Enjoy Rome**, Via Varese 39 (☎445.1843), which has a free room-finding service and left-luggage deposit, and will also advise on where to eat, drink and party, if you so wish. Their information is in any case more up-to-date and reliable than that handed out by the tourist office. They run an emergency line to call if you get into trouble, open until 10pm each evening, and they're also worth contacting when it comes to moving on, since they also operate a room-finding service for places beyond Rome.

Accommodation

Rome in season is as crowded as you might expect, and, although the city has a huge number of **hotels**, along with several **hostels**, during the height of the summer it's not unusual to find nearly everywhere full. Book in advance if you can; if you can't, make straight for the tourist office or *Enjoy Rome* (see opposite) to save your legs. You may be offered a room by touts at Stazione Termini, but these are only usually hotel rooms in the middle to upper price bracket; in any case you should only accept if the offerer is carrying proper identification, and make sure you establish the (full) price beforehand, in writing if necessary.

Hotels

Many of the city's cheaper **hotels** are handily located close to Termini station, and you could do worse than hole up in one of these: the streets both sides of the station – Via Amendola, Via Principe Amedeo, Via Marghera, Via Magenta, Via Palestro – are stacked full of cheap hotels, and some buildings have several pensions to choose from, though you should be somewhat circumspect in the streets to the southwest of the station, parts of which can be a little *too* unsavoury, especially if you're a woman travelling alone. If you want to stay somewhere more central and more picturesque, there are hotels in the *centro storico*, some of them not that expensive, but again be warned that they might be full during the summer – best phone in advance before heading down there. Consider also staying across the river in the Borgo district around the Vatican – a pleasant neighbourhood, nicely distanced from the hubbub of the city centre proper, and handy for the Vatican and Saint Peter's; or even in the lively streets of Trastevere, on the same side of the river.

Around Stazione Termini

Cervia, Via Palestro 55 (☎491.057). Pleasant rooms in a lively *pensione* in the same palazzo as the *Restivo* and *Mari*. ⑤.

Eureka, Piazza della Repubblica 47 (☎482.5806). Housed in the dingy crescent above the metro station and McDonalds, the Eureka has a certain character, with enthusiastically artexed walls coupled with decaying frescoes and tarnished candelabra. ⑤.

Gexim, Via Palestro 34 (☎446.0211). Pleasant, recently decorated and clean rooms in an appalling-looking palazzo a short walk from Termini. ⑤.

Katty, Via Palestro 35 (☎444.1216). One of the cheaper options east of the station. ④.

Liberiano, Via S. Prassede 25 (☎482.8804). Just off Piazza Santa Maria Maggiore, this is very friendly, and comfortably far from the worst of Termini's sleaze.

Mari, Via Palestro 55 (☎446.2137). Clean rooms in a friendly hotel across the landing from the *Restivo*, run by three women.⑤.

Mari II, Via Calatafimi 38 (☎474.0371). Owned by the same people as the *Mari*, and equally clean, though poorly situated on a nasty little alley close to a porno cinema. ⑤.

Marsala, Via Marsala 36 (☎445.6861). Handily situated two-star, 50m from the station. Very clean, very good value. ⑥.

Papa Germano, Via Calatafimi 14 (☎486.919). Friendly and cheap hotel that is very popular, so best book in advance. ④.

Perugia, Via del Colosseo 7 (☎679.7200). Reliable hotel, situated on a peaceful but central street. ⑤.

Restivo, Via Palestro 55 (☎446.2172). Spotless rooms in a small *pensione* run by a sweet old lady. She stays up until all guests are safely back home, so it's best avoided if you're planning to party into the small hours. ⑤.

Romano, Largo C. Ricci 32 (☎679.5851). Well-priced hotel in a central location, at the Forum end of Via Cavour. ④.

Rosetta, Via Cavour 295 (☎488.1598). A marginally more upmarket choice but a nice location close to the Colosseum. ⑤.

Tony, Via P. Amadeo 79d (☎446.6887). Lovely, very friendly, family-run hotel two minutes' walk from Termini. Triples and four-bedded rooms too. ⑤.

Villafranca, Via Villafranca 9 (☎444.0364). Decent, recently refurbished three-star hotel. ⑦.

Vulcania, Via Cavour 117 (☎488.4915). Good-value two-star hotel. ⑤.

Around the centre

Abruzzi, Piazza della Rotonda 69 (☎679.2021). Bang in front of the Pantheon, and as such you pay for the location. But not as pricey as you'd think. ⑤.

Fiorella, Via del Babuino 196 (☎361.0597). Garish rooms in a small *pensione* just below Piazza del Popolo. ⑤.

Jonella, Via della Croce 41 (☎679.7966). Basic rooms in a swanky location on one of the shopping streets below Piazza di Spagna. ⑤.

Della Lunetta, Piazza del Paradiso 68 (☎686.1080). An unspectacular hotel but in a nice location close to Campo dei Fiori. ⑥.

Mimosa, Via Santa Chiara 61 (☎654.1753). Clean if slightly scruffy rooms in a good position, popular with groups of visiting students, close to Santa Maria sopra Minerva and the Pantheon. ⑤.

Navona, Via dei Sediari 8 (☎686.4203). Perfectly placed *pensione* run by an Italian-Australian couple. ⑤.

Piccolo, Via dei Chiavari 32 (☎654.2560). In a nice part of town, central but very quiet, with pleasant, clean rooms. ⑤.

Pomezia, Via dei Chiavari 12 (☎686.1371). Down the street from the *Piccolo*, with slightly more expensive double rooms. ⑥.

Primavera, Piazza San Pantaleo 3 (☎654.3109). Simple rooms in a small *pensione* overlooking Corso Vittorio Emanuele, a couple of minute's walk from both Piazza Navona and Campo de' Fiori. ⑤.

Scalinata di Spagna, Piazza Trinita' dei Monti 17 (☎6840.0986). One of the few hotels in Rome really worth splashing out on, housed in an eighteenth-century villa at the top of the Spanish Steps. Comfortable and unpretentious, many of the rooms are furnished with antiques, and some have terraces with wonderful views over the city. ⑧.

Sole, Via del Biscione 76 (☎654.0873). Almost overlooking Piazza del Campo dei Fiori, one of the nicest city centre locations. ⑤.

Across the river: Trastevere and the Vatican

Alimandi, Via Tunisi 8 (☎384.548). Close to the Vatican, a nicely furnished old place with good-value doubles, all with telephone and radio. ⑥.

Carmel, Via G. Mameli 11 (☎ 580.9921). Pleasant rooms, most with private bathroom and two with their own terrace, at the southern end of Trastevere. There's also a leafy roof terrace for all guests. Don't arrive on spec as the owner closes if she's not expecting anyone. ⑥.

La Rovere, Vicolo Sant'Onofrio 5 (☎654.0739). Affable small Trastevere *pensione* that is handily placed for Saint Peter's. ⑤.

Manara, Via Luciano Manara 25 (☎581.4713). The place to come if you want to be in the heart of Trastevere. Friendly too, and not at all expensive. ④.

Hostels, convents and student accommodation

Ostello del Foro Italico, Viale delle Olimpiadi 61 (☎323.6279). Rome's official *IYHF* hostel, with dorm beds for around L13,000 a head, including breakfast, if you're a member; membership cards are on sale if you're not. Not particularly central or easy to get to from Termini: take bus #492 or metro line #A to Ottaviano, then bus #32. From the centre take metro line #A to Piazzale Flaminio, then bus #48. They won't take phone bookings direct, although you can make advance reservations through *AIG*, Via Cavour 44 (Mon–Thurs 7.30am–7pm, Fri 7.30am–3pm; ☎487.1152). ①.

Ottaviano, Via Ottaviano 6 (☎383.956). Privately run hostel that offers beds in basic dorms. A short walk from the Vatican. ①.

Pensionato Concezioniste di Lourdes, Via Sistina 113 (☎474.5324). A swankily located convent – a couple of minutes' walk from the Spanish Steps – with singles and doubles for women who can put up with a 10.30pm curfew. Not cheap, though. ④.

Raccuia, Via Treviso 37 (☎883.1406). A *pensione* rather than a hostel, clean and family-run, a short walk from the Policlinico metro stop. However, as there's a flat rate for doubles and triples – L25,000 – it's a great deal if there are two or three of you.

Sandy, Via Cavour 136 (☎483.121). Run by the same folk as the *Ottaviano* (see opposite), with a similar set-up and identical prices.

Student accommodation. During high season (end July–end-Aug) the university rents out vacated student accommodation in single or double rooms. There are sites at Viale Ministero Affari Esteri 6 and Via Cesare de Lollis 20. Either ask at the tourist office or contact *AIG* – address opposite. Best book a month in advance. ③.

Suore Pie Operaie, Via di Torre Argentina 76 (☎686.1254). This place offers the cheapest beds in the centre, although you need to book well in advance, and there's a 10.30pm curfew. It's also open to women only. ①.

Villa Santa Cecilia, Via Argeleto 54–58 (☎5237.1688). Twenty minutes by metro from Termini, a religious-run hostel/hotel with singles, doubles, triples and four-bedded rooms, all with private bath. Metro stop Magliana, on line #B, where you change for Lido and the overground train to Vitinia. ④.

YWCA, Via C. Balbo 4 (☎488.0460). For women only, but more conveniently situated than the *IYHF* hostel, ten minutes' walk from Termini. A mixture of singles and doubles, along with three- and four-bedded rooms. Midnight curfew. ④.

Camping

All Rome's **campsites** are some way out of the city and, although easy enough to get to, not especially cheap. The closest site is *Camping Flaminio*, 8km north of the centre on Via Flaminia Nuova (☎333.2604); bus #202, #204 or #205 from Piazzale Flaminio, which is connected with Termini by metro line #A; it's open from the beginning of March until the end of October. In the opposite direction, close to the sea in Ostia, *Camping Capitol*, Via di Castelfusano 195 (☎566.2720), is better equipped and actually slightly less expensive, as well as being open all year, although it's much further out – take a train to Ostia Lido and then bus #05.

The City

Rome's city centre is divided neatly into distinct blocks. The warren of streets that makes up the **centro storico** occupies the hook of land on the left bank of the River Tiber, bordered to the east by Via del Corso and to the north and south by water. From here Rome's central core spreads east: across Via del Corso to the major shopping streets and alleys around the **Spanish Steps** down to **Via Nazionale**; to the major sites of the **ancient city** to the south; to the huge expanse of the **Villa Borghese** park to the north. The left bank of the river is oddly distanced from the main hum of this part of the city, home to the **Vatican and Saint Peter's**, and to the south of these, **Trastevere** – even in ancient times a distinct entity from the city proper and still with a reputation for separatism, as well as the city centre's liveliest concentration of nightlife.

For most of this, you'd be mad to risk your blood pressure in any kind of vehicle, and really the best way to see the city centre and points east to Termini is to walk. The same goes for the ancient sites, and possibly the Vatican and Trastevere – although for these last two you might want to jump a bus going across the river. Keep public transport for the longer hops, down to Testaccio, EUR or the catacombs, or other scattered attractions around the centre's outskirts.

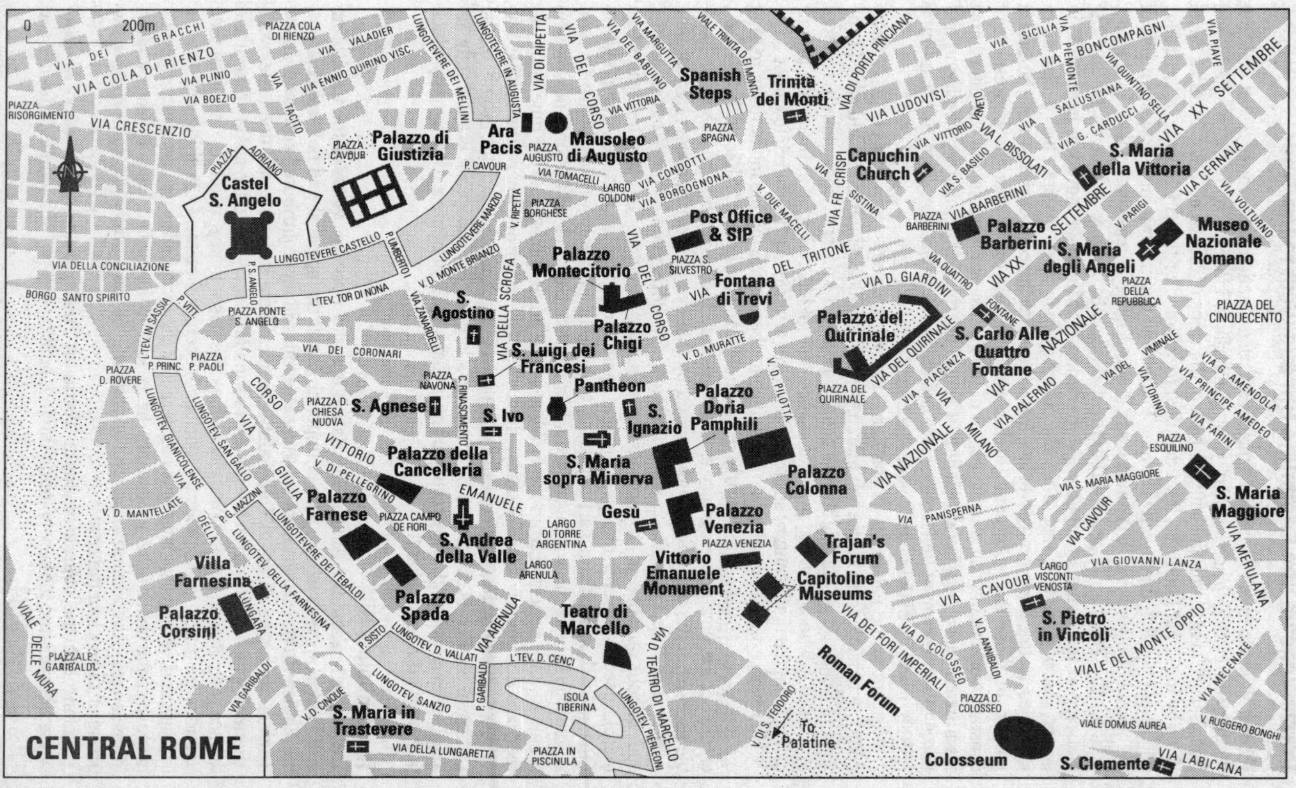
CENTRAL ROME
0
200m
Castel S. Angelo
Palazzo di Giustizia
Ara Pacis
Mausoleo di Augusto
Spanish Steps
Trinità dei Monti
Capuchin Church
S. Maria della Vittoria
Museo Nazionale Romano
S. Maria degli Angeli
Palazzo Barberini
S. Carlo Alle Quattro Fontane
Palazzo del Quirinale
Post Office & SIP
Fontana di Trevi
Palazzo Montecitorio
Palazzo Chigi
Pantheon
S. Ignazio
Palazzo Doria Pamphili
Palazzo Colonna
S. Luigi dei Francesi
S. Agostino
S. Ivo
S. Agnese
Palazzo della Cancelleria
S. Andrea della Valle
S. Maria sopra Minerva
Gesù
Palazzo Venezia
Vittorio Emanuele Monument
Capitoline Museums
Trajan's Forum
Roman Forum
To Palatine
Colosseum
S. Clemente
S. Pietro in Vincoli
S. Maria Maggiore
Teatro di Marcello
Palazzo Farnese
Palazzo Spada
Villa Farnesina
Palazzo Corsini
S. Maria in Trastevere
ISOLA TIBERINA
VIA DEL CORSO
VIA NAZIONALE
VIA XX SETTEMBRE
VIA CAVOUR
VIA DEI FORI IMPERIALI
CORSO VITTORIO EMANUELE
VIA GIULIA
VIA DELLA CONCILIAZIONE
VIA COLA DI RIENZO
VIA CRESCENZIO
VIA MERULANA
VIA LABICANA
VIA DEL TRITONE
VIA VENETO
VIA LUDOVISI
VIA SISTINA
VIA DEL BABUINO
VIA DI RIPETTA
VIA CONDOTTI
VIA D. TEATRO DI MARCELLO
VIALE DELLE MURA
VIA DELLA LUNGARETTA
LUNGOTEVERE IN AUGUSTA
LUNGOTEVERE DEI MELLINI
PIAZZA NAVONA
PIAZZA VENEZIA
PIAZZA DEL CINQUECENTO
PIAZZA DELLA REPUBBLICA
PIAZZA CAVOUR
PIAZZA RISORGIMENTO

Piazza Venezia, the Capitoline Hill and west to the Tiber

Piazza Venezia is not so much a square as a road junction, and a busy one at that. But it's a good central place to start your wanderings, close to both the medieval and Renaissance centre of Rome and the bulk of the ruins of the ancient city. Flanked on all sides by imposing buildings, it's a dignified focal point for the city in spite of the traffic, and a spot you'll find yourself returning to time and again. Forming the western side of the piazza, the **Palazzo di Venezia** was the first large Renaissance palace in the city, built for the Venetian Pope Paul II in the mid-fifteenth century and for a long time the embassy of the Venetian republic. More famously, Mussolini moved in here while in power, occupying the vast *Sala del Mappamundo* and making his declamatory speeches to the huge crowds below from the small balcony facing on to the piazza proper. In those days the palace lights would be left on to give the impression of constant working in what was the centre of the Fascist government and war effort; now it's a much more peripheral building, a venue for the odd temporary exhibition and home to a **museum** of Renaissance arts and crafts (Mon–Sat 9am–2pm, Sun 9am–1pm; L8000), made up of the magpie-ish collection of Paul II.

Adjacent to the palace on its southern side, the church of **San Marco** (daily 9am–noon), accessible from Piazza San Marco, is a tidy basilica rebuilt in 833 and added to by various Renaissance and eighteenth-century popes. It's a warm, cosy church, restored by Paul II – who added the graceful portico and gilded ceiling – with an apse mosaic dating from the ninth century showing Pope Gregory offering his church to Christ.

However, everything pales into insignificance beside the marble monstrosity rearing up across the street – the **Vittorio Emanuele Monument** or "Altar of the Nation", erected at the turn of the century to commemorate the Unification and about as likeable as most of the other buildings inspired by that event. Most Romans refer sardonically to it as "the Typewriter", while American GIs christened it "the Wedding Cake"; and without question it's a pompous, overweening structure, too big, too white (the marble used will never mellow with age), and altogether too boastful. King Vittorio Emanuele II, who it's in part supposed to honour, probably wouldn't have thought much of it either – he was by all acounts a modest man; indeed the only person who seems to have benefited from the building is the prime minister at the time, who was (perhaps not entirely coincidentally) deputy for Brescia, from where the marble was supplied. Incidentally, the equestrian statue of the king, behind the Tomb of the Unknown Soldier, is claimed to be the world's largest (its moustache is apparently 3m long) – though perhaps the greatest irony is that all this honours a royal dynasty which produced just four monarchs.

The Capitoline Hill

The real pity about the Altar of the Nation is that it obscures views of the **Capitoline Hill** behind – once, in the days of Imperial Rome, the spiritual and political centre of the Roman Empire. Apart from anything else, this hill has contributed key words to the English language: "Capitol", obviously, derives from this site, as does the word "money", which comes from the temple to Juno Moneta which once stood up here and housed the Roman mint. The Capitoline was also a key point in medieval and Renaissance times: the flamboyant fourteenth-century dictator, Cola di Rienzo, stood in triumph and seven years later was murdered by the mob here – an uncharacteristically humble statue marks the spot where he is said to have died; and, a century after, Michelangelo was commissioned to redesign the site as a symbol of Rome's regeneration after the sack of the city.

On the left, the church of **Santa Maria in Aracoeli** (daily 7am–noon & 4pm–sunset) crowns the highest point on the hill, built on the site of a temple to Jupiter and reached by a flight of steps erected by Cola di Rienzo in 1348. It's a steep climb to the top of these, and you might find it easier to approach the church via the **cordonata**, an elegant, gently rising flight to the right, designed by Michelangelo. Whichever way you go, the church is worth it, one of Rome's most ancient, with some fine, humane frescoes by Pinturicchio recording the life of San Bernadino – realistic tableaux of landscapes and bustling town scenes. The church is also known for its role as keeper of the so-called "Bambino", a small statue of the child Christ, carved from the wood of a Gethsemane olive tree, that is said to have healing powers and was traditionally called out to the sickbeds of the ill and dying all over the city, its coach commanding instant right of way through the heavy Rome traffic. The bambino is still appealed to from time to time and still enjoys the privileges normally accorded to foreign dignitaries (though he now apparently prefers to travel by taxi); the rest of the time he sits in a chapel at the eastern end of the church, bejewelled and smug and wrapped in luxurious swaddling clothes.

At the top of the cordonata, topped with two Roman statues of Castor and Pollux, the **Piazza Campidoglio** is one of Rome's most elegant squares, also designed by Michelangelo in the 1550s for Pope Paul III, who was determined to hammer Rome back into elegant shape for a visit by Charles V – which makes it even odder that the zealots of the Unification should have wanted it hidden behind the hideous white marble typewriter. In the centre of the square Michelangelo placed a statue of Marcus Aurelius on horseback, which had stood unharmed for years outside San Giovanni in Laterano because it was believed to be of the emperor Constantine. The statue has recently been restored, but sadly hasn't been placed back on its plinth, instead occupying a glass case in the palace museum on the left. Otherwise, though, the square is much as Michelangelo planned it, focusing on the **Palazzo Senatorio**, now Rome's town hall, at the far end, and flanked by the two branches of one of the city's most important museums of antique art – the **Capitoline Museums** (Tues–Sat 9am–1.30pm, Sun 9am–1pm; summer Tues also 5–8pm & Sat 8–11pm; winter Tues & Sat also 5–8pm; L10,000, free on last Sun of each month).

Of these, it's the **Palazzo del Museo Capitolino**, on the left, which really steals the show, and if you only have time for one of the two you should really make it this. It's much smaller, but on its first floor concentrates some of the best of the city's Roman and Greek sculpture into half a dozen or so rooms and a long gallery crammed with elegant statuary. There's a remarkable, controlled statue of the *Dying Gaul*, a Roman copy of a Hellenistic original; a naturalistic *Boy with Goose* – another copy; an original grappling depiction of *Eros and Psyche*; a *Satyr Resting*, after a piece by Praxiteles, that was the inspiration for Hawthorne's book, the *Marble Faun*; and the red marble *Laughing Silenus*, another Roman copy of a Greek original. Walk through, too, to the so-called *Sala degli Imperatori*, with its busts of Roman emperors and other famous names – a young Augustus, a cruel Caracalla, a portrait of Helena, the mother of Constantine, reclining gracefully. And don't miss the *Capitoline Venus*, housed in a room on its own – headless now, but a coy, delicate piece, again based on a work by Praxiteles.

The same ticket will get you into the **Palazzo dei Conservatori** across the square (though it must be on the same day) – a larger, more varied collection, with more ancient sculpture but later pieces too. Littered around the courtyard are the feet and other fragments of a gigantic statue of Constantine. Inside, in various first-floor wings, there are friezes and murals showing events from Roman history, a couple of enormous statues of popes Innocent X and Urban VIII, the exquisite *Spinario* – a Hellenistic work from the first century BC showing a boy plucking a thorn from his foot – and the sacred Roman statue of the wolf suckling the twins, thought to be originally an Etruscan work. Look, too, for the so-called *Esquiline Venus* and *Capitoline Tensa* – the latter a reconstructed chariot in bronze; and the soft *Muse Polymnia* and a gargantuan Roman copy of *Athena*. The second floor holds Renaissance painting – numerous works by Reni and Tintoretto, a vast picture by Guercino that used to hang in Saint Peter's, some nice small-scale work by Carracci, especially an early *Head of a Boy*, Caravaggio's *Gypsy and Fortune Teller* and a handful of Velazquez and Van Dyck portraits.

After seeing the museums, walk around behind the Palazzo Senatorio for a view – Rome's best – of the Forum and across to the Colosseum beyond. On the right, Via del Monte Tarpeio follows, as its name suggests, the brink of the old **Tarpeian Rock**, from which traitors would be thrown in ancient times – so-called after Tarpeia, who betrayed the city to the Sabines. To the left, the road skirts the Forum down to the little church of **San Pietro in Carcere** (daily 9am–noon & 2–6.30pm), built above the Mamertine Prison of ancient Roman times where spies, vanquished soldiers and other enemies of the state were incarcerated, and where Saint Peter himself was held. Steps lead down into the murky depths of the jail, where you can see the bars to which he was chained, along with the spring the saint is said to have created to baptise the other prisoners down here. At the top of the staircase, hollowed out of the honeycomb of stone, is an imprint claimed to be of Saint Peter's head as he was tumbled down the stairs. It's an unappealing place even now, and you won't be sorry to leave – through an exit cunningly placed to lead you through the gift shop.

West from Piazza Venezia

Via del Plebiscito forges west from Piazza Venezia, a dark, rather gloomy thoroughfare that's almost permanently jammed up with traffic. About 300m down, flanking the north side of **Piazza dei Gesù**, is the dark-grey decaying bulk of the **Palazzo Altieri**, a monster of a project in its time which – a Pasquinade of the time quipped – looked set to consume Rome by its very size. One compassionate act, though, was for the Altieri pope, Clement X, to build around the house of an old woman who refused to make way for the palace: the two spyhole windows that were left can still be seen above the ground-floor windows, three windows to the right of the main entrance. Lording it over the piazza proper (said, incidentally, to be the windiest in Rome), the church of **Gesù** (daily 6.30am–12.30pm & 4–7.15pm) is a typical Baroque church of the Counter-Reformation, and of the Jesuit order: high and wide, with a single-aisled nave and short transepts edging out under a huge dome – ideal for the large and fervid congregations the Jesuits wanted to draw; indeed it has served as the model for Jesuit churches everywhere. The facade is by Giacomo della Porta, the interior the work of Vignola. Today it's still a well-patronised church, notable for its size (the glitzy tomb of the order's founder, Saint Ignatius, is topped by a huge globe of lapis lazuli – the largest piece in existence) and the richness of its interior (sumptuous would be an understatement), especially the paintings of Baciccia in the dome and the ceiling's ingenious trompe l'oeil, which oozes out of its frame in a tangle of writhing bodies, flowing drapery and stucco angels stuck like limpets.

Continuing west, **Corso Vittorio Emanuele** opens out onto **Largo di Torre Argentina**, a good-sized square frantic with traffic circling around the ruins of four (Republican era) temples and the channel of an ancient public lavatory, now home to a thriving colony of cats and not open to the public. There's not a lot to see here – it's more a place to wait for a bus than to deliberately linger – but on the far side of the square, the **Teatro Argentina** was in 1816 the venue for the first performance of Rossini's *Barber of Seville* – not a success at all on the night, Rossini apparently booed into taking refuge in Bernasconi's pastry shop next door. Built in 1731, it still hosts the greater part of Rome's opera productions; it is also thought, incidentally, to stand on the spot where Caesar was assassinated.

Campo de' Fiori and around

From Largo Argentina you can either push on down Corso V. Emanuele, or cut left towards the Tiber and right at Piazza Cairoli into the network of streets that centres on Campo de' Fiori. Taking the Corso route, you pass the church of **Sant' Andrea della-Valle** (daily 7.30am–noon & 4.30–7.30pm), which has the distinction of sporting the city's second tallest dome (after Saint Peter's), built by Carlo Maderno. A little further down, on the left, the Piccola Farnesina palace, built by Antonio Sangallo the Younger, holds the **Museo Barracco** (Tues–Sun 9am–1pm, Tues & Thurs also 5–7.30pm; L3750), a small but fine-quality collection of ancient sculpture that was donated to the city at the turn of the century by one Baron Barracco. The palace itself was actually never anything to do with the Farnese family; it in fact got its name from the lilies on the outside, which were confused with the Farnese heraldic lilies. There's another museum in the eighteenth-century Palazzo Braschi opposite, home of the **Museo di Roma**, which displays an assortment of exhibits relating to the history of the city from the Middle Ages to the present day. There are paintings showing the city during different eras, frescoes from demolished palaces and the open railway carriage that the nineteenth-century Pope Pius IX used for journeys out of the city – though this has been closed for restoration for years.

Crossing over once again, the grand **Palazzo di Cancelleria** was the seat of the papal government that once ran the city. From behind, the streets lead down to **Piazza Campo de' Fiori**, in many ways Rome's most appealing square, home to a morning fruit and veg market and with the restaurants and cafés that flank it on every side busy pretty much all day. No one really knows how the square got its name – "field of flowers". One theory holds that it was derived from the Roman Campo Martius which used to cover most of this part of town; another claims it is after Flora, the mistress of Pompey, whose theatre used to stand on what is now the northeast corner of the square – a huge complex by all accounts, which stretched right over to Largo Argentina, where Julius Caesar was cut down by Brutus (you can still see the foundations in the basement of the *Da Pancrazio* restaurant, on the tiny Piazza del Biscione). Later it was an important point on papal processions between the Vatican and the major basilicas of Rome (notably San Giovanni in Laterano), and a site of public executions. The most notorious killing here is remembered by the statue of **Giordano Bruno** in the middle of the square. Bruno was a late sixteenth-century rationalist who followed the teachings of Copernicus and was denounced to the Inquisition; his trial lasted for years under a succession of different popes, and finally, when he refused to renounce his philosophical beliefs, he was burned at the stake.

Just south of the Campo, **Piazza Farnese** is a quite different square, with great fountains spurting out of lilies – the Farnese emblem – into marble tubs brought from the Baths of Caracalla, and the sober bulk of the **Palazzo Farnese** itself, now the French Embassy. It was begun in 1514 by Antonio di Sangallo the Younger and finished off after the architect's death by Michelangelo, who added the top tier of windows and cornice. It's a pity you can't get in here: the building holds what has been called the greatest of all Baroque ceiling paintings, Caracci's *Loves of the Gods*, finished in 1600. Make do instead with the Palazzo Spada, back towards Via Arenula, and the **Galeria Spada** inside (Tues–Sat 9am–2pm, Sun 9am–1pm; L4000; guided tour, in Italian, Sat 11am), though its four rooms, decorated in the manner of a Roman noble family, aren't spectacularly interesting unless you're a connoisseur of seventeenth- and eighteenth-century Italian painting. Best are a few portraits by Reni, works by the odd Italian-influenced Dutch artist (Van Scorel, Honthorst) and, among bits and pieces of Roman statuary, a seated philosopher. The building itself is better: its facade is frilled with stucco adornments, and, left off the courtyard, there's a crafty trompe l'oeil by Borromini – a tunnel whose actual length is multiplied about four times through the architect's tricks with perspective.

Behind the Farnese and Spada palaces, **Via Giulia**, which runs parallel with the Tiber, was built by Julius II to connect the Ponte Sisto with the Vatican. The street was conceived as the centre of papal Rome, and Julius commissioned Bramante to line it with imposing palaces. Bramante didn't get very far with the plan, as Julius was soon succeeded by Leo X, but the street became a popular residence for wealthier Roman families, and is still packed full with stylish palazzi and antique shops.

The Jewish Ghetto and around

By way of contrast, cross over to the far side of Via Arenula and you're in the old **Jewish Ghetto** of the city, a crumbling area of narrow, switchback streets and alleys, easy to lose your way in, and with a strong sense of lingering age. There was a Jewish population in Rome as far back as the early days of the empire, which with the accruing of Middle Eastern colonies eventually swelled to around 40,000. Revolts in the colonies led to a small tax on Jews and a special census, but they were never an especially persecuted group, and were only effectively ghettoised here in the mid-sixteenth century when Pope Paul IV issued a series of punitive laws that forced them into what was then one of Rome's most squalid districts: a wall was built around the area and all Jews (with chilling echoes of future events) had to wear yellow caps and shawls. Sadly the area has recently become a target for Nazi skin vandalism.

The main artery of the Jewish area is **Via Portico d'Ottavia**, principal thing to see the vast nineteenth-century **Synagogue** on the river, which houses a permanent exhibition on the Roman Jewish community (Mon–Thurs 9.30am–2pm & 3–5pm, Fri 9.30am–2pm, Sun 9.30am–12.30pm; L4000). Take a look, also, at the **Fontana delle Tartarughe** or "tortoise fountain" on the tiny Piazza Mattei, a delightful late sixteenth-century creation perhaps restored by Bernini.

Via Portico d'Ottavia leads down to the **Portico d'Ottavia**, a not terribly well preserved second-century BC gate, rebuilt by Augustus and dedicated to his sister in 23 BC, that was the entranceway to the adjacent **Teatro di Marcello**. This has served many purposes over the years: begun by Julius Caesar, finished by Augustus, it was pillaged in the fourth century for the construction of the Ponte Cestio and not properly restored until the Middle Ages, after which it became a formidable fortified palace for a succession of different rulers, including the Orsini family. Now, although the theatre itself is in bad need of repair, the old Orsini fortress on top has been converted into exclusive apartments.

Between the theatre and the river lies the broad open space of **Piazza della Bocca della Verità**, home to two of the city's better-preserved Roman temples – the **Temple of Portunus** and the **Temple of Hercules Victor**, long known as the temple of Vesta because, like all vestal temples, it is circular. Both date from the end of the second century BC, and although you can't get inside, and they can't help but look a little neglected in the middle of what is yet another busy traffic spot, they're actually fine examples of republican-era places of worship; and the Temple of Hercules Victor is, for what it's worth, the oldest surviving marble structure in Rome. More interesting is the church of **Santa Maria in Cosmedin** on the far side of the square (daily 9am–noon & 3–5pm), a typically Roman medieval basilica with a huge marble altar and surround and a colourful and ingenious Cosmati-work floor – one of the city's finest. Outside in the portico and giving the square its name is the **Bocca della Verità** ("Mouth of Truth"), an ancient Roman drain cover in the shape of an enormous face that in medieval times would apparently swallow the hand of anyone who hadn't told the truth. It was particularly popular with husbands wanting to test the faithfulness of their wives.

There are more ancient remains opposite the square, out on the Tiber, where the **Ponte Rotto** (Broken Bridge) is all that remains of the first stone bridge to span the river – built between 179 and 142 BC – since its collapse at the end of the sixteenth century.

Isola Tiberina

The **Ponte Fabricio** further down, which links the Tiber bank to the **Isola Tiberina**, has fared rather better, built in 62 BC and the only classical bridge to remain intact without help from the restorers (the Ponte Cestio, on the other side of the island, was partially rebuilt in the last century). As for the island, it's a calm escape from the city centre proper, its originally tenth-century church of **San Bartolomeo** worth a peep on the way across the river to Trastevere, especially if you're into modern sculpture – one of the priests here is a highly thought-of sculptor, and the church holds some wonderful examples of his elegant, semi-abstract religious pieces.

The Centro Storico

You need to walk a little way north from the Capitoline Hill to find the real city centre of Rome, the **centro storico**, which makes up the greater part of the roughly triangular knob of land that bulges into a bend in the Tiber, above Corso Vittorio Emanuele. This area was the old Campus Martius of Roman times, outside the main body of the ancient city, a low-lying area that was mostly given over to barracks and sporting arenas together with the odd temple. Later it became the heart of the Renaissance city, and nowadays it's the part of the town that's densest in interest, an unruly knot of narrow streets and alleys that holds some of the best both of Rome's classical and baroque heritage, and its street- and nightlife.

The boundary of the historic centre to the east, **Via del Corso** is Rome's main street, the old Via Lata of ancient Rome, so called because of its exceptional width and now holding its principal shops and cutting straight through the heart of the city's centre. On its far side it gives onto the swish shopping streets that lead up to Piazza Spagna; on the western side the web of streets tangles its way right down to the Tiber. Walking north from Piazza Venezia, the first building on the left, the Palazzo Doria Pamphilj, is one of the city's finest Rococo palaces, and nowadays holds the **Galleria Doria Pamphilj** (entrance in Piazza Coll. Romano; Tues & Fri–Sun 10am–1pm; L5000). This is one of many galleries open to the public housed in palaces belonging to old Roman patrician families, and is probably the best, at least for the quality of its collection. The Doria-Pamphilj family still lives in part of the building, and you can visit a carefully selected group of private apartments – a cosily furnished library, a couple of salons filled with busts of the family and the ballroom – which takes just half an hour and for an extra L3000 isn't really worth it. As for the paintings, these are only numbered and to know what you're looking at it's necessary to invest in a catalogue (L4000). Among a rich group of works, including Rome's best concentration of Dutch and Flemish paintings, there are canvases by Caravaggio, one catching the bones and skin of the body with a heavy chiaroscuro not unlike Michelangelo (indeed, it's said Caravaggio painted this after seeing the Sistine Chapel ceiling). A small room off the main gallery holds Velazquez's painting of the Pamphilj pope, Innocent X, an irritable character regarding the viewer with impatience. Bernini's bust of the same man is quite different, the pope seemingly about to erupt into laughter.

The next left after the palace leads into **Piazza Sant'Ignazio**, an odd little square, laid out like a theatre set and dominated by the facade of the church of **Sant'Ignazio** (daily 7.30am–noon & 4–7.15pm): a spacious structure with a marvellous Baroque ceiling by Pozzo showing the entry of Saint Ignazio into paradise. The saint isn't actually buried here (he's in the Gesù church a little way south) but it's worth looking in just for the ceiling, a spectacular work employing sledgehammer trompe l'oeil effects, notably in the mock cupola painted into the dome of the crossing. Stand on the disc in the centre of the nave for the truest sense of the ingenious rendering of perspective (directly underneath it just looks wrong): figures in various states of action and repose, conversation and silence fix you with stares from their classical pediment.

Cut through Via di Seminario from here and you're standing right in front of the **Pantheon** (summer daily 9am–6pm; winter 9am–4pm; free) on Piazza della Rotonda, easily the most complete ancient Roman structure in the city, and with the Colosseum visually the most impressive. Though originally a temple that formed part of Marcus Agrippa's redesign of the Campus Martius in around 27 BC – hence the inscription – it's since been proved that this building was the work of the Emperor Hadrian, finished around the year 125 AD. It's a formidable architectural achievement even now, its dome still – apart from the Palazzo dello Sport in EUR (built for the 1960 Olympics) – the largest in Rome. Like the city's other Roman monuments, it would have been much more sumptuous in its day. Consecrated as a Christian structure in 609 AD, and dedicated to Santa Maria ad Martiri in allusion to the Christian bones that were found here, its bronze roof was stripped soon after, and the bronze from the ceiling of the portico was removed by Pope Urban VIII to be melted down for the baldachino in Saint Peter's and the cannons of the Castel Sant'Angelo. (Interestingly, some later found its way back here when after Unification the cannons were in turn melted down to provide materials for the tombs of the new Italian kings, which are in the building.) Inside you get the best impression of the engineering expertise of Hadrian: the dimensions of the dome and height are precisely equal, the hole in the centre of the dome – from which shafts of sunlight descend to illuminate the musty interior – a full 9m across. Most impressively, there are no visible arches or vaults to hold the whole thing up; instead they're sunk into the concrete of the walls of the building. Again, it would have been richly decorated, the coffered ceiling heavily stuccoed and the niches filled with the statues of gods. Now, apart from the sheer size of the place, the main thing of interest is the tomb of Raphael, between the second and third chapel on the left, inscribed by the writer and priest Bembo: "Living, great Nature feared he might outvie Her works, and dying, fears herself may die." The same kind of sentiments might well have been reserved for the Pantheon itself.

There's more artistic splendour on view behind the Pantheon, though Bernini's **Elephant Fountain** doesn't really prepare you for the church of Santa Maria sopra Minerva beyond. The fountain is Bernini's most endearing piece of work, if not his most characteristic: a cheery elephant trumpeting under the weight of the obelisk he carries on his back – a reference to Pope Alexander VII's reign, and supposed to illustrate the fact that intelligence should support wisdom. **Santa Maria sopra Minerva** is Rome's only Gothic church (daily 7am–noon & 4–7pm), and worth a look for just that, though its soaring lines have since been heavied by marble and frescoes. Built in the late thirteenth century on the ruins of a temple to Minerva, it is also one of Rome's art-treasure churches, crammed with the tombs and self-indulgences of wealthy Roman families. Of these, the Carafa chapel, in the south transept (open again after a lengthy restoration), is the best known, holding Filippino Lippi's fresco of *The Assumption*, a bright effervescent piece of work, below which one painting shows a hopeful Carafa (the religious zealot, Pope Paul IV) being presented to the Virgin Mary by Thomas Aquinas; another depicts Aquinas confounding the heretics in the sight of two beautiful young boys – the future Medici popes Leo X and Clement VII (the equestrian statue of Marcus Aurelius, still not in place on the Capitoline Hill, is just visible in the background). You should look too at the figure of *Christ bearing the Cross*, on the left-hand side of the main altar, a proud serene work that Michelangelo completed in 1521 specially for the church.

Cut through from here towards Piazza Navona, passing on the way the church of **Sant'Ivo** (open Sun am only), accessible from the courtyard of the Palazzo della Sapienza, and, from the outside at least, one of Rome's most impressive churches, with a playful facade designed by Borromini. Though originally built for probably the most famous Barberini pope, Urban VIII, the building actually spans the reign of three popes. Each of the two small towers is topped with weird, blancmange-like groupings, the symbol of the Chigi popes, and the central cupola spirals helter-skelter-fashion to its zenith, which is crowned with flames, which is supposed to represent the sting of the Barberini bee, the family's symbol.

Just beyond, **Piazza Navona** is in many ways the central square of Rome, an almost entirely enclosed, and pedestrianised, sausage-shaped space fringed with cafés and restaurants, which through most of the year is thronged with tourists, street artists and pigeons. It's a place that more or less everyone sees at some point on a visit to Rome, a focus both for political demonstrations and some of the city's most expensive food – and, in *Tre Scalini* on the western side, some of the city's most delicious chocolate ice cream. Really, the best time to come is at night, when the inevitably tourist-geared flavour of the place is at its most vibrant, crowds hanging out around the fountains or clocking the scene while nursing a pricey drink on the terrace of one of the chi-chi bars. But there's plenty to see by day too. The space actually follows the lines of the Emperor Domitian's arena, principal home to the sports and chariot races that took place in the Campus Martius. Until the mid-fifteenth century the ruins of the arena were still here, overgrown and disused, but the square was given a facelift in the mid-seventeenth century by Pope Innocent X, building most of the grandiose palaces that surround and commissioning Borromini to design the church of Sant'Agnese on the west side. The story goes that the thirteen-year-old Saint Agnes was exposed naked to the public in the stadium, her punishment for refusing to marry, whereupon she miraculously grew hair to cover herself. This church, typically squeezed into the tightest of spaces by Borromini, is supposedly on the spot where it all happened.

The **Fontana dei Quattro Fiumi** opposite, one of three that punctuate the square, is by Borromini's arch-rival, Bernini; the story goes that all the figures are shielding their eyes in horror from the church – Bernini was an arrogant man who never had time for the work of the less successful Borromini. The fountain itself, however, is no mean creation, each figure supposed to represent one of the four great rivers of the world – the Nile, Danube, Ganges and Plate – though only the horse, symbolising the Danube, was actually carved by Bernini himself. The grand complexity of rock is topped with an obelisk brought here from the Circus of Maxentius by Innocent X – which explains the ancient Roman inscriptions.

Bernini also had a hand in the fountain at the southern end of the square, designing the central figure of the "Moro" or Moor. Just west of here, the small space of **Piazza Pasquino** isn't quite what you'd expect from the scene of centuries of satire, but the battered torso of Pasquino itself, anonymous poker of fun at the rich and famous during the Middle Ages, still stands in the corner, the most famous among a number of so-called "talking statues" of Rome, on which anonymous comments on the affairs of the day would be attached – comments which had a serious as well as a humorous intent. Pasquino gave us our word "pasquinade", but nowadays the graffitied comments and photocopied poems that occasionally grace the statue are usually lacking in wit. "The finest piece of ancient sculpture in Rome", Bernini called it, though now Pasquino is so knocked about it's hard to tell what he meant.

Beyond are some of Rome's liveliest streets, narrow and noisy at night, holding some of the city's most vigorous restaurants and bars. Thread your way through to **Via dei Coronari**, home to a sizeable few of Rome's antique dealers, and back east across the northern end of Piazza Navona – where, sealed behind glass, there are the only visible remains of Domitian's arena. Beyond here, the Renaissance facade of the church of **Sant'Agostino** (daily 7.45–noon & 4.30–7.30pm) takes up one side of a drab piazza of the same name: not much to look at from the outside but with a handful of art treasures that might draw you in – among them Raphael's vibrant fresco of *Isaiah*, Sansovino's craggy *Saint Anne, Virgin and Child*, and, in the first chapel on the left, a *Madonna and Pilgrims* by Caravaggio; to see this properly you need to drop L500 into a box to switch on the lights. There's more work by Caravaggio down Via della Scrofa, in the French national church of **San Luigi dei Francesi** (daily 7.30am–12.30pm & 3.30–7pm, Thurs pm only; L200 to illuminate the paintings), in the last chapel on the left: early works, describing the life and martyrdom of Saint Matthew, the best of which is the *Calling of Saint Matthew* on the left wall – Matthew the dissolute-looking youth on the far left, illuminated by a shaft of sunlight. Caravaggio's first public commission, these paintings were actually rejected at first, partly on grounds of indecorum, and it took considerable reworking by the artist before they were finally accepted.

From the church cut back to Piazza della Rotonda and beyond to Piazza Montecitorio and the **Palazzo di Montecitorio**, home since 1871 of the Italian parliament – though the building itself is another Bernini creation. The obelisk in the centre of the square was brought to Rome by Augustus and set up in the Campus Martius, where it formed the hand of a giant sundial. Just beyond, the **Palazzo Chigi** flanks the north side of **Piazza Colonna**, official residence of the Prime Minister. The **Column of Marcus Aurelius** that gives the square its name was originally erected in 180–190 AD to commemorate military victories in northern Europe, and, like the column of Trajan which inspired it, decorated with reliefs depicting the aspects of the campaigns. There are actually steps spiralling up inside the hollow core to the top, but you need to get permission to climb them.

Three hundred metres or so further on down Via del Corso and left, **Via della Ripetta** was laid out by Leo X to provide a straight route out of the city centre from the old river port area here. A little way up, the **Mausoleum of Augustus** was the burial place of the emperor and his family, now closed to the public and these days no more than a peaceful ring of cypresses, circled by paths, flowering shrubs and the debris of tramps. On the far side, enclosed in a glass box between the river and the mausoleum, the **Ara Pacis Augustae** (summer Tues–Sat 9am–1pm, Tues & Sat also 3–7pm, Sun 9am–12.30pm; winter Tues–Sat 9am–1pm, Sun 9am–12.30pm; L3750) or "Altar of Augustan Peace" is a more substantial – and recognisable – Roman remain, built in 13 BC to celebrate Augustus's victory over Spain and Gaul and the subsequent peace it established. Much of this had been dug up piecemeal over the years, but the bulk of it was found during the middle half of the last century. It was no easy task to put it back together: excavation involved digging down to a depth of 10m and freezing the water table, after which many other parts had to be retrieved from museums the world over. But it's a superb example of Imperial Roman sculpture and holds on its fragmented frieze the portraits of many familiar names, most shown in the victory procession itself, which is best preserved on the eastern side. The first part is almost completely gone, but the shape of Augustus is a little more complete, as are the figures that follow – first Tiberius, then the priests with their skull-cap headgear, then Agrippa. The women are, respectively, Augustus's wife Livia, daughter Julia, and niece Antonia, the latter caught simply and realistically turning to her husband. Around their feet run various children clutching the togas of the elders, the last of whom is said to be the young Claudius.

The oval-shaped space at the far end of Via di Ripetta is **Piazza del Popolo**, a dignified square and meeting of roads designed by Valadier in 1814 that provides an impressive – and very French – entrance to the city, all symmetry and grand vistas. During summer, the steps around the obelisk and (if you're wealthy enough) the bars on either side, are popular hang-outs. But the square's real attraction is the unbroken view it gives all the way back down Via del Corso through the centre of Rome to glimpse the central columns of the vulgar Vittorio Emanuele Monument.

On the far side of the piazza, hard against the city walls, the church of **Santa Maria del Popolo** (daily 7am–noon & 4–7.30pm) holds some of the best Renaissance art of any Roman church. The church was originally erected here in 1099 over the burial place of Nero, in order to sanctify what was believed to be an evil place, and rebuilt for the last time during the fifteenth century. Inside it holds frescoes by Pinturicchio in the south aisle and the Bramante-designed apse which in turn boasts two fine tombs by Andrea Sansovino. The penultimate chapel in the northern aisle, the Chigi chapel, was designed by Raphael for Agostino Chigi in 1516 – though most of the work was accomplished by other artists and not finished until the seventeenth century. Michelangelo's protégé, Sebastiano del Piombo, was responsible for the altarpiece, and two of the sculptures in the corner niches, of Daniel and Habakkuk, are by Bernini. But it's two pictures by Caravaggio which get the most attention, in the left-hand chapel of the north transept. These are typically dramatic works – one, the *Conversion of Saint Paul*, showing Paul and horse bathed in a beatific radiance, the other, the *Crucifixion of Saint Peter*, showing Peter as an aged but strong figure, dominated by the muscly figures hoisting him up. Like the same artist's paintings in the church of San Luigi dei Francesci (see p.589), both works were considered extremely adventurous in their time, their heavy chiaroscuro and deliberate realism too much for the church authorities, who rejected them out of hand.

East of Via del Corso

The area immediately southeast of Piazza del Popolo, fast under the heights of the Villa Borghese gardens and stretching down as far as the Spanish Steps and around, is travellers' Rome, historically the artistic quarter of the city, for which eighteenth- and nineteenth-century Grand Tourists would make in search of the colourful, exotic city, lending the area a distinctly cosmopolitan air. Keats and Giorgio de Chirico are just two people who used to live on Piazza di Spagna; Goethe had lodgings in nearby Via Condotti; and institutions like *Caffè Greco* and *Babington's Tea Rooms* were the meeting-places of a local artistic and expat community for close on a couple of centuries. Today these institutions are gradually giving ground to more latter-day traps for the tourist dollar: *American Express* and McDonalds have a high profile in the area, Via Condotti and around is these days strictly international designer territory, with some of Rome's fanciest stores, and the local residents are more likely to be investment bankers than artists or poets. But the air of a Rome being discovered, even colonised, by foreigners remains, even if most of them are more likely to be flying-visit InterRailers than short-term residents.

Piazza di Spagna and around

Via del Babuino, which leads south from Piazza del Popolo, sets the tone for the area, in the Sixties the core of a thriving art community and home to the city's best galleries and a fair number of its artists, until high rents forced out all but the most successful. Now it supports a prosperous trade in antiques. At its southern end is **Piazza di Spagna**, a long thin straggle of a square almost entirely enclosed by buildings and centring on the distinctive boat-shaped **Barcaccia** fountain, the last work of Bernini's father. It apparently remembers the great flood of Christmas Day 1598, when a barge from the Tiber was washed up on the slopes of Pincio hill close by. At the southern end of the square, a **column** commemorates Pius IX's nineteenth-century official announcement of the dogma of the Immaculate Conception – more controversially so than ever these days, since an *American Express* scheme to donate L200 or so from every card used in Rome towards its restoration raised the heckles of Protestant visitors. The **McDonalds** restaurant, opposite, provoked similar reactions a few years back, this time from Romans, when plans were unveiled to open another branch of the world's most ubiquitous fast-food chain on one of Rome's most historic squares. That McDonalds is here now is proof that the American multinational won, but it's to the city's credit that it's one of the most discreet examples you'll ever see.

Facing directly onto the square, opposite the fountain, the **Keats-Shelley Memorial House** (Mon–Fri 9am–1pm & 2.30–5.30pm; L4000), where the poet John Keats died in 1821, now serves as an archive of English-language literary and historical works and a museum of manuscripts and literary mementoes relating to the Keats circle of the early nineteenth century – namely Keats himself, Shelley, Mary Shelley and Byron (who at one time lived across the square). Among many bits of manuscript, letters and the like, there's a silver scallop shell reliquary containing locks of Milton's and Elizabeth Barrett Browning's hair, while the poet's death mask, stored in the room where he died, catches him in resigned grimace. Keats didn't really enjoy his time in Rome, referring to it as his "posthumous life": he was tormented by his love for Fanny Browne, and he spent months in pain before he finally died, confined to the rooming house with his artist friend Joseph Severn, to whom he remarked that he could already feel "the flowers growing over him".

As for the **Spanish Steps**, which sweep down in a cascade of balustrades and balconies beside the house, the only thing that is Spanish about them is the fact that their architect, Alessandro Specchi, was also responsible for the facade of the nearby Spanish Embassy, which gave the square and steps their name. In the last century they were the hang-out of young hopefuls waiting to be chosen as artists' models; nowadays the scene is not much changed, as the venue for international posing and fast pick-ups late into the summer nights. At the top, adding to the international flavour of the square is the **Trinità dei Monti**, a largely sixteenth-century church designed by Carlo Maderno and paid for by the French king. Its rose-coloured Baroque facade overlooks the rest of Rome from its hilltop site, and it's worth clambering up just for the views. But while here you may as well pop your head around the door for a couple of faded works by Daniel da Volterra, notably a soft flowing fresco of *The Assumption* in the third chapel on the right, which includes a portrait of his teacher Michelangelo. His *Deposition*, across the nave, is also worth a glance, though it's hard to see under the current dim lighting. Poussin considered it the world's third greatest painting (Raphael's *Transfiguration* was, he thought, the best), painted from a series of cartoons by Michelangelo.

South of Piazza di Spagna

From the church you can either continue left along past the Villa Medici, now housing the French Academy, to the Pincio terrace and the gardens of the Villa Borghese (see p.603), or head south down Via Sistina to **Piazza Barberini**, a busy traffic junction at the top end of the shopping street of Via del Tritone – named after Bernini's **Fontana del Tritone**, which gushes a high jet of water in the centre of the square. The fountain lends a unity to the square in more ways than one: traditionally this is the Barberini quarter of the city, a family who were the greatest patrons of Gianlorenzo Bernini, and the sculptor's works in their honour are thick on the ground around here. He finished the Tritone fountain in 1644, going on shortly after to design the **Fontana delle Api** ("Fountain of the Bees") at the bottom end of Via Veneto. Unlike the Tritone fountain you could walk right past this, a smaller, quirkier work, its broad scallop shell studded with the bees that were the symbol of the Barberinis.

A little way up Via Veneto, the Capuchin church of **Santa Maria della Concezione** was another sponsored creation of the Barberini, though it's not a particularly significant building in itself, only numbering Reni's androgynous *Saint Michael Trampling on the Devil* among its treasures. The devil in the picture is said to be a portrait of Innocent X, whom the artist despised and who was apparently a sworn enemy of the Barberini family. But the Capuchin cemetery (daily 9am–noon & 3–6pm; compulsory "donation"), on the right of the church, is one of the more macabre – and bizarre – sights of Rome. In this the bones of 4000 monks coat the walls of a series of chapels, a monument to "Our Sister of Bodily Death", in the words of Saint Francis, that was erected in 1793. The bones cover the walls in abstract patterns or as fully clothed skeletons, their faces peering out of their cowls in various twisted expressions of agony – somewhere between the chilling and the ludicrous.

Via Veneto itself, which bends north from here up to the southern edge of the Borghese gardens, is a cool, materialistic antidote to the murky atmosphere of the

Capuchin grotto, its pricey bars and restaurants, once the haunt of Rome's Beautiful People, made famous by Fellini's *La Dolce Vita* but now the home of high-class tack and overpriced sleaze, not to mention the fortified bulk of the US Embassy on the right. Anita Ekberg probably wouldn't be seen dead here these days, and you'd really do better to retrace your steps back to Piazza Barberini and push on up Via delle Quattro Fontane. Just off to the right of here, **Via Rasella** was the scene of an ambush of a Nazi military patrol in 1944 that led to one of the worst Italian wartime atrocities – the reprisal massacre of 300 Romans in the catacombs outside the city. The bullet-holes in the house on the corner of Via Bocaccio remain as a kind of memorial. Oddly enough, Mussolini had a flat on Via Rasella in which he would entertain his mistresses.

On the other side of the road, the **Palazzo Barberini** is home to the **Galleria di Arte Antica** (Tues–Sat 9am–2pm, Sun 9am–1pm; L6000), currently undergoing a massive restoration, although the galleries inside remain open. It displays a rich patchwork of mainly Italian art from the early Renaissance to late Baroque period in the palace's converted rooms. In addition to canvases by Tintoretto, Titian and El Greco, highlights include Fra Filippo Lippi's warmly maternal *Madonna and Child*, painted in 1437 and introducing background details, notably architecture, into Italian religious painting for the first time; and Raphael's beguiling *Fornarina*, a disputed painting in fact, claimed by some experts to be the work of a pupil, though Raphael's name appears clearly on the woman's bracelet; everyone likes to believe the woman, Margherita Luti, the daughter of a Trasteveran baker, was Raphael's mistress. But perhaps the most impressive feature of the gallery is the building itself, worked on at different times by the most favoured architects of the day – Bernini, Borromini, Maderno – and the epitome of Baroque grandeur. The *Salone*, certainly, is guaranteed to impress, its ceiling frescoed by Pietro da Cortona in one of the best examples of exuberant Baroque trompe l'oeil work there is, a manic rendering of *The Triumph of Divine Providence* that almost crawls down the walls to meet you.

Continue on up Via delle Quattro Fontane and you're at another scaffolding-sheafed seventeenth-century landmark, the church of **San Carlo alle Quattro Fontane** (Mon–Fri 9am–12.30pm & 4–6pm, Sat 9am–12.30pm). This was Borromini's first real design commission, and in it he displays all the ingenuity he became known for, cramming the church elegantly into a tiny and awkwardly shaped site that apparently covers roughly the same surface area as one of the main columns inside Saint Peter's. Outside the church are the four **fountains** that give the street and church their name, each cut into a niche in a corner of the crossroads that marks this, the highest point on the Quirinal Hill. Walk west from here and you're passing the blank featureless wall of the **Palazzo del Quirinale**, a sixteenth-century structure that was the official residence of the popes until Unification, when it became the royal palace. It's now the home of Italy's president and not open to the public, but you can appreciate its exceptional siting from the **Piazza del Quirinale** at the far end on the right, from which views stretch right across the centre of Rome.

Hidden among the tight web of narrow, apparently aimless streets below is one of Rome's more surprising sights, easy to stumble upon by accident – the **Fontana di Trevi**, a huge, very Baroque gush of water over statues and rocks built onto the backside of a Renaissance palace that's fed by the same source that surfaces at the Barcaccia fountain in Piazza di Spagna. There was a Trevi fountain around the corner in Via dei Crociferi, a smaller, more modest affair by all accounts, but Urban VIII decided to upgrade it in line with his other grandiose schemes of the time and employed Bernini to design an alternative. This wasn't carried out until Niccolo Salvi started work on the fountain in 1723, and even then it took 39 years to finish the project. Salvi died in the process, his lungs shot by the time spent in the dank waterworks of the fountain.

The Trevi fountain is now, of course, the place you come to chuck in a coin if you want to guarantee your return to Rome (though you might remember Anita Ekberg throwing herself into it in *La Dolce Vita*), and, newly restored, it's one of the city's most vigorous outdoor spots to hang out of an evening. Opposite, the grubby little church of **Santi Vicenzo ed Anastasio** is the parish church of the Quirinal Palace and, bizarrely, holds in marble urns the hearts and viscera of the 22 popes who used the palace as a papal residence. A short stroll directly south from here brings you to the **Galleria Colonna**, Via del Pilotta 17 (Sat only 9am–1pm; L5000), part of the Palazzo Colonna complex and, although outranked by many of the other Roman palatial collections, worth forty minutes or so if only for the chandelier-decked Great Hall, where most of the paintings are displayed. Best on the whole is the gallery's collection of Dughet landscapes (Poussin's brother-in-law), but other works which stand out are Carracci's early – and unusually spontaneous – *Bean Eater* (though this attribution has since been questioned), a *Narcissus* by Tintoretto, and a *Portrait of a Venetian Gentleman* caught in supremely confident pose by Veronese.

Via Nazionale and east

Five minutes from the gallery, **Via Nazionale** begins its long straight route east, connecting Piazza Venezia and the centre of town with Stazione Termini and the districts beyond. A focus for much development after Unification, its heavy, overbearing buildings, like those on Via XX Settembre, were constructed to give Rome some semblance of modern sophistication when it became capital of the new country. Most are now occupied by department stores and boutiques. At the top end, **Piazza della Repubblica**, formerly Piazza d'Esedra, is typical of this nineteenth-century regeneration, a stern, once dignified but now rather tawdry semicircle of buildings given over to cheap hotels, fast-food joints and travel agents, and centring on a fountain surrounded by languishing nymphs.

The square actually occupies part of the site of Diocletian's Baths, the remains of part of which lie across the square in the church of **Santa Maria degli Angeli** – not Rome's most welcoming church but giving the best impression of the size and grandeur of Diocletian's bath complex. It's a huge, open building, used these days for official occasions, state visits and the like, with an interior standardised after a couple of centuries of piecemeal adaptation (started by an aged Michelangelo) by Vanvitelli in a rich eighteenth-century confection. The pink granite pillars are, however, original, and the main transept formed the main hall of the baths; only the crescent shape of the facade remains from the original caldarium (it had previously been hidden by a newer facing), the vestibule (the tepidarium) and main transept. The meridian which strikes diagonally across the floor here was, until 1846, the regulator of time for Romans (now a cannon shot is fired daily from the Janiculum Hill).

Michelangelo is also said to have had a hand in modifying another part of the baths, the courtyard which makes up part of the **Museo Nazionale Romano** behind the church (Tues–Sat 9am–2pm, Sun 9am–1pm; L3000) – entrance off Piazza dei Cinquecento. This could be a very good museum – its collection of Greek and Roman antiquities is superb and second only to the Vatican – but like many Roman museums it suffers from under-funding. For the past year or so, only a couple of rooms have been open, and the entire collection is supposed to be moving to the Palazzo Massimo across the way, already snazzily revamped in its honour. So far nothing has happened, so be sure to enquire what's open *before* you cough up the admission fee. Of the items worth paying for, there are some good mosaics at the top of the stairs, stucco work from the ruins of an Augustan-era villa discovered in the grounds of the Villa Farnesina, and in a separate room an almost entirely complete set of frescoes from a country villa which belonged to Augustus's wife, Livia, representing an orchard dense with fruit and flowers and patrolled by partridges, doves and other birds. The museum is also home of the so-called Ludovisi Throne, a fifth-century BC Greek work embellished with a delicate relief depicting the birth of Aphrodite.

Through the trees of the museum garden, you can faintly discern the low white shape of **Stazione Termini** and the bus-crammed hubbub that is **Piazza dei Cinquecento** in front. The latter is probably the city's biggest open space and the focal point for all kinds of traffic – most buses pass through here, the two metro lines converge at Termini and it's a good place to find taxis. As for the station itself, it's an ambitious piece of modern architectural design that works very well, completed in 1950 and entirely dominating the streets around with its low-slung self-consciously modern lines – a fine place to arrive.

Beyond Termini, heading east past the buildings of the Policlinico and the university, the neighbourhood of **SAN LORENZO** spreads from the far side of Via Tiburtina to the railway tracks, a solidly working-class district that retains something of its local air. The area takes its name from the church of **San Lorenzo fuori le Mura** (daily 3.30–6.30pm; tours every half-hour), further up Via Tiburtina, one of the seven great pilgrimage churches of Rome, oddly sited to the side of the main road in front of the enormous **Campo Verano** cemetery – since 1830 the burial-place of all Catholics in Rome, and in itself worth a visit for the grandiose tombs in which many of them are laid. The church is a typically Roman basilica, fronted by a columned portico and with a lovely twelfth-century cloister to its side. The original church here was built over the site of Saint Lawrence's martyrdom by Constantine – the saint was reputedly burned to death on a gridiron, halfway through his ordeal apparently uttering the immortal words, "Turn me, I am done on this side." Where the church of San Lorenzo differs is that it is actually the combination of three churches built at different periods – one a sixth-century reconstruction of Constantine's church by Pelagius II, which now forms the chancel, another a fifth-century church from the time of Sixtus III, both joined by a basilica from the thirteenth century by Honorius II. Inside there are features from all periods, though inevitably heavier on the later one – a Cosmati floor, thirteenth-century pulpits and a paschal candlestick. The mosaic on the triumphal arch is a sixth-century depiction of Pelagius offering his church to Christ; while below stairs, catacombs lead a dank path from the pillars of Constantine's original structure to the Romanesque cloister and its well-tended garden.

North of Termini

A short walk north of Piazza della Repubblica, the church of **Santa Maria della Vittoria** on Via XX Settembre (daily 6.30am–noon & 4.30–7.30pm) was built by Carlo Maderno and has an interior that is one of the most elaborate examples of Baroque decoration in Rome – almost shockingly excessive to modern eyes, its ceiling and walls pitted with carving, statues crammed into remote corners like an over-stuffed attic. The church's best-known feature, Bernini's carving of *Ecstasy of Saint Theresa*, the centrepiece of the sepulchral chapel of Cardinal Cornaro, continues the histrionics – a deliberately melodramatic work which features a theatrically posed Saint Theresa against a backdrop of theatre-boxes on each side of the chapel, from which the Cornaro cardinals murmur and nudge each other as they watch the spectacle.

Beyond the church **Via XX Settembre** spears out towards the Aurelian Wall – not Rome's most appealing thoroughfare by any means, flanked by the deliberately faceless bureaucracies of the national government, erected after Unification in pompous anticipation of Rome's ascension as a new world capital. The street itself was the route by which Garibaldi's troops entered the city on September 20, 1870, and the place where they breached the wall is marked with a column. At the end of XX Settembre, the **Porta Pia** was one of the last works of Michelangelo, erected under Pope Pius IV in 1561. The other side of busy Corso d'Italia (in effect forming part of the central ring road which girdles the city centre), the luxury villas which line the wide boulevard of **Via Nomentana** have long been home to some of the city's more illustrious names, not least the nineteenth-century **Villa Torlonia** on the right, which was in 1925 donated by its owner, the banker Prince Giovanni Torlonia, to Mussolini to use as long as he needed it. You can't visit the house but the grounds are open to the public.

Further up Via Nomentana is the church of **Sant'Agnese fuori le Mura** (daily 7am–noon & 4–8pm), dedicated to the same saint who was martyred in Domitian's Circus in 303 AD (see "Piazza Navona" p.589). To get into the church, walk down the hill and through the courtyard to the narthex of the building, which apart from some very out-of-place later fixtures is much as it was built by Honorius I in the seventh century, when he reworked Constantine's original structure. The apse mosaic is Byzantine in style and contemporary with Honorius's building, showing Agnes next to the pope, who holds a model of his church. Out of the narthex the custodian will lead you down into the **catacombs** that sprawl below the church, which are among the best preserved and most crowd-free of all the city's catacombs. Indeed if you only have time for one set of catacombs during your stay in Rome (and they really are all very much alike), these are among the best.

After the catacombs the guide will show you a further part of what is really a small complex of early Christian structures, the church of **Santa Constanza**, which more than any other building in Rome, perhaps, illustrates the transition from the pagan to Christian city in its decorative and architectural features. Built in 350 AD as a mausoleum for Constantia and Helena, the daughters of the Emperor Constantine, it's a round structure which follows the traditional shape of the great pagan tombs (consider those of Hadrian and Augustus elsewhere in the city), and the mosaics on the vaulting of its circular ambulatory – fourth-century depictions of vines, leaves and birds – would have been as at home in a Roman *domus* as they were in a Christian church.

South of Piazza Venezia

From Piazza Venezia **Via dei Fori Imperiali** cuts south through the heart of Rome's ancient sites, a soulless boulevard imposed on the area by Mussolini in 1932. Before then this was a warrren of medieval streets that wound around the ruins of the ancient city centre, but as with the Via della Conciliazione up to Saint Peter's, the Duce preferred to build something to his own glory rather than preserve that of another era. The plan was to create a huge archaeological park which stretched right down to the catacombs on the Via Appia Antica, but this was never carried out; the scheme has since been revived, but rather half-heartedly, and for the moment much of the ancient city remains unexcavated, buried beneath the road.

Via dei Fori Imperiali is used for the odd military parade, and it's a useful link for traffic between the Colosseum and Piazza Venezia. But its main pedestrians are tourists, rooting about among the ancient sites. Of these, the original Roman Forum, the Palatine Hill beyond, and of course the Colosseum are the principal things to see, all off to the right of the main road. In addition to these, though, scattered along on either side of Via dei Fori Imperiali, are the remains of various imperial forums, built after the forum proper had become too small to accommodate the needs of the ever-expanding city.

One of the major victims of Mussolini's redesign was the **Forum of Trajan** on the left side of the road, in its day the most sumptuous of the imperial forums but now fairly unrecognisable. The main section is no more than a sunken area of scattered columns to the left of the road, fronting the semicircle of **Trajan's Markets** (Tues–Sat 9am–1.30pm, Sun 9am–1pm; L3000), a tiered ancient Roman shopping centre that's accessible from Via IV Novembre. Behind, the **Torre delle Milizie** is said to be the tower from which Nero watched Rome burning, although given that it is medieval in origin this would have been impossible; indeed the most prominent – and intact – relic of Roman times around here is nearer Piazza Venezia – **Trajan's Column**, erected to celebrate the emperor's colonisation of Dacia (modern-day Romania). Though difficult to see, the column's reliefs illustrate the highlights of the Dacian campaign.

The Roman Forum and Palatine Hill

Summer Mon & Wed–Sat 9am–6pm, Sun 9am–noon, Tues 9am–1pm; winter Mon, Wed & Sat 9am–3pm, Sun 9am–noon, Tues 9am–1pm; L10,000.

Cross the road from here and you're outside the very partially excavated remains of the **Forum of Caesar** – just a few piles of broken columns really – and the entrance to the main part of the **Roman Forum** and the **Palatine**. These are very near the top of most visitors' things to see in Rome, and it's rare that you'll be alone; but for many it's also one of the city's most disappointing sites, and you need an imagination and some small grasp of history to really appreciate the place at all.

Certainly both sites hold some of the most ruined Roman ruins you'll see: the area was abandoned for so long that there's very little that remains anything like intact. But this five or so acres was the heart of the Mediterranean world, and is a very real and potent testament to a power which ruled a large chunk of the earth for close on five centuries, and whose influence reverberates right up to the present day – in language, in architecture, in political terms and systems, even in the romance that the last couple of hundred years have lent to its ruins. Even in ancient times Rome was a very large city, stretching out as far as the Aurelian Wall in a sprawl of apartment blocks or *insulae*. But the Forum was its centre, home to its political and religious institutions, its shops and market stalls, and a meeting-place for all and sundry – which it remained until the Imperial era, when Rome's increased importance as a world power led to extensions being built nearby. The Forum never really recovered from this: neglect set in, a fire in the third century AD destroyed many of the buildings, and although the damage was repaired, Rome was by this time in a general state of decay, the coming of Christianity only serving to accelerate the process, particularly with regard to its pagan temples and institutions. After the later downfall of the city to various barbarian invaders, the area was left in ruin, its relics quarried for the construction in other parts of Rome during medieval and Renaissance times and the odd church or tower being constructed *in situ* out of the more viable piles. Excavation of the site didn't start until the beginning of the nineteenth century, since when it has continued pretty much without stoppage: you'll notice a fair part of the site, particularly up on the Palatine, closed off for further digs.

THE ROMAN FORUM

The **Via Sacra** runs directly through the core of the Forum, from below the Capitoline Hill in the west to the far eastern extent of the site and the Arch of Constantine (where there's a handy exit for the Colosseum), the best-known street of ancient Rome, along which victorious emperors and generals would ride in procession to give thanks at the Capitoline's Temple of Jupiter. At the bottom of the hill, the scattered rows of towering columns mark an array of temples dedicated to various gods and emperors, though there's precious little left of any other part of the buildings. Better preserved, just in front, the **Arch of Septimus Severus** was constructed in the early second century AD to commemorate the emperor's tenth anniversary in power. The friezes on it recall not only Severus but his son, Caracalla, who ruled Rome with a reign of undisciplined terror for seven years; there's a space, too, where Severus's other son Geta was commemorated: he was joint-ruler of the empire after his father's death but Caracalla soon had him murdered and removed his name from the arch altogether.

Next to the arch, the **Rostra** faces the grassy, wide-open scatter of paving, dumped stones and beached columns that makes up the central portion of the Forum, the place where most of the life of the city was carried on, and in ancient times usually crowded with politicians, tribunes and traders. Nearby, the black, fenced-off paving of the **Lapis Niger** marks the traditional site of the tomb of Romulus, the steps beneath leading down to a monument that was considered sacred ground during Classical times. Behind, the **Curia** is one of the few whole structures in the forum, a huge barnlike building with a plain pediment that was begun in 80 BC, restored by Julius Caesar soon after and rebuilt by Diocletian in the third century AD. The Senate met here during the Republican period, and augurs would come to announce the wishes of the gods. For years the Curia served as a church, only reverting to its original form earlier this century.

More columns and stones mark more temples and basilicas along the northern side of the Forum, notably the **Basilica Emilia**, back by the entrance, from which you can easily discern the original shape of the building, and the **Basilica Julia** on the other side of the forum. Next to the Basilica Julia, the columns of the **Temple of Castor and Pollux**, cocooned in scaffold and netting, is one of the site's oldest remains, dating back to 430 BC and dedicated to the divine twins who appeared miraculously to ensure victory for the Romans in a key battle. Just behind, the church of **Santa Maria Antiqua** formed the vestibule to the Emperor Domitian's palace on the Palatine Hill, and was the first ancient building to be converted for Christian worship. The church is now normally kept closed, and unfortunately you can't get very close to it at all.

Beyond here, crouching under the brow of the Palatine Hill, huge monolithic remains are still being excavated; better to turn in the opposite direction for the **House of the Vestal Virgins**, a second-century AD reconstruction of a building originally built by Nero. The cult of the Vestal Virgins was an important one in ancient Rome: the six women who lived here were charged with the responsibility of keeping the sacred flame of Vesta alight always; if it should go out, the woman responsible was scourged; if she should lose her chastity, she was scourged and then buried alive (the man was merely flogged). Not surprisingly, it wasn't a job too many young girls were eager to take up, although the Vestals enjoyed many privileges and the palace was very comfortable: four floors of rooms around a central courtyard, with the round **Temple of Vesta** at the near end. The rooms are mainly ruin now, though they're fairly recognisable on the Palatine side, and you can get a good sense of the shape of the place from the remains of the courtyard, still with its pool in the centre and fringed by the statues or inscribed pedestals of the women themselves.

Opposite the Vestals' house, the neat round **Temple of Romulus**, from the fourth century AD, has also been sanctified and serves as vestibule for the church of **Santi Cosma e Damiano** behind, which sports a wide and majestic sixth-century apse mosaic showing Christ and the Apostles (entrance on Via dei Fori Imperiali). Just past the temple, a short arcade leads round to the **Basilica of Constantine and Maxentius**, which rises up towards the main road – in terms of size and ingenuity probably the forum's most impressive remains. It was begun by Maxentius and continued by his co-emperor and rival, Constantine, after he had defeated him at the Battle of the Ponte di Milvio in 312 AD. It's said that Michelangelo studied the hexagonal coffered arches here when grappling with the dome of Saint Peter's, and Renaissance architects in general apparently used its apse and arches as a frequent model.

From the basilica the Via Sacra climbs more steeply, past a series of ruins no one has been able to positively identify to the **Arch of Titus**, which stands commandingly on a low arm of the Palatine Hill, looking one way down the remainder of the Via Sacra to the Colosseum, and back over the forum proper. This is the only arch you can currently get close to, unencumbered by scaffolding and with inside reliefs showing the spoils of the sacking of Jerusalem being carried off by eager Romans.

THE PALATINE HILL

Turning right at the Arch of Titus takes you up to the **Palatine Hill**, supposedly where the city of Rome was founded and holding some of its most ancient ruins. It's a pleasanter site to tour than the forum, larger, greener and more of a park – a good place to have a picnic and relax after the rigours of the stones below. In the days of the Republic, the Palatine was the most desirable address in Rome (from it is derived our word "palace"), and the big names continued to colonise it during the Imperial era, trying to outdo each other with ever larger and more magnificent dwellings.

Following the main path up from the forum, the **Domus Flavia** was one of the most splendid residences, and although it's now almost completely ruined, the peristyle is easy enough to identify, with its fountain and hexagonal brick arrangement in the centre. To the left, the top level of the gargantuan **Domus Augustana** spreads to the far brink of the hill – not the home of Augustus as its name suggests, but the private house of any emperor (or "Augustus"). You can look down from here on its vast central courtyard with mazelike fountain, and wander to the brink of the deep trench of the **Stadium**. On the far side of the stadium, the ruins of the **Baths of Septimus Severus** cling to the side of the hill, the terrace giving good views over the Colosseum and the churches of the Celian Hill opposite; down below is another entrance/exit to the site.

Walking in the opposite direction from the Domus Flavia, steps lead down to the **Cryptoporticus**, a long thin passage built by Nero to link his Domus Aurea on the far side of the Colosseum (see overleaf) with the Domus Augustana and other Palatine palaces, and decorated along part of its length with well-preserved Roman stucco-work. You can go either way along the passage: a left turn leads to the **House of Livia**, originally believed to have been the residence of Livia, the wife of Augustus, though now identified as simply part of Augustus's house (the set of ruins beyond). Its courtyard and some of the inner rooms are decorated with scanty frescoes.

Turn right down the passage and up some steps on the left, and you're in the **Farnese Gardens**, among the first botanical gardens in Europe, laid out by Cardinal Alessandro Farnese in the mid-sixteenth century and now a tidily planted, shady retreat from the exposed heat of the ruins. The terrace here looks back over the forum, while the terrace at the opposite end looks down on the church of San Teodoro, across to Saint Peter's, and down on the new excavations immediately below – the traces of an Iron Age village that perhaps marks the real centre of Rome's ancient beginnings.

The Colosseum, the Celian Hill and east to San Giovanni in Laterano

Immediately outside the Forum site, the fourth-century **Arch of Constantine** marks the end of the Via Sacra, the friezes on its inside pillaged from other, earlier monuments. Across the way from here, the **Colosseum** (Mon, Tues & Thurs–Sat 9am–1hr before sunset, Sun & Wed 9am–1pm; free, L6000 for the upper tier) is easily Rome's most awe-inspiring ancient monument, and one which – unlike the Forum – needs little historical knowledge or imagination to deduce its function. Originally known as the Flavian Amphitheatre, it was begun by the Emperor Vespasian around 72 AD and finished by his son Titus about eight years later – an event celebrated by 100 days of continuous games. The Romans flocked here for many things: gladiatorial contests were the big attraction, designed to prime soldiers for real combat, but there were other, equally cruel spectacles, pitting man against animal, even animal against animal – rhinos against elephants, say, or buffaloes against bears. The unifying factor was violence: the slaughter, of animals especially, was huge, leading to the extinction of entire species in Africa; and although gladiators earned big money – and great fame – by fighting in the Colosseum, the tussles were often to the death.

The games were eventually outlawed in the fifth century and, pillaged over the centuries for stone to build some of Rome's grandest palaces (the Barberini and Cancelleria palaces, even Saint Peter's, all used stone from here), the Colosseum is not much more than a shell now, eaten away by pollution and cracked by the vibrations of cars and metro. (A major restoration project, expected to take the best part of ten years and financed in part by the *Banca di Roma*, has just begun, during which it is hoped to keep the Colosseum open to the public.) The floor of the arena has gone entirely, exposing the labyrinth of tunnels beneath, from which the animals would be hoisted into view; around the outside, the arches would originally have held statues, and there are gaping holes where metal brackets linked the great blocks together. The basic structure of the place is easy to see, however, and has served as a model for stadiums around the world ever since. You'll not be alone in appreciating it, and during summer the combination of people and scaffolding can make a visit more like touring a contemporary building-site than an ancient monument. But visit late in the evening or early morning before the tour buses have arrived, travel up a level to get a real sense of the size of the building, and the arena can seem more like the marvel it really is.

The animals that died in the Colosseum were kept in a zoo up on the **Celian Hill**, just behind the arena, the furthest south of Rome's seven hills and probably its most peaceful, clothed almost entirely in woodland and with the gorgeous park of **Villa Celimontana** at its heart. You can get in here by way of the entrance on Piazza di Navicella, a little way down Via Claudia, and you could do worse than take a stroll through. But if you'd rather see some churches, follow Clivo di Scauro from the square, around the edge of the park up to the summit of the hill and the church of **Santi Giovanni e Paolo** (daily 8am–noon & 3.30pm–5.30pm), marked by its colourful campanile and set in a peaceful square that's a neat bubble of medieval facades. Originally founded by a Roman senator called Pammachius, this is in a way a memorial to conscientious objection, dedicated to two dignitaries in the court of Constantine who were beheaded here in 361 AD after refusing military service. The relics of their house are downstairs, although this is currently closed for restoration – around twenty rooms in all, frescoed with pagan and Christian subjects. In the church, the railed-off square in mid-nave marks the supposed place of martyrdom.

From the church the road descends under a succession of brick arches to the church of **San Gregorio Magno** on the left, in a commanding position above the traffic drone of the road below, and looking over to the lollipop pines of the Palatine Hill opposite. Again, it's the story behind the place that's most interesting. It was from here that Saint Gregory dispatched Saint Augustine in the early seventh century to convert England to Christianity, and though the rather ordinary Baroque interior shows little evidence of it now the chapel of the saint does have a beautifully carved altar showing scenes from his life, and there's a room which contains his marble throne.

Back at the Colosseum, it's a short walk east down Via San Giovanni in Laterano to the church of **San Clemente** – a light, white twelfth-century basilica that encapsulates better than any other the continuity of history in the city. It's in fact a conglomeration of three places of worship. The ground-floor church is a superb example of a medieval basilica: its facade and courtyard face east in the archaic fashion and there are some fine, warm mosaics in the apse. Downstairs (daily 9am–12.30pm & 3.30pm–6.30pm; L1000), there's the nave of an earlier church, dated back to 392 AD, with a frescoed narthex showing, among other things, the *Miracle of San Clemente*, one of the first popes, believed to have been ordained by Saint Peter. And at the eastern end of this church, steps lead down to a third level, the remains of a Roman house – a labyrinthine set of rooms including a Mithraic temple of the late second century, drippy and dank and centring on an altar of Mithras.

Continuing down the same street brings you out eventually at the Basilica of **San Giovanni in Laterano** (open all day), officially Rome's cathedral and the former seat of the pope until Unification – after which the pope took refuge in the Vatican and only emerged when the Lateran Treaty of 1929 accorded this and the other patriarchal basilicas extra-territorial status. There has been a church on this site since the fourth century, the first established by Constantine, and the present building, reworked by Borromini in the mid-seventeenth century, evokes – like San Clemente – Rome's staggering wealth of history, with a host of features from different periods. The doors to the church, oddly enough, were taken from the Curia or Senate House of the Roman Forum. Inside, the first pillar on the left of the right-hand aisle shows a fragment of Giotto's fresco of Boniface VIII, proclaiming the first Holy Year in 1300, while further on, a more recent monument commemorates Sylvester I – "the magician pope", bishop of Rome during much of Constantine's reign – and incorporates part of his original tomb, said to sweat and rattle its bones when a pope is about to die. Kept secure behind the papal altar are the heads of Saint Peter and Saint Paul, the church's prize relics. Outside, the cloisters (daily 9am–5pm; L1000) are one of the most pleasing parts of the complex, decorated with early thirteenth-century Cosmati work and with fragments of the original basilica arranged around in no particular order, including a remarkable papal throne assembly and various papal artefacts (not least the vestments of Boniface VIII) in a room off to the side.

Adjoining the basilica is the **Lateran Palace**, home of the popes in the Middle Ages and also formally part of Vatican territory. Next door, the **Baptistery** (daily 9am–1pm & 3–5pm) is the oldest surviving baptistery in the Christian world, an octagonal structure built during the fifth century that has been the model for many such buildings since. There are more ancient remains on the other side of the church, on Piazza di Porta San Giovanni, foremost among which is the **Scala Santa** (daily 6.15am–12.15pm & 3.30–7.15pm), claimed to be the staircase from Pontius Pilate's house down which Christ walked after his trial. The 28 steps are protected by boards, and the only way you're allowed to climb them is on your knees, which pilgrims do regularly – although there is also a staircase for the non-faithful alongside. At the top, the chapel of **San Lorenzo** holds an ancient (sixth–seventh century) painting of Christ said to be the work of an angel, hence its name – *archeiropoeton*, or "not done by human hands".

Across the far side of the square, the **Porta San Giovanni** marks the Aurelian Wall, one of the city's grander gateways. If it's a Saturday morning, you could visit the **clothes market** on Via Sannio; otherwise follow the wall on the city side by way of Viale Carlo Felice to another key Roman church, **Santa Croce in Gerusalemme**, one of the seven pilgrimage churches of Rome, built on the site of the palace of Constantine's mother Saint Helena to house the relics of the true cross she had brought back from Jerusalem. The building is mainly Baroque in style following an eighteenth-century renovation, but the relics of the cross are stored in a surreal Mussolini-era chapel at the end of the left aisle, and the Renaissance apse mosaics, recording the discovery of the fragments, are very fine indeed. North of here towards the rail tracks, the **Porta Maggiore** is probably the most impressive of all the city gates, built in the first century AD to carry water into Rome from the aqueducts outside.

The Esquiline Hill and north to Termini

On the far side of the main road from the Colosseum, the **Esquiline Hill** is the highest and largest of the city's seven hills and was one of the most fashionable residential quarters of ancient Rome. After the fire of 64 AD, Nero began to build a huge palace here, the **Domus Aurea** or "Golden House", the like of which Rome had never seen before. The facade was supposed to have been coated in solid gold, there was hot and cold running water in the baths, one of the dining rooms was rigged up to shower flowers and natural scent on guests, and the grounds – which covered a full square mile – held vineyards and game. Nero didn't get to enjoy his new home for very long, however – he died a couple of years after it was finished, and his successor, Vespasian, tore it down in disgust, draining one of its lakes and building the Colosseum on top.

Later Trajan built his baths on top of the rest of the complex, and it was pretty much forgotten about until the wall paintings were discovered by Renaissance artists, including Raphael, who was influenced by them when working in the Vatican palace.

The ruins of Nero's Golden House are only partially excavated and are closed to the public, while tramps sleep in the relics of Trajan's Baths. The Esquiline Hill's principal feature of interest is for the moment the church of **San Pietro in Vincoli** (daily 6.30am–12.30pm & 3.30–7pm) on the northern side – one of Rome's most delightfully plain churches, nestled in its own, normally tranquil, square. As its name suggests, San Pietro was built to house an important relic, the chains of Saint Peter from his imprisonment in Jerusalem, to which were added those that bound him when a prisoner in Rome. These can still be seen under the canopy in the apse. But most people come for the tomb of Pope Julius II in the southern aisle, which occupied Michelangelo on and off for much of his career and was the cause of many a dispute with Julius and his successors. Michelangelo reluctantly gave it up to paint the Sistine Chapel, and never again found the time to return to it for very long, being always at the beck and call of the latest pope, who had little interest in promoting the glory of one of his predecessors. He never finished the tomb, but the figure of Moses, pictured as descended from Sinai to find the Israelites worshipping the golden calf, and flanked by the gentle figures of Leah and Rachel, is one of the artist's most captivating works, the rest of the composition – completed by later artists – dull and static by comparison.

Steps lead down from San Pietro to **Via Cavour**, a busy central thoroughfare which carves a route between the Colosseum and Termini station. It's a good place to eat cheaply, especially up near the station, though the quality of the food is nothing special. After about half a kilometre the street widens to reveal the basilica of **Santa Maria Maggiore** (daily 9am–6.30pm), one of the city's four great basilicas, and inside one of Byzantine Rome's best preserved relics – a fact belied by the eighteenth-century casing that encloses it. Unlike the other great places of pilgrimage in Rome, Santa Maria Maggiore was not built on any special Constantinian site, but instead went up during the fifth century after the Council of Ephesus recognised the cult of the Virgin and churches venerating Our Lady began to spring up all over the Christian world. Inside, the basilica survives intact, its broad nave fringed on both sides with strikingly well-kept mosaics, most of which date from the church's construction and tell, in comic strip form, of incidents from the Old Testament. The Sistine chapel, on the right, holds the elaborate tomb of Sixtus V, while the equally fancy Pauline chapel has a venerated twelfth-century Madonna topped with a sculpted panel showing the legendary tracing of the church's plan after a snowfall – an event celebrated every August 5 with a pontifical mass.

There are two other, smaller churches worth seeing in the neighbourhood. Behind Santa Maria, off Via Merulana, the ninth-century church of **Santa Prassede** occupies an ancient site, where it's claimed Santa Prassede harboured Christians on the run during the Roman persecutions. She apparently collected their blood and placed it in a well where she was later buried; a slab in the floor of the nave marks the spot. In the southern aisle, the Chapel of Saint Zeno was built by Pope Paschal I as a mausoleum for his mother, Theodora, and is decorated with marvellous ninth-century mosaics.

On the other side of Via Cavour, the church of **Santa Pudenziana** on Via Urbana has equally ancient origins, dedicated to Santa Prassede's supposed sister and for many years believed to have been built on the site where Saint Peter lived and worshipped – though this has since been entirely discredited. There were for years two relics in the church, the chair which Saint Peter used as his throne and the table at which he said mass, though both have long gone – to the Vatican and Saint John Lateran respectively. But the church still has one feature of ancient origin, the superbly stylised fifth-century apse mosaics – apparently the oldest in Rome.

Having seen this group of churches you can either push on up to Termini station or make a left down Via Carlo Alberto to **Piazza Vittorio Emanule II**, the centre of a district which became known as the "quartiere piemontese" when the government located many of its major ministeries here after Unification. The arcades of the square, certainly, recall central Turin, as do the heavy palatial buildings which surround it. But otherwise it's hard to imagine the area as a centre of the nation's government: the palaces are dilapidated and converted to cheap apartments, and the park in the middle is the refuge of junkies and homeless people, who leave a scattered refuse of syringes and empty bottles. Around the square and in the streets beyond, the **market** is one of the city's cheapest, the stalls clogging the pavements selling food, cheap clothes and secondhand furniture.

Villa Borghese and north

Immediately above the Piazza del Popolo, the Pincio Hill marks the edge of the city's core and the beginning of a collection of parks and gardens that forms Rome's largest central open space – the **Villa Borghese**, made up of the grounds of the seventeenth-century pleasure palace of Scipione Borghese, which were bought by the city at the turn of the century. It's a vast area, and its woods, lakes and grass criss crossed by roads are about as near as you can get to peace in Rome without making too much effort. There are any number of attractions for those who want to do more than just stroll or sunbathe: a boating lake, a zoo – a cruel affair well worth avoiding – and some of the city's finest museums.

The **Pincio Hill** isn't formally part of the Villa Borghese, but its terrace and gardens, laid out by Valadier in the early nineteenth century and fringed with increasingly decrepit-looking Classical statues (pinching bits is a major Roman sport), give fine views over the roofs, domes and TV antennae of central Rome, right across to Saint Peter's. Walking south from here, there are more gardens in the grounds of the **Villa Medici**, though as the villa is home to the French Academy these days, they can only be visited on selected days.

The Galleria Borghese

The Villa Borghese proper lies across the far side of the Aurelian Wall and the sunken road that follows it. The best place to make for first, if you want some focus to your wanderings, is the **Casino Borghese** itself, on the far eastern side, which was built in the early seventeenth century and turned over to the state when the gardens became city property in 1902 as the **Galleria Borghese** (Tues–Sat 9am–2pm, Sun 9am–1pm; L4000). Made up of an assortment of works collected by Cardinal Scipione Borghese, only the ground floor of the villa is open for the moment, but it contains the very best of the museum's sculpture collection, made up of a mixture of ancient Roman items and seventeenth-century works. Not surprisingly, Bernini, a protege of Borghese, dominates, his work the essence of Italian Baroque, not least in the bust of his patron, which typically brings its subject to life. Other rooms house more dramatic works. There's an *Aeneas and Anchises*, carved with his father when he was fifteen; a coolly virtuoso *Rape of Proserpine*, in a room surrounded by busts of Roman emperors; and best of all his *Apollo and Daphne*, a dramatic, poised work that captures the split second when Daphne is transformed into a laurel tree, her fingers becoming leaves, her legs tree trunks, while Apollo looks on helplessly. In the next room, Bernini's *David* is a self-portrait of the sculptor aged 25, said to have been carved from a mirror held for him by Scipione Borghese himself; while the centrepiece of the following gallery, *Pauline Borghese*, remembers another member of the family, whose daring portrait by Canova depicts her reclining as Venus on a couch, the thin drapery leaving little to the imagination. Pauline Borghese, the sister of Napoleon and married (reluctantly) to a Borghese prince, was a shocking woman in her day, with grand habits. There are tales of her jewels and clothes, of the Negro who used to carry her from her bath, of the servants she used as footstools, and of course her long line of lovers. The statue was considered outrageous by everyone but herself: when asked how she could have posed almost naked she simply replied: "Oh, there was a stove in the studio."

The collection of art on the upper floor – when it eventually re-opens – should be well worth the extra L4000 you can expect to be charged for entry. There are fine works by Raphael, including a *Deposition*; Caravaggio is represented by a dissolute self-portrait, an emaciated *St Jerome* and the *Madonna dei Palfrenieri* featuring the Madonna stamping on a snake; and Titian by *Sacred and Profane Love*. There is also a famous *Portrait of a Man* by Antonello da Messina, along with paintings by Andrea del Sarto, Lucas Cranach, Palma the Elder, Veronese and Giovanni Bellini.

The Villa Borghese's other museums

The Villa Borghese's two other major museums are situated across the other side of the park, along the Viale delle Belle Arti. Of these, the **Galleria Nazionale d'Arte Moderna** (Tues–Sat 9am–2pm, Sun 9am–1pm; L8000) is probably the least compulsory, its huge lumbering Neoclassical building housing a collection that isn't really as grand as you might expect – a wide selection of nineteenth- and twentieth-century Italian (and a few foreign) names. The nineteenth-century collection, on the upper floor, is currently closed, which is little hardship as the twentieth-century works are far more appealing. Names you might recognise include Modigliani, De Chirico, Giacomo Balla, Boccione and other Futurists, along with the odd Cezanne, Mondrian and Klimt.

The **Villa Giulia**, ten minutes' walk away in the direction of Via Flaminia, a harmonious collection of courtyards, loggias, gardens and temples put together in a playful Mannerist style for Pope Julius III in the mid-sixteenth century, is perhaps more of an essential stop, since it is home to the **Museo Nazionale di Villa Giulia** (Tues–Sat 9am–2pm, Sun 9am–1pm, Wed 9am–7pm; L8000). This is Rome's, indeed the world's, primary collection of Etruscan treasures, and a good introduction (or conclusion) to the Etruscan sites in Lazio, which between them contributed most of the artefacts on display here. It's not an especially large collection, and as such it's worth taking the trouble to see the whole. It splits roughly in two, the left side holding artefacts from the sites north of Rome – Tarquinia, Cerveteri, Veio – and the right those from the south – Nemi, Praeneste (Palestrina). The sculpture is a must: strong, dignified, highly personalised works, best among which is the group of *Apollo and Herakles*, from Veio, and the remarkable *Sarcophagus of a Married Couple* from Cerveteri – on which the figures' features are sharply rendered as portraiture. Other highlights include the *Cistae* recovered from tombs around Praeneste – drumlike objects, engraved and adorned with figures, that were supposed to hold all the things needed for the care of the body after death. In the same room, look too at the marvellously intricate pieces of gold jewellery, delicately worked into tiny horses, birds, camels and other animals.

North of the Villa Borghese

The area north of Villa Borghese is the posh **PARIOLI** district – one of Rome's wealthiest neighbourhoods though of little interest to anyone who doesn't live there – except, that is, if you feel like going on an ice cream pilgrimage (see; *Gelaterie and Paticcerie*). Immediately east stretches the enormous expanse of the **Villa Ada**, connected with Villa Borghese by Via Salaria – the old trading route between the Romans and Sabines, so called because the main product transported along here was salt. The Villa Ada was once the estate of King Vittorio Emanuele III and is about as interesting as any park – a bucolic enough place to while away an afternoon but otherwise not really worth the special journey from the centre of town. The **Catacombe di Priscilla** (Tues–Sun

8.30am–noon & 2.30–5pm; L6000), which you can reach from Via Salaria, are the only real thing to see, the (obligatory) guided tours taking you through a frescoed labyrinth of tunnels to see what is claimed as the earliest known painting of the *Virgin and Child*, believed to date from the latter part of the second century – although in fact it's more likely simply a picture of a mother and child, both of whom were probably buried here.

On the far side of the Parioli district the Tiber sweeps around in a wide hook-shaped bend. These northern outskirts of Rome aren't particularly enticing, though the **Ponte Milvio**, the old originally Roman footbridge where the Emperor Constantine defeated Maxentius in 312 AD, still stands and provides wonderful views of the meandering Tiber, the city springing up green on the hills to both sides, the river running fast and silty below. On the northern side of the river, **Piazzale di Milvio** sports a market and a handful of cheap *birrerias* and restaurants, and is just ten minutes' walk – past the huge Foreign Ministry building – from the **Foro Italico** sports centre, one of the few parts of Rome to survive intact pretty much the way Mussolini planned it. This is still used as a sports centre, but it's worth visiting as much for its period value as anything else. At the centre, there's a fountain surrounded by mosaics of muscle-bound figures indulging in healthful sporting activities, which gives onto an avenue, past the ski slope, patched with more mosaics revering the Duce. Either side of the fountain are the two main stadiums: the larger of the two, the **Stadio Olimpico** on the left, was used for the Olympic Games in 1960 and is still the venue for Rome's two soccer teams on alternate Sundays; the smaller, the **Stadio dei Marmi** ("stadium of marbles"), is a typically fascist monument, ringed by sixty great male statues, groins modestly hidden by fig leafs, in a variety of elegantly macho poses.

The south of the city

On its southern side, the Palatine Hill drops suddenly down to the **Circo Massimo**, a long, thin, green expanse bordered by heavily trafficked roads that was the ancient city's main venue for chariot races. The arena could apparently hold a crowd of around 200,000 betting punters, and if it was still even half intact could no doubt have matched the Colosseum for grandeur. As it is, a litter of stones at the Viale Aventino end is all that remains.

Across the far side of Piazza di Porta Capena, on the right on the corner of Via Antonina, the **Baths of Caracalla** (Tues–Sat 9am–5pm, Mon & Sun 9am–1pm; L6000) are much better preserved, and they give a far better sense of the scale and monumentality of Roman architecture than most of the extant ruins in the city; looking at what's left of this huge complex, there's no doubt that the Romans believed in building *big*. The baths are no more than a shell now, but the walls still rise to very nearly their original height. There are many fragments of mosaics – none spectacular, but quite a few bright and well preserved – and it's easy to discern a floor plan. As for Caracalla, he was one of Rome's worst and shortest-lived rulers, and it's no wonder there's nothing else in the city built by him. The baths are nowadays used for opera performances during the summer (one of Mussolini's better ideas), which is a good, if pricey, way to see them at their most evocative.

The Aventine Hill, Testaccio and the Protestant Cemetery

Otherwise, if you're here during the day, it's a good idea to cross back over Viale Aventino after seeing the baths and scale the **Aventine Hill** – the southernmost of the city's seven hills and the heart of plebeian Rome in ancient times. These days the working-class quarters of the city are further south, and the Aventine is in fact one of the city's more upscale residential areas, covered with villas and gardens and one of the few places in the city where you can escape the traffic. A short way up Via Santa Sabina, the church of **Santa Sabina** (daily 6.30am–12.45pm & 3.30–7pm) is a strong contender for

Rome's most beautiful basilical church: high and wide, its fifth-century nave and portico left mercifully free from the tampering of centuries. Look especially at the main doors, which are contemporary with the church and boast eighteen panels carved with Christian scenes, forming a complete illustrated Bible, which includes one of the oldest representations of the Crucifixion in existence. Santa Sabina is also the principal church of the Dominicans, and it's claimed that the orange trees in the garden outside which you can glimpse on your way to the restrained cloister are descendants of those planted by Saint Dominic himself. Whatever the truth of this, the views from the gardens are splendid – right across the Tiber to the centre of Rome and Saint Peter's.

There are other churches on the Aventine, and in any case it's a nice place to wander, following the road south past the **Priorato di Malta**, one of the city's several buildings belonging to the Knights of Malta, which has a celebrated view of the dome of Saint Peter's through its main gate keyhole. On the far side of Via Marmorada, below, the solid working-class neighbourhood of **TESTACCIO** groups around a couple of main squares, a tight-knit community with a market and a handful of bars and small trattorias that was for many years synonymous with the Mattatoio or slaughterhouse that sprawls down to the Tiber just beyond. In recent years the area has become a trendy place to live, and property prices have soared, leading to some uneasy contradictions, vegetarian restaurants opening in an area still known for the offal dishes served in its traditional trattorias, and gay and alternative clubs standing cheek-by-jowl with the car-repair shops in the caves hollowed into Monte Testaccio. The slaughterhouse, or **Mattatoio**, once the area's main employer, is closed now and used for the occasional gig or rave, along with the city's horse and carriage drivers and an old people's day centre, and for years there has been talk of sprucing it up into a Covent Garden-like affair of shops and restaurants. Up until now nothing has happened, and it's likely to remain as it is for some time to come.

Opposite the slaughterhouse, **Monte Testaccio**, which gives the area its name, is a 35-mtere-high mound created out of the shards of Roman amphorae that were dumped here over some 600 years. It's an odd sight, the ceramic curls clearly visible through the tufts of grass that crown its higher reaches, the bottom layers hollowed out by the workshops of car and bike mechanics. The hill is officially closed, but you may be able to climb up over the wall by no. 52.

On the opposite side of Via Zabaglia, Via Caio Cestio leads up to the entrance of the **Protestant Cemetery** (daily except Wed 8am–11.30am & 3.20–5.30pm; free), one of the shrines to the English in Rome, and a fitting conclusion to a visit to the Keats-Shelley house on Piazza Spagna, since it is here that both poets are buried, along with a handful of other well-known names. It's a small and surprisingly tranquil enclave, crouched behind the mossy pyramidal **tomb** of one Caius Cestius – a local landmark. Keats lies next to his friend the painter, Joseph Severn, in a corner of the old part of the cemetery near the pyramid, his stone inscribed as he wished with the words "whose name was writ in water". Severn died much, much later than Keats but asked to be laid here nonetheless, with brushes and palette. As for Shelley, his ashes were brought here at Mary Shelley's request and interred after much obstruction by the papal authorities in the newer part of the cemetery, at the opposite end. Edward Trelawney lies next door, Gramsci on the far right-hand side in the middle – though if you're at all interested in star-spotting you should either borrow or buy the booklet from the entrance.

From here it's a longish walk or short bus ride back into the centre of town. With energy to spare, you could make a long detour back following the length of the **Aurelian Wall**, built by the Emperor Aurelia in 275 AD to enclose Rome's seven hills, the best-preserved stretch of which runs between Porta San Paolo and Porta San Giovanni – a fairly lengthy hike, but it leaves you about a kilometre from the Colosseum. Failing that, you could take the metro from Piramide station further south to San Paolo fuori le Mura or EUR.

Further south: San Paolo fuori le Mura, EUR and Tre Fontane

Two kilometres or so south of the Porta San Paolo, the basilica of **San Paolo fuori le Mura** is one of the four patriarchal basilicas of Rome, occupying the supposed site of Saint Paul's tomb, where he was laid to rest after being beheaded at Tre Fontane (see overleaf). Of the four, this basilica has probably fared the least well over the years. It was apparently once the grandest of them all, connected to the Aurelian Wall by a mile-long colonnade made up of 800 marble columns, but a ninth-century sacking by the Saracens and a devastating fire in 1823, when a couple of cack-handed roofers spilt burning tar, which left it almost entirely destroyed, means that the church you see now is largely a nineteenth-century reconstruction, sited in what is these days an unenticing neighbourhood of apartment blocks and factories.

For all that, it's a very successful if somewhat clinical rehash of the former church, succeeding where Saint Peter's tries but ultimately fails by impressing with sheer size and grandeur: whether you enter by way of the cloisters or the west door, it's impossible not to be awed by the space of the building inside, its crowds of columns topped by round-arched arcading. Some parts of the building did survive the fire. In the south transept, the paschal candlestick is a remarkable piece of Romanesque carving, supported by half-human beasts and rising through entwined tendrils and strangely human limbs and bodies to scenes from Christ's life, the figures crowding in together as if for a photocall. The bronze doors were also rescued from the old basilica and date from 1070, as was the thirteenth-century baldachino, under which Saint Paul's remains are supposed to lie. The arch across the apse is original too, embellished with mosaics; and the Cosmatesque cloister, just behind here, is probably Rome's finest, its spiralling, mosaic-encrusted columns enclosing a peaceful rose garden. Just off here, the Relics Chapel houses a dustily kept set of semi-august relics and the pinacoteca shows engravings depicting San Paolo before and after the fire.

From San Paolo, Via Ostiense leads south to join up with Via Cristoforo Colombo which in turn runs down to **EUR** (pronounced "Ai-oor") – the acronymic label for the district known as the "Esposizione Universale Roma", reachable on bus #93 from Termini or on metro line #B. This is not so much a neighbourhood as a statement in stone: planned by Mussolini for the aborted 1942 World's Fair and not finished until well after the war, it's a cold, soulless grid of square buildings, long vistas and wide processional boulevards linked tenuously to the rest of Rome by metro but light years away from the city in feel. Come here for its numerous museums, some of which *are* worth the trip, or if you're interested in modern city architecture and planning; otherwise stay well clear.

The great mistake about EUR is that it's not built for people: the streets are wide thoroughfares designed for easy traffic flow and fast driving, shops and restaurants are easily outnumbered by offices and museums, and those that there are – along the main drags of Viale Beethoven and Viale Europa – are high-priced clothes stores and upscale eateries. Of the buildings, the postwar development of the area threw up bland office blocks for the most part, and it's the prewar fascist-style constructions that are of most interest. The **Palazzo di Civiltà di Lavoro** in the northwest corner stands out, Mussolini-inspired architecture at its most assured – the "square Colosseum" some have called it, which sums up its mixing of modern and classical styles perfectly. To the south, **Piazza Marconi** is the nominal centre of EUR, where the wide, classically inspired boulevards intersect to swerve around an obelisk in the centre.

All the museums are within easy reach of here. On the square itself, the **Museo delle Arti e delle Tradizioni Popolari** (Mon–Sat 9am–2pm, Sun 9am–1pm; L4000) is a run-through of applied arts, costumes and religious artefacts from the Italian regions – though, as ever, all is labelled in Italian; bring a dictionary. The **Museo Preistorico e Etnografico** (same times as above; L6000) is unquestionably complete, and arranged in manageable and easily assimilable order, but its prehistoric section is mind-numbingly exhaustive; the ethnographic collection does something to relieve things, with artefacts from South America, the Pacific and Africa, and much is well worth skimming. The **Museo dell'Alto Medioevo** in the same building (Tues–Sat 9am–2pm, Sun 9am–1pm; free) concentrates on artefacts from the fifth century to the tenth century – local finds mainly, including some beautiful jewellery from the seventh century and a delicate fifth-century gold fibula found on the Palatine Hill. But of all the museums, of most interest is the **Museo della Civiltà Romana** (Tues–Sun 9am–1.30pm, Tues & Thurs also 4–7pm; L4000), which has among numerous ancient Roman finds a large-scale model of the fourth-century city – perfect for setting the rest of the city in context.

The perfect antidote to the sense of alienation induced by EUR is just a short walk away, at the **Abbazia delle Tre Fontane** (open all day), a complex of churches founded on the spot where Saint Paul was martyred; it's said that when the saint was beheaded his head bounced and three springs erupted where his head touched the ground, and the churches were sited at these spots. In those days it was a malarial area, and was soon abandoned, but in the second half of the last century Trappist monks drained the swamp and planted eucalyptus trees in the vicinity; they still distill a eucalyptus chest remedy here, sold at the small shop by the entrance.

As for the churches, they were rebuilt in the sixteenth century and restored by the Trappists. They're not particularly outstanding buildings, appealing more for their peaceful location, which is relatively undisturbed by visitors, than any architectural distinction. On the right, the church of **Santa Maria Scala Coeli** owes its name to a vision Saint Bernard had here: he saw the soul he was praying for ascend to heaven; the Cosmatesque altar where this is supposed to have happened is in the crypt. Beyond, the church of **San Paolo alle Tre Fontane** holds the pillar to which Saint Paul was tied, and a couple of mosaic pavements from Ostia Antica.

Via Appia Antica: the catacombs

During classical times the **Via Appia** was the most important of all the Roman trade routes, the so-called "Queen of Roads", carrying supplies right down through Campania to the port of Brindisi. It's no longer the main route south out of the city – that's Via Appia Nuova from Porta San Giovanni – but it remains an important part of early Christian Rome, its sides lined with the underground burial cemeteries or **catacombs** of the first Christians.

Laws in ancient Rome forbade burial within the city walls – most Romans were cremated – and there are catacombs in other parts of the city. But this is by far the largest concentration, around five complexes in all, dating from the first century to the fourth century, almost entirely emptied of bodies now but still decorated with the primitive signs and frescoes that were the hallmark of the then-burgeoning Christian movement. Despite much speculation, no one really knows why the Christians decided to bury their dead in these tunnels: the rock here, tufa, is soft and easy to hollow out, but the digging involved must still have been phenomenal, and there is no real reason to suppose that the burial places had to be secret – they continued to bury their dead like this long after Christianity became the established religion. Whatever the reasons, they make intriguing viewing now. You can get to the main grouping on bus #118 from the Colosseum (Via Celio Vibenna): the three principal complexes are within walking distance of each other, though it's not really worth trying to see them all – the layers of shelves and drawers aren't particularly gripping after a while.

Via Appia Antica begins at the **Porta San Sebastiano**, built in the fifth century, a little way on from which the church of **Domine Quo Vadis** signals the start of the catacomb stretch of road. Legend has this as the place where Saint Peter saw Christ while fleeing from certain death in Rome and asked "Where goest thou, Lord ?", to which Christ replied that he was going to be crucified once more, leading Peter to turn around and accept his fate. Continuing on for a kilometre or so you reach **San Calisto**

(Thurs–Tues 8.30am–noon & 2.30–5pm; L6000), the first catacombs of any significance, burial place of all the third-century popes (of whom San Calisto was one), whose tombs are preserved in the papal crypt, and the site of some well-preserved seventh- and eighth-century frescoes. A little way west from here, the catacombs of **Domitilla** (Wed–Mon 8.30am–noon & 2.30–5pm; L6000) are quieter than those of San Calisto, and adjoin the remains of a fourth-century basilica erected here to the martyrs Achilleus and Nereus. The labyrinth itself is Rome's largest, stretching for around 17km in all, and contains more frescoes and early wall etchings.

The catacombs of **San Sebastiano** (Fri–Wed 9am–noon & 2.30–5pm; L6000), 500m further on, are probably best for a visit, situated under a (much-renovated) basilica that was originally built by Constantine on the spot where the bodies of the apostles Peter and Paul are said to have been laid for a time. Downstairs, half-hour tours wind around dark corridors showing signs of early Christian worship – paintings of doves and fish, a contemporary carved oil lamp and inscriptions dating the tombs themselves. The most striking features, however, are not Christian at all, but three pagan tombs (one painted, two stuccoed) discovered when archaeologists were burrowing beneath the floor of the basilica upstairs. Just above here, Constantine is said to have raised his chapel to Peter and Paul, and although Saint Peter was later removed to the Vatican, Saint Paul to San Paolo fuori le Mura, the graffiti collected above records the fact that this was indeed, albeit temporarily, where the Apostles rested.

Trastevere and the Janiculum Hill

Across the river from the centre of town, on the right bank of the Tiber, the district of **TRASTEVERE**, a small, tightly knit neighbourhood sheltered under the heights of the Janiculum Hill, was the artisan area of the city in classical times, neatly placed for the traded goods that came upriver from Ostia and were unloaded nearby. Later, during the Middle Ages and the Renaissance period, it became Rome's main immigrant quarter, first for Jews (who later migrated across the river to the Ghetto) and after that for other migrants to the city. Today the percentage of immigrants here is much less – they're more likely to be holed up in the poor suburbs on the city's outskirts – but Trastevere still sees itself as a place apart from the rest of the city. The Roman dialect is at its most exaggerated here, with many distinctive vernacular words – there was even a nineteenth-century school of dialect poets based in Trastevere. And the neighbourhood celebrates its independence from Rome proper every year with its *Festa Noiantri* ("We Others"), which takes place in July.

Actually, Trastevere is becoming more and more absorbed into the city of Rome. As a traditionally dissenting voice, the district has been exploited over the last few decades as the city's alternative focus, home to much of its most vibrant and youthful nightlife – something which has made the typical Trasteverini increasingly hard to find; indeed most simply can't afford to live here anymore. Nonetheless it still feels distinctly distanced from the city across the water, its narrow streets and closeted squares peaceful in the morning and vigorous by night; and it still hosts Rome's most intriguing market by far, and (and, if you know where to look) some of its best restaurants.

The obvious way to approach Trastevere is to cross over from Isola Tiberina, which leaves you five minutes from the heart of the neighbourhood's life. But on a Sunday it's worth walking over the Ponte Subiaco to Porta Portese, from which the **Porta Portese** fleamarket stretches down Via Portuense to the Trastevere railway station in a congested medley of antiques, old motor spares, cheap clothing, trendy clothing and assorted junk. Come early if you want to buy, or even move – most of the bargains have gone by 10am, by which time the pack of people can be intense – and afterwards stroll north a little way up Via Anicia to the church of **Santa Cecilia in Trastevere** (daily 10am–noon & 4–6pm), a cream, rather sterile church – apart from a pretty front courtyard – whose antiseptic eighteenth-century appearance belies its historical associations. A church was originally built here over the site of the second-century home of Saint Cecilia, whose husband Valerian was executed for refusing to worship Roman gods, and who herself was subsequently persecuted for Christian beliefs. The story has it that Cecilia was locked in the caldarium of her own baths for several days but refused to die, singing her way through the ordeal (Cecilia is patron saint of music). Her head was finally half hacked off with an axe, though it took several blows before she finally died. Below the high altar, Stefano Maderna's limp, almost modern statue of the saint shows her incorruptible body as it was found in 1599, swathed in a golden robe, with three deep cuts in her neck, a fragile, intensely human piece of work which has helped to make Cecilia one of the most revered of Roman saints. To the side, you can descend to the excavations of the baths (make a small offering for the light), though hints at restoration have robbed these of any atmosphere and there's little to mark out what's what. Only the caldarium itself, on the other side of the church down a small passageway off the right aisle, is clearly marked.

Santa Cecilia is situated in the quieter part of Trastevere, on the southern side of **Viale Trastevere** – the wide boulevard which cuts through the centre of the district. There's more life on the far side of here, centred – during the day at least – around two main squares. The first, **Piazza San Cosimato**, holds a lively produce market every morning except Sunday, after which the action transfers to **Piazza Santa Maria in Trastevere**, a short walk north – the heart of old Trastevere, named after the church in its northwest corner. The church of **Santa Maria in Trastevere** (daily 7am–12.40pm & 3–7pm) is held to be the first Christian place of worship in Rome, built on a site where a fountain of oil is said to have sprung on the day of Christ's birth. The greater part of the structure now dates from 1140, after a rebuilding by a Trastevere pope, Innocent II. These days people come here for two things. The church's mosaics are among the city's most impressive: those on the cornice were completed a century or so after the rebuilding, and show the Madonna surrounded by ten female figures with lamps – once thought to represent the Wise and Foolish Virgins. Inside, there's a Cosmatesque pavement of spirals and circles, and apse mosaics contemporary with the building of the church – Byzantine-inspired works depicting a solemn yet very sensitive parade of saints centring on Christ and Mary.

Cutting north through the back streets towards the Tiber, the **Palazzo Corsini** is an unexpected cultural attraction on this side of the river, built orignally for Cardinal Riario in the fifteenth century, rebuilt in the eighteenth century, and nowadays housing the other half of the **Galleria Nazionale di Arte Antica** (Tues–Sat 9am–2pm, Sun 9am–1pm; L6000), which it shares with the Palazzo Barberini – though it's in fact a much less essential stop than the Barberini collection, including paintings by Caravaggio, Reni, Flemish artists, and Pozzo's designs for the trompe l'oeil ceiling of Sant'Ignazio, which you may have seen across the river.

More interesting is the **Villa Farnesina** across the road (Mon–Sat 9am–1pm; free), built during the early sixteenth century by Baldassare Peruzzi for the Renaissance banker, Agostino Chigi, and known for its Renaissance murals. Inside you can view the Raphael-designed painting of *Cupid and Psyche* in the now glassed-in loggia, completed in 1517 by the artist's assistants, Guilio Romano, Francesco Penne and Giovanni da Udine. Vasari claims Raphael didn't complete the work because his infatuation with his mistress was making it impossible to concentrate, and says that Chigi arranged for her to live with the painter in the palace while he worked on the loggia. More likely he was simply so overloaded with commissions that he couldn't possibly finish them all. He did, however, manage to finish the *Galatea* next door, which he fitted in between his Vatican commissions for Julius II; "the greatest evocation of paganism of the Renaissance", Kenneth Clark called it. The other paintings in the room are by Sebastiano del Piombo and the architect of the building, Peruzzi, who also decorated the upstairs *Salone delle Prospettive*, which shows trompe l'oeil views of Rome – one of the earliest examples of the technique.

The Janiculum Hill

From the Villa Farnesina, it's about a fifteen-minute walk up Via Garibaldi (bus #41 goes up from Piazza delle Rovere) to the summit of the **Janiculum Hill** – not one of the original seven hills of Rome but one of the highest in the city, with easily the best and most accessible views over the centre. About halfway up, on the right of Via Garibaldi, you pass the church of **San Pietro in Montorio** (daily 9am–noon & 4–7pm), built on a site once – now, it's thought, wrongly – believed to have been the place of the saint's crucifixion. The church itself isn't of much interest and in any case is often closed (its one draw, Raphael's *Transfiguration* which used to hang in the apse, was removed to the Vatican in 1809). But the little **Tempietto** in the courtyard on the right is one of the Renaissance's seminal works, built by Bramante at the turn of the fifteenth century and one of his earliest creations in Rome. Built on the supposed precise spot of Saint Peter's martyrdom, the small circular building – it holds a maximum of ten people – is like a classical temple in miniature, perfectly proportioned and neatly executed. The courtyard that surrounds it was supposed to have been remodelled on circular lines to complete the effect, but this was never carried out.

The Janiculum was the scene of a fierce 1849 set-to between Garibaldi's troops and the French, and the white marble **memorial** opposite the church remembers all those who died in the battle. A little further up the hill, the **Acqua Paola** gushes water at a bend in the road, constructed for Paul V with marble from the Roman Forum. At the top, the **Porta di San Pancrazio** was built during the reign of Urban VIII, and today it marks the turn-off for the grounds of the **Villa Doria Pamphilj**, which stretch across the back side of the Janiculum Hill. This is the largest and most recent of Rome's parks, laid out in 1650 and acquired for the city in the Seventies. It's a good place for a picnic, but most people continue straight on up the hill along the **Passeggieta del Gianicolo** to the peak of the hill. At the top, on Piazzale Garibaldi itself, the equestrian monument to Garibaldi is an ostentatious work from 1895 and marks the spot, just below, from which a cannon is fired at noon each day for Romans to check their watches. Further on, the fiery statue of Anita Garibaldi recalls the important part she played in the 1849 battle and marks her grave; opposite are some of the best of the vistas over the city, its brown and orange roofs punctured by the blue-grey of domes and green splashes of its hills.

Descending from here towards the Vatican and Saint Peter's, follow some steps off to the right and, next to a small amphitheatre, you'll find the gnarled old oak tree where the sixteenth-century Italian poet **Tasso** whiled away his last days. Further down the hill, past the Jesuit children's hospital, the church of **Sant'Onofrio** (open mornings only) sits on the road's hairpin, its L-shaped portico fronting the church where Tasso is buried and, on the right, the city's plainest but most delightful small cloister, above which are ranged the rooms of the Franciscan cloister where he died. You can visit the poet's cell, which holds some manuscripts, his chair, his death mask and personal effects.

Across to the Vatican: Castel Sant'Angelo, Saint Peter's and the Vatican Museums

On the right bank of the Tiber, directly across from Rome's historic centre, the **VATICAN CITY** was established as an independent sovereign state in 1929, a tiny territory surrounded by high walls on its far, western side and on the near side opening its doors to the rest of the city and its pilgrims in the form of Saint Peter's and its colonnaded piazza. Saint Peter's and the part of the palace kept up as the Vatican Museums are open to the public, and you don't need to pass through any entrance formalities to visit them.

In addition to these it's possible to visit the **Vatican Gardens**, though only on organised tours. There are tours daily (except Wed and Sun in summer, Sat only in winter) at 10am; price L15,000. You can book these in advance at the **Vatican Information Office** (Mon–Sat 9am–noon & 2–5pm; ☎698.4466), where you'll also find lots of bumph, detailed guides and postcards, which you can post from one of a couple of portacabins in the square if you want a Vatican postmark – and speedier delivery than the notoriously bad Italian service. Finally, you can also, if you wish, attend a **papal audience**: these happen once a week, usually on Wednesdays at 11am in the Audiences Room, and are by no means one-to-one affairs (in summer they're normally held in the summer papal residence in Castel Gandolfo, south of Rome). You can often get a place on one if you apply not more than a month and not less than two days in advance to the Prefettura della Casa Pontificia, 00120 Citta del Vaticano (☎6982).

Crossing the river: Castel Sant 'Angelo and Piazza San Pietro

The best route to the Vatican and Saint Peter's is across **Ponte Sant'Angelo**, flanked by angels carved to designs by Bernini (his so-called "breezy maniacs"). On the far side is the great circular hulk of the **Castel Sant'Angelo** (Mon–Sat 9am–1pm, Sun 9am–noon, Mon also 2–6.30pm; L8000), burial place of the Emperor Hadrian, and in later times the papal city's main fortified defence. Designed by Hadrian himself, the mausoleum was a grand monument, faced with white marble, surrounded with statues and topped with cypresses, designed "to form a black pyramid high in the sky". It was renamed in the sixth century, when Pope Gregory the Great witnessed a vision of Saint Michael here that ended a terrible plague. Later the castle's impressive fortifications and position were not lost on the papal authorities, who converted the building for use as a fortress and built a passageway to link it with the Vatican as a refuge in times of siege or invasion – a route utilised on a number of occasions, most notably when Clement VII sheltered here for several months during the Sack of Rome in 1527. Even now a papal suite is still kept furnished in case of need. Inside, some rooms hold swords, armour, guns and the like, others are lavishly decorated with grotesques and paintings, while below dungeons and storerooms are testament to the castle's grisly past as the city's most notorious Renaissance prison – Benvenuto Cellini and Cesare Borgia are just two famous names to have been held here. Upstairs the official papal apartments, accessible from the terrace, are extravagantly decorated with frescoes depicting Michael sheafing his sword and lewd friezes crammed with naked bodies in various poses of revelry, amid paintings by Poussin, Jordaens and others.

The military still lays claim to the Castel Sant'Angelo, and would like to turn it into a museum of post-Unification history, but for the moment it remains papal property. The surrounding neighbourhood, too, the **BORGO**, which stretches up towards Monte Mario, was once all the pope's land, though it was incorporated into the city of Rome at the end of the sixteenth century. The names of many of the streets still have the "Borgo" prefix, which stemmed from the area's one-time colonisation by Saxon pilgrims – the word "Borgo" is a mutation of their word "burh" – and they are remembered by the old hospital and church of **Santo Spirito in Sassia** on Via di Penitenzieri. The church was founded in 726 by the resident Saxon population and rebuilt in the sixteenth century by Antonio di Sangallo the Younger.

Beyond here, the approach to Saint Peter's – **Via della Conciliazione** – is disappointing: typically, Mussolini swept away the houses of the previously narrow street and replaced them with this wide sweeping avenue, and nowadays Saint Peter's somehow looks too near, the vast space of Bernini's **Piazza San Pietro** not really becoming apparent until you're on top of it – the people sitting on the steps of the basilica (moved at intervals by keen attendants) not much more than dots in the distance. In tune with the spirit of the Baroque, the church was supposed to be even better hidden than it is now: Bernini planned to complete the colonnade with a triumphal arch linking the two arms, so obscuring the view until you were well inside the square, but this was never carried out and the arms of the piazza remain open, symbolically welcoming the world into the lap of the Catholic church. The obelisk in the centre was brought to Rome by Caligula in 36 AD, and it stood for many years in the centre of Nero's Circus on the Vatican Hill (to the left of the church); according to some theories it marked the site of Saint Peter's martyrdom. It was moved here in 1586, when Sixtus V ordered it be erected in front of the basilica – a task which took four months and was done in silence, on pain of death. Either side, the two fountains are the work of Carlo Maderno (on the right) and Bernini; in between, the exact centres of the two ellipses which make up the piazza's oval shape give ingenious views of the four-rowed colonnade as a single line of columns.

Saint Peter's Basilica

The piazza is so impressive, you can't help but feel a little let down by the basilica of **Saint Peter's** (daily 7am–7pm; free), its facade – by no means the church's best feature – obscuring the dome that signals the building from just about everywhere else in the city. Built to a plan initially conceived at the turn of the fifteenth century by Bramante and finished off, heavily modified, over a century later by Carlo Maderno, Saint Peter's is a strange hotchpotch of styles, bridging the gap between the Renaissance and Baroque eras with varying levels of success. It is, however, the principal shrine of the Catholic church, built as a replacement for the rundown structure erected here by Constantine in the early fourth century on the site of Saint Peter's tomb, and as such can't help but impress, worked on by the greatest Italian architects of the sixteenth and seventeenth centuries and occupying a site rich with historical significance.

In size, certainly, Saint Peter's beats most other churches hands down. Unlike most other Christian structures (though like a number in Rome), Saint Peter's actually faces west rather than east, since this was the way pagan basilicas, which the first Christian churches followed, were orientated. Bramante had originally conceived a Greek cross plan rising to a high central dome, but this plan was altered after his death and only revived with the (by then) very elderly Michelangelo's accession as chief architect. Michelangelo was largely responsible for the dome, but he too died shortly afterwards and, under orders from Pope Paul V, Carlo Maderno took over changing the church quite radically by again exchanging the Greek Cross for a Latin Cross, which had the advantage of being more practical for large congregations. Nor did it have the pagan associations of the original shape and followed more directly the plan of Constantine's original basilica. But it completely unbalanced all the previous designs, not least in the way it obscured the dome (which he also modified) from view in the piazza. The inside, too, is very much of the Baroque era, largely the work of Bernini, who created many of the most important fixtures.

INSIDE SAINT PETER'S

You need to be properly dressed to enter Saint Peter's, which means no shorts, mini-skirts or short sleeves – a rule that is very strictly enforced. Inside on the right is Michelangelo's other legacy to the church, his **Pietà**, completed at the opposite end of his career – when he was just 24 – and now, following an attack by a vandal a few years back, strangely removed from the life of the rest of the building behind glass. Looking at the piece, its fame comes as no surprise: it's a staggeringly sensitive and individual work, and an adept one too, placing the limp body of a grown man across the legs of a woman with grace and ease. Etched into the strap across Mary's chest are words proclaiming Michelangelo's authorship – uncharacteristic of the sculptor and apparently done after he heard his work, which had been placed in Constantine's basilica, misattributed by passers-by.

As you walk down the nave, the size of the building becomes more apparent – and not just because of the shrill bronze comparisons with the sizes of other churches alongside. The **dome** is breathtakingly imposing, no question, rising high above the supposed site of Saint Peter's tomb and with balconies decorated with reliefs depicting the basilica's so-called "major relics" – Saint Veronica's handkerchief, adorned with a miraculous image of Christ, the lance of Saint Longinus which pierced Christ's side and a piece of the True Cross. Close by, on the right side of the nave, the bronze statue of **Saint Peter** is another of the most venerated monuments in the basilica, carved in the thirteenth century by Arnolfo di Cambio and with its right foot polished smooth by the attentions of pilgrims. Bronze was also the material used in Bernini's **baldachino**, the centrepiece of the sculptor's Baroque embellishment of the interior, a massive 85 feet high (the height, apparently, of the Palazzo Farnese), cast out of metal pillaged from the Pantheon roof in 1633. It's an almost grotesque piece of work actually, at least to modern eyes, its wild spiralling columns unwittingly copied from the former canopy. But it has the odd personal touch, not least in the female faces and beaming baby carved on the plinths – said to be done for a niece of Bernini's patron, Urban VIII, who gave birth at the same time as the sculptor was finishing the piece.*

Bernini's feverish sculpting decorates the apse, too, his **cattedra** enclosing the supposed (though doubtful) chair of Saint Peter in a curvy marble and stucco throne, surrounded by the doctors of the church and puffs of cloud ascending into the heavens. To the right, the tomb of Urban VIII is less grand but more dignified, though more interesting is Bernini's monument to **Alexander VII** in the south transept, with its skeleton struggling underneath the heavy marble drapes and significantly clutching an egg-timer. This is Baroque at its most melodramatic, even most political. On the left sits Mercy, on the right, Justice, the foot of which rests on a globe and specifically on England – where, according to Bernini, justice was most needed at the time.

There are innumerable other tombs and works of art in the basilica, and you could spend hours inspecting each one. But you'd do better to be more selective. An entrance off the aisle leads to the **treasury** (daily 9am–5.30pm; L3000), which along with more recent additions holds those artefacts left from the earlier church – a spiral column (the other survivors form part of the colonnade around the interior of the dome), a wall-mounted tabernacle by Donatello, a rich blue and gold dalmatic that is said once to have belonged to Charlemagne (though this has since been proved doubtful) and the massive, though fairly ghastly, late fifteenth-century bronze tomb of Sixtus IV by Pollaiolo – which as a portrait is said to be very accurate. There's also, for those frustrated by glass and distance, a plaster copy of Michelangelo's *Pietà*. Back at the central crossing, steps lead down under Bernini's statue of Saint Longinus to the **Crypt**, where a good number of popes are buried in grandiose tombs – in the main those not distinguished enough to be buried up above. None are particularly interesting and you can't turn back, so leave this for your route out. Far better to cross over to the opposite side of the church for the **ascent to the roof and dome** (May–Sept daily 8am–6pm; Oct–April daily 8am–5pm; without lift L4000, with lift L5000) – though you'll probably need to queue. You can ascend to the vertiginous gallery around the interior

* The baldachino and confessio just in front are supposed to mark the exact spot of the **tomb of Saint Peter**, and excavations earlier this century did indeed turn up – directly beneath the baldachino and the remains of Constantine's basilica – a street of Roman tombs, with inscriptions confirming that the Vatican Hill was a well-known burial ground in classical times. Whether the tomb of Saint Peter was found is less clear: a shrine was discovered, badly damaged, that agrees with some historical descriptions of the saint's marker, with a space in it through which ancient pilgrims placed their heads in prayer. Close by, the bones were discovered of an elderly but physically fit man, and although these have never been claimed as the relics of the apostle, speculation that they are has always been strong. It is possible to visit the Vatican necropolis but you must get official permission; contact the office on Piazza San Pietro (see p.612) for details.

of the dome, and afterwards go out onto the roof to look down from behind the huge statues on the grasp of Bernini's piazza below. From the inner balcony a series of steps and ramps lead eventually to the lantern at the top of the dome, from which the views over the city are as glorious as you'd expect.

The Vatican Museums

Mon–Sat 8.45am–1.45pm; Easter period & July 1–Sept 30 Mon–Fri 8.45am–5.45pm, Sat 8.45am–1.45pm; closed Sun all year, except last Sun of each month, which is also free; L12,000; guidebook 15,000.

A five-minute walk out of the northern side of the piazza takes you up to the only part of the Vatican Palace you can visit independently, the **VATICAN MUSEUMS** – quite simply, the largest, richest, most compelling and perhaps most exhausting museum complex in the world. If you found any of Rome's other museums disappointing, the Vatican is probably the reason why: so much booty from the city's history has ended up here, from both Classical and later times, and so many of the Renaissance's finest artists were in the employ of the pope, that not surprisingly the result is a set of museums so stuffed with antiquities as to put most other European collections to shame.

As its name suggests, the Vatican Palace actually holds a collection of museums on very diverse subjects – displays of classical statuary, Renaissance painting, archaeological and Egyptian sections, not to mention displays of books, old maps and the furnishings and decorations themselves. There's no point in trying to see them all, at least not on one visit, there's simply too much; just seeing one tenth of the total exhibits could take you half a day. You'd do far better to select what you want to see and aim to return another time if you can. Above all, be conservative – the distances between different sections alone can be vast and very tiring.

It's worth taking account of the official, colour-coded **routes** through the museums, which are constructed for varying amounts of time and interest and can take you anything from 45 minutes to the best part of a day. It's a good idea to follow these, at least in part, since it's easy to get lost and in any case you'll get around quicker if you're heading roughly in the same direction as the crowds. The only features you really shouldn't miss are the Raphael Stanze and the Sistine Chapel; these are included in all suggested routes.

MUSEO EGIZIO, CHIARAMONTI, BRACCIO NUOVO, PIO-CLEMENTINO

The **Museo Egizio**, founded in the nineteenth century by Gregory XVI, has some vividly painted mummy cases and a shrivelled mummy, along with *canopi*, the vessels into which the entrails of the deceased were placed. There's also a partial reconstruction of the *Canopos Serapeum*, or Temple to Serapis, from Hadrian's Villa near Tivoli, along with a statue of his favourite, Antinous. Antinous drowned close to the original temple in Egypt, and in his memory Hadrian had a replica built in the garden of his villa.

The **Museo Chiaramonti** and **Braccio Nuovo** hold Classical sculpture, although they are the Vatican at its most overwhelming – close on a thousand statues crammed into two long galleries that you need a keen eye to sort through meaningfully. The 300-metre long Chiaramonti gallery is especially unnerving, lined as it is with the chill marble busts of hundreds of nameless, blank-eyed ancient Romans, along with the odd deity. It pays off to have a leisurely wander, for there are some real characters here: sour, thin-lipped matrons with their hair tortured into pleats, curls, coils and spirals; kids, caught in a sulk or mid-chortle; and ancient old men with flesh sagging and wrinkling to reveal the skull beneath. Around the corner, the **Braccio Nuovo** holds a bizarre statue depicting the Nile, whose yearly flooding was essential to the fertility of the Egyptian soil. It is this aspect of the river which is here represented: crawling over the hefty river god are sixteen babies, thought to allude to the number of cubits the river needed to rise to fertilise the land.

The small **Museo Pio-Clementino**, back at the top of the Chiaramonti, is more interesting. Here you'll find the Cortile di Belvedere, a small courtyard which holds some of the best of the Vatican's classical statuary, including the serene *Apollo Belvedere*, a Roman copy of a fourth-century BC original, and the second-century BC *Laocoon* – two statues which influenced Renaissance artists more than any others. The *Laocoon* especially, which was discovered under Nero's Golden House in 1506 and depicts the treacherous priest of Apollo being crushed with his sons by serpents, lays claim to be the most famous Classical statue ever, referred to by Pliny and written about by Byron – who described its contorted realism as "dignifying pain". The **Museo Gregoriano Etrusco**, above, holds sculpture, funerary art and applied art from the sites of southern Etruria – a good complement to the Villa Giulia. Especially worth seeing are the finds from the Regolini-Galassi tomb, discovered near Cerveteri, which include some gorgeously excessive jewellery, a bronze bed, the reconstructed fragments of a funeral chariot, and, presumably to stave off boredom in the after-life, a set of dice.

TO THE RAPHAEL STANZE

The **Raphael Stanze** lie at the opposite end of the building to the entrance and – if you want to make straight for them – can be reached by way of a long hike through the west wing (green route C); the route in itself takes in a fair quantity of interest. For example, there's the **Gallery of Candelabra**, with a marvellous collection of Roman sculptures that includes the candelabra that gives the gallery its name; three rooms of **tapestries**, woven in Brussels after designs by Raphael's pupils; and, most engagingly, a **Map Gallery** with sixteenth-century wall maps showing cities and reliefs of Italy and the islands of the Mediterranean. But it's the Raphael Rooms themselves which are the real prize, although only two – the *Stanza di Eliodoro* and *Stanza della Segnatura* – were actually decorated by Raphael himself.

The **Stanza di Eliodoro** was painted by Raphael for Pope Julius II, and its principal painting, the *Expulsion of Heliodorus from the Temple*, is an exciting piece of work packed with action, in which the figures on the right seem ready to jump into the room; it's also an allusion to the military success of Julius II, captured on the left in portrait. Not to be outdone, Leo X, Julius's successor, in the *Meeting of Atilla and Saint Leo* opposite, ordered Raphael to substitute his head for that of Julius II, turning the painting into an allegory of the Battle of Ravenna at which he was present; thus he appears twice, as pope and (confusingly) as the equally portly Medici cardinal just behind. The *Deliverance of Saint Peter* is an undisguised reference to the captivity of Leo after the same battle, portraying him as both victim and martyr in the same room, but is most impressive for its radiant lights over the slumbering Peter, and contrasting soft glows on the armour. Opposite, over the inner window (and using the window shape to heighten the effect of a flight of steps), the *Mass at Bolsena* shows Julius again on the right, pictured in attendance at a famous thirteenth-century miracle in Orvieto where real blood issued during a mass said by a doubting priest: the composition is neat, the colouring rich, the onlookers kneeling, turning, gasping, as the miracle is realised.

The next room, the **Stanza della Segnatura** or Pope's study, is probably the best known – and with good reason. Raphael decorated this between 1512 and 1514, the subjects again the choice of Julius II, and it comes close to the peak of the painter's art composed with careful balance and harmony. The *School of Athens*, on the near wall as you come in, steals the show, a representation of the "Triumph of Scientific Truth" (to pair with the *Disputation of the Sacrament* opposite, which is a reassertion of religious truth) in which all the great minds from antiquity are represented. Plato and Aristotle discuss philosophy in the background, spread across the steps is Diogenes, lazily ignorant of all that is happening around him, while to the right Raphael cheekily added a solitary, sullen portrait of his rival Michelangelo, who was working on the Sistine Chapel at the time, almost next door.

The last room, the **Stanza Incendio**, was the last to be decorated, and in a sense it brings together three generations of work. The ceiling was painted by Perugino, Raphael's teacher, and the frescoes were completed to Raphael's designs by his pupils (notably Giulio Romano), most striking of which is the *Fire in the Borgo*, facing the main window – an oblique reference to Leo X restoring peace to Italy after Julius II's reign.

THE SISTINE CHAPEL

Steps lead down from here to the **Sistine Chapel**, a huge barnlike structure, built for Pope Sixtus IV in 1481, which serves as the pope's official private chapel and the scene of the conclaves of cardinals for the election of each new pontiff. The **wall paintings** down each side wall are contemporary with the building, depictions of scenes from the lives of Moses and Christ by – among others – Perugino (the *Keys to St Peter* and the *Calling of Peter and Andrew*), Botticelli (*Cleansing of the Leper*) and Ghirlandaio (*Resurrection*), and in any other church they would be pored over very closely indeed. But it's the ceiling frescoes of Ghirlandaio's pupil, Michelangelo, depicting the **Creation**, that everyone comes to see: as famous a work of art as there is on earth, executed almost singlehanded (though there have been recent disputes about this) in a sustained burst of creative energy over a period of about four years. It depicts scenes from the Old Testament, starting with the *Drunkenness of Noah* at the eastern end and working back to *Creation of Light* above the altar wall – the sides decorated with figures from Christian and pagan theology. Oddly enough Michelangelo hadn't wanted to do the work at all: he considered himself a sculptor, not a painter, and was more eager to get on with carving Julius II's tomb (now in San Pietro in Vincoli) than the ceiling, which he regarded as a chore. Julius, however, had other plans, drawing up a design of the twelve Apostles for the vault and hiring Bramante to design a scaffold for the artist from which to work. Michelangelo was apparently an awkward, solitary character: before he had barely begun painting, he had rejected Bramante's scaffold as unusable, fired all his staff and dumped the pope's scheme for the ceiling in favour of his own. But the pope was easily his match: there are all kinds of tales of the two men clashing while the work was going on – Michelangelo would lock the doors at crucial points, ignoring the pope's protestations to see how it was progressing; and legend has the two men at loggerheads at the top of the scaffold one day, resulting in the pope striking the artist in impatience.

Julius II lived only a few months after the Sistine Chapel ceiling was finished, but the fame of the work he had commissioned soon spread far and wide. Certainly, it's staggeringly impressive, all the more so for its recent restoration (financed by a Japanese TV company to the tune of $3 million in return for world TV rights), which has lifted centuries accumulated soot and candle grime off the paintings to reveal a much brighter, more vivid painting than anyone thought existed. The restorers have also been able to chart the progress of Michelangelo as he moved across the vault. Images on fresco must be completed before the plaster dries, and each day a fresh layer of plaster would have been laid, on which Michelangelo would have had around eight hours or so before having to finish for the day. Comparing the different areas of plaster, it seems the figure of Adam, in the key *Creation of Adam* scene, took just four days; God, in the same fresco, three days.

Restoration work, again financed by Japanese TV, is now underway on the fresco of the **Last Judgement**, on the west wall of the chapel, painted by Michelangelo more than twenty years later, and it will be interesting to see how its murky colours come up afterwards – although it's reckoned the work will last until 1994. Michelangelo wasn't especially keen to work on this either – he was still engaged on Julius II's tomb, under threat of legal action from the late pope's family – but Pope Paul III was keen to complete the decoration of the chapel. It was another five years' work, again alone, but the painting is probably the most spirited, most inspired and most homogeneous large-scale painting you're ever likely to see, the technical virtuosity of Michelangelo taking a back seat to the sheer exuberance of the work, fashioning the human body into a finely captured set of exquisite poses: even the damned, even the aged prophets, appear as a celebration of the human form. Perhaps unsurprisingly the painting offended some and even before it was complete Rome was divided as to its merits, especially regarding the etiquette of introducing such a display of nudity into the pope's private chapel. But Michelangelo's response to this was unequivocal, lampooning one of his fiercer critics with ass's ears and an entwined serpent in the bottom right-hand corner of the picture. Later the pope's zealous successor, Pius IV, objected to the painting and would have had it removed entirely had not Michelangelo's pupil, Daniele da Volterra, appeased him by carefully – and selectively – adding coverings to some of the more obvious nude figures, earning himself forever the nickname of the "breeches-maker". Although the Vatican is unwilling to release any information about the restoration, it seems that the breeches will remain, since it's claimed that the restorers have discovered nothing but bare plaster beneath them.

THE APPARTAMENTO BORGIA

On the upper level, above the Raphael Rooms and Sistine Chapel, the **Appartamento Borgia** – small draughty rooms that have little hint of papal luxury about them – sport a fairly dreadful collection of modern religious art, although the ceiling frescoes in the *Salla dei Santi*, by Pinturrichio, are worth seeing, typically rich in colour and detail and dominated by a large portrait said to be Lucrezia Borgia as Saint Catherine. The room was reputedly the scene of a decidedly un-papal party to celebrate the first of Lucrezia's three marriages, which ended up with men tossing candies down the fronts of the women's dresses.

PINACOTECA, GREGORIANO PROFANO, PIO CRISTIANO, ETNOLOGICO

The **Pinacoteca** is housed in a separate building on the far side of the Vatican's main spine, and ranks possibly as Rome's best picture gallery, with works from the early to High Renaissance. Among early work, there are pieces by Crivelli, Lippi and Giotto – best a triptych of the *Martyrdom of SS Peter and Paul* which captures everyone's attention. There are the rich backdrops and elegantly clad figures of the Umbrian School painters, Perugino and Pinturrichio. And Raphael has a room to himself, including the unfinished *Transfiguration*, painted at the end of his life, that hung above the artist as he lay in state. Leonardo's *Saint Jerome*, in the next room, is unfinished too, but it's a remarkable piece of work, Jerome a rake-like ascetic torn between suffering and a good meal. Caravaggio's *Descent from the Cross*, however, gets more attention, a warts'n'all canvas that is imitated successfully by Reni's *Crucifixion of Saint Peter* in the same room.

Leaving the Pinacoteca leaves you well placed for the grouping of further museums in the modern buildings around. The **Museo Gregoriano Profano** holds more classical sculpture, mounted on scaffolds for all-round viewing, including Roman funerary work, notably the Hatieri tomb friezes, which show backdrops of ancient Rome and realistic portrayals of contemporary life. It's thought the Hatieri were a family of construction workers and that they grabbed the opportunity to advertise their services by including reliefs of the buildings they had worked on (including the Colosseum), along with a natty little crane, on the funeral monument of one of their female members.

The adjacent **Museo Pio Cristiano** has intricate early Christian sarcophagi and, most famously, an expressive third-century AD statue of the *Good Shepherd*. And the **Museo Missionario Etnologico** displays art and artefacts from all over the world, collected by Catholic missionaries, and is obviously inspired by the Vatican's desire to poke fun at non-Christian cults, as well as slap itself on the back for its own evangelical successes.

Drinking and eating

Drinking is not something Romans do a lot of – at least not in public. **Eating out** is a different matter, and in a city of comparatively scarce nightlife is one of the things you'll spend a lot of time doing – mainly in Italian restaurants, though we've included some brief listings of non-Italian eateries too, some varieties of which (notably Chinese) have been booming of late. We've also listed a handful of places serving **snacks** – though most bars serve *panini* and *tramezzini* – and the best of the city's **gelaterie** and **pasticcerie**, together with a checklist of **late- and all-night drinking** places. For **gay** and **women's** drinking and nightlife, see the "Nightlife" heading.

Bars

You'll find a **bar** on every corner in Rome, but as with the rest of Italy most are functional daytime haunts, not at all the kinds of places you'd want to spend an evening. To get around the licensing laws, many of Rome's evening drinking places are run as private clubs (usually known as *centri culturali*), a device which means you may be stung for a membership fee – particularly where there's music – though as a one-off visitor some places will let you in without formalities.

Many drinking spots are slick and expensive excuses for people to sit and pose, but most have the advantage of staying open late – sometimes until 4am in summer, almost always until around 1am. **Prices** generally are over the odds – reckon on about L6000 (and upwards) for a medium (40cl) beer, more for anything really fancy. The only slightly cheaper places you'll find are the odd **birreria** or a handful of relaxed and reasonably priced **wine bars**.

Central

Caffè Greco, Via Condotti 86. Founded in 1742 and patronised by, among others, Casanova, Byron, Goethe and Stendhal. Today it's a tourist joint of dubious cleanliness and quality. Curiosity value only.

Bar della Pace, Via della Pace 5. Just off Piazza Navona, this is *the* summer bar, with outside tables full of Rome's self-consciously beautiful people. Quietest during the day, when you can enjoy the nineteenth-century interior – marble, mirrors, mahogany and plants – in peace, although the prices and rather snooty staff may put you off altogether.

Camilloni, Piazza Sant'Eustachio 54. One of three or four bars to claim the best coffee in Rome (*Eustachio* across the street is another). Busy until late but otherwise unexceptional. A few tables on a quiet but not particularly scenic piazza. Great *tartufo* ice cream.

Cul de Sac, Piazza del Pasquino 73. Bustling and atmospheric wine bar in two narrow rooms, both invariably packed. Wines from every Italian region at relatively low prices, and good snacks served from antique marble bar at the front. Open lunchtime and 8pm until midnight.

Druid's Den, Via San Martino ai Monti 28. Appealing Irish pub with a genuine Irish feel (and Irish owners). Mixed expat/Italian clientele, but not just for the homesick. Cheap and lively, with occasional impromptu music – good for an evening out in its own right. Open 8pm–1am.

Enoteca Cavour, Via Cavour 313. At the forum end of Via Cavour, a lovely old wine bar that makes a handy retreat after seeing the ancient sites. Lots of wines and delicious (though not cheap) snacks and salads.

Enoteca Piccolo, Via del Governo Vecchio 75. Intimate candlelit wine bar with a dozen wines by the glass and many more by the bottle.

Fiddler's Elbow, Via dell'Omarta 43. Another Irish bar but roomier than *Druid's* and with a decidedly more Latin feel. Open 5pm–1am.

The Fox, Via Monterone 19. Small, boozy *birreria* behind Largo Argentina with some expats and a high-volume jukebox.

Gelocremeria, Via della Pigna 58. A quiet, no-frills bar still with Fifties fittings. Good for a sit-down during the day without being ripped off, and a welcome refuge from the Pantheon's nearby tourist traps. Closes early.

Goldfinch, Via Pollarola 31. Tucked behind Campo de' Fiori behind an unmarked door, this place fills up after midnight with an eclectic mix of well-oiled drinkers, lonely gays and local artisans, along with some of the Campo's more odd-ball denizens. Open from around 10pm until 4am.

Latteria, Via del Gatto. Old-fashioned dairy shop which serves gigantic bowls of hot chocolate and caffé latte. Frequented by eccentric locals during the day, but packed in the evening with arty, alternative types and English priests from the nearby seminary.

Miscellanea, Via Paste s/n. The boozy hangout of US students in Rome, and inevitably packed at night. Reasonable prices and the best-value sandwiches in town – jaw-breaking doorsteps for L4000. Open lunchtime until 4am.

Pasticceria Farnese, Via de' Baullari, corner Piazza Farnese. Popular with business types and beautiful young things, but actually not expensive, and a pleasant place to come for breakfast or lunch, as well as evening drinks. Good cappuccino and *cornetti*, and excellent *pizza romana*. Free seating at the window bar, but you might want to pay to sit outside on a warm evening for the view of the graceful Palazzo Farnese.

Picasso, Piazza della Pigna 23. Cool, but not too pretentious, *Picasso* hosts the occasional art exhibition and performance arts event, as well as playing an interesting and eclectic mix of music. Perch on a bar-stool rather than taking a table to avoid paying extra for service. Open from 9pm.

Taverna di Bacco, Via della Pace 1. Amiable little haunt just around the corner from the rather pretentious *Pace*, where you can drink a wide range of bottled beers to an accompaniment of jazz. Tables outside in summer. Open 7.30pm–4am.

La Tazza d'Oro, Via degli Orfani. Straight off Piazza del Pantheon. Coffee shop that by common consent sells Rome's best cup of coffee. Closed in the evening.

Tempera, Via di San Marcello 19. Centrally situated behind Piazza Venezia, this is potentially Rome's best *birreria*, with cheap beer, good pub-type food and a convivial atmosphere.

La Vetrina, Via della Vetrina 20. One of a few bars scattered around the centre where the clubbing crowd congregates before moving on to the main event of the night. Lively atmosphere, and a good place to check out the latest dance-floor fashions. Usually piles of fliers for the clubs on the bar, many of which will get you in at a discount. Opens about 10pm.

Vineria, Campo de' Fiori 15. Long-established bar/wine shop patronised by lefties, ageing hippies, bikers and expats who spill out onto the pavement outside, perching on Vespas and the bonnets of parked cars, or tables in summer. Due to the foreign contingent, drinking is heavier than in most Roman bars. Open evenings all year and lunchtimes too in summer.

Trastevere

La Scala, Piazza della Scala. The most popular Trastevere birreria – big, bustling and crowded, with a Texan ranch-meets-McDonalds decor. Pub food, cheap beer and occasional (dire) music.

Caffe' del Marzio, Piazza Santa Maria in Trastevere 14b. A little expensive if you sit at the outisde tables, but then you *do* have a great view of Santa Maria's glinting mosaics and of the eclectic life of the piazza. Open 7am–2am.

Melvyn's, Via della Politeama 8. Big, noisy and slightly tatty bar that packs in the punters for videos and live music. A good place to start an evening, but can get slightly dodgy later on.

Pub-Birreria, Vicolo del Cinque 31a. Exactly what it says, an easy-going *birreria* that's worth a visit for the frescoed ceilings alone. Some pub food.

Bar San Calisto, Piazza San Calisto 4. Dingy-looking dive with a smoky side room full of card-playing old men and their dogs, which attracts a crowd of hardened drinkers late at night and is periodically closed down after drugs raids. The occasional fight notwithstanding, it's a great place to drink: the booze is cheap, and you can sit at outside tables for no extra cost. Things are slightly less demi-mondeish during the day, and it's perfectly OK to bring your own sandwich or pizza slice. They also do wonderful ice cream. Open 7am–1am.

San Michele aveva un gallo, Via di San Francesco a Ripa XX. Bleak decor, but good snacks and salads and mid-priced wine and beer. Recently opened, and as yet not too crowded.

Caffe' della Scala, Via della Scala 4. Pleasant, not-too-hectic little bar which usually plays jazz. Open 8am–1pm & 5pm–1.30am.

Trastè, Via della Lungharetta 76. Refined meeting-place for the young and cultured Trastevere crowd. Emphasis more on fancy teas than getting well-oiled. Good for informal eating.

Testaccio

Aldebaran, Via Galvani 54. Laid-back cocktail bar (250 to choose from) around the corner from the nightspots of Via di Monte Testaccio. Open 9pm–2.30am.

Caffe' del Seme e la Foglia, Via Galvani 18. Pleasantly low-key café popular with Testaccio trendies and students from the nearby music school. Good for sandwich lunches during the day, and in the evenings a mellow place to relax before visiting the area's more energetic offerings. Open 7am–1.30am.

Gelaterie and Pasticcerie

Alberto Pica, Via della Seggiola 12 (between Ponte Garibaldi and Piazza Arenula). Fresh fruit sorbets are the house speciality, with a hundred-flavour assortment. Open 8am–1am. Closed Sun.

Bella Napoli, Corso Vittorio Emanuele II 248. Excellent Neapolitan pastries (most famously ricotta-filled *sfogliatella*, served warm in the mornings). Attracts a fairly sedate crowd, but it's not expensive, and you can sit for no extra cost at the tables in the front.

Bernasconi, Largo Argentina 1. One of the oldest and busiest *pasticcerie* in town. Also a central daytime bar.

Ciampini, Piazza San Lorenzo in Lucina 29. A café which serves a decadent, velvety chocolate ice cream, along with good sandwiches. If you can afford it, sit on the terrace to watch the beautiful poseurs passing to and from the nearby designer shopping streets.

Dagnino, in an arcade off Via E. Orlando, near Piazza Repubblica. Wonderful Forties bar/*pasticceria* with Sicilian specialities and wide range of general goodies.

La Dolce Roma, Via del Portico d'Ottavia 20b. An Austro-American bakery at the heart of the Jewish ghetto, whose tempting goodies include carrot cake, choc-chip cookies, cheesecake and apple strudel.

Il Forno del Ghetto, Via del Portico d'Ottavia 2. Marvellous Jewish bakery whose unforgettable "pizze giudie" guarantees long queues from around 5pm. It's a kind of rock-cake, crammed with dried and candied fruit, traditionally eaten standing outside the shop.

Gelateria della Palma, Via della Maddalena 20. Designer ice cream in suitably stylish surroundings. 104 flavours including fig, pomegranate, avocado, After Eight and muesli. Currently Rome's best. Open 8am–2am. Closed Wed.

Giolitti, Via dei Uffici del Vicaro 40. An Italian institution which once had a reputation – now lost – for the country's top ice cream. Still pretty good, however, with a choice of 70 flavours. Open 7am–2am. Closed Mon.

Palazzo del Freddo di Giovanni Fassi, Via Principe Eugenio 65/7. A wonderful, airy 1920s ice cream parlour, well worth the trek down from Piazza Vittorio. Brilliant fruit ice creams and good milkshakes.

San Filippo, Via di Villa San Filippo 8–10. Way out of the centre at Parioli, but worth the trip for what are perhaps the best ice creams in the city.

Tre Scalini, Piazza Navona. Renowned for its absolutely remarkable *tartufo* – death by chocolate.

Valzani, Via del Moro 37. One of the oldest of the city's pastry shops, still keeping up the traditions.

Snacks and self-service

Virtually every bar and caffé in town sells sandwiches and *pizza romana* (cheese and prosciutto sandwiched between white pizza bread and best eaten toasted). If money is tight you can picnic off bread, tomatoes, salad and ricotta bought from street markets and bakeries (the cheapest cheese) for around L2000 a head, and reckon on spending around L1000 for a can of fizz or beer in a grocery, less than that from the Standa, the most central supermarket, on Viale Trastevere. Expect to pay upwards of L3000 for a decent-sized pizza slice from one of the many *pizza al taglio* or *pizza rustica* outlets scattered throughout the city.

Central

Caffe Capranica, Piazza Capranica 104. Down-at-heel environment but a cheap place to eat in an otherwise expensive area.

Corso Chianti, Via del Gesù 88. Old-world wine shop with a few tables at the back. The good food, cheap prices and friendly service mean it's always busy. Come at noon for lunch. Recommended.

Il Delfino, Corso V. Emanuele 67. Central and very busy caféteria right on Largo Argentina with huge choice of snacks and full meals. Good for a fast fill-up between sights.

Enoteca Nibbi, Via Emilia 42. One of few reasonable places to lunch near Via Veneto. Sandwiches made to order, and wine served by the glass, both consumed on your feet as you're elbowed by the area's business people.

Filetti di Baccala, Largo dei Librari 88. A fish and chip shop without the chips. Paper-covered Formica tables, cheap wine, beer and fried cod.

Caffe' Fiume, Via Salaria 57. Ritzy Art Nouveau café which does one of the best *tavola caldas* in town, and more than merits the ten-minute walk from the Galleria Borghese. There's also a superb range of salads and generously filled sandwiches, and, as it's off the beaten tourist track, prices are pretty reasonable.

Forno, Via delle Muratte 8. 7am–2.30pm & 4–9pm. Closed Thurs pm and all day Sun in winter, open daily in summer. The last thing you'd expect just by the Trevi Fountain – a well-priced sandwich bar, bakery and grocery store rolled into one.

Paneformaggio, Via Ripetta 7–8. Some hot dishes, filled croissants and huge range of rolls and pastries. Takeaway or small space at the bar.

Pizza al Taglio, Via del Governo Vecchio 28. Unnamed bakery in which the Paladini family have been making wood-oven baked *pizza bianca* since 1914. It gets chock-full at lunchtime, but it's well worth queueing for the scrumptious customised pizzas. Fillings – mozzarella, ricotta, prosciutto, bresaola, rughetta – are laid out on the marble bar, and you simply order the combination you want.

Pizza Italia, Corso d'Italia 103. A bit out of the way, but only about ten minutes' walk from the Galleria Borghese. It's worth the effort for thin, crispy-based pizza with strange toppings such as corn, smoked salmon and *puntarella* with anchovies.

Pizzeria, Campo de' Fiori 39. Great little *pizza al taglio* place, serving especially good *pizza fredda* (cold pizza with salady toppings like mozzarella, tomato and basil or tuna, rughetta and tomato). Small *tavola calda* as well, with good, gooey *suppli*.

Around Termini

Bar Camilloni, Via A. Depretis 77a. Hot and cold buffet, and sandwiches – a convenient place to break after seeing Santa Maria Maggiore. No extra charge for sitting down.

Cottini, Via Merulana 286–7. Good-value *tavola calda*, and a mouthwatering selection of cakes and pastries, right opposite Santa Maria Maggiore.

Nadia e Davide, Via Milano 33. On a side street off Via Nazionale, one of the city's better *pizza al taglio* joints, with some relatively unusual toppings.

Trimani, Via Cernaia 37. Classy wine bar good for a lunchtime tipple and gastronomic indulgence. A fixed lunch for L19,500 might not seem good value for a mixed plate of cheeses and salamis, dessert and wine, but this is real quality food! If you can't afford this, individual dishes go for around L8000; wines start at L3000 a glass.

Vatican and around

Antico Forno, Borgo Pio 8. The best of a number of places to snack on this cobbled street below Saint Peter's. Unusual *pizza al taglio*, including truffle and mozzarella, zucchini flowers and anchovies and chocolate. Standing room only.

Michelangelo Food, Viale dei Bastioni 4. A daft name and noisy adolescent crowd notwithstanding, this place serves great crepes. A good post-museum treat.

Restaurants

Rome's culinary specialities sound pretty unappetising – tripe (*trippa*), brain (*cervello*) and baby calf intestines (*pagliata* or *pajata*) – but they crop up on most menus. A rather less stomach-churning speciality is artichoke (*carciofi*), which come deep-fried and crispy (*alla giudea*), as well as with pasta (*carciofi e ricotta* is a revelationary combination). Rome is also blessed with some good, honest pizzerias, churning out thin, crispy-based pizza from authentic wood-fired ovens. House wine is usually drinkable, especially the white from the Castelli Romani, although most Romans dilute it, as their ancient ancestors did, with water.

There are lots of good places to eat in the **centro storico**, and it's still surprisingly easy to find places which are not tourist traps – prices in all but the really swanky places remain pretty uniform throughout Rome. The area around **Via Cavour** and **Termini** is packed with cheap eateries, although some of them are of dubious cleanliness, and, if you're staying in the area, you might do better heading up to the student area of San Lorenzo, where you can often eat far better for the same money. South of the centre, the **Testaccio** neighbourhood is also well endowed with good, cheap trattorias, while, across the river, **Trastevere** is Rome's traditional restaurant ghetto, even though the number of authentic trattorias has decreased greatly over recent years.

Central

L'Antico Carbonaro, Vicolo di Monte Vecchio 27. Legendarily brusque service, but worth putting up with for an excellent fettucine with artichokes.

Baffetto, Via Governo Vecchio 114. A tiny, highly authentic pizzeria that has long been a Rome institution, though it now tends to be swamped by tourists. Amazingly it's still good value, and has tables outside in summer, though you'll always have to queue.

La Carbonara, Piazza di Campo de' Fiori 23. The most expensive of the square's restaurants, but always busy, with plenty of outdoor seating and an excellent selection of antipasti.

Da Mario, Piazza del Coppelle 51. Good, simple Roman restaurant, close to the Pantheon but undiscovered by most tourists, that does a reasonably priced set menu.

Edy, Vicolo del Babuino 4. A mellow candlelit trattoria in which the quality of the food merits the slow service. Unforgettable fettuccine with ricotta and artichokes, and excellent tiramisu.

Da Francesco, Via della Fossa 29. Amiable pizzeria-trattoria which keeps its kitchen open to just before midnight. Great choice of help-yourself antipasti, and memorable pizza with smoked salmon.

Grappolo d'Oro, Piazza della Cancelleria 80. Curiously untouched by the hordes in Campo dei Fiori. Genuine Roman cuisine and traditional trattoria feel. Was featured in a *New Yorker* article as the epitome of Rome.

Il Corallo, Via del Corallo 10. Modern, friendly restaurant which attracts a lively mixed crowd and serves a choice and quality of food – especially pizzas – that's way above average. Trendy and consequently not especially cheap, but recommended nonetheless.

Da Giggetto, Via del Portico d'Ottavia 21a. Roman-Jewish fare, like deep-fried artichokes, *baccalà*, and *rigatoni con pagliata*, along with good non-offal pasta dishes, eaten outside in summer by the ruins of the Portico D'Ottavia. Not cheap, but worth the splurge.

L'Insalata Ricca, Largo di Chiavari 85. Anglo-American presence in a relaxed and slightly out of the ordinary place. Interesting salads, as name suggests, some wholefood options and reasonably priced Italian fare. There's a less crowded second branch, *L'Insalata II*, on Piazza Pasquino.

Al Leoncino, Via del Leoncino 28. Cheap, hectic and genuine pizzeria, little known to out-of-towners.

La Montecarlo, Vicolo Savelli 12. Hectic pizzeria owned by the daughter of Baffetto, and serving similar crispy, blistered pizza. Tables outside in summer. Be prepared to queue.

Pallaro, Largo del Pallaro 15. Old-fashioned trattoria serving a set daily menu, including wine, for L25,000. A good option when you're starving.

Pierluigi, Piazza de' Ricci (off Via Monserrato). Good seafood antipasti and great pasta dishes, eaten in fine weather on a little lamplit piazza. Attracts a pretty well-heeled crowd, along with a fair number of tourists, but not too expensive if you skip the *secondo*. No menu, and the day's offerings are reeled off at top speed.

Romanesca, Piazza di Campo de'Fiori 40. On the Campo, so inevitably it attracts some tourists, but it's used by market traders too and retains a thoroughly Roman atmosphere.

Sora Margherita, Piazza delle Cinque Scuole 30. Open weekday lunchtimes only, a tiny trattoria in the heart of the Jewish quarter. Good, cheap, home-made pasta and gnocchi, and desserts from the nearby bakery. No sign outside – look for the doorway with plastic streamers.

Trattoria, Via del Governo Vecchio 18. Utterly plain, quiet, cheap and straightforward – a rare survivor of Rome as it was. Completely untouched by tourists or the city's gilded youth.

Trattoria da Luigi, Piazza Sforza Cesarini 23. Pleasant no-nonsense restaurant off Corso V. Emanuele that has tables outside on a shady piazza. Nice antipasto table.

Trattoria Polese, Piazza Sforza Cesarini 39. Plainer and smaller than *Da Luigi* across the square, but equally good value and also with tables outside.

Termini, San Lorenzo

La Diligenza Rossa, Via Merulana 271. Low-priced, convivial eatery just beyond Santa Maria Maggiore that's normally full of locals.

Formula 1, Via degli Equi 13. Justifiably popular San Lorenzo pizzeria, with tables outside in summer. Delicious pizza *all'Ortalana* (with courgettes, aubergines and peppers) and good courgette flower fritters.

Hosteria Angelo, Via Principe Amedeo 104. Quiet trattoria with a neighbourly atmosphere that is rare around here. Below-average prices and an above-average menu. Probably best choice this side of the tracks.

Hosteria L'Archetto, Via F. Turati 106. Clean, small and straightforward, with big choice (including pizzas) and a touch cheaper than its neighbours.

Hosteria da Bruno, Via Varese 29. Shade more pricey than others in the area, but quieter and – tellingly – with no English menu. One to think about if you're staying nearby. Closed Sun.

Pizza Economica, Via Tiburtina 44. This well-named restaurant is a legend among the cheaper Rome eateries.

Le Maschere, Via degli Umbri 8–14. Another studenty San Lorenzo pizzeria, again with outside tables in summer. The house speciality is pizza *La Maschera*, topped with hot peppers, garlic and anchovies.

Pizzeria-Steak House, Via Montebello 77. Despite the odd and rather ominous name, a good-value restaurant with clean white interior with fresh flowers on the tables, a clear menu, with choice of four "tourist meals" which for once are worth thinking about and good service – all something of a rarity hereabouts.

Tram Tram, Via dei Reti 44–46. Trendy, animated and unpretentious San Lorenzo restaurant, serving some fine pasta dishes, notably seafood lasagne, and unusual salads. There's also a bar if you want to carry on drinking after dinner.

Trastevere

Osteria dell'Aquila, Via Natale del Grande 52. Amiable Abbruzese-Roman restaurant which has been run for the past thirty years by three sisters. Home-made gnocchi and fettuccine, and pizza in the evenings.

Trattoria da Augusto, Piazza de Renzi 15. Relaxed and genuine restaurant in a quiet piazza off the tourist beat. Recommended.

Ivo, Via di San Francesco a Ripa 157. *The* Trastevere pizzeria. Arrive early to avoid a chaotic queue. Recommended, but in danger of becoming a caricature. Open 6–11pm. Closed Mon.

La Fraschetta, Via di San Francesco di Ripa 134. The calmer alternative to *Ivo*, less well known, with good pizzas and above-average desserts. Closed Mon.

Popi-Popi, Via delle Fratte di Trastevere. Good place to eat in summer, when there's a good quantity of tables outside. Not expensive either.

Trattoria G. Ficini, Via Natale del Grande 10. Slightly plastic but serving good, cheap pizzas cooked in a big wood-fired oven. Another alternative to *Ivo* round the corner.

Trattoria Il Generale, Via del Moro 1a. Opposite *Mario's*, and often empty as a result, but food is good and cheap. Atmosphere Roman and relaxed. Cheap Castelli wine.

Vatican and around

L'Abbruzzese, Via dei Gracchi 27. Friendly, family-run restaurant serving Abbruzzese dishes like *maccheroni alla chitarra* and *ravioli* stuffed with ricotta and spinach in a tomato and basil sauce. Set menu for L20,000.

Osteria dell'Angelo, Via G Bettolo 24. Above-average traditional Roman food, in a highly popular restaurant run by an ex-rugby player. It's safer to book (☎389.218).

Testaccio

Il Cantinone, Piazza Testaccio. Typical Testaccio neighbourhood restaurant – raucous and cheap, and serving excellent food. Bus #27 or tram #30.

Gennargentu, Via Ostiense 21–3. Excellent Sardinian pizzeria, and a handy place to eat before heading to the clubs of Monte Testaccio.

Piccolo Alpino, Via Orazio Antinori 5. Chaotic family-run trattoria justly famous for its fettucine with peas, mushrooms and cream, and other pasta dishes, but also serving good pizza.

Lo Scoppetaro, Lungotevere Testaccio 7. Traditional Testaccio trattoria, specialising in offal dishes, and frequented by enough outsiders for you not to feel too intrusive.

Non-Italian restaurants

Centro Macrobiotico Italiano, Via delle Vite 14. Predictable vegetarian with a L5000 membership charge. Cheap after that, with a relaxed but somewhat soulless air; and it's open lunchtimes only, noon–3pm.

Dionyssos, Via della Pelliccia 4. Rome's only Greek restaurant, and pretty good apart from the *meze*.

Dragon Garden, Via del Boschetto 41. Run by an Italo/Chinese couple, and probably the best-value Chinese in the city. Slow service but worth waiting for.

Hosteria Africa, Via Gaeta 28. Arguably the city's most interesting food, and the first culinary sign of Rome's new Ethiopian and Somalian population.

Lotus, Via Vespasiano 25. Out of the way, extra-cheap Sri Lankan restaurant.

Mar Rosso, Via Conte Verde 62. Cheap restaurant where you can eat Ethiopian style, sitting at a low table and scooping the spicy food with pieces of hot African bread, or at conventional tables with a knife and fork.

Margutta, Via Margutta 119. Upmarket, super-tasteful vegetarian that serves generous helpings albeit at rather high prices, although we have had reports of poor service.

Sorya Mahal, Piazza Trilussa. Reckoned to be the best Indian restaurant in Rome. Reasonably priced set vegetarian and meat- and fish-based menus, eaten in a garden in summer. Open evenings only.

Nightlife

Roman **nightlife** still retains some of the smart ethos satirised in Fellini's *Dolce Vita*, and designer-dressing up is still very much a part of the mainstream scene. Entrance prices to the big **clubs**, however, tend to be high, although seasoned clubbers can usually charm their way past the bouncers; and, if Roman friends ask you join them in a night's clubbing, they'll more than likely be able to get you in for free. There are also a few smaller, more alternative nightspots, where your travel-crumpled clothes will be perfectly acceptable; and, although these can still be pretty expensive, with a flier (see "Bars", *La Vetrina*, p.620) you can often get a discount on the entrance charge.

In summer, very little happens in Rome itself, with most clubs either closing down or moving to alternative premises on the beaches of Ostia and Fregene. However, **live music** continues, and summer is a particularly good time to catch major **jazz** artists, who often stop off in Rome on their way to or from the Umbria Jazz Festival. The chances of catching major **rock and pop** gigs are slimmer, with most UK and US bands preferring to play the trendier cities up north, although there's usually at least one prestige gig per month, and you should keep an eye out for up-and-coming US and UK indie bands playing some of the city's more alternative venues. As for more cultural pursuits, Rome's *Estate Romana* festival means that there's a good range of **classical music, opera, theatre** and **cinema** running throughout the summer, although obviously much of plays and films are inevitably of little interest if you don't speak Italian.

Information and tickets

For **what's on information** the city's best source of listings is *Trovaroma*, a free supplement published with the Thursday edition of *La Repubblica*. It's in Italian, but it's easy to make sense of what's happening. The daily arts pages of the main Rome newspapers – *La Repubblica* and *Il Messagero* – can also be useful references, and there are rather scanty English-language listings in free magazines like *Wanted in Rome* and *Metropolitan*, as well as the free tourist office booklet, *Carnet di Roma*.

The first stop for **tickets** should be *Orbis* at Piazza Esquilino 37 (☎474.4776), although you'll also find box offices at the following shops: *Babilonia*, Via del Corso 85 (☎678.6641); *Rinascita*, Via delle Botteghe Oscure 1 (☎679.7460); *Ricordi*, Viale Giulio Cesare 88 (☎372.0215); *Disfunzioni Musicali*, Via degli Etruschi 4 (☎446.1984). Phone and credit card bookings have still not caught on in Rome, and you usually need to go in person, although it's obviously wise to phone first to check the tickets you want are available. ("C'e l'ha biglietti per...").

Discos and clubs

Rome's **discos and clubs** cover the range. There are vast glitter palaces with stunning lights and sound systems, predictable dance music and an over-dressed, over-made-up clientele – good if you can afford it and just want to dance (and observe a good proportion of Romans in their natural Saturday night element). But there are also places that are not much more than upmarket bars with music, and other, more down-to-earth places to dance, playing a more interesting selection of music to a younger, more cautious-spending crowd. There is, too, a small group of clubs which cater specifically for gay or lesbian customers. Whichever you prefer, all tend to open and close late, and some charge a heavy entrance fee, the more spectacular places as much as L50,000.

Clubs

Alien, Via Velletri 13 (☎841.2212). Currently the hippest disco in Rome. Art shows, performance art and exhibitions as well as lots and lots of house music.

L'Argonauta, Lungotevere degli Artigiani s/n (☎556.5440). Vaguely alternative club on a boat, moored just below the Ponte Testaccio. A wide range of music, an infectious atmosphere, and what is probably the sweatiest dance floor in town. You can, however, cool down at the tables on the top deck. Expect to queue to get in.

Batello Ubriaco, Via dei Leutari 34. Youthful bar with music that changes nightly; the name means "drunken boat" – hence the kitsch boat-fronted bar and underwater effects (seaweed, starfish and ultraviolet lighting) which grace the small dance floor. Again, it's a place to go before hitting the main clubs, and a source of discounts on entrance. Open 10.30pm–2am.

Black Out, Via Saturnia 18 (☎759.6791). The only club in Rome to devote a night to US and UK indie bands (currently on Fridays) and consequently popular with American and British students.

Frankie Go, Via Schiapperelli 29 (☎322.1252). Some of the most narcissistic DJs you'll ever have the misfortune to encounter, with a clientele to match. House and garage, interspersed with the occasional theme night.

Gilda, Via Mario de'Fiori 97 (☎678.4838). A slick and stylish club, the focus for the city's minor (and would-be) celebs.

Piper 90, Via Tagliamento 9 (☎855.5398). Established in the Seventies by singer Patty Pravo, the Piper has survived by undergoing a reincarnation every season. Different nightly events (fashion shows, screenings, parties, gigs and the like) and a smart-but-casual mixed-aged crowd. Heavy pick-up scene.

Soul II Soul, Via dei Fienaroli 30B (☎581.3249). Small, intimate Trastevere club, and one of the few to attract an equal black/white crowd. Some brilliant DJs on the pay roll, playing a skilfully mixed assortment of soul, dance, ragamuffin and African music.

Lesbian and gay clubs

Angelo Azzurro, Via Cardinale Merry del Val (☎580.0472). Relaxed gay club with music, small rooms and discreet lighting. Patronised by a fairly mixed crowd.

L'Alibi, Via Monte Testaccio 44 (☎574.3448). Predominantly but not exclusively male venue that's one of Rome's best gay clubs. Downstairs cellar disco and upstairs open-air bar.

Il Castello, Via di Porta Castello 44 (☎686.8328). Club which often hosts gay and, occasionally, lesbian nights. Details usually in *Trova Roma*.

Joli Coeur, Via Sirte 5 (☎839.3523). Gay club which currently hosts a lesbian night on Saturdays, but phone before you go to check it's still running.

Panico, Via del Panico 17 (entrance on Vicolo della Campanella). Lesbian evening from 5pm on Sundays, with food, drink, snooker and a disco. Relaxed atmosphere and a fair amount of cruising.

Live music

Rome's **rock scene** is a relatively limp affair, especially compared to the cities of the north, focusing mainly on imported product and the big venues. Summer sees local bands giving irregular free concerts in the piazzas, but the city is much more in its element with **jazz**, with lots of venues and a wide choice of styles performed by a healthy array of local talent. There's a massive **Latin music** scene, too, particularly Brazilian. As for other kinds of music, **opera** here has long been overshadowed by Milan but is improving, while **classical music** can be heard at a number of venues all over the city, most atmospherically in concert series organised in its churches.

Rock and pop

Alpheus, Via del Commercio 36 (☎574.7826). Recently opened venue off Via Ostiense with space for three simultaneous events – usually a disco, concert and exhibition or piece of theatre. Studenty crowd.

Circolo degli Artisti, Via Lamarmora 28 (☎446 4965). Venue housed in part of the old milk distribution centre, in an extremely unsavoury location just below Termini. Good range of gigs, and frequent discos. Membership L5000, after which entrance is free for discos, although you will be charged for concerts.

Club Picasso, Via di Monte Testaccio 63 (☎574.2975). Live music nightly – rock, blues and funk. Free on Fridays.

Forte Prenestino, Via Delpino 14. Squatted anarchist club way out in eastern suburbs. Rock, cinema and alternative events, most of them free. Look out for posters. Buses #14, #19, #516.

Caffè Latino, Via Monte Testaccio 96 (☎574.4020). Multi-event Testaccio club that has varied live music, along with cartoons, films, and cabaret. Best at weekends when it gets more crowded.

Melvyn's, Via Politeama 8 (☎581.3300). Roman bands of every musical shade play nightly at this popular Trastevere bar. Open until 4am. Closed Sun.

Palaeur. Immense sports arena out in EUR that's the automatic choice for visiting mega-stars. Appalling acoustics and usually packed. Metro line #B or bus #93 from Termini.

Tenda Pianeta, Viale de Coubertin. One of Rome's two permanent tent venues, hosting mainly semi-famous Italian groups, and the odd ethnic show or festival. Bus #95 from Piazza Venezia, or tram #19.

Tenda Strisce, Via Cristofo Colombo 393 (☎541.0196). The other tent, a middle-sized stage for non-mainstream bands, both foreign and Italian. Bus #93.

Uonna Club, Via Cassia 871. Well out of town, but one of the most adventurous rock venues, with a punk/Gothic slant. Foreign cult groups, and if not the best of the Roman bands, certainly the most original.

Jazz and Latin

Alexanderplatz, Via Ostia 9 (☎372.9398). Reliable club/restaurant with free entry except when there's star-billing. Closed Mon.

Big Mama, Vicolo San Francesco a Ripa 18 (☎581.2551). Trastevere-based jazz/blues club of long-standing hosting nightly acts. Membership L5000; admission L10–20,000. Closed July–Oct.

Blatumba, Piazza in Piscinula 20 (☎589.6421). Small, inviting club that stages authentic Latin American acts. Very busy Fri and weekends. Open 10pm until late. Closed Mon. Admission L10,000, including first drink.

El Charango, Via Sant'Onofrio 28 (☎687.9908). Currently best of the Latin clubs and heavily patronised by the city's South American population.

Folkstudio, Via Frangipane 42 (☎487.1063). Jazz, poetry, folk, singer-songwriters and occasionally avant-garde classical music.

Fonclea, Via Crescenzio 82a (☎689.6302). Long-running jazz/salsa outfit fitted out like a British pub that has live music most nights.

Music Inn, Largo dei Fiorentini 3 (☎654.4934). Legendary Rome club – the city's oldest – in the smoky den mould. Music still lives up to past reputation and prices are reasonable. Membership L5000; admission L10–20,000. Open Thurs–Sun. Closed July to Sept.

Saint Louis, Via del Cardello 13a (☎474.5076). Modern club known for serious, high-quality music. Admission free, but cover charge of L3000 on the first drink. Closed Tues and July–mid-Sept.

Yes! Brazil, Via San Francesco a Ripa 103 (☎581.7332). Brazilian-staffed bar with live Latin music nightly.

Classical and opera

Rome's own orchestras are not of international standard, and the city attracts far fewer prestigious orchestras and artists than you might expect of a capital. Year-round, the focus of the classical music scene is the **Accademia di Santa Cecilia**, which stages concerts by its own orchestra (Rome's best), and by visiting orchestras and artists. Orchestral concerts are held at the auditorium at Via della Conclilazione 4 (☎581.2551), just down the road from Saint Peter's. Chamber recitals are usually held at the Accademia's headquarters at Via dei Greci 18 (box office at nearby Via Vittoria 6; ☎678.0742).

Of the city's other orchestras, the **Accademia Filarmonica** usually performs at the Teatro Olimpico, Piazza Gentile da Fabriano 17 (☎323.4890), and the **RAI** orchestra and chorus at the Auditorium del Foro Italico, Piazza Lauro De Bosis (☎368.6625). In addition, there are a number of musical associations which organise concert seasons: **ARCUM** (☎721.6558), whose concerts are usually held at the Sala Baldina on Piazza Campitelli; the **Istituzione Universitaria dei Concerti** (☎361.0051), who perform at the Aula Magna of the Sapienza University, Piazzale Aldo Moro 2, and the Auditorio del San Leone Magno, Via Bolzano 38; and the **Gonfalone**, Oratorio del Gonfalone, Via del Gonfalone 32 (☎687.5952). Comprehensive details can be found weekly in *Trova Roma*, and monthly in the tourist office's free *Un Ospite a Roma* and *Carnet di Roma*. The city's **churches** also host a wide range of choral, chamber and organ recitals, all widely advertised and many of them free. In addition there are sponsored **Sunday morning concert cycles**, like the *Italcable* one at the *Teatro Sistina*, Via Sistina 129 (☎4770.4664), between November and April. Ideally you should pick tickets up during the week, but there are usually people unloading spare seats on the morning.

Rome's **opera** scene bases around the **Teatro dell'Opera** on the corner of Via Torino and Piazza Beniamino Gigli (☎488.1755), between November and May. Tickets, priced from L25,000, go on sale two days before the performance at 10am–1pm and 5–

7pm. In summer the season moves outdoors to the remains of the Roman baths at **Terme di Caracalla**, a beautiful and suitably spectacular location for what are usually productions on an epic and madly lavish scale – *Aida* is the repertoire's mainstay. Purists should be prepared for a carnival atmosphere and plenty of unscheduled intervals.

Film

Rome's only English-language cinema is the **Pasquino** in Trastevere, a homely affair on Vicolo del Piede (☎580.3632). It shows recent general releases, with a programme which changes every few days, and a popular late-night screening that goes out around 10.30pm. Tickets are currently L7000. The only alternative to this is films dubbed into Italian, many of which, if you can cope with the language, come out several months ahead of their British release. Ticket prices for first runs are about L10,000. You'll find major listings in all the newspapers, which also include a section on film clubs, where – very occasionally – English-language films go out as matinee; look for the words "in inglese". The best bets for these are the **Labirinto**, Pompeo Magno 27 (☎321.6283), and the excellent **Grauco Cineclub**, Via Perugia 34 (☎782.2311).

Listings

Airlines *Alitalia*, Via Bissolati 13 (☎65.643); *British Airways*, Via Bissolati 54 (☎479.991); *TWA*, Via Barberini 67 (☎47.211). Note that most other airlines are in one of these two streets, or very close by.

Airport enquiries Fiumicino ☎65.951; Ciampino ☎794.491. If time's tight or there's four of you, it's worth considering a limousine service to Fiumicino; a flat fare of L75,000 gets you a silver Mercedes. Information from the offices in Termini.

American Express Travel office and exchange facilities at Piazza di Spagna 38 (☎67.641). Open Mon–Fri 9am–5pm, Sat 9am–noon.

Baths Use the facilities at the *Albergo Diurno* in Stazione Termini.

Beaches Rome's nearest beach is at Lido di Ostia, half an hour away by train, and this is where the tourist board will try to point you. Don't listen to them, and make instead for either Anzio or Nettuno an hour to the south of the city by frequent (hourly) train from Termini, where you'll find clean, if fairly crowded beaches, and, at Anzio especially, excellent seafood. See below, "The southern Lazio coast" for more details.

Books The *Lion Bookshop*, Via del Babuino 181 (☎322.5837), is the city's biggest and best-stocked English-language bookstore, and has an English-speaking staff for enquiries. Try also the *Economy Book Center*, Via Torino 136 (☎474.6877), which has a good stock of new and used English-language paperbacks. Be warned, however, that both places are pricey, and that you may find the same thing cheaper at *Feltrinelli*, Via Orlando 83.

Bus enquiries *ATAC* (☎4695.4444); *ACOTRAL* (☎591.5551). Rebibbia (☎406.7849; Tivoli, Subiaco); Via Lepanto (☎386.196; Cerveteri, Civitavecchia, Bracciano area); EUR Fermi (☎592.0402; Nettuno, Anzio, southern Lazio coast); Anagnina (☎722.2153; Castelli Romani); Saxa Ruba (☎332.8333; Viterbo and around).

Camera repair *Vasari*, Piazza della Repubblica 61 (☎481.4505), is a centrally placed store that repairs most kinds of camera.

Car rental *Avis*, Piazza Esquilino 1 (☎470.1216); *Hertz*, Via Veneto 156 (☎321.6831); *Maggiore*, Via Po 8 (☎854.8698).

Car repair ☎116 for emergency breakdown service. Otherwise consult the telephone directory for specialised repair shops.

Dentist The *Ospedale di Odontoiatria G. Eastman*, Viale Regina Elena 287b (☎445.4851), has a 24-hour emergency service. If you're an EC citizen be sure to take your E111 form, which entitles you to buy a "ticket" for a consultation – currently L15,000.

Embassies *Australia*, Via Alessandria 215 (☎832.721); *Canada*, Via G.B. De Rossi 27 (☎841.5341); *New Zealand*, Via Zara 28 (☎440.2928); *Great Britain*, Via XX Settembre 80a (☎482.5441); *Ireland*, Via Largo Nazareno 3 (☎678.2541); *USA*, Via Veneto 119 (☎46.741).

Emergencies ☎113. The central police station is at Via San Vitale 15 (☎4686).

Exchange For exchanging currency and travellers' cheques out of banking hours, there are two offices at Termini station, one on the upper level, another down below (Mon–Sat 8.30am–7.30pm). You could also try *Thomas Cook* at Piazza Barberini 21d (Mon–Sat 8am–6pm), and Via della Conciliazione 23 (Mon–Sat 8am–6pm, Sun 9am–5pm), where you can also save on commission if you're exchanging *Thomas Cook* travellers cheques. Otherwise there's *Frama*, Corso Vittorio Emanuele II 106 (Mon–Fri 8.30am–1.30pm & 3–5pm, Sat 9am–1pm), or the *Cambio* at Via San Vincenzo 20, near the Trevi fountain (daily 9am–8pm)

Football Rome's two teams, *Roma* and *Lazio*, play at the Stadio Olimpico, on Via del Foro Italico (☎36.851), on alternate Sundays. The stadium is reachable by way of metro line #A to Ottaviano, then bus #32. Unsurprisingly, feelings run high between the two teams, and derby games are big – and sometimes violent – occasions. Until recently, *Roma* (supporters middle-class, establishment) were clearly the better side, but *Lazio* (supporters poorer, more working-class) have in recent years built a dynamic side of international stars, not least among which is Britain's Paul Gascoigne, and are challenging the long-established supremacy of *Roma*. For the record, the Lazio supporters traditionally occupy the Curva Nord end of the ground, the Roma fans the Curva Sud. *Enjoy Rome*, Via Varese 39 (☎445.1843), can get tickets for Roma games; for tickets to see Lazio, contact *Lazio Point*, Via Farina 24 (☎482.6688).

Hospital In case of emergency ☎462.371 or ☎113. Otherwise the most central hospital is the Policlinico Umberto I, Viale del Policlinico (☎492.341).

Laundry You can get washes done at Via Montebello 11; reckon on paying around L15,000.

Left luggage At Stazione Termini 7am–9pm; L1500 per item per day.

Libraries The British Council, Via della Quattro Fontane 20, has a lending library and mounts film-showings and other events in English (Mon–Fri 10am–1pm & 2–6pm, Sat 10am–1pm). The library is, however, closed during summer and you must produce proof of residence to join (and pay L40,000), although anyone can use it for reference. There's also a library at the English church of Santa Susanna, Via XX Settembre 14 (open Sun & Thurs mornings, Wed afternoons), with a good noticeboard for finding work, accommodation, etc.

Lost property For property lost on a train call ☎4730.6682, on a bus ☎581.6040.

Newspapers You can normally buy English newspapers the same day of publication from news-stands at Termini, Piazza Colonna or on Piazza Barberini.

Pharmacies The following pharmacies are open all night: *Internazionale*, Piazza Barberini 49 (☎482.5456); *Piram*, Via Nazionale 228 (☎488.0754); *Spinedi*, Via Arenula 73 (☎654.3278).

Post office The main post office is on Piazza San Silvestro (☎6771); post and telegraphic enquiries on ☎160. Opening times Mon–Fri 8.30am–9pm, Sat 8.30am–noon. Telegrams can be sent at any time, day or night, on ☎679.5530.

Radio *Radio Centro Suona* (101.3 FM), plays better music than most of the local radio stations.

Swimming pools There is an open-air public pool, *Piscina delle Rose*, Viale America 20, in EUR (metro line #B), naturally open during summer only. For a list of other public pools, contact the *Ufficio di Sport e Turismo* at Via Capitan Bavastro 94 (☎5790.2214).

Telephones You can make international calls and pay afterwards at Stazione Termini (7am–midnight) and the main post office, Piazza San Silvestro (8.30am–11.30pm). Expect long queues, especially in the evening and on Sundays.

Touring Club Italiano Head office at Via Ovidio 7 (☎687.4603).

Tours A number of companies run organised trips around the city centre, though these are, for the most part, over-priced. For general orientation and a glance at the main sights, you can either take tram #30, which passes most places of interest on its route, or join the daily *ATAC* bus tour, which (between April and September) leaves Termini at 2.30pm and costs L6000 per person – excellent value.

Train enquiries Stazione Termini (information booth open daily 7am–11.30pm; ☎4775); Stazione Tiburtina (☎423.972); Stazione Ostiense (☎575.8748); Stazione di San Pietro (☎631.391); Stazione Trastevere (☎4730.5628); Piazzale Flaminio/Roma-Nord line (☎361.0441).

Travel agents *CTS* are at Via Genova 16 (☎46.791) and Corso Vittorio Emanuele II 297 (☎687.2672), for discount tickets, though you may find better deals at *Viaggiare*, Via San Nicola da Tolentino 18 (☎474.6751), who also have some English-speaking staff.

Women's Rome The women's bookshop – *Al Tempo Ritrovato* – on Piazza Farnese is the best place to go for contacts and to find out what's happening from its noticeboard.

Out from the city: Tivoli and Ostia

You may find there's quite enough of interest in Rome to keep you occupied during your stay. But Rome can be a hot, oppressive city, its surfeit of churches and museums intensely wearying, and if you're around long enough you really shouldn't feel any guilt about freeing yourself from its weighty history to see something of the countryside around. Two of the main attractions visitable on a day trip are, it's true, Roman sites, but just the process of getting to them can be energising. **Tivoli**, about an hour by bus east of Rome, is a small provincial town famous for the Travertine quarries nearby and its fine ancient Roman villa and landscaped gardens and parks. **Ostia**, in the opposite direction from the city near the sea, and similarly easy to reach on public transport, is the city's main seaside resort (though one worth avoiding) and home of the port of Rome in classical times, the site of which is well preserved and worth seeing. Bear in mind, too, that a number of **other places in Lazio** – Lake Bracciano and the Etruscan sites north of Rome, the Castelli Romani, Palestrina and Subiaco, and parts of the southern coast – are close enough to the city to make a feasible day trip, especially if you have access to a car. See the relevant headings for details.

Tivoli

Just 40km from Rome, perched high on a hill and looking back over the plain, **TIVOLI** has always been something of a retreat from the city. In Classical days it was a retirement town for wealthy Romans; later, during Renaissance times, it again became the playground of the monied classes, attracting some of the city's most well-to-do families out here to build villas. Nowadays the leisured classes have mostly gone, but Tivoli does very nicely on the fruits of its still-thriving travertine business, exporting the precious stone worldwide (the quarries line the main road into town from Rome), and supports a small airy centre that preserves a number of relics from its ritzier days.

The Town

Most people head first for the **Villa d'Este** (summer daily 9am–1hr before sunset; L5000), across the main square of Largo Garibaldi – the country villa of Cardinal Ippolito d'Este that was transformed from a convent by Pirro Ligorio in 1550 and is now often thronged with visitors even outside peak season. It's the gardens rather than the villa itself – a parade of dim, scruffy rooms decorated with faded Mannerist murals – that they come to see, peeling away down the hill in a succession of terraces: probably the most contrived garden in Italy, but also the most ingenious, almost entirely symmetrical, its carefully tended lawns, shrubs and hedges interrupted at decent intervals by one playful fountain after another. In their day some of these were quite ingenious – one played the organ, another imitated the call of birds – though nowadays the emphasis is on the quieter creations. There's the central, almost Gaudi-like Fontana di Bicchierone by Bernini, one of the simplest and most elegant; on the far left, the Rometta or "Little Rome" has reproductions of the city's major buildings and a boat holding an obelisk; while perhaps the best is the Fontana del Ovato on the opposite side of the garden, fringed with statues, behind which is an arcade, rather dank, in which you can walk.

The Villa d'Este is an expensive way to spend an hour, and if you're short of time or money, you may prefer to visit the **Villa Gregoriana** (daily 9am–1hr before sunset; L2500), a park with waterfalls created when Pope Gregory XVI diverted the flow of the river here to ease the periodic flooding of the town in 1831. It's less well known and less touristed than the d'Este estate, with none of the latter's conceits, its vegetation lush and overgrown, descending into a gashed-out gorge over 60m deep. There are two main waterfalls – the larger *Grande Cascata* on the far side, and a small Bernini-designed one at the neck of the gorge. The path winds down to the bottom of the canyon and the water, scaling the drop on the other side past two grottoes, where you can get right up close to the pounding water, the dark, torn shapes of the rock glowering overhead. It's harder work than the Villa d'Este – don't go lightly down to the bottom of the gorge, it's a long way back up the other side – but in many ways more rewarding; the path leads up on the far side to an exit and the substantial remains of a **Temple of Vesta**, which you'll have seen clinging to the side of the hill. This is now incorporated into the gardens of a restaurant, but it's alright to walk through and take a look, and the view is probably Tivoli's best – down into the chasm and across to the high green hills that ring the town.

The Villa Adriana

Once you've seen these two sights you've really seen Tivoli – the rest of the town is nice enough but there's not that much to it. But just outside at the bottom of the hill, fifteen minutes' walk off the main Rome road (ask the Rome–Tivoli bus to drop you or take the local *CAT* #4 from Largo Garibaldi), the **Villa Adriana** (daily 9am–1hr before sunset; L8000) casts the invention of the Tivoli popes and cardinals very much into the shade. This was probably the largest and most sumptuous villa in the Roman empire, the retirement home of the Emperor Hadrian for a short while between 135 AD and his death three years later, and it occupies an enormous site. You need time to see it all; there's no point in doing it at a gallop, and with the rest of Tivoli it makes for a long day's sightseeing – set out *early*.

The site is one of the most soothing spots around Rome, its stones almost the epitome of romantic, civilised ruins. The imperial palace buildings proper are in fact one of the least well-preserved parts of the complex, but much else is clearly recognisable. Hadrian was a great traveller, and a keen architect, and parts of the villa were inspired by buildings he had seen around the world. The massive *Pecile*, for instance, through which you enter, is a reproduction of a building in Athens. And the *Canopus*, on the opposite side of the site, is a liberal copy of the sanctuary of Serapis near Alexandria, its long, elegant channel of water fringed by sporadic columns and statues leading up to a *Temple of Serapis* at the far end. Nearby, a museum displays the latest finds from the usually ongoing excavations, though most of the extensive original discoveries have found their way back to Rome. Walking back towards the entrance, make your way across the upper storey of the so-called *Pretorio*, a former warehouse, and down to the remains of two bath complexes. Beyond is a fishpond with a *cryptoporticus* winding around underneath and behind that the relics of the emperor's imperial apartments. The *Teatro Marittimo*, adjacent, with its island in the middle of a circular pond, was the place to which it's believed Hadrian would retire at siesta time to be sure of being alone.

Practicalities

Buses leave Rome for Tivoli every half an hour from Rebibbia station – journey time 45 minutes. In Tivoli, the **bus station** is outside the Villa Gregoriana, though you can get off earlier, on the main square of Largo Garibaldi, where you'll find the **tourist office** (Mon–Sat 8am–6pm; ☎0774/21.249) that has free maps and information on **accommodation** if you're planning to stay over.

Ostia

There are two Ostias: one an over-visited seaside resort, the so-called Lido di Ostia, which is well worth avoiding; the other, one of the finest ancient Roman sites – the excavations of the port of Ostia Antica – which are on a par with anything you'll see in Rome itself and easily merit a half-day journey out.

Lido di Ostia

The **LIDO DI OSTIA**, reachable by overground train from Magliana metro station on line #B, has for many years been the number-one seaside resort for Romans and has suffered accordingly. The beaches here are notorious: dangerously filthy and bordering some equally murky water, and mostly sectioned off as private stretches stacked with over-priced bars that you have to pay to enter.

As for the town, it's on the whole a poor outpost of the city with little, if anything, to recommend it. All in all, even if you're desperate for a swim you'd really be better off travelling further afield to, say, ANZIO or NETTUNO – both of which are only an extra half an hour by train away from the city.

Ostia Antica

The stop before Lido di Ostia on the train from Rome, the site of **OSTIA ANTICA** marked the coastline in Classical times, and the town which grew up here was the port of ancient Rome, a thriving place whose commercial activities were vital to the city further upstream. The excavations (daily 9am–1hr before sunset; L8000) remain relatively unvisited; indeed until the 1970s the site was only open one day a week and few people knew – or even cared – that the port had been quite well preserved by the Tiber's mud. But it's an evocative site, still free of the bustle of tourists, from which it's much easier to reconstruct a Roman town than any amount of pottering around the Forum.

It's also very spread out, so be prepared for a fair amount of walking. From the entrance, the **Decumanus Maximus**, the main street of Ostia, leads west, past the **Baths of Neptune** on the right (where there's an interesting mosaic) to the town's commercial centre, otherwise known as the **Piazzale di Corporazione** for the remains of shops and trading offices that still fringe the central square. These represented commercial enterprises from all over the ancient world, and the mosaics just in front denote their trade – grain merchants, ship fitters, ropemakers and the like.

Flanking one side of the square, the **theatre** has been much restored but is nonetheless impressive, enlarged by Septimus Severus in the second century AD to hold up to 4000 people. On the left of the square, the **House of Apulius** preserves mosaic floors and, beyond, a dark-aisled *mithraeum* with more mosaics illustrating the cult. Behind here – past the substantial remains of the *horrea* or warehouses that once stood all over the city – the **Casa di Diana** is probably the best-preserved private house in Ostia, with a dark, mysterious set of rooms around a central courtyard, and again with a *mithraeum* at the back. You can climb up to its roof for a fine view of the rest of the site, afterwards crossing the road to the **Thermopolium** – an ancient Roman café, complete with seats outside, a high counter, display shelves and even wall paintings of parts of the menu.

North of the Casa di Diana, the **Museum** (daily 9am–1pm) holds a variety of articles from the site, including wall paintings depicting domestic life in Ostia and some fine sarcophagi and statuary. Left from here, the **Forum** centres on the **Capitol** building, reached by a wide flight of steps, and is fringed by the remains of baths and a basilica. Continuing on down the main street, more **Horrea** superbly preserved and complete with pediment and names inscribed on the marble merit a detour off to the right; although you can't enter, you can look into the courtyard. Beyond, the **House of Cupid and Psyche** has a courtyard you can walk into, its rooms clearly discernible on one side, a colourful marbled floor on the other.

NORTHERN LAZIO

Northern Lazio is a quite different entity from the region south of the capital. Green and wooded in its central areas, its steadily more undulating hills hint at the landscapes of Tuscany and Umbria further north. There are few large centres, though, and interest is sparse: with determination (and, in some cases, a car), you can see much of it on day trips from Rome. Foremost among the area's attractions is the legacy of the **Etruscans**, some of whose most important sites, scattered along the southern stretch of coast, are readily accessible by road or rail – necropoli mainly, but the only remains of a civilisation which ruled the area for close on a thousand years. The **coast** itself is of very little appeal until you get close to the Tuscan border, and if you want to swim you'd be better off doing so inland, around lakes **Bracciano**, **Vico** or **Bolsena** – happy hunting-grounds for hot and bothered Romans on summer weekends. Between these, **Viterbo** is the main centre, a dour provincial town that can make a good base for visiting both the lakes and the region's **Mannerist villas and gardens**, though all over this central area bear in mind that touring without your own transport can be a full-time job. Over to the east, **Rieti** is the big centre, a rather bland and deservedly unvisited town on the way to Abruzzo. Beyond it lie the **lakes and mountains** of Terminillo and Amatrice, scenically spectacular, but again virtually out of reach unless you have your own transport.

Etruria and the coast

D. H. Lawrence had pretty much the last word on the plain and low hills stretching north from Rome towards the Tuscan border: "A peculiarly forlorn coast," he lamented, "the sea peculiarly flat and sunken, lifeless looking, the land as if it had given up its last gasp and was now forever inert." His *Etruscan Places*, published in 1932, is one of the best introductions to both the Etruscans and their cities, which, one or two beaches excepted, are the only good reasons for venturing out here.

Fregene and Ladispoli

For a so-called resort, **FREGENE** is one of the grimmest places imaginable. First main stop on the train out of Rome, its 4km of **beaches** – twenty years ago Lazio's trendiest – are plagued by mosquitos, blighted by the usual commercial tat, and only very slightly redeemed by huge stands of umbrella pines. Romans pile out here mainly for the fish restaurants. The sand's marginally cleaner and less crowded than at Ostia, but the gravy-coloured water fails every health and safety test going. Sunbathing slumbers are also disturbed by jets flying out of Fiumincino down the coast, and for decent, almost deserted beaches, you'd do better to stay on the train.

Neighbouring **LADISPOLI** is even worse, summed up by Lawrence in a thumbnail sketch that's still spot-on sixty years later: "Ladispoli is one of those ugly little places on the Roman coast," he wrote, "consisting of new concrete villas, new concrete hotels, kiosks and bathing establishments; bareness and non-existence for ten months in the year, seething solid with fleshy bathers in July and August . . . desecration put upon desolation."

Cerveteri

The station at Ladispoli also serves **CERVETERI**, which provides the most convenient first taste of the Etruscans if you're commuting from Rome. Buses also run to the town from Via Lepanto. Once at the station be warned that it's a seven-kilometre hike to the centre, and buses timetabled to shuttle passengers into town don't always materialise.

There's been a settlement here since the tenth century BC, when it was already known to the Greeks as an important trading centre. Cerveteri, the Roman *Caere*, was among the top three cities in the twelve-strong Etruscan federation, its wealth derived largely from the mineral riches of the **Tolfa hills** to the northeast – a gentle range which give the plain a much-needed touch of scenic colour. In its heyday the town spread over 8km (something like thirty times its present size), controlling territory that stretched for 50km up the coast. The rot set in from 351 BC, when it became a dependency of Rome, having failed, like most of Etruria, to maintain a neutrality with the new power.

The present town is a thirteenth-century creation, dismissed by Lawrence – and you can't blame him – as "forlorn beyond words". On arrival, make straight for the Etruscan **necropoli**, just a kilometre away and signposted from the central piazza (May–Sept Tues–Sun 9am–7pm; Oct–April Tues–Sat 9am–4pm, Sun 11am–4pm; L6000; maps L1000). The Etruscans constructed a literal **city of the dead** here, weird and fantastically well preserved, with complete streets and houses, some formed as strange round pillboxes carved from the living rock – almost Egyptian in feel – others still covered in earth to create the tumuli effect that ripples over the surrounding plateau. The general span of the graves is seventh to first century BC: as far as anyone can make out, women were buried in separate small chambers within the "house" – easy to distinguish – while the men were laid on death beds (occasionally in sarcophagi) hewn directly from the stone. Slaves were cremated and their ashes placed in urns alongside their masters – civilised by comparison with the Romans, who simply threw their slaves into mass burial pits. The twelve or so show-tombs – lying between the two roads that bisect the city – are grouped together beyond the entrance; they close in random rotation, so it's difficult to know in advance which ones are going to be open. If possible don't miss the **Tomba Bella** (Tomb of the Bas-Reliefs); **Tomba dei Letti Funebri** (Tomb of the Funeral Beds) and the **Tomba dei Capitalli**.

If the tombs whet your appetite (and you could spend an hour or so wandering about), you might head back to town and take in the **Museo Nazionale di Cervéteri**, at the top of the old quarter in the sixteenth-century **Castello Orsini** (Tues–Sun 9am–1pm & 4–7pm; L6000). Two large rooms contain a fraction of the huge wealth that was buried with the dead – vases, sarcophagi, terracottas and a dull run of miscellaneous day-to-day objects; most of the best stuff has been whisked away to Rome.

Civitavecchia

The only reason to break a journey in **CIVITAVECCHIA**, 30km north, is to change trains, or to pick up a ferry to Sardinia. It's an ugly and forgettable port that is otherwise best avoided, with little to see beyond a small **Museo Archeologico** right in the centre of town on the corner of Largo Plebiscito, just off Viale Garibaldi (Tues, Thurs, Sat 9am–1pm).

The **ferry docks** are in the centre of the town at the end of Viale Garibaldi, ten minutes' walk from the train station at the other end. There's a **tourist office** between the two at Viale Garibaldi 40 (Mon–Fri 8.30am–1.30pm & 4.30–7.30pm, Sat 8.30am–1pm; ☎0766/25.348). If you are heading to Sardinia by ferry, try to do so on a night crossing, since by doing that you save yourself the dubious pleasure of spending a night in the town. Should you get stuck, however, there are two functional **hotels**, the *Miramare*, immediately right of the station at Viale della Repubblica 6 (☎0766/26.167; ④), and, on the other side of the small town centre, the not nearly so well situated *Traghetto* on Via Braccianese Claudia (☎0766/29520; ⑤). As for **eating**, there are lots of cheap trattorias and pizzerias along the seafront Viale Garibaldi, and there's not much to choose between them – the *Santa Lucia*, Viale Garibaldi 34, close by the tourist office, does decent pizzas. Just back from the water, off Largo Plebiscito on Via Zara, *Trattoria Sora Maria* is a nice place that's good for fish.

Going to Sardinia, there are daily crossings to Golfo Aranci (8hr), and one each to Olbia (8hr), Cagliari (14hr) and Arbatax (9hr). The cheapest rides tend to be with *FS*, who run ferries to Golfo Aranci that in theory coincide with the main train connections from Rome and Genova. *Tirrenia* operate bigger and pricier boats to Olbia, Cagliari and Arbatax. In the summer when half of Italy wants to get to the island, you should make bookings several months in advance, whoever you're travelling with, even if you're on foot. The tourist office sells tickets for both lines, but you can book ahead from many travel agents both in the town and in other parts of Italy.

Tarquinia

TARQUINIA is the most touted of the Etruscan necropoli, and as such it can't help but come as a disappointment. The town itself, though partly walled, with an evocative crop of medieval towers, is a fairly unappealing place. However, the museum, though a little overrated, is much better for a recent refurbishment; and the site, though rather spread out, can be quite evocative as long as there aren't too many fellow visitors around.

The Town

There's not much in Tarquinia that merits any degree of attention. Apart from its old fortified district, which commanded the town approaches for several centuries and holds within its walls a twelfth-century Romanesque church, **Santa Maria di Castello** – notable for its rib vaulting, the first known example in Italy – it's the **Museo Nazionale Tarquiniense**, right on the main town square of Piazza Cavour, just inside the city walls (Tues–Sat 9am–2pm, Sun 9am–1pm; L8000, ticket gives admission to site too), that draws the crowds. It's not a large museum, and is all the better for that and for the fact that it is sensitively housed in an attractive Gothic-Renaissance palazzo. The ground-floor rooms contain some superb sculpted sarcophagi, many decorated with warm and human portraits of the deceased, while upstairs there are some lovely Etruscan gold jewellery, painted ceramics, bronzes, candlesticks, figures and heads, including the renowned winged terracotta horses (fourth century BC), probably from a temple frieze – a striking example of the Etruscans' skill in decorative carving. As well as fine views over the countryside around down to the sea, the top floor is home to the gift shop, and, probably the most impressive part of the museum, some of the best of the wall paintings from the nearby necropolis – relocated here due to their on-site deterioration, and kept under wraps much of the time even in the museum (you may have to ask to see them). Though in general in a pretty sorry state, a couple are very bright and realistic: one shows the lithe forms of dancers and musicians; another depicts athletes running and jumping, and a chariot race.

The Site

It's the **necropolis** itself (Tues–Sun 9am–2pm; L8000, free with museum ticket), though, which really makes the journey worthwhile, a warren of graves spread across a plateau on the southeast edge of the town – all that's left of a city that was once the artistic, cultural and probably political capital of Etruria. Founded in the tenth century BC, its population has been estimated at 100,000, declining gradually from the fourth century BC with the growing influence of Rome. Etruscan cities were built almost entirely of wood, so most vanished quickly – and those that didn't were redeveloped by the Romans, making this one of the few extant remnants of a culture that was around for something like 1000 years.

Excavations started in 1489, the first recorded in modern times, since when 6000 tombs have been uncovered (900 in 1958 alone), with many more apparently still to be unearthed. Grave-robbing is common (thieves are known as *i tombaroli*), and there are patrols. Also, the recent increase in the number of visitors means that only limited numbers are open at any time. As for getting there, there are about four buses a day, or it's a fifteen-minute walk: take Via Umberto I from Piazza Cavour, pass through the Porta Romana, skip the roundabout (Piazza Europa) and follow Via IV Novembre/Via delle Croci up the hill and the site is on the left.

Etruscan burial places were often straight copies of houses (here less literally so than at Cerveteri) and filled with the clutter of daily life to provide the dead with all they would need in the afterlife. But the Tarquinia tombs have something else besides – **wall paintings**, the oldest of which date from about the seventh century or eighth century BC. There's been much speculation on the purpose and style of these. The earliest paintings emphasise mythical and ritualistic scenes, but later works from the fourth century to sixth century – in the Orco, Auguri, Della Caccia and Della Pescia tombs – show greater social realism, giving an insight into the habits, customs and scenes from the life of the deceased. The style of these later works is a mixture of Greek, indigenous Etruscan and even Eastern influences, their ease and fluidity pointing to a civilisation that was at the pinnacle of its development. The Greek aspects are particularly important, representing the only allusions to Hellenistic monumental painting, a form which otherwise has vanished largely without trace. From the fourth century BC decadence sets in, with the appearance of increasingly morbid and purely necromantic drawings.

Practicalities . . . and Tarquinia Lido

Tarquinia's train station is 2km below the town centre, connected with the central Barriera San Giusto, hard up against the city walls, by regular local bus; buses from Viterbo and Rome also drop you in Barriera San Giusto. The **tourist office** is just through the city gate on Piazza Cavour (Mon–Sat 8.30am–12.30pm & 4–6pm; ☎0766/856.384) and doles out maps of the town and other information.

There are few places to **eat** and even fewer places to **stay** in town; indeed if you want to stay you're really better off in Tarquinia Lido (see below), where there's more choice. As for **eating**, there's a cosy trattoria-pizzeria, *Campanari*, at Piazza Cavour 11, and *Il Bucchero*, around the corner at Via XX Settembre 27, does decent pasta dishes and pizzas – and is the closest Tarquinia comes to any sort of nightlife. Failing that, there's the more upscale *Arcadia* at Via Mazzini 6 (avoid the grubby *Cucina Casarecchia* over the road). Perhaps the most atmospheric place to drink is *Osterina il Grottina*, a rather dingy cavelike bar at Alberata Dante Aligheri 8 that serves wine siphoned out of barrels piled in the corner.

Tarquinia Lido, reachable by hourly bus from Barriera San Giusto via the *FS* station, is home to most of Tarquinia's real action. The *Albergo Miramare*, Viale dei Tirreni 36 (☎0766/88.020; ④), has reasonably priced double rooms, and there are three huge **campsites** here – and at Riva di Tarquinia to the north – hosting great herds of holiday-makers. The beaches are inevitably heavily developed, with restaurants, discos, sports facilities, "pubs", even cinemas, but might be just what you're looking for after dismal Tarquinia proper. The best bet, though, is to round off a day-trip with a quick dip and head back to the station.

North to the Tuscan border

Continuing north offers more peaceful opportunities for camping, though you'll probably want to skip **MONTALTO DI CASTRO**, a quiet but unexciting hilltop village famous throughout Italy for its huge, half-built nuclear power station. The plant became a *cause célèbre* for the country's emergent Green Party, and was at the heart of the 1987 referendum which voted against the country's nuclear power programme. After much government double-dealing it's now – at vast cost – going to be converted to either oil or natural gas. If you really want to sleep in the eerie shadow of nuclear reactors, there are seafront **campsites** at Montalto Marina and Pescia Romana.

VULCI, some 11km inland, is another **Etruscan site**, but despite the presence of an estimated 15,000 tombs, has next to nothing to see. Many of the tumuli have been ransacked and left to decay, though there's ample scope for scrambling around what's left. North of the remains is the **Ponte d'Abbadia**, a single-arched Roman-Etruscan bridge over a pretty ravine and next to a ninth-century abbey that houses a small collection of finds from the local necropoli.

The best and quietest of the **beaches** on this coast are at **CHIARONE**, singled out in a report as enjoying the first unpolluted water north of Rome. Fifteen kilometres of unbroken sand stretch emptily towards the Argentario peninsula, with a **lagoon** midway down at Burano, and plenty of opportunities for camping in the dunes. Things get grubby on shore as the summer wears on, but the gentle shelving seabed makes for good swimming, and all it takes for complete solitude on the sand is a few minutes' walk. A handful of Grosseto-bound trains stop nearby (90min from Rome), where you'll find a shop and a couple of bars. The beach lies fifteen minutes' walk from the station, with an obvious **bar and campsite** at the end of the road.

With a car from Chiarone it's possible to visit one of Italy's oddest and increasingly well-known works of modern art, **Il Giardino dei Tarocchi** or the Tarot Garden – a huge set of monumental sculptures by Niki de Saint Phalle, most famous for the "Fontaine Stravinsky" (with Jean Tinguely) in Paris. Ten years in the making, it's a whimsical mixture of Gaudi and sheer fun, is loved by children and admired by grown-ups, and is definitely worth the detour. The brightly coloured, mirror-covered pieces are clearly visible inland from the Via Aurelia: to reach them it's a 5km drive on the road from Chiarone to Pescia Fiorentina. As it is still only a cult attraction, opening times are restricted to summer weekends.

Lago di Bracciano and around

The closest of northern Lazio's lakes to Rome, **Lago di Bracciano** fills an enormous volcanic crater, a smooth, roughly circular expanse of water that's popular – but not too popular – with Romans keen to escape the summer heat of the city. It's nothing spectacular, with few real sights and a landscape that verges on the dull, but its shores are fairly peaceful even on summer Sundays, and you can eat excellent lake fish in its restaurants. You can also combine a visit with a side trip to the Etruscan site of Veio on the way – though you'd need a a car and a full day to do justice to both.

The lake's main settlement is the town of **BRACCIANO** on the western shore, about half an hour by train from Rome San Pietro (direction Viterbo). It's a small town, dominated by the imposing **Castello Orsini-Odelscalchi** (guided tours summer Tues–Sun 10am–noon & 3–6pm; winter Tues–Sun 9am–noon & 3–5pm; L7000), a late-fifteenth-century structure now privately owned by the Odelscalchi family, whose outer walls, now mostly disappeared, contained the rectangular piazza of the medieval town. Nowadays it's rather rundown, the interior home to rusting suits of armour and faded frescoes, but the view from the ramparts is worth the admission price alone.

The best place to **swim** in the lake is from the sandy **Lido di Bracciano**, below Bracciano town. You can hire a boat and picnic offshore; and the nearby trattorias are good and inexpensive. There are also good restaurants at TREVIGNANO and ANGUILLARA, best of which is the *Belvedere* just beyond the Piazza del Commune in Anguillara, which has a large terrace that gives magnificent views over the village.

Veio

Midway between Lake Bracciano and Rome, 2km beyond the turn-off for Bracciano, **Veio** (summer daily 9am–7pm, winter Tues–Sun 9am–2pm; L4000) was the largest of the twelve cities of the Etruscan League, at its height between the eighth century and sixth century BC. Nowadays, however, it's one of the least appealing of the Etruscan sites – spread over a wide area and not at all well-preserved. Captured by the Romans in 396 BC, its chief attraction is its *Sanctuary of Apollo*, the remains of which constitute the most important example of an Etruscan temple yet found – although its terracotta roof decorations and the statue of Apollo itself have long since been removed to the Villa Giulia in Rome. A good sign board explains things (in Italian), and a map helps you make out what's what. But it's a bleak site and for the most part hard work for all but the most dedicated lovers of the Etruscans.

Lago di Vico and around

The smallest but most appealing of north Lazio's lakes, and the only one deemed worthy of being declared a nature reserve, **Lago di Vico** is another former volcanic crater, ringed by appreciable mountains, the highest of which – Monte Fogliano – rises to 963m on the western shore. The **Via Ciminia** traverses the summit ridges, and is a popular scenic drive – dotted with restaurants, but there's a quieter road lower down (closed to cars) which skirts closer to the shoreline. The flatter northern edge, marshy in places, is a spot for discreet unofficial **camping**.

Getting around this part of Lazio is a sweat, and in an ideal world you'd have your own transport. Buses between Viterbo and Rome skirt the area, and two rickety branch rail lines spear around the lake from ORTE. With careful scrutiny of the timetables both can just about be made to work for you. One of the rail lines ties in to the Rome–Viterbo line at CAPRANICA, with halts at Ronciglione and Caprarola; the other winds up to Viterbo via Bomarzo.

Caprarola: the Palazzo Farnese

Over and above the lake's sheer prettiness, there's not much besides the odd attractive village and a scattering of Roman and Etruscan remains – none terribly interesting in their own right, but worthwhile if you can string several together. More properly deserving of individual attention is the Palazzo Farnese at **CAPRAROLA**, which, like the villas at Bagnaia and Bomarzo (see p.643), counts among the high points of seventeenth-century Italian Mannerism.

The town is pleasant enough, owing its present prosperity to vast hazlenut groves which blanket the surrounding countryside, though you can't help feeling the place is simply an excuse for the **palace**, which stands huge and imposing at the top of the steep main street (summer daily 9am–7pm; spring daily 9am–6.30pm; winter daily 9am–5pm; L4000). If you're keen on the period, the building is clearly a masterpiece – Stendhal described it as a building where "architecture married Nature". Begun by Antonio di Sangallo the Younger for Pierluigi Farnese in the early 1520s, it was originally more a castle than a palace, situated at the centre of the lands belonging to the Farnese family. Later, Cardinal Alessandro Farnese took up residence here, in 1559 hiring Vignola to modify the building while retaining the peculiar pentagonal floor-plan. Vignola was an inspired choice. Apprenticed at Fontainbleau, responsible for crucial advances in sixteenth-century garden design, he was among the most accomplished architects of the late Renaissance, and exemplifies the Mannerist style at its best in his creation at Caprarola, which celebrates the period's values of superiority of art over nature, style over substance, together with a self-satisfied, almost gloating eulogising of the patron's virtues.

Most of the palace's five floors are closed to the public; indeed only the *piano nobile* is open, and there's no escaping a certain seediness which seems to have overtaken the place of late, both in the fag-ends and graffiti in the curving forecourt, and in the state rooms themselves, which have lost all their furniture, suffering a cold, unlived-in feel as a result. There are frescoes from 1560, most of them by the brothers Zuccaro chronicling the Farnese family's greatness, much lauded as the building's highlight (though some are embarrassingly crude and others terribly knocked about), and a monumental spiral staircase up to a circular courtyard that gives on to the main rooms of the *piano nobile*, huge and heavy with its thirty pairs of columns, which is considered one of Vignola's best moments. The first and last rooms are perhaps the best, however, the first with a super-embellished grotto-like fireplace and pictures of local communities like Caprarola itself (the central scene is an imaginary one), the last, the *Sala del Mappomondo* – about the only place not given over to glorifying the Farnese clan – decorated with huge painted maps of the known world and a wonderful ceiling fresco of the constellations.

Outside there are twin **gardens**, divided into a south-facing summer terrace and an east-facing winter terrace, with plants and design appropriate to each. Look out for the artificial grotto and the stalactites, brought from a real cave and stuck on. Beyond is a **park**, some of it open at least a few times daily (at 10am, 1.30pm and 3pm), the rest a summer hideaway for the Italian president.

Practicalities

There's an infrequent **train** to Caprarola from Orte (35min), though the town's train station is a stiff forty-minute walk from the town. For the centre bear left from the station, turn right at the T-junction and keep walking straight ahead. You're probably better off using Viterbo as a base and taking the reasonably frequent **bus** from there, a pleasant ride through the wooded hills of the Monti Cimini which takes half an hour or so and leaves you at the foot of the main street, a ten-minute walk from the palace at the top. In any case Caprarola only has one **hotel**, the *Farnese*, a modern building way out on the Viterbo side of town (the Viterbo bus goes right past) that should be kept for emergencies only. For **food**, there's the *Trattoria del Cimino* midway down the main street at Via F. Nicolai 44, and a pizzeria off to the left of Piazza Romei in front of the palace.

South of the lake

South of Caprarola lies a trio of towns, each good for about half an hour if you've got your own transport. **RONCIGLIONE** is closest, its old quarter nicely situated over one of the small east-running **ravines** that cut through the area. Turner thought it picturesque enough to paint, though Dickens later described it as "a little town like a large pig-sty". These days it's the self-styled "Gateway to Etruria" and claims to be the birthplace of Pontius Pilate, though a couple of churches aside there's little to see; the **tourist office** at Corso Umberto 22 can fill you in further.

SUTRI, 6km south, has more solid attractions, enclosed by part medieval, part Etruscan walls, with odd traces of cyclopean gateways. The site itself – on a rocky tufa outcrop between valleys – is one typically chosen by the Etruscans, and it's an Etruscan site that provides the town's one real draw: an **amphitheatre** south of the town off the main Via Cassia, carved completely from the solid rock. Later adapted by the Romans, it had seating for 6000, and though now overgrown is a neat antidote to over-restored theatres elsewhere in Italy. Back along the Cassia towards the old town a left-hand track across the river takes you to **Madonna del Parto** – rarely open, but an extremely ancient church, again carved from the rock, and probably converted first from old Etruscan tombs and subsequently from a Mithraic temple.

NEPI is another outcrop village, perched over three valleys on the road to CIVITA CASTELLANA. Principal attraction is the eleventh-century Romanesque **Basilica of Sant'Elia**, 2km away to the east, a pleasant cypress-surrounded spot, with traces of an eighth-century church and twelfth-century frescoes in the apse.

Back up the Cassia to VETRALLA, and there are a couple of good **walks** nearby. If you feel ambitious, one follows an old railway from Capranica to Civitavecchia, cutting through the **Tolfa hills**, a two-to-three-day excursion. The others – more of a doddle – leave from the medieval village of BLERA (bus from Viterbo or Tarquinia): one takes in the **Etruscan necropoli** to the north (2hr), the other is a more scenic wander through the wooded ravine to BARBARANO ROMANO (3hr).

Viterbo and around

The capital of its province, and indeed of northern Lazio as a whole, **VITERBO** is easily the region's most historic centre, a medieval town that during the thirteenth century was once something of a rival to Rome. It was, for a time, the residence of popes, a succession of whom relocated here after friction in the capital. Today there are some vestiges of its vanquished prestige – a handful of grand palaces and churches, an intact set of medieval walls – but the town is a rather shabby place, refreshingly untouched by much tourist traffic but only really worth staying in if you're keen to visit the surrounding area. If you aren't, it's worth knowing that buses and trains run frequently from Rome (buses are fastest) and you can comfortably see the town in a day.

The Town

If there is a centre to Viterbo it's **Piazza del Plebiscito**, an appropriately named square girdled almost entirely by the fifteenth- and sixteenth-century buildings that make up the town's council offices. The lions that echo each other across the square are Viterbo's symbol, and you'll see them repeated, in grandiose echoes of Venice, all over town. You can look in on the fine Renaissance courtyard of the main, arcaded building of the **Palazzo Comunale**, and climb the stairs from here to view a *Pietà* by Sebastiano del Piombo. You can also view the council chamber itself (accessible through the modern extension, by the door under the bridge), decorated with a series of murals depicting Viterbo's history from Etruscan times in a weird mixture of pagan and Christian motifs – a mixture continued across the square in the church of **Sant'Angelo**, which holds a Roman sarcophagus on its facade.

There are a number of directions you can walk from the piazza. Most interesting is to take a left off the square down Via San Lorenzo, which leads past the pretty Piazza di Gesù, where there's a small market, to the macabrely named Piazza del Morte. Left from here takes you through Viterbo's oldest quarter, the **Quartiere Pellegrino** – a tight mess of hilly streets hinged onto the arched axis of Via San Pellegrino. It's a nice neighbourhood, home to a number of art and antique shops, but half an hour should be more than enough time to see it all. In the opposite direction, Piazza San Lorenzo is flanked by the town's most historic group of buildings, most notably the **Palazzo Papale** itself, a thirteenth-century structure whose impressive site, looking over the green gorge that cuts into central Viterbo, is best appreciated from its open Gothic loggia. You can peep into the Great Hall, venue of the election of half a dozen or so popes, but otherwise the palace is closed to the public, and you have to content yourself with a wander into the **Duomo** opposite, a plain Romanesque church that has a fine Cosmatesque floor and an understated beauty unusual among Italian churches.

Walking east from Piazza del Plebiscito, Via Roma soon becomes **Corso Italia**, Viterbo's main shopping street and the scene of a busy *passeggiata* of an evening. At its far end, steps lead up from Piazza Verdi to the nineteenth-century church of **Santa Rosa**, which holds the saint's corpse in a chapel in the south aisle – a faintly grotesque, doll-like figure with a forced grin, dressed up in a nun's habit; for a close-up view ring the bell on the right-hand side of the church entrance and someone will let you into the chapel itself (Mon–Sat 8.45am–12.15pm & 4.30–6pm). A good time to be in Viterbo is September 3, when the so-called "macchina" of Santa Rosa is carried through the streets of the town to the accompaniment of much revelry and, later, fireworks.

After this, the rest of Viterbo can't help but seem a bit sinister, and in any case you've seen it all except for one quarter. This is at the top of the hill above Piazza Verdi. Follow Via Matteotti up to **Piazza della Rocca**, a large square dominated by the fierce-looking **Rocca Albornoz**, home of the small **Museo Nazionale** (Tues–Sat 9am–2pm, Sun 9am–1pm; L4000), whose archaeological collection includes displays of Roman and Etruscan artefacts unearthed locally. Just off the opposite side of the square, the church of **San Francesco** is also worth a quick look, a high and unusually plain Gothic church that is the burial place of two of Viterbo's popes – Clement IV and Adrian V – both laid in now heavily restored but impressive Cosmatesque tombs on either side of the main altar.

Practicalities

Unusually for a small town, Viterbo has two **main train stations** – one, Porta Romana, situated just outside the Porta Romana to the south of the town centre, around fifteen minutes' walk from Piazza del Plebiscito, and another, Porta Fiorentina, on Viale Trento just north of the city walls, close by Piazza della Rocca and handier for hotels and the centre of town. There's also a station serving the **ACOTRAL** Roma-Nord line, next door to Porta Fiorentina, where trains from Rome's Piazzale Flaminia station arrive. There's a **tourist office** on Piazza Caduti (Mon–Sat 8.30am–2.30pm; ☎0761/346.363), two minutes down Via F. Ascenzi from Piazza del Plebiscito, which has free maps of Viterbo and the surrounding area and information on **accommodation**. Close by, Via della Cava, which winds up to Piazza della Rocca, has a couple of Viterbo's inexpensive hotels: the *Milano*, Via della Cava 54 (☎0761/340.705; ④), is the cheapest, though it is in truth a bit of a dump; with a little more money you might be better off at the *Roma*, down the street at Via della Cava 26 (☎0761/227.274; ⑤), which isn't greatly more expensive. **Eating** isn't tremendously difficult. *Schenardi*, Corso Italia 11, is one of the nicest places for a lunchtime snack or a drink, and later on there are a number of cheap pizzerias on Via Matteotti and Via della Cava, most of them offering special menus to the conscripts that come into town from the army camp just outside Viterbo. More specifically, *La Scaletta*, Via Marconi 43, does reasonably priced pizzas, while *Tre Re*, Via Marcel Gattesco 3, off Piazza dell'Erbe, is a cosy place, popular with locals, that makes a good venue for trying local specialities. If you're keen to splurge, the *Enoteca la Torre*, Via delle Torre 5, is Viterbo's culinary highlight: a slightly precious place that is something of a haunt of local yuppies, but which serves wonderful food that is not overly costly, especially if you select sparingly from the five or six courses normally on offer – and go easy on the huge and pricey wine list.

Around Viterbo: Bagnaia, Bomarzo and Tuscania

Viterbo makes by far the best base besides Rome for seeing much of northern Lazio, especially the places that aren't really feasible on a day trip from the capital. The Mannerist villas of Caprarola (see p.639) and Bagnaia are a short distance away and easily reached on public transport, as are – from the same era – the bizarre gardens of

Bomarzo, and the shores of Lake Bolsena. Less excitingly, Viterbo is also connected by regular bus with Tuscania, the dull centre of a very dull locality.

Bagnaia

BAGNAIA, about 5km east of Viterbo, isn't much of a town, but like Caprarola further south it's completely dominated by a sixteenth-century palace, the **Villa Lante**, whose small but superb **gardens** are considered Vignola's masterpiece, and one of the supreme creations of Renaissance garden art – "the most lovely place of the physical beauty of nature in all Italy or in all the world", according to Sachaverell Sitwell. The villa is easily seen from Viterbo, using the hourly **buses** from the small bus station on Piazza Martiri dei Ungheri, by the tourist office, or less frequent trains of the Roma-Nord line.

A short walk up the hill from the main square, the **villa** is actually two villas, built for a pair of cardinals twenty years apart, but symmetrically opposed as part of the same architectural plan. Only open on the big public holidays, they're nothing much to write home about, and in contrast to Caprarola it's the **gardens** that take pride of place – some of the best preserved from the period, and a summing up of Mannerist aspirations. The main group lie behind the villas, ranged over five gently sloping terraces, and are only open in the company of a guide (May–Aug daily 9am–7.30pm; March–April & Sept–Oct daily 9am–5.30pm; Nov–Feb daily 9am–4pm; tours every half-hour; L4000). An attempt at a stylised interpretation of the natural world, they were an ambitious project, even by the standards of the time, depicting the progress of a river from its source in the hills to its outlet in the sea – represented here by a large *parterre*. The route takes in various watery adventures – waterfalls, lakes and the like – and among numerous fountains and low hedges there are plenty of humorous (or plain silly) touches, such as a maiden whose breasts spout water, a cascade designed as an elongated crayfish, and the so-called "wetting sports" – hidden sprays of water that drenched unsuspecting onlookers and were a big favourite of Mannerist funsters. Only the guide gets to play with these.

The adjoining **park**, through which you're free to wander, has an even more ambitious narrative, attempting to describe, through horticulture, the progress of civilisation from primitive times to the glories of the sixteenth century. In true Mannerist style almost as much weight is given to allegory as to architecture, both here and on the villas. The various square motifs that appear around the buildings, for example, were supposed to represent the perfection of Heaven brought to earth.

Bomarzo

Twelve kilometres northeast of Bagnaia, the village of **BOMARZO** is home to another Mannerist creation, the **Parco dei Mostri** (daily dawn–dusk; L8000) – and a greater contrast to the former's restrained elegance would be hard to find. It's still ostensibly a garden, but one look at the tangled wood and its huge, completely crazed sculptures is enough to see that this is Mannerism gone mad. Salvador Dali loved the surreal flavour of the place, even making a film here, and its strange other-worldly qualities – like a sixteenth-century theme park of fantasy and horror – have made it one of northern Lazio's primary tourist attractions.

Built in 1552 by the hunch-backed Duke of Orsini, the *Sacro Bosco* or "Sacred Wood", as he called it, set out to parody Mannerist self-glorification by deliberate vulgarity. It knocked the intellectual pretentions of the day by mocking idealised Arcadian retreats from society and Art's supposed "triumph" over Nature, while retaining typically Mannerist calculated attempts at sensationalism. Apparently built by Turkish prisoners captured at the Battle of Lepanto (though this seems a doubtful Christian rationalisation of the park's "heretical" features), the park has an Etruscan influence too, manifest in the plentiful urns and pine cones, and its madder moments are said to have been induced by a popular epic of the time, Ariosto's *Orlando Furioso*, a tale of lost sanity. The giant warrior at the entrance tearing apart a woodcutter comes from the story, a symbol of Orlando's madness, and deeper into the park an English prince pours Orlando's brains down an elephant's trunk – another symbol apparently, this time of the restoration of sanity. There are many other dank, mossy sculptures – tortoises, elephants, Moby Dick, a mad laughing mask, dragons, nymphs, butterflies and plenty of things you couldn't put a name to. And there's a Doric temple which makes a deliberate dog's dinner of all Classical conventions. Legend has it that the Duke's wife took one look and dropped dead of heart failure.

Six **buses** a day run from Viterbo to Bomarzo, from where the Parco dei Mostri is a signposted ten-minute walk. You can also get here by **train** – the nearest station is Attigliano-Bomarzo, on the Orte-Montefiascone-Viterbo link, but this is a 5km walk from the park.

Tuscania

Sheep and then more sheep are the only thing to break the monotony of the wide, desolate country between Viterbo and Tarquinia. The only thing, that is, apart from **TUSCANIA**, a strange, open-plan town announced by a fine avenue of cypresses and distinguished by a long-ranging spread of medieval walls and some well-preserved towers. Its largely Renaissance centre is attractive and almost unvisited, and it's a charming town in its way. But the real point of a visit lies in the two justly celebrated **Romanesque churches** on the eastern edge of the town, close to the rocky outcrop of the old Etruscan settlement.

From the central Piazza Basile take the Via Clodia until the unmistakable bulk of **San Pietro** looms into view. Considered one of the gems of the Italian Romanesque, it's an essentially thirteenth-century construction with eighth-century fragments of Lombard origin. Fronted by a threadbare grass piazza – giving an odd courtyard effect – it's also flanked by the remains of a Bishop's Palace, and two sturdy towers, the whole church having once been fortified as part of the town's defensive scheme. The facade's marble embellishments – look out for the dancer and a man being strangled by a snake – may well come from an Etruscan temple. The interior is solemn and airy, with huge blunt pillars supporting curious notched arches, a feature known in Italian as *dentati* (literally "toothed"), and early twelfth-century frescoes in the transept, somewhat the worse for wear after an earthquake in 1971.

The town's other focal point, **Santa Maria Maggiore,** is a stone's throw away down the hill, a less gracious affair than San Pietro, despite the fact that it deliberately repeats some of its features and was built over the same period. The arched marble doorway is a carbon copy, probably added by Pisan sculptors in the twelfth century; the rest of the ruddy stone facade is largely Gothic, only the left portal preserving the zigzags of Norman motif. Inside is the usual bare simplicity of the Romanesque – stone walls, the odd fresco, and most remarkably, a font designed for total immersion.

The rest of the town is decidedly less impressive, boasting only a small **archaeological museum**, housed in the cloisters of Santa Maria di Rosa on Via XX Settembre (Tues–Sun 9am–1.30pm & 2.30–6pm; free). In addition to the predictable Etruscan display, there's a collection of twelfth- to seventeenth-century ceramics, many taken from the walls of local houses.

Lago di Bolsena and around

Heading north from Viterbo by road, there's little choice but to take the Via Cassia to **MONTEFIASCONE**, an ugly journey, not improved by opting for the train, which runs alongside. If you're **hitching** and want to move out of the area fast, there's a new dual carriageway (not marked on all maps) from just north of Viterbo, linking up with the *Autostrada del Sole* (A1) at Orte.

Montefiascone itself rears up high, perched on the rim of an old volcanic crater, an Etruscan city and possibly the site of a huge temple to Voltumna – a sort of Houses of Parliament for the heads of the twelve-city Etruscan Federation. The seventeenth-century **Duomo** is immediately striking, a huge octagonal pile that totally dominates the skyline, though it's less interesting than the twelfth-century church of **San Flaviano** a little way out of town on the road to Orvieto. An extraordinary Romanesque work, consisting of two interconnected but opposite-facing basilicas, the lower church contains several fourteenth- and fifteenth-century frescoes, as well as the tomb of Bishop Giovanni Fugger, who reputedly died from knocking back too much of the local wine, *Est!Est!Est!*. Bumph from the **tourist office**, Via Verentana 4, regales you with other unlikely legends surrounding the brew and has details of accommodation, including a **campsite**, the *Amulasanta*, Via del Lago 77 (☎85.294), out on the MARTA road at PRATO RONCONE.

Buses run from Montefiascone to ORVIETO, and to most points on **Lago di Bolsena** – a popular destination whose hotels and restaurants tend to make their pitch in German and English, though it rarely gets overcrowded. If you want to be away from the crowds and plan on spending some time here, head for the less-visited western shore – better for camping rough, and more picturesque into the bargain. The lake, Lazio's biggest, occupies the remains of a broad volcanic crater. The surrounding soil is immensely fertile, and there's a super-mild micro climate, with most of the shores intensely cultivated as a result. Dante praised the quality of its eels, though fishermen today are hampered by the so-called *sesse* – odd tide-like variations in the lake's level.

CAPODIMONTE, on the southern shore, is one of the more developed spots, an attractive town which pushes into the lake on a half-wooded peninsula. The only sight worth a mention is the sixteenth-century **Castello Farnese**, an octagonal tower commanding the tip of the promontory, but there's good **swimming** from a tree-lined shore, and boat trips run out to the **Isola Bisentina**, which sports Etruscan tombs, five frescoed chapels, and another Farnese villa – the summer retreat of several popes. The nearest **campsite** is 1500m away at SAN LAZZARO (open May–Sept; ☎88.102).

On the opposite shore, **BOLSENA** is the lake's main focus, a relaxed and likeable place that's worth a stop even if you don't intend to hang around. Medieval nooks and alleyways run off the single main drag, with a well-preserved fourteenth-century **castle** perched over the western end. The thirteenth-century church of **San Francesco** adds character to the town's main Piazza Matteotti, and occasionally hosts concerts and small exhibitions, and the eleventh-century **Santa Cristina** conceals a good Romanesque interior behind a wide Renaissance facade added in 1494. Santa Cristina was the daughter of the town's third-century Roman prefect, who tortured her as a Christian, eventually throwing her into the lake with a stone round her ankles. Miraculously the stone floated and saved her life, becoming marked with the imprint of her feet – though she died from further mistreatment aged just 12. The stone makes up the altar of the *Cappella del Miracolo*, off the left-hand aisle – an altar which also starred in the Miracle of Bolsena (see "Vatican Museums", earlier in this chapter), when a sceptical priest was assured of the mystery of transubstantiation by real blood. Adjoining the chapel is the Grotta di San Cristina, once part of early Christian catacombs.

Set back a kilometre from the lake, the town itself tends to shut down come nightfall, when the **bars and restaurants** on the shore get into full swing. The closest of the **campsites**, most of which are out of town, is the *Lago*, open all year round, at Viale Cadorna 6 (☎0761/799.191); *La Pineta*, open May to September, is a kilometre away at Viale Diaz 48 (☎0761/799.801). The cheapest hotel is the *Italia*, Corso Cavour 53 (☎0761/799.193; ④). For full details call in at the **tourist office** on Piazza Matteotti.

To the east of Bolsena stretches an extraordinary, almost lunar landscape, pitted with deeply eroded **canyons**, some wooded but most just bare, wasted slopes. At its heart lies the tiny village of **CIVITA**, known as "la città che muore" – the city which is dying – due to the erosion of the rock below it. People have been emigrating from here since the sixteenth century, leaving a population today of around seven and a strange eerily deserted village that's slowly becoming a tourist attraction in its own right. Apparently an Italian computer company has plans to buy up the place wholesale, but for the moment it's worth a visit just for its very weirdness. Stranded evocatively on an isolated rocky outcrop, the only access is from the nearby village of BAGNOREGIO.

Due north of the lake, **SAN LORENZO NUOVO** is just one of many villages you'll pass through if you're continuing up by road to SIENA. It's not a town of monuments, but it does come as a pleasant surprise if you are passing through. A planned settlement, centred on an octagonal piazza, it was constructed in 1774 to house the inhabitants of the village of San Lorenzo, who had been forced to move by the malaria that once ravaged the entire lake shore. By some architectural freak the design was copied from a suburb of Copenhagen. If you have time and transport, hilltop **GRADOLI**, a few kilometres west, is at the heart of a big wine area, and has another palace built by the Farnese family. A rough road just beyond, from LATERA, leads to the **Lago di Mezzano**, a beautiful and highly recommended spot if you're travelling with a tent.

Rieti and around

Pleasantly situated, but thoroughly dull, **RIETI** is capital of Lazio's largest province, occupying the plumb geographical centre of Italy – and with a plaque in Piazza di San Rufo to prove it. In the days of the Romans this was a key region – the so-called *Umbilicus Italiae* – with the Via Salaria or "Salt Road" forming an essential route for trading salt (extracted at Ostia) with the Sabines who lived up in these hills. But nowadays it's on its last legs, with the second lowest population density in the country (after Aosta), and a drift from the land that's more often associated with the South. Three-quarters of the rural population has moved from the countryside since 1950, most of them to Rome, and it doesn't look like changing: poor communications have deterred any sort of industrial initiative – something which is to the visitors' if not the locals' advantage, leaving Rieti's mountain-ringed plain almost entirely unscarred by factories or housing.

The Town

At best Rieti is somewhere to while away an hour waiting for a bus, so don't be fooled by the tourist office's artful pictures of medieval walls and arches – the only traces of the medieval town you'll find are the **Duomo** and the **Palazzo Vescovile** off the main street, and a short stretch of twelfth-century wall to the north of the centre. For those planning serious walking or camping trips it's worth visiting the main **EPT**, 50m from the duomo at Via Cintia 87, who have maps of the town and, more importantly, detailed routes for **high level walks** around Terminillo. With their help you also shouldn't have problems planning a tour of the four **Franciscan monasteries** around Rieti, all connected one way or another with important episodes in the saint's life. They're all scenic enough, though without a special interest in Saint Francis you may not find them terribly exciting. The most famous is at **GRECCIO**, where Francis created the first ever Christmas crib, a real-life nativity with cows and all, for the benefit of local peasants.

Practicalities

Rieti's **train** and **bus station** is just north of the town centre on the far side of Viale L. Morroni. By **train** from Rome it's around three hours to Rieti: there's no direct link and you have to change at Terni (and sometimes Orte) for a line that eventually continues to L'Aquila and Sulmona. Several **buses** a day ply back and forth to Rome, though they tend to take around the same amount of time. If you need **to stay**, the *Serena*, Viale della Gioventu 17 (☎0746/270.930; ⑤), is probably the cheapest option close to the centre of town, and has a few cheaper unbathed rooms. If you want to be in the centre itself, try the *Europa*, Via San Rufo 49 (☎0746/495.149; ⑥), which also has some cheaper rooms. You can **eat** cheaply at *Il Pappomondo*, Piazza Cavour 63, a cheap pizzeria close to the river; or, with a little more money, try *Bistrot*, on Piazza San Rufo, a family-run place whose adventurous and varied menu changes daily.

Around Terminillo

Less than 20km from Rieti, reachable by way of a heart-stopping bus ride, **TERMINILLO** lies amidst 2000m-high mountains and scenery of almost Alpine splendour, a winter ski-resort that likes to think of itself as something of an elite tourist centre. As such it's dominated by clusters of big modern hotels, ski lifts and associated winter sports paraphernalia. Terminillo is not an especially attractive place, more a string of ski-centres than a town, with facilities that seem rather out of place and redundant in summer, but there's plenty of off-season scope for walking and climbing in the hills around, including a series of refuges if you want to do more than stroll.

There's a **tourist office** in Via Covemese at Terminillo/Pian de Valli (☎0746/61.121), which can advise on **accommodation**. There's a **youth hostel,** the *Ostello della Neve*, at Terminillo/Campoforogna (☎0746/261.169; ①). **Hotels** start in the two-star bracket: go for *Il Ghiacciolo* in Campoforogna (☎0746/261.240; ④) or the *Regina* in Pian de Valli (☎0746/261.375; ④). The **Club Alpino Italiano**, Via Garibaldi 264b, has advance details of some of the most challenging hikes in the countryside around.

If you've just turned up on the off-chance, one tremendous and manageable low-level hike you can make is by way of **La Valle Scura**, 12km across country to SIGILLO. If you plan on trekking off into the wilderness, bear in mind that many slopes away from the ski-runs are thickly wooded, especially in the Vallonina towards Leonessa, and you often have to get quite high before finding open country. Another good base for hikes is **AMATRICE**, easily hitchable from Terminillo, a rather drab grid-iron town laid out in 1529, famous only for having given birth to a pasta dish, the spicy *spaghetti all'amatriciana*. Behind, the Monti della Laga rise to seriously high peaks – 2400m up – which continue on into Abruzzo's Gran Sasso D'Italia. The **tourist office** at Via Madonna della Porta 19 issue a detailed map with several marked paths, most of which start from rough roads above the hamlets of SAN MARTINO and CAPPRICCHIA. If you're staying, the cheapest **hotel** is the two-star *La Conca* on Via della Madonnella (☎0746/85.267; ④).

The Sabine Hills

THE SABINE HILLS, south of Rieti, are an altogether softer option than the mountains to the east. For an area so close to Rome they suffer only a trickle of tourism – partly because there are no big sights and partly because it's difficult to get around in what is an area of small villages and secondary roads. If you decide to bother with the region it'll be for the scenery, the best of which is east of the Via Salaria around **Lago del Turano** and **Lago del Salto**, where the village of **ROCCA SINIBALDA** provides a focus – though it's not really more than a fortified castle, surrounded by high wooded hills. Northeast of here, a great swathe of desolate country centres around Monte Nuria (1888m) and Monte Moro (1524m) – walking and backpacking territory mostly, with the small **Lago Rascino** providing a wild and unspoilt target, particularly if you're camping.

On the other side of the Via Salaria, many of the villages have been doubly destroyed, first in the Fifties by people emigrating to Rome, and then more recently – ironically – by richer Romans returning to buy up holiday homes. They still look much as they've always done – small self-contained nuclei on the tops of low hills – but varying degrees of medieval character are about all they've got going for them. The rolling countryside in between – looking like a higher version of the Cotswolds – is still moderately pretty. One undoubted highlight in a lacklustre area is the old Benedictine abbey at **FARFA**, situated in fine olive-covered countryside 6km from FARO – to which it's connected by an *ACOTRAL* bus service. Founded in the fifth century and endowed by Charlemagne, it was one of the single most powerful abbeys in Europe for a while, with a huge economic base, a merchant fleet, even its own army, and rights to Aquila, Molise, Viterbo, Spoleto, Tarquinia and Civitavecchia – central Italy in effect. By the end of the Middle Ages, however, it was in decline, and most of its early medieval splendour has since been submerged under fifteenth- and sixteenth-century additions. The **Abbey Church** is stacked with various treasures, and a few eleventh-century frescoes survive in the belltower, but the new **museum** is the main focus, collecting together parts of the Abbey's heritage as well as local archaeological fragments. Most fascinating is the **Cures Pillar**, a sixth-century BC Sabine inscription found in a local river bed in 1982. It's the only example known, and, still undeciphered, it remains an emblem for studies of the previously ignored Sabine culture.

SOUTHERN LAZIO

The saying goes that the Italian South begins with the first petrol station south of Rome, and certainly there's a radically different feel to the **southern part of Lazio**, the green wooded hills north of the city having given way to a mix of flat marshy land and harsh unyielding mountains that has a poor, desperate look in places. Many skate straight through the area on their way south to Naples, and you may want to do the same. But if you've time, the **coast** is worth taking in on a more unhurried route south: its resorts, especially **Terracina** and **Sperlonga**, are fine places to take it easy after the rigours of the capital, and the **Pontine Islands**, a couple of hours offshore, are (out of high season at least) among Italy's most undiscovered treasures. **Inland**, too, the landscape can be rewarding: the towns of the **Castelli Romani** are the most accessible taste of the region, easily assimiliated on a day trip from Rome; **Subiaco** and the **Ciocaria** region to the south are more remote, but hold some of Lazio's most inspiring scenery – broad tree-clad hills and valleys sheltering small towns unknown to many tourists.

The Castelli Romani and Alban Hills

Just free of the sprawling southern suburbs of Rome, the thirteen towns that make up the **Castelli Romani** date back to medieval times, since when these hills – the **Colli Albani** – have served as an escape for the rich and powerful from the summer heat of the city. It's a wine-growing area (the vines grow easily on the volcanic soil), and is now pretty heavily built-up, most of the towns ringed by unprepossessing new suburbs; and summer weekends can see Romans trooping out in huge numbers for lunch at local trattorias. But if you avoid the rush-hour times and peak season holidays, the region is still worth the journey, either as a day trip from Rome or on the way south through Lazio. By car, there are two obvious routes, both starting with Frascati and Grottaferrata and then spearing off at Marino along either the eastern or western side of Lago Albano. On public transport, buses for the area leave from the terminus opposite the Metro station Subaugusta (line #A).

Frascati, and east of Lago Albano

At just 20km from Rome, **FRASCATI** is the nearest of the Castelli towns and also the most striking, dominated by the majestic **Villa Aldobrandi** (Tues–Sun 9am–1pm; free), built by Giacomo della Porta in 1598 for one Cardinal Aldobrandi. Since it still belongs to the family you can't actually get inside, but the **gardens** are open to the public on application to the tourist office on Piazza Marconi. These are somewhat neglected these days, and sadly the potentially spectacular water garden at the rear of the villa is often switched off. But the view from the terrace in front of the house is superb, with Rome clearly visible on a clear day. Frascati is also about the most famous of the Colli Albani wine towns: ask at the tourist office for details of local wine producers that run tours and tastings; or have lunch at the *Spartaco* restaurant on Viale L. Bonaparte, where you can eat outside in summer.

The tourist office will also tell you about **Tusculum**, beautifully sited on a hilltop just outside Frascati, which was a favourite retreat of Roman patricians. Cicero had a villa here, but the resort was destroyed in 1191 by Pope Celestine III, the inhabitants moving down the hill to modern-day Frascati, and most of the Roman remains seem to have disappeared forever beneath the undergrowth. There's a small theatre, and the views, again, are fine.

Three kilometres or so down the road, **GROTTAFERRATA** is also known for its wine and its eleventh-century **Abbey** – a fortified Basilian (Greek Orthodox) monastery surrounded by high defensive walls and a now empty moat. It's a timeless spot, the little church of Santa Maria inside with a Byzantine-style interior decorated with thirteenth-century mosaics and, in the chapel of Saint Nilus off the right aisle, frescoes by Domenchino. Through the inner courtyard there's a small museum (Tues–Sun 8.30am–noon & 4.30–6pm; free) displaying Classical and medieval sculptures.

MARINO, another 4km further on, isn't a particularly attractive place, though its wine is perhaps the region's best after Frascati, and is distributed free on the first Sunday of October during its *Sagra dell'Uva* festival. From here, the scenic Via dei Laghi skirts the eastern rim of **Lago Albano** before reaching the turn-off for **NEMI**, built high above the tiny crater **lake** of the same name. The village itself isn't much to write home about, but a cobbled road leads down to fields of strawberries which lie between the steep walls of the crater and the shores of the lake and make a good place to picnic. The town is known for its strawberries, in fact, and celebrates this each June in the *Sagra delle Fragole*. On the northern shore of the lake you'll notice a large hangar-like building, which contains the scanty remains of two Roman ships said to have been built by Caligula. Signs at nearby GENZANO would have you believe there's something exciting to see; in fact the museum there has been closed indefinitely for some time.

Before you reach Nemi, a winding road leads up from Via dei Laghi to **Monte Cavo**, at 949m the second highest of the Colli Albani, and topped with the masts and satellite dishes of the Italian military – who operate from nearby Ciampino airport. There used to be a hotel here, a former Passionist convent, but the building is now derelict, and the summit is much less of a tourist attraction than it used to be. A temple to Jupiter once stood here, but now the only extant antiquity is the Via Sacra, which, about 1000m from the top, emerges from dense undergrowth, snaking down through the woods for a kilometre or so before disappearing again into thick bush.

On the far side of Monte Cavo, the road bears right for **ROCCA DI PAPA**, at 680m the highest of the Castelli Romani towns, and one of its most picturesque, with a medieval quarter tumbling down the hill in haphazard terraces, and motor traffic at a (forced) minimum. The large main square, Piazza Repubblicca, is modern and dull; instead, make for the small Piazza Garibaldi, a lively place in summer with a bar and restaurant, and soak up the views.

West of Lago Albano

Leaving Marino, the road joins up with the old Roman Via Appia, which travels straight as an arrow down the west side of Lago Albano. **CASTEL GANDOLFO** is the first significant stop, named after the castle owned by the powerful twelfth-century Genevose Gandolfi family and now best known as the summer retreat of the pope – though John Paul II is said to prefer visiting the mountains further north during the summer months, much to the disgruntlement of the town. At over 400m above the rim of Lago Albano, it's a pleasantly airy place, but inevitably papal business predominates, especially on Sundays when the pope traditionally gives a midday address between July and September from the courtyard of the Papal Palace. Unless you want to see the pope, it's best to avoid this. You can visit the **palace** and its gardens, originally built by Carlo Maderno in 1624, but you need a special permit from the director. Better, if it's hot, to take advantage of the lake: there's a pleasant **Lido** just below the town, from where, if you've the energy, you can make an on-foot circuit of the whole lake in about two hours.

From Castel Gandolfo a panoramic road leads to **ALBANO LAZIALE**, probably the most appealing of the towns along the Via Appia, its large Piazza Mazzini looking south to the lovely Villa Communale park, with sketchy remains of a villa that once belonged to Pompey. The town also has other Roman remains. Along the high street, Corso Matteotti, the church of **San Pietro** was built over the foundations of the baths of a Roman garrison, which you can see built into the walls. Opposite, the **Palazzo del Comune** (daily 9.30am–1.30pm & 4.30–7.30pm) houses a small but quality archaeological collection including Roman artefacts found locally. Walk out also to the **Tomb of Horatii and the Curiatii**, just outside town on the Ariccia road, whose strange "chimneys" date from the Republican era. There's an **amphitheatre** too, on the hill above – in heavy ruin now, and currently closed, but once with room for 15,000 spectators.

The Via Appia continues on to **ARICCIA** across the nineteenth-century **Ponte di Ariccia** – from where you can see the arches of the old Roman viaduct just below – into the central piazza of the town, a well-proportioned square embellished with Bernini's round church of **Santa Maria dell'Assunzione**. **GENZANO**, 2km further on, also has a pleasant medieval centre, built around Piazza Frasconi, from where a road leads to the edge of Lake Albano's crater and sweeps down to the shore through dense woods. The town is the scene of the yearly *Infiorata* in May, when Via Italo Belardi, which scales the hill from the piazza, is carpeted with flowers. **VELLETRI**, though larger, is scarcely more interesting, its largely modern centre rebuilt after extensive war damage and with a Baroque cathedral, the fourteenth-century Torre del Trivio and a small archaeological museum among its scant sights.

Palestrina, Subiaco and the Ciociaria

Considering its proximity to the capital, it's a surprise that the southeastern rim of Lazio isn't more discovered; in fact it's one of Italy's least-known areas to tourists, for the most part a poor region of low hills edging into the mountains of the Abruzzi which is bypassed by those heading south on the fast *Autostrada del Sole*.

Palestrina

PALESTRINA was built on the site of the ancient *Praeneste*, originally an Etruscan settlement and later a favoured resort for patrician Romans. "Cool Praeneste", as Horace called it, was the site of an enormous Roman Temple of Fortune, whose foundations more or less determine the extent of the modern town centre, which is stepped up the hillside in a series of terraces constructed on the different levels of the once vast edifice – the ruins of which you can see at every turn.

Buses run to Palestrina about every 30–45 minutes from Rome and take about an hour, dropping you on Via degli Arcioni, from where you have to walk up to the steep town centre. You can see this in no time. There's a much-changed **Duomo** with fragments of a Roman road at the top end of the right aisle and a copy of Michelangelo's *Pietà di Palestrina* – the original, sadly, is now in Florence. And the stepped streets of the place are appealing enough for some casual strolling. But you have to climb to the top of the town for the real attraction – the **Palazzo Colonna-Barberini**, which houses the **Museo Nazionale Archaeologico Prenestino** (daily 9am–3.30pm; L6000). Originally built in the eleventh century and greatly modified by Taddeo Barberini in 1640, this occupies the uppermost level of the Temple of Fortune, now largely modernised inside and containing a slightly faded display of artefacts. Among a number of Roman pieces, there's a torso of a statue of Fortune in slate-grey marble, other bits from the temple and funerary *cistae* much like those displayed at the Villa Giulia in Rome.

At the top, the museum's prize exhibit is the marvellous first-century BC *Mosaic of the Nile*, which depicts the flooding of the river with a number of Egyptian scenes of life along the waterway from the source to the delta. Look closely and you'll notice a wealth of detail: there's a banquet going on under the vines on the left, soldiers and priests are grouped in front of the Serepaeum on the right, while the source of the river among the mountains is pictured at the top of the mosaic, where hunters and wild animals, labelled with Greek lettering, congregate. Outside the museum, your ticket admits you to the top **terrace** of the temple, the ruins of which command fine views over the surrounding countryside.

Subiaco

Around 15km northeast of Palestrina, **SUBIACO** (accessible by bus from Tivoli or direct from Rome), is beautifully set, pyramided around a hill topped by the Rocca Abbazia castle, close to Mount Liviato – Lazio's premier ski resort. It grew up originally as a purpose-built settlement to accommodate workmen building Nero's grand villa nearby (very thin traces of which survive), and later, during the fifth century, became the chosen contemplative base of Saint Benedict, who lived a life of seclusion and prayer in a cave on the slopes of a nearby mountain. Saint Benedict left after three years to found the monastery at Montecassino (see overleaf), but his legacy lives on in the town, in the shape of two monastic complexes just outside.

The **Convento di Santa Scolastica** (9am–12.30pm & 4–7pm; free) is the closer (and larger) of the two, about 25 minutes' walk out of town following the Ienne road from the main bus stop and following the signs off to the left before the bridge. Dedicated to Benedict's sister, it's been heavily restored over the years: the facade, with the Benedictine motto *Ora et Labore* over the entrance, isn't original and the only features of any real age in the church inside are two cipolin marble pillars from Nero's villa. The two cloisters, though, are delightful, the first one of the oldest Gothic works in Italy, lushly planted and fragrant, the second a Cosmati work with lovely arcades of pillars.

Continuing up the same road, the landscape grows more dramatic, after about fifteen minutes reaching the **Convento di San Benedetto** (daily 9am–12.30pm & 3–6pm; free) – a complex of two churches, chapels and other buildings clasping the rocky hillside on the precise site of Saint Benedict's cave. This is much the more interesting of the two monasteries: its church divides into several levels, the upper part decorated with fourteenth-century frescoes of the schools of Siena and Perugino, the lower leading into the *Sacro Speco* – the actual cave where Saint Benedict lived, now left in its natural condition but for a serene statue by Raggi, a disciple of Bernini. From here a spiral staircase leads up to the chapel of San Gregorio – often closed, but containing a thirteenth-century picture of Saint Francis that's reckoned to be one of the oldest ever portraits. In the other direction, stairs lead down to another chapel, from which Benedict would preach to shepherds, and a terrace which looks out on to the so-called "Holy Rose Tree" – actually a three-aisled bush that's said to have been created by Saint Francis from a bramble.

Practicalities

You can comfortably see Subiaco and its monasteries on a **day trip** from Rome: the bus journey takes around two hours and you can arrive in the town by lunchtime, eat, visit the monasteries in the afternoon and take an evening bus back to Rome (the last one leaves at 7.30pm).

The town's location may, however, make you want to linger: there's a reasonable **hotel** in the centre of town, the *Aniene*, Via Cavour 18 (☎85.565; ③), which also has an adequate **restaurant**. And if you're **heading south** there's an early bus out to Frosinone – from where you can get train or bus connections on to other points in Lazio and Campania. The **tourist office** at Via Cadorna 57 (Mon 8am–2pm, Tues–Sat 8am–2pm & 3.30–7.30pm, Sun 9am–noon) has full details.

The Ciociaria

From Subiaco the road heads south into a region known as the **Ciociaria**, a relatively remote corner of Lazio that takes its name from the sandals – *ciocie* – worn here in days gone by. It's hilly country, and historic too, settled several centuries before the Romans by the Hernici tribe who built inaccessible and heavily fortified towns, the remains of which – due to the shrewd Hernici policy of allying themselves with Rome – can still be seen today in the form of the extraordinary cyclopean walls of their citadels, quite unlike anything else in Italy.

The first town you come to, **FIUGGI**, is a spa resort whose bottled mineral water you will probably have already noticed in supermarkets, and which attracts health-conscious Italian tourists throughout the summer. For all that it's not an especially appealing place, its spa facilities, gardens and sports halls chic and pricey places that are either overflowing with crowds or (in winter) entirely dead.

From Fiuggi there's a choice of two routes, either west to Anagni or south to Alatri. **ANAGNI**, a former Hernici stronghold, is a well-preserved old place that produced a number of medieval popes from its powerful local Segni family, including Boniface VIII, whose **palace** here was invaded in 1303 by representatives of Philip IV of France when he attempted to assert the absolute authority of the papacy. There's not much left of the palace, which is now mostly modern, but a statue of Boniface stands on the outside of Anagni's **Duomo**, an imposing Romanesque basilica dating from the eleventh century. Inside there's a fine Cosmatesque pavement, a thirteenth-century baldachino, some thirteenth-century frescoes in the crypt and a treasury containing some of the pontifical effects of Pope Boniface.

In the opposite direction, **ALATRI** – the Hernici *Aletrium* – preserves its cyclopean walls from the sixth century BC, massive fortifications, still very much intact, and built long before the more sophisticated stone-cutting techniques of the Romans. The town's streets wind around the citadel at the top, cut by two square gateways (the arch hadn't yet been invented when this was built), inside of which the cathedral and Episcopal Palace stand on the site of the Hernici's ancient temples, since lost. The views, incidentally, are terrific.

FERENTINO, 10km west, also sports a good set of walls, though a hybrid one, modified by the Romans. You can get up to the old citadel here too, though it's some way from the modern town's station, and the Roman temples and cathedral there are seldom open. **FROSINONE**, 10km or so further south, is the main town of the Ciociaria, but is of little interest, a bland sprawling place with no obvious centre and barely any remains of the Hernici settlement. But it's a good place to pick up bus and train connections on to other points in Lazio and Campania: buses run west to Priverno from here, near to which you can pick up trains south or north and see Fossanova Abbey; and trains connect Frosinone's *FS* station (way out of town but connected by bus), with Naples, Cassino and Caserta.

Buses take about fifty minutes to reach **PRIVERNO**, another hilltop town with a pretty main square flanked by a Gothic town hall and a duomo from 1283 which apparently holds the relics of Saint Thomas Aquinas. About 5km outside the town, an hour or so's walk or reachable by regular bus from Piazza XX Settembre, the **Abbey of Fossanova** (summer daily 8am–noon & 4–7.30pm, winter daily 3.30–5.30pm) was where Aquinas died in 1274, en route between Naples and Lyon – a monastery of the Cistercian order that may tempt you off the road if you're waiting for a train at the nearby Priverno-Fossanova railway station, 2km beyond. It's a fairly tame complex on the whole, much restored, but its thirteenth-century Burgundian Gothic church is a refreshingly plain affair after the gaudiness of most Italian churches. A door leads from here out to a plain Romanesque cloister, with a garden in the centre and a chapter house off to one side, with wide windows through which lay brothers could watch the services (the corridor on the far side of the cloisters was for their use). A door to the left leads through a small separate courtyard to the guest wing where, at the northern end, Saint Thomas is supposed to have breathed his last.

Further south: Cassino and the Abbey of Montecassino

The town of **CASSINO**, fifty minutes down the railway line from Frosinone, is the site of another important monastery, the **Abbey of Montecassino** (daily 8am–noon & 3.30–6pm; free), founded in 529 by Saint Benedict after he left Subiaco (see p.651), on a spot to which he was guided by three ravens. This was for many years one of the most important and influential monastic complexes in the Christian world, its monks spreading the word as far away as Britain and Scandinavia and developing the tradition of culture and learning that was at the core of the Benedictine order. Over the years it has been repeatedly destroyed: its strategically vital position perched high on a mountaintop between Rome and Naples has been fought over by a succession of invaders, culminating in 1944 when Allied troops clashed with German forces in a battle that lasted nearly six months. The abbey was the key to the German presence in this part of Italy, and the Allies eventually bombed it to ruins in May 1944, losing over 1000 Polish lives in the process. It was rebuilt soon after, and the austere medieval style of its buildings has been followed faithfully, but it's really more impressive for its siting than for itself: much of the complex is not open to the public, and its sterile white central courtyard is engaging only for the views it gives over the surrounding hills and the Polish war cemetery below. The church, off here, in a hideously ornate Baroque style, has a small museum (L2000) containing incunabula, old manuscripts and suchlike. But otherwise you really feel that Montecassino's glory days firmly ended with the war.

The **town** below was fairly comprehensively destroyed too, and has very little appeal. There's a **tourist office** on Via Condotti (Mon–Sat 8.30am–2pm), on the opposite side of the centre to the train and bus station, and another at Corso della Repubblica 23 (Mon–Sat 9am–noon & 4–7pm). Buses scale the mountain to the abbey at 9.45am and 3.45pm each day – though if you miss one it's fairly easy to hitch. If you need to stay, hotels are at least cheap – pick up a list from the tourist office.

The southern Lazio coast

The Lazio **coast** to the south of Rome is a much more attractive proposition than that to the north. Its towns are more attractive, the water is less polluted, and in the further reaches, beyond the dreary flats of the Pontine Marshes and Monte Circeo, the shoreline begins to pucker into cliffs and coves that hint gently at the glories that await in Campania further south – all good either for day-trips and overnight outings from the city, or for a pleasant wayward route to Naples.

Anzio and Nettuno

About 40km south of Rome, and easily seen on a day trip, **ANZIO** is the first town of any note, centre of a lengthy spread of settlement that focuses on a lively central square and a busy fishing industry. Much of the town was damaged during a difficult Allied landing here on January 22, 1944, to which two military cemeteries (one British, one, at nearby Nettuno, American) bear testimony. But despite a pretty thorough rebuilding it's a likeable resort, still depending as much on fish as tourists for its livelihood. The town's seafood **restaurants** are reason enough to come, crowding together along the harbour and not unreasonably priced, and the **beaches**, which edge the coast on either side, don't get unbearably stuffed outside of August. Anzio is also a possible route on to the islands of Ponza or Ischia, or Naples, for which **hydrofoils** leave daily in summer – ask for timings at the tourist office in the harbour (daily 9am–12.30pm & 5–8pm, closed Wed & Sat pm).

NETTUNO, a couple of kilometres down the coast (and walkable by the coast road), is more of the same, but with slightly less beach space and water that's not so clear and calm. Again it's a mostly modern town, but there's a well-preserved old quarter, still walled, with a couple of trattorias on the main square – information from the **tourist office** on Via Gramsci, just off the main square (Mon–Sat 9am–1pm & 4–7pm).

The Pontine Marshes, Monte Circeo and San Felice

Beyond Anzio and Nettuno lie the **Pontine Marshes**, until sixty years ago a boggy plain prone to malaria that was populated by few except water buffalo. Julius Caesar had planned to drain the area but was assassinated before he could carry out his plan, and it was left to Mussolini to reclaim the region in 1928 – in a scheme that built a series of spanking new towns and provided acres of fertile, fresh farmland.

LATINA lies at the centre of the development, the provincial capital, founded in 1932, and centre of the thriving local agricultural economy, though of little interest now save for its transport connections. If you do end up here, it's instructive to at least have a brief walk around the town centre, which is something of a monument to Fascism, large open squares and sturdy-looking buildings interrupting broad avenues radiating out with classical uniformity from the central Piazza del Popolo.

The area around **SABAUDIA**, another new town 20km away on the coast, gives some impression of what the marshes were like before they were drained, poised between two lagoons that make up the coastal Lago di Sabaudia. A large area to the north of the town, the Salve del Circeo, four coastal lakes, the huge bulk of Monte Circeo to the south and the offshore island of Zannone together form the **Parco Nazional del Circeo**, set up in 1934 to preserve something of the marshes' wildlife and almost sinister natural beauty. It's a fine spot for birds: all kinds of water species can be seen here – herons, buzzards, storks, fish hawks, and rare species like the peregrine falcon and Cavaliere d'Italia; and the flora includes eucalyptus groves, oaks, elms, ash and wild flowers in spring.

Monte Circeo itself lies to the south of Sabaudia across several kilometres of gleaming water, the sandy beach coming to an end at the sixteenth-century **Torre Paola**, set at the entrance of a canal linking Lago di Sabaudia to the sea. There's a little pier usually occupied by a group of fishermen, from where the road turns inland and skirts the northern slopes of the mountain, passing through splendid woods. After about 4km a road branches off to the right and rounds the mountain to emerge at **SAN FELICE CIRCEO**, a picturesque village of pretty stone houses bleached yellow by the sun that can be a fairly trendy spot in summer, its marina chock-a-block with fancy motor launches and yachts and its sandy beaches crowded with glistening oiled bodies. The small **Piazza Municipio** has a tourist office and a local museum, open in July, August and September, from behind which a road winds its way up to the summit of the **mountain** and the site of an ancient **temple**. Not surprisingly, the views are marvellous. There's a large carpark at the top, with a bar open in summer, near to which is the entrance to the sparse relics of a Roman town – *Circeii* – and its rather better preserved cyclopean walls, not unlike the constructions in the Ciociaria (see p.652).

Back in the village you can rest up on the beaches or hire a boat out to the famous **Grotta della Maga Circe** – though this is only possible in season. For quieter swimming-spots, take the road towards the lighthouse, the "Faro di Torre Cervia", which after a couple of kilometres reaches a secluded rocky spot – great for snorkelling. It's handy, too, for the *Il Faro* hotel a little further on, which has a **restaurant** serving good seafood on its sea-facing terrace.

Terracina

A further 15km down the coast from San Felice (buses half-hourly), or, if you're coming from Rome, a short train ride on the local line from Priverno, **TERRACINA** is an immediately likeable little town, divided between a tumbledown old quarter high on the hill above and a lively newer area by the sea. During Classical times it was an important staging-post on the Appian Way, which reaches the sea here; nowadays it's primarily a seaside resort, and one of the nicest along this stretch of coast, with good, ample beaches and frequent connections on to the other points of interest around.

The Town

Terracina splits into two distinct parts, the old town on the hill and the new town below, whose main street, Via Roma, is a continuation of Via Appia, cutting through the town to the sea. The centre of the old quarter is **Piazza Municipio**, which occupies the site of the old Roman forum and now focuses on the colonnade of the town's **Duomo**, with its elegant mossy campanile. It's an endearing little church with a fine mosaic floor and a beautiful mosaic-studded pulpit, built over the remains of a Roman temple, some of which are visible inside.

Terracina's main attraction, and rightly so, is the **Temple of Jupiter Anxurus**, which crowns the hill above the town. Take the steps up from Piazza Municipio onto Via Anxur and follow this for 200m, from where you can either follow the winding road to the top (forty minutes) or, 100m after the sign to the temple, turn off right and climb up by way of a rocky path – which takes half as long. There's a bar at the top for recovering after the climb. The temple is believed to date back to the first century BC and was connected to Terracina by some lengthy walls, although all that's now visible is the base of the structure, in the form of an arched terrace from which the views are stupendous – Terracina boxed neatly below and the bay curving round on either side.

Practicalities

If you're staying, there are a number of reasonably priced **hotels**, best of which is the very pleasant and friendly *Hegelberger*, up in the old town at Via San Domenico 2 (☎0773/701.697; ④); in the lower town there's the strangely named *For You*, right next to the beach at Viale Circe 116 (☎0773/730.914; ⑤), and the cheaper *Vittoria*, Piazza

Mazzini 1 (☎0773/727.603; ④), although both may insist on half-board. The nearest **campsite** is the *Costazzurra* (☎0773/702.589), a fifteen-minute walk south along the coast road.

The **tourist office**, just off Piazza Mazzini (July–Sept daily 9am–noon & 5–7pm; rest of the year daily 9am–noon; ☎0773/727.759), has more information, hotel lists and a map of the town. **Bikes** are for hire at *Caccia e Pesca*, Via Roma 9, for around L8000 a day. For **eating** you could do worse than stop in at *Pizzeria Marino* on Piazza Repubblica, whose low-priced pizzas are very popular locally; if you don't fancy pizza, the *Miramare*, Viale Circe 32, at the end of Viale Vittoria, is also cheap and has a convivial terrace. In the old town, try the excellent *Vesuvio* on Via San Domenico. As for the **beaches**, apart from a scrubby oval of beach in the centre of town, they stretch north pretty much indefinitely from beyond the main town harbour, and are large enough not to get overcrowded.

The coast to Campania: Sperlonga, Gaeta, Formia, Minturno

The coast south of Terracina is probably Lazio's prettiest stretch, the cliff punctured by tiny beaches signposted enticingly from the road. **SPERLONGA**, built high on a rocky promontory, is a fashionable spot locally, its whitewashed houses and narrow streets more Greek than Italian in feel, and sadly given over entirely to tourists during summer (though cars are not allowed into the centre). There are some excellent restaurants specialising in seafood, and a few pricey *pensioni*, but these are often full and you might find it easier to hole up in Terracina and come to Sperlonga for the day (half-hourly buses). The beach, certainly, is worth stopping for, a lengthy stretch of sand to the south with the town as backdrop and abundant space.

Between Sperlonga and Gaeta the coast steepens markedly, with yet more appealing beaches, and, if you're camping, any number of handy campsites. A couple of kilometres from Sperlonga, there's a small museum and the remains of the **Villa of Tiberius** (open year-round; sunrise–sunset) – worth a stop if you're independently mobile. The house was built around a large ornamental pool which extends into a large grotto in the cliff face. The museum holds finds from the villa, centrepiece of which is a large complex group of statues in the style of the Vatican's *Laocoon* (see "Rome", p.616), possibly by the same sculptors.

Some 10km further on, **GAETA** signals the beginning of its broad bay from its high castle-topped headland, an appealing place at first sight (especially from the southern side), piled up untidily onto the head of its defensive rock. The fortress here was impregnable: it resisted Gothic and Saracen invaders and the town flourished under the Normans, some of its architecture dating back to that time – and earlier. The tiny church of **San Giovanni al Mare**, by the water, hails from the tenth century; and on the summit of Monte Orlando, now a park, there's the classical tomb of one **Munatius Plancus**, the founder of Lyons, decorated with a frieze showing scenes of battle. Close by, a **terrace** gives fine views over the Serapo bay below, next to which the small church of **Santuario del Crocifisso** is built on a boulder breaching the chasm of Montagna Spaccata, literally suspended a few hundred feet above the sea.

But for all this, it's Gaeta's modern-day role as a naval port that colours the place most significantly. Much of the old town is closed off to the public (parts of the port and the castle itself) and the quayside bars advertise "burgers and chips" to visiting American servicemen off the warships often docked in the harbour. The main square, **Piazza del Municipio**, flanks the portside and is a lively enough spot, with a small market; and there's a **tourist office** (for maps) on Piazza XIX Maggio. But you'd do best to visit Gaeta for the **beaches** north of the headland – though be warned that these, especially the closest *Spiaggia di Serapo*, can get quite packed and have been bought up almost exclusively by restaurants.

Around the bay, hard under the glowering backdrop of the Monti Aurunci, **FORMIA** is not much better, a largely modern town that was an important resort during Roman times. Cicero had a villa here, at which he was murdered by Mark Antony's soldiers in 44 AD after opposing the triumvirate that had succeeded Caesar. There are **beaches** to the north of the town centre, and a **tourist office** just behind the central Piazza Mattei (Mon–Fri 8.30am–1.30pm, Sat 9am–noon). But otherwise Formia is more a stopover than a stop in itself, with plentiful connections on to Naples, Rome and inland to Cassino, and regular ferries and hydofoils to Ponza. If you're taking an early boat, the *Ariston* at Via Cristoforo Colombo 19 (☎0771/7700.405; ⑥) is the most convenient **hotel** to the harbour, but is expensive and rather characterless; the *Marino*, Piazza Marconi 5 (☎0771/771.940; ④), is much cheaper, and not a great deal less convenient. For **food**, try *Muro di Nerva* a little way north of the *Ariston* hotel on the right of the main Viale dell'Unità d'Italia – friendly and with excellent fish.

A few kilometres south of Formia – and the next stop on the train – **MINTURNO** is the last town before the Campania border, a maze of tiny lanes and vaulted streets oddly reminiscent of an Arab *medina*. Its massive crumbling **castle**, on the main square, was owned until the middle of this century by the Carraciolo-Carafa dynasty; a plaque on the west wall recalls a visit by Saint Thomas Aquinas in 1272. Behind, the town's **Duomo** is a Norman structure not unlike that of nearby Sessa Arunca or Ravello, with a similar colourfully mosaiced pulpit. About 4km south of town are the ruins of the ancient Roman port of **Minturnae** (daily 9am–6pm; L5000), a once flourishing town that became depopulated as this low-lying area grew more malarial. Most striking among the rubble are the remains of a large amphitheatre, below which there's a small antiquarium containing finds from around the site and a broken-down aqueduct that runs for 2km southwest. A worthy stop if you're travelling south by car; otherwise stay on the train for Naples.

The Pontine Islands

Scattered across the sea between Rome and Naples, the **Pontine Islands** are one of Italy's least well-known island groupings, relatively unvisited by all except Italians. Volcanic in origin, only two are inhabited, **Ponza** and **Ventotene**, of which only Ponza supports any kind of tourist industry. Visit between June and the end of August and you'll find this well developed, many people coming here as an alternative to crowded Cápri; at any other time the island is yours for the asking.

As for **getting to the islands**, you can reach **Ponza** from a number of points on the mainland during the summer. From **Formia**, there are year-round services every day except Wednesday consisting of a twice-daily ferry and a twice-daily hydrofoil. There are also year-round ferries once daily from **Terracina** (twice daily in July and August), and at least twice-daily hydrofoils from **Anzio** between June and September. From each port, prices for ferries are around L20,000 return, for hydrofoils about double that – although they take under half as long.

To reach **Ventotene** from the mainland you can go from **Formia** or **Anzio**: ferries run once daily, though at variable times, hydrofoils twice daily every day except Tuesday. You can also travel on from **Ponza to Ventotene** by hydrofoil twice daily, every day.

Ponza

Even **PONZA**, the main island of the Pontine group, is manageably small, a sharp, rocky hunk of land just five miles end to end and at its widest point a mile across. Ferries sail to **PONZA TOWN**, one of the most beautiful small towns along this coast, which is heaped around its bay in a series of neat pastel-coloured pyramids, its flat-roofed houses focusing on the pink semicircle that curls around the fishing harbour.

It's a marvellous place to rest up for a while: designer boutiques and souvenir shops are still thin on the ground, and although there's not a lot specifically to see on the island, the town is a fun place to wander through, particularly at *passeggiata* time, when the crowds turn out to parade along the yellow-painted **Municipio** arcade of shops and cafés. To laze and swim, there's a small **beach** in the town, which is clean, and it's a ten-minute walk to the other side of the island to the **Chiaia di Luna** beach: a sheer sickle of cliff lined by a slender rim of sand – though be warned that the waves here are much choppier than those on the mainland-facing side of the island.

The only other real settlement on the island is **LA FORNA**, a wide green bay dotted with huddles of houses. There's a beach here, but a small dirty one, and you'd be better off following the path down from the road around the bay to the rocks and swimming from there: the water is lovely and clear, and, with the so-called **Piscina Naturale**, perfect for sheltered swimming when the fishing boats have finished for the day. For really secluded swimming, you can also take a boat from here (L7000 per person return) around the headland to **Spiaggia Santa Lucia**, where you're likely to have the beach to yourself.

Settlement straggles on from La Forna towards the sharp northern end of the island, where the road ends abruptly and a steep stony path (to the right) leads down to more rocks from which you can swim.

PRACTICAL DETAILS

The **tourist office** in Ponza Town (daily 9am–1pm & 4–8pm; ☎0771/80.031), up the hill from the *Banco di Napoli* on the right side of the harbour, has maps and accommodation lists. You may well be accosted with offers of **rooms** as you get off the ferry: if so, L60,000 a double is a fair price; if not, the woman at Via Chiaia di Luna 8 (☎0771/80.043) takes in visitors for a negotiable fee. Of the island's **hotels**, the cheapest in Ponza Town is the *Luisa*, on Via Chiaia di Luna (☎0771/80.128; ⑥); *Gennarino al Mare*, next to the town beach (☎0771/80.071; ⑧), is much more expensive but worth the splurge, and it has its own restaurant. In La Forna, the *Ortensia* (☎0771/808.922; ⑥) is the best option. **Getting around**, there's an island bus service connecting Ponza Town with other points on the island, including La Forna, roughly hourly. You can rent scooters from a place by the main harbour, by the first tunnel, for L60,000 a half-day. Motorboats, too, are a good (sometimes the only) way of seeing the most dramatic parts of the island: L70,000 a day from a number of outlets around the harbour.

For **food** you're spoilt for choice: there are plenty of restaurants in Ponza Town and most are good, albeit expensive. Try *Al Delfino Blu* in the harbour, which serves the local speciality of *zuppa di lenticchie* (lentil soup); the *Ippocampo*, in the Municipio above, does good pasta and fish; or the *Gennarino al Mare* hotel has a good restaurant.

Ventotene

The only other inhabited Pontine island, **VENTOTENE** is quite separate from Ponza, situated a fair way south, flatter and much less lush and green. It's much smaller, too, and although it makes a nice stop on a leisurely route to Naples, it's unlikely to detain you for long – though if you do want to stay, there are a couple of hotels. The single town – village really – has a population of around 500, its dusty piazza home to a museum displaying finds from an imperial era villa, remains of which you can see spread over the headland to the left of the village. On the other side, there's a small beach of grey volcanic sand.

travel details

Trains

Frosinone to: Cassino (12 daily; 1hr 10min); Caserta (8 daily; 1hr 10min); Naples (6 daily; 1hr 55min).

Priverno-Fossanova to: Terracina (10 daily; 40min).

Rome (Termini) to: Cerveteri (11 daily; 45min); Civitavecchia (8 daily; 45min); Tarquinia (5 daily; 3hr 30min); Anzio/Nettuno (hourly; 1hr); Latina (hourly; 35min); Priverno-Fossanova (hourly; 1hr); Formia (hourly; 1hr 25min); Naples (hourly; 2hr 30min); Florence (hourly; 2–3hr 30min); Bologna (12 daily; 3hr 20min); Milan (12 daily; 3hr–5hr 40min); Ancona (8 daily; 3hr 15min–6hr); Pescara (4 daily; 3hr 40min); L'Aquila (5 daily; 4hr 40min).

Rome (Laziale) to: Bracciano (8 daily; 40min); Palestrina (5 daily; 35min); Anagni (14 daily; 55min); Viterbo (6 daily; 2hr).

Rome (Ostiense) to: Ostia Lido (every 20min; 30min).

Rome (San Pietro) to: Bracciano (8 daily; 40min); Viterbo (6 daily; 1hr 45min).

Rome (Piazzale Flaminia/Roma Nord line) to: Viterbo (5 daily; 2hr 45min).

Buses

Frosinone to: Priverno (hourly; 50min).

Rome (Anagnina) to: Palestrina (every 30min; 1hr).

Rome (EUR Fermi) to: Sabaudia (12 daily; 1hr 30min); San Felice (12 daily; 2hr); Terracina (hourly; 2hr).

Rome (Rebibbia) to: Subiaco (hourly; 2hr); Tivoli (every 15min; 45min).

Rome (Via Lepanto) to: Cerveteri (every 30min; 1hr); Civitavecchia (20 daily; 1hr 30min); Tarquinia (10 daily; 2hr).

Rome (Saxa Rubra) to: Viterbo (6 daily; 1hr 30min).

Terracina to: Cassino (1 daily; 2hr 30min); Sperlonga (half-hourly; 30min); Formia (half-hourly; 1hr); Sabaudia (hourly; 1hr); San Felice Circeo (half-hourly; 30min).

Viterbo to: Bagnaia (hourly; 20min); Bomarzo (6 daily; 40min); Caprarola (6 daily; 30min); Civitavecchia (5 daily; 1hr 20min); Tarquinia (8 daily; 1hr); Tuscania (14 daily; 30min).

Subiaco to: Frosinone (3 daily; 2hr).

Ferries

Civitavecchia to: Golfo Aranci (2 daily; 9hr); Olbia (1 daily; 7hr); Calgliari (1 daily; 13hr).

Formia to: Ponza (2 daily; 2hr 30min); Ventotene (2 daily; 2hr 10min).

Terracina to: Ponza (2 daily; 1hr).

Hydrofoils

Anzio to: Ponza (3 daily; 1hr 10min); Ventotene (2 daily; 1hr 10min).

Formia to: Ponza (2 daily; 1hr 15min); Ventotene (2 daily; 1hr 15min).

Ponza to: Ventotene (2 daily; 40min).

CHAPTER TWELVE

ABRUZZO AND MOLISE

One region until 1963, **Abruzzo** and **Molise** – previously just plain Abruzzi – together make Italy's transition from North to South. Both are sparsely populated mountainous regions prone to earthquakes, and both have always been outside the mainstream of Italian affairs. You could spend a whole and very varied holiday in **Abruzzo**. Bordered by the Appenines, it holds some of Italy's wildest terrain: silent valleys, vast untamed mountain plains and abandoned hill-villages, as well as some great historic towns, many of them rarely visited by outsiders. But this is only half the story: the Abruzzese have done much to pull their region out of the poverty trap, developing resorts on the long, sandy Adriatic coastline and exploiting the tourist potential of the large, mountainous National Park – actions you may balk at until you see the poverty and neglect of Molise.

Molise is still manifestly a part of the South, its countryside gentler than Abruzzo, its mountains less forbidding, and its villages and towns less appealing – either modern and functional to withstand the shock of earthquakes, or rotting into quiet ruin due to lack of funds and organisation. The lasting impression is one of despair and of a people unused to outsiders, let alone foreigners. You may, however, pass through on your way south to Puglia, and it's feasible to stop off for a few days in the seaside town of Térmoli, visit one of Italy's least-visited Roman sites, Saepinum, or go hiking in the Matese mountains on the border with Campania. Don't expect to rush through, though; getting around in both regions on public transport demands patience and the careful studying of bus and train timetables.

ABRUZZO

Over the last century or so **Abruzzo** has become better known for its emigrants than for itself. These number Dante Gabriele Rossetti, film star Alan Ladd, and, most recently, Madonna, whose ancestors left Abruzzo to seek their fortunes in Britain and America. They left behind them hilltop villages and medieval towns overlooked by mountain ranges in which wolves, bears and chamois roamed and legends of witches and werewolves persisted.

Abruzzo has now entered the twentieth century, but although its coast is lined by a string of lucrative resorts, and its wolves, rounded up, enclosed and demystified, have become a major tourist attraction in its **National Park**, there are still vast tracts of unspoilt countryside and villages where life is hard and strangers a novelty. There's a strong, unshakeable sense of the provincial here, and although the region's costumes, crafts and festivals are now popular tourist attractions, there is little hype, and you could almost believe that the traditions are perpetuated as much for the locals as for their power to attract revenue.

L'Aquila, at the foot of Gran Sasso, and **Sulmona** just to its south, are the most visited of Abruzzo's historic towns. Both are good bases: Sulmona is convenient if you're coming by train from Rome, L'Aquila if you're approaching from Umbria. The hill-villages around L'Aquila are worth visiting if you're based here for any length of time: those below the **Gran Sasso**, the Appenines' highest peak, are deeply rural places, where time can seem to have stopped in the fifteenth century; **Bominaco**, to the east, has two impressive churches, one a perfect and pristine example of the Romanesque, the other covered with Byzantine-style frescoes. The rail route from the Marche runs down the coast, through Abruzzo's numerous grid-plan resorts – none of them anything special, but adequate sun-and-sand stopovers. The only resort really worth considering is **Pineto**, with a pine-fringed beach and bus connections inland to the sleepy old town of **Atri**, whose cathedral holds a stunning cycle of frescoes.

South of Sulmona, Abruzzo is more traditional. In **Scanno** the women wear costumes that – like the Scannese – originated in Asia Minor, and make intricate lace on cylindrical cushions known as *tómbole*. Just down the road, **Cocullo** is a scruffy hill-village that on the first Thursday in May hosts one of Europe's most bizarre religious festivals – draping a statue of the local saint with live snakes and parading it through the streets.

L'Aquila

At first sight **L'AQUILA** seems a severe city. Overlooked by the bulk of the Gran Sasso, which cuts it off from the coastal province of Téramo, its sombre grey stone resists even the strongest of sunlight, creating an atmosphere of almost Teutonic austerity. Founded by a German emperor, its brooding northern air is apt, while the story of its foundation is worthy of a Grimm fairy tale. In 1242 Frederick II drew together the populations from 99 Abruzzo villages to form a new city. Each village built its own church, piazza and quarter: there's a medieval fountain with 99 spouts; and the town hall clock still chimes 99 times every night.

L'Aquila may no longer be the city of 99 churches, most of them having been destroyed in earthquakes, but two magnificent ones remain. And the city itself is a brighter place than you might expect – an appealing blend of ancient and modern, with a university, smart shops, bustling streets and a daily market where you can buy anything from black-market cassettes to traditional Abruzzese craftwork.

Arrival, information and accommodation

L'Aquila's **train station** is some way out of the centre, connected with the main part of town by regular buses. Long-distance **buses** stop on Piazza Battaglione Alpini, at the beginning of the old centre's main street, Corso Vittorio Emanuele. The **information booth** there has bus timetables covering L'Aquila province. The most convenient of L'Aquila's **tourist offices** is on Piazza Santa Maria Paganica (Mon–Fri 8am–2pm & 4–6pm, Sat 8am–2pm; ☎0862/410.808); there's another at Via XX Settembre 8 (Mon–Sat 9am–1pm & 3.30–6.30pm, also open Sun in summer), and a *Centro Turistico di Gran Sasso*, next to the Banca di Napoli on Corso Vittorio Emanuele (Mon–Sat 9am–1pm & 3.30–6.30pm; ☎0862/22.146), which has information on the province as well as the town. Hiking information can be gleaned from *Club Alpino Italia*, Via XX Settembre 17 (daily 7–8pm).

The main drawback of L'Aquila is its lack of cheap **hotels**, and you should definitely book in advance if you're planning to stay. The *Aurora*, Via Cimino 21 (☎0862/22.053; ③), off Piazza Duomo, and the *Orazi*, Via Roma 175, a goodish walk from Piazza Annunziata (☎0862/69.545; ③), are the cheapest options. If you can afford a little more, your first choice should be the atmospheric old *Sole*, Largo Silvestro dell'Aquila 4 (☎0862/24.041; ④); if that's full, there's the modern, functional *Castello* on Piazza Battaglione Alpini (☎0862/419.147; ⑥) as a last resort.

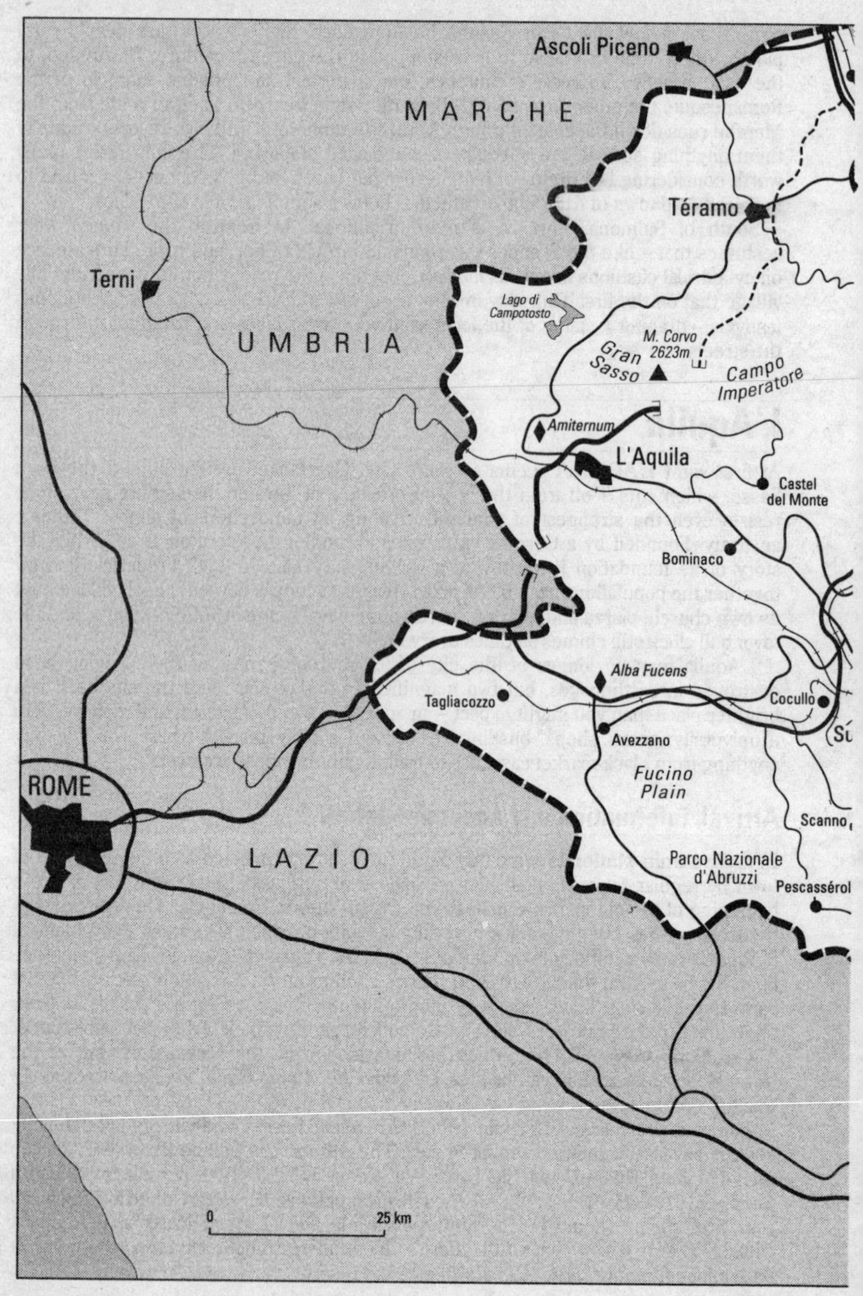
Ascoli Piceno
MARCHE
Téramo
Terni
Lago di Campotosto
UMBRIA
M. Corvo 2623m
Gran Sasso
Campo Imperatore
Amiternum
L'Aquila
Castel del Monte
Bominaco
Alba Fucens
Tagliacozzo
Cocullo
Avezzano
Fucino Plain
ROME
Scanno
LAZIO
Parco Nazionale d'Abruzzi
Pescassérol
0
25 km

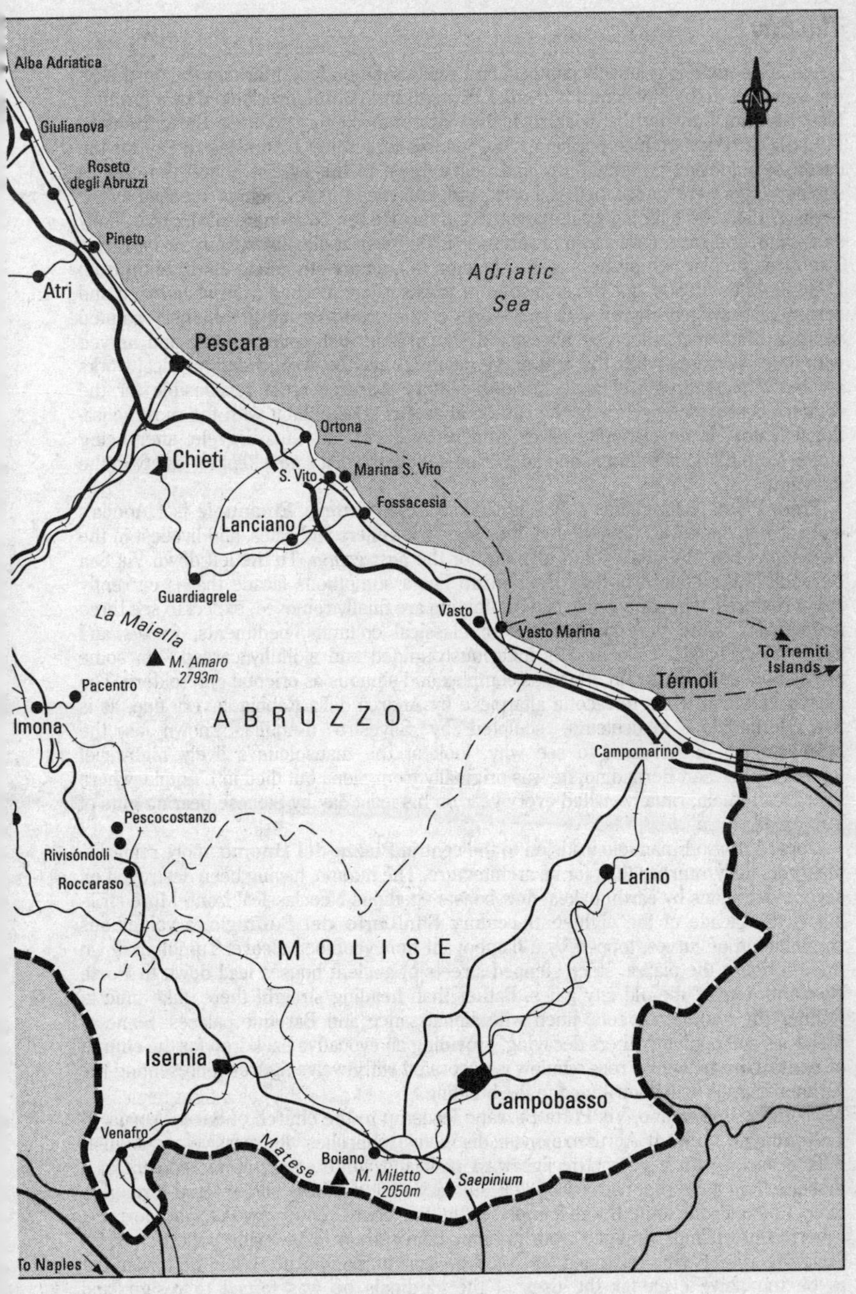
Alba Adriatica
Giulianova
Roseto degli Abruzzi
Pineto
Atri
Adriatic Sea
Pescara
Ortona
Chieti
S. Vito
Marina S. Vito
Fossacesia
Lanciano
Guardiagrele
Vasto
Vasto Marina
To Tremiti Islands
La Maiella
M. Amaro 2793m
Pacentro
Imona
ABRUZZO
Térmoli
Campomarino
Pescocostanzo
Rivisóndoli
Roccaraso
Larino
MOLISE
Isernia
Campobasso
Venafro
Matese
Boiano
M. Miletto 2050m
Saepinium
To Naples

The City

L'Aquila's **centre** is relatively compact and easily seen on foot. Marking the northeastern entrance to the city centre is **Piazza Battaglione Alpini**, overlooked by a formidable **Castello**, built by the Spanish in the sixteenth century to keep the citizens of L'Aquila in order after an uprising. The Spanish forced the L'Aquilans to pay for the castle by imposing an annual tax and heavy fines. In the Fascist period the castle's surroundings were landscaped as a park, and, following the devastation wreaked by the Nazis in 1943, the building was renovated and the **Museo Nazionale d'Abruzzo** (daily 9am–2pm, open afternoons also in summer; L3000) established in the former barracks. The most popular exhibit here is the skeleton of a mammoth, found about 14km from L'Aquila in the 1950s, but the collection of works of art rescued from abandoned and earthquake-ravaged churches is also worth a brief visit. Among the clumsily painted wooden Madonnas, those by Silvestro d'Aquila stand out, spare, ascetic and nerved with inner strength, while the best of the paintings are the dreamy and mystical works attributed to Andrea Delitio, a fifteenth-century Abruzzo artist responsible for the region's best fresco cycle – in the cathedral at Atri. The exhibit with the most sensational history is an elaborate silver crucifix by Nicola da Guardiagrele: after being stolen from L'Aquila's duomo and auctioned at Sotheby's, it's now kept for safety in the museum.

From Piazza Battaglione Alpini, arcaded **Corso Vittorio Emanuele** is L'Aquila's main street, lined with upmarket clothes shops, jewellers and cafés, and liveliest in the evenings when L'Aquila's youth turn out for the *passeggiata*. To the left down Via San Bernadino, the church of **San Bernadino** has a sumptuous facade that is currently being restored; when the gauze and scaffolding are finally removed, expect to see three magnificent white tiers bedecked with classical columns, pediments, friezes and inscriptions. Inside, its ceiling is luxuriously gilded and skilfully carved – in some places bold and chunky, in others as complex and sinuous as oriental embroidery. The glazed blue and white terracotta altarpiece by Andrea della Robbia is very fine, as is San Bernadino's mausoleum, sculpted by Silvestro d'Aquila, known as the Michelangelo of Abruzzo; to see why, look at the mausoleum's lively high-relief figures. As for San Bernadino, he was originally from Siena but died in L'Aquila, where his relics remain, ritually visited every year on his feast day by Sienese bearing gifts of Tuscan oil.

Corso Vittorio Emanuele leads on to the central **Piazza del Duomo**, more remarkable for its daily **market** than for its architecture. The duomo, having been destroyed on several occasions by earthquakes, now boasts a tedious Neoclassical front. More striking is the facade of the eighteenth-century **Santuario del Suffragio**, a voluptuous combination of curves, topped by a flamboyant honeycombed alcove. Tumbling down the hill below the piazza, steep stepped streets of ancient houses lead down to **Porta Bazzano**, one of the old city gates. Rather than heading straight there, take time to wander the abutting streets, lined with Renaissance and Baroque palaces. Some of these are still opulent, others decaying, providing an evocative backdrop for the church of **Santa Giusta**, whose rose window is decorated with twelve figures representing the various artisans who contributed to the building.

From Porta Bazzano, Via Porta Bazzano leads up to the church of **Santa Maria di Collemaggio**. One of Abruzzo's most distinctive churches, its massive rectangular bulk is faced with a geometric jigsaw of pink and white stone, more redolent of a mosque than a church, pierced by delicate, lacy rose windows and entered through a fancy Romanesque arch. It was founded in the thirteenth century by Peter of Morrone, a hermit unwillingly dragged from his mountain retreat to be made pope by power-hungry cardinals who reckoned he would be easy to manipulate. When he turned out to be too naive even for the uses of the cardinals he was forced to resign, and

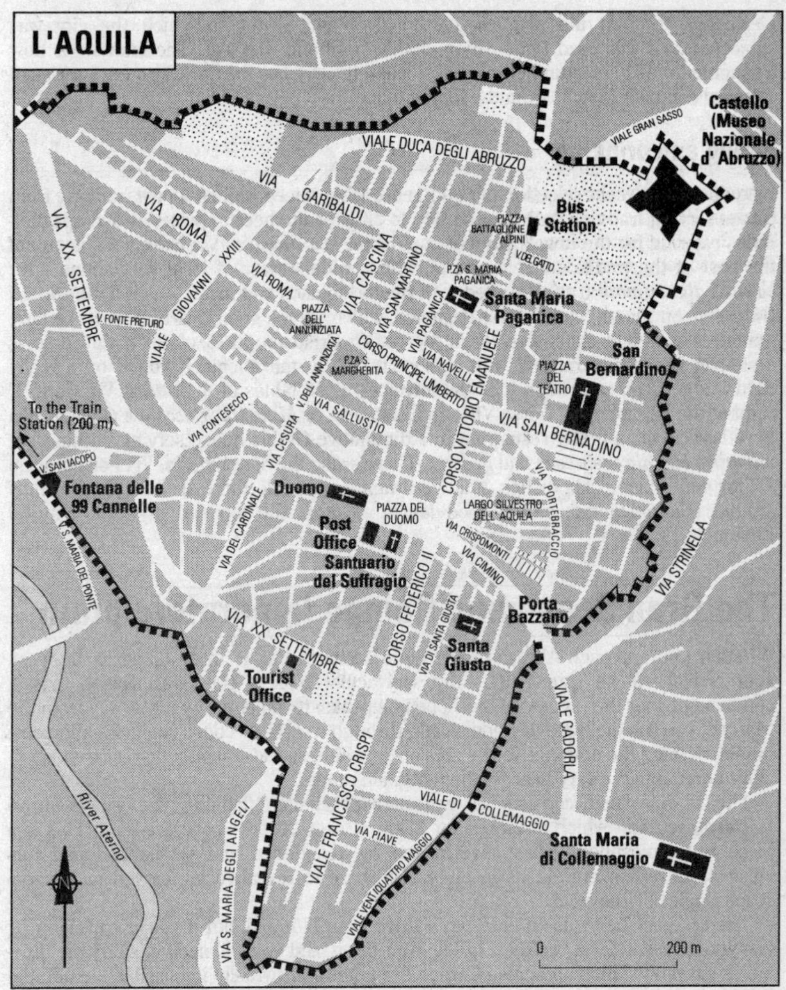

posthumously compensated for the ordeal by being canonised. Thieves stole his relics in April 1988, intending to hold them to ransom, but they were soon safely retrieved and returned to their grandiose Palladian-style sarcophagus. One of the few things Peter managed to do during his short reign was to install a Holy Door in the church – opened every year on August 28, when sinners pass through it to procure absolution.

Finally there's L'Aquila's best-known sight, the unique 99-spouted fountain, **Fontana delle 99 Cannelle**, outside the town centre close to the train station, tucked behind the medieval **Porta Riviera**. Set around three sides of a sunken piazza, overlooked by abandoned houses and the tiny church of **San Vito**, the water pours from an unknown source through 93 toby-jug gargoyles (six are undecorated), each a symbol for one of the villages that formed the city. This constant supply of fresh water sustained the

L'Aquilans through the plagues, earthquakes and sieges to which the city was subjected, and was used for washing clothes until after the war. The fountain is now frequented mostly on summer evenings, when it serves as the backdrop for a series of classical concerts (details from the tourist office).

Eating and drinking

L'Aquila has a decent selection of good, reasonably priced **places to eat**, ranging from places serving traditional Abruzzese fare to cheap and cheerful pizzerias and spaghetterias catering for the town's student population. *La Mimosa*, Via Navelli 22, is one of the best of the traditional restaurants, with a wide variety of local specialities – try *bauletti alla mimosa* (ravioli stuffed with ricotta, spinach and meat) – as is *Trattoria del Giaguaro*, on Piazza Santa Maria Paganica, which serves good hearty Abruzzese fare; neither is especially expensive. *Stella Alpina*, Via Crispomonti 15, off the main Corso, is a simple, family-run trattoria with a more run-of-the-mill menu. If you're on a really tight budget, you can rough it at the formica-topped tables of *Il Gatto* at Via Gatto 1, right at the beginning of Corso Vittorio Emanuele, or *Minestra, Baccalá e Gnocchi*, Via Fortebraccio 49, a pretty restaurant in a diminutive Gothic house serving nothing but *minestra*, *baccalá* (salt cod) and *gnocchi*. There's also the *Spaghetteria*, Via Fortebraccio 27, for good-value pasta dishes. If all you want is a **snack**, there are lots of *alimentari* around Piazza Duomo, and a good *tavola calda* at the top end of Corso Vittorio Emanuele.

The Gran Sasso and Campo Imperatore plain

Whether you approach Abruzzo from the Marche in the north or Rome in the west, your arrival will be signalled by the spectacular bulk of the **Gran Sasso** massif, containing by far the highest of the Appenine peaks. If you come by motorway from the Marche, you'll actually travel underneath, through a recently constructed ten-kilometre tunnel, passing the entrance to the area's worst-kept secret – an atomic research laboratory bored into the very heart of the mountain range.

The massif itself consists of two parallel chains, flanking the vast **Campo Imperatore** plain which stretches for 27km at over 2000m above sea-level. This is a bleak but atmospheric place, overlooked by abandoned and semi-abandoned hill-villages, its rolling grasslands in places laid bare to reveal rocks, carved into moonscape ripples by the wind.

The itinerary below is an easy day's drive from L'Aquila, but if you're travelling by bus you'll need at least two days to see everything, and you will need to study the timetables carefully. Hitching across Campo Imperatore is virtually impossible outside the summer months, and even then it's not easy; if you're without your own transport you may have to content yourself with viewing the plain by cable car and taking buses up to the hill-villages from L'Aquila via the less interesting southern route.

Fonte Cerreto and the Corno Grande

The first leg, however, is easy. Bus #6 from L'Aquila's Corso Vittorio Emanuele runs regularly up to **FONTE CERRETO**, the gateway to Campo Imperatore – basically two hotels, a restaurant and a campsite clustered around a cable car station. Most of these were built in the Thirties as part of Mussolini's scheme to keep Italians fit by encouraging them to take exercise in the mountains. Ironically he was imprisoned here in 1943, first at the *Villetta* inn in Fonte Cerreto, and then at the *Albergo-Rifugio Campo*

Imperatore, a grim hotel at the top of the cable car route. Apparently it was with some trepidation that Mussolini stepped into the cable car, enquiring whether it was safe and then hastily covering his cowardice by adding, "Not for my sake, you understand, because my life is over. But for those who accompany me." *Il Duce* apparently spent his days at the hotel on a diet of eggs, rice, boiled onions and grapes, contemplating suicide. Hitler came to his rescue, dispatching an ace-pilot to airlift him out in a tiny aeroplane, which is supposed to have terrified Mussolini almost as much as the cable car.

The cable car which so terrified Mussolini has recently been replaced by a new one, though you can still stay at his prison hotel; it is not, however, especially cheap. Fortunately there's more realistically priced accommodation at the *Ostello Campo Imperatore* (☎0862/411.202; ①), which occupies the old cable car station. Alternatively, you could sleep in the *Duca degli Abruzzi rifugio* (2388m), a short walk beyond. It's run by the Rome branch of the *Club Alpino Italia* (☎06/654.3424), and is now the most popular starting-point for assaults on the Gran Sasso's highest peak, the **Corno Grande** (2912m).

Outside the summer months, the ascent of Corno Grande, which is the Gran Sasso's highest peak and at all times includes some fairly killing scree-climbing and alarming descents, should only be attempted by experienced climbers. Perhaps the most challenging route is the tough trek from the *Ostello Campo Imperatore* right across the mountain range, taking in the Corno Grande, sleeping over at the *Rifugio Franchetti* (☎0861/95.634), also open June to mid-September, and then walking across to the Arapietra ridge. From here a ski-lift will take you down to the ugly ski resort of PRATI DI TIVO – which nevertheless offers some of the best views of Gran Sasso – from where you can get a bus to the town of Teramo. If you're going to do any of the Gran Sasso trails, you'll need the *CAI* Gran Sasso d'Italia map, and should check out weather conditions from the *CAI* office in L'Aquila.

The Campo Imperatore plain

For non-hikers the road continues from Fonte Cerreto across **Campo Imperatore**, whose weird rock formations have been prime fodder for film-makers over the years, masquerading as everything from the surface of Mars to a remote region of Tibet. Film crews and the occasional hiker apart, the only people you're likely to meet here are nomadic shepherds, who bring their flocks up to the plain for summer grazing after wintering in the south – a practice that has been going on since Roman times. Although the sheep are now transported by lorry rather than on foot, a peep in one of the shepherd's shacks sprinkled across the plain suggests that their living standards have changed very little.

The plain is fringed with hilltop villages, some with a few hotels and villas, others virtually abandoned. **CASTEL DEL MONTE** is a medieval village, heavily fortified and crowned with a ruined castle and church, that is now a minor tourist attraction. It was the scene of a chilling incident early this century when workmen discovered caves underneath them, filled with clothed skeletons seated on cane chairs. This was the traditional way of burying the village's dead until 1860, when an outbreak of cholera alerted the inhabitants to the health hazard. All the skeletons that could be found were burned; those that weren't were lost forever when the cave was set alight and later filled in. As for the rest of the village, the steep streets and dark tunnels were designed to slow down invaders; windows, strategically placed high up, enabled the inhabitants to chuck hot oil down on the heads of unwelcome visitors. It's still not a particularly welcoming place. Visitors are viewed as a useful source of revenue, but be prepared, especially out of season, to be stared at; and women can expect to feel uncomfortable when they enter the bars.

If you want to stay over, there are two **hotels**: the *Miramonti* (☎0862/938.142; ③) and the slightly cheaper *Della Pineta* (☎0862/938.263; ③). There are also some **private rooms** to rent – ask at the *Comune* on the main square for details.

If you can't cope with suspicious stares, head instead to **ROCCA CALASCIO**, a honey-pale castle crumbling above a completely abandoned village. The bus from L'Aquila passes by, dropping you at the bottom of the hill, and there's no reason why you shouldn't camp out in one of the deserted houses. You can catch a bus in the morning back to L'Aquila, or on to **SAN STEFANO DI SASSANIO** – a Medici stronghold in the fifteenth century, still with Tuscan-style loggias and Medici coats of arms stuck on the dilapidating and semi-abandoned houses. There's a **youth hostel** here too, open July–mid-September (☎0862/89.203; ①).

North of L'Aquila: Amiternum and San Vittorino

The countryside to the north of L'Aquila is undistinguished. **Lago di Campotosto**, encircled by bland hills smeared with small tourist resorts, is one of the town's most popular nearby attractions, but is really just an uninteresting artificial lake, regularly restocked with fish to keep the anglers happy. Closer to L'Aquila, and accessible by bus, are the theatre and amphitheatre surviving from the Sabine, and later Roman, city of **Amiternum** (daily 9am–1.30pm; L4000), now used for concerts and plays in the summer. Above Amiternum, **SAN VITTORINO** is hardly one of Abruzzo's more appealing villages, but it has a series of **catacombs** underneath its church that make for a dank and spooky way to pass an hour, with skulls and bones spilling out of coffin-shelves and the remains of Saint Vittorino stuffed underneath an altar. Someone called Buci has the key to these – he lives in a brown house with a glass porch opposite three shacks near the entrance of the village. Get here on the last Sunday in May and you can join in an underground procession through the passages.

South to Sulmona: Bominaco

From L'Aquila, the SS17 follows the ancient route of the local shepherds across the saffron fields south to Sulmona. If you have your own transport, it's worth making a short detour on the way to see two of Abruzzo's most beautiful churches at **BOMINACO** (also accessible by bus from L'Aquila). The village itself is an inauspicious knot of grubby houses, but the endearingly skewwhiff and lichen-mottled facade of **San Pellegrino** conceals floor-to-ceiling frescoes in vivid hues reminiscent of a peacock's plume. There's also an intriguing thirteenth-century calendar, with the signs of the zodiac looking down over lists of religious festivals and miniatures of men engaged in supposedly typical activities for the time of year – boozing in January, chopping wood in February, sleeping in March . . ..

The church of **Santa Maria dell'Assunta**, just beyond, has a more coolly refined exterior, but its aloofness is tempered by monsters carved at the bases of the windows – notably a chimera with the face of a diabolic lion, flexing its talons and flicking its serpentine tail. Inside, the creamy-white carvings are so exquisitely precise that it seems the mason has only just put down his chisel. In fact they're 800 years old. There's been some restoration, but this is scarcely discernible, and the lack of the usual cracks and crumblings is uncanny. This is particularly striking in the extraordinary free-standing column, consisting of two entwined rolls of stone so supple and sensuous that you expect them to dimple to the touch. To get the keys, you'll need to search out the custodian. His house is tucked behind a garage bearing the number two on the left of the main street; if he's out, try the village's bars.

Sulmona and around

Flanked by bleak mountains, and bristling with legends about its most famous son, Ovid, **SULMONA** is a rich and comfortable provincial town owing its wealth to gold jewellery and sugar almonds. An atmospheric little place, with a dark tangle of a historical centre lined with imposing palaces, its sights can be seen in a day, but the town makes a good base for exploring the surroundings, and you may want to stay longer.

Arrival, information and accommodation

Arrive in Sulmona **by bus** and you'll be dropped at the Parco Fluviale, just down the hill from the western end of the main street, Corso Ovidio. The **train station** is about 2km outside the centre of town; bus #A runs from the station along Corso Ovidio. The **tourist office** (Mon–Sat 8.30am–2pm; ☎0864/53.276), with maps and leaflets on the town, is at Via Roma 21.

The most atmospheric of the town's affordable **hotels** is the *Italia* (☎0864/52.308; ④) just behind Piazza XX Settembre – clean, comfortable and convenient, and numbering Puccini among its first guests. Among cheaper options are the *Stella*, on Via Mazzara, off Corso Ovidio (☎0864/52.653; ③), a relaxed, family-run establishment, and the *Traffico*, Via degli Agghiacciati 17 (☎0864/54.080; ③).

The Town

Corso Ovidio, Sulmona's main street, cuts through the centre from the park-side bus terminus, leading up to **Piazza XX Settembre**, an intimate square that's home to the art nouveau **Gran Caffè**. Nowadays the elegant twists and curlicues of the wrought-iron lamps on its terrace have a soundtrack of blipping video games, but it makes a nice spot for sipping a drink. A couple of minutes back up Corso Ovidio, the **Annunziata** is Sulmona's architectural showpiece, a Gothic-Renaissance palazzo adjoining a flamboyant Baroque church. Its steps are these days a hang-out for the town's lads during the evening *passeggiata*, but once they would have been crowded with Sulmona's ill and destitute: the Annunziata housed a hospital, a pharmacy and a store of grain, donated by the rich and shared out to the needy. It was established by a confraternity to take care of the citizens from birth until death, and most of the external decoration is designed to remind onlookers of the life process: around the first door is a tree of life; a frieze with scenes of birth, marriage and death stretches right across the facade; a wheel of life stands above an ornate window; and statues of saints gaze piously down from pedestals, firmly placing the symbolism in a Christian context. The most intriguing statue, however, is just inside the entrance: Ovid, metamorphosised from pagan poet of love into an ascetic friar. Inside the Annunziata is a small **museum** (Tues–Sun 10am–1pm, Aug also 4–6pm; free), with examples of work by Sulmona's Renaissance goldsmiths – a tradition which continues here today, as evidenced by the number of jewellers' shops along the Corso.

The Corso's **shops** are also full of Sulmona's other great product – *confetti*, a confection of sugar almonds twisted with wire and ribbons into elaborate flowers. Through ingenious marketing the Sulmonese confetti barons have made gifts of their sugar almond sculpture de rigueur at christenings and confirmations throughout Catholic Europe. At Abruzzese weddings bride and groom are painfully pelted with loose white confetti. Most apparent in the Corso's shops, however, are the brashly coloured giant daisies designed to tempt kids and tourists.

Beyond Piazza XX Settembre, the weighty Romanesque portal of **San Francesco delle Scarpe** was the only part of the church solid enough to withstand the 1703 earthquake. The church gets its name – delle Scarpe means "with the shoes" – from the fact that Franciscans wore shoes instead of sandals like other orders of monks. Opposite, the impressive Gothic aqueduct, built to supply water to the town and power to its wool mills, ends at a fifteenth-century fountain, the **Fontana del Vecchio**, named for the chubby-cheeked old man on top. On the other side of the aqueduct is **Piazza Garibaldi**, a vast square dominated by the austere slopes of Monte Morrone, on which the hermit, Pietro Morrone, lived until he was dragged away to be made pope (see p.664). The former nunnery in the corner is being renovated as a museum of Abruzzo's nomadic shepherds – take a look at the courtyard, where there's a tiny door outside which unmarried mothers were permitted to abandon their babies.

For centuries, women suffering from the opposite problem – infertility – would visit a Roman ruin outside the town known as **Ovid's Villa**, where they would pray to the poet, who was seen as some kind of fertility god. A stone phallus then lay upon the steps, and although archaeologists have now put paid to the myth by identifying the ruin as a temple of Hercules, the site is still evocative – beneath a rocky crag topped by a monastery, with fine views over the valley to the Maiella massif; and there's a well-preserved mosaic pavement decorated with leaping dolphins. To get there, take a bus to Bagnatura/Badia, get off after the prison and walk up the hill. The Ovid connection continues behind the prison, in the **Fonte d'Amore** where – the Sulmonese claim – Ovid was caught making love to a fairy or (for sceptics) to the Emperor Augustus' granddaughter.

Eating and drinking

Sulmona has some excellent, reasonably priced **restaurants**. Nicola, the chef at the *Italia* on Piazza XX Settembre, bases his dishes on traditional Abruzzese fare, but is ever inventing new variations – try his fresh cannelloni stuffed with ricotta and various secret ingredients – and it isn't all over-priced. *Al Quadrivio*, Via Mazzara 38, also serves up some memorable food, like *carrati* – homemade bucatini with fresh tomato – while *Mafalda* at Via Solimo 20 is enjoyable in summer, when you can eat dishes like *maccheroni alla chitarra* in its walled garden. *Cesidio*, Via Solimo 25, can be a bit hit-and-miss, but it too does some great pasta dishes, good crepes – even a truffle-based lasagne. The best ice cream is to be had at *Schiazzo*, at the western end of Corso Ovidio, and for late-night boozing there are a couple of pseudo "pubs" – the *Papillon*, at Viale Stazione Introdacqua, though this is a bit of a walk from the centre, and the quintessentially Italian *Black Bull*, across the river by the Ponte Capograssi.

Around Sulmona: the western slopes of Maiella

The beautiful **Maiella** mountain range rises high above Sulmona, its steep wooded slopes and red and gold cliffs giving way to an upland plain as smooth as a cricket field. With your own transport you could explore it in a day; by bus, you either have to make a very early start or sleep over in one of the many villages with facilities for tourists. There are regular buses to some villages, and if you're stuck it's easy enough to hitch.

One of the easiest places to reach is **PACENTRO**, a drab little village topped by a castle, most famous these days for the fact that the grandparents of Madonna emigrated from here. Pacentro had its fifteen minutes of fame back in the late-1980s, when the mayor (who just happened to own the village's only pizzeria) decided to erect a statue to the pop star. The Church, feeling that Madonna was hardly an ideal role model for young girls, objected, and nothing ever came of the plan – though for a short while the village became accustomed to visits by armies of tabloid hacks.

Pacentro is once again quiet, and you might be better off heading instead to the mountain-top forest of **Bosca Sant'Antonio** on the bus route to Pescocostanzo. As well as walking and picnicking, you can also rent horses, and if you want to stay over the *Hotel Sant'Antonio* (☎0864/67.101; ⑤) has reasonable doubles. Alternatively, after a morning in the woods you could move on to **PESCOCOSTANZO**, a well-preserved village with steep grey and white stone streets lined with craft workshops selling lace, gold filigree, wrought-iron work and woven rugs and bedspreads. As the sprawl of Swiss-style apartments on the periphery might have warned you, it's also an extremely popular winter and summer resort. The best of the local crafts are to be found in the **Collegiata**, a fifteenth-century church at the head of the main street, with a magnificently carved and gilded Baroque ceiling and some superb wrought-iron work – lifelike putti and curling, delicate flowers incorporated into the iron chapel screen and the lampholders. The **tourist office** (Mon–Sat 9am–1pm & 4.30–6.30pm, Sun 9am–1pm) is on the main square, next to a café, and there's also a **youth hostel** on Corso Roma (☎0864/641.247; ①).

There's little reason for visiting the other villages, now suffocated by purpose-built resorts, unless you're going **skiing** or want somewhere cheaper to stay. The major centres for skiing are **CAMPO DI GIOVE**, **RIVISONDOLI** and **ROCCARASO**. These are connected to Sulmona by (admittedly few) trains as well as by bus, and accommodation prices are not high. At Campo di Giove, you could stay at the *Del Lago* (☎0864/40.107; ⑤), *Fonte Romana* (☎0864/40.111; ⑤), or *Locanda D'Amico* (☎0864/40.120; ⑤); at Rivisondoli there's the *Monte Pratello* (☎0864/69226; ③) and *La Botte* (☎0864/69129; ③); and Roccaraso is home to the *Italia* (☎0864/62174; ④) and the *Locanda Duca Degli Abruzzi* (☎0864/62176; ④). The **tourist office** at Roccaraso (Mon–Sat 9am–1pm) has details.

South of Sulmona: Cocullo and Scanno

A tatty hill-village, connected by rare trains and even rarer buses with Sulmona, **COCULLO** is understandably neglected by outsiders for 364 days of the year. However, on the first Thursday in May it's invaded by TV crews, journalists, deformed beggars, buskers, street-vendors and what seems like half the population of central Italy. Market stalls sell everything from digital watches to spit-roast pork, and the roads – and on occasions even the nearby motorway – are crammed with parked cars and flustered traffic police. The reason for all this activity is Cocullo's weird **festival of snakes**, an annual event celebrated in memory of San Domenico, the patron saint of the village, who allegedly rid the area of venomous snakes back in the eleventh century.

It's an odd affair, a mixture of the modern and archaic. Everyone pours into the main square, while a wailing mass is relayed from the church over aged tannoys, competing with pulsing pop music and the cries of the beggars. After the service a number of snake-charmers in the crowd drape a wooden statue of Domenico with a writhing mass of live but harmless snakes, which is then paraded through the streets in a bizarre celebration of the saint's unique powers (he was apparently good at curing snake-bites too). Actually, it is thought that Cocullo's preoccupation with snakes dates back to before the advent of Domenico. In the pre-Christian era, local tribes worshipped their goddess Angitia with offerings of snakes, and it seems too much of a coincidence that Domenico's powers also related to the creatures. Scholars have attempted to rationalise the festival by drawing a parallel between snakes shedding their skins and the ancient Cocullans shedding their paganism for Christianity – but whatever the origins, Cocullo's festival is today more than anything a celebration of Domenico's power to attract enough tourist lucre in a day to keep the village going for a year. Incidentally, if you're suffering from toothache, Domenico is also reckoned to have the power to cure it, the only snag being that you have to ring the church bell with the rope in your teeth.

Lago di Scanno . . . and Scanno

Twenty kilometres down the road, but most easily reached by bus from Sulmona, Scanno is another popular tourist destination, reached by passing through the narrow and rocky Saggitario Gorge, past the glassy green **Lago di Scanno**. There's a **campsite** here, *I Lupi* (☎0864/740.100), with boats and horses for rent, and a good restaurant, the *Trattoria sul Lago*. Perched over the lake is a church, **Madonna del Lago**, encrusted with ex-votives and with the cliff as its back wall. If you're planning on staying over, be warned that the campsite is normally packed out in summer, especially during August.

A couple of kilometres beyond, **SCANNO** itself is a well-preserved medieval village encircled by mountains. At most times of the year, although especially in the summer season, women can be seen wearing their local costume – long pleated skirts, either heavy and dark or richly brocaded, a black velvet bodice and an embroidered fez with coils of cord looped behind to conceal the hair. The hat, and the fact that at Scannese weddings the women squat on the floor of the church, has led scholars to believe that the Scannese originated in Asia Minor; Scannese jewellery also has something of the Orient about it – large, delicately filigreed earrings, and a star, known as a *presuntuosa*, given to fianceés to ward off other men. If you want to watch a goldsmith at work, go to the jewellers round the corner from the tourist office on the main square. There's a shop on Via Roma selling Scannese costumes, and if this doesn't tempt you, the mountain cheeses, hams and salami and the sticky Scannese cakes on sale in the main café probably will. Scanno is also linked by chair lift to a small **ski resort** – worth going up just for the view of lake and mountains, especially at sunset.

Every August Scanno holds a **classical music festival**, and on January 17 a **lasagne festival** – more properly called the *Festa di San Antonio Abate*, involving the cooking of a great cauldron of lasagne and beans outside the door of the church, which is then blessed and doled out with a somewhat unholy amount of pushing, shoving and squabbling. For the rest of the year you'll have to make do with the **restaurants**, best of which is *Agli Archetti* on Via Silla. If you're **staying over** the cheapest options are the *Eden* (☎0864/74.328; ③) or the *Pensione Nilde* (☎0864/74.359; ④).

Southwest Abruzzo and the National Park

Heading west towards Rome from Sulmona, road and railway skirt the **Fucino Plain**, an endless, unreal and utterly flat expanse of agricultural land whose only landmarks are the satellite dishes of *Telespazio*, Italy's biggest telecommunications complex. The Fucino was once Italy's third largest lake, and is the largest lake in the world to have been artificially drained. Attempts to empty it began nearly two thousand years ago. The *Marsi* tribe who lived on its shores, fed up with the fact that it flooded every time the mountain snows melted, managed to persuade Emperor Claudius to build a six-kilometre-long outlet tunnel, designed to transfer the water from the lake into a nearby valley. On the day of the draining, the shores and surrounding mountains were packed with spectators: the proceedings were inaugurated by a mechanical Triton who rose up from the lake blowing a trumpet, whence a mock battle ensued, with warships manned by condemned criminals, after which Claudius gave the signal for the outlet gates to be opened. Unfortunately, the tunnel couldn't cope with the vast volume of water, and thousands of spectators, including members of the Imperial party, only narrowly escaped being washed away. Frederick II attempted to open up the tunnel in 1240, but the lake was only finally drained in 1875, as much to gain agricultural land as to solve the flooding problem – though it has brought associated problems. The climate has grown humid, misty and mosquito-ridden, and it's clear that lakeside tourist developments would have been far more profitable than agriculture.

Avezzano, Alba Fucens and Tagliacozzo

Fringing the plain are **CELANO**, a pretty village crowned by a turreted toytown castle, and **AVEZZANO**, an unfortunate city that was destroyed – along with 10,000 inhabitants – by an earthquake in 1915. It was rebuilt, but flattened again by World War II bombings. It's since been reconstructed, but is a bland garden city, and the only reason for a visit is to get a bus out to the substantial ruins of a Roman colony at *Alba Fucens*, or south to the Abruzzo National Park (see below).

Buses to **Alba Fucens** leave from outside the train station; there are around nine daily going there, about five coming back – phone *Arpa* for precise times (☎0836/26.561). Make sure that your bus goes right on to Alba Fucens and not just to Massa d'Albe, dropping you at the far end of the village of **ALBE**, a straggle of prefabs from where you can either wander around the site alone or be shown round by a guide, who will give you a down-to-earth (Italian) commentary.

Alba Fucens

Alba Fucens was a garrison town of about 30,000 inhabitants, founded by the Romans in 304 BC to keep the surrounding tribes in check. Aerial photographs have identified remains spreading over three square kilometres, but only the area nearest to Albe has been excavated. The main street of the town, Via Valeria, originally ran to Rome, 68 Roman miles away, according to a milestone on the town's edge. Walking down the parallel street, you reach the marketplace, still with the walls and arches of the small shops that used to surround it. Beyond is a bar, consisting of a sink with pipes through which hot wine with honey and pine-resin was dispensed; behind are the steam baths – you can see the holes in the raised pavement through which the steam rose. A good many statues, most notably a gargantuan marble Hercules, were also found, but these are now kept at Chieti's archaeology museum (see p.678). Further on, above the amphitheatre, the beautiful Romanesque church of San Pietro has some excellent Cosmatesque inlaid and twisted marble decoration.

Tagliacozzo

Twenty minutes beyond Avezzano by train is **TAGLIACOZZO**, a picturesque town with an unspoilt Renaissance core, nestling beneath a pine-wooded cliff. There's not a lot to see here, but it's a much pleasanter base for Alba Fucens than Avezzano, with some gorgeous small squares enclosed by fourteenth- and fifteenth-century houses, a tangle of narrow streets and alleys, and the church of San Francesco, with its paper doily rose window and column capitals carved with twisting flowers and leaves. Above the church is the impenetrable **Palazzo Ducale** and the small **Teatro Thalia** – named, like Tagliacozzo itself, after the Greek muse of theatre. The story goes that the town was founded by Greeks from Mount Parnassus: next to San Francesco is a church dedicated to two Greek saints, Cosmo and Damiano, and there are supposedly still traces of Greek in Tagliacozzo's dialect.

There's a **tourist office** on Piazza Argoli which has leaflets and a map of the town (Mon–Sat 9am–1pm & 4–6pm; ☎0863/610.318); if you want to stay overnight, the cheapest **hotel** is *La Lucciola* on Via della Giorgina (☎0863/6501; ④). You'll have no problem finding **somewhere to eat**: *Petit Restaurant chez Nunzia*, Via XXIV Maggio 6, parallel with Viale Aldo Moro, is good, friendly and family-run, and serves a type of pasta known as *strozza preti* which means "priest-strangler".

The Parco Nazionale dell'Abruzzo

At four hundred square kilometres, the **Parco Nazionale dell'Abruzzo** is Italy's third largest national park, and holds some of its wildest mountain land, providing a hunter-free haven for wolves, brown bears, chamois and a pair of royal eagles, along with some great walking. Sadly, it's become rather overdeveloped: **CIVITELLA ALFEDENA**, on the shores of the artificial Lake Barrea, has its wolves, stripped of the mystery that made stories of werewolves so prevalent around these parts, lazing placidly behind barbed wire to prevent them mating with local dogs; everywhere you'll see the park's cute logo – a brown bear looking as daft and cuddly as Winnie the Pooh; and the central village, **PESCASSÉROLI**, is surrounded by campsites and fake Tyrolean holiday flats and hotels, mainly full of coachloads of schoolkids and German pensioners.

However, you can get away from all this if you're prepared to hike; and if you're not there's little point in coming to the park at all. There's no free camping, just certain fields laid aside for anyone who can cope without facilities, and between April and September the numbers coming here can be immense. If you want more comfort, you'll have to put up with everything-but-the-kitchen-sink car campers, or with their heartier but less hardy compatriots in a hotel. The trick is to treat the twee tourism as a joke, take advantage of the comprehensive information service, and get walking as quickly as possible: as soon as you get away from the tourist villages, and their nearby short tracks that would be negotiable in stilettos, the wild Appenine beauty really makes itself felt.

Information and walking routes

There is an **information office** in Pescasséroli, which also has a **museum** to fill you in on the park's flora and fauna, and others in **OPI**, **VILLETTA BARREA**, **BARREA** and Civitella Alfedena (each open daily 10am–noon & 3–7pm), with leaflets outlining specific walks. These take less than an hour, and are gentle and very popular. They can also sell you a map (L8000) on which all routes are marked, along with an indication of the difficulty involved (F=easy, M=moderate, D=difficult), the time needed, and the flora and fauna you're likely to see on the way. There are getting on for a hundred **walking routes**, starting from 26 letter-coded points, so making a choice can be difficult. The following are just suggestions, taking into account the ease of reaching the starting-point by bus.

From point #F, near Opi, there's a two-hour walk through the **Valle Fondillo** – one of the loveliest parts of the park but best done very early morning, to avoid other hikers and have a small chance of seeing bears. If you do see a bear, take care, keep quiet and don't panic – they've never harmed a tourist but are nevertheless extremely strong, and will attack if under threat. Alternatively, from the same point you can climb **Mont'Amaro** (1862m) for great views over to Lake Barrea. Another good climb is up **Monte Tranquillo** (route #C3 from point #C) about a kilometre out of Pescasséroli, taking the road to the left on entering the village, past the *Hotel Ivy*. The mountain (1841m) is crowned by a small sanctuary, dedicated to the black Madonna of Tranquillo. From the summit you can either retrace your steps or take path #Q3 into the **next valley**, where's there's a campsite, and tracks leading into the remoter reaches of the park. Your best chance of seeing some of the park's chamois is to take path #I1, turning left just before the youth hostel at Civitella Alfedena, and through the forested **Valle de Rosa**, until the forest gives way to the grassy slopes where the chamois graze. A path zigzags from here up the slope to **Passo Cavuto**, and beyond to the *Rifugio Forca Resuni* (see opposite for information on *rifugi*). From here a path (#K6) descends into the **Valle Iannanghera** – where you may see bears – and back to Civitella Alfedena. This circuit should take 5–6 hours.

Accommodation and other practicalities

Pescasséroli is the least pleasant of the park's villages, but it is fairly well served by buses (from Avezzano, and from Castel di Sangro on the border with Molise) so you may find it a convenient place to stay. In high season, there's little chance of finding a

room on arrival; you need to book at least a month in advance. The cheapest places are *Al Castello*, on Via Gabriele d'Annunzio off the main piazza (☎0863/910.757; ④), and *Peppe di Sora*, across the river on Viale B. Croce (☎0863/91.908; ④). Campers should manage to find space on one of the four **campsites**, of which the simplest to reach is *dell' Orso* (☎0863/91.955) on the main approach road (SS83); this also has a hostel, open all year, but again you'll need to book well in advance. Of the other sites, *Marsicano* (☎0863/912.356) is closer to the village on the SS83; *Sant'Andrea* (☎0863/912.173) is to the left off the SS83; and *Panoramica* (☎0863/912.257) is out of the village at the foot of the *funivia* up to M. Vitelle. If you plan on staying for a week or more, the **tourist office** on Via Piave (Mon–Sat 9am–1pm & 4.30–6.30pm), a right turn off the main street, has a list of families who rent out rooms; again, in the summer, contact the tourist office about a month before you plan to come.

Among the other villages, Civitella Alfedena has a **youth hostel**, *Le Torri* (☎0864/641.247; ①), and a camping area, *Wolf* at Sotto i Cerri (☎0864/89.336). Villetta Barrea also has a **hostel** (☎0864/89134), and Barrea, at the far end of the lake, has a hostel, *Le Vicenne* (☎0864/88.348), and two campsites – *Colle Ciglio* (☎0864/88.348), half a kilometre along the road to Alfedena, and *La Genziana* (☎0864/88.101), convenient for walk-point #K up to the tiny mountain Lago Vivo or the larger Lago Montana Spaccata.

The best of the park's **restaurants** are expensive, and it's often a better bet to picnic, though in most villages you'll find fairly cheap pizza and pasta. If you can afford to splash out a bit, *Boselli*, on Via Lungo Sangro in Pescasséroli, serves traditional food and isn't too pricey. For splurges, try *Il Pescatore* in Villetta Barrea; or, slightly cheaper, *Alle Vecchie Arcate*, on Via della Chiesa in Pescasséroli.

Northeast Abruzzo: Téramo and around

Rising from the Adriatic and rolling towards the eastern slopes of the Gran Sasso, the landscape of northeast Abruzzo is gentle, and its inland towns are usually ignored in favour of its long, sandy and highly popular coastline. **TÉRAMO**, capital of the province of the same name, is a modern town with an elegant centre harbouring a couple of Roman ruins and a treasure-filled cathedral. Not much to draw you, but Teramo does have good bus and train connections with the northern Abruzzo coast, and if you're heading for the sea you may well pass through. **Buses** stop at **Piazza Garibaldi**, to which the **train station** is linked by regular city buses. Just off the piazza, on Via del Castello, is the **tourist office** (Mon–Sat 8am–2pm) and a cheap **hotel**, the *Castello* (☎0861/247.582; ④).

Even if you're just passing through, it's worth looking in on Téramo's main attraction, the **Duomo**, at the top of Corso San Giorgio, behind whose patchy facade lies a remarkable silver altarfront. It's worth squatting down for a good look at this (ask the sacristan to switch the lights on). Crafted by the fifteenth-century Abruzzese silversmith Nicola da Guardiagrele – also responsible for the statues of Mary and Gabriel that flank the church doorway – it has 35 panels with lively reliefs of religious scenes, starting with the *Annunciation*, and moving through the New Testament, punctuating the narrative with portraits of various saints. Nicola was famous enough to feature in a sumptuous polyptych by a Venetian artist, Jacobello del Fiore, in a Baroque chapel to the left. Set into an ornate gilded frame are static portraits of saints, in rich blue, red and gold gowns, flanking the *Coronation of the Virgin*, and beneath it a model of Téramo, set against a gilded sky, with Nicolo wearing a monk's habit on the left, Jacobello in the red gown on the right.

To the right of the duomo, Via Irelli leads to the heart of Roman Téramo, with fragments of the **amphitheatre**, and the more substantial walls of the **theatre**, where two of the original twenty entrance arches remain. Just behind Piazza Garibaldi is the town's modest **museum** (Mon–Sat 10am–1pm; L500), whose collection of local art over the centuries includes two appealing works – a lovely almond-eyed Madonna by a local fifteenth-century artist, Giacomo da Campli, and Campli's *Madonna Enthroned with Saints* – a polyptych in which the colours are lucid and the forms almost sculpted.

The northern Abruzzo coast

The **northern Abruzzo coastline** isn't at first sight the region's most appealing stretch, its ribbon of sand hugged for most of its considerable length by road and railway, studded with grids of beach umbrellas and flimsy cabins and lined with concrete-box apartment blocks and hotels. However, the beaches are good and frequently palm-fringed, there are plenty of campsites, and though the resorts may look bland they can be fun – especially if you're weary of travel or culture.

The coastal rail line ensures that access to the resorts couldn't be easier, though finding a hotel can be a problem, as the cheaper ones tend to be closed out of season, and they get booked up in advance for most of the summer – your best bet at most of the coastal towns is to head straight for the tourist office on arrival.

The northern Abruzzo resorts

ALBA ADRIATICA is the most northerly of the Abruzzo resorts – a good place to stop off if you're heading on to Marche. **GIULIANOVA** has a rather forlorn old town perched above its resort quarter, although its five campsites (bus #1 or #4 from opposite the train station) and connections with Téramo make it a useful stop-off if you want a last swim before heading inland. Ten kilometres further south, **ROSETO DEGLI ABRUZZO** is modern and undistinguished, but has views up the Vomano valley towards the Gran Sasso. **PINETO** is without doubt the most attractive option, a well-organised resort with a palm-lined beach and every hotel clearly signposted from the railway station. It's also a good base for visiting Atri (see below). There are lots of **campsites**, and of the many **hotels** the *Azzura al Mare* at Via Venezia 1 (☎085/949.1462; ④) and the *Maria*, Via Morandi 2 (☎085/949.2065; ④), both charge about the same. If everywhere is full, consult the **tourist office**, Viale Gabriele d'Annunzio 123 (Mon–Sat 9am–noon & 4–7pm; ☎085/949.1745), who should be able to advise on where the vacancies are.

Atri

The approach to **ATRI**, about 10km inland from Pineto, is like travelling through the background of a Renaissance painting, with gently undulating hills planted with orderly olive groves giving way to a surrealist landscape of sleek clay gullies known as *calanchi*, water-eroded into smooth ripples, wrinkles and folds. Regular buses make the trip from Pescara and Téramo as well as Pineto, and it's a journey that's undeniably worth making. Atri's duomo contains Abruzzo's greatest cycle of frescoes, and the town itself, with its narrow stepped and bridged streets, is one you're likely to be reluctant to leave.

Buses drop you near **Porta San Domenico**, the town's only surviving defensive gate. To get to the centre, walk through the gate and cut down one of the narrow side streets to the main street which leads up to the central piazza, dominated by the thirteenth-century **Duomo**. Its facade is understated, pierced by a rose window and perforated by the holes in which scaffolding beams were slotted during construction. The inside is similarly simple, with patches of frescoes on the brick columns and – visible through glass set into the floor of the apse – an octagonal mosaic pavement decorated with sea-horses, dolphins and fish, from the Roman baths over which the church was built. The duomo's highlight, however, is the cycle of **fifteenth-century frescoes** by Andrea Delitio on the apse walls. Delitio has been called the Piero della Francesca of Abruzzo for his sophisticated use of architecture and landscape; but in contrast to Piero's cool intellectualism and obscure symbolism, Delitio places the religious scenes in realistic contexts. *The Birth of Mary*, for example, has servants giving the newly born baby a bath; in the vault the four Evangelists are placed in natural settings, the animals that are the emblems of the saints behaving as domestic pets; and back on the walls, the lives of the rich – especially in the *Dinner at Cana* and *Presentation in the Temple* – contrast with the lives of the poor, notably Mary, Joseph and the shepherds in the *Nativity*. The most emotionally charged scene is the *Slaughter of the Innocents*, in which the horror is intensified by the refined Renaissance architectural setting and the fact that the massacre is coolly observed from a balcony by Herod's party of civic bigwigs. One opulently dressed slaughterer slices a child with chill, technical accuracy as if it were a joint of meat; another holds a child upside down by the ankles, while the mothers weep wretchedly over the tiny corpses.

For a touch of light relief, head back up the right-hand aisle to see a piece of Renaissance kitsch – a font with four oversized frogs clinging to the basin. In the cloisters is the entrance to a cavernous Roman cistern, and there are more Roman relics outside the cathedral – the foundations of what was possibly a dye-works, complete with a vat. There's also a small **archaeological museum**; to visit, you need to phone the cathedral librarian, Bruno Trubiani, at lunchtime (☎085/87.241).

Really the best thing to do in Atri is just wander around, strolling out to the belvedere for views, nosing into the many churches, or simply sitting in a café and watching the small-town life around you. You may well want to stay the night, and there's a great **hotel** – three-star quality at one-star prices – the *San Francesco* (☎085/87.287; ③), housed in an ex-convent next to the church of San Francesco on Corso Adriano. The best **restaurant** is *La Campana d'Oro*, on Piazza del Duomo.

Pescara

The main town and resort of the Abruzzo coast is **PESCARA**, a bustling, modern place that's probably the region's most commercial and expensive city. Now that ferries to the former Yugoslavia are no longer running, there's not much point in coming; if you're looking for somewhere to sunbathe there are much nicer places. But there's a chance you might pass through for the train or bus connections.

Architecturally, Pescara isn't a distinguished town. In fact, its most striking sight is the central **train station**, strangely enough the most up-to-date in Italy, with a slick network of slinky escalators, smoked-glass screens and non-slip black rubber pavements. Opposite, the main street, **Corso Umberto**, is lined with designer boutiques and packed with the label-conscious Pescarese, who also hang out in the elegant cafés on **Piazza Rinascita**, known as Pescara's *salone*. If you've time to kill, you could visit the city's new museum, the **Museo delle Gente d'Abruzzo** on Via delle Caserme (Tues–Sun 9am–noon), devoted to the life and popular traditions of the region, or visit the birthplace of the poet and mentor of Mussolini, **Gabriele d'Annunzio**, on Corso Manthone (Tues–Sat 9am–1pm). Otherwise, just go to the **beach**, the development of which stretches for an unrelenting 16km.

Practicalities

Pescara has two **train stations**, though until peace returns to the former Yugoslavia you only need to use one, Stazione Centrale (the other, Porta Nuova, is only for ferry connections). Conveniently, **buses** to Rome (quicker than the train) and Naples leave from outside Stazione Centrale.

If you need to stay (and you should really try to avoid this if possible), there's a **campsite**, the *Internazionale* (☎085/65.653), open May to September, on Lungomare Colombon – bus #10 from the train station. Most of the **hotels** are on the beach front north of the river, although you can sleep more cheaply at somewhere like the *Corso* (☎085/422.4210; ④) opposite the train station, or in the area south of Corso Umberto; try the *Bristol*, Via Trento 122 (☎085/374.126; ④), or the *Centrale*, Via Firenze 283 (☎085/421.1772; ④). For **eating**, try the *Cantina di Jazz*, Via delle Caserme 61, which does great Abruzzese food, or if it's full, *La Lumaca*, down the road at no. 51.

Chieti, Guardiagrele and Lanciano

Just twenty minutes by train from Pescara, **CHIETI** is a pleasanter place to stop over between trains. It holds Abruzzo's best museum by far, with an extensive collection of finds from the region, and the town itself, though not particularly attractive, has a relaxed and appealing provincial air. Give it a night at most, then move on.

Coming by train you arrive at Chieti Scalo, from where it's a short journey on bus #1 up the hill to Chieti proper, 5km away, which spreads over a curving ridge and has great views of the Maiella and Gran Sasso – and, when it's clear, out to sea. Buses arrive at **Piazza Vittorio Emanuele** alongside the ugly and much-reconstructed cathedral, from where the main **Corso Marrucini** cuts through the town centre to **Largo Trento e Trieste**. Behind the post office, off Via Spaventa, are the remains of three little Roman temples. However, it's the **Museo Nazionale Archaeologico di Antichitá** (daily 9am–1.30pm) which is of most interest, laid out in a dignified villa encircled by a park beyond Piazza Trento e Trieste. It holds finds from Abruzzo's major sites: there's a Roman portrait-bust of an old man, in which the stone appears as soft, wrinkled and flaccid as real skin; a massive and muscly white marble Hercules from the temple at Alba Fucens (see p.673); and a metal and uncomfortably narrow bedstead from a tomb at Amiternum. If you've seen Amiternum, look also at the frieze showing how its amphitheatre would have looked in the first century, packed with bloodthirsty spectators at the gladiatorial games. Upstairs, don't miss the *Capestrano Warrior*, a statue of a Bronze Age soldier with a body so curvaceous that there's a question mark over its gender. There's no doubt about the sexes of the occupants of Bronze Age tombs, as you'll see in the adjacent rooms – the men were buried with armour and weapons, the women with jewellery, kitchen utensils, spindles, and in one case even a nail-brush. For more insight into prehistoric hygiene, head for the extraordinary exhibition about Palaeolithic dental health, conclusions about diet being drawn from the state of the Palaeolithic teeth.

Practicalities

The **tourist office is** on Via Spaventa, just off Corso Marrucino (Mon–Fri 9.30am–12.30pm & 4–6pm, Sat 9.30am–12.30pm). For **sleeping**, there's a reasonable hotel a few minutes walk from Piazza Vittorio Emanuele: the *Marrucino* on Via dei Veneziani, off Corso Marrucini (☎0871/330.081; ③). If you're not bothered about your own teeth, sample Chieti's sweet and gooey speciality, *Torrone di Fichi Secchi* (nougat with dried figs), before you leave. More practically, there are good-value full **meals** at the *Trattoria Nino* on Piazza Trento e Trieste, and, somewhat livelier, fairly cheap pizzas at the *Magico Alvermann Video Pub* on the Corso.

Near Chieti: Guardiagrele and Lanciano

From Chieti, most people head south to the lovely historical town of **LANCIANO**, taking in the smaller town of **GUARDIAGRELE** on the way if they have a car. The latter town enjoyed a literal golden age in the fifteenth century, when it was home to

Nicola da Guardiagrele, a gold- and silversmith whose ornate crucifixes and altar-fronts can be seen in churches and museums throughout Abruzzo. Guardiagrele itself, however, has only one piece by Nicola – a silver processional crucifix in the church of **Santa Maria Maggiore**. The church's external fresco of Saint Christopher, by another great fifteenth-century Abruzzo artist, Andrea Delitio (see p.677) was supposed to bring travellers good fortune. It had its own share of luck in 1943 when it escaped being destroyed by the German soldiers who smashed the church's portico.

Lanciano, some 18km east of Guardiagrele, holds one of Abruzzo's most enticing and best-preserved historical quarters and is well worth the onward journey. Indeed, its handful of cheap hotels make it a feasible alternative base for this part of the region.

As Italy's main producer of needles and host of an important wool and cloth fair, Lanciano was a major commercial centre during the Middle Ages, and the main **Piazza Plebiscito**, in the words of a contemporary, was invariably crowded with "peasants in red and blue jackets, Jews in yellow sashes, Albanians, Greeks, Dalmatians and Tuscans: there was an assortment of languages, it was a muddle, a nightmare. . . ." The square is not much quieter now, a chaotic junction where the cathedral balances on a reconstructed **Roman bridge** – a testament of even earlier prosperity, built in the time of Emperor Vespasian to give easy access to the merchants of the Roman era.

Corso Roma leads out of the piazza and up to the church of **San Francesco**. Behind its austere rectangular facade are the relics of one of the more improbable miracles of the Catholic church, the *Miracolo Eucaristico*. Contained in two reliquaries are five coagulated globules of blood and a fragment of muscular heart tissue, both 1200 years old. The story goes that during a communion service in the eighth century the bread became flesh and the wine blood in order to prove Christ's presence to a doubting monk. The relics have been forensically analysed by the Vatican's scientists, right down to their trace minerals, and the findings are presented in an exhibition, in which it is verified that the relics are indeed human blood and flesh, and that they both have the same blood group (AB) as that traced on the now discredited Turin shroud.

From the church, Via Fieramosca and Via Finamore climb up to the **Torri Montanare**, a bulwarked, multi-towered and crenellated stronghold as grim and impenetrable as when it was built in the eleventh century to protect the town's newly built residential quarters. You can walk along the walls, for great views of the Maiella mountain range, or descend to Via Santa Maria Maggiore to explore the appealingly crumbling houses of the medieval quarter, **Civitanova**, and Lanciano's most interesting church, **Santa Maria Maggiore**. Its Gothic portal, surrounded by a series of columns carved into twists, zigzags and tiny leaves and flowers as elaborate as piped icing, is slightly crumbled, while inside there's a silver processional cross by Nicola da Guardiagrele, delicately decorated with biblical reliefs and hanging with silver incense baubles.

A few streets further on, a long flight of steps decends towards the centre. This marks the boundary of **Ripa Sacca**, the medieval Jewish ghetto – a series of the narrowest of stepped streets spanning out like ribs from a barely wider central spine. Here eighty Jewish families lived, obliged to observe a strict curfew, allowed to follow only certain professions, and forced to identify themselves by wearing a yellow sash at all times. A handful of the original houses remain on Via and Vico Santa Maria Maggiore, but even the later houses are in character. Below is the large and scruffy Piazza Garibaldi, and from there a flight of steps climbs up to Via degli Agorai, which was named after its fifteenth-century needlemakers. The same street skirts another wanderable quarter, **Lancianovecchia**, not as old as its name suggests, but still something of a centre for the town's artisans.

Practicalities

Lanciano's **train station**, where **buses** also stop, is at the head of a broad avenue, off which Corso Trento e Trieste runs down to Piazza Plebiscito, where there's a tourist office (Mon–Sat 9am–1pm, Sun 10am–1pm). If you're staying overnight, Lanciano's cheapest and most convenient **hotel** is the *Allegria* on Via Fieramosca (☎0872/24.154; ④) – also a good bet for a reasonable meal; otherwise there's the *Alba* (☎0872/714.640; ④), just off Viale del Mare, though this is slightly more expensive; take bus #1 from Piazza Plebiscito and get off after the FINA garage. The nicest place to eat is the *Allegria*, housed in a sixteenth-century palazzo on Via Fieramosca, which does excellent pasta.

The southern Abruzzo coast

The coast south of Pescara is less developed than the northern stretch; the long ribbon of sand continues, followed by the train line and punctuated with mostly small resorts. The largest, **FRANCAVILLA AL MARE**, is a characterless place, basically a continuation of Pescara. **ORTONA**, further along, is of most interest for its daily summer ferries to the Trémiti Islands (see Chapter Fourteen, *Puglia*), its mainly reconstructed centre dominated by the shell of a castle and the massive dome of its cathedral. The town was at the centre of a six-week battle in 1943, fought over the territory between the Sangro and Mora rivers, which ended in the German occupation of Ortona and the deaths of thousands of British soldiers; there's a military cemetery 3km south of Ortona on the banks of the Moro.

On the other side of the river lies **SAN VITO**, a small resort and fishing centre, with a pebbly beach and rocky coast. From here you can take a bus or – more fun – the gradient-scaling small-gauge railway inland to Lanciano (see above), or continue down the coast to the equally small resort of **FOSSACESIA**. There's only one, rather expensive, hotel here, but a 2km-walk inland is a **campsite**, *Shanty Boy* (☎0872/60135), open year-round. Just before you reach the site is the creamy-gold Romanesque church of **San Giovanni in Venere**, which owes its name to the fact that it was built over a Roman temple dedicated to Venus the Conciliator and is visited by anyone seeking the return of peace within their family. The church, with its finely carved sandstone door and triple apse, is superbly sited among the undulating fields above the coast and is still a favourite outing for Abruzzo families – harmony now being sought by the treat of a slap-up meal in the swanky restaurant outside the church. If you're visiting at the weekend or during holidays and want the church to yourself, aim to get there at lunchtime, while everyone else is safely ensconced behind plates of pasta.

Vasto

VASTO, further south, close to the border with Molise, is a fine old city, overlooking the resort of **VASTO MARINA**. There are boats in the summer to the Trémiti Islands, plenty of campsites, and a handful of reasonable hotels along the broad sandy beach – palm-lined and beach-hutted in the centre, wilder and rockier to the north.

Though its sights are pretty run-of-the-mill, Vasto is a nice place to hang out for a while. Buses from the train station run along the seafront and to the upper town, whose rooftops and campanili rise above palms and olive groves. The centre of town is **Piazza Rossetti**, its gardens dominated by the chunky **Castello Calderesco**. The piazza is named after Gabriele Rossetti, a local eighteenth-century poet who is better known as the father of the Pre-Raphaelite poet, Dante Gabriele Rossetti.

Just off the piazza, next to the small **Duomo**, stands the **Palazzo d'Avalos**, its Renaissance splendour still perceivable through its scruffiness. This was once the home of the poet and friend of Michelangelo, Vittoria Colonna, who was famous in her time for the bleak sonnets she wrote after her husband's death; nowadays it houses the town's **museum**, which is currently closed for restoration. The best of its exhibits are some bellicose second-century bronzes, a third-century warrior with an arm missing, and a collection of Greek coins – evidence of Vasto's early importance as an international trading city.

Alongside the palazzo, **Piazza del Popolo** is home to a **tourist office** (Mon–Sat 9am–12.30pm & 4.30–6.30pm), and opens onto a panoramic promenade that takes you to Vasto's most memorable sight, the door of the church of **San Pietro**, surrounded by Romanesque twists and zigzags, standing isolated against a backdrop of sky, sea and trees, the rest of the church having been destroyed in a landslide.

Pleasant as the upper town is, most of the action is down by the beach in **VASTO MARINA**, and it's here that you're more likely to want to stay. There's another **tourist office** on the seafront (daily 9am–12.30pm & 5–8.30pm; ☎0873/801.751), and numerous **campsites** along the coast, of which the *Sea Garden* (0873/801.097) is the most central. The cheapest of the many **hotels** here are the *Cigno Bianco*, on Via Donizetti, above the train station (☎0873/801.753; ④), and *La Bitta*, close to the beach on Lungomare Cordella (☎0873/801.979; ④). If you do want to stay in the upper town, try either *Dei 7*, on Via San Michele, to the left of the centre by the public gardens (☎0873/609.23; ④), or the *Palizzi* on the busy Corso Mazzini (☎0873/2361; ④). As for **eating and drinking**, there are loads of pizzerias and "pubs" in Vasto Marina, although you might prefer to consider splashing out at *Lo Scudo*, in the upper town at Via Garibaldi 39, which does good fish.

MOLISE

Molise is the most recently created and least-known of Italy's regions. Gentler, less rugged and much poorer than Abruzzo, it has more in common with southern than central Italy. Much of the region still seems to be struggling out of its past, its towns and villages victims of either neglect or overdevelopment. The old hill-villages, which look so enticing from a distance, are on closer inspection either collapsing and rotting, or suffocated by bland housing estates. And the cities, **Isernia** and **Campobasso**, are large and bland, fringed with factories erected by northern money that has been lured here by the low price of land and labour.

But Molise has its compensations. Just as the twentieth-century industrial tycoons have invaded Molise, scattering it with formula-built Anytowns, so, over 2000 years ago, the Romans charged into the region, forcing the native Italic Samnite tribes to leave their small villages and live in equally formula-built settlements. Molise still has a scattering of low-key Roman ruins – most interestingly at **Saepinum**, Italy's most complete example of a Roman provincial town and a site that's still well off the beaten tourist track. Wandering among the ruins, and looking out over the green fields to the mountains beyond, you get some inkling of what it must have been like for Italy's first Grand Tourists.

It's a region of contrasts, too. Traditions that would have been ancient two hundred years ago persist even in the boom-towns. In many a new apartment block, Benetton-clad girls will be making lace alongside their grandmothers, and in the village of **Ururi**, settled by Albanian refugees in the fourteenth century, there's an annual chariot race, as barbaric as anything the Romans dreamed up.

Finally there's the sheer physical aspect of the place. Forty percent of Molise is covered by **mountains**, and although they are less dramatic than Abruzzo's there are masses of possibilities for hiking. A must is the trail up **Monte La Gallinola** in the **Matese** mountains, from where on a clear day the whole of the peninsula, from the Bay of Naples to the Adriatic, stretches out before you.

Isernia and around

An air of tragedy hangs over **ISERNIA**. It was severely damaged for the eighth time by an earthquake in 1984, and the few remaining streets of its old town are scarcely visible behind the tunnels of scaffolding that support them. They cluster round a desolate square, Piazza X Settembre, where the skeletons of houses destroyed in a bombing raid on September 10, 1943, overlook a monument to the 4000 who were killed – an anguished nude ankle-deep in fractured tiles, bricks and gutters. Abutting all this is the new town, a soulless grid of apartment blocks built more to last than to charm.

Isernia's one attraction is the **Museo Nazionale della Pentria e Isernia** (Tues–Sun 9am–1pm; free), in the heart of the old town at Piazza S. Maria 8. In 1979 local road-builders unearthed traces of a million-year-old village here, the most ancient signs of human life yet found in Europe. The exhibits are backed up by computer programmes in four languages, including English, which reconstruct the village and put the ancient civilisation in context. Contrary to the misleading publicity, there were no human remains found, just weapons, traps, traces of pigment thought to have been used as body paint, and animal bones, laid out to create a solid platform on the marshy land for the village.

Though unattractive in itself, Isernia can be a useful starting-point for exploring the rest of Molise: **buses** to local villages leave from Via XXIV Maggio, parallel with Corso Garibaldi, and longer-distance buses, including those to Rome and Naples, from outside the train station. Avoid sleeping over, if you can, as the cheapest **hotel** is the *Sayonara*, at Via G. Berti 132 (☎0865/50.992; ⑤), the second street parallel to Corso Garibaldi. The **eating** prospects are better: there's a good traditional restaurant, *Taverna Maresca*, in the old town on Corso Marcelli. If you're on a budget, their pasta-, bean- or polenta-based first courses are filling and cheap; if you're not, you can then gorge yourself on roast kid or lamb cooked in various mysterious but delicious ways.

Around Isernia

The countryside **around Isernia** is lush and gentle, at its best in spring, when the meadows are sprinkled with wild flowers. The valleys are headed by hill-villages, most of them rundown places ringed with new housing estates, and the rewards of exploring are principally those of being the first foreigner to have visited in ages. This is not always the most comfortable of experiences, and women can expect to be stared at, cat-called or even kerb-crawled – there's no chance of anonymity in a village where every-one knows everyone else. Getting around, too, isn't easy: buses are organised around the school day, which means you'll have to leave either very early in the morning or at around 2pm – after that there may be no other bus until the next day.

Just outside **PIETRABBONDANTE**, northeast of Isernia, are the remains of a pre-Roman Samnite village, notably a well-preserved theatre set in a green field at the foot of Monte Caraceno. Further along the road, **AGNONE** is best known for the fact that it produces, as it has for the last thousand years, church bells. The **Marinelli Pontifical Foundry** still makes bells in the traditional way, using a priest to bless the molten bronze as it's poured into the mould, which supposedly ensures that the bell's tones will be pure. If you're into metalwork, Agnone is also famous for its coppersmiths, most of whom work on the main street.

To the west of Isernia, the bus calls at **CERRO AL VOLTURNO**, crowned by one of Molise's more spectacular castles, almost growing out of the grey rock on which it is perched. A few kilometres further on is **CASTEL SAN VINCENZO**, another pretty-from-a-distance hill-village: get off the bus below the village at the *Cartiera* (paper mill) and walk along the road to the left for about one kilometre, until you come to the abbey of **S. Vincenzo al Volturno** – a much-reconstructed complex, with a crypt covered by a complete cycle of ninth-century frescoes in rich Byzantine colours, the only surviving example of ninth-century Benedictine art. **Be warned**, though, that the abbey is very rarely open – so check at Isernia's tourist office before leaving.

South of the abbey, but most easily accessible by train from Isernia, is the village of **VENAFRO**, topped by a derelict castle, and with a Roman amphitheatre (just by the railway station) that was converted into an oval piazza in the Middle Ages. The piazza, dry and dusty, is less startling for its architecture than for its squalor and neglect – the Roman arcades now lead into dilapidated shacks, and, usually deserted, it resembles more a pre-gunfight western movie set than an ancient site. For real spaghetti-western action, however, you need to be in Molise at the beginning of August, when the village of **MONTENERO VAL COCCHIARA**, north of Cerro al Volturno, holds an annual **rodeo**.

Campobasso, Saepinum and the Matese

Home of a top-security prison and the National Caribinieri School, **CAMPOBASSO**, the regional capital, is about as appealing as you'd expect – a modern, rather faceless town that was once known for its cutlery industry. It's a good base, though, for the remarkable ruins at **Saepinum**, and if you're around in early June, its Corpus Christi *Sagra dei Misteri* procession is a spectacular event. Citizens are dressed as saints, angels and devils, inserted into Heath-Robinsonish contraptions and transported, seemingly suspended in mid-air, through the streets.

At any other time of the year there really isn't much to see. There is supposed to be a museum of Samnite antiquities opening soon – at least that's what the *comune* has been claiming for the past five years – but until then the steep alleys of the small, old upper town are a mild diversion and lead up to a couple of Romanesque churches – **San Bartolomeo**, which has eerily contorted figures carved around its main door, and **San Giorgio**, whose entrance displays a dragon surrounded by stylised flowers. The views at least are extensive, though they consist mostly of Campobasso's suburban sprawl. And there's little point carrying on up the hill to the monastery and sixteenth-century castle: the monastery is modern, and the castle now a weather station.

Should you need to sleep over, the cheapest **hotel** is outside the centre on the road to Térmoli – the *Tricolore* (☎0874/63.190; ④). The **tourist office** on Piazza Vittoria in the new town has details of local events and bus routes to elsewhere in the province (Mon–Sat 8am–2pm, June–Aug also 4–6pm; ☎0874/415.662).

Saepinum

It's **Saepinum**, a ruined Roman town to the south, close to the border with Puglia, that makes the stopover in Campobasso worthwhile. Three kilometres from the nearest village, surrounded by a lush plain fringed with the foothills of the Matese mountains, it's the best example in Italy of a provincial Roman town – and is tourist-free.

The main reason Saepinum is so intact is that it was never very important: nothing much ever happened here, and after the fall of the Roman Empire it carried on as the sleepy backwater it had always been – until the ninth century when it was sacked by Saracens. Over the centuries its inhabitants added only a handful of farms and cottages, incorporating the odd Roman column or architrave, and eventually moved south to the more secure hilltop site of present-day Sepino. Some have now moved back and have rebuilt the farms and cottages on Saepinum's peripheries, contributing if anything to the site's appeal. Their sheep graze below an ancient mausoleum, chickens scratch around the walls, and the only sounds are from the geese and white peacocks in their tiny smallholdings.

To get to Saepinum from Campobasso, try to take a bus that stops at ALTILIA, right outside the site. Unfortunately there are only a couple a day, and you may have to go to SEPINO and walk the 3km to Saepinum unless you can persuade the driver to detour to the "zona monumentale" – they sometimes will.

The Site

Entrance to Saepinum is through the **Porta Terravecchia**, one of the town's four gates, from which you can follow the *cardus maximus*, still paved with the original flags, to the crossing with the *decumanus* – centre of town and home to the public buildings and trading quarters. On the left, grass spills through the cracks in the pavement of the **forum**, now used by the few local kids as a football pitch, bordered by the foundations of various municipal bulidings: the *comitium*, the *curia*, a temple, baths, and in the centre a fountain with a relief of a griffin. Beyond the forum, on the left of the *decumanus*, the **Casa Impluvio Sannitico** contains a vat to collect rainwater, from the Samnite town that stood on the site before the Romans sacked it in 293 BC. Beyond lies the **Porta Benevento**, adjoining which is one of the two **museums** (both Tues–Sun 9am–1pm) documenting the process of excavation, and with a section on more recent rural traditions. Until quite recently the village was passed through, as it had been for over 2000 years, by nomadic shepherds, moving their flocks between their winter grazing lands in the south and summer pastures in Abruzzo. The *trattura*, as it's called, still takes place, but by lorry and motorway. Further along the road is what must have been a welcome, if bizarre, landmark for generations of shepherds – an enormous stone cylinder resembling a modern water tower that is in fact the mausoleum of one of Saepinum's Roman citizens.

Back down the *decumanus* on the other side of the crossroads is the well-preserved **Basilica** that served as the main courthouse. Beyond is the most interesting part of the town – the octagonal *macellum* (marketplace), with its small stone stalls and central rain-collecting dish, and a series of houses fronted by workshops, with the small living quarters behind. This leads down to the best-preserved gate, the **Porta Boiano**, flanked by cylindrical towers and statues of prisoners celebrating some victory over barbarian invaders. Following the walls around, you reach the **theatre** and the second **museum**, which contains fragments of sculpture.

The Matese

One of Italy's least visited mountain ranges, scattered with high plains, forests and lakes, the **Matese** stretches between Molise and Campania. Wolves still wander its woods, and the peaks are home to eagles, falcons and hawks. The streams are well stocked with fish and the valleys full of the much-coveted *porcini* mushrooms.

Trains running between Isernia and Campobasso stop at **BOIANO**, a pleasant town overlooked by a densely wooded hill crowned with the remains of a castle. If you want to stay, the *Hotel Mary*, Via Barcelona 21 (☎0874/778.375; ⑤), and *Hotel Risi*, on Via Croce (☎0874/782.128; ⑤), are both reasonably priced. The town is a good starting-point for the hike (around 2hr) up **Monte Gallinola** – best done on a clear day when the views take in Italy's eastern and western coastlines. The road leads from beyond the central Piazza Pasquino up to a *rifugio*; from here a steep road, later a footpath, climbs through a forest to the Costa Alta, a mile-high pass whose views are good – though nothing compared to what you'll see when you get to the summit. The path then leads across ski-slopes to the base of Monte la Gallinola, where a track leads up to the top, from which you look down over the Lago del Matese, and, if weather permits, get the much-touted panoramic view.

You can, of course, see something of the Matese in more comfort, either taking a bus to the winter sports centre of **CAMPITELLO MATESE** from either Boiano or

Campobasso; or, if Campitello's generally pricey accommodation options don't suit, staying over at the *Matese* (☎0874/780.378; ⑤) at **SAN MASSIMO**, northwest of Boiano. From Boiano, take the road marked Castellone and San Massimo, and, coming down from the mountains, take the left branch when the road forks.

Towards the coast: Larino and the Albanian villages

Halfway between Campobasso and Térmoli, **LARINO** is considerably more attractive than most Molise towns, its medieval centre clasped in the valley, relatively untouched by the concrete and pace of the modern industrial town that supports it. The highlight is its cathedral, but there are also some minor Roman relics in its small museum and a neglected amphitheatre in the modern town.

To the left of the **train station**, Via Gramsci leads down to old Larino. The main street widens out at Piazza Vittorio Emanuele and the old town's one, ultra-cheap **hotel**, the *Albergo Moderno* (☎0874/822.895; ③). Backing onto it is the **Palazzo Comunale**, whose **museum** (mornings only) contains the *Ara Frentana*, a pre-Roman sacrificial altar, large Roman mosaics and a hoard of coins. Close by is the **Duomo**, built in the early fourteenth century just after the town had been flattened by an earthquake and sacked by the Saracens, with an intricately carved Gothic portal. The interior is unremarkable, but the rickety steps and precarious ladders up the sixteenth-century campanile give good views.

The oldest part of the town starts beyond the duomo, but, appealing as the houses and steep alleys are, it is the glimpses of centuries-old streetlife which are more memorable – women making lace and preparing vegetables outside their houses, while the kids play at their feet and the men do absolutely nothing unless they're boozing in the bar.

If you take a bus from Piazza Vittorio Emanuele to the upper city, you'll jump a couple of centuries in five minutes. Modern Larino is a bustling place, built on the site of the original Samnite/Roman town. The large and overgrown **amphitheatre** (off Via Viadotto Frentano) gives some idea of the importance of early second-century BC *Larinum*, though apart from this the mosaic pavement off Viale Molise and a few fragments of walls, behind the Scuola Materna off Viale Giulio Cesare, are hardly sufficient clues to how Larino once looked.

The Albanian villages

URURI, 12km from Larino, and **PORTOCANNONE**, closer to the coast, are isolated villages, most easily reached by bus from Térmoli (although you could hitch from Larino). Their isolation is such that 600 years after their ancestors emigrated from Albania, the locals still speak an Albanian-Italian dialect incomprehensible to outsiders. Portocannone's Romanesque church contains an icon of the Madonna of Constantinople, brought over by the original emigrés, and in Ururi, at the beginning of May, a **festival** is staged: a fierce and furious race through the village streets on gladiator-style carts, pulled by bulls and pushed by men on horseback with spiked poles. It's a ruthless business: the horses are fed beer before the race to excite them, and although the riders are supposed to push only the back of the carts, they are not averse to prodding the flanks of the bulls, who have already been given electric shocks to liven them up. The race itself is terrifying, but unforgettable, with bulls, carts and spikes hurtling past the frenzied crowds. There are almost inevitably injuries, and at least one person has been killed. If you want to go, the tourist offices at Campobasso or Térmoli will have the precise date.

The Molise coast

The brief stretch of the **Molise coast** is less developed than Abruzzo's. Its only real town, **TÉRMOLI**, a fishing port and smart, attractive resort, makes for a relaxing place to spend a few days. The beach is long and sandy, the modern town has browsable shops, and the old town, walled and guarded by a castle, an interesting cathedral. It's also departure point for ferries (all year) to the Trémiti Islands, and, in summer, to Vasto in Abruzzo and Gargano in Puglia.

Térmoli is the place where Italian and Central European time is set – from the observatory inside the stark castle built above the beach in 1247 by Frederick II. Beyond the castle the road follows the old walls around the headland, holding what's left of the old town, focus of which is the **Duomo**. This is most notable for its Romanesque exterior, decorated all the way round with a series of blind arcades and windows – a feature introduced by Frederick II's Norman-influenced architects. Inside are the relics of Saint Timothy, best known for the letters he received from Saint Paul, who advised him on how to go about converting the Greeks. That he ended up in Térmoli is thanks to Térmolese crusaders, who brought his bones back from Constantinople as a souvenir. The Térmolese hid them, fearing that if the Turks ever succeeded in penetrating the city they would seize and destroy them. In fact the relics were hidden so well they weren't discovered until 1945, during restoration work to repair bomb damage (the sacristan will show you them).

Térmoli's **tourist office** (Mon–Sat 8am–1pm; ☎0875/706.754) is tucked into a grotty car park beside the **bus station**. The cheapest **hotel** is *Al Caminetto* (☎0875/52.139; ④) on the coast road, SS Europa 2, served by hourly buses from the train station; on the same route is the **campsite**, *Cala Saracena* (☎0875/52.113). If you want to be closer to the train station, the *Villa Ida*, on Via M. Milano (☎0875/706.666; ④), isn't greatly more expensive. While here you should certainly have a meal in one of Térmoli's seafood **restaurants**. The prices at *Da Pasquale*, on Via Fratelli Brigada, and at *Blutuff*, on Lungomare Columbo, are not too steep; and there are plenty of pizzerias and simple trattorias along Via Fratelli Brigada, the seafront and the parallel Via V. Emanuele III, if you want somewhere cheaper.

travel details

Trains

Avezzano to: Tagliacozzo (15 daily; 15min).

Campobasso to: Térmoli (10 daily; 1hr 45min).

L'Aquila to: Sulmona (11 daily; 1hr); Terni (11 daily; 2hr 10min).

Pescara to: Ancona (37 daily; 2hr); Giulianova (11 daily; 30min); Pineto (11 daily; 15min); Rome (8 daily; 3hr 30min); Sulmona (18 daily; 1hr 30min); Térmoli (19 daily; 1hr 40min); Vasto (15 daily; 1hr).

Sulmona to: Avezzano (14 daily; 1hr 20min); Campo di Giove (9 daily; 45min); Isernia (3 daily; 2hr 30min); Rivisondoli (9 daily; 1hr); Roccaraso (9 daily; 1hr 10min).

Téramo to: Giulianova (4 daily; 25min).

Térmoli to: Foggia (23 daily; 1hr).

Buses

Atri to: Pescara (12 daily; 55min); Pineto (12 daily; 25min); .

Avezzano to: Albe (9 daily; 30min); Pescasséroli (10 daily; 1hr 30min).

L'Aquila to: Bominaco (4 daily; 30min); Castel del Monte (5 daily; 1hr); Rome (16 daily; 2hr 30min); Sulmona (6 daily; 1hr); Téramo (6 daily; 1hr 20min).

Pescara to: Áscoli Piceno (6 daily; 2hr 45min); Atri (13 daily; 55min); Chieti (every 20min; 40min); L'Aquila (9 daily; 1hr 30min); Lanciano (15 daily; 1hr 25min); Sulmona (5 daily; 1hr 30min).

San Vito to: Lanciano (7 daily; 30min).

Sulmona to: Cocullo (2 daily; 30min); Pacentro (9 daily; 20min); Scanno (8 daily; 50min).

Téramo to: Atri (3 daily; 1hr).

CHAPTER THIRTEEN

CAMPANIA

The region immediately south of Lazio, **Campania** marks the real beginning of the Italian South or *mezzogiorno*. It's the part of the South too, perhaps inevitably, that most people see, as it's easily accessible from Rome and home to some of the area's (indeed Italy's) most notable features – Roman sites, spectacular stretches of coast, tiny islands. It's always been a sought-after region, first named by the Romans, who tagged it the *campania felix*, or "happy land" (to distinguish it from the rather dull *campagna* further north), and settled down here in villas and palatial estates that stretched right around the Bay.

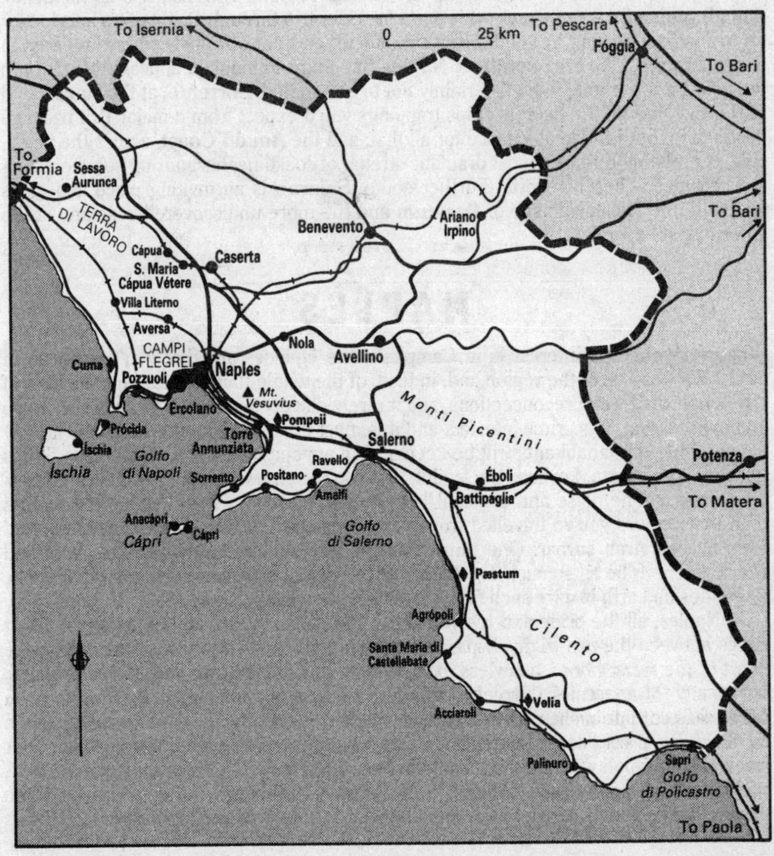

You might, of course, find this hard to believe now, and anyone coming in search of the glories of the Bay of Naples is likely to be disappointed. Industry has eaten into the land around the city as to render it almost unrecognisable, and even in the city the once-grand vistas are often hindered by cranes and smoke-belching chimneys. Most people take one look and skate right out again, disappointed at such a grimy welcome.

But give the area time. **Naples** is the obvious focus, an utterly compelling city (to say the least) and dominating the region in every way. At just two and a half hours by train from the capital, there's no excuse for not seeing at least this part of Campania, though of course you need a fair few days to absorb the city properly, and once established it's a base for some remarkable attractions. The **Bay of Naples**, certainly, is dense enough in interest to occupy you for a good week: there are the ancient sites of Pompeii and Herculaneum, just half an hour outside – probably Italy's best-preserved and most revealing Roman remains; there is the odd, volcanic **Campi Flegrei** area to the north of the city; and of course there are the islands, **Cápri**, **Ischia** and **Prócida** – swarmed over by tourists these days but, with Cápri, at least, so beautiful that a day there is by no means time squandered.

Inland Campania is by contrast a poor, unknown region for the most part, but the nearby towns of **Cápua** and **Caserta** repay visits and are easily seen on day trips. Similarly **Benevento**, an old stop on the Roman route to Bríndisi, has its moments, though you might want to make this part of a wider trip through Campania's interior (or on to Puglia), bearing in mind that it's a difficult and not obviously rewarding area to travel through. The area **south of Naples** has more immediate appeal – beach bum territory on the whole, though certainly not to be avoided. **Sorrento**, at the far east end of the Bay, has all the beer 'n' chips trappings you'd expect from a major Brit package destination, but is a likeable place for all that; and the **Amalfi Coast**, across the peninsula, is probably Europe's most dramatic stretch of coastline, harbouring some enticing – if crowded – beach resorts. Further south, **Salerno** is an inviting place and gives access to the Hellenistic site of **Paestum** and the more undiscovered coastline of the **Cilento** just beyond.

NAPLES

Whatever your real interest is in Campania, the chances are that you'll wind up in **NAPLES** – capital of the region and, indeed, of the whole Italian South. It's the kind of city people visit with preconceptions, and it rarely disappoints: it is filthy, it is very large and overbearing, it is crime-infested, and it is most definitely like nowhere else in Italy – something the inhabitants will be keener than anyone to tell you. In all these things lies the city's charm. Perhaps the feeling that you're somewhere unique makes it possible to endure the noise and constant harassment, perhaps it's the feeling that in less than three hours you've travelled from an ordinary part of Europe to somewhere that feels like an Arab bazaar. One thing, though, is certain: a couple of days here and you're likely to be as staunch a defender of the place as its most devoted inhabitants. Few cities on earth inspire such fierce loyalties.

In Naples, all the pride and resentment of the Italian South, all the historical differences between the two wildly disparate halves of Italy, draw into focus. This is the true heart of the *mezzogiorno*, a lawless, petulant city that has its own way of doing things. It's a city of extremes, fiercely Catholic, its streets punctuated by bright neon Madonnas cut into niches, its miraculous cults regulating the lives of the people much as they have always done. Football, too, is a religion here: the celebrations went on for weeks after Napoli wrested the Italian championship from the despised North in 1987, and you'll still see "Grazie Napoli" graffiti around, although the team has hit some harder times of late. Music, also, has played a key part in the city's identity: there's long been a Naples style, bound up with the city's strange, harsh dialect – and, to some extent, the long-established presence of the US military: American jazz lent a flavour to Neapolitan traditional songs in the Fifties; and the Seventies saw one of Italy's most concentrated musical movements in the urban blues scene of Pino Daniele and the music around the radical Alfa Romeo factory out at Pomigliano.

Some history

There was a settlement here, *Parthenope*, as early as the ninth century BC, but it was superseded by a colony formed by the Greek settlers at nearby Cumae, who established an outpost here in 750 BC, giving it the name *Neapolis*. It prospered during Greek and later Roman times, escaping the disasters that befell the cities around and eventually declaring itself independent in 763 – which it remained for close on 400 years, until the Normans took the city in 1139. The Normans weren't here for long: like the rest of this region, the city soon came under the rule of the Hohenstaufen dynasty, who stayed rather half-heartedly until 1269, when their last king, Conradin, was beheaded in what's now Piazza del Mercato, and the Angevins took over the city. With one exception – Robert the Wise, who was a gentle and enlightened ruler and made the city a great centre for the arts – the Angevin kings ruled badly, in the end losing Naples to Alfonso I of Aragon in 1422, thus establishing a Spanish connection for the city for the next 300 years, until Charles of Bourbon arrived in 1734. Neither the Spanish nor the French were very good for the city, like all great colonialists taking much and contributing little. But it's they who have left most mark on the city today, both in their grand architecture and the history that goes with it. Under the French the city became one of the most populated in Europe, and one of the most iniquitous, setting a trend which still holds good today. For the rest of Europe, Naples was the requisite final stop on the Grand Tour, a position it enjoyed not so much for its proximity to the major Classical sites as for the ready availability of sex. Naples was for a long time the prostitution capital of the continent, and its reputation drew people from far and wide, giving new meaning (in the days when syphilis was rife) to the phrase "See Naples and die".

More recently, Naples and its surrounding area have been the recipient of much of the money that has poured into the South under the *Cassa per il Mezzogiorno* scheme and its industry is spreading, if not exactly booming. But the real power in the area is still in the hands of organised crime or the Camorra: much of the coastline west of the city – to Bagnoli – was built by Camorra money, and, though it's not at all publicised, little happens that matters here without the nod of the larger families. Not surprisingly, much government money has found its way into their hands too, with the result that there's been little real improvement in the living standards of the average Neapolitan: a very high percentage remain unemployed, and a disgraceful number still inhabit the typically Neapolitan one-room *bassi* – slums really, letting in no light and housing many in appallingly overcrowded conditions. A little over ten years ago there was a cholera outbreak in part of the city, and it is perhaps only a matter of time before the same thing happens again: Naples produces more rubbish than any other city in the world, and yet its refuse-collecting is abysmally inefficient. The notorious city government has long been too at odds with itself to do anything about all this, and even if it tried would probably be thwarted by the interests of the Camorra. For how much longer the city can limp on is anybody's guess, and for the moment Naples is either romanticised by its aficianados or vilified by its opponents – neither standpoint likely to much help the people who live here.

The Naples **area telephone code is** ☎081.

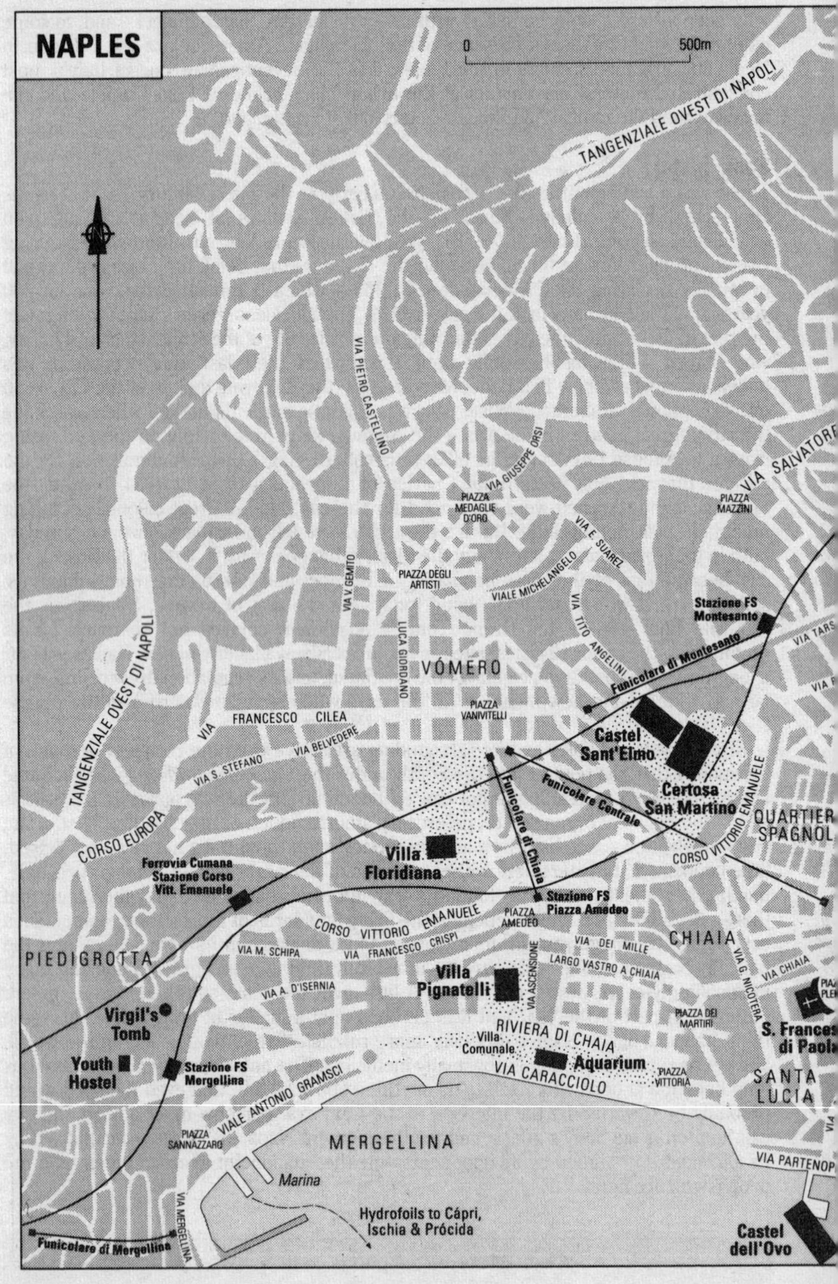
NAPLES
0
500m
TANGENZIALE OVEST DI NAPOLI
VIA PIETRO CASTELLINO
VIA GIUSEPPE ORSI
VIA SALVATORE
PIAZZA MEDAGLIE D'ORO
PIAZZA MAZZINI
VIA E. SUAREZ
VIALE MICHELANGELO
PIAZZA DEGLI ARTISTI
VIA V. GEMITO
VIA TITO ANGELINI
Stazione FS Montesanto
LUCA GIORDANO
VÓMERO
Funicolare di Montesanto
TANGENZIALE OVEST DI NAPOLI
VIA FRANCESCO CILEA
PIAZZA VANVITELLI
VIA BELVEDERE
VIA S. STEFANO
Castel Sant'Elmo
Funicolare di Chiaia
Funicolare Centrale
Certosa San Martino
CORSO VITTORIO EMANUELE
QUARTIER SPAGNOL
CORSO EUROPA
Villa Floridiana
Ferrovia Cumana Stazione Corso Vitt. Emanuele
Stazione FS Piazza Amedeo
PIAZZA AMEDEO
CORSO VITTORIO EMANUELE
CHIAIA
VIA M. SCHIPA
VIA FRANCESCO CRISPI
VIA DEI MILLE
PIEDIGROTTA
VIA ASCENSIONE
LARGO VASTRO A CHIAIA
VIA CHIAIA
Villa Pignatelli
VIA A. D'ISERNIA
VIA G. NICOTERA
Virgil's Tomb
PIAZZA DEI MARTIRI
RIVIERA DI CHIAIA
S. Frances di Paol
Villa Comunale
Youth Hostel
Stazione FS Mergellina
Aquarium
VIA CARACCIOLO
PIAZZA VITTORIA
SANTA LUCIA
VIALE ANTONIO GRAMSCI
PIAZZA SANNAZZARO
MERGELLINA
VIA PARTENOP
Marina
Hydrofoils to Cápri, Ischia & Prócida
VIA MERGELLINA
Castel dell'Ovo
Funicolare di Mergellina

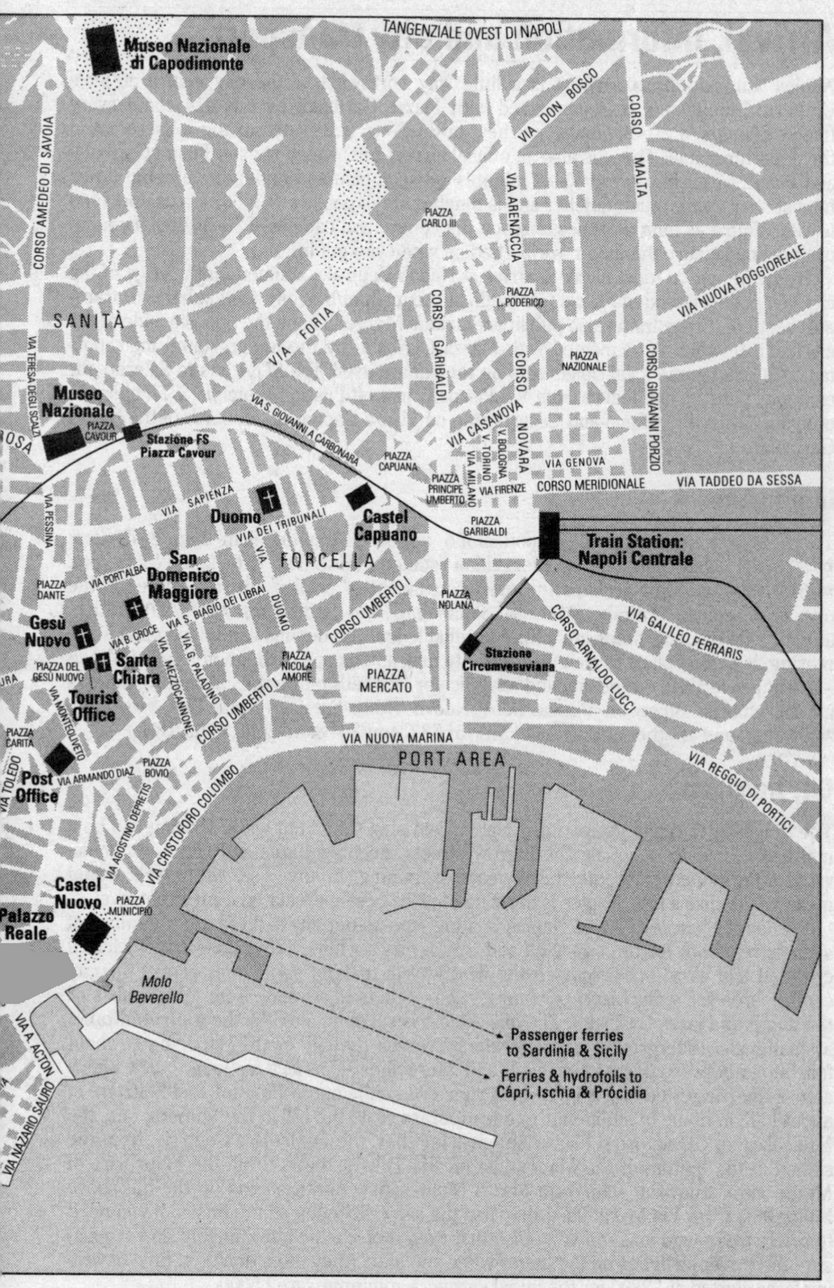
TANGENZIALE OVEST DI NAPOLI
Museo Nazionale di Capodimonte
CORSO AMEDEO DI SAVOIA
VIA DON BOSCO
CORSO MALTA
VIA ARENACCIA
PIAZZA CARLO III
PIAZZA L. PODERICO
CORSO GARIBALDI
VIA NUOVA POGGIOREALE
SANITÀ
VIA FORIA
CORSO NOVARA
PIAZZA NAZIONALE
CORSO GIOVANNI PORZIO
VIA TERESA DEGLI SCALZI
Museo Nazionale
PIAZZA CAVOUR
Stazione FS Piazza Cavour
VIA S. GIOVANNI A CARBONARA
VIA CASANOVA
V. TORINO
V. BOLOGNA
VIA MILANO
VIA GENOVA
PIAZZA CAPUANA
PIAZZA PRINCIPE UMBERTO
VIA FIRENZE
CORSO MERIDIONALE
VIA TADDEO DA SESSA
VIA PESSINA
VIA SAPIENZA
Duomo
VIA DEI TRIBUNALI
Castel Capuano
PIAZZA GARIBALDI
Train Station: Napoli Centrale
San Domenico Maggiore
FORCELLA
VIA DUOMO
PIAZZA DANTE
VIA PORT'ALBA
VIA S. BIAGIO DEI LIBRAI
CORSO UMBERTO I
PIAZZA NOLANA
CORSO ARNALDO LUCCI
VIA GALILEO FERRARIS
Gesù Nuovo
VIA B. CROCE
Santa Chiara
PIAZZA DEL GESÙ NUOVO
VIA MEZZOCANNONE
VIA G. PALADINO
PIAZZA NICOLA AMORE
PIAZZA MERCATO
Stazione Circumvesuviana
VIA MONTEOLIVETO
Tourist Office
PIAZZA CARITÀ
VIA NUOVA MARINA
PORT AREA
VIA REGGIO DI PORTICI
Post Office
VIA ARMANDO DIAZ
PIAZZA BOVIO
VIA TOLEDO
VIA AGOSTINO DEPRETIS
VIA CRISTOFORO COLOMBO
Castel Nuovo
PIAZZA MUNICIPIO
Palazzo Reale
Molo Beverello
VIA A. ACTON
VIA NAZARIO SAURO
Passenger ferries to Sardinia & Sicily
Ferries & hydrofoils to Cápri, Ischia & Prócidia

Arrival, information and city transport

Naples' **Capodochino airport** is a little way northwest of the city centre at Viale Umberto Maddalena. It is connected with Piazza Garibaldi by bus #14 about every fifteen minutes, a 20–30-minute journey; buy tickets (L1000) from the tobacconist in the departures hall. There is also an official airport bus, which runs to Piazza Garibaldi and Piazza Municipio every 30–40 minutes between 6am and midnight, although to be honest it isn't very much quicker and is much more expensive (L3000). Taxis, too, tend to take almost as long as buses to reach the centre, and can cost L20–30,000; if you do use one, make sure the meter is switched on when you get in.

By train, you're most likely to arrive at Napoli Centrale, situated on the edge of the city centre at one end of Piazza Garibaldi, at the main hub of city (and suburban) transport services. Some trains also pull in to Stazione Mergellina, on the opposite side of the city centre, which is connected with Piazza Garibaldi by the underground metropolitana. City and some local buses stop on the square itself; the *SITA* bus to Salerno, for example, pulls up and leaves from Via Pisanelli, just off Piazza Municipio; *CTP* buses to outlying towns like Cápua and Caserta stop on Piazza Capuana, just north of the Piazza Garibaldi.

Information

There is a tourist desk at Capodochino airport (Mon–Fri 8am–2pm & 5–7pm; ☎780.5761), and another at Mergellina station (Mon–Fri 8am–2pm & 5–7pm; ☎761.2102), although perhaps the most convenient of Naples' **tourist offices** is the one in Stazione Centrale (Mon–Sat 9am–8pm, Sun 9am–1pm; ☎268.779), which, although its opening times are a little unreliable and the queues can be long and slow-moving, is a good place to pick up a free city map and a copy of the monthly *Qui Napoli* – a useful reference on the city and an indicator of what's on. In the city centre, there is another tourist office on Piazza Gesù Nuovo (Mon–Sat 9am–7pm, Sun 9am–3pm; ☎406.289), and another at Piazza dei Martiri 58 (Mon–Fri 8am–2pm; ☎405.311).

City transport

The only way to really **get around** Naples and stay sane is to **walk**. Driving can be a nightmare, and to negotiate the narrow streets, hectic squares and racetrack boulevards on a moped or scooter takes years of training. In any case, *not* to walk would mean you'd miss a lot – Naples is the kind of place best appreciated from street level.

For longer journeys – and Naples is a big, spread-out city – there are a number of alternatives, both for the city itself and the Bay as a whole. City **buses** are efficient if crowded and slow, but are much the best way of making short hops across the city centre: fares are a flat L1000 per journey; buy tickets in advance from tobacconists or the booth on Piazza Garibaldi. The bus system is supplemented by the **metropolitana**, a small-scale underground network which crosses the city centre, stopping at about four stops between Piazza Garibaldi and Mergellina – perfect for long, quick jumps across the congested city centre – and runs eventually out to Pozzuoli and Solfatara in about half an hour. In addition, three **funiculars** scale the hill of the Vómero: one, the Funicolare di Chiaia, from Piazza Amedeo; another, the Funicolare Centrale, from the station at the bottom of Via Mattia, just off Via Toledo; and a third, the Funicolare di Montesanto, from the station on Piazza Montesanto. Another runs up the hill above Mergellina from Via Mergellina; they use the same ticketing as the buses. If you need to take a **taxi** – and you should realise that even they can be interminably slow – make sure the driver switches on the meter when you start (they often don't); at time of writing fares started at L2800 for the initial journey – minimum fare L5000.

USEFUL BUS ROUTES

#CD Piazza Garibaldi–Piazza Dante–Piazza Carlo III–Piazza Garibaldi

#CS Piazza Garibaldi–Piazza Carlo III–Piazza Dante–Piazza Garibaldi

#106 Piazza Garibaldi–Piazza Municipio–Riviera di Chiaia–Mergellina

#140 Piazza Gesù–Piazza Plebiscito–Piazza Vittoria–Mergellina–Posillipo

#152 Piazza Garibaldi–Piazza Municipio–Piazza Vittoria–Mergellina–Pozzuoli

#440 (night bus) Piazza Garibaldi–Corso Umberto–Via Partenope–Riviera di Chiaia–Mergellina–Posillipo

For details on the frequency of the rail lines, see "Travel Details".

For solely **out-of-town trips** – around the Bay in either direction – there are three more rail systems. The **Circumvesuviana** runs from its station on Corso Garibaldi right round the Bay of Naples about every half-hour, stopping everywhere, as far as Sorrento, which it reaches in about an hour. The **Ferrovia Cumana** operates every twenty minutes from its terminus station in Piazza Montesanto west to Pozzuoli and Baia. And the **Circumflegrea** line runs, again from Piazza Montesanto, west to Cuma – again about every twenty minutes. Ticketing for all these depends on where you're going, but as a rough guide, you can expect to pay around L4000 if you're going all the way to Sorrento on the Circumvesuviana, L1500 or so as far as Ercolano.

Accommodation

Accommodation prices in Naples may come as a refreshing change after the north of Italy, but they're still not cheap, and the city being the kind of place it is you need to choose carefully between the cheaper dives. A good many of these are conveniently situated around Piazza Garibaldi, spitting distance from the train station and not badly placed for the rest of town; others group on the far side of the *centro storico*, near the university. The station tourist office may point you somewhere good (it's certainly worth enquiring); if not, just follow the listings below – and don't, whatever you do, go with one of the touts outside the station. It's unlikely you'll be getting into anything dangerous but it *is* a possibility and in any case the hotel room probably won't be up to much. Incidentally, if you can, try to book somewhere in advance, especially in high season, when the city – like everywhere else in Italy – gets crowded. Finally, it's worth knowing that the Naples youth hostel, and some of the hotels, offer cheap deals on ferry tickets to the islands; if they don't tell about them, it's normally worth enquiring.

Hotels

Ambra, Via Mezzacanone 109 (☎552.9256). Handy for the university and consequently often full. But the low prices and central location mean it's worth a try. ④.

Ausonia, Via Caracciolo 11 (☎682.278). A more upscale choice altogether, and neatly placed on the far side of town, convenient for hydrofoils to the islands. Bus #106. ⑦.

Casanova, Via Venezia 2 (☎268.287). Station-area hotel run by an affable management team. Pleasant, clean rooms, low prices, and a communal roof terrace. ④.

Crispi, Via Crispi 104 (☎668.048). Well-established budget hotel close to the Mergellina metropolitana stop. ⑤.

Ginevra, Via Genova 116 (☎283.210). Welcoming place just to the right of the station that has fairly basic rooms looking onto a large plant-filled courtyard. Very handy if you're catching an early train. ④.

Imperia, Piazza Luigi Miraglia 386 (☎459.347). Friendly hotel with English-speaking management and a marvellous location in the heart of old Naples, a short walk from Piazza Dante. Unspectacular but clean rooms, all with shared facilities; the only drawback is its location at the top of five arduous flights of stairs. Perhaps the best option in this price range. ③.

Odeon, Via Silvio Spaventa (☎285.656). Two-star hotel with decent doubles with TV, just two minutes from the station, off Piazza Garibaldi. ⑤.

Orchidea, Corso Umberto 7 (☎551.1676). A good central location, not far from the ferry port and just a short bus ride from Stazione Centrale. Large rooms, all with private bath. ⑥.

San Pietro, San Pietro ad Aram 18 (☎553.5914). Recently upgraded hotel just off Corso Umberto on the right., just after you leave Piazza Garibaldi. ⑤.

Zara, Via Firenze 81 (☎287.125). A rather seedy location, but very close to the station, and the rooms are nice enough. ④.

Hostels and campsites

The cheapest place of all to stay in Naples is the official **youth hostel**, *Ostello Mergellina*, Salita della Grotta 23 (☎761.2346), in a nice location, if somewhat removed from the life of the city centre, and offering two-, four- and six-bedded rooms. The drawbacks are an 11.30am curfew and a three-day maximum stay during July and August. Take the metropolitana to Mergellina or bus #152 from Piazza Garibaldi.

There are a number of **campsites** within a feasible distance of Naples. The closest is the *Vulcano Solfatara* site in Pozzuoli at Via Solfatara 161 (☎526.7413), open between April and October; bus #152 runs right there from Piazza Garibaldi, or take the metropolitana to Pozzuoli and walk ten minutes up the hill. Out of these months, you're probably best off going to one of the other sites around the Bay – perhaps at Pompeii, or, rather nicer, Sorrento, neither of which is more than an hour out from the city. See the relevant headings for details.

The City

Naples is a surprisingly large city, and a sprawling one, with a centre that has many different focuses. The area between Piazza Garibaldi and Via Toledo, roughly corresponding to the old Roman *Neapolis* (much of which is still unexcavated below the ground), makes up the old part of the city – the **centro storico** – the main streets still following the path of the old Roman roads. This is much the liveliest, most teeming part of town, an open-air *casbah* of hawking, yelling humanity that makes up in energy what it lacks in grace. Buildings rise high on either side of the narrow, crowded streets, cobwebbed with washing; there's little light, not even much sense of the rest of the city outside – certainly not of the proximity of the sea.

But the insularity of the *centro storico* is deceptive, and in reality there's another, quite different side to Naples, one that's much more like the sunwashed Bay of Naples murals you've seen in cheap restaurants back home. **Via Toledo**, the main street of the city, edges the old centre from the **Palazzo Reale** up to the **Archaeological Museum** and the heights of **Capodimonte**; to the left rises the **Vómero**, with its fancy housing and museums, and the smug neighbourhood of Chiaia, beyond which lies the long green boulevard of **Villa Comunale**, stretching around to the district of **Mergellina** and **Posillipo**: all neighbourhoods which exert quite a different kind of pull – that of an airy waterfront city, with views, seafood eaten *al fresco* and peace and quiet.

Piazza Garibaldi to Via Toledo: the centro storico

However you actually get to Naples, there's a good chance that the first place you'll see is **Piazza Garibaldi**, a long, wide square criss-crossed by traffic lanes that cuts into the

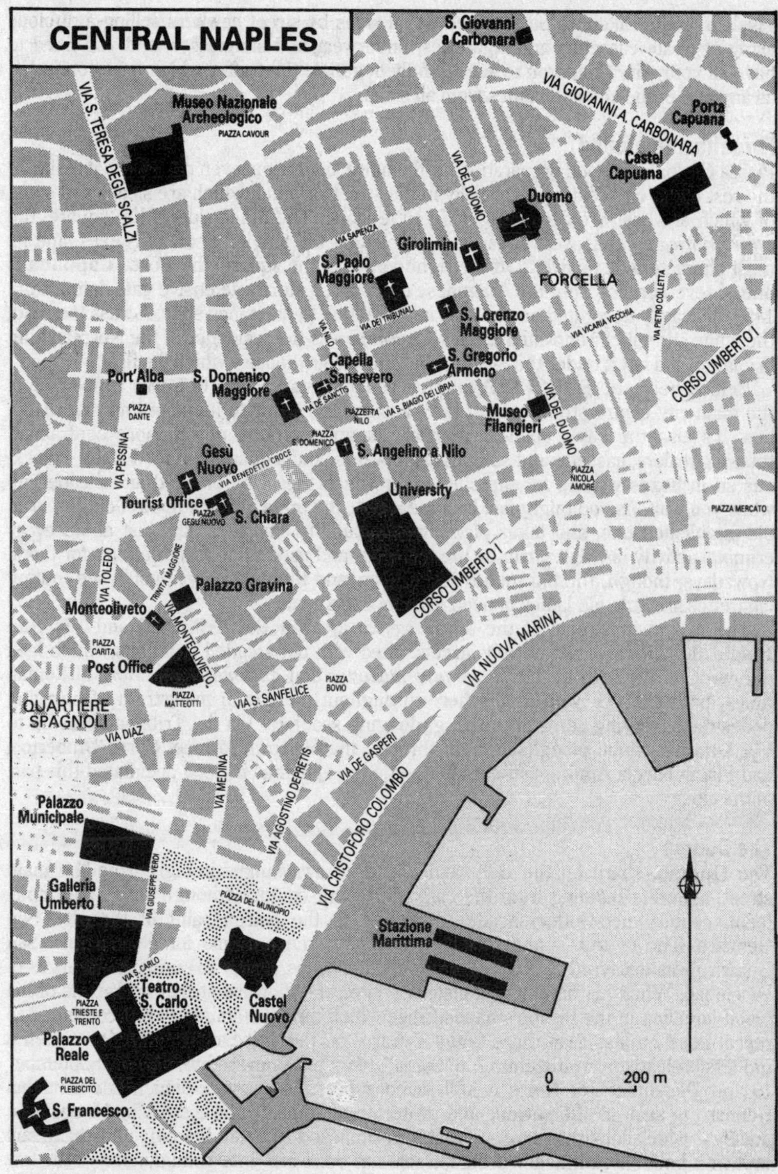

city centre from the modern train station. It's the city's transport hub – most of the city buses leave from here, as do the metropolitana and Circumvesuviana lines – and one of its most hectic junctions; indeed it's Piazza Garibaldi, perhaps more so than any other part of the city, that puts people off Naples. The buildings aren't particularly distinguished, you're likely to be accosted on all sides by street hawkers selling a dubious array of pirate cassettes and cigarettes, underwear and sunglasses, and you need to have all your wits about you to successfully negotiate the traffic, which is as congested as any part of the city and comes from all sides.

Forcella and around

Piazza Garibaldi is good preparation for the noise, confusion, even menace that make up the rest of the city centre – especially in the streets around, which are sleazy and some of which are best avoided at night if you're alone. The other side of the square, the *centro storico* spreads west as far as Via Toledo – the tangled heart of Naples, and its most characteristic quarter. Off the right corner of the square, the **Porta Capuana** is one of several relics from the Aragonese city walls, a sturdy defensive gate dating from 1490, delicately decorated on one side in Florentine Renaissance style. Across the road, the white and much renovated **Castel Capuano** was the residence of the Norman king William I, and later, under the Spanish, became a courthouse – which it still is.

Behind here, the **FORCELLA** quarter, which spreads down to Corso Umberto I, is the main city centre stronghold of the Camorra and home to its most important families. It's also the city's open-air **market**, stamping-ground of yet more contraband tobacco dealers, cassette and sunglasses hawkers, and a quantity of food stalls – chickens sit in boxes waiting for the chop, after which they'll be plucked and cleaned up while you wait. As you might fast become aware, the trade in black market ciggies is an old-established one, and takes place throughout the city. It is, like just about every criminal activity in Naples, run by the Camorra, and used to be a high earner for them. Nowadays, though, the big money is in drugs, and the only people you'll see touting cigarettes are little old ladies in need of a few extra cents.

The two main streets of the *centro storico* are **Via dei Tribunali** and **Via San Biagio dei Librai** – two narrow streets, lined with old arcaded buildings, which lead due west on the path of the *decumanus maximus* and *ducumanus inferiore* of Roman times, both charged with atmosphere throughout the day, a maelstrom of hurrying pedestrians, revving cars and buzzing, dodging scooters. Via dei Tribunali cuts up to **Via Duomo**, which ploughs straight through the old town to meet Corso Umberto I and Piazza Nicola Amore, laid out after a cholera epidemic in 1884 decimated this part of the city.

The Duomo

The **Duomo**, sharp on the right and is tucked away unassumingly from the main street, a Gothic building from the early thirteenth century (though with a late nineteenth-century neo-Gothic facade) dedicated to the patron saint of the city, San Gennaro. The church – and saint – are key reference points for Neapolitans: San Gennaro was martyred at Pozzuoli, just outside Naples, in 305 AD under the purges of Diocletian. When his body was transferred here, tradition has it that two phials of his blood liquefied in the bishop's hands, since which time the "miracle" has continued to repeat itself no less than three times a year – on the first Saturday in May (when a procession leads from the church of Santa Chiara to the cathedral) and on September 19 and December 16. There is still much superstition surrounding this event: San Gennaro is seen as the saviour and protector of Naples, and if the blood refuses to liquefy – which luckily is rare – disaster is supposed to befall the city, and many still wait with bated breath to see if the miracle has occurred. Interestingly, one of the few times this century Gennaro's blood hasn't turned was in 1944, an event followed by Vesuvius's last eruption. The last time was in May 1988, the day after which Naples lost an important football match to their intense rivals, Milan.

The miraculous liquefaction takes place during a special mass in full view of the congregation – a service it's perfectly possible to attend (see box for a note on proce-

THE MIRACLE OF SAN GENNARO

If you're in Naples at the right time it's possible to attend the service to witness the **liquefaction of San Gennaro's blood**, but you must be sure to arrive at the cathedral early. The mass starts at 9am and queues begin to form two hours before that; arrive much after 7am and there's a chance you won't get in. Once the line of carabinieri have opened up the church everyone will make a dash for the front; for a good view of the proceedings you'll have to join them – and pushing and shoving is, incidentally, very much part of the procedure. The atmosphere in the church throughout the service is a boisterous one. The preliminary mass goes on for some time, the chancel of the church ringed by armed policemen and flanked by a determined press and photographic corps, until a procession leads out of the saint's chapel holding the (still solid) phial of the blood aloft, to much applause and neck-craning, and cries of "Viva San Gennaro". After ten minutes or so of emotional imprecations the reliquary is taken down from its holder and inspected – at which point, hopefully, it is declared to tumultuous applause and cheering that the saint's blood is indeed now liquid, and the phial is shaken to prove the point. Afterwards the atmosphere is a festive one, stallholders setting up outside the church and the devout queueing up to kiss the phial containing the liquefied blood – a process which goes on for a week.

dure), though the church authorities have yet to allow any close scientific examination of the blood or the "miraculous" process. Whatever the truth of the miracle, there's no question it's still a significant event in the Neapolitan calendar, and one of the more bizarre of the city's institutions.

The first chapel on the right as you walk into the cathedral is dedicated to San Gennaro and holds the precious phials of the saint's blood and his skull in a silver bust-reliquary from 1305. On the other side of the church, the basilica of Santa Restituta is almost a church in its own right, officially the oldest structure in Naples, erected by Constantine in 324 and supported by columns that were taken from a temple to Apollo on this site. The baptistery, too, contains relics from very early Christian times, including a late fifth-century structure preserving fragments of contemporary mosaics and a font believed to have been taken from a temple to Dionysus. Downstairs, the crypt of San Gennaro is one of the finest examples of Renaissance art in Naples, founded by Cardinal Carafa and holding the tombs of both San Gennaro and Pope Innocent IV.

Spaccanapoli

Across Via Duomo, Via Tribunali continues on past **Piazza Girolamini**, on which a plaque marks the house where, in 1668, Giambattista Vico was born – now ironically the home of a well-known Camorra family. Vico was a late-Renaissance Neapolitan philosopher who advanced theories of cyclical history which were far ahead of their time and still echo through twentieth-century thinking: James Joyce's *Finnegans Wake* was based on his writings. Vico lived all his life in this district and was buried in the church of **Girolamini** (entrance on Via Duomo).

Further on down Via Tribunali, on the left, the church of **San Lorenzo Maggiore** is a light, spacious Gothic church, unspoiled by later additions and with a soaring Gothic ambulatory at its apse – unusual in Italy, even more so in Naples, where garishly embellished church interiors are the order of the day. It's a mainly fourteenth-century building, though with a much later facade, built during the reign of the Angevin king Robert the Wise on the site of a Roman basilica – remains of which are in the cloisters. In a way it was at the centre of the golden age that Naples enjoyed under Robert, the focus of its cultural activity. Petrarch stayed for a while in the adjacent convent, and Boccaccio is said to have met the model for his Fiammetta, believed to be Robert's daughter, during Mass here.

You're now in the city's busiest and most architecturally rich quarter, the so-called **Spaccanapoli** or "split-Naples" that's the real heart of the old city. Cut down to its other main axis, **Via San Biagio dei Librai** by way of **Via San Gregorio Armeno**, one of the old city's most picturesque streets, lined with places specialising in the making of *presepi* or Christmas cribs. This is a Neapolitan tradition, kept up to this day, and the workshops along here start turning out the often-inventive creations well before Christmas – the last courtyard on the left is a good place to see one of them in action if you're here at the right time of year. Almost opposite is the arched portal of the church of **San Gregorio Armeno**, a sumptuous Baroque edifice with frescoes by the late seventeenth-century Neapolitan artist Luca Giordano, not to mention two stupendously ornate gilded organs, one on each side of the nave. Up above the south aisle, you'll notice a series of grills, through which the Benedectine nuns of the **Chiostro di San Gregorio Armeno** next door would view the services. You can visit the courtyard of the convent (entrance up the street and on the left; daily 9.30–11.30am), which is a wonderfully peaceful haven from the noise outside, planted with limes and busy with nuns quietly going about their duties.

There's more work by Giordano back on Via Duomo, at no. 288 in the **Museo Filangieri** (Tues–Sat 9am–2pm, Sun 9am–1pm; L4000), housed in the knobbly fifteenth-century Palazzo Cuomo and made up of the collection of Prince Gaetano Filangieri, reassembled after the original collection was burned by the Nazis in 1943. Giordano was easily the most prolific of all the Neapolitan painters, known as *Luca fa presto* or "Luca paint quickly" for his astonishing output. He was the pupil of another well-known Neapolitan painter, Jose Ribera (otherwise known as "Il Spagnoletto"), whose work is also here, alongside the canvases of his contemporary and similar stylist Mattia Preti, and an assortment of porcelain, old manuscripts and other bits and pieces.

More compellingly, west down Via San Biagio leads to the **Largo di Corpo di Nilo**, where a Roman statue of a reclining old man is a representation of the Nile, sculpted in Nero's time, and has a habit, it's claimed, of whispering to women as they walk by. The church nearby, **Sant'Angelo a Nilo**, has sculpture by Michelozzo and Donatello, the first Renaissance work to be seen in Naples. Further on, **Piazza San Domenico Maggiore** is marked by the **Guglia di San Domenico** – one of the whimsical Baroque obelisks that were originally put up after times of plague or disease, built in 1737. The **church** of the same name flanks the north side of the square, an originally – though much messed about – Gothic building from 1289, one of whose chapels holds a miraculous painting of the *Crucifixion* which is said to have spoken to Saint Thomas Aquinas during his time at the adjacent monastery.

North of here, Via de Sanctis leads off right to one of the city's odder monuments, the **Capella Sansevero** (Mon–Sat 10am–1.30pm & 5–7pm, Sun 10am–1.30pm, closed Tues am; L4000), the tomb-chapel of the di Sangro family decorated by the sculptor Guiseppe Sammartino in the mid-eighteenth century. The decoration, at least, is unique, the centrepiece a carving of a dead Christ, laid out flat and covered with a veil of stark and remarkable realism, not least because it was carved out of a single piece of marble. Even more accomplished is the veiled figure of *Modesty* on the left, and, on the right, its twin *Disillusionment*, in the form of a woeful figure struggling with the marble netting of his own disenchantment. Look, too, at the effusive *Deposition* on the high altar, and the memorial above the doorway which shows one Cecco di Sangro climbing out of his tomb, sword in hand. You might also want to take a look downstairs. The man responsible for the chapel, Prince Raimondo, was a well-known eighteenth-century alchemist, and down here are the results of some of his experiments: two bodies under glass, their capillaries and most of their organs preserved by a mysterious liquid developed by the prince – who, incidentally, was excommunicated by the pope for such practices. Even now they make for gruesome sights – not for the queasy.

Continuing west, Via San Biagio becomes Via San Benedetto Croce, named after the twentieth-century philosopher who spent much of his life in this neighbourhood, living in the palace at no. 12. A little way down, the street broadens out at Piazza del Gesù Nuovo, centring on another ornate **Guglia**, much larger than the San Domenico one, and dating from 1750. On the right, the **Gesù Nuovo** church is most notable for its lava-stone facade, originally part of a fifteenth-century palace which stood here, prickled with pyramids that give it an impregnable, prison-like air. The inside is as gaudy as you might expect, in part decorated by the Neapolitan-Spanish painter Ribera.

Facing the Gesù church, the church of **Santa Chiara** is quite different, a Provençal-Gothic structure built in 1328 that was completely gutted during the last war and rebuilt with a bare Gothic austerity that's pleasing after the excesses opposite. There's not very much to see inside, only the tombs of the Angevin monarchs in the last chapel on the right, including Robert the Wise at the altar, showing the king in a monk's habit. But the attached convent, established by Robert's wife, Sancia, has a **cloister** (entrance to the left of the church: daily 8.30am–12.30pm & 4–6.30pm) that is truly one of the gems of the city, a shady haven lushly planted and furnished with benches and low walls covered with colourful majolica tiles depicting bucolic scenes of life outside.

Corso Umberto I, Piazza Municipio and the Palazzo Reale

Off the far left corner of Piazza Garibaldi, **Corso Garibaldi** runs down to the sea, past the main Circumvesuviana terminal and, on the right, the **Porta Nolana**, a solid-looking Aragonese gateway that signals the entrance to Naples' main fish market – a grouping of streets lined with a wonderful array of stalls piled high with wriggling displays of fish and seafood. Behind, towards the water, the church of **Santa Maria del Carmine** dates back to the thirteenth century and is traditionally the church of the poor in Naples, particularly fishermen and mariners – the main port area is close by. Axel Munthe, the Swedish writer and resident of Cápri, used to sleep here after tending to victims of the 1884 cholera outbreak.

Just west, the still war-damaged **Piazza del Mercato** was for centuries home to the city's scaffold, and is a bleak, dusty square even now. There's little to detain you in this part of town, and you may as well cut back up to **Corso Umberto I**, which spears through the old part of the city, a long straight journey from the seedy gatherings of prostitutes and kerb-crawlers at its Piazza Garibaldi end, past many of the city's more mainstream shops, to the symmetrical **Piazza Bovio** and its elegant seventeenth-century Fontana del Nettuno.

From Piazza Bovio it's a short walk down to **Piazza del Municipio**, a busy traffic junction that stretches from the ferry terminal on the water up to the Palazzo Municipale at the top, dominated by the brooding hulk of the **Castel Nuovo** opposite – the "Maschio Angioino" – erected in 1282 by the Angevins and later converted as the royal residence of the Aragon monarchs. The entrance incorporates a triumphal arch from 1454 that commemorates the taking of the city by Alfonso I, the first Aragon ruler, and shows details of his triumph topped by a rousing statue of Saint Michael. These days the castle is mainly taken up by the offices of the Naples and Campania councils, but part is given over to the **Museo Civico** (Mon–Fri 9am–2pm, Sat 9am–1.30pm, Sun closed; free), comprising a rather dull collection of frescoes and sculpture in chapel, and an array of silver and bronze objects. Even if you don't want to visit the museum, it's worth sauntering into the courtyard for the fine views of the harbour from the far side.

Just beyond the castle, on the left, the **Teatro San Carlo** is an oddly unimpressive building from the outside; inside, however, you can see why this theatre was the envy of Europe when it opened in 1737 in time for Charles of Bourbon's birthday, for whom it was built. It's still the largest opera house in Italy, and one of the most distinguished in the world. Opposite, the **Galleria Umberto I** has fared less well over the years, its high arcades, erected in 1887, remarkably empty of the teeming life that characterises the rest of Naples, and in the evening even something of a danger spot. Its rather downbeat collection of shops can't compete with those of, say, Milan's Galleria, built ten years earlier – though you'll still pay way over the odds in its rather grotty cafés.

Come out of the Galleria and you're on **Piazza Trieste e Trento**, more a roundabout than a piazza, whose life you can watch while sipping a pricey drink on the terrace of the sleek **Caffè Gambrinus**. To the left, **Piazza del Plebiscito** is another attempt at civic grandeur gone badly wrong, its curve of columns – modelled on Bernini's piazza for Saint Peter's in Rome – shabby and belittled by the expanse of cars which use the square as a parking space, not to mention the buses which line up in front. The church of **San Francescó di Paola** in the centre is no great success either, a copy of the Pantheon in Rome, whose attempts at Classical majesty are thwarted by the traffic and graffiti – and only really work once you're standing under the impressively enormous dome.

Opposite, the **Palazzo Reale** (Mon–Sat 9am–2pm, Sun 9am–1pm; L6000) manages better than most of the buildings around here to retain some semblance of its former glories, though it's a bland, derivative building for the most part and even a bit of a fake, thrown up hurriedly in 1602 to accommodate Philip II on a visit here and never actually occupied by a monarch long-term. Indeed it's more of a monument to monarchies than monarchs, with the various dynasties that ruled Naples by proxy for so long represented in the niches of the facade, from Roger the Norman to Vittorio Emanuele II, taking in among others Alfonso I and a slightly comic Murat on the way. Upstairs, the palace's first-floor rooms are decorated with fine Baroque excesses of gilded furniture, trompe l'oeil ceilings, great overbearing tapestries and lots and lots of undistinguished seventeenth- and eighteenth-century paintings. Best bits are the chapel, on the far side of the central square (you may have to ask someone to open this for you), with its finely worked altarpiece; the little theatre – the first room on the right – which is refreshingly restrained after the rest of the palace; and the terrace, which gives good views over the port and the forbidding Castel Nuovo. Look also at the original bronze doors of the palace at the bottom of the dwarfing main staircase, cast in 1468 and showing scenes from Ferdinand of Aragon's struggle against the local barons. The cannonball wedged in the bottom left-hand panel dates from a naval battle between the French and the Genoese that took place while the former were pillaging the doors from the palace.

Just south of Piazza del Plebiscito, Via Santa Lucia curves around towards the sea, the main artery of the **SANTA LUCIA** district – for years the city's most famed and characteristic neighbourhood, site of a lively fish market and source of most of the *O Sole Mio*-type cliches about Naples you've ever heard. It's a much less neighbourly place now, home to most of the city's poshest hotels on the streets around and along the seafront Via Partenope, though one or two decent restaurants make it a better than average place to come and eat. Down on the waterfront, a grouping of seafood restaurants cluster around the grey mass of the **Castel dell'Ovo** or "egg-castle" – so named because of the story that it was built over an egg placed here by Virgil in Roman times: Colosseum-like, if the egg breaks then Naples will fall. Actually it was built by the Hohenstaufen king Frederick II and extended by the Angevins, and nowadays belongs to the military and is off-limits to ordinary visitors. But you can walk over the short causeway that connects its small island to the mainland and eat at one of the surrounding restaurants – which make an atmospheric if not always culinarily memorable place to spend the evening; *La Bersagliera* on the landward side is best.

From Piazza Trieste e Trento to Capodimonte

Piazza Trieste e Trento marks the beginning of the city's main shopping street, **Via Toledo** – or, to give it its official name, Via Roma – which leads north in a dead straight line, climbing the hill up to the National Archaeological Museum and separating two very different parts of Naples. To its right, across as far as Piazza Gesù Nuovo, the streets and buildings are modern and spacious, centring on the unmistakable mass of the Fascist-era central **Post Office**. The streets to the left, on the other hand, scaling the footslopes of the Vómero, are some of the city's most narrow and crowded, a grid of alleys that was laid out to house Spanish troops during the seventeenth century and is hence known now as the **Quartiere Spagnoli**. It's an enticing area, at least for visitors, in that it's what you expect to find when you come to Naples, with the buildings so close together as to barely admit any sunlight. But it's as poor a part of Italy as you'll find, home to the notorious Neapolitan *bassi* – one-room windowless dwellings that open directly onto the street – and as such a national disgrace.

Further up Via Toledo, just north of Piazza Carità on the edge of the old part of the city, the church of **Monteoliveto** was rebuilt after a sound wartime bombing, but it holds some of the city's finest Renaissance art, including a sacristry frescoed by Vasari, a rather startling almost life-size *pietà* of eight figures by Guido Mazzoni (the faces are said to be portraits) and two sculptural works by Antonio Rossellino – a nativity scene and the tomb of Mary of Aragon, daughter of Ferdinand I.

Continuing on up the hill, **Piazza Dante** is another Neapolitan square which looks as if it has seen better days, designed by Luigi Vanvitelli during the eighteenth century and cutting an elegant semicircle off to the right of the main road that focuses on the pumps of a small, grimy petrol station and a statue of Dante splotched with graffiti. There are a couple of restaurants here, and it's a turnaround point for buses, but otherwise – unless you want to cut through the seventeenth-century **Port'Alba** into the old part of the city – you may as well push on up the street to the archaeological museum, housed in a grandiose late sixteenth-century army barracks on the corner of Piazza Cavour.

The Museo Archeologico Nazionale

Naples isn't really a city of museums – there's more on the streets that's worth observing on the whole, and most displays of interest are kept *in situ* in churches, palaces and the like. However, the **Museo Archeologico Nazionale** (Tues–Sat 9am–2pm, Sun 9am–1pm; L8000; reachable direct by bus #110 from Piazza Garibaldi) is an exception, home to the Farnese collection of antiquities from Lazio and Campania, and the best of the finds from the nearby Roman sites of Pompeii and Herculaneum. Sadly, some parts of the museum are often closed "for restoration" and there's a good chance you won't be able to see it all; plus none of the exhibits are labelled, making identification at best difficult. But the most impressive sections are usually open, and it would be a shame to miss them, especially if you intend visiting the sites themselves.

The ground floor of the museum concentrates on sculpture from the **Farnese collection**, displayed at its best in the mighty Great Hall, which holds Imperial-era figures like the *Farnese Bull* and *Farnese Hercules* from the Baths of Caracalla in Rome – the former the largest piece of classical sculpture ever found. The mezzanine floor at the back holds the museum's collection of **mosaics** – remarkably preserved works all, giving a superb insight into ordinary Roman customs, beliefs and humour. All are worth looking at – images of fish, crustacea, wildlife on the banks of the Nile, a cheeky cat and quail with still-life beneath, masks and simple abstract decoration. But some highlights to look out for include a realistic *Battle Scene* (no. 10020), the *Three Musicians with Dwarf* (9985), an urbane meeting of the *Platonic Academy* (124545), and a marvellously captured *Group of Soothsayers* (124666) giving a dour and doomy consultation.

Upstairs through the *Salone della Meridiana*, which holds a sparse but fine assortment of Roman figures (notably a wonderfully strained *Atlas* and some demure female figures – Roman replicas of Greek originals), a series of rooms holds the **Campanian Wall Paintings** that are the museum's other major draw after the mosaics – lifted from the villas of Pompeii and Herculaneum, and rich in colour and invention. There are plenty here, and it's worth devoting some time to this section – some of the smallest and most easily missed works are among the most exquisite. Among those to look out for are a paternal *Achilles and Chirone* (9109); the *Sacrifice of Iphiginia* (9112) in the next room, one of the best preserved of all the murals; the dignified *Perseus Frees Andromeda* (8998); and *Theseus Victorious over the Minotaur* (9043), showing the strong figure of Theseus as the subject of much wonder and admiration. Look out too for the group of four small pictures in the first main room, best of which is a depiction of a woman gathering flowers entitled *Primavera* – a fluid, impressionistic piece of work capturing both the gentleness of spring and the graceful beauty of the woman.

Beyond the murals are the actual **finds from the Campanian cities** – everyday items like glass, silver, ceramics, charred pieces of rope, even foodstuffs (petrified cakes, figs, fruit and nuts), together with a model layout of Pompeii in cork. On the other side of the first floor, there are finds from one particular house, the **Villa dei Papiri** in Herculaneum – sculptures in bronze mainly. The *Hermes at Rest* in the centre of the second room is perhaps the most arresting item, rapt with exhaustion, but around are other adept statues – of athletes, suffused with movement, a languid *Resting Satyr*, the convincingly woozy *Drunken Silenus*, and, in the final room, portrait busts of soldiers and various local big cheeses.

Piazza Cavour and Sanità

To the left of the archaeological museum as you come out, **Piazza Cavour** is a busy traffic junction and bus stop. A short walk east, off Via Foria, lies the **Orto Botanico** (Mon–Fri mornings, by appointment only; ☎449.759), founded in 1807 and a detour worth making if you're interested in such things. Perhaps more intriguing is the enormously long facade of the **Albergo dei Poveri** alongside, a workhouse built in 1751 that has been empty for years and forms a vast, oddly derelict landmark along the top side of **Piazza Carlo III**.

North of Piazza Cavour, you can stroll up through the old quarter of **SANITÀ**, following the tangle of streets for ten minutes or so up to the church of **Santa Maria della Sanità** on the piazza of the same name, a Dominican church from the early seventeenth century whose design was based loosely on Bramante's for Saint Peter's in Rome. There are paintings by Giordano and other Neapolitan artists inside, if you can get in, although perhaps of more interest are the **Catacombe di San Gaudioso** underneath, an intriguing early-Christian burial ground full of skeletons and other slightly bizarre features, including the fifth-century tomb of Saint Gaudioso, who was known, apparently, as the "African", due to the fact that he was a fifth-century bishop from North Africa.

Lifts link Sanità with Corso Amedeo up above, the main road up to Capodimonte. Walk under the bridge through to the rest of the teeming district, home to a couple of the city centre's larger hospitals and, close by one of them, another burial place, the **Catacombe di San Gennaro** (tours Fri, Sat & Sun 9.30am, 10.15am, 11am & 11.45am; L4000), behind the huge Madre del Buon Consiglio church. These were only discovered recently, next to the originally eighth-century church of San Gennaro in Moenia, and hold early Christian frescoes and mosaics, newly restored and amazingly bright. Continuing the death theme is the **Cimitero della Fontanelle** (open last Sat of the month only), made up of caverns containing the bones and skulls of – so it's said – plague victims, some of which have been "adopted" by visitors over the years in a weird kind of ex-voto cult. The cemetery is a good ten-minute walk from the bridge over Corso Amedeo, following Via della Sanità at first, then Via Fontanelle to its end; or bus #105 goes right there from Via Duomo.

The Palazzo Reale di Capodimonte

At the top of the hill, accessible by buses #110 or #127 from Piazza Garibaldi, or #160 or #161 from Piazza Dante, the **Palazzo Reale di Capodimonte** – and its extensive grounds – was the royal residence of the Bourbon King Charles III, built in 1738 and now housing the picture gallery of the Naples museum, the **Museo Nazionale di Capodimonte** (Tues–Sat 9.30am–2pm, Sun 9.30am–1.30pm; L8000). The royal apartments, on the first floor, are smaller and more downbeat than those at Caserta (see "Inland Campania", p.726), and in many ways more enjoyable, not least because you can actually walk through the rooms freely. That said, you'll need a keen interest in the Bourbon dynasty to want to linger: high spots are the ballroom, lined with portraits of various Bourbon monarchs and other European despots, and a number of rooms of porcelain, some painted with local scenes and one in particular a sticky confection of Chinese scenes, monkeys and fruit and flowers from the Capodimonte factory here.

Upstairs, the picture gallery holds a superb collection of Renaissance paintings, though once again parts sporadically close down for restoration. Assuming all is open, there is a good group of Flemish works, including a couple of Brueghels – *The Misanthrope* and *The Blind* – and two triptychs by Joos van Cleve. Early Italian rooms take in canvases by Perugino and Pinturicchio, an elegant *Madonna and Child with Angels* by Botticelli and Lippi's soft, sensitive *Annunciation*. Later paintings include a room full of Titians, with a number of paintings of the shrewd Farnese Pope Paul III in various states of ageing and the lascivious *Danae*; Raphael's austere portrait of *Leo X* and a worldly *Clement VII* by Sebastiano del Piombo; and Bellini's impressively coloured and composed *Transfiguration*.

Chiaia, Villa Communale, Mergellina and Posillipo

Via Chiaia leads west from Piazza Trieste e Trento into a quite different Naples from the congested *vicoli* of the *centro storico* or Quartiere Spagnoli, lined with the city's fanciest shops and bending down to the **Piazza dei Martiri** – named after the nineteenth-century revolutionary martyrs commemorated by the column in its centre. This part of town, the **Chiaia** neighbourhood, displays a sense of order and Classical elegance which is quite absent from the rest of the city centre, its buildings well preserved, the people noticeably better heeled – although the upper part of the district, which spreads up the hill towards Vómero, is as maze like and evocative as anywhere in the city.

From Piazza dei Martiri, you can stroll down to the waterfront and **Villa Communale**, Naples' most central city park and the place from where it's possible to appreciate the city best as a port and seafront city, the views stretching right around the Bay from the long lizard of its northern side, rising up on the right, to the gloomy shape of Vesuvius in the east – godlike behind the cranes and far-off apartment blocks of the sprawling industrial suburbs.

The park is girdled by the hum of the omnipresent Naples traffic but it makes a nice way to walk around the Bay to Mergellina, particularly in the early evening when the lights of the city enhance the views. On the way you might want to take in the century-old **Aquarium** (Tues–Sat 9am–5pm, Sun 9am–2pm; L3000), though its rather glum collection of tanks containing fish, turtles, eels, octopuses and rays, together with a revolting array of pickled marine life, may put you off your dinner. Across from here, on the other side of Riviera di Chiaia, the gardens of the **Villa Pignatelli** (Mon–Wed 9am–2pm,Thurs–Sat 9am–7.30pm, Sun 9am–1pm; L4000) are a peaceful alternative to the Villa Communale, and the house itself, now a museum, is kept in much the same way as when it was the home of a prominent Naples family and a turn-of-the-century meeting place for the city's elite. It's tastefully furnished and by Naples standards low-key, its handful of rooms holding books, porcelain, the odd painting and a set of photos signed by various aristocrats and royal personages.

Villa Communale stretches around the Bay for a good mile, at the far end of which lie the harbour and main square – Piazza Sannazzaro – of the **Mergellina** district, a good place to come and eat at night and a terminus for hydrofoils to the Bay's islands. There's not a lot else here, only the dense **Parco Virgiliano** (9am–1pm) north of Piazza Sannazzaro, which holds the spot where the Roman poet Virgil is supposed to be buried, marked by a Roman monument. To get there, follow the Salita della Grotta from the other side of the tunnel off Piazza Piedigrotta. Of the other neighbourhoods nearby, the **Fuorigrotta** district, the other side of the Mergellina hill, is not of interest unless you're going to a football match, since it's home to Napoli's San Paolo Stadium (see "Listings" for details). Ditto **Posillipo**, further along the shore, which is an upmarket suburb of the city stacked with fat villas and pockets – though, again, people do come out here to eat.

Vómero

Like Chiaia below, and Mergellina to the west, **VÓMERO** – the district topping the hill immediately above the old city – is one of Naples' relatively modern additions, a light, airy and relatively peaceful quarter connected most directly with the teeming morass below by funicular railway. It's a large area but mostly residential, and you're unlikely to want to stray beyond the streets which fan out from each of the three funicular stations, centering on the grand symmetery of **Piazza Vanvitelli**.

Come up on the Montesanto funicular (see map) and you're well placed for a visit to two of the buildings which dominate Naples, way above the old city. Five minutes' walk away, the **Castel Sant'Elmo** (Tues–Sun 8am–8pm; free) occupies Naples' highest point and is an impressive fortification, a fourteenth-century structure once used for incarcerating political prisoners and now lording it grandly over the streets below. Though still in use primarily as a military fortification, it nowadays hosts exhibitions, concerts and an annual antiques fair, as well as boasting the very best views of Naples.

Beyond the castle, the fourteenth-century **Certosa San Martino** has the next-best views over the Bay, and is also accessible, now being home to the **Museo Nazionale di San Martino** (Tues–Sat 9am–2pm, Sun 9am–1pm; L6000). Much of this, too, often appears to be under restoration, but the monastery itself, throughly Baroqued in the seventeenth century, and the views from its cunningly constructed terrace, are well worth the entrance fee – short of climbing Vesuvius as good a vista of the entire Bay of Naples as you'll get. The church, on the left of the entrance, is typically garish Baroque, with a colourful pavement and an *Adoration of the Shepherds* by Reni above the altar. In the museum proper, there are paintings by Neapolitan masters – Ribera, Stanzione, Vaccaro – and other rather dusty bits and pieces rescued from churches and the odd minor aristocrat, as well as historical and maritime sections displaying models of ships, and documents, coins and costumes recording the era of the Kingdom of Naples. The Baroque cloisters are lovely, though again rather gone to seed. The display of *presepi* or Christmas cribs is probably the most remarkable – and unique – aspect of the museum, the craft of which is peculiar to the city and continued avidly today (see p.698).

There's another museum up here, ten minutes' walk away in the Neoclassical **Villa Floridiana**, close to the Chiaia funicular, whose lush grounds (daily 9am–7.30pm) might make a good place for a picnic. The **Museo Duca di Martino** (Tues–Sat 9am–2pm, Sun 9am–1pm; L4000) is, however, of fairly specialist interest, a porcelain collection such as you've never seen before, varying from the beautifully simple to the outrageously kitsch – hideous teapots, ceramic asparagus sticks and the like. There are examples (of course) of Capodimonte and Meissen, and eighteenth-century English,

French, German and Viennese work – as well as a handful of pieces of Qing dynasty Chinese porcelain and Murano glass, and exquisite non-ceramic items like inlaid ivory boxes and panels. On the whole, a small museum that's worth taking in before salivating over yet another view, this time from just below the villa.

Eating, drinking and nightlife

It's arguable that **Neapolitan cuisine** is Italy's best – simple dishes cooked with fresh, healthy ingredients that have none of the richness or pretentions of the North. Also, as Naples is not primarily a tourist-geared city, most restaurants are family-run places used by locals and as such generally serve good food at reasonable prices. Seafood is good, as is all pasta (Naples is the home of spaghetti), and specialities include *spaghetti alle vongole*, *zuppa di cozze* (steamed mussels served with hot pepper sauce) and *pasta e fagiole* – frugal dishes originally but nowadays firmly in the mainstream. Naples is also the home of the pizza, and there's no better place in Italy to eat it, at a solid core of almost obsessively unchanged places that still only serve the (very few) traditional varieties. Eating on your feet, too, is nowhere difficult. Or you can pick something up from the city's streetmarkets – La Forcella or the fish market at Porta Nolana.

Cakes, snacks, ice cream

Attanasio, Vico Ferrovia, off Via Milano. Bakery that specialises in *sfogliatelle* (ricotta-stuffed pastries).

Gambrinus, Via Chiaia 1–2. The oldest and best-known of Neapolitan cafés, founded in 1861. Not cheap, but its aura of peeling gentility – and outside seating at one of the city's busiest spots – may appeal.

Motta, Via Toledo 152. Large and basic café serving both sit-down and take-away food and drink.

Scaturchio, Piazza San Domenico. Another elegant old Naples standard, it's been serving coffee and pastries in the heart of Spaccanapoli for decades. Has a small back room but mainly a place to grab a quick coffee and pastry and move on.

Scimmia, Piazza Carità 4. Centrally placed *gelateria* that's held in very high regard locally, with an even wider range of flavours than usual.

Restaurants and pizzerias

Alle Brace, Via S. Spaventa 14–16. Good, cheap alternative just off Piazza Garibaldi, which has well-priced pasta dishes and main courses.

Bellini, Via Santa Maria di Constantinopoli 80. One of the city's most famous and longest established restaurants. Great pizzas and a very good selection of other, especially seafood, dishes – and with a great convivial outside terrace on the street.

Bersagliera, Borgo Marinaro. Fine food, though inevitably you pay for the location, slap next to the Castel dell'Ovo, and for the "*O Sole Mio*" minstrels who wander between the tables.

Brandi, Salita Sant'Anna di Palazzo 1–2, off Via Chiaia. One of Naples' most famous pizzerias, said to be where they invented the *pizza margherita* in 1889 in honour of the visiting Queen Margherita of Savoy. Very friendly, serving pasta and (excellent) pizzas from L6000.

California, Via Santa Lucia 101. Another Naples institution, though a rather different one, serving a menu that's an odd hybrid of American and Italian specialities. Best for its full American breakfasts.

Canterbury, Via Ascensione 6. Strangely named Chiaia restaurant near the Pignatelli museum that is one of the best-value places in the area. Pasta dishes are particularly good – try the *penne alla vodka* (!).

Dante e Beatrice, Piazza Dante 44. A long-established restaurant that trades slightly on its reputation, not least in its rather brusque service, although its menu of traditional Naples specialities is still not at all expensive – and you can eat outside.

Da Gennarino, Via Capuana alla Medelena 1–2. Again among the best pizzerias in the city, well situated (opposite the Porta Capuana) for hungry arrivals by train. A new branch now on Piazza Garibaldi, on the corner of via Spaventa.

Gorizia, Via Bernini 29. Unpretentious Vomero restaurant close to the Centrale and Chiaia funicular stops that does good antipasti, great mini-pizzas as well as good selection of main courses. Try the speciality of the house – veal wrapped around prosciutto and mozarella.

Lombardi a Santa Chiara, Via B. Croce 59. Another well-known and well-respected pizza restaurant, and with a varied menu besides pizza.

O Marenaro, Via Casanova. Around the corner from Piazza Garibaldi, opposite the *CTP* bus station, this is a great place to try *zuppe di cozze*, with a couple of tables outside.

Da Michele, Via Cesare Sersale 1–3. Tucked away off Corso Umberto I in the Forcella district, this is the most determinedly traditional of all the Naples pizzerias, offering just two varieties – *marinara* or *margherita*. Don't arrive late, as they sometimes run out of dough.

Da Pasqualino, Piazza Sannazzaro 79. Inexpensive Mergellina restaurant with outdoor seating and great seafood and pizzas.

Da Peppino Avellinese, Via S. Spaventa 31. The most welcoming and best value of the many options on and around Piazza Garibaldi. Used by tourists and locals alike.

Port'Alba, Via Port'Alba 18. Old-established pizzeria just off Piazza Dante that has a wide menu besides its excellent pizza. Said to be the oldest pizzeria in Italy.

Spaghetteria, Via G. Paladino 7. Inexpensive plates of pasta in a youthful restaurant patronised by students from the nearby university.

Umberto, Via Alabardieri 30–31. A long-time popular choice among the professional classes of the Chiaia district, serving marvellous food in somewhat smooth and old-fashioned surroundings that belie the moderate prices.

Trianon (da Ciro), Via P. Colletta 46. Forcella pizzeria that is a nearby rival to *Da Michele* (above), but serving a wider range of pizzas.

Al Triunfo Mario, Vico Il Duschesca 10. Great, cheap and popular eatery just off the Porta Capuana end of Piazza Garibaldi. Cheap pizza and pasta, and spit-roast chicken. Always full of locals and workers.

Nightlife: bars, clubs, culture

Naples isn't a city with a café scene as such, although recent years have seen the growth of a number of new **bars**, some with occasional live music, especially in the old part of the city. One of the most spectacular additions to the nightlife scene is *Intra Moenia*, a rather bookish bookshop by day that at night transforms itself into one of Naples' trendier cafés, with tables spreading right across the square; it has a low-key food menu too. Close by, *Murat*, Via Bellini 5, and the *Gauguin* opposite often have live music, especially on Fridays, as does the *Notting Hill* on Piazza Dante, which is a bit of a reggae and rap hang-out. Not too far away in the opposite direction, Via Paladino, by the university, has a clutch of fashionable drinking haunts, the nicest of which is perhaps the *Vineria del Centro*, Via Paladino 8, although you pay for the very un-Italian pubby atmosphere; the *Frame Café*, virtually next door, is OK too, and has live music every Wednesday. For something a little different, there's *Riot*, housed in an old palazzo on Via San Biagio dei Librai, close to Via Duomo, popular with a self-consciously alternative crowd. Outside the old city, many of the city's Bright Young Things congregate around Piazza Amedeo in Chiaia, where the underground *Cervezeria La Salsa* can get very crowded indeed, especially on weekends for its live bands. The *Guernica* just up Via del Parco Margherita on the right is perhaps a quieter place for a drink, and sometimes has art exhibitions, and the piano bars and pseudo-pubs along Via Martucci are popular, although prices are through the roof. The *East India Company* has good pizzas.

As for **clubs**, you may have to travel around the Bay for the best of these, ideally with your own transport, since some of the best of the area's discos are situated in the beach areas north or south of the city. *Havana Club*, in Pozzuoli at the Tangenziale exit, is one the most popular places, especially in summer. Others include *Play-off*, in Lucrino, near Pozzuoli, and *Le Dune*, in Licola. In Naples itself there's the *Virgilio* open-air disco in Posillipo, just below the Parco della Rimembranza, or try *Chez Moi*, Parco Margherita 13.

If you're more into serious **culture** than late-night dancing, there's the *Teatro San Carlo*, whose opera season runs from December to May, while the rest of the year is given over to classical concerts and ballet (box office open daily 10am–1pm & 4.30–6pm; ☎797.2331).

Listings

Airlines *Alitalia*, Via Medina 41–42 (☎542.5111); *British Airways*, Piazza Municipio 2 (☎400.144); *TWA*, Via Partenope 23 (☎764.5828).

Airport enquiries ☎780.5763.

Books English-language books from *Universal*, Rione Sirignano 1.

Bus enquiries *CTP* station, Piazza Porta Capuana, for Caserta, Cápua, etc (☎554.0507); Piazza Garibaldi, for Benevento, Avellino, etc (☎334.677); *SITA*, for Salerno (☎552.2176).

Car rental Many of the larger car-rental firms group along along the seafront near the Castel dell'Ovo. *Avis*, Via Partenope 32 (☎764.5600); *Europcar*, Via Partenope 38 (☎764.5070); *Hertz*, Via Partenope 29 (☎764.5533); *Maggiore*, Via Cervantes 92 (☎552.1900). They all also have desks at Stazione Centrale and at the airport.

Consulates *UK*, Via Crispi 122 (☎663.511); *USA*, Piazza della Repubblica (☎583.8111).

Emergencies ☎113. The main police station is at Via Medina 75 (☎794.1111).

Exchange Outside normal banking hours you can change money and travellers cheques at the booth inside Stazione Centrale (daily 7am–9pm).

Football The Stadio di San Paolo in Fuorigrotta is the home of the Serie A Napoli side, recent championship winners but at time of writing going through a bit of a lean patch, despite having South Americans of the class of Fonseca and Careca in the side. To get to the ground, take the Ferrovia Cumana from Montesanto to Mostra and the stadium is right in front of you.

Funerals Death is big business in Naples, and if you're lucky you can still see the incredibly ornate traditional black hearses pulled by teams of horses on the streets of the city – the preferred way to go of Neapolitan fat cats and higher-ranking Camorra members. There are other, equally bizarre Neapolitan customs regarding death: a white hearse, for example, means a child or virgin has died; and despite official discouragement some corpses are still dug up by their families after burial, in a bizarre celebration of the dead centring on All Souls Day – November 2.

Hospital ☎751.3177 or go to the Guardia Medica Permanente in the Palazzo Municipio, open 24hr.

Left luggage At Stazione Centrale (open 24hr).

Lottery Along with San Gennaro and Diego Maradona, the lottery is a fanatically observed institution in Naples. Winning the lottery is seen, in a way, as the ultimate triumph over the system, and superstitions around it are rife – to the extent that there's even a book, *La Smorfia*, which interprets the meaning behind each lottery number. There are also people, called *assisti* (literally "guided ones"), who claim to have supernatural access to knowledge of what the winning numbers are to be. If you're keen to see the lottery draw, it's made every Saturday noon at the Ufficio Lotto on Via San Biagio dei Librai, to the accompaniment of much noise and hysteria.

Pharmacy Late-night pharmacies work on a rotation system. ☎192 for addresses of current ones, or look in *Il Mattino*. There's also a pharmacy at Stazione Centrale open Mon–Sat 8am–8pm.

Post office The main post office is in the enormous building on Piazza Matteotti, just off Via Toledo (Mon–Fri 8am–7.40pm, Sat 8.30am–noon).

Taxis There are taxi ranks at the train station, on Piazza Dante and Piazza Trieste e Trento; or phone ☎556.4444, ☎556.0202, ☎552.0200 or ☎210.200.

Telephones There is an ASST at Stazione Centrale (open 24hr), though large queues form early evening. The ASST, Via Depretis 40 (also open 24hr), is quieter; SIP in Galleria Umberto (Mon–Sat 8am–9.30pm) is usually chaos.

Tours The Naples tourist office run guided tours of various parts of the city every Sunday morning beginning at 10.30am; details direct from one of their offices. You can also tour underground Naples if you wish; tours, run by *LAES* (☎400.256), leave from Bar Gambrinus every Saturday and Sunday at 10am, and take you through sewers and passageways that date back as much as 4000 years. In summer you can also cruise Naples harbour by boat at night; departures leave Mergellina harbour twice each Saturday between mid-July and the end of August, three times on Sunday; in September just three times each Sunday evening. Price L6000 per person; tickets are available at the embarkation point or from the Piazza del Gesù tourist office. A number of companies also offer guided tours of places of interest outside the city – Pompeii, Cápri, Ischia and suchlike – lasting either a half or full day. Try *CIT*, Piazza Municipio 70 (☎552.5426), or *Aritur*, Piazza Trieste e Trento 7–8 (☎416.630).

Train enquiries Phone ☎ 553.4188 or go to the information booths at the station and be prepared to queue (daily 7.30am–10pm).

Travel agents *CTS*, Via A. de Gasperi 25 (☎552.0074), for discount tickets, budget flights, etc.

THE BAY OF NAPLES

For the Romans, Campania and particularly the **Bay of Naples** was the land of plenty, a blessed region of mild climate, gorgeous scenery and an accessible location that made it a favourite vacation and retirement area for the city's nobility. Patrician Rome built villas here by the score – Hadrian had a house at Baia, for example – and towns like **Pompeii** and **Herculaneum** were among the richest in the Imperial era: the "Bay of Luxury", Cicero called it. Later, when Naples became the final stop on northerners' Grand Tours, the Bay became no less fabled, the relics of its heady Roman period only adding to the charm for most travellers.

It's a charm which is easy to detect – the landscape is still there and still as impressive, and the offshore islands of **Cápri**, **Ischia** and **Prócida** are no less enticing than they ever were, if immeasurably more crowded. But the fact is that these days it's hard to tell where Naples ends and the countryside begins. Northern money and Camorra speculation mean that the city now sprawls around the Bay in an industrial and residential mess that is quite at odds with the region's popular image, and whatever it was once like, the environment close to the city is pretty much beyond recall. You need to head some way out of the city before reaching anywhere you might want to stay for longer than an afternoon, especially if you want to swim. Even if the water is clean, the proximity of the Bay's industry will make you think it isn't; and it's only when you reach **Sorrento** in the east, **Pozzuoli** in the west, or any of the islands, that you really feel free of it all. Luckily this is easy by way of the extra-urban train services out of Naples (see "City Transport", p.693), or one of the Bay's plentiful ferry connections: most of the places mentioned below are convenient for day trips – though many obviously demand longer.

West from Naples: Pozzuoli and the Campi Flegrei

The area around Naples is one of the most unstable in the world. Vesuvius is only the best known of the many and varied examples of volcanic activity in the province, the most concentrated instances – volcanic craters, hot springs, *fumaroles* – being northwest of the city in the region known as the **Campi Flegrei** (Fiery Fields). This is the *Phlegrean Fields* of Classical times, a mysterious place in turn mythologised by Homer and Virgil as the entrance to Hades and eulogised as the Elysian Fields for its beauty.

These days most of the mystery is gone – like most of the Bay, the presence of Naples dominates in the form of new building and suburbs – and much of the volcanic activity is extinct. But parts of the area still retain some of the doomy associations that first drew the ancients here, and there are some substantial remains of their presence – not to mention some of the best and most accessible of Naples' nearby beaches.

Pozzuoli and the Solfatara

The first town that can really be considered free of Naples' sprawl is **POZZUOLI**, which sits on a stout promontory jutting out from the slender crescent of volcanic hills behind. It's a workaday little place, nothing special but likeable enough, with ferry connections to the islands of Prócida and Ischia. And although you wouldn't want to stay here (unless you're a camper; see "Accommodation", p.694), it's a good first stop before travelling on to the rest of the Campi Flegrei. You can get there from Naples on the metropolitana from Piazza Garibaldi, or on the Ferrovia Cumanarail line from Montesanto station; both take about twenty minutes. Bus #152 also runs direct from Piazza Garibaldi.

Pozzuoli has suffered more than most of the towns around here from the area's volcanic activity. Twenty years ago a minor tremor caused a number of buildings to collapse, and subsidence is still a major – and carefully monitored – problem. The best time to come is on Sunday, when the whole town turns out for the morning fish market, afterwards eating lunch in one of the many waterfront restaurants – *Dal Capitano* and *A Lampara* are both good. In town there are a number of relics of the Romans' liking for the place. The **Antifeatro Flavio** (daily 9am–4pm; L4000), on Via Domiziana just north of the centre, was at one time the third largest in Italy and is still reasonably well preserved, although some parts are shut off to the public – a little illicit clambering over fences might enable you to get a better sense of the place. Not far from here, beyond the Cumana station between Via Roma and Via Sacchini, a **Temple of Serapide** sits enclosed within a small park, flooded for much of the year but the rest of the time accessible – and in fact since proved to be not a temple at all but a market hall from the first century AD. It's pretty ruined, but it is still possible to make out the shape of the building, its three freestanding marble columns eaten away halfway up by shellfish.

Just north of town, ten minutes' walk up the hill from the metropolitana/*FS* station (bus #152 from Naples stops outside), the **Solfatara** (daily 8.30am–7pm; L4500) is further, and tangible, evidence of the volcanic nature of the area, the exposed crater of a semi-extinct volcano – into which you can walk – that hasn't erupted for a couple of thousand years; in fact, it was a major tourist attraction in Roman times too. Not surprisingly, it's a weird place: steam rises from the rocks around and the grey-yellow ground is hot to the touch (and sounds hollow to the stamp), emitting eerily silent jets or *fumaroles* that leave the air pungent with sulphurous fumes. Some of the *fumaroles* have been covered artificially with brick, creating an almost unbearably warm, sauna-like environment into which you can bend if you can stand it, while others are just left open. You can hire a guide (from L16,750) to steer you clear of the dangerous parts, but it's not really necessary – there's a clearly marked route and it's far more fun exploring the site on your own.

A short, three-minute walk further up the hill on the right, the sixteenth-century **Santuario di San Gennaro** (Mon–Fri 9am–noon & 4.30–8pm) was built on the supposed site of the martyrdom of Naples' patron saint, and holds a stone stained with splashes of his blood (he was beheaded) which apparently glows when his blood liquefies in Naples, which it does three times a year – see box on p.697, "The Miracle of San Gennaro".

Baia, Bacoli, Capo Miseno and Cumae

The next town along from Pozzuoli, reached in fifteen minutes by train from the Cumana station, by the Temple of Serapide, is **BAIA**, a small port with a tiny, rather unattractive bit of beach and a set of Imperial-era Roman ruins piling up on the hill above. This was one of the Bay's most favoured spots in Roman times, a trendy resort at which all the most fashionable of the city's patricians had villas: the Emperor Hadrian died here in 138 AD and Nero was rumoured to have murdered his mother in Baia.

Immediately behind the station, remains of some enormous Roman baths leave you in no doubt of the town's function in ancient times. Steps lead up from the station square to the entrance to the **excavations** (Tues–Sun 9am–1hr before sunset; L4000) of a Roman palace of the first to the fourth century AD, structured across several levels. It's hard to tell what's what – the site is very ruined and there's little or no labelling – but it's an evocative location, and can afford a happy hour of stumbling around among the stones and passages. Follow the steps down from the entrance level to the first terrace of the palace: the rooms on the right contain patches of Roman stucco-work depicting birds and mythical creatures and a statue of Mercury, beheaded by vandals a decade ago. Below are the remains of a small theatre, and an open space – a former *piscina* – bordered on one side by a pretty loggia now used for summer drama performances.

There are more ruins inland from Baia at **Lago d'Averno**, where Agrippa constructed a military harbour in 37 BC. The lake itself is the *Lake Avernus* of antiquity, a volcanic crater that the Greeks believed – and Virgil later wrote – was the entrance to Hades: birds flying over were said to suffocate with the toxic fumes that rose from the lake's murky waters, and sacrifices were regularly made here to the dark deities that lurked beneath the gloomy surface. Today it's more cheerful, no longer surrounded by thick forest (this was cut down by Agrippa), although there's not really any other reason to come – the water of the nearby sea is much more enticing for swimming.

A few kilometres down the coast from Baia, **BACOLI** has more Roman remains, an underground Roman reservoir, the **Piscina Mirabile**, and a small stretch of beach – more appealing than Baia's. However, if it's **beaches** you're after you'd be well advised to stay on the bus until **MISENO**, where, just beyond the lake of the same name, there's a very broad strand. You'll not find it empty by any means, but it's large enough to find yourself a space – and beach bars and restaurants abound.

If you've the energy, you can make the stiff climb to **Capo Miseno** from here, an almost level-topped hump at the furthest tip of the Campi Flegrei, though it's only really worth it if the weather's clear – the views back to Naples and up the coast to Gaeta are the main attraction. Otherwise push up to **CUMAE**, home to one of the most lauded of the ancient sites hereabouts.

The town of **Cumae** was the first Greek colony on the Italian mainland, a source of settlers for other colonies (Naples was originally settled by Greeks from Cumae) and a centre of Hellenistic civilisation. Later it was home to the so-called Cumaean Sibyl, from whom Tarquinius purchased the Sibylline Books that laid down the laws for the Republic. The **site** (Tues–Sun 9am–1hr before sunset; L4000), a short walk from the bus stop, is spread over a large area and not at all comprehensively excavated. But the only part you're likely to want to see forms a tight nucleus close to the entrance. The best-known feature is the *Cave of the Sibyl*, a long dark corridor that was home to the most famous of the ancient oracles. Rectangular in shape, with light admitted from a series of niches in the western wall, the Sibyl used to dispense her wisdom from the three large chambers at the far end of the forty-foot passageway, the most famous occasion being when Aeneas came here to consult her – an event recorded by the lines of Virgil posted up either side of the entrance.

But the best of Cumae is still to come. Climb up the steps to the right of the cave entrance and follow the winding Via Sacra past a constructed belvedere on the left and the fairly scanty remains of a temple on the right to the Acropolis. Here you'll find the remains of a temple to Jupiter, but it's the views that you really come for: from the far side of the temple way south across the shellfish-filled **Lago Fusaro** and the bottom corner of the coast; and, if you clamber down from the other side of the temple, north up the curving coast to the Gulf of Gaeta.

The coast north of Cumae

The coast north of Cumae up to the Lazio border is known as the **Costa Domiziana**, after the Roman road that leads north from here to join up with the Via Appia, and looks, at least from the heights of Cumae itself, enticingly empty – which it can be if you've a car to reach its more isolated spots. But most of the resorts along this stretch of coast are polluted and over-developed and hard to recommend for any kind of visit. **PINETA A MARE** is the closest resort to Cumae and fairly typical – tacky, rather dirty, and, according to local newspaper reports, something of a haunt of warring drug dealers. **BAIA DOMIZIA**, further north, close to the Lazio border, is much the same.

East from Naples: Ercolano to Sorrento

The coast **east from Naples** is no better, perhaps even a little worse than the coast west of the city – the Circumvesuviana train edging out through derelict industrial buildings and dense housing that squeezes ever closer to the track. Most people come here for the ancient sights of Herculaneum and Pompeii, or to scale Vesuvius – or they skip the lot for the resort town of Sorrento. All are easy day trips, though Sorrento is worth a little more time, and is a good base for seeing some of the Amalfi coast.

Ercolano: Vesuvius and the site of Herculaneum

The first real point of any interest is the town of **ERCOLANO**, the modern offshoot of the ancient site of *Herculaneum*, which was destroyed by the eruption of Vesuvius on August 2, 79 AD. It's worth stopping here for two reasons: to see the excavations of the site and to climb to the summit of Vesuvius – to which buses run from outside the railway station. A word of warning, though: if you're planning to both visit Herculaneum and scale Vesuvius in one day (and it is possible), be sure to see Vesuvius first, and set off reasonably early – buses stop running up the mountain at lunchtime, leaving you the afternoon free to wander around the site.

Herculaneum

Situated at the seaward end of Ercolano's main street, the site of **Herculaneum** (daily 9am–1hr before sunset; L8000) was discovered in 1709, when a well-digger accidentally struck the stage of the buried theatre. Excavations were undertaken throughout the eighteenth and nineteenth centuries, during which period much of the marble and bronze from the site was carted off to Naples to decorate the city's palaces, and it wasn't until 1927 that digging and preservation began in earnest. Herculaneum was a residential town, much smaller than Pompeii, and as such it makes a more manageable site, less architecturally impressive and less outside the modern mainstream (Ercolano virtually abuts the site), but better preserved and more easily taken in on a single visit. Archaeologists held for a long time that unlike in Pompeii, on the other side of the volcano, most of the inhabitants of Herculaneum managed to escape. However, recent discoveries of skeletons in various poses of horror suggests otherwise, and it's now believed that most of the town's population was buried by huge avalanches of volcanic mud, which later hardened into the tufa-type rock that preserved much of the town.

Many of the houses on the site are kept locked, and you may have to ask one of the many attendants to open them up for you (in return for a tip). There are always plenty of guides hanging around, some English-speaking: if you feel you can afford it, they'll take you around the whole site; if you can't, tag along discreetly with an English-speaking group.

Because Herculaneum wasn't a commercial town, there was no central open space or forum, just streets of villas and shops, cut as usual by two very straight main streets which cross in the centre. Start your tour just inside the entrance at the bottom end of Cardo III, where you'll see the **House of the Argus** on the left, a very grand place judging by its once-impressive courtyard – although even this is upstaged by the size of the place across the street, the so-called **Hotel**, which covers a huge area, though you can only really get a true impression of its size from the rectangle of stumpy columns that made up its atrium. Further up, Cardo III joins the Decumanus Inferiore, just beyond which it's the large **Thermae** or bath complex which dominates – the domed *frigidarium* of its men's section decorated with frescoes of fish, its *caldarium* containing a plunge bath at one end and a scallop-shell apse complete with washbasin and water pipes. The women's section has a well-preserved mosaic of Neptune and glass shards in its window that are original. On the far side of the baths, across Cardo IV, the **Samnite House** and **House of the Wooden Partition** are both worth a peek inside, the Samnite House in particular, whose atrium is one of the most attractive in Herculaneum, with a graceful blind arcade all the way round and a hole in the roof still decorated with animal spouts. Next door but one, in the **House of the Carbonised Furniture**, there's a room with the marital bed still intact and portraits of the gent and lady of the house nearby – the former, in the room to the right, marked by a satyr, the latter voluptuously posed on the left-hand wall of an alcove. Close by, the dining room has pictures of Roman dishes – chicken, mushrooms and the like – while on the left as you enter there's a kitchen with an oven in the corner, and a toilet on the other side. Beyond, the **House of the Neptune Mosaic** holds another sparklingly preserved mosaic floor, again including portraits of the owners of the household, and flower and vegetable frescoes which served in lieu of a garden; the concrete hatch to the right was a *vomitarium*, which allowed guests to relieve themselves of excess food before proceeding to the next course of their meal. Under the house is a **wine shop**, stocked with amphorae and with a coiled rope left as it stood when disaster struck.

Turning right at the top of Cardo IV takes you around to Cardo V and most of the rest of the town's **shops** – a variety of places including a baker's, complete with ovens and grinding mills, a weaver's, with loom and bones, and a dyer's, with a huge pot for dyes. Behind the ones on the left you can see the **Palestra**, where public games were held, although it's not actually possible to reach this. Further down on the right, the shop on the corner of Cardo V and Decumanus Inferiore has a well-preserved counter and urns for cereals or somesuch merchandise; another, further down Cardo V on the right, has a Priapic painting behind its counter. Cutting through to Cardo IV, from here, the **House of the Wooden Partition** preserves its original partition doors under glass – evidence that it was the home of a poorer class of person than many of the buildings here. The next-door **House of Opus Craticium** is a very well-preserved example of a plebeian artisans' residence, and would have been divided into separate apartments; it gives a good impression of its original plaster and wood construction, complete with the overhang on the streetfront. At the bottom end of Cardo IV, the **House of the Mosaic Atrium**, at the bottom, was a grand villa in its day and retains its mosaic-laid courtyard, corrugated by the force of the tufa. Behind here, the **House of the Deer** on Cardo V was another luxury villa, its two storeys built around a central courtyard and containing corridors decorated with richly coloured still-lifes, and, as the centrepiece of one of its rooms, a bawdy statue of a drunken Hercules seemingly about to piss all over the visitors.

Close by, from the end of Cardo IV, a covered passageway leads down to another **baths** building on the left, which is in fact one of the most impressive – and intact – structures in Herculaneum, complete with extremely well-preserved stucco work, and a pretty much intact set of baths; it also has a complete original Roman door, the only one in Herculaneum that wasn't charred by fire. Its damp mustiness makes it certainly the most evocative stop on a tour of the site, although it is prone to regular flooding and sadly often out of bounds altogether.

Mount Vesuvius

Since its first eruption in 79 AD, when it buried the towns and inhabitants of Pompeii and Herculaneum, **Mount Vesuvius** has dominated the lives of those who live on the Bay of Naples, its brooding bulk forming a stately backdrop to the ever-growing settlements that group around its lower slopes. It's a still active volcano, the only one on mainland Europe. There have been more than a hundred eruptions over the years, but only two others of real significance – one in December 1631 that engulfed many nearby towns and killed 3000 people; and the last, in March 1944, which caused widespread devastation in the towns around, though no one was actually killed. The people who live here still fear the reawakening of the volcano, and with good reason – scientists calculate it should erupt every thirty years or so, and it hasn't since 1944. It's carefully monitored, of course, and there is apparently no reason to expect any movement for some time. But the subsidence in towns like Ercolano below is a continuing reminder of the instability of the area, incidentally one of southern Italy's most densely populated; and it's odd that there are no emergency plans as to what to do in case of an eruption.

There are two ways of making the **ascent**. There are six *SITA* buses a day from Ercolano train station (currently at 7.35am, 9.20am, 11.20am, 12.35pm, 3pm & 4.50pm) to a car park and huddle of souvenir shops and cafés close to the crater throughout the morning. This costs L4000 return, and is much the easiest and cheapest way of working things, although there are plenty of taxis eager to take you up and wait while you see the crater for around L50,000 all-in. If you have more energy, or have missed the bus and don't have that kind of money, you can also take a local bus (#5) from the roundabout near the train station to the end of the line and walk from there – a good couple of hours to the crater, though a nice walk. One way of doing it might be to walk up and take the bus back down (the last one descends at 5.50pm). The walk is certainly a pleasant one, winding through the fertile lower slopes of the volcano, covered with vines and olives, past the main lava flows of the 1944 eruption as far as the car park, which sits just above the greenery among the bare cinders of Vesuvius's main summit.

The walk up to the crater from here takes about half an hour, a stony stroll across reddened, barren gravel and rock on marked-out paths, though with nothing on your right to prevent you falling down the smooth side of the mountain – take care. At the top (admission L4500), the crater is a deep, wide, jagged ashtray of red rock swirled over by midges and emitting the odd plume of smoke, though since the last eruption effectively sealed up the main crevice this is much less evident than it once was. You can walk most of the way round, but again take it easy – the fences are old and rickety, and not to be relied upon.

The Bay to Sorrento

Beyond Ercolano the Bay doesn't really pick up: it's still hard to distinguish much countryside between the towns – most of which sadly seem more in tune with their proximity to the city than to the sea. **TORRE DEL GRECO**, the first place you reach, is famous for its coral industry, and you can still buy coral jewellery here, but the business is threatened by the polluted nature of the waters of the Bay.

Further along, **TORRE ANNUNZIATA** is no more appealing at first sight, though about half a kilometre from the railway station there's a recently excavated **Roman villa** that was covered, and preserved, by the 79 AD eruption. It was a sumptuous residence in its time, part of a suburb of Pompeii known as *Oplontis*, with elegant loggias, murals and graceful gardens, which have been reconstructed in the style of their day.

By the time you reach **CASTELLAMMARE DI STABIA**, a few kilometres further round the Bay, the houses have begun to thin out a little. But the town isn't any more appetising for all that, dominated by the ships and gantries of the Italian navy's military harbour here. Oddly enough, Castellammare is the kind of place people still come for a holiday, or at least for a cure: its spas are well known hereabouts and draw many for their healing properties. From the Circumvesuviana station you can take the funicular (every 40min; L8000 return) up to the top of **Monte Faito** (1100m), a ten-minute journey that gives predictably dazzling views, although you need to walk for fifteen minutes or so at the top to get clear of the trees. However, on the whole you'd do better not to tarry here at all, instead hurrying on south to Salerno or west to Sorrento – both feasible jumping-off points for the Amalfi coast.

Pompeii

The other Roman town to be destroyed by Vesuvius – **Pompeii** – was a much larger affair than Herculaneum, and one of Campania's most important commercial centres in its day. After a spell as a Greek colony, Pompeii came under the sway of the Romans in 200 BC, later functioning as both a monied resort for wealthy patricians and a trading town that exported wine and fish products, notably its own brand of fish sauce. A severe earthquake destroyed much of the city in 63 AD, and the eruption of Vesuvius sixteen years later only served to exacerbate what was already a desperate situation.

Vesuvius had been spouting smoke and ash for several days before the eruption and in fact most of the town had already been evacuated when disaster struck: out of a total population of 20,000 it's thought that only 2000 actually perished, asphyxiated by the toxic fumes of the volcanic debris, their homes buried in several metres of volcanic ash and pumice. Pliny, the Roman naturalist, was one of the casualties – he died at nearby Stabiae (now Castellammare) of a heart attack. But his nephew described the full horror of the scene soon after in two vivid letters to the historian Tacitus, who was compiling a history of the disaster, describing the sky as turning dark "as a sealed room".

In effect the eruption froze the way of life in Pompeii as it stood at the time – a way of life that subsequent excavations have revealed in precise and remarkable detail; indeed Pompeii has probably yielded more information about the ordinary life of Roman citizens during the Imperial era than any other site: its social conventions, class structure, domestic arrangements and its (actually very high) standard of living. Some of the buildings are even covered with ancient graffiti, either referring to contemporary political events or simply to the romantic entanglements of the inhabitants; and the full horror of their way of death is apparent in plaster casts made from the shapes their bodies left in the volcanic ash – faces tortured with agony, or shielding themselves from the dust and ashes.

The first parts of the town were discovered in 1600, but it wasn't until 1748 that excavations began, continuing more or less without interruption – after 1860 under the auspices of the Italian government – until the present day. Most of the site has now been uncovered, and much is very complete, though bear in mind that most of the best mosaics and murals (from Herculaneum too) have found their way into the archaeological museum in Naples, and that as you can only see a small proportion of those found *in situ*, visits to both sites really need to be supplemented by an additional one to the museum.

The Site

The **site** of Pompeii (daily 9am–1hr before sunset; L10,000) covers a wide area, and seeing it properly takes half a day at the very least; probably you should devote most of a day to it and take plenty of breaks – unlike Herculaneum there's little shade, and the distances involved are quite large: flat comfortable shoes are a must.

All of this makes Pompeii sound a bit of a chore – which it isn't. But there is a lot to see, and you should be reasonably selective: many of the streets aren't lined by much more than foundations, and after a while one ruin begins to look much like another. Again, many of the most interesting structures are kept locked and only opened when a large group forms or a tip is handed over to one of the many custodians. To be sure of seeing everything you could take a tour, but as large groups are one of the main features of Pompeii this will probably be the least of your problems. Indeed you're more likely to be struck by how neglected the site is these days.

Entering the site from the Pompeii-Villa dei Misteri side, the **Forum** is the first real feature of significance, a long, slim open space surrounded by the ruins of what would have been some of the town's most important official buildings – a basilica, temples to Apollo and Jupiter, and a market hall. Walking north from here, up the so-called Via di Mercurio, takes you towards some of the town's more luxurious houses. On the left, the **House of the Tragic Poet** is named for its mosaics of a theatrical production and a poet inside, though the "Cave Canem" (Beware of the Dog) mosaic by the main entrance is more eye-catching. Close by, the residents of the **House of the Faun** must have been a friendlier lot, its "Ave" (Welcome) mosaic outside beckoning you in to view the atrium and the copy of a tiny bronze dancing faun (the original is in Naples) that gives the villa its name.

On the street behind, the **House of the Vettii** is one of the most delightful houses in Pompeii, and one of the best maintained, a merchant villa ranged around a lovely central peristyle that gives the best possible impression of the domestic environment of the city's upper middle classes. The first room on the right off the peristyle holds the best of Pompeii's murals actually viewable on site: the one on the left shows the young Hercules struggling with serpents; another, in the corner, depicts Ixion tied to a wheel after offending Zeus, while a third shows Dirce being dragged to her death by the bull set on her by the song of Antiope. There are more paintings beyond here, through the villa's kitchen in a small room that's normally kept locked – erotic works showing various techniques of lovemaking (Greek-style, woman on top; Roman-style, man on top) together with an absurdly potent-looking statue of Priapus from which women were supposed to drink to be fertile; phallic symbols were also, it's reckoned, believed to ward off the evil eye.

Cross over to the other side of the site for the so-called **new excavations**, which began in 1911 and actually uncovered some of the town's most important quarters, stretching along the main Via dell'Abbondanza. The **Grand Theatre**, for one, is very well preserved and is still used for performances, overlooking the small, grassy, column-fringed square of the **Gladiators' Barracks** – not in fact a barracks at all but a refectory and meeting-place for spectators from the nearby amphitheatre. Walk around to the far left side of the Grand Theatre, down the steps and up again, and you're in front of the **Little Theatre** – a smaller, more intimate venue also still used for summer performances, and with a better kept corridor behind the stage space. As for the **Amphitheatre**, it's one of Italy's most intact and accessible, and also its oldest, dating from 80 BC. It's pleasantly overgrown now but once had room for a crowd of some 12,000 – well over half the town's population. Next door, the **Palestra** is a vast parade ground that was used by Pompeii's youth for sport and exercise – overgrown too now, but still with its square of swimming pool in the centre. It must have been in use when the eruption struck Pompeii, since its southeast corner was found littered with the skeletons of young men trying to flee the disaster.

One last place you shouldn't miss at Pompeii is the **Villa dei Misteri**, outside the main site, a short walk from the Porta Ercolano and accessible on the same ticket. This is probably the best preserved of all Pompeii's palatial houses, an originally third-century BC structure with a warren of rooms and courtyards that derives its name from a series of paintings in one of its larger chambers: depictions of the initiation rites of a young woman into the Dionysiac Mysteries, an outlawed cult of the early Imperial era. Not much is known about the cult itself, but the paintings are marvellously clear, remarkable for the surety of their execution and the brightness of their tones and colours. They follow an obvious narrative, starting with the left-hand wall and continuing around the room with a series of freeze-frames showing sacrifice, flagellation, dancing and other rituals, all under the serene gaze of the mistress of the house.

Practicalities

To **reach Pompeii from Naples**, take the Circumvesuviana to Pompeii-Scavi-Villa dei Misteri – about thirty minutes; this leaves you right outside the western entrance to the site. The Circumvesuviana also runs to Pompeii-Santuario, outside the site's eastern entrance, or you can take the roughly hourly mainline train (direction Salerno) to the main Pompeii *FS* station, on the south side of the fairly characterless modern town, which stretches east from the amphitheatre entrance.

It makes most sense to see the site from Naples, and there's really no need to stay overnight, though if you get stuck or are planning to move on south after seeing Pompeii, there are plenty of **hotels** in the modern town, and a large and well-equipped **campsite** – *Zeus* (☎081/861.5320), open all year, right outside the Pompeii-Villa dei Misteri station. Talk to modern Pompeii's **tourist office** at Via Sacra 1 (Mon–Sat 8am–2pm; ☎081/850.7255), just off the main square, for more details. There's also a **tourist office** (☎081/861.0913) outside the site on Piazza Esedra (turn right outside Pompeii-Villa dei Misteri station), which has a plan of the site and other information.

Sorrento

Topping the rocky cliffs close to the end of its peninsula, the last town of significance on this side of the bay, **SORRENTO** is solely and unashamedly a resort, its inspired location and mild climate drawing foreigners from all over Europe for close on 200 years. Ibsen wrote part of *Peer Gynt* in Sorrento, Wagner and Nietzsche had a well-publicised row here, and Maxim Gorky lived for over a decade in the town. Nowadays it's strictly package-tour territory, but really none the worse for it, with little of the brashness of its Spanish and Greek equivalents but all of their vigour, a bright, lively place that retains its southern Italian roots. Cheap restaurants aren't hard to find; neither – if you know where to look – is reasonably priced accommodation; and there's really no better place outside Naples itself from which to explore the rugged peninsula (even parts of the Amalfi coast) and the islands of the Bay.

Sorrento's centre is **Piazza Tasso**, built astride the gorge that runs through the centre of town; it was named after the wayward sixteenth-century Italian poet to whom the town was home and has a statue of him in the far corner. There's nothing much to see in Sorrento itself, but it's nice to wander through the streets which feed into the square, some of which are pedestrianised for the lively evening *passeggiata*. The local **Museo Correale di Terranova**, housed in the airy former palace of a family of local counts at the far end of Via Correale (April–Sept daily Mon & Wed–Sat 9am–12.30pm & 5–7pm, Sun 9.30am–12.30pm; Oct–March Mon & Wed–Sat 9am–12.30pm & 3–5pm, Sun 9am–12.30pm; L5000), might kill an hour or so, with its examples of the local inlaid wood *intarsio* work – most of it much nicer and more ingenious than the mass-produced stuff you see around town – along with various paintings of the Neapolitan school, the odd foreign canvas, including an obscure Rubens, lots of views of Sorrento and the Bay of Naples, and various locally unearthed archaeological knick-knacks. Otherwise the town is entirely given over to pleasure, and there's not much else to see, although it's nice to linger in the shady gardens of the **Villa Communale**, whose terrace has lovely views out to sea, and peek into the small thirteenth-century cloister of the church of **San Francesco** just outside, planted with vines and bright bougainvillea – a peaceful escape from the bustle of the rest of Sorrento.

Strange as it may seem, Sorrento isn't particularly well provided with **beaches**, and in the town itself you either have to make do with the small strips of sand of the **Marina Piccola** lido, right below the Villa Communale gardens and accessible by a lift or steps, or the rocks and tiny, crowded strip of sand at **Marina Grande** – fifteen minutes' walk or a short bus ride (roughly every 30min) from Piazza Tasso. Both places cost around L3500 a head for the day, plus charges for parasol and chair rental, although there is a small patch of sand, immediately right of the lift exit at Marina Piccola, that is free. If you do come down to either of these spots, it's a good idea to hire a pedal-boat (around L15,000 an hour) and get free of the shore, since they can get busy.

If you don't fancy the crowds in Sorrento, you can try the beaches further west. Twenty minutes' walk from the centre of Sorrento along Via del Capo (which is the continuation of Corso Italia), or a short bus ride from Piazza Tasso, there are a couple of options. You can either walk ten minutes or so from the bus stop down the Ruderi Villa Romana Pollio to some nice rocks, swathed with walkways, around the ruins of a Roman villa; or you could stroll 100m further west and take a path off to the right past the *Hotel Dania*, which shortcuts in ten minutes or so to **Marina Puolo** – a short stretch of beach lined by fishing boats and a handful of trattorias.

Practicalities

Sorrento's **train station** is located in the centre of town, five minutes from the main Piazza Tasso along the busy Corso Italia. There's a **tourist office** in the large yellow *Circolo dei Forestieri* at Via Luigi de Maio 35, just off Piazza San Antonino (Mon–Sat 8.30am–2pm & 4.30–7.30pm; ☎081/878.2229), which has maps and details on accommodation; the travel offices on Piazza San Antonino can deal with bus and ferry enquiries and reserve tickets. Incidentally, if you don't want to rely on public transport, *Sorrento*, Corso Italia 210 (☎081/878.1386), close by the train station, rent cars and scooters, and *Guarracino*, Via Sant'Antonino 19 (☎081/878.1728), just off the piazza of the same name, rent bicycles.

Accommodation isn't really a problem, although during peak season you should definitely book in advance. There's an official **youth hostel** at Via B. Capasso 5 (☎081/878.1783), five minutes' walk from the train station: to get there walk out of the station and turn right on the main road – Via B. Capasso is 200m down on the left. There are also a number of centrally placed inexpensive **hotels**, perhaps the most convenient of which are the *Nice*, Corso Italia 249 (☎081.878.1650; 416+), and the *City*, Corso Italia 221 (☎081/877.2210; ④), although they are fairly basic. In the opposite direction from the train station, the *Mara*, Via Rota 5 (☎081/878.3665; ④), in a modern block around the corner from the youth hostel, is a good, cheap bet if all else is full. A notch up in price, just the other side of Piazza Tasso, the *Hotel del Corso*, Corso Italia 134 (☎081/878.1299; ⑤), is very pleasant, with lovely airy rooms; also good is the slightly more expensive *Savoia*, near the train station at Via Fuorimura 48 (☎081/878.2511; ⑤). If you want to be by the sea, the *Loreley et Londres*, Via Califano 12 (081/807.3187; ⑤), situated in a lovely ancient building high on the cliffs on the eastern edge of the town centre, is wonderful value, as is the *Elios*, on the other side of town, ten minutes' walk from the centre at Via del Capo 33 (☎081/878.1812; ⑤), with wonderful sea views and private parking. Among **campsites**, the closest option is the *Nube d'Argento* site, close by the *Elios* at Via del Capo 12 (☎081/878.1344); if that's full, try the *Santa Fortunata*, about five minutes further on at Via del Capo 39 (☎081.878.2405).

As for **eating**, you're spoilt for choice. If you just want a snack, *Bar Rita*, Corso Italia 219, can't be bettered, with a wide array of sandwiches, cakes and other delicious lunch items. For a full meal, the *Trattoria-Pizzeria da Gigino*, Via degli Archi 15, is a great no-nonsense choice, with excellent pizzas and good pasta and main courses. The *Sant' Antonino*, around the corner on Via Santa Maria delle Grazie, off Piazza Sant'Antonino, is good, with excellent pizzas, and has a garden as well, while the *Parruchiano*, Corso Italia 71, is an enormous restaurant, very popular locally, with fine food and a wonderful enclosed garden setting. *La Fenice*, Via degli Aranci 11, is also very good, and has a lively atmosphere. If you want a scenic eating option, try the *Minervetta*, whose terrace restaurant perches a little way along Via del Capo on the right.

For just **drinking**, *Bar Ercolano*, right on Piazza Tasso, isn't as pricey as you'd think and is vibrantly sited. For late-night boozing, the "pubs" along Corso Italia are as good a place as any: try the *English Inn*, Corso Italia 55, and *Chaplin's*, almost opposite. The terrace bar in the *Circolo dei Foristeri* is a genteel place to drink, and has ultra-romantic nighttime views, not to mention a dance floor. For somewhat more up-to-date sounds, the *Kalimera* disco, at the end of Via del Capo (right by the bus stop), is a convivial local joint.

The Islands

Guarding each prong of the Bay of Naples, the islands of Cápri, Ischia and Prócida between them make up the best known group of Italian islands. Each is a very different creature, though. **Cápri** is a place of legend, home to the mythical Sirens and a much-eulogised playground of the super-rich in the years since – though now settled down to a lucrative existence as a target for day-trippers from the mainland. Visit by all means, but bear in mind that you have to hunt hard these days to detect the origins of much of the purple prose. Similarly with **Ischia**, predominantly package-tour territory now and just as crowded, primarily with German sunseekers who colonise the place during the summer months. Only **Prócida**, the smallest of the islands and probably the least interesting – though the best venue for fairly peaceful lazing – remains reasonably untouched by the high season

Cápri

Sheering out of the sea just off the far end of the Sorrentine peninsula, the island of **Cápri** has long been the most sought-after part of the Bay of Naples. During Roman times Augustus retreated to the island's gorgeous cliffbound scenery to escape the cares of office; later Tiberius moved the Imperial capital here, indulging himself in legendarily debauched antics until his death in 37 AD. After the Romans left, Cápri was rather neglected until the early nineteenth century, when the discovery of the Blue Grotto and the island's remarkable natural landscape coincided nicely with the rise of tourism, and the island has never looked back, attracting a steady flow of artists and writers and, more recently, inquisitive tourists, ever since. The English especially have always flocked here: D. H. Lawrence and George Bernard Shaw were among more illustrious visitors, Graham Greene and Gracie Fields have (or had) houses here; and even Lenin visited for a time after the failure of the 1905 uprising.

Cápri tends to get a mixed press these days, the consensus being that while it might have been an attractive place once, it's been pretty much ruined by the crowds and the prices. And Cápri *is* crowded these days, mainly with Germans and Americans (though the Brits continue to hold their own), and in July and August, and on *all* summer weekends, it would be sensible to give it a miss. But reports that the island has been irreparably spoilt are way overstated. Ischia is just as busy, Prócida isn't nearly as interesting

GETTING TO THE ISLANDS

Ferries and **hydrofoils** are run by three companies: *Caremar*, who operate ferries and hydrofoils from the main harbour at the bottom of Piazza Municipio; *SNAV*, who run hydrofoils from Mergellina; and *Linee Lauro*, who operate ferries and hydrofoils from both places. Between them, they depart for all of the islands from Naples, Pozzuoli and Sorrento, with some connections from Salerno, Amalfi and Positano. Whichever you take, day trips are quite feasible; usually the last connection delivers you back on the mainland in time for dinner. On foot, you can simply buy tickets when you turn up from the offices at the port; in general it's better to buy a single rather than a return ticket since it doesn't work out more expensive and you retain more flexibility on the time you come back. The following is to give a rough idea of frequencies during the summer, and you should either check with the local tourist office or buy a copy of *Il Mattino* for specific timings. Or phone the companies direct: *Caremar* (☎081/551.3882); *Linee Lauro* (ferries ☎081/551.3236, hydrofoils ☎081/761.1004); *SNAV* (☎081/761.2348).

HYDROFOILS

Naples (Molo Beverello)–Cápri (6 daily; 40min).
Naples (Molo Beverello)–Ischia (6 daily; 50min).
Naples (Molo Beverello)–Prócida (6 daily; 35min).
Naples (Megellina)–Cápri (12 daily; 40min).
Naples (Mergellina)–Ischia (12 daily; 40min).
Naples (Mergellina)–Forio (Ischia) (6 daily; 50min).
Naples (Mergellina)–Casamicciola (Ischia) (4 daily; 50min).
Naples (Mergellina)–Prócida (4 daily; 30min).
Salerno–Cápri (via Amalfi and Positano) (3 daily; 1hr).
Sorrento–Ischia (via Naples) (2 daily; 1hr).
Sorrento–Cápri (6 daily; 20min).
Casamicciola (Ischia)–Prócida (4 daily; 30min).

FERRIES

Naples (Molo Beverello)–Cápri (6 daily; 1hr 15min).
Naples (Molo Beverello)–Ischia (12 daily; 1hr 20min).
Naples (Molo Beverello)–Prócida (5 daily; 1hr).
Pozzuoli–Ischia (4 daily; 1hr 40min).
Pozzuoli–Casamicciola (Ischia) (5 daily; 1hr 50min).
Pozzuoli–Prócida (4 daily; 1hr 10min).
Ischia–Prócida (4 daily; 40min).
Sorrento–Cápri (5 daily; 50min).
Salerno–Cápri (via Amalfi) (1 daily; 2hr).
Salerno–Ischia (via Amalfi and Positano) (1 daily; 2hr 30min).

– or beautiful – and it would be hard to find a place with more inspiring views. It's expensive, too, especially if you sit and drink on its main squares. But prices aren't really any higher than other major Italian resorts, and you can cut out the inflated expense of accommodation by visiting on a day trip; indeed a couple of these and you can see all of the island comfortably.

Marina Grande, Cápri town and around

Ferries and hydrofoils dock at **MARINA GRANDE**, the waterside extension of the island's main town, which perches on the hill above. You can take boats to the Blue Grotto from here (see p.721), and there's a tourist office which doles out maps and other information, as well as any number of pricey waterside cafés and restaurants. It is, however, quickly exhausted, and you may as well take the **funicular** (daily 6.35am–10pm; L1500 one-way) up the steep hill to Cápri town itself; if the funicular is too crowded (as it surely will be in high season) you can also walk, which takes about twenty minutes; follow the road up from the far end of the harbour, from where steps lead all the way up across the crisscrossing road.

CAPRI is the main town of the island, nestled between its two mountains, its houses connected by winding, hilly alleyways that give onto the dinky (almost toytown) main square of **Piazza Umberto**, crowded with café tables and, invariably, a lot of people. Sit on the steps and eat your lunch and watch the drinkers and diners digging deep for the (undeniable) ambience.

Of things to see in or near Cápri, the **Certosa San Giacomo** (Tues–Sun 8am–2pm; free) on the far side of the town is a rundown old monastery with a handful of paintings, a couple of shapeless Roman statues dredged up from the deep and an odd, overgrown cloister given over in part to a music school. To the right of the monastery, the **Giardini Augustos** give tremendous views of the coast below and the towering jagged cliffs above, and from there you can wind down to either the beach below (rocks really), or, beyond, to **MARINA PICCOLA** – a small huddle of houses and restaurants around a few patches of pebble beach: reasonably uncrowded out of season, though in July or August you might as well forget it. Marina Piccola is also accessible by bus.

Up above the Certosa, and a further pleasant walk fifteen minutes through Cápri town, the **Belvedere del Cannone** has marvellous views, especially over the **Faraglioni** rocks to the left and Marina Piccola to the right. Further out of Cápri town, there are two walks worth doing out to the eastern edge of the island. One, up to the ruins of Tiberius's villa, the **Villa Jovis** (daily 9am–6pm; L4000), is a steep thirty-minute hike from Piazza Umberto following Via Botteghe out of the square and Via Tiberio up the hill. It was here that Tiberius retired in 27 AD to lead a life of vice and debauchery and to take revenge on his enemies, many of whom he apparently had thrown off the cliff-face. You can see why he chose the site: it's among Cápri's most exhilarating, with incredible vistas of Ischia, Prócida and the Bay; on a clear day you can even see Salerno and beyond. There's not much left of the villa, but you can get a good sense of the shape and design of its various parts from the arched halls and narrow passageways that remain. Below, there's another villa, the more recent **Villa Fersen** of one Count Fersen-Adelsward, a gay Swedish millionaire who built the house early this century apparently to entertain pick-ups from the town. Its gates are locked, the building in a sad state of disrepair, but the adventurous may want to clamber in for a hunt around.

The other walk is to the **Arco Naturale**, an impressive natural rock formation at the end of a high, lush valley, a 25-minute hike from Cápri town, again following Via Botteghe out of the square but branching off up Via Matermania after ten minutes or so; you can get quite close to the arch due to the specially constructed viewing platforms. Just before the arch, steps lead down to the **Grotta di Matermania**, ten minutes away down quite a few steps – a dusty cutaway out of the rock that was converted to use a shrine to the Sybil by the Romans. Steps lead on down from the cave, sheer through the trees, before flattening into a path that you can follow back to the **Tragara Belvedere**, and, eventually, Cápri town – reachable in about an hour.

Anacápri and around

The island's other main settlement, **ANACÁPRI**, is more sprawling than Cápri itself and less obviously picturesque, its main square, **Piazza Vittoria**, flanked by souvenir shops, bland fashion boutiques and restaurants decked with tourist menus – Cápri without the chic. During the season, a chair lift operates from Piazza Vittoria up to **Monte Solaro** (daily 9am–1hr before sunset; L6000), shifting you up to the summit of the mountain at 596m high, the island's highest point, in about twelve minutes. At the top there's only a ruined castle and a café, but the location is very tranquil and the views are marvellous.

A short walk away from Piazza Vittoria down Via G. Orlandi, the church of **San Michele** is the village's principal sight, its tiled floor painted with an eighteenth-century depiction of the Fall that you view from an upstairs balcony – a lush work after a drawing by the Neapolitan painter Solimena, in rich blues and yellows, showing cats, unicorns and other creatures.

Continuing in the same direction, a good 45-minute hike away starting off down Via Lo Pozzo (or reachable by bus every twenty minutes from Piazza Vittoria), the **Blue Grotto** or "Grotta Azzura" is probably the island's best-known feature – though also its most exploitative, the boatmen here whisking visitors onto boats and in and out of the grotto in about five minutes flat. The grotto is quietly impressive, the blue of its innards caused by the sun entering the cave through the water, but it's rather overrated, and the process is all over so quickly as to be barely worth the trip down here, let alone the extortionate fees. Technically, you can swim into the cave – it's not the exclusive preserve of the boatmen, though they'll try to persuade you otherwise – but the route through is so busy that unless you're a strong swimmer it's not advisable to try. Incidentally, it's also possible to take a boat trip to the grotto direct from Marina Grande (see p.719), though the prices mean it's an even more expensive way to get here. (Entrance: L4000, plus L6000 for the rowing boat; taking a boat direct from Marina Grande costs an additional L6900, more on Sun.)

Time is much better spent walking in the opposite direction from Piazza Vittoria, past a long gauntlet of souvenir stalls to Axel Munthe's **Villa San Michele** (daily 9am–6pm; L4000), a light, airy house with lush and fragrant gardens that is one of the real highlights of the island. The Swedish writer Munthe lived here for a number of years, and it's filled with his furniture and knick-knacks, as well as Roman artefacts ingeniously incorporated into the villa's rooms and gardens. Busts and bronzes abound: one statue of Hermes was given to Munthe by the city of Naples in thanks for his work in the city during the cholera epidemic of 1884 (see "Naples" p.699); Corinthian capitals are converted as coffee tables, other surfaces topped with intricate Cosmati mosaic-work.

Practicalities

There are **tourist offices** in Marina Grande (Mon–Sat 8am–8pm; ☎081/837.0634), on Piazza Umberto in Cápri town (Mon–Sat 8am–8pm, Sun 8.30am–2.30pm; ☎081/837.0686), and in Anacápri on Via G. Orlandi (Mon–Sat 9am–1pm & 3–6.30pm; ☎081/837.1524). **Getting around** the island, there is a decent bus service connecting all the main centres – Marina Grande, Cápri, Marina Piccola, Anacapri – every fifteen minutes; buses also run regularly down to the Blue Grotto from Anacápri; tickets cost L1500.

You'd be well advised not to **stay overnight** on Cápri: in peak season space is extremely limited, and the prices are through the roof; day trips here from Naples or Sorrento are in any case easy. If you are keen to stay, however – and the island certainly is a lot quieter after the day-tripping crowds have gone home – you could try the *Quattro Stagioni*, Via Marina Piccola 1 (☎081/837.0041; ⑤) or the centrally placed *Stella Maris*, Via Roma 27 (☎081/837.0452; ⑤). If they are full, *La Prora*, very appealingly situated up above the *Stella Maris* on Via Castello (☎081/837.0281; ⑤), is an exceedingly pleasant place to stay. If you don't mind staying in Anacápri, the *Villa Eva*, Via La Fabbrica 8 (☎081/837.2040; ④), is perhaps the best-value place to stay on the island, a welcoming family-run hostel/hotel; to get there, phone from Piazza Vittoria and they'll pick you up.

Even if you don't stay, **eating** can be an expense, and you might prefer to knock yourself up a picnic lunch: in Cápri town there is a supermarket and a bakery a little way down Via Botteghe off Piazza Umberto, and well-stocked *salumerie* at Via Roma 13 and 30. For sit-down food, one of the best places is *Da Gemma*, under the arches of old Cápri at Via Madre Serafina 6, a friendly, long-established place with a windowed main room overlooking the bay – good for seafood, and not that pricey. Down below, *Moscardino* on Via Roma is a central but surprisingly inexpensive restaurant in a good location, as is *Di Giorgio* almost next door, while on the other side of Piazza Umberto, *Pizzeria Aurora*, on Via Fuorlovado – the continuation of Via Botteghe – is pretty good value too.

Ischia

Largest of the islands in the Bay of Naples, **Ischia** rises out of the sea in a series of pointy green hummocks, downbeat sister to more glamorous Cápri and these days the favoured playground of German and Scandinavian tourists, who flock in increasingly huge numbers during peak season to its beach resorts, thermal springs and therapeutic sands. It's not hard to see why its reputation has always been poorer than Cápri's: it's not nearly so beautiful, and there's not a lot here that's all that historic. But you can at least be sure of being alone in exploring parts of its mountainous interior; and if you're after a straight bit of beach lounging and don't want to stray too far from Naples, it might just be the place.

There are buses around the island from Ischia Porto every thirty minutes in both directions, stopping just about everywhere; they run on two circular routes, the CS and CD, basically one in each direction. Tickets cost L1500 and are valid for half an hour or an hour.

Ischia Porto and Ischia Ponte

The main town of Ischia is **ISCHIA PORTO**, where most of the ferries dock, a long straggle of hotels, boutiques and beach shops fronted by patches of beach and punctuated by cafés serving *wurst* and hamburgers to the large crowds of young Germans. There are a couple of beaches in Ischia Porto, one to the right of the port, **Spiaggia San Pietro**, accessible by following Via Buonocore off Via Roma, and another, small affair, the inexplicably named **Spiaggia degli Inglese**, on the other side of the port, reachable by way of the small path which leads over the headland from the end of Via Jasolino.

Otherwise the main thing to do is to window-shop and stroll along the main Corso Vittoria Colonna, either branching off to a further beach, the **Spiaggia dei Pescatori**, or following it all the way down to the other part of Ischia's main town, **ISCHIA PONTE**, a quieter and less commercialised centre. Here the focus is the **Castello Aragonese** (daily 9am–7pm; L5000, plus L1000 for the lift to the top), which crowns an offshore rock but is accessible from a short causeway. Vittoria Colonna, the Renaissance poet and close friend of Michelangelo, spent much of her life here, following the seizure of her family's land by Alexander VI. The citadel itself where she lived is rather tumbledown now and closed to the public, but below is a complex of buildings, almost a separate village really, around which you can stroll. There's the weird open shell of a cathedral destroyed by the British in 1804, a prison that once held political prisoners during the upheavals of the Unification, and the macabre remnants of a convent, in which a couple of dark rooms ringed with a set of commode-like seats served as a cemetery for the dead sisters – placed here to putrefy in front of the living members of the community.

Ischia Porto's helpful **tourist office** is right by the quayside ferry ticket offices (Mon–Sat 9am–2pm & 3–8pm; ☎081/991.146); the **bus terminus**, with buses going to all other parts of the island, is right behind here. If you're planning on **staying** in the island's main town, the *Monastero*, in the castello in Ischia Ponte (☎081/992.435; ⑤), is perhaps the most atmospheric choice you could come up with, and is not too pricey, although being in Ischia Ponte it's a bit distanced from the liveliest parts of the island. There's certainly more life in Ischia Porto, where the *Rosita*, Via Quercia 38 (☎081/993.875; ⑤), is a good-value alternative, a large place in a lush garden, two minutes from the bus terminus – as is the clean and appealing *Antonio Macri*, off the portside at Via Jasolino 96 (☎081/992.603; ④). Not too much more expensive, and almost as handy, is *Il Crostolo*, Via B. Cossa 2 (☎081/991.094; ⑤), a short walk from the bus terminus on the main road. For **eating**, the *Mastù Peppe*, right by the tourist office and ferry quay, is cheap and quite good; with a little more money, try *Gennaro*, across the harbour at Via Porto 64. In Ischia Ponte, *Pirozzi*, Via Seminario 47, does great pizzas and has lovely views over the Bay and the castello.

Casamicciola Terme, Lacco Ameno, Forio

The island is at its most developed along its northern and western shores – heading west from Ischia Porto. The first village you reach, **CASAMICCIOLA TERME**, is a bland spa centre with many hotels and a crowded central beach – though you can find a quieter one on the far side of the village. Ibsen spent a summer here, and the waters are said to be full of iodine, but otherwise you may as well push on to **LACCO AMENO**, a brighter little town, again with a beach and with spa waters that are said to be the most radioactive in Italy.

FORIO sprawls around its bay, another growing resort that is quite pretty behind its tawdry seafront of bars and pizzerias, focusing around the busy main street of Corso Umberto. Out on the point on the far side of the old centre (turn right at the far end of Corso Umberto), the **Chiesa Soccorso** is a bold, whitewashed landmark from which to survey the town, a simple church, one of whose chapels preserves a wooden crucifix discovered among the rocks below after a storm in the early 1500s.

There are good **beaches** either side of Forio: the **Spiaggia di Chiaia** a short walk to the north and the **Spiaggia di Citara** a somewhat longer walk to the south along Via G. Mazzella. Both are decent stretches of sand – with some free areas – and make Forio a base worth considering. If you do stay, the *Pensione di Lustro*, right in the centre at Via Filippo di Lustro 9 (☎081/997.163; ⑤), is probably the nicest place to stay, and is very reasonably priced. The *Nettuno*, Via C. Piro 1 (☎081/997.140; ④), is a bit less expensive but not as nice; the *Villa Serena*, up in the heart of the old town on Via Vecchia (☎081/997.661; ④), is somewhere in between the two. When you get **hungry**, the *Tinaia*, Via M. Verde 39, does middling pizzas and pasta dishes in an affable garden setting.

Sant'Angelo and around

Ischia is pleasantest on its southern side, the landscape steeper and greener, with fewer people to enjoy it. **SANT'ANGELO** is probably its loveliest spot, a tiny fishing village crowded around a narrow isthmus linking with a humpy islet that's out of bounds to buses, who drop right outside. It's inevitably quite developed, centring on a square and harbour crowded with café tables and surrounded by pricey boutiques; but if all you want to do is laze in the sun it's perhaps the island's most appealing spot to do so. There's a reasonable **beach** lining one side of the isthmus that connects Sant'Angelo to its islet, as well as the nearby stretch of the **Spiaggia dei Maronti**, about a kilometre east, which is accessible by plentiful taxi boats from Sant'Angelo's harbour (L2000–3000), or on foot in about 25 minutes – take the path from the top of the village. This is long enough to make it possible to get a bit of space to yourself, and you can of course just head for an empty spot. However, taxi boats will drop you at one of a number of specific features: one, the **Fumarole**, is where steam emerges from under the rocks in a kind of outdoor sauna; further along close by a couple of hotels is a path that cuts inland through a mini-gorge to the **Terme Cavascura** (daily 8.30am–1.30pm & 2.30–6pm; L10,000), where hot springs have been harnessed for you to pamper yourself thoroughly.

Up above Sant'Angelo looms the craggy summit of Ischia's now dormant volcano, **Monte Epomeo**. Ischia Porto-bound buses make the twenty-minute trip up to **FONTANA**, a superb ride, with wonderful views back over the coast, from where you can climb up to the summit of the volcano. Follow the signposted road off to the left from the centre of Fontana: after about five minutes it joins a larger road; after another five minutes take the left fork, a stony track off the road, and follow this up to the summit – when in doubt, always fork left and you can't go wrong. About a fifty-minute climb in all, perhaps an hour, it's a steep haul and at times quite testing, especially at the end when the path becomes no more than a channel cut out of the soft volcanic rock. However, there are a couple of scenically placed cafés in which to gather your energies at the top, and the views from its craggy summit are stunning – right around the island and back across to the sprawl of Naples. Bear in mind, too, that you can drive to within about twenty minutes of the summit, leaving your vehicle by the signs for the military exclusion zone, if you don't think you can manage it there and back on foot; you can also rent a mule in Fontana; reckon on paying up to L30,000 each way for this, though.

There are plenty of places to **stay** in and around Sant'Angelo; the cheaper places tend to be outside the village proper. Up in SUCCHIVO, ten minutes' walk back in the direction of Forio (the bus passes right by), *Casa Nicola* (☎081/907.165; ④) and, next door, *Casa Guiseppina* (☎081/907.830; ④), on the main road, are both excellent. Down in Sant'Angelo itself, the *Conchiglia* (☎081/999.270; ⑤) is good too but a little pricier and definitely noisier. When it comes to **eating**, you might be wise to walk up to the next village along from Succhivo, PANZA, where the *Da Leopoldo* restaurant is famous around these parts for its Ischian specialities (rabbit, great sausages, good antipasto table), cosy atmosphere and moderate prices. It is, however, a bit difficult to find – follow Via S. Gennaro from the main square of Panza for about ten minutes; it's a little way past the *Hotel Al Bosco*. In Sant'Angelo itself you could do worse than stoke up on the fine pizzas at the unpretentious *Da Pasquale*, up in the old centre of the village; everywhere else is much of a muchness.

Prócida

A serrated hunk of volcanic rock that's the smallest and nearest island to Naples, **Prócida** has managed to fend off the kind of tourist numbers that have flooded into Cápri and Ischia; and arriving here it's easy to see why. It lacks the spectacle, or variety, of both islands, though it more than compensates with the extra room and extra peace. With a population of just 10,000, there are few real population centres, its main town, **MARINA GRANDE** – where you arrive by ferry – an oddly rundown conglomeration of houses rising from a pastel-painted waterfront to a network of steep streets winding up to the fortified tip of the island – the so-called **Terra Murata**. Part of this is given over to a rather forbidding prison, now closed, but it's worth walking up anyway to see the abbey church of **San Michele** (Mon–Fri 9am–noon & 3.30–6.30pm), whose domes are decorated with a stirring painting by Giordano of Saint Michael beating back the Turks from Prócida's shore. The views, too, from the nearby belvedere are among the region's best, taking in the whole of the Bay of Naples, from Capo Miseno bang in front of you right around to the end of the Sorrentine peninsula and Cápri on the far left.

For the rest, Prócida's appeal lies in its opportunities to swim and eat in relative peace. There are **beaches** in Marina Grande itself, on the far side of the jetty, and, in the opposite direction, beyond the fishing harbour, though both are fairly grubby. Similarly, **Spiaggia Chiaia**, just beyond the fishing harbour of nearby CORICELLA, is a reasonable bathing beach but isn't very large and can get crowded. You can walk there, or the Chiaioella bus stops nearby.

On the whole if you want to swim you're better off making the fifteen-minute bus journey from Marina Grande to **CHIAIOELLA**, where there's a handful of bars and restaurants around a pleasant, almost circular bay and a long stretch of sandy beach that is the island's best. By taking the road up from behind the beach you can cross over the bridge (the gate is usually left open) onto the islet of **Vivara**, a nature reserve, very peaceful and overgrown, that is a refreshingly bucolic affair after the rest of the island, where the settlement is pretty much continuous.

Practicalities

The **tourist office** is by the water in the ferry terminal building (daily 9.30am–1pm & 4–8pm; ☎081/896.9624), close by where the buses stop; it has free maps and advice on accommodation. For **getting around**, a bus service connects Marina Grande with Chiaioella roughly every twenty minutes and coincides with all ferry and hydrofoil arrivals. There's not much choice if you want to **stay**: there are only three hotels, together with a couple of *pensione*. Chiaioella is probably your best bet, where you can stay at the *Riviera* hotel, ten minutes' walk from the beach at Via G. de Procida 36 (☎081/896.7197; ⑤) – the bus goes right by – or, slightly more conveniently, the *Crescenzo*, right on the waterfront at Via M. Chiaioella 33 (☎081/896.7255; ⑤). If these are full, there's the *Celeste Residence*, between the *Riviera* and the harbour on the left, at Via Rivoli 6 (☎081/896.7488; ⑤). Be aware that at all of these places you *must* book in advance. If you're **camping**, there are five sites on the island, most within easy walking distance of the sea: try one of the two on Via IV Novembre, the *Caravella* (☎081/896.9230), open May to September, and the *Vivara* (☎081/896.9242), open June to September – both around 200m from the sea. To get to them, take the Chiaioella bus and get off at Piazza Olmo.

Eating is rather easier. In Marina Grande, restaurants line the waterfront Via Roma: *La Medusa*, opposite the ferry terminal, is not cheap but is very good; *Ipanema*, a little further down at no. 68, is a long-standing favourite; or you could eat at the cheapest option, the very friendly *Cantinone da Zio Luigi*, at Via Roma 55, a popular locals' joint. In Chiaioella, you could try *Il Galeone*, right by the bus stop between the Bay and the beach.

INLAND AND SOUTHERN CAMPANIA

Away from the coast Campania's appeal fades. The **interior** is a poor and remote region that few tourists visit – quite different from the populous and much-lauded coast. Large towns are few, travel can be slow and unless you're spending a long time in the area, or are an enthusiast for obscure ancient sites, there's not much of interest anyway. What places there are that might appeal – the royal palace at **Caserta**, the Roman amphitheatre at **Cápua**, the ancient town of **Benevento** – are best seen on a day trip from Naples.

The **south** of the region, on the other hand, holds some of Campania's real gems. The **Amalfi coast** is as spectacular a bit of shoreline as Italy has to offer, and worth a visit for just that, though you may find the tourist presence in high season a bit offputting. **Salerno**, at the far end of this stretch, is a genial working port and a jumping-off spot for the less-developed **Cilento** coast that stretches all the way to the Basilicata border. Inland from here is also very undeveloped and difficult to reach without your own car. But it can be a rewarding area, its high hills and valleys sheltering some supremely unspoilt routes and villages.

North of Naples: Caserta, Cápua and around

There's not much to draw you to the territory immediately north of Naples. The towns just outside the city – Casoria, Afragola, Acerra – are collectively known as the **"Triangle of Death"** for their Camorra connections and make up a bleak conurbation of poor housing and industrial messiness.

Caserta

Further inland, a short train or bus ride direct from Naples, **CASERTA**, incongruously surrounded by a sprawl of industrial complexes and warehouses that stretches all the way back to Naples, is known as the "Versailles of Naples" for its vast eighteenth-century royal palace, which utterly dominates the town. There's not much point in coming here if you don't want to see this; if you do, be sure to also see the old village of **Caserta Vecchia**, 10km north of the modern town, where the population lived before the building of the palace. To get there by car, more or less the only way, do a left onto Piazza Vanvitelli from the palace and carry straight on to the edge of town, following the road from there up into the hills. It's now almost entirely deserted but is a bucolic antidote to Caserta's soulless streets and has a twelfth-century cathedral that is a fine example of southern Norman architecture. There are a couple of restaurants up here geared to wedding parties and Sunday excursionists from Naples and Caserta: try *A Marchesina*, on the right of the street which leads off the square from under the church tower; they do hearty sandwiches and strong local wine.

The Palazzo Reale

The palace and its grounds are royal creations on the grandest of scales and made a fitting setting for the signing of the German-Italian armistice in 1945. Begun in 1752 for the Bourbon King Charles III to plans drawn up by Vanvitelli, and completed a little over twenty years later, it's an awesomely large complex, built around four courtyards, with a facade 245m long, nestling between two curving brick arms and overlooking a massive, classically ordered square. However, it's ultimately a dull structure that substitutes size for inspiration. Only the majestic central staircases up to the **royal apartments** (Mon–Sat 9am–1.30pm, Sun 9am–12.30pm; L6000) hit the right note. And the apartments themselves are a grand parade of heavily painted and stuccoed rooms, sparsely furnished in Empire style, some with great, overbearing Classical statues, and all, in their brazen, overstated display of wealth, pretty disgusting – not least in the smug portraits of the Bourbon dynasty, especially the one of the podgy Francis I with his brat-like children. There's little point in singling out anything of special significance: there isn't anything really, and it's the feel of the building and its pitiless overstatement that are the real attractions.

Behind the palace, the **gardens** too are classically ordered and on no less huge a scale, stretching out behind along one central three-kilometre-long axis and punctured by myth-inspired fountains. The main promenade is longer than it looks from the palace (it's a good half an hour's walk or a free bicycle ride), and regular buses make the round trip, dropping you off at selected intervals along the way and turning round by the main cascade at the top, which depicts Diana turning Actaeon into a stag. Walk to the top, look back at the palace, hop on a bus . . . and depart.

Santa Maria Cápua Vetere, Cápua and around

Regular buses run from Caserta, either from the bus/train station or the stop just to the left as you exit the palace, down to **SANTA MARIA CÁPUA VETERE** – a not especially pleasant journey past jutting signs, petrol stations and rundown housing. There's not a blade of grass in sight, and the feeling is one of grinding, hapless urban poverty. There's not much to Santa Maria itself either, but in its day this originally Etruscan, later Samnite, city, then known as *Cápua*, was the second city of Italy, centre of the rich and important region of Campania and famous for its skill in working bronze. Its first-century AD **amphitheatre** was once the largest in Italy after the Colosseum, and parts of it remain on the far side of town, a right turn shortly after

Piazza San Francesco d'Assisi. In its day this held a reputed Roman gladiator school and barracks, and it was here that the gladiators' revolt, led by Spartacus, broke out in 73 BC – a revolt that was only put down after two years and four lost battles. The amphitheatre now is less well preserved than the Colosseum (though better than Pozzuoli's), having lost most of the surrounding tiers – and many of the remaining ones have been concreted over. But the network of tunnels underneath survives reasonably intact, and is accessible. You can also ask for the keys to a nearby **Mithraeum** across the road, down Via Antifeatro and then left down Via Morelli – one of the best preserved in the country and redolent with the bizarre, bloodletting rites that accompanied the cult of Mithraism.

There are heaps of rubble and a handful of artefacts dotted around the amphitheatre, not least a large piece of mosaic, but most of the finds have found their way to the **Museo Provinciale Campano** in **CÁPUA**, 4km down the road (Tues–Sat 9am–2pm, Sun 9am–1pm; free) – a smaller town than Santa Maria, settled by refugees when the original city was plundered in 856 by Saracens. Sited on the broad curve of the Volturno River, it's a marginally more attractive place than Santa Maria, but it's not really worth the trek (or even bus ride) if you're without a car.

The area northwest of Cápua, the **Terra di Lavoro**, is a flat, fertile plain that's one of Campania's prime agricultural regions, yielding a healthy array of fruit and supporting plentiful herds of mozzarella-producing buffalo. The main town, **SESSA ARUNCA**, has a pleasant centre of narrow arched streets and a Romanesque cathedral which has a pulpit similar to those at Salerno and Ravello. But otherwise there's not a lot to persuade travellers to stop, and most push straight on to Formia or Rome.

Benevento

BENEVENTO, further inland than Cápua or Caserta and reachable in about an hour and half from Naples by bus, was another important Roman settlement, a key point on the Via Appia between Rome and Brindisi and as such a thriving trading town. Founded in 278 BC, it was at the time the farthest point from Rome to be colonised, and even now it has a remote air about it, circled by hills and with a centre that was (pointlessly) bombed to smithereens in the last war and even now seems only half rebuilt. Its climate also ranks among southern Italy's most extreme.

Buses from Naples drop you on the main square, where the **Duomo** is an almost total reconstruction of its thirteenth-century Romanesque original; what's left of its famous bronze doors, believed to be Byzantine, is now stashed inside. Left from here, the main street, **Corso Garibaldi**, leads up the hill, a once elegant thoroughfare lined with ancient palaces. Off to the left about halfway up, the **Arch of Trajan** is the major remnant of the Roman era, a marvellously preserved triumphal arch that is refreshing after the scaffolding and netting of Rome's arches, since you can get close enough to study its friezes. Built to guard the entrance to Benevento from the Appian Way, it's actually as heavy-handed a piece of self-acclaim as there ever was, showing the Emperor Trajan in various scenes of triumph, power and generosity. Further up Corso Garibaldi, the **Museo Sannio**, in the cloister behind the eighth-century church of Santa Sofia (Mon–Sat 9am–1pm; free), holds a selection of Roman finds from the local area, including a number of artefacts from a temple of Isis – various sphinxes, bulls and a headless statue of Isis herself. There are also terracotta votive figurines from the fifth century BC, and the cloister itself has capitals carved with energetic scenes of animals, humans and strange beasts – hunting, riding and attacking.

There are more bits and pieces from Roman times scattered around the rather battered old quarter of town, the **Triggio** – reached by following Via Carlo Torre off to the left of the main road beyond the cathedral. The **Bue Apis**, at the far end of Corso Dante, is another relic from the temple of Isis, a first-century BC sculpture of a bull. And in the heart of the old quarter there are the substantial remains of a **Teatro Romano** built during the reign of Hadrian – though it's been a little over-restored for modern use. In Hadrian's time it seated 20,000 people, rather less today as the upper level remains mossily decrepit, but it's still an atmospheric sight – like most of Benevento relatively unvisited by tourists and looking out over the green rolling countryside of the province beyond.

Practicalities

Benevento is roughly 60km from Naples and **buses** run roughly every two hours from Piazza Garibaldi – an hour-and-a-half trip. **Trains** stop down the hill from the centre and are in any case slower and more infrequent. Benevento is easily seen on a day excursion and there's no need **to stay**, but if you're pushing on east to Foggia and Puglia (to which there are regular train connections), or if you get stuck, the *Genova*, at Viale Principe di Napoli 130 (☎0824/42.926; ⑤), is an adequate hotel. For **food**, if you're just here for the day you're likely to be content with the snacks, pizza and *tavola calda*-style dishes at *Pizzeria Romana*, next door to the cathedral on the corner of Via Carlo Torre. For evening eating there are adequate restaurants dotted on and around the main Corso Garibaldi.

The Amalfi coast

Occupying the southern side of Sorrento's peninsula, the **Costiera Amalfitana** lays claim to being Europe's most beautiful stretch of coast, its corniche road winding around the towering cliffs that slip almost sheer into the sea. By car or bus it's an incredible ride, and if you're staying in Sorrento especially it shouldn't be missed on any account; in any case the towns along here hold the beaches that Sorrento lacks. The coast as a whole has become rather developed, and these days it's in fact one of Italy's ritzier bits of shoreline, villas atop its precarious slopes fetching a bomb in both cash and kudos. But the cliffs are so steep, and the towns' growth so inevitably constrained, that it seems unlikely that the Amalfi coast can ever become completely spoilt.

Coming **from Sorrento**, buses normally join the coast road a little way **west of Positano**. If the coast road is closed, however, which it is from time to time due to landslides and forest fires, the bus from Sorrento will take the alternative route, via Castellammare and Agerola, right over the backbone of the Sorrentine peninsula, which is itself a journey worth making – the bus zigzagging down the other side in a crazy helter-skelter of hairpin bends to join the road a few kilometres **west of Amalfi**.

Positano, Praiano and the Grotta dello Smeraldo

There's not much to **POSITANO**, only a couple of decent beaches and a great many boutiques and souvenir shops. But its location, heaped up in a pyramid high above the water, has inspired a thousand picture postcards and helped to make it a monied resort that runs a close second to Cápri in the celebrity stakes. Since John Steinbeck wrote up the place in glowing terms back in 1953, the village has enjoyed a fame quite out of proportion to its tiny size. Franco Zefferelli is just one of many famous names who have villas nearby, and the people who come here to lie on the beach consider themselves a cut above your average sun-worshipper.

Positano is of course expensive, and an overnight stay isn't especially recommended, although its beaches are nice enough and don't get overly crowded. The main one, the Spiaggia Grande right in front of the village, is OK, although you'll be sunbathing among the fishing boats unless you want to pay over the odds for the pleasanter bit on the far left; there's also another, larger stretch of beach, Spiaggia del Fornillo, around the headland to the west, accessible in five minutes by a pretty path which winds around from above the hydrofoil jetty – although its central section is also a pay area. Nonetheless the bar-terrace of the *Puppetto* hotel, which runs along much of its length, is a cheaper place to eat and drink than anywhere in Positano proper.

Buses to Positano drop off at the top of the village, from where it's a steep walk down or a short bus ride (every 30min) to the little square at the bottom end of Via Cristoforo Colombo, five minutes' walk from the seafront; **ferries** and **hydrofoils** from Cápri, Naples, Amalfi and Salerno pull in at the jetty just to the right of the main beach. There's a helpful **tourist office** just back from the beach by the church steps (daily 8am–2pm; ☎089/875.067). If you're keen to stay, the *Bougainville*, right by the bus stop (☎089/875.047; ⑤), is very pleasant and very central; less central, but handy for the Fornillo beach on Via Fornillo, are the *Maria Luisa* (☎089/875.023; ④), the *Casa Guadagno* (☎089/875.042④), or the slightly more expensive *Vittoria* (☎089.875.049; ⑤). Consider also the *Puppetto* hotel (☎089/875.087; ⑤), which is very enticingly placed right by the beach. For **food**, *Chez Black*, right behind Positano's beach, is a long-established restaurant whose pizzas, though relatively pricey, are the closest you'll get to a budget sit-down lunch in this location. Just around the corner, *O Capurale* is worth a try too and isn't too expensive whatever you have. On an extra tight budget, it's worth knowing about the *alimentari* by the tourist office at the foot of the church steps.

PRAIANO, a little further along to the east, squeezed into a cleft in the rocks, is smaller than Positano but these days is often no less congested; indeed it's becoming more so as its status as fashionable resort increases. There is a small patch of beach, together with a couple of sandy coves close by, but food and rooms are again quite pricey, especially if you want to stay right in Praiano itself. Try the *Tranquillità* **campsite** (☎089/874.084), up above the village off the main road, which also rents out bungalows, or the nearby *Continental* hotel (☎089/874.089; ④), which also has a good **restaurant**.

Shortly after Praiano you pass the **Furore** gorge, which gashes into the mountainside just above the coast road, and a little further along, about 4km out of Praiano (reachable direct by taxi boat from either Praiano or Amalfi), the **Grotta dell Smeraldo** (daily 9am–5pm; L4000), one of the most highly touted local natural features. An elevator gets down to the level of the grotto, where you can tour the green-hued interior by boat – a mildly impressive but certainly not unmissable sight which includes a rather startling sub-aquatic nativity scene.

Amalfi

Set in a wide cleft in the cliffs, **AMALFI**, a mere 4km or so further east, is the largest town and perhaps the highlight of the coast, and much the best place to base yourself. It has been an established seaside resort since Edwardian times, when the British upper classes found the town a pleasant place to spend their winters. Actually Amalfi's credentials go back much further: it was an independent republic during Byzantine times and one of the great naval powers, with a population of some 70,000; Webster's *Duchess of Malfi* was set here, and the city's traders established outposts all over the Mediterranean, setting up the Order of the Knights of Saint John of Jerusalem. Amalfi was finally vanquished by the Normans in 1131, and the town was devastated by an earthquake in 1343, but there is still the odd remnant of Amalfi's past glories around today, and the town has a crumbly attractiveness to its whitewashed courtyards and alleys that makes it fun to wander through.

The Town

The **Duomo**, at the top of a steep flight of steps, utterly dominates the town's main piazza, its decorated, almost gaudy facade topped by a glazed tiled cupola that's typical of the area. The bronze doors of the church came from Constantinople and date from 1066. Inside it's a mixture of Saracen and Romanesque styles, though now heavily restored, with a major relic in the body of Saint Andrew buried in its crypt, though the cloister – the so-called **Chiostro del Paradiso** (daily 9am–1pm & 3–8pm; L1000) is the most appealing part of the building – oddly Arabic in feel, with its whitewashed arches and palms.

Almost next door to the duomo, in the **Municipio**, you can view the *Tavoliere Amalfitana*, the book of maritime laws which governed the republic, and the rest of the Mediterranean, until 1570. On the waterfront, the old **Arsenal** is a reminder of the military might of the Amalfi republic, and its ancient vaulted interior now hosts art exhibitions and suchlike. In the opposite direction you can follow the main street of **Via Genova** up through the heart of Amalfi and out the other side, to where the town peters out and the gorge narrows into the **Valle dei Mulini**, or "Valley of Mills", once the centre of Amalfi's high-quality paper industry. There's not much to see here nowadays, despite the grandiose claims inferred by name, and it's hard to find a mill that is still functioning – although there is a shop on the left that makes and bottles its own lemon liqueur, a speciality of the region.

Practicalities

Amalfi's most immediate focus is along the seafront, a humming, cheerfully vigorous strand given over to street stalls, a car park for the town's considerable tourist traffic, and an acceptably crowded **beach**, although once again the best bits are pay-areas only. There's a supremely unhelpful **tourist office** (Mon–Sat 8am–2pm & 4–7pm; ☎089/872.619), which may not even have so much as a map but it's worth a try; close by, at Corso delle Repubbliche 27, there's a **post office**. If you do want to stay – and Amalfi is the best place along this coast to find accommodation – there are a number of fair-priced **hotels**, the cheapest of which by far is the *Proto*, off Via Genova down Salita dei Curiali (☎089/871.003; ③), although this is somewhat grim. It's worth splashing out a bit extra for either the *Lidomare*, tucked away up to the left of the main square at Via Piccolomini 9 (☎089/871.332; ⑤), or the centrally placed *Sant'Andrea* on the main square (☎089/871.145; ⑤), both of which are pretty reasonable considering their locations. You might also consider staying in the adjacent village of Atrani (see below). As for **eating**, *Trattoria da Gemma*, a short walk up Via Genova on the left, has a small, carefully considered menu, strong on fish and seafood, and a lovely terrace overlooking the street, although it's not one of the town's cheaper places. *Il Tari*, a little further up on the left after Via Genova has become Via P. Capuano, *is* cheap and not at all bad; while *Il Mulino*, right at the top of the main street, ten minutes' walk from the duomo, is an inexpensive family-run place used by locals that does good pizza and pasta dishes. Back in the centre of town, *Da Barracca*, left off the main square past the *Sant'Andrea* hotel on its own small piazza, is an old, established place with good food – especially fish dishes – at moderate prices. If all you want is a snack, the *Green Bar*, Via P. Capuano 46, has sandwiches, pizza slices, *calzone* and the like.

Atrani

A short walk around the headland (take the path off to the right just before the tunnel through the *Zaccaria* restaurant), **ATRANI** is an extension of Amalfi really, and was indeed another part of the maritime republic, with a similarly styled church sporting another set of bronze doors from Constantinople, manufactured in 1086. It's a quiet place, which benefits from all the attention bestowed upon its neighbour, with a pretty, almost entirely enclosed little square, Piazza Umberto, giving onto a usually gloriously peaceful (and free) patch of sandy **beach** – hard to believe the bustle of Amalfi is just around the corner. Another good reason for coming here is that it has a great **place to stay** in the *A Scalinatella*, Piazza Umberto 12 (☎089/871.492; ① & ④), hostel and hotel – a friendly, family-run establishment that offers excellent-value hostel beds and regular private rooms in various different buildings around town. The same people also own the *Piazzetta* **restaurant** on the main square, which has good, moderately priced food and offers a special low-priced student menu.

Ravello

The best views of the coast can be had inland from Amalfi in **RAVELLO**: another renowned spot, "closer to the sky than the seashore" wrote Andre Gide – with some justification. Ravello was also an independent republic for a while, and for a time an outpost of the Amalfi city-state; now it's not much more than a large village, but its unrivalled location, spread across the top of one of the coast's mountains, 1100 feet up, makes it more than worth the thirty-minute bus ride up from Amalfi – although, like most of this coast, the charms of Ravello haven't been recently discovered. Wagner based part of *Parsifal*, one of his last operas, on the place; John Huston filmed his languid movie *Beat the Devil* in the town (a film in which the locations easily outshine the plot) and Gore Vidal is just one of the best known of many celebrities who spend at least part of the year here.

Buses drop off on the main **Piazza Vescovado**, outside the **Duomo**: a bright eleventh-century church, renovated in 1786, that's dedicated to Sant Pantaleone, a fourth-century saint whose blood – kept in a chapel on the left-hand side – is supposed to liquefy like Naples' San Gennaro twice a year on May 19 and August 27. It's a richly decorated church, with a pair of bronze doors, twelfth century, cast with 54 scenes of the Passion; inside, attention focuses on a monumental *ambo* of 1272, adorned with mosaics of dragons and birds on spiral columns supported by roaring lions, and with the coat of arms and the vivacious profiles of the Rufolo family, the donors, on each side. The superb bust, downstairs in the crypt, is also said to be a portrait of Sig. Rufolo, alongside a collection of mosaics and reliquaries from the same era.

The Rufolos figure again on the other side of the square, where various leftovers of their **Villa Rufolo** (daily 9.30am–1pm & 3–7pm; L2000) scatter among rich gardens overlooking the precipitous coastline. If the crowds put you off – and you certainly won't be alone here – turn left by the entrance and walk up the steps over the tunnel for the best (free) view over the shore, from where it's a pleasant stroll through the back end of Ravello to the main square. Failing that, walk in the opposite direction to the **Villa Cimbrone** (daily 9am–1hr before sunset; L3000), ten minutes away, whose gardens, laid out by an obscure Yorkshire aristocrat earlier this century, spread across the furthest tip of Ravello's ridge. Most of the villa itself is not open to visitors, though it's worth peeking into the crumbly, flower-hung cloister as you go in and the open crypt down the steps from here – probably the only crypt with views over cliffs and open sea. But the gardens are entirely accessible, dotted with statues and leading down to what must be the most gorgeous spot in Ravello – a belvedere that looks down to Alatri below and the sea beyond.

Practicalities

Buses run up to Ravello from Amalfi roughly hourly from the seafront car park. It's not really worth staying – accommodation is much cheaper in Amalfi – but if you can't tear yourself away the **tourist office** on Piazza Vescovado (Mon–Sat 8am–8pm, Sun 8am–2pm; ☎089/857.977) has information on rooms. There are some marvellous places **to eat**, all doing their best to exploit the location, one of the best of which is the *Garden* through the tunnel off the main piazza on via Chiunzi, which has a wonderfully panoramic terrace. The *Cumpa Cosimo* restaurant at via Roma 44 is good too, with decent local food and wine at moderate prices.

Amalfi to Salerno

The coast road maintains the attack on the senses beyond Amalfi, though the resorts grow less exclusive and for the most part less appealing. Around 4km beyond Atrani, **MINORI** is a pretty village with an appealing network of narrow streets behind its short treelined seafront and grey sandy **beach**. The remains of a Roman **villa** (daily 8am–8pm; free), dating from the first century AD, lie just off the main road into town from Amalfi, opposite the *Hotel Settebello*. They were discovered in 1932, and part of the site still lies unexcavated under the houses beyond, but you can visit the sunken peristyle, with its fish pond at one end, and the remains of a nymphaeum; and there's a couple of rooms housing an assortment of finds. If you want to stay in Minori, there are a few reasonable alternatives, the most affordable of which is the *Albergo Capri*, the large building on Via Dietro la Chiesa (☎089/877.417; ④), which starts from the arch supporting the church's belltower, just back from the far end of the seafront. For **food**, try *La Botte*, around the corner from the Roman villa on Via S. Maria Vetrano, where you can sit outside if you wish. The **tourist office** (Mon–Sat 9am–noon & 4–7pm), on the main square of Piazza Umberto, has all the information you need.

MAIORI, 2km beyond Minori, is quite a different place altogether – a much louder, brasher place indeed than anywhere along the Amalfi coast, straggling along its huge stretch of beach for a kilometre or more in a long line of beach bar and restaurants. It's not especially enticing, particularly bearing in mind the rest of the coast, and you'd be well advised to move on, although it might be a place to base yourself if everywhere else is full. If you do stay, the *Pensione Rosa*, in a modern apartment building a block back from the seafront on Via degli Orti(☎089/877.031; ④), and *Pensione Vittoria*, right by the sea on the corner of Corso Regina (☎089/877.652; ④), are both very convenient if you're here for the sea. When it comes to **food**, *Mammato*, right on the seafront, is a long-running favourite with good fish and pizzas.

After Maiori you may as well stay on the bus as far as **CETARA**, a tiny fishing village clasped tightly at the end of its narrow valley that has another very small beach, three restaurants and a hotel – the *Cetus* (☎089/261.388; ⑥) – which has lovely rooms and a superb location perched on top of its own sandy cove, just past the village. A little further on, **VIETRI SUL MARE** is a larger and livelier town, split between its old centre heaped up towards the main road, the centre of a long-standing local ceramics industry, and a rather soulless waterfront area down below with numerous lidos lining its undeniably fine grey sand beach. It's not a place to linger, but if you have an hour or so to kill you should visit the **Solimene** factory, housed in an amazing bulbous tiled building on the Salerno road (daily 9am–10pm) – the bus goes right past – whose shop is a treasure trove of brightly coloured mugs, jugs, pots and bowls. You can also wander into the workshop next door for a brief look at how it's done.

Salerno and south

Capital of Campania's southernmost province, **SALERNO** has much of the scruffy, disorganised charm of Naples: a busy, dirty port city that's well off most travellers' itineraries and so holds a good supply of cheap accommodation – making it a good base for both the Amalfi coast and the ancient site of Paestum further south. During medieval times the town's medical school was the most eminent in Europe. More recently, it was the site of the Allied landing of September 9, 1943 – a landing which reduced much of the centre to rubble. The subsequent rebuilding has restored neither charm nor efficiency to the town centre, which is an odd mixture of wide, rather characterless boulevards and a small medieval core full of intriguingly dark corners and alleys. But the town's siting, strung along the top of its gulf and looking across to the sheer wall of the Amalfi coast, is fine.

Arrival, information and accommodation

Salerno's **train station** lies at the southern end of the town centre on Piazza Vittorio Veneto. City and local **buses** pull up here; those from Paestum and further south arrive and leave from Piazza Della Concordia, down by the waterside nearby; buses from Amalfi or Naples use the *SITA* bus station at Corso Garibaldi 119.

For information, there's a **tourist office** on the corner outside the train station (daily 9am–1pm & 5–7pm; ☎089/231.432), which has free maps, hotel lists and information on the Salerno area. If you're staying, there's a **youth hostel** about fifteen minutes' walk south from the station at Via Luigi Guercio 112 (☎089/790.251; ①); follow Via Torrione left out of the station and then do a left under the rail line up Via S. Mobilio; it's the second street on the right. Alternatively, the town's cheaper **hotels** are handily placed along (or just off) Corso V. Emanuele, which leads north into the town centre from the station, namely the *Santa Rosa*, at Corso V. Emanuele 16 (☎089/225.346; ④), and the *Salerno*, across the road at Via G. Vicinanza 42 (☎089/224.211; ④); there's also the cheaper *Cinzia*, further up at Corso V. Emanuele 74 (☎089/232.773; ③), though this is rather uninviting.

The Town

There isn't a great deal to see in Salerno, but it's pleasant to wander through the vibrant streets of the centre, especially the ramshackle old medieval quarter which starts at the far end of Corso V. Emanuele, with **Via dei Mercanti** as its main axis. To the right up Via Duomo, the **Duomo** (daily 9am–noon & 4–7pm) squeezes into the congested streets, an enormous church built originally in 1076 by Robert Guiscard that is dedicated to San Matteo. Like the cathedrals of the Amalfi coast, the main features are yet another set of bronze doors from Constantinople, and, inside, two elegant mosaic pulpits dating from 1173 and a similarly decorated paschal candlestick. The crypt holds the body of Saint Matthew himself, brought here in the tenth century. Outside, the courtyard is cool and shady, its columns plundered from Paestum, centring on a gently gurgling fountain.

Outside, turn right at the bottom of the steps for the **Museo del Duomo** which, although its opening times are erratic, is worth a hammer on the door to see its large altar-front, embellished with ivory panels in the late eleventh century and the largest work of its kind in the world. Failing that, turn left out of the church, left at the bottom of the steps, left again and then first right, and 100m or so further on is the **Museo Provinciale** (daily 9am–1pm & 5–7.30pm; L5000) – a fairly dull museum occupying two floors of a much-restored Romanesque palace that displays a deadening array of fossils and fragments of ancient sculpture from the surrounding area.

Eating and drinking

Salerno isn't a tourist town and it shows in the choice of **eating places**. If all you want is a bite at lunchtime, there is a good *tavola calda*, *Pranz Express*, at Corso V. Emanuele 15, and the fruit and vegetable market off to the left just before the end of Corso V. Emanuele is a good source for picnics, as are the *alimentari* and *panificio* outside the station by the *Plaza* hotel. Among sit-down options, the nearby *Trattoria Rosalia*, tucked away at Via degli Orti 22, a right turn off Corso V. Emanuele immediately after Via Diaz, is a reliable and inexpensive restaurant, used by locals, serving decent fish and seafood. Other than that, there are a number of places in and around the old town, and on the main roads – Via Roma and Lungomare Trieste – that sweep around by the sea. *Pizzeria Vicolo delle Neve*, in one of the scruffiest streets in the old city – left off Via dei Mercanti about 50m past the duomo – is a deliciously downbeat place with both pizzas and local specialities; *Il Caminetto*, five minutes' away at Via Roma 230, is very cheap and friendly; while in between the two at Via Roma 184, *Ristorante Santa Lucia* is the elegant haunt of Salerno's young and trendy.

Incidentally, if you fancy a **swim** Salerno does have a scrappy bit of beach but swimming from there isn't recommended. Better to make the short bus journey to Vietri (see p.732), or even south to Paestum and make a day of it.

Paestum

About an hour's bus ride south of Salerno, the ancient site of **Paestum** (site and museum 10am–1hr before sunset; L5000) spreads across a large area at the bottom end of the **Piana del Sele** – a wide, flat plain grazed by buffalo that produce a good quantity of southern Italy's mozzarella cheese. Paestum, or *Poseidonia* as it was known, was founded by Greeks from Sybaris in the sixth century BC, and later, in 273 BC, colonised by the Romans, who Latinised the name. But by the ninth century a combination of malaria and Saracen raids had decimated the population and left the buildings deserted and gradually overtaken by thick forest, and the site wasn't rediscovered until the eighteenth century during the building of a road through here. It's a desolate, open place even now ("inexpressibly grand", Shelley called it), mostly unrecognisable ruin but with three golden-stoned **temples** that are among the best preserved Doric temples in Europe. Of these, the Temple of Neptune, dating from about 450 BC, is the most complete, with only its roof and parts of the inner walls missing. The Basilica of Hera, built a century or so earlier, retains its double rows of columns, while the Temple of Ceres at the northern end of the site was used as a Christian church for a time – though it's now sectioned off from the public. In between, the forum is little more than an open space, and the buildings around are pure rubble. But the **museum**, across the road, holds finds from the site and around, including a set of archaic period Greek metopes from another temple at the mouth of the Sele River, a few miles north – brutish, rather crude scenes of fighting and hunting mainly. Much else is dull stuff, but you should see the fourth-century ceramics and the tomb paintings at the back of the building, one of which, from the so-called "Tomb of the Diver", a graceful and expressively naturalistic piece of work, is possibly the only extant example of Greek wall painting.

Practicalities

It's perfectly feasible to see Paestum on a day trip from either Salerno to the north or Agrópoli to the south (see opposite) – to which it's much nearer. However, you can also stay in one of the many **hotels** or **campsites** that are strewn along the sandy shore beyond the site. The **tourist office** on the main road close to the site entrance (Mon–Sat 8am–2pm; ☎0828/811.016) has details. Or just walk down to the beach (about fifteen minutes) and take your pick: the *Santa Lucia* (☎0828/811.133; ④) and *Poseidonia* (☎0828/811.066; ④) are among the cheaper **hotels**, close by the site to the left of where the main road hits the beach. Most of the **campsites** are much of a muchness: the *Apollo* (☎0828/811.178) and *Mare Pineta* (☎0828/811.086) are two of the most central, to the right of the main beach road and well signposted. As for the **beach** itself, the development behind it is fairly tacky, and it's a bit grimy in places. But space, even in peak season, is rarely too much of a problem.

The Cilento

Immediately south of Paestum, the coastline bulges out into a broad mountainous hump of territory known as the **Cilento** – one of the remotest parts of Campania, thickly wooded with olives and chestnuts. The region divides into two distinct parts: inland, which is still wedded to a fairly traditional way of life, and the coast, which is where tourists go – although even in the main resorts you'll find far fewer people than further north.

The Cilento coast

After the sands of the Piana del Sele, the Cilento coast is fairly rocky territory, more suited to scuba-diving than sunbathing, though it does have sandy moments. **AGRÓPOLI**, the first town you reach, fifteen minutes out from Paestum, is a good base for the ruins (buses every hour), and its blend of the peaceful old quarter, heaped on a headland, and the new modern centre down below makes for a nice place to spend a few days, with a vivacious main street *passeggiata*. The beaches aren't great – dirty on the north side of town, crowded to the south in the Lido di Trentova – but you can swim from the flat rocks in the harbour and the water's perfectly clean. For **accommodation**, the *Hotel Carola* (☎0974/823.005; ⑤) in the harbour is central and has attractive double rooms with balconies. Agrópoli is also on the main Salerno–Reggio railway line.

Buses from Salerno run down the coast as far as the next town of Santa Maria di Castellebate, 8km south, but if you've time and energy it's preferable to walk, taking the **dirt road** from behind the Lido di Trentova's tennis courts, which skirts the hillsides past abandoned farmhouses, above rocky bays, eventually becoming a fairly good-quality track a little way before **SANTA MARIA DI CASTELLEBATE**. This is another small resort, with a small harbour and bus connections south, along one of the most isolated stretches of the Cilento coast. There's a long **beach** of clean, golden sand just north of the town, the so-called "Lago" area, close to where the path from Agrópoli comes out, with a number of inexpensive **hotels and campsites**. The *Pizzeria Zia Rosa* (☎0974/961.506; ⑤) is the cheapest place to stay; *La Duna* (☎0974/965.168) and *Trezene* (☎0974/965.013) are the best value of several campsites.

SAN MARCO, three kilometres or so further along from Santa Maria, is a picturesque, very active fishing village which supplies fish to most of the villages along this part of the coast, though its tiny centre can get very crowded in summer. A narrow track leads from here down to **PUNTA LICOSA**, where there's a small harbour fringed by rocks from which you can swim. The offshore reef that's topped by a lighthouse is inhabited by lizards said to be of a unique species. From here you can either return to San Marco or follow the track around to **OGLIASTRO MARINA**, an attractive little village with a hotel and cheap *pensione* (*Da Carmine*) and some indifferent restaurants – and a long, rather dirty beach that in summer attracts a good number of holidaymakers.

The facilities, and the beaches, improve the closer you get to **ACCIAROLI**, about 10km further south – one of the Cilento's larger resorts and a port for the hydrofoils which ply the coast during summer. The railway joins the shoreline again at **MARINA D'ASCEA**, a fairly indifferent resort but surrounded by hotels and campsites, especially along the lengthy sand beach which stretches north to Marina del Casalvelino.

Close by, **MARINA DI VELIA** gives access to the site of **Velia** (daily 9am–1hr before sunset; L5000) – comprising the ruins of the Hellenistic town of *Elea*, founded around 540 BC and an important port and cultural centre, home to its own school of philosophy. Later it became a favourite holiday resort for wealthy Romans, Horace just one of many who came here on the advice of his doctor. The decline of Velia parallels that of Paestum – malarial swamp rendering much of the area uninhabitable – though the upper reaches were lived in until the fifteenth century. There, however, the comparison ends: the remains of Velia are considerably more decimated than those of Paestum and the town was never as crucial a centre, with nothing like as many temples. At the centre of the ruins the "Porta Rosa", named after the wife of the archaeologist who conducted the first investigations, is one of the earliest arches ever found – and the first indication to experts that the Greeks knew how to construct such things. Up from here, the Acropolis has relics of an amphitheatre and a temple, together with a massive Norman tower – visible for some distance around.

Outside the site there's a restaurant, the *Casa Bianca*, and beyond here a small beach – though this can get crowded in summer. The beaches further down the coast near **PISCIOTTA** are better, and the town itself is a lively place of an evening. **PALINURO**, too, further south, is worth a stop, named after the legendary pilot of the *Aeneid*, who is supposed to have been buried here. It's a more cosmopolitan spot than anywhere else on the Cilento coast, and so can be packed out. But the harbour area retains a certain fishing port authenticity, and it's a good alternative to Agrópoli, both as a base for the site of Velia and a beach-bumming spot. There are a number of **campsites** and **hotels** around – the *Sant'Anna* (☎0974/931.159; ④) and *Parigino* (☎ 0974/931.027; ④) are the most affordable places, though bear in mind that in August it is essential to book in advance. For **food**, you can either eat adequately in two restaurants in the upper part of town – the *Corniglia* or *La Carminella*, on Capo Palinuro overlooking the sea. Or blow your last few lire at the *Da Carmelo* restaurant, 2km south of town, whose fish and seafood is said to be the best for miles around.

The last real resort, **MARINA DI CAMEROTA**, is less busy than Palinuro and has a shingly beach, three campsites and a couple of hotels – the *Pollina* (☎0974/932.051; ④) is good value. **POLICASTRO BUSSENTINO**, too, is a quiet resort, with a crumbly *centro storico* and a shingle beach in a majestic setting, clasped by the high walls of the Golfo di Policastro. Or you can push straight on to **SAPRI** – not much of a place in itself, but with an outstanding restaurant in *A Cantina I Mustazz* on the main town square, Piazza Plebiscito, at which you can sample traditional Cilento cooking at its best and at very reasonable prices.

Inland Cilento

Inland the Cilento is lonely and often inaccessible, especially if you don't have your own transport. The train cuts through part of the region but doesn't stop, buses are few and far between and in any case there's only a couple of proper roads winding across the rocky mountainsides. There are also few large settlements and little in the way of accommodation – although the countryside can be gorgeous, offering some splendidly panoramic routes, fine mountain walks and spectacular gorges and caves.

There are a number of villages you might structure a long day's car journey around. In the north, the caves of **CASTELCIVITA** (L4000) form just one of several systems that riddle the Cilento, discovered by two brothers who got lost here in 1889 – one of whom died as a result, while the other was found to have gone totally insane. Guided tours every half-hour wind past intricate stalactites and under clusters of bats; whatever the weather outside, bring a jumper – it can get cold.

About 10km further south (though much longer by road), the village of **ROSCIGNO VECCHIO** is an example of a typical Cilento village from the turn of the century, deserted now following a landslip but with a small museum of Cilento rural life in its old church. Back towards the coast, **VALLO DELLA LUCANIA**, a little way inland from Velia, is an example of the more prosperous recent years here, the largest town inland and a lively place with a busy *passeggiata* of an evening. Three kilometres outside, **NOVA VELIA** is a tiny village overshadowed by 1705-metre-high **Monte Sacro**, at the top of which is a **sanctuary** which has been a place of pilgrimage since

1323 – an odd, very remote complex of dormitories and churches and even a small post office that's open from the end of May until the beginning of October. With luck you should be able to stay the night.

travel details

Metropolitana

Principal stops: Piazza Garibaldi—Piazza Cavour–Montesanto–Piazza Amedeo–Mergellina–Piazza Leopardi (Fuorigrotta)–Campi Flegrei–Cavalleggeri d'Aosta–Bagnoli–Pozzuoli.

Circumflegrea (information: ☎551.3328)

Connects Naples Montesanto with Cuma, Lido Fusaro, Torregaveta. Departures every 20min.

Circumvesuviana (information ☎779.2444)

This line runs between Naples and Sorrento, with many stops around the southern part of the Bay, roughly every 20min.

Ferrovia Cumana (information ☎551.3328)

Connects Naples Montesanto with Fuorigrotta, Agnana, Bangoli, Pozzuoli, Baia, Fusaro, etc. Departures every 20min.

Trains

Benevento to: Foggia (8 daily; 1hr 20min).

Naples to: Agrópoli (10 daily; 1hr 15min); Benevento (5 daily; 2hr); Caserta (every 30min; 45min); Foggia (4 daily; 3hr); Formia (hourly; 1hr); Paola (Calabria) (every 2hr; 3hr); Rome (hourly; 2hr 30min); Salerno (hourly; 45min); Sapri (12 daily; 2hr); Santa Maria Cápua Vetere/Cassino (8 daily; 30min/1hr 30min).

Salerno to: Paestum/Agrópoli (6 daily; 40min/50min); Sapri (6 daily; 2hr 30min).

Buses

Naples to: Benevento (6 daily; 1hr 30min); Cápua (hourly; 1hr 15min); Caserta (every 20min; 1hr); Salerno (every 30min); Sant'Agata dei Goti (1 daily; 1hr 30min).

Sorrento to: Amalfi (12 daily; 1hr 30min); Positano (12 daily; 40min); Salerno (12 daily; 2hr 45min).

Salerno to: Agrópoli (hourly; 1hr 15min); Amalfi (hourly; 1hr 10min); Naples (every 15–30min; 1hr); Positano (every 1–2hr; 2hr); Sorrento (every 1–2hr; 2hr 45min); Vietri (every 20min; 20min); Paestum (hourly; 1hr).

Agrópoli to: Acciaroli (6 daily; 55min); Salerno (hourly; 1hr 15min); Paestum (hourly; 15min); Santa Maria di Castellebate (hourly; 30min); Sapri (1 daily; 3hr 30min).

Ferries

Naples to: Sorrento (3 daily ferries/6 daily hydrofoils; 1hr 15min/40min); Palermo (1 daily at 8.30pm; 10hr 30min); Cagliari (every Sun & Wed at 5.30pm; 15hr 30min); Aeolian Islands/Milazzo (every Wed & Sat at 9pm; 12hr); Reggio/Catania/Siracusa/Malta (every Thurs at 8.30pm; 7hr/24hr).

For details of ferry and hydrofoil connections between Naples, the Amalfi coast and Salerno and the islands, see "Getting to the Islands", p.719.

CHAPTER FOURTEEN

PUGLIA

Puglia is the long strip of land, 400km from north to south, which makes up the "heel" of Italy. It was for centuries a strategic province, colonised, invaded and conquered (like its neighbours, Calabria and Sicily), by just about every major power of the day: from the Greeks through to the Spanish. As elsewhere in the South, each ruling dynasty left its own distinctive mark on the landscape and architecture, often changing the face of the province completely – as with the surviving traces of Roman agricultural schemes and the fortified medieval towns. There's no escaping some of the historical influences in Puglia. Perhaps most distinctive are the Saracenic kasbah-like quarters of many towns and cities, the one at **Bari** the biggest and most atmospheric. The Normans covered Puglia with splendidly ornate cathedrals; there's one at **Trani** which skilfully blends many strands of regional crafts work from north and south. And the Baroque exuberance of towns like **Lecce** and **Martina Franca** are evidence of the Spanish legacy. But if there's one symbol of Puglia that stands out, it's the imposing castles built by the Swabian, Frederick II, all over the province – foremost of which are the **Castel del Monte** and the remnants of the palace at **Lucera**.

Despite these attractions, Puglia is still very much a province through which you pass on the way elsewhere, an echo of the Middle Ages when crusaders stopped off en route to the Holy Land. Today the cities, including Bari, have little that's characteristic enough to warrant long stays: **Táranto** and its surroundings have fought a losing battle with the local steel industry, while **Bríndisi** is known and visited only for its ferry connections with Greece. Nevertheless, there's a geographical diversity to Puglia which can be very attractive, given the time to get away from the main train routes. The very southern tip, the **Salentine peninsula**, is rocky and dry, more Greek than Italian, while there's plenty of barren mountain scenery in the undulating plateau of **Le Murge**, in the centre of the province. The best escape, though, is to the north, to the mountains, forests and beaches of the **Gargano promontory**, slowly opening up to holidaymakers seeking some of the finest unpolluted sand and sea to be found anywhere on the Adriatic.

Getting around Puglia by public transport is fairly easy, at least as far as the main towns and cities go. *FS* **trains** connect nearly all the major places, while small, private lines head into previously remote areas – in the Gargano and on the edges of Le Murge. Most other places can be reached by **bus**, though as ever services are often infrequent or inconveniently early – a problem which can only really be solved by taking, or renting, your own **car**. Incidentally, if you're on your way **to Greece**, it's worth noting that you don't have to leave from Bríndisi: there are year-round departures from Bari and seasonal ferries from **Otranto**, south of Lecce.

Foggia and the Tavoliere

The broad sweep of the **Tavoliere plain** stretches from the Basilicata border to the edge of the Gargano massif – flat, fertile lands that are southern Italy's wheat bowl – and the source of much of the country's pasta. It was the Romans who attempted the first intense cultivation of the area, parcelling the land up into neat squares for distribution to its pensionable centurions. This lent the land its chessboard appearance, from

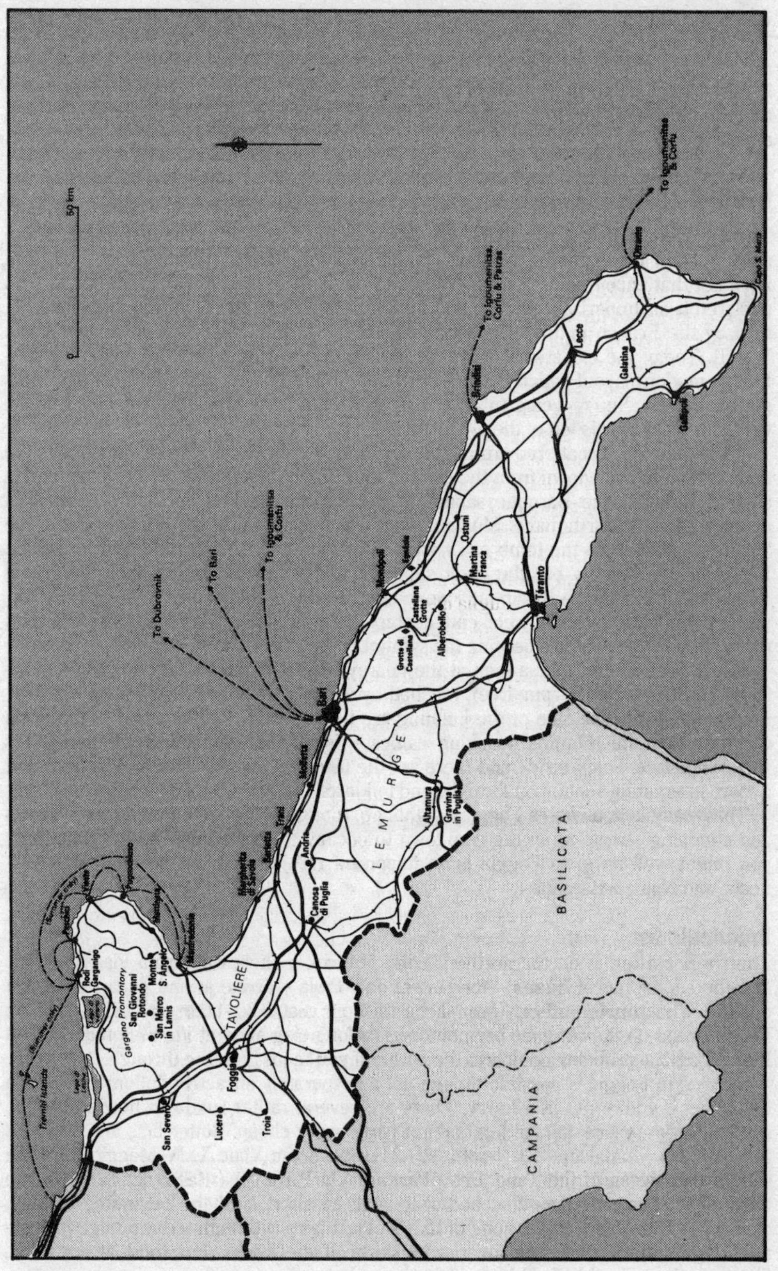
0
50 km
To Dubrovnik
To Bari
To Igoumenitsa & Corfu
To Igoumenitsa, Corfu & Patras
To Igoumenitsa & Corfu
Tremiti Islands
(Summer only)
Rodi Garganico
Gargano Promontory
San Giovanni Rotondo
San Marco in Lamis
Monte S. Angelo
Manfredonia
Margherita di Savoia
Barletta
Trani
Molfetta
Andria
Canosa di Puglia
Bari
Monopoli
Grotte di Castellana
Castellana Grotte
Alberobello
Martina Franca
Ostuni
Taranto
Brindisi
Lecce
Galatina
Gallipoli
Otranto
Altamura
Gravina in Puglia
L E M U R G E
TAVOLIERE
Foggia
Lucera
Troia
San Severo
BASILICATA
CAMPANIA

which the Tavoliere takes its name, but for the centurions the gift was a mixed blessing. Foggia province proved to be an unhealthy place, an earthquake-prone swampland rife with malarial mosquitos, and settlements here suffered from disease and disaster in fairly equal proportions. It wasn't until the advent of irrigation schemes in the 1920s that the mosquitos lost their malarial bite and the area began to take on its present rich appearance.

Foggia

The Tavoliere's main town, **FOGGIA**, looms out of the plain without warning, a fine starting-point for exploring northern Puglia and the Gargano promontory though in itself not that encouraging a stop. Although Foggia flourished under Frederick II, who declared it an Imperial residence and built a palace here, the town was devastated in turn by the French in 1528, an earthquake in 1731, and Allied bombs during World War II. Today the city's streets are all reassuringly earthquake-proof, wide and low-built, a modern layout which is handsome enough but doesn't make for a lot of investigative interest. You're going to have to search hard in between the tree-lined boulevards for what little is left of the old town.

What there is, is scattered around the **Duomo**, left off Corso Vittorio Emanuele, the main drag that runs down from the central, fountained Piazza Cavour. The cathedral is an odd Romanesque–Baroque sandwich, the top part tacked on in the eighteenth century after the earthquake. Much of what was once notable about it was lost in the 'quake – particularly the tomb of Charles I of Anjou and a receptacle said to contain Frederick II's heart – but the crypt survived, and it features some finely decorated Romanesque capitals. A Byzantine icon, now housed in a chapel next to the presbytery, was reputedly discovered by eleventh-century shepherds in a pond upon which burned three flames; these flames became the symbol of the city.

While you're here, take a look at the nearby **Museo Cívico** on Piazza Nigri (daily 9am–1pm, Tues also 5–7pm; free), reached by walking on down the Corso to Via Arpi. Incorporated into the side of the building are three portals, one of which – the Porta Grande, with the thoughtful-looking eagles – is all that remains of Frederick II's Imperial palace. Duck inside and there are the usual regional archaeological finds and a more interesting section on local life and folklore.

That really is it, as far as Foggia's sights go, though there are enough green spaces and shopping streets up in the new town to occupy any remaining time – something you might well have, as Foggia is an important rail junction on the main Bologna–Lecce and Naples–Bari lines.

Practicalities

The **train station** is on the northern edge of town, a short walk from Piazza Cavour and the centre. Local **buses** – for Lucera and Troia – arrive at and depart from just outside. The **tourist office** (Mon–Fri 8am–2pm, Sat 8.30–11am; ☎23.650), bad on Foggia, good on the Gargano promontory, is a long slog away at Via E. Perrone 17, off Piazza Puglia – probably not worth the bother if you're just passing through.

Staying in Foggia is possible though not a desperately attractive option; Lucera is a better bet if you're not in a hurry. There are several rather rundown hotels near the station, but most are uninspiring and not particularly cheap. Better bets are the *Hotel Bologna*, Via Monfalcone 53 (☎0881/621.341; ④), down Viale XXIV Maggio from the station then second right, and *Hotel Venezia*, Via Piave 40 (☎0881/622.621; ④), the third right. The only time that bed space will be short is at the beginning of May, during the **Fiera di Foggia** – one of Italy's oldest fairs, although today a huge international agricultural affair held on the outskirts of the town. For **food** at any time, *Trattoria Santa Lucia*, Via Trieste 57, is a good bet and not at all expensive.

Lucera

Just eighteen kilometres west, within easy reach of Foggia (hourly buses), **LUCERA** is a far better introduction to Puglia, a small town with a bright and bustling centre in the process of being carefully restored. Once the capital of the Tavoliere, it has a distinct charm, its vast castle dominating the landscape for miles around. It was once a thriving Saracen city: Frederick II, having forced the Arabs out of Sicily, resettled 20,000 of them here, on the site of an abandoned Roman town, allowing them complete freedom of religious worship – an almost unheard of act of liberalism for the early thirteenth century.

Buses arrive in Piazza del Popolo, from where it's only a short walk up Via Gramsci to the **Duomo**, which marks the centre of the medieval walled town. It's a dark, rather miserable building built on the site of a mosque that was destroyed by the Angevins, who massacred the Arabic inhabitants of Lucera in the early fourteenth century. At the end of Angevin rule, little remained of the Islamic-influenced buildings which once adorned the town. However, although the buildings may have been destroyed, the Angevins didn't alter the Arabic layout of Lucera and there's a powerful atmosphere here – best appreciated by wandering the narrow streets of the old town, peering into the lived-in courtyards and alleyways. Close to the cathedral, a little way down Via de Nicastri, is the **Museo Cívico** (Tues–Sun 9am–1pm, Wed & Fri also 3–6pm; L1500), well stocked with Greek pottery and their Puglian copies. There are some fine mosaics and terracotta heads too, and the bust of a Greek youth said – rather optimistically – to be that of Alexander the Great.

Other sights are all outside the old centre, most notably the **Castello** (Tues–Sun 7.30am–2.20pm; free), built by Frederick and designed to house a lavish court which included an exotic collection of wild beasts. To get there from Piazza Duomo, follow Via Bovio and Via Federico II to Piazza Matteotti and look for the signs. The largest in southern Italy after Lagopésole in Basilicata, the castle commands spectacular views over the Tavoliere, stretching across to the foothills of the Appenines to the west and the mountains of Gargano to the east. Contained within the walls and towers, a kilometre long, are the suggestive remains of Frederick's great palace, fragments of mosaic work and fallen columns peering out of a dense undergrowth of wild flowers.

Stopping over in Lucera wouldn't be a bad thing. There's an excellent **hotel**, the *Albergo Al Passeto*, at Piazza del Popolo 30 (☎0881/941.124; ④). Built into the old walls of Lucera, it has a fine **restaurant** too.

Troia

Frequent buses also make the short ride (from either Lucera or Foggia) to **TROIA**, 18km due south of Lucera. The locals seem curiously blasé as to the origin of their village's name (it means "slut" in Italian), and no one is able to offer a reasonable explanation – it's possible that it's named after the more famous Troy, now in Turkey. Whatever the reason, the Troiani atone for the name by having five patron saints, whose statues are paraded around town in procession every July 9.

At all other times of the year the highlight in Troia – an otherwise quiet, dusty village – is the fine **Duomo**, an intriguing eleventh-century blend of Byzantine and Apulian–Romanesque styles, with a generous hint of Saracen influence, too. The great bronze doors are covered with reliefs of animals and biblical figures, while above, surrounded by a frenzy of carved lions frozen in stone, is an extraordinary rose window. Distinctly Saracen in flavour, the window resembles a finely worked piece of oriental ivory, being composed of eleven stone panels, each one delicately carved. There's more exact detail inside too, including a curiously decorated pulpit and some ornate capitals.

West and south of Foggia

Well off the beaten track in Foggia province are some of the most handsome hilltop villages in this part of Italy. Most are little visited and requests for information about them are likely to be met with a blank gaze at the tourist office. Indeed, although the area is slowly beginning to open up to visitors, it's still very much a quiet backwater of forests and hills.

Most remote is the scattering of settlements which lies to the **west of Lucera**, in the gentle **Monti di Daunia**. The inhabitants are Albanian in origin, first arriving in the fifteenth century to help fight the French and later as refugees fleeing from the Turks. It's hard to get here without your own transport, and there's not a lot here if you do.

South of Foggia is more interesting. **BOVINO**, near the Campanian border, is a small and distinctly medieval village, with fragments of Roman fortifications and a thirteenth-century cathedral looking out over a fine landscape of undulating wooded slopes. The snag is that Bovino is an alarmingly steep 7km climb away from its train station, and if you're travelling by train **ORDONA**, over to the east, is probably an easier target. The ancient Daunic people of the Tavoliere once had a town here, sited on the banks of the river Carapelle, which was destroyed by Pyrrhus (who used elephants) in the third century BC. Over what was left the Romans built *Herdonia*, large parts of which still survive. The **site** (open at all times; free) is a short walk south from the present village of Ordona, and there are the obvious remains of a forum and a small amphitheatre, as well as scantier pieces of a small basilica and two temples.

Manfredonia

By Puglian standards, **MANFREDONIA** is a new town, a mere 600 years old, founded – as the name suggests – by Manfred, illegitimate son of Frederick II. The Austrians struck the first blow of World War I on Italian soil here, by bombing the town's station in 1915, but this is really – apart from recent demonstrations against chemical waste dumping in the port – Manfredonia's only claim to fame. The town is seen more as the gateway to the Gargano promontory and most people pass quickly through. Still, what the town lacks in historical sights is more than made up for by its sandy beaches, which stretch for miles down the coast.

The easiest way to reach Manfredonia is by train from Foggia: from the **station**, turn right and it's a short walk along Viale Aldo Moro to Piazza Marconi. Just across the square, Corso Manfredi leads down to the **tourist office** (Mon–Sat 8am–2pm), good for maps and information on the Gargano area. Further down Corso Manfredi, the **Castello** was started by Manfred and extended by the Angevins. Its huge bastions were added in 1607 by the Spanish to stave off a Turkish attack: they failed to do so, the Turks landing in 1620, ravaging the hapless inhabitants and destroying much of the town – though most of the protective walls still survive.

The castle now houses the **Museo Nazionale** (Tues–Sun 9am–1pm & 3–5pm; free), largely devoted to Daunic finds from the seventh and sixth centuries BC, particularly several stone slabs or *stelae*, thought to be tombstones, richly carved with images of armoured warriors, female figures and scenes from daily life.

Practicalities

If you're going to use Manfredonia as a base, there's no shortage of **accommodation**. The most reasonable option is the *Albergo San Michele*, Via degli Orti 10 (☎0884/21.953; ④). If this is full, the nearby *Albergo Santa Maria Grazie*, Piazza d'Acquisto 5 (☎0884/22.465; ④), has similarly priced though shabbier rooms.

There are plenty of places **to eat** too, best of which is the *Trattoria Il Baracchio*, Corso Roma 38 – traditional Puglian dishes and a cheapish *pranzo turistico*. Otherwise, try the *Al Fuego*, Via G. di Palma 36, signposted down a side street off Corso Manfredi, a little way down on the right from the tourist office.

The beach: Siponto

SIPONTO, 3km south down the coast from Manfredonia, was once a thriving medieval port. But constant malarial attacks and damaging earthquakes have left it with little beyond its good sandy **beaches** to draw you – all an easy ten-minute walk from Manfredonia's train station. They're signposted from town and in high summer you can expect them to be packed to the gills.

Siponto is also a fairly useful place **to stay** if you don't fancy Manfredonia. The cheapest choice is the *Ninfa Marina* on the Lungomare del Sole (☎0884/541.551; ③). There are **campsites** strung out south along the coast, the nearest 4km from town, although you'll probably have to walk there; check with the tourist office in Manfredonia.

The Gargano promontory

The **Gargano promontory** rises like an island from the flat plains of the Tavoliere, geographically and culturally different from the rest of Puglia. Its landscape is remarkably diverse: beaches and lagoons to the north, a rocky, indented eastern coast and a mountainous, green heartland of oaks and beech trees – reminiscent of a Germanic forest rather than a corner of southern Italy. For centuries the promontory was extremely isolated, visited only by pilgrims making their way along the valley to Monte Sant'Angelo and its shrine. Nowadays tourism has taken off in a big way, especially on the coast around Vieste, although much of the interior remains supremely unspoiled and quiet. There are plans to turn the whole peninsula into a national park, something that would help protect Gargano from overbearing development.

Approaches to the promontory are pretty straightforward. *FS* trains run from Foggia to Manfredonia on the southeast side of Gargano, from where it's only 16km by bus to Monte Sant'Angelo, and there are buses straight up the coast as well. Alternatively, in the north of the region, *Ferrovia del Gargano* (*FG*) operates **trains** between San Severo and Péschici-Calanelle, from where a bus connects with Péschici. Note that most *FG* stations are quite a distance from the towns and villages they serve, so always go for the connecting bus if there is one.

Getting around can be a little more tortuous. **Buses** are run by three companies: *SITA* serves the inland towns and operates the inland route to Vieste; *ATAF* runs a coastal route to Vieste; while *FG* runs the trains and connecting buses in northern Gargano, roughly between San Severo and Péschici. See "Travel Details" for more information. There is also a **daily ferry service** (April–September) connecting Manfredonia, Vieste, Péschici and Rodi Garganico with each other and the Trémiti Islands.

Monte Sant'Angelo and the pilgrim route

Just north of Manfredonia, perched almost 800m up in the hills, **MONTE SANT'ANGELO** is the highest – and coldest – settlement in the Gargano. Pilgrims have trudged up the switchback paths and roads for centuries to visit the spot where the archangel Michael is said to have made four separate appearances, mostly at the end of the fifth century – making the sanctuary here one of the earliest Christian shrines in Europe and one of the most important in Italy. Today, the pilgrims come by bus, and the major festivals on May 8 and September 29 every year attract locals from miles around who turn up in traditional dress.

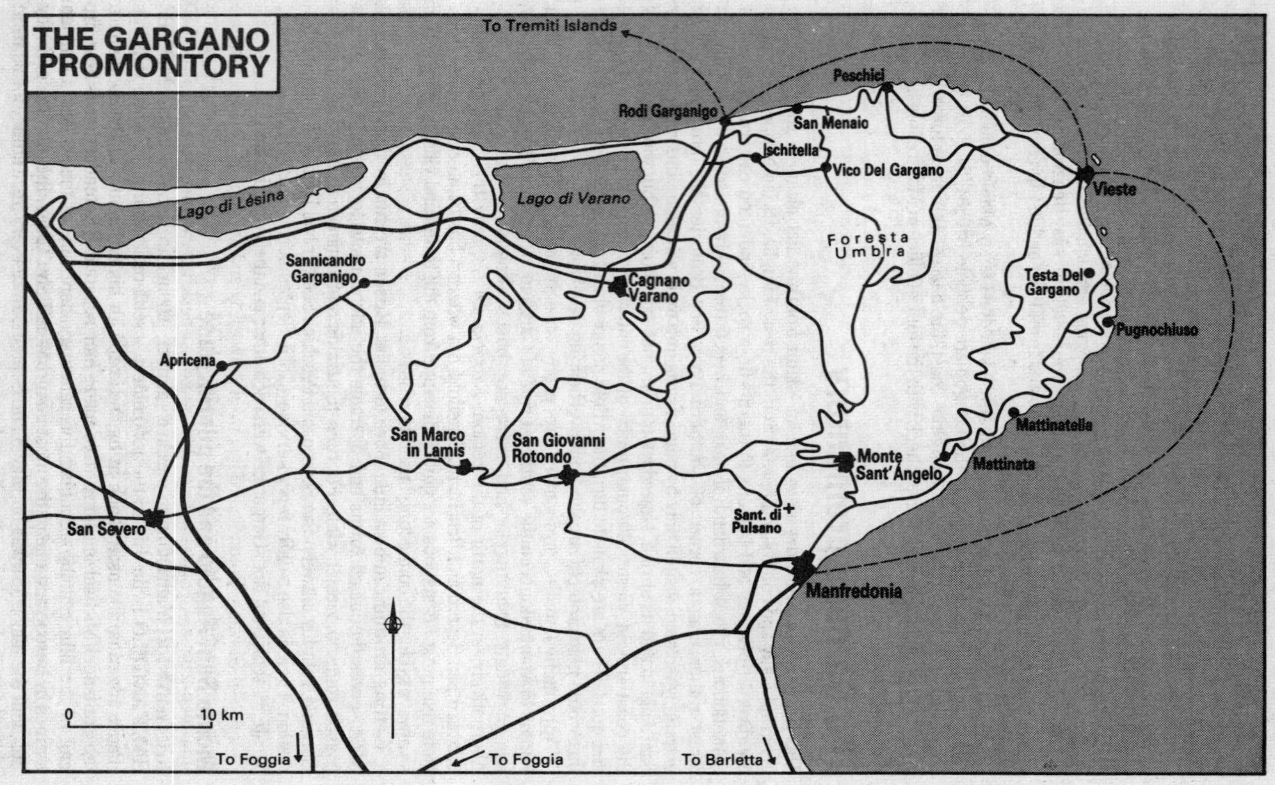
THE GARGANO PROMONTORY
To Tremiti Islands
Rodi Garganigo
Peschici
San Menaio
Ischitella
Vico Del Gargano
Vieste
Lago di Lésina
Lago di Varano
Foresta Umbra
Sannicandro Garganigo
Cagnano Varano
Testa Del Gargano
Pugnochiuso
Apricena
Mattinatella
San Marco in Lamis
San Giovanni Rotondo
Monte Sant'Angelo
Mattinata
Sant. di Pulsano
San Severo
Manfredonia
0
10 km
To Foggia
To Foggia
To Barletta

The **bus** – which runs every two hours from Manfredonia – drops you in Piazza Duca d'Aosta, from where you should follow the road uphill to the edge of the old town and the Via Reale Basilica, where you'll find the **Santuario di San Michele** itself (daily 10am–dusk). Apart from a lean octagonal thirteenth-century campanile, the sanctuary seems rather plain on the outside, but from the small courtyard on the right a flight of stone steps leads down to the grotto – heralded by a magnificent pair of eleventh-century bronze doors, made in Constantinople, that form the entrance to the church built on the site of the cave in which the archangel first appeared (in 490). Opposite the campanile, another set of steps leads down to the nearby ruins of the **Chiesa di San Pietro**, behind which is the so-called **Tomba di Rotari** – an imposing domed tower once thought to be the tomb of Rothari, a seventh-century Lombard chieftain who was converted to Christianity. More prosaically, it's more likely to have been a twelfth-century baptistry; the large baptismal font is just on the right as you enter the tower. Little remains of the church itself, wrecked by an earthquake, but look out for the rose window – a Catherine wheel of entwined mermaids.

Back on Via Reale Basilica, it's an easy clamber up to the ruined Norman **Castello** for good views over the town and valley. From here, you can cut down through the narrow whitewashed streets of the old town to Piazza San Francesco d'Assisi and the **Museo Tancredi** (Mon–Sat 8am–2pm, May–Sept also 3–7pm; L1000), an arts and crafts museum housed in a fine, old, vaulted building.

Practicalities

You can pick up information at the tourist office (Mon–Sat 9am–1pm & 4–6pm), just off Piazza Duca d'Aosta at Via C. Durazzo 2. They have a glossy booklet on the town which includes a useful map. If you're going to stay overnight (though don't count on available beds at the main pilgrimage times), the best bet for **accommodation** is the spotlessly clean *Albergo Moderno*, Via Leone Gargánico 34 (☎0884/61.331; ④); bear right at the tourist office and walk downhill – the hotel is on your left. Otherwise, there's **hostel** accommodation at the well-sited *Casa del Pellegrino* on Via Carlo d'Angio (☎0884/62.396 – L20,000 a head out of season, a rip-off L45,000 July to Sept). **Eating** is straightforward at a number of places along Via Reale Basilica: *Trattoria Paradise* has an outdoor garden; for pizzas *Pizzeria al Castello* is the local choice.

The pilgrim route: San Giovanni Rotondo

The ancient **pilgrim route** weaved its way along the Stignano valley between San Severo in the west and Monte Sant'Angelo and until comparatively recently was the only road that linked the villages of the Gargano interior. With your own transport, it's still a good route to explore a couple of the region's most important religious centres. By public transport, though, the service and connections are sketchy. With this in mind, if you want to follow any part of the pilgrim route by bus, you'll probably have to do so by going back to Manfredonia.

Certainly, direct bus services between Monte Sant'Angelo and the first village on the route, San Giovanni Rotondo, are inconveniently early and infrequent, and the village is better connected by bus with Manfredonia, a *SITA* service from there making around fourteen trips a day. Nestling under the highest peak hereabouts, Monte Calvo, **SAN GIOVANNI ROTONDO** is no mean religious centre itself; it's the burial place of Padre Pio, a local priest who died in the 1960s. At a time of reform for the Catholic Church, Padre Pio caused consternation in the Vatican with his apparently effortless ability to appear before cardinals in Rome while asleep in San Giovanni Rotondo: there's no escaping his frail portrait throughout the Gargano peninsula, but it's especially prominent here. The town takes its name from the **Rotonda di San Giovanni**, a building of indeterminate origin or purpose at the edge of the old town – like the Tomba di Rotari, it's thought to have been a baptistry, built on the site of an earlier pagan temple.

Nine kilometres further west, and looking splendidly out over the Tavoliere plain, **SAN MARCO IN LAMIS**, though considerably smaller than San Giovanni, is dominated by a huge sixteenth-century monastery. Every Good Friday the town holds a noisy and lively affair, of pagan origin, called the **fracchie**, when huge bundles of burning wood are hauled through the streets.

Vieste and the Costa Gargánica

About 15km north of Manfredonia, the road tunnels under a mountain to emerge in a softer, greener landscape. **MATTINATA**, a small but popular resort with good campsites, sits back from the coast, overlooking olive groves and pine trees which drop down gently to a magnificent stretch of beach. Beyond Mattinata the road splits: one branch (which the *SITA* bus takes) winds its way through the eastern part of the Foresta Umbra (see overleaf) to Vieste; the coastal route (and the *ATAF* bus) runs up to **PUGNOCHIUSO**, a panoramic bay dominated by a vast *Club Med* holiday village. If you're interested, one of the easiest of the local **hiking trails** starts close by. The path is clearly marked off the Mattinata–Pugnochiuso road, about 3km north of BAIA DI ZAGARE, and the trail (around 3km each way) runs sharply down to a beach, the *Spiaggia di Vignanótica*. To reach the start of the trail, take the *ATAF* bus from Mattinata for Pugnochiuso/Vieste and ask to be let off at Località Mégoli.

Vieste

VIESTE juts out into the Adriatic on two promontories, the most easterly point of the Gargano peninsula. Fifty years ago there wasn't even a proper road here, but today Vieste, with its excellent beaches, is the holiday capital of Gargano (and Puglia), particularly popular with German tourists who pack the streets and sand in the summer months. Despite this it has managed to survive as a lively and inviting town, with, in addition to its active nightlife, enough of historical interest around to warrant at least a short stop – certainly if you're killing time before taking the ferry from here to the offshore Trémiti Islands.

The **old town** sits on the easternmost of the two promontories, at the tip of which stands the **Chiesa di San Francesco**, once a thriving monastery, and a **trabucco** – a mass of beams, winches and ropes still used by fishermen to catch mullet. Made of wood, these structures are a feature peculiar to the rocky Gargano coast, probably Phoenician in origin, and the principle at least is straightforward. As mullet swim head to tail, a live mullet is attached to a line and used to entice others to swim over a net suspended below, which is then hoisted up to the platform.

From the church, climb up Via Mafrolla, walking into the old town to Piazza Seggio. Straight ahead, Via Duomo is site of the so-called **Chianca Amara**, the "bitter stone", where as many as 5000 local people were beheaded when the Turks sacked the town in 1554. Further down, beyond the stone, the **Cattedrale**, eleventh-century in origin but tampered with in the eighteenth century, is a cool retreat from the fierce glare of the sun in the whitewashed streets; and beyond here the **Castello** is another of Frederick II's installations – owned by the military now and not open to the public, but giving good views over the beaches and town.

You **arrive** by bus at Piazza Mazzoni, to the west of the town centre; bear right from here along Viale XXIV Maggio, which becomes Corso Lorenzo Fazzini – the main street. On Piazza Kennedy, in the centre of the old town, there's a **tourist office** (Mon–Fri 9am–12.30pm & 5.30–7pm). Though there's no shortage of accommodation, **staying over** in Vieste, at least in the summer, can be very expensive. Try to avoid August if you can, when prices increase threefold. The best deals you'll find are *Pensione al Centro Storico*, Via Giolitti 4 (☎0884/707.030; ⑤), and *Albergo Vela Velo*,

Lungomare Europa 19 (☎0884/706.303; ⑤), around 500m north of the castle along the shore. For **food**, the strangely named *Box 19*, Via Santa Maria di Merino 19, is very highly thought-of, and fairly moderately priced.

There are also regular ferry connections to the **Trémiti Islands** from Vieste (see overleaf). There are daily, early-morning departures throughout the summer and tickets cost around L19,000 one way. *Gargano Viaggi* at Piazza Roma 7 is the best place to buy them.

Around Vieste

There are a number of day trips worth making **around Vieste**. The most obvious move is to the **beaches**: there's a small one between the promontories, a second, *San Lorenzo*, to the north, and a third, *Pizzomunno*, just south of town – of which the last is much the nicest. Best of all, though, and certainly less crowded, is the marvellous *Scialmarino* beach, 4km up the coast towards Péschici – walkable if you don't have transport.

Otherwise, Vieste is an excellent base for seeing the grotto-ridden **coastline** around the Testa del Gargano, south of town, though the only way to do it properly is on an organised trip. Excursion boats for the grottoes leave from next to San Francesco church at 8.30am and 2.30pm, a three-hour trip; tickets, which cost around L15,000, are again available from *Gargano Viaggi* (see above) .

Péschici and northern Gargano

Atop its rocky vantage point overlooking a beautiful sandy bay, **PÉSCHICI** is without doubt the pick of all the towns and villages in the Gargano: although it has undergone some development in recent years, it is less touristy, less expensive and more attractive than Vieste, and well worth visiting while it remains that way. Though originally built in 970 as a buffer against Saracen incursions, its labyrinth of tiny streets and houses sporting domed roofs has a distinctly Arabic tinge. There's nothing to do beyond beach-lazing, although the town does make a good base for exploring parts of the coastline nearby – an interesting mixture of caves and defensive medieval towers. The easiest trips are to the grotto at **San Nicola**, 3km east of town (some buses), or 5km west to the **Torre di Monte Pucci** for some fine coastal views.

The *FG* **train** line ends at Calanelle, a few kilometres west of Péschici but connected to the town by a bus. This, and other **buses**, drop you in the newer part of Péschici from where it's a short walk down to Corso Garibaldi, the main street. For information there's a **tourist office** (Mon–Sat 9am–noon & 4.30–8pm) just off the Corso, on Via XXIV Maggio. For **accommodation**, the *Locanda Al Castello*, Via Castello 29 (☎0884/964.038; ⑤), is nice, and the tourist office has lists of **private rooms** available in town. There's also a **campsite**, *the Baia San Nicola* (☎0884/964.231), 2km east of town along the coast at Punta San Nicola. For **eating**, there's an expensive but excellent restaurant in the *Locanda Al Castello*, with good home cooking; or, more cheaply, try *Fra Stefano* at Via Forno 8.

The **ferry** from Manfredonia to the Trémiti Islands makes a stop at Péschici's tiny port, down below the old town. Buy **tickets** at Corso Garibaldi 49. There are daily departures in summer, currently at 10.05am, L8800 one way.

West along the coast

Sticking with the coast, there's a mass of white sandy beaches stretching from San Menaio to **RODI GARGANICO** – originally a Greek settlement ("Rodi" is derived from Rhodes), and nowadays, with its beaches and fast hydrofoil links with the Trémiti Islands, a highly popular resort in summer. Again, it's full and expensive in August, but come a couple of months either side and it can be delightful. From here, road and rail line skirt the large **Lago di Varano**, a once-malarial swamp which swallowed the ancient Athenian town of Uria in the fourth century BC. The region around the lake, its villages traditionally poor and backward, is probably the least visited part of the Gargano promontory – though the lake itself is full of eels and attracts a great variety of birdlife, particularly curlews and warblers. Further west, the thin **Lago di Lésina** is a highly saline shallow lagoon, cut off from the sea by a 27km stretch of sand dunes. It's still mercifully free from development – unlike the northern spit of Varano, which is slowly beginning to fill with campsites.

Alternatively, from Cagnano Varano the *FG* train line cuts southwest, skirting the promontory, inland to **SAN SEVERO**, a small market town known for its wines but otherwise not a place where you'll want to do much more than change transport. The *FG* line ends in San Severo, from where you can pick up mainline trains down to Bari and the occasional bus to San Marco in Lamis in Gargano's interior.

Inland Gargano: Vico del Gargano and the Foresta Umbra

The **interior** of the Gargano promontory can make a cool break from its busy coast, though it's not possible to see much of it without your own transport. **VICO DEL GARGANO** is the nicest of the villages and firmly off the beaten track, sited on a hill surrounded by citrus groves and with a creakingly ancient centre full of steep, tangled streets. It's also right on the edge of the **Foresta Umbra** (or "Forest of Shadows") which stretches right across the centre of the Gargano massif – 11,000 hectares of pines, oaks and beeches, hiding a rich variety of wildlife, roe deer especially. It's the last remnant of an ancient forest which once covered most of Puglia. There are numerous marked **walks** through the forest and a **Centro di Vísita** in the middle which doles out advice and information. **Public transport** is a bit thin on the ground. During July and August, a twice-daily bus runs from Rodi Gargánico to the Centro di Vísita, leaving Rodi in the morning and returning in the afternoon. There's also a daily *SITA* bus (Mon–Sat) between Vico del Gargano and Manfredonia, passing through the forest. If you do get stranded in the forest, hitch towards Vico del Gargano or Monte Sant'Angelo, as the Vieste road is pretty dead.

The Trémiti Islands

A small group of islands 40km off the Gárgano coast, the **Trémiti Islands** – Isole Trémiti – are almost entirely given over to tourism in the summer, when the tiny population is swamped by visitors. Despite this, the islands remain relatively unspoilt, the sea is crystal clear, and the beaches are some of the best in Puglia.

Oddly enough, the islands were traditionally a place of exile and punishment in the past. Augustus banished his granddaughter Julia to the islands, while Charlemagne packed his father-in-law off here (minus eyes and limbs) in the eighth century. Monks from Montecassino, on the mainland, first set about building a formidable fortress-abbey on one of the islands in the eleventh century, which managed to withstand frequent assault by the Turks. Later, during the eighteenth century, the islands returned to their old role as a place of confinement for political prisoners, though the Bourbons, concerned at the decline in the local population, shipped in 200 women from the Neapolitan taverns to encourage a recovery.

The 7.15am **ferry** (mid-April–Sept) from Manfredonia calls at Vieste, Péschici and Rodi Gargánico, before reaching the islands at San Nicola; the full one-way trip costs L28,000, though from Rodi Gargánico it's only L11,500 (see "Travel Details"). There are also services from Vasto and Ortona and out of season an infrequent service from Térmoli; see Chapter Twelve, "Abruzzo and Molise".

The Islands

The main Trémiti group consists of three islands: San Nicola, San Domino – the biggest – and Capraia, of which only the first two are inhabited. **Ferries** all arrive at **SAN NICOLA**, where you can wander around the monastic fortress and the tiny church of **Santa Maria a Mare**, built by the monks in the eleventh century on the site of an earlier ninth-century hermitage. San Nicola is rugged and rocky with no beaches, although there is nude bathing on its east side and good swimming to be had off the whole island.

Ignore the offers of pricey boat trips to the other islands and instead take the ferry to **SAN DOMINO** for just L5000. It's a greener island than its neighbour, its pines offering a welcome shade from the heat. Although there is a sandy **beach** – *Cala delle Arene* – on the northeast side of the island, it gets packed in the summer. Your best bet is to follow the signs for the *Villagio TCI*, and make for the west of the island and its quieter coves. You can buy **maps** from souvenir shops. **Accommodation** on the islands is limited to San Domino and is largely full-board only, especially in high season (July & Aug). Prices for this are as high as you might expect: count on L80,000 a night per person. The Municipio holds a list of **private rooms**; or you could try the small *Albergo La Nassa* (☎0882/663.075; ④) or *Albergo Gabbiano* (☎0882/663.044; ④), though it's essential to book ahead for these. A cheaper alternative is to **camp** at the *Villagio TCI*, open all year: you can rent tents if you haven't brought your own, for around L18,000 a night. Bear in mind, too, that provisions have to be brought in from the mainland, so **eating out** can be a costly exercise – bring a picnic.

Along the coast to Bari

The first part of the coastal route south from Manfredonia is unremarkable, flat lands given up to saline extraction. You won't, anyway, be able to come this way by train or bus – though there is a direct coastal road for drivers. First stop, by rail at least, isn't until **MARGHERITA DI SAVOIA**, at the edge of the Tavoliere, a small town producing ninety percent of the country's salt. Beyond here, though, the rest of the coastline is easily accessible by public transport, with most places stops on the main Bologna–Lecce rail line. It's a varied stretch and there are two enjoyable stops, at Trani and Molfetta.

Barletta

The first place that's really worth a stop is **BARLETTA**, nearly 60km from Manfredonia – an indifferent and rather shabby town really, but meriting some attention if you happen to be passing on the last Sunday in July, when it's the venue of one of Puglia's largest medieval pageants, the **disfida**. The event re-enacts an occasion in 1503 when thirteen Italian knights challenged thirteen French knights to a duel for control of the besieged town. They had been drinking together and, following a brawl, the Italians won and the siege was lifted.

For the rest, Barletta's dowdy atmosphere says little about its former importance as a medieval crusader port, the only relic of its earlier days a 5m-high statue in the town centre known as the **Colosso** – said to be the largest Roman bronze in existence, and a relic from the Venetian sacking of Constantinople in 1204. Towering dourly over pedestrians on Corso Vittorio Emanuele, its identity is a mystery, although most money is on Marcian, one of the last Eastern Roman emperors. Over the way from here, the thirteenth-century **Basilica di San Sepolcro** has been restored to its original thirteenth-century simplicity, though the only other place of real interest is the **Museo Cívico de Nittis** at Via Cavour 8 (Tues–Sun 9am–1pm; free). This houses the usual regional archaeological finds and, as a bonus, displays a large collection of paintings by the nineteenth-century artist Giuseppe de Nittis, a local lad who spent most of his short but prolific life in Paris, painting under the influence of the Impressionists.

Practicalities

The **tourist office** at Via Gabbiani 4 has information on the town (Mon–Fri 8am–1pm & 4–6pm, Sat 8am–1pm). You can **eat** at the reasonable *Bella Napoli*, Corso Garibaldi 127, near the museum, and **sleep** at the *Pensione Prezioso*, Via Teatini 11 (☎0883/520.046; ④).

Trani

Thirteen kilometres down the coast from Barletta, **TRANI** is a very different kind of place, with a cosmopolitan air not found in any of the other towns nearby. One of the most important medieval Italian ports, it was a prosperous trading centre with a large mercantile and Jewish community, during the Middle Ages rivalling Bari as a commercial port and in the fourteenth century powerful enough to take on the domineering Venetians.

Twentieth-century Trani is still a prosperous place, its elegant buildings spruce and smart. Centrepiece of the town is the cream-coloured eleventh-century **Duomo**, overlooking the sea on a large open piazza at the edge of the old town. Dedicated to San Nicola Pellegrino, it consists of no less than three churches, stacked on top of each other like an inverted wedding cake – the facade austere, but lightened by a pretty rose window. Inside it has been restored to its original Norman state, the stark nave displaying a timbered ceiling, while near the presbytery fragments of a twelfth-century mosaic have been uncovered. Below the vaulted crypt is the earlier church of Santa Maria della Scala whose marble columns are Roman, while further down the *Ipogea di San Leucio* is an early Christian underground chamber dating from the sixth century. Back outside, the **Castello** is visible from Piazza Duomo, currently under restoration after years of service as a prison. A wander through the adjacent streets gives an impression of the medieval city, not least in the names which echo the town's mercantile and Jewish origins – Via Sinagoga, Via Doge Vecchia and Via Cambio ("Street of the Moneychangers"). The **Palazzo Cacetta** on Via Ognissanti is a rare example of fifteenth-century Gothic architecture; the **Chiesa di Ognissanti**, close by, was a twelfth-century chapel of the Knights Templar, once part of a hospital for injured Crusaders. Sadly, it's unlikely to be open but hang around and someone may appear with a key.

Practicalities

If you're going to stick around in Trani, the **tourist office** is at Via Cavour 140 (Mon–Fri 8.30am–1pm, Sat 8.30–11am), just down the road from the **train station**, which is at the far end of Via Cavour; there's also a tourist information kiosk on the central Piazza della Repubblica. Further along towards the sea, opposite the public gardens, the *Albergo Lucy* on Piazza Plebiscito has **rooms**(☎0883/41.022; ④). For **snacks and lunches**, *La Citadella* in Via Amadeo is a tiny *rosticceria* with modest prices. Otherwise do your **eating** in *La Darsena*, right on the harbour near Piazza Quercia, at Via Statuti Marittimi 98 – great fresh fish – or get pizzas in the *Antica Cattedrale*, just behind the duomo, which has tables outside in the piazza in summer.

Molfetta

The last stop worth making on this stretch of coast is at **MOLFETTA**, a working port, unashamedly non-touristy and all the better for it, with a twelfth-century **Duomo** that's a mishmash of styles from the Romanesque and Byzantine eras and a tiny alleywayed old centre – once an island – that's home to one of the biggest fishing fleets on the southern Adriatic. There are no beaches as such, but it's a busy, evocative place, its waterfront active with visiting ships and thronged by an evening *passeggiata* that sweeps down to the docks to watch the gorgeous sunsets over the Adriatic. You probably won't want to stay, but if you do there's one central **hotel**, the *Tritone* on Lungomare M. Colonna (☎080/911.069; ⑤). If you need to **eat** and are feeling flush, try the *Bistrot*, Corso Dante 33 – upwards of L30,000 a head but worth it. For **snacks** the *Al Duomo*, next to the duomo, has outdoor tables, ideal for watching Molfetta amble by.

Bari

Commercial and administrative capital of Puglia, a university town and the Mezzogiorno's second city, **BARI** has its fair share of interest. But although an economically vibrant place, it harbours no pretensions about being a major tourist attraction. Primarily people come here to work, or to leave for Greece on its many ferries.

Bari was already a thriving centre when the Romans arrived. Later the city was the seat of the Byzantine governor of southern Italy, while under the Normans Bari rivalled Venice, both as a maritime centre and, following the seizure of the remains of Saint Nicholas, as a place of pilgrimage. Since those heady days Bari has declined considerably. Its fortunes revived briefly in 1813 when the King of Naples foisted a planned expansion upon the city – giving the city its contemporary gridded street pattern, wide avenues and piazzas. And Mussolini instituted a university and built numerous examples of strident fascist architecture. But the city was heavily bombed during the last war, and today its vigorous centre is a symbol of the South's zeal for commercial growth at the expense of much local colour.

Arrival and information

Bari is a fairly compact city, running from the train station in the gridded new city, down to the bulging old centre, the *citta vecchia*, in just ten blocks. There are several **train stations** in Bari. The main *FS* station is in Piazza Aldo Moro, on the southern edge of the modern centre, and serves both regular *FS* trains and those of the private *Ferrovia del Sud-Est* (*FSE*) line. Nearby, there's a separate station for trains on another private line, the *Ferrovia Bari-Nord* (*BN*), while *Ferrovia Calabro-Lucane* (*FCL*) trains leave from a station on Corso Italia; see "Listings", p.755, for destinations. **Buses** complicate the issue even further: from the coastal towns north of Bari you'll arrive at Piazza Eroi del Mare; *SITA* buses from inland and southern towns pull up in Piazza Aldo Moro; while the private rail lines' bus services – *FCL* and *FSE* – leave respectively from stations on Corso Italia and Largo Ciaia. Again, see "Listings".

Ferries from Igoumenitsa, Corfu and Patras (Greece) all use the Stazione Marittima, next to the old city, connected with the main *FS* railway station by bus #20. The **airport** is about 9km out of the city, an *Alitalia* bus connecting with arrivals and dropping at Via Calefati 3.

Getting around, you're best advised to walk – not a bad option in such a small city. **Buses** are bright orange and run from 5.30am until around midnight, mostly focusing on Piazza Aldo Moro. Tickets cost a flat L700 for each trip.

The **tourist office** is at Piazza Aldo Moro 33, to the right of the main train station (Mon–Fri 8.30am–1pm, Sat 8.30–11am; ☎524.2244) and has maps of the city; ask also for the monthly magazine *Ecobari* which has the only decent plan of the old city. If you're stopping over in Bari between June and August and are under 30, you might want to take advantage of a special scheme run by the *CTS* youth travel agency and

OTE – a tourist promotion agency – which allows free travel on city buses and the possibility of accommodation for two nights at a total cost of L40,000 per person. Further information from *CTS* (for address; see "Listings").

A **word of warning**: the Barese take a positive delight in portraying the old city as a den of thieves, and certainly strolling through the narrow alleys with your camera in full view isn't particularly wise. Bag snatching by young kids on mopeds (the *topini*, or "little mice") isn't as rife as it once was, but neither is it extinct. Keep your wits about you.

Accommodation

Though Bari has its share of crummy hotels, finding somewhere cheap **to sleep** can be tricky. The cheapest places close to the station are the *Loizzo*, Via Crisanzio 46 (☎080/521.1284; ④), and the slightly more expensive *Pensione Giulia*, Via Crisanzio 12 (☎080/521.6630; ⑤); a more upscale choice near the station is the *Adria*, right out of the station on Via Zuppetta (☎080/524.6699; ⑥), though make sure they don't fob you off with an inward-facing room. Close to the old town, Via Calefati has a number of choices, including the *Darinka* at Via Calefati 15 (☎080/235.049; ④), and, in the same building, the *Bristol* (☎080/521.1503; ⑦), which is a good option if you have a little more money. If you don't mind the trek out of town, there's a decent **youth hostel** near the beach at PALESE, 8km up the coast (☎080/320.082; ①). Open all year except the last two weeks of December, you can reach it on bus #1 from Piazza Aldo Moro; get off at the Villaggio dell'Aeronautica and walk 300m. You can **camp** for free between June and September if you're under 30 at *Pineta San Francesco*, on the outskirts of the city – reachable on bus #5 from the main train station, bus #1 from Corso Cavour. Out of season, the nearest **campsite** is 6km south of the city on the SS16 – *Camping San Giorgio* (☎080/491.175); bus #12 from Teatro Petruzzelli.

The City

There's not a lot to the **new city** of Bari, bar a good museum or two. Its straight streets are lined with shops and offices, relieved occasionally by the odd piazza and bit of greenery, best of which is the starting-point of the evening *passeggiata*, **Piazza Umberto I** – usually full of stalls selling jewellery, books and prints. Off the piazza, the university building holds an excellent **Museo Archeologico** (Mon–Sat 9am–1pm; free), with a good selection of Greek and Puglian ceramics and a solid collection of artefacts from the Daunic, Messapian and Peucetic peoples – Puglia's earliest inhabitants. Afterwards, cut to the right for tree-lined **Corso Cavour**, Bari's main commercial street, which leads down to the waterfront. Right along here, in the Palazzo della Provincia, the **Pinacoteca Provinciale** (Mon–Sat 9am–1pm & 4–8pm, Sun 9am–1pm; free) is a local art collection of mainly southern Italian stuff, twelfth- to nineteenth-century, with strong work by the fifteenth-century Vivarini family.

The old city

Quite clearly it's the **old city** which is Bari's more entrancing quarter, a jumble of streets at the far end of Corso Cavour that's possibly the most confusing place to walk around in southern Italy. Its labyrinth of seemingly endless passages weaving through courtyards and under arches was originally designed to spare the inhabitants from the wind and throw invaders into a state of confusion. This it still does admirably, and even with the best of maps you're going to get lost.

Of specific sights there are few. The **Basilica di San Nicola** (daily 9am–1pm & 5–7pm), in the heart of the old city, was consecrated in 1197, as an inscription at the side of the main door testifies, to house the relics of the saint plundered a century earlier

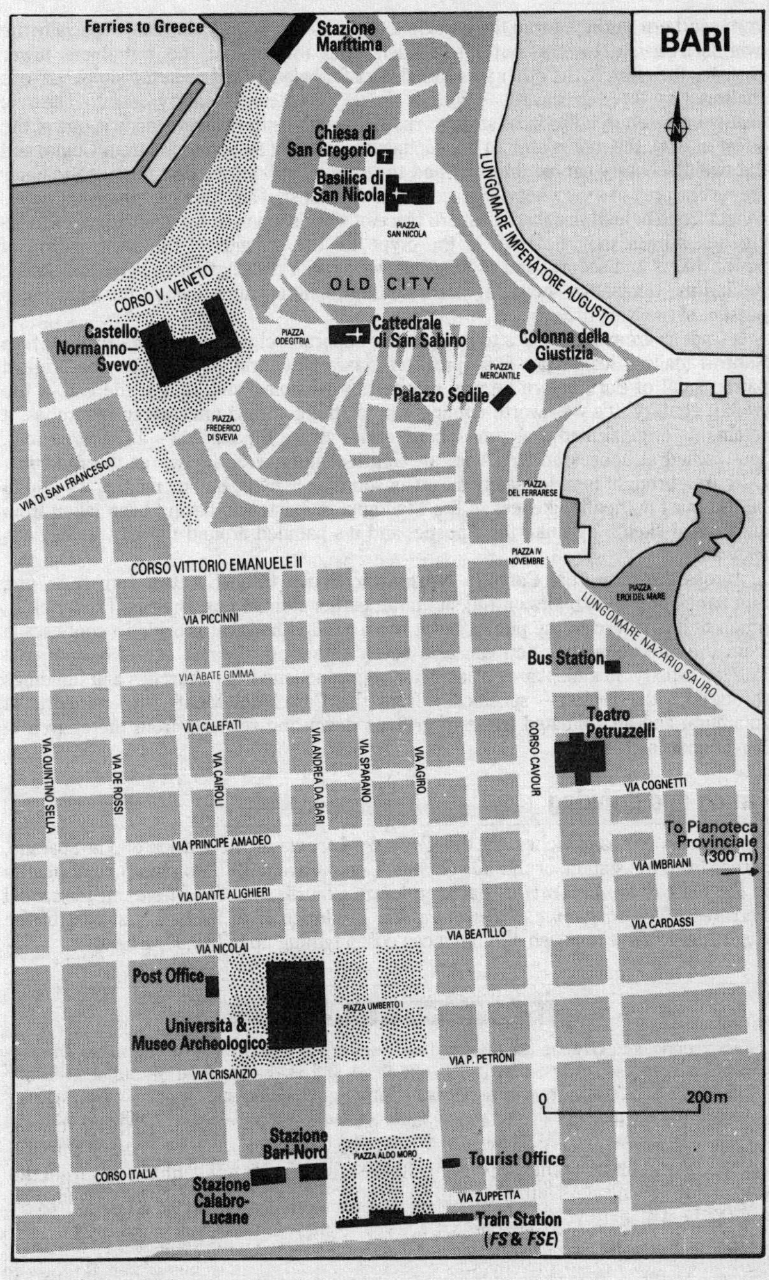
BARI
Ferries to Greece
Stazione Marittima
Chiesa di San Gregorio
Basilica di San Nicola
PIAZZA SAN NICOLA
LUNGOMARE IMPERATORE AUGUSTO
OLD CITY
CORSO V. VENETO
Castello Normanno–Svevo
PIAZZA ODEGITRIA
Cattedrale di San Sabino
Colonna della Giustizia
PIAZZA MERCANTILE
Palazzo Sedile
PIAZZA FREDERICO DI SVEVIA
VIA DI SAN FRANCESCO
PIAZZA DEL FERRARESE
PIAZZA IV NOVEMBRE
CORSO VITTORIO EMANUELE II
PIAZZA EROI DEL MARE
LUNGOMARE NAZARIO SAURO
VIA PICCINNI
Bus Station
VIA ABATE GIMMA
Teatro Petruzzelli
VIA CALEFATI
VIA QUINTINO SELLA
VIA DE ROSSI
VIA CAIROLI
VIA ANDREA DA BARI
VIA SPARANO
VIA AGIRO
CORSO CAVOUR
VIA COGNETTI
To Pianoteca Provinciale (300 m)
VIA PRINCIPE AMADEO
VIA IMBRIANI
VIA DANTE ALIGHIERI
VIA CARDASSI
VIA BEATILLO
VIA NICOLAI
Post Office
PIAZZA UMBERTO I
Università & Museo Archeologico
VIA P. PETRONI
VIA CRISANZIO
0
200m
Stazione Bari-Nord
PIAZZA ALDO MORO
Tourist Office
CORSO ITALIA
Stazione Calabro-Lucane
VIA ZUPPETTA
Train Station (FS & FSE)

from southern Turkey. From the outside it all looks thoroughly Norman, especially the twin fortress-like towers, but it's a misleading impression: the right-hand tower predates the church, the other was added later for balance, and even the simple nave is shattered by three great arches and an ornate seventeenth-century ceiling. The real beauty of the church lies in its stonework: the twelfth-century altar canopy is one of the finest in Italy, the motifs around the capitals the work of stonemasons from Como; and the twelfth-century carved doorway and the simple, striking mosaic floor of the choir are lovely, prey to a very heavy Saracen influence. Best of all is the twelfth-century episcopal throne behind the altar, a superb piece of work supported by small figures wheezing beneath its weight. Down in the crypt are the remains of the saint, patron of pawnbrokers and sailors (and of Russians, who made the pilgrimage here until 1917). Behind the tomb-altar, the richly decorated fourteenth-century icon of the saint was a present of the King of Serbia.

It's not far from the basilica to Bari's other important church, the **Cattedrale di San Sabino** (daily 8.30am–1pm & 5–7pm), off Piazza Odegitria, dedicated to the original patron saint of Bari, before he was usurped by Nicholas, and built at the end of the twelfth century. It's well worth coming just for the contrast: uncluttered by arches, it retains its original medieval atmosphere, and – unlike the basilica – a timbered roof. The cathedral houses an icon, too, an eighth-century work known as the *Madonna Odegitria*, brought here for safety from Constantinople by Byzantine monks. It's said to be the most authentic likeness of the Madonna in existence, having been taken from an original sketch by Luke the Apostle, and it's paraded around the city at religious festivals.

Across the piazza the **Castello Normanno-Svevo** (Mon–Sat 9am–1pm & 3–7pm, Sun 9am–1pm; L4000) sits on the site of an earlier Roman fort. Built by Frederick II, much of it is closed to the public, but it has a vaulted hall that provides a cool escape from the afternoon sun. You can also see a gathering of some of the best of past Puglian artistry, in a display of plaster-cast reproductions from churches and buildings throughout the region – specifically from the Castel del Monte, the cathedral at Altamura, and an animated frieze of griffons devouring serpents from the church of San Leonardo at Siponto.

Eating and drinking

For snacks and sandwiches try the *Caffe del Levante* at the corner of Via Sparano, across from the station, or the *Bar Oceano*, Corso Cavour 49. Two **cheap restaurants** in the old city are *Le Travi di Buco*, on Largo Chiurlia, and *Da Nicola*, off Piazza del Ferrarese. The *Ristorante al Pescatore*, Via Frederico II di Sveia 8, just east of the castle, does marvellous fish, though it can cost anything up to L40,000 a head.

ONWARDS TO GREECE

Ferry services to **Greece** are operated by *Ventouris* – contactable through *Pan Travel*, Via San Francesco d'Assisi 95 (☎080/524.4388) and at the Stazione Marittima (☎080/218.493 or 521.1726). They run services to Corfu, Igoumenitsa and Patras. On foot, prices range from around L40,000 one way to Igoumenitsa/Corfu to L45,000–60,000 one way to Patras; you'll pay L70,000-plus for a cabin, and upwards of L60,000 for a small car. Passengers also pay an embarcation tax of L11,000 per person and L11,000 per car.

Travel agents around town often have a wide variety of offers on **tickets**, including *CTS* (address opposite), who give a ten percent discount on student/youth fares. *InterRail* pass holders get discounts too; see *Basics*. Once you've got your ticket, you must report to the relevant desk at the Stazione Marittima at least two hours before departure.

Listings

Beach The nearest beach is north of the city; take bus #1 from Teatro Petruzzelli to Palese/Santo Spirito.

Buses *FCL* to Basilicata (from Corso Italia 6); *FSE* to Bríndisi (from Largo Ciaia); Marozzi to Rome (from Corso Italia 3).

Exchange Outside banking hours in Piazza Aldo Moro, outside the main train station .

Post office The main office is behind the university in Piazza Battisti (Mon–Fri 8am–7.30pm, Sat 8.30am–noon).

Telephone There's an *ASST* office by the train station on Piazza Aldo Moro (daily 8am–9pm).

Trains Of the three private lines operating out of Bari, *FSE* run to Castellana Grotte, Martina Franca and Alberobello; *BN* connect Bari with Bitonto, Andria and Barletta; the *FCL* line goes to Altamura, Gravina, and Matera and Potenza in Basilicata.

Travel agents *CTS*, Via Dante 111 and Corso Italia 3 (☎080/523.2716).

Le Murge

Rising gently from the Adriatic coast, **Le Murge** – a low limestone plateau – dominates the landscape to the south and west of Bari. Around 50km wide and 150km long, it's generally divided into "Low" and "High" Murge: the further away from the coast you are, the higher and more barren it gets. The towns in the region are not natural holiday destinations: the area is sparsely populated, especially further inland, and the small settlements that exist are rural backwaters with a slow pace of life. But they do make an interesting day out from the more popular coastal towns, or a good stopover if you're heading for the region of Basilicata. There are some buses and trains from Bari, but, as always, without your own car travelling very extensively can be difficult.

The Low Murge

The main town of the Low Murge is **ANDRIA**, a large agricultural centre easily reached from Barletta or Bari that's at its best on market day (Monday) – though it otherwise has little to hold you. It was, though, a favourite haunt of Frederick II, who was responsible for the main local attraction these days, the **Castel del Monte**, 17km south – the most extraordinary of all Puglia's castles and one of the finest surviving examples of Swabian architecture (Mon–Sat 9am–1pm & 3–7pm, Sun 9am–1pm; L4000). Begun by Frederick in the 1240s, it is a high, isolated fortress precisely built around an octagonal courtyard in two storeys of eight rooms. A mystery surrounds its intended purpose. Although there was once an iron gate which could be lowered over the main entrance (as tell-tale grooves in the portal show), there are no other visible signs of fortification, and the castle may have served as a mere hunting lodge. Nonetheless the mathematical precision involved in its construction, and the preoccupation with the number eight, have excited writers for centuries. It's argued the castle is in fact an enormous astrological calendar, also that Frederick may have had the octagonal Omar mosque in Jerusalem in mind when he designed it; but despite his recorded fascination with the sciences, no one really knows. There is only one record of its use. The defeat of Manfred, Frederick's illegitimate son, at the battle of Benevento in 1266, signalled the end of Swabian power in Puglia; and Manfred's sons and heirs were imprisoned in the castle for over thirty years – a lonely place to be incarcerated.

Sadly, there is only one bus a day from Andria (at 7am, for Spinazzola), stopping at Castel del Monte and returning to Andria from there at 11.15am.

The rest of the Low Murge

West of Andria, on the edge of the Low Murge, **CANOSA DI PUGLIA** used to be a thriving commercial centre but has never really recovered from its destruction by the Saracens, and today it's an aged, broken-down old place, only worth a stop for its **Duomo** – uninteresting from the outside but with a wealth of treasures in its beautiful eleventh-century interior. The bishop's throne behind the altar, carved with plants and animals and supported by a couple of rather fed-up looking elephants, dates from 1079. Adjacent is a tomb with a solid bronze door, richly engraved in an Arab fashion, its occupant Bohemond – the son of the Norman Robert Guiscard.

About the same distance east of Andria (but best reached by hourly bus from Molfetta), the old centre of **RUVO DI PUGLIA** is a more attractive stop, with a quiet, timeless atmosphere. In the autumn, the pavements of the old town are strewn with almonds, spread out to dry in the sun as they have been for centuries. The town was also famous once for its pottery, the locals strong on copying Greek designs to great effect. Just across from the **tourist office** (Mon–Fri 9am–1pm), the **Museo Jatta** in Piazza Bovio houses a dusty collection of the homemade stuff as well as some beautiful Greek originals – like a fifth-century BC *krater* depicting the death of Talos – though it's been closed for the past couple of years. If it is still closed, Ruvo's thirteenth-century **Duomo**, tucked into the tightly packed streets of the town's old quarter, is well worth time. Its beautiful portal is guarded by animated griffons balancing on fragile columns, while recent work has restored the interior to its original state – exposing some of the sixteenth-century frescoes which used to cover the walls. What distinguishes Ruvo's cathedral, though, is the sheer amount of decoration that survives on the outer walls, like the rose window and the arches tapering off into human and animal heads.

There's a similar cathedral in **BITONTO**, just a few kilometres out of Bari (20min by train), again with fiercely animated portals and a thirteenth-century pulpit with a bas-relief depicting Frederick and his family. Bitonto is also the centre of olive oil production in Puglia and is a fairly attractive place to visit anyway; pottering around the maze-like medieval centre makes for a pleasant afternoon's escape from the city noise of Bari.

The High Murge

Around 45km south of Bari (and reachable by train), **ALTAMURA** is the largest town in the High Murge, an originally fifth-century BC settlement fortified by the Peucetians – parts of whose town still remain. You'll see bits of the walls as you come in from the station, over 4m thick in places. Destroyed by the Saracens, the ancient town lay abandoned until the thirteenth century when Frederick restocked a new settlement with Greeks, and built the high walls from which the town derives its name.

Altamura's most interesting feature is its **Duomo**, a mixture of styles varying from Apulian–Romanesque to Gothic and Baroque. The original thirteenth-century structure was badly damaged by an earthquake and suffered further in the sixteenth century when it was restyled: the portal and rose window were moved round to what had been the apse, and a couple of campaniles were tacked on – the pinnacles added later when Baroque was all the rage. Thankfully, the intricately carved medieval portal survived the switch, while the interior is still suitably austere. Take a look, too, at the tiny church of **San Niccolò dei Greci**, built by the Greek colonists in the thirteenth century and in which they celebrated their Orthodox religion for over 400 years. It's on Corso Federico di Svevia.

Twelve kilometres west, not far from the border with Basilicata, lies **GRAVINA IN PUGLIA** – a castle-protected town which clings to the edge of a deep ravine. During the early barbarian invasions the locals took refuge in the caves along the sides of the ravine, a move which seems to have paid off until the arrival of the Saracens, who promptly massacred every cave-dwelling inhabitant. Under the Normans, though, the shattered town settled down to a quieter life as a fiefdom of the wealthy pope-producing Orsini family, whose mark – an enormous spread eagle – is all over town. In the dilapidated old quarter, the cave-church of **San Michele dei Gratti**, a dark, dank affair hewn out of the rock, holds bones that are said to be the remains of victims of the last Saracen attack, almost a thousand years old. (The church is currently closed but the caretaker, Signora Cascarano, lives nearby.) The **museum** (Mon–Sat 9am–2pm) in Piazza Santomasi contains some artefacts from the excavations of the ancient town abandoned to the invaders. But more engaging, certainly if you couldn't get into San Michele, is the reconstruction of San Vito Vecchio, another cave-church, set up on the ground floor with some remarkable tenth-century Byzantine frescoes.

Down the coast from Bari: to Monópoli and the Ruins of Egnázia

The coast south of Bari is a rocky stretch, with rock-built villages perching above tiny sandy coves. Just ten minutes by *FS* train from Bari (or bus #12 from Piazza Aldo Moro), **TORRE A MARE** provides one of the easiest escapes from the city, situated on a rocky crag high above two large caves, though its ease of access from Bari means it can get quite crowded. There'll be fewer people around another twenty minutes on, at **POLIGNANO A MARE**, which, despite some newfound tourists, remains fairly low-key. It's a small port, with a tiny medieval centre, perching on the edge of the limestone cliffs here. Polignano is best reached by train, although there is a bus service, run by *FSE*, from Largo Ciaia in Bari.

MONÓPOLI, 8km further down the coast, was, like Polignano, once controlled by the Venetians, a trading centre originally populated by the ancient Egnazians, whose maritime know-how lives on in what is still a large commercial port. Other than the goings-on at the dockside, there's not a lot to see, though the old town is worth wandering through, its steep narrow streets revealing fragments of its Venetian past. A brief scout around might take in the **Museo della Cattedrale** on Largo Cattedrale (daily 8am–noon & 4–7pm; L2000), which contains some beautiful examples of religious art, including a tenth-century Byzantine reliquary, and the tiny chapel of **Santa Maria Amalfitana**, tucked away on Largo Plebiscito – built in the twelfth century by wealthy merchants from Amalfi on the site of an earlier cave-church, which is now the crypt.

The ancient city of Egnázia

There's more of interest south of the town, at the site of the ancient city of **Egnázia**, or *Gnathia* (daily 8.30am–sunset; free), easily reached by bus from Monópoli's Villa Comunale (direction "Torre Canne"). Egnázia was an important Messapian centre during the fifth century BC, fortified with over 2km of walls, large parts of which still stand in the northern corner of the ruined town – up to 7m high. It was later colonised by the Greeks and then the Romans (in 244 BC), who built a forum, amphitheatre, a colonnaded public hall and temples: one was dedicated to Syria, a goddess popular with the early Romans who – according to Lucian – was worshipped by men dressed as women. Horace is known to have dropped by here to see the city's famous altar, which ignited wood without a flame.

At the turn of the first century AD, the Emperor Trajan constructed the **Via Egnatia**, a road which ran down to Bríndisi and continued from what is now Durres in Albania, via Thessaloniki, right the way to Constantinople, marking Egnázia's importance as a military and commercial centre. Parts of the road survive, running alongside the Roman public buildings. With the collapse of the Roman Empire, however, the city fell to subsequent Barbarian invasions, and was almost completely destroyed by the Gothic king Totila in 545 AD. A community struggled on here, seeking refuge in the Messapian tombs, until the tenth century when the settlement was finally abandoned. There's a new **museum** (summer Mon–Sat 8.30am–1.30pm & 3–6.30pm; winter Mon–Sat 8.30am–1.30pm; L2000) on the site housing a fascinating array of artefacts, including examples of the distinctive earthenware for which the ancient town was prized, uncovered during excavations that are still underway.

The FSE line: Castellana Grotte to Martina Franca

Meandering lazily down towards the **Valle d'Itria** and – finally – to TÁRANTO, the *Ferrovia Sud-Est* passes through some of the prettiest of Puglia's landscapes. The olive gradually loses ground to vineyards, cherry and peach orchards, neatly partitioned off by dry stone walls. About 40km out of Bari are the **Grotte di Castellana** (daily April–Sept 8.30am–12.15pm & 2.30–6pm; rest of the year 9am–noon & 2–5pm; L20,000, students L15,000), a spectacular set of underground caves. The barren limestone terrain of Le Murge, which touches the region, swallows rivers whole (south of the Ofanto, near Barletta, few rivers make it to the sea), producing a landscape cut by deep ravines and pitted with caverns and grottoes. At Castellana, a lift takes you down to the largest of the caverns, *La Grave*, 60m below ground, which was used as the local rubbish dump until its accidental discovery in 1938. From here, there's over a kilometre of strangely formed caves to explore, variously named according to shape, ending in the most impressive of them all, the *Caverna Bianca* – a shimmering sea of stalagmites and stalagtites.

To **get to the caves**, simply follow the signs from the station; the grotto is about two kilometres southwest of town. **Tours** leave roughly every hour and take around an hour and three quarters. There are also cheaper, one-hour trips and evening tours at 9pm in August.

PUTIGNANO, next stop down the line, marks the beginning of the Valle d'Itria. It's really only worth a call if you happen to be in the area when its riotous carnival explodes at the beginning of February. But there is a grotto here, too, if you haven't already had your fill – this one of glistening pink alabaster, about 1km north of town, signposted *Grotta di Putignano*.

After Putignano the natural gives way to the constructed, and **trulli** come to dominate the landscape: cylindrical, whitewashed buildings with grey conical roofs which taper out to a point or sphere, often adorned with painted symbols. Confined to this part of Puglia, their ancient origins are obscure, though few today date back more than a couple of hundred years. Apart from their intrinsic beauty, there seems no special reason for building houses like this, and certainly no reason for them popping up here – though many theories abound, one claiming that the dome-shaped houses are much cooler in the baking Puglian summers. Certainly they make full use of local building materials and are remarkably easy to adapt: when you need more room, you simply knock a hole in the wall and build another next door. See *Contexts* for more.

If you want to take a closer look, **ALBEROBELLO** is the best place to get off, where there's a large local concentration of *trulli* – around 1500 cluttering Alberobello's narrow streets – although there is a certain amount of tourist exploitation to go with it. Most are south of the town centre, on and around Largo Martellotta, past the tourist office from the station. Just a few kilometres south, **LOCOROTONDO**, which owes its name to its circular layout, gives good views over the whole area, speckled with red- and grey-roofed *trulli* in a sea of olives, vines and almond trees.

Martina Franca

The *trulli* are still plentiful by the time you reach **MARTINA FRANCA**, a surprising town with a tangible Moorish flavour. Reputed to have been founded by Tarentine settlers fed up with constant Saracen attacks during the tenth century, it was the Angevin prince of Táranto who bolstered the community in the early fourteenth century by granting it certain tax privileges. The town derives its name from this – *franca* meaning duty or stamp. Today its centre shelters within an unprepossessing approach of tower blocks, a medieval core adorned with some of the most subtle and least overbearing examples of architecture from the Baroque period you'll find.

There's a spasmodic bus service from the **train station** up to the centre of town; otherwise you'll have to walk – left out of the station and up Viale della Liberta to Corso Italia, which leads to the old town centre, marked by the so-called **Porta di Santo Stefano**. Through here, Piazza Roma is dominated by the vast **Palazzo Ducale**, dating from 1688 and now housing the town hall, but with a handful of rooms open to the public most mornings – most of them smothered in classically eighteenth-century Arcadian murals by a local artist. Just across the square the **tourist office** (Mon–Fri 9.30am–1pm & 4.30–7.30pm, Sat 9.30am–1pm) has good maps of the town. From here narrow Via Vittorio Emanuele leads right into the old town and Piazza Plebiscito, fronted by the vast Baroque facade of the **Chiesa di San Martino**, an eighteenth-century church built on the site of an earlier Romanesque structure, of which only the campanile survives. From adjacent Piazza Immacolata you can either bear left down Via Cavour, with its Baroque palazzi and balconied streets, or wander further into the old town, the roads running around the edge of the surviving fourteenth-century town walls offering an excellent panorama of the Valle d'Itria, with its neatly ordered fields dotted with *trulli*. Indeed, if you're further interested in finding out about life in the *trulli*, there's a **Museo della Civiltà dei Trulli**, 7km from Martina Franca on the road to Ceglie Messapico.

Visits to Martina Franca are best if they coincide with the **Festivale della Valle d'Itria**, held from the end of July until the first week in August, one of the most important events on the Italian musical calendar, with opera, classical, jazz music and the like. Although tickets aren't cheap, it's a congenial and unpretentious event. Information is available from the festival office in the Palazzo Ducale.

The cheapest **hotel** in town is the *Hotel da Luigi* on Via Táranto (☎080/901.324; ④), – though at festival time you won't even get a room here. If your budget is tighter than this, it'll have to be the **youth hostel**, the *Ostello Papa Martino*, 6km south of town on the Táranto road at SAN PAOLO (☎080/700.052; ①); take the *FSE* bus for Táranto from Piazza Crispi, off Corso Italia. As for **eating**, you'll get an excellent meal at *La Tavernetta*, Corso Vittorio Emanuele 30, though the food is cheaper down Corso dei Mille (off Corso Italia) – try the *Scacco Matto*, at no. 26, for pizzas. Or head straight for the town's best pizzas at *La Panca*, Via Spirito Santo 14, off Via Bellini.

Táranto

There are numerous legends connected with the origins of **TÁRANTO**. It was variously founded by the Spartan deity Phalanthus; Taras, the son of Neptune; or – perhaps more likely – illegitimate Spartans born while their fathers were away fighting. Whatever the truth is, Taras, as it was known to the Greeks, was a well-chosen site and soon became the first city of Magna Graecia, renowned for its wool, its oysters and mussels, and its dyes – the imperial purple was the product of decayed Tarentine molluscs. Resplendent with temples, its acropolis harboured a vast bronze of Poseidon that was one of the wonders of the ancient world. Sadly, little remains of ancient Taras or even of later Roman Tarentum, their monuments and relics confined to the great museum in the modern city. After being destroyed by the Romans, Táranto was for years little more than a small fishing port, its strategic position on the sea only being recognised in Napoleonic times. It was home to the Italian fleet after Unification, and consequently heavily bombed during the last war, since when attempts to rejuvenate the town have left its medieval heart girdled by heavy industry, including the vast *Italsider* steel plant which throws its flames and lights into the skies above.

Finding your way around is easy. The city divides neatly into three distinct parts: the northern spur is the industrial part of town, home of the steel works and train station. Cross the Ponte di Porta Napoli and you're on the central island containing the old town. And the southern spur contains the modern city centre (the *Borgo Nuovo*), the administrative and commercial hub of Táranto, linked to the old town by a swing-bridge.

The City

In Greek times the island holding the **old town** wasn't an island at all but part of the southern peninsula, connected by an isthmus to the southern spur. Here the Greeks raised temples and the acropolis, while further south lay the residential districts. There's one extant fragment of ancient Táranto – the Doric **columns**, re-erected in a corner of **Piazza Castello**, which once adorned a temple of Poseidon. The rest of the tiny island is a mass of poky streets and alleyways, buttressed by scaffolding seemingly to prevent the whole place from falling down. The Aragonese **Castello** (now owned by the navy and closed to the public) at the southern end surveys the comings and goings of warships and fishing boats. The narrow canal they slide through, between the city's two inland "seas", was built in the late nineteenth century, on the site of the castle's old moat. "Seas" is a bit of a misnomer: the *Mare Piccolo* is really a large lagoon, home to Táranto's famous oysters and the Italian navy; and the *Mare Grande* is really a vast bay, protected by sea walls and the offshore fortified island of San Pietro.

At the heart of the old town lies the eleventh-century **Cattedrale**, which once did duty as a mosque – dedicated to Táranto's patron saint, Cataldo (Cathal), a seventh-century Irish monk who on returning from a pilgrimage to the Holy Land was so shocked by the licentiousness of the town's inhabitants that he decided to stay and clean the place up. His remains lie under the altar of a small chapel which bears his name – "a jovial nightmare in stone", Norman Douglas thought. As for the rest of the church, recent restoration has stripped away most of the baroque alterations and fragments of a Byzantine mosaic floor have been revealed. The columns of the nave, too, are ancient, pillaged from the temples that once stood on the island, their delicately carved capitals depicting tiny birds nestling among the stone foliage. A few blocks away, check out the city's **fish market**, on Via Cariati, a lively affair where the best of the local catch is displayed: octopi lie dazed, clams spit defiantly at you, while other less definable creatures seem preoccupied with making a last dash for freedom before the restauranteurs arrive – some of the city's finest restaurants are just across the road.

It's a short walk across the swing-bridge to Táranto's **modern centre** – though this, like Bari's, has limited charms, its wide streets laid out on a grid pattern that forms the centre of Táranto's *passeggiata*, around piazzas Vittoria and Archita. Nearby, the **Villa Peripato** was *the* place for the Tarentini to take their early evening stroll at the turn of the century, but today's gardeners seem to be fighting a losing battle with the undergrowth.

The only real attraction in this part of town – and it's a gem – is the **Museo Nazionale** at Corso Umberto I 41 (Mon–Sat 9am–2pm, Sun 9am–1pm; L6000), which offers a fascinating insight into the ancient splendour of Taras. With something in excess of 50,000 pieces of Greek terracotta alone, it's one of the largest collections anywhere in the world; be wary of trying to see too much – the more noteworthy of the

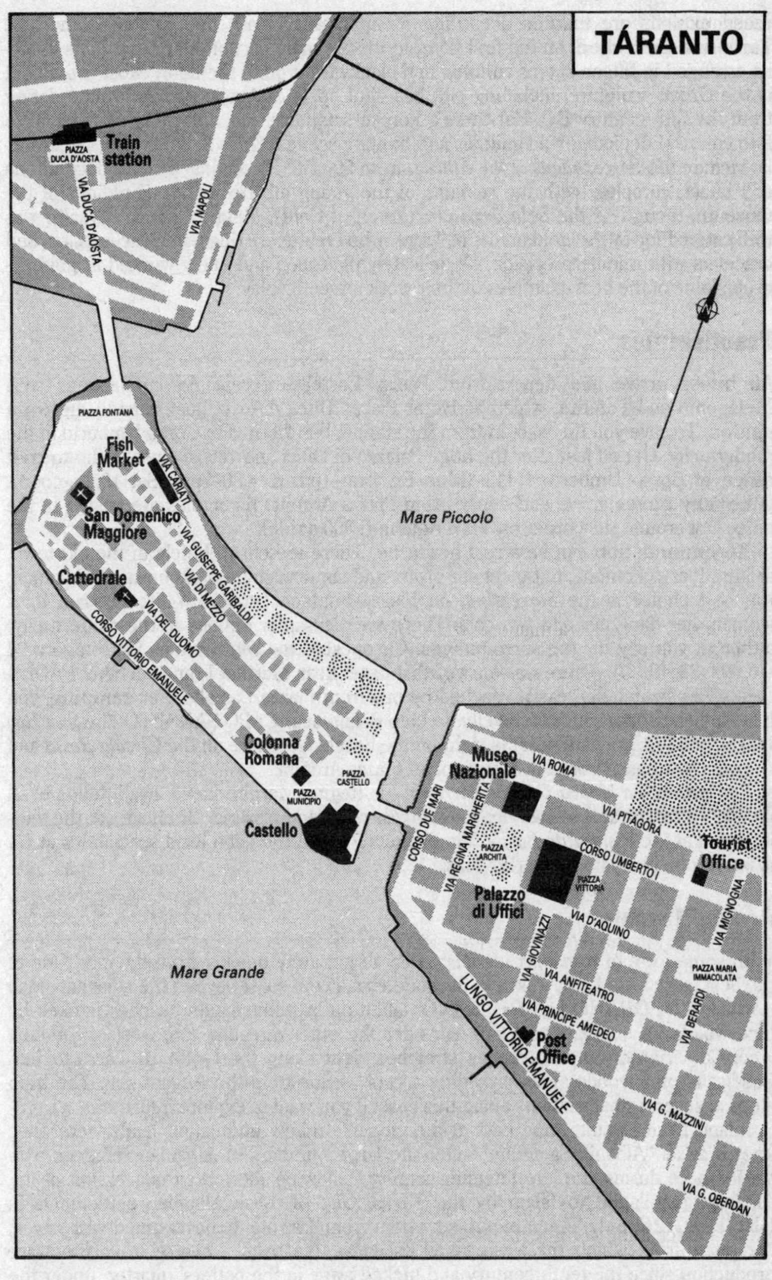
TÁRANTO
Train station
PIAZZA DUCA D'AOSTA
VIA DUCA D'AOSTA
VIA NAPOLI
PIAZZA FONTANA
Fish Market
VIA CARIATI
San Domenico Maggiore
VIA GIUSEPPE GARIBALDI
VIA DI MEZZO
Cattedrale
VIA DEL DUOMO
CORSO VITTORIO EMANUELE
Mare Piccolo
Colonna Romana
PIAZZA CASTELLO
PIAZZA MUNICIPIO
Castello
Museo Nazionale
VIA ROMA
VIA PITAGORA
CORSO DUE MARI
VIA REGINA MARGHERITA
PIAZZA ARCHITA
CORSO UMBERTO I
PIAZZA VITTORIA
Tourist Office
Palazzo di Uffici
VIA D'AQUINO
VIA MIGNOGNA
VIA GIOVINAZZI
PIAZZA MARIA IMMACOLATA
Mare Grande
VIA ANFITEATRO
VIA PRINCIPE AMEDEO
VIA BERARDI
LUNGO VITTORIO EMANUELE
Post Office
VIA G. MAZZINI
VIA G. OBERDAN

cased exhibits are marked according to importance, with one to four stars. The **Tarentine Collection**, on the first floor, forms the main part of the museum, its exhibits arranged in fifteen rooms running anti-clockwise around the floor. Most prominent is the Greek sculpture, including two beautiful busts of Apollo and Aphrodite dating from the fifth century BC. But there's Roman scuplture, too, and mosaics (second to fifth century) depicting wild animals and hunting scenes. Finds from the city's necropolis include the *Sarcophagus of the Athlete*, from 500 BC, its original painted decorations still intact, complete with the remains of the young athlete within. Highlight of the museum, though, is the *Sala degli Ori* (Room of Gold). Magna Graecia's wealth was well catered for by the goldsmiths of Taras, who created earrings, necklaces, tiaras and bracelets with minute precision, all delicately patterned and finely worked in gold filigree. Some of the best examples of their work are on display.

Practicalities

All **buses** arrive and depart from Piazza Castello, except *FS* connections with Metaponto and Potenza, which arrive at Piazza Duca d'Aosta, just outside the **train station**. To save you the walk in from the station, bus #8 runs to Corso Umberto in the modern city. Get off just after the huge Palazzo di Uffici and you're close to the **tourist office** at Corso Umberto I 113 (Mon–Fri 9am–1pm & 4.30–7pm, Sat 10am–noon). Other **city buses** arrive and depart from Piazza Archita: timetables are posted in the office just around the corner on Via d'Aquino (L800 a ride).

Accommodation can be a real headache. There are cheap hotels in the old town, around Piazza Fontana, but most are grotty and some even possibly unsafe for women; the best choice is the *Sorrentino*, on Piazza Fontana (☎099/407456; ③), run by a woman, her daughter and two cats. There are pleasanter options in the modern city, although you pay for the surroundings. Cheapest is the *Imperiale* at Via Pitagora 94 (☎099/433019; ⑤). There's also a **youth hostel** near Martina Franca at SAN PAOLO (see p.759 for details), easily reached by bus from Piazza Castello. For **camping**, you have to head 10km south of the city, to Lido Bruno near CAPO SAN VITO: the *Sun Bay* (☎099/532.172; open all year) is right on the beach. Get there on the *Circola Rossa* and *Circola Nera* buses from Via d'Aquino, off Piazza Archita.

For **eating**, *La Nuova Grande Birreria*, Via Regina Margherita 43, is all things to all people – a restaurant, self-service joint, *távola calda* and pizzeria. Or check out the tourist menu at the *Ristorante Basile*, Via Pitagora 76, and the good local specialities at *Da Mimmo*, one block up at Via Giovinazzi 18.

Around Táranto

With some form of transport it's fairly easy to get away quickly from the city. One of the best targets, and only 13km to the southeast, is the coast beyond the adjacent small towns of **LEPORANO** and **PULSANO**, taken up by white sandy beaches flanked by pine woods. If you want to swim, consider the other direction too, west of the city, where a series of empty beaches stretches right along the **Golfo di Táranto** into Basilicata, pine woods again providing a cool escape from the August sun. The train stops at several small stations along this coast if you want to explore it further.

Inland from Táranto, due east of the city, the mildly undulating lands were once known as as "Albania Salentina", after the large numbers of Albanian refugees who settled here during the late fifteenth century, following the forced conversion of the Albanian population to Islam by the Turks. One of these Albanian settlements is **GROTTAGLIE**, only fifteen minutes by train from Táranto, honeycombed with caves, the *grotte* from which the town takes its name. It's been a centre of earthenware production since the tenth century and tucked away in the potters' quarter, under the shadow of Grottaglie's massive fourteenth-century castle, they're still making convincing replicas of ancient Greek ceramics. The town's roofs, walls and pavements – in fact any part of the town with a flat surface – are covered with stacks of earthenware pots, plates and amphorae.

Northwest of Táranto: ravines and cave-churches

Inland and **northwest** of the city, the scenery changes dramatically, gorges and ravines marking a landscape that's closer to that of Basilicata than Puglia. **MASSAFRA**, about 15km from Táranto (regular trains), is split in two by a ravine, the *Gravina di San Marco*, lined with grottoes dating mainly from the ninth to the fourteenth century. Many contain cave-churches, hewn out of the rock by Greek monks and decorated with lavish frescoes. Unfortunately, many are difficult to get to and badly signposted, but there are some that are relatively easily accessible, on the edge (quite literally) of the old town on Via del Santuario. A Baroque staircase runs down to the eighteenth-century **Santuario della Madonna della Scala**, built onto an earlier cave-church, which features a beautiful fresco of a Madonna and Child, dating from the twelfth to the thirteenth century – beyond which more steps lead down to an eighth-century crypt. The nearby **Cripta della Buona Nuova** houses a thirteenth-century fresco of the Madonna and a striking painting of Christ Pantocrator. About 200m away, at the bottom of the ravine, is a mass of interconnected caves known as the **Farmacia del Mago Greguro**, now in a pretty pitiful state but once used by the medieval monks as a herbalist's workshop.

Fifteen minutes further west by train, **CASTELLANETA** clings to the edge of another ravine, 145m deep and 350m wide, commanding some spectacular views over the Golfo di Táranto and the mountains of Basilicata. It, too, has a sprinkling of cave-churches, though it's better known as the birthplace of Rudolph Valentino – to whom the locals have erected a statue on the windy town square.

Easily the most spectacular of the ravine towns is **LATERZA**, close to the border of Basilicata. You can reach the town by *FSE* bus from Táranto's Piazza Castello. It's situated on the edge of one of the largest gorges in Puglia, 10km long, 200m deep and 500m wide in places – a Puglian "Grand Canyon", complete with buzzards and kites. Like the other ravine towns, the walls are scoured with cave-churches, over 180 of them dating from the eleventh century, of which about thirty can be visited. Contact the *Vigili Urbani* in town for information.

Bríndisi

Switching seas (Ionian to Adriatic), **BRÍNDISI** lies 60km east of Táranto, once a bridging point for crusading knights and still strictly a place for passing through. The natural harbour here, the safest on the Adriatic coast, made Bríndisi an ideal choice for early settlers. In Roman times, the port became the main crossing point between eastern and western empires, and later, under the Normans, there came a steady stream of pilgrims heading east towards the Holy Land. The route is still open, and now Bríndisi – primarily – is where you come if you're heading for Greece from Italy. First impression on arriving is that the entire town is full of shipping agents. This, when all is said and done, is the town's main business. But even if you're leaving the same night you'll almost certainly end up with time on your hands. You could just while away time in a bar or restaurant down the main Corso Garibaldi but the old town is pretty compact, and, although it isn't brimming with ancient monuments, has a pleasant, almost oriental, flavour about it – and a few things to see tucked down its narrow streets. And the town's *passeggiata* is one of the South's best.

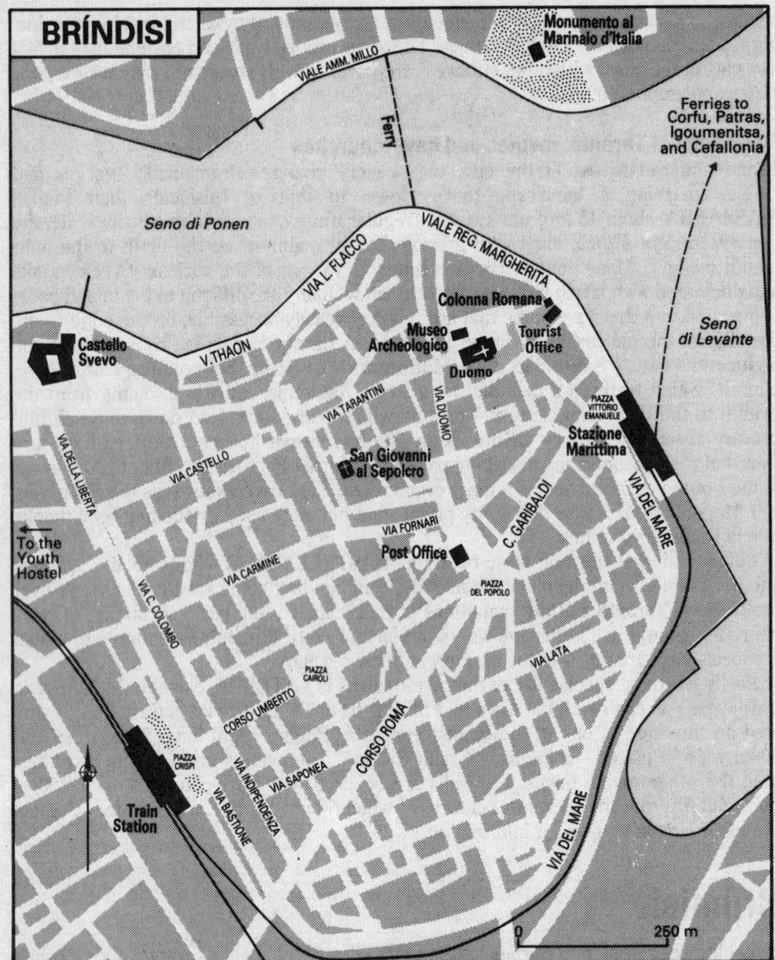

The town and around

At the top of a broad flight of steps known as the *Scalinata Virgiliana* (Virgil's Steps), the19m-high **Colonna Romana** dates back to the first century BC and marked the end of the ancient Via Appia, which ran all the way from the Porta Capena in Rome. A marble tablet in the corner of the piazza marks the supposed site of the house in which Virgil died, in 19 BC. Via Colonne, with its seventeenth- and eighteenth-century palazzi, runs up to the **Duomo** – a remarkable building, if only for the fact that it's survived seven earthquakes since its construction in the eleventh century. Just outside, the **Museo Archeologico Provinciale** (Mon–Sat 8.30am–1pm; free) stores ornaments and statues from the necropoli that lined the Via Appia in Roman times, as well as finds from the excavations at Egnázia. Follow Via Tarentini from here and bear left for the tiny round church of **San Giovanni al Sepolcro**, an eleventh-century baptistry. It's a little dark and decrepit inside, but you can just make out some of the original thirteenth-century frescoes. And there are more frescoes, this time a century earlier, in the **Chiesa di Santa Lucia**, just off Piazza del Popolo.

If you've got the time, take the little **ferry** which runs from Viale Regina Margherita, the *Seno di Ponente* (tickets L200 from the *Casalmare* office on the harbour), over the water to the **Monumento al Marinaio d'Italia**, erected in the 1930s as a memorial to Italian sailors. A lift runs up the 52m-high rudder-like edifice and gives some excellent views over town and coast. Bríndisi's most important medieval monument, though, is further afield: the **Chiesa di Santa Maria di Borgo Casale** – a 3km bus ride from town; take bus #3 (for the airport) and ask the driver when to get off. Built by Philip of Anjou at the end of the thirteenth century, it's an odd mixture of styles, the facade an Arabic mass of geometric patterns, worked in two shades of sandstone, and the portal with an almost Art Deco touch to it. The stark interior is rescued from gloom by some fourteenth-century frescoes depicting allegorical scenes relating to the Day of Judgment, a vision of hell designed to scare the living daylights out of the less devout.

Practicalities

Arriving by ferry at the **Stazione Marittima** leaves you on Via del Mare, from where it's a few minutes' walk to Piazza Vittorio Emanuele and the bottom of Corso Garibaldi, and another twenty minutes up to the **train station** the other side of the town centre in Piazza Crispi. The twice-daily **bus service** linking Bríndisi with Rome and Naples arrives at and departs from near the tourist office on Viale Reg. Margherita. The **airport** is 5km north of town and connected with the train station by regular *Alitalia* buses. For transport around town, lots of **buses** run down Corso Umberto and Corso Garibaldi (L700 a ride); **taxis** sit in ranks outside the train station. There's a helpful **tourist office** on Viale Regina Margherita (Mon–Sat 8.30am–12.30pm & 4.30–7.30pm).

Nearly all the ferries leave in the evening so **accommodation** isn't usually a problem. If you need to stay, the rock-bottom option is the *Locanda Doria* on Via Fulvia (☎0831/26.453; ③), but it's way out of town – walk down Via Appia to Via Arione and Via Fulvia is the second on the right. More central – and more expensive – are the *Hotel Villa Bianca*, Via Armengol 23 (☎0831/25.438; ③), and the *Venezia*, Via Pisanelli 6 (☎0831/25.411; ③). There are fairly cheap rooms, too, at the *Hotel Europa*, Piazza Cairoli 5 (☎0831/528.546; ④). The nearest **campsite** is *Camping Pineta al Mare* (☎0831/968.057), 18km northeast of town on the coast road, reached during the summer by local buses – details from the *STP* office on Piazza Cairoli. There's also a **youth hostel**, 2km out of town at Via Brandi 2 (☎0831/413.123; ①), reachable on bus #3 or #4 from the train station.

It's not difficult to **eat** cheaply in Bríndisi; the whole of Corso Umberto and Corso Garibaldi (particularly the port end) is smothered in bars and restaurants staffed by waiters who will chase you down the street with copies of the menu. You should be able to grab a complete meal for under L20,000. One favourite is the *Pizzeria L'Angoletto*, Via Pergola 3, just off Corso Garibaldi, which has outdoor tables and cheap local wine.

Listings

Exchange To buy/sell Greek drachmas, avoid the numerous exchange offices in town and stick to the banks, who shouldn't clobber you with exorbitant charges – though they might need persuading to deal with you. *Banco di Napoli* and *Credito Italiano* are both on Corso Garibaldi. The exchange office at the Stazione Marittima is open on Saturdays until 9pm, and the one at the main train station on Sundays too.

Hitching To get out of the city, ask around at the harbour as there's a steady stream of traffic, particularly around 10am and again at 4–5pm when the ferries arrive.

Post office Main office on Piazza Vittoria (Mon–Fri 8am–7.30pm, Sat 8.30am–noon).

Showers Public showers (L3000) beneath Piazza Cairoli.

Telephones There are *SIP* offices at Via XX Settembre 6 and the Stazione Marittima (both open daily 9am–8pm).

ONWARDS TO GREECE: FERRIES, TICKETS AND SOME TIPS

AGENTS

There is a staggering array of **agents** selling ferry tickets to Greece and you must take care to avoid getting ripped off. Ignore the touts clustered around the train station, who specialise in selling imaginary places on nonexistent boats, and *always* buy your ticket direct from the company's office or an approved agent. The **most reliable agencies** are *Hellitalia*, Via del Mare 6 (☎0831/222.988), and *UTAC Viaggi*, Via Cesare Braico 8, off Corso Umberto near the station (☎0831/560.780). *Grecian Travel*, Via Bastioni San Giorgio 20 (☎0831/222.884), can also handle bookings through to Turkey, Israel and Egypt, and give advice on the more seaworthy seasonal offers which crop up. **Peak period** (roughly mid-July to mid-August) is calamitous, and less reputable agents make crass overbookings: book well in advance or travel a month either side of these dates, when things are appreciably better.

FERRY COMPANIES

Ferry companies can't always be trusted either. Many appear overnight in July and August operating craft of questionable seaworthiness. A rough guide (though there are honourable exceptions) is that nearly all the reliable companies' ferries sail at night (between 9 and 10.30pm); only the pirates depart during the day. The companies listed below are not necessarily the cheapest, but their ferries will at least get you there: *Adriatica*, on the first floor of the Stazione Marittima (☎0831/523.825), to Corfu, Igoumenitsa and Patras; *Hellenic Mediterranean Lines*, Corso Garibaldi 8 (☎0831/528.531), destinations as above, and to Cefalonia, Paxi and Itaca with connections for Lefkada and Zakynthos included in the price; *Fragline*, Corso Garibaldi 88 (☎0831/521.589), to Corfu, Igoumenitsa and Patras. For full **schedules** get a timetable from the companies concerned, and see "Travel Details" at the end of this chapter. Roughly, though, *Adriatica* run virtually daily throughout the year; the others operate daily services between March and October.

PRICES AND OTHER THINGS

Prices vary considerably according to season. On the whole, *Adriatica* are the most expensive, *Fragline* the cheapest; you're looking at upwards of L50,000–70,000 one way in low/middle season to Corfu/Igoumenitsa or Patras, though less than double that for returns. *EurRail* pass holders go free, *InterRail* pass holders get a thirty percent discount; motorbikes go free in low season with *Fragline*. Everyone pays an **embarkation tax** – currently L10,000.

Leaving Italy, you must present your boarding card to the authorities at the Stazione Marittima (first floor); do it as soon as you have your ticket to avoid the crowds. Then, you should go to the terminal **at least two hours** before ship's departure, and make sure that any stopover you are making on the way to Patras is clearly marked on your ticket. Don't forget to **stock up on food and drink** in Bríndisi's supermarkets, as there are some serious mark-ups once on board.

West of Bríndisi: Ostuni

If you're stuck in Bríndisi for long enough, **OSTUNI**, 40km northwest of the town, represents a much better way of passing the time than moping around the centre and, just 35 minutes away by train, is one of the most stunning small towns of southern Italy. Situated on three hills at the southernmost edge of Le Murge, and an important Greco-Roman city in the first century AD, its old centre spreads across the highest of the hills, a gleaming white splash of sun-bleached streets and cobbled alleyways, dominating the plains below. The maze of streets makes for a fascinating amble and there are some exceptional views – particularly from Largo Castello over the woods to the north. Bits of cavorting rococo twist out of unexpected places, a reminder of Ostuni's erstwhile Spanish rulers – including an ornamented eighteenth-century obelisk, 21m high, dedicated to Saint Oronzo, which stands on the southern edge of the old town. Here, in Piazza Libertà, the **tourist office** dish out a useful map with suggested walks through the medieval maze of the old town.

Ostuni's proximity to a popular sandy coastline, 7km away, makes budget **accommodation** tricky to find. The *AAST* can help with private rooms in town, or you can go for one of two rather pricey hotels: the *Hotel Orchidea Nera* on Corso Mazzini (☎0831/301.366; ④), or the *Rex*, at Via G. di Vittorio 12 (☎0831/972.143; ④), for much the same price. For **eating**, there are a number of excellent restaurants in Ostuni, both higher up in the old town and in the new part, where *El Dorado*, Via F. Ayroldi 2, comes particularly recommended.

Of the **coastal resorts** accessible from Ostuni, there's more happening at **OSTUNI VILLANOVA** than OSTUNI MARINA: if you want to stay here, go for the *Baia del Re* at Villanova (☎0831/970.144) – doubles L60,000 a night.

Lecce and the Salentine peninsula

A fast 40km south from Bríndisi, Baroque **Lecce** is a place to linger, with some diverting Roman remains and a wealth of fine architecture scattered about an appealing old town area. It's also a good starting point for excursions further into the **Salentine peninsula**, which begins south of the city. Following its long association with traders and settlers, the landscape here begins to take on a distinctive Greek flavour, a mildly undulating region planted with carob, prickly pear and tobacco. The Adriatic coast is pitted with cliffs, topped with ruined watchtowers, with rugged coves and caves right the way down to the **southern cape**. The hinterland, by comparison, is more barren, although there's again a Greek element to it, with its tiny, sun-blasted villages growing out of the dry, stony, red earth and the flat-roofed houses painted in bright pastel colours.

Lecce

Whether or not you like the Baroque style, you can't fail to be impressed by the exuberant building styles on display in **LECCE**. Previously prey to opportunist attack, the city began a settled era signalled by the defeat of the Turkish fleet at Lepanto in 1571. The subsequent arrival of religious orders (Jesuits, the Teatini and Franciscans) brought an influx of wealth which was reflected in the building of opulent churches and palazzi, and it's this architectural extravagance that still pervades today's city. The flowery style of "Leccese Baroque" owed as much to the materials to hand as to the skills of the architects: the soft local sandstone could be intricately carved and then hardened with age. Unfortunately, modern pollution is in danger of ruining many of the buildings, keeping the mass of stonemasons and carpenters who still work in Lecce well occupied.

The City

Start in **Piazza Sant'Oronzo**, the hub of the old town, named after the first-century bishop of Lecce who went to the lions under Nero. His bronze statue lurches unsteadily from the top of the **Colonna di Sant'Oronzo** which once stood at the end of the Via Appia in Bríndisi. It resurfaced here in 1666 to honour Oronzo, who was credited with having spared the town from plague ten years earlier. The south side of the piazza is taken up by the weighty remains of the **Anfiteatro Romano**, which probably dates from the time of Hadrian. In its heyday it seated 20,000 spectators, and it's still used in summer for concerts and plays. Sadly, though, most of its decorative bas-reliefs, of fighting gladiators and wild beasts, have been removed to the town's museum for safe-keeping, and nowadays it looks rather depleted.

The best of Lecce's Baroque churches are all a short distance from Piazza Sant'Oronzo. The finest, certainly the most ornate, is the **Basilica di Santa Croce**, just to the north, whose florid facade, the work of the local architect Antonio Zimbalo, took around 150 years to complete, its upper half a riot of decorative garlands and flowers around a central rose window. The **Church of Santa Chiara**, in the opposite direction on Piazza V. Emanuele, is similarly loaded down with ornament, its interior full of little chapels groaning with garlands and gilt. There's more Baroque extravagance on offer on Via Vittorio Emanuele, where the **Church of Sant'Irene** houses the most sumptuous of Lecce's Baroque altars – lavishly frosted and gilded, and smothered with decoration. Nearby, facing onto Piazza del Duomo, the **Seminario** holds an impressively ornate well, carved stone masquerading as delicately wrought iron. Next door, the balconied **Palazzo Vescovile** adjoins the **Duomo** itself, twelfth century in origin but rebuilt entirely in the mid-seventeenth century by Zimbalo. He tacked on two ornate facades and an enormous five-storeyed campanile that towers 70m above the square; you'll need to track down the sacristan to be let in.

There's further work by Zimbalo in the **Church of San Giovanni Battista** (or del Rosario), by the Porta Rudiae in the southwest corner of town – the ornate facade and twisting columns fronting some extremely odd altars, dumpy cherubim diving for cover amid scenes resembling an exploding fruitbowl. But if the Baroque trappings of the town are beginning to pall, there's the odd relic from other eras too, not least a well-preserved **Teatro Romano** near the church of Santa Chiara, the only one of its kind to be found in Puglia, with its rows of seats and orchestra floor still remarkably intact. There's also the fine Romanesque church of **Santi Nicola e Cataldo**, built by the Normans in 1190, with a cool interior that reveals a generous hint of Saracen influence in the arches and the octagonal rounded dome. Little remains of the frescoes that once covered its walls, though an image of San Nicola can be found on the south side, together with a delicately carved portal. One more stop you should make, near the railway station on the other side of town, is the **Museo Provinciale** (Mon–Fri 9am–1pm & 3.30–5.30pm, Sun 9am–1pm; free), which has finds from the old Roman town, including decorative panels from the amphitheatre, and some religious gold and silverwork.

Practicalities

Regional **buses** arrive at the Porta Napoli, or at the *FSE* bus station on Via Adua. **Trains**, both *FS* and *FSE*, use the same station, a kilometre south of the centre, at the end of Via Oronzo Quarta. The sixteenth-century **Palazzo Sedile**, on Piazza Sant'Oronzo, holds the **tourist office** (Mon–Sat 9am–1pm & 5.30–7.30pm).

The cheapest **place to stay** is the *Albergo Faggiano*, near the castle at Via Cavour 4 (☎0832/42.854; ④), though it's pretty basic; if your budget will run to it, give yourself a treat and book in at the *Patria*, opposite the church of Santa Croce (☎0832/29.431; ⑦), an elegant hotel wholly in keeping with Lecce's Baroque flavour. Otherwise, the tourist office can help you find a private room in someone's home. The nearest **youth hostel** is the *Ostello per la Gioventu Adriatico*, on the beach in MARINA DI SAN CATALDO

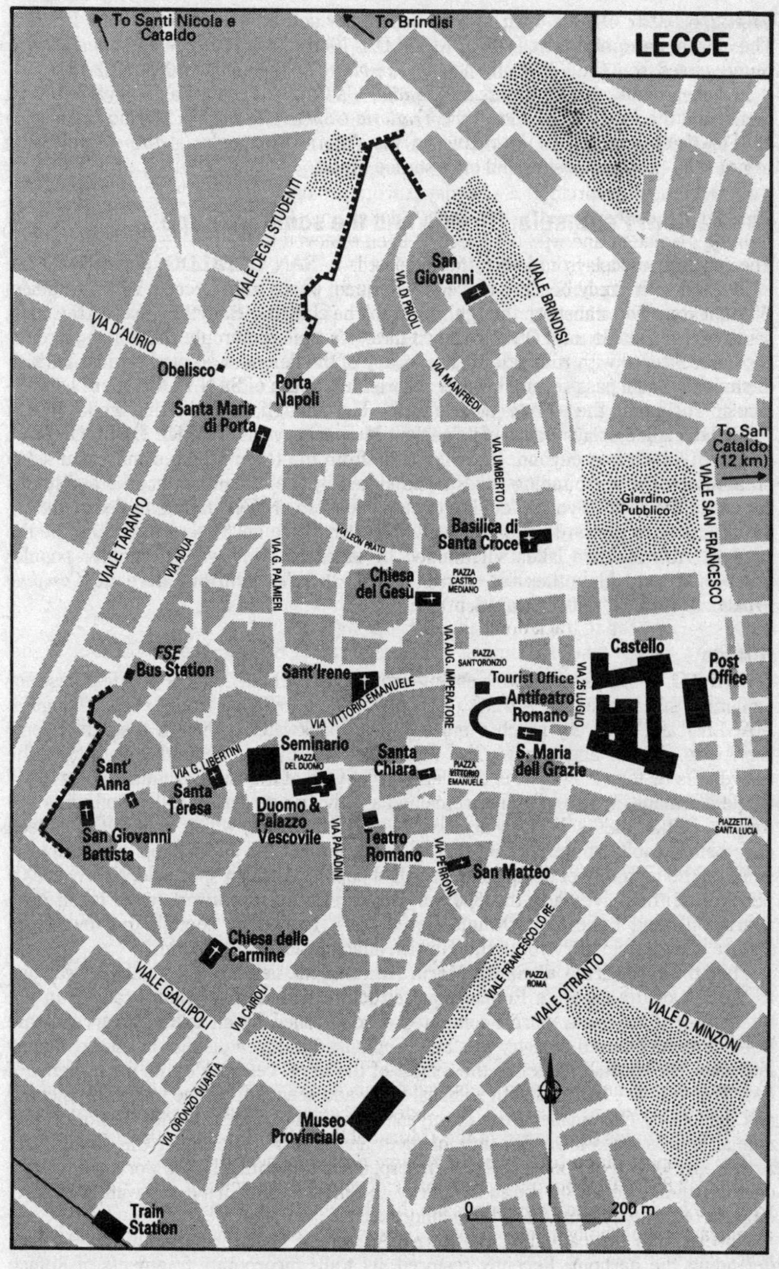

LECCE
To Santi Nicola e Cataldo
To Bríndisi
To San Cataldo (12 km)
VIALE DEGLI STUDENTI
VIA D'AURIO
Obelisco
Porta Napoli
Santa Maria di Porta
San Giovanni
VIA DI PRIOLI
VIALE BRINDISI
VIA MANFREDI
VIA UMBERTO I
Giardino Pubblico
VIALE SAN FRANCESCO
Basilica di Santa Croce
VIA LEON PRATO
VIA G. PALMIERI
VIALE TARANTO
VIA ADUA
Chiesa del Gesù
PIAZZA CASTRO MEDIANO
PIAZZA SANT'ORONZIO
Castello
Post Office
FSE Bus Station
Sant'Irene
VIA VITTORIO EMANUELE
VIA AUG. IMPERATORE
Tourist Office
VIA 25 LUGLIO
Antifeatro Romano
S. Maria dell Grazie
Seminario
PIAZZA DEL DUOMO
VIA G. LIBERTINI
Santa Chiara
PIAZZA VITTORIO EMANUELE
Sant' Anna
Santa Teresa
Duomo & Palazzo Vescovile
VIA PALADINI
Teatro Romano
VIA PERRONI
San Matteo
San Giovanni Battista
PIAZZETTA SANTA LUCIA
Chiesa delle Carmine
VIALE FRANCESCO LO RE
PIAZZA ROMA
VIALE OTRANTO
VIALE D. MINZONI
VIALE GALLIPOLI
VIA CAIROLI
VIA ORONZO QUARTA
Museo Provinciale
0
200 m
Train Station

(☎0832/650.026; ①). It's open May to September and buses run from Viale Bríndisi. The closest **campsite** is at TORRE RINALDA, 10km north of Lecce and open all year round; buses from the Villa Comunale to *Camping Torre Rinalda* (☎0832/652.161).

For cheap **eats**, the *Ristorante da Claudio*, Via Cavour 11, does a good-value tourist menu; and the food's good, too, at the *Trattoria Gambero Rosso*, Via Marino Brancaccio 16. For quick **snacks**, *La Rusticana* on Via Vittorio Emanuele (at the side of Santa Irene) sells excellent pasties and olive-stuffed bread.

The Eastern Peninsula: Otranto and the southern cape

The quickest escape from Lecce to the coast is to **SAN CATALDO**, popular with the locals, and with sandy beaches served by frequent buses from Lecce's Villa Comunale. Without your own transport, though, you won't be able to see anything else of the coast south of San Cataldo until Otranto. If you have, it's a pleasant route south along a rocky shoreline littered with ruined towers, a legacy of the defences erected against Turkish incursions. You'll pass several low-key resorts. Just south of **SAN FOCA** there's a spectacular rockpool, the *Grotta della Poesia*, big enough to swim in; while **ROCA VECCHIA** still displays traces of its ancient Messapian walls. **TORRE DELL'ORSO**, a couple of kilometres beyond, takes its name from the tower which stands on a stony promontory, the surrounding coves pockmarked by the remains of houses and tombs cut out of the rock. If you're looking to stay, the *Casa del Turista* at San Foca (☎0832/841.006; ④) is right on the coastal road. Between Torre dell'Orso and Otranto lie the **Lagi di Alimini**, two lakes surrounded by extensive pine woods, another popular green stop on this otherwise barren coast; there's **camping** here at *Camping Frassanito* (☎0833/85.005; May–Sept).

Otranto

OTRANTO, a minuscule town nestling around its harbour, makes an ideal base for exploring this part of the Adriatic. It's only an hour by train from Lecce (change at MAGLIE) and still very much a quiet Puglian backwater – though a summer ferry service to Greece and a new *Club Med* affair nearby are beginning to attract the crowds. Its history, however, is decidedly grim. One of the last Byzantine towns to fall to the Normans, in 1070, Otranto remained a thriving port for crusaders, pilgrims and traders. But in 1480 a Turkish fleet laid siege to the town, which held out for fifteen days before capitulating. It's said that as a punishment the archbishop, upon capture, suffered the indignity of being sawn in half, a popular Turkish spectacle. Nearly 12,000 people lost their lives and the 800 survivors, refusing to convert, were taken up a nearby hill and beheaded. Otranto never really recovered, though the town does feature one glorious survivor of the Turkish attack inside its cathedral.

This, the **Cattedrale di Santa Maria Annunziata**, lies down a small alleyway just to the left of the castle, a Romanesque structure with a rose window added in the fifteenth century and a marble-columned nave adorned by an extraordinary **mosaic floor**, a multicoloured tapestry in stone. Composed in three distinct but interconnecting parts, the mosaic stretches the length of the nave, centring on its main theme of the "Tree of Life", adorned with zodiacal signs and scenes from the medieval calendar and flanked by two smaller trees in the aisles depicting biblical scenes. Historical and animal figures are shown as a mix of myth and reality – Alexander the Great, King Arthur, the Queen of Sheba, crabs, fish, serpents and mermaids. The work of a twelfth-century monk, for all its rough simplicity the mosaic provides a captivating picture, empowered by a delightful child-like innocence.

Not far from the cathedral, the town's Aragonese **Castello** juts out into the bay, defending the harbour. Recently restored, its walls incorporate fragments of Roman and medieval inscriptions, while Charles V's coat-of-arms looms from its portal. Outside on a dusty square, old men still play a highly animated form of *boules*, impervious to passers-by. Out on the southern edge of town is the hill, covered with cypress trees, where the survivors of the Turkish siege were beheaded. At the top of the hill, the sixteenth-century **Chiesa di San Francesco di Paola** holds inscriptions of the names of the victims, together with a vivid description of the terrible events of July 1480.

If you want **to stay** in Otranto, your best bet is the *Pensione Bellavista*, Via Vittorio Emanuele 16 (☎0836/86.359; ④). The nearest **campsite** is signposted from the port, *Campeggio Hydrusa* (☎0836/801.255), open May to August. There are some excellent **fish restaurants** in town, like *Il Gambero* at the Porta Terra. Also, there's a variety of musical and theatrical events in Otranto throughout summer, usually centred around the castle, and an annual **festival** commemorating the "800 Martyrs" on August 13–15. Details and other information are available from the **tourist office**, Via Rondachi 8, near the cathedral (Mon–Fri 9am–1pm & 4.30–6pm).

If you're heading **to Greece**, *R Line* operates a ferry to Corfu and Igoumenitsa between June and late September, Monday to Friday at 10.30pm. Tickets cost L80,000 one way: buy them from the office at the port.

To the southern cape

From Otranto, all the way down to the cape at Santa Maria di Leuca, the coastline is steep and rugged. **CAPO D'OTRANTO**, five kilometres south of Otranto, is the most easterly point on the Italian peninsula, topped by a lighthouse and the rather desolate ruins of a seventh-century abbey. On a clear day there's a commanding view across the Straits, the mountains of Albania visible about 80km away. (On seriously clear days they say you can even see Corfu, 100km away.) **CASTRO**, about 30km down the coast, is the nicest of the towns around here. Fortified by the Aragonese in the twelfth century, it lies slightly inland, 100m above the small fishing hamlet of Castro Marina, the rocky creek serving as a harbour – and reputedly the landing place of the Trojan hero Aeneas. The area hereabouts is full of grottoes, the most spectacular and easiest to reach the **Grotta Zinzulusa**, a little way north of Castro Marina. An iridescent mass of stalactites and stalagmites, its dark waters are home to a rather odd species of blind fish. If you feel confident enough to explore a grotto by swimming, ask around in **MARINA D'ANDRANO** (about 6km down the coast from Castro Marina) for the unsignposted **Grotta Verde**, which is splendidly phosphorescent.

There isn't really much to draw you down as far as **SANTA MARIA DI LEUCA**, a somewhat barren spot that's a fitting "land's end", with a scattering of Neolithic remains and an uninspiring marina. The once-supposed "end of the world" is marked by the tiny church of **Santa Maria Finibus Terrae**, built on the site of an ancient temple dedicated to Minerva, which stands perched on the white limestone cliffs. But it's all a bit of an anticlimax: even the cape isn't really the southernmost point, that distinction going to the Punta Ristola, a little to the west. You can get down this far, or at least as far as GAGLIANO DEL CAPO, by train: it's at the end of the *FSE* rail line, just 5km from the cape, and hitching the rest should be possible in the summer months.

The Western Peninsula: Galatina, Nardo and Gallipoli

About half an hour down the rail line from Lecce, **GALATINA** is one of the most intriguing of the Salentine towns. It remained a key Greek colony well into medieval times, while retaining Greek customs and language up until the present century. Today, it's an important centre of the Italian tobacco industry, with much of the weed grown in the fields around, as well as being famed for its excellent local wine.

Most interestingly, Galatina is the only place in the Salentine where the phenomenon of **tarantulism** still survives. Once a year, on the feast day of saints Peter and Paul (June 28/29), the devout gather at the church dedicated to the saints to perform a ritual – the origins of which go back to the outbursts of mass hysteria that swept Europe in the wake of frequent plagues from the fourteenth century onwards. Victims of the dreaded tarantula bite would come here to give thanks for their survival from the spider's venom. Actually, the tarantula itself wasn't the culprit, but another smaller spider. In any case, the bite induced hallucinogenic symptoms, vomiting and paranoia, and those bitten believed that the only way to survive was to sweat the poison out of the system. This gave rise to a frenzied dance, which could last for days. During the nineteenth century the tarantella, as it was known, was modified into the colourful, popular dance that you see here today.

Fifteen kilometres west of Galatina, reachable by train, **NARDO** is a busy little town with a long and turbulent history of sackings, rebellions and occupations. Despite that, the centre of town, based around Piazza Antonio Salandra and Piazza San Domenico, retains some fine buildings in a more or less preserved state: there's an odd amalgam of ornately sculpted palazzi and bold facades, a fortified town hall and an eighteenth-century *guglia*, or obelisk, similar to the one in Ostuni.

By way of contrast, first impressions of **GALLIPOLI** are fairly uninspiring. The new town sprouted on the mainland once the population outgrew its original island site in the eighteenth century, and all that remains of the once-beautiful city (the *Kalli-pollis*) of the Greeks is a rather weatherbeaten fountain, which sits in the new town near the bridge. Over the bridge, the old town itself is a maze of meandering and twisting white-washed streets, tiny tomatoes hanging on the walls to dry, providing a sudden blaze of colour alongside the fishing nets. Only the familiar Aragonese castle, which squats in one corner of the island, serves as a reminder that this is still Italy.

The Beaches

There are some excellent **beaches** along this part of the coast, all fairly accessible by bus from Gallipoli. The *Baia Verde*, just to the south of the town, is highly popular in summer, though the beaches to the north, near the tiny villages of **SANTA CATERINA** and **SANTA MARIA AL BAGNO**, are better. Although there's been a spate of hotel building in recent years, this stretch remains one of the quietest spots in southern Italy, making it a good place to rest up for a while and see the coast. For **accommodation in Gallipoli**, try the *Pensione Pescatore* on Riviera C. Colombo (☎0883/473.656; ④), overlooking the sea in the old quarter; and there are a couple of good **campsites** nearby, both 3km from town at TORRE SABEA.

travel details

Trains

Altamura to: Gravina in Puglia (13 daily; 12min).

Bari to: Altamura (13 daily; 1hr 10min); Andria (hourly; 1hr); Barletta (hourly 1hr 10min); Bitonto (hourly; 20min); Bríndisi (hourly; 2hr); Grotte di Castellana/Putignano/Alberobello/Locorotondo/Martina Franca (*Ferrovia Sud-Est*; hourly; 50min/1hr/1hr 30min/1hr 40min/1hr 50min); Gravina in Puglia/Spinazzola (3 daily; 1hr 15min/1hr 45min); Lecce (hourly; 2hr 45min); Molfetta/(14 daily; 25min); Naples/Rome (4–6 daily; 4hr 30min/6hr); Ostuni (hourly; 1hr); Ruvo di Puglia (hourly; 40min); Táranto (hourly; 2hr); Torre a Mare/Polignano a Mare/ Monopoli (hourly; 10min/30min/35min); Trani (14 daily; 40min).

Barletta to: Canosa di Puglia (9 daily; 1hr).

Bríndisi to: Lecce (hourly; 50min); Ostuni (hourly; 35min).

Foggia to: Bari (hourly; 1hr 30min); Barletta (hourly; 40min); Manfredonia (9 daily; 30min);

Molfetta (hourly; 1hr 5min); San Severo/Péschici (5 daily; 40min/2hr 15min); Trani (hourly; 50min).

Lecce to: Bari (hourly; 2hr); Gallipoli (9 daily; 1hr); Otranto (7 daily; 1hr); Gagliano del Capo (10 daily; 1hr 30min); Rome (1 daily; 9hr 30min).

Martina Franca to: Táranto (8 daily; 40min).

San Severo to: Péschici (7 daily; 1hr 40min).

Táranto to: Bari (16 daily; 2hr 20min); Grottaglie (11 daily; 15min); Massafra/Castellaneta (12 daily; 15min/30min); Metaponto/Reggio di Calabria (3 daily; 50min/6hr); Bríndisi (12 daily; 1hr).

Buses

Bari to: Andria (7 daily; 1hr 30min); Canosa di Puglia (11 daily; 2hr 10min) Molfetta/Trani/Barletta (3–4 hourly; 40min/1hr 5min/1hr 25min); Margherita di Savoia (8 daily; 1hr 45min).

Foggia to: Manfredonia (8–10 daily; 50min); Vieste (5 daily; 2hr 45min).

Manfredonia to: Bari (1 daily; 2hr 20min); Monte Sant'Angelo (every 2hr; 55min); San Giovanni Rotondo (14 daily; 40min); San Marco in Lamis (10 daily; 1hr); Vico del Gargano (2 daily; 2hr 15min); Vieste (2 daily; 1hr 40min).

Molfetta to: Ruvo di Puglia (hourly; 30min).

Péschici to: Rodi Garganico (3 daily; 35min); San Severo (1 daily; 3hr); Vico del Gárgano (1 daily; 45min).

Rodi Garganico to: Vico del Gargano/Foresta Umbra (2 daily; 40min/1hr 5min).

Vico del Gargano to: Ischitella (9 daily; 15min).

Vieste to: Foggia (2 daily; 2hr 45min); Manfredonia (3 daily; 1hr 40min); Péschici (9 daily; 45min).

Ferries

Manfredonia to: the Vieste/Péschici/Rodi Garganico/Tremiti Islands (mid-June–mid-Sept 1 daily; early June & late Sept 4 weekly; April–mid-May 2 weekly; 2hr/3hr/3hr 40min/5hr 20min).

International ferries

There's usually at least one daily service from Bríndisi to the Greek ports throughout the year; services increase between April and September; and mid-June to August is peak season with several sailings a day to most destinations.

Bríndisi to: Corfu/Igoumenitsa (at least 1 daily; 9hr 30min/11hr); Patras (at least 1daily; 7hr); Paxi (1 daily; 13hr); Ithaca (1 daily; 17hr); Cefalonia (1 daily; 18hr).

Bari to: Corfu/Igoumenitsa/Patras (June–Sept 1 daily , otherwise 3 weekly; 12hr/13hr/26hr).

Otranto to: Corfu/Igoumenitsa (June–Sept 5 weekly; 9hr 30min/13hr).

CHAPTER FIFTEEN

CALABRIA AND BASILICATA

More than any other of the regions of the Italian South, **Calabria** and **Basilicata** represent the quintessence of the *mezzogiorno*. Culturally impoverished, underdeveloped and – owing to emigration – sparsely populated, these rural regions were long considered only good for taxation, and even then they were mismanaged. The feudal era didn't really die here until the Bourbons were ejected at Unification, and remnants of the older society persist in the exaggerated use of titles and the widespread system of patronage. Respect for authority coexists with a deep scepticism, an apathy and inertia vividly described by Carlo Levi in his *Christ Stopped at Eboli* – a book that for many Italians was the introduction to the very deep problems besetting the *mezzogiorno*.

Indeed, this area is if anything even more marginalised than it was before Unification, when it was at least the geographical centre of the Bourbon state, and today talk of the Two Nations of Italy is most strikingly manifest in what can seem a very distant region from the emphatically European North – to which its people provide a reluctant supply of cheap labour. But despite the lingering of attitudes on both sides that perpetuate this gulf, much has changed in the South, to the extent that the picture drawn in Levi's book would hardly be recognised today, thanks largely to a massive channelling of funds since the war to finance huge irrigation and land-reclamation schemes, industrial development and a modern system of communications, all helping to set the southern economy on its feet. Unemployment remains the highest in the country, and emigration is still very much a reality, but malaria has been eradicated, previously unproductive land made fertile, and construction is underway everywhere – though often hand-in-hand with the forces of organised crime and with frequently dire consequences for the physical aspect of the land.

On the whole it is the landscape that's the main reason for coming to Basilicata and Calabria. Artistically they are the most barren regions in Italy, but the combination of mountain grandeur and a relatively unspoilt coastline, often in close proximity, are a unique attraction, and one only beginning to be exploited by the tourist industry. The **main cities – Reggio**, **Catanzaro**, **Potenza** – are useful as transport hubs only, although **Matera**, the second city of Basilicata, holds a distinctive feature in its Sassi – cavelike dwellings in the heart of the town that were until relatively recently occupied by the poorest of its townspeople. And **Cosenza**, halfway down the Tyrrhenian coast, has a charm of a kind and can make a vibrant stopoff if you're beach-bumming. Of the coasts, it's the **Tyrrhenian** that is the more obviously appealing, with spots like **Maratea**, **Tropea** and **Scilla** well on their way to becoming discovered. The **Ionian** coast, on the other hand, can be bleak and is visited mainly for its **ancient sites** – relics from the days when the area was an important colonial corner of Magna Graecia. Inland, Italy's boot rises to a high and rugged core, ranging from the Norman strongholds of Basilicata to the forested slopes of the **Sila massif** around Cosenza and the craggy wilderness of **Aspromonte**, long the haunt of brigands and their *mafiosi* descendants.

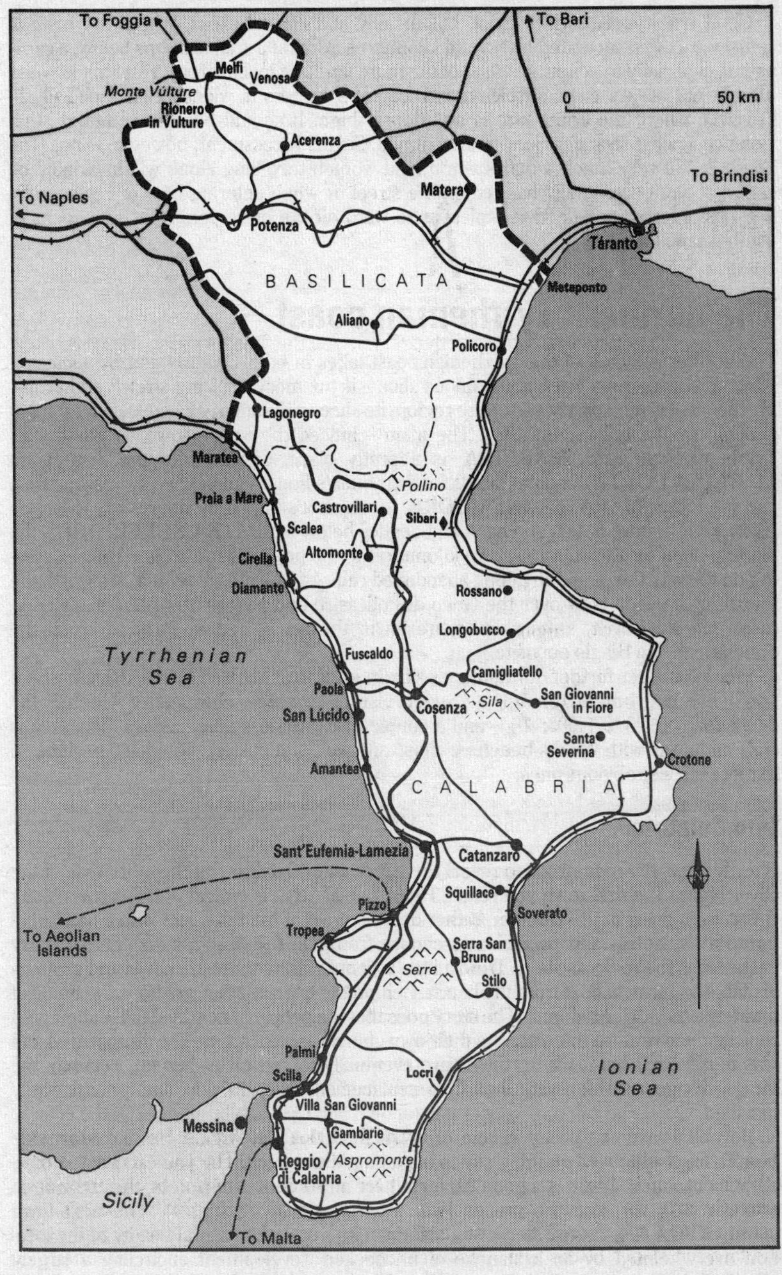
To Foggia
To Bari
Melfi
Venosa
Monte Vúlture
Rionero in Vulture
0
50 km
Acerenza
To Brindisi
Matera
To Naples
Potenza
Táranto
BASILICATA
Metaponto
Aliano
Policoro
Lagonegro
Maratea
Pollino
Praia a Mare
Castrovillari
Sibari
Scalea
Altomonte
Cirella
Rossano
Diamante
Longobucco
Tyrrhenian Sea
Fuscaldo
Camigliatello
Paola
Cosenza
Sila
San Giovanni in Fiore
San Lúcido
Santa Severina
Crotone
Amantea
CALABRIA
Sant'Eufemia-Lamezia
Catanzaro
Squillace
Pizzo
Soverato
To Aeolian Islands
Tropea
Serra San Bruno
Serre
Stilo
Palmi
Ionian Sea
Locri
Scilla
Villa San Giovanni
Messina
Gambarie
Reggio di Calabria
Aspromonte
Sicily
To Malta

Good **transport** services exist, but in hilly and coastal areas, where the historic centres are often separated by several kilometres from their train stations below, a car is useful, especially to penetrate some of the more far-flung inland areas. Hitching is possible but not always easy: suspicion and fear of strangers is widespread, especially in Calabria, where the crime rate is notoriously high. It should be added, though, that violence against strangers is very uncommon. Sexual harassment, however, is not. The South is still very much a man's world, and women travelling alone will invariably be stared at and occasionally hassled on the street or when entering bars or restaurants. See *Basics* for some effective expletives to ward off the more persistent specimens of southern manhood.

The northern Tyrrhenian coast

The northern stretch of the Tyrrhenian coast takes in both Calabria and Basilicata, of which the former – a brief mountainous slice – is the most inspiring stretch and probably the most visited part of the entire region, its sheer cliffs and rocky coves refreshingly unspoilt by the holiday industry. The main – indeed the only – town on Basilicata's Tyrrhenian seaboard, **MARATEA**, is a pretty place, divided into the districts of **MARATEA PORTO**, a quaint huddle of fishermen's houses and expensive restaurants, and the larger **MARATEA INFERIORE**, to which it's linked by hourly bus. Maratea Inferiore has more hotels and bars, and nestles below **MARATEA SUPERIORE** – the starting-point for the climb (a steep kilometre) to the peak of **Monte San Biagio**, passing on the way the straggling, long-abandoned ruins of **Maratea Vecchia**. It's worth the effort for the wide view over the Golfo di Policastro and a close-up of Maratea's enormous marble Christ, arms akimbo, frozen in the act of setting forth to crush the Santuario di San Biagio opposite.

Five kilometres further down, there's a **train station** at **MARATEA MARINA**, where you'll also find **hotels** (though not much else of appeal) – cheapest of which is the *Marisdea* (☎0973/879.003; ⑦) – and a couple of **campsites** near the sea. The area is well endowed with sandy **beaches**: most are well signposted, but don't hesitate to explore the less obvious ones.

Into Calabria

Shortly after, the road drops to reveal the flat coast of Calabria, on the other side of the River Noce. The first town you reach, **PRAIA A MARE**, is typical of the resorts along this coast – lively in the summer, rather dead the rest of the time, and with a handful of **campsites, hotels** and **pizzerias** to choose from. On the beach, a sixteenth-century castle faces the rocky **Isola di Dino** a little way out, where there are caves and grottoes visitable by hiring a boat from the beach. Behind the town another **grotto** is the home of a widely venerated Madonna. The story goes that the people of nearby AIETA attempted repeatedly to remove this image to their own church, but each time she disappeared and was found back here, where they were eventually forced to let her be. Recently the image disappeared forever, though a replacement was quickly and pragmatically installed.

Beyond Praia, the pretty village of **SAN NICOLA ARCELLA** has a lovely wide **beach**, from which – through a series of passages and a tunnel – you can get to other, emptier beaches. There is a good **pizzeria** here and a couple of **hotels**, the *Brillantino* (☎0985/3280; ④), and the pricier *Villa Principe* (☎0985/3125; ⑥). The next town south, **SCALEA**, is quite different – Calabria at its worst, the natural beauty of the location overwhelmed by an avalanche of unchecked development encircling a largely abandoned old quarter. Stop here to visit the ruins of the Norman/Aragonese castle and a frescoed eleventh-century Byzantine chapel, bombed by both sides during the war (the *famiglia* Grisolia holds the key). Then move on.

South of Scalea, excavations are under way on the banks of the River Lao that may bring to light the remains of ancient **Laos**, colonised by the Sybarites following the destruction of their city (see"Sibari", p.797). The seaside town of **CIRELLA** was also a Sybarite colony, devastated by Hannibal, then Romanised, though the theatrical ruins of **Cirella Vecchia**, overlooking the SS18, are of a later date, the result of a French bombardment in 1806 (though local lore attributes other, more sinister explanations, most notably a plague of ants). From behind the ruins a road leads to the hilltop villages of GRISOLIA and MAIERA, close together on the map but actually divided by a gully, across which you may hear conversations being conducted from one village to the other.

Five kilometres down the coast, **DIAMANTE**, glistening on its small promontory, is a chic seaside town, rather arty, its narrow whitewashed lanes adorned with vast and striking modern murals – though it's looking rather faded these days. A brief walk away from the seafront and over a bridge, *Il Giardino* is an averagely priced **pizzeria** where you can sit outside and eat good seafood.

BELVEDERE MARITTIMO, some 10km down the coast, overlooks its unexceptional marina from a spur a little way inland; it's an imposing and elegant town, full of greenery and having little of the air of neglect typical of Calabria's older centres. Eat at the *Perrera Trattoria* (well marked), and visit its impressive **castle**, originally a Norman construction but rebuilt under the Aragonese, whose coat-of-arms can be seen above the main gate. Its restoration is being planned, and for the moment you can only get in between 6pm and 8pm daily.

CITTADELLA has good **beaches** and the grand *San Michele* hotel just beyond – one of the last of an Edwardian generation of hotels, with a golf course and a lift down to the beach at the base of the cliff. Further down, **CETRARO** has a decent bar, the *Caffè Muliti*, on Via Macchia di Mare, where you can sit outside and cool off from the beach with an ice cream or beer. **GUARDIA PIEMONTESE** was once the home of a community of Protestant refugees from the north of Italy who were brutally suppressed by the Inquisition in 1560, as the name of one of the gates round the still partly intact city walls recalls: *Porta della Strage*, "Gate of the Slaughter". From here, with the wind blowing in the right direction, you can't fail to notice the musty odours emitted from nearby **TERME LUIGIANE**, a popular hot springs.

Paola . . . and south

Next down the coast, **PAOLA**'s size and importance is partly due to its function as the main rail and road junction for Cosenza, partly to its **Santuario di San Francesco di Paola**, in a ravine above the town. San Francesco spent most of his life in the town and, as Calabria's principal saint, is venerated throughout the South. People visit the shrine at all times in the year, but particularly during the week leading up to the May 4 **festa** – when a fair occupies the town, with daily festivities culminating in the carrying of his statue into the sea and a grand display of fireworks on the beach at midnight. There are several **hotels** and **trattorias** around the station by the sea and a good **pizzeria** near the central piazza above – *Renato*, in via del Cannone – though if you want to sleep over, **SAN LÚCIDO**, 6km south, is more attractive. The *Hotel Irma* (☎0982 81330; ④), near the seafront, is a nice place to stay, and close by there's one of the best **trattorias** in the region, *La Rupe*, on the cliff in the old centre.

The series of small towns and villages that follow are all split between the original centres located higher up from the shore and more modern marinas – good for beaches but visually uninteresting. The older villages are difficult to get to but, if you can manage it, are worth the hike. **FIUMEFREDDO** has cobbled streets leading to a pleasant lookout perched above a sheer drop and a strange and dilapidated **castle** – a good place for picnics. **BELMONTE**, just beyond, has a mausoleum – easily visible as you pass below – dedicated to its greatest son, **Michele Bianchi**, one of the *quadrumvirate* of Fascists who marched on Rome in 1922, and for a while Mussolini's deputy. **AMANTEA** is the largest and liveliest of the chain, with beaches (either in the town itself or 3km south) and a wide choice of **eating places**; try the *Lanterna Rossa* on the main shopping street of the lower part of town, Via Margherita. If you feel like staying, the *Pensione Margherita* is on the same street (☎0982/41.337; ③). As for things to see, there's the fifteenth-century church and convent of **San Barnardino di Siena**, with majolica decoration and a sculpture by Gagini, up towards the old town, and a fine **castle** overlooking the town – easily visible and always accessible (free). If you like castles, there's another one nearby; take the turning at CÁMPORA SAN GIOVANNI for CLETO, close to the Savuto River.

Cosenza and around

COSENZA, Calabria's first town of any size if you're travelling from the North, is also the region's most interesting, and makes a useful base to explore the surrounding area, particularly the **Sila** mountains. Historically it has always played an important role in the commercial and intellectual life of Calabria (Norman Douglas wrote, with characteristic hyperbole, "for acute and original thought this town can hardly be surpassed by any other of its size on earth"), and recently the town has generated a degree of wealth which – while still some way below most of Italy – has in the last twenty years or so literally transformed the landscape. New construction, much of it featureless and ugly, has sprouted everywhere, while its recently established university is expanding fast, helping to create a new and strong regional awareness and self-confidence.

Completely enclosed by mountains – the Sila on the east, the Catena Costiera separating it from the sea to the west – Cosenza is the meeting point of two rivers, the Crati and the Busento. Somewhere beneath the latter, tradition has the burial place of **Alaric the Goth**, the barbarian who gave the western world a jolt when he finally managed to prise open the gates of Rome in 410 AD. Struck down for his sins by malaria while on his way south, he was interred here along with his booty, and the course of the river deviated to cover the traces, lending Cosenza a place in history and giving rise to countless (and fruitless) projects to discover the tomb's whereabouts.

The Town

The two rivers form a neat division between old and new Cosenza, with the main artery of the newer town, **Corso Mazzini**, running off south from their junction. This is the liveliest place to be, but most of the things worth seeing are located in the old part, the **centro storico**, a compact knot of steps and alleys rising up to a sturdy Swabian castle. Much of the old town has been abandoned in favour of the newer suburbs to the north, and the area is unfairly denigrated as a ghetto, the haunt of *mafiosi*, delinquents and prostitutes. But there's a tranquillity here that the rest of the town lacks, and more character and charm than most other places in Calabria.

From Piazza Valdesi on the far side of the bridge, Corso Telesio leads off into the old quarter's confusion of narrow streets. This main road of the area is named after Cosenza's most famous son, **Bernardino Telesio**, the sixteenth-century humanist philosopher and major influence on the other great Calabrian philosopher, Tommaso Campanella. Halfway up, Cosenza's stately **Duomo** stands in a square of tall dilapidated palaces. Consecrated on the occasion of Frederick II's visit to the city in 1222, its Provençal Gothic style was later modified by Baroque accretions – though sporadic

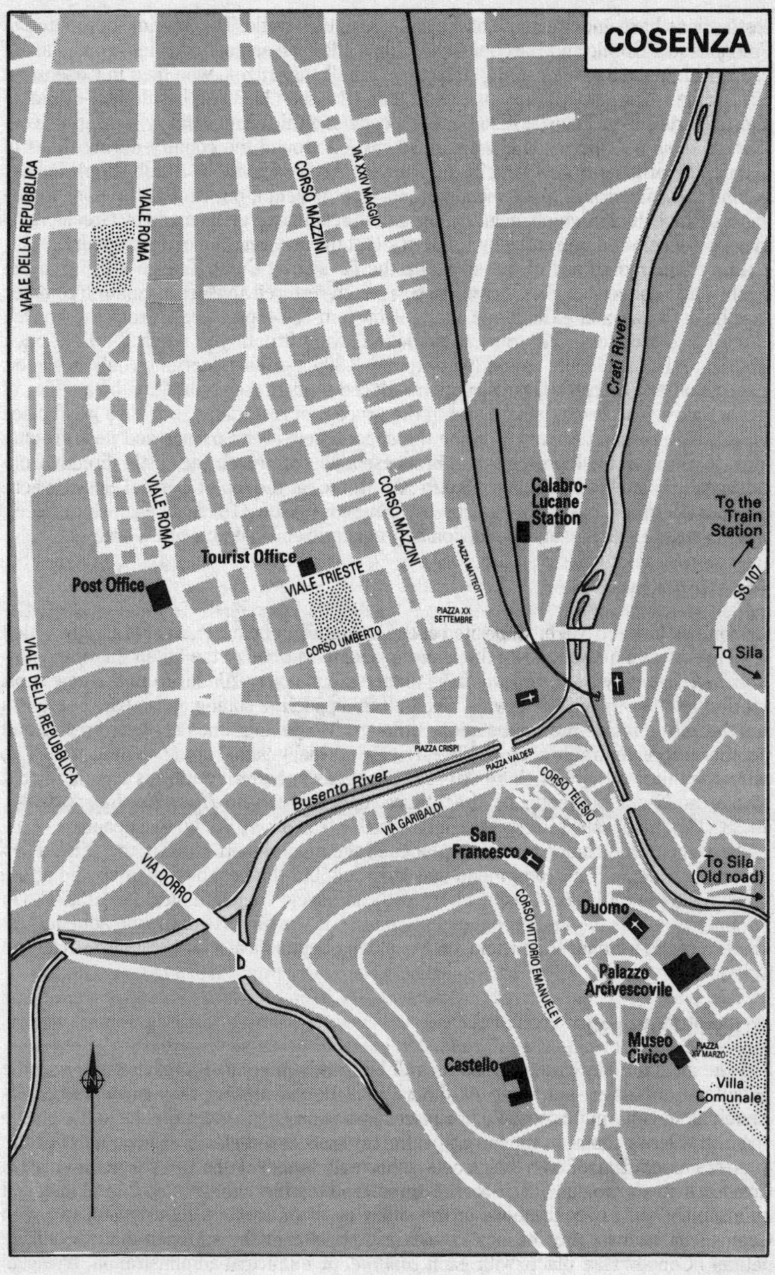
COSENZA
VIALE DELLA REPUBBLICA
VIALE ROMA
CORSO MAZZINI
VIA XXIV MAGGIO
Crati River
Calabro-Lucane Station
To the Train Station
SS 107
To Sila
Tourist Office
Post Office
VIALE TRIESTE
CORSO UMBERTO
PIAZZA MATTEOTTI
PIAZZA XX SETTEMBRE
PIAZZA CRISPI
PIAZZA VALDESI
CORSO TELESIO
Busento River
VIA GARIBALDI
VIA DORRO
San Francesco
To Sila (Old road)
CORSO VITTORIO EMANUELE II
Duomo
Palazzo Arcivescovile
Museo Civico
PIAZZA XV MARZO
Villa Comunale
Castello

restorations have undone much of the damage to the facade. The interior – a mixture of Romanesque, Gothic and Baroque styles – has a Roman sarcophagus in a good state of preservation and a stone carving depicting Isabella of Aragon, who died in Cosenza in 1271 while returning with her husband Philip III – seen kneeling beside her – from an abortive crusade in Tunisia. Also here is a copy of a thirteenth-century Byzantine icon, the *Madonna del Pilerio*, which was once carried around the country during times of plague; the original is now kept in the **Palazzo Arcivescovile** or Archbishop's Palace, behind the cathedral. This is eventually to be a museum, but ring at the door to see some of the exhibits, which include a Byzantine reliquary crucifix made by Greek craftsmen in Palermo and presented by Frederick II at the consecration of the cathedral.

From the Duomo any of the alleys on the far side of Corso Telesio lead up to the church and convent of **San Francesco**, a much-restored thirteenth-century complex that holds occasional exhibitions (daily 9am–1pm & 4–6pm; free). From the church climb up to the Corso Vittorio Emanuele, following it until you reach the little track leading to the formidable **castle** (9am–1pm & 3.30pm–sunset; mornings only in winter; free), another Frederick II construction reduced to its present condition by a series of earthquakes. The inside is bare and in the process of restoration, but it's a good place for a breath of clean air and to enjoy the superb view over Cosenza and its surroundings. If you want to skip seeing San Francesco, you can reach the castle directly from Cosenza's most elegant square, **Piazza XV Marzo**, at the top of Corso Telesio, where the **Accademia Cosentina** houses the **Museo Civico** (Tues–Sat 9am–1pm; free), which sports a rather scanty collection of prehistoric and classical bric-a-brac.

Practicalities

Arriving by bus you will be deposited at the **bus station** below Piazza Fera, from which it's a twenty-minute walk down the length of Corso Mazzini to the hotels and the *centro storico*. Arriving by train, you will have to take a bus (every 20min) from the new **train station** a little way outside town – tickets from inside the station at the bar. There is a **tourist office** inside the train station, although its opening times are very erratic, and another, more central branch at Viale Trieste 50 (daily 9am–1pm & 4–7pm; ☎27.821), although this is rather unhelpful. Most of Cosenza's **accommodation** is around the old station in Piazza Matteotti: on the square itself there's the *Hotel Excelsior* (☎0984/74.383; ④); the *Bruno* at Corso Mazzini 27 (☎0984/73.889; ④) is slightly cheaper.

There is a wide choice of **eating places** in the modern part of town: the *Pizza d'Oro* on Via 24 Maggio has a long menu and a garden, but the best deal is to be had at the small **trattoria** on Piazza Crispi, where you can have a complete meal for L13,000. On summer evenings the most congenial place to be is the **birreria** at the old aqueduct, at the end of the winding Via Arnone off Viale della Repubblica, with great views over the valley.

Around Cosenza

People spending any time in Cosenza will be mostly interested in excursions into the **Sila** (see opposite), but some of the villages dotted around the surrounding hills shouldn't be ignored. Especially in summer, when the heat and humidity settle on the town, the focus tends to move out of the city and into the hills, where most of the Cosentine population have their roots and family homes. With the village population swollen too by emigrants back for the summer, the streets are thronged until late, and at night the view over the bowl of the valley is magnificent, a glittering theatre with even Cosenza managing to look romantic. It is also in the summer that the village **festas** normally take place, with each *comune*, or municipal administration, trying to outdo the others in terms of spectacle and expense.

The villages of the **Presila**, on the eastern slope of the valley, have a reputation for late-night revelry and some good **pizzerias** (the best is in PEDACE, *U'Fuccularu*) and **birrerias** (try *Le Demon Rouge* in SPEZZANO DELLA SILA, with quite respectable food). On the other side of the valley the hilltop village of **RENDE** holds the prize for the tidiest village in the region, and it has good views, a **birreria** and a **restaurant**. Opposite Montalto, on the other side of the autostrada and the Crati River, five kilometres above LUZZI, stands the **Abbazia di Sambucina** – a Cistercian abbey founded in the twelfth century and long the centre of this order of monks throughout the South. It has a good portal (rebuilt in the fifteenth century) and the original presbytery.

There are buses to all of these places from the **bus station** in Cosenza below Piazza Fera, though they normally stop at nightfall. Another interesting (but slow) way to get to the Presila during the day (and beyond, into the Sila) is by the **trenino** of the Calabro–Lucane (*FCL*) line, which you can take from a small (unmarked) station behind Cosenza's old station three times a day, offering some marvellous glimpses over the Cosenza Valley, as the train twists and grinds up the mountain through woods and over rivers. It completes the 76km journey to SAN GIOVANNI IN FIORE in just over two hours, twice the time it would take by road, with return tickets at L5000, last departure at 2pm. Make sure of the return times, though, if you don't want to get stranded.

The Sila

Covering the widest part of the Calabrian peninsula, the **Sila** massif is more of an extensive plateau than a mountain range, though the peaks on its western flank reach heights of nearly 2000m. It's divided into three main groups, the Sila Greca, Sila Grande and Sila Piccola, the last two of which are little more than an administrative division, while the former – although the least entrancing scenically – is distinguished by the Albanian villages from which it takes its name.

At one time the Sila was one huge forest and was exploited from earliest times to provide fuel and material for the construction of fleets, fortresses and even for church-building in Rome, resulting in a deforestation that helped bring about the malarial conditions that for centuries laid much of Calabria low. The cutting of trees is now strictly controlled, and since the regional government recognised the potential of the area and imposed restrictions on building and hunting, there is plenty here for the outdoors enthusiast, in summer as a relief from the heat of the towns or coasts and in winter for downhill or cross-country skiing. The other seasons have their own charms: spring, when the woods are a riot of wild flowers, and autumn, for the full gamut of decaying colour and – a local speciality – wild mushrooms.

The Sila Greca

Deforestation has had the most devastating effect on the **Sila Greca**, the most northerly part of the massif, leaving mainly cultivated rolling highlands in place of the dense woods. But the area is easily accessible from the Ionian coast or the autostrada inland, and if you have a car is worth the detour to investigate some of the **Albanian villages** scattered around these hills. These mountain communities have their origin in the fifteenth century, when colonies of Albanians in flight from Muslim invasions were allowed to settle in some of the poorest areas of the peninsula by Irene, princess of Bisignano and daughter of **Skanderbeg** – the Albanian warrior-king, whose fiery image adorns many a main square in these parts. The villages retain to this day the shabby, untended look of straitened circumstances, visually unexciting and with few buildings or treasures of great artistic merit. **SAN DEMETRIO CORONE** is the most interesting, containing an Italo-Albanian *Collegio* charged with the task of guarding what remains of the Albanian heritage. Annexed to this is the church of **Sant'Adriano**, a structure that still shows elements of its Byzantine and Norman origins, including some Norman paving depicting the various animals which roamed the woods that once covered these hills – lions, serpents and panthers. Really, though, it's the annual festivals that show these villages at their best, and you should try to make your visit coincide with one if you can. Along with the opportunity to see their elaborate costumes and hear some gutsy singing, it may be the only chance of hearing the authentic language – a fifteenth-century version of modern Albanian – which has only recently been replaced by *calabrese* dialect as the everyday language in these parts. Festivals take place in the villages of Santa Sofia (July 15 & 16), San Cosmo (September 26 & 27), Vaccarizzo (March 31–April 2), and San Giorgio (April 2).

The Sila Grande

Densely forested, and the highest, most extensive part of the Sila range, the **Sila Grande** has Calabria's main **ski slopes** as well as the region's three principal **lakes** – all artificial (for hydroelectric purposes) and much loved by fishing fanatics who come out in force at weekends. The best base for day trips is Cosenza, but if you want to spend any time up here it would be advisable either to camp in the Sila or stay in one of the small towns there. These vary greatly. **SAN GIOVANNI IN FIORE**, in the heart of the Sila, is the biggest town in the area, but also the dreariest. More interesting is **LONGOBUCCO**, atmospherically enclosed at the bottom of a narrow valley directly below the national park of La Fossiata (see below). There is one **hotel** here, the *Stella* (☎0983/72082; ④). For winter-sports enthusiasts and summer trekkers alike, **CAMIGLIATELLO**, well connected by bus with Cosenza, is the best known of the resorts, a straggling little town wholly given over to tourism, with three ski slopes of its own and another at nearby Moccone, facilities for hiring equipment and tuition, and a confusion of hotels, restaurants and souvenir shops. In season there is an abundance of **hotels**, but they can be expensive; for moderate rates try the *Miramonti* (☎0984/578.343; ④) or *La Pineta* (☎0984/578.001; ④). For a good **trattoria**, the aptly named *Si Mangia Bene e Si Spende Poco* in Moccone has a well-deserved reputation. For hiking information, the **tourist office** is on Via Roma.

From Camigliatello, walk or hitch the 15km to **Lago Cecita**, best starting-place for expeditions to **La Fossiata**, a conservation area that resembles a national park on the American model, with tidy wooden fences along the roads and numerous picnic spots. It is always possible to find your own space, but it's a good idea, too, to follow the planned routes set out by the *Forestale* – paths can run out on you when you least expect it. Camping in the area is forbidden except in the **campsite** near Lake Cecita, but there are many opportunities to hide away undiscovered if you pitch your tent after dark; the foresters are primarily concerned about littering and the danger of fires (a real risk in the summer).

Get hold of a brochure with map and explanations of the area from one of the bars around here, or from the **tourist office** in Camigliatello, Cosenza or – if all else fails – the offices of the *Corpo Forestale* in Cosenza (Viale della Repubblica 26). You need to understand Italian to read the route descriptions, and the map is useless for discovering where to find the paths, but it can be helpful as a broad guide to their relative lengths and for switching from one to another.

Camigliatello is also a useful starting-point for a ramble that takes in the area's highest peaks, following the *strada delle vette*, snowbound in the winter months, for 13km through pine and beech woods before forking off and up to the three peaks of Monte Botte Donato (1928m). The road continues on down to Lake Arvo and the resort of **LORICA**, from which it is a shorter distance to Botte Donato. Or you can save the sweat and take the chair lift from the *località* Cavaliere, a little outside the main town.

Lorica, like Camigliatello, is dedicated to tourism in the height of the winter and summer seasons, but its lakeside location makes it a more relaxed spot, with lots of places for picnicking under the pines and observing the antics of the curious black squirrels that inhabit them. The town is connected with Cosenza by **bus**, arriving in the morning and going back in the afternoon, and there are two **campsites** (one inside, the other just outside the town), and several **hotels** – though only one, the *Belvedere* (☎0984/997.016; ④), is open all year round.

The Sila Piccola

Bounded by Lago Ampollino in the north, Catanzaro and the Ionian coast in the south, the **Sila Piccola** is the region's most densely forested section, centring on the **Foresta di Gariglione** – much reduced from its extent at the turn of the century but still impressively thick, with fir, beech and the gigantic turkey oak from which it derives its name. Its designation as national park protects it from further plundering, though it is not so well adapted for walking as La Fossiata. Apart from the odd resort, it's a sparsely populated area, and most of its villages are in any case unattractive. Only **SANTA SEVERINA**, on the eastern fringes, is worth a stop – an originally Byzantine fortified town built on a hilltop and dominated by a Norman castle. The **Cattedrale** here has an eighth-century Byzantine **baptistery** off its left aisle, with an original font. On the other side of the main piazza the **castle** was rebuilt by Robert Guiscard on the ruins of a Byzantine stronghold. Now occupied by an infants' school but open to visitors, its well-preserved battlements look out over the district known as the *Marchesato*, a former vast feudal domain surrounding Crotone and belonging to the Ruffo family, one of the main landowning dynasties in Calabria.

Further south, **BELCASTRO** – also watched over by a Norman castle – claims to be the birthplace of Saint Thomas Aquinas, whose family once held the town in fief. Further down the SS109, the mountain village of **TAVERNA** has long historical associations, but is best known today as the home of Calabria's foremost seventeenth-century painter, **Mattia Preti**, whose Spanish-looking paintings can be seen in four of the local churches, particularly **San Domenico** – in which, in a corner of his portrait of *St John the Baptist*, is a self-portrait. From here it's 25km down a winding road to the regional capital of CATANZARO.

The southern Tyrrhenian coast

The province of Catanzaro begins at the Savuto River, and from here down to Reggio the SS18, autostrada and main rail line all run parallel, tracing the coast together apart from the stretch of the Tropea promontory. Immediately after the river, a few kilometres inland from the resort of LIDO DI FALERNA, the hill-village of **NOCERA TIRINESE** (hitch or bus from the station on the coast) is famed for the flagellants that paint the streets red every Easter – a religious festival, not at all laid on for tourists, that grips the whole village with fervour. Wailing processions sway through the streets, and teams of two sprint between churches, one holding a cross, the other slapping himself systematically with a spiked brush, after which his blood is splashed over the doors of the houses to protect those within – not to be washed off until it happens naturally with the rain. It is one of the few cases of this kind of ritual bloodletting still to be found in the South, worth catching if you're around here at the right time.

Further down the coast, between Capo Súvero (marked by its lighthouse) and LIDO DI GIZZERIA, is a fine **swimming spot**, a sandy spit with a freshwater lake close by, surrounded by palms and bamboo – though it can only be a matter of time before the site is earmarked for development. The plain that stretches east from here, the **Piana**

di Sant'Eufemia, is the narrowest part of the Calabrian peninsula, much of it reclaimed only in the last hundred years from malarial swamp: the mosquitos remain but they no longer carry the disease. SANT' EUFEMIA-LAMEZIA is the **rail and road junction** for CATANZARO and the Ionian coast. Heading south on the motorway you begin a slow ascent on the long viaduct that is one of the engineering feats of the *Autostrada del Sole*, the views growing more inspiring as it rises above the coast to the high tableland of the Tropea promontory.

Pizzo and the Tropea promontory

Following the railway or the SS18, the picturesque little town of **PIZZO** is a good place to spend some time, neatly placed for the **beaches** around Tropea and with an albeit sporadically open clifftop **youth hostel** (*pizzo* in dialect means rock) converted from a castle built in 1486 by Ferdinand I of Aragon – inside which you can see the room in which the French general **Murat** was imprisoned, and the yard where he was shot in October 1815. Murat, one of Napoleon's ablest generals, met his ignominious end here after attempting to rouse the people against the Bourbons and reclaim the throne of Naples given to him by Napoleon; the people of Pizzo ignored his haughty entreaties and he was arrested and court-martialled.

If you intend staying at the hostel it's a good idea to phone first to check on vacancies (☎0963/231.551); if it's full, there's the *Sonia* on Via Phangi (☎0963/531.315; ④), or – an expensive alternative – the *Hotel Murat* overlooking the main square (☎0963/531.006; ⑦). There are numerous **places to eat**, including a couple of pizzerias in the main square (*Il Porticato* is one) and in Piazzetta Garibaldi the trattoria *Il Ritrovo*, along the main shopping street, Corso Garibaldi – as well as several other places in the port below. Between April and July try the tuna or swordfish, for which Pizzo is a fishing centre.

The Tropea promontory

Pizzo is also a starting-point for the coastal rail line that rings the **Tropea promontory**; trains run from a separate **station** near the port (if you've come down from the north you'll need to have changed at LAMEZIA). The first stop, **VIBO MARINA**, is the major port and industrial centre of this stretch of coast, with a regular peak-season boat service to the Aeolian Islands (see Chapter Sixteen, "Sicily"). Some 10km above the port and served by the mainline station of Pizzo-Vibo Valentia, the larger town of **VIBO VALENTIA** has a history that goes back to Greek times, when it was known as **Hipponion** (fragments of whose walls are still standing 2km north of town). Because of its strategic importance, Vibo has always held a prominent position in Calabria's history: under Murat it was a provincial capital with a flourishing cultural life, inhabited by grandees whose memory survives in the street names and in the many surviving palaces – all now in a state of decay that contributes to the town's rather shabby aspect. It's a place to be passed through rather than stopped at, with a small **Museo Archeologico** in Piazza Garibaldi (summer Tues–Sat 9am–1pm & 3–5pm, Sun 9am–1pm; winter Tues–Sat 9am–2pm, Sun 9am–1pm; free), soon to be enlarged but currently containing items from the Greek and Roman sites in the area, and a Norman **castle** reachable on a path which winds up behind – under restoration, but you may be able to enter and admire from its massive walls the view over the coast and the rolling countryside behind.

Inland from here (connected by frequent buses), the village of **SORIANO** is dominated by the ruins of the church and monastery of **San Domenico** – one of the largest and richest houses of the Dominican Order in Europe until it was wrecked by earthquakes in 1659 and 1783. The monastery produced four popes, two of whom can be seen on canvas in the modern adjoining church, along with a miraculous portrait of

Saint Dominic said to be painted by no human hand. The majestic ruins still manage to render an idea of the size and wealth of the complex, which must have once striven to out-dazzle the nearby Carthusian monastery at Serra San Bruno (see p.802).

On the other side of Vibo the golden sands of Tropea stretch invitingly into the Tyrrhenian Sea – one of the least spoilt and most picturesque parts of Calabria. Take your choice among the numerous **campsites** and **beaches**, mostly clean and sandy, though relatively crowded at the height of the season. Try *La Rocchetta* at BRIATICO, with its ruined watchtower and scattered fishing boats, or those around SANTA DOMENICA.

TROPEA itself can claim to be the prettiest town on the whole of the Tyrrhenian coast, and the most fashionable, with a seaside charm missing from many of the other Calabrian resorts, and one which is not yet entirely eroded by the annual influx of tourists. The buildings have character without being twee – see particularly the lovely Norman **cathedral** at the bottom of Via Roma, whose interior harbours a couple of unexploded American bombs from the last war (each accompanied by a grateful prayer to the Madonna), a Renaissance ciborium and a statue of the Madonna and Child from the same period. The views from the upper town over the sea and the church of **Santa Maria dell'Isola** on its rock are superb, and on a clear day you will see the cone of Stromboli and perhaps some of the other Aeolian Islands looming out of the horizon. There are good beaches all around and more trattorias per square metre than in any other town in Calabria, and in season at least plenty of choice of **accommodation** – though it may be wise to book all the same. Try the *Hotel Miramare* on the road heading south out of town (☎0963/61.570; ⑥), which is closed in winter; open all year round is the *Virgilio* (☎0963/61.978; ⑥) in Viale Tondo.

Further around the promontory, **CAPO VATICANO** is a complex of some of the most popular beaches, including **Grotticelle** – spacious enough to get away from the bustle and with a **campsite** immediately above and a clean hotel, the *Grotticelle* (☎0963/663.157; ⑤). To the south of here, the road teeters high above the sea before reaching **NICOTERA**, built in its present position by Robert Guiscard. It has a couple of small **museums**, a **cathedral** with work by Antonello Gagini, and a **marina** below – a pleasant place to eat outside in the summer. There are wide beaches too, with a couple of **campsites** at their southern end.

South to Reggio

From Nicotera there are some long views to be had stretching south over the **Piana**, Calabria's second plain of any size and dedicated to olive cultivation. The towns here are mostly new and unattractive, partly due to the fact that the area is one of the most seismically active in Italy – the epicentre of the notorious 1783 earthquake was at nearby Oppido. The small Tropea rail line connects with the main line at ROSARNO, beyond which **PALMI** holds an interesting **museum complex** in **La Casa della Cultura Leonida Repaci**: a newly built cultural centre and exhibition hall a little way above the town (take Via San Giorgio, close to the exit onto the SS18). It includes the best collection of folklore items in Calabria and a museum of art and sculpture with work by Modigliani, De Chirico, Guttuso and Carlo Levi (Mon–Fri 8am–2pm, Mon & Wed also 3–6pm; free).

From Palmi the tall TV mast on the northern tip of Sicily is already visible, but the best view of Sicily and the Calabrian coast (thought by Leslie Gardiner in his *South to Calabria* to be "perhaps the finest viewpoint in southern Italy") is some 5km down the road, at **Monte Sant'Elia**, the first elevation of the Aspromonte massif. From this balcony, perched on cliffs that plunge vertically down to the sea, you can see the two volcanoes of Etna and Strómboli on a clear day; there is a **campsite** behind, and a tourist village. The spot is believed to have been named after Sant'Elia Spelaeotes, who lived in these parts (in a cave, which can be visited on the road leading into Aspromonte from Melicucca) and whose body, when he died aged 94, proved unburnable by the Saracens. Earlier, when his body was washed, the water was used for curing another holy man's toothache. "Virtues," he said, however, "are better than miracles".

From here south, the proximity of Sicily becomes the dominant feature looking out to sea, and the stretch of the autostrada that dives down to Villa San Giovanni can claim to be one of the most panoramic in Italy, burrowing high up through mountains with the Straits of Messina glittering below. By train or following the old road, you skirt the so-called *Costa Viola*, passing through BAGNARA, famous for its swordfish, and **SCILLA**, ancient Scylla, with a fine sandy **beach** and lots of action in the summer. This was the location of one of the two dreaded monsters (possibly whirlpools) mentioned as a threat to mariners in the **Odyssey**, the other being Charybdis, corresponding to the modern Cariddi located 6km away on the other side of the Strait. Unquestionably the best place to stay in Scilla is the **youth hostel**, located in the castle that separates the beautiful people on the main beach from the fishing village to the north. Open from April to the end of September, it is likely to be full at the height of the season so phone first to check on availability (☎0965/75.4033). The best alternative is the *Pensione Le Sirene* (phoning also advisable in summer: ☎0965/75.4121; ④). Otherwise, a blind eye is turned on those who want to sleep on the beach (the southern end).

From Scilla it's just 9km to **VILLA SAN GIOVANNI** (frequent buses), worth stopping at only as a point of embarkation for Sicily. The state-run *FS* **ferries** leave from directly behind the station and arrive at Messina **train station** in about forty minutes. More frequent are the private *Caronte* ferries (left out of the station and under the rails), leaving approximately every fifteen minutes and pulling in closer to the entrance to the *autostrada*. This is the one the lorry drivers take, so it's also useful if you're hitching. There's also a hydrofoil service from Villa to the Aeolian Islands (twice a day). If you're heading for Reggio, take a train or one of the hourly *Salzone* **buses** from outside the station.

Reggio and around

The southernmost province of Calabria – **Reggio** – is, in some ways, the apotheosis of all that makes the Italian South so distinctive. Encapsulating many of the problems to be found throughout the region, it is the place, as Joan Didion once said about California, where hope runs out. But, unlike the American West, the response here is despair. Significantly, emigration from this part of Italy has long been the highest, and continues to be high, though with the narrowing of the international job market the number of escape routes is constantly diminishing. At the same time the land itself, once the heart and soul of the southern peasant culture and economy, is increasingly being abandoned in the face of low returns and high expectations – no one expects to share in the get-rich-quick society by tilling fields. Misery and delinquency are more evident here than in other parts of the South, earthquakes more frequent, the landscape more extreme in all ways, with dilapidated villages lying stranded among mountains, which are themselves torn apart by wide *fiumare*, or riverbeds – empty or reduced to a trickle for nine-tenths of the year, but swelling with the melting of the winter snows to destructive torrents.

Reggio di Calabria

REGGIO DI CALABRIA, the provincial capital, was originally the first of the ancient Greek settlements on the Italian mainland, and today, with a population of over 170,000, is the town in the region that most resembles a city. It also has all the

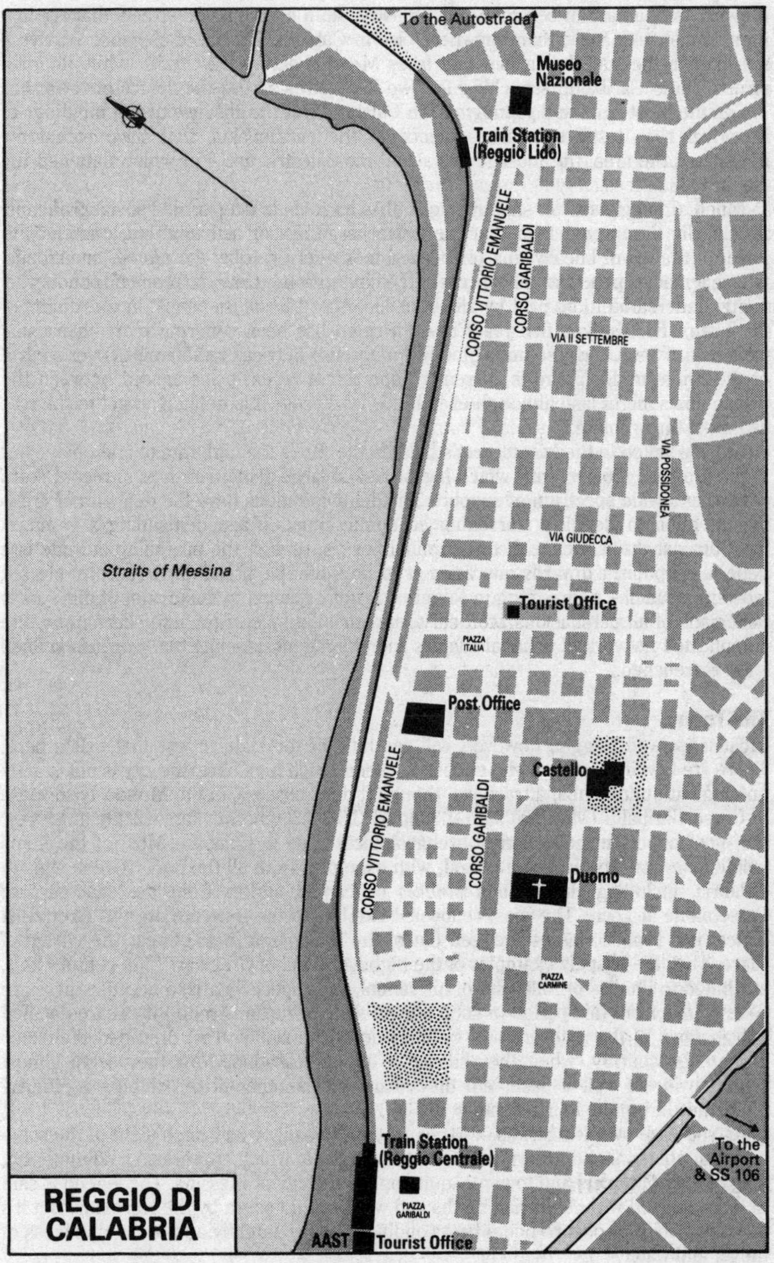

To the Autostrada
Museo Nazionale
Train Station (Reggio Lido)
CORSO VITTORIO EMANUELE
CORSO GARIBALDI
VIA II SETTEMBRE
VIA POSSIDONEA
VIA GIUDECCA
Straits of Messina
Tourist Office
PIAZZA ITALIA
Post Office
Castello
CORSO VITTORIO EMANUELE
CORSO GARIBALDI
Duomo
PIAZZA CARMINE
Train Station (Reggio Centrale)
To the Airport & SS 106
PIAZZA GARIBALDI
AAST Tourist Office
REGGIO DI CALABRIA

drawbacks of an urban centre: heavy industry, slum housing, and streets that are in a more ramshackle state than anywhere else in Calabria. Traces of elegance survive – not least in the superb seafront that faces Messina across the Straits, while its main street, Corso Garibaldi, stretching for two kilometres across the centre of town, has one of the most animated *passeggiatas* in Calabria. But the absence of any buildings of historical note testifies to the violence of the earthquakes that have repeatedly devastated the area, the most recent – and most destructive – of which flattened the city in 1908.

Much of Reggio's air of shabby neglect has its roots in deep-seated social problems, specifically the stranglehold that the Calabrian Mafia, or **'ndrangheta**, continues to have on the town. Locally this phenomenon is referred to as the *piovra*, or octopus, whose tentacles penetrate all aspects of the city's life (*tangente*, or protection money, is tacitly understood to be paid by all shopkeepers and business people in most parts of the town). For the last five years or so, Reggio has been suffering more than usual from its activities, the result of a bloody *faida* (feud) between rival families over control of the drugs trade. There is currently hope that a recent truce agreed between the protagonists might last, although even if this is effective it is unlikely to get to the root causes of the problem.

Closely linked to the *'ndrangheta*'s hold on the city is the high rate of unemployment in the province (25 percent), which has provoked large demonstrations in recent years attracting a wide spectrum of support. The demonstrations have the dual aim of drawing attention to Reggio's worsening economic situation and demanding a common front against the influence of the criminal bosses, though the prevailing attitude is a general scepticism towards any attempt to improve the situation. A recently elected left-wing council – a rare thing in Reggio – is not expected to make a lot of difference: politicians of all persuasions are held to be intrinsically corrupt, and *clientelismo*, the complicated network of political favours and obligations, is – like the *'ndrangheta* itself – too entrenched.

The Town

Most visitors to Reggio, however, will see little of the state of war that exists here. There are few, in any case, who choose to spend much time here: the city is not exactly bulging with unmissable attractions, though it does possess, in the **Museo Nazionale** in Corso Garibaldi (Mon–Sat 9am–1.30pm & 3.30–7.30pm, Sun 9am–12.30pm; L6000), the most important collection of archaeological finds in Calabria. Most of the items inside date from the Hellenic period, with examples from all the major Greek sites in Calabria, including the famous *pinakes* or carved tablets from the sanctuary of Persephone at Locri. The most renowned exhibits in the museum are the **Bronzi di Riace**: two bronze statues dragged out of the Ionian Sea in 1972 near the village of Riace. They are shapely examples of the highest period of Greek art (fifth century BC), attributed to Phidias or followers of his school, and especially prized because there are so few finds from this period in such a good state of repair. Around them are detailed explanations of the recovery and cleaning-up of the statues that preceded their tour around the country, when they caused a minor sensation. Now they seem almost forgotten in the well-lit basement they share with another prize exhibit – a philosopher's head from the fourth century BC.

As you gaze over the Straits of Messina, you probably won't catch sight of the semi-mythical phenomenon known as the **Fata Morgana**, which appears as a shimmering, magical city of turrets and towers – quite unlike the city of Messina. The legend is said to be connected with Arthurian myths and was brought south by the Normans. But it's an extremely rare occurrence – best conditions are apparently an absolute stillness of the air and water.

Practicalities

If you're travelling by train, get off at **Reggio Lido** for the port or museum. Buses end up at the **Reggio Centrale** station a kilometre or so down, which is where you'll find most of the hotels, including the *Albergo San Giorgio* at Via Gaeta 9 (☎0965/99.464; ④). A little further out, there's the excellent-value *Locanda degli Ulivi* at Via Eremo Botte 30 (☎0965/890.133; ③), though it's often full, and, on the same street, a **campsite**: for both take bus #7 or #8 from Piazza or Corso Garibaldi. There is a **youth hostel** at SCILLA (see p.786), for which buses from Piazza Garibaldi leave hourly until 8pm. There is a small **tourist office** in the bus station, and a larger one at Corso Garibaldi 329 (Sun–Fri 8am–1pm & 2–8pm, Sat 8am–noon; ☎21.171). There are several eating places around Piazza Carmine (behind the Duomo), best of which is the *Trattoria Toscano* in Via Muratori.

From Reggio's port you can reach MESSINA in fifteen minutes by hydrofoil; by car you have to go from Villa San Giovanni (see p.786). A regular hydrofoil service also leaves daily for the AEOLIAN ISLANDS; see "Travel Details" for frequencies and journey times.

Aspromonte

Most visitors to Reggio province leave without having ventured into the great massif of **Aspromonte**, the last spur of the Appennines on the tip of Italy's boot, and displaying an even more pronounced dialogue between mountain scenery and seascape than elsewhere in Calabria. You can be on a beach and a ski slope within the same hour, passing from the brilliant almost tropical vegetation of the coast to dense forests of beech and pine that rise to nearly 2000m. The physical aspect of the range varies enormously, depending on which side you enter from: coming up from the Tyrrhenian coast you pass through endless groves of olive that are the thickest and tallest in the region, whereas on the Ionian side the mountains have the empty, arid look of desert peaks.

Santo Stefano: Giuseppe Musolino

Access is easiest from the Tyrrhenian side, from BAGNARA or GALLICO, from which frequent buses leave for Delianuova or Gambarie. The most scenic route is the SS184 from Gallico, which winds through profusely terraced groves of vine and citrus to the village of **SANTO STEFANO**, famous as the birthplace and resting-place of the last of the great brigands who roamed these parts, **Giuseppe Musolino**. Occupying a sort of Robin Hood role in the popular imagination, Musolino was a legend in his own lifetime, the last thirty years of which he spent in jail, and, finally, a lunatic asylum – the penalty for having led the Carabinieri on a long and humiliating dance up and down the slopes of Aspromonte during his profitable career.

While he was alive, he was warmly regarded by all who might otherwise have paled at the mention of brigandage, and even now he is seen as a local hero. A policeman in the village described him to me as "una persona onestissima" – the most honest of people. Musolino's victims were rich, or corrupt, or informers, and he was never known to refuse a plea for help from those in need. It is hard to know how much is myth, but the romantic aura that surrounds him is partly due to the fact that brigandage, with which the region was rife during the Bourbon period and for which the tormented mountainscape of Aspromonte provided a natural refuge, was also a political gesture of rebellion and little to do with the organised crime that has succeeded it. Just above the village, in the cemetery, you can see Musolino's grave, now renovated but until recently daubed with the signatures of people come to pay their respects.

Gambarie: skiing and walking

GAMBARIE, a little further up amid thick woods, is a fully fledged holiday town, used as a skiing resort in the winter and a cooling-off place for overheated *reggini* (from Reggio) in the summer. There is a **ski slope** from the top of **Monte Scirocco** (1660m), connected by a sporadically working chair lift, and a small choice of **hotels**, cheapest of which is the *Don Basco* (☎0965/743.107; ③). Ask here or at any of Gambarie's larger hotels about hiring facilities for skiing equipment. When the mountain is not snowbound, Gambarie is also a good base for walks in the area: for Aspromonte's highest peak, **Montalto** (1955m), start down along the SS183 towards Melito, turning off left after three or four kilometres onto a broken road, after which it's another 16km to the top, marked by a bronze statue of Christ gazing steadily out over the Straits of Messina – a memorable view. If you still have any energy there is another track that descends steeply to the *santuario* of **Madonna di Polsi**, inhabited only by the monks of the monastery there. A large **fair** takes place here every year on the first two days of September – an unashamedly pagan event that involves the slaughter and sale of large numbers of goats. The monastery can put you up, or else camp in the area.

Delianuova and the coastal route

Continuing on down along the SS183 will bring you eventually to the Ionian coast at MELITO DI PORTO SALVO, a tortuous but highly scenic route with views over towards Sicily. Going up the same road from Gambarie (in the opposite direction) leads along a plain and through more forest to **DELIANUOVA**, another resort, though not as busy as Gambarie, with a trattoria, a birreria and one **hotel**, the *Aspromonte 2001* (☎0966/963.012; ⑤). Another path from here leads up to Montalto (about a five-hour hike). Halfway between Gambarie and Delianuova, a turn-off on the right will take you to the **Cippo Garibaldi**, a modern monument in the woods commemorating the spot where the hero, having emerged from his retirement in the summer of 1862 with the intention of marching on Rome, was ignominiously captured by the troops of King Vittorio Emanuele, in whose name he had raised the banner.

The **coastal route** along Italy's toe-tip also offers some interesting excursions into Aspromonte, road and rail line running south out of Reggio through the series of small nondescript towns adorned by a profusion of cactus, agave, banana trees and date palms, and surrounded by the extensive plantations of citrus that are a feature of the Reggio area. Look out in particular for the *bergamot*, a fruit resembling a yellow orange whose essence is used as a base for expensive perfumes – one of the principal exports of this area, and until recently, because of the precise conditions required for its cultivation, not found anywhere else in the world.

Campsites abound along this coast, attached to sandy beaches in varying states of cleanliness. Immediately after the *La Tegara* site, the village of **PENTEDATTILO** owes its name to the Greek meaning "five-fingered", on account of the curiously shaped rock on which it stands. Norman Douglas likened it more to an upturned molar, and Edward Lear, travelling through the area in 1848, thought it "perfectly magical" – though its old Byzantine centre has recently been abandoned in favour of a new and ugly town just below.

You are now in the **Zona Grecanica**, named after the villages on these southern slopes of Aspromonte that were settled by Greeks some two thousand years ago and that still retain some traces of the Greek language in the local dialect. One such village is **BOVA**, perched on a crag 15km inland from its seaside satellite, BOVA MARINA – a remote place, with a view justifiably described by Lear as "truly magnificent", although the thick oak forests he saw then no longer exist. From the remains of the **castle** at the top, you can map out some alluring excursions into the wild country around: there are no hotels here but the countryside is one of the loveliest and most isolated parts of Aspromonte, with plenty of opportunity for camping. Around the corner of the coast, another route into Aspromonte takes you by way of the village of **SAN LUCA**, known to *calabresi* as the home of the writer **Corrado Alvaro,** whose novels (*Gente di Aspromonte* is one) describe the lives of the people living in these mountains. It's also known for its reputation as a *'ndrangheta* stronghold: the triangle of land between the villages of San Luca, Plati and Cimina is a favourite area for holding kidnap victims, often for months at a time, and is periodically – usually following accusations of apathy on the part of the government – a target for army operations to root out the hiding places. From San Luca a road continues up, leading after 20km to the Santuario della Madonna di Polsi (see opposite) and from there to the peak of Montalto. The road is asphalted for only half the way and careers up some pretty hairy mountainsides, but is worth the sweat for the truly Himalayan landscape and the numerous possibilities for picnicking and walking. Local people will warn you against travelling alone in these parts . . ..

Potenza and around

Basilicata's regional capital, **POTENZA**, has suffered more than most southern towns from the effects of earthquake and war, which have robbed it of much of its historical heritage. There is still considerable restoration work continuing after the last 'quake, in November 1980, adding to the dust and commotion that fill the town's centre, and it's not the most pleasant place to be during the heat of summer. The mainland's highest provincial capital, built on a spur between two valleys, it's also rather spread out, with most of the modern districts at the bottom of the hill, a brisk walk down rickety stairways or a short ride on one of the city's frequent buses (pay on board), and most of what's worth seeing in the old town above. The narrow and animated **Via Pretoria** is the main street, partly pedestrianised and at its best during the nightly *passeggiata*. Beyond that Potenza's interests don't amount to much. The church of **San Francesco** contains a Byzantine-style icon of the *Madonna del Terremoto* – though even this is sometimes locked up – and the modern quarter of *Rione Santa Maria*, north of the centre, is home to the **Museo Archeologico Provinciale**, which holds the region's most important collection of finds from the prehistory of Lucania, although it's been closed for some time and nobody seems to know when it will re-open.

Practicalities

Potenza has three **train stations**, all connected but not all serving the same routes. The central Potenza Città station links only with Potenza Inferiore, on the other side of town, which has trains to Metaponto, Taranto, Foggia and Battipaglia; the Stazione Superiore in Rione Santa Maria serves stops to Foggia; the independent *FCL* line, across the tracks from here, serves Bari and places around Potenza. Most **buses** leaving for destinations within Basilicata leave from Piazza Crispi; buses for Salerno, Naples and Rome leave from Piazza Bologna. There is a **tourist office** at Via Alianelli 4 (Mon–Fri 9am–1pm & 4–7pm, Sat 9am–1pm).

Potenza's cheapest **place to sleep** is *La Casa dello Studente* in Piazza Don Bosco (☎0971/442.708; ③). Closer to the centre is the *Albergo Miramonti* at Via Caserma Lucana 30 (☎0971/22.987; ⑤). If you want **to eat**, you can do so well and cheaply in the *Trattoria Satriano*, a dark and airless basement frequented by students, just off Piazza Matteotti.

Around Potenza

The best reason for coming to Potenza is to see some of the smaller towns and villages of inland Basilicata, most of which are conveniently situated on the main routes to – or from – the outside world.

South: Grumentum and Moliterno

To the south, just inside the border with Campania and close to a lake formed by the damming of the River Agri, lies ancient **Grumentum**, one of the principal cities of Roman Lucania and the site of two victories over the Carthaginians, most memorably that of 207 BC when Hannibal lost 8000 of his men and four elephants. At two spots along a narrow country lane (well signposted) are the remains of a theatre, a basilica, baths and an amphitheatre, with fragmentary mosaics among the ruins of the houses. A large **museum** on the site (Tues–Sun 9am–2pm; free) displays some of the finds, though sadly not the so-called "Siri bronzes", which have been in London since 1833.

Following the destruction of the town by the Saracens between 872 and 975, many of Grumentum's inhabitants fled to the nearby town of **MOLITERNO**, a few kilometres up the road, later a Norman stronghold that guarded the western approaches into Basilicata. The birthplace of a clutch of *literati*, it possesses the remains of the **castle** and several mediocre churches.

North: Acerenza

It's the region to the north of Potenza which is the most interesting historically, with several towns from the Norman era and some good examples of their brand of hybrid architecture. All are connected by bus with Potenza, and most are on the main Potenza–Foggia rail line. The venerable stronghold of **ACERENZA**, northeast of Potenza, is the one exception, although it does have a station on the Bari line a few kilometres below the town itself, connected by a regular bus service to the top. It's worth the effort for the grand panorama and its famous **Cattedrale**, from which it is thought the name of Basilicata derives (it was the bishop of this basilica who exercised jurisdiction over the territory around). Constructed in the eleventh century but rebuilt in its present Romanesque form in 1281, probably by French architects, the cathedral has an interesting exterior, though the cupola at the top is a recent addition, following the earthquake of 1930. Inside, its crypt is a rare example of the impact of the Renaissance in Basilicata.

Castel Lagopésole and Monte Vulture

West of here, following the main road north out of Potenza towards Foggia, the massive castle of **Castel Lagopésole** (daily dawn–dusk; free) is visible long before you reach it, dominating the surrounding country and dwarfing the village at its base. This was the last and greatest of Frederick II's castles, and was said to be his favourite for the rich hunting-grounds in the woods around (now farmland), though the building itself was still unfinished by the time of the emperor's death in 1250. You can visit the chapel and some of the royal apartments. Note the two sculpted heads on the outside of the keep, one representing Beatrice, Frederick Barbarossa's second wife, the other Barbarossa himself (Frederick II's grandfather), on whom you may just distinguish the ass's ears for which he was famous.

North of here, the truncated cone of **Monte Vulture** becomes increasingly evident – the only volcano east of the Appennines and now a national park with a large range of fauna and flora. A road leads up through thick woodland to two lakes that occupy the former crater – **lago grande** and **lago piccolo** – separated by a thin strip of land entirely given over to bars, pizzerias and souvenir shops, the area being a favourite for weekend trippers from Naples and Foggia. Signs exhort visitors to be tidy to no avail, ruining what is a genuine beauty spot. If you want to stay over, there are several **hotels** and two **campsites**, one right on the shore of the lago piccolo.

Melfi

From the lakes a road runs down to the historic town of **MELFI**, long a centre of strategic importance, taken by the Normans in 1041 and their first capital in the south of Italy. It was in the formidable **castle** at the top of the town that Pope Nicholas II formally recognised the conquests of Robert Guiscard over the Byzantines and Saracens, thereby legitimising the piratical Normans and confirming their place in the embattled history of the South. It was here also that Guiscard imprisoned his first wife Alberada, and from where, in 1231, Frederick II issued his *Constitutiones Augustales*, reckoned to be the most comprehensive body of legislation promulgated since the time of Charlemagne. Repeatedly damaged by earthquake, the castle is currently undergoing restoration work but is normally the home of a **museum** (Tues–Sun 9am–1pm & 3–7.30pm; L4000) housing prehistoric finds and objects from the Greek, Roman and Byzantine eras. The most celebrated item is a Roman sarcophagus from the second century, the so-called *sarcofago di Rapolla*, on which are carved five statuettes of gods and heroes and the image of the dead girl, reclining on cushions.

Just off via Vittorio Emanuele, near the centre of town, is the **Duomo**, twelfth century but rebuilt following earthquakes. After the 1930 'quake, a Byzantine-style fresco of a Madonna and Child was brought to light, which you can see in a chapel to the right of the altar. The cathedral's campanile has miraculously survived the various cataclysms: the two black stone griffons symbolised the Norman hegemony in the South and are now visible everywhere in Melfi, having been adopted as the town's emblem.

On the other side of Piazza Municipio there is a decent **pizzeria**, *La Tavernetta*, in Via Nitti. By turning right at the *Municipio* you can find a cheap **hotel** – *Il Barbato* (☎0972/24.477; ③).

Venosa

If Melfi preserves the appearance of a dark medieval town, **VENOSA** has an attractive airiness, a harmonious place, rich with historical associations. Known in antiquity as *Venusia*, it was in its time the largest colony in the Roman world, and much is made of the fact that it was the birthplace of Quintus Horatius Flaccus, known to Italians as *Orazio* and to the English as **Horace** (65–8 BC); his supposed house lies past the cathedral on the right. Venosa's web of narrow streets is full of reminders of the town's long past. The tomb of the Roman general Marcellus, ambushed and killed by Hannibal here in 208 BC, is off Via Melfi. Five minutes' walk away, the formidable **castello** dominates the spacious and arcaded Piazza Umberto, from which the main street – Via V. Emanuele – leads to a small **archaeological zone** holding the sketchy remains of some Roman baths and a palaeo-Christian baptistery. But Venosa's real attraction is the adjoining **Abbazia della Trinità**, a complex of churches begun in the mid-eleventh century that was the resting place of a number of Norman bigwigs, including Robert Guiscard, who is buried along with four of his brothers and his divorced first wife Alberada in the oldest part of the abbey, the *Chiesa Vecchia*, dating from 1059. Alberada's tomb is the only one that has survived. Backing on to the older church, the *Chiesa Nuova* was begun fifty years later, a gigantic construction that was too ambitious to ever be properly finished – only the lower part of the walls and the apse were completed.

There are numerous places to **eat** at Venosa, most of them in the new part of town, and a good, cheap **hotel**, the *Orazio* (☎0972/31.135; ⑤), on the main street between Piazza Orazio and the cathedral.

Matera and around

The interior of the **province of Matera** has a great deal in common with Potenza province – a wide, empty terrain, much of it given over to agriculture and pasture, much of it good for nothing in particular. Rundown, depopulated, its bare clay hills appear, in Levi's words, "a sea of white, monotonous and treeless", dotted with solitary villages that are cut off from each other and the rest of the world. Little to recommend for an action-packed tour, then, but plenty of the timeless atmosphere portrayed by film-makers like Rosi and Bertolucci.

Matera

The town of **MATERA** itself is unique, with a degree of culture and elegance unusual by southern standards and, in its **Sassi** – dwellings dug out of the ravine in tiers – one of the country's oddest urban features. The *Sassi* are abandoned now, an eerie troglodyte enclave occupying the lower regions of the city. But until thirty years ago this part of the city was still populated by the poorest of the *materani*.

During the 1950s and 1960s, fifteen thousand people were forcibly removed from the *Sassi* and rehoused in modern districts on the outskirts of town. Since then the area has been officially cleaned up (some *Sassi* have been sealed with cement to prevent their former inhabitants from returning), and although a certain squalor still hangs about some parts, it's a far cry from the dense malaria-ridden area of thirty years previous. Levi's sister, in *Christ Stopped at Eboli*, compared the *Sassi* to Dante's *Inferno*, horrified by their disease-ridden inhabitants. "Never before have I seen such a spectacle of misery," she said. They had "the wrinkled faces of old men, emaciated by hunger, with hair crawling with lice and encrusted with scabs. Most of them had swollen bellies and faces yellowed and stricken with malaria." Pursuing her, they begged not for coins but for quinine.

The Town

Divided into two sections – the *Sasso Caveoso* and *Sasso Barisano* – the *Sassi* district can be entered from a number of different points around the centre of town, some signposted, some not. The **Strada Panoramica dei Sassi**, newly built with an eye to tourism, skirts through both zones and is a useful reference point, but you need to leave this to penetrate the warren and its *chiese rupestri* or **rock-hewn churches**. One, **Santa Maria de Idris**, perched on the conical Monte Errone that rises in the midst of the *Sassi*, has frescoes dating from the fourteenth century, Another, the tenth-century **Santa Lucia alle Malve** in the so-called Albanian quarter (settled by refugees in the fifteenth century), has Byzantine-style frescoes dating from 1250. Others are on the far side of the ravine – detailed itineraries can be obtained at the tourist office.

The more animated face of the old town has its centre at **Piazza Vittorio Veneto**, a large and stately square which in the evening is cleared of traffic and given over to a long procession of shuffling promenaders. The *materani* take their evening *passeggiata* seriously, and the din of the crowds rising up out of this square can be like the noise from a stadium. Matera's modern quarters stretch out to the north and west of here, but most of the things worth seeing are along the Via San Biagio and Via del Corso.

Winding off from the bottom end of the piazza, the narrow Via del Corso leads down to the seventeenth-century church of **San Francesco d'Assisi**, whose ornate Baroque style was superimposed on two older churches, traces of which, including some eleventh-century frescoes, can be visited through a passage in the third chapel on the left. In the main church are eight panels of a polyptych by Bartolomeo Vivarini, set above the altar. Behind San Francesco, on Piazza Sedile, the imposing structure on the right was formerly a convent, then the town hall, and is now a conservatory dedicated to the eighteenth-century composer Egidio Duni, a native of Matera who settled in Paris, where he was largely responsible for popularising Neapolitan comic opera among the pre-revolutionary aristocracy. Via Duomo leads off to the right, a good place to view the sprawling *Sassi* below. The **Duomo**, which effectively divides this area into two, was built in the late thirteenth century and retains a strong Apulian-Romanesque flavour. Between the figures of Peter and Paul on the facade is a sculpture of the patroness of

Matera, Madonna della Bruna. Her feast day, the *Sagra di Santa Bruna*, is celebrated on July 2, when her statue is carried in procession three times round the piazza before being stormed by the onlookers, who are allowed to break up the papier-mâché float and carry off bits as mementos.

From Piazza San Francesco, continue down into Via Ridola to admire the elliptical facade of the **chiesa del Purgatorio**, gruesomely decorated with skulls. A little further on is the **Museo Ridola**, housed in the ex-monastery of Santa Chiara and containing an extensive selection of prehistoric and classical finds from the Matera area (Tues–Sat 9am–2pm, Sun 9am–1pm; free).

Practicalities

Matera is on the *FCL* line, the **station** for which is on Piazza Matteotti, where buses also stop. The **tourist office** is at Via de Viti fe Marco 9, off Via Roma (Mon–Fri 8am–2pm & 3–7pm, Sat 8am–2pm; ☎212.488). The **SIP** telephone office and the **main post office** are in Via del Corso.

The most convenient **place to stay** in Matera is the *Albergo Roma*, at Via Roma 62 (☎0835/333.912; ③); the *President*, Via Roma 13 (☎0835/335791; ⑤), is pricier, while the *Piccolo* at Via de Sariis 11 (☎0835/212.336; ⑥) and the elegant *Albergo Italia* in Via Ridola (☎0835/333.961; ⑦) – with its own restaurant – are more expensive still.

Matera's **restaurants** tend to be expensive, but the food is good. Try the *Trattoria Lucana* in Via Lucana for a quality meal. There is a pizzeria in Piazza Sedile, and a much rowdier affair, *La Panca*, a bit further out from the centre, in Via Giolitti (ten minutes' walk up Via Annunziatella). For a snack and a bit of atmosphere, the basement cavern, *Il Grottino*, in Via San Biagio, does food and local wine. There's also a pizzeria, *Il Castello*, below the Angevin castle, where you can eat outside.

Around Matera

A short distance from Matera and connected by rail, the hilltop town of **MONTESCAGLIOSO** was once a Greek settlement and is now the site of a magnificent ruined eleventh-century Benedictine abbey, the **Abbazia di Sant'Angelo**. There are good views from here over the Bradano Valley. On the same line is the lively medieval town of **MIGLIONICO**, with a finely preserved bastion at one end, fifteenth century, with views all around. It was here in 1481 that the *congiura dei baroni* was held, a meeting of rebellious barons who formed a league in opposition to Ferdinand II of Aragon, from which the castle assumed the name, *Castello del Malconsiglio*.

The SS7, which heads west from here, is the old Via Appia, and is a far preferable route to the newer road which runs parallel. Tracing the ridge between the Bradano and Basento valleys, it takes in a number of good stopoffs. **TRICARICO** is another old hilltop village, quite important in its time, with a **duomo** originally constructed by Robert Guiscard. Further south, **ALIANO** is the village in which Carlo Levi set *Christ Stopped at Eboli*. Called Gagliano by Levi, it's reachable by bus from PISTICCI, on the Matera line. Apart from the yellow "welcome" sign on the outskirts of the village and a general air of well-being, the place has not significantly changed since he was there. Nothing is missing: the church, the piazza where the Fascist mayor gave his regular addresses to the impassive peasants, which gives onto the steep drop of the *fossa del bersagliere* and a striking view over the Agri and the "endless sweep of clay, with the white dots of villages, stretching out as far as the invisible sea" that Levi knew so well. You can see the rather grand house where he stayed at the bottom of the village ("away from the gaze of the mayor and his acolytes"), nearby which is a **museum** (Mon–Sat 10.30am–12.30pm & 5–7pm, Sun 9.30am–12.30pm; free) housing some personal items of Levi's and articles of folkloric interest.

The northern Ionian coast

From Táranto to Reggio, the **Ionian coast** is a mainly flat sandy strip, sometimes monotonous but less developed than the Tyrrhenian side of the peninsula, and with cleaner water. The **northern** section, from **Metaponto** to **Capo Colonna**, consists of a mountainous interior backing onto an empty seaboard, punctuated only by holiday resorts, a plethora of campsites – overflowing, in the summer months, with legions of Italians – and some notable historical sites. Of these, the most significant are connected with the periods of Greek occupation, the most recent of which was that of the Byzantines, who administered the area on and off for 500 years, leaving their traces most strikingly in the hilltop town of **Rossano**. A thousand years earlier, the clutch of Greek colonies collectively known as *Magna Graecia* rose and fell, of which *Metapontion*, *Sybaris* and *Croton*, all on this stretch of the Ionian coast, were some of the greatest. Although only the first of these has been properly excavated, there are museums in all, describing an era that was – culturally and intellectually – the brightest moment in the history of Basilicata and Calabria.

The Basilicata coast

The most extensively excavated of the Greek sites, and the only place of any real significance on the Ionian coast of Basilicata, is at **METAPONTO**, an important road and rail junction connecting the coastal routes between Táranto and Reggio with the interior of Basilicata – to Potenza by train and Matera by bus. *Metapontion* was settled in the eighth century BC and owed its subsequent prosperity to the fertility of the surrounding land – perfect for cereal production (symbolised by the ear of corn stamped on its coinage) and its position as a commercial centre. Pythagoras, banished from Croton, established a school here in about 510 BC that contributed to an enduring philosophical tradition. The city's downfall came as a result of a series of catastrophes: absorbed by Rome, embroiled in the Punic Wars, sacked by the slave-rebel Spartacus, and later desolated by a combination of malaria and Saracen raids.

Lido di Metaponto – and the site

Metaponto today is a straggling, amorphous place, comprising train station, beaches and ruins. Arriving at the station, you're three kilometres from the **LIDO DI METAPONTO**, where there are sandy, well-equipped **beaches** and **campsites**. For those who don't want to sleep under canvas, three of these – the *Lido*, *Magna Grecia* and *San Marco* – also have bungalows available; all have their own beaches and the bigger ones have tennis, discos and other facilities. Otherwise the only moderately priced **hotel** is the *Oasi* (☎0835/741.930; ③), in Viale Olimpia, 1km from the station off the Lido road – very cheap but only open June to September.

For the first batch of ruins, take the next turning on the right after the Lido junction (coming from the station), and follow the narrow lane down to the wide site – signposted **Zona Archeologica** – which has the remains of a theatre and a Temple of Apollo Licius. The latter is a sixth-century BC construction that once possessed 32 columns, but you need some imagination to picture its original appearance. In a better state of preservation is the **Temple of Hera**, or *Tavole Palatine*, 2–3km north, where the main SS106 crosses the Bradano (take one of the buses to Táranto from Metaponto station). With fifteen of its columns remaining, it is the most suggestive remnant of this once mighty state. A good selection of other survivals can be seen at the **Antiquarium** just in front (daily April–Sept 9am–1pm & 3.30–6.30pm; Oct–March 8am–1pm & 3–5pm; L4000), whose items are displayed on a rotating basis, but should include numerous examples of fourth- and fifth-century statuary and ceramics. The aerial photographs with accounts of the excavations are interesting, and look out for examples of the famous coins.

Policoro

There's a more extensive collection of antiquities at the **Museo Nazionale della Siritide**, 25km down the coast, just behind the village of **POLICORO**. The museum (daily 9am–1pm & 3–7.30pm, winter until 6pm; L4000) contains some fascinating material taken from the zone between the Sinni and Agri rivers, in its time one of the richest areas on this coast and site of the two Greek colonies of **Siris** and **Heraclea**. The first of these, after which the museum is named, reached such a position of wealth and eminence that the other colonies were persuaded to gang together in the middle of the sixth century BC to put an end to Sirian ambitions, with devastating consequences. Heraclea was founded on the same spot by Tarentines in 432 BC with the aim of driving a wedge between the Achaean cities of Metapontion and Sybaris to the north and south. It was here that Pyrrhus, king of Epirus, first introduced elephants to the Romans, and although winning the first of two battles in 280 BC, suffered such high losses that he declared another such victory would cost him the war – so bequeathing to posterity the term "Pyrrhic victory".

Into Calabria: Sibari and Rossano

Shortly after crossing the Sinni River you enter Calabria, skirting the base of the lofty Monte Pollino. Look out for the **castle** at **ROCCA IMPERIALE**, built by Frederick II in the style of Lagopésole and Lucera. Imposing from a distance, its state of abandon becomes more obvious as you approach, but the views from its crumbling walls are impressive. Further inland, at the medieval village of **ORIOLO**, there's another **castle**, this one fifteenth century and in a better state of preservation, from which you can continue inland into Basilicata and the woods around SENISE, or loop back to the coast at ROSETO, the site of another of Frederick II's castles, prominent at the side of the road. In Norman times this spot marked the boundaries between the territories controlled by Robert Guiscard and his brother Roger.

Sibari

The mountainous slopes soon give way to the wide **Piana di Sibari**, the most extensive of the Calabrian coastal plains, bounded by Pollino to the north, the Sila Greca to the west and the Sila Grande in the south. The rivers flowing off these mountains, which for centuries kept the land well watered and rich, also helped to transform it into a stagnant and malarial mire, and although land reclamation has restored the area's fertility, without visiting the museum and excavations at **Sibari** you could pass through the area with no inkling of the civilisation that once flourished on these shores.

Long one of the great archaeological mysteries tantalising generations of scholars, the site of ancient *Sybaris* was only definitely identified in the late 1960s, when aerial and X-ray photography confirmed that the site previously known to be that of Roman Thurium was also that of Sybaris. There are in fact three separate levels of construction that have been unearthed here, one Greek and two Roman, each on top of the other. However, the great riches that the excavations were expected to yield have never been found; there have been too many other settlements on this same spot, not to mention the marauders who made regular visits through the centuries.

The wealth of the city – said to number 100,000 in population and have dominion over half a million – was only one factor in its fame, around which myth and documentary evidence have combined to produce a colourful muddle of anecdotes. The city's laws and institutions were apparently made to ensure the greatest comfort and wellbeing of its citizens, including the banning from the city of all noisy traders, such as metalworkers, and the planting of trees along every street for shade. Cooks were so highly prized that they were apparently bought and sold in the marketplace for great sums and were allowed to patent their recipes, while inventions ascribed to the

Sybarites include pasta and the chamberpot. This was all too much for the Crotonians, who, under their general Milo (more famous as a much-garlanded Olympic athlete) sacked and destroyed the city in 510 BC, diverting the waters of the river over the site to complete the job.

The **excavations** lie across the rail lines some 4km south down the new (coastal) SS106. On the left stands the new museum destined to house all finds from each of the local sites, but until that time they live in a low shack (daily 9am–2pm & 4pm–7pm; free) across the road, on the banks of the River Crati. Most of the excavations belong to the Roman period, but something of the earlier site might still be turned up – the silt and sand of the river bed has yet to be explored properly, work having been effectively halted for the last fifteen years due to shortage of funds. Of the Roman city, the remains are at least impressively displayed and maintained, including baths, a patrician's house with mosaics, and a *decumanus* (claimed to be the widest in existence). Just off the site, a small room contains individual finds including some Greek exhibits, mainly ceramic shards, though nothing that would have raised much excitement in the imaginations of the numerous enthusiasts who have passed this way.

Pathirion and Rossano

There are remnants from more recent times further south, near the village of **SANTA MARIA DEL PATIRE**, where the **Monastery of Pathirion** sits among groves of olive and holm-oak at the end of a road built by Austrian prisoners during World War I. Its well-preserved church – a simple basilica – has sweeping views over the Sibari plain and the mountains around, but is the only intact relic of the monastery, which lies in ruins below – an extensive complex that had its centre at nearby Rossano and rivalled the holy mountain of Athos as a centre of monastic learning.

Twelve kilometres away, the resort of **ROSSANO SCALO** has far outstripped its parent-town of **ROSSANO** in terms of size and bustle, and most of the holiday-makers who frequent its **beach** and **campsite** never even get round to visiting the hilltop town, 7km up an awkward winding road – something which has helped to preserve the old centre from excessive development. The foremost Byzantine centre in the south, Rossano was the focus of a veritable renaissance of literature, theology and art between the eighth century and eleventh century, a period to which the town's greatest treasures belong. Its majolica-tiled **Cattedrale** is an Angevin construction largely rebuilt after the 1836 earthquake, but has a much-venerated ninth-century Byzantine fresco, *Madonna Achiropita*, whose Greek epithet, meaning "not painted by hand", refers to its divine authorship (there are several of these in Italy). Behind the cathedral, the **Museo Diocesano** (Mon–Sat 10am–noon & 5–7pm; L2000), contains the famed *codex purpureus Rossanensis*, or Purple Codex, a unique sixth-century manuscript on reddish-purple parchment illustrating the life of Christ. The book, which was brought from Palestine by monks fleeing the Muslim invasions, is open at one page, but you can leaf through a good copy and see, among other things, how the Last Supper was originally depicted, with Christ and his disciples not seated but reclining on cushions round the table, and all eating from the same plate. Other items in this tiny museum include a fifteenth-century icon painted on both sides and formerly at Pathirion, and several pieces of silverware of superb artistry. Walk out, also, to the little church of **San Marco**, at the end of Corso Garibaldi on the edge of town, a tenth- or eleventh-century construction with a strong Middle Eastern flavour, its five cupolas surrounded by palms and giving way to a terrace that's a fine lookout over the gorge below. For the key, apply to the *famiglia* Federico at Via Vallone S. Marco 37.

The *Associazione Ruscianum* in Piazza Anargiri has more information on Rossano and around. For **hotels**, you've got to go to the lower town, but they aren't cheap. Try the *Scigliano* (☎0983/21.848; ⑤), 50m up from the level crossing, or the *Murano*

(☎0983/21.788; ⑥), in Lido Sant'Angelo right by the sea. There's also a **campsite** in town. Just off Piazza Anargiri is a reasonable **pizzeria/trattoria** at Via Martucci 4; and there's another one, *La Botte*, in Via San Nilo off the higher end of the square.

Crotone and around

South of Rossano there is an empty stretch of beaches; inland, the vineyards of Ciro, the source of Calabria's best-known **wine**. Crossing the River Neto into the fertile **Marchesato** region, the approach to **CROTONE** (the ancient Greek *Croton*) is signalled by a smoky industrial zone – not the most alluring entry into a city but a rare thing in Calabri, and testimony to the town's continuing significance in the region's economy.

Crotone

The site of ancient *Croton* has been entirely lost, but in its day this was among the most important colonial settlements of Magna Graecia, overshadowed by its more powerful neighbour Sybaris but with a school of medicine that was famous throughout the classical world and closely linked with the prowess of the city's athletes, who regularly scooped all the honours at the Olympic Games back in Greece. In 530 BC the mathematician and metaphysician Pythagoras took up residence in Croton and established an aristocratic party based on his ideas which eventually gained control here, though the political turmoil that resulted from the sack of Sybaris led to their banishment from the city. Croton went on to be the first of the Greek cities in Calabria but was increasingly destabilised by internal conflicts and the external threat of the encroaching barbarians, eventually being destroyed by the Romans. A resurgence of sorts occurred in the thirteenth century when it was made the main town of the Marchesato region, a vast agricultural territory – extending from the Neto to the Simeri rivers – held by the powerful Ruffo family of Catanzaro. But its prosperity was always hindered by the scourge of malaria, which poisoned every initiative and debilitated its people.

George Gissing, visiting in 1897, called Crotone "a squalid little town", and it's not much better now, most of its seafront given over to industry – though the view isn't so bad once you get past the port, and it's a good base for the beaches that spread to the south and for the Greek ruins at Capo Colonna. There's not a lot to see in Crotone itself. The **Duomo**'s Black Madonna is paraded through the town out to Capo Colonna at midnight on the third Sunday in May (it's transported back by sea the following night); and at the other end of the Corso, the church of the **Immacolata** has a good ossiary in its crypt, containing hundreds of neatly piled skulls grinning under electric candle-light. Continuing up Via Risorgimento, the modern **Museo Archeologico Statale** (July–Sept Tues–Sat 9am–1pm & 3.30–7pm, Sun 9am–1pm; free) displays fragments from the excavations at Crotone and its various colonies and items from Capo Colonna. Further up from the museum is the **Castello** (closed), locally called Charles V's but actually constructed by the Spanish viceroy Don Pedro di Toledo in 1541, and today still surrounded by various palazzi of the Spanish nobility.

Arriving by **train** you will need to take either a taxi or bus the 3km to the centre of town, Piazza Pitagora, and most of the **hotels**. The small and clean *Pensione Ruffo* in Via Ruffo is a good choice (no phone; ④), or there's the slightly cheaper *Albergo Pace*, on Via Cutro (☎0962/22.584; ④). There is no shortage of **pizzerias** in this part of town: opposite the *Pace* hotel, the *Mery* pizzeria cooks its pizzas in a wood-fired oven, while the area around Via Nicoletta has dozens of places, of varying standards and prices. For something more than a pizza, try the *Ristorante Da Peppino* in Largo Umberto (especially good for seafood) at one end of Corso Vittorio Emanuele, the main street in the older part of town.

On from Crotone: Capo Colonna, Capo Rizzuto and La Castella

From the bus office in Via Ruffo, there is one morning departure a day to SANTA SEVERINA (see p.783), but to get to the famed column at **Capo Colonna** on Calabria's extreme eastern point, you have to walk the 11km along the coast. The column is a solitary remnant of a vast structure which served as the temple for all the Greeks in Calabria. Dedicated to Hera Lacinia, it originally possessed forty eight of these Doric columns and was the repository of immense wealth before being repeatedly sacked as Magna Graecia and Hellenism itself declined. The object of Gissing's pilgrimage to Crotone, and a feature of his fevered visions as he lay on his sick bed (he eventually left without seeing it), it remained forever a mirage for him as he strained his eyes on the Crotone seafront, as unattainable as his attempts to recapture the glories of ancient Greece.

There are some excellent **bathing spots** not far south of here. **CAPO RIZZUTO** is a spit of land, not excessively developed and with plenty of sandy or rocky inlets to swim from. In winter it is dead, but it can get quite feverish in the height of summer and difficult to find space in the **hotels** or **rooms to rent**. Nearby **LE CASTELLA** is another busy holiday spot, but not yet strangled by tourism. It would be hard to spoil the beautifully sited Aragonese **castle** on an islet just off the main town (daily 8am–8pm; free). You can climb up its restored tower or swim off the rocks around it. A good beach stretches out to the right, with places allocated for tents. The **hotels** tend to be expensive, but there's an official **campsite**, and it's worth asking around for **rooms**. If you're flush you could try *Il Corsaro* (☎0962/795.178; ⑥); if not, there's the more modest *Onde Blu* (☎0962/795.029; ④).

The Southern Ionian coast

The southern part of Calabria's Ionian seaboard is less developed than the rest of the region, perhaps because it's less interesting scenically and most of the seaside towns and villages strung along it are unappealing. If you like sandy **beaches**, though, this is where to find them – either wild and unpopulated, or, if you prefer, glitzy and brochure-style, as at **Soverato**. At **Locri** there is the best collection of Greek ruins in the region, and, overlooking the coast a short way inland, the craggy medieval strongholds of **Squillace**, **Gerace**, and **Stilo**, with its jewel of Byzantine church-building, the **Cattolica**. Further inland, solace from the hard road may be found in the hills and cool forests of the **Serre**.

Catanzaro

One of the more major resorts is **CATANZARO LIDO**, a bustling, rather overworked place with a variety of hotels and eating-places. It's not a place to hang around in, but you might want to push up to **CATANZARO**, perched on a hilltop just out of sight of the coast. Regular buses leave from outside the main station every twenty minutes or so, and trains on the Calabro-Lucane line operate hourly from an anonymous white building up the road.

Despite its fine position, the appeal of Calabria's regional capital is hard to grasp. A crowded, overdeveloped, traffic-ridden city, it's a useful base for the Sila Piccola and is within a short ride of some five-star beaches, but is otherwise best avoided. It has much in common with its northern neighbour, Cosenza, and perhaps for this reason they share an implacable rivalry. Both are inland mountain towns within sight of the Sila range, although Catanzaro also has a view over the sea, from which frequent strong winds keep the town relatively free of the sticky heat that can clog Cosenza during the summer months. Both towns have also been subject to repeated devastations of human and natural causes, though Catanzaro has suffered the most, being almost entirely demolished by a 1783 earthquake and robbed of any residual character by postwar property speculation.

Piazza Matteotti separates the older from the newer end of the city, and is terminus for most of the buses from outside town. Corso Mazzini leads off from the square, an animated stream of cars and people around which is almost everything that is worth seeing in Catanzaro – though, to be frank, it doesn't amount to much. Step into the huge eighteenth-century Baroque church of the **Immacolata** to see four of the few remaining examples of the work of the Neapolitan Caterina de Iuliani: biblical scenes modelled in wax, rather difficult to make out clearly because they need to be kept away from excessive heat and light. Behind the town hall, **Villa Trieste** is a tranquil public garden on the edge of the ravine, the haunt of card-players and couples in clinches, and with views over one of the two viaducts that tether Catanzaro to the surrounding hills – much used for suicides, they say, before the higher *viadotto* was built on the other side. The nearby **Museo Provinciale** (Thurs & Fri 10am–noon; free) is just three rooms containing a good coin collection, various artefacts from local digs and some paintings.

Practicalities

An **overnight stay** in Catanzaro isn't recommended, but if you get stuck there are a couple of basic *locandas* – the *Locanda Pompea*, Via Poerio 32, behind the *Upim* supermarket (no phone; ④), and *Locanda Mario*, on Piazza Galluppi (no phone; ④). More comfortably, there's the slightly pricier *Belvedere* in Via Italia (☎0961/29812; ④). An interesting place **to eat**, or just sit for a quick snack or glass of wine, is the old *bettola*, or wine shop, in Vicolo San Rocchello. Recently converted to suit modern tastes without altogether sacrificing its old character, it's a place to sample a variety of local specialities and cheap wine, and a complete meal shouldn't cost more than L20,000.

Squillace and around

Continuing on down the Ionian coast, the **Roccelletta del Véscovo di Squillace** lies some hundred metres up the side-road signposted San Floro and Borgia – a rather grand name for a shell of an old basilica, partly restored, situated in an olive grove on the left of the road. Once the second largest church in Calabria (after Gerace), it still has a mighty impact on the unsuspecting viewer for its sheer size. It is of uncertain date, though probably Norman in origin, founded by Basilian monks. Much of the building material used in its construction came from the remains of the Roman town of *Scolacium*, the excavations of which (theatre, amphitheatre and some baths) are not yet open to the public but may be spied by walking on through the olive grove. A museum is also planned.

Five kilometres further, at LIDO DI SQUILLACE, is the turnoff for the old town of **SQUILLACE**, 8km up in the hills, once an important centre but now just a mountain village, rather isolated on its high crag from the currents of Calabrian life. There are lofty views to be enjoyed over the Gulf and beyond Catanzaro as far as the Sila Piccola, and the **castle** (open only in the summer months) is one of the most romantic collections of ruins in Calabria. But the place is probably most renowned for its associations with **Cassiodorus**, whose monastery was located in the vicinity – though all trace of it has long since disappeared. Cassiodorus (480–570) was learned secretary to the Ostrogoth, Theodoric, and used his position to preserve much of Italy's classical heritage against the onset of the Dark Ages and the book-burning propensities of the Christians. Retiring to spend the last thirty years of his life in seclusion here, Cassiodorus composed histories and collections of documents which have been of invaluable use to historians.

Inland to the Serre

South of Squillace, the golden sands of the resorts of **COPANELLO** and **SOVERATO** beckon, two towns which are increasingly attracting the international market. The private lidos hold sway here, charging L5000–10,000 for a day under a parasol on a clean **beach** with access to a bar; there are no cheap **hotels**, but plenty of swimming, dancing and summer madness. From Soverato, buses leave for the leafy uplands of the **Serre**, a little-known area that's well worth a visit for its lush green slopes and shady glens. In its thick beech and oak forest it's still possible to see black-faced *carbonari* making charcoal in the traditional way, cooking the wood in conical ovens resembling dozens of miniature smoking volcanoes.

As far as **hotels** are concerned, you won't find any outside **SERRA SAN BRUNO**, a secluded village in the heart of the Serre where the Soverato bus stops. This is the most visited place in the area, mainly because of the famous Carthusian abbey twenty minutes' walk south of town. The **Certosa di Santo Stefano del Bosco** was built on land granted by the Norman Count Roger in 1090 to Saint Bruno, the founder of the strict Carthusian order who lent his name to the village. The abbey grew in wealth and influence, accumulating vast portions of land in Calabria and Sicily, but was almost completely destroyed by a series of earthquakes in 1783. Rebuilt, it is still going strong, although much reduced from its former glory; one of the monks – who recently died – was rumoured to be one of the American airmen who flew on the atomic-bomb missions to Japan. Men only can visit the ruins of the old monastery inside (ring the bell) from 11am to noon and 4 to 5pm every day except Sunday.

A couple of kilometres further down the road, the little church of **Santa Maria del Bosco** stands on the site of the first church founded here by Saint Bruno. You can see the cave where the saint is said to have prayed, and a pond with his statue kneeling in the middle. Legend has it that when the saint died in 1101 he was buried on this spot, the spring gushing forth when his bones were later dug up to be transferred to the abbey. The water is prized by devotees, who gather to bathe here on Whit Monday, when a statue of Saint Bruno is brought from the abbey.

The coast to Locri

South of the developed lidos around Soverato, the coast assumes a bare, empty look that it keeps until the outskirts of Reggio, though with views of the distant mountains of the Serre and Aspromonte to stave off monotony. On the far side of Monasterace a turnoff where the bus stops leads to **STILO**, 11km up the side of the rugged Consolino mountain. An influential centre at different periods, Stilo is best known for the tiny tenth-century Byzantine temple, the **Cattolica** (daily 9am–8pm, or until sunset in winter; free, but tip), which can be reached by car by taking the first hairpin on the right at the end of the village, or on foot by climbing a series of alleys from the village's main street, Via Tommaso Campanella. Once a base for hermits and Basilian monks in the south of Calabria, this perfectly proportioned temple has little remaining inside of its former glory, apart from some damaged frescoes and four slim, upturned columns taken from an older temple. The name of **Tommaso Campanella** occurs everywhere in Stilo, a reminder of the village's links with this Dominican friar and utopian philosopher. Campanella was hounded by the Inquisition principally for his support of the Copernican model of the solar system, although his idealistic views didn't endear him to the champions of orthodoxy either. The shell of **San Domenico** church, part of the convent where he lived, can be seen by following Via Campanella to the Porta Stefanina at the end of the village. Halfway along the road, look into the thirteenth-century **Duomo**, its ogival Gothic portal the only part remaining from the original construction. Note, too, along with other Byzantine and Norman reliefs, the surreal pair of feet stuck onto the wall on the left of the door, taken from a pagan temple and symbolising the triumph of the Church.

There is one **hotel** in Stilo, the *San Giorgio* at Via Citarelli 8 (☎0964/731153; ⑤), just off the main Via Campanella. Occupying a seventeenth-century cardinal's palace and furnished in period style, it looks expensive but is really excellent value, equipped with a swimming pool and with wide views over the Ionian from its spacious terrace. Run by a Milanese acting company who stage performances on the premises, it's unarguably the most unusual hotel in Calabria.

Continuing south, you pass the resort of **RIACE**, where the Bronzi di Riace were found (see p.788), although the most famous classical ruins on this coast are at **Locri Epizefiri**, some 3km beyond the town of **LOCRI**. Founded at some time in the seventh century BC, the city of *Locris* was responsible for the first written code of law throughout the Hellenic world. Its moment of glory came in the second half of the sixth century when, assisted by Castor and Pollux, 10,000 Locrians defeated 130,000 Crotonians on the banks of the River Sagra, 25km north. Busy founding colonies and gathering fame in the spheres of horse rearing and music, the city was an ally of Syracuse but eventually declined during Roman times. The walls of the city, traces of which can still be seen, measured some five miles in circumference, and the excavations within are now interspersed over a wide area among farms and orchards. Transport would be useful for some of the more far-flung features, though many can be visited on foot without too much effort, including a fifth-century BC Ionic temple, a Roman necropolis and a well-preserved Graeco-Roman theatre. In any case make a stop at the **museum** (daily 9am–1pm & 4–6pm; free) to consult the plan of the site. Inside you can examine the most recent finds, including a good collection of **pinakes**, or votive ceramics – though some of the best items have been appropriated by the Museo Nazionale at Reggio.

When the Saracens devastated Locris in the seventh century AD, the survivors fled inland to found **GERACE**, on an impregnable site which was later occupied and strengthened by the Normans. At the end of a steep and tortuous road 10km up from modern Locri, its ruined **castle** stands at one end of the town on a sheer cliff, as inaccessible now as it ever was. Easier to visit is the **Duomo**, founded in 1045 by Robert Guiscard, enlarged by Frederick II in 1222 and today still the biggest church in Calabria. Its simple and well-preserved interior has twenty columns of granite and marble, each different and with various capitals; the tenth on the right in *verde antico* changes tone according to the weather. Two other churches from the same period that are worth a look are **San Francesco** and **San Giovanello**, at the end of Via Cavour (to the left of the Duomo's main entrance), both showing an interesting mix of Norman, Byzantine and Saracenic influences.

travel details

Trains

Cosenza to: Naples (2 daily; 5hr); Paola (hourly; 20min); Rome (2 daily; 7hr).

Matera to: Bari (*Ferrovia Calabro–Lucane*; 12 daily; 1hr 30min).

Paola to: Naples (15 daily; 5hr); Rome (15 daily; 7hr).

Potenza (Inferiore) to: Battipaglia (6 daily; 2hr); Foggia (10 daily; 2hr 30min); Táranto (10 daily; 2hr 10min).

Reggio to: Naples/Rome (15 daily; 6hr/8hr).

Buses

Cosenza to: Catanzaro (8 daily; 1hr); Reggio (6 daily; 2hr); Rome (1 daily; 6hr).

Matera to: Potenza (3 daily; 1hr).

Potenza to: Matera (2 daily; 1hr); Naples (4 daily; 2hr); Rome (2 daily; 3hr 30min).

Ferries and hydrofoils

Reggio to: Catania/Siracusa (3 weekly; 3hr 15min/6hr 30min); Messina (hourly; 15min).

Villa San Giovanni to: Messina (every 30min; 45min).

CHAPTER SIXTEEN

SICILY

I like Sicily extremely – a good on-the-brink feeling – one hop and you're out of Europe . . .

D.H. Lawrence in a letter to Lady Cynthia Asquith, 1920.

The Sicilians aren't the only people to consider themselves, and their island, a separate entity. Coming from the Italian mainland, it's easy to spot that **Sicily** (Sicilia) has a different feel, that socially and culturally you *are* all but out of Europe. Occupying a strategically vital position, and as the largest island in the Mediterranean, Sicily's history and outlook are not those of its modern parent but of its erstwhile foreign rulers – from the Greeks who first settled the east coast in the eighth century BC, through a dazzling array of Romans, Arabs, Normans, French and Spanish, to the Bourbons seen off by Garibaldi in 1860. Substantial relics of these ages remain: temples, theatres and churches are scattered about the whole island. But there are other, more immediate hints of Sicily's unique past. A hybrid Sicilian language, for a start, is still widely spoken in the countryside; the food is noticeably different, spicier and with more emphasis on fish and vegetables; even the flora echoes the change of temperament – oranges, lemons, olives and palms are ubiquitous.

Sicily also still promotes a real sense of **arrival**. The standard approach for those heading south from the mainland is to cross the Straits of Messina, from Villa San Giovanni or Reggio di Calabria: this way, the train-ferry pilots a course between *Scylla* and *Charybdis*, the twin hazards of rock and whirlpool that were a legendary threat to sailors. Coming in by plane, too, there are spectacular approaches to either of the coastal airports at Palermo and Catania.

Once on land, deciding **where to go** is largely a matter of time. Inevitably, most points of interest are on the coast: the interior of the island is often mountainous, always sparsely populated and relatively inaccessible. The capital **Palermo** is a memorable first stop, a bustling, noisy city with an unrivalled display of Norman art and architecture and Baroque churches, combined with a warren of medieval streets and markets. From modern and earthquake-ravaged **Messina**, the most obvious trips are to the chic resort of **Taormina** and the lava-built second city of **Catania**. A skirt around the foothills, and even up to the craters of **Mount Etna**, shouldn't be missed on any visit to the island; while to the south sit **Siracusa**, once the most important city of the Greek world, and a baroque group of towns centring on **Ragusa**. The south coast's greatest draw is the Greek temples at **Agrigento**, while inland, **Enna** is typical of the mountain towns that provided defence for a succession of the island's rulers. Close by is **Piazza Armerina** and its Roman mosaics, and to the west, most of Sicily's fishing industry – and much of the continuing Mafia activity – focuses on the area around **Trápani**. To see all these places, you'll need at least a couple of weeks – more like a month if you want to travel extensively inland, a slower and more traditional experience altogether.

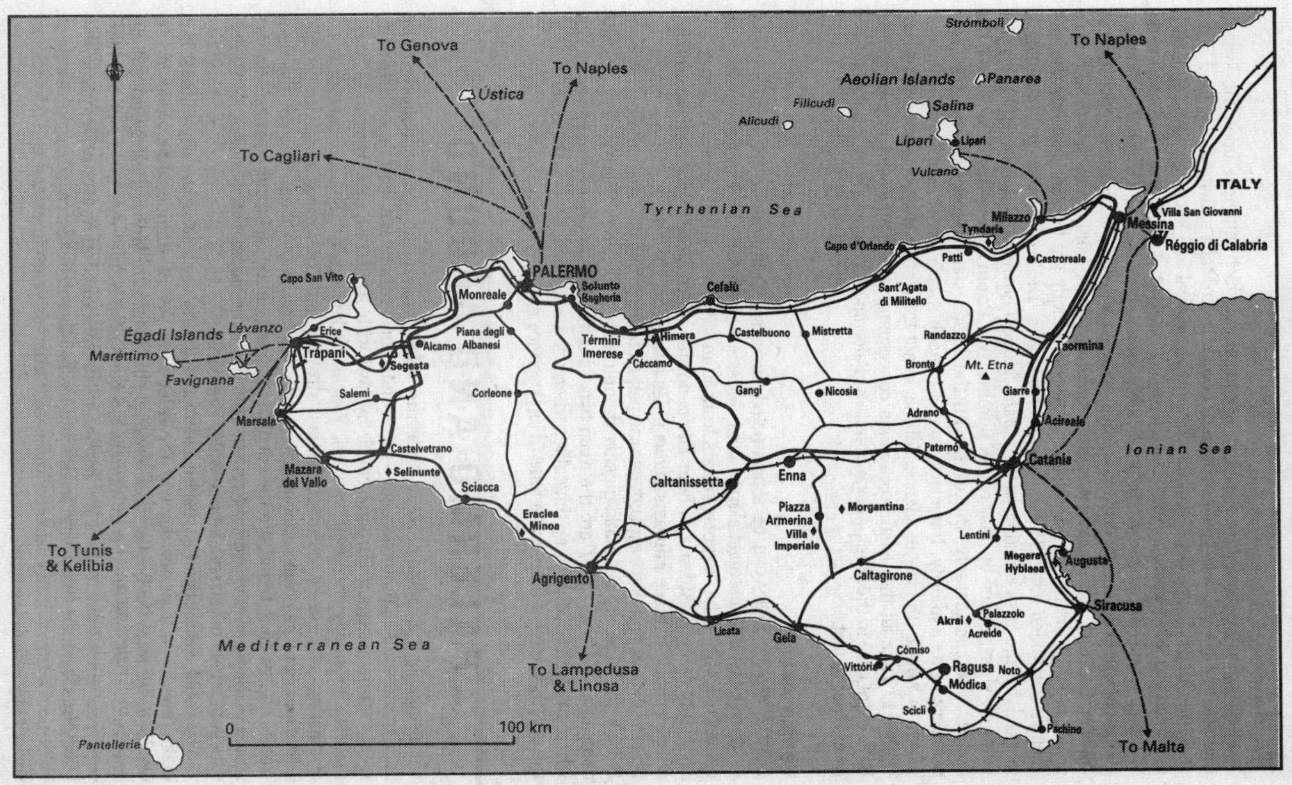
To Genova
To Naples
Ústica
To Cagliari
Strómboli
To Naples
Aeolian Islands
Panarea
Filicudi
Salina
Alicudi
Lipari
Lipari
Vulcano
ITALY
Tyrrhenian Sea
Milazzo
Villa San Giovanni
Messina
Tyndaris
Réggio di Calabria
Capo d'Orlando
Patti
Castroreale
PALERMO
Capo San Vito
Solunto
Bagheria
Monreale
Cefalù
Sant'Agata di Militello
Égadi Islands
Lévanzo
Erice
Piana degli Albanesi
Términi Imerese
Himera
Castelbuono
Mistretta
Randazzo
Marèttimo
Trápani
Alcamo
Taormina
Segesta
Cáccamo
Bronte
Mt. Etna
Favignana
Salemi
Corleone
Gangi
Nicosia
Giarre
Adrano
Marsala
Acireale
Castelvetrano
Paternò
Ionian Sea
Mazara del Vallo
Selinunte
Catania
Enna
Caltanissetta
Sciacca
Piazza Armerina
Morgantina
Eraclea Minoa
Villa Imperiale
Lentini
To Tunis & Kelibia
Megara Hyblaea
Augusta
Agrigento
Caltagirone
Siracusa
Akrai
Palazzolo
Acreide
Licata
Gela
Mediterranean Sea
Cómiso
To Lampedusa & Linosa
Vittória
Ragusa
Noto
Módica
Scicli
0
100 km
Pachino
Pantelleria
To Malta

The Mafia

Whatever else the **Mafia** is, it isn't an organisation which impinges upon the lives of tourists, and it's unlikely you'll come into contact with Mafia activity of any kind. That said, the Mafia does exist – and for very real historical and social reasons. But what began as an early medieval conspiracy, to protect the family from oppressive intrusions of the state, has developed along predictable lines. Throughout the twentieth century, alongside the endemic poverty, Sicily has endured a system of allegiance, preferment and patronage of massive self-perpetuating proportions, from which few local people profit. Most of the towns and villages of western Sicily are tainted, and Palermo and Trápani have been noted Mafia centres for decades. The recent escalation of violence, marked by the assassination of anti-Mafia judge **Giovanni Falcone** in May 1992, followed shortly after by that of his number two **Paolo Borsellino**, has raised the temperature considerably. But even with the Italian state traumatised by this cruel mockery of its authority, travellers won't be much aware of the problem, due to the power of *omertà*, the law of silence. All this is not to say that **petty crime** won't make itself felt. Take all the usual precautions concerning your money and valuables, and have extra care in the cities – certain parts of Palermo and Catania have reputations it's as well not to test.

Getting around

Getting around Sicily can be a protracted business. **Trains** along the northern and eastern coasts (Messina–Palermo and Messina–Siracusa) are extensions of – or connected with – the "express" trains from Rome/Naples, which means that they are invariably delayed. At least an hour late is normal. Also, Sicily's geographical oddities often conspire to place railway stations miles away from the relevant town – check the text for details, and don't expect your rail passes to be as much use as on the mainland. **Buses**, as usual, are generally quicker though more expensive. There's no single bus company – *SAIS* and *AST* are the main two – but the local tourist office can point out where to catch what. Pick up timetables wherever you go and, despite the assertions to the contrary, expect there to be little (if any) service anywhere on a Sunday.

PALERMO AND AROUND

Unmistakably the capital of Sicily, **Palermo** is fast, brash, loud and exciting. Here the Sicilian fusion of all things foreign – art, architecture, culture and lifestyle – exists at its most extreme: elegant Baroque cheek by jowl with Arabic cupolas, Byzantine street markets swamping medieval warrens, Vespas parked against Spanish palazzi. It's a fascinating place to be, as much for just strolling and consuming as for its specific attractions. But Palermo's monuments, when you can get to them through the tight streets and swirling traffic, are the equal of anything on the mainland: the city's unique series of Baroque and Arabic-Norman churches, the unparalleled mosaic work and excellent museums all stand much wider comparison.

You could easily spend a week in Palermo without ever leaving the city's limits. But make time for at least one day trip: the capital has several traditional bolt-holes if you want a break from the bustle, most obviously the heights of **Monte Pellegrino** and the fine beach at **Mondello**. If your interest has been fired by the city's great Norman heritage, you won't want to miss the famous medieval cathedral of **Monreale**, just a few kilometres west. Or year-round ferries and hydrofoils run to **Ústica**, 60km northwest of Palermo – a tiny volcanic island with enough impressive grottoes and coastal walks to occupy any remaining time.

Palermo

In its own wide bay underneath the limestone bulk of Monte Pellegrino, and fronting the broad, fertile Conca d'Oro (Golden Shell) valley, **PALERMO** is stupendously sited. Originally a Phoenician, then a Carthaginian colony, this remarkable city was long considered a prize worth capturing. Named Panormus (All Harbour), its mercantile attractions were obvious, and under Saracen and Norman rule in the ninth to twelfth centuries Palermo became the greatest city in Europe – famed for the wealth of its court, and peerless as a centre of learning. There are plenty of relics from this era, but it's the rebuilding of the sixteenth and seventeenth centuries that shaped the city as you see it today.

It's worth making Palermo your first stop in Sicily. It's the island's main transport centre, and it boasts Sicily's greatest concentration of sights. Quite apart from the Arab influence in its finest churches, there's more than a hint of the city's eastern past in its undisciplined centre, a sprawling, almost anarchic mass with no real focus: great pockets of medieval alleys, munificent nineteenth-century piazzas, twentieth-century bomb-sites and contemporary office blocks conspiring to confuse what is essentially a straightforward street grid. Money from Rome and from the European Community has been earmarked for a redevelopment of the city centre but it's difficult to see that ever happening: this is partly due to the age-old system of kickbacks for contracts and tenders to bent politicians and the Mafia, which would cream off much of the money. One of the few to stand up against this state of affairs was **Leoluca Orlando**, Palermo's mayor until his deposition by his own Christian Democrat party in 1990. Now leader of his own anti-Mafia and anti-Masonic party, **La Rete**, Orlando has moved on to the national stage, doubtless retaining his place on the Mafia's hit list. Meanwhile Palermo itself is once more abandoned to graft and corruption.

Essential city stops are all pretty central, and if you are disciplined enough you could get around them in a couple of days. Paramount are the hybrid **Cattedrale** and nearby **Palazzo dei Normanni** or Royal Palace, with its superb, mosaic-decorated chapel, the **Cappella Palatina**; the glorious Norman churches of **La Martorana** and **San Giovanni degli Eremeti**; the Baroque opulence of **San Giuseppe dei Teatini** and **Santa Caterina**; and three magnificent **museums** – inspiring collections of art, archaeology and ethnography.

This historical jumble of treasures has its downside. Many people have continued to live in their medieval ghettoes, unemployment is endemic, the old port largely idle and petty crime commonplace. Some areas can be positively dangerous if you're not careful, and every *pensione* owner will warn you to watch your money and camera. There are no Third World extremes here but – like parts of the southern mainland – plenty of glaring contrasts with the wealthy north of Italy.

The Palermo area telephone code is ☎091.

Arrival, information and transport

Palermo's **airport** is at Punta Raisi, 31km west of the city, from where fairly regular buses (fifteen daily) run into the centre, stopping outside the Politeama Garibaldi theatre on Via I. La Lumia, then at the train station; first bus is at 5.40am, last bus 9.30pm, journey time 45 minutes (L4500). Taxi fares for the same trip run to around L60,000 per car (though you might be able to negotiate a lower price), so night flight arrivals may prefer to wait for the first bus of the day.

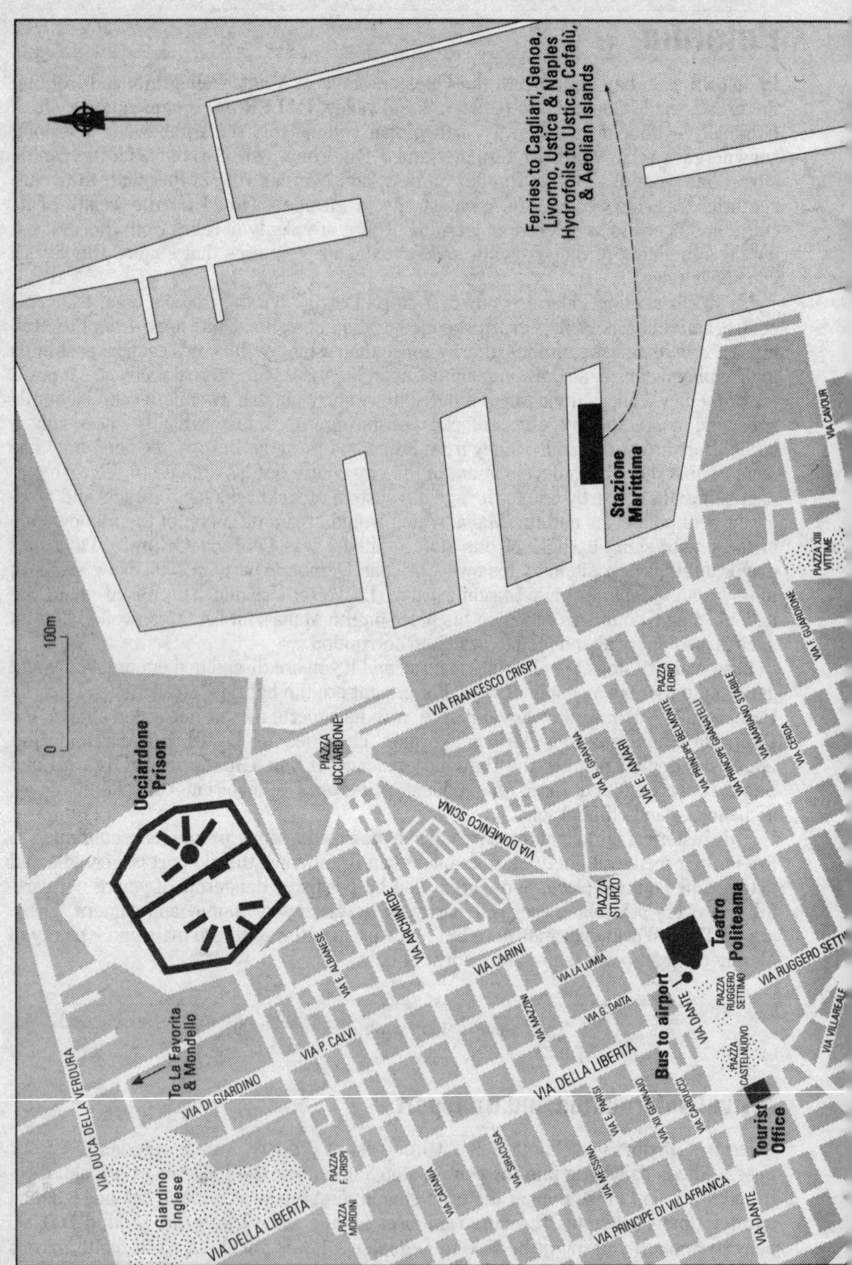

Ferries to Cagliari, Genoa, Livorno, Ustica & Naples
Hydrofoils to Ustica, Cefalù, & Aeolian Islands
Stazione Marittima
Ucciardone Prison
0
100m
PIAZZA UCCIARDONE
VIA FRANCESCO CRISPI
VIA CAVOUR
PIAZZA XIII VITTIME
VIA F. GUARDIONE
PIAZZA FLORIO
VIA PRINCIPE BELMONTE
VIA PRINCIPE GRANATELLI
VIA PRINCIPE MARIANO STABILE
VIA CERDA
VIA E. AMARI
VIA B. GRAVINA
VIA DOMENICO SCINA
PIAZZA STURZO
Teatro Politeama
VIA RUGGERO SETTIMO
VIA ARCHIMEDE
VIA E. ALBANESE
VIA CARINI
VIA LA LUMIA
Bus to airport
PIAZZA RUGGERO SETTIMO
VIA DANTE
VIA G. DAITA
VIA MAZZINI
VIA VILLAREALE
PIAZZA CASTELNUOVO
VIA DELLA LIBERTA
VIA P. CALVI
To La Favorita & Mondello
VIA DUCA DELLA VERDURA
VIA DI GIARDINO
VIA E. PARISI
VIA XII GENNAIO
VIA CARDUCCI
Tourist Office
Giardino Inglese
PIAZZA F. CRISPI
PIAZZA MORDINI
VIA CATANIA
VIA SIRACUSA
VIA MESSINA
VIA PRINCIPE DI VILLAFRANCA
VIA DANTE
VIA DELLA LIBERTA

CENTRAL PALERMO
La Cala
Porta Felice
Santa Maria della Catena
FORO ITALICO
Palazzo Chiaramonte
PIAZZA MARINA
Giardino Garibaldi
Galleria Regionale
La Gancia
Santa Maria di Miracoli
PIAZZA DELLA KALSA
Villa Giulia
Botanical Gardens
VIA LINCOLN
VIA ARCHIRAFI
S. Theresa
VIA DI SPASIMO
LA KALSA
PIAZZA MAGIONE
La Magione
Palazzo Aiutamicristo
VIA GARIBALDI
CORSO DEI MILLE
Stazione Centrale
Telephone Office
PIAZZA GIULIO CESARE
Bus to airport
VIA ORETO
VIA R. GREGORIO
VIA P. BALSAMO
VIA MAQUEDA
VIA ROMA
Palazzo S. Croce
VIA DIVISI
VIA MILANO
VIA GORIZIA
VIA M. SANTO
VIA TORINO
VIA TRIESTE
VIA S. ROSALIA
PIAZZA DELLA REVOLUZIONE
VIA SCHIAVUZZO
VIA PATERNOSTRO
PIAZZA CROCE DI VESPRI
VIA ALLORO
San Francesco d'Assisi
VIA MERLO
VIA BOTTAI
CORSO VITTORIO EMANUELE
VUCCIRIA
VIA CALA
Oratorio di San Lorenzo
PIAZZA CASSA DI RISPARMIO
Santa Caterina
PIAZZA PRETORIA
Municipio
La Martorana
PIAZZA BELLINI
San Cataldo
Quattro Canti
San Giuseppe del Teatini
PIAZZA BOLOGNI
Università
VIA DELL'UNIVERSITÀ
PIAZZA CASA PROFESSA
Il Gesù
VIA PONTICELLO
VIA DI BOSCO
PIAZZA DEL CARMINE
Carmine
PIAZZA BALLARO
San Nicolò
ALBERGHERIA
CORSO TUKORY
VIA ALBERGHERIA
San Giorgio
Oratorio di Santa Zita
Oratorio del Rosario
VIA MELI
San Domenico
PIAZZA SAN DOMENICO
VIA ARGENTERIA
VIA GAGINI
Museo Archeologico
Palazzo delle Poste (Post Office)
VIA MONTELEONE
VIA BANDIERA
VIA BARI
VIA NAPOLI
VIA VENEZIA
VIA CAVOUR
VIA N. COZZO
VIA S. SPINUZZA
VIA BARA OLIVELLA
VIA DELL'OROLOGIO
VIA TRABIA
VIA MAQUEDA
VIA A. AMICO
Sant'Agostino
VIA CANDELAI
VIA DEL CELSO
PIAZZA VERDI
Teatro Massimo
Telephone Office
PIAZZA UNGHERIA
VIA PIGNATELLI ARAGONA
VIA VOLTURNO
VIA SAN GREGORIO
VIA SANT'AGOSTINO
PIAZZA BEATI PAOLI
Cattedrale
PIAZZA CATTEDRALE
Palazzo Sclafani
PIAZZA SAN GIOVANNI
VIA PORTA DI CASTRO
VIA A. MONGITORE
CAPO
Palazzo Arcivescovile
Villa Bonnano
CORSO CALATAFIMI
Porta Nuova
PIAZZA VITTORIO
Palazzo dei Normanni
VIA DEI BENEDETTINI
San Giovanni degli Eremiti
CORSO RE RUGGERO
PIAZZA INDIPENDENZA
Parco d'Orleans
To La Cuba & Monreale (8 km)
To Convento dei Cappuccini
Palazzo di Giustizia
PIAZZA VITT. EMANUELE ORLANDO
To La Zisa
VIA CARNI
PIAZZA S. FRANCESCO DI PAOLA
VIA LATINI
VIA CLUVERIO

Trains all pull in at the Stazione Centrale, at the southern end of Via Roma, close to the cheap accommodation; buses #14, #15, #16 and #19, from outside the station, connect with the modern city. Other country- and island-wide **buses** operate from terminals all over Palermo; full details in the "Listings" section. All **ferry and hydrofoil** services dock at the Stazione Maríttima, just off Via Francesco Crispi, from where it's a ten-minute walk up Via E. Amari to Piazza Castelnuovo.

Information

Palermo's main **tourist office** is at Piazza Castelnuovo 34 (Mon–Fri 8am–8pm, Sat 8am–2pm; ☎586.122 or 583.847); it has big free maps of the city and province, and a booklet (*Palermo Hotels*) containing full accommodation lists. There are other smaller offices, which can at least provide maps: at the airport (Mon–Sat 8am–8pm), Stazione Centrale (Mon–Fri 8am–8pm, Sat 8am–2pm), Stazione Maríttima (summer Mon–Sat 9am–1.30pm), and in Piazza Sepolcro (Mon–Sat 8am–2pm), below the church of San Cataldo. For more complete **city listings** and a rundown of what's on, pick up a copy of *Un Mese a Palermo*, a free arts and entertainment guide issued monthly and available from the tourist offices.

City transport

Palermo is very much a city in which to **walk**, but you'll find getting around exclusively on foot exhausting and impractical. The **city buses** (run by *AMAT*) are easy to use, covering every corner of Palermo and stretching out to Monreale and Mondello. There's a flat fare of L1000 and you buy tickets from the glass booths outside Stazione Centrale or at the southern end of Viale della Libertà, in *tabacchi* and wherever else you see the *AMAT* sign; validate one in the machine at the back of the bus every time you ride. There's a discount if you buy twenty tickets at once (L12,000). Buses run up until around 11pm, when night-services take over on all the main routes – generally once an hour. Main city **bus ranks** are outside Stazione Centrale, in Piazza Castelnuovo/Piazza Ruggero Settimo, along Corso Vittorio Emanuele and along the southern stretch of Viale della Libertà. Otherwise, don't be afraid of jumping into a **taxi** (ranks outside the train station and in other main piazzas), a cheap and safe way to get around at night – just make sure the meter is switched on.

Accommodation

Nearly all the reasonable budget **hotel accommodation** in Palermo is on and around the southern ends of Via Maqueda and Via Roma, roughly in the area between Stazione Centrale and Corso Vittorio Emanuele. Here there are often several places in the same block, usually cheaper the higher the floor. Beyond the Corso the streets begin to widen out and the hotels get more expensive, though there a few exceptions.

Best choices along **Via Roma** are the *Albergo Concordia* at no. 188 (☎617.1514; ③), the *Diana* also at no. 188 (☎329.959; ③), and the *Serena* (☎281.731; ③) at no. 72 – very friendly and with big rooms. The *Albergo Olimpia* at no. 18 (☎616.1276; ③), with rooms overlooking Piazza Cassa di Risparmio, is off to the right just before Corso Vittorio Emanuele.

On **Via Maqueda**, the large block at no. 8 conceals the *Eden* (☎616.7455; ③), the *Sud* (☎617.5700; ③), and the *Vittoria* (☎616.2437; ④). One of the most atmospheric hotels in Palermo is the *Orientale* at no. 26 (☎616.5727; ④), a few cavernous rooms in a marble-studded palazzo. For more modern rooms and facilities, try the *Alessandra*, Via Divisi 99 (☎616.7009; ③), at the corner with Via Maqueda.

Elsewhere in the city, a couple of good budget options are the *Castelnuovo*, right on Piazza Castelnuovo (☎334.072; ③), and the *Albergo Odeon*, Via E. Amari 140 (☎332.778; ③), opposite the Politeama theatre.

If you're **camping** you'll have to take bus #28 from the Politeama theatre out to SFERRACAVALLO, 13km northwest, where there are two all-year sites: the *Trinacria* on Via Barcarello (☎530.590), and the cheaper *Ulivo* on Via Pegaso (☎533.021). Don't even think of **sleeping rough** in the centre of the city – if the thieves don't get you, the police will.

The City

Historical Palermo sits compactly around one central crossroads, the **Quattro Canti**, and within the four quarters that it delineates: southwest and the **Albergheria**, northwest and the **Capo** quarter beyond the cathedral, northeast and the **Vucciria** and old harbour, and southeast and **La Kalsa**. In these areas you'll find virtually all the surviving ancient monuments and buildings of the city, a confusing chronological jumble. Each quarter, too, retains something of its medieval character in a system of rundown labyrinthine streets and alleys which speak volumes about the quality of life behind the rich churches and sights. Don't be unnecessarily wary though – most areas are never anything less than perfectly safe in the daytime.

Around the Quattro Canti

Heart of the old city is the **Quattro Canti**, or "Four Corners", erected in 1611: not so much a piazza as a dingy Baroque crossroads that divides old Palermo into its quadrants. You'll pass this junction many times, awash with traffic, newspaper vendors sitting under the ugly fountain water spouts, and it's worth one turn around to check the tiered statues – respectively a season, a king of Sicily and a patron of the city – in each concave "corner".

On the southwest corner (entrance on Corso Vittorio Emanuele), **San Giuseppe dei Teatini**, begun in 1612, is the most harmonious of the city's Baroque churches. Inside there's a wealth of detail – especially in the lavish side chapels – given plenty of contrasting space by 22 enormous supporting columns in nave and dome. Outside, across Via Maqueda, is **Piazza Pretoria**, floodlit at night to highlight the nude figures of its great central fountain, a racy sixteenth-century Florentine design since protected by railings to ward off excitable vandals. The piazza also holds the restored Municipio, plaque-studded and pristine, while towering above both square and fountain is the massive flank of **Santa Caterina** (open at 10am for short visits, Sun only), Sicilian Baroque at its most exuberant, every inch of the enormous interior covered in a wildly decorative, pustular relief-work, deep reds and yellows filling in between sculpted cherubs, Madonnas, lions and eagles.

You enter Santa Caterina from **Piazza Bellini**, just around the corner, the site of two more wildly contrasting churches. The little Saracenic red golfball domes belong to **San Cataldo**, a squat twelfth-century chapel on a palm-planted bank above the piazza. Never decorated, it retains a good mosaic floor in an otherwise bare and peaceful interior. The understatement of this little chapel is more than offset by the splendid interior of the adjacent **La Martorana** (Mon–Sat 8.30am–1pm & 3.30–7.30pm, Sun 8.30am–1pm; closes 5.30pm in winter) – one of the finest survivors of the medieval city. With a Norman foundation, the church received a Baroque going-over – and its curving northern facade – in 1588. Both, happily, don't detract from the power of the interior, entered through the slim twelfth-century campanile, which retains its ribbed arches and slender columns. Inside, on and around the columns supporting the main cupola, is a series of spectacular **mosaics**, animated twelfth-century Greek works. A gentle Christ dominates the dome, surrounded by angels, the Apostles and the Madonna to the sides. The colours are still strong, the admirable craft work picked out by the sun streaming in through the high windows. Two more original mosaic panels have been set in frames on the walls just inside the entrance to the church: a kneeling George of

Antioch (the church's founder) dedicating La Martorana to the Virgin and King Roger being crowned by Christ – the diamond-studded monarch contrasting with a larger, more dignified Christ.

The Albergheria and the Palazzo dei Normanni

The district just to the northwest of the train station – the **Albergheria** – can't have changed substantially for several hundred years. A warren of tiny streets and tall leaning buildings, it's an engaging place to wander in, much of the central area taken up by a street market which conceals several fine churches too. Via Ponticello leads down past the Baroque church of **Il Gesu** (daily 7–10.30am & 5–6.30pm), first Jesuit foundation in Sicily and gloriously decorated inside, to **Piazza Ballarò** – along with adjacent **Piazza del Carmine** the focus of a raucous daily market, with bulging vegetable stalls, unmarked drinking shops and some very basic snack stalls.

At the westernmost edge of the quarter, over Via Benedettini, is the Albergheria's quietest haven, the deconsecrated church of **San Giovanni degli Eremiti** (Mon, Thurs & Sat 9am–2pm, Tues, Wed & Fri 9am–1pm & 3–5pm, Sun 8.30am–2pm; free) – St John of the Hermits. Built in 1132, it's the most obviously Arabic of the city's Norman relics, with five ochre domes topping a small church that was built upon the remains of an earlier mosque. A path leads up through citrus trees to the church, behind which lie its celebrated late thirteenth-century cloisters – perfect twin columns enclosing a wild garden.

From San Giovanni it's a few paces to the main road, where, if you turn right and then veer left up the steps, you'll climb out of the fast traffic to gaze on the vast length of the **Palazzo dei Normanni** or Palazzo Reale (Mon & Fri–Sat 9am–12.30pm; free). A royal palace has always occupied the high ground here, above medieval Palermo. Originally built by the Saracens, the palace was enlarged considerably by the Normans, under whom it housed the most magnificent of medieval European courts – a noted centre of poetic and artistic achievement. Sadly, there's little left from those times in the current structure. The long front was added by the Spanish in the seventeenth century and most of the interior is now taken up by the Sicilian regional Parliament (which explains the security guards and the limited opening hours).

To see anything of the interior you have to take a **tour**. Present yourself at the gate (for times, see above) and a guide steers you through the **Royal Apartments**, two flights up, including the so-called *Sala di Ruggero*, decorated with lively twelfth-century mosaics of hunting scenes. You then descend a floor to the beautiful **Cappella Palatina** (Mon–Sat 9am–noon & 3–5pm, Sun 9–10am & noon–1pm; closed Wed afternoon), central Palermo's undisputed artistic gem. The private royal chapel of Roger II, built between 1132 and 1143, its interior is immediately overwhelming – cupola, three apses and nave entirely covered in twelfth-century **mosaics** of outstanding quality. As usual, it's the powerful representation of Christ as Pantocrator which dominates the senses, bolstered here by other secondary images – Christ blessing, open book in hand, and Christ enthroned, between Peter (to whom the chapel is dedicated) and Paul. Unlike the bright pictures of La Martorana the mosaics here give a single, effective impression, fully expressing the faith that inspired their creation.

The Cattedrale, the Capo and the modern city

Spanning Corso Vittorio Emanuele, on the far side of the Royal Palace, the early sixteenth-century **Porta Nuova** commemorates Charles V's Tunisian exploits, with suitably grim and turbaned figures adorning the western entrance. This gate marked the extent of the late medieval city, and the long road beyond heads to Monreale.

The Corso runs back towards the centre, past the huge bulk of the **Cattedrale** (daily 7am–noon & 4.30–6.30pm; free) – a more substantial Norman relic than the palace. It's an odd building in many ways, due to the less than subtle alterations of the late eighteenth century which added the dome – completely out of character – and spoiled the fine lines of the tawny stone. Still, the triple-apsed eastern end and the lovely matching towers are all original, dating from 1185. And despite the Catalan-Gothic facade and arches, there's enough Norman carving and detail to rescue the exterior from mere curiosity value. The same is not true, however, of the inside: grand enough but cold and neoclassical, the only items of interest are the fine portal and wooden doors (both fifteenth century) and the royal **tombs**, containing the mortal remains of some of Sicily's most famous monarchs – among others, Frederick II and his wife Constance. There's also a **treasury** (L1000) to the right of the choir: a sumptuous collection which includes a jewel- and pearl-encrusted skull cap and three simple, precious rings, all enterprisingly removed from the tomb of Constance of Aragon in the eighteenth century.

From the cathedral you can bear left, around the apses, and up into the **CAPO** quarter, one of the oldest areas of Palermo and another tight web of poor streets, unrelieved by space or greenery. Just around the corner from Piazza del Monte is the fine **Chiesa di Sant'Agostino** (Mon–Sat 7am–noon & 4–6pm, Sun 7am–noon), built in the thirteenth century. Above the main door (on Via Raimondo) there's a gorgeous latticework rose window; inside, some calm sixteenth-century cloisters; and – along Via Sant'Agostino, behind the market stalls – a sculpted fifteenth-century doorway attributed to Domenico Gagini.

The stalls of the market (mostly clothes) along **Via Sant'Agostino** run all the way down to Via Maqueda, the streets off to the left gradually becoming wider and more nondescript as they broach the area around the late nineteenth-century **Teatro Massimo**. Strictly neoclassical in style, this is a monumental structure, supposedly the largest theatre in Italy. But it's impossible to judge, since it remains closed indefinitely for restoration.

The theatre marks the dividing line between old and new Palermo and beyond here there's little that's vital, though plenty that is grand and modern. Via Maqueda becomes **Via Ruggero Settimo**, which cuts up through the gridded shopping streets to the huge double square made up of **Piazza Castelnuovo** and **Piazza Ruggero Settimo**. Dominating the whole lot is Palermo's other massive theatre, the **Politeama Garibaldi**, which houses the city's **Galleria d'Arte Moderna** (Tues–Sat 9am–noon & 3–8pm; L2000) – a collection of Sicilian art and sculpture.

The Vucciria, archaeological museum and old harbour

Via Roma, running from Stazione Centrale, is a fairly modern addition to the city, all clothes and shoe shops: parallel to Via Maqueda it offers a second chance for orientation if you get lost in the narrow alleys between the two. It's nothing like as interesting as Via Maqueda, its buildings mostly tall apartment blocks concealing hotels, but stick with it as far as the church of Sant'Antonio. Behind here – down the steps – is the sprawling **market** of the **Vucciria**: winding streets radiating out from a small enclosed piazza, wet from the ice and waste of the groaning fish stalls. There's a couple of excellent restaurants, some very basic bars and all manner of food and junk on sale. Other than early morning when the action is at its most frenzied, lunchtime is a good time to stroll around here – the stallholders take a break at card schools set up around packing cases and trestle tables, or simply fall asleep amongst their produce.

The northern limit of the market is marked by the distinctive church of **San Domenico** (daily 7.30–11.30am, plus Sat & Sun 5–6.30pm), with a fine eighteenth-century facade that's lit at night to great effect, and an interior of tombs containing a horde of famous Sicilians. Parliamentarians, poets and painters, they're of little interest to foreigners except to explain the finer points behind Palermitan street naming. The **oratory** behind the church (*Oratorio del Rosario*; ring for entry at Via dei Bambinai 16) contains stucco work by Serpotta and a masterful Van Dyck altarpiece, painted in 1628 before the artist fled Palermo for Genova to escape the plague.

From Piazza San Domenico, Via Roma continues north, passing (on the left) Palermo's main post office, the gargantuan **Palazzo delle Poste**. Built by the Fascists in 1933, it's a monstrous concrete block, a wide swathe of steps running up to ten unfluted columns which run the length and height of the building itself. The empty pretension of the post office is put to shame by the sixteenth-century convent behind, which now houses the **Museo Archeologico Nazionale** (Mon–Sat 9am–1.30pm, Sun 9am–12.30pm plus Tues & Fri 3–6pm; L2000): a magnificent collection of artefacts, mainly from the western half of the island, displayed on two main floors.

Two cloisters hold anchors and other retrieved hardware from the sea off the Sicilian coast, Egyptian and Punic remains in rooms to either side, and Roman sculpture – notably a giant enthroned Zeus. In rooms at the far end of the cloisters are numerous carved *stelai* and other inscribed tablets, and reconstructions of the assembled stone **lion's head water spouts** from the so-called "Victory Temple" at Himera (fifth century BC), the fierce animal faces tempered by braided fur and a grooved tongue which channelled the water. There are also finds from the temple site of Selinunte, on the southwest coast of the island, highpoint of which – indeed of the museum – is the **Salone di Selinunte**, a room which gathers together the richly carved metopes from the various known temples. Sculpted panels from the friezes which adorned the temples, the metopes are appealing works of art depicting lively mythological scenes: earliest, sixth-century BC, are ones representing the gods of Delphi, the Sphynx, the rape of Europa, and Herakles and the Bull. But it's the friezes from Temples C and F which really catch the eye, vivid fifth-century BC works – like Perseus beheading the Medusa with a short sword. Upstairs has plenty to occupy a lengthy dawdle too: lead water pipes with stopcock retrieved from a site at Termini Imerese, some 12,000 votive terracotta figures, and two bronze sculptures – the believable figure of an alert ram (third century BC), once one of a pair, and the glistening, muscular study of Hercules subduing a stag, found at Pompeii.

The contrasts in style and surroundings begin again in earnest if you cross back over Via Roma and head towards the water. The church of **Santa Zita**, on quiet Via Squarcialupo, suffered gravely during the war, though it has since been restored, and is justly known for its marvellous **oratory** (ring the bell 11am–noon, or ask in the church in front, San Mamiliano, 8–11am & 4–5.30pm): repository of one of Serpotta's finest works – the Battle of Lepanto – and some rich mother-of-pearl benches. Striking wealth indeed when you step back outside and consider the neighbourhood, the depressed inertia of whose streets spreads to the thumb-shaped inlet of the old harbour, **La Cala**. Once the main port of Palermo, stretching as far inland as Via Roma, the rot set in during the sixteenth century when silting caused the water to recede to its current position. All the heavy work eventually moved northwards to docks off the remodelled postwar streets, and La Cala has been left to the few fishing boats that still work out of Palermo.

La Kalsa and the Galleria Regionale

There's a markedly different character to the southeastern quarter of old Palermo. Worst hit by the war and allowed to decay since, these are some of the poorest streets in the city, within some of the most desolate urban landscapes imaginable. But, alongside the bombsites, you'll find a number of Palermo's most remarkable buildings and churches – and a surprising amount of greenery.

Indeed, Palermo's only central park, **Villa Giulia**, is just a few minutes' walk along Via Lincoln from the train station: an eighteenth-century garden that provides a welcome escape from the traffic. Attractions include planned, aromatic gardens, a kiddies' train, bandstand, deer and ducks and a botanical garden (Mon–Fri 9am–noon, Sat 9–11am).

Cut back to Piazza Garibaldi and walk north, turning off down Via Magione for the church of **La Magione** (Mon–Sat 7–11am & 4–6pm, Sun 7.30am–12.30pm), one of the city's more graceful spots, approached through a palm-lined drive. Built in 1151, the simple Norman church was subsequently given to the Teutonic knights as their headquarters by Henry VI. Today, it's strikingly sparse, inside and out, the reason clear as you step around the back to look at the finely worked apse: you're standing on the very edge of **La Kalsa**, an area subjected to saturation bombing during World War II, owing to its proximity to the port. Planned by the Saracens, the quarter (its name is from the Arabic *khalisa*, meaning pure) looks old, shattered and – even in daylight – vaguely threatening. Parts are no more than a huge bombsite, with scarred and gutted buildings on all sides, and on maps it just appears as a blank space. It goes without saying that this is one of Palermo's more notorious areas, with young pickpockets on speeding Vespas adding to the thrills.

Beyond Piazza della Kalsa is Via Alloro with, at its seaward end, the **Palazzo Abatellis**, a fifteenth-century palace revamped since the war to house Sicily's **Galleria Regionale** (Mon–Sat 9am–2pm, Sun 9am–1pm, plus Tues, Thurs & Fri 3–8pm; L2000), a stunning medieval art collection. Inside, there's a simple split – sculpture downstairs, paintings upstairs, the one exception to which, a magnificent fifteenth-century fresco of the *Triumph of Death*, is displayed in the former chapel, coating an entire wall. It's a chilling study by an unknown (possibly Flemish) painter in which Death is cast as a skeletal archer astride a galloping, spindly horse, trampling bodies planted by his arrows. The other masterpiece on the ground floor is among the works of fifteenth-century sculptor Francesco Laurana (room 4), whose white marble bust of Eleonora of Aragon is a calm, perfectly studied portrait.

Upstairs there's no shortage of excellent Sicilian work, including a fourteenth-century Byzantine mosaic of the Madonna and Child, and paintings and frescoes from the fifteenth century vivid in their portrayal of the coronation of the Virgin, a favourite theme. This floor, too, contains a collection of works by Antonello da Messina (1430–79), including three small portraits of saints Gregory, Jerome and Augustine and the celebrated *Annunciation*, a placid depiction of Mary, head and shoulders covered, right hand slightly raised.

Via Paternostro, which runs west off Via Alloro, curves north passing the striking thirteenth-century church of **San Francesco d'Assisi** (daily 7–11am), whose portal, picked out with a zigzagged decoration, is topped by a wonderful rose window. The harmonious design is, for once, continued inside too: all the Baroque trappings have been stripped away to reveal a pleasing stone interior, some of the chapels showing excellently worked arches. To the side of the church (at Via Immacolatella 5) is the renowned **Oratorio di San Lorenzo**, harbouring stucco scenes from the lives of Saint Lawrence and Saint Francis by Serpotta. Sadly it's likely to remain closed for some drastic restoration work in the forseeable future.

Nearby, Corso Vittorio Emanuele runs straight down to the water, ending in the Baroque gate, **Porta Felice**, begun in 1582 as a balance to the Porta Nuova to the west. The whole area beyond the gate was flattened in 1943, and has since been rebuilt as the ugly **Foro Italico** promenade, from where you can look back over the harbour to Monte Pellegrino. Back beyond the Porta Felice, around the corner from the large **Palazzo Chiaramonte**, second largest of Palermo's palaces and ex-headquarters of the Inquisition, is the engaging **Museo delle Marionette** at Via Butera 1 (Mon–Sat 9am–1pm & 4–7pm; L2000), the definitive collection of puppets, screens and painted scenery in Palermo. Come on Saturdays in the summer and there's a free traditional puppet show (*Spettacolo dei pupi*) at 5pm. Like all Sicilian puppet displays, it's great fun – plenty of action, clashing armies and buckets of blood as Roland (Orlando), Rinaldo and friends fight off the Saracen hordes.

The outskirts

Even if you don't have the time to see everything in the old centre there are several targets beyond – on the outskirts of the modern city – which warrant investigation. Some, in fact, shouldn't be missed on any visit to Palermo; others have a low-key interest for fans of the Norman period – while one is decidedly ghoulish, for the strong of stomach only.

The third of Palermo's showpiece museums lies on the edge of **La Favorita**, a large park around 3km from Piazza Castelnuovo (bus #14 or #15 from Viale della Libertà). The **Museo Etnografico Pitrè** (9am–1pm; closed Fri; L2000) is *the* vital exhibition of Sicilian folklore and culture on the island. There's all the work traditionally associated with Sicily – a wealth of carts painted with bright scenes from the story of the Paladins, a reconstructed puppet theatre (with performances in the summer; ask at the tourist office), and dozens of the expressive puppets, scenery backdrops and handbills lining the walls. Fascinating, too, are the other Sicilian artefacts, including a whole series of intricately worked terracotta figures, dolls and games, bicycles, painted masks, even a great, flowery iron bedstead.

To be thorough in tracking down the rest of central Palermo's **Norman relics** entails a lot of fairly fruitless scurrying around the southern and western parts of the city. Most of what survives is often locked or under restoration. Bus #24 runs west to **La Zisa** (from the Arabic, *el aziz*, "magnificent"), a huge palace begun by William I in 1160, with a fine exterior and marvellously rich Islamic interior (Tues–Sun 9am–2pm, plus Tues & Fri 3–6pm; free). Closer to the centre, about 1km beyond Porta Nuova at Corso Calatafimi 100, is **La Cuba** (Wed & Sun 9am–noon), the remains of a slightly later Norman pavilion that formed part of the same royal park as La Zisa, now tucked inside an army barracks. Best excursion, though, is south to the eleventh-century church of **San Giovanni dei Lebbrosi** (Mon–Sat 4.30–6.30pm, Sun 8–11.30am), reachable on bus #11, #26 or #31 from the northern end of Corso dei Mille. Just off the Corso, at Via Cappello 38, it's one of the oldest Norman churches in Sicily, reputedly founded in 1070 by Roger I – its squat tower topped by a red dome, a second dome beyond over the apse, the windows just narrow slits.

For real attention-grabbing stuff, take bus #27 from Corso Vittorio Emanuele southwest to Via Pindemonte. Close by, in Piazza Cappuccini, the **Convento dei Cappuccini** (Mon–Sat 9am–noon & 3–5pm; donation expected) retained its own burial ground for several hundred years, placing its dead in catacombs under the church. Later, others were also interred here, right up until 1881. The bodies (some 8000 of them) were preserved by various chemical and drying processes – including the use of vinegar and arsenic baths – and then placed in niches along corridors, dressed in the suit of clothes that they provided for the purpose. Descending into the catacombs is like having a walk-on part in your own horror film. The rough-cut stone corridors are divided according to sex and status, different caverns reserved for men, women, the clergy, doctors, lawyers and surgeons. Suspended in individual niches, the bodies are vile, contorted, grinning figures – some decomposed beyond recognition, others complete with skin, hair and eyes fixing you with a steely stare. Those that aren't lined along the walls lie in stacked glass coffins, and – to say the least – it's an unnerving experience to walk among them. Follow the signs for the sealed-off cave which contains the coffin of two-year-old Rosalia Lombardo, who died in 1920 but looks like she's simply asleep, thanks to a series of embalming injections.

Eating and drinking

For **breakfast and snacks**, best stops are at the *Extra Bar*, Via Ruggero Settimo 107, the *Ferrara*, just to the left of the train station in Piazza Giulio Cesare, and the *Bar Self Service*, Corso Vittoria Emanuele 244 – the last two also offering cheap complete lunches. For authentic Sicilian fast food, *Antica Foccacceria San Francesco*, Via A. Paternostro 58 (off Corso Vittorio Emanuele), is an old-time pizzeria with marble-topped tables. **Markets** all offer a variety of typically Sicilian takeaway food – boiled octopus, liver-filled bread rolls and cooked artichokes – as well as fruit and vegetables. Best is the Vucciria, off Via Roma between Corso Vittorio Emanuele and the San Domenico church. And there's a *Standa* **supermarket** at the junction of Via Ruggero Settimo and Via Generale Magliocco.

The most popular **pizza** restaurants get packed at the weekends, full of young people intent upon a night out rather than just a meal. Easily best is the *Pizzeria Italia*, Via Orologio 54 (off Via Maqueda), where large queues develop quickly. Or try the slightly fancier *Trattoria dal Pompiere* at Via Bara 107, the next parallel street north. More expensive, with a full restaurant menu, is *Peppino* at Piazza Castelnuovo 49, whose management also runs *Bellini* in Piazza Bellini – pricey, but with outdoor tables in the shadow of La Martorana church.

For full-blown **meals**, the city's best bargain is *Trattoria-Pizzeria Enzo*, Via Maurolico 17/19, close to the train station – excellent food, hefty portions and daft prices. Next door, *Luigi Basile* has similarly priced food, including pizza and good local wine. More expensive, but worth every lira, are two restaurants renowned for their *cucina casalinga*: the *Primavera*, Piazza Bologna 4, is close to the cathedral and fills quickly; the *Stella*, Via Alloro 104, has outdoor seating in a lovely courtyard. The *Shanghai* (not Chinese but Italian) has a restaurant terrace overlooking the Vucciria market at Vicolo dei Mezzani 34. **Non-Italian food** is all but impossible to find in Palermo, but try the *Al Duar*, Via E. Amari 92, for cheap couscous and the like.

Bars and nightlife

The strangest thing about Palermo's fast lifestyle is that it stops at 8pm. Apart from a perfunctory *passeggiata* between the Teatro Massimo and Piazza Castelnuovo, everything is quiet outside after dark. In summer, most young people head for Mondello (see below) and buses run there and back all night. Still, for an outdoor, early evening **drink**, **Via Principe di Belmonte** is a good spot – closed to traffic, and with several popular places – for coffees and beers. There are a couple of other central options too, notably the *Pinguino*, Via Ruggero Settimo 86, which has excellent ice cream, famous milkshakes and a rank of non-alcoholic cocktails. Or try *Liberty*, a spaghetteria on Via Cerda, off Via Maqueda, which serves food and is open until late.

If it's **discos** and **video bars** you're after, what exists is all in the new, northern section of the city, along Viale Strasburgo, or along Via Generale Arimondi (beyond the Giardino Inglese). Otherwise, there are **cinemas** on Via Cavour and Via E. Amari, and an English Film Club which shows new releases at the *Metropolitan Cinema*, Viale Strasburgo 356 (☎502.278) – it gives a fifty-percent *ISIC* discount.

Listings

Airport bus Fifteen daily departures to Punta Raisi airport from the terminal at Via I. Lumia, behind the Politeama theatre; first bus at 5.30am, last bus at 9.30pm; L4500, 45min. Enquiries on ☎580.457.

American Express Via E. Amari 40 (Mon–Fri 9am–1pm & 4–7pm, Sat 9am–1pm; ☎587.144).

Bookshops Large selection of English books from *Feltrinelli*, Via Maqueda 457, opposite Teatro Massimo.

Buses *AST*, Piazza Lolli/Piazza Marina (for Bagheria, Ragusa, Comiso, Corleone, Modica, Termini Imerese); *Camilleri*, Via P. Balsamo 32 and *Cuffaro*, Via Lincoln 42 (both for Agrigento); *SAIS*, Via P. Balsamo 16 (for Rome, Caltanissetta, Catania, Enna, Piazza Armerina, Gela, Messina, Siracusa, Noto, Cefalù, Termini Imerese); *Segesta*, Via P. Balsamo 26 (for Rome, Trápani).

Car rental *Avis*, Via Principe di Scordia 12/14 (☎333.806); *Europcar*, Via Cavour 77 (☎321.949); *Hertz*, Viale Michelangelo 200 (☎204.277); *Interrent*, Via Cavour 61 (☎328.631); *Maggiore*, Via Agrigento 27/33 (☎625.9286).

Consulates The US consulate is at Via Vaccarini 1 (☎302.590). For other nationals, the nearest consulates are in Naples or Rome.

Exchange For exchange services outside normal banking hours, there are offices at Punta Raisa airport (daily 6.45am–1.45pm & 2.30–8pm) and Stazione Centrale (daily 7.30am–12.30pm & 2.30–8pm).

Ferry companies *Grandi Traghetti* to Genova and Livorno (Via M. Stabile 179; ☎587.832); *Siremar* to Ustica (Via Crispi 120; ☎582.403); *SNAV*, Via Principe Belmonte 5 (☎586.533); *Tirrenia* to Naples and Cagliari (Palazzina Stella Maris, at the port on Via Crispi; ☎602.1111).

Gay information Contact *ARCI Gay* (☎324.917/8), at the cultural wing of the Communist Party's youth section, Via Genova 7.

Hospital *Civico Regionale Generale*, Via Carmelo Lazzaro (☎606.1111). For emergency first aid ☎288.1411.

Left luggage Stazione Centrale (open daily 24hr; L1300 per day); Stazione Maríttima (daily 7–11am, 12.30pm–5pm & 7–8pm; L1500 per day).

Newspapers English newspapers and magazines from the newsagents at the southern corner of Via Ruggero Settimo and Piazza Castelnuovo.

Pharmacist All-night service at Via Roma 1, Via Roma 207 and Via Principe di Belmonte 110.

Police Tourist police at Piazza Vittoria (☎210.111).

Post office Main post office is the Palazzo delle Poste on via Roma (Mon–Fri 8.10am–7.30pm, Sat 8.10am–1.30pm).

Taxis To call a cab ☎513.311. Otherwise ranks in all the main squares.

Telephones Offices at Via Lincoln, directly opposite the train station (open 24hr); Piazza Ungheria (daily 8am–8pm), off Via Ruggero Settimo; and Via Principe di Belmonte 92 (daily 8am–8pm). Reverse charge calls from the first office only.

Train enquiries Call ☎616.1806/4808 daily 7am–10pm.

Travel agents *CTS*, Via Sammartino 79 (Mon–Fri 9am–1pm & 4–7.30pm; ☎332.209).

Women's movement Contact *ARCI Donna*, Via Dante 44 (☎588.994) or *Unione delle Donne Italiane*, Via XX Settembre 57 (☎329.604).

Around Palermo

Palermo is a busy city with few quiet spaces and fewer parks, so any respite is welcome. Even on just a short visit to the city, try not to miss any of the trips below – all easy day (or half-day) excursions.

Monte Pellegrino and Mondello

Splitting the city from the bay at MONDELLO (see below) is **Monte Pellegrino**, to which the ride itself is as good a reason as any to go (bus #12 from Via Filipo Turati, opposite the Politeama theatre) – an impressive route through a green belt of trees, cacti and scrub, and with views over Palermo and its plain. The bus drops you at the **Santuario di Santa Rosalia**, a cave in the hillside where the bones of the city's patroness were discovered. A chapel was promptly built over the entrance in 1625: supposedly miraculous water trickles down the walls, channelled and collected by steel plates, and fancy lighting illuminates a bier containing a statue of the saint, around which there's invariably a scrum. A small road to the right of the chapel leads to the summit, a half-hour's walk, affording more splendid views, while paths and trails cover the rest of the mountain top.

If this isn't your bag, the other obvious trip from central Palermo is the short (11km) run to **MONDELLO**, a small seaside resort tucked under the northern bluff of Monte Pellegrino. It features one of Sicily's best stretches of sand (as opposed to the more usual stones), the two-kilometre beach curving round to a tiny working harbour and the remnants of a medieval tower. There's a line of restaurants overlooking the water and the fish, naturally, is temptingly fresh. Alternatively, you could grab some of the excellent snack food from the waterfront stalls and hit the beach. It's often crowded, but summer nights at Mondello are fun, the real scene of Palermo's *passeggiata*. In winter it's more laid-back, and rarely very busy, but the restaurants and snack stalls are still open and it's usually warm enough to swim. To get to Mondello, take bus #3, #14 or #15 (or, summer only, bus #6) from Stazione Centrale or Viale della Libertà – a half-hour ride.

Monreale

Whether or not you get to mountain or beach, there's no excuse for missing Sicily's most extraordinary medieval mosaics in the cathedral at **MONREALE** (Royal Mountain). This small hill-town, 8km southwest of Palermo, commands unsurpassed views down the Conca d'Oro valley, the capital shimmering in the distant bay. Bus #9 or #8/9 runs frequently from Piazza dell'Indipendenza, the journey up the valley taking twenty minutes. From the bus stop follow Via Roma up to Piazza Vittorio Emanuele, where Monreale's Norman **Duomo** (daily 8am–12.30pm & 3.30–6.30pm) flanks one side. The rather severe, square-towered exterior – though handsome enough – is no preparation for what's inside: the most impressive and extensive area of Christian medieval mosaic work in the world, the apex of Sicilian-Norman art.

The cathedral, and the town that grew up around it in the twelfth century, both owe their existence to young King William II's rivalry with his powerful Palermitan archbishop, the Englishman Walter of the Mill. William endowed a new monastery in his royal grounds in 1174; the abbey church – this cathedral – was thrown up in a matter of years. This haste accounts for the splendid uniformity of the cathedral's most famous relic, its interior art a galaxy of coloured mosaics bathed in a golden background.

The **mosaics** were almost certainly executed by Greek and Byzantine craftsmen, and they reveal a unitary plan and inspiration. Once inside, your eyes are drawn immediately over the wooden ceiling to the all-embracing half-figure of Christ in benediction in the central apse: an awesome and pivotal mosaic, the head and shoulders alone almost twenty metres high. Underneath sit an enthroned Virgin and Child, attendant angels and, below, ranks of saints, each individually and subtly coloured and identified by name. Interesting here is the figure of Thomas à Becket (marked *SCS Thomas Cantb*), canonised in 1173, just before the mosaics were begun, and presumably included as a political show of support by William for the papacy. The nave mosaics are no less remarkable, an animated series that starts with the Creation (to the right of the altar) and runs around the whole church. Most scenes are instantly recognisable: Adam and Eve, Abraham on the point of sacrificing his son, a positively jaunty Noah's ark; even the Creation, shown in a set of glorious, simplistic panels portraying God filling his world with animals, water, light . . . and Man.

Ask at the desk by the entrance to climb the **tower** (L2000) in the southwest corner of the cathedral – an especially attractive idea as the steps give access to the roof, leaving you standing right above the central apse – an unusual and precarious vantage point. It's also worth visiting the **cloisters** (Mon–Sat 9.30am–1.30pm, Sun 9am–12.30pm; L2000), part of William's original Benedictine monastery. The formal garden is surrounded by an elegant arcaded quadrangle, 216 twin columns supporting slightly pointed arches – a legacy of the Arab influence in Sicilian art. No two capitals are the same, each a riot of detail and imagination: armed hunters doing battle with winged beasts; flowers, birds, snakes and foliage. Entrance to the cloisters is from Piazza Guglielmo, in the corner by the right-hand tower of the cathedral.

Ústica

A volcanic, turtle-shaped island 60km northwest of Palermo, **ÚSTICA** is one of the more appealing destinations for a quick trip away from the city. Colonised originally by the Phoenicians, the island took its name from the Latin *ustum*, or "burnt", a reference to its blackened, lavial appearance. Exposed and isolated, it had a rough time throughout the Middle Ages, its scant population repeatedly harried by pirates who used the island as a base. Even as late as the 1890s the few inhabitants were nearly all exiled prisoners. Today, Ústica's fertile uplands are just right for a day's ambling, while the rough coastline is touted as a skin-diver's paradise, the clear water bursting with fish, sponges, weed and coral. Easy, too, is to take a boat trip through Ústica's rugged grottoes and lava outcrops. The little port of **ÚSTICA TOWN**, where the boats dock, features a museum devoted to underwater finds from the area, a bank, a dozen restaurants and a handful of places to stay. All these facilities sit around a sloping double piazza, just five minutes' walk uphill from the harbour.

Ferries and **hydrofoils** operate roughly once or twice daily from Palermo (from the Stazione Maríttima), the cheapest summer passage around L15,000 one way by ferry, with hydrofoils twice the price in less than half the time. (Tickets from *Siremar* or *SNAV* – see Palermo listings.) If you want to stay overnight on Ústica, ask about **private rooms** at the **tourist office**, Piazza Vito Longo (daily 9am–1pm & 6–8pm; ☎844.9190) or in the *Bar Centrale* on the piazza. There are also two cheap **hotels**: the *Clelia*, Via Magazzino 7 (☎844.9039; ④), and the *Locanda Castelli*, Via San Francesco 16 (☎844.9007; ③). Best place to **eat** is *Da Mario*, opposite the Bar Centrale, a small, simple trattoria where superb fish dinners with wine cost around L25,000.

THE TYRRHENIAN COAST

From Palermo, the whole of the rugged **Tyrrhenian coast** is accessible by rail and road, offering at times a spectacular ride past deserted coves and rocky beaches. Aside from spots of interest at and around **Bagheria** and **Termini Imerese**, the first real attraction is **Cefalù**, a beach resort and cathedral town. Vital stops beyond are few, though the quiet seaside towns further east are all nice enough for a short break. Also, buses run inland from the larger resorts, providing access to the northern **mountain chains**, the Madonie and the Nebrodi. Worth some time are most of the hill-towns here, especially **Caccamo** and **Castroreale**, quiet airy places with castles and good hiking at hand. Sadly, the easternmost part of the coast, around **Milazzo** – Sicily's second largest port – is fairly grim and industrial. However, there's an easy escape to the desolate **Aeolian Islands**, easily visible from much of the Tyrrhenian coast, reached by ferries and hydrofoils from Milazzo.

Bagheria, Solunto, Termini Imerese and Caccamo

Although it's tempting to head straight for Cefalù, there are some enticing stops before that – all easily seen on day trips from Palermo if that's where you're based. Road and railway cut eastwards, across Capo Zafferano, to reach the rural town of **BAGHERIA**, a ten-minute ride by train. Scattered across town, a seventeenth- and eighteenth-century summer retreat, is a series of (largely neglected) Baroque country villas, on which the city's nobility stamped their mark. Most are privately owned, and closed, but you can get into the **Villa Palagonia** (Mon–Fri 9am–12.30pm & 5pm–1hr before sunset, Sat & Sun

11am–12.30pm & 4pm–1hr before sunset; L1000) on Piazza Garibaldi, noted for its menagerie of eccentric gargoyles. The villa is ten minutes' walk from the train station. You may as well combine a trip to Bagheria with a tour around the Graeco-Roman town at **SOLUNTO** (the ancient *Solus*), one stop further on the train (the station is called SANTA FLAVIA-SOLUNTO-PORTICELLO). The **site** (daily 9am–1hr before sunset; L2000) is about half-an-hour's walk from the station, beautifully stranded on top of Monte Catalfano. There's a **museum** at the entrance, as well as the impressive remains of Roman houses (some with mosaics) and shops, a well-preserved *agora* and a fragmentary theatre – all looking down on the small bay below, guarded by the medieval **Castello di Solanto**.

Another twenty minutes on, **TERMINI IMERESE** has an upper town whose cliff-edge belvedere is another excellent vantage point for views of the curving shore. The grand piazza holds a seventeenth-century cathedral studded with four sixteenth-century statues, and take a look in the **Museo Civico** (Tues–Sun 9am–2pm; L2000), over the other side of the piazza, which gathers together remains from the ancient Greek site of Himera, 20km to the east. Termini, after a prosperous Greek and Carthaginian period, was also a Roman spa, and in the shaded, congested lower town are the remains of the former baths, covered now by a modern hotel, the *Albergo delle Terme*, close to the little port. Termini would be a fair place to spend the night: there's a scrappy beach and a couple of cheap **places to stay** – most basic is the *Locanda Roma*, at Vicolo di Stefano 12 (☎091/814.1566; ③). The nearest **campsite**, *Torre Battilamano* (☎091/814.0044), is at BUONFORNELLO, 15km east of town; take the bus from outside the train station.

Buses from Termini's train station also run regularly to **CACCAMO**, 10km south. The small town, a jumble of little houses astride a rocky hill, is dominated by a sturdy, battlemented twelfth-century **fortress**, its sheer walls built on a crag which falls away down into the valley below. Though it's propped up by scaffolding, you should at least be able to climb up to the gates of the castle for views over the steeply stepped streets; for entrance, try ringing at the door of the custodian at Corso Umberto 6.

Cefalù

Despite the recent attentions of *Club Med* and a barrage of modern building outside town, **CEFALÙ** remains a fairly small-scale fishing port, partly by virtue of its geographical position – tucked onto every available inch of a shelf of land underneath a fearsome crag, the *Rocca*. Roger II founded a mighty cathedral here in 1131 and, as befitting one of the most influential early European rulers, his church dominates the skyline, the great twin towers of the facade rearing up above the flat roofs of the medieval quarter. Naturally, it's the major attraction in town, but most visitors are as tempted by Cefalù's fine curving sands – the main reason why the holiday companies have moved in in such great numbers in recent years. Still, it's a pleasant town, nothing like as developed as Sicily's other package resort, Taormina.

The **Duomo** (Mon–Sat 8am–noon & 3–7pm, Sun 7am–1pm & 3.30–8pm) was built – partly at least – as Roger's thanks for fetching up at Cefalù's safe beach in a violent storm. Inside, covering the apse and presbytery, are the earliest and best preserved of the Sicilian church mosaics, dating from 114. The **mosaics** follow a familiar pattern. Christ Pantocrator dominates the central apse, underneath is the Madonna flanked by archangels, and then the Apostles. Although miniscule in comparison with those at Monreale, these mosaics are equally effective and, most interestingly, display a quite marked artistic tradition. Forty years earlier than those in William's cathedral, they are thoroughly Byzantine in concept: Christ's face is elongated, the powerful eyes set close together, the outstretched hand flexed and calming.

In high season, when Cefalù's tangibly Arabic, central grid of streets is crowded with tourists, you'd do best to visit the cathedral early in the morning to find it empty. The rest of the time, the long sandy **beach** beyond the harbour beckons. A couple of places are worth venturing to, however. The **Museo Mandralisca** (daily 9am–12.30pm & 3.30–6pm; L4000), at Via Mandralisca 13 (across from Piazza Duomo), has a wry *Portrait of an Unknown Man* by the fifteenth-century Sicilian Master Antonello da Messina. And **La Rocca**, the mountain above the town, holds the megalithic so-called Tempio di Diana, from where paths continue right around the crag, inside medieval walls, to the sketchy fortifications at the very top.

If you want to **stay** over, choose between the bargain rooms at *Locanda Cangelosi*, Via Umberto I 26 (☎0921/21.591; ③), and the seafront *Riva del Sole* on Via Lungomare (☎0921/21.230; ⑤). Best place to **eat** on a budget is the *Arkade Grill*, Via Vanni 9 (off Corso Ruggero), which has a small Tunisian menu as well as cheapish pasta and good local wine. For more elegant dining, the friendly *La Brace*, Via XXV Novembre, serves a wonderful three-course meal for around L40,000. The **tourist office** is on the main street at Corso Ruggero 7 (Mon–Fri 8am–2pm & 4.30–7.30pm, Sat 8am–2pm), and has free maps and accommodation lists.

The coast to Milazzo, and inland routes

The best stretches of the Tyrrhenian coast all lie east of Cefalù: clean stony beaches backed for the most part by extensive orange and lemon groves. The train stops at several small, attractive seaside resorts, where there's often cheap accommodation, and there are buses south, into the hills, from various points on the coast.

Frequent trains stop at **SANTO STEFANO DI CAMASTRA**, a ceramics town and small-time resort, where there's a cheap *locanda*, the *U Cucinu*, at Via Nuova 75 (☎0921/31.106; ③). Another 30km east, **SANT'AGATA DI MILITELLO** has a small working fishing fleet, which means excellent fish in the local restaurants. The busy summer resort has a long pebbled beach and you can stay here at the *Locanda Miramare*, Via Cosenz 3, next to the train station (☎0941/701.773; ③).

Further down the coast, rounding the cape, there are good **beaches** at CAPO D'ORLANDO itself, and from PATTI's main square you can catch a bus (3 daily) to **TINDARI** and the ruins of ancient **Tyndaris** (daily 9am–1hr before sunset; free). Originally founded in 396 BC, it was one of the last Greek settlements in Sicily and retains its Greek walls. Most of the remains, though, are Roman, including some house ruins and a theatre with splendid views over the sea, together with finds collected in a museum (daily 9am–2pm; free).

There's not much else to stop for before Milazzo; indeed the better destinations are all south and inland, away from the increasingly built-up coast. The SS185 cuts one of the grandest routes on the island, climbing gently into the hills to **NOVARA DI SICILIA**. Creakingly medieval, the small town offers terrific views and a certain fascination in just wandering the decrepit streets and alleys. A closer target is the hill-town of **CASTROREALE**, to the northeast, just 8km south of BARCELLONA train station on the coast – to which it's connected by seven daily buses. This is another extraordinarily sited town, defended in past days by the fourteenth-century castle of Frederick of Aragon, the tower of which survives on top of the pile. It does duty these days as an *IYHF* **youth hostel** (April–Oct; ☎090/974.6398; ①), though it's been under restoration recently and may still be closed. Even if you can't stay the night, Castroreale is well worth seeing and provides ample opportunity for aimless wandering through the stepped streets, past badly restored sixteenth-century churches and fine nobles' houses.

Milazzo

At the base of a thin spit of land poking into the Tyrrhenian Sea, **MILAZZO** is not the sort of place you're likely to make a beeline for. Disfigured by a giant oil refinery, the coast around is noisy and smelly. However, it's the main port of departure for the Aeolian Islands, which means, at best, a couple of hours in town awaiting the ferry/hydrofoil – at worst a night in one of the numerous cheap hotels. Try the *Cosenz* in Via Cosenz (☎090/928.2996; ③), or, nearer the port, the *Capitol*, Via G. Rizzo 23 (☎090/928.3289; ④).

If there's time to kill, you can poke around the restored **castle** (guided tours roughly hourly; free) which sits inside a much larger and older walled city, complete with its own cathedral. Ticket offices, opposite the docks, have all the information on departures to the islands: hydrofoils are more frequent, twice as quick and twice as expensive as the ferries; in winter, rough weather can disrupt the schedules – be prepared for cancellations. The **train station** is a ten-minute (signposted) walk from the port, and **buses** from Messina stop right on the harbour front.

The Aeolian Islands

Volcanic in origin, the **Aeolian Islands** lead a precarious existence in the buffeted waters off the northern Sicilian coast. They are named after Aeolus, the Greek god who kept the winds he controlled shut tight in one of the islands' many caves. According to Homer, Odysseus put into the Aeolians and was given a bag of wind to help him home, but his sailors opened it too soon and the ship was blown straight back to port. More verifiably, the islands were coveted for their mineral wealth, the mining of obsidian (hard glass-like lava) providing the basis for early prosperity. Later their strategic importance attracted the Greeks, who settled on Lípari in 580 BC. The Greeks' powerful fleet kept rivals at bay until the islands fell to the Carthaginians, who in turn were pushed out by the Romans in 252 BC. Thereafter began a period of decline: the islands became a haven for pirates and a place of exile, a state of affairs that continued right into the twentieth century with the Fascists exiling their political opponents to Lípari.

It's only comparatively recently that the islanders stopped scratching a subsistence living and started welcoming tourists. Emigration had virtually depopulated some of the islands, and even now the more remote ones are sorely stretched to maintain a decent living. That said, you'll not be alone if you come to the islands during the summer months, the central group – Vulcano, Lípari and Salina – pretty well known to a gradually increasing crowd of devotees. Lípari, particularly, is expensive in high season, rapidly becoming rather a hip resort. But get out to the minor isles or come in blustery winter for a taste of what it was like twenty – or a hundred – years ago: unsophisticated, rough and beautiful.

Getting there is easiest from Milazzo (see above), with year-round ferries and hydrofoils connecting the port with all the islands. There are summer services, too, from Naples, Reggio di Calabria and Messina, and from Palermo and (sometimes) Cefalù. **Getting around** in summer is easy as ferries and hydrofoils link all the islands. In winter, services are reduced and in rough weather cancelled altogether, particularly on the routes out to Alicudi and Filicudi. You can take cars to Lípari and Salina but bikes are better, something that's true for all the islands. Most islands have plenty of **accommodation**, though you'll often pay over the odds for a room, but note that the only **campsites** are on Lípari, Vulcano and Salina – and that camping rough elsewhere is illegal. **Food** prices, too, verge on the exclusive, so if you're only going for a short visit, take your own and avoid the pricey restaurants.

Vulcano

Closest to the Sicilian mainland, **VULCANO** is the first port of call for ferries and hydrofoils – around an hour and a half on the slowest crossing. The last volcanic explosion here was in 1890; you can walk up to the main crater from the harbour, **PORTO DI LEVANTE**, in around an hour. A second hike is to **Vulcanello**, the volcanic pimple just to the north of the port, thrown up out of the sea in 183 BC, and there's good walking to be had around the rest of the island, too. Less energetically, just fifteen minutes' walk from Porto di Levante, across the neck of land separating it from Porto di Ponente, there's an excellent black-sand **beach**. On the way you'll pass Vulcano's sulpherous mud baths and the hot springs which bubble into (and warm) the sea. There are cheapish **rooms** at Porto di Levante: popular places are *Casa Fioritan* on Via Levante (☎090/985.2006; ④) and *Casa Sipione* (June–Sept; ☎090/985.2034; ④) at the end of a path beside the church – try to ring before you arrive. The **campsite** (*Sicilia*; ☎090/985.2164), near the port, is only open from June to September.

Lípari

There are regular daily hydrofoil services from Vulcano on to **LÍPARI**, by far the most popular of the islands – and the most diverse. The group's main port and capital, **LÍPARI town** is a thriving little place prettily bunched between two harbours, **arrival** at which is one of *the* island experiences: hydrofoils dock at the Marina Corta, a tiny harbour formed by a church-topped mole and dwarfed by the castle that crowns the hill above; ferries steam straight past, around the mighty sixteenth-century walls of the fort, to dock at the Marina Lunga, a deep-water harbour which curves around to the north as a long beach.

It's the upper town within the fortress walls, the **Castello**, which is the main focus of interest. Finds from the site, which has been continuously occupied since Neolithic times, have enabled archaeologists to date other Mediterranean cultures. Alongside the well-marked **excavations**, there's a tangle of dilapidated churches flanking the main cobbled street, and several buildings (including the seventeenth-century bishop's palace) which make up the separate arms of the **Museo Eoliano** (Mon–Sat 9am–2pm, Sun 9am–1pm; free) – a lavish collection of Neolithic pottery, late Bronze Age artefacts, and Greek and Roman vases and statues, most of it dug up outside. Down below, the streets wind around the base of the fortified hill and down to the harbours. The town is reliant upon tourism these days – as the restaurants and craft shops testify – but it's all fairly small-scale, even now. There's plenty of **accommodation**, though the cheap hotels – like the *Locanda Salina*, Via Garibaldi 18 (☎090/981.2332; ④), and the *Europeo*, Via Vittorio Emanuele 98 (☎090/981.1589; ⑤) – tend to fill early in the day in high season. Ask around in the harbour bars for **rooms**; you should get something with a shower and a kitchen from L45,000 a double. There's also a **youth hostel** (☎090/981.1540; ①) in the castle. If you're **camping**, Lípari's only site, the *Baia Unci* (April–Sept; ☎090/981.1909), is at CANNETO, 3km away – connected by at least nine buses daily from the **bus terminal** at Marina Lunga. The **tourist office**, Corso Vittorio Emanuele 239 (Mon–Sat 8am–2pm & 4.30–7.30pm), has free maps and accommodation lists; there's also an office at Marina Corte.

The **rest of the island** is easy to reach on a network of regular **buses**. **CANNETO**, a fishing village with a pebbled beach and a couple of hotels, is a good excursion. From here the road climbs north, passing an excellent sandy beach (the Spiaggia Bianca) a couple of kilometres out of Canneto, before reaching the stony beach at **PORTICELLO**.

West of Lípari, the road clambers up the hill to **QUATTROCCHI** ("Four Eyes"), a three-kilometre hike which ends in glorious and much photographed views over Vulcano and the spikey *Faraglioni* rocks which puncture the sea between the two islands. Keep on the road to **PIANOCONTE**, which has a couple of popular pizza restaurants, good in the evening, and just before the village, a side road slinks off down to the old Roman thermal baths at **SAN CALOGERO**. This is a particularly fine walk, across a valley and skirting some impressive cliffs.

Salina and Panarea

North of Lípari, **SALINA**'s two extinct volcanic cones rise out of a fertile land which produces capers and white *malvasia* wine by the bucketload. Again, it's excellent walking country (though there are bus services between the main villages) and you get some marvellous vantage points over the other islands. Boats arrive either at the main port, **SANTA MARINA DI SALINA** – hotels and **rooms** – or on the south coast at **RINELLA**, a little fishing village. There's **accommodation** here too, and a **campsite**, the *Tre Pini* (April–Oct; ☎090/984.2155), as well as boat trips to the most interesting of Salina's grottoes, ranged along the southern coast.

PANAREA, to the east, is the smallest of the Aeolians but easily the most scenic. Only 3km by 1.5km, it packs plenty of small, fairly cheap hotels into **SAN PIETRO**, one of the three settlements, though it's wise to ring ahead in summer; try the *Locanda Stella Maris* (☎090/983.042; ④) or the *Locanda Roda* (☎090/983.006; ④). Half an hour's walk south of San Pietro is the island's one sandy **beach** and, high above here on the other side, **Punta Milazzese**, where a Bronze Age village of 23 huts was discovered in 1948. The site is thought to have been inhabited since the fourteenth century BC, and pottery found here (displayed in Lípari's museum) shows a distinct Minoan influence. Elsewhere, there are hot springs at San Pietro and, at **CALCARA** to the north, a beach and sea that sometimes steam – one effect of the island's *fumarole*.

Strómboli

Despite the regularity of the volcanic explosions which throw up noise and flashes – and occasionally chunks of rock – throughout the day, people have always lived on **STRÓMBOLI**. It's a famous phenomenon, but not as frightening as it sounds. All the action is limited to one volcanic trail (the Sciara del Fuoco), on the northwest side of the volcano, and the eastern villages – white houses standing out against the green slopes – are safely settled. Most of the many hotels and rooms to let on Strómboli are here, in the adjacent parishes of San Vincenzo, San Bartolo and Piscita, often grouped together as **STRÓMBOLI** town and these days something of a chic resort. Just to the north, beyond Piscita, is the island's main beach, of jet black sand. Boats dock a short distance from San Vincenzo, while an island service also calls at **GINOSTRA** on the southwestern side of Strómboli: a tiny hamlet closer to the craters, with one *locanda*, the *Petrusa* (☎090/981.2305; ④) and a few rooms to let.

A footpath from Piscita leads to an **observatory**, far enough if all you want is a view of the volcano. Otherwise, it's another three or four hours' climb (following the marks on the rocks) to the **summit** (924m), from where the nightly natural fireworks show is seen to best effect. Guides are available, though there's no reason why you shouldn't do it alone: it's not dangerous and it's easy enough to find your way. Do, though, take warm clothes and a torch, and a sleeping bag if you're going to stay until dawn – well worth it on the less blustery days.

THE IONIAN COAST: MESSINA TO SIRACUSA

It's Sicily's eastern **Ionian coast** which draws most visitors, the summer mob attention merited by some of the island's most exciting sights – natural and constructed. Likely arrival point is **Messina**, which receives a constant stream of ferries bearing trains across the Straits from Calabria. **Taormina**, most chic of the island's resorts and famed for its remarkable Graeco-Roman theatre, is an hour's train ride south and lava-built **Catania**, Sicily's second city, is another hour beyond: both places (indeed the whole of this part of the coast) are dominated by the massive presence of **Mount Etna**, Europe's highest volcano. A road and a narrow-gauge, single-track railway circumnavigate the lower slopes of Etna, passing through a series of hardy towns surrounded by swirls of black rock spewed from the volcano. Further south, out of the lee of Etna, lie traces of the ancient Greek cities which once lined the southeastern coast. **Megara Hyblaea** has the most extensive remains, and the route concludes in **Siracusa** – formerly the most important and beautiful city in the Hellenistic world.

Messina and south

MESSINA may well be your first sight of Sicily; and – from the ferry – it's a fine one, the glittering town spread up the hillside beyond the sickle-shaped harbour. Sadly, the image is shattered almost as soon as you step into the city, bombed and shaken to a shadow of its former self by a record number of disasters. Plague, cholera and earthquakes all struck throughout the eighteenth and nineteenth centuries, culminating with the great earthquake of 1908 which killed 84,000 people, levelled the city and made the shore sink by half a metre overnight. Allied bombing raids in 1943 didn't help, undoing much of the post-earthquake restoration.

Today, the remodelled city guards against future natural disasters, wide streets and low, reinforced concrete buildings marching off in all directions. Not surprisingly, it is a pretty dull spectacle, and most of what interest there is resides in Messina's active port area. Take time at least to walk up Via I Settembre from the train station to Piazza del Duomo. The traffic-strewn paved square was laid out in the eighteenth century, while the **Duomo** itself is an elegant reconstruction of the medieval cathedral built by Roger II. The facade retains its grand doorways and some original sculpture: inside, most of what you see – from the marble floor to the painted wooden ceiling – has been retouched and rebuilt. The detached **campanile** reputedly contains the largest astronomical clock in the world. Be there at noon and you get the full show, a visually impressive panoply of moving gilt figures including a crowing cock, roaring lion and a succession of doves and angels accompanying the Madonna.

Much of what was saved from the various disasters now resides in the **Museo Regionale** (Mon–Sat 9am–1.30pm & 3–5.30pm, Sun 9am–12.30pm; L2000), 3km out of town – a 45-minute walk along Via della Libertà or a #8, #27 or #28 bus from the train station. A great deal has been painstakingly stuck and plastered back together in this beautifully laid-out museum, including a couple of Caravaggios, commissioned by the city in 1604. There are also damaged works by Antonello da Messina, a few good Flemish pieces and the city's rescued archaeological remains as well.

Practicalities

Trains all use the **Stazione Centrale** by the harbour, adjacent to the **Stazione Maríttima** – where the train-ferries from Calabria dock. Other **ferries** and **hydrofoils** (to and from Villa San Giovanni/Reggio di Calabria, the Aeolian Islands and Naples) dock at quays further to the north, around the port and along Via Vittorio Emanuele and Via della Libertà. *SAIS* **buses** for Taormina and Catania leave from outside the train station, while those for Milazzo (for boat services to the Aeolian Islands) depart from the nearby *Giuntabus* office at Via Terranova 8 (at the corner of Viale San Martino). The **tourist office** (Mon–Sat 9am–1pm) is just outside the train station, on Piazza della Repubblica, good for free maps and Aeolian Island ferry timetables.

Unless you arrive late in the day, it's hardly necessary to **stay over** in Messina. Still, there are several very cheap options, including one, the *Roma* (☎090/675.566; ③), right on Piazza del Duomo. Other budget hotels are all close to the train station, two on Via N. Scotto, an alley to the left of Piazza della Repubblica. There's a **campsite,** *Il Peloritano* (☎090/348.496; May–Oct), out beyond Punta del Faro on the northern coast; take bus #28 to RODIA from the train station. For **eating**, the *Trattoria Firenze* is good value, close to the station, on Via del Vespro, across Piazza della Repubblica.

The coastal route south – and some hill villages

Try to take the train, rather than the slower bus, **south from Messina**, since the line follows the rough, stony shore pretty much all the way: on a clear day there are spanking views back over to Calabria.

SANTA TERESA DI RIVA is the first recognisable resort, with an oversized beach, though it's nothing to shout about. The straggling village is more attractive as a jumping-off point for the foothills of the **Monti Peloritani**, the long mountain range that cuts south from Messina. Buses from Santa Teresa twist the 4km up to **SAVOCA**, a peaceful hill village, evocatively sited up in the clouds. Houses and three churches perch precariously on the cliff sides in clumps, a tattered castle topping the pile. Signs in the village point you to the **Cappuccini monastery** whose catacombs (*catacombe*; April–Sept daily 9am–1pm & 4–7pm; Oct–March Tues–Sun 9am–noon & 3–5pm; free) maintain a selection of mummified bodies, two to three hundred years old, in niches, dressed in their eighteenth-century finery, the skulls of less complete colleagues lining the walls above. More offbeat delight is at hand in the village's *Bar Vitelli*, used as the scene of Michael Corleone's wedding breakfast in Coppola's film *The Godfather*; there's a still of Marlon Brando inside, terrace tables outside. Two kilometres on, **CASALVECCHIO SICULO** has even better valley views from its terraces, and is the nearest village to the Norman monastery of **San Pietro e Paolo**, a twenty-minute hike away. Built in the twelfth century, its battlemented facade and double domes are visible from quite a distance, and the church betrays a strong Arabic influence.

Taormina

TAORMINA, high on Monte Tauro and dominating two grand sweeping bays below, is Sicily's best-known resort. The outstanding remains of its classical theatre, with Mount Etna as an unparalleled backdrop, arrested passing travellers when Taormina was no more than a medieval hill village: Goethe and D.H. Lawrence are the two big names touted by the tourist office, Lawrence so enthusiastic that he lived here (1920–23) in a house at the top of the valley cleft behind the theatre. Although international tourism has taken its toll over recent years, Taormina still retains much of its small-town charm. The one main traffic-free street is an unbroken line of fifteenth- to nineteenth-century palazzi and small, intimate piazzas, and there is an agreeably crumbly castle and lines of flower-filled balconies. The downside is that between June and August it's virtually impossible to find anywhere to stay, and the narrow alleys are filled shoulder-to-shoulder with tourists. April, May or September are slightly better, but to avoid the crowds completely come between October and March, when it's often still warm enough to swim.

In summer, you could see the whole of town and the theatre in a short afternoon. **Trains** pull up at Taormina-Giardini station (left-luggage office) on the water's edge, way below town. It's a very steep thirty-minute walk up to Taormina (turn right out of the station and then, after 200m, left through a gap in the buildings, marked *Centro*). Much better (certainly if you have luggage) is to arrive by bus or take one of the fairly frequent local buses that pick up outside the train station. The **bus terminal**, where they all stop, is on Via Pirandello in Taormina itself: bear left up the road from the terminal, turn through the Porta Messina, and the main street, **Corso Umberto I**, lies before you. The useful **tourist office** (Mon–Fri 8am–2pm & 2.30–7.30pm, Sat 8am–noon) is in the fourteenth-century Palazzo Corvaja, off Piazza Vittorio Emanuele, the first square you come to. Pick up a free map, accommodation listings and bus timetables, and programmes for summer events in the theatre.

It's the **Teatro Greco** (daily 9am–1hr before sunset; L2000) – signposted from just about everywhere – that you should make your way to first, if only to acquaint yourself with Taormina's remarkable siting: southern Calabria, the Sicilian coastline and snow-capped Etna are all visible. That it was founded by Greeks in the third century BC is the extent of the theatre's Hellenistic connections, for the existing remains are almost entirely Roman. It was rebuilt at the end of the first century AD, when Taormina thrived under Imperial Roman rule, and the reconstruction changed the theatre's character entirely. The impressive Roman scene building, for example, is Sicily's only surviving example but can only have obscured the views of Etna – presumably a major reason for the theatre's original siting. Likewise, the stage and lower seats were cut back to provide more room and a deep trench dug in the orchestra to accommodate the animals and fighters used in Roman gladiatorial contests. In July and August the theatre hosts an international film festival and various concerts; tickets and information from the tourist office.

There are a few other Roman vestiges around town, including a much smaller **Odeion** (originally used for musical recitations) next to the tourist office. Really, though, Taormina's attractions are all to do with strolling the flower-decked streets and alleys, and window shopping in the converted ground floors of the mansions along the Corso. Centre of town is Piazza IX Aprile, with its restored twelfth-century **Torre dell'Orologio** and terrace overlooking Etna and the bay – though don't sit down at the inviting outdoor cafés unless you have a substantial bankroll. Give yourself time to hike up to the **Castello** by way of a stepped path which leads up from the main road behind the tourist office, from where you can continue on to **CASTELMOLA**, 5km above and seemingly growing out of its severe crag. It's about an hour's climb to the village (though there are buses), while another couple of hours beyond are the heights of **Monte Venere** (885m) – take the path behind Castelmola's cemetery – for the last word in local panoramas.

Practicalities

Finding a **bed** in summer is a time-consuming business without a reservation. Only a handful will be both available and affordable, so start looking early. Good possibilities are along **Via Bagnoli Croce** (alongside the public gardens): cheap rooms at no. 66 (very small but with incredible roof-terrace views; ③), nos. 124–126 (☎0942/23.878; ③), above the pizzeria, and no. 88 (*Villa Pompei*, ☎0942/23.812; ④). A big step up in price gets you a room at the pleasant *Pensione Elios* at no. 98 (☎0942/23.431; ⑥). Other options are *Villa Liliana*, Via Dietro Cappuccini 4 (☎0942/24.373; ④), close to the tourist office; and, more expensive but with excellent views, the *Pensione Svizzera*, at Via Pirandello 26 (☎0942/23.790; ④), just up from the bus terminal. For a family-run place, the *Pensione Villa Greta* (0942/28.286; ⑤) is warmly recommended – it's ten minutes' walk out of town on the road up to Castelmola, and has superb baclony views as well as a dining room with good home cooking.

If everywhere is full, you'll have to try nearby Giardini-Naxos (also a good place to eat, see opposite) or **camp**. The campsite, *San Leo* (☎0942/24.658), open all year, is on the cape below town (next to the *Grande Albergo Capo Taormina*): take any bus running between Taormina and the train station.

Eating in Taormina can also be terribly expensive. The only vaguely cheap trattoria is the basic but good *Trattoria da Nino*, Via Pirandello 37, while *Il Baccanale* in Piazza Filea (end of Via Bagnoli Croce) has outdoor tables and similar prices. For decent pizzas and pasta in lively surroundings, there's *Mamma Rosa*, Via Naumachie 10, and *La Botte*, Piazza Santa Domenica 4. More upmarket is the formal *Giova Rosy Senior*, Corso Umberto 38, where a full meal runs to L40,000 – the stuffed squid is especially good. Otherwise, there's an indoor **market** off Via Dietro Cappuccini (Mon–Sat mornings) and a *Standa* supermarket outside the Porta Catania.

Taormina's beaches – and Naxos

The **coastline** below town is appealing, no question – a mixture of grottoes and rocky coves – but too many of its beaches are either private lidos (which you have to pay to use) or simply too packed in summer to be much fun.

Closest beach to town is at **MAZZARO** with its much-photographed islet. There's a **cable car** service (L1000) which runs every fifteen minutes from Via Pirandello, and a steep path which starts just below the cable car station. If you're still searching for a bed there's a dozen small **hotels** here, though get the tourist office to ring for you first. The beach-bars and restaurants at **SPISONE**, north again, are also reachable by path from Taormina, this time from below the cemetery in town. From Spisone, the coast opens out and the beach gets wider. With more time you might explore **LETOJANNI**, a little resort in its own right with rather more ordinary bars and shops, a few fishing boats on a sand beach, two campsites and regular buses and trains back to Taormina.

Roomier and better for swimming are the sands south of Taormina at **GIARDINI-NAXOS**, and to a lesser extent at the holiday village of RECANATI, beyond. Be prepared to pay to use the beach, a few hundred lire for access, a couple of thousand for a sunbed. The wide curving bay of Giardini – easily seen from Taormina's terraces – was the launching-point of Garibaldi's attack on the Bourbon troops in Calabria (1860) and, as significantly, the site of the first Greek colony in Sicily. An obvious stop for ships running between Greece and southern Italy, it was the site of a settlement in 734 BC, named Naxos after the Naxian colonists. It was never very important, and the **excavations** (daily 9am–1hr before sunset; free) are very low-key – a long section of ancient, lava-built city wall, two covered kilns and a sketchy temple. But it's a pleasant walk there through the lemon groves (bus from Taormina to Naxos/Recanati and follow the signs, *Scavi*). Right on the cape, Capo Schiso, in between two restaurants, is an inconspicuous **Museo Archeologico** (Mon–Sat 9am–2pm, Sun 9am–1pm; free) housing some of the finds.

Giardini itself, the long town backing the good beach, is an excellent alternative source of accommodation and food. Prices tend to be a good bit cheaper than in Taormina and in high season, if you arrive by train, it's probably worth trying here first. Recommended **places to stay** are *La Sirena*, Via Schiso 36 (☎0942/51.853; ⑤), by the pier with views over the bay, and the central *Villa Pamar*, Via Naxos 23 (☎0942/52.448; ④), behind the tourist office. For **eating**, the best and the cheapest is the restaurant-pizzeria attached to the seafront *Lido Europa* (opposite the Chiesa Immacolata); good pizzas and fresh pasta are also to be had at *Fratelli Marano*, Via Naxos 181. For terrace seating and views of the bay, visit *Da Angelina* on Via Schiso, by the pier – it does fine fish soup. **Buses** run half-hourly to Giardini, the last one at 9.30pm; last one back to Taormina at 9pm from the stop outside the *Lido Europa*.

Around Mount Etna

Mount Etna's massive bulk looms over much of the coastal route south from Taormina. One of the world's largest volcanoes, it really demands a separate visit, but if you're pushed for time you'll have to content yourself with the ever more imminent views of its eastern flank as you head along the coast to Catania. With time, you can make the circular route to Catania on the slow train around the volcano, the **Circumetnea** – one of Sicily's most interesting rides – and stop off on the **volcano** itself. Reaching the lower craters below the summit is eminently possible, on foot or by mountain-bus – either way a thrilling experience.

South down the coast: Acireale, Aci Trezza and Aci Castello

The train is best if you're travelling directly to Catania, a fast route which hugs the coast. The only major town on the way is **ACIREALE**, 35km south of Taormina. Well sited a couple of kilometres above the rocky shore, and a noted spa centre, Acireale was rebuilt directly over the old lava streams after the 1693 earthquake. Aside from the views along the coast from its pretty public garden, the town's worth a stop for its several striking examples of Sicilian Baroque in the crowded central streets. A good time to come is at *Carnevale* (February/March), when Acireale hosts one of Sicily's best festivals, with flower-decked floats and fancy dress parades clogging the streets for five noisy days.

Acireale takes its name from the local river Aci, in Homeric myth said to have appeared following the death of the shepherd Acis at the hands of the giant, one-eyed cyclops Polyphemus. Other nearby villages take the name too, like **ACI TREZZA** and **ACI CASTELLO**, a few kilometres south (both reachable on the Messina–Catania bus route). Between the two, just offshore, the jagged points of the **Scogli dei Cicopli** stand: Homer wrote that the now blinded Polyphemus slung these rocks, broken from Etna, at Ulysses as he and his men escaped from the cyclops in their ships. The three main sharp-edged islets present an odd sight, and it's a good half day's entertainment to get off the bus at Aci Trezza and walk the couple of kilometres south along the rough coast to Aci Castello. The **Castello** itself (Tues–Sun 9am–1pm & 3–5pm, summer 5–7.30pm; free) is a terrific thirteenth-century building that rises above the sea in splinters from a volcanic rock crag. In summer the rough, lava-scattered coastline around town is popular for sunbathing and swimming, while Aci Castello has a couple of small restaurants, handy for lunch. Very frequent buses connect the two villages with Catania.

The Circumetnea railway: Giarre-Riposto to Catania

If you don't have the time to reach the summit of Etna, then the **Circumetnea** railway provides some alternative volcanic thrills. A private line, 114km long, it runs around the base of the volcano through fertile vegetation and the strewn lava from more recent eruptions – a marvellous ride. The line begins in the twin town of **GIARRE-RIPOSTO**, thirty minutes by train or bus from Taormina; mainline *FS* trains will drop you in Giarre, from where it's a short walk down Corso Italia to the station of Riposto, where the Circumetnea line starts. Rail passes are not valid on this route, and if you make the entire trip to Catania, allow five hours; tickets L6500 one way, L12,500 return.

The closest town to the summit is **RANDAZZO**, a dark medieval town built entirely of lava. Although dangerously near Etna, Randazzo has never been engulfed; when the 1981 eruption saw it on the point of evacuation, the lava-flow finally stopped just outside town. Poke around the gloomy streets – dingily authentic despite the fact that much of the town has been heavily restored after being bombed to bits in 1943, when it figured as the last Sicilian stronghold of the Axis forces.

If you want to break the journey around Etna then Randazzo is probably the place to stay, despite the fact that the only **accommodation** is uninspiring: the tatty *Motel Scrivano* (☎095/921.126; ⑤), behind the *Agip* petrol station on Via Regina Margherita. You could, anyway, give Randazzo a couple of hours and pick up the next Circumetnea train for Catania – or the regular branch line (rail passes valid) to Taormina-Giardini.

Mount Etna: the ascent

Fine though the journey and views are, circling **Etna** by road or rail can only be second best to an ascent, a spectacular trip worth the effort – though without your own transport that effort can be considerable. At 3323m, Etna is a fairly substantial mountain, with the fact that it's also one of the world's biggest active volcanoes only adding to the draw. Some of the eruptions have been disastrous: in 1169, 1329 and 1381 the lava reached the sea; in 1669 Catania was wrecked and its castle surrounded by molten rock; while this century the Circumetnea railway line has been repeatedly ruptured by lava flows and, in 1979, nine people were killed on the edge of the main crater.

This unpredictability means that it's no longer possible to get close to the main crater. An **eruption** in 1971 destroyed the observatory supposed to give warning of such an event; another in 1983 brought down the cable car which provided access to the crater. The cable car may have reopened by now, but at the time of writing access was by 10km of rough track. The volcano was in an almost continual state of eruption throughout most of 1991 and 1992, when the US navy joined Italian forces in attempts to stanch the lava flow by dropping concrete blocks into the fissures from helicopters. All this is not to say you'll be in any danger, provided you heed the warnings as you get closer to the top.

There are several **approaches** to the volcano and, with a car, some of the best scenery is on the north side of the volcano, taking the road that leads up from Linguaglossa. On **public transport**, though, you'll need to come via **NICOLOSI**, on the southern side of Etna and a hour from Catania by bus. A winter ski resort and last main stop before the steeper slopes begin, it's a good place to pick up information. The small town **information office** is at Via Etnea 65 (daily 8.30am–1pm, summer also 4–7.30pm), the main road that runs through Nicolosi. There are several **hotels** too, a couple in town, the rest on the road out, as well as a **campsite** – all signposted and detailed on full lists available from the information office.

Although there are frequent buses to Nicolosi from Catania, only one (8.05am from outside Catania train station) continues to **Rifugio Sapienza**, the mountain refuge-cum-hotel that marks the end of the negotiable road up the south side of Etna. Everywhere here the slopes are dotted with earlier, spent craters, grass covered on the lower reaches, like black pimples further up. At the car park beyond the road there's a line of souvenir shops, a couple of restaurants and the *Rifugio Sapienza* (☎095/911.062; ④) itself. Arriving on the early morning bus, you'll have enough time to make the top and get back for the return bus to Catania – it leaves around 4pm from the refuge. Failing that, cadging a lift down with someone isn't impossible.

There are two ways **up the volcano** from the refuge. You can either take one of the tough-looking *SITAS* **minibuses** from outside the old cable car station (April–Oct/Nov only; L35,000), a two-hour return trip which gives you half an hour clambering around just below the main crater. Or you can **walk**, following the rough minibus track. Really it all depends on finances and time: walking up will take between three and four hours, the return obviously a little less. However you go, take warm clothes, good shoes or boots and glasses to keep the flying grit out of your eyes.

As you climb, the ground under your feet is alternately black, grey or red depending on the age of the lava. The more recent stuff lies in great folds, earlier minor craters signposted as you climb. The highest you're allowed to get (on foot or in the bus) is 2900m, and though there's only a rope across the ground to prevent you from climbing further, it would be foolish to presume that nothing serious would happen to you if you did – gaseous explosions and molten rock are common this far up. From the turn-around point for the minibus you look up to the summit, smoke puffing from the south-east crater immediately above. Higher still is the main crater: depending on the weather conditions you'll see smoke from here too and, if you're lucky, spitting explosions. If you've walked, you'll be glad of the **bar** set up in a wooden hut here, one of the odder places in the world to get a cappuccino.

Catania

First impressions don't do much at all for **CATANIA**, on an initial encounter possibly the island's gloomiest spot. Built from black-grey volcanic stone, its central streets can feel suffocating, dark with the shadows of grimy, high Baroque churches and palazzi; and the presence of Etna dominates everywhere, in the buildings, in the brooding vistas you get of the mountain at the end of Catania's streets – even the city's main street is named after the volcano.

Yet fight the urge to change buses and run: Catania is one of the most intriguing, and historic, of Sicily's cities. Some of the island's first Greek colonists settled the site as early as 729 BC, becoming so influential that their laws were eventually adopted by all the Ionian colonies of Magna Graecia. Later, a series of natural disasters helped shape the city as it appears today: Etna erupted in 1669, engulfing the city, the lava swamping the harbour, which was then topped by an earthquake in 1693 that devastated the whole of southeastern Sicily. The swift rebuilding was on a grand scale, and making full use of the local building material, Giovanni Vaccarini, the eighteenth-century architect, gave the city a lofty, noble air. Despite the neglect of many of the churches and the disintegrating, grey mansions, there's still interest in what, at first, might seem intimidating. Delving about throws up lava-encrusted Roman relics, surviving alongside some of the finest Baroque work on the island.

Arrival, information and transport

The **train station**, for all mainline train arrivals, is in Piazza Giovanni XXIII, northeast of the centre. If you're changing on to the round-Etna train, the **Circumetnea terminus** is on Corso delle Province, just off Corso Italia. The **airport**, Fontanarossa, is 5km south of the city, entry point of most charter flights to Sicily; if you're not on a package and don't have a bus to meet you, bus #24 leaves from right outside for Piazza del Duomo and the train station (see below for bus fares). Taxis from the airport to the centre cost about L25,000. **Regional buses** to and from Acireale, Nicolosi, Etna (Rifugio Sapienza) and Lentini all park on the other side of Piazza Giovanni XXIII; buses to and from Piazza Armerina stop on Via Luigi Sturzo, just to the left of the square; most other regional and **island-wide buses** stop in Piazza Bellini, a few minutes' walk from Piazza del Duomo.

Immediately outside the train station you'll find ranks of **city buses**: #27, #29, #33, #36 and #42 run into the centre at Piazza del Duomo. **Tickets** are valid for one journey (L1000) or two hours (L1500), bought from the booth by the ranks.

There's a **tourist office** (summer daily 8.30am–8.30pm; winter Mon–Fri 9am–1pm & 4–7pm; ☎095/531.802) inside the train station, with accommodation listings, maps and English-speaking staff; and there's also an information office at the airport (Mon–Fri 9am–noon & 1–8pm).

The City

Catania's main square, **Piazza del Duomo**, is a handy orientation point and stop for most city buses: Via Etnea steams off north, lined with the city's most fashionable shops and cafés; fish market and port lie behind to the south; train station to the east; the best of the Baroque quarter to the west.

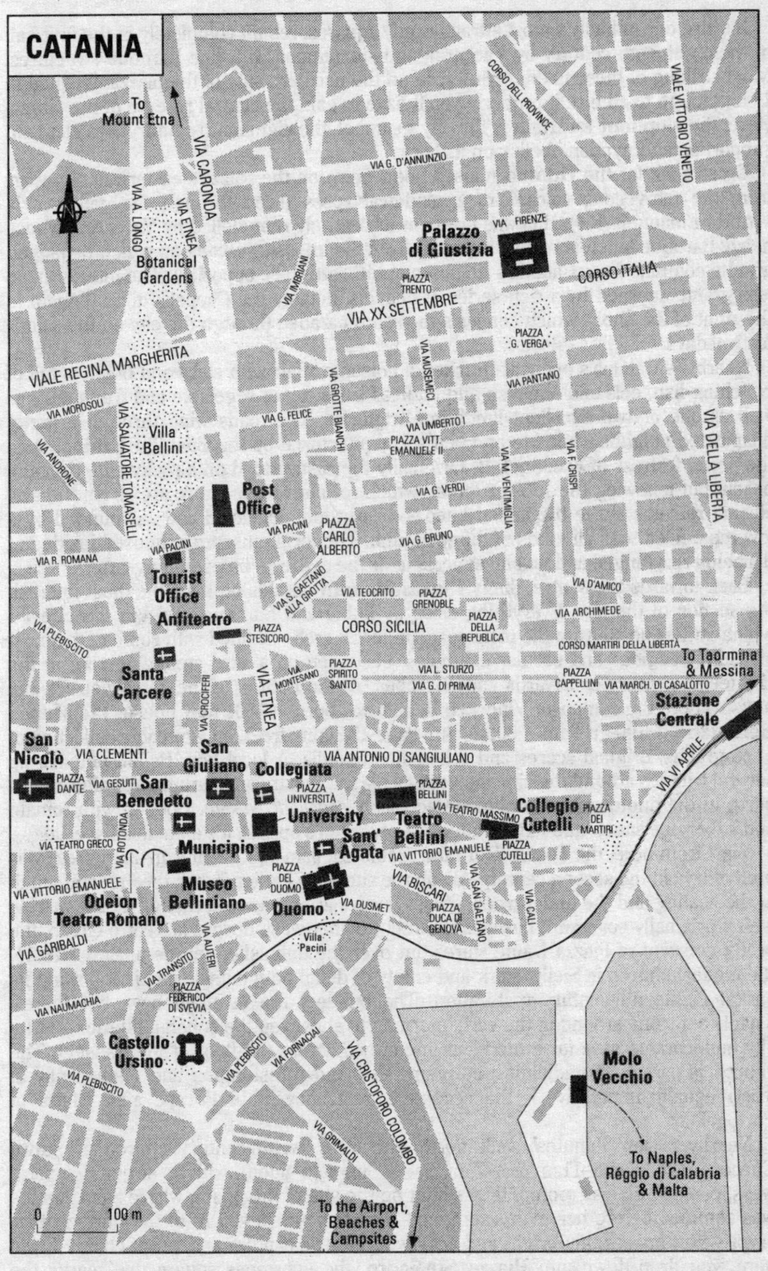
CATANIA
To Mount Etna
VIA CARONDA
VIA A. LONGO
VIA ETNEA
Botanical Gardens
VIA G. D'ANNUNZIO
CORSO DELL PROVINCE
VIALE VITTORIO VENETO
VIA FIRENZE
Palazzo di Giustizia
VIA IMBRIANI
PIAZZA TRENTO
CORSO ITALIA
VIA XX SETTEMBRE
PIAZZA G. VERGA
VIALE REGINA MARGHERITA
VIA MUSEMECI
VIA GROTTE BIANCHI
VIA PANTANO
VIA MOROSOLI
VIA G. FELICE
VIA UMBERTO I
PIAZZA VITT. EMANUELE II
VIA ANDRONE
VIA SALVATORE TOMASELLI
Villa Bellini
VIA M. VENTIMIGLIA
VIA F. CRISPI
VIA DELLA LIBERTA
Post Office
VIA G. VERDI
VIA PACINI
PIAZZA CARLO ALBERTO
VIA G. BRUNO
VIA R. ROMANA
VIA PACINI
Tourist Office
VIA S. GAETANO ALLA GROTTA
VIA TEOCRITO
PIAZZA GRENOBLE
VIA D'AMICO
VIA ARCHIMEDE
Anfiteatro
PIAZZA STESICORO
CORSO SICILIA
PIAZZA DELLA REPUBLICA
VIA PLEBISCITO
CORSO MARTIRI DELLA LIBERTÀ
To Taormina & Messina
Santa Carcere
VIA CROCIFERI
VIA ETNEA
VIA MONTESANO
PIAZZA SPIRITO SANTO
VIA L. STURZO
VIA G. DI PRIMA
PIAZZA CAPPELLINI
VIA MARCH. DI CASALOTTO
Stazione Centrale
San Nicolò
VIA CLEMENTI
San Giuliano
VIA ANTONIO DI SANGIULIANO
VIA VI APRILE
Collegiata
PIAZZA DANTE
VIA GESUITI
San Benedetto
PIAZZA UNIVERSITÀ
PIAZZA BELLINI
University
Teatro Bellini
VIA TEATRO MASSIMO
Collegio Cutelli
PIAZZA DEI MARTIRI
VIA TEATRO GRECO
VIA ROTONDA
Municipio
Sant' Agata
VIA VITTORIO EMANUELE
PIAZZA CUTELLI
VIA VITTORIO EMANUELE
Museo Belliniano
PIAZZA DEL DUOMO
VIA BISCARI
VIA SAN GAETANO
VIA CALI
Odeion Teatro Romano
Duomo
VIA DUSMET
PIAZZA DUCA DI GENOVA
Villa Pacini
VIA GARIBALDI
VIA AUTERI
VIA TRANSITO
PIAZZA FEDERICO DI SVEVIA
VIA NAUMACHIA
Castello Ursino
VIA PLEBISCITO
VIA FORNACIAI
VIA CRISTOFORO COLOMBO
Molo Vecchio
VIA PLEBISCITO
VIA GRIMALDI
To Naples, Réggio di Calabria & Malta
0
100 m
To the Airport, Beaches & Campsites

It's also one of Sicily's most attractive city squares, rebuilt completely in the first half of the eighteenth century by Vaccarini and surrounded with fine Baroque structures. Most striking of these is the **Municipio** on the northern side of the piazza, finished in 1741, though to admire it properly you'll have to gain the central reserve of the piazza. Here, the **elephant fountain** is the city's symbol, the eighteenth-century lava elephant supporting an Egyptian obelisk on its back.

Cross back for the **Duomo** (closed noon–5pm) on the piazza's eastern flank. Apart from the marvellous volcanic-rock medieval apses (seen through the gate at Via Vittorio Emanuele 159), this was pretty much entirely remodelled by Vaccarini, whose heavy Baroque touch is readily apparent from the imposing facade on which he tagged granite columns from Catania's Roman amphitheatre (see opposite). The interior is no less grand: adorned by a rich series of chapels, notably the Cappella di Sant'Agata to the right of the choir, which conceals the relics paraded through the city on the saint's festival days.

Nearby is Catania's open-air **market**, a noisome affair with slabs and buckets full of twitching fish, eels and shellfish and endless lanes full of vegetable and fruit stalls, as well as one or two excellent lunchtime trattorias. The roads wind through a pretty dilapidated neighbourhood to an open space punctured by the **Castello Ursino**, once the proud fortress of Frederick II. Originally the castle stood on a rocky cliff, over the beach, but following the 1669 eruption, which reclaimed this entire area from the sea, all that remains is the blackened keep – desperately neglected and surrounded by a low moat filled with all kinds of dumped junk. The local museum is housed inside but it's being rearranged and no one expects it, or the castle, to be open for years.

Back towards the centre, dingy **Piazza Mazzini** heralds perhaps the most interesting section of the city. Everything close by is big and Baroque, and **Via Crociferi** – which strikes north from the main road, under an arch – is lined with some of the most arresting religious and secular examples, best seen on a slow amble, peering in the eighteenth-century courtyards and churches. At the bottom of the narrow street, the house where the composer Vincenzo Bellini was born in 1801 now houses the **Museo Belliniano** (Mon–Fri 9am–1.30pm, Sun 9am–12.30pm; free), an agreeable collection of photographs, original scores and other memorabilia. A local boy, Bellini notches up several tributes around the city, including a piazza, theatre and park named after him, a berth in the duomo and the ultimate accolade, *spaghetti Norma*. Cooked with tomato and aubergine sauce, and named after one of Bellini's operas, it's a Catanian speciality.

West from here, the **Teatro Romano** (Mon–Sat 8am–5pm, Sun 8am–2pm; free) was built of lava in the second century AD on the site of an earlier Greek theatre, and much of the seating and the underground passageways are preserved, though all the marble which originally covered it has disappeared. Further west, down Via Teatro Greco, the pretty crescent of Piazza Dante stares out over the unfinished facade of **San Nicolò**, the biggest church in Sicily, stark and empty of detail both outside and in following its partial eighteenth-century restoration. The builders are in again now, but there's usually someone around in the early morning to show you the echoing interior – virtually undecorated save for a meridian line drawn across the floor of the transept. The church is part of the adjoining **convent**, also under restoration and (statistically at least) equally impressive – the second largest convent in Europe after Mafra in Portugal.

Nearby, a few minutes' walk north, the little twelfth-century church of **Santo Cárcere** (Mon–Fri 8–11am & 4–7pm, Sat & Sun 8am–noon), with its strong defensive walls, couldn't be less roomy. It was built on the site of the prison where Saint Agatha was confined before her martyrdom, and a custodian lets you in to the third-century crypt – now appealingly bright and cosy with electric candles and velvet chairs. From here, you drop down into **Piazza Stesicoro**, the enormous square that marks the modern centre of Catania, one half of which is almost entirely occupied by the closed-off, sunken, black remains of Catania's **Anfiteatro Romano**, dating back to the second or third century AD. The amphitheatre could hold around 16,000 spectators, and from the church steps above you can see the seating quite clearly, supported by long vaults.

Accommodation, eating and drinking

There are lots of **places to stay** in Catania, and some real bargains if you hunt around. *Pensione Gresi*, Via Pacini 28 (☎095/322.709; ④), is one of the nicest, and the *Rubens*, Via Etnea 196 (☎095/317.073; ④) is also good for around the same price. Best of the rest is the *Ferrara*, Via Umberto 66 (☎095/316.000; ④), though it fills quickly. If you want to stay around Piazza del Duomo, try the *Savona*, Via Vittorio Emanuele 210 (☎095/326.982; ④). There are three **campsites** (with lidos and cabins available) a short way south of the city on Lungomare Kennedy; take bus #24, #27 or #D (the last in summer only) from the train station or Via Etnea.

You'll rarely do better for **eating** than in Catania, where fresh fish is a speciality. The *Ristorante Rapido*, Via Corridoni 17, off Via Pacini, is probably Catania's best – great at lunch, with a L15,000 *pranzo completo*. Worth trying too is the *Trattoria Calabrese*, on Via Penninello, down the steps at the end of Via Crociferi. For a more expensive meal, *Ristorante Finocchiaro*, off Piazza dell'Università at Via Reina 13, has excellent *antipasti* and unusual local dishes. Of the **bars**, handiest is the *Bar Università* in Piazza dell'Università, which sells good milkshakes and fresh fruit drinks; the *Centrale*, Via Etnea 123, is a busy *tavola calda* with a full range of snacks.

Listings

Airport Enquiries ☎095/349.837. Note that buses from Catania to Agrigento and Enna make a stop at the airport. Direct services, too, from the airport to Taormina/Messina and Milazzo (for the Aeolian Islands).

American Express c/o *La Duca & C.*, Via Etnea 63 (☎095/316.155).

Car rental *Hertz* and *Holiday Car Rental* at the airport; *Avis*, Via San Giuseppe La Rena 87 (☎095/347.116); *InterRent*, Via Firenze 104 (☎095/444.063).

Emergencies ☎095/375.050 for an ambulance.

Ferry tickets *Tirrenia Società Navigazione*, Piazza Grenoble 26 (☎095/316.394) for services to Naples, Reggio di Calabria, Siracusa and Malta.

Hospital First aid at the following hospitals: *Garibaldi*, Piazza S. Maria di Gesu (☎095/322.216); *Santa Marta*, Via Clementi 36 (☎095/317.668); *S. Tomaselli*, Via Passo Gravina 185 (☎095/333.703).

Left luggage At the train station, open 24hr, L1500 per day.

Pharmacies Night pharmacies at Via Etnea 274, Via Vittorio Emanuele 54 and Corso Italia 105.

Post office Via Etnea 215, close to the Villa Bellini; Mon–Sat 8am–8pm.

Telephones *SIP* at Corso Sicilia 67; daily 8am–8pm.

Travel agency *CTS*, Viale Regina Margherita 4c.

The plain of Catania

Compared to the interest further north, there's a real paucity of places if you're looking for another halt before Siracusa. Trains and buses cut right across the **Piana di Catania**, known to the Greeks as the Laestrygonian Fields after the cannibalistic Laestrygones who were reputed to live there: it's a pretty ride but with absolutely no reason to get off until **LENTINI**, half an hour or so out of Catania. Lentini was founded in 728 BC, probably to restrict any further northward expansion by the Corinthians in Siracusa. Built far inland, unusual for a Greek colony, it prospered before succumbing to the Romans under Marcellus, who slaughtered some 2000 of the inhabitants in 214

BC. The ancient city – some defences, a necropolis and part of a main gate – lies between Lentini and nearby CARLENTINI, a twenty-minute walk north from the centre, or take bus #1 or #2 from Lentini's train station. The local **Museo Archeologico** in Lentini's Piazza del Liceo (Mon–Sat 9am–2pm, Sun 9am–1pm; free), holds the finds and a reconstruction of the gate, a necessary first stop before seeking out the remains on the ground.

If this doesn't grab you then trains and direct buses from Catania run around the southern spur of the Golfo di Catania to **AUGUSTA**, oil port and naval base. It's more pleasant than it sounds, built (like Siracusa) on a small islet connected to the mainland, and there are beach resorts to the north, one at BRUCOLI together with a fifteenth-century castle. But the real reason to stay would be as a base for visiting the nearby site of **MEGARA HYBLAEA**, around 10km south, across the bay. Founded by Greeks a few years before Siracusa, the city enjoyed a fair living from sea-trade and pottery until destroyed by first Gelon in 483 BC and later the Romans. The large **site** (always open) shows a Doric temple, some tombs and houses, an eighth-century BC *agora*, as well as a small **museum** (Mon–Sat 9am–2pm, Sun 9am–1pm; free) with plans, photos and some finds. Unfortunately, it's not easy to get to without your own transport: the only possibility is to take a local train from Augusta to MEGARA-GIANNALENA, from where it's a fair hike, though you could reduce it to a kilometre by walking along the rails and climbing up at the road bridge.

The last stretch of the journey to Siracusa, by train especially, is a nightmare of **rampant industrialisation**. As far as PRIOLO, the track skirts the largest concentration of chemical plants in Europe, a stinking, Meccano-built mesh of pipes and tanks that has irreversibly polluted the local sea and air. People living in the coastal villages have had to be evacuated and their houses destroyed, the environment deemed unfit for human habitation.

Siracusa

It's hardly surprising that **SIRACUSA** (ancient Syracuse) – an easily defendable offshore island with fertile plains across on the mainland and two natural harbours – should attract the early Greek colonists, in this case Corinthians who settled the site in 733 BC. Within a hundred years, the city was so powerful that it was sending out its own colonists to the south and west; and later Siracusa was the island's main power base – indeed, the city's history reads as a list of Sicily's most famous and effective rulers.

Some history

Syracuse first assumed its almost mythic eminence under **Gelon**, the tyrant of Gela, who moved his rule to the city in 485 BC to increase his power: it was he who began work on the city's Temple of Athena, later to become the Christian cathedral of Syracuse. It was an unparalleled period of Greek prosperity in Sicily, while the extent of a wider Siracusean influence was indicated by the defeat of the Etruscans (474 BC), who had been causing trouble for Greek towns on mainland Italy. It was a growing influence which troubled Athens, and in 415 BC a fleet of 134 triremes was dispatched to take Syracuse – only to be blockaded and the fleet destroyed. Those who weren't slaughtered as they ran were imprisoned in the city's stone quarries.

Under **Dionysius the Elder**, the city became a great military base, the tyrant building the first of the Euryalus forts and erecting strong city walls. As the leading European power, Syracuse more or less retained its prime position for two hundred years until it was attacked by the Romans in 215 BC. The subsequent two-year siege was made long and hazardous for the attackers by the mechanical devices contrived by **Archimedes** – who, as the Romans finally forced victory, was killed by a foot soldier.

From this time, Syracuse withered in importance. It became, briefly, a major religious centre in the early Christian period, but for the most part its days as a power were done: it was sacked by the Saracens and most of its later Norman buildings fell in the 1693 earthquake. Passed by until this century, the city suffered a double blow in World War II when it was bombed by the Allies and then, after its capture, by the Luftwaffe in 1943. Luckily, the extensive ancient remains were little damaged, although decay and new development have reduced the attractions of the modern city. It's an essential stop on any tour of the island, but it's getting daily more difficult to picture the beautiful city which Plutarch wept over when he heard of its fall to the Romans.

Some **orientation** pointers are useful. The original Greek settlement was on the fortified island of **Ortygia**, compact enough to see in a good half-day's stroll and almost completely late medieval in character. The Greek city spread onto the mainland in four distinct areas: **Achradina**, over the water from Ortygia, was the city's commercial and administrative centre, and today encompasses the new streets which radiate out from the train station; **Tyche**, to the northeast, was residential and now holds the archaeological museum and the city's extensive catacombs; **Neapolis**, to the west, is the site of the fascinating archaeological park based on ancient Syracuse's public and social amenities; while **Epipolae** stretched way to the northwest, to the city's outer defensive walls and the Euryalus fort.

Arrival and information

You'll **arrive** in Siracusa in any one of a number of places. The **train station** is on the mainland, about a twenty-minute walk from either Ortygia or Neapolis. If you're not staying, then dump your bags in the **left luggage office** in the station (open 24hr; L1500 a day) and strike off for one or the other. *AST* **buses** arrive in Piazza della Poste, just over the bridge on Ortygia, where there's also an office doling out timetables for regional and city bus services. *SAIS* buses stop just around the corner, in Via Trieste. **Ferries**, from Naples, Reggio di Calabria and Catania, and for Malta, dock right on the Foro Vittorio Emanuele; tickets and info from *Tirrenia-Adriatica*, Viale Mazzini 4 (☎0931/65.684).

The main **city bus** stops are in Piazza Archimede and Largo XXV Luglio on Ortygia, and along Corso Umberto on the mainland. One ride will cost you L600. For free maps, accommodation listings, details about the performances in the Greek theatre, and other **information**, visit the **tourist office** (Tues–Sun 9am–2pm) at Via Maestranza 33, or inside the train station (Mon–Sat 9am–1pm and 3–7pm). The main **post office** is in Piazza delle Poste; **telephones** (8am–8pm) are at Via Brenta 35, close to the train station.

Central Siracusa: Ortygia and Achradina

A fist of land with the thumb downturned, **ORTYGIA** stuffs more than 2700 years of history into a space barely one kilometre long and half a kilometre across. The island was connected to the mainland at different times by causeway or by bridge: today you approach over the wide Ponte Nuovo to Piazza Pancali, where the sandstone remnants of the **Tempio di Apollo** sit in a little green park surrounded by railings. Erected around 570 BC in the colony's early years, it was the first grand Doric temple to be built in Sicily, though there's not much left to provoke the senses: a few column stumps, part of the inner sanctuary wall and the stereobate can be made out.

Follow Via Savoia towards the water and you fetch up on the harbour front, an active place overlooking the main harbour, the Porto Grande. Set back from the water, a curlicued fifteenth-century limestone gateway, the **Porta Marina**, provides one entrance into the webbed streets of the old town. The walk uphill ends on a terrace looking over the harbour, from where you slip down to a piazza encircling the **Fonte Aretusa**,

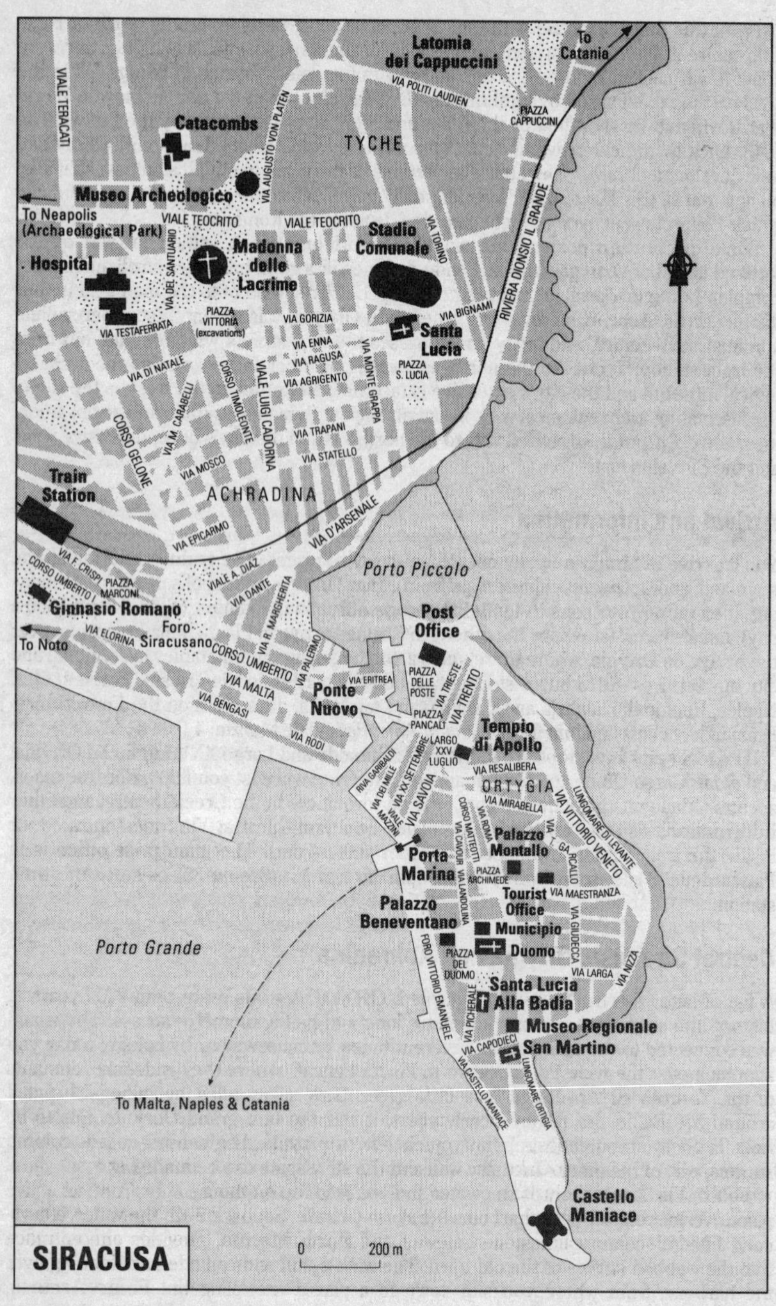

Latomia dei Cappuccini
To Catania
VIA POLITI LAUDIEN
PIAZZA CAPPUCCINI
VIALE TERACATI
Catacombs
VIA AUGUSTO VON PLATEN
TYCHE
Museo Archeologico
To Neapolis (Archaeological Park)
VIALE TEOCRITO
VIALE TEOCRITO
Stadio Comunale
VIA TORINO
RIVIERA DIONSIO IL GRANDE
Hospital
VIA DEL SANTUARIO
Madonna delle Lacrime
PIAZZA VITTORIA (excavations)
VIA TESTAFERRATA
VIA GORIZIA
VIA BIGNAMI
Santa Lucia
VIA ENNA
VIA RAGUSA
PIAZZA S. LUCIA
VIA DI NATALE
CORSO TIMOLEONTE
VIALE LUIGI CADORNA
VIA MONTE GRAPPA
VIA AGRIGENTO
VIA M. CARABELLI
CORSO GELONE
VIA TRAPANI
VIA STATELLO
VIA MOSCO
Train Station
ACHRADINA
VIA EPICARMO
VIA D'ARSENALE
VIA F. CRISPI
CORSO UMBERTO I
PIAZZA MARCONI
VIALE A. DIAZ
Porto Piccolo
VIA DANTE
VIA R. MARGHERITA
Ginnasio Romano
Foro Siracusano
To Noto
VIA ELORINA
CORSO UMBERTO
Post Office
VIA PALERMO
VIA ERITREA
PIAZZA DELLE POSTE
VIA TRIESTE
VIA TRENTO
VIA MALTA
VIA BENGASI
Ponte Nuovo
PIAZZA PANCALI
Tempio di Apollo
VIA RODI
LARGO XXV LUGLIO
VIA RESALIBERA
RIVA GARIBALDI
VIA DEI MILLE
VIA XX SETTEMBRE
VIA SAVOIA
ORTYGIA
VIALE MAZZINI
CORSO MATTEOTTI
VIA ROMA
VIA MIRABELLA
VIA CAVOUR
LUNGOMARE DI LEVANTE
VIA VITTORIO VENETO
Palazzo Montalto
VIA GARCALLO
Porta Marina
PIAZZA ARCHIMEDE
VIA LANDOLINA
Tourist Office
VIA MAESTRANZA
Palazzo Beneventano
Municipio
Duomo
VIA GIUDECCA
PIAZZA DEL DUOMO
FORO VITTORIO EMANUELE
Porto Grande
VIA LARGA
VIA NIZZA
Santa Lucia Alla Badia
VIA PICHERALE
Museo Regionale
VIA CAPODIECI
San Martino
VIA CASTELLO MANIACE
LUNGOMARE ORTIGIA
To Malta, Naples & Catania
Castello Maniace
SIRACUSA
0
200 m

probably the most enduring of Siracusa's romantic locations. The freshwater spring – incidentally now neither fresh nor a spring – fuelled an attractive Greek myth: the nymph Arethusa, chased by the river god Alpheus, was changed into a spring by the goddess Artemis and, jumping into the sea off the Peloponnese, reappeared as a fountain in Siracusa. Actually, there are natural freshwater springs all over Ortygia, but the landscaped, papyrus-covered fountain – complete with fish and ducks – is undeniably pretty. Admiral Nelson took on water supplies here before the Battle of the Nile, though you'd be better advised to sip a coffee in one of the cafés nearby.

The old town's roads lead on, down the "thumb" of Ortygia, as far as the **Castello Maniace** on the island's southern tip. Thrown up by Frederick II in 1239, the solid square keep is now a barracks and is off-limits to visitors. Back on the main chunk of Ortygia, the severe thirteenth-century Palazzo Bellomo houses the **Museo Regionale d'Arte Medioevale e Moderna** (Tues–Sun 9am–1pm; L2000), an outstanding collection of medieval art. There are some wonderful pieces in here, including notable works by the omnipresent Gagini family and a damaged fifteenth-century *Annunciation* by Antonello da Messina, the museum's most famous exhibit.

Ortygia's most obvious attractions, though, surround the **Piazza del Duomo**, the island's most appealing spot. The piazza is an elongated space from which impressive buildings radiate out up either flank, including the seventeenth-century **Municipio** with the remains of an early Ionic temple in its basement. This was abandoned when work began on the most ambitious of all Siracusa's temples, the **Tempio di Atena**, which was raised in the fifth century BC and now forms the basis of the duomo. In the normal run of things it might be expected to have suffered the eventual ruination that befell most of the Greek temples in Sicily. Yet much of it survives, thanks to the foundation in the seventh century AD of a Christian church which incorporated the temple in its structure – thus keeping the masonry scavengers at bay. The **Duomo** itself (closed noon–4pm) makes the grandest statement about Ortygia's continuous settlement, with twelve of the temple's fluted columns, and their architrave, embedded in its battlemented Norman wall. Inside, the nave of the Christian church was formed by hacking eight arches in the *cella* walls.

Buses run from Largo XXV Luglio over Ponte Nuovo and into **ACHRADINA**, the important commercial centre of ancient Syracuse. Although nowadays there's little of interest here, you may find yourself staying in one of the hotels scattered around its modern streets. The **Foro Siracusano** was the site of the *agora*, the marketplace and public square, and there are a few remains still to be seen – though the dominant feature is the war memorial in its garden, a Fascist monument of 1936. The only other ancient attraction left in the area is the **Ginnasio Romano**, off Via Elorina behind the train station: not a gymnasium at all, but a small first-century AD Roman theatre – partly sunken under moss-covered water – and a few pieces of a temple and altar.

Tyche and Neapolis: archaeological museum and park

TYCHE, north of the train station, is mainly new and commercial, and if you want to see the best of Siracusa's archaeological delights you might as well take the bus straight from Ortygia and save your legs. Buses #1, #4, #6 and #12 (not Sun) leave from Piazza XXV Luglio, #11 from Corso Umberto – all running up Corso Gelone. Get off at Viale Teocrito and signposts point you east for the archaeological museum and west for Neapolis. It's best to take the museum first: it's good for putting the site into perspective and is unlikely to be packed first thing in the morning.

The **Museo Archeologico** (Tues–Sat 9am–1pm, Sun 9am–12.30pm; L2000) is Sicily's newest and most spectacular archaeological museum. There is almost indescribable wealth here, starting with geological and prehistoric finds, moving through entire rooms devoted to the Chalcidesian colonies (Naxos, Lentini, Zancle) and to

Megara Hyblaea, and finally to the main body of the collection: an immensely detailed catalogue of life in ancient Syracuse and its sub-colonies. Most famous exhibit is the *Venus*, at the entrance to the Syracuse section: a headless figure arising from the sea, the clear white marble almost palpably dripping. Attempt also to track down the section dealing with the temples of Syracuse; fragments from each (like the seven lion-gargoyles from the Tempio di Atena) are displayed alongside model and video reconstructions. There's an explanatory diagram at the entrance to the circular building and everything is colour coded: pick the sector you're interested in and follow the arrows, prehistory starting just to the left of the entrance.

NEAPOLIS, to the west, is now contained within a large **Parco Archeologico** (daily 9am–2hr before sunset), reachable on bus #4, #5 or #6 from Largo XXV Luglio. Although you don't pay for the initial excavations, seeing the Greek theatre and quarries – easily the most interesting parts – costs L2000, paid at a separate entrance. The **Ara di Ierone II**, an enormous altar of the third century BC on a solid white plinth, is the first thing you see, across the way from which is the entrance to the theatre and quarries. The **Teatro Greco** is very prettily sited, cut out of the rock and looking down into trees below. It's much bigger than the one at Taormina, capable of holding around 15,000 people, though less impressive on the whole. But the theatre's pedigree is impeccable: Aeschylus put on works here, and around the top of the middle gangway are a set of carved names which marked the various seat blocks occupied by the royal family. Greek dramas are still played here in even-numbered years, as wooden planking over the surviving seats testifies.

Walk back through the theatre and another path leads down into a leafy quarry, the **Latomia del Paradiso**, best known for its unusually shaped cavern that Dionysius is supposed to have used as a prison. This, the **Orecchio di Dionigi** (or "Ear of Dionysius") is a high, S-shaped cave 65m long: Caravaggio, a visitor in 1586, coined the name after the shape of the entrance, but the acoustic properties are such that it's not impossible to imagine Dionysius eavesdropping on his prisoners from a vantage point above. A second cave, the **Grotta dei Cordari**, used by the ancient city's ropemakers, is shored up at present.

Keep your ticket from the theatre and Latomia del Paradiso, as it will also get you into the elliptical **Anfiteatro Romano**, back up the main path past the altar and through a gate on your right; you have to see this last. A late building, dating from the third century AD, it's a substantial relic with the tunnels for animals and gladiators clearly visible. Again, some of the seats are inscribed with the owner's names.

Castello Eurialo

If it's hot and crowded, better targets are a few kilometres to the west of the city – the military and defensive works begun under Dionysius the Elder, designed to defend ancient Syracuse from land attack. Added to and adapted over a couple of centuries, they basically consisted of a great wall which defended the ridge of **Epipolae** (the city's western limit), and the massive **Castello Eurialo** (Mon–Sat 9am–6pm, Sun 9am–1pm; free) – *the* major extant Greek fortification in the Mediterranean.

There are three defensive trenches, the innermost leading off into a system of tunnels and passages. Climb up to the castle proper, its long keep and the lower walls and towers providing hearty views over the oil refineries and tankers of the coast north of the city, and over Siracusa itself. Clambering around the castle and the defensive walls is good fun, and the youth hostel just up the road from the castello (see opposite) is a fine alternative to staying in the packed central city.

Bus #9, #10 and #11 run from the Corso Gelone, outside the archaeological park, to the village of BELVEDERE; the site is just before the village, on the right, a fifteen-minute ride.

Practicalities

Accommodation choices aren't spectacular and in high season you must make an advance reservation. A popular choice on Ortygia is the *Gran Bretagna*, Via Savoia 21 (☎0931/68.765; ⑤), or you could ask around the several cheaper hotels on the way in from the train station: try the *Centrale*, Corso Umberto 141 (☎0931/60.528; ④) or the *Hotel Milano*, Corso Umberto 10 (☎0931/66.981; ③). The *Pensione Al Pantheon*, Foro Siracusano 22 (☎0931/22.985; ③) is a friendly alternative – it's at the back of the Foro Siracusano, signposted off the main road. The private **youth hostel** out at Belvedere, Via Epipoli 45 (☎0931/711.118; ①), is open all year round, and serves meals. The nearest **campsite**, *Agriturist* (all year; ☎0931/721.224), is 5km away – take bus #34 or #35 from Corso Umberto.

Many of Siracusa's **restaurants** are overpriced, but there are some good-value places. *Pizzeria Savoia*, Via Savoia 17, is cheap if not exactly cheerful, while *Da Egidio*, Via Savoia 18, is a workers' trattoria with basic, filling lunches. *Spaghetteria do Scogghiu*, Via Scina 11, has a huge selection of cheap pasta and is popular at night. *Pescomare*, just off Piazza del Duomo at Via Londolina 6, serves pizzas and fish in an atmospheric, plant-filled old courtyard. For staggeringly good local dishes, take a taxi or hike out to the rustic *Ristorante Jonico A Rutta e Ciauli*, Riviera Dionisio Il Grande 194, where a meal of superb antipasti and fresh fish costs around L60,000. Good **bars** and cafés are easy to come by, two of the best the outdoor *Porta Marina*, on the Foro Vittorio Emanuele, and the *Bar Del Ponte*, at the end of the Ponte Nuovo on Ortygia – a good breakfast stop.

THE SOUTHERN COAST AND THE INTERIOR

It's tempting to give Sicily's long **southern coast** a miss, especially if you're short on time. But to do so would be to ignore some of the most appealing places on the island. The whole region, coast and hinterland, marks a welcome break from the volcanic fixation of the blacker lands to the north: here the towns are largely spacious and bright, strung across a gentler, unscarred landscape that rolls and pitches down to the sea.

Sicily's southeastern bulge was devastated by a calamitous seventeenth-century earthquake and the inland rebuilding, over the next century, was almost entirely Baroque in concept and execution. **Ragusa** dominates, a splendid town on two levels, the older lower town much abandoned but still with its share of grandiose buildings. Elsewhere, similar vigorous Baroque towns mushroomed, like little **Modica** to the south and – the undisputed gem – **Noto** to the east.

Down on the **coast** itself there's a line of small-town resorts which stretches from the southeastern cape, **Capo Passero**. There are good beaches but often the coastline is marred by industrial development and pollution; the only place that's not a resort and worth a stop is **Gela**, which retains its extensive Greek fortifications. More vital, further west, is **Agrigento**, sitting on a rise overlooking the sea above its famed series of Greek temples.

Slow cross-country trains and limited exit motorways do little to encourage stopping in the island's **interior**, but it's only here that you really begin to get off the tourist trail. Much of the land is burned dry during the long summer months, sometimes a dreary picture, but in compensation the region boasts some of Sicily's most curious towns. **Enna** is the obvious target, as central as you can get, the blustery mountain town a pace apart from the dry hills below. There are easy trips to be made from here, north into the hills, and south to **Piazza Armerina** and the fabulous Roman mosaics, and to airy, ceramic-studded **Caltagirone**.

Ragusa and the southeast

The **earthquake of 1693**, which destroyed utterly the towns and villages of southeastern Sicily, had one positive and lasting effect. Where there were ruins, a new generation of confident architects raised new planned towns in an opulent Baroque style. All were harmonious creations, Catania the grandest, Noto the most eagerly promoted by the tourist board. But there is a bagful of other towns too, less visited but all providing surprising pockets of grandeur amid the bare hills and deep valleys of the region.

Ragusa

Best base for any exploration of the area is **RAGUSA**, a busy and likeable provincial capital with an encouraging, friendly atmosphere. The destructive earthquake split the city in two: the old town of Ragusa Ibla, on a jut of land above its valley, was comprehensively flattened, and within a few years a new town emerged, on the higher ridge to the west. Ibla was stubbornly rebuilt around its medieval ruins, while its new rival developed along grander, planned lines. All the business and industry relocated in the prosperous upper town, where oil is the latest venture – derricks scattered around modern Ragusa's higher reaches.

It's here, in the **upper town**, that you'll arrive. All **buses** stop outside the **train station** and a left turn takes you along the main road and over the exposed Ponte Nuovo, spanning a huge cleft in the ridge. All the interest in modern Ragusa is on the other side, the gridded Baroque town slipping off to right and left on either side of the steeply sloping Corso Italia. To the right, down the Corso on a wide terrace above Piazza San Giovanni, stands the **Duomo**, conceived on a grand, symmetrical scale. Finished in 1774, its tapered columns and fine doorways are a fairly sombre background to the vigorous small-town atmosphere around. Back towards the train station, underneath the *Standa* supermarket, there's an important **Museo Archeologico** (Mon–Sat 9am–2pm, Sun 9am–1pm; free) dealing mainly with finds from the archaeological site of Kamarina (sixth century BC) on the coast to the southwest.

But it's **RAGUSA IBLA**, the original **lower town**, where you'll probably while away much of the day, its weatherbeaten roofs straddling the outcrop of rock about twenty minutes' walk away. Main attraction, the church of **San Giorgio**, stridently placed at the top of Piazza Duomo, is one of the masterpieces of Sicilian Baroque, built by Rosario Gagliardi and finished in 1784. The glorious three-tiered facade, sets of triple columns climbing up the wedding cake exterior to a balconied belfry, is an imaginative work, though typically not much enhanced by venturing inside. As with Gagliardi's other important church in Modica (see opposite), all the beauty is in the immediacy of the powerful exterior.

The whole town – deathly quiet at lunchtime – is ripe for aimless wandering. Gagliardi gets another credit for the elegant rounded facade of **San Giuseppe** in Piazza Pola, a few steps below the duomo, while Corso XXV Aprile continues down past abandoned palazzi to the **Giardino Ibleo** (daily 8am–8pm) – gardens which mark the very edge of the spur on which the town is built. If you can't face the walk back to the upper town, bus #1 or #3 makes the trip, hourly, from Piazza Pola.

Practicalities

Sadly, there's nowhere to stay in Ragusa Ibla, and even up in the main part of town **accommodation** is limited to a very few fairly expensive hotels. The cheapest, *San Giovanni*, Via Traspontino 3 (☎0932/621.013; ⑤), is at the train station end of the lower Ponte dei Cappuccini. There's a good, basic **restaurant** in Via San Sebastiano, the *Trattoria Ragusana*, with large, full meals for around L20,000. The *Caffè Trieste*, Corso Italia 76–78, is a decent **café-bar** with an enticing savoury snack and pastry selection.

Comiso, Módica and Noto

The best of the rest of the Baroque southeast can be seen in easy trips from Ragusa. If you came from the west you might already have passed through **COMISO**, its green centre dominated by the twin domes of two impressive churches. If you didn't, the journey in itself is worth making, up over a barren 600m-high plateau looking away to the distant sea. The wild countryside hereabouts continues to impress as you head beyond Ragusa, the route to **MÓDICA**, half an hour to the south, a case in point. As the bus swirls down past Ragusa Ibla and climbs through some rugged hills, all the vegetation seems to have been pulled into the valleys below, the tiered slopes bare and rocky. Modica itself is an enjoyable place to spend half a day. A powerful medieval base of the Chiaramonte, the upper town is watched over by the magnificent eighteenth-century facade of **San Giorgio**, a worthy rival to the church of the same name in Ragusa Ibla. It's thought that Gagliardi was responsible for this too: the elliptical facade is topped by a belfry, the church approached by a symmetrical double staircase which switchbacks up across the upper roads of the town.

But the real highlight of any tour of the Baroque southeast is further afield. **NOTO** is easily the most harmonious post-earthquake creation, and for a time, in the mid-nineteenth century, it replaced Siracusa as that region's provincial capital. Indeed, despite its architectural identification with the Baroque towns around Ragusa, Noto is best reached **from Siracusa** – around half an hour's journey by bus or train. Planned and laid out by Giovanni Battista Landolina, adorned by Gagliardi, there's not a town to touch Noto for uniform excellence in design and execution, but sadly it's in a very sorry state nowadays. Pollution has crumbled the stone so much that virtually every building of note is shored up by scaffolding to prevent further deterioration. The main Corso is now closed to traffic and its buildings largely obscured by a rack of buttressing, which will remain in place for a long time, reducing much of Noto's visual impact.

Underneath the metalwork, the Corso is lined with some of Sicily's most captivating buildings, all a rich honey colour – from the flat-fronted church of **San Francesco**, on the right, along as far as Piazza XVI Maggio and the graceful, curving church of **San Domenico**. And Piazza Municipio is arguably Sicily's finest piazza: perfectly proportioned, tree-planted expanses flank the raised, twin-towered **Duomo** (closed noon–4pm), finished in 1770, itself hemmed in by two palaces of remarkable decorative quality. Opposite, the **Municipio** (or Palazzo Ducezio) is flanked by its own green spaces, the arcaded building presenting a lovely, simple facade of columns and long stone balconies. Head up the steep **Via Corrado Nicolaci**, an eighteenth-century street which contains the extraordinary **Palazzo Villadorata** (no. 18), its six balconies supported by a panoply of griffons, galloping horses and fat-cheeked cherubs.

Staying in Noto wouldn't be a bad alternative to Siracusa, though you'll have to move sharp to get a room at the *Albergo Stella*, Via F. Maiore 44 (☎0931/835.695; ④), on the corner of Via Napoli. You can eat at the straightforward *Trattoria Giglio*, just to the side of the municipio at Piazza Municipio 8–10. Get free maps and further information from the **tourist office** in Piazza XVI Maggio (daily April–Oct 9am–8pm; Nov–March 8am–2pm & 4–6pm).

West to Gela

Most of the coastal section west of Capo Passero is pretty inaccessible without your own transport. Even then, to be frank, there's not a lot worth stopping for, the odd seaside town awash with new holiday apartments but little individual character. The railway line touches down at POZZALLO and trains then loop north, through Modica, Ragusa and Comiso before cutting back down to the coast at Gela.

GELA couldn't present a worse aspect as the train edges into town, through a petrochemical mess of futuristic steel bubbles and pipes. There are fine dune-backed beaches in the vicinity but there must be serious doubts about the cleanliness of the water. Once, though, Gela was one of the most important of the island's Hellenic cities, founded in 688 BC, and under Hippocrates and Gelon rivalled even Siracusa as the island's political hub. But, smashed by the Carthaginians, ancient Gela was abandoned to the encroaching sands. Modern Gela was the first Sicilian town to be liberated in 1943, but otherwise – beyond an excellent archaeological museum and a fine set of defensive walls – is almost entirely without interest.

If you want to see these, best leave your bags at the train station left-luggage office – there's really no need to stay longer than half a day. Outside the station (also where buses pull up) turn right down the main road and, at the junction, bear right for the town centre and the main Corso Vittorio Emanuele, at either end of which are Gela's two sights. To the left, a twenty-minute walk, Gela's **Museo Archeologico** (daily 9am–1.30pm; free) is notable largely for its excellent collection of painted vases: mainly seventh- to fifth-century BC, the black-and-red jugs and beakers were Greek Gela's speciality. Outside the museum a small acropolis has been uncovered, a few walls and a single temple column from the fifth century BC. There are more archaeological remains at the other end of town – along the Corso and then a left fork into Via Manzoni, which runs parallel to the sea as far as the red gates of the site, a hefty three- to four-kilometre walk. Here, at **Capo Soprano**, is a remarkable series of **Greek fortifications** (daily 9am–1hr before sunset; free) dating from the fourth century BC. Preserved by the sand, the walls stand nearly eight metres high in parts, made up of perfectly fitted stone blocks topped by a storey of brick – now covered in protective glass panels. It's a beautiful site, waves crashing onto a particularly fine duned stretch below.

Agrigento

Though handsome, well sited and awash with medieval atmosphere, **AGRIGENTO** is not visited for the town. The interest instead focuses on the substantial remains of Pindar's "most beautiful city of mortals", a couple of kilometres below. Here, strung out along a ridge facing the sea, is a series of Doric temples – the most captivating of Sicilian Greek remains and a grouping unique outside Greece.

The Site

In 581 BC colonists from nearby Gela and from Rhodes founded the city of Akragas between the rivers of Hypsas and Akragas. They surrounded it with a mighty wall, formed in part by a higher ridge on which stood the acropolis (and, today, the modern town). The southern limit of the ancient city was a second, lower ridge and it was here, in the so-called "Valley of the Temples", that the city architects erected their sacred buildings during the fifth century BC.

A road winds down from the modern city to the **VALLE DEI TEMPLI**, buses dropping you at a car park between the two separate sections of archaeological remains, the eastern and western zones. The **eastern zone** is unenclosed and is at its crowd-free best early morning or late evening. A path climbs up to the oldest of Akragas's temples, the **Tempio di Ercole** (Herakles). Probably begun in the last decades of the sixth century BC, nine of the original 38 columns have been re-erected, everything else scattered around like a waiting jigsaw puzzle. Retrace your steps back to the path which leads to the glorious **Tempio della Concordia**, dated to around 430 BC: perfectly preserved and beautifully sited, with fine views to the city and the sea, the tawny stone lending the structure warmth and strength. That it's still so complete is explained by its conversion (in the sixth century AD) to a Christian church. Restored to its (more or less) original layout in the eighteenth century, it's kept its lines and slightly tapering columns, although – sadly – it's fenced off to keep the crowds at bay. The path continues, following the line of the ancient city walls, to the **Tempio di Giunone** (or Hera), an engaging half-ruin standing at the very edge of the ridge. The patches of red visible here and there on the masonry denote fire damage, probably from the sack of Akragas by the Carthaginians in 406 BC.

The **western zone** (daily 9am–1hr before sunset; free), back along the path and beyond the car park, is less impressive, a vast tangle of stone and fallen masonry from a variety of temples. Most notable is the mammoth construction that was the **Tempio di Giove**, or Temple of Olympian Zeus. The largest Doric temple ever known, it was never completed, left in ruins by the Carthaginians and further damaged by earthquakes. Still, the stereobate remains, while on the ground, face to the sky, lies an 8m-high *telamone*: a supporting column sculpted as a male figure, arms raised and bent to bear the temple's weight. Other scattered remains litter the area, including the so-called **Tempio dei Dioscuri** (Castor and Pollux), rebuilt in 1832 and actually made up of unrelated pieces from the confused rubble on the ground.

Via dei Templi leads back to the town from the car park via the excellent **Museo Nazionale Archeologico** (Tues–Sat 9am–1.30pm & 3–5pm, Sun 9am–1.30pm; free) – the bus passes by outside. The extraordinarily rich collection is devoted to finds from the city and the surrounding area; best displays are the cases of vases (sixth to third century BC) and a reassembled *telamone* stacked against one wall. Nip over the road on the way out for the **Hellenistic-Roman quarter** (daily 9am–1hr before sunset; free), which contains lines of houses, inhabited intermittently until the fifth century AD, many with mosaic designs still discernible.

The modern city

It would be a mistake not to scout round modern Agrigento, modern only in comparison with the temples. Thoroughly medieval at its heart, its tiny stepped streets and fine churches look down over the Valle dei Templi and beyond to the sea. The main street, **Via Atenea**, starts at the eastern edge of the old town, above the train station, the streets off to the right harbouring ramshackle palazzi and the church of **Santa Maria dei Greci**. Built over a Greek temple of the fifth century BC, the flattened columns are visible in the nave, while an underground tunnel reveals the stylobate and column stumps, all part of the church's foundations.

Practicalities

Trains arrive at the edge of the old town and city buses leave from outside in Piazza Marconi to the temples, the campsite and Porto Empedocle (for ferries to the Pelagie Islands; see overleaf). **Buses** from elsewhere in Sicily will drop you at the terminal in Piazza Roselli, near the post office. The **tourist office**, Via Atenea 123 (Mon–Sat 8am–2pm & 5–7pm), has hotel listings and maps.

Finding **somewhere to stay** in Agrigento shouldn't be a problem, except perhaps in peak season. The *Concordia*, Piazza San Francesco 11 (☎0922/56.266; ④), has some smart doubles, or try the *Belvedere*, Via San Vito 20 (☎0922/20.051; ④). You can **camp** 5km away at the coastal resort of SAN LEONE, at *Internazionale San Leone* (April to Sept; ☎0922/416.121); bus #10 from outside the train station. For **eating**, the food and local wine is excellent at *La Forchetta*, next door to the *Concordia* hotel, but not particularly cheap, unless you ask for the unadvertised *menu turistico*. If you're budgeting, you can't beat the L15,000 pasta, pizza and drink combination at *La Corte degli Sfizii*, a trendy little eaterie on Cortile Contarini, an alleyway above Via Atenea.

Eraclea Minoa

From Agrigento you're well poised for moving on into western Sicily, and frequent buses get you to Sciacca in around two and a half hours. If you can, though, first drop in on the other important local Greek site, **ERACLEA MINOA**: originally named Minoa after the Cretan king Minos, who chased Daedalus from Crete to Sicily and founded a city where he landed. The Greeks settled here in the sixth century, later adding the tag Heraklea. A buffer between the two great cities at Akragas, 40km to the east, and Selinus, 60km west, Eraclea Minoa was dragged into endless border disputes, but in spite of this it flourished. Most of the remains date from the fourth century BC, Eraclea Minoa's most important period, three hundred years or so before the town declined.

The **site** (daily 9am–1hr before sunset) is finely sited right on the coast, at the mouth of the river Platani. Apart from the good **walls**, once 6km long, which survive in interrupted sections, the main attraction is the sandstone **theatre**, and certain of the finds are held in a small on-site **museum**. It's all well worth the trip, and there's a **beach** and the *Eraclea* **campsite** (May–Oct; ☎0922/847.310) near the ruins, as well as a couple of bars with **rooms** to rent. But, without wheels of some description you're going to have to do some tough walking to get here. Take any bus running between Agrigento and Sciacca and ask the driver to let you off at the turning; it's 5km west of MONTALLEGRO, on the SS115, and the site is another 4km from there. Heading on, west from the site turning, you should be able to flag down a bus going to Sciacca.

The Pelagie Islands

The remote and barren **PELAGIE ISLANDS** (Isole Pelagie) are simply that – dry rocks, south even of Malta and bang in the middle of the Mediterranean. Throughout history they've been neglected, often abandoned, their only days of importance destructive ones: in 1943 the Allies bombed the main island, Lampedusa, prior to springing into Sicily; and Colonel Qadhafi of Libya provided a repeat performance in 1987 when he retaliated against the American bombing of Tripoli by despatching missiles (off-target it turned out) at Lampedusa's US base. That said, the only danger you're likely to face now is a rough sea crossing from Porto Empedocle.

Most travellers will **get to the islands** by ferry from **PORTO EMPEDOCLE**, the ugly port town 6km south of Agrigento: buses run there hourly (#8, #9 or #10 from outside Agrigento's train station). It costs around L40,000 one way to Linosa, L50,000 to Lampedusa, and the journey takes six to eight hours; tickets can be bought from the harbour-side *Siremar* office and travel agents in Agrigento. The only way to cut this time would be to **fly** from Palermo to Lampedusa; around L100,000 one way for the hour's flight, L125,000 for a weekend return.

Ferries call first at **LINOSA**, a volcanic islet, a pretty quiet place with four extinct craters, some lavial beaches and not much else in the way of sights. The only village has a few hundred inhabitants, rather fewer cars and a minimal road system. There is one **hotel**, the *Algusa* (☎0922/972.052; ⑥), at which you should really make a reservation in advance if you want to stay, and an unofficial **campsite**. The other ferry stop is at **LAMPEDUSA**, 50km south and much bigger. Around 4000 people live here, mostly in the town of the same name, most making their living from fishing, though more and more tourists are arriving every year. It's a flat, dry island with more in common with Africa than Europe, the main attraction the beaches and the sea – bitingly clean and offering easily the best swimming and skin-diving in the Mediterranean. You should have no trouble finding somewhere to stay on Lampedusa: most of the many **hotels** are a few minutes' walk from the port, and many have double rooms for under L40,000. There's an official **campsite**, too, *La Roccia* (all year; ☎0922/970.055), at Cala Greca.

Inland to Enna

The most scenically rewarding parts of Sicily's **interior** are in the east, primarily the hill towns and villages that lie in a wide half-circle to the north of Enna – which is where you should head if you want to see the region by public transport.

Coming from Agrigento, however, there are several worthwhile routes – most only practicable for mobile travellers. One route goes by way of **SANT'ANGELO MUXARO** (daily buses from Agrigento), beyond which begins the most convoluted **approach to Palermo**, the twisting road climbing up to 1000m at PRIZZI, from where there are occasional bus services down to **CORLEONE**. A fairly large town for these parts, it lent Mario Puzo's fictional Godfather, Don Corleone, his adopted family name – and it's the name of one of Sicily's most notorious real-life Mafia clans. There is a bus from Corleone to Palermo, another 60km, though drivers won't want to miss the diversion into the higher hills around **PIANA DEGLI ALBANESI**: one of the most interesting of Sicilian towns, a fifteenth-century Albanian colony whose Greek Orthodox inhabitants still wear the costume and speak the tongue of their ancestors. Any celebration brings out the festive garb, but the best time to visit is at Easter when the local ceremonies form a marked contrast to the island's Catholic rites. At other times of the year entertainment is limited, though a stroll down the steep main street – Via Giorgio Kastriota – reveals street signs in Albanian and gives a glimpse of the town's three churches. Only 25km from Palermo, Piana degli Albanesi could also be seen on a day trip from the capital; regular buses leave from outside the train station; the last one back to Palermo leaves at 7.45pm.

The other option from Agrigento, better if you want to head on to the most appealing parts of the interior, is the **route to Enna**. There's a local bus service which connects up the nearer places, while trains make the journey too, up through gentle, tree-planted slopes and then across the hilltops. At **CANICATTI** the line splits, trains running south to Licata, on the coast. Better to keep on to **CALTANISSETTA**, capital of its province and a brisk modern town, which (with its couple of hotels) is a possibility for day-tripping to Enna and Piazza Armerina (see overleaf); the bus timetables, for once, are kindly disposed. Caltanissetta's only tangible attraction is the worthy **Museo Civico** (Mon–Fri 9am–1.30pm, Sat 9am–noon), on Via Napoleone Colajanni, close to the train station, which contains some of the earliest of Sicilian finds, including vases and Bronze Age sculpted figures. From Caltanissetta it's a short bus ride to Enna – don't take the train as Enna's train station is way outside town.

Enna

From a bulging V-shaped ridge almost 1000m up **ENNA** lords it over the surrounding hills of central Sicily. The approach to this doughty mountain stronghold is still as formidable as ever, the bus climbing slowly out of the valley and looping across the solid crag to the summit and the town. For obvious strategic reasons, Enna was a magnet for successive hostile armies, who in turn besieged and fortified the town, each doing their damnedest to disprove Livy's description of Enna as *inexpugnabilis*.

Despite the destructive attention, most of Enna's remains are medieval and in good nick, with the prize exhibit the thirteenth-century **Castello di Lombardia** (daily 9am–1pm & 3–7pm; free), dominating the easternmost spur of town. A mighty construction with its strong walls complete, it guards the steep slopes on either side of Enna, its six surviving towers (out of an original twenty) providing lookouts. From the tallest, the Torre Pisana, the magnificent views take in Enna itself, some rugged countryside in all directions and, if you're lucky, Mount Etna.

In the centre of town virtually all the accredited sights lie stretched out along and around **Via Roma**, which descends from the castle. It's a narrow street, broken by small piazzas – one of which fronts the hemmed-in **Duomo**, dating in part from 1307. The spacious sixteenth-century interior (usually open afternoons) features huge supporting alabaster columns, the bases and capitals of which are covered with an amorphous, writhing mass of carved figures. Outside, behind the apses, the **Museo Alessi** (Mon–Sat 9am–1pm; free) fields a rich collection of local church art, old coins and the impressive contents of the cathedral's own treasury. There's a second museum too, equally good, the **Museo Archeologico** (Mon–Sat 9am–1.30pm, Sun 9.30am–1pm; free), just over the way in Piazza Mazzini: covering Neolithic to Roman times and including a fine series of painted Greek vases.

Via Roma slopes down to the rectangular **Piazza Vittorio Emanuele**, focal point of the evening *passeggiata*. Off here, there's a long cliff-edge belvedere, while the bottom of the piazza is marked by the plain, high wall of the **Chiesa di San Francesco**, whose massive sixteenth-century tower previously formed part of the town's system of watchtowers. This linked the castle with the **Torre di Frederico**, which stands in isolation in its little park in the largely modern south of the town. An octagonal tower 24m high, it's a survivor of the alterations to the city made by Frederick of Aragon who added a (now hidden) underground passage linking it to the castello.

Practicalities

Overnight stays in Enna have to be at the *Grande Albergo Sicilia* in Piazza Colaianni (☎0935/500.850; ⑤), below the duomo off Via Roma. Alternatively, you can take a bus 9km south to **PERGUSA**, supposedly the site of Pluto's abduction of Persephone to the Underworld. These days the famed Lago di Pergusa is encircled by a motor-racing track, alongside which are several new hotels, the two cheapest being on the Enna road: the *Miralago* (☎0935/541.272; ③) and *La Pergola* (☎0935/541.733; ③). There's a **campsite** here too, just off the race track. Buses depart hourly from San Francesco church until 8.30pm; the last service from Pergusa to Enna is at 9pm.

As for **eating**, back in Enna the *Ristorante Familiare*, Via S. Agata 123 (near San Francesco), is recommended and cheap; the *Grotta Azzurra*, Via Colajianni (between Piazza Matteoti and Piazza Vittorio Emanuele), is more adventurous but still reasonably priced.

All long-distance **bus services** use the bus terminal in the new town; to get into the centre, turn right and follow Corso Sicilia around until the road forks, then bear right into Piazza Vittorio Emanuele. Enna's **train station** is an unfortunate 5km below town, an impossibly long and steep walk, though a bus connects roughly hourly with the town centre. Information, as well as a good free map of Enna, is available at the **tourist office** in Piazza Garibaldi (Mon–Sat 8.30am–1.30pm).

North of Enna

Some of the most fascinating, unsung towns of the Sicilian interior are within easy reach of Enna: to the north, along roads which wind either over mountain ranges to the Tyrrhenian coast or en route to the foothills of Mount Etna. Both directions provide spectacular rides and, unlike destinations further west, are feasible by bus.

Closest to Enna, across the valley and accessible by regular buses from Enna's bus and train stations, is medieval **CALASCIBETTA**, its tightly packed buildings perched above a sheer drop on the eastern side. Buses run further east from Enna, too, to **AGIRA**, again well sited with sparkling views down over the surrounding hills. The bus route continues through REGALBUTO and, eventually, to Catania, a journey that strikes through land that was fiercely contested during the short Sicilian campaign of World War II.

If you can time it right, three *SAIS* buses a day link Agira with **TROINA**, a tortuous 30km ride to Sicily's highest town (1120m). Hardly surprisingly, the journey there is the real event. Without a car you'll probably have to retrace your steps as the two onward routes – east to Cesaro and west to **NICOSIA** – are long, mountainous hauls, not to be hitched lightly. Nicosia, though, can be reached by bus from Enna, changing at Leonforte (as well as directly from Palermo), another momentous ride rewarded by an ancient medieval town of cracked palazzi and the remains of a Norman castle. It's an evocative little place, worth an **overnight stop** if you can: there's an extremely cheap *locanda*, *La Greca*, at Via della Pace 6 (☎0935/638.258; ③), with its own good restaurant, off the main street.

Piazza Armerina and around

To the **south of Enna**, less than an hour away by bus, **PIAZZA ARMERINA** lies amid thick tree-planted hills, a quiet, unassuming place mainly seventeenth- and eighteenth-century in appearance, its skyline pierced by towers, the houses huddled together under the joint protection of castle and cathedral. All in all, it is a thoroughly pleasant place to idle around, though the real local draw is an Imperial Roman **villa** which stands in rugged countryside at Casale, 5km southwest of Piazza Armerina. Hidden under mud for 700 years, the excavated remains reveal a rich villa, probably a hunting lodge and summer home, decorated with polychromatic mosaic floors that are unique in the Roman world for their unrivalled quality and extent.

Seeing the villa and mosaics might well entail spending the night in Piazza Armerina, but neither of the two **hotels** is cheap: the *Selene*, in the lower new town at Viale Generale Gaeta 30 (☎0935/682.254; ④), is friendlier and more central than the similarly priced *Park Hotel Paradiso* (☎0935/680.841; ④), 2km west of Piazza Armerina, beyond the Norman church of Sant'Andrea. The **tourist office** (Tues–Fri 8am–2pm & 4.30–7.30pm, Mon & Sat 8am–2pm) is at Via Cavour 15, just off central Piazza Garibaldi, and they can provide a map.

The Villa Imperiale

To **get to the villa** from Piazza Armerina, there's a minibus service from Piazza Generale Marescalchi, daily (except Sun) at 1.30pm, which passes the turnoff for the villa, 1km beyond. Otherwise you'll have to walk or hitch, usually an easy enough proposition. (Coming **from Caltanissetta**, currently the daily 8.30am bus gets to Piazza Armerina at 9.50am; return at 4.05pm.) Note that the return bus from Mazzarino passes the turnoff at around 3.30pm.

The **Villa Imperiale** (daily 9am–1hr before sunset; L2000) dates from the early fourth century BC and was used right up until the twelfth century when a mudslide kept it largely covered until comprehensive excavations in the 1950s. It's been covered again since to protect the mosaics, a hard plastic and metal roof and walls designed to indicate the original size and shape, while walkways lead visitors through the rooms in as logical an order as possible. The mosaics themselves are identifiable as fourth-century Roman-African school, which explains many of the more exotic scenes and animals portrayed; they also point to the villa having had an important owner, possibly Maximianus Herculeus, co-emperor with Diocletian.

The **main entrance** leads into a wide courtyard with fountains, where the **thermae** (baths) group around an octagonal *frigidarium* and a central mosaic showing a lively marine scene. A walkway leads out of the baths and into the villa proper, to the massive central court or **peristyle**, whose surrounding corridors are decorated with animal head mosaics. From here, a balcony looks down upon one of the villa's most interesting pictures, a boisterous **circus scene** showing a chariot race. Small rooms beyond, on either side of the peristyle, reveal only fragmentary geometric patterns, although one contains probably the villa's most famous image, a two-tiered scene of **ten girls**, realistically muscular figures in Roman "bikinis" taking part in various gymnastic and athletic activities.

Beyond the peristyle, a long, covered corridor contains the most extraordinary of the mosaics: the **great hunting scene**, which sets armed and shield-bearing hunters against a panoply of wild animals. Along the entire 60m length of the mosaic are tigers, ostriches, elephants, even a rhino, being trapped, bundled up and down gangplanks and into cages, destined for the Games back in Rome. The square-hatted figure overseeing the operation is probably Maximianus himself: his personal area of responsibility in the Imperial Tetrarchy was North Africa, where much of the scene is set.

Other rooms beyond are nearly all on a grand scale. The **triclinium**, a dining room with three apses, features the labours of Hercules, and a path leads around the back to the **private apartments**, based around a large basilica. Best mosaics here are a **children's circus**, where tiny chariots are drawn by colourful birds, and a **children's hunt**, the kids chased and pecked by the hares and peacocks they're supposed to snare.

Caltagirone

CALTAGIRONE, an hour's ride southeast from Piazza Armerina, is one of the least known of Sicily's inland towns, with a fine central body of monumental buildings that dates from the rebuilding after the 1693 earthquake. As the town is a noted centre of ceramics, the effect is lightened by tiled decoration found all over Caltagirone, most effectively as flowers and emblems flanking both sides of a bridge (the Ponte San Francesco) on the way into the centre. The grandest statement, though, is made by the 142 steps of **La Scala**, which cut right up one of Caltagirone's hills to a church at the top, the "risers" in between each step covered with a ceramic pattern, no two the same. There's a good-value **place to stay** in the *Casa Donato*, Via Portosalvo 22b (☎0933/25.684; ⑤), close to the hospital in the new town.

TRÁPANI AND THE WEST

The **west** of Sicily is a land apart. Skirting around the coast from **Trápani** – easily the largest town in the region – it looks immediately different: the cubic whitewashed houses, palm trees, active fishing harbours and sunburned lowlands seem more akin to Africa than Europe; and historically, the west of the island has always looked south. The earliest of all Sicilian sites, the mountain haunt of **Érice**, was dominated by Punic influence, the Carthaginians themselves entrenched in **Marsala**, at Sicily's westernmost point, for several hundred years; while the Saracen invaders took their first steps on the island at **Mazara del Vallo**, a town still strongly Arabic at heart. The Greeks never secured the same foothold in Sicily's west as elsewhere, although the remains at **Segesta** and **Selinunte** count among the island's best.

Trápani

Out on something of a limb, **TRÁPANI** is not the most enticing of Sicilian cities, more a port of call than a stop in itself. Today, the obvious move is to jump a hydrofoil to the offshore Égadi Islands (see overleaf), or a ferry on to Tunisia. But throughout the early Middle Ages Trápani was a rich trading centre, halfway point for Tunis and Africa. However, all the medieval activity counts for nothing today, and despite the recent revitalisation of the huge salt pans to the south of town, Trápani is in firm decline: the old centre of town has been depopulated, most people moving to the gridded hinterland of modern Trápani. But you might end up spending time here if you're on your way either to Érice or Segesta, and there's enough left of the old town to occupy the hours waiting for a bus or ferry.

The Town

Trápani's **old town**, broadly speaking the area west of the train station, sports a mix of often incongruous architectural styles, something that harks back to Trápani's past as a complex medieval Mediterranean trading centre. It's particularly true of the medieval Jewish quarter, a wedge of hairline streets and alleys that holds one of the city's most characteristic buildings, the **Palazzo della Giudecca** on Via Giudecca – sixteenth-century, with a stone-studded tower and finely wrought Spanish-style Plateresque windows. Just up from here, Trápani is at its most engaging, Corso Italia preceding a confused set of three piazzas, enlivened by their surrounding churches: one doorway of the sixteenth-century **Chiesa di Santa Maria di Gesu** (Via San Pietro) is defiantly Renaissance in execution, and further up, on Piazzetta Saturno, the church of **Sant'Agostino** is even earlier, fourteenth century and retaining a Gothic portal and delicate rose window – and doing service during the day as a local art gallery.

Off the Piazzetta, Via Torrearsa neatly splits the old town. West of here Trápani's layout becomes more regularly planned, while the main drag and shopping street, the elegant **Corso Vittorio Emanuele**, changes name a couple of times as it runs towards the **Torre di Ligny** – utmost point of the scimitar of land that holds the old town. The squat tower hides Trápani's only other museum, an archaeological collection of fairly dull content, but the water here is clean enough should you to want to swim off the rocks. Finish off your circuit at the daily **market**, at the northern end of Via Torrearsa – fish, fruit and veg sold from the arcaded Piazza Mercato di Pesce, and with several lively bars in the area.

Celebrations and processions at Easter in Trápani are given added piquancy by the carriage around town on Good Friday of the **Misteri**, a group of life-sized eighteenth-century wooden figures representing scenes from the Passion. At other times they are on display in the exuberantly sculpted **Chiesa del Purgatorio** (Mon–Sat 10am–noon & 4–6pm, Sun 10am–noon; free), on Via Dom Giglio, near the junction with Via Francesco d'Assisi.

Except when arriving, you hardly need to set foot in the newer parts of the city. The only incentive is the interesting **Museo Nazionale Pepoli** (Mon–Sat 9am–1.30pm, Sun 9am–12.30pm, plus Tues, Thurs & Fri 3–6.30pm; L2000), a good 3km bus ride away in the drab heart of modern Trápani: take bus #1, #10 or #11 from Corso Vittorio Emanuele, Via Libertà or Via Garibaldi, and get off at the garden outside the Santuario Santissima Annunziata, the fourteenth-century convent which houses the museum. Approached through bird-filled cloisters, the collection includes a bit of everything, from Gagini statuary and local archaeological finds to delicate seventeenth-century coral craftwork, some nice prints and drawings, and a grim wooden guillotine of 1789.

Practicalities

Come to Trápani by land from the east of the island and you'll arrive in the modern part of town: most **buses** (including those to and from Érice) pull up at the terminal in Piazza Malta; **trains** stop just around the corner in Piazza Umberto I. Exceptions to the rule are the fast **buses** for Palermo and Agrigento, which leave from Piazza Garibaldi. **Ferries/hydrofoils** for the Égadi Islands, Pantelleria, Cagliari and Tunis dock at the adjacent Molo di Sanita. For information, accommodation listings and free maps, visit the **tourist office** in Piazzetta Saturno (Mon–Sat 9am–1pm & 2–8pm, Sun 9am–noon).

Finding **somewhere to stay** at Easter will be tricky, unless you book well in advance, but at other times rooms are easy to come by. Best of the cheaper hotels is the *Messina*, Corso Vittorio Emanuele 71 (☎0923/21.198; ③), but it's often booked out; if it's full try the *Maccotta* on Via degli Argentieri (☎0923/28.418; ③), which costs only slightly more. The nearest **campsite** is a twenty-minute bus ride away at LIDO VALDÉRICE (April–Sept; ☎0923/73.086) – there are five to seven buses daily.

Eating is particularly good in Trápani. The *Trattoria Safina*, opposite the train station at Piazza Umberto I, is both cheap and excellent; for fine pizzas seek out *Pizzeria Mediterranea*, Corso Vittorio Emanuele 195, opposite Piazza Jolanda – a takeaway joint with a couple of rooms at the back.

Érice and Segesta

The nearest and most exhilarating ride from Trápani is to **ÉRICE**, forty minutes away by bus. It's a mountain town with powerful associations: creeping hillside alleys, stone buildings and silent charm. Founded by Elymnians, who claimed descent from the Trojans, the original city was known to the ancient world as Eryx, and a magnificent temple, dedicated to Venus Erycina, Mediterranean goddess of fertility, once topped the mountain. Though the city was considered impregnable, Carthaginian, Roman, Arab and Norman forces all forced entry over the centuries. But all respected the sanctity of Érice: the Romans rebuilt the temple and set 200 soldiers to serve as guardians of the shrine; while the Arabs renamed the town Gebel-Hamed, or Mohammed's mountain.

If it's fine, the views from the terraces of Érice are stupendous – over Trápani, the slumbering whales of the Égadi Islands and on clear days as far as Cape Bon in Tunisia. Scout around the town at random: the most convoluted of routes is only going to take you a couple of hours and every street and piazza is a delight. You enter through the Norman **Porta Trápani**, just inside which the battlemented fourteenth-century campanile of the **Chiesa Matrice** did service as a lookout tower for Frederick III of Aragon. From here there's no set route, though passing through pretty **Piazza Umberto** with its couple of outdoor bars is a good idea; and a natural start or finish could be made at the ivy-clad Norman **Castello** at the far end of town. This was built on the site of the famed ancient temple, chunks of which are incorporated in the walls.

Hardly surprisingly, **staying** in Érice means paying through the nose and booking in advance. The one relatively cheap choice, the *Edelweiss*, is in Cortile Padre Vincenzo, a cobbled alley off Piazzetta San Domenico (☎0923/869.158; ⑤). More economical is the **youth hostel** (☎0923/869.144; ①), outside the town walls on Viale delle Pinete, but it's usually open July and August only – check with the helpful **tourist office** (daily 8.30am–2pm & 4.30–7pm) on Viale Conte Pepoli, which also dishes out maps. There are private **rooms to rent** at Via A. Palma 7 (☎0923/869.185; ④). If you're coming for the day you may want to bring a picnic since **restaurant** prices in Érice are vastly inflated. However, there have been reasonable reports of the *Re Aceste*, Viale Conte Pepoli 45, whose terrace overlooks the plain below town.

The Temple of Segesta

If time is limited, it's hard to know which to recommend most: the heights of Érice or Trápani's other local draw, the temple at **Segesta**. Although unfinished, this Greek construction of 424 BC is one of the most inspiring of Doric temples anywhere and, along with the theatre, virtually the only relic of an ancient city whose roots – like those of Érice – go back to the twelfth century BC. Unlike Érice, though, ancient Segesta was eventually Hellenised and spent most of the later period disputing its borders with Selinus to the south. The temple dates from a time of prosperous alliance with Athens, the building abandoned when a new dispute broke out with Selinus in 416 BC.

The site is unenclosed, with steps rising past a café and car park to the **temple** itself, crowning a low hill. From a distance you could be forgiven for thinking that it's complete: the 36 regular white stone columns, entablature and pediment are all intact, and all it lacks is a roof. However, get closer and you see just how unfinished the building is: stone studs, always removed on completion, still line the stylobate, the tall columns are unfluted and the *cella* walls are missing. Below the car park, a road (open to cars; daily 9am–1hr before sunset) winds up through slopes of wild fennel and marigolds to the small **theatre** on a higher hill beyond. The view from the top is justly lauded, across green slopes and the plain to the sea, the deep blue of the bay a lovely contrast to the theatre's white stone – not much damaged by the stilted motorway snaking away below.

Without your own transport **getting to Segesta** involves some walking, though nothing too off-putting. The two daily **trains** from Trápani to Palermo make a stop at SEGESTA-TEMPIO, from where it's a twenty-minute walk uphill. To return, unless you make the 11.57am back from Segesta-Tempio, you'll have to walk from the site car park to the station of **CALATAFIMI**, signposted 4km away (the town itself is a further 4km away), from where more frequent trains connect with Trápani. There's also a cheap **hotel** in Calatafimi, the *Mille Pini*, Piazza F. Vivona 2 (☎0924/951.260; ③), if you wanted to stay the night in the quiet surroundings.

The Égadi Islands

Of the various islands, islets and rock stacks that fan out from the west coast of Sicily, the three **Égadi Islands** (Isole Égadi) are best for a quick jaunt – connected by ferry and hydrofoil with Trápani. Saved from depopulation by tourism, in season at least you're not going to be alone, certainly on the main island, Favignana. But a tour of the islands is worthwhile, not least for the caves that perforate the splintered coastlines. Out of season things are noticeably quieter: come between April and July and you may witness the bloody *Mattanza*, an age-old slaughter in this noted centre of tuna fishing.

All **transport** (ferries and hydrofoils several times daily in summer) to the islands departs from Trápani's Molo di Sanita; tickets are available from the office on Via Ammiraglio Staiti or (hydrofoil tickets only) from the booth on the dockside. Though less frequent, ferries are, as always, much cheaper.

FAVIGNANA, island and port town, is first stop for the boats from Trápani, a good base since it has virtually all the accommodation and the Égadi's only campsites. Only 25 minutes by hydrofoil from the mainland, the island attracts a lot of day-trippers, keen to get onto its few rocky beaches. But get out of the main port and it's easy enough to escape the crowds, even easier if you've brought a bike. (There's a bike rental shop, *Isidoro*, at Via Mazzini 40; around L5000 a day.) Caves all over the island bear prehistoric traces and many are accessible if you're determined enough. Otherwise, the two wings of the island invite separate walks; best is the stroll around the eastern part, past the bizarre ancient quarries at Cala Rossa and taking in Lido Burrone, the island's best beach, only 3km from the port. Cheapest **hotel** is the *Egadi*, Via C. Colombo 17 (☎0923/921.232; ③), right in the centre of Favignana town, and there are two **campsites** to the east of town – an easy walk and both well signposted.

LEVANZO, to the north, looks immediately inviting, its white houses against the turquoise sea reminiscent of the Greek islands. The steep coast is full of inlets and, again, is riddled with caves. One, the **Grotta del Genovese**, was discovered in 1949 and contains some remarkable Palaeolithic incised drawings, 6000 years old, as well as later Neolithic pictures. To arrange to see the cave you'll have to contact the guardian, Giuseppe Castiglione, who lives at Via Calvario 11 (☎0923/921.704), near the hydrofoil quay – about an hour's walk from the village. There are two **hotels** on Levanzo, both just above the only road; cheaper is the *Paradiso* (☎0923/924.080; ④), though in summer you have to pay half- or full-board. However, you should be able to get rooms in private houses if you ask around the port.

MARÉTTIMO, furthest out of the Égadi Islands, is the place to come for solitude. Very much off the beaten track, it's reached by only a few tourists. More white houses are scattered across the rocky island, while there's a bar in the main piazza and two restaurants. The spectacular fragmented coastline is pitted with rocky coves sheltering hideaway **beaches**, and there are numerous gentle **walks** which will take you all over the island. Again, although there are no hotels on Maréttimo you should be able to rent a room by asking at the café in the main square.

Trápani to Palermo: the coastal route

Frequent buses run the first section of the route from Trápani, cutting away from the coast until reaching **SAN VITO LO CAPO** at the very nib of the northwestern headland. There are some good sands nearby, while the cape itself is only a stride away; and there are three **campsites** too – best value are *La Fata* (☎0923/972.133) and *Soleado* (☎0923/972.166), both open June to September. San Vito is a popular local holiday spot and you don't have to camp – there are several fairly cheap *pensioni* in the village too, as well as trattorias and bars catering to the summer crowds. The *Sabbia d'Oro*, behind the church at Via Santuario 49 (☎0923/972.508; ④), is a decent enough place to **stay**, or you could walk 500m up the main Via Savoia then turn left onto Via Mulino, where three places offer rooms. You can **eat** reasonably at *Da Peppe*, Via Savoia 13, where pasta, pizza and wine weighs in at under L25,000.

You'll have to return to Trápani for onward transport. Buses or, more frequently, **trains** cut across the headland to **CASTELLAMMARE DEL GOLFO**, another popular resort. There are a couple of upmarket hotels here if you want to stay, but a more attractive option is to catch the twice-daily bus (or walk/hitch the 10km) north to **SCOPELLO**. Gavin Maxwell lived in this tuna-fishing centre, for several months in the early 1950s, an experience he recorded in his classic account of Sicilian life, *The Ten Pains of Death*. Scopello is still a fairly unspoiled fishing village, prettily sited, with more campsites around and – 3km inland at Scopello di Sopra – a choice of cheap **hotels**.

East of here (and the train from Trápani stops at every town before Palermo) it's a strange – often unpleasant – coastal mixture of industrialisation and tourist development. The wide and fertile gulf provides some good views though, and there's the occasional beach that beckons. The last few towns that line the gulf, **BALESTRATE**, **TRAPPETO** and, inland, **PARTINICO** are more interesting for what they were, and to some extent still are – infamous centres of Mafia influence and social and political neglect. **Daniel Dolci**, a social reformer of remarkable persistence, first came to Trappeto in 1952 from wealthy northern Italy. He was appalled. "Looking all around me, I saw no streets, just mud and dust. Not a single drugstore – or sewer. The dialect didn't even have a word for sewer." Dolci inaugurated a programme of self-help among the local people, building community and cultural centres, promoting local education – things that cut right across the traditional areas of influence in the Mafia-ridden west of Sicily. It's a story told in the words of the local people in Dolci's extraordinary book *Sicilian Lives*: vital reading if you intend to pass this way.

Marsala and Mazara del Vallo

Another section of the western rail loop runs **south from Trápani** down the coast, pretty much within sight of the sea all the way, trains ploughing across the cultivated plain, past white, squat houses and distant burned hills. The region flaunts its tangible non-Greek heritage even more in **MARSALA**, 10km on, which takes its name from the Arab *Marsah-el-Allah*, the port of Allah. Once the main Saracenic base in Sicily, since the late eighteenth century Marsala has been better known for the dessert wine that carries its name, something every bar and restaurant will sell you.

The centre of Marsala is extremely attractive, a clean sixteenth-century layout that's free of traffic and littered with high, ageing buildings and arcaded courtyards. But – pleasant as the town is – save your exploratory legs for two excellent museums. The most central, behind the cathedral at Via Garraffa 57, is the **Museo degli Arazzi** (daily 9am–1pm & 4–6pm; L2000), whose sole display is a series of eight enormous hand-stitched wool and silk tapestries depicting the capture of Jerusalem – sixteenth century and beautifully rich, in burnished red, gold and green. Afterwards, walk out to the cape (follow the main Via XI Maggio to Piazza della Vittoria and bear left towards the water); one of the stone-vaulted warehouses that line the promenade holds the equally impressive **Museo Marsala** (Mon–Sat 9am–2pm, Wed, Sat & Sun 3–6pm; free). An archaeological museum of quality, its major exhibit is a reconstructed Punic warship rowed by 68 oarsmen, probably sunk during the First Punic War and found in 1971. Finds from the ship are on display in the hall while other bits and pieces are from the excavated site (mostly Roman) of *Lilybaeum* (daily 9am–1hr before sunset), around the corner from the museum.

Half an hour further on, **MAZARA DEL VALLO**, one of the most powerfully atmospheric of Sicilian towns, is Italy's most important fishing port and a place of equal distinction for the Arabs and Normans who dominated the island a thousand years ago. The first Saracen gain in Sicily, Mazara was Arabic for 250 years until captured by Count Roger in 1075: the island's first Norman parliament met in the town 22 years later, a relic of that period the tiny pink-domed Norman chapel of **San Nicolò**, a little way upriver from the harbour. All around, though, the atmosphere is pungently Arabic, North Africans crewing the colourful fishing boats which block the harbour and river, the old city *kasbah* revitalised and a *hamman* advertised in Piazza Bagno. Wandering around the harbour area is easily the most rewarding thing to do in Mazara although you can spend an enjoyable hour or so as well on the seafront promenade and poking around the **Museo Civico** (Mon–Sat 9am–1pm) in Piazza del Plebiscito, just off Mazara's main square.

Castelvetrano to Sciacca

There's very little else to stop for around the western coast; even less inland, which is crossed by one major road, the SS188 which runs from Marsala to SALEMI, centre of a prosperous winemaking region. But the southernmost chunk of Sicily's western bulge is easily reached by train and has several places worth more than a cursory glance if you have the time.

CASTELVETRANO isn't necessarily one of them. If anyone stops at all, it's to take in the nearby Greek ruins at Selinunte (see overleaf), though this can be much better done from the coastal fishing village next to the site. But the centre of Castelvetrano is handsome and you may be intrigued enough by the story of Sicily's most famous bandit, **Salvatore Giuliano**, to want to stop. Less a Robin Hood figure than a political pawn caught between the regrouping Mafia and the Sicilian separatists after World

War II, Giuliano got a sympathetic press – and much covert support – from the local people hereabouts. But like all true folk heroes he was eventually betrayed, his bullet-riddled body found in one of Castelvetrano's courtyards in 1950.

If you're **staying overnight** to see Selinunte, the *Hotel Ideal*, Via Partanna 26 (☎0924/901.454; ③), is the budget choice. A better idea, though, is to take a bus from the station down to **MARINELLA** on the coast (7 daily; 20min), where there are several **hotels**. The ones overlooking the excellent beach are expensive, but the *Pensione Costa D'Avorio*, at Via Stazione 5 (☎0924/46.207; ③), is a good budget choice, and you may well be offered **rooms** as you get off the bus, which is perhaps the best idea of all. There are two **campsites** on the main Castelvetrano road (the bus passes them both), though no one minds if you camp out at the Mare Pineta; left from the station and follow the signs to the tree-backed **beach**. There are plenty of **restaurants** on the main village road – *Lido Azzurro* has a decent antipasto buffet and windows overlooking the sea.

Selinunte

The most westerly of the Hellenic colonies, the Greek city of *Selinus* – **SELINUNTE** in modern Italian – reached its peak in the fifth century BC when a series of mighty temples were erected. A bitter rival of Segesta, whose lands lay adjacent to the north, the powerful city and its fertile plain attracted enemies hand over fist, and it was only a matter of time before Selinus caught the eye of Segesta's ally, Carthage. Geographically vulnerable, the city was sacked by Carthaginians, any recovery forestalled by earthquakes which later razed the city. Despite the destruction, which left the site completely abandoned until it was rediscovered in the sixteenth century, the ruins of Selinus have exerted a romantic hold ever since.

The **site** of Selinus is set back behind the main part of Marinella village, split into two parts, with temples in each, known only as Temples A–G. The first stop is at the **East Group**, just over the railway line, the entrance through a car park and open all the time (free). Shrouded in the wild celery which gave the ancient city its name, the temples are in various stages of reconstructed ruin: the most complete the one nearest the sea (Temple E), the northernmost (Temple G) a tangle of columned wreckage six metres high in places. The road leads down from here, across the (now buried) site of the old harbour to the second part of excavated Selinus, the **acropolis** (daily 9am–1hr before sunset; L2000), a site containing what remains of the other temples (five in all), as well as the well-preserved city streets and massive, stepped walls which rise above the duned beach below. Temple C stands on the highest point of the acropolis, and there are glorious views from its stones out over the sparkling sea: from this temple were removed some of the best metopes, now on show in Palermo's archaeological museum.

Sciacca

FS **buses** leave from outside Castelvetrano train station six times daily for Sciacca, picking up at the abandoned Selinunte station in Marinella village. **SCIACCA**'s upper town is skirted by good medieval walls which form high sides to the steep streets, rising to a ruined Spanish castle. Below, the lower town sits on a clifftop terrace overlooking the harbour, a place where it's easy to while away time drinking in the coastal views. Hot springs at **Monte San Calogero**, 8km from town, kept the Romans healthy and are still in use. Get there on bus #5 every hour and a half from Sciacca; check on details in the **tourist office**, Corso Vittorio Emanuele 84.

Sciacca would be a nice place to stop over – there's an active harbour here and some good beaches close by – and the *Paloma Bianca*, Via Figuli 5 (☎0925/25.837; ④), has inexpensive rooms, though half-board is often obligatory in summer. There are also a couple of **campsites** 4km west of town at Contrada Foggia, off the SS115 (direct bus June–Sept).

Pantelleria

Forty kilometres nearer to Tunisia than to Sicily, **PANTELLERIA** is the most singular of Sicily's outlying islands. Volcanic, it has been settled since Neolithic times and later supported a Phoenician colony in the seventh century BC. Its strategic position kept it in the mainstream of Sicilian history for years: developed as one of the main Mediterranean bases by the Fascists during World War II, Pantelleria was bombed without mercy by the Allies in May 1943 as they advanced from North Africa. In part, this explains the morose appearance of the island's main town (also called Pantelleria) – thrown up in unedifying concrete.

There's more than enough that's attractive on the rest of the island, though, to compensate. You're going to have to walk to most places, not something you should tire of through a fertile countryside covered in vineyards and the traditional houses or *dammuso*. Skirted by dry stone walls, they are domed, a throwback to the buildings of Neolithic times. Major landmark on the island – visible from the ships heading for Malta – is the spent volcano, **Montagna Grande** (836m), to the summit of which there's a track from the old town of Siba. At some stage refresh yourself with the local wine: the island's myriad vineyards produce *Tanit*, a rightly appreciated raisin wine.

Practicalities

You **arrive** in the main town and port of Pantelleria. Ferries from Trápani do the journey in five hours for around L35,000 one way and there's generally one a day in summer. There are also daily flights from Trápani and Palermo, which tourist discounts can make a viable option – weekend returns cost as little as L60,000. A bus connects airport arrivals with Pantelleria town.

Accommodation is fairly expensive; best budget choice is the *Miryam* on Corso Umberto I (☎0923/911.374; ④), with the *Agadir*, on Via Catania (☎0923/911.100; ④), a good second. There's no campsite on the island and camping rough is impractical given the terrain and the lack of water. Better to contact an agency dealing in stays in the volcanic stone *dammuso* houses that are unique to the island: try *Dammuso* on Contrada San Vito (☎0923/911.827). Don't expect **food** to be cheap either, though you should try the local speciality, a sort of fish couscous.

travel details

Trains

Catania to: Caltagirone (9 daily; 2hr); Enna (9 daily; 1hr 30min); Gela (9 daily; 2hr 40min); Messina (every 40min; 1hr 30min); Palermo (4 daily; 3hr 15min); Randazzo (11 daily; 2hr 10min); Siracusa (hourly; 1hr 30min); Taormina (13 daily; 1hr).

Enna to: Catania (9 daily; 1hr 20min).

Messina to: Catania (every 40min; 1hr 30min); Cefalù (16 daily; 2hr 45min); Palermo (16 daily; 3hr 30min–6hr); Taormina (every 40min; 1hr).

Palermo to: Agrigento (11 daily; 2hr 30min); Castelvetrano (10 daily; 2hr); Catania (5 daily; 3hr 10min); Enna (5 daily; 2hr); Marsala (10 daily; 3hr); Mazara del Vallo (10 daily; 2hr 30min); Messina (16 daily; 3hr 30min–6hr); Milazzo (16 daily; 3hr); Términi Imerese (hourly; 35min); Trápani (20 daily; 2–4hr).

Ragusa to: Gela (7 daily; 1hr 20min); Módica (12 daily; 25min).

Randazzo to: Riposto (8 daily; 1hr 15min).

Siracusa to: Catania (18 daily; 1hr 30min); Gela (3 daily; 4hr); Messina (14 daily; 3hr); Noto (11 daily; 40min); Ragusa (6 daily; 2hr 20min).

Taormina to: Catania (13 daily; 45min); Messina (every 30min; 1hr); Randazzo (3–5 daily; 1hr); Siracusa (13 daily; 2hr 15min).

Trápani to: Castelvetrano (10 daily; 1hr 10min); Marsala (10 daily; 25min); Mazara del Vallo (10 daily; 50min); Segesta-Tempio (3 daily; 30min).

Buses

Agrigento to: Porto Empédocle (every 30min; 20min); Trápani (2 daily; 3hr 30min).

Castelvetrano to: Marinella (7 daily; 20min); Marsala (7 daily; 40min); Mazara del Vallo (7 daily; 20min); Trápani (7 daily; 1hr 30min).

Catania to: Agrigento (2–4 daily; 2hr 50min); Caltagirone (7 daily; 1hr 30min); Gela (7 daily; 2hr); Messina (6–12 daily; 3hr 10min); Nicolosi (hourly; 40min); Noto (5 daily; 2hr 15min); Piazza Armerina (5 daily; 2hr); Ragusa (4–8 daily; 3hr); Siracusa (7 daily; 1hr 15min).

Enna to: Catania (3–7 daily; 1hr 20min); Gela (1–2 daily; 1hr 40min); Piazza Armerina (1–2 daily; 45min).

Messina to: Catania (5–11 daily; 3hr); Giardini-Naxos (4 daily; 55min); Randazzo (4 daily; 2hr 15min); Taormina (every 30min; 1hr 30min).

Milazzo to: Messina (hourly; 40min).

Palermo to: Agrigento (3–4 daily; 2hr 15min); Bagheria (hourly; 20min); Catania (hourly; 2hr 40min); Cefalù (2 daily; 1hr); Enna (2–4 daily; 1hr 50min); Messina (1 daily; 4hr 30min); Piana degli Albanesi (2–9 daily; 30min); Siracusa (4 daily; 4hr 45min); Términi Imerese (5 daily; 40min); Trápani (hourly; 1hr 45min).

Ragusa to: Módica (every 30min; 20min).

Siracusa to: Caltagirone (1 daily; 2hr); Catania (7 daily; 1hr 15min); Noto (every 30min; 40min); Piazza Armerina (1 daily; 2hr 30min); Ragusa (8 daily; 1hr 30min).

Taormina to: Castelmola (5–6 daily; 20min).

Trápani to: Érice (5–11 daily; 40min).

Ferries

Most of the services detailed here refer to the period from June to September; you should expect frequencies to be greatly reduced outside these months, especially to the Aeolian Islands.

Catania to: Naples (1 weekly; 15hr); Réggio di Calabria (3 weekly; 3hr 15min); Siracusa (3 weekly; 2hr 15min).

Lampedusa to: Trápani (2 weekly; 10hr); Pantelleria (1 weekly; 6hr).

Lípari to: Alicudi (5 weekly; 3hr 45min); Filicudi (5 weekly; 2hr 25min); Milazzo (4 daily; 2hr); Naples (5 weekly; 14hr); Salina (1–2 daily; 50min); Vulcano (4 daily; 30min).

Messina to: Reggio di Calabria (10 daily; 50min); Villa San Giovanni (every 20min; 35min).

Milazzo to: Alicudi (4 weekly; 6hr); Filicudi (4 weekly, 4hr 30min); Lípari (2 daily; 2hr 15min); Salina (2 daily; 3hr 30min); Vulcano (2 daily; 1hr 30min).

Palermo to: Cágliari (1 weekly; 12hr 30min); Genoa (4 weekly; 23hr); Livorno (3 weekly; 18hr); Naples (1 daily; 11hr); Ústica (6–7 weekly; 2hr 45min).

Porto Empédocle to: Lampedusa (1 daily; 8hr 15min); Linosa (1 daily; 6hr).

Trápani to: Cágliari (1 weekly; 11hr); Favignana (6–7 weekly; 55min); Lampedusa (2 weekly; 10hr 30min); Lévanzo (6–7 weekly; 1hr 40min); Maréttimo (6–7 weekly; 2hr 50min); Pantelleria (6–7 weekly; 5hr).

Hydrofoils

Again, most of the services below are greatly reduced outside summer.

Cefalù to: Lípari (3 weekly; 2hr 10min); Palermo (3 weekly; 1hr 10min); Vulcano (3 weekly; 1hr 50min).

Lípari to: Alicudi (4 daily; 1hr 30min); Capo d'Orlando (3 daily; 1hr); Cefalù (3 weekly; 2hr 10min); Filicudi (4 daily; 1hr); Messina (4 daily; 1hr 30min); Milazzo (every 30min; 55min); Naples (1 daily; 5hr 30min); Palermo (2 daily; 3hr 30min); Panarea (10 daily; 30min); Reggio di Calabria (4 daily; 2hr); Salina (12 daily; 15min); Sant'Agata (3 daily; 1hr 30min); Strómboli (10 daily; 1hr); Vulcano (every 45min; 10min).

Messina to: Lípari (2–4 daily; 3hr); Naples (1 daily; 6hr); Reggio di Calabria (every 40min; 15min); Vulcano (2–4 daily; 1hr 45min).

Milazzo to: Alicudi (1 daily; 2hr 30min); Filicudi (1 daily; 2hr); Lípari (every 30min; 55min); Naples (1 daily; 4–6hr); Panarea (6 daily; 2hr 30min); Salina (8 daily; 1hr 25min); Strómboli (6 daily; 3hr); Vulcano (every 30min; 40min).

Palermo to: Cefalù (3 weekly; 1hr 10min); Lípari (1–2 daily; 3hr 30min); Naples (3 weekly; 5hr 20min); Ústica (1–2 daily; 1hr 15min).

Pantelleria to: Trápani (3 weekly; 2hr 15min).

Trápani to: Favignana (10 daily; 20min); Lévanzo (10 daily; 35min); Maréttimo (10 daily; 1hr 5min); Naples (3 weekly; 6hr 45min); Pantelleria (3 weekly; 2hr 15min); Ústica (3 weekly; 2hr 30min).

Ústica to: Capri (3 weekly; 5hr 30min); Favignana (3 weekly; 2hr); Naples (3 weekly; 4hr); Trápani (3 weekly; 2hr 30min).

Flights

Palermo to: Lampedusa (2 daily; 45min); Pantelleria (1 daily; 35min).

Trápani to: Pantelleria (2–3 daily; 30min).

CHAPTER SEVENTEEN

SARDINIA

A little under 200km from the Italian mainland, slightly more than that from the North African coast at Tunisia, **Sardinia** is way off most tourist itineraries of Italy: D.H. Lawrence found it exotically different when he passed through here in 1921 – "lost," as he put it, "between Europe and Africa and belonging to nowhere." Your reasons for coming will probably be a combination of plain curiosity and a yearning for clean beaches. Relatively free of large cities or heavy industry, Sardinian beaches are indeed some of the cleanest in Italy, and are on the whole uncrowded, except perhaps for peak season, when ferries bring in a steady stream of sun-worshippers from what the islanders call *il continente*, or mainland Italy. But Sardinia offers plenty besides sun and sea – the more so if you are prepared to penetrate into its lesser-known interior.

Although not known for its cultural riches, the island holds some surprises, not least the remains of the various civilisations that passed through here. Its central Mediterranean position ensured that it was never left alone for long, and from the Carthaginians onwards the island was ravaged by a succession of invaders, each of them leaving some imprint behind: Roman and Carthaginian ruins, Genoan fortresses, a string of lovely Pisan churches, not to mention some impressive Gothic and Baroque architecture. Perhaps most striking of all, however, are the remnants of Sardinia's only significant native culture, known as the **nuraghic** civilisation after the 7000-odd *nuraghi* which litter the landscape. These mysterious, stone-built constructions, unique to Sardinia, are fairly difficult to see without your own transport, but make the effort to visit at least one during your stay – or failing that, drop in on the museums of Cágliari or Sássari to see the lovely statuettes and domestic objects left by this culture.

On the whole, Sardinia's smaller centres are the most attractive, but the capital, **Cágliari** – for many the arrival point – shouldn't be written off. With good facilities for eating and sleeping, it makes a useful base for exploring the southern third of the island. The other main ferry port is **Olbia** in the north, little more than a transit town but well geared for accommodation and conveniently close to the jagged northern coast. The **Costa Smeralda**, a few kilometres distant, is Sardinia's best-known resort area, and lives up to its reputation for opulence. The prices may preclude anything more than a brief visit, although there are campsites for those outside the ranks of the super-rich.

Both Olbia and Cágliari have airports, as does Sardinia's main package destination of **Alghero** – a fishing port in the northwest of the island that has been known to British holidaymakers for years, yet retains a friendly, unspoiled air. But Alghero's main attraction is its Spanish ambience, a legacy of long years in which the town was a Catalan colony, giving it a wholly different feel from the rest of the island. Inland, **Nuoro** has impressive literary credentials and a good ethnographical museum. As the biggest town in Sardinia's interior, it also makes a useful stopover for visiting some of the remoter mountain areas, in particular the **Gennargentu** range, covering the heart of the island. This is where you can find what remains of the island's traditional culture, best embodied in the numerous village **festivals**.

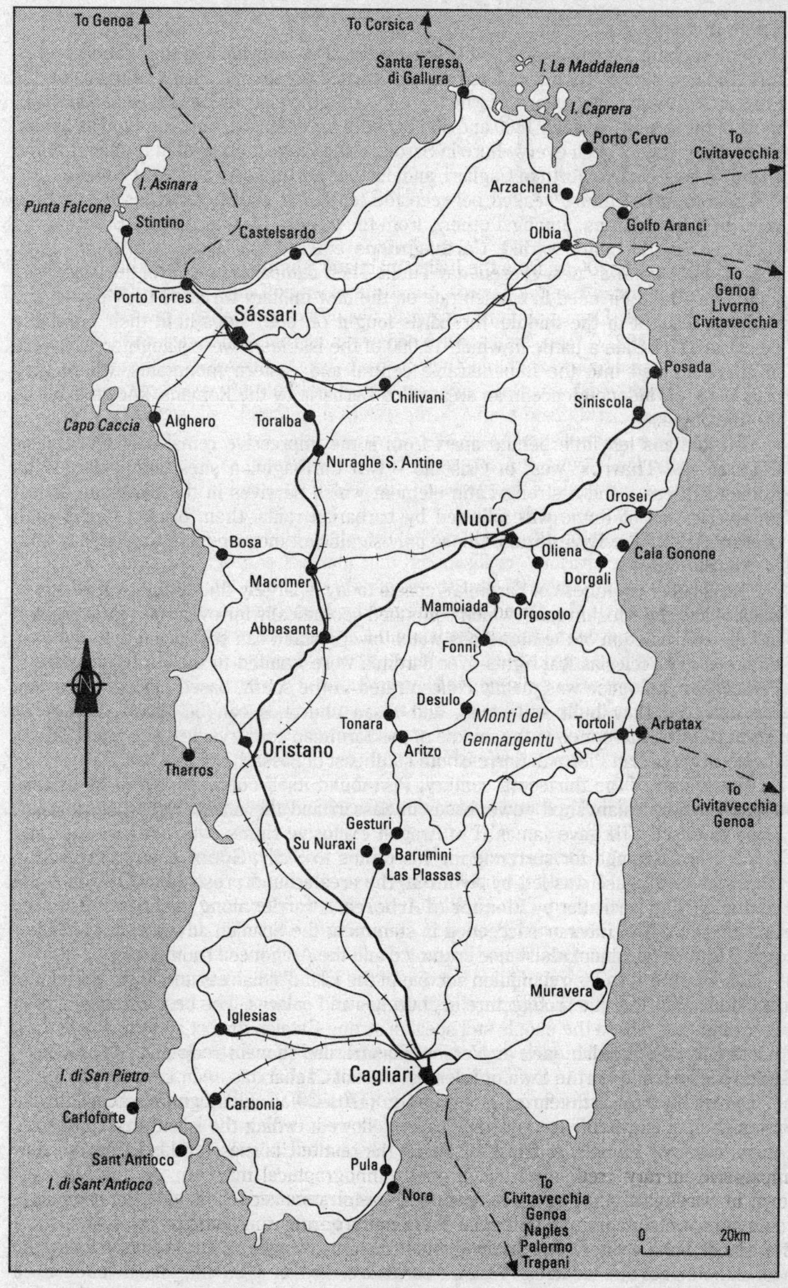
To Genoa
To Corsica
Santa Teresa di Gallura
I. La Maddalena
I. Caprera
Porto Cervo
To Civitavecchia
I. Asinara
Punta Falcone
Stintino
Castelsardo
Arzachena
Golfo Aranci
Olbia
To Genoa Livorno Civitavecchia
Porto Torres
Sássari
Posada
Chilivani
Siniscola
Capo Caccia
Alghero
Toralba
Nuraghe S. Antine
Orosei
Nuoro
Bosa
Oliena
Cala Gonone
Dorgali
Macomer
Mamoiada
Orgosolo
Abbasanta
Fonni
Desulo
Monti del Gennargentu
Tonara
Tortoli
Arbatax
Aritzo
Oristano
Tharros
To Civitavecchia Genoa
Gesturi
Su Nuraxi
Barumini
Las Plassas
Muravera
Iglesias
Cagliari
I. di San Pietro
Carbonia
Carloforte
Sant'Antioco
I. di Sant'Antioco
Pula
Nora
To Civitavecchia Genoa Naples Palermo Trapani
0
20km

Some history

Anyone seeking the true Sard identity must refer all the way back to the island's prehistory, the one period when it enjoyed an undisturbed prosperity. Plenty of traces of this era survive, most conspicuous of which are the rough constructions known as *nuraghi*, most of them built between 1500 and 500 BC both for defensive purposes and as habitations. They can be seen everywhere in Sardinia, the biggest ones all in the heart of the island: at **Su Nuraxi**, north of Cágliari, and, further north, **Losa** and **Sant'Antine**.

This nuraghic culture peaked between the tenth and eighth centuries BC, trading with the **Phoenicians**, amongst others, from the eastern Mediterranean. But from the sixth century the more warlike **Carthaginians** entered the scene, with their capital less than 200km away near present-day Tunis. Their campaign to control the island was halted only by their need to concentrate on the new military threat to their power, the Romans. Caught in the middle, the Sards fought on both sides until their inevitable defeat in 177 BC, in a battle in which 12,000 of the islanders were slaughtered. A core of survivors fled into the impenetrable central and eastern mountains, where they retained their independence in an area called Barbaria by the Romans, known today as the **Barbágia**.

The Romans left little behind apart from some impressive remains at **Nora**, near Cágliari, and **Tharros**, west of Oristano – two Carthaginian sites later enlarged by Roman settlers – and a strong Latin element which survives in the Sardinian dialect today. The fall of Rome was followed by barbarian raids, then, briefly, in the sixth century AD, by the **Byzantines**, whose only significant monument is Cágliari's church of **San Saturnino**.

The relative emptiness of Sardinia's coasts today is largely due to the twin effects of malaria and the Muslim raids which continued sporadically for over 500 years, prompting the construction of the numerous watchtowers which can still be seen. In the eleventh century ecclesiastical rights over Sardinia were granted to the rising city-state of Pisa. **Pisan** influence was mainly concentrated in the south, based in Cágliari, where the defences they built still stand, and Pisan churches can be found throughout Sardinia, often marooned in the middle of the Sardinian countryside – like Santa Trinità di Saccárgia or San Pietro di Sorres, both southeast of Sássari.

By the end of the thirteenth century, Pisa found itself out-manoeuvred by its rival **Genoa**, which established power-bases in Sássari and the north. But when, in 1297, Pope Boniface VIII gave James II of Aragon exclusive rights over both Sardinia and Corsica in exchange for surrendering his claims to Sicily, **Spain** entered the scene. The islanders' cause was led by **Arborea**, the area around present-day Oristano, and championed in particular by **Eleanor of Arborea**, a warrior along the lines of Boadicea and Jeanne d'Arc. Eleanor succeeded in stemming the Spanish advance, but after her death in 1404 Sardinian resistance crumbled and the Aragonese triumphed.

Traces of Spain's long dominion survive in the island's dialects and in the sprinkling of Gothic and Baroque architecture in churches and palaces. The best example of both is at **Alghero**, where the people still speak a strong Catalan dialect and the whole town has the air of a Spanish enclave. Nearby **Sássari** also shows strong Spanish influence, as do the festivities in the town of **Iglésias**, west of Cágliari.

During the War of the Spanish Succession (1701–20), Cágliari was bombarded by an English fleet and briefly occupied. Treaties followed, ceding the island first to Austria, then to Victor Amadeus, Duke of Savoy. His united possessions became the new **Kingdom of Sardinia**.

The years that followed saw a new emphasis on reconstruction, with the opening of schools, investment in industry and agriculture, and the building of roads, most famously the **Carlo Felice highway** that runs the length of the island – today the SS131. But Savoy's quarrels became Sardinia's, and in 1793 the island found itself threatened by **Napoleon**, who led an unsuccessful attempt at invasion in 1793. Later, **Nelson** spent fifteen months hovering around the island's coasts in the hunt for the French fleet that led up to the rout at Trafalgar in 1805. Throughout this long wait, during which Nelson never once set foot on shore, he sent a stream of letters to London urging that steps be taken to secure Sardinia – at the time the only neutral shore in this part of the Mediterranean: "God knows," he wrote, "if we could possess one island, Sardinia, we should want neither Malta, nor any other."

Garibaldi embarked on both his major expeditions from his farm on one of Sardinia's outlying islands, **Caprera**, and the Kingdom of Sardinia ended with the **unification of Italy** in 1861. Since then, Sardinia's role as part of a modern nation-state has not always been easy. The phenomenon of **banditry**, for example, associated with the hinterland and the Gennargentu mountains in particular, was largely the continuation of old habits into the new age. Outbreaks of lawlessness were ruthlessly suppressed, but there was little money available to improve the root causes of the problem, nor much interest in doing so.

Ironically, it was Mussolini who initiated some of the most far-reaching land reforms, including the harnessing and damming of rivers, the draining of land, the introduction of agricultural colonies from the mainland, and the founding of the new towns of **Carbónia** and **Fertília**.

After World War II, Sardinia was granted the same autonomous status as Sicily, Valle d'Aosta and Alto-Adige, allowing control over such areas as transport, tourism, police, industry and agriculture. The *Cassa per il Mezzogiorno* fund was extended to Sardinia, and the island was saturated with enough DDT to rid it of malaria forever. But despite the improvements, much rancour is still felt towards a central government which has imposed on the island, among other things, one of the largest NATO concentrations in the Mediterranean. Campaigning against this presence, and ultimately for complete independence from Rome, albeit with limited popular support, is the **Partito Sardo d'Azione**, or Sardinian Action Party.

Getting to Sardinia

There are frequent daily **flights** from the Italian mainland to the island's three airports, at Cágliari, Olbia and Fertília (for Alghero and Sássari). The flights, which take about an hour, are run by *Alitalia*'s internal arm, *ATI*, and Sardinia's own *Alisarda* and *Air*

FERRIES TO SARDINIA

From	To	Line	No. per week	Duration
Civitavecchia	Olbia	Tirrenia	7	8hr
Civitavecchia	Golfo	Aranci FS	7	8hr
Civitavecchia	Arbatax	Tirrenia	2–3	9hr
Civitavecchia	Cágliari	Tirrenia	7	14hr
Genoa	Porto Torres	Tirrenia	7	12hr
Genoa	Olbia	Tirrenia	3–7	13hr
Genoa	Arbatax	Tirrenia	2	18hr
Genoa	Cágliari	Tirrenia	2 (June–Sept only)	20hr
La Spezia	Olbia	Tirrenia	7	11hr
Livorno	Golfo Aranci	Sardinia	4–7 (April–Sept only)	10hr
Livorno	Olbia	Navarma	4–7 (April–Sept only)	9hr
Naples	Cágliari	Tirrenia	1–2	15hr
Palermo	Cágliari	Tirrenia	1	14hr
Trápani	Cágliari	Tirrenia	*1*	*12hr*
Tunis	Cágliari	Tirrenia	1	37hr

Sardinia. Cheaper but slower are the overnight **ferries** from mainland Italy (Civitavecchia, Genoa, Livorno, Naples) – as well as from Sicily, Tunis, Corsica and France. If you're travelling by car, remember that it is essential to book well in advance: sailings in July and August can be fully booked up by May. Prices range from L42,000 to L150,000 per person, depending on season and type of accommodation: a berth costs a minimum of L60,000. A vehicle will cost a minimum of L70,000 for a small car in low season. Note that *Navarma* and *Sardinia Ferries* offer fifty percent discounts for vehicles on certain dates if you book your return when you buy your outward-bound ticket.

Getting around the island

Once arrived, you can rely on a good network of public transport to get you round all but the remoter areas. On the roads there is the island-wide bus network run by *ARST* and the private *PANI* for longer hauls between towns, while trains connect the major towns of Cágliari, Sássari and Olbia, with smaller narrow-gauge lines linking with Nuoro and Alghero.

CAGLIARI AND THE SOUTH

Cágliari has been Sardinia's capital at least since Roman times and is still its biggest town, with the busiest port and the greatest concentration of industry. Intimidating as this may sound, Cágliari is no urban sprawl: its centre is small and compact enough to be easily manageable on foot, offering both sophistication and charm in the raggle-taggle of narrow lanes crammed into its high citadel.

Viewing Cágliari from the sea at the start of his Sardinian sojourn in 1921, D.H. Lawrence compared it to Jerusalem: ". . . strange and rather wonderful, not a bit like Italy." The main attractions here are the **museum** with its unique collection of nuraghic statuettes, the city walls with their two **Pisan towers** looking down over the port, and the **cathedral** – all within easy distance of each other in the old centre. There is also a sprinkling of Roman remains, including an impressive **amphitheatre**. More evocative ruins from this period can be seen 40km out of town at **Nora**, the most complete ancient site on the island. Other places worth visiting from Cágliari include the famous *nuraghe* of **Su Nuraxi**, a compelling sight surrounded by the brown hills of the interior. Off the coast west of Cágliari are moored the islands of **Sant'Antíoco** and **San Pietro**, while the Spanish-tinged town of **Iglésias** makes an appealing inland destination during its flamboyant Easter festivities.

Cágliari

Rising up from its port and crowned by an old centre squeezed within a protective ring of Pisan fortifications, **CÁGLIARI** is less frenetic than any town of equivalent size on the mainland, with a population of nearly a quarter of a million spread around its modern outskirts, where new blocks of flats have mushroomed in the last twenty years. Is setting is enhanced by the calm lagoons (*stagni*) behind the city and along the airport road, the habitat for cranes, flamingos and cormorants. In the centre, the evening promenades along Via Manno are the smartest you'll see in Sardinia, dropping down to the noisier Piazza Yenne and Largo Carlo Felice, around which most of the shops, restaurants, banks and hotels are located. At the bottom of the town, the arcades of Via Roma shelter shops and bars, in between which the Senegalese traders jostle for pavement space.

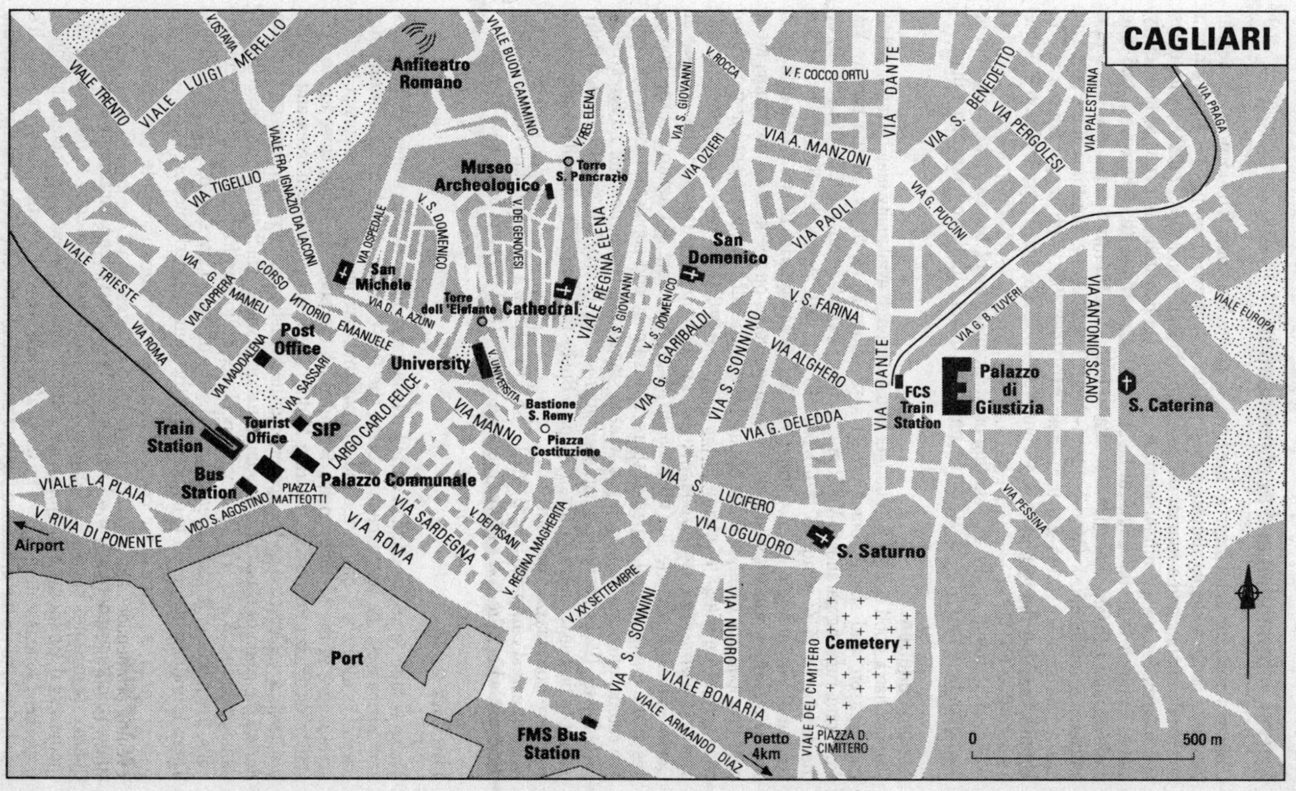
CAGLIARI
V. OSTAVIA
VIALE LUIGI MERELLO
VIALE TRENTO
Anfiteatro Romano
VIALE BUON CAMMINO
V. REG. ELENA
Torre S. Pancrazio
Museo Archeologico
VIA TIGELLIO
VIALE FRA IGNAZIO DA LACONI
V. S. DOMENICO
V. DEI GENOVESI
VIA OSPEDALE
San Michele
VIA D. A. AZUNI
Torre dell' Elefante
Cathedral
VIALE REGINA ELENA
V. S. GIOVANNI
V. S. DOMENICO
VIA S. GIOVANNI
V. ROCCA
VIA OZIERI
San Domenico
V. F. COCCO ORTU
VIA A. MANZONI
VIA PAOLI
VIA DANTE
VIA S. BENEDETTO
VIA PERGOLESI
VIA PALESTRINA
VIA PRAGA
VIA G. PUCCINI
VIALE TRIESTE
VIA G. MAMELI
CORSO VITTORIO EMANUELE
VIA CAPRERA
VIA ROMA
Post Office
VIA MADDALENA
VIA SASSARI
University
V. UNIVERSITA
Train Station
Tourist Office
SIP
LARGO CARLO FELICE
VIA MANNO
Bastione S. Remy
Piazza Costituzione
VIA G. GARIBALDI
VIA S. SONNINO
V. S. FARINA
VIA ALGHERO
VIA G. DELEDDA
VIA G. B. TUVERI
VIA ANTONIO SCANO
VIALE EUROPA
FCS Train Station
Palazzo di Giustizia
S. Caterina
Bus Station
PIAZZA MATTEOTTI
Palazzo Communale
VIALE LA PLAIA
V. RIVA DI PONENTE
VICO S. AGOSTINO
Airport
VIA ROMA
VIA SARDEGNA
V. DEI PISANI
V. REGINA MAGHERITA
VIA S. LUCIFERO
VIA LOGUDORO
S. Saturno
VIA PESSINA
V. XX SETTEMBRE
VIA S. SONNINI
VIA NUORO
Cemetery
VIALE DEL CIMITERO
PIAZZA D. CIMITERO
Port
VIALE BONARIA
VIALE ARMANDO DIAZ
FMS Bus Station
Poetto 4km
0
500 m

Arrival, information and accommodation

Cágliari's **port** lies in the heart of the town, opposite Via Roma. The **airport** sits beside the city's largest *stagno*, fifteen minutes' bus ride west of town. The airport has a bureau de change and a **tourist office** (Mon–Fri 9am–6pm; ☎070/240.200) with maps and information on accommodation. A free bus service into town runs at least every ninety minutes from 6.20am until 8.55pm to Piazza Matteotti; otherwise a taxi ride costs around L15,000. Piazza Matteotti also holds the **bus and train stations** and a tourist information kiosk (Mon–Sat 9am–2pm). The Stazione Maríttima at the port also has a tourist office (Mon–Sat 9am–2pm; ☎070/668.352), with bigger offices at Via Mameli 97 (Mon–Sat 9am–2pm & 4–7pm; ☎070/664.195) and Piazza Defennu 9 (same hours; ☎070/663.207).

Piazza Matteotti is also the starting-point for most **local buses**: tickets are sold at the booth here for L1100, or L1500 for unlimited travel within two hours of purchase.

Accommodation

Cágliari has a good selection of budget **hotels**, though availability may be restricted in high season, and single rooms are at a premium at all times. In the narrow Via Sardegna, running parallel to Via Roma, try the *Centrale* at no. 4 (☎070/654.783; ④) or the nearby *La Perla* at no. 18 (☎070/669.446; ④), with almost identical rooms. At the far end of Via Sardegna, the *Londra* at Via Regina Margherita 16 (☎070/669.083; ④) is run by a London woman who's lived seventeen years on the island – the rooms are a mite cramped but clean, and the atmosphere is friendly. A convenient but far pricier choice right on Piazza Matteotti is the *Moderno* (☎070/660.306; ⑦), or else try the nearby *Quattro Mori* (☎070/668.535; ⑤). Further up from the port, the *Firenze* at Corso Vittorio Emanuele 50 (☎070/653.678; ③), like most of Cágliari's cheap hotels, lies at the top of several flights of stairs, but it's cosy and popular – though with only five rooms, often full. Finally, if you want to stay near a beach, head for *La Sirenetta* at Viale Poetto 192 in Poetto, Cágliari's summer suburb (☎070/370.332; ④), though don't expect to find space here in July or August. Buses (marked "P") take fifteen minutes to get there from Piazza Matteotti.

The nearest **campsite** is at QUARTU SANT'ELENA, a 45-minute bus ride east along the coast, where the *Pini e Mare* (June–Sept; ☎070/803.107) has bungalows as well.

The City

There is little to see in Cágliari's traffic-thronged modern quarters beyond the banks and businesses, the one exception being the fifth-century church of **San Saturnino**, Sardinia's oldest and one of the most important surviving examples of early Christian architecture in the Mediterranean. Stranded on the busy Via Dante close to the FCS station on Piazza Repubblica, looking Middle Eastern with its palm trees and cupola, the basilica was erected on the spot where the Christian martyr Saturninus met his fate during the reign of Diocletian. Around the sturdy walls, which withstood severe bomb-damage during World War II, lie various pieces of flotsam from the past: four cannon-balls, fragments of Roman sarcophagi and slabs of stone carved with Latin inscriptions. There is nothing of interest to detain you in the church's stark interior.

The Castello

Almost all the wandering you will want to do in Cágliari is encompassed within the old quarter, sometimes known as "Castello." The most evocative entry to this is from the monumental **Bastione San Remy** on Piazza Costituzione, whose nineteenth-century Imperialist tone is watered down by the graffiti and weeds sprouting out of its walls. It's worth the haul up the grandiose flight of steps inside for Cágliari's best views over the port and the lagoons beyond. Sunset is a good time to be here, or whenever you feel like a pause from sightseeing-fatigue, as its shady benches are extremely conducive to a twenty-minute siesta.

From the bastion, you can wander off in any direction to enter the intricate maze of Cágliari's citadel, traditionally the seat of the administration, aristocracy and highest ecclesiastical offices. It has been little altered since the Middle Ages, though the tidy Romanesque façade on the **Cattedrale** in Piazza Palazzo is in fact a fake, added in this century in the old Pisan style. The structure dates originally from the thirteenth century but has gone through what Lawrence called "the mincing machine of the ages, and oozed out Baroque and sausagey."

Inside, a couple of massive stone **pulpits** flank the main doors: they were crafted as a single piece around 1160 to grace Pisa's cathedral, but were later presented to Cágliari along with the same sculptor's set of lions, which now adorn the outside of the building. Other features of the cathedral that are worth a glance include the ornate seventeenth-century tomb of Martin II of Aragon (in the left transept), the presbytery, which is the entrance to a small museum, and the **crypt**. Hewn out of the rock, little of this subterranean chamber has been left undecorated, and there are carvings by Sicilian artists of the Sardinian saints whose ashes were said to have been found under the church of San Saturnino in 1617. Also here are the tombs of the wife of Louis XVIII of France, Marie-Josephine of Savoy, and the infant son of Vittorio Emanuele I of Savoy and Maria-Teresa of Austria, Carlo Emanuele, who died in 1799.

The cathedral stands in one corner of the square, flanked by the eighteenth-century **Governor's Palace**, formerly the palace of the Piedmontese kings of Sardinia, though rarely inhabited by them, and by the graceful archbishop's palace – both the work of the same architect, Davisto, in 1769.

At the opposite end of Piazza Palazzo a road leads into the smaller Piazza Indipendenza, site of Sardinia's **Museo Archeologico Nazionale** (Mon 9am–1.30pm, Tues–Sat 9am–1.30pm & 3.30–6pm, Sun 9am–12.30pm; L4000), a must for anyone interested in Sardinia's past. The island's most important Phoenician, Carthaginian and Roman finds are gathered here, including busts and statues of muses and gods, jewellery and coins, and funerary items from the sites of Nora and Tharros. But everything pales beside the museum's greatest pieces, from the Sardinia's **nuraghic** culture.

Of these, the most eye-catching is a series of bronze statuettes, ranging from about six to eighteen inches in height, spindly and highly stylised, but packed with invention and quirky humour. The main source of information about this phase of the island's history, these figures represent warriors and hunters, athletes, shepherds, nursing mothers, bulls, horses and wild animals. Most were votive offerings, made to decorate the inside of temples, later buried to protect them from the hands of foreign predators.

The museum is in the process of being transferred a short distance away to Piazza dell'Arsenale, where the **Cittadella dei Musei** has been recently inaugurated on the site of the former royal arsenal, with the aim of housing all the city's principal museums. A plaque in the square records the visit made by Cervantes to Cágliari in 1573, shortly before his capture and imprisonment by Moorish pirates.

Off the square stands the **Torre San Pancrazio**, from which it's only a short walk to Via dell'Università and the **Torre dell'Elefante**, named after a small carving of an elephant on one side. Together these formed the main bulwarks of the city's defences, erected by Pisa after it had wrested the city from the Genoans in 1305, though the towers did not stop the Aragonese from walking in just fifteen years later. Both have a half-finished look about them, with the side facing the old town completely open.

Nearby, Viale Buon Cammino leads to the **Anfiteatro Romano**. Cut out of solid rock in the second century AD, the amphitheatre could hold the entire city's population of about 20,000. Despite the decay, with much of the site cannibalised to build churches in the Middle Ages, you can still see the trenches for the animals, the underground passages and several rows of seats. However, apart from special occasions, the theatre is closed to visitors not holding a special permit from the town hall, though you can see a good part just by walking round it.

Poetto

When you need a break and a bathe, head for the suburb of **Poetto**, a fifteen-minute bus ride from Piazza Matteotti past Cágliari's Sant'Elia football stadium. Poetto has six kilometres of fine sandy beach, with small bars and showers conveniently nearby; some stretches are lidos where you pay a standard daily rate (about L5000) for entry and use of deck chairs and umbrella.

One end of the strip, rearing above a small marina, is the **Sella del Diávolo**, or "Devil's Saddle," aptly describing the shape of the rock that juts into the sea, most of it now a military zone and therefore off limits. The name is connected with a legend relating how the Archangel Gabriel won a battle here against the devil himself. The name of Cágliari's gulf, Golfo degli Angeli, is also a reference to this celestial tussle.

Eating, drinking and nightlife

Poetto in summer is a blitz of bars, pizzerias, fairgrounds and ice cream kiosks – a good place to while away an evening. Cágliari itself is the place for **restaurants**, most clustered around Via Sardegna. *Da Serafino*, with entrances at both Via Sardegna 109 and Via Lepanto 6, is extremely good value and popular with the locals. The *Trattoria-Pizzeria* at Via dei Mille 16 is a bit touristy but always open. Seafood-lovers will do well at the *Stella Marina di Montecristo*, at the end of Via Sardegna, where it meets Via Regina Margherita. Away from the port area, try *Il Gatto*, just off Piazza del Cármine at Viale Trieste 15, for something a little more upmarket – seafood or meat dishes, all immaculately prepared.

For a **snack** and a beer, drop in on *Il Merlo Parlante* in Via Portascalas, an alley off Corso Vittorio Emanuele, where you can find drink, music, *panini* and a mynah bird (after which the pub is named) that can whistle *Colonel Bogey* in three keys. Down by the port, the bars on Via Roma make good breakfast-stops, while there are several decent pizza and sandwich joints in the alleys running off it.

Listings

ACI Via Carboni Boi 2 (☎070/492.308).

Airlines *Alitalia*, Via Caprera 12 (☎070/60.101); *Alisarda*, Via Rossi (☎070/669.161); *Ati*, Aeroporto Elmas (☎070/240.079).

Airport Elmas airport ☎070/240.047.

Bicycle rental Piazza Paolo VI (summer only).

Consulates *Netherlands*, Viale Regina Margherita 8 (☎668.094); *UK*, Via San Lucífero 87 (☎070/662.755). There is no US or Canadian consulate.

Car rental *Autonoleggio Catte*, Via Roma 189 (☎070/657.245); *Avis*, Via Sonnino 87 (☎070/668.128); *Caralis*, Via Santa Margherita 12 (☎070/652.913); *Hertz*, Piazza Matteotti 1 (☎070/668.105).

Ferries *Tirrenia*, Via Campidano 1 (☎070/666.065).

Festivals Sant'Efisio: May 1–3, including a procession to the saint's church at Nora.

Hospital Via Peretti 21 (☎070/2000).

Post office Piazza del Cármine (Mon–Sat 8am–7pm).

Telephones Via Angioy, open 24hr.

Travel agents *CTS*, Via Balbo 4 (☎070/488.260); *Sardamondial*, Viale Regina Margherita 8 (☎070/668.094); *Viaggi Orru*, Via Roma 95 (☎070/657.954).

Nora

The easiest excursion you can make from Cágliari is to the waterside archaeological site at **NORA**, 40km south of the city. In July and August two daily *ARST* buses follow the coast past Sardinia's biggest industrial complex at SARROCH, where the second-biggest refinery in the Mediterranean imports eighteen million tonnes of oil annually, mainly from Libya. At other times of the year you'll have to get off at PULA (10 buses daily), and then walk the 3km to the sea. It's worth going to Pula anyway, as the village **museum** (daily April–Oct 9am–8pm; Nov–March 9am–12.30pm & 2–5pm) gives some explanation of the Nora finds: the L3000 ticket is good for both site and museum.

Founded by the Phoenicians and settled later by Carthaginians and Romans, **Nora** (daily April–Oct 9am–8pm; Nov–March 9am–noon, 3–6pm) was abandoned around the third century AD, possibly as a result of a natural disaster. It is now partly submerged under the sea, with the remains on land including houses, Carthaginian warehouses, a temple, baths with some well-preserved mosaics, and a theatre in an equally good state of repair. The rest is rubble, though its position on the tip of a peninsula gives it plenty of atmosphere. Outside the archaeological site stands the rather ordinary-looking eleventh-century church of Sant'Efísio, site of the saint's martyrdom and destination of Cágliari's three-day Mayday procession.

Behind the church is an exquisite sandy bay, lapped by crystal-clear water. There is also a small **hotel** nearby, *Su Guventeddu* (☎070/920.9092; ④), although Pula has more choice – pick of them being the *Quattro Mori* at Via Cágliari 10 (July–Sept; ☎070/920.9124; ④).

The coast south has some of Sardinia's most exclusive hotels, including the massive *Forte Hotel Village* complex and the *Is Molas* hotel, with its championship golf course. Beyond, the coastal road offers terrific views over a deserted cliff-hung coastline, sheltering small sand beaches; you need a car to get to them.

Su Nuraxi and around

If you have no time to see any other of Sardinia's *nuraghi*, make a point of visiting **SU NURAXI**, the biggest and most famous of them and a good taste of the primitive grandeur of the island's only indigenous civilisation. The snag is access: the site lies a kilometre outside the village of BARUMINI, 50km north of Cágliari, to which there are only two daily *ARST* buses, which stop here en route to Désulo and Samugheo.

Just south of Barúmini you'll see the extraordinary conical hill of **Las Plassas**, with the fragments of a twelfth-century **castle** sticking up like broken teeth on its round peak – a landmark for miles around.

Three kilometres further on, turn left at Barúmini's main crossroads and walk the last leg to Su Nuraxi. Its dialect name means simply "the *nuragh*" and not only is it the biggest nuraghic complex on the island, but it's also thought to be the oldest, dating probably from around 1500 BC. Comprising a bulky fortress surrounded by the remains of a village, Su Nuraxi was a palace complex at the very least – possibly a capital city. The central tower once reached 21m (now shrunk to less than 15m), and its outer defences and inner chambers are connected by passageways and stairs. The whole complex is thought to have been covered with earth by Sards and Carthaginians at the time of the Roman conquest, which may account for its excellent state of preservation: if it weren't for a torrential rainstorm that washed away the slopes in 1949, the site may never have been revealed at all. The site is free and open every day during daylight hours; there's a restaurant and bar nearby.

Just north and west of Barumini extends the high plain of **Giara di Gésturi**, the last refuge of Sardinia's wild ponies. You'll need a little luck and a lot of cunning to spot these small, shy creatures, but in any case it's an excellent spot for walking, at an altitude of around 600m. Again, though, the problem is access. Dedicated hikers can explore a good part of the plain on foot from the village of Gésturi, a stop on the Cágliari–Désulo and Cágliari–Samugheo bus routes. Spring is the best season to visit, when the area is a stopover for migrating birds.

West of Cágliari: Sant'Antíoco and San Pietro

On the mainland, only two places west of Cágliari warrant a stopoff: **IGLESIAS**, surrounded by abandoned mine-shafts but best known for its numerous churches and Spanish-flavoured Holy Week celebrations; and nearby **CARBONIA**, a coal-mining centre founded by Mussolini as "Mussolinia" in 1936 – its regimented streets and planned workers' houses are still imbued with the Duce's presence. Both are connected to Cágliari by the *FMS* line, and from Iglesias there are bus connections to PORTOSCUSO, the port for ferries to **San Pietro**. This island, and neighbouring **Sant'Antíoco**, can just about be visited from Cágliari in a day, but you'd do better staying over. Although well-frequented holiday destinations in summer, the islands have not yet become too developed; in fact accommodation is on the scarce side, and if you're thinking of staying, be sure to book ahead.

Sant'Antíoco

SANT'ANTÍOCO, the larger of the southwest islands, is linked by causeway to Sardinia's coast and served by six daily *FMS* buses, which leave from the terminal at Via Cristóforo Colombo 24, behind Piazza Deffenu (2hr; L8000). Halfway across the causeway you'll see two stones sticking out of the water: named *Su Para* and *Sa Mongia* – "the monk" and "the nun" – they are supposed to be two lovers turned to stone by divine intervention when attempting to escape from the island.

The port area of the island's town (also called Sant'Antíoco) is just on the other side of the causeway. Nelson's flagship, the *Vanguard*, put in here shortly before the Battle of the Nile in 1798, severely damaged from a storm. The vessel was re-rigged in four days, though Nelson deplored the fact that, on account of Sardinia's recently declared neutrality in the French Revolutionary War, the ship's company was not allowed ashore. "We are refused the rights of humanity," he wrote to Lady Nelson.

The core of the upper part of Sant'Antíoco has been continuously inhabited since Phoenician times and was an important base both for the Carthaginians and the Romans, commanding the whole of Sardinia's southwest coast. The twelfth-century church of **Sant'Antíoco** here was built over Christian **catacombs**, which were in turn enlarged from an existing Carthaginian burial place; you can visit these dingy corridors, with authentic skeletons and reproductions of ceramic objects unearthed during excavation, on a guided tour (Mon–Sat 9am–noon & 3–6pm, Sun 3–7pm; L5000).

Near the church entrance stands a statue of Saint Antiochus, plainly showing his Mauretanian origins; his feast day, on the second Sunday after Easter, is a four-day affair with traditional songs, poetry recitations, dancing, fireworks and a procession to the sea.

Outside the church, a signpost points down a side-road to a **Punic tophet**, an extensive burial site dedicated to the Carthaginian goddess Tanit, which once covered the entire hill where the old city now stands. The numerous scattered urns were long thought to contain the ashes of sacrificed first-born children, but this is now thought to have been Roman propaganda: the urns, it seems, contained the cremated remains of children still-born or dead from natural causes. There are also the well-preserved ruins of a temple here, and an excellent little **museum** (site and museum open 9am–noon & 3.30–7pm in summer; closes 6pm in winter; L5000).

The best of Sant'Antíoco's **hotels** is the centrally located *Moderno* (☎0781/83.105; ⑤). Other hotels are out of town, mostly along the northern coast road to the small resort of CALASETTA, the ultimate destination of the *FMS* bus from Cágliari. There are also **campsites** here, for example *Camping Vacanze* (☎0781/88.218), just before Calasetta, open all year round.

San Pietro

Every day six **ferries from Calasetta** do the five-kilometre hop to **SAN PIETRO** (40min; L1500): if you're in a car, make sure you're in the ferry queue in good time, as summer sees a lot of congestion.

San Pietro's dialect is pure Piedmontese, two and a half centuries after the Savoyan king Carlo Emanuele III invited a colony of Ligurians to settle here after their eviction from the island of Tabarca, near Tunisia. The settlers were later abducted back to Tunisia in one of the last great pirate raids, but they were lucky enough to be ransomed back. The island's only town, **CARLOFORTE** (named after the king), is attractive and lively in summer, and is close to various panoramic beauty spots and mainly rocky beaches.

The island's few **hotels** are concentrated in Carloforte. Best choice is probably the *Hieracon*, fairly central at Via Cavour 63 (☎0781/854.028; ⑥), though the *Passero*, Via Nazionale 117 (☎0781.961225; ③) is cheaper. Availability is extremely limited in summer, but if you are stuck without a booking, ask around for **rooms for rent**. There is a **campsite** at LA CALETTA (May–Sept; ☎0781/852.112), 8km from Carloforte and accessible by bus.

ORISTANO AND NUORO

Sardinia's smallest province, Oristano, was created as recently as 1975 out of bits hacked off the provinces of Cágliari and Nuoro, but it roughly corresponds with the much older entity of Arborea, the medieval *giudicato* which championed the Sardinian cause in the struggle against the Spaniards. Then as now, **Oristano** was the region's main town, and today it retains more than a hint of medieval atmosphere.

Far older is the Punic-Roman town of **Tharros**, similar to Nora in appearance and worth a visit if you haven't seen that other site. Even older traces are to be seen at **Abbasanta**, where the nuraghic remains of **Losa** give an insight into Sardinia's prehistory. North up the coast, the predominant flavour at the riverside town of **Bosa** is again medieval, with its sturdy fort overlooking a lovely unspoilt stretch of coastline.

Bosa is the only west-coast point of the province of Nuoro, which covers most of Sardinia's interior and its barren eastern coast. This area is little travelled by tourists, which no doubt has helped to preserve here the last remnants of Sardinia's traditional culture as well as a largely unspoiled natural environment. Scattered over the woodland and pasturage are isolated villages, of which the provincial capital, **Nuoro**, is only a larger, drabber version, though it is a useful transport junction and base for excursions.

Oristano

ORISTANO is a flat, initially unprepossessing place, whose old walls have been mostly replaced by busy boulevards. However, the centre has a relaxed and sophisticated ambience, and although it is four kilometres from the sea, the town is attractively surrounded by water, its lagoons and irrigation canals helping to make this a richly productive agricultural zone. The southern lagoon, the **Stagno di Santa Giusta**, is one of the two homes of Sardinia's flamingo population: if they're not at Cágliari they're bound to be here, sharing the water with the coracle-like flat-bottomed boats still used by the lagoon's fishermen.

The Town

In the heart of the town is Oristano's central symbol, the marble statue of **Eleonora d'Arborea**, presiding over the piazza named after her. Eleanor was the *giudice* of the Arborea region from 1384 to 1404, and is the best-known and best-loved of Sardinia's medieval rulers, having been the only one who enjoyed any success against the island's aggressors. Ensconced in the last of Sardinia's *giudicati* to remain independent of the Aragonese, Eleanor united local resistance, and, despite the desertion of her husband Brancaleone Doria to the enemy, succeeded in negotiating a treaty in 1388 that guaranteed her a measure of independence. She later backed this up by a tactical alliance with the Genoans, and it was with Genoan help that Brancaleone, returned to the fold, managed to occupy Sássari on her behalf.

Eleanor's military achievements collapsed soon after her death from plague in 1404, though the most enduring benefit of her reign survived her by several centuries: the formulation of a **Code of Laws** (*Carta di Logu*), first mooted by her father Mariano IV but embodied by Eleanor in a legal document in 1395. Covering every aspect of civil legislation, this document was adopted in 1421 by the Aragonese and extended throughout the island. As the eighteenth-century English lawyer and traveller John Tyndale put it: "The framing of a body of laws so far in advance of those of other countries, where greater civilisations existed, must ever be the brightest ornament in the diadem of the Giudicessa." Eleanor's statue, carved in 1881, shows her bearing the scroll on which the laws were written, while inset panels depict her various victories.

Although it's called the **Casa di Eleonora**, the fine house at Via Parpáglia 4 (left off Via La Marmora, which leads off the piazza) could not have been her home, as it was built over a century after her death. She is unequivocally buried in the fourteenth-century church of **Santa Chiara**, in the parallel Via Garibaldi.

From Piazza Eleonora d'Arborea, the narrow pedestrianised Corso Umberto leads up to Piazza Roma, where pavement bars are clustered around the base of the **San Cristóforo** bastion, erected by the *giudice* Mariano II in 1291, and the fulcrum of Oristano's fortifications. The only other survivor of these defences is the smaller

SA SARTIGLIA

The rituals of Oristano's flamboyant **Sa Sartiglia** perhaps originated with knights on the Second Crusade, who in the eleventh century may well have imported the trappings of Saracen tournaments to Sardinia. In the period of the Spanish domination, similarly lavish feasts were held for the ruling knights at regular intervals throughout the year. In time, these celebrations took on a more theatrical aspect and became merged with the annual Carnival – the Sa Sartiglia is now a three-day festival that closes the Carnival period, ending on Shrove Tuesday. Highlights of this costumed pageant include horseback parades and trials of equestrian prowess, all judged by a white-masked arbiter known as **Su Componidori**. Selected from among the "knight" contestants, the *Componidori* represents the continuation of the *giudice*'s role, and is decked out in a bizarre pastiche of medieval garb – the process of dressing him is itself a highly formal ceremony, conducted in public at the beginning of each day.

In fact all the participants are masked and costumed, and the whole affair exudes a theatrical spirit unrivalled by any of Sardinia's other festivals. Climax of the proceedings is the joust after which the festival is named, when the mounted contestants attempt to lance a ring, or *sartiglia*, suspended in the air, charging towards it at full gallop. Make sure you've got accommodation sorted out if you're planning to stay over.

Portixedda ("little gate") tower, a squat, neglected thing at the bottom of Via Mazzini (off Via Roma).

Oristano's **Duomo** stands in a spacious square up Via Duomo, which is behind Piazza Eleonora. Though started in the thirteenth century, most of the present duomo is a Baroque renovation, retaining only parts of the apses from its original construction. With the fourteenth-century onion-roofed bell-tower and the next-door seminary, it forms an atmospheric ensemble.

At the other end of Via Duomo stands the nineteenth-century church of **San Francesco**, incorporating the remains of a much older Gothic building. The space in front, merging with Piazza Eleonora d'Arborea, forms the main arena for Oristano's annual *Sa Sartiglia* (see box).

Practicalities

Oristano's **train station** is at the eastern end of town, a half-hour walk from the centre, or linked by a local bus every forty minutes or so. The *ARST* **bus** station is on Via Cágliari, while *PANI* buses pull in at Via Lombardia, twenty minutes from the centre down Via Tirso. Opposite the *ARST* station is the main **tourist office**, a fifth-floor office (Mon–Fri 9am–noon & 5–8pm; Sat 9am–noon); there is another, handier office on Via de Castro (same hours).

Accommodation

Oristano is badly off for **accommodation**, with just five hotels listed, and these often full. The cheapest and friendliest is also the most difficult to find – the *Píccolo Hotel* at Via Martignano 19 (☎0783/71.500; ④), in an area of unmarked streets behind Piazza Martini, near Via del Cármine. A convenient choice near the train station is the expensive *Cama*, in Via Vittorio Véneto (☎0783/74.374; ⑥). Closer to the centre is the *Isa* in Piazza Mariano (☎0783/78.040; ⑤), rundown and bland but a useful last resort.

The nearest **campsite** is 6km away at MARINA DI TORRE GRANDE, Oristano's lido. The *Torre Grande* site (May–Sept; ☎0783/22.008), 150m from the sea, is reachable on the frequent buses from the *ARST* bus station.

Eating and drinking

Oristano is better off for **restaurants**, among the cheapest of which is *Trattoria Gino* off Piazza Roma, offering traditional Sardinian items like *ravioli sardi* (made with butter and sage) and *sebadas* (cheese-filled pastry-cases topped with honey). The *Stella Marina* at Via Tirso 6 is a good venue for seafood, and Via Tirso has a couple of other choices, both inexpensive: *Trattoria Gino* and *Ristorante Tirso*, the latter good for fish. Cheapest of all is *La Torre*, a pizzeria-restaurant on Piazza Roma, with a wood-fired oven. You might finish your meal with a glass of Oristano's celebrated **Vernaccia**, a strong dessert wine that is one of Sardinia's finest.

Tharros

Many people come to Oristano just to visit the Punic and Roman ruins at **THARROS**, twenty-odd kilometres from Oristano and served by two *ARST* buses daily. Like Nora, Tharros is pitched on a limb of land surrounded by water, though in this case it's a clenched fist, dominated by a sturdy Spanish watchtower. The peninsula forms part of the mouth of the Golfo di Oristano and was settled by Phoenicians as early as 800 BC. Tharros grew under Carthaginian occupation and then, after 238 BC, was revitalised by the Romans, who furnished it with the baths and streets that you see today. The town was finally abandoned in 1070 in favour of the securer Oristano, then a small village.

The **site** (daily 8am–1pm & 4–7pm; free) consists mostly of Punic and Roman houses arranged on a grid of streets, of which the broad-slabbed Decumanus Maximus is the most impressive. Another, the Cardo Maximus, has a deep open sewer visible alongside it. But the first things you'll notice on first entering the site are the solitary remnants of a first-century BC Roman temple, with only two of its four Corinthian columns still upright. There are also baths and fragments of mosaics from the Roman city, and a wall and remains of a tophet from the earlier Punic settlement. Like Nora, there is much more submerged under the water, sunk as a result of subsidence.

Near the site stands the fifth-century church of **San Giovanni di Sinis**, which vies with Cágliari's San Saturnino for the title of oldest Christian church in Sardinia. Further back up the road towards Oristano (signposted off the Tharros road) is the sanctuary of **San Salvatore**, whose main interest is in a subterranean fourth-century chamber dedicated to Mars and Venus, complete with faded frescoes of Venus, Cupid and Hercules – ask the custodian to let you see it.

The sanctuary is the focus of a wild **festival** on the first weekend of September, the main feature of which is a race run at dawn to the village of CABRAS, 8km away, by the town's boys. Barefoot and clad in white shirts and shorts, they bear aloft the statue of San Salvatore in a re-enactment of a frantic rescue mission undertaken four centuries ago to save the saint from Moorish attackers.

Bosa

North of Oristano, a brief bus ride from the rail and road junction of MACOMER takes you to **BOSA** and the coast. Stranded in the middle of one of Sardinia's last remaining stretches of deserted coastline, and so far overlooked by the tourist industry, the town huddles on the banks of the Temo river around a hilltop castle. The sense of remoteness is in large part due to the encircling mountains, a terrain which proved useful to the western governments which used **Capo Marárgiu**, 10km to the north, as a training ground for the anti-communist commando ring recently exposed in the so-called Gladio scandal.

From the riverside the corridor-like streets of the old district, **Sa Costa**, follow the contours up the hillside, one above the other, full of medieval gloom. To explore these backstreets, take any road leading up from the **Cathedral**, on the northern side of Bosa's one bridge. Keep climbing for about twenty minutes to reach Bosa's **castle** (daily 10am–1pm & 4–7pm, closing earlier in winter; free), erected by the Malaspina family in 1122 – there's also a road that skirts the back of town, leading round to the castle gate.

From the castle ramparts you can pick out the ex-Cathedral of **San Pietro**, an eleventh-century construction with a lovely Gothic facade added by Cistercian monks a couple of hundred years later. From the bridge, it's a two-kilometre walk to the church. In the other direction, **BOSA MARINA** lies five kilometres downstream on what was the town's original site before its inhabitants decided to shift to a more defensible position. Today it is a conventional minor resort with a small choice of hotels and trattorias, its tiny port and beach in the lee of the former islet of Isola Rossa, now linked to the mainland by a bridge and guarded by a sullen Spanish watchtower.

Practicalities

Bosa's **tourist office** is in Via Ciusa, off Piazza Gioberti (Mon–Sat 10am–1pm & 4–7pm). Most of the **hotels** are in Bosa Marina, though Bosa does have one fine old palazzo just over the river, *Sa Pischedda* (☎0785/373.065; ④). The hotels at Bosa Marina are all close to the sea and much of a muchness, though it does have one of Sardinia's rare **youth hostels**, in Via Sardegna (☎0785/374.380; ①); it's scrupulously clean and not linked to the IYHF, so you don't have to be a member.

Nuoro and the interior

Heading east from Macomer on the private *FCS* line, you can reach **Nuoro** in around two hours; the alternative is to take a *PANI* bus all the way from Oristano (4 daily; 2hr). The huge central province of Nuoro has little in common with Sardinia's modern sun-and-sand image. For many, though, it's the most interesting part of the island, dotted with small and isolated villages which have never known the heel of foreign conquerors. Their inhabitants have retained a fierce sense of independence and loyalty to their traditions, and this is especially true in the ring of once almost impenetrable **Gennargentu mountains**, centred on the island's highest peak, **La Mármora** (1834m). These mountains form the core of the **Barbágia** region, called Barbaria by the Romans who, like their successors, were never able to subdue it, foiled by the guerrilla warfare for which these hidden recesses proved ideal.

Nuoro

"There is nothing to see in Nuoro: which to tell the truth, is always a relief. Sights are an irritating bore," wrote D.H. Lawrence, though he forgot to mention the town's superb position beneath the soaring peak of Monte Ortobene and opposite the sheer and stark heights of Sopramonte. In many respects **NUORO** is little different from the other villages of the region, but no place on the island can match its extraordinary literary fame. This was the town Lawrence made for in his Sardinian excursion of 1921, when it appeared to him "as if at the end of the world, mountains rising sombre behind." The best-known Sard poet, **Sebastiano Satta** (1867–1914) was Nuorese, as was the author **Grazia Deledda** (1871–1936), who won the Nobel Prize for Literature in 1927 in recognition of a writing career devoted to the day-to-day trials and passions of the local villagers. For **Salvatore Satta** (1902–75) – no relation to Sebastiano – "Nuoro was nothing but a perch for the crows," as he wrote in his semi-autobiographical masterpiece, *The Day of Judgement*, his only work, published posthumously to great acclaim. This century little has changed in this insular town despite the unsightly apartment blocks, administrative buildings and banks superimposed upon it.

Nuoro's **old quarter** is the most compelling part of town, spread around the pedestrianised hub of **Corso Garibaldi**, along which the *passeggiata* takes place. After poking around this area, the only other attraction lies in the impressive collection in the town's Museo Etnografico (Tues–Sat 9am–1pm & 3–6/7pm, Sun 9am–1pm; free) on Via Antonio Mereu, a ten-minute walk from the Corso on the other side of Piazza Vittorio Emanuele. The museum has Sardinia's most comprehensive range of local costumes, jewellery, masks, carpets and other handicrafts, arranged in a modern purpose-built complex.

As many as 3000 of the costumes are aired at Nuoro's biggest annual **festival**, the **Sagra del Redentore**, usually taking place on the penultimate Sunday of the month and involving participants from all over the island, but especially the villages of the Barbágia. The dancing and dialect singing may have become somewhat contrived and institutionalised, but it's one of the most vibrant events on the island's calendar.

Practicalities

Nuoro's **train station** is a half-hour walk from the centre of town along Via La Mármora. The *PANI* buses stop at Via Brigata Sássari (parallel to Via La Marmora), while *ARST* buses stop in Piazza Vittorio Emanuele in the old town. Nuoro is hopelessly ill equipped for tourists: its few **hotels** are antiquated, grubby and usually full. The efficient **tourist office** on Piazza Italia (Mon–Fri 9am–1pm & 4–7pm, Sat 9am–1pm) has a list of private rooms that may be the best option for a short stay. Otherwise try Signora Iacobini's unofficial hotel at Via Cedrino 31, off Piazza Italia (☎0784/30.675;

⑤), or the *Mini Hotel* in the centre of town, at Via Brofério 31 (☎0784/33.159; ⑤) – though it's overpriced, the chances are you won't be staying long enough to get too depressed about it.

As with accommodation, Nuoro is not particularly well off for **restaurants**. The best choice and most popular with the Nuorese is the excellent pizzeria-restaurant *Da Gesuino*, at Viale Ciusa 53, on the western end of town. For a lunch-time snack, there's a handy sit-down **bar** on Via Mereu, between the museum and the duomo.

Monte Ortobene

From Nuoro's Piazza Vittorio Emanuele you can take a local bus (3–10 daily) up to the summit of **Monte Ortobene**, 8km away, from where there are striking views over the gorge separating Nuoro from the Sopramonte massif. This is the venue for Nuoro's **Festa del Redentore** on August 29, when a procession from town weaves up the mountain to the bronze **statue** of the Redeemer at the top (955m). Poised in an attitude of swirling motion, the statue is probably the best vantage point, with dizzying views down to the valley floor. The woods round about are perfect for walks and picnics, and there are possibilities for horse-riding at the signposted *Locanda Sedda Ortai*. Delicious – but pricey – local fare can be had at the *Fratelli Sacchi* on Monte Ortobene, also signposted off the only road up the mountain.

Oliena

The nearest village to Nuoro is **OLIENA** (10 buses daily from Nouro), 12km distant on **Monte Corrasi** and visible across the deep valley south of the provincial capital. Rising to 1349m, this dramatically rugged limestone elevation forms part of the Sopramonte massif, famed as the haunt of bandits until relatively recently. Oliena itself prefers its reputation as the producer of one of the island's best wines, a dry, almost black concoction which turns lighter and stronger over the years.

Organised trips around Sopramonte's caves and crags kick off from Oliena. Contact Fabrizio Serri on Via Falae Nodi (☎0784/285.222 – after 1.30pm), or the *Cooperativa Turística Enis*, just outside town in Località Maccione (☎0784/288.363).

Orgósolo

Deeper into the mountains, at the end of a straggly eighteen kilometre road from Oliena, **ORGÓSOLO** is stuck with its label of bandit capital of the island. The clans of Orgósolo, whose menfolk used to spend the greater part of the year away from home with their flocks, have always nursed an animosity towards the settled crop-farmers on Barbágia's fringes, a tension that occasionally broke out into open warfare. On top of this there was the tension between rival clans, expressed in large-scale sheep-rustling and bloody vendettas, such as the *disamistade* (enmity) which engulfed Orgósolo at the beginning of this century. The feud arose from a dispute over the inheritance of the village's richest chieftain, Diego Moro, who died in 1903, and lasted for fourteen years, virtually exterminating the two families involved. Between 1901 and 1954, Orgósolo – population 4000 – achieved an average of one murder every two months.

Perhaps the village's most infamous son is **Graziano Mesina**, the so-called "Scarlet Rose", who won local hearts in the 1960s by robbing only from the rich to give to the poor and only killing for revenge against those who had betrayed him. Roaming at will through the mountains, even granting interviews to reporters and television journalists, he was eventually captured and incarcerated in Sássari prison. Escaping in 1968, he was recaptured near Nuoro and flown by helicopter the same day to appear on television in Cágliari. Mesina last surfaced in July 1992, when he was dispatched to Sardinia from a mainland prison to help negotiate the release of Farouk Kassam, an eight-year-old boy held hostage for seven months in the Barbágia.

Saddled with this semi-legendary background, it is inevitable that Orgósolo should be the destination of a constant dribble of visitors hoping to find some traces of its violent past amid the shabby collection of breeze-blocked grey houses – whose poverty seems a world apart from the whitewashed luxury of the Costa Smeralda, only a couple of hours' drive away. But the villagers have obliged the tourists by providing a vivid collection of **murals**, some of them covering whole houses and shops, portraying village culture, most illustrating the oppression of the landless by the landowners or demanding Sardinian independence. One of them seems intended to shock unsuspecting newcomers: a scarlet face painted onto a rock below the entrance to the village, as if lurking in wait.

Except on Sundays there are between five and ten buses to Orgósolo from Nouro, so it's not necessary to stay over. Should you want to, however, the cheapest **hotel** is the *Petit* on Via Mannu (☎0784/402.009; ③).

The Barbágia

There are dozens of small villages like Orgósolo in the **BARBÁGIA**, interconnected by twisting mountain roads and still, as Salvatore Satta described them in the early years of the century, "minuscule settlements as remote from one another as are the stars." The elderly folk in these tight communities are just about the only people on the island who still routinely wear the traditional local costumes, which otherwise are most likely to be seen during one of the numerous small festivals that punctuate the year. Each village has at least one, for which preparations are made months in advance.

MAMOIADA, 11km west of Orgósolo, is the scene of a highly pagan carnival romp, when masked *mammuthones* representing hunted animals march through the streets, decked in sheepskin with their backs arrayed with rows of jangling goat-bells. **OTTANA**, on the northern fringes of the area – and reckoned to be the dead centre of Sardinia – vies with Mamoiada for its masked and horned carnival horrors. **FONNI**, due south of Mamoiada and at 1000m the island's highest village, has a less gruesome costumed procession in its festival of the Madonna dei Mártiri, held on the Monday following the first Sunday in June.

Each of these villages is primarily a shepherds' community, whose isolated circumstances and economic difficulties in the postwar years led to widescale emigration and, among those who stayed behind, a crime wave. Sheep-rustling and internecine feuding were replaced by the infinitely more lucrative practice of the **kidnapping** and ransoming of wealthy industrialists or their families. This phenomenon reached epidemic proportions during 1966–68 when scores of *carabinieri* were drafted into the area to comb the mountains for the hide-outs, rarely with any success. After a lull in the kidnaps, there has been a resurgence recently, with the front pages dominated by the case of Farouk Kassam, who was kidnapped on the Costa Smeralda and held for seven months, suffering the severance of part of his ear to speed up the ransom payment.

Nowadays, shepherds send their children to university, or they go to seek work in mainland Italy and don't come back. They leave behind slowly atrophying village communities whose salvation is deemed to lie in a greater awareness of their tourist potential as centres for outdoor activities. The **Gennargentu** chain of mountains – the name means "silver gate," referring to the snow that covers them every winter – have the island's only **skiing** facilities on the island's second-highest peak of **Monte Bruncu Spina** (1829m).

Practicalities

Various Barbágia villages offer accommodation from which to explore the region, all of them connected by bus with Nouro and with each other. Nearest to Nouro is **FONNI**, 33km south (5–10 buses from Nouro Mon–Sat), where there is the three-star *Cualbu* (☎0784/57.054; ⑥). **DESULO**, a further 26km south (2–3 buses daily) has a couple of hotels: the *Gennargentu* (☎0784/61.270; ⑤) and *La Nuova* (☎0784/61.251; ③). At **TONARA**, 14km to the west (2–3 buses), you'll find a trio of small hotels: the *Belvedere* (☎0784/63756; ④); *Il Noccioleto* (☎0784/63.923; ④); and *Su Toni* (☎0784/63.420; ④). Finally, **ARITZO**, 15km south of both Desulo and Tonara, has a choice of six hotels, of which the most reasonable are the *Moderno*, on Via Kennedy (☎0784/629.229; ⑤), and *La Capannina*, on the same street (☎0784/629.121; ⑤).

These villages all make good bases for **mountain treks**, best undertaken in spring and summer. From Désulo, for example, it is possible to reach the area's highest peak, La Mármora, by a twelve-kilometre path. Along the way you may see wild pigs, vultures and deer, though you would be lucky to spot one of the rare mouflon, an elegant wild goat with long curved horns – its numbers have been decimated by hunting. For fuller details on walks, you can obtain a handy booklet from Nuoro's tourist office.

The eastern coast

Nuoro province's long **eastern seaboard** is highly developed around the resorts of Siniscola and Posada, but further south it preserves its desolate beauty, virtually untouched apart from a couple of isolated spots around **Orosei** and **Cala Golone**, and, further down, the small port of **Arbatax**. Frequent daily buses connect Cágliari and Nuoro with Tortolì, which is close to Arbatax. Tortolì and Arbatax are also on the narrow-gauge railway which follows an inland route to Cágliari; the full rail journey from the coast to Cágliari takes seven dawdling hours.

Dorgali and Cala Gonone

Centre of the renowned **Cannonau** wine-growing region, **DORGALI** attracts a lot of tourists in summer, both for its craftwork and on account of the recent growth of Cala Gonone, a small port 10km away. Dorgali's restaurants and hotels are generally cheaper than its neighbour's: the cheapest is the *San Pietro* (☎0784/96.142; ⑤).

CALA GONONE is reached going south out of town and turning left into the tunnel that brings you through the mountain wall, from which the road plunges down to the bay. Beautifully sited at the base of the 900-metre-high mountains, this once tiny settlement was until recently accessible only by boat. Now hotels and villas dominate the scene, though these have not entirely spoilt the sense of isolation, and it is worth a visit if only to take advantage of the numerous boat tours to the secluded coves up and down the coast. Among the best are **Cala Luna** and **Cala Sisine**, though if you are here for a short time you would do well to choose a tour that combines pauses at these swimming stops with exploration of the deep grottoes that pit the shore.

Most famous of these is the **Grotta del Bue Marino** – touted as the last refuge of the Mediterranean monk seal, or "sea ox", in Italian waters. Whether or not you see them, it's a good expedition anyway, as this is one of Sardinia's most spectacular caves, a luminescent gallery filled with remarkable natural sculptures, resembling organ pipes, wedding cakes and even human heads – one of them is known as *Dante*, after an imagined resemblance to the poet.

Thirteen **hotels** are listed for Cala Gonone, so there's no shortage of choice. Near the port are the *Cala Luna* (☎0784/93.133; ⑥), the *Bue Marino* (☎0784/93.130; ④) and the *Píccolo* (☎0784/93.232; ⑥); most others don't have seafront views. There's a choice of eateries too, ranging from fast food to gourmet parlours. In the latter category, the *Miramare*, on Lungomare Palmasera, is rated highly.

Hikes from Cala Gonone and Dorgali

South of Cala Gonone lies one of Sardinia's last truly unspoilt tracts: swerving inland along the ridge of the Flumineddu River, walled on the other side by the Sopramonte massif, the new road brings you into a majestic mountain landscape, devoid of human life. Stefano Ardito, in his *Backpacking and Walking in Italy*, outlines two long-distance hikes in these wild parts, which he describes as among the best in the whole Mediterranean basin.

One of these walks – a two- to three-day hike – follows the coast **from Cala Gonone** to Cala Sisine, at which point the route wanders inland, up the Sisine canyon, as far as the solitary church of San Pietro, from which a track leads down to BAUNEI. The second, shorter hike follows the course of the Flumineddu River **from Dorgali** and takes you after a couple of hours into the **Gorruppu gorge**, though further exploration requires mountaineering skills and even dinghies to negotiate the small lakes in the heart of the gorge, which terminates at Baunei.

Tortolì and Arbatax

From Baunei the road descends steeply to **TORTOLÌ**, 5km inland from the port of **ARBATAX**, which is little more than a paper factory, a few bars and a port from where ferries ply to Genoa and Civitavecchia two or three times weekly. The small beach here is famous for its red rocks, but there are better bathing spots outside town – especially south, where there is a series of sand and rock beaches at **Lido Orri**. The seafront **tourist office** (summer daily 9am–7pm, open sporadically in winter) has information on sea **excursions** from Arbatax, including the Grotta del Bue Marino for L50,000 (see above). The *Tirrenia* office, for advance **ferry tickets**, is on the right after the tourist office kiosk (Mon–Fri & Sun 9am–1pm & 4–7.30pm, Sat 9am–1pm, plus Sun & Wed 10pm–midnight); you can also buy tickets on the day of departure from the booth at the port.

There are several small hotels in the Arbatax area, most of them difficult to reach on foot. Best value are the *Villagio Telis* (☎0782/667.126; ⑥) and the *Supersonic* (☎0782/623.512; ⑤), both a couple of kilometres south of the port in the Frailis area. Tortolì also has a small selection, cheapest being the *Splendor* on Viale Arbatax (☎0782/623.037; ④).

OLBIA, GALLURA AND THE COSTA SMERALDA

The largest town in Sardinia's northeastern wedge, **Olbia** owes its recent phenomenal growth to the huge influx of tourists to one of the Mediterranean's loveliest stretches of coast, the **Costa Smeralda**, whose five-star development transformed the economy of the entire island. Elsewhere on the coast it's still possible to have fun without having stacks of money: there are miles of shoreline still undeveloped and a profusion of minor islands, over sixty in all, which you can explore on various boat tours. A daily ferry service from **Palau** links the biggest islands of **Maddalena** and **Caprera**, while further west **Santa Teresa di Gallura** boasts some wonderful coves and beaches.

This indented northern shore fringes the region of **Gallura**, whose raw red and wind-sculpted granite mountains imbue the area with its unique edge-of-the-wilderness appeal. There is a hidden world within here that most tourists never discover, thickly forested with the cork-oaks which, after tourism, provide most of Gallura's revenue.

Olbia

When the English barrister John Tyndale visited **OLBIA** in the 1840s, he compared its Greek name, meaning "happy," with the state he found it in: "A more perfect misnomer, in the present condition of the town, could not be found. . . . The whole district suffers severely from intemperie. The wretched approach across these marshes is worthy of the town itself. The houses, none of which have an elegant or neat appearance, are built mostly of granite, and are whitewashed, as if to give a greater contrast to the filth and dirt within and around them."

The "intemperie" of which Tyndale complained was malaria, which, together with the marshes and the filth, has long vanished as a result of the land-drainage schemes and DDT-saturation of the 1950s. Olbia today is once more a happy place, enjoying its new-found income from the tourists pouring through the docks and airport. Few of these tourists stay, however, for Olbia – the least Sardinian of all the island's towns – is awash with traffic and ugly apartment blocks which spoil what might once have been an attractive seafront. All the same its numerous bars and restaurants are generally crowded with tourists, sailors from the port and US service personnel from the NATO base on Palau and the Maddalena archipelago, who venture into town to spend their dollars and stalk the main Corso Umberto.

If you're stuck for an afternoon here, you might as well visit Olbia's only item of historical interest, the little basilica of **San Símplicio**, on the street of the same name. The simple granite structure is set in a piazza apart from Olbia's bustle, making it a good spot for a sit-down. Claimed to be the most important medieval monument in the whole of Gallura – a region hardly famed for its artistic heritage – the church formed part of the great Pisan reconstruction programme of the eleventh and twelfth centuries. Its murky interior has three aisles separated by pillars and columns recycled from Roman constructions, and even the stoup for the holy water was formerly an urn that once held cremated ashes. Along the walls is an array of Roman funerary slabs, with fragments of inscription still visible on some.

The church is the venue for Olbia's biggest *festa*, six days of processions, costumed dancing, poetry recitations, traditional games and fireworks around May 15, commemmorating San Símplicio's martyrdom in the fourth century.

Practicalities

Ferries from Civitavecchia, Genoa and Livorno dock at the former island of Isola Bianca, now connected by a two-kilometre causeway along which you can walk or take an hourly #3 bus. For frequencies of service, see the box on p.863. There are *Tirrenia* offices at the port (daily 8.30–11.30am & 4.45–11pm; ☎0789/24.691) and at the bottom of Corso Umberto (Mon–Sat 8.30am–1pm & 4.30–6pm), where at no. 187 you'll find the *Navarma* office (☎0789/27.927). *Sardinia Ferries* for Livorno leave from Golfo Aranci, 15km up the coast (8 buses daily); their office in Olbia is at Corso Umberto 4 (☎0789/25.200). Book early for all departures.

Olbia's **airport** is connected by hourly buses (#2) to the central Piazza Regina Margherita; tickets cost L1300, and can be bought from the airport bar. Taxis cost about L15,000. **Trains** for Sássari and Cágliari run several times daily from the station just off Corso Umberto, where there is a **left-luggage office** (daily 6am–10pm). There is also a station at the ferry quay, though not all trains stop here. The *ARST* **bus station** is round the corner on the Corso.

The helpful **tourist office** is on Via Piro, a side street running off the Corso (June–Sept Mon–Sat 8.30am–1pm & 4–6pm, Sun 9am–1pm; Oct–May closed Sat afternoons and all day Sun; ☎0789/21.453).

There is a good selection of **hotels** in Olbia, though mostly on the expensive side. Best choices are the two hotels on Via Garibaldi, parallel to Corso Umberto: the

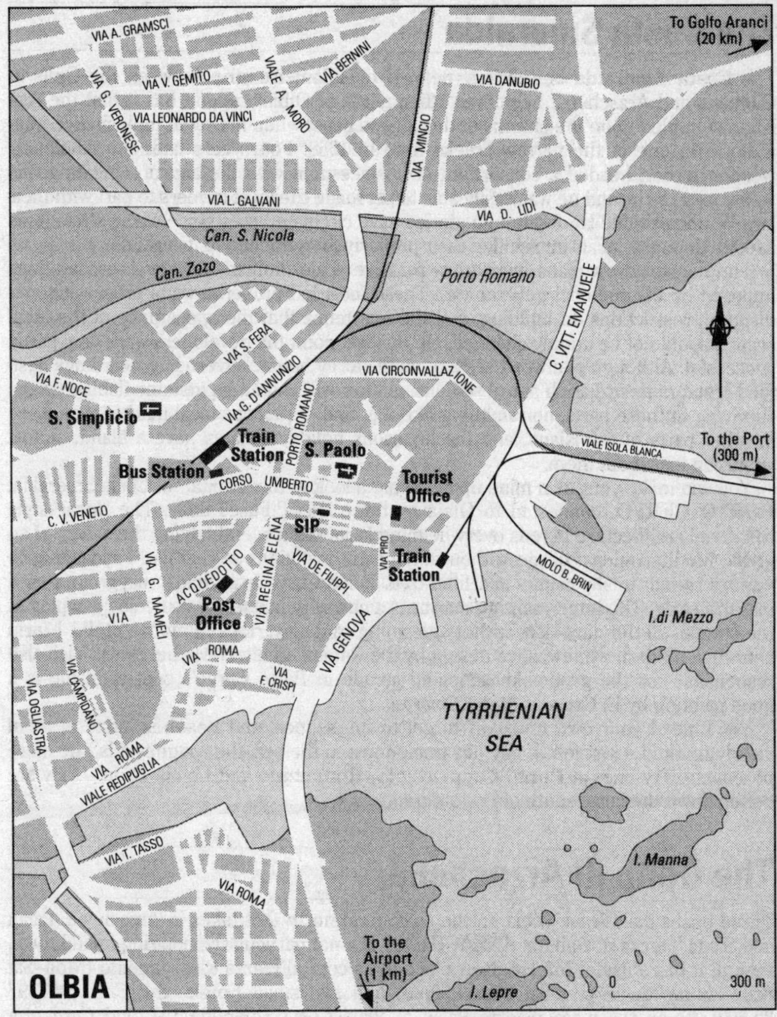

Terranova (☎0789/22.395; ④) and the *Minerva* (☎0789/21.190; ④) – both accepting only half-board guests in August, adding L10,000 to the bill. The nearest **campsite** is 10km south of town in Multa Maria, served by two buses daily (June–Sept; ☎0789/36.009).

As for **eating**, the small and elegant *Zhanto*, just off the Corso on Via delle Terme, offers excellent value and is always busy with locals. For a decent pizza, try the subterranean *La Lanterna*, off the other side of the Corso on Via Olbia: their speciality is a vegetarian pizza. Good for breakfast is the *Caffè Cosimino* on Piazza Margherita; the only café with fresh cornetti, it sports faded photos of old Olbia on the walls.

The Costa Smeralda

The **Costa Smeralda** is a strictly defined ten-kilometre strip between the Gulfs of Cugnana and Arzachena, beginning 10km north of Olbia. Legend has it that the Aga Khan stumbled upon the charms of this jagged coast when his yacht took shelter from a storm in one of the narrow creeks here in 1958. Four years later the fabulously wealthy tycoon headed a consortium of businessmen with the aim of exploiting this wild coastal strip, and he was easily able to persuade the local farmers to part with their largely uncultivable land – though stories have circulated ever since of the stratagems used to dupe the locals into selling their property for a fraction of its value.

The consortium's plans were on a massive scale, limited only by the conditions imposed by the regional government. These included proper sewage processing and disposal, restrictions on building, and the insistence that the appearance of the landscape should not be unduly changed. On this last point the developers were only partly successful. Although you won't see any multi-storey hotels, advertising hoardings, fast-food restaurants or garish petrol stations, neither will you find a genuine fishing village surviving in these parts, nor anything like the kind of raucous local markets you'll see in other parts of the island, and the luxurious holiday villages have a bland, almost suburban feel about them.

You can make your own mind up by taking a look at the "capital" of Costa Smeralda, **PORTO CERVO**, connected to Olbia by three *ARST* buses daily. The "local"-style rustic red architecture here is overwhelming in its artifice, embodying the dream of an idyllic Mediterranean village without any of the irritations of real life. Fascinating to wander round, totally crime- and litter-free, Porto Cervo is a child's playground on a massive scale. The huge yachting marina is a curiosity in itself, if you enjoy gawping at the baubles of the ultra-rich, with its gleaming ranks overlooked by the **Stella Maris** church, a modern whitewashed design by the Roman architect Michel Busiri Vici, also responsible for the grotto-like shopping arcade in Porto Cervo's centre. Inside is a good painting by El Greco, a *Mater Dolorosa*.

You'll need your own transport to get to the sequestered **beaches**, none of them clearly marked – just follow any dirt track down to the sea, the rougher it is, the more promising. Try ones at **Punta Cappricciolo, Romazzino** and **Liscia Ruia** – they are dotted down the coast south of Porto Cervo.

The Golfo di Arzachena

Three buses daily leave Olbia on the coast road north that takes in Arzachena, Palau and Santa Teresa di Gallura. **ARZACHENA** is a not particularly inspiring inland town, though it has a useful **information** office in its central Piazza Risorgimento (Mon–Sat 8am–1.30pm & 3–7pm; Sat 8am–1.30pm) and two small **hotels**: the *Citti* (☎0789/82.662; ⑤) on the main road to Palau at Viale Costa Smeralda 197, and *Casa Mia* (☎0789/82.790; ④), with a restaurant, off the Olbia road at Via Torricelli 3.

Outside the luxury zone but sharing many of the Costa Smeralda's natural advantages, the **Golfo di Arzachena** is a deep narrow bay with facilities concentrated around the resort village of **CANNIGIONE** – a small fishing port and yachting resort linked by frequent buses with Arzachena. Virtually all Cannigione's hotels cost upwards of L80,000 per night – the cheapest is the *Baja* on Via Nazionale (☎0789/88.010; ⑥), which like all the others is open from May to October only.

A couple of kilometres beyond Cannigione, the road curves round the side of the bay to LACONIA, dotted with villas, hotels and a couple of **campsites**: the *Golfo di Arzachena* (May–Oct; ☎0789/88.101) and the *Villaggio Isuledda* (March–Oct; ☎0789/86.003), better equipped and right on the shore, with excellent bathing spots.

The Maddalena Islands

From PALAU, 10km up the coast from Cannigione, ferries leave every 45 minutes or so for the main island of the Maddalena archipelago, **La Maddalena**, from which you can reach **Caprera**, the island on which Garibaldi spent the last third of his life. Be warned that it's a hectic bustle for tickets (L2000 per person, L5000 for a medium-sized car), and long queues are common.

La Maddalena

It takes twenty minutes to cross what Nelson called "Agincourt Sound" from Palau to the port and sole town on **LA MADDALENA**. The town, bearing the same name as the island, is a cheerful place with a population of about 15,000, swollen by a large number of Italian and US sailors who lend the town a garrison feel. Their headquarters are on the eastern side of town, a drab area of barracks and sentries, though the main military installations and submarine base are situated on the neighbouring island of Santo Stéfano – briefly captured by Napoleon in 1793 in an abortive attempt to take Sardinia.

The **tourist office** is on the seafront road, Via XX Settembre (Mon–Fri 8am–2pm & 4–7pm, Sat 8am–2pm). The town is not particularly well off for **hotels**; cheapest are the *Arcipélago* at Via Indipendenza Traversa 2 (☎0789/727.328; ⑤), and the state-run *Il Gabbiano* at Via Giúlio Césare 20 (☎0789/737.007; ⑤). Addresses of **rooms** to rent are available from the tourist office, or you could ask around in bars. There are also two **campsites**: *Il Sole*, on Via Indipendenza (all year; ☎0789/727.130), and *Maddalena* in the Moneta district, facing Caprera (June–Sept; ☎0789/738.333).

Buses run to various parts of the island from near the Bank of Sardinia at the end of Via XX Settembre, every fifteen minutes in summer (every two hours in winter). A good way of getting round the island is by **bike**, for rent from a small shop near the tourist office (L35,000 per day), or by **moped** (L60,000). The island invites aimless wandering and offers a variety of sandy and rocky beaches in mostly undeveloped coves. The beaches on the northern and western coasts are most attractive, particularly those around the tiny port of MADONETTA, 5km west of Le Maddelena, and at CALA LUNGA, 5km north of town.

Caprera

Between October and May half of **CAPRERA** is closed off for military purposes, but there is always plenty of space left to roam this protected woody parkland, which is undeveloped apart from Garibaldi's house in the centre and a Club-Med complex that offers the island's only tourist facilities.

Giuseppe Garibaldi (1807–82) came to live in Caprera in 1855, after a twenty-year exile from Italy. It was from here that he embarked on his spectacular conquest of Sicily and Naples in 1861, accompanied by his thousand red-shirts, and it was here that he returned after his campaigns to resume a simple farming life. Having bought the northern part of the island for £360, he spent much of his time writing his memoirs and some bad novels. His neighbour was an Englishman named Collins, with whom he had some celebrated disagreements concerning their wandering goat-herds, as a result of which Garibaldi built a wall dividing their properties, which can still be seen. After Collins' death in 1864 a group of English admirers provided the money for Garibaldi to buy the rest of Caprera from his ex-neighbour's family.

The **museum** (Tues–Sat 9am–1pm, Sun 9am–12.30pm; L6000) is in Garibaldi's old house, the elegant South American-style **Casa Bianca**, which has been preserved pretty much as he left it. Visitors are escorted past the bed where he slept, a smaller one where he died, various scrolls, manifestos and pronouncements, a pair of ivory and gold binoculars given to him by Edward VII and a letter from London, dated 1867, conferring on him honorary presidency of the National Reform League. A stopped clock and a wall-calendar indicate the precise time when he died.

The tour ends with Garibaldi's tomb in the garden, its rough granite contrasting with the more pompous tombs of his last wife and five of his children. Garibaldi had requested to be cremated, but following the wishes of his son Menotti his corpse was stuffed. In 1932, fifty years after his death, his tomb was opened to reveal the body perfectly intact.

Santa Teresa di Gallura

There are two ways of moving on to **SANTA TERESA DI GALLURA**, Sardinia's most northerly port: by boat from La Maddalena (1 daily; L4000), and by bus from Olbia, passing a succession of lovely bays, some dramatic rocky coastline, and a handful of campsites. Santa Teresa's **tourist office** is on the main Piazza Vittorio Emanuele (Mon–Fri 9am–1pm, 4–7pm; Sat 9am–1pm); there is also a summer-only booth down by the port. *Navarma*, *Tirrenia* and *Saremar* operate ferries from here to Bonifacio in Corsica (2–8 daily; 1hr; L15,000).

Of Santa Teresa's plentiful central **hotels**, the best is perhaps the *Scano* on Via Lázio (☎0789/754.447; ⑤). There are several more hotels outside town, where they are best placed to take advantage of some of Sardinia's most alluring **beaches**, all with superb views over to Corsica, just 11km away. To the east, **Punta Falcone** and **La Marmorata** are popular spots, while 3km west of Santa Teresa, **Capo Testa** is one of Sardinia's finest bathing localities, a rocky promontory surrounded by turquoise sea. A decent **hotel** is the *Da Colomba* at Capo Testa, which, like most here, is open in summer only (☎0789/754.272; ④).

SASSARI, ALGHERO AND LOGUDORO

The western half of the province is a green, fertile region, hilly rather than mountainous, though the hills get craggier and more dramatic as you move south and east from **Sássari**, the provincial capital. Sássari is for many the island's most interesting town, with its crowded medieval centre and teeming modern squares. As a holiday destination, however, it has limited appeal, being inland and lacking enough entertainment to justify more than a couple of afternoons or evenings here. More popular is **Alghero**, the island's oldest resort as well as its major fishing port. Further inland, the heartlands of the old *giudicato* of **Logudoro**, the "Land of Gold", offer some fine examples of Pisan architecture, their refinement in sharp contrast to the ramshackle but equally grand *nuraghi*, of which the area has a rich selection.

Sássari

Sardinia's second city, **SÁSSARI** has 110,000 inhabitants, less than half Cágliari's population, yet it thinks of itself as the most important, most elegant, most up-to-date town on the island. Historically, while Cágliari was Pisa's base of operations during the Middle Ages, Sássari was the Genoan capital, ruled by the Doria family, whose power reached throughout the Mediterranean. Under the Aragonese it became an important centre of Spanish hegemony, and the Spanish stamp is still strong, not least in its

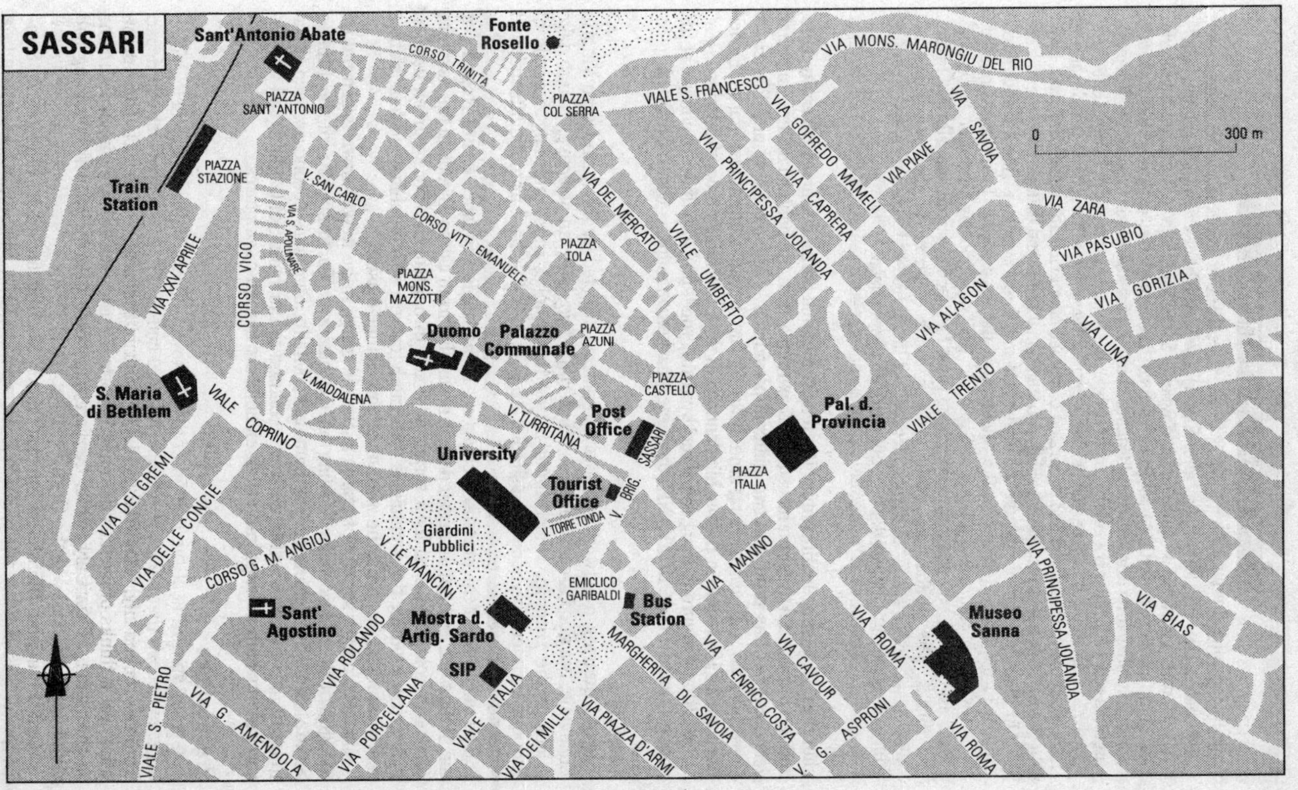
SASSARI
Sant'Antonio Abate
Fonte Rosello
PIAZZA SANT 'ANTONIO
CORSO TRINITA
PIAZZA COL SERRA
VIALE S. FRANCESCO
VIA MONS. MARONGIU DEL RIO
0
300 m
Train Station
PIAZZA STAZIONE
V. SAN CARLO
VIA S. APOLLINARE
CORSO VITT. EMANUELE
VIA DEL MERCATO
VIALE UMBERTO I
VIA PRINCIPESSA JOLANDA
VIA CAPRERA
VIA GOFREDO MAMELI
VIA PIAVE
VIA SAVOIA
VIA ZARA
VIA PASUBIO
VIA GORIZIA
VIA LUNA
VIA ALAGON
VIALE TRENTO
VIA XXV APRILE
CORSO VICO
PIAZZA TOLA
PIAZZA MONS. MAZZOTTI
Duomo
Palazzo Communale
PIAZZA AZUNI
PIAZZA CASTELLO
S. Maria di Bethlem
V. MADDALENA
VIALE COPRINO
V. TURRITANA
Post Office
SASSARI
Pal. d. Provincia
University
PIAZZA ITALIA
Tourist Office
V. BRIG.
V. TORRE TONDA
Giardini Pubblici
VIA DEI GREMI
VIA DELLE CONCIE
CORSO G. M. ANGIOJ
V. LE MANCINI
EMICLICO GARIBALDI
Bus Station
VIA MANNO
VIA PRINCIPESSA JOLANDA
VIA BIAS
Sant' Agostino
Mostra d. Artig. Sardo
SIP
VIA ROLANDO
VIA ENRICO COSTA
VIA CAVOUR
VIA ROMA
Museo Sanna
MARGHERITA DI SAVOIA
VIALE S. PIETRO
VIA G. AMENDOLA
VIA PORCELLANA
VIALE ITALIA
VIA DEI MILLE
VIA PIAZZA D'ARMI
V. G. ASPRONI
VIA ROMA

SÁSSARI'S FESTIVALS

One of Sardinia's showiest festivals – the **Cavalcata** – takes place in Sássari on **Ascension Day** (the fortieth day after Easter), the highlight of a month of cultural activities. Northern Sardinia's equivalent to Cágliari's Sant'Efisio festival, it attracts hundreds of richly costumed participants from villages throughout the province and beyond. Originally staged for the benefit of visiting Spanish kings or other dignitaries, it lapsed until its revival forty years ago by, of all people, the local branch of the Rotary Club. The festival is divided into three stages, the morning featuring a horseback parade and a display of the embroidered and decorated costumes unique to each village, followed by a hectic *palio*, or horse race, and ending with traditional songs and dances.

On the afternoon of **August 14** there is a much more local affair– **I Candelieri**, linked to the Pisan devotion to the Madonna of the Assumption. It became a regular event when an outbreak of plague in Sássari in 1652 mysteriously abated on the eve of the feast of the Assumption, since when the ritual has been repeated annually as a token of thanks. The rumbustious event involves bands of *gremi*, or medieval guilds of merchants, artisans and labourers, decked out in Spanish-style costumes and bearing gigantic wooden "candlesticks," 8m tall, through the old town.

churches. In the sixteenth century the Jesuits founded Sardinia's first **university** here, and the intellectual tradition has survived, particularly in the political sphere. In recent years, Sássari has produced two national presidents – Antonio Segni and Francesco Cossiga – as well as the long-time head of the Italian Communist Party, Enrico Berlinguer (1922–84) – a cousin, incidentally, of the Christian Democrat Cossiga.

Note that if you're coming to Sássari by **train**, you'll probably have to change at the nondescript town of CHILIVANI, sometimes marked on maps as Ozieri-Chilivani.

The City

The **old quarter**, a network of alleys and piazzas bisected by the main Corso Vittorio Emanuele, is a good area for aimless wandering. If you want an objective, though, take a look at the **Duomo**, whose florid facade is Sardinia's most imposing example of Baroque architecture, added to a simpler Aragonese-Gothic base from the fifteenth and sixteenth centuries.

The only other item worth searching out is the late-Renaissance **Fonte Rosello**, at the bottom of a flight of dilapidated steps accessible from Corso Trinità, in the northern part of the old town. Fed by a spring in which throngs of the city's women used to scrub their clothes, the fountain is elaborately carved with dolphins and four statues representing the seasons, the work of Genoese stone-masons.

Connected by a series of squares to the old quarter, the **newer town** is centred on the grandiose Piazza Italia. Leading off the piazza is Via Roma, site of the **Museo Sanna** (Mon–Sat 9am–2pm, Sun 9am–1pm; L4000), Sardinia's second archaeological museum. It's a good substitute if you've missed the main one at Cágliari, and like the Cágliari museum its most interesting exhibits are nuraghic sculptures.

Practicalities

The **train station** is at the bottom of the old town's Corso Vittorio Emanuele, with a luggage deposit that closes at 8.45pm. All local and *ARST* **buses** arrive at and depart from the semicircular Emiciclo Garibaldi, south of the tourist office. *PANI* buses run from Via Bellieni 5, just off Via Roma. Free buses connect **Fertília airport** with the *Alitalia* office at Via Cágliari 30; they are scheduled to coincide with incoming and outgoing flights.

Sássari's **tourist office** is on the first floor of Via Brigate Sássari 19 (Mon–Fri 8am–1.45pm & 3.30–6.30pm; ☎079/231.331), near Piazza Italia. **Staying** in Sássari can be a real problem, and you'd do well to ring ahead to ensure availability. The best budget option is the tumbledown *Pensione Famiglia* at Viale Umberto 65 (☎079/239.543; ③); otherwise try the *Giusy* (☎079/233.327; ④) conveniently near the station on Piazza Sant'Antonio. On the other hand, you'll find a good range of **restaurants** in town: try *Da Peppina*, in Vícolo Pigozzi, an alley off Corso Vittorio Emanuele – a good place to sample the local speciality of horsemeat. Nearby, at no. 148 on the Corso, is the *Pizzeria al Corso*, serving other things besides pizzas. For a bit more class, try the arty, candle-lit *Liberty* further up the Corso on Piazza Sauro.

Around Sássari: inland Logudoro

Inland from Sássari there are few places you would consider staying, but there are a couple that are well worth a stop en route to somewhere else – though a car is generally necessary. In the middle of the **Logudoro** countryside, right on the main Sássari–Olbia SS 597 some 15km from Sássari (and also glimpsable from the Sássari–Chilivani train), rises the unmissable tall bell-tower of **Santa Trinità di Saccárgia**, its striking zebra-striped facade marking its Pisan origins. Built in 1116, the church owes its remote location to a divine visitation, informing the wife of the *giudice* of Logudoro that she was pregnant. It has survived remarkably well, with lovely Gothic capitals at the top of the porch as you enter the rather gloomy interior, where there is little to distract attention from the stark walls apart from some faded thirteenth-century frescoes.

There is another Pisan relic 30km south of Sássari – the twelfth-century church of **San Pietro di Sorres**, perched on a bluff with sweeping views, near the villages of BONNANARO and BORUTTA. Formerly a cathedral, the church shows more French influence in its ornate style than Sardinia's other Pisan churches, being grander and tidier, though the interior is disappointing.

A couple of kilometres further on, the road leads straight past one of the island's greatest prehistoric monuments, the **Nuraghe Sant'Antine** (daily 9am–sunset; free). Located in the heart of the so-called Valle dei Nuraghi, an area liberally dotted with the ancient structures, this one stands only a few hundred metres from TORRALBA train station, making the site easily visitable. Of the dozens here, this nuraghic palace is the biggest and most impressive, hence its common name **Nuraghe Majore**, and is thought to date back to the fourteenth century BC. Overlooking the scattered ruins of a village as well as later Carthaginian and Roman additions, the central complex consists of three external bastions connected by a defensive wall, grouped around the original massive three-storey tower, with walls up to five metres thick and sixteen high.

The **Museo di Torralba** (daily summer 9am–1pm & 3–7pm; winter 8am–2pm; L3000), two and a half kilometres away in Torralba village, features a small collection of finds from the site as well as a model of the *nuraghe*'s original appearance and details of its excavation. There are also rooms devoted to the local costume, with fascinating old photos of the everyday dress of the people of Logudoro.

Alghero

ALGHERO is a very rare Italian phenomenon: a tourist town that is also a flourishing fishing port, giving it an economic base entirely independent of the summer masses. The predominant flavour here is Catalan, owing to a wholesale Hispanicisation that followed the overthrow of the Doria family by Pedro IV of Aragon in 1354, a process so thorough that it became known as "Barcelonetta". The traces are still strong in the old town today, with its flamboyant churches, wrought-iron balconies and narrow cobbled streets named in both Italian and Catalan. Beyond the stout girdle of walls enclosing

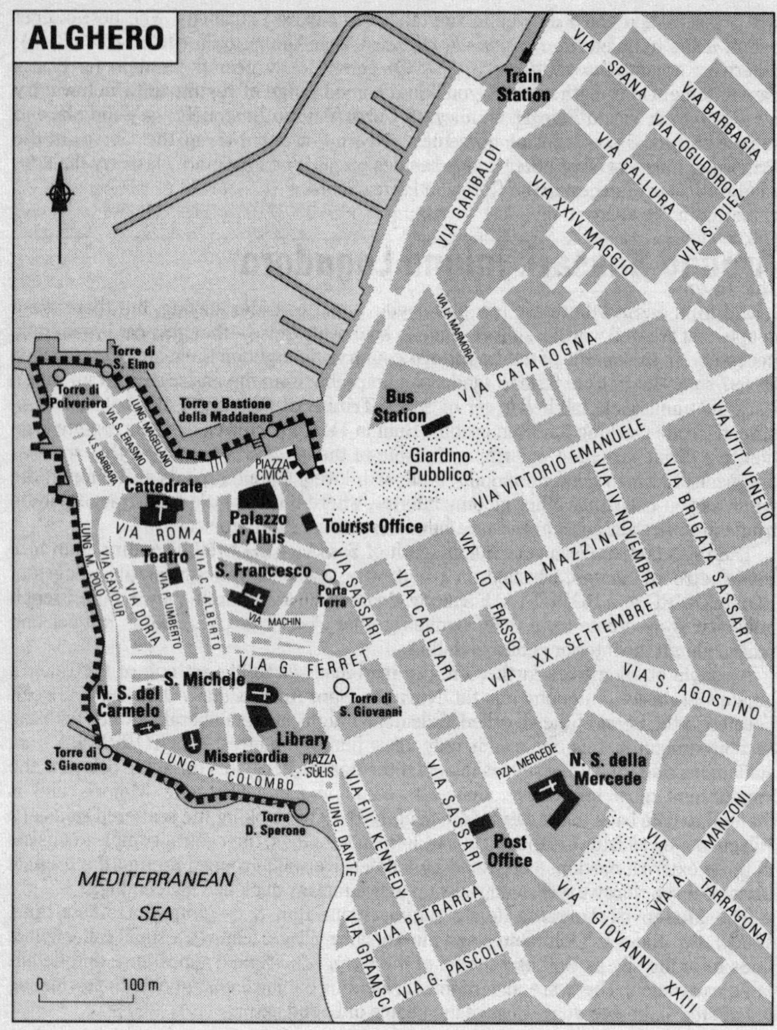

this historic core, the new town's grid of parallel streets have little of interest except their restaurants and hotels.

Arrival and accommodation

Trains linked with Sássari arrive some way out of the centre, connected to the port by shuttle buses. **Buses** arrive in Via Catalogna, on the Giardino Púbblico. Alghero's efficient **tourist office** is on the corner of the Giardino Púbblico, its multilingual staff equipped with reams of maps, accommodation lists and tour details (May–Sept daily 8am–8pm; Oct–April Mon–Sat 8am–2pm; ☎079/979.262).

Alghero's best-value **hotel** is the *San Francesco* (☎079.979.258; ④), in the heart of the old town at Via Machin 2, just behind San Francesco church; each of its clean and quiet rooms has a bathroom. If it's full, try the *Normandie*, on Via Enrico Mattei in the newer part of town, between Via Kennedy and Via Giovanni XXIII (☎079/975.302; ③). Two kilometres out of town, *La Mariposa* **campsite** (April–Oct; ☎079/950.480) has direct access to the beach. Alghero's *Giuliani* **youth hostel** (April–Oct; ☎079/930.353; ①) is actually 6km along the coast at FERTILIA, reachable by local bus. Ring first to check availability.

A good way to get around the town and its environs is by **bike**: *Cicloexpress* at Via Lamarmora 39 (also at the port in summer) charge L50,000 per day for a Vespa, L25,000 for a moped, L12,000 for a bicycle.

The Town

A walk around the old town should take in the series of seven defensive **towers** which dominate Alghero's centre and its surrounding walls. From the **Giardino Púbblico**, the **Porta Terra** is the first of these massive bulwarks – known as the Jewish Tower, it was erected at the expense of the prosperous Jewish community before their expulsion in 1492. Beyond is a puzzle of lanes, at the heart of which the pedestrianised Via Carlo Alberto, Via Principe Umberto and Via Roma have most of the bars and shops. At the bottom of Via Umberto stands Alghero's sixteenth-century **Cattedrale**, where Spanish viceroys stopped to take a preliminary oath before taking office in Cágliari. Its unprepossessing entrance is round the other side on Via Manno; inside, the lofty nave's alternating pillars and columns rise to an impressive octagonal dome.

Most of Alghero's finest architecture dates from the same period, and is built in a similar Catalan-Gothic style. Two of the best examples are a short walk away: the **Palazzo d'Albis** on Piazza Cívica, and the elegantly austere Jewish palace **Palau Reial** in Via Sant'Erasmo.

Outside the old quarter, most of the tourist activity revolves around the **port**, its wide quay nudged by rows of colourful fishing boats and bordered by bars. The town's beaches begin further north, backed by hotels, many of the older ones converted from villas formerly owned by the expatriate community of central Europeans who fled here after World War I.

Neptune's Grotto

The best of the excursions you can take from the port is to **Neptune's Grotto**, with departures several times daily in summer: tickets cost L15,000, not counting the entry charge to the grotto. The fifteen-minute boat ride west along the coast takes you past the long bay of Porto Conte as far as the point of **Capo Caccia**, where the spectacular sheer cliffs are riddled by deep marine caves. They include the **Grotta Verde** and **Grotta dei Ricami** – visited on some tours – but the most impressive is the **Grotta di Nettuno** (daily April–Sept 9am–6pm; Oct–March 9am–2pm; L9000), a long snaking passage delving far into the rock, into which half-hour tours are led, single-file, on the hour every hour, past dramatically lit and fantastical stalagmites and stalactites.

A cheaper alternative to the boat is to take a **bus** to Capo Caccia from the main bus terminal (L3000). Once you are deposited at the end of the line, there's a 654-step descent down the Escala del Cabirol, a highly scenic route whose Catalan name means "goat's steps," presumably a reference to the only animal that could negotiate the perilous path before the construction of the stairway in 1954. On the way back, leave some time before the bus leaves for a well-earned ice cream at the bar opposite the bus stop.

Eating and drinking

Alghero's **restaurants** are renowned for their fish and seafood, always fresh, inventively prepared and tastefully presented – spring and winter are the best seasons. The *Corsaro* on Via Columbano is an excellent choice, as are *La Lépanto* on Via Carlo

Alberto and *Da Pietro*, at Via Machin 20, though none could be described as budget places. For cheaper meals, you're better off trying the right-angled streets of the new town, for instance Via Mazzini, where the *Ristorante Mazzini*, at no. 59, serves decent fare at modest prices and has a wood-fired oven for pizzas. For snacks, the fast-food joints by the port aren't bad.

There is an abundant supply of decent **bars** to repair to when required. The *Mill Pub* in Via Maiorca has live music nightly at 11pm, but the best venue is the vaulted *Totem* pub at Via Minerva 22, with good sounds and atmosphere.

Stintino and Pelosa

The tiny village of **STINTINO**, on Sardinia's northwestern tip, was until recently nothing more than a remote jumble of fisher cottages jammed between two narrow harbours. Fortunately its discovery by the tourist industry has not drastically altered it, and it remains a small, laid-back village and the only centre in the tongue of land forming the western arm of the **Golfo di Asinara**. Most of the sunning and swimming takes place further up the coast at La Pelosa, but the only cheapish **accommodation** in the area is in Stintino itself: the *Lina* (☎079/523.071; ⑤) at Via Lepanto 38, or the *Silvestrino* (☎079/523.007; ⑥) at Via Sássari 12, which has an excellent trattoria, specialising in lobster soup. You can also **rent rooms** in Stintino for about L30,000 per person. One **bus** runs from Alghero to Stintino at noon each day, going via Sássari.

Five kilometres up the road from Stintino a collection of tourist villages clutter up the otherwise idyllic promontory of **La Pelosa** – reached by taxi or hired bike from Stintino. Hotels and self-catering apartments back some of Sardinia's most deluxe **beaches**, with views out to the isles of Piana and the larger, elongated **Asinara**, only known habitat of a miniature white ass from which the island takes its name. Close though it is, Asinara is unfortunately out of bounds, having been a prison-island since the end of the last century, when its inhabitants were moved to Stintino.

travel details

Trains

Alghero to: Sássari (10 daily; 50min).

Arbatax to: Cágliari (1–2 daily; 7hr).

Cágliari to: Arbatax (1–2 daily; 7hr); Macomer (7 daily; 2hr); Olbia (4 daily; 5hr); Oristano (7 daily; 1hr–1hr 30 min); Sássari (4 daily; 4hr).

Olbia to: Cágliari (4 daily; 5hr); Macomer (4 daily; 2hr); Oristano (4 daily; 3hr); Sássari (10 daily; 2hr).

Oristano to: Cágliari (7 daily; 1hr–1hr 30 min); Macomer (10 daily; 1hr); Olbia (4 daily; 3hr); Sássari (7 daily; 2–3hr).

Sássari to: Alghero (10 daily; 50min); Cágliari (6 daily; 4hr); Macomer (6 daily; 2hr); Olbia (10 daily; 2hr); Oristano (6 daily; 3hr).

Macomer to: Nuoro (4 daily; 2hr).

Nuoro to: Macomer (4 daily; 2hr).

Buses

Alghero to: Bosa (5 daily; 45min); Sássari (10 daily; 50min).

Cágliari to: Macomer (5 daily; 2hr); Nuoro (4 daily; 3hr); Oristano (5 daily; 1hr); Sássari (7 daily; 3hr 15min–4hr).

Macomer to: Bosa (3 daily; 30min); Cágliari (5 daily; 2hr); Nuoro (4 daily; 1hr); Oristano (5 daily; 50min); Sássari (4 daily; 1hr 15min).

Olbia to: Arzachena (5 daily; 1hr 15min); Palau (5 daily; 1hr 30min); Porto Cervo (5 daily; 45min); Santa Teresa di Gallura (5 daily; 2hr); Sássari (2 daily; 2hr).

Oristano to: Cágliari (5 daily; 1hr); Macomer (4–5 daily; 1hr); Nuoro (4–5 daily; 2hr); Sássari (4 daily; 2hr 15min).

Sássari to: Alghero (10 daily; 50min); Bosa (4 daily; 2hr 20min); Cágliari (5 daily; 4hr); Olbia (2 daily; 2hr); Stintino (4–5 daily; 1hr 10min).

Ferries

Arbatax to: Civitavécchia (2–3 weekly; 9hr); Genoa (2 weekly; 18hr).

Cágliari to: Civitavécchia (1 daily; 14hr); Genoa (2 weekly in summer; 20hr); Naples (1–2 weekly; 15hr); Palermo (1 weekly; 15hr); Trápani (1 weekly; 12hr); Tunis (1 weekly; 37hr).

Golfo Aranci to: Civitavécchia (1 daily; 8hr); Livorno (4–7 weekly; 10hr).

Olbia to: Civitavécchia (1 daily; 8hr); Genoa (3–7 weekly; 13hr); La Spezia (1 daily; 11hr); Livorno (4–7 weekly; 9hr).

Porto Torres to: Genoa (1 daily; 12hr); Toulon (April–Sept 1 weekly; 16hr).

Santa Teresa di Gallura to: Bonifacio (2–8 daily; 1hr).

PART THREE

THE CONTEXTS

HISTORICAL FRAMEWORK

A specific Italian history is hard to identify. Italy wasn't formally a united country until 1861, and the history of the peninsula after the Romans is more one of warring city states and colonisation and annexation by foreign powers. It's almost inconceivable now that Italy should fragment once again, but the regional differences remain strong and have even, in recent years, become a major factor in Italian politics.

EARLY TIMES

A smattering of remains exist from the Neanderthals who occupied the Italian peninsula half a million years ago, but the main period of colonisation began after the last Ice Age. Evidence of **Paleolithic** settlements dates from this time, around 20,000 BC, the next development being the spread of **Neolithic** tribes across the peninsula, between 5000 and 6000 years ago. More sophisticated tribes developed towards the end of the prehistoric period, beteen 2400 and 1800 BC; those who left the most visible traces were the **Ligurians** (who inhabited a much greater area than modern Liguria), the **Siculi** of southern Italy and Latium, and the **Sards**, who farmed and raised livestock on Sardinia. More advanced still were migrant groups from the eastern Mediterranean, who introduced the techniques of working copper. Later, various **Bronze Age** societies (1600–1000 BC) built a network of farms and villages in the Apennines, and on the Sicilian and southern coasts, the latter population trading with Mycenaeans in Greece.

Other tribes brought Indo-European languages into Italy. The Veneti, Latins and Umbrii moved down the peninsula from the north, whilst the Piceni and the Messapians in Apulia crossed the Adriatic from what is now former Yugoslavia. The artificial line between prehistory and history is drawn around the eighth century BC, with the arrival of the **Phoenician** alphabet and writing system. Sailing west along the African coast, the Phoenicians established colonies in Sicily and Sardinia, going on to build trade links between Carthage and southern Italy. These soon encouraged the arrival of the **Carthaginians**, who set themselves up on Sicily, Sardinia and the Latium coast, at the same time as both **Greeks** and **Etruscans** were gaining influence.

ETRUSCANS AND GREEKS

Greek settlers colonised parts of the Tuscan coast and the Bay of Naples in the eighth century BC, moving on to **Naxos** on Sicily's Ionian coast, and founding the city of Syracuse in the year 736 BC. The colonies they established in Sicily and southern Italy came to be known as **Magna Graecia**. Along with Etruscan cities to the north they are the earliest Italian civilisations leaving substantial buildings and written records.

The Greek settlements were hugely successful, introducing the vine and the olive to Italy, and establishing a high-yielding agricultural system. Cities like **Syracuse** and **Tarentum** were wealthier and more sophisticated than those on mainland Greece, dominating trade in the central Mediterranean, despite competition from Carthage. Ruins such as the temples of **Agrigento** and **Selinunte**, the fortified walls around **Gela**, and the theatres at Syracuse and Taormina on Sicily attest to a great prosperity, and *Magna Graecia* became an enriching influence on the culture of the Greek homeland – Archimedes, Aeschylus and Empedocles were all from Sicily. Yet these colonies suffered from the same factionalism as the Greek states, and the cities of Tarentum, Metapontum, Sybaris and Croton were united only when faced with the threat of outside invasion. From 400 BC, after Sybaris was razed to the ground, the other colonies went into irreversible economic decline, to become satellite states of Rome.

The **Etruscans** were the other major civilisation of the period, mostly living in the area between the **Tiber** and **Arno** rivers. Their language, known mostly from funerary texts, is one of the last relics of an ancient language common to the Mediterranean. Some say they arrived in Italy around the ninth century BC from western Anatolia, others that they came from the north, and a third hypothesis places their origins in Etruria. Whatever the case, they set up a cluster of **twelve city states** in northern Italy, traded with Greek colonies to the south and were the most powerful people in northern Italy by the sixth century BC, edging out the indigenous population of Ligurians, Latins and Sabines. Tomb frescoes in Umbria and Lazio depict a refined and luxurious culture with highly developed systems of divination, based on the reading of animal entrails and the flight of birds. Herodotus wrote that the Etruscans recorded their ancestry along the female line, and tomb excavations last century revealed that women were buried in special sarcophagi carved with their names. Well preserved chamber tombs with wall paintings exist at **Cerveteri** and **Tarquinia**, the two major sites in Italy. The Etruscans were technically advanced, creating new agricultural land through irrigation and building their cities on ramparted hill tops – a pattern of settlement that has left a permanent mark on central Italy. Their kingdom contracted, however, after invasions by the **Cumans**, **Syracusans** and **Gauls**, and was eventually forced into alliance with the embryonic Roman state.

ROMAN ITALY

The growth of **Rome**, a border town between the Etruscans and the Latins, gained impetus around 600 BC from a coalition of Latin and Sabine communities. The **Tarquins**, an Etruscan dynasty, oversaw the early expansion, but in 509 BC the Romans ejected the Etruscan royal family and became a **republic**, with power shared jointly between two consuls, both elected for one year. Further changes came half a century later, after a protracted class struggle that resulted in the **Law of the Twelve Tables**, which made patricians and plebeians equal. Now stabilised, the Romans set out to systematically conquer the northern peninsula, and after the fall of **Veii** in 396 BC, succeeded in capturing **Sutri** and **Nepi**, towns which Livy considered the "barriers and gateways of Etruria". Various wars and truces with other cities brought about agreements to pay harsh tributes.

The **Gauls** captured Rome in 390, refusing to leave until they had received a vast payment, but this proved a temporary reversal. The Romans took **Campania** and the fertile land of **Apulia** after defeating the **Samnites** in battles over a period of 35 years. They then set their sights on the wealthy Greek colonies to the south, including Tarentum, whose inhabitants turned to the Greek king, **Pyrrhus of Epirus** for military support. He initially repelled the Roman invaders, but lost his advantage and was defeated at **Beneventum** in 275 BC. The Romans had by then established their rule in most of southern Italy, and now became a threat to Carthage. In 264 they had the chance of obtaining **Sicily**, when the Mamertines, a mercenary army in control of Messina, appealed to them for help against the Carthaginians. The Romans obliged – sparking off the **First Punic War** – and took most of the island, together with Sardinia and Corsica. With their victory in 222 BC over the Gauls in the Po valley, all Italy was now under Roman control.

They also turned a subsequent military threat to their advantage, in what came to be known as the **Second Punic War**. The Carthaginians had watched the spread of Roman power across the Mediterranean with some alarm, and at the end of the third century BC they allowed **Hannibal** to make an Alpine crossing into Italy with his army of infantry, horsemen and elephants. Hannibal crushed the Roman legions at Lago Trasimeno and Cannae (216 BC), and then halted at Capua. With remarkable cool, considering Hannibal's proximity, **Scipio** set sail on a retaliatory mission to the Carthaginian territory of **Spain**, taking Cartagena, and continuing his journey into **Africa**. The Carthaginians recalled Hannibal, who was finally defeated by Roman troops at **Zama** in 202 BC. It was another fifty years before Carthage was taken, closely followed by all of Spain, but the Romans were busy in the meantime adding **Macedonian Greece** to their territory.

These conquests gave Roman citizens a tax-free existence subsidised by captured treasure, but society was sharply divided into those enjoying the benefits, and those who were not. The former belonged mostly to the **senatorial party**, who ignored demands for reform by their opposition, the **popular party**. The radical reforms sponsored by the tribune **Gaius Gracchus** came too close to democracy for the senatorial party, whose declaration of martial law was followed by the assassination of Gracchus. The majority of people realised that the only hope of gaining influence was through the army, but **General Gaius Marius**, when put into power, was ineffective against the senatorial clique, who systematically picked off the new regime.

The first century BC saw **civil strife** on an unprecedented scale. Although Marius was still in power, another general, **Sulla**, was in the ascendancy, leading military campaigns against northern invaders and rebellious subjects in the south. Sulla subsequently took power and established his dictatorship in Rome, throwing out a populist government which had formed while he was away on a campaign in the east. Murder and exile were common, and cities which had sided with Marius during their struggle for power were punished with massacres and destruction. Thousands of Sulla's war veterans were given confiscated land, but much of it was laid to waste. In 73 BC a gladiator named **Spartacus** led 70,000 dispossessed farmers and escaped slaves in a revolt, which lasted for two years before they were defeated by the legions.

JULIUS CAESAR AND AUGUSTUS

Rome became calmer only after Sulla's death, when **Pompey**, another general, and **Licinus Crassus**, a rich builder, became masters of Rome. Pompey's interest lay in lucrative wars elsewhere, so his absence from the capital gave **Julius Caesar** the chance to make a name for himself as an orator and raiser of finance. When Pompey returned in 60 BC, he made himself, Crassus and Caesar rulers of the **first Triumvirate**.

Caesar bought himself the post of consul in 59 BC, then spent the next eight years on campaigns againt the **Gauls**. His military success needled Pompey, and trouble began. Pompey eventually turned against his colleague, giving Caesar the chance to hit back. In 49 BC he crossed the river **Rubicon**, committing the offence of entering Roman territory with an army without first informing the Senate, but when he reached the city there was no resistance – everyone had fled, and Caesar became absolute ruler of Rome. He spent the next four years on civil reforms, writing his history of the Gallic wars, and chasing Pompey and his followers through Spain, Greece and Egypt. A group of enemies within the Senate, including his adopted son **Brutus**, conspired to murder him in 44 BC, a few months after he had been appointed ruler for life. **Octavian**, Caesar's nephew and heir, Lepidus, and Marcus Antonius (**Mark Anthony**) formed the **second Triumvirate** the following year. Again, the arrangement was fraught with tensions, the battle for power this time being between Anthony and Octavian. While Anthony was with **Cleopatra**, Octavian spent his time developing his military strength and the final, decisive battle took place at **Actium** in 31 BC, where Anthony committed suicide.

As sole ruler of the new regime, Octavian, renaming himself **Augustus Caesar**, embarked on a series of reforms and public works, giving himself complete powers despite his unassuming official title of "First Citizen".

THE EMPERORS

Tiberius (AD 14–37), the successor to Augustus, ruled wisely, but thereafter began a period of decadence. During the psychopathic reign of **Caligula** (37–41) the civil service kept the empire running; **Claudius** (41–54) conquered southern Britain, and was succeeded by his stepson **Nero** (54–68), who murdered his mother Agrippina and his wife Octavia, moving on to violent persecution of the **Christians**. Nero committed suicide when threatened by a coup, leading to a rapid succession of four emperors in the year 68. The period of prosperity during the rule of the **Flavian** Emperors (Vespasian and his sons Titus and Domitian) was a forerunner for the **Century of the Antonines**, a period named after the successful reigns of Nerva, Trajan, Hadrian, Antonius and **Marcus Aurelius**. These generals consolidated the empire's infrastructure, and created an encouraging environment for artistic achievement. A prime example is the formidable bronze equestrian statue of Marcus Aurelius in Rome – a work not equalled in sophistication until the Renaissance.

A troubled period followed under the rule of Marcus Aurelius' son **Commodus** (180–93) and his successors, none of whom were wholly in control of the legions. Artistic, intellectual and religious life stagnated, and the balance of economic development tilted in favour of the north, while the agricultural south grew ever more impoverished.

BARBARIANS AND BYZANTINES

In the middle of the third century, incursions by **Goths** in Greece, the Balkans and Asia, and the **Franks** and **Alamanni** in Gaul foreshadowed the collapse of the empire. **Aurelian** (270–75) re-established some order after terrible civil wars, to be followed by **Diocletian** (284–305), whose persecution of Christians produced many of the Church's present-day saints. **Plagues** had decimated the population, but problems of a huge but static economy were compounded by the doubling in size of the army at this time to about half a million men. To ease administration, Diocletian **divided the empire** into two halves, east and west, basing himself as ruler of the western empire in Mediolanum (Milan). This measure brought about a relative recovery, coinciding with the rise of **Christianity**, which was declared the state religion during the reign of **Constantine** (306–337). **Constantinople**, capital of the eastern empire, became a thriving trading and manufacturing city, while Rome itself went into decline, as the enlargement of the senatorial estates and the impoverishment of the lower classes gave rise to something comparable to a primitive feudal system.

Barbarians (meaning outsiders, or foreigners) had been crossing the border into the empire since 376 AD, when the **Ostrogoths** were driven from their kingdom in southern Russia by the **Huns**, a tribe of ferocious horsemen. The Huns went on to attack the **Visigoths**, 70,000 of whom crossed the border and settled inside the empire. When the Roman aristocracy saw that the empire was no longer a shield against barbarian raids, they were less inclined to pay for its support, seeing that a more comfortable future lay in being on good terms with the barbarian successor states.

By the fifth century, many legions were made up of troops from conquered territories, and several posts of high command were held by outsiders. With little will or loyalty behind it, the empire floundered, and on New Year's Eve of 406, Vandals, Alans and Sueves crossed the frozen Rhine into Gaul, chased by the Huns from their kingdoms in what are now Hungary and Austria. Once this had happened, there was no effective frontier. A contemporary writer lamented that "the whole of Gaul is smoking like an enormous funeral pyre". Despite this shock, worse was to come. By 408, the imperial government in **Ravenna** could no longer hold off **Alaric** (commander of Illyricum – now former Yugoslavia), and he went on to **sack Rome** in 410, causing a crisis of morale in the west. "When the whole world perished in one city," wrote Saint Jerome, "then I was dumb with silence."

The bitter **end of the Roman Empire** in the west came after **Valentinian III**'s assassination in 455. His eight successors over the next twenty years were finally ignored by the Germanic troops in the army, who elected their general **Odoacer** as king. The remaining Roman aristocracy hated him, and the eastern emperor, **Zeno**, who in theory now ruled the whole empire, refused to recognise him. In 488, Zeno rid himself of the Ostrogoth leader **Theodoric** by persuading him to march on Odoacer in Italy. By 493, Theodoric had succeeded, becoming ruler of the western territories.

A lull followed. The Senate in Rome and the civil service continued to function, and the remains of the empire were still administered under Roman law. Ostrogothic rule of the west continued after Theodoric's death, but in the 530s the eastern emperor, **Justinian**, began to plan the reunification of the Roman Empire "up to the two oceans". In 536 his general **Belisarius** landed in Sicily and moved north through Rome to Ravenna; complete reconquest was achieved in 552, after which the empire remained virtually intact for 500 years.

During this time the **Christian Church** developed as a more or less independent authority, since the Emperor was at a safe distance in Constantinople. Continual invasions had led to an uncertain political scene in which the **bishops of Rome** emerged with the strongest voice – justification of their primacy having already been given by Pope Leo I (440–461), who spoke of his right to "rule all who are ruled in the first instance by Christ". A confused period of rule followed, as armies from northern Europe tried to take more territory from the old empire.

LOMBARDS AND FRANKS

During the chaotic sixth century, the **Lombards**, a Germanic tribe, were driven southwest into Italy. Rome was successfully defended against them, but by the eighth century the Lombards were extending their power throughout the peninsula. In the middle of that century the **Franks** arrived from Gaul. They were orthodox Christians, and therefore acceptable to Gallo-Roman nobility, integrating quickly and taking over much of the provincial administration. The Franks were ruled by the Merovingian royal family, but the mayors of the palace – the Carolingians – began to take power in real terms. Led by **Pepin the Short**, they saw an advantage in supporting the papacy, giving Rome large endowments and forcibly converting pagans in areas they conquered. When Pepin wanted to oust the Merovingians, and become King of the Franks, he appealed to the pope in Rome for his blessing, who was happy to agree, anointing the new Frankish king with holy oil.

This alliance was useful to both parties. In 755 the pope called on the Frankish army to confront the Lombards. The Franks forced them to hand over treasure and 22 cities and castles, which then became the northern part of the **papal states**. Pepin died in 768, with the Church indebted to him. According to custom, he divided the kingdom between his two sons, one of whom died within three years. The other was Charles the Great, or **Charlemagne**.

An intelligent and innovative leader, Charlemagne was proclaimed King of the Franks and of the Lombards, and patrician of the Romans, after a decisive war against the Lombards in 774. On Christmas Day of the year 800, Pope Leo III expressed his gratitude for Charlemagne's political support by crowning him **Emperor of the Holy Roman Empire**, an investiture that forged an enduring link between the fortunes of Italy and those of northern Europe. By the time Charlemagne died, all of Italy from south of Rome to Lombardy, including Sardinia, was part of the huge **Carolingian empire**. The parts which didn't come under his domain were Sicily and the southern coast, which were gradually being reconquered by Arabs from Tunisia, and Apulia and Calabria, colonised by Byzantines and Greeks.

The task of holding these gains was beyond Charlemagne's successors, and by the beginning of the tenth century the family was extinct and the rival Italian states had become prizes for which the western (French) and eastern (German) Frankish kingdoms competed. Power switched in 936 to **Otto**, king of the eastern Franks. Political disunity in Italy invited him to intervene, and in 962 he was crowned emperor; Otto's son and grandson (Ottos II and III) set the seal on the renewal of the Holy Roman Empire.

POPES AND EMPERORS

On the death of **Otto III** in 1002, Italy was again without a recognised ruler. In the north, noblemen jockeyed for power, and the papacy was manipulated by rival Roman families. The most decisive events were in the south, where Sicily, Calabria and Apulia were captured by the **Normans**, who proved effective administrators and synthesised their own culture with the existing half-Arabic, half-Italian south. In **Palermo** in the eleventh century they created the most dynamic culture of the Mediterranean world.

Meanwhile in Rome, a series of reforming popes began to strengthen the church. **Gregory VII**, elected in 1073, was the most radical, demanding the right to depose emperors if he so wished. **Emperor Henry IV** was equally determined for this not to happen. The inevitable quarrel broke out, over a key appointment to the archbishopric of Milan. Henry denounced Gregory as "now not pope, but false monk"; the pope responded by excommunicating him, thereby freeing his subjects from their allegiance. By 1077 Henry was aware of his tactical error and tried to make amends by visiting the pope at **Canossa**, where the emperor, barefoot and penitent, was kept waiting outside for three days. The formal reconciliation thus did nothing to heal the rift, and Henry's son, **Henry V**, continued the feud, eventually coming to a compromise in which the emperor kept control of bishops' landownership, while giving up rights over their investiture.

After this symbolic victory, the papacy developed into the most comprehensive and advanced centralised government in Europe in the realms of law and finance, but it wasn't long before unity came under attack again. This time, the threat came from **Emperor Frederick I** (Barbarossa), who besieged many northern Italian cities from his base in Germany from 1154. **Pope Alexander III** responded with ambiguous pronouncements about the imperial crown being a "benefice" which the pope conferred, implying that the emperor was the pope's vassal. The issue of papal or imperial supremacy was to polarise the country for the next two hundred years, almost every part of Italy being torn by struggles between **Guelphs** (supporting the pope) and **Ghibellines** (supporting the emperor).

Henry's son, **Frederick II**, assumed the imperial throne at the age of three and a half, inheriting the Norman **Kingdom of Sicily**. Later linked by marriage to the great **Hohenstaufen** dynasty in Germany, he inevitably turned his attentions to northern Italy. However, his power-base was small, and opposition from Italian *comunes* and the papacy snowballed into **civil war**. His sudden death in 1250 marked a major downturn in imperial fortunes.

THE EMERGENCE OF CITY STATES

Charles of Anjou, brother of King Louis IX of France, defeated Frederick II's heirs in southern Italy, and received **Naples** and **Sicily** as a reward from the pope. His oppressive government finally provoked an uprising on Easter Monday 1282, a revolt that came to be known as the **Sicilian Vespers**, as some two thousand occupying soldiers were murdered in Palermo at the sound of the bell for vespers. For the next twenty years the French were at war with **Peter of Aragon**, who took Sicily and then tried for the southern mainland.

If imperial power was on the defensive, the papacy was in even worse shape. Knowing that the pontiff had little military backing or financial strength left, **Philip of France** sent his men to the pope's summer residence in 1303, subjecting the old man to a degrading attack. Boniface died within a few weeks; his French successor, Clement V, promptly moved the papacy to **Avignon**.

The declining political power of the major rulers was countered by the growing autonomy of the cities. By 1300, a broad belt of some three hundred virtually **independent city states** stretched from central Italy to the northernmost edge of the peninsula. In the middle of the century the population of Europe was savagely depleted by the **Black Death** – brought into Europe by a Genovese ship returning from the Black Sea – but the city states survived, developing a concept of citizenship quite different from the feudal lord-and-vassal relationship. By the end of the fourteenth century the richer and more influential states had swallowed up the smaller *comunes*, leaving four as clear political front runners. These were **Genova** (controlling the Ligurian coast), **Florence** (ruling Tuscany), **Milan**, whose sphere of influence included Lombardy and much of central Italy, and **Venice**. Smaller principalities, such as Mantua and Ferrara, supported armies of mercenaries, ensuring their security by building impregnable fortress-palaces.

Perpetual vendettas between the propertied classes often induced the citizens to accept the overall rule of one *signore* in preference to the bloodshed of warring clans. A despotic form of government evolved, sanctioned by official titles from the emperor or pope, and by the fifteenth century most city states were under princely rather than republican rule. In the south of the fragmented peninsula was the **Kingdom of Naples**; the **States of the Church** stretched up from Rome through modern-day Marche, Umbria and the Romagna; **Siena**, **Florence**, **Modena**, **Mantua** and **Ferrara** were independent states, as were the **Duchy of Milan**, and the maritime republics of **Venice** and **Genova**, with a few odd pockets of independence like Lucca, for example, and Rimini.

The commercial and secular city states of late-medieval times were the seed bed for the **Renaissance**, when urban businessmen (such as the Medici) and autocratic rulers (such as Federico da Montefeltro) enhanced their status through the financing of architectural projects, paintings and sculpture. It was also at this time that the Tuscan dialect – the language of Dante, Petrarch and Boccaccio – became established as Italy's literary language; it later became the nation's official spoken language.

By the mid-fifteenth century the five most powerful states – Naples, the papacy, Milan, and the republics of Venice and Florence – reached a tacit agreement to maintain the new balance of power. Yet though there was a balance of power at home, the history of each of the independent Italian states became inextricably bound up with the power politics of other European countries.

FRENCH AND SPANISH INTERVENTION

The inevitable finally happened when an Italian state invited a larger power in to defeat one of its rivals. In 1494, at the request of the Duke of Milan, **Charles VIII of France** marched south to renew the Angevin claim to the Kingdom of Naples. After the accomplishment of his mission, Charles stayed for three months in Naples, before heading back to France; the kingdom was then acquired by **Ferdinand II of Aragon**, subsequently ruler of all Spain.

The person who really established the Spanish in Italy was the Habsburg **Charles V** (1500–1558), who within three years of inheriting both the Austrian and Spanish thrones bribed his way to being elected Holy Roman Emperor. In 1527 the imperial troops sacked **Rome**, a calamity widely interpreted at the time as God's punishment to the disorganised and dissolute Italians. The French remained troublesome opposition, but they were defeated at Pavia in 1526 and Naples in 1529. With the treaty of Cateau-Cambresis in 1559, Spain held Sicily, Naples, Sardinia, the Duchy of Milan and some Tuscan fortresses, and they were to exert a stranglehold on Italian political life for the next 150 years. The remaining smaller states became satellites of either Spanish or French rule; only the papacy and Venice remained independent.

Social and economic troubles were as severe as the political upheavals. While the papacy combatted the spread of the **Reformation** in northern Europe, the major manufacturing and trading centres were coming to terms with the opening up of the Atlantic and Indian Ocean trade routes – discoveries that meant that northern Italy would increasingly be bypassed. Mid-sixteenth-century **economic recession** prompted wealthy Venetian and Florentine merchants to invest in land rather than business, while in the south high taxes and repressive feudal regimes produced an upsurge of banditry and even the raising of peasant militias – resistance that was ultimately suppressed brutally by the Spanish.

The seventeenth century was a low point in Italian political life, with little room for manoeuvre between the papacy and colonial powers. The Spanish eventually lost control of Italy at the start of the eighteenth century, when as a result of the War of the Spanish Succession, Lombardy, Mantua, Naples and Sardinia all came under Austrian control. The machinations of the major powers led to frequent realignments in the first half of the century. Piedmont, ruled by the Duke of Savoy, Victor Amadeus II, was forced in 1720 to surrender Sicily to the Austrians in return for Sardinia. In 1734 Naples and Sicily passed to the Spanish Bourbons, and three years later the House of Lorraine acquired Tuscany on the extinction of the Medici.

Relatively enlightened Bourbon rule in the south did little to arrest the economic polarisation of society, but the northern states advanced under the intelligent if autocratic rule of Austria's **Maria Theresa** (1740–80) and her son **Joseph II** (1780–92) who prepared the way for early industrialisation. Lightning changes came in April 1796, when the French armies of **Napoleon** invaded northern Italy. Within a few years the French had been driven out again, but by 1810 Napoleon was in command of the whole peninsula, and his puppet regimes remained in charge until Waterloo. Napoleonic rule had profound effects, reducing the power of the papacy, reforming feudal land rights and introducing representative government to Italy. Elected assemblies were provided on the French model, giving the emerging middle class a chance for political discussion and action.

UNIFICATION

The fall of Napoleon led to the Vienna Settlement of 1815, by which the Austrians effectively restored the old ruling class. **Metternich**, the Austrian Chancellor, did all he could to foster any local loyalties that might weaken the appeal of unity, yet the years between 1820 and 1849 became years of revolution. Uprisings began in Sicily, Naples and Piedmont, when **King Ferdinand** introduced measures that restricted personal freedom and destroyed many farmers' livelihoods. A makeshift army quickly gained popular support in Sicily, and forced some concessions, before Ferdinand invited the Austrians in to help him crush the revolution. In the north, the oppressive laws enacted by **Vittorio Emanuele I** in the Kingdom of Piedmont sparked off student protests and army mutinies in Turin. Vittorio Emanuele abdicated in favour of his brother, Carlo Felice, and his son, **Carlo Alberto**; the latter initially gave some support to the radicals, but Carlo Felice then called in the Austrians, and thousands of revolutionaries were forced into exile. Carlo Alberto became King of Piedmont in 1831. A secretive, excessively devout and devious character, he did a major volte-face when he assumed the throne by forming an alliance with the Austrians.

In 1831 further uprisings occurred in Parma, Modena, the Papal States, Sicily and Naples. Their lack of coordination, and the readiness with which Austrian and papal troops intervened, ensured that revolution was short-lived but even if these actions were unsustained, their influence grew.

One person profoundly influenced by these insurgencies was **Giuseppe Mazzini**. Arrested as Secretary of the Genovese branch of the *Carbonari* (a secret radical society) in 1827 and jailed for three months in 1830, he formulated his political ideology and set up **"Young Italy"** on his release. Among the many to whom the ideals of "Young Italy" appealed was **Giuseppe Garibaldi**, soon to play a central role in the **Risorgimento**, as the movement to reform and unite the country was known.

Crop failures in 1846 and 1847 produced widespread **famine** and **cholera outbreaks**. In Sicily an army of peasants marched on the capital, burning debt collection records, destroying property and freeing prisoners. Middle- and upper-class moderates were worried, and formed a government to control the uprising, but Sicilian **separatist** aims were realised in 1848. Fighting spread to Naples, where **Ferdinand II** made some temporary concessions, but nonetheless he retook Sicily the following year. At the same time as the southern revolution, serious disturbances took place in Tuscany, Piedmont and the Papal States. Rulers fled their duchies, and Carlo Alberto altered course again, prompted by Metternich's fall from power in Vienna: he granted his subjects a constitution and declared war on Austria. In Rome, the pope fled from rioting and Mazzini became a member of the city's republican triumvirate in 1849, with Garibaldi organising the defences.

None of the uprisings lasted long. Twenty thousand revolutionaries were expelled from Rome, Carlo Alberto abdicated in favour of his son Vittorio Emanuele II after military defeats at the hands of the Austrians, and the Dukes returned to Tuscany, Modena and Parma. One thing which did survive was Piedmont's constitution, which throughout the 1850s attracted political refugees to this cosmopolitan state.

CAVOUR AND GARIBALDI

Nine years of radical change began when **Count Camillo Cavour** became Prime Minister of Piedmont in 1852. The involvement of Piedmontese troops in the Crimean War brought Cavour into contact with Napoleon III at the Congress of Paris, at which the hostilities were ended, and in July 1858 the two men had secret talks on the "Italian question". Napoleon III had decided to support Italy in its fight against the Austrians – the only realistic way of achieving unification – as long as resistance was non-revolutionary. Having bargained over the division of territory, they waited for a chance to provoke Austria into war. This came in 1859, when Cavour wrote an emotive anti-Austrian speech for Vittorio Emanuele at the opening of Parliament. His battle cry for an end to the *grido di dolore* (cry of pain) was taken up over Italy. The Austrians ordered demobilisation by the Piedmontese, who did the reverse.

The war was disastrous from the start, and thousands died at Magenta and Solferino. In July 1859, Napoleon made a truce with the Austrians without consulting Cavour, who resigned in fury. Provisional governments remained in power in Tuscany, Modena and the Romagna. Cavour returned to government in 1860, and soon France, Piemonte and the papacy agreed to a series of plebiscites, a move which ensured that by mid-March of 1860, **Tuscany** and the new state of **Emilia** (Duchies of Modena and Parma plus the Romagna) had voted for **union with Piedmont**. A secret treaty between Vittorio Emanuele and Napoleon III ceded Savoy and Nice to France, subject to plebiscites. The result was as planned, no doubt due in part to the presence of the French army during voting.

Garibaldi promptly set off for Nice with the aim of blowing up the ballot boxes, only to be diverted when he reached Genoa, where he heard of an **uprising in Sicily**. Commandeering two old paddle steamers and obtaining just enough rifles for his thousand Red Shirts, he headed south. More support came when they landed in Sicily, and Garibaldi's army outflanked the 12,000 Neapolitan troops to take the island. After that, they crossed to the mainland, easily occupied Naples, then struck out for Rome. Cavour, anxious that he might lose the initiative, hastily dispatched a Piedmontese army to **annexe the Papal States**, except for the Patrimony around Rome. Worried by the possibility that the anti-church revolutionaries who made up the Red Shirt army might stir up trouble, Cavour and Vittorio Emanuele travelled south to Rome, accompanied by their army, and arranged plebiscites in Sicily, Naples, Umbria and the Papal Marches that offered little alternative but to vote for annexation by Piedmont. After their triumphal parade through Naples, they thanked Garibaldi for his trouble, took command of all territories and held elections to a new parliament. In February 1861, the members formally announced the **Kingdom of Italy**.

Cavour died the same year, before the country was completely unified, since Rome and Venice were still outside the kingdom. Garibaldi marched unsuccessfully on Rome in 1862, and again five years later, by which time Venice had been subsumed. It wasn't until Napoleon III was defeated by Prussia in 1870 that the French troops were ousted from Rome. Thus by 1871 **unification** was complete.

THE WORLD WARS

After the *Risorgimento*, some things still hadn't changed. The ruling class were slow to move towards a broader based political system, while living standards actually worsened in some areas, particularly in Sicily. When Sicilian peasant farmers organised into *fasci* – forerunners of trade unions – the prime minister sent in 30,000 soldiers, closed down newspapers and interned suspected troublemakers without trial. In the 1890s capitalist methods and modern machinery in the Po Valley created a new social structure, with rich *agrari* at the top of the pile, a mass of farm labourers at the bottom, and an intervening layer of estate managers.

In the 1880s Italy's **colonial expansion** began, initially concentrated in bloody – and ultimately disastrous – campaigns in Abyssinia and Eritrea in 1886. In 1912 Italy wrested the Dodecanese islands and Libya from Turkey, a development deplored by many, including **Benito Mussolini**, who during this war was the radical secretary of the *PSI* (Partito Socialista Italiano) in Forlì.

WORLD WAR I AND THE RISE OF MUSSOLINI

Italy entered **World War I** in 1915 with the chief aims of settling old scores with Austria and furthering its colonial ambitions through French and British support. A badly equipped, poorly commanded army took three years to force Austria into defeat, finally achieved in the last month of the war at Vittorio Veneto. Some territory was gained – Trieste, Gorizia, and what became Trentino-Alto Adige – but at the cost of over half a million dead, many more wounded, and a mountainous war debt.

The middle classes, disillusioned with the war's outcome and alarmed by inflation and social unrest, turned to Mussolini, now a figurehead of the right. In 1921, recently elected to parliament, Mussolini formed the *Partito Nazionale Fascista*, whose *squadre* terrorised their opponents by direct personal attacks and the destruction of newspaper offices, printing shops, and socialist and trade union premises. By 1922 the party was in a position to carry out an insurrectionary "March on Rome". Plans for the march were leaked to Prime Minister Facta, who needed the king's signature on a martial law decree if the army were to meet the march. Fears of civil war led to the king's refusal. Facta resigned, Mussolini made it clear that he would not join any government he did not lead, and on October 29 was **awarded the premiership**. Only then did the march take place.

Zealous *squadristi* now urged Mussolini towards **dictatorship**, which he announced early in 1925. Political opposition and trade unions were outlawed, the free press disintegrated under censorship and Fascist takeovers, elected local governments were replaced by appointed officials, powers of arrest and detention were increased, and special courts were established for political crimes. In 1929, Mussolini ended a sixty-year feud between

Church and State, by reorganising the **Vatican** as an autonomous church state within the Kingdom of Italy. (As late as 1904, anyone involved in the new regime, even as a voter, had been automatically excommunicated.) By 1939, the motto "Everything within the State. Nothing outside the State. Nothing against the State" had become fact, with the government controlling the larger part of Italy's steel, iron and ship building industries, as well as every aspect of political life.

WORLD WAR II

Mussolini's involvement in the **Spanish Civil War** in 1936 brought about the formation of the **"Axis"** with Nazi Germany. Italy entered **World War II** totally unprepared and with outdated equipment, but in 1941 invaded Yugoslavia to gain control of the Adriatic coast. Before long, though, Mussolini was on the defensive. Tens of thousands of Italian troops were killed on the Russian front in the winter of 1942, and in July 1943 the Allied forces gained a first foothold in Europe, when Patton's American Seventh Army and the British Eighth Army under Montgomery landed in Sicily. A month later they controlled the island.

In the face of these and other reversals Mussolini was overthrown by his own Grand Council, who bundled him away to the isolated mountain resort of Gran Sasso, and replaced him with the perplexed **Marshal Badoglio**. The Allies wanted Italy's surrender, for which they secretly offered amnesty to the king, Vittorio Emanuele III, who had coexisted with the Fascist regime for 21 years. On September 8 a radio broadcast announced that an **armistice** had been signed, and on the following day the Allies crossed onto the mainland. As the Anglo-American army moved up through the peninsula, German divisions moved south to meet them, springing Mussolini from jail to set up the **republic of Salò** on Lake Garda. It was a total failure, and increasing numbers of men and women from Communist, Socialist or Catholic parties swelled the opposing partisan forces to 450,000. In April 1945 Mussolini fled for his life, but was caught by partisans before reaching Switzerland. He and his lover, Claretta Petacci, were shot and strung upside down from a petrol station roof in Milan's Piazzale Loreto.

MODERN TIMES

A popular mandate declared Italy a **republic** in 1946, and Alcide de Gasperi's **Democrazia Cristiana** (DC) party formed a government. He remained in power until 1953, sustained by a succession of coalitions. Ever since then, the regular formation and disintegration of governments has been the norm, a political volatility that reflects the sharp divisions between rural and urban Italy, and between the north and the south (or *mezzogiorno*). A strong manufacturing base and large-scale agriculture have given most people in the north a better material standard of living than previous generations, but the south still lags far behind, despite such measures as the establishment in 1950 of the *Cassa del Mezzogiorno* development agency, which has pumped much-needed funds into the region.

During the 1950s Italy became a front-rank industrial nation, massive firms such as *Fiat* and *Olivetti* helping to double the Gross Domestic Product and triple industrial production. American financial aid was an important factor in this expansion, as was the availability of a large and compliant workforce, a substantial proportion of which was drawn from the villages of the south.

The DC at first operated in alliance with other right-wing parties, but in **1963**, in a move precipitated by the increased politicisation of the blue-collar workers, they were obliged to share power for the first time with the **Partito Socialista Italiano** (PSI). The DC politician who was largely responsible for sounding out the socialists was **Aldo Moro**, the dominant figure of Italian politics in the 1960s. Moro was prime minister from 1963 to 1968, a period in which the economy was disturbed by inflation and the removal of vast sums of money by wealthy citizens alarmed by the arrival in power of the PSI. The decade ended with the "autunno caldo" (hot autumn) of 1969, when strikes, occupations and demonstrations paralysed the country.

In the 1970s the situation worsened even further: bankruptcies increased, inflation hit twenty percent, and unemployment rocketed. More extreme forms of unrest broke out, instigated in the first instance by the far right, who were almost certainly behind a bomb which killed sixteen people in Milan in 1969. **Neo-**

fascist terrorism continued throughout the next decade, reaching its hideous climax in 1980, when 84 people were killed and 200 wounded in a bomb blast at Bologna train station. At the same time, a plethora of left-wing terrorist groups sprang up, many of them led by disaffected intellectuals at the northern universities. The most active of these were the **Brigate Rosse** (Red Brigades). Founded in Milan in 1970, they reached the peak of their notoriety eight years later, when they kidnapped and killed Aldo Moro himself. A major police offensive in the early 1980s nullified most of the *Brigate Rosse*, but a number of hardline splinter groups are still in existence, as was proved in 1988 by the murder of an aide of the prime minister.

Yet the DC government survived, sustained by the so-called "historic compromise" negotiated in 1976 with **Enrico Berlinguer**, leader of the **Partito Comunista Italiano** (PCI). By this arrangement the PCI – polling 34 percent of the national vote, just three points less than the DC – agreed to abstain from voting in parliament in order to maintain a government of national unity. The pact was rescinded in 1979, and after Berlinguer's death in 1984 the PCI's share of the vote dropped to around 27 percent. The combination of this collapse of popular support and the collapse of the Communist Bloc led to a realignment of the PCI under the leadership of **Achille Occhetto**, who has turned the party into a democratic socialist grouping along the lines of left-leaning parties in Germany or Sweden – a transformation encapsulated by the party's new name – the **Partito Democratico della Sinistra** (Democratic Party of the Left).

In its efforts to exclude the left wing from power, the DC has been obliged to accede to demands from minor parties such as the **Radical Party**, which gained eighteen seats in the 1987 election, one of them going to the porn star Ilona Staller, better known as La Cicciolina. Furthermore, the DC's reputation was severely damaged in the early 1980s by a series of scandals, notably the furore surrounding the activities of the **P2** masonic lodge, when links were discovered between corrupt bankers, senior DC members, and fanatical right-wing groups. As its popularity fell, the DC was forced to offer the premiership to politicians from other parties. In 1981 Giovanni Spadolini of the Republicans became the first non-DC prime minister since the war, and in 1983 **Bettino Craxi** was installed as the first premier from the **Partito Socialista Italiano** (PSI), a position he held for four years.

Even through the upheavals of the 1970s the national income of Italy continued to grow, and there developed a national obsession with **Il Sorpasso**, a term signifying the country's overtaking of France and Britain in the economic league table. Experts disagree as to whether *Il Sorpasso* has actually happened (most think it hasn't), and calculations are complicated by the huge scale of tax evasion and other illicit financial dealings in Italy. All strata of society are involved in the withholding of money from central government, but the ruling power in this **economia sommersa** (submerged economy) is the **Mafia**, whose contacts penetrate to the highest levels in Rome. The most traumatic proof of the Mafia's infiltration of the political hierarchy came with the murders of anti-Mafia judges **Giovanni Falcone** and **Paolo Borsellino**, whose killers could only have penetrated the judges' security with the help of inside information.

The murders of the immensely respected Falcone and Borsellino might well come to be seen as marking a fault-line in the political history of modern Italy. Italians are now deserting the DC in droves and are offering their support to parties that have sprung into existence within the last few years. A major beneficiary of this accelerating disillusionment with the establishment is Leoluca Orlando's **La Rete** ("Network"), founded specifically to counter the Mafia in Sicily, but rapidly evolving into a coalition of groups opposed to the vested interests in the country's town halls and businesses. Even more successful is the right-wing **Lega Nord** whose autocratic leader, **Umberto Bossi,** has capitalised on northern frustration with the state, which they see as supporting a corrupt south on the back of the hard-working, law-abiding north. Bossi and his supporters used to talk of secession, but the Northern League's official aim is now a federation, with Italy divided into two or three parts. Formerly a marginalised firebrand, Bossi is now the most feared man in Italian politics. The newer **Democratic Alliance**, led by the more circumspect **Mario Segni** offers a less divisive alternative to middle-of-the road voters.

In 1992 the new government of **Giuliano Amato** – a politician untainted by any hint of corruption – instigated the biggest round-up of Mafia members in nearly a decade, issuing some 200 arrest warrants in "Operation Leopard". However, this was nothing compared to the arrest in Palermo, at the beginning of 1993, of Salvatore "Toto" Riina, the Mafia *capo di tutti capi* (boss of bosses) and the man widely believed to have been behind the Falcone and Borsellino killings. The arrest of Riina followed the testimony of numerous supergrasses, whose evidence might at last bury the reputations of key members of the establishment. For example, it has come to light that a murdered associate of **Giulio Andreotti** – three times prime minister – had been the Mafia's man in Rome, a top-level fixer who would arrange acquittals from the Supreme Court in exchange for support. Bettino Craxi once called Andreotti a fox, adding "sooner or later all foxes end up as fur coats".

But Craxi himself is now in deep trouble as a result of huge **bribery scandals** that broke in 1992. It is alleged that the Socialists and their Christian Democrat allies have shared out bribes from major civil contractors in Milan (Craxi's power base), Venice and Florence, splitting the kickbacks on a percentage related directly to the parties' representation on the city councils. The personal reputations of Craxi and ex-foreign minister Gianni de Michelis are in tatters, and the Socialist party – previously regarded as cleaner than the DC – has seen its support plummet since the heyday of Craxi's government. As the old parties get further mired in allegations of corruption, the balance of power in Italy is shifting towards Bossi and the other newcomers, whose influence increases with every ballot and every resignation.

ITALIAN PAINTING AND SCULPTURE

Italy's contribution to European painting and sculpture far surpasses that of any other nation. This is in part due to the triumph of the Renaissance period, but Italy can also boast many other remarkable artistic achievements, ranging from the seventh century BC to modern times. The country's fragmented political history has led to strong regional characteristics in Italian art: Rome, Pisa, Siena, Florence, Milan, Venice, Bologna and Naples all have distinctive and recognisable traditions.

THE ETRUSCANS

Italian artistic history begins with the **Etruscans**, whose culture spanned the seventh to the first centuries BC. Etruscan art was distinct from that of Greece, then the dominant nation both politically and artistically, though in many other respects it consistently shows the impact of contemporary trends in Greece. Many of the finest Etruscan **sculptures** date from the sixth century BC. Among the best examples, both now in the Villa Giulia in Rome, are the *Apollo and Herakles* from Veio, and the *Sarcophagus of a Married Couple* from Cerveteri, the reclining figures of the latter a typical motif of Etruscan art – the faces realistic and expressive, with prominent eyes and enigmatic smiles, but otherwise little attention paid to human anatomy. Depictions of animals, both real and imaginary, were also common, most famous among which are the *Chimera* from Arezzo, now in the Museo Archeologico in Florence, and Rome's own emblem, the *She-Wolf* in the Palazzo dei Conservatori – both from the fifth century BC.

Surviving Etruscan **wall paintings** are surprisingly numerous, especially considering that (apart from a few at Paestum) all of their Greek counterparts in Italy have vanished. The most outstanding array is in Tarquinia, which preserves examples ranging from the sixth to the first century BC; another fine group is at Chiusi. These paintings were at first of a religious or magic nature, initially intending to provide an amenable environment for the dead man. Later, visionary views of the afterlife were attempted. With their bold drawing, bright colours and lively details, they have an immediate visual appeal.

THE ROMANS

Like the Etruscans, the **Romans** were heavily indebted to the Greeks for their art forms, happily adapting Greek models to suit their own purpose, though they had little taste for the aesthetic values which had played such a key role in Greek art. Admittedly, the great heroic statues of the Greeks were highly prized. Many were brought to Rome, while others were extensively imitated and copied, and some of the most famous pieces of Roman **sculpture** – the *Apollo Belvedere* and the *Venus of Cnidos* in the Vatican, the *Medici Venus* in the Uffizi – are actually Roman copies of lost Greek originals, though they are successful pieces of work in their own right.

The empire's own contribution to artistic development is exemplified by Roman **portraiture**, which usually eschewed idealisation in favour of an objective representation of the physical features, typically showing a bony facial structure, bare forehead, pursed lips and large eyes. Only occasionally, as in the reigns of Augustus and Hadrian, was this image softened. Marble portrait busts have survived in vast quantities, but the bronze equestrian statues – a particularly effective means of stressing the power and aura of the emperor – were later melted down. Only that of Marcus Aurelius in Rome survives.

The Romans also made full and varied use of relief sculpture, not least in the carvings used to adorn the front of **sarcophagi**, their main form of funerary art, and on the **triumphal arches** and **columns** erected to celebrate military victories. Some of these, like Trajan's Column in Rome, which dates from the second century AD, display a virtuoso skill and attention to detail in their depiction of great deeds and battles.

In the domestic environment, **wall paintings** were an essential feature, though relatively few survive. In Rome itself, there are the *Esquiline Landscapes* and *Aldobrandini Wedding* and the frescoes from the Villa Livia, while the best examples are those preserved in the towns of Pompeii and Herculaneum after their submersion by the eruption of Mount Vesuvius in 79 AD. Some of these remain *in situ*, notably the spectacular paintings in the Villa dei Misteri; others have been moved to the Museo Nazionale in Naples. In general, a huge range of subject matter was tackled – landscapes, portraits, still lifes, mythologies and genre scenes – while both realistic and stylised approaches to the depiction of nature were attempted.

EARLY CHRISTIAN ART

The **early Christian** period saw an almost total rejection of sculpture, other than for sarcophagi, though the remarkable wooden doors of Santa Sabina in Rome – featuring the earliest known representation of the Crucifixion – are a notable exception. The earliest murals were created in the Roman catacombs, and show no great stylistic innovation, but increasingly Christian painters began to render a sense of expression to the facial features, in order that the emotions of pain, sorrow and ecstasy could be depicted, along with a richly symbolic pictorial vocabulary. But the early Christians favoured **mosaics** rather than frescoes as a medium. This painstaking art form had hitherto been associated with floor decoration, but it proved ideal for the decoration of the early churches, its inappropriateness for the depiction of movement in many ways responsible for the rigid artistic forms which took an increasing grip. The earliest surviving cycle, in Santa Maria Maggiore in **Rome**, dates from the second quarter of the fifth century, and is fairly small-scale. The slightly later group in the Mausoleo di Galla Placidia in **Ravenna**, the city which had by then assumed the status of capital of the western empire, are more monumental, their daring geometric patterns, elaborate imagery and sublime colouring representing perhaps the first great milestone of Christian art.

Ravenna continued as a centre of artistic innovation when a century later it became in effect the Italian capital of **Byzantine** culture and politics. Many magnificent mosaic cycles were created, and three sets in particular far surpass in quality anything produced in Constantinople itself, or indeed anywhere else in its empire: the church of San Vitale, where the mosaics are the central focus of the architecture itself; Sant'Apollinare Nuovo, whose two frieze processions were quite unlike anything previously seen in Italian art; and the church of Sant'Apollinare in Classe, whose apse mosaics exude a matchless sense of peace and mystery.

THE MIDDLE AGES

Italy at first played a rather subsidiary role in the Europe-wide re-emergence from the Dark Ages. The **Byzantine tradition** proved surprisingly durable, particularly in Venice and Sicily, which both retained strong trading links with Constantinople. Throughout the twelfth century, Byzantine craftsmen proved that the art of mosaic was far from exhausted, providing works that are worthy successors to those at Ravenna in the Cappella Palatina of Palermo and the duomos of Cefalù and Monreale, and of course the Basilica of San Marco in Venice.

Many Italian **fresco cycles** of the period still show traces of Byzantine influence, and the style was also a feature of the great eleventh-century Benedictine art movement fostered by the abbey of Montecassino. Sadly, nearly all the products of this school have vanished, though the murals in Sant'Angelo in Formis near Capua give an approximate idea of what they must have looked like.

Because of the cost of frescoes, from the second quarter of the twelfth century **panel paintings** became increasingly important, particularly in Tuscany. Subjects fell into three main categories: the Madonna and Child with saints; the portrait of a saint surrounded by scenes from his life; or the *Christus Triumphans*, a large painted crucifix showing an open-eyed Christ with outstretched hands.

The art of **sculpture** was initially slow to revive after its long period in the doldrums, but it came to occupy a crucial role throughout Europe during the Romanesque period, with Lombard and Emilian masons playing a key role in its dissemination. Just after the turn of the twelfth century, a master by the name of **Wiligelmo** carved at Modena what may well be the earliest of the great cathedral porches – a form that was to become one of the outstanding features of European medieval art. His bas-reliefs feature expressive figures grouped with considerable narrative skill, and they suggest at least some familiarity with classical works. The same sculptor may also have carved the magnificent episcopal throne in San Nicolò in Bari. **Nicolò**, a pupil of Wiligelmo, seems to have been responsible for most of the other great portals of northern Italy – those of the Sacra di San Michele, San Zeno in Verona, and the cathedrals of Verona, Ferrara, Piacenza and Cremona. Towards the end of the century, this style was developed in and around Parma by **Benedetto Antelami**, who created the graceful *Deposition* relief in the cathedral, the profuse and lively decoration of the baptistery.

THE PRECURSORS OF THE RENAISSANCE

The distinction between **Gothic** and **Renaissance**, so marked in the painting and sculpture of other countries, is very blurred in Italy. In the mid-thirteenth century, what is normally considered one of the key planks of the Renaissance – the rediscovery of the full sense of form, beauty and modelling characteristic of classical art – had already occurred with the statues of the Porta Romana in **Capua**, fragments of which are preserved in the town's museum. These were commissioned by Emperor Frederick II, who wished to revive memories of the grandeur that was Rome. Increasingly, Italians came to believe that it was northern barbarians who had destroyed the arts, which it was now their own duty to revive.

A sculptor of south Italian origin who was doubtless familiar with the work at Capua, **Nicola Pisano** (c.1220–84), developed this style, in four major surviving works – the pulpits of the Pisa Baptistery and the Duomo in Siena, the Arca San Domenico in Bologna and the Fonte Gaia in Perugia. His figures have a sure sense of volume, with varying levels of relief used to create an illusion of space. **Arnolfo di Cambio** (c.1245–1310), his assistant on some of these projects, developed the mix of classical and Gothic features in his own works, which include the famous bronze *St Peter* in Rome, and the *Tomb of Cardinal de Braye* in San Domenico in Orvieto. The latter defined the format of wall tombs for the next century, showing the deceased lying on a coffin below the Madonna and Child, all set within an elaborate architectural framework.

Of even greater long-term significance was the achievement of **Giovanni Pisano** (c.1248–1314), who abandoned his father's penchant for paganism, adopting instead new and dramatic postures for his figures which were quite unlike anything in the previous history of sculpture. This is nowhere more evident than in the statues he created for the facade of the Duomo in Siena, which are placed high up rather than round the portals, and are a world away from their static counterparts on French cathedrals.

It was only in the last three decades of the thirteenth century that Italian painters finally began to break away from the time-honoured Byzantine formulas, a new sense of freedom initiated by **Pietro Cavallini** (active 1273–1308) in Rome and developed by the Florentine **Cimabue** (c.1240–1302), who introduced rounded forms to his fresco of *The Madonna of St Francis* in the lower church at Assisi. His masterpiece, the Passion cycle in the church above, is sadly ruined, but enough remains to give evidence of the overwhelming tragic grandeur it must have once possessed.

Whereas Cimabue's works are still rooted in the Byzantine tradition, and make no attempt to break away from a flat surface effect, a huge leap was made by his pupil and fellow Florentine, **Giotto di Bondone** (1266–1337), whose innovations were to define the entire subsequent course of Western art. Giotto decisively threw off the two-dimensional restrictions of painting, managing to give his pictures an illusion of depth. Thanks to having better materials at his disposal than Cimabue, his *Life of St Francis* in the upper church at Assisi has survived in good condition, as has his decoration of the Scrovegni Chapel in Padua. These two great cycles are the best examples of Giotto's genius in all its many facets. Among these are such basic principles as a sense for the significant, unencumbered by surplus detail; the convincing treatment of action, movement, gesture and emotion; and total command over technical matters like figure modelling, foreshortening, and effects of light and shade.

THE FOURTEENTH & EARLY FIFTEENTH CENTURIES

In spite of these momentous developments, the path towards the Renaissance was not to follow a continuous or consistent course. Indeed, the leading local school of painters in the fourteenth century was not that of Florence, but of neighbouring **Siena**, which had very different preoccupations. This had a great deal to do with the father figure, **Duccio di Buoninsegna** (c.1255–1318), who did not go along the revolutionary path of Giotto, but instead breathed a whole new life into the Byzantine tradition. Duccio's sense of grandeur is well conveyed by the central panel of his masterpiece, the *Maestà* in the Museo dell'Opera del Duomo of his native city. However, it is the small scenes of this vast altarpiece which bring out his best quality: that of a masterful storyteller, adept at arrangement, grouping and the depiction of expression, feeling and movement. Colour, which in Giotto is merely used to bring out the forms, becomes a leading component in its own right.

In spite of the presence in the city of the vibrant statues of Giovanni Pisano, subsequent Sienese painters found Duccio's narrative art the more potent model. **Simone Martini** (c.1284–1344) began his career by painting a fresco counterpart of Duccio's *Maestà* in the Palazzo Pubblico, though his most celebrated work in this building, the commemorative *Equestrian Portrait of Guidoriccio da Fogliano*, is now widely regarded as a fake. His refined, graceful style depended above all on line, colour and decorative effects – seen to best effect in the cycle of *The Life of St Martin* in the lower church in Assisi and in the sumptuous, cunningly designed *Annunciation* in the Uffizi. The latter was painted in collaboration with his brother-in-law **Lippo Memmi** (d.1357), who independently painted the *Maestà* in the Palazzo Pubblico in San Gimignano, and may also have been responsible for the dramatic New Testament frescoes in the Collegiata of the same town, traditionally ascribed to the otherwise unknown **Barna**.

Another Sienese painter who worked at Assisi was **Pietro Lorenzetti** (active 1306–45); his frescoes there show the impact of Giotto, and have a sense of pathos which is uncharacteristic of Sienese painting. His brother **Ambrogio Lorenzetti** (active 1319–47) was a more original artist, whose main achievement was the idiosyncratic *Allegory of Good and Bad Government* in the Palazzo Pubblico, which shows painting being used for a secular, didactic purpose for the first time and raises the landscape background to a new, higher status, with an awareness of perspective uncommon for this date. The other notable Sienese sculptor of the period was the mysterious **Lorenzo Maitani** (c.1270–1330), who is associated with one work only – the wonderfully lyrical reliefs on the most sumptuous facade in Italy, that of the Duomo in Orvieto.

In **Florence**, meanwhile, a whole group of painters consciously followed Giotto's style, without materially adding to it. The most talented was **Maso di Banco**, who was particularly skilled at conveying the master's sense of plastic form, while the most faithful was **Taddeo Gaddi** (d.1366), whose son **Agnolo Gaddi** (d.1396) carried the Giottesque tradition on to nearly the end of the century. **Bernardo Daddi** (c.1290–1349), on the other hand, combined this tradition with aspects of the Sienese style. The sculptor **Andrea Pisano** (c.1290–1348) succeeded Giotto as master mason of the Campanile. The reliefs he executed for it, plus the bronze door he made for the Baptistery, translate Giotto's pictorial language back into a three-dimensional format.

A reaction against the hegemony of the Giottesque style came with **Andrea Orcagna** (c.1308–68) who was equally prominent as a painter and sculptor, developing a flowery, decorative idiom seen to best effect in the tabernacle in Orsanmichele. The paintings of Orcagna and his school re-established the hierarchical tradition of the Byzantines, and rejected the importance of spatial depth.

At the very end of the fourteenth century, the **International Gothic** style, originating in the Burgundian courts, swept across Europe. This introduced a new richness to the depiction of landscape, animals and costume, though it was unconcerned with intellectual matters. Its dissemination in Italy was largely due to **Gentile da Fabriano** (c.1370–1427), whose *Adoration of the Magi* in the Uffizi (one of his relatively few surviving compositions) shows the gorgeously opulent surface effects of this style at its best. Another leading practitioner was **Masolino da Panicale** (c.1383–1447), who is best known for having begun the famous fresco cycle in Santa Maria del Carmine in Florence. In the same city, the new movement influenced **Lorenzo Monaco** (c.1372–1425), whose work bridges the Florentine and Sienese traditions.

International Gothic took a particularly firm grip in Verona, chiefly through **Antonio Pisanello** (1395–1455). The latter's fame rests partly on his prowess as a medallist, and only a tantalising handful of his paintings remain, notably the frescoes in the Veronese churches of Sant'Anastasia and San Fermo, and the Palazzo Ducale in Mantua, which magically evoke the idealised courtly world of fairy tales. Numerous drawings prove these were based on patient observations of nature – something that was to be a key element in the unfolding of the Renaissance.

THE FLORENTINE RENAISSANCE

A date often given for the start of the **Renaissance** is 1401, when the Florentine authorities announced a public competition for the right to make a second door for the Baptistery. Candidates had to submit a trial piece of *The Sacrifice of Isaac*, a stiff test presenting problems of narrative, expression, movement and spatial arrangement, in which scenery, animals and both nude and draped figures had to be adequately depicted. The most audacious solution, which can be seen in the Bargello, was provided by **Filippo Brunelleschi** (1377–1446), who in the process fully mastered the science of perspective. He failed to win, and in disgust gave up sculpture in favour of architecture, but the new possibilities opened up by his command over visuals, and the impetus they provided for other artists to experiment and discover, mark the transition from medieval art to modern.

Brunelleschi's mantle was taken over by **Donatello** (c.1386–1466), who began his long career by creating a new kind of freestanding statue to adorn Florence's churches, which became the artistic symbol of the city. These heroic, larger-than-life figures are shown with their feet planted firmly on the ground, displaying facial expressions of great energy and concentration. A typical example is the *St George* made for Orsanmichele, below which was placed an extraordinary carving of the saint slaying the dragon which uses the art of perspective for the first time in stone sculpture, as well as pioneering the technique of very low relief. With the bronze *David*, now in the Bargello, Donatello helped bring the nude – the ultimate figurative challenge – back into the mainstream of art; and he also revived another lost art, the bronze equestrian statue, with the *Monument to Gattamelata* in Padua.

The victor of the Baptistery door competition was **Lorenzo Ghiberti** (1378–1455), who thereafter devoted almost his whole life to the project. Ghiberti initially showed no interest in perspective, and remained loyal to most of the old Gothic formulas, his first set of doors merely refining Andrea Pisano's techniques. However, his second set of doors, known as the *Gates of Paradise*, show how his style evolved under the influence of classical antecedents, creating a sense of space and illusion, and imbuing the grouping and characterisation of the figures with a gently lyrical touch.

Donatello's collaborator **Nanni di Banco** (c.1384–1421) was another to achieve an individual mix of the Gothic and Renaissance idioms, notably in *The Four Saints* on Orsanmichele. Another architect-sculptor, **Bernardo Rossellino** (1409–64), created in the *Monument to Leonardo Bruni* in Santa Croce the prototype of the sort of niche tomb that was to prevail for the rest of the century.

Luca della Robbia (1400–82) began his career as a sculptor of marble and bronze, working in a classically derived style, but a very different one from the essentially serious approach of his contemporaries. However, after Luca invented the art of glazed terracotta, he abandoned other forms of sculpture, laying the foundation for a highly lucrative family business which was continued by his nephew **Andrea della Robbia** (1435–1525).

The painter **Masaccio** (1401–28) belongs with Brunelleschi and Donatello as a key figure of the early Renaissance. His *Trinity* fresco in Santa Maria Novella must have startled his contemporaries, its perfect sense of depth and perspective giving the illusion of peering into the solid wall on which it was painted. Masaccio collaborated with Masolino, most notably in the fresco cycle in Santa Maria del Carmine. In this, the scenes are pared down to the essentials; the figures have a heroic quality and dignity, with their gestures depicted at the moment of maximum intensity. A single source of light is used, with shadows cast accurately.

Fra' Angelico (1387/1400–55), like Ghiberti in sculpture, combined new techniques with the Gothic tradition. A devout Dominican monk, his pictures show a rapt, heavenly vision. Colour is a telling ingredient: Angelico's ethereal blue was inimitable, the rest of his palette hardly less fetching. Frescoes in the cells of his own monastery of San Marco, intended as aids to contemplation, rank as his most important body of work. Late in his career, Angelico was called to the Vatican, where he frescoed the Cappella Niccolina, employing a style which had by then lost all Gothic traces.

Fra' Filippo Lippi (c.1406–69) gradually moved away from the style of his master Masaccio to develop a greater sense of drama, seen to best effect in the frescoes in the cathedral at Prato. His later panels show a highly personal, mystical vision, characterised by wistful Madonnas, playful children and poetic landscapes. Fra' Angelico's only follower of note was **Benozzo Gozzoli** (c.1421–97), whose work lacks any sense of profundity, but possesses undeniable decorative charm, best seen in the frescoes in the Palazzo Medici-Ricardi in Florence.

The city's most eccentric painter was **Paolo Uccello** (1396–1475), who was obsessed by the problems of perspective and foreshortening. His *Sir John Hawkwood* in the Duomo was a deliberate piece of *trompe l'oeil*, though its effect is marred by the use of different vantage points, a characteristic common to his paintings, in which he tried to find as many lines as possible to lead the eye inwards. **Domenico Veneziano** (1406–61) was one of the most admired artists of the day, but only a few works by him survive, notably the serene *St Lucy Altar* in the Uffizi, which shows his talent for spatial arrangement and gentle, pastel-like colouring. **Andrea del Castagno** (c.1421–57), in contrast, favoured harsh, strong colours, and an exaggerated dramatic pose for his figures, as can be seen in *The Last Supper* in Sant'Apollonia. In the series of *Famous Men* in the Uffizi he initiated a Florentine trend by vividly translating on to canvas the late sculptural types of Donatello.

Halfway through the century, a new versatility was brought to Florentine art by **Antonio Pollaiuolo** (c.1432–98), who was active as a painter, sculptor, engraver, goldsmith and embroidery designer. Pollaiuolo was renowned for the advances he made in the depiction of anatomy and movement; he was also one of the first to grapple with the next great challenge facing Renaissance painters, namely how to move beyond making all parts of a picture accurate and realistic, while at the same time creating a satisfying compositional whole. Another painter-sculptor was **Andrea del Verrocchio** (c.1435–88), whose fame as a teacher has unfairly drawn attention away from his own wide-ranging achievements. His *Christ and St Thomas* on Orsanmichele shows crafty compositional skills in fitting two statues into a space intended for one, and marks a move away from classicism, as does his equestrian *Monument to Bartolommeo Colleoni* outside San Zanipolo in Venice. Other Florentine sculptors of this period preferred a much softer approach. **Desiderio da Settignano** (1428–64) made sensitive busts of women and children, and used Donatello's technique of low relief to create scenes of the utmost delicacy. **Mino da Fiesole** (1429–84), **Antonio Rossellino** (1427–79) and **Benedetto da Maiano** (1442–97) showed broadly similar preoccupations, all concentrating on grace and beauty of line.

Subjects drawn from classical mythology became an increasingly important part of the repertoire of Florentine painters in the second half of the fifteenth century, in large part due to the humanist culture fostered at the court. One of Italy's most distinctive artists, **Sandro Botticelli** (c.1445–1510), created the most famous and haunting images in this field, notably *The Birth of Venus* and *Primavera*, both now in the Uffizi. His late work shows a deliberate archaism, perhaps as a result of the religious fanaticism of the time.

Filippino Lippi (1457/8–1504), the result of Fra' Filippo's affair with a nun, came to fame with his completion of Masaccio's frescoes in Santa Maria del Carmine. He developed a style based on that of Botticelli, though with a more consciously antique feeling. Another painter with pagan tastes was the reclusive **Piero di Cosimo** (c.1462–1521), who was at his best in enigmatic mythological scenes. Meanwhile, vivid new frescoes were created for Florence's churches by **Domenico Ghirlandaio** (1449–94), whose works are now chiefly remembered for their documentary interest, being filled with portraits of contemporary notables and vivid anecdotal details.

THE 15TH CENTURY ELSEWHERE IN ITALY

Although the fifteenth century brought a rich crop of artists working throughout Italy, including many places which previously had little tradition of their own to draw on, no other city came near to matching the depth and consistency of the fifteenth-century Florentine school.

However, although the technical innovations pioneered in Florence were to have an enormous influence, they were by no means slavishly followed. Sienese painters proved the continuing vitality of the colourful narrative approach of the previous century, modified by the impact of International Gothic. The works of **Sassetta** (c.1392–1450), which are often impregnated by a sense of mysticism, do make some concessions to the new theories of spatial composition, but this is an essentially subordinate feature. The finest Sienese artist of the century was the sculptor **Jacopo della Quercia** (1374–1438), whose style is essentially linear, though with classical tendencies modified by knowledge of the most advanced northern European art of the day. He was given important public commissions in his native city, such as the overall supervision of the Baptistery font and the Fonte Gaia. However, his masterpiece is his last work, the reliefs on the facade of San Petronio in Bologna, which show a vigorous approach fully comparable with those of the great Florentines. His main follower was the Florentine-born **Agostino di Duccio** (1418–81), another sculptor heavily dependent on line, whose work abounds with nervous energy. His masterpiece, executed in collaboration with **Matteo de'Pasti** (c.1420–67), is the joyous series of low reliefs in the Tempio Malatestiano in Rimini.

Another artist associated with the Rimini project was the Tuscan **Piero della Francesca** (1410/20–92), who cast an overwhelming influence over the development of painting in central Italy. A painstaking worker, Piero was also active as a mathematician, hence the importance of perspective and symmetry in his compositions. His figures are painted with a cool sense of detachment yet have a grave, monumental beauty. Piero was also one of the great painters of light, in the blue skies which illuminate his gentle landscapes, and in more dramatic effects, such as in *The Dream of Constantine*, part of his most substantial commission – the fresco cycle in San Francesco, Arezzo.

Melozzo da Forlí (1438–94) was the closest follower of Piero della Francesca, showing a similar interest in perspective, and apparently inventing a favourite Renaissance trick device called *sotto in su* an extreme form of illusion in which figures painted on a ceiling appear to float in space. Another inventive pupil of the same master was **Luca Signorelli** (1450–1523), who developed the ideas of dramatic movement pioneered by Pollaiuolo. In spite of obvious defects, such as harsh colours, stiff drawing and a tendency to overcrowd his compositions, Signorelli was responsible for some of the most heroic paintings of the day. His profound knowledge of anatomy was to be an enormous influence on the succeeding generation, and he used the nude to achieve the most spectacular effects, notably in the frescoes in Orvieto's Duomo.

Pietro Perugino (1445–1523), probably yet another pupil of Piero, developed in a quite different way from Signorelli, producing calm altarpieces featuring soft and beautifully rounded figures set against serene Umbrian landscapes. His collaborator **Bernardino Pinturicchio** (c.1454–1513) was a purely decorative artist whose work has no pretensions to depth, but which is nearly always fresh and pleasing, particularly in his larger schemes such as the Libreria Piccolomini in the Duomo in Siena.

The first important Renaissance painter in northern Italy was **Andrea Mantegna** (c.1431–1506), who represents the apogee of classical influence. Steeped from an early age in the art of the Romans, Mantegna's ideal vision of the antique world permeates nearly all his work, even becoming the predominant element in many of his sacred compositions, together with a phenomenal technical skill, and daring use of unorthodox vantage points – best seen in the grief-laden *Dead Christ* in the Brera, Milan. In total contrast is the exuberant decoration for the *Camera degli Sposi* in Mantua, one of the artist's few works based on direct observation rather than classical inspiration.

Padua in the mid-fifteenth century became an important training ground for artists, thanks to the early successes of Mantegna, and the ten-year stay of Donatello. One of its offshoots was the group of painters active in Ferrara: **Cosmè Tura** (c.1431–95), **Francesco del Cossa** (1435/6–77) and **Ercole de' Roberti** (1448/55–96). Tura's figures are highly charged, with mannered poses and claw-like hands, typically set against fanciful architecture very different from the idealised townscapes painted by other Renaissance artists. Cossa's outline is sharper, his figures energetic rather than theatrical, his colours more resplendent; he too favoured architectural backgrounds, particularly of ruins. Roberti's essentially small-scale style combines something of the pathos of Tura with Cossa's emphasis on colour and line.

Also trained in Padua was the Brescian **Vincenzo Foppa** (1427/30–1515/6), who subsequently became the leader of the Milanese school. His best works have a certain grandeur of conception, and a subdued sense of colouring. His main follower was **Ambrogio Bergognone** (1450/60–1523), who is particularly associated with the Certosa di Pavia. This great building project was also the main outlet for the talents of the leading Lombard sculptors of the day, notably **Giovanni Antonio Amadeo** (1447–1522), whose other main work is the decoration of the Cappella Colleoni in Bergamo.

Venice, as always, remained something of a law unto itself. Even in mid-century, the sculptures of **Bartolomeo Bon** (c.1374–1464/7) and the crowded panels of **Michele Giambono** (active 1420–62) showed the city's continuing preference for late-Gothic forms. Something of a transition can be seen with the **Vivarini** family – **Antonio** (c.1419–80), his brother **Bartolomeo** (c.1430–91) and his son **Alvise** (c.1445–1505) – who gradually introduced a sense of spatial perspective and an increased attempt at characterisation. **Carlo Crivelli** (c.1430–95) was also associated with them. One of the most inventive and idiosyncratic artists of the day, Crivelli abandoned Venice, preferring commissions from churches in small towns in Marche, which he executed in a deliberately archaic style. His altarpieces are claustrophobically opulent, characterised by strong drawing, rich colours, elaborate detail and a superfluity of decoration, with incidental still lifes a common ingredient.

Another, and far more influential, artistic dynasty was that of the **Bellini** family – **Jacopo** (c.1400–70) and his sons **Gentile** (c.1429–1507) and **Giovanni** (c.1430–1516). The last-named was the most significant, standing as a major influence on Venetian painters to come. Though influenced by his brother-in-law Mantegna, Bellini's overall effect is very different, with a soft beauty of both colour and outline. He painted a seemingly endless series of variations on subjects such as the *Madonna and Child* and *Pietà*, yet always managed to make each very different. His larger altarpieces concentrate attention on the foreground, and arrange the figures in such a way that there is a parallel plane behind, rather than the more usual receding landscape. Gentile Bellini was essentially a history painter who epitomised the penchant for highly detailed depictions of Venetian life.

Vittore Carpaccio (c.1460–1523) continued this narrative tradition, and two complete cycles by him can still be seen in the city: that of *St Ursula* in the Accademia, and of *St George and St Jerome* in the Scuola di San Giorgio degli Schiavoni. A love of the picturesque also pervades his altarpieces, which generally give due prominence to fantastic landscapes and resplendent Renaissance buildings.

Venetian Renaissance sculpture was dominated by yet another dynasty, the **Lombardo** family: **Pietro** (c.1438–1515) and his sons **Antonio** (c.1458–1516) and **Tullio** (c.1460–1532). Their strongly classical style was particularly suited to funerary monuments, the best of which are in San Zanipolo. They were also talented decorative carvers, as can be seen in the interior scheme for their own church of Santa Maria dei Miracoli.

Closely associated with the Venetian school was the only important southern Italian painter of the Renaissance, **Antonello da Messina** (c.1430–79), who spent the last years of his life in the city. Antonello's style is derived in large part from fifteenth-century Flemish artists, and it was through contact with their work that he introduced oil painting to Italy. His pictures have a strong sense of pathos, and some of his most arresting images are simple devotional pictures, which follow the same format he favoured for his secular portraits.

THE RENAISSANCE

Just as the beginning of the Renaissance is linked to the specific circumstances of the competition for the Florence Baptistery doors, so the climactic part of the era, known as the High Renaissance, is sometimes considered to have started with the mural of *The Last Supper* in Santa Maria delle Grazie in Milan, painted in the last years of the fifteenth century by **Leonardo da Vinci** (1452–1519). Apart from its magnificent spatial and illusive qualities, this painting endowed each of the characters with identifiable psychological traits, and successfully froze the action to capture the mood of a precise moment. His use of *sfumato*, a blurred outline whereby tones gradually but imperceptibly changed from light to dark, was of crucial importance to his ability to make his figures appear as living beings with a soul – a technique best seen in his portraits.

In Florence, the most original painter of the generation after Leonardo was **Fra' Bartolommeo della Porta** (c.1474–1517), who was caught up in the religious fanaticism which also influenced Botticelli. As a device to stress the otherness of the divine, he clad the figures in his religious compositions in plain drapery, rather than the colourful contemporary costumes which had hitherto been fashionable. He also did away with elaborate backgrounds and anecdotal detail, concentrating instead on expression and gesture. **Mariotto Albertinelli** (1474–1515), who worked with him in the same workshop in San Marco that had once been run by Fra' Angelico, painted in a broadly similar but less austere manner. **Andrea del Sarto** (1486–1530), on the other hand, was the one Florentine artist who shared the Venetian precept of colour and shade as being the most important ingredients of a picture. His figures are classical in outline, aiming at a balance of nuance, proportion and monumentality.

These Florentines, however, stood very much in the shadow of **Michelangelo Buonarroti** (1475–1564), with whom the Renaissance period reaches its climax. Michelangelo's first love was the creation of marble statues. He had little interest in relief, and none at all in bronze or clay, believing that the slow building up of forms was too simple a task for a great artist. His technique is illustrated most graphically in the unfinished *Slaves* in Florence's Accademia, who seem to be pushing their way out of the stone. The colossal early *David*, also in the Accademia, shows his mastery of the nude, which thereafter became the key focus of his art. In spite of claiming to be a reluctant painter, Michelangelo's single greatest accomplishment was the frescoing of the ceiling of the Sistine Chapel, one of the world's most awe-inspiring acts of individual human achievement. Its confident and elated mood is offset by the overpowering despondency of *The Last Judgment* on the end wall, painted three decades later. His later works are more abstract, as seen in the *Pietàs* in the Museo dell'Opera in Florence and the Milan Castello, which contrast sharply with the formal beauty of his youthful interpretation of the scene in St Peter's.

Raphael (1483–1520) stands in almost complete antithesis to his rival Michelangelo, though the personal friendships he forged with his powerful patrons were as significant in raising the status of the artist as was the latter's less compromising approach. A pupil of Perugino, he quickly surpassed his teacher's style, going to Florence where he became chiefly renowned for numerous variants of *The Madonna and Child* and *The Holy Family*. Raphael also developed into a supreme portraitist, skilled at both the psychological and physical attributes of his sitters. His greatest works, however, are the frescoes of his Roman period, notably those in the *Stanze della Segnatura* in the Vatican and the Villa Farnesina. Raphael's late works show him moving towards a large-scale, more dramatic and mannered style, but his early death meant that the continuation of this trend was left to his pupils.

Closely related to the classicising tendency of Raphael is that of the Florentine-born sculptor **Andrea Sansovino** (c.1467–1529), whose grandiose tombs in Santa Maria del Popolo in

Rome, with standing effigies of the Virtues, set the tone for sixteenth-century funerary monuments. His pupil **Jacopo Sansovino** (1486–1570) took his name and carried on his tradition, spending the latter part of his career in Venice, where although principally active as an architect, he also made monumental sculptures which are inseparable from the buildings they adorn. **Sebastiano del Piombo** (c.1485–1547), on the other hand, stood as a direct rival to Raphael in Rome, striving to transfer Michelangelo's heroic manner to panel painting. In this, he was only variably successful, though he was a highly sensitive portraitist.

Meanwhile **Antonio Correggio** (1489/94–1534) managed to carve out a brilliant career for himself in Parma. His three ceiling frescoes there develop the illusionistic devices of Mantegna, marking Correggio out as a precursor of the Baroque. One of the great painters of mythological scenes, he was also a relentless explorer of the dramatic possibilities of light and shade. Another fine exponent of the contrasts of light was the Ferrarese **Dosso Dossi** (1479/90–1542), a romantic spirit who created fantastic landscapes peopled with gorgeously dressed figures.

The golden period of Venetian painting, ushered in by Bellini, continued with his elusive pupil, **Giorgione** (1475–1510), whose short life is shrouded in mystery. One of the few paintings certainly by him is *The Tempest* in the Venice Accademia, whose true subject matter baffled even his contemporaries. In it, the figures are, for the first time in Italian art, completely subsidiary to the lush landscape illuminated by menacing shafts of light. The haunting altarpiece in the Duomo of his native town of Castelfranco Veneto is also almost certainly his, but many other paintings attributed to him may actually be by one of many painters who maintained something of his poetic, colourful style. Some of these, notably **Vincenzo Catena** (c.1480–1531) and **Palma il Vecchio** (c.1480–1528), developed recognisable artistic personalities of their own. **Lorenzo Lotto** (c.1480–1556) was the most distinctive of this circle, travelling widely throughout his career, assimilating an astonishing variety of influences.

Giorgione's influence is also marked in the early works of **Titian** (c.1485–1576), the dominant personality of the Venetian school and one of the most versatile painters of all time. His art embraced with equal skill all the subjects that were required by the Renaissance – altarpieces, mythologies, allegories and portraits. Even more than Michelangelo, he was able to pick and choose his patrons, and was the first artist to build up a truly international clientele. As a portraitist of men of power, Titian was unrivalled, setting the vocabulary for official images which was to prevail until well into the seventeenth century. His complete technical and compositional mastery is already apparent in relatively early works such as the *Assumption* in I Frari, the first example of what was to become a Venetian speciality: a panel painting specially designed to fit an architectural space. Towards the end of his life, Titian abandoned his bravura and brilliant palette in favour of a very free style, stretching the possibilities of oil paint to their very limits.

Giovanni Antonio Pordenone (1483/4–1539) was a provincial north Italian painter strongly influenced by Giorgione and Titian. More obviously in direct descent from the Venetian masters was the school of Brescia. **Giovanni Girolamo Savoldo** (active 1508–48) showed particular adeptness at light effects, and was a pioneer of night scenes, while **Alessandro Moretto** (c.1498–1554) was one of the most incisive portraitists of the Renaissance, and seems to have been responsible for introducing the full-length form to Italy. His altarpieces are more variable, but often have a suitably grand manner.

THE HIGH RENAISSANCE

The perfection of form achieved in the late Renaissance was the culmination of centuries of striving. As artists could not hope to improve on the achievements of Michelangelo and Raphael at their peak, they had to find new approaches. As a result, **Mannerism** was born. This was a deliberately intellectual approach, aimed at flouting the accepted rules, notably by distorting the senses of scale and perspective, exaggerating anatomical details, adopting unlikely poses for the figures, and using unnaturally harsh colours.

One artist commonly labelled a Mannerist is **Giulio Romano** (c.1492–1546), one of the most gifted of Raphael's assistants, whose frescoes in the Palazzo del Te in Mantua, which he himself built, show the style at its most bravura, notably in *The Fall of the Giants*, occupying a room to itself. A leading light in the adoption of Mannerism in Florence was **Rosso Fiorentino** (1494–1540), together with **Jacopo Pontormo** (1494–1556) and **Agnolo Bronzino** (1503–72). Pontormo, a brilliant draughtsman, was the most talented of this group, an able decorator and an inquiring if understated portraitist. Bronzino was highly prolific, but only his portraits of royal and noble personages have much appeal today, their detachment, concentrating more on the beauty of their clothing, casting an enormous influence on official portraitists down the centuries. **Giorgio Vasari** (1511–74), originally from Arezzo, was responsible for many of the frescoes in the Palazzo Vecchio, although he is now chiefly famous for his series of biographies of artists, which marked the birth of art history as a discipline.

Another Florentine Mannerist whose writings have helped secure his fame is the sculptor **Benvenuto Cellini** (1500–71), the author of a racy *Autobiography* which offers a fascinating insight into the artistic world of the time. Though he was successful in finding favour at courts all over Europe, only a few of his sculptures, all of a very high quality, survive. The *Bust of Cosimo I*, in the Bargello, marks the departure of the portrait from realism, creating instead a new heroic image. His *Perseus*, in the Loggia dei Lanzi, forms a fitting counterpart to Donatello's late *Judith*, and completely outclasses the *Hercules and Cacus* in the square outside by his rival **Baccio Bandinelli** (1493–1560).

By far the most influential Florentine Mannerist, however, was **Giambologna** (1529–1608), a sculptor of French origin. His favourite medium was bronze, and he established a large workshop which churned out miniature replicas of his most important compositions. These typically show figures in combat, and are designed for the spectator to walk around, rather than examine from only one viewpoint. His most famous image is the typically androgynous *Mercury*; in a conscious rebuttal of the approaches of both Donatello and Michelangelo, this figure appears to float in the air, in the boldest attempt ever made by a sculptor to defy the laws of gravity.

One of the most individualistic Mannerists was **Domenico Beccafumi** (1484/6–1551), who provided a somewhat unusual end to the long line of Sienese painters, though his emphasis on colour was utterly typical of that city. He was a master of decorative effect, as witnessed by his illusionist frescoes in the Palazzo Pubblico, and his large altarpieces for Sienese churches, which show a particular concern for light and shade, perspective effects, and deep emotions. In Parma, the paintings of Francesco Mazzola, known simply as **Parmigianino** (1503–40), retained something of the consciously refined approach of Correggio, with their exaggeratedly sinuous figures, though his portraits reveal considerable spiritual insight. His decorative scheme for Santa Maria della Steccata typifies the Mannerist penchant for surplus ornament and demonstrates the fertility of his imagination.

Venice, as ever, followed its own distinctive late-Renaissance path, having no taste for the sort of Mannerism practised elsewhere in Italy. **Jacopo Tintoretto** (1518–94) aimed at an ideal based on the drawing of Michelangelo and the colour of Titian, though in fact the heroic style he forged had only superficial resemblances to his mentors. To heighten the sense of drama, he used a battery of other methods: unorthodox vantage points, elongated figures, and unexpected positioning of the main subject on the canvas.

In strong contrast to Tintoretto, the other leading Venetian painter of the day, **Paolo Veronese** (1528–88), was a supreme decorator on a grand scale. Indeed, some of his best work was conceived for architectural settings, such as San Sebastiano in Venice and the Villa Barbara in Masèr. Veronese's love of pomp and splendour, however, is carried over into his easel paintings, which revel in warm, glowing colours and monumental figures, with little sense of gravitas. He fell foul of the Inquisition as a result of the inclusion of German soldiers (which put him under suspicion of Protestant sympathies) and other anachronistic and surplus detail in a huge banquet scene (now in the Venice Accademia) purporting to represent *The Last Supper*. He responded by changing the title to *A Feast in the House of Levi*.

Alessandro Vittoria (1525–1608), a pupil of Jacopo Sansovino, embellished Venice's churches with sculptures that have much in common with Mannerist productions elsewhere in Italy, but are more classically modelled. **Jacopo Bassano** (1510/19–92) was trained in the city, but preferred to work in the provincial town after which he takes his name, where he was by far the most remarkable of a dynasty of painters. As a setting for his religious panels, he painted the small town and country life of his day as it really was. He also popularised the inclusion of animals and heaped piles of fruit and vegetables – features eagerly taken up by later northern European artists – and was a superb painter of light and shade, using heavy dabs of colour and strong chiaroscuro.

Another remarkable artist working well away from the main centres was **Federico Barocci** (1535–1612) of Urbino. His paintings were painstakingly executed, their soft rounded forms mirroring the comforting religious image propagated by the Counter-Reformation, and with an emphasis on light and movement that was to some extent anticipatory of the Baroque to come.

THE BAROQUE AGE

The leadership of Italian art away from the sterility of late Mannerism came initially from cities which had hitherto played a minor role in its development. Bologna was the first to come to prominence, through the academy founded there in 1585 by members of the **Carracci** family – **Ludovico** (1555–1619), **Agostino** (1557–1602) and **Annibale** (1560–1609). This was by no means the first attempt to set up a training school for artists, a concept rendered necessary by the blow the Renaissance had dealt to the old workshop tradition, but it was far more successful than any previous venture. Annibale was easily the greatest and most versatile artist of the three, breathing a whole new life into the classical tradition. His frescoes in the Palazzo Farnese in Rome offer a fresh and highly imaginative approach to mythological scenes, as well as being brilliant examples of illusionism. A more serious intent is noticeable in the artist's canvases, which introduce an emotional yet untheatrical content to well-ordered religious subjects. He was also a major landscape painter, pioneering the sort of luscious scene with a subsidiary subject from the Bible or classical literature which was later to be developed in Rome by the great French painters, Claude and Poussin.

An entirely different but equally novel approach was taken by **Michelangelo da Caravaggio** (1573–1610), whose violent and wayward life led him from Milan to Rome, Naples, Malta, Sicily and most of the way back again. Caravaggio was the great master of chiaroscuro effects, which he used to even more dramatic purpose than Tintoretto. He also used what seemed like shock tactics to his patrons in the Church, stripping away centuries of idealised tradition to present biblical stories as they might have seemed at the time. Real-life peasants, beggars, ruffians and prostitutes were all used as models for the figures, to enhance the realistic impact. His original canvases for commissions such as those for the Roman churches of San Luigi dei Francesi and Santa Maria del Popolo were sometimes rejected, though he always managed to find a private buyer. His impact on the great European Golden Age of seventeenth-century painting was immense, spawning whole schools of Dutch and French derivatives, along with Rembrandt, Rubens, and most of the great Spanish masters.

In Italy, Caravaggio's art had an immediate impact on the older **Orazio Gentileschi** (1563–1639), who was particularly keen on its tenebrist effects. The Mantuan **Bartolomeo Manfredi** (c.1580–1620/1) extended the master's style to such genre subjects as card games and soldiers in guardrooms. And Caravaggio's style was brought to Naples by **Giovanni Battista Caracciolo** (c.1570–1637), inspiring the city's painters to raise Naples from its traditionally marginal position in Italian art to a place, throughout the seventeenth century, at the very forefront.

The first important follower of the Carracci in Bologna was **Guido Reni** (1575–1642). In the nineteenth century, Reni was ranked as one of the supreme artists of all time, but suffered a slump in reputation when a reaction against artistic sentimentality set in; it is only very recently that his genuine gifts for the expression of feeling have been given their proper due. Among other Carracci pupils, **Domenichino** (1581–1641) was a faithful follower of the style, extending its hold on Rome, though he was better at its more decorative and idealised aspects. **Guercino** (1591–1666) merged the classical and realistic styles, imbuing chiaroscuro effects with a subtlety very different to that favoured by Caravaggio and his followers.

Giovanni Lanfranco (1582–1647), originally from Parma, combined the Carracci style with elements borrowed from Correggio. His frescoes in Rome and Naples have a greater sense of movement and technical trickery than those Domenichino was painting at the same time, and mark the beginnings of High Baroque painting. In turn, his own work was made to seem out-of-date by **Pietro da Cortona** (1596–1669), who introduced a sense of fantasy and freedom that was far more ambitious than anything previously attempted. His ceiling in the Palazzo Barberini presented the illusion of opening on to the heavily populated heavens above, with figures seen *sotto in su* – apparently teeming down into the hall below. For a century, this was to be the sort of monumental painting favoured in Rome; it was also spread to Florence by Cortona himself, by means of a series of frescoes in the Palazzo Pitti.

The High Baroque style was essentially a Roman phenomenon, born out of the super-confident mood in the world capital of Catholicism as a result of the success of the Counter-Reformation. Its overwhelmingly dominant personality was **Gianlorenzo Bernini** (1598–1680), a youthful prodigy who had created a wholly new sculptural language while still in his early twenties. Such works as *David* and *Apollo and Daphne*, both in the Villa Borghese, were the first great marble statues since Michelangelo, yet in their independence of form showed a decisive rejection of the concept of belonging to the block from which they were carved, drawing the spectator into the scene and asserting the primacy of the emotions – a key concept of the Baroque. Though only an occasional painter (he in fact spent more time as an architect), Bernini adopted painterly techniques for his work, using different materials for contrast, exploiting sources of light, and using illusionist techniques, producing a drama best seen in *The Ecstasy of St Theresa* in Rome's Santa Maria della Victoria, which goes so far as to recreate the atmosphere of a theatre by the inclusion of a gallery of onlookers.

So overwhelming was the impact of Bernini's art, that most other sculpture of the period is but a pale imitation of it. One of the few sculptors not to be overawed was the Tuscan **Francesco Mochi** (1580–1654), who made two magnificent equestrian monuments in Piacenza. **Alessandro Algardi** (1595–1654) of Bologna managed a brilliant career in Rome as a bitter rival of Bernini, promoting a sculptural version of the Carracci style.

In Venice, the versatile Genovese **Bernardo Strozzi** (1581–1644) tried to revive memories of the great sixteenth-century masters. His exuberant early works are generally more successful, showing the influence of Rubens: they typically have very free brushwork, luminous colours and pronounced modelling. In Naples, **Massimo Stanzione** (1585–1656) combined something of the approaches of Carracci and Caravaggio, though his most original works are his detailed, colourful portraits. A much more aggressively Caravaggesque idiom is apparent in the work of **Artemisia Gentileschi** (c.1597–1651), daughter of Orazio, who was particularly adept at lurid subjects. She enjoyed a remarkable degree of independence and status for a woman of her day, and has attracted a great deal of attention from modern feminists, having a fair claim to the title of "the greatest ever female painter". **Salvator Rosa** (1615–73) painted landscapes that have a wild, mystical quality very different from those of the classical painters of Bologna and Rome. Characteristically, they are populated by bandits or witches, or have an allegorical theme. **Mattia Preti** (1613–99), who originally hailed from the artistic backwater of Calabria, painted some of the most effective canvases in Caravaggio's idiom, excelling at its tenebrist aspects. His later work is more influenced by Roman Baroque, using brighter colours and pronounced spatial effects. In these, he resembles **Luca Giordano** (1632–1705), the main Neapolitan painter of the second half of the century. Giordano was renowned for his ability to paint quickly, and he ranks among the most prolific artists of all time. His output employs a whole variety of styles and is uneven in quality, but shows remarkable technical facility. The last major Baroque painter active in Naples was **Francesco Solimena** (1657–1747), whose large crowded compositions show the full theatricality of the style.

Meanwhile, the Roman vogue for spectacular illusionistic ceilings was continued by **Giovanni Battista Baciccia** (1639–1709), who was warmer in colour and even more audacious in approach than Pietro da Cortona.

His most famous decoration is that in the Gesù, which boldly mixes painted and stucco figures. An even greater command of pyrotechnics, however, was displayed by the Jesuit **Andrea Pozzo** (1642–1709) on the ceiling of Sant'Ignazio, whose illusion is designed to be seen from only one specific point.

THE EIGHTEENTH CENTURY

The decline of Italian art in many of its most celebrated strongholds gathered pace in the eighteenth century, a slump from which only Venice and Rome stood apart. In the case of the former, its pre-eminence was due to a revival of its grand decorative tradition after a century's gap. This gave it a leading position in European **Rococo**, the ornate derivative of late Baroque.

An updated version of the style of Veronese was first fostered by **Sebastiano Ricci** (1659–1734), whose work is superficially similar to Veronese's, but has an airier, lighter feel. A more individual approach is apparent in the work of **Giovanni Battista Piazzetta** (1683–1754), an outstanding draughtsman whose joyful and harmonious paintings give the impression of a free and easy approach, yet which were actually the result of meticulous planning. Venice also boasted a notable female portraitist in **Rosalba Carriera** (1675–1757), who was the first artist to use pastel as an independent medium.

By far the most accomplished exponent of Venetian Rococo, and one of the greatest decorative artists of all time, was **Giovanni Battista Tiepolo** (1696–1770). His work is best seen in an architectural setting, where his illusionistic approach compares favourably with those of the earlier Roman artists in its colour, handling, spatial awareness, sense of fantasy and depth of feeling. The finest schemes were made for foreign patrons (in Würzburg and Madrid), but there are some excellent examples in Udine, Vicenza and Stra, and several in Venice itself, notably the Palazzo Labia and Ca'Rezzonico.

His son, **Giovanni Domenico Tiepolo** (1727–1804), aided him on many projects and painted in a broadly similar style, though he had a more obvious eye for satire. Also active in Venice were a number of painters who specialised in painting views of the city as mementoes for its aristoctatic visitors. The best known of these was **Antonio Canaletto** (1697–1738), whose images, often painted on the spot and with the use of a camera obscura, have defined the popular conception of the buildings and lifestyle of Venice ever since. However, they are an idealised representation, with spatial arrangements and even individual buildings altered. Canaletto's nephew, **Bernardo Bellotto** (1721–80), closely followed his style and applied it to cities all over Europe, but took a more literal approach, stressing topographical exactness. A more sombre, musing mood is present in the Venetian views of **Francesco Guardi** (1712–93), who used a darker palette. His emphasis on transitory light effects foreshadowed the French Impressionists, while his figures have a greater vivacity than those of Canaletto. Genre scenes were also much in demand with visiting tourists, and **Pietro Longhi** (1702–85), who had a limited technique but ready sense of humour, vividly characterised the Venetian life of his day for the benefit of this market.

Among non-Venetian painters, the Genovese **Alessandro Magnasco** (1677–1749) is particularly distinctive, often combining into one picture his two favourite themes of mannered landscapes ravaged by the elements and ecstatic monks at prayer. In Rome, the tourist demand for views was met by **Giovanni Paolo Panini** (c.1692–1765/8), who painted both the ruins of the classical period and the modern buildings of the day. These are surpassed, however, by the grandiose large-scale etchings of **Giovanni Battista Piranesi** (1720–78), which fully exploit the dramatic contrasts of light and shade possible in the black-and-white medium.

The latter can be seen as an early manifestation of **Neoclassicism**, a movement which began in the middle of the century, inspired partly by a reaction against Baroque excesses, and partly by the excitement caused by the discovery of Pompeii and Herculaneum, though many of its leading exponents were foreigners resident in Rome. Neoclassicism aimed at the complete revival of the arts of the ancients, a trend that was particularly marked in sculpture, which had a far larger legacy to borrow on than painting. It is best seen in the works of **Antonio Canova** (1757–1822), which show great beauty in modelling, though a certain frigidity in the depiction of emotions. His statues are often highly erotic in effect: the several monuments he made in honour of Napoleon include life-sized nude depictions, one of which is now in the Brera, Milan.

THE NINETEENTH AND TWENTIETH CENTURIES

If the eighteenth century was a lean time for Italian art, the nineteenth century was even worse, Paris becoming the overwhelmingly dominant European trendsetter. **Francesco Hayez** (1791–1882) was just about the only native painter of note at work in the first half of the century, continuing the Neoclassical manner in his history scenes and highly finished portraits. The Europe-wide Romantic movement made little impact on the Italian imagination, although the country's scenery was to be a potent source of inspiration for visiting foreigners.

Just after the middle of the century, there arose a group of Italian painters based in Florence, known as the **Macchiaioli**, who held more modern and definable aims. Their name derives from the Italian word for a blot, as they made extensive use of individual patches of light and dark colour, which was used to define form, in opposition to the super-smooth Neoclassical approach then in vogue. The guiding spirit of the movement was **Giovanni Fattori** (1825–1908), who painted scenes of military life (based on his experiences fighting in the Wars of Independence of 1848–9) and broad landscapes using very free brushwork and compositional techniques. The group's chief theorist, **Telemaco Signorini** (1835–1901), came to be influenced by the painting of Corot and the Barbizon School, and later followers moved to Paris, to become accepted as peripheral members of the Impressionist circle.

These painters are overshadowed by **Amedeo Modigliani** (1884–1920), the only Italian artist born in the last two hundred years to have gained truly universal recognition. Although most of his adult life was spent in Paris, Modigliani's work is recognisably Italian, being rooted in the tradition of the Renaissance and Mannerist masters. Primitive African art, then being appreciated in Europe for the first time, was the other main influence on his highly distinctive and essentially linear style. His output consists almost entirely of sensuous reclining female nudes, and strongly drawn, psychologically penetrating portraits.

In 1909 an attempt to break France's artistic monopoly was launched – ironically enough, in Paris – by the **Futurists**, who aimed to glorify the dynamism of the modern world, including the key role of warfare. Their approach was similar to the recently-founded Cubist movement in aiming to reproduce several sides of an object at the same time, but differed in wanting to convey movement as well. **Umberto Boccioni** (1882–1916) was the most resourceful member of the group, which never recovered from his death in World War I – for which, true to his principles, he had volunteered. His erstwhile colleagues later developed in different directions. **Giacomo Balla** (1871–1958) painted in a variety of styles, ranging from the academic to the abstract. **Gino Severini** (1883–1966) joined the Cubists after the latter had become more interested in colour, but then turned to mural and mosaic decorations before reverting towards the end of his life to a sense of fantasy characteristic of his Futurist phase. **Carlo Carrà** (1881–1966) did a complete about-face from his Futurist origins, aiming to revive the representationalism of the old Italian masters.

Carrà teamed up in 1917 with **Giorgio de' Chirico** (1888–1978) to form **Pittura Metafisicia**, which reacted against both the mechanical approach of Cubism and Futurism's infatuation with the modern world, cultivating instead a nostalgia for antiquity. The movement, which established a school in Ferrara, was influenced by Surrealism, and in particular a penchant for the presence of unexpected, out-of-place objects. De'Chirico's *Metaphysical Interiors* show rooms littered with all the fetishes of modern civilisation; architectural forms of a strange and rigid nature are another recurring theme in his work of this period, though like Carrà he later abandoned this in favour of a consciously archaic approach.

Among other Italian painters of the twentieth century to have gained an international reputation, **Giorgio Morandi** (1890–1964), who was strongly influenced by de'Chirico, specialised in haunting still lifes – very precisely drawn and often in monochrome. Also touched by the Metaphysical tradition was **Filippo de Pisis** (1896–1956). His huge output is experimental in nature, often exploring sensation and the unexpected; consequently, it is highly uneven in quality. The Sicilian **Renato**

Guttuso (1912–87) also focused on dramatic subjects, this time with political intent. His early works expressed his opposition to Fascism; in 1947, he helped to found *Fronte Nuovo delle Arti*, which aimed to link art to revolution. Italy's leading practitioner of abstraction is **Alberto Burri** (b.1915), best known for his collages of waste materials with a thick blob of red or black paint.

Modern Italian sculptors have been more successful than painters in reinterpreting Italy's heritage in a novel way. **Giacomo Manzù** (b.1908) has aimed to revive the Italian religious tradition, in a highly personal manner reminiscent of Donatello, whose technique of very low relief he has used extensively. His best known work is the bronze door of St Peter's on the theme of Death, a commission awarded following a highly contentious competition in 1949. **Marino Marini** (1901–80) specialised in another great theme of Italian art, that of the equestrian monument – examples of his work are now displayed in a museum specially devoted to Marini in Florence – while the portraits and female nudes of **Emilio Greco** (b.1913) stand as an updated form of Mannerism.

Gordon McLachlan

ITALIAN ARCHITECTURE

Even if Italy's architecture has not been so consistently influential as its painting and sculpture, the country still boasts a remarkable legacy of historic buildings, an almost unbroken tradition stretching back over more than 2500 years. As in the other arts, strong regional distinctions are evident in most of the main architectural periods.

THE GREEKS AND ETRUSCANS

The earliest important structures still standing in Italy were built by the peninsula's **Greek** colonisers of the sixth century BC. These exhibit the same qualities characteristic of the classical architecture of Greece itself: a strong but simple outline, a rigorous adherence to balanced proportions, a total unity of design featuring a logical system of horizontals and verticals, and extensive use of decoration to emphasise the structure. This architecture, which principally made use of marble, was based on three great **classical orders**, each of which consisted of an upright column, sometimes resting on a base, topped by a capital and an entablature of architrave, cornice and frieze.

Doric, the grandest and plainest of these orders, was used for the **temples** which are the chief glory of the Greek style, dedicated to gods yet always human in scale, never rising very high, nor appearing in any way overblown. A fine group can be seen on the Italian mainland at **Paestum**; the others – at Agrigento, Selinunte, Segesta and Syracuse – are in **Sicily**. They are older and less refined than the Parthenon in Athens, but their state of preservation compares favourably with any of their counterparts in Greece. Significantly, the Temple of Concord in Agrigento, the most complete of all, was saved by being transformed into a Christian church, while the Temple of Athena in Syracuse was incorporated into the Duomo, where it still remains.

The Greeks were also inveterate builders of open-air **theatres** – generally set against hillsides, with seats for the spectators hollowed out of the rock. Syracuse's Greek theatre is one of the best preserved of its period; that of Taormina, with the peerless backdrop of Mount Etna, also dates back to the Greeks, but was extensively remodelled by the Romans.

A very different form of architecture was practised during the same period in central Italy by the **Etruscans**, but unfortunately little Etruscan architecture remains above ground, as their Roman conquerors engaged in a deliberate programme of obliteration. The few surviving examples include the city walls of Volterra and Cortona, from the sixth century BC, and the gateways at Volterra and Perugia, from about three centuries later. However, Etruscan **tombs** survive in abundance, mainly at Cerveteri and Tarquinia in northern Lazio.

THE ROMAN PERIOD

In architecture, as in many other fields, the **Romans** borrowed from and adapted Greek models. Just as was the case with other art forms, however, their approach to building shows marked differences, particularly in their preference for order and usefulness above beauty. Functional building materials were favoured, and only from the time of Augustus, which marked the softening of the Roman image, are marble and stucco much in evidence, and then usually for facing purposes only. Furthermore, towns were laid out wherever possible in a regular planned grid format, to the model of a military camp.

Although they used the three Greek orders (preferring the Corinthian, with its elaborate acanthus leaf capital), and invented two more of their own, the Romans relegated the column from the essential structural role it had performed under the Greeks to one that was merely decorative. Instead, they concentrated on solid constructions, employing the rounded forms of the arch and dome, and focusing attention on the end walls. **Vaulting** was the Romans' major contribution to architectural development. Their use of concrete rather than timber frames enabled them to span much larger spaces, and build much higher, than the Greeks had ever done; indeed, their achievements were unequalled until the nineteenth century. Accordingly, they were able to create an architecture which perfectly expressed their own preoccupations of power and glory.

Roman architecture once dominated Europe, showing no appreciable regional variations, and many of the most impressive individual monuments still standing lie outside Italy. However, the most important ensembles are to be found in **Rome** itself, its original seaport of **Ostia**, and the residential towns of **Pompeii** and **Herculaneum** (which were both submerged by the massive eruption of Mount Vesuvius). The heart of a Roman city was its **forum**, a square usually set at the intersection of the two main streets. Its buildings were the focus of all the main aspects of public life: worship, politics, law, finance, trading, shopping and meeting. In time, it often became too small for all these functions: the Roman Forum itself, which largely dates from the days of the Republic, is an extreme case in point, and successive emperors found it necessary to lay out separate new forums in the city.

Each forum usually contained several **temples**, of which notable examples survive in Palestrina, Tivoli, Assisi and Brescia. At first, these tended to follow the Greek model, with the front entrance given due prominence, and often preceded by a flight of steps. Later, circular designs were increasingly favoured, as with the Temples of Vesta in Rome. A circular design was also chosen for the **Pantheon** in Rome, which is not only the greatest temple of all, and the only complete building to have survived from the days of Imperial Rome, but is also one of the all-time masterpieces of both engineering and architecture, its dome still one of the largest in the world.

The main public building in Roman towns was the **basilica**, which was used for meetings and administration. In many respects, it was rather like a Greek temple turned inside out, consisting of a large hall terminating in an apse, with aisles to the side, often bearing galleries and with a sloping vault which was lower than that of the main section. No complete examples survive in Italy, but some idea of the development of this type of building can be had by comparing the fragments of the basilicas of Trajan and Maxentius in Rome, which are nearly two centuries apart in date. The former was colonnaded, and had a flat wooden roof, while the latter (as can clearly be seen in the surviving aisle) had a sturdy concrete vault borne by five massive piers.

In the field of leisure, the **thermae** played a key role. These vast edifices had hot, warm and cold baths, as well as halls for all kinds of other activities, those of the Emperors Caracalla and Diocletian, both in Rome, from the third and fourth centuries AD, providing the most potent reminder of their splendour. Roman **theatres** differed from those of the Greeks in being constructed above ground, and in having a semicircular *orchestra*. The Teatro de Marcello, completed under Augustus, is the only survivor in Rome itself; it is also notable for marking the use of superimposed orders in architecture for the first time. However, the Romans as a rule much preferred the atmosphere of their **amphitheatres**, which were used to stage gladiatorial contests and other public spectaculars. These were elliptical in shape, and of very solid construction, using a variety of materials. The outer wall, pierced by rows of arches, had a massive effect; inside, the seats were grouped in tiers. Rome's so-called Colosseum is the best-preserved; others are to be found in Verona, Cápua, Pozzuoli and Pompeii. Proof of the durability of these monuments is provided by the fact that they are still in use.

Roman **houses** fall into three main categories. The *domus* or town dwelling was grouped symmetrically around an atrium and one or more peristyle courts. A more rambling plan characterises the *villa*, a patrician country residence which tended to be decorated with porticoes and colonnades, and have rooms specially aligned to catch both the sun and the shade. Poorer Romans lived in *insulae*, tenement-type constructions with several floors, which were often vaulted throughout and grouped symmetrically in streets and squares. Few Roman

palaces remain. The most important is the misleadingly named Villa Adriana in Tivoli, replete with fantastical recreations of buildings the Emperor Hadrian had seen on his travels, along with grottoes, terraces and fountains. From a century earlier, Nero's fabled Domus Aurea in Rome survives only in part.

Roman law forbade burial inside the city walls, and the Via Appia became the favoured site, lined by cylindrical, tower-like **mausoleums**, the finest being that of Cecilia Metella. A similar but larger structure, of the Emperor Augustus, was the first to be built in the city centre. Another in honour of Hadrian was by far the most spectacular funerary monument built by the Romans, but was later converted into the Castel Sant'Angelo.

The **triumphal arch** was a specifically Roman creation, usually erected to celebrate military victories and richly adorned with bas-reliefs, the whole surmounted by a large sculptural group, usually of a horse-drawn triumphal chariot. Several of these arches can be seen in Rome; others are in Ancona, Aosta, Benevento, Rimini and Susa.

Another Roman invention was the **aqueduct**, which was built to transport water to the towns. These were undecorated and purely functional, with the water running down a very gentle gradient along a channel at the top. Nonetheless, they often have a majestic sweep, particularly when the lie of the land dictated the building of several tiers. Traces of aqueducts can be seen south of Rome, though the most impressive surviving examples are in other countries. The Romans also excelled at building **bridges**. There were eleven spanning the Tiber in the capital in imperial times; these have mostly been replaced or altered, but the Pons Fabricius remains substantially intact. Other bridges which have changed little are the graceful Ponte di Solesta in Ascoli Piceno, which is of a single arch only, and the five-arched Ponte di Tiberio in Rimini.

EARLY CHRISTIAN AND BYZANTINE

The **early Christians** in Italy initially had to practise their religion in private houses and underground in **catacombs** hollowed out of the living rock. Those in Rome are the most famous, but other impressive groups can be seen in Naples and Syracuse. When Christianity was legalised and officially adopted by the Roman Empire, it was hardly surprising that its architecture should base itself very directly on secular imperial models. In particular, **churches** adopted a basilican format. They were generally raised over the graves of martyrs, whose tombs were kept in the crypt, directly below the high altar. In time, they would invariably be orientated towards the east, though in the early churches it was quite normal to face exactly the opposite way. For the interior, columns were often taken from demolished secular buildings.

In **Rome** itself, much the best-preserved church of this time is Santa Sabina, which dates from the fifth century. Its exterior is of a stark simplicity, the plain brick walls pierced only by large windows; the interior shows the move towards regular columns. The larger contemporary basilicas of Santa Maria Maggiore and San Paolo fuori le Mura, though both much altered down the centuries, still clearly show the variations in the basilican plan. **Transepts** were introduced, as a result of a conscious desire to simulate the shape of the Cross; double aisles were also employed, except at Santa Maria Maggiore. Also of this period is San Giovanni in Laterano, which pioneers the Italian preference for a separate, octagonal **baptistery**.

The basic basilican style flourished in the city for centuries, and little in the way of development is discernible between the seventh-century Sant'Agnese and the ninth-century Santa Maria in Cosmedin, or even the twelfth-century San Clemente, though the last is unusually archaic.

The next significant buildings are those of the subsequent imperial capital, **Ravenna**. These are understandably more famous for the resplendent mosaics which adorn their interiors, but they are also of major architectural significance, marking the appearance in Italy of the **Byzantine** style, whose most distinctive characteristic was the development of the dome. Under the Romans, this by necessity had to rest on a circular base; by the use of pendentives, the Byzantines were able to erect a dome on square foundations. The earliest of the surviving Ravenna monuments, the Mausoleum of Galla Placida, dating from about 430, provides a good illustration of this. The church of San Vitale, an ingenious design of an octagon within an octagon, is also remarkable. The other churches here are basilican in form; a curiosity is that the apse is semicircular inside, but has a polygonal exterior. Their cylindrical **campaniles** were added later, probably in the ninth century. These are the earliest freestanding bell towers – from then on, a popular characteristic of Italian churches – to have survived, though the form was actually pioneered in Rome.

Italy's most purely Byzantine buildings are to be found in the Venetian lagoon, whose prosperity was dependent on its eastern trade. The Duomo of **Torcello**, originally seventh-century but extensively remodelled in the early eleventh century, is the oldest of these; Santa Fosca on the same island is in the same style. However, the Byzantine heritage is seen to best effect in the basilica of San Marco in **Venice** itself. This was also much altered in the eleventh century, but the basic layout of the original ninth-century building, modelled on the Church of the Holy Apostles in Constantinople, was preserved. With its five bulbous domes, its Greek-cross plan and sumptuous mosaic decoration it stands as the supreme Byzantine monument of its time.

ROMANESQUE

The European emergence from the Dark Ages in the tenth and eleventh centuries is associated in architecture with the **Romanesque** style, which in Italy draws heavily on the country's own heritage. Features not commonly found in other countries include a continued attachment to the basilical plan, and to cupolas raised on domes, the use of marble for facing, the presence of separate baptisteries and campaniles, and the employment of the arch for decorative rather than purely structural reasons.

Strong regional variations are apparent. The churches of the **Lombard plain** most resemble those of northern Europe, and were among the most internationally influential. Their most dominant features are their tall, stately towers, which are unbuttressed and adorned with pilaster strips. They usually have a projecting vaulted porch on the facade, resting on a base of lions, above which a wheel window serves as the principal source of light for the nave. Decoration is otherwise concentrated in the apse, which often has an open dwarf gallery and corbels delicately carved with grotesque heads. Rib vaulting – revolutionary in its day – was sometimes used inside. The Duomo in **Modena** is particularly outstanding, as are the characteristic trios of duomo, campanile and baptistery at **Parma** and **Cremona**.

All these are surpassed by the highly distinctive style of **Pisa**, which can be seen all over the city but is particularly associated with the Piazza del Duomo, which adds a burial ground (the Camposanto) to the normal group of three, and has the rare advantage of a spacious verdant setting away from the commercial centre. Although the ensemble was begun in the mid-eleventh century and only finished three hundred years later, it shows a remarkable sense of unity. The buildings all have marble facing, and their exteriors, in a design conducive to catching wonderful light effects, have open arcaded galleries, which rise all the way to the facade gable – and all the way round the building. A broadly similar approach was adopted in the neighbouring cities of **Lucca** and **Pistoia**.

An even more idiosyncratic Romanesque style was fostered in the earliest surviving buildings of **Florence** – the Baptistery, San Miniato and Santi Apostoli, plus the Badia in Fiesole. The overall layout of these buildings is typical enough of the time, but the continued use of mosaics and marble panelling in the interiors is suggestive of the Byzantine era, while the overall elegance of form shows a debt to Roman models.

In **southern Italy** there was a marriage of Byzantine and Romanesque styles, as can be seen at San Nicola in Bari and the duomos of Salerno, Amalfi, Troia, Trani, Molfetta and Bitonto. An even more intoxicating mix is found in **Sicily**, where the island's traditions were freely welded into an exotic confection which is wholly unique. Sturdy Norman towers are often found in concert with Byzantine domes and mosaics and Saracenic horeshoe arches and stalactite vaulting. The Duomo of **Monreale** – and in particular its fabulous cloister with dazzling mosaics and richly carved capitals – is particularly outstanding. Those of **Cefalù** and **Palermo** are also notable, as are three surprising parish churches, all in the capital – La Martorana, San Cataldo and San Giovanni degli Eremiti. The same city also has two outstanding palaces which show the same mix of styles: the Palazzo dei Normanni and La Zisa.

THE GOTHIC PERIOD

The **Gothic** style, which placed great emphasis on light and verticality, and was associated with the pointed arch, rib vault, flying buttress and large traceried windows, progressed from its mid-twelfth-century French origins to become the dominant architectural force of medieval Europe. But although it was used in Italy from the early thirteenth century to the early fifteenth century, its lifespan here was far shorter than elsewhere, and the forms it took quite different from those of other countries. In many ways, Italy was wholly unsuited to the Gothic, which remained essentially a northern European creation. The pointed arch was foreign to a country steeped in classicism, while the hot climate meant that only small windows were required, or interiors would become stifling. For the same reason, the giant portals of northern Gothic were unwanted; moreover, the large numbers of statues in the round they required were anathema to a nation reared on relief carvings.

In Italian Gothic architecture the emphasis is still on the **horizontal**: buildings seldom rise very high, and often have wooden roofs rather than stone vaults. **Colour** plays a far more important role than in any other country, walls covered with marble facing, mosaics and frescoes. A great deal of attention was lavished on **facades**, but these were again often purely decorative, with no architectural relationship to the structure behind. Many of the most characteristic features of Gothic, such as soaring steeples and graceful pinnacles, flying buttresses and elaborate vaults, are hardly to be found in Italy at all.

As elsewhere in Europe, the spread of the plain early-Gothic style in Italy is associated with the reforming Cistercian order of monks. The abbey of **Fossanova**, which was complete by the first decade of the thirteenth century, is an outstanding example of their architecture, as well as an unusually complete example of a medieval monastic complex. In a similar manner are the monasteries of San Galgano near Siena (now in ruins) and the collegiate church of Sant'Andrea in Vercelli. However, the most outstanding early-Gothic church in Italy is the basilica of San Francesco in **Assisi**, which was built in the wake of the saint's death in 1226. It is a wholly original, symbolical design, with the lower church dark and mysterious, the upper light and airy, each provided with ample wall space which in time was duly filled with appropriate fresco cycles.

Nothing quite like San Francesco was ever built again, but the churches of the Franciscan and Dominican orders became a dominant feature of many cities. In accordance with the emphasis placed on preaching, these were typically barn-like structures, intended to hold a large congregation. They were invariably of brick, but differed considerably in plan. The most imposing are the late-thirteenth-century Santa Croce and Santa Maria Novella in **Florence**, and their fourteenth-century counterparts in **Venice** – I Frari and San Zanipolo.

Only one modest Gothic church (Santa Maria sopra Minerva) was ever built in Rome. Nonetheless, the relatively few important building projects of the period generally took on a spectacular nature. The Duomo in **Siena** is arguably the most sumptuous Gothic cathedral ever built, and boasts a resplendent facade in which sculptures were used in a wholly unorthodox and challenging way. **Florence**'s Duomo has gained world fame through its Renaissance dome, but in essentials it is a highly inventive Gothic design, whose final shape had already been determined by the mid-fourteenth century. Its detached campanile, unbuttressed and faced with coloured marbles and reliefs illustrates the continuing Italian preference for this form. **Orvieto** shows the tendencies of Italian Gothic at its most extreme: the interior architecture is plain, and remarkably close in spirit to an early Christian basilica, whereas the facade surpasses even Siena's for ornateness, with its narrative bas-reliefs, brightly coloured marbles and mosaics. Only the Duomo of **Milan**, begun in the late fourteenth century but only finally completed in the nineteenth century, uses much of the stock vocabulary of northern European cathedral architecture, no doubt due to the fact that German masons were partly responsible for its construction. Yet even here the gleaming white marble and pronounced geometric nature of the design are wholly Italianate.

The scale of this project seems to have inspired that of the nearby Certosa of **Pavia**, the most extensive monastic complex in the country. Here, however, notice was paid to changing artistic tastes, with the result that it progressively moved away from its Gothic origins. San Petronio in **Bologna**, which was started around the same time, was a parish church intended to rival any cathedral, and to surpass them all in length. Work, however, was abandoned on the belated completion of the nave. From a century earlier, another idiosyncratic design worthy of mention is the pilgrimage church of Il Santo in **Padua**. This has an essentially Gothic plan, even including a French-style chevet with radiating chapels. However, the facade is derived from the Lombard Romanesque, while the seven large domes are evidence of the continued attraction of Byzantinism.

In the field of military architecture, the most imposing thirteenth-century **castles** were built in southern Italy by Emperor Frederick II, most impressive of which is the celebrated **Castel del Monte**, which combined classical and Gothic elements in a plan of monotonous regularity, with an octagonal shape used for towers, perimeter walls and courtyard. Frederick's castle at **Lucera** was transformed later in the century by the Angevins, who also built the Castel Nuovo in **Naples** – later altered to serve as a palace in succeeding centuries.

Among fourteenth-century constructions, the Fortezza at **Volterra** is an archetypal medieval castle set high on a hill, with cylindrical keep, round towers, massive outer walls and machicolations. Of the palatial fortresses begun around this time, those of **Mantua**, **Ferrara** and **Verona** are particularly outstanding, the last guarded by a strongly fortified **bridge** over the Adige. Italy's other famous Gothic bridge, the Ponte Vecchio in Florence, presents a total contrast, with jewellers' shops along its length.

In the late thirteenth century, the rise of civic pride led to a passion for building majestic **town halls**, often crowned by a slender tower. The most imposing are the Palazzo Pubblico in Siena and the Palazzo Vecchio in Florence. These same cities, along with many more in central Italy, are rich in Gothic **mansions** of the patrician class. However, the most distinctive residences in the country were built in **Venice**. The Ca' d'Oro is the most refined, whereas the Ca' Fóscari and Palazzi Giustinian have a compensating monumental grandeur. All were modelled on the **Palazzo Ducale**, arguably the greatest secular European building of its time, which ingeniously combines Gothic and Islamic styles on its exterior walls, with evidence of the classical influence in its courtyards and interiors.

THE EARLY RENAISSANCE

The Gothic style maintained a firm hold over northern European architecture until well into the sixteenth century. In **Florence**, however, it had been supplanted by the second decade of the fifteenth century by the new, classically derived **Renaissance** style, which soon spread throughout Italy. Its conquest of the rest of Europe, if belated, was absolute, establishing an architectural vocabulary which remained unchallenged until the nineteenth century, and still maintains a footing even today. From here on, the history of architecture becomes a history of architects. Previously, major buildings had been designed and built by lodges under masons whose fame was seldom wide or long lasting. To some extent this had been modified in Italy by the appointment of famous painters and sculptors for the most prestigious commissions. This trend continued in the Renaissance period – and was undoubtedly a factor in ensuring that all major buildings were aesthetically pleasing, a casual relationship which was lost in later centuries. However, architecture shed its dilettante connotations, and was henceforth professional in outlook, with full-time practitioners emerging for the first time.

Both the format of modern architecture and the profession of architect were in many respects the single-handed creation of **Filippo Brunelleschi** (1377–1446). Having been unsuccessful in the competition for the Florence Baptistery doors, he turned away from his original training as a sculptor, devoting himself to a careful study of the building practices and techniques of the ancients. He subsequently won another major local competition, that for the Duomo's dome. It was only by reviving Roman methods of herringbone brickwork, and by inventing suitable hoisting machinery, that Brunelleschi was able to give the final shape to this otherwise Gothic construction, which ever since has served as the focal point of the city, and provided a model for all subsequent domes. In his key original buildings – the Ospedale degli Innocenti, the churches of San Lorenzo and Santo Spirito and the Cappella Pazzi –

Brunelleschi seems to have been inspired as much by the distinctive Romanesque legacy of his native city as by ancient Rome. His designs are majestic but uncomplicated; they are entirely original, and in no sense an archaeological revival of any previous style.

Two more Brunelleschi innovations – a new type of urban palace, and a central plan for church design – are best illustrated in buildings by **Michelozzo di Bartolommeo** (1396–1472). The Palazzo Medici-Riccardi established the form of Florentine mansions for the rest of the century – a severe facade with rusticated stonework in the basement and smooth ashlar upstairs, an overhanging cornice, and a compensatingly light inner courtyard. In the church of Santi Annunziata, Michelozzo modelled the tribune on a circular Roman temple in the first centrally planned church design to be built in the Renaissance period; with Santa Maria delle Grazie in **Pistoia** he extended this concept to the entire building. His light and airy library in San Marco is a mould-breaker in its own right; its format of a central nave flanked by aisles was used throughout the Renaissance.

Even more influential was **Leon Battista Alberti** (1404–72). One of the most complete personifications of Renaissance Man, Alberti was above all a writer and theorist, the author of the first architectural treatise since Roman times; he designed buildings, but always relied on other architects to build them. Far more archaeological in taste than Brunelleschi, he set out to give new life to such Roman forms as triumphal arches and pedimented temple fronts. He also articulated the theory of harmonic proportions, which, in emulation of musical intervals, adopted certain ratios of measurement – first put into practice in the facade of Santa Maria Novella. With the Palazzo Rucellai, he solved the problem of how to make the facades of Florentine palaces seem less austere and Gothic in feel by the simple expedient of introducing thin pilaster strips. Alberti's most original creations, however, are outside Florence. Although unfinished, his design for the Tempio Malatestiano in **Rimini** is a magnificent fragment, cloaking the old Franciscan church with a covering inspired by the same town's great Roman monuments. An even more resplendent facade was designed for Sant'Andrea in **Mantua**. Its elements are carefully repeated in the interior, a vast space which daringly omits aisles in favour of a single nave with side chapels.

Bernardo Rossellino (1409–64), who was the builder of the Palazzo Rucellai, used its basic form again in the Palazzo Piccolomini in **Pienza**, where he was also responsible for the duomo. This was part of the most ambitious planning scheme of the day, the laying out of a complete new papal town. Like many subsequent Renaissance projects, it remains incomplete, available funds so often failing to match the grandeur of inspiration. The creation of ideal towns was the main preoccupation of **Antonio Averlino Filarete** (c.1400–69), the second main architectural theorist of the day. He himself built very little, other than part of the Castello Sforzesco and the huge, symmetrical Ospedale Maggiore, both in **Milan**.

Of the next generation of Florentine architects, **Giuliano da Maiano** (1432–90) introduced the Renaissance style to Siena with the Palazzo Spannochi, and also built the duomo in **Faenza**. The last phase of his career was spent in **Naples**, where he was responsible for the Porta Capuana and chapels in the church of Monteoliveto. **Giuliano da Sangallo** (1445–1516) was the first to apply Renaissance principles to the layout of villas, and his work in Florence includes the Palazzo Strozzi, the most ambitious palace of the century, and the heavily antique cloister of Santa Maria Maddalena dei Pazzi, in which Ionic columns boldly take the place of arches.

The most complete and refined early-Renaissance palace was built in the comparative obscurity of **Urbino**, where a cultivated humanist court flourished. **Luciano Laurana** (c.1420–79), an obscure architect of Dalmatian origin, is credited with the overall plan, as well as the building of the elegant courtyard, and the ornate chimneypieces and doorways which are key features of the interior. Also attached to Urbino was the Sienese **Francesco di Giorgio Martini** (1439–1501/2), who is thought to have built the exquisite loggia overlooking the hills, as well as two domed churches: San Bernardino in Urbino itself and Santa Maria del Calcinaio in Cortona. Like many other Renaissance architects, he worked extensively on military projects, specialising in hilltop castles with pioneering defences against artillery. **Ferrara** was another small court where the Renaissance prospered, thanks in large part to an ambitious extension to the town designed by **Biagio Rossetti** (1447–1516), which included numerous churches and palaces, the most original of which is the Palazzo dei Diamanti, named after the diamond shapes used on its facade. **Venice** remained attached to the Gothic style until the 1460s. When the Renaissance finally took root, it was given a pronounced local accent, with hangovers from Byzantinism in the preference for rich surfaces and mystical spatial effects. Architects still enjoyed nothing like the prestige they had gained in Florence, and it was only as a result of nineteenth-century research that **Mauro Coducci** (c.1440–1504) emerged from obscurity to be identified as the builder of many of the city's best buildings of this time – the churches of San Michele in Isola, San Giovanni Crisostomo and Santa Maria Formosa. His rival **Pietro Lombardo** (c.1435–1515) was less concerned with the central tenets of the Florentine Renaissance than with using them to update the Venetian-Byzantine tradition. The tiny church of Santa Maria dei Miracoli, for which he and his sons also made the decoration, shows his highly ornate style at its best.

THE HIGH RENAISSANCE AND MANNERISM

The ornate facades characteristic of the Venetian Renaissance were to some extent repeated all across northern Italy, notably in the early buildings of **Donato Bramante** (1444–1514) in **Milan**. These include the church of San Satiro, which ingeniously incorporates a ninth-century chapel and makes up for the lack of space to build an apse by including a convincing *trompe l'oeil* of one; the centrally planned east end of Santa Maria delle Grazie, which completely outclasses the Gothic nave; and a series of cloisters for Sant'Ambrogio.

With the French invasion of the city in 1499, Bramante fled to **Rome**, where his enthusiasm coincided nicely with the papal authorities' desire to rebuild the city in a manner worthy of its imperial heyday, and the **High Renaissance** in architecture was born. This centred on the demolition of the fourth-century basilica of **St Peter's**, and its replacement by a vast new church. Bramante provided a design that was the ultimate in central planning, a Greek cross with four smaller Greek crosses in its arms. This project took well over a century to complete, by which time Bramante's plan had been altered out of all recognition, with only the piers of the dome surviving. Bramante's surviving masterpiece in Rome is the tiny Tempietto of San Pietro in Montorio, whose grandeur is out of all proportion to its size.

Bramante's position as leading architect in Rome was taken over by **Raphael** (1483–1520). His painting activities left him little time for this, but his few buildings were enormously influential. The Chigi chapel in the church of Santa Maria del Popolo brought to fruition the interest in centralised temples first evident in his early panel of *The Marriage of the Virgin* (now in the Brera). It is deliberately set apart from the rest of the church, and opulently adorned with statues, bronze reliefs, paintings, marbles and mosaics, its richness reflecting that of the patron, the papal banker. His pupil **Giulio Romano** (c.1492–1546) was active mainly in **Mantua**, where he consciously distorted the elements of classical architecture, thus beginning the Mannerist style. The Palazzo del Te establishes an organic unity between house and garden, as well as between architecture and interior decoration. The artist's own house in the same city is very different but equally inventive, while his design for the Duomo is an early example of a building concerned above all with effect, the intention being to "suck" the viewer towards the high altar.

Baldassare Peruzzi (1481–1536), originally from Siena, built the most graceful of Rome's High Renaissance palaces, the Villa Farnesina, which is arguably the outstanding secular monument of the time, featuring an unusual U-shaped plan with two superbly frescoed ground floor loggias and an upstairs hall with illusionistic architectural perspectives. The Palazzo Massimo alle Colonne from late in his career successfully overcomes the difficulties of its sloping site by means of a highly original convex facade. Peruzzi also built the pentagonal Villa Farnese in Caprarola in collaboration with **Antonio da Sangallo the Younger** (1485–1546), with whom he also worked on St Peter's. Sangallo's most important independent work, however, is the strongly classical Palazzo Farnese, the most spectacular Roman palace of its time.

Michelangelo Buonarroti (1475–1564) only took up architecture in middle age. His approach was in direct contrast to Alberti's, using plans only as a rough guide, and making constant changes throughout the period of execution. None of his major buildings were finished in his lifetime: his earliest commissions in **Florence** – San Lorenzo's Sagrestia Nuova (which forms a piece with his own sculptures) and the Biblioteca Laurenziana (where every element of the decoration is closely tied to the architecture) – already show an original approach to building. Like Giulio Romano, he adopted an entirely new attitude to space, and turned the vocabulary of classicism to suit his own ends. In **Rome**, he invented the giant order – columns and pilasters rising through two or more storeys – for his palaces on the Piazza dei Campidoglio. Other major projects were the conversion of the central hall of the Baths of Diocletian into the church of Santa Maria degli Angeli, and the work on St Peter's.

The High Renaissance was introduced to **Venice** by **Jacopo Sansovino** (1486–1570), who fled from Rome after its sacking by French troops in 1527. Sansovino quickly became the leading architect in the city, and erected a series of public edifices – the Zecca, the Loggetta and the Libreria Sansoviniana – which transformed the area around San Marco. The last-named is one of the most joyous, festive designs of the Renaissance, a highly successful compromise between classical precision and Venetian love of surface ornament.

Michele Sanmicheli (c.1484–1559) spent much of his career on military projects, building the fortifications of his native **Verona**, including three dignified gateways, and the Fortezza at the entrance to Venice's Lido. He also built very grandiose palaces in both cities, which are especially notable for their facades of richly detailed stonework: the Palazzo Grimani on the Canal Grande and the Palazzo Bevilacqua in Verona are among the finest. The Cappella Pellegrini in San Bernardino, Verona, develops the idea of Raphael's Cappella Chigi, while the later pilgrimage church of Madonna di Campagna in the same city is one of the most ambitious centrally planned churches of the sixteenth century.

Italy's most erudite and internationally influential architect was the Paduan **Andrea Palladio** (1508–80), who distilled features from all his great predecessors, welding them into a distinctive personal style. Palladio is associated above all with the city of **Vicenza**, which he adorned with a magnificent series of palaces, beginning with the so-called Basilica. In a spectacular piece of conjectural archaeology in the same city, he built the Teatro Olimpico, the first permanent theatre since the days of antiquity. The villas he created for aristocratic clients in the surrounding countryside were much imitated elsewhere; indeed, they served as the model for British country houses until well into the nineteenth century. In the most famous, La Rotonda, Palladio put the architect's ideal of a central plan to secular use for the first time, and introduced identical temple-like fronts on all four sides of the building.

Genoa developed a distinctive architectural character of its own during the High Renaissance thanks to **Galeazzo Alessi** (1512–72), who made the most of the sloping sites common to this hilly city. His huge palaces typically feature monumental staircases and courtyards set on different levels. He also designed the commanding hilltop church of Santa Maria di Carignano, which borrows Bramante's plan for St Peter's.

In **Florence**, the Mannerist style took firm root in the wake of Michelangelo. **Bartolomeo Ammannati** (1511–92) is best known for his additions and amendments to the Palazzo Pitti, which more or less determined its final form, and for the graceful Ponte San Trinità. **Bernardo Buontalenti** (c.1536–1608) was the city's quirkiest architect, celebrated mainly for the grottoes in the Bóboli Gardens and his designs for court spectaculars. Yet he also worked in a conventional idiom, as witnessed by the Fortezza del Belvedere, the Tribuna of the Uffizi and the facade of San Trinità.

Both Ammannati and Vasari also worked in Rome in collaboration with **Giacomo Barozzi da Vignola** (1507–73) on the Villa Giulia, the city's finest expression of the Mannerist delight in architecture mingled with landscape gardening. Vignola also succeeded Michelangelo as architect of St Peter's, but his chief importance lies in the way he prepared the ground for the new Baroque style. The Gesù, mother church of the Jesuits, the order on whom the Counter-Reformation was to depend so much, was Vignola's most important commission, and one which was imitated all round the world. His design was based on Alberti's Sant'Andrea in Mantua, eliminating the aisles and using the nave pilasters and lighting effects to draw the eye towards the high altar.

Vignola died before the Gesù was complete, leaving the facade to be built by **Giacomo della Porta** (c.1537–1602). This imperious front places emphasis on the portal, and presents a highly unified design in which every component plays an essential role. Della Porta was also responsible for the construction and final shape of the dome of St Peter's, making it more ornate than Michelangelo had intended.

While Rome moved confidently into a new era, the High Renaissance was kept alive in northern Italy by Palladio's most faithful follower, **Vincenzo Scamozzi** (1552–1616). He completed many of Palladio's unfinished designs, and added the brilliant perspective stage set to the Teatro Olympico. Many of his original works imitate Palladio's most famous buildings: he built a broadly similar theatre at Sabbioneta, and modelled San Nicola da Tolentino in Venice on Il Redentore.

THE BAROQUE

Although it may be difficult to pinpoint the exact period when **Baroque** began, it is recognisably a distinctive style in its own right. Politically, its birth is inexorably linked to **Rome**, a city which needed to reflect in a wealth of new buildings the brash, self-confident mood it had acquired as a result of the Counter-Reformation, its architecture expressing both the pomp and mystery of the religious approach then being propagated. Architects became concerned with daring spatial effects, with rendering movement by the use of curvaceous lines and dazzling tricks of light, and with rich decoration of which painting and sculpture were integral components.

The first architect to build wholly within the new idiom was **Carlo Maderno** (1556–1629). Maderno's reputation has been sullied by his association with a major architectural failure, the completion of St Peter's by the addition of a nave and facade, which destroyed the balance of the Greek-cross plan and masked the view of the dome. Yet Maderno was really only marginally at fault: the clergy had always disliked the democratic nature of centrally planned churches, and it was the new hieratic spirit of the age which prompted the need for the extensions. The highly original facade of Santa Susanna and the dome of Sant'Andrea della Valle prove that Maderno was actually a highly capable designer. He also started Rome's most important seventeenth-century palace, the Palazzo Barberini, though this was much altered by later hands.

The overall appearance of Baroque Rome is due above all to **Gianlorenzo Bernini** (1598–1680). Like Michelangelo, Bernini only took up architecture in mid-career, by which time he had established his reputation as the leading sculptor of the day. His fusion of the arts was to be one of the keynotes of the Baroque. His principal architectural achievements were in the field of town planning: he revamped the Piazza Navona, in the centre of which he placed a monumental fountain to his own design. Most brilliant of all was his surprisingly simple rearrangement of the square in front of St Peter's into an oval shape, with two sets of colonnades grouped to symbolise the embracing arms of the Church. The nearby Scala Regia is an equally clever design, with the steps, columns and vault all diminishing in size towards the summit to give a far greater feeling of grandeur than the restricted space would seem to allow.

Francesco Borromini (1599–1667), at first Bernini's assistant, but later his bitter rival, was the most daring and inventive Baroque architect. His attitude to decoration was very different to Bernini's, whose sculptural training he did not share. To him, architecture was sculpture in its own right, and he treated the entire wall surface plastically, favouring monochromal effects instead of colours. Even in his first commission, San Carlo alle Quattro Fontane, Borromini showed his total disregard for convention, creating a stunning spatial design based on a complex series of shapes, with two equilateral triangles resolved into an oval at the level of the dome, and a circle in the lantern above. The facade, added later, was highly influential in its mixed use of concave and convex effects. Most of Borromini's subsequent buildings suffered from the handicap of having been begun by other architects. Nevertheless, he achieved many highly unusual effects, notably in Sant'Ivo della Sapienza, and in the seemingly independent towers flanking the dome of Sant'Agnese, a motif that was subsequently much imitated. Borromini's most prestigious commission was the internal remodelling of San Giovanni in Laterano, which transformed the early Christian basilica into a vast Baroque temple.

The third main architect of Baroque Rome was **Pietro da Cortona** (1596–1669). Surprisingly, Cortona desisted from the union of the arts beloved of Bernini, preferring instead whitewashed interior walls. Nonetheless, his mature work combines elements from both Borromini and Bernini: the facade of Santa Maria della Pace, for example, makes considerable play with concave and convex shapes, yet takes this further by rearranging the square in which it is set to form a kind of foyer.

Elsewhere in Italy, only a handful of seventeenth-century architects stand comparison with their Roman contemporaries. One of these was **Francesco Maria Ricchino** (1583–1658), whose buildings in **Milan** bear direct comparison with the most progressive designs in Rome. **Bartolommeo Bianco** (c.1590–1657) adorned **Genova** with some of the century's finest palaces, proving a worthy successor to Alessi in the way he turned the sloping ground to his advantage.

The leading Baroque architect in **Naples** was the Lombard **Cosimo Fanzago** (1591–1678), whose early buildings, notably the cloisters of the Certosa di San Martino, are restrained and classically inspired. Another south Italian centre for a distinctively exuberant, wilful form of Baroque was the little town of **Lecce**, which was adorned with a series of churches and public buildings by a group of architects whose leading light was **Giuseppe Zimbalo** (active 1659–86).

The only major Baroque architect in **Venice** was **Baldassare Longhena** (1598–1682). His fame rests chiefly on the votive church of Santa Maria della Salute, whose distinctive domed silhouette makes the most of its prominent site. Longhena also built two of the Canal Grande's finest palaces, the Ca' Pésaro and the Ca' Rezzonico, though here he did little more than update Sansovino's forms.

Turin, which had previously played no significant part in Italian art and architecture, progressively took over from Rome as the leading centre of the Baroque. **Carlo di Castellamonte** (1560–1641) drew up an ambitious plan of the city, and built the Piazza San Carlo as its centrepiece. Even more significant was the arrival of the monk **Guarino Guarini** (1624–83), who was a brilliant mathematician as well as architect. Guarini was unusual among Italians in his interest in both Gothic and Islamic styles of building, but the prime influence on his development was Borromini. He used his mathematical skills to inflate the Roman architect's essentially small-scale approach into the grand manner in such commissions as the Collegio dei Nobili and the Palazzo Carignano. Both San Sidone, built at the east end of the Duomo to house the Turin Shroud, and San Lorenzo feature fantastic conical domes and pyrotechnic spatial effects using a wide variety of shapes.

After a gap of a generation, Turin attracted another remarkable architect, the Roman-trained Sicilian **Filippo Juvarra** (1678–1736). In a twenty-year sojourn in the city, he was responsible for a wealth of buildings, including the planning of new districts, churches, palaces and countryside villas. His imposingly sited Superga basilica combines the pilgrimage church and monastery in a single unit, and is by far the finest of its type in Italy, fully worthy of comparison with its central European counterparts. However, Juvarra's masterpiece is the Palazzina di Stupinigi, an extravagantly decorous villa which uses a triaxial hexagonal design instead of the conventional rectangle.

In **Sicily**, the disastrous earthquake of 1693 led to a wholesale demand for new buildings. Accordingly, the island is richly endowed with flowery late-Baroque creations which are the nearest Italian equivalents to French and German Rococo. Essentially, they are derivative in nature, paying a heavy debt to Borromini as well as to the Churrigueresque style of Spain. The most individual architect was **Giovan Battista Vaccarini** (1702–68), who was particularly associated with the laying out of **Catania**. However, the much smaller planned town of **Noto** provides an even more visually satisfying ensemble.

NEOCLASSICISM

The **Neoclassical** style, which reacted against the sumptuousness of late Baroque by returning to the most basic principles of classicism, is generally considered to have begun in **Rome** in the mid-eighteenth century. Yet long before that, while the century was still young, a number of architects in **Venice** had decisively moved against Baroque excesses, notably **Giovanni Scalfarotto** (1690–1764), whose San Simone Piccolo is demonstrably derived from the Pantheon.

Giovanni Battista Piranesi (1720–78) did more than anyone to popularise the Neoclassical approach in Rome. His inspired large-scale engravings of the city's ruins rank among the all-time masterpieces of graphic art, and were to have a wide circulation. His theoretical writings asserted the superiority of the architecture of Classical Rome over Greece, and advocated a reinterpretation of its forms as the basis for a new style. As a practising architect, Piranesi is known only for Santa Maria del Priorato, a heavily symbolical church for the Knights of Malta, set in a pentagonal square.

A remarkable synthesis of late Baroque and Neoclassicism was achieved by **Luigi Vanvitelli** (1700–73) in the colossal royal palace of **Caserta**, whose ornate apartments with their long vistas show all the swagger of the old style, whereas the exterior has all the calm restraint of the new. His pupil **Giuseppe Piermarini** (1734–1808) became the leading Neoclassical architect in **Milan**, where he designed several severe palaces with long, unadorned facades, along with what became Italy's most prestigious opera house, La Scala.

Another celebrated theatre, La Fenice in **Venice**, is the best-known building by the city's most committed exponent of Neoclassicism, **Giannantonio Selva** (1751–1819). A certain French influence pervades the work of **Giuseppe Valadier** (1762–1839), who was given responsibility for remodelling the interiors of the cathedrals of Spoleto and Urbino while still in his twenties. Later he was based in Rome, where his commissions included the triumphal arch on the Ponte Milvio and the laying out of the Piazza del Popolo.

As with the other visual arts, architecture in Italy was in the doldrums for most of the nineteenth century. Because of the all-pervasiveness of the classical tradition, there was little of the confident modern reinterpretation of other styles which characterises northern European building of this period. Only **Giuseppe Japelli** (1783–1852) stands as an exception to this. His masterpiece, the Caffè Pedrocchi in **Padua**, is firmly Neoclassical, but its extension is neo-Gothic, while his Teatro Verdi in the same city is based on Rococo, and his villas are modelled on Palladio.

The nineteenth century also saw some impressive examples of town planning. One of these was in **Trieste**, where the waterfront area was redesigned. In **Turin**, the work of the previous century was continued by the laying out of the Piazza Vittorio Veneto and Piazza Carlo Felice at opposite ends of the city. Later, **Alessandro Antonelli** (1798–1888) adorned the city with a huge iron supported tower, the Mole Antonelliana, originally intended as a synagogue, but converted into a museum.

The most original piece of planning was in **Milan**, whose status as the commercial hub of the emergent nation-state is symbolised by the construction of the Galleria Vittorio Emanuele II by **Giuseppe Mengoni** (1829–77) – Italy's first important example of design in iron and glass, and the initiator of a trend for covered shopping areas throughout Europe.

With the accomplishment of complete Italian unification in 1870, **Rome** had to be supplied with new streets and buildings worthy of a great modern capital; inevitably, the most monumental classical style possible was chosen, and it was only a partial success. The most strikingly visible – if not the most aesthetically pleasing – late-Neoclassical addition to the city's patrimony is the huge white marble Monument to Vittorio Emanuele II by **Giuseppe Sacconi** (1853–1905).

THE TWENTIETH CENTURY

A reaction against the nineteenth-century infatuation with the past came with the unashamedly modernist **Art Nouveau** movement, whose glittering, sinewy forms dominated European architecture and design in the early years of the new century. In Italy, where it was known as **Lo Stilo Liberty**, its impact was less extensive than in most other countries, and also more restrained, deriving above all from the Viennese Secession. **Giuseppe Sommaruga** (1867–1917) was the most talented exponent; his surviving buildings include the Casa Castiglione and Clinica Colombo in **Milan**, and the Hotel Tre Croci near **Varese**.

Of far more long-lasting significance to the overall direction of Italian architecture were the visionary **Futurist** designs of **Antonio Sant'Elia** (1888–1916), especially his *Città Nuova*, which envisaged a vibrant high-rise metropolis of the future dominated by technological commercial activities and rapid transport systems operating on several levels. Sant'Elia's death in World War I meant that none of this was ever built, save for the posthumously erected and much simplified War Memorial in **Como**. The executant architect for this was **Giuseppe Terraini** (1904–43), a member of the *Gruppo Sette*, which comprised seven of Italy's most progressive interwar architects, all strongly influenced by the ideas promulgated by the Bauhaus in Germany and Frank Lloyd Wright in America. Terraini built several other buildings in Como, the most original of which was the Casa dei Fascisti, the local Fascist Party headquarters.

In spite of its unpleasant associations, **Fascist** architecture is sometimes of good quality. The status of **Rome** as the national capital meant that it again became the centre of the most ambitious projects, including some appalling examples of planning, the worst of which was the opening up of the Via della Conciliazione linking St Peter's to the Tiber. This exacerbated the flaws caused by the previous failure to build the third wing of Bernini's Piazza, and has spoiled its element of surprise ever since.

New prestige schemes were generally supervised by Mussolini's favourite architect, **Marcello Piacentini** (1881–1960). When left to his own devices – as in the Stadio dei Marmi, with its coarse echoes of Imperial Rome – Piacentini produced the most distasteful monuments of the period. His EUR project, south of the city, was interrupted by World War II, and completed after the fall of Fascism in a modernised Neoclassical manner.

The most internationally celebrated Italian architect of the twentieth century was **Pier Luigi Nervi** (1891–1979). He popularised the use of reinforced concrete, which enabled a greater variety of design than was possible with the steel leads favoured in so many other countries. His celebrated aircraft hangars were destroyed during the war, but the Municipal Stadium in **Florence**, with its helical staircase, survives as an example of his early work. Among his prestigious postwar commissions are exhibition halls in **Turin**, whose amazing wide-span vaults recall the lost hangars; the buildings for the 1960 Olympic Games in **Rome**; and the Papal Audience Chamber in the Vatican.

Nervi also provided the engineering core of Italy's most famous skyscraper, the Torre Pirelli in Milan by **Gio Ponti** (1891–1979), a prolific and versatile designer. **Giovanni Michelucci** (b.1891), who built the Instituto di Mineraolgia in the same complex, was shortly afterwards responsible for the highly stylised train station in **Florence**. In the 1960s, he built just outside the same city one of the century's most striking churches, the expressionistic San Giovanni sull'Autostrada del Sol, dedicated to the men who had died constructing the motorway. Two more impressive examples of railway architecture, both designed by several hands, are the grandiosely Neoclassical station in **Milan**, dating from the Fascist epoch, and its modernist, utopian counterpart in **Rome**, which ranked as the most prestigious architectural project in the aftermath of World War II.

Gordon McLachlan

ITALIAN VERNACULAR ARCHITECTURE

Architecture isn't just about palaces and churches, and it's interesting to see how domestic architecture has developed, especially with regard to the siting and layout of small towns and farming settlements, both of which have had at least as much impact on the landscape of Italy as the country's better-known monumental architecture.

THE HILL TOWNS

Throughout the Middle Ages in Italy, the countryside was unsafe and unhealthy and the land in many places remained uncultivated, either swamp or barren. As late as the fifteenth century, wolves still prowled within a few miles of Florence, in a landscape populated largely by brigands and deer. The topography of the countryside, with its abundance of hills and mountains rising steeply from fertile plains provided natural sites for fortified settlements which could both remove the population from the malarial swamps and bandits and preserve the limited fertile land for cultivation.

In the period of their greatest expansion – between the twelfth and fourteenth centuries – **hill towns** sprang up all over. Many were superimposed on early Etruscan cities – **Chiusi** and **Cortona** – or cave dwellings, as in **Sorano**. **Matera**, Basilicata, grew from a very early settlement of grottoes formed by the natural erosion of volcanic rock (tufa) along the side of a high ravine. The houses that evolved from these caves (called I Sassi – literally "rocks") remained in use until 1952 when they were condemned. Though most hill towns were built within high and sometimes battlemented perimeter walls, the fortress aspects of many sites obviated the need for additional protection. Houses in **Pitigliano** (in Tuscany), for example, rise like a natural extension of the rock outcropping on which they sit. The sheer drop afforded by these sites (often extended by the use of towers) enabled inhabitants to make good use of gravity by dropping a crushing blow onto the heads of enemies attempting to scale the walls. It also facilitated a precipitate (if practical) dispatch of the dead as well as a simple form of rubbish disposal. After the revolution in fortifications between the thirteenth and fifteenth centuries, and the introduction of gunpowder and cannon reduced the need for enormous vertical drops, towers grew shorter and were adapted to newer methods of warfare.

Although many hill towns were genuinely self-contained communities, the countryside remained under the political and economic control of the cities and of the Comunes, Grand Dukes and Church officials who ran them, particularly in North and Central Italy. Each city-state set up satellite towns of its own, to protect trade routes (whether at sea or on land), or to operate as garrisons for soldiers, weaponry and food in case of war (or civil insurrection). Siena established the fortified hill town of **Monteriggioni** in the early thirteenth century along an important route from Rome into France which also passed through **San Gimignano**. **San Miniato** was also set up as a fortified town by Emperor Frederick II (still quarrelling with the papacy) to take advantage of and protect this same route. At roughly the same time, Florence founded similar frontier outposts, setting up **San Giovanni Valdarno, Scarperia** and **Firenzuola**, all within ten years. Fewer towns emerged in the South during this period, partly because there were fewer cities: of the 26 Italian towns with populations of more than 20,000 in the thirteenth century, only three were in the South.

Hill towns share many features, whatever the impetus for their original development. They are almost always densely built settlements, constructed with materials found on or near their site, helping to give the impression of arising naturally from their geological foundations. They usually rely on just one or two simple dwelling types endlessly repeated. **Strómboli**, off the north coast of Sicily, is an example of the rich effects created by repetition of a single, very basic dwelling type, in this case a simple cube. In most hill towns, houses are built right up to the edge of – and often open out directly onto – the narrow passageways and streets. This reflects the more integral links between the productive activities of the medieval household (carried out on the ground floor) and the street immediately outside which not only became an extension of the works inside but also served as a kind of shop, linked to a wider network of merchants, traders and exchange. Altogether, many more functions were carried out publicly in the streets, traces of which are still visible in the surviving evidence of public fountains and wash-houses, wells, and communal ovens. Streets in medieval hill towns were even more crowded than they are today; houses had overhanging wooden balconies, used to dry and store a variety of foods. Supports for these balconies (or the holes which held them) can still be seen on the fronts of many houses.

Taken together, hill towns still preserve a great deal of their medieval character. The very characteristics which made them useful for purposes of defence and isolation made them unsuitable for later growth and redevelopment in response to changing circumstances. There are exceptions – in the late-fifteenth century the village of Corsignano near Montepulciano was transformed into the little Renaissance town of **Pienza** to commemorate the birthplace of Pope Pius II. But in general, there is much less evidence of urban planning, or the country's more recent economic history, in hill towns.

SETTLEMENTS OF THE PLAIN

Though variations abound, the basic types of settlements in the plains and coastal areas reveal a great deal about the impact of urban political and economic activity on the development of the countryside. Distinct waves of development correspond to changes in the fortunes of city merchants and in the accumulation of capital required for agricultural investment. Accumulation, in turn, depended on economic prosperity and on relatively long and uninterrupted periods of peace.

Just as the economic incentive for rural development derived from the towns, so did the house types used by the first intrepid petty noblemen in setting up agricultural holdings after centuries of disuse and stagnation. The **house-tower** (*la casa-torre*), which spread first through the Mugello, Chianti and Casentino districts between the thirteenth and fifteenth centuries, was really a transplanted version of the tall, square, fortified city house, using construction techniques borrowed from urban models, particularly from the fortified towns of Bologna, Perugia, and Siena. The defensive character of the house-tower can be read from the thickness of its walls, from its restricted openings high off the ground and from its height.

Over successive centuries, the house-tower gradually lost its defensive character, re-emerging as a **dove tower** (*la torre columbaia*), protruding from the centre of a new form of extended dwelling which had been wrapped around it. Doves and pigeons were not only adept at killing snakes and consuming weeds but also provided valuable meat for the table and dung for agricultural use. Though this functional role gradually fell away, the dove tower became a ubiquitous feature of domestic architecture across almost all of Central and Southern Italy, and still remains an important decorative element in contemporary villas.

The house to which the dove tower belongs is the **casa della mezzadria**, the classic Renaissance country villa, widespread across Tuscany, Umbria and the Marche as well as other areas in central and northern Italy. Usually square in plan, it was built using a combination of brick, stone and terracotta under a tent-like roof with the dove tower at its apex. Depending on its location and the urban models to which it harks back, it might boast a portico at ground level (typically Florentine), and a loggia at first-floor level (typically Arentine), or neither a portico nor loggia but a flat wall on the front facade (more common in the area around Siena).

The house derives its name from the system of sharecropping by which most of the land was farmed. Under this system, *la mezzadria* (based on the word *mezza* – "half"), the peasant farmer, in exchange for half the seed, yielded up half the annual produce to his landowner. This gave the landlord no incentive either to invest in stock or to introduce new agricultural methods. At the same time, it impoverished the labour force, compelled by increasing debt to supply free labour – which was used, among other things, to build the main house. Used only occasionally by the landlord, the house was the primary residence of the estate manager (*il fattore*), who was the agent and overseer of urban capital invested in the countryside. Because this system paid workers in kind rather than in cash, it inevitably tied agriculture to the limited production of subsistence goods and so failed to encourage specialisation (based on natural advantages) and the commercial innovations that modern agriculture required.

By contrast, the alluvial plain across north and central Italy encouraged specialisation very early on. To be made arable, it required large-scale investment in the reclamation and irrigation of land, something that was first undertaken by the Benedictines and Cistercians in the eleventh to thirteenth centuries. The enormous commercial enterprises which subsequently appeared to cater for commercial markets in rice, silk and dairy products, bore some resemblance to the monasteries whose functions they replaced and extended. Square in plan and built around a massive enclosed courtyard which could extend to 150 metres or more on a side, the architecture of the farming complex (*la casa della Pianura Padana*) was often stark with high rectangular porticoes supported by square columns sometimes running along three sides of the enclosed interior space.

Normally, the estate accommodated four basic elements which were architecturally distinct; the owner-manager's house which was more elaborate in design and often taller than the other buildings; housing for workers, tenement-like in character, with external balconies running along the upper floors used to dry and store crops like rice; stables for cows and other animals; and stables for horses with hay lofts above. This last is a feature easily recognisable at great distances because of the often striking patterns of brickwork used to create large grates for the ventilation of hay. The overall operation of this kind of enterprise was convincingly portrayed in the film *Tree of the Wooden Clogs*, set in nineteenth-century Lombardy. Today many of these courtyards are inhabited by independent small farmers, each cultivating their own smallholding. Others are abandoned. On the eastern side of the plain, around the Ferrara district, where agriculture has become most mechanised, the stables and storage areas of enclosed-court complexes have become truly vast.

In central and southern Italy (particularly Campania and Puglia), the **masseria** is a more common type of farming settlement. Dominating vast tracts of land which were derived from feudal estates and ultimately from the landed properties of the Roman emperors (*latifondia*), these complex structures are massive in bulk and set in isolated countryside where they are entirely closed to the outside world. Consisting of a dense cluster of separate building elements which were often vertically prominent, *masserie* were sometimes enclosed by a high perimeter stone wall with round turrets built in for defense purposes. They could, however, also consist of a lower grouping of buildings more loosely bound within a larger area. At its largest a *masseria* virtually operated as a self-contained village incorporating church, school, medical clinic and shop within its precinct, in addition to accommodating the full range of agricultural requirements for stabling, housing (of day labourers called *braccianti*) and a wide variety of storage. In their purest, least-altered form, village *masserie* are still visible on the mountain slopes of Sicily. A later parallel to these large farms are the eighteenth- and nineteenth-century worker villages like **San Leucio** near Caserta, set up by the Bourbon Ferdinand IV at the end of the eighteenth century to promote silk weaving; and **Crespi**, built on the Adda in Lombardy by Critoforo Crespi and devoted to the cotton industry.

Trulli, found along the coast of Puglia and inland, form one of the most remote, curious and ancient types of farm settlement in Italy. Of uncertain origin that might be Cretan or North African, appearing in Italy some time between 2000 and 1000 BC, *trulli* consist of clusters of single circular rooms, each covered by a conical roof made of overlapping rough stone tiles and topped by decorative symbolic pinnacles. Built as primitive agricultural communities, the profusion of conical roofs (each dwelling contributing two or three) produces a startling effect on the landscape.

At the more modest end of the spectrum, the house of the **independent farmer** (*la casa colonica*) is to be found all over Italy, adapted to local materials and customs. Of simpler construction, it often consists of a kitchen and bedrooms sitting on top of animal sheds and agricultural stores (common in central and north Italy), but equally, the barn and house might form separate wings or entirely separate buildings, as is typically found along the slopes of the Appenines running the entire length of the country.

Ellen Leopold

MAFIA, 'NDRANGHETA, CAMORRA: SOCIALISED CRIME IN SOUTHERN ITALY

"And the Mafia – what's this Mafia that the newspapers are always talking about?'

"Yeah, what is the Mafia, after all?" Brescianelli chimed in.

"It's a very complicated thing to explain", Bellodi said, "It's . . . incredible, that's what it is"

Leonardo Sciascia, *The Day of the Owl*

Few modern social phenomena have been more misinterpreted and misunderstood than the **Mafia**, **'ndrangheta** and **camorra**, the three names designating organised criminal activity in **Sicily**, **Calabria** and **Naples**. In some sense it is no surprise that there should be misunderstandings. Numerous hindrances lie in wait for the would-be Mafia observer. Most important of these may be the secrecy in which the Mafia shrouds itself, a secrecy the Mafia ensures through the vow of silence known as *omerta*, which surrounds all those who, however unwillingly, come into contact with it.

An example, at 2am, July 10, 1988, three associates of the Camorra boss Antonio Bardellino were gunned down on the streets of his hometown of Aversa, just outside Naples, by members of a rival clan. The gunfight lasted thirty minutes. A few minutes after the last shots were fired, the police arrived. While they removed one of the corpses from the street, a man in a nearby apartment opened his window to ask in a derisory tone – "anything happen down there?" As Leonardo Sciascia shows in his penetrating portrait of the Mafia world cited above, one knows better than to be a witness to a Mafia crime.

Another, less dramatic, hindrance to making sense of the Mafia, 'ndrangheta and camorra is the complexity of these phenomena. They *are* distinct organisations, based in particular territories, but they also have numerous common characteristics, not to mention continuous dealings with one another. The Mafia and 'ndrangheta especially have similar, interwoven, histories – unless otherwise specified, in this article the term Mafia will be used to indicate them both. The Neapolitan camorra, for all its similarities, is something of a case unto itself, and will be considered separately below.

Until recently organised crime was mostly viewed as a *southern* problem, an issue of "special" interest to those with a criminal curiosity. But in recent years it has become clear that these organisations are thoroughly enmeshed in the fibre of Italian society as a whole, and that understanding Italy is hardly possible without reference to them. Certainly they are not something that can be eradicated with one trial, defeated in one year or even in ten; indeed to move beyond the Mafia would require the total transformation of Italian society, politics and economic life. Those that ask what shape Italy will have in the 21st century will therefore also need to ask what role the Mafia, 'ndrangheta and camorra will play in it.

MAFIA AND 'NDRANGHETA

The one thing most mafiologues agree on is that the Mafia as a thing, as a noun, *does not exist*. When a defendant in a 1960s Mafia trial was asked if he belonged to the Mafia he responded, "I don't know what the word means". This criminal was not so much evading the question as confessing a real perplexity. Mafiosi never call themselves, or one another, mafiosi, but rather *amici* (friends) or *uomini d'onore* (men of honour). In the words of one noted mafiologue, the defendant above "knew individuals who are called mafiosi, not because they belong to a secret sect but rather because they behave in a particular fashion, that is in a Mafia-like fashion".

What does it mean to behave in a Mafia-like fashion? "It means *to make oneself respected, to be a man of honour*, capable of vindicating by force any offence against his enemy," writes another Mafia expert, Pino Arlacchi. Honour and respect clearly have rather different meanings here than what most people are accustomed to. A man is an *uomo d'onore* when he acts according to the prevailing codes of courage, cleverness and ferocity, never hesitating to resort to violence and trickery in imposing his will upon others.

What gradually emerges from this portrait, however, is a sort of confusion between the Mafia as a "state of mind, a philosophy of life, a moral code, prevailing among all Sicilians" (Luigi Barzini), and organised criminal activity, delinquency and social deviance. In southern Italy, the border between the two is often unclear.

Two aspects of southern Italian culture in particular seem to have contributed to the birth and development of the Mafia as a criminal organisation. The first is the generally positive value which this culture has attributed to assertiveness, aggression and the ability to impose one's will on others. The meek, mild and naive may be saints in their afterlives, but in this life they are, quite simply, fools. The fundamental Neapolitan phrase, *ca'nisciun e'fesso* (I'm no fool – you won't get the best of me), sums up the constant awareness of dominance and submission in which the southern Italian lives.

A second, related aspect is the southern Italian attitude towards the state. Even today, the relationship of the southern Italian (and of many northern Italians as well) to the state is one of profound distrust. The state, its institution and laws, are not something in which one participates as a citizen but are rather things which challenge the citizen's independence, interfering with his family's sacred autonomy. This attitude towards the state may have its origins in the long succession of invading powers that ruled southern Italy over the centuries (Norman, French, Catalan, etc). And also in the distance that separated the mass of peasant-farmers (*contadini*) working on huge estates (*latifondi*) from their absentee landlords residing in Naples or Palermo. Certainly Unification did little to help matters in the South, transferring as it did the capital from Naples to Rome and replacing the Bourbon monarchy with the Turin-based House of Savoy. Whatever the case, the space of distrust between citizen and State is the space in which the Mafia has prospered.

ORIGINS AND DEVELOPMENT

However, there is much more to the Mafia than this, and a look at more recent history shows that Mafia criminality is no longer what it used to be. The Mafia has come a long way from the traditional, feudal ways of the nineteenth century to become an entrepreneurial Mafia moving in the circles of international finance, and of drugs and arms dealing. With this transformation has come a change in the Mafia's relationship to society at large, from one of widespread sympathy and support to that of dismay and alienation.

The word "Mafia" first appears in written documents around the time of Italian Unification, and, although its etymological origins are debatable, many speculate that it derives from the arabic word *mu'afah* meaning "protection". In 1863 a play entitled *I Mafiusi della Vicaria*, based on the life of a Palermo prison, was a roaring success among the high society of Sicily's capital, giving the word its first extensive usage: when the city rose against its new Italian rulers three years later, the British consul described a situation where secret societies were all-powerful: "*Camorre* and *maffie*-elected *juntas* share the earnings of the workmen, keep up intercourse with outcasts, and take malefactors under their wing and protection."

The Mafia's appearance at this time is historically significant, its rise paralleling that of the young Italian state. Indeed, in the words of Leonardo Sciascia: "a history of the Mafia would be none other than the history of the State's complicity – from the Bourbons to the Savoys to the Republic – in forming and encouraging this unproductive and parasitic class of power."

Which isn't to say it hadn't existed before in a different form. Early versions of the Mafia were to be found in the Sicilian countryside during the long centuries of foreign rule. This vast, mountainous island was virtually impenetrable to the distant authorities in Naples, Madrid or elsewhere, and "law and order" had to be maintained by local, semi-official authorities. The Bourbons, for example, in the early nineteenth century entrusted their campaign against brigands and bandits to "companions at arms", which consisted of ex-brigands who would be pardoned in return for assistance in helping to catch and prosecute their old friends, the brigands at large. Usually, however, these "companions", instead of catching the brigands would negotiate a kind of peaceful settlement between the bandit who had committed some theft and the offended party. In this way local social harmony was maintained without the direct intervention of central government.

Another early Mafia activity was that of a certain type of rural "middleman" who handled negotiations between property owners, landlords, sharecroppers and dayworkers. During the first half of the nineteenth century, the great estates were divided up numerous times in the crown's attempt to challenge the power of local barons and proprietors. The early mafiosi grew fat off the tensions that these social changes generated, intimidating sharecroppers into accepting unfavourable contracts and dayworkers into accepting low wages, while persuading proprietors and landlords to cede control over their land to them, so fulfilling the important social function of mediation. As E.J. Hobsbawm noted: "we can't say that the Mafia was imposed upon the Sicilians by someone. In a certain sense it expressed the needs of all the rural classes and served their interests in varying ways."

The main characteristic of the traditional, rural Mafia, then, is that of the mediation of social conflict. And by the late nineteenth century these mediators had turned into true mafiosi with well-established codes of honour and a semi-formal, though unwritten, form of organisation. Though much has changed in the Mafia world, its organisation, based on the family, is much the same today as it was one hundred years ago.

The Mafia *family*, however, is not really a domestic unit at all, but a conglomeration of people, some blood-relations and others not, who gather together in the pursuit of illicit aims. Each family takes on the name of the village it comes from (Corleone, for example) or the quarter of a city which it controls (in Palermo – Ciaculli, Santa Maria di Gesù, Porta Nova, etc). Above the families is something called the *commission*, a kind of governing body made up of representatives from all the major groupings. In each family there is a body of "soldiers", presided over by lieutenants, who are in turn presided over by the *capo* or *padrino* ("godfather") and his assistants. Families, in turn, ally themselves in *cosche*, meaning the crown of the artichoke (symbolising the solidarity of many), which act in coordination with other *cosche*, all of which together form the *onorata societa*, the totality of organised crime in Sicily.

All this sounds much neater than in fact it is. Periods of peace, when everyone feels comfortable in their place, when territories are respected and pacts observed, are relatively rare. More often there are wars between and within families, and between and within *cosche*.

There is little or no documentary proof of the "Honoured Society's" rise to power, but most writers agree that between the 1890s and 1920s its undisputed boss was **Don Vito Cascio Ferro**, who presided over a period of unprecedented Mafia peace. Don Vito generated such fear and respect (virtual synonyms in the world of the Mafia) that no theft occurred in Palermo of which he did not receive a substantial cut. Already at this time the Sicilian underworld and its younger cousin in America, the "Black Hand", or *Cosa Nostra* (meaning literally "our thing"), were well coordinated. When Joe Petrosino, head of the Italian squad of the New York Police Department, secretly arrived in Palermo to study the relations between the *onorate societa* and the Black Hand, Don Vito was there at the waterfront to shoot him down. Don Vito later declared, "in all my life I've only killed one person, and I did it selflessly . . . Petrosino was a courageous adversary – he deserved to die in dignity, not by the hand of just any old assassin".

The rise to power of the American Mafia at this time was no accident. Mafia-style groupings and loyalties flourished among the hundreds of thousands of Sicilians who emigrated to America in the early decades of this century, emigrants who had need of their own forms of social and economic security in a country where they lacked the full franchise. In addition to this the Sicilian Mafia had suffered considerable (if temporary) setbacks at the hands of the Fascist authorities and many mafiosi fled to the US for safer operations.

Ferro's career ended with Mussolini's anti-Mafia purges, instigated to clear the ground for the establishment of a vigorous Fascist structure in Sicily. Il Duce sent the legendary prefect, **Cesare Mori**, to Sicily, granting him almost limitless powers to suppress the Mafia. Most importantly, Mori understood that the only way to beat the Mafia was on its own terms: "if the Sicilians are afraid of the mafiosi, I'll show them that I'm the meanest mafiosi of them all." He had understood that in the Sicily of the time it was indeed necessary to fight fear with fear.

This brief, Fascist chapter in the campaign against the Mafia foreshadows certain aspects of the debate over what legal and governmental forms the fight against the Mafia should take today. In particular it raises the question of how much the law should be circumvented by authorities in the attempt to wage an effective fight against the Mafia, and to what extent "extraordinary powers" should be granted to combat this "extraordinary" form of criminality. While opponents of the more "repressive" approach exemplified by Mori agree that the Mafia can be more effectively fought with the tools of repression, they ask at what cost to society as a whole? The fight against terrorism in the late 1970s and early 1980s is a dark example of a fight that was won at the cost of civil liberties, when hundreds of innocent men and women were put in jail.

If Mori, the Fascist, on the one hand, did much to reduce the powers of the Mafia, the Americans, on the other, did a good deal to restore them. When the Allies prepared for their landing in Sicily in 1943, they relied on the Mafia for crucial intelligence information and logistical support for the execution of Operation Husky. One of these informers was **Lucky Luciano**, with whom the US Navy consulted frequently while he was serving his thirty- to fifty-year prison sentence. Luciano not only provided them with important information and connections for the American landing in southwest Sicily but helped them to catch a group of Nazi saboteurs who were operating in New York. After the war the US expressed their gratitude by letting him go free, sending him to his home country where, in Naples, he would play a key role in developing links between the Sicilian, Neapolitan and American underworld.

The most important connection with which Luciano provided the allies was that of **Don Calógero Vizzini**, head of the Mafia of all Sicily during and immediately after the war. Don Caló was instrumental in clearing the way for the American landing and, afterwards, in helping the Allied Military Government establish itself in Sicily. In order to maintain political control of the island the Allies relied heavily on the Mafia: of the 66 cities on the island, 62 were entrusted either to mafiosi or men connected with the Mafia. **Don Vito Genovese**, the figure on which Mario Puzo modelled Don Corleone in *The Godfather*, was one of these men. After helping the Americans, and the Mafia, to consolidate their power in Sicily, Genovese returned to the US to become head of the American Cosa Nostra.

The Mafia was left in a good position to take advantage of the extraordinary economic growth which Italy underwent in the first two postwar decades. Moreover, in the South there was a key novelty which helped the Mafia secure its economic and political base: billions of dollars of government funding were sent here for an "extraordinary intervention" designed to modernise the region and bring it up to par with the wealthy North. The Mafia exploited the situation with ruthless efficiency, landing crucial and lucrative government contracts by intimidating all competitors into not even tendering bids. Needless to say, the Mafia-firm bid would be two to three times the appropriate amount necessary to complete the job.

THE NEW MAFIA

It was during these years that the Mafia underwent a fundamental transformation, from a predominantly rural organisation with a role of mediation, to an active criminal society, with its powerbase in the cities, and interests in construction, real estate and drugs smuggling. The modern Mafia may keep up a "clean and legal" front, but the economic basis for their civilised decorum is predominantly drugs and, to a lesser extent, the arms trade, kidnapping and extortion. In the 1950s the Mafia helped to found and develop an international drug market which extended its influence to all four corners of the globe. Experts estimate that more than half of the world's heroin trade is controlled in Palermo. The dizzying profits are "laundered" – invested in legal activities, all traces of their illicit origin having vanished.

Part of the Mafia's postwar success, then, can be traced to the ability to become "entrepreneurs" in high-risk, high-profit international trade while maintaining a respectable social front as businessmen in both the local and national economy. The strength of the Mafia organisation would not make sense, however, without the presence of another factor which explains its ability to continue to recruit *new* mafiosi. The chronic unemployment which has plagued southern Italy in recent decades has ensured that there will always be a reserve army of idle, able-bodied men who have been denied access to legal employment. And to these unemployed men, an invitation to work for the Mafia is often an offer they simply can't refuse.

In almost complete symbiosis with the culture and economy of southern Italy, the Mafia has thus established itself in every area of politics and society, obtaining a more modern form of bourgeois respect, based not on fear but economic power. It is a form of economic power, however, whose costs to society are high, which diverts human energy, initiatives and funds from the public sphere where they can be more democratically managed and accounted for. Also, the plague of drug addiction on which the Mafia grows fat, and its perennial family wars, have thoroughly traumatised both Sicilian and Italian society. The death count has grown too high for the people to remain sympathetic with these mafiosi who, stripped of all folklore and Hollywood hype, reveal themselves for what they are: rapacious criminals bent on personal accumulation at all costs.

The state responded to the growing power of the Mafia with a **Parliamentary Commission** that sat between 1963 and 1976, which posed enough of a threat to the underworld to provoke a change of tactics by the Mafia, who began to target state officials in a sustained campaign of terror which continues to this day. In 1971 Palermo's chief public prosecutor, Pietro Scaglione, became the first in a long line of **illustrious corpses** – *cadaveri eccellenti* – which has included journalists, judges, lawyers, left-wing politicians and police chiefs. A new peak of violence was reached in 1982 with the ambush and murder in Palermo's city centre of **Pio La Torre**, regional secretary of the Communist Party in Sicily, who had proposed a special government dispensation to allow lawyers access to private bank accounts.

One of the people attending La Torre's funeral was the new Sicilian prefect of police, **General dalla Chiesa**, a veteran in the state's fight against the Red Brigade, and whose dispatch promised new action against the Mafia. He began investigating Sicily's lucrative construction industry, which proved an effective means of investing drug profits. His scrutiny of public records and business dealings threatened to expose one of the most enigmatic issues in the Mafia's organisation: the extent of corruption and protection in high-ranking political circles, the so-called **Third Level**. But exactly one hundred days after La Torre's death, dalla Chiesa was gunned down, together with his wife, in Palermo. The whole country was shocked, and the murder revived questions about the depth of government commitment to the fight. In his engagement with the Mafia, dalla Chiesa had met with little local cooperation, and had received next to no support from Rome, to the extent that his son had accused the politicians of isolating his father. The Italian president and senior cabinet ministers were present at the prefect's funeral, and were pelted with coins by an angry Sicilian crowd – an expression of disgust which has since been repeated at the funerals of other prominent anti-Mafia fighters.

THE MAXI-TRIALS . . . AND THE OUTLOOK

This new, more critical attitude to the Mafia is emerging throughout Italian society. A scandal in 1981, surrounding the so-called "Propaganda Due" (P2) masonic lodge, also helped to mobilise public opinion against the Mafia when it was discovered that numerous high-ranking politicians, bankers, military men and even members of the Vatican were involved in a secret masonic organisation with Mafia connections. A year later, the first anti-Mafia law in history was passed by the Italian parliament.

Of equal import has been the recent wave of *pentitismo*, of "repentance" or confession, in which, for the first time, the age-old code of *omerta* has been broken. For the first time mafiosi are revealing the secrets of their organisation, breaking the promise they make during their initiation as mafiosi, when they declare, "may my flesh burn if I do not maintain this promise". **Tommaso Buscetta**, a high-ranking Mafia member, was one of the first to break with *omerta*, setting in motion the Palermo "maxi-trials" or *maxiprocessi* in 1986, the largest ever held against the Mafia. Never before had so high-ranking a member of the *commis-*

sion turned on his "friends". His revelations about the most intimate high-level dealings of the *onorata societa* were a breakthrough for the campaign against the Mafia both in Italy and in the US, and led to important prosecutions against members of the massive heroin and cocaine network between Palermo and New York known as the "pizza connection".

The decisions taken by the "maxi-trial" court in Palermo in December of 1987 were hailed as a substantial, if partial, victory of the forces of law and order in Italy. The fears of most seasoned Mafia fighters, however, were soon confirmed: as soon as the media-hype surrounding the "maxi-trial" ended, and the public – and government – turned its attention to other matters, the Mafia went back to business as usual. The Mafia fighters (judges, special investigators, police, parliamentary commissions), deprived of all-important media attention and government support, once again were engaged in a losing battle.

For the first seven months of 1988 the Mafia problem seemed, indeed, to fade out of sight. But in mid-summer something quite unexpected happened which thrust the issue back on the front pages. Giovanni Falcone, a bright, young member of the special anti-Mafia "pool" of judges in Palermo, issued an accusation against the government's handling of the fight against the Mafia, and against the head of the pool, Antonino Meli. Falcone maintained that the government and anti-Mafia organisations had become lax, returning, he implied, to a form of complicity with the Mafia.

What was at stake in Falcone's accusation, and in the debate which immediately grew around it, were two approaches to the campaign: that of the veteran Antonino Meli, who proposed to conduct investigations through the normal bureaucratic channels, without making waves; and that of Falcone himself, who proposed to take chances, legal and otherwise, asking for a staff of crime-fighters exclusively trained in Mafia affairs, and also for special measures, and special funds.

This local debate soon became a national polemic, involving parliament and the Supreme Court. And during the same period the Mafia itself further awakened the public to the debate's urgency, carrying out a series of ruthless killings of both Mafia members and public officials. In the autumn of 1988 this clamorous situation resulted in a new, stepped-up government committed to the fight against the Mafia. Parliament granted vast, unprecedented powers to the High Commissioner for the Fight Against the Mafia, Domenico Sica, making him the most powerful anti-Mafia commissioner in postwar history: the use of a branch of the Italian Secret Service, legal clearance to perform wire-tappings, to spy on individuals suspected of Mafia activity, to confiscate funds of suspected mafiosi, and access to information on all citizens in the files of public offices and banks.

Since the late-Eighties the battle against the Mafia has, if anything, intensified, the Mafia responding, with typically brutal efficiency, with a new series of **murders** of prominent officials. The first of these was that of **Salvatore Lima**, a former mayor of Palermo turned Euro-MP who was in the Mafia's pocket; he was killed perhaps as a warning to any other establishment figures who were seen to be not adequately "protecting" their Cosa Nostra paymasters. Shortly after, the Mafia turned its attention to two of its most prominent opponents, the judges **Giovanni Falcone** and **Paolo Borsellino**. The nation was appalled that two such well-known anti-Mafia figures could be disposed of so easily, and the anti-Mafia mood intensified in direct proportion to the growing anti-Establishment mood in the country: it was only the politicians that allowed the Mafia to continue to exist and prosper, the thinking went, so why not get rid of them, and the rest, surely, would follow? It is this mood of disillusionment with the Italian political establishment that the ex-mayor of Palermo, Leoluca Orlando, was beginning to tap with his anti-Mafia party, **La Rete** ("Network"), although it must be said that the separatist parties of the Lega Nord were benefitting too.

The murders led to a special Carabinieri unit being sent to Sicily in a calculated show of force by the state – something which might have seemed a somewhat empty gesture but for the arrest, in January 1993, of **Salvatore Riina**, or "Don Toto", after 24 years on the run. Riina sat at the head of the Cosa Nostra, the *capo di tutti capi* ("boss of all bosses"); it was he who was largely responsible for turning it into the sophisticated multinational corporation it is today, expanding into the lucrative global drugs trade and laundering the profits worldwide; he too who probably ordered the murders of Pio la Torre, Della Chiesa, Falcone and Borsellino. Riina will undoubtedly already have been replaced, and in any case may still be able to wield considerable power from his prison cell. However, there is a belief that his arrest could be a turning point in the fight against the Mafia, a sign that the political establishment has finally lost patience with the Cosa Nostra and its murderous deeds – it is said, after all, that until his arrest Riina walked around the streets of Corleone quite openly, and could have been picked up at any time, should anyone have wanted to do so.

Above all the arrest of Riina might be the chance at last to bury the reputations of key members of the Italian establishment. There are without question many in high places who have much to fear from any revelations that Riina may come up with, and the backlash against organised crime has potentially devastating implications for the postwar Italian political concensus. It has, for example, come to light that a murdered associate of Giulio Andreotti ("the fox", and three times prime minister) had been the Mafia's man in Rome, a top-level fixer who would arrange acquittals from the Supreme Court in exchange for support. Perhaps most importantly the idea that the Cosa Nostra is invincible does really seem to be a thing of the past.

THE CAMORRA

Though in recent years the Neapolitan **Camorra** has in many ways become indistinguishable from the Mafia and 'ndrangheta, executing similar illicit activities in the drug trade, extortion, building speculation and suchlike, and often working in collaboration with them, its origins are quite distinct from its southern cousins. While the Mafia and 'ndrangheta were predominantly rural phenomena until World War II, the camorra has always been an urban animal, a secret underworld organisation of gambling and gaming. Today, a main camorra activity is that of the clandestine lottery, which shadows the official one run by the state. Instead of buying an official ticket you buy one printed by the camorra. The winning numbers are those drawn by the official lottery, only the camorra version has a number of advantages: if you win you're paid immediately (instead of waiting a year or two); and, clearly, you pay no taxes.

Though the Mafia has outshone, or outshot, the camorra over the past century, the camorra is much older and was already a well-established and ill-reputed criminal society at the beginning of the nineteenth century. In the bustling Bourbon capital there were great sums of wealth to be controlled by aspiring men of the underworld, and there were few commercial transactions in the city of which the camorrista did not get a substantial cut, known as the *taglio* or *tangente*. Even today, a great number of Neapolitan businesses pay a monthly sum to the camorra for "protection" – which of course means protection from the camorra itself.

Until World War II the camorra was a relatively traditional organisation, performing the familiar social functions of mediation and the maintenance of a kind of social harmony, by whatever violent and parasitic means. With the profound transformations in postwar Naples, and the arrival of the American-trained gangster **Lucky Luciano**, the camorra turned to the traffic in contraband cigarettes and drugs. Like the Mafia, the camorra has become entrepreneurial, and the name of the clan which commanded Naples until recently, the New Organised Camorra, suggests that the new Neapolitan underworld is structured more like a commercial firm than a family.

Still, at the same time as the camorra rule is to retain its business in all corners of the globe, its cardinal rule is to maintain its connection to the culture of the region, to the popular quarters of Naples. Such is the case of the Giuliano family, the clan based in Forcella, the district near the railway station, which controls the centre of Naples. Though members of the family have become millionaires many times over, comfortably moving in the international circles of high society, the family still lives in the centre of one of Naples' most degraded quarters, in a *basso*, or one-room, groundfloor apartment whose name is synonymous with poverty. A friend from Forcella once explained it like this: "These camorristi, for however powerful they become, realise that outside of their quarter, their territory, they're nobodies, provincial hoods. They stay here because this is where they count, this is where their respect and control is beyond dispute."

The "traditional", neighbourhood character of such a camorra clan as the Giuliano family raises a paradox, however, a kind of clash between good neighbourliness and delinquency. By producing and dealing heroin, the camorra, Giulianos included, have brought upon Naples (as elsewhere in Italy) one of the great social tragedies in contemporary Italy. The used needles that litter the streets of Naples are the unnerving, unmistakable proof of this epidemic.

This paradox came home to the Giuliano family in the autumn of 1987 when one of their own, seventeen-year-old Ciro, died of a heroin overdose. What followed was unprecedented: the grandfather/godfather of the family forbade the funeral to take place in his native quarter, making it pass through a street behind Forcella. He wanted to signal to his "people" that something was wrong, that something had to change. This strange admonition, however, did not deter the thousands of mourners from following the funeral cortege, and the 25 limousines bearing flowers from "friends" made clear that it wasn't just any seventeen-year-old who had died.

The other unprecedented aspect of this incident was the reaction of Nunzio Giuliano, the boy's father. Soon after his son's death, Nunzio began a campaign (in the papers, in public gatherings) against the heroin trade and the camorra's perpetration of it – in general terms, taking care not to incriminate any kin. Many see this as a possible turning point in the camorra's operations in Naples, while others, less optimistic, view it as little more than an act of showmanship, a piece of theatre, to divert attention from the real workings of the camorra and an embarrassing family tragedy.

Relatively cut off from the reintensification of Mafia and 'ndrangheta violence in 1988, the camorra has, thus far, also been spared the stepped-up investigations of the anti-Mafia commission. While the various anti-Mafia parliamentary laws and measures include the camorra in their jurisdiction, in recent years the camorra has taken a lower profile in the Naples area, falling short of some of the bolder acts of violence committed by the Mafia and 'ndrangheta. Far from being cause for relief, however, this may well mean that the camorra is finding new, more "acceptable" ways of inserting its illicit activities into the social and economic life of Naples.

Nelson Moe

ITALIAN CINEMA

From the earliest days of the cinema, the Italians have always been passionate movie-lovers and movie-makers. But it was with their films of the postwar period, and the shift from studio-based films to the use of the country's actual town and landscapes, that Italy came to the forefront of world cinema. Their style and technique were ground-breaking, and the use of real locations added a dimension, a mood, which made Italian cinema linger longer in the memory. The endless expanse of the Po Valley plain in *Obsession*, the steaming sulphur springs outside Naples in *Voyage to Italy*, the deserted, off-season seaside resort of Rimini in *I Vitelloni*, created an atmosphere that could never have been achieved in a studio.

THE BACKGROUND

The Italians were once famous for their silent costume epics, pre-World War I dramas that had monumental backdrops and crowd scenes – a leftover from the Italian grand opera tradition. They were often set in the period of the Roman Empire, anticipating the Fascist nostalgia for ancient Rome by at least a decade. **Giovani Pastrone**'s *Cabiria* (1913), set in Babylon, was the most sophisticated and innovative of these, with spectacular sets and lighting effects that the American director D.W. Griffiths imitated in his masterpiece *Intolerance* (1916). This borrowing of Italian expertise by Hollywood gave the Taviani brothers the story for their *Good Morning Babylon* (1984).

But even in its early stages the Italian cinema was handicapped by the economic problems that would always keep it lagging behind its rivals, the Americans. The reason for this was not simply lack of funds, but also an inability on the part of the government to realise what a moneyspinner the indigenous film-making talent could be, and what the unregulated influx of foreign films into Italy would mean for the home market.

In addition to this, the Americans themselves began making films in Italy, attracted by the cheap labour, the locations, and the quality of Italian light, so gutting the already fragile indigenous industry. An American film team arrived in 1923 to make an epic version of *Ben Hur*. Three years previous to this, 220 films were made in Italy; by 1927 the number had dropped to around a dozen a year.

The Fascist regime (1922–43) was surprisingly slow to recognise the potential, both economic and propagandist, of the cinema. But in 1934 Mussolini did begin to support it financially. He also limited the number of foreign imports, had film added to the arts festival in Venice, and in 1937 inaugurated "Cinecitta", the film studio complex just outside Rome. From 1938 to 1944 the proportion of Italian productions against imports rose rapidly, though home-produced films would never account for more than a third of the total number of films distributed in the country.

Films made during the Fascist period featured glorious victories from the past (the Romans again), and from the present – the war in Ethiopia, for example. During this time, not all movies were vehicles for propaganda, though no films could be made that were overtly critical of the regime. Most popular at the time were the escapist, sentimental, "white telephone" films, so-called because the heroine would have a gleaming white telephone in her boudoir, Hollywood-style – a touch of the exotic for the average Italian at the time, who never even saw such a thing, let alone owned one, in real life.

Italians were not, however, cut off from what was going on in world cinema between the wars, and the ideas and techniques of Eisenstein and, even more so, of French directors, particularly Renoir, Pagnol and Carne, began to filter through. Likewise with literature: probably the biggest single influence on the emerging generation of Italian film-makers was the American novel. Hemingway, Faulkner and Steinbeck spoke directly to the young generation: their subjects were realistic, their stylistic approach was fresh, even raw, and the emotion seemed genuine.

It was not surprising, then, that the late 1930s and early 1940s should see an element of documentary-style realism creep into film-making. Contemporary social themes were addressed; non-professional actors were sometimes used. Directors – even those with the official stamp of approval – made the occasional realistic documentary, with none of the bombast or gloss of the typical Fascist film. It was on films such as these that future neo-realist directors such as Visconti, Rossellini and De Sica, and the writer Zavattini, did their apprenticeships, learning techniques that they would draw on a few years later when they would be allowed to unleash their creative imaginations.

A film made in 1943 caused a considerable stir. When it was first shown, Mussolini's son, Vittorio, walked out exclaiming "This is not Italy!". But Mussolini allowed it to be distributed anyway, probably because there was nothing politically controversial in it. This was **Luchino Visconti's** *Obsession*, an unauthorised adaptation of the American novel *The Postman Always Rings Twice* by James M. Cain. Visconti transposed this low-life story of adultery and murder to Northern Italy, the characters playing out their seedy tragedy in the relentlessly flat landscape of the Po Valley and among the surreal carnival floats in Ferrara (a favourite town of the surrealist painter Giorgio de Chirico). It showed two ordinary people in the grip of a violent passion, so obsessed with each other that they bring about their own destruction. The original negative was deliberately destroyed when the official film industry was moved north to Mussolini's Saló Republic on Lake Garda.

Obsession was something new in the Italian cinema. It had an honesty and intensity, a lack of glamour, that pointed the way to the "neo-realist" films of the immediate postwar period.

THE NEO-REALISTS

The end of the war meant the end of the Fascist domination of everything, including the film industry; but Italy was left emotionally as well as physically shattered. It now seemed important to film-makers to make sense of the intense experience the Italian people had undergone, to rebuild in some way what had been destroyed.

As the tanks were rolling out of Rome in 1945, **Roberto Rossellini** cobbled together the bare minimum of finances, crew and equipment and started shooting *Rome, Open City*. He used real locations, documentary footage, and low-grade film, and came up with a grainy, idiosyncratic style that influenced not only his Italian contemporaries, but also the American *film noirs* of the late 1940s, and the grittily realistic films of the early 1950s – as well as the French New Wave of the 1960s.

Neo-realism had no manifesto, but its main exponents – Rossellini, De Sica and Visconti – had the following aims, even if they didn't always stick to them: to show real people rather than conventional heroes (using non-actors), real time, real light, real places (shooting on location, not in studios). Their intention was to present the everyday stuff of life and not romantic dreams.

Unusually for an "art" film, *Rome, Open City* was a box office hit. It had a good emotional, even melodramatic, story, with touches of humour, and packed a terrific moral punch. Set in a downbeat quarter of occupied Rome, it is about a partisan priest and a communist who join forces to help the resistance; a collaborator betrays them, and he is taken off to a labour camp by the Nazis while his fiancée (Anna Magnàni) is shot down while running after him. The Nazis are depicted as effeminate and depraved, while the partisans – including a band of children – are the true heroes, though taken as a whole the film's impact is ambiguous, and Rossellini seems to pursue immediacy at the expense of making political statements.

This was the first in Rossellini's so-called "war trilogy". It was followed by *Paisa* (1946), which traced the Allied Occupation north from Sicily to the Po Valley, in six self-contained episodes; and the desolate *Germany, Year Zero* (1947), set in the ruins of postwar Berlin, about a child whom circumstances push to suicide.

In these, as in other neo-realist films, children are seen as the innocent victims of adult corruption. **Vittorio De Sica**'s *Shoeshine* (1946) is an anatomy of a friendship between two Roman boys, destroyed first by black-marketeers, then by the police. A young boy is also the witness to his father's humiliation in De Sica's *Bicycle Thieves* (1948) – also set in the poorer quarters of Rome – when he sees him steal a bicycle out of desperation (a bicycle means getting his job back) and immediately get caught. The child's illusions are dashed, and it's society's fault for not providing the basic human requirements. At the time *Bicycle Thieves* was called the only truly Communist film of the postwar decade, but in retrospect the message, as in *Rome, Open City*, seems politically ambiguous. Crowds are seen as hostile and claustrophobic, and the only hope seems to lie in the family unit, which the hero falls thankfully back on at the end.

This conflict between Catholic and Marxist ideology is a recurrent theme in Italian cinema, from Rossellini through to Pasolini, and the Taviani brothers in the 1980s, and it's often this that gives their films their necessary tension. More than anyone, Visconti exemplifies this dichotomy. Born an aristocrat in the famous Milanese family, and sentenced to death for being an anti-Fascist in 1944, he was influenced by the writings of Antonio Gramsci, and right up until his death in 1976 veered between two milieux for his films – the honest, suffering sub-proletariat, and the decadent, suffering upper classes.

In 1948 Rossellini made a version of the nineteenth-century Sicilian author Giovanni Verga's novel about a family of fishermen who are destroyed through a series of circumstances, *The House by the Medlar Tree*, which he called *The Earth Trembles*. It was shot on location on the stark Sicilian coast, using an entire village as cast, speaking in their native Sicilian (with an Italian voice-over and subtitles). He adapted the story to incorporate a Marxist perspective, but this fades from view in the pervading atmosphere of stoic fatalism, closer to Greek tragedy than to the party line.

Something else that detracted from the intended message was the sophisticated visual style. Stunning tableaux such as the one where the wives, dressed in black, stand waiting for their husbands on the skyline, looking out to sea, prompted Orson Welles to remark that Visconti shot fishermen as if they were Vogue models. Indeed, style constantly threatened to overtake content in Visconti's work, culminating in the emotionally slick *Death In Venice* (1971).

THE END OF NEO-REALISM

By the early 1950s, neo-realism was all but dead. Social problems no longer occupied centre stage, and film-makers now concentrated on the psychological, the historical, even the magical side of life. There were several reasons for this, not least that the trauma of World War II had receded, and cities (and lives) were being rebuilt. As Rossellini said in 1954, "you can't go on making films about heroism among the rubble for ever". Directors wanted to move on to new themes. Another reason for the break was government intervention. The cinema industry was in the doldrums, and the Christian Democrat minister Giulio Andreotti had banned any more neo-realist films from being made on the grounds that social criticism equalled Communism. The Cold War was just beginning.

Neo-realist films had in any case, with one or two exceptions, rarely been good box office. Of Italian-made films, the general public tended to prefer farces, historical dramas, or comedies. The Neapolitan comic actor **Totò** – who had a colossal career spanning scores of films and several decades – was a particular favourite. In *Toto looks for a Home* (1949), he and his family search for somewhere to live in the postwar ruins of Rome, in a comic variation on a neo-realist theme. It was a sign of the times that people preferred to laugh at their problems rather than confront them.

De Sica meanwhile had moved on from the unremitting pessimism of *Bicycle Thieves*, to a fantastic fable set in Milan, *Miracle in Milan* (1950), about a young man who is given a white dove which can grant the wishes of everyone living in his slummy suburb. Surreal special effects are used to good effect, for example in a shot of the hero and heroine flying high above the pinnacles of Milan cathedral on a broomstick. The moral is still a neo-realist one, but with a change of emphasis: art and imagination can help your problems disappear for a while, but won't solve them.

In 1954 **Visconti** made *Senso*, another adaptation of a nineteenth-century novel but worlds away from *The Earth Trembles*. It opens to the strains of Verdi, in the Venice opera house, the Fenice, one night in 1866, and is Visconti's view of the politically controversial Unification, portrayed through the lives of a few aristocratic individuals. It was a theme he would explore again in *The Leopard* (1963). *Senso* was the first of Visconti's historical spectaculars, and the first major Italian film to be made in colour.

THE FIFTIES AND AFTER

Neo-realism was dead, but the next generation of film-makers – Fellini, Pasolini, Bertolucci, Antonioni, Rosi – could not help but be influenced at first by its ideals and techniques, though the style each of them went on to evolve was highly personal.

Federico Fellini, for one, saw neo-realism as more a world-view than a "school". His early films, such as *La Strada* (1954), follow a recognisably realistic storyline (unlike his later movies), but the whole feeling is different to the films of the 1940s. His characters are motivated by human values rather than social ones – searching for love rather than solidarity.

All through his long career Fellini used films as a kind of personal notebook in which to hark back to his youth. *I Vitelloni* (1953) is set in an unrecognisable Rimini, his birthplace, before the days of mass tourism; *Amarcord* (1974) is again set in Rimini, this time under Fascism. He also explores his own personal sexual fantasies and insecurities, as in *Casanova* (1976), and *The City of Women* (1980).

But Fellini isn't all nostalgia and sex. There are philosophical themes that run right through his work, not least the gap between reality and illusion. The heroine of *The White Sheikh* (1952) falls in love with the Valentino-type actor playing the romantic lead for "photo romance" comics (being shot on the coast outside Rome), and has her illusions dashed when reality intervenes and he makes a bungling attempt to seduce her. *Casanova* too is an oddly (and deliberately) artificial-looking film. It wasn't shot in the real Venice, and the water in the lagoon is in fact a shaken plastic sheet – an odd backlash against the real landscapes of the neo-realists.

Religion is also a theme in Fellini's work, and he's at his best when satirising the Roman Catholic church, as in the grotesque clerical fashion parade in *Roma* (1971), or the malicious episode in *La Dolce Vita* (1960) where a couple of children claim to have had a vision of the Virgin Mary, and create the press event of the month.

Pier Paolo Pasolini, murdered under mysterious circumstances in 1975, was a practising Catholic, a homosexual and a Marxist, as well as a poet and novelist. His films reflected this cocktail of ideological and sexual tendencies, though in a less autobiographical way than Fellini. They're also far more disturbing and challenging: *Theorem* (1968) intercuts shots of a spiritually empty middle-class Milanese family, which the mysterious young stranger insinuates himself into, with desolate scenes of a volcanic wasteland. *The Gospel According to Matthew* (1963) is a radical interpretation of a familiar story (and an excellent antidote to Zeffirelli's syrupy late-Seventies *Jesus of Nazareth*) in which Jesus is not a man of peace but the champion of the sub-proletariat and the enemy of hypocrisy. It was filmed in the surprisingly biblical-looking landscape of the poorer regions of southern Italy – Puglia and Calabria – and used the peasants of the area in the cast. Pasolini's *Decameron* (1971) was a record hit at the box office because of its explicit sex scenes, though the director's intention had been political rather than salacious, with Boccaccio's fourteenth-century tales transposed from their original middle-class Florentine setting to the Naples of the sub-proletariat.

Otherwise, the real box-office earners in the 1960s and 1970s were the so-called "spaghetti westerns", shot in the Arizona-look-alike interior of Sardinia, the best of which were directed by **Sergio Leone**. Equally popular were detective stories, and soft porn.

Bernardo Bertolucci started out as Pasolini's assistant, and shared his politics, though his own films are more straightforward and accessible. *The Spider's Strategem* (1969), filmed in the strange, star-shaped Renaissance town of Sabbioneta near Mantua, was the first of many feature films sponsored by RAI, the Italian state TV network, the anatomy of a destructive father-son relationship with constant flashbacks between the Fascist era and the present day. Another early film, *The Conformist* (1970), adapted from the novel by Moravia, had the spiritually empty hero (or rather, anti-hero) search for father-substitutes in Fascist Rome – again a dream-like jumble of flashbacks. *The Conformist* was Bertolucci's first step on the path to world recognition; subsequent projects, from *Last Tango in Paris* (1971), through *1900* (1976), *La Luna* (1979), the Oscar-winning *The Last Emperor* (1988) and the ill-judged *The Sheltering Sky* (1990) have made him one of the country's commercially most successful directors.

Michelangelo Antonioni again had a neo-realist background, but in the films he made in the 1960s and 1970s he shifted the emphasis from outward action and social realism to internal and psychological anguish. The locations he chose – the volcanic landscape of Sicily for *L'Avventura* (1964), the bleak townscape of industrial Milan in *La Notta* (1961), the impersonal Stock Exchange building in Rome for *The Eclipse* (1962), the alienating oil refineries and power plants at Ravenna for *The Red Desert* (1964) – were perfect settings for his almost cinematic equivalents of existential novels.

The Neapolitan director **Francesco Rosi** made a series of semi-documentary "inquiry" films attacking various aspects of the Italian establishment: the Sicilian mafia in *Salvatore Giuliano* (1962), the building mafia in Naples in *Hands Over the City* (1963), the army in *Just Another War* (1970), and vested interests of all kinds in *The Mattei Affair* (1972). Not that these are dry analyses of Italian society: the viewer has to sort through the pieces of evidence – the newsreel footage, the half-heard comments, the absence of comment – to come to his or her own conclusions about the truth, in kind of do-it-yourself mystery stories.

Later on, in the late 1970s and 1980s Rosi went in a more personal direction. *Christ Stopped at Eboli* (1979) is a surprisingly unincisive critique of "the problem of the South", set in a poverty-stricken mountain village in Basilicata. *Three Brothers* (1980) looks at three different political attitudes, as the brothers of the title, reunited for their mother's funeral back home in Puglia, argue, reminisce and dream. Oddly enough, in 1983 Rosi made a completely apolitical film of the opera *Carmen*.

This was a national trend. Hardly any of the major films of the last twenty years have attacked political targets, even after the explosion of the P2 scandal in the early 1980s. Instead there has been a looking back to their recent past. Italian cinema of the last two decades has been dominated by foreign co-productions and TV-sponsored films, which has inevitably led to a loss of national identity – though Italy does remain a cinema-going nation, its audiences less eroded by the successive onslaughts of television, video and TV deregulation than elsewhere. **Ermanno Olmi**'s *Tree of the Wooden Clogs* (1978) has a Bergamasque cast speaking dialect with Italian subtitles, and did well at the box office worldwide. Also prominent among current Italian directors are the **Taviani brothers**, whose *Padre Padrone* (1977), set in Sardinia, and *Kaos* (1984), an adapation of Pirandello stories shot in scenic Sicily, are loving of the Italian landscape and redolent of a time past. Both films, together with *Good Morning Babylon* (1986), have put the brothers' work centre-stage internationally.

Nostalgia has become the keynote in recent years, typified by **Giuseppe Tornatore**'s Oscar-winning *Cinema Paradiso* (1988), shot in the director's native village near Palermo. Much of the film comprises flashbacks to the boyhood years of the central figure, Salvatore, who goes on to become a successful film director; he returns to the village for a funeral, to find that the magical Cinema Paradiso of his childhood is about to be razed to make way for a car park. Similarly, in **Ettore Scola**'s *Splendor* (1989), the owner of the cinema in a small provincial town is forced to sell up to a property developer because of declining audiences and debt. This is, however, a far less saccharine film than *Cinema Paradiso*, and is less a lament for a lost past than a tirade against the impoverishing aspects of TV-culture. Despite the predominantly backward-looking themes, the future looks promising. New film schools and production houses have been set up, state and private sponsorship is often available even for first-time projects, and no fewer than 150 new directors have emerged during the last decade, indicating one of the healthiest film industries in Europe.

Sheila Brownlee

ITALIAN POPULAR MUSIC: GREATEST HITS

At the beginning of this century, Italy had one of the richest and most diverse traditions of folk music of any European country. Nearly a century of industrial, mass-market life and entertainment have done much to level this tradition, and it takes the keenness of the folklorist or anthropologist to find live folk music in Italy today, and determination to locate available recordings in record shops. When you do find it, however, live or recorded, it is always worth the effort.

What *has* happened musically during these years, in particular after World War II, is the cultural colonisation of Italy by the US and UK. And yet however strong these influences have been, the Italians have tended to make their own styles, often creating striking fusions. What follows is an extremely partial listing of Italian music since the war, a listing of those artists which have been popular in Italy *and* which have offered some special, Italian contribution to the pop music genre.

NAPLES AFTER THE WAR

The history of postwar Italian popular music may well begin in Naples in 1944, with the arrival of the Allies. Here the occupying Americans created a kind of Dixieland in exile with their officers' clubs and cafés. For at least a century before Naples had been a goldmine of popular music, providing the nation with such favourites as *O sole mio* and *Funicule Funicula*, and a long line of some of Italy's most distinctive and passionate singer-songwriters which continues to this day. The meeting of these two traditions, the Black American and Neapolitan, is perhaps the single most important factor in the making of contemporary Italian pop music. One man in particular, the pianist and singer-songwriter **Renato Carosone**, played a key role in this fusion. Carosone did much to import the Dixieland-swing sound into Italy during the 1950s. But he always did so with an ironic twist, ridiculing the Italian mania for America even as he fuelled it. In one of Carosone's best-known songs he chides his compatriots, "you want to play the American, but tough luck, kid, you were born in Italy".

THE FIFTIES

During the Fifties, another kind of song was taking form across the rest of the country, one vaguely reminiscent of the cabarets, but with a more sweetened, romantic sound. It was a style that took much from the singing of Peggy Lee, Frank Sinatra, and other American singers of the era. **Ornella Vanoni** and **Gino Paoli**, often singing together, are the best example of this kind of music, whose hits have become a part of the Italian collective musical memory. Together with Paoli and Vanoni, the sound of singers **Domenico Modugno** (of *Volare* fame), **Peppino di Capri** and **Mina**, has come to be associated with a particular moment in Italian history: the economic boom of the late 1950s and early 1960s.

This style of music, it might be added, though usually in watered-down form, was the music of "San Remo", the annual popular Italian music festival. To trace the popular musical consciousness of Italy you need only listen to the hits that came out of that festival.

THE SIXTIES

A spirit of restlessness, of rock, swept over the music scene of the 1960s, an international phenomenon but with a local, Italian accent. A specifically Italian kind of folk-rock is one of the most successful expressions of the decade. The songs of **Luigi Tenco** mark a kind of fusion between the San Remo sound and that of the new folk-rock. **Fabrizio De André, Francesco Guccini**, and, a little later, **Francesco De Gregori** are all noted for their combination of fine folk guitar music with poetic, and often political, lyrics. At the same time **Gabriella Ferri** mixed the tradition of Roman folk songs and cabaret in her spirited singing.

Out of the late Sixties emerged one of Italy's most original and popular singer-songwriters, **Lucio Dalla**. For twenty years, his songs, teeming with the sounds of every pop genre, have cast a humorous and ironic gaze at Italian society. The Italians appreciate Dalla's playful self-portraits and love him like few other performers. In 1988, Dalla and **Gianni Morandi**, a more romantic singer from the ranks of San Remo, joined forces to take Italian audiences on a nostalgic tour through two decades of their hits.

THE SEVENTIES

During the 1970s the sounds of heavy rock erupted onto the Italian music scene, partly in the shape of "progressive " bands such as: **Premiata Forneria Marconi** ("PFM"), who enoyed a fair amount of success outside Italy with their slightly pompous blend of jazz and rock; **Banco**, memorable for their huge lead singer, Francesco di Giacomo, if nothing else; and other, more political acts. These were the "anni di piombo", the "years of lead" or "hot" years of terrorism and social unrest, and the popularity of certain of these bands, like **Area** and **Stormy Six**, was tied to the radical politics of their music. Area in particular were a rallying point for young activists and intellectuals. Their legacy, however, is as much musical as it is political. With its Greek leader, Demetrios Stratos, Area sought to elaborate a musical style that was not limited to an Italian/US-UK fusion, but which opened itself to the various musical traditions of the Mediterranean, in particular those of the Balkan and the Arab countries.

At the same time that Area was looking to the Mediterranean to create a new form of hard rock, two groups based in Naples, **Nuova Compagnia di Canto Popolare** and **Musica Nova**, were looking in that direction in an effort to revive long-forgotten traditions of southern Italian folk music. For the past ten years the group, **Gruppa Operaio é zezi**, composed of workers at the Alfa Sud auto plant outside Naples, has given a political accent to this folk revival, setting contemporary political lyrics to ancient folk songs which they perform at rallies.

Out of the two dominant tendencies in Naples during the 1970s – the Mediterranean folk revival on the one hand, and American blues and rock on the other – came some of the most interesting musicians on the scene today. Though these performers have come to be grouped together by the label, "new Neopolitan sound", theirs is not one sound but many. **Pino Daniele** is certainly the foremost of these, fusing American rock, blues and funk with Neapolitan lyricism, American slang and Neapolitan dialect. Saxophonist **James Senese**, while collaborating with Daniele, is also a fine jazz musician in his own right. The music of **Tullio De Piscopo**, **Edoardo** and **Eugenio Bennato**, and **Teresa De Sio** are all marked in different ways by a mingling of folk and pop styles.

THE EIGHTIES

The most distinctive performers of the 1980s offer a sampling of many of the styles mentioned above, often carrying them to new heights of sophistication and self-consciousness. **Gianni Nanini**'s rock songs tend to be musically rather traditional, but her husky voice and risqué lyrics have earned her a wide following. **Franco Battiato** bases his music on an unmistakeable personal style: aloof, slick and synthesised. Recently he too has turned to the folk heritage, writing songs in his Sicilian dialect which make use of various elements of Sicilian folk music.

The most innovative group of "ethno-rock" today is the Florence-based **Litfiba**. Seeking to create a new musical language based on Mediterranean traditions, Litfiba blend together Italian, Arab, Latin, Balkan and "dark" sounds in their striking compositions.

As if to turn back the clock to the immediate postwar years, piano man **Paolo Conte** takes the traditions of American swing and French cabaret as his chief inspirations. Decidedly retro, his clever, moody songs have attained considerable international success. The work of

TV showman and clarinetist, **Renzo Arbore**, trained in the Neapolitan school of the postwar years, is also nostalgic, displaying that mixture of American musical style and lyrical irony so common to Italian music. But most importantly, Arbore has shown that Italy, and Italian music, has entered the age of mass media. As the creator of smash hit "variety" shows *Quelli della Notte* and *Indietro Tutta*, he reminds us that music in Italy has become in large part a video phenomenon, and that here, perhaps even more than in other countries, those that successfully make music are usually those that also make the best show of it.

More recent musical output has been less Italian, more international, with bands like **Black Box** and **Starlight** specialising in dance music that could have come from just about any country, their clever synthesis of smooth production, soul-roots and hypnotic rhythms bringing success to Italian music worldwide. The other big global success from Italy in recent years has been **Zucchero**, the gravel-voiced if rather middle-of-the-road soul/blues singer in mould of Joe Cocker who has performed with Paul Young, U2 and many other big rock names.

Nelson Moe

MODERN ITALIAN LITERATURE

Modern Italian literature tells the traveller a part of a story which we might call the "making of modern Italy", the transformation of a traditional, rural society into a modern, industrialised nation. One of the keys to appreciating the country's literature is to understand the interplay of regionalism, nationalism and internationalism which to this day has been a dynamic force in Italian social and cultural life – though, for the Anglo-American reader, one of the main expressions of this interplay, the tension between local dialect and standard Italian, is caught imperfectly in translation. For a complete rundown on what *is* available in translation, see "Books", which follows.

TOWARDS NATIONAL LITERATURE

Italian modern literature arguably begins around the time of Unification (1861), although to start here would be to ignore two writers who in some way inaugurated the literature of the new Italy some decades before, **Giacomo Leopardi** (1798–1837) and **Alessandro Manzoni** (1785–1873).

A poet and philosopher from the Marche, Giacomo Leopardi's obsession with fading youth has earned him the title of pessimist. But if, for Leopardi, "all is vanity", then human imagination is infinitely precious, for through it people create the illusions which allow them to live from day to day. To the suffering poet who sees through these illusions, the poetic imagination offers, if not happiness, at least the comfort that from these worldly sufferings he has created a kind of eternal music. Leopardi published many of his finest poems in the volume *Canti*.

Through the diversity and force of Alessandro Manzoni's writings, and his long career spanning more than half a century, this Milanese writer has profoundly shaped the Italian reading public's sense of literature and language. His magnum opus, *The Betrothed*, is no summertime thriller – indeed Italian high school students, who spend a full year reading it, cringe at its mention – but it masterfully weaves together a romance of young lovers and a vast panorama of historical drama, all suffused by a deep religious sense of human destiny.

Most significantly, Manzoni's novel is the key literary intervention in the much-debated *questione della lingua*, the question over what kind of language would be Italy's national language. As only two to four percent of the total population could speak Italian in 1861 (the rest spoke regional dialects), this issue was in the forefront of all writers' minds. The two editions of *The Betrothed* mark the country's contorted attempt to move from linguistic regionalism to nationalism: the 1827 edition was written in a rather thick Milanese dialect, but in 1841 he published an edition which he had "rinsed in the Arno"; that is to say, he had rewritten the novel employing contemporary Florentine, the language which he and many others deemed the most appropriate for the young nation. Manzoni's view, in fact, became the dominant one, and the Italian taught in schools today is still modelled in part on Florentine.

THE SICILIAN EPIC OF GIOVANNI VERGA

The tension between regional and national language is also a prominent feature of the work of Italy's other great nineteenth-century novelist, **Giovanni Verga** (1840–1922). Again, the literary culture and language of Florence and Milan exert an irresistible influence on this writer – it was to these two cities that the young author went to seek his literary fortune – but it is Verga's native Sicily which becomes the scene for his most powerful novels and short stories; and it is, moreover, his fusion of the Sicilian dialect and Milanese-Florentine literary idiom which remains one of his most notable achievements.

Many of Verga's works – *Life in the Fields and Rustic Stories*, for instance – focus on the life of Sicilian peasants and artisans, acutely representing the world-view of that traditional society. *The House of the Medlar Tree* and *Master Don Gesualdo* are, however, in Verga's own words ". . . the sincere and dispassionate study of how the first restlessness for affluence in the poorest, most humble conditions is probably born and develops". In these two grand novels, Verga examines the turmoil which takes place in late-nineteenth-century Sicilian society as it gradually finds itself more and more part of a modern European state and the international capitalist system.

Verga has been an important mentor for later generations of Italian writers, and his success in writing about the poor, marginal elements of Italian society, as well as his particular form of realism, *verismo*, were to be a model for the movement known as neo-realism between 1930 and 1950.

NINETEENTH-CENTURY POETRY IN DIALECT

One of the things that distinguishes Italian poetry from Italian prose writing, and, above all, from the poetry of all other European literatures is the large portion of it which is written in dialect. In other words, a great part of "Italian" poetry is not, in fact, in Italian. This creates peculiar difficulties for both poets and readers, and tends to restrict a dialect poet's readership and reputation to his native city and region, or at best to certain Italian cognoscenti. Three of the greatest poets of nineteenth-century Italy are relatively unknown outside of the country: **Carlo Porta** (Milan, 1775–1821), **G.C. Belli** (Rome, 1793–1863) and **Salvatore Di Giacomo** (Naples, 1860–1934), each of whom provide powerful evocations of the spirit and life of their cities. Today, after half a century of relative dormancy, Italian dialect poetry is alive and well in the verses of Albino Pierro, Tonino Guerra, Franco Loi, Ignazio Butita, and others.

NINETEENTH-CENTURY WOMEN'S WRITING

If dialect poets have existed somewhat on the margins of "official" Italian literary culture, they certainly have not been alone. Women writers too have been largely ignored over the years by the Italian cultural establishment, even though some of the most successful writers during the late nineteenth century in Italy were women. Publishing serially in newspapers, **Carolina Invernizio** (1858–1916) thrilled her petit-bourgeois north Italian readers with such tales as *The Bastard, The Infamous, Dreams of Adultery*, and *The Train of Death.* **Matilde Serao** (1856–1927) was another popular writer who wrote stories varying between impassioned and astute social observation, and baroque melodrama based on the tumultuous, desperate life of late-nineteenth-century Naples. **Grazia Deledda** (1871–1936), one of the few female recipients of the Nobel Prize for Literature (1926), wrote most of her numerous novels about her native Sardinia. Her prose style, which owes much to Verga and the French realists but exhibits a heightened interest in her characters' state of mind, make her a kind of link between the literature of nineteenth- and twentieth-century Italy.

SVEVO AND THE DRAMA OF THE MIND

A detailed examination of human psychology marks much of the prose writing of the early 1900s. Italy's great turn-of-the-century master of the tragi-comic machinations of the human psyche, **Ettore Schmitz** (1861–1928), went by the name of **Italo Svevo**, and his choice of a pseudonym reveals a good deal about his own mind's make-up. Italo Svevo means "the Italian-Swabian", that is "the Italian-German". Svevo spent most of his life in his native Trieste, a city which, until the end of World War II, had been the main port of the Habsburg Austrian Empire. Trieste, with its mixed population of Italians, "Swabians", Slavs and Jews, was a city whose ethnic and political identity was in flux, and this instability comes out in profoundly personal, psychological terms in Svevo's writing. With irony and humour he achieves an incisive analysis of the middle-class, middle-European mind. Indeed, Svevo was one of the first writers to incorporate the insights of psychoanalysis into the novel. For those who have ever struggled to give up smoking, the opening of *The Confessions of Zeno* is not to be missed.

PROPHETS OF DECADENCE

The critique of realism implicit in the writings of Italo Svevo becomes bold and explicit in the work of Nobel Prize-winning dramatist **Luigi Pirandello** (1867–1936). Part and parcel of this was Pirandello's critique of positivism, the dominant cultural ideology of late-nineteenth-century Italy. Pirandello opposed the positivist faith in the ability to analyse "reality" scientifically and objectively (which lay behind much of realist writing, such as Verga), showing instead the subjective qualities of human experience, and the way in which "reality" is determined in fact by social convention.

Whether in such grand plays as *Six Characters in Search of an Author* or *Henry IV*, in the novels *The Late Mattia Pascal* and *The Old and Young*, or his numerous short stories, Pirandello's writing expresses a crisis which is at once cultural and political. Pirandello's works investigate the psychology both of his native, rural Sicily and of metropolitan Rome, and he is a striking example of how the different cultural layerings of region, nation and the world can come together to produce a literature of both local and global resonance.

Behind Pirandello's challenge to the stable appearances of bourgeois reality, its conventions and hypocrisies, lies his affirmation of the dynamism of human existence, of the crucial role that the will, or willpower, plays in determining the shape of the world – a world that in the early twentieth century was undergoing a radical transformation.

Willpower was also a philosophical trademark of that most flamboyant of Italian intellectuals, **Gabriele D'Annunzio** (1863–1938) – writer, playboy and rabble-rouser. His artistic, amorous and political activities found a kind of dramatic unity as, at every turn, he attempted to embody the Nietzschean "Superman". Like his colleague Giovanni Pascoli – and, in England, Oscar Wilde and Arthur Symons – D'Annunzio explored the aesthetic dissolution of Western European Civilisation, breaking down "sense" into sonorous sensuality in his poetry.

D'Annunzio was, moreover, one of the first Italian writers to appreciate the effects that industrialisation and the mass media had on the writer's role in society. In this he found the company of **Filippo Tommaso Marinetti** (1876–1944), the founder of the Futurist Movement in 1909. Marinetti took things a step further, however, proposing to destroy art and literature as we know it, replacing it with the aesthetics of modern technology and machinery. For Marinetti and the Futurists the beauty of a sonata or poem was far surpassed by that of a machine gun. Indeed they were not so much interested in beauty as in speed, power and violence.

WRITERS IN OPPOSITION

Such prominent cultural figures as Pirandello, D'Annunzio and Marinetti reached the height of their careers during the early years of Fascism in Italy. In different ways, their ideas and actions entwined with the development of Fascism.

At the same time, a generation of younger writers grew up through Fascism, acquiring a new sense of the social function of culture in opposition to it. For some, like **Ignazio Silone** (1900–1978) and **Carlo Levi** (1902–1975), their exile at the hands of Fascist authorities drew their attention to the poorest, marginal areas of Italy. From his exile in Switzerland, Silone wrote about his native Abruzzo, and about the struggle to bring social justice to this mountain area, in such books as *Bread and Wine* and *Fontamara*. Levi was from Turin, raised in the same industrial and metropolitan milieu in which Antonio Gramsci was politically active. Levi's exile in a small village in Basilicata opened his eyes to the existence of a world which, he wrote, "had been denied History and Government", where "the peasant lives out the immobility of his existence in misery and solitude". It was in fact Levi's *Christ Stopped at Eboli*, published in 1946, which awakened the Italian people to the problem of the underdeveloped South, *la questione meridionale*.

Conversation in Sicily, the masterpiece of yet another fine Sicilian writer, **Elio Vittorini** (1908–1966), expresses a more oblique critique of Fascism. The voyage of the novel's alienated young protagonist from the northern industrial city where he works to his island home (and mother) becomes a search for the authenticity of personal memory and communal tradition which stands in clear contrast to the pretence of the Fascist present.

Vittorini is often associated with the Piemontese writer **Cesare Pavese** (1908–1950): both wrote narratives about their native regions in a deeply lyrical and personal-mythical style; both were avid readers of American literature and changed the Italian literary landscape with their translations of it; and both came to be seen as the precursors of the literary "tendency" known as neo-realism.

In a hybrid style of myth and realism, Pavese's novels (as well as an unusual volume of poetry, *Working Tired*) dramatise the trauma of an Italian society in transition from the slow, steady rhythms of an agrarian existence to the shock and speed of the urban, technological age – a trauma which Pavese experienced first-hand in his frequent passage between Turin and the outlying countryside, Le Langhe, where he was born. This trauma, and that of Fascism, proved too much for Pavese, who took his own life in 1950.

NEO-REALISM

The term neo-realism was first used in 1931 to describe the "new" style of Moravia's *The Time of Indifference* and Alvaro's *People of Aspromonte.* A novelist and Communist intellectual from Calabria, the work of **Corrado Alvaro**(1895–1956) has yet to be adequately presented to the English-speaking public. **Alberto Moravia** (1907–92), on the other hand, is one of the best-known Italian writers in the UK and US. He burst onto the scene with *The Time of Indifference* at the age of 22 in 1929 and, with *Agostino* in 1944, *Two Women* in 1957, and numerous recent works, he was the most prolific presence on the Italian literary scene.

The term neo-realism was applied to Moravia's and Alvaro's novels as an indication of a new interest in social content and history, an interest that seemed to go against the prevailing mood of "decadent" formalism of the early 1930s.

Neo-realism, however, only became a dominant trend in the decade following World War II. As a cultural tendency or "state of mind", neo-realism arose out of the need to make sense of the social and economic ruins in which Italy found itself at the end of the war, and out of the intellectuals' desire for social commitment and civic purpose. Neo-realist writers tended to focus on the life of the provincial, lower classes, of peasants and farmers especially from the South, making frequent use of local dialect and idioms in their prose. In different ways, the works of Alberto Moravia, Elio Vittorini, Cesare Pavese, Vasco Pratolini, Carlo Levi and Corrado Alvaro manifest neo-realist characteristics. However, it was in Italian cinema, with the films of Rossellini, De Sica, Visconti et al that neo-realism achieved greatest artistic success and international acclaim (see "Italian Cinema").

HERMETIC POEMS AND OTHERS

Neo-realists, in different ways, attempted to confront society and politics directly in their writings, to break open what they viewed to be the dense, obscure literary productions that had proliferated under Fascism. The prime polemical target of the neo-realists was that of **Hermeticism**, a term that came to be associated with the poetry of **Giuseppe Ungaretti** (1888–1970), **Eugenio Montale** (1896–1981) and **Salvatore Quasimodo** (1901–1968), the latter two Nobel Prize winners. If these three poets were "guilty" of a difficult, oblique style, they also lay claim to having written some of the finest Italian lyrics of this century. Ungaretti's verses pare down the sufferings of World War I trench warfare, and of life's daily vicissitudes, into brilliant, imagistic compositions. Montale evokes a world of metaphysical breakdown, where man stands godless and alone in the storm of existence (*The Storm and Other Poems* is the title of one of Montale's collections of poetry). Quasimodo, at first the most "hermetic" of the three, later converted to a more overtly social kind of poetry. Today, **Andrea Zanzotto** (born 1921) is probably the most articulate descendant of the Hermetic lineage. In striking contrast with the Hermetic tendency, **Umberto Saba** (1883–1957), the Jewish bard of Trieste, offers a rare example of simplicity and directness in Italian poetry.

LATER FICTION: C.E. GADDA

One prose writer in particular stands out for his intelligent opposition to the neo-realist aesthetic, **Carlo Emilio Gadda** (1893–1973) of Milan. Gadda objected to the seriousness and moral rigidity of the neo-realists, and to their attempt to grasp reality "as it is". He instead saw the world as a welter of sexual energy in which humans, caught between the forces of desire and repression, try desperately to get some satisfaction. In *Acquainted with Grief* and *That Awful Mess on Via Merulana*, Gadda brilliantly demonstrates his conviction that the only way to represent such a world is through parody and pastiche, through a baroque profusion of styles which does not so much grasp reality as show how people "deform" reality according to their own desires.

REWRITING HISTORY

While the debate over neo-realism raged during the first postwar decade, **Giuseppe Tomasi Di Lampedusa** (1896–1957), far removed from the fray, set to meditating on the effects of the Unification in his native Sicily, meditations which would take the form of his novel, *The Leopard*. Published posthumously in 1958, *The Leopard*'s preoccupation with social immobility and its critique of the concept of progress underlying the Unification provoked the "committed" intellectuals of the day into heated debate over its significance. Its publication and ensuing debate in some sense mark the end of the neo-realist aesthetic.

Around the same time, **Elsa Morante** (1918–1986) was writing another kind of history, the history of a child's awakening to adulthood on the island of Prócida in *The Island of Arthur*, though in later years she too turned to an overt reflection on Italian history in *History: A Novel*. Like *The Leopard*, *History* provoked heated discussion of the question of historical interpretation, and of the relationship between literary representation and historical events. *History* also marks a significant moment in the history of Italian publishing: it is the first Italian book to have been published (by Einaudi) in coordination with a widespread publicity campaign. Within a few months of its appearance in 1974 it sold 600,000 copies.

Another history, one commonly viewed as marginal to mainstream Italian history, is that of the Italian Jews. Giorgio Bassani, Primo Levi and Natalia Ginzburg all explore, in different contexts and from different perspectives, the experience of being an Italian Jew. For **Giorgio Bassani** (born 1916), in *The Garden of the Finzi-Contini*, this context is the bourgeois milieu of Ferrara under Fascism. **Primo Levi**'s (1919–1987) writings focus primarily on his experience of the Nazi concentration camps, of which *If This Is A Man*, his first book, is perhaps the most powerful; and **Natalia Ginzburg** (born 1916), in *Family Sayings*, turns her attention to the daily experience of home and family.

CONTEMPORARY WRITING

The two Italian writers with the keenest sense of the passage of Italian society into the contemporary world of consumerism and the mass media are **Pier Paolo Pasolini** (1922–1975) and **Italo Calvino** (1923–1985), and the contrast between them is illuminating. Pasolini, who had one of the most refined sensibilities for the "poetry" of rural, peasant society, especially for its dialects (he wrote exquisite poems in his native dialect of Friuli), also experienced the impact of the modern age in the most violent, traumatic fashion.

So much of Pasolini's writing can be read as his attempt to come to terms with the positive and negative aspects of the rapid progress towards modernisation which was bringing an end to the local, dialect-based cultures of agrarian Italy. In the novels *The Ragazzi* and *A Violent Life*, Pasolini grapples with this process in the underworld of the Roman suburbs; his long poem, *The Ashes of Gramsci*, is a more meditative treatment of the same Roman theme. Following Gramsci's footsteps, Pasolini explored the historical necessity of forming a *national* culture, at the same time lamenting the homogenisation of Italy's regions which accompanied this formation. The Italy which took form during these years was a nation in which the majority could speak a standard Italian, light years away from the fragmented, dialect-speaking country at the time of Unification.

Though Pasolini, as a film director, lived out of the realisation that the new Italy would be a predominantly audio-visual (and not literary) society, it was Italo Calvino who displayed the sharpest awareness of the necessity, and possible benefits, of these changes. In books like *Marcovaldo*, *Invisible Cities* and others, Calvino expresses some of the possibilities inherent in the contemporary moment of the metropolis and mass media. While never detached from a critique of capitalism's nefarious effects on human life, Calvino's writing (such as his experimentations with science fiction in *Cosmicomics*) works out new ways of humanely and humorously coping with the modern world. His constructive and pragmatic vision contrasts neatly with Pasolini's tragic and elegiac one.

Umberto Eco (born 1932) is another writer who has reflected upon the role of literature in the age of telecommunications: Eco's observations on these phenomena are found in his various essays on the semiotics of everyday life (on

Snoopy, James Bond, television quiz shows, etc). It was by writing the international best-seller, *The Name of the Rose*, however, that he best demonstrated his understanding of the tastes and tendencies of the present era, though there were many who found this theological thriller a sterile synthesis of cultural trends. Its follow-up, the massively hyped *Foucault's Pendulum*, has again attracted accusations of hollowness, and is certainly one of the least-read best sellers of recent years.

One of Italy's finest modern novelists, **Leonardo Sciascia** (1912–91), takes a different approach to the contemporary moment. Writing again and again about his native Sicily, Sciascia has made of that island what he calls "a metaphor of the modern world". Whether writing on the Mafia, reflecting on obscure events in Sicilian history or investigating the assassination of prime minister Aldo Moro, Sciascia displays how passionate attention to a local, "provincial" reality can have international significance. An equally strong sense of place informs the work of another Sicilian novelist, **Gesualdo Bufalino** (born 1920), whose celebrated debut novel, *The Plague Sower*, was over thirty years in gestation.

Among younger Italian writers, Antonio Tabucchi, Fabrizia Ramondino, Aldo Busi, Gianni Celati and Daniele Del Giudice suggest promising new directions for Italian literature – and new articulations of an "Italianicity" poised between region, nation and the world on the verge of the 21st century.

Nelson Moe

BOOKS

A comprehensive background reading list for Italy would run on for dozens of pages, and would include a vast number of out-of-print titles. Most of our recommendations are in print, and those that aren't shouldn't be too difficult to track down. Wherever a book is in print the UK publisher is given first in each listing, followed by the publisher in the US – unless the title is available in one country only, in which case we have specified the country.

TRAVEL AND GENERAL

Vincent Cronin *The Golden Honeycomb* (Harvill in UK & US). Disguised as a quest for the mythical golden honeycomb of Daedalus, this is a searching account of a sojourn in Sicily in the 1950s. Although overwritten in parts, it has colourful descriptions of Sicily's art, architecture and folklore.

Charles Dickens *Pictures from Italy* (Granville/Ecco). The classic mid-nineteenth-century Grand Tour, taking in the sights of Emilia, of Tuscany and Rome, and of Naples, in elegant, measured and incisive prose.

Norman Douglas *Old Calabria* (Century in UK). The chronicle of Douglas's travels around the South in the early part of this century. Evocative and descriptive, though riven with digressions. See also the slightly earlier *Siren Land* (o/p), which focuses on Cápri and Sorrento; and *South Wind* (o/p), a comical, if now rather dated novel set very obviously on Cápri, which the author knew well.

Wolfgang Goethe *Italian Journey* (Penguin in UK & US). Revealing for what it says about the tastes of the time – Roman antiquities taking precedence over the Renaissance.

Henry James *Italian Hours* (Century/Ecco). Urbane travel pieces from the young James; perceptive about particular monuments and works of art, superb on the different atmospheres of Italy.

D.H. Lawrence *D.H. Lawrence and Italy* (Penguin in UK & US). Lawrence's three Italian travelogues collected into one volume. *Sea and Sardinia* and *Twilight in Italy* combine the author's seemingly natural ill-temper when travelling with a genuine sense of regret for a way of life almost visibly passing away – classic travel writing, supremely evocative of the spirit of place. *Etruscan Places*, published posthumously, consists of his more philosophical musings on Etruscan art and civilisation, and remains much the most illuminating book to read on the period.

Norman Lewis *Naples '44* (Eland/Pantheon). Lewis was among the first Allied troops to move into Naples following the Italian surrender in the last war, and this is his diary of his experiences there. Part travelogue, part straight journalism, this is without question the finest thing you can read on World War II in Italy – and, despite its often bleak subject matter, among the most entertaining.

Mary McCarthy *The Stones of Florence/Venice Observed* (Penguin in UK & US). A mixture of high-class reporting on the contemporary cities and anecdotal detail on their histories; one of the few accounts of these two cities that doesn't read as if it's been written in a library.

James Morris *Venice* (Faber/Harcourt, Brace). Some people think this is the most acute modern book written about any Italian city, while others find it unbearably fey. At least give it a look.

H.V. Morton *A Traveller in Italy, A Traveller in Rome* and *A Traveller in Southern Italy* (all o/p). Morton's leisurely and amiable books were written in the 1930s, long before modern tourism got into its stride, and their nostalgic charm has a lot to do with their enduring popularity. But they are also packed with learned details and marvellously evocative descriptions.

William Murray *Italy: the Fatal Gift* (o/p). Murray spent several years in Italy shortly after the last war, and this is a collection of essays inspired by his time there, and many return visits since. Skilfully combining personal anecdote and contemporary Italian history and politics, it's perhaps the most insightful and immediate introduction to the country and its people you can buy – though sadly it's for the moment only available in North America.

Eric Newby *Love and War in the Apennines* (Picador/Penguin). Anecdotal, oddly nostalgic account of the sheltering of the author by local people in the mountains of Emilia-Romagna in the closing months of World War II.

Tobias Smollett *Travels through France and Italy* (OUP in UK & US). One of the funniest travel journals ever written – the apotheosis of Little Englandism, calling on an unmatched vocabulary of disgust at all things foreign.

HISTORY, POLITICS AND SOCIETY

The Longman History of Italy. This eight-volume series covers the history of Italy from the end of the Roman Empire to the present, each instalment comprising a range of essays on all aspects of political, social, economic and cultural history. Invaluable if you've developed a special interest in a particular period.

Luigi Barzini *The Italians* (Penguin/ Macmillan). Long the most respected work on the Italian nation, and rightly so. Barzini leaves no stone unturned in his quest to pinpoint the real Italy.

Judith C. Brown *Immodest Acts* (OUP in UK & US). Subtitled "The Life of a Lesbian Nun in Renaissance Italy", this is a fascinating glimpse into the life of an aristocratic woman of the period.

Jerome Carcopino *Daily Life in Ancient Rome* (Penguin in UK & US). Detailed but never dull, this is a seminal work of Roman social history.

Daniel Dolci *Sicilian Lives* (Writers and Readers/Pantheon). Dolci's formidable record of the lives of the Sicilians he met when he moved to Trappeto in the early 1950s. Short accounts told in their own words, it's at once a moving and depressing document.

Alan Friedman *Agnelli and the Network of Italian Power* (Mandarin/New American Library). Agnelli publicly didn't like this when it came out, and no wonder. Friedman's book is the first piece of journalism to properly pull no punches on the dynastic and anti-democratic power network that is at the heart of Italian society. If you're intrigued by the inertia of Italian postwar politics, it's a must.

Edward Gibbon *The History of the Decline and Fall of the Roman Empire.* Awe-inspiring in its erudition, Gibbon's masterpiece is one of the greatest histories ever written, and one of the finest compositions of English prose. The full work is published by Dent in six volumes and Random House in three, but Penguin issue a decent abridgement.

Michael Grant *A History of Rome* (Faber/ Scribner). Straightforward and reliable summary of an impossibly complicated story.

Christopher Hibbert *Rome: The Biography of a City* (Penguin in UK & US). The history of Italy's capital made easy. As ever, Hibbert is readable and entertaining, but never superficial, providing by far the most comprehensive brief account of the city through the ages yet published.

Christopher Hibbert, *Venice: The Biography of a City* (Grafton/Norton). The usual highly proficient Hibbert synthesis of a vast range of secondary material. Very good on the changing social fabric of the city, and has more on twentieth-century Venice than most others. Excellent illustrations too.

Christopher Hibbert *Garibaldi and his Enemies* (Penguin in UK & US). A popular treatment of the life and revolutionary works of Giuseppe Garibaldi, thrillingly detailing the exploits of "The Thousand" in their lightning campaign from Marsala to Milazzo.

Valerio Lintner *A Traveller's History of Italy* (Windrush Press/Interlink). Brief history of the country, from the Etruscans right up to the present day. Well written and sensibly concise, it could be just the thing for the dilettante historian of the country. Lots of tables and chronologies for easy reference.

Allan Massie *The Caesars* (Cardinal in UK). Readable introduction to the subject, drawing heavily on Suetonius.

John Julius Norwich *The Normans in Sicily* (Penguin in UK & US). Accessible, well-researched story of the Normans' explosive entry into the south of Italy and their creation in Sicily of one of the most brilliant medieval European civilisations. Just as stimulating is his *A History of Venice* (Penguin in UK & US), the most engrossing treatment of the subject that's available.

Giuliano Procacci *History of the Italian People* (Penguin in UK & US). A comprehensive history of the peninsula, charting the development of Italy as a nation-state.

Donald Sassoon *Contemporary Italy* (Longman in UK & US). Slightly academic background on the country and its institutions.

Denis Mack Smith *The Making of Italy 1796–1866* (Macmillan/Holmes & Meier). Admirably lucid explanation of the various forces at work in the unification of Italy. The same author has also written excellent biographies of Cavour (Methuen £6.95) and Mussolini (Grafton £4.95).

Dennis Mack Smith *Italy and its Monarchy* (Yale in UK & US). Learned and entertaining account of Italy's short-lived monarchy, whose kings ruled the country for less than a century. Reveals Vittorio Emanuelle II and co. as a bunch of irresponsible and rather dim buffoons that the country was glad to be rid of.

CRIME

Pino Arlacchi *Mafia Business* (Verso/Routledge). Dry and academic account of how the Mafia moved into big business, legal and illegal, its argument contained in the book's subtitle *The Mafia Ethic and the Spirit of Capitalism*. The author has served on the Italian government's Anti-Mafia Commission, which makes him supremely qualified to judge accurately the Mafia's cutting edge.

Christopher Duggan *Fascism and the Mafia* (Yale in UK & US). Well-researched study of how Mussolini put the Mafia in their place. Duggan uses this account for his thesis that there's no such thing as the Mafia, that it was dreamed up by Italians seeking a scapegoat for their inability to control the delinquent society.

Giovanni Falcone, *The Truth about the Mafia* (Fourth Estate in UK). The most incisive analysis of the *mafioso* mentality, by the investigating magistrate assassinated by the mob in May 1992.

Norman Lewis *The Honoured Society* (Eland/Hippocrene). Famous account of the Mafia, its origins, personalities and customs. Certainly the most enjoyable introduction to the subject available, though much of it is taken up with the story of banditry – really a separate issue – and his lack of accredited sources leaves you wondering how much is conjecture.

Claire Sterling *The Mafia* (Grafton/Touchstone). Thorough piece of Mafia scholarship, showing to a disturbing degree just how little Mafia power has been eroded by the state's onslaught of recent years.

ART, ARCHITECTURE AND ARCHAEOLOGY

Michael Baxandall *Painting and Experience in Fifteenth-Century Italy* (OUP in UK & US). Invaluable analysis, concentrating on the way in which the art of the period would have been perceived at the time.

Anthony Blunt *Artistic Theory in Italy 1450–1600* (OUP in UK & US). Cogent summary of the aesthetic ground rules of Renaissance art, but – contrary to the impression given by the writer's patrician tone – far from the last word.

Jacob Burckhardt *Civilisation of the Renaissance in Italy* (Penguin in UK & US). Nineteenth-century classic of Renaissance scholarship.

J.R. Hale (ed.) *Concise Encyclopaedia of the Italian Renaissance* (Thames & Hudson in UK & US). Exemplary reference book, many of whose summaries are as informative as essays twice their length; covers individual artists, movements, cities, philosophical concepts, the lot.

Frederick Hartt *History of Italian Renaissance Art* (Thames & Hudson in UK & US). If one book on this vast subject can be said to be indispensable, this is it. In view of its comprehensiveness and acuity, and the range of its illustrations, it's something of a bargain.

Howard Hibberd *Bernini* (Penguin in UK & US). Standard overview of the life and work of the central figure of Roman Baroque.

Michael Levey *Early Renaissance* (Penguin in UK & US). Precise and fluently written, and well illustrated; probably the best introduction to the subject. Levey's *High Renaissance* (Penguin £5.95) continues the story in the same style.

Cyril Mango *Byzantine Architecture*; **Hans Erich Kubach** *Romanesque Architecture*; **Louis Grodecki** *Gothic Architecture*; and **Christian Norberg-Schulz** *Baroque Architecture* and *Late Baroque and Rococo Architecture* (all Faber/Rizzoli). Though these volumes in the Faber/Rizzoli *History of World Architecture* series don't deal exclusively with Italian architecture, they provide a full context within which to place Italy's contribution to the movements.

Peter Murray *The Architecture of the Italian Renaissance* (Thames & Hudson in UK & US). Begins with Romanesque buildings and finishes with Palladio – valuable both as a gazetteer of the main monuments and as a synopsis of the underlying concepts. For a more detailed discussion of those ideas, the standard work is Rudolf Wittkower's *Architectural Principles in the Age of Humanism* (Academy £12.95).

Peter and Linda Murray *Art of the Renaissance* (Thames & Hudson in UK & US). Serviceable thumbnail sketch, useful for preparing the ground before a trip to Italy.

T.W.Potter *Roman Italy* (British Museum Publications/University of California). Learned illustrated survey of Roman society based on archaeological sources. Essential reading if you're interested in the period.

Frank Sear *Roman Architecture* (Batsford/Cornell). As thorough an account as the lay reader could want; good plans and diagrams.

John Shearman *Mannerism* (Penguin in UK & US). The self-conscious art of sixteenth-century Mannerism is one of the most complex topics of Renaissance studies; Shearman's brief discussion analyses the main currents, yet never oversimplifies nor becomes pedantic.

Giorgio Vasari *Lives of the Artists* (Penguin in UK & US). Two-volume abridgement of the sixteenth-century artist's classic work on his predecessors and contemporaries. Includes essays on Giotto, Brunelleschi, Mantegna, Leonardo, Michelangelo, Raphael, and more. The first real work of art history and still among the most penetrating books you can read on Italian Renaissance art.

Rudolf Wittkower *Art and Architecture in Italy 1600–1750* (Penguin in UK & US). Exhaustive and sometimes laborious survey of the period; best borrowed from a library.

SPECIFIC GUIDES

Burton Anderson *Guide to Italian Wine* (Mitchell Beazley/Simon & Schuster). Comprehensive pocket guide to the regional wines and winemaking techniques of Italy.

Stefano Ardito *Backpacking and Walking in Italy* (Bradt/Hunter). Selective guide to walking all over Italy.

Stefano Ardito (ed.) *A Piedi in Piemonte / Lombardia / Emilia-Romagna / Toscana / Abruzzo / Lazio* (Edizione Iter). Available in Italy and not in English, but with a basic grasp of the language, easy enough to follow, and with lots of very detailed hiking routes of varying standards of difficulty.

Tim Jepson *Wild Italy* (Aurum in UK). Recently published guide to the flora and fauna of the Italian peninsula.

Gillian Price *Walking in the Dolomites* (Cicerone). Lively and informative specialised guide to the best walks in the Dolomites. Cicerone also publish guides to Alta Via 1 & 2 and various "Via Ferrata".

Victoria Pybus & Rachael Robinson *Live and work in Italy* (Vacationwork). Accessible and informative handbook on all aspects of living and working in Italy.

William Ward *Getting it Right in Italy* (Bloomsbury/Trafalgar Square). Sassy observations on contemporary Italy.

ANCIENT LITERATURE

Catullus *Poems* (Penguin in UK & US). Although his name is associated primarily with the tortured love poems addressed to Lesbia, Catullus also produced some acerbic satirical verse; this collection does full justice to his range.

Cicero *Selected Works* (Penguin in UK & US). The rhetorical prose of Cicero was for many Renaissance scholars the paragon of literary style, and his political ideas provided similarly fertile material for discussion. Penguin publish half a dozen volumes of his work.

Juvenal, *Sixteen Satires* (Penguin in UK & US). Savage attacks on the follies and excesses of Rome at the end of the first century and start of the second.

Livy *Early History of Rome* (Penguin in UK & US). Lively chronicle of the city's evolution from the days of Romulus and Remus; Penguin also publish later instalments of those parts of Livy's history that have survived, including the gripping *War with Hannibal*.

Marcus Aurelius *Meditations* (Penguin in UK & US). The classic text of Stoic thought, written by one of the few Roman Emperors it's easy to admire.

Ovid *Metamorphoses* and *Erotic Poems* (both Penguin in UK & US). The mythical tales of the *Metamorphoses* have been so frequently quarried by artists that they can be enjoyed both as literature and as a key to some of the masterworks of Renaissance and later art. His elegiac love poems have a sexual candour that makes them seem almost modern.

Petronius *Satyricon* (Penguin in UK & US). Fragmentary, spicy narrative written by one of Nero's inner circle; Fellini's film of the same name gives a pretty accurate idea of the tone.

Plautus *Pot of Gold, and other plays* (Penguin in UK & US). The most popular playwright of his time, whose complicated plots provided a model for Renaissance comedies such as *The Comedy of Errors.*

Seneca *Four Tragedies and Octavia* (Penguin in UK & US). Violent, fast-paced drama from Nero's one-time tutor; the only plays to have survived from the Roman Empire.

Suetonius *The Twelve Caesars* (Penguin in UK & US). The inside story on such vile specimens as Caligula, Nero and Domitian; elegantly written and appalling.

Tacitus *Annals of Imperial Rome* (Penguin in UK & US). Covers much of the terrain dealt with by Suetonius, but from the stance of the diligent historian and serious moralist.

Virgil *The Aeneid* (Penguin in UK & US). The central work of Latin literature, depicting the adventures of Aeneas after the fall of Troy, and thus celebrating Rome's heroic lineage.

ITALIAN CLASSICS

Ludovico Ariosto *Orlando Furioso* (Penguin in UK & US). Italy's chivalrous epic, set in Charlemagne's Europe; has its exciting moments, but most readers would be grateful for an abridged version.

Giovanni Boccaccio *The Decameron* (Penguin in UK & US). Set in the plague-racked Florence of 1348, this assembly of one hundred short stories is a fascinating social record as well as a constantly diverting comic sequence.

Baldassare Castiglione *The Book of the Courtier* (Penguin in UK & US). Written in the form of a series of dialogues held in the court of Urbino, this subtle, entertaining book defines all the qualities essential in the perfect gentleman; the idealistic converse of Machiavelli.

Benvenuto Cellini *Autobiography* (Penguin in UK & US). Shamelessly egocentric record of the travails and triumphs of the sculptor and goldsmith's career; one of the freshest literary productions of its time.

Dante Alighieri *The Divine Comedy* (OUP in UK & US). No work in any other language bears comparison with Dante's poetic exegesis of the moral scheme of God's creation; in late medieval Italy it was venerated both as a book of almost scriptural authority and as the ultimate refinement of the vernacular Tuscan language. Numerous translations have been attempted – the OUP edition is clear, and has the original text facing the English version. One of the better translations, Laurence Binyon's, is printed in full in the *Portable Dante* (Penguin in UK & US).

Leonardo da Vinci *Notebooks* (OUP in UK & US). Miscellany of speculation and observation from the universal genius of Renaissance Italy; essential to any understanding of the man.

Niccolo Machiavelli *The Prince* (Penguin in UK & US). A treatise on statecraft which actually did less to form the political thought of Italy than it did to form foreigners' perceptions of the country; there was far more to Machiavelli than the *realpolitik* of *The Prince*, as is shown by the selection of writings included in Penguin's anthology *The Portable Machiavelli* (£5.95).

Alessandro Manzoni *The Betrothed* (Penguin in UK & US). The classic nineteenth-century Italian novel, focusing on the collisions of love and class. First published in 1823, it was reissued in 1840 after Manzoni had improved its diction through the study of the Tuscan dialect.

Petrarch (Francesco Petrarca) *Selections from the Canzoniere* (OUP in UK & US). Often described as the first modern poet, by virtue of his preoccupation with worldly fame and secular love, Petrarch wrote some of the Italian language's greatest lyrics. This slim selection at least hints at what is lost in translation.

Marco Polo *Travels* (Penguin in UK & US). Buttonholing account of Polo's journey to the court of Kublai Khan, and his seventeen-year stay there; engaging even when the stories are clearly fanciful.

MODERN LITERATURE

Giorgio Bassani *The Garden of the Finzi Continis* (Quartet/Harcourt, Brace). Gentle, elegiac novel, set in the Jewish community of

Ferrara during the Fascist period, on the eve of the mass deportations to Germany. Infused with a sense of regret for a Europe that died with the war.

Gesualdo Bufalino *The Plague Sower* (Collins Harvill/Aradinos); *Blind Argus* (Collins Harvill/Marsilio) and *Night's Lies* (Collins Harvill/Atheneum). Sicily's most esteemed living writer since the death of Sciascia, Bufalino arrived late on the literary scene, publishing his first novel, *The Plague Sower*, when he was into his sixties. Translations are now keeping pace with his output, which has augmented the reputation made by his remarkable debut.

Aldo Busi *Seminar on Youth*; *Confessions of a Panty-Hose Salesman* and *Sodomies in Twelve Point* (all Faber/Farrar, Strauss & Giroux). Busi is something of an *enfant terrible* in the Italian literary world, but his tales of gay escapades around northern Italy go beyond the mere showy; indeed his somewhat impenetrable style masks a humanity and wit that is rare in much recent Italian fiction.

Italo Calvino *If on a Winter's Night a Traveller* (Minerva/Harcourt, Brace). Calvino's fiction became increasingly concerned with the nature of fiction itself, and this involuted, witty novel marks the culmination of the process. His first three anti-realistic novels are published in one volume by Minerva in the UK, under the title *Our Ancestors*. Others include *Castle of Crossed Destinies*, *Invisible Cities*, *Difficult Loves* and *Mr Palomar* (all Picador/Harcourt, Brace).

Ann & Michael Caesar (ed.) *The Quality of Light* (Serpent's Tail). Recently published anthology of contemporary Italian writers, including work by Primo Levi and Gianni Celati, as well as many other less well-known writers like the starkly realistic Pier Vittorio Tondelli.

Gianni Celati *Voices from the Plains* (Serpent's Tail/Consort). Chance encounters on a walk down the Po provide the focus for these atmospheric tales. The four understated novellas in *Appearances* (Serpent's Tail in UK) pay similarly close attention to the specific locales of Emilia Romagna.

Luciano de Crescenzo *Thus Spake Bellavista* (Picador/Grove). Not really classifiable as straight fiction, more a collection of short tales and rambling discussions on Naples, the north-south divide, and the meaning of liberty. As a commentary on the Southern question, it's a useful supplement, although de Crescenzo has a tendency to romanticise his native city.

Gabriele D'Annunzio *Halcyon* (Carcanet in UK). Self-regarding dandy, war hero and worshipper of Mussolini, D'Annunzio was perhaps the most complex figure of twentieth-century Italian literature; this extended lyric sequence – a troubled idyll set on the Tuscan coast – contains much of his finest poetry.

Umberto Eco *The Name of the Rose* (Minerva/Warner). Allusive, tightly plotted monastic detective story. Perhaps the best-selling high-brow novel of the Eighties. See also his latest, equally hyped work, *Foucault's Pendulum* (Picador/Ballantine).

Carlo Emilio Gadda *That Awful Mess on Via Merulana* (Quartet/Brazillier). Superficially a detective story, this celebrated modernist novel is so dense a weave of physical reality and literary diversions that the reader is led away from a solution rather than towards it; it has the sort of status in Italian fiction that *Ulysses* has in English.

Natalia Ginzburg *Family Sayings* (Carcanet/Arcade). The constraints of family life are a dominant theme in Ginzburg's writing, and her own upbringing is the source material for this characteristically rigorous yet lyrical work.

Giuseppe di Lampedusa *The Leopard* (Collins Harvill/Pantheon). The most famous Sicilian novel, written after the war but recounting the dramatic nineteenth-century transition from Bourbon to Piedmontese rule from a aristocrat's point of view. A good character-study and rich with incidental detail, including some nice description of the Sicilian landscape.

Carlo Levi *Christ Stopped at Eboli* (Penguin/Farrar, Strauss & Giroux). First published in 1945, this novel, set in a remote region of Basilicata, to which Levi was exiled under the Fascists, was the first to awake modern Italy to the plight of its southern regions.

Primo Levi *If This is a Man/The Truce* (Abacus/Summit) – published as *Survival in Auschwitz*; *The Periodic Table* (Abacus/Schocken). Levi's training as a chemist saved his life in Auschwitz, and the first two books here – his first – record the horrors he experienced both in captivity and after the war. The anti-morality of the Third Reich and its repercussions are the recurrent subjects of Levi's later works, every one of which is distinguished by an unwavering exactitude of recollection and judgment.

Elsa Morante *History* (o/p). Capturing daily Roman life during the last war, this is probably the most vivid fictional picture of the conflict as seen from the city. Her first novel, *Arturo's Island*, is published by Picador in the UK.

Alberto Moravia *Roman Tales* (o/p). Collection of stories, first published in the Fifties, which attempt to show the underbelly of a city rapidly changing. Evocative both of the city and its people. *The Conformist* (o/p) is a psychological novel about a man sucked into the amorality of Fascism by his desperation to conform; *The Woman of Rome* (o/p) is an earlier work, a teeming and sensual novel, centred on the activities of a Roman prostitute.

Pier Paolo Pasolini *A Violent Life* (Carcanet/Pantheon). This super-naturalistic evocation of life in the slums areas of Rome caused a scandal when it was published in 1959. The critics have got used to it now, and the late author's novel is considered one of the classics of Italian postwar fiction. See also the collection of short stories, *Roman Nights and Other Stories* (Marlborough Press), and *A Dream of Something* (Quartet) – Pasolini's pastoral tale of growing up in Friuli in the late Forties.

Cesare Pavese *The Moon and the Bonfire; The Devil in the Hills* (Sceptre in UK). Exploring the difficulties of achieving an acceptance of one's past, the *Moon and the Bonfire* was written shortly before Pavese's suicide at the age of 42; the *Devil in the Hills* is an early collection of tales of adolescence in and around Turin.

Luigi Pirandello *Six Characters in Search of an Author* (Methuen/Dee); *The Late Mattia Pascal* (Dedalus/Eridanos) and *Short Stories* (Quartet in the UK). His most famous and accomplished work, *Six Characters...*, written in 1921, contains many of the themes that dogged Pirandello throughout his writing career – the idea of a multiple personality and the quality of reality. *The Late Mattia Pascal* is an early novel (1904), entertainingly written despite its stylistic shortcomings; while the collection of short stories is perhaps the best introduction to Pirandello's work you can buy.

Umberto Saba *Ernesto* (Paladin in UK). Lyrical autobiographical novel by the Triestine poet, recollecting youth and homosexuality. Marvellous translation.

Leonardo Sciascia *Sicilian Uncles*; *The Wine Dark Sea* (both Paladin in UK); *Candido* (Carcanet/Harcourt, Brace) and *The Day of the Owl & Equal Danger* (Paladin/Godine). Economically written, Sciascia's short stories are packed with incisive insights into the island's quirky ways, and infused with the author's humane and sympathetic views of its people. Recently published in hardback is his *1912 + 1* (Carcanet), which is a fictionalised attack on the work of Gabriele D'Annunzio.

Ignazio Silone *Bread and Wine*; *Fontamara*. Though out of print as we went to press, these are two modern Italian classics. *Fontamara* tells the tale of a small village driven to revolt against its landlords and the Fascist thugs sent to enforce their rule; *Bread and Wine*, a more introspective work, examines the parallels between Silone's political commitment and religious belief.

Italo Svevo *Confessions of Zeno* (Penguin/Random). Complete critical indifference to his early efforts so discouraged Svevo that he gave up writing altogether, until encouraged by James Joyce, who taught him English in Trieste. The resultant novel, *The Confessions*, is a unique creation, a comic portrait of a character at once wistful, helpless and irrepressible.

Giovanni Verga *Short Sicilian Novels* (Dedalus/Hippocrene); *Cavalleria Rusticana* (Dedalus/Greenwood) and *I Malavoglia* or *The House by the Medlar Tree* (Dedalus/University of California). Verga, born in the nineteenth century in Catania, spent several years in various European salons before coming home to write his best work. Much of it is a reaction against the pseudo-sophistication of society circles, stressing the simple lives of ordinary people, though they're occasionally drawn with a heavy smattering of "peasant passion", with much emotion, wounded honour and feuds to the death.

Elio Vittorini *Conversation in Sicily* (Quartet in UK). A Sicilian emigrant returns from the north of Italy after fifteen years to see his mother on her birthday. The conversations of the title are with the people he meets on the way, local villagers and his mother, and reveal a poverty- and disease-ridden Sicily, though the scenes are affectionately drawn. In the US, New Directions publish an excellent anthology of his writings, *A Vittorini Omnibus*.

LANGUAGE

The ability to speak English confers prestige in Italy, and there's often no shortage of people willing to show off their knowledge, particularly returned *emigrati*. However, even in the main cities and resorts you'll need to use at least some Italian, and in more remote areas you may find no one speaks English at all.

PRONUNCIATION

Wherever you are, it's a good idea to master at least a little **Italian**, a task made easier by the fact that your halting efforts will often be rewarded by smiles and genuine surprise. In any case, it's one of the easiest European languages to learn, especially if you already have a smattering of French or Spanish, both of which are extremely similar grammatically.

Easiest of all is the **pronunciation**, since every word is spoken exactly as it's written, and usually enunciated with exaggerated, open-mouthed clarity. The only difficulties

ITALIAN WORDS AND PHRASES

BASICS

Good morning	*Buon giorno*	Tomorrow	*Domani*
Good afternoon/ evening	*Buona sera*	Day after tomorrow	*Dopodomani*
Good night	*Buona notte*	Yesterday	*Ieri*
Hello/goodbye	*Ciao (informal; to strangers use phrases above)*	Now	*Adesso*
		Later	*Più tardi*
		Wait a minute!	*Aspetta!*
		In the morning	*di mattina*
Goodbye	*Arrivederci*	In the afternoon	*nel pomeriggio*
Yes	*Si*	In the evening	*di sera*
No	*No*	Here (there)	*Qui/La*
Please	*Per favore*	Good/bad	*Buono/Cattivo*
Thank you (very much)	*Grázie (molte/mille grazie)*	Big/small	*Grande/Píccolo*
		Cheap/expensive	*Económico/Caro*
You're welcome	*Prego*	Early/late	*Presto/Ritardo*
Alright/that's OK	*Va bene*	Hot/cold	*Caldo/Freddo*
How are you?	*Come stai/sta? (informal/formal)*	Near/far	*Vicino/Lontano*
		Vacant/occupied	*Líbero/Occupato*
I'm fine	*Bene*	Quickly/slowly	*Velocemente/ Lentamente*
Do you speak English?	*Parla inglese?*		
I don't understand	*Non ho capito*	Slowly/quietly	*Piano*
I don't know	*Non lo so*	With/without	*Con/Senza*
Excuse me	*Mi scusi/Prego*	More/less	*Più/Meno*
Excuse me (in a crowd)	*Permesso*	Enough, no more	*Basta*
I'm sorry	*Mi dispiace*	Mr . . .	*Signor . . .*
I'm here on holiday	*Sono qui in vacanza*	Mrs . . .	*Signora . . .*
I'm English/Scottish/ Welsh/Irish	*Sono inglese/ scozzese/gallese/ irlandese*	Miss . . .	*Signorina . . .*
I live in . . .	*Abito a . . .*	(*il Signor, la Signora, la Signorina* when speaking about someone else)	
Today	*Oggi*		

you're likely to encounter are the few **consonants** that are different from English:

c before e or i is pronounced as in **ch**urch, while **ch** before the same vowel is hard, as in **c**at.

sci or **sce** are pronouced as in **sh**eet and **sh**elter respectively. The same goes with **g** – soft before e or i, as in **g**eranium; hard before h, as in **g**arlic.

gn has the ni sound of our o**ni**on.

gl in Italian is softened to something like li in English, as in stal**li**on.

h is not aspirated, as in **h**onour.

When **speaking** to strangers, the third person is the polite form (ie *Lei* instead of *Tu* for "you"); using the second person is a mark of disrespect or stupidity. It's also worth remembering that Italians don't use "please" and "thank you" half as much as we do: it's all implied in the tone, though if in doubt, err on the polite side.

All Italian words are **stressed** on the penultimate syllable unless an **accent** (´ or `) denotes otherwise, although accents are often left out in practice. Note that the ending *-ia* or *-ie* counts as two syllables, hence *trattoria* is stressed on the *i*. Generally, in the text we've put accents in whenever it isn't immediately obvious how a word should be pronounced – though you shouldn't assume that this is how you'll see the words written in Italian: for example, in *Maríttima*, the accent is on the first *i*.

You'll find variations in **dialect** all over the country. Neapolitan especially can be difficult to understand, and the Sicilian dialect is different enough from conventional Italian as to be an almost separate language. But everywhere people will slip into more orthodox Italian if they see you're a foreigner.

DRIVING

Left/right	*Sinistro/Destro*	No entry	*Senso vietato*
Go straight ahead	*Sempre diritto*	Slow down	*Rallentare*
Turn to the right/left	*Gira a destra/sinistra*	Road closed/up	*Strada chiusa/guasta*
Parking	*Parcheggio*	No through road	*Vietato il transito*
No parking	*Divieto di sosta/Sosta vietata*	No overtaking	*Vietato il sorpasso*
		Crossroads	*Incrocio*
One way street	*Senso único*	Speed limit	*Limite di Velocità*

SOME SIGNS

Entrance/exit	*Entrata/Uscita*	To let	*Affítasi*
Free entrance	*Ingresso líbero*	Platform	*Binario*
Gentlemen/ladies	*Signori/Signore*	Cash desk	*Cassa*
WC	*Gabinetto*	Go/walk	*Avanti*
Vacant/engaged	*Libero/Occupato*	Stop/halt	*Alt*
Open/closed	*Aperto/Chiuso*	Customs	*Dogana*
Arrivals/departures	*Arrivi/Partenze*	Do not touch	*Non toccare*
Closed for restoration	*Chiuso per restauro*	Danger	*Perícolo*
Closed for holidays	*Chiuso per ferie*	Beware	*Attenzione*
Pull/push	*Tirare/Spingere*	First aid	*Pronto soccorso*
Out of order	*Guasto*	Ring the bell	*Suonare il campanello*
Drinking water	*Acqua potabile*	No smoking	*Vietato fumare*

ITALIAN NUMBERS

1	uno	9	nove	17	diciassette	50	cinquanta	200	duecento
2	due	10	dieci	18	diciotto	60	sessanta	500	cinquecento
3	tre	11	undici	19	diciannove	70	settanta	1000	mille
4	quattro	12	dodici	20	venti	80	ottanta	5000	cinquemila
5	cinque	13	tredici	21	ventuno	90	novanta	10,000	diecimila
6	sei	14	quattordici	22	ventidue	100	cento	50,000	cinquantamila
7	sette	15	quindici	30	trenta	101	centuno		
8	otto	16	sedici	40	quaranta	110	centodieci		

ACCOMMODATION

Hotel	*Albergo*
Is there a hotel nearby?	*C'è un albergo qui vicino?*
Do you have a room . . .	*Ha una cámera . . .*
for one/two/three people	*per una/due/tre person(a/e)*
for one/two/three nights	*per una/due/tre nott(e/i)*
for one/two weeks	*per una/due settiman(a/e)*
with a double bed	*con un letto matrimoniale*
with a shower/bath	*con una doccia/un bagno*
with a balcony	*con una terrazza*
hot/cold water	*acqua calda/freddo*
How much is it?	*Quanto costa?*
It's expensive	*È caro*
Is breakfast included?	*È compresa la prima colazione?*
Do you have anything cheaper?	*Ha niente che costa di meno?*
Full/half board	*Pensione completa/mezza pensione*
Can I see the room?	*Posso vedere la cámera?*
I'll take it	*La prendo*
I'd like to book a room	*Vorrei prenotare una cámera*
I have a booking	*Ho una prenotazione*
Can we camp here?	*Possiamo campeggiare qui?*
Is there a campsite nearby?	*C'è un camping qui vicino?*
Tent	*Tenda*
Cabin	*Cabina*
Youth hostel	*Ostello per la gioventù*

QUESTIONS AND DIRECTIONS

Where? (where is/are . . . ?)	*Dove? (Dov'è/Dove sono)*
When?	*Quando?*
What? (what is it?)	*Cosa? (Cos'è?)*
How much/many?	*Quanto/Quanti?*
Why?	*Perché?*
It is/there is (is it/is there . . . ?)	*È/C'è (È/C'è . . . ?)*
What time is it?	*Che ora è/Che ore sono?*
How do I get to . . . ?	*Come arrivo a . . . ?*
How far is it to . . . ?	*Cuant'è lontano a . . . ?*
Can you give me a lift to . . . ?	*Mi può dare un passaggio a . . . ?*
Can you tell me when to get off?	*Mi può dire scendere alla fermata giusta?*
What time does it open?	*A che ora apre?*
What time does it close?	*A che ora chiude?*
How much does it cost (. . . do they cost?)	*Quanto costa? (Quanto cóstano?)*
What's it called in Italian?	*Come si chiama in italiano?*

TRAVELLING

Aeroplane	*Aeroplano*	Bicycle	*Bicicletta*	On foot	*A piedi*
Bus	*Autobus/pullman*	Ferry	*Traghetto*	Bus station	*Autostazione*
Train	*Treno*	Ship	*Nave*	Railway station	*Stazione ferroviaria*
Car	*Macchina*	Hydrofoil	*Aliscafo*	Ferry terminal	*Stazione maríttima*
Taxi	*Taxi*	Hitch-hiking	*Autostop*	Port	*Porto*

A ticket to . . .	*Un biglietto a . . .*
One-way/return	*Solo andata/andata e ritorno*
Can I book a seat?	*Posso prenotare un posto?*
What time does it leave?	*A che ora parte?*
When is the next bus/train/ferry to . . . ?	*Quando parte il prossimo pullman/treno/traghetto per . . . ?*
Do I have to change?	*Devo cambiare?*
Where does it leave from?	*Da dove parte?*
What platform does it leave from?	*Da quale binario parte?*
How many kilometres is it?	*Quanti chilómetri sono?*
How long does it take?	*Quanto ci vuole?*
What number bus is it to . . . ?	*Che número di autobus per . . . ?*
Where's the road to . . . ?	*Dové la strada per . . .*
Next stop please	*La prósima fermata, per favore*

PHRASEBOOKS AND DICTIONARIES

The best of the **phrasebooks** are *Harrap's Italian Phrase Book*, which has useful vocabulary sections and menu readers, and the *Penguin Italian Phrase Book*. Among dictionaries, *Collins* publish a comprehensive series: their *Gem* or *Pocket* dictionaries are fine for travelling purposes, while their *Concise* is adequate for most language needs.

GLOSSARY OF ARTISTIC AND ARCHITECTURAL TERMS

AGORA Square or market place in an ancient Greek city.

AMBO A kind of simple pulpit, popular in Italian medieval churches.

APSE Semicircular recess at the altar (usually eastern) end of a church.

ARCHITRAVE The lowest part of the entablature.

ATRIUM Inner courtyard, usually of a Roman house.

BALDACHINO A canopy on columns, usually placed over the altar in a church.

BELVEDERE A terrace or lookout point.

CALDARIUM The steam room of a Roman bath.

CAMPANILE Bell tower, sometimes detached, usually of a church.

CAPITAL Top of a column.

CATALAN-GOTHIC Hybrid form of architecture, mixing elements of fifteenth-century Spanish and Northern European styles.

CHIAROSCURO The balance of light and shade in a painting, and the skill of the artist in depicting the contrast between the two.

CELLA Sanctuary of a temple.

CHANCEL Part of a church containing the altar.

CIBORIUM Another word for *Baldachino*, see above.

CORTILE Galleried courtyard or cloisters.

CORNICE The top section of a classical facade.

COSMATI WORK Decorative mosaic work on marble, usually highly coloured, found in early Christian Italian churches, especially in Rome. Derives from the name Cosma, a common name among families of marble workers at the time.

CRYPT Burial place in a church, usually under the choir.

CUPOLA Dome.

CYCLOPEAN WALLS Fortifications built of huge, rough stone blocks, common in the pre-Roman settlements of Lazío.

DECUMANUS MAXIMUS The main street of a Roman town. The second cross-street was known as the *Decumanus Inferiore*.

ENTABLATURE The section above the capital on a classical building, below the cornice.

EX-VOTO Artefact designed in thanksgiving to a saint. The adjective is *ex-votive*.

FRESCO Wall-painting technique in which the artist applies paint to wet plaster for a more permanent finish.

LOGGIA Roofed gallery or balcony.

METOPE A panel on the frieze of a Greek temple.

MITHRAISM Pre-Christian cult associated with the Persian god of Light, who slew a bull and fertilised the world with its blood.

NAVE Central space in a church, usually flanked by aisles.

PANTOCRATOR Usually refers to an image of Christ, portrayed with outstretched arms.

PIANO NOBILE Main floor of a palace, usually the first.

POLYPTYCH Painting on several joined wooden panels.

PORTICO Covered entrance to a building.

PRESEPIO A Christmas crib.

PUTTI Cherubs.

RELIQUARY Receptacle for a saint's relics, usually bones. Often highly decorated.

SGRAFFITO Decorative technique whereby one layer of plaster is scratched to form a pattern. Popular in sixteenth-century Italy.

STEREOBATE Visible base of any building, usually a Greek temple.

STUCCO Plaster made from water, lime, sand and powdered marble, used for decorative work.

THERMAE Baths, usually elaborate buildings in Roman villas.

TROMPE L'OEIL Work of art that deceives the viewer by means of tricks with perspective.

TRYPTYCH Painting on three joined wooden panels.

GLOSSARY OF ITALIAN WORDS AND ACRONYMS

ITALIAN WORDS

ALISCAFO Hydrofoil.

ANTIFEATRO Amphitheatre.

AUTOSTAZIONE Bus station.

AUTOSTRADA Motorway.

CAPPELLA Chapel

CASTELLO Castle.

CENTRO Centre.

CHIESA Church.

COMUNE An administrative area; also the local council or town hall.

CORSO Avenue or boulevard.

DUOMO/CATTEDRALE Cathedral.

ENTRATA Entrance.

FESTA Festival, holiday.

FIUME River.

FUMAROLA Volcanic vapour emission from the ground.

GOLFO Gulf.

LAGO Lake.

LARGO Square.

LUNGOMARE Seafront road or promenade.

MARE Sea.

MERCATO Market.

MUNICIPIO Town hall.

PAESE Place, area, country village.

PALAZZO Palace, mansion, or block of flats.

PARCO Park.

PASSEGGIATA The customary early evening walk.

PIANO Plain.

PIAZZA Square.

SANTUARIO Sanctuary.

SENSO UNICO One-way street.

SOTTOPASSAGGIO Subway.

SPIAGGIA Beach.

STAZIONE Station.

STRADA Road.

TEATRO Theatre.

TEMPIO Temple.

TORRE Tower.

TRAGHETTO Ferry.

USCITA Exit.

VIA Road (always used with name, eg Via Roma).

ACRONYMS

AAST Azienda Autonoma di Soggiorno e Turismo.

APT Azienda Promozione Turistica

ACI Automobile Club d'Italia.

DC Democrazia Cristiana; the Christian Democrat party.

EPT Ente Provinciale per il Turismo (provincial tourist office); see also *APT* and *IAT*.

FS Italian State Railways.

IVA Imposta Valore Aggiunto (VAT).

MSI Movmento Sociale Italiano; the Italian Fascist party.

PDS Partito Democratico della Sinistra; the former Italian communist party.

PSI Partito Socialista Italiano; the Italian Socialist party.

RAI The Italian state TV and radio network.

SIP Italian state telephone company.

SS Strada Statale; equivalent to a British "A" road, eg SS18.

GLOSSARY OF ITALIAN STREET NAMES

Italian streets form a kind of outdoor pantheon of historical figures. A jumble of artists, thinkers, politicians, generals and saints, in roughly equal proportions, intersect with each other in blind disregard for sense or chronology. The mad mix of heroes (and a very few heroines) constantly reminds the visitor of just how much Italians relish their past. Almost all of the following appear in every major Italian city.

Bassi, Ugo (1801–1849). A priest from Bologna who, as a fervent and eloquent supporter of Garibaldi and his cause, became one of its most important martyrs when he was condemned to death and shot by the Austrians.

Bellini. The name of both a Venetian family of fifteenth-century painters (Jacopo and sons Gentile and Giovanni) and a nineteenth-century Sicilian composer of operas (Vicenzo), best known for *Norma* and *La Sonnambula*.

Bertani, Agostino (1812–1886). A Milanese doctor, who organised the medical and ambulance services for Garibaldi's campaigns and became one of his closest associates and shrewdest strategists.

Bixio, Nino (1821–1873). Loyal companion-at-arms to Garibaldi, who enlisted and disciplined civilian volunteers to fight some of the critical battles of the Unification era.

Buonarroti, Filippo (1761–1837). Tuscan revolutionary and friend of Robespierre, who was involved with Gracchus Babeuf in the short-lived Conspiracy of Equals in Paris, May 1796.

Calatafimi. First decisive battle in Garibaldi's Sicilian campaign, May 1860.

Cappuccini. Monks whose characteristic brown robes and peaked white hoods have lent their names to the Italian coffee drink with hot milk.

Carducci, Giosue (1835–1907). Patriotic poet of the Risorgimento who won the Nobel Prize for literature in 1907.

Cavour, Camillo di (1810–1861). Prime Minister of Piemonte who relied on diplomatic cunning to promote the interests of his Northern kingdom in the unification of Italy.

Crispi, Francesco (1819–1901). Reforming prime minister of the late nineteenth century.

D'Annunzio, Gabriele (1863–1938). Nationalist writer who refurbished Italy's past with sex and violence and who lived out some of his fantasies as a Fascist military adventurer.

Dante Alighieri (1265–1321). Medieval Italian poet known for his three-part poem, *The Divine Comedy*.

Depretis, Agostino (1813–87). Italian prime minister on three occasions during the late nineteenth century. His administrations are remembered for the stagnation and corruption they engendered.

De Gasperi, Alcide (1881–1954). A prominent anti-Fascist imprisoned by Mussolini, and the first Catholic Prime Minister of modern Italy in 1945, aligning his country with the West by joining NATO.

Foscolo, Ugo (1778–1827). Nineteenth-century poet, dramatist and critic who left Venice under Austrian rule to settle in England where he became a commentator on Petrarch, Dante and Bocaccio.

Garibaldi, Giuseppe (1807–1882). Italy's unquestioned nationalist hero, and the tag on most Italian towns' most prominent boulevards or squares. Streets are full of his exploits and the supporting cast of comrades (see Bassi, Bertani, Bixio, Calatafimi, Le Mille, Turr).

Giolitti, Giovanni (1842–1928). Prime minister five times between 1892 and 1921. He sponsored an electoral reform bill which extended male suffrage and won workers the right to organise and strike.

Goldoni, Carlo (1707–1793). Venetian dramatist much influenced by Moliere, who wrote more than 250 comedies.

Gramsci, Antonio (1881–1937). One of the founders of the Italian Communist Party. Arrested by Mussolini in 1928 and held until just before his death, his influential writings from prison on the political role of culture and intellectuals remain controversial fifty years on.

Leopardi, Giacomo (1798–1837). A lyric poet plagued by ill-health and melancholy whose patriotic verses were taken up by the Unification.

Machiavelli, Nicolo (1469–1527). Political scientist and author of *The Prince* whose name outside Italy has become synonymous with unprincipled political opportunism.

Manin, Daniele (1804–1857). Leader of a revolution in Venice which proclaimed a republic in March 1948 and was overrun by the Austrians shortly thereafter.

Manzoni, Alessandro (1785–1873). Liberal Catholic writer and playwright whose historical novel *I promesi sposi (The Betrothed)*, set in seventeenth-century Milan, is still required reading in Italian schools.

Marconi, Guglielmo (1874–1937). Developer of the wireless system, sending messages across the Straits of Dover in 1899 and across the Atlantic in 1901.

Matteotti, Giacomo. A Socialist in the Italian Parliament who was murdered by Fascist thugs for his public denunciation of the 1924 elections which gave Mussolini majority control. In what has become known as Mussolini's Watergate, the incident had a brief chance of stopping Il Duce in his tracks – but didn't.

Mazzini, Giuseppe (1805–1872). Propagandist of Italian Unification whose influence was spread through the organisation Young Italy (*Giovine Italia*) which he founded to promote the national cause.

I Mille (The Thousand). The name given to the largely untrained band of civilian volunteers (made up of students, workers, artists, journalists and every kind of adventurer) who were mobilised in 1860 for Garibaldi's successful Sicilian campaign.

Puccini, Giacomo (1858–1924). A member of the fifth generation of a family of professional musicians, and composer of many popular operas, including *Madame Butterfly*, *La Bohème* and *Tosca*.

Quattro Novembre (November 4). Anniversary of the 1918 victory in the war.

Ricasoli. An ancient and distinguished Tuscan family name. The nineteenth-century Baron Ricasoli (an ally of Cavour and very briefly prime minister) has been eclisped by the relatively greater prominence of his family's vineyards, known particularly for their Chianti.

Ricci, Matteo (1552–1610). Early Italian missionary to China.

Risorgimento. The nineteenth-century movement to unify Italy and liberate the country from foreign domination.

Savonarola. A fifteenth-century Dominican friar and prophet of doom, who inspired a famous book-burning (which included Boccaccio's *Decameron* among the forbidden texts), and was himself burned in 1498.

Togliatti (1893–1964). Co-founder (with Gramsci and others) of the Italian Communist Party, which, in 1956, adopted his programme for an "Italian Road to Socialism".

Turr, Stefan. A Hungarian colonel in Garibaldi's army and close associate who helped acquire arms for the volunteer army (The Thousand) to mount the campaign in Sicily.

Umberto I and II. Kings of Italy, respectively, between 1878 and 1900 and for a brief period in 1946.

Vasari, Giorgio (1511–1574). The father of modern art history, whose *Lives of the Artists* traced the story of art from ancient Rome through to his own contemporary – and fellow Tuscan – Michelangelo.

Venti Settembre (September 20). The day Italian troops stormed into Rome in 1870, marking the final stage of unification.

Venticinque Aprile (April 25). Anniversary of the 1945 liberation.

Ventiquattro Maggio (May 24). Date in 1915 when Italy declared war on Austria-Hungary.

Verdi, Giuseppe (1813–1901). Hugely popular and prolific composer of operas who became a national hero.

Vespri Siciliani. Massacre of the Angevin French in Sicily in 1282, carried out (according to legend) while vesper bells were ringing, in retaliation for the savage colonisation of the island by the Angevin. Verdi used the story for an opera in 1855.

Vittorio Emanuele II and III. Respectively, the first king of unified Italy, from 1861 to 1878, and from 1900 until 1946. Very often the main street of towns are named after Vittorio Emanuele II – an overly grand accolade for a dull and unenlightened ruler.

Volturno. A river near Capua, and the name given to an important battle led by Garibaldi against the Bourbons in October 1860.

INDEX

NOTES

NOTES

NOTES

NOTES

NOTES

NOTES